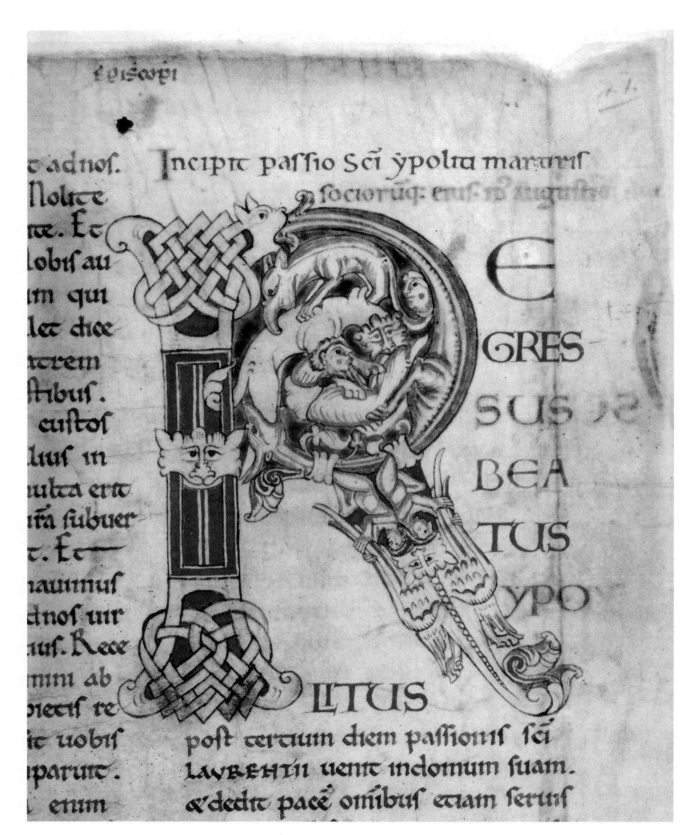

An illuminated letter "R" from the Legenda sanctorum *manuscript at Canterbury Cathedral.*
(© Angelo Hornak/CORBIS)

NEW CATHOLIC ENCYCLOPEDIA

NEW CATHOLIC ENCYCLOPEDIA

SECOND EDITION

12
Ref–Sep

GALE®

THOMSON
— ✳ —™
GALE

Detroit • New York • San Diego • San Francisco • Cleveland • New Haven, Conn. • Waterville, Maine • London • Munich

in association with
THE CATHOLIC UNIVERSITY OF AMERICA • WASHINGTON, D.C.

The New Catholic Encyclopedia, Second Edition

Project Editors
Thomas Carson, Joann Cerrito

Editorial
Erin Bealmear, Jim Craddock, Stephen Cusack, Miranda Ferrara, Kristin Hart, Melissa Hill, Margaret Mazurkiewicz, Carol Schwartz, Christine Tomassini, Michael J. Tyrkus

Permissions
Edna Hedblad, Shalice Shah-Caldwell

Imaging and Multimedia
Randy Bassett, Dean Dauphinais, Robert Duncan, Leitha Etheridge-Sims, Mary K. Grimes, Lezlie Light, Dan Newell, David G. Oblender, Christine O'Bryan, Luke Rademacher, Pamela Reed

Product Design
Michelle DiMercurio

Data Capture
Civie Green

Manufacturing
Rhonda Williams

Indexing
Victoria Agee, Victoria Baker, Sylvia Coates, Francine Cronshaw, Lynne Maday, Do Mi Stauber, Amy Suchowski

LIBRARY OF CONGRESS CATALOGING-IN-PUBLICATION DATA

New Catholic encyclopedia.—2nd ed.
    p. cm.
        Includes bibliographical references and indexes.
        ISBN 0-7876-4004-2
        1. Catholic Church—Encyclopedias. I. Catholic University of America.
   BX841 .N44 2002
   282' .03—dc21
   2002000924

ISBN: 0-7876-4004-2 (set)
0-7876-4005-0 (v. 1)
0-7876-4006-9 (v. 2)
0-7876-4007-7 (v. 3)
0-7876-4008-5 (v. 4)

0-7876-4009-3 (v. 5)
0-7876-4010-7 (v. 6)
0-7876-4011-5 (v. 7)
0-7876-4012-3 (v. 8)
0-7876-4013-1 (v. 9)

0-7876-4014-x (v. 10)
0-7876-4015-8 (v. 11)
0-7876-4016-6 (v. 12)
0-7876-4017-4 (v. 13)
0-7876-4018-2 (v. 14)
0-7876-4019-0 (v. 15)

Printed in the United States of America
10 9 8 7 6 5 4 3 2 1

For The Catholic University of America Press

Foreword

This revised edition of the *New Catholic Encyclopedia* represents a third generation in the evolution of the text that traces its lineage back to the *Catholic Encyclopedia* published from 1907 to 1912. In 1967, sixty years after the first volume of the original set appeared, The Catholic University of America and the McGraw-Hill Book Company joined together in organizing a small army of editors and scholars to produce the *New Catholic Encyclopedia*. Although planning for the NCE had begun before the Second Vatican Council and most of the 17,000 entries were written before Council ended, Vatican II enhanced the encyclopedia's value and importance. The research and the scholarship that went into the articles witnessed to the continuity and richness of the Catholic Tradition given fresh expression by Council. In order to keep the NCE current, supplementary volumes were published in 1972, 1978, 1988, and 1995. Now, at the beginning of the third millennium, The Catholic University of America is proud to join with The Gale Group in presenting a new edition of the *New Catholic Encyclopedia*. It updates and incorporates the many articles from the 1967 edition and its supplements that have stood the test of time and adds hundreds of new entries.

As the president of The Catholic University of America, I cannot but be pleased at the reception the NCE has received. It has come to be recognized as an authoritative reference work in the field of religious studies and is praised for its comprehensive coverage of the Church's history and institutions. Although Canon Law no longer requires encyclopedias and reference works of this kind to receive an *imprimatur* before publication, I am confident that this new edition, like the original, reports accurate information about Catholic beliefs and practices. The editorial staff and their consultants were careful to present official Church teachings in a straightforward manner, and in areas where there are legitimate disputes over fact and differences in interpretation of events, they made every effort to insure a fair and balanced presentation of the issues.

The way for this revised edition was prepared by the publication, in 2000, of a Jubilee volume of the *NCE*, heralding the beginning of the new millennium. In my foreword to that volume I quoted Pope John Paul II's encyclical on Faith and Human Reason in which he wrote that history is "the arena where we see what God does for humanity." The *New Catholic Encyclopedia* describes that arena. It reports events, people, and ideas—"the things we know best and can verify most easily, the things of our everyday life, apart from which we cannot understand ourselves" (*Fides et ratio,* 12).

Finally, I want to express appreciation on my own behalf and on the behalf of the readers of these volumes to everyone who helped make this revision a reality. We are all indebted to The Gale Group and the staff of The Catholic University of America Press for their dedication and the alacrity with which they produced it.

Very Reverend David M. O'Connell, C.M., J.C.D.
President
The Catholic University of America

Preface to the Revised Edition

When first published in 1967 the *New Catholic Encyclopedia* was greeted with enthusiasm by librarians, researchers, and general readers interested in Catholicism. In the United States the *NCE* has been recognized as the standard reference work on matters of special interest to Catholics. In an effort to keep the encyclopedia current, supplementary volumes were published in 1972, 1978, 1988, and 1995. However, it became increasingly apparent that further supplements would not be adequate to this task. The publishers subsequently decided to undertake a thorough revision of the *NCE,* beginning with the publication of a Jubilee volume at the start of the new millennium.

Like the biblical scribe who brings from his storeroom of knowledge both the new and the old, this revised edition of the *New Catholic Encyclopedia* incorporates material from the 15-volume original edition and the supplement volumes. Entries that have withstood the test of time have been edited, and some have been amended to include the latest information and research. Hundreds of new entries have been added. For all practical purposes, it is an entirely new edition intended to serve as a comprehensive and authoritative work of reference reporting on the movements and interests that have shaped Christianity in general and Catholicism in particular over two millennia.

SCOPE

The title reflects its outlook and breadth. It is the *New Catholic Encyclopedia,* not merely a new encyclopedia of Catholicism. In addition to providing information on the doctrine, organization, and history of Christianity over the centuries, it includes information about persons, institutions, cultural phenomena, religions, philosophies, and social movements that have affected the Catholic Church from within and without. Accordingly, the *NCE* attends to the history and particular traditions of the Eastern Churches and the Churches of the Protestant Reformation, and other ecclesial communities. Christianity cannot be understood without exploring its roots in ancient Israel and Judaism, nor can the history of the medieval and modern Church be understood apart from its relationship with Islam. Interfaith dialogue requires an appreciation of Buddhism and other world religions, as well as some knowledge of the history of religion in general.

On the assumption that most readers and researchers who use the *NCE* are individuals interested in Catholicism in general and the Church in North America in particular, its editorial content gives priority to the Western Church, while not neglecting the churches in the East; to Roman Catholicism, acknowledging much common history with Protestantism; and to Catholicism in the United States, recognizing that it represents only a small part of the universal Church.

Scripture, Theology, Patrology, Liturgy. The many and varied articles dealing with Sacred Scripture and specific books of the Bible reflect contemporary biblical scholarship and its concerns. The *NCE* highlights official church teachings as expressed by the Church's magisterium. It reports developments in theology, explains issues and introduces ecclesiastical writers from the early Church Fathers to present-day theologians whose works exercise major influence on the development of Christian thought. The *NCE* traces the evolution of the Church's worship with special emphasis on rites and rituals consequent to the liturgical reforms and renewal initiated by the Second Vatican Council.

Church History. From its inception Christianity has been shaped by historical circumstances and itself has become a historical force. The *NCE* presents the Church's history from a number of points of view against the background of general political and cultural history. The revised edition reports in some detail the Church's missionary activity as it grew from a small community in Jerusalem to the worldwide phenomenon it is today. Some entries, such as those dealing with the Middle Ages, the Reformation, and the Enlightenment, focus on major time-periods and movements that cut across geographical boundaries. Other articles describe the history and structure of the Church in specific areas, countries, and regions. There are separate entries for many dioceses and monasteries which by reason of antiquity, size, or influence are of special importance in ecclesiastical history, as there are for religious orders and congregations. The *NCE* rounds out its comprehensive history of the Church with articles on religious movements and biographies of individuals.

Canon and Civil Law. The Church inherited and has safeguarded the precious legacy of ancient Rome, described by Virgil, "to rule people under law, [and] to establish the way of peace." The *NCE* deals with issues of ecclesiastical jurisprudence and outlines the development of legislation governing communal practices and individual obligations, taking care to incorporate and reference the 1983 *Code of Canon Law* throughout and, where appropriate, the *Code of Canons for the Eastern Churches*. It deals with issues of Church-State relations and with civil law as it impacts on the Church and Church's teaching regarding human rights and freedoms.

Philosophy. The Catholic tradition from its earliest years has investigated the relationship between faith and reason. The *NCE* considers at some length the many and varied schools of ancient, medieval, and modern philosophy with emphasis, when appropriate, on their relationship to theological positions. It pays particular attention to the scholastic tradition, particularly Thomism, which is prominent in Catholic intellectual history. Articles on many major and lesser philosophers contribute to a comprehensive survey of philosophy from pre-Christian times to the present.

Biography and Hagiography. The *NCE,* making an exception for the reigning pope, leaves to other reference works biographical information about living persons. This revised edition presents biographical sketches of hundreds of men and women, Christian and non-Christian, saints and sinners, because of their significance for the Church. They include: Old and New Testament figures; the Fathers of the Church and ecclesiastical writers; pagan and Christian emperors; medieval and modern kings; heads of state and other political figures; heretics and champions of orthodoxy; major and minor figures in the Reformation and Counter Reformation; popes, bishops, and priests; founders and members of religious orders and congregations; lay men and lay women; scholars, authors, composers, and artists. The *NCE* includes biographies of most saints whose feasts were once celebrated or are currently celebrated by the universal church. The revised edition relies on Butler's *Lives of the Saints* and similar reference works to give accounts of many saints, but the *NCE* also

provides biographical information about recently canonized and beatified individuals who are, for one reason or another, of special interest to the English-speaking world.

Social Sciences. Social sciences came into their own in the twentieth century. Many articles in the *NCE* rely on data drawn from anthropology, economics, psychology and sociology for a better understanding of religious structures and behaviors. Papal encyclicals and pastoral letters of episcopal conferences are the source of principles and norms for Christian attitudes and practice in the field of social action and legislation. The *NCE* draws attention to the Church's organized activities in pursuit of peace and justice, social welfare and human rights. The growth of the role of the laity in the work of the Church also receives thorough coverage.

ARRANGEMENT OF ENTRIES

The articles in the *NCE* are arranged alphabetically by the first substantive word using the word-by-word method of alphabetization; thus "New Zealand" precedes "Newman, John Henry," and "Old Testament Literature" precedes "Oldcastle, Sir John." Monarchs, patriarchs, popes, and others who share a Christian name and are differentiated by a title and numerical designation are alphabetized by their title and then arranged numerically. Thus, entries for Byzantine emperors Leo I through IV precede those for popes of the same name, while "Henry VIII, King of England" precedes "Henry IV, King of France."

Maps, Charts, and Illustrations. The *New Catholic Encyclopedia* contains nearly 3,000 illustrations, including photographs, maps, and tables. Entries focusing on the Church in specific countries contain a map of the country as well as easy-to-read tables giving statistical data and, where helpful, lists of archdioceses and dioceses. Entries on the Church in U.S. states also contain tables listing archdioceses and dioceses where appropriate. The numerous photographs appearing in the *New Catholic Encyclopedia* help to illustrate the history of the Church, its role in modern societies, and the many magnificent works of art it has inspired.

SPECIAL FEATURES

Subject Overview Articles. For the convenience and guidance of the reader, the *New Catholic Encyclopedia* contains several brief articles outlining the scope of major fields: "Theology, Articles on," "Liturgy, Articles on," "Jesus Christ, Articles on," etc.

Cross-References. The cross-reference system in the *NCE* serves to direct the reader to related material in other articles. The appearance of a name or term in small capital letters in text indicates that there is an article of that title elsewhere in the encyclopedia. In some cases, the name of the related article has been inserted at the appropriate point as a *see* reference: (*see* THOMAS AQUINAS, ST.). When a further aspect of the subject is treated under another title, a *see also* reference is placed at the end of the article. In addition to this extensive cross-reference system, the comprehensive index in volume 15 will greatly increase the reader's ability to access the wealth of information contained in the encyclopedia.

Abbreviations List. Following common practice, books and versions of the Bible as well as other standard works by selected authors have been abbreviated throughout the text. A guide to these abbreviations follows this preface.

The Editors

Abbreviations

The system of abbreviations used for the works of Plato, Aristotle, St. Augustine, and St. Thomas Aquinas is as follows: Plato is cited by book and Stephanus number only, e.g., Phaedo 79B; Rep. 480A. Aristotle is cited by book and Bekker number only, e.g., Anal. post. 72b 8–12; Anim. 430a 18. St. Augustine is cited as in the Thesaurus Linguae Latinae, e.g., C. acad. 3.20.45; Conf. 13.38.53, with capitalization of the first word of the title. St. Thomas is cited as in scholarly journals, but using Arabic numerals. In addition, the following abbreviations have been used throughout the encyclopedia for biblical books and versions of the Bible.

Books

Acts	Acts of the Apostles
Am	Amos
Bar	Baruch
1–2 Chr	1 and 2 Chronicles (1 and 2 Paralipomenon in Septuagint and Vulgate)
Col	Colossians
1–2 Cor	1 and 2 Corinthians
Dn	Daniel
Dt	Deuteronomy
Eccl	Ecclesiastes
Eph	Ephesians
Est	Esther
Ex	Exodus
Ez	Ezekiel
Ezr	Ezra (Esdras B in Septuagint; 1 Esdras in Vulgate)
Gal	Galatians
Gn	Genesis
Hb	Habakkuk
Heb	Hebrews
Hg	Haggai
Hos	Hosea
Is	Isaiah
Jas	James
Jb	Job
Jdt	Judith
Jer	Jeremiah
Jgs	Judges
Jl	Joel
Jn	John
1–3 Jn	1, 2, and 3 John
Jon	Jonah
Jos	Joshua
Jude	Jude
1–2 Kgs	1 and 2 Kings (3 and 4 Kings in Septuagint and Vulgate)
Lam	Lamentations
Lk	Luke
Lv	Leviticus
Mal	Malachi (Malachias in Vulgate)
1–2 Mc	1 and 2 Maccabees
Mi	Micah
Mk	Mark
Mt	Matthew
Na	Nahum
Neh	Nehemiah (2 Esdras in Septuagint and Vulgate)
Nm	Numbers
Ob	Obadiah
Phil	Philippians
Phlm	Philemon
Prv	Proverbs
Ps	Psalms
1–2 Pt	1 and 2 Peter
Rom	Romans
Ru	Ruth
Rv	Revelation (Apocalypse in Vulgate)
Sg	Song of Songs
Sir	Sirach (Wisdom of Ben Sira; Ecclesiasticus in Septuagint and Vulgate)
1–2 Sm	1 and 2 Samuel (1 and 2 Kings in Septuagint and Vulgate)
Tb	Tobit
1–2 Thes	1 and 2 Thessalonians
Ti	Titus
1–2 Tm	1 and 2 Timothy
Wis	Wisdom
Zec	Zechariah
Zep	Zephaniah

Versions

Apoc	Apocrypha
ARV	American Standard Revised Version
ARVm	American Standard Revised Version, margin
AT	American Translation
AV	Authorized Version (King James)
CCD	Confraternity of Christian Doctrine
DV	Douay-Challoner Version

ERV	English Revised Version	NJB	New Jerusalem Bible
ERVm	English Revised Version, margin	NRSV	New Revised Standard Version
EV	English Version(s) of the Bible	NT	New Testament
JB	Jerusalem Bible	OT	Old Testament
LXX	Septuagint	RSV	Revised Standard Version
MT	Masoretic Text	RV	Revised Version
NAB	New American Bible	RVm	Revised Version, margin
NEB	New English Bible	Syr	Syriac
NIV	New International Version	Vulg	Vulgate

R

REFLECTION

From the Latin *reflexio* (from *re-flectere,* to bend back), the return of an agent or power upon its own operation or upon itself. Though the concept can apply to any spiritual operation or power (such as the will), it usually refers to knowledge. Four types of cognitive reflection may here be distinguished: (1) psychological, or knowledge one has of one's own operation, power, and self, both in direct singular awareness and in scientific and universal knowledge; (2) epistemological, or consciousness of the grounds for judging, for recognizing the possession of truth, and for certitude; (3) logical, or reflection upon the status of apprehended natures in thought with their consequent properties and relations there; and (4) ontological, or a simple return to the objects of knowledge for further and more detailed inspection and analysis.

Greek and Augustinian Views. Aristotle recognized that there is a certain reflex knowledge even in sense, for man perceives that he sees, hears, etc. (*Anim.* 425b 12). Self-knowledge more properly belongs to the INTELLECT, which is itself intelligible (430b 24). The highest form of being is pure intelligence, or thought, and its characteristic and exclusive activity is "thinking thought," i.e., knowing itself (*Meta.* 1074b 33–35; cf. 1072b 19–20, 23).

NEOPLATONISM stressed this self-regarding aspect of intellect, or mind. PLOTINUS said of his second hypostasis, intelligence, that it not only has knowledge, especially of the intelligible world, but that it essentially knows itself and its own act (*Enneads* 5.3.1–10). It is its own first and proportioned object in which everything else in known. In PROCLUS the doctrine of return upon self becomes more prominent. Everything that returns upon itself must be incorporeal and self-subsistent (*Elements of Theology* 16–17, 42–43), and such a being returns not only upon its activity but also upon its essence (44), particularly in self-knowledge (83). Every intelligence knows itself immediately (167) and, in knowing anything, by the same act knows that it knows (168). The influence of Proclus reached the Latin West in the late 12th century through the 9th-century Arabian compilation and digest known as the *LIBER DE CAUSIS,* long attributed to Aristotle. There the schoolmen read that an intelligence, in knowing anything else, at the same time knows itself and its own essence (13) and "returns completely to its own essence" (15).

St. AUGUSTINE, before Proclus but influenced by Plotinus, held for the presence of the soul to itself and a consequent self-intuition (*Trin.* 9.3.3, 10.7.10, 10.9. 12–13, 14.4.7). There is a habitual self-awareness always with man in "memory," or consciousness (14.6. 8–9, 8.11). Man is aware of his activities of remembering, willing, thinking, and judging (10.10.13, 11.14); and even if he doubts or errs, he knows that he is living (*ibid.*).

In the Middle Ages the influence of Augustine continued to be strong. St. BONAVENTURE, for example, held that the soul is immediately present to itself and by nature knows itself intuitively (*In 2 sent.* 19.1.1 sed contra 7; cf. *In 1 sent.* 3.2.2 ad 1, 2 ad 2; *Itin. ment.* 3.1–2); for it belongs to the nature of an intellectual substance to know itself in a complete return (*De don. Spir. Sanct.* 8.20; *In Hexaem.* 12.16).

Doctrine of Aquinas. The influence of Augustine, of the *Liber de causis,* and of Aristotle converged in St. THOMAS AQUINAS to produce an elaborate doctrine.

Psychological Reflection. Spiritual substances and immaterial powers, because immaterial, have complete reflection (*De ver.* 22.12; *In 2 sent.* 19.1.1). This applies to the WILL as well as to cognition (*De ver.* 22.12): the will wills its own act and its own good. Even in SENSE KNOWLEDGE there is a certain return, as man knows his own sensing, though not by the external senses but by a distinct internal power (*In 3 anim.* 2.284–87, 13.391; *De ver.* 1.9, 10.9). Only the intellect has a complete cognitive return, knowing besides its objects its acts, itself, and its own nature (*Summa theologiae* 1a, 87.3; *In 3 sent.* 23.1.2; *C. gent.* 2.49, 4.11). It also knows whatever is in the soul

(ST 1a2ae, 112.5 ad 1), especially its means of knowing such as the intelligible species (ST 1a, 85.2) and its habits (*De ver.* 10.9). Through his intellectual acts too man knows himself and his own existence (*De ver.* 10.8; *In 9 eth.* 11.1908; *C. gent.* 2.75). In this knowledge there is a determinate order: first the direct object is known, then the act of knowing it, and finally the intellect itself (ST 1a, 87.3, 14.2 ad 3).

The soul's concrete awareness of its own act explains man's intellectual knowledge of material singulars. Knowing directly, by ABSTRACTION, the immaterial and universal, the intellect can know the singular only indirectly. By knowing its act of apprehending the universal nature, and in this the intelligible species and its abstraction from and dependence upon the PHANTASM, which presents a singular object, the intellect sees the universal nature in a singular subject. Thus it is by a certain reflection upon the phantasm (*reflexio super phantasma*) that the singular is known (*De ver.* 2.6, 10.5; *In 3 anim.* 8.712–713; ST 1a, 86.1).

An important distinction is made between the reflection of immediate consciousness and the reflective consideration that yields a quidditative, scientific, and universal knowledge of the soul, the intellect, and its acts (*De ver.* 10.8, 9; *C. gent.* 2.75, 3.46; ST 1a, 87.1). In immediate CONSCIOUSNESS, what is primarily given is the existence of one's own singular act currently going on; but implicit in this awareness is the existence of oneself, one's soul, and the intellect, and also the nature of the act, of the power, and of the soul. For what is known is an act of a determinate sort, and it is apprehended concretely, as it is; and consequently the subject and principles of this are also implicitly apprehended as of a determinate sort (*De ver.* 1.9; *In 3 sent.* 23.1.2 ad 3). But this knowledge is not explicit; it is in simple APPREHENSION only and not in reflexive judgment; and especially it is not universal, i.e., of the nature of understanding, intellect, and soul as such. In explicit, judgmental, and universal reflection the nature, or QUIDDITY, of the soul is known from that of its power, the intellect; that of the intellect, from its act, UNDERSTANDING; and this, from its object. The soul, for instance, is known to be immaterial because the intellect is an immaterial power; the immateriality of the intellect is known from the "quality," or nature of its act; and that of the act from the immateriality of its object, especially because it is a universal nature (*see* SOUL, HUMAN 4; SPIRIT). Such quidditative psychological knowledge is not spontaneous and easy but "most difficult" (*De ver.* 10.8 ad 8 contr.) and the result of a "diligent and penetrating inquiry" (ST 1a, 87.1; cf. 2). (*See* INTROSPECTION.)

Epistemological Reflection. Spontaneous psychological reflection is the basis of a reflection that gives a knowledge of the possession of TRUTH and consequently yields CERTITUDE. In judging, the intellect affirms or denies something of something else. The JUDGMENT is known to be warranted because what is apprehended about the thing (the predicate) is known to belong to the thing (the subject); for the intellect knows the act of apprehending and its nature, knows that what it has apprehended is derived from the thing and expresses some aspect of the thing, and consequently knows that it is the nature of its act, and of itself as the principle of the act, to come into conformity with the thing that is made its object (*De ver.* 1.9; *In 1 perih.* 3.6 and 9; *In 6 meta.* 4.1236). This is an awareness of truth and the basis of certitude.

Logical Reflection. This differs from psychological reflection in that the "secondary objects of understanding" with which logic is concerned are not the acts, intelligible species, and concepts "according to the existence which they have in the knower," which psychology studies (*De ver.* 10.4, 2.5 ad 17), but "secondary intentions which follow upon the manner of understanding" (*De pot.* 7.9; *In 4 meta.* 4.574; *In 1 anal. post.* 20.5). They are views of the primary intentions or concepts not considered subjectively but objectively, according to what is represented, that is, the apprehended natures, and the condition that these natures have in the mind as a result of being apprehended, e.g., universality or the fact of being a genus. Formed by the intellect, these intentions are attributed to the natures that are known, not as these natures exist in reality, i.e., in singular things, but precisely as known, i.e., as existing in the mind (*De pot.* 7.6).

Modern Doctrines. The whole philosophy of R. DESCARTES is built upon self-awareness, or reflection. Its basic principle, which alone is found indubitable, is *Cogito ergo sum:* "I think, therefore I am" (*Discourse* 4; *Medit.* 2; *Prin.* 1.7). By thinking he means every event of immediate consciousness within man, such as understanding, willing, imagining, and sensing (*Prin.* 1.9; *Medit.* 2, 3; *Replies* 2 Arg. def. 1; 3.2). Thought is known by the mere fact of thinking; and even when all else is doubted, in the act of doubting the fact of thinking cannot be doubted; and at the same time the thinker is known as existing and as a thinking thing (*res cogitans*), a substance whose whole essence, or nature, is simply to think (*Discourse* 4; *Medit.* 2, 3; *Replies* 2.4; 5.2.4; *Prin.* 1.7). Descartes even refers to the self simply as thought (*cogitatio*), meaning, however, not simply the operation but the thing or nature so operating (*Replies* 3.2; *For Arnauld,* July 29, 1648). There is accordingly much ambiguity in his usage of the word "thought"; and thinking for him is not distinctively intellectual. The self-awareness that attends it, however, is intellectual and spiritual.

J. LOCKE makes more direct mention of reflection as a principle in his philosophy than does Descartes, for he lays down as the exclusive sources of man's knowledge sensation and reflection (*Essay* 2.1.2–4). Reflection is "the perception of the operations of our own mind within us, as it is employed about the ideas it has got," that is, such operations as "perception, thinking, doubting, believing, reasoning, knowing, willing" (*ibid.*) and "remembrance, discerning, reasoning, judging, knowledge, faith, etc." (2.6). Simple ideas of these operations are formed, but these ideas as such seem to play relatively little part in the subsequent explanation of knowledge. And reflection has almost no role in the constitution of the objective content of man's knowledge. On the perception of one's own existence Locke sounds almost exactly like Descartes: "If I doubt of all other things, that very doubt makes me perceive my own existence, and will not suffer me to doubt that. . . . If I know I doubt, I have as certain perception of the existence of the thing doubting, as of that thought which I call 'doubt'. . . . In every act of sensation, reasoning, or thinking, we are conscious to ourselves of our own being" (4.9.3). This self-awareness does not lead Locke, however, to any ample knowledge of the nature of the soul; for man is "in the dark concerning these matters" (2.27.27).

G. W. von LEIBNIZ defines reflection as "an attention to that which is in us" (*New Essays*, Introd. 4) and holds that it is by reflection, or self-consciousness, that the human soul is distinguished from inferior monads (*Monadology* 30; cf. 15, 19, 23, 29). The soul or mind, moreover, contains the whole universe within itself and is a mirror of the whole and an image of God (*Principles of Nature and of Grace* 13–14; *Monad.* 56–57, 60–62). Thus through reflection upon itself and reasoning it knows everything else. Attractive as this doctrine may be, it takes insufficient account of man's experience of the process of knowing and of the effort and steps involved.

Phenomenology and Existentialism. Reflection of a somewhat different sort plays an important role in PHENOMENOLOGY, a philosophy or method of philosophizing that professes to be a radical, unprejudiced, and detailed description of experience or "pure consciousness," particularly as propounded by E. HUSSERL. The data of experience are scrutinized precisely as experience; neither the objects nor the subject are considered in their ontological reality but only as exhibited or manifested: objects are viewed only as objects and the subject just as a center of pure consciousness evoked and conditioned by what it is conscious of. This requires a reflection that is called "transcendental" and is distinguished from "natural" reflection, which includes both immediate consciousness of one's acts of perception, recall, and predication as well as the studied introspection of psychology; this new type

observes and makes explicit the content of these acts of consciousness (*Cartesian Meditations* 1.15; *Ideas* 38, 45, 77–78, 108, 150) from the viewpoint of its formal structure, essence, or "meaning" (*Ideas* 3–5, 129–131). This would make the reflection ontological rather than psychological, except that it is not concerned with the existence, or reality, of the object. And this reflection reveals the transcendental "I," which is not "a human Ego *in* the universal, existentially posited world, but exclusively a subject *for* which this world has being" (*Ideas*, Introd. to Eng. ed.; cf. 33, 46, 49, 50, 80, 92, 115; *Cartes. Med.* 1.11; 4.30–33, 36). The subject is constituted in constituting the object, the world of its own experience. For Husserl himself, phenomenology tended toward idealism, though this does not seem to be a necessary consequence. The faithful acceptance of the data of experience and the careful analysis and description of its contents can prove a solid beginning for philosophy; but its sufficiency for a complete philosophy has been questioned or denied by most of his followers, who have gone on in the various directions of psychology, psychoanalysis, ethical inquiry, and especially existentialism (see M. MERLEAU-PONTY, "What Is Phenomenology?" *Cross Currents* 6 (1956) 59–70).

In EXISTENTIALISM attention is focused not only on human existence but on the experience of this existence. S. A. KIERKEGAARD stresses the SUBJECTIVITY of the existence of the individual, which is known by direct experience but cannot be expressed to another in universalized and systematized thought. Each one not only knows his own existence but must be himself (*Either/Or* 2, 150); but the "immediate" man, immersed in other things and without reflection, cannot do this (*Sickness unto Death* 80–81). Reflection, which is presupposed by consciousness (*Johannes Climacus* 2.1, 151), is needed to bring out distinctness and individuality (*ibid.* 150–53) and also to attain the inwardness of a conscious, ethical, and religious man (*Postscript* 169–224). Existentialist philosophers have tended to place a chasm between subject and object and, in stressing subjective knowledge, to eliminate or minimize essences, thereby abolishing the principle of INTELLIGIBILITY of things. Gabriel Marcel has resisted this tendency. He considers thought as self-transcendence (*Being and Having* 30) and propounds a twofold reflection. Primary reflection is turned toward the objective content of knowledge as independent of the act of thinking in order to inspect and analyze; it could accordingly be classified as ontological. Secondary reflection, directed toward the primary, considers the content precisely as given in the act of experiencing and, without denying the value of primary reflection, recuperates the original unity and reveals the self-transcendence of the self and founds OBJECTIVITY (*Du refus à l'invocation* 34; *Philosophy of Existence* 14).

See Also: INTENTIONALITY; KNOWLEDGE, PROCESS OF; SPECIES, INTENTIONAL.

Bibliography: J. P. RUANE, "Self-Knowledge and the Spirituality of the Soul in St. Thomas," *New Scholasticism* 32 (1958) 425–442. J. D. MCKIAN, "The Metaphysics of Introspection According to St. Thomas," *ibid.* 15 (1941) 89–117. G. P. KLUBERTANZ, "St. Thomas and the Knowledge of the Singular," *ibid.* 26 (1952) 135–166. C. V. PAX, "Philosophical Reflection: Gabriel Marcel," *ibid.* 38 (1964) 159–177. B. ROMEYER, *Saint Thomas et notre connaissance de l'esprit humain* (2d ed. Archives de philosophie 6.2; Paris 1932). J. DE FINANCE, *Cogito carsésien et réflexion thomiste* (*ibid.* 16.2; 1946); "Being and Subjectivity," *Cross Currents* 6 (1956) 163–178. J. WÉBERT, "'Reflexio': Étude sur les opérations réflexives dans la psychologie de Saint Thomas d'Aquin," *Mélanges Mandonnet,* 2 v. (*Bibliothèque Thomiste* 13, 14; 1930) v. 1.

[R. W. SCHMIDT]

REFLEX PRINCIPLES

A general rule intended to provide indirect or reflex certainty about the morality of a contemplated course of conduct when sufficient direct certainty cannot be obtained from an investigation of the problem in itself. We shall consider: (1) the use of reflex principles in general, and (2) some reflex principles in particular.

The Use of Reflex Principles in General. Frequently a person is in doubt as to the morality of an action that he is thinking of performing. Is there a law forbidding it, or is he morally free to perform it? In other words, which should prevail, law or liberty? His first duty, if he wishes to perform the act, is to seek direct certainty as to its morality. This he can do by examining the nature and circumstances of the action, in the light of reason, faith, and the teaching of the Church or by seeking counsel from one more learned than himself. But even when he has made such an investigation, proportionate in its thoroughness to the importance of the problem, he may still remain in doubt. He finds that there are probable reasons in favor of law and probable reasons in favor of liberty. In such a situation he may sometimes change his practical doubt into indirect or reflex certainty in favor of liberty by the use of reflex principles. (For the exceptions to this rule *see* MORALITY, SYSTEMS OF). These are general norms of conduct, applicable to all fields of morality, enabling one to act with "the liberty of the glory of the sons of God" (Rom 8.21), without fear of formal sin, even though the action he performs may be a material sin. The basis of this doctrine is the reasonable conviction that the God of mercy and goodness does not always oblige men to obey a law binding them with any degree of probability however slight. There are different schools of thought among Catholic theologians as to the measure of probability an opinion in favor of liberty must possess before one can render it practically certain by the use of a reflex principle, but all admit the use of reflex principles to solve practical doubts of conscience in favor of liberty when the opinion for liberty possesses some particular degree of probability. (These same principles hold when a person doubts whether he is obliged to perform an act or may omit it.)

Some Reflex Principles in Particular. The best known and most widely used reflex principle is "A doubtful law does not bind" (*Lex dubia non obligat*). This principle is admitted by all theologians, though it is not understood by all in the same sense. The probabilists consider a law doubtful even when the opinion for law is definitely more probable than the opinion for liberty, whereas the probabiliorists and the equiprobabilists believe that in such a case the preponderance of the opinion for law renders it practically certain.

Another reflex principle is "In a doubt the possessor is to be favored" (*In dubio melior est conditio possidentis*). This principle had its origin in matters of justice, when there was a doubt as to ownership. It is reflected in a more popular form in English as "Possession is nine-tenths of the law." It is used especially in equiprobabilism, when the probabilities for liberty and law are approximately equal. When the doubt concerns the existence of the law (whether there is a law, whether this person is bound by law, etc.), equiprobabilists say, liberty is in possession and may be followed; when the doubt concerns the cessation of the law (whether it has been fulfilled, whether it has been dispensed with, etc.), the law is in possession and must be obeyed.

Other reflex principles are "From what commonly occurs a prudent presumption can be drawn" (*Ex communiter contingentibus prudens fit praesumptio*), and "Everything done is presumed to have been rightly done" (*Omne factum praesumiter rite factum*). The former will help a person who regularly repels temptation when he is in doubt as to whether or not he has consented to a particular temptation. The latter will assist one who has made a careful general confession but who now doubts whether he has included a particular sin of the past.

Prümmer says (1:336) that all reflex principles can be reduced to this one: "In a doubt the side having the presumption is to be favored" (*In dubio standum est pro quo stat praesumptio*).

See Also: DOUBT, MORAL; MORALITY, SYSTEMS OF.

Bibliography: D. M. PRÜMMER, *Manuale theologiae moralis,* ed. E. M. MÜNCH (Barcelona 1945–46) 1:332–336. B. H. MERKELBACH, *Summa theologiae moralis,* 3 v. (Paris 1938) 2:85–89. ALPHONSUS LIGUORI, *Theologia moralis,* ed. L. GAUDÉ, 4 v. (Rome

1905–12) 1:40–89. A. TANQUEREY, *Synopsis theologiae moralis et pastoralis,* 3 v. (new ed. Paris 1930–31) 2:419.

[F. J. CONNELL]

REFORMATION, PROTESTANT (IN THE BRITISH ISLES)

The English Reformation was intricately bound up with dynastic politics. It began when HENRY VIII (1491–1547), unable to secure a male heir from his 24-year marriage to CATHERINE OF ARAGON, divorced and married Anne Boleyn. Although Henry officially severed ties between the English Church and Rome, the Reformation in England is generally seen as having been completed by Henry's daughter ELIZABETH I (1533–1603). By 1590, Elizabeth had secured England's place within the ranks of Protestant countries and the majority of English men and women were united in their opposition to the re-establishment of Catholicism. The English Reformation had become a fact that was to affect the modern history of Great Britain, Europe, and the West.

The 16th century was a time of quickening change in Europe and the Channel did not keep the effects of these transformations from England. The 95 theses on indulgences, while intended by Martin LUTHER as a routine challenge to formal scholastic debate, were elaborated into a declaration of independence, and neither the Christian Church nor Christendom itself was ever the same again. At the moment when the religious revolution began, other changes already had announced the birth of the modern world. Gunpowder altered the methods of warfare and shifted the centers of political power because no longer could the armored man on horseback count on automatic military superiority. The use of the printing press had demonstrated by 1517 how swiftly and cheaply information might be disseminated. Renaissance HUMANISM had already produced all over Europe a group of critical and restless intellectuals, and the pendulum of European economic preponderance was swinging for the first time in recorded history away from the Mediterranean to the Atlantic seaboard, as Portuguese sailors opened cheaper and safer trade routes to the Orient and Spanish adventurers ransacked the wealth of the newly found continents.

Economic and Political Change in England. The medieval alliance in English economic and political life between static rural feudalism and the protectionist guild-directed towns was fast disappearing. The possibilities of commerce, particularly in wool production, and of small industry, which could escape the restrictions of the local guilds, led to a new partnership between enterprising landlords and provincial business men or London merchants who could provide domestic and foreign markets. In the new economy some vast fortunes were accumulated at the cost of considerable social dislocation. In a land where nine of ten inhabitants were directly engaged in farming, much unrest arose from the practice of enclosure, whereby the landlord fenced off the village common lands, plowed them, and planted wheat, or converted arable land into sheep pasture. The resultant eviction of tenants led to riots, protests, and even statutes in opposition.

The Englishman of Luther's generation witnessed political alterations no less dramatic. The kings of England had enjoyed during the Middle Ages a much greater control over their feudal realms than sovereigns on the Continent, yet in Tudor times, when an absolute monarch could be found in every European capital, it was ironic that whoever wore the crown in Westminster had to remember that the king of England, though below no man, was below the law. Nevertheless, with the Tudors (1485–1603), the English monarchy attained a power and prestige seldom known before and certainly never known since. This achievement was the triumph of Henry VII (reigned 1485–1509), shrewd, grasping, and meticulous, who brought peace and stability to a kingdom harassed for more than a century by foreign and civil wars and general distress; of his son, Henry VIII (reigned 1509–47), who concealed behind a soft, self-indulgent exterior a will of iron and not a small talent for the workings of government; and of his granddaughter, Elizabeth I (reigned 1558–1603), perhaps the most skillful woman politician in the history of the West.

The Tudors, however, were never able to employ fully those absolutist principles of sovereignty contained in the Roman law and so commonly accepted on the Continent. Though they secured an important advantage in that at Henry VII's accession in 1485 large numbers of feudal barons had been killed or discredited by the aristocratic Wars of the Roses, and though they were ingenious in asserting financial independence, still ultimately all had to turn to Parliament for money, usually receiving less than demanded. In the final analysis the Tudor monarchs were allowed more political power because instead of disregarding cherished English institutions, they learned to manipulate them with unmatched skill. The willingness of 16th-century Englishmen to follow their rulers proved the deciding factor when the religious crisis arose. Because it was precipitated not by a theologian but by a ruler, it took a radically different direction from its counterpart on the Continent. Questions of doctrine, matters of primary importance to Luther and Calvin, were secondary in England to personal and political considerations. Henry VIII remained convinced that the sacramental system was the normal efficacious means of salvation for the Christian, and therefore rejected the Continental Reformers' fundamental tenet. Elizabeth, more inclined than her father to treat religion as an abstraction, would probably have kept the Mass in England had she judged it politically advantageous.

Englishmen, however, were not uninterested in the theological controversies raging round them. Not long after 1517, small but intense groups of genuine English Lutherans began to appear in London and environs. Devotees of the new doctrinal views surrounded the Tudors, and during the reign of the child king, Edward VI (reigned 1547–53), were effective in creating a truly Protestant England. But the real architects of the religious change, Henry and Elizabeth, were professionally concerned with politics and economics. In England, therefore, the order of events was rather the reverse of that on the Continent. Henry VIII's primary objective was control over the judicial machinery and the financial resources of the Church, not deviation from traditional doctrine.

Provision of Benefices. The polity of the English Church had few of the features of centralization familiar today. Its finances appeared inextricably bound to the medieval system of land tenure, at a time when that system was being transformed by commercial and monetary revolution. Increasingly, churchmen, like their lay contemporaries, tended to think of their ''income'' no longer in terms of bushels of wheat, but in terms of money payments. Ancient feudal practice conflicted with newer ideas about financial and constitutional organization, especially in the key issue of appointment of ecclesiastical personnel. Attached to every diocese, parish, or monastic community was a source of income to support the cleric in the performance of his religious functions. Though the bishop possessed sole right to confer sacramental power on a priest, he did not have an unrestricted right to place him in a parish of his diocese. The parish, and no less the diocese and monastery, was an economic as well as a spiritual entity, whose revenue came for the most part from the land.

Hence, besides the ecclesiastical superior, the nobleman whose ancestor had originally endowed the parish with a parcel of land also controlled clerical appointments. Between himself and every priest who enjoyed a living on his land existed a feudal contract to be renewed each time the benefice fell vacant. The nobleman was no less interested in the appointment to the parish when, as the economy changed, its endowment brought cash rents instead of baskets of produce. The protection of that nobleman's rights prompted the legislation that ultimately made possible the kind of reformation Henry VIII brought to England. The 14th-century Statutes of PROVI-

SORS and PRAEMUNIRE checked in England the papacy's attempt to gain more direct control over the appointment to benefices. They made it a crime to invoke papal aid in securing a benefice contrary, to the wishes of the local patron, and defined the king's court as the final legal arbiter in cases involving ecclesiastical appointments. These laws, which, to a large degree, delivered the machinery of the Church into the hands of the king, did not deny the pope's theoretical control over any ecclesiastic anywhere. They simply maintained the feudal principle that centralization was a corruption. Feudal lawmakers could hardly feel otherwise, since the whole structure of their economic and political life was built upon the supremacy of the locality.

Pope and King. The pope's position was equally defensible. Landed patrons disregarded the spiritual qualifications of candidates to benefices, and as a result Christian communities were afflicted with unworthy and uneducated clerics. The nobles retorted that those priests who appeared with a papal license to a benefice were not noticeably better than those who sought the approbation of the landed patron, and that the papacy was really engaged in a money-making venture, since the papal court charged a fee for every petition it satisfied with a benefice. The Statutes of Provisors and Praemunire, in the tradition of MAGNA CARTA, regarded the king as the first feudal baron of the realm. But the English Lords and Commons, particularly after 1485, found that the laws they had passed were rarely enforced, because the king found it more to his advantage to use them as a threat. Clerics continued to secure benefices with papal licenses, but none was named to whom the king objected, and only his candidates became bishops. Thus, for more than 100 years before the accession of Henry VIII, the kings of England were blessed with a clergy, and thus a large part of the literate population, completely submissive. They had at the same time the use of a free civil service, for a clergyman who served the crown could be easily rewarded with a benefice. The popes, on their side, received theoretical recognition of their prerogatives and some concrete financial considerations as well. This latter was attractive to the Renaissance popes with their luxurious tastes and expensive political ambitions.

The Dynastic Marriage. Royal personages ruled by reason of their blood, and one of their favorite tools of diplomacy was marriage. No treaty could be sealed, no war concluded, without such alliances. No prince dreamed of choosing a mate for himself, and often he was betrothed before he had reached the age of reason. Thus it was agreed as early as 1492 that six-year-old Arthur, Prince of Wales (1486–1502) and heir to Henry VII, should wed seven-year-old Catherine (1485–1536), fourth daughter of Ferdinand and Isabella. Nine years later, November 14, 1501, the ceremony was performed at St. Paul's, London, to the delight of King and people. Four months afterward Prince Arthur died. The Spanish-English diplomatic connection, to which the marriage had given expression, still appeared mutually beneficial, and so negotiations were opened between the two courts with a view toward new nuptials between the widowed Princess and her brother-in-law, Henry, now heir presumptive to the English throne. A serious obstacle, however, stood in the way of the proposed union. Catherine and Henry were related to one another by AFFINITY in the first degree, because Catherine had been the wife of Henry's deceased brother. The Church's law on this point was severe, and it was almost unheard of that two Catholics so related would be allowed to marry.

Henry VII and Ferdinand sought a dispensation from this strict law; it was granted in 1503 by Julius II, though six years passed before it was used. Meanwhile, Henry VII followed a devious course, assuring Ferdinand of his constant interest in the Spanish match, and, at the same time, watching for proposals that might be more advantageous politically. The unfortunate Catherine lived on in England, her dreary widowhood made more grim by her father-in-law's miserly restrictions and her father's apparent indifference. At Henry VII's death, the new king immediately announced to his Council his intention to marry Catherine. Any objection based upon affinity was dismissed because of the papal dispensation and Catherine's solemn declaration that her marriage to Arthur had never been consummated. The archbishop of Canterbury witnessed their exchange of vows June 3, 1509, and the coronation followed three weeks later. Henry VIII had just turned 18; his bride was six years older. Most Englishmen were pleased with their vigorous and intelligent young king, the firm alliance with the rising power of Spain against the ancient French enemy, and the new queen whose charm and virtue had already won a devotion from her people that would not be lost even in the days of her deepest troubles.

A Decree of Nullity. Five children were born to the royal couple, only one of whom, the Princess Mary (1516–58), survived infancy. Such domestic tragedy for the head of a ruling family such as the Tudors, who had come to power by conquest only a generation before, presented concern. The survival of his dynasty weighed heavily upon Henry's mind, but that this serves as adequate explanation for the king's extra-marital liaisons may be doubted. One of his mistresses bore him a son in 1519. Another, Mary Boleyn, closely related to the powerful Duke of Norfolk, was married to one of his gentlemen when Henry was tired of her, a fate that provided a ready example for Mary's younger sister Anne, when her own charm infatuated the king. Anne made it clear that

if she could not be his wife she would not be his mistress. By 1526 the possibility of making her his wife was absorbing almost all of Henry's attention. Divorce, in the sense of the termination of a marriage validly contracted and consummated, did not then or ever figure in the king's calculations. What he sought, and what finally he gave himself, was a declaration of nullity, a definitive legal statement that his marriage to Catherine had never been valid. Could the dispensation of 1503 be successfully challenged? If Julius II could not or should not have given the dispensation, then the degree of affinity between Henry and Catherine still existed and rendered true Christian matrimony impossible in their case.

Wolsey's Failure. Early in 1527 the king placed his "great matter" in the charge of Cardinal Thomas WOLSEY, Archbishop of York, Lord Chancellor, and papal legate. Wolsey could stand as the archetype of self-seeking churchmen of Renaissance Christendom. As legate Wolsey acted almost independently of Rome, thus providing for his sovereign a useful and ominous precedent. Because Wolsey did not know, at first, that Henry intended Anne Boleyn to be queen, the King's desire for an annulment was not unwelcome. The Tudors, with scanty resources and a small population, could not compete with the continental titans, the Valois of France and the Hapsburgs of Spain and Austria. But an English policy of shifting alliances might give England a position more significant than her means alone could have won. This policy Henry and Wolsey had adopted, though in their hands it had enjoyed a singular lack of success. Now, when Wolsey was in the midst of negotiating a new treaty with the French, the diplomatic possibilities of a marriage between his master, free of Catherine, and a French princess struck him immediately. Two things, however, he did not know: first, that he had once again chosen the losing side in the Continental struggle, for the French cause lay prostrate almost everywhere in Europe; and second, that Henry meant to have Anne Boleyn and his own way, over all obstacles.

From 1527 to 1529 Wolsey exerted pressure on Clement VII, even when he learned that Henry's passion for Anne ruled out a French marriage. He saw now that his career, perhaps his life, depended upon the success of the suit, which had a certain prima facie strength. The dispensation of 1503 was unusual. Henry had given diplomatic support to the papacy, and he could hope, as Defender of the Faith (a title won from Rome in recognition of his book against Luther, *Assertio septem sacramentorum* in 1521), that he would receive a friendly hearing; Julius II had granted the dispensation on the grounds, among others, that certain international advantages would accompany the marriage. If the phrases of this grant were rhetorical only, then the dispensation was invalid and the marriage, too. He could argue further that Julius, though Vicar of Christ, had no power to permit a man to marry his brother's widow in the face of Scripture. But Wolsey knew how unsound this position was, with one ambiguous Old Testament passage (Lv 20.2) easily balanced by another (Dt 25.5).

Soon after negotiations opened, Clement was further handicapped by imprisonment. From the fateful sack of Rome on May 6, 1527, until November, he was the captive of Catherine's nephew, Charles V. To envoys from the King he made promises, thus hoping that somehow the trouble would go away. After delays, he named Lorenzo CAMPEGGIO as Wolsey's colleague in the trial proceedings. Campeggio arrived in London in October 1528 with secret instructions to keep the business from solution. In January 1529 Henry threatened schism if Campeggio did not speed the proceedings. The pressure on the Pope mounted as Charles, whose armies controlled Italy, reminded him that he expected his aunt to receive unbiased treatment. Catherine appealed to Clement for a fair trial and weakened her husband's case by producing a brief, signed by Julius II, with none of the technical flaws alleged to have invalidated the dispensation in Henry's possession. In the summer of 1529 Clement could procrastinate no longer and recalled the case to Rome for special hearing. Henry, feeling betrayed by Wolsey's assurance and Clement's promises, avenged himself upon his minister. Wolsey was dismissed in 1529, banished in disgrace to his diocese, in which he had never resided, and died November 30, 1530.

Royal Supremacy. The king charged that Wolsey had broken the Statute of Praemunire by exercising in England a foreign jurisdiction, namely, that of papal legate. Henry confronted the Parliament in November 1529. Through his new Lord Chancellor, Sir Thomas MORE, significantly a layman, he requested suitable legislation against the abuses of the clergy. During the next month the members of Parliament passed several acts aimed at clerical practices that had nettled them and their ancestors for generations: arbitrary fees set by bishops for probate of wills; nonresidence, pluralism, and secular business engaged in by clerics; and the mortuary rights exercised against deceased parishioners. The king was not a step closer to his goal, but the anticlerical spirit of this Reformation Parliament placed in his hand an indispensable tool. Since the legal authority claimed by the Church had blocked his way, he would absorb it into the authority of the state. He would become "under God, the Supreme Head" of the Church in England.

To overturn with legality loyalties and procedures 1,000 years old, he needed the support of his high court of Parliament. As a prelude to the new legislation, Henry,

by threatening to invoke the penalties of Praemunire, extracted from the clergy, with scarcely a demur, a formal submission on May 16, 1532. This surrender was later confirmed by statute in a series of parliamentary acts that reached flood tide in the two sessions of 1534, when it became the law of the realm that no longer was it heresy to deny the pope's divinely instituted supremacy, that the pope had no more rights than any other foreign bishop with regard to ecclesiastical appointments and dispensations, that the king was the Supreme Head of the English Church, and that to deny this was treason. Finally, in the Succession Acts, it was defined that the marriage between Catherine and Henry, or any like it, was against God's law, "any foreign dispensations notwithstanding," and that the marriage between Anne and Henry was "undoubtful, true, sincere, and perfect." It was further decreed that every adult should swear an oath in support of the contents of these Acts, with stern penalties for those who refused. For Anne Boleyn was now Queen Anne, after her secret marriage to the king in January 1533, and her coronation on June 1 by Thomas CRANMER, Henry's new archbishop of Canterbury.

Catherine, now styled Dowager Princess of Wales, had been banished to a rural exile. On March 23, 1534, Clement VII, as a last exercise in futility and anticlimax, decreed that Catherine was indeed Henry's true wife and ordered her restoration as queen.

The Supression of the Traditional Church. Henry VIII accomplished his seizure of the Church's administration with remarkably little resistance, but not without some bloodshed. The servant girl Elizabeth BARTON, the "Nun of Kent," was executed on April 20, 1534, for preaching against the divorce; the priors of the Charterhouses of London, Beauvale, and Axholme, John HOUGHTON, Robert LAWRENCE, and Augustine WEBSTER, together with the Brigitine Richard REYNOLDS and the pastor of Islesworth, John Haile, were tortured to death on May 4, 1535; John FISHER, Bishop of Rochester, and Thomas More, after dubious trials, suffered martyrdom on June 22 and July 6, 1535, respectively (*see* ENGLAND, SCOTLAND, AND WALES, MARTYRS OF). But the nation as a whole, whether it approved or not, remained quiet. The King's lieutenant was Thomas CROMWELL, a man of keen intelligence and without a trace of scruple. Under his direction the crown explored the possibilities of exploiting the Church. Taxes and fees, once paid to the Roman court, now poured into the royal coffers. The monasteries were suppressed, first the small ones (1536) and then the large (1539), 800 houses in all. Their lands, plate, and other valuables were confiscated, thus setting in motion a massive redistribution of wealth. In October 1536, Robert Aske, a London lawyer, led an insurrection in protest. Calling it the PILGRIMAGE OF GRACE, he marched on

York, drove out the King's tenants, and returned expelled nuns and monks to their houses. The pilgrims grew to 35,000, but after Aske's execution on July 12, 1537, they were scattered by forces of the Duke of NORFOLK.

Edward VI. On Henry's death, Jan. 28, 1547, the kingdom passed from his firm hand into that of a child of ten years. Under the reign of the sickly boy, Edward VI, son of Henry's third wife, Jane Seymour, continental Protestantism was able to take hold. During the lifetime of Henry, justification by faith alone and the consequent rejection of the sacramental system stood no chance. His Six Articles Act of June 1539 prescribed hanging or burning for those who denied transubstantiation, Communion under one species, the value of Masses for souls in purgatory, auricular confession, clerical celibacy, or the binding force of solemn vows of chastity. During Edward's reign of six years, however, Protestant divines became influential.

In the summer of 1547 the government placed in the hands of the clergy the *First Book of Homilies,* much of it composed by Cranmer himself, in which the fundamental Protestant doctrines were thoroughly explained. These dogmatic lessons were to be read as instruction from the pulpit on Sunday. The next spring *The Order of Communion* appeared, an English adaptation of the Lutheran Communion rite that, as the directives stated, was to be added to the Mass on Communion days. It provided for the reception of Communion under both species, and explicitly dispensed communicants from the prior need of the Sacrament of Penance. Then, on January 21, 1549, Parliament gave its blessing to the most revolutionary venture so far, *The BOOK OF COMMON PRAYER.* It replaced the Missal, the Breviary, and all the rest of the old Church's liturgical books. Written in singularly graceful language, it furnished a service of great linguistic beauty and manageable length.

The introduction of the Prayer Book on Pentecost Sunday 1549 provoked riots. But they were put down, and Somerset, blamed for the crisis, was replaced in power by John Dudley, Earl of Warwick (1502?-53). In 1552 Cranmer, with the approval of Dudley, now Duke of Northumberland, produced a revision of the Prayer Book, a catechism for children, and in the next year a formal statement of belief, *The Forty-Two Articles of Religion.* Edited by Cranmer and the Bishop of London, Nicholas RIDLEY, the articles were to be accepted under threat of severe penalties and were so radically Protestant that an orthodox Lutheran would have rejected much of what they contained. Edward VI died July 6, 1553, and his eldest sister, Mary, daughter of Catherine of Aragon, became the new monarch.

Marian Restoration. The possibility of the accession of Catholic MARY TUDOR led to an attempted *coup d'etat.* Northumberland, Cranmer, and Ridley succeeded in persuading the Council to declare Lady Jane Grey, Mary's 16-year-old cousin, queen; but their rebellion, lacking public support, collapsed in a few days. Mary Tudor, now queen at 37, had known little but distress since the day, more than 25 years before, that her father had repudiated her mother and had declared Mary herself illegitimate. Now, as queen, she could find few in England whom she could trust. The Council, the bench of bishops, the lay lords had all been involved in one way or another in the assault upon her religion and herself. Her choice of a chancellor, the gifted Stephen Gardiner, Bishop of Winchester, was a good one; but Mary knew that Gardiner, though no Protestant in the continental sense, had accepted the Royal Supremacy, and had been an active agent of Henry VIII in the divorce. She turned for guidance to the members of her mother's family, the Hapsburg Emperor Charles V and his son, Philip of Spain, despite their single-minded dynastic interests. On July 25, 1554, a marriage was celebrated between Mary and Philip, 11 years her junior, that proved disastrous for the Queen and the nation. Philip cared little for her and after his father's abdication in October 1555 turned his attention completely to continental politics. Though Philip and his entourage were intensely unpopular in England, Mary loyally supported her husband's anti-French policy and declared war upon France in 1557. In spite of allied successes, the French captured Calais in January 1558. The loss of this Channel port, which had been in English hands for two centuries and which recalled the glorious days of the Black Prince and Henry V, was a blow to English pride from which the Queen never recovered. Against this background of disappointment and failure, Mary worked to undo the religious reformation of her father and brother. By the end of 1554 the religious statutes of the previous 20 years had been repealed. Pope Julius III commissioned Cardinal Reginald POLE (1500–58) legate to England with sweeping powers to restore the Catholic religion. A kinsman of Mary and once her father's intimate, Pole had exiled himself from his homeland at the time of the divorce. He came to his new task with the reputation of an ascetic, scholar, and diplomat. He had been lately legate to the Council of TRENT. But because he was known to oppose the Spanish marriage, Charles V placed every obstacle in his path. Pole did not reach England or assume his duties as legate and archbishop of Canterbury until October 1554. Even after his arrival the work of restoration proceeded with tragic slowness. The chief complication was the new pope, the erratic and bitterly anti-Spanish PAUL IV, who imagined that Pole, since he served a queen wedded to a Spanish husband and Spanish policy, might well be a heretic. He canceled Pole's legatine commission and summoned him back to Rome in April 1557. Though Pole managed to evade the order, much of his effectiveness disappeared.

Ineffective though Pole might have been, the Marian regime is remembered chiefly not for that but for the persecutions. Between February 1555 and November 1558, 273 men and women were burned to death for heresy. This total included the five bishops: Thomas Cranmer, Hugh Latimer, Nicholas Ridley, Robert Ferrar, and John Hooper; 16 other clergymen; and a handful of gentlemen. But for the most part the victims were peasants and artisans. Most suffered in London and the southern counties-nearby under statutes passed 150 years before. The law directed that once it had been determined by a bishop's court that an individual held unorthodox beliefs and refused to abjure them, an officer of the crown should "receive" him and "before the people in a high place cause him to be burned, that such punishment may strike fear into the minds of others . . . ." That Queen Mary burned heretics did not shock her contemporaries. Those who condemned her did so because, in their judgment, she burned the wrong people, the very elect of God. Society in those days, as surely in Calvin's Geneva as in Mary's London, considered nobody so dangerous to the commonweal as the heretic. It was also taken for granted that no heretic held his views in good faith, and that he was, therefore, a willful criminal. Add to these social convictions a penal code harsh beyond modern imagination—in England, capital punishment was inflicted for a list of felonies running to several hundred—and a necessary backdrop is drawn behind the infamous "Fires of Smithfield."

Nevertheless, Mary's persecution evidenced elements of unusual horror and futility, unmatched in intensity by anything heretofore in English history. Furthermore, those who suffered belonged largely to a social class that could do Mary or the work of Catholic restoration little harm. The wealthy mostly fled abroad, with little government interference, free to intrigue and to await a fairer day. Finally, general religious sentiment was profoundly damaged by the cynicism of the officers who enforced the statutes. Heresy laws had been framed for the protection of the Catholic community threatened by a hostile minority. But the whole English nation had formally abandoned the Catholic faith 20 years before the first Protestant martyr suffered in 1555. The police who ferreted him out, the bishop who determined the heterodoxy of his views, the sheriff who bound him to the stake had all accepted at least some of the things for which their victim was burned. Farmers and shopkeepers went to their deaths because they had believed what their clergy and lawmakers had been telling them for two decades about the pope and the Mass. In the persecution that brought her unhappy fame Mary demonstrated a typical Tudor ruthlessness and a curiously un-Tudor fanaticism, but at least the charges of hypocrisy and opportunism must be laid at other doors.

Elizabeth I. Mary died on Nov. 17, 1558, and was succeeded by her half-sister, Elizabeth. With each change of government, Elizabeth had had to shift her theological alliances, and during Mary's reign she outwardly practiced Catholicism. For some weeks, therefore, it remained unclear what course she would follow in ecclesiastical affairs. By Christmas, however, all doubts were dispelled, and the Parliament that convened a month later was presented with a government program calling for the reestablishment of Henry's and Edward's religious legislation and the repeal of Mary's. After four months of maneuver the Elizabethan Acts of Supremacy and Uniformity, which once more made the English sovereign a kind of local pope and imposed upon the nation a Protestant form of worship, received the royal assent (May 8, 1559). Resistance to it came immediately from two sides and continued. The Catholics who fought the losing battle in the Parliament of 1559 proved to be more resolute than their ancestors of a generation before. All the bishops and many of the lower clergy now refused to follow the direction of the government. Elizabeth deprived them of their offices and replaced them with men more pliable. Catholic laity who refused to attend the Protestant services she fined and restricted with increasing severity as the years passed. But she made traitors of them, not martyrs as Mary would have done in like circumstances. Not that Elizabeth hesitated to shed blood, and in great quantity, wherever her religious policy went unaccepted; for example, in 1569, after the failure of the Rising of the North, a mismanaged and half-armed protest against the heretical policies of the government, no less than 800 men were executed for their part in a "rebellion" whose military operations had produced five fatalities.

This and similar savage reprisals persuaded most Englishmen of Elizabeth's generation that conformity was necessary for survival. As they attended the Protestant service on Sunday, Catholics could soothe their consciences with the thought that what had been taken away had once been restored and might be restored again. Their sons, however, who did not remember the marching and countermarching between 1534 and 1559, were much more prepared to accept the government's story that acceptance of the settlement was both a religious and a patriotic duty and that it represented no fundamental change in England's traditional faith. But this myth seemed threatened during the later years of the reign by the post-Tridentine Catholic revival, reflected in England by the work of the secular and Jesuit missionary priests. Excommunicated by PIUS V in 1570 through the bull *Regnans*

Excelsis, Elizabeth reacted, especially after 1577, with a brutal determination that sent 183 Catholics to their deaths and many more to torture, mutilation, and exile.

The second source of opposition came from the more radical Protestants, soon to be lumped together under the name PURITANS. They quickly discovered that Elizabeth was not prepared to go nearly so far as they wanted in the task of cleansing the English church of papistry. They disliked her retention of the episcopal structure and sternly disapproved of the continued liturgical use of vestments and ceremonial, all of which, they said, was but an aspect of the pomp and display of the Roman Antichrist. They also had serious misgivings, as did their continental mentors, about the Queen's defined position in the church, "Supreme Governor of this realm . . . as well in all spiritual . . . causes as temporal." The bitter lesson they had to learn in the years after 1559 was that Elizabeth considered the pope not as Antichrist but as a political enemy. She did not share their zeal for the establishment of God's kingdom, as they conceived it, and she abhorred their notions of an evangelical theocracy on the Zurich or Geneva model. It was the political value of her position as head of the English church that Elizabeth prized most highly. To protect this supremacy she used the devoted talents of William Cecil (Lord Burghley, 1520–98), her confidant for 40 years, a ruthless secretary of state who saw that religious unity was a needed prelude to England's movement toward greatness, and Sir Francis Walsingham (1530?-98), an alarmist intriguer who saw spies everywhere and who was largely responsible for bringing about the execution of Mary, Queen of Scots. Conformity Elizabeth demanded, and obedience she insisted upon. However divergent Englishmen's views might be on points of doctrine, they had to conform to the government approved 39 Articles and be content with them. For Elizabeth, as for Henry VIII, reformation of religion in England meant primarily that the State should control the Church.

Bibliography: R. B. MERRIMAN, *Life and Letters of Thomas Cromwell,* 2 v. (Oxford 1902). J. A. MULLER, *Stephen Gardiner and the Tudor Reaction* (New York 1926). K. W. M. PICKTHORN, *Early Tudor Government: Henry VIII* (Cambridge, England 1934). C. H. GARRETT, *The Marian Exiles: A Study in the Origins of Elizabethan Puritanism* (Cambridge, England 1938). G. MATTINGLY, *Catherine of Aragon* (Boston 1941). H. M. SMITH, *Henry VIII and the Reformation* (New York 1962), Anglican view. E. T. DAVIES, *Episcopacy and the Royal Supremacy in the Church of England in the XVI Century* (1950). J. D. MACKIE, *The Earlier Tudors* (New York 1952). J. E. NEALE, *Queen Elizabeth* (New York 1934; repr. 1959); *Elizabeth I and Her Parliaments,* 2 v. (New York 1959). G. R. ELTON, *The Tudor Revolution in Government* (Cambridge, England 1953); *New Cambridge Modern History* (2d ed. London-New York 1957–) 2:226–250. H. F. M. PRESCOTT, *Mary Tudor* (rev. ed. New York 1953). L. B. SMITH, *Tudor Prelates and Politics, 1536–1558* (Princeton 1953). N. SYKES, *The English Religious Tradition* (London 1953). P. HUGHES, *The Reformation in England,* 3 v. in 1 (5th, rev. ed. New York 1963), most reliable history of the English Reformation. S. C. CARPENTER, *The Church in England, 1597–1688* (London 1954). C. READ, *Mr. Secretary Cecil and Queen Elizabeth* (New York 1955); ed., *Bibliography of British History: Tudor Period, 1485–1603* (2d ed. New York 1959); *Lord Burghley and Queen Elizabeth* (New York 1960). H. C. PORTER, *Reformation and Reaction in Tudor Cambridge* (Cambridge, Eng. 1958). D. KNOWLES, *The Religious Orders in England,* 3 v. (Cambridge, England 1948–60) v.3, best reference for the religious orders. M. D. R. LEYS, *Catholics in England, 1559–1829: A Social History* (London 1961). W. R. TRIMBLE, *The Catholic Laity in Elizabethan England, 1558–1603* (Cambridge, MA 1964). G. BARRACLOUGH, *Papal Provisions* (Oxford 1935). L. PASTOR, *The History of the Popes from the Close of the Middle Ages,* 40 v. (London-St. Louis 1938–61) v.9–15. E. G. RUPP, *Studies in the Making of the English Protestant Tradition* (Cambridge 1947). A. H. THOMPSON, *The English Clergy* (Oxford 1947). A. G. DICKENS, *The English Reformation* (New York 1964). W. A. CLEBSCH, *England's Earliest Protestants, 1520–35* (New Haven 1964). P. COLLINSON, *The Religion of Protestants* (Oxford 1982). C. HAIGH, *The English Reformation Revised* (Cambridge 1987). R. O'DAY, *The Debate on the English Reformation* (New York 1986). J. J. SCARISBRICK, *The Reformation and the English People* (Oxford 1984).

[M. R. O'CONNELL]

REFORMATION, PROTESTANT (ON THE CONTINENT)

The term reformation as a restoration of an original form or norm was in common use throughout the Middle Ages. Renovation, restitution, regeneration, rebirth (RENAISSANCE), and many other expressions described the same general concept. The call for reform of the Church became more insistent in the late-medieval period. In part, the popularity of apocalyptic views of history from the twelfth century onward helped fuel the sense of urgency about reform at this time. Prophetic movements promoted the notion that the Church was experiencing a constantly worsening decline and deterioration from its early Christian state. Rising expectations, deepening piety, and the perennial appeal of monastic asceticism also fed the reforming impulse. To understand the onset of the sixteenth-century Reformations, movements more dynamic and transforming than the many medieval reforms that preceded them, we must separate perception from reality. The evidence is scanty to suggest that corruption and abuse were worse in the fourteenth- and fifteenth-century Church than they had been in the twelfth or thirteenth. Throughout Europe there were many places where ecclesiastical functions were efficiently executed and where clerical discipline was widely respected. Yet the Western Church was vulnerable to criticism on a variety of fronts because it was an enormous, international institution that performed cure of souls, but also fulfilled important social, economic, and political functions. To many, these worldly aims seemed in conflict with the institution's religious and sacramental mission.

While the idea of reform was common in Europe around 1500, Martin Luther and the other early evangelical reformers rarely used the term "reformation" to describe the movement they initiated. These early sixteenth-century reformers desired a restoration of the primitive Christian Gospel, which in their view, had been obscured through centuries of human innovation. Luther's view often discounted the human ability to effect change in the Church, and instead insisted that it was the Word of God that would accomplish reform in God's own time. Luther's reserve in adopting the term "reformation" to describe the evangelical movement may help to explain why the word Reformation was not used to describe his work until a century and a half following his death. [see V. L. Von Seckendorf, *Commentarius historicus et apologetic de Lutheranismo seu de reformatione* (1688–92)]. In the eighteenth century the term was extended to describe the reform movements that followed the work of John Calvin, and from the nineteenth century onward, the word "Reformation" has commonly been used to designate the rise and growth of Protestantism in the sixteenth century.

Causes of the Reformation

The roots of the Continental Reformation are primarily religious and reach back into the later Middle Ages. Several features of the doctrines of WYCLIF, HUS, the WALDENSES and unorthodox fifteenth-century theologians anticipated the later attacks of Luther and other early Protestant reformers. These included criticisms of transubstantiation, priestly status, the wealth and political power of the Church, and the corruption of biblical teaching. No direct lineage existed, however, between these figures and the later reformers. Instead the early evangelicalism of Luther, Zwingli, and others was the result of their search for religious truths that occurred within an orthodox context.

Philosophical Climate. The scholasticism of the later Middle Ages, particularly in its Ockhamist and nominalist forms, was incisive in the development of Protestant theology (*see* NOMINALISM). The *via moderna,* as late scholasticism was called, contrasted with the *via antiqua* of St. Thomas Aquinas. The reformers accepted some of the new philosophical and theological presuppositions of the nominalists, while disregarding others. The nominalist school denied the validity of universals, insisting instead that theological concepts were mere names created to describe certain ideas and things revealed in the Word of God. Most nominalists drew a sharp distinction between God's absolute power, the *potentia absoluta,* and the ordering power, the *potentia ordinata,* He had displayed in Creation and revelation. By virtue of his "absolute power," God could have created the world in an infinite number of ways, but His Word revealed the covenant He had established with humankind. The duty of the theologian, according to the nominalists, was not to deploy reason to understand God's absolute power, but to illuminate the nature of these promises.

Through his education at the University of Erfurt, a center of the *via moderna,* Martin Luther came in contact with these nominalist teachings. Although he would eventually come to distance himself from Ockham and nominalism in the years after 1515, the school's emphasis on the limits of human reason and on a covenantal theology left a residue in his work, as it did in other sixteenth-century reformers.

Role of Scripture. There is no doubt of the beginning of a Biblical revival in the later Middle Ages. The scriptures were widely available to scholars in the Vulgate and in a good number of vernacular translations. Further, a movement toward the study of the Scriptures in their original languages can be discerned among the humanists and theologians of the later fifteenth century. This return to the sources could produce controversy, as in the famous Reuchlin Affair that began in 1506 when the humanist Johannes REUCHLIN (1455–1522), author of a Hebrew grammar, attacked the converted Jew Johannes PFEFFERKORN for his attempts to destroy Jewish manuscripts he considered dangerous to Christians. Reuchlin's persecution by members of Germany's Dominicans resulted in the championing of his cause by humanists from throughout Europe and did nothing to retard the deepening study of the Bible in its original tongues. It did produce ill feelings, though, that persisted even as the Reformation began. In 1516 ERASMUS published a Greek version of the New Testament, and a subsequent corrected version of the Vulgate. Although Erasmus's Greek edition may not have been of the same caliber as that contained in the *Complutensian Polyglot* (1502), edited by Cardinal Francisco XIMENES DE CISNEROS, his commentary emphasized the popular concept of the "philosophy of Christ" and downplayed medieval sacramental theology. His undermining of the scriptural foundations for the sacrament of penance, in particular, would win admirers among early evangelical reformers.

State of Religion among the Laity. The requirements for participation in the late-medieval Church had largely been drawn by the Fourth Lateran Council (1215) and included among their hallmarks annual attendance at the sacraments of penance and the Eucharist. The evidence suggests that in most parts of Europe lay attendance did not exceed the yearly duties of Lent and Easter, the one commonly shared way in which most people came into contact with the Church. Baptism and confirmation were also important events in the life of all Europeans, since they functioned as religious events, but also as important rites of passage that marked off various life stages. Differences of emphasis in religious life have long been identified between the countryside, where the vast majority of the population lived, and Europe's burgeoning cities. Preaching in the towns and the ministration of the friars meant that city dwellers were probably more effectively indoctrinated in "official" Church teaching than were country people. Urban confraternities, too, provided a way for the laity to practice some of the offices and devotions normally undertaken only by the clergy. In the countryside priests were nevertheless vital members of the village community who were called upon to deliver benedictions, perform exorcisms, lead rogations and other rites that aimed to insure communal life. It is a mistake, though, to draw the distinction between town and country as one of a dichotomy between a ritualistic and superstitious rural religion, and a doctrinal and sacramental urban one. Superstition was common to both spheres. In Europe's towns, moreover, mortality was always high, and in each generation immigrants from the surrounding countryside renewed the population. The religious practices noted in the countryside, with their emphasis on perpetuating and insuring the community, also pervaded Europe's cities.

Other distinctions have been observed between elites and people in the religious life of the later Middle Ages. Again, these differences should not viewed as hard and fast, since the late-medieval Church held out a variety of ways in which those without means could deepen their devotion. Still, the endowing of anniversary masses, the establishment of religious houses, enrollment in confraternities, the praying of the hours, and the amassing of indulgences—all important signs of late-medieval devotion—could generally only be practiced by those who possessed sufficient financial resources and leisure. The dichotomy between elites and people begins to break down when we realize that many nobles, patricians, and merchants—those possessed of the amenities of time and money—often evidenced little interest in these religious practices.

Scholars have long debated the precise character of late-medieval lay piety and its relationship to the subsequent Reformation. Some have argued that the institutional hierarchy of the Church ignored the needs of Europe's laity, and as a result a low level of knowledge and devotion existed among Europeans at the close of the Middle Ages. In this way the Reformation, and the later Catholic response, the Counter Reformation, have been interpreted as events that accomplished a final, effective "Christianization" of Europe. Others have judged the late-medieval Church to be too intrusive and demanding, an institution that fostered a vigorous, but ultimately un-

satisfying piety. Such generalizations prove perilous for several reasons. They evaluate late-medieval religion against the subsequent Reformation. During the sixteenth century Protestant Reformers relied on propaganda and polemic to attack the Church and in the process, they sometimes obscured the character of late-medieval religion. The documentary evidence suggests that many fifteenth-century Europeans found adequate spiritual sustenance within the Church, while others were indifferent to it. For some, like Luther, the Church's teachings produced doubt and anxiety, even as for others, they were a source of consolation. The Church was, in other words, too large and diverse an institution to allow for such generalizations.

Clerical Abuse and Corruption. *The papacy.* On the eve of the Reformation abuse and corruption continued to exist within the Church, as it had for centuries. From 1309 to 1378 the papacy had resided in voluntary exile in the French city of Avignon, followed by a 40-year schism in which first two, then three, popes had simultaneously demanded the allegiance of Catholic Christendom. In the century between 1417 and 1517 the papacy also become involved in numerous dynastic intrigues, both in Italy and throughout Europe.

The AVIGNON PAPACY, the period that subsequently was dubbed the "Babylonian Captivity," has long been synonymous with a growing worldliness within the papal court. The Avignon popes, though French, did not capitulate to the French monarchy, but by reason of their residence at Avignon (a fief of Naples which since 1228 had acknowledged the papacy as overlord) they were able to maintain feudal independence. The personal lives of the Avignon popes were not scandalous except for nepotism and they did attempt reform. The most significant development of the period was the great increase in the machinery of papal government, that is in the pope's Curia, and the equally large increment in papal taxation, which touched the entire Church and caused irritation. The sums collected helped to sustain the temporal power of the papacy.

The Great Schism (1378–1417) damaged the prestige of the Church hierarchy when it presented the spectacle of rival popes mutually excommunicating each other and their adherents (*see* WESTERN SCHISM). Eventually, the Council of Constance (1414–1418) acted to heal this breach, but the survival of CONCILIARISM within the Church was the result and this movement continued to be a challenge to papal authority. The most extreme supporters of conciliar theory advocated the establishment of a permanent Church council at Rome, a move that would have, in effect, made the pope a constitutional monarch.

Despite such problems the papacy revived by the second half of the fifteenth century, and its prestige and authority were generally well respected by 1500. If the papal court was a worldly place, filled with pomp and luxury and tolerant of sexual immorality, most Western Christians knew little about these things. The pope, it is also true, was an important Italian prince, who warred and intrigued against other princes and powers in the peninsula. But for most Renaissance Europeans, it seemed natural that the papacy must enjoy its share of political power so that the Church might be safeguarded from the challenges of secular kings and princes.

Ecclesiastical hierarchy. It is not easy to generalize about the conditions of the episcopate on the eve of the Reformation. Saintly, reforming bishops existed alongside corrupt and worldly ones. In many places in Western Europe, admission to a cathedral chapter, the pool from which most bishops were selected, was restricted to those from verifiable noble lineages. In some places one had to demonstrate, not only the noble births of one's parents, but of grandparents and great-grandparents as well. In other places bishoprics were awarded to those who had served royal interests. In these circumstances the episcopacy's goals were often more aristocratic and worldly than spiritual. The households of bishops and cathedral chapters were also seen as a path to professional advancement by humanists and university-educated clergy. Bishoprics could be looked upon primarily as sources of income, and in the inflationary spiral of the later Middle Ages, it was sometimes necessary for churchmen to acquire several sees to support themselves. The Reformation itself may be said to have begun out of just these circumstances. The precipitating Indulgence Controversy of 1517 arose from the pluralism of ALBRECHT of Brandenburg. Upon his election to the Archbishopric of Mainz, Leo X allowed Albrecht to retain the Sees of Magdeburg and Halberstadt at a tax of 10,000 ducats above the pallium fee of 14,000 ducats for the See of Mainz. To reimburse the Fugger banking house, Leo X allowed him to retain half of the returns from the preaching of St. Peter's indulgence in his territory.

In the Holy Roman Empire and in Italy, in particular, many bishops were also temporal authorities as well. These figures, known as prince bishops, were consequently more often concerned with the political interests of their territories than they were with spiritual matters. Often deputies performed the religious functions of their offices. Since these territories were usually quite small, the machinery of state bureaucracy and defense exacted a heavy burden upon their peasant populations, who bore the lion's share of the cost of financing these states. Between 1475 and 1525 a number of peasant rebellions occurred in the Holy Roman Empire and some were protests against the governments of Germany's prince bishops.

Lower Clergy. Below the episcopal government were the members of the secular clergy, who served as parish priests, vicars, and chantrists. Although great differences existed in the living conditions and educational level of priests, the lower clergy was the clerical proletariat of the Church. Seminaries for the training of the clergy would not be created until the post-Tridentine era, and thus most priests learned their craft by apprenticing themselves to those whom already held clerical offices. Many understood relatively little about Church teachings and some priests were illiterate and had learned the Mass merely by rote. This situation was likely most pronounced among the chantrists, who were paid only to say masses for the dead. Since the GREGORIAN REFORM of the eleventh and twelfth centuries, the Western Church had redoubled its campaign against clerical marriage and clerical concubinage (the keeping of mistresses by priests). By the time of the Reformation the ban against clerical marriage had been generally established throughout Europe. The Church had experienced less success, though, in outlawing clerical concubinage, and it persisted unevenly throughout Europe. In some regions— England, the Netherlands, Northern France—the requirement of clerical celibacy seems to have been generally respected. In more remote and mountainous regions, however, many priests kept concubines. Diocesan governments often dispensed priests from their vows of celibacy through the imposition of an annual concubine tax. This casual attitude toward celibacy was a corruption of the standard set by the Gregorian Reform. But in those places where the custom of keeping concubines was widespread, the laity seems to have accepted the practice as the natural state of affairs, preferring priests who had a helpmate and sexual partner to those who were strictly celibate.

Many members of the lower clergy lived in poverty, the revenues of the benefice they held, if there was any benefice at all, went almost entirely to some person or corporation higher in the ecclesiastical power structure for which they were simply vicars. This numerous class of vicars and chantrists—some churches had many— lived on small benefices in exchange for which they were obliged to say Mass and the Office for particular intentions. Still others were unbeneficed and complaints about the sale of the sacraments from these quarters can be found. Many bishops expressed little interest in this category of the clergy and control was a matter of indifference.

Religious Communities. The same breadth of financial circumstances and religious observances as well as problems of oversight that have been noted among the secular clergy prevailed in religious communities. There were both exemplary and lax communities. In many cases monasteries and convents, having amassed rich endowments in previous centuries, admitted their novices primarily from the nobility, the urban patriciate, or the merchant class. Royal abbeys, and in the German Empire imperial foundations, controlled vast tracts of land and exercised temporal rule over thousands of peasants. In these cases conditions were sometimes similar to the territories of prince bishops. Reports of worldly behavior in monasteries and convents—dancing, gaming, and so forth—were common at the end of the Middle Ages. Still the monastic ideal of a life spent in ascetic self-denial was alive and well, too. Numerous "observant" reform movements developed in fifteenth-century Europe with many following a similar pattern of development. A charismatic founder convinced an existing order to take over a rundown or abandoned monastery that he and his followers then built into a model of strict observance of the order's rule. In time, imitators reformed their houses along similar lines or invited advisers from the initial observant house to reform them. The most successful of these Observant movements occurred among the Augustinians, particularly among the group known as the Windesheim, Congregation, which grew out of the devotional movement known as the Brethren of the Common Life. Founded in 1387 in the Dutch town of Windesheim, the congregation established its control over more than 83 houses. In Germany a similar reform movement also occurred among the Augustinian Eremites, and eventually affected Martin Luther, who was a member of the Eremites' houses at Erfurt and Wittenberg. It has long been debated whether the piety practiced by these Augustinian reform movements, the Modern Devotion (*devotio moderna*), influenced the later Reformation. Members of the Brethren of the Common Life wrote numerous devotional tracts that advocated intense self-examination and a life of prayer and Bible reading. Their writings influenced numerous humanists and later reformers, including Erasmus and Luther. In the main, though, the Modern Devotion was extremely traditional and demonstrates that monastic asceticism continued to have great appeal to those seeking to undertake a vocation at the end of the Middle Ages.

Influence of Humanism. The word HUMANISM, a nineteenth-century term derived from the Latin *studia humanitatis* or "humane studies," was primarily an educational philosophy, rooted in the study of languages, rhetoric, moral philosophy, and history. While no humanist creed or manifesto existed, many of the generation of Northern Renaissance humanists who came to maturity around 1500 advocated the reform of the Church and biblical and patristic study, even as they criticized clerical corruption, scholastic theology, and popular superstition. These attacks were most widely broadcast through the work of the "Prince of Humanists" Erasmus, who, it was

charged in the sixteenth century "laid the egg that Luther hatched." Erasmus, like many other humanists of his generation, would not admit his relationship to the developing Reformation, but a number of his younger disciples were won over to its cause in the 1520s and 1530s. Many of these, including Philipp MELANCHTHON, Ulrich ZWINGLI, Martin BUCER, and John CALVIN, would come to play dynamic roles in the development of Protestantism. Differences of emphasis and theology continued to separate many humanists from evangelicals. While humanism was an elite and learned movement, for instance, Protestantism appealed to a mass audience. Despite these distinctions, it is difficult to imagine the Reformation's success without the preparation that humanism provided in its criticisms of the Church or its turn to focus on the study of the Bible.

German Reformation

The Reformation in Germany began with Luther's campaign against indulgences and would eventually result in the formation of a new evangelical church. Luther was once seen as the great formative personality in the creation of sixteenth-century Protestantism. More recently scholars have come to realize that, while Luther's influence was important, he was only the first and most prominent of a vast number of evangelical reformers active upon the early sixteenth-century scene.

The Development of Luther's Doctrine. Luther had entered the monastery of the Augustinian Eremites at Erfurt in 1505 and passed the next decade of his life wrestling with the central problem of his spiritual life: how he could find a merciful God and achieve assurance of his salvation. During this period his study turned, in particular, to the Epistles of St. Paul, particularly those to the Romans and Galatians. By 1516 Luther had emerged as one of Germany's most brilliant biblical scholars, and now as a professor at the new University in Wittenberg in Saxony, he took on the task of academic reform. During 1516, Luther, a theologian trained in the scholastic traditions of nominalism, began to criticize scholastic theology publicly and to promote a new view of justification. Luther taught that good works did not make a man righteous, but that one who had been made righteous performed good works. While this was a radical departure from late-medieval orthodoxy, Luther's teachings seem to have gone unnoticed, that is, until he criticized the selling of indulgences during the autumn of 1517. As a priest, Luther had learned of the methods that indulgence sellers were using in nearby territories, and on October 31 he wrote Albrecht of Brandenburg, the Archbishop of Mainz, to warn him that if the abuses did not stop, he would be forced to speak out against them. At the same time he prepared the 95 theses, a document intended to become the subject of an academic disputation. It remains an open question as to whether Luther posted these theses on the door of the castle church at Wittenberg, as legend has long suggested. Certainly, he circulated the theses privately, and although he had not intended to have them published, they soon appeared in unsanctioned editions printed in five cities throughout the empire. By the following spring reaction against the theses grew more intense, as Johannes TETZEL, Albrecht of Brandenburg's chief indulgence preacher, and other members of Germany's Dominicans lobbied Rome for Luther's condemnation. Leo X (1475–1521) responded by dispatching Cardinal CAJETAN (1469–1534) who attempted unsuccessfully to secure Luther's recantation. A staged disputation between Luther, Eck, and Karlstadt, held in June 1519, confirmed Luther's opponents and supporters in their positions, even as it extended Luther's notoriety throughout the empire.

Despite his problems with church authorities Luther remained actively engaged in his academic pursuits during 1520, publishing a number of defenses of his positions. Three of these, in particular, were widely circulated, and were to exercise a profound effect on the subsequent evangelical movement. The first, *The Address to the Christian Nobility of the German Nation*, advocated that the German nobility should take on the task of reforming the church in their territories. The second, *The Babylonian Captivity of the Church*, outlined a new theology of the sacraments, arguing that only baptism, communion and perhaps a reformulated penance could be said to have clear scriptural justification. And the third, *The Freedom of a Christian*, defended his teachings on justification, arguing that those who received faith through God's grace were simultaneously justified and sinful, and that their good works were the product, not the cause, of their justification. These treatises were widely circulated in the early 1520s and spread the Reformer's message far beyond Saxony. These works did not present a systematic theology. Luther's close associate, Philipp Melanchthon, undertook the task of ordering Luther's ideas into a definitive statement for the evangelical cause, when in 1521 he published the *Loci Communes*, the Reformation's first systematic theology. By that date, Luther's denial of the infallibility of Church councils and his burning of the papal bull condemning his heresies had led to his formal excommunication, and he was summoned to an imperial diet at Worms to respond. In Worms, Luther still refused to recant and as a result, he was placed under the imperial ban. This ban would continue to plague Luther for the rest of his life since it limited his travel to Saxony and other neighboring friendly states within the empire. The ban thus prevented Luther from taking a direct role in the many discussions that

would aim to heal the breach between evangelicals and Catholics during the coming decades. Luther had been prudent, however, to request a safe conduct to attend the imperial diet, and as he left Worms, he was kidnapped as part of a plan hatched by his protector the Saxon Elector Frederick the Wise. He was spirited away to the Wartburg castle near Eisenach, and there for the next two years he devoted himself primarily to completing a German translation of the Bible.

Diffusion of Evangelical Ideas. The extraordinary events of the years 1517–1521 had transformed a scholastic dispute into an international controversy that resonated far beyond the confines of the academy. At the same time a number of preachers and reformers had appeared who promoted doctrines that were either similar to Luther's or more radical in their implications. This rapid diffusion and multiplication of religious positions made the Reformation difficult to suppress. To the south, Ulrich Zwingli had begun a reform of Zürich's church establishment as early as 1518. By 1522 and 1523, radical reformers like Andreas Karlstadt and Thomas Müntzer came to promote ideas more extreme than either Zwingli's or Luther's. The appearance of ANABAPTISM further clouded the religious landscape. In Germany's semi-autonomous imperial cities the evangelical message spread quickly during the 1520s and 1530s. In the cities of Southern Germany many local reformers emerged, or towns bowed to popular pressure for reform and appealed to Wittenberg or to Zürich for advisors to aid them in their efforts. Nuremberg, Strassburg, and somewhat later Augsburg emerged as the first leaders of this urban evangelicalism, but within the first two decades of the Reformation, upwards of two thirds of the empire's 65 imperial cities initiated reforms of their church establishments. Although their populations were a tiny fraction of the empire's total population, Germany's imperial cities were far more important than mere size would indicate. These towns were one of the backbones of the Holy Roman Empire, providing CHARLES V (1500–1558, ruled 1519–1556) with his major source of revenue for administering his government. Further, these imperial cities were important arenas for debate, centers of commerce, trade, and learning, and markets for agricultural goods. Since 1499, the Empire had been engaged in conflicts with a confederation of its Swiss cantons that had declared their independence in 1495. The fear of appearing disloyal to the emperor helps to explain the essentially conservative nature of many urban reforms during the 1520s and 1530s. While some town's initially turned toward the Zürich reformer Zwingli, most eventually came to favor Luther's more conservative approach. In addition, most town councils modulated their response to growing popular demands for reform, allowing just enough evangelical teaching and innovation to satisfy their populations. This initial stage of the Reformation in the cities aimed to translate the liturgy into the vernacular, reform the sacraments, establish "biblical" preaching, and abolish monastic institutions.

The unfolding events of the 1520s fed the ruling class's fears of rebellion. Already in 1523, several hundred members of Germany's imperial knights, a servile order of nobility, had taken up Luther's charge to reform the Church and initiated a series of raids against several prince bishops. The revolt was soon suppressed, but not without the destruction of more than twenty noble castles. One year later, an outbreak of rural rebellion began in the southwest along the upper Rhine, and quickly spread into the central and southern empire. This "Peasants' War" came to attract supporters beyond the rural peasantry as Anabaptists and other radicals as well as members of the urban proletariat joined the movement. In March 1525, representatives of the rebellion met in Memmingen and adopted the "Twelve Articles" as their manifesto, and thousands of copies of the document circulated in more than 25 editions printed during the coming months.

In April 1525 Luther responded to the rebellion by publishing his *Admonition to Peace*, a document that indicted both the nobility for their oppression and the peasantry for their rebellion. As the violence increased, however, Luther reissued the *Admonition* in June 1525 with a new addendum titled *Against the Robbing and Murderous Hordes of the Peasantry*. Now Luther advised the peasant movement's swift and decisive repression. The Reformer's response, unpopular among many of his supporters including Melanchthon, was to produce a measure of disaffection from the evangelical cause in the German countryside during the coming years.

The Magisterial Reformation. In Germany's imperial cities the reforming impulse had usually come from the populace writ large, not from the ruling class, and town councils adapted themselves gradually to the demands for Church reform. In the empire's territorial states, greater distance separated rulers from their people, and princes, fearing reprisals from the empire, were even slower to adopt reform measures. Still in the 1520s the Reformation did make inroads into the important territories of East Prussia, Brandenburg-Ansbach, Electoral Saxony, and Hesse. By 1546, 23 territories had adopted reformed Church ordinances, an impressive number, but still only ten percent of the secular states within the empire. As Luther's homeland, Saxony continued to take the lead in fashioning the reforming methods many territorial states came to use. Saxon universities at Wittenberg and somewhat later at Jena became important seminaries for the training of Lutheran pastors. In the years following

the Peasants' War, a more authoritarian pattern of reform emerged. In 1527, the Elector Johann the Constant of Saxony introduced the Reformation in his territory by imitating a practice of the medieval Church, the Visitation. Philipp Melanchthon provided the instructions that the state's Visitors were to use in examining ministers and laity, and a complete inventory of religious practices and beliefs was made in the countryside. The results of this first Saxon Visitation pointed up the low level of religious knowledge, even indifference that existed in the territory, and a scheme for mandatory primary education and catechizing of youth was the eventual result. It remains an open question as to how effective education was as a vehicle for indoctrinating youth in evangelical principles. Lutheran educational schemes, with their heavy emphasis on the rote memorization of catechetical formulas, seem to have been widely unpopular among the populace. Still such measures were to be imitated by the major Protestant and Catholic reform movements of the sixteenth century. The remaining hallmarks of this territorial reformation included the obligatory adoption of Luther's reformed and translated liturgy and the suppression of the territory's monasteries and convents, sometimes over the vigorous protests of their religious. In the cities the abolition of benefices and monastic foundations had often been used to establish community chests for social welfare. But in the territories, these resources usually flowed into princes' coffers. In this and other ways the adoption of the Reformation allowed sixteenth-century princes, who were increasingly jealous of their prerogatives, to establish greater fiscal and political control over their territories. The sixteenth-century Reformations did produce princes who seem to have motivated primarily by these political considerations. It would be a mistake, though, to stress mere political advantage as most rulers' sole motivation. Most expressed sincere religious convictions while acting on political opportunities.

In addition, politics both hindered and permitted the spread of evangelical teaching within the empire's territorial states. In the 1520s, the Holy Roman Empire's religious issues were never more than secondary to Charles V, who was distracted by problems throughout his numerous possessions. These included sporadic revolts from his Spanish and Netherlandish subjects, wars in Italy waged against the French and the papacy, and the threat of the Turks in Eastern Europe. Charles V's absence from Germany allowed the formation of leagues among the empire's princes. Under the Emperor's brother, Archduke Ferdinand of Austria, Catholic princes organized themselves into one such league during the summer of 1524, while a Lutheran alliance followed in 1526. In 1526, both leagues converged to lobby the imperial diet at Speyer. The result was a decree that, while prohibiting religious innovation, left the enforcement of the Diet of Worms's prohibition of 1521 against the spread of Luther's teachings up to the individual consciences of Germany's princes. The religious issue was to be postponed until a national or general council could address it. The Diet of Speyer in 1529 changed these provisions by annulling the earlier decree and prohibiting further innovations. In Lutheran principalities, the Catholic clergy were to retain their rights and incomes, and Catholic worship was to be allowed. Against this measure seven princes and 14 imperial cities protested on April 19, 1529, and thereafter they became known as "Protestants." In the coming decades politics continued to cloud efforts at reconciliation.

Failure of Religious Reconciliation. An attempt was made to heal the religious division at the Diet of Augsburg (1530) presided over by Emperor Charles V. Melanchthon prepared an irenical statement of Lutheran doctrine, the Confession of AUGSBURG, which was approved by Luther and signed by seven Protestant princes and two cities. Four southern German cities in opposition produced the *Confessio Tetrapolitana,* a document influenced by the spiritual and symbolic eucharistic doctrines of Zwingli. Despite earnest negotiations, the attempt at reconciliation failed. The Protestants were called upon to accept the final decree of the Diet, which if enforced would have restored Catholicism. Instead the Protestants in 1531 formed the SCHMALKALDIC LEAGUE, an alliance of seven princes and 11 cities. The Emperor, preoccupied by the Turkish threat, was forced to grant them immunity and toleration until the Peace of Frankfurt of 1532. During the coming nine years, the Emperor was again absent from Germany and the Lutheran cause strengthened through reformations enacted in the territories of Württemberg, Pomerania, Dessau, the Duchy of Saxony (Albertine Saxony), the Electorate of Brandenburg and many more cities. Under the aegis of the Emperor, theological conversations continued at the Colloquies of Regensburg in 1541 and 1546, but without success. The atmosphere of mistrust and bad faith had grown through two decades of bitter polemic, now hindering doctrinal agreement and leading eventually to the Schmalkaldic War (1546–47). But politics also came to aid Charles V in his attempts to suppress the Protestant league, since he was able to secure the support of the evangelical Duke Moritz of Albertine Saxony. Maurice abandoned the Schmalkaldic League in support of Catholicism after he secured a promise from Charles V that he might succeed to control neighboring Electoral Saxony. In 1547 Charles V won a decisive victory against Protestant forces at Mühlberg. The Schmalkaldic League was dissolved, and Charles V was briefly master of the religious situation. He attempted to settle at least provisionally the differences between

Protestants and Catholics with a compromise, the Interim of Augsburg of 1548 (*see* INTERIMS). The Interim's moderate Catholic reform position, however, pleased neither Protestants nor Catholics. His erstwhile ally, Moritz of Saxony, having secured the position of an imperial elector through his previous political maneuvers, now defected again and joined forces with a small band of Protestant princes. In March 1552, the brief Prince's War they staged against the Hapsburg's led to the abandonment of the policies of the Interim. The religious issues were to be resolved through a compromise formulated at the next imperial diet, held at Augsburg in 1555. Through the Peace of AUGSBURG Lutheranism achieved legal recognition, and the princes were allowed to determine the religion of their territories. Lutheranism's growth was to be tolerated within the imperial cities, although the towns were expected to tolerate Catholic worship within their walls as well. No other religious group (e.g. Calvinism) was recognized. A further important provision, the "ecclesiastical reservation," specified that any bishop or abbot who adopted the Augsburg Confession would be required to surrender his territory.

Lutheranism outside Germany. Lutheranism was not to remain a reformation force only within the boundaries of Germany. It spread throughout Northern Europe easily, and even in places where it did not become the dominant reformation settlement, it influenced later reform movements.

France. The importance of the diffusion of Lutheranism in France is not to be found in the persistence of any Lutheran group but rather in the preparation that Lutheran ideas laid for the acceptance of the Reformed Churches of Calvin. Lutheranism spread through the printed writings of Luther, Melanchthon, and their followers, and by means of French students who went to Wittenberg, and German and Swiss students who came to the university of Paris. It met opposition, but repression was intermittent due to political reasons and the reluctance of Francis I to stigmatize indiscriminately as heretics all those with reformist ideas. For even before the Reformation, an orthodox reform group (the Circle of Meaux) had appeared with the desire of purifying the Church in France, though some of its members later joined the Reformation. Many other intellectuals imbued with Erasmian ideals were eager for reform. Before the arrival of Calvin, the lines between orthodox and heterodox were not clearly drawn despite condemnations of Lutheranism by the University of Paris.

Netherlands. The Lutheran Reformation also attracted disciples in the Low Countries, especially in urban centers such as Antwerp. It had to compete early on with SACRAMENTARIANISM and anabaptism; eventually the growth of Calvinism supplanted all these movements (*see* REFORMED CHURCHES; NETHERLANDS REFORMED CHURCH).

Italy. In Italy, the situation was different. Calvinism was less congenial to the Italians than the very moderate form of Lutheranism that began to circulate in many cities, for example, Venice and above all Naples, where a reforming circle gathered around the Spanish humanist Juan de VALDÉS. As in the case of the Circle of Meaux, certain members of this group became Protestants. There were also a number of spectacular conversions of notable Italian clerics to Protestantism: Bernardino OCHINO, Pier Paolo VERGERIO, and Peter Martyr Vermigli, but each of these figures eventually left Italy and thus did not develop a widespread following. After Trent through the agency of the Inquisition, Lutheranism disappeared in Italy. As in Spain, the Inquisition succeeded in preventing almost completely the infiltration of Protestantism.

Scandinavia. In Scandinavia, the state furthered progress of the Reformation. A priest, Olaus PETRI, who had studied at Wittenberg, and who had married a few months before Luther, openly preached Lutheran doctrine in Sweden. King Gustavus I Vasa, who was ultimately responsible for the official acceptance of Lutheranism in his kingdom, approved both his teaching and his marriage. The Riksdag of Västerås in 1527 broke the ties of the Swedish Church with Rome. The moderate Synod of Oerebro in 1529 laid the foundations for the Swedish form of Lutheranism. In 1535 Laurentius Petri, brother of Olaus and an ardent Lutheran, became archbishop of Uppsala; he can justly be called the reformer of Sweden. There was Catholic resistance, even beyond the Riskdag of Västerås in 1544, which had proclaimed the kingdom evangelical, but gradually the entire country adopted a conservative Lutheranism.

The Reformation was likewise introduced into Denmark and established by the agency of the crown. King Christian II, who was deposed in 1523, had encouraged the propagation of Lutheran doctrine. His successor, Frederick I, made Hans TAUSEN, a Wittenberg-trained Lutheran, his personal chaplain. Tausen, "the Danish Luther," became the leading exponent of the new doctrine in Denmark. The Diet of Odense in 1527 gave protection and recognition to both Catholics and Lutherans, but with the King favoring Lutheranism and the nobles acquiring ecclesiastical properties, the Reformation made rapid progress. The final triumph of Protestantism came following a three-year civil war that began at the death of Frederick I in 1533. Christian III, who became king in 1536, called Luther's friend Johann BUGENHAGEN to organize the Danish Church. Though only a priest himself, Bugenhagen undertook to consecrate seven other priests

as the new Church's superintendents. Thus in contrast to the Swedish Church, the episcopacy did not prevail in Denmark, as it had not in Protestant Germany either. The King himself became the head of the Danish Church in a manner similar to the Anglican reforms being worked out in England at roughly the same time. Through the Danish conquest of Norway, the Lutheran Reformation was imported there along the same lines. In Iceland also, once a colony of Denmark, Lutheranism was successfully introduced despite resistance.

Finland, which was under the rule of Sweden, gradually became completely Lutheran. The Lutheran Reformation had penetrated early into the other Baltic states, especially in those cities where there were German-speaking populations. Estonia, Livonia, and Kurland also witnessed forms of Lutheran Reformation. After the collapse of the authority of the Order of the Teutonic Knights in the region, these countries came under the control of Sweden, Denmark, and Poland respectively and their Lutheran Church ordinances were safeguarded.

Elsewhere in Eastern Europe it was not monarchs who introduced Lutheranism, but rather German-speaking burghers. Some members of the nobility in Poland, Lithuania, Bohemia, and Hungary were attracted to Lutheranism, but eventually Calvinism was to attract considerably more adherents in these countries.

The Development of Reformed Christianity

The Reformation in Switzerland and parts of Southern Germany came to develop different theological and political teachings and thus it constitutes a separate chapter in the history of the continental Reformation. The Zwinglian reform and the Calvinist, which virtually supplanted it, belong to that branch of Protestantism customarily called "Reformed," in contrast to the Lutheran or Evangelical and to the forms of Radical Protestantism.

Zwingli and the Reform at Zürich. While Ulrich Zwingli was theologically indebted to Luther in some respects, he was an independent thinker very much influenced by humanism and the ideas of Erasmus as well. His assessments of the effects of original sin were less pessimistic than Luther's; he was less tolerant of the medieval Church's liturgy and ceremonialism. Zwingli's ideas about the relationship between Church and state tended towards the theocratic. His insistence upon the mere symbolic presence of Christ in the Eucharist could not be resolved with Luther's retention of the doctrine of the real presence, and the two eventually parted company. (*See* EUCHARIST.)

Growth of Zwinglianism. Due to the success of the Reformation in Zürich and to the widespread desire of

Swiss burghers to be free of episcopal control, Zwingli-anism expanded swiftly through the German-speaking cantons of Basel, Berne, and St. Gall, as well as else-where. The forest cantons resisted, and were eventually successful in retaining Catholicism, but in 1531 Zwingli was killed on the battlefield during one of these conflicts. The leadership of the church in Zürich passed to Heinrich BULLINGER, who eventually prevailed in establishing the eucharistic doctrine of Calvin throughout the Zwinglian churches of Switzerland. They retained only the Church organization that Zwingli had instituted.

Bucer and Strasbourg. The *Confessio Tetrapoli-tana,* presented by the four cities of Strassburg, Con-stance, Memmingen and Lindau to the Diet of Augsburg in 1530, had been written by Martin BUCER, the leading reformer of Strassburg. Bucer was in general agreement with many of the puritanical features of Zwinglianism and he came to exercise an influence, not only upon his city Strassburg, but upon the ideas of John Calvin too. The Archbishop of Canterbury Thomas CRANMER called him to England in 1549 and in the two years before his death, Bucer helped shape the course of the English Ref-ormation, first by serving as a theological adviser and later as Regius Professor at Cambridge. Both Bucer's and Zwingli's reform programs contributed importantly to the religious life of Southern German and Swiss cities, too. In time, however, their influence was to be overshad-owed by the development of the Lutheran Confession in Germany and the advent of Calvinism in Switzerland.

Calvin's Theology

Calvin accepted and codified the theology of Luther, but with a number of shifts in emphases. Calvin em-braced the idea of the sinner's sanctification following justification, something that Luther sometimes denied and always tended to downplay. He also rejected Luther's notion of consubstantiation, that is, that the elements of communion were accompanied ''with'' the physical body and blood of Christ. Calvin came to an imaginative fusion of both Lutheran and Zwinglian ideas concerning the Eucharist. He rejected Zwingli's purely symbolic teachings concerning communion, but agreed that the body of Christ was not made physically present in com-munion. At the same time Calvin upheld Luther's notion of a real presence, insisting that after the reception of the sacrament, Christ's spiritual presence came to suffuse the believer. While Luther, Zwingli and Calvin all stressed the majesty of God, Calvin's theology came to accentuate the remoteness of the Creator from His creatures. And while both Luther and Calvin stressed the principle of *sola scriptura* (scripture alone), Luther had been tolerant of customs and traditions that did not expressly violate divine law. Calvin, on the other hand, argued for a more

thorough reformation and purification of the Church based upon scriptural warranty for all Church practices. Thus God's law, as well as a rigorous organization of the Christian community, assumes a prominence in Calvin's theology.

The Institutes. In contrast to Luther whose literary output was prodigious, Calvin was a systematic theolo-gian, and the essence of his doctrine can be gleaned from a single book, the *Institutes of the Christian Religion.* From the first Latin and French editions in six chapters (1536), through successive Latin and French editions constantly augmented, the work became by its last edition in Calvin's lifetime (1564) an ingenious summa of Prot-estantism that comprised four books and 80 chapters. Translated into a number of other languages, it had an in-comparable role in the diffusion of Calvinism. (*See* INSTI-TUTES OF CALVIN.)

Calvinism in France. Calvinism gradually replaced Zwinglianism in the Protestant regions of Switzerland. Similarly in France, it tended to supplant Lutheran influ-ences, which had prepared the way for it. The first nation-al synod of the Reformed Church was held in Paris in 1559. Intermittent periods of toleration had permitted Calvinism to grow into a sizable minority. The Wars of Religion (1562–98) in France were of unparalleled feroc-ity, but eventually gave way to a compromise position. Through the Edict of NANTES (1598), Calvinists were granted a limited degree of religious toleration and civil equality. During the course of the next century these rights were gradually restricted until Louis XIV revoked the Edict in 1685. Under severe harassment, most French Calvinists emigrated or converted to Catholicism. A small minority managed to survive, though, and they were eventually granted religious freedom during the French Revolution.

The Low Countries. Calvinism also replaced Lu-theranism as an influence in the northern provinces of the Low Countries. Calvinist Church organization did not rely upon the aid of princes, and thus its institutions pene-trated into the Dutch cities quite readily. Calvinism came to play a role in the northern provinces' rebellion against Spanish authority, and once independent, the provinces became the strongest Reformed Protestant power on the continent.

Germany & Eastern Europe. In Germany, Calvin-ism made inroads in the Electoral Palatinate in 1562 and in several smaller territories thereafter. The presence of Calvinism within the empire provoked bitter controversy and elicited polemical attacks from Lutheran theologians and preachers. By the end of the sixteenth century, Cal-vinism had won converts in some princely families and even among the Lutheran Confession's theologians and pastors. Calvinism, though, would not be legally recognized until the ratification of the Peace of WESTPHALIA in 1648. In Eastern Europe, the Reformed religion often replaced Lutheranism. In Hungary and Bohemia especially, Calvinists were to develop into strong minorities.

The Radical Reformation. Calvinism, less conservative than Lutheranism in advocating religious change, was itself conservative when compared to the program of the Radical Reformation. Under this term are included many widely scattered and differing groups such as the Zwickau Prophets of Thomas Müntzer (1489–1525), the Swiss Brethren of Balthasar HUBMAIER (1485?–1528), the Jorists of David JORIS (1500–56), the Familists of Hendrick NICLAES (1502–80), the Hutterite Brethren of Jakob Hutter (d. 1536), the Melchiorites of Melchior HOFFMAN (1500–43), and the Mennonites of Menno Simons (d. 1561). This list, however, comprises only a small fraction of the many Radical Reformation sects active in sixteenth- and seventeenth-century Europe. Despite variant doctrines most agreed in their common commitment to the doctrine of "Scripture alone," and their acceptance of the necessity of resting worldly influences. Most pursued the ideal of a "gathered" Christian community, and most were passive, if not always pacifist. Their refusal to submit to oaths and vows was usually interpreted as a sign of political resistance, and Protestants and Catholics consequently persecuted them alike. Social and economic grievances played a role in the formation of many of these sects, but the leadership of the Radical Reformation included devout humanists, pious biblical Christians, and rationalists, as well as some fanatical extremists.

Three main groups stand out in the history of the Radical Reformation: Spiritualists, Anabaptists, and Rationalists. The first group tended to repudiate the real presence, the efficacy of infant baptism, and outward ceremonies and rites. The second and most important group was derisively called Rebaptizers or Anabaptists. They held that infant baptism was unscriptural, and differed from the Spiritualists mainly in the degree to which they insisted on the rebaptism of adult Christians. The cities of Zürich, Nuremberg, Augsburg, and Strassburg, as well as the Low Countries and Moravia were early centers of their activity. An attempt to set up a millenial New Jerusalem at Münster in Westphalia in 1534–35 led to their brutal repression. There, Bernhardt Rothmann, chaplain of St. Mauritz Church near the city, and Bernhardt Knipperdollink, a prosperous cloth merchant from within the town walls, were won over to Anabaptism. By February 1534 Knipperdollink had been elected Münster's burgermeister and Anabaptism was made the city's official religion. Jan Mattyssoon, a former baker from Haarlem, and his disciple, Jan Bokelszoon, a Dutch tailor known as

John of Leyden, joined Knipperdolinck's reform program. Their dream of a Christian commonwealth with equality of goods shared in common soon proved untenable. The city's bishop, Franz von Waldeck, laid siege to the town, recapturing it on June 24, 1535. The final group of radical reformers, the Rationalists, attracted the fewest adherents and was bitterly persecuted. They denied the divinity of Christ, and included the Spaniard Michael SERVETUS, and the Socinians in Poland (*see* SOCINIANISM).

Consequences of the Reformation

The force of the Reformation was felt in all spheres of society and extended far beyond the geographical boundaries of Europe.

Geographic Divisions. In the resultant religious division of Europe into Catholic, Lutheran, and Reformed, Catholicism's greatest strength was now to be concentrated in the Latin countries. Significant pockets of Catholic strength persisted in Ireland, Poland, Hungary, and parts of German-speaking Europe. But by the seventeenth century the character of Catholicism was beginning to change because of the dominance of the Mediterranean countries in the life and government of the Church. In addition, the fracture of Europe into three (and if one includes Anglicanism, four) combative religious confessions ended the medieval reality of a united Western Christendom.

Confessional Disputes. The Reformation and subsequent Counter Reformation often bred bitter hatred both within and between the confessions. For more than thirty years after his death, doctrinal infighting ensued between the German theologians who followed Luther. By 1580, the Lutheran Churches throughout the Holy Roman Empire adopted the Formula of CONCORD, Lutheranism's last great creedal statement. The Reformed churches in Europe generally formulated their confessional statements for communities within their national boundaries, such as the Confessio Czengerina of 1557–58 for Hungary, the Confessio Gallicana of 1559, the Confessio Belgica of 1561, and others (*see* CONFESSIONS OF FAITH, PROTESTANT). CALVINISM, too, experienced its own internal rivalries and stresses throughout the later sixteenth and seventeenth centuries.

As a result of the Reformation, Catholicism weathered a period of theological confusion, a confusion that was in large part resolved by the Council of TRENT (1545–1563). Trent's decrees did not designate the Protestant reformers by name, hoping to leave open the door for future discussions, but the Council nevertheless condemned Protestant teaching. It helped as well to establish a body of doctrine that would give unity and stability to modern Catholic theology. And its impact on modern Catholic Church government and organization was immeasurable.

Sacramental De-emphasis and Individualism. In many parts of Europe official state forms of Protestantism retained much of their medieval inheritance. In Lutheranism and Anglicanism, in particular, the fabric of medieval ritual and ceremonial continued to live on until the modern period. Yet the Protestant religions of the sixteenth century had also won many adherents through their emphasis on the gospel, the scriptures, and a personal faith as well as their de-emphasis of the sacraments and priestly orders. These were radical departures from the traditions of the Church, and they have been seen as helping to destroy the strongly communal religious experience of late-medieval religion. Certainly, in both the evangelical and Reformed traditions, human salvation was now seen as something that was accomplished individually, worked out "with fear and trembling" between the sinner and God.

Similarities of the Post-Reformation Churches. Scholars of the sixteenth-century Reformations and Counter Reformation have recently realized the many essential political and social similarities that existed among the post-Reformation churches. Through a process of confessionalization Europe came to be carved up into mutually exclusive and competing religions in which states heightened their efforts to control religious beliefs and practices. This enhanced authority of the state over religious life was a reality in both Catholic and Protestant countries. Most states moved to enforce printed confessions and Church ordinances as the standard of orthodoxy. Those who deviated from these norms were often bitterly persecuted. At the same time religious heterodoxy grew in most of Europe during the seventeenth century, pointing up the ultimate failure of state-directed religious policies. Rising literacy rates and improving educational systems meant that more and more people could examine the scriptures and Christian texts on their own. In addition, a growing skeptical climate toward the end of the seventeenth and the beginning of the eighteenth centuries, aided in part by the rise of modern scientific mentalities, was to make it increasingly difficult for the state to enforce a single set of beliefs. Religious heterodoxy increased in the eighteenth and nineteenth centuries; at the same time the process of confessionalization had helped to create enduring religious identities and divisions among Europeans, as certain rituals, symbols and beliefs came to be identified with a particular confession's most firmly held convictions. Calvinism, with its emphasis on biblical law, became identified as a religion of the book whose adherents practiced the most spare and severe style of worship; early-modern Catholicism, on

the other hand, emerged in the minds of non-Catholics as a religion of ritual, the sacraments, and the saints.

Movement toward Ecumenism. This identification of religious teachings with cultural identities helped to sustain bitter rivalries between Protestants and Catholics into the nineteenth and twentieth centuries, long after most Westerners had lost a precise knowledge of the Reformation and Counter Reformation's intricate theological controversies. At the same time, however, Protestant ecumenism emerged as a movement that tried to heal the divisions that existed among its various religious traditions, a movement that would result in the formation of the World Council of Churches in 1948. During the pontificates of Pius XII, John XXIII, Paul VI, and John Paul II, the Catholic Church has again entered into these discussions, although a unified Christendom continues to be more a desire than reality.

Bibliography: P. BLICKLE, *The Revolution of 1525,* T. A. BRADY and H. C. E. MIDELFORT, ed. and trans. (2nd ed., Baltimore, 1985). J. BOSSY, *Christianity in the West 1400–1700* (Oxford, 1985). T. A. BRADY, *Turning Swiss* (Cambridge, 1985). E. CAMERON, *The European Reformation* (Oxford, 1991). B. MOELLER, *Imperial Cities and the Reformation,* H. C. E. MIDELFORT and M. U. EDWARDS, trans. (Philadelphia, 1972). H. OBERMAN, *Luther: Man Between God and the Devil* (New Haven, 1989). S. OZMENT, *The Reformation in the Cities* (New Haven, 1975). G. STRAUSS, *Luther's House of Learning* (Baltimore, 1978). T. TENTLER, *Sin and Confession on the Eve of the Reformation* (Princeton, 1978).

[P. SOERGEL/W. S. BARRON, JR.]

REFORMED CHURCHES

Part I: Europe

The term "Reformed Churches" designates those churches that in the early development of Protestantism adopted the tenets and ecclesiastical organization of Huldrych ZWINGLI, Martin BUCER, Heinrich BULLINGER, and John CALVIN. Because Calvin's doctrinal principles ultimately became dominant, the Calvinist Church is identified with the Reformed Church, although Calvin was not the first but a subsequent influence in its growth. The presbyteral type of church government characteristic of the Reformed Churches affected the progress of Protestantism also in Great Britain and America, so that PRESBYTERIANISM traces its origins to these reformers, although it has developed its own distinctive marks. Originally the word "reformed" was used indiscriminately by all the established churches having common cause against Rome, including Lutherans; but the disputes over Christ's presence in the elements of the Last Supper, which grew grave in 1529, separated the Lutherans from the Reformed. The Reformed movement began in Switzerland and spread rapidly to Germany, the Netherlands, England, Wales, Scotland, Hungary, Poland, and America.

Switzerland. The Evangelical program of Huldrych Zwingli was already active in Zurich in 1516, thereby antedating that of Martin Luther. Switzerland offered advantages to the reformers because of its political structure, in which all affairs including religious policy were determined by a group elected to govern within each federated canton. Thus success could be facilitated by gaining control of the Council and the votes of the community. This Zwingli achieved through public religious debates with the Catholic clergy preceding elections. Beginning with 1523, Zurich and then Basel voted for the new religion. Bern made the change in 1528 and was followed by other cantons. Calvin, who had his own church firmly established at Geneva by 1536, met with Guillaume FAREL and Bullinger in Zurich in 1549. There they formulated the Zurich Consensus concerning the Real Presence, so that by 1580 Zwinglianism and Calvinism became the Reformed Church. This assured the predominance of French Protestantism in the Swiss cantons until the Enlightenment of the 18th century, when German influence grew stronger. In 1920 the Federation of Swiss Evangelical Churches was organized with membership from all 22 cantons. This union with its many commissions and groups such as the *Junge Kirche* and the *Heimstätte* allowed the penetration of Evangelical Christianity into all aspects of society.

Germany. The Reformed movement in Germany made its start in the Rhineland, specifically in Strassburg, through the preaching of the Zwinglian Evangelist, Mattäus Zell. Its growth there began in 1521 and extended to 1549, when the INTERIM of CHARLES V restored Roman Catholicism. Catholicism continued to dominate through the devastation of the THIRTY YEARS' WAR (1618–48) and the francophile episcopates of Charles Egon and Wilhelm Egon von FURSTENBERG. When Protestantism returned to Strassburg it was in a Lutheran form. From 1521 to 1549, however, Swiss Reformed theology flourished at Strassburg under the protection of Elector Frederick III of the Palatinate. From Heidelberg University issued the HEIDELBERG CATECHISM of 1563, which became the standard creedal expression for all Reformed Churches. From Strassburg as the center, the movement spread along the cities of the Rhine and into the rest of Germany. It suffered reverses during the religious wars but gained explicit recognition at the Peace of WESTPHALIA in 1648, when Switzerland was also accorded independence from the Empire. The large emigration brought on by Louis XIV's revocation of the Edict of NANTES in 1685 also swelled the number of Reformed in Germany, though they never became a serious threat to the influence of Lu-

theranism on German Protestantism, especially not in the periods of Pietism and the Enlightenment. In the late 19th century and early 20th century, the German Reformed Churches experienced a revival of interest in social works and missionary activity, though they suffered a decline during World War II. Today much of the territory in which they were strongest lies in the eastern part of Germany.

The Netherlands. The Reformed Church came to the Netherlands in about 1560 and gained popularity because of its appeal to the rising middle class and its sympathy with William of Orange in his struggle against the Hapsburgs for home rule. In 1584 when the war for independence was won, Reformed theology was accepted and defended in the *Remonstrance* by Bisschop, a disciple of ARMINIUS, at the Synod of Dort (*see* CONFESSIONS OF FAITH, PROTESTANT). Disagreement with its standard of doctrine has brought schisms, so that by the 19th century many Reformed theologians and pastors had departed from the Synod of Dort and regarded Christianity principally as a code of morality. The Netherlands Reformed Church (*De Nederlandse Hervormde Kerk*) is the oldest and most traditional group today and is generally considered the national church, although there are two influential secessionist branches, the Christian Reformed Church (*De Christelijke Gereformeerde Kerken*) and the Reformed Churches in the Netherlands (*De Gereformeerde Kerken in Nederland*). In 1944 one-quarter of the congregations and one-third of the clergy of the Reformed Churches in the Netherlands split and formed the Reformed Adhering to Article 31 of the Church Order of Dort (*De Gereformeerde Kerkonderhovdende Art. 31 k.o.*). (*See* NETHERLANDS REFORMED CHURCH.)

France. The Reformed Church appeared in France in 1555 and held its first synod in 1559. The impetus came from Geneva, where Calvin, Farel, and Theodore BEZA eyed their homeland as a mission field, sending evangelists to France by the hundreds. The French Reformed Church, whose members were called HUGUENOTS, adopted Calvinism as a basic body of dogmas, but freely altered it. Their history was troubled during the Wars of Religion (1562–94), until Henry IV granted religious tolerance by the Edict of Nantes (1598). Upon the revocation of the Edict (1685), they were forced underground or emigrated. They regained their rights after the Revolution of 1789. France's recovery of Alsace-Lorraine after World War I augmented the number of Reformed, as well as Lutherans within her borders, and furthered the need for strong and unified organization. In 1905 the Reformed Church separated into the orthodox and conservative *Église Réformée Évangélique* and the *Églises Réformées Unies,* which were liberal. Mediation between these branches has been attempted. In 1939 a union of Reformed, Methodist, and several Free Churches made up the *Églises Reformées de France.*

Hungary. After the Battle of Mohács in 1526 and the death of King Louis II in the same year, Hungary became the scene of contest over the succession between Ferdinand of Hapsburg, brother of Charles V, and John Zápolya. In the warfare that followed, Transylvania turned to Calvinism, and by 1563 the Hungarian Reformed Church accepted the Calvinistic Confession, the Heidelberg Catechism, and elements of Puritan belief brought back by ministers studying in England. At the end of the 16th century Hungary was 90 percent Protestant. Through Hapsburg political pressure and the work of the Jesuits, the influence of the Reformed Church was lessened, so that by the 19th century the Reformed numbered less than one-fifth of the population. The Treaty of Trianon on June 4, 1920, further diminished their membership by the transfer of territory to Czechoslovakia, Rumania, and Yugoslavia.

Poland. The Reformation entered Poland in 1518 when James Knade, a monk who renounced his vows, preached Lutheranism. In 1540 Calvinism appeared and caused a breach among Catholic clergy. James Uchánski, Archbishop and Primate of Poland, advised that a national church be established. By 1573 the Reformation had spent its force and through the activity of the Jesuits, the Reformed Church movement diminished.

Other Countries. In Scotland the Reformed faith, known as Presbyterianism, was established by John KNOX in 1560, and 30 years later was recognized as the official religion of Scotland (*see* SCOTLAND, CHURCH OF). It began its spread also in the Union of South Africa in 1562 and became officially adopted in 1859 as the Reformed Church of South Africa. It is found in Wales and England, Northern Ireland (*see* IRELAND, CHURCH OF), the republics of former Yugoslavia, the Czech and Slovak republics, Romania, Ukraine, throughout Africa, Oceania, Asia, and the Americas (*see* REFORMED CHURCHES IN NORTH AMERICA).

Bibliography: J. DILLENBERGER and C. WELCH, *Protestant Christianity Interpreted through Its Development* (New York 1958). H. J. GRIMM, *The Reformation Era, 1500–1650* (New York 1954). K. S. LATOURETTE, *Christianity in a Revolutionary Age: A History of Christianity in the Nineteenth and Twentieth Centuries,* 5 v. (New York 1958–62) v.2, 4. H. G. HAGEMAN, *Pulpit and Table* (Richmond, Va. 1962); "Reformed Worship: Yesterday and Today," *Theology Today* 18 (1961) 30–40. D. SINOR, *History of Hungary* (New York 1959) 184–187. I. RÉVÉSZ, *History of the Hungarian Reformed Church,* tr. G. A. F. KNIGHT (Washington 1956). *Cambridge History of Poland,* ed. W. F. REDDAWAY et al., 2 v. (Cambridge, Eng. 1941–50).

[J. A. LEAHY/EDS.]

Part II: North America

Reformed Churches are descendants of the church of John Calvin, and therefore collateral relations of the Presbyterian bodies in Europe and America. But whereas Presbyterianism is mainly an Anglo-Saxon development through the Scot John Knox, the Reformed groups derive from Calvin directly. Their immediate ancestors are the Calvinists in France, Switzerland, and the Low Countries (*see* CALVINISM). Although they are concentrated in the U.S., Reformed congregations have been established also in Latin America, principally in Mexico.

History. The Reformed Churches emerged in North America as a direct result of the business migration of Calvinists from Holland, sponsored by the Dutch East India Company. At first they were only scattered groups along the Hudson River, but in 1628 they organized at New Amsterdam what has become the oldest church in America with an uninterrupted ministry. In 1792 they broke away from the parent body in Holland and held their first general synod two years later. Insistence on keeping the Dutch language in preaching and the liturgy retarded the church's growth and alienated some of its younger members, but no grave doctrinal crisis arose until the 19th century.

To understand this crisis it is necessary briefly to retrace the European origins of the Christian Reformed Church, which, together with the Reformed Church in America, accounts for 90 per cent of the Reformed membership in the U.S. After the troubles of the Napoleonic era in the Netherlands, William I reorganized the Dutch (Calvinist) Church, but in the process took over so much control that a conservative reaction set in. In 1834 a secession of strict Calvinist ministers started a church of their own. Social and economic conditions in the Netherlands forced the secessionists to migrate to the U.S. One group went to Holland, Mich., in 1846, where they were invited to enter into a loose merger with the Reformed Church in America.

Almost from the day the union was effected, some leaders in the conservative party were dissatisfied. Their basic fear was the same that had motivated those who had seceded in the Netherlands 20 years before. Believing themselves to be the true heirs of the Reformed position, they argued that continued association with the Reformed Church in America would entangle them in embarrassing alliances with churches of other beliefs. They felt that instruction in the seminary tended to weaken the Reformed tradition and that the laity needed to be better instructed in their creedal inheritance. But the most crucial factor was the lodge question, i.e., whether members of the Reformed Church may belong to such lodges as the Freemasons and continue in good standing in the church. The

Reformed Church in America tolerated lodge membership and, in the eyes of the conservatives, belittled its significance. When the final break came in 1857, grievance over the existence of Freemasonry in the Reformed Church in America was decisive. In 1857 four congregations with about 750 people left the Reformed Church in America to form what eventually became the Christian Reformed Church in America. A steady tide of immigrants from the Netherlands gradually swelled the membership.

Since 1857, each of the two main branches has developed a history of its own. The Reformed Church in America remained concentrated in the East, mainly New York and New Jersey, and in the Middle Western states of Michigan and Illinois. The General Synod meets annually, with headquarters in New York City. An elaborate missions program sponsors operations in the U.S. and in foreign countries. The Reformed Church in America has cooperated actively with the WORLD COUNCIL OF CHURCHES. Its representatives have given exceptional leadership in the National Council of the Churches of Christ in the U.S.A.

With its strong emphasis on doctrinal orthodoxy, the Christian Reformed Church developed along different lines. More concerned with integrating religion and education, and more compact in geographical distribution, the church promoted a system of Christian day schools from elementary through secondary and college grades. The Society for Christian Instruction on a Reformed Basis was organized in 1892 to federate the dozen schools in existence at that time. At its first meeting, the society recommended that all Christian schools should be owned and operated by the parent society. This departure from parochialism is generally credited with having produced the nation's most extensive program (80 percent) of religion-centered education in the Reformed tradition.

Also consistent with its stress on doctrinal integrity, the Christian Reformed Church has engaged in such projects as neighborhood evangelism, home mission work, catechism instruction to children and adult converts, and church publications with an appeal to denominational loyalty. The preamble to the constitution of a national youth organization illustrates this emphasis on distinctively religious values: "recognizing the desirability and necessity of uniting the youth of Calvinistic churches for service in the Kingdom of God, and the need of guidance and direction in this work in order that the youth of the church, as well-prepared servants of the Lord, may recognize Jesus Christ as King and serve Him always and everywhere, the Young Calvinist Federation of North America is established."

Unlike the Reformed Church in America, the Christian Reformed body is centered in smaller cities, mostly in the Middle West but also along the West Coast and in Canada. The largest single contingent is in Michigan, around Grand Rapids, Holland, and Kalamazoo.

Bibliography: W. D. BROWN, *My Confession of Faith* (New York 1941). H. G. HAGEMAN, *Lily Among Thorns* (Grand Rapids 1953). Christian Reformed Church Centennial Committee, *One Hundred Years in the New World: The Story of the Christian Reformed Church,* ed. H. J. KUIPER (Grand Rapids 1957). J. KROMMINGA, *The Christian Reformed Church: A Study in Orthodoxy* (Grand Rapids 1949). B. KRUITHOF, *The Meaning of My Confession of Faith* (Grand Rapids 1951). L. NIXON, *The Doctrinal Standards of the Reformed Church in America* (Grand Rapids n.d.); *Reformed Standards of Unity* (Grand Rapids 1957). M. SCHOOLAND, *Children of the Reformation: The Story of the Christian Reformed Church* (Grand Rapids 1958). F. S. MEAD, S. S. HILL and C. D. ATWOOD, eds., *Handbook of Denominations in the United States*, 11th ed (Nashville 2001).

[J. A. HARDON/EDS.]

REFORMED EPISCOPAL CHURCH

A denomination formed in 1873 as a result of a revolt by a small group of Protestant Episcopalians of Low Church sympathies. Bp. George David Cummins of Kentucky, a former Methodist, became the presiding bishop of the new church. Cummins, who belonged to the evangelical LOW CHURCH faction of the Episcopal Church, had objected to the increased use of liturgical vestments, ornaments and rituals that arose from the Anglo-Catholic Tractarian movement. The immediate occasion for the schism was a union communion service at the Fifth Avenue Presbyterian Church in New York City in which Bishop Cummins and the then dean of Canterbury, England, participated. Both were severely criticized by fellow Episcopalians for their action. Cummins called a meeting on Dec. 2, 1873, attended by seven clergymen and 20 laymen; the result was the establishment of the Reformed Episcopal Church. This action climaxed a long debate over ritualism and sacramentalism in the Protestant Episcopal Church.

The dissenters held that the episcopal form of church government was an ancient and desirable polity, but did not rest on divine command. They affirmed their adherence, with some reservations, to the THIRTY-NINE ARTICLES of ANGLICANISM and rejected the beliefs in TRANSUBSTANTIATION and baptismal regeneration.

The Reformed Episcopal Church recognizes the spiritual authority of ministers of all other Protestant denominations. It receives clergymen from other denominations into its ministry without reordination. At the same time, this church claims to stand in the apostolic succession and to maintain that only bishops have the right to confirm and ordain. Worship is liturgical and is based on the BOOK

OF COMMON PRAYER. However, the Reformed Episcopal Church revised that book, deleting and changing some elements and words that it considered objectionable because of a sacerdotal emphasis. Thus "priest" was changed to "minister" throughout the Book of Common Prayer; prayers for the dead were removed from holy communion and the burial service; and the phrase "now regenerate" was taken out of the baptismal service. Unlike those of the Protestant Episcopal Church, the Reformed Episcopal bishops do not form a separate house at the triennial general council.

Bibliography: F. S. MEAD, S. S. HILL and C. D. ATWOOD, eds., *Handbook of Denominations in the United States*, 11th ed (Nashville 2001).

[W. J. WHALEN/EDS.]

REFORMKATHOLIZISMUS

Reformkatholizismus is a term coined in 1898 by Josef Müller to describe a loosely united movement within the Catholic Church in Europe, mainly in Germany, that was active from the end of the 19th century to about World War I. It was known also as Critical Catholicism and Present–day Catholicism (*Gegenwartskatholizismus*). Its leading figures, who did not work in close conjunction with one another, were mostly scholarly priests and ardent Catholics; the best known among them were Hermann SCHELL, Albert EHRHARD, Philipp Funk, Franz X. KRAUS, Josef Müller, Carl MUTH, and Josef Wittig. Their aims were political, social, and cultural as well as pastoral and disciplinary. In general they sought to rid Catholicism of the ghetto mentality ensuing on the KULTURKAMPF and to narrow the chasm between the Church and modern culture by bringing the Church abreast of recent advances in science, history, and Biblical research, by utilizing more fully the methods and accomplishments in these fields, and by assuming a more positive and cooperative attitude toward progress in natural knowledge. Not all agreed on the specific means to attain these ends. Some opposed the trend toward increasing centralization of power in the PAPACY and hierarchical authoritarianism, while demanding, with a certain degree of ANTICLERICALISM, greater independence for the laity and a minimum of clerical direction. Others were hostile to NEOSCHOLASTICISM and Neothomism. There were demands to abolish the Index of Forbidden Books and even clerical CELIBACY (a demand prominent in the Diocese of Rottenburg). Reformkatholizismus differed from MODERNISM, at least in the latter's heretical aspects, but its program suffered from the spirit pervading the Church after the condemnation of Modernism and the development of INTEGRALISM. Works of Funk, Müller, and Schell were placed on the Index.

Bibliography: W. SPAEL, *Das katholische Deutschland im 20. Jahrhundert* (Würzburg 1964). W. VON LOEWENICH, *Modern Catholicism,* tr. from Ger. by R. H. FULLER (London 1959). Y. M. J. CONGAR, *Vraie et fausse réforme dans l'église* (Paris 1950). A. HAGEN, *Der Reformkatholizismus in der Diözese Rottenburg, 1902–1920* (Stuttgart 1963); *Lexikon für Theologie und Kirche²*, ed. J. HOFER and K. RAHNER (Freiburg 1957–65) 8:1085. W. REINHARD, *Lexikon für Theologie und Kirche¹*, ed. M BUCHBERGER, 10 v. (Freiburg 1930–) 8:705–707. G. MARON, *Die Religion in Geschichte und Gegenwart³* 7 v. (Tübingen 1957–65) 5:896–903.

[E. J. DUNNE]

REFRIGERIUM

Refrigerium is the Latin equivalent of the Greek ἀνάψυξις (refreshment), used among pagans and early Christians to signify both spiritual solace and the banquet celebrated for the memory or well–being of a deceased person, near his tomb. The word is used in the Old Testament (Ps 65.11; Wis 4.7; Jer 6.16) and in the New Testament story of the rich man requesting of Lazarus that he freshen his tongue (Lk 16.24), as well as by St. Paul, who says that Onesiphorus frequently gave him refreshment (2 Tm 1.16).

A Greek inscription of the 3rd century B.C. speaks of "cold water from the spring of Mnemosyne for the refreshment of the deceased" [*Incriptiones graecae* (Berlin 1873–) n.638]; while in an epitaph found at Praeneste a certain Syncratius requests that all his friends refresh themselves in cheerful spirit [*Corpus inscriptinum latinarum* (Berlin 1863–) 14.3323].

In the late 2nd–century *Passio* of SS. Felicity and PERPETUA, the martyrs speak of taking refreshment; and TERTULLIAN used the word explicitly of a wife praying that her husband's soul might enjoy eternal refreshment: *pro anima eius orat et refrigerium interim adpostulat ei* (*De monog.* 10). Among the inscriptions found in the catacombs, many speak of a soul *in pace et in refrigerium* [in peace and refreshment; E. Diehl, *Inscriptiones Christianae latinae veteres,* 3 v. (Berlin 1925–31) 2722]; in the catacomb of St. Agnes: *spiritus in refrigerium* (the soul in refreshment; *ibid.* 3407); and in that of Praetextatus: *Deus Christus omnipotens refrigeret spiritum tuum* (*ibid.* 1102). This meaning is also expressed in the *memento* of the deceased in the Canon of the Mass: *Ipsis Domine et omnibus in Christo, quiescentibus locum refrigerii, lucis et pacis ut indulgeas deprecamur* (To them, O Lord, and to all resting in Christ, we beg you to grant a place of refreshment, light and peace).

The custom of holding a banquet after the burial of a relative or friend, as well as the celebration of the anniversary of death near the tomb or mausoleum with a commemorative meal, was common among the Greeks and Romans (Tertullian, *Apologeticus,* 39). It was observed also among the Jews (Tb 4.18). The same custom was followed by the early Christians, as is attested by the discovery in the catacombs of St. Sebastian of a *triclia,* or banquet room, on the walls of which were *graffiti* (inscriptions) signifying that pilgrims had satisfied a vow by celebrating a *refrigerium* there in honor of SS. Peter and Paul, or near Peter and Paul. Between the late 3rd and early 4th centuries hundreds of such *graffiti* were scribbled on the wall. There are also pictorial representations of a *refrigerium* in several tombs. Commodianus advises: *si refrigerare cupis animam, ad martyres i* (if you wish to refresh your soul, go to the martyrs; *Inst.* 2; *Carm.* 17.19).

By the end of the 4th century, however, this custom, which earlier had frequently been accompanied by almsgiving to the poor and other acts of piety, had degenerated into an occasion of scandal; and both Ambrose (*De Elia* 17) and Augustine felt constrained to take measures against it (*Epist.* 20.10).

Bibliography: H. LECLERCQ, *Dictionnaire d'archéologie chrétienne et de liturgie,* ed. F. CABROL, H. LECLERCQ, and H. I. MARROU, 15 v. (Paris 1907–53) 14.2:2179–90. R. AUDOLLENT, *Mélanges offerts à L. Havet* (Paris 1909) 595–599. P. DE LABRIOLLE, *Bulletin d'ancienne littérature et d'archéologie chrétiennes* 2 (1912) 214–219. F. GROSSI-GONDI, *Römische Quartalschrift für christliche Altertumskunde und für Kirchengeschichte* 29 (1915) 221–249. A. M. SCHNEIDER, *Refrigerium* (Freiburg 1928). T. A. KLAUSER, *Die Cathedra im Totenkult der heidnischen und christlichen Antike* (Münster 1927).

[F. X. MURPHY]

REGALIA

Regalia are royal possessions in general, but in legal contexts those "temporalities" that were held by bishops and abbots as feudal dependents of the secular order, and in virtue of which secular rulers claimed by "regalian right" the patronage of bishopries and abbacies as well as the revenues of these during vacancies. Regalian rights originated in feudal conceptions and are seen first in France toward the end of the 10th century. Introduced into England by King WILLIAM II Rufus during the vacancy caused by the death of LANFRANC (1089), they were later extended, despite papal opposition, to practically all English bishoprics. In Germany they were claimed and exercised by Emperor HENRY V (1106–25), but ceased in effect after the death of Frederick II (1250); in France they were an abiding source of friction between the king and powerful territorial lords. Regalia, whether lands, towns, castles, or cities, involved bishops in a double alliance; for bishops were in charge of the pastoral care, yet committed to various secular duties such as judgeships or military service. The problem, which was one of the main issues of the INVESTITURE STRUGGLE, was, if anything, made more acute by the Concordat of Worms (1122), since this countenanced an oath of fealty to the emperor as well as imperial investiture. A way out of the dilemma would have been, as Pope PASCHAL II (1099–1118) was convinced, for bishops to renounce temporalities altogether and live off their TITHES; but this was difficult to implement in an era when benefices were no longer viewed solely in relation to the offices they were originally meant to support. In some modern states regalia are now in the hands of the state; in Italy regalian rights passed to the state by law in 1860, but were abolished in the Lateran Pacts of 1929.

Bibliography: EADMER, *Historia novorum,* ed. M. RULE in *Rerum Britannicarum medii aevi scriptores,* 244 v. (New York 1964–) 81; 27. J. B. SÄGMÜLLER *Die Bischofswahl bei Gratian* (Cologne 1908). A. DEELEY, "Papal Provision and Royal Rights of Patronage in the Early Fourteenth Century," *English Historical Review* 43 (1928) 497–527. M. HOWELL, *Regalian Right in Medieval England* (London 1962). C. J. CAMPBELL, "Temporal and Spiritual Regalia during the Reigns of St. Louis and Philip III," *Traditio* 20 (1964) 351–383.

[L. E. BOYLE]

REGAN, AGNES GERTRUDE

Lay leader; b. San Francisco, Calif., March 26, 1869; d. Washington, D.C., Sept. 30, 1943. Her parents were James Regan, secretary to the first archbishop of San Francisco, and Mary Morrison Regan. After attending St. Rose Academy and the San Francisco Normal School, Agnes taught in the city school system, and was a member of the board of education. In 1920, she went to Washington, D.C., and served until 1941 as first executive secretary of the National Council of Catholic Women. From 1921 to 1943, she was also assistant director of the National Catholic School of Social Service, a major project of the council.

Regan established a practical program for realizing the idea, basic in the founding of the National Catholic Welfare Conference, that the laity should be informed, unified, and encouraged to work actively for Church and country. She saw the freedom of modern women as increasing their obligation to society, and urged Catholic women to organize at the parish, diocesan, and national levels so that they could contribute to social betterment. Under her leadership the council was a sponsoring organization of the National Interracial Conference held in Washington in 1920 to consider race problems.

Out of her active concern for sound family life, she became a staunch supporter of federal housing legisla-

Max Reger. (©Bettmann/CORBIS)

tion. She worked for closer relationships with the people of Latin America, and brought young women from these countries to study at the School of Social Service.

Bibliography: L. R. LAWLER, *Full Circle: The Story of the National Catholic School of Social Service* (Washington 1951).

[D. A. MOHLER]

REGER, MAX

Late romanticist composer and conductor; b. Brand (Bavaria), Germany, March 19, 1873 (baptized Johann Baptist Joseph Maximilian); d. Leipzig, May 11, 1916. Reger received his early music instruction from his mother, and after three years (1886–89) as organist at the Weiden Catholic church, he continued his training at the Wiesbaden conservatory, where H. Riemann directed his studies to Bach and Brahms, thus laying the groundwork for his apparently complex contrapuntal style. In 1910 he was appointed teacher of composition, theory, and organ at the Munich Akademie der Tonkunst. There he renounced Riemann's influence and declared himself a ''progressivist,'' and so drew critical attacks from all sides. In 1911 he became director of the court orchestra at Meiningen and restored it to its previous distinction under Hans von Bülow. When at the Duke of Meiningen

died in 1913 Reger retired to Jena to compose. Although contemporaries considered him a harmonic innovator, he was actually a traditionalist. His extraordinary technical facility led him to produce numerous works of inordinate length, thick texture, and complicated counterpoint; yet there is nothing in his music that is not paralleled in the works of Richard WAGNER and Richard Strauss, and an almost desperate preoccupation with sonority for its own sake betrays his basic lack of inspiration. Reger's output includes no music for the Catholic liturgy, but his attractive organ chorales are frequently heard in Catholic churches. For the Lutheran service he produced chorale arrangements, German motets, and sacred songs for small choir. His gigantic setting of Psalm 100 for chorus, organ, and orchestra is a concert work.

Bibliography: *Sämtliche Werke,* ed. the Max Reger-Institut, 35 pts. in 18 v. (Bonn 1954–62). F. W. STEIN, *Thematisches Verzeichnis der im Druck erschienenen Werke von M. R.* (Leipzig 1953). E. REGER, *Mein Leben mit und für Max Reger* (Leipzig 1930). S. KALLENBERG, *Max Reger* (Leipzig 1930). E. SEGNITZ, *Max Reger: Abriss seines Lebens und Analyse seiner Werke* (Leipzig 1922). A. WIRTH, *Die Musik in Geschichte und Gegenwart,* ed. F. BLUME (Kassel-Basel 1949–) 11:119–132. E. BLOM, *Grove's Dictionary of Music and Musicians,* ed. E. BLOM 9 v. (5th ed. London 1954) 7:91–99. P. H. LÁNG, *Music in Western Civilization* (New York 1941). A. SALAZAR, *Music in Our Time,* tr. I. POPE (New York 1946). I. BREDENBACH, ''Zur Agogik in der Orgelmusik des 19. Jahrhunderts, dargestellt an einem Choralvorspiel Max Regers (op. 67, 25),'' *Musik und Kirch* 66 (1996) 234–43. M. DRUDE, ''Stichworte und Randbemerkungen zu Regers Harmonik,'' *Musiktheorie* 11 (1996) 111–23. D. HARRISON, ''Max Reger's Motivic Technique: Harmonic Innovations at the Borders of Atonality,'' *The Journal of Music Theory* 35 (1991) 61–92. M. KUBE, ''(K)eine Schmonzette: Max Regers *Mariä Wiegenlied* op. 76/52,'' *Musik und Kirche* 69 (1999) 160–63. T. MÄKELÄ, ''Zwischen Inspiration und Imitation: Max Regers Streichsextett opus 118 und das *Schott-Konzert* des Reger-Schülers Aarre Merikanto (1893–1958) im Vergleich,'' *Die Musickforschung* 48 (1995) 369–94. B. MEISCHEIN, ''Max Regers Orgelwerke und ihre Ausgaben,'' *Ars Organi* 45 (1997), 78–84. S. POPP, ''Melancholische Konfessionen für Kirche und Konzertsaal zu Max Regers *Einsiedler* Op. 144a,'' *Kirchenmusikalisches Jahrbuch* 75 (1991) 63–77.

[A. MILNER]

REGIMINIS APOSTOLICI

A bull of ALEXANDER VII dated Feb. 15, 1665, that renewed the condemnations previously directed against C. JANSEN and prescribed the signing of a formulary that condemned the five propositions censured by Innocent X in 1653, recognizing that they had been extracted from *Augustinus* and that they had been condemned in the very sense of Jansen. This signature was demanded of all ecclesiastics, religious women, and members of the teaching profession. In fact, this bull ratified those measures that the Assembly of the Clergy in France had already taken in 1655, 1656, and 1661; it therefore effected little change in the already existing situation. Four bishops, however, who were favorable to Jansenism, of whom the most noted were Nicolas Pavillon, Bishop of Alet, and Henry Arnauld, Bishop of Angers and brother of Antoine Arnauld, published the bull in their mandates in which they introduced the famous distinction between *droit* and *fait*. In 1667 the Holy Office condemned these mandates and named a commission to proceed against the four bishops, an action that provoked violent reactions in the French episcopate.

Bibliography: H. DENZINGER, *Enchiridion symbolorum,* ed. A. SCHÖNMETZER, (Freiburg 1963) 2020.

[L. J. COGNET]

REGINA CAELI LAETARE

The Marian antiphon traditionally sung at the conclusion of the hour of Compline during Paschaltide; since 1742, by decree of Benedict XIV, it has also been used to conclude the ANGELUS during the same season. Its earliest appearance is as the Magnificat antiphon for the octave of Easter in a MS of the Local Roman chant tradition, dating from *c.* 1200 [text only in J. M. Thomasius, *Opera Omnia,* ed. A. F. Vezzosi (Rome 1749), 4]. Its use as a concluding antiphon for Compline dates from about the mid-13th century. Two melodic settings, both in mode VI, are given in current editions of the Roman chant books. The first and more elaborate of these is the one traditionally associated with the text (probably early 13th century); it differs entirely from the melody found in the MS of the local Roman tradition, the music of which seems to have been used only in Rome and its environs. The second, simpler setting emerged during the later decades of the 17th century and probably was composed by Henri Dumont.

Bibliography: W. B ÄUMKER, *Das Katholische deutsche Kirchenlied,* v.2 (Freiburg 1883; repr. Hildesheim 1962). S. BÄUMER, *Histoire du bréviaire,* tr. and rev. R. BIRON, 2 v. (Paris 1905). G. REESE, *Music in the Renaissance* (New York 1959). G. REESE, *Music in the Middle Ages* (New York 1940). J. MEARNS, J. JULIAN, eds., *A Dictionary of Hymnology* (New York 1957) 2:954. F. L. HARRISON, *Music in Medieval Britain* (New York 1958). H. THURSTON. *Familiar Prayers,* ed. P. GROSJEAN (Westminster, Md. 1953).

[R. J. SNOW]

REGINALD, VALERIUS

Jesuit moral theologian, known also as Regnault and Raynauld; b. Usie in the diocese of Besançon, France, in 1543 or 1545; d. Dôle, 1623. After completing his ecclesiastical studies at Paris where he studied under Johannes MALDONATUS and Juan de MARIANA, among others, he entered the society in 1573. Then followed a long and brilliant teaching career in the society's colleges, notably at Dôle, where he taught moral theology for 20 years. His *Praxis fori paenitentialis* (Lyons 1616) ranks among the classics of CASUISTRY.

Bibliography: C. SOMMERVOGEL et. al., *Bibliothèque de la Compagnie de Jésus* 6:1591–96; 9: 798. R. BROUILLARD, *Dictionnaire de théologie catholique* 13.2:2115–17.

[R. A. COUTURE]

REGINALD OF CANTERBURY

Latin poet and Benedictine monk; b. ''Fagia,'' probably the present Faye-la-Meuse, Poitou, France, *c.* 1040; d. soon after 1109. Where he was educated, though supposedly the abbey school of Noyers, is still a matter of conjecture, and it is only probable that he was professed at BEC. He had certainly, however, become a monk of ST. AUGUSTINE'S ABBEY, Canterbury, by 1092. Reginald wrote accomplished Latin verse and was familiar with the work of at least some of the classic poets. His name is associated with that of HILDEBERT OF LAVARDIN, to whom he lent his poems. His principal work is a life of St. Malchus, a Syrian hermit, written in some 4,000 lines of Leonine hexameters.

Bibliography: T. WRIGHT, ed., *The Anglo-Latin Satirical Poets and Epigrammatists of the 12th Century* 2 v., *Rerum Britannicarum medii aevi scriptores* 59, 1872, 2:259–267. L. R. LIND, *The Vita sancti Malchi of Reginald of Canterbury* (Urbana, IL, 1936). W. HUNT, *The Dictionary of National Biography from the Earliest Times to 1900* (London 1885–1900) 16:863–864. A. SCHMITT, *Lexikon für Theologie und Kirche,* ed. J. HOFER and K. RAHNER (Freiburg 1957–65) 8:1090.

[P. BLECKER]

REGINALD OF ORLÉANS, BL.

Also known as Reginald of St. Gilles; Dominican preacher; b. Orléans, France, 1183; d. Paris, Feb. 1, 1220. Reginald took the doctorate in Canon Law at the University of Paris in 1206 and taught there for the next five years. In 1212 he was elected dean of the canons of Saint-Aignan, Orléans. St. DOMINIC received him into his order in 1218 after a nearly mortal illness during which Our Lady is said to have appeared and shown Reginald the DOMINICAN habit. On Reginald's return from a pilgrimage to the Holy Land Dominic sent him to Bologna, where he erected a priory at the Church of St. Nicholas of the Vines (now San Domenico). In the summer of 1219 he was sent to Paris to help the young Dominican foundation at the university. He died the following February. Acclaimed for his preaching and holy life, he was beatified by Pius IX in 1875.

Feast: Feb. 17 (formerly Feb. 12).

Bibliography: J. QUÉTIF and J. ÉCHARD, *Scriptores Ordinis Praedicatorum.* (Paris 1719–23) 1.1:89–90. H. SCHEEBEN, *Der heilige Dominikus* (Freiburg 1927). G. GIERATHS, *Lexikon für Theologie und Kirche,* ed. J. HOFER and K. RAHNER (Freiberg 1957–65) 8:1099. M. H. VICAIRE, *Saint Dominic and His Times,* tr. K. POND (New York 1965).

[M. MARKOWSKI]

REGINALD OF PIPERNO

Theologian; b. Piperno, Italy; d. Anagni, 1290. After joining the Roman province of the Dominican Order, he met THOMAS AQUINAS in 1259. Reginald became secretary, constant companion, confessor, and intimate friend of Aquinas. He accompanied Aquinas on all his journeys and gave his funeral oration at Fossanova. He finished Aquinas's commentaries on St. Paul's Epistles, the Gospel according to St. John, and the *De anima* of Aristotle. He is probably also the author of the supplement to the third part of the *Summa theologiae* of Thomas; this supplement was taken from Aquinas's commentary on the *Sentences* but arranged in the manner of the *Summa.* Reginald succeeded his friend in the chair of theology at Naples. Aquinas had dedicated to Reginald the *Compendium theologiae,* the *De substantiis separatis,* and the *De iudiciis astrorum.*

Bibliography: J. QUÉTIF and J. ÉCHARD, *Scriptores Ordinis Praedicatorum* (New York 1959) 1.1:382, M. GRABMANN, *Die Werke des heiligen Thomas von Aquin* (3d ed. Münster 1949) 70–76, 265–267, 298–301. A. WALZ, *Lexicon für Theologie und Kirche,* ed. J. HOFER and K. RAHNER (Freiburg 1957–65) 8:1098–99.

[A. WALZ]

REGINO OF PRÜM, COLLECTION OF

Regino was born about 840 probably in Altrip, near Speyer. He entered the monastery of Prüm in the Eifel (Rhine mountains); was elected abbot after the abdication of Abbot Farabert in 892; resigned in 899; and was appointed abbot of St. Martin's in Trier on the initiative of Abp. Ratbod of Trier. He died there in 915.

Regino was the author of three works: (1) *De harmonica institutione,* preface to a corrected new edition of the Trier *Antiphonarium;* (2) *Chronicon,* a universal chronicle from the birth of Christ to 906, dedicated to Bp. Adalbero of Augsburg; (3) *Libri duo de synodalibus causis et disciplinis ecclesiasticis,* a practical vademecum for

episcopal visitations and circuit court, composed at the suggestion of Archbishop Ratbod and dedicated to Archbishop Hatto of Mainz. This work in fact covers the entire area of episcopal diocesan administration and provides a vivid and graphic source for the study of ecclesiastical life of the period because of its detailed treatment of the matters with which it deals. Book one treats of ecclesiastical persons and things. It begins with 96 questions that were to serve as guidelines for the bishop on the occasion of parochial visitations. The following 455 chapters provide the legal basis for the precepts and prohibitions whose contravention is examined in the circuit court. Book two deals with the laity. Its 454 chapters contain procedural regulations, 89 questions, and a copious description of the various delicts and their penalties.

The sources used were generally of Roman origin and those deriving from the Carolingian Reform: canons and decrees from the *HISPANA COLLECTIO* and especially the *HADRIANA COLLECTIO;* canons from Frankish councils; 14 fragments from the FALSE DECRETALS; numerous texts from the Fathers of the Church, ecclesiastical writers, and monastic rules; fragments from the *Breviarium Alaricianum* and its interpretation; and texts from genuine and forged collections of capitularies. Regino altered many of the texts to make them better serve his purposes. He was full of the dominant thought of the Carolingian reform and specially anxious for a close tie with the Roman Church. His work had only limited success in the 10th century, but when BURCHARD OF WORMS used it in the following century, it was assured of a great and lasting influence.

Bibliography: Editions. F. G. A. WASSERSCHLEBEN (Leipzig 1840). Literature. P. FOURNIER, ''L'Oeuvre canonique de Réginon de Prüm,'' *Bibliothèque de l'École des Chartes* 81 (1920) 4–44. P. FOURNIER and G. LEBRAS, *Histoire des collections canoniques en occident depuis les fausses décrétales jusqu'au Décret de Gratien,* 2 v. (Paris 1931–32) 1:244–268. G. FLADE, ''Germanisches Heidentum und christliches Erziehungsbemühen in Karolingischer Zeit nach R. von P.,'' *Theologische Studien und Kritiken* 106 (1934–35) 213–240. R. NAZ, *Dictionnaire de droit canonique,* ed. R. NAZ, 7 v. (Paris 1935–65) 7:533–536. W. HELLINGER, ''Die Pfarrvisitation nach R. von P.,'' *Zeitschrift der Savigny-Stifug für Rechtsgeschichte, Kanoistische Abteilung* 48 (1962) 1–116; 49 (1963) 76–137. P. HOFMEISTER, *Lexikon für Theologie und Kirche,* ed. J. HOFER and K. RAHNER, 10 v. (2d, new ed. Freiburg 1957–65) 8:1099–1100.

[G. MAY]

REGIS, JOHN FRANCIS, ST.

Missionary to the French Huguenots; b. Fontconverte, Diocese of Narbonne, southeastern France, Jan. 31, 1597; d. La Louvesc (Ardèche), Dec. 31, 1640. Under the care of his devout parents, Jean, a successful merchant, and Marguerite de Cugunhan, he developed an interest in study and prayer. At 14 he began formal studies at the Jesuit college at Béziers, and, on Dec. 8, 1616, he entered the Society of Jesus; he was ordained at Toulouse in 1631. A tireless missionary, he devoted the ten remaining years of his life to the conversion of the Huguenots, visiting hospitals and prisons, reviving the faith of lax Catholics, assisting the needy, bringing the hope of Christ to wayward women, and preaching to children and the poor. His influence reached all classes and brought about a lasting spiritual revival throughout France. Among the cities and mountain towns that felt his zeal were Montpellier, Le Cheylard, Privas, the Doux valley, Fay-le-Froid, Montregard, Montfaucon, and Le Puy. The numerous miraculous cures effected during his lifetime continued after his death, whereupon he was immediately venerated as a saint by thousands who sought his intercession. John Baptist VIANNEY, Curé d'Ars, ascribed his vocation and his accomplishments to Regis.

In 1712 a Jansenist priest, L. Maille, circulated a report that John Francis Regis had been dismissed from the Society of Jesus just before his death. A commission, appointed by Clement XI, examined the official records and declared the story pure invention. Regis was proclaimed blessed by Clement XI on May 18, 1716, and declared a saint by Clement XII on April 5, 1737. The church of La Louvesc, where his body is entombed, received the title and privileges of a basilica in 1888. Here in 1830, Jean Pierre Étienne Terme (d. 1834), priest of the Diocese of Viviers, and Marie Victoire Thérèse COUDERC instituted a group of women into the Sisters of St. Francis Regis, known today as the Religious of the CENACLE.

Feast: June 16; July 2 (Jesuits).

Bibliography: F. DE CURLEY, *Saint Jean-François Régis* (Paris 1893). L J. M. CROS, *Saint Jean-François Régis* (Paris 1894). L. PIZE, *La Perpétuelle mission de Saint François Régis* (Paris 1923). J. VIANEY, *Saint François Régis* (Paris 1914). G. GUITTON, . . . *Saint Jean François Régis* (Paris 1937). A. S. FOLEY, *St. Regis, a Social Crusader* (Milwaukee 1941; Mobile, Ala. 1961). A. BUTLER, *The Lives of the Saints*, rev. ed. H. THURSTON and D. ATTWATER, 4v. (New York 1956) 2:558–61. J. N. TYLENDA, *Jesuit Saints & Martyrs* (Chicago 1998), 458–60.

[J. G. BISCHOFF]

REGIS, PIERRE SYLVAIN

French Cartesian philosopher, b. La Salvetat de Blanquefort in the Diocese of Agen, 1632; d. Paris, Nov. 1, 1707. Regis attended the Cartesian conferences given in Paris by J. Rohault (1620–75), and then gave some himself at Toulouse (1661), Montpellier (1671), and Paris, but suspended them at the request of the archbishop of Paris in 1680. He waited until 1690 before publishing

his *Cours entier de philosophie ou système général selon les principes de M. Descartes* (3 v. Paris). He defended Descartes against the *Censure* of P. D. HUET in his *Réponse . . .* (1691) and against J. B. DU HAMEL in his *Réponse aux réflexions critiques . . .* (1692). He answered the *Réponse* of N. MALEBRANCHE to his criticisms in the *Système* through a few letters in the *Journal des Savants* (1694). Named to the Academy of Sciences in 1699, he published *L'Usage de la raison et de la foi* (1704), containing a refutation of Spinoza's ethics, and a *Traité de l'amour de Dieu* (1705), together with a Latin discourse on history. He influenced Cartesian DUALISM in the direction of EMPIRICISM and defended the real union of body and soul. His physics was mechanistic; he also taught a moral philosophy based on self–love and a political science based on absolute power in the tradition of T. HOBBES.

See Also: CARTESIANISM.

Bibliography: F. C. BOUILLIER, *Histoire de la philosophie cartésienne,* 2 v. (3d ed. Paris 1868) 1:517–527. N. MALEBRANCHE, *Oeuvres complètes,* ed. A. ROBINET, v. 17.1 (Paris 1960) 238–255.

[G. RODIS-LEWIS]

REGUERA, EMMANUEL DE LA

Jesuit mystical theologian; b. Diocese of Burgos, 1668; d. Rome, 1747. Reguera entered the Society of Jesus in 1682, and after teaching philosophy and theology for many years he was called to Rome to act as a revisor general for the society. He published a work entitled *Praxis theologiae mysticae, opusculum selectum auctore P. Michaele Godinez . . . hispanice primum editum, nunc vero latine redditum et plenis commentariis . . . illustratum* (2 v. Rome 1740, 1745). This was much more than a translation into Latin of Godinez's *Práctica de la theología mystica* (1681); it added to that small work an extensive and valuable commentary. Reguera's *Praxis* was one of the finest *summae* of mystical theology of the 18th century, but its merit was somewhat obscured by the order and method he imposed on himself by electing to construct his treatise on the basis of the work of Godinez. Dominikus Schramm, OSB, in his *Institutiones theologiae mysticae* (Augsburg 1774 and many times reprinted) provided a résumé of the *Praxis* that put the doctrine of Reguera in better order. It was through this résumé that the *Praxis* was best known and exercised its influence. Reguera was among the revisors general appointed to examine the *Direttorio mistico* of G. B. SCARAMELLI and favored its publication.

Bibliography: J. DE GUIBERT, *La Spiritualité de la Compagnie de Jésus* (Bibliotheca Instituti Historici 4; Rome 1953), Eng.

The Jesuits: Their Spiritual Doctrine and Practice, tr. W. J. YOUNG, ed. G. E. GANSS (Chicago 1964).

[P. K. MEAGHER]

REGULA MAGISTRI

An anonymous and heterogeneous collection, in two parts, of spiritual precepts and practical legislation governing monastic life. The whole constitutes a *regula monachorum* or rule for monks that was undoubtedly in actual practice in one or more monastic establishments, as indicated by its bulk: a prologue of 57 lines (in the only complete MS, Paris, Bib. Nat. lat. 12205), and a *thema* of 314 lines and 95 chapters, many of which exceed 100 lines each. It was most probably compiled in the early part of the sixth century in the region south of Rome (present day Latium).

The *Regula Magistri* (RM) is a document of great value to the student of monastic institutions and early liturgical observance of the BENEDICTINES. Although St. Benedict is nowhere mentioned in the RM, it is of particular interest to note that certain passages are identical, word for word, with the BENEDICTINE RULE. Hence there arose a great deal of controversy as to which of the two rules is the more ancient. In all probability, both are derived independently from still earlier sources. It should be noted that some of the material appearing in the RM seems to have little relevance to the cenobitic life, and may well be derived from primitive, Eastern, ascetic sources, e.g., the account of the *gyrovagi* or wandering monks in ch. I, "De generibus monachorum." There are also many echoes of John CASSIAN, who introduced Eastern practice into southern Gaul in the early 5th century. The above Paris MS, is, itself, not later than *c.* 700, i.e., earlier than any MS we possess of the Benedictine Rule. Furthermore, there are extracts of the RM in Paris, Bib. Nat. lat. 12634, which may date from an even earlier period.

The RM may be studied in the diplomatic edition prepared by H. Vanderhoven and F. Masai, in collaboration with P. B. Corbett, *Aux Sources du monachisme Bénédictin I, Publications de Scriptorium III* (Brussels-Paris 1953), which has extensive prolegomena (5–123). For a comparison of the the RM and the Benedictine Rule, see T. Fry, ed., *The Rule of St. Benedict in Latin and English with Notes* (Collegeville, Minnesota 1981); G. Penco, *S. Benedicti Regula introduzione, testo, apparati, traduzione e commento* (Florence 1958); and A. de Vogüé, *La Communauté et l'abbé dans la Règle de Saint Benoît* (Bruges 1961). On the language of the RM, see P. B. Corbett, *The Latin of the Regula Magistri* (Louvain 1958).

Bibliography: M. ALAMO, ''La Règle de Saint Benoît éclairée par sa source, la Règle du maître,'' *Revue d'histoire ecclésiastique* 34 (1938) 740–55. J. PÉREZ DE URBEL, ''Le Maître et Saint Benoît,'' *ibid.* 756–64. H. VANDERHOVEN, ''S. Benoît a-t-il connu la Règle du Maître?'' *ibid.* 40 (1944–45) 176–87. B. CAPELLE, ''Le Maître antérieur à S. Benoît?,'' *ibid.,* 41 (1946) 66–75. A. GENESTOUT, ''La Règle du Maître et la Règle de S. Benoît,'' *Revue d'ascétique et de d'archéologie* 21 (1940) 51–112. J. FROGER, ''La Règle du maître et les sources du monachisme Bénédictin,'' *ibid.* 30 (1954) 275–88. F. MASAI, ''La Règle de S. Benoît et la *Regula Magistri,*'' *Latomus* 6 (1947) 207–29. M. CAPPUYNS, ''L'Auteur de la *Regula Magistri:* Cassiodore,'' *Recherches de théologie ancienne et médiévale* 15 (1948) 209–68. P. BLANCHARD, ''La Règle du maître et la Règle de Saint Benoît,'' *Revue Bénédictine* 60 (1950) 25–64. B. STEIDLE, ed., *Regula Magistri, Regula S. Benedicti: Studia monastica (Studia anselmiana* 44; 1959). A. DE VOGÜÉ, *La Règle du maître,* 2 v. (Paris 1964), Latin text and French tr. L. EBERLE, *The Rule of the Master* (Cistercian Studies Series 6, Kalamazoo, Michigan 1977).

[P. B. CORBETT/EDS.]

REICHENAU, ABBEY OF

A former Benedictine monastery in the old Diocese of Constance in south-western Germany (Latin, *Augia Dives*). CHARLES MARTEL founded a Benedictine abbey on the island of Reichenau in Lake Constance in 724 and entrusted it to its first abbot, St. PIRMIN. The nucleus of the present cloisters was the Carolingian cathedral of Mittelzell, built by Abbot Hatto I (806–822 or 823). At the same time, Bp. Egino of Verona (d. 802) erected the second Carolingian basilica for the monastery in Niederzell, modeling it on S. Maria in Cosmedin in Rome. In 896 Abbot Hatto III (888–913) founded the canonry of Oberzell, where the church was decorated in the third quarter of the 10th century with the famous and still well-preserved Ottonian fresco cycle.

The monastery began to flourish under the fourth abbot, Arnefried, who in 736 became also bishop of Constance. This personal union lasted till 782. Abbot Hatto I was simultaneously bishop of Basel; and Abbot Hatto III, archbishop of Mainz. The ecclesiastical importance of the abbey was still further enhanced by the translation of the relics of St. MARK, which Reichenau obtained in 830 from Bp. Ratold of Verona (d. 847), and of the head of St. GEORGE obtained by Abbot Hatto III. The monastery's period of greatness arrived under Abbot Alawich II (997–1000), who was granted pontifical rights and the privilege of papal abbatial consecration by GREGORY V.

Reichenau's position in the field of scholarship was outstanding. Its library and school, founded by Abbot Wallo (786–806), were especially flourishing under the direction of WALAFRID STRABO (d. 848) and later of HERMANNUS Contractus (d. 1054). Under Abbot BERNO

(1008–48) Reichenau's illumination work attained European fame. The expressionistic Reichenau style was influenced by contemporary BYZANTINE practice and was distinguished by strong animation of ornamentation, disembodiment of figures, and the brilliance of its internal color. About the middle of the 11th century a decline set in as a result of poor economic management of the monastery. In 1535 the abbey was incorporated into the Diocese of Constance, and in 1802 it was secularized. The various churches, however, remain in large part intact.

Bibliography: BERTHOLD VON REICHENAU, *Die Briefe des Abtes Bern von Reichenau,* ed. F. J. SCHMALE (Stuttgart 1961). K. GRÖBER, *Die Reichenau* (Karlsruhe 1938). T. MAYER, ''Die Anfänge der Reichenau,'' *Zeitschrift für die Geschichte des Oberrheins* 101 (1953) 305–352. O. FEGER, *Geschichte des Bodenseeraumes,* 2 v. (Lindau 1956–58). A. KNOEPFLI, *Kunstgeschichte des Bodenseeraumes* (Constance 1961–). K. MARTIN, *Die ottonischen Wandbilder der St. Georgskirche Reichenau-Oberzell* (Constance 1961). L. H. COTTINEAU, *Répertoire topobibliographique des abbayes et prieurés,* 2 v. (Mâcon 1935–39) 2:2427–30.

[W. GRAPE]

REICHERSBERG, MONASTERY OF

Under Augustinian canons; on the Inn River in the Diocese of Linz (before 1784 part of the Diocese of Passau), Upper Austria; the patron is St. Michael. It was founded in 1084 by Werner of Reichersberg (d. 1086), who entered the cloister after the death of his wife and son, and again by Abp. Conrad I of Salzburg (1105–47), who restored the possessions seized by an antibishop (of Salzburg), built the cloister (1122), consecrated the church (1126), and called in canons from the thriving monasteries of Saxony. Reichersberg was known also for the activity and writings of GERHOH and his brother Arno, who assisted Conrad in the Gregorian reform. Provost Paul Tellenpeck (1415–68) had historical sources collected and a register begun. After a fire in 1624, cloister and church were rebuilt (1625–44) and enlarged (1663–1704); they contain noteworthy frescoes, stuccowork, and sculpture. The provost has been mitered since 1654. The monastery was suppressed (1810–16) and since 1907 has belonged to the Austrian Congregation of Canons Regular of the Lateran; in 1964 it had 20 priests and two clerics and cared for 12 parishes.

Bibliography: G. WEISS, *Lexikon für Theologie und Kirche,* ed. M. BUCHBERGER, 10 v. (Freiburg 1930–38) 8:731–732; *Geschichte und Sehenswürdigkeiten des Stiftes Reichersbergs* (Ried 1934). B. F. MITTERER, *Die Reichersberger Chorherren* (Vienna 1950).

[M. H. SCHMID]

Thomas Reid. (Archive Photos)

REID, THOMAS

Philosopher, founder of the SCOTTISH SCHOOL OF COMMON SENSE; b. Strachan, near Aberdeen, April 26, 1710; d. Glasgow, Oct. 7, 1796. Reid was a professor at the University of Aberdeen from 1752 to 1764, when he succeeded Adam SMITH in the chair of moral philosophy at Glasgow.

The method of observation and analysis limited to sensorial experience is typical of Reid and his school: the mind knows itself by observing and analyzing the various faculties and constitutive principles of man, in order not to go beyond phenomena and thereby to renounce explaining their origins (metaphysical agnosticism). The validity of sensible knowledge, the existence of the perceiving subject, and belief in the existence of external objects are all inexplicable yet basic principles of human nature. ''The mind has a certain faculty of inspiration or suggestion . . . to which we are debtors for an infinite number of simple notions, which are neither impressions nor ideas, as well as for a good number of basic principles of belief'' (*Inquiry* 2.7). Sensation and perception are basic acts of knowledge; through them man knows the primary (objective) and secondary (subjective) qualities of things. In perception, the immediate object of the mind is not the idea but the thing. Ideas do not exist, and to admit them is to accept the skeptical consequences of G. BERKELEY and D. HUME that is, to deny matter, spiritual substance, and the principle of causality—truths made indisputable by common sense (*Essays* 2.9). Sensation is infallible and attests to the objectivity of the qualities existing in an object, the essence of which man does not know, since he cannot know material or spiritual substance; he knows only extension, motion, etc., which are neither ideas nor impressions, nor can they exist without something extended or moved. Perception, moreover, has immediate evidence, not demanding reasoning for its proof. Man perceives an object and immediately there arises in him the invincible belief that he and the object exist. All reasoning is based upon this belief, which is first and independent of reasoning. It is an innate suggestion that, not explaining anything because man cannot explain anything, makes him believe in everything and gives him confidence in his faculties, without which he cannot think or act. Common sense should not conform to philosophy, but the latter to the former.

Thus, Reid thought that he had resolved the problem about the objectivity of knowledge and reality against the idealists or impressionists. Yet, like I. KANT, he made dogmatic assumptions and thereby hardly departed from Kant's apriority.

Bibliography: Works. *An Inquiry into the Human Mind, on the Principles of Common Sense* (London 1764); *Essays on the Intellectual Powers of Man* (Edinburgh 1785); *Essays on the Active Powers of Man* (Edinburgh 1788). Literature. F. C. COPLESTON, *History of Philosophy* (Westminister, Md. 1946–) v. 5, *Hobbes to Hume* (1959) 364–373. M. M. ROSSI, *Enciclopedia filosofica*, 4 v. (Venice-Rome 1957) 3:1928–35. M. F. SCIACCA, *T. Reid* (Brescia 1945); *La filosofia di T. Reid* (Naples 1935).

[M. F. SCIACCA]

REIFFENSTUEL, ANACLETUS (JOHANN GEORG)

Theologian, canonist; b. Tegernsee, Bavaria, July 2, 1642; d. Freising, May 10, 1703; entered the Bavarian Province of the Franciscan order in 1658. He served as professor of philosophy, theology, and canon law, and held various offices within his order. The bishop of Freising appointed him director of episcopal educational establishments; in this capacity he organized and cataloged the episcopal and capitular libraries of that diocese.

His *Theologia moralis,* which first appeared in 1692, was published in about 30 editions. Reiffenstuel's most notable work was the *Ius canonicum universum,* published in 1700, which, following the basic divisions of the Decretals of Gregory IX, provides a clear and scientific explanation of the law. Except for Hostiensis and Du-

randus, Reiffenstuel did not directly utilize the older decretalists, but primarily those of the 15th century, especially Panormitanus. In a series of questions, the *Ius canonicum* treats the entire field of canon law, embracing the decrees of the Council of Trent, the papal constitutions issued after the council, and the practice of the Roman Curia. Its principal merit besides its completeness and extent is its excellence, which made it a standard work of reference for later canonists. This work alone accords Reiffenstuel a high place among canonists and scholars. In addition, he is the author of a *Vita S. Francisci Solani* and a treatise *De caeremoniis et ritibus ecclesiasticis.*

Bibliography: A. TEETAERT, *Dictionnaire de théologie catholique,* ed. A. VACANT et al., 15 v. (Paris 1903–50; Tables générales 1951–) 13.2:2126–30. J. OBERMAYR, *Die Pfarrei Gmund am Tegernsee und die Reiffenstuel* (Freising 1868) 388–400.

[D. W. BONNER]

REILLY, WENDELL

Sulpician priest and Biblical scholar; b. North Hatley, Quebec, Canada, March 25, 1875; d. Baltimore, Maryland, Oct. 7, 1950. In 1895 Reilly entered the Grand Séminaire, Montreal and was ordained on July 31, 1898, in Sherbrooke, Quebec. After higher studies in theology and Scripture for two years at the Institut Catholique, Paris, he began his teaching career at St. Mary's Seminary, Baltimore. In 1901 he resumed his study of Oriental languages at the Catholic University of America in Washington, D.C. The following year he spent in the Sulpician novitiate at Issy, France, where he received the degree of S.T.D. from the Institut Catholique. From 1903 to 1907 he taught at St. John's Seminary, Brighton, Massachusetts, and then was sent to Jerusalem to continue his scriptural studies at the École Biblique. His studies were completed in Rome where he was awarded the degree of S.S.D. by the Pontifical Biblical Commission, the first American to earn this degree. Returning to the U.S., he taught at St. John's Seminary (until 1911) and then at St. Mary's Seminary again (until his retirement in 1947).

Reilly was one of two Americans chosen to work on the Westminster revision of the Bible, for which he translated and commented on St. John's Gospel. He was also one of the founders of the Catholic Biblical Association of America, a member of its committee on revision, and an editor of the NT translation (1941) published by the Confraternity of Christian Doctrine, for which he translated the Epistle to the Ephesians. He was cofounder and first editor–in–chief (1939–47) of the *Catholic Biblical Quarterly,* to which he contributed many articles, and cofounder and first moderator (1924–49) of *The Voice,* a magazine published by St. Mary's Seminary for its students and alumni.

Bibliography: *The Catholic Biblical Quarterly* 13 (1951) 86.

[C. J. NOONAN]

REIMARUS, HERMANN SAMUEL

Deist exegete; b. Hamburg, Germany, Dec. 22, 1694; d. Hamburg, March 1, 1768. After being an instructor of philosophy at Wittenberg (1719–23) and the rector of a Protestant church in Wismar (1723–27), for the rest of his life he was professor of Oriental languages at the Gymnasium Johanneum in Hamburg. Early influenced by C. WOLFF and the English Deists (*see* DEISM), Reimarus was opposed both to the French rationalists, such as J. O. de La Mettrie, who scoffed at the idea of NATURAL LAW, and to the defenders of traditional Biblical Christianity, as he showed in his first works, *Die vornehmsten Wahrheiten der natürlichen Religion* (Hamburg 1754) and *Die Vernunftlehre* (Hamburg 1756). Although personally pious and attentive to the externals of Protestantism, he based his faith on reason alone, and the only miracle that he admitted was creation itself.

In his endeavor to make Christianity entirely "reasonable," i.e., totally free of the miraculous and the supernatural, Reimarus spent 20 years on the composition of his most influential work, the *Apologie oder Schutzschrift für die vernünftigen Verehrer Gottes,* in two voluminous manuscripts, an earlier one and a revised one. Fearing the consequences of publication, however, he left the work unpublished. After his death, his children lent a copy of the earlier manuscript to G. E. LESSING, who published seven abstracts ("fragments") of it under the title *Fragmente eines Wolfenbüttelschen Ungenannten* (Berlin 1774–78); (1) On Sufferance of the Deists, (2) On Decrying Reason from the Pulpit, (3) The Impossibility of a Revelation That All Men Could Reasonably Believe, (4) The Passage of the Israelite through the Red Sea, (5) That the Books of the OT Were Not Written to Reveal a Religion, (6) On the Resurrection Story, and (7) On the Aim of Jesus and His Disciples. The publication of the abstracts soon produced the so-called *Fragmentenstreit* (quarrel about the fragments), in which they were attacked not only by the conservative Protestant J. M. Goeze, but also by the liberal J. S. Semler and others. The main controversy was waged over the seventh abstract. In it Reimarus maintained that Jesus was a mere man who had messianic illusions and preached a simple, practical morality in preparation for the imminent establishment of the kingdom of God; after His death, His disciples stole His body, preached that He had risen, and founded a com-munity with a newly developed Christology. Although most of Reimarus's theories had no lasting influence, the question that he raised concerning the historical value of the Gospels for the life of Jesus is still a live issue.

Bibliography: F. MUSSNER, in *Lexikon für Theologie und Kirche,* ed. J. HOFER and K. RAHNER, 10 v. (2d new ed. Freiburg 1957–65) 8:1137–38. H. HOHLWEIN, in *Die Religion in Geschichte und Gegenwart,* 7 v. (3d ed. Tübingen 1957–65) 5:937–938. F. L. CROSS, *The Oxford Dictionary of the Christian Church* (London 1957) 1148. A. C. LUNDSTEEN, *Hermann Samuel Reimarus und die Anfänge der Leben-Jesu-Forschung* (Copenhagen 1939).

[L. F. HARTMAN]

REIMS

The capital of an arrondissement in the department of Marne, northeast France; since the 3d or 4th century the seat of a metropolitanate. In 2001 the archdiocese had 76 parishes, three churches or mission stations, 168 secular and 14 religious priests, 58 members of men's religious institutes, 306 members of women's religious institutes, and 20 permanent deacons. There were 594,000 Catholics in a population of 608,356; it is 6,931 square kilometers in area.

City. Reims (Gallic *Durocortorum*) was the capital of the Gallic *Remi,* a tribe that gave the city its name in the 3d century. It was a major Gallo-Roman *civitas* at the junction of routes from Lyons to Great Britain and from Paris to Lorraine, but it lost importance when Paris became the capital and crossroads of France. After the ruinous mid-3d-century barbarian invasions, Reims was fortified and became the main defense point against the Germans, the capital of *Belgica II,* a city of soldiers and officials. Christianity probably appeared there early. Gregory of Tours mentions Timothy and Apollinaris as 3d-century martyrs in Reims, which probably had a bishop by 300. Imbetausius at the Council of ARLES (314), 4th in a later episcopal list, is the first certainly known bishop. The first Christian community and the first basilica were in the southeast suburb.

St. Nicasius, slain by either Vandals (407) or Huns (451), built the first cathedral, within the walls. CLOVIS, to whom St. REMIGIUS had sent a letter on his accession (481), occupied Reims after the battle of Soissons (485–486); and king and bishop became good enough friends for Remigius to be entrusted with Clovis' religious instruction and baptism at Reims (496 or 506?). Reims thus became the religious cradle of the Frankish monarchy, a fact of basic importance in its history.

In the 6th and 7th centuries Reims held within its walls, for reasons of security, the Abbeys of Saint-

Roman arch dating from the 3rd century A.D., near the church of St.-Remi, at Reims, France. (©Angelo Hornak/CORBIS)

Thierry, SAINT-REMI, Saint-Pierre-les-Dames, and Saint-Pierre *in civitate,* as well as a hospital. Moreover, there were schools, famous in Gallo-Roman times. To judge from these establishments, the Church seems to have been the largest landowner in the city of 60 to 75 acres. Royal privileges assured the Church's predominance, despite confiscations by CHARLES MARTEL; immunity was accorded (575–583) and confirmed (625, 711–715, 769–794, and after).

Reims's bishops were of major importance in Carolingian times. Gilles, closely involved in the intrigues of the Merovingian kings, was deposed at the synod of Metz (590). St. Nivard (649–672) founded the monastery of Hautivilliers. St. Reolus founded that of Orbais *c.* 680. Rigobert (698–743), godfather of Charles Martel, became entangled with him later. Abel (743–748) was the first to use the title archbishop. TURPIN (753–800) gave his name to the hero of the *Chanson de Roland.* EBBO (816–845), a counselor of the rebel sons of Louis the

Pious, was expelled from Reims and died as bishop of Hildesheim. HINCMAR (845–882), the most famous of Reims's bishops, rebuilt his cathedral (862). Despite depradations the Church of Reims at this time was rich: 17 basilicas, four abbeys, a hospital, and a cathedral chapter founded *c.* 800. Several Carolingian kings were consecrated in Reims, which at times became a royal residence. Norman incursions made the bishops rebuild the fortifications (*c.* 885), torn down at the time of Ebbo. In 940 Louis IV gave the archbishop the *comitatus* (rights of a count) of the *civitas.* Thus began the important temporal sovereignty of the archbishop of the city.

In the 10th and 11th centuries arose merchant suburbs (a commune in the 12th, with a charter from the archbishop in 1182), and the famous episcopal school was established. Reims's ties with political life were close. Archbishop Adelbero (969–987) was the great elector of Hugh Capet (987); Gerbert (991–995), formerly director of the episcopal school, later became Pope Sylvester II.

In feudal days Reims was above all the city of consecration of kings. A bull of Sylvester I (999) gave its archbishops a monopoly of the consecration. All the Capetian kings but nine were consecrated at Reims. At Charles VII's consecration (1429), probably the most important, JOAN OF ARC, who sought and obtained the consecration by her victories, was present, standard in hand. Charles X was the last king consecrated (1825). Cardinal de La Roche Aymon, who consecrated Louis XVI in 1775, had baptized, confirmed, married, and given first Communion to the young king—testimony of the marriage of the royalty with the Church of Reims. The consecration comprised four main ceremonies: oaths of the king, consecration, crowning, enthroning with popular acclaim—followed by a Mass at which the king received Communion under both species. The anointings, nine in all, were made with the miraculous chrism of the Holy Ampulla (brought by an angel to St. Remigius for the baptism of Clovis). A banquet at the archbishop's palace followed the ceremony. A day or so later the king would touch the sores of those ill with scrofula (adenitis), of which there were 2,500 at the consecration of Louis XVI. The king, fasting, said "I touch you; may God cure you."

Feudal archbishops came from the foremost families. Two were sons of kings, four others were royal princes; five (1533–1641) belonged to the ducal family of Lorraine. Popes often visited Reims: Stephen V (816), Leo X (1049), Callistus II (1119), Innocent II (1131) who presided at a council attended by St. Bernard, and Eugene III (1148) at another council with St. Bernard. Noteworthy archbishops include GERVASE (1055–67), SIMON OF CRAMAUD (1409–13), and Robert (1493–97) and Guillaume (1497–1507) BRIÇONNET.

After undergoing 49 months of bombardment that destroyed 12,000 of its 14,000 houses in World War I, Reims suffered again in World War II. But it still has beautiful monuments. The Cathedral of Notre-Dame was built (1211–1311) on the location of the old cathedral of St. Nicasius and Hincmar's cathedral (490 ft long, 201 ft wide at the transept, a nave 125 ft high, and towers 267 ft high). It was restored after World War I, thanks in large part to Rockefeller's contribution. Its statues equal the most beautiful of the Greeks. The Church of Saint-Remi (11th–15th century), formerly the abbey church, is almost as beautiful as the cathedral. Practically nothing remains of the former episcopal palace, destroyed in World War I.

Reims had flourishing schools very early. The College of Good Children, founded c. 1245 to educate clerics, was made a university with four faculties by Cardinal Charles of Lorraine (1548). The exempt cathedral chapter, which shared seigneurial rights with the bishop, furnished the Church with five popes, 23 archbishops, and 53 cardinals; St. BRUNO the Carthusian belonged to it. St. John Baptist de LA SALLE (1651–1719) was a canon of Reims; G. Marlot (1596–1667) was a historian of the city; Denis PETAU (1583–1652) was professor at the Jesuit College; and Thierry RUINART (1657–1709) was born in Reims.

Archdiocese. The diocese (*Remensis*) does not compare with the city. Reims has been a metropolitan see since the creation of *Belgica II*. At the time of the official *Notitia Galliarum* (c. 400) its suffragans were Soissons, Châlons, SAINT-QUENTIN (or NOYON), Arras, CAMBRAI, Senlis, Beauvais, AMIENS, Thérouanne, and Boulogne. Disrupted by the Germanic invasions, the province gradually restored itself in the 6th and 7th centuries. St. Remigius founded the See of Laon. When diocesan boundaries were redrawn in 1559, Reims lost Cambrai, Arras, and Tournai. At the end of the Old Regime its suffragans were Soissons, Châlons, Senlis, Laon, Noyon, Beauvais, Amiens, and Boulogne. Suppressed by the CONCORDAT OF 1801, the see was restored in 1822 with its present suffragans.

Among its archbishops are Cardinal Thomas Gousset (1840–66, a theologian, revived the tradition of provincial synods (Soissons 1849, Amiens 1853, Reims 1857) and multiplied institutions of Catholic education; J. B. Landriot (1867–74) preached and wrote; Cardinal L. H. Luçon (1906–30) remained calm through the bombardments of World War I; Cardinal Emmanuel Suhard (1930) became archbishop of Paris in 1940. Archbishops of old had the titles of duke, peer, *legatus natus* of the Holy See, and primate of Belgian Gaul.

Besides Saint-Remi, former abbeys include Saint-Basle (scene of a council in 991), Mouzon (councils in 948, 995, 1147), Saint-Nicaise (founded 6th or 7th century on the tomb of St. Nicasius, suppressed in 1792), and Igny.

The oldest historian of Reims is FLODOARD, canon of Reims (d. 966), who wrote a remarkable *Historia Remensis ecclesiae*.

Bibliography: G. MARLOT, *Histoire de la ville, cité et université de Rheims*, 4 v. (Reims 1843–46). F. VERCAUTEREN, *Étude sur les civitates de la Belgique seconde* (Brussels 1934). G. BOURGEOIS, *Le Duché de Reims, première pairie de France* (Paris 1944). L. BRÉHIER, *La Cathédrale de Reims* (Paris 1916). M. RENARD, *Notre-Dame royale. Tableaux du sacre de Louis XVI à Reims* (Paris 1927). M. L. B. BLOCH, *Le Rois thaumaturges* (Strasbourg 1924). G. TEISSIER, *Le Baptême de Clovis* (Paris 1964). G. ALLEMANG, *Lexikon für Theologie und Kirche*, ed. J. HOFER and K. RAHNER (Freiburg 1957–65); suppl., *Das Zweite Vatikanishe Konsil: Dokumente und Kommentare*, ed. H. S. BRECHTER et al. (1966) 8:1139–41. G.

A child, believed to be the reincarnation of Kalou-Rimpoche, at a Buddhist temple in Sonada, India. (©Daniel Lainé/CORBIS)

BAILLAT *Reims* (Paris 1990). R. HAMMAN-MACLEAN, *Die Kathedrale von Reims* (Stuttgart 1993). P. DESPORTES *Diocèse de Reims* (Turnhout 1998). FLODOARD OF REIMS *Historia Remensis ecclesiae*, ed. M. STRATMANN (Hannover 1998). *Annuario Pontificio* (2001) 500.

[E. JARRY]

REINCARNATION

Belief in reincarnation seems to have originated in India and to have been introduced into HINDUISM from the tenets of the earlier inhabitants in about the 6th century B.C. According to this doctrine the souls of all living beings, plants, animals, men, and even gods, are subject to a perpetual cycle of rebirth (*saṁsāra*). By the law of KARMA, the condition of a soul in this life is determined by its action in the past. A soul rises in the scale of being by performance of good deeds and descends by evil deeds, but in either case there is no finality. Even the gods must die when the universe is dissolved and be born again when a new creation begins. This doctrine must be judged, however, in the light of the corresponding beliefs that all creation is *māyā,* that is, ultimately unreal. The purpose of life is to realize the unreality of the world of becoming and to attain liberation (*mokṣa*) in the world of absolute Being. This doctrine, common to Hinduism, BUDDHISM, and JAINISM, gradually spread from India to the West.

[B. GRIFFITHS]

REINERT, PAUL C.

Jesuit, educator and university president. b. Boulder, Colorado, Aug. 12, 1910; d. St. Louis, Missouri, July 22, 2001. One of six sons born to Francis and Emma (Voegtle) Reinert, he joined the Society of Jesus in 1927. After receiving an A.B. (1933) and M.A. (1934) from St. Louis University, he served for a time as registrar at St. Mary's College, Kansas. He earned a Ph.D. at the University of Chicago (1944) and that same year was assigned to St. Louis University where he served as dean of the College of Arts and Sciences (1944–48), vice president (1948–49), and president (1949–74). Reinert was instrumental in obtaining the admission of the first African-American students to the university (and thus the first such students admitted to a historically white university in a former slave state).

Reinert's tenure as president spanned 25 years, a seminal period in the history of the university and of all American higher education. Reinert found himself confronted with the challenges of the postwar flood of students into higher education, curricular innovation and expansion, the overlapping roles of university president and rector of the local Jesuit community, and the admission of women as regular students. In addition, the city of St. Louis faced urban decline during these years, accompanied by ''white flight'' and continued racial tensions. Reinert committed the university to remain in its urban setting and became a leader of efforts to revitalize the inner city of St. Louis, pairing these endeavors with expansion of the university campus and the creation of programs designed to attract minority students.

In 1967, under Reinert's direction, St. Louis University became the first Catholic university to reorganize its board to include lay trustees, initiating a trend that transformed Catholic higher education. While critics complained that, along with the appointment of lay professionals to high ranking university positions, Reinert was diluting the Jesuit character of the institution, others saw a broadening of the university's vision and a reaffirmation of the original Ignatian educational mission, and pointed to the increased national status of the university and its service to the community.

Reinert served as a consultant to several Catholic educational institutions and on many national commissions on education. He was the recipient of many awards and honorary doctorates. Following his retirement as president he served as the university's Chancellor (1974–1991) and Chancellor Emeritus (1991–2001), remaining an articulate spokesman for Catholic higher education and for social justice.

Reinert's publications include *The Urban Catholic University* (1970), *To Turn the Tide* (1972), and *Seasons of Change: Reflections on Half a Century at Saint Louis University* (with Paul Shore) (1996).

[P. SHORE]

REINHOLD, HANS A.

Liturgical innovator; b. in Hamburg, Germany, 1897; d. Pittsburgh, Pa., 1968. He was educated at Freiburg, Innsbruck, Münster, and the Pontifical Institute of Archaeology in Rome. During World War I he served as an artilleryman on both the Eastern and Western fronts, and, after being wounded, in the intelligence corps. He tried his vocation as a Benedictine at Maria Laach, but was advised not to continue, and in 1925 was ordained priest for the Diocese of Osnabrück. In his autobiography

he lists as the strongest influences in his formation Romano Guardini, the Jesuits at Innsbruck, and Abbot Ildefons Herwegen, Prior Albert Hammenstede, and Dom Odo Casel of Maria Laach. Assigned to organize an apostolate to German seamen at Bremerhaven and Hamburg, he began such liturgical experimentation (dialogue Mass, Mass facing the people, nocturnal celebration of the Easter Vigil) as was startlingly novel at the time. Not long after Hitler rise to power he was threatened with arrest and prosecution for criticizing Nazi leaders and politics, and escaped to England in 1935. A year later he came to New York to work for the placement in the United States of German Catholic refugees, but found himself under suspicion in ecclesiastical circles because of his alleged sympathy with communism and with liturgical reform. Incardinated at last in the Archdiocese of Seattle (later, when that diocese was erected, in the Diocese of Yakima), he founded a seamen's club, served as a curate, and was pastor at Sunnyside, Washington, from 1944 to 1956. Misunderstandings with his bishop led to his requesting a leave of absence. After long illness and painful sufferings in the spirit, he was received by Bishop John Wright in Pittsburgh.

By temperament Reinhold was timid and sensitive—characteristics which were aggravated by his misfortunes—but seemed unable to evaluate the effect his own outspokenness had on others, especially his superiors. This forthright style, however, was very effective in his writings, which appeared through many years in *Commonweal* and *Orate Fratres* (later *Worship*) and in several books, advocating not only liturgical reform but also social reform as deriving from liturgical awareness and participation, and reaching out to allied topics in catechetics, art and architecture, and theology. He lectured widely, having achieved a mastery of idiomatic English. He served on the first board of directors of the Liturgical Conference and presented a paper at the annual national Liturgical Week for many years. He helped to organize the Vernacular Society of America and attended international meetings of liturgical scholars in Europe, where the reforms that were later adopted by Vatican Council II were first proposed and endorsed.

Bibliography: Works of Reinhold. *The Soul Afire: Revelations of the Mystics,* ed. (New York 1944). *Churches, Their Plan and Furnishing,* with P. F. ANSON (Milwaukee 1948). *The American Parish and the Roman Liturgy* (New York 1958). *Bringing the Mass to the People* (Baltimore 1960). *The Dynamics of Liturgy* (New York 1961). *Liturgy and Art* (New York 1966). *H.A.R.: The Autobiography of Father Reinhold* (New York 1968).

[W. J. LEONARD]

REISACH, KARL AUGUST VON

Archbishop, cardinal, count; b. Roth, near Eichstätt, Germany, July 6, 1800; d. Contamine (Savoie), France, Dec. 16, 1869. After studying law at Heidelberg, Göttingen, and Landshut, Reisach obtained a doctorate in law (1821). He then attended the German College in Rome (1824–29), was ordained (1828), and received a doctorate in theology (1829). In 1830 he was appointed prefect of studies at the College of Propaganda in Rome. He became bishop of Eichstätt (1836), coadjutor (1841), and then archbishop of Munich and Freising (1846). At Eichstätt he established a minor seminary and also reorganized the major seminary. During the COLOGNE MIXED MARRIAGE DISPUTE, he played an important role as confidant of the pope and of the kings of Bavaria and Prussia.

In Munich after 1846, he became intimately involved in the conflict over the government's use of the placet in Bavaria. He strongly upheld the Church's freedom at the first German bishops' conference in Würzburg (1848) and at the Bavarian bishops' meeting in Freising (1850). The conflict with the Bavarian government led to his transfer to Rome in 1855, when he was raised to the cardinalate.

Because of his agreeable personality, he was chosen to negotiate the concordats with Württemberg (1857) and Baden (1859), which were not ratified by the legislatures of these two states. Reisach became minister of education for the STATES OF THE CHURCH (1862) and a member of several Roman Congregations. In 1865, he was in appointed president of the preparatory commission for VATICAN COUNCIL I and in 1867 president of the commission for Church–State questions. In 1868 he became cardinal bishop of the suburbicarian See of Sabina. He was named a council president (Nov. 27, 1869), but died before exercising this office.

Bibliography: H. RALL, *Lexikon für Theologie und Kirche*, ed. J. HOFER and K. RAHNER (Freiberg 1957–65) 8:1151–52.

[V. CONZEMIUS]

REITZENSTEIN, RICHARD

Classical scholar and historian of Hellenistic religion; b. Breslau, April 2, 1861; d. Göttingen, March 3, 1931. The major part of his career was spent in his professorships at Strassburg (1893–1911) and at Göttingen (from 1914). At Strassburg the history of Hellenistic religion became his main interest. As a representative of the religio-historical school, he approached all religious phenomena in the ancient world from the viewpoint of comparative religion, and he tended to be extreme in his syncretistic interpretations. In 1904 he published his first major work in the religious field, a study on the *Poimandres,* the first treatise in the *Corpus Hermeticum.* He exaggerated, however, the Egyptian influence upon it. His most famous contribution, *Die hellenistischen Mysterienreligionen* (Leipzig 1910; 3d ed. 1927), greatly overemphasized the relation of the mystery religions to and their influence on early Christianity. In his *Das iranische Erlösungsmysterium* (Bonn 1920) he became a champion of *Paniranismus,* and he continued to maintain this position in his last major work, *Studien zum antiken Synkretismus aus Iran und Griechenland* (Leipzig 1926).

Bibliography: W. SCHATZ, *Lexikon für Theologie und Kirche,* ed. J. HOFER and K. RAHNER, 10 v. (2d, new ed. Freiburg 1957–65) 8:1155. C. COLPE, *Die Religion in Geschichte und Gegenwart,* 7 v. (3d ed. Tübingen 1957–65) 5:951. E. FRAENKEL et al., *Festschrift R. Reitzenstein* (Leipzig 1931), with list of his publications. K. PRÜMM, *Religionsgeschichtliches Handbuch für den Raum der altchristlichen Umwelt* (2d ed. Rome 1954) 544–546.

[A. CLOSS]

RELATION

Relation, from the Latin, *relatio (referre, relatum),* means a reference, bearing, or towardness, and relative signifies the substantive meaning of something so ordered or referred. The Greeks devised a technical phrase for relation to emphasize the preposition ''to'' or ''toward,'' viz., πρός τι (Lat. *ad aliquid*), which may be translated as ''toward something.'' This article treats of the historical development of the concepts of relation and the relative, with emphasis on Greek, scholastic, and modern thought, and then offers a summary comparison of historical and doctrinal interest to thinkers in the scholastic tradition.

Origins in Greek Thought. The principal philosophers in the ancient Greek tradition who contributed to the development of the concepts of relation and the relative were PLATO, Aristotle, and PLOTINUS.

Plato. In the *Sophist* (esp. 242B–254B) the Eleatic stranger and Theaetetus, personifying the materialist and idealist currents respectively, consider the former's conception of being as ''the changing.'' Advancing this notion from what resists touch to what naturally possesses a power of acting or undergoing action, thence to power itself—taken for a distinctive sign of being (247B)—the dialectic finally introduces ''soul'' as a unifying principle (253B). Thus thought, as recognizing both movement and rest without becoming either, affords a principle resolving their opposition. This exposure of the three distinct genera—being, movement, and rest—when linked with the notions of ACTION AND PASSION, returns again to power, the sum of the properties outwardly expressive of the inward, incommunicable nature. Thought, then, provides a reach into something more than the isolated self-identity of the three genera of forms in their mutual distinctiveness and reciprocal relevance. From this emerge two more forms: selfhood or identity and nonselfhood or otherness. This last, grounded on power, is the basis for the Platonic teaching on relation.

The different applications of the πρός (to, toward) of ordinary discourse, summed up in πρός τι (toward something), are gradually unified in the *Sophist,* through the variant forms πρὸς ἄλλα and ἕτερον ἀεὶ πρὸς ἕτερον, in the distinct genus θάτερον (255C–D).

Aristotle. In the, *Categories,* book 1 of the *Organon,* Aristotle distinguishes τὰ πρός τι (relatives) as the third of his CATEGORIES OF BEING. A provisional (6a 36–37) and later revised (8a 32–33) definition of relatives sets forth the distinction between "being said of another" and "being actually related to another," which for Aristotle are not the same (8a 34). This is made more explicit in the *Metaphysics* (1020b 25–1021 b 11), where a studied treatment of the relative is given. Here a threefold division of relatives is proposed as complete: (1) that of the double to the half, the triple to the third, and, generally, the multiple to the multiplied and the container to the contained; (2) the "what can heat" to "what can be heated," the "what cuts" to "what is cut," and, in general, the active to the passive; (3) the measurable to the measure, the knowable to knowledge, and the sensible to sense.

The first are said "according to number" or "according to unity," the former giving the proportions derived from any continuous quantity, the latter the unities of SUBSTANCE (same), QUANTITY (equal), and QUALITY (similar). The second also is twofold, based on the distinction of POTENCY AND ACT: "what can heat" to "what can be heated," potential; "what heats" to "what is heated," acting. These vary also as to time: past, as father to son; future, as an action referred to what will be done. Even the incapable and the invisible are mentioned here.

The third mode troubles all later commentators, some even correcting the text to read "measure to measurable," since the parallels, "knowable" and "sensible," actually are what measure knowledge and sense. Further, whereas the *Categories* proposes all relatives as reciprocal, even using this as a critical premise (12b 20), in the *Metaphysics* Aristotle gives a distinct classification of πρός τι that explicitly excludes reciprocity.

Yet, since universal reciprocity is a demand for correlative terms (not mutual relationship), one can hold that in treating of relative terms Aristotle is attending mainly

to one aspect of the measurable, the knowable, and the sensible—themselves peculiar terms in that each is so named not from anything intrinsic to it but from an external referent: a dependency in being, relatively named. The other two classes furnish extremes, each incorporating its own entitlement to being relatively named. "Measurable," by naming only a terminal function for another's reference, viz, the measure's, becomes a distinctive relative not signifying like the bilaterally related examples of the other two sets.

Plotinus. In his sixth Ennead, tract. 1–3, Plotinus refutes the Aristotelian genera by attacking their univocities, and exposes the equivocity of relation by applying it beyond any single category. But carrying the Platonic analysis toward Aristotle, he further fixes motion between action and passion, linking the power of Plato with the potency of Aristotle: ". . .arts (like boxing) as dispositions of the soul are qualities, as outwardly orientated they are active, and as directed to an outside object they are relative" (1.12). He also relegates being to the "higher realm" and lists becoming in the categories, thereby reducing the whole "lower realm" to two genera, one comprising matter, form, and composite, and the other relation (3.3).

Scholastic Development. Among the scholastics, relation is generally first distinguished as a distinct category of ACCIDENT, having its being in a subject not absolutely but in respect to another. This they call "predicamental" relation. Then, confronted with other relations no less real but not fitting this accidental category (e.g., means, appetite, creation), they named these "transcendental" in contrast. Still other relations, abundantly used but not explicitly classified by Aristotle (e.g., sign, universal, predicate), remain, and these were standardized as "relations of reason." The last include all nonreal or logical relations, and thus are distinguished from "real" relations, which embrace both the predicamental and the transcendental.

Transcendental Relations. Christian philosophers, exposed to cases of real relation that could not be classified as accidental, as in the Holy TRINITY and CREATION, enumerated such transpredicamental relations as transcendental. Either they anchored these in tradition as the third mode identified in Aristotle's *Metaphysics,* or they based their distinction on the expression *relativum secundum dici vel secundum esse* (relative as to speech or as to reality), which was formulated from Aristotle's double definition, but has been abusively wielded to the present day despite the teaching of St. Thomas Aquinas (*De pot.* 7.10. ad 11). A typical, scholastic manualist definition of this relation calls it "the order included in some absolute essence" [J. Gredt, *Elementa Philosophiae Aristotelico-Thomisticae* (Freiburg 1937) 1:154–155].

Predicamental Relations. Predicamental relations, whether taken as real *secundum esse* or as the first two Aristotelian modes based on quantity or on action and passion, are defined as real accidents, distinct from substance, whose whole nature consists in reference to another. Beyond this definition, however, little unanimity obtains.

Foundations of Relations. Most divergencies stem from basic tenets regarding the foundation of relations and the distinction between relations and their foundations. Classical THOMISM distinguishes the relation itself from the extremes (subject and term) and the foundation, sometimes reducing extremes and foundation to the material and formal causes of the reference constituting the relation.

If relations are really distinct from their foundations, then differences in foundation provide causal difference for the kinds of relation; but if relations are really no more than the underlying absolutes, merely viewed and hence named relatively, then relatedness is a being of reason (logical) and the supporting essence the only real entity. On such a basis nominalists generally reject the "ancient" predicamental relation and call the foundation "transcendental relation" (*see* NOMINALISM).

Persuaded of the real identity of relation with its foundation, F. SUÁREZ is ranged rather with the nominalists and therefore unable to see how St. Thomas or DUNS SCOTUS can distinguish predicamental and transcendental relations (*Meta. disp.* 2.37.2). (*See* SUAREZIANISM).

Relation in the Modern Period. For most modern thinkers, theories of relation were reducible to the problem of knowledge of relation, as a result of the dismissal of SUBSTANCE and CAUSALITY from true objectivity. The resulting schools may be conveniently classified under the titles of EMPIRICISM, criticism, and IDEALISM (*see* CRITICISM, PHILOSOPHICAL).

Empiricism. The empiricism of John LOCKE, reducing knowledge of substance to knowledge of qualities, distinguishes primary and secondary qualities, with only the primary ones known surely, but in a general way, and without any discoverable connections between them and secondary qualities. By making the generality of an IDEA a function of the second operation of the mind, "relating," Locke reduces signification to nothing but a relation added by mind. Knowledge, defined as only "perception of the connexion and agreement, or disagreement and repugnancy of any of our ideas," thus shifts from the idea to the relation between ideas. Types of judgment then follow the various relations of agreement or disagreement, yielding two further divisions distinguished as mental and concrete connections. (*See* KNOWLEDGE, THEORIES OF.)

These last, ideal relations and relations among matters of fact, become the "invariable" and "variable" relations of HUME, with only the former rendering any strict knowledge, since they alone are purely ideal. Invariable relations are twofold: those belonging to intuition (qualitative), and those to demonstration (quantitative). This makes mathematics the only strict science, and leaves to fallible "moral reasoning" the existential world of matters of fact, thus effecting a dichotomy between ideal demonstration and experimental belief.

Criticism. Kant, marking the two sides of this chasm as the *ratio veritatis* (explanation of ideal essence) and the *ratio existendi vel actualitatis* (fact of a thing's reality), distinguishes analytic method from analytic judgment, and the order of logical relations of ideas from the order of relevance of these to actual relatives. Because Kant holds that up-down and near-far are not really relations between parts of reality, but to us and through us are related to some absolute frame, he is led to space and time as forms of the mind, coordinates for the singular and sensible. Universal concepts of the understanding, on the other hand, have no such frames; hence, for him, there are two irreducible kinds of knowledge. Avoiding Hume's path to SKEPTICISM, he is led to look to a kind of knowledge independent of experience, hence to pure knowledge, thence to pure reason.

Reversing the relationship of mind and thing, making the former measure rather than measured, Kant fixes the a priori forms of his categories. These, taken either absolutely or relatively, "unschematicized" or "schematicized" by imagination to relate to sense intuition, form the basis for the distinction between phenomenal and noumenal concepts. His list of categories includes quantity, quality, relation, and modality, with relation including substantiality, causality, and interaction. The corresponding judgments show "all the relations of thought in judgment" gathered under relations of predicate-subject (categorical), cause-effect (hypothetical), and of sub-membership. But instead of the traditional predicate as related to subject, this transcendental method now centers on the pure relations between, whether these be analytic (regressive) or synthetic (progressive).

Following that of Kant, the modern emphasis remains on the relations rather than on the terms treated as correlatives, becoming ever more pronounced in both modern physics and modern mathematics, where the old primacy of substance yields to function, and logic becomes a calculus of relations.

Idealism. SCHELLING declares that both dogmatism (Descartes through Spinoza) and criticism (Kant through Fichte) failed in their attempts: the former to reduce subject to absolute object, the latter to reduce object to absolute subject. Favoring criticism, his solution dissolves the distinction of both subject and object in the absolute. How Schelling's theory of relation directs this may be seen from the first and last of his five metaphysical principles: the law of identity, based on the ubiquitous bond of ground and consequent; and the law of reciprocity, ruling that every nature is revealed in its opposite. The underlying unity of opposition should resolve by ever diminishing distinction into the identity of the ABSOLUTE. A dynamic PANTHEISM results from the two logical functions of the first principle: every relation between ground and consequent produces a predication of identity (so the pantheism); but also conversely, every predication of identity discloses, then, a process from ground to consequent (hence, the EMANATIONISM or DYNAMISM).

HEGEL is disappointed with this indifferent absolute: "calling a cow black because seen at night." For him, three steps involving relation escape the abstractness and vacuity of ordinary universals: (1) the "concrete universals," grasping mutual relations, express the unity in difference and the interrelatedness of actual things; (2) the roles of "negativity" and "mediation" determine otherness, negation exposing relations to what an idea is not (supplementing its abstractness and making it concrete), while mediation relates it to all other points of reference for systematic connections; (3) the positive result by negation-of-negation comes through the triadic dialectic: thesis, first stage of the concrete universal, which negated gives antithesis, which in turn negated completes the mediation in synthesis, itself a new thesis for further development. Hegel sees this system of organic relations of concretion as justified in that this is just the way one must expect Absolute Spirit to be evolving if It is self-developing.

Relation in Logic: A Comparison. The whole of Aristotelian logic concerns relations. Taking "intention" for relation, the intellect's registration of reality can be viewed as "intentional," related to reality as measured to measure. This is St. Thomas's view of the material and formal aspects presented by logical relations. "First intentions" are the (real) relations whereby man variously engages the real. "Second intentions" arise from the subsequent mutual relevance of these concepts for their distinction and ordering: genus-species, subject-predicate, *etc.* (*See* INTENTIONALITY; PREDICABLES; CONCEPT.)

LOGIC is both the art of reasoning and the science of second intentions. Rules controlling the intentionalities of reasoning from the formal side are easily mastered as an art; the rules for integrating second intentions with their material ground in first intentions pertain to the more advanced consideration of the science. The first without the other leads to a mere formal RATIONALISM,

as history sadly attests; but the latter, fully taken, is so taxing as to be commonly forfeited.

What Hume did to experience (reducing it to relations of ideas), and Kant to the notion of substance (subsuming it under his category of relation) frustrates any retrace of logical intentions to real intentions, thus transforming the nature of logic. If judgments and their expression in propositions be concerned only with the interlinking relations, neglecting the terms, as Locke held, relationality rather than intentionality becomes the new subject of logic. Such relations are commonly distinguished according to symmetry, transitivity, and reflexivity. Symmetrical and asymmetrical differ as the simultaneous and the prior; transitive and intransitive differ as "on the right" and "next to." Rules of inference treat symmetrical statements as convertible (*A* is simultaneous to *B*, *B* is simultaneous to *A*), and explore the consequences of transitivity and intransitivity as expounded by William JAMES and systematized by Boole, DE MORGAN, RUSSELL, WHITEHEAD, et al.

An adaptation of modern symbols as a shorthand for traditional consequences is often treated in scholastic manuals; however, such algebraic manipulation of symbols seems inadequate by itself to capture and control the intricate causalities required for philosophical demonstration. Although considerable advances have thereby been made in the area of formal logic, and therefore in dialectic, the material logic of demonstration remains concerned with a real, causal level that is itself irrelevant to this relational calculus.

Critique and Evaluation. Plato's identification of the other and its reciprocity with the same or self opens a wedge between his absolutes, which Aristotle notes in commenting that if all the Ideas were absolutes, the idea of relation would itself be repugnant (*Meta.* 991b 15–18). Aristotle's mind cannot be measured by the *Categories* alone. His *Metaphysics,* treating relatives (not relations as such), distinguishes correlatives named for a relatedness from their own standpoint, from others named only because of a relatedness found in their opposite: thus confounding all the commentators who confuse "relation" with the "relative." Plotinus, reverting to Forms, fails to see merit in the Aristotelian categories; but his attack on the univocity of relation highlights its analogous nature, a source of later difficulties and solutions.

Thomistic Doctrine on Relation. Among the scholastics, St. Thomas alone seems to emend Aristotle's teaching with precision. His capital texts, the *Commentary on the Metaphysics* and the *De potentia,* qq. 7–8, give a fully developed doctrine of both relatives and relation. Composite substance—that analyzed through the categories—furnishes two basic accidents, quantity (from its matter) and quality (from its form), twin sources of all real relations, which also underlie the causality of action and passion. His reduction of all the real to these two fonts alone is constant, and almost invariably he invokes the authority of the *Metaphysics*. But he does not exclude real relation from the third mode (nor does he exclude logical relations from the others). Most important is his postponement of any such question until first having indicated the unique relative that is wholly indebted to its correlative even for being named relatively. Whatever relatedness this correlative involves must be reducible, precisely as real, to the real causality founding the other two modes, but now taken transcendentally—i.e., not limited to the univocal senses of the categories, where action means transitive action and quantity means corporeal dimensiveness. That action, for instance, admits of transpredicamental extension by analogical transference is commonly understood; such relations simply follow this transference. And such correlatives, always in diverse genera or orders, disclose the root of their onesidedness in their basic dependence, itself often springing from a causal reference that makes them real.

The Relatedness of Knowledge. The problem of the knowledge of relation that engages modern thinkers as EPISTEMOLOGY is, for St. Thomas, essentially the relation of KNOWLEDGE, an instance of measurable to measure. The very name and notion of OBJECT demand this specification of the immanent activity of knowledge by some external reality. Crucial to the critical problem, therefore, is the totality of progressively immanent causality from the sensed to its being understood. For all of this the "third mode" alone, since committed to a diversity of orders, hardly suffices. Antecedent causalities in action and passion, and even in quantity, integrate the Thomistic analysis, making a circuit from the physical-physiological immutation by sense qualities, through the relational transition to perceptual-spiritual immutation of the internal senses, to the intellect's reflexive attainment of this objective content *with the relations themselves.* (See KNOWLEDGE, PROCESS OF.)

The correlation of the modern primary and secondary sense qualities (the common and proper SENSIBLES) with relatives of the first two modes, and these with the internal and external SENSES, is thus prerequisite to any examination of comprehension by the INTELLECT.

Relation and Analogy. But not only is the study of relatives prior to that of relation; the search for relations also exceeds any limited presentation in terms of "relative terms." Besides the relationship designated by every preposition, and the order and reference signified by relative terms, sometimes words are intentionally made relational to encompass some observable unity while still allowing for variation.

Such is the nature of analogical signification, basically the naming of correlatives by an identical term to signify their relational community. Denying such a relationship means either taking the name equivocally for the several applications (allowing for no causal connection) or taking it univocally (allowing for no oppositional distinction). Further attention to relations between relations (or proportions of proportions) results in "proportionality," an analogy reducible to the sharing of a common name on the part of comparable extremes of diverse sets because of relatedness within the sets. (*See* ANALOGY.)

A further stage of analogical import arises in inferences drawn from this relational interplay between elements in proportionality. Because $a:b::c:d$ (genus is to difference as matter is to form), then by permutation or transumption, $a:c::b:d$ (genus is to matter as difference is to form). St. Thomas frequently uses this dialectical device to set up parallels like the following: just as genus is taken from the matter of the subject, so difference derives from the form, thereby exposing the underlying causality that justifies the permutation.

Current Positions. Later scholastics, lacking critical knowledge of Thomistic texts, seem to have passed on something less. And the modern manualists claiming this tradition usually constrain themselves by their method to excluding necessary but delicate analogies. Their position on relation generally ruins their doctrine of analogy, thus reciprocally spoiling their doctrine on relation also.

Classical modern thinkers, rejecting the Wolffian version of SCHOLASTICISM, sacrificed centuries of attainment to make new starts. But starts that stop short of substance or cause, intelligence or sense, can find only rational relations and logical analogies disassociated from the real, and thus futile for philosophy. This heritage prevails in the current developments of LOGICAL POSITIVISM, as present problems in PERSONALISM keep alive Plato's "self" and "other." Enrichment awaits all in the doctrines of PERSON, knowledge, and analogy, as properly explained through the Thomistic notion of relation. But the warning of history is here: not only more, but different doctrine is available in masters like Aristotle and St. Thomas; it is hazardous to substitute their simplifiers.

See Also: RELATIONS, TRINITARIAN; RELATIVISM; ORDER; ACCIDENT; SIMILARITY.

Bibliography: V. MATHIEU, *Enciclopedia filosofica*, 4 v. (Venice-Rome 1957) 4:26–41. A. KREMPEL, *La Doctrine de la relation chez saint Thomas* (Paris 1952) reviewed by M. A. PHILIPPE in *Bulletin Thomiste* 9 (1955) 363–69 and *Revue des sciences philosophiques et théologiques* 42 (1948) 265–75. M. J. ADLER and R. M. HUTCHINS, eds., *The Great Ideas*, 2 v. (Great Books of the Western World 2–3; Chicago 1952). R. EISLER, *Wörterbuch der philosophischen Begriffe*, 3 v. (4th ed. Berlin 1927–30) 2:668–87.

[B. MATTINGLY]

RELATIONS, TRINITARIAN

Ever since Thomas Aquinas's elaboration of Trinitarian theology (*Summa theologiae* I, pp. 27–43), scholastic theology structures its tract on the Trinity along four basic concepts: procession, RELATION, PERSON, and mission, in this logical order. By procession is meant the origination of the Son from the Father by way of the intellect (generation) and the origination of the Spirit from the Father and/through the Son by way of the will (spiration). These PROCESSIONS are used to explain how God can be one ''substance'' or ''nature'' and yet three ''persons'' at the same time without self-contradiction. These two processions give rise to four ''real'' relations in the deity but only three ''opposed'' relations, which are called ''persons.'' The two missions refer to the visible sending of the Son into the economy of salvation in the Incarnation, and the invisible sending of the Spirit at the Pentecost.

Processions of origination presuppose that there is a real distinction between the principle or source from which the term proceeds (e.g., the father) and the term that originates from the principle or source (e.g. the son). ''Real'' here is opposed to mental or logical. A logical or mental distinction is one that is created by the mind between two realities but does not exist in fact. For example, one can make a distinction in one's mind between Jesus as the Word of God and as the Son of God, but there is no real distinction between the Word of God and the Son of God because both are the same reality. In this case the relation between the Word of God and the Son of God is only mental.

On the other hand, a real distinction is one that exists in the extramental world and is often based on some kind of action between the two realities. For example, the distinction between father and son is a real distinction, just as that between son and father, that is, a distinction between two real objects based on the fact of generation. Consequently, the relations between father and son are real relations. Note that real relations are always reciprocal, that is, between x and y and between y and x.

In summary, real relations imply three things. First, there must be at least two terms that are related to each other. Secondly, there is the ground or basis for this relation which can be of different kinds, the most obvious of which is origination. Thirdly, there is the relationship itself, which is always double, that links the two terms together. This relationship however does not exist in itself and by itself; to use the language of Aristotle, relation is not a substance but an accident. It does not subsist in itself but exists in another. If x and y are really related to each other, the relationship exists both in x and in y. Relations are to be-in (*esse in*).

Esse in and *esse ad*. There is an important sense in which relations can be said to be not only to be-in (*esse in*) but also to be-toward (*esse ad*). This is particularly true of relations in human beings. Through relationships human persons are open outward to others, have a dynamic orientation toward them, give themselves to them and receive them in return in love and commitment, and in so doing constitute a community of spouses, parents and children, friends, and citizens. In a true sense, humans become fully persons only in and through these relationships. For humans to be person is to be interpersonal.

Applied to the Trinity, the relations between the Father and the Son, between the Son and the Father, between the Father/Son and Spirit, and between the Spirit and Father/Son are real relations because the relations are based on the two processions of GENERATION and SPIRATION. The Father's relation to the Son is termed ''Fatherhood'' (paternity), the Son's relation to the Father ''Sonship'' (filiation), the relation of the Father and the Son to the Spirit ''active spiration,'' and the Spirit's relation to the Father and the Son ''passive spiration.'' These four divine relations are real.

Of these four real relations scholastic theology points out that only three are ''opposing relations'' in the sense that they are set over against one another in terms of origination. These are: fatherhood, sonship, and passive spiration. That is, only the Father and the Son face each other, and together they face the Spirit. The active spiration of the Father and the Son, which originates the Spirit (the passive spiration), does not constitute an opposing relation by itself since it is simply the already existing relation between the Father and the Son. Consequently, there are only three ''persons'' in God.

Despite illuminating analogies between relations in the Trinity and those in humans, there is a fundamental difference between them. As pointed out above, relations in humans exist not in and by themselves but only in another reality (*esse in*). They are, in other words, accidents and not substances. Fatherhood does not exist by itself; rather, it is a relation that a person possesses toward another. It is of course an existentially important qualification but does not define what a human person essentially is. Indeed, a person still is human without being a father, and one can cease being a father without ceasing to be human.

In God, however, there is no real distinction between SUBSTANCE and ACCIDENT, between EXISTENCE and ESSENCE. God does not have a relation but is the relation. Relations do not exist *in* God's substance but are *identical* with the divine substance. Divine relations are therefore said to be *subsistent* relations. They are the distinct ways in which God is: the divine nature existing in the relation of fatherhood is God the Father, the divine nature existing in the relation of sonship is God the Son, and the divine nature existing in the relation of spiration (as the Father's and Son's mutual gift and love) is God the Spirit. In God relation is pure *esse ad*, pure facing-each-other, pure being-oriented-toward-each-other, pure self-giving-and-receiving-another. Divine persons are persons par excellence, the perfect and asymptotic models of ''personality'' for human persons.

Many modern theologians emphasize the priority of relations over substance in God and consequently in humans as well. The ''one God'' refers to the Father and not to the common divine substance. It is the relations between the Father and the Son, and the relations between the Father and the Son and the Spirit that constitute who God is. It is the dynamic interrelationship of the divine persons that Greek and Latin theologians refer to when they speak of divine PERICHORESIS and *circumincessio* (and somewhat more statically *circuminsessio*) respectively (*see* CIRCUMINCESSION). In the beautiful words of Augustine: ''They [the three divine persons] are each in each and all in each, and each in all and all in all, and all are one'' (*De Trinitate* 6, 12).

Bibliography: K. RAHNER, *The Trinity*, tr. J. DONCEEL (New York 1974). W. J. HILL, *The Three-Personed God* (Washington, DC 1982). T. MARSH, *The Triune God: A Biblical, Historical, and Theological Study* (Mystic, CT 1994). G. O'COLLINS, *The Tripersonal God: Understanding and Interpreting the Trinity* (New York 1999). C. LACUGNA, *God for Us: The Trinity & Christian Life* (San Francisco 1991). E. JOHNSON, *She Who Is* (New York 1993). D. COFFEY, *Deus Trinitas: The Doctrine of the Triune God* (New York 2000).

[P. C. PHAN]

RELATIVISM

Like many terms ending in ''ism,'' the term relativism is used somewhat loosely in philosophy; a view is generally said to be relativistic if it maintains that there are no absolute principles in some order of knowledge (e.g., epistemology, metaphysics, history, or mathematics), or in the moral order, or in the aesthetic order. It denies that any of some class of statements is absolutely true, or that anything is absolutely right or good, or that anything is absolutely beautiful; and asserts that judgments vary according to the subjects who make them at different times, or in different places, or under some other circumstances. The subject whose judgments are relative may be thought of either as an individual person, or as a universal subject (man); the first usage is generally characteristic of ancient Greek relativism, and the second of various modern relativisms (*see* SUBJECTIVISM). Relativists are often called skeptics when they deny that what appears true to one subject and false to another can ever be shown to be either absolutely true or absolutely false (*see* SKEPTICISM).

Apart from a brief sketch of cultural and ethical relativism near the end, this article is limited to a discussion of some of the major philosophers who, in treating of the nature of knowledge and reality, have adopted positions often called relativist. A chronological sequence is followed.

Greek Relativism. In the history of ancient philosophy the idea of ''true knowledge'' was first made explicitly relative by the SOPHISTS, the most notable figure among whom was Protagoras of Abdera (fl. *c.* 450–440 B.C.) who enunciated the *homo mensura* doctrine: ''Man is the measure of all things, of things that are that they are, and of things that are not that they are not.'' This doctrine is based on the ''deceitfulness'' of the senses and on the fact of disagreement in philosophy and religion. It is generally interpreted as meaning that *each* man is the measure of all things; that there is no objective truth in virtue of which one man is right and the other wrong, since a man's own peculiar nature is intimately involved in every judgment; and that therefore contradictory statements can be made on any subject and each can be true according to circumstances. (Cf. Plato's Dialogues: *Protagoras, Theaetetus,* and *Sophist.*)

The basic error of Sophist relativism is SENSISM, the identification of all knowledge with sense knowledge. While an adequate critique of this position is impossible here, one may point out that the assertion, ''What appears true to one person may appear false to another,'' is not warranted by the typical examples adduced in its support. ''Socrates is sitting'' and ''Socrates is not sitting'' may both be true without contradiction. The apparent relativity is due to incomplete formulation of the propositions: when time and place are specified it is easy to see that there is no contradiction between ''Socrates is sitting in the kitchen at three P.M.'' and ''Socrates is not sitting in the kitchen at three-fifteen P.M.'' And the statement, ''What is true for me may be false for you'' gains its plausibility from the fact that a statement *about me* may be true while a similar statement *about you* may be false.

Origins of Modern Relativism. In the genesis of modern relativism the Copernican theory played a role of great importance by showing, contrary to popular belief and to the traditional Ptolemaic system, that the earth revolved around the sun and was thus not the absolute center of the universe. Giordano BRUNO argued that though to man's senses the sun appears to move and the earth does not, motion is relative to the position of the observer: to an observer on the sun the earth would appear to move. To follow sense-bound reason is to take as objective what is really relative from the higher point of view of mystical intuition.

In providing reasons for doubting the value of all previous philosophies, Michel de MONTAIGNE in his *Apology for Raimond Sebond* (1580) played an important role in setting the stage for modern philosophy. Thus the intellect is untrustworthy, mainly because of its dependence on the utterly untrustworthy human senses, "the greatest foundation and proof of our ignorance"; and to show this he repeats the arguments of classical Pyrrhonian skepticism (*see* PYRRHONISM). There is no way out of this skeptical intellectual despair; but in practice one ought stoically to rely on "universal reason," expressed in tradition and the customary social order, as a guide to life; and one ought to cease looking for intellectual support for what is held by faith, since Protestant reliance on reason surely leads to nothing but radical doubt and uncertainty.

One effect of the work of Galileo GALILEI (1564–1642) was to cast doubt on the truths of traditional philosophy, and implicitly to question the value of any nonmathematical methodology in attaining truth. There should be no philosophical investigation of final causes; man cannot penetrate to "the true and intrinsic essence of natural substance"; and only primary qualities (number, motion, rest, figure, etc.), which can be given precise quantitative formulation, are the true and real accidents of bodies and can be studied; secondary qualities (colors, tastes, odors, etc.) have only a subjective reality in the sensing subject. Galileo left the way open to the denial of the possibility of attaining extrascientific truth, a denial found in the radical empiricism of David HUME.

Empiricist and Rationalist Versions. Hume's philosophy can be seen as an attempt to establish the foundations of a genuinely empirical study of human nature—an investigation equivalent, for Hume, to determining what solutions would be given to traditional problems if the methodological limitations of Newtonian mechanics were imposed on philosophy as a whole. It follows that any book not devoted either to mathematics or to "experimental reasoning concerning matter of fact and existence," such as a work on metaphysics or theology, can contain "nothing but sophistry and illusion" and one should "commit it then to the flames." Agreeing with his empiricist predecessors, John LOCKE and George BERKELEY, that the immediate objects of the mind are its own contents or perceptions, he found it impossible to transcend these and found himself holding a radical PHENOMENALISM: man's perceptions and their subjective connections are all he knows and all he can hope to know. One cannot even know whether there is an external world or a personal self, for any inference from subjective impressions to something beyond has only subjective validity. Both senses and reason are so fallible that no science can possibly be founded on them. "Shall we then establish it as a general maxim that no refin'd or elaborate reasoning is ever to be receiv'd? . . . By this means you cut off entirely all science and philosophy" (*Treatise,* 1.4.7). Hume thus bore witness to the dilemma of radical EMPIRICISM: throw metaphysics into the fire, and science must follow; save science from the flames, and you cannot but save some metaphysics.

Immanuel KANT attempted in his *Critique of Pure Reason* (1781) to restore the bridge between sense perception and nonprobable intellectual knowledge, the bridge so effectively cut by Hume with his critique of CAUSALITY. But the Kantian solution, noetic hylomorphism, is itself relativistic in that the forms of sensibility and the categories of understanding are part and parcel of reality as man knows it: intersubjective reality is constituted by the application of a priori forms and categories to the manifold of perception. Kant saw no way of saving REALISM, for if intellect wholly depends on sense, it is forever sense-bound and Humean skepticism is the outcome; he was thus led to adopt a rationalistic position, substituting a priori elements for innate ideas. It is clear that Kant's "Copernican Revolution," as he called it, proved too much. Not only is Newtonian physics erroneously made definitive scientific knowledge, but "pure natural science" becomes the *necessary* result of man's mental digestive and organizing system and, as Karl Popper has remarked, it becomes impossible to explain why Newton's discovery had not been made earlier [*Conjectures and Refutations* (New York 1963) 95].

John Passmore has written, "The main tendency of 19th-century thought was towards the conclusion that both 'things' and facts about things are dependent for their existence and their nature upon the operations of a mind. . . . They all agreed that if there were no mind there would be no facts; they disputed, only, about what there *would* be—the Absolute, sensation, or a stream of experience. . . . Yet none of these writers. . . was prepared explicitly and consistently to assert that facts are merely recognized by a mind, not *made* by it." [*A Hundred Years of Philosophy* (London, Gerald Duckworth & Co. Ltd., 1959) 175.]

Positivism. The relativism of Auguste COMTE is embedded in his positivist thesis that all knowledge consists in a description and correlation of the facts of observation; any attempt at explanation in theological terms or in terms of metaphysical natures and essences should be abandoned as belonging, according to Comte's historical hypothesis, to one of the earlier and now outmoded stages of man's evolution to POSITIVISM.

British Relativists. The associationist phenomenalism of J. S. MILL led him to define matter as the permanent possibility of sensation and the external world as the world of possible sensations succeeding one another according to laws (''Berkeley's Life and Writings,'' 1871); even mathematical propositions are generalizations from experience and subsequent experience (*see* ASSOCIATIONISM). Mill's opponent, Sir William HAMILTON, was famous as an exponent of ''the philosophy of the conditioned'' or ''the relativity of knowledge.'' For him, although man is directly conscious of independently existing qualities of mind and matter, he has no direct acquaintance with mind-in-itself or matter-in-itself; and he knows things only as they are related to his experience of them, not as they exist in themselves. Herbert SPENCER believed that Hamilton was right in asserting that nothing in its ultimate nature can truly be known, and that man has no definitive consciousness of anything but the Relative; but wrong in concluding that man can know nothing of the nonrelative. Spencer held that one could reason to an Unknowable, Incomprehensible Power that is the source of phenomena, which he associated with the law of evolution. He identified evolution and progress in such a way as to claim that ''progress is not an accident, not a thing within human control, but a beneficent necessity.''

T. H. Green (1836–82) maintained that all reality lies in relations, and that since relations exist for a thinking consciousness, the real world must be a world made by (external) Mind, yet somehow constituted by man's mind qua participant in the eternal consciousness. F. H. BRADLEY believed that things are a finite being's distortion of reality: man's ordinary judgments are ''riddled with contradictions,'' and so attain mere Appearance, since Green was right in maintaining that thought is by nature relational; only in the Absolute, ''an all-embracing, suprarational . . . experience'' are appearances transcended [*Essays on Truth and Reality* (Oxford 1914) 249].

Pragmatism and Other Influences. For the pragmatist William JAMES both things and facts about things are tools made by the mind to come to grips with the endlessly flowing stream of experience. It is unnecessary to suppose that either things or consciousness, considered as entities, exist: ''Consider what effects, that might conceivably have practical bearings, we conceive the object of our conception to have. Then, our conception of these effects is the whole of our conception of the object.'' The proponent of secular HUMANISM, F. C. S. Schiller (1864–1937), went beyond James in denying that ''there is an external world given independently of us and constraining us to recognize it''; for both truth and reality, are man-made, and Protagoras was perfectly right in maintaining that ''man is the measure of all things.''

Today PRAGMATISM is strongest in the writings of social theorists, an application of relativism strikingly found in the writings of John Dewey and his followers. Perhaps the most influential American educational theorist of the first half of the 20th century, Dewey insisted that education be both practical and liberal: devoted to learning *how* to change the world for the *better,* though by ''better'' Dewey means that which is pragmatically relative to what is discovered experimentally.

Three other influences might be considered as leading to the apparent weakening of absolutist positions in the 20th century: (1) the development of modern mathematics, especially of non-Euclidean geometries, which seem to cast the shadow of relativity over what was traditionally regarded as the very paradigm of science; (2) the work of some theorists in logic who tended to identify logic with mathematics; and (3) the fall of classical physics as a result of relativity and quantum theory.

One significant contemporary relativist position is that of Marxist polylogicism, which asserts that the logical structure of a man's mind is correlated to membership in his socioeconomic class. Another important relativist school of thought is that of LOGICAL POSITIVISM, which develops and refines the phenomenalism of the British empiricists. Its thesis is that a material thing is a group of actual and possible sense data, for to say of a material thing that it exists is to say that it is possible to perceive it.

Critical Evaluation. The various positions that can appropriately be called relativistic are, to that extent, negative in character, involving a denial that such-and-such absolutes can be attained or known. An adequate critique of any of these positions can be given only by showing which absolutes can be successfully defended, and how; such a task obviously cannot be accomplished here. But it may prove useful to indicate briefly some objections to which phenomenalism, a historically important and currently popular form of relativism, is open.

As a theory of perception, phenomenalism is a doctrine about the relations between material objects and sense data, i.e., what one immediately and directly experiences. It maintains, in an ontological form, that a material thing is the permanent possibility of sensation (J. S. Mill), or the class of its appearances (B. RUSSELL); or, in the contemporary linguistic idiom, that statements about material objects are reducible to, or translatable into, statements about sense data. A realist would question: (1) the fundamental assumption that the only immediate objects of perception are sense data; (2) the possibility, even in principle, of carrying out the reductionist translation, both because of the lack of verbal means and because the appearances associated with a given material object are infinitely numerous and complex; (3) the possibility of explaining the causal influence of unobserved material things that are only clusters of possible sense data—e.g., one cluster of possible sense data, the water at the bottom of a well, emits an actual noise when another cluster of possible sense data, an unobserved and so hypothetical stone, strikes it [cf. H. H. Price, *Perception* (London 1932)]; (4) the possibility of formulating laws of nature as laws of regularity among sense data; and (5) the possibility of a reductionist translation without presupposing the physical order and without using a concept of the physical order in the very translation.

Ethical Relativism. From the time of Herodotus, civilized man has been aware of the existence of what are apparently differing value systems and ethical codes. This awareness was the occasion for the development of what is today called cultural or sociological relativism, defined as the view that different groups of people have different moral standards, and that the same act may be thought right by one group and thought wrong by another. To claim this is not to make the further claim that both groups are equally right: for one might maintain that though each group *believes* its standards right, this is not to say that both groups *are* right.

Though the very existence of fundamental moral disagreements is controverted [cf. K. Duncker, "An Enquiry into the Psychology of Ethics," *Mind* 48 (1939) 39], let us suppose that such disagreements do exist. If one now maintains that conflicting moral principles are equally correct, he will be known as an ethical relativist. An ethical relativist, then, is a cultural relativist who maintains there is no rational method of determining which of any conflicting positions is right, and so neither is rationally preferable and each is equally right. An ethical relativist must maintain that there is no one governing principle that justifies different practices in different societies; a utilitarian, for example, cannot be an ethical relativist because he will maintain that differing moral codes can be tested by the principle of utility and shown to be comparatively better or worse.

A widely held version of ethical relativism maintains that to speak of ethical codes as more or less justified is senseless, on the ground that ethical statements are noncognitive, being nothing more than expressions of emotion, wishes, exhortations, or commands. Another important relativist position is that of some existentialists, who claim that to think of morality as being a matter of rules or codes is mistaken, for each moral situation so differs from any other that a rationally justified decision is impossible.

An adequate critique of ethical relativism would entail a discussion of NATURAL LAW. But quite briefly, ethical relativist positions are open to the following major objections: (1) all propositions comparatively assessing moral standards and codes whether past, present, or future, would be rendered meaningless; and (2) once the notion of a standard for the whole of humanity is dismissed, there is no logical stopping-place short of separate individual standards arbitrarily adopted, and every judgment to the effect that one man is morally better or morally worse than another becomes meaningless.

See Also: KNOWLEDGE, THEORIES OF; ETHICS, HISTORY OF; RELATION.

Bibliography: A. ALIOTTA, *Enciclopedia filosofica,* 4 v. (Venice-Rome 1957) 4:1–11. M. J. ADLER, ed., *The Great Ideas: A Syntopicon of Great Books of the Western World,* 2 v. (Chicago 1952); v.2, 3 of *Great Books of the Western World* 2:569–587. *La Relativité de notre connaissance* (Louvain 1948). J. A. PASSMORE, *A Hundred Years of Philosophy* (London 1957). A. ALIOTTA, *Il Relativismo, l'idealismo e la teroia di Einstein* (Rome 1948). R. H. POPKIN, *The History of Scepticism from Erasmus to Descartes* (Assen 1960). E. MAY, *Am Abgrund des Relativismus* (3d ed. Berlin 1943). S. E. ASCH, *Social Psychology* (New York 1952). P. W. TAYLOR, *Normative Discourse* (Englewood Cliffs, NJ 1961), esp. ch. 6. G. V. HINSHAW, "Epistemological Relativism and the Sociology of Knowledge," *Philosophy of Science* 15 (1948) 4–10.

[R. L. CUNNINGHAM]

RELATIVISM, MORAL

The term "relativism" is often associated with certain styles of moral reasoning common in contemporary literature. However, the term, as it is used, has two quite different meanings which should be carefully distinguished.

Relativism as Subjectivism. First, moral relativism can be taken as synonymous with, or at least correlative to, subjectivism, with the moral subject or agent as the sole criterion of right or wrong. A relativistic moral theory, in this sense, would be a theory denying objective morality as a whole for it contends that the sole and exclusive source of moral value is the intention of the agent, the person's inner commitment to behaving out of loving or generous motives. Relativism, then, identifies morality with motivation; it sees the virtues as descriptions of styles of moral intending rather than as characteristics of moral action. Thus it rejects entirely the concept of "intrinsic value" as a constituent of moral judgment.

Relativism of this first sort is identified with the work of Joseph Fletcher who affirms that it is reductively a form of philosophical nominalism for it claims that the objective moral value denominating specific acts does not really reside in those acts, but solely in the intentions. Arbitrarily a "name" (moral classification) is projected onto modes of behavior.

Relativism with Objective Morality. Relativism, however, can have quite a different meaning: in this second meaning it is a moral theory that sees moral value as objective but not unchanging. This sort of relativism affirms that moral value is not solely the product of human intention, that actions have value in and of themselves. But it refuses to conclude that the value of specific actions is always and in all contexts, exactly the same. Rather it affirms that an action wrong in one context might well be right in another. The reasoning involved is that morality precisely requires doing what is truly good; what is good in one context, however, might not be good in another. Thus, for example, responsible use of money would be quite different for the married man of limited means and the wealthy bachelor; proper sexual behavior is quite different for the married woman and the single woman. In these cases, then, it can be said that moral value is ''relative,'' but relative to the facts of the case, not purely to the intention of the agent.

This second sort of relativism does not reject objective morality; it rejects immutable morality. Its ultimate basis is the belief that the world is a dynamic, not static, reality and that moral value is consequently also changeable, though always objective.

Debates regarding the extent to which morality is relative (in this second sense) are not really debates about morality at all. They are debates about the nature of the world. If the world is static, then moral values will be rather absolute and unchanging. If, however, the world is dynamic and evolving, then moral values will be seen more as objective-but-relative.

Bibliography: C. CURRAN, ''Natural Law,'' and ''Utilitarianism, Consequentialism, and Moral Theology,'' *Themes in Fundamental Moral Theology* (South Bend, Ind. 1977) 27–80, 121–144. J. FLETCHER, *Situation Ethics* (Philadelphia 1966). J. FLETCHER and H. MCCABE, ''The New Morality,'' *Commonweal*, 84 (14 Jan. 1966) 427–440. J. FUCHS, *Human Values and Christian Morality* (Dublin 1970). R. MCCORMICK, *Ambiguity in Moral Choice* (Milwaukee 1974); ''Notes on Moral Theology,'' *Theological Studies* 32 (1971) 80–97; 35 (1975) 85–100. T. O'CONNELL, *Principles for a Catholic Morality* (New York 1978).

[T. E. O'CONNELL]

RELICS

The material remains of a saint or holy person after his death, as well as objects sanctified by contact with his body. Only late in its history did the word relics, or *reliquiae,* assume a religious meaning. The Greek word *leipsana* and the classic Latin *reliquiae* originally signified any mortal remains; but the Catholic Church employs the word to distinguish the body or whatever remains of a holy person after death, as well as objects that had actual contact with the saint's body during his lifetime. Real (or first-class) relics include the skin and bones, clothing, objects used for penance, instruments of a martyr's imprisonment or passion; while representative relics are the objects placed in contact with the body or grave of a saint by the piety of the faithful or by circumstance.

ORIGIN OF THE VENERATION

Veneration for the dead, or the religion of remembrance, was common among almost all peoples. In many instances some attempt was made to render the departed present by means of an object in which it was believed something of the deceased remained. Among certain ancient peoples this developed into the custom of erecting elaborate funereal monuments and using them for commemorative gatherings, frequently with some religious significance. Though no special honor was paid their relics, care was taken to preserve the ashes or bodies of deceased in graves, tombs, or urns.

Early Christian Practice. Scriptural texts supporting the cult of relics are few and not explicit (Ex 13.19; 1 Kgs 13.21). While the Mosaic Law recognized the veneration of the dead, especially of deceased heroes, it is not certain that this practice had a religious character. The instances of Elisha (2 Kgs 13.21) and Elijah (2 Kgs 2.14) offer certain grounds for such cult; but Jewish fear of contamination by idolatrous practices finally suppressed human representation and material attachment in such matters. One looks in vain to seek a justification for the cult of relics in the Old Testament; nor is much attention paid relics in the New Testament. In the Book of Revelation the author recommends that the faithful and martyrs be left to rest in peace (Rv 11.13). Despite this, although the Apostles inherited Jewish diffidence regarding relics, the new converts in the time of St. Paul disputed about objects that belonged to the Apostles and recognized as miraculous agents clothing that they had touched (Acts 19.12).

St. Polycarp. In the middle of the second century there was an unambiguous instance of the veneration of relics in the history of the martyrdom of St. POLYCARP. The authenticity of this *passio* is beyond question, for the document was written soon after the martyrdom (156 or 157). As the pagans had great respect for the dead, ordinarily they allowed burial even to condemned criminals. But in the case of a crime against the majesty of the state or its ruler, that is, treason, the magistrates could forbid surrender of the body to claimants. As Christians were accused of this crime in refusing to worship the emperor or other state gods, claimants often had to resort to stealth to obtain the bodies of martyrs for burial. Christians and pagans alike showed respect for the dead, but in the recital of Polycarp's martyrdom a new note appears: from a private and implicit veneration there is a change to a public and explicit cult of the remains of the saint. The citizens of Smyrna proclaimed their devotion to the relics of their holy bishop before the whole Church in the Roman Empire.

The magistrate had refused to surrender the body because he did not think it proper to allow Christians "to create a new Christ." Then, having succeeded in obtaining the remains, the Christians of Smyrna felt required to justify their action; and this they did by underlining the subordinate character of the veneration rendered to the martyrs. Polycarp's relics were honored in a religious context in consideration of his holiness as "a disciple and imitator of Christ." Each year, on the anniversary of his martyrdom, the faithful celebrated his memory in the place where he was buried.

Ritual Development. During the persecutions the veneration of the relics of martyrs spread quickly and does not seem to have been opposed by the Christian hierarchy. However, no liturgy accompanied this development until the third century. Relics were simply collected and piously buried. In the mid-third century CYPRIAN OF CARTHAGE justified the veneration of the instruments of the martyrs' sufferings by saying the bodies of Christ's prisoners sanctified their chains (*Epist.* 13); and in the fourth century St. BASIL OF CAESAREA described the official ceremonies held on a martyr's anniversary.

The Alexandrian theologians, on the other hand, were reticent about the veneration of relics since their teaching avoided anything having to do with external cult. ORIGEN seems to have regarded the practice as a pagan sign of respect for a material object. At Rome, however, in the course of the persecutions relics were soon associated with liturgical cult. Since the veneration of the dead was the only cult that could be practiced freely at Rome during times of persecution, the Christians assembled near the tombs to render homage to their dead. Occasionally these gatherings were accompanied by a liturgical celebration. After the peace of Constantine I this practice grew, and churches were built over the graves of the martyrs beginning with the basilicas of St. Peter on the Vatican and that of St. Paul on the Via Ostia. It is not known, however, whether the Eucharist was celebrated on the tombs of the martyrs before the end of the third century.

Theological Consideration. In the course of the 4th and 5th centuries the veneration of martyrs' relics grew as a liturgical cult and received theological justification through recourse to the doctrine of the mystical body by MAXIMUS OF TURIN (*Sermo* 77). At the same time evidence is available for the veneration offered by the faith-

Woman kissing a relic of St. Ronan, Lacronan, Brittany. (©Charles & Josette Lenars/CORBIS)

ful to relics that is on a par with modern practices. The tombs of martyrs were opened, and relics were distributed in the form of *brandea,* or objects that had touched the actual body or bones. These *brandea* were enclosed in little cases and hung round the neck (*see* RELIQUARIES).

Patristic Doctrine. With SS. Basil and John Chrysostom in the East and SS. Ambrose and AUGUSTINE in the West the theology of the cult of relics received its formal development, but adversaries of the practice were not lacking. A principal attack came from Vigilantius of Toulouse in Gaul, who criticized the basic principles of the cult of relics, declaring that it constituted nothing less than idolatrous adoration, even though Christian authors had already pointed out the explicit difference between the cult of *latria* (worship) and of *doulia* (veneration). St. JEROME (347–420) in his *Contra Vigilantium* answered the main objections, defending the cult of relics with an appeal to Scripture, ecclesiastical tradition, and the miracles worked by God through the relics of the saints.

The Finding of the Relics of St. Stephen, in two registers, fresco painting, 1547. (©Archivo Iconografico, S.A./CORBIS)

After Jerome, the Fathers attempted to clarify the relation between God and the saints and their earthly relics. Four different points of view are proposed in justification of this veneration: The faithful see the saints in the relics they venerate; this is the thought of St. EPHREM THE SYRIAN, THEODORET OF CYR, Maximus of Turin, and many others. As the martyrs were saints on earth, their bodies were likewise sanctified. John Chrysostom and Basil of Caesarea insist rather on the blood of the martyrs and the sensible record of their sufferings as stimuli to the courage of the faithful. The excellence of the martyrs renders their relics precious, and the relics are a reminder that these saints should serve as models for all.

GREGORY OF NAZIANZUS, St. Augustine, Paulinus of Nola, Ambrose, and Pope LEO I (440–461) justify relics on the testimony of the miracles God works through their instrumentality. Glory is to be given to God alone; but since God's power is manifest in relics, they can be venerated. This idea resulted in two opposing developments in HAGIOGRAPHY: the legends that had no other purpose than edification of the faithful; and the notion that the more extraordinary the miracles, the holier were the relics and the more efficacious the intercession of the martyr with God. Historical criticism in the patristic period busied itself with establishing the authenticity of the miracles

since the power of the relics rested not so much on the presumed sanctity of the martyrs as on the miraculous signs that God worked in their favor. The final justification rests on a human appraisal of relics: they are the remains of friends who as saints are close to God. Both Augustine and Gregory of Nyssa emphasize this aspect of the cult of relics.

Middle Ages. In the 7th century ISIDORE OF SEVILLE made a résumé of patristic teaching in his *De Ecclesiae officiis* (1.25.1–6). But in practice, among the barbarian peoples recently Christianized, the principal interest of relics centered on the miracles and prodigies associated with their cult, particularly on the day of a martyr's commemoration, as attested by GREGORY OF TOURS in his *De gloria martyrum* (31). The Council of Gangra in Asia Minor (A.D. 343) excommunicated those who despised the cult of relics (c.20); and the Council of Carthage (401) counseled the destruction of churches in which no relics were honored (c.14). But in 675 the Council of Braga called the attention of the bishops to abuses connected with relics.

Eastern Christian Practice. The care for the relics of martyrs and saints differed considerably in the West and East. In the Christian East the holy bodies were exhumed, dismembered, and transported from place to place, as in the case of the transferal of relics of St. Babylas in 351. Already in the 4th century such translations were surrounded with solemn ceremonies; and emperors desired to have their reigns marked by such occasions. The great cities of Constantinople, Alexandria, and Antioch were enriched with relics taken from lesser sanctuaries. By the fifth century the dismemberment of body and of bones became an accepted practice.

Western Practice. In the West a different development took place. The Theodosian Code contained severe penalties against the spoliation of graves. Hence transferal of remains was considered the equivalent of the violation and profanation of tombs, and the popes became strong advocates of this point of view. Hence translation of the remains of a saint was an exceptional happening and had to be dictated by strong reasons or effected clandestinely, as in the case of the FOUR CROWNED MARTYRS brought from Pannonia in the 5th century. Certain churches in Italy, however, did not accept the strict Roman discipline in this matter, and at Brescia St. GAUDENTIUS enriched his church with a treasury of relics (*Patrologia Latina* 20:959–971).

In the 8th century Roman severity was relaxed and Paul I (757–767) and Paschal I (817–824) authorized a large number of translations. This practice quickly spread through Italy and beyond and resulted in the dismemberment and dispersal of the bodies of the saints. Outside

Italy, where martyrdoms had been rare, the matter became complicated by a proliferation of *brandea* or substitute relics in private and public cult until the Carolingian Age, when the cult of relics of confessors or non-martyr saints became frequent. Likewise the acclaim of relics that accompanied the translations in the East was achieved by pilgrimages in the West and had a great influence on the economic, cultural, and social development of Western Europe.

John Damascene. With the outbreak of ICONO-CLASM, the diversity of thought and practice in the Christian East and West became more marked. In the East, after the theological settlement of the Iconoclastic dispute at the Council of NICAEA II (787), the cult of relics as well as of images had a considerable development. St. JOHN DAMASCENE brought stability to the doctrine of the veneration of relics in the East. He taught that God gave the relics of saints to the Church as a means of salvation and that it was necessary to give them honor as representing the saints, the friends of Christ, the sons and daughters of God. So the cult of relics was actually an extension of the honor due to God alone. This became the viewpoint of orthodox theologians generally, and the remains of the saints received an honor secondary to the cult due to God. Only the sects springing from MANICHAEISM thereafter attacked the principle involved in this veneration. In the 11th century, however, the cult of icons in Byzantium became more important than that given to relics, and the theology of relic veneration, as well as the folklore, poetry, and homiletic development, received no further stimulus. Not until the 17th century did an Orthodox theologian, Stephan Yavorsky, show an interest in the question of relics.

Translations and Dispersals. In the West the cult of relics advanced with the development of the Middle Ages. Relics were multiplied by division of larger pieces, by the discovery of new relics, and by falsifications. In the 11th century the Church was forced to protect relics by legislating for the authorization of translations, particularly in consideration of the Norman and Mongol invasions. This dispersal occasioned an increasing number of relics as is illustrated by the case of St. Philibert of Beaulieu, whose remains were carried by the monks fleeing before the Norman invasion and parceled out in the various monasteries they founded before coming to rest at Tours. It likewise gave rise to an extraordinary commerce. Translations of relics at times assumed the proportions of an export enterprise, then of a regular trade, particularly as regards Rome.

Pilgrims and Princely Visitors. During the eighth and ninth centuries guidebooks for pilgrims in Rome gave visitors indispensable indications for their visits to

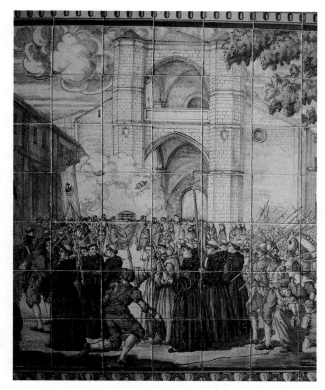

"Procession of the Relics of Saint Benedict through the Streets of Valladolid," Spanish ceramic tiles. (©Archivo Iconografico, S.A./CORBIS)

the city's all but abandoned suburban cemeteries. Visitors to the CATACOMBS were led to believe by their own piety or the suggestion of charlatans that they stood in the midst of great collections of the bodies of the saints. The catacombs were thus considered an inexhaustible mine for relics, which until the time of GREGORY I (590–604) had been protected by the civil laws. This reserve was succeeded by great audacity. Popes now gave royal and important visitors whole bodies of the martyrs, and monastic founders were convinced that the stability and celebrity of their foundations depended on the relics in their treasury. Likewise it was considered necessary to strengthen the faith of new nations, such as the Saxons, recently won to the faith by introducing the cult of relics among them as a stimulus to their piety and a preventative against their reversal to the cult of their old idols.

Papal authority made an effort to prevent or control this dispersal, but popes frequently were powerless to prevent such phenomena as the formation, in the ninth century, of a corporation that specialized in the discovery, sale, and transport of relics to all parts of Europe. This was possible because the ancient Roman cemeteries had been abandoned at this epoch and were visited only occasionally by pilgrims. One of the more successful of these entrepreneurs of relics was the deacon Deusdedit, who showed a deep sympathy for the importunings of barbarian princes and ecclesiastics so desirous of possessing relics that were evidently misprised in Rome. Deusdedit had the administration of the third cemeterial region of Rome, which covered the areas of Casalina (*Labicana*), Prenestina, and Tiburtina, with the cemetery of SS. Peter and Marcellinus. In 827 he made his first journey through the Germanic countries with a listing of the relics possibly transferable. EINHARD and RABANUS MAURUS were among his more important clients.

But Deusdedit and his brothers who continued the practice did not always have honest partners or imitators. Thus in the case of the martyr St. HYACINTH, whose bones were considered a primary treasure in the Abbey of Seligenstadt for over 1,000 years, it was discovered in 1845 that the true Roman martyr's remains were still intact in a grave in the cemetery of St. Hermes. Paschal I finally ordered the abandonment of the catacombs and the transfer of relics to the churches of Rome; but the transport was not conducted with proper care and many of these bones are now unidentifiable.

Crusaders. During the Crusades the commerce in relics reached a new high. In 1204, with the taking of Constantinople, a great number of relics were captured by the Latin army; and successively, Antioch, Jerusalem, and Edessa were sacked, and the relics sent back to enrich the churches and cathedrals of medieval Europe. Actually the Crusaders were more interested in the possession of the relics themselves than in their commercial value. This is evidenced by the fact that frequently they did not carry off the rich reliquaries in which they discovered the relics. But false relics were also multiplied in increasing numbers, both by enterprising charlatans and in the course of transport, theft, and exchange of captured relics. To offset this practice, horror stories and legends concerning the fate of relic falsifiers were put into circulation. In 1274 the Council of LYONS prohibited the veneration of new relics without the approbation of the pope.

Late Medieval Practice. Once a relic was discovered and authenticated it was placed as close as possible to the altar in a church or chapel. The tombs of the martyrs were actually considered altars; and the bodies of saints were no longer buried but exposed to be seen and touched in tombs made into sumptuous reliquaries and placed above or behind the altar. It soon became indispensable for the dedication of an altar that it contain relics of the martyrs; and the proprietor of a new church had to request of the pope or the bishop of the place the relics of the saint in whose honor the church was to be dedicated (*Liber diurnus romanorum pontificum*).

The cult of relics in the Middle Ages was dependent on the great stock put in their efficacy. Celebrated shrines gave rise to gigantic pilgrimages with the arrival of immense crowds on certain feast days or during the whole course of the year. The pilgrimages to St. James of Compostela in Spain are a key to the literary, artistic, and cultural understanding of the Middle Ages, in the opinion of the art historian É. Mâle.

Not only PILGRIMAGES but PROCESSIONS with the relics of saints in the streets gave rise to special feasts, fairs, and events that attracted crowds of people and had a great effect on the exchange of ideas, information, styles, and customs. And almost all civic events were activated with an appeal to the city's relics, from the taking of oaths to the conclusion of pacts and treaties. Likewise in the case of saints called upon as protectors against disease, their relics were frequently applied to the parts of the bodies of the sick. Abuses were inevitable; but theologians recognized the impossibility of controlling them and paid more attention to the doctrine than to the practice of the faithful.

Abuses. Denunciatory voices were not entirely lacking, however. At the very time when enormous churches were being erected and Masses organized in honor of the saints, Guibert of Nogent attacked the superstitions connected with relics in his *De pignoribus sanctorum.* St. BERNARD OF CLAIRVAUX denounced the pride in their relics and the bad faith of the Cluniac monks, while PETER THE VENERABLE contented himself with explaining the traditional teaching that justified the cult of relics (*Sermo* 4). The LATERAN COUNCIL IV recognized the problems raised by both clergy and laity in this matter and repeated the teaching of the Council of Nicaea II.

Liturgy. In the liturgy the action of the hierarchy proved more effective, and the Roman rituals never included a feast in honor of the relics of a saint even though Rome permitted certain dioceses and religious orders to celebrate the feast of *Sancta Maria ad martyres.* In the 10th century a salutation was directed to the altar relics at the beginning of Mass; but allusions to relics are rare in the prayers of the canonical hours or in the antiphonaries and lectionaries. On the contrary, triumphal hymns and homilies honoring saints and martyrs were tolerated, while the great veneration of relics was indicated by the position that was assigned them on the altars.

Scholastic Theology. The teaching of the scholastic theologians does not differ greatly from that of the Fathers. The first redactors of *summae* gave no special attention to relics, mainly because PETER LOMBARD had not treated them in his *Sentences.* The commentators contented themselves with protests against abuses; but THOMAS AQUINAS dedicated a question in his *Summa theologiae* to the problem (3a, 25.6). Summing up John Damascene, he took as point of departure the vivid sense of the human element involved. The saints belong to Christ; they are the sons and daughters of God and as a consequence serve as intercessors with God for the living. Every relic is thus a record of the saint. As God works miracles through relics, relics have a direct relationship with the saints, with Christ, and with God. It is thus the saints who are the direct object of honor, of which their relics are but the sensible signs.

St. Thomas thus concluded that relics in themselves have no sanctifying power; but they do "excite to love, by signifying the love that is achieved through the relic."

On second consideration, he tended to accept a certain extrinsic value by way of the physical proximity of a relic in its relation to the body of a saint. Saints are the temples and instruments of the Holy Spirit in their whole person. They continue to be so in a secondary fashion in the remains of their bodies still on earth. Thus the body of a saint deserves honor for itself; and it follows that relics deserve more veneration than do images. The miracles worked by God are irrefutable proofs of this fact. God is the principal and primary object of worship (*latria*), while the saints and their relics deserve veneration (*doulia*). Thomas finally sought to justify the so-called representative or substitute relics that have been in true contact with actual relics; but he stressed the necessity of avoiding every semblance of superstitious practice.

This last consideration was taken up by later scholastics whose principal consideration was the axiom *in medio virtus*. At the same time, however, the precursors of the Protestant reform began to raise voices against the cult of relics. John HUS considered the practice idolatrous; and his criticism was repeated by John Wyclif and, a century later, by all the reformers. Luther considered the cult of relics as mainly a lucrative invention of the Roman Church and contrary to the Word of God as manifest in the Scriptures. Calvin proved more moderate and confined his attack to false relics.

Responding to Protestant criticisms, the Council of TRENT in a decree issued in its 25th session made no reference to Scripture but appealed to the Apostolic tradition and the constant practice of the Church. Trent repeated the condemnations of previous councils against those who denied the licitness and legitimacy of the veneration of relics.

Suárez. After Trent F. SUÁREZ was the first theologian to return to the question of relics (*Sum. theol.* 18.654). He collected the common teaching and added his critical observations particularly regarding the traditions of the churches of Rome, Constantinople, Antioch,

and Milan. He found proof of the excellence of relics in the dignity invested in the bodies of the saints, an argument built on that of St. Augustine. Contrary to St. Thomas he held that the relation between the saint and his relics is not to be sought in physical continuity or in actual contact with the remains but in the reason on which the moral dignity of the relic is based. He likewise gave diverse value to relics in accordance with their relative importance. When they are reduced to specks of powder, it is unbecoming to preserve them.

Bellarmine and Billuart. Some 17th- and 18th-century theologians felt that the veneration of relics was inferior to the cult of the saints; still others put the two on a par, distinguishing between relative *doulia* to the relics and absolute to the saint in heaven. This was the opinion of Robert BELLARMINE in his *De Ecclesia triumphanti* (2.3; 3.203–211). The most interesting observations in this period were made by Cardinal Billuart (1685–1757) in his *De Incarnationis diss.* (23.4). He made a distinction between relics, based on his discussion of images. Materially considered, relics have no right to veneration; but in their formal aspect, as representative of the saint whose remains they are, they are worthy of the same veneration that is due to the saint. They are only distinguished from the saint whom they represent by the modality of being immobile and inanimate; but actually they constitute one sole entity with the saint. Hence the dignity of the relic is the same as that of the saint.

The relic in itself as an object, however, does possess value of sanctification in so far as it was once in direct contact with the saint. The dignity with which the Church invests a relic thus has a true foundation, and the veneration is based on a true autonomous title. This last consideration was advanced to justify the veneration of relics whose title to authenticity could no longer be ascertained but whose cult was both ancient and venerable. But such cult is not the same as that offered to a saint and can be considered *doulia* only in an improper sense.

MODERN CARE OF RELICS

While the piety of the faithful and the zealous care of curators preserved the greater number of relics handed down from the past, the revolts and sequestration of churches and monasteries that swept Europe in the wake of the French Revolution and continued to the end of the 19th century caused the disappearance of large collections of relics. But the wars of religion, the revolutions, and occasional uprisings in missionary territories occasioned many martyrdoms among both missionaries and converts, thus providing modern relics whose authenticity cannot be questioned. Likewise the progress achieved by Christian archaeology has enabled scholars to provide means for controlling the study of ancient relics. In this process certain ancient relics have been excluded, such as those of St. PHILOMENA, whose name was removed (18 April 1961) from the Calendar of Saints by the then Congregation of Rites. An excellent guide in this connection is provided by the *Acta Sanctorum* of the Bollandists. In the preface to the life of each saint information is provided concerning the principal sites where the holy person's relics are preserved, and an attempt is made at identifying the value of the tradition involved.

Bibliography: S. DITCHFIELD, ''Martyrs on the Move: Relics as Vindicators of Local Diversity in the Tridentine Church,'' *Martyrs and Martyrologies* (Oxford 1993) 283–94. C. DOHERTY, ''The Use of Relics in Early Ireland,'' *Ireland and Europe* (Stuttgart 1984) 89–101. P. J. GEARY, ''The Ninth-Century Relic Trade: A Response to Popular Piety,'' *Religion and the People, 800–1700* (Chapel Hill, North Carolina 1979) 8–19. T. JOHNSON, ''Holy Fabrications: The Catacomb Saints and the Counter-Reformation in Bavaria,'' *Journal of Ecclesiastical History* 47 (1996) 274–97. G. LENHOFF, ''The Notion of 'Uncorrupted Relics' in Early Russian Culture,'' *Christianity and the Eastern Slavs, Vol. 1* (Berkeley, California 1993) 252–75. B. R. MCCANE, ''Bones of Contention: Ossuaries and Reliquaries in Early Judaism and Christianity,'' *Second Century* 8 (1991) 235–46. J. M. MCCULLOH, ''The Cult of Relics in the Letters and Dialogues of Pope Gregory the Great: A Lexicographical Study,'' *Traditio* 32 (1976) 145–84. O.F.A. MEINARDUS, ''A Study of the Relics of Saints of the Greek Orthodox Church,'' *Oriens Christianus*, Vol. 54 (Wiesbaden 1970) 130–279. P. C. MILLER, '''Differential Networks': Relics and Other Fragments in Late Antiquity,'' *Journal of Early Christian Studies* 6 (1998) 113–38. D. W. ROLLASON, ''Relic-Cults as an Instrument of Royal Policy c. 900–c. 1050,'' *Anglo-Saxon England,* 15 (Cambridge 1986) 91–103. W. TABBERNEE, '''Our Trophies Are Better Than Your Trophies': The Appeal to Tombs and Reliquaries in Montanist-Orthodox Relations'' *Studia patristica* 31 (1997) 206–17. A. THACKER, ''Cults at Canterbury: Relics and Reform under Dunstan and His Successors,'' *St Dunstan* (Woodbridge, England 1992) 221–45; ''Saint-Making and Relic Collecting by Oswald and His Communities,'' *St Oswald of Worcester* (London 1996) 244–68.

[F. CHIOVARD/EDS.]

RELIGION

This article is concerned with the basic nature of religion as such and with the common elements found in the various religions of mankind.

Problems of Definition

A precise but comprehensive definition is difficult. The problem can be examined best by considering religion from several different points of view or under several distinct aspects.

Nominal Definition and the Universal Fact of Religion. The etymology of the Latin word *religio* is disputed. Some have tried to connect *religio* with other Latin terms (*relegere, religare, reeligere, relinquere*), but each

scholar has been influenced by his personal ideas, and no accord has been reached. Philological investigation of the use of the word has revealed some interesting aspects of Roman religiosity, which was characterized by a scrupulous attention to all signs or manifestations of invisible powers or forces. But the problem becomes much more complicated when one wishes to examine the phenomenon of religion in cultures that do not use the Latin word. The languages that have an equivalent general term are rare, and the terms selected for comparison have turned out, ordinarily, to be descriptions merely of one of the duties considered essential by the respective civilization. In fact, there are very few cultures in which the question of the essence of religion has been formally raised; as a general rule, each takes its own religion as an obvious norm. Furthermore, the same thing happened in the development of the science of religions itself. In the 19th century some scholars maintained that there were peoples without religion, until it was recognized that such investigators had simply failed to find religion, as they themselves conceived religion, among certain primitive tribes.

Empirical Definition. Even when it was once admitted that all peoples have a religion, the question remained: how could investigation be carried on if the investigators had no precise idea of the object of their research? This was a purely theoretical question, which in practice did not hamper scholarly investigation. As in the case of other sciences, the science of religions began with working hypotheses, which were more or less exact and which were gradually corrected in the process of research itself. In the end it was possible for this science to isolate and delimit empirically a specific object proper to it.

In the totality of human experiences and activities the religious phenomenon presents itself as irreducible to any other category save its own and as definitely and always belonging to its own category and *no other*. At the same time every religion implies a choice that is so total and exclusive, affecting as it does the personal destiny of every human being in irrevocable fashion even where no clear notion of a transcendent absolute exists, that no religion seems able to tolerate its inclusion in the cadre of a general definition. Therefore, for the religious man, the definition of religion could be only that of his own religion. Actually the disagreement or diversity is such that the outsider can operate only with a selection of a minimum of statistical religious data that will be admitted by any of the existing religions.

Religious-minded men, concerned with the problem of general accord, will appeal instinctively to a revelation. It is clearly established that there are civilizations, however, among which it is necessary to include all the ''primitives'' and also the major polytheistic groups, that profess theoretical and practical relativism in matters of religion and affirm that no one religion in particular, but all religions together, fulfill the religious function of mankind in the world and before God. And those who, like Plato and the Aztecs, awaited a future revelation adopted the same attitude regarding their contemporary world. Accordingly, to come to closer grips with the problems, it seems necessary to distinguish between the religions founded on a revelation in the strict sense and other religions.

Theological Definition. In the case of revealed religions, which are at the same time religions of salvation, the problem of definition seems simple, for it is given by REVELATION itself, at least implicitly. Revelation indicates specifically under what conditions a man can fulfill his destiny and be saved. The theology of the SALVATION of unbelievers indicates precisely under what conditions the individuals who do not know the revelation can participate in salvation. But the interpreters of the revelation do not say whether there are really any nonrevealed religions that deserve the name of religion. The special polemical character of the inspired writings that criticize the pagan religions do not permit on the basis of their arguments a definitive judgment to be passed on the religions in question.

The revealed religions, however, do not make salvation the primary end and immediate object of religion. From the subjective point of view, religion is a virtue that leads man to render to God the homage that is due to Him. As an objective manner of behavior and concrete manifestation of virtue, it comprises belief in one God, personal and infinite in His attributes; an attitude of absolute respect and submission; exterior acts that express this belief and this attitude in worship; and, as required by all exterior human activity, institutions to regulate that activity.

Historical Definition. There is a science of religions, however, that is a branch of anthropology. This science does not teach the norms of the true religion, and it is not occupied solely with the institutions that have come from revelation. It includes within its scope what men have come to employ, so to speak, as substitutes for revelation, along with many contradictions that baffle science itself. Yet it is precisely the tentative efforts of science in themselves that make possible a better grasp of the whole amplitude of the problems of man and religion.

On the level of the collection of documents to be studied, science ought to begin, then, with a very broad conception of its object and thus let nothing escape it that may sometime be able to clarify an aspect of the religious phenomenon. The definition of the latter, accordingly, will be entirely pragmatic, and will embrace belief, rite, and institution that occupy in a group the place that revelation reserves for religion. Furthermore, it is well known how difficult it is to enter into the spirit of an environment in which one has not been reared. Hence it is rash to try to decide too quickly whether this or that conception is closely connected or not with what other religions believe and practice. This kind of judgment and distinction can be made only after long work and study.

Phenomenological Approach

It is possible, it seems, to employ a criterion that is less pragmatic, negative, or exterior, for marking out or defining the object of research. A specific domain may be circumscribed, once that is distinct, e.g., from metaphysics and techniques, by a characteristic aspect inherent in all that is religious in the broadest sense of the term and that is proper to itself. This is the concept of "the sacred."

The Sacred. The SACRED is opposed to the profane. Although the majority of primitive and ancient peoples never separated the two domains in their interpretations and usages, they distinguished them sharply enough by their different psychological reactions. The sacred, as distinct from the profane, represents an order of reality, the presence of which commands man's attention and at the same time escapes him; it is simultaneously desired and regarded with awe. In other words, it possesses an essentially ambivalent character, which makes man feel at once irresistibly attracted by its grandeur and frightened by its superiority.

This double character of the sacred, which R. Otto called *fascinans* and *tremendum,* is one of the keys to the discovery and interpretation of religious phenomena. But research becomes science only from the moment it occupies itself with putting order into the material collected and when it succeeds, by comparison and distinction, in producing a classification. It is then necessary to select from the categories obtained that which should be called religion. The discussions that have agitated the science of religion for more than a century demonstrate clearly that all that was believed "to take the place of religion" cannot be included in its essence and its history. Many essential facts of history have changed category as progress has been made in understanding.

Religion and Magic. One of the facts to emerge clearly from the constant revision of ideas mentioned is this: two kinds of phenomena exist that can indeed occupy the place of religion but that assume conceptions of the world and of the position of man that are diametrically opposed, namely, religion and MAGIC. The fact that so many theories have been advanced to explain the hypothetical passage of one to the other by an evolutionary process and the fact also that the civilizations that claim to include magical practices in religion had to invent myths to explain this inconsistency show that both science and religions perceive an essential difference between religion and magic.

The opposition between them is clearly evident from both their respective conceptions of the order of the world and of man's attitude in this world. Magic believes in an ensemble of automatic forces that gives the man who knows their techniques an unconditional efficacy or power independent of every other will except his own. Religion, on the other hand, acknowledges a universe that always remains, and one in which man always remains, dependent on a good will that is absolutely beyond the reach or power of techniques effective in themselves. Even if man, in order to reconcile the two conceptions, claims that he has received his knowledge and power from the divinity, who then loses control over them in such cases, there is an implication that the feeling of an ultimate dependence that one tries to avoid is still present. This distinction made, the inductive work required to determine the constituent elements of religion becomes feasible.

Double Usage of the Term "Religion." The science of religions always studies religion and magic together because their opposition clarifies problems. For the sake of simplification, the two continue to be studied under the one heading, religion, and the specific religion studied is even defined according to the proportion and combination of the two in the theory and practice of its environment. This is the pragmatic usage, the broad sense of the term, and it is so employed in the expression *science of religions*.

But on a different level of research, science is not merely concerned with each "religion." It tends to make comparisons and then to distinguish and establish constants in order to define religion more precisely as a system of coherent phenomena, distinct from other concurrent phenomena, and in opposition to magic in particular. It is not yet a philosophy of religion but rather a synthesis of historical data. Few peoples have produced a conscious and critical elaboration of these elements. Therefore, it is precisely the function of the science of religions to explain in their name, without misrepresenting them, what they conceive implicitly, namely, the precise content and trends of their religious feeling, which is often complex but coherent in practice—their religion in the strict and exact sense.

Content of Religions

At the outset it is essential to consider a matter of basic importance, namely, the object of religion and the conception of this object.

Object of Religion. Religion is opposed to the anarchy of magic by an attitude of dependence that is felt and accepted within definite limits. This attitude itself, therefore, assumes a certain conception of its object. Investigation shows that this attitude is always directed to a reality superior to man, a reality that is beyond the control of man's will and all the forces of nature. Those who maintain that this reality is merely the projection of the attitude itself emphasize at least that such an attitude and such an object are connected and that man does not have the choice or decision.

This reality belongs to the category of the sacred, with its characteristic ambivalence. But while magic tries, in spite of the fear it provokes, to make itself master of the sacred in order to use its power, religion sees in fear a reason for respect because it sees in the attraction of the sacred a reason for acknowledgment or surrender. This is accepted dependence. The difference, however, is not only in the subjective attitude, but in the object itself, because it is conceived in a different manner.

Specialists in the science of religions believed for some time that there were two successive attitudes in the history of religion. According to this view man first tried to control the sacred by "incantation," and often-repeated failure then forced him to resign himself to "invocation." This is the theory of "From Spell to Prayer," according to the formula of R. R. Marset (1866–1943). A knowledge of the facts, which was less distorted by evolutionary theory, then suggested that man in all periods felt inclined to try one method or the other—a procedure that is closer to the historical and psychological truth. But invocation, PRAYER—the religious act par excellence—assumes that the sacred is conceived as having ears for hearing, a heart for understanding, and a freedom to reply—in brief, that the sacred is regarded as a person. Furthermore, it may be noted in passing that an act such as prayer implies that man by his reason did not merely construct an object of thought as a logical response to a question on existence, a first principle. It was necessary also that, in some manner, he should "feel" it as living, for otherwise, he would not have prayed to it. As U. von Wilamowitz-Moellendorff (1848–1931) once said, "Zu einem Begriff betet kein Mensch" (No man prays to a concept).

Vagueness in the Concept of Divinity. It must be kept in mind, however, that religion finds expression not only in prayer but also in sacrifice, purifications, and consecrations, whose mechanism of efficacy and objective presuppositions are much more ambiguous than in the case of prayer. They can leave the personal character of the divine very vague. Likewise, the much Divine (Θεῖον), the One, the Logos, the Brahman, etc., may well inspire a strong feeling of complete dependence; but all these seem to be limited to the representation of a transcendent order that is hardly favorable to dialogue, but an order that men seek to recognize and to venerate by a strict submission.

In this case, however, one notes quickly a discord between speculative conceptions and the religious attitude in which the personal representation unfailingly reappears. Whether this situation results from psychological need or is due to the power of religious experience is not clear. Yet this Absolute, the alleged impersonal divine force, is prayed to in moving fashion by the Sioux as Wakonda, by the emperor of China as Heaven, or by the Stoic Cleanthes as Zeus. Perhaps this inconsistency exists only for modern Westerners, who find difficulty in thinking of the personal except in anthropomorphic terms. More deeply, however, it is perhaps the religious sense itself that perceives that this lofty Reality is so different from all other human experiences that it cannot be included in any of the contradictory categories of Western thought. On the other hand, the knowledge that man has of this Reality is so closely connected with the immensity of the universe and its order—impressive even for a primitive in his own little universe—with this All that is at once calm and agitated, that man, as the whole history of religions bears witness, is led to hesitate constantly between the personal and the impersonal, looking now at the one and now at the other according to the circumstances in which he believes that he encounters, or desires to approach, the one or the other. The religious sense itself influences him to respect what he knows of the nature of the sacred reality without imposing his own ideas upon it. Nevertheless, a historical description of the manner in which men conceive the object of their acts of submission and homage cannot assume a rigorous and exclusive precision. In any case, the inclusion of a strict notion of person would limit to an extreme degree the range of a historical definition of the object of religion. On the other hand, the personal aspect always makes itself felt.

Transcendence and Unicity of the Object of Religion. The same ambiguity marks the question of the transcendence and unicity of the object of religion. These are two interdependent aspects, and in their regard the majority of religions are uniformly vague. Just as very few cultures are concerned about the absolute origin of the universe, although they consider it vitally important to fit man into the totality of the universe that actually exists, so also, like the ancient philosophers, they are much more conscious of the sovereignty of divinity than of the need of defining its internal nature. The chief preoccupation of religions that are not strictly and aggressively monotheistic is the multiplicity of the elements or relations that mark man's dependence. Concrete expression is given to these relations under the form of spirits or gods.

At first sight it would seem rather easy to oppose *polytheism* and *monotheism.* But when one begins to interpret images and names, this opposition between the one and the many frequently eludes precise analysis. The Great Gods of many African peoples can bear collective names and not belong to the grammatical class of animate beings, and yet they are treated as persons. Similarly, in the most highly developed religions of the Greco-Roman world and the ancient East there is a constant intermingling of notions of many individual gods and of unique divinity. One gets the impression that the sovereignty of the gods, which is their essential prerogative, is a collegiate sovereignty, with or without hierarchy, in which each god is absolute ruler of a part of reality, and all the gods together are absolute Master of the universe in its totality. In worship each god, when he is invoked, seems to be regarded as the momentary expression of all divinity (Kathenotheism), and in popular piety one god is in practice given a place above all others as the equivalent of all (HENOTHEISM). Accordingly, many ethnologists in dealing with very primitive peoples do not hesitate to state that some of their gods appear as "hypostases" of the cosmic God, as a remote foundation or beginning from which they do not separate themselves completely. Perhaps a total manifestation of Divinity, always identical with itself, is beyond the range of human experience. In fact, the knowledge of the divine that men have is always acquired through perception in depth of particular aspects of the universe. Hence the TRANSCENDENCE of the divine is never perceived except through its immanent manifestations.

Philosophy is primarily concerned with examining thoroughly and describing precisely each and every aspect of experience. Religion, on the other hand, is concerned essentially with taking a thing just as it thinks that it perceives it, and it adopts practical behavior to it in accordance with this perception. But even the ancient philosophers, although deliberately remaining very close to myth, which among ancient peoples gave expression to constructions of reality actually experienced, were always tempted by the idea that impersonality and indetermination were characteristic of transcendence, while its manifestations in the universe could only be limited and therefore multiple.

On the basis of historical investigation, apart from revelation, it must be concluded as very probable that transcendence and a certain unicity are consciously present even when a multiplicity of gods is recognized and that, in spite of its various manifestations in the universe, divinity remains entirely other and, above all, sovereign.

It is only as a result of reactions of very complex origin that the monotheistic religions rejected other systems and thus opposed in a consistent and strict manner every tendency that would lead to involvement in cosmic manifestations—especially biological and immanent manifestations—of the absolute Reality, transcendent and unique, and regarded before all as sovereign.

Attitudes. It is easy to see that the manner in which religion is conceived determines man's attitude toward it. As a matter of fact there is necessarily a reciprocal reaction between religious representations and attitudes, and scientific observation can hardly do more than note a complex ensemble in which it is difficult to distinguish what is tendency or trend and what is experience. But to suppose that everything in religion is merely a subjective projection is an opinion that is not based on science but reflects rather philosophical criticism. On the contrary, the fact that the divine is represented as personal, endowed with consciousness, freedom, and initiative, seems to indicate clearly that men feel themselves really at grips with objective forces of a spiritual character: religiously minded men have thought even that God is not so much the object of religion as its subject, the active agent who determines even man's own initiative. In revealing Himself in a certain manner, He actually directs even man's reaction. It is very likely for this reason that in religions that are strictly theistic there is recourse also to divination in order to know exactly in a given case what the Divinity expects of man or will, on His side, accept.

Submission to a person considered as superior and free necessarily includes respect in the state of dependence. But some pagans have gone even further. Sometimes they give feminine titles to God without, however, making him a mother goddess. But the great majority of those who believe in a Sky God, i.e., the most transcendent form of the divine, call him Father. This name, however, does not allude to creation or to any kind of filiation but rather to the nature of his general comportment toward man and that of man toward him. Again, fear can be dominant when the transcendence of the divine is associated with cosmic manifestations like the great calmness of the sky and its violent storms. Yet one should not forget that a terrible mother goddess, such as the Hindu goddess Kali, is at the same time a beloved mother. Reasoning is certainly not the determining factor in such cases, but rather man's experience in his daily life in the world. At a lower level, yet very close to the one just mentioned, God can be conceived in a manner little different from the spirits of nature, those manifestations of multiple and contradictory forces that are anthropopathic, i.e., having the same feelings or passions as man. In this case even respect disappears, and transcendence is reduced to a low level. Magic can take the upper hand.

These last phenomena mark the limit of religious facts and go even beyond it. If there were not other nuances and other conceptions, which come into play at the same time, it would no longer be possible in these instances to speak of religion in the strict sense of the term.

Expression by Religious Rites. An interior attitude, especially if it is felt with at least some intensity, is expressed normally by gestures, words, or actions. These manifestations should be the starting point for the observer who wishes to study the spiritual content of religions. At any rate, they are of prime importance for verifying the affirmations obtained by questions, discussions, or literary speculations in which the presence of the stranger and the judgments that are unconsciously suggested by his attitudes exercise a marked influence on the spontaneity and sincerity of statements made.

It is well established that there are no civilizations without religious rites. These rites may be reduced to the minimum, even to the point that many inexperienced observers do not perceive them, especially if they are spontaneous, and have little that is formalistic or ceremonial about them. Such is the case in the majority of the religions of the primitives with regard to the Supreme Heavenly Being.

Prayer. Prayers are found everywhere and range from spontaneous invocations without fixed formulas to hymns of literary character, which cannot always be successfully distinguished from incantations. They are addressed to all entities that a religion conceives as representing the divine in any manner. They relate to all needs and desires and may include moral and spiritual values. Even among the pagans, and perhaps especially among the primitives, there are prayers stressing social justice, individual virtues, and unity.

Sacrifice. But the rite that is most significant and at the same time most difficult to analyze is sacrifice. The term is often employed to designate rites that are very dissimilar and ambiguous. But in such a phenomenon, since it is a human act, what ought to be decisive respecting a definition is the interior attitude of the subject and then, indirectly, the nature of the Being to which appeal is made. The sovereign gods only, either alone or on a sharing basis, are objects of sacrifices. These sacrifices are direct offshoots of the primitive offerings of first fruits of the chase or gathering. Accordingly, they are acts whereby man deprives himself of his goods in order to recognize by so doing the absolute rights of divinity over his property and over himself. But when excessive anthropomorphism enters into the representation of the divine or when the destruction of goods is made to satisfy inferior beings, eventually there is no longer any idea of true sacrifice. There is then a question rather of gifts that are sent on their way by death or fire to the world of spirits. Between these two extremes all ambiguities are possible. If the same word is applied to all cases in which there is destruction of property or offering, it loses all precise meaning and designates an aspect that is merely exterior and material. Hence it is necessary to distinguish sacrifices, offerings, gifts, presents, contracts (*do ut des*), magic, blackmail, etc.

Passage Rites. Another rich category of rites comes from the ambivalence of the sacred, namely, passage rites, i.e., purifications, consecrations, and other precautions that are intended to protect the man who approaches the sacred or who leaves the domain of the sacred to return to the profane world. In this case, especially, it is difficult to draw the line between religion and magic because the interested parties themselves do not try to define precisely their interior attitude. This is the situation particularly respecting "confessions," "taboos," or interdicts, the meaning of which depends entirely on the circumstances and on the mentality of the milieu.

Feasts and Ceremonies. Finally, the extremely important category of rites, or rather of cycles of rites, namely, that of feasts and ceremonies, is difficult to classify as religious in the strict sense. But these rites must be studied carefully if one wishes to get a precise idea of the religious phenomenon. They are passage-rites in one of their aspects, but the passage in question is no longer that from the sacred to the profane or vice versa. They celebrate and effect rather the passage of an individual or of a group, or of all nature, from one state to another—age, religious or social function, or season. Their internal structure leads scholars to classify them more and more as mystery rites because of the parallel with the Hellenistic mysteries. From the religious point of view it is to be noted that these rites disregard, but do not exclude, the idea of homage or invocation to a divinity. On the other hand, they express a deep and strongly felt submission to a superior cosmic order, which is often characterized by greater intensity than submission to God. Their function is to subject all growth in man and nature to a process of total renewal of being. This process is carried out ordinarily under the form of various symbols of death and rebirth. The complete acceptance of the conditions of human existence exhibits subjectively all the characteristics of the religious attitude. But, objectively, these rites are marked by the absence of the worship of divinity, for the sovereign will and intervention of divinity are not evoked. The "gods," if mentioned at all, are only models who were the first themselves to experience the operation of the cosmic law of renewal.

These rites, despite their aspect of dependence, are easily exposed to magic interpretations and deformations, which are all the more dangerous because they corrupt a highly spiritual element. Their danger is inherent in the fact that the universal structure to which man recognizes that he belongs and to which he wishes to be closely joined is not explicitly represented as an order willed by God. On the other hand, it seems that religious life can gain in depth only where, as in Christianity, the mysterical rite is an integral part of the worship of God. There is then no longer question of mysteries but of sacraments.

Mythology. A separate place must be given to mythology. At the outset it is necessary to understand "myth" in the correct sense that has only recently become clear. MYTH is the normal form for expressing the content of religion before the elaboration of philosophical definitions, and even side by side with them. Myth is also rite. It cannot be said that a myth is always the explanation of a rite or that every rite postulates a myth. The recitation itself of the myth is a rite, as is shown by the conditions required for communicating it: secrecy, night, ceremonies, etc. The myth seeks to give expression to religious experience without separating it from the concrete elements of that experience. To maintain this connection is properly the function of symbols. Only the myth projects this experience beyond actual and profane time in order to emphasize the absolute value attributable to it.

Religion in Relation to the Individual and Society

After the explanation of the objective elements (representations) and subjective elements (attitudes) of religion, which are both expressed by exterior acts (rites), it must now be emphasized that because of the importance of the social factor in the life of men, especially in the realm of expression, religions necessarily have a social aspect. The significance of the social expression of religion is brought out by the latest classification of types of religion into tribal, national, and universal. The first two types show clearly that the religious experience of individuals, which is the basis of all religious life, becomes a religion, i.e., an institution that leaves a trace in history, only if other individuals participate in it. This participation is the guarantee and necessary sanction of the objectivity and authenticity of the private experience. In the two types mentioned the collectivity whose sanction is decisive is the natural collectivity (cultural or political) whose exclusive solidarity encompasses strictly the life of the individuals concerned.

But the need of collective sanction, even outside the revealed religions, is much more evident in the universal religions that rise in some way on the ruins of the natural collectivities whose authority has been shattered by the contact and mingling of cultures. Religious experience and its exigencies remain, but they seek their collective guarantee in a collective organization proper, founded on the one religion only, and with its specialized officers.

Priesthood. Priesthood, however, is earlier than the universal religions. It is not found, it is true, at the tribal stage, at which there are specialists for the efficacious rites of magic and ANIMISM, while the relation with the supreme divinity remains the prerogative of tribal members, each acting for himself and for the natural groups for which he is responsible. Priesthood appears first in the national religions as a specialization of all religions functions, after the manner of specialization of political functions. Just as the nation develops out of the political centralization occasioned by foreign aggression or by the initiative of individuals who, in order to assure their domination over their group and neighboring groups, make use of a power that was acknowledged in their case as needed for the protection of tribal territory, so this new unity embraces generally a nonhomogeneous collection of cultural groups that had traditionally been independent.

This new situation calls for a religious justification in accordance with the mentality of tribal cultures. Political power, which is of profane origin, seeks an alliance with the natural representatives of these groups. These representatives are stripped of their political functions, but by way of compensation they are invested, in the name of these groups, with the specialized religious function. A universal reflex is to be noted in ancient civilizations in this respect: a religious solidarity is reestablished when the cultural solidarity is destroyed. At the tribal stage secret societies then have their birth. At the national stage, the sacerdotal function comes into being. In the universal religions the priesthood becomes completely independent, at least in essence, of the political power, and vice versa. Even in these religions, however, some mutual understandings are necessary and are deliberately sought in order to take into account the religious mentality of the masses and to regulate the conflicts of authority and interest between specialists.

Prophetism. Yet in this evolution of the sociology of religions toward specialization of functions, reactions in an opposite direction are not lacking. On the religious plane prophetism makes its appearance, and its characteristic note is universality. PROPHETISM may be described as a protest of the individual conscience against the excesses of specialization. The PROPHET himself, however, needs collective sanction. If he gets it within his own group, he becomes a reformer; if not, he will become the founder of a new religion more independent of the cultural or political structures of his milieu.

But in this connection it is necessary to correct the sociological classification of religions since the term "universal religion" is ambiguous. In fact, universality is inherent in genuine religious experience. Hence, even in the most primitive religions, as soon as they give an important place to the personal Sky God, universality is present, since they consider, often in a touching manner, that their cult is necessary for the maintenance of the whole universe, including other religions and cultures. This kind of thinking, however, does not limit itself to the creation of a single universal religion, but it continues to regard every religion as charged with a function in the whole. It has a prophetic tendency, but this confines itself to stressing the necessity of individual religious experience by visions (Native North Americans) or by ecstasy (shamanism; *see* SHAMAN AND MEDICINE MAN).

The prophet is not only universal in his outlook but tends to pass beyond the national religion into a single universal religion by the deepening of his experience in respect to the transcendent Creator or Sky God. Such a universal religion is opposed to the utilitarian or egoistic preoccupations of the specialists or of societies closed in upon themselves.

Morality. The problem of the relations between religion and morality must be situated in a similar perspective (*see* RELIGION AND MORALITY). If morality is identified with fidelity to the individual conscience to the point of excluding all collective sanctions and all objective norms, one may be tempted to consider tribal or national religions as completely amoral. Correspondingly, universal religions will be relegated to the domain of strictly private life. But if it is considered that tribal and national religions arise in groups in which the individual feels that he is truly himself, both in security and defined by function only in the perfect solidarity of the group, it follows that the group's religion and its morality are completely identified. The one expresses and effects the desired integration of the individual into the human group; and the other, his integration and that of the group into the universe. Man and society regard themselves as members of this universe. It should be noted, furthermore, that the individual desires this integration intensely, for it gives him a meaning. And this integration is not purely passive or impersonal, since even in the most strictly clannish religions the protest of the individual expresses itself in his belief—so surprising to the ethnologist—in the "distant god," who is invoked in precise terms as a recourse against the community that has become unjust. There is no effective revolt but solely an appeal to the transcendent witness because the experience of life teaches daily the necessary reality and practical primacy of group solidarity.

On the other hand, if it is true that the apparent history of human societies is that of a "progressive laicization," there are grounds for questioning the rationalistic optimism of the 19th century and for observing, furthermore, that the so-called rational system of morality influences consciences only to the extent that they are sustained, however unknowingly, by religious values still widespread in the milieu that follows it. Such a system of morality collapses as soon as individuals change their milieu without taking their religion with them, just as every detribalized individual finds himself without moorings and lost.

Salvation. The sociological classification of religions and the corrections required have been covered sufficiently. It is necessary to pass to other distinctions that, strictly, concern aspects only of religions. These aspects are wrongly regarded as being capable in themselves of defining a religion, such as monotheism, polytheism, and animism. They are only ingredients, however, the combination of which characterizes each particular religion. Yet there is one aspect that appears to be more specific, namely, the idea of salvation. Some think that every religion is a salvation religion, while others hold that only universal religions can be salvation religions. The former, however, can find the idea of salvation in all religions only on condition that they recognize that, in tribal religions in particular, the idea of salvation is entirely implicit. The tribal religions do not have a pessimistic metaphysics that would teach the necessity of a savior since they propose and effect a perfect integration of individuals into their group and into their universe, in order that they may participate in their values, without separating the sacred and the profane. The attitude of these religions is not one of preoccupation with saving or transforming their world but of maintaining it, and themselves with it, by adhering scrupulously to its actual structures.

It is to be emphasized that Christianity does not belong in either category. It is not solely a religion of salvation, but a religion of redemption.

Origin and Evolution of Religion

The analysis presented above has eventually led to the question—at least in simplified form—of the origin and historical variations in religion. Since the prehistoric documentation is obviously inadequate by its very nature, it is necessary to employ ethnological comparisons as much as possible to clarify origins. It may be stated without qualification that no culture, however primitive and backward, has been found that does not have ideas on divinity, spirits, human survival, and supernatural forces, along with corresponding rites. The problem of religion seems indeed to be identical with the problem of man (hominization).

The whole evolution of religion seems to be summed up in a diversification of syntheses and proportions of the same universal elements. Apart from a few notable exceptions, a certain parallelism is evident between the inordinate development, on the one hand, of magic, animism, fertility rites, and finally, polytheism, and on the other, the cultural changes that have produced civilizations that became more and more complex in their economic and political techniques. The great civilizations belong to general history rather than to the history of religions since they, in particular, have only developed further a political and philosophical heritage that was constituted in its entirety before history. Revealed religions alone pose specific problems, since they constitute conscious reactions against the tendencies of evolution. The Bible, and to some extent Zarathushtra, go very definitely against the trend of their contemporary milieus. All else that can be said on these subjects falls in the sphere of philosophy and theology, and not in that of sciences such as anthropology and sociology.

See Also: RELIGION (IN PRIMITIVE CULTURE); RELIGION, PHILOSOPHY OF; RELIGION, SOCIOLOGY OF.

Bibliography: General works. H. PINARD DE LA BOULLAYE, *L'Étude comparée des religions,* 3 v. (3d ed. Paris 1931). G. MENSCHING, et al., *Die Religion in Geschichte und Gegenwart,* 7 v. (3d ed. Tübingen 1957–65) 5:961–975, 986–991, with good bibliog. F. KÖNIG, ed., *Religionswissenschaftliches Wörterbuch* (Freiburg 1956). F. KÖNIG, ed., *Christus und die Religionen der Erde: Handbuch der Religionsgeschichte,* 3 v. (2d ed. Vienna 1961). P. TACCHI VENTURI, *Storia delle religioni,* 2 v. (4th ed. Turin 1954). M. BRILLIANT and R. AIGRAIN, eds., *Histoire des religions,* 5 v. (Paris 1953–56). F. HEILER, *Erscheinungsformen und Wesen der Religion* (Stuttgart 1961). A. BRUNNER, *Die Religion* (Freiburg 1956). M. ELIADE, *Patterns in Comparative Religion,* tr. R. SHEED (New York 1958). M. ELIADE and J. KITAGAWA, eds., *The History of Religions: Essays in Methodology* (Chicago 1959). J. WACH, *The Comparative Study of Religions* (New York 1958). P. SCHEBESTA, *Der Ursprung der Religion* (Berlin 1961). W. SCHMIDT, *Der Ursprung der Gottesidee,* 12 v. (Münster), v. 1 (2d ed. 1926), v. 2–12 (1925–55). Special works. R. CAILLOIS, *L'Homme et le Sacré* (2d ed. Paris 1953). B. HÄRING, *Das Heilige und das Gute* (Freiburg 1950). M. ELIADE, *The Sacred and the Profane,* tr. from Fr. W. R. TRASK (New York 1959); *Myths, Dreams, and Mysteries,* tr. from Fr. P. MAIRET (New York 1960); *Birth and Rebirth,* tr. from Fr. W. R. TRASK (New York 1958). R. OTTO, *The Idea of the Holy,* tr. J. W. HARVEY (2d ed. New York 1958). R. ALLIER, *Magie et religion* (Paris 1935). C. H. RATSCHOW, *Magic und Religion* (2d ed. Gütersloh 1955). T. OHM, *Die Liebe zu Gott in den nichtchristlichen Religionen* (Krailling, Ger. 1951). A. KIRCHGÄSSNER, *Die mächtigen Zeichen: Ursprünge, Formen und Gesetze des Kultes* (Freiburg 1959). B. MALINOWSKI, *Magic, Science and Religion* (New York 1955). R. WILL, *Le Culte,* 3 v. (Paris 1925–35). F. HEILER, *Das Gebet: Eine religionsgeschichtliche und religionspsychologische Untersuchung* (5th ed. Munich 1923). A. VORBICHLER, *Das Opfer auf den uns heute noch erreichbaren ältesten Stufen der Menscheitsgeschichte* (Mödling

1956). A. E. JENSEN, *Myth and Cult among Primitive Peoples,* tr. M. T. CHOLDIN and W. WEISSLEDER (Chicago 1963). J. DE VRIES, *Forschungsgeschichte der Mythologie* (Freiburg 1961). P. RADIN, *The World of Primitive Man* (New York 1960).

[J. GOETZ]

RELIGION (IN PRIMITIVE CULTURE)

Investigations in cultural anthropology and the comparative study of RELIGION have led scholars to advance numerous and varied theories to account for the origins and universality of religious phenomena in human societies. This article presents a brief review of the main trends in the development of these theories and a consideration of some of the principal religious ideas and practices found in primitive societies.

Theoretical Interpretations

Mid-20th-century investigations of religion in preliterate or barely literate societies reveal a renewed emphasis on the nature and meaning, rather than on the origin and social function, of religion. Interpretative studies of religious SYMBOLISM, MYTH AND MYTHOLOGY, ritual, SACRAMENTS, and SACRIFICE, made by reputable anthropologists, have appeared with increasing frequency. This shift in emphasis can be explained partly in terms of the sociology of knowledge and partly as reflecting a growing realization of the inadequacy of theoretical frameworks once considered as established.

Evolutionist Hypothesis. Many early students of primitive religion were savants belonging to the 19th-century European middle class, from whose perspective the socioeconomic history of mankind appeared to be a triumphal march toward ever-greater material prosperity and rational enlightenment. It was natural for them to regard Charles DARWIN and T. H. Huxley as their major prophets and to view the history of thought as an evolutionary process of emancipation from magical and religious categories, through those of increasing philosophical refinement, to unchallenged scientific RATIONALISM.

Tylor. Sir Edward Tylor, for example, in *Primitive Culture* (2 v. London 1871) held that religion began with universal belief in ghosts and spirits (animism) and that by degrees men arrived at the notion of one universal Spirit animating all things. Tylor's scheme left no room for revelation but only for progressive generalization as human society embraced ever-wider social aggregates.

Frazer. Sir James George Frazer, in the manner although not with the matter of his positivist predecessor Auguste COMTE, claimed in *The Golden Bough* (2 v. London 1890) that mankind had passed through three broad intellectual stages: MAGIC, religion, and SCIENCE. According to Frazer the earliest men thought that by magical procedures, imitating natural processes or utilizing the "law of sympathy," they could compel events to comply with their desires. It was when such procedures did not work that they invented religion. They conceived religion not as the manipulation of impersonal supernatural powers immanent in phenomena but as the supplication of supernatural persons. Spell became prayer, and the kill became the sacrifice. Religion explained more cogently than magic why its practices sometimes failed to bring about the desired results. Since deities and spirits were persons, they possessed the attributes of persons; they had likes and dislikes toward mortals, they could give or withhold favors at will. Ethically, Frazer argued, religion was on a higher level than magic, since the success or failure of a prayer might hinge on the moral state of the petitioner. Nevertheless, religion also failed men, since their attempts to persuade the divine beings to give them benefits were frequently uncertain in their outcome. Finally, the vanguard of mankind, having learned all too slowly from past errors, had discovered the scientific method, which gave understanding of the real causes of events, by which the events could be controlled. Religion for Frazer, like the state for Marx, was to wither away in the sun of this scientific enlightenment. This was a doctrine that scientists of Frazer's time found flattering.

Freud and Durkheim. In the early 20th century scientific humanists such as Sigmund FREUD and Émile DURKHEIM continued to speculate about the origin and evolution of religion. Freud's etiological myth is well known. He derived religion (and even culture) from the dominance of the father in a postulated primordial horde and from remorse (commemorated in sacramental rituals of many types) when the father was murdered, out of sexual jealousy, by the young males. This was the origin of the Oedipus complex and of all subsequent religious development. Durkheim found in TOTEMISM of the Australian aboriginal variety "the earliest form" of religion. The animal eaten by the totemic group was in his view the master symbol of that group itself. Through its consumption each member of the group partook of its unifying power, and all became "members of one another" instead of a mere assemblage of separate individuals. For Durkheim totemism was a stage of social evolution through which all more advanced societies had passed. Successive religious refinements, such as animism, polytheism, and monotheism, were but modalities of the totemic principle: all man's gods are but man-created symbols of society itself.

All these theories, and others too numerous to mention, had one common feature: they treated religion as an illusion that originated in "the childhood of the race" and passed through successive stages until men had either outgrown it completely or so tinged it with philosophical and ethical elements as to make it a "religion of humanity" divested of its supernatural "errors."

Functionalist Hypothesis. Scientific cultural evolutionism—which was inconsistent with the Marxist view that "force is the midwife of progress"—received a sharp setback in the West as a result of World War I and its consequences. It recovered somewhat in the materialistic evangelism of Leslie White and his school of American neoevolutionists. But the millions of dead and the mutual barbarities wrought by "civilized" men in the war made progress appear less inevitable than the earlier Darwinians had supposed.

Practical Interest in Cultural Anthropology. It became apparent that change was not always "progressive" but might lead to anarchy and *anomie*. Those Western nations especially that governed large impoverished colonial populations became concerned to maintain their stability rather than encourage radical changes that might have a violent outcome. Great Britain, in particular, developed the notion of "indirect rule" in its overseas territories, whereby a share of political and judicial authority was delegated to indigenous leaders, to chiefs, headmen, and religious functionaries. In order to rule through these authorities it became necessary to understand to some extent the structure of the social systems in which they operated. Consequently some encouragement was given to anthropological research.

Interdependence of Religion and Society. Anthropologists came to see their task as "exhibiting the systematic interconnections" in the social relationships and social institutions found in the tribal societies at any given time. Emphasis was laid on the "social function" of a given institution in contributing to the "cohesion" of the total system. Students of primitive religion sharing this bias, such as Bronislaw Malinowski and A. R. Radcliffe-Brown, saw religion, especially in its ritual aspect, as what has been described as "a sort of all-purpose social glue," for cementing together fractured social relationships or for binding together different types of institutions. In the Trobriand Islands of the western Pacific Malinowski endeavored to show how magical ritual served to coordinate and regulate cooperative human behavior in a variety of hazardous and uncertain social and economic undertakings, such as open-sea fishing, agriculture, and overseas trading expeditions. Radcliffe-Brown argued that ritual expresses in its symbolism certain values, upon the acceptance of which the proper functioning of society depends.

Functionalist analyses stressed the close interdependence of society and religion, the latter being regarded as a kind of servomechanism to the former. The question asked was always: what is the "function" of a given religious belief, or ritual performance, or myth in the maintenance of "social solidarity"? In such an intellectual climate it was not considered "meaningful" to inquire about the meaning but only about the function of such phenomena. Differences between religions, as expressed in doctrine, symbolism, and liturgical forms, were reduced to the single functional requirement that "religion makes for social cohesion (or social solidarity)."

"Meaning" Versus "Function." Anthropologists have begun to concede a greater degree of autonomy, and even validity, to religious systems. This has been due partly to the study of religion in pluralistic and changing societies, in which its function in maintaining social solidarity is by no means so obvious as in isolated traditional communities. The proliferation of new sects, the rise of millenarian movements, the persistence of religious forms in groups undergoing rapid changes in social structure—all these have underlined the need for a new approach based on a consideration of what is *meant* by religious beliefs and symbols. The work of such philosophers and sociologists as A. N. WHITEHEAD, Ernst CASSIRER, Suzanne Langer, and P. A. Sorokin in the field of symbolism, and the anthropological field studies of E. E. Evans-Pritchard, Godfrey Lienhardt, and Clifford Geertz have been crucial in restoring to its former prominence the notion that "ritual is a language for saying things which are felt to be true and important but which are not susceptible of statement in scientific terms" [J. Beattie, *Other Cultures* (London 1964) 239].

Religion in Multifunctional Communities

The preoccupation of earlier scholars with functional aspects of religion may well be attributable to certain features of social organization in small-scale communities living close to the margin of bare subsistence and possessed of only limited technological equipment. The major types of human purposive activities that are broadly classified as religious, political, legal, economic, etc., in preliterate societies are hardly specialized as separate associational structures (each with its appropriate sets of beliefs, aims, concepts, techniques, and procedures) but remain, as it were, embedded in the total community.

Multiplex Character of Social Relations. Social relationships in such communities tend to be *multiplex,* i.e., each serves a plurality of interests at the same time. Thus an elder may be at once head of a lineage (in the kinship system), headman of a village (in the politicojural system), overseer of the village's productive and distributive activities (in the economic system), and priest of the ancestral cult (in the religious system). These aspects of life overlap, interpenetrate, and concern the same persons. Thus all types of activities are saturated, as it were, with religious and moral implications, at any rate more fully than in modern societies characterized by a complex division of labor, in which social relationships, increasingly associational in type, tend to serve single interests. Objective comparative study of religious systems indicates that a major note of religious belief and practice is the achievement of what might be called subliminal unity. This type of unity is quite distinct from the reconciliation of interests, rational and utilitarian, that may be brought about by legal, political, or economic institutions. It relates rather to the establishment, through prayer, liturgical action, sacrifice, communion rites, and the use of symbolism, of a state of rapport or corporate solidarity between Deity or Spirit (whether singular or conceived of as a unanimous group) and a congregation-in-worship, on the one hand, and between the individual members of that congregation, on the other. When the congregation is identical with the kin group, the local community, the polity, and the economic unit, the function of its religious institutions may easily be mistaken for ''the promotion or maintenance of social solidarity.'' Yet it is not the fact of unity but the nature, or quality, or dimension of unity that is in question. At what level of being or experience do the participants in ritual seek to be bound together? What is the meaning, rather than the function, of their joint worship? There are many dimensions of ''solidarity,'' and it is this crucial multiplicity that Durkheim and his followers did not adequately comprehend, or else tried to reduce to the single mysterious essence ''the social *sui generis.*''

Varieties of Religious Ideas and Behavior. In multifunctional communities the quintessentially religious tends to be tinctured with evaluations, imagery, sentiments, rules, customs, life styles, etc., derived from experience in economic, political, domestic, legal, and other types of situations—in each instance colored by a particular natural, social, and ecological environment. The great catalytic sentence ''Render, therefore, to Caesar the things that are Caesar's and to God the things that are God's'' (Mk 12.17) is not heard so as to be understood in such communities. God, or the gods, are translated into Caesarean terms and take on the attributes of power figures in political, domestic, economic, and legal situations where the utilitarian interests of the group and its component individuals tend to be paramount. Nevertheless, as even such an agnostic humanist as Paul Radin has often pointed out, it is possible to discern in very many ''primitive'' religions traces of mystical and philosophical thought that appear to be unalloyed by Caesarean considerations, as in cases of prayers and myths of a monotheistic cast set in polytheistic religious contexts.

In societies with a low degree of technological development and division of labor, with multiplex social relationships, with total personal involvement in almost every relationship, and in which kinship is an irreducible principle of social organization, it is perhaps not surprising to find close interdependencies between the system of religious beliefs and practices and other cultural systems. It should also occasion little astonishment that the powers of nature and of human and animal disease should figure predominantly in religion. With poor technological control over the environment and inadequate knowledge of empirical causation, everyday existence is surrounded by unpredictable and menacing hazards that cannot be effectively dealt with or curbed. Such perils appear to be autonomous entities and are conceived of as arbitrary and capricious personalities. The tendency to personify natural powers may well be connected with the personal character of multiplex social relations, whereas the tendency to spiritualize almost every force that can affect human beings may be linked with man's inability to bring practical resources to bear against them. Spiritual personalities may be coped with by entreaty, sacrifices, and the symbolic activities of ritual, where forces known to be impersonal and uncontrollable would evoke only despair and helplessness.

Cults of the Dead. There are manifold varieties of what Tylor called ANIMISM (to which he assigned a pivotal position in his treatment of the origin of religion; his ''minimal definition'' of religion was indeed ''a belief in spiritual beings''). These varieties may be reduced to two main categories: beliefs about the spirits of the dead and beliefs about nature spirits (including those of disease). Cults of the dead take many forms but, again, may be broadly regarded as falling under two heads: ghost placation and ancestor veneration. In the former the spirits of the dead are regarded as inimical ghosts who bring illness or other misfortune on the living. Such spirits are not thought of as genealogically interlinked with the living but as the supernatural residues of powerful, rich, or important individuals. What is left after death is not usually the humane aspect of personality but the individual's accumulated grudges against the living. The aim of ritual in this case is to detach the living victim from his dead persecutor by propitiation or exorcism.

In many societies in Africa, China, and elsewhere, however, the cults of ANCESTOR WORSHIP are addressed to the congregation's known and named forebears whose links of kinship to the living and to each other are not only remembered but are of structural importance to the living in their daily interactions. Such cults are found especially in societies that attach a high value to unilineal descent as a vertebral principle of social organization. They assign beneficent as well as punitive characteristics to the dead; indeed, when the dead punish it is to remind their living kin to ''live well'' and morally together. The aim of many rites performed on behalf of ancestral ''shades'' is to ''cause the ancestors to be remembered,'' as the Ndembu of Zambia phrase it. The importance of commemoration may be structural and jural as well as exemplifying piety. For in such societies lineage ancestors several generations back may constitute indices of the distinct lineage subdivisions of which the community is composed. The segmentation of society into its jural and economic subgroups may thus be validated and sustained by regular performances of ancestral ritual.

Not all societies with strong lineage-organization have ancestral cults, however, while others lacking lineages of any depth venerate their immediate forebears. Examples of the former may be found in the Nuer and Dinka tribes of the Sudan; of the latter, among the Thai-Lao of Thailand. Thus it is by no means inevitable that lineage-based societies should possess ancestral cults, although there is a marked tendency for this to be the case.

The High God. Cults of the dead may coexist with beliefs in a creator spirit, or High God, as in many parts of Africa, e.g., among the Lunda and Luba of the Congo; Ila, Bemba, and Tonga of Zambia; Fon, Nupe, and Ashanti of West Africa; Zulu and Basuto of South Africa. Not infrequently the term for the High God is of wide provenience, cutting across tribal boundaries, e.g., *Nzambi* and *Kalung'a* in West Central Africa, *Mulungu* in East Africa, and *Leza* in East Central Africa. Sometimes, as among the Interlacustrine Bantu, the ancestors are regarded as intermediaries between their living kin and the High God. Although the Supreme Being is often regarded as ''otiose,'' as having refrained from intervening in the cosmos after having created it, it is sometimes held, as among the Nupe, that He gave men a set of automatically efficacious rituals to set right breaches and disturbances of the moral, social, and natural orders. Even in societies without cults of the dead, including many with crude and presumably very ancient cultures, such as those of the Bushmen of southwest Africa and some Australian aboriginal tribes, research by Wilhelm SCHMIDT, Wilhelm Koppers, and others of the Vienna school has demonstrated fairly conclusively that beliefs in High Gods, if not positive monotheism, are well established.

Polytheism. Polytheism tends to flourish in societies relatively well endowed technologically and especially where the natural habitat is diversified. Each god is associated with a province of nature and may also become the representative of a cluster of ideas and sentiments relat-

ing to certain culturally defined aspects of social and psychical life. Or the gods may be connected with man's attempts to control his physical environment. As Raymond Firth has written, ''The departmental gods of the Maori are invoked each in his own sphere—the god of the sea for fishing and ocean voyaging, the god of the forests for bird-snaring and canoe-building, the god of agriculture for successful planting and harvests'' [*Human Types* (London 1941) 177]. Often the gods are arrayed in a hierarchy, forming a pantheon. Such a hierarchy may closely replicate in its structure the political structure of the state, as in the case of the Fon of Dahomey, described by M. J. Herskovits and Paul Mercier.

Cults of the dead, ancestral veneration, and polytheistic hierarchies can be shown to be closely interconnected with kinship, political, and economic structures. High Gods, however, whether they are found in association with these religious phenomena or alone, are less easily related to their sociocultural context. Rather they provide protophilosophical explanations of the origins of the cosmos and of mankind. Where there are myths about them such myths attempt to answer the following kinds of question: Why are we here? Where do we come from? For what purpose? Why do we act in this way? Why do we die? Very frequently no formal worship is paid to the High God, no prayers are offered to Him. He remains, as it were, a latent *Deus absconditus* in a religious system largely conceived and symbolically expressed in a set of analogies with human social and economic orders. Primitive monotheism or the concept of an otiose High God (*Deus otiosus*) in the background of a system of active lesser deities or ancestral shades or both represents a qualitatively distinct stratum of religious belief. The passive High God foreshadows the active High God of the Judeo-Christian monotheistic tradition.

Syncretism and Revelation in the Ancient East. These two strands of religious development, the gods of embodied society and the God of faith, remain distinct but interwoven in many religious systems. Their significant separation may best be traced by examination of the religions of ancient MESOPOTAMIA, Asia Minor, Syria, the Iranian plateau, and EGYPT, the seed beds of the ancient civilizations and, indeed, as modern scholarship is coming to realize, of many complex West and East African societies. It was in these areas that the higher living religions first appeared *in nuce*. In the ancient state systems of Egypt and Mesopotamia the later neolithic emphases on female fertility and, later still, bull symbolism, which probably appeared first in an animistic context, have clearly developed into the worship of mother goddesses and their spouses—universal gods of the sky and fertility in taurine guise.

Syncretist Cults. In Egypt the male solar deity, as the heavenly father of the pharaoh, took precedence over the mother goddess as life giver. This stood, as E. O. James has memorably demonstrated, in marked contrast to the religious beliefs of Mesopotamia, where the mother goddesses were regarded as the actual source of life. In the course of time, as the ancient agricultural civilization spread from southwestern Asia to Egypt, western Europe, and India, the Goddess, the Magna Mater, tended to become an increasingly syncretistic deity, incorporating many local goddesses of maternity and fertility. For example, Isis, the "goddess of many names," became the most popular of Egyptian deities in the Hellenistic period and was identified with the allied foreign goddesses, Silene and Io, Demeter, Aphrodite, and Pelagia (*see* ISIS AND OSIRIS). In the Roman Empire her worship spread everywhere until she lost her original Egyptian character. Other composite deities of that period in the Near East included a virile Young God, regarded as both the son and husband of the Goddess, who united in a single figure the properties of what were once local gods, such as Baal, Adonis, Tammuz, Hadad, Aleyan, and El. He combined the attributes of a storm god, a weather god, a bestower of fecundity, a vegetation deity, a sky god, and a sun god. These syncretistic cults of Goddess and Young God, paired or separate, were associated with much ritual license, goaded by such sensory stimuli as frenzied dancing, wild music, and sexual symbolism, in the hope of obtaining communion with the source of life and vitality in a condition of ecstatic abandonment and mystical communion. On account of their disorderly character such rites were frequently condemned officially in the Greco-Roman world, although they had such deeply entrenched popular support that during the Roman imperial period the cult of the Goddess, in a rather more decorous and restrained form, compelled state recognition.

Relation to Mundane Order. It has been noted that, in societies with multiplex social relationships, there is a high degree of consistency between mode of subsistence, social and political structure, and religious system. Indeed, one can go a long way in the analysis of a religious system if one accepts Radin's hypothesis that religion is "one of the most important and distinctive means for maintaining life-values." "As these vary," he asserts, "so will the religious unit vary." Among the most prominent "life-values" Radin places the desire for success, for happiness, and for long life. Religion, since it is concerned with maintaining these and the secular institutions that also promote them, is not a thing apart from mundane life nor is it essentially a philosophical inquiry into the nature of being and becoming. "It only emphasizes and preserves those values accepted by the majority of a group at a given time" [*Primitive Religion: Its Nature and Origin* (New York 1937) 5].

There is evident support for this position in the vast literature on primitive and prehistoric societies, with their rites to ensure the fertility of crops, animals, and men and to maintain the institutions of secular society. The cults of ancient Egypt and Mesopotamia, too, exemplify Radin's hypothesis. James, in his discussion of the Tammuz cultus in Syria, explicitly relates its main features to ecological factors. "Behind the cultures," he writes, "lay the emotional needs of everyday life, created by the environmental conditions, in which rain was the principal necessity in the absence of an effective system of inundation and irrigation as in the Nile Valley. Without an adequate rainfall the land could not give her increase, and the social and religious structure of Mesopotamia and Syria was very largely determined by the need of rain and fertility" [*The Ancient Gods* (London 1960) 306].

Uniqueness of Judaism. But the external differences between primitive and ancient religions, largely determined by ecological and political conditions, resolve into substantial identity when these religions are compared with JUDAISM. This strongly monotheistic religion stands out in marked contrast to the polytheism and syncretic monolatries of all the other Semitic- and Hamitic-speaking peoples of the ancient East. James has characterized succinctly the contribution made by the Hebrew prophets: "They insisted on a standard of conduct that would satisfy the demands of an ethically righteous God who had shown man what is good, and what is required of him: to do justice and to love mercy and to walk humbly with his God . . . . The transcendent majesty of God inspired awe, loyalty and obedience, which introduced a new standard of the good life . . . . Moral goodness was a quality that had to be won in conflict with evil, whether evil be interpreted theologically in terms of sin, biologically as an inheritance from man's forebears, human or animal, or sociologically as a result of the demoralization of society and its institutions, beliefs and customs" (*ibid.* 275). This was not a religion that would change radically with alterations in the economic and social structures with which it would be associated. It was destined to preserve its basic principles and ethical and legal precepts throughout innumerable historical vicissitudes and in a variety of economic and social milieus. It is no mere reflection or expression of the way men organize themselves in the pursuit of "human life-values" but rather the voice of God Himself, speaking to and through His prophets. It is what C. H. Dodd has described as "the entry into history of a reality beyond history" [*History and the Gospel* (London 1938) 181].

See Also: RELIGION; RELIGION, SOCIOLOGY OF.

Bibliography: J. BEATTIE, *Other Cultures: Aims, Methods and Achievements in Social Anthropology* (New York 1964). J. M. COOPER, "The Origin and Early History of Religion," *Primitive*

Man 2 (1929) 33–52. E. DURKHEIM, *The Elementary Forms of the Religious Life,* tr. J. W. SWAIN (London 1915; repr. Glencoe, IL1954). M. ELIADE, *Patterns in Comparative Religion,* tr. R. SHEED (New York 1958). E. E. EVANS-PRITCHARD, *Nuer Religion* (Oxford 1956). J. G. FRAZER, *The Golden Bough,* 12 v. (3d ed. London 1911–15). S. FREUD, *Totem and Taboo* (New York 1918). C. J. GEERTZ, ''Ritual and Social Change: A Javanese Example,'' *American Anthropologist* 59 (1957) 32–54. E. O. JAMES, *The Ancient Gods* (New York 1960). B. MALINOWSKI, *Magic, Science and Religion* (Boston 1948; repr. New York 1954). A. R. RADCLIFFE-BROWN, ''Religion and Society,'' *Journal of the Royal Anthropological Institute* 75 (1945) 33–43. P. RADIN, *Primitive Religion: Its Nature and Origin* (New York 1937). W. SCHMIDT, *The Origin and Growth of Religion,* tr. H. J. ROSE (2d ed. London 1935). E. B. TYLOR, *Primitive Culture,* 2 v. (London 1873; New York 1958).

[V. TURNER]

RELIGION, PHILOSOPHY OF

The title of courses taught mainly in non-Catholic colleges and universities, dealing with a variety of topics ranging from the history, sociology, and psychology of religion to problems in epistemology and metaphysics; also, in modern schools of philosophy since the time of Kant, commonly regarded as a branch of philosophy concerned with a critical evaluation and analysis of religion. This article presents a historical survey of the thought of modern philosophers on the subject of religion, and then gives a systematic analysis of the meaning of ''philosophy of religion'' when used to designate a category of knowledge.

Historical Survey

Immanuel KANT (1724–1804), influenced by the EN-LIGHTENMENT and by D. HUME, rejected traditional metaphysics and natural theology as transcending the proper limits of human reason. For traditional metaphysics Kant substituted a metaphysics based on the moral law that exists in the minds of all people. Man's awareness of the moral law and his duties under it enable him to postulate the existence of God and the immortality of the soul. Thus religion is based on an autonomous ethics; religious faith is a trust in the promises of the moral law. Kant was more or less indifferent to other aspects of religion, e.g., religious practices and dogmas, except as they could be brought within the limits of practical reason and subordinated to ethics. Mysticism received little sympathy, since for him the divine presence exists only in man's awareness of his freedom and obligations under the moral law.

Post-Kantian Idealism. Following Kant, J. G. FICHTE (1762–1814) also associated religion closely with ethics. Religious faith is faith in a moral order and obedience to the moral law. In *The Vocation of Man* (1800), Fichte identified the moral world order with the Absolute as infi-

nite will and reason. The religious man is aware that the divine life exists within him; his true and moral vocation is a love for the divine rather than for the finite and sensible. As infinite, God lacks personality—for personality implies finitude. Traditional theism is rejected for a kind of ambiguous pantheism. The more significant contribution of Fichte is his ethical idealism.

F. SCHELLING (1775–1854), although a disciple of Fichte, argued in his *Philosophy and Religion* (1804) for a personal God revealed to the individual consciousness. Creation was regarded as a kind of cosmic fall away from the Absolute. The end of creation is the historical triumph of good over evil. In history Schelling found an empirical confirmation of a religious philosophy. God reveals himself to man in the history and development of the religious consciousness. Christianity is the culmination of historical religion and mythology, for the truth and aim of mythology is revelation, especially as known through Christ.

F. D. E. SCHLEIERMACHER (1768–1834), a Protestant clergyman and theologian, separated religion radically from ethics and metaphysics. He held that the essence of religion and the basis of faith lies in a feeling of dependence. The intellectual element is not entirely excluded, for it is the function of philosophical theology to conceptualize the religious side of self-consciousness. God transcends human concepts, however, and religion remains fundamentally a matter of the heart rather than of the understanding. As a liberal theologian, Schleiermacher considered theology to be more symbolical than doctrinal.

G. W. F. HEGEL (1770–1831) set forth his basic religious ideas in the *Phenomenology* (1807) and the *Lectures on the Philosophy of Religion* (1832). God, the Absolute, is identified with Spirit or Reason. Religion is one form of knowing the Absolute, and in the dialectic it passes through three principal stages: natural religion, artistic religion, and revealed or spiritual religion. To these correspond the religions of the Orient, of Greece and Rome, and of Christianity. Although it is the highest form of religion, Christianity is not absolute truth. Philosophy is a higher manifestation than religion in the dialectical development of the Absolute. Religion is thus subordinated to philosophy. Both philosophy and religion are concerned with God, but the concern is expressed differently—philosophy is a manifestation of reason, whereas religion is a manifestation of the religious consciousness through faith and love.

Later Development. Later idealism is represented principally by John Caird (1820–98), a British philosopher, and Josiah ROYCE (1885–1916), an American philosopher. Caird declared that the primary concern of religion is with objects of devotion and spiritual enjoyment, while philosophy's aim is intellectual knowledge. Religious knowledge is concerned with revelation and authority; beyond the competence of reason it is identified with feeling and faith. In *The Religious Aspect of Philosophy* (1885) Royce distinguishes between the theological and the ethical. The former is a theory of faith that requires a critical and even a skeptical approach. The latter has for its objective a morality of harmony that requires only the Biblical precept ''Thou shalt love thy neighbor as thyself.'' The justification of religion as an ethical idealism led Royce to develop a system of absolute idealism in which the partial finite self finds the fulfillment of its experience in an Absolute Experience, identified with God as Absolute Person and Infinite Self. The impact of idealism on American philosophies of religion is apparent also in the work of such men as W. E. Hocking (1873–1966) and W. M. Urban (1873–1952).

Personalism. The personalist movement represents a modification of absolute idealism. Originating with G. H. Howison (1834–1916), it has been represented by such philosophers as Borden P. Bowne (1847–1910), E. S. BRIGHTMAN (1884–1953), and Ralph Flewelling (1871–1960). Its principal characteristics are a spiritual pluralism, an emphasis upon God and finite individuals as persons, and the notion of a finite theology and its implications for the problem of evil (*see* PERSONALISM).

Materialism. L. A. FEUERBACH (1804–72), a materialist and leader of left-wing HEGELIANISM, argued in the *Essence of Christianity* (1841) that religion is an illusion, a dream of the human mind. God is no more than the attributes man finds in himself and hence the proper worship of man is man. This form of religious humanism had considerable influence on Karl MARX.

Positivism. Auguste COMTE (1798–1857), the founder of POSITIVISM, held that human knowledge passes through three stages: the theological, the metaphysical, and the scientific or positive. Truth and certitude are attained only in the last stage, where the religion of humanity is conceived as replacing the worship of God in the first stage. Humanity is the sum total of all dead, living or future beings who in one way or another have worked for the progress and happiness of man. Positivist dogmas, religious rites, and even a religious calendar were worked out by Comte for this worship of humanity.

Phenomenology. PHENOMENOLOGY is largely a method for describing the experiences or data of CONSCIOUSNESS. It was employed in philosophy by Edmund HUSSERL, and its expression in the philosophy of religion has been well represented by Rudolph OTTO (1869–1937), and Max SCHELER (1874–1928). In the *Idea of the Holy* (1917), Otto argues in Kantian fashion that the holy is an a priori category. It is impressed upon the religious consciousness and makes possible a religious interpretation of experience. Such an experience is characterized by a numinous feeling, an emotional state leading to an intuition of the manifestations of eternity. The numinous also signifies the *mysterium tremendum et fascinans,* the Wholly Other, the feeling of awe and fear contributing the promise of an exaltation similar to the experiences of the mystics.

Scheler's phenomenology is directed to the affective life of man, to the a priori structure of feelings. As the basis of feelings, values are arranged hierarchically from the sensible, vital, and spiritual to the religious values that include the holy and the unholy. The notion of religious value is further developed in *On the Eternal in Man* (1921), where it is brought out that man as a person transcends nature and his religious experience is perfected in God as the source of love. Moral values constitute, for Scheler as for St. Augustine, the ordering of human love to the highest values.

Existentialism. S. A. KIERKEGAARD (1813–55), the father of modern EXISTENTIALISM, sought to replace the Absolute of Hegel with the existential reality of the individual. Existence is prior to essence; truth is subjective and to be achieved in the inner experience of the individual rather than by reason and objective knowledge. Faith is the encounter of the existing individual with God. Faith is a venture and a risk for the individual rather than a doctrine. The truth of Christianity is not to be found in theoretical knowledge or in argumentation, but is something to be appropriated in the passionate inwardness of the individual.

Martin Buber (1878–1965) argues in his *Eclipse of God* (1953) that religion is based on the ''I-Thou'' relationship whereas philosophy is based on the ''I-It'' relationship. Religious faith begins with the ''fear of God,'' with the dread uncertainty man has of his existence. Through faith man establishes an existential relationship with God, an ''I-Thou'' relationship in which he can meet with God as a Person. The philosophical relationship is wholly objective and can result only in the eclipse of God.

Pragmatism. William JAMES (1842–1910) rejected any intellectual approach to religion. The truth of religious beliefs rests for him upon the values they contribute to humanity's concrete everyday experience. Religious ideas are true if they make human lives more meaningful. In *The Varieties of Religious Experience* (1902), James held that there is an empirical confirmation of religious experience and ideas. He himself believed that deity is finite and can only be considered as a ''something'' greater than man.

Henri BERGSON (1859–1941) has been termed an "intuitional pragmatist." He claimed that God is a creative life force that one may intuit within his experience. In *Two Sources of Morality and Religion* (1932), he declared there is a closed religion, that of myth and ritual, which is static and defensive; contrasted to it is the open or dynamic religion, the religion of the mystic whose religious genius leads him to an intuitive grasp of God and effects the union of the soul with God.

Maurice BLONDEL (1861–1949), although associated with modernism, remained a loyal Catholic. In his philosophy of action he developed a dialectic that necessitated the supernatural. God is both immanent and transcendent, but man can bridge the gap between the natural and the supernatural through God's grace and His action toward man. Only in action that is not mere will but the whole of man's activity can God be affirmed and attained by the individual. It is action that gives reality to the intellectual arguments for God's existence and to any understanding of God.

American Naturalism. George SANTAYANA (1863–1952) maintained that the supernatural is merely an extension of the natural. Nature is materialistic and mechanistic and religion is merely "human experience interpreted by human imagination." Religious beliefs are not to be taken literally; they belong to the sphere of poetry and their function is to express human moral ideals in mythical and poetical images. God is only a symbol for human ideals.

A. N. WHITEHEAD (1861–1947), an "idealistic naturalist," maintained that God has both a primordial and a consequent nature. By the former He knows the eternal objects that serve to mediate between Himself and the world. God is neither infinite nor omnipotent; He is the final but not efficient cause of all things. In his consequent nature, God is immanent in, and develops with, the world. God as a principle of concretion overcomes the Platonic dualism in the metaphysics of Whitehead; involved in becoming and the struggle to overcome evil, God is "the great companion, the fellow sufferer who understands."

John Dewey (1859–1952) rejected the supernatural completely and was extremely critical of traditional religion. His book, *A Common Faith* (1934), is essentially a plea for a divine reality as a symbol representative of all human ideals. The function of religious faith is that of unifying men in the pursuit of the highest ideals.

Charles HARTSHORNE (1897–2000) was both a disciple of Whitehead and an original thinker. He rejected any conception of "Other-Worldliness" and claimed that God must be found within the world process; here He realizes and perfects His unchanging essence within the context of a developing experience. This relationship of God with the world is described as a PANENTHEISM. Religious humanism is rejected; Hartshorne argued that a true humanism must be based on a recognition of God and an awareness of God's love and His total involvement with His creatures.

Systematic Analysis

What kind of knowledge the "philosophy of religion" may be depends in part upon the meaning of "philosophy of." Through analysis, possible meanings are here considered in order to discover whether the philosophy of religion can be identified with one of them.

Possible Meanings. In the "philosophy of X" the reference may be to X as a kind of being. It is in this sense that one speaks of the philosophy of nature or the philosophy of history. In this case there is a kind of knowledge that is a synthesis of two other kinds of knowledge, one of which is an ontological discipline, e.g., metaphysics or theology based upon revelation. If the reasoning by which a proposition of the philosophy of nature is obtained may be thought of as the conclusion of a syllogism, then the minor premise would be a proposition of the natural sciences and the major premise would be a philosophical (or metaphysical) proposition. Evidently the philosophy of religion is not this kind of knowledge, for the term religion refers to neither being nor existence.

The "philosophy of X" may refer to knowledge about a kind of knowledge. Reference may be to a group of philosophical disciplines, the group being defined in terms of the relevance of philosophical principles to some other kind of knowledge. An instance of this would be the "philosophy of science." In this case the X refers to the kind of knowledge known as positive science. The term philosophy refers to the logical, epistemological, and metaphysical principles that are implied by, or presupposed to, the positive sciences. It is evident that the philosophy of religion cannot be identified with this meaning.

In the "philosophy of X" the X may refer to a kind of human activity, and philosophy then has reference to the philosophical principles that function normatively or regulatively for this kind of activity. The "philosophy of education" would be an example of this kind of meaning. Education is not a kind of knowledge, but rather a kind of human activity. The philosophy of religion can hardly be identified with this meaning, for what usually goes under that name pretends to be at least concerned with the existential. Furthermore, religion is not to be associated with human activity in the sense that education is.

Natural Theology. The conclusion thus far would seem to be that the philosophy of religion must be, and yet cannot be, identified with any one of the three aforementioned meanings. A solution might be suggested by reconsidering the first meaning, in which case the *X* is existential. If so, then the philosophy of religion becomes identical with the "philosophy of God," which in turn means what has been called "natural theology." However, certain difficulties attend this interpretation. A systematic analysis of the meaning of the philosophy of religion can neither be arbitrary nor completely nonhistorical. Depending upon the possible relations of faith and reason to each other, there have been three interpretations of the meaning of natural theology.

(1) After the Reformation some Protestants considered natural theology to be the kind of knowledge about the finite, natural world that could be secured as the result of a deduction from the teachings of revelation. In this case natural theology was neither an autonomous subject nor one that was a synthesis of other kinds of knowledge. It was really a name for an aspect of the theology of revelation. The philosophy of religion can hardly be identified with this movement of thought.

(2) Stemming from the realistic theism of St. THOMAS AQUINAS is the view of natural theology as a relatively autonomous discipline on the level of reason, but presupposing revelation and open to suggestions from it (*see* THEOLOGY, NATURAL; CHRISTIAN PHILOSOPHY). In this view natural theology is the completion of metaphysics, yet in content dependent wholly upon human reason. Natural theology, in this meaning of the phrase, is a kind of knowledge about being, namely, God. If the philosophy of religion is identified with this meaning, then it becomes merely a synonym. However, it would be at least historically inaccurate to make the philosophy of religion synonymous with natural theology. Moreover, it would be an easy way of escaping the problem at hand.

(3) Natural theology may also be considered not only to be autonomous, but also to be a substitute for theology based upon revelation. Such it was for DEISM, sometimes called the "religion of reason." However, this product of the Enlightenment was itself ambiguous and took two forms, the one Kantian and the other pre-Kantian. In the pre-Kantian form the argument was not from a metaphysical analysis of finite things to God, but rather from a false analogical view of the physical world to God. This view of the religion of reason tended to be unstable and negative. Its chief value seems to have been that of a weapon against the Church, a kind of anticlericalism.

Religion of Reason. In the Kantian form the religion of reason became a kind of agnosticism and skepticism. Certainly the religion of reason in terms of Kant's *Die*

Religion innerhalb der Grenzen der blossen Vernunft is not a kind of knowledge. In fact, neither of these forms of the religion of reason is compatible with the notion of natural theology. This was later demonstrated in the development of religious thought, although one could have known on rational grounds alone that the denial of a theology based upon revelation would ultimately lead to a denial of any kind of theology at all.

The conclusion would now seem to be that the philosophy of religion cannot be identified with any movement of thought before Kant, nor even with KANTIANISM itself. Even the expression "philosophy of religion" itself came into being after the age of Kant, and hence can be understood only in terms of the kind of IDEALISM that is based upon the philosophy of Kant.

There were two main constituents in the Kantian revolution. In the first place, there was a blurring over of the distinction between making and knowing. A real world was still assumed by Kant, but it cannot be known. The phenomenal world can be known—but only because, in the process of knowing it, man helps to make it. In the second place, metaphysics in any realistic sense was eliminated once and for all as impossible. In terms of strict Kantianism there could be no place for the philosophy of religion, which is not possible unless acceptance of metaphysics is possible. The same can be said for all of the post-Kantian movements of a positivistic nature that were current throughout the 19th century.

However, the matter was somewhat different with the development of post-Kantian idealism of the Hegelian kind. No longer was reason considered to be "pure," because in a sense it helps to fashion its own content; in fact, it helps to make the world. In the second place, one has a clear view of the meaning of the priority of reason over faith—a clear view in the sense that there was a consistency in the Hegelian thesis that enabled it to avoid the instability of the pre-Kantian position. Also, one can find a clear meaning of the philosophy of religion. For Hegel the philosophy of religion investigates the process of the Absolute. If so, the question may now be asked whether the philosophy of religion is a kind of knowledge. The language remains the same, but the concepts were radically changed. Two instances may be cited.

(1) If reason helps to make the world, rather than to discover truths about it, then the meaning of revelation, as the object of faith, could hardly find a place in the new idealistic system. And equally incompatible would be the traditional theistic conception of God.

(2) Implicit, and often explicit, in the new idealism was the notion of man and God cooperating in making the world. Because of the use of the word "idealism,"

it is sometimes forgotten that this idea was essentially new. The philosophy of LEIBNIZ is called "idealistic," but this label is accurate only as regards the "stuff" of reality. Leibniz did not break down the distinction between making and knowing. The same can be said for the old idealisms in the Orient. Even classical Hinduism was relatively realistic. With respect to being, knowing, and making, Oriental idealism can accurately be called a "religious philosophy," but not "a philosophy of religion" in the Hegelian sense.

An Ideological Substitute. The conclusion must be drawn that, insofar as the expression "philosophy of religion" is to have any reference at all, it is as the post-Kantian idealistic substitute for natural theology in pre-Kantian realism. If this is what the philosophy of religion is, then it is not a kind of knowledge—unless one is prepared, in the name of Hegelian idealism, to repudiate all past philosophy. This may seem to be an exaggeration. However, Hegelianism, just as much as the later philosophy of Feuerbach and Marx, was the ultimate philosophy to deny philosophy. Philosophy is unique among all the disciplines in that only it can deny itself. Nevertheless a "metaphysics" that denies the possibility of metaphysics cannot, without pure equivocation, be called by the same name. Hence, it is not the case that the Judaic-Christian God and the Absolute are merely different conceptions of the same referent. Rather, they are radically different in conception because they do not refer to the same "thing."

The Kantian revolution, however, requires a similar inversion in the meaning of other terms, e.g., reason, revelation, philosophy, theology, logic, nature, essence, and existence. Hence, it is not at all an arbitrary act to designate the philosophy of the 19th century by some new term, as Henry Aiken has done when he calls the 19th century the "Age of Ideology." A more accurate statement, then, as to what the philosophy of religion is would be to say that it is an ideological substitute for a natural theology—understanding, of course, the universe of discourse which is that of idealistic *Weltanschauungen.* The "philosophy of religion," then, became an expression reflecting a contradiction: it was presumably a category in the order of knowing, and yet it did not refer to any kind of systematic knowledge. A kind of knowledge is open-ended and developing, and is that to which various thinkers make contributions. Idealistic *Weltanschauungen,* on the contrary, are closed and final and confined to the individual "systems" of the thinkers. As such, ideologies can be compared only by way of similarities, or studied developmentally by ways of showing, in a literary fashion, the various personal influences. In this case the history of philosophy becomes the "history of ideas."

Curricular Category. With the decline of Hegelian idealism and realistic Protestant theologies, and with the concomitant rise of liberal Protestantism, secularism, and government-owned schools, the expression "philosophy of religion" has taken on a quite different meaning in the 20th century. It has often become a category of "the order of teaching and learning." All curricular categories are of this order. They are institutional categories, and as such they may or may not refer to any kind of knowledge.

See Also: RELIGION; RELIGION, SOCIOLOGY OF.

Bibliography: F. C. COPLESTON, *History of Philosophy* v.6, *Wolff to Kant* (Westminster, Md. 1960); v.7, *Fichte to Nietzsche* (Westminster, Md. 1963). G. GRANERIS, *Enciclopedia filosofica* (Venice-Rome 1957) 4:43–59. J. B. METZ, *Lexikon für Theologie und Kirche,* ed. J. HOFER and K. RAHNER, (2d new ed. Freiburg 1957–65) 8:1190–93. N. H. SØE and W. TRILLHAAS, *Die Religion in Geschichte und Gegenwart* (3d ed. Tübingen 1957–65) 5:1010–21. J. A. MOURANT, ed., *Readings in the Philosophy of Religion* (New York 1954). W. O. MARTIN, *The Order and Integration of Knowledge* (Ann Arbor 1957); *Metaphysics and Ideology* (Milwaukee 1959). J. MACQUARRIE, *Twentieth Century Religious Thought* (New York 1963).

[W. O. MARTIN]

RELIGION, SOCIOLOGY OF

The study of the relationship of RELIGION to social structures and social processes. It includes the study of the relation of religion to social stability, to social change, and to the functional problems of a SOCIETY. It includes also the study of the internal structure, development, and functional problems and dilemmas of religious organizations and institutions, and their relation to other social institutions. The term thus designates a specialized field of sociology, wide in scope, in which results and findings are reported in works of great variety.

Scope

Until recently the sociology of religion did not attract great scholarly attention. Although important and even basic works had been published in Europe in an earlier period, American research in the sociology of religion did not begin on any real scale until the time of World War II. Since then, interest in the field has grown considerably, whether measured in terms of number of workers involved, number of studies published, or number of courses offered at American colleges and universities. This growth reflects the growing popularity of sociology and of the social sciences generally in American thinking, education, and policy formation in business and government. It reflects also an increase in scholarly concern with religion in academic life. Finally, it represents an increasing appreciation by people in religious organizations and church work generally of the potential contribution of the social sciences in the confrontation and solution of contemporary problems by religious bodies.

Sources of Interest in the United States. In the United States, two groups of workers have made important contributions to the field, academic sociologists who have approached religion with predominantly sociological interests and concerns, and men in religion, often in Protestant seminaries, who have used sociology to further their understanding of the religious situation and its problems both past and present. A number of Catholic sociologists, clerical, religious, and lay, have shared with those in Protestant seminaries an interest in sociological research and sociological theory as means of enriching their understanding of religious problems and developments. In methods and in aims these groups have tended to converge, to influence each other, and to unite in one body of scientific workers in the field. In Europe some attempt has been made to distinguish "religious sociology," as an empirical study ancillary to the pastoral work of the Church, from the "sociology of religion," as an objective scholarly study of religious behavior uncommitted to immediate practical ends viewed in terms of commitment to a particular faith. Such a distinction has not gained acceptance in America.

Catholic Participation. In an earlier period American Catholic sociologists were often concerned with clarifying for themselves the relation between the basic assumptions of sociological theory as the conceptual framework of an empirical social science, and Catholic philosophical and theological views of the nature and meaning of man. The early issues of the *American Catholic Sociological Review,* which first appeared in 1940, as well as a number of books and theses from this period testify to the significance of this effort for those involved. Although the issue is still discussed among Catholic sociologists, the development of events has solved many of the earlier problems. Within sociology the spread of the influence of Max WEBER has led to a view of human action that recognizes the significance of meaningful and normative elements and repudiates narrow behaviorism and dogmatic POSITIVISM. On the Catholic side, a more mature appreciation of the problems involved and a greater involvement in the general intellectual life of the discipline have prevented earlier sectarian tendencies from becoming dominant. As a result there has not developed any attempt to create a "Catholic sociology" or a "Catholic sociology of religion"; Catholic workers in the field share with others significant common elements in their understanding of the discipline, its theory, and its methods.

Diversity of Interests. The sociology of religion has produced a vast spectrum of studies, and it exhibits a variety of concerns and emphases. Works in the field include Émile DURKHEIM's study of elementary religious forms among Australian aborigines; anthropological monographs on nonliterate cultures, such as that of Bronislaw Malinowski on the Trobriand Islands or A. R. Radcliffe-Brown on the Andamans; Max Weber's work on the importance of religious ideas in economic development; Ernst TROELTSCH's study of the relation between Christianity and the world, and its sociological consequences; H. Richard NIEBUHR's study of denominationalism in America; the work of Liston Pope and Bryan Wilson on sects; Will Herberg's analysis of Protestantism, Catholicism, and Judaism in the United States; monographs on Mormonism by Thomas F. O'Dea and on Conservative Judaism by Marshall Sklare; Robert N. Bellah's work on Japanese religion; Joseph Fichter's study of a southern United States parish, John Donovan's study of the role of the Catholic priest, and Scherer's of the Lutheran minister; the studies of Gabriel Le Bras and Fernand Boulard on the geography of religious practice among French Catholics; Andrew Greeley's study of religion and social mobility; and Seymour Lipset's concern with religion and politics. This list is merely suggestive, but its variety is striking indeed.

Nature of Sociological Investigation. All these studies have in common a concern with an empirical study of some aspect of religious life; each of them, to one degree or another, represents an attempt to apply the analytical methods and practical research techniques of sociology to the study of religious phenomena. Approaching religion as observable human activity, meaningful in that it is infused with and influenced by ideas and attitudes, the sociologist of religion employs explicit concepts and propositions in the analysis of observed empirical data. The concepts used comprise a conceptual scheme or body of theory in the scientific sense; this is useful in formulating problems, designing empirical studies, and analyzing the data obtained from such studies for the purpose of understanding and prediction. Whereas such a body of theory makes empirical work more significant by relating it to central interests shared in the discipline, the empirical work checks, reforms, deepens, and develops the theoretical structure itself. Although this conceptual instrument is in a comparatively early stage of development, some degree of sophistication has been reached. The main outline of this body of concepts presented here is drawn chiefly from the work of a minority of significant contributors, especially from Durkheim, Weber, Troeltsch, Joachim Wach, and Talcott Parsons.

Relative Autonomy of Social Systems. Sociology is the study of those uniformities of human behavior that cannot be understood simply as effects of the motivation of individual actors or of the ideas and values of the CUL-TURE of a society. There is a relatively autonomous level of social structure, related to and integrated with both individual motivation and cultural elements, but best understood in terms of its own relative autonomy. This social structure displays a systematic quality; it is revealed as a social system whose integration is patterned and orderly, and whose elements have functional significance for each other and for the system as a whole. One important element in sociological analysis is investigation of the functional significance of various kinds of social institutions and human behavior. In presenting the theoretical body of concepts in the sociology of religion, it is well to begin with this fundamental aspect—functional theory and functional analysis. Moreover, in its application to the study of religion, functional analysis indicates with considerable salience one important characteristic of the role of religion in social life and underlines its inherent character and operational importance in the human situation. Finally, acknowledgment of the limitations of functionalism leads directly to consideration of a more sophisticated model, which utilizes the insights of Weber and others and makes possible a more adequate approach to the sociological study of religion.

Sociology and Religious Values. Sociology is a value-free science and does not claim competence to judge the validity of religion in general or of particular religions. The sociology of religion commences with the study of religion as one kind of observable meaningful human activity; it attempts to understand the content and point of view of the religion being studied; and focusing upon the level of social structure, it examines the problems and dilemmas characteristic of this realm of human life. Among the empirical disciplines, sociology is but one, although an important one, among those relevant to the study of religion. It stands in close relation to both history and psychology: to history, because structural analysis must be understood in the context of the unique course of events in which a social system is formed, and social change must be seen in the setting of long-term historical trends; to psychology, since human motivation and human propensities to respond and to adjust are significant elements in the functioning of social structures as well as in their emergence and dissolution. The sociology of religion is also enriched by those disciplines that study the content of religious beliefs, since a sociology of meaningful behavior must appreciate the definition of the situation of action held by the groups being observed and studied. Hence, for the sociology of religion, theology and the content of commitments of faith are data that must be understood to the extent that they enter into human action by affecting both men's definitions of situations and their motivational structure (although their validity is beyond the competence of sociological analysis).

Functional Theory and Analysis

Sociological functionalism presents an analytical model in which human societies are seen as social systems, that is, as on-going, patterned equilibria of social institutions. Through such institutions human behavior is patterned on the basis of normative consensus, and such consensus is itself integrated into the world view of the culture and internalized in the motivational structure of individuals. The social system is made up of subsystems or institutional complexes that involve a patterned and legitimated allocation of functions, resources, facilities, and rewards, both material and nonmaterial. The social institutions, resting upon normative consensus, pattern and restrain human activity, including force and violence. Such institutions are interdependent with each other and with the social system as a whole. Thus functional analysis does not seek simplified cause and effect relationships, but rather recognizes multiple causation and the feedback of effect upon cause in a systemic frame of reference. Within such a model the functional questions arise: what is the contribution of each part, each institutional complex or aspect thereof, to maintenance of the structure of the whole, and what is the reciprocal relationship between the parts themselves and between them and the whole?

Functional Significance. In these terms religion is seen as one kind—a strategically important and unique kind—of institutionalized behavior having functional significance for the social system. This functional significance may be manifest, that is, recognized by the human actors themselves, or it may be latent, i.e., unrecognized by them. Although functional theory has given more emphasis to positive contributions to the functioning of the social system, it has also recognized that elements of the system may be dysfunctional as well. Hence functional theory raises the question: what is the contribution of religion to the functioning of the social system?

Functional theory also distinguishes two kinds of needs that characterize men in society. Men must act in a practical manner to ensure group survival; human action must be instrumental or adaptive to some degree. But men also have expressive needs, needs to act out emotions and to enter relationships. In the course of their problem-solving activities, their instrumental or adaptive behavior, men also express basic needs and characteristics. Thus out of their interaction there emerge relationships, patterns of expectations, forms of respect and deference, and expressive rituals that are valued in themselves, and not simply as means to ends. With respect to them, too, the functional question may be asked: what is the contribution of religion to the satisfaction of the expressive and adaptive needs of men?

Men act in terms of what W. I. Thomas called their definition of the situation, the existential and normative attributes of their condition as they understand them. In so acting men develop culture, a fabric of existential and value meanings, central to which is a basic definition, explicit or present by implication, of the structure and meaning of the human condition. Culture is integrated with social structure and with individual motivation in terms of the goals and ends valued and the norms patterning the proscriptions and prescriptions of the social order. The functional question arises again: what is the contribution of religion to culture and its integration?

Religion and the Human Situation. These three versions of the functional question bring into the purview of sociological theory certain of the most central characteristics of the human situation, characteristics that are of strategic significance for the development and maintenance of social systems. First, it is seen that religion is concerned with something beyond the empirical, that it transcends empirical adaptive experience. Second, it is recognized that religion is not only beyond empirical knowledge in a cognitive and problem-solving sense, but is concerned with relationship rather than problem-solving, with the acting out of attitudes and responses rather than with adaptation in the face of environmental challenges. Thus religion transcends instrumental action; it allows expression and patterns the realization of important expressive needs. Human life confronts men with aspects of reality and with problems and dilemmas that cannot be handled in terms of adaptive empirical knowledge alone. Moreover, in solving adaptive problems men establish patterns of allocation and function—in the development of political and economic institutions, for example—that demand discipline and inhibition, cause deprivation, and inflict frustration on various strata of society that are differentiated in the process. Often such difficulties cannot be changed, for some measure of inequality and differential allocation appears inescapable; indeed, it seems to be an analytical element of the very conception of social order. Yet such hardships must be rendered acceptable and legitimated in terms of a larger understanding of the human situation and its attributes and ends.

Contexts of Uncertainty and Impossibility. The most crucial of the aleatory and frustrating elements that are derived from the insufficiency of adaptive techniques and from the inherent consequences of the functioning of social systems—elements that transcend tested empirical knowledge and practical control—are those associated with contexts of uncertainty and impossibility. The uncertainty context refers to the inherent and fundamental contingency characteristic of human existence. Even with advanced technology and increasing control over conditions of life, men find the possibility of disappointment lurking everywhere, and often in situations in which human interests are deeply involved—"the best laid plans of mice and men gang aft agley." The impossibility context refers to the fact that certain misfortunes are humanly unavoidable; they include suffering, illness, death, and the evils that human beings intentionally or unintentionally inflict upon each other. These are the phenomena that theology classically has discussed as the "problem of evil"; they are considered sociologically in terms of their functional consequences for human society.

Functional theory recognizes the way in which both the uncertainty and impossibility contexts lead men beyond the everyday life of the workaday world. At such a beyond men come to confront the deeper—the ultimate—meaning of the human condition. Here human knowledge and mundane forms of social relations are proved totally insufficient either for providing solutions to problems or as modes of adjustment to unavoidable evils. Thus men are propelled to "breaking points" in mundane experience, and questions are raised that can be answered only by going beyond the empirical world of mundane experience.

Religion and the Sacred. Further, since man is not simply *homo faber,* since men are not beings that simply adapt to their environment for survival's sake, expressive needs require satisfaction and men must enter into relationships and act out responses. Such needs find outlets in the everyday world, but they also point beyond it. Durkheim has shown that men respond to reality not simply as something profane and mundane, but that they perceive another aspect of what they experience and react to it in a different modality of response. Men respond to an aspect of reality as sacred; they experience it as radically heterogeneous from the profane and give it intense awe and respect. The sacred, despite its localization in a tremendous variety of vehicles and occasions, is felt to lie beyond the appearances of things. It is something that not only elicits awe but also attracts and nurtures the worshiper. Sacred forces are seen as both propitious and dangerous, as powers that lie behind appearance and sustain being and life. The response to the sacred is the religious response, and in religion human experience breaks beyond the everyday. Thus, both in responses to the sacred and in reactions at the breaking points of personal life there is transcendence of the everyday in attitude and relationship. The religious response originates in a limit situation that transcends empirical knowledge and everyday social forms, and involves an awareness of a sacred ground of experience that elicits reaction in a relational rather than manipulational mode of response.

Implications for Social Systems. The problems of men when they are propelled into limit situations beyond everyday experience have great functional significance for societies. If the questions raised by the impossibility and uncertainty contexts are not answered meaningfully, the worth and value of human effort are rendered doubtful.

At these breaking points, what Weber called the problem of meaning is raised in its sharpest and most poignant form. It is not simply an intellectual problem, but one in which many-sided human involvement and concern are necessarily implicated. If no mode of adjustment to the frustrations and deprivations inherent in the allocations fundamental to every society is found, the established goals and norms of the society are called into question. This means that individual morale founders, the meaning of life is lost, the legitimacy of norms and the worth of ends are undermined, and society can no longer exist. Life raises for men questions that go beyond the limits of empirical knowledge and confronts them with problems that cannot be met adequately within the context of everyday relationships and modes of adjustment. Religion provides an answer, a relationship, and a mode of adjustment precisely in this limit situation.

If in this limit situation men can enter into a relationship with a sacred ground of existence and experience, and if a view of empirical reality can be developed in terms of that transcendent and sacred relationship, then both security and meaning, both adjustment and hope, can be found and maintained. Then the threat to human action and human association that life presents in limit situations can be met. Then indeed all is not in pieces and all coherence is not gone. Then are disappointment, injury, and tragedy rendered meaningful and acceptable. In relation to the deeper sacred ground men can act out their needs for a deeper relationship on which both security and worth can be based. Thus religion solves a fundamental functional problem for human societies by relating men to a supraempirical, sacred beyond. However this sacred is conceived and conceptualized in different cultures and religions, in pointing to it as the highest common factor in the relation between religion and society Durkheim has supplied an insight of great sociological significance.

Functions of Religious Rites. Functional theory calls attention not only to the attempts of men to enter into a relationship with the sacred realm, but also to their efforts to manipulate the sacred forces and bend them to human will in the service of human aspirations. Such manipulation of the sacred comprises the sphere of MAGIC. In distinguishing religion from magic Malinowski and others have shown that men resort to magic in those endeavors that lie outside the range of human control in any secure sense and in which danger is great. Thus the Trobriand Islanders were found to utilize magic in deep-sea fishing with its combination of personal danger and uncertainty of results, but not in lagoon fishing, which was both safe and predictable. Malinowski also showed that, although magic is a manipulative affair, religion and the religious rite involve an acting out for its own sake and not for the sake of manipulation and control.

Both the cultural anthropologists and Durkheim point out that religious rites reassert the basic value consensus of the group, act out its solidarity, and thus reenact and renew the cohesiveness of the group itself. Durkheim indeed went so far in stressing this important function of the religious cult as to see the object of worship—the sacred realm itself, or in the higher religions, God—as the projection and hypostatization of society itself. Thus Durkheim thought that in worship a society worships itself and thereby renews itself. Sociological theory today recognizes the great importance of the functional insight of Durkheim. Religious ritual in acting out and expressing attitudes toward the sacred reasserts norms and values that are often strategic to the integration of society, and it reinforces and strengthens social solidarity. There is much profundity in Durkheim's stress on the social character of much of religious activity. Yet his formulation of religion as group self-worship is crude and unacceptable.

Evaluation of Functionalism. Seen from the perspective of functional theory, religion maintains the social system by providing an answer to the problem of meaning, by justifying socially accepted goals, by renewing solidarity through ritual and cult, by deepening the acceptance of norms through their sacralization, and by providing some catharsis for frustration and making it understandable in the context of a larger religious view and a deeper religious relationship to the sacred beyond. To paraphrase the anthropologist Edward Sapir and the sociologist Durkheim, in the religious relationship human consciousness is secured and human association made possible.

Contributions. In brief, functional analysis calls attention to two fundamental aspects of the social role of religion. It shows the functional significance of religion to society in terms of its relation to the impossibility and uncertainty contexts. It shows how religion answers the problem of meaning in terms of its ramified implications for the continued functioning of societies and how it reinforces norms and strengthens solidarity. Thus functional explanations mark a distinct advance in the social sciences over those theories, based on and influenced by a naïve implicit positivism, that were common at the beginning of the 20th century, in which religion was viewed as absurd prescientific fantasy, characteristic of the ignorance and error of underdeveloped peoples or unenlightened strata. Such explanations also mark a considerable advance in comparison with theories that propounded or sought simple and sovereign causal factors to explain social phenomena.

Limitations. Yet functional theory alone presents an incomplete and inadequate sociological model for the analysis of the relation of religion to social structure and processes. Its fundamental insights were derived largely from studies of nonliterate societies at least a generation ago and are consequently inadequate for the study of the world religions and of the situation and condition of religion in complex societies. It throws little light on the problems involved in the developmental sequences or the internal functioning of the world religions, or on the complicated relationships between religious and other institutions in complex societies—e.g., between church and state, church and education—that have been the cause and occasion of severe conflict in many countries.

Moreover, while functional theory provides insights of indisputable importance into the structure and function of human groups, it has never refined these insights to provide any criteria for estimating or measuring the degree of positive or negative functionality to be accorded to religious phenomena under various societal conditions. Although it has recognized that there are dysfunctional as well as functional consequences of religious phenomena for human societies, it has emphasized the latter. It tends to direct attention to the contribution of religion to stability and to resistance to change, and to neglect the importance of religion as the setting of innovation and as an element promoting change.

Functional theory does not provide any significant insights into the process of the SECULARIZATION of culture, which has been so markedly developed in modern times and which is the fundamental characteristic of the current religious situation. Consequently it has not directed attention to the study of religion surrogates in secular movements of a social or national character. Such movements perform in contemporary societies many of the functions formerly performed by religion and attributed to religion in the functionalist model, although they are based on less than ultimate experience in which the sacral elements are often disguised or latent. Prophetic religion and its creative consequences and the functional equivalent of prophecy in secular religion-surrogate movements are both neglected.

Importance. Yet the importance of functional theory cannot be denied. It formulates and makes explicit certain fundamental characteristics of the relation of religion to society—religion as concerned with the sacred, as a relational mode of orientation, as a transcendent phenomenon made functional in the limit situation, as providing an answer to the problem of meaning and a mode of adjustment for frustration, and as sacralizing norms and legitimating institutions. These fundamental dimensions must be included in any analytical model for the sociological study of religion. All analytical models must be constructed on this groundwork. Functional theory has provided the basis on which more sophisticated models of analysis can be built. The quite justifiable emphasis on function has unfortunately tended to keep some sociological investigators from paying sufficient attention to the content of the religious experience and the doctrines and institutions derived and secondarily developed from it. Such a foreshortening of the sociological view results in a failure to recognize and comprehend many significant functional problems internal to religious organization and its development.

Developmental Theory

There exists in sociological theory a body of concepts more adequate for the analysis of religion in complex societies and of the problems involved in the development of the founded religions. The works of Weber, Troeltsch, Wach, and Parsons, among others, are the chief sources for these ideas.

Role of Religion in Social Change. Weber recognized the seriousness and importance of man's religious interests and activities, and the causal significance of religious ideas affecting human action and historical development. Unlike the functionalists who emphasized the contribution of religion to social stability, Weber investigated the role of religion in social change and the development of societies. He saw religious experience and religious thought as the sphere in which men broke through to more rational, more profound, and more adequate definitions of the human situation. This interest was the source of his concern with the charismatic leader and the prophet and his work on charisma and prophecy as sociological factors.

Charisma and Institutionalization. Weber saw charisma as characteristic of leaders who exhibit unusualness, creativity, and spontaneity in specific ways and who either through their preaching or their mode of being, or both, issue calls that attract followers and form the nucleus of religious movements. Such movements stand in important ways outside the everyday, the traditional and established forms of social life. Religious charisma possesses a sacred character and is specifically alien to routinized forms of social relations and to economic life. As recognized by Weber, charisma in the pure state is inherently unstable; therefore, the requirements of continuity result in the establishment of new social forms and new social institutions. Weber called attention to the importance of succession crises in this kind of development. After the originating charismatic moment there develops, in Weber's phrase, a routinization of charisma in which the charisma of status and office replaces the earlier unroutinized dynamic forms. This transformation is both a diminution and containment of the charisma within structured roles, rites, and procedures. The routinization of charisma may proceed in either a rational direction, giving rise to social structures of a *gesellschaftliche,* or modern, kind, or in a traditional direction characterized by more diffuse *gemeinschaftliche* social organization. It may develop in a way that combines both of these, as may be seen in the early Church with its emphases on both rationality and tradition.

Religion as a Causal Influence in History. Troeltsch's treatment of the relation between Christianity and the societies and cultures in which it existed in Europe developed further generalized categories of sociological analysis. Both Weber and Troeltsch insisted on the reality of religious interests and their causal influence in human history, in contrast with contemporary Marxist writers who reduced religious interests to socioeconomic interests and saw religion as an epiphenomenon. Troeltsch showed religious interests, religious ideas, and the social conditions in the context of which the Church exists and develops, as all exerting causal influences. The adjustment of the Church to classical society is seen as the result of Christian ideas and values, of the propensities and needs of the social strata that Christianity attracted, and of the need of the developing organization of the Church. Thus he produced a sociological model of analysis that gives adequate weight to both external and internal views of development, and recognizes the multiplicity of factors involved.

Religion and Complex Societies. In his monographs on the world religions, Weber showed that religious orientations, ideas, and values must be reckoned with as one factor involved in economic development, and under certain circumstances, as the crucial factor. He attempted to show that some Asian societies, such as China and India, were in important economic and material respects at least as prepared for the development of modern capitalism as was Europe. He explained the priority of capitalistic development in Europe by the presence in European society of certain elements in its religious outlook that fostered ethical and economic rationality.

Further, Weber explored the multiple relations characterizing religion and social structure, the differential appeal of different religious ideas to different social strata, and the importance of the inner differentiation of the

religious community itself. He saw lower classes showing a tendency to embrace religious doctrines promising salvation, whereas ruling and successful classes desired doctrines legitimating their functions and justifying their status. He showed that lower middle classes, especially artisans, tend to develop rational ethical religion, whereas peasants and warriors show a much greater affinity for magical phenomena. Yet he emphasized that these were tendencies or propensities for affinity and not causally determining in any definitive sense, for a religious doctrine once established is capable, because of the elements of universality it contains, to appeal to various and diverse social strata; and even in its initial state its appeal may be widespread among varied social strata. With respect to the internal differentiation of religious bodies themselves, Weber stated that the development of rational theology must await as its necessary, though not necessarily its sufficient, condition the development of a priesthood enjoying a status apart from the laity. He also recognized the significance of the secularization of culture and of such movements as 19th-century socialism and 20th-century nationalism as religion surrogates.

Thus there is developed a scheme of analysis that deals adequately with ideas, interests, and social structure, both in the religious community and in the general society, and also with the relations between the society and the religious body, with a degree of adequacy for studying complex situations. It is a scheme that eschews reductionism and simple causal hypotheses of the single factor variety, and that makes possible the delineation of complex empirical phenomena. The content of religious doctrines, both their world views and their ethics, the social setting of religious groups and their social composition, and the internal structure of religious bodies are all seen as important factors.

Typologies of Religious Groups. Troeltsch explored the types of adjustment Christianity made to its social world in four spheres of experience: family life, economic activities, political power, and intellectual endeavor. He found in the Christian value system a basis for both acceptance and rejection of the ''world'' in this sense. Both responses are also found empirically, each in its own particular sociological form. Troeltsch saw the ''church'' form as the embodiment of an acceptance, however qualified, of society and culture, and the ''sect'' form as the embodiment of revolt against such a compromise. These concepts have been widely used in sociological research and have been refined in the writings of R. E. Park and E. W. Burgess, Georg Simmel and Leopold von Wiese, Niebuhr, Wilson, and others. The church form is characterized by membership in fact on the basis of birth, administration of the means of grace and its sociological concomitants, hierarchy and dogma, inclusiveness of social structure often coinciding with ethnic or geographical boundaries, universalist orientation to the conversion of all, and a tendency to compromise with and adjust to the world. The sect is a more exclusive and ascetic group characterized by separatism from the world and often defiance of it, exclusiveness in social composition and in attitude, emphasis upon a conversion experience previous to membership, and voluntary election or joining.

Although sectarianism is a protest against the compromise with the world made by churches, the sect itself tends to become routinized with time. The term denomination has been used in a technical sense to apply to such a routinized sect. Wilson has shown how sects may successfully resist routinization and accommodation over a long period of time. Wiese and Howard Becker have introduced another type of religious grouping, the cult, in which religion is more private and personal and which does not itself achieve secure viable long-term establishment. Wach has introduced another type called by him the independent group, a semiecclesiastical body that begins as a sect but develops in a churchlike direction. Although Wach suggested the Mormon Church as an example of this type, O'Dea has shown that the Mormons, acting on the model of Biblical Israel, under propitious American 19th-century conditions, produced a new religious quasiethnicity and became a "people" possessing both identity and homeland.

Although the concepts "church" and "sect" developed by Troeltsch have been fruitfully utilized and considerably refined in American sociology, his concern with more individualized responses has been neglected. Troeltsch did not propose simply a church-sect dichotomy, but a church-sect-mysticism trichotomy with reference to the response of religion to the world. Troeltsch saw mysticism as an individualized response capable of expressing indifference or revolt with respect to established religious forms. Its importance in religious history has been enormous. Today secular analogues of this response are also important, as may be seen in certain philosophical movements, such as EXISTENTIALISM. The neglect of this aspect of Troeltsch's work is a loss to the sociology of religion.

Developmental Sequences. Wach has developed the insights presented above in delineating the developmental sequence for founded religions. Starting with Rudolf OTTO's treatment of the holy in the religious experience, which in important ways parallels and complements that of Durkheim, Wach proposed a scheme of analysis that shows the religious movement proceeding from its charismatic moment of origin to the full development of an ecclesiastical structure on three levels—

ideational, cultic, and organizational. Thus religious ideas, religious rites, and religious organizations are seen as three interpenetrating aspects of a single developing entity. Wach introduced the idea of "protest" as a universal category of analysis for the understanding of religious movements. Adjustments to the world, specifications of doctrine, and developments in liturgy and in church organization are of differential significance to various strata of society and of the religious body itself. Some groups are unable to accept these developments and are moved to protest against them. Protest may develop into movements that secede from the parent body, or it may be organized and directed from within the parent body.

Parsons has done much to emphasize and make highly explicit the assumptions and implications of functional theory and to emphasize the role of ideas, and of religious ideas particularly, in social life. He has been an important figure in promoting the assimilation of Weber's contributions in American sociology, both through his early translations of Weber and his own later theoretical work. The work of Weber, Troeltsch, Wach, and Parsons has been supplemented by that of a host of others who have tested, refined, and developed a body of concepts that today equips the sociology of religion with considerable theoretical sophistication and empirical skill.

Implications

Wach's paradigm of the developmental sequence in the world religions opens up great possibilities of integrating work in the sociology of religion with that done by students in a number of fields. One example may be seen with respect to the studies of symbolism and myth by Ernst CASSIRER, Andrew Lang, Mircea Eliade, Gerardus van der LEEUW, the school of Carl JUNG, and others. This work is closely related to sociological concern with the development of doctrine and the practice of cult and their functional significance.

Relation to Special Fields of Sociology. Moreover, specialists in other areas of sociological interest have contributed both in their theoretical construction and in their empirical findings materials of great utility to the sociology of religion. The institutionalization of religion produces formal organizations, often with a hierarchical structure. Much of the sociological study of formal organizations in economic, political, and military spheres offers models of analysis and empirical generalizations of utility to the study of religious organization. The study of social disorganization and its effects on societies and personality structures has added to knowledge of the role of religion as a factor reintegrating social life. The study of the accommodation, assimilation, and conflict involved in intergroup relations and in the Americanization of immigrants and their descendants provides models for the study of religious conflict, and often considerable data as well, since in America ethnic and religious groups are closely interrelated. The study of politics and voting behavior reveals the importance of religious identity as a factor in general political alignments and offers significant material to the sociology of religion. The same may be said for studies of achievement and social mobility that have been concerned with the religious factor. A similar relation exists between the sociology of religion and the sociology of KNOWLEDGE, as Durkheim early recognized. Finally, the sociology of religion makes complementary contributions to the sociological study of movements and institutions other than religion that are based upon situationally transcendent ideals, such as the many religion surrogates in contemporary society.

Relation to Theology. The general relationship between the sociology of religion and theology has been indicated above. Sociology is an empirical social science that does not make judgments concerning the substance of theological matters or commitments of faith. The content of theology is treated as a source of data insofar as the sociological investigator must become familiar with the world view of the religion being studied and its ethical position. For theology, the sociology of religion offers data on the development of religious movements and the role and function of religion in various societal contexts; hence it contributes to theology data both on religion as a human phenomenon and on human behavior generally.

Like all empirical sciences, sociology assumes its own angle or perspective of vision and develops in its own autonomous fashion its methodology and techniques. The 19th-century idea of formulating ''hierarchies of sciences''—itself received from earlier periods of Western thought—has tended to lose relevance and consequently to lose favor in the intellectual climate of scientific endeavor. The relationship of various sciences is one rather of cross fertilization and dialogue than of subordination or subsidiarity. Although many problems of concern to the philosophy of knowledge remain, the older idea that empirical sciences were ranged under and worked in terms defined by philosophical or theological views and positions has been progressively abandoned.

It is significant in this respect that the declaration on the relationship of the Catholic Church to non-Christian religions approved by VATICAN COUNCIL II is based first of all on a historical and sociological interpretation of empirical facts: ''Men expect from the various religions answers to the unsolved riddles of the human condition, riddles that move the hearts of men today as they did in olden times: What is man? What is the meaning, what is the purpose of our lives? What is the moral good and what is sin? What are death, judgment and retribution after death? What, finally, is the ultimate, inexpressible mystery which encompasses our existence, which is the fountain as well as the destiny of our being?'' This basic core of religion comprises what sociologists have been concerned with in terms of the problem of meaning and its functional significance for human society. The declaration continues: ''Ever since primordial days, numerous peoples have had a certain perception of that hidden power which hovers over the course of things and over the events that make up the lives of men'' (*De Ecclesiae Habitudine ad Religiones Non-Christianas*). Here the sociologist recognizes the content of the sacred treated by Durkheim and accepted in sociological theory as central to an understanding of religion on the sociological level.

Generalization and Findings. What has been presented above, in addition to the chief interests and scope of the sociology of religion, is its theory in the sense of analytical models providing contexts for the conduct of empirical investigations. What is to be said about generalizations concerning religious behavior based on the findings of such studies? This is the second important aspect of theory. It is clear that a number of generalizations—concerning the probable sequence of development, the functional significance of religion to social stability, its role in influencing innovation and change, the relationship between religious ideas and historical developments, the possible options open to religious movements and their probable consequences, to name the most important—have been integrated into theory as a result of empirical study. They stand as probable bases for drawing conclusions and formulating hypotheses for empirical study. They are significant and important. It remains true, however, that insufficient attention has been given to systematization of theory with respect to the empirical generalizations of various degrees of validity found in the literature of the field. The field stands in need not only of more and better empirical studies, but also of a more systematic and critical integration of theory, especially through the incorporation of empirical generalizations derived from past empirical work into the theoretical model for future use in analysis and for further testing, verification, and refinement.

See Also: RELIGION; RELIGION (IN PRIMITIVE CULTURE); RELIGION AND MORALITY.

Bibliography: General Theoretical Background. E. DURKHEIM, *The Elementary Forms of the Religious Life*, tr. J. W. SWAIN (London 1915; repr. Glencoe, Illinois 1954). C. Y. CLOCK, ''The Sociology of Religion,'' *Sociology Today,* ed. R. K. MERTON et al. (New York 1959) 153–177. B. MALINOWSKI, *Magic, Science and Religion* (Boston 1948; repr. New York 1954). T. PARSONS, *The Structure of Social Action* (2d ed. Glencoe, Illinois 1949); ''The

Theoretical Development of the Sociology of Religion,'' *Essays in Sociological Theory* (2d ed. Glencoe, Illinois 1954) 197–211. L. SCHNEIDER, ed., *Religion, Culture and Society* (New York 1964). E. TROELTSCH, *The Social Teaching of the Christian Churches,* tr. O. WYON, 2 v. (New York 1931; repr. 1956). J. WACH, *Sociology of Religion* (London 1947). M. WEBER, *The Protestant Ethic and the Spirit of Capitalism,* tr. T. PARSONS (London 1930); *The Theory of Social and Economic Organization,* tr. A. M. HENDERSON and T. PARSONS (New York 1947); *The Religion of China,* ed. and tr. H. H. GERTH (Glencoe, Illinois 1951); *Ancient Judaism,* tr. H. H. GERTH and D. C. MARTINDALE (Glencoe, Illinois 1952); *The Sociology of Religion,* tr. E. FISCHOFF (Boston 1963). O. R. WHITLEY, *Religious Behavior: Where Sociology and Religion Meet* (Englewood Cliffs, New Jersey 1964). J. M. YINGER, *Religion, Society, and the Individual: An Introduction to the Sociology of Religion* (New York 1957). Special Substantive Treatments. R. N. BELLAH, *Tokugawa Religion: The Values of Pre-Industrial Japan* (Glencoe, Illinois 1957). F. BOULARD, *An Introduction to Religious Sociology,* tr. M. J. JACKSON (London 1960). J. J. KANE, *Catholic Protestant Conflicts in America* (Chicago 1955). G. E. LENSKI, *The Religious Factor* (Garden City, New York 1961). R. LEE and M. E. MARTY, eds., *Religion and Social Conflict* (New York 1964). H. R. NIEBUHR, *The Social Sources of Denominationalism* (New York 1929). T. F. O'DEA, *The Mormons* (Chicago 1957). M. SKLARE, *Conservative Judaism* (Glencoe, Illinois 1955). K. W. UNDERWOOD, *Protestant and Catholic* (Boston 1957). B. R. WILSON, *Sects and Society* (Berkeley 1961). T. F. O'DEA, *The Sociology of Religion* (Englewood Cliffs, New Jersey 1966).

[T. F. O'DEA]

RELIGION, TEACHER OF

Charged with the instruction and formation of others in religious doctrine and practice, the religion teacher differs from other teachers not simply in the subject with which the teaching is concerned, but also by possession of a particular charism from God and a derivative authority in the religious assembly. This article confines its attention to the teacher of the Judeo-Christian religion.

Old Testament. In the OT, Israel, as a community taught by Yahweh, never forgot its patriarchal origins in its emphasis on parents as the first teachers of religion (Dt 4.9; 6.6–7; 11.19; 32.46). While the mother gave the rudiments of the moral education that might extend even into the adolescence of the child (Prv 1.8; 6.20; 31.1), the father, having marked his son with circumcision as the sign of the covenant (Gn 17.12; Lv 12.3; cf. Lk 2.21), performed the sacred duty of communicating the history of salvation (Ex 10.2; 12.26–27; 13.8). The paternal role in religious education was so marked that it explains how priests, who were also teachers of sacred doctrine, came to be called father (Jgs 17.10; 18.19). The familial character of the religious teacher is stressed as well in the liturgical setting; the sacrifice was offered in the temple, but it was at the domestic table during the Passover meal that the child asked and the father responded on the meaning of the sacred event commemorated.

Fathers and the Patriarchs, however, were not the sole teachers of religion in Israel. Moses' mission as lawgiver involved the teaching of religion and indeed divine assistance in that sacred task (Ex 4.12). The teaching apostolate was likewise confided to Aaron and his Levites, i.e., to the priesthood (Lv 10.11). The Prophets were in a rather special sense teachers of religion; without hierarchic office, their teaching authority apparently was derived from some direct, charismatic experience of the divine with a consequent mandate to communicate the divine message. Then the sages of Israel, whose religious teachings are preserved in the Wisdom literature of the Old Testament, were teachers not only of purely religious doctrine, but of secular prudence as well. Finally, Israel had its rabbis as interpreters of the Torah. In the DIASPORA, especially after the destruction of the Temple, Jewish teachers had formal schools (the elementary house of the book and the more advanced house of study for adolescent boys) besides the synagogue or house of prayer. The elementary teacher was a voluntary worker whose pay was poor, but who was ennobled so by the glory of the divine word that the Talmud wanted him venerated as God Himself was venerated.

New Testament. The logia reserved the title of teacher for the Christ alone (Mt 23.10), and the Disciples were forbidden the title of teacher (Mt 23.8). Moreover, other NT writers (1 Jn 2.27; 1 Pt 2.9; cf. Heb 8.11; Jn 6.45) see in the advent of the Spirit the fulfillment of the prophecies that there would no longer be need of teachers (Is 54.13; Jer 31.34). Yet Jesus permitted others to call Him teacher (Jn 13.13) and sent His disciples to teach all men to observe the things He had commanded them (Mt 28.19). The early Church also recognized distinct persons as teachers of religion (Acts 13.1; 1 Cor 12.28; Eph 4.11). St. Paul, who sees his own apostolate as teaching (2 Tm 1.11), admonishes parents on their role as teachers of religion (Eph 6.1–4) and instructs Timothy and Titus on their task of teaching (1 Tm 4.11, 13, 16; 2 Tm 1.13; 4.2; Ti 1.9; 2.1, 7).

The paradox may be resolved by a consideration of the response of faith to the Christian teacher. Jesus is *the* Teacher as the complete Word of the Father (cf. Heb 1:1–2). While His spoken word reached only the few of His time and place, His Spirit teaches all truth (Jn 16.13) to all united to Him in Baptism and in faith. The Cenacle on the Pentecost after the Resurrection is only the first and visible advent of the Spirit. The activity of Christ through His spirit continues forever throughout the world until His return. Nevertheless, just as the Sacraments are needed for the visible extension of Christ's sanctifying mission throughout the ages to all nations, so also the proclamation of His word by preachers and deeper instruction in the meaning of that word require other teachers of religion.

Primitive church. This work of teaching the religion of Christ (*magisterium*) is the responsibility of the Church, especially the Apostles (not just the Twelve) who are themselves both disciples and witnesses of Christ. The appointed successors of the Apostles in the primitive Church were called names other than teacher (e.g., overseers, comforters), which were not altogether synonymous but are now almost impossible to distinguish. As the Church assumed more definite organizational structures, sharper distinctions gradually emerged. These teachers (*didaskaloi;* see *Didache* 13.2; 15.2; *Epistle of Barnabas* 1.8; 4.9; Hermas, *Visiones* 3.5.1; *Similitudines* 9.15.4) seem to have been soon absorbed into the clergy, the bishop taking the duty of principal teacher, a role he most often performed in a liturgical context, that is, in homilies on the Gospel and other Scripture texts. Some of the teaching of the great bishops and Fathers is preserved in catechetical discourses and sermons, e.g., the instructions delivered by St. Cyril of Jerusalem to those preparing for Baptism and to those who had just been baptized [see F. L. Cross, *St. Cyril of Jerusalem's Lectures on Christian Sacraments* (London 1951) and *The Great Catechetical Discourse of St. Gregory of Nyssa,* tr. J. R. Shawley (London 1917)]. Even in this period of a more or less formal catechesis in the Church, the parental teacher of religion was not forgotten. St. John Chrysostom's *Address on Vainglory and the Right Way for Parents to Bring Up Their Children* (tr. M. L. W. Laistner, Ithaca 1951) not only insists on the obligation but instructs parents in method. [*See* CHURCH, II (THEOLOGY OF).]

Teachers of theology. From the beginning, there appears some distinction between the catechist who prepared the catechumen for Baptism and the teacher of a more advanced and deeper study of the faith already received. The problem of a Christian gnosis, a confrontation and harmony of the Christian message and human, secular knowledge in the same teacher, is etched more sharply in the catechetical school of Pantaenus at Alexandria and in its derivatives at Antioch and Edessa. CLEMENT OF ALEXANDRIA in his *Paedagogus* (tr. Simon P. Wood, *Christ the Educator,* New York 1954) shows this development from persuasion and formation to instruction. Origen, like his predecessors, began as a catechist, but as sophisticated converts returned for further instruction after Baptism, he and others turned to a more refined, often subtle and allegorical exegesis of Scripture and to the uses of philosophy. The Eastern Fathers, especially the two Gregories, expected the teacher of religion to be well versed in non-Christian culture; Western Fathers, such as Jerome and Gregory the Great, not to mention

Tertullian, were suspicious of pagan learning. The significant historical fact is that Christian teachers remained in pagan schools, and the Christian teachers of religion did not yet attempt to teach in their own schools anything but religion.

St. AUGUSTINE (354–430), in his earlier career as teacher and later life as bishop, as well as in his writings, both theoretical and practical, on teachers, represents the acme of patristic teaching, at least in the West. To leave aside his own observations in the *Confessions* and in the *De magistro* as only indirectly pertinent, careful attention should be given to his *De doctrina christiana* (tr. John Gavigan, New York 1947) and *De catechizandis rudibus* for important insights into the character and function of the teacher of religion. The latter is addressed to the deacon Deogratias of Carthage, who had requested from the bishop of Hippo some advice on first instructions for the catechumens. The reply concerns itself with the catechist himself, who is always being taught even as he teaches. He is especially warned against discouragement with the *rudes* (the very young and the very simple under instruction). The teacher of religion is to be cheerful in countenance and bearing as he presents sacred history to the catechumens, who may be variously disposed. The *De doctrina christiana* is more concerned with the formation of the teacher than with the art of pedagogy. A program for the exploitation of every human means possible to understand the sacred text is proposed, and there as in other places, such as the *Enchiridion de fide, spe et caritate,* St. Augustine provides models for religion teachers.

Monastic teachers. Among the monks of the 4th century, the *apa* (the Coptic term for father) was first of all the teacher of other solitaries and cenobites who came to him as one experienced in the ways of ascesis and mystical experience. At times in the later development of monasticism, children were taken in to be taught by the monks, but this practice was generally discouraged except under the legal fiction of preparation for the monastic life. The monks for a long time were laymen and unlettered; any presumption on their part to assume a teaching office in the Church was sternly rebuked by the bishops. However, as the institution of monasticism developed, especially in the West, into a more lettered and erudite society, and as more monks received Holy Orders, it was quite natural for the monks to become teachers to the unlettered. A further evolution of religious life provided the Church with a new type of religion teacher; the friars of the high Middle Ages were apostolic in character. They derived their way of life not simply from the monks but from the canons regular, the cathedral clerics who were often teachers, and ultimately from the primitive Christian community described in the Acts of the Apostles. The friars, although they began with popular preaching, quite naturally gravitated toward the newly founded universities.

Teachers of religion in universities. The masters and doctors of the medieval institutions of learning owed much of their ancestry to their Greco-Roman predecessors; the teacher of Catholic truth, whom St. Thomas Aquinas mentions in the first sentence of his *Summa,* owes more to St. Paul and to Christ. The theologians with their precision based on Scripture and common sense carefully distinguished their own role. Private exhortation, that personal admonition that is a call to repentance, is every Christian's business. The university teacher of sacred doctrine, however, must be scientifically competent to carry on a purely objective and intellectual teaching (St. Thomas, *Summa theologiae* 2a2ae, 177.2; 3a, 55.2; IV *Sent.* 6.2.2 ad 2; *In 1 Cor.* 11.2; 14.7; *In 1 Tim.* 2.3; *In Tit.* 2.3). Moreover, the instruction of the little ones was carried on not only by devoted parish priests but by the ambient culture of stone and stained glass. The prescriptions concerning the teaching of religion in the constitutions of John Peckham, who became archbishop of Canterbury in 1279, may at times have been more honored in the breach, but there were good Christian parents, devoted parsons, and the marketplace preaching of the friars. Like St. Augustine, the scholastic teachers theorized on the nature of their operation (e.g., Hugh of Saint-Victor's *Treatise on the Pursuit of Learning;* John of Salisbury's *Policraticus* and *Metalogicon;* Aquinas, *Summa theologiae* 1a, 1; 117.1; *De Ver.* 11.1), seeing the teacher as an external principle assisting the principal and divine Teacher acting from within.

Post-Tridentine period. A partial cause of the Reformation was the paucity and poor quality of teachers of religion. While the earlier humanists and the later Protestant reformers attempted to ameliorate the situation on their terms, the Church drew on its own resources. Besides Tridentine decrees on the teaching of religion, there were new religious orders devoted in particular to this work of mercy. St. Ignatius for one was quick to see that the Church needed a learned body of disciplined teachers who would not only teach the humanities but order them to the greater glory of God in the souls of the pupils. The emphasis that the RATIO STUDIORUM of the Jesuits put on the teacher of religion bore fruit in the work of such men as St. Peter Canisius. The Brothers of the Christian Schools (1695) founded by St. John Baptist de la Salle were most influential as teachers of religion to poor and ignorant boys, not only in France but throughout the world. Numerous congregations of women also were founded for the specific purpose of the religious education of children and young women. The Confraternity of Christian Doctrine (1562) used lay teachers for the instruction of children in Sunday schools. Protestants also used lay instructors, and the Bible teacher represented an important contribution to the teaching of the Protestant religion.

Twentieth century. In the years leading up to the Second Vatican Council, greater emphasis was put on the teaching role of parents. Although the council emphasized the obligation of parents to educate their children in faith, it recognized the importance of schools in religious education and those who undertake a teaching career in the name of the Christian community (*Gravissimum educationis* 3, 5). The words of the council echo in "guidelines for reflection and renewal" published by the Congregation for Catholic Education (1988). The congregation describes the religion teacher as "the key, the vital component, if the educational goals of the [Catholic] school are to be achieved." Because their effectiveness is closely tied to their personal witness, teachers of religion "must be men and women endowed with many gifts, both natural and supernatural." They must have "a thorough cultural, professional, and pedagogical training, and they must be capable of genuine dialogue" (n. 96). The distinction made by the Congregation between religious instruction and catechesis (n. 68) is repeated in the *General Directory for Catechesis* (1997) which further describes the characteristics of religious instruction and the need for interdisciplinary dialog (n. 73–74).

Bibliography: The teacher of religion is usually treated indirectly and in passing in works on Christian education, catechesis, etc. For OT, see R. DE VAUX, *Ancient Israel, Its Life and Institutions,* tr. J. MCHUGH (New York 1961). NT. Y. M. J. CONGAR, *Lay People in the Church,* tr. D. ATTWATER (Westminster, Md. 1957). The Fathers. H. I. MARROU, *A History of Education in Antiquity,* tr. G. LAMB (New York 1956) 419–465. General. G. SLOYAN, ed., *Shaping the Christian Message* (New York 1958; pa. 1963). R. MASTERSON, ed., *Theology in the Catholic College* (Dubuque, Iowa 1961). M. SAUVAGE, *Catéchèse et Laïcat* (Paris 1962). U. VOLL, "The Teacher in the Church" (*Proceedings of the North American Liturgical Week*; Philadelphia, Pa. 1964); "The Sacred Teacher," in *Proceedings of the Society of Catholic College Teachers of Sacred Doctrine* 10 (1964) 7–138. CONGREGATION FOR CATHOLIC EDUCATION, *The Religious Dimension of Education in a Catholic School: Guidelines for Reflection and Renewal* (Rome 1988). P. W. CAREY and E. C. MULLER, eds., *Thelological Education in the Catholic Tradition* (New York 1997).

[U. VOLL/EDS.]

RELIGION, VIRTUE OF

The supernatural, infused, moral habit that inclines us to give to God the worship that is due Him as Supreme Being and as Creator and Lord of the universe.

Nature of the Virtue. The virtue of religion is a potential part of the virtue of justice. That is, while not being justice strictly so-called (strict justice between God and creatures, as also between children and parents, is not possible), religion is a virtue annexed or akin to justice. Justice is the virtue that gives to each his due. Religion gives to God the homage and service that are His due.

While there has been much discussion of the question whether or not religion is a theological virtue, theologians are in general agreement with St. Thomas Aquinas that religion is not a theological but a moral virtue. Some criticize Aquinas's argumentation, and many seek to give religion a preeminent position in the catalogue of virtues; but all are agreed that it is not to be ranked with faith, hope, and charity. F. Suárez places the virtue of religion immediately after his study of the theological virtues and makes it head the list of moral virtues. While St. Thomas prefers to place the virtue of religion within his study of justice, he does admit that the virtue of religion holds a special rank among the moral virtues (see *Summa theologiae* 2a2ae, 81.5–6, 8).

Further, St. Thomas holds that the supernatural virtues are not hermetically compartmentalized. Rather, they interpenetrate one another. Thus the virtue of religion can use faith and hope as materials subservient to the ends of religion as, e.g., when one believes something out of reverence for God. On the other hand, charity can command the virtue of religion, as when one performs a religious duty out of love for God.

Perhaps more insistence might be given to the fact that, in the exercise of the supernatural virtue of religion, the virtue of piety has an important part to play. Man's relationship to God, even when religion is concerned, is not that of servant to master. It is rather that of son to father; or more correctly, it is that of both son and servant. While these two roles are simultaneous, they are governed by two distinct, though interpenetrating, virtues. While combining them in daily living, it is good not to confuse them in theological discussion.

Although it is itself a moral virtue, religion has a preeminent role among the virtues of that kind. Every just man is religious because justice demands that the rights of God be respected before those of any others. Without proper attention to the duties of religion, one cannot be properly oriented toward the duties to neighbor or to self. It is rather the fulfillment of this primary duty that ensures proper balance and perspective for carrying out other duties required by justice.

Its Acts. The acts of the virtue of religion are both interior and exterior. The modern liturgical revival has made much of this. God, who is Creator of both body and soul, must be acknowledged by the whole man. This acknowledgment is not something that God needs, but rather it is a demand of justice and human psychology. In every aspect of human life, both body and soul have their share. It would indeed be strange if man were to be only half human in the worship of God.

The reason for interior worship is given by the Gospel: "God is a spirit and they who worship Him must worship in spirit and in truth" (Jn 4.24). The reason for exterior worship is a psychological one. Whatever man experiences fully he expresses in some exterior way. Exterior expression is the means of both manifesting and fostering the interior experience. There are two interior acts of the virtue of religion: DEVOTION and PRAYER. Devotion is the very heart of religion, and prayer is the surrender of the mind to God in a service of contemplation. Devotion is of special importance to the virtue of religion since it acts as a prime mover, setting into motion the religious activity dependent upon it. Devotion is nothing else but readiness to serve God. This disposition of the will is what inclines a man to worship. Prayer is an activity of the practical intellect, which seeks the achievement of certain effects through certain causes. In the case of prayer, the favor for which one prays is sought through the power of God. The causality of prayer lies ultimately in its being a submission to the ordination of Providence to give certain spiritual favors only when they have been requested in humble prayer.

There are three kinds of exterior acts of the virtue of religion: gestures of the body, gifts made to God, and the use of sacred things. Gestures of the body St. Thomas specifically calls ADORATION, and he points out that these gestures would have no worth at all except in virtue of the interior devotion that prompts them. Among gifts made to God, Aquinas numbers offerings and VOWS. Of special importance among offerings is sacrifice, which is reserved to God alone; it is the outward sign of man's dependence upon God for all things, and especially for the gift of life itself. Oblations and TITHES are other forms of offerings. The use of Sacraments and the use of the Sacred Name (e.g., in OATHS, invocations, and adjurations) constitute the use of sacred things St. Thomas had in mind. He does not devote space to a discussion of the use of Sacraments in his treatment of religion, but he does lay down a principle that has inspired many a liturgist: God is worshiped not only by what is given to Him, but also by man's reception of things from God. To receive a Sacrament is to profess one's faith. The use of Sacraments can therefore be considered an act of homage to God.

An age that has rediscovered the meaning of worship and its place in the Christian life must of necessity rediscover the importance of the virtue of religion, for it is "the inner life of worship." Without a deep practice of this virtue, liturgical worship is reduced to mere formalism.

Bibliography: J. W. CURRAN, *Dictionnaire de spiritualité ascétique et mystique. Doctrine et histoire*, ed. M. VILLER et al. (Paris 1932–) 3:716–727. C. M. MAGSAM, *The Inner Life of Worship* (St. Meinrad, Ind. 1958). F. SUÁREZ, *Opera omnia* (Vivès ed. v.13–14) *De religione*. THOMAS AQUINAS, *Summa theologiae* 2a2ae, 81–100.

[E. R. FALARDEAU]

RELIGION AND MORALITY

It is often claimed that morality became connected with religion only at a relatively late date. But H. Bergson has shown that ancient religions may be called amoral only "if religion such as it was at first is used for a comparison with morality in the form that it assumed later," and that, inversely, men have been able to claim success in constructing an independent morality only in milieux where religion continued to exercise an influence on consciences without their owners' being aware of the fact.

Group morality. In primitive civilizations the sacred and the profane, although they are distinguished, are never separated; but conscience seems entirely merged in the collective conscience. The sense of good and evil is completely socialized in this case, and social solidarity includes relations with the dead, the invisible powers, and the elements of the cosmos. As an example, incest is universally forbidden, but it is also deeply feared as inevitably entailing catastrophes in all nature. Actions that do not produce confusion or harm in the human and cosmic solidarity are not regarded as bad, and, conversely, any action that disturbs their order is blameworthy, even if it is involuntary. Thus, cosmic morality is completely identified with cosmic religion. Natural law in the modern sense does not seem to apply, because nature is thought of in a different manner.

Yet here it is necessary to make a slight qualification in this statement. It is more just to say that primitive man submits to the sanction demanded by the collectivity. He agrees with the collectivity if it declares that he is blameworthy or guilty, even if he has no knowledge of having committed the act charged. This, however, does not prevent protest on the part of the individual conscience. It is precisely at this moment that the idea of God as the supreme judge naturally reappears: "God sees me" or this is "God's business." But even that leads to a fatalistic submission to the verdict of the group. The latter, moreover, does not act to punish a guilty member, but to suppress a danger.

In primitive societies, the person is not a subject of rights and duties. He is rather a member of a whole, and his reason for existence is his function in the whole. The individual does not pass judgment on advantages or disadvantages; he fulfills his function and in that way gives full meaning to his existence. He is an individualist but not in the modern sense. He seeks to be distinguished from others, but this is accomplished by attracting attention through his conformity to the patterns of his society. A right such as that of property is thought of as legal only if it is put at the service of the community. And the feeling of existential solidarity is so strong through daily experience, that each accepts his function, even if it should be to serve as a victim in a human sacrifice. Protest expresses a kind of astonishment and a hope, but such protest does not lead to revolt.

Development of individual morality. The individual begins really to be distinguished from his function only in heterogeneous civilizations, where he can pass from one group to another within a complex collectivity, or dream of a different society because he has some vague knowledge of other existing civilizations. Then, however, in order to justify his protest and to orient his conduct and leave his group, he has to establish his existence upon an absolute norm, God, or even reason, if indeed reason is conceivable as a norm without God. In other words, reference to the All is no longer identified with the human group and its milieu but is situated beyond it.

A choice can be made between religion and reason. However, the apotheosis of Reason showed what it could do in the days of Robespierre, and again in the early 20th century, when supporters of reason thought that it could resume the antireligious battle "with greater spirit than Voltaire" (S. Reinach). There is no question, meanwhile, of the individual's returning to the morality of the group, race, party, or *raison d'état*. The protest of Antigone was representative of an advance in ethics, but it was not the first. On the other hand, morality itself needs a collective sanction that is none other than religion. One appeals from a collective order to another collective conscience and gets an inkling of what the universal religions offer to man, namely, a court that judges both individuals and collectivities. And the tension between the socialized collective conscience and a more profound collective conscience has made equilibrium in human societies possible and disposed humanity for its movement forward.

See Also: MORALITY; RELIGION, VIRTUE OF.

Bibliography: H. BERGSON, *Les Deux sources de la morale et de la religion* (Paris 1932). L. LÉVY-BRUHL, *L'Expérience mystique et les symboles chez les Primitifs* (Paris 1938); *Les Carnets* (Paris 1949) 80–85, 182–184. P. RADIN, *The World of Primitive Man* (New York 1953; reprint 1960). B. HÄRING, *Das Heilige und das Gute* (Freiburg 1950).

[J. GOETZ]

RELIGIONS, COMPARATIVE STUDY OF

"Comparative religions" is understood here in the broader, nondisciplinary sense in order to include some important contributions of the past two decades. While the concept of function, which focused on the relation of religious phenomena to their social and cultural contexts, was a prominent tool in the study of religions throughout the first half of this century, in recent research it has been eclipsed by a concern with "structure," the logical relationships obtaining among religious phenomena within a specific context.

Though he did field work in South America, C. Lévi-Strauss, the leading proponent of structuralist anthropology, is interested primarily in the universal structures of the human mind. He seeks the unconscious framework of relations which underlies superficial facts. Lévi-Strauss characterizes primitive thought, not by its intellectual poverty, but by its demand for order, and has pursued the "logics of myth" in his four volumes of *Mythologiques* by showing "not how men think in myths, but how myths operate in men's minds without their being aware of the fact." His slighting of context has been criticized, but Lévi-Strauss' bold comparative endeavor merits serious attention.

Mary Douglas, though less concerned with universal structures, has illuminated the conceptions of order which inform beliefs about pollution and taboo in societies as diverse as those of ancient Israel and contemporary Africa. Building on the idea that "dirt" is essentially something that is out of place, she has shown that those beliefs "have as their main function to impose system on an inherently untidy reality." She also argues, in *Natural Symbols*, that particular visions of the social order will be expressed in characteristic attitudes toward the body in a given culture.

Like Douglas, Victor Turner proposes a theoretical approach which facilitates comparisons of a broad range of data. Enlarging upon A. van Gennep's observation that most rituals display a threefold structure of separation-transition-reincorporation. Turner has concentrated on the qualities of the middle phase. During that "limited period," all structures typical of daily life are suspended; the actors become a homogeneous group, and the feeling of *communitas* which the ritual engenders confirms both the underlying sentiment of essential equality and the necessity for role- and status-differentiation in society. Turner also discusses how particular symbols can be manipulated to convey ideological messages in *rites de passage* and other cultural situations.

Georges Dumézil echoes the concern with system in his work on Indo-European mythology. An adherent of *la méthode sociologique*, Dumézil has found a remarkable coherence of outlook in the mythical literature of ancient India, Iran, Italy, Germany, Scandinavia, and Ireland. He identifies as the principle of coherence the tripartite division of human and divine society into royal, warrior, and cultivator strata. Although the specifically Indo-European character of that ideology has been questioned, the main lines of Dumézil's challenging synthesis remain unshaken.

Among others in sociology, B. Wilson, through his studies on various contemporary religious movements, has influenced comparative studies of religions. Others might be mentioned, but those examples from several disciplines serve to confirm the persistence of a long-standing task for *Religionswissenschaft*. Despite its periodic claims to autonomy, it has always had and must continue to incorporate the findings of any discipline which seriously attempts the study of religions.

See Also: RELIGION, SOCIOLOGY OF; RELIGION (IN PRIMITIVE CULTURES).

Bibliography: M. DOUGLAS, *Natural Symbols* (London 1970); *Purity and Danger* (London 1966); ed., *Rule and Meanings* (Harmondsworth, England 1973). G. DUMÉZIL, *L'idéologie tripartite des Indo-Européens* (Brussels 1958); *Mythe et épopée* 1 (Paris 1968); 2 (Paris 1971); 3 (Paris 1973). E. LEACH, *Claude Lévi-Strauss* (New York 1970). C. LÉVI-STRAUSS, *The Savage Mind* (Chicago 1966); *Structural Anthropology* 1 (New York 1963); 2 (New York 1976). C. S. LITTLETON, *The New Comparative Mythology* (rev. ed., Berkeley 1973). J. Z. SMITH, "Birth Upside Down or Right Side Up?" *History of Religions* 9 (1970) 281–303; "Adde Parvum Parvo Magnus Acervus Erit," *History of Religions* 11 (1971) 67–90. V. TURNER, *The Forest of Symbols* (Ithaca, N.Y. 1967); *The Ritual Process* (Chicago 1969); *Dramas, Fields, and Metaphors* (Ithaca, N.Y. 1975). B. WILSON, *Sects and Society* (London 1961); *Magic and the Millennium* (London 1973); *Contemporary Transformations of Religion* (London 1976).

[E. V. GALLAGHER]

RELIGIOUS (MEN AND WOMEN)

A religious is a member of the Christian faithful who follows the evangelical counsels of poverty, chastity, and obedience by profession of vows, living a life in common in an institute of consecrated life in a manner of life approved by the Church. Those who are members of secular institutes, which are also institutes of consecrated life, differ from religious in that they do not necessarily live a life in common and they do not give the same manner of public witness. Members of societies of apostolic life live a style of life that resembles religious, but the former do not profess vows.

Before the Second Vatican Council, many religious lived rather similar lives with similar schedules, customs, spirituality, prayer, and the like. With the Second Vatican Council, there came a directive to institutes to rediscover their roots and to return to the charism of their founder or foundress. With the 1983 *Code of Canon Law*, there came a new emphasis on proper law and subsidiarity. Thus, religious life began to manifest a variety of forms based upon the unique charism, mission, and situation of each religious institute.

Nonetheless, all religious in whatever institute they may live do live lives with important elements in common. Most notably, all are bound by the three evangelical COUNSELS: OBEDIENCE, POVERTY, and CHASTITY. The evangelical counsels are a means to the most important goal of a religious, following Christ. While many of the externals and practices surrounding these counsels have changed, their essentials continue to form the foundation of religious life.

Religious Vows (c. 607). Religious profess a vow of obedience recognizing that the competent religious superior has the right to exercise authority. Superiors are to exercise this authority in a spirit of dialogue, treating the religious as a member of a family rather than a subject. Religious find their model of obedience in Christ who always fulfilled the will of the Father. The religious and the superior are to collaborate in discerning God's will, considering the good of the religious and the institute. This collaboration ends with the decision of the superior if the two cannot reach a common agreement. The living of this counsel is a challenge to a secular need for autonomy and individualism.

Religious profess a vow of chastity which is meant to free the religious for a greater love of Christ and others. Again, the model for this counsel is Christ who gave away his life in love for all persons. While the essence of living this counsel has not altered, much of its rationale has deepened; the emphasis is not on a denial of self but rather on being available to others and being free for apostolic work. Some externals associated with this practice have been discarded; for example, the principles that religious must always be together and should not have close friendships with persons of the other gender. It is recognized that healthy celibates should have authentic friendships with women and men. Following this counsel sets the religious apart from a secular society that sees love solely from a physical or romantic perspective or as a commodity.

The vow of poverty means that religious cannot use property for their own benefit. Whatever a religious acquires, with some exceptions, is acquired for the institute. The model for this counsel is Christ who was rich but for our sake became poor. It is also following the gospel command of Christ to the rich young man to go, sell ev-erything, give it to the poor and follow Christ. Religious who follow a solemn vow tradition renounce both the acquisition and the use of property. Religious who follow a simple vow tradition renounce only the use, such that any property to which they may be entitled is still owned by them, but is administered by another. In following this counsel, religious should be like Christ who depended on the providence of God. The practice of poverty probably seems less strict than it had been; since most religious have apostolates and duties outside their religious houses, and since many must from time to time travel significant distances, most religious must use credit cards and they have access to larger amounts of cash than previously. Nonetheless religious making use of such community funds are expected to live a simple lifestyle. There is also a communal dimension to this counsel since the institute and its members are to be concerned about the poor and work to alleviate their needs. Living out this counsel is a challenge to the consumerism and materialism of society.

Rights and Obligations (cc. 662–72). Most religious live a life in common. Some religious for reasons of apostolate or study or health do not live in a community, but this is not intended as a permanent situation. Small local communities are less institutional, with greater likelihood that there may be few, if any, members home at any one time. This is frequently accompanied with less emphasis on community liturgy and prayer.

Religious houses must have a cloister or enclosure, an area that is reserved to the religious alone. This is done so that religious may have space and quiet for prayer and study. The superior may allow others to enter the enclosure on occasion. Often, areas that may have once been commonly enclosed such as dining rooms and community rooms may now be open to visitors. For many institutes, their charism of HOSPITALITY means inviting others into their houses so that they are not so separated from neighbors and those whom they serve.

It is traditional for religious to wear a habit or a distinctive medallion or logo that identifies their affiliation to a particular institute. The constitutions of the institute define the distinctive garb.

Religious are expected to have a strong life of prayer. The living of the evangelical counsels is rendered much more difficult if the religious does not have a strong relationship with God through prayer.

Many religious institutes are CONTEMPLATIVE, which means that their members spend much of their day celebrating the liturgy of the hours, participating in Mass, and engaging in private prayer. Most of these groups are cloistered and do not as a rule have apostolates outside the enclosed area. Other institutes have what may be called an active apostolate, such as teaching, health care, or parish work. The nature of the apostolate very much affects the nature and way of life within the institute.

The religious institute is obligated to provide its members with what they need to live and fulfill their vocations. What is necessary may vary from institute to institute depending on its proper law.

Recent Trends. Among the more recent trends in religious life is a decline in vocations among most institutes. This is coupled with an increase in the average age of the membership. Many institutes have had to give up many apostolates and change the way that the charism of the institute is expressed in the apostolates that it retains. The decline in numbers also can affect the quality or manner of community life.

Since the Second Vatican Council many religious and religious institutes have manifested a deep concern for SOCIAL JUSTICE. In many cases they believe that it is not enough to provide charitable assistance to the needy, but that they must also work to counteract systemic injustice and inequality in the societies in which they minister. A number of religious work to raise the consciousness of members of their institute and society at large about matters of peace, justice, and the environment.

Religious Clerics. Consecrated life is neither clerical nor lay; nonetheless many religious orders are clerical or lay. Many orders of religious men consist of either clergy alone or priests and lay brothers, the latter being members who profess the vows but are not ordained. These clergy are incardinated in their orders, not in a diocese; the major superior is usually a local ordinary under canon law. Religious clergy often work within a diocese and so are subject to the diocesan bishop in terms of their ministry to the people in the diocese, as well as being subject to their religious superiors in terms of living their religious life. A clerical order is ordinarily under the supervision of clerics; ordinarily the priests and brothers in such orders are essentially equal but the lay brothers cannot hold certain offices.

Bibliography: VATICAN II, "Decree on the Up-To-Date Renewal of Religious Life" (*Perfectae caritatis*), Oct. 28, 1965 (in *Acta Apostolicae Sedis* 58 [1966] 702–12). JOHN PAUL II, apostolic exhortation *Vita consecrata,* March 25, 1996 (in *Acta Apostolicae Sedis* 88 [1996] 377–486). D. FLEMING and E. MCDONOUGH, eds., *The Church and Consecrated Life—The Best of the Review* (St. Louis 1996). P. PHILIBERT, ed., *Living in the Meantime* (New York 1994). C. YUHAUS, ed., *Religious Life: The Challenge for Tomorrow* (New York 1994).

[P. SHEA]

RELIGIOUS, CANON LAW OF

Religious Institutes are one of the two forms of consecrated life delineated in the *Code of Canon Law* (cc. 573–731). The code first treats both religious institutes and secular institutes (cc. 573–606), then each separately (religious institutes in cc. 607–709 and secular institutes in cc. 710–730). Canon 573 describes life consecrated through the profession of the evangelical counsels of poverty, chastity and obedience as a stable form of life by which the Christian faithful strive to follow Christ more closely through the Holy Spirit and are entirely dedicated to God for building up the Church and the salvation of the world; those so consecrated seek perfection of charity in furtherance of the kingdom of God and are an outstanding sign in the Church of heavenly glory to come.

Canon 607 describes the nature of religious life as a manifestation to the whole Church of a marriage brought about by God and a sign of the future age through the consecration of the whole person. By this consecration, religious bring to perfection a complete gift of themselves to God through which their entire life becomes a continuous worship of God. This canon describes a religious institute as an organization in which its members, according to its proper law, pronounce public religious vows, either perpetual or temporary; if the latter, the temporary vows are to be renewed before their expiration. The members of the religious institute are to lead the life of brothers or sisters in common.

Historically, the fundamental concept of religious life can be traced to the response of the early Christians to the urging of Christ to strive after evangelical perfection. In the desert, in hermitages, in individual homes and in monasteries, they sought to put his teachings into practice in their lives, and ultimately this led to acknowledgment of their religious way of life by the law of the Church. The first official recognition of the general law came in the Council of Chalcedon (451) when it was decreed that no religious institute could be established without the permission of the local bishop. Consecrated life gradually developed, was adapted throughout history and received a new impetus for renewal from the Second Vatican Council which in the document *Perfectae caritatis* urged the various institutes to return to their roots and their original charism. In doing this, they were to revise their particular law according to their true charism and the teachings of the council.

Religious institutes are either pontifical or diocesan, depending on the ecclesiastical authority that erected them and has authority over them. Some institutes are clerical, having entirely or primarily clerics as members and consequently certain rights and restrictions concerning their leadership. Other institutes are lay, having solely lay members. Institutes in which the members are both cleric and lay but are not subject to the certain of the rights and restrictions that apply to clerical institutes are recognized as ''mixed.'' Monastic institutes are the subject of certain unique provisions. Institutes are also described as contemplative or apostolic depending on the type of apostolate or purpose that they have.

Consistent with the principle of subsidiarity, great importance is paid to the proper law of the institute in the form of constitutions and statutes for the entire institute and individual provinces if the institute organizes itself this way. The code leaves many matters for proper law to delineate. This means that the law applicable to an individual religious institute can better reflect its charism, mission and unique situation.

Governance (cc. 617–640). The code describes the authority that all superiors are to exercise in terms of service, providing that they should treat those under their authority as children rather than subjects, promoting voluntary obedience and displaying a willingness to listen. Nonetheless, the superiors have the authority to act for the common good of the institute if a superior and subject cannot agree on an issue.

Monastery, convent, priory and friary are among the various names used to indicate a religious house which must be erected in accordance with canon law and consequently is the subject of certain rights. Individual religious are ordinarily assigned to a specific religious house under the authority of a local superior. This local superior is in turn subject to the authority of a major superior called a provincial, if the institute is divided into provinces, or a major superior called a general superior or supreme moderator, if the institute is not so divided; if the institute is divided into a province, all the provincials are subject to the authority of a general superior or supreme moderator. Major superiors and supreme moderators or general superiors are each to be advised by a council. The general chapter of an institute holds supreme authority in the institute according to the proper law of the institute; the general chapter meets every few years to elect leadership, determine policies, propose amendments in proper law and decide matters of greater importance.

All religious are subject to the supreme authority of the Church and are bound to obey the pope as their highest superior in virtue of the vow of obedience. Ordinarily, the pope leaves the government of an institute to its own superiors. If the Holy See is involved in a decision affecting religious, this is ordinarily done through the Congregation for Institutes of Consecrated Life and for Societies of Apostolic Life which is the administrative office of the Holy See that handles issues related to religious life.

While institutes, provinces and houses can acquire and administer temporal goods, they must do so according to the requirements of canon law; they are to avoid any appearance of wealth. There are specific rules governing the alienation of temporal goods and depending on the value of the goods involved, permission of various superiors and even of the Holy See may be required. There are similar laws governing mortgages and the encumbering of property.

Membership and formation (cc. 641–661). The code sets forth several qualifications for membership which include that a candidate must have completed seventeen years of age, not be bound by vows of matrimony, not already be a member of another institute of consecrated life or society of apostolic life and not be under the influence of force, grave fear, or malice. The proper law of the institute may set other qualifications, many of which may deal such matters as physical and mental health.

The code provides for a period of formation before a candidate may eventually make perpetual profession of vows. Proper law covers the preparation for entering novitiate, often called postulancy. NOVITIATE is a period of at least a year during which the novices begin their life in the institute by means of a program so they can understand the vocation proper to the institute, experience life within the institute, and form their minds in its charism; it is a period during which the novices and those entrusted with their formation discern their intentions and suitability for life in the institute. A novice can freely leave novitiate or be dismissed. At the end of novitiate, if a novice is judged fit for religious life, then the novice may make temporary profession. A major superior can also extend the duration of novitiate of a novice but not beyond six months.

By religious profession, members are committed to follow the evangelical counsels by public vow and are incorporated into the institute. Temporary profession lasts a limited period of time defined in the law of the institute: not less than three years nor more than six. Competent authority can extend this period in individual cases but not beyond nine years. During this time the member in temporary vows lives the life of the institute but is still undergoing formation during which the member and those in charge of formation determine the religious's suitability for the institute. Temporary profession is renewed from time to time. With the approval of the competent authority according to the law of the institute, a member may make perpetual profession providing, among other requirements, that the religious is at least twenty-one years old and has been in temporary vows for at least three years. The code makes it clear that formation does not end when one takes perpetual vows, but continues throughout the life of the religious.

Obligations and rights (cc. 662–671). The supreme rule of life for religious is comprised of following Christ as found in the Gospels and as delineated in their proper law. It follows that their primary duty is prayer by such means as the Mass, Eucharistic devotions, reading of scripture, liturgy of the hours, the marian rosary, an annual retreat, private prayer, an examination of conscience and frequent confession. Religious must use discretion regarding communications media and they are to avoid what may be harmful to their vocation.

Religious are to live in their own religious house, but they may be absent with permission for periods exceeding a year for reasons of health, studies or apostolate. All houses are to have an area of enclosure or cloister—always reserved to members alone—which must be adapted to the character of the institute. Monasteries of nuns entirely devoted to contemplative life must observe papal cloister according to the norms of the Holy See.

Before first profession religious are to cede administration of what goods they may own to another. Before perpetual profession religious must renounce their goods fully and they must make a will. There are two traditions with regard to the vow of poverty, the solemn vow tradition and the simple vow tradition. In institutes which follow a solemn vow tradition, the religious must renounce ownership and use of all property. In institutes which follow a simple vow tradition, the religious may retain the ownership of their goods, but they must renounce the use of goods and cede the administration of the goods to another; the goods that such a religious continues to own but not use are sometimes called patrimony. Whatever religious acquire by means of their own effort or by reason of their work on behalf of the institute is acquired for the institute.

Religious are to wear the habit of the institute, which is specifically designated garb, as a public witness to their consecration and poverty. Clerics of an institute which does not have a proper habit are to wear clerical dress according to the norm of canon law. Religious are not to accept offices or duties outside the institute without the permission of the appropriate superior. All religious are also bound by specified obligations of clerics.

The institute has an obligation to supply its members with all those things necessary to fulfill their vocation according to the proper law of the institute.

Apostolate (cc. 673–683). The primary APOSTOLATE of all religious consists of their witness of consecrated life. The code emphasizes that contemplative institutes hold a distinguished place in the Church and their mem-

bers are not to be summoned to serve in more active apostolates. Institutes dedicated to the works of the apostolate are to be imbued with an apostolic spirit, and a religious spirit must influence their apostolic action; apostolic action must always be carried out in communion with the Church. The code also stresses the value of lay institutes.

Religious ordinarily work within a diocese and must obey the bishop in those matters that concern care of souls, public exercise of divine worship and other works of the apostolate. Religious who serve in an apostolate outside the institute must also obey their own religious superiors and remain faithful to the discipline of the institute. Given the potential for some conflict in this area, bishops and religious superiors are to cooperate and organize apostolic works through mutual consultation. If a religious is to serve in a diocesan apostolate, the diocesan bishop is to appoint the religious after the religious superior has proposed or presented the religious for appointment. The diocesan bishop may conduct visitation in apostolates of the religious institutes in which the Christian faithful are ordinarily served, but they do not have this right with regard to schools that serve exclusively the institute's own students.

Separation (cc. 684–704). If religious desire to transfer from one institute to another, they must have the consent of the supreme moderator and council of each institute and they must undergo a period of formation before joining the new institute. If a religious wishes to transfer from a religious institute to a secular institute or a society of apostolic life, or vice versa, then the consent of the Holy See is also required. A religious in temporary vows can freely depart when the period of the vows expires. Otherwise, the consent of the competent authority is required.

If a religious for a serious reason wishes to leave the institute for a temporary period, then the supreme moderator can grant a decree of exclaustration for not more than three years with the consent of the council. If exclaustration is sought for more than three years, then the Holy See for institutes of pontifical right and the diocesan bishop for institutes of diocesan right must grant it. Only the Holy See can grant exclaustration for nuns. For grave reasons the Holy See (for institutes of pontifical right) or the diocesan bishop (for institutes of diocesan right) can impose exclaustration on a member of the institute upon the petition of the supreme moderator and council. A religious on exclaustration remains a member of the institute and remains dependent upon the religious superiors and also the local ordinary, especially if the religious is a cleric, but the religious is freed from obligations that are inconsistent with the situation of being on outside the community on exclaustration.

For serious reasons, a religious can petition for an indult of departure from the supreme moderator and the council; departure must be approved by the Holy See for institutes of pontifical right and by the diocesan bishop of the house to which the religious is assigned. If the religious seeking departure is a cleric, then he must first find a bishop who will incardinate him or receive him experimentally.

An institute may dismiss a member for a serious reason; the institute must either show a violation of certain canons or a continuing incorrigibility in violating other obligations of religious life. A religious may only be dismissed after the institute has followed a prescribed process of dismissal, which includes a right of defense of the religious. The supreme moderator must issue the decree of dismissal after obtaining the consent of the council and it must be confirmed by the Holy See or diocesan bishop of the house to which the religious is assigned, depending on whether the institute is pontifical or diocesan.

Eastern law code (cc. 410–572). In the *Code of Canons of the Eastern Churches*, monastic life provides the pattern for religious orders and congregations. The Eastern code appears to approach religious institutes more from a historical paradigm, recognizing the historic influence of monasticism, while the Latin code seems to have a more abstract organization for religious institutes. The Eastern code tends to legislate in more detail, whereas the Latin code seems to allow more topics to be handled under proper law. The Eastern code necessarily differs because of the different hierarchical structure, so that, for example, there are institutes of pontifical, patriarchal or eparchial right. The Eastern code also seems to give more authority over the internal life within monasteries to the Apostolic See, patriarchs and eparchs than the Latin code gives to the Holy See and bishops.

Bibliography: VATICAN II, ''Decree on the Up-To-Date Renewal of Religious Life'' (*Perfectae caritatis*), Oct. 28, 1965 [in *Acta Apostolicae Sedis*, 58 (1966) 702–712]. *New Commentary on the Code of Canon Law*, eds., J. BEAL et al., (New York 2000). *Selected Issues in Religious Law—Bulletin on Issues of Religious Law 1985–1995*, ed., P. COGAN, (Washington 1997). *A Handbook on Canons 573–746*, eds., J. HITE et al., (Collegeville, Minn. 1985). R. MCDERMOTT, ''Two Approaches to Consecrated Life: The Code of Canons of the Eastern Churches and the Code of Canon Law,'' *Studia Canonica*, 29 (1995) 193–239.

[P. SHEA]

RELIGIOUS, CONSTITUTIONS OF

Constitutions (or constitution) are the fundamental code of the proper law of a religious institute, drawn up by the members and sanctioned by competent ecclesiastical authority (*Codex iuris canonici c.* 587 §2). The constitutions of religious institutes provide constitutive or essential norms that reflect the sacred patrimony of the institute (*c.* 578). Some constitutions draw upon the inspiration of the holy founder contained in the institute's rule (Augustinian, Basilian, Benedictine, Franciscan) that guides the spirituality of the members. The Congregation for Institutes of Consecrated Life and Societies of Apostolic Life (CICL) approves the constitutions for religious institutes of pontifical right (*c.* 587 §2; 593), and the diocesan bishop of the principal seat approves those of diocesan right after he has consulted any other bishops to whose diocese the institute has spread (*c.* 587 §2; 594; 595 §1). In some clerical exempt religious institutes, it is required and sufficient that the changes be approved by the general chapter of the institute which has ecclesiastical power of governance (*c.* 596 §2). Constitutions supplement the universal law for a particular religious institute, inasmuch as they protect its vocation and identity (*c.* 587 §1). The constitutions of a religious institute should not be contrary to the universal law, unless the variance is authorized by the Apostolic See.

The constitutions contain the designs of the founder or foundress regarding the nature, purpose, spirit, and character of the institute, as well as its sound traditions approved by competent ecclesiastical authority (*c.* 578). Besides norms that explicate the spiritual patrimony of the institute, this fundamental code includes principal norms of governance, discipline of the members, formation, incorporation, and the object of the sacred vows (*c.* 587 §1). Both spiritual and juridic elements can be joined in the constitutions, but there should not be a multiplication of unnecessary norms (*c.* 587 §3). Norms established by the competent authority of an institute and collected in other codes (directories, statutes) are also part of the proper law of the religious institute. These lesser or complementary norms should be reviewed periodically and adapted by the competent authority of the institute in accord with the needs of places and times (*c.* 587 §4).

Changes or amendments in constitutions are approved by ecclesiastical authorities only after they have been recommended by a two-third vote of the general chapter of the particular religious institute. While the diocesan bishop of the principal seat approves the constitutions, confirms changes, and dispenses from the disciplinary norms of the constitutions in particular cases for an institute of diocesan right, he cannot approve nor confirm changes reserved to the Apostolic See (*c.* 595).

At religious profession, members assume the observance of the three evangelical counsels by public vow and are incorporated into the institute with rights and obligations defined by law (*c.* 654). All religious have as their supreme rule of life the following of Christ (*sequela Christi*) as proposed in the gospel and expressed in their constitutions (*c.* 662). Superiors fulfill their function and exercise their power in accord with the norm of universal and proper law (*c.* 617). Constitutions often incorporate divine or ecclesiastical laws; likewise, they contain fundamental norms pertaining to the religious life. A religious who would transgress the constitutions in a grave, external, imputable, and juridically proven matter could, after formal canonical warnings and the administrative process set forth in the universal law, be dismissed from the religious institute (*c.* 694–701). Ordinarily, the disciplinary norms of the constitutions which are not precepts of God or the Church or the essential obligations of the evangelical counsels do not of themselves bind under pain of sin. However, the habitual transgressions of disciplinary norms out of contempt or laxity would certainly be blameworthy.

Code of Canons of the Eastern Churches. In the CCEO the fundamental code of a monastery is the typicon (*c.* 414 §1, 1°), while that of a religious order or congregation is referred to as statutes (*c.* 414 §1, 1°; 511 §1). The competent ecclesiastical authority who approves these laws and changes, or dispenses from the norms in a particular case and for a single occasion, is the eparchial bishop with respect to monasteries and congregations of eparchial right (*c.* 414 §1 1°). If a congregation of eparchial right has extended to other eparchies, the eparchial bishop of the principal house is bound to consult with the eparchial bishops in whose eparchies the houses are located (*c.* 414 §3). A patriarch has this authority with respect to orders and congregations of patriarchal right which have their headquarters within the territorial boundaries of the Church over which he presides (*c.* 414 §2). The Congregation for the Eastern Churches has authority over all other orders, monasteries, and congregations that are not of eparchial right (*c.* 414 §2). However, approval of changes or amendments to norms approved by a higher authority cannot be approved by a lesser ecclesiastical authority (*c.* 414 §1, 1°). Superiors of monasteries, orders, and congregations are bound by a grave obligation to see that the members committed to their care direct their lives in accord with the proper typicon or statutes (*c.* 421). Likewise, each religious is obliged to tend to perfection in arranging his or her life in accord with the typicon or statutes in fidelity to the intention and determinations of the founder (*c.* 426).

[R. MCDERMOTT]

RELIGIOUS, EXEMPTION OF

The exemption of religious, in the 1983 *Code of Canon Law*, refers to the possibility of the pope exempting a religious or secular institute or a society of apostolic life from the governance of local ordinaries and subjecting it to himself alone or to another ecclesiastical authority (cc. 591, 732). Thus far, this is a mere theoretical possibility, because the pope has not used this provision since the 1983 code took effect. This code eliminated all remaining distinctions in law between exempt and nonexempt religious that had developed over many centuries and was codified in the 1917 *Code of Canon Law*.

The Former Law. In the 1917 code, religious exemption was granted by law or by pontifical privilege. All the religious orders of "regulars" (those with solemn vows) were exempt by law, namely, the orders of monks, canons regular, mendicants, and the Jesuits. Some congregations of simple vows were granted this privilege by the pope. Monasteries of cloistered nuns were exempt from the local ordinary's jurisdiction, provided they were accountable to a male superior of the order, but even then they had fewer rights than the male orders and were subject to the local ordinary in more respects. The 1917 code granted various powers and rights to the exempt, but none of these is unique to the old exempt orders anymore.

In the law of the 1917 code, superiors and chapters in clerical exempt institutes had the power of jurisdiction; the other institutes did not (c. 501, §1). The major superiors of clerical exempt institutes were ordinaries, which gave them all the powers of an ordinary in the law. In 1964, Pope Paul VI granted several faculties, formerly reserved to the exempt, to the general superiors of nonexempt, pontifical, clerical institutes and societies, including the power of jurisdiction (*Cum admotae*, Nov. 6, 1964, *AAS* 59 [1964] 374–79). The 1983 code removed all other distinctions among clerical major superiors. All clerical major superiors of pontifical right are ordinaries and exercise the power of governance. All have equal powers in the universal law (cc. 134, §1; 596, §2).

In the former law, major superiors of clerical exempt institutes could establish semipublic oratories in their houses, as well as secondary oratories in the house or an institution connected with it (1917 c. 1192). Non-exempt religious needed the permission of the local ordinary to establish a semi-public oratory. In the 1983 code, this difference is abolished; any ordinary can establish an oratory (c. 1223).

Under the law of the 1917 code, houses of regulars were completely exempted from the canonical visitation of the local ordinary. In 1966, Paul VI gave the right to local ordinaries to conduct the visitation of churches of exempt religious and of their semi-public oratories that were regularly used by the faithful (*Ecclesiae sanctae*, I, Aug. 6, 1966, *AAS* 58 [1966] 757–75, no. 38). In the 1983 code, all religious are subject to the same provisions on visitation by the bishop (c. 683). The bishop has no right to visit the houses of any pontifical right institutes for matters concerning internal governance and discipline. The bishop is obliged to conduct a visitation of their churches; their oratories, if the faithful regularly come to them for the liturgy; their works of religion or charity; and their schools, except for schools open only to their own members (c. 683).

In the former law, exempt religious had to observe special judicial procedures for the dismissal of a member in perpetual vows (1917 cc. 654–68). The non-exempt followed a simpler procedure. In 1974, a decree of the Sacred Congregation for Religious and Secular Institutes determined that exempt religious were to observe the same dismissal process as the non-exempt (*Processus judicialis*, Mar. 2, 1974, *AAS* 66 [1974] 215). The 1983 code likewise has only one procedure for all institutes (cc. 694–704).

Other differences between exempt and non-exempt religious in the 1917 code included laws on the superior who could punish violations of the cloister, grant faculties for preaching and hearing confessions, issue dimissorial letters, dispense from non-reserved private vows, grant permission to a priest to perform an exorcism, and remit censures reserved to the bishop or to the ordinary (1917 cc. 1338; 875; 964, 2&°; 1313, 2&°; 1151; 2253, 3&°). None of these differences between exempt and non-exempt institutes exists in the current law.

Exemption Today. Except for the hypothetical possibility in c. 591 of the pope granting an exemption, nothing remains in the current universal law of the traditional differences between exempt and non-exempt religious. The changes in the law began at Vatican II, with the council decreeing that exemption "does not prevent religious being subject to the jurisdiction of the bishops in the individual dioceses in accordance with the general law, insofar as is required for the performance of their pastoral duties and the proper care of souls" (*Christus Dominus* 35). In 1966, Pope Paul VI established new laws governing the relations between local ordinaries and religious, and the exempt and non-exempt were treated alike (*Ecclesiae Sanctae* I, 22–40). The 1978 document of the Sacred Congregations for Religious and Secular Institutes and for Bishops, *Mutuae relationes*, spoke of a "renewed awareness of exemption." The exempt were not to be thought of as subject to the pope alone, but they "should cultivate above all special attachment to the Roman Pontiff and to the bishops . . ." (*Directives for the Mutual Relations Between Bishops and Religious in the Church,* May 14, 1978 [Washington: USCC], no. 22).

During the process of revising the 1917 code in the 1970s, the commission (*coetus*) on religious law stated its intention to eliminate obsolete norms and those that treated men's and women's institutes unequally. It specifically mentioned exemption and its juridical consequences as being obsolete and inappropriate (Pontifical Commission for the Revision of the Code of Canon Law, *Schema of Canons on Institutes of Life Consecrated by Profession of the Evangelical Counsels* [Washington: USCC, 1977] 11). Accordingly, the 1983 code no longer distinguishes between the regular orders with solemn vows and the congregations with simple vows, between the exempt and the non-exempt. The law continues to differentiate between clerical and lay institutes (c. 588). Only clerical major superiors are ordinaries and have the powers of ordinaries in law.

Exemption is not an operative principle in the 1983 code. It has been replaced by "the rightful autonomy of life" of all religious and secular institutes and societies of apostolic life (cc. 586, 732). This means that members of these institutes and societies have considerable freedom in controlling their own internal governance and discipline in keeping with their nature, purpose, spirit, character, and sound traditions (c. 578). All members of these institutes and societies, whether of pontifical right or diocesan right, are subject to the diocesan bishop in three areas: the care of souls, the public exercise of divine worship, and other works of the apostolate (c. 678, §1). Institutes and societies of diocesan right are additionally subject to a closer supervision by the diocesan bishop in the same ways that pontifical institutes and societies are subject to the Holy See (cc. 593–95).

Bibliography: E. FOGLIASSO, "Exemption des Religieux," *Dictionnaire de droit canonique*, v.5 (Paris 1953) colls. 646–65. G. GHIRLANDA, "Iusta autonomia et exemptio Institutorum religiosorum: fundamentum et extensio," *Periodica* 78 (1989) 113–42. J. M. HUELS, "The Demise of Religious Exemption," *The Jurist* 54 (1994) 40–55. D. J. KAY, *Exemption: Origins of Exemption and Vatican Council II* (Rome 1990).

[J. M. HUELS]

RELIGIOUS BROTHERS CONFERENCE

Founded as the National Assembly of Religious Brothers in 1971. The name was changed to the National Association of Religious Brothers in 1996, and the present name in 2000. The Religious Brothers Conference is the only organization in the American Church designed specifically to be of service to religious brothers. The organization is composed of individual memberships from brothers throughout the U.S. and from other parts of the world. The Conference is directed by a national board and elected office. An executive Secretary conducts the daily business of a national office.

Brothers' Voice, a newsletter of the Conference is published five times a year for its members. An annual national meeting is sponsored in different parts of the U.S. The organization seeks to project a strong national image for the religious brother, and maintains a close working relationship with every Catholic organization.

In relation to the needs of the Church and the needs of religious brothers for their continued growth in their religious life and their service to the Church, the Conference seeks to encourage the development of the spiritual life of all brothers; to promote increased awareness among brothers of their ministerial power for good; to publicize the unique vocation of brothers; to provide a means for brothers to help shape the direction of their religious life; to heighten brothers' concerns with and involvement in the needs of the Church and society; and to improve communication among brothers and to provide liaison with the various organizations of the Catholic Church. The headquarters of the Conference is in Chicago, Ill.

[W. BILTON/EDS.]

RELIGIOUS EDUCATION (ARTICLES ON)

The articles in the *New Catholic Encyclopedia* under the headings RELIGIOUS EDUCATION, RELIGIOUS EDUCATION ASSOCIATION, and RELIGIOUS EDUCATION MOVEMENT use religious education as a generic term descriptive of a range of activities associated with learning about religious beliefs and practices. Related to these entries is a cluster of articles that in some cases overlaps and complements the above, and in some cases describes religious indoctrination that for some is incompatible with true religious education. This latter cluster is grouped under some cognate of catechesis. They include three entries on the history of catechesis, CATECHESIS (EARLY CHRISTIAN); CATECHESIS (MEDIEVAL) and CATECHESIS (REFORMATION). Important in the history of catechesis are the CONFRATERNITY OF CHRISTIAN DOCTRINE and MUNICH METHOD IN CATECHESIS. The article CATECHISMS is complemented by entries describing specific catechisms, CATECHISM OF THE CATHOLIC CHURCH, CATECHISM OF THE COUNCIL OF TRENT, and CATECHISMS IN COLONIAL AMERICA. Another genre of catechetical works is described under the headings GENERAL DIRECTORY FOR CATECHESIS and CATECHETICAL DIRECTORIES, NATIONAL. The general entry describing the role and tasks of the CATECHIST is complemented by biographies of a large number of individuals, some canonized and some beatified, who authored catechisms and worked as catechists. A number of associations to assist catechists in their work

include the INTERNATIONAL COUNCIL FOR CATECHESIS and the NATIONAL CONFERENCE OF CATECHETICAL LEADERSHIP. Another cognate, CATECHUMENATE traces the history of that institution and describes the modern form that is closely related to the liturgy, the sacraments of initiation, and sacramental practice in general. This relationship is explored in detail under the heading LITURGICAL CATECHESIS and to some extent FIRST COMMUNION and INFANT BAPTISM.

[B. L. MARTHALER]

RELIGIOUS EDUCATION

Religious education is understood in several ways. As a generic term it serves as an umbrella for a variety of pedagogical activities associated in one way or another with religion, e.g., formation, instruction, socialization, schooling, moral development, catechesis, bible study, teaching theology. In recent years it has also acquired a specific meaning, describing a particular field or discipline of academic study which investigates the theory and practice of the activities mentioned. In this latter sense religious education is perceived as ''a special work demanding focused scholarship, unique training programs, and personnel'' (Lee 8).

Origins of the Discipline. Several factors caused scholars to take a more systematic and theoretical approach to religious education. By the end of the 19th century the public school, a firm support of the Protestant tradition in the U.S., was well on its way toward secularization. The burden of religious education, therefore, fell more and more on the family, churches, Sunday and vacation schools, and similar institutions. Such Protestant writers as George Albert Coe, Paul Vieth, William Clayton Bower, Luther Weigle, Lewis Sherrill, H. Shelton Smith, and James Smart subjected religious education endeavors to a critical examination. In Roman Catholic circles a certain dissatisfaction with the conventional method of rote memorization of the catechism, the emergence of kerygmatic theology in the 1930s, and the blossoming of the liturgical movement in the 1950s raised theoretical questions about the nature and purpose of religious education. The need to address theoretical issues became more clearly defined in the 1960s when The Catholic University of America, Marquette, Fordham, Notre Dame, and other Catholic universities began to offer graduate programs.

Theoretical Approaches. It is possible to identify four theoretical approaches to religious education among contemporary Roman Catholic writers.

The Theological Approach. This accepts the premise of the 1972 *General Catechetical Directory* that religious education is a form of the ministry of the Word (1972 GCD 17). The nature and purpose of religious education are defined in terms of transmitting creed, code, and cult. Religion is carried on under the direction of the Church's teaching authority.

The Social Science Approach. The designation describes religious education as the process by which religious behavior is facilitated. It argues that religious education must be grounded in learning theory and the empirical research of the social sciences. It emphasizes teaching or instruction which is defined as a prime means ''of promoting learning more rapidly, of helping to effect the retention of learned behaviors for a longer period, and facilitating the translation of learned behaviors into the personal lifestyle of the student'' (Lee 8).

The Socialization Approach. A third approach sees religious education as a process of socialization. The term is used, by different authors, to mean: (1) the nurture of a personal religious identity and integrity; (2) the process whereby a person is initiated and assimilated into a particular religious community; or (3) the acquisition of a religious symbol system. The first understands socialization as it is used by psychologists; the second as in sociology; and the third as in anthropology, where it is also called acculturation. Religious educators who take this approach insist to a greater or lesser degree on all three aspects. The Rite of Christian Initiation of Adults is based on a socialization model of catechesis.

The Educational Approach. This theory holds that education is essentially religious. In this context education is carefully distinguished and sometimes totally dissociated from schooling. Education is understood as the systematic planning of experience for growth in human understanding. It is religious insofar as it examines the deepest meaning of the origin and destiny of the world and finds its expression in social gestures—symbols and behaviors.

Evaluation. The differences in these four approaches can be most readily seen in the way they define the relationship of religion to education. The theological model takes religion—creeds, code, and cult—as the content to be taught; its educational philosophy and procedures are largely unexamined. The social-science model puts religion and education in dialogue with one another so that religious education is responsive to psychology, sociology, and anthropology, as well as to theology. The socialization model takes creed, code, and cult not so much as the content but as the means whereby individuals and communities acquire religious identity in a particular tradition; they create what they represent. The educational model separates institutional religion from education so that while Christian education and catechesis are legiti-

mate ministries of the Church, they are not properly speaking dimensions of religious education.

While this taxonomy is based on the works of contemporary Catholic authors, there are also Protestant scholars who advocate each of the above approaches. Whatever must be said of the philosophical assumptions and theories which underlie them, in practice these approaches are not mutually exclusive.

Bibliography: H. W. BURGESS. *An Invitation to Religious Education* (Mishawaka, Ind. 1975). J. M. LEE, *The Shape of Religious Instruction* (Dayton 1971). M. J. TAYLOR, ed., *Foundations for Christian Education in an Era of Change* (Nashville 1976). P. O'HARE, ed., *Foundations of Religious Education* (New York 1978). T. GROOME, *Christian Religious Education* (San Francisco 1980). K. R. BARKER, *Religious Education, Catechesis, and Freedom* (Birmingham, Ala. 1981). M. HARRIS, *Fashion Me a People: Curriculum in the Church* (Louisville, Ky. 1989). I. V. CULLY and K. B. CULLY, *Harper's Encyclopedia of Religious Education* (San Francisco 1990). T. H. MORRIS, *The RCIA: Transforming the Church: A Resource for Pastoral Implementation*, rev. and updated ed. (New York 1997).

[B. L. MARTHALER]

RELIGIOUS EDUCATION ASSOCIATION

The Religious Education Association (REA) was founded in 1903 as part of a larger progressive movement to improve education in the United States. The background to the movement was the alliance that had been formed in the 1840s between the common (public) school and the Sunday school. Major social and economic changes at the end of the nineteenth century brought increasing doubts about the effectiveness of the Sunday School. Many Protestant leaders saw the need for a realignment of efforts.

The main leadership in founding the REA was provided by William Rainey Harper, president of the University of Chicago. The intellectual leader of the movement was unquestionably George Albert Coe. The first meeting of the REA brought together 400 college presidents, political leaders, church administrators and religious thinkers. The keynote address was given by John Dewey on the importance of the new field of psychology. This first meeting generated great optimism that the time was ripe for educational change. The REA had three ambitious aims: 1) To create cooperation among Catholic, Protestant and Jewish educators in the United States and Canada 2) To bring the teaching of religion into the public school 3) To professionalize church education in the local congregation.

In this same decade, the NATIONAL CATHOLIC EDUCATIONAL ASSOCIATION was founded, a sign that the Catholic church had reservations about the REA. Only a few Reform Jews became active members of the Association. Most Protestants, especially the Evangelicals, did not join. As a result, the REA became mostly identified as a liberal Protestant organization.

The REA has never really flourished even while it continued to hold national conferences. Its most notable achievement has been the journal *Religious Education* which has been continuously published throughout the century. The hope to professionalize church education was frustrated by the Depression of the 1930s. The viability of a church position called Director of Christian Education suffered a setback from which it has never recovered in most denominations. In addition, the theological shift in Protestant theology after the Second World War called into question the liberal aims of religious education. In the public school, Bible reading and the recitation of the Lord's Prayer continued until the 1960s, but any attempt to introduce religious instruction faced formidable opposition.

The REA received a big boost in 1965 with the entrance of large numbers of Roman Catholics. The largest national conferences of the Association occurred in the late 1960s and early 1970s, and there were also regional conferences. At that time a related organization, the Association of Professors and Researchers in Religious Education, was founded. Although APRRE evolved from within the structure of the National Council of Churches, it has functioned as a professors' section of the REA, contributing to the journal and co-sponsoring national conferences.

Compared to many Catholic and Evangelical organizations, the REA always had a small membership that continues to provide an ecumenical setting for educational discussion and the hope of greater cooperation among religious groups in the future.

Bibliography: G. A. COE, *A Social Theory of Religious Education* (New York: 1920). S. SCHMIDT, *History of the Religious Education Association* (Birmingham: 1983).

[G. MORAN]

RELIGIOUS EDUCATION MOVEMENT

A movement that emerged in the United States in the 1890s. As the Sunday School movement began to wane, Protestant educators attempted to reconfigure their educational efforts. The RELIGIOUS EDUCATION ASSOCIATION was formed with the ambitious intention of bringing religion and education into a dynamic, new relation.

The choice of the term religious education was a sign of the ecumenical intentions of the Protestant founders of the movement. Catholic and Jewish educators were invited to join the movement but only a small number did. The more conservative part of Protestantism was also wary of the movement and evangelical Protestants retained their own separate organizations. Very quickly, therefore, religious education became the equivalent of liberal Protestant education.

A separate religious education movement in the Catholic church had its beginnings in the 1930s. The focus of this movement was the life of Jesus as recounted in the New Testament. In Europe, a biblical and liturgical movement had been launched at the beginning of the century. The effects of this movement were not apparent in the United States until the 1950s. Dissatisfaction with the question-answer approach of the traditional catechism led to the "kerygmatic movement" with its emphasis on salvation history in the Old Testament and the announcement of the gospel in the New Testament. Textbooks for religion classes in Catholic schools showed this new emphasis in the early 1960s.

With the founding of graduate programs of religious education at Catholic universities and colleges before and after the Second Vatican Council, religious education became recognized as an area of academic study. At the CATHOLIC UNIVERSITY OF AMERICA, the graduate program of Religious Education, under the leadership of Gerard Sloyan, provided direction for this movement in the 1960s. Similar programs were started at Fordham University, Marquette University, Manhattan College, the University of Notre Dame, Boston College, and more than a dozen other Catholic colleges.

When the Catholic school system began to shrink in the late 1960s, a movement was begun to professionalize parish-based education. Parishes began to hire men and women who had earned degrees in religious education. For the first ten years, the role had various names. The 1975 publication of *The DRE Book* by Maria Harris helped to establish the name of the position as Director of Religious Education. This movement quickly became a significant part of the church's educational work.

As a result of these developments, religious education in the Catholic church came to be closely identified with parish education. Many parishes replaced the term Confraternity of Christian Doctrine with religious education. New efforts in adult education were also included under religious education. Somewhat illogically, the Catholic school and religious education were often seen to be alternatives that were in competition for financial support.

At the same time that religious education was coming into general use in the Catholic church it was declining in use among Protestant churches. The 1950 book *The Clue to Christian Education* by Randolph Crump Miller is often cited as signaling the end of the religious education movement. Henceforth, Protestant seminaries and congregations would call their educational work by the name of "Christian education," a title that has continued to the present.

In English-speaking countries outside the United States, religious education usually takes its meaning from a movement that began in England during the 1940s. Under the leadership of Archbishop William Temple, religious education was given a legal standing. Every county (state) school in England and Wales was to provide religious education. The Education Act of 1944 defined religious education as comprised of two parts: a daily exercise of collective worship and religious instruction according to an agreed syllabus. The requirement of prayer was controversial from the start and schools often downplayed its observance. One result has been that religious education became equivalent to the religious instruction element, and most commonly the term refers to the subject taught in the state schools.

In the United States the courts have almost never referred to religious education; courts usually refer to "religious instruction" as the sectarian activity that is forbidden by law. But it is usually assumed by editorial writers, politicians and textbook makers that religious education is unconstitutional. When the United States Supreme Court in the 1960s outlawed religious exercises in public schools, it encouraged the study of religion. However, the movement to include religion in public schools has always distanced itself from religious education, even though academic instruction in religion could be logically included in religious education.

At the beginning of the 21st century, the pattern of religious education shows no signs of coalescing into a single, logical meaning. Catholic, Protestant, Jewish and other religious groups continue to refer to their educational activities with terms that are thought to be more specifically appropriate to the group. In the Catholic church, catechesis, initiation and formation have particular connotations that are related to sacramental life. Nevertheless, Catholics are the most frequent users of the term religious education both in referring to parish based programs and to the general field of study.

Protestant churches nearly always refer to Christian Education, except in settings where there is conversation with Catholics and Jews. There has been a great deal of conversation between Protestants and Catholics since 1965 and cooperation in publishing ventures. The Religious Education Press, founded by James Michael Lee, published the works of Protestant and Catholic scholars.

Thomas Groome's *Christian Religious Education* in both its title and its content provided a meeting place for discussion by Catholics and Protestants.

Jews occasionally use the term religious education, especially when in conversation with Christians. Jews in Israel use the term more often than do Jews in the United States. The only groups that use religious education as their usual way to refer to education are those outside the mainstream, either to the left or the right. Unitarian-Universalists have consistently used the term for over a century; more recently the Unification church speaks of religious education. The point of convergence of such disparate groups is their aim to transcend traditional differences among religions and achieve for the first time a universal religion.

Despite the limitations in its hundred-year history, religious education has often provided an umbrella term for interreligious dialogue. In the United States, Roman Catholics, Jews, Protestants, Orthodox Catholics, and recently some Buddhists and Muslims have been able to converse about religious education and at times engage in cooperative educational projects. The Association of Professors and Researchers in Religious Education has provided a forum for Catholic, Protestant and, in recent years, Jewish academics.

In England the ecumenical possibilities of religious education, which was the reason for Archbishop Temple's choice of the term in the 1940s, began to be realized in curriculum developments of the 1960s. John Hull at the University of Birmingham spearheaded the development of school curricula that include study of the major religions of the world. This ecumenical approach to religious education in schools is now present in parts of Canada, Australia, New Zealand, South Africa, and Ireland. It has also had some influence in Norway, Sweden, the Netherlands, Germany and Eastern Europe. An International Seminar on Religious Education, with members from 25 nations, has been meeting regularly since 1978.

Bibliography: T. GROOME, *Christian Religious Education* (San Francisco 1980). M. HARRIS, *The DRE Book* (New York 1975). J. HULL, *New Directions in Religious Education* (London 1982). G. MORAN, *Religious Education as a Second Language* (Birmingham 1989). M. ROSENAK, *Commandment and Concern: Jewish Religious Education in Secular Society* (Philadelphia 1987). P. SCHREINER, ed., *Religious Education in Europe* (Munich 2000). I. V. CULLY and K. B. CULLY, *Harper's Encyclopedia of Religious Education* (San Francisco 1990).

[G. MORAN]

RELIGIOUS HABIT

A religious habit is the distinctive attire or dress proper to a particular religious institute. From early times the basic religious habit generally consisted of a tunic that was secured by a cincture or belt; a scapular; and a hood. Most religious women wore a veil and wimple instead of the hood. This remained the model of religious attire until the rise of apostolic religious congregations in the sixteenth century, and still obtains in some of the contemplative, cloistered orders.

From the outset, the habit adopted by any religious institute served several purposes. First, and most basically, it identified the individual wearing it as a member of a particular group. Then, very often within an institute, differences in the habit distinguished those in leadership positions from the others, or distinguished brothers from clerics or those in solemn vows from those in simple vows. The habit was also worn as an expression of spirituality that reflected the values and charism of the institute and its separation from the world. Finally, the habit was an essential piece of the common life of religious, and a means of assuring the observance of poverty.

History. Saint Pachomius (294–346), who introduced cenobitical monachism in Egypt, was the first to establish definite provisions regarding monastic attire. The Pachomian habit consisted of a sleeveless linen tunic, held together by a cincture, a tanned goatskin or sheepskin cloak, and a small thin cape to which was connected a hood bearing a special badge of the monastery. Saint Basil the Great (329–79), who observed the conditions of monastic life while journeying in Egypt, succeeded in adopting a special garb for the monks of the Eastern Church. For Saint Basil the habit was an effective instrument to make a monk realize his station in life and to keep him from indecorous conduct. John Cassian (350–447) gives a detailed description of the monk's garb. While insisting on the utility of dress appropriate to monastic life, he explains the mystical significance of each item—cincture, hood, tunic, scarf, cape and goatskin.

Fourth-century writers record many testimonies on the ceremony of veiling virgins and the garb of female religious. Saint Ambrose related that his sister Marcellina received the "robe of virginity" from the hands of Pope Liberius (352–366) in Rome. Elsewhere, Saint Ambrose recounted that many young women came to be veiled in Milan.

The first pontifical directive dealing explicitly with the wearing of the religious habit is the epistle of Pope Celestine (423–32), written in 428. Celestine reprimanded clerics who attempted to introduce the monastic garb as a distinctive garb for the clergy of Gaul. Saint Benedict (480?–543), the father of Western monasticism, summarized his directions regarding the monk's clothing in chapter 55 of his Rule. Their attire was to be dictated ac-

Carthusian Nun in a Novice's habit, 18th century. (©Gianni Dagli Orti/CORBIS)

cording to the circumstances of the place and the nature of the climate in which they live according to the discretion of the abbot. In a temperate climate a cowl and a tunic were deemed sufficient plus a scapular for work and stockings and shoes. The color and texture of the clothes were not a concern except that they be such as can be bought cheaply.

According to early monastic custom the habit was not usually assumed until the novitiate was over; consequently, the practice of the Congregation of Cluny in having its novices wear the entire habit, with the exception of the hood or cowl, was a deviation from previous monastic practice. Later the *Regula Bullata* of Saint Francis (1223) describes the "habit of probation" given to candidates. It consisted of two tunics without the capuche (hood); the cord, trousers, and cape. Franciscans did not wear a scapular and the habit, modelled on the pilgrim's garb, substituted a cord for the belt (cincture). Professed friars—those who had "promised obedience"—wore the capuche and "in case of necessity" shoes. In the Middle

Ages color became a distinguishing feature of the habits worn by mendicants. In England, Franciscans were known as the Grey friars, Domincans as Black friars and Carmelites as White Friars.

The apostolic congregations that developed in the sixteenth century modelled their attire on the dress of clerics rather than the habits of monks or mendicants. The Jesuit Constitutions, for example, set down only three conditions for clothing: that it be appropriate, that it conform to clerical dress in the locality, and that it be in keeping with the vow of poverty. In practice this meant, the Jesuits wore cassocks but there was a certain latitude in color. Most wore black or grey, but in Aragon some wore violet and possibly brown.

Similarly, the newer congregations of women usually adapted the contemporary dress of the locality, in some cases dressed as ordinary women of the countryside. Saint Vincent de Paul, carefully distinguishing the Daughters of Charity from cloistered nuns does not speak of a habit except to say their veil is to be ''holy modesty'' (*The End and Fundamental Virtues of the Institute*, ch. 1). Both Elizabeth Seton, in the United States, and Cornelia Connelly, in England, adopted the simple black ''widow's weeds'' common at the time (nineteenth century). Thus many did not adopt a habit in the monastic sense, but a style of dress that only became uniform with the passage of time because it was not changed or adapted. The distinctive garb of the Missionaries of Charity founded by Mother Teresa of Calcutta in the twentieth century is an adaptation of the cotton sari worn by women in India.

Legislation. Among the papal and conciliar enactments, the Fourth Council of Constantinople (869–70) may be the first to have regulated the wearing of the habit. According to canon 27 monks who were raised to the episcopate were liable to the severe penalty of deposition for laying aside the monastic habit. The Fourth Council of the Lateran (1215) reaffirmed canon 27, but it was the constitution *Ut Periculosa* in the time of Pope Boniface VIII (1294–1303) that had the force of universal law by reason of its inclusion in the *Liber Sextus*. *Ut Periculosa* forbade regulars to remove their religious garb under pain of excommunication *latae sententiae*. It remained the fundamental source of law and served as the basis for the various disquisitions on the habit up to, through and after the Council of Trent. Commentators continued to discuss the conditions required to incur the excommunication of Boniface VIII for the temerarious removal of the religious garb.

At the end of the 19th century Pope Leo XIII published the Constitution *Conditae a Christo* that gave bishops the legal right to found new religious institutes, and shortly afterward the Congregation of Bishops and Regulars published its *Normae*, or directives, for the foundation of institutes of simple vows. These latter directed that a detailed description of the habit adopted by any new institute be included in constitutions sent for approbation to Rome. After application had been made to the Holy See for approval of constitutions, alterations in the form of the habit were prohibited without authorization from the Congregation of Bishops and Regulars. It was the desire of the Holy See to curb the odd forms of religious habit that were being adopted. Notwithstanding the *Normae*, adequate control was not attained over the practices of the religious institutes. Consequently, Pope Saint Pius X (1903–14) issued the *motu proprio Dei Providentis*, demanding that bishops consult the Holy See before they founded institutes. Explicit information had to be transmitted to Rome regarding the name, founder, purpose, scope, and religious habit of prospective institutes. The Pontiff wished to check the establishment of new congregations that would have no specific difference from extant ones but would merely employ a new name or new form of religious habit.

In the 1940s Pope Pius XII (1939–58) counseled a prudent modification of the garb of sisters in keeping with the demands of reason, hygiene, and well-ordered charity. At the time his exhortations went unheeded for the most part, and it was not until Vatican Council II 20 years later that religious heeded the call to modify, and in many instances, discard the habit entirely, except for some type of sign or symbol which would identify the wearer as a member of a particular congregation. This was the result of the interpretation of *Perfectae Caritatis*, the Vatican document on the renewal of religious life, which stated ''The religious habit, as a symbol of consecration, must be simple and modest, at once poor and becoming. In addition, it must be in keeping with the requirements of health and it must be suited to the times and place and to the needs of the apostolate. The habits, both of men and of women, which are not in conformity with these norms ought to be changed'' (number 17). *Renovationis Causam*, the *Instruction on the Renewal of Religious Life* dealing with formation, issued in 1969, stated only that ''As for the habit of the novices and other candidates to the religious life, the decision rests with the General Chapter.''

The Code of Canon Law of the Latin church, promulgated in 1983, states that religious are to wear the habit of the institute, made according to the norm of proper law, as a sign of consecration and as a witness to poverty. Clerical religious, that is, priests who are religious, if they belong to an institute which does not have a proper habit, are to wear the clerical dress mandated by the episcopal conference norms and legitimate local custom (c. 669).

The Code of Canons of the Eastern Churches has similar norms for monks and other religious, stating that they should wear the monastic habit in and outside of the monastery or the house, in accord with their statutes and the norms of the eparchial bishop.

Bibliography: D. M. HUOT, "Summus Pontifex Pius XII et accomodata renovatio in statibus perfectionis," *Apollonaris* 32 (1959) 360–68. G. ROCCA, ed., *La Sostanza dell'Effemero: gli abiti degli Ordini religiosi in Occidente* (Rome 2000).

[R. M. SERMAK/C. BARTONE]

RELIGIOUS OF JESUS AND MARY

A religious community of women (RJM, Official Catholic Directory, #3450) with papal approbation, founded in Lyons, France, in 1818, by Claudine Thévenet (Mother Mary St. Ignatius, 1774–1837). The Religious of Jesus and Mary (RJM) devote themselves principally to Christian education and to mission work. The constitutions of the congregation, based on the Rule of St. Ignatius of Loyola, received papal approval in 1847. The motherhouse was transferred to Rome in 1903. The community spread successively to Spain, England, Canada, the U.S., Switzerland, Ireland, Argentina, Germany, Mexico, and Cuba. In 1842 the sisters opened their first foreign mission in India, where they later expanded to Pakistan. Subsequently other missions were founded in Canada, Algeria, Spanish Guinea, Gabon, Colombia, Bolivia, Uruguay, New Zealand, Haiti and Mexico.

After coming to the U.S. in 1877, the sisters established themselves at Fall River, Mass. The U.S. provincialate is in Mt. Rainier, MD. In the U.S., the sisters are engaged in academic education, catechetics, pastoral ministries and social outreach.

[M. B. A. HAMELIN/EDS.]

RELIGIOUS ORDERS, ANGLICAN-EPISCOPALIAN

In 16th-century England an act of Queen ELIZABETH I dissolved the religious houses refounded by MARY TUDOR. An Anglican mixed community, founded by Nicholas Ferrar, existed at Little Gidding, Northamptonshire, between 1625 and 1646. Several attempts were made to establish Anglican so-called Protestant monasteries and Colleges of Maids during the 17th and 18th centuries, but none succeeded.

The modern revival of the religious life in the Anglican Communion started with the foundation of the Sisterhood of the Holy Cross (London 1845). After 1848, more than 100 female communities were established in Great Britain and Ireland, the majority devoted to active works of mercy and charity or to teaching. Approximately 30 male communities were founded in Britain after J. H. NEWMAN's short-lived "monastery" at Littlemore, Oxford (1842). While many of the Anglican religious orders in Great Britain witnessed a declining number of vocations, this was compensated by the growth of religious orders in the worldwide Anglican communion, especially in Africa.

According to the 2002–03 Anglican Religious Communities Year Book, there were about 2,500 religious (950 men and 1,550 women) in the worldwide Anglican Communion, distributed as follows: 420 in Africa (50 men, 370 women); 95 in Asia (25 men, 70 women); 825 in Australasia and the Pacific (600 men, 225 women); 800 in Europe (175 men, 625 women); 360 in North America and the Caribbean (100 men, 260 women). The accompanying table shows the breakdown of international orders.

Bibliography: P. F. ANSON, *The Call of the Cloister* (rev. ed. London 1964), full bibliog. for Anglican religious communities. A. M. ALLCHIN, *The Silent Rebellion: Anglican Religious Communities 1845–1900* (London 1958). F. BIOT, *The Rise of Protestant Monasticism,* tr. W. J. KERRIGAN (Baltimore 1963). S. C. HUGHSON, *An American Cloister* (6th ed. West Park, N.Y. 1961). *A Directory of the Religious Life. . . in the Church of England* (2d ed. Society for Promoting Christian Knowledge; 1957). *Guide to the Religious Communities of the Anglican Communion* (3d ed. London 1963). *Religious Communities in the Episcopal Church and in the Anglican Church of Canada* (3d ed. West Park, N.Y. 1964). *Anglican Religious Communities Year Book 2002–2003* (Norwich, England 2001).

[P. F. ANSON/EDS.]

RELIGIOUS TEACHERS FILIPPINI

A congregation of women religious (MPF; Official Catholic Directory #3430) with papal approbation. One of the earliest teaching communities of sisters in Italy, it was founded by St. Lucy FILIPPINI and Cardinal Marc' Antonio BARBARIGO, Bishop of Montefiascone, a city north of Rome, Italy. In 1692 the Cardinal asked Lucy to head the schools he had organized for the education of young girls. Twelve years later he devised a set of rules to guide Lucy and her followers in the religious life. The sisters were to be dedicated to providing Christian training for the children of the common people. As the community grew, it attracted the attention of Clement XI who, in 1707, called Lucy to Rome to found schools there.

In 1910, five sisters arrived in the U.S. Their destination was St. Joachim parish, Trenton, N.J., and their mis-

	Anglican-Episcopalian Religious Orders
AFRICA	
Lesotho	Community of the Holy Name, Lesotho Province (CHN, estb. 1962, women)
	Society of the Precious Blood, Priory of Our Lady, Mother of Mercy (SPB, estb. 1905, women)
Madagascar	Fikambanan'ny Mpanompovavin l Jesoa Kristy (FMJK, Society of the Servants of Jesus Christ, estb. 1985, women)
Mozambique	Community of St Paul (CSP)
South Africa	Community of Jesus' Compassion (CJC, estb. 1993, women)
	Community of St John the Baptist (CSJB)
	Community of St Michael & All Angels (CSM&AA, estb. 1874, women)
	Community of the Holy Name, Zulu Province (CHN, estb. 1969, women)
	Community of the Resurrection of our Lord (CR, estb. 1884, women)
	Society of St John the Divine (SSJD, estb. 1874, women)
Swaziland	Community of St Peter (CSP)
Tanzania	Chama Cha Mariamu Mtakatifu (CMM, Community of St. Mary of Nazareth and Calvary, estb. 1946, women)
Zimbabwe	Chita che Zita Rinoyera (CZR, Holy Name Community, estb. 1935, women)
	Chita che Zvipo Zve Moto (CZM, Community of the Gifts of the Holy Fire, estb. 1977, mixed community of nuns and friars)
	Community of the Blessed Lady Mary (CBLM, estb. 1983)
	Community of the Divine Compassion (CDC, estb. 1986)
	Community of the Holy Transfiguration (CHT, estb. 1982, women)
ASIA	
Bangladesh	Brotherhood of the Epiphany (BE, estb. 1879, men)
	Christa Sevika Sangha (CSS, Handmaids of Christ, estb. 1970, women)
	Sisterhood of St Mary (estb. 1929, women)
India	Brotherhood of the Ascended Christ (BAC, estb. 1877, men)
Japan	Community of Nazareth (CN, estb. 1936, women)
Malaysia	Community of the Good Shepherd (CGS, estb. 1978, women)
South Korea	Daughters of St Francis (DSF)
	Korean Franciscan Brotherhood (KFB, estb. 1994, men)
	Order of St Benedict, Pusan (OSB, estb. 1993, women)
	Society of the Holy Cross (SHC, estb. 1925, women)
EUROPE	
Ireland	Community of St John the Evangelist (CSJE, estb. 1912, women)
UK	Alton Abbey, Benedictine Community of Our Lady & Saint John (OSB, estb. 1884, men)
	Community of All Hallows (CAH, estb. 1855, women)
	Community of St Andrew (CSA, estb. 1861, women)
	Community of St Clare (OSC, estb. 1950, women)
	Community of St Denys (CSD, estb. 1879, women)
	Community of St Francis (CSF, estb. 1905, women)
	Community of St John Baptist (CSJB, estb. 1852, women)
	Community of St John the Divine (CSJD, estb. 1848, women)
	Community of St Laurence (CSL, estb. 1874, women)
	Community of St Mary the Virgin (CSMV, estb. 1848, women)
	Community of St Peter (CSP, estb. 1861, women)
	Community of St Peter of Horbury (CSPH, estb. 1858, women)
	Community of the Companions of Jesus the Good Shepherd (CJGS, estb. 1920, women)
	Community of the Glorious Ascension (CGA, estb. 1960, men and women)
	Benedictine Community of the Holy Cross (CHC, estb. 1857, women)
	Community of the Holy Family, St. Mary's Abbey (CHF, estb. 1898, women)
	Community of the Holy Name–UK Province (CHN, estb. 1865, women)
	Community of the Reparation to Jesus in the Blessed Sacrament (CRJBS, estb. 1869, women)
	Community of the Resurrection (CR, estb. 1892, men)
	Community of the Sacred Passion (CSP, estb. 1911, women)
	Community of the Servants of the Cross (CSC, estb. 1877, women)
	Community of the Servants of the Will of God (CSWG, estb. 1953, men and women)

EUROPE (cont.)

UK
    Community of the Sisters of the Love of God (SLG, estb. 1906, women)
    Ewell Monastery (Anglican Cistercian, estb. 1966, men)
    Oratory of the Good Shepherd (OGS, estb. 1913, men)
    Order of St Benedict, Burford Priory (OSB, estb. 1941, men and women)
    Order of St Benedict, St. Mary of the Cross, Edgware (OSB, estb. 1866, women)
    Order of St Benedict, Elmore Abbey (OSB, estb. 1914, men)
    Order of St Benedict, Malling Abbey (OSB, estb. 1891, women)
    Order of the Holy Paraclete (OHP, estb. 1915, women)
    Sisterhood of the Epiphany (SE, estb. 1902, women)
    Sisters of Charity (SC, estb. 1869, women)
    Society of All Saints Sisters of the Poor (ASSP, estb. 1851, women)
    Society of Our Lady of the Isles (SOLI, estb. 1984)
    Society of Our Lady St Mary (SLSM)
    Society of St Francis, European Province (SSF, estb. 1921, men)
    Society of St John the Evangelist, Cowley Fathers (SSJE, 1866, men)
    Society of St Margaret (SSM, estb. 1855, women)
    Society of the Franciscan Servants of Jesus & Mary (FSJM, estb. 1935)
    Society of the Holy Trinity, Ascot Priory (SHT, estb. 1848)
    Society of the Precious Blood, Burnham Abbey (SPB, estb. 1905, women)
    Society of the Sacred Cross (SSC, estb. 1914, women)
    Society of the Sacred Mission (SSM, estb. 1893, men)
    Society of the Sisters of Bethany (SSB, estb. 1866, women)

NORTH AMERICA

Canada
    Sisterhood of St John the Divine (SSJD, estb. 1884, women)
USA
    Community of St John Baptist (CSJB, estb. 1874, women)
    Community of St Mary (CSM, estb. 1865, women)
    Community of the Holy Spirit (CHS, estb. 1952, women)
    Community of the Transfiguration (CT, estb. 1898, women)
    Order of Julian of Norwich (OJN, estb. 1985, men and women)
    Order of St Anne, Bethany Convent (OSA, estb. 1910, women)
    Order of St Benedict, Servants of Christ Priory, Phoenix, AZ (OSB, estb. 1968, men)
    Order of St Benedict, St. Gregory's Abbey, Three Rivers, MI (OSB, estb. 1939, men)
    Order of St Helena (OSH, estb. 1945, women)
    Order of the Holy Cross (OHC, estb. 1884, men)
    Order of the Teachers of the Children of God (TCG, estb. 1935)
    Sisterhood of the Holy Nativity (SHN, estb. 1882, women)
    Society of All Saints Sisters of the Poor (ASSP, estb. 1872, women)
    Society of St Francis, American Province (SSF, estb. 1919, men)
    Society of St John the Evangelist, Cowley Fathers (SSJE, estb. 1866, men)
    Society of St Margaret, Boston, Mass. (SSM, estb. 1873, women)
    Society of St Paul (SSP, estb. 1958, men)

OCEANIA-PACIFIC

Australia
    Benedictine Community of Christ the King (CCK, estb. 1933, women)
    Community of the Holy Name (CHN, estb. 1888, women)
    Order of St Benedict, St. Mark's Priory, Camperdown (OSB, estb. 1975, men and women)
    Little Brothers of Francis (LBF, estb. 1987, men)
    Australia Sisters of the Incarnation (SI, estb. 1911, women)
    Society of the Sacred Advent (SSA, estb. 1892, women)
Australia/New Zealand   Society of St Francis (SSF, estb. 1921, men)
Melanesia
    Community of the Sisters of Melanesia (CSM, estb. 1980, women)
    Melanesian Brotherhood (MBH, estb. 1925, men)
New Zealand   Community of the Sacred Name (CSN, estb. 1893, women)
Papua New Guinea   Congregation of the Sisters of the Visitation of Our Lady (CVL, estb. 1964, women)
Solomon Islands   Society of St Francis, Pacific Province (SSF, estb. 1921)

sion was to serve the needs of neglected Italian immigrants. Had it not been for Thomas Joseph Walsh, then bishop-elect of Trenton, the difficult circumstances of the early years would have constrained the sisters to return to Italy. In 1918 Mother Ninetta Ionata, the leader of the group and later superior general, appealed to him for help. In 1920 he purchased Villa Victoria, on the banks of the Delaware River in New Jersey, to serve as a motherhouse and novitiate. Ten years later, Villa Walsh, an estate on Tower Hill in Morristown, N.J., became the new motherhouse and novitiate for the U.S. province of St. Lucy, and the site of the community's high school, school of music, and college.

Over the years in the U.S., the sisters have become engaged in academic education, catechetics, daycare centers, parish ministries, retreats, pastoral ministries, social outreach and foreign mission work. There are two American provinces: St. Lucy Filippini Province (headquartered in Morristown, NJ) and Queen of Apostles Province (headquartered in Bristol, CT). The generalate is in Rome.

[M. MARCHIONE/EDS.]

RELIQUARIES

Containers for safeguarding and exhibiting the relics of saints; they first appeared with the development of the veneration of RELICS. Among the oldest known are small casket-form boxes of silver found in the church of St. Nazarius in Milan and the famous ivory Samagher reliquary of Pola, Yugoslavia. The façade of the latter shows the *confessio* and apse of the fourth-century Constantinian basilica of St. Peter, enabling modern archeologists to reconstruct the interior lineaments of the original church. An earlier example (*c.* 315) of an ivory casket-type reliquary, preserved in the Reliquary Museum at Brescia, is decorated with a cycle of Old and New Testament scenes.

Rings and Crosses. The discovery of the true cross in Jerusalem by St. Helena, of the relics of St. Stephen the Protomartyr, the bodies of SS. Gervasius and Protasius at Milan, and those of the Forty Martyrs frozen to death under Licinius (*c.* 320) in the East, as well as the wide dispersal of relic particles of the true cross, said by PAULINUS OF NOLA to cover the whole world (*Epist.* 32.11), caused the rapid appearance of many types of reliquaries, including rings, amulets, and *encolpia* (small round containers suspended on a chain about the neck and worn upon the breast). Crosses of gold, silver, or crystal were used to contain pieces of the true cross (*Peregr. Aether.* 37.1–2), such as the silver-plated copper cross of Justinian (sixth century) in the Treasury of St. Peter's,

Rome, and the cross of Gregory I (603) in the Theodolinda Treasury at Monza. The use of precious metals for reliquaries is attested in the late fourth century by St. Jerome (*Adv. Vigil.* 5) and at the start of the fifth by Prudentius (*Perist.* 11.184–8).

Table and "Speaking" Reliquaries. Between the seventh and nineth centuries various forms of reliquaries came into existence. Among the Merovingians a burse-form reliquary was made of cloth with the relic woven into it. An example of this type can be found in the National Museum of Nürnberg, Germany. There were, too, pocket reliquaries of rich metal, conveniently carried on one's person. A seventh-century example is in the Abbey of Saint Moritz, and one from the eighth century is in the former State Museum in Berlin. Reliquaries were also constructed in table form, that is, the relics were imbedded in small tables decorated with enamel, jewels, or paintings. Table reliquaries containing a piece of the true cross are to be found at the cathedral of Limburg (*c.* 950), the palace of Henry II in Munich (*c.* 1024), and the church of St. Matthias in Trier (*c.* 1220).

So-called "speaking reliquaries" were fashioned to symbolize the relics they contained. Examples are the hornshaped reliquary of St. Hubertus, patron of the hunt, in the church of St. Servatius in Maastricht, Holland, and the nail-shaped and the crown-of-thorns-shaped reliquaries in Trier. In the early 12th century, reliquaries were often shaped like parts of the body: a leg, an arm, or especially a head or bust. There are famous bust reliquaries of the Apostles Peter and Paul at the Lateran in Rome, of St. JANUARIUS in Naples, and of St. Zenobius in the cathedral of Florence. A famous head reliquary of St. John the Baptist (15th century) adorns the cathedral of Aosta, Italy; and the silver head reliquary of St. Andrew, brought to Rome for safekeeping under Pope Pius II (1464), was returned to the cathedral at Patras by Pope Paul VI (1964).

In the Form of Buildings. A few notable reliquaries took the form of gabled buildings or shrines and reflect the architectural patterns of the period of their construction. Following the Maas-Rhein school of architecture with Godefroid of Claire, Nicholas of Verdun, and Hugo of Oignies, there is the Shrine of the Three Kings in the treasury of the cathedral of Cologne (*c.* 1200), constructed after the supposed relics of the Magi were captured in the storming of Milan (1162) and carried off to Cologne. This is a magnificent silver shrine (nearly six feet long and four-and-a-half feet wide) that resembles a church with a nave and two aisles. Of slightly later date (*c.* 1230) and of Gothic design is the resplendent Marienschrein at Aachen. Towers and other building forms were used during the late Middle Ages, and the Renaissance artists bent their talents to the construction of finely jeweled reliquaries. In the baroque period glass casings for bones reconstructed in bodily form became common, and the relics were exhibited beneath the altar in the full clothing of a bishop, monk, or nun. The form of modern reliquaries is a modest capsule with a glass lid, although ostensorial types are still common, usually for exhibiting large relics or groups of relics on an altar.

Bibliography: H. S. CRAWFORD, *Journal of the Royal Society of Antiquarians of Ireland,* 53 (1923) 74–93, 151–176. M. S. BYNE, *Forgotten Shrines of Spain* (Philadelphia 1926). J. BRAUN, *Die Reliquiare des christlichen Kultes und ihre Entwicklung* (Freiburg 1940), bibliog. A. GRABAR, *Martyrium,* 2 v. and portfolio (Paris 1943–46). A. LIPINSKY, *Münster* 15 (1962) 353–375, Bologna reliquaries. F. J. DÖLGER, *Antike und Christentum,* v.3 (Münster 1932) 81–116.

[J. M. FARNIK/EDS.]

REMBERT OF BREMEN-HAMBURG, ST.

Monk, second archbishop of Bremen-Hamburg; d. Bremen, Germany, June 11, 888. At an early age Rembert (or Rimbert) entered the monastery of Turholt near Bruges in Flanders, where he first met St. ANSGAR, first archbishop of Hamburg, and became his constant companion. Rembert, consulted by Ansgar on the choice of his eventual successor, was asked to accept the archbishopric himself. Although he refused at first, Rembert finally accepted, and his consecration after Ansgar's death (865) was approved by Louis II the German. Pope Nicholas I conferred the PALLIUM on him. Soon thereafter—as Ansgar had desired—Rembert was formally received as a monk at CORVEY. Tradition holds that Rembert made missionary journeys as far north as Sweden during his many years as archbishop, but this is disputed. Because of a foot ailment he accepted ADALGAR OF BREMEN as his coadjutor. He was buried near the cathedral church in Bremen. A life of Rembert was written *c.* 900 (*Monumenta Germaniae Historica: Scriptores* 2:765–775). Rembert's biography of Ansgar (*Monumenta Germaniae Historica: Scriptores* 2:683–725) is a valuable historical document and character sketch.

Feast: Feb. 4.

Bibliography: *Acta Apostolicae Sedis* Feb. (Rome) 1:559–571. O. H. MAY, *Regesten der Erzbishiöfe von Bremen,* v.1 (Hanover 1928) 15–19. A. HAUCK, *Kirchengeschichte Deutschlands* (Berlin-Leipzig 1958) 2:708. G. G. MEERSSEMAN, *Rembert van Torhout* (Brugge 1943). ADAM OF BREMEN, *History of the Archbishops of Hamburg-Bremen,* tr. F. J. TSCHAN (New York 1959). *Geschichtsschreiber der deutschen Vorzeit* v.22 (1939), v.44 (1962), lives of Rembert and Ansgar. A. RÖPCKE, *Pro memoria Remberti* (Husum 1990).

[V. A. SCHAEFER]

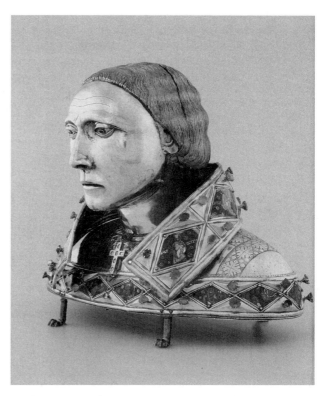

"Reliquary Bust of St. Donato" by Donadino da Brugnone. (©Elio Ciol/CORBIS)

REMESAL, ANTONIO DE

Dominican chronicler; b. Villa de Allariz, Galicia, Spain, date unknown; d. probably Zacatecas, Mexico, after February 1627. He was a member of a noble family and studied at the Colegio de San Sebastián, Salamanca. There he became a distinguished linguist, proficient in Greek, Latin, and Hebrew. He came to America in 1613 with Alonso de Galdo, bishop of Comayagua. On his arrival in Guatemala, Remesal settled at the Dominican convent in Santiago de los Caballeros. He apparently began his historical investigations at once, but also gained a reputation as a preacher and a scholar. He encountered the animosity of the dean of the cathedral, Felipe Ruiz del Corral, who was also commissary of the Inquisition. Remesal's major work, the *Historia de la Provincia de San Vicente de Chiapa y Guatemala,* was finished in Oaxaca, and the author then went to Spain, where he received a royal cedula authorizing its publication June 1, 1619. The work met with resistance in Guatemala, where Ruiz del Corral tried to prevent its circulation by denouncing it to the Inquisition as branding all priests as bastards and all nobles as adulterers and traitors to the king. The Holy Office eventually found no cause to destroy the history, but in the meantime Remesal underwent two periods of confinement.

A 14th-century Venetian reliquary, detail showing St. Erasmus in relief with border of diamonds and rosettes, gold and silver, located in the treasury, Cattedrale di Santa Eufemia, Grado, Italy. (©Elio Ciol/CORBIS)

The history is an extensive chronicle, patiently and exactly done. Remesal used archival materials and oral tradition and reproduced both civil documents, including royal cedulas, and ecclesiastical ones. The work is divided into 11 books. It begins with the conquest of Mexico and Central America and the pioneer missionary activities that accompanied it. Book 5 has much material on the natives of Chiapas, as does book 7, which discusses native character and rights, ways of life, and the problems involved in conversion. In addition to the history of the Dominicans, the work contains also much information on the Mercedarians in Chiapas and Guatemala.

Bibliography: A. DE REMESAL, *Historia general de las Indias occidentales y particular de la gobernación de Chiapa y Guatemala,* 2 v. (2d ed. Guatemala City 1932). F. FERNÁNDEZ DEL CASTILLO, *Fray Antonio de Remesal* (Mexico City 1920).

[J. HERRICK]

REMIGIO DE' GIROLAMI

Dominican theologian and preacher; b. Florence, 1235; d. there, 1319. Known also as Remi of Florence, he came from one of the foremost families of the city, the Chiaro Girolami. While studying arts at the University of Paris, he entered the Dominican Order at Saint-Jacques *c.* 1268. He is thought to have been a disciple of St. THOMAS AQUINAS, whom he certainly knew at Paris and whose doctrine he later followed. Before 1275, while still a dea-

con, he began his long teaching career as lector at Santa Maria Novella in Florence. In 1284 he was preacher general for Florence, and in 1294 he was prior of Santa Maria Novella. During his second assignment to Paris, he read the *Sentences* (1300–02) before receiving license to incept directly from BONIFACE VIII in 1302. Two *Quodlibeta* date from his regency, which continued at least until 1304, when BENEDICT XI invited him to lecture in the curia in Perugia. He was provincial of the Roman province (1309–10) and again prior of Santa Maria Novella in 1313. He lived to celebrate his 50th anniversary as a Dominican.

The bulk of his writings, 24 treatises, of which only one has been edited, are preserved in Florence (Bibl. Naz. 910 C. 4). Among the more important treatises are *De modis rerum, De bono communi, De peccato usurae, De via paradisi,* and an alphabetically ordered *Quaestiones theologicae* (Bibl. Naz. G. 3. 465). His lectures on Romans and 1 Corinthians are preserved in Florence (Bibl. Naz. G. 4. 936). There is some evidence for considering him one of the "teachers" of DANTE ALIGHIERI in the sense that Remigio's lectures were open to Florentine citizens, and Dante's *Convivio* seems to have been inspired by Remigio.

Bibliography: P. GLORIEUX, *Répertoire des maîtres en théologie de Paris au XIIIᵉ siècle* 1:177–179. C. VASOLI, *Enciclopedia filosofica* 4:63. M. GRABMANN, "Fra Remigio de' Girolami O.P., discepolo di S. Tommaso d'Aquino e maestro di Dante," *Scuola cattolica* 5–6 (1925) 267–281, 347–368; *Mittelalterliches Geistesleben,* v.1 (Munich 1926) 361–373, 10:764–765.

[P. GLORIEUX]

REMIGIUS OF AUXERRE

Carolingian humanist and theologian; b. *c.* 841; d. Paris, 908. Remigius (Remi) became a Benedictine at the monastery of Saint-Germain at Auxerre where HEIRIC OF AUXERRE was his teacher. When Heiric died, Remi assumed his teaching post. He later taught at Reims (after 862) and at Paris, where he had ODO OF CLUNY as his pupil.

Remi's labors, the fruit of earlier Carolingian learning, continued the work of reviving classical letters begun by ALCUIN, "Dunchad," and JOHN SCOTUS ERIGENA. Since he was trained in the methodology of Laon, Reims, and Auxerre, which called for compiling, commenting, and writing glosses, Remi was the author of numerous glosses and commentaries on Latin authors (Cato, Terence, Vergil, Juvenal, PRUDENTIUS, Sedulius, Persius, and BEDE), on several late ancient grammarians (Priscian, Donatus, Phocas, and Eutyches), and on the liberal arts, especially the *De Nuptiis* of Martianus Capella. John, the biographer of Odo of Cluny, appears to be the source for the claim that Remi also wrote glosses on the pseudo-Augustine's *Dialectica* (cf. Manuscript in Paris Bib. Nat. Lat. 12949, f. 12–22 v).

As a theologian Remi expounded the *Opuscula Sacra* of BOETHIUS, wrote a commentary on Boethius's *De consolatione philosophiae*, explained Genesis and the Psalms, and wrote homilies on St. Matthew. It is not clear just where Remi stood on the much-disputed question concerning UNIVERSALS, but his glosses on Martianus Capella suggest a position inclining to and influenced by that of Erigena. The latter's influence is also pronounced in Remi's exposition of Boethius's *Opuscula Sacra*.

Bibliography: *Opera*, J. P. MIGNE, ed., *Patrologia latina*, 217 v. (Paris 1878–90) 131:52–970. "Epistolae," *Monumenta Germaniae Historica*, (Berlin 1826–) 7.2:635–640. M. MANITIUS, *Geschichte der lateinischen Literatur des Mittelalters*, 3 v. (Munich 1911–31) 1:504–519; 2:808–809; 3:1063. C. E. LUTZ, ed., *Remigii Autissiodorensis Commentum in Martianum Capellam, Libri I–II* (Leiden 1962). M. CAPPUYNS, "Le Plus ancien commentaire des *Opuscula Sacra*. . ." *Recherches de théologie ancienne et médiévale* (1931): 237–272. J. R. GEISELMANN, "Der Einfluss des Remigius von Auxerre auf die Eucharistielehre des Heriger von Lobbes," *Theologische Quartalschrift* 114 (1933): 222–244. A. VACCARI, "Il genuino commento ai Salmi di Remigio di Auxerre," *Biblica* 26 (1945): 52–99. P. COURCELLE, "Étude critique sur les commentaires de la *Consolation* de Boèce," *Archives d'histoire doctrinale et littéraire du moyen-âge* 14 (1939): 56–65; "La Culture antique de Remi d'Auxerre," *Latomus* 7 (1948): 247–254. R. B. C. HUYGENS, "Remigiana," *Aevum. Rassegna di scienze storiche linguistiche e filologiche* 28 (1954): 330–344. C. E. LUTZ, "Remigius' Ideas on the Classification of the Seven Liberal Arts," *Traditio* 12 (1956): 65–86. M. L. W. LAISTNER, *Thought and Letters in Western Europe, A.D. 500 to 900* (New York 1957). L. SCHEFFCZYK, *Lexikon für Theologie und Kirche*, ed. J. HOFER and K. RAHNER (Freiburg 1957–65) 8: 1223–1225.

[L. E. LYNCH]

REMIGIUS OF LYONS, ST.

Archbishop of Lyons; d. Lyons, France, Oct. 28, 875. He was chaplain of the Emperor LOTHAIR I and of King Charles II, and became archbishop of Lyons in 852. His episcopacy was marked by lengthy involvement in controversies with civil authorities over church property and with ecclesiastical authorities over doctrinal issues. Remigius was particularly active in the PREDESTINATION issue, and it is in that connection that his name is most frequently mentioned. Though not sympathetic to the theories of GOTTSCHALK, Remigius opposed also Gottschalk's famous adversary, Abp. HINCMAR OF REIMS, for he felt that neither writer had done full justice to the thought of St. AUGUSTINE on the subject. Remigius, something of a reformer, took an active part in the Councils of Valence (855), Langres and Savonnières (859), and Thuzey (860). The authenticity of the works ascribed to Remigius has been seriously doubted. In 1287 his relics were translated to the cathedral in Lyons.

Feast: Oct. 29.

Bibliography: *Acta Sanctorum* Oct. 12:678–699. B. LAVAUD, *Dictionnaire de théologie catholique*, ed. A. VACANT et al., 15 v. (Paris 1903–50; Tables générals 1951–) 12:2901–35. H. PELTIER, *Dictionnaire de théologie catholique*, ed. A. VACANT et al., 15 v. (Paris 1903–50; Tables générals 1951–) 13:2379. É. BROUETTE, *Lexikon für Theologie und Kirche*, ed. J. HOFER and K. RAHNER, 10 v. (2d, new ed. Freiburg 1957–65) 8:1225–26.

[J. F. FAHEY]

REMIGIUS OF REIMS, ST.

Also known as Remi or Remy, bishop, "Apostle of the Franks"; b. either at Cernay or Laon, France, *c.* 437; d. Reims, France, Jan. 13, *c.* 533. He was the scion of an influential Gallo-Roman family, his mother being St. Cilinia (feast: October 21) and his younger brother St. Principius (feast: September 25); his father was Aemilius, count of Laon. He was educated at Reims, and his learning and sanctity were such that he was chosen bishop of the city in his 22d year. The most notable event of his nearly 100-year life was the conversion of CLOVIS, the pagan king of the Franks. As a result of his territorial aggrandizements in Gaul, the king had come into conflict with the Alamanni. Hard pressed by this people, Clovis had vowed to embrace the faith of his wife, St. CLOTILDE, if the God of the Christians would grant him victory. He prevailed in 496 at the battle of Tolbiac (Tolbiacum or Zülpich, near Cologne), and was baptized by Remigius on Christmas 498 or 499, with the aid of Clotilde and St. VEDAST. Clovis became known as the eldest son of the Church and was of inestimable influence in the subsequent history of Christianity in the West. Remigius himself seems throughout his career to have been a distinguished administrator and missionary, for with papal approval he set up bishoprics at Tournai, CAMBRAI, Therouanne, Arras, and LAON. Illustrative of his influence is the oft-told story of how he successfully interceded with Clovis for the return of the sacred vessels stolen from the church of Soissons. He is credited with four *Letters* (*Patrologia Latina* 65:963–970); a *Testament* (*Patrologia Latina* 65:970–976), appearing in a longer and interpolated form and a shorter form in metrical prose; and a *Vita* from shortly before his death, not extant. Two of the four *Letters* are to Clovis, a third has to do with Remigius's defense of his own actions regarding an offending priest named Claudius, and the fourth is to the bishop of Tongres. His *Sermones* (not extant) won the admiration of SIDONIUS APOLLINARIS (9.70). The account of the baptism of Clovis is found in GREGORY OF TOURS' *Historia Francorum* (2.3), and lives of the saint were written by HINCMAR OF REIMS (*Monumenta Germaniae Historica: Scriptores rerum Merovingicarum* 3:239–349) and Venantius FORTUNATUS [*Acta Sanctorum* Oct. 1(1765) 128–1301]. His relics were translated by Pope LEO IX to the Abbey of SAINT-REMI in 1049.

Feast: Oct. 1 (translation); Jan. 13 (Reims).

Bibliography: *Acta Sanctorum* Oct. 1 (Venice 1765) 59–187. *Bibliotheca hagiographica latina antiquae et mediae aetatis*, 2 v. (Brussels 1898–1901; suppl. 1911) 7150–73. H. JADOT, *Bibliographie des ouvrages concernant la vie et le culte de saint Remi* (Reims 1889–90). É. D'AVENAY, *Saint Remi de Reims, apôtre des Francs* (Lille 1896). A. HAUDECOEUR, *Vie populaire de Saint Remi, évêque de Reims et apôtre des Francs* (Abbeville 1896). L. LEVILLAIN, "La Conversion et le baptême de Clovis," *Revue d'histoire de l'Église de France* 21 (Paris 1935) 161–192. A. VAN DE VYVER, "La Victoire contre les Alamans et la conversion de Clovis," *Revue Belge de Philologie et d'Histoire* 15 (1936) 859914; 16 (1937) 35–94; 17 (1938) 793–813. ABBÉ DESSAILLY, *Authenticité du grand testament de Saint Remi* (Paris 1996). H. LECLERCQ, *Dictionnaire d'archéologie chrétienne et de liturgie* (Paris 1907–53) 14.2:2231–37, L. RÉAU, *Iconographie de l'art chrétien* (Paris 1955–59) 3:1144–47. É. BROUETTE, *Lexikon für Theologie und Kirche,* ed. J. HOFER and K. RAHNER (Freiburg 1957–65); suppl., *Das Zweite Vatikanishe Konsil: Dokumente und Kommentare,* ed. H. S. BRECHTER et al. (1966) 8:1226–27.

[W. C. KORFMACHER]

REMIGIUS OF ROUEN, ST.

Frankish archbishop; d. Rouen *c.* 772. A natural son of CHARLES MARTEL, he was educated at Court and created archbishop of ROUEN in succession to Rainfroi *c.* 754. His brother, PEPIN III, sent him on a political mission to Pope PAUL I in 760, during which he visited also King DESIDERIUS OF THE LOMBARDS. One result of this mission was the introduction of the Roman chant and liturgy into the French Church, under Pepin and then CHARLEMAGNE (*see* GALLICAN RITES). Remigius brought Roman monks back with him to instruct his diocese in GREGORIAN CHANT and liturgical practice. A legend says that Remigius was entrusted with the task of transferring the relics of St. BENEDICT from Fleury (SAINT-BENOÎT-SUR-LOIRE) to MONTE CASSINO, but that he was prevented from doing so by a miracle. He was present at the council at ATTIGNY in 765. His body was transferred from Rouen cathedral to Saint-Médard of Soissons, and then back to Saint-Ouen at Rouen in 1090, subsequently disappearing in the sack of that abbey by the Huguenots, 1562. His name was inserted in the calendar of saints of the Rouen Breviary on Jan. 19, 1627.

Feast: January 19.

Bibliography: E. MARTÈNE and U. DURAND, *Thesaurus novus anecdotorum,* 5 v. (Paris 1717) 3:1665–70. B. DE GAIFFIER, *Analecta Bollandiana* 23 (1904) 197, for a 13th-century vita. *Acta Sanctorum* Jan. 2:599–600. A. R. COLLETTE, *Histoire du bréviaire de Rouen* (Rouen 1902). H. NETZER, *L'Introduction de la messe romaine en France sous les carolingiens* (Paris 1910). J. L. BAUDOT and L. CHAUSSIN, *Vies des saints et des bienheureux selon l'ordre du calendrier avec l'historique des fêtes,* ed. by the Benedictines of Paris, 12 v. (Paris 1935–56); v. 13, suppl. and table générale (1959) 1:384–385.

[P. B. CORBETT]

REMIREMONT, ABBEY OF

Chapter of noble women in the town of Remiremont, France, former Diocese of Toul, modern Diocese of Saint-Dié. The abbey was founded *c.* 620 by St. Romary (Romaricus) on the summit of "Saint Mont" in the southern Vosges. Originally it was a double MONASTERY in the filiation of LUXEUIL, following the Rule of St. COLUMBAN and practicing the *Laus perennis,* i.e., continuous chanting of the Office by alternating choirs. The men's monastery disappeared fairly early, perhaps during the 9th century. The women's monastery was transferred to the valley between 814 and 821, about the same time it adopted the BENEDICTINE RULE. During the 11th century the abbey was transformed into a chapter of CANONESSES that accepted only the daughters of the highest nobility. Common life and vows disappeared; only the abbess promised to observe celibacy. There were several attempts at reform, especially under the Abbess Catherine of Lorraine *c.* 1620, but all failed. The chapter was suppressed during the French Revolution. When the women's monastery was transferred to the valley in the 9th century, "Saint-Mont" was occupied by hermits who became CANONS regular *c.* 1100 and gave the place to the BENEDICTINES in 1623.

Bibliography: L. H. COTTINEAU, *Répertoire topobibliographique des abbayes et prieurés,* 2 v. (Mâcon 1935–39) 2:2442–43. A. DIDIER-LAURENT, "L'Abbaye de Remiremont . . .," *Mémoires de la Société d'archéologie Lorraine et du musée historique Lorrain* 47 (1897) 259–498. G. DURAND, *L'Église Saint-Pierre des Dames de Remiremont,* 2 v. (Epinal 1929-31). E. HLAWITSCHKA, *Studien zur Äbtissinnenreihe von Remiremont* (Saarbrücken 1963). V. A. BERGEROT, "L'Organisation et le régime intérieur de chapitre de Remiremont du XIIIe au XVIIIe siècle," *Annales de l'Est* 13–17 (1899–1903), *passim.*

[J. CHOUX]

REMONSTRANTS

The name given to the followers of Jacobus ARMINIUS, who continued to propound the less rigid views of Calvinism that Arminius had upheld in his theological writings and disputes. After his death, these disciples met in convention at Gouda (1610) and succeeded in producing in written form the substance of Arminius's teaching. The five articles in this petition became known as the *Remonstrantie,* and those who adhered to these articles became known as Remonstrants.

They stressed that the atonement was intended for all men, that man needs grace, yet is able to resist it and can even lose it. Those who opposed such views, known as Gomarists after their leader, Franciscus Gomarus, met the *Remonstrantie* with a *Contra-Remonstrantie,* in which they renewed their staunch adherence to the strict doctrines of Calvinism and likewise condemned their adversaries for heretical tendencies.

The Remonstrant group was under the leadership of Simon Episcopius (Biscop), a former pupil of Arminius and later a professor of theology at the University of Leyden (1612–18). Both sides took part in conferences held at The Hague and at Delft, but they found no solution. In fact, the dissensions led to further disturbances forcing the States-General to prohibit continents or sermons on such doctrines. Yet despite efforts of the government to maintain mutual tolerance, matters grew worse. Riots ensued.

Eventually, Maurice of Orange openly championed the cause of the Contra-Remonstrants and arrested and even executed some of the Remonstrant leaders. Finally, in 1618–19 a national synod met at Dort (Dordrecht) with representatives of the Dutch Reformed Churches and those of the REFORMED CHURCHES from other parts of Europe present. Instead of being allowed to sit as equals, the Remonstrants were practically placed on trial for their advocacy of doctrines unfavorable to the majority of the ministers and people of Holland. The members of the synod drew up 93 canonical rules and confirmed the authority of the Belgic Confession and the Heidelberg Catechism. In accordance with the judgment of the synod, 200 Remonstrant ministers were deprived of office and 80 were exiled by the States-General.

About 1622 Simon Episcopius had written a *confessio,* which embodied the doctrine of the Remonstrants. By 1630 the Arminians were allowed to live in any part of Holland and to build churches and schools, having already founded the town of Friedrichstadt in Schleswig. It was not until 1795 that they first received official recognition. Although numerically small today, the Arminians have been influential insofar as their teaching is especially evident in the doctrines of groups of Baptists, Methodists, and Calvinists, as well as other evangelical bodies.

Bibliography: D. NOBBS, *Theocracy and Toleration: A Study of the Disputes in Dutch Calvinism from 1600–1650* (New York 1938). J. REGENBOOG, *Geschichte der Remonstranten,* 2 v. (Lemgo, Germ. 1781–84). P. SCHAFF, *Bibliotheca symbolica ecclesiae universalis: Creeds of Christendom,* 3 v. (New York 1877). P. GEYL, *The Netherlands Divided 1609–1648,* tr. S. T. BINDOFF (London 1936).

[L. F. RUSKOWSKI]

"Virgin and Child," detail of High Renaissance painting attributed to Raphael. (©Burstein Collection/CORBIS)

RENAISSANCE

The term used to designate the period of European history beginning in Italy in the 14th century and extending into the 16th. Since it originated in connection with what was considered a "rebirth" of letters and art, those fields have often been emphasized in the study of the Renaissance, and some would prefer to confine the term to such usage. There was, however, a general cultural transition at this time, and historians therefore have concerned themselves also with the period's political, religious, economic, and social changes. They have felt justified in using the term Renaissance to refer to the transitional pe-

"Guidobaldo della Rovere," oil on canvas painting by Bronzino.

riod as a whole. In France, England, and Germany, the movement in question began in the latter half of the 15th century rather than in the 14th. The Renaissance beginning in Italy in the 14th century brought about fundamental changes in the course of which many ideals, attitudes, and institutions that had been predominant during the medieval period were modified or replaced. This article is concerned with describing the nature of those changes in the cultural, political, and religious areas, with emphasis upon the role of the Church in this transitional age, and upon the impact of the age upon the Church.

DEVELOPMENT OF THE RENAISSANCE CONCEPT

To understand the nature of the Renaissance, a necessary first step is to see how the term came into existence and the circumstances of its development. It is immediately apparent that the rise of the concept of the Renaissance is closely connected with the rise of the concept of the Middle Ages. It is likewise apparent that the writers of the 14th and 15th centuries who first developed these concepts were thinking primarily of conditions and changes in the realms of literary style and the visual arts, though they did occasionally make remarks about religious, political, and other factors as being also involved.

Petrarch. PETRARCH (1304–74) seems to have been the first to refer to the period between his own times and

ancient Rome as the "Dark Ages." He designated as "ancient history" the period before the adoption of Christianity by the Roman emperors, and as "modern history" the events "from that time to the present." He declined to write about this "modern period" from the 4th to the 14th century because it offered "so few famous names," because it was simply a period of "darkness." [See T. E. Mommsen, "Petrarch's Conception of the 'Dark Ages'" *Speculum* 17 (1942) 226–242.]

Boccaccio and Villani. BOCCACCIO (1313–75) considered that his age was witnessing a great increase of illustrious men, who wished to "raise up again . . . the oppressed art of poetry." The first of these was Dante (1265–1321), though he reached the sacred spring of poetry "not by the path that the ancients had followed, but by certain byways entirely unknown to our ancestors." After him came Petrarch, who did "follow the ancient path," and thus "opened the way for himself and for those who wished to ascend after him" (Ross and McLaughlin 123–126). Filippo Villani (1325–1405) expresses views similar to those of Boccaccio. He states in his *Liber de civitatis Florentiae famosis civibus* that Claudian (d. *c.* 408) was perhaps the last of the poets of the ancient world. After him, "almost all poetry decayed, because of the weakness and avarice of the emperors, and also because art was no longer prized, since the Catholic faith began to abhor the figments of poetic imagination as a pernicious and vain thing." The revival of poetry came with Dante, "who recalled it from an abyss of shadows into the light" [quoted in W. K. Ferguson, "Humanist Views of the Renaissance," (*American Historical Review* 4) 19]. In a parallel way, Villani held that painting had been "almost extinct" until Cimabue (1240–1302) recalled it to natural similitude, and Giotto (d. 1336) "restored painting to its ancient dignity and greatest fame" (*ibid.* 20).

Leonardo Bruni. With Bruni (*c.* 1370–1444) the political factor is more fully developed: the decline and subsequent revival of poetry are directly attributed to the decline and the revival of political liberty. In his *Vita di Messer Francesco Petrarca* he states that "after the liberty of the Roman people had been lost through the rule of the emperors . . . the flourishing condition of studies and of letters perished, together with the welfare of the city of Rome." Then, connecting the recovery of liberty with the recovery of literature, he observes that "when the liberty of the Italian people was recovered, by the defeat of the Lombards, the cities of Tuscany and elsewhere began to revive, and to take up studies, and somewhat to refine the coarse style." He considered that the recovery was feeble and slow until the time of Dante, and that the really significant recovery had begun only with Petrarch. Petrarch's style was not perfect, but he opened the way to perfection by recovery of the works of Cicero (see Ross and McLaughlin 127–130). It is apparent that there is a considerable chronological divergence in regard to his views as to the time of the recovery of liberty and that of the recovery of literature.

Bearing upon this matter also are references in Bruni's *Historiarum Florentini populi libri xii,* in which he states that the recovery of liberty by the Italian cities came when the emperors confined their attention in Italy to only brief campaigns, allowing the cities to concern themselves more with freedom and less with imperial power. This suggests the 12th-century victories of the Italian communes over the emperors—a considerable time before the literary revival that he sees in Petrarch. One of the basic problems in interpreting the Renaissance is essentially connected with this divergence. The 12th and 13th centuries, which saw the rise of relatively free, self-governing communes, produced literature that the humanists disliked, while the literary revival they praised took place in 14th- and 15th-century Italy, when most of the free communes had come under despotic princes or small oligarchies of wealthy businessmen.

Vasari. Giorgio Vasari (1511–74), who coined the word *rinascita* (rebirth), expressed views similar to those of Bruni in his famous *Lives of the Painters,* first published in 1550. Although beginning with Cimabue, he gives an introductory section explaining his views on earlier art, describing its rise and perfection in the ancient world, and then its decline, beginning about the time of Constantine. For him, medieval art was unworthy because it was unclassical. He wished to discuss art before Cimabue in an introductory way merely in order that the readers might see that, just as it is with human beings, so also it is with the arts: they "have their birth, growth, age, and death." He hoped his readers would thereby "be enabled more easily to recognize the progress of the renaissance [*rinascita*] of the arts, and the perfection to which they have attained in our own time" (quoted in Ferguson, *The Renaissance in Historical Thought,* 62).

Luther. It is understandable that the deprecatory view of the Middle Ages among the humanists and art historians would continue in the historical opinions of the leaders of the Protestant Reformation especially in the light of Luther's theological objections to medieval philosophy and theology. Luther also saw the literary Renaissance as preparing the way for his religious revival. It is perhaps understandable, too, that the 18th-century Enlightenment, in view of the hatred of the Church that is evident in many of its leaders, would continue the deprecatory view of medieval civilization.

Voltaire. In his *Essai sur les moeurs et l'esprit des nations, et sur les principaux faits de l'histoire, depuis*

"Etienne Chevalier and St. Stephen," painting by Jean Fouquet, 1450. (©Francis G. Mayer/CORBIS)

Charlemagne jusqu'à Louis XIII, published in 1756, Voltaire expressed his strong dislike of medieval Latin (which he considered barbarous), of medieval religion, and of the culture of the period in general. Scholasticism, he considered as a "bastard off-spring of the philosophy of Aristotle, poorly translated and poorly understood, which had done more harm to reason and to polite studies than had the Huns and Vandals." In contrast to that darkness, he held that human intelligence began to revive in Italy about the end of the 13th century and the beginning of the 14th. As a cause for this, he noted the wealth of Italy, coming from the commerce of her cities. He emphasized the importance of Florence in this revival, and spoke with great praise of the Medici rule there.

Voltaire noted not only the revival in intelligence, but also the moral shortcomings of Renaissance men, the widespread assassinations, poisonings, and such; but this did not disturb him, for he viewed Renaissance irreligion as a factor in the destruction of Christianity; he held this to be a gain, since he considered the loss of religion as a necessary step for the progress of reason.

Hegel. The interpretation of the Renaissance in G. W. F. Hegel's *Philosophie der Geschichte* (1837) and *Geschichte der Philosophie* (1833–36) is similar to that of Voltaire. For HEGEL the Middle Ages meant a period

Interior courtyard of College de France, Monument of Bude, c. 19th Century, by Jean-Francois Chalgrin, Paris. (©Paul Almasy/CORBIS)

of despiritualization of religion through emphasis upon mere externals of ceremony and scholastic thought, so that life in this world was devoid of spiritual content. The medieval Church and feudalism made freedom impossible. An antithesis to this came at the end of the Middle Ages, as men became free again, ''having the power of exercising their activity for their own objects and interests.'' It is at this time, also, that there was a new birth, a ''revival of the arts and sciences which were concerned with present matter, the epoch when the spirit gains confidence in itself and its existence, and finds its interest in its present.'' Hegel's interpretation was reflected in the dramatic phrase used by Jules Michelet in his *Histoire de France.* In the seventh volume of this work, which he entitled *La Renaissance* (1855), he said that the 16th century must be considered as the age that brought about, more than any previous age, ''the discovery of the world and the discovery of man.''

An echo of Hegel's interpretation is found also in Georg Voigt's *Die Wiederbelebung des classischen Altertums* (1859), which noted ''the corporative tendency'' as the characteristic that especially distinguished the Christian Middle Ages, when the great men who arose ''—seem so only as representatives of the system in which they lived.'' In contrast, he saw Petrarch as the example of the Renaissance humanist who broke through the bonds of the corporative tendency, and in whom ''individuality and its rights stood forth strong and free with a claim to the highest significance.''

Burckhardt. The full development of this line of interpretation, coming down from the Renaissance humanists themselves, through Voltaire, Hegel, and others, was presented in 1860 in Jacob Burckhardt's work, *Die Kultur der Renaissance in Italien.* He credited the Renaissance with the beginning of individuality, and the beginning of the objective treatment of this world. He granted that there had been some examples of ''free personality'' in medieval Italy, but for the most part, he saw the Middle Ages as a period when a ''ban'' had been ''laid upon human personality.'' But, ''at the close of the 13th century Italy began to teem with individuality.'' Medieval men had been ''dreaming or half awake'' under a veil woven of ''faith, illusion, and childish prepossession.'' Then, in Renaissance Italy this veil first melted into air, and ''an objective treatment and consideration of the state and of all the things of this world became possible.'' Burckhardt considered that the chief cause for the birth of individualism and objectivity was the political condition in Italy, which had developed from the conflicts between emperors and popes. In 14th-century Italy the state became a ''calculated, conscious creation . . . a work of art.'' The illegitimacy of the princely governments and the conflicts within the republics provided the possibility of success to the man who could ''make good his claims by personal merit.'' If he were sufficiently resourceful, able, and unscrupulous, he would succeed, no matter what his other shortcomings—the illegitimacy of his birth, the illegality of his position, the flaunting of tradition or accepted conventional morality.

In ''the character of these states, whether republics or despotisms, lies not the only but the chief reason for the early evolution of the Italian in the modern man,'' As to the moral crisis that he considered a part of this movement, he did not welcome it in the same way that Voltaire did, but considered that the ''excessive individualism'' of the Renaissance Italian came upon him not ''through any fault of his own, but rather through an historical necessity.'' And so, it was in itself ''neither good nor bad, but necessary.'' Hence, he considered the political situation in Italy rather than the revival of antiquity as the chief cause for the Renaissance. Indeed, though he admitted that Renaissance developments were ''colored in a thousand ways by the influence of the ancient world,'' yet the ''essence of the phenomena might still have been the same without the classical revival.''

MODIFICATIONS OF THE BURCKHARDT INTERPRETATION

Burckhardt's interpretation in many of its aspects had been developing from the age of the Renaissance humanists. A different view, however, already began to appear in the Romantic school in the early 19th century.

One may or may not agree with these Romantics in their glorification of chivalry, Gothic architecture, and medieval life in general. But, after F. CHATEAUBRIAND's *Le Génie du Christianisme* (1802), and works of others of this school, such as F. SCHLEGEL, Mme. de Staël (1766–1847) and Walter Scott, there was a growing consciousness that there was another point of view than that which insisted upon the absolute superiority of classical literature and art. Chateaubriand insisted upon the superiority of medieval culture because he was convinced that Christianity gave a truer, more fruitful basis for understanding human nature and emotions, and for the depiction of them in literature and art than had the beliefs underlying the literature and art of the classical world.

20th-Century Reevaluations. In addition to the reaction of the Romantics, 20th-century historians, such as C. H. Haskins, J. de Ghellinck, L. Thorndike, É. GILSON, C. DAWSON, and others provided convincing evidence that the medieval period, and especially from 800 on, cannot be correctly described as ''Dark Ages.'' Nor can it be maintained that medieval men were blind in regard to the nature of man or the world about them. Medieval men had a much better understanding of and appreciation for classical Latin literature than the Renaissance humanists suspected. One who reads the works and letters of Alcuin (d. 804), Lupus of Ferrières (d. *c.* 862), and John of Salisbury (d. 1180) is impressed not only with the extent of their knowledge of ancient literature, but also with their enthusiasm and understanding of the importance of such studies. One who investigates medieval architecture and sculpture and reads the studies that É. MÂLE, among others, has made of them, will hardly fail to be impressed with medieval man's consciousness of the world about him, as reflected in the exact depiction of plants in the details of Gothic sculpture. The profundity of Dante's understanding of human nature could hardly have come about if Dante and the men from whom he drew his intellectual and spiritual roots had been separated from reality by the ''veil . . . woven of faith, illusion, and childish prepossession'' of which Burckhardt spoke.

Consequently, a study of the works of medieval men and of recent historians who have devoted themselves to the intellectual history of the Middle Ages makes it clear that the Michelet-Burckhardt formula of attributing to the Renaissance the *discovery* of the world and of man is an exaggeration that is false. It is, nevertheless, true that the men of the Renaissance placed a much greater and more exclusive emphasis upon man and this world than had medieval men. This tendency is discernible first, perhaps, in the works of the 14th- and 15th-century humanists.

RENAISSANCE HUMANISTS

At the outset it should be noted that there were links of a professional nature between the Renaissance human-

Christ on the cross, detail from Italian Renaissance Processional Cross. (©Elio Ciol/CORBIS)

ists (*see* HUMANISM) and their medieval predecessors. P. O. Kristeller has stated that the Renaissance humanists were ''the professional heirs and successors of the medieval rhetoricians, the so-called *dictatores*. . . ,'' the professional writers of the Middle Ages, who wrote letters and prepared documents of various kinds in accordance with the *ars dictaminis* (''Humanism and Scholasticism in the Italian Renaissance,'' in Kristeller 100–103). Thus, there is a marked similarity in function between Petrus de Vineis, who served the Emperor Frederick II as *dictator*, and Coluccio Salutati, the humanist chancellor of Florence from 1375 to 1406. When Salutati was given Florentine citizenship in 1400 he was cited as one skilled in the *ars dictaminis* (see Hay 121 n.3).

As R. Weiss has pointed out (*The Dawn of Humanism in Italy*), it must be noted, too, that a large proportion of the early humanists were connected with the legal profession in some way. Thus, Lovato dei Lovati (d. 1309), who made a study of the meters of Seneca's tragedies, was a Paduan jurist, and Geri d'Arezzo (d. *c.* 1339), whom Salutati considered an important precursor of Petrarch, was a doctor of civil law. Albertino Mussato (1261–1329) of Padua, the most important of these early humanists, who wrote the Senecan tragedy, *Ecerinis*, and who was crowned poet laureate in 1315, was also connected with the law. The *Ecerinis* deals with the 13th-century tyrant Ezzelino da Romano, and apparently Mussato hoped to influence the Paduans to oppose the aggressive moves of the Can Grande della Scala. It would be unwise, however, to attempt on this basis a generalization respecting the political aspirations of these early humanists, because a great deal more research work still remains to be done concerning them (Weiss *Il primo secolo dell'Umanesimo*, 10).

Petrarch. Difficulties in the interpretation of the works of Francesco Petrarca, or Petrarch (1304–74) are of a different type. He wrote a great deal, and some of his statements are confused and contradictory. But there does seem to be in him, in spite of his egocentrism, a charitable concern to help his fellow men. He believed that effective communication was essential, the right word must be found, and for this purpose the works of classical Latin literature were the perfect models. He was convinced that men should help their fellow men, and that the spirits of men can be helped especially through effective discourse. Learning how to use right words comes from study of the classics. This was the objective, the *studia humanitatis,* for Petrarch, and to pursue such studies was the justification he would probably offer for his life of retirement, for the solitude he loved. (See Garin 27–31.) His emphasis upon the importance of classical Latin rhetoric is seen in his work *On His Own Ignorance and That of Many Others,* in which he agrees that in Aristotle's *Ethics* he sees virtue "egregiously defined and distinguished by him and treated with penetrating insight," all of which causes him to know a little more than he knew before. But, he says, "I myself remain the same." The trouble with Aristotle is that "his lesson lacks the words that sting and set afire the urge toward love of virtue and hatred of vice or, at any rate, does not have enough of such power. He who looks for that will find it in our Latin writers, especially in Cicero and Seneca . . ." (tr. H. Nachod, in Cassirer 103).

There is nothing in Petrarch's attitude that is anti-Christian; on the contrary, he seems to be inspired by sincere Christian charity. But he is not satisfied with the medieval emphasis upon the theological. When his friend, Luigi Marsili, an Augustinian, was going away to study theology, Petrarch wrote to him, urging him to follow the example of Lactantius and St. Augustine in conjoining the *studia humanitatis* with *studia divinitatis,* and thus to continue working for the construction of a *pia philosophia* (see Garin 36). His conviction of the superiority of classical literature was such that it was natural enough for him to consider the civilization that produced medieval literature, different as it was, the "Dark Ages."

As to his political views, Petrarch centered all his hopes in Rome, believing that the world had never seen such peace and justice as it had when it had one head, and that head was Rome. He was enthusiastic about Cola di Rienzo until the more fantastic aspects of his activities began to be demonstrated. It seems, too, that Petrarch expected the papacy to make of the *Pax romana,* a *pax christiana,* and the fact that the popes were in Avignon, removed from Rome—where he thought they should be—disturbed him greatly. One historian has even gone so far as to suggest that "Humanism was forged in the Catholic pathos generated by the seventy years of Babylonian captivity" (G. Toffanin 112).

In regard to dictatorship, as opposed to republicanism, Petrarch had been critical of Caesar in his *Africa,* but praised him in his later *Historia Julii Caesaris.* He even became friendly with the Visconti tyrants of Milan, and decided to reside there in 1353. Boccaccio, the devoted follower of Petrarch in so many matters, nevertheless reproached him for this. Boccaccio lived long enough in Florence to become attached to its republican traditions, as Petrarch had not.

Boccaccio. Giovanni Boccaccio (1313–75) had moved to Florence in 1340, after having spent some time in Naples. He entered into the cultural life of the city, and served as an important link in emphasizing the contribution of Petrarch. In addition to his *Decameron* and other productions of a similar nature, Boccaccio did very serious scholarly work in classical Latin literature and culture and was one of the first to promote the study of Greek. He devoted himself especially to the preparation of treatises that would assist readers in understanding classical authors, such as his work on mythology, *De genealogiis deorum gentilium.*

Salutati and Civic Humanism. In 1375, the year of Boccaccio's death, Coluccio SALUTATI (1331–1406) the disciple of Petrarch and Boccaccio, became chancellor of Florence, and continued to foster their influence in that city. His writing reveals the development of the humanist movement into the civic humanism that was so important in Florence. His humanist attitude is seen in an exchange of letters he had with the Dominican Giovanni DOMINICI on the values and dangers of the new humanistic trends. Dominici was a formidable opponent, for he was well informed and fully aware of the value of the classics for mature students, but was opposed to placing so much emphasis upon them in the education of the young. Salutati was in agreement that Christianity came first, and had no intention of saying anything contrary to the Faith. But he was convinced of the value of the new attitudes. He maintained that the *studia humanitatis* and *studia divinitatis* were interrelated, and a true and complete knowledge of the one could not be had without the other (see Emerton 341–377).

In one of his letters he expressed his conviction on the superiority of the active life, in behalf of family, friends, and the state. In writing to a friend who was planning to become a monk he said: "Do not believe . . . that to flee from turmoil, to avoid the view of pleasant things, to enclose oneself in a cloister, or to isolate oneself in a hermitage, constitute the way of perfection. . . Without doubt you, fleeing from the world, can fall from heaven to earth, while I, remaining in the world, can raise my heart to heaven." Consequently, Salutati advised his friend to do those things "necessary for the family, pleasing to friends, salutary for the state . . ." (tr. in Brucker 35–36). As in the case of Petrarch, there is here no rejection of Christian doctrine as such, but there is a rejection of the ascetic ideal that had held so high a place in the medieval period.

Civic Humanism of Bruni. The trend toward civic humanism, which is evident in Salutati, reached perhaps its fullest expression in the works of Leonardo Bruni. Although born in Arezzo, Bruni spent most of his mature years in Florence. He studied Greek under Manuel Chrysoloras there, and came also under the influence of Salutati. After service in the Roman Curia from 1405 to 1415, Bruni returned to Florence, where he became chancellor in 1427, a post he held until his death. The numerous Greek works translated by him included the *Ethics* and the *Politics* of Aristotle. These works very likely confirmed him in his belief that the study of politics must have a central place in the educational process, since that study is connected with the bringing of happiness, not just to one man but to the entire population. He considered that the study of politics should be a part of moral philosophy, and that in the classics of the ancient world one could obtain knowledge of those things that concern life and morality, and which, therefore "are called *humanitatis studia,* inasmuch as they perfect and elevate man" (quoted in Garin 53). Cicero was recommended for such studies, but Lactantius, St. Augustine, and the other Fathers were mentioned also.

Boccaccio had praised Petrarch, together with Dante, for the restoration of poetry. Bruni went further and hailed Petrarch as the founder of a new discipline of literary studies. While these 15th-century humanists had progressed sufficiently to realize that Petrarch's *Africa* could not match the poetic achievements of Vergil's *Aeneid,* Bruni nevertheless praised Petrarch as the one who restored the humanities to life when they were already extinct, and "opened for us the path upon which we could cultivate learning" (quoted from *Dialogi ad Petrum Paulum Histrum,* in Baron 1:237).

Perhaps the most remarkable presentation of his civic humanism is found in the funeral oration that Bruni composed in 1428, eulogizing Nanni degli Strozzi, a general who had been important in the Florentine coalition that prevented the Visconti tyranny from dominating northern Italy. The oration is a Renaissance counterpart of the funeral oration in which Pericles— as reported in Thucydides—had praised the free institutions of Athens. Florence, said Bruni, had "revived and rescued from ruin Latin letters, which previously had been abject, prostrate, and almost dead." It had been Florence, too, that had brought back knowledge of Greek letters, which for more than 700 years had fallen into disuse in Italy. "Finally, the *studia humanitatis* themselves, surely the best and most excellent of studies, those most appropriate for the human race, needed in private as well as public life, and distinguished by a knowledge of letters befitting a free born man—such *studia* took root in Italy after originating in our city" (quoted in Baron 1:362–363).

Reflections of Humanism in Renaissance Art. Some observers consider that the paintings of Masaccio (c. 1401–28), such as the "Tribute Money" and the "Expulsion of Adam and Eve" in the Brancacci Chapel in Florence, reflect an emphasis upon man, parallel to that which is found in the writings of these humanists. It would seem, too, that the interior of the Chapel of San Lorenzo, designed by Brunelleschi (1377–1446), the Florentine architect, emphasizes the dominance of man in this world, just as clearly as the high nave of Chartres Cathedral emphasizes the otherworldliness of medieval civilization. Theophilus (10th century), in writing about the nature of art, stated that the achievement in art is "in glorifying the Creator in His Creature, in causing God to be admired in His works." [See E. De Bruyne, *Études d'esthétique médiévale* 2 (Bruges 1946) 413–417.] There is no trace of such a view in Leon Battista Alberti (1404–72), who in his *Della Pittura* wrote that "The object of painting is to earn favor and goodwill and praise." It is man, the artist, not the Creator, who has become important in this 15th-century view (see Chabod 182–183).

Filelfo. It should be realized that not all Renaissance humanists advocated civic humanism in the same way as Salutati and Bruni. There were those also who served the tyrants and princes, and there were those who did not place emphasis upon the active life. When Cosimo de' MEDICI returned from exile in 1434, Francesco Filelfo (1398–1481) left FLORENCE and then spent much of his time writing in opposition to Florence and the Medici. He went to Milan, where he placed his scholarly services at the disposal of the Visconti tyrants. He served the Ambrosian republic during its short life in Milan, and then Francesco SFORZA, after he gained control of the government in 1450. In his earlier life Filelfo had spent seven years in Constantinople, and when he returned to Italy in 1427, brought back a large number of Greek manuscripts, as well as a member of the Chrysoloras family as his first wife. Nevertheless, in his *De morali disciplina libri quinque,* he did not emphasize the active life or civic humanism of Salutati and Bruni, but praised wisdom, which he defined as knowledge of things divine. Wisdom contemplates the eternal and immutable, rather than the temporal and mobile (see Rice 50—53). Bruni had praised the republican freedom of Florence, but Filelfo wrote his epic poem, the *Sfortias,* to glorify the most successful of the *condottieri,* Francesco Sforza, who had gained control of Milan solely by military ability, unscrupulousness, and force.

Pontano. Pontano (1426–1503) was similar to Filelfo in many respects. He had served the tyrannical Aragonese kings of Naples, and received many favors from them. Yet, when the Aragonese were overthrown by the French in 1494–95, Pontano was ready with an oration in honor of Charles VIII of France. Also, in contrast to Bruni and Salutati, in his *De prudentia,* Pontano insisted that the prudent man, skilled in civic affairs and business cannot be the wise man who concerns himself with investigating the principles and causes of things (see Rice 53–57).

POLITICAL DEVELOPMENTS IN ITALY

It would seem, then, that Bruni's civic humanism cannot serve as a general definition of Renaissance humanism, though it certainly was a very important development within that movement (see Kristeller, in Helton 35). That Bruni's thought developed in the way that it did must be considered as due in large part to the historical actuality of Florence, which had taken the lead in the later 14th and earlier 15th century in defending central Italy and preventing it from falling completely under the domination of the Visconti tyrants of Milan (see Baron *passim*). It may well be that "the Renaissance would have been nipped in the bud if Florence had become a provincial town within an Italian kingdom under despotic Viscontean rule" (Baron 383–384).

However, throughout Italy, except for Florence and Venice, the trend of the 14th century was from relatively free communes to one man rule of the *signorie* and princes. And, although there is much to be said in favor of the government of Florence or Venice when compared with tyrannies like those of the Visconti, it is nevertheless true that from the early 14th century, Florence and Venice were ruled by small oligarchies of wealthy businessmen rather than by the citizens generally. Furthermore, however much the Florentines might complain about the aggression of the Visconti, the Florentines themselves were little different, as they brought the other areas of Tuscany under their control.

Milan. The Visconti had gained control of Milan in 1278, and, except for about ten years in the early 14th century, had held it constantly until 1447. After the short-lived Ambrosian republic, Francesco Sforza (d. 1466) gained control in 1450, and he and his descendants ruled, except for the period of French control in the early 16th century, until 1535. The Della Scala family, which controlled Verona, had by 1335 reached out to gain also Vicenza, Treviso, Padua, Parma, Reggio, and Lucca. Other princes and despots of the 14th and 15th centuries included the Este family of Ferrara, the Malatesta of Rimini, and the Bentivoglio family of Bologna. The House of Anjou, which had ruled the Kingdom of Naples since the 13th century was replaced by Alfonso the Magnanimous of Aragon (d. 1458) in 1442, and it would be difficult to imagine a government more tyrannical than that of his illegitimate son Ferrante (d. 1494).

Florence under the Medici. In Florence the executive power was in the hands of a kind of city council—the eight priors and the gonfalonier of justice. The priors were selected by the guilds, but from the early 14th century, a majority of places were allotted to the Seven Greater Guilds, made up of the very wealthy, such as the bankers and great merchants. The Lesser Guilds, including lower tradesmen such as bakers and shoemakers, were allotted only a minority of places. Furthermore, from the 1320s, the priors were picked by lot, their names being pulled out of an election bag at two-month intervals. The trick in controlling the government was to have charge of the committee that determined which names would be allowed to go into the election bag, and which would be excluded on one pretext or another. In this way the oligarchy could see that enemies did not become priors and that friends did. In 1378 there was a revolt of the *ciompi,* as the wool carders were called, and this led to lower-class control of the government for a short time. But, by 1382 the wealthy oligarchy, led by the Albizzi family, was back in control, which it maintained until 1434, when Cosimo de'Medici (d. 1464) returned from exile.

Cosimo de'Medici held public office for only three terms of two months each, but in effect he was in complete control as the dictator of the city from 1434 to 1464: On the one hand, he was able to see to it that only names of Medici supporters got into the election bags, and that enemies of his regime had their taxes raised so high that they had no alternative but to move out of the city, as happened to Giannozzo Manetti. On the other hand, Cosimo spent much of his great wealth in the patronage of arts and letters, so that Florentines could be proud of their city and thank the Medici for making it so beautiful and famous. It appears to have been Cosimo's money and influence that caused the general council that had opened in Ferrara in 1438 to be moved to Florence in 1439. One of the Greek delegates was Georg Gemistos Plethon, whose lectures on Plato were important in initiating the great interest in Platonic philosophy among the Florentines. This interest led to Cosimo's patronage of Marsilio Ficino (1433–99), who later was provided with a monetary allowance and a home near the Medici Villa Careggi.

Important also in the maintenance of Cosimo's position was the successful foreign policy he pursued. In the years following his return from exile in 1434 he continued the alliance with Venice, for protection from the aggression of Filippo Maria Visconti of Milan (1412–47). But after the death of this last of the Visconti, Cosimo broke the link that had existed with Venice and allied himself with Francesco Sforza. Cosimo realized that Venice was now more of a menace than Milan. He perceived, also, that Sforza would make an excellent ally, since he would need Cosimo's financial support, whereas Venice would not. Venice soon saw the wisdom of coming to terms with Milan (Peace of Lodi, 1454) and of joining in a league with Florence and Milan. By 1455 the papacy and Naples joined with the above three states. The Italian League thus formed was able to keep out foreign invaders and maintain comparative peace within the peninsula. Historians have usually given Cosimo de'Medici chief credit for the formation and maintenance of this system, though recent studies have held that Francesco Sforza and Pope Pius II (1458–64) were equally important, if not more so, in keeping up a steadfast opposition to French interference [see V. Ilardi, "The Italian League, Francesco Sforza and Charles VII (1454–61)," in *Studies in the Renaissance,* 6 (1959) 129–166].

Cosimo had been willing to maintain his control by such indirect methods, and without changing the constitution of the city, but his grandson Lorenzo the Magnificent (d. 1492), who directed affairs after the death of his father Piero (1469), made changes assuring his dictatorial power. In 1480 Lorenzo established a Council of Seventy. This Council, which included Lorenzo and friends of the Medici, and which had the right to fill its own vacancies as they occurred, had the power to appoint committees from its own members, to handle foreign affairs, defense, internal security, and finance. Lorenzo's power became constantly more dictatorial until the time of his death. There are indications that he helped his declining financial position by tapping the treasury of the state, and there were murmurings that he dipped into various savings funds, such as the state dowry fund, which the citizens had built up.

Later Florentine Cultural Developments. Florence's later chancellors—Marsuppini, appointed in 1444, Poggio in 1453, and Benedetto Accolti in 1458—became merely ornamental, while Bartolomeo Scala, appointed in 1464, devoted himself chiefly to praising the Medici. In contrast to Salutati, who had insisted upon the importance of the active life in preference to the ascetic ideal,

Marsilio FICINO (1433–99), an ardent student of Plato and the founder of the Platonic Academy in Florence, insisted upon the superiority of the mind and spirit of man over the body and all things material. He was convinced that the farther behind the mind can leave the body, the more perfect it is. As man goes about his intellectual activities, studying the liberal arts, astronomy, music, and poetry, "in all these arts the mind of man despises the service of the body, since the mind is able at times, and can even now begin, to live without the help of the body" (tr. J. L. Burroughs, in Ross and McLaughlin 387–392). PICO DELLA MIRANDOLA (1463–94) was a member of this group in Florence, but his interests did not stop with Platonism or Neoplatonism; he was interested also in Aristotle as well as in Arabic and Hebraic works. Because of his conviction of the unity of truth, he believed that apparently contradictory philosophies really share in a common truth. Paralleling Ficino's emphasis upon the spirit, Pico explains, in his *Oration of the Dignity of Man,* that man is the only creature whose life is determined not by nature, but by his own free choice. Ficino's desire to get away from the material is probably best reflected in the paintings of Sandro Botticelli (d. 1510), with his stress upon unembodied line and movement (see Berenson 111–112).

THE PAPACY AND THE RENAISSANCE

The Renaissance confronted the papacy with a difficult political problem: the aggressive expansion of the nearby Italian states would be achieved at the expense of the Papal States, unless adequate means of defense could be found by the militarily weak popes. In this crisis some popes resorted to means that were too much like those in vogue at the time and which have been labeled "Machiavellian."

Nicholas V. The cultural development of the Renaissance presented a much more subtle danger and one that was not immediately apparent. NICHOLAS V (1447–55) was a leading patron of Renaissance humanists and artists. Understandably, he considered that the center of the religious world should look the part and should also be the center of the cultural world. His wholesale patronage, however, resulted in his bringing of certain humanists into the papal service whose personal lives and writings left much to be desired on moral grounds. Among them was Lorenzo Valla mentioned above. In his dialogue *De voluptate,* Leonardo Bruni defended the Stoic point of view; Antonio Beccadelli (Panormita; 1394–1471), author of the immoral *Hermaphroditus,* defended the Epicurean view; while Niccolò de'Niccoli (d. 1437), the famous collector of manuscripts, defended the Christian view. Niccoli's defense of the Christian view won out in the debate, but Valla presented the Epicurean view so vividly that some have considered that it represented his personal belief. If this work is read together with Valla's *De professione religiosorum,* in which he attacks the whole idea of monasticism, it appears that Valla's position is that whatever comes from nature is good and praiseworthy. On the other hand, he considered continence unnatural and therefore wrong. He seems to have considered pleasure man's highest good.

Immediate Successors of Nicholas V. Ludwig von Pastor considered that within the Renaissance there were two tendencies, the Christian and the pagan (*Geschichte der Päpste* 1:14–15), and he emphasized the fact that despite the immorality, obscene literature, and Machiavellian diplomacy of the age there were also a great many remarkable saints. PIUS II (1458–64) understood the pagan tendency in the movement better than had Nicholas V, who had been something of a dilettante; Pius II had himself been a leading humanist writer. Consequently, Pius was not quite so lavish in his patronage. Under PAUL II (1464–71) some of the worst pagan aspects of the movement began to appear in the Roman Academy, led by Pomponius Laetus. Paul understandably looked upon this development with disfavor, and in the quarrel that resulted, a political conspiracy was planned and was said to include a plot to murder the Pope. After discovery of the plot, however, Pomponius Laetus and Platina were arrested.

SIXTUS IV (1471–84) has been criticized because of his extensive NEPOTISM. Actually, it was imperative for him to gain control of the cities throughout the Papal States that were held by local despots who allied themselves with enemies of the papacy at will. It seemed to Sixtus that his only safe course was to install his nephews in such cities. When Lorenzo de'Medici, who was interested in expansion toward the Adriatic, tried to interfere, the Pazzi conspiracy of 1478 to overthrow the Medici was planned by a nephew of the Pope, but with the Pope's knowledge. Pastor provided ample documentation to prove that Sixtus directed that murder should not be employed, but Giuliano, the brother of Lorenzo, was nevertheless killed.

Alexander VI. Innocent was followed by the worst of the Renaissance popes, ALEXANDER VI (1492–1503). The immorality of his personal life is indisputable. It was Alexander VI's ruthless, immoral son, Cesare Borgia, whom MACHIAVELLI (1469–1527) praised in *The Prince.* Machiavelli maintained that a prince who tries to be good in the midst of so many who are not good is bound to fail. Hence he warned that a prince who insists on keeping his promises will not be successful. Some historians have attempted to explain away what Machiavelli wrote in *The Prince,* claiming that he meant it only as a satire, and that

his true, democratic thought is to be found in his *Discourses on the First Decade of Livy.* Actually, the same basic principles are to be found in the *Discourses.* For example, in book 1, ch. 9, he praises Romulus for killing his brother, insisting that it should be put down as a general rule that "reprehensible actions may be justified by their effects, and when the effect is good, as it was in the case of Romulus, it always justifies the action."

Julius II and Leo X. The last great popes in the Renaissance tradition were JULIUS II (1503–13) and LEO X (1513–21). Despite the brilliance of their reigns from the cultural point of view, the Renaissance in Italy was beginning to be overshadowed by developments elsewhere in Europe. The sack of Rome in 1527 and the momentous happenings north of the Alps marked the beginning of a new age, especially in politics and religion.

RENAISSANCE IN SPAIN AND NORTH OF THE ALPS

The Renaissance in the strict sense was an Italian movement. In its spread to Spain and to the countries north of the Alps, it encountered new political, cultural, and religious conditions and accordingly took on a somewhat different aspect. It should be observed also that it was the later Italian Renaissance that exercised the major influence outside Italy.

Printing and the Renaissance. The art of printing was developed in Germany *c.* 1450 and therefore antedated the impact of the Renaissance in that area. The new art was soon carried into Italy, and presses were established at Rome, Venice, and other cities. It was not received with any great enthusiasm by certain humanists at first, and was opposed, understandably, by the professional scribes, but long before 1500 the printed book replaced the manuscript as the normal form of book production. The invention of printing created a revolution in the dissemination of learning, the effects of which would be difficult to exaggerate. The spread of Renaissance writings and ideas within Italy and outside Italy was now rapid and effective and the whole program of education at all levels was put on a new foundation. A careful study of the printed books before 1500 reveals concretely both the spread of the new learning and, at the same time, the vitality of the late medieval cultural tradition.

Spain. The Renaissance crossed the Pyrenees when such Italian humanists as Pomponio Montovano, Lucio Marineo Siculo (d. 1533), and Pietro Martire d'Anghiera (d. 1526) were welcomed as lecturers in Castile. Owing to the inclusion of the Low countries in the Spanish empire, there were intimate contacts also between Spanish humanism and northern humanism. Enthusiasm for the new learning produced the great scholar Antonio de Nebrija (1444–1522). The Complutensian Polyglot Bible was prepared at the University of Alcalà under the patronage of Cardinal Francisco XIMÉNEZ DE CISNEROS. Juan Luis VIVES of Valencia challenged the medieval dialecticians and composed new rules of literary style and influential theories of education.

Renaissance in the North. France and England, although among the first kingdoms to feel their growth into nationhood, largely as a result of the 100 Years' War, resisted humanism and other features of the Renaissance longer then other areas of Northern Europe. Like Germany, they were governed by a rural nobility that clung to the traditions of courtly chivalry. However, clerics and officials of the crown in their visits to Italy occasionally brought back an enthusiasm for the new learning. Hence, some humanists were invited into the employ of wealthy patrons or into the schools and universities. But it was not until the last quarter of the 15th century that cultural contacts were extensive. Besides literary interest in the classics, the northern Renaissance developed a practical and pedagogical character that included a critical study of the manuscripts of Scripture, patristic literature, and a corresponding impatience with scholastic method. Moreover, they were strong advocates of ecclesiastical reform.

England. In England, William Grocyn, student of the two greatest Greek stylists, Angelo Poliziano (1454–94) and Demetrius Chalcondyles (1424–1511), brought his own knowledge of Greek to a perfection that won praise even from the refugee scholars from Constantinople. The lectures of John COLET (1467?–1519) at Oxford witness the new insistence upon textual studies and historical exegesis of the New Testament, especially of St. Paul's letters, rather than upon the prevailing allegorical interpretation. Colet founded St. Paul's School in London as a center of the new theology. What Colet was doing for theology, Thomas LINACRE (1460?–1524) achieved in medicine. His Greek he had learned in the household of Lorenzo the Magnificent, where he was tutored with Giovanni, the future Pope Leo X. He translated some of his treatises of the Greek physicians, especially Galen, into Latin and later founded the Royal College of Physicians. It was Linacre who taught Greek to St. Thomas MORE, whose own mastery of classical and English prose produced some of the finest examples of Renaissance writing, especially the *Utopia,* where wit and gravity vie in an indictment of society.

Germany. The decentralized political structure of Germany favored the academic rivalry out of which several centers of humanism emerged. The Rhenish scholar Rodolphus Agricola and Johann von DALBERG, Bishop of Worms, promoted a classical revival at Heidelberg. Lud-

wig Dringenberg (d. 1490) made Schlettstadt the humanistic axis of the Upper Rhine. Nürnberg, long known as a trading market, was becoming the "Florence of Germany" through the scholarly reputations of Herman (1410–85) and Hartman (1440–1514) Schedel and the patronage of Willibald PIRKHEIMER. The generous favor of Emperor Maximilian I led to the formation of literary academies by Conrad Celtis and Johannes Cuspinian and the rise of such scholars as Conrad Peutinger, leading antiquary and epigraphist of Augsburg. Jakob Wimpfeling of Schlettstadt, the "Schoolmaster of Germany," was surrounded by a growing circle of scholars at Strassburg, as was Maternus Pistoris (d. 1534) at Erfurt.

Investigation of Latin and Greek texts soon included scriptural and exegetical writing. Johannes TRITHEMIUS, Abbot of Sponheim, among his copious writings, dealt with the Fathers and with Scripture; Johann REUCHLIN of Pforzheim (1455–1522), professor at Ingolstadt and Tübingen, traced philological errors in earlier transcriptions of the Bible. Ridicule was heaped upon the techniques of the scholastic theologians in the *Epistolae obscurorum virorum* and in the *Narrenschiff* of Sebastian Brandt.

ERASMUS of Rotterdam was the greatest and most influential representative of the new learning in the north. Outstanding as a classical and patristic scholar, he made important contributions in the textual study of the Bible. He was a severe critic of the contemporary Church and of scholastic theology, and an ardent advocate of reform, but he regarded Luther's revolt as a calamity and refused to support it.

France. Guillaume Budé (1468–1540), a friend of Erasmus and distinguished Hellenist and specialist in antiquities, was a founder of the new learning in France. He was appointed royal librarian by Francis I and was largely responsible for the founding of the Collège de France (1530) by that king. Patristic and scriptural studies were given a new and critical direction by Lefèlvre d'Étaples (c. 1450–1537) and other scholars influenced by him.

The Renaissance in Recent Historical Work. Scholars continue to explore the cultural, artistic, and intellectual legacies of the Italian Renaissance and the national movements it helped produce in Northern Europe. In recent decades historians have returned again to debate humanism's precise influence upon the cultural life of Renaissance cities. Following the work of Hans Baron some have stressed the decisive role that "civic humanism" played in shaping the values of Renaissance culture. Others have seen humanism's penetration of the world of the Renaissance as more problematic and diffuse. The researches of Paul Kristeller, Charles Trinkaus, and others have stressed that the *studia humanitatis* was primarily an educational and rhetorical movement. As such, they have stressed that humanism's influence was often more conservative and traditional than dynamic or modern. Despite these ongoing debates about the precise character of Renaissance humanism, few would deny that the Renaissance did produce new approaches to art, literature, learning, and politics. Above all, a new view of humankind and its place and role in the world seems to have been one of the era's most distinctive contributions to the modern world.

Bibliography: W. K. FERGUSON, *The Renaissance in Historical Thought* (Boston 1948); *Europe in Transition: 1300–1520* (Boston 1963). P. O. KRISTELLER, *Renaissance Thought* (New York 1961). H. BARON, *The Crisis of the Early Italian Renaissance: Civic Humanism and Republican Liberty in an Age of Classicism and Tyranny,* 2 v. (Princeton 1955). E. GARIN, *L'Umanesimo italiano: Filosofia et vita civile nel Rinascimento* (Bari 1952). G. TOFFANIN, *History of Humanism,* tr. E. GIANTURCO (New York 1954). H. RÖSSLER, *Europa im Zeitalter von Renaissance, Reformation und Gegenreformation, 1450–1650* (Munich 1956). D. HAY, *The Italian Renaissance in Its Historical Background* (Cambridge, England. 1961). G. A. BRUCKER, ed., *Renaissance Italy* (New York 1958). J. B. ROSS and M. M. MCLAUGHLIN, eds., *The Portable Renaissance Reader* (New York 1953). E. CASSIRER et al., eds., *The Renaissance Philosophy of Man* (Chicago 1948). E. EMERTON, *Humanism and Tyranny: Studies in the Italian Trecento* (Cambridge, MA 1925). M. P. GILMORE, *The World of Humanism, 1453–1517* (New York 1952). F. CHABOD, *Machiavelli and the Renaissance,* tr. D. MOORE (Cambridge, MA 1958). B. HATHAWAY, *The Age of Criticism: The Late Renaissance in Italy* (Ithaca, NY 1962). E. F. JACOB, ed., *Italian Renaissance Studies* (New York 1960). G. SAITTA, *Il pensiero italiano nell' Umanesimo e nel Rinascimento,* 3 v. (Bologna 1949–51). E. F. RICE, *The Renaissance Idea of Wisdom* (Cambridge, MA 1958). B. BERENSON, *The Italian Painters of the Renaissance* (5th rev. ed. New York 1959). A. RENAUDET, *Humanisme et Renaissance* (Geneva 1958). R. WEISS, *The Dawn of Humanism in Italy* (London 1947); *Il primo secolo dell'Umanesimo* (Rome 1949). B. L. ULLMAN, *Studies in the Italian Renaissance* (Rome 1955). T. HELTON, ed., *The Renaissance: A Reconsideration of the Theories and Interpretations of the Age* (Madison, WI 1961). A. SAPORI, *L'età' della rinascita, secoli XIII–XVI* (Milan 1958). L. PASTOR, *The History of the Popes from the Close of the Middle Ages,* v.1–3 (London–St. Louis 1938–61). R. AUBENAS and R. RICARD, *L'Église et la Renaissance, 1449–1517* (*Histoire de l' église depuis les origines jusqu'à nos jours* v.15; 1951). G. BRUCKER, *The Civic World of Early Renaissance Florence* (Princeton 1977). L. MARTINES, *Power and Imagination* (New York 1979). A. RABIL, JR., *Renaissance Humanism,* 3 v. (Philadelphia 1988). C. NAUERT, JR., *Humanism and the Culture of Renaissance Europe* (Cambrige 1995). J. SIEGEL *Rhetoric and Philosophy in Renaissance Humanism* (Princeton 1968). C. TRINKAUS *In Our Image and Likeness* (Chicago 1970).

[W. W. WILKINSON]

RENAISSANCE PHILOSOPHY

While historians continue to debate when the Renaissance began or whether it began at all, there is no doubt that the style of philosophy was rather different in 1600 than it had been in the middle of the 14th century. There is no single philosopher of this time who compares

in importance to Plato, Aristotle, Augustine, and Aquinas, or Descartes, Hume, and Kant; yet the period is significant as the time of transition when the medieval world ceased to be and the modern secular world began. The word secular is important. The leading thinkers of the Renaissance were for the most part believing, practicing Christians; nevertheless, they contributed to the development of a way of thinking not opposed to theology but no longer in the service of theology. Their problems were still the traditional problems of the Christian tradition: God, man's immortality, morals, predestination, and free choice; but their treatment indicated a difference of style that was no longer medieval, yet not quite modern. While they must be studied as individuals, it can be conceded that, if they have anything in common, it is their HUMANISM.

As P. O. Kristeller has often noted, the term "humanism" has been used in a wide, not too discriminating sense, whereby every appreciation of any human value has been stamped humanistic. Actually the word "humanism" is derived from the phrase *studia humanitatis,* which refers to the study of the humanities; and in the slang of the 15th century a student of the humanities was a *humanista*. Five subjects especially composed the educational curriculum of the *humanista*: grammar, rhetoric, poetry, history, and moral philosophy. Such a course of study was not entirely unlike that of the cathedral schools of the Middle Ages, but there were differences. The *humanista* was less concerned with the logic, natural science, and metaphysics of the scholastic curriculum; and with the passing of time, increasing attention was paid to the classical authors of Greece and Rome, whose works served both as models of expression and as objects of analysis. In this respect Francesco Petrarch is considered a leading figure of the Italian Renaissance.

Petrarch. Although he knew little Greek, PETRARCH was aware of Rome's debt to Greek learning. He was an enthusiastic manuscript hunter, and he integrated his love of classical learning with his own hunger for fame. Still he was religious, and in his reflections in his *Ascent of Mont Ventoux* he reprimanded himself in Augustinian fashion for his weakness and vanities. As a transitional figure from the medieval to the Renaissance world, he forecasts the shape of trends to be developed by others.

Valla. If Petrarch may be considered the most outstanding humanist of the 14th century, Lorenzo VALLA would be a strong contender for that title in the 15th. Valla's wide-ranging contributions to history, philology, and rhetoric mark him as a Renaissance man of many abilities: he wrote *De elegantia linguae latinae* (1444), exposed the so-called DONATION OF CONSTANTINE as a fake, translated Herodotus and Thucydides, and applied some of the newer philological techniques to the study of Scripture. In addition he made worthwhile contributions to philosophy with his dialogues *On Pleasure* (1431), in which the Christian position wins out but the Epicurean view is treated with sympathy; *Dialectical Disputations* (1439), in which his rejection of the current Aristotelian school is apparent; and *On Free Will* (1435–43), in which the key problem of God's foreknowledge, human freedom, and predestination is explored. Later, in their disputes on the same topic, Erasmus and Luther were to refer to Valla's treatment of the question. Valla held that God's foreknowledge and man's freedom were not incompatible, but when pressed that God's knowledge expressed His predestination, he retreated from the question as an unresolvable mystery.

Cusa. Cardinal NICHOLAS OF CUSA combined in his life work the activity of a papal diplomat busy with the problems of Church councils and the contemplation of a mystic philosopher. His thought on God and the universe reflects the Neoplatonic tradition previously expressed by JOHN SCOTUS ERIGENA and Meister ECKHART, which Cusa integrated with a mathematical imagery that dwells on the paradoxes of the infinite. The title of his main work, *De docta ignorantia* (1440), indicates the combining of opposites that is his key to understanding reality. Just as a straight line can be regarded as the circumference of a circle of infinite radius, so God is the maximum and minimum of all things. Cusa presents something more than the medieval negative theology; he breaks with the Aristotelian categories, which judged the universe to be a closed sphere with the earth at the center. For him the universe is an infinite sphere whose circumference is nowhere and whose center is everywhere. While he made no scientific discovery himself, his high ecclesiastical rank and his emancipation from the categories of contemporary scholasticism encouraged his readers in the next century, e.g., Copernicus, to express themselves in ways that did lead to scientific breakthroughs. Though he wrote many treatises, Cusa is most famous for his expression of learned ignorance.

Ficino. Renaissance PLATONISM centers around Florence and the gentle figure of Marsilio FICINO. Trained in the humanities, philosophy, and medicine, Ficino was encouraged in his research on Plato by Cosimo de' Medici, who donated a villa at Careggi for the "Platonic Academy." After translating from Greek to Latin the writings of Hermes Trismegistus (1463), Ficino began the translation of Plato's *Dialogues,* which he completed before 1469, the year he wrote his commentary on the *Symposium.* He later translated some writings of Porphyry and Proclus, as well as of Pseudo-Dionysius and Plotinus. In addition to the tremendous contribution Ficino made to Western learning by making so much Platonic thought

"Peter Paul and Philip Rubens with Justus Lipsius and John van Woverius," painting by Peter Paul Rubens. Also known as "The Four Philosophers."

available in Latin, he presented his own philosophy, a blend of Christian wisdom and Platonism, in his *Theologia Platonica,* which he wrote between 1469 and 1474. Ficino attempted an elaborate description of a hierarchical universe ranging from God to primary matter and focusing on man at the center. Preoccupied with man's immortality, Ficino stressed that man's happiness comes when he is freed from his mortal body and attains God. He recognized that the Christian doctrine of the resurrection of the body will return the soul to a temperate immortal body far different from the one in which it now dwells. This argument for immortality made a profound impression on some of the 16th-century philosophers and is thought to have been influential in leading to the pronouncement of personal immortality as a dogma by the Lateran Council in 1513. Ficino's theory of friendship, his doctrine of Platonic love, was influential, especially in Renaissance literature. Friends should be united in a mutual respect that has its binding element in their common love of God. The true lover loves the other for the sake of God. Here is reflected the Christian Platonism of Ficino, who was honored with a monument in the cathedral of Florence after his death.

Pico della Mirandola. Although associated with Ficino's Platonic Academy, Count Giovanni PICO DELLA

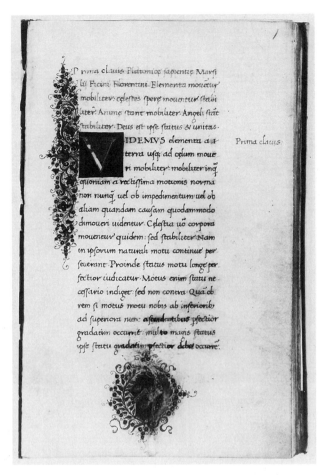

Manuscript folio, first page, from "Claves Platonicae Sapientiae," c. 1480, by Marsilio Ficino.

MIRANDOLA was more interested in discovering the truth that underlay or was common to Platonism, Aristotelianism, ARABIAN PHILOSOPHY, and the Jewish CABALA. Pico believed that different systems expressed different parts of the truth. By studying mystical Jewish writings and attempting to show their harmony with Christian thought, he prepared the way for the studies of J. REUCHLIN. In his famous *Oration,* prepared for delivery on what was to be a debate on some 900 theses he had proposed, Pico began by a special affirmation of the dignity of man and went on to stress the harmony among his philosophical predecessors. Whereas Ficino was more committed to Platonism, Pico appreciated Aristotle as well and defended his scholastic interpreters. Though Pico did not achieve his ideal of the intellectual reconciliation of Plato and Aristotle, later generations have honored him for his work in philosophy and Scripture commentary, the *Heptaplus,* an analysis of Genesis.

Pomponazzi. Just as contemporary philosophy resists characterization by a word or by one movement, so too Renaissance philosophy is a strand composed of many threads. While Platonism was enjoying a revival through the work of Ficino, the universities remained the stronghold of a secular ARISTOTELIANISM concentrated on its natural and biological aspects. Various schools of interpretation flourished side by side: AVERROISM, THOMISM, SCOTISM, and Alexandrianism. In such a milieu Pietro POMPONAZZI prided himself on his attempt to express the real Aristotle. Thus, while accepting the Church's teaching on personal immortality, he argued in *On Immortality* (1516) that such a doctrine could not be established on philosophical, i.e., Aristotelian, principles. The intellectual soul's need for phantasms precluded it from ever functioning as a separated soul after death. To the objection that mortality required immortality, Pomponazzi replied, like the Stoics, that virtue was its own reward and evil its own punishment. Pomponazzi was concerned also with predestination and free choice; he attempted to analyze these questions in a naturalistic fashion that led him to conclusions different from those of his professed faith. He took care, however, to accept as a matter of faith the teachings of the Church; but this did not prevent the condemnation of his work. Something of the vitality of Renaissance Aristotelianism is to be seen in the controversies in which such philosophers as Giovanni Crisostomo JAVELLI, Tommaso de Vio CAJETAN, Gasparo CONTARINI, Alexander Achillini (1463–1512), and Agostino NIFO participated.

Telesio. While the Aristotelian tradition flourished in 16th-century Italy, it continued to engender reactions against itself. Such philosophers as Telesio, Patrizi, and Bruno repudiated the shortcomings they believed they saw in Aristotle and attempted to correct his mistakes with their own analyses. In *De rerum natura* (Naples 1565) Bernardino TELESIO rejected matter and form and tried to explain nature in terms of matter and force, hot and cold. He asserted that man has a material spirit that vivifies his body and, in addition, a soul created by God and infused into the body. He attempted to break with Aristotle and build another natural philosophy on an empirical basis.

Patrizi. Whereas Telesio's interests were physical and biological, the interests of Francesco Patrizi were literary and mathematical. He wrote treatises on history, *Della historia* (1560), and on poetics, *Della poetica* (1586), and lectured in Rome on Platonic philosophy. He translated Philoponus's commentary on Aristotle's *Metaphysics* (1583), Proclus's *Elements of Theology* and *Elementatio physica* (1583), and various treatises attributed to Hermes Trismegistus. He edited in Latin the so-called *Theology of Aristotle* (1591), accepting as genuine this work judged by Thomas Aquinas to be Neoplatonic. In mathematics he wrote works on geometry and on physical space, *Nova de universis philosophia* (1591). In general, Patrizi preferred Plato to Aristotle, and his achievement in having a chair of Platonic philosophy in Rome went against the contemporary trend at the universities.

Bruno. The tragic and dramatic circumstances surrounding the death of Giordano BRUNO, executed for heresy after a long investigation by the Inquisition, have made him a martyr to the cause of free thought. "One of the leading and most influential thinkers of the Renaissance" (Copleston), he combined Cusa's Neoplatonism and the Hermetic tradition with the implications of the new astronomy of Copernicus into a philosophy that approached pantheism but never bluntly asserted it. For Bruno there was an infinite number of solar systems giving one infinite universe in which God vivified the matter as the soul principle vivifies the body. Bruno anticipated Spinoza by making God immanent in the material substance of the universe yet somehow transcendent as its cause. In this system man loses his substantiality, except in the sense that he is a particular manifestation of the infinity of God. In his reaction against Aristotle, Bruno anticipated developments in modern philosophy and science, but it is doubtful that he caused them.

Agricola. What Petrarch was to Italian humanism, Rodolphus Agricola was to German humanism. More of a rhetorician than a philosopher, Agricola preferred Cicero to Aristotle; in *De inventione dialectica* (1479) he stressed discovery rather than judging. Along with his contributions to educational reform, he concerned himself with history and translations. Sacred Scripture was his interest when he died at age 41, a religious person faithful to his Church and unaffected by events on the eve of the Reformation.

Reuchlin. Johann Reuchlin, called Capnion by his associates, is regarded as the seed from which the strong tradition of Hebrew studies in Germany grew. A thorough humanist, Reuchlin became intrigued with the magic symbolism of the Jewish CABALA while studying in Italy. Like Pico, he sought to use this tradition in support of Christianity, combining number wisdom with the strong Neoplatonic tendencies he inherited from Nicholas of Cusa. When overly zealous Christians proposed destroying Hebrew books in order to promote the conversion of the Jews, Reuchlin bravely defended the value of Hebrew knowledge in *Angenspeigl* (1511). Both Luther and Erasmus appreciated Reuchlin's learning; but when the crisis of the Lutheran break came toward the end of his life, he chose to remain Catholic rather than join the reformers.

Erasmus. Desiderius ERASMUS is rightly regarded as the greatest figure of the Northern Renaissance, but his

Bernardino Telesio.

contribution to philosophy was slight. A tremendous worker at humanistic studies, he ardently applied his learning to the service of religion with an edition of the New Testament in Greek, editions of Church Fathers, such as St. Jerome, and a moral treatise, *Enchiridion militis christiani* (The Handbook of the Christian Soldier, 1501). His collection of classical proverbs, *Adagia*, was a best seller, and his *Praise of Folly* (1509) was both a tribute to his friend Thomas More and a satiric comment on the foibles and failings of the churchmen of his day. Because he had been caustic toward various religious practices that detracted from Christian piety as he envisioned it, many expected him to favor Martin Luther at the time of the latter's break with Rome. But Erasmus attacked Luther's denial of free choice in *Diatribe de libero arbitrio* (1524).

Reflecting somewhat the position of St. Thomas Aquinas on free choice, Erasmus went beyond that and argued that, since man really cannot settle these matters of freedom and foreknowledge, he must assume freedom, because the consequences of assuming determinism would be disastrous. The general public, never too well behaved in the first place, would abandon all moral restraint if it no longer feared being held responsible for its actions. Erasmus then struggled with difficult scriptural passages that seemed to indicate that God "hardened the hearts'' of some and caused others to repent. This work provoked Luther to reply with his polemical *De servo arbitrio* (1525). Erasmus is not to be measured in terms of his philosophical ability but by the scholarship he accomplished.

Paracelsus. One of the thinkers most difficult to classify in 16th-century thought is the strange Swiss physician-philosopher who called himself Philippus Aureolus Paracelsus. He was born Theophrastus Bombastus von Hohenheim and was trained by his father in medicine, alchemy, and astrology. His bombastic writings challenged accepted medical knowledge but mixed magic and the occult with an appreciation of differences in chemical compounds and elements and their effect upon health. He is thought to have served as one of the models for Faust.

Böhme. Jakob BÖHME, German mystic and philosophical theologian, attempted through his devotional writings to resolve the problem of good and evil in reality. He was remarkably productive, writing books on religious devotion (*The Way to Christ*) and works of speculative philosophy that sought to understand how the multiplicity of the world arose out of the unity of God (*On the Three Principles,* 1619). Later philosophers, as diverse as A. Schopenhauer, M. Heidegger, and N. A. Berdîaev, acknowledge his influence; and such church groups as the Quakers are part of his legacy in religious practice.

Machiavelli. Though scholars vary in their estimates of the political morality of Niccolò MACHIAVELLI, they agree on his significance as a political thinker. When a change of political power in Florence forced Machiavelli into early retirement, the world of humanistic learning gained a reporter, historian, and shrewd analyzer of political power. In his commentary on Livy's History, *Discorsi sopra la prima deca di Tito Livio* (1515–19?), Machiavelli combined a sense of the appropriate historical anecdote with an ability to delineate the political troubles of contemporary Italy. He longed for his country to achieve the national unity that was growing in France, England, and Spain, but he grieved over the impossibility of this task so long as the Church ruled the central section of Italy. His social comments were caustic and cynical, but his patriotism is unquestioned. In *Il Principe* (written 1513, first published 1532) Machiavelli provided future rulers with a handbook that described the technique of grasping and retaining power in predatory society. While the book is in the tradition of the medieval treatises *On the Governance of Rulers,* it is unlike them in its frankly amoral character. J. Maritain argues that the techniques of *Il Principe* can promise only short-term success and its ruthless pragmatism cannot be the basis of promoting

a stable society, for Machiavelli's *virtù* is an aggressive daring, a talent for opportunism, not a form of justice.

In all his writings, the political treatises, the *Art of War,* and *Florentine Histories,* Machiavelli regards human nature as brutal, avaricious, power hungry, and collectively cowardly. He appears to be echoing in the political sphere the corrupted man of the Reformers.

Bodin. While Machiavelli is associated with amorality in political thinking, the French political philosopher Jean Bodin is associated with the reapplication of natural law to political questions. Living and writing in the context of civil wars arising out of the post-Reformation religious disputes, Bodin strongly emphasized the need of a sovereign power as the ultimate source of authority in society, but for him the sovereign remained subject to moral law. In *Six livres de la République* (1576) Bodin maintained that the family is the foundation of society and that certain fundamental rights of liberty and property belong to the subject. Bodin reflected also on the nature of history in *Methodus ad facilem historiarum cognitionem* (1566). This attention to the nature of historical writing and study is a mark of the emerging modern mind in contrast to the medieval chronicler, who was not so time conscious. Another modern note was the element of biblical criticism Bodin displayed in the colloquy *Heptaplomeres* (written toward the end of his life but not published until 1841), wherein a Catholic, a Calvinist, a Lutheran, a Muslim, a Jew, a Deist, and an Epicurean discuss religious questions, seeking some common denominator. Their agreement lies in rejecting atheism; tolerance of religious differences is implied to be the solution to the divisions plaguing the sixteenth century.

Vives. Juan Luis VIVES was the Spanish contemporary of Erasmus and, like him, was concerned with education and man. He is famous for a functionalist approach to psychology. In *De anima et vita libri tres* (Basel 1538), he sought to study man's actions rather than to follow the classical writers who explained man's nature. His analysis of memory and forgetfulness represents a contribution to Renaissance psychology. Like Erasmus, Vives employed his humanistic gifts in the service of Christian learning, for example, in *De veritate fidei Christiane* (1543).

Ramus. Pierre de la Ramée, or Peter RAMUS, is noted for his opposition to Aristotle and his criticism of scholasticism. His thesis at the College of Navarre was ''Everything Aristotle Taught Is False'' (1536), and in *Aristotelicae animadversiones* (1543) and *Dialecticae partitiones* (1543) he revised the approach to the teaching of logic. Ramus emphasized logic as part of the arts of expression; and while it is said that his dialectic cannot be taken seriously by any competent logician, his influence on the teaching of rhetoric and dialectic in the late 16th and the 17th century, in Europe and then in America, was tremendous. Hundreds of editions of his *Dialecticae* were published, and it is through his influence as a textbook author that he is significant rather than from any intrinsic merit in his system. Appointed by Francis I in 1551 to be regius professor of eloquence and philosophy (a title he designed himself), he enjoyed the life of controversy he engendered. However, becoming a Protestant sometime after 1562, he suffered disqualification from his official position. He was murdered in the rioting of the St. Bartholomew's Day Massacre.

Lipsius. While Pomponazzi and Montaigne used Stoic themes in their philosophy, Justus LIPSIUS (or Joest Lips, as this Flemish humanist and philologist was also called) is considered the most thoroughgoing student and expositor of STOICISM in the Renaissance. Born a Catholic, Lipsius accepted Lutheranism and Calvinism at times when the conditions of his employment as a teacher required it. He returned to Catholicism during his later years as a professor at Louvain, but some of his contemporaries found it difficult to forgive what they regarded as religious inconstancy. The truth seems to be that Lipsius was not theologically minded; rather, he concentrated on the exposition of Stoic thought integrated with the Christianity he had inherited.

In *De Constantia* (1584), *Politicorum* (1589), *Manuductio ad stoicam philosophiam* (1604), and *Physiologia stoicorum* (1604), Lipsius showed his growth in the understanding of Stoic belief, which, as J. Saunders has shown, he reconciled with Christianity: "Living according to Nature came to mean living according to Right Reason, or according to Virtue, and hence to mean seeking after God, who himself becomes the all important Object or End." In situations where Stoic practice tended to conflict with Christianity, for example, in accepting suicide, Lipsius preferred the Christian position. In his revival of Stoicism, Lipsius greatly influenced Montaigne, P. CHARRON, and Francis BACON.

Montaigne. Michel Eyquem de MONTAIGNE is almost a distillation of Renaissance philosophy. While only in his late thirties, he retired to his estate in Bordeaux to study himself. He published his reflections, observations, and his conversations about his reading and experience under the title *Essais* (3 v. 1582–88); these thoughts represent the reaction of a learned and cultivated man to the confusion and suffering brought on by the Reformation and the wars of religion that followed it. Montaigne expressed the Renaissance's preoccupation with man; "I study myself more than any other subject; that's my metaphysics; that's my physics." In his relaxed musings, he expressed the humanistic learning he had acquired from his boyhood by calling on a wide range of classical authors as witnesses in support of his insights. But the controversies of the time made him skeptical of the conflicting philosophies, and he rejected their dogmatism. His motto *Que scay-je?* (What do I know?) states his philosophy; in *The Apology for Raymond Sebond* he brought to bear his most critical comments to show the poverty of human reason and the uncertainty resulting from the conflict of authorities about the fundamental problems of life. Montaigne was no revolutionary: "Wherefore it will become you better to confine yourself to the accustomed routine, whatever it is, than to fly headlong into this unbridled license"—given man's inability to know what is better, he should conserve what he has. As Gilson remarked, Montaigne's humility is the wisdom of the acceptance of oneself. This is an indication also of his Stoicism, and the tranquillity it promises is the Pyrrhonian *ataraxia*.

The essential characteristics of Renaissance philosophy consist in its being a period of transition. By the time the thinkers surveyed in this article had exerted their influence, medieval thought had come to its end and the setting was provided for the beginning of modern philosophy.

See Also: PHILOSOPHY, HISTORY OF, 4; ARISTOTELIANISM; PLATONISM.

Bibliography: P. O. KRISTELLER, *Eight Philosophers of the Italian Renaissance* (Stanford, Calif. 1964). L. W. SPITZ, *The Religious Renaissance of the German Humanists* (Cambridge, Mass. 1963). F. C. COPELSTON, *History of Philosophy,* v. 3. (Westminster, Md. 1953). J. D. COLLINS, *A History of Modern European Philosophy* (Milwaukee, Wis. 1954), on the Renaissance background with bibliog. A. MAURER, *Medieval Philosophy* (New York 1962), studies on Ficino, Pico, and Pomponazzi. É. H. GILSON and T. D. LANGAN, *Modern Philosophy: Descartes to Kant* (New York 1963), on Montaigne. J. H. RANDALL, *The Career of Philosophy from the Middle Ages to the Enlightenment* (New York 1962). A. R. CAPONIGRI, *Renaissance to the Romantic Age (A History of Western Philosophy* v. 3; Chicago, Ill. 1963). F. CHABOD, *Machiavelli and the Renaissance,* tr. D. MOORE (New York 1965), with extensive bibliog. chapter. J. O. RIEDL, ed., *A Catalogue of Renaissance Philosophers, 1350–1650* (Milwaukee, Wis. 1940). W. J. BOUWSMA, *The Interpretation of Renaissance Humanism* (Service Center for Teachers of History, Amer. Historical Assoc. pamphlet 18; Washington 1959). M. P. GILMORE, *The World of Humanism, 1453–1517* (New York 1952). *The Renaissance Philosophy of Man,* ed. E. CASSIRER et al. (Chicago, Ill. 1948). G. DE SANTILLANA, ed., *The Age of Adventure* (New York 1956). E. GARIN, *La cultura filosofica del Rinascimento italiano* (Florence 1961). G. SAITTA, *Il pensiero italiano nell'Umanesimo e nel Rinascimento,* 3 v. (Bologna 1949–51). R. POPKIN, *A History of Scepticism from Erasmus to Descartes* (rev. ed. New York 1964). J. SAUNDERS, *Justus Lipsius: The Philosophy of Renaissance Stoicism* (New York 1955). F. A. YATES, *Giordano Bruno and the Hermetic Tradition* (Chicago 1964). D. M. FRAME, *Montaigne: A Biography* (New York 1965).

[D. J. FITZGERALD]

RENAN, JOSEPH ERNEST

Orientalist and philosopher; b. Trégiuer, Brittany, France, Feb. 28, 1823; d. Paris, Oct. 2, 1892. When Ernest (as he was ordinarily called) was only five years old, the corpse of his fisherman father was found on the seashore at Esqui. Thereafter the youth owed much to the devoted interest that his sister Henriette, 12 years his senior, took in him. Through her intervention, after his early education in the parochial school at Regier, he received a scholarship to study at the Sulpician minor seminary of St. Nicolas da Chardonnet, then recently founded by F. DUPANLOUP. He continued his studies for the priesthood at the major seminaries of Issy and Saint Sulpice, Paris. In the latter place he studied Scripture, Hebrew, and Syriac under A. M. Le Hir. But in 1845 he gave up the idea of becoming a priest. After a short stay at the Oratorian college in Stanislas, he took the post of prefect of studies at the school of M. Crouzet. There he began his lifelong friendship with one of the students who was to become an illustrious chemist, P. E. M. Berthelot. Meanwhile, he continued his university studies and received the degree of fellowship in philosophy.

In 1848 he published his first work, the *Histoire des langues sémitique,* which won for him the Prix Volney and made him known as an Orientalist in the scientific world. It was at this time also that he wrote the *Avenir de la Science,* which, however, was not published until 1890. The period of October 1849 to June 1850 he spent on an archeological mission in Italy. In 1851 he was appointed to a post in the manuscript department of the Bibliothèque Nationale in Paris, and in 1852 he received the doctorate in literature. In 1856 he married the niece of the artist Ary Scheffer. From 1860 to 1861 he was engaged in an archeological expedition in Phoenicia. There he began his famous *Vie de Jésus* (Life of Jesus), and there also his sister Henriette, who had urged him to write this work, died. Appointed a professor of Hebrew at the Collège de France in 1862, he made bold in his opening lecture to speak of Jesus as merely ''an incomparable man.'' The scandal and protestations caused by this cost him this professorship until 1870, when, at the fall of the Empire, he was reinstated. After a second archeological expedition in the East from 1864 to 1865, he was chosen in 1879 to take the place of Claude Bernard in the Académie Française, and in 1879 he became the director of the Collège de France. His funeral, held at the expense of the state, was a purely civil affair.

Among his abundant literary production, his chief work is *L'Histoire de origines du christianisme* in seven volumes, embracing (1) *Vie de Jésus* (1863), (2) *Les Apôtres* (1868), (3) *Saint Paul* (1869), (4) *L'Anté-christ* (1873), (5) *Les Évangiles et la seconde génération chré-* tienne (1877), (6) *L'Église chrétienne,* and (7) *Marc-Aurèle et la fin du monde antique* (1881). The style of Renan's language was largely responsible for the attraction that his works held for his contemporaries and later generations; his writings are always clear and smooth, rhythmic and interesting. While he made lasting contributions as a Semitic philologist, his value as a historian and exegete is much less—mostly that of a dilettante. Dazzled by the new science of the 19th century and the novel higher criticism of the Bible, Renan exchanged his Christian faith for skepticism, rationalism, and romanticism. Although he often changed his opinions on many points, he remained steadfast on one—the denial of the supernatural, the divinity of Christ, and the existence of a transcendent God.

Bibliography: *Oeuvres complètes,* ed. H. PSICHARI, 9 v. (Paris 1947–60). J. CHAIX-RUY, *E. Renan* (Paris 1956), with full bibliog. of Renan's works. W. F. BARRY, *Ernest Renan* (New York 1905). L. F. MOTT, *Ernest Renan* (New York 1921). M. J. LAGRANGE, *Christ and Renan: A Commentary on Ernest Renan's ''The Life of Jesus,''* tr. M. WARD (New York 1928).

[A. M. MALO]

RENAUDOT, EUSÈBE

Orientalist, historian of liturgy; b. Paris, July 20, 1648; d. Paris, Sept. 1, 1720. The oldest of 14 children, and son and grandson of prominent physicians, Renaudot entered the ORATORIANS but withdrew and remained in minor orders, deeply religious and somewhat austere. With his knowledge of Syriac, Coptic, and Arabic, he combined an interest in theology and Church history. Part of his time was taken up with consultations on diplomatic affairs at the French court, and from 1680 he was editor of the *Gazette de France,* a family property by royal privilege.

Elected to the French Academy in 1689, he was 62 when he began to publish his materials on Oriental Church teaching and practice in liturgy and ritual. His *Liturgiarum orientalium collectio* (2 v. Paris 1715–16) provided the West with a large repertory of liturgical texts of the various Eastern rites in Latin translation. There is in it some mixing of Maronite and West Syrian (Jacobite) materials, and most of the liturgies have been critically studied since his day; but this work and his volumes on the *Perpetuité de la foi catholique de l'Eglise* (between 1708 and 1713) were important reference works in the fields of liturgy and sacramental theology. He also published a history, drawn from Arabic sources, of the Coptic Church of Alexandria, and the text and translation of early Arab seafarers' accounts of India and China. He left his library to the Benedictines of Saint-Germain-des-

Prés. Some of his unpublished translations were later employed in H. Denzinger's *Ritus orientalium* (2 v. Würzburg 1863–64).

Bibliography: A. RAES, *Lexikon für Theologie und Kirche*, ed. J. HOFER and K. RAHNER (Freiberg 1957–65) 8:1236. H. LECLERCQ, *Dictionnaire d'archéologie chrétienne et de liturgie*, ed. F. CABROL, H. LECLERCQ and H. I. MARROU (Paris 1907–53) 14.2:2369–72. J. CARREYRE, *Dictionnaire de théologie catholique*, ed. A. VACANT et al. (Paris 1903–50) 13.2:2381–83. A. VILLIEN, *L'Abbé Eusèbe Renaudot* (Paris 1904).

[P. W. SKEHAN]

RENO, DIOCESE OF

The diocese of Reno, NEVADA (*Dioecesis Renensis*), which encompassed the entire state of Nevada, was originally established in 1931 during the pontificate of Pope Pius XI. In 1976, during the time of Pope Paul VI, it was redesignated as the diocese of Reno-Las Vegas. In 1995 Pope John Paul II divided the diocese into the diocese of Reno in the western part of the state and the diocese of LAS VEGAS in the southern part. The first bishop of Reno was Thomas K. Gorman, who served from 1931 until 1952 when he was appointed coadjutor bishop of Dallas. His successor, Robert J. Dwyer served from 1952 to 1966 when he was named archbishop of Portland, Oregon, and he in turn was succeeded in 1967 by Bishop Joseph Green who resigned for reasons of health at the end of 1974. It was during the time of Bishop Norman F. McFarland who first served as apostolic administrator (1974–76) that Pope Paul VI redesignated the diocese Reno–Las Vegas. McFarland served until he was transferred to the diocese of Orange, California in 1987. Bishop Daniel F. Walsh, first named bishop of Reno–Las Vegas in 1987, became bishop of the newly established diocese of Las Vegas in 1995, and Bishop Phillip F. Straling, the bishop of San Bernardino, California, was installed as the sixth bishop of Reno.

At the time of the division, Catholics in Nevada numbered about 432,970, the largest single religious group in the state. The Reno diocese covers the twelve northern counties in the state. The diocesan newspaper is the *Northern Nevada Catholic*. It is a suffragan see of the Archdiocese of San Francisco.

[J. FILTEAU/EDS.]

RENZI, ELISABETTA, BL.

Foundress of the Sisters of Our Lady of Sorrows (*Istituto Maestre Pie dell'Addolorata*); b. Nov. 19, 1786, Saludecio (near Rimini), Italy; d. Aug. 14, 1859, Coriano, Italy. Elisabetta's wealthy, noble parents sent her to the Poor Clare monastery at Pietrarubbia for her education. Upon completing her studies, she entered the same convent with their permission (1807). Renzi and her sisters were exclaustrated when the monasteries were suppressed by Napoleon before she could make her vows. From that time until 1824, Elisabetta engaged in charitable activities while living at home. Recognizing the need to provide youth with a Christian education in a society increasingly hostile to religion, she began teaching at a school for girls in Coriano near Rimini (April 1824). When Saint Maddalena CANOSSA declined to assume responsibility for the school and suggested that Elisabetta was the better candidate, Renzi gathered a group of women to undertake the task (1828). The association eventually became a religious congregation, approved by the Holy See, Dec. 10, 1839, dedicated to education and care of the neglected in the villages of Romagna. Elisabetta, who was declared venerable in 1988 and beatified by John Paul II, June 18, 1989, is buried in the chapel of the mother house at Coriano.

Bibliography: *Acta Apostolicae Sedis* (1989): 764. *L'Osservatore Romano*, English ed. July 10, 1989, 4.

[K. I. RABENSTEIN]

REORDINATION

The question of reordinations reflects one of the great theological issues from the 3rd and 4th centuries onward. Essentially the debate concerned the power of the Church over Sacraments administered outside the Church. Were they valid Sacraments? Should Baptism and Orders administered by heretics and schismatics be repeated? This use of the term "reordination" should be distinguished from two other possible uses: (1) the view of some theologians of the reformed churches that the power of orders can be lost and so validly reputed, and (2) reordination in cases where the first ceremony was clearly null, e.g., lack of proper form or matter. This article is not concerned with these uses.

The traditional teaching of the Catholic Church, defined by the Council of Trent [H. Denzinger, *Enchiridion symbolorum*, ed. A. Schönmetzer (32d ed. Freiburg 1963) 1622], is that Orders once validly conferred cannot be reiterated, for the character is indelible. In the case of unworthy ministers, the traditional view, the one that has been the "common and certain" doctrine of all approved authors since the 13th century (St. Thomas, *Summa theologiae*, Suppl. 38.2; Cappello, 275), is that Orders conferred by heretics, provided due matter, form, and intention are observed, are valid. Thus the mere fact of heresy or unworthiness in the minister does not invalidate the Sacrament. Hence there can be no reordination unless, of course, other factors intervene. Thus, if Anglican orders are excluded, it is because Catholic teaching insists that there is some defect of form and intention, considered indispensable by the Council of Trent (*ibid.*, 1624). Eastern Orthodox Churches generally stress more strongly the connection between right faith and right Sacraments.

The history of the Church records a number of occasions, and certainly many doubtful ones, when Orders conferred in a proper manner, but by an unworthy minister, have been condemned as useless and were therefore repeated. The doctrine behind this attitude is identified with St. CYPRIAN's (d. 258) teaching (see Saltet 11–34). It had some strong adherents in the Middle Ages, e.g., HUMBERT OF SILVA CANDIDA (d. 1061) in his *Libri tres adversus simoniacos* (1054–58). The majority, however, opposed the invalidity theme, and their arguments were identified with the doctrine of St. AUGUSTINE (d. 430) recognizing the validity of orders conferred by heretics [*Contra epist. Parmeniani*, 2.28; *Corpus scriptorum ecclesiasticorum latinorum* (Vienna 1866–) 51:79–80]. Such ministers on being reconciled to the Church were not to be reordained. (Whether they would be allowed the exercise, i.e., lawful use, of their Orders, was a different matter.) Conciliar legislation supported this view, which was held by the majority throughout the period of controversy.

The number of reordinations was not, in fact, very large, if we bear in mind the period of time involved (*see* Saltet or Amann). We shall consider only the problem of cases in which the popes ordered ministers to be reordained whose Orders would today be regarded as valid. Thus the Roman Synod of 769 declared null the ordinations conferred by the false pope Constantine II; and Stephen IV (d. 772) reordained the bishops. Sergius III (d. 911) ordered all those ordained by FORMOSUS (d. 896) to be reordained. In 964 the ordinations conferred by Leo VIII, who had usurped the papacy, were annulled by John XII (d. 964). During the 11th century reordination was particularly associated with the "heresy" of SIMONY. The validity of simoniacal orders was greatly discussed from Leo IX (d. 1054) onward. Hence Leo IX ordered certain simoniacs to be reordained. HUMBERT and St. PETER DAMIAN (d. 1072) expressed opposite viewpoints, but it was the latter who set the general tone for the 11th century. Despite some opposing views, especially among the canonists of Bologna, the doctrine of the validity of Sacraments independent of the probity and faith of the minister became universally admitted by the 13th century.

How is one to explain these "reordinations"? Three solutions have been suggested. The first assumes them to be examples of a "temporary deformation of doctrine"; the second holds that reordinations were valid because the Church has the power to determine the conditions in which the power of Orders may be validly exercised. Neither explanation is satisfactory, especially the second, which is against accepted teaching. The third and more likely solution is that the significance of the term "reordination" has not been sufficiently examined. Moreover, the term commonly used to describe unworthy Orders (*irritae*) is too often mistakenly translated as "invalid" when it really meant "illicit." Again there are few recorded instances of reordination. Where there are such instances, they usually occurred in times of political and ecclesiastical conflict, e.g., at the time of the INVESTITURE STRUGGLE. In some cases reordination obviously referred not to the Sacrament but to the canonical institution. Certain popes, e.g., Leo IX, acted unwisely under pressure, but it is clear that the magisterium and infallibility were not involved. Despite Saltet's fundamental work, there is need today for the whole question to be reexamined.

Bibliography: L. SALTET, *Les Réordinations* (Paris 1907). J. TIXERONT, *Holy Orders and Ordination*, tr. S. A. RAEMERS (St. Louis 1928). V. FUCHS, *Der Ordinationstitel von seiner Entstehung bis auf Innocenz III* (Bonn 1930). É. AMANN, *Dictionnaire de théologie catholique*, ed. A. VACANT et al., 15 v. (Paris 1903–50; Tables générales 1951–) 13.2:2385–2431. F. M. CAPPELLO, *Tractatus canonicomoralis de sacramentis iuxta codicem iuris canonici*, v. 4 (3d ed. Rome 1951), 4. H. LENNERZ, *De sacramentis Novae Legis in genere* (Rome 1950). B. LEEMING, *Principles of Sacramental Theology* (Westminster, Md. 1956). A. VANNESTE, "La Sainteté et la foi du ministre et du sujet des sacrements," *Ephemerides theologicae Lovanienses* 39 (1963) 5–29. J. GILCHRIST, "*Simoniaca haeresis* and the Problem of Orders from Leo IX to Gratian," *Proceedings of the 2d International Congress of Medieval Canon Law Held at Boston, August 1963* (Vatican City 1964).

[J. GILCHRIST]

REPARATION

The term reparation lends itself to a variety of meanings in both the profane and religious contexts. It may signify the action of repairing or keeping in repair, and when so used by a theologian or religious writer it designates the whole work of restoring men to the FRIENDSHIP OF GOD. This usage is close to the root meaning of the word, yet it is not as common as that in which reparation designates compensation for an injury. This is the usual meaning given reparation by theologians. In moral theology its use implies restitution for a personal injury for which the compensation cannot be measured exactly. In ascetical theology or devotional writing reparation designates the effort to make amends for insults given to God by sin, one's own or another's. In dogmatic theology the idea of reparation enters into the attempt to find a theological explanation of Redemption or, more specifically, to clarify the notion of satisfaction.

Related to Sin. In the history of dogma the concept of reparation is intimately bound to the notion of sin as a personal injury or insult to God (*see* SIN, THEOLOGY OF). Adam had been constituted the moral head of the human race, and his sin not only alienated mankind from God but was also a personal injury or insult to God because it deprived Him of what is His by strict right. By sinning, Adam offered the supreme insult to God and accomplished the downfall of mankind. These effects of Adam's sin have, moreover, been compounded by the sins of his descendants.

Man is subject to the consequences of sin, which is a reality of his history. The first consequence of sin is guilt (called *reatus culpae*), which separates man from God and makes him an enemy of his Creator. The second consequence is a penalty (*reatus poenae*) for the injury done to God. Sin in the nature of things is enmity to God and must therefore be abandoned before one can be restored to His friendship. It also appears clear from the history of God's relationship to man that sin is followed by a penalty that must be paid (*see* e.g., Gn 3.16–19). That is to say, to obtain forgiveness reparation must be made; one must restore to God what he has deprived Him of and make amends for the insult done to Him (*see*, e.g., 2 Sm 24.10–25).

God's reaction to sin is often described in terms of anger and the punishment of sin as His revenge. One is face to face with a mystery that Scripture presents in metaphors. These anthropomorphic expressions are indispensable but are not meant to carry the whole burden of God's message. Misunderstanding of this has led to serious distortions of the idea of satisfaction and reparation for sin. The reformers, certain Catholic preachers, and popular spiritual writers taught that Jesus Christ became the object of the wrath of His Father and suffered the torments of the damned to satisfy retributive justice as a penal substitute for sinful man. In reaction to this distorted and exaggerated view of God's wrath, liberal Protestant theology has denied any idea of reparation.

The consideration of God's infinite holiness and His eternal immutability precludes the imperfections of retributive justice. God's love initiates all movements of reconciliation; it is not caused by them. In spite of this it is clear from the first pages of Genesis that sin is hateful to God and is punished. Even after sin was forgiven and the sinner turned again to God, punishment was often inflicted to expiate for the offense against God. The Old Testament especially points to a close connection between sin and a penalty (*see* Nm 16.25–35; 2 Chr 29.6–9; Ps 77(78) and 108(109); Jer 15.1–9).

Sin is a personal offense against God; it makes the sinner an enemy of God; it is the death of the soul and delivers the sinner into the slavery of Satan. Added to these effects, which follow upon sin, there is a debt of the sinner to God. Because the original state of friendship was completely gratuitous, its restoration when lost was completely beyond man's power. The initiative had to come from God. God planned the restoration in Jesus Christ, who for His part embraced His Father's will perfectly. Thus as the second Adam He restored all things in Himself and reversed the course of action taken by the first Adam. Further, whatever debts had been incurred were wiped out by the humble and obedient submission of Jesus to His Father's will in His Passion and death.

An Attempt to Explain. The introduction of the notion of reparation is an attempt to explain how the Passion and death of Christ effected man's Redemption. The organization and synthesis of this theology took place first in the *Cur Deus Homo* of St. ANSELM OF CANTERBURY. For him reparatory satisfaction became necessary from the fact of sin. While rejecting this note of necessity, Catholic theology has followed St. Anselm's lead in explaining the redemptive work of Christ. In the past there often was an overemphasis on the penal aspects of the material sufferings involved. The Son of God became the substitute of His fellow men as the object of the wrath of His Father. These ideas are not contained in St. Anselm nor in the works of the great scholastics, who adopted and modified his theory. Satisfaction is not punishment, nor is reparation found in the sufferings themselves but in the humility and love and obedience found in submission to the sufferings.

The Redemption is God's love in operation. The Son of God became the Son of Man to wipe out the decree against men by reversing the pride and disobedience of Adam in His humble and obedient death. In this there was vicarious satisfaction and reparation made possible by the Redeemer's identification and solidarity with the redeemed rather than by substitution. There is a judgment upon sin that Jesus Christ took upon Himself and removed from mankind. The themes of the Suffering Servant (Is ch. 53; Acts 8.32–35), the LAMB OF GOD (Jn 1.29; 1 Pt 1.19), obedience restoring what had been lost by the disobedience, all point to reparation. There is more to men's Redemption than reparation; however, there is an aspect of this saving work that can hardly be explained in any other way.

Duty. Reparation is a wider notion than that of EXPIATION in that its burden is not only the removal of sin and guilt and penalty, but the reestablishment of all things in Christ. The duty of reparation, then, is the obligation of a Christian to share in the redemptive mission of Jesus

Christ, who, by His obedience to the will of His Father in Heaven, especially by the offering of His life on the cross, merited eternal salvation for all men. Every Christian is personally involved in Christ's sacrifice, for he is baptized in his death (Rom 6.3–4), and those who are spiritually alive through that death may not live only for themselves (2 Cor 5.15). St. Peter, therefore, offered the suffering Jesus as an example to be followed not only by the chosen few but by all who are Christians (1 Pt 1.18–2.20).

This duty of sharing in the Savior's work of Redemption may be fulfilled in many ways. Such reparation is contained, actually or virtually, in the mere carrying out of the Commandments of God and of the Church. By reason of one's association in the priesthood of Christ by Baptism (*see* St. THOMAS AQUINAS, *Summa Theologiae,* 3a, 62.2), all of the day's actions can be merged with Christ's redemptive action. In this connection, recent popes have recommended the offering of the day's activities as a way to share in the reparation achieved by the Savior on the cross (e.g., Pius X, April 9, 1911, *Acta Apostolicae Sedis* 3:345; Pius XII, Sept. 27, 1956, *ibid.* 48:674–677, and May 19, 1957, *ibid.* 49:415). Also, attendance at Mass with the intention, even obscure, of being united to Christ's sacrifice is a special means for sharing in His work of reparation.

In modern times, especially by the renewal of the ancient devotion to the humanity of Christ (*see* SACRED HUMANITY, DEVOTION TO), in the symbol of His love for man, the Sacred Heart, the Church has promoted among the faithful the practice of reparation. Many prayers of reparation, several acts of reparation, and the morning offering mentioned above have been richly indulged. Also, the canonization of saints, such as Rose of Lima, Thérèse of Lisieux, and Gabriel Possenti, who devoted their lives to reparation, has furthered this spirit.

See Also: RESURRECTION OF CHRIST, 2; SATISFACTION OF CHRIST; SOTERIOLOGY; REDEMPTION.

Bibliography: J. RIVIÈRE, *Dictionnaire de théologie catholique,* ed. A. VACANT et al., 15 v. (Paris 1903–50; Tables générales 1951) 13.2:1912–2004; *The Doctrine of the Atonement,* tr. L. CAPPADELTA, 2 v. (St. Louis 1909). L. HÖDL, *ibid.* 4:683–685. H. F. DAVIS et al., *A Catholic Dictionary of Theology* (London 1962) 1: 189–198. *Encyclopedic Dictionary of the Bible,* tr. and adap. by L. HARTMAN (New York 1963) from A. VAN DEN BORN, *Bijbels Woordenboek* 167–175, 2032–40, 2218–32. J. BONSIRVEN, *The Theology of the N.T.,* tr. S. F. L. TYE (Westminster, Md. 1963). L. CERFAUX, *Christ in the Theology of St. Paul,* tr. G. WEBB and A. WALKER (New York 1959). W. F. HOGAN, *Christ's Redemptive Sacrifice* (Englewood Cliffs, N.J. 1963). S. LYONNET, *De peccato et redemptione* (Rome 1957–), "Conception paulinienne de la rédemption," *Lumière et vie* 7 (1958) 35–66. PHILIPPE DE LA TRINITÉ, *What is Redemption?* tr. A. ARMSTRONG (New York 1961).

M. MELLET, "The Redemption" in *The Historical and Mystical Christ,* ed. A. M. HENRY, tr. A. BOUCHARD (Theology Library 5; Chicago 1958) 147–207. G. OGGIONI, "Il mistero della redenzione," *Problemi e orientamenti di teologia dommatica,* v.2 (Milan 1957) 236–343. E. F. SIEGMAN, "The Blood of Christ in St. Paul's Soteriology," in *Proceedings of the Second Precious Blood Study Week, 1960* (Carthagena, Ohio 1962) 11–35. E. TESTA, "La sotereologia de s. Paolo causa della sua cattività," *Studii biblici francescani* 8 (1957–58)113–214. PIUS XI, "Miserentissimus Redemptor," *Acta Apostolicae Sedis* (Rome 1909–) 20:165–178. PIUS XII, "Caritate Christi Complusi," *Acta Apostolicae Sedis* (Rome 1909) 24:177–194. C. MARMION, *Christ in His Mysteries* (London 1939) 248–265. R. GARRIGOU-LAGRANGE, *The Three Ages of the Interior Life,* tr. M. T. DOYLE, 2 v. (St. Louis 1947–48) 2:497–510. *Enchiridion Indulgentiarum* (Vatican City 1950) 178–179, 256–257.

[A. A. MAGUIRE/P. F. MULHERN]

REPENTANCE

Repentance and penance are imperfect and unsatisfactory equivalents of μετάνοια of the Greek New Testament and *poenitentia* of the Latin Vulgate. The Greek form directly signifies the change of mind or of heart that occurs in conversion. The Latin *poenitentia,* with which the Vulgate (often joining with it some form of the verb *agere*) translates the Greek term, connotes regret for one's past sins as well as penalties undertaken on their account; it represents penance as something to be done, a work to be performed. By contrast, Protestant insistence upon the idea of μετάνοια (translated by "repentance" in the AV) in the sense of the beginning of a new life, a new way of looking at things and feelings about them, has often been understood as requiring no special attitude with regard to moral lapses of the past. For the teaching of Catholic theology that sorrow and regret for past sins is always included in true conversion, *see* CONTRITION.

See Also: CONVERSION, I (IN THE BIBLE); PENANCE, SACRAMENT OF; REPARATION.

[T. A. PORTER/EDS.]

REPETTO, MARIA, BL.

Sister of Our Lady of Refuge of Mount Calvary; b. Nov. 1, 1807, Voltaggio, northern Italy; d. Jan. 5, 1890, Genoa, Italy. Maria, the eldest child of Giovanni Battista Repetto and his wife Teresa Gozzola, helped raise her siblings. Of the nine children, five girls became religious sisters and one boy a priest. At age 22 Maria became a cloistered nun of Our Lady of Refuge in Genoa. There she served the community in various offices (infirmarian, laundress, laborer), but became known as a portress of unwearying charity and wisdom. She nursed the sick of Genoa through the cholera epidemics of 1835 and 1854.

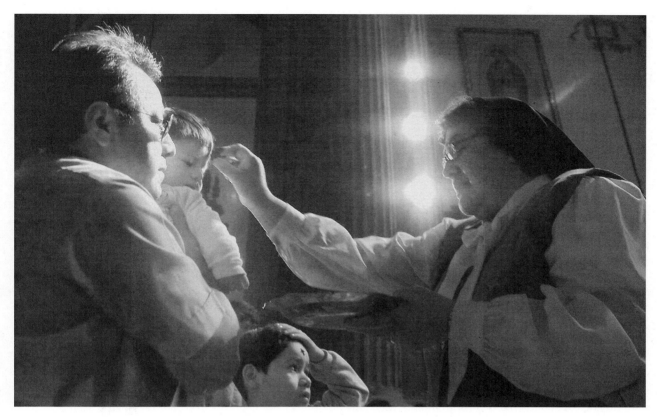

A nun marks the forehead of a child on Ash Wednesday ceremonies marking Lent, the opening of 40 days of contemplation and repentance before Easter, Mexico City Cathedral. (AP/WideWorld Photos)

Revered for her holiness while she lived, her body was interred in the chapel of Our Lady of Refuge of Mount Calvary.

During Repetto's beatification (Oct. 4, 1981), Pope John Paul II recalled her words: "Jesus must be contemplated, loved, and served in the poor, at all moments of our life." Patroness of Genoa.

Feast: Jan. 5.

Bibliography: *Acta Apostolicae Sedis* (1982): 1100–03. *L'Osservatore Romano,* English ed. 41 (1981): 1, 12.

[K. I. RABENSTEIN]

REPINGTON, PHILIP (REPYNGDON)

Former Wyclifite, bishop; d. Lincoln, 1424. A CANON REGULAR of St. AUGUSTINE and a doctor of theology (1382), he emerged from obscurity as a supporter of John WYCLIF's Eucharistic teaching. In 1382 Archbishop William COURTENAY became dissatisfied with the dilatoriness of the Oxford chancellor Robert RYGGE in dealing with Wyclif and ordered the Oxford Carmelite Peter Stokes to promulgate a condemnation of 24 theses drawn from Wyclif's writings. At this invasion of the university's freedom, Rygge defiantly invited Repington to give the university sermon on the Feast of Corpus Christi. In his sermon Repington stoutly maintained Wyclif's orthodoxy. Rygge was immediately hailed before the Blackfriars' synod and the king's council, and he abjectly submitted: he published the condemnation of Wyclif's theses and suspended Wyclif, Nicholas HEREFORD, and Repington until they should be purged of heresy.

Repington and Hereford both appealed to John of Gaunt, but without success. Before the synod they were evasive in their answers and were given a week to state their position unequivocally. On failing to appear, they were excommunicated; they then protested and appealed to Rome. Courtenay ignored the appeal and solemnly excommunicated them on July 13. Repington made his abjuration in November of 1382, and one cannot doubt the sincerity of his change of mind. He became a close friend of the orthodox King Henry IV. In 1404 he was made bishop of Lincoln. He was chancellor of Oxford in 1397, and from 1400 to 1403. In 1408 he was made cardinal. He resigned his see in 1419. His sermons are unedited.

Bibliography: C. L. KINGSFORD, *The Dictionary of National Biography from the Earliest Times to 1900,* 63 v. (London 1885–1900) 16:912–914. K. B. MCFARLANE, *John Wycliffe and the Beginnings of English Nonconformity* (New York 1953). J. H. DAHMUS, *The Prosecution of John Wyclyf* (New Haven, Conn. 1952). A. B. EMDEN, *A Biographical Register of the University of Oxford to A.D. 1500,* 3 v. (Oxford 1957–59) 3:1565–1567.

[J. E. HEALEY]

REPROBATION

Reprobation is the withdrawal by God of SUPERNATURAL gifts during life or of glory after death. The latter is meant here. So understood, reprobation includes God's knowledge of those who will be lost and His decree to damn them. This decree supposes final sin and its permission by God. Reprobation is God's supernatural providence over those who are lost. The reprobate are called ''foreknown,'' not ''predestined,'' for no one is destined to sin. The term reprobation is used only of adults in Catholic theology, they only being capable of personal sin.

Reprobation is conceived either positively, the intention to punish, or negatively, the intention to deny a person glory, as an undue gift, expressed in three ways: the intention to exclude one from glory, or not to elect one, or to omit one from it.

Positive reprobation of adults in the order of time consequent on their death in personal mortal sin is theologically certain, for it is a dogma of faith that sinners are punished in time [H. Denzinger, *Enchiridion symbolorum,* ed. A. Schönmetzer (Freiburg 1963) 1002], and what God does in time He decrees in eternity. All who admit divine providence admit this positive reprobation. It follows also from the description of the Last Judgment, which is found in Mt 25.41–46.

But the theological problem concerns the eternal order of intention. Does God first, antecedently to the foreseen death of some, absolutely intend to punish them and consequently will that they die in sin (antecedent positive or negative reprobation)?

SUPRALAPSARIAN (antelapsarian) Calvinists held that God always intended to punish some. INFRALAPSARIAN (sublapsarian, postlapsarian) Calvinists and Jansenists held that God did so after He foresaw men merely contracting ORIGINAL SIN. Catholic theologians unanimously reject these doctrines as false, being in contradiction with God's will to save all, even fallen men, prior to some foreseen condition.

Catholic theologians raise a like question about negative reprobation in the order of intention. Does God absolutely intend to deny glory to some, as an undue gift, and consequently refuse them final efficacious GRACE, permitting their death in sin?

Most non-Molinists hold God absolutely intends to deny some men glory, as an undue gift, because this fits the divinely preestablished order of the universe and the degree in which He wills His glory manifested; they disagree whether this occurs before or after the contraction of original sin. Some, who otherwise follow Molina, hold the same absolute divine intent, but that it is for other reasons known to God alone, it being a necessary sequel to God's absolute choice of the elect. Strict Molinists reject any form of antecedent reprobation.

The effect of consequent reprobation can be only punishment after death; that of antecedent reprobation can be also privation of efficacious grace and permission of sin during life.

Catholic theologians all agree that God antecedently to some condition wills to save all men. They disagree whether in the order of intention this be simply death in sin or some prior consideration; hence their disagreement concerning antecedent negative reprobation.

See Also: MOLINISM; BÁÑEZ AND BAÑEZIANISM; PERSEVERANCE, FINAL; PREDESTINATION OF GOD; PROVIDENCE OF GOD.

Bibliography: H. LENNERZ, *De Deo Uno* (Rome 1955). R. GARRIGOU–LAGRANGE, *The One God,* tr. B. ROSE, (St. Louis 1943).

[F. L. SHEERIN]

REPUTATION, MORAL RIGHT TO

Reputation is the esteem in which a person is held by his fellows for praiseworthy qualities that he is considered to possess. Praiseworthy qualities consist in moral, intellectual, physical, or merely external perfections. A person is said to have a right to his reputation in the same way that he has a right to his other possessions. Any violation of a person's right to his reputation constitutes a violation of the moral order. Because ''a good name is more precious than great riches'' (Prv 22.1), it is a more serious offense to deprive a person of his good name than to rob him of his other possessions. All theologians agree that a person has a moral right to his reputation. They all agree that violations of the person's rights are sins of injustice.

There is disagreement over the reasons for a person's right in justice to his good name, especially when the good name is not based on reality.

Kinds of Good Name. Theologians make certain distinctions concerning a person's good name. One distinction has reference to the way in which a person's fellows have come to esteem him. If the person is admitted to ordinary social relationships in business and other fields as an honest person, simply because nothing dishonest is known about him, he possesses a good reputation in a negative sense. If, on the other hand, the person is esteemed as honest because his honest actions have become publicly known, he possesses a good reputation in a positive sense.

Applying the notion of moral right to the way in which a person attains a good name, there is no difficulty in concluding that everyone has a right to his good reputation in the negative sense, or the right to be admitted to ordinary social relationships, until at least there is clear evidence that he is undeserving of this. On the other hand, we are not obliged to grant anyone a good reputation in the positive sense unless his actions have merited or produced this exceptional esteem.

A second and more important distinction pertains to the factual basis for a person's good reputation. If a man is considered honest and in reality is honest, he has a true good name. If, however, a man is considered honest and actually is dishonest, he has a false good name. A storekeeper, for instance, who is accepted in business relationships as honest but who has secretly doctored his scales has a false good name. In applying the notion of moral right to the factual basis for a good name, theologians agree that a person whose good name is based on factual qualities has an unconditional right to his good name. Thus, an honest judge has an unconditional right to his reputation for honesty. There are no circumstances that would justify a person's deliberately declaring the judge dishonest.

Right to a False Good Name. Disagreement arises concerning the reason why a person who has a false good name possesses a right in justice to his public reputation. The difficulty has long troubled theologians. Various solutions have been proposed, in both former and recent times.

Earlier Thought. Earlier theologians pointed out that the discord, strife, and countless other harmful effects resulting from unnecessary revelations of the crimes of others would be detrimental to the common good; the very existence of society would be threatened if such revelations were not forbidden. There is no doubt that these things are true, but the fact that society would suffer countless bad effects unless this act were forbidden does not establish the individual's right in strict justice to his good name. The most that the argument proves is that unnecessary revelations of blackening truths would be a violation of one's obligation to promote the common good. This obligation, however, pertains to the virtue of legal

justice rather than to commutative justice. Hence, the argument does not show that the person's right in justice to his good name is violated. In like manner, the argument maintaining that "one who has a false good reputation is in peaceful possession of his good name and to deprive him of it without reason would be a violation of the virtue of justice" does not establish a reason for the action's being contrary to justice. Peaceful possession certainly does not give one the same rights as ownership.

Later Thought. The later arguments give a more adequate solution to the problem. One view maintains that certain rights are conferred by God and are based on the nature of man. According to this view, one has a right to those things necessary for him to live in accordance with his human nature. By nature, man is a social being, and to live as such, nothing is more necessary to him than at least ordinary acceptance in his social encounters. Ordinary acceptance by one's fellows is, in reality, nothing more than a good reputation, in the negative sense. Hence, everyone has a God-given, natural right to a good name in this negative sense of the term. This theory has the advantage of establishing a moral right in strict justice for a good name.

The more difficult problem is whether this natural right is lost by a grave sin or crime. According to this same view, the right to a good name is not lost by any grave sin or crime, but only by certain offenses. Since the right to a good name consists in being admitted to ordinary social relationships, one forfeits his right to this acceptance whenever the offense committed has been such that harm could come to society if he were freely admitted to certain relationships at this time. Thus, one who is secretly a swindler would constitute a danger to society if he were admitted to normal relationships in business. By reason of the nature of his conduct he has forfeited (at least for the time being) his right to be accepted as an honest man. However, in other instances in which a person's conduct has been sinful, but not of a nature that makes his ordinary acceptance a danger to society, he retains his basic right to his reputation. Thus, someone who knows some gossip about another may not reveal it, unless it can be said that continued ignorance of the facts could make the person a danger to society. In other words, the person retains his right to ordinary social relationship because his offense in no way conflicts with this relationship.

Another view differs somewhat from the above in that it attempts to establish a more proximate title to ownership of a false good name. According to this view, reputation, in one way or another, is a product of one's personal industry. Just as a man is esteemed for his honesty because his actions have become a matter of public knowledge, so also a person obtains a right to his good name if he has deliberately refrained from any public act that would adversely affect his good reputation. In this view the person retains his right to his good name not simply because the truth is unknown but because he has refrained from public actions that would have a detrimental affect on his reputation. The right of the person is conditional, being forfeited only when the continued ignorance of his sinful act could make his normal acceptance in social relationships harmful to society (*see* DETRACTION).

The advantage of these recent solutions is that there are reasons that establish a person's right in strict justice to his good name, even when the good name is not based on reality. At the same time, it is shown that the right is conditional and ceases to be operative when it would conflict with moral rights of an equal or greater moral urgency.

Bibliography: D. M. PRÜMMER, *Manuale theologiae moralis,* ed. E. M. MÜNCH (Freiburg-Barcelona 1955). B. H. MERKELBACH, *Summa theologiae moralis* (Paris 1949). THOMAS AQUINAS, *Summa Theologiae* 2a2ae, 73–74. H. DAVIS, *Moral and Pastoral Theology,* rev. and enl. ed. by L. W. GEDDES (New York 1958). K. B. MOORE, *The Moral Principles Governing the Sin of Detraction* (Washington 1950).

[K. B. MOORE]

REQUIEM MASS

Requiem Masses, or Masses for the dead, are celebrated as suffrages for the souls of the deceased. The name Requiem Mass is derived from the first words of the entrance antiphon: *Requiem aeternam dona eis Domine.*

Origin. From earliest times Christians have celebrated Masses for their dead. Several second-century sources mention this celebration of the Eucharist, for example, the *Apology* of Aristides [H. J. M. Milne, ''A New Fragment of the Apology of Aristides,'' *Journal of Theological Studies* 25 (1923–24) 75] and the apocryphal Acts of John [M. J. James, *The Apocryphal New Testament* (3d ed. Oxford 1945) 245]. Tertullian repeatedly refers to the celebration of the eucharist on the anniversary of death (*De Corona* 3, *Patrologia Latina* 2:79; *De Castitate* 11, *ibid.* 2:926; *De Monogamia* 10, *ibid.* 2:942).

During the first centuries Masses were celebrated on certain days after the death and burial. Masses on the third day and on the anniversary were common and remained so in all rites. Masses on the 7th and 30th days were traditional in the Latin rite, while the Eastern churches observed the 9th and 40th days. In the fourth century, funeral Masses were celebrated in Rome, as was noted by St. Augustine (*Conf.* 9.12.32; *Patrologia Latina* 32:777), but the celebration of Masses on the days after the burial continued to be the general practice. Funeral Masses were never customary in the East, but they became general in the West during the early Middle Ages. In time, they came to be considered the principal part of the burial rite and were prescribed by liturgical law.

Liturgical research has not yet determined the precise date when a special formulary was first adopted for Masses for the dead. The use of the apocryphal 4 Esdras indicates that this took place not later than the sixth century. The Leonine Sacramentary already contained five sets of prayers for the dead; the Gelasian, 13 sets. During the early Middle Ages formularies increased rapidly. From among this wealth of texts the reform of Pius V selected a single formulary, that used by the Roman Curia, offering a limited variety of readings and prayers.

Older texts of the Requiem Mass can be understood correctly only if it is remembered that the early Christians saw in death primarily the final identification of the Christian with Christ in His death and Resurrection and the beginning of the life of glory. The ''eternal rest,'' for example, of the Introit and Gradual (4 Esdras 1.34; this verse, like the entire first two chapters, is considered a Christian addition) intimates eternal happiness and the vision of God. The Preface for the dead, which had its origin in the fifth-century Mozarabic liturgy and was inserted into the Roman Missal in 1919, emphasizes the joyful aspects of the Resurrection. In keeping with the piety of the High Middle Ages, the twelfth-century Sequence *DIES IRAE,* however, stresses fear of judgment and condemnation. Its traditionally accepted authorship by the Franciscan THOMAS OF CELANO (d. *c.* 1250) was disproved by the discovery of an earlier, somewhat different twelfth-century version. The Offertory antiphon with its plea for deliverance from hell is best explained as a prayer that was originally recited before death.

Previous to the Missal of Pius V (1570), a great variety of texts for the Proper was in use; since that date only one set of texts for all Masses for the Dead is prescribed. The texts assigned by the Missal of Pius V were Introit, *Requiem aeternam* (Eternal Rest); Gradual, *Requiem aeternam* (Eternal rest); Tract, *Absolve, Domine* (Absolve, O Lord); Sequence, *Dies irae* (Day of Wrath); Offertory, *Domine Jesu Christe* (Lord Jesus Christ); Communion, *Lux aeterna* (May Light Eternal).

Origin of the Requiem. The Introit text is probably the most ancient component of the currently used requiem Propers. The fact that it is taken from the Apocryphal Fourth Book of Esdras, which was held as canonical until the late fifth century, indicates that it must have been introduced into the liturgy no later than *c.* 490. Certain of the other texts currently used may have been introduced in the sixth and seventh centuries. The earliest preserved complete sets of Propers for Masses of the Dead, however, date only from the tenth century, when, through the monastic influence of the Abbey of Cluny, the cult of all the dead was established under the form of a solemn commemoration on November 2.

The rapid spread and growth of this cult resulted in the creation of a great number and variety of formularies. Well over 100 different texts, including some Alleluias, can be found assigned to Masses for the Dead in the medieval chant manuscripts of the tenth through the fourteenth centuries. Slightly more than half of these texts were written specifically for use in connection with the cult of the dead. The others were simply borrowings from Mass formularies assigned to Sundays or to weekdays in Lent.

Thus the Gradual *Si ambulem,* for example, which was widely used, was borrowed from the Saturday of the third week of Lent. These borrowed texts retained their original chant melodies; for new texts either entirely new music was composed (the most frequent procedure) or a preexistent melody was adapted. For example, the Introit *Si enim credimus* utilized the melody of the Introit *Sicut oculi* for the Monday of the first week of Lent; and the Gradual *Qui Lazarum,* that of the Gradual *Beata gens,* from the seventeenth Sunday after Pentecost. The vast majority of these texts gradually fell into disuse during the fourteenth and early fifteenth centuries, and hardly more than a dozen were in general use during those years of the Renaissance that preceded the Missal of Pius V.

Polyphonic Versions. The earliest polyphonic settings of the Requiem Mass date only from the last third of the fifteenth century. The first of these seems to have been composed by Guillaume DUFAY; it has not been preserved, however, and the only knowledge of it comes from a reference to it in the composer's will. The earliest preserved setting, that of Okeghem (*c.* 1485–90), consists of all of the sung items then used in France, both Proper and Ordinary, from the Introit through the Offertory; it is not known whether the remaining three items were lost or simply never written. Some anonymous and isolated items, apparently from about the same time, are found in certain Italian sources.

Of some 40 settings of the Requiem Mass surviving from the sixteenth century, the most notable are those by Brumel, La Rue, Fevin, G. Fogliano(?), Prioris, Richafort, Sermisy, Clemens, Morales, Certon, Bonefont, Clereau, Guerrero, Kerle, Vaet, Monte, Du Caurroy, Lassus, Mauduit, Asola, Palestrina, and Victoria, in addition to certain anonymous settings. Several of these compos-

ers produced two or more Requiem Masses, and in several cases their Requiem Masses were among their most inspired works. Most of these share certain characteristics, such as the tendency to create music for both the Ordinary and the Proper and to incorporate the original chant melodies into the polyphonic texture.

Three essential traditions evolved in the selection of texts: the Italian, Spanish, and French. In general, all three adopted the same Introit (*Requiem aeternam*), Offertory (*Domine Jesu Christe*), and Communion (*Lux aeterna*) texts. There were, however, consistent variants in certain phrases of the Offertory text. The chief distinguishing features of the traditions are to be found in the Lesson chants. The Italian tradition usually chose the Gradual *Si ambulem,* the Tract *Absolve, Domine,* or *Sicut cervus,* and almost always included the Sequence *Dies irae.* The Spanish tradition favored the Gradual *Requiem aeternam* and the Tract *Sicut cervus,* and omitted the Sequence. In France, also, the Sequence was omitted, the Gradual selected was *Si ambulem,* and the Tract was *Sicut cervus.* It did not become customary to add a polyphonic composition for the Responsory *Libera me, Domine* until after the Missal of Pius V.

Baroque Requiems were composed in the new *stile concertato* and the *stile antico.* The first setting to utilize all of the features of the new style was that of Monteverdi, Grillo, and Usper, performed on May 25, 1621, in memory of Cosimo II, Grand Duke of Tuscany; it exerted great influence on later works, such as those by Biber, Kerll, and C. Strauss, all of which call for a large chorus and orchestra. As a general rule, neither the Requiems in the *stile concertato* nor those in the *stile antico* (e.g., the outstanding work by A. Scarlatti) made use of material derived from the traditional chant melodies; the few exceptions are limited to the Sequence *Dies irae.* Important French baroque composers of Requiem Masses or portions thereof are Lully, Charpentier, Campra, and Gilles. In the late baroque and early classic Austrian tradition, the most significant version is that by Mozart.

Another period opened with the Requiem setting by Gossec (1760). Highly romantic in concept, it led the way for nineteenth-century composers who intended their Requiems more for the concert hall than for the church. To this group belong Cherubini (1836), Berlioz (1837), Verdi (1874), Fauré (1887), and Dvořák (1890). Nineteenth-century composers who wrote primarily for liturgical purposes include Bruckner (1845), Liszt (1868), and Saint-Saëns (1878). One of the most significant twentieth-century settings intended for liturgical use is that of Duruflé (1947). There are also several important nonliturgical works of the nineteenth century that derive their inspiration from the Requiem in some sense and are analogous to it in purpose. These include Brahms' *Deutsches Requiem* (1867), Ravel's *Tombeau de Couperin* (1914–17), Berg's *Violin Concerto* (1935), Honegger's *Symphonie liturgique* (1946), and Britten's *Sinfonia da Requiem* (1940) and *War Requiem* (1963).

Bibliography: A. C. RUSH, *Death and Burial in Christian Antiquity* (Washington 1941). T. MAERTENS and L. HEUSCHEN, *Doctrine et pastorale de la liturgie de la mort* (Bruges 1957). ''Les Funérailles chrétiennes,'' *Maison-Dieu* 44 (1955).

[A. CORNIDES/R. SNOW/EDS.]

RERUM DEUS TENAX VIGOR

The office hymn that was historically sung at the hour of None in the Divine Office. It shows in form and language that it was by the same author who composed *RECTOR POTENS, VERAX DEUS* (Sext) and *Nunc Sancte nobis Spiritus* (Terce). All three are possibly the work of St. AMBROSE. This hymn, like *Rector potens,* is so correct in form that it suffered the change of only one word for the 1632 revision of the Roman BREVIARY. C. Blume questions the attribution of these hymns to St. Ambrose and classifies them under what he calls *Hymnodia Hiberno-Celtica.* Accentual rhythm, alliteration, and rhyme are characteristics that suggest a Celtic origin. Simonetti denies that the three hymns are Ambrosian, but Szövérffy disagrees. As in *Rector potens,* the first verse of the *Rerum Deus* is an invocation; the second, a petition. None (3 o'clock), the traditional hour of the Lord's death, may have suggested the reference to death. God is invoked as unchanging yet guiding the day in its course; He is begged to grant light in the evening of life so that eternal glory may be the reward of a holy death. Mearns studied the manuscript tradition; Julian gives some account of the MSS and lists 18 translations.

Bibliography: H. T. HENRY, ''Hymns of the Little Hours,'' *American Ecclesiastical Review* 3 (Sept. 1890) 204–209. *Analecta hymnica* 50:19–20; 51.xx–xxii. V. ERMONI, *Dictionnaire d'archéologie chrétienne et de liturgie,* ed. F. CABROL, H. LECLERCQ, and H. I. MARROU (Paris 1907–53) 1.1:1347–52. J. JULIAN, ed., *A Dictionary of Hymnology* (New York 1957) 956. J. MEARNS, *Early Latin Hymnaries* (Cambridge, Eng. 1913) 74. A. S. WALPOLE, ed., *Early Latin Hymns* (Cambridge, Eng. 1922) 111–112. M. SIMONETTI, ''Studi sull'innologia popolare cristiana dei primi secoli,'' *Atti dell'Accademia nazionale dei Lincei: Memorie Classe di scienze morali, storiche e filologiche,* ser. 8, 6 (1952) fasc. 6. F. J. E. RABY, *A History of Christian-Latin Poetry from the Beginnings to the Close of the Middle Ages* (Oxford 1953) 131–140. J. SZÖVÉRFFY, *Die Annalen der lateinischen Hymnendichtung* (Berlin 1964–65) 1:51.

[A. J. KINNIREY]

RERUM NOVARUM

Encyclical letter of LEO XIII issued May 15, 1891; the first of the great social encyclicals. Its appearance marked the bestowal of significant papal approval on the then emergent Catholic social movement. Its formulation of Catholic social principles owed much to the work of the Fribourg Union, established in 1885 by Cardinal G. MERMILLOD. But there is considerable evidence that Leo's approach was also affected by the practical attitudes toward labor and agrarian problems of Cardinals James GIBBONS in the U.S. and Henry Edward Manning in England, and Abp. William Joseph WALSH of Dublin. First drafted by Cardinal Francesco Zigliara, the encyclical was revised according to the pope's instructions by his secretaries, further corrected by Zigliara, and finally by Leo himself. The English translation was prepared by Manning and circulated in America, Ireland, and all other English-speaking countries. Despite the descriptive title ''On the Condition of Workers,'' *Rerum novarum* is in fact a social charter of the broadest scope.

The encyclical may be divided into five parts. The first is an examination of the solution to the social question advanced by socialism, which was currently attracting much support in the working class. In rejecting it Leo developed a classical set of arguments establishing the natural right to private property. Four in number, they were derived in turn from man's power of self-direction in virtue of his intelligence and foresight, his personal independence, his mastery of his energies, and finally his right to found a family and his duty to care for it. The second part outlines the role of the Church in social affairs, without which, the pope said, no practical solution could be found. It is the task of the Church to keep ever before men's minds the truths that certain inequalities are inevitable, that to suffer and endure is the lot of man, and that man's final end is not here but hereafter. The third part is devoted to a positive exposition of the social action of the Church, which is concerned not alone with the soul of man but indirectly also with the body. Poverty is not a good in itself and every effort should be made to alleviate it through the practice of charity and the promotion of justice. The role of the state in the matter is outlined in the fourth part, in which the Pope rejected *laissez faire.* The state has functions in relation to the protection of private property; the forestalling of strikes, insofar as possible; the regulation of conditions of work; the seeing to it that employees receive a just wage; and the encouragement by the law of a wide distribution of property. A final part emphasized the beneficial activity of voluntary organizations, such as trade unions and Church bodies of various kinds devoted to social action.

Bibliography: Official Latin text in *Acta Leonis* XIII, 4 (1894) 177–209. English translation in D.J. O'BRIEN and T.A. SHAN-

NON, eds., *Catholic Social Thought: The Documentary Heritage* (Maryknoll, NY 1992) 14-39. L. WATT, *A Handbook to Rerum Novarum* (Oxford 1941). J. MÍGUEZ BONINO, ''*Rerum novarum*: One Hundred Years,'' *Ecumenical Review* 43 (1991) 392–442. D.J. O'BRIEN, ''A Century of Catholic Social Teaching: Contexts and Comments,'' in J.A. COLEMAN, ed., *One Hundred Years of Catholic Social Thought* (Maryknoll, NY 1991) 13–24. J.A. COLEMAN and G. BAUM, eds., *Rerum novarum: A Hundred Years of Catholic Social Teaching* (Philadelphia 1991). E.L. FORTIN, ''''Sacred and Inviolable': *Rerum novarum* and Natural Rights,'' *Theological Studies* 53 (1992) 203–33. F.P. MCHUGH, et al., eds., *Things Old and New: Catholic Social Teaching Revisited* (Lanham, MD 1993). P. FURLONG and D. CURTIS, *The Church Faces the Modern World : Rerum novarum and Its Impact* (Hull, Eng. 1994). T.O. NITSCH, et al., eds., *On the Condition of Labor and the Social Question One Hundred Years Later* (Lewiston, NY 1994).

[J. NEWMAN]

RESCH, PETER ANTHONY

Author; b. Chicago, IL, Feb. 27, 1895; d. Kirkwood, MO, April 29, 1956. He received his B.A. (1919) from the University of Dayton, Ohio, and was ordained and received the S.T.D. at Fribourg, Switzerland (1926). He was superior of MARIANIST seminarians (1943–46) and provincial of the St. Louis province (1946–56). His publications include *Marianist Meditations* (2 v. Kirkwood 1936), *Our Blessed Mother* (Milwaukee 1947), *Shadows Cast Before* (Kirkwood 1948), *The Prayer Life of a Religious* (New York 1948), *A Life of Mary, Co-Redemptrix* (Milwaukee 1954), *One Hundred Years of Educational Foundations by the Brothers of Mary in America* (Kirkwood 1949), and *La doctrine ascétique des premiers maîtres égyptiens de quatrième siècle* (Paris 1931). He translated Henri Lebon's *The Marianist Way* (2 v. Kirkwood 1951) and Emil Newbert's *Our Mother* (St. Meinrad 1953), contributed articles to Catholic periodicals, and wrote numerous religious pamphlets.

[G. J. RUPPEL]

RESCRIPTS

Rescripts are written replies from competent ecclesiastical authorities in answer to requests for privileges, dispensations, favors, or information. The use of rescripts dates back to the early Church, but the legal institute took form in the 12th century and derives from Roman law.

Although requests may be oral, they are expected to be in writing, and the answer will also be written. Rescripts from the Roman Curia are issued in the form of apostolic bulls, briefs, or simple rescripts. Generally, they contain a summary of the petition, an outline of the reasons why they are being issued, and a third section in which the actual response concerning some point of law is given or the favor requested is granted or denied. To this last section may be appended any conditions that are to be observed. The present law deals mainly with the right to request, validity, interpretation, execution, and revocation of rescripts.

All who are not explicitly forbidden by law may freely petition rescripts (*Codex iuris canonici* c. 60). Rescripts may be sought and obtained for another, even without the latter's knowledge and consent (*Codex iuris canonici* c. 61; *Codex Canonum Ecclesiarium Orientalium* c. 1528). Unless otherwise stated, the validity of such a rescript does not depend upon its acceptance; but the recipient is under no obligation to make use of the favor received.

Validity. Whenever conditions are added to rescripts, the nature of the subject matter, the requirements of law, or the very force of the words used may make it clear that such conditions are essential for validity. Otherwise, only those conditions are essential for validity that are introduced by such expressions as ''if,'' ''provided that'' (*si, dummodo*), or words of similar meaning. Truth in the recitals (*preces*) of the petition is an implied condition for the lawfulness of every rescript. Misrepresentation of the truth by suppression (*subreptio*) or positive falsification (*obreptio*) of the facts and circumstances may not render a rescript invalid or ineffective (*Codex iuris canonici* c. 63; *Codex Canonum Ecclesiarium Orientalium* c. 1529). Accidental errors in the name of the recipient, his or her place of residence, or subject matter invalidate a rescript only when, in the judgment of the ordinary, there is serious doubt regarding the identity of the person or the matter in question (*Codex iuris canonici* c. 66).

Before a favor refused by one congregation or office of the Roman Curia can be granted validly in a rescript by another congregation or office, or by the another competent authority, the consent of the congregation or office with which the matter was first taken up must be obtained, without prejudice to the rights of the Sacred Penitentiary in matters involving the internal forum (*Codex iuris canonici* c. 64). A favor denied by the vicar general cannot be obtained validly from the bishop without mention of the refusal, and should the bishop refuse a favor, his consent is necessary before a valid rescript granting the said favor can be obtained from the vicar general (*Codex iuris canonici* c. 65 §3; *Codex Canonum Ecclesiarium Orientalium* c. 1530). One is not to seek from another ordinary a favor denied by one's own ordinary without mention of refusal, and, before granting the favor, the second ordinary should ask of the first the reasons for the refusal (*Codex iuris canonici* c. 65 §1).

Interpretation. When the meaning of the words of a rescript is clear, no interpretation is really necessary. An initial attempt must be made to understand every rescript according to the proper meaning of its terms. Common usage, or the use a term receives in law, generally determines the proper, ordinary meaning of the words. Rescripts are not to be extended to include persons, cases, or things not expressed in the proper meaning of the words. Before the meaning of a rescript is considered objectively doubtful, it should be read carefully and every reasonable effort made to comprehend the meaning intended.

In real doubt, rescripts that pertain to legal suits and the administration of justice, those that restrict a person's rights, those adverse to the acquired rights of others, and those contrary to the law in such a way as to favor private persons are to be strictly interpreted. All other doubtful rescripts are to be given a broad interpretation, and the words are to be understood in the widest sense of their proper meaning (*Codex iuris canonici* c. 36; *Codex Canonum Ecclesiarium Orientalium* c. 1512 pp. 1–2).

Execution. Rescripts are issued directly to the recipient (*in forma gratiosa*) or through the medium of an executor (*in forma commissaria*). When no executor is used, rescripts take effect the moment they are issued. Rescripts requiring execution become effective from the time of the execution.

The executor must inspect the rescript and satisfy himself regarding its authenticity and integrity. He must proceed according to his instructions, fulfill all conditions, and follow the proper form of procedure. At times the decision whether a rescript should be executed is left to the prudent and conscientious discretion of the executor. When the executor is without such discretionary power, he must proceed to the execution of the rescript, unless it is clear that the rescript is invalid for some reason (e.g., *subreptio* or *obreptio*), that the conditions appended have not been fulfilled, or that the rescript cannot be upheld because of another grave reason. In any of these cases the executor shall immediately suspend execution and inform the grantor (*Codex iuris canonici* c. 41; *Codex Canonum Ecclesiarium Orientalium* c. 1522). The executor is free, according to his prudent judgment, to substitute another for himself, unless substitution is forbidden, some person has been designated substitute, or the executor has been chosen for his personal qualifications (*Codex iuris canonici* c. 43; *Codex Canonum Ecclesiarium Orientalium* c. 1524). The successor in the executor's dignity or office may execute all rescripts except those for which the executor was chosen by reason of his special skills (*Codex iuris canonici* c. 44; *Codex Canonum Ecclesiarium Orientalium* c. 1525). A mistake made in the execution of a rescript may be remedied by executing the rescript anew (*Codex iuris canonici* c. 45; *Codex Canonum Ecclesiarium Orientalium* c. 1526).

Cessation. Rescripts may be permanent or they may cease by the lapse of the specified time for which they were given, by the fulfillment of a resolutory condition, by renunciation by the recipient, or by revocation through a special act of the grantor. A revoked rescript remains in force until the recipient has been informed of the revocation. A law contrary to a rescript normally does not revoke it (*Codex iuris canonici* c. 73; *Codex Canonum Ecclesiarium Orientalium* c. 1513 §1). The vacancy of the Holy See or a diocese does not cancel or nullify a rescript, unless the contrary is made clear (*Codex iuris canonici* c. 46; *Codex Canonum Ecclesiarium Orientalium* c. 1513 §2). If a rescript contains a privilege or dispensation instead of a simple favor, the canons on dispensations and privileges must also be observed (*Codex iuris canonici* c. 75).

Bibliography: R. NAZ, *Dictionnaire de droit canonique*, ed. R. NAZ, 7 v. (Paris 1935–64) 7:607–635. T. L. BOUSCAREN and A. C. ELLIS, *Canon Law* (3d rev. ed. Milwaukee, WI 1957) 56–63. A. G. CICOGNANI, *Canon Law* (2d rev. ed. Westminster, MD 1947). G. MICHIELS, *Normae generales jurist canonici. Commentarius libri I. Codex iuris canonici,* 2 v. (2d ed. Paris-Turnai-Rome 1955) 2:279–479. D. E. ADAMS, *The Truth Required in the 'Preces' for Rescripts* (Catholic University of America, CLS 392; Washington 1960). B. C. GERHARDT, *Interpretation of Rescripts* (Catholic University of America, CLS 398; Washington 1959). W. H. O'NEILL, *Papal Rescripts of Favor* (Catholic University of America, CLS 57; Washington 1930). A. VAN HOVE, *Commentarium Lovaniense in Codicem iuris canonici 1,* v.1–5 (Mechlin 1928–); v.1, Prolegomena (2d ed. 1945) 1.4.

[B. C. GERHARDT]

RESPECT

Esteem, reverence, or honorable regard. In the New Testament this attitude is frequently recommended as desirable among Christians in general, and special emphasis is assigned to it with reference to those in authority. James is vigorously opposed to the undue deference given to the rich man by the rest of the Christian community, perhaps because he noted in his time that the primitive democracy of the spirit taught in the Acts of the Apostles and alluded to in St. Paul was disappearing.

Moral theologians speak of respect with reference to persons of outstanding goodness and dignity, and as a part of the virtue of piety which involves reverence to family and country. Thus it is associated more with justice and the external respect seasonably accruing to persons, than to charity, which involves an attitude of love based on divine goodness and kinship with God.

Respect is concerned positively .with the exhibition of appropriate signs of respect and negatively with the avoidance of discourtesy, offensive words, and actions which would have the effect of dishonoring another. Normally, offenses of this type would be considered of slight moral importance. However, on the grounds that honor and dishonor are to be estimated in terms of the dignity of the one so treated, it is possible that disrespect could be serious. The more common type of disrespect in modern society appears in the inhuman attitude of employers to employees and of racial groups for one another.

See Also: PIETY, FAMILIAL.

Bibliography: THOMAS AQUINAS, *Summa theologiae* 2a2ae, 102. F. ROBERTI et al., comps., *Dictionary of Moral Theology,* ed. P. PALAZZINI et al., tr. H. J. YANNONE et al. from 2d Ital. ed. (Westminster, Md. 1962).

[W. HERBST]

RESPIGHI, OTTORINO

20th-century composer famed for his orchestral colorism; b. Bologna, July 9, 1879; d. Rome, April 18, 1936. Following musical studies at the Liceo Musicale of Bologna (1891–99), he was active until 1908 as violinist, but continued to study composition, first under Rimsky-Korsakov in St. Petersburg (now Leningrad), then under Max Bruch in Berlin. From 1913 on he taught composition at the conservatory of Santa Cecilia in Rome, for two years as its director. In 1932 he was elected to the Italian Royal Academy. Eclectic in his approach, he was associated for a time with the movement around Casella and Malipiero to revive Italian neoclassic instrumental music, and he produced a number of transcriptions of 17th- and 18th-century works. In his most successful style, notably in the symphonic poems *The Fountains of Rome* (1917) and *The Pines of Rome* (1924), he used a more conservative harmonic language and the sumptuous orchestration identified with Richard Strauss. At the same time his interest in Gregorian chant (encouraged by his wife and former pupil, the composer Elsa Olivieri Sangiacomo), emerges in the modal melodies of many works from *c.* 1920. The opera *Lucrezia* (1935) and *Concerto a cinque* (1934) tend toward linear structure and reduced performing media, thus approaching the progressive features of style prevailing among his contemporaries. Among his operas, *Maria Egiziaca* (1931), first produced at Carnegie Hall, New York City, is probably the best known.

Bibliography: E. RESPIGHI, *Ottorino Respighi,* tr. G. MORRIS (London 1962). R. DE RENSIS, *Ottorino Respighi* (Turin 1933). P. ALVERÀ, *Portraits of Greatness: Respighi* (New York 1986). L. BRAGAGLIA and E. RESPIGHI. *Il Teatro di Respighi: Opere, Balli e Balletti* (Rome 1978). A. CANTÙ, *Respighi Compositore* (Torino

Ottorino Respighi.

1985). D. M. RANDEL, ed., *The Harvard Biographical Dictionary of Music* (Cambridge 1996). N. SLONIMSKY, ed. *Baker's Biographical Dictionary of Musicians* (8th ed. New York 1992). J. C. G. WATERHOUSE *The New Grove Dictionary of Music and Musicians* ed. S. SADIE (New York 1980).

[H. BRAUNLICH]

RESPONSA, JEWISH

The responsa literature consists of published answers to written questions directed to rabbinic authorities over a span of 17 centuries. The term responsa is the Latin word for ''answers''; in Hebrew this literature is called *šeʾēlôt utešûbôt,* ''questions and answers.'' It is the practical supplement to the two other types of rabbinical literature—the explanatory commentaries and novellae on the TALMUD (such as those of RASHI and other commentators) and the codes that summarized the law in the maze of debate and coordinated the related laws found in separate places. In the early days, before the compilation of the Talmud, the oral law was a mass of tradition passed down by word of mouth through the generations. When a particular case required expert advice on a specific interpretation of the law, a written request for a ruling was directed to the distant central authority. At first the place of authority was Palestine. Later, after completion of the

Talmud, the center of learning and authority shifted to Babylonia, where the Geonim (*see* GAON) headed the academies of Sura and Pumpeditha (from the 6th to the 11th century). The Gaonic responsa were brief, concise, and authoritative. In the middle of the 11th century the Gaonic period came to an end, and the era of the Rishonim (early rabbinic authorities) began. As the academies and books spread Talmudic knowledge and understanding over a broader area, responsa correspondence evolved to an intrascholarly legalistic level, resulting in full rabbinic essays and monographs.

The general structure included: (1) statement of the case; (2) indication of the relevant law, as recorded in one of the codes; (3) discussion of such contradictory opinions on a subject in the codes that compel reexamination of the basic Talmudical discussion from which the law is derived; (4) an analysis of passages in the Talmud containing principles possibly relevant to a case at hand. The principle is tested by being subjected to seemingly contradictory opinions in the Talmud. Having withstood the test, the principle is then applied to the case. This pattern, with variations according to time and place, was regularly followed.

The spotlight of importance highlighted the respondents of first one country and then another as the centers of learning shifted with the progress of history. Spain and its logical, scientific school produced men such as Solomon ben Adret (1235–1310), the author of 7,000 responsa. In France the grandson of Rashi, Rabbenu Tam (1100–71), achieved great fame. In Germany Rabbi Meir of Rothenburg (1220–93) answered questions of concern to entire communities. In 15th-century Turkey, the haven for emigrants from Spain after the expulsion, Joseph CARO was prominent. Remnants of many responsa from this era and the previous Gaonic era were discovered in the Cairo GENIZA. At the end of the 15th century the era of the later rabbinic authorities (Aharonim) began. The religious community in Poland was being developed; Talmudic schools were set up. Solomon Luria (1510–73) was famous in this period, as was Moses Isserles (1525–72). The responsa of this era were lengthier, for they quoted extensively from the responsa of the Rishonim.

In the 19th and 20th centuries, as emigration to America began and the emigrants found themselves facing a different life, they wrote to their familiar rabbis in eastern Europe for advice on how to proceed. Isaac Elhanan Spektor (1817–96), Rabbi of Kovno, became world-renowned for his responsa. New inventions and circumstances in the modern era raised new questions. Railroads brought up questions regarding travel on the Sabbath. Tobacco posed a problem as to whether smoking is permitted on the holidays. Electric dishwashers, radios, telephones, doorbells, microphones all raised questions concerning usage on the Sabbath. Prayers in the vernacular were questioned, mixed seating, etc. There have been rulings in every field: philosophy of religion, astronomy, mathematics, chronology, and geography, as well as interpretations of difficult passages in the Bible, MISHNAH, and Talmud. Side remarks inserted regarding historical circumstances through the ages have become valuable as source material for Jewish and general history, customs, moral climate, etc. Case law has come to carry as much weight as code law. The Jewish legal system is still flexible and adaptable due to the responsa of the past and present.

Bibliography: S. B. FREEHOF, *The Responsa Literature* (Philadelphia 1955). J. Z. LAUTERBACH, *Jewish Encyclopedia* 11:240–250. M. ELON, *Mavo Lemishpat Halvri* (Jerusalem 1963) 317–338. B. COHEN, *Kuntres Hateshubot* (Budapest 1930).

[E. SUBAR]

RESPONSIBILITY (IN THE BIBLE)

In the ancient Semitic world, collective responsibility was often practiced in its cruder forms; and, as part of a common heritage, it became a significant basis for society and law in the world of the Old Testament. With the insight gained from revelation and experience, the concept of collective responsibility was refined; and this was effected especially by due recognition of individual responsibility. In the New Testament it is explicitly revealed that the principle of the solidarity of the human race, an instance of collective responsibility, stands at the center of the economy of salvation.

This article will treat in order: the common Semitic attitude of collective responsibility; instances of collective responsibility in the Old Testament, the growth of the concept of individual responsibility in the Old Testament, and, finally, the solidarity of the human race in salvation history.

Common Semitic Attitude. In the ancient Near East, a man was looked upon more as a member of his social group than as an individual person. This was due especially to the fact that in nomadic communities the tribe's fight for subsistence bound its members so closely together that each member was filled with the same community spirit. The ideas, engendered by such community spirit, when applied to criminal law, held a man responsible for the deeds of another of his group, particularly of his family. Perhaps the best example of this was the law of blood vengeance. In the Code of Hammurabi there are noteworthy examples: "If a man struck another man's daughter and caused her to have a miscarriage . . . if she died, they shall put his daughter to death'' (209–210); ''If a builder built a house for a man but did not make his work strong and as a result the house collapsed . . . if this cause the death of the son of the owner of the house, they shall put to death the son of the builder'' (229–230); ''If a man held another man's son as pledge for a debt and the son dies from beating or abuse, they shall put to death the son of the distrainer'' (115–116).

Primitive notions about collective responsibility were slow in changing. Even in postexilic times the popular idea that the presence of a great sinner on a ship endangered all the travelers was commonly accepted (Jon 1.7); and among the Medes and Persians it was customary for the children to be punished for the sins of their parents (Dn 6.25; Est 9.10, 14). That such primitive notions were still current in Christ's time is seen in the narrative about the man born blind (Jn 9.2).

Collective Responsibility in Old Testament. In the Old Testament there are many examples of God punishing or rewarding a group for the acts of one individual. The sin of Adam is most noteworthy. Although the Old Testament does not explicitly teach the doctrine of ORIGINAL SIN, it does teach a certain solidarity with Adam; all men share in punishment for Adam's sin. Implicit in the punishment of Cain is the punishment of his offspring (Gn 4.13–14). The curse brought forth by the shameless behavior of Ham falls on his son Canaan (Gn 9.18–27). Because of the unwilling fault of Pharao, his whole house is struck (Gn 12.15–20). Their wives and children share in the punishment of Dathan and Abiram (Nm 16.27). The family of Achan, although they did not share in his sinful violation of the ban, shared his punishment (Jos 22.20). In the Book of Judges it is in accordance with the idea of collective responsibility that the stereotyped formula of sin, punishment, repentance, and liberation sums up current history. In Exodus 20.5 the punishment of children for their parents' violation of the First Commandment is threatened: ''I the Lord, your God, am a jealous God, inflicting punishment for their fathers' wickedness on the children of those who hate me down to the third and fourth generation; but bestowing mercy on the children of those who love me and keep my commandments'' (Ex 20.5–6; 34.7; Nm 14.18; Dt 5.9)

As stated in the passage just quoted from Ex 20.6, God blesses the descendants of a virtuous individual for many generations. There are many instances of this: Noah's family shares his salvation in the ark (Gn 7.1); Lot's family accompanies him out of Sodom (Gn 19.12); and, the descendants of Caleb share in his blessings in the land (Dt 1.36). If ten just men could have been found in Sodom and Gomorrah, God would have spared the city (Gn 18.22–32).

The covenant relationship to God, whereby the Israelites stood as one body before God, i.e., as a church (qāhāl), made the people all the more conscious of collective responsibility. Until the time of the Exile, the Israelite considered his reward or punishment from God not so much a response from God to his individual actions, but as common participation in the response given by God to the whole people.

Individual Responsibility. Yet, the correct understanding of collective responsibility does not exclude a strong feeling of individual responsibility; indeed, some of the oldest stories in the Old Testament show clearly that God punished or rewarded the individual as an individual for his deeds. There are many punitive laws in the Pentateuch based on the principle of individual responsibility. In Dt 24.16 (dealing with human, not with divine justice as in Ex 20.5), there is a protest against the punishment of the children for their parents' sins: ''Every one shall die for his own sin.''

But it was the preaching of the Prophets that emphasized individual responsibility, thus correcting the cruder notions of collective responsibility common to their world. During the Exile, the inherited view whereby children suffer full punishment for the sins of their parents began to be questioned. The older theology had been synthesized into a proverb: ''Fathers have eaten green grapes, thus their children's teeth are on edge'' (Ez 18.2). Ezekiel, in response, answers that any sinner can be saved, if he does penance, and that if ''Noah, Daniel, and Job were in it [the land], as I live, says the Lord God, I swear that they could save neither son nor daughter; they would save only themselves by their virtue'' (14.20). Thus Ezekiel becomes the champion and, so to say, the theorist of individual responsibility. A similar reaction against the more primitive notions of collective responsibility is found in Jer 31.30 (although perhaps not written by him, but a later addition based on Ez 18.2): ''Through his own fault only shall anyone die: the teeth of him who eats the unripe grapes shall be set on edge'' (Prv 24.12; Sir 16.14).

Solidarity in Economy of Salvation. Considering the Exile experience in the light of collective responsibility, it is not surprising that the concept of vicarious suffering of the future Messiah, based on the principle of solidarity, should be explicitly expounded in the SUFFERING SERVANT SONGS (Is 52.13–53.12). For Pauline theology in the New Testament, although the role of Christ as the Servant of the Lord was recognized (Phil 2.7), the central Old Testament text used for explaining the reality of human solidarity in Christ's redemption was the fall of Adam (see Rom 5.12–19; 1 Cor 15.22). For the Christian religion, the whole of theology ultimately is summed up in the intervention of two persons: the one (Adam) in whom all men fell, and the other (Jesus Christ) in whom alone man can be saved. The New Testament, insisting on a solidarity with the risen Christ through personal faith, satisfies both the demand of individual retribution and the law of human solidarity in sin and salvation (see Rom 5.19; 1 Cor 15.21–22; Eph 4.25; 1 Cor 12.26; etc.).

See Also: RETRIBUTION.

Bibliography: L. V. A. BOURGEOIS, . . . *Solidarité* (3d ed. Paris 1902). J. LAROCHE, *La Rétribution sous l'ancienne alliance* (Cahors 1904). H. BÜCKERS, ''Kollektiv und individualvergeltung im Alten Testament,'' *Theologie und Glaube* 25 (1933) 273–286. H. W. ROBINSON, ''The Hebrew Conception of Corporate Personality,'' *Beiträge zur Wissenschaft vom Alten (und Neuen) Testament* 66 (1936) 49–62. *Encyclopedic Dictionary of the Bible,* tr. and adap. by L. HARTMAN (New York 1963) 2032–36.

[M. RODRÍGUEZ]

RESPONSORIAL PSALM

The name applied in the General Instruction on the Roman Missal (GIRM) to the psalm after the first (Old Testament) reading in the 1969 revision of the Roman Rite of the Mass. Originally, the psalm was performed by cantor and assembly in alternation, in the following fashion: a cantor sang verses of the psalm, and the assembly responded to them with a fixed refrain. As the music became more elaborate, the refrain consisted only of the final part of the responsory and was called the *repetenda.* The musical and textual form was as follows: R, V1, R, V2, R, etc. Its liturgical function was that of a meditative assent to the preceding scriptural reading. Thus, the GRADUAL and ALLELUIA were originally responsorial chants. By the middle ages, the ancient responsorial psalm evolved into a highly stylized musical piece that was sung by the choir or cantor without any congregational response.

The 1969 revision of the Roman Rite of the Mass restored the ancient practice of singing the responsorial psalm as ''integral part of the liturgy of the word.'' (GIRM 19). GIRM 20 insists that ''as a rule the responsorial psalm should be sung.'' It goes on to explain that there are ''two established ways of singing the psalm after the first reading: responsorially and directly. In responsorial singing, which, as far as possible, is to be given preference, the psalmist, or cantor of the psalm, sings the psalm verse and the whole congregation joins in by singing the response. In direct singing of the psalm there is no intervening response by the community; either the psalmist, or cantor of the psalm, sings the psalm alone as the community listens or else all sing it together'' (GIRM 20). To reinforce the understanding that the re-

sponsorial psalm is ''an integral part of the liturgy of the word,'' the General Instruction prescribes that the responsorial psalm ''is sung or recited by the psalmist or cantor at the ambo'' (GIRM 22).

[R. G. WEAKLAND/EDS.]

REST

(GR. μονή, ἠρεμία; Lat. *quies, mansio, status*), the opposite of motion. It is the privation of motion in that which is receptive of motion but is not actually being moved. Rest in an initial state (*terminus a quo*) is contrary to the motion that proceeds from it, but there is no strict contrariety between motion and rest in a terminating state (*terminus ad quem*), since rest is the end and perfection of motion, the state of actuality to which motion tends. Likewise, motion is the cause of rest, and something is not the cause of its contrary. Motion and rest are in the same subject, although not both together.

There is a rest corresponding to each type of motion, so that a being may be in motion in one respect and simultaneously at rest in the possession of some state acquired by a different kind of motion. SUBSTANTIAL change is not only absence of change.

Rest is measured by TIME, not by the indivisible now. Strictly speaking, only motion is measured by time, since time is the number of motion according to before and after. A body in the state of rest is a mobile being, and its repose has come about as the result of a motion and will cease when a contrary motion occurs. The duration of the repose between two such motions is measured by means of the duration of the motion of some other body.

Like motion, rest can be either natural and according to nature or unnatural and forced. Rest can be understood in an extended sense. When an agent ceases acting, it is said to come to rest. The mind rests in contemplation of truth and the appetites in the possession of good. The state of equilibrium is not so much rest as the balancing off of opposite forces. Homeostasis is a state of dynamic equilibrium that tends to maintain itself in living beings.

See Also: MOTION; REALITY.

Bibliography: ARISTOTLE, *Phys.*, bk. 5, ch. 6. THOMAS AQUINAS, *In 5 phys.* 9–10.

[M. A. GLUTZ]

RESTITUTION

From the Latin *restituere,* meaning to restore something, to set it up where it had been. In moral theology restitution is an act of commutative justice whereby property is restored to one who has been deprived of it by unjust damage or theft. Not every giving back of something can be called restitution. The restoration of a thing to a person who once owned it but who for some reason lost ownership of it for a time is not restitution. It could be an act of charity, kindness, or liberality, but it would not, in the strict sense, be restitution, not being an act of commutative justice nor presupposing a violated right.

Restitution, then, is the repairing of an injury, the righting of a wrong. The wrong in question could be either theft of something belonging to a person or the damaging of his property. There are, therefore, two grounds of restitution: (1) the possession of something belonging to another and (2) damage done to the property of another. That stolen property no longer exists because it has been exhausted in use by the thief is not a circumstance that excuses from restitution; for in using, spending, or giving away what he has stolen, the thief has spared his own property and thus continues to be ''richer'' and in virtual possession of his unjust gain.

The obligation to make restitution is founded on natural law. Given ownership as a true right, if a person is deprived by theft or unjust damage of what is his, what he has lost must be restored to him to balance the scales of justice. To deny that this is morally necessary is to deny the inviolability that is a property of true rights. A thing is said to cry out for its owner—*res clamat domino*. The injustice continues until it is repaired. Not just the original theft of a thing is wrong, but the retention of it by the thief is equally unjust and is, in effect, a prolongation of the act of injustice.

This obligation of natural law is enforced by the Seventh Commandment of the Decalogue: ''You shall not steal'' (Ex 20.15). To the obligation of restitution there was added in the Old Law the further obligation of satisfaction: ''When a man steals an ox or a sheep and slaughters or sells it, he shall restore five oxen for the one ox, and four sheep for the one sheep'' (Ex 21.37). This disposition of Hebraic law points to two elements in an act of theft or damage: there is an imbalance of justice caused by the act; and there is guilt of the crime incurred by its performance. Restitution of what was taken remedies the inequity; punishment—in the instance cited, the exaction of more than was taken—is to make amends for the guilt of the crime.

An obligation to restitution may be modified by the good, bad, or dubious faith of one in possession of something belonging to another.

Circumstances of Restitution. The general rule is that restitution should be made to the person who has been injured and that it should be made as soon as is morally possible. The inequity arising from the injustice is not remedied by giving the property to one who was not the owner; unnecessary delay in making restitution prolongs the act of injustice; it might possibly do further harm to the injured party. Restitution need not be made openly or in a way that might cause the offending party's guilt to become known. It can be made secretly, anonymously, or even in the form of a gift, provided this can be done without causing the one to whom restitution is made to feel obligated to give a gift in return. An employee can make restitution to an employer by doing extra work for which he is not compensated.

When the injured party or his whereabouts is unknown, restitution should be made to the poor. This is not an exception to the general rule that restitution should be made to the person who has been injured. It is rather a way of disposing of the property according to the wishes of the rightful owner, who is presumed to want his property to be used in the interests of the poor if it cannot be restored to him personally.

Causes Excusing from Restitution. Certain reasons will justify the deferring of restitution, either for a time or permanently. Impossibility, physical or moral, is the chief cause justifying a temporary postponement. It is physical when restitution simply cannot be made; it is moral when it cannot be made without grave hardship, provided the hardship involved in making the restitution is notably greater than that which would be suffered by the injured party in being made to wait for the return of his property. When the impossibility has passed, restitution must be made without further delay. The causes that permanently absolve from the obligation are: (1) condonation, which is the remission of the debt granted expressly or tacitly by the one to whom it is owed; (2) compensation, which occurs when what one owes another is counterbalanced by what the other owes him; (3) composition, which is the remission of the debt granted by the Holy See where restitution is owed for ecclesiastical property or where the creditors are unknown.

Restitution Owed by Cooperators in Injustice. Not only the perpetrator of an injustice, but those who cooperate with him may also be bound to restitution. Moralists distinguish two general kinds of cooperation, positive and negative.

Positive Cooperation. This can take different forms. (1) If one cooperates by inducing another by counsel or persuasion to do an injustice, he is bound, if the principal agent does not do so, to repair all the harm done in consequence of his counsel or persuasion. If he retracts his counsel before the act has been committed, he is not obligated to restitution. Cooperation by way of praise, flattery, ridicule, etc., is reducible to cooperation by counsel, and the same general rule regarding restitution is applicable to it. (2) If one cooperates by commanding or ordering a subordinate to do an injury, he is bound, even before the actual agent, to repair all the harm done under his orders. (3) A cooperator by consent is bound to restitution to the extent to which the consent contributed effectively to the perpetration of the injustice. (4) One who cooperates by sheltering an evil doer or receiving stolen goods is bound to restitution so far as his cooperation results in preventing the injured party from receiving the compensation that is due to him. (5) A cooperator by actual participation is obligated to make restitution for the harm of which he was the efficacious and culpable cause. If his cooperation was essential to the injury, he is obligated equally and *in solidum* with the other essential cooperators for the whole harm done, i.e., he is bound only to his proportionate share in the repair of the harm if the others are prepared to shoulder their responsibility, but he is bound to repair the whole wrong himself if the others refuse to make restitution. If the different cooperators act in a conspiracy aimed at effecting the whole damage, each conspirator is bound *in solidum* with the others to repair the total damage, and each, if the others default, must take full responsibility. But if the cooperators act without conspiracy and each independently of the others effects some harm, each is obligated only to the repair of the harm he has done individually.

Negative Cooperation. The negative cooperator, i.e., one who is bound in justice to prevent injury to another and fails to do so, is bound to restitution if he could have prevented the injustice without incurring unreasonable risk or difficulty. A person may be bound in justice to prevent an injury either by reason of his office or of some contractual obligation, e.g., a parent with respect to the controllable behavior of his children, a policeman, a watchman. A negative cooperator, however, is bound to restitution only when the actual perpetrator of the act, or others more positively implicated in it, fail to meet their obligation.

Order in Which Cooperators Are Bound. In the case of theft, the obligation to restitution rests primarily upon the unjust possessor of the stolen thing, and he must restore it to its owner. He has a right to expect compensation from the one from whom he bought it, provided he acquired it in good faith. If the thing no longer exists, the person who profited most by the theft is considered the possessor. After the possessor, the obligation falls upon the *mandans,* i.e., the one under whose orders or command the theft was committed. Effective persuasion is considered equivalent to command. Next are bound the actual thief and those actively associated with him in the commission of the act. Among these there may be a prior-

ity of responsibility depending upon the nature of the participation of each. Some may be leaders or may contribute to the crime in an essential way. Finally responsibility falls upon the negative cooperators. Except for the unjust possessor, the order is substantially the same in the case of unjust damage. The above order is applicable in ordinary cases. Extraordinary circumstances may alter it in particular cases.

Bibliography: THOMAS AQUINAS, *Summa theologiae* 2a2ae, 62. N. JUNG, *Dictionnaire de théologie catholique,* ed. A. VACANT et al., 15 v. (Paris 1903–50) 13.2:2466–2501. H. NOLDIN, *Summa theologiae moralis,* rev. A. SCHMITT and G. HEINZEL, 3 v. (Innsbruck 1961–62). B. H. MERKELBACH, *Summa theologiae moralis,* 2:284–342. H. DAVIS, *Moral and Pastoral Theology,* rev. and enl. ed. by L. W. GEDDES (New York 1958) 2:284–323.

[A. DOOLAN]

RESTITUTION, EDICT OF

Proclamation of FERDINAND II (1619–37), Mar. 6, 1629, apex of imperial power and Catholic reaction during the THIRTY YEARS' WAR. Following the defeat of Frederick V, Elector Palatine, and the failure of Danish intervention in the struggle between the Hapsburgs and the Protestant Union, Emperor Ferdinand II seized the opportunity to restore Catholic influence and strengthen Hapsburg control throughout the Holy Roman Empire. Without consulting the imperial diet (Reichstag), Ferdinand issued an edict nullifying the alienation of all church lands since the Convention of Passau in 1552, calling for restitution to their rightful owners. The emperor also authorized the new proprietors to expel all those who would not embrace the religious preference of the ruler of the territory, thus reaffirming the principle of *cujus regio ejus religio.* All Protestant sects except Lutherans of the AUGSBURG CONFESSION (1530) were outlawed, especially that of the Calvinists. Ferdinand's unconstitutional decree relaxed Protestant control of the archbishoprics of Magdeburg and Bremen; the bishoprics of Minden, Verden, Halberstadt, Lübeck, Merseburg, Naumburg (these last three, however, were retained by the Elector of Saxony), Brandenburg, Havelberg, Lebus, and Kammin; and many monasteries and smaller foundations. Enforced by imperial commissioners from whom there was no appeal, the decree expelled thousands of peaceful citizens from their homes. The edict also stiffened Protestant resistance and encouraged Swedish intervention against Hapsburg religious and absolutist policies.

Bibliography: C. V. WEDGWOOD, *The Thirty Years' War* (New Haven 1939). C. J. FRIEDRICH, *The Age of the Baroque, 1610–1660* (New York 1952). K. REPGEN, LexThK2 8:1257–58.

[P. S. MCGARRY]

RESURRECTION, GRECO-ORIENTAL

Resurrection is the act on the part of a being, human or divine, whereby he rises again from the dead, with or without the body, as the same individual. This doctrine of resurrection is therefore distinct from that of TRANSMIGRATION OF SOULS.

Greco-Roman paganism found resurrection difficult to accept. The two chief characteristics that distinguished Greek gods from men were happiness and immortality; man was regularly regarded as the union of two discrete entities, a soul and a body, of which the former, but not the latter, was often believed to survive death. The dissolution of the body was regarded, with resignation, as inevitable. This view of man is quite different from that found in the Old Testament, where man is regarded not as a duality, but as an animated body (a unity). This concept of man is more hospitable to belief in resurrection.

Accordingly, Greco-Roman ideas on resurrection were quite different from those of the Christian. The chief Greek god who was believed to die and live again was DIONYSUS, and he was recognized to be of non-Greek origin. When he was introduced into the Orphic Mysteries (*see* MYSTERY RELIGIONS, GRECO-ORIENTAL), the result was belief in transmigration, not resurrection in the proper sense. In the later mystery religions, resurrection was often referred to, but only in a metaphorical sense. In the Mysteries of Isis, for example, the initiate experienced a symbolic death, followed by a moral rebirth in this world (*quodam modo renatos,* Apuleius, *Met.* 11.21). The new life began, not with physical death, but at the time of initiation, and so is analogous to Christian Baptism. Physical death thus ceased to be significant, compared to spiritual rebirth. Similar doctrines, symbolizing a complete break with the initiate's previous life, occur in the Mysteries of Attis and in the rite of TAUROBOLIUM. The Mithraic doctrine of immortalization, 'απαθανατισμός, refers only to a temporary union with the divine during a rite [see A. Dieterich, *Eine Mythrasliturgie* (3d ed. Leipzig 1923) and M. P. Nilsson *Geschichte der griechischen Religion* (Munich 1955–61) 2: 658]. It is thus analogous to ὁμοίωσις θεῷ, the effort to make oneself like the gods, first mentioned by Plato (*Theaetus* 176b) and elaborated in NEOPYTHAGOREANISM and the Hermetic documents. In later Greco-Roman antiquity, the corporeal aspect of death was pushed more and more into the background: punishments and purifications of the dead were no longer said to take place within the earth, but in the upper air.

Gods who were believed to have died and been reborn were more common in the Near East. In Babylon there was the vegetation god Tammuz, and possibly Bel-Marduk, but there was no belief in personal resurrection. In Egypt the soul was believed to leave the dead body for limited periods. This was clearly not the work of gods, but of men, who enabled the soul to continue its life by proper care of the body. There was no expectation of bodily resurrection in this world. Similarly, in the cult of the vegetation god Adonis, whose worship spread from Byblus to Cyprus and to the Greco-Roman world at large, there is no evidence of belief in personal resurrection.

In at least two striking aspects, these Oriental beliefs differ from biblical teachings. First, several dying gods were associated with the annual death and rebirth of vegetation. The hymns to Tammuz, for example, often associate his death with the withering of plants in summer; in fact, the month Tammuz was in midsummer. Second, most of these gods were associated with a goddess who mourned her favorite's death and assisted his resurrection: Tammuz with Ishtar, Osiris with Isis, Adonis with Astarte (Aphrodite), and Attis with Cybele. In these respects, and in its strong moral emphasis, the fully developed Christian doctrine is quite unlike the so-called Greco-Oriental parallels.

The closest real parallel occurs in later portions of the AVESTA. There the soul is judged for the first time three days after death and is then rewarded or punished. After thousands of years there will be a general resurrection of soul and body and a second judgment, after which the evil, now purified, and the good will live in a new world. This doctrine probably goes back to the time of the Achaemenids, and was certainly in existence when 2 Maccabees was written, with its explicit reference to resurrection of the body. However, the Jewish concept is not borrowed from Persian religion, but is to be regarded as a parallel phenomenon.

Bibliography: G. BERTRAM and A. OEPKE, *Reallexikon für Antike und Christentum* (Stuttgart 1941) 1:919–938. G. J. BOTTERWECK et al., *Lexikon für Theologie und Kirche,* ed. J. HOFER and K. RAHNER (Freiburg 1957–65) 1:1042–52. W. VON GODEN et al., *Die Religion in Geschichte und Gegenwart* (Tübingen 1957–65) 1:688–698. M. P. NILSSON, *Geschichte der grieschishen Religion* (Munich 1955–61) 2:610, 657–664. F. NÖTSCHER, *Altorientalischer und alttestamentlicher Auferstehungsglauben* (Würzburg 1926). A. T. NIKOLAINEN, *Die Auferstehungsglauben in der Bibel und ihrer Umwelt,* 2 v. (Helsinki 1944–46). J. LEIPOLDT, *Sterbende und auferstehende Götter* (Leipzig 1923).

[H. S. LONG]

RESURRECTION OF CHRIST

1. In the New Testament

Faith in the resurrection of JESUS of Nazareth as the divinely caused aftermath of his ministry and crucifixion that established him as Jewish Messiah and reigning Lord

"The Resurrection of Christ," oil painting by Giovanni Bellini, 1475–1479, collection of the Staatliche Museen, Berlin. (©Francis G. Mayer/CORBIS)

"The Resurrection," fresco painting by Piero della Francesca, 1463–1465, the Pinacoteca Communale, Sansepolcro, Italy. (©Archivo Iconografico, S.A./CORBIS)

of the universe permeates the thought of the NT. Apart from the resurrection-faith, there would have been no Christian community, no NT, and scarcely any historical memory of Jesus of Nazareth. The NT contains a variety of literary formulations of this resurrection-faith: discourses, termed "kerygmatic speeches" (Acts 2.14–36; 3.12–26; 4.8–12; 5.29–32; 10.34–43; 13.16–41) that assert and substantiate the resurrection-claim; confessional formulae (Phil 2.11; Rom 10.8b–9; 1 Cor 12.3; Rom 8.34; 1 Thes 1.9–10; Rom 1.1–5) expressing the Christian community's conviction of the resurrection; a tradition of the original apostolic witness (1 Cor 15.3–5) not only testifying to the resurrection but explaining its religious significance; Christological hymns (Phil 2.6–11; Col 1.15–20; Eph 1.20–22; 1 Tm 3.16; 1 Pt 1.18–22; Heb 1.3–4) inspired by the resurrection-faith; prophecies of death and resurrection (Mk 8.31; 9.31; 10.32–34 and parallel places) ascribed to Jesus himself; and finally narratives concerning the resurrection that form the conclusion of each GOSPEL (Mk 16.1–8, 9–20; Lk 24.1–53; Mt 28.1–28; Jn 20.1–29; 21.1–23).

The resurrection narratives with which each Gospel closes contain material not present in the kerygmatic speeches, confessional formulae, traditional apostolic testimony, Christological hymns, and Gospel prophecies. This narrative material invariably follows the same pattern—a visit of women to the tomb of Jesus followed by accounts of appearances of the risen Christ. The accounts of the women's visit differ considerably in detail, and the appearance stories in each Gospel are entirely different from the same type of stories in the other three Gospels.

The differences between the resurrection narratives and other formulations of the resurrection-faith in the NT have presented a persistent challenge to NT scholarship. Vatican Council II encouraged biblical scholars to pursue their research for the purpose of bringing the religious meaning of the Scriptures into ever sharper focus (*Dei Verbum* 23). With this objective in view, contemporary NT scholarship has undertaken a critical reassessment of the NT material bearing on the resurrection of Christ. This article concerns itself first with Paul's use of the apostolic tradition in 1 Cor 15.1–8 and second with the kerygmatic speeches in Acts. Consideration of this material supplies the actual NT foundation for the understanding of the resurrection narratives. Finally, the article makes an assessment of the resurrection narratives themselves.

First Cor 15.1–8 and the resurrection narratives.

From the standpoint of the chronology of NT literature, 1 Cor 15.1–8 is the earliest written statement concerning the apostolic testimony to the resurrection of Christ. Writing about 54 to 56 A.D., St. Paul uses the apostolic tradition to address himself to the question of the resur-

rection of the dead, in which some Corinthian Christians had lost faith (1 Cor 15.12). He reminds them that the resurrection-faith that created their community did not involve the acceptance of a marvelous display of divine power simply in favor of the crucified Jesus of Nazareth by means of which a personal glorious afterlife was granted him. What was proclaimed to them and what they accepted was that Christ "died for our sins according to the Scriptures," i.e., Christ accepted the death of the cross as God's will for the remission of sins of which all peoples throughout human history are guilty, as the OT makes clear (1 Cor 15.1–3); and that Christ "was raised . . . according to the Scriptures," an event that occurred and was made known in time ("on the third day"), 1 Cor 15.4, i.e., the manifestation of the resurrection of Christ had for its purpose God's communicating to people like themselves that in Christ's death and resurrection he was carrying to completion his plan to save humanity from the disastrous effects of sin, of which death is the chief (1 Cor 15.54–57). To deny the resurrection of the dead as the beginning of an everlasting afterlife in the full integrity of the person is to remove all religious significance from God's act in raising Christ and to render Christian faith in his person meaningless: "If there is no resurrection of the dead, Christ himself has not been raised" (1 Cor 15.13), i.e., if the dead are not restored to a life with God as the final result of the remission of their sins, neither was Christ himself restored to a life with God, for it was the prevalence of sin itself that caused his death. If Christ did not overcome the sins that caused his death, he did not overcome death and consequently was not raised.

But according to the apostolic testimony, Christ was in reality raised from the dead (1 Cor 15.20), the divine sign that he did overcome sin and death. That God in fact raised him from the dead was manifested to Cephas and to the Twelve (1 Cor 15.5). To this testimony of the original apostles, the Twelve, Paul adds a list of others who had a similar experience of the risen Christ through which they understood his overcoming of sin and death: the five hundred brethren (1 Cor 15.6); James, the administrator of the Jerusalem community; and "all the apostles," probably a different group from the Twelve, who because of their experience of the risen Christ were mandated apostles by the Twelve. Paul concludes by adding himself to the list of apostolic witnesses to Christ's resurrection and its religious significance, a fact of which, no doubt, he had already informed the Corinthians when he established their community.

Scholars disagree as to whether 1 Cor 15.3–5 alludes to, or shows that, Paul was aware of the tradition of the empty tomb. His text certainly makes no clear allusion to this tradition. The fact that the Jewish conception of the human person required both body and spirit and that on this basis the Apostle would naturally have assumed an empty tomb, does not constitute an argument for a reference in 1 Cor 15.4 (''he was buried'') to the specific tradition of the empty tomb in the resurrection narratives. It seems to be a necessary inference that in Paul's understanding, the apostolic preaching of the resurrection of Christ did not incorporate the datum of the empty tomb.

Although in 1 Cor 15.5–8 Paul insists that the resurrection-faith is based upon the testimony of witnesses to the risen Christ, he makes no reference to accounts of the experiences of the witnesses. The Greek verb *ōphthē* used successively in each verse of the passage to designate a particular, personal, and special encounter with the risen Christ by Cephas, the Twelve, the five hundred brethren, James, all the apostles, and Paul can be translated as ''was seen by'' or ''appeared.'' Even if with the majority of NT scholars one prefers ''appeared,'' one cannot deduce the nature of the appearances from this verb. The most that can be concluded from it is that the experience of the risen Christ to which the verb makes reference had both objective and subjective elements, i.e., the verb implies more than a mere internal visionary experience, but does not necessarily imply the same kind of objective presence of Christ that was the recipients' experience of the objective presence of the historical Jesus. From the fact that the experiences of the risen Christ were apparently different in nature from their experience of the historical Jesus, it does not follow that they were any less intense and meaningful than the encounter with the Jesus of the ministry. The effect upon Paul of his experience of the risen Christ on the road to Damascus (Acts 9.1–9; 22.6–11; 26.12–18)—the intensity of his apostolic life (1 Cor 9.1–27) and his steadfastness in the face of extreme hardship (2 Cor 11.22–29)—shows that the encounter with the risen Christ could be more intense and meaningful than even a daily relationship with the Jesus of the ministry.

The lack of reference to accounts of the appearances of the risen Christ in 1 Cor 15.5–8 indicates that the original apostolic proclamation of the resurrection did not include a narrative form recapitulating these appearances. Since in the final analysis the apostolic preaching of the resurrection rested on the authority of God (cf. 1 Cor 15.15), the recital of appearances of the risen Christ would add nothing substantial to the assertion of his resurrection. Such recitals would have diverted attention away from the risen Christ to the Twelve and the phenomenon of their experiences of him.

Kerygmatic speeches in Acts and the resurrection narratives. Luke's Gospel and Acts contain the perimeters of the NT resurrection-faith without any attempt on the author's part to fuse them. Luke's Gospel ends with the narrative form of the women's visit to the tomb followed by appearance narratives (Lk 24.1–53). Although Acts 1.3 speaks in strong terms of the appearances of the risen Christ to the Twelve, the kerygmatic speeches (cf. the listing above) make no mention of actual appearances. Nor do they make any reference to the empty tomb.

The material of the kerygmatic speeches coheres with the Pauline formulation of the apostolic proclamation in 1 Cor 15.3–5. Each of the speeches contains the same central assertion: ''God raised Jesus'' (Acts 2.32; 3.15; 4.10; 5.30; 10.40; 13.30). In 1 Cor 15.4 the formulation in the passive mood (''was raised on the third day . . .'') is the Jewish way of avoiding the use of the divine name while clearly attributing the action to God. Thus in the kerygmatic formulations of both Paul and Luke, the resurrection of Christ is placed outside the sphere of human observation and investigation. Its reality is declared to be knowable only if one accepts it as a communication of God, its author.

In Acts, Luke chooses the Greek term *martyres*, witnesses, to characterize the role of the Twelve toward the risen Christ. In the Greek world the term *martys*, witness, carried both the sense of ''eyewitness,'' or of one who could testify to a fact from personal experience, as well as the meaning of expert testimony in the case where testimony concerned truths not empirically verifiable and requiring special knowledge or education. Utilizing this twofold meaning of *martys*, Luke depicts the Twelve as witnesses to the risen Christ from divinely given personal experience of him and from divinely endowed insight into the religious meaning of his resurrection (Acts 2.32–36; 3.15–23; 5.32; 10.40–43; 13.31). In 1 Cor 15.3–8 Paul combines *ōphthē*, ''appeared,'' with use of the dative case for the persons to whom the manifestation of the risen Christ was made. Thus he clearly has the idea, though not the language, of witnesses to the risen Christ. When in 1 Cor 15.3 he observes, ''I handed on to you what I also received'' concerning Christ's death for sin and his resurrection, both according to the Scriptures, he is referring to the divinely endowed insight of Cephas and the Twelve as a group into the religious meaning of Christ's resurrection. In substance, the concept of the apostolic preaching in the Lucan speeches and in Paul's formulation of it in 1 Cor 15 are in harmony. Whereas Paul, aiming in 1 Cor 15.1–8 to focus attention on the personal relationship created by Christ's death and resurrection between Christ and every human being, contents himself with a sweeping reference to the OT Scriptures as manifesting God's will fulfilled in Christ, Luke, whose purpose in Acts is to describe the apostolic address to nonbelievers, cites the OT Scriptures explicitly (e.g., Ps

16.8–11 in Acts 2.25–28; Ps 110.1 in Acts 2.34–35; Dt 18.15–16 in Acts 3.22–23).

Conclusion. According to 1 Cor 15.1–8 and Luke's presentation of the kerygmatic speeches in Acts, the resurrection-faith of the NT Christian communities originated from the authoritative assertion of the Twelve, of Paul, and of other apostles that they had been the recipients of a divinely caused experience of the risen Christ. The salient thrust of their testimony was that the risen Christ reigned in the realm of God, a vantage point from which he demanded the faith and adherence of humanity. The orientation of the apostolic preaching was toward the otherworldly status and power of the risen Christ. It did not direct attention to the actual experiences of the witnesses who were the recipients of God's self-communication concerning his action toward the crucified, dead, and buried Jesus of Nazareth.

Nonetheless, Paul's use of *ōphthē* and Luke's use of *martys* to convey the connection between the apostolic assertion of the resurrection and the experience on which the assertion was based imply a relationship between the original preachers of the resurrection-event and the person of the risen Christ. This terminology of Paul and Luke has traditionally led theologians to conclude that a real experience of the risen Christ was the root cause of the apostolic testimony to his resurrection. The experience itself was the creative force that produced the resurrection-faith, first in the apostles, next through them in others who became the Christian community. In recent years, some exegetes and theologians have proposed a different interpretation of the NT data: that it was the teaching of the historical Jesus that produced the resurrection-faith, either by way of theological reflection upon his historical teaching and person together with a factor of divine revelation somehow associated with the theological reflection, or simply by way of theological reflection upon the memory of Jesus of Nazareth and his religious significance. This interpretation of the NT data, while in some respects worthy of further discussion, is not as yet sufficiently well founded or developed to be given serious consideration here. Its principal value is that it points to the usefulness of taking seriously the question of the interaction between the resurrection-faith of the apostles and their experience of the historical Jesus. It remains to be seen whether this particular avenue of research will succeed in contributing to the understanding of the origin of the resurrection-faith in the NT.

Resurrection narratives. It is already clear that these narratives, as well as their component parts, did not originate for the purpose of creating a faith-community centered on the risen Christ. As is the case with the four Gospels as a whole, the resurrection narratives are addressed to Christian communities whose faith in Jesus Christ is established, and, in the particular instance of his resurrection, on the ground of the apostolic testimony. The evangelists composed the four Gospels in order to support the faith of Christians. In general they have the same objective in the resurrection narratives.

The Women's Visit to the Tomb of Jesus. The visit is narrated in Mk 16.1–8; Lk 24.1–10; Mt 28.1–8; Jn 20.1–2. The differences of detail in each evangelist's presentation of the women's visit to Jesus' tomb are remarkable. In Mk 16.1 they proceed to the tomb "to anoint him"; in Lk 24.1 they bring "spices" or "aromatic oils," but for what particular purpose is not stated; in Mt 28.1 they come to "view" or possibly "to observe" the tomb; in Jn 20.1 Mary Magdalene simply "comes" to the tomb. In Mk 16.3 the women are concerned about the difficulty of rolling back the heavy stone sealing the tomb, a detail not included in the other three accounts. In Mk 16.4 and Lk 24.2, when they find the tomb open, they enter it; but in Jn 20.1–2 Mary Magdalene, making the same discovery, does not enter it. In Mt 28.1–4 the women's entrance to the tomb is blocked by an angel, who subsequently, however, invites them to determine for themselves that it is empty (Mt 28.6).

The dress of the angels varies from one Gospel to another. Mk 16.5 describes a young man dressed simply in white—a figure unconvincingly explained by some NT scholars as a representative of the risen Christ or of a Christian neophyte; Lk 24.4 speaks of two angels in shining garments, while Mt 28.3 depicts a figure whose facial features are like lightning and whose clothing is snow-white; Jn 20.12 laconically notes the presence of two angels dressed simply in white.

The function of the angels varies in the four Gospel accounts of the women's visit to the tomb. In Mk 16.6 and Mt 28.6 the angel informs the women of the empty tomb, whereas in Lk 24.3 and Jn 20.11–13 the women make the discovery themselves. In Mk 16.7 and Mt 28.7 the angel instructs the women to inform Jesus' disciples of his resurrection and that they will see him in Galilee; in Lk 24.6–7 the women are reminded of Jesus' prophecies of his crucifixion and resurrection on the third day as if these prophecies in Lk 9.22; 9.43–44; 18.31–34 were directed to the women. In Jn 20.13 the angels make no response to Mary Magdalene's plaint that Jesus' body had been stolen from the tomb.

The women's reaction to the angelic message at the tomb varies from Gospel to Gospel: in Mk 16.8 they flee from the tomb in fear and astonishment and "say nothing to anyone"; in Lk 24.9–10 they report their experience at the tomb to the apostles; in Mt 28.8 they leave the tomb in a holy fear but with joy and set out to report to Jesus' disciples; in Jn 20. 13–14 Mary Magdalene poses no question to the angels concerning the whereabouts of Jesus' body, her main concern.

The variations among the evangelists in their depiction of the women's visit to Jesus' tomb, remarkable as they are in themselves, become even more astonishing in the light of the fact that Luke and Matthew availed themselves of the Gospel of Mark as a source and guideline for the composition of their own Gospels (a literary relationship among the synoptic evangelists that the majority of contemporary NT scholars consider to be established). On this supposition, it follows that neither Luke nor Matthew viewed their variations from Mark as anything other than instructive for the faith of the Christian community.

The single constant in the four Gospel accounts of the women's visit to the tomb is their discovery that it was open and empty. In John's Gospel, Mary Magdalene eventually verifies the emptiness of the tomb, her original inference (Jn 20.1–2), by personal inspection (Jn 20.11–13). Contemporary NT scholars continue to debate the historical veracity of the tradition of the open-empty tomb. Unlike the resurrection of Christ and the apostolic experience of the person of the risen Christ, the tradition of the open-empty tomb is a direct object of historical assessment.

Since the tradition was not put forward by the apostolic preaching as a basis for the resurrection-faith, its origin cannot be accounted for out of such a purpose. In all four Gospels the open-empty tomb is linked with the accounts of Jesus' burial. Although it was Roman practice to leave the corpse of the crucified to decompose on the cross or to be devoured by animals, the Roman authority, having regard for Jewish sensibilities concerning the respect due a human corpse (cf. Dt 21.22–23), permitted immediate burial of crucified Jews. Jn 19.31 has certain (unnamed) leaders of the Jews requesting Pilate to have the *crurifragium*, the breaking of the legs, performed upon Jesus and the two men crucified with him, so as to hasten their deaths and permit their burial before the Sabbath (in Jn, also the feast of the Passover). It was perhaps as a member of this delegation from the Sanhedrin that Joseph of Arimathea sought and received from Pilate charge of Jesus' corpse. At least in Judea it lay within the jurisdiction of the Roman procurator to grant the corpse of the crucified Jew to relatives or friends for the purpose of interment.

Joseph was not a relative or friend of Jesus (in Mk 15.43 he is a "prominent counsellor"; in Lk 23.50 he is a "counsellor, a good and just man"; in Mt 27.57 he is a disciple of Jesus; in Jn 19.38 he is a secret disciple). On what precise grounds he won custody of the corpse from the procurator can only be conjectured, for the evange-

lists supply no information on this point. In the case of one executed for a political offense, as was Jesus on suspicion of sedition, the procurator ordinarily refused such a request when it was made by one who was not a relative of the deceased. Perhaps the fact that Pilate acceded to Joseph's petition is one of the reasons why the evangelists emphasize Pilate's judgment that Jesus was innocent of sedition (Mk 15.12–15; Lk 23.13–16; Mt 27.18–19, 23–24; Jn 19.4–6). Since the Jews considered the burial of their dead, even of those executed in connection with violations of the OT Law, to be a sacred duty, it is not surprising that Joseph, as a member of the Sanhedrin, a man of stature and, as a Jew, a man of religious concern, (Mk 15.43) assumed a responsibility that Jesus' relatives and friends were unwilling or unable to undertake. Those adjudicated to be violators of the OT Law, as was the case with Jesus (Mk 14.62–64 and parallels) and the two robbers crucified with him (Lv 19.13), were normally interred in a burial ground reserved for them and located at some distance from the city where executions took place. Among the Jews, burials on the Sabbath were strictly forbidden: Joseph's choice of his own tomb (Mt 27.59–60) provided a site close enough to Golgotha that permitted interment before the Sabbath. The two robbers may have been buried with Pilate's consent by relatives or friends also near Golgotha.

The Gospel depiction of Jesus' burial is in accord with both Roman and Jewish practice concerning the final disposition of the corpse of a crucified Jew. The opinion that the burial took place in the burial ground reserved for criminals, advanced by a minority of NT scholars, lacks substantiation in the evidence. Further, on this hypothesis the women's presence as witnesses to the burial in Joseph's tomb (Mk 15.47; Lk 23.55; Mt 27.61) becomes difficult to explain, since women's testimony was not considered of value either in Jewish or Roman culture. Their testimony was simply inadequate to supplant the supposed fact of burial in a common graveyard in favor of an honorable interment in Joseph's tomb.

From a historical point of view, there is no reason to dispute the accuracy of the statements in the Synoptic Gospels attributing to the women knowledge of the location of Jesus' tomb (Mk 16.1; Lk 24.1; Mt 28.1; cf. also Jn 20.1) with which each evangelist begins his account of the women's visit. The differences among the evangelists on the women's motives for visiting the tomb may well be due in part to an actual difference of motives among them and in part to the discrepancies of detail among witnesses with which historians are familiar. It was established Jewish custom to honor the tombs of the dead. Since Jesus had in fact received honorable burial, but without any marks of affection or respect from his followers, it is not unnatural that these women, who had witnessed the humiliation of the cross (Mk 15.40; Lk 23.49; Mt 27.55–56; Jn 19.25), were determined somehow to compensate for this deficiency, whether by placing aromatic materials at the tomb or, should it have turned out to be possible, around the enshrouded corpse of Jesus. Each evangelist's mention of the women's motives serves to concentrate attention upon the unexpected drama of their visit: their objectives could not be carried out, for the tomb was open and empty. Only Mt (28.2) offers the explanation that it was an angel who opened the tomb. The other evangelists leave the reader to share in the women's mystification at this turn of events (Mk 16.3–4; Lk 24.2; Jn 20.1–2).

In the Synoptic Gospels, the explanation for the open-empty tomb is made by an angel or angels: the crucified Jesus has been raised by God. The angelic announcement then looks backward to prophecies ascribed to Jesus (in Lk and Mt to the passion-resurrection prophecies; in Mk to the reunion in Galilee spoken of in 14.28) and forward to his appearances to his disciples (Mk 16.6–7; Lk 24.5–7; Mt 28.5–7). The tradition of the women's discovery of the open-empty tomb (upon which the resurrection narrative of the Fourth Gospel at first centers its entire attention, Jn 20.1–13) is interpreted in the Synoptic Gospels by use of the apostolic proclamation that the crucified Jesus was buried and raised by God (cf. 1 Cor 15.4). The Twelve, the original proclaimers of this divine act, are replaced by angels: whether the proclamation be apostolic or angelic, it is the message of God. On this note Mark's Gospel, whether by design or by accident, originally concluded (Mk 16.1–8). The evangelist's stress on the women's silence (Mk 16.8; ". . . they said nothing to anyone . . .") need not be understood in a sense so absolute as to exclude "the disciples and Peter" (Mk 16.7). Neither Luke (24.9) nor Matthew (28.8) took Mk 16.8 to mean that the women did not report their experience at the tomb to the disciples and Peter. For Mark the women are witnesses to the burial of Jesus and to the open-empty tomb, but they are not among the original apostolic witnesses to Christ's resurrection, a function reserved to the disciples and Peter (cf. Mk 13.9–11).

Luke's inclusion of a reaction of skepticism in response to the women's report (Lk 24.9, 11, 22–24) may be in part theologically motivated (to exclude the discovery of the open-empty tomb as a basis for the apostolic proclamation of Christ's resurrection) and in part a literary technique to introduce the reader to the lengthy account of the appearance of the risen Christ to the two disciples on the way to Emmaus. Jn 20.3–10 presents a favorable reaction to Magdalene's report: in consequence of it Peter and the beloved disciple visit the tomb and are impressed by the fact that the cloths that had enshrouded

Jesus' corpse are lying neatly in place. Lk 24.12 (a passage that contemporary textual critics incline to accept as authentic) reflects the same tradition, but told of Peter alone. Matthew's Gospel does not include a reaction of Jesus' disciples to the report intended by the women (Mt 28.8).

Mt 28.4 interweaves the story of the guarding of Jesus' tomb (Mt 27.62–66) with the women's visit. This evangelist's portrayal of the women's visit is set in the context of apocalyptic, a literary technique that emphasized the revelatory aspect of an event and intimated its special importance for the future. Apocalyptic features in Matthew's portrayal of the women's visit are the earthquake, the descent of the angel of the Lord, the OT representative of Yahweh (Mt 28.2), the lightning-like appearance of the angel's facial features (Mt 28.3), and the paralysis of the guards (Mt 28.4). The address of the apocalyptic angel to the women, appointing them emissaries to Jesus' disciples (Mt 28.5–7), places greater emphasis on their function as witnesses than is the case in the other three Gospels. Perhaps Matthew intended to contrast the women's acceptance of the resurrection-proclamation and its rejection by certain leaders of the Jewish community.

The guarding of the tomb (requested by a Jewish leadership unaware of Jesus' passion-resurrection prophecies, and not until the day after his burial), the defeat of the guards by the apocalyptic angel (a pre-Matthean or Matthean figure depicted to interpret the open-empty tomb), and therefore the payment of the guards to secure their silence (Mt 28.11–15) cannot be understood as historical data. Since this material, however, is taken seriously in Mt, the possibility suggests itself that neither the Christian story of the guarding of the tomb, nor the Jewish story of the disciples' theft of the corpse, nor the Christian story of the payment of the guards were originally historical assertions but forms of theological debate, probably (but not necessarily) over the religious significance of the open-empty tomb. But what precisely such a theological debate might have centered upon is not presently ascertainable.

The Christophanies. Appearances of the risen Christ are described in Mk 16.7; Lk 24.13–53; Mt 28.9–10; 16–20; Jn 20.11–18; 19–29; 21.1–23.

(a) *Mk 16.7.* Some contemporary NT scholars interpret the "seeing" of the risen Christ by the disciples and Peter (Mk 16.7a) as a reference to the parousia to occur in Galilee. The text, however, refers the reader to Mk 14.28: "But after I am raised I will go before you into Galilee." When Mk 16.7 observes, ". . . there," i.e., in Galilee, "you will see him as he told you," the reference is simply to Christ now risen from the dead. Parousia-passages speak of "seeing" the Son of Man (Mk 14.62; 13.26), i.e., the risen Christ, in the role of judge. Before the judgment at the parousia is to take place, the disciples' function is to preach the risen Christ who demands faith now (Mk 13.9–11), a situation that is to be evaluated when he appears as the Son of Man of Dn 7.13–14 for the final judgment (Mk 13.26). Mk 16.7 speaks of the disciples and Peter seeing the risen Christ as the prelude to their mission of Mk 13.9–11. The language of Mk 16.7 has at least one christophany in view, as is also the case with each person or groups of persons mentioned in 1 Cor 15.5–8 and in the kerygmatic speeches in Acts. It is not possible to determine whether or not Mark intended to record a christophany as the conclusion to his Gospel. However peculiar it may seem that his Gospel does in fact conclude without a christophany, this omission accords with the form of the apostolic proclamation in 1 Cor 15.5–8 and in the kerygmatic speeches in Acts, where it is sufficient for the audience to know that christophanies have occurred. It has also to be kept in mind that Mark's readers could easily have been in possession of a tradition of one or several christophanies to which the evangelist simply chose to allude.

(b) *Lk 24.13–32.* The Appearance to the Disciples on the Way to Emmaus is a narrative quite skillfully written. It is linked to the women's visit to the tomb (the two disciples discount the women's report on the ground that no one has seen Jesus alive, Lk 24.22–24) and to the appearance to Peter from which the Eleven and others have learned of Jesus' resurrection (Lk 24.33–34). Paradoxically, the disciples who refuse the women's report because Jesus has not been seen alive do not recognize him (Lk 24.16). Their surprise that the traveler who now accompanies them is apparently unaware of the importance of the crucifixion and death of Jesus of Nazareth (Lk 24.18–21) is matched by the traveler's surprise that they have not understood the tragedy of this prophet in terms of the OT Scriptures (Lk 24.25–27). The disciples' sadness (Lk 24.17) begins to dissipate as a result of their confrontation with the Scriptures under the guidance of the traveler (Lk 24.28–29). The meal to which they had been looking forward in his company terminates when bread is broken and given them by the traveler: the mysteriousness of non-recognition becomes the mysteriousness of recognition; but with recognition he vanishes from their sight (Lk 24.30–31). Their report in Jerusalem is overshadowed by the announcement of the Eleven and others that "the Lord has really been raised and has appeared to Simon" (Lk 24.34).

In this narrative of Luke the experience of the two disciples surpasses that of the women, who do not see the risen Christ but have a vision of angels affirming "that he was alive" (Lk 24.23). But it falls short of the experience of Simon to whom "the Lord . . . appeared" (Lk 24.34). Luke uses the verb *ōphthē* of the appearance, as does Paul in 1 Cor 15.5–8 of all the appearances he mentions. In Paul this verb supposes that Christ appears as one who has received a glorious afterlife from which he reigns over the Christian community. The two disciples discover at Emmaus that Jesus of Nazareth (Lk 24.19) is indeed alive. But Peter discovers that he is alive and raised by God as "the Lord." The two disciples recognize him; Peter understands also his identity.

The Emmaus narrative has to be understood within the limitation placed upon it by Luke. The two disciples only begin to perceive that the suffering of Jesus possesses religious meaning when the traveler explains the Scriptures to them (Lk 24.25–27). Even when they did not recognize him, his explanation cast the suffering of Jesus of Nazareth in a new and impressive light (Lk 24.32). Their recognition of him at "the breaking of the bread" (Lk 24.30–31, 35) is certainly a Eucharistic allusion, but it does not imply the fullness of understanding. Rather the fullness of understanding is a requirement for a share in the Eucharistic meal. It is this understanding they begin to acquire from the declaration of the disciples at Jerusalem that "the Lord . . . has appeared to Simon."

As NT scholars have shown, Luke composed the Emmaus narrative from at least two sources. He also reworked these sources to highlight the historical ministry of Jesus (Lk 24.19), the passion-resurrection prophecies (Lk 24.20, 21b), the Christian use of the OT Scriptures (Lk 24.25–27), the Eucharist (Lk 24.35), and the apostolic proclamation of the resurrection of Christ (Lk 24.34). Thus his Emmaus narrative presents a compendium of factors that are essential to the formation of Christian faith. Luke was more interested in the religious significance of the Emmaus appearance than in the phenomenon of the appearance itself.

(c) *Lk 24.36–53.* The Appearance to the Eleven is a narrative composed of three distinct parts: the appearance of the risen Christ (Lk 24.36–43); the mission mandate (Lk 24.44–49); and the departure of Christ (Lk 24.50–53). To maintain the literary continuity of his resurrection narrative as a whole, Luke places this appearance-story in the context of the report of the Emmaus disciples (Lk 24.36). The story is concerned with the disciples' recognition of Christ as corporeally risen and objectively present before them: it is not his spirit or a phantom that they see (cf. Acts 23.9), as the marks of his wounds attest (Lk 24.39a); nor are they undergoing a subjective vision, for they can touch him if they wish (Lk 24.39b). Jesus eating broiled fish before them (Lk 24.41–43) is obviously intended by Luke to indicate his bodily resurrection, but how this implication follows is unclear unless one supposes that as the host he shared the fish with them (cf. Acts 10.41). Since the story as a whole is introduced by mention of the disciples' panic and fright, a strange reaction in view of their knowledge of two appearances of Jesus, it becomes all the more clear that Luke wishes to emphasize the corporeal and objective reality of these appearances of the risen Christ, especially because he has had to acknowledge the Emmaus disciples' passage from non-recognition to recognition.

The mission mandate is a compressed summary of the kerygmatic speeches in Acts, followed by mention of the gift of the Holy Spirit enabling the disciples to perform the mission (Lk 24.49; cf. Acts 1.5 for the meaning of the ''promise of the Father'').The departure scene seems to be introduced with the priestly blessing of the risen Christ (cf. Heb 8.1; Sir 50.19–21). Whether there is explicit mention of an ascension in Lk 24.51 (''he was taken up to heaven'') depends upon the authenticity of this clause in the Greek text. The reading has the support of good MSS, of Acts 1.2, and Lk 24.52a (''they fell down to do him reverence''), which is consistent with it.

(d) *Mt 28.9–10.* The Appearance to the Women seems, from a literary standpoint, a poorly placed christophany. Mary Magdalene and ''the other Mary'' (Mt 28.1) have been instructed by the angel to inform the disciples of Jesus' resurrection and of a meeting with them in Galilee. As they are on their way to fulfill this commission, Jesus appears to them. Two observations may be made on the literary location of this brief narrative. In both Luke and John the appearance of Christ to the Eleven (or Twelve), Jesus' chosen disciples, is preceded by a christophany to others that prepares the Eleven for the experience of the risen Christ: the Emmaus disciples in Luke, who report to the Eleven and Mary Magdalene in John, who also makes a report (Jn 20.18). It seems then that Matthew's literary location of the appearance to the women follows a tradition that christophanies were first experienced by those outside the group constituting Jesus' chosen disciples and reported to them. Second, the instruction of the risen Christ to the women speaks of ''my brethren'' (Mt 28.10), not of the ''disciples'' as in Mt 28.7. ''Brethren'' is the common Christian term in the NT for a fraternal relationship. Consequently, the message of the risen Christ from the women to the disciples implies his forgiveness of their desertion of him. As in Luke and John, a prior christophany in Matthew prepares for the appearance of the risen Christ to his chosen disciples.

(e) *Mt 28.16–20.* This Appearance to the Eleven in Mt presents the most solemn christophany in the resurrection-narratives. It takes place on an undesignated mountain in Galilee (a favorite place for significant events in Mt: Jesus' temptation, 4.8; the Sermon on the Mount, 5.1; Jesus' prayer after the feeding of the five thousand and before the sea-walking, 14.23; Jesus' healing of a multitude of sick, 15.29; and the Transfiguration, 17.1). What precise symbolism, if any, the evangelist attached to the mountain is undetermined. Strangely, at the appearance of Christ the Eleven worship him but some ''doubted.'' The majority of NT scholars no longer interpret this doubt by translating ''had doubted'' (impermissible in view of the aorist tense of the Greek verb). Some consider it to be a reference to earlier doubts among the Eleven; but if such was the evangelist's viewpoint, it is difficult to understand why he did not indicate that the doubts were now dissipated. A plausible explanation is that Matthew makes use of the tradition of doubt among Jesus' disciples concerning his resurrection to criticize the doubts of the Christian community of his own time, a point that may also be made in Mk 16.14.

The words of the risen Christ portray a structure of the Christian community that combines divine and human authority: the full authority of the risen Christ residing in the realm of God is shared in history by the Eleven. In turn they are to share it by making disciples in all nations. These disciples are to be united to the triune God through Baptism; and, beginning with the Eleven, whatever Jesus has taught (as recorded in Mt) is to be carried out by the Eleven and by the disciples in all the nations. In this very mission, the risen Christ will be mysteriously present as long as human history endures. The text of this mandate in Mt 28.18–20 is related to Dn 7.13–14 and probably also to Ps 110.1. The exact conceptual relationship between these OT passages and this passage in Mt remains, however, uncertain.

(f) *Jn 20.11–18.* The Appearance to Mary Magdalene is a christophany in which the theme of non-recognition occurs. But unlike Luke's Emmaus-narrative, it is given a practical explanation: Magdalene takes Jesus for the gardener because she assumes that he is dead and that his corpse has been taken from the tomb and buried elsewhere (Jn 20.11–15). Her recognition occurs when Jesus calls her by name (Jn 20.16). Since there has been a previous conversation, it is not simply the sound of Jesus' voice that causes the recognition but his knowledge of her. While in Luke the mysteriousness lies in the non-recognition, in John it lies in the recognition. Evidently, Magdalene assumes that the risen Christ is to resume his past relationship with his disciples (probably, the import of ''Don't cling to me,'' Jn 20.17). Jesus corrects her assumption by instructing her to inform his disciples that he is ascending to his Father. By focusing attention on the ascension, the evangelist prepares the way for Jesus' gift of the Spirit to the Twelve.

(g) *Jn 20.19–29.* The Appearance to the Disciples and to Thomas concludes the Fourth Gospel. In the narrative of the appearance to the disciples (Jn 20.19–23), their recognition of the risen Christ results from the perception of his wounds, at the sight of which the disciples rejoice (Jn 20.20). Their recognition and rejoicing are theologically based: in John the cross is the beginning of Jesus' glorification (Jn 13.31–32), and by means of it he will attract the world to himself (Jn 12.32). With his appearance to them, the disciples begin to understand the truth of his words and rejoice that he is about to achieve this goal. However, the achievement is to be brought about in history by themselves. Having understood the religious significance of the cross and resurrection, they are capable of receiving and exercising the mission mandate (Jn 20.21–23): they are given the Spirit so that they might exercise discernment and authority to forgive men's sins or to withold forgiveness in the name of Christ, a power that the evangelist leaves unspecified and therefore probably conceives broadly. The fact that he makes no mention of Jesus' departure suggests that he wishes to give particular prominence to the mission mandate.

The narrative of the appearance to the unbelieving Thomas (Jn 20.24–29) is a dramatic conclusion to the Gospel, which has been written in support of Christian faith: ". . . that you may believe that Jesus is the Christ, the . . ." (cf. Jn 20.30–31). The drama results from his absence when the christophany occurred. He refuses the disciples' testimony to the christophany and its religious significance, taking the position that unless he has the opportunity to judge for himself and on his own terms, he will not believe (Jn 20.24–25). The occurrence of the subsequent christophany with the disciples again behind locked doors (Jn 20.26; cf. Jn 20.19) does not mean that the risen Christ physically passed through locked doors, but that the physical construction of things does not preclude his objective presence. The reality and communicative force of Christ's presence are so compelling, that Thomas makes the supreme confession: "My Lord and my God" (Jn 20.28).

In the opinion of contemporary NT scholars, the story of the unbelieving Thomas was inspired by the tradition of the doubt among the Twelve (Lk 24.41; Mt 28.17; Mk 16.14) and the difficulties of some Christians in holding to the resurrection-faith at a time when the original witnesses to the risen Christ had died out. It was, of course, always known that actual witnesses were few in number and that the resurrection-faith arose out of the apostolic testimony. The story of the unbelieving Thomas dwells upon the latter fact: that it was through the apostolic word, accepted as the word of God (cf. 1 Thes 2.13), that the Christian community originated. Although the original witnesses are no longer with the community, the power of their word remains with it. The blessing or *macarism* (a Jewish way of speaking of one's good fortune in having accepted God's word, cf. Lk 1.45; 10.23) that concludes the story (Jn 20.29) does not contrast those who believed as the result of a christophany with those who believed without having experienced a christophany. The blessing is an instruction that both groups of believers are equally fortunate. The resurrection-faith lies at the heart of the Christian community, and both groups enjoy the same understanding of it. The double manner of its origin is the work of God.

(h) *Jn 21.1–23.* The narrative of the Appearance to the Disciples at the Sea of Tiberias is an addition to the Fourth Gospel, made (unlike Mk 16.9–20) before its publication, as its universal presence in the MS tradition shows. Generally speaking, its purpose is to reflect upon the roles played by Simon Peter and the beloved disciple of the Fourth Gospel (Jn 13.23; 19.26; 20.2) in the development of the Christian community. The supposition of the narrative is that both Simon Peter and the beloved disciple are dead. It is composed of two parts: an account of the appearance of the risen Christ on the shore of the Sea of Tiberias—a later name for the Sea of Galilee—(Jn 21.1–14); and an account of a conversation between Christ and Simon Peter on this occasion (Jn 21.15–23).

The appearance of Christ is set in the context of a fishing scene and in the framework of the disciples' non-recognition of him. When he suggests where they should cast the net, they do not recognize him. But after a strikingly large catch (Jn 21.6), the beloved disciple realizes that the person on the shore is "the Lord" and so informs Simon Peter (Jn 21.7). Once on shore and breakfasting at Christ's invitation, the group of disciples recognize him (Jn 21.12). The principal point of the story is that the beloved disciple leads Simon Peter to the recognition of the risen Christ. NT scholars recognize a Eucharistic allusion in Jesus' giving of the bread and fish to the disciples (Jn 21.13), but perhaps the allusion occurs by way of reference to Jn 6.11, where Jesus performs the same action for the purpose of the feeding of the five thousand. After the feeding, an instruction of Jesus follows, ending in a confession by Simon Peter (Jn 6.68–69). An instruction of Jesus now follows that focuses on Simon Peter.

The instruction is a mission mandate directed to Peter alone as in Mt 16.18–19. Three times Jesus requires him to confess his devotion, now to the risen Christ (almost certainly an allusion to the insistent tradition of his triple denial); and three times Jesus commands him to care for those who believe in him—imaged as "lambs" and "sheep"—(Jn 21.15–17). Since the leading function here given Peter is conveyed in symbolic language, its exact nature and extent cannot be set out in neat, concrete terms. It is acknowledged that his performance of the role of shepherd given him led to his martyrdom (Jn 21.18–19). The role of the beloved disciple, on the other hand, was to serve Christ in another way, one that involved preaching and teaching, but not martyrdom. It is probable that the conversation between Jesus and Peter in Jn 21.21–23 has the purpose of presenting John the Apostle as one who, like Peter, but without Peter's specific mandate from Christ, exercised a pastoral ministry of preaching and teaching that is of enduring significance for the Christian community and to which the Fourth Gospel stands as the lasting witness.

Concluding observations. The resurrection narratives contain no allegations or claims that in themselves constitute an object of historical research. From beginning to end the narratives are theological statement. Behind them lies an assumption of divine action in history. But this assumption is neither systematic nor unsystematic philosophical or theological speculation. It is an assumption unrelated to any religious thought, whether philosophical or theological, including the thought of the OT Scriptures and of Judaism itself, that preceded it. The assumption is specific: that God raised Jesus of Nazareth who was crucified, died, and was buried as a seditionist under Pontius Pilate and manifested him to be reigning in his own realm as the salvific Lord of creation. The assumption itself is historically undemonstrable: only its context, the crucifixion of Jesus of Nazareth on grounds of sedition, is an object of historical evaluation. Although the assumption itself was not the net result of religious speculation of any kind and was not presented in terms of the historically demonstrable, it was not without its own historical context: the assertions of specific people to be the divine appointees to witness to the risen Christ and to his religious reign. Except on the assumption of the divine action in history testified to by specific people as divinely appointed witnesses, a testimony that is presumed to be accepted, the resurrection narratives carry neither conviction nor intelligible meaning.

Once the presupposition of the resurrection narratives is accepted, however, they acquire meaning that is both forceful and challenging. The sequel to the burial of Jesus of Nazareth in accordance with the customs of the time is the natural mystery of the open-empty tomb. But the resurrection narratives do not permit this natural mystery to hold the field of thought. It is elevated to the plane of the resurrection itself by angelic messengers: a natural explanation for this natural mystery is denied from the outset. Even in John's Gospel, the empty tomb is not a cause for weeping (Jn 20.13). The resurrection narratives show no interest in supplying data that leave no room for doubt about the empty tomb. They reflect a point of view that it was more important to provide a theological expla-

nation for this phenomenon, than to supply historical information guaranteeing the emptiness of the tomb. The fact that a theological explanation was invariably offered shows at least that it was the Christian conviction that the tomb was found to be empty.

The variety of the christophanies reveals the same theological preoccupation as the variety of the accounts of the empty tomb: a phenomenon occurred that also required interpretation. In the instance of the christophanies, the phenomenon was the personal manifestation of the risen Christ to chosen witnesses. The content of the christophanies as they exist in the resurrection narratives seems to be due in part to the function carried out in their lifetimes by at least some of the recipients and in part to the catechetical needs of the Christian community. There is no need to assume that the risen Christ parceled out specific directions to a variety of people who then compared notes. St. Paul asserts that after his experience of the risen Christ on the road to Damascus, he felt no need to consult with the apostles in Jerusalem (Gal 1.15–17). That some form of communication took place between the risen Christ and the chosen witnesses is plausible and is indicated by Luke (Acts 1.3; 10.41). But such communication could bear only upon the immediate future and would in itself require interpretation in the course of time. The fact that the resurrection narratives offer a variety of interpretations of christophanies indicates that the appearances of the risen Christ took place, but in such a way as to require interpretation.

The literary classification of the christophanies remains unsettled. They have been categorized according to their setting (Jerusalem or Galilee), according to their content (recognition or mission), and according to their purpose (personal or apostolic).

Bibliography: P. BENOIT, *Passion et Résurrection du Seigneur* (Paris 1966). J. BLINZLER, "Die Grablegung Christi," in E. DHANIS, ed., *Resurrexit: Actes du Symposium International sur la Résurrection de Jésus* (Rome 1974) 56–107. E. L. BODE, *The First Easter Morning* (Rome 1970). R. E. BROWN, *The Virginal Conception and Bodily Resurrection of Jesus* (New York 1973); *The Gospel according to John*, XIII–XXI (New York 1970). C. H. DODD, "The Appearance of the Risen Christ: A Study in Form-Criticism of the Gospels," *More New Testament Studies* (Grand Rapids, MI 1968). R. H. FULLER, *The Formation of the Resurrection Narratives* (New York 1971). J. P. GALVIN, "Resurrection as *Theologia crucis Jesu*: The Foundational Christology of Rudolf Pesch," *Theological Studies* 38 (1977) 513–524. X. LÉON-DUFOUR, *Résurrection de Jésus et méssage pascal* (Paris 1971). W. MARXSEN, *The Resurrection of Jesus of Nazareth* (Philadelphia, PA 1970). C. F. D. MOULE, ed., *The Significance of the Message of the Resurrection for Faith in Jesus Christ* (Naperville, IL 1968). B. RIGAUX, *Dieu l'a ressuscité: Exégèse et théologie biblique* (Gembloux, Belgium 1973). L. SCHENKE, *Auferstehungsverkündigung und leeres Grab* (Stuttgart 1968). P. SEIDENSTICKER, *Die Auferstehung Jesu in der Botschafft der Evangelisten* (Stuttgart 1967). H. STRATHMANN, "Martys," G. KITTEL, *Theological Dictionary of the New Testament* 4:474–508.

P. DE SURGY, P. GRELOT, et al., *La Résurrection du Christ et l'exégèse moderne* (Paris 1969).

[C. P. CEROKE]

2. Theology of

The meaning of the Resurrection has never been so fully understood as during apostolic times. The Resurrection was the source and the object of faith; the theology of the time was a theology of the paschal mystery. It is not the purpose of the present section to follow the evolution of the early ideas and to determine what is peculiar to each author of the New Testament but, in keeping with the demands of theology, to endeavor by a proper arrangement of the Scripture texts to grasp the very mystery of the Resurrection. The elements of synthesis furnished by Scripture are grouped under two main heads.

RISEN CHRIST, UNIVERSAL SAVIOR

Some texts concern Christ constituted universal savior by the Resurrection (objective Redemption). They show in the Resurrection the fulfillment of eschatological SALVATION and determine the relations between the Resurrection and the death of Christ, between the Resurrection and the INCARNATION.

Resurrection and the Final Coming of the Kingdom. Jesus had announced the KINGDOM OF GOD, that is, the final advent of the dominion of God. He had taken the title of SON OF MAN, which, in the evocation of Daniel chapter 7 and the connections that Jesus established between this title and "the Day," appears to be an eschatological title: it characterizes Jesus as the perfecter of the world (Mt 10.23; 19.28; 25.31; 26.64; Mk 8.38; 13.26; Lk 11.29–32; 12.8–9, 40; 17.24, 26–30; 18.8; 21.36). It is certain that, according to the Synoptic tradition, the coming of the kingdom is connected with "the coming" of Jesus [see K. H. Schelkle, *Die Passion Jesu in der Verkündigung des NT* (Heidelberg 1949) 199]. It would take place when the Son of Man "would come" with power [R. Schnackenburg, *God's Rule and Kingdom,* tr. J. Murray (New York 1963) 177]. Between the kingdom and the Son of Man in His coming there exists a real identity, so much so that the two terms, kingdom and Son of Man, can be interchanged (cf. Mk 8.39 and Mt 16.28; Lk 18.29 and Mt 19.28; Mt 25.34 and 41). The power and the glory whose sudden appearance in the world constitutes the eschatological coming of God are proper to Jesus in His "coming." This final coming of the kingdom, which is also that of the Son of Man, is already contained in germ in the miracles (Lk 10.18, 23–24; 11.20), and it is certain that Jesus spoke of it as being very near (Mt 10.23; Mk 8.38–39; 13.30; Lk 12.54–56; 22.16–18).

In saying "But first he [the Son of Man] must suffer many things and be rejected by this generation" (Lk 17.25), He links the final coming (verse 24) with His death, not as to something merely presupposed but by an internal bond (see Mk 10.37–38; Lk 19.12, 15). The announcement of the death and the Resurrection of the Son of Man (Mk 8.31; 9.9–12, 30; 10.32–34) pertains to the preaching of the eschatological kingdom: it means that it is through death and then in a Resurrection that Jesus will enter into the glory of the kingdom (Luke 24.26, 46). Jesus thus fulfills the prophecy of Daniel chapter 7 on the heavenly coming of the Son of Man through that of the Suffering Servant.

The account of the Last Supper (see Lk 22.14–20) is the summit and point of crystallization of the Synoptic thought on the kingdom: here this appears imminent (verses 16–18, 29–30), like a meal, but one that will be a pasch and a completed pasch (v.16), a repast in the joy of a new world (Mk 14.25). In this narrative, kingdom and Eucharist are placed in the same perspective and thus receive mutual clarification one from the other. In the light of the Eucharist, which is image and mysterious realization of the kingdom, one discovers that the nourishment of the eschatological banquet is none other than Christ in His oblation for the multitude. Here, then, again the kingdom is linked with the Person of Jesus and His death pertains to the mystery of this kingdom.

Before His Passion, Jesus said: ". . . hereafter you shall see the Son of Man sitting on the right of the Power and coming upon the clouds of heaven" (Mt 26.64). The reference to Daniel chapter 7 is evident, where the advent of the Son of Man means the advent of an eternal empire. The Son of Man "comes" henceforth through death, into the glory (Lk 24.26) and the omnipotence (Mt 28.18) that in the eyes of the early Church are synonyms for the coming of the kingdom (cf. Mk 10.37 and Mt 20.21; Mk 8.38 and 8.39; 1 Thes 2.12).

Unique Coming. Scripture does not say explicitly that the kingdom has come in the Resurrection. But it is certain that the coming was considered very near, linked with death and identical with the coming of Jesus in glory and power. It is also certain that primitive thought knew only one coming of the kingdom, in the one and final "coming" of Christ. The later transformation of "the coming" into a "return" and the notion of successive PAROUSIAS is not in keeping with early thought and beclouds it. Theology has the right to conclude that the coming of the kingdom in which is the eschatological fullness of salvation is identical with the mystery of the Resurrection.

For Saint John, more explicitly than for the Synoptics, the Hour of Christ is at the same time that of His Passion and that of His final consummation (Jn 12.31–32; cf. 5.25 and 17.1–3).

It is significant that after the Resurrection the Apostles no longer announced the kingdom to come, but the risen Christ. The Resurrection is considered as the advent of salvation; it forms the principal object (Acts 2.22–36; 4.8–12), indeed the only object (4.33), of the message of salvation. It is no longer the preparation for eschatological events (Acts 17.31; 1 Thes 1.10), but the termination of history (Acts 13.32–33), the final accomplishment (Acts 13.34) of every promise of salvation (Acts 13.32; 26.6, 22–23) from that made to Abraham (Acts 3.25–26) to that made to David (Acts 2.31). The coming of the Son of Man is henceforth a reality (Acts 7.55–56). Jesus has become the Messiah-Lord (Acts 2.36), elevated to the throne of David (Acts 2.30–31), at the right hand of God (Acts 2.33–34). All salvation is in Him (Acts 4.11–12).

Kyrios and Pleroma. The characteristic title of the risen Christ is that of *Kyrios* (Lord). It was given to Christ with the same meaning it had when applied to God (Phil 2.9; Jn 20.28) in the fullness of His sovereignty. It is the Resurrection that has established Jesus in this Lordship (Acts 2.24–36; Mt 28.18; Rom 10.9; Phil 2.9–11). In view of the realism the Semites attached to the name, the granting of the sovereign Name means that the Resurrection was not merely a vivification but rather a divinization, the total assumption of the man Jesus in God and in His attributes [see Saint Ambrose, *De excessu fratris sui Satyri* 2.91, *Corpus scriptorum ecclesiasticorum latinorum* 73:299; *Summa theologiae* 3a, 55.2]. Such an affirmation contains an unfathomable mystery that justifies the most surprising assertions of the New Testament on the risen Christ's manner of being and acting.

It seems also that Saint Paul was thinking of the Resurrection and not of the Incarnation in the beginning when he said that "it has pleased God the Father to make dwell in him the fullness" (Col 1.19), to make it dwell there "bodily" (Col 2.9), that is, it seems, in the body of the risen Christ [see L. Cerfaux, *Christ in the Theology of St. Paul*, tr. G. Webb and A. Walker (New York 1959) 427]. The term fullness (πλήρωμα, pleroma), borrowed here from popularized Stoicism [see J. Dupont, *Gnosis* (Bruges 1949) 453–76], designates the whole plenitude of being and of creative and saving power that is in God and, through God, in the world [see *Theodori episcopi mopsuesteni in ep. b. Pauli commentarii*, ed. H. B. Swete (Cambridge 1880 1:275–76]. This divine and cosmic totality God was pleased to concentrate in Christ in raising Him from the dead [see P. Benoit, "Corps, tête et plérôme dans les ép. de la captivité," *Revue biblique* 63 (1956) 31–44]. In this plenitude, Christ has become the summit and term of creation, but also the root where all begins (1 Cor 8.6; Col 1.16). For all men the end and salvation consist in participating in this plenitude (Col 2.9; Eph 1.23; 4.10, 13, 15).

This Lordship and plenitude make the Resurrection the eschatological event. It has already been seen that the power and the glory of the Lordship (Rom 1.4; 2 Thes 2.14) are eschatological attributes (1 Thes 2.12; 2 Thes 2.14). The divinization by the granting of the Name and the universal acclamation of the Resurrected (Phil 2.9–11) express the Parousia triumph of Christ. The text of Isaiah 45.23 used in Phil 2.10 to describe the paschal exaltation describes in Rom 14.11 the last judgment. The submission of the cosmic powers obtained in the glorification of Christ (Eph 1.20–21) is, according to 1 Cor 15.24–25, the effect of the final triumph. Thus it is established that the Resurrection constitutes the advent of the kingdom of heaven that Jesus had announced as near.

Scripture, however, recognizes multiple effects, ranged in time, of the unique Parousia—coming with Easter; in the Church (Jn 14.18–20); coming manifested by the destruction of Jerusalem, of the adversary who is already at work in Paul's time (2 Thes 2.6–8); etc. The theologian concludes from this that the final mystery, already realized in all its power in the sole Person of Christ, ought henceforth to be communicated to the Church and imposed on the world.

Spirit-Flesh Antithesis. The difference between the new being of Christ and His earthly being is expressed in the antithesis *Spirit* and *flesh*. The Spirit is the heavenly reality (Jn 3.3–5; 1 Cor 2.12; 1 Pt 1.12); in it resides the sanctity and power of God (Lk 1.35; Acts 1.8; 10.38; Rom 15.13, 19; 1 Thes 1.5); it is the vivifying "glory" of God, while carnal man deprived of the Spirit is said to be "deprived of the glory of God" (Rom 3.23). Glory, strength, Spirit are associated in many texts (see 1 Cor 15.43–45) and constitute one and the same reality. All that which defines God [power, life, holiness, spirituality (Jn 4.24), love] is proper to the Spirit: it is the expression of the divine transcendence and, for man, the gift of the Spirit is eschatological salvation (Rom 8.11, 23; Eph 1.13–14). The flesh, on the contrary, denotes man in an existence closed to God, deprived of the Spirit, a stranger to the kingdom (1 Cor 15.50).

Christ, then, who had lived according to the flesh (Rom 1.3) and "died by the flesh" and by its weakness, God has raised up by the power that is the Spirit (2 Cor 13.4; 1 Pt 3.18; Rom 8.11), by His glory (Rom 6.4) that is the Spirit. The divine resuscitating action is the total effusion of the Spirit, into which Christ was entirely transformed to the point of becoming Himself "a vivifying spirit" (1 Cor 15.45), in some way identified with the Spirit: "Now the Lord is the spirit" (2 Cor 3.17). Not that Christ, in the eyes of Saint Paul, would henceforth be an ethereal impersonal substance, as a liberal exegesis has claimed. It is the same Christ, previously asleep in death, who has "been awakened" (cf. Greek of Rom 4.25) and who "arose again" (ἀνάστασις). But the Spirit has communicated to Christ His own manner of divine being, and that is a profound mystery. In the context of 2 Cor 3.17, the Spirit was opposed to a written document (γράμμα), that is, to the ancient economy, devoid of vivifying substances (2 Cor 3.6); Christ who "is the spirit" is presented because of this as the concentration of all the vivifying, sanctifying, celestial reality that is the Spirit and of whom the rest, according to Col 2.17, was but a shadow projected by the body. Here is found the reaffirmation of the assumption of Christ in God, that "the plenitude" is in Him, that He has become the total and final reality; but with a more immediate reference to the salvation of men, for the Spirit is communication (2 Cor 13.13) and sanctification (2 Thes 2.13; 1 Cor 6.11). In this Christ-spirit, the vivifying action is essential to His being; he is the "vivifying spirit" (1 Cor 15.45), the communicative fullness (2 Cor 3.18). The unique effusion of the Spirit, concentrated on Christ, ought to reach all men, as the Resurrection of Christ was for them (2 Cor 5.15).

According to Saint John, the gift of the Spirit depends on the exaltation of Jesus (Jn 7.39; 16.7); for, on the one hand, the Spirit is the reality from on high (Jn 3.3, 5), and, on the other, it is the corporal humanity of Jesus that is the means of communion with celestial reality (the body is the rock from which springs forth the water of the Spirit, Jn 7.37–39; the bread of heavenly life, Jn 6.51; the temple of the New Testament, Jn 2.21). It was necessary that Jesus, even in the body, be exalted in the Father that from His immolated and celestial body there might spring forth the waters of the Spirit (see Jn 7.37–39; 19.34 and 20.22). On Easter, He gave the Spirit (Jn 20.22).

Relationship between the death and Resurrection. The glory of Christ is linked with His death by a necessary bond: it is the end of a movement accomplished in His death. Saint Luke speaks of a departure (Lk 9.31), of a taking up (Lk 9.51) to God; the Resurrection is the purpose of the death (Lk 24.26; Jn 10.17). For Saint John, the death is a passage (Jn 13.1, 3; 14.12; 16.5, 10, 28), a lifting up above the earth (Jn 3.14; 12.32), an ascension into heaven (Jn 3.13; 6.63; Rv 12.5). This ascension is not local, it is a transformation. Saint John mentions the points of departure and arrival: Jesus passed "from this world to the Father" (Jn 13.1). During His earthly existence, Jesus became adapted to this world, deprived of His glory (Jn 17.5), and, because of this, far removed from the Father. By His death, He entered into the bosom of His Father (Jn 13.32), into His glorious sanctity (Jn 17.1, 5, 19). The redeeming death is essentially divine exaltation of Jesus.

Justification. Saint Paul points out that the earthly existence of Jesus was in relation to sin. For this was an existence according to the flesh (Rom 1.3); and the flesh, closed to the spirit (Gal 5.17) and therefore to the vivifying holiness of God, is for this reason "a flesh of sin" (Rom 8.3) and of death (Rom 7.24). Although of a divine condition, Christ had been a man like others (Phil 2.7), subject to slavery (Phil 2.7), to that of the Law (Gal 4.4), in a flesh like to that of sin (Rom 8.3). "Made sin for us" (2 Cor 5.21) because of His flesh, He needed the holiness of the Spirit in which man is "justified" (1 Tm 3.16). His death was a death to the flesh, to sin (Rom 6.10), and to the Law (see Gal 2.19), because through it He entered into the holiness and power of the Spirit (Rom 1.4). The redeeming act constitutes a process of justification in Christ as well as of divinization (Rom 6.10).

Sacrifice. Considered as a sacrifice, Redemption appears as a giving by Christ of Himself (Eph 5.2). The Epistle to the Hebrews sees this giving as a movement that carries Christ from the earthly sphere (Heb 9.11–12) through the veil of His flesh (10.20) into the divine sanctuary. His entrance into the sanctuary and His sitting at the right hand of God (12.2) expresses a divinizing transformation that the Epistle calls "the consummation" (Heb 2.10; 5.9). According to Jn 17.19, the sacrifice is a "sanctification," which transfers the victim from a profane existence into divine holiness. The glorification, then, pertains to the sacrifice: it is its result, the acceptance in God of the victim offered in death. It ought to be concluded that death for Christ constituted the entrance into total communion with God.

Summary. Consequently, the death is essentially related to the glorification, without which it would have no redemptive meaning, nor be a sacrifice; for a giving does not exist if it is not accepted, and a movement without a term is inconceivable. One understands, therefore, 1 Cor 15.17, "If Christ has not risen . . . you are still in your sins."

Salvation was a personal drama with Christ. The effect of His death, the total object of His merit, was His Resurrection. It was He who, thanks to His death, was "saved from death" (Heb 5.7). For others, the death of Christ is advantageous because of the glory to which it leads (Heb 2.9; 5.9).

Redemptive merit is not understood according to the law of *do ut des,* but (cf. Saint Thomas, *De ver.* 29.7) as the physical and moral disposition to receive the gift of God. The death was total submission (Phil 2.8; Rom 5.19), complete disponibility for the divine plenitude; the purpose of the sufferings was to prepare this receptivity (Heb 2.10; 5.8). Thus the merit is in the death (Phil 2.9; Heb 2.9), and the Resurrection is the divine gift that corresponds to this receptivity. That is why, even in Saint John (Jn 12.28; 13.32; 17.1), the Resurrection is almost always the work of the Father.

The redemptive act was not a gift offered to God to appease Him. Since He is love, God took the initiative in saving (Jn 3.16; Eph 1.9). It is Jesus who welcomed the gift of God. Even if the sacrifice was a giving, it was a giving of self, that is, acceptance of the dominion of God. For sin means opposition to God, the refusal of His saving justice (Rom 10.3); the sinner is characterized by his withdrawal (Lk 15.4–20) and by the absence of God's glory in him (Rom 3.23) [see S. Lyonnet, *De peccato et redemptione,* v.1, *De notione peccati* (Rome 1957) 81–82, 90]. Christ satisfied divine justice, offended by the refusal to receive it, when He allowed Himself to be filled with it to the point of "becoming justice" (1 Cor 1.30). Expiation does not consist of compensatory suffering; according to Scripture, it is God who expiates, that is, wipes out sin [see L. Moraldi, *Espiazione sacrificale e riti espiatori nell'ambiente biblico e nell AT* (Rome 1956) 265–66]. The Spirit of the Resurrection is the expiation of the sins of the world; He frees the flesh of sin (Jn 1.29 and 20.22–23).

In a theological system where Redemption is understood as a gift of infinite value made by Christ in compensation for offenses, the death is not necessary; it is even declared useless, since every action of Christ is of infinite value. If, because of scriptural evidence, one attributes salvation to death, it is not so much to death itself as to the circumstances that preceded it (suffering, etc.). In paschal theology, the death appears necessary, in keeping with Sacred Scripture; for salvation is God who gives Himself, and it is by death that Christ opened Himself to this infinite gift.

Relationship between the Resurrection and Incarnation. To say that the death was an entrance into total communion with God is to affirm that the Incarnation began in Christ a history whose termination was the Resurrection. The glory pertains to the definition of the Incarnation (Jn 1.14); now, although Christ experienced passing glorification on earth (Jn 2.11; 11.4), only the Hour brought Him the glory that was His (Jn 17.1–5). The definition of the Incarnation given in Jn 10.36 comprises two elements: the consecration by which Jesus is in God, and the mission that brought Him among men.

Now according to Jn 17.19, it is by death that Christ is consecrated in God; for, if by an initial consecration He is already in heaven, one with the Father (Jn 3.13; 10.30, 38), He must, nevertheless, still go to the Father (Jn 14.12) and ascend into heaven (Jn 6.63). On earth He is not then in His full truth, which is to be: "the Son in the bosom of the Father" (Jn 1.18).

As regards the mission: it is simultaneously to the world and to the death in which He is lifted up that, according to Jn 3.14–16, Christ is delivered up. His coming includes a departure: "I go away and I come" (Jn 14.28). He goes away in order to come.

In the same manner, the effects of salvation, proper to the Incarnation, are produced only in glory: by the Incarnation Jesus is the light that gives life to the faithful (Jn 8.12), but in His exaltation (Jn 3.14–15; 8.28; 17.1–3); by the Incarnation, He is the living font, bread from heaven, resurrection of the dead, but in His exaltation (cf. Jn 4.14 and 7.37–39; 6.33 and 6.63–64; 11.25 and 17.1–3). Scripture recognizes therefore a development of the mystery of the Incarnation in Christ.

Saint Paul says in turn that Christ "was constituted Son of God in power by the resurrection" (Rom 1.4); the resurrecting act of the Father is a divine generation (Acts 13.33). The Epistle to the Hebrews calls Christ Son of God, high priest according to the order of Melchizedek; it sees Him in His "consummation" (glorification). The affirmations of the Epistle to the Hebrews about the Incarnation concern in general Christ glorified (cf. Heb 5.5–6 and 5.9–10; 6.20).

It is therefore in the history of the Incarnation that Redemption was achieved: salvation is communion with God, by divine Incarnation, realized in its plenitude in the Resurrection. It would be the duty of theology to define this real progress of the Incarnation, in such a way that the truth of the divinity of Christ on earth would in no way be weakened.

Resurrection and Death Eternal Realities. Although because of its circumstances (empty tomb, apparitions, etc.) the Resurrection was included in history (H. Denzinger, *Enchiridion symbolorum,* ed. A. Schönmetzer, 3436; cf. 1 Cor 15.4), it is in itself an eschatological fact that remains ever present. For it is an action of divine plenitude [the granting of the Name (Phil 2.9), of the pleroma (Col 1.19; 2.9)]; it is the final consummation (Heb 2.10; 5.9), and therefore eternal. The texts that show in the Resurrection the blossoming of the divine filiation permit the theologian to understand Acts of the Apostles 13.33 in the deepest sense: "He has raised up Jesus, as it is written . . . 'Thou art my Son, this day have I begotten thee.'" The Resurrection proceeds from the mystery of the eternal generation. Thus it is made clear that every follower who is united in Christ is "raised up with" Him (Col 2.12–13; Eph 2.5–6). For he is united to Him the moment the Father engenders Him; he becomes a new creature (2 Cor 4.16; 5.17; Col 3.10), he is born (Ti 3.5), because Christ, to whom he is united, is placed at the original point of His newness, in the filial beginning that is the Resurrection.

To this permanent vivification by God there corresponds a simultaneous permanence of the death. For

Saint John, the term for "the exaltation above the earth" is the cross (Jn 12.32–33; 3.14); this is the eternal place of glorification [W. Thüsing, *Die Erhöhung und Verherrlichung Jesu im Johannesevangelium* (Münster 1960) 31–33]. It is then in death that Christ is glorified. The Hour when Christ's destiny is accomplished is simultaneously death and glorification. The death is the moment of plenitude when "all is consummated" (Jn 19.30). In Jn 19.31–37 the image of the eternal Christ is presented. He is pierced through (v.37; 20.27), the lamb of which no bone is broken—for He is upright in death (Rv 5.6)—nevertheless, a lamb forever immolated (*ibid.*). From His side flow together the blood of immolation and the water, symbol of the Spirit of glory (Jn 7.37–39). It is thus that He will be eternally seen (Jn 19.37; Rv 1.7; 5.6). Never has Christ been healed of His mortal wounds (Jn 20.20, 27); the faithful steep their garments in His blood (Rv 7.14), receive the sprinkling of His blood (Heb 12.24; 1 Pt 1.2). In the narrative of the Last Supper, the heavenly banquet, celebrated in the joy of a new wine, is illustrated by the Eucharist, where the immolated Christ is offered as food. Heb 8.1–5 supposes an eternal sacrifice. According to Saint Paul, whoever enters into communion with Christ dies with Him (Rom 6.3) and also "rises with" Him. All this proves that death is integrated into the glory of Christ.

The perdurance of the death is explained by the connection of the death to the Resurrection. The death is meritorious of glory, disponibility in relation to the divine plenitude; it is a gift made to God at the moment that this giving becomes a reality, that is, in God's glorifying acceptance of it; it is the end of Christ's carnal state through its transformation into the spiritual state. That is why it does not precede, in time, glorification but coincides with it (first of all with the glorification of His soul, into which His body is then drawn). Now the glorification is a permanent actuality; it therefore maintains Christ in the redemptive death with which it coincides, in His disponibility for glory, at the summit of His giving.

Fullness of Incarnation. The paschal mystery is in every sense the fullness of the Incarnation. Even in His corporal humanity, Christ is entirely begotten by the Father; He is relation to the Father, situated as He is at the height of His offering; He is transformed into the Spirit in which the divine attributes are expressed, and even in His humanity He is the font of the Spirit (Jn 7.37–39). Because the death and Resurrection are the affirmation of the divine filiation, it is there that Jesus is beloved of the Father (Jn 10.17); it is there (Acts 13.33) or in the anticipation of the paschal mystery (baptism, Transfiguration) that He is proclaimed the beloved Son. It seems that the death was virtually included in the Incarnation from the beginning; according to Phil 2.7–8, it was the ultimate

expression of the initial despoilment. For since this despoilment meant submission to God, it pertained to the Incarnation. At its end, but also, it seems, at its beginning, the Incarnation is a mystery of death and glory.

SALVATION COMMUNICATED TO MEN

In addition to the texts concerning Christ as constituted universal savior by the Resurrection (objective Redemption, treated above), there are other texts concerning the integration of men into this principle of salvation (subjective Redemption). Salvation is realized in Christ alone, with whom it is identified (1 Cor 1.30); men will not be saved except by communion with Christ in this salvation. These texts show that the paschal Christ has become communicable to men, that the Church is the Body of Christ in the paschal mystery, that salvation is attained by means of communion with the paschal mystery, that the eschatological realities are the plenitude of communion with the paschal mystery, and that all creation takes part in the paschal mystery.

Christ Glorious in condition of communicating Himself. The Resurrection that brought about salvation in Christ also puts this salvation at the disposal of men. While remaining an individual being, Jesus henceforth is continually communicating Himself. In the Synoptic Gospels, He appears in His glorious coming as a "corporative personality," in the strongest sense of the term; He contains in Himself the kingdom (cf. Mt 26.64 and Dn chapter 7). The narrative of the Last Supper shows this kingdom united in a paschal repast, of which the Eucharistic communion is the Sacrament on earth. Less explicit, the Acts of the Apostles says, however, that Christ is risen for men and sent to men (Acts 3.26; 26.23), that He has become the author of life (Acts 3.15) and cornerstone of the house (Acts 4.11). According to Saint Paul, Christ was raised up for men (2 Cor 5.15), "for our justification" (Rom 4.25), which seems to mean that the resuscitative action of God was destined to effect men's salvation. Formerly limited by His body to one race, Jesus became a universal being, capable of uniting the multitude in Himself (Gal 3.28; Col 3.11), a new Adam, father of eschatological humanity (1 Cor 15.45–49). His Lordship is ordered to the Church (Eph 1.22). The title Head comes to Christ through the Resurrection (Col 1.18) and refers to an organic bond with the Church. The Spirit is communion; transforming Christ, it makes Him "a life-giving spirit" (1 Cor 15.45), of which the essence is to give life.

According to Saint John, Christ "comes" hereafter to His disciples; He draws them to Himself in His exaltation (Jn 12.32). Formerly a solitary grain, now a full ear of wheat (Jn 12.24), He becomes the temple of the new people (Jn 2.19–21). He is open to the faithful by His very being, just as the being of the Father is open to the Son (Jn 14.20). His transcendence, which is expressed in the formula ''I Am'' is salutary in itself. Ordinarily this divine name was coupled with a predicate that emphasized its soteriological character: ''I Am the resurrection (Jn 11.25), the bread of life (Jn 6.35), the true vine (Jn 15.1). . . .'' But it is in the lifting up that this (Jn 8.28) and its salutary character are affirmed. It is then that Jesus is the bread eaten (Jn 6.51, 63–64) and that the vine bears those fruits in which the glory of God takes concrete form (cf. Jn 15.5 and 8; 12.24–28). Henceforth His disciples are His brothers, sons of His Father (Jn 20.17). The glorious Christ is savior by His very being.

Church, Body of Christ Dead and Risen Again. The resuscitating action of God that makes Christ communicable is thus creative of the Church. The latter is like the space in which Christ exists and lives; it is filled with Him (Eph 1.23; Col 2.9; 3.11), so much so that it is identified with His risen humanity and is called the ''body of Christ.'' The interpretation that sees in 1 Cor 12.12–13 (cf. Rom 6.3; Gal 3.27–28); 1 Cor 6.15–17; 10.16–17; and also Eph 1.23; 5.28–32 a union identifying the faithful with the physical and ''spiritual'' body of Christ appears exegetically certain and is in accord with patristic thinking, especially when it considers the Church, as does Saint Paul [1 Cor 10.16–17; 11.25: ''this cup is the New Establishment (see Jer 31.31; Is 42.6; 49.8)] in the perspective of the Eucharist. It is the Spirit (Rom 8.9–10; 1 Cor 12.13) of the Resurrection that integrates the faithful with the Body of Christ, in one communion of being (Rom 6.5; 12.5; Gal 3.27–28) and of life (Rom 6.11, 23), which Saint Paul ordinarily designates by the phrase ''in Christ'' or ''Christ in us.'' Having become one Body with Christ, they are also ''one spirit'' (1 Cor 6.17) with Him who is ''spirit,'' benefiting by the effusion of the Spirit that has resuscitated Him. They are sons of Abraham through incorporation in his Offspring, inheriting His blessing actualized in the Resurrection (Acts 3.25–26), which is the Spirit (Gal 3.14). Thus salvation realized in Christ becomes in turn personal for them.

This incorporation is also an association with the salvation present in its actuality in Christ. The believer is seized by the resuscitating action of God (Eph 2.5; Col 2.13). He is overcome by it in communion with the very death of Christ (Rom 6.3–4; Col 2.12). He communes with the redeeming act that historically is placed in the time of Pontius Pilate and that he encounters in its actuality in Christ glorified. While distinguishing between objective and subjective Redemption, paschal theology considers the latter as a communion with the former.

Christian existence is thus located in the mystery of the Redemption (Rom 6.3–11; 8.17; 2 Cor 4.10–12; Gal 2.19–20; Phil 3.10; 2 Tm 2.11); the Church is the Body of Christ in the redemptive mystery.

Man saved is a new creature (2 Cor 5.17; Eph 2.15; 4.24) created in the Resurrection of Christ. This means that he belongs to a new genus: a child of God (Gal 3.26–27) in Christ made ''the Son of God by the Resurrection'' (Rom 1.4), dead to the flesh (Rom 8.9) and freed from sin (Rom 8.1), because he has been given life in the Spirit (Rom 8.2). This also means that he is a brand-new creature, in a fresh newness of being, his newness being the opposite to his old self (Rom 6.4–6; 7.6). Christian by birth in the Spirit (Ti 3.5), who is absolute newness and plenitude, he does not swerve from what he is by his birth, as he is under the action of God, who raised up Christ; he advances in this newness (2 Cor 4.16) unto the day when he arrives at adulthood by total birth, in the Resurrection of Christ.

The ethical situation of the believer is also new. Incorporated in the risen Christ, he is freed from the earthly Law and subjected to the source of the risen life, the Spirit (Rom 7.1–6); this is the moral law of the New Testament (Rom 8.2; Saint Thomas Aquinas, *In epist. ad Rom.* 8 lect. 1; *Summa theologiae* 1a2ae, 106.1). While containing both the Mosaic and the natural law, this law is different: contrary to the Mosaic Law, imposed from outside, it is immanent in the faithful (Rom 5.5); contrary to the law of nature, it is transcendent, being the holiness of God; contrary to both one and the other, it is a law of evolution, of a physical supernatural transformation, for it is a law of resurrection in the death of the flesh (Rom 6.2–5; Col 3.1–4). The moral effort roused by the Spirit of the Resurrection (Rom 8.13; Gal 5.16) seeks to extend through ''the earthly members'' the mysterious transformation realized in Baptism (Col 3.1–5) and prepares the final resurrection (Rom 6.2–8). Before being an obligation, this law is a salutary gift; it is therefore beatifying in itself. Since it is the Holy Spirit, it is the love and power of God; that is why moral effort is not the affirmation of man but his gift of self and acquiescence with the resuscitating action of God. Charity is the adequate expression of this law; it expresses communion with Christ in one Body, death to selfish flesh, the life of the Spirit of love. It is ''the new commandment,'' i.e., eschatological, ''the law of Christ,'' who, in death to Himself, has been given to God for the multitude in the love of the Spirit.

Means of communion with paschal mystery. To give to men the salvation that exists in Him, Christ has created means of communion with the paschal mystery.

The Apostles are created as such in the paschal mystery (Jn 17.19; 20.21–22; Gal 1.1); they are sent forth from the time Christ is glorified (Mt 28.18–19; Lk

24.46–47), and filled with the Spirit (Acts 1.8; Jn 20.22; cf. 7.37–39), they proclaim the risen Christ (Acts 1.22; 2.32; 4.33) and His death (1 Cor 1.23). While Christ, pre-eminent Apostle (Heb 3.1), is no longer connaturally present in the world (cf. Acts 10.41), precisely from the moment of His essential sending through His Resurrection (Acts 3.26; 26.23), the Apostles become by their word and their person the organs of His presence in the world and of His contact in the death and Resurrection (2 Cor 4.6–12; 13.4). Through them, men enter into communion with Christ dead and risen again (Rom 10.8–10; 2 Cor 2.15–16; Col 1.25–29).

All the Sacraments draw their strength from the paschal mystery [Vatican II, *Constitution on the Sacred Liturgy* 61; *Acta Apostolicae Sedis* 56 (1964) 116–17]. The two Sacraments of which Scripture speaks more explicitly, Baptism and the Holy Eucharist, sanctify insofar as they are means of communion with Christ in His paschal mystery. By Baptism man submits to the action of the Spirit (1 Cor 6.11), of whom the water is the symbol (Is 32.15; 44.3–4; Jn 3.5; Ti 3.5). This Spirit is given in union with Christ (cf. Jn 9.7 and 7.37–39) in one Body (Rom 6.3, 5; Gal 3.27; 1 Cor 12.13) and by participation in His Resurrection in one same death (Rom 6.3–11; Col 2.11–13; the sprinkling of His blood, spoken of in 1 Pt 1.2 and Heb 10.22 is related to Baptism).

The Eucharist is, from all evidence, paschal communion. The faithful eat the body of Christ and turn into it (1 Cor 10.16–17). This body is immolated (1 Cor 11.24–26; Jn 6.52) but also glorified in the Spirit (a spiritual food, 1 Cor 10.3–4; Jn 6.63–64), every sacrificial repast supposing the preliminary "sanctification" of the victim. Since Christ, because of His glorification, continues in an enduring way in the supreme moment of His sacrifice (for His death coincides with this always actual glorification and is eternalized by it), the Eucharistic celebration is the very sacrifice of Christ, the unique sacrifice, made sacramentally present to the Church. Thus the Church, which communicates with the body of Christ, becomes itself the Body of Christ in His sacrifice.

These Sacraments, and especially the Eucharist, which, as Sacrament of the kingdom, throws light on all Christian reality, place before the theologian the question of whether all the Sacraments do not act except as means of communion in the paschal mystery. The remission of sin, for example, is achieved, according to Scripture, not by the application of the merits of Christ (with application understood in a juridic sense), but by communion with Him in His death and Resurrection.

Man engages himself by faith in the paschal mystery that is offered to him by means of the Apostles and the Sacraments. The object of faith is not in the first place a complex of doctrines but rather God, who has raised up Jesus for men (Rom 4.24; 10.9; Col 2.12; 1 Pt 1.21), and the risen Christ, in whom is revealed (Jn 17.1–3; Col 1.15) this God who saves. As regards the doctrinal complex, it is developed by reflection on the paschal mystery in which it is contained [cf. O. Cullmann, *Les Premières confessions de foi chrétiennes* (Paris 1948)]. The believer confesses that "Jesus is Kyrios" (Rom 10.9; 1 Cor 12.3; Phil 2.11). Christ, in His Resurrection, is so truly the essential object of faith that if the Resurrection had not taken place faith would be without content and efficacy (1 Cor 15.14); its efficacy stems from its content, and the latter is the Resurrection that justifies men (Rom 4.24–25). The believer says yes to God, who reveals Himself by resuscitating Christ for men, and thus submits to the action of God, who raises him up with Christ (Col 2.12) in the death of the flesh (Phil 3.8–11). Faith is itself the effect of this glory (cf. Jn 3.14–16 and 12.32) that justifies men (Rom 4.25), making believers of them.

This assent to salvation is continued by moral effort. The ultimate means of receiving strength from the Resurrection are, according to Saint Paul, weakness (2 Cor 12.9), suffering (2 Cor 4.10–12), and death (2 Tm 2.11). The faithful die with Christ (2 Tm 2.11), "leaving the world for God" (Saint Ignatius of Antioch, *Pros Romaious* 2.2, cf. 6.1; *The Fathers of the Church: A New Translation*, ed. R. J. Deferrari et al., 109, 110).

Full realization in the Church of paschal mystery. At the Parousia, the Church will participate in the fullness of salvation realized in the Resurrection of Christ (2 Thes 2.14). The difference between Easter and the Parousia is not to be found in Christ, to whose power the latter adds nothing, but in the Church, for which Easter was a beginning and a hope, and the Parousia the full realization. All eschatological events are to be found ontologically in the mystery of the Resurrection.

Resurrection of the Faithful. Constituting the inevitable consequence of the resuscitating action of God in Christ is the resurrection of the faithful. The glory of Christ has such necessary ecclesial dimensions that to deny the resurrection of the faithful would be to deny that of Christ (1 Cor 15.13). The glorification of the faithful does not demand a new display of power: they are risen by INCORPORATION IN CHRIST (Rom 6.5), "together with" Him (2 Tm 2.11). For the resuscitating intervention of God is unique and applies to Christ. In Baptism, the faithful have been "resuscitated with" by an initial gift of the Spirit that calls for the complete gift, the Redemption of the body (Rom 8.11, 23; Eph 1.13–14). Now they are subjected according to their whole being to the "power [that effects] the resurrection of Christ" (Phil 3.10), absorbed in the eschatological mystery.

With the resurrection of the faithful, the action of God in Christ has attained its effects. For the end of this action is the salvation of the Church (Rom 4.25; 2 Cor 5.15; Eph 1.18–23). This salvation, then, is henceforth complete: the filiation is perfect (Rom 8.19, 23); formerly hindered by the body (1 Cor 15.50), the sons have entered into their heritage; the Church realizes in perfection its definition as the Body of Christ, the repository of His riches (Eph 1.23; cf. 4.13). By His victory over "the last enemy," death, Christ has imposed His dominion on the entire world (1 Cor 15.25–26).

Cosmic Unity. The other effects of the Parousia are obtained by this resuscitating action that bestows final salvation on the faithful. The material universe is freed from "corruption," thanks to the "revelation of the sons of God," for its Fall was in man, and its Redemption consists in enjoyment of the "liberty of the glory of the children of God" (Rom 8.19–22). The harmful Powers have been overcome (1 Cor 15.24), for it was in men and their universe incompletely saved that these Powers were able to set themselves against the Lordship of Christ. In Christ, cosmic unity (Col 1.20) and submission of the Powers (Eph 1.21–22) were already realized; they remained incomplete, however, because the resurrection of the Church was not achieved. The Church is, with Christ, the crucible of the eschatological transformation of the word; the Parousia that determines the destiny of the world is the paschal mystery totally communicated to the Church.

Judgment. It seems that the last judgment should be included in this ultimate saving intervention of God. This judgment had been announced as an event to be realized at the coming of Christ (Mt 3.11–12). Several texts suggest or affirm that it was pronounced in the coming of Christ, which is nothing else than His glorification. In Mt 26.64, Jesus announces His glorification while evoking Daniel chapter 7 and Psalms 109 (110).1, where the judgment of God is described; Acts of the Apostles (10.41–42; 17.31) brings the Resurrection of Jesus and the final judgment together; for John (12.31) Jesus' Hour is that of His exaltation and last judgment. In fact, according to Scripture, the JUSTICE OF GOD is His holiness and saving power (in the New Testament it is, in the final analysis, the Holy Spirit Himself who is holiness and saving power); it does not operate according to legal procedure but by creating justice, that is, by creating salvation in men. In the Resurrection, all the justifying power of God has burst forth, so that "justified in the Spirit" (1 Tm 3.16), Christ Himself becomes the justice of God (1 Cor 1.30). Henceforth the justice of God is also exerted over other men: it makes them just in their union with Christ (Rom 3.21–26; 8.1). It is exerted at the present time (Rom 3.21), but the fullness of this salvation is re-

served for the end (Gal 5.5). It is exerted by vivification, as in Christ; the believer is always judged by passing from death to life (Jn 5.24). That is why Saint John does not separate justifying power from the vivifying power of Christ (5.21–29). According to Saint Paul, the justice of the Day effects final salvation (Gal 5.5) that, as is known, is identical with the Resurrection. To account for these elements (the last judgment realized in the glorification of Christ, the vivifying effect of justice, the saving character of the Day for the faithful), theology does not look upon the judgment of the faithful as if it were a human trial; theology situates it in the justifying action of God, who raises up the dead together with Christ (*see* JUDGMENT, DIVINE).

Punishment and Reward. Those who have "rebelled against justice" (Rom 10.3) are condemned by this justice of salvation—by being excluded from justice, from the Spirit, and from the kingdom (cf. Gal 6.8; 1 Cor 15.50). This condemnation is not merely privation; the Lord has subdued all with His power (1 Cor 15.25; 2 Thes 1.8–9), leading the world toward its end, the risen Christ (cf. Col 1.16, 20). It is in His redeeming Lordship, in the power of His saving Resurrection (*Summa theologiae* 3a, 56.1 ad 3), as Son of Man (Jn 5.27) who has no power of condemnation (Jn 3.17; 12.47), that Christ raises up those "who have done evil" (Jn 5.29). For them the effect of the supreme action of salvation will be a resurrection of damnation (Jn 5.29; cf. Dn 12.2): opposed to the salvation of which they will nevertheless be created by the resuscitating power of Christ, they will exist in total contradiction to their own being. Thus hell would appear to be an effect of the salvific power of the risen Christ and of the refusal set against this power.

The theology of heaven ought to be developed beginning with the notion of the kingdom. The latter is a personal reality to Christ, who did not enter there as into a place; His entry into heaven is identical with His glorification. Men's heaven is in Christ glorified. They enter into it through the paschal communion. Thus the kingdom appears in the narrative of the Last Supper: a paschal banquet of the faithful with Christ (Lk 22.15). This explains why Saint Paul and Saint John do not distinguish the Ascension of Christ from His glorification; why men could not enter heaven before Christ's glorification (Heb 11.40), but do enter it as soon as they participate in His glory (Lk 23.43; cf. Saint Ambrose, *Expositio in Lucam* 10; *Corpus scriptorum ecclesiasticorum latinorum* 32.4:500). They are "in heaven" insofar as, living "in Christ," they have "risen with him" (Eph 2.6). Already in the Church, particularly in the Eucharistic celebration, they participate in this banquet of the immolated and glorified body that without a veil they will celebrate in the heavenly kingdom (cf. *Enchiridion symbolorum* 1649; Ignatius of Antioch, *Pros Romaious* 7.3).

Resurrection of Christ and creation of the world. In its eschatological form, the world is then created by the action of God who raises up Christ. Being all fullness Himself (Col 1.19), Christ "fills" the Church to the highest degree (Eph 1.23; Col 2.9) and beyond it the universe (Eph 4.10). This dominion over the world is exerted over the being of things, His Lordship being that of God Himself (Phil 2.9). Saint Paul expressly recognizes in Christ a creative causality (1 Cor 8.6). This is not exerted only on the world at its term, but also in its progress toward its term. "The beloved Son . . . image of the invisible God, firstborn of all creation, in whom and for whom all is created" (Col 1.14–16), is not the Word in His preexistence but Christ in His glory. If it is true that "all fullness" of being and of power has come to abide in Him (Col 1.19), nothing then could exist except in dependence on Christ. This causality does not include any chronological priority over creation; the glorified Christ is, on the contrary, the final term of the world. The theologian ought to understand the creative action of God in Christ after the manner of a call, of an attraction to final plenitude. We have recognized in the Resurrection the mystery of the Incarnation in its achievement. Dependent on Christ's glory, creation depends on the mystery of the Incarnation; it is in His divine glorious birth, where He is entirely assumed into the mystery of the Word, that Christ is the primordial source of the world. We also know that the glory of Christ is essentially redemptive, that the cosmic Lordship is affirmed in death. It seems, then, that the mystery of creation is to be found in that of Redemption.

Conclusion. The study of the Resurrection has taught us that salvation is none other than God who communicates Himself. He communicates Himself in Jesus by the Incarnation and when this Incarnation has arrived at its plenitude through the death. This salvation realized in Christ is extended to men in their union with Christ. Man's work is to consent, with Christ in His death, to the saving gift of God.

Mystery of communion, the Resurrection is also a ferment of unity for Christian thought. Source and center of the theology of apostolic times, it very soon lost its central place because there was not seen in it the eschatological event, the plenitude of salvation; furthermore the death of Christ began to be considered as a payment of debt and not as an entrance into communion; it was isolated from the Resurrection and had imputed to it alone a redemptive role. The role attributed to the Resurrection reduced it henceforth to prolonging the mediatory existence of Christ, to being an exemplary cause of justifica-

tion and the motive of credibility of faith [cf. D. M. Stanley, *Ad. historiam exegeseos Rom. 4.25, Verbum Domini* 29 (1951) 261, 258, 274]. To Saint Thomas belongs, nevertheless, the credit for seeing in the Resurrection the instrumental efficient cause of the resurrection of souls and bodies (*In epist. ad Rom.* 4 lect. 3; *Summa theologiae* 3a, 56.1–2). The misunderstanding of the central reality was no doubt the cause of the parceling out of theological thought, and it will no doubt be one of the benefits of the theology of the Resurrection to restore this thought to unity. "There are many things," says Saint Thomas, "to be meditated on in Him [Christ] but especially the Resurrection; everything is ordered to it, particularly the whole economy of the Christian religion" (*In epist. 2 ad Tim.* 2 lect. 2).

See Also: ESCHATOLOGY, ARTICLES ON; JESUS CHRIST, ARTICLES ON; MYSTICAL BODY OF CHRIST; PASSION OF CHRIST, II (THEOLOGY OF); REDEMPTION; RESURRECTION OF THE DEAD; SACRIFICE OF THE CROSS; SATISFACTION OF CHRIST; SOTERIOLOGY.

Bibliography: A. MICHEL, *Dictionnaire de théologie catholique: Tables générales*, ed. A. VACANT et. al. 2:2553–54, 2598–2655. J. SCHMITT and K. RAHNER, *Lexikon für Theologie und Kirche*, ed. J. HOFER and K. RAHNER, 1:1028–35, 1038–41. R. MARLÉ and A. KOLPING, *Handbuch theologischer Grundbegriffe*, ed. H. FRIES 1:130–45. J. COMBLIN, *La Résurrection de Jésus-Christ* (Paris 1959). C. DE CONDREN, *The Eternal Sacrifice*, tr. A. J. MONTEITH (London 1906). F. X. DURRWELL, *The Resurrection: A Biblical Study*, tr. R. SHEED (New York 1960). N. FUGLISTER, *Die Heilsbedeutung des Pascha* (Munich 1963). G. KOCH, *Die Auferstehung Jesu-Christi* (Tübingen 1959). W. KÜNNETH, *Theologie der Auferstehung* (4th ed. Munich 1951). A. M. RAMSEY, *The Resurrection of Christ* (Philadelphia 1946; rev. ed. London 1961). K. H. RENGSTORF, *Die Auferstehung Jesu: Form, Art und Sinn der urchristlichen Osterbotschaft* (Witten 1952). J. SCHMITT, *Jésus ressuscité dans la prédication apostolique* (Paris 1949). D. M. STANLEY, *Christ's Resurrection in Pauline Soteriology* (*Analecta biblica* 13; 1961). "Christus victor mortis," papers of the third Theology Week at the Gregorian University, in *Gregorianum* 39 (1958) 201–524. F. HOLTZ, "La Valeur sotériologique de la résurrection du Christ selon s. Thomas," *Ephemerides theologicae Lovanienses* 29 (1953) 609–45. K. RAHNER, "Dogmatische Fragen zur Osterfrömmigkeit," in *Schriften zur Theologie* 4 (Einsiedeln 1960) 157–72. B. VAWTER, "Resurrection and Redemption," *The Catholic Biblical Quarterly* 15 (1953) 11–23.

[F. X. DURRWELL]

RESURRECTION OF THE DEAD

This article discusses the resurrection of the dead as it is taught in the Bible and in theology.

1. IN THE BIBLE

In the Apostles' Creed the Christian professes faith in the resurrection in two distinct, but intimately connect-

''*The Raising of Lazarus*'' *by Rembrandt van Rijn.* (©Historical Picture Archive/CORBIS)

ed, articles: "the third day He arose again from the dead;" and "I believe . . . the resurrection of the body." The latter is the subject of this section, which discusses: (1) the biblical use of the term "resurrection"; (2) the basis and background of this belief in the Old Testament (OT); (3) the OT doctrine on the resurrection; and (4) the faith of the New Testament (NT) in the resurrection of the dead.

Biblical Use of Term. The teaching of the OT on man rests upon the definition of him given in the creation narrative of Gn 2.7. A creature whose life is the exclusive gift of God, whose body and spirit come from God, man remains always for the Israelite mind a "living being," a total whole. Consequently, man in the Bible is not thought of as that composite entity so familiar to Greek anthropology, but is viewed rather as a totality.

A normal consequence of this totality is the fact that the biblical notion of the resurrection is in no way comparable to the Greek idea of immortality. It was precisely the Hebrew conception of the body and the Hebrew notion of life that provided a favorable soil for the later development of the doctrine of the resurrection. In the biblical framework of ideas, the whole person falls into the power of death; and, if there is any possibility of deliverance from its power, then the formulation of such a possibility would have to be not in terms of the natural immortality of the soul but in the affirmation of a belief in a supernatural deliverance of the whole person from the implacable dominion of death.

To investigate such a belief in the OT, it must be borne in mind that there is no one biblical term reserved for resurrection and that such words actually used to convey the idea are often ambiguous, particularly so in the Hebrew of the Masoretic Text. Thus, for example, the NT uses two basic verbs for resurrection: ἀνιστάναι and ἐγείρειν. Both verbs do occur in the Septuagint (LXX); the former as an equivalent of no less than 14 and the latter of some 17 various Hebrew verbs or verb forms. The use of the substantive ἀνάστασις is quite frequent in the NT (occurring 42 times there as against six times in the LXX) and gives us some indication of the preponderance and importance of the notion in Christian revelation. Such statistical indications, however, could be misleading, especially in the OT, where, aside from the fact that we have to deal with both the Hebrew of the Masoretic Text and the Greek of the LXX, we have to keep constantly in mind that a hope, as it arises and hesitantly seeks precision, rarely, if ever, finds distinct, technical formulations to express its object.

Basis and Background of the Belief. The vernal rebirth of nature and the cyclic succession of death and life formed the basis of naturalistic cults in the ancient Near East. It is not surprising to see among the cultic elements that constituted the celebration of the seasonal pattern in the ancient world the element of the return of a dead god to life. This is so, for instance, in the cults of TAMMUZ in Babylon, of Osiris in Egypt (*see* ISIS AND OSIRIS), of the Hittite Telipinu and the Canaanite BAAL. The communal import of such rituals in agricultural and pastoral communities is readily understandable; for, in the mind of their peoples, the religious dramatization of seasonal recurrences assured the very efficacy of the cycle of death and life that was so essential for survival.

Dying and Rising Gods. Of course, it is not at all surprising that Israel, living in such close contact with its neighbors, should have known of the cults of a god who died and rose annually. Israel's history bears all too unmistakably the marks of such abominations as the idolatrous service of "the Baals and the Ashtaroth, the gods of Aram, the gods of Sidon, the gods of Moab, the gods of the Ammonites and the gods of the Philistines" (Jgs 10.6; see also 11.30–40).

The terebinths and the groves (Is 1.29), the pagan plants and the foreign vine slips (Is 17.10), the cakes for the queen of heaven and the libations poured out to strange gods (Jer 7.18), consort with harlots and the offering of sacrifice with prostitutes (Hos 4.14), the women who weep for Tammuz (Ez 8.14), and the god in whom women delight (Dn 11.37)—all bear eloquent witness to the noxious extent of Israel's contact with its neighbors, to say nothing of the compelling fascination that fertility cults exerted upon the Israelites. Nor were the trials of the Babylonian Exile sufficient to exorcize that "rebellious people, who walk in evil paths . . . offering sacrifices in the groves and burning incense on bricks, living among graves and spending the night in caverns" (Is 65.2–4).

Israel's Reaction. But the very abomination of such practices is guarantee against the adoption of their underlying beliefs as a basis for the formulation of a doctrine on the resurrection. It seems a truism to say that the errant ways of Israel were not enshrined into a theological doctrine by the sacred authors. However intimate Israel's contact with its neighbors, the possibility of their resurrection myths directly influencing OT doctrine on the subject seems quite remote. The prophets' vigilant fulminations against idolatry, the periodic purges of religious cult and practice, and the grim procession of national tragedies do not make such direct influence on the actual doctrine very likely. Nevertheless, the possibility of a negative influence by way of reaction against the idolatrous cults, by a greater stress on Yahweh's dominion over life and death, is more likely and cannot be dismissed. Nor, of course, can linguistic borrowings be wholly discounted.

From the very beginning, OT monotheism makes a clear break with the ambient mythologies and their accompanying rituals. Too hasty identification of similarities in expression, too facile establishment of causal nexus between Israel's faith and its neighbors' beliefs cannot but be disastrous. (See P. Follet's mordant but hardly unjustified criticism of T. Gaster's *Thespis* in *Biblica* 33 [1952] 139–142.) The immutable principle of the OT is the unique God's total dominion over life and death: "I alone am God. . . . It is I who bring both death and life" (Dt 32.39; and see 1 Sm 2.6 and the triumphant monotheism of the "Book of Consolation," Is 40–55). This principle is defended against the almost irresistible onslaught of idolatry and idolatrous practices; and its defense could well have been the basis of a still more important assertion for our purpose, namely, Yahweh's power over Sheol itself. "The nether world and the abyss lie open before the Lord" (Prv 15.11; Jb 26.5–6; Am 9.2; Ps 138[139].8; and cf. Jer 23.23–24).

Persian Influence. There is yet another source of influence that, though perhaps quite real and direct, is not at all easy to assess. The relations of the Jews with their Persian rulers were excellent, as is attested by Ezra and Nehemiah. Moreover, although preexilic texts favoring subsequent development are not altogether lacking, still OT doctrine on the resurrection does show remarkable progress after contact of the Jews with the Persians. Of them it has been said, "Outside of Judaism and Christianity, it is impossible to find in antiquity so true, so noble, so ideal a belief in the resurrection of the body . . . as is to be found in the scriptures of Ancient Iran" (A. V. W. Jackson, *Zoroastrian Studies: The Iranian Religion and Various Monographs* [New York 1928] 3). At the start of the twentieth century, W. Bousset judged Iran's influence on Jewish belief in the resurrection as primordial (*Die Religion des Judentums* [Göttingen 1902; 3d ed. 1926] 507–517); and, at mid-century, H. Birkeland asserted the same opinion. (*See* PERSIAN RELIGION, ANCIENT.) The question, however, is not as simple today as it seemed to Bousset; and the problem at present is by no means solved.

It is quite easy to see in Zoroastrianism, for example, the mortal combat between the good principle, AHURA MAZDA, and the evil spirit, Ahriman, ending on the last day in the triumph of good, the annihilation of evil, and the general resurrection of the dead. (*See* ZOROASTER [ZARATHUSHTRA].) What is not easy at all to determine is the time at which various parts of Iran's religious corpus were written or the exact religion of the Achaemenian monarchs to whom the Jews were subject (see H. S. Nyberg, *Die Religion des alten Iran* [Leipzig 1938]; J. Duchesne-Guillemin, *La religion de l'Iran ancien* [Paris 1962]; E. Herzfeld, "Die Religion der Achaemeniden,"

Revue de l'histoire des religions 113 [1936] 21–41). Until such questions receive the precise answers they deserve, a greater caution must be exercised in determining the extent of Jewish borrowings from the Iranian doctrine of the resurrection.

Old Testament Doctrine. The life of man, prized as a good above all goods, was acknowledged by Israel as God's gift to man, a gift totally dependent upon Him. Though death was accepted as a normal fact, as man's appointed end, it was no less under God's dominion than life itself, for "the Lord killeth and maketh alive: he bringeth down to hell and bringeth back again" (1 Sm 2.6; see also Dt 32.39 and Tb 13.2). This dominion of Yahweh was manifested in Elijah's raising of the widow's son to life (1 Kgs 17.17–24), the similar miracle worked by Elisha (2 Kgs 4.31–37), and the more marvelous one worked by Elisha's bones (13.21).

God as Savior. Yahweh's dominion over life and death was no less evident in His power to heal man's illness, to cure his ills, and to deliver him from his enemies. Various Psalms uttered in times of distress and sickness call upon this power of God (Ps 3; 31 [32]; 37 [38]; 101 [102]). They acknowledge His might that brings up from the netherworld and preserves from going down into the pit, rescues from the depths of Sheol and redeems life from destruction, bestows upon man the gifts of life and health (Ps 29 [30].4; 85 [86].13; 102 [103].3–4; and see Is 38.17). Yet, however wondrous those divine deeds were, they remained but a temporary reprieve from the dark and inevitable reign of death. A far more beatific lot was that of Enoch who "walked with God and was seen no more, because God took him" (Gn 5.24; cf. Hb 11.5), and that of Elijah who was taken up to heaven in a fiery chariot (2 Kgs 2.11).

Union with Yahweh remained an end desired by the just: "with you I shall always be . . . in the end you will receive me in glory" (Ps 72 [73].23–24). "God will redeem me from the power of the nether world by receiving me" (48 [49].16). From the midst of his distress, the Psalmist calls upon Yahweh and is delivered from "the breakers of death . . . the destroying floods . . . the cords of the nether world . . . the snares of death" (17 [18].5–7). Upon this might of Yahweh was founded the hope of final union with Him, the expectation of being always "before his face." The Psalm that best expresses this confidence in Him who "will not abandon my soul to the nether world, nor will you suffer your faithful one to undergo corruption" (15 [16].10) proves in its Greek version to be an invaluable aid for the Apostolic preaching of the Resurrection of Christ (Acts 2.25–31; 13.34–37).

It will be noted, especially in the Psalms cited above, that this divine tutelage over life and death is a soteriological function. Just as sickness and death are seen in a larger context of sin, so too healing and life are seen in a context of salvation. This salvation was generally regarded in the beginning as the deliverance of a people, a communal event; and, understandably enough, the initial attempts to express this people's hope in the resurrection exhibit the same characteristics. (*See* SALVATION HISTORY [HEILSGESCHICHTE].)

Resurrection in the Prophets. The OT employs a series of prophetic texts to translate this collective hope of Israel into some sort of comprehensive image. Thus, Hosea's "on the third day he will raise us up, to live in his presence" (6.2; and see 13.14) can rightly be described as a *völkisch-nationale Wiederherstellung* (Botterweck in *Lexikon für Theologie und Kirche,* 1:1044), for it does see this recall to life as a national conversion to Yahweh. Similarly, death and destruction are seen as the nation's afflictions for its sins and infidelities toward Him (see Is 1.5–9). The hope of a future and permanent restoration rests on Yahweh's promise to "raise up the fallen hut of David . . . wall up its breaches, raise up its ruins, and rebuild it as in the days of old" (Am 9.11). "He who remains in Sion and he that is left in Jerusalem will be called holy: every one marked down for life in Jerusalem" (Is 4.2–6).

The seed of this hope of final deliverance lies in that "scanty remnant" (Is 1.9) whose return to the land is Israel's return to life. After the Exile, Yahweh raises His people even as in Ezekiel's vision He brings the dry bones to life (Ez 37.1–14). The Lord's promise that "your dead shall live, their corpses shall rise" (Is 26.19; see also 51.17 and 60.1) is a promise of national deliverance from death and extinction. The notion of a resurrection remains, at this stage in Israel's history, at the service of the hope for the reestablishment of an unending reign and a definitive prosperity of the Chosen People. Even should the faithful remnant fall prey to the powers of Sheol, a day will come when, like Yahweh's faithful servant, it "shall see the light in fullness of days" (Is 53.11; although most exegetes of this passage agree that here there is no explicit reference to the resurrection).

The ideas of the so-called Apocalypse of Isaiah (Is 24.1–27.13) on this point are still the subject of dispute among exegetes (see *Lexikon für Theologie und Kirche,* 1:1043; Sutcliffe, 126–128; and *Dictionnaire de la Bible,* 4:680). But such passages as "your dead shall live, their corpses shall rise" (Is 26.19) and "he will destroy death forever" (25.8) cannot be wholly discounted as stages in the development of the doctrine on the resurrection. Though it is difficult to determine whether the value of such passages is in their being an image or an affirmation, they do contribute this important note to the evolution of the doctrine: they set it within an eschatological framework. The eschatological banquet and the banishment of death, the end of sorrow and tribulation are images of the end of time (Is 25.6–8; cf. Rev 7.17 and 21.4) and of the advent of salvation.

In the Postexilic Period. In the centuries that followed the Exile, what had previously been an expression of hope in a national restoration became a clear assertion of the eventual resurrection of the individual. Yahweh's might could surely snatch the dead from Sheol; His mercy will not let His own languish there always, but will call them to be before His face forever. Divine justice will be satisfied in this world or the next. It was reflection on this divine justice, setting forth the problem of the suffering just, particularly in the Book of JOB, that contributed so much to the eventual evolution of the OT doctrine on the resurrection.

Although the original Hebrew text of Jb 19.25 is poorly preserved, this passage hardly refers to individual resurrection, as is clear from the context of the whole book. Yet in its yearning for justice and its conviction that this justice will be ultimately satisfied, it did serve as a prelude to the explicit affirmation of the resurrection in Daniel and 2 Maccabees. Faith in the resurrection of the dead seems to have been Yahweh's gift to a people who had become a nation of martyrs.

The violent persecution of Antiochus IV Epiphanes raised the question of the lot of the saints martyred for the faith. The apocalypse of DANIEL gave the response that thenceforth became a common, though not universal, possession of Israel: "Many of those who sleep in the dust of the earth shall awake; some shall live forever, others shall be an everlasting horror and disgrace" (Dn 12.2). Daniel thus uncovered the profound sense latent in the Torah and the Prophets, affirming a resurrection that was no longer merely the restoration of a nation but the individual recompense of personal merit.

The author of 2 Maccabees reiterates this conviction, giving it, as it were, its historical setting in the glorious martyrdom of the brothers: "the King of the world will raise us up, who die for his laws, in the resurrection of eternal life . . . the Creator of the world that formed the nativity of man and that found out the origin of all, he will restore to you again in his mercy, both breath and life, as now you despise yourselves for the sake of his laws" (2 Mc 7.9, 23).

Finally, the Book of WISDOM, written shortly before our era, not only presupposes this doctrine throughout, but attempts to give it, in its third part (ch. 11–19), a solidly reasoned basis. In a midrash on the wonders of Exodus, as "subtle" as it is "luminous," the author of

Wisdom sets forth a cosmosoteriology implicit in Exodus. He erects upon it an argument that probably, upon close literary analysis of the chapters, would have to be linked with the author's theory of the salvation of the body, if the last section of his book is to make any sense at all. (See P. Beàuchamp, ''Le Salut corporel des justes et la conclusion du livre de la Sagesse,'' *Biblica* 45 [1964] 491–526.)

In the apocalyptic literature and the pseudepigrapha that proliferated around the Christian era, the doctrine of the resurrection of the body (at least, of the just) became an established one (see Jubilees 23.30–31; Enoch 22.13; 91.10; 100.5; Testament of Juda 25.1, 4; of Zebulun 10.2; and of Benjamin 10.6–8). It appears in the writings of the Qumran sectaries (see *Hôdâyôt [Thanksgiving Hymns]* 3:19–23; 11:10–14; 8:26–30), though there it is rather ambiguous because of the heavy admixture of tenets on the immortality of the soul. The doctrine occurs frequently also in rabbinic literature. (For abundant testimony see in *Kommentar zum Neuen Testament,* 4:2, the excursus on ''Allgemeine oder teilweise Auferstehung der Toten?'' especially pp. 1172–98.) The well-known division of opinion on it between the Pharisees and the Sadducees is recorded by Flavius Josephus (*B.J.* 2.8.14; *Antiquities* 18.1, 3) and recalled in the NT: ''For the Sadducees say that there is no resurrection, and that there are no angels or spirits, whereas the Pharisees believe in both'' (Acts 23.8; see also Mt 22.23).

Faith of the New Testament. The Book of Acts bears witness to the focal position occupied by the Resurrection of Christ in the primitive catechesis and the KERYGMA of the early Church. Peter's discourses proclaimed God's might that raised up Christ, ''having loosed the sorrows of hell'' (Acts 2.24; 3.15). Paul's disputations with the Epicureans and the Stoics of Athens centered around the ''resurrection of the dead'' (17.18, 32); and before his Pharisee and Sadducee accusers, he flatly stated, ''it is about the hope and the resurrection of the dead that I am on trial'' (23.6).

What was a final milestone in revelation in the OT becomes in the NT the foundation of Apostolic preaching and the basis of Christian faith. Here the idea of the resurrection of the dead takes on a hitherto unsuspected precision and assumes capital importance in the life of the Christian community, both in its cultic expression and its creedal formulations. The NT doctrine of the resurrection is in continuity with what preceded it and rejoins the initial intuition of the OT in asserting God's dominion over life and death. That is why St. Paul is at pains to stress the ''according to the Scriptures'' before undertaking his exposition in 1 Corinthians ch. 15. Throughout the NT, however, all affirmations on the resurrection radiate as from one luminous source: the fundamental event of the RESURRECTION OF CHRIST, ''the first-fruits of those who have fallen asleep'' (1 Cor 15.20).

In the Synoptics. The Gospel of St. Mark records a verity fundamental to all subsequent understanding of the true meaning of the resurrection: God is not the God of the dead but of the living (12.27). By citing Ex 3.6 in this context, the argument for the resurrection not only is based upon a central text of the OT, but it is also linked with a fundamental revelation of the Old Covenant that is perfected in the New. All error on the resurrection, therefore, is ultimately attributable to ignorance of the Scriptures and of the power of God (Mk 12.24).

Jesus' reply to the question put to him by the Sadducees (Mt 22.23–33 and parallels), in addition to setting forth the basic principle for the correct understanding of the doctrine of the resurrection, presupposes the all-important fact of the identity between the dead and the risen person. Without this identity of person, the very question put to Jesus by the Sadducees would be meaningless. The Resurrection narratives are at pains to highlight this identity in the case of the risen Lord Himself. This is an essential aspect of the doctrine because it affirms the reality of the individual's destiny. That is why, in this context, St. Luke speaks of ''those who shall be accounted worthy of that world and of the resurrection of the dead'' (20.35–36). Ultimately, the divine JUDGMENT on the last day derives its personal significance and its urgency from this fact.

As the Synoptic narratives advance toward the events of the Passion and the Resurrection, they mark a progress toward the final victory over death itself; and it is in the eschatological perspective of this victory that the closing events of Christ's life on Earth must be viewed. Moreover, all the healing narratives of Christ's public ministry are an anticipation of the final victory. They are incursions into the domain of death, no less than the raising of Jairus's daughter (Mk 5.21–23, 35–43) and of the widow's son (Lk 7.11–15) are signs that herald its definitive overthrow.

The faith context of the MIRACLES in the Bible should help us understand why the NT, when it speaks of the resurrection of the dead, stresses the resurrection of the just and of the believers. Life is God's gift to the believing just; death is the lot of the unrighteous. It was by no means easy for Jesus' contemporaries to comprehend how the unjust and the unbelievers could really rise to life. Nevertheless, the NT not only presupposes this resurrection of the unrighteous as well as of the just (e.g., Mt 11.24; Rev 20.12–13), but asserts it quite clearly in Acts 24.15 and Jn 5.29: ''They who have done good shall come forth to the resurrection of life; but they who have done evil unto the resurrection of judgment.''

In the Pauline Epistles. Aware of his fidelity to the tradition he received (1 Cor 15.3–4), Paul sets Christ's Resurrection as the foundation of his teaching, indeed as the very foundation of Christian belief: "Now if Christ is preached as risen from the dead, how do some among you say there is no resurrection of the dead? But if there is no resurrection of the dead, neither has Christ risen; and if Christ has not risen, vain then is our preaching, vain too is your faith" (1 Cor 15.12–14). There is an intimate interdependence between the resurrection of the dead and the Resurrection of Christ; our faith in the latter must include our faith in God's power to accomplish the former, "for if we believe that Jesus died and rose again, so with him God will bring those also who have fallen asleep through Jesus" (1 Thes 4.14; 2 Cor 13.4). The Resurrection of Christ and that of the Christian are both worked not only by the same power of God (1 Cor 6.14) but also by the same Spirit who dwells in us (Rom 8.11). "For we know that he who raised up Jesus will raise up us also with Jesus" (2 Cor 4.14). The link between the two is so close that to deny one is to deny the other, "for if the dead do not rise, neither has Christ risen" (1 Cor 15.16).

St. Paul emphasizes the Resurrection of Christ and, consequently, that of the Christian as the work of the Father: "Now God has raised up the Lord and will also raise us up by his power" (1 Cor 6.14; 1 Thes 1.10). Christian witness is a witness to God the Father who raised Jesus from the dead (Gal 1.1; 1 Cor 15.15). Christian faith is faith in Him who "raised Jesus our Lord from the dead" (Rom 4.24; 10.9). The Resurrection, moreover, is a manifestation of the power of God: Christ "lives through the power of God"; and, by implication, so too will the Christian (2 Cor 13.4). It is the expression of God's will that calls sinful men from the power of death to take part in the new life of the resurrection.

Through baptism Christians are even now called to this new life of the resurrection, called "to walk in newness of life" (Rom 6.4–11). In this basic Sacrament of Christian life, the Christian is buried with Christ and in Him rises again "through faith in the working of God who raised him from the dead" (Col 2.12; Eph 2.1 and 5). Though he is even now "a new creature" (2 Cor 5.17), though he is at present spoken of as raised and seated together in heaven in Christ Jesus (Eph 2.6; Col 2.12; 3.1–4), the Christian must nevertheless await the total and definitive triumph at the final consummation, "the end when he delivers the kingdom to God the Father" (1 Cor 15.12, 23–28).

Having set forth the fundamental elements of our faith in the resurrection, St. Paul turns to the question of its mode: "How do the dead rise? with what kind of body do they come?" (1 Cor 15.35–55). The answer to this question remains, in the final analysis, a mystery; and, even though to answer it Paul marshals his own peculiar vocabulary (vv. 46–49), calls forth nature's imagery (vv. 36–38), has recourse to the physics of his day (vv. 40–41), and cites the Prophets (vv. 47, 55), nevertheless, he concludes with a true theologian's only attitude before a mystery: "Thanks be to God who has given us the victory through our Lord Jesus Christ" (15.57). One thing, however, must be insisted upon throughout St. Paul's exposition: no matter how true and how great the difference is between what is "sown" and what "rises," there is true and real identity.

Were this identity between the body that is "sown" and the body that "rises" not true, the Christian's participation in the life of the risen Christ would be meaningless here and hereafter. The paschal character of Christian life and the certitude of the hope that impels it forward (Col 3.1–2) dominate the moral life of Christians (3.5–4.6). Because he already bears within him the pledge of this future life, the Christian is secure in his hope of the final resurrection (Rom 8.22–25; Phil 3.11–14). He awaits eagerly the Lord "who will re-fashion the body of lowliness, conforming it to the body of his glory" (Phil 3.20–21). On the last day that life that is now "hidden in Christ with God" will appear in the clarity of glory (Col 3.4).

In St. John's Gospel. For the author of the fourth Gospel, Christ's work is ζωοποίησις: "In him was life" (Jn 1.4), and He was sent into the world "that those who believe in him may not perish; but may have life everlasting" (3.16). He can, with sovereign power, say, "Thy son lives" (4.50); "Rise, take up thy pallet and walk" (5.8); "Lazarus, come forth!" (11.43); for "as the Father raises the dead and gives them life, even so the Son also gives life to whom he will" (5.21). It is the Father's will that He should raise up those whom the Father had given Him (6.39, 40, 44). He is the living bread; and those who eat of this bread will not die (6.50), for they have life everlasting, and He will raise them up on the last day (6.55).

Even though, unlike St. Paul, John emphasizes the resurrection as the work of the Son, his whole Gospel bears witness to the fact that all the work of the Son, including the resurrection, is in obedience to the Father's will. God gave His only-begotten Son, "that those who believe in him may not perish, but may have life everlasting" (3.16). This life is Christ's gift to men; it is, ultimately, the gift of Himself to them; for He is not only the life by which they live now, but also the resurrection: "I am the resurrection and the life" (11.25).

In the fourth Gospel the narrative of the raising of Lazarus constitutes a high point in the revelation of the mystery of resurrection. The actual event constitutes both a sign and a fulfillment of "thy brother shall live" (11.23). Its fulfillment was in the coming forth of him who was dead; but that coming forth was symbolic of a future life, a sign of a resurrection unto life everlasting. The whole narrative reveals a peculiar modality of the gift of life by presenting it as a triumph over death. It is, as it were, an exegesis of "he who believes in me, even if he die, shall live" (11.25). Nowhere in the NT is this total reversal of the order of our mortality more clearly revealed than here. This whole section (11.1–44) is fundamentally a sign of Christ's triumph in the Resurrection: His victory over death through death itself. It was indeed expedient that "one man die for the people" (11.50; see also 11.15).

"For this is the will of my Father who sent me, that whoever beholds the Son, and believes in him, shall have everlasting life, and I will raise him up on the last day" (6.40). Henceforth, Christian life here on Earth is an anticipated resurrection, a life of faith in the risen Christ, a life of hope in the final triumph of living and reigning with Him (Rev 20.4). According to the life they lead here on Earth they will be judged (20.12, 13). Only then, on that last day, will they behold "a new heaven and a new earth" (21.1). They will then hear a loud voice proclaiming the end of things past, the final fulfillment of all promises, and the realization of all signs: "Behold the dwelling of God with men, and he will dwell with them. . . . And they will be his people, and God himself will be with them as their God. And God will wipe every tear from their eyes. And death shall be no more" (21.3–4; see also Ex 25.8 and Jn 1.14).

Bibliography: A. OEPKE, "ἀνίστημι," G. KITTEL, *Theologisches Wörterbuch zum Neuen Testament* (Stuttgart 1935–) 1:368–372. *Encyclopedic Dictionary of the Bible,* tr. and adap. by L. HARTMAN (New York 1963), from A. VAN DEN BORN, *Bijbels Woordenboek* 2022–32. J. SCHMID, *Lexikon für Theologie und Kirche,* ed. J. HOFER and K. RAHNER, 10 v. (2d, new ed. Freiburg 1957–65) suppl., *Das Zweite Vatikanische Konzil: Dokumente und Kommentare,* ed. H. S. BRECHTER et al., pt. 1 (1966) 1:1042–48. H. BIRKELAND, "The Belief in the Resurrection of the Dead in the Old Testament," *Studia Theologica* 3.1 (1949) 60–78. E. F. SUTCLIFFE, *The Old Testament and the Future Life* (Westminster, MD 1947). R. MARTIN-ACHARD, *De la Mort à la résurrection d'après l'Ancien Testament* (Paris 1956). C. LARCHER, "La Doctrine de la résurrection dans l'Ancien Testament," *Lumière et vie* 3 (1952) 11–34. J. GUILLET, "Les Sources scripturaires de la foi en la résurrection de la chair," *Bible et vie chrétienne* 2 (1953) 40–54. B. VAWTER, "Resurrection and Redemption," *Catholic Biblical Quarterly* 15 (1953) 11–23.

[S. B. MARROW]

2. THEOLOGY OF

Even though the tenet of the Creed, "I believe in the resurrection of the dead," has been an integral element in the Christian faith from the very beginning, yet a more ready response from Christians for many centuries to the question of man's fate after death has been, "I believe in the immortality of the soul." This response appears to be the outgrowth of two factors that have played major roles in the development of the belief in the resurrection of the dead.

The first of these elements is traceable to a questionable approach to NT eschatology [see ESCHATOLOGY (IN THE BIBLE)]. Christians for too long have tended to look merely to the future, to the things "of the other world," counting the things of earth as nothing, as mere shadows of the true realities to come and valueless when the perfect heavenly things shall have arrived. The vision of this world's destruction has led Christians to reject it as far as possible, and where not possible, to put up with it in a spirit of renunciation, penance, and mortification. The true sense of eschatology, therefore, is lost, for the NT (especially St. John) insists that the kingdom of God is present, that Jesus never really left, but represents the definitive intervention of God. The risen Christ is present and active through the Sanctifier, the HOLY SPIRIT, in the Church. The end time (ἔσχατον), therefore, has already come (*see* INCARNATION; TEMPORAL VALUES, THEOLOGY OF).

The second element entering into the formation of "traditional" theology of the resurrection has been the influence of Platonic and Neoplatonic thought, and its insertion into the very core of Christian theology. The gradual development of an eschatology that looked too longingly to the future was possible in the measure that Platonism furnished an understanding of the SOUL-BODY RELATIONSHIP that allowed the Christian to speculate freely about the separated soul, without impelling him simultaneously to make provisions for the material principle in man (*see* PLATONISM; NEOPLATONISM).

Gradually, therefore, the eschatological structure arose: DEATH was the separation (liberation) of the soul from the body. The body reverted to the earth from where it had originated; the soul was judged either worthy of eternal union with God if at death it were in the state of GRACE and needed no purification (or punishment) before *seeing* God, or else, deserving of eternal punishment because of mortal sin, its state at death. Even though the doctrine thus presented spoke only of the soul, and not the person, yet theologians affirmed "essential" beatitude for the just at death, since the BEATIFIC VISION in its totality could be enjoyed by the soul whose potentialities for knowledge and love were enormously enhanced through its separation from the body. They could likewise speak of the separation of the soul from God as the essential element of hell. The destiny of the body in this whole other-world existence, whether it contributed to the glorification of the just, or made some sense out of physical torture for the damned, was generally considered something secondary and accidental in the total picture. Possible difficulties about the fate of the human *person* the whole while were solved by perhaps too facile references to the transcendental relationship of soul to body after death.

In such a context the resurrection of the body, albeit a professed truth of the Christian faith, gradually faded out of the forefront of the eschatological picture. The emphasis in Catholic theology for many centuries has been simply to explain how it comes to pass. Experience of aspects of death has taxed the theological imagination to explain God's restoring bodies that have been totally corrupted through cremation, cannibalism, etc. In other words, the questions in theology have dealt more with the philosophic-scientific aspects of the resurrection of the body than with its place in the harmonious totality of Christian revelation. There is, therefore, a much needed reemphasis on the resurrection of the dead, or the body, as an indispensable event in the economy of SALVATION. The *person* in Christian reality is the object of Redemption and salvation; the full Christian HOPE is in the resurrection-glorification of the *person* (enfleshed SPIRIT). [*See* PERSON (IN THEOLOGY).] Until such time as this comes to pass every man in some sense is in a state of expectation. The basis of this Christian hope is the faithful conviction that salvation is a share in the Christ-life and the Christ-event. The paschal mystery, therefore, forms the core of the understanding of Christian revelation: just as Christ's redemptive action included death-resurrection-glorification, so man's share in the Christ-life involves him in the same necessary transition or passage (pasch) through death (transformation) to resurrection-glorification. An eschatology that sets its sights exclusively on the soul as the immortal element in man runs the risk of misconceiving these fundamental Christian truths. The resurrection of the body must not be considered an adjunct to the Christian's destiny; it cannot be an afterthought to the salvation of the soul.

Doctrine of the Teaching Church. In many ways over the centuries the Church in conciliar and other official pronouncements has proposed the resurrection of the dead as a truth revealed by God (H. Denzinger, *Enchiridion symbolorum,* 11, 30, 76, 150, 801, 859). The language used is not always uniform: sometimes profession of faith is in the resurrection of the flesh, sometimes in the resurrection of the body, and at times in the resurrection of the dead. The later conciliar assemblies accentuate the identity of the risen body. A general conclusion from the documents of the teaching Church is that there will be a resurrection, that it will be for all men, and that all men will arise with the same bodies they now have. It is to this resurrection that the Church from the very beginning has been the believing witness.

Witness of Christian Tradition. It can be said quite definitely that there is hardly any truth of Christian revelation that is so openly and clearly taught by the Fathers and Christian writers as the resurrection of the body. Indeed, it is the very keystone of Christianity, mirroring as it does the Resurrection of the Lord. By the time of Lateran Council IV (1215) the developed teaching of Christian tradition regarding the resurrection of the body received definitive formulation in its essential elements, that is, that there will be a resurrection, that it will be universal for the just and unjust alike, and that all men will rise with the same bodies they now possess (H. Denzinger, *Enchiridion symbolorum,* 801).

The fact of the resurrection and its universality not only formed an integral part of the Christian's profession of faith from the very beginning, but was defended *ex professo* in various writings of the early Fathers and Church writers (Didache, St. Polycarp, St. Athenagoras, Theophilus of Antioch, Tertullian). The later insistency on the identity of the resurrected body grew out of the Christian reaction in the 4th and 5th centuries to Origen's earlier assertions that resurrected bodies were composed of ethereal matter.

Theological Reflections. It must be affirmed with deliberate insistence before all else that man's continuance in existence forever cannot be proved from, neither is it derived from, nor supported by, philosophy. Philosophy might prove the immortality of the soul, or spiritual element, in man (arguments from its spirituality to its simplicity, from its independence of matter, from the culmination of an evolutive process in spirit existence, etc.), but Christianity professes faith in the resurrection of the body, of the man, the enfleshed spirit, and this can come only from God's revealed Word and man's immersion into Christ's own death-resurrection. Once this is clear, then it is valid and, within limits, useful and necessary to inquire into the manner of this resurrection and related problems.

The most general approach of the theologian must be to demonstrate that the mystery of the resurrection introduces a certain fulfillment into the Christian conscience. The man who is committed to God in Christ Jesus through the Sanctifier, the Holy Spirit, is assured through his commitment that he will live forever. It is God's love for man, therefore, that guarantees the resurrection of that body which at death appears to fade out of the eschatological perspective. If forced to formulate an argument for his faithful conviction, the Christian might respond: God loves me. But God is eternal. Therefore I will live forever (not my soul, but I). The great movement of the whole of creation toward Christ, the New Adam, after its progressive decline through the Old Adam, is crowned by the resurrection of the body, the final victory of each individual (through Christ's death-resurrection) over death, which gained dominion in the person of the first Adam. By the same token the resurrection of the damned seals forever their totally free movement away from Christ and the Christian community. The existence of the resurrection of the body, then, lends universal harmony to the totality of Christian revelation.

The question, finally, of the manner of the resurrection is truly the object of speculative theology. Perhaps no explanation is completely satisfying. As prototypes, of course, the Resurrection of Christ and the ASSUMPTION OF MARY heighten one's expectation, but add little enlightenment as to the exact manner of the Christian's resurrection. The fact is that men will arise with their own bodies in a glorified state (*see* GLORIFIED BODY). The general principle to be accentuated here is that man is a composition of both a material or visible element and a spiritual or angelic element, that is, flesh and spirit; man represents a unique relationship between spirit and matter. This will continue forever, but still man will be changed, since at the resurrection a new and different relationship between spirit and matter (glorification in the case of the just) will exist. But he will still be this individual, this human being. It is the traditional view in theology that the spiritual principle in man is responsible for the identity that characterizes him as this man forever. Whatever the speculative analysis of the resurrection, the risen body guarantees man, as man, an eternal existence in union with, or separated from, God through Christ in unity with the Holy Spirit.

See Also: ESCHATOLOGY, ARTICLES ON.

Bibliography: A. MICHEL, *Dictionnaire de théologie catholique,* ed. A. VACANT, 15 v. (Paris 1903–50; Tables générales 1951–) 13.2:2501–71. W. VON SODEN et al., *Die Religion in Geschichte und Gegenwart,* 7 v. (3d ed. Tübingen 1957–65) 1:688–698. H. CORNÉLIS et al., *The Resurrection of the Body,* tr. M. JOSELYN (Notre Dame, IN 1964). K. RAHNER, *On the Theology of Death,* tr. C. H. HENKEY (Quaestiones Disputatae 2; New York 1961). R. TROISFONTAINES, *I Do Not Die,* tr. F. E. ALBERT (New York 1963) 279–295. H. KÜNG, *Eternal Life?: Life after Death as a Medical, Philosophical, and Theological Problem,* tr. E. QUINN (New York 1991, c1984). G. A. MALONEY, *The First Day of Eternity: Resurrection Now* (New York 1982). V. KESICH, *The First Day of the New Creation: The Resurrection and the Christian Faith* (Crestwood, NY 1982). T. PENELHUM, *Immortality* (Belmont, CA 1973). P. BENOÎT and R. MURPHY, eds., *Immortality and Resurrection* (New York 1970). J. RATZINGER, *Eschatology: Death and Eternal Life,* tr. M. WALDSTEIN (Washington, DC 1988).

[H. M. MCELWAIN]

RESURRECTIONISTS

The Congregation of the Resurrection (CR, Official Catholic Directory #1080) received its name from the original members who pronounced their first vows on the feast of the Resurrection, 1842, in the catacombs of St. Sebastian in Rome. The founders were three young Polish scholars, Bogdan Janski, Peter Semenenko, and Jerome Kajsiewicz, who had returned to the practice of their Catholic faith only a few years earlier. Inspired by the French Catholic lay apostolate movement headed by Count Charles MONTALEMBERT, Jean LACORDAIRE, and Frédéick OZANAM, the three founders attempted a similar work among their compatriots in Paris. There in 1836 with a few companions, they began leading a common life under the direction of Janski. Never ordained, he died in Rome before his community made first vows and before Semenenko became the first superior general. The three cofounders, Janski, Semenenko, and Kajsiewicz, are buried in the Church of the Resurrection adjacent to the mother house in Rome.

Although the congregation encountered many reverses, its members were soon working in Italy, France, Canada, Turkey, Bulgaria, the U.S., Poland, and Austria. They received the decree of praise in 1860; final approval of the constitutions was granted in 1902. Later, at the request of Pius XII, the Resurrectionists established missions in Bermuda, Bolivia, and Brazil. The motherhouse is in Rome.

In 1857 Father Eugene Funcken left Rome for Canada and began work in the Catholic settlement of St. Agatha, Ontario. Headquarters were later moved to a neighboring town then called Berlin, later the city of Kitchener. Work in the U.S. began in 1865 at Parisville, MI, and spread the following year to Texas. In 1870 a permanent mission was established in Chicago, IL, and in 1871 the Canadian Resurrectionists, complying with an earlier request of Bp. William McCloskey of Louisville, assumed control of St. Mary's College, founded in 1821 by Rev. William Byrne. The U.S. provincialate is in Chicago, IL.

Bibliography: L. LONG, *The Resurrectionists* (Chicago 1947).

[A. A. RUETZ/EDS.]

RETRIBUTION

Repayment for moral guilt or virtue. Recompense for injustices was exacted by human custom and law in Biblical history, just as rewards were allotted by human agents in return for good actions. This article's main concern, however, is to examine the evolution of Biblical thought and expression concerning divine retribution, or how the Judeo-Christian God was considered to reward virtue and to punish vice.

Old Testament Retribution

Israelite ideas about God's rewards and punishments for moral actions were limited, almost until the Christian Era, to sanctions given in this world (*see* AFTERLIFE, 2) and, for the most part, they focused on divine recompense to the whole group rather than to individual persons.

RETRIBUTION IN THIS WORLD

OT rewards were mainly material, and, even when they were spiritual, e.g., a closer friendship with God, they ceased with death. [*See* DEATH (IN THE BIBLE).] In SHEOL (abode of the dead) the dead could no longer praise God; the just who died were united with the unjust in a common lot (Jb 3.13–19). Observers of the Mosaic LAW would enjoy a long and prosperous life in the promised land and would die surrounded by their numerous progeny (Dt 5.16; 6.1–3, 10–15). Pentateuchal and prophetic doctrine proclaimed only earthly rewards or punishments for those who fulfilled or transgressed the obligations of God's COVENANT (Jer 11.1–12). In the SAPIENTIAL BOOKS rewards for good conduct were all of a temporal nature—wealth and honor, land and possessions, and healthy, numerous children, whereas the folly of wickedness brought sudden and early death (Prv 8.17–21; 10.27; 22.22–23). Only in the latest OT books was the notion of reward connected with life after death.

Repayment for the crime or virtuous act of an individual affected the group to which the person belonged. Hebrew tribal background was a source of this idea, but a more important reason was that God had chosen the Israelites and made a religious pact with them, not as individuals, but as a collective entity, His holy people (*see* ELECTION, DIVINE). Consequently, God was conceived of as punishing the group for one person's sin and as rewarding it for another's good action.

Collective Punishment for Individual Fault. The obvious example of solidarity in punishment is the story of the fall of man (Gn ch. 3), but there are many others. Cain's murder brought a crescendo of corruption on his whole line. Simeon and Levi, by their violent revenge (Gn 34.25–31), were the remote causes for the dispersion of their tribes throughout Israel (49.5–7). Achan's violation of the ban (anathema) led to the obliteration of his whole family (Jos 6.27–7.1, 24–26). Even King DAVID, by his adultery followed by murder, doomed the son of the adulterous union to death and his royal line to perpetual warfare and violence (2 Sm 12.7–14). Not only a person's descendants but even the whole nation could be punished for the sin of one of its members, as in the cases of Achan (Jos 22.20), Saul (2 Sm 21.1), and David (2 Sm ch. 24).

The classical statement of punishment meted out by Yahweh on the presumably innocent children of evil men is found in Ex 34.7, in a context, however, that makes sure to highlight His mercy and forgiveness "for a thousand generations." One is confronted here with thought patterns of a nomadic, tribal solidarity in fortune and misfortune, good and evil, merit and guilt. The custom of BLOOD VENGEANCE, which found its excessive expression in Lamech's savage poem (Gn 4.23–24), is another example of such solidarity. A society without a police force or courts of law needed such a custom as a deterrent to crime. Its origin was even attributed to God in the story of Cain; very likely, the token or mark given Cain by God made it apparent to anyone who wished to harm him that he belonged to a tribe that would avenge his murder severely (Gn 4.15–16). Later in Israel's history the law of exact retaliation (Ex 21.24) introduced a wise control over indiscriminate vengeance that could decimate whole tribes and families. By demanding in Israel a compensation exactly equal to an injury, this law, which seems so harsh now, curbed excessive revenge and concentrated the people's attention on the precise crime and its perpetrator rather than on the whole group to which the criminal belonged. It was a step toward the separation of the innocent from the guilt brought upon a group by a single offender and affected the Israelite idea of the JUSTICE OF GOD in avenging sin. [*See* SIN (IN THE BIBLE).] As tribal influences gradually died out with the coming of the monarchy and more developed government by statute (*see* ISRAEL, 3), collective retribution gave way to a more discriminating justice that found its expression in Dt 24.16 and its application in 2 Kgs 14.6, where Joash refrains from slaying the children of his father's murderers. The advanced principle had been stated, "Only for his own guilt shall a man be put to death" (Dt 24.16), but the older customs continued to be practiced, and what was of timeless value in the basic idea of the contagion of sin and solidarity in guilt continued to evolve [Ps 108 (109). 9–16; Sir 41.5–9; Wis 3.16–19].

Collective Reward Merited by an Individual. Group solidarity in the achievements and rewards of just individuals was the logical converse of solidarity in an individual's punishment. This happier aspect of a person's involvement with his family, tribe, and nation was exemplified by the Deluge and the common lot of his family with the just NOAH, by the blessings promised to the Patriarch ABRAHAM for his posterity, and, through it for all mankind, by the immunity granted Rahab's family (Jos 2.17–18), and by many other examples. In fact, God's willingness to show mercy and forgive sins because of the loyalty of a few or only of one person revealed His nature more accurately to the Israelites than did His punishment (Ex 32.11–14; 33. 12–17; 34.6–7a). Thus, in Jer 5.1 and Ez 22.30, God would forgive and spare Jerusalem, were only one just man discovered there. The bargaining between Abraham and God over Sodom was based not on the personal value of each just man, but on how few just men would be needed to win pardon for all their wicked compatriots; Abraham did not even ask that the just men be spared individually, although God later spared Lot's daughters because of their just father (Gn 18.23–33; 19.12–15). Finally, the suffering of one man, described in the Songs of the SUFFERING SERVANT, was going to save the whole nation (Isaia ch. 53). Here the solidarity of God's people in punishment for one man's sin is paradoxically reversed; the mysterious servant of the Lord, an innocent individual, at least in the author's description of him, receives the punishment due the many—and thereby, justifies the many by bearing their guilt. God's mercy and forgiveness, in view of one man's loyalty, is granted the whole group. This oracle was the OT's deepest delving into the mystery of God's collective reward in consideration of the good actions and faithfulness of one individual; it is no wonder that the prediction was not understood until it had been realized in Christ's salvific death and Resurrection.

Retribution for a Whole Group's Guilt or Virtue. The judgment of God [*see* JUDGMENT, DIVINE (IN THE BIBLE)] upon mankind in general for its collective sinfulness is described in the etiological stories of the flood and the TOWER OF BABEL. (*See* ETIOLOGY.) Smaller groups were punished for collective guilt, e.g., the people of Sodom and Gomorra, the tribe of Benjamin (Jgs ch. 19–20), CANAAN and the Canaanites (Dt 9.5), and the Israelites themselves (Jer ch. 2; Is 1.2–9). The Prophets from Amos to Ezechiel constantly warned God's people of their collective infidelity to the covenant, which would bring upon them, first, the destruction of the Northern Kingdom and, then, of JUDAH. Only a small REMNANT OF ISRAEL would eventually be saved (Am 3.12; 5.15; 9.8–10; Is 10.20–23; Ez ch. 9). Editorial additions of the DEUTERONOMISTS to their great collection (Joshua to 2 Kgs) can be easily distinguished by the theme that all the catastrophes that ever afflicted Israel were due to God's punishment for its collective infidelity to His pact (Jos 24.19–20; Jgs 2.11–15; 1 Kgs 8.33–40; 2 Kgs 17.7–18; Dt 28.15–46). That just men were caught in this collective retribution was accepted with difficulty and without an adequate explanation (Gn 18.25; Ez 21.1–10). This problem led, especially in Ezechiel and the wisdom literature, to a greater emphasis on individual guilt and merit.

Individual Retribution. The Hebrew words for retribution came from the basic experience of a man earning wages or gain as the result of a pact or contract entered into with someone who desired his services. When this concept was transferred to the relationship between God and man, it was adapted to Israel's experience with God, and retribution became the result of God visiting His people to reward or punish His servant in consideration of the way His bondsman fulfilled his service. In this way the principle was evolved that God would repay every man according to his works (1 Sm 26.23; Prv 12.14; Is 59.18; Sir 51.30; Rom 2.6). That this principle involved the individual in its collective horizon from the very beginning is evident from the most ancient Mosaic penal codes that were sanctioned by God and often adjudicated by ORDEAL (Nm 5.11–31). That an individual's crime or virtuous act affected the group to which he belonged only tended to heighten his concern for the results of his actions. There were, however, many cases in which the individual was repaid for his own action, without any apparent retribution for his group. So, Er and Onan died because of their wickedness (Gn 38.7–10); whereas Shiphrah and Phuah were rewarded by God for protecting Hebrew infants (Ex 1.15–20).

Both during and after the period of the scourge of the Exile of Israel the idea of collective punishment evolved so that greater concern was given to an individual's responsibility for his actions before God. If one was to live or die (the perspective was still limited to this side of the tomb), it was to be the result of one's own virtuous or evil deeds. The sinner could repent, do good, and live; the just man could turn to sin and die (Ez ch. 18). What had already been clearly expressed in the story of Abraham's bargaining with God over Sodom, ''Far be it from you to do such a thing as kill the just with the wicked, treating just and wicked alike!'' (Gn 18.25), became with Ezechiel and the wisdom writers a common teaching for enticing individual Israelites to return to God and act justly so that they might receive, as individuals, His rewards. God had ''no pleasure in the death'' of the sinner; He wanted everyone to ''return and live'' (Ez 18.32). When such a principle was applied solely to temporal sanctions without any hope of a retribution beyond the tomb, it soon became evident that it ran contrary to man's experience. The just man did not always live; in fact, for the most part, the just were oppressed and downtrodden by evil men, while God remained aloof in His heavens. The stage had been set for the revelation of God's plan for rewarding and punishing men beyond the confines of their mortal life.

RETRIBUTION IN THE FUTURE WORLD

The greatest advance toward conceiving that human justice or evilness had to wait until after death before being requited by God was made by a remarkable man whose name has not been recorded, the author of the book of JOB.

The Problem in Job and Ecclesiastes. The author of the Book of Job attacked frontally a traditional teaching because it gave rise to more problems than it answered. Job's innocence is affirmed by God Himself before He allows Satan to test him by taking away every shred of temporal reward. As a result the consequent dialogue between Job and his friends clearly indicates the author's problem: just men who are miserable in this life (and most of them are) must of necessity encounter God Himself whom they know is just but whom they also feel in their flesh is acting unjustly. The author eventually capitulates to the traditional view by having Job vindicated by God with twice as many material blessings than before, but this is only because he cannot formulate a solution to his basic problem, except the unfathomable mystery of God. God alone knows the answer to the obvious injustices to which the innocent succumb. With Job the author makes every innocent man confronted with a death he did not deserve desire to stand up on some vague day beyond his death to receive a human awareness of God's vindication (Jb 19.23–29). He does not say that such an event will ever happen, but he knows that such a desire is in the heart of every just man faced with an unwarranted death. God's benign creativity seems to be canceled out by His cruel governance of human destiny in which the just are never fully vindicated for their service to Him. Yet God is just. What, then, is the solution? It is, at least, God Himself who hides Himself in a whirlwind and from it demands man to submit to His mysterious plans.

The anthologist who composed the Book of ECCLESIASTES faced more bitterly and less profoundly the same problem. He was very much aware that the just suffered in life while the wicked prospered (Eccl 7.15; 8.10, 14). Death above all, death and oblivion, is the common lot of all men, good and evil alike (8.16–9.10). A concrete horror of death is his contribution to the evolution of retribution; everything in life, all the rewards held up to the Israelite have no meaning when confronted by death; everything flattens out and there is no lasting pleasure. A Christian is startled not so much at Qoheleth's bitterness as at the fact that the Israelites had to wait so long a time to hear it expressed. From about the time of Ecclesiastes the thought of Jews took another turn and longed for the never ending happiness hidden behind all their concrete symbols for the happy life with their God.

Intimations of a Resurrection of the Dead. A few intimate friends of God had already attempted to pierce these symbols in order to reach God Himself. They knew God was good, full of loving loyalty to His promises, but, oppressed and suffering as they were, they never experienced the concrete pleasures contained in the traditional symbols for happiness. Yet their faithful Lord had held out to them these rewards; the only solution was to hope, blindly, in His goodness. Their return of filial loyalty to God and the joy in sorrow that it made them experience led them to desire to be with Him forever, despite the frustration of their human experience. Thus Jeremiah, at his loneliest, when he complains most bitterly against the degradation brought on him by his faithful service to God, still realizes that God is with him and will, somehow and at sometime, reward him (Jer 15.10–21; 20.11–13). The sapiential poet of Psalm 72(73) penetrates, with Jeremiah, God's mystery and affirms confidently, against his experience, that God will, Himself, be the just person's reward, his "portion forever," even though his flesh now groans in pain; while he is with God, he has no desire for earthly pleasures, and to be apart from God is to perish [Ps 72(73).23–28]. Psalm 15(16) clarifies this teaching by expressing a trust that the just man's close friendship with God will be prolonged beyond the threat of the grave and he will enjoy a happy life at God's side indefinitely [Ps 15 (16).8–11]. Perhaps this Psalmist did not have so clear an insight into the blessed afterlife reserved for the just as has been claimed by some, but his longing to be with God has nothing material connected with it, and he fears death only because it will destroy his friendship with God. His is a definitive step toward a belief in the resurrection of the just. Almost as an answer to the bitterness of Ecclesiastes and his reluctant satisfaction with this world's pleasures the sage of Psalm 48(49) concludes that wealth and earthly splendor are traps that lead men to be content with this life and the death that must follow it, while the poor but wise and upright man is much better off, for God will redeem him from the power of the abode of the dead, snatching him away from death's rule [Ps 48(49).14–16]. The need of the impoverished and oppressed upright man for God's vindication, therefore, evoked from him a blind but confident cry that God would, indeed, prove His fidelity and justice despite death's universal reign.

A resurrection of Israel as a whole had already been conceived by Ezekiel in his Vision of the Dry Bones (ch. 37) and, later, by the Apocalypse of Isaiah (Is 26.19), but this was only a figure for God's restoration of the Israelite people after the Exile. Yet, the images were there in their tradition, and when the poor of Yahweh were suffering the terrible persecution of the second century B.C., they recalled the images from the depths of their need for Yahweh's vindication, and one of them shouted out at his executioner that the King of the world would raise all of them up to an eternal life for having died for His laws (2 Mc 7.9). Daniel's message, given about the same time, contains a more explicit teaching: those who are asleep in the dust will awaken, some to receive eternal life, the others to live in eternal horror. (*See* RESURRECTION OF THE DEAD, 1.)

Immortality in the Book of Wisdom. Because of the Biblical concept of man as a unit and not as a composite made of body and soul, the Israelites did not conceive of the soul as a subsistent element of man, destined to have a separate existence after the death of the body. [*See* MAN, 1; SOUL (IN THE BIBLE).] It was only very late in their history that Greek psychological influences on Alexandrian Judaism led the author of the Book of WISDOM to postulate some kind of happy and vital existence for the just who died prematurely and after an unhappy mortal life. Yet this author is still thoroughly Jewish in his monistic ideas and does not classify the body as the soul's prison from which the best that is in man escapes at death. The immortality that he offers as the just person's reward is one that is based essentially on the Israelite God's creative power and His hatred of death (Wis 1.12–15); it is an immortality that comes to the total man so that he may enjoy God's friendship forever in the traditional Israelite context of the DAY OF THE LORD (Wis ch. 3–5). Here the desire of the Psalmists [Ps 15(16).10; 48(49).16; 72(73).24] has received a more explicit statement in terminology redolent of Jewish eschatology and only slightly akin to Greek ideas about immortality; yet, it is remarkable that this somewhat Hellenized Jew of Alexandria says nothing about a resurrection of the just or of the wicked, although such a belief had already been stated in the Book of Daniel a century before he wrote and had been carried to Alexandria from Palestine by 2 Maccabees. Perhaps, already, a resurrection of dead, just men for their reward had become a laughingstock to certain elements of Hellenized Judaism as it was for the SADDUCEES and for Paul's audience at Athens (Acts 17.32). A definitive doctrine about retribution after death had to wait for the proclamation of Christ's victory over sin and death before it could evoke a longing response of faith from those who saw in Christ the fulfillment of OT desires.

Retribution in the New Testament

The problem of temporal reward and punishment did not disappear as soon as Christians believed that the ultimate retribution for just and wicked alike would come at the PAROUSIA of the Lord Jesus.

TEMPORAL RETRIBUTION

The recompense for following Jesus was nothing other than the possession of the kingdom of God (Mt 5.1–11). This kingdom, however, was to have two stages in its existence, one in this world, governed by the Lord Jesus through the Holy Spirit, the other in heaven, the final kingdom that would come only after the Son had submitted everything, which had been subjected to Him in His kingdom, to the Father (1 Cor 15.24–28; Mt 16.27–28; 10.23; 24.30, 34; 26.64).

In the first stage it would be a sufficient reward for Christ's disciple to be like His master in suffering and service (Mt 10.24–25, 37–39; Mk 10.41–45). In fact, a disciple's happiness on earth was to consist in being insulted and persecuted as Christ had been, for then he knew that his recompense was great in heaven (Mt 5.11–12; Acts 5.40–41; 21.13; 1 Pt 4.13–19; Rom 5.3–4; 2 Cor 12.9–10). Earthly rewards, even the honor accorded holy persons by others, were not to be desired by the Christian whose repayment for virtue was being stored up for him in the secrecy of the Father's realm (Mt 6.1–6). The unjust rich, however, would find that they were completely bankrupt on the Last Day (Jas 5.1–6; Lk 12.16–21; 16.19–26). In the matter of temporal need Christ's disciple must abandon himself completely to God's loving concern; after all, the kingdom itself has been given to him (Lk 12.22–32; Mt 6.25–33). Luke, especially, emphasized that the basic principle of Christian foresight and prudence was the complete detachment from earthly wealth (Lk 14.28–33; 16.1–13). When he prays, the Christian should ask not for what other men are anxious to gain but for whatever good things the Father, who is good, wants to give him, above all, the Holy Spirit (Mt 7.7–11; Lk 11.9–13). The only passage in the NT that seems to offer earthly rewards to Christ's disciples is Mk 10.30: those who have left all to follow Jesus will "receive now in the present time a hundredfold as much, houses, and brothers, and sisters, and mothers, and children, and lands—along with persecutions . . . ." However, the obvious parabolic overstatement of this saying, combined with the "along with persecutions," indicates that Christ promises His disciples not a superabundance of material wealth or mere human relations but the supereminent spiritual benefits that will accrue to them even in the present age from being conformed to Him in suffering and poverty, in other words, the graces of Redemption and justification.

Temporal punishment for evil was a more apparent form of retribution for the first stage of God's kingdom. An incestuous Corinthian was delivered to Satan to suffer pain in his physical life so that his spiritual life might be saved on the Day of the Lord (1 Cor 5.2–5). Paul interpreted that the diseases and deaths among the Corinthians were punishments for their irreverent and selfish practices at the celebration of the LORD'S SUPPER (1 Cor 11.30–34). He also warned them against false worship by recalling the sudden punishments meted out to idolaters in the OT (1 Cor 10.6–10, 22). Testing the Holy Spirit by a lie brought instant death to an early Christian couple (Acts 5.1–11).

Jesus, Himself, foretold that the coming of the Son of Man with power would bring about the destruction of Jerusalem before the generation He was addressing passed away (Lk 21.5–36, especially v. 32; Luke, more clearly than Matthew or Mark, distinguished between the coming of the Son's kingdom through the retributive destruction of Jerusalem, the definitive closing of the old order, resulting from its rejection of the Messiah, and the Son's coming on the Last Day to establish His Father's kingdom, described in Lk 17.22–37). Punishment for sin on earth remained, therefore, an important Christian theme that found its fullest expression throughout the book of Revelation, whereas earthly material reward for good actions was hardly, if at all, put forth as a legitimate Christian motive for virtue.

RETRIBUTION AND THE CHRIST MYSTERY

The solidarity of Jesus Christ with the sinfulness of, and the punishment due, all mankind, revealed by the mystery of His salvific death and Resurrection, changed forever humanity's concept of repayment from God for services rendered. Henceforth, mankind was forced to admit, in order to attain happiness, that eternal reward was not due to it apart from Jesus' action. Man's ultimate happiness depended on the acceptance of God's favor manifested to him in Christ's propitiatory death, i.e., on his acceptance by faith of the justifying value and gratuitous nature of Jesus' submission to the Father's will (Rom 3.21–26). Retribution, then, takes on a meaning that identifies it more with Redemption and reconciliation than the just repayment for service given. [See REDEMPTION (IN THE BIBLE)]. A completely innocent man had become sin on behalf of all sinners, i.e., the rest of mankind (2 Cor 5.21). As a result, the Christian can no longer conceive that his ultimate happiness is something due him, except in so far as he is united to Christ, the perfect servant of God. Christ's reward, His Resurrection, exaltation, and His eternal human life with God, is strictly due Him, in accord with the contract He entered into with His Father (Phil 2.5–11). By His obedience the Son freely submitted to the Father's demand for justice in view of mankind's sinfulness, and by being lifted up on the cross He drew to Himself a new human race that could perfectly serve the Divinity through Him (Jn 12.32–33; Rom 5.12–19). The service offered the Father by this new humanity in and through the Son is being and will continue to be rewarded by the life of the Spirit, by which Christians work out their ultimate salvation while on earth (Rom ch. 8); and ultimately, it will be rewarded by the resurrection to an incorruptible life with Christ (1 Cor ch. 15) for each individual. In the world the Christian's union

with Christ is already, in a true sense, a participation in the life Christ now leads (Rom 6.1–11; Col 3.1–4). A Johannine theme bears the same message: those who believe in God's Word, who come to the Light and accept Jesus' death as the glorification of the Son of Man, have already been reborn from on high and possess, already, eternal life. For those others who do not accept Him there is only darkness, and the wrath of God already rests upon them (Jn 3.16–21, 31–36). Reward and punishment have become the acceptance or refusal of God's gift in Christ Jesus.

Bibliography: *Encyclopedic Dictionary of the Bible*, tr. and adap. By L. HARTMAN (New York 1963), from A. VAN DEN BORN, *Bijbels Woordenboek* 2032–40. C. WIÉNER, in *Vocabulaire de théologie biblique*, ed. X. LÉON-DUFOUR (Paris 1962) 919–925. P. E. DAVIES, *The Interpreters' Dictionary of the Bible*, ed. G. A. BUTTRICK (Nashville 1962) 4:71–74. E. WÜRTHWEIN, *Theologisches Wörterbuch zum Neuen Testament*, G. KITTEL, (Stuttgart 1935–) 4:710–718. J. GUILLET, *Themes of the Bible*, tr. A. J. LAMOTHE (Notre Dame, Ind. 1960) 24–170. F. HORST et al., *Die Religion in Geschichte und Gegenwart* (3d ed. Tübingen 1957–65) 6:1343–49. W. STÄRK, *Vorsehung und Vergeltung* (Berlin 1931). A. M. DUBARLE, *Les Sages d'Israël* (Paris 1946) 46–173. E. F. SUTCLIFFE, *Providence and Suffering in the Old and New Testaments* (London 1953). P. VAN IMSCHOOT, *Théologie de l'Ancien Testament,* 2 v. (Tournai 1954–56) 303–314.

[J. E. FALLON]

RETZ, JEAN FRANÇOIS PAUL DE GONDI DE

Prelate, controversial churchman and politician, rival and opponent of Cardinal MAZARIN; b. Montmirail, Sept. 20, 1613; d. Paris, Aug. 24, 1679. Paul, as well as others of the De Gondi children, was tutored by Vincent de Paul. Against his inclinations, Paul was marked for the priesthood at an early age, being given a canon's stall at Notre Dame when he was 13 years old. His intelligence and excellent education were attested when at age 18 he published a book called *La Conjuration du Compte Jean-Louis de Fièsque,* which disclosed his love of intrigue. His subsequent support of the Count of Soissons in his plots against RICHELIEU indicated the turn his career was to take.

Ecclesiastical Career. In 1643 he was appointed coadjutor to his uncle, Archbishop Gondi of Paris, and he was consecrated as titular archbishop of Corinth. As coadjutor of Paris he continued his political activities, became the power behind the Fronde, and openly patronized the Jansenist party. He hoped to supplant Cardinal Jules Mazarin, and so the two churchmen were involved in mutual hostilities for some 20 years. In the contest with Mazarin, he showed his ''fine Italian hand,'' taking delight in Machiavellian tactics, intrigue, and clandestine meetings, and appealing to the emotions of the Parisians, with whom he was very popular. Despite his excessive involvement in politics, Retz's opposition to Mazarin did endear him to Pope Innocent X, who offered him in 1650 the opportunity to become cardinal. His efforts to obtain approval of the French court for the cardinalate forced him into a temporary *rapprochement* with Mazarin. This Retz accomplished by siding with Mazarin against Prince Louis II de Condé, leader of the Fronde, who was pressing for a final test of strength with the crown. On Sept. 21, 1651, Retz's actions bore fruit; the council, under Mazarin's control, approved his nomination as cardinal.

The expected allegiance of Retz in the feud with Condé was not forthcoming, for he now resumed his opposition to Mazarin despite the fact that he continued to revile Condé at court. Matters were brought to a head when Mazarin was exiled temporarily to appease the Fronde and the populace. Upon his return in late 1652, Mazarin became more powerful than ever; he broke the power of the Fronde and turned to the disposal of Retz. The ambitious Cardinal de Retz was offered the post of representative to Rome, a type of face-saving exile, but he delayed too long in making up his mind and Mazarin had him imprisoned on Dec. 19, 1652. The years of Retz's imprisonment paradoxically proved to be two very important years of his life. During that time, while he languished in the dungeons of Vincennes, he was championed by Pope Innocent X, who knew it was Retz's colleague, Mazarin, who had imprisoned him. Innocent X urged Louis XIV to free Retz, but meanwhile he referred the matter to the College of Cardinals. Protests from French bishops and from Rome failed to move Mazarin, who was now firmly established in power. Mazarin at one point offered Retz freedom if he would resign as coadjutor of Paris, an offer Retz declined, saying he would rather die in prison than resign. The imprisoned cardinal became the subject of a new controversy between Mazarin and the Jansenists, who expressed sympathy for Retz. The situation was radically changed when on March 21, 1654, the archbishop of Paris died, and Retz automatically became archbishop. Retz was then pressed by Louis XIV to resign and was offered in recompense the income of seven abbeys yielding 120,000 livres. Retz resigned but Innocent X refused to accept the resignation knowing it was under pressure.

On Aug. 8, 1654, Retz succeeded in breaking out of prison and escaping to Spain. The pope approved of his escape and assured him of his protection. Mazarin, on the other hand, ordered the rearrest of Retz and took measures to deprive him of the archiepiscopal see of Paris, but Pope Innocent X in November of 1654 received the exiled cardinal with full honors in Rome. Retz then retracted his resignation of the Paris see and took up residence in Rome, whence he assailed Paris with letters that were publicly burned by Mazarin. While in Rome between 1654 and 1662 Retz continued to engage in ecclesiastical affairs and in European politics.

Last Years. After Mazarin's death on March 9, 1661, Retz wished to return to France, but Louis XIV refused to receive him unless he resigned the archbishopric of Paris. This he did in 1662; he then received the previously mentioned income and took up residence at the Abbey of Saint-Denis. His career became one of loyal service to Louis XIV, especially in the latter's relations to the Holy See. He succeeded in warding off condemnations and excommunications resulting from the Gallican controversy. As cardinal, he traveled to Rome for three conclaves, those that elected Clement IX in 1667, Clement X in 1670, and Innocent XI in 1676. Retz received eight votes at the last-mentioned conclave. The last four years of his life gave evidence of a remarkable spiritual conversion. In 1675 he became a penitent at the Benedictine Monastery of Saint-Mihiel, and that same year he resigned his cardinalate. In a letter to the pope he stated that he wished by becoming a monk at Saint-Mihiel to make up for the harm done to the Church by his evil conduct in the past. Pope Clement X refused his resignation, but Retz remained in isolation at Saint-Mihiel for three years, scarcely leaving the monastery. He spent the last year of his life at Saint-Denis. During his last years he founded an institute for young girls attached to the Ladies of Charity. He also completed his *Mémoirs,* a valuable source of information about court and ecclesiastical life during his times.

Bibliography: H. R. GUGGISBERG, *Die Religion in Geschichte und Gegenwart,* 7 v. (3d ed. Tübingen 1957–65) 5:1073. F. ALBERT-BUISSON, *Le Cardinal de Retz: Portrait* (Paris 1954). L. BATIFFOL, *Le Cardinal de Retz* (Paris 1927). F. R. DE CHANTELAUZE, *Le Cardinal de Retz et l'affaire du chapeau,* 2 v. (Paris 1878); *Le Cardinal de Retz et ses missions diplomatiques à Rome* (Paris 1879). A. GAZIER, *Les Dernières années du Cardinal de Retz* (Paris 1875). P. G. LORRIS, *Le Cardinal de Retz, un agitateur au XVIIe siècle* (Paris 1956). D. OGG, *Cardinal de Retz* (London 1912). J. T. DE CASTELNAU, *Retz et son temps* (Paris 1955).

[J. W. BUSH]

REUCHLIN, JOHANN

German humanist, Hebrew scholar; b. Pforzheim, Feb. 22, 1455; d. Bad Liebenzell, Germany, June 30, 1522. He studied liberal arts at Freiburg im Breisgau, Paris (beginning Greek there), and Basel, and then law at Orléans and Poitiers (licentiate, 1481). Next he accompanied Duke Eberhard of Württemberg to Italy, where he met Marsilio FICINO. He received a Doctor of Laws degree from Tübingen and remained in the service of Duke Eberhard. In 1490 he made a second Italian trip, meeting PICO DELLA MIRANDOLA. On a mission to the imperial court at Linz (1492), he continued his study of Hebrew. The accession of an unfriendly duke drove Reuchlin to Heidelberg (1496), where he associated with humanists such as Jakob Wimpfeling. In 1498 he made his third Italian trip. He next became judge of the Swabian League (1502–13). Later he held professorships at Ingolstadt (1520–21) and Tübingen (1521–22). Despite his busy public career, Reuchlin was always the humanist. In 1475 he published a Latin dictionary, and later he made translations from Greek. At Heidelberg he wrote two Latin comedies, *Henno* and *Sergius.* He was seeking to recover ancient wisdom, but in his view all true wisdom stemmed ultimately from the Hebrew revelation. Hence he was one of the first to attempt mastery of Hebrew. He not only succeeded in learning it, but also produced the books that firmly established Hebrew studies in Germany: *De rudimentis hebraicis* (1506) and *De accentibus et orthographia linguae hebraicae* (1518). He was seeking ancient wisdom and thought he had found it in Jewish CABALA, which inspired his *De verbo mirifico* (1494) and *De arte cabalistica* (1517). These two works, though tending toward a potentially dangerous syncretism, aimed to demonstrate the truth of Christianity with the aid of Cabala. The most famous episode in Reuchlin's life was his controversy with the converted Jew Johannes PFEFFERKORN and the Dominicans of Cologne. Pfefferkorn had urged the destruction of all Hebrew books. Consulted by the emperor, Reuchlin argued (1510) that such a measure would be both unjust and disastrous for Christian scholarship. Pfefferkorn denounced him in *Handspiegel,* and Reuchlin replied bitterly in *Augenspiegel* (1511). The issue broadened when the inquisitor Jacob van Hoogstraten, OP, tried to convict Reuchlin of heresy. In 1516 Pope Leo X suspended the case and enjoined silence. After the Reformation had created a new mood, Leo issued a mandate (June 20, 1520) condemning the *Augenspiegel.* Long before this, however, the case became the symbol of a bitter struggle between conservative scholastic theologians and defenders of the new humanistic studies. Reuchlin called the humanists to his support (*see* HUMANISM, CHRISTIAN). The result was a flood of pamphlets, of which the most famous was the savage satire *EPISTOLAE OBSCURORUM VIRORUM.* Despite his difficulties with the theologians, Reuchlin was consistently obedient to Rome and cool toward Luther and toward his own nephew MELANCHTHON.

Bibliography: J. REUCHLIN, *Briefwechsel,* ed. L. GEIGER (Tübingen 1875). L. GEIGER, *Johann Reuchlin: Sein Leben und seine Werke* (Leipzig 1871). L. W. SPITZ, *The Religious Renaissance of the German Humanists* (Cambridge, Mass. 1963) 61–80. M. KREBS,

Johann Reuchlin, woodcut engraving. (Archive Photos)

ed., *Johannes R., 1455–1522: Festgabe seiner Vaterstadt Pforzheim zur 500. Wiederkehr seines Geburtstages* (Pforzheim 1955).

[C. G. NAUERT, JR.]

REUSCH, FRANZ HEINRICH

Ecclesiastical historian and theologian; b. Brilon in Westphalia, Germany, Dec. 4, 1825; d. Bonn, March 3, 1900. Reusch attended the Universities of Bonn (1843–45), Tübingen (1845–46), and Munich (1846–47), studied privately at Brilon (1847), then entered the seminary in Cologne (1848) where he was ordained (1849). After serving as chaplain at St. Alban's in Cologne (1849–53), he went to Bonn as a lecturer (1854–58) and became professor of Old Testament exegesis in 1858.

He played a prominent part in the foundation of the *Kölnische Blätter* (*Kölnische Volkzeitung* from 1869). From 1866 to 1877 he was editor of the *Theologisches Literaturblatt,* which provided critical surveys of theological publications. Apart from newspaper articles and translations of works by NEWMAN and WISEMAN, Reusch's writings before 1870 dealt with Old Testament exegesis, chiefly with the deuterocanonical books. His *Einleitung in das Alte Testament* appeared in 1859. In 1862 his account of the final chapters of Genesis and their relation to contemporary natural sciences appeared as *Bibel und Natur* (Eng. tr., 2 v. 1886). Catholics regarded these two works highly, but Protestants found little in them to praise.

Reusch refused to accept the definition of papal infallibility by VATICAN COUNCIL I and was excommunicated by the archbishop of Cologne (1872). He joined the OLD CATHOLICS, took charge of their parish in Bonn, and served as vicar-general to Joseph Reinkens, the first Old Catholic bishop. Reusch was not an extremist and limited his protest to what he termed "Romanism" in the Catholic Church. The reformist trend among the Old Catholics displeased him. When they abolished clerical celibacy in 1878, he resigned his offices and joined DÖLLINGER in passive protest against papal infallibility, but did not return to the Church.

Modern Church history, rather than exegesis, was Reusch's major scholarly interest in the second half of his life. He produced a work on Luis de LEÓN in 1873 and another on Galileo Galilei in 1879. His famous two-volume study of the Index, *Index der verbotenen Bücher* (1883–85), has not been superseded. In conjunction with Döllinger, he published *Geschichte der Moralstreitigkeiten in der römisch-katholischen Kirche seit dem 16. Jahrhundert* (2 v. 1889), which remains the sole comprehensive explanation of the modern disputes among Catholics concerning moral theology. Reusch also published two collections of articles by Döllinger after the latter's death. Reusch was a profound scholar, an untiring worker, and a zealous, morally upright priest. His convictions concerning papal infallibility were sincere.

Bibliography: L. K. GOETZ, *Franz Heinrich Reusch* (Gotha 1901). J. E. B. MAYOR, *Franz Heinrich Reusch* (Cambridge, Eng. 1901). F. H. MENN, "Reusch als Schriftsteller," *Revue internationale de théologie* 14 (1906) 38–72, 462–468, 729–744; 15 (1907) 75–93, 462–480. R. BÄUMER, *Lexikon für Theologie und Kirche*, ed. J. HOFER and K. RAHNER (Freiberg 1957–65) 8:1267.

[V. CONZEMIUS]

REVELATION, BOOK OF

The Book of Revelation, generally placed last in the New Testament canon, is known in many Catholic Bibles as the Book of the Apocalypse, which in Greek means "revelation." This article treats the book's authorship and canonicity, occasion, date of composition, contents, unity, the character of the visions, and methods of interpretation, but first it addresses the question of the Book's literary genre.

Apocalyptic Genre. One of the most debated points has been the literary genre of Revelation. It has tradition-

ally been assumed that Revelation belongs to the genre of Apocalyptic works. It exhibits many characteristics of this genre: mythological influences, dualism, the role of angels and Satan, a rich symbolic matrix and an emphasis on the eschaton.

In spite of these similarities, Revelation lacks one of the most critical elements of APOCALYPTIC works: pseudonymity. Apocalyptic works are normally attributed to famous individuals of antiquity. To explain the time lag between when they were supposedly written and when they appeared, the author posits a sealing up of the book until the author's day (Dn 12.9). The author of Revelation, however, openly calls himself John and never speaks of a sealing (in fact, the opposite in Rv 22.10). The suggestion that the author might be attributing the book to John, the apostle, is discounted by some (A. Yarbro Collins) who argue that the author never gives identifying information such as genealogies (as in 2 Ezr 1.1–3) or historical references to the apostle John's life (as is done with Paul's role in the PASTORAL EPISTLES). These arguments, although impressive, are not entirely conclusive. The reference to Patmos in Rv 1.9, for example, might be a reference to a contemporary tradition in the early Church concerning John. Furthermore, the book expresses a certain urgency because the events described are already in process. The fact that the revelation was not sealed might be due to the urgency of proclaiming it in light of the impending eschaton.

Many of those who argue that the book is not apocalyptic suggest that it belongs to a prophetic genre (Aune, Hill, Schüssler-Fiorenza). The author describes his work as a prophecy (1.3; 22.7, 10, 18, 19), and in this prophetic role he affirms and corrects the seven churches of Asia Minor (2–3). He contrasts his true prophetic status to that of the false prophets Jezebel and Balaam. Finally, the seven angels of the seven churches could be local prophets who were to communicate and interpret the message to their communities.

The question remains, however, whether the author of Revelation wanted to make a distinction between the apocalyptic and prophetic genres. He shows tendencies of both, as well as influences from Wisdom literature (Vanni) and Greek drama (Blevins). He is similarly eclectic with his theology. In addition to the traditional attribution of the book to Johannine theology, Schüssler-Fiorenza has documented considerable Pauline influences. Thus, while accepting elements from the various genres and theologies, the author seems to have been producing his own original synthesis which defies easy classification.

Authorship and Canonicity. When giving his name as John (1.1, 4, 9. 22.8) the author identifies himself as

An illustration of a scene from Revelation Chapter 16. (©Historical Picture Archive/CORBIS)

a Christian prophet (22.6, 9; see also 1.3; 10.11). An early tradition equates him with John the Apostle: the Gnostic *Apocryphon of John* (*c.* A.D. 150 or earlier), Justin Martyr (*c.* 160), Irenaeus (*c.* 175), the MURATORIAN CANON (*c.* 200), Tertullian (*c.* 200), and Clement of Alexandria (*c.* 200). Despite this persistent tradition, nowhere does the author claim the identification JOHN THE APOSTLE. About this time the ALOGOI, led by the Roman priest Caius, in reaction to the abuse of Apocalypse by the Montanists, ascribed both the Gospel according to St. John and Revelation to the heretic Cerinthus and denied their canonicity. Though St. DIONYSIUS OF ALEXANDRIA (d. 264) considered Revelation an inspired writing, he questioned its apostolic authorship because of literary and theological considerations similar to those that prompt most modern scholars to posit different authors for the Fourth Gospel and Revelation. Dionysius' arguments are reproduced by Eusebius (*Ecclesiastical History* 7:25; *Sources Chrétiennes* 41:204–210), who also credits John the Pres-

byter with the writing of Revelation (*ibid.*, 3.39.5; *Sources Chrétiennes* 31:154–155). Between A.D. 300 and 450 a number of the Fathers of the Church in the East, especially of the Antiochian School, excluded Revelation from the Canon. During the same period, however, it was accepted in the West and in the East by Athanasius, Cyril of Alexandria, Basil, Gregory of Nyssa, and others, all of whom assumed apostolic authorship of the book. In final analysis it seems hardly probable that both the Fourth Gospel and the Book of Revelation were authored by the same person.

Occasion. Like other APOCALYPTIC literature, John's was occasioned by a religious crisis. He wrote to encourage Christians, in the first instance those of Asia Minor, to be steadfast even to martyrdom in the face of the social, economic, and legal pressures that made it increasingly difficult to avoid taking part in pagan religious practices, especially emperor worship. Many had become disheartened and disillusioned because the glorious return of Christ, His PAROUSIA, which they had been eagerly expecting, seemed to recede farther and farther from the horizon of their hope.

John himself had been exiled to the penal island of Patmos for having borne witness to the word of God (Rv 1.9–10), probably for preaching Christianity and refusing to participate in the state religion. Intensely worried over the fate of the churches (5.4), he was caught up in rapture on a certain Sunday and received supernatural assurances from the glorified Jesus, whom he saw; these he was commanded to write on a scroll and send to seven important churches of Asia Minor (1.10–20). The visions and auditions granted him reminded the Christians that Jesus is Lord of all history, both as Son of God and as Redeemer; He is as truly present in the churches even now, though invisibly, as He will be in His Parousia, which is certain to come. The trials that Jesus' followers are suffering have been foreseen and foreordained; many more will be called to suffer martyrdom before the end. Pagan Rome, however, is doomed to destruction, and a glorious future of unending happiness awaits all those who suffer with patient endurance.

Date of Composition. Most commentators, ancient and modern, think that the Book of Revelation received its present form in the last years of the reign of Domitian (81–96). Internal evidence can be adduced that confirms this external consensus. Some scholars, however, believe that the historical background of Revelation was the reign of either Nero [54–68; the cryptograph 666 in Rv 13.18 is probably the name Nero by gematria; *see* NUMEROLOGY (IN THE BIBLE)] or Vespasian (69–79). The simplest explanation of the enigmatic statement in 17.9 that ''five [emperors] have fallen'' indicates the reign of Vespasian.

A combination of both views is proposed by several authors: either the present Revelation resulted from the fusion of two earlier apocalypses (see below), or John resorted to the popular apocalyptic device of antedating his work, i.e., though writing under Domitian he adopted the standpoint of the time of Nero or Vespasian.

Contents. The introduction (1.1–20) includes a superscription (1.1–3); an epistolary introduction (1.4–6), like those of the Pauline Epistles; a solemn assurance of the Parousia (1.7–8); and the historical occasion of the work; the first prophetic investiture of John (1.9–20). The body of the book contains two main sections of unequal length: (1) the letters to the seven churches of Ephesus, Smyrna, Pergamum, Thyatira, Sardis, Philadelphia, and Laodicea (ch. 2–3); and, (2) the main section that recounts a number of visions that are sometime referred to as ''the apocalypse of the future'' (ch. 4–22). An epilogue (22.6–21) confirms in Christ's words what has been previously promised.

The Seven Letters. The letters to the seven churches of Asia Minor provide an opportunity for the author to address specific problems in these communities. They are a type of examination of conscience conducted by Jesus. Ephesus is commended for its faithfulness and scolded for its lack of charity, possibly referring to an over zealous attempt to preserve orthodoxy which has led to judgmentalism and division. Smyrna and Philadelphia are encouraged to remain faithful in the face of persecution organized by the Jews. Sardis and Laodicea are warned that they must give clear witness to the truth and not allow themselves to be complacent. The Christians of Ephesus, Pergamum, and Thyatira are warned about those with Gnostic tendencies who visit or reside in their communities.

The call in all seven of these letters is to faithful endurance. It is a theme which forms the core of the message of Revelation: trust in God and be faithful to him until the end.

The Church and Judaism. The visions of the main section are partly parallel and fall into two clearly defined sections: the Church and Judaism (*ch. 4–11*), and the Church and the ANTICHRISTS. The preparatory vision in heaven (ch. 4–5) serves as a second prophetic investiture for the revelation of God's interventions from the Resurrection of Christ to the fall of Jerusalem, including the rejection of the Jews and assurance of their ultimate conversion. Transported to the heavenly temple, John sees in God's hand a seven-sealed scroll, containing the divine decrees that govern all history. Only Christ as Redeemer can open and disclose the contents of the scroll. As the first four seals are successively broken (ch. 6), four horsemen appear—white [representing either the victory of the Gospel (cf. Mk 13.10) or imperialism], red (war), black (famine), and pale green (pestilence and death); the scene is like that in Jesus' apocalyptic discourse (Mk 13.5–8 and parallels, especially Lk 21.8–11). The opening of the fifth seal discloses the martyrs praying for a hastening of divine judgment and vengeance upon their persecutors, while the sixth introduces upheavals in nature, described in current apocalyptic clichés. An intermediate vision (ch. 7) shows how the elect, both Jewish and Gentile Christians, are preserved from the punitive aspect of the plagues.

The seventh seal, silence in heaven (8.1), ushers in the seven apocalyptic trumpets, introduced by a vision that depicts them as the answer to the prayers of Christians (8.2–6). The first four trumpets (8.7–12) herald calamities reminiscent of the PLAGUES OF EGYPT, though it is futile to ask what specific realities the seer had in mind. An eagle (8.13) warns that the last three trumpet blasts are to be special woes. The fifth shows a huge infernal invasion, while the sixth summons a vast demonic horde from the Euphrates to destroy a third of mankind (9.1–20). S. Giet here finds apocalyptic allusion to different phases of the Jewish War of A.D. 66–70.

A second intermediate vision (10.1–11) prepares for the universal character of the revelations to follow and includes a third prophetic investiture of John, that to the Gentiles, symbolized by the eating of a small scroll (10.8–11). This vision, however, anticipates (as frequently in Revelation), since John has not yet finished his predictions regarding Judaism.

The measuring of the Temple and the preaching, death, and resurrection of the two witnesses (11.1–14) depict parabolically the temporary rejection of the Jews, the witness of the Church through ''Moses and the Prophets'' to Christ in the face of Jewish opposition to Him, and the final conversion of the REMNANT OF ISRAEL, referred to also in Rom 9–11, especially 11.25–29. The seventh trumpet depicts the culmination of the covenant in the opening of heaven (11.15–19).

The Church and the Antichrists (ch. 12–19). Seven ''signs'' seen by John portray various aspects of the conflict between the Church and anti-God forces, as incarnate initially in pagan, emperor-worshiping Rome. The Church is presented as the WOMAN CLOTHED WITH THE SUN, who gives birth to the Messiah, whom the great red dragon, Satan (cf. Gn 3.15), tries in vain to destroy; the Church is driven underground (12.1–6). The heavenly counterpart of this battle shows Michael casting Satan to earth (12.7–12), where he pursues the woman, divinely protected in the desert (12.13–18). Satan calls up two lieutenants: the ''beast from the sea,'' the political antichrist, the Roman Empire with its emperor worship (13.1–10); and the ''beast of the earth,'' the philosophical and theological antichrist (13.11–18).

As in 7.1–17, an intermediate vision portrays the heavenly security of the faithful with the Lamb (Christ) on Mount Sion (14.1–5). Three angels successively warn all mankind to fear God, predict the fall of Babylon-Rome, and threaten eternal damnation (14.6–11). A heavenly voice proclaims that the faithful who have died even now enjoy their reward (14.12–13). An anticipatory vision shows the Last Judgment, the reprobation of the wicked, and the ingathering of the elect (14.14–20).

After a brief introductory scene (15.1–8), the final septenary of plagues is hurriedly described as the outpouring of the wrath of God from seven bowls. The effects that follow remind the reader, though in heightened form, of the Egyptian plagues and the first four trumpets (16.1–12). Probably they create a dramatic effect rather than specify concrete happenings of the future. Between

the sixth and seventh bowls three frog-like evil spirits summon the kings of the earth for the great final battle with the forces of God (16.14–16). After the last bowl, Babylon-Rome falls amid great upheavals in nature (16.17–21).

Once more the fall of Babylon is depicted, now under the image of the great harlot who leads the world astray and persecutes the Christians (17.1–18). Her destruction is dwelt upon with relish (18.1–24) and hailed by heavenly songs of triumph (19.1–10). Seated upon a white horse, Christ appears, His garments red with His own blood, or, according to many interpreters, with the blood of His enemies (19.11–16). Again the destruction of the beasts is proclaimed (19.17–21).

Next Satan is chained, the millennium (*see* MILLENARIANISM) is rapidly mentioned, and Satan is unloosed but summarily defeated along with his followers and cast into hell after the judgment (20.1–15).

The Consummation (21.1–22.5). The new heaven and the new earth (21.1–8) and the heavenly Jerusalem, of which God and the Lamb are temple and sun, with the river and tree of life, are the figures used to disclose final glory, which the elect enjoy for all eternity.

Unity. The inconsistencies and repetitions in the Book of Revelation have often raised the question: Is this a single composition or a conflation of more than one writing? Impressed by the uniformity of style and vocabulary and the closely knit character of the work, most scholars judge that Revelation is the work of one author. M. E. Boismard has revived and modified the opinion of R. Charles that both divergences and unity of style can be accounted for by distinguishing two apocalypses, both written by the same disciple of John the Apostle. Boismard dates what he calls Text 1 from a time toward the end of Vespasian's reign; Text 2, the reign of Nero; the letters of ch. 2–3, that of Domitian. The fusion of the three parts was made by another writer, who slightly retouched his sources [M. E. Boismard, ''L'Apocalypse ou les Apocalypses de saint Jean?'' *Revue biblique* 56 (1949) 507–541].

Character of the Visions and Literary Form. Do the visions of Revelation purport to be a precise description of what John actually saw and heard? Or are they merely a literary device, as in the case of the noncanonical apocalyptic writings and probably also of the Book of DANIEL? The first alternative must be ruled out because of the inconsistencies and contradictions, the improbable images that this would involve. The second alternative, while it would not militate against the admittedly inspired nature of the book, yet fails to account for the realism of the descriptions and the impression conveyed that the writer seriously intended to report a supernatural mystical experience.

Accordingly, many students of Revelation today hold that John actually had a supernatural vision (or visions) with accompanying revelations from Christ that he was told to write down. When he carried out this order, he naturally resorted to the apocalyptic literary form, because it was the best-known vehicle, using symbols and imagery of every kind, to report as best he could experiences that defied the limitations of human speech.

One characteristic of the Book of Revelation that must be stressed is its use of the OT. It has been computed that in the 404 verses of Revelation, 518 OT citations and allusions are found, 88 of them from Daniel; 278 of the 404 verses are made up of reminiscences of Scripture, especially (besides Daniel) Isaiah, Jeremiah, Ezekiel, Zechariah, Psalms, and Exodus. Revelation is, then, a re-reading of the OT in the light of the Christian event. There is also good reason to surmise, with Origen, that the scroll that John saw (5.1–8) is the OT. Christ alone could open it because it finds in Him its ultimate meaning. The Christological reading of the Scriptures is, in the last analysis, the answer to the anguished questions and problems that faced the churches in John's day and in all times.

Methods of Interpretation. A. Feuillet has classified the systems of interpretation relevant to this study ("Les diverses méthodes d'interprétation de l'Apocalypse . . . ," *Ami du Clergé* 71 [April 27, 1961] 257–270). The labels he attached to the five different systems summarized here indicate emphasis of each.

Recapitulation. This method goes back to VICTORINUS OF PETTAU (martyred under Diocletian); it was adopted by Tyconius, Augustine, and other commentators, medieval and modern. In its most developed form, that of E. B. Allo, it may be summarized thus: the septenaries of the seals (6.1–8.1) and the trumpets (8.2–9.21) describe the future of the world from the glorification of Christ to the Last Judgment, mentioned as early as 11.15–18, with emphasis upon world events. The section 12.1–21.8 covers the same period, but centering on the role of the Church. The millennium describes the same period from another viewpoint (20.1–15), and even the description of the heavenly Jerusalem (21.1–22.5), though it offers a transcendent image of the Church, takes in the Church both on earth and in heaven, under the regime of grace as well as of glory.

While there is much truth in this reading of Apocalypse, the evidence of chronological progression rules out the sweeping nature of Allo's parallelism. It seems true, nevertheless, that while alluding to specific events of his time and of the past and predicting the future to the end of the world, John has in mind some succession of events, which he sees, perhaps, less as individual facts than as "laws" that mark God's dealing with mankind and the Church through all ages.

World History. JOACHIM OF FIORE (d. 1201) popularized the system that sees in the septenaries of Revelation seven periods in the history of the Church; Nicholas of Lyra (d. 1340) systematized this exegesis and gave it a stricter chronology. Again and again, in various forms, it has been proposed, even in modern times, especially in popularizations. Because it was based upon a misunderstanding of prophecy and of the apocalyptic genre, it has had to be revised and corrected whenever events belied previous conclusions drawn from it.

Eschatological. The originator of this interpretation was Francisco de RIBERA, whose commentary appeared in 1591; it has been called the beginning of scientific study of Revelation. Ribera held that only the first five seals refer to the primitive Church down to the reign of Trajan. The last seals and the rest of the book have to do with the end-time. Since then this system has been favored by many commentators, some of whom assume that John thought the Parousia near and did not reckon with the possibility of a long future for the Church.

Historicizing. To some extent this method is at opposite poles from the eschatological. Inaugurated by J. Henten in the middle of the 16th century, it holds that at least part of Revelation refers to contemporary or past events. Henten interpreted ch. 6–11 as referring to the abrogation of Judaism, ch. 12–19 as referring to the destruction of paganism. Modern proponents of this view differ in regard to the amount of contemporary or past material they find in Revelation.

Liturgical. John intended his work to be read in the liturgical service of the churches (1.3). Revelation is admittedly full of references and allusions both to the liturgy of the OT and to the Christian Eucharistic service. John receives his inaugural vision on a Sunday, possibly during the liturgical service. He is invited up to heaven (ch. 4), where a cosmic service of praise and adoration takes place that is reminiscent of OT inaugural visions (cf. Isaiah ch. 6, where the vision takes place in the Temple, and Ezekiel ch. 1–3) as well as the Christian service (the throne of the bishop surrounded by the 24 elders suggesting the sanctuary setting of the ancient Eucharistic service). The description of the heavenly Jerusalem (ch. 20–21) is also cast in liturgical forms. Again, the hymns scattered throughout Revelation are probably echoes of Christian hymns at the seer's time. That the structure of Revelation itself was modeled upon the early liturgy has been argued by M. H. Shepherd, *The Paschal Liturgy and the Apocalypse, Ecumenical Studies in Worship* 6 (Richmond, Va. 1960).

See Also: APOCALYPSE, ICONOGRAPHY OF;
APOCALYPTIC MOVEMENTS.

Bibliography: A. FEUILLET, *L'Apocalypse: État de la question* (Bruges 1963), introductory problems to date and thorough bibliog. E. B. ALLO, *Saint Jean: L'Apocalypse* (3rd ed., Paris 1933); *Dictionnaire de la Bible,* suppl. ed. L. PIROT, et al. (Paris 1928) 1:306–325. E. LOHSE, *Die Offenbarung des Johannes* (Das Neue Testament Deutsch 11; 8th ed. Göttingen 1960). S. GIET, *L'Apocalypse et l'histoire* (Paris 1957). J. BLEVINS, ''The Genre of Revelation,'' *Review and Expositor* 77 (1980) 393–408. G. CAIRD, *A Commentary of the Revelation of St. John the Divine* (New York 1966). D. HILL, ''Prophecy and Prophets in the Revelation of St. John,'' *New Testament Studies* 18 (1971–72) 401–418. J. LAMBRECHT, ed., *L'Apocalypse johannique et l'Apocalyptique dans le Nouveau Testament* (Louvain 1980). R. MOUNCE, *The Book of Revelation* (Grand Rapids, Mich. 1977). E. SCHÜSSLER-FIORENZA, *The Book of Revelation: Justice and Judgment* (Philadelphia 1985). J. SWEET, *Revelation* (Philadelphia 1979). U. VANNI, ''La Riflessione Sapienziale come atteggiamento ermeneutico costante nell'Apocalisse,'' *Rivista Biblica Italia* 24 (1976) 185–197; *La Struttura letteraria dell'Apocalisse* (Rome 1971). A. Y. COLLINS, *Crisis and Catharsis: The Power of the Apocalypse* (Philadelphia 1984).

[E. F. SIEGMAN/J. WINKLER]

REVELATION, CONCEPT OF (IN THE BIBLE)

Primarily, revelation is the act of God, seen in the progressive unfolding of His eternal plan of salvation in Christ, by which He manifests and communicates Himself to people, calls the Church into being, and invites the loving response of assent and obedience; secondarily, it is the body of truth that is made known through God's unfolding plan. The nature of revelation can be seen both in the OT and in the NT.

Revelation in the OT

Under this heading will be considered the hidden God and His revelation of Himself through His word and through His entrance into history.

The Hidden God. God is, above all else, holy (Is 6.3), which means that He is entirely ''other,'' exalted above men, transcendent, inaccessible. He dwells in the heavens (Gn 28.12–13; Dt 26.15; 1 Kgs 8.30); no one can see His face and live (Ex 19.21; 33.20; Dt 18.16); He is shrouded in darkness in the Holy of Holies and even in theophanies (Ex 20.21; Dt 4.11; Ps 80[81].8; 1 Kgs, 8.12); He is a hidden God (Is 45.15). The NT concurs (see Mt 11.27; Lk 10.21–22; Jn 1.18; 6.46; 1 Tm 6.16; 1 Jn 4.12).

The author of Wisdom (1st century B.C.) is the first to assert clearly that men can come to know God through reason—but he then blames them for not worshiping Him (Wis 13.1–9). St. Paul, in the NT, argues in much the same way (Acts 14.15–17; 17.22–31; Rom 1.18–32); the Gentile may have the law of God in his heart (Rom 2.14–15), but all have sinned (Rom 3.23); before the time of revelation in Christ the Gentiles lived in ''times of ignorance'' (Acts 17.30), for the world did not come to knowledge of God by human wisdom (1 Cor 1.21). Thus biblical authors admit the possibility of a knowledge of God derived by reasoning from creation, but assert that, historically, it had not led to a personal knowledge, i.e., one expressed by worship and moral commitment. Much less was God's particular plan of salvation known through reason; it was somewhat hidden even from the Angels (1 Pt 1.12). The Israelites did, in fact, believe that creation revealed God (Ps 18[19].2–5; 103[104]), because it was viewed as subservient to His will and as controlled directly by Him: the phenomena of creation were looked upon as acts of God. Thus, a storm could be a theophany (Ps 28[29]); calamities such as famine (2 Sm 21) or plague (2 Sm 24) manifested His anger; a flight of quail (Nm 11.31), a timely wind (Ex 14.21), or a hailstorm (Jos 10.11—''the Lord hurled great stones'') marked His providential intervention. This approach was valid for the Hebrew who had already met God the Creator and now contemplated Him in His works, even though it did not distinguish between the natural and the supernatural.

Revelation through God's Word. The transcendent invisible God who can be known but imperfectly by reason shows merciful condescension by revealing Himself to man. God's will to reveal is attested by specific texts (Am 3.7; Is 45.19; Nm 12.6; Dt 18.15–18; Dn 2.47; Sir 42.19) and by a wide variety of terms and expressions. God uncovers or reveals (*gālâ*) some truth or quality (in *qal* or *piel*) or Himself (*niphal*); He makes Himself known (*niphal* of *yāda‘*) or causes another to know (*hiphil*); He appears (is seen— *niphal* of *rā'â*) or makes someone to see a fact, His glory, a vision (*hiphil*); He causes someone to hear His word, voice, judgment (*hiphil* of *šāma‘*); He announces (*higgîd*); He speaks (*dibbēr*); He says (*'āmar*); His word (*dābār*) comes to the prophets. The *niphal* of the verb often has some divine force or quality as subject, such as word, glory, arm, or salvation.

It is God, acting as a person, who takes the initiative in communicating Himself to men. To seek revelation through divination, necromancy, and other forms of magic was strictly forbidden (Dt 18.9–14), though one might seek (*dāraš, šā'al*) an answer from a qualified spokesman of God, such as a priest or prophet.

Revelation is accomplished primarily by means of God's ''word.'' Even when God came to man in dream, vision, or THEOPHANY, it was still, often enough, His word that clarified the event's meaning (Jer 1.11–14; Am 7.7–9; Dn 7.15–18; Ex 19.9–11). Priest, PROPHET, and sage spoke God's word, but in differing manner and degree (Jer 18.18).

The Word of the Law. The Ten COMMANDMENTS in particular are called words (Ex 34.28; Dt 4.13; 10.4), but the term includes also other legislation (Dt 4.2). By a prophetic experience Moses understood the response that God required of the people He had called out of Egypt, and the laws he mediated were for them a valid expression of God's moral will. Much of the legislation of the Pentateuch came from later times and was evolved in priestly circles, where it continued to develop, in the spirit of the Mosaic legislation, into a law code that would ever more perfectly reveal God's moral will. In this further development, the influence of prophetic teaching was incalculable.

The Prophetic Word. For the Hebrew mind, the word had a dynamic reality (Is 40.6–8; 55.10–11). The word that was spoken by the prophet was the Lord's word (e.g., the formula ''the word of the Lord came to X''; Is 38.4; Jer 28.12) and partook of all the might of His will. But how did this word come to them? One should not think of an audible message; much less can it be imagined that the word was literally placed in Jeremiah's mouth (Jer 1.9). These expressions indicate the prophet's conviction that he was speaking the message of the Lord. The prophet had experienced the holiness, personality, and will of God in an inexpressible way (Is 6; Jer 1; Ez 1–2), a way that set him apart from his fellows; he was conscious of having been admitted to the council of God (Jer 23.18, 22). It was in the light of this experience that he viewed the concrete historical situation and pronounced God's judgments and promises to the men of his time.

Unlike the word of the false prophet (Jer 23.16–32), the true prophet's message cannot be explained as the product of inclination, environment, or political insight. He was a man under compulsion to speak a message not his own (Jer 1.6–7; 20.7–9; Am 3.8) to men who would gladly have been rid of him (Jer 26.7–15; Ez 3.4–11; Am 2.11–12; 7.10–13) and from whom his vocation cut him off (Is 8.11–15; Jer 15.17). If he foretold doom to a naive, optimistic, conscienceless people, it was not that he had less faith than they in the mighty power of the Lord to deliver, but because he knew His will. The objective validity of the prophet's conviction that he spoke the word of God was often established in part, at least, by the criteria that led many to accept his message even in his own day: conformity to a mature and truthful conception of God's nature, His demands, and Israel's own inspired tradition (Dt 13.1–6), fulfillment of prophecy (Dt

18.15–22; Jer 28.5–9), and, rarely, miracles (1 Kgs 18.30–39). The final guarantee of their validity, however, rests on the inclusion of their collected oracles in the canon of inspired Scripture.

The Word of Wisdom. Especially in later passages of the sapiential books, wisdom is seen as something much deeper than mere practical advice and is presented as divinely revealed: it belongs to God alone and is hidden from the eyes of man (Job 28), is given to men as a gift (Prv 2.6; Jb 32.8–9; Sir 1.1), and has divine qualities (Wis 7.25–27). Although wisdom, understood in this sense, came to be identified with the Law (Sir 24.22), the development of its meaning owed a great deal to prophetic teaching with which the wisdom writers were deeply imbued. In fact, wisdom was often an application of prophetic teaching (concerned largely with the nation) to the individual.

God's Revelation through History. The secular historian may not feel compelled to admit any special intervention of God in the history of Israel; the escape of slaves, conquest, exile, and restoration are events that can be analyzed and understood, especially since many of the miracles that made them possible are susceptible to naturalistic explanations. The biblical authors, however, believed that in these events the hand of God was revealed. But because such knowledge is by faith, it rests, not upon the events alone, but upon a divinely inspired interpretation of them.

Because the Judeo-Christian revelation is historical in nature, it rests upon the historical event as upon the very material of which it is composed. Yet the external event, no matter how impressive, needs the word before it can adequately reveal God's action and plan; this word is supplied by prophets, i.e., God's spokesmen. The biblical texts in which the events are described already bear the (spokesmen's) interpretation of the events. To describe the deliverance from Egypt as accomplished by the mighty hand of God (Ex 6.1; 32.11) is already an interpretation that refuses to view the events as merely natural phenomena (e.g., the ten plagues). The origin and validity of the interpretation is, of course, all important.

Israelite tradition named Moses as the great leader and first prophet through whom the new faith was mediated, for it was he who explained to the chosen people the significance of the events of the Exodus and even of the fiery theophany on Mt. Sinai (Ex 19.3–21; 20.18–21; Dt 5.22–27). What was affirmed in the accounts of Moses' ascent into the mountain (Ex 19.3, 20; 24.12–18) and his intimate association with the Lord (Ex 33.7–23; Nm 12.6–8; Dt 34.10) was the religious experience that enabled Moses to know and to communicate to the chosen people the significance of what the Lord had done for them. The prophets, in their interpretation of events, were led by God in the same path trodden by Moses. They gave interpretation not only of events past and present but even of those they confidently predicted. From the whole there emerged God's plan of salvation, to be completed only in the NT.

Prophetic interpretation of Israel's history of this kind was incorporated into the historical books of the Bible (see 2 Kgs 17.7–23; 21.10–15). The fact that revelation proceeded by way of God's unfolding plan meant that revelation itself was a progressive thing and that there was a constant, objective increase in its content. This included an ever deeper awareness of God's nature, of His mercy, power, wisdom, and justice. Individual elements of the plan already foreshadowed the whole, e.g., the Exodus, which began the constant theme of deliverance through God's mighty acts (Is 10.25–27; 40.3; 41.17–20; 43.16–21; Jn 8.12; 1 Cor 10.1–12; Rv 15.2–3). The action was irreversible, not cyclical, and would move to a climax understood as "the Day of the Lord" by the prophets (Is 11.11; 12.1; Am 9.11; Jl 3.1–5; Is 26.20–27.13); it would mark the establishment of the kingdom of God on Earth.

Revelation in the NT

God's word in Christ, the Spirit of truth in the Apostles, and human response, referred to in the NT, give further insight into the nature of revelation.

The Word of God in Christ. God, who had formerly spoken through the prophets now spoke through His Son (Heb 1.1–2), whom God sent in the fullness of time (Gal 4.4) and in whom all the promises found their "Yes" (2 Cor 1.20). With the coming of Christ the final age is initiated, the redemptive act of God is accomplished. In His person and work Christ is the perfect revelation and supreme condescension of the transcendent God. It is He whom the prophets foretold (1 Pt 1.10–12).

In the Synoptics. Christ is presented as prophet and as Son of God, whose coming both heralds and inaugurates the kingdom of God, the final age in God's plan of salvation. His exorcisms and cures indicate that the dominion of Satan has been brought to an end and has given place to that of God (Mt 12.25–28; Mk 3.23–26; Lk 11.17–20), while His preaching and parables reveal the nature of the kingdom (Mt 5–7; 13.1–51). His true nature is known only to the Father, who reveals it to the humble, particularly to the Apostles; and the Father is in turn revealed by Jesus (Mt 11.25–27; 16.17; 17.1–5). He foretells His death, Resurrection (Mk 8.31–33; Mt 16.21–23; Lk 9.22), and return in glory (Mk 14.62) and interprets the meaning of His work (Mk 10.45; Lk 24.25–27, 44).

In St. Paul. As in the Synoptics, the advent of Christ marks the final age in God's plan of salvation, but Paul is more concerned with the "mystery" of Christ than with His visible earthly career. By the term "mystery" (μυστήριον) Paul means the unfathomable truth of salvation in Christ, a truth formerly hidden, though foretold by the prophets, and which has now been revealed by God (Rom 16.25–26; 1 Cor 2.7, 10; Eph 1.9–10; Col 1.26; cf. 1 Pt 1.10–12). Basically it refers to God's saving act in Christ and can be equated with Paul's gospel (Eph 6.19), though often it is applied to partial aspects of it (1 Cor 15.51; Eph 3.4–6; 5.32). It is identified with the wisdom of God (1 Cor 1.23–25; 2.7; Col 2.2–3).

God Himself reveals the mystery of Christ: cf. the use of ἀποκαλύπτειν (to reveal—Eph 3.5) and ἀποκάλυψις (revelation—Rom 16.25; Eph 3.3), used always with God as the agent, or in the passive—a reverential way of indicating the divine activity. Other verbs are used in a sense close to that of ἀποκαλύπτειν (sometimes with the Apostles as grammatical subject, as God's agents): γνωρίζειν (to make known—Eph 1.9; 3.3; 6.19; Col 1.27); φωτίζειν (to enlighten—Eph 3.9); φανεροῦν (to manifest—Col 1.26).

This revelation takes place in two stages that mark the beginning and end of the final age, which is now present: the beginning, known by the elect through faith, is accomplished in the Passion and Exaltation of Christ (Rom 1.16–17; 3.21–22; Gal 1.16; Eph 3.3, 5; Col 1.26; 2 Tm 1.10); the end will be manifest to all in the PAROUSIA (παρουσία, ἀποκάλυψις, ἐπιφάνεια), which will be preceded by the revelation of antichrist (2 Thes 2.3, 6, 8). This "Day of the Lord," expected by the prophets, will reveal Christ's glory and the glorious salvation of the faithful (Rom 8.18, 23; 2 Cor 4.13–14; Col 3.4; 1 Thes 4.14–18; 2 Thes 1.10) as well as God's wrath against sinners (Rom 2.5, 8; 1 Thes 1.10)—realities that in fact are already present in a partial and hidden manner.

The conception of revelation as a deposit (παραθήκη) that is to be guarded is found also in 1 Tm 6.20; 2 Tm 1.14; see also the insistence on "sound doctrine" in 1 Tm 1.10–11; 6.3; 2 Tm 1.13.

In St. John. Although St. John does not use ἀποκαλύπτειν except in an OT citation, many other significant terms do occur. He presents Christ as the visible revelation of the invisible Father and makes significant use of φανεροῦν (to manifest—Jn 1.31; 2.11; 3.21; 9.3; 17.6), φῶς (light), φωτίζειν (to enlighten—1.9), γνωρίζειν (to make known—15.15; 17.26).

God has never been seen (Jn 1.18; 6.46; 1 Jn 4.20); it is precisely to reveal Him that Christ has come (1.18; 17.2–3—where knowledge of the Father is identified with eternal life, the gift Jesus has come to confer). Jesus is able to manifest the Father because, divine and preexistent with Him (1.1–2, 18), He came into the world (1.9; 3.2, 19, 31; *passim*), having been sent by the Father (4.34; 5.23; *passim*). The mission of Christ is attested by the witness of John the Baptizer (1.7, 15, 32–34; 5.33), by His own works (5.36), by the Scriptures (5.39), and especially by the Father (5.37; 8.18). Christ is able to bear witness to Himself (8.14, 18) and to the truth (18.37), and the words He speaks are God's words (3.34; 7.17; 8.26, 28, 38, 40). He reveals the Father because He is the visible embodiment of God's work. He sees the works of the Father, works when He works, and, just as the Father does, He gives life and He judges (5.17–22, 27; cf. 9.3). His miracles are signs because of the deep meaning they carry (2.11, 23; 4.54; *passim*). His glory is the very glory of the Father (1.14, 51; 2.11; 12.41; 17.5, 22, 24). So fully is He the manifestation of God among men that all must honor Him as they do the Father (5.23). To see Him is to see the Father (14.9), for He and the Father are one (10.30). So perfectly does He reveal the Father that He can be called simply "the Word" (1.1, 14; 1 Jn 1.1).

The Spirit of Truth and the Apostles. Only by the preaching of divinely commissioned agents can people enter by faith into the saving work of Christ (Rom 10.14–15). Yet even at the time of the Ascension the Apostles were far from understanding the true nature of the kingdom established by Christ that was still to be evolved to its full stature (Acts 1.6). Their baptism by the Holy Spirit sent by Christ was needed before they could begin the work entrusted to them (Acts 1.5, 8; 2.1–41). As Christ had promised (Jn 14.26; 16.13), by the guidance of the Spirit the Apostles took important new steps (Acts 10.19–48; 13.2–3) whose significance they fully understood through the Spirit's enlightenment (Acts 11.15–18; cf. 1 Cor 2.10–16; Eph 3.3–6). By the sending-forth of the Apostles directed by the Holy Spirit, witness was given to enable people to believe (Acts 5.32; cf. Jn 15.26–27); by it, too, the Church was established to carry on the same work for all time and to make universal the revelation that until then had been confined to one nation (Mt 28.19–20; Mk 16.19–20).

Man's Response. God does not speak in a vacuum but to human beings, and a response is expected. If God "makes to hear" and "makes to know," then we are expected to "hear" and to "know"—but in the biblical sense of these words. "To hear" is not restricted to audition; it includes loving obedience as well (Ex 3.18; Is 28.12; Jer 11.10; Ez 2.5; Mt 18.17; Lk 16.31). "To know" is a word that summarizes biblical spirituality and includes love and election on God's part, love, obedience, and faithful adherence on man's (Is 19.21; Jer 31.34; Hos 2.21–22, 13.4; Am 3.2 "favored"; Jn 10.14–15; 17.3;

Phil 3.10; 1 Jn 2.3). This response of loving assent and obedience is termed "faith." It is a challenge that faces each generation, each individual (Dt 5.3); the choice is free but is by no means presented on a take-it-or-leave-it basis (Dt 30.19; Is 7.9; Jn 6.29–50; 8.24). The clearest example of what is meant by the challenge of revelation and the response of faith is St. Paul's conversion. When the mystery of Christ was revealed to him (Gal 1.15–16), he considered that he had been "laid hold of" by Christ and pressed on to lay hold of the divine prize (Phil 3.12–14).

See Also: DREAM; MYSTERY (IN THE BIBLE); NECROMANCY; ORACLE (IN THE BIBLE); PROPHETISM (IN THE BIBLE); SALVATION HISTORY (HEILSGESCHICHTE); URIM AND THUMMIM; WORD OF GOD.

Bibliography: *Encyclopedic Dictionary of the Bible,* tr. and adap. by L. HARTMAN (New York 1963), from A. VAN DEN BORN, *Bijbels Woordenboek* 2040–46. M. VERENO and R. SCHNACKENBURG, *Lexikon für Theologie und Kirche,* ed. J. HOFER and K. RAHNER, 10 v. (2d, new ed. Freiburg 1957–65) 7:1104–09. S. H. HOOKE, *Alpha and Omega: A Study in the Pattern of Revelation* (London 1961). W. PANNENBERG, ed., *Offenbarung als Geschichte* (Kerygma und Dogma, Beiheft 1; Göttingen 1961). W. BULST, *Revelation,* tr. B. VAWTER (New York 1965). H. D. MCDONALD, *Ideas of Revelation: An Historical Study A.D. 1700 to A.D. 1860* (London 1959); *Theories of Revelation: An Historical Study, 1860–1960* (London 1963). J. BAILLIE, *The Idea of Revelation in Recent Thought* (New York 1956). H. SCHULTE, *Der Begriff der Offenbarung im Neuen Testament* (Munich 1949). H. W. ROBINSON, *Inspiration and Revelation in the Old Testament,* rev. L. H. BROCKINGTON and E. A. PAYNE (Oxford 1946). C. H. DODD, *The Bible Today* (Cambridge, Eng. 1947) 98–121. H. E. BRUNNER, *God and Man,* tr. D. CAIRNS (London 1936) 103–135. J. J. O'ROURKE, "Romans 1, 20 and Natural Revelation," *Catholic Biblical Quarterly* 23 (1961) 301–306. R. E. BROWN, "The Pre-Christian Semitic Concept of 'Mystery,'" *ibid.* 20 (1958) 417–443. E. O'DOHERTY, "The Organic Development of Messianic Revelation," *ibid.* 19 (1957) 16–24. J. L. MCKENZIE, "The Word of God in the Old Testament," *Theological Studies* 21 (1960) 183–206. O. G. LORETZ, *Die Wahrheit der Bibel* (Freiburg 1964). J. J. COLLINS, "Natural Theology and Biblical Tradition: The Case of Hellenistic Judaism," *Catholic Biblical Quarterly* 60 (1998) 1–15. D. PATRICK, *The Rhetoric of Revelation in the Hebrew Bible* (OBT; Minneapolis 1999). L. G. PERDUE, "Revelation and the Problem of the Hidden God in Second Temple Wisdom Literature," *Shall Not the Judge of All the World Do What Is Right? Studies in the Nature of God in Tribute to James L. Crenshaw,* ed. D. PENCHANSKY and P. L. REDDITT (Winona Lake, Ind. 2000) 201–222.

[J. JENSEN]

REVELATION, FONTS OF

"Fonts of revelation" is a technical term used by theologians of recent centuries to designate the authoritative sources of Christian doctrine. Although the Church Fathers and medieval theologians regularly treated Scripture and tradition as authentic sources, the problem of their respective dignity and mutual connection did not become acute until the time of the REFORMATION. LUTHER, followed by many other PROTESTANTS, took the position that Scripture alone was the final authority, and that the tradition of the Church, as expressed in creeds, dogmas, liturgy, and the like, had to be tested against Holy Scripture. The *Epitome* in the Lutheran *Book of Concord* (1580) begins with the lapidary statement: ''We believe, teach, and confess that the prophetic and apostolic writings of the Old and New Testaments are the only rule and norm according to which all doctrines and teachers alike must be appraised and judged.'' The Anglican William Chillingworth in 1638 asserted: ''The Bible, I say, and the Bible only, is the religion of protestants!'' (*Works* [Philadelphia 1844], 480–81).

Responding to Lutherans and other Protestants, the Council of TRENT taught in 1546 that the gospel promised of old through the prophets in the Sacred Scriptures and promulgated by Jesus Christ was ''the source [*fontem*] of every saving truth and rule of conduct.'' This truth and this rule, the council then declared, were received by the apostles either by word of mouth from Jesus Christ or by inspiration of the Holy Spirit and are contained ''in the written books and in unwritten traditions'' that have come down to us from the apostles. The books of Scripture and the apostolic traditions, since they alike come from Christ and the Holy Spirit, are to be received ''with the same sense of loyalty and reverence'' (DS 1501).

During the next several centuries, Catholic theologians, apologists, and catechetical writers commonly professed a ''two-source'' theory, namely, that the revelation of Christ is contained partly in Holy Scripture and partly in sacred TRADITION. Perhaps this was the meaning intended by the Fathers at Trent, but the council did not actually teach that any revealed truth was contained either in Scripture alone or in tradition alone. A previous draft of Trent's decree had stated that the truth of the gospel is contained ''partly in written books and partly in written traditions,'' but the words ''partly'' were stricken from the final text. To satisfy the demands of Trent it would therefore be sufficient to say that the word of God is accessible in two ways. It is transmitted both through Scripture and through apostolic tradition, two channels that are to be held in the same reverence insofar as both attest with divine authority to the same gospel.

In the ecumenical climate of the 20th century the cleavage between the Catholic and Protestant positions became less sharp. Protestant Scripture scholars recognized that Holy Scripture depends heavily on a prior oral tradition, of which it is a privileged sedimentation. Protestants also recognized that they themselves read Scripture in the light of tradition, and that it is practically impossible to bypass tradition and approach Scripture, as it were, for the first time. In the words of Paul Tillich, ''the radical biblicistic attitude is a self-deception. No one is able to leap over two thousand years of church history and become contemporaneous with the writers of the New Testament, except in the spiritual sense of accepting Jesus as the Christ'' (*Systematic Theology*, 1:36).

The WORLD COUNCIL OF CHURCHES, through its Faith and Order Commission, responded to this more positive attitude toward tradition on the part of Protestants. It was affected also by the traditionalism of the Orthodox, since several important Orthodox churches had been admitted to membership in 1951. Finally, it was influenced by the new climate of cooperation with Roman Catholic scholars. The Faith and Order Commission accordingly launched in 1954 an in-depth study of the problem, and as a result produced an important report on ''Scripture, Tradition, and traditions,'' accepted at the Fourth World Conference on Faith and Order in Montreal in 1963. Acknowledging the indispensability of tradition, this report stated: ''We exist as Christians by the Tradition of the gospel (the *paradosis* of the *kerygma*) testified in scripture, transmitted in and by the church through the power of the Holy Spirit. Tradition taken in this sense is actualized in the preaching of the word, in the administration of the sacraments and worship, in Christian teaching and theology, and in mission and witness to Christ by lives of the members of the Church.'' By this declaration the Montreal statement distanced itself from those Protestants who thought it possible to appeal to ''Scripture alone,'' but the statement did not provide a clear rule for distinguishing between merely human traditions and divine or apostolic Tradition (which it spelled with a capital T).

On the Catholic side the Second VATICAN COUNCIL manifested the effects of the ecumenical movement on Catholic theology. The first draft of the Constitution on Revelation began with a chapter on ''The Two Sources of Revelation'' (*De duplici revelationis*) that was sharply criticized at the first session in November 1962 and was withdrawn by order of Pope John XXIII. The new text, composed in 1963 and several times revised, became in November 1965 the dogmatic constitution *Dei Verbum*. It insisted on the inseparability of Scripture and tradition, which together ''form one sacred deposit of the word of God'' (DV 10). In line with previous Catholic teaching, however, the constitution affirmed: ''It is not from sacred Scripture alone that the Church draws her certainty about everything that has been revealed'' (DV 9). In other words, even if all revealed truth is in some way contained in Scripture, tradition is needed to grasp it with the required assurance.

Tradition, therefore, has an intimate relationship with sacred Scripture. Vatican II viewed both Scripture and tradition not statically, as depositories containing particular truths, but rather dynamically, as ways in which God converses with his People (DV 8 and 21). Scripture itself is actively handed down (''traditioned'') in the Church. Tradition, moreover, consists not simply in oral and written statements but in the total life and practice of the praying and believing Church. Tradition in this sense is viewed as necessary, not least for the identification of the canonical Scriptures. ''Through the same tradition the Church's full canon of the sacred books is known, and the sacred writings themselves are more profoundly understood and unceasingly made active in her'' (DV 8).

Regarding the relative dignity of Scripture and tradition, Vatican II repeated the assertion of Trent that the two are to be received with the same sense of devotion and reverence (DV 9), inasmuch as apostolic tradition is, like Scripture, a form of the word of God. On the other hand, Scripture enjoys a certain priority, since the very text of Scripture is the word of God (DV 24), whereas tradition is a more elusive reality. Particular traditions, which may be thought to be apostolic, have to be sifted and evaluated in order to determine their authenticity. Scripture, as the divinely guided expression of God's word in human language, has a certain critical function over against all other expressions. Thus there is a sense in which Catholics, as well as Protestants, can speak of Scripture as being finally normative. But while tradition cannot contradict the true meaning of Scripture, Scripture cannot be confidently identified or authoritatively interpreted without the help of tradition.

In answer to the question raised at Montreal about how to distinguish genuine tradition from merely human and possibly distorted traditions, Catholics refer to a variety of tests, such as conformity with Scripture, coherence with Catholic tradition as a whole, harmony with the norms for worship (the *lex orandi*), acceptability to the community of believers (the *sensus fidelium*), agreement with the past teaching of popes and councils, and the approval of the contemporary magisterium. Exegetes and theologians by their preparatory study help the judgment of the Church to mature (DV 12). According to Vatican II, the task of authentically interpreting the word of God, as found in Scripture or tradition, is entrusted to the living magisterium, which exercises its authority in the name of Jesus Christ (DV 10).

Some theologians look upon Scripture as the true source and regard tradition as a succession of commentaries upon it. Although unexceptionable in what it affirms, this position tends to be reductive. Tradition does not first arise from the study of Scripture. Having existed even before Scripture was written, it accompanies Scripture at every stage of history as a kind of surrounding atmosphere. Tradition, therefore, gives a perspective for biblical interpretation deeper than merely philological exegesis. Some elements of Christian faith, barely hinted at in Holy Scripture, may be more vividly attested by tradition.

In the early centuries it may have been possible to identify certain particular traditions as coming from the apostles by word of mouth. Theologians speculate that doctrines such as infant baptism and the perpetual virginity of Mary may have been transmitted in this way. But at the distance of many centuries scientific history can no longer establish the apostolic origin of these doctrines. Thus the concept of tradition as a source of factual information, parallel with and alongside of Holy Scripture, has been losing favor.

In recent centuries the theology of tradition has been taking on new features. Authors such as Johann Adam MÖHLER, John Henry NEWMAN, and Maurice BLONDEL have propounded the thesis that authentic tradition is sustained and illuminated in the Church by the Holy Spirit, and gives rise to a ''sense of the faith'' on the part of committed members of the Church. Vatican II adopted this dynamic concept of tradition. ''This tradition which comes from the apostles develops in the Church with the help of the Holy Spirit. For there is a growth in understanding of the realities and the words that have been handed down. . . . As the centuries succeed one another, the Church constantly moves forward toward the fullness of divine truth until the words of God reach their complete fulfillment in her'' (DV 8).

In the 16th century the burning question was whether the finally decisive authority was single or double. Was it Scripture alone or Scripture together with apostolic traditions? In the 20th century theologians asked how best to use both Scripture and tradition in order to find the word of God in them. Christians of many different ecclesial affiliations involved themselves in the effort to reexamine Scripture in the light of their own traditions, and to evaluate their traditions in the light of Scripture. Protestants, Catholics, and Orthodox have been engaged in similar pursuits and have come to understand each other better. As Christianity enters the third millennium, the churches may hope to be further enriched both by their own traditions and those of other ecclesial bodies as they listen to one another and prayerfully read the Scriptures they hold in common.

Bibliography: J. P. MACKEY, *The Modern Theology of Tradition* (New York 1963). K. RAHNER, ed., ''Scripture and Tradition,'' *Encyclopedia of Theology: The Concise Sacramentum Mundi* (New

York 1975), 6:54–57, with bibliog. Y. M.-J. CONGAR, *Tradition and Traditions* (New York 1967). A. DULLES, *The Craft of Theology*, 2d ed. (New York 1995). H. C. SKILLRUD and others, eds., *Scripture and Tradition: Lutherans and Catholics in Dialogue IX* (Minneapolis 1995).

[A. DULLES]

REVELATION, PRIMITIVE

The term primitive revelation has generally meant a body of supernatural truths revealed to man at the beginning of the human race and passed down over the centuries, with remnants of this revelation embedded in primitive religions. This conception of primitive revelation, most closely associated with the name of H. F. R. de LAMENNAIS, arose in the 19th century in reaction to rationalism. In the 20th century it was given support by the work of Wilhelm SCHMIDT, whose aim was "to describe the first glimmering of SUPERNATURAL Revelation, more properly referred to as primitive revelation; and to show its obscuration by the Fall of Man, together with its subsequent fate" [W. Schmidt, *Primitive Revelation*, tr. J. Baierl (St. Louis 1939) 3].

Primitive revelation, however, may have a wider significance, namely all pre-Judaic revelation of God. Catholic theology must accept this kind of primitive revelation because: (1) the first chapters of Genesis testify to it; (2) God wills all men to be saved, and the existence of such a salvific will implies the possibility of FAITH in a supernatural revelation. That there was supernatural revelation before the Patriarch ABRAHAM is a necessary conclusion; but the origin, form, and content of such revelation is far from clear. The first definition stated above finds practically no defenders in mid-20th century. A better understanding of the Biblical story opens other possibilities, and the findings of anthropological sciences make the passing down of truths from the first man all but inconceivable.

Although this question has yet to receive adequate treatment by theologians, the following principles would seem to be the basis for a solution. The supernatural revelation to the first man need not have taken place through verbal utterances of God or through extraordinary events. That ADAM had a PRETERNATURAL gift of knowledge does not imply that he had more than a fragmentary knowledge of revelation. Furthermore, the existence of revelation at later periods of history need not stem from this first revelation. Both the first man and subsequent men may have attained divine revelation by the GRACE of God through their own experiences.

Because man lives in an order of grace and is directed to a supernatural DESTINY, it is possible that his moral experience could indicate to him a more than natural ideal, thus bringing about an implicitly supernatural knowledge of divine things. The natural and supernatural orders must not be confused, but neither are they to be separated; and all man's experiences are in a world of sin and grace. The pointers to such a revelation, arising in the life of the individual, could be preserved and developed in religious institutions and myths so that the possibility of supernatural faith would not depend entirely on the isolated experience of the individual. Christianity thus recognizes that primitive religion may be the vehicle of true religious, even supernatural, knowledge, though such knowledge is in constant danger of being distorted or destroyed.

See Also: RELIGION (IN PRIMITIVE CULTURE); SYMBOL IN REVELATION.

Bibliography: "Uroffenbarung," *Lexikon für Theologie und Kirche*[2], ed. J. HOFER and K. RAHNER, 10 v. (Freiburg 1957–65): suppl., *Das Zweite Vatikanische Konzil: Dokument und Kommentare*, ed. H. S. BRECHTER et al., pt. 1 (1966) v.10. G. GLOEGE, *Die Religion in Geschichte und Gegenwart* 7 v. (Tübingen 1957–65) 6:1199–1203. H. VORGRIMLER, *Lexikon für Theologie und Kirche*, ed. J. HOFER and K. RAHNER, 10 v. (Freiburg 1957–65) 7:1115–16. M. VERENO et al., *ibid.* 7:1104–15. J. R. GEISELMANN, H. FRIES, ed., *Handbuch theologischer Grundbegriffe*, 2 v. (Munich 1962–63) 2:242–250. A. LANG, *Religions-Wissenschaftliches Wörterbuch*, ed. F. KÖNIG (Freiburg 1956) 604–607. W. KOPPERS, *ibid.,* 189–203. K. RAHNER and H. VORGRIMLER, *Kleines theologisches Wöterbuch* (Freiburg 1961) 372–373.

[G. MORAN]

REVELATION, THEOLOGY OF

The English word is derived from the Latin *revelare,* meaning to unveil or disclose. In common usage, even outside a religious context, revelation means a sudden and unexpected receipt of knowledge of a profoundly significant character, especially that which gives the recipient a new outlook on life and the world. It frequently designates the free action whereby one person confides his inner thoughts and sentiments to another, enabling the latter to enter into his spiritual world. In theology the term generally denotes the action by which God communicates to creatures a participation in His own knowledge, including His intimate self-knowledge. Such a communication is SUPERNATURAL since it transcends all that a creature could discover by its native powers. Some authors use the term in a wider sense to include "natural" or "general" revelation, that is, the knowledge of divine things that God imparts through nature and conscience. This usage has the advantage of making it clear that all man's knowledge of God depends on God's free initiative. But to avoid repeating what is said elsewhere (*see* THEOLOGY, NATURAL), we shall here speak only of supernatural revelation.

No adequate theology of revelation can be derived by mere analysis of the formal, abstract notion. The Christian view emerges from a concrete consideration as presented in Scripture and tradition (*see* TRADITION [IN THEOLOGY]). Building on the biblical idea of revelation, this article first surveys the main statements of the Catholic magisterium and then sketches a general theory of revelation as understood in modern Catholic theology.

Documents of the Church

Until recent centuries the existence and knowability of revelation were taken for granted by Christians; little was therefore said concerning revelation as such.

Refutation of error. Church decisions were concerned rather with specifying the contents of revelation in answer to particular heresies. In the Middle Ages it was repeatedly declared against Manichaean denials that the same God had spoken in the Old Testament and in the New Testament (e.g., H. Denzinger, *Enchiridion symbolorum* [32d ed. Freiburg 1963] 685, 790, 854). Lateran IV, amplifying this point, affirmed in 1215 that God had given His ''salutary doctrine'' to the human race ''through Moses and the holy Prophets and His other servants, according to a most orderly disposition of times,'' culminating in the action by which ''the only-begotten Son of God, Jesus Christ . . . more evidently disclosed the way of life'' (*ibid.* 800–801).

The Council of Trent touched incidentally on the nature of revelation in its discussion of the divinely authoritative sources of doctrine. The Christian gospel, said the council, having been ''previously promised by the Prophets in the Holy Scriptures,'' was first promulgated by Jesus Christ with His own lips. Then it was disseminated by the Apostles on the basis of what they had heard from Jesus Christ and been taught by the Holy Spirit (*ibid.* 1501).

In the nineteenth century, a number of fundamental errors concerning revelation and faith were condemned. The fideists were censured for their view that FAITH was not solidly supported by the evidences of credibility (cf. *ibid.* 2751–2756, 2765–2769) (*see* FIDEISM). The rationalists and agnostics were reprobated for denying respectively the possibility and knowability of revelation (cf. *ibid.* 2901–2907) (*see* RATIONALISM; AGNOSTICISM). Likewise rejected was the semirationalist position, which maintained that once human reason had developed to full maturity all the Christian dogmas could be established by human science and philosophy, without appeal to authority (cf. *ibid.* 2856, 2909) (*see* SEMIRATIONALISM).

Positive teaching. The Church's doctrine regarding the possibility, existence, and nature of revelation was most authoritatively set forth by Vatican I, which canonized the doctrine that human knowledge is of two distinct orders: natural knowledge—reason—and supernatural knowledge—revelation (*ibid.* 3004, 3015). Although human reason is able to attain some knowledge of God by its natural light, God has graciously consented to reveal Himself and His eternal decrees in a supernatural way (*ibid.* 3004). This revelation has a twofold aim. First, it permits the most important naturally knowable truths of religion to be grasped by all, with full certitude, and without admixture of error. Secondly, it enables man as an intelligent creature to orient himself to the supernatural end for which God has destined him (*ibid.* 3005). (*See* DESTINY, SUPERNATURAL.) If man had a merely natural destiny, revelation would be only morally necessary, but in view of man's gratuitous call to the intuitive vision of God, revelation is absolutely necessary for SALVATION. The revealed object accordingly contains not only truths that human reason could discover by its own efforts, but also, more importantly, divine mysteries that could by no means be grasped without revelation (*ibid.* 3015, 3041). These mysteries, even after their revelation, remain so hidden in God that man can apprehend them only obscurely in this life (*ibid.* 3016) (*see* MYSTERY [IN THEOLOGY]).

Vatican I dealt with the relations between revelation and reason. Reason, it affirmed, can discern no absurdity in the fact or contents of Christian revelation (*ibid.* 3017, 3027). Indeed it can establish the reasonableness of believing, thanks to the abundant signs of credibility, notably miracles and prophecies (*ibid.* 3009, 3014, 3019, 3033). Once the act of faith has been made, reason can ponder fruitfully on the data of revelation. If this meditation is made with due diligence, piety, and modesty, reason can achieve a very profitable, though limited, understanding of mysteries themselves. Such an understanding can arise from comparing the revealed mysteries with one another, with man's last end, and with things naturally known (*ibid.* 3016).

The Modernist heresy at the opening of the twentieth century gave occasion for further clarifications. The Roman magisterium declared that revelation is not a mere emotion or sentiment welling up from the depths of the subconscious; it has a definite intellectual content accepted not on the basis of intrinsic evidence, but on the authority of the revealing God (*ibid.* 3542). Such acceptance is commended by the external signs of credibility, especially miracles and prophecies, which have not lost their efficacy for the modern mind (*ibid.* 3539). Revelation, moreover, was complete in apostolic times (*ibid.* 3421). The Dogmas of the Church are revealed truths (*ibid.* 3422); they do not evolve in the course of time into dogmas having another sense (*ibid.* 3541) (*see* MODERN-ISM).

Vatican II devoted an entire dogmatic constitution, *Dei Verbum,* to the subject of revelation. The doctrine of that council will be closely followed in the exposition that follows.

Theological Reflection

From the time of the ENLIGHTENMENT until the mid-twentieth century, a heavily apologetic slant was given to the treatise on revelation. Primary attention was focused on what reason, unaided by faith, could demonstrate concerning the possibility, fittingness, and knowability of revelation. Contemporary theology is more concerned with exploring from a position within faith the nature and attitudes of revelation. This inquiry is favored by the interests and achievements of the twentieth century with regard to the theory of language, communication, symbolism, and interpersonal relations (*see* APOLOGETICS, 2).

Modern Protestant scholarship has given added impetus to the study of revelation. Biblical scholars such as C. H. Dodd, Oscar Cullmann, and Alan Richardson have called attention to the historical dimension of revelation, as witnessed by the mighty deeds of God recounted in Scripture. Dialectical theologians such as Karl Barth and Emil Brunner have stressed the mysterious attributes of God's word to man, which cannot be fully captured in human concepts and language (*see* DIALECTICAL THEOLO-GY). Existential theologians such as Rudolf Bultmann and Paul Tillich have pointed out the value of revelation in liberating man from the anxieties and pettiness of ordinary existence (*see* EXISTENTIAL THEOLOGY). In general it may be said that recent Protestant theology tends to look on revelation primarily as event and experience. Catholic theologians, without ignoring these aspects, are more concerned with safeguarding the doctrinal and transmissible features, as accentuated in the documents of the Church.

The contemporary theologian will find valuable elements for a theory of revelation in the Greek Fathers and in St. Augustine. Among the scholastic doctors St. Thomas Aquinas has contributed most importantly to the field in his treatises on faith and prophecy (*Summa Theologiae* 2a2ae, 1–16; 171–178).

Aspects of revelation. The Judeo-Christian revelation, which primarily concerns us here, is the noetic component of God's total work of REDEMPTION. Through revelation man becomes a sharer in the knowledge proper to God, inchoatively on earth, definitively in the life after death. Revelation therefore introduces man into the blessedness of God's own life. If he is to view reality, as it were, through God's eyes, man's mental horizons must be enlarged; otherwise he would reduce God's message to purely human perspectives. Therefore, revelation has a subjective aspect, consisting in the inner transformation of man's apprehensive faculties. This modification, however, occurs when the divine message comes from without through a definite intervention of God in history. The subjective and objective aspects of revelation are inseparable, but the former are more explicitly treated under the headings of GRACE and FAITH. We shall therefore focus primary attention on the objective side, considering first the process by which revelation comes to man and then the inner structure of the revealed datum.

Process of revelation. Two phases may be distinguished—the original communication of God's message to man and its subsequent transmission.

Immediate Revelation. According to Christian belief, immediate revelation was given in biblical times to the Prophets and Apostles (*see* PROPHECY [THEOLOGY OF]; APOSTLE.) The prophetic experience sometimes involved external sensation, dreams, visions, imaginary words, and even the direct infusion of new ideas, but none of these elements, according to St. Thomas, is essential. The primary and indispensable element is the illumination of the Prophet's understanding, giving him a divine insight into the meaning of what is presented to his mind (*Summa Theologiae* 2a2ae, 173.2; *C. gent.* 3.154).

The Apostles received revelation through the spoken words of Christ, in the context of His conduct. But in order for these words to take on the value of revelation, the recipients had to be inwardly attracted and enlightened by grace (Mt 16.17; Jn 6.64, 66). Some of the Apostles were later favored by ecstatic experiences (Acts, ch. 9 and 10; 2 Cor 12.1), but such experiences are not constitutive of apostleship as such, which depends rather on personal association with the risen Lord and on a special commission from Him.

According to the Bible, revelation comes primarily through the word of God. The word may be spoken or written symbol, or it may be an interior utterance whereby God articulates His message in the consciousness of the recipient. But the word of God, in Hebrew thinking, is not merely a vehicle of knowledge. Besides being noetic, it is dynamic: it effects what it signifies (cf. Is 55.10–11; Heb 4.12).

Even human words, as understood in modern speech-theory, are not devoid of efficacy. When one person addresses another or opens up his heart to him, the other becomes personally involved. If he responds appropriately in faith and trust, a new interpersonal relationship is established. God's revelatory word opens up to the believer a salutary communion with God and with his fellow believers. St. John of the Cross, in his *Ascent of Mount Carmel* (2.31), connects the sanctifying power of God's word with its dynamic efficacy [E. Allison Peers, ed., *The Complete Works of St. John of the Cross* (London 1934–35) 1.218–219].

The word of God, in its full biblical sense, includes God's revelatory deeds. The early books of the Bible describe numerous THEOPHANIES (e.g., the burning bush, the pillar of fire) in which God visibly manifests His presence. The whole Bible bears witness to the salvific and punitive actions by which God intervenes in history. These deeds have value not simply as confirmatory signs, bearing out the Prophets' declarations, but also as significant gestures. They are themselves revelatory, at least when accompanied by the commentary of prophetic interpretation. Words and deeds are closely interconnected; only in their mutual union do they constitute the full event of revelation. In the words of Vatican II, "the deeds wrought by God in the history of salvation manifest and confirm the teaching and realities signified by the words, while the words proclaim the deeds and clarify the mystery contained in them" (DV 2).

Mediated Revelation. The Prophets and Apostles received revelation not for their own sake but for the people of God. They were conscious of a divine mandate to hand on the message faithfully. This they did primarily through their preaching; and authorized preaching in the Church continues to be a vehicle of revelation. Like the original divine word, the preached word is charged with mysterious power. Besides its objective reality, it has a spiritual dimension which gives it value as God's word. The Fathers (Augustine, Gregory the Great) and St. Thomas (*De ver.* 27.3 ad 12) look upon Christian preachers as instruments or disposing causes in the transmission of revelation. Their human words became revelatory when the grace of God fecundates the minds of their hearers (*see* PREACHING, III [THEOLOGY OF]).

The inspired words of Scripture likewise convey revelation. Not all the biblical writers were immediate recipients of revelation. Some of them merely wrote down what they had learned from ordinary experience or from the testimony of others. Many statements in the Bible, taken in themselves, are merely secular pieces of information, and in that sense not revelation. But the entire Bible, according to Catholic faith, was composed under a divine impulse (or charism) known as inspiration. Therefore it constitutes a divinely guaranteed objectification of the religious consciousness of God's people in its supernaturally guided existence, lived out under the impact of progressive revelation. In this sense, the whole Bible is revelatory. Some theologians hold that the Bible, like the preached word, has quasi-sacramental value; that is, that one who reads or hears it under favorable circumstances receives grace to enter into a new relationship with God in faith. The Bible becomes in fullest actuality the word of God when it is being read in a spirit of faith.

The same combination of word and deed already noted in the original communication of revelation is characteristic of its further transmission. The Prophets often preach by dramatic actions (e.g., ch. 20 of Isaiah; ch. 27 of Jeremiah; Hos 1.2–9). So too, in the Church the Christian revelation is transmitted not only by spoken and written sentences but by the liturgy and by the whole conduct of Christians, which reflects the teaching of Christ and visibly incarnates His grace at definite points of space and time.

Stages of revelation. The Judeo-Christian revelation was given progressively in the course of centuries. St. Thomas distinguishes three great periods of sacred history—before the Mosaic law, under the law, and under grace; these he connects with the great revelations made respectively to ABRAHAM, MOSES, and the Apostles (*Summa Theologiae* 2a2ae, 174.6). The revelation was from its inception public; it was addressed not simply to individuals but to a whole people. The Israelite revelation in the Old Testament period was particular, being directed to a single nation, rather than, like Christianity, to all mankind. Moreover, it was preparatory for it pointed forward to a later fulfillment. From a Christian point of view, the Old Testament revelation appears as totally ordered toward Christ and the Church by way of type and prophecy. Christ Himself is depicted in the New Testament in terms borrowed from the Old Testament. He is the second Adam, the new Moses, the SON OF DAVID, the MESSIAH, the Servant (*see* SUFFERING SERVANT, SONGS OF THE), SON OF MAN, SON OF GOD. Jesus Himself declares that the great personages of the Old Testament looked forward to His coming (Mt 13.16–17; Jn 5.45; 8.56).

Vatican II stated that Christ is "the Mediator and at the same time the fullness of all revelation" (DV 2). This full revelation is present in Christ not only objectively but subjectively. Revelation should not be thought of as merely objective, existing outside of human minds. At its most perfect, it exists in the human intellect of Christ, which grasps the divine as fully as a finite mind can grasp it. Because Jesus as man was totally receptive to God's word and perfectly faithful to His vocation as witness, He gave supreme expression to God's message for mankind. And this He did by both words and deeds. "Because Christ Himself is the Word of God, the very deed of the Word is a word to us" [Augustine, *In evang. Ioh.* 24.2 (*Corpus Christianorum. Series latina* 36:244)].

Through the teaching and life of Christ—including His Passion and glorification—God communicates in an unsurpassable way His message of pardon and reconciliation, manifesting His eternal attributes and freely chosen attitudes toward man. When it is said that the DEPOSIT of faith was closed with the Apostles, this does not have the merely negative meaning that God decides to say nothing more. It has a positive aspect inasmuch as God has so completely expressed Himself in the Christ-event that any real addition would be superfluous. Whatever comes later has no function except to illumine the meaning of what Christ said and did and was.

Although Christians await no further public revelation within history (Vatican II, DV 4), much remains to be done by way of clarification. To penetrate more deeply the meaning of the deposit is the ceaseless task of theologians and of the Church (cf. H. Denzinger, *Enchiridion symbolorum* [32d ed. Freiburg 1963] 3020, quoting St. Vincent of Lerins). But since mystery is the very heart of revelation, theological understanding does not aim to remove the essential obscurity of faith or render the revealed datum evident to reason (*see* DOGMATIC THEOLOGY). So long as man remains on earth, he must be content to walk by faith, reverently inclining his mind and will before the Word of God. At the end of time, faith will issue into vision, and the revelation will be clearly perceived by the help of the LIGHT OF GLORY.

Contents of revelation. The contents are described by Vatican I as "God Himself and the eternal decrees of His will" (*ibid.* 3004). Vatican II teaches that "God chose to reveal Himself and to make known to us the hidden purpose of His will" (DV 2). The mighty deeds of God are the central theme of the confessions of faith found in the Old Testament (e.g., ch. 7 and 26 of Deuteronomy) and in the earliest Christian preaching (e.g., ch. 2 and 10 of Acts). The focal message of the Old Testament is the liberation of Israel from the slavery of Egypt through Moses; that of the New Testament, the deliverance of mankind from the death of sin through Jesus Christ. In the course of centuries, this "recital theology" was gradually supplemented by more abstract, ontological formulas, as needed to settle questions that came up at a later stage of reflection. The successive creeds and dogmatic declarations of the Church exhibit this trend. The intelligible content of the Church's dogmas, according to the Catholic view, is not an addition to revelation, but is an authentic aspect of the revealed datum itself (cf. *ibid.* 3011).

In the final analysis, one believes in neither the salvific events nor the doctrines for their own sake, but in God who manifests Himself through these. The primary object of revelation is God Himself in His gracious approach to man. Because revelation includes this element of divine encounter, it can never be fully contained in dogmatic propositions (cf. *ibid.* 3886). Thanks to his faith-relationship to the Light of the World (Jn 8.12), the Christian is inwardly renewed in his mind (Rom 12.2).

Church and revelation. The Apostles hold a unique status in SALVATION HISTORY by reason of their immediate contact with the Incarnate Word (1 Jn 1.1) and their Pentecostal experience. The post-apostolic Church receives revelation dependently on them, through Scripture and tradition. The Church is commissioned to preserve, defend, and interpret the contents of faith, adapting the presentation to the capacities and needs of successive ages. As this process continues, the implicit contents of the deposit are progressively unfolded. The explicitation is not a mere matter of logical deduction from the primitive formulas. Thanks to the Spirit of Christ that animates it, the Church enjoys a kind of "connaturality" with the revealing God and a privileged insight into His word. In proclaiming dogmas, the Church therefore speaks with prophetic authority (*see* DOCTRINE, DEVELOPMENT OF).

Revelation outside the Church. Judaism continues to profess the revelation given under the Old Testament. Islam accepts certain elements from Judaism and Christianity. Non-Catholic Christian communities retain and teach large portions of the Christian revelation and can, to that extent, communicate authentic revelation to their adherents. Through the inspirations of the Holy Spirit, who is operative among them, non-Catholic Christians can achieve valid insights into the Gospel and in this way contribute to the development of doctrine. Since the whole patrimony of Christ, according to Catholic belief, was passed on to the Catholic Church, the presence of revealed truth in these other confessions is a bond between them and Catholicism (*see* Vatican II, *Decree on Ecumenism*, 2-3).

Can revelation be present in other religions, independently of any influence upon them of biblical religion? Formerly it was widely believed that elements of the primitive revelation made to Adam or Noah had been kept alive in these religions, but this theory, in the light of what is now known about the antiquity of man, has been largely abandoned (*see* REVELATION, PRIMITIVE). However, few would deny that God in some way reveals Himself to the unevangelized. Since supernatural faith is absolutely necessary for salvation, no other view seems fully compatible with God's universal salvific will. St. Paul seems to take it for granted that God has revealed Himself to the pagans of Paul's time (Acts 14.16; Rom 1.19–20; 2.14–15). And St. Thomas, as is well known, maintained that every man can make an act of justifying faith when he reaches moral maturity (cf. *Summa*

Theologiae 1a2ae, 89.6). It is therefore probable that the non-Judaic religions embody certain reflections of a supernatural experience of God. Vatican II, in its *Declaration on Non-Christian Religions,* speaks of them as being based on a certain perception of the divine (NA 2). Unlike the biblical revelation, these religious expressions are not protected against serious distortion. But thanks to the elements of truth they contain, the non-biblical religions may be providential channels of grace for those who have had no opportunity to hear an accurate and persuasive presentation of the gospel.

Private revelation. Since it is the object of a separate article, private revelation requires only a brief mention here to point out how it differs from the public revelation of which we have been speaking (*see* REVELATIONS, PRIVATE). Whatever God has communicated since apostolic times to privileged souls can add nothing to the deposit of Christian faith. Private revelations of this character may be granted for the personal good of individuals and also to stir up among Christians a more faithful adherence to the gospel. St. Thomas holds that prophetic revelation, insofar as it is ordered to doctrine, ceased with the Apostles, but that such revelation, insofar as it is directive of human action, will always continue (*Summa Theologiae* 2a2ae, 174.6 ad 3). In view of the dangers of delusion, fraud, exaggeration, and the like, reports of private revelations should be treated with caution. The Church never teaches that their contents must be accepted on a motive of divine faith, but sometimes it certifies that they contain nothing contrary to sound faith and morals.

Demonstrability of revelation. As declared by Vatican I and by John Paul II in his encyclical *FIDES ET RATIO,* God has furnished sufficient external signs to render the assent of faith fully reasonable. Without being able to give apodictic proofs of the truth of Christianity, reason can prepare for, and support, the decision of faith. Philosophy can show that the idea of revelation contains no absurdity. Why should God not be able to communicate with man? Considering man's actual condition, as attested by human history and personal experience, a revelation would unquestionably be a great source of encouragement and guidance to man on his earthly pilgrimage; it seems entirely worthy of a beneficent God.

The philosophy of religion can specify to some extent the form that a divine revelation might be expected to take. God would undoubtedly accommodate His revelation to man's nature; He would speak so that man could hear. But man is by nature a historical and social being. He fulfills himself through free personal actions unfolding in time, interrogating the experience of his contemporaries and forbears. It seems likely, therefore, that God would communicate to man in a social and historical manner—through spatio-temporal symbols (words) given and transmitted in history. The religious inquirer, therefore, should turn to history to look for signs of whether God has spoken.

Apologetics can carry the investigation a stage further. It can assess the value of the various signs of credibility and exhibit the prudence of believing. But in view of the complexity of the evidences, the astounding and mysterious contents of the Christian message, and the heavy demands that it makes on fallen nature, apologetics will hardly be able to bring a man to the point of professing Christianity. The firm assent of salutary faith does not directly result from the arguments of credibility but from the grace of God.

See Also: SYMBOL IN REVELATION; REVELATION, CONCEPT OF (IN THE BIBLE); FAITH AND REASON; MIRACLES (IN THE BIBLE); MIRACLES (THEOLOGY OF); REVELATION, VIRTUAL.

Bibliography: Catholic Literature. R. LATOURELLE, *Theology of Revelation* (Staten Island, N.Y. 1966). E. SCHILLEBEECKX, *Revelation and Theology,* 2 v. (New York 1967–1968). K. RAHNER, *Hearers of the Word* (New York 1969). A DULLES, *Revelation Theology: A History* (New York 1969); *Models of Revelation* (Garden City, N.Y. 1983). A. SHORTER, *Revelation and Its Interpretation* (London 1983). H. DE LUBAC, *La Révélation divine* (Paris 1983). Protestant Literature. J. BAILLIE, *The Idea of Revelation in Recent Thought* (New York 1956). H. D. MCDONALD, *Ideas of Revelation: An Historical Study, A.D. 1700 to A.D. 1860* (London 1959); *Theories of Revelation: An Historical Study, 1860–1960* (London 1963). H. R. NIEBUHR, *The Meaning of Revelation* (New York 1941). H. E. BRUNNER, *Revelation and Reason,* tr. O. WYON (Philadelphia 1946). P. TILLICH, *Systematic Theology,* 3 v. (Chicago 1951–63) v. 1. W. PANNENBERG et al., *Revelation as History* (New York 1968). G. FACKRE, *The Doctrine of Revelation* (Edinburgh 1997).

[A. DULLES]

REVELATION, VIRTUAL

Truths of FAITH and morals that are not formally revealed either explicitly or implicitly but that are necessary to guard and to explain the deposit of revealed truth. Although distinct from the truths of the revealed deposit, they are said to be "revealed" because they possess an objective connection with revealed truth. The magisterium determines the extent of the connection and indicates it by the solemnity with which it proposes the truth, e.g., by papal bull, or by the censure attached to its denial, e.g., excommunication.

Revelation is "virtual" because deduced from formally revealed truths of faith and morals by means of a naturally known proposition in virtue of some relationship of causality or fittingness: e.g., the Church, in order to guard the supernaturality of revelation, has defined that faith gives a different and higher knowledge of God than does natural science (H. Denzinger, *Enchiridion symbolorum*, ed. A. Schönmetzer, 3015). Also, a revealed proposition may be applied to a particular fact: e.g., Saint Peter has successors who possess supreme teaching authority in the Church, and Pius XII was such a successor with this authority.

The Church has traditionally taught, and consistently practiced doctrinal intervention in defining, truths of faith and morals that are not directly and formally revealed but that are necessary for the integrity of the Christian message. Especially does it condemn errors that imperil revealed truth, and it declares as true those facts and truths that are connected with the preserving and explaining of Christian DOGMA. Nicaea I (325) declared that a heretic could be the minister of valid Baptism (*Enchiridion symbolorum* 127), while Pius XII defined the matter and form for Holy Orders (*Enchiridion symbolorum* 3859). Many truths have been defined that do not pertain directly and immediately to the DEPOSIT OF FAITH. They are propositions that express a concept not formally and immediately contained in the terms of a revealed proposition but that the Church expects its members to accept on divine faith. In this sense they are conceptually and propositionally distinct from the revealed deposit. This is possible because revelation contains mysteries that the intellect cannot fully comprehend. Since the time of the Apostles there has been no new public revelation; it is "closed," yet the revealed mysteries are "open" to a deeper understanding and avoidance of misunderstanding. Pius XII did not "reveal" anything by determining the matter and form of Orders, but he did determine for the future what part of the ceremony would essentially constitute the Sacrament.

Saint Thomas Aquinas, one of the first to do so, distinguished a double object of faith (*Summa theologiae* 1a, 32.4; 2a2ae, 11.2.): one composed of truths directly and principally believed, e.g., articles of the Apostles' Creed, the other composed of truths indirectly and secondarily believed insofar as their denial would lead to a denial of a revealed truth, e.g., faith gives a higher knowledge of God than does natural science. Sixteenth- and seventeenth-century theologians such as D. Báñez, Gregory of Valencia, and J. de Lugo applied this distinction to the magisterium, later theologians adopted it, and ecclesiastical documents expressed it, e.g., Syllabus of Errors of Pius IX (Dec. 8, 1864). Present-day theologians distinguish formally revealed truth, i.e., directly and immediately revealed, from that which is virtually revealed, i.e., indirectly and mediately. Modern emphasis on development of dogma has necessitated a greater precision in terms to clarify the limits of formally revealed truth.

Divisions. Virtual revelation is divided according to its connection with revealed truth, a relationship of either necessity or fittingness.

Necessity. Certain truths or facts are connected to formal revelation by a relationship of absolute necessity insofar as they are needed to preserve its very sources, e.g., the determination of the canon of Scripture. Others are connected by moral necessity insofar as they are needed for the Church to attain its primary end of guarding and explaining the deposit of faith, e.g., the condemnation of J. Hus's error that neither Peter nor his successors are head of the Church (*Enchiridion symbolorum* 1207, 1210). It includes: the condemnation of statements directly or indirectly contrary to revealed truth, and contingent facts that happened after the close of revelation but that are necessary to guard or explain the truths of faith and morals as particular applications of a universal revealed proposition, e.g., Pius XII was truly Pope.

Fittingness. Other truths and facts are not directly connected to revelation, yet to reason illuminated by faith they appear connected with eminent fittingness, e.g., the theological conclusion that the human soul of Christ always enjoyed the beatific vision. The pope, using his full authority as head of the Church, may approve them as matters of faith, morals, or worship that are suitable for leading souls to the truth and holiness of God, or he may condemn propositions contrary to them. His authority guarantees infallible safety to these pronouncements, though not infallible truth. So Pius XII denounced the hypothesis of polygenism as applied to man's origin, since it is not apparent how it can be reconciled with the Church's teaching on original sin and hence cannot safely be held by Catholics (*Enchiridion symbolorum* 3897). This is the secondary teaching message of the Church, and the truths pertain more remotely to virtual revelation. They are accepted on ecclesiastical, or mediate, faith.

Some truths are even further removed from direct connection with the deposit of faith, e.g., various problems of the moral life of spouses, rights and obligations of workers and employers, peace among nations. In teaching such truths the pope may not intend to apply the full force of his prudential authority in a universal manner, and then such truths are not proposed infallibly nor are they a part of virtual revelation.

Opinions. Are the truths connected to formal revelation by a relationship of absolute necessity an intrinsic part of the revealed deposit or annexed to it from outside, i.e., are they really part of formal or of virtual revelation? The Church has irrevocably and infallibly declared the truth of these propositions and expects its members to accept them on faith. It has not declared that they are revealed but leaves it to the theologians to determine just how these truths may be connected to the revealed deposit. There are three principal opinions. (1) All truths that have been infallibly and irrevocably declared as true are, and always have been, a part of the formally revealed deposit, as the implicit is contained in the explicit. It suffices to analyze the extension of the subject or the comprehension of the predicate of the revealed proposition. Hence, all truths defined irrevocably and infallibly are an intrinsic part of the revealed deposit and demand divine faith, e.g., the necessity of confessing all mortal sins committed after Baptism; Vatican Council I was an ecumenical council (C. Vollert). (2) Truths infallibly and irrevocably declared by the Church may be a part of virtual revelation insofar as they have an intrinsic connection with the formally revealed deposit, but are conceptually distinct from it and are obtained by means of some other naturally known truth, e.g., Christ, as true God and true man, had two wills (*Enchiridion symbolorum* 500). It is accepted on divine faith and may be declared as revealed by the Church (F. Marín-Sola). This also applies to an individual under a universal revealed proposition, e.g., Christ died to save all men, therefore He died to save me (C. Journet, K. Rahner). (3) A third position differs from the second by expressing the connection between formal and virtual as one that is necessary for the proper preserving and explaining of revealed truth, rather than as an intrinsic one: e.g., determination of the canon of Scripture, determination of the matter and form of Orders, solemn canonization of saints. Nor may the Church declare such truths to be revealed, though it may and does oblige its members to accept them on divine, or theological, faith (L. Ciappi).

Conclusion. Virtual revelation is distinct from formal revelation. Both dogmatic facts and theological conclusions pertain to virtual revelation and may be defined as infallibly true on divine faith, infallibly safe to follow on ecclesiastical faith, or recommended as fitting.

See Also: REVELATION, THEOLOGY OF; DOCTRINE, DEVELOPMENT OF.

Bibliography: E. DUBLANCHY, ''Dogme,'' *Dictionnaire de théologie catholique,* ed. A. VACANT et al., 15 v. (Paris 1903–50) 4.2:1639–47; ''Église,'' *ibid.* 2199–2200. C. JOURNET, *The Church of the Word Incarnate,* v.1, tr. A. H. C. DOWNES (New York 1955) 338–53. B. J. F. LONERGAN, *Divinarum personarum conceptionem analogicam* (Rome 1959) 28–51. F. MARÍN-SOLA, *L'Évolution homogène du dogme catholique,* 2 v. (2d ed. Fribourg 1924) v.1. K. RAHNER, ''The Development of Dogma,'' *Theological Investigations,* tr. C. ERNST, v.1 (Baltimore 1961) 39–77. R. RICHARD, ''Rahner's Theory of Doctrinal Development,'' *Catholic Theological Society of America. Proceedings,* 18 (New York 1963) 157–89. C. VOLLERT, ''Doctrinal Development,'' *ibid.* 12 (1957) 45–74.

[A. E. GREEN]

REVELATIONS, PRIVATE

Besides the public revelation that was completed at the death of the last Apostle and that gave to the Church the deposit of faith, there were in the course of Christianity private revelations. Their meaning and their role in the life of the Church can be understood from their history and theology.

History. The Prophets of the Old Testament generally exercised a public function and a permanent ministry as Yahweh's spokesmen for the public evelation. There is little evidence of private revelations in the Old Testament, though there may have been instances among the groups of Prophets mentioned, e.g., in 1 Samuel 10.10–13. In the New Testament, even during the lifetime of the Apostles, Saint Paul testifies that there were in the nascent Church CHARISMS, which are more or less extraordinary gifts of grace granted for the common good of all to persons with no official function in the Church (1 Cor 12.7–11; 28–30; Rom 12.6–8; Eph 4.11–13). Among these gifts is mentioned that of prophecy, or of speaking in the name of God (1 Cor 12.10; Rom 12.6; Eph 4.11). Those receiving such a gift were inspired preachers and may be considered bearers of a revelation in the proper sense of the term. This is what is now called private revelations.

In post-Apostolic times also there is evidence for the existence of such Prophets, (e.g., in *Didache* 15.1 or in the *Pastor of Hermas* 11.7). The visions in the *Pastor* bear witness to the belief of the early Church in such revelations. Overconfidence in these charisms led, in the 2d century, to the formation of the Montanist sect, which advocated the guidance of the Paraclete (and this included so-called private revelations) in preference to the direction of the Church authorities. TERTULLIAN is a well-known example of the type of deviation that was to recur periodically in the shape of illuminist movements, for example, the Alumbrados in Spain (16th and 17th centuries) and the Illuminati of Bavaria (18th century). (*See* ILLUMINISM.) Even apart from these extremes, tension in relations between the hierarchy and the charismatics is a feature not only of early Church history but, in varying degrees, of all times.

The Church was never for long without saints or holy persons who received from God authentic private revelations. In medieval times there were great mystics like Saint HILDEGARDE (d. 1179), Saint GERTRUDE THE GREAT (d. 1301), and Saint BRIDGET OF SWEDEN (d. 1373), who wrote books of revelations. More spectacular, in a way, were those persons called by private revelation to a mission in the Church, such as Saint CATHERINE OF SIENA (d. 1380) who brought about the return of Pope Gregory X from Avignon to Rome. Others commissioned by private revelation to work for the erection of a liturgical feast were Blessed Juliana of Cornilion (d. 1258) for the feast of Corpus Christi, and Saint Margaret Mary AL-ACOQUE (d. 1690) for the Feast of the Sacred Heart. In another class of private revelations, also generally involving a mission, are the modern Marian apparitions, among which Lourdes and Fatima are best known. There are also the ''revelations'' of the mystics and saints, often unconnected with any visible mission but providing spiritual guidance for the Church, such as the two Carmelite mystics, Saint Teresa of Avila and Saint JOHN OF THE CROSS.

An important fact in ecclesiastical history, easily explained by the possible and actual harm connected with questionable revelations, is the control that the Church authorities have tried to exercise over these charismatic phenomena. In medieval times, the writings of many persons favored with visions and revelations were approved by Church authorities. In modern times the hierarchy gave its approval to some well-known private revelations such as those concerning the Miraculous Medal (1830), La Salette (1846), Lourdes (1858), and Fatima (1917). That approval is sometimes withheld. In a series of 22 Marian apparitions between the years 1931 and 1950, only two were approved (Beauraing and Banneux, Belgium), six remained undecided, and the remaining 14 were rejected [*Clergy Monthly* 17 (1952) 271–72]. There have been cases of wholesale fraud and pathological self-delusion. Examples of this are Miguel de MOLINOS, Madame GUYON, the Illuminati and Alumbrados, and Mère Marie Yvonne [d. 1951; see *Études* 307 (1960) 106–07]. Moreover, even in the case of genuine private revelations, it often happens that in the writings relating them, truth and error so blend that the discrimination between authentic and spurious elements becomes difficult. Augustin POULAIN, in *Graces of Interior Prayer,* examines 32 cases of saints and mystics in whose authentic revelations, approved by the Church, human error and illusion are mixed; and he includes such saints as Catherine of Siena, Gertrude, and VINCENT FERRER. Moreover, there are, in the writings of genuine charismatics, besides the divine message, particulars of time and place that do not belong to the message but were added by the writers. They themselves are generally unable to make a distinction between the divine and the human element.

Theology. The existence of authentic private revelations is, from the facts of history and the Church's approval, beyond doubt. The number of spurious revelations, which may well be greater than that of the recorded authentic ones, does not disprove this. There were always private revelations among the charismatic graces that the Holy Spirit bestows on some members of the Church for the common good. These revelations are called private

not because they were intended only for the individual persons to whom they were granted (for every charismatic grace is ''communal''), but because they are not part of the public or official revelation. As for their nature, so far as they are ''revelations''—a formal communication from God infusing into the minds of the charismatics the supernatural knowledge that He wants them to transmit to the Church—the essence of private revelations does not differ from that of the public revelation. The same kind of divine inspiration or prophetic light, elevating the minds of the chosen persons and enabling them to perceive and know what is naturally above the power of their reason, is operative in the charism of prophecy, whether in private or in public revelations (see Thomas Aquinas, *Summa theologiae* 2a2ae 171.1–2). The difference between the two lies elsewhere.

Role in the Church. Private revelations have no bearing on the deposit of faith. They do not, theologians are agreed, contain new doctrine for belief by divine and Catholic faith (*see* FAITH). When it is further asked: Can and must these revelations be believed privately by divine faith? the answer is generally: Only those to whom these revelations are addressed can, and when they have sufficient certainty of the facts, must give an assent of divine faith. As for other people who come to know the revelations from the charismatics, the more common opinion is that they are not obliged and are not able to believe them by divine faith. This opinion was challenged by Karl Rahner, on the ground that no greater guarantee can be required for divine faith in private revelations than for faith in the public revelation: in both cases the moral certainty of the fact is sufficient. The question is perhaps more academic than practical, considering the specific purpose of private revelations. Though they are not meant to present new doctrines, private revelations do play a positive role in the life of the Church. They are a part of the normal, if more or less extraordinary, guidance of the Church by the Spirit of Christ, not unlike that which the same Spirit provides through the inspirations of grace for the life of individual Christians. Their purpose is to point out and to urge a practical manner of applying, in the particular circumstances of the changing times, some one or other teaching of faith or morals. Rahner explains that while the public revelation is meant to teach a doctrine expressed in a statement, private revelations transmit a command. The first is to be believed, the second to be done. This is evident, for example, from the revelations of the Sacred Heart to Saint Margaret Mary that led to the establishment of the feast, or from the Lourdes apparitions that introduced the pilgrimages to that shrine.

Attitude of the Church. The Church's attitude toward private revelations confirms this view. Her great caution, not to say diffidence, in the face of new and extraordinary phenomena, is well known; and it is justified by the all-too-frequent error, illusion, and even fraud that steal into them. But the Church does believe that there are genuine private revelations. If after due examination she is satisfied that the facts are trustworthy and the probability of error or fraud is excluded, she gives her official approval. This, however, does not entail any obligation for the faithful; nor is it a direct invitation to believe these revelations. It does not guarantee the truth of the facts but ''means nothing more than the permission to publish [these divine communications] after due examination, for the instruction and spiritual benefit of the faithful. . . . These revelations demand an assent of human belief according to the rules of prudence, when these rules present them as probable and devoutly believable'' (Benedict XIV). Accordingly, theologians conclude, the Church's approval implies that the revelations considered contain nothing contrary to the faith and to morality, that they may be made known in publications, and that the faithful are given permission to believe them with caution.

There is, however, a more positive side to this approval. The very fact that the approval is given after careful examination by experts in such matters is a guarantee that humanly speaking there is sufficient reason for a prudent assent. There is no rashness in so believing. Yet, even then it is well to remember that the reports on the revelations may contain, beside the genuine divine message, inaccuracies and misinterpretations; the Church's approval does not guarantee the truth of every detail.

The Church goes beyond mere approval; she also takes account of private revelations in her pastoral guidance of the faithful and in her liturgy. This is only natural. Charismatic graces such as private revelations are a normal manifestation of the presence of the Spirit of Christ in the Mystical Body and of His continued guidance of the Church. Naturally they are adapted to the varying needs of the Church. Without bringing anything new to the Catholic faith, they draw attention to what in the faith is likely to meet the particular needs of the times. Thus the Church instituted the liturgical Feasts of the Sacred Heart of Jesus and of the Immaculate Heart of Mary at the prompting of private revelations. These revelations, nonetheless, were only a secondary motivation of the Church's action. The doctrinal foundations of the new devotions are found not in the new, but in the ancient public revelation. Pius XII made this clear as regards the devotion to the Sacred Heart, in his encyclical *Haurietis aquas* (May 15, 1956).

Attitude of the Faithful. The theology of private revelations and of the Church's approval provides clear pastoral guidance for the faithful. Their attitude should be the same as that of the Church. First, it should be one

of caution, of awareness that illusion and error easily enter into the writings of even genuine and approved mystics and saints. To sift the wheat from the chaff is a delicate task better left to experts in the theology and psychology of mystics. When reading books of revelations or reports on visions and apparitions, the wise rule is not to draw on them for spiritual guidance, unless it be something the Church has approved and teaches independently of them. What is singular and not in keeping with the common teaching of spiritual and theological writers must inspire caution and distrust, as also what tends to satisfy unnecessary curiosity. One should beware of overeagerness for extraordinary facts. A craving for the marvelous and the sensational is not in keeping with the mind of the Church. It exposes one to the danger of not heeding her decisions in these matters, although she has the right and the duty to judge of their nature and truth. Such eagerness for the marvelous must not be mistaken for a sign of a true Catholic sense, which lies in following the Church's official guidance. Nor is there any need for one to desire these charismatic graces for himself. Private revelations of themselves do not sanctify those who receive them; they are meant for the common good of the Church and are no sure sign of personal holiness. A desire for private revelations is generally unhealthy and, as history shows, leads to pitiful or disastrous deviations. But when private revelations have been recognized as authentic by the Church and have proved their genuineness in the fruits for the spiritual life of her members, then it is right, after her example, to heed their message and to learn the practical lesson that the Spirit of Christ teaches through them. Not to do so would be to neglect a grace given for the spiritual good of the members of the Church. However, even while accepting them we should keep a discriminating mind, subordinating these directives to the teaching of the deposit of faith proposed by the Church. This is and remains the doctrinal foundation of Catholic life and spirituality. ''Guided by the Magisterium of the Church, the *sensus fidelium* knows how to discern and welcome in these revelations whatever constitutes an authentic call of Christ or his saints to the Church'' (*CCC* 67).

See Also: REVELATION, THEOLOGY OF; FAITH; MYSTICAL PHENOMENA.

Bibliography: BENEDICT XIV, *De servorum Dei beatificatione et beatorum canonizatione*, v.1–7 of *Opera omnia*, 17 v. in 20 (new ed. Prato 1839–43) 2:32; 3:53. A. F. POULAIN, *The Graces of Interior Prayer*, tr. L. L. YORKE SMITH (10th French ed. St. Louis 1950) 299–399. GABRIELE DI SANTA MARIA MADDALENA, *Visions and Revelations in the Spiritual Life*, tr. by a Benedictine of Stanbrook Abbey (Westminster, Md. 1950). K. RAHNER ''Les Révélations privées,'' *Revue d'ascétique et de mystique* 25 (1949) 506–14; *Visionen und Prophezeiungen* (2d ed. enl. Quaestiones disputatae 4; Freiburg 1958). L. LOCHET, *Apparitions of Our Lady: Their Place* *in the Life of the Church,* tr. J. BOYLE (New York 1960). H. HOL-STEIN, ''Les Apparitions mariales,'' *Maria* 5 (1958) 755–78. P. DE LETTER, ''The Meaning of Lourdes,'' *Clergy Monthly* 22 (1958) 3–16.

[P. DE LETTER/EDS.]

REVERENCE (OBSERVANTIA)

A term used here, not in its general meaning, but as a somewhat less than satisfactory translation of the Latin *observantia* of Catholic moral theologians. It is the proper name of the virtue inclining a man to satisfy his obligation of RESPECT and submission toward those superior to himself in dignity and authority. It is like piety, which disposes one to render the debt of reverence and submission to his parents, except that the persons revered by this virtue are those endowed with an official dignity and authority. A person in a position of authority in the state, for example, shares according to the measure of his office in the excellence and principality of the state itself, and on account of this, respect and, when he commands within the limits of his authority, submission are due to him— respect because of his official position and dignity; submission because of his authority.

Observantia is closely associated with OBEDIENCE, but differs from it in being concerned more with securing a general attitude of submission, while obedience has for its object the execution of specific commands. It is also associated with the virtue of respect (*DULIA*), differing from it in requiring the tribute of respect for the specific excellence of authority, while *dulia* pays respect to any excellence or superiority.

As is the case with other moral virtues, failure by way of either defect or excess is possible. Defect consists in the withholding of due respect or submission; excess, in their exaggeration.

Bibliography: THOMAS AQUINAS, *Summa theologiae* 2a2ae, 102.

[W. HERBST]

REVISIONIST THEOLOGY

In the broadest sense, ''revisionist theology'' refers to such recent theological movements as process theism and various forms of political and LIBERATION THEOLOGY (i.e., feminist, black and Third World as well as the work of other individual theologians. What is characteristic of and common to such diverse forms of theological reflection is their attempt to reformulate from various critical perspectives the meaning and truth-claims of the Christian tradition's central theological and Christological affirmations.

In the narrowest sense, revisionist theology refers to a specific formal model of the method of fundamental theology. The term itself was first put forward by David Tracy in *Blessed Rage For Order* and this text remains the primary source for the most refined and detailed exposition of the model. For Tracy, a revisionist fundamental Christian theology is best described as philosophical reflection on the meanings present in common human experience and those present in the Christian tradition. The broad and the narrow senses of the term are not unrelated. Revisionist theology as a formal model of theological method is characterized by a specific understanding of the web of commitments which define the standpoint of the individual theologian's approach to the Christian faith. This methodological commitment at the level of fundamental theology finds its embodiment in the sphere of systematic theology, and to a greater or lesser extent, in the theological movements noted above.

For revisionist theology the primary commitment of the Christian theologian as theologian is to the community of scholarly inquiry and its respective canons of inquiry (i.e., philosophical, historical, literary-critical, ideological-critical, etc.) and the morality of critical inquiry: a resolve to defend methodological canons in a public manner, to assert only that for which warrants are provided, and a willingness to follow the evidence wherever it may lead in the spirit of open inquiry. The theologian's primary loyalty to the tradition as Christian theologian lies in a commitment to the investigation of the present meaning and defensibility of the truth-claims of that tradition.

Critical Corrective. This understanding of the task of the theologian is aptly called revisionist because it represents a critical corrective to the dominant neo–orthodox understanding of the task of theology described by Paul Tillich through the ''method of correlation.'' According to Tillich, the task of the theologian is to show that the Christian message contains answers to the questions implied in the human situation. The revisionist maintains that such a correlation is insufficiently critical—indeed, it is simply a juxtaposition—as it derives the questions for theology from one source (the human situation) and its answers from another (the Christian message) and does not allow for a correlation and interplay of the principal questions *and* answers of each source.

In this criticism revisionist theology reaffirms the commitment to the principal values, cognitive claims, and existential faiths of classic liberal theologies. Yet revisionist theology affirms these through the correctives of post-liberal neo-orthodox and radical theologies. Revisionist theology self-consciously acknowledges first, the naiveté and optimism of liberal theology regarding the reconciliation of Christian faith and modern culture. Second, it accepts the description of the cognitive, ethical, and social ambiguity of the contemporary world as articulated by both neo–orthodoxy and post-Enlightemnent schools of secular thought. Third, given the criticism of the method of correlation, revisionist theology remains disenchanted with the final neo–orthodox defense of theism through a retrieval of God as the "Wholly Other." The revisionist therefore accepts the criticisms—which is not to say the conclusions—of a radical theology which rejects orthodox, liberal and neo–orthodox defenses of theism as incompatible with the affirmation of an authentic, illusionless secularity. Fourth, it seeks to preserve within theological reflection the polyvalent nature of the dominant symbols of Christian faith along with an acknowledgement of the hermeneutical and social conditions of all human understanding. Revisionist theology is thus defined by its commitment to the articulation and critical correlation of both a reinterpreted post-modern consciousness which recognizes the antinomies of the Enlightenment and a reinterpreted Christianity which recognizes the crisis of the meaningfulness of Christian faith today.

In the execution of this task, revisionist theologians have especially relied upon the resources of the process thought of Whitehead and Hartshorne, hermeneutical theory, deconstructive structuralism and various schools of ideology–critique in an attempt to formulate a reconciliation and critical correction of both modernity and the Christian tradition.

See Also: DECONSTRUCTIONISM.

Bibliography: D. TRACY, *Blessed Rage For Order* (New York 1975); *The Analogical Imagination* (New York 1981); *Plurality and Ambiguity* (San Francisco 1987). S. OGDEN, *The Reality of God* (New York 1966). V. A. HARVEY, *The Historian and the Believer* (New York 1966). G. KAUFMAN, *God the Problem* (Cambridge 1972). J. L. SEGUNDO, *The Liberation of Theology* (New York 1976). L. GILKEY, *Reaping the Whirlwind* (New York 1976). J. B. COBB and D. R. GRIFFITY, *Process Theology: An Introductory Exposition* (Philadelphia 1976). J. METZ, *Faith in History and Society* (New York 1980). R. R. REUTHER, *Sexism and God–Talk* (Boston 1983). E. S. FIORENZA, *Bread Not Stone* (Boston 1984). C. BOFF, *Theology and Praxis* (New York 1987).

[J. A. COLOMBO]

REVIVALISM

An approach to religion designed to stimulate interest by appealing principally to the emotions. It was a characteristic feature of 17th-century German PIETISM and 18th-century English Methodism (*see* WESLEY, CHARLES; WESLEY, JOHN; WHITEFIELD, GEORGE). This method of religious instruction was brought to colonial America, where Jonathan EDWARDS made religious emotion theologically and intellectually respectable during the GREAT AWAKENING. During the Second Awakening in the early years of the 19th century, revivalism grew to maturity.

The Second Awakening began as a Presbyterian movement, but eventually it was the METHODISTS and BAPTISTS who found its techniques appropriate to their goals and doctrines. Most characteristic of this movement were the camp meetings and the circuit riders. On the frontier, particularly in the West, people gathered from miles around to spend a few days coping with their religious problems and, incidentally, enjoying the rare opportunity of social life so lacking because of their isolation. The first planned camp meeting was held in Logan County, Ky., in July 1800 as the result of the activity of Rev. James McGready. Born of Scotch-Irish parents in Pennsylvania, McGready was licensed to preach in 1788, when he was about 30 years old. He moved to North Carolina, and then to Kentucky in 1798. Described by contemporaries as ugly and uncouth, he nevertheless attracted wide attention by his earnestness, zeal, and impassioned preaching. In 1824 revivalist Charles Grandison FINNEY began a notable 20-year preaching career in the area north of the Ohio and Potomac Rivers. Although ordained by the Presbyterians, he pursued his own way both theologically and otherwise.

The camp meeting generally took place in August or early fall at a cleared location in the forest. The participants came prepared to camp out for several days. The natural confusion of so many adults and children, along with the necessary animals, added to the effect of the impassioned preaching of the ministers and resulted in a scene of emotional chaos. The "falling exercise," in which the subject lost consciousness, was generally considered a clear manifestation of the power of God in the hearts of man. Other physical phenomena, of more questionable efficacy, were "the jerks," "the laughing exercise," "the barking exercise" in which the sinner treed the devil, and "the singing exercise." Despite the many abuses connected with these meetings and the ridicule they inspired, they nevertheless served as a social and religious outlet for the frontiersman. Camp meetings continued through the 19th century, but after the Civil War the locations generally became summer resorts or were used for sedate religious conferences. Supplementing the camp meetings was the effort of the circuit rider, who went anytime and anywhere sinners were in need of being saved. With their saddle bags stuffed with Bibles and tracts, these missionaries visited nearly every hovel on the frontier and were a key factor in the spread of the Methodist Church.

MAIN SQUARE OF THE DUCK CREEK METHODIST EPISCOPAL CHURCH CAMP MEETING, DURING SERVICE, NEAR CINCINNATI.

Preacher delivers sermon to the crowd in the main square of Duck Creek Methodist Episcopal church, near Cincinnati, Ohio.
(©CORBIS)

The great U.S. revival, which followed the financial panic of 1857, launched Dwight Lyman MOODY, the greatest of the professional revivalists, who worked under the Young Men's Christian Association during the Civil War. His major evangelistic career began immediately after the war, and included very successful tours of Great Britain as well as of the U.S. With the aid of his hymn leader, Ira David Sankey, Moody brought to the rapidly growing cities the revivalist methods of frontier religion. Leadership next passed to William Ashley (Billy) SUNDAY, a reformed baseball player with a great talent for dramatization. World War I was followed by a new type of revivalism, which featured physical as well as spiritual healing; no meeting was complete without its "miracles." At mid-20th century the leading revivalist was William Franklin (Billy) Graham (1918–), whose gigantic, organized cooperative meetings were designed to increase the membership of the local churches.

Bibliography: B. A. WEISBERGER, *They Gathered at the River* (Boston 1958). C. A. JOHNSON, *The Frontier Camp Meeting* (Dallas 1955). W. W. SWEET, *Revivalism in America* (New York 1944).

[E. R. VOLLMAR]

REVIVISCENCE, SACRAMENTAL

A validly administered Sacrament of the Church, if it is unproductive of grace because of some impediment or *obex* in the recipient, is said to revive when the obstacle is subsequently removed; that is, the Sacrament confers the grace by virtue of the initial validly administered rite. Reviviscence of sacramental power requires: that the obstacle be removed, for example, by sincere contrition; that the Sacrament have been validly administered; that the rite have left in the recipient some real effect; and that God will in His mercy that this be the sacramental action. This is the general teaching of theologians with respect to Baptism, Confirmation, Orders, Anointing of the Sick, and Matrimony. Some theologians extend the doctrine to the Eucharist and Penance.

The belief implicit in this teaching, that Sacraments confer some real effect other than grace, is derived from the early Church's practice of not repeating some Sacraments, notably Baptism and Orders, once validly administered. From this practice St. Augustine (d. 430) derived and developed his teaching of the sacramental character. His frequent assertions that although Sacraments received unworthily do not avail for salvation, yet do so immediately upon the recipient's repenting, are the clearest expression of reviviscence in the teaching of the Fathers of the Church.

With the renewal of interest in sacramentology in the Middle Ages, given impetus by disputes about simoniacal ordinations, the Church approved theologians' distinguishing in a Sacrament the external rite (*sacramentum tantum*), the symbolic reality (*sacramentum et res*), and the grace (*res tantum*). Some theologians think that the symbolic reality that the recipient receives as a real effect from a validly administered Sacrament causes the giving of grace after the obstacle has been removed; others speak of the real effect left in the soul as a disposition for grace; others, as an impression in the faculties of the soul; still others, as a modification of the baptismal character.

Theologians usually assign the symbolic reality, i.e., the character of Baptism, Confirmation, and Orders, and the *vinculum,* or interior sacramental bond, of Matrimony, as the cause of grace in reviviscence. They deduce the will of God from this, that if reviviscence were not His will, original sin could never be removed in one who receives Baptism validly, but unworthily. Moreover, the faithful would never receive the grace of those states of life into which Confirmation, Orders, and Matrimony admit them. Most theologians reason that the real effect of the Anointing of the Sick is a consecrating of the sick to God's mercy during a particular illness; and the ritual for conditional administration seems to confirm this opinion. Much less agreement exists among theologians as to whether the Eucharist and Penance also in some sense "revive."

Bibliography: B. LEEMING, *Principles of Sacramental Theology* (new ed. Westminster, Md. 1956). F. SOLÁ, "De sacramentis initiationis Christianae," *Sacrae Theologiae Summa* (*Biblioteca de autores cristianos* 4; 1953) 183–185. A. MICHEL, *Dictionnaire de théologie catholique*, ed. A. VACANT et al., (Paris 1903–50) 13.2:2618–19.

[P. L. HANLEY]

REVIVISCENCE OF MERIT

The question of the reviviscence of MERIT is really a question of the extent of God's forgiveness of sinners. Does God restore to a repentant sinner all the merit that had been acquired during previous years of faithful service or not? It is a question of condign merits, not of congruous, which may be likened to a gratuity given in consideration of service. Does God's mercy extend so far as to restore previously acquired merits, which had been lost through mortal sin? The question depends entirely upon the free will of God. How extensive is His forgiveness?

Restoration of Merit. The restoration of past merits together with the forgiveness of mortal sin has always been the unanimous and certain teaching of theologians.

A positive argument in favor of reviviscence is found in the Council of Trent (*Enchiridion symbolorum*, 1545, 1582), which declared that supernatural good works, performed in the state of grace, lead the just person who dies in the state of grace to eternal life. There is no requirement that sanctifying grace be never lost in the meanwhile.

Again there is the teaching of Pius XI, in his apostolic letter of May 29, 1924, *The Infinite Mercy of God*, which announced the Holy Year of 1925. In it he teaches: "For all who by doing penance carry out the salutary commands of the Apostolic See, during the great jubilee, regain and receive entirely the abundance of merits and gifts that they had lost by sin . . ." (*Enchiridion symbolorum*, 3670). This statement is certainly not restricted to the occasion of the jubilee.

The revival of merit thus seems to be well established by the Church. It does not regard God, offended by sin, as bearing any grudge against or being ungenerous to repentant sinners. But it is difficult to find any specific teaching on this precise point in Scripture. Ez 18.21 and 33.12, Gal 3.4, and Heb 6.9–10 are sometimes cited. But the words of Ezechiel are not about the recovery of merit lost by sin; the passages in Galatians and Hebrews refer to merit formerly acquired, but it is not clear that they refer to believing sinners. The Parable of the Prodigal Son (Lk 15.11–32), and various texts of the Fathers, speak of the restoration of goods lost by sin but not clearly of goods acquired by personal merit. It seems that, as often happens, Scripture and the Fathers have left no clear evidence; this evidence must come instead from other sources.

Evidently the question of the revival of merit depends on the free will of God; it can therefore be settled only by an authentic interpreter of that, such as the Church, clarifying the attitude of God toward forgiven sinners as He has revealed it. But once this has been done theological reason can show the reasonableness of the revival of merit. This was accomplished by St. Thomas (*Summa theologiae* 3a, 89.5), who developed the idea that merit lost by sin can revive, for the only obstacle to its revival is removed by repentance. The works that gave rise to it have passed, but they remain in the acceptance of God. Man's subsequent sin does not efface this acceptability but only impedes its execution for as long as the impediment to the revival of merit remains.

Measure of Restoration. The question of the measure of the restoration of merits, whether they be restored in whole or only in part, is a disputed one. Three opinions, which have been diversely described, are current among theologians and may be stated as follows. The first opinion holds that a sinner, newly justified, does not receive any essential reward beyond what is due to his disposition when repentant, but that the reward is now due both to his conversion and to his previous merit. The second opinion holds that merits revive not in their original fullness but only in a degree proportionate to one's disposition at the time of repentance. This proportion is computed differently by different theologians. The third opinion asserts that merits revive in their totality, so that a penitent, dying immediately after repentance, receives not only the reward proportionate to the actual disposition at the time of repentance but also all that was due in the past in previous states of grace.

When these three opinions are compared with one another, it seems that the first practically does away with the act of reviviscence, the second preserves it, but arbitrarily restricts it, while the third really does honor to the generosity of God and the completeness of His forgiveness. Such seems to be the generosity of a forgiving God.

See Also: GOOD WORKS; IMPUTATION OF JUSTICE AND MERIT; SALUTARY ACTS.

Bibliography: B. BERAZA, *De gratia Christi* (2d ed. Bilbao 1929). C. BOYER, *Tractatus de sacramento paenitentiae . . .* (Rome 1942). S. GONZÁLEZ, *Sacrae theologiae summa*, ed. FATHERS OF THE SOCIETY OF JESUS, PROFESSORS OF THE THEOLOGICAL FACULTIES IN SPAIN, 4 v. *Biblioteca de autores cristianos* (Madrid 1945) 3.3:347–352. L. LERCHER, *Institutiones theologiae dogmaticae* (5th ed. Barcelona 1951).

[F. L. SHEERIN]

REVOLUTION OF 1688 (ENGLAND)

The events of 1688–89, when William and Mary replaced James II on the English throne, produced a decisive shift in the relationship between monarch and parliament. Hitherto the latter had owed its existence to

Mary II (1662–1694), Queen of England, Ireland and Scotland. (Archive Photos)

the former; henceforth the obligation was reversed. William and Mary were granted the crown only after agreeing to conditions laid down in the DECLARATION OF RIGHTS, made statutory in the Bill of Rights and underlined by a remodeled coronation oath, pledging them to govern ''according to the Statutes in Parliament agreed on.'' These limitations sought to curb conduct such as that by which James II had undermined parliament's legislative power and the position of the established Church. These encroachments were added to personal grievances that prompted their victims to a more ardent opposition than they might otherwise have undertaken. James brought his downfall upon himself largely through his headlong drive for religious equality, heedless of the warnings of the Pope, the papal nuncio, Louis XIV, Cardinal Howard, and leading Catholic laymen.

James compelled many of those most disposed to be loyal to him, Anglican tories whose watchword was ''Church and King,'' to choose between their Church and their King; when they chose the former, his cause was lost. Many grievances, some unreasonable, some self–interested but some well founded, were awakened: distaste for a standing army and disquiet at its quota of Catholics, anger among the nobility over their loss of command of the militia, anxiety at inconvenient enquiries into the handling of recusancy revenues (which were ordered to be refunded), resentment at dismissal from administrative positions, and the subsequent appointment of Catholics and nonconformists. Many disapproved of James's attempt (by means of a questionnaire in the autumn of 1687) to make potential M.P.'s commit themselves on the question of penal law repeal; and indignation arose at the King's treatment of the universities (especially his imposition of a Catholic president and fellows upon Magdalen College, Oxford). In addition there was fury at the prosecution of seven Anglican bishops who refused to promulgate the second Declaration of Indulgence, granting religious toleration to Catholic and Protestant dissenters. James may have been aiming at general toleration and not at a Catholic despotism, but his methods lent themselves all too readily to the latter construction, particularly at a time when Irish massacres of Protestants, the "Popish Plot," and Louis XIV's revival of the persecution of Huguenots (culminating in the revocation of the Edict of Nantes in 1685) were in all men's minds. Such additional factors as the opening of Catholic chapels and schools, the wearing of religious garb by Catholic clergy, the preaching of a sermon at a court of assize by a Jesuit (at Hertford), the use of Bath Abbey for Catholic ceremonies, and the occasional anti–Protestant sermon intensified the impatience and suspicion with which James's rule was regarded and made for a general acceptance of the Revolution. It was not, however, until after the birth of an heir to the throne on June 10, 1688 (characteristically, James announced that the Pope was to be his godfather), that positive action was taken against the King. Hitherto, mounting indignation had been tempered by the knowledge that both his immediate successor, his elder daughter, Mary, and her sister Anne were devout Anglicans; the rule of the Catholic King was accepted as a temporary and probably short–lived aberration (by 1688 James had already attained the age at which his predecessor had died.) The prince's birth, however, augured a succession of Catholic monarchs.

On June 30, the day that the seven bishops were acquitted amid tumultuous rejoicing (in which the army, significantly, participated), seven men—neither representative nor, at that time, politically important—invited William of Orange to invade England to uphold the "religion, liberties and properties" of the people. On November 5, William landed in Devon; James marched westward to meet him, but defections among those he most trusted (e.g., John Churchill and Princess Anne) so disheartened him that he returned to London, sent the Queen and baby prince to France, and followed them on December 23. In the last months of 1688 anti-Catholic feeling showed itself in nationwide attacks on Catholics and on their property, and three of the four vicars apostolic and numerous priests were imprisoned.

Legislation of 1689 subjected Catholics to fines and imprisonment for refusing the oaths of allegiance and supremacy, expelled them from London, confined them to their dwelling places, authorized the search of their homes for weapons, and ordered the sale of papists' horses worth over £5. After the immediate crisis had passed, however, these laws were enforced only spasmodically and the same applied to the levying of the double land tax, imposed on Catholics in 1692. William III's claim that he came not to persecute Catholics but to protect Protestants, although only a minor motive (his principal purpose was to gain English support against Louis XIV) was, on the whole, borne out by events. Catholics were, nevertheless, subject to numerous political disabilities, which produced apostasies among the Catholic nobility and gentry during the ensuing century.

Bibliography: G. DAVIES, ed., *Bibliography of British History, Stuart Period, 1603–1714* (Oxford 1928). C. L. GROSE, *A Select Bibliography of British History, 1660–1760* (Chicago 1939). G. N. CLARK, *The Later Stuarts* (2d ed. Oxford 1955). D. OGG, *England into the Reigns of James II and William III* (Oxford 1955). J. P. KENYON, *The Stuarts* (London 1958), brilliant and perceptive; *The Nobility in the Revolution of 1688* (Kingston upon Hull, Eng. 1963); *Robert Spencer, Earl of Sunderland* (London 1958). F. C. TURNER, *James II* (New York 1948). M. P. ASHLEY, "Is there a Case for James II?" *History Today* 13 (1963) 347–352. L. PINKHAM, *William III and the Respectable Revolution* (Cambridge, Mass. 1954). G. M. STRAKA, *Anglican Reaction to the Revolution of 1688* (Madison 1962). D. C. DOUGLAS, ed., *English Historical Documents* (London 1953–) v. 8 *1660–1714*, ed. A. BROWNING. W. C. COSTIN and J. S. WATSON, comps., *The Law and Working of the Constitution: Documents,* 2 v. (London 1952) v.1 *1660–1783.* G. M. STRAKA, ed., *The Revolution of 1688. . . .* (Boston 1963). H. E. BELL and R. L. OLLARD, "King James II and the Revolution of 1688: Some Reflections on the Historiography," *Historical Essays, 1600–1750* (London 1964).

[J. A. WILLIAMS]

REX GLORIOSE MARTYRUM

The office hymn which was formerly sung at Lauds in the common office for several martyrs. The author is unknown, but Walpole thinks that this hymn, the *DEUS, TUORUM MILITUM,* and the *JESU, REDEMPTOR OMNIUM* are all by the same person because they are similar in language. They are written in iambic dimeter, yet with a strong accentual rhythm; this feature, and particularly the sophisticated use of rhyme, point to Celtic origin. The verses of each strophe are in rhyming couplets, the rhyme sometimes of two syllables, yet often inexact, a style characteristic of the 6th century. In the 1632 revision of the Roman BREVIARY, this hymn suffered several changes (six words). The hymn invokes Christ, the glorious king of martyrs, reward of confessors, who guides to eternal life those who despise the things of earth. He is asked to lend a kindly ear to our petitions as a reward for the celebration of the martyrs' triumph.

Bibliography: *Analecta hymnica* 51:128–129. A. S. WALPOLE, ed., *Early Latin Hymns* (Cambridge, Eng. 1922) 384–385. J. MEARNS, *Early Latin Hymnaries* (Cambridge, Eng. 1913) 75. F. J. E. RABY, *A History of Christian-Latin Poetry from the Beginnings to the Close of the Middle Ages* (Oxford 1953) 131–140. J. SZÖVÉR-FFY, *Die Annalen der lateinischen Hymnendichtung* (Berlin 1964–65) 1:214; 2:453. J. CONNELLY, *Hymns of the Roman Liturgy* (Westminster MD 1957) 148–149.

[A. J. KINNIREY]

REX SEMPITERNE CAELITUM

The office hymn that was historically prescribed for Matins at Easter time. This hymn is the *Rex aeterne domine* cited by BEDE as an example of rhythmical rather than metrical verse. He describes it as beautifully composed, with a resemblance to iambic verse. It seems to have been composed in the 5th or early 6th century, since it is prescribed by CAESARIUS OF ARLES and AURELIUS OF RÉOMÉ. Its rhythmical character and use of assonance and rhyme suggest Celtic origin. The hymn is part of a longer composition celebrating the whole redemptive work of Christ. From the 10th century, the first seven stanzas were taken to form an Easter hymn. The text of these stanzas underwent extensive revision in the 1632 revision of the Roman BREVIARY.

Bibliography: *Analecta hymnica* 51:5. BEDE, *De arte metrica* in *Grammatici latini*, ed. H. KEIL, 7 v. (Leipzig 1857–80) 7:258. S. G. PIMONT, *Les hymnes du bréviare romain*, 3 v. (Paris 1874–87) 3:93–100. J. JULIAN, ed., *A Dictionary of Hymnology* (New York 1957) 958. J. MEARNS, *Early Latin Hymnaries* (Cambridge, Eng. 1913). A. S. WALPOLE, ed., *Early Latin Hymns* (Cambridge, Eng. 1922) 211–217. C. S. BALDWIN, *Medieval Rhetoric and Poetic* (New York 1928) 107–118. F. J. E. RABY, *A History of Christian-Latin Poetry from the Close of the Middle Ages* (Oxford 1953) 131–140. J. CONNELLY, *Hymns of the Roman Liturgy* (Westminster, MD 1957) 92. J. SZÖVÉRFFY, *Die Annalen der lateinischen Hymnendichtung* (Berlin 1964–65) 2:453.

[A. J. KINNIREY]

REY, ANTHONY

Educator and chaplain in the Mexican War; b. Lyons, France, March 19, 1807; d. near Ceralvo, Mexico, Jan. 19, 1847. Although Rey had first prepared himself for a business career, he entered the Jesuit college of Fribourg, Switzerland, and in 1827 he joined the society. After his ordination, he taught at Fribourg and at Sion in Valais. In 1840 he was sent to the U.S. and appointed professor of metaphysics and ethics at Georgetown College, Washington, D.C. Three years later he was transferred to St. Joseph's Church, Philadelphia, Pa., and subsequently served as assistant to the Jesuit provincial of the Maryland province, pastor of Trinity Church in Georgetown, and vice president of Georgetown College (1845). During the Mexican War (1846–48), Rey was appointed a chaplain in the U.S. Army and assigned to serve on the staff of Gen. Zachary Taylor, where he frequently exposed himself to enemy fire in order to minister to the wounded and dying soldiers. After the successful siege at Monterrey, he preached to the rancheros of the area and, against the advice of experienced U.S. officers, set out on a mission to Matamoros. He was last known to have preached to a mixed Mexican-American congregation at Ceralvo. Within a few days of his sermon at Ceralvo, Rey's body was discovered, pierced with lances; it is conjectured that he was murdered by a band of guerrillas.

[J. Q. FELLER]

REYES SALAZAR, SABÁS, ST.

Martyr, priest; b. Dec. 5, *c.* 1879–83, at Cocula, Jalisco, Archdiocese of Guadalajara, Mexico; d. Apr. 13, 1927 (Wednesday of Holy Week), Tototlán, Guadalajara, Diocese of San Juan de los Lagos. Sabás came from a poor family, studied in Guadalajara's seminary, then transferred to the diocese of Tamaulipas, where he was ordained (1911). At the beginning of the revolution, he returned to Guadalajara to minister in various parishes, primarily forming catechists. Despite the outbreak of anti-clerical persecution, he continued working in Tototlán. When federal troops attacked as he was returning from a baptism, he found refuge for two days before he was discovered by Izaguirre's troops. In vain they tortured him with fire to elicit the hiding places of Francisco Vizcarra and other priests, then riddled his body with bullets. His body rests in the church at Tototlán. Fr. Reyes was both beatified (Nov. 22, 1992) and canonized (May 21, 2000) with Cristobal MAGALLANES [*see* GUADALAJARA (MEXICO), MARTYRS OF, SS.] by Pope John Paul II.

Feast: May 25 (Mexico).

Bibliography: J. CARDOSO, *Los mártires mexicanos* (Mexico City 1953). J. DÍAZ ESTRELLA, *El movimiento cristero: sociedad y conflicto en los Altos de Jalisco* (México, D.F. 1979).

[K. I. RABENSTEIN]

REYNOLDS, RICHARD, ST.

English Bridgettine priest, martyr; b. Devon, *c.* 1487; hanged, drawn, and quartered at Tyburn (London),

May 4, 1535. At the age of 16 he went to Cambridge, where, receiving his A.B. (1506) and his M.A. (1509), he became a fellow of Corpus Christi College. His particular interest in the Scriptures led to the D.B. in 1513, when he was also appointed University Preacher. This same year he became a Bridgettine monk at Syon Abbey, Isleworth, the last of the large medieval monastic foundations and the only house of the order in England. Little is known of his next 20 years beyond his reputation as a preacher and spiritual counselor. When Henry VIII began his divorce proceedings, Reynolds was consulted by many who were perplexed about the "King's great matter," as well as about the prophecies of Elizabeth BARTON, the Holy Maid of Kent. Barton was executed in April 1534, but before her arrest she had visited Syon several times; according to the depositions of St. Thomas More, Reynolds had distrusted her. Anxious to secure the backing of Syon, the King sought its submission, but agents of Cromwell failed.

Sometime before April 20, 1535, Reynolds was arrested and with three Carthusian priors, John HOUGHTON, Robert LAWRENCE and Augustine WEBSTER, was imprisoned in the Tower, where, when visited by Cromwell, he spoke fearlessly against the king's supremacy over the Church. On April 28 he was indicted on the charge of high treason at Westminster, and found guilty by a jury that had been intimidated by Cromwell and the king's secretary. On May 4 all four were hanged, drawn, and quartered at Tyburn. From the window of his cell Thomas MORE watched them passing to their execution, and remarked to his daughter, "Lo, dost thou not see, Meg, that these blessed fathers be now as cheerfully going to their deaths as bridegrooms to their marriage."

Reynolds was beatified by Pope Leo XIII on Dec. 29, 1886, and canonized by Paul VI on Oct. 25, 1970 as one of the Forty Martyrs of England and Wales.

Feast: May 11 (Archdiocese of Westminster, Bridgettine nuns); Oct. 25 (Feast of the 40 Martyrs of England and Wales); May 4 (Feast of the English Martyrs in England).

See Also: ENGLAND, SCOTLAND, AND WALES, MARTYRS OF.

Bibliography: D. KNOWLES, *The Religious Orders in England* 3:214–218. F. R. JOHNSTON, *Bl. Richard Reynolds* (Postulation Pamphlet; London 1961). A. HAMILTON, *The Angel of Sion* (n.s. 1905). R. CHALLONER, *Memoirs of Missionary Priests,* ed. J. H. POLLEN (rev. ed. London 1924; repr. Farnborough 1969). B. CAMM, ed. *Lives of the English Martyrs . . . ,* 2 v. (New York 1904–14). A. BUTLER, *The Lives of the Saints,* ed. H. THURSTON and D. ATTWATER (New York 1956) 2:277–280. J. GILLOW, *A Literary and Biographical History or Bibliographical Dictionary of the English Catholics from 1534 to the Present Time* (New York 1961) 5:408–409.

[G. FITZHERBERT]

RHAZES (RAZES, AL-RĀZĪ)

Rhazes is the Latin for al-Rāzī, physician, scientist, and philosopher whose full name in Arabic was Abū Bakr Muḥammad ibn Zakarîya al-Rāzī. The details of his life and the dates of his birth (*c.* 865) and death (923 or 925) are not well established.

Life and Works. His ethnic name, al-Rāzī relates to the city of Rayy, once Rages (Rhagae), which was important in the eastern caliphate under Islam; it was situated near Teheran, the present-day capital of Iran. Until the age of 30 (some say 40), Rhazes was interested in music and chemistry (alchemy). Thereafter, he became interested in medicine. According to some, this interest was brought about by the weakened condition of his eyes, variously attributed to his chemical experiments or to a lash of the whip. But according to his admirer, the great scientist al-Bīrūnī, Rhazes' blindness was due to deficiencies in his diet and to excesses in his way of life. This may explain the marked interest Rhazes had in matters of diet, as evidenced by the writings preserved in manuscript that he has left on this subject. Rhazes enjoyed a wide reputation as a physician; he was made head of a hospital in Rayy and later held a similar position in Baghdad.

Rhazes is the author of more than 100 works of various sizes, of which a work on alchemy, *Kitāb alAsrār,* and three on medicine, *Kitāb al-Ḥāwī, Kitāb al-Ṭibb al-Manṣūrī,* and *Kitāb al-Jadarī wa'l-Ḥaṣba,* were widely known during the Latin Middle Ages. *Kitāb al-Asrār* (The Book of Secrets) was translated in the twelfth century by Gerard of Cremona. The *Ḥāwī* "Continens," was translated in the thirteenth century by Sālim ibn Faraj, under the title *Liber Elhavi.* The *Manṣūrī, "Liber Almansoris,"* so called because it was dedicated to a prince of the Sāmanid dynasty, Manṣūr ibn Isḥāq, has had several editions since the last part of the fifteenth century. The *Kitāb al-Jadarī wa'l-Ḥaṣba* was translated into Latin, Greek, French, and English; the last-named translation was by W. A. Greenhill, *A Treatise on Smallpox and Measles* (Sydenham Society, London 1848). Rhazes' treatise on stones in the bladder and kidneys was edited and translated into French by P. de Koning (Leiden 1896).

The following medical aphorisms are among those attributed to Rhazes: "Whenever you can treat medically with foods, do not use medicines; and whenever you can treat by using a simple medicine, do not use a compound." "When the physician is learned and the patient obedient, how short the malady's persistence!" "Let your treatment of an incipient illness be such that it will not cause the patient's strength to fail."

Philosophy. To the Arabs, Rhazes was known as *al-ṭabīb,* "the physician," and not so much as a philosopher. This may be due to the fact that his writings belong overwhelmingly to the field of medicine; this in turn may account for the fact that the study of his philosophy was neglected until very recently. [*See* Schraeder, *Zeitschrift der deutschen morgenländischen Gesellschaft* 79 (1925): 228–235; S. Pines, *Beiträge zur islamischen Atomenlehre* (Berlin 1936) 34–36; *Abu Bekr Muhammedis fil. Zachariae Rhagensis opera philosophica fragmentaque quae supersunt,* ed. P. Kraus, Fuad I University, Faculty Publications, fasc. 22 (Cairo 1939)].

In Rhazes' metaphysics there are five eternal principles: the creator, the soul, matter, time, and space. Against the prevailing doctrine of the Muslim philosophers, and in agreement (though not intentional) with the Muslim theologians, he denies the eternity of the world. Metempsychosis, for which he was criticized by the Andalusian theologian Ibn Hazm (d. 1064), was a central doctrine in Rhazes' philosophy. The liberation of the soul from the body is brought about by the creator who endows the soul with intelligence (*'aql*) enabling it to study philosophy, the only means it has of liberating itself from the body. The end of the world will come about once all the individual souls have liberated themselves from their bodies. Rhazes' metaphysics manages to put him in simultaneous conflict with both philosophers and theologians in Islam.

Rhazes' cosmology is characterized by an atomic theory close to that of DEMOCRITUS, but differing from that of the later atomists of the Ash'arite school of Moslem theology [*see* ASH'ARĪ, AL-]. For Rhazes, atoms have extension, and the void has a positive character. The elements (five in number) come into being from the different proportions in which the atoms and the voids have combined. The property of a body depends on the number of the atoms in proportion to the number of voids.

Rhazes' ethics commends a full life. While avoiding excesses, one need not condemn the passions. Pleasure does not have a positive character; it is merely the normal state after pain, as health after sickness. The highest form of living belongs to the philosopher, who, like the creator, treats men with justice and kindness. In contrast to the later AVERROËS (IBN RUSHD), Rhazes saw no possibility of conciliation between philosophy and religion. In the former he saw a supreme way of life, and in the latter the cause of wars.

See Also: ARABIAN PHILOSOPHY.

Bibliography: L. LECLERC, *Histoire de la médecine arabe,* 2 v. (Paris 1876). E. G. BROWNE, *Arabian Medicine* (Cambridge, Eng. 1921). G. SARTON, *Introduction to the History of Science,* 3 v. in 5 (Baltimore 1927–48) 1:609. F. M. PAREJA, *Islamologia* (Rome 1951) 697. For fuller bibliog., C. BROCKELMANN, *Geschichte der arabischen Literatur,* 2 v. (2d ed. Leiden 1943–49) 1:267–271; suppl. 1:417–421. J. D. PEARSON, *Index Islamicus* (Cambridge, Eng. 1958) 167–168, studies by P. KRAUS, M. MEYERHOF, J. RUSKA, and others. AL-RĀZĪ, *The Spiritual Physick of Rhazes,* tr. A. J. ARBERRY (London 1950), a popular ethical work.

[G. MAKDISI]

RHEINAU, ABBEY OF

Former Benedictine abbey on an island in the Rhine River, Zurich, Switzerland. Founded probably in the early 9th century, Rheinau had extensive possessions by 852 and in 858 came under royal protection with the right to elect its abbot. New lands were received, and the abbey's immunity was confirmed by Otto I (972) and Henry III (1049); Henry IV placed it under the bishop of Constance (to 1067). Bishop GEBHARD III (1088–1110) introduced the HIRSAU reform. The three-nave, three-apse basilica of Our Lady and St. Peter and the chapel of St. FINTAN (an Irish monk at Rheinau 851–878) were completed in 1114. The scriptorium flourished in the 12th century. The decline of the abbey in the 13th and 14th centuries was associated with economic difficulties and feudal lords; in 1455 the abbey came under the Swiss Confederation. Abandoned for a while (1529–31) during the Reformation, Rheinau joined the Swiss Benedictine Congregation (1602) under Gerold I Zurlauben (1598–1607). Its peak was reached under Gerold II Zurlauben (1697–1735), when scholarship flourished and a baroque church (1707) and a conventual building and library (1717) were built. Moritz HOHENBAUM VAN DER MEER, the historian, was at Rheinau (1734–95). Suppression by the French Revolution (1799–1803) was followed by a prohibition to accept novices (1836) and secularization by Zurich (1862). The abbey was converted to use as a mental institution; its library and archives went to Zurich.

Bibliography: R. HENGGELER, *Monasticon Benedictinum Helvetiae* 2 (Einsiedeln 1933) 163–402. H. FIETZ, ed., *Die Kunstdenkmäler des Kantons Zürich,* v.1 (Basel 1938) 225–362. H. G. BUTZ, *Die Benediktinerabtei Rheinau im Zeitalter der Gegenreformation* (Diss. Zurich 1954). G. HÜRLIMANN, *Das Rheinauer Rituale* (Fribourg 1959). W. HILDEBRANDT, in *Dictionnaire historique et biographique de la Suisse,* v.5 (Neuchâtel 1930) 465–467. U. ENGELMANN, *Lexikon für Theologie und Kirche,* ed. J. HOFER and K. RAHNER, 10 v. (2d, new ed. Freiburg 1957–65) 8:1274. L. H. COTTINEAU, *Répertoire topobibliographique des abbayes et prieurés,* 2 v. (Mâcon 1935–39) 2:2457–58. O. L. KAPSNER, *A Benedictine Bibliography: An Author-Subject Union List,* 2 v. (2d ed. Collegeville, MN 1962) 2:253–254.

[A. MAISSEN]

RHEINBERGER, JOSEF GABRIEL VON

Composer, organist, teacher; b. Vaduz, Lichtenstein, March 17, 1839; d. Munich, Nov. 25, 1901. Rheinberger revealed precocious musical talent when he began his piano studies at five years of age. At seven he served as church organist and at eight composed a three-part Mass with organ accompaniment. After harmony studies under P. Schmutzer at Feldkirch, in 1851 he enrolled at the Munich Conservatory, where he studied organ with Herzog, piano with Leonhard, and counterpoint with J. J. Maier. Thereafter he taught at the conservatory from 1855 to 1859, and then at the Royal Music School, and was assistant director of the court opera from 1865 to 1867. In subsequent years he was a royal professor and inspector of school music, director of the court chapel, and director of the oratorio society. He was named to the nobility of Bavaria in 1894, and received a doctorate from the University of Munich in 1899. Employing his solid background and mastery of composition, he wrote prolifically for both instrumental and vocal media, much of his output comprising Masses, motets, cantatas, and other religious forms. His organ works, especially the sonatas, rank among the best for that instrument from the romanticist period. A renowned and much sought-after teacher, he influenced many younger composers. His American pupils included George W. Chadwick (1854–1931) and Horatio Parker (1863–1919), both of whom became distinguished members of the Boston group of composers.

Bibliography: T. KROYER, *Joseph Rheinberger* (New York 1916). H. GRACE, *The Organ Works of Rheinberger* (London 1925); *Grove's Dictionary of Music and Musicians*, ed. E. BLOM 9 v. (5th ed. London 1954) 7:145–149. J. A. FULLER-MAITLAND, *Masters of German Music* (London 1894). A. WÜRZ, *Die Musik in Geschichte und Gegenwart*, ed. F. BLUME (Kassel-Basel 1949–) 11:377–381. D. M. RANDEL, ed., *The Harvard Biographical Dictionary of Music* (Cambridge 1996) 741–742. N. SLONIMSKY, ed. *Baker's Biographical Dictionary of Musicians*, Eighth Edition (New York 1992) 1504. H. WANGER, ed., *Rheinberger: Sämtliche Werk Supplement 2, Leben und Werk in Bildern* (Stuttgart 1998). M. WEYER, *Die Orgelwerke Josef Rheinbergers: Ein Handbuch für Organisten* (Wilhelmshaven 1994). A. WÜRZ, ''Joseph (Gabriel) Rheinberger'' in *The New Grove Dictionary of Music and Musicians*, vol. 15, ed. S. SADIE, (New York 1980) 791–792.

[I. WORTMAN]

RHETORIC

The discipline, traditionally enumerated among the LIBERAL ARTS, concerned with persuasion or engendering credence. Since it has no proper subject matter and no inherent restrictions on what means it can or should employ, its notion tends to vary with the philosophy with which it is associated. Sometimes, however, rhetoric itself is taken as the basis of entire philosophy (M. Nizolius, 1498–1576), and at others it is excluded from philosophy as a hallmark of sophism (Plato).

Various Views. The verbal and the mental are two aspects of rhetoric that may be taken as poles between which the variations assumed by the discipline are to be apprehended. When the verbal aspect predominates and the rhetorician's emphasis is on effective speech, criticism is characteristically moral. Either rhetoric is dismissed as a somewhat empty concern with verbal ornamentation; or, if the rhetorician is a figure to be reckoned with, it is argued that man is not ''the measure of all things'' (Protagoras) and that true self-knowledge leads to principles transcending the merely human. When a cosmological identification of such principles takes place, rhetoric shares with poetry the condemnation of being inferior to philosophy, this frequently accompanied by paradoxical use of poetic devices, such as Plato's, to express a philosophy that excludes poets. The refutation by rhetoric of this attempt to devaluate its importance has ordinarily been to urge the human irrelevance of cosmological speculation—the mistake of Socrates, according to Cicero, was separating wisdom and eloquence—and at the same time to dissociate the rhetorician's active participation in human affairs from the fancies and falsehoods of the poet.

Christian thinkers have evaluated the verbal aspect of rhetoric somewhat differently. The preeminence in so many senses of the Word of God accounts for the subordination of the rhetoric of human words—in the thought of the converted professor of rhetoric, St. AUGUSTINE— not to a cosmological, but to a personal Principle (confer, *Doctr. christ.* 4.1.1–4.7.11; *Mag.* 3.5–6, 11.36–12.46). The change from belief to Christian faith, the development of theology and the issuing forth of the independent scientific certitudes of philosophy provide the background against which the vicissitudes of rhetoric, conceived in relation to the other liberal arts, can be traced through the intellectual history of the Middle Ages. For St. THOMAS AQUINAS, for example, rhetoric is a part of LOGIC leading the mind to a state that is neither full-blown opinion or conviction on the one hand, nor estimation based almost wholly on manner of representation on the other. These are the offices of DIALECTICS and POETICS respectively, whereas rhetoric induces a kind of suspicion that does not exclude the contrary possibility (*In anal. post., proem.* 6).

Throughout the history of Western thought rhetoric or some of its devices has been a part of logic or dialectics. This is not so much because the verbal aspect is preempted or devalued by wisdom, philosophy, science, or some other discipline as because the devices of rhetoric belonging to its mental aspect prove attractive to some philosophers at certain critical junctures. When the larger analogical contexts become doubtful or subject to dispute, or when univocal definitions become difficult to establish, rhetoric has often seemed to offer appropriate resources.

Rhetorical Devices. The rhetorical distinction between definite and infinite questions, the former having a name and time attached and the latter arrived at by removal of these (Cicero, *Partitiones oratoriae* 9, 18, 30), has sometimes been invoked as a means of first approach to otherwise resistant data, or has been used along with its subdistinctions to order transcendental considerations in metaphysics.

Once the kind of question has been settled on by a rhetorician, his most characteristic device, namely, place or topic (*locus, topos*), can be brought into use. Places can be characterized as sets of recurrent patterns that oratorical encounters are likely to embody. Running over these in preparing his case, the orator can locate both his opponent's position and possible lines of argument and his own most effective lines of argument and refutation. Lists of places in the rhetorical tradition are customarily divided into common places, that is, those common to all situations and proper places, those appropriate either to kinds of questions (Cicero) or to kinds of oratory (Aristotle) and distinguished according to type of audience as forensic, deliberative, or epideictic (display). A familiar example of both questions and places in a short, though mixed, list is the set of CIRCUMSTANCES— *quis, quid, ubi, cur, quomodo, quando, quibus auxiliis*—that has a long history of use in Canon Law, moral theology and journalism.

The notion of rhetorical place can be presented by contrasting the treatments of DEFINITION in rhetoric and dialectics. Dialectics in many of its versions (for example, Aristotle's or Agricola's) employs places, not infrequently taking over those to be found in the lists of rhetoric; but even when dialectics does not use places, its characteristic movement, often rather far ranging, is centripetal with regard to definition or some approximation of this. For rhetoric, definition is one of the places or topics, along with others, such as cause, consequences and contrary. Rhetoric proceeds to definition by explication rather than by narrowing. Unfolding parts or divisions carries out defining (Cicero, *Topica* 5), the idea being that definition in some matter or affair may provide some room for possible argument in the course of presentation.

Rhetorical Argument. It is in argument that the interest of the great classical rhetorics of Aristotle and Cicero lies. Their predecessors had devoted too much

attention either to the verbal side of the art (Aristotle), or to the judging of statements (Cicero), whereas the prior or more important aspect is the invention of arguments. The arguments, for which the places serve as a means of inventing, are for example, corresponding to INDUCTION in logic or dialectics, and enthymeme, the counterpart of DEDUCTION. While manuals of logic have for centuries described enthymeme as a SYLLOGISM with some unexpressed member, for Aristotle it is what is in the mind (Gr. ἐνθυμεῖσθαί, to keep in mind) of the judge or the audience, and for Cicero, what is in his forensic opponent's mind, that dictates what the argument should be.

Treatises on rhetoric, however much they may emphasize the invention of argument, do not neglect the further elements on whose proper synthesis effective rhetorical practice depends. Collocation or arrangement of introduction (*exordium*), division of the issue (*partitio*), the argument (*confirmatio*), the refutation of the opponent's argument and peroration need to be looked after. Elocution or the choice of effective language and memorization require attention. Above all, in the view of the greatest orator of antiquity, Demosthenes, the speech needs delivery (*actio*).

The dependence of rhetoric for its persuasive effect is traditionally not confined to the words or the thought or to the combining of the two. Rhetoric relies on the confluence of these with the character of the orator and the emotions (*motus animi*) of his audience. The chief rhetorical fallacy would be ineffectiveness. On the other hand, the union in mutual appropriateness of so many elements—thoughts, words, actions and men—in rhetorical practice at its greatest has sometimes suggested itself as a moral ideal. For Quintilian, moral education would be moral training; and in Cicero's dictum, the good life would be like a good speech.

Recent Interest. Contemporary attention to rhetoric has largely concentrated on the history of the discipline (R. McKeon). Sometimes it is said that many of the matters included in the classical treatises on rhetoric have been absorbed by the subject matters of psychology and the social sciences. In recent decades, however, the question has been raised whether closer study and adaptation of the devices of rhetorical theory might not contribute to the considerations of problems in literary theory (K. Burke), poetics (J. Paulhan), linguistic theory (I. A. Richards) and ethics, politics and jurisprudence (C. Perelman).

See Also: ARGUMENTATION.

Bibliography: C. S. BALDWIN, *Ancient Rhetoric and Poetic* (New York 1924; reprint Gloucester, Mass. 1959). K. BURKE, *A Rhetoric of Motives* (New York 1950). I. A. RICHARDS, *The Philosophy of Rhetoric* (New York 1936). R. MCKEON, ''Poetry and Philosophy in the Twelfth Century: The Renaissance of Rhetoric," *Critics and Criticism: Ancient and Modern,* ed. R. S. CRANE (Chicago 1952) 297–318; "Rhetoric in the Middle Ages," *ibid.* 260–296. P. A. DUHAMEL, "The Function of Rhetoric as Effective Expression," *Journal of the History of Ideas,* 10 (1949) 344–356. C. PERELMAN and L. OLBRECHTS-TYTECA, *Rhétorique et philosophie: Pour une théorie de l'argumentation en philosophie* (Paris 1952). J. PAULHAN, *Les Fleurs de Tarbes: ou, La Terreur dans les lettres* (Paris 1941).

[G. F. DRURY]

RHO, GIACOMO

Jesuit missionary, mathematician, and reformer of the Chinese calendar; b. Milan, Italy, Jan. 29, 1592; d. Beijing, China, April 27, 1638. Rho entered the Society of Jesus Aug. 24, 1604, and was ordained by Cardinal Robert Bellarmine at Rome. He taught mathematics at Milan until his departure for the Far East in 1620 with 44 companions. His arrival at Macau coincided with an attack on the city by the Dutch, who were driven off by artillery directed by Rho. In 1624 he entered China and soon gained a firm command of the language. His religious writings in Chinese embraced such topics as fasting, the corporal works of mercy, and prayer. In 1631 his knowledge of mathematics led to his being appointed to the Imperial Bureau of Astronomy in Beijing where he labored with Father Johann Adam SCHALL VON BELL on the calendar reform until his death. Rho's contribution to this vast project was some 17 tracts on astronomical subjects. His work was in the tradition of Father Matteo RICCI, who hoped to convert the Chinese to Christianity by the means of science.

Bibliography: C. SOMMERVOGEL et al., *Bibliothéque de la Compagnie de Jésus* (Brussels–Paris 1890–1932) 6:1709–18; 9:803–804. L. PFISTER, *Notices biographiques et bibliographiques sur les Jésuites de l'ancienne mission de Chine 1552–1773* (Shanghai 1932–34) 1:188–191.

[J. V. MENTAG]

RHODE ISLAND, CATHOLIC CHURCH IN

Rhode Island is the smallest state in the United States (1,212 square miles) and the eighth smallest in population (1,048,319). It is the most Catholic of states, however, with 635,590 Catholics making up 61 percent of its population. Founded by Roger WILLIAMS (1603–83) as an enclave of religious tolerance, and confirmed as such by the royal charter of 1663, Rhode Island became a haven for every sort of religious dissenter, even a few Catholics. However, by a statute of the General Assembly in 1719, not removed until 1783, Catholics were excluded from full citizenship. The first public Mass said in Rhode Island was at Newport in 1780 for the funeral of the commander of the French fleet sent to help the colonists in the War of Independence.

Rhode Island was first under the jurisdiction of Bishop CARROLL of Baltimore and then under the bishops of Boston, first Jean CHEVERUS (1808–23) and then Benedict FENWICK (1825–44). In 1844 the Vermont-born convert, William Barber Tyler, was created the first bishop of Hartford (which included all of Connecticut and Rhode Island) with his cathedral and residence at Rhode Island's capital of Providence. With Tyler's death in 1849, Irish-born Bernard O'REILLY became the second bishop, but his ship was lost at sea on a return trip from Europe in 1856. Francis P. MCFARLAND, a native-born son of Irish immigrants, became the third bishop of Hartford in 1858. When in 1872 the diocese of Providence was created, it included all of Rhode Island and, until 1904, southeastern Massachusetts. Thomas F. Hendricken (1827–86), a zealous Irish-born priest who once dreamed of being a missionary in the Far East, was its first bishop.

Until the 1820s Catholics were few and far between, with priests making periodic trips to the scattered Catholic population. The first permanent church in Rhode Island, now St. Mary's, was founded in Newport in 1828; the second, also St. Mary's, was erected in 1829 in Pawtucket; and in 1837 the parish of SS. Peter and Paul, which would become the cathedral, was established in Providence. The growth of the Church was primarily due to the transformation of the state from a mercantile and agrarian economy to one based primarily on manufacturing in metals and textiles, and the need for cheap labor to maintain it. The factories and mills of Providence and the Blackstone and Pawtuxet valleys in the northern half of the state drew mostly Catholic immigrants in great numbers, with the Irish being the first and largest group.

The influx of the Irish, which would become a flood in the late 1840s, led to a transformation of the state's population so that the Irish made up nearly three out of every eight people by 1865. This led to the growth of anti-immigrant and anti-Catholic feeling. The constitution of 1843, by retaining property requirements for voting by naturalized foreign-born citizens while removing them for the native-born, was designed to disfranchise Irish Catholics. In the 1855 elections the nativist Know-Nothings swept the state, winning five of every seven votes. Their anti-Catholicism seems to have been based primarily on religious and cultural issues, lacking the economic aspect that was so important, for example, in Massachusetts. The Know-Nothings (*see* KNOW-

Providence College, Providence, Rhode Island. (©Bob Rowan; Progressive Image/CORBIS)

NOTHINGISM) were soon eclipsed by the newly born Republican party which, while eschewing the Know-Nothings' anti-Catholic sentiments, absorbed most of their supporters. While the old English stock became the pillar of the Republican party, the Irish became wedded to the Democratic party. In 1888, with the Bourn Amendment, the property qualification was removed. By then the Republicans saw the virtue of using newer immigrants, particularly the French Canadians, as a counter to the Democratic Irish. While the first Catholic governor was the Irish Democrat, James H. Higgins (1906), the second was the French Canadian Republican Aram J. Pothier (1908). While the sectarian violence that was seen in other places never occurred in Rhode Island, the divisions were deep and long-lasting, and anti-Catholic bigotry continued well into the next century.

The demands of the Civil War led to an expansion of mills and factories and the need of workers to fill them. This was the beginning of the next great immigration, the French Canadians: between 1860 and 1910 over 35,000 came to Rhode Island. The city of Woonsocket became the "Quebec of New England." They were like the Irish both in the firmness of their Catholicism and their nationalism, and in their fusion of the two, creating their own national parishes, schools and organizations to preserve their language and culture. However, they did not get along well with the Irish, who considered them a threat to their jobs, or with the Irish-dominated Church, which pushed for much greater centralization and Americanization.

Other major Catholic immigrant groups followed: from the late 1880s, the Italians, and from 1900, Poles and Lithuanians. The Portuguese long had a presence in the state, especially from the whaling days, but in the 1870s, and particularly after 1890, they came in great numbers. The Portuguese were divided by their place of origin: the Azores, Cape Verdes, and mainland Portugal. Syrians (Melkite and Maronite) and Ruthenians also immigrated to the state, though in much smaller numbers. National parishes were created for all these groups. The enactment of the national origins quota system (1924) and the decline of the mills (from 1923) led to a great decline in immigration. In more recent years, however, there has been some Catholic immigration, though not to the high degree of the earlier groups, from the Portuguese islands, Hispanics from Latin America, and to a lesser extent refugees from Southeast Asia. Except for the Portuguese from Cape Verdes, for whom a national parish was created in 1979, these groups have been cared for within already existing parishes.

In its early years Rhode Island was missionary country and depended on the financial support of foreign missionary societies and from priests from Ireland. By the late 1860s the Church was able to maintain itself, to start building churches and schools on their own, and to find vocations among themselves. This was less true for the newer immigrant groups, and finding priests for them was often difficult and a source of friction. Even if priests could be found who spoke their language, national pride or cultural differences could get in the way. While Catholics were at the bottom of the social ladder, and the overwhelming majority of Catholics were laborers whose jobs depended on the vagaries of the business cycle, some had prospered and had become professionals and businessmen themselves. The growing wealth and security of the Church was manifested by Bishop Hendricken's beginning the construction of a magnificent new cathedral in 1878. While only consecrated in 1889, its first Mass was for Hendricken's funeral in 1886. Another manifestation of stability was Hendricken's founding of the *Weekly Visitor* in 1875, which would eventually become the diocesan newspaper under the name the *Providence Visitor*— and which has become the state's second largest newspaper with a circulation of 40,000.

The death of Hendricken led to the appointment of Matthew Harkins (1845–1921), whom Archbishop John Ireland once called "my ideal type of bishop." He was a learned and able Boston priest, under whose tenure the diocese experienced phenomenal growth. On his arrival there were 39 parishes and 63 diocesan priests in Rhode Island, and when he gave up the administration of the diocese in 1919 to his coadjutor, Bishop William A. Hickey (1869–1933), there were an additional 62 parishes (a majority of them national parishes) and 207 diocesan priests, all but one of whom were ordained during his episcopacy. He also created an extensive system of charitable institutions. To better serve the non-English speaking faithful he brought in the Scalabrini Fathers, the Marist Fathers, the Holy Ghost Fathers, and the Missionaries of the Sacred Heart. The Brothers of the Sacred Heart and 20 different congregations of women religious entered the

state, joining the Sisters of Mercy, the Society of the Sacred Heart, the Ursulines, the Religious of Jesus and Mary, and the Christian Brothers in the work of education. Following the decrees of the Third Plenary Council of Baltimore (1884) which mandated parochial schools, Harkins created a Diocesan School Board and pushed for the construction of schools wherever feasible. By 1921 there were 41 parish schools, three academies for young men and five for young ladies. As the capstone of this educational system Harkins wished to create a Catholic college. The Jesuits had taken on a parish in Providence (1876) in the hope that they would eventually open a college, but when they left the state in 1899, Harkins had to look elsewhere. Eventually the Dominican friars agreed to staff such a college, and in 1919 Providence College opened with 71 students. It has become a flourishing coeducational school, still run by the Dominicans, of some 3,600 students on a 105-acre campus in the city of Providence. Harkins also cared for the educational quality of his priests. He raised the standards for accepting young men as seminarians and sent many of his young priests for further studies to universities in Europe and America. He was an early supporter of The Catholic University of America, in Washington, D.C., and became a trustee in 1903.

Among the other orders that entered the diocese at this time were also the Trappists (1900) and the Benedictines (1919). The Trappists moved from Nova Scotia to Lonsdale on land donated by Harkins but moved to Spencer, Massachusetts, after their monastery burned down in 1949. The Benedictines of Portsmouth Priory (raised to an abbey in 1969) have remained and direct a flourishing, coeducational, preparatory school, first opened in 1926. Harkins had studied with the English Benedictines for a year in the English College at Douai, France, before going to train with the Sulpicians in Paris. When Father Leonard Sargent, a convert priest on his way to join an English abbey, broached the subject of founding a Benedictine house in the state, Harkins was enthusiastic, and when Sargent returned, Harkins not only gave him permission to set up a house at Portsmouth but also supplied $5,000 to make the foundation possible.

At Harkins's death, his coadjutor, Hickey, immediately became the ordinary, and while some 16 parishes were created during his tenure, he gave greater emphasis to the consolidation and improvement of already existing institutions. He was extremely active, however, in the area of education, creating 14 parish schools, and expanded the size of already existing schools. He also reorganized the establishing and funding of the high schools. He was an aggressive fundraiser, raising a million dollars for his high school fund and vast sums for diocesan charitable institutions in his centralized annual Catholic Charity Fund Appeal. With the beginning of the Great Depression, Hickey speeded up church construction work so as to provide jobs, and in order to relieve immediate needs for food and clothing he directed that branches of the St. Vincent de Paul Society be established in every parish.

It was Hickey's centralization of Catholic high schools and their funding that led to a rebellion of the ultranationalists among the French Canadians, led by Elphege Daignault of Woonsocket, who saw it as a threat to their separate existence, customs, and way of life. In 1924 they began a French-language newspaper, *La Sentinelle,* to promote their views and be "on the watch" against assimilationist trends. In 1925 they appealed to Rome against Hickey's "illegal assessment" of parish funds. When their petition was denied, they appealed in 1927 to the civil courts (unsuccessfully) and began a boycott of all contributions to the Church. All those who had appealed to the civil courts were excommunicated by Hickey in April 1928, and *La Sentinelle* was put on the Index. The controversy gained national attention and led to much bitterness and division in the French Canadian community. By February, 1929, virtually all of those excommunicated, including Daignault, had capitulated and the conflict was over.

The 1930s were a turning point for Rhode Island Catholics, for it marked their ascent to political power. From the 1850s till the 1930s the state had been dominated by a Yankee Republican oligarchy supported by wealthy businessmen and rural voters. From the 1920s, a disenchantment among French Canadians and Italians began toward the Republicans. This was partly due to the negative Republican reaction to the major strikes that punctuated this period. It was also due to the revival of nativism. This nativism was seen in the rise of the avowedly anti-Catholic KU KLUX KLAN (even in Rhode Island), in the immigration restriction laws of 1922 and 1924, and in the Peck Act passed by the Republican General Assembly in 1922, which prohibited school instruction for the basic subjects in languages other than English. The Peck Act was never enforced and it was repealed in 1925, but it intensified the distaste for the Republicans. The presidential election of 1928 was the political "coming of age" for Catholics in the state. The Catholic Al Smith was only the second Democrat to have carried the state since the founding of the Republican party. But the voting showed a polarized electorate, with Smith doing very badly in the Yankee areas and extremely well in the Catholic ethnic ones. Also, there was a substantially larger turnout in the Catholic ethnic districts. In 1928 the restrictive qualifications for voting in city council elections were also removed. While the Great Depression and New Deal continued the political transformation

of the state, it was not until the "Bloodless Revolution" of 1935, when the Democratic administration forced through the General Assembly a massive reorganization of the state government, that the structures that kept the Yankee minority in power were removed and the triumph of the Catholic ethnics was made complete.

Francis P. Keough (1890–1961), a priest of Hartford, was made bishop at Hickey's death in 1933 and remained until he was made archbishop of Baltimore in 1947. When he arrived there were 328,528 Catholics, 270 diocesan priests and 95 religious priests, and when he left there were 427,364 Catholics, 344 diocesan priests and 145 religious priests. In his time 15 new parishes, four high schools, and 14 elementary schools were founded. In 1939 he founded a minor seminary in Warwick Neck, and in 1947 the Sisters of Mercy founded Salve Regina College in Newport which is now a successful coeducational school of some 1,800 students.

Russell J. McVinney (1898–1971) was named the fifth bishop of Providence in 1948—the first Rhode Island native to hold that position. The first part of his tenure witnessed a period of remarkable growth, with the construction of 28 parishes and 40 schools, especially in the suburbs and the growing rural areas of the state. The school system reached its peak at this time with 106 out of 154 parishes having a parish school. The expansion in education, however, led to the need for lay teachers and tuition payments for the first time. He opened a new hospital, Our Lady of Fatima, in 1954, a diocesan retreat house at Narragansett in 1952, and a youth retreat center at Peace Dale in 1954. He also expanded the seminary and he founded a diocesan congregation of Sisters, Sisters of Our Lady of Providence (1955), and a society of diocesan brothers, Brothers of Our Lady of Providence (1959).

The final decade of his tenure was as tumultuous and painful as the first part was stable and prosperous. It coincided with the profound social changes of the 1960s and early 1970s as well as the Civil Rights Revolution, the Vietnam War and its protests, and the changes occasioned by the Second Vatican Council. Even before this, with the decline of ethnic enclaves and the movement to the suburbs, Catholics had become far more assimilated to American middle-class life and its mores. Bishop McVinney, while he was essentially politically and religiously conservative, took a leading role in the movement for political and economic rights of minorities and the poor, and was a strong advocate of the Fair Housing laws passed by the General Assembly in 1965. He also dutifully implemented the changes following the Council, always attempting to be faithful to a proper understanding of the Council and the postconciliar directives. In this period there began a profound decline in religious and priestly vocations, with many religious leaving their orders (the Sisters of Our Lady of Providence were dissolved at this time) and even many priests leaving the active ministry. Among those leaving was McVinney's auxiliary since 1964, Bishop Bernard M. Kelly, who resigned on June 14, 1971. Two months later McVinney died, and in December, 1971, Louis E. Gelineau (b. 1928), the vicar general of the Diocese of Burlington, Vermont, was appointed bishop.

Bishop Gelineau reorganized the administrative structures of the diocese so as to emphasize the pastoral dimension of his office, to increase participation of the clergy and people in its running, and to develop strategic planning. The decline in Mass attendance and in priestly and religious vocations continued, as did resignations from the priesthood and religious life. With the decline in numbers of teaching religious, more lay faculty had to be hired and schools became much more expensive. From 1968 schools started to close: some 65 elementary schools and 12 high schools either closed or merged with other schools. Enrollments continued to decline until 1980 when the first increase appeared since 1963. The seminary also experienced declining enrollment: in 1989 the high school seminary closed, and in 1975 the college seminary began sending its students to Providence College, the college seminary itself moving to Providence in 1983. While a few new parishes were established, changing demographics also led to the merging of some: in the late 1990s a number of parishes were merged in Warwick, Central Falls, and Woonsocket. In 1995 Bishop Robert E. Mulvee (b. 1930), bishop of Wilmington, Delaware, was appointed coadjutor, and in 1997, with the retirement of Bishop Gelineau, he became the seventh bishop of Providence.

The statistics for 2000 show that the state had 157 parishes, 307 diocesan priests (of which 202 are active in the diocese), 133 religious priests, 96 permanent deacons, 688 sisters, 133 brothers, 12 Catholic high schools, and 46 Catholic elementary schools.

Bibliography: P. T. CONLEY and M. J. SMITH, *Catholicism in Rhode Island: The Formative Era* (Providence 1976). R. W. HAYMAN, *Catholicism in Rhode Island and the Diocese of Providence: 1780–1886* (Providence 1982); *Catholicism in Rhode Island and the Diocese of Providence: 1886–1921* (Providence 1995).

[P. SCOTTI]

RHODES, ALEXANDRE DE

Jesuit missionary to Indochina, b. Avignon, March 15, 1593; d. Nov. 5, 1660. Shortly after his ordination in 1618, de Rhodes was granted by Superior General Mutio

Vitelleschi the permission to go to the mission in Japan. De Rhodes's dream of being a missionary in Japan was not to be realized. Because of persecutions in Japan, de Rhodes's superiors thought it wise not to send him there. Instead, they dispatched him to Cochinchina.

With regard to the political situation of VIETNAM in the 17th century, although there was a king of the Lê dynasty, he was in fact nothing more than a puppet, and real power lay in the hands of two clans; the north, known to the West as Tonkin, was under the Trinh clan, and the center, known then as Cochinchina, under the Nguyen clan. Continuous warfare was conducted between the two rival clans for total control of the country with no definitive results. De Rhodes's entire ministry in Vietnam was carried out during this struggle for power between Tonkin and Cochinchina.

De Rhodes's First Mission in Cochinchina (1624–1626). There were three Jesuit residences in Cochinchina when de Rhodes arrived in the country— Hoi An, Thanh Chiem, and Nuoc Man (Qui Nhon). He was assigned to that of Thanh Chiem to study the language under the guidance of Francisco de Pina. Meanwhile Andrea Palmiero, the Jesuit visitor, was planning to send missionaries to Tonkin. In July 1626, de Rhodes and Père Marques were recalled to MACAU to prepare for their mission in Tonkin.

De Rhodes's Mission in Tonkin (1627–1630). On March 1627, the two missionaries embarked a Portuguese merchant ship for Tonkin and arrived at Cua Bang (today Ba Lang) on March 19, 1627. Shortly afterwards, they met Lord Trinh Trang, who was on his way to wage war against Cochinchina. When Lord Trinh Trang returned in defeat from his military expedition, the missionaries accompanied him to Thang Long (modern Hanoi), the capital, and there began their mission in earnest. The great number of conversions aroused the opposition of eunuchs, Buddhist monks, and the concubines dismissed by their husbands who decided to become Christian. One of the monks accused the missionaries of joining in a plot against Lord Trinh Trang. As a result, on May 28, 1628, Lord Trinh Trang issued a decree forbidding his subjects, under pain of death, to meet with the missionaries and to embrace the religion they preached.

However, the lord tolerated the presence of de Rhodes and Marques in the hope that they would attract Portuguese traders. When the Portuguese ships had not come during the sailing season, the lord expelled the missionaries. In March 1629, they left for the south with the plan to return to Macau. However, in November, when two Jesuits, Gaspar do Amaral and Paul Saito, arrived, de Rhodes and Marques returned to the capital in their company. At first, Lord Trinh Trang tolerated their presence, but after six months, when the Portuguese ship returned to Macau, he ordered them to embark the ship and leave the country.

In May 1630, de Rhodes left Tonkin, never to return. He had worked there for more than three years. By numerical standards alone, his mission had been a huge success: when he left, there were 5,602 Christians. Banished from Tonkin, de Rhodes returned to Macau and stayed there for ten years during which he taught theology at the Madre de Deus College and looked after Chinese Christians. However, in 1639, events in Cochinchina once again made de Rhodes's missionary experience highly desirable. There were then some 15,000 Christians and 20 churches in central Vietnam. In 1639, the lord of Cochinchina, Nguyen Phuoc Lan, who suspected that the missionaries had assisted his brother's rebellion against him, ordered the seven Jesuits to leave the country.

De Rhodes's Second Mission to Cochinchina (1640–1645). Eager to continue the mission in Cochinchina, the new visitor Antonio Rubino canvassed for someone to send there. De Rhodes volunteered and was accepted. De Rhodes's second mission to Cochinchina was divided into four trips and lasted a total of 50 months from 1640 to 1645. As a whole, it was far more difficult and eventful than his mission in Tonkin. Four times he was exiled from the country. During that time, he baptized some 3,400 people, not counting the baptisms administered by his catechists. Compared with his mission in Tonkin which produced 5,602 conversions, de Rhodes's second mission in Cochinchina produced significantly fewer, though it was much longer and much more strenuous (50 versus 38 months). On July 3, 1645, sentenced to perpetual exile from Cochinchina, de Rhodes left Vietnam for Macau.

Return to Rome and the Establishment of the Hierarchy in Vietnam. De Rhodes's superiors in Macao decided that a man of his experience could render a vast service to the missions by going back to Europe to fetch spiritual and temporal help. In December 1645, de Rhodes began his return journey to Rome. Immediately after his arrival on June 27, 1649, he set out to realize his plan of having a hierarchy established in Vietnam. On Sept. 11, 1652, de Rhodes left for Paris where he found three priests of the *Société des Bons Amis* who were judged worthy candidates for the episcopacy, among whom was François PALLU. On learning that Rome was about to send French bishops to Vietnam, Portugal voiced fierce opposition. Meanwhile the Jesuit General, believing that de Rhodes's presence in the project of establishing a hierarchy in Vietnam would prevent it from being realized, decided to make him superior of the Jesuit mission in Persia. On Nov. 16, 1654, de Rhodes left Mar-

seilles for his new mission where he died on Nov. 5, 1660.

Achievements. Though not the first to arrive in Vietnam, de Rhodes is often proclaimed the founder of Vietnamese Christianity. No doubt he deserves this accolade. First, he carried out a highly successful mission in both parts of Vietnam, Tonkin and Cochinchina. Secondly, besides two priceless memoirs on the Vietnamese society in the seventeenth century and on the beginnings of Vietnamese Christianity, he published the earliest Vietnamese books in Romanized script (*quoc ngu*)— the *Dictionarium annamiticum, lusitanum, et latinum ope Sacrae Congregationis de Propaganda Fide in lucem editum ab Alexandro de Rhodes è Societate Jesu, ejusdemque Sacrae Congregationis Missionario Apostolico* (Rome 1651), and the *Cathechismus pro iis, qui volunt suscipere Baptismum, in Octo dies divisus. Phep giang tam ngay cho ke muan chiu phep rua toi, ma beao dao thanh duc Chua Bloi. Ope sacrae Congregationis de Propaganda Fide in lucem editus. Ab Alexandro de Rhodes è Societate Jesu, ejusdemque Sacrae Congregationsi Missionario Apostolico* (Rome 1651). Thirdly, he successfully lobbied for the establishment of a hierarchy in Vietnam. Thanks to his persistent efforts, on Sept. 9, 1659, two bishops, Pallu and Pierre Lambert DE LA MOTTE, were appointed apostolic vicars of Tonkin and Cochinchina respectively.

Bibliography: Q.C. DO, *La mission au Viet-Nam 1624–30 et 1640–45 d'Alexandre de Rhodes, S.J. avignonnais.* (Diss., Sorbonne, 1969). P.C. PHAN, *Mission and Catechesis: Alexandre de Rhodes and Inculturation in seventeenth-century Vietnam* (Maryknoll 1998).

[P. C. PHAN]

RIARIO

Family of papal *nipoti* that originated in modest circumstances at Savona in Liguria and rose to prominence through the marriage of Paolo Riario to Bianca, sister of Francesco della Rovere, later Pope SIXTUS IV. Elected pope in 1471, Sixtus promoted the careers of his Riario and DELLA ROVERE nephews, partly through excessive family feeling, partly to strengthen his difficult political position at Rome.

Pietro, cardinal; b. 1445; d. Rome, Jan. 5, 1474. Son of the pope's sister, Pietro followed his uncle into the FRANCISCANS. He was made cardinal Dec. 16, 1471, aged only 25. He accumulated benefices (including bishoprics and abbacies) of great value and lived in lavish ostentation. While his patronage of artists and scholars offers a partial mitigation, his personal immorality was notorious.

Girolamo, brother of Pietro; b. 1443; d. Forlì, April 14, 1488. Girolamo remained a layman, but also profited from NEPOTISM. The first step was his marriage (1477; betrothal 1472) to Caterina, natural daughter of Galeazzo Maria SFORZA, Duke of Milan. Sforza created him Count of Bosco, and Sixtus conferred the lordship of Imola on him. After Pietro's death, Girolamo became the closest adviser of his uncle. He was a prime mover of the infamous PAZZI conspiracy against the MEDICI and the ensuing war. In 1480, taking advantage of a disputed succession among the Ordelaffi dynasty, he made himself lord of Forlì. He became deeply involved in the feuds of aristocratic factions at Rome, siding with the ORSINI against their enemies the COLONNA. After his uncle's death, his influence waned, but he survived as lord of Imola and Forlì until conspirators murdered him. His widow preserved the throne for their son Ottaviano until 1500 when Cesare BORGIA overthrew her and she fled to Bologna.

Raffaele, cardinal; b. 1461; d. Naples, July 9, 1521. Raffaele was the son of Valentina Riario (niece of Sixtus IV) and Antonio Sansoni, but bore the Riario name. The pope made him cardinal (Dec. 10, 1477) when he was only 17. He nearly perished in the popular reaction against the Pazzi conspirators at Florence in 1478, being there innocently at the time. He was a notorious pluralist, accumulating bishoprics and other high offices. Under Pope Alexander VI he avoided Rome, but the election of JULIUS II, his uncle, ended his period of disfavor. In 1517 he was implicated in Cardinal Alfonso Petrucci's conspiracy against Pope LEO X, but he was pardoned after paying a heavy indemnity.

Alessandro, cardinal; b. 1543; d. Rome, July 18, 1585. One of the Riario-Sforza of Bologna, Alessandro was notable for his piety and legal learning, becoming an *uditore* in the apostolic CAMERA and patriarch of Alexandria (1570). Pope GREGORY XIII created him cardinal in 1578, and in 1580 sent him as legate to Portugal in a vain attempt to prevent the annexation of that country by PHILIP II OF SPAIN.

Bibliography: L. PASTOR, *The History of the Popes from the Close of the Middle Ages* (London-St. Louis 1938–61) 4:231–255, 300–330, 348–388; 5–8 *passim;* 19:227, 359–361; 21 *passim.* K. A. FINK, *Lexikon für Theologie und Kirche,* ed. J. HOFER and K. RAHNER (Freiberg 1957–65) 8: 1280–81. A. CAMPANA, *Enciclopedia Italiana di scienzi, littere ed arti* (Rome 1929–39) 29:200. G. B. PICOTTI, *ibid.* 200–201.

[C. G. NAUERT, JR.]

RIBADENEYRA, PEDRO DE

Historian, ascetical writer, and disciple of IGNATIUS OF LOYOLA; b. Toledo, Nov. 1, 1526; d. Madrid, Sept. 22, 1611. When in Rome as a page of Cardinal Alexander Farnese, he entered the Society of Jesus (Sept. 18, 1540). After studies at the University of Padua (1545–49), he taught at Palermo and at the Germanicum, Rome. Having been ordained in 1553, he was in the Netherlands from 1556 to 1560, where he consolidated the society and made a name as a preacher. He was in England in the winter of 1558–59. Between 1560 and 1572 he filled many important administrative offices in the society in Italy, but ill health compelled his return to Spain in 1573. From then until his death he was chiefly occupied in writing. Best known of his classic Castilian works are his life of St. Ignatius, a history of the schism in England, and the *Flos Sanctorum* (Lives of the Saints).

Bibliography: *Obras escogidas del padre Pedro de Rivadeneira,* ed. V. DE LA FUENTE (Madrid 1868). *Historias de la contrarre-forma,* ed. E. REY (Madrid 1945). *Monumenta historica Societatis Jesu* (Madrid 1894– ; Rome 1932–), esp. *Monumenta Ribadeneyra.* C. SOMMERVOGEL et al., *Bibliothèque de la Compagnie de Jésus,* 11 v. (Brussels-Paris 1890–1932; v. 12, suppl. 1960) 6:1724–58. J. M. PRAT, *Histoire du Père Ribadeneyra, discipline de saint Ignace* (Paris 1862). A. ASTRAIN, *Historia de la Compañía de Jesús,* 7 v. (Madrid 1902–25). *Enciclopedia de la Religión Católica,* ed. R. D. FERRERES et al., 7 v. (Barcelona 1950–56) 6:730–732.

[F. COURTNEY]

RIBERA, FRANCISCO DE

Exegete and professor of Sacred Scripture; b. Villacastín near Segovia, Spain, 1537; d. Salamanca, Nov. 24, 1591. In 1570, when he was already a priest and doctor in theology, he entered the Society of Jesus. He dreamed of imitating St. Jerome's eremitic dedication to the sacred sciences, but his life as a Jesuit in Spain was spent in missionary activity and scholarship, including 16 years at Salamanca teaching Scripture. His renowned Biblical exegesis, prayerfulness, penance, and zeal for souls gained the attention of St. Teresa of Avila, and he became her confessor and first biographer.

His commentaries demonstrate wide patristic erudition and, for his century, pioneered in proposing the unique literal sense of a scriptural passage. They include principally: *In librum XII prophetarum minorum commentarii sensum . . . historicum moralem et persaepe allegoricum complectentes* (Salamanca 1587); *In librum XII prophetarum commentarii selecti historici* (Salamanca 1598); *In epistolam ad Hebraeos commentarii* (Salamanca 1598); and *In evangelium secundum Iohannem commentarii* (Lyons 1623). In addition, the University of Salamanca library possesses many manuscripts of his exegesis. His one biography, *La vida de la madre Teresa de Jesús* (Salamanca 1590), has often been reproduced.

Bibliography: C. SOMMERVOGEL et al., *Bibliothèque de la Compagnie de Jésus,* 11 v. (Brussels-Paris 1890–1932; v. 12, suppl.

1960) 6:1761–67. H. HURTER, *Nomenclator literarius theologiae catholicae*, 5 v. in 6 (3d ed. Innsbruck 1903–13) 3: 238–240. A. AS-TRAIN, *Historia de la Compañía de Jesús en la Asistencia de España*, 7 v. (Madrid 1902–25) 4:48–50. F. STEGMÜLLER, *Lexikon für Theologie und Kirche*, ed. J. HOFER and K. RAHNER, 10 v. (2d, new ed. Freiburg 1957–65) 8:1282.

[T. T. TAHENY]

RIBET, JÉRÔME

Mystical theologian and writer; b. Aspet, Haute-Garonne, France, Jan. 16, 1837; d. Algiers, May 29, 1909. After entering the seminary at Toulouse in 1859, he completed his studies at the College of Saint-Sulpice in Paris, where he entered the Sulpicians and was ordained in 1863. For 20 years he taught philosophy and then theology at Clermont, Lyons, Rodez, and Orléans. In 1885 he left the Sulpicians to act as secretary to the bishop of Châlons and then returned to his diocese, where he was curê at Saman for about ten years. He spent his last years in retirement and writing, residing at various places.

Ribet accepted without question, as did his contemporaries, the essential distinction between asceticism and mysticism and the particular vocation to mystical states. In his principal work, *La mystique divine distinguée des contrefaçons diaboliques et des analogies humaines* (3 v. Paris 1879–83), he treats mystical contemplation and its stages, mystical phenomena distinct from and external to contemplation, such as visions and revelations, and examines their causes. Although sometimes insufficiently critical, Ribet's discussion of the discernment of phenomena was an important contribution in his day. His other writings include *L'ascétique chrétienne* (Paris 1887).

Bibliography: E. LEVESQUE, *Dictionnaire de théologie catholique*, ed. A. VACANT et al. (Paris 1903–50) 13.2:2659–60. P. POURRAT, *Christian Spirituality*, tr. W. H. MITCHELL et al., 4 v. (Westminster, Md. 1922–55) 4:506–507.

[J. C. WILLKE]

RICCARDI, PLACIDO, BL.

Benedictine priest; b. Trevi, Italy, June 24, 1844; d. Rome, March 14, 1915. He was baptized Tommaso. After studying philosophy at the Angelicum in Rome, he joined the Benedictines in Rome at the Abbey of SAINT PAUL-OUTSIDE-THE WALLS (1867) and took the name Placido. In 1870 he was arrested for not presenting himself for military service, and was sentenced by a military tribunal in Florence to a one-year imprisonment as a desert-er. The following month he was released from prison and placed in the army. After a month's service he was declared incapable of military service and dismissed. Thereupon he returned to his abbey and was ordained (1871). After spending several years there in various positions, he became in 1884 vicar for his abbot at S. Magno d'Amelia, a convent of Benedictine sisters juridically dependent on St. Paul's. In 1885 he returned to Rome as master of novices. He went again to S. Magno in 1887 as spiritual director for the sisters, and became highly esteemed as confessor for the clergy of that area. In 1895 he became rector of the ancient basilica in Farfa. His zealous labors there as pastor for the local faithful and his care for the pilgrims to Farfa gained him the title of apostle of the Sabine region. Serious illness caused him to spend his last three years in Rome. He was beatified in 1954.

Feast: March 14.

Bibliography: P. GRANFIELD, ''Blessed Placid Riccardi,'' *American Benedictine Review* 5 (1954) 299–305. I. SCHUSTER, *Profilo Storico del beato Placido Riccardi* (Milan 1954). J. L. BAUDOT and L. CHAUSSIN, *Vies des saints et des bienheureux selon l'ordre du calendrier avec l'historique des fêtes,* ed. by the Benedictines of Paris, 12 v. (Paris 1935–56); v. 13, suppl. and table générale (1959) 228–234.

[V. A. LAPOMARDA]

RICCI, LORENZO

Eighteenth general of the Jesuits at the time of the expulsion of the society from the Bourbon states and its suppression by Clement XIV (July 31, 1773); b. Florence, Aug. 2, 1703; d. Castel Sant' Angelo, Rome, Nov. 24, 1775. The Ricci family was among the oldest and most renowned in Florence. One of Lorenzo's brothers was canon of the cathedral and another served as chief magistrate of the Grand Duchy of Tuscany.

Early Life. Lorenzo attended Cicognini College, conducted by the Jesuits at Prato near Florence, and entered the novitiate of Sant' Andrea in Rome (1718). His extreme youth proved no disadvantage to his pursuit of learning or his practice of religious discipline, and after distinguishing himself in philosophy as well as the humanities, he was assigned to teach rhetoric and philosophy at the Jesuit College in Siena. After resuming his studies in Rome in 1731, he was selected for a public defense of the entire field of theology, an assignment in which he acquitted himself brilliantly.

After his ordination and his completion of formal studies, Ricci was appointed to the theological faculty of the Roman College, and there he pronounced the four vows of solemn profession Aug. 15, 1736. He continued teaching theology until 1751, when he was appointed spiritual director of the Roman College; he served in that capacity until 1755. In that year he became secretary to the newly elected general, Aloysius Centurione, and after the latter's death (Oct. 7, 1757), while Marquis Sebastião POMBAL was preparing the first devastating attack on the society from Lisbon, Father Ricci was chosen general on May 25, 1758, by the 19th General Congregation. Announcement of the choice was received with mixed reactions. One group of those conspiring to destroy the Jesuits is reported to have exulted, ''Ricci, Ricci, now we have them!'' Many members of the order and apprehensive friends thought that someone more active in public affairs and more alert to the Bourbon menace should have been chosen. Whatever the merit of these opinions, the selection of a general was to prove notably less significant than the choice of the next two popes.

Ricci and the Papacy. CLEMENT XIII became pope just six weeks after Ricci's election, and during the 11 years of his pontificate the two worked unremittingly to protect the Church and the society from their common enemies. Clement XIII, besides issuing the brief ''Apostolicum Pascendi,'' vigorously defending the order and adding an impressive endorsement to those of his predecessors, directed to rulers and ministers 150 letters that carried additional support and served notice to Voltairian agitators and the Bourbon states that he would not be forced into suppressing the order. The pope counseled Ricci to be ''silent, patient, and prayerful,'' evidently judging that reticence and meekness would best counteract the fierce hostility that bold missionary ventures, zealous aggressiveness, and daring rebukes of dissolute kings had occasioned. Ricci not only observed the pope's admonitions as faithfully as his responsibilities would permit, but made silence, patience, and prayer the prevailing theme of his letters to his fellow Jesuits. Annoying instances of interception of, or tampering with, his mail and the use of clumsy forgeries by enemies discouraged his use of the normal channels of communication. Despite these difficulties, he managed to deliver some stern remonstrances to those intent on destroying the order, and to refute each new or reedited diatribe as it appeared. The famous response ''Sint ut sum ant non sint'' (Let them continue as they are or cease to be), which peremptorily rejected the French proposal that an autonomous aggregation of Jesuits be formed for France, although mistakenly credited at times to Ricci rather than to Clement XIII, expresses a tenacity of purpose that was a notable attribute of both men.

Even when his subjects had been driven from Portugal, from France, and finally from Spain and Naples by the Bourbon conspiracy, Ricci cherished the hope that the

order would continue to flourish elsewhere, even if this were to require preternatural intervention. The assistant for Italy, Father Timoni, an indomitable optimist, did much to sustain a hope that was destined to be verified only by the remnant of the order that survived in White Russia, where CATHERINE II refused to promulgate the brief of suppression.

Clement XIII died on Feb. 2, 1769, as the result of the shock caused by a vicious threat of removal from the papacy, seizure of the Papal States, and schism if he delayed the suppression any longer.

Suppression by Clement XIV. Disquieting rumors that the factional tensions in the electoral conclave centered on the fate of the Jesuits severely tested Ricci's hopes, and the memory that he had personally sponsored Fra Giovanni Ganganelli for the cardinalate ten years before did not carry any reassurance when it was announced that he was to be consecrated as CLEMENT XIV. The demands that had hastened the death of Clement XIII then assailed the more pliant Clement XIV, and to appease the clamorous Bourbon governments, he became harsh toward those Jesuits exiled in, or seeking sanctuary in, the Papal States. His publication of statements about the necessity of maintaining Church-State amity even at the cost of certain ''sacrifices'' was obviously designed to serve as a prelude to the suppression ordered by the brief ''Dominus ac Redemptor,'' which was presented to Ricci on Aug. 16, 1773.

Father Ricci and his assistants were arrested and held for a day at the Roman College before their removal to CASTEL SANT' ANGELO on Sept. 23, 1773. There Ricci was to spend the two remaining years of his life under such close confinement that word of the death of his secretary, imprisoned nearby, did not reach him for six months. The tedious hearings to which he was subjected to satisfy the vindictiveness of the Bourbon courts not only exonerated him but thoroughly discredited the canards about buried treasure and dark conspiracies that had been fabricated to justify the suppression. Despite Ricci's advanced age and broken health, which made his narrow confinement and the boarding-up of his cell window superfluous precautions, Clement XIV refused any relaxation of custodial vigilance, explaining that it was maintained for ''reasons of safety.''

PIUS VI, who succeeded Clement after a conclave that again centered on the attitudes of candidates toward the Jesuits, had several years earlier detected and exposed one of the forged letters originating in Spain but purporting to have come from Ricci in Rome. Pius VI was considering a plea for the release of Ricci when death freed the prisoner. The pope arranged an elaborate funeral in S. Giovanni de' Fiorentini, where the body lay in state until the funeral Mass and burial in the church of the Gesù in the vault reserved for generals of the order.

Bibliography: G. C. CORDARA, *De suis ac suorum rebus . . . usque ad occasum S. I. commenatarii,* ed. G. ALBERTOTTI (Turin 1933). J. CRÉTINEAU-JOLY, *Clément XIV et les Jésuites* (Paris 1847). B. DUHR, *Geschichte der Jesuiten in den Ländern deutscher Zunge,* 4 v. in 5 (St. Louis 1907–28); ''Lorenzo Ricci,'' *Stimmen der Zeit* 114 (1928) 81–92. C. SOMMERVOGEL et al., eds., *Bibliothèque de la Compagnie de Jésus* (Brussels-Paris 1890–1932) 6:1785–92. L. PASTOR, *The History of the Popes from the Close of the Middle Ages* (London-St. Louis 1938–61) v.36, 37, 38. L. KOCH, *Jesuiten-Lexikon: Die Gesellschaft Jesu einst und jetzt* (Loovain-Heverlee 1962) 1535–39.

[R. F. COPELAND]

RICCI, MATTEO

Italian Jesuit, eminent missionary scientist, founder of the modern Chinese Church, and pioneer of cultural relations between Europe and China; b. Macerata, March of Ancona, Oct. 6, 1552; d. Beijing, China, May 11, 1610. When 16 he was sent to Rome for higher studies, but instead of embracing the legal profession as intended by his father, he entered Sant' Andrea novitiate on Aug. 15, 1571, and a year later began university courses at the Roman College, where his professor of mathematics was the celebrated Christopher CLAVIUS. Having had his mind long set on the order's expanding Asian missions, he set out for Portugal on May 18, 1577, and the following spring sailed from Lisbon with the annual fleet to the East Indies, reaching Goa on Sept. 13, 1578. There he applied himself to theology until the early months of 1582 and was ordained at midpoint of his studies (at Cochin on July 25, 1580).

Conquest through Learning. By this time there was in process a radical change in mission policy respecting the Middle Kingdom, hermetically sealed off to outsiders beyond a periodic mercantile fair at Canton. Alessandro VALIGNANO, the Jesuit visitor in the Far East, had matured a bold, farsighted plan to break through China's isolationism by engaging the Chinese intelligentsia on its own level of language, social customs, and superior talent. To prepare himself for this master enterprise, Ricci's fellow Jesuit in Rome and Goa, Pompilio (Michele) Ruggieri, was summoned to Macao in 1579. After intensive language study, he conducted several exploratory conversations in nearby Guangdong Sheng cities. No sooner had Ricci completed his theology than he too was ordered to Macao to help Ruggieri. He reached the Portuguese colonial outpost on Aug. 7, 1582, and the following year, on September 10—a date thereafter memorable in China mission annals—the two pioneer missionaries settled at Chaoking (Chao-ch'ing), seat of

Matteo Ricci. (©Bettmann/CORBIS)

the friendly *Tsung-tu* or viceroy of the two provinces of Guangdong Sheng and Guangxi, who had in fact welcomed them there. It was at the prefect's insistence that, to lessen suspicions of their intent, the foreign immigrants adopted the garb of Buddhist monks. Two years later, in May 1585, they dedicated a small church and residence.

Honored Scientist. ''Blue-eyed and with a voice melodious like a bell,'' as a Chinese gazette of the day described him, Ricci instantly made his reputation as a scientist of astonishing versatility. Demonstration of such novelties as Venetian prisms, European books, paintings and engravings, sundials, clocks, and projection of maps attracted a steady stream of the educated. Further, designed and displayed there for the first time, his remarkable World Map, ''Great Map of Ten Thousand Countries,'' perfected by later retouches, effected a revolution in traditional Chinese cosmography by delineating China's proper area relative to global dimensions. It was the first of a series of what became Ricci's major contribution to China, namely, the composition of works in

Chinese on various subjects—mathematics, apologetics, literature, catethetics—comprising altogether more than 20 during his years of fruitful activity. Of his many works, the treatise *T'ien-chu shih-i* (The True Meaning of the Lord of Heaven) stands out as his *magnum opus* and a lasting contribution to Confucian-Christian dialogue.

Thus was set the pattern of evangelization that Ricci would unfalteringly pursue to the end. His vision was to win the intellectual masters of Confucian society, using the ascendancy of learning as a magnet. To critics at home who clung to old-fashioned concepts of mission objectives, Ricci wrote that the scientific apostolate he and his associates had initiated in China was worth far more than making thousands of piecemeal converts, for it was the means that would eventually lead to the "universal conversion of the whole kingdom *en bloc*"—mighty China as a Christian unit. His role in the reciprocal transmission of European-Chinese cultures, praised by all students of history, must be viewed in this spiritual perspective.

Western Mandarin. Ousted from Zhaoqing through a replacement of viceroys, the two fathers settled at Shaochow, farther north in Guangdong Sheng (Aug. 26, 1589). There Ricci made his most significant move to that date. Discarding Buddhist attire, which had proved a hindrance in his dealings with Confucian students, he moved directly into the social stratum of the professional literati. From then on he was "Doctor from the Great West Ocean," wearing the ceremonial square bonnet and the silk robes of the Confucian scholar. Ricci could accordingly lecture authoritatively to his numerous clientele from a position of equality and receive for himself and the Christian culture he represented the amenities of the mandarin bureaucracy. The timing of this move was providential. Valignano, the ever-vigilant strategist, had all along been urging his protégé to strike out to the chief administrative and scholastic centers of the country, the southern capital of Nanjing, and after that, imperial Beijing itself, the residence of the Ming court. Greater responsibility, as well as freedom of action, was accorded Ricci by his appointment on Aug. 4, 1597, as superior and director of Jesuit personnel and works in China, which thus were freed from links with Macau that had become undesirable. At last, with considerable personal fame, influential contacts, and a singular mastery of Chinese thought and action, Ricci felt himself equipped for the high adventure Valignano wanted him to undertake. His determined march northward to the seat of empire and the decade of impressive service he there rendered Church and adopted country under the shadow of the appreciative Wan-li sovereign constitute China mission history's most dramatic chapter.

Entrance to Imperial Beijing. There were two milestones in Ricci's progress. Starting out from Nanchang, metropolis of Jiangxi, where three years earlier he had founded a permanent midway post, Ricci reached the walls of Beijing for the first time on Sept. 7, 1598, but, his entrance blocked by intriguing officials, he was forced back to Nanjing, his new headquarters; then, two years later, accompanied by the youthful Spaniard Diego Pantoja, he was again at the gates seeking admission. Spectacularly, and armed with an imperial summons, the two pilgrims from the West Ocean rode into the capital on Jan. 24, 1601, presented their gifts to the throne, were granted right of residence, and were allotted a subsidy for their avowed exploration of mathematics and astronomy. Helped by these natural aids, they would bring the Gospel to the highest non-Christian civilization in that age.

Last Years. Once securely established in Beijing and hard at his academic work, Ricci had only a brief span of life left to pursue his transcendent objective of a China turned Christian vertically, from the top down. Despite his mounting prestige at court, the noble friendships he formed, and the undeniable authority he commanded in the circles of the learned, these terminal years were burdened with toil and tensions that undermined his constitution and, as he himself confessed, made him old and white-haired before his time. Forewarned by this condition, he reflected on how best to secure permanency for the project on which he had so long concentrated his moral and intellectual energies. Shortly before the fatal decline of 1610, he confided to the fathers that he felt that his death at the height of his career would be the greatest benefit he could render the fledgling China Church. He meant, it seems, that he envisioned his tomb standing forever visible to the Chinese people he loved. It was a prophetic sentiment. His grave outside the city walls was the gift of the Emperor, the Son of Heaven, and was honored with imperial consecration. Known throughout the realm as Li Mat'ou, this missionary scholar from the West became and has remained one of the most respected foreign figures in Chinese history.

Western students of Chinese science and civilization acknowledge in Matteo Ricci a rare combination of endowments: Renaissance humanism brought to its finest and illumined by unusual qualities of mind and heart, a rich Italian temperament in which the disciples of Confucius admired their own ideal of suavity and tact, profound appreciation of Chinese cultural and moral values and the possibility of their integration with the European heritage under the aegis of Catholic philosophy, and an exemplary priestly and apostolic commitment that inspired unbounded zeal. This combination was the key to his life's splendid vocation and ranks him as "one of the most remarkable and brilliant men in history" [J. Needham, *Sci-*

ence and Civilization in China (2d ed. Cambridge 1961) 1:148].

See Also: CHINESE RITES CONTROVERSY.

Bibliography: For a Chinese-English critical edition of Matteo Ricci's *T'ien-chu shih-i* (True Meaning of the Lord of Heaven) see: *The True Meaning of the Lord of Heaven*, tr. D. LANCASHIRE and P. HU KUO-CHEN, ed. E. J. MALATESTA (St. Louis 1985). For other collections of his writings, see: *Opere storiche . . . ,* ed. P. TACCHI-VENTURI, 2 v. (Macerata, Italy 1911–13), memoirs and extant correspondence; *Fonti Ricciane,* ed. with notes by the sinologist P. M. D'ELIA 3 v. (Rome 1942–49), lacks the correspondence; before these works the memoirs were known through the Latin, *De christiana expeditione apud Sinas . . . ,* tr. N. TRIGAULT (Augsburg 1615) or later vernacular versions. Eng. from Trigault's Latin, *China in the 16th Century,* tr. For studies of his life and work, see: L. J. GALLAGHER (New York 1953). G. H. DUNNE, *Generation of Giants* (Notre Dame, Ind. 1962) E. DUCORNET, *Matteo Ricci* (Paris 1992). D. E. MUNGELLO, *The Chinese Rites Controversy: Its History and Meaning* (Nettetal 1994). J. D. SPENCE, *The Memory Palace of Matteo Ricci* (New York 1984). J. D. YOUNG, *East-West Synthesis: Matteo Ricci and Confucianism* (Hong Kong 1980).

[F. A. ROULEAU/EDS.]

RICCI, SCIPIONE DE'

Bishop of Pistoia; b. Florence, Italy, Jan. 9, 1741; d. Rignana, near Florence, Dec. 27, 1809. During his studies at the Roman College he became acquainted with persons of Jansenist tendencies. As a student later at the University of Pisa he came under the influences of the ENLIGHTENMENT, the GALLICANISM of the French APPELLANTS, and rigid AUGUSTINIANISM. After ordination (1766) he returned to FLORENCE and frequented the company of men interested in religious studies but opposed to the Roman Curia. As vicar-general of the Archdiocese of Florence (1775–80) he did not hide his sympathies, similar to those of Count Dupac de Bellegarde, a French abbot and an adherent of the schism of UTRECHT; of Giovanni Lami, a disciple of Freemasonry and the Enlightenment; and of Pietro Tamburini, professor of theology at Pavia; and other promoters of JANSENISM in Italy. Because of his friendship with Leopold I, Grand Duke of Tuscany, Ricci became bishop of Pistoia, then united with the See of Prato (1780). Heeding the advice of French appellants and the schismatic bishops of Utrecht, he introduced into his diocese radical changes in ecclesiastical discipline, studies, administration, and liturgy. He also caused writings of Italian and foreign Jansenists to be printed and widely diffused. He condensed in 57 propositions the ecclesiastical changes that found expression in the Synod of PISTOIA (1786). At the ensuing national assembly of the bishops of the Grand Duchy held in Florence (1787), Ricci sought to create a schismatic church, but the bishops disavowed the decrees of Pistoia. Popular reaction against these innovations caused Ricci to flee and then to resign his diocese (1791).

Scipione de' Ricci.

After Pius VI condemned the Synod of Pistoia in the apostolic constitution *AUCTOREM FIDEI* (1794), Ricci was evasive but finally submitted "purely and simply." His submission to Pius VII in 1805 he considered "a grammatical sacrifice." He was a friend of the French constitutional priests GREGOIRE, Mouton, and Clement; but this did not prevent his leading an irreproachable and pious private religious life. During his final years, spent in confinement in Rignana, he composed his memoirs, which testify to his ambivalent personality. Although he lacked a solid theological training and was somewhat mediocre culturally, he was animated by grandiose reform aspirations. His prestige was due to his episcopal dignity and to his friendship with Leopold, who desired social reforms and changes favorable to his absolutist aims. Ricci was influenced by Jansenism, Gallicanism, FEBRONIANISM, and JOSEPHISM. His outlook revealed also the anticurial spirit of SARPI, the ardor of SAVONAROLA, and the zeal for reforming religion common in 18th-century Italy and found in men such as MURATORI and Lambertini (Benedict XIV). Aspirations for modernization, hagiographical and liturgical revisions, ecclesiastical and cultural reforms, and desires to purify even legitimate forms of piety found in Ricci a heretical and schismatic deviation and a lack of discipline that rendered precarious such innovations as translations of the Missal and prayers, new norms for a just distribution of ecclesiastical goods and honors, and changes in clerical education and in catechetical instruction.

Bibliography: *Memorie di S. de' Ricci vescovo di Pistoia e Prato scritte da lui medesimo e pubblicate con documenti,* ed. A. GELLI, 2 v. (Florence 1865). N. RODOLICO. *Gli amici e i tempi di S. de' R.* (Florence 1920). B. MATTEUCCI, *S. de' R.: Saggio storico teologico sul giansenismo italiano* (Brescia 1940), with full bibliog. I. CARREYRE, "Synode de Pistoie," *Dictionnaire de théologie catholique,* ed. A. VACANT et al., 15 v. (Paris 1903–50; Tables Générales 1951–) 12.2:2134–2230. L. PASTOR, *The History of the Popes From the Close of the Middle Ages,* 40 v. (London-St. Louis 1938–61): v.1, 6th ed.; v.2, 7th ed.; v.3–6, 5th ed.; v.7–8, 11–12, 3d ed.; v.9–10, 4th ed.; v.13–40, from 1st German ed. *Geschichte der Päpste seit dem Ausgang des Mittelalters,* 16 v. in 21. (Freiburg 1885–1933; repr. 1955–) v. 39. L. WILLAERT, *Lexikon für Theologie und Kirche,* ed. J. HOFER and K. RAHNER, 10 v. (2d, new ed. Freiburg 1957–65) 8:524–525.

[B. MATTEUCCI]

RICCI, VITTORIO

Dominican missionary, prefect apostolic of Formosa (Taiwan) and southern China; b. Fiesole, near Florence, Italy, Jan. 18, 1621; d. Parian, near Manila, Philippines, Feb. 17, 1685. After studying at Fiesole and after later studies and teaching in Rome, Ricci met Juan Bautista MORALES, who interested him in the missions. As Morales's procurator in Rome, he obtained the CHINESE RITES decree (1645) and aided him in establishing the University of Manila. In 1648 Ricci went to the Philippines, where he carried on missionary work among the Chinese of Parian. In July 1655 he moved to Amoy (Fukien), China, where he served as procurator of the Spanish Dominicans. There he gained the confidence of Koxinga, "lord of the seas," a pirate who sent Ricci to the Philippines to demand their submission to his rule. Ricci did not return to Amoy until after Koxinga's death (1661). As prefect apostolic of Formosa and southern China, he performed many delicate missions in China, Taiwan, and the Philippines in an effort to establish peace among the Spanish, Dutch, and natives, all of whom were vying for control of the area. After one such mission in 1666, Ricci was seized by Governor Salcedo of Manila and imprisoned for treason. After Salcedo's removal, Ricci was freed and resumed his important religious tasks. The manuscript of his principal work, *Hechos de la Orden de Predicadores en el Imperio de China,* was completed in 1667.

Bibliography: B. M. BIERMANN, *Die Anfänge der neueren Dominikanermission in China* (Münster 1927). J. M. GONZÁLEZ, *Un Misionero diplomático: Vida del padre Vittorio Ricci* (Madrid 1955).

[B. M. BIERMANN]

RICE, EDMUND IGNATIUS, BL.

Married educator, founder of the Irish Christian Brothers and the Presentation Brothers; b. June 1, 1762, near Callan (Westcourt), Co. Kilkenny, Ireland; d. Aug. 29, 1844, at Mount Sion, Waterford.

The fourth of the seven sons of the wealthy farmer Robert Rice and his wife Margaret, Rice attended the Catholic school at Moat Lane, Callan, which despite the provision of the iniquitous penal laws, the authorities suffered to exist. After preparing at Kilkenny for a business career, he went to Waterford in 1778 to serve as apprentice to his uncle, Michael Rice, a successful export and import trader, and, after the latter's death, became sole proprietor. Edmund married in 1785, but his wife, Mary Elliot, died suddenly in 1789 during a hunting trip.

The death of his wife was a turning point in Rice's life. At first he thought of entering a contemplative order on the Continent or the nearby Cistercian monastery at Mellary, but his brother, an Augustinian who had but just returned from Rome, discountenanced the idea. Rice, thereupon, devoted himself to the extension of his business. Some years later, however, he again desired to become a religious, then decided that his vocation was among the oppressed, poverty–stricken, and uneducated Irish Catholics. He provided for his only daughter and gave up his business career in order to dedicate himself to the service of God.

In 1796, he sought authorization from Pius VI to create a society to provide free education for poor boys. With papal encouragement and the permission of the bishop, Rice and three disciples opened a school in Waterford (1803). In 1809 they took vows and formed a religious society following the rule of the Presentation Sisters of Cork. This arrangement proved unsatisfactory, because each house was autonomous as to personnel and finances and subject directly to the local bishops. At the urging of Daniel Murray, then auxiliary bishop of Dublin, Rice successfully petitioned Pius VII to permit the adoption of the rule of the Christian Brothers, founded by St. John Baptist de La Salle. Rice made his religious profession once more, this time as Brother Ignatius (1821). He was then elected the first superior general of the Irish Christian Brothers.

As a citizen he was distinguished for his probity, charity, and piety; he was an active member of a society established in the city for the relief of the poor. He was known to be an intensely committed yet modest and spiritual man. Following his peaceful death, Rice was interred in the monastery cemetery (Mt. Sion) in Dublin and marked with a simple stone. Since then a chapel was erected on the site.

At Rice's beatification (Oct. 6, 1996), John Paul II called him "an outstanding model of a true lay apostle and a deeply committed religious. The love which he first gave to his young wife and which, after her untimely death, he always showed for his daughter, blossomed into a host of spiritual and corporal works of mercy, as he helped the clergy of his parish meet the pressing needs of his fellow citizens oppressed by poverty and the weight of anti-Catholic legislation."

Feast: May 5.

Bibliography: *L'Osservatore Romano*, English edition, no. 27 (1996): 12–13. *A Time of Grace—School Memories: Edmund Rice and the Presentation Tradition of Education*, ed. by J. M. FEHENEY (Dublin 1996). A CHRISTIAN BROTHER, *Edmund Ignatius Rice and the Christian Brothers* (New York 1926). D. BURTON, *Edmund Rice, Merchant Adventurer* (London 1964). J. D. FITZPATRICK, *Edmund Rice* (Dublin 1945). D. KEOGH, *Edmund Rice* (Portland, Oregon 1996). D. RUSHE, *Edmund Rice: The Man and His Times* (Dublin 1981). P. R. WILSON, *Educating Street Kids: A Ministry to Young People in the Charism of Edmund Rice* (New York 1991).

[J. H. VAUGHAN]

RICE, LUTHER

Founder of the General Missionary Convention of the Baptist Denomination; b: Northboro, Mass., March 25, 1783; d. Edgefield, S.C., Sept. 25, 1836. He prepared for the Congregational ministry at Williams College and Andover Seminary, Massachusetts, where he was instrumental in awakening interest in foreign missions. In 1812 he was ordained and sailed for India as one of the first group of American missionaries. Arriving independently at the same conclusions on faith before Baptism as those of a colleague, the Rev. Adohiram Judson, Rice was rebaptized at Calcutta by English Baptist missionaries. Returning to America in 1813, he persuaded local Baptist associations to unite in a nationwide missionary society. The General Missionary Convention, meeting at Philadelphia, Pa., on May 18, 1814, established the Baptist Board for Foreign Missions and agreed to reconvene every three years. Since the convention was the only centralized Baptist agency, Rice sought to make it responsible for home missions and educational activities. He won its support for a theological school (now Andover Newton) and for Columbian College (now George Washington University, founded in 1822 at Washington, D.C.). Baptist financial troubles forced Rice to resign as treasurer of Columbian College in 1826, and thereafter the work of the convention was confined to foreign missions.

Bibliography: J. B. TAYLOR, *Memoir of Rev. Luther Rice . . .* (Richmond 1843; 2d ed. Nashville 1937). R. G. TORBET, *A History of the Baptists* (rev. ed. Valley Forge 1963).

[R. K. MACMASTER]

RICH, RICHARD

Lord chancellor; b. St. Laurence Jewry, London, 1496?; d. Rochford, Essex, June 12, 1567. A student at Cambridge and the Middle Temple, Rich seems to have led a dissipated youth. He was a good lawyer, however, and served on several royal commissions. He also represented Colchester in the "Reformation Parliament" (1529–36). Knighted and appointed solicitor general in 1533, Rich loyally supported Henrician policies. His evidence, based on private interviews with Thomas MORE and John FISHER, was instrumental in securing their conviction. More accused Rich of perjury, a charge history has sustained. Henry VIII rewarded Rich with honors, especially the chancellorship of the court of augmentations. Speaker of the parliament that met in 1536, he was second to Thomas CROMWELL in his influence and assisted him in suppressing the monasteries.

Rich grew wealthy on these spoils. He also managed to survive Cromwell's demise in 1540 and quickly adapted his policies to fit his sovereign's mood. Created a baron and lord chancellor (1548), he soon deserted the Protector Somerset for the cause of John Dudley, Earl of Warwick. Resigning the chancellorship in 1551, Rich retired to Essex. A halfhearted supporter of Lady Jane Grey, he soon declared for Queen Mary, thus surviving another change of regime. Rich fostered Catholic practices in Essex and persecuted Protestants. At Elizabeth's accession, he swore his loyalty, but refused to accept the Act of Uniformity (1559). An ambitious and greedy politician, Rich has been criticized by historians as a man of skill who was also an unscrupulous timeserver.

Bibliography: A. F. POLLARD, *The Dictionary of National Biography from the Earliest Times to 1900* (London 1885–1900) 16:1009–12. P. HUGHES, *The Reformation in England* (New York 1963). R. W. CHAMBERS, *Thomas More* (Westminster, Md. 1949). H. F. M. PRESCOTT, *Mary Tudor* (rev. ed. New York 1953).

[P. S. MCGARRY]

RICHARD, GABRIEL

Missionary; b. Saintes, France, Oct. 15, 1767; d. Detroit, Sept. 13, 1832. He entered the Society of Saint-Sulpice and was ordained in October 1791 at Issy, near Paris. For a very brief period, he taught at the Sulpician seminary there, but the anticlerical policies of the French Revolutionary government forced him and three of his confreres, Ambrose Maréchal, François Ciquard, and François Matignon, to leave France. On June 24, 1792, the group arrived in Baltimore, where the Sulpicians staffed the newly established St. Mary's Seminary. Because he was not needed in Baltimore, Richard was given missionary assignments at Prairie du Rocher and Kaskaskia, Illinois, where he labored for six years. After his transfer to Detroit in 1798, he was responsible also for the missions of Wisconsin and Michigan. So successful were his efforts that in 1801 more than 500 persons were ready for Confirmation when Bishop Pierre Denaut of Quebec visited Detroit.

In 1804 Richard established an academy for girls and a seminary at Detroit, but a fire the following year destroyed both institutions, as well as Richard's church and rectory. Within three years the church was rebuilt and six primary schools and two girls' academies were erected. Always interested in education, Richard was instrumental in the founding of the University of Michigan in Ann Arbor in 1817 and served there as vice president and professor. He is remembered also for a series of lectures on religious subjects given in 1807 at the request of the governor and other officials of the Michigan Territory.

In 1808 Richard visited Baltimore, where he secured a printing press and type. The next year, he published the *Michigan Essay or Impartial Observer,* the first paper in Michigan. During the next three years, he published seven books dealing with education and religion. After the British victory at Detroit in the War of 1812, Richard was taken to Canada and imprisoned at Sandwich, although he was given many liberties. When released, he returned to Detroit and rebuilt his missions. In 1823 he was elected as a representative to the U.S. Congress, the only Catholic priest ever to hold a seat in the House of Representatives. He was befriended by Henry Clay, who often translated the Sulpician's faulty English for the benefit of the House. Richard lost his bid for reelection in 1826 mainly because of the opposition of several of his parish trustees. A year later, when the Holy See issued a brief erecting the Diocese of Detroit, Richard was named first bishop. But his nomination was suppressed, and Detroit remained without a bishop until 1833, six months after Richard's death during a cholera epidemic.

Bibliography: G. PARÉ, *The Catholic Church in Detroit, 1701–1888* (Detroit 1951). P. GUERIN, *Le Martyr de la Charité ou Notice sur Mr. G. Richard, Missionaire* (Paris 1850), with excerpts from R.'s letters. F. WOODFORD and A. HYMA, *Gabriel Richard: Frontier Ambassador* (Detroit 1958). D. MAST, *Always a Priest: The Life of Gabriel Richard, S.S.* (Baltimore 1965). L. COOMBS and F. BLOUIN, JR., *Intellectual Life on the Michigan Frontier: The Libraries of Gabriel Richard and John Monteith* (Ann Arbor 1985). L. TENTLER, *Seasons of Grace: A History of the Catholic Archdiocese of Detroit* (Detroit 1992).

[J. Q. FELLER]

RICHARD DE LA VERGNE, FRANÇOIS MARIE

Cardinal, archbishop of Paris; b. Nantes, March 1, 1819; d. Paris, Jan. 28, 1908. After theological studies at Saint-Sulpice, Paris, he was ordained (Dec. 21, 1844) and made graduate studies in theology in Rome (1846–49). Returning to Nantes, he became secretary to the bishop and vicar-general (1850–69). After Bishop Jacquemet's death (1869) he preached parish missions. As bishop of Belley (1872–75) he began the beatification process for the Curé of Ars. He became coadjutor to Cardinal Guibert (May 7, 1875), succeeded him as archbishop of Paris (July 8, 1886), and was named cardinal (May 24, 1889). In this post he showed no favor toward the Third Republic or the RALLIEMENT, but in the face of an anticlerical government he zealously defended the religious congregations threatened with expulsion, the cause of Catholic education, and that of the Church itself at the time of the law separating Church and State (1905). This law caused him to be expelled from his see some months before his death. The foundation and organization of the Institut Catholique in Paris owes much to him. He was one of the first to oppose LOISY. The Roman decree *LAMENTABILI* contains 18 propositions taken almost verbatim from Richard's memorial to the Holy See concerning Modernism. Richard was known for his asceticism, modesty, and mildness joined to firmness. Besides pastoral letters he published several works.

Bibliography: H. L. ODELIN, *Le Cardinal Richard: Souvenirs* (2d ed. Paris 1922). M. CLÉMENT, *Vie du Cardinal Richard* (Paris 1924). J. RUPP, *Histoire de l'Église de Paris* (Paris 1948). R. SCHERER, *Lexikon für Theologie und Kirche,* ed. J. HOFER and K. RAHNER, 10 v. (2d, new ed. Freiburg 1957–65) 8:1294–95.

[R. LIMOUZIN-LAMOTHE]

RICHARD DE MORES (RICARDUS ANGLICUS)

Important English canonist, priest, and Augustinian canon; b. Lincolnshire, date unknown; d. Dunstable (Diocese of Lincoln), Apr. 9, 1242.

Life. He was the first canonist of English origin to teach at the school of Bologna, where he also published a number of influential writings in the last decade of the twelfth century. In the tradition of the schools, he was known merely as ''Richard the Englishman,'' and many wrong guesses as to his identity have been made over the centuries by historians and bibliographers of canon law. It is now established that he was Richard de Mores (or Morins), prior of the Augustinian canons at Dunstable from 1202 to his death, and author of a substantial portion of the Dunstable Annals. He left a record of his long tenure as prior, but of his early years we know only what can be deduced from his canonistic writings. He first studied the arts before turning to law. His first canonical treatise places him in a group of Anglo-Norman canonists in Paris (*c.* 1186–87); given the date of his death, he would not have been much older than 25 at that time. About ten years later he was regent master in Bologna. During the interval he may or may not have taught for some time in England, but in all probability he had connections with the civil law glossators of the Vacarian School in Oxford. In Bologna he completed within a brief span of years a surprising number of works. Since none of these contain any reference to the decretals of INNOCENT III (1198–1216), we may presume that Richard was back in England by 1198. He was a canon of the Augustinian house of Merton when elected prior of Dunstable in 1202. He was ordained to the priesthood on Sept. 21, 1202. Matters of administration, visitations, and commissions entrusted to him by pope and king, by legates and bishops, filled the second half of his life, except for one brief interval. On his way back from the Fourth Lateran Council (1215) he remained in Paris for a year to attend courses in theology. In 1239, three years before his death, and when he was close to 80 years of age, he acted as one of the judges in a controversy between London and Canterbury on the metropolitan's right of visitation.

Writings. The canonistic works of Richard de Mores all antedate his long years in office as prior of Dunstable; with the exception of his *Summa de ordine iudiciario,* they exist only in manuscript tradition. In 1965 critical editions of the other canonistic works were in preparation for the *Monumenta Iuris Canonici* under the general editorship of the Institute of Medieval Canon Law. *Summa questionum,* written in Paris (*c.* 1186–87), probably represents a formal course of *questiones* given on Fridays (*questiones veneriales* in one of the manuscripts); this book of his youth is closely related to the anonymous Anglo-Norman *summa, Omnis qui iuste* (*Lipsiensis*) and the *Summa questionum* of master HONORIUS, both of the same period and school. Later, in Bologna, Richard did not include it in the list he gave of his writings in the prologue to the *Distinctiones* (below). The works of his Bolognese years were all completed *c.* 1196 to 1198, although they were probably much longer in preparation. They are *Summa brevis,* an elementary introduction (consisting partly of mnemonic verse) to GRATIAN'S *Decretum; Distinctiones decretorum,* one of his most important works (at least 16 manuscripts are preserved today), systematically presenting the concepts and problems contained in the *Decretum* in the form of analytical diagrams; *Argumenta* or *Notabilia decretorum,* probably lost; *Summa de ordine iudiciario,* a treatise on canonical procedure that was widely read and annotated in its day (for editions, see bibliography); *Casus decretalium,* a summary of the contents, chapter by chapter, of Bernard of Pavia's *Breviarum extravagantium*—the compilation of decretals that had just then been adopted in Bologna as a new subject in the curriculum (known later as *Compilatio I*); *Apparatus decretalium,* one of the first and most influential commentaries of glosses on the new compilation and an important source for TANCRED'S *Glossa ordinaria* on *Compilatio I* and, indirectly, for BERNARD OF PARMA'S *Glossa ordinaria* on the decretals of GREGORY IX; and *Generalia* or *Brocarda,* general maxims and commonplaces drawn from the texts of the new compilation, each rule presented with a string of pros and cons and a dialectical solution of the antinomies. Richard published his *Generalia* both as part of the *Apparatus decretalium* and as a separate collection.

Bibliography: *Magistri Ricardi Anglici ordo iudiciarius ex codice Duacensi . . . ,* ed. C. WITTE (Halle 1853). L. WAHRMUND, ed., "Die Summa de ordine iudiciaris des Ricardus Anglicus," in *Quellen zur Geschichte des römisch-kanonischen Processes im Mittelalter,* v. 2.3 (Innsbruck 1915). "Annales prioratus de Dunstaplia" in *Annales Monastici,* v. 3, ed. H. R. LUARD, *Rerum Britannicarum medii aevi scriptores,* 244 v. (London 1858–96; repr. New York 1964–) 1866. F. GILLMANN, "R. A. als Glossator des Compilatio I," *Archive für katholisches Kirchenrecht* 107 (1927): 575–655. S. KUTTNER, *Repertorium der Kanonistik* (Rome 1937) 222–227, 323–325, 398, 417–418. J. C. RUSSELL, *Dictionary of Writers of Thirteenth-Century England* (New York 1936) 111–113, the first to identify the canonist as Richard de Mores. S. KUTTNER and E. RATHBONE, "Anglo-Norman Canonists of the Twelfth Century," *Traditio* 7 (1949–51): 329–339, 353–358. C. LEFEBVRE, "Recherches sur les manuscrits des glossateurs de la Compilatio Iª: L'Oeuvre de R. A.," *Congrès de droit canonique médiéval, . . . 1958* (Louvain 1959). E. M. MEIJERS, *Études d'histoire du droit,* ed. R. FEENSTRA and H. F. FISCHER, v. 3 (Leiden 1959) 278–279. S. KUTTNER, *Dictionnaire de droit canonique,* ed. R. NAZ, 7 v. (Paris 1935–65) 7:676–681, full bibliog.

[S. KUTTNER]

RICHARD FISHACRE

English Dominican theologian; b. Diocese of Exeter; d. Oxford, 1248. The first Dominican to study theology at the University of Oxford, he incepted under ROBERT BACON, his master and intimate friend, before 1240, and continued to teach there until his death. He introduced a new method of teaching, separating theological questions from moral instruction, using the *Sentences* in his magisterial lectures (*lectiones ordinariae*) and relegating *moralitates* to the Biblical course. This innovation displeased Bp. ROBERT GROSSETESTE [*Epistolae,* ed. H. R. Luard (London 1861) 346–347], but INNOCENT IV requested that Fishacre be encouraged, not hindered, from lecturing *ordinarie* on the *Sentences.* His unpublished commentary on the *Sentences,* the first to issue from Oxford, manifests considerable skill in theological, philosophical, scientific, and medical matters. Although he frequently quoted Aristotle and the ''Aristotelians,'' he followed the current Augustinian tradition on knowledge, divine illumination, and the hylomorphic composition of spiritual substances. On plurality of forms and other difficult problems he did not commit himself, but rather attempted to reconcile Aristotle with Augustinianism. His principal sources were St. BERNARD OF CLAIRVAUX, ALEXANDER OF HALES, HUGH OF SAINT-CHER, and Grosseteste. His influence was great both at Oxford and at Paris, notably on SIMON HINTON, ROBERT KILWARDBY, RICHARD RUFUS OF CORNWALL, WILLIAM OF MELITONA, St. BONAVENTURE, and indirectly on St. ALBERT THE GREAT. He was a remarkable preacher. Besides several sermons, which have survived, he is credited by NICHOLAS TREVET with *Postillae* on the first 70 Psalms, ''most beautiful, intermingled with sweetest moralities'' (Trevet, *Annales* 230); *Quodlibeta;* two treatises *De paenitentia;* and *De fide, spe et caritate.*

Bibliography: D. A. CALLUS, ''Introduction of Aristotelian Learning to Oxford,'' *Proceedings of the British Academy* 29 (1943) 229–281. A. B. EMDEN, *A Biographical Register of the University of Oxford to A.D. 1500* (Oxford 1957–59) 2:685–686. F. PELSTER, ''Das Leben und die Schriften des Oxforder Dominikanerlehrers Richard Fishacre,'' *Zeitschrift für katholische Theologie* 54 (1930) 518–553. D. E. SHARP, ''The Philosophy of Richard Fishacre,'' *The New Scholasticism* 7 (1933) 281–297. W. A. HINNEBUSCH, *The Early English Friars Preachers* (Rome 1951) 364–369. F. STEGMÜLLER, *Repertorium biblicum medii aevi* (Madrid 1949–61) 5:7266–69; *Repertorium commentariorum in Sententias Petri Lombardi* (Würzburg 1947) 1:718.

[D. A. CALLUS]

RICHARD FITZRALPH

Archbishop, theologian, controversialist whose views influenced John WYCLIF; b. Dundalk, Ireland, *c.* 1300; d. Avignon, Nov. 10, 1360. After studies at Oxford, Fitzralph spent a short period at Paris. He was chancellor of Oxford University (1332–34). Thereafter he held a series of benefices, and in 1346 became archbishop of Armagh. He was well known at Avignon (*see* AVIGNON PAPACY), preached several times before the papal court, and took part in current controversies about the BEATIFIC VISION, the Armenians, and the privileges of the MENDICANT ORDERS. As archbishop he quarreled with the friars and was cited to Avignon after a series of outspoken sermons against them in London (1356–57), but he died before the case was decided. A canonization process, begun in 1399, was dropped, but a shrine and cult to ''St. Richard of Dundalk'' are found as late as 1545.

Bibliography: Sources. R. FITZRALPH, *Defensorium curatorum* (Louvain 1475?); *Summa . . . in questionibus Armenorum*

(Paris 1512); *De pauperie Salvatoris,* in *Iohannis Wycliffe de dominio divino,* ed. R. L. POOLE (London 1890). **Literature.** R. L. POOLE, *The Dictionary of National Biography from the Earliest Times to 1900,* 63 v. (London 1885–1900) 7:194–198. E. AMANN, *Dictionnaire de théologie catholique,* 15 v. (Paris 1903–50) 13.2:2667–2668. A. GWYNN, *Studies* 22 (1933): 389–405, 591–607; 23 (1934): 395–411; 24 (1935): 25–42, 558–572; 25 (1936): 81–96; 26 (1937): 50–67. L. L. HAMMERICH, *The Beginning of the Strife between R. Fitzralph and the Mendicants* (Copenhagen 1938). A. B. EMDEN, *A Biographical Register of the University of Oxford to* A.D. *1500,* 3 v. (Oxford 1957–59) 2:692–694. G. LEFF, *R. F.: Commentator of the ''Sentences''* (Manchester, Eng. 1964).

[M. B. CROWE]

RICHARD GRANT OF CANTERBURY

Archbishop, also known as Le Grand or Wethershed; date of birth unknown; d. Aug. 3, 1231. Chancellor of Lincoln cathedral (1221–29), he was provided to Canterbury by GREGORY IX on Jan. 19, 1229, and was consecrated on June 10. The bull of provision refers to his reputation in the schools, which was known at the Papal Curia. Possibly he is to be identified with the ''Ricardus Anglicus'' who was regent in theology at Paris in 1218. As archbishop he was engaged in a sharp dispute with the justiciar, Hubert de Burgh; he went to Rome to plead his case, but died on the way home and was buried in the house of the Friars Minor at S. Gemini (Umbria).

Bibliography: J. C. RUSSELL, *Dictionary of Writers of 13th-Century England* (New York 1936) 115–116. M. GIBBS and J. LANG, *Bishops and Reform, 1215–1272* (London 1934; repr. 1962). P. GLORIEUX, *Répertoire des maîtres en théologie de Paris au XIII siècle* (Paris 1933–34) 1:118.

[C. H. LAWRENCE]

RICHARD KNAPWELL (CLAPWELL)

English Dominican, known variously as Cnapwell, Klapwell, etc., famous for his role in the Oxford controversies over THOMISM; b. Knapwell, Cambridgeshire, date unknown; d. Bologna, *c.* 1288. He was *baccalaureus sententiarius c.* 1280 and master of theology at Oxford in 1284. His *Notabilia* (or notes) *in 1 sententiarum* attest to his hesitation to accept Thomism fully, but also to his adoption of some of its theses, for example, the simplicity of the soul; his *Correctorium Corruptorii ''Quare''* shows him as one of its staunchest defenders.

Correctorium ''Quare.'' Scholars now agree on Knapwell's authorship of the *correctorium ''Quare,''* although F. Pelster ascribed it to the Dominican THOMAS OF SUTTON. It is the most complete of all the *CORRECTORIA.* From Aquinas's own writings Knapwell proved that the Franciscan ''correction'' was based on a failure to grasp the Thomist doctrine, which, correctly understood, is philosophically and theologically sound. On Oct. 29, 1284, JOHN PECKHAM confirmed the prohibition (1277) of ROBERT KILWARDBY and proclaimed the unicity thesis a dangerous error (*see* FORMS, UNICITY AND PLURALITY OF). Following the suggestion of his provincial, WILLIAM DE HOTHUM, that philosophical problems in which neither opinion is inconsistent with Catholic teaching should be defined in solemn disputation rather than by condemnation or prohibition, Knapwell discussed the vexed question "Whether faith about the essence of human nature united to the Word requires us to posit plurality of forms." He advanced 42 arguments for the pluralist opinion and 41 for the unicity view. In his solution he stated first the difficulty of the problem, viz, the difference of opinion between famous masters, especially between the two most famous (Aquinas and Kilwardby). Since both were Catholics and neither was a heretic, he defended them both; at the outset, however, he declared that the unicity thesis as understood by Aquinas was not erroneous. Next, he proposed three principles on which the solution depended and on which all disputants should agree: the nature of dimensive quantity, of symbolic quality, and of transformation. He then examined the evidence advanced for and against, explained each argument objectively and impartially, tried to reconcile both opinions, and, proclaiming both solutions equally Catholic, concluded: "all this is said without dogmatizing, and without detriment to a better opinion."

Reaction. A report of the proceedings was sent to Peckham. Twelve propositions were chosen from Knapwell's question and declared heretical. Knapwell was personally charged with teaching heresies and particularly with preferring as a more probable opinion that "no difficulty follows if there were in Christ, as man, one form." Knapwell did not appear, but his provincial entered a formal protest as to the incompetence of the court and appealed to the pope. On April 30, 1286, the archbishop, with his suffragans, withdrawing Knapwell's name and reducing the 12 articles to eight, pronounced them heretical in themselves or in their implications. The thesis of the unicity of form was expressly condemned as heretical and as a source of heresies (art. 8). Its supporters were excommunicated. Knapwell was accused of having asserted that "in these matters one is not bound to follow the pope's, or the Fathers' authority, but only the Bible, or necessary reason" (art. 7). This he vigorously denied [see Godfrey of Fontaines's *Quodlibet* 3.5, ed. M. de Wulf and A. Pelzer (Louvain 1904) 198; for the identity of Knapwell with *magister valens, see* P. Glorieux, *Recherches de théologie ancienne et médiévale* 12 (1940): 143–145]. Knapwell left for Rome, and his appeal was heard, as one may gather from Peckham's letter to the bishop of Lincoln (March 28, 1287) requesting urgent information about it. But before the matter was settled, the pope died, and his successor, Nicholas IV, a Franciscan, silenced Knapwell on Feb. 15, 1288. Knapwell went to Bologna, where he died. Peckham's action was considered by his contemporaries as harsh and *ultra vires*, and he knew it. On his own confession, the matter was reserved to the Holy See.

Against Peckham's expectations and pressures, Rome never condemned the unicity thesis. On the contrary, St. Pius X declared in 1914, almost in the same terms of the condemnation (cf. art. 8), that this thesis is one of the fundamental tenets of the Thomist synthesis, and as such is to be held and taught in the schools as *tuta* and *secura* [*Acta Apostolicae Sedis* 6 (1914): 385].

Bibliography: For Knapwell's writings, F. J. ROENSCH, *Early Thomistic School* (Dubuque 1964) 39–40. D. A. CALLUS, *The Condemnation of St. Thomas at Oxford* (2d ed. Oxford 1955); "The Problem of the Unity of Form and Richard Knapwell," *Mélanges offerts à Étienne Gilson de l'Academie française* (Toronto 1959). F. STEGMÜLLER, *Repertorium commentariorum in Sententias Petri Lombardi*, 2 v. (Würzburg 1947) 716. W. A. HINNEBUSCH, *The Early English Friars Preachers* (Rome 1951) 342–356, 389–391. F. PELSTER, *Zeitschrift für katholische Theologie* 52 (1928): 473–491. A. B. EMDEN, *A Biographical Register of the University of Oxford to A.D. 1500* (Oxford 1957–59) 2:1058.

[D. A. CALLUS]

RICHARD OF BURY

Bishop, royal official, bibliophile; b. near Bury-St.-Edmunds, Jan. 24, 1287; d. Durham, April 14, 1345. Born of a landowning family, Richard of Bury or Richard Aungerville studied at Oxford from 1302 to 1312, when he received the first of the enormous number of ecclesiastical benefices that he was to enjoy during the rest of his life, many of them being held in plurality by virtue of royal favor and papal PROVISION. In the same year (1312) his appointment as clerk in the royal treasury set him on a career of service to Edward II and Edward III as a financial expert and diplomat. As diplomat he constantly visited the courts of Europe, including the papal court at AVIGNON (1333) where he met PETRARCH. Even after becoming bishop of DURHAM in 1333 he was continuously engaged in the King's affairs (e.g., he served as chancellor, 1334–35), yet proved himself a kindly and conscientious pastor in his diocese. During his last years, he was able to devote himself more completely to collecting books, the real passion of his life, as witness his *Philobiblon,* a work remarkable in its use of the CURSUS, every clause being laced together in a concatenation of some 19,000 clausulae. He also compiled a *Libor epistolaris,* a formulary of belles lettres collected by Richard and including treatises of otherwise unknown Italian *dictatores.*

Bibliography: R. AUNGERVILLE, *The Philobiblon,* ed. A. TAYLOR (Berkeley 1948); *Liber epistolaris,* ed. N. DENHOLM-YOUNG (Oxford 1950). N. DENHOLM-YOUNG, ''Richard de Bury,'' *Transactions of the Royal Historical Society,* 4th ser., 20 (1937) 135–168. A. B. EMDEN, *A Biographical Register of the Scholars of the University of Oxford to A.D. 1500,* 3 v. (Oxford 1957–59) 1:323–326.

[D. NICHOLL]

RICHARD OF CAMPSALL

English secular theologian of Oxford; b. *c.* 1285; d. Oxford, *c.* 1350. Originally a fellow of Balliol College, he became a fellow of Merton College by 1306. Receiving his degree of master of arts by 1308, he studied theology and became regent master in theology by 1322. Throughout his life he was active in academic affairs as proctor and frequent delegate of the university. Present at the excommunication of the mayor of Oxford by the chancellor on Dec. 19, 1325, he was empowered by the chancellor to absolve the mayor on Jan. 10, 1326. He wrote questions on the first three books of the *Physics,* as well as *Notabilitates* on the whole *Physics;* these are not known to be extant. Existing works are *Quaestiones super librum Priorum Analyticorum,* a *Logica valde utilis et realis contra Ocham,* and 16 *Dicta* on contingency and divine foreknowledge. Campsall reacted to the influences of both DUNS SCOTUS and WILLIAM OF OCKHAM, but he remained an independent thinker. He was buried in the choir of Merton College chapel.

Bibliography: E. A. SYNAN, ''Richard of Campsall, an English Theologian of the 14th Century,'' *Mediaeval Studies* 14 (1952): 1–8; ''R. of C.'s First Question on the *Prior Analytics,*'' *Mediaeval Studies* 23 (1961): 305–323; ''Sixteen Sayings by R. of C. on Contingency and Foreknowledge,'' *Mediaeval Studies* 24 (1962): 250–262; ''The Universal and Supposition in a *Logica* Attributed to R. of C.,'' *Nine Mediaeval Thinkers: A Collection of Hitherto Unedited Texts,* ed. J. R. O'DONNELL (Toronto 1955). A. B. EMDEN, *A Biographical Register of the University of Oxford to A.D. 1500,* 3 v. (Oxford 1957–59) 1:344–345. G. C. BRODRICK, *Memorials of Merton College, with Biographical Notices of the Warden and Fellows* (Oxford 1885) 175.

[E. A. SYNAN]

RICHARD OF CANTERBURY

Or Richard of Dover, Benedictine monk, successor to Abp. Thomas BECKET; d. Feb. 16, 1184. Richard, a Norman by birth, was of considerable importance in the development of Canon Law in England (*see* CANON LAW, HISTORY OF, 4). Educated at Christ Church, Canterbury, where he became a monk, he was later chaplain to Abp. THEOBALD OF CANTERBURY. From 1157 he was prior of St. Martin's, Dover. His election to the See of Canterbury on June 3, 1173, though canonical, was contested; after a successful appeal, he was consecrated by Pope Alexander III on April 7, 1174, and appointed legate in his own province. Though he believed in cooperation with the lay power and was never extreme in his defense of the liberties of the Church, he was efficient and active in ecclesiastical administration and resolutely upheld the rights of his see. At Westminster in 1175 he presided over one of the earliest English provincial councils and promulgated some important canons. As judge delegate, legislator, and promoter of an influential decretal collection, he helped to build up a corpus of decretal law of permanent value.

Bibliography: *Materials for the History of Thomas Becket,* ed. J. C. ROBERTSON, 7 v. (*Rerum Brittanicarum medii aevi scriptores* 67; 1875–85) 7:561–564. W. HUNT, *The Dictionary of National Biography from the Earliest Times to 1900,* 63 v. (London 1885–1900) 16:1077–80. R. FOREVILLE, *L'Église et la royauté en Angleterre sous Henri II Plantagenet* (Paris 1943) 371–387, 517–524. C. R. CHENEY, *From Becket to Langton* (Manchester, Eng. 1956). C. N. L. BROOKE, ''Canons of English Church Councils in the Early Decretal Collections,'' *Traditio* 13 (1957) 471–479. C. DUGGAN, *Twelfth-Century Decretal Collections and Their Importance in English History* (London 1963).

[M. CHIBNALL]

RICHARD OF CONINGTON

English Franciscan theologian; d. Cambridge, 1330. His name is first mentioned in a document of 1300 when, along with John DUNS SCOTUS and 20 other Franciscans, he was presented to the bishop of Lincoln for faculties to hear confessions. A doctor of theology, he incepted at Oxford (*c.* 1305–07) and then became lector at the Cambridge friary (1308–10). He was the 16th provincial minister of the English province of Franciscans (1310–16). He assisted at the Council of VIENNE (1311–12) and with Martin of Alnwick took part in the great debate with the Franciscan SPIRITUALS. At this time also he wrote his treatise on evangelical poverty, *Beatus qui intelligit,* a work that brought an ironic reply from UBERTINO OF CASALE (*see* POVERTY CONTROVERSY). In 1322 Richard prepared his *Responsiones ad conclusiones domini papae,* a dialogue between friar and pope regarding difficulties that could arise from the papal bull *Ad conditorem cartonum* (*see* JOHN XXII, POPE). No trace of Richard's Commentary on the *Sentences* remains (though L. WADDING referred to a copy in the Vatican Library). V. Doucet drew attention to eight *Quaestiones disputatae* and two *Quodlibeta* attributed to Richard that include questions on creation, knowledge of God, univocity and equivocity, beatitude, will, intellect, etc. Doctrinally, Richard seems to stand midway between Aristotelianism and Augustinianism. He is quoted by WILLIAM OF ALNWICK, Godfrey of England (Cornwall?), Robert of Walsingham, JOHN

BACONTHORP, and PETER THOMAE. Richard spent his last years at Cambridge, where he is buried.

Bibliography: S. DUMONT, ''William of Ware, Richard of Conington, and the *Collationes Oxonienses* of John Duns Scotus,'' in *John Duns Scotus* (Leiden 1996) 59–85. S. BROWN, ''Richard of Conington and the Analogy of the Concept of Being,'' in *Festgabe fur P. Dr. Valens Heynck, OFM zur Vollendung des 60 Lebensjahres, Franziskanische Studien* 48 (1966) 297–307.

[T. C. CROWLEY]

RICHARD OF GRAVESEND

Bishop of Lincoln; d. Stow Park, Lincolnshire, England, Dec. 13, 1279. A native of Kent, he became dean of Lincoln, 1254, and then bishop, 1258. Gravesend assisted Simon de Montfort in negotiations for Anglo-French peace (1258). He supported the Provisions of Oxford, sided with Montfort against King Henry III in the Barons' War, and represented Montfort in negotiations leading to temporary peace (1263). The papal legate Ottobuono Fieschi, later Pope ADRIAN V, suspended him for supporting Montfort (1266), but Gravesend, already reconciled with Henry, visited Rome and obtained absolution from Pope CLEMENT IV. Archbishop JOHN PECKHAM rebuked him (1279) for instituting overly harsh measures against pluralists in Lincoln diocese, and taking advantage of constitutions issued by Peckham in order to do so. Gravesend, whom MATTHEW PARIS calls ''worthy'' and ''useful,'' was closely associated with ADAM MARSH. He is buried in Lincoln Cathedral.

Bibliography: *Annales Monastici,* ed. H. R. LUARD, 5 v. (*Rerum Brittanicarum medii aevi scriptores* 36) v. 1, 3, 4. M. PARIS, *Chronica majora,* ed. H. R. LUARD, 7 v. (*Rerum Brittanicarum medii aevi scriptores* 57; 1872–83) v. 5. *Rotuli Ricardi Gravesend, dioecesis Lincolniensis,* ed. F. N. DAVIS (London 1925). C. L. KINGSFORD, *The Dictionary of National Biography from the Earliest Times to 1900,* 63 v. (London 1885–1900) 8:441–442. F. M. POWICKE, *King Henry III and the Lord Edward,* 2 v. (Oxford 1947). A. B. EMDEN, *A Biographical Register of the Scholars of the University of Oxford to A.D. 1500,* 3 v. (Oxford 1957–59) 2:803–804. M. GIBBS and J. LANG, *Bishops and Reform, 1215–1272* (London 1934; repr. 1962).

[R. W. HAYS]

RICHARD OF GRAVESEND

Bishop of London; b. Kent, England; d. Fulham, London, Dec. 9, 1303. He was the nephew of RICHARD OF GRAVESEND, bishop of LINCOLN from 1258 to 1279, in whose household he began the church career during which he advanced from protégé of Henry of Sandwich, bishop of LONDON (1262–73), to become bishop of London himself (May 1280). During his 23 years in that important see, he could be counted on to oppose the metropolitan claims of JOHN PECKHAM, archbishop of CANTERBURY, challenging especially the court of Canterbury's jurisdiction over any case arising within the bounds of the London Diocese. When other suffragan bishops found themselves in opposition to Peckham, they could expect the support of Gravesend, who aligned himself with Thomas of Cantelupe, bishop of Hereford, in 1281–82 and with GODFREY GIFFARD, bishop of Worcester, in 1284 and 1289. As for his cathedral, ST. PAUL's, Gravesend instituted the office of subdean as an officer to fulfill the dean's duties during the dean's absences, and, being a man of some scholarly tastes, he ordered that the chancellor of the cathedral must be a bachelor or doctor of theology and must lecture on theology or at least engage such a lecturer. Gravesend's library, which further indicates his scholarly interests, is listed in what is probably the earliest extant priced book catalogue. On the political scene, the bishop was commissioned by the Synod of Canterbury (Feb. 5, 1281) to persuade King Edward I to release from prison the litigious son of Simon de Montfort of Barons' War fame, Amaury de Montfort, a cleric whom Edward had held prisoner since 1275. From 1289 to 1290 Gravesend was abroad on the King's business; in 1293 he was Edward's envoy to King PHILIP IV OF FRANCE concerning attacks on French shipping from the Cinque Ports; in 1294 and 1296 he attended royal weddings abroad; and in 1297 he was one of the councilors of Prince Edward (II) while the king was in France. The bishop was buried in St. Paul's, but his tomb has been destroyed. He was able to advance the ecclesiastical careers of his nephew, Richard of Gravesend, who became treasurer of St. Paul's in 1310, and of his nephew, STEPHEN OF GRAVESEND, who succeeded him as bishop of London (1319–38).

See Also: LONDON, ANCIENT SEE OF.

Bibliography: C. L. KINGSFORD, *The Dictionary of National Biography from the Earliest Times to 1900* 8:442–443. K. EDWARDS, *The English Secular Cathedrals in the Middle Ages* (Manchester, Eng. 1949) 152, 203. D. L. DOUIE, *Archbishop Pecham* (Oxford 1952), *passim.* F. M. POWICKE, *The Thirteenth Century* (2d ed. Oxford 1962) 330–331; 486–487. A. B. EMDEN, *A Biographical Register of the University of Oxford to A.D. 1500* 2:804–805.

[M. J. HAMILTON]

RICHARD OF KILVINGTON

English philosopher, theologian, and controversialist; b. Diocese of York; d. London, by 1362. He was educated at Oxford (M.A. by 1331; B.Th. by 1335; D.Th. by 1350); canon of York, 1353; canon of St. Paul's, London, 1354; and dean of St. Paul's, 1354. In July of 1339, he was one of the envoys sent to negotiate with King Philip

VI of France; between 1342 and 1344 he was, with his friend RICHARD FITZRALPH, a member of the household of RICHARD OF BURY, Bishop of Durham. As Fitzralph's ally in the antimendicant campaign of 1356 and 1357, he took a leading part in his controversy with the Franciscan Roger of Conway on evangelical poverty, but the treatises on this subject attributed to him seem to be no longer extant (*Pro Armachano contra fratres, Contra Rogerum Conway, Contra mendicitatem otiosam*). Also attributed to him are *Questiones de generatione et corruptione,* a *Commentary on the Sentences, Tractatus de intencionibus et remissionibus potenciarum, Sophismata, Sermo de adventu Domini,* and probably *Decem questiones morales super X libros Ethicorum Aristotelis.* He is buried at St. Paul's.

Bibliography: A. B. EMDEN, *A Biographical Register of the University of Oxford to A.D. 1500,* 3 v. (Oxford 1957–59) 2:1050–1051. C. L. KINGSFORD, *The Dictionary of National Biography from the Earliest Times to 1900,* 63 v. (London 1885–1900) 11:353; F. STEGMÜLLER, *Repertorium commentariorum in Sententias Petri Lombardi,* 2 v. (Würzburg 1947) 1:347, where he is wrongly described as an Austin friar. On Kilvington's part in the antimendicant controversy, see A. GWYNN, "Archbishop Fitzralph and the Friars," *Studies* 26 (1937): 50–67. On Kilvington as philosopher, see A. LANG et al., eds., *Aus der Geisteswelt des Mittelalters,* 2 v. (Münster 1935).

[T. P. DUNNING]

RICHARD OF MIDDLETON (MEDIAVILLA)

Franciscan philosopher and theologian, honored with the title of *Doctor solidus;* b. c. 1249; d. Reims, March 30, 1302. Some hold that he is of English origin; others hold that he is French. On Sept. 20, 1295, he was elected provincial minister of the province of France [see H. Lippens, *Archivum Franciscanum historicum* 37 (1944) 3–47], a fact, however that does not settle the question of his nationality.

The earliest certain date in his life is 1283, when, together with other theologians, Richard was appointed to examine the writings of PETER JOHN OLIVI. In that year he held the degree of bachelor, but by the following year he had become a doctor of theology. He probably studied at Paris under Pietro Falco, WILLIAM DE LA MARE, and MATTHEW OF AQUASPARTA. From 1284 to 1287 he was *magister regens* of the Franciscan studium in Paris. He is last heard of in 1296 when he was near Naples in the company of St. Louis of Toulouse.

Richard's principal work is his commentary on the *Sententiae* of PETER LOMBARD. He wrote also 45 *Quaestiones disputatae,* mostly unpublished, and three series of

Quodlibeta that reflect the problems discussed by HENRY OF GHENT, GODFREY OF FONTAINES, GILES OF LESSINES, and GILES OF ROME. Four of his sermons are extant. Richard's interest in the experimental sciences may be indicative of an English background. He often uses arguments drawn from experience and favors induction. In general, he remains faithful to Augustinian-Bonaventurian views, but on some points he tends toward Thomism or proffers personal opinions. He held that intellectual knowledge proceeds from abstraction, through the work of the *intellectus agens,* without a special divine illumination. He also attributed to matter the smallest degree of actuality so that, if God willed, matter could exist even without a form.

See Also: FORMS, UNICITY AND PLURALITY OF.

Bibliography: S. BROWN, "Richard of Middleton, OFM on Esse and Essence," *Franciscan Studies* 8 (1976) 49–76. P. VAN VELDHUIJSEN, "Richard of Middleton on the Question Whether the World Could Have Been Eternally Produced by God," in J. B. M. WISSINK, ed., *The Eternity of the World in the Thought of Thomas Aquinas and His Contemporaries* (Leiden 1990), 69–81. M. HENNINGER, "Hervaeus Natalis and Richard of Mediavilla," in J. J. E. GRACIA, ed., *Individuation in Scholasticism* (Albany 1994) 299–318. L. COVA, *Originale Peccatum e Concupiscentia in Riccardo di Mediavilla* (Rome 1984), bibliography. A. PEREZ-ESTEVEZ, *La Materia, De Avicena a la Escuela Franciscana: Avicena, Averroes, Tomas de Aquino, Pecham, Marston, Olivo, Mediavilla, Duns Escoto* (Maracaibo 1998), bibliography.

[G. GÁL]

RICHARD OF SAINT-VICTOR

Theologian, mystical writer; b. probably Scotland, date unknown; d. March 10, 1173. A Regular Canon of the Abbey of Saint-Victor, Paris, Richard of Saint-Victor was a major mystical writer of the second half of the twelfth century, who contributed also to theology, exegesis, and school and homiletic literature. Like all of the leading figures in the early years of the Abbey's history, little is known of Richard's life; he was probably from Scotland and most likely entered the Abbey near the middle of the twelfth century. He was subprior and became prior in 1161. He played an important role in the interior life of the Abbey of Saint-Victor as prior and as its leading spiritual guide in the third quarter of the twelfth century. His influence was strongest in the literature of contemplation. BONAVENTURE's *Itinerarium mentis in Deum* shows Richard's influence, as does Bernardino of Laredo's *Ascent of Mount Sion.* The author of the *Cloud of Unknowing* draws upon passages from *The Twelve Patriarchs (Benjamin major).*

Richard was strongly influenced by the effective founder of the Victorine school of exegesis, theology, and mysticism, HUGH OF SAINT-VICTOR (d. 1141). Richard's *Liber Exceptionum* is based on Hugh's *Didascalicon* and *Chronicon*, while his mysticism builds on Hugh's practice of using biblical images, such as Noah's Ark, as symbolic structures to represent the mystic's path to contemplative ecstasy. In exegesis, Richard gave attention both to allegory and to the literal sense of Scripture. Like other Victorine exegetes, Richard consulted Jews and Jewish sources for the literal sense of Hebrew Scripture, but in *De Emanuele* Richard strongly criticizes what he sees as Andrew of Saint-Victor's Judaizing literal interpretation of Isaiah 7:14. Richard's treatise on Ezekiel's visions of the Jerusalem Temple (*In visionem Ezechielis*) contains a strong justification for interpreting Ezekiel's description of the Temple literally (as opposed to the exegesis of Gregory the Great) and also presents in the manuscripts some of the first medieval architectural drawings showing the elevation of a building. His commentary on the Revelation of John analyzes four kinds of vision (ordinary [trees, the sea]; the deeper meaning of scripture [the burning bush symbolizing Mary's virginity]; images in visionary experience; imageless visionary experiences) and situates John's visions in the Apocalypse as falling into the third kind. In theology Richard developed a distinctive argument for the necessity of God as a Trinity, based on an analysis of the nature of love (*De Trinitate*). In the Revelation commentary and elsewhere Richard shows a knowledge of the ideas of DIONYSIUS THE PSEUDO-AREOPAGITE, a knowledge mediated through the writings of Hugh of Saint-Victor.

Richard's two major contemplative treatises are *The Twelve Patriarchs* (*Benjamin major*) and *The Mystical Ark* (*Benjamin minor*). In *The Twelve Patriarchs* Richard takes the patriarch Jacob, his two wives, their two handmaidens, and the 12 sons and one daughter of the four women to symbolize the rational soul (Jacob), the faculties of the mind (the four women; will, sensation, imagination, reason) and the stages of discipline of body and mind that lead to contemplative ecstasy (the 13 children). The dynamic progression of the narrative of births, etc., provides Richard with a rich canvas on which to unfold his ideas concerning the development and psychological dynamics of the spiritual life. In *The Mystical Ark* (the Ark of the Covenant) Richard again uses a set of biblical images to explore both structure and development in the mystical life. The "construction" of the Ark and the two accompanying Cherubim presents the materials to develop a six-stage division of the mind's "ascent" to contemplative ecstasy, or "alienation of mind" (*alienatio mentis*) which is an experience of divine presence, mediated in the "emptiness" in the space above the Ark and between the two Cherubim in the visualization of biblical images. Richard made extensive spiritual commentaries on Psalms. But again and again he was drawn back to the dynamics of the spiritual life in works such as: *De exterminatione mali et promotione boni* (using the symbol of the 12 stones on which the Hebrews crossed the Jordan into the Promised Land), *De eruditione interioris hominis* (using the dream of Nebuchadnezzar to explore again the dynamics of the spiritual life) and *De quatuor gradiabus violentae charitatis* (a brilliant exploration of the centrality and transforming power of love in the mystical quest). All address the subtle processes and culmination of the life of discipline in quest of divine presence.

See Also: VICTORINE SPIRITUALITY.

Bibliography: Works. RICHARD OF SAINT-VICTOR, *Omnia opera. Patrologia Latina,* ed. J. P. MIGNE (Paris 1878–90) 196. *De Trinitate,* ed. J. RIBAILLIER, TPMA 6 (Paris 1958). *De statu interioris hominis,* ed. J. RIBAILLIER, *Archives d'histoire doctrinale et litéraire du moyen-âge* 34 (1967) 7–128. *L'Édit d'Alexandre ou les trois processions,* ed. J. CHATILLON and W.-J. TULLOCH, TPMA 5 (Paris 1958). *Liber exceptionum,* ed. J. CHATILLON, TPMA 5 (Paris 1958). *Opuscules théologiques,* ed. J. RIBAILLIER, TPMA 15 (Paris 1967). *Selected Writings on Contemplation,* tr. C. KIRCHBERGER (New York 1957). *The Twelve Patriarchs, The Mystical Ark, and Book Three on the Trinity,* tr. G. A. ZINN (New York 1979). *Les quatre degrés de la violente charité,* ed. G. DUMEIGE (Paris 1955). *Les douze Patriarches ou Benjamin Minor,* tr. J. CHATILLON and M. DUCHET-SUCHAUX, Sources chrétiennes 419 (Paris 1997). Studies. M.-A. ARIS, *Contemplatio: Philosophische Studien zum Traktat Benjamin Maior des Richard von St. Victor: Mit einer verbesserten Edition des Textes,* Fuldaer Studien (Frankfurt am Main 1996). S. CHASE, *Angelic Wisdom: The Cherubim and the Grace of Contemplation in Richard of St. Victor,* Studies in Spirituality and Theology 2 (Notre Dame and London 1995). J. CHATILLON, "Les quatre degrés de la charité d'apres Richard de Saint-Victor (I)," *Revue d'ascétique et de mystique* 20 (1939) 237–264; "Les trois modes de la contemplation selon Richard de Saint-Victor," *Revue du moyen-âge latin* 4 (1948) 23–52, 343–366; "Richard de Saint-Victor," *Dictionnaire de Spiritualité,* 13.593–654. G. DUMEIGE, *Richard de Saint-Victor et l'idée chrétienne de l'amour* (Paris 1952). R. JAVELET, "Thomas Gallus et Richard de Saint-Victor mystiques," *Recherches de théologie ancienne et médiévale* 19 (1962) 206–233. G. A. ZINN, "Personification Allegory and Visions of Light in Richard of St. Victor's Teaching on Contemplation," *University of Toronto Quarterly* 46 (1977): 190–214; "Book and Word: The Victorie Background of Bonaventure's Use of Symbols," *S. Bonaventura (1274–1974),* 2.143–169 (Grottferrata 1973).

[G. A. ZINN]

RICHARD OF SWYNESHED

Oxford philosopher, fl. 1340–55; also known as Swineshead, or Suisseth, and sometimes confused with ROGER OF SWYNESHED. Richard was a secular master, a native of the Lincoln Diocese, born probably in Swineshead, southeast of Lincoln. He was certainly a fellow of Merton College by 1344, and in 1349 was involved in the tumultuous election of John Wylyot to the chancellorship. On March 29, 1354, he was ordained deacon to the title of fellowship, and was still a member of the college in 1355. His fame rests mainly on the often-printed *Liber calculationum,* written before 1355. Within a few decades the author, whose name was lost in confusion, was known as "the Calculator." His renown was greater among mathematicians than among philosophers or humanists. The mathematician G. Cardano (1501–76) included him among the 12 greatest thinkers of all time; and LEIBNIZ wrote (1696): "I would also like to edit the writings of Suisset, commonly known as the Calculator, who introduced mathematics into scholastic philosophy." In scholastic thought his concern was not with traditional problems of Aristotelian physics, nor with linguistic problems of NOMINALISM. Rather, it was with problems of proportionality in accelerated motion, density, rarity, gravity, heat, and other divisible qualities. His work prepared the way for infinitesimal calculus. *See* SCIENCE (IN THE MIDDLE AGES).

Bibliography: P. DUHEM, *Études sur Léonard de Vinci* 3 v. (Paris 1955) 3:412–417, 451–460 and *passim.* M. CLAGETT, *The Science of Mechanics in the Middle Ages* (Madison, Wis. 1959). A.B. EMDEN, *A Biographical Register of the University of Oxford to A.D. 1500,* 3 v. (Oxford 1957–59) 3:1836–37.

[J. A. WEISHEIPL]

RICHARD OF WALLINGFORD

Abbot, inventor; **b.** Wallingford, Berkshire, *c.* 1292; d. May 23, 1336. He was the son of William, a smith in Wallingford; he studied at Oxford, first in the arts faculty and then in theology. Having entered the BENDICTINES at ST. ALBANS *c.* 1315, he was appointed abbot in 1328 by papal provision, a year after his first election to the office was declared invalid. As abbot, a position he held until his death, he was a stern disciplinarian and was concerned with the improvement of the finances of the abbey. He is famous for his invention of an astronomical clock, "Albion," which indicated the times and seasons as well as the movements of the sun, moon, and other planets, and for his writings on mathematical and astronomical subjects, several of which are still in manuscript. These include a treatise on the *Albion, Exafernon pronosticorum temporis, De eclipsi solis et lunae, De computo, De sinubus et arcubus, Quadripartitum,* and *Rectangulum.* He also wrote a treatise on the general statutes of the Benedictine Order. He died of leprosy.

Bibliography: C. L. KINGSFORD, *The Dictionary of National Biography from the Earliest Times to 1900,* (London 1885–1900) 16:1091–93. A. B. EMDEN, *A Biographical Register of the University of Oxford to A.D. 1500,* 3 vol. (Oxford 1957–59) 3:1967. L. THORNDIKE and P. KIBRE, *A Catalogue of Incipits of Mediaeval Scientific Writings in Latin* (new ed. Cambridge, Mass. 1963).

[P. KIBRE]

RICHARD RUFUS OF CORNWALL

Franciscan theologian and philosopher; b. England; d. Oxford, *c.* 1260. Richard entered the order in Paris in 1238, already a master of arts, and was ordained in England the next year. He commented on the *Sententiae* of Peter Lombard, first at Oxford (1250–53) and later at Paris. For his Oxford commentary, which covers the first three books, Richard had at hand the respective commentaries of ALEXANDER OF HALES, HUGH OF SAINT-CHER, and RICHARD FISHACRE. The Paris commentary is a critical condensation of St. Bonaventure's commentary. It is likely that Richard wrote also a voluminous commentary on Aristotle's *Metaphysics* (Cod. Vat. Lat. 4538). In 1256 he left Paris for Oxford to serve as *magister regens* of the Franciscan studium there.

Richard possessed an acute and critical mind and an excellent knowledge of Aristotle. On more than one point he anticipates John DUNS SCOTUS. The universal has for him a double aspect: *species abstracta,* which exists in the mind, and *natura communis,* which exists extramentally in individuals. All of creation demonstrates the existence of the Creator. Richard denies the validity of the ONTOLOGICAL ARGUMENT, but admits (as Duns Scotus did later) that from the possibility of *ens a se* one can conclude to its existence. He professes a pronounced VOLUNTARISM. He introduces among the powers of the soul a distinction that is considered to be the first indication of Scotus's formal distinction. Theses common to the Augustinian-Franciscan school, such as divine illumination and the hylomorphic composition of spiritual creatures, are also found in his writings.

Bibliography: T. NOONE, "Roger Bacon and Richard Rufus on Aristotle's Metaphysics," *Vivarium* 35 (1997) 251–65. R. WOOD, "Angelic Individuation according to Richard Rufus, St. Bonaventure, and St. Thomas Aquinas," in *Individuum and Individualitat im Mittelalter* (Berlin 1996) 209–29. P. RAEDTS, *Richard Rufus of Cornwall and the Tradition of Oxford Theology* (Oxford 1987). G. GÁL, "Opiniones Richardi Rufi Cornubiensisa a censore reprobatae," in *Franciscan Studies Annual* 8, 1975 (St. Bonventure, N.Y. 1976) 136–93.

[G. GÁL]

RICHARDSON, LAURENCE, BL.

Priest and martyr; *vere* Johnson; b. Great Crosby, Lancashire, England; d. hanged, drawn, and quartered at Tyburn (London), May 30, 1582. Laurence, the son of Richard Johnson, was a fellow at Brasenose College, Oxford (*c.* 1569–72) before beginning his seminary studies at Douai. He was ordained at Cateau-Cambresis (March 23, 1577), then left for the mission field in Lancashire (July 27, 1577). En route to France he was arrested in

London and held in Newgate Prison until his indictment on Nov. 16, 1581. Thereafter he was committed to the Queen's Bench Prison and condemned (Nov. 17, 1581) on the trumped up charge of conspiring against the Crown in Rome and Rheims. Following his sentencing, he was held in the Tower of London where he had no bedding for two months. He was beatified by Pope Leo XIII.

Feast of the English Martyrs: May 4 (England).

See Also: ENGLAND, SCOTLAND, AND WALES, MARTYRS OF.

Bibliography: B. CAMM, ed., *Lives of the English Martyrs,* (New York 1905), II, 500–35. R. CHALLONER, *Memoirs of Missionary Priests,* ed. J. H. POLLEN (rev. ed. London 1924; repr. Farnborough 1969), I, nos. 12, 13, 14. J. H. POLLEN, *Acts of English Martyrs* (London 1891).

[K. I. RABENSTEIN]

RICHARDSON, WILLIAM, BL.

Priest, last martyr under Elizabeth I; *alias* Anderson; b. Wales (Vales), near Sheffield, West Riding, Yorkshire (per Challoner) or in Lancashire (per Valladolid diary), England; hanged, drawn, and quartered at Tyburn (London), Feb. 17, 1603. He studied for the priesthood (1692–94) at Valladolid, Spain, and was ordained at Seville in 1594. He was betrayed by a trusted friend, arrested at Clement's Inn, imprisoned at Newgate, and prosecuted hastily. At his execution about a week after his apprehension, he prayed for the queen, then died cheerfully. He was beatified by Pius XI on Dec. 15, 1929.

Feast of the English Martyrs: May 4 (England).

See Also: ENGLAND, SCOTLAND, AND WALES, MARTYRS OF.

Bibliography: R. CHALLONER, *Memoirs of Missionary Priests,* ed. J. H. POLLEN (rev. ed. London 1924; repr. Farnborough 1969). J. H. POLLEN, *Acts of English Martyrs* (London 1891).

[K. I. RABENSTEIN]

RICHELIEU, ARMAND JEAN DU PLESSIS DE

Cardinal, minister, and head of the royal council of Louis XIII from 1624 to 1642; b. Paris, Sept. 9, 1585; d. Paris, Dec. 4, 1642. He prepared the way for absolute monarchy in France and for French predominance in Europe.

His father, Francois du Plessis, was at the court of Henry III and died in 1590 in the service of HENRY IV.

Armand Jean Du Plessis de Cardinal Richelieu, engraving.

His mother, Suzanne de la Porte, was the daughter of a lawyer in Parlement and lady in waiting to the queen. On his father's death Richelieu's mother withdrew from Paris to begin the education of her five children. In 1597 Armand began his studies in the humanities at the University of Paris and then, after studies in philosophy, went to the military academy to prepare for a military career. In 1605 his older brother Alphouse, destined for the bishopric of Luçon, which Henry IV reserved to the family, became a Carthusian, and Richelieu began studies in theology to prepare himself for the bishopric. In 1606 he went to Rome and obtained his bulls of institution with a dispensation for his age (21). After being consecrated bishop on April 17, 1607, he returned to defend a thesis in theology at the Sorbonne. The next year he left for Luçon, where he worked to restore the material and moral ravages of the Wars of Religion. He convoked a synod, began a seminary, called in the Capuchins and Oratorians, and wrote his *Instruction du chrétien,* with lessons on the articles of the Credo to be read by pastors in Sunday instructions and notes for the clergy as well. He was elected deputy of the clergy for the Estates General of 1614 and gave the concluding address to the King, calling for acceptance of the Council of Trent, the naming of ecclesiastics to the royal council, and religious toleration for Protestants. After gaining the good graces of the queen mother, MARIE DE MÉDICIS, he became secretary of state in 1616. With the fall of her favorite, Concini, Richelieu was exiled to Avignon but then recalled to work for her reconciliation with King Louis XIII. He received the cardinal's hat in 1622 for his success. In April 1624 Louis XIII yielded to his mother's request and reappointed Richelieu to the council, of which he became head a few months later, coming into the trust and esteem of the King. The first successes of his policy strengthened his position, which at first was uncertain, but also aroused the ill will of the queen mother, who in 1630 asked the King to choose between Richelieu and her. Richelieu was on the point of being dismissed when he definitely regained the confidence of Louis XIII (Nov. 11, 1630, *journée des dupes*). Marie de Médicis went abroad and Richelieu governed without a rival.

Although his health suffered from his work and his excessive nervous tension, Richelieu brought to the King's service an incomparable intelligence and an adamant will. When he took office, France was threatened with internal division and confronted abroad by the House of HAPSBURG and its gains in Europe. In 18 years these dangers were overcome.

Domestic Policy. Henry IV had to give Protestants not only freedom of conscience but considerable political privileges as well, in particular garrisoned fortresses, such as the port of La Rochelle. The Protestants constituted a kind of federated republic within the monarchy and prepared to receive foreign help. In 1628, after a 14-month siege that he personally directed, Richelieu took La Rochelle, and the next year occupied the last Protestant strongholds. The Edict of Alais in 1629 abolished the political privileges of the HUGUENOTS while leaving them religious freedom.

The fight against the rebellious nobility took longer. Richelieu and the King mercilessly eradicated the plots of discontented nobles, which often were supported by the King's brother, Gaston d'Orlélais. Chalais in 1626 conspired against Richelieu, Montmorency in 1632 raised a rebellion in Languedoc, Cinq-Mars in 1642 signed a treaty with Spain, and his friend, de Thou, failed to denounce him—and they were beheaded. Richelieu also had the King enforce laws that made duelling punishable by death (Montmorency-Bouteville was executed in 1626). Apart from the punishment of conspiracy, in the provinces, where *commissaires en mission* or intendants kept an eye on governors, parlements, and provincial Estates, several castles were razed in conformity with the wishes of the Estates General. Crushing taxation frequently gave rise to popular revolts fostered or tolerated by local notables. In 1639 Chancellor Séguier himself was dispatched to Normandy to put down the revolt of the *va-nu-pieds,* and for a while the parlement of Rouen was suspended. Finally the Parlement of Paris, which tended to control royal authority by its remonstrances and the modification of royal laws, had to yield. An edict of 1641 placed strict limitations on Parlement's traditional right of remonstrance.

Foreign Policy. Amid this tension of national energies Richelieu began the fight to bring to a halt Hapsburg successes. His aim was to weaken the house of Austria and restore equilibrium in Europe to the advantage of France and her allies—not, as one often reads, to give France a frontier on the Rhine. He began by giving diplomatic support and subsidies to all the enemies of Spain. In England in 1625 he arranged the marriage of Louis XIII's sister and Charles I, who earlier had sought a Spanish Infanta. In Switzerland, Richelieu restored Protestant Grisons to power in the Valtelline, where Catholic inhabitants had rebelled with Spanish support. Valtelline Pass gave Milan communications with Spanish possessions to the north. In Italy, Richelieu sought to unite all the independent states, including the papacy, in an anti-Spanish league, and he forced a passage through the Duchy of Savoy to assure the duke of Nevers the inheritance of Mantua, which the Emperor Ferdinand II contested (1629–30). He supported the Dutch against Spain, and Mansfeld and Christian IV, King of Denmark, against the Emperor. He loosed the King of Sweden, Gustavus II Adolphus, against the Emperor (Treaty of Bärwald, January 1631). At the same time he sought to detach Catholic Bavaria from the Emperor's cause (Treaty of Fontainebleau, May 1631). The incursion of Gustavus into Germany with his consequent victories put an end to FERDINAND II's efforts for monarchial centralization and Catholic restoration. Gustavus's death at Lützen (November 1632) freed Richelieu of an ally who had become dangerous but forced him to go to war openly. Louis XIII had already occupied Lorraine when the Swedish defeat at Nordlingen forced Richelieu to send French armies not yet prepared into combat (war declared on Spain, May 19, 1635). Burgundy was invaded and Paris threatened (1636). For several years victory and defeat alternated on land and sea. But Richelieu reorganized the army and gradually built a navy, which was nonexistent when he came to power. Military success came after 1640: Spain was busied with revolts in Portugal and Catalonia, and French armies advanced in Artois to the north and in Rousillon to the south. The treaties of WESTPHALIA and the Pyrenees, concluded by Jules MAZARIN, later brought to fulfillment the political work of Richelieu.

These successes were not the result of armed force alone. The cardinal's diplomacy probably played a greater role. Richelieu as a matter of principle negotiated ceaselessly. His agents crossed Europe constantly on all kinds of missions: to strengthen old alliances and gain new ones and to bring back reports. His most noteworthy aide in this was Father Joseph (LE CLERC DU TREMBLAY).

Richelieu's political work was not limited to Europe. The navy allowed him to send expeditions overseas and to found French settlements in the Antilles, Senegal, Madagascar, and especially in Canada. England had taken advantage of the break with France at the time of the capture of La Rochelle to occupy French settlements in the St. Lawrence Valley. Richelieu regained them in 1632 and founded the Company of 100 Associates to develop the new lands (New France). He sent Capuchins and Jesuits to convert the natives, who were to be treated as Frenchmen.

The World of Letters. Richelieu's respect for public opinion and the power of the press was still more modern. He was concerned with the press and himself wrote works and accounts of events to defend his policy before France and the world. The *Mercure François* and the *Gazette* under his control and with his collaboration became quasi-official journals. His concern for French letters was more disinterested. He founded and was the first protector of the Académie Française. In 1622 the Sorbonne made him guardian, and he rebuilt all its buildings and endowed it with the chapel in which he is buried.

Religious Character. The religious character of the cardinal, the ally of Protestants, has been much debated. As bishop of Luçon, he was a model pastor. When he became minister, he resigned his see but considered himself somewhat the head of the Church in France. One of his first concerns was to reunite the Protestants. Devout Catholics were disappointed in his religious policy, for Richelieu felt that in matters of conscience, constraint should be avoided, and he maintained the religious liberties of the Edict of NANTES. But he worked, and had others work, to win Protestants by persuasion, fostering missions in Calvinist areas and protecting the controversialist Veron. After publishing in 1618 *Les principaux points de la foi catholique défendus contre . . . les quatre ministres de Charenton,* he worked through his whole ministry at his *Traité . . . pour convertir ceux qui se sont séparés de l'Église,* which appeared only after his death and in which he sought to convert Protestants with the help of Scripture, the Fathers, and Protestant authors as well. His relations with Rome were at times strained, due to his Protestant alliances, his attempts to obtain a cardinalate for Father Joseph and later for Mazarin, his attempt to consolidate the orders of Cluny, Cîteaux, and the Premonstratensians under one head, his plan to dominate the French clergy by obtaining a long-term legate in Paris, and the taxation he imposed on the clergy.

He was fortunate to have to deal with Urban VIII, who was favorable to France and only reluctantly put up with Spanish hegemony in Italy. Besides, Richelieu had given testimony of his faith. He made E. RICHER retract his anti-Roman theses, he made peace between the bishops and the religious orders, and he looked for a middle way in the dispute between Gallicans and Ultramontanes. He ordered the imprisonment at Vincennes of the abbot of Saint-Cyran, a reformer with imprecise and suspect doctrines. Richelieu's *Traité de la perfection du chrétien* (a rather dry expression of the traditional doctrine of Catholic asceticism) and the consecration of France to the Blessed Virgin (by Louis XIII in 1637, but inspired by Richelieu) open perspectives on his religious character, which remains to be studied.

Richelieu left a *Political Testament* (ed. Paris 1947); *Memoirs* (3 v. 1837–38, 10 v. 1907–31); and letters, instructions, and papers (8 v. 1853–77).

Bibliography: G. HANOTAUX and DE LA FORCE, *Histoire du Cardinal de Richelieu,* 6 v. (Paris 1893–1947). H. BELLOC, *Richelieu: A Study* (Garden City, N.Y. 1929). K. J. BURCKHARDT, *Richelieu: Der Aufstieg zur Macht* (Munich 1936). V. L. TAPIÉ, *La France de Louis XIII et de Richelieu* (Paris 1952).

[P. BLET]

RICHER, EDMOND

French canonist and theorist of Gallicanism; b. Chesley, near Chaource, then in the Diocese of Langres, Sept. 15, 1559; d. Paris Nov. 29, 1631. From a poor peasant family, he worked as a domestic at the Collège du Cardinal Lemoine during his studies there. Attaining his doctorate at the Sorbonne (*c.* 1590), he was named rector of the Collège du Cardinal Lemoine in 1595, and in 1602, syndic of the Sorbonne. In defending the rights of the university against the encroachments of the religious orders, especially the Jesuits, he professed a basic and intransigent GALLICANISM. The publication of his treatise *De ecclesiastica et civili potestate* (Paris 1611) earned him the hostility of the nuncio Ubaldini and of Cardinal du Perron, who procured the condemnation of his book and had him deposed from his office (1612). The controversies continued, and Richer by way of many booklets had to defend his positions, especially against the ultramontanist professor André Duval. Finally, RICHELIEU intervened and forced Richer to sign a half-retraction of his book on Dec. 7, 1629. In his various works, Richer claims the superiority of the councils over the popes; the pope is only the ministerial head of the Church; the deposit of revelation should be confided to the faithful, as well as the hierarchy; the bishops should have immediate jurisdiction, independent of the pope; and temporal governments should be absolute masters in their own domain. These ideas were adopted by the Jansenists of the 18th century.

Richer is the author also of an edition of Jean Gerson (Paris 1606) and a *Historia conciliorum generalium* (Cologne 1880).

Bibliography: E. PUYOL, *Edmond Richer*, 2 v. (Paris 1876). H. RAAB, *Lexikon für Theologie und Kirche*, ed. J. HOFER and K. RAHNER (Freiburg 1957–65) 8:1299. H. R. GUGGISBERG, *Die Religion in Geschichte und Gegenwart*, 6 v. (Tübingen 1957–63) 5:1093. J. CARREYRE, *Dictionnaire de théologie catholique*, 15 v. (Paris 1903–50) 13.2:2698–2702, bibliog.

[L. COGNET]

RICHTER, FRANZ XAVER

Prominent composer of the Mannheim school; b. Holleschau (Moravia), Dec. 1, 1709; d. Strasbourg, Sept. 12, 1789. After musical studies, probably in Vienna and Italy, Richter became concurrently vice chapelmaster to the prince-abbot of Kempten (Allgäu) and Elector Karl Theodor of the Palatinate in 1740, from which year dates his productive career as composer and teacher. After 22 years at the Mannheim court chapel (1747–69), he became cathedral choirmaster in Strasbourg. His early compositions were for the church; at Mannheim his creative activity naturally centered upon orchestral and chamber music in the current of the Bohemian-Mannheim development; and at Strasbourg he returned to his first genre, creating a sacred style similar in form, texture, and sonority, in sweetness and expressivity, to the Bohemian symphonic style (as in the work of V. J. Tomášek, J. L. Dusek, A. Gyrowetz, and J. A. and L. A. Koželuch), but also related to the Viennese baroque church tradition, especially in the aria movements of his cantata Masses. Together with these characteristics of the newer music, a stricter style along the principles of J. J. FUX may also be found, and his *Missa Laetare in contrapuncto posita* (1744) is a masterpiece of *stile antico,* heavily laden with canons, fugues, mirror fugues, and multiple counterpoints. In all he composed more than 40 Masses and 50 motets, as well as many cantatas, Office music, and other vocal works. In his theoretical works he followed Fux and M. Spiess, who placed the resources of *stile antico* and *stile moderno* at the service of an intensified mode of expression for church music.

Bibliography: W. BARTH, *Die Messenkomposition Franz Xaver Richters 1709–1789* (Munich 1941). W. GÄSSLER, *Die Sinfonie von F. X. Richter* (Munich 1941). F. X. MATTHIAS, "Thematischer Katalog der im Strassburger Münsterarchiv aufbewahrten kirchenmusikalischen Werke F. X. Richters," *Riemann-Festschrift,* ed. C. H. MENNICKE (Leipzig 1909). R. MÜNSTER, *Die Musik in Geschichte und Gegenwart*, ed. F. BLUME (Kassel-Basel 1949–) 11:455–460. *Baker's Biographical Dictionary of Musicians*, ed. N. SLONIMSKY (5th, rev. ed. New York 1958) 1338. D. M. RANDEL, ed., *The Harvard Biographical Dictionary of Music* (Cambridge 1996) 743. J. REUTTER, *Studien zur Kirchenmusik Franz Xaver Richters (1709–1789)* 2 vols. (Frankfurt am Main 1993). N. SLONIMSKY, ed., *Baker's Biographical Dictionary of Musicians, Eighth Edition* (New York 1992) 1507–1508. R. WÜRTZ, "Franz Xaver Richter" in *The New Grove Dictionary of Music and Musicians, vol. 15,* ed. S. SADIE, (New York 1980) 846–847.

[K. G. FELLERER]

RICKABY, JOSEPH

Jesuit philosopher and theologian; b. Everingham, Yorkshire, Nov. 20, 1845; d. North Wales, Dec. 18, 1932. He studied at the University of London prior to entrance into the Society of Jesus at Manresa, then lectured in ethics and natural law at Stonyhurst from 1879 to 1896. His work there led him to write *Moral Philosophy* in 1888, a sharp, polemical defense of the doctrine of Aquinas against EMPIRICISM and HEGELIANISM. Between 1896 and 1899 he served the society in both Oxford and London, and in 1899 joined the staff at Campion Hall, Oxford, where he remained until 1924. In 1905 he published an annotated translation of St. Thomas's *Summa contra gentiles,* which proved to be his most representative work. After 1926 Rickaby retired to St. Bueno's College, North Wales. His last work was a translation of Rodriguez's *Christian Virtues and Perfection.* Between 1870 and 1930 he published 60 articles in the *Month* and wrote nearly 30 books. (*See* SCHOLASTICISM)

Bibliography: *Month* 161 (1933) 170–175. J. J. DELANEY and J. E. TOBIN, *Dictionary of Catholic Biography* (Garden City, N.Y. 1961) 991.

[F. J. ROENSCH]

RICKE, JODOCO

Franciscan missionary, builder and educator; b. of a noble family of Ghent, Belgium, 1495; d. Popayan, New Granada, 1575. According to Diego de Trujillo, he came to Peru from Nicaragua while Pizarro was still at Túmbez waiting to go to Cajamarca to meet the Inca. Ricke came to Quito with his fellow citizen Pedro Gosseal, in the retinue of Don Pedro de Alvarado. Although he is not included in the list of those who took up domicile in Quito, his name appears among those to whom ground-plots were distributed. About 30,000 square meters were assigned to the Franciscans for the church, monastery, and garden, on the site where the palace of the Inca had been located. Friar Jodoco drew up the plan of the church and the buildings and directed construction until most of the work was finished. He was the leader in the founding and operation of the Colegio de San Andrés, which trained the native peoples in all types of crafts and trades. In both educational and construction work, he had as collaborators his fellow countrymen Pedro Gosseal, Germán de Alemán, and Jácome Flamenco, and he was helped by educated natives headed by Jorge de la Cruz Mitima and his son Francisco Morocho. Civezza says that Friar Jodoco taught the natives to plow with oxen, to make yokes and carts, to do arithmetic, to read and write in Spanish, to play musical instruments, and to sing both with the pipe organ and unaccompanied.

Bibliography: J. M. VARGAS, *Arte quiteño colonial* (Quito 1944). J. G. NAVARRO, *Artes plásticas ecuatoréanas* (Mexico City 1945).

[J. M. VARGAS]

RICOEUR, PAUL

Philosopher; author and lecturer; b. Valence, France, Feb. 27, 1913. Baptized into the Reformed community, Ricoeur's early life is bound up with the loss of both his parents, his mother six months after his birth, his father during World War I. His early philosophical education at the University of Rennes brought him into contact with the reflexive philosophy of Lachelier and Lagneau with their concern for the grounds of authentic subjectivity. This concern was to become the touchstone of his later philosophy.

At the Sorbonne for doctoral studies Ricoeur became part of the Friday sessions of Gabriel MARCEL, the Christian existentialist philosopher, who introduced him to the works of Edmund HUSSERL and PHENOMENOLOGY. After becoming agrégé in 1935, he married his childhood friend, Yvonne Lejas, and began to teach first in Colmar, then in Lorient. Ricoeur was drafted into the army in the general mobilization and became a prisoner of war in the early stages of the Second World War. He was interned in several camps in Pomerania until 1945. There he read the works of Karl JASPERS, translated in the margin *Ideen I* of Husserl, and taught philosophy to his fellow prisoners. The results were published in the postwar years: *Karl Jaspers et la philosophie de l'existence* (with Mikel Dufrenne) (1947), *Gabriel Marcel et Karl Jaspers: philosophie du mystère et philosophie du paradoxe* (1948), and the translation of *Ideen I* (1950). During the same time his interest in political philosophy led him to read Hegel. Between 1945 and 1948 he taught at Cévenol college in Chambon-sur-Lignon during which time he became known as an expert in Husserl's phenomenology [see his collection of articles in Husserl (1967)]. In 1948 he was awarded the chair of philosophy at the University of Strasbourg. While there, he defended his doctoral thesis on the phenomenology of the will [*Le volontaire et l'involontaire* (1950); *Freedom and Nature* (1966)] and contributed frequently to the periodicals Christianisme social and Esprit.

Toward Hermeneutical Phenomenology. In his doctoral dissertation Ricoeur projected his life's work. Guided by the famous Husserlian *epochē*, a bracketing-out procedure in order to arrive at the roots of phenomena, he understood the task of such a phenomenology of the will as (1) a pure phenomenology of the will abstracted from the question of the fault (negation, evil) and transcendence [*Le volontaire et l'involontaire*]; (2) a phenomenology of evil as seen through human fallibility [*L'homme faillible* (1960), *Fallible Man* (1965)] and through the myths and symbols of evil, sin, and guilt [*La symbolique du mal* (1960), *The Symbolism of Evil* (1967)]; (3) a poetics of the will: a reflection on the human self as responsible, fragile, between sameness and ipseity, as other, and as grace and gift of freedom [see Ricoeur's most recent works on textual and practical hermeneutics, temporality, narrativity, metaphor, imagination, action/passion and the self, and the Bible].

In 1956 Ricoeur accepted a position at the Sorbonne and began to live in a commune (Murs Blancs), inspired by the social mission of Christianity. Experiencing deeply the malaise of the university, he transferred in 1966 to Nanterre, briefly accepting the post of dean (1969–70). In the turmoil of the democratization movement at Nanterre, he was physically attacked and the leftist philosophical community was so violent in their rejection of him that he expatriated himself to the University of Louvain. Three years later, he returned to Nanterre, but he also began to commute to North America (Montreal, Yale, and especially Chicago). Philosophically these were fruitful years. He kept up a constant dialogue with the major currents of thought in the 60s and 70s such as Freudian psychoanalysis, STRUCTURALISM, DECONSTRUCTION, and Anglo-American analytic philosophy. His own philosophical roots became more firmly established in the erstwhile reflexive philosophy (Nabert), the hermeneutical phenomenology configured out of Husserl, GADAMER, and HEIDEGGER, the action theory of Habermas, and analytic philosophy. These gave rise to a number of books: *De l'interprétation* (1965), *Freud and Philosophy* (1970); *La métaphore vive* (1975), *The Rule of Metaphor* (1977); *Temps et récit*, volumes 1–3 (1983,1984,1985), *Time and Narrative*, volumes 1–3 (1984, 1985, 1988), and *Soi-même comme un autre* (1990), *Oneself as Another* (1992); *Amour et justice. Liebe und Gerechtigkeit* (1990); and an avalanche of articles, the most important of which are collected in *Histoire et verité* (1955, 1964, 1990), *History and Truth* (1965); *Le conflit des interpétations* (1969), *The Conflict of Interpretations* (1974); *A l'école de la phénoménologie* (1986); *Du texte à l'action* (1986), *From Text to Action* (1991); *Lectures 1: Autour de la politique* (1991); *Lectures 2: La contrée de la philosophie* (1992); *Lectures 3:*

Aux frontières de la philosophie (1994); *Le juste* (1995); *Réflexion faite* (1995); *Penser la Bible* (with A. Lacocque) (1998), *Thinking Biblically* (1998).

Distinctive Traits. First among the distinctive traits of Ricoeur's philosophy must be mentioned his respectful dialogue with conflicting philosophies. Ricoeur believes strongly in the dialectic process of truth. Truth, he believes, is not immediately available. It can be searched out in terms of the traces found in the writings of those who have most intensely struggled with the question of truth. Conflicting philosophies are probed not to execute a coup de grâce, but to exploit their sometimes unspoken, constructive potential. His philosophy forges its own path in debate with the foremost philosophers of the second half of the 20th century: Heidegger, Husserl, Lévinas, Sartre, Lévi-Strauss, Lacan, Althusser, Gadamer, Habermas, Derrida, and Davidson.

Second, interpreters of Ricoeur have found it difficult to uncover a unifying theme. Ricoeur has compared himself to an intellectual bricoleur, answering questions left unanswered by his previous writings or occasioned by the themes of congresses and symposia. This so-called tinkering with a wide range of topics has led commentators to understand Ricoeur through such themes as the hermeneutical method, the imagination, the subject, language, ethics, literary theory, meaningful action. However, aided by Oneself as Another, it is possible to trace an underlying trajectory of a practical philosophy. From his earliest project of a philosophy of the will, Ricoeur has consistently sought, however great the detours, to outline the possibilities of authentic subjectivity. This search for a practical philosophy led him originally from phenomenology to hermeneutics and later from primacy of language to primacy of action. Although subscribing to an intense suspicion of the deceptive claims of rationality and despite the current privileging of negation and nothing, Ricoeur upholds the possibility of the affirmation of life, the desire and effort of human existing, and the human projection of truth, happiness, and pleasure. His is a philosophical witness to Augustinian hope. This renewed practical philosophy is at core an ethical venture: the search for the good life lived in just institutions with and for others. In Oneself as Another this leads to a hermeneutics of the self: a search for what remains after the demise of the Cartesian self-constituting ego and of the proclaimed death of the self by deconstructionism in the 20th century.

A third trait is Ricoeur's disavowal of any attempt to totalize. He renounces Hegel's great narrative of the final synthesis. In his early writings he fulminates against the violent totalizations of state and church. Human knowing and action in history are only mediately available and demand the endless detours by way of its signs and traces. For Ricoeur philosophy is hermeneutical. Its epistemology and ontology are attestations of belief and conviction in the truthfulness of the self. Its politics is a politics of fragility. Its religious witness is a testimony to the "available believable" in the face of the ravages of evil and suffering in the 20th century. This capacity to engage the current intellectual climate with suspicion but without skepticism may well be Ricoeur's enduring attraction.

Ricoeur's prodigious activity and his brilliant engagement of the philosophical debate gained for him the recognition in France as one of the foremost contemporary philosophers. Elsewhere, particularly in North America, Ricoeur steadily increased his influence particularly among theologians and literary critics.

See Also: HERMENEUTICS.

Bibliography: P. ANDERSON, *Ricoeur and Kant: Philosophy of the Will* (Atlanta 1993). S. H. CLARK, *Paul Ricoeur* (London 1990). B. DAUENHAEUR, *Paul Ricoeur: The Promise and Risks of Politics* (Lanham, Md. 1998). F. DOSSE, *Paul Ricoeur: Le sens d'une vie* (Paris 1997). D. JERVELINA, *The Cogito and Hermeneutics: The Question of the Subject in Ricoeur* (Dordrecht 1990). D. E. KLEMM and W. SCHWEIKER, eds., *Meanings in Texts and Actions: Questioning Ricoeur* (Charlottesville 1993). O. MONGIN, *Paul Ricoeur* (Paris 1994). J. PUTTI, *Theology as Hermeneutics: Paul Ricoeur's Theory of Text Interpretation and Method in Theology* (San Francisco 1994). J. VAN DEN HENGEL, *The Home of Meaning: The Hermeneutics of the Subject of Paul Ricoeur* (Lanham 1982). K. J. VANHOOZER, *Biblical Narrative in the Philosophy of Paul Ricoeur* (Cambridge 1990). F. D. VANSINA, *Paul Ricoeur: A Primary and Secondary Bibliography (1935–1984)* (Leuven 1985).

[J. VAN DEN HENGEL]

RICOLDUS DE MONTE CROCE

Missionary and writer; b. Florence *c.* 1243; d. Florence, Oct. 31, 1320. He entered the Dominicans at S. Maria Novella, Florence, in 1267 and taught at Pisa, Prato, and Florence (1272–88). In 1288 he began his journey to the East, traveling to Acre, to Galilee, and as far as Baghdad. He worked for the reunion of the JACOBITES in Mosul, and of the NESTORIANS in Baghdad, where he disputed also with the Muslims. While in the capital (1291) he received the news of the fall of Acre and saw booty from the captured city pass through the markets of Baghdad. The fall of Acre occasioned his *Epistolae ad ecclesiam triumphantem,* a series of letters of lamentation addressed to Our Lord, the Blessed Virgin Mary, and the saints, and to Nicholas of Hunnapes, the patriarch of Jerusalem, who had just been killed in the defense of Acre. While in the East he wrote also an *Itinerarium,* in which he left an account of his journeys and of his reflections on the various peoples and customs he had encountered. This work contains the first Western Christian account of the MANDAEAN sect. The date of his return to Europe is uncertain, but he was back in Florence by Oct. 10, 1301. His *Impugnatio Alcorani* dates probably from the period 1301–11 and was widely used by later Catholic apologists against the errors of ISLAM. It was published with slightly varying titles in a number of the late 15th- and early 16th-century editions. In 1315 Ricoldus was given the title of preacher general by his order. Five years later he died at S. Maria Novella.

Bibliography: Works. *Epistolae V ad ecclesiam triumphantem,* ed. R. RÖHRICHT in *Archives de l'Orient latin* 2 (1884) 258–296; *Confutatio Alcorani,* Gr. tr. D. KYDONES in *Patrologia Graeca* 154:1035–1152; *Itinerarium,* ed. J. C. M. LAURENT in *Peregrinatores medii aevi quatuor* (Leipzig 1864). Literature. P. MANDONNET, *Revue biblique* 2 (1893) 44–61, 182–202, 584–607. U. MONNERET DE VILLARD, *Il Libro della peregrinazione nelle parti d'oriente di frate Ricoldo da Montecroce* (Rome 1948). J. QUÉTIF and S. ÉCHARD, *Scriptores Ordinis Praedicatorum* (Paris 1719–23) 1.2:504–506. H. C. PUECH, *Revue d'histoire des religions* 135 (1949) 250–254. A. WALTZ, *Lexikon für Theologie und Kirche* 2 8:1303–04. *Archivum Fratrum Praedicatorum* 8–30 (1938–60), *passim.*

[P. M. STARRS]

RIDDER, CHARLES H.

American journalist and publisher; b. New York City, June 11, 1888; d. Poughkeepsie, N. Y., Oct. 10, 1964. He was the son of Henry and Lena (Croker) Ridder and was related on the maternal side to Robert Emmet, the Irish patriot; his father had been cofounder of the New York *Catholic News.* After graduation from De Witt Clinton high school (1905) and Packard College (1908), he entered journalism and joined the staff of the *Catholic News* (1910) to gain experience in all phases of publishing. In 1914 he married Alice Lytle; they had four sons and a daughter. At his father's death (1936), Ridder, who was general manager of the *News,* became its publisher, a post he retained until his death.

He was a member of the Catholic Press Association (CPA), which he served as treasurer and from 1938 to 1940 as president, and he aided materially in the establishment of the National Catholic Welfare Conference (NCWC) News Service, which developed out of the CPA News Service. Active in organizing and supporting lay charitable work in New York, he was one of the founders of the first Catholic boys' club in that city. When this organization later developed into the Catholic Youth Organization, Ridder was a member of its original board of directors. He was also a member of the board of the Casita Maria Settlement in East Harlem, founded by Elizabeth Sullivan, whom Ridder married (1944) three years after the death of his first wife.

Ridder's historical interests were extensive. He was treasurer of the U.S. Catholic Historical Society (1943–53) and its two-term president (1954–56); he contributed to its *Historical Records and Studies.* Twice knighted by Pius XII—Knight of Malta (1950) and Knight of the Holy Sepulchre (1952)—he was honored again by John XXIII, who made him Knight of the Holy Sepulchre with Star in 1959.

[L. GILHOOLEY]

RIDLEY, NICHOLAS

Bishop of Rochester and London and prominent English reformer; b. Unthank Hall near Willemoteswick, Northumberland, c. 1500; d. Oxford, Oct. 16, 1555. As a descendant of an ancient family of knights, he was educated at Cambridge, where he received the master of arts (1516). After further study at the Sorbonne and at Louvain, he returned to Cambridge as a fellow of Pembroke Hall (c. 1530); chaplain to Thomas CRANMER, Archbishop of Canterbury (1537); vicar of Herne, Kent (1538); master of Pembroke Hall (1540); and chaplain to Henry VIII (1540). As proctor to Cambridge (1534), Ridley had signed the decree against papal supremacy; and a few months after the accession of King Edward VI, he was made bishop of Rochester (1547) through Cranmer's influence. He was one of the principal theologians among the English reformers and was instrumental in establishing Protestantism at Cambridge. He assisted in compiling the Book of COMMON PRAYER. Upon becoming bishop of London (1550), he ordered all altars in his diocese removed and replaced with tables. He denied the doctrine of transubstantiation. He supported Lady Jane Grey in 1553 as King Edward's successor, and soon after Queen Mary's accession, he was arrested. He was tried for heresy and convicted, and with Hugh LATIMER he was burned at the stake before Balliol Hall, Oxford.

Bibliography: *Works,* ed. H. CHRISTMAS (Cambridge, Eng. 1841), with biographical sketch. P. HUGHES, *The Reformation in England,* rev. ed., 3 v. in 1 (New York 1963). L. B. SMITH, *Tudor Prelates and Politics, 1536–1558* (Princeton 1953). M. SCHMIDT, *Die Religion und Geschichte und Gegenwart,* 6 v. (Tübingen 1957–63) 5:1099. S. LEE, *The Dictionary of National Biography from the Earliest Times to 1900,* 63 v. (London 1885–1900) 16:1172–1175.

[D. J. GUNDERSON]

RIEVAULX, ABBEY OF

Former English Cistercian abbey (Rievallis, Rievallensis abbatia), founded in 1131 by Walter Espec with monks from CLAIRVAUX, sent by St. BERNARD with his

Ruins of Rievaulx Abbey, North Yorkshire, England. (©Eric Crichton/CORBIS)

secretary, William, at their head. It lay three miles north of Helmesley in the Archdiocese of York. It soon made foundations at Wardon in Bedfordshire (1135), MELROSE in Scotland (1136), DUNDRENNAN in Scotland (1142), Revesby in Lincolnshire (1143), and Rufford in Nottingham (1146–48). Under its third abbot, AELRED, the community grew until it numbered 150 monks and 500 lay brothers: the buildings soon became too small, and new ones were erected, the old church forming the transept of the new. A strong literary tradition, formed by the first abbot, William, was fostered by Aelred, who wrote historical, philosophical, and theological works; it was continued into the 13th century by Walter Daniel, Aelred's biographer, by Thorald, Maurice of Durham, and Matthew of Rievaulx. The library catalogue mentions others also who left behind glossed psalters. Historical writing was discouraged by Ernaldus, eighth abbot, though he stimulated WILLIAM OF NEWBURGH, a neighboring Augustinian, to undertake such work; poetry, though condemned by the general chapter of 1199, lingered on a little longer.

Rievaulx always held a commanding place among the Cistercians of the north of England, and its abbots were constantly called upon to carry out commissions both for the general chapter and for the king. Its period of greatest expansion covered the 12th and 13th centuries. At the beginning of the 14th century it suffered greatly from depredations by the Scots, particularly in 1322 when King Edward II, surprised during a meal there, fled to York for safety, leaving his silver plate and treasures at the monastery. The pursuing Scots plundered and destroyed the abbey, its buildings, and belongings. During the 15th century the abbots shared with the abbots of FOUNTAINS the office of reformer for the northern province; reports of their activities, sent annually to the abbot of CÎTEAUX, are preserved in the archives at Dijon. They fostered the *studium* of St. Bernard at OXFORD, and a monk of Rievaulx, John Pomfret, was supervisor there *c.* 1456. At the time of the Dissolution, Edward Kirkby, the abbot, not being well disposed toward the impending religious changes, was removed from his post by the royal commissioners. The community would not accept this as a canonical deposition and refused to elect a successor. The abbot of Byland was ordered by the king to install another abbot; when only seven out of 23 monks would agree to vote, Richard Blyton of Rufford was intruded. The house finally surrendered Dec. 3, 1538, its value being £278 10s.

Bibliography: W. DUGDALE, *Monasticon Anglicanum* (London 1655–73) 5:274–286. *Cartularium abbathiae de Rievalle ordinis cisterciensis,* ed. J. C. ATKINSON (Surtees Society 83; Newcastle 1889). *Yorkshire Star Chamber Proceedings* (Yorkshire Archaeological Society 45; 1911). J. M. CANIVEZ, ed., *Statuta capitulorum generalium ordinis cisterciensis,* 8 v. (Louvain 1933–41). *The Victoria History of the County of York,* ed. W. PAGE, 4 v. and index (London 1907–13) v.3. C. H. TALBOT, "The *Centrum Sententiae* of Walter Daniel," *Sacris erudiri,* 11 (Bruges 1960) 266–383.

[C. H. TALBOT]

RIGBY, JOHN, ST.

Serving man, lay martyr; b. Harrock, near Wigan, Lancashire, England, *c.* 1570; d. St. Thomas' Watering's, Southwark, June 21, 1600. He came from a family of respected lineage, though impoverished through its years of loyalty to Catholicism. His lack of formal education and his destitution forced him to enter domestic service. While in the employ of a Protestant household, he occasionally conformed by attending their religious services. Later as a gentleman servant of the Catholic Huddlestons of Sawston Hill, near Cambridge, he came in contact with Father John GERARD, then a prisoner in the Clink. Gerard's influence and the example of the Huddlestons effected a reconciliation of Rigby with the Church, either through Gerard or St. John JONES. Rigby desired to become a Jesuit lay brother, though there is no record of any formal entrance into the Society of Jesus. This desire may have been inspired by the example of St. Nicholas OWEN, who built a hiding hole at Sawston. About two years after Rigby's reconciliation, he was sent to the Middlesex sessions of the Old Bailey to plead the illness of his master's widowed daughter, Mrs. Fortescue, as the reason for her nonappearance on a recusant charge. His firm answers impressed the aldermen; and when asked about his own religion, Rigby in his direct way replied that he had been reconciled to Catholicism, which was a capital offense. He was sent to Newgate prison, and after interrogations in which he rejected pardon on the condition of his attendance in the queen's church, he was sentenced to death. On his way to execution he was met by the Earl of Rut-

land, who admired his courage and counseled him in vain to conform. In his execution, which was performed with barbarity, his strong physique prolonged the agony. After the hangman had cut him down he stood dazed, and when pushed over was heard to say distinctly "God forgive you. Jesus, receive my soul." A man standing by pressed his heel on Rigby's throat to stop further speech. Rigby was beatified by Pius XI on Dec. 15, 1929, and canonized by Paul VI on Oct. 25, 1970 as one of the Forty Martyrs of England and Wales.

Feast: June 21; Oct. 25 (Feast of the 40 Martyrs of England and Wales); May 4 (Feast of the English Martyrs in England).

See Also: ENGLAND, SCOTLAND, AND WALES, MARTYRS OF.

Bibliography: J. GERARD, *The Autobiography of a Hunted Priest,* tr. P. CARAMAN (New York 1952). *Seven Lancastrian Martyrs* (Postulation Pamphlet; London 1960). A. BUTLER, *The Lives of the Saints,* ed. H. THURSTON and D. ATTWATER (New York 1956) 2:611–612. R. CHALLONER, *Memoirs of Missionary Priests,* ed. J. H. POLLEN (rev. ed. London 1924; repr. Farnborough 1969), 238–45. T. WORTHINGTON, *A Lancashire Man: The Martyrdom of John Rigby of Southwark,* ed. C. A. NEWDIGATE (London 1928). J. GILLOW, *A Literary and Biographical History or Bibliographical Dictionary of the English Catholics from 1534 to the Present Time* (New York 1961) 5:420. J. E. PAUL, *Blessed John Rigby* (Postulation Pamphlet; London 1964).

[G. FITZHERBERT]

RIGGS, THOMAS LAWRASON

First Catholic chaplain at Yale University, New Haven, Conn.; b. New London, Conn., June 28, 1888; d. New Haven, April 26, 1943. He was the son of Elisha Francis Riggs, known for his charitable works and for his advocacy of a restored Gregorian chant. After his early education at home, Riggs was prepared for college at Westminster School in Simsbury, Connecticut. At this Episcopal institution, his religious instruction was cared for by Father Maurice McAuliffe, later bishop of Hartford and close friend and spiritual counselor of Riggs.

After receiving an A.B. from Yale (1910) and an M.A. from Harvard University, Riggs returned to Yale as an instructor in English. During World War I, he joined the Yale Ambulance Corps and became an officer in Intelligence Interallié to do work at the peace conference. His awareness of the impact of war upon Europe's Christian cultural tradition prompted his choice of a priestly vocation. He began theological studies at the Catholic University of America in 1919, and he completed them under McAuliffe at St. Thomas Seminary in Hartford.

After ordination in 1922, Riggs received episcopal approval for residence near Yale and a limited chaplaincy there. In 1934, when McAuliffe became bishop of Hartford, the situation was reviewed and permission given for the construction of More House as a chapel and cultural center for Catholics at Yale. Meanwhile, Riggs had been active as a lecturer in behalf of the liturgical movement. He was a founder and contributor to *Commonweal,* a Catholic weekly published by laymen, and a participant in the interfaith work of the National Conference of Christians and Jews. But his greatest enthusiasm was for the design and construction of More House.

In his last years Riggs was a fellow of Calhoun College at Yale. Although without regular faculty status, he was in frequent demand as an authority in matters relating to Catholic belief and tradition. In 1963, Yale honored Father Riggs by establishing the T. Lawrason Riggs Professorship of Religion, the first endowed chair for Roman Catholic studies in a nonsectarian American university for a professor on permanent appointment.

[J. T. FARRELL]

RIGORISM

Rigorism is the moral system according to which, in every doubt of conscience as to the morality of a particular course of conduct, the opinion for law must be followed. In other words, one may act for liberty only when the arguments for this course are certain. The view was defended in the 17th century by the Jansenists, particularly by John SINNICH, an Irishman who taught at Louvain, in his book *Saulus ex-Rex.* The system eliminates the use of reflex principles and hence cannot be called a moral system in the present-day sense. Rigorism exaggerated the adage: "In a doubt the safer side is to be followed." This is correctly applied only to a practical doubt, not to a speculative doubt that can be resolved into practical certainty for liberty by the prudent use of reflex principles. Rigorism was condemned in 1690 by Alexander VIII, who listed among Jansenistic teachings the doctrine of Sinnich: "It is not lawful to follow a probable opinion, even if it is most probable among probable opinions" (H. Denzinger, *Enchiridion symbolorum,* ed. A. Schönmetzer [32d ed. Freiburg 1963] 2303).

See Also: MORALITY, SYSTEMS OF; DOUBT, MORAL; REFLEX PRINCIPLES; CONSCIENCE.

Bibliography: D. M. PRÜMMER, *Manuale theologiae moralis,* ed. E. M. MÜNCH, 3 v. (10th ed. Barcelona 1945–46) 1:338. J. AERTNYS and C. A. DAMEN, *Theologia moralis,* 2 v. (16th ed. Marietti 1930) 1:101. M. ZALBA, *Theologiae moralis compendium,* 2 v. (Madrid 1958) 1:673.

[F. J. CONNELL]

RIMED OFFICE

The designation "rimed office" has come into use only in recent years and is somewhat inexact. It refers to the series of ANTIPHONS and RESPONSORIES used at Vespers, Matins, and the daily hours of a liturgical feast (*see* DIVINE OFFICE, ROMAN). The texts involved are written in verse and set to music in a more florid style than that of GREGORIAN CHANT. The expression "rhythmic office" is broad, suggesting not only rhymed texts, but also texts that may be written in metrical or accentual verse without rhyme. The term *historia* also has been used for such offices, since most of them utilize "historical" texts, such as the *vita* or *passio* of a saint. Each series of antiphons and responsories is composed in the order of the modes from I to VIII. For the ninth piece, mode I is used again. This apparent organization is superficial, for only the last notes of the pieces obey the modal system, and everything else in them seems closer to tonal music, or even folk song.

Origin. Rimed offices appeared toward the end of the ninth century and were used to provide texts for newly established feasts. As the practice spread, new offices were composed to replace others already in use, and even for some parts of the temporal cycle, such as Trinity Sunday. In general the "historical" text employed was divided into antiphons and responsories and slightly changed to fit into a poetic scheme such as metrical verse, accentual verse, or rhymed prose. Sometimes the text was taken whole without any additions, but more often it was mixed with material from many sources.

Sources and Editions. Rhythmic offices, being perfectly liturgical, were included in numerous breviaries and antiphonaries containing the night hours, as well as in other sources. G. M. Dreves devoted nine volumes of his *Analecta Hymnica* to texts of rhythmic offices (v.5, 13, 18, 24, 25, 26, 28, and 45a). Although this edition is incomplete, it remains the only source for a methodical study. An analysis of these volumes was made by U. Chevalier in his *Repertorium Hymnologicum,* but the two works taken together still reveal many lacunae and errors.

History and Earliest Evidence. The Offices of St. Stephen and St. Lambert, written by Stephen of Liège, are generally regarded as the oldest evidence of the practice of composing rimed offices; the MS containing them is of the tenth century and seems to have been written during Stephen's lifetime or soon after his death in 920 (A. Auda). Some efforts along this line, such as an Office of St. Peter by HUCBALD OF SAINT-AMAND, were certainly made earlier (R. Weakland). This office used the *vita* of the saint without any modifications; that of St. Stephen transformed it into metrical verse with some assonance. Metrical offices can be found that span more than a century; it appears that composition in this genre was concluded, toward the beginning of the 11th century, with the series of antiphons attributed to Robert the Pious, *Pro fidei meritis* (S. Corbin, *Essai sur la musique . . .* 339), and the compositions of Fulbert of Chartres (Y. Delaporte). Accentual verse appeared in the 11th century, bringing with it rhyme and a style that became more and more studied, and even affected, especially under the influence of Leonine verse. During the next two centuries there was an immense proliferation of these series, but when the religious orders with strong centralized organization appeared (the Dominicans in particular), a sort of sclerosis afflicted the rhythmic office. Among the Dominicans, offices were still composed, but from the 13th century forward they were based on the offices for St. Dominic and St. Peter Martyr and introduced no new music (S. Corbin, "L'Office de la conception de la Vierge . . ." 62). Rhythmic offices were removed from the Roman rite by the Council of Trent, but they survive in the liturgy of the orders.

Research Methods. In the past these offices were edited one by one, without reference to other offices and even without a study of previous editions of the same office. Yet they had often undergone certain alterations in passing from church to church. The order of responsories might be changed, disturbing the order of the modes, or pieces might at times be replaced. Such alterations are historically useful in their own way, and sometimes permit identification of the church where they originated. Also, melodies were borrowed from other offices, as in the Office for Corpus Christi, for which the adaptations were meticulously indicated in one of the earliest texts: Paris, Bibliothèque National, fonds latins 1143 (L. M. J. Delaissé, 235; pl. 27 has indications in the margin of the borrowed melodies). It would be impossible to discuss the rimed office without considering such borrowings. On the other hand, the offices may be sorted, according to certain norms of compositions not yet investigated, into a Norman group, an Alsatian group, and a Flemish group.

Bibliography: *Analecta hymnica* (Leipzig 1886–1922) v.5, 13, 18, 24, 25, 26, 28, 45a. U. CHEVALIER, *Repertorium hymnologicum* (Louvain-Brussels 1892–1921). L. EISENHOFER and J. LECHNER, *The Liturgy of the Roman Rite*, tr. A. J. and E. F. PEELER from the 6th German Edition, ed. H. E. WINSTONE (New York 1961). G. REESE, *Music in the Middle Ages* (New York 1940). W. APEL, *Gregorian Chant* (Bloomington, Ind. 1958). A. AUDA, *L'École musicale liégeoise au X e siècle: Étienne de Liége* (Brussels 1923). S. CORBIN, *Essai sur la musique religieuse portugaise au moyen âge* (Paris 1952); "L'Office de la conception de la Vierge . . . dominicain d'Aveiro," *Bulletin des études portugaises* 13 (1949) 105–166. R. WEAKLAND, "The Compositions of Hucbald," *Études grégoriennes* 3 (1959) 155–163. Y. DELAPORTE, "Fulbert de Chartres et l'école chartraine de chant liturgique au XIe siècle," *ibid.* 2 (1957) 51–81. L. M. J. DELAISSÉ, "A la recherche des origines de 'office du Corpus Christi," *Scriptorium* 4 (1950) 220–239.

[S. CORBIN]

RINALDI, FILIPPO, BL.

Salesian priest; b. May 28, 1856 at Lu near Monferrato, Piedmont, Italy; d. Dec. 5, 1931, Turin, Italy.

The eighth of the nine children of the farmers Christoforo Rinaldi and Antonia Brezzi, Rinaldi attended the Salesian school at nearby Mirabello for a short time in 1866. Rinaldi became a priest because of the persistence of (St.) John BOSCO, who recognized his vocation. Rinaldi began religious studies with the Salesians at Sampierdarena in spring 1877 and proved to be an outstanding student. From Sampierdarena he went to the novitiate at San Benigno Canavese (1879), where the novice master chose him as his assistant. Rinaldi pronounced his vows in 1880, then continued his studies of philosophy and theology, and was ordained priest in 1882. Immediately thereafter he was placed in charge of late vocations at Mathi (1883–88), then Turin.

Father Rinaldi was sent to Sarria, Spain (1889–92), to assist the rector. There he established schools and two new houses (Gerona and Santander), and attracted many vocations, including that of the future saint St. Joseph CALASANCTIUS. Thereafter he was provincial for Iberia (1892–1901), during which he set up sixteen houses in Spain and three in Portugal; founded *Lecturas Catolicas*, a weekly newspaper for youth, as well as a library for students; and fostered the expansion of the Daughters of Mary Help of Christians in Spain.

In 1901, Rinaldi returned to Turin when he was chosen prefect general, an office he held for twenty years under Rectors General Michael Rua and Paul Albera. He spurred the spiritual development and the commitment of Salesian cooperators by promoting congresses and organizing reunions of past pupils. In spite of his other work, Rinaldi was a popular confessor and spiritual director and taught regularly at the Foglizzo seminary.

On May 24, 1922, Father Rinaldi was elected the third successor of John Bosco. He directed the Salesians with perspicacity in answer to the appeal of Pope PIUS XI, with special reference to the Asian and Eastern missions. He opened the Cardinal Cagliero Institute (1922 at Ivrea) to train new missionaries, and similar training centers at Penango (1925), Foglizzo (1926), Astudillo, Spain (1928), Shrigley, England (1929), and elsewhere, and fostered missionary vocations in various ways to staff the new missions in Porto Velho, Brazil (1926), Madras and Krishnagar, India (1928), Japan (1928), and Ratburi, Siam (Thailand, 1930).

He also served as apostolic delegate to the Daughters of Mary Help of Christians and encouraged their expansion, as well as that of the Don Bosco Union among teachers. During his tenure as rector general, Don Bosco was beatified (June 2, 1929). The order grew from 6,000 to 10,000 members during Rinaldi's tenure and added over 250 new houses.

This dynamic leader of the Salesians died at age seventy-five. His cause was initiated in 1947 and ended in his beatification by John Paul II, April 29, 1990.

Feast: Dec. 5 (Salesians).

Bibliography: Works. *Quaderno Carpanera*, verbali redatti da Luigina Carpanera, *Documenti e testi* V, (Rome 1980). *Don Rinaldi ci parla ancora* (Palermo 1984). Literature. *Lo spirito di Don Bosco nel cuore del beato Don Rinaldi*, ed. S. MAGGIO (Turin 1990). R. ALBERDI, *Don Filippo Rinaldi en Barcelona-Sarriá (1889–92)* (Barcelona 1990). A. L'ARCO, *Il Beato Filippo Rinaldi* (Castellammare di Stabia, Italy 1990). J. M. BESLAY, *Le Pere Rinaldi* (Lyons 1950). T. BOSCO, *Profili di santità* (Turin 1977). *Die Güte Don Boscos in Person*, tr. R. DAFELMAIR (Vienna 1990). L. CÀSTANO, *Don Rinaldi. Vivente immagine di Don Bosco* (Turin 1980). *Beato Don Filippo Rinaldi* (Turin 1990). E. CERIA, *Vita del Servo di Dio Sac. Filippo Rinaldi terzo successore di San Giovanni Bosco* (Turin 1951). M. COLLINO, *Il beato Filippo Rinaldi e l'Istituto delle Figlie di Maria Ausiliatrice* (Rome 1990). E. DAL COVOLO, *Il beato don Filippo Rinaldi, maestro di profondità interiore, testimone di vita* (Rovigo 1990). L. DALCERRI, *Un maestro di vita interiore* (Rome 1990). A. FANTOZZI, *Un uomo di fede Don Filippo Rinaldi* (Rome 1990). P. M. RINALDI, *Sospinto dall'amore* (Turin 1979, 1990). *By Love Compelled: The Life of Blessed Philip R., Third Successor of St. John Bosco* (New Rochelle, N.Y. 1992). *Droga milosci* (Krakow 1992). P. SCHINETTI, *La spiritualità di Don Filippo Rinaldi e la Volontaria di Don Bosco oggi* (Rome 1986). *Acta Apostolicae Sedis* (1990) 578.

[K. I. RABENSTEIN]

RINALDI, ODORICO (RAYNALDUS)

Oratorian priest and historical scholar; b. Treviso, Italy, June 1594; d. Rome, Jan. 22, 1671. He pursued his studies in Parma and Padua and in 1618 entered the Oratory in Turin. He was twice elected superior general of that congregation. Rinaldi was distinguished for his scholarship as well as for his personal piety, and through his historical work he rendered inestimable services to the Church. At the request of Pope Innocent X he undertook the continuation of the *Annales Ecclesiastici* inaugurated by his fellow Oratorian, Cardinal Caesar BARONIUS, in the previous century as a refutation of the errors and calumniations against the Church in the well-known Lutheran CENTURIATORS of Magdeburg. The work of Baronius had ended with the accession of Pope Innocent III in 1198 (v. 1–12); Rinaldi, who is generally recognized as the ablest continuator of Baronius, extended the work from 1198 to 1565 (v. 13–22) in a series of volumes

published in Rome (1646–77). His work marks an advance over that of Baronius in the publication of new and important documentary materials. He also published excerpts from his own work and that of Baronius in Latin and Italian. An abridgment of his own work, in three volumes, was published in Rome in 1670. Rinaldi declined Pope Innocent X's offer of the directorship of the Vatican Library. The significance of the work of Baronius and Rinaldi is reflected in their careers as historiographers who pioneered in the critical evaluation and use of source materials.

Bibliography: A. MARCHESAN, *Lettere inedite di Oderico Rinaldi* (Treviso 1896). W. WERBECK, *Die Religion in Geschichte und Gegenwart*, 6 v. (Tübingen 1957–63) 5:807.

[A. M. CHRISTENSEN]

RINGS, LITURGICAL USE OF

Rounded ornaments, mainly of metal or precious stone, usually worn on the finger, lip, neck, nose, ankle, arm, or ears as a symbol of religious or magic power, or used for exchange or value and adornment among ancient peoples, as well as a pledge of loyalty and trust. Ancient rings of marble, ivory, crystal, and metal have been discovered in almost every culture. Many were ornamented with gems, jewels, stones, pearls, and enamel. In ancient Egypt, Mycenae, Cyprus, and among the Celts, golden rings with markings for dismemberment were used as instruments of exchange or money; later, in Egypt particularly, the facing on a ring was used as a seal for the authentication of documents. This last practice was common in Israel and Greece and was adopted by the Romans, from whom the Christians borrowed it; this use has continued to the present day.

Bible and Early Church. The OT frequently refers to the use of gold or metal rings as ornaments, and many have been discovered in ancient Palestinian tombs. Arm, foot, and nose rings are mentioned in Genesis (24.22), Isaiah (3.18–21), Ezekiel (16.11–12), and Ecclesiastes (11.22). Pharaoh invested Joseph with a ring to signify his dignity (Gn 41.42), and Saul's arm ring was evidently a sign of rank (2 Sm 32.2). Women wore earrings, but the custom was also indulged in by men (Nm 31.50). The ancient Romans at first limited the use of finger rings to senators and high officials, but by 216 B.C., knights could wear them, and in the republic, it became general custom to wear signet, betrothal (*anulus pronubus*), wedding, and birthday (*anulus natalicius*) rings.

Tertullian complains about the luxurious use of rings by Christians (*De cultu fem.* 1.9), and Cyprian (*De hab. virg.* 21) and Jerome (*Epist.* 107.5) caution against this vanity. CLEMENT OF ALEXANDRIA distinguishes between the images on rings that were of pagan or immoral character and those permitted to Christians, such as the fish or dove as signs of Christian hope, the ship and anchor as symbols of heavenly security, and the lamb, lion, *Orans,* and *Monogram* of Christ as laudable symbolism. Later, pictures of Christ and the saints adorned Christian rings, and some were fitted with RELIQUARIES and worn round the neck. Gnostic rings usually carried a magic or religious formula and were considered amulets. Costly rings have been found in the tombs of Germanic and Frankish nobles of the 7th century, and during the Renaissance, artists prided themselves on turning out precious and luxuriously ornamented rings.

Liturgical Rings. St. Augustine speaks of the bishop's ring as a seal (*Epist.* 127.59), and it is probably from this practical usage that rings became a sign of the episcopal office. Isidore of Seville mentions the bishop's ring and staff in the course of the consecration and installation ceremonies (*De eccl. off.* 2.5.12; *Patrologia Latina,* ed. J. P. Migne [Paris 1878–90] 83:783), and so does the Council of Toledo IV in 633 (28; *Patrologia Latina,* 84:374–375). It was used in Gaul in the 9th century, according to a letter from Charles the Bald in 867 to Nicholas I (*Patrologia Latina,* 124:874). Rings eventually became a sign of the bishop's marriage to his see, and in the 10th century, the wearing of rings by bishops became an accepted custom. Innocent III tells us that bishops use the ring as a *fidei sacramentum,* that is, as a contract of love and faith between them and their church. The use of a ring was granted to the abbot of Monte Cassino by Leo IX (*Patrologia Latina,* 182:832).

The pope has three official rings: one for ordinary usage, the pontifical ring for ceremonies, and the ring of the Fisherman. The latter, the *anulus piscatoris,* is the gold seal ring that the cardinal *camerlengo* places on a new pope's finger. On it is the pope's name and an engraving of St. Peter in a boat fishing (Lk 5.10). It has been used for sealing briefs from the 15th century and is ceremoniously destroyed by the *camerlengo* on the death of the pope. The cardinal's ring is presented to him by the pope in the first consistory the cardinal attends after his elevation. Abbots wore rings from the 12th century with papal permission, and more generally from the 15th century. Some cathedral chapters and, since the 10th century, clerics in orders having doctoral degrees in theology, philosophy, or Canon Law may wear a ring designating their office or achievement. St. Ambrose witnesses to the right of consecrated virgins to wear a ring; and since the 14th century, many orders of professed nuns and sisters wear rings as a sign of their complete dedication to Christ.

Wedding Rings. The Christian use of wedding rings developed from the Roman custom of betrothal rings.

15th-century papal ring. (©Archivo Iconografico, S.A./CORBIS)

They are mentioned by GREGORY OF TOURS in the 6th century (*Vitae patrum* 20) and were widespread among the Visigoths and Lombards. In later times, husband and wife gave each other rings in pledge of their union and fidelity. In the old Roman Ritual, however, there is only the ceremonial for the ring given to the bride by the groom. Custom in this matter differed widely. Wearing the wedding ring on the third finger of the left hand seems to be connected originally with pronouncing the Trinitarian formula over the thumb and first two fingers so that the Amen was pronounced on the third finger.

Other Uses. In the 15th century, rosary rings with ten beads for each decade came into use, and this type of ring has been revived in modern times.

Bibliography: H. BATTKE, *Geschichte des Ringes* (Baden-Baden 1953). J. A. MARTIGNY, *Des Anneaux chez les premiers chrétiens* (Mâcon 1858). G. F. KUNZ, *Rings* (Philadelphia 1917). J. R. MCCARTHY, *Rings Through the Ages* (New York 1945).

[F. X. MURPHY/J. NABUCO/EDS.]

RINUCCINI, GIOVANNI BATTISTA

Archbishop of Fermo, papal nuncio to Ireland; b. Rome, Sept. 15, 1592; d. Fermo, Dec. 13, 1653. Rinuccini was born of noble Florentine stock. He was educated by the Jesuits and later studied law at Bologna and Perugia, obtaining his doctor's degree at Pisa. He entered the papal service, and at the age of 33 became archbishop of Fermo in the Marches (1625). Twenty years later, when Innocent X decided to send a fully accredited nuncio to the Irish Confederate Catholics, he chose the experienced and devoted Rinuccini.

The Irish Catholics had taken arms in 1641 to defend their political and religious rights, and the following year they had formed a political confederacy to which Urban VIII had accredited a papal envoy, Pier Francesco SCARAMPI. When Rinuccini arrived on Oct. 22, 1645, a serious crisis had arisen because some of the Anglo-Irish leaders among the Catholics were pressing for a political agreement with King Charles I that would grant very limited toleration to the Catholic religion, with no public recognition or adequate guarantees.

On the advice of Scarampi and the Irish bishops, Rinuccini decided on strong measures. At the synod of Waterford in August of 1646, all supporters (mostly Anglo-Irishmen) of the agreement with the king were declared excommunicated. By this bold stroke Rinuccini secured the rejection of the proposal and the imprisonment of those who had attempted to negotiate its acceptance. Shortly afterward, however, on the advice of some of the bishops, but against that of Scarampi, he agreed to their release and readmission to the political life of the Catholic confederates.

During the next two years the confederate armies were unsuccessful, and by 1648 their only effective military force was the army of the "Old Irish" (intransigent opponents of compromise) under Owen Roe O'Neill. The Anglo-Irish leaders, unwilling to accept O'Neill's hegemony, gradually maneuvered Rinuccini into a position whereby his demands for adequate guarantees for the Catholic religion could be identified with political support for the "Old Irish" party in the Confederation. Rinuccini tried hard to avoid such an identification, but he made some serious misjudgments in the spring of 1648, culminating in another excommunication of the Anglo-Irish leaders on May 27, and this time they did not succeed in winning sufficient public support.

Rinuccini was forced to retire to Galway, while at the headquarters of the Confederation in Kilkenny events developed outside his control. In January of 1649, a peace agreement was signed between the Confederates and the Marquis of Ormond, the king's representative. It included a hard-fought and, in the end, ambiguous agreement on terms for the Catholic religion, that, even if more favorable, would not have satisfied Rinuccini. He sailed from Galway on Feb. 25, 1649.

His mission was unsuccessful, but it may be doubted if anyone could have imposed a satisfactory solution on the complicated question of religious and political allegiances in 17th-century Ireland. On his return to Italy he retired to his see of Fermo where he died.

Bibliography: M. J. HYNES, *The Mission of Rinuccini* (Dublin 1932). T. L. COONAN, *The Irish Catholic Confederacy and the Puritan Revolution* (New York 1954). S. KAVANAGH, ed., *Commentarius Rinuccinianus*, 6 v. (Dublin 1932–49).

[P. J. CORISH]

RIORDAN, PATRICK WILLIAM

Archbishop of SAN FRANCISCO; b. Chatham, New Brunswick, Canada, Aug. 27, 1841; d. San Francisco, Dec. 27, 1914. His parents, Matthew and Mary Riordan, of Kinsale, Ireland, moved to Chicago, Illinois, when Patrick was seven years old. He attended St. Mary of the Lake University and graduated from the University of Notre Dame in 1858. Selected as one of the first 12 students of the North American College in Rome, Riordan left for Europe in 1859 to enter the Propaganda Seminary with the understanding that he would transfer to the American College when it opened on December 7 of the same year. For reasons of health he left Rome and studied first at the College of the Holy Ghost, Paris, and then at the American College, Louvain, Belgium, where he received his licentiate in sacred theology in 1866, having been ordained at Mechlin, Belgium, on June 10, 1865.

Riordan served at St. Mary of the Lake as professor of canon law and dogmatic theology until 1868 when he became pastor at Woodstock, Illinois, and successively at Joliet and at St. James in Chicago in 1871. In 1883 he was named coadjutor archbishop of San Francisco with the right of succession to Archbishop Joseph S. Alemany and succeeded to the see on Dec. 28, 1884.

Riordan participated actively in the Third Plenary Council of Baltimore in 1884 and spoke against the establishment of irremovable rectors in the western states as a premature move for missionary territory. He was named president of the commission of prelates for the Native American and African American missions and served on the commission for the study of secret societies. He supported the establishment of national churches wherein immigrants could hear their mother tongue and in his own archdiocese formed Italian, Spanish, Slavonian, Portuguese, French, and German churches. He built St. Mary's Cathedral in 1891.

Riordan led the campaign to exempt churches from the taxation that had been imposed by the State of California in 1868. By a narrow margin the churches were granted tax exemption on Nov. 6, 1900, although church schools remained taxable. The problem of the PIOUS FUND had vexed the bishops of California since 1869 when the Mexican government defaulted on its payment of indemnities to the Catholic Church in California. Riordan was named to bring the case before the Hague Tribunal, where he and Garrett McInerney won a unanimous decision in favor of the Church in the first case of international arbitration brought before that tribunal. The Mexican government defaulted in 1913 and has ignored the Hague decision ever since.

Riordan initiated an archdiocesan fund drive for St. Patrick's Seminary, Menlo Park, entrusting it to the Sulpician Fathers from Baltimore. This mother seminary opened in 1898, serving the entire West as the only diocesan major seminary for more than a quarter of a century.

Riordan constantly appealed to clergy and laity to work together in close harmony for the salvation of souls, particularly to effect the conversion of non-Catholics. His sermons were marked by an irenic spirit and his public statements on moral and social matters attracted attention in the daily press. His fluency in six languages endeared him to the immigrants flocking to California.

Bibliography: T. J. BRENNAN, "Archbishop Riordan," *Records of the American Catholic Historical Society of Philadelphia* 26 (1915): 47–54.

[M. J. HURLEY]

RIPA, MATTEO

Missionary, educator; b. Eboli (Salerno), Italy, March 29, 1682; d. Naples, March 29, 1746.

Matteo Ripa, son of a noble family, began his studies in 1697 at Naples. In 1701 he became a cleric; after his ordination (1705) he went to Rome to prepare for the foreign missions. Clement XI, in 1707, named him one of a group sent to take the red hat to Monsignor de Tournon, legate *a latere* to the Chinese emperor. Ripa arrived in Macau in 1710, remained there some months after the death in July of de Tournon, and then studied Chinese at Canton until the next year, when he went to the imperial court at Beijing. He found favor with the emperor, Hsüan-yeh, and was able, while acting as court painter, to perform some missionary work in spite of the general curtailment of Catholic missionary activity because of the Chinese rites controversy. He was in regular correspondence with the Congregation for the Propagation of the Faith during these years, and in 1717 he was named a prothonotary apostolic in recognition of his services. He acted as intermediary between the Emperor and Monsignor Mezzabarba, newly appointed papal legate, when he arrived in 1720.

When Hsüan-yeh died (1722), court intrigue intensified and Ripa was the victim of harassment by the Chinese and discrimination by some of the missionaries. Discouraged, he returned to Italy in 1723 with five Chinese, who became the first students in a school Ripa founded in Naples for the education of missionaries. In 1732 Clement XII formally approved the school and made Ripa's group a congregation of secular priests. The school came to be known as the Chinese College; there Ripa, called the Chinese Apostle, died. His foundation prepared priests for the missions until it was suppressed by the government in 1860. Ripa's valuable account of his work was published posthumously.

Bibliography: *Storia delea fondazione dalla Congregazione e del Collegio de' Cinese sotto il titolo della S. Famiglia de G. C., scritta dallo stesso fondatore M. Ripa e dei viaggi da lui fatti*, 3 v. (Naples 1832). A. S. ROSSO, *Apostolic Legations to China of the 18th Century* (South Pasadena 1948). A. THOMAS, *Histoire de la Mission de Pékin* (Paris 1923).

[P. F. MULHERN]

RIPALDA, JUAN MARTÎNEZ DE

Jesuit theologian; b. Pamplona, Navarre, 1594; d. Madrid, April 26, 1648. He entered the Society of Jesus in 1609. After the usual course of studies, he began his teaching career in 1619 at Monforte, where he lectured in philosophy for four years. He then went to Salamanca, where for many years he held the chair of dogmatic theology with great renown. From Salamanca he was summoned by royal decree to teach moral theology at the Imperial College of Madrid. He was later appointed censor to the Inquisition, and confessor of Philip IV's favorite, De Olivares, whom he followed upon his exile from Madrid in 1643. Ripalda was a good religious, noted for his innocence. A keenness of mind and clarity of expression made up for his lack of physical strength. He is ranked with Lugo among the best theologians of Spain at the time, and perhaps of all Europe. Some of his more notable theological opinions are: (1) Prescinding from the actual Divine Law and considering only natures, faith obtained by contemplation of created things would be sufficient for salvation, although assent comes only through grace. (2) The formal object of faith is God's faithfulness, constancy of will, and efficacy of power. (3) The sense BAIUS gave his propositions was condemned as well as the words. (4) God can create a being to whom supernatural grace is due. (5) Supernatural grace is conferred for every good act; thus every good natural act is accompanied by a supernatural act. (6) The Divine maternity of Mary is itself formally sanctifying.

Ripalda's principal work is *De ente supernaturali disputationes in universam theologiam* (v.1 Bordeaux

1634; v.2 Lyons 1645; v.3 *Adversus Bajanos,* Cologne 1648). This work includes many questions not treated in standard texts. The last volume elicited an anonymous attack, attributed to Sinnich, *P. Joannis Martinez. . . Vulpes capta per theologos. . . Academiae Lovaniensis.* His other published works are: *Expositio brevis literae Magistri Sententiarum* (Salamanca 1635), and the *Tractatus theologici et scholastici de virtutibus, fide, spe et charitate* (Lyons 1652). There are two collections of his works: Vives (8 v. Paris 1871–73), Palmé (4 v. Rome 1870–71). Another work, *Discurso sobre la elección de successor del pontificado en vida del pontifice* (Seville), is attributed also to him. Several other writings are preserved in manuscript at Salamanca and at the Biblioteca Nacional.

Bibliography: C. SOMMERVOGEL et al, *Bibliothèque de la Compagnie de Jésus,* 11 v. (Brussels–Paris 1890–1932; v. 12 suppl. 1960) 5:640–643. H. HURTER, *Nomenclator literarius theologiae catholicae,* 5 vol. in 6 (3d ed. Innsbruck 1903–13) 3:928–930. P. DE RIBADENEIRA, *Bibliotheca Scriptorum Societatis Jesu* (Rome 1676). A. ASTRAIN, *Historia de la Compagñia de Jesús en la asistencia de España,* 7 v. (Madrid 1902–25) v.5. G. R. DE YURRE, "La teoría de la maternidad divina, formalmente santificante en Ripalda y Scheeben," *Estudios Marianos* 3 (1944) 255–286. A. ARBELOA EGÜES, *La Doctrina de la predestinación y de la Gracia eficaz en Juan Martinez Ripalda* (Pamplona 1950). N. ANTONIO, *Bibliotheca hispana nova,* 2 v. (Madrid 1783–88) 1:736–737. P. DUMONT, *Dictionnaire de théologie catholique,* ed. A. VACANT et al., 15 v. (Paris 1903–50; Tables générales 1951–) 13.2:2712–37.

[J. E. KOEHLER]

RIPOLL, ABBEY OF

An important former Benedictine monastery dedicated to the Blessed Virgin, situated in north Ripoll (*Rivipolli, Rivipullo*) in Catalonia, Diocese of Vich. It was founded (*c.* 880) by Count Wilfrid I of Barcelona, who subsequently enriched the monastery with gifts of books, silver, gold, and jewels for liturgical vessels. The abbey was expanded in the 10th century by the addition of cells, enclosure wall, scriptorium, and a mill, and MONTSERRAT became a daughterhouse. Agapetus II gave Ripoll papal protection (951), and in 1011 Sergius IV granted full exemption. It reached its greatest material and intellectual development under the noble Abbot Oliva (1008–46), who was bishop of Vich (1018–46). A new church was built (1032) and consecrated; the cloisters were enlarged and scholarship was encouraged. Count Bernard II of Besalù, a relative of Oliva, made Ripoll a dependency (1163–72) of SAINT-VICTOR IN MARSEILLES after Oliva's death. Perhaps disagreement over this step was instrumental in the Count's decision to transfer the family burial place to Poblet. At any rate, the change caused Ripoll's fame to decline. In the early 16th century the abbey joined a congregation of 30 Benedictine houses in Aragon and Roussillon. Further decline set in as a result of the appointment of commendatory abbots (among them the future ALEXANDER VI) and on account of the sufferings caused by the wars of the 17th and 18th century. In 1835 during the Carlist wars the monastery was destroyed, and whatever MSS of its famous archival collection had not been sent to Paris or Barcelona were burned. The abbey church, reconstructed as a parish church (1887) on the old plans, retains the original great Romanesque doorway, the cloisters, and sections of the seven apsidal chapels.

Bibliography: P. F. KEHR, ed., *Papsturkunden in Spanien,* 2 v. in 4 (Berlin 1926–28) 1.1:120–125. R. BEER, "Die Handschriften des Klosters Santa Maria de Ripoll," *Sitzungsberichte der Akademie der Wissenschaften in Wien* 155.3 (1908); 158.2 (1908). R. ABADAL, *Analecta Montserratensia* 9 (Montserrat 1962). J. J. BAUER, *Lexikon für Theologie und Kirche,* ed. J. HOFER and K. RAHNER, 10 v. (2d, new ed. Freiburg 1957–65) 8:1319–20. *Enciclopedia de la Religión Católica,* ed. R. D. FERRERES et al., 7 v. (Barcelona 1950–56) 6:757–759.

[C. M. AHERNE]

RIPOLL MORATA, FELIPE, BL.

Priest, martyr of the Spanish civil war; b. Sept. 14, 1878, Teruel, Spain; d. Feb. 7, 1939, "Can Tretze" of Pont de Molins (near Gerona), Spain. Felipe, son of a poor family, was educated and ordained a priest for the diocese of his birth. He then served consecutively as professor, spiritual director, and rector of the seminary. Upon the elevation of Anselmo POLANCO to bishop of Teruel (1935), Father Ripoll was appointed his vicar general. The following year the Spanish Church experienced its most severe persecution. Undaunted, the bishop of Teruel and Father Ripoll remained with their flock. In 1938 Bishop Polanco was arrested for refusing to withdraw his name from a document signed by his brother Spanish bishops that condemned the persecution of the Church by the Republican Army. Father Ripoll joined him in jail for thirteen months, until the Republican forces were in retreat. The two were taken as hostages and shot in a gorge near Gerona. Fr. Ripoll's body rests in the cathedral of Teruel together with those of his bishop. They were beatified by John Paul II, Oct. 1, 1995.

Feast: Feb. 7.

Bibliography: V. CÁRCEL ORTÍ, *Martires españoles del siglo XX* (Madrid 1995). J. PÉREZ DE URBEL, *Catholic Martyrs of the Spanish Civil War, 1936–1939,* tr. M. F. INGRAMS (Kansas City, Mo. 1993). *L'Osservatore Romano,* English ed. 40 (1995): 1–3.

[K. I. RABENSTEIN]

RIPON, ABBEY OF

Early English monastic foundation about 20 miles northwest of York (Latin, *Ad Ripam;* OE, *In Hrypum*). The foundation of the abbey is credited to a group of Celtic monks from MELROSE, led by Abbot Eata, on land given by Alcfrith, subking of Deira, *c.* 651. CUTHBERT OF LINDISFARNE was a member of this early community and his famous "miracle of the heavenly loaves" occurred at Ripon. Declining to institute the Roman practices demanded by Alcfrith, the Celtic monks abandoned the house (*c.* 661), which was then given to WILFRID OF YORK, who established the BENEDICTINE RULE there. One of Wilfrid's first disciples at Ripon was the later "Apostle of Frisia," WILLIBRORD. Although Wilfrid soon after became bishop of York, Ripon remained the place he "loved better than any other place" during his stormy career, and it was there that he passed his last years and was later to be buried (709). The first abbey church, dedicated to St. Peter, was built by Wilfrid before 678, and its crypt, called "Wilfrid's Needle," is still extant under the present cathedral, which was commenced in the second half of the 12th century. The original monastic buildings and church were destroyed *c.* 948 during King Edred's wars against the Danes. The abbey was rebuilt and populated with monks later in the century by Abp. OSWALD OF YORK as part of the monastic revival. Before the Norman Conquest, however, the monks were replaced by CANONS REGULAR. This foundation was dissolved under HENRY VIII. In 1604 Ripon was refounded as an Anglican collegiate church; in 1836 the church became the cathedral of the Anglican Diocese of Ripon.

Bibliography: BEDE, *Ecclesiastical Historiography* 3.25; 4.12; 5.19. EDDIUS, *The Life of Bishop Wilfrid,* ed. and tr. B. COLGRAVE (Cambridge, England 1927), *passim.* A. H. THOMPSON, "Collegiate Church of St. Peter and St. Wilfrid, Ripon," *The Victoria History of the County of York,* ed. W. PAGE, 4 v. and index (London 1907–13) 3:367–372. R. L. POOLE, "St. Wilfrid and the See of Ripon," *English Historical Review* 34 (1919). F. L. CROSS, *The Oxford Dictionary of the Christian Church* (London 1957) 1167.

[R. D. WARE]

RISORGIMENTO

Nationalist movement in 19th-century Italy culminating in the unification of the country by 1870. Its origins can be traced to the intellectual ferment of the 18th-century ENLIGHTENMENT and to the influence of the FRENCH REVOLUTION. Ignoring the liberal and national aspirations of many Italians, the Congress of Vienna in 1815 gave Austria a dominant position over an Italy divided into seven states. This settlement caused widespread antagonism. After many failures and disappointments, Austrian control was finally ended and a national Italian state achieved. The *risorgimento* falls into two distinct periods: 1815 to 1848 and 1849 to 1870.

EARLIER PERIOD

Revolutionary unrest characterized these years. Immediately after the Congress of Vienna, Italians began vain demands for liberal reforms and constitutional guarantees. From 1831 the idea of unifying the peninsula gained support among intellectuals. Secret societies, such as the CARBONARI and Mazzini's Young Italy, organized conspiratorial activities and prepared the revolutions of 1820 1821, 1831, and 1848. The 1820s were dominated by the Carbonari and the 1830s and 1840s by the extreme, revolutionary, republican followers of Mazzini, but the 1840s witnessed the emergence of a moderate, liberal, Catholic group that looked to the papacy for leadership in a future confederation of Italian states. Among the leaders of this group were Manzoni, Capponi, Cattaneo, Ricasoli, ROSSI, Mamiani, Tommaseo, VENTURA, Balbo, and GIOBERTI. It was composed mostly of devout, practicing Catholics, who were trying to reconcile their religious sentiments and loyalty to the Church with their desire for political liberty and representative government. When Cardinal Mastai-Ferretti became Pope Pius IX in 1846, they turned to him for leadership. "Viva Pio Nono" became the cry of many Italian patriots, especially after the papal allocution (Feb. 10, 1848) that concluded with the words, "God bless Italy." Until 1848 it was widely believed that Pius IX supported the cause of Italian independence. In fact, his policies added impetus to a movement that later the pope was unable to control or to stop.

Revolutions erupted across Europe in 1848 and reverberated throughout Italy. Popular pressure forced rulers to grant constitutions. An effort was made to form an Italian coalition against Austria, but Pius IX and Ferdinand II of Naples withdrew their troops, and the small army of Piedmont-Sardinia was defeated by Austria at the battles of Custozza and Novara. Subsequently the independent revolutionary governments in Milan, Venice, and Rome were suppressed one by one. By 1849 Austria was victorious. It had reestablished its rule over Lombardy and Venetia and had restored to Tuscany, Modena, and Parma rulers subservient to its policies. The recent constitutions were quickly revoked everywhere, except in Piedmont-Sardinia.

LATER PERIOD

A decrease in revolutionary activity and the emergence of the Kingdom of Piedmont-Sardinia as leader in the drive for unity marked the later period. The 1848 debacle influenced subsequent developments. Its violence

"The Proclamation of the Republic of Venice in 1848," 19th-century painting by V. Giancomelli. (©Archivo Iconografico S.A./ CORBIS)

impressed on Pius IX the incompatibility between his role as head of the universal Church and his support of Italian liberal national aspirations. These events created a rift between the Church and the *risorgimento,* which was henceforth anticlerical and openly in favor of unification. A realignment of forces occurred throughout the peninsula as Mazzini's influence waned. Piedmont-Sardinia initiated a program of internal political and economic reforms and became the haven for political exiles from all parts of Italy. Moreover, the able leadership and diplomacy of Camillo Benso di CAVOUR, its prime minister, who held power almost uninterruptedly from 1852 until his death in June 1861, gained the support of most Italian liberals and patriots, with the exception of Mazzini and a few of his diehard followers. In 1858 the Italian National Society, organized by many of the former republican leaders of the 1848 revolts, espoused the monarchial leadership. Cavour's diplomacy disavowed revolution and gained recognition abroad for Italy's national aspirations. In 1855 Piedmont-Sardinia entered the Crimean War against Russia and sent a small army to fight in the Crimea. This enabled Cavour to attend the Congress of Paris in 1856 with the great European powers. After the Pact of Plombières, which assured Cavour French support against Austria, war broke out in 1859 between Austria and Piedmont-Sardinia. Austria was defeated and ceded Lombardy. Within a few months Piedmont-Sardinia succeeded in annexing most of central Italy, including parts of the STATES OF THE CHURCH. The expedition of GARIBALDI added the southern part of the peninsula. Early in 1861 the new kingdom of Italy (with Turin as its capital) was officially proclaimed, although Pius IX retained control of the Eternal City with the protection of French troops. Austria still held Venetia. Most Italian patriots agreed that the *risorgimento* would remain incomplete until Rome became part of the new kingdom and until Austria relinquished Venetia. The latter event occurred in 1866, when Italy allied with victorious Prussia against Austria. Rome fell into Italian hands in 1870, after France recalled its soldiers to meet the threat of Prussian attack. By 1870 the *risorgimento* could be considered finished, even though some claim that its completion did not occur until the acquisition of *Italia irredenta* (Italian territory still in Austrian hands) after World War I.

The *risorgimento* was mainly a political movement, but it can be interpreted also as a national revival that made Italy part of the 19th-century Western state system and civilization. As such, the movement posed serious religious problems, for with few exceptions all who participated in it were practicing Catholics, from the leaders of the 1821 revolts to General Cadorna, who occupied Rome in 1870. The split between the Church and the national and liberal movement began in 1848 and gained momentum after 1855, when the first Piedmontese anticlerical laws were passed. From then on, Catholics who were also patriots were faced with a serious crisis of conscience. This created many problems for the new state and had serious consequences for Italy and its people until the schism was healed by the LATERAN PACTS of 1929 (*see* ROMAN QUESTION).

Bibliography: A. MONTI, *Pio IX nel Risorgimento italiano* (Bari 1928). R. ALBRECHT-CARRIÉ, *Italy from Napoleon to Mussolini* (New York 1950). E. P. NOETHER, *Seeds of Italian Nationalism 1700–1815* (New York 1951). D. MACK SMITH, *Cavour and Garibaldi, 1860: A Study in Political Conflict* (Cambridge, Eng. 1954). R. GREW, *A Sterner Plan for Italian Unity: The Italian National Society in the Risorgimento* (Princeton 1963). A. C. JEMOLO, *Chiesa e stato in Italia negli ultimi cento anni* (Turin 1948); *Church and State in Italy, 1850–1950,* tr. D. MOORE (Philadelphia 1960). D. MASSÈ, *Cattolici e Risorgimento* (Milan 1961). E. ROTA, ed., *Questioni di storia del Risorgimento e dell' unità d'Italia* (Milan 1951). *Nuove questioni di storia del Risorgimento e dell' unità; d'Italia* (Milan 1962). L. SALVATORELLI et al., ''Il problema religioso del Risorgimento,'' *Rassegna storica del Risorgimento* 43 (1956) 193–345, 413–589, proceedings of the 33d *Congresso di Storia del Risorgimento,* 1954. E. ARTON et al., ''Il problema politico del cattolicesimo nel Risorgimento,'' *Rassegna storica Toscana* 4.3–4 (1958), proceedings of the 11th *Convegno of the Società toscana per la storia del Risorgimento,* 1958. R. AUBERT, *Le Pontificat de Pie IX* (Fliche-Martin 21; 2d ed. 1964).

[E. P. NOETHER]

RIST, VALERIUS

Franciscan missionary to Indochina; b. Neuburg, Jan. 6, 1696; d. Nhatrang, Cochin China, Sept. 15, 1737. In 1712 he joined the Reformed Franciscans of Bavaria. In 1721 he entered the S. Pietro in Montorio missionary college, Rome, and in 1722 left to found a mission in Johore, Malaya. When he was refused entry on May 11, 1724, he went to Cambodia, where he worked from October of 1724 to August of 1728. He was sent by the Con-

gregation de Propaganda Fide to Kuang-chou, China, enduring a shipwreck on the way. In July of 1730 he became pro-vicar of Cambodia and Laos. On Oct. 1, 1735, he was named titular bishop of Mindonium and coadjutor to Bishop Alessandro Alessandri, vicar apostolic of Cochin China and Cambodia, and was consecrated by him on April 28, 1737, at Hué. He was buried at Nhatrang, center of his apostolate. Despite conflicts of jurisdiction with missionaries of other institutes, he converted many pagans, almost completed a catechism in Cambodian that has since perished, and compiled an itinerary of his travels.

Bibliography: E. SCHLUND, *Nach Cochinchina* (Trier 1911). B. LINS, *Geschichte der bayerischen Franziskanerprovinz* (Munich 1926). B. H. WILLEKE, *Lexikon für Theologie und Kirche,* ed. J. HOFER and K. RAHNER (Freiburg 1957–65) 8:1321–1322.

[F. MARGIOTTI]

RITA OF CASCIA, ST.

''Saint of Desperate Cases''; b. Roccaporena near Cascia, Umbria, 1377; d. May 1447. After her husband had been murdered and her children had died, she entered the new Augustinian convent of Santa Maria Magdalena (now S. Rita) in Cascia. A mystic of the cross, she bore Christ's bloody thorn in her forehead for 15 years before her death. Because of her reputation for sanctity and miracles, her body and original coffin were transferred in 1457 to a decorated sarcophagus that still exists. Inside this sarcophagus is traced the bishop's *recognitio cultus* of 1457. She was beatified July 16, 1626, and canonized May 24, 1900. The sources for her life include the short versified life on the sarcophagus of 1457, the biographical introduction of the original list of miracles after 1457 included in her beatification process, and the authentic 15th-century painting with six medallions portraying some events of her life. This painting was described in the beatification process. The iconography of the saint is based on the 15th-century painting as well as on two pictures on the sarcophagus. A new basilica containing the body of the saint was erected in 1946. It is combined with a monastery, school, hospital, and orphanage and is a pilgrim center.

Feast: May 22.

Bibliography: *Acta Sanctorum* May 5:224–234. A. MORINI, ''La cassa funebre di S. Rita da Cascia,'' *Archivio per la storia ecclesiastica dell'Umbria* 3 (1916) 75–80. F. CAMPO DEL POZO, *Vida de S. Rita de Cascia* (Zamora 1998). A. GORINI, *La devozione a S. Rita de Cascia in Liguria* (Cascia 1997).

[F. ROTH]

RITES, CONGREGATION OF

On Jan. 22, 1588, Sixtus V established a Congregation of Sacred Rites and Ceremonies as a part of his systematic arrangement of the Roman congregations. Before long the distinct Ceremonial Congregation assumed responsibility for the ceremonial of the papal court and from that time the Congregation of Sacred Rites remained practically unchanged until the end of the 19th century.

The work of the Congregation fell naturally into two categories: (1) worship in general, including supervision over rites, restoration and reform of ceremonies, reform and correction of liturgical service books, solution of controversies, concession of feasts of saints; and (2) the processes of beatification and canonization. Once the liturgical books authorized by the Council of Trent were published, the Congregation did not substantially reform them until the 20th century, so that its liturgical activity is represented principally by decrees and responses to difficulties rather than by revision of the liturgy.

In order to balance the Congregation's traditional preoccupation with beatification and canonization, Leo XIII added two commissions: (1) the Liturgical Commission (1891) to codify past decrees and to advise the Congregation on liturgical questions; and (2) the Historico–liturgical Commission (1902) to settle historical questions, with special reference to the eventual reform of the liturgical books. Pius X added a third commission, for ecclesiastical music, in 1904.

In the general reform of the Curia by Pius X (1908), the Congregation of Rites was restricted in its competence to matters directly related to sacred worship (in addition to the cult of the saints, as before). Questions of precedence and of the discipline of the sacraments (as distinct from the rite of the sacraments) were transferred to other congregations.

A further reorganization was decreed by Pius X in 1914. He suppressed the three attached commissions and set up two sections of the Congregation itself, one for beatification and canonization, the other for sacred rites. Still later, Pius XI strengthened the Congregation by establishing a third, historical, section in 1930. Its purpose is to engage in historical research necessary for beatification and canonization processes and for the emendation of the liturgical books.

In order to resume the liturgical reform initiated by Pius X, Pius XII in 1948 established a new body attached to the Congregation, the Pontifical Commission for the General Restoration of the Liturgy. This commission undertook a partial revision of the Roman Missal, Breviary, and Pontifical. The reform of all the liturgical books of the Roman rite, which was decreed on Dec. 4, 1963, by Vatican Council II, was entrusted by Paul VI to a new body, the *Consilium* for the Implementation of the *Constitution on the Sacred Liturgy* rather than to the Congregation of Rites (*motu proprio Sacram liturgicam,* Jan. 25, 1964). The general reform of the Roman Curia by Paul VI in 1967 left the Congregation of Rites relatively unaffected. In the apostolic constitution, *Sacra Rituum,* dated May 8, 1969, the Congregation of Rites was divided into two separate entities: the Congregation for Divine Worship and the Congregation for the Causes of Saints.

See Also: DIVINE WORSHIP AND THE DISCIPLINE OF THE SACRAMENTS, CONGREGATION FOR.

Bibliography: F. R. MCMANUS, *The Congregation of Sacred Rites* in *Catholic University of America Canon Law Studies* 352 (Washington 1954). *Decreta authentica Congregationis Sacrorum Rituum,* 7 v. (Rome 1898–1927).

[F. R. MCMANUS/EDS.]

RITSCHL, ALBRECHT

German Protestant theologian; b. Berlin, Mar. 25, 1822; d. Göttingen, Mar. 20, 1889. Son of Carl Ritschl (1783–1858), bishop and general superintendent of the Evangelical Church in Pomerania, Albrecht Benjamin Ritschl von Hartenbach studied philosophy and theology at Tübingen and other German universities and became lecturer (1846) and then professor (1852) of New Testament studies and patristics at the University of Bonn. In 1864 he moved to the University of Göttingen as professor of theology and served for a time as chancellor. Ritschl's thought and writings came to exercise an immense influence upon the German theological faculties at Giessen, Tübingen, Marburg, Berlin, and Leipzig, and upon Protestantism throughout the world. A Ritschlian school emerged in the second half of the nineteenth century.

Originally Ritschl subscribed to HEGEL'S interpretation of the early Church's development as presented by the TÜBINGEN SCHOOL, particularly by F. C. BAUR, Ritschl's former teacher. In the second edition of *Die Entstehung der altkatholischen Kirche* (1857; 1st ed. 1850), in which it was evident that his patristic studies had led him to distrust the speculative-idealistic understanding of history and theology and to advocate instead a nonmetaphysical exposition of sacred scripture and dogma. Ritschl was the first theologian to take seriously and to utilize fully the philosophy of I. KANT, especially the *Critique of Practical Reason.* According to Ritschl, ontological statements in theology should give way to value judgments, since theology must focus on ethical and moral realities; it cannot operate with deductions from the *Ding an sich*. After abandoning all forms of natural theology, Ritschl based his system on the revelation in Jesus Christ as the perfect manifestation of the love of God. Ritschl would not permit ontological or metaphysical questions about the natures of Jesus. Instead he proposed a personalistic and moral query about the meaning of Christ for men. Consistent with this viewpoint, Ritschl criticized harshly the ontological Christology and soteriology of the early Fathers of the Church. His approach influenced Adolf von HARNACK, Friedrich Loofs, and other Protestant historians, as well as some Catholic theologians.

The notion of JUSTIFICATION was central in Ritschl's theology. In this regard he followed Luther and anticipated Rudolf Bultmann. Justification, in Ritschl's opinion, should not be conceived in juridical terms, but as the divine act of lifting the ''guilt-consciousness,'' which is simultaneously sin and punishment. This ''lifting away'' does not mean that God merely forgets sin, for it causes men to believe that God is no longer to be ''distrusted'' as if his wrath were on man. The result of this trust is reconciliation, full harmony between God and man. Ritschl stressed that God justifies the sinner, not the righteous; yet he emphasized also that God's sole purpose with mankind is moral perfection as revealed by Jesus. This ideal of a moral rule over the entire world Ritschl called the kingdom of God. The realization of divine love in men's lives should be manifested in love for the neighbor; this in turn should be exercised by fulfilling the duties of one's state in life (*Beruf*). These ideas found their mature expression in *Die christliche Lehre von der Rechtfertigung und Versöhnung* (3 v. 1870–74; 3d ed. 1888–89; Eng. tr. 1872–1900).

Many conservative theologians and some liberal ones understandably assailed severely Ritschl's theology, whose impact was most noticeable on later theologians, who did not fully agree with it. Among them were Wilhelm Herrmann, Ernst Troeltsch, and perhaps Karl Barth, who was Ritschl's sternest critic.

Bibliography: *Genealogisches Handbuch des Adels,* v. 26 (Limburg 1961) 307–314, origin and history of Ritschl family. O. RITSCHL, *Albrecht Ritschls Leben,* 2 v. (Bonn 1892–96), with full bibliog. J. ORR, *The Ritschlian Theology and the Evangelical Faith* (2d ed. London 1898); *Ritschlianism* (London 1903). R. MACKINTOSH, *Albrecht Ritschl and His School* (London 1915). K. BARTH, *Die protestantische Theologie im 19. Jahrhundert* (2d ed, Zollikon-Zurich 1952). H. O. WÖLBER, *Dogma und Ethos: Christentum und Humanismus von R. bis Troeltsch* (1950). C. WALTHER, ''Der Reich-Gottes-Begriff in der Theologie R. Rothes und A. Ritschls,'' *Kerygma und Dogma* 2 (1956) 115–138. D. L. MUELLER, *An Introduction to the Theology of Albrecht Ritschl* (Philadelphia 1959). E. SCHOTT, *Die Religion in Geschichte und Gegenwart,* 7 v. (3rd ed. Tübingen 1957–65) 5:1114–17.

[D. RITSCHL]

Albrecht Ritschl.

RITTER, JOSEPH

Cardinal; b. New Albany, Indiana, July 20, 1892; d. St. Louis, June 10, 1967. Ritter attended St. Meinrad Seminary and was ordained to the priesthood at the Abbey Church on May 30, 1917. He served as rector of the Cathedral of Saints Peter and Paul in Indianapolis until he was ordained an auxiliary bishop of the diocese on March 28, 1933. He succeeded to the diocese on March 24, 1934, and became first archbishop of Indianapolis on Dec. 19, 1944. He was appointed archbishop of St. Louis to succeed the late Cardinal John Joseph Glennon on July 20, 1946. In the consistory of Jan. 16, 1961, he was created cardinal priest of the Church of the Holy Redeemer and St. Alphonsus.

During the first year of his tenure as archbishop of St. Louis, Ritter instructed his pastors to end segregation in Catholic schools for the opening of the 1947 school term. He turned aside the objection of dissenting Catholics who threatened to obtain a court injunction against integration with the warning that they risked automatic excommunication under canon law for impeding an ordinary in the exercise of his pastoral office. He supported and encouraged organizations of the laity and the lay retreat movement and became a leading spokesman for liturgical renewal, twice hosting the National Liturgical Conference meeting at St. Louis (1948 and 1964).

Appointed to the Central Preparatory Commission for the Second Vatican Council, Ritter attended every session of the council and was elected vice president of the Commission for the Clergy. In the aftermath of the council, Ritter was appointed by Pope Paul VI to the Consilium on Sacred Liturgy to help prepare the norms for implementation of the Council's liturgical directives. He spent the final years of his life working to make Vatican II a living reality in his archdiocese, laboring for the establishment of human and civil rights and providing vigorous ecumenical leadership.

[J. W. BAKER]

RITUAL, ROMAN

The Ritual (*Rituale*) is the liturgical book containing texts for several non-eucharistic liturgies intended generally for presbyteral use, some other sacramental celebrations (e.g. baptism, matrimony, penance, anointing of the sick) and other services (e.g. funerals).

The development of the Ritual as a separate liturgical book was a complex one in late antiquity and the medieval period. As was the case with the sacramentary and the pontifical, early rubrics for the celebration of some ritual services were preserved as individual *ordines*, or in collections of the *ordines romani*. Again like the sacramentary and the pontifical, individual ritual celebrations were next recorded in *libelli*, small booklets prepared for specific services. These *libelli* were later collected and bound together in more complete volumes for use at specific churches. However, the ritual material was often bound with other liturgical services that in later centuries would be separated into distinct volumes. There were several kinds of these "hybrid" books: one can find many examples of early medieval pontifical-rituals, collectar-rituals, sacramentary-rituals, and even breviary-rituals. The development is further complicated by the presence of ritual material in liturgical books intended for monastic use (especially monasteries involved in the wider *cura animarum*) as well as books prepared for cathedral and parochial churches. Even the titles of these volumes varied: *sacerdotale, manuale,* or *agenda,* among others, are all terms used for this volume, until the name *rituale* became the standard among the printed editions of the sixteenth century.

The Council of Trent (1545–1563) called for papal supervision in the preparation of revised liturgical books. An earlier volume by Albert Castellani (the *Liber Sacerdotalis,* 1523) and a revision project already substantially underway (1575–1602) both supplied the groundwork for the Tridentine *Rituale Romanum* (RR). One of the last of the Tridentine books to appear, the RR was published in 1614 and recommended for adoption by all Roman Catholic dioceses. However, many of these in Europe chose to retain their own ritual books, and it was not until the nineteenth century that the adoption of the RR was more strictly mandated. The volume itself contained twelve "titles," or sections; the sacraments of baptism, confirmation, penance, extreme unction (and funeral liturgy), and matrimony were all included, as well as a section containing various blessings, another on processions, and a final title on exorcisms.

The RR was retained, with two expansions/revisions (1752, 1925) until the middle of the twentieth century. The liturgical reforms mandated by the Second Vatican Council (1962–1965) included a reform of the other sacramental rites and services contained in the old Ritual. The *editiones typicae* of these rites were published as follows:

> *Ordo Baptismi parvulorum* (1969; *editio typicae altera* 1977), *Ordo celebrandi matrimonium* (1969, *editio typicae altera* 1990), *Ordo exsequiarum* (1969) *Ordo professionis religiosae* (1970), *Ordo initiationis christianae adultorum* (1972), *Ordo unctionis infirmorum eorumque pastoralis curae* (1972), *Ordo paenitentiae* (1973), *De sacra communione et cultu mysterii eucharistici extra missam* (1973), *Ritus ad deputandum ministrum extraorinarim sacral communionis* (1973), *De benedictionibus* (1984), *De Exorcismis et Supplicationibus Quibusdam* (1999).

In addition to the Roman Ritual, other ritual material can be found in the PONTIFICAL, the liturgical book used when a bishop presides, e.g. confirmation and ordination.

Bibliography: P.-M. GY, "Collectaire, rituel, processionnel," *Revue des Sciences Philosophiques et Théologiques* 44 (1960) 441–469. E. PALAZZO, *A History of Liturgical Books: From the Beginning to the Thirteenth Century,* trans by M. BEAUMONT (Collegeville, MN *Liturgical Press,* 1998). C. VOGEL, *Medieval Liturgy: An Introduction to the Sources,* trans and rev W. G. STOREY and N. K. RASMUSSEN, O.P. (Washington, DC 1986).

[J.M. PIERCE]

RITUAL STUDIES

Ritual studies, sometimes called "ritology," is an emerging field which attracts scholars from such diverse disciplines as anthropology, psychology, religious studies, psychiatry, biology, sociology, and the performing arts. In *Beginnings in Ritual Studies* (1995), Ronald Grimes, a major authority in the new field, indicated that its originality consists not in the fact that people are studying ritual, but in their attempt to do so in a way which brings a variety of methodological perspectives into dialogue within a cross cultural and comparative context. The American Academy of Religion (AAR) has provided a forum for that discussion; in 1977 the AAR held the first Ritual Studies Consultation as part of its annual meeting.

Ritual studies is a field of some complexity, a factor due largely to its interdisciplinary nature. In an attempt to identify and classify works in the field, Grimes collected 1,600 sources and grouped them under four major categories: ritual components, ritual types, ritual descriptions, and general works in various field clusters (1984, 1985). The sub-headings under each of the first two categories illustrate the great number of topics open to exploration. Under ritual components Grimes lists the following: action, space, time, objects, symbol and metaphor, group, self, divine beings, and language. Among ritual types he includes: rites of passage, marriage rites, funerary rites, festivals, pilgrimage, purification, civil ceremonies, rituals of exchange, sacrifice worship, magic, healing rites, interaction rites, meditation rites, rites of inversion, and ritual drama. Although action is one among many ritual components, Grimes assigns it a place of primacy in the study of ritual. Theodore Jennings agrees and emphasizes the role played by bodily action in the knowledge attained by people through their participation in ritual. Much work remains to be done in elaborating methods to facilitate the study of ritual action.

Relation to Liturgical Studies. While the study of liturgy engages scholars in the exploration of questions from a variety of theoretical and methodological standpoints, it has been suggested that the unifying principle and distinguishing characteristic of liturgical theology is its focus on the living worship of the Church. Since liturgy is a form of ritual action which embodies that worship, it would seem that liturgical scholars have a place within the broader field of ritual studies. The dialogue between liturgy and cultural anthropology emerged in North America, in the wake of the liturgical reforms initiated by the Second Vatican Council. Criticism of some aspects of the reformed Roman Catholic liturgy by such anthropologists as Mary Douglas and Victor TURNER has revealed a certain lack of sensitivity to the nature of ritual in the process of reform. A growing desire on the part of some liturgical scholars to investigate such topics as ritual celebration, ritual symbols, and the process of ritual change led them to venture into the field of cultural anthropology. This interdisciplinary move was supported within the NORTH AMERICAN ACADEMY OF LITURGY.

Until recently liturgical scholars engaged in the study of rites centered their attention on liturgical books or texts as their chief source material. There is a growing recognition among scholars of the need to expand this focus to include liturgical/ritual performance as a source for liturgical theology, liturgical spirituality, and pastoral liturgy. Several attempts to study liturgical performance have already been made. Phase Two of the Notre Dame Study of Catholic Parish Life (1983) included empirical descriptions of liturgical celebrations as part of its data. Also, the Ritual/Language/Action Study Group of the North American Academy of Liturgy has pursued an interest in the study of ritual first expressed in 1976. In recent years the group has been concerned with the question of methodology. Instruments designed by members of the group for the purpose of studying liturgical performance have been used in actual field research and reports have been made at the annual meetings. The experience has provoked a number of questions which are being studied by those engaged in the project.

Diversity of Approaches. Many students of ritual have directed their attention to the study of symbols, but the diversity of symbol theories has made this a difficult task. There is an emerging criticism of the overdependence of symbol theory on linguistic models and a realization that more attention must be directed to symbolic action. Although the study of symbolism occupies a place of primacy in the field, there are some who would challenge this and who question the attention given to the quest for symbolic meaning.

The study of ritual in relation to society remains an area of great interest, and the works of Mary Douglas and Victor Turner continue to command attention. In *Natural Symbols* (1970) Mary Douglas argued that the propensity for ritual and the body symbolism inherent in ritual are factors that can best be understood when placed in correlation with a more basic set of social relationships. She offered a formula for classifying those relationships that attempted to discern the relative strength or weakness of a society in terms of ''group,'' recognized by boundaries, and ''grid,'' the rules regulating the relationship of an individual with others in the group. Much of her research since then has been directed toward working with and refining this group-grid diagram as a tool to be used in cultural analysis.

Victor Turner's contribution to the field of ritual studies is manifold. This becomes especially apparent when one attends to the development that took place in his own thought. A brief description of this journey can be found in the prologue to *On the Edge of the Bush: Anthropology as Experience*, a collection of Turner's essays edited posthumously by his wife and collaborator, Edith Turner. Turner began his field work after having been trained within the British structural-functionalist school of anthropology. That gave him a predisposition to view ritual symbols as the reflection or expression of social structure. However, his own experience of studying ritual within its social context persuaded him of the inadequacy of this approach.

Turner's investigation led him to formulate a theory of society as a dynamic process which incorporates dimensions of structure and anti-structure. He presented ritual as a process within the larger social process and emphasized the creative and transformative capabilities of ritual symbols. Turner credited Arnold van Gennep's identification of the liminal or transitional stage of rites of passage with providing inspiration for his own processual view. The notion of drama was central to his understanding of the social process, and he even ventured into the field of theater in pursuit of a richer understanding of performance.

Before he died in 1983, Turner had found a new area of interest in the work of those who were investigating the neurobiology of ritual. He discovered there some possible biological foundations for his hypothesis about the manner in which ritual symbols operate. This encounter also led him to see a need for further dialogue between those involved in brain research and those engaged in the study of culture. Turner's own work presents a good illustration of the complexity of the field of ritual studies.

Methodological Considerations. Those who venture into the field and attempt to study ritual performance face the tasks of gathering, reporting, and interpreting data. Each has its own problems. Should one approach the ritual with a list of categories or questions for the purpose of focusing one's attention, or should one go without such a framework? If one chooses the former approach, on what basis does one choose the categories and questions? What is the balance between participation and observation in one who is attempting to be present as a participant-observer? The task of reporting is equally complex because it means choosing an appropriate style and making decisions about content and degree of detail. Finally, the work of interpretation calls for the choice of a particular theoretical framework and engages one in the exploration of such problems as the meaning of interpretation and the role of the interpreter in the whole process.

The *Journal of Ritual Studies* promotes interdisciplinary collaboration among scholars engaged in the study of ritual. It is concerned with such topics as theories of ritual, the biological bases of ritual, methods for studying ritual, ritual and myth, ritual texts, and specific types of ritual. Such a forum provides a stage for a new phase in the development of the field.

Bibliography: C.M. BELL, *Ritual Theory, Ritual Practice* (New York 1992). *Ritual: Perspectives and Dimensions* (New York 1997). M. COLLINS, ''Critical Ritual Studies: Examining an Intersection of Theology and Culture,'' *The Bent World: Essays on Religion and Culture,* ed. R. MAY (1981) 127–147. E. G. D'AQUILI, ''The Myth-Ritual Complex: A Biogenetic Structural Analysis,'' *Zygon* 18 (1983) 247–269. M. DOUGLAS, *Cultural Bias* (London 1978). R. L. GRIMES, *Beginnings in Ritual Studies* (Columbia, SC 1995); *Research in Ritual Studies: A Programmatic Essay and Bibliography* (Metuchen 1985); ''Sources for the Study of Ritual,'' *Religious Studies Review* 10 (1984) 134–145; *Reading, Writing, and Ritualizing: Ritual in Fictive, Liturgical, and Public Places* (Washington, D.C. 1993); *Readings in Ritual Studies* (Upper Saddle River, N.J. 1996); *Ritual Criticism: Case Studies in its Practice, Essays on its Theory* (Columbia, S.C. 1990). T. W. JENNINGS, ''On Ritual Knowledge,'' *The Journal of Religion* 62 (1982) 111–127. M. SEARLE, ''The Notre Dame Study of Catholic Parish Life,'' *Worship* 60 (1986) 312–333. E. L. B. TURNER, ''Encounter With Neurobiology: The Response of Ritual Studies,'' *Zygon* 21 (1986) 219–232. V. TURNER, ed., *Celebration: Studies in Festivity and Ritual* (Wash., D.C. 1982); *On the Edge of the Bush: Anthropology as Experience,* ed. E. L. B. TURNER (Tuscon 1985).

[M. M. KELLEHER]

RIVADAVIA, BERNARDINO

Argentine political figure; b. Buenos Aires, May 20, 1780; d. Cádiz, Spain, Sept. 2, 1845. Rivadavia studied philosophy and for two years theology in his native city. After backing the revolution in 1810, he rose the following year to the position of secretary of war in the Second Triumvirate, in which he was the leading spirit. In 1820 he was appointed minister of government and foreign affairs of the province of Buenos Aires. In 1826 he attained the presidency of the republic but lost it in 1827.

Rivadavia was an outstanding civic leader and originator of Argentine institutions. He was a reformer by temperament and sought to reform the Church. Having been steeped in Bourbon regalism and influenced by GRÉGOIRE and De Pradt, whom he encountered in France, Rivadavia maintained a religious policy that tended to make the Church dependent upon the state. According to his concept, whatever pertained to discipline fell within the province of the State. Gallican and semi-Jansenist ideas, then very much in vogue among the clergy of repute around him, supported this position and allowed him to limit papal interventions in support of episcopal powers and, still more, in powers of the state. On the basis of these principles, while minister he introduced in the legislature of Buenos Aires a plan of ecclesiastical reform that included (1) abolition of ecclesiastical judicial power, (2) replacement of tithes by a Church budget, (3) reduction and reorganization of the cathedral chapter, (4) suppression of monasteries and confiscation of their property, and (5) prohibition of the taking of vows thereafter in the two convents of women religious. The opposition of the legislature, which sought reform but not suppression of the religious orders, succeeded in saving one of the three largest monasteries in Buenos Aires, the Franciscan, which thus kept alive the mendicant tradition in the province.

It was not Rivadavia's idea, at its most extreme, to create a schismatic church, separate from Rome. He maintained, however, that before entering upon official relations (he tolerated private ones) with the Vatican and drawing up a concordat with it, the country should erect its own ecclesiastical institutions and acquire abroad some degree of standing that would permit it to obtain from the Holy See recognition of its legislation on religious matters.

Bibliography: A. TONDA, *Rivadavia y Medrano: Sus actuaciones en la reforma eclesiástica* (Santa Fé, Argentina 1952); *El deán Funes y la reforma de Rivadavia* (Santa Fé, Argentina 1961). G. GALLARDO, *La política religiosa de Rivadavia* (Buenos Aires 1962).

[A. TONDA]

RIVER BRETHREN

Popular name for the Brethren in Christ Church, so named because its members first met at a point along the Susquehanna River in Lancaster County, Pa. In 1710 groups of Swiss MENNONITES began to settle near the Susquehanna; later other German sectarians, such as the German Baptist Brethren (Dunkers), arrived. [*See* CHURCH OF THE BRETHREN (DUNKERS)]. Influenced by pietistic REVIVALISM, members from these religious communities, along with some German Lutherans and Reformed, grouped informally as UNITED BRETHREN and began to conduct fellowship meetings in various parts of Lancaster County. The ''brotherhood down by the river,'' or River Brethren, ultimately broke away from the other United Brethren because of differences over the form of baptism and rituals.

The River Brethren followed a way of life similar to that of the Mennonites or Dunkers. Their churches were loosely organized; however, when the Civil War draft began to take members of the sect into the army, the River Brethren were forced to devise a more formal organization to protect conscientious objectors. The sect took the name Brethren in Christ in 1863. Their theology represents a synthesis between PIETISM and the Anabaptist-Mennonite heritage. They stress the necessity of an immediate assurance of salvation through personal experience. Early in the 20th century the sect adopted the Wesleyan doctrine of entire sanctification. With these doctrinal positions, the Brethren in Christ allow only adult baptism; the candidate for baptism is immersed three times. The sect stresses simplicity of life and plain dress, anoints the sick with oil, opposes secret societies, and emphasizes pacifism.

Bernardino Rivadavia, painting.

Bibliography: F.S. MEAD, S.S. HILL and C.D. ATWOOD, eds., *Handbook of Denominations in the United States*, 11th ed (Nashville 2001).

[W. J. WHALEN/EDS.]

RIVIER, MARIE-ANNE, BL.

Also known as Anne-Marie or Marinette, foundress of the Sisters of the Presentation of Mary; b. Dec. 19, 1768, Montpezat-sous-Bauzon, France; d. Feb. 3, 1838, Bourg-Saint-Andéol, Diocese of Viviers, France; beatified by Pope John Paul II, May 23, 1982.

Marie-Anne Rivier, who had been crippled by a fall as a toddler, was miraculously healed through the faith of her mother and the intercession of the Blessed Virgin Mary (1774).

By age 18, Rivier had opened a parish school, tended abandoned children, and engaged in evangelization. After the outbreak of the French Revolution, Rivier organized secret assemblies on Sundays.

On Nov. 21, 1796, the feast of the Presentation of Mary in the Temple, when the French Revolution was dissolving existing congregations, Rivier and four companions founded a community in the small village of

Thueyts, Ardèche, France. With the assistance of Father Pontannier, they consecrated themselves to God and to the education of youth. Neither the Reign of Terror nor the absence of human assistance prevented them from spreading and expanding their apostolate to include adult education and, in 1814, orphanages. The motherhouse was established at Bourg-Saint-Andéol (1819). At the death of Marie-Anne Rivier, who was known for her faith, expansive joy, and courage, the congregation had 141 houses.

The sisters arrived in Canada, Oct. 18, 1853, at the invitation of the first bishop of St. Hyacinthe, Jean-Charles Prince, and began their first mission in the United States at Glens Falls, New York, in 1873.

Bibliography: A.-C. PELLESCHI, *Une parole de feu* (Paris 1983). T. REY-MERMET, *In the Strength of Her Vision*, tr. G. DANSEREAU (Manchester, NH 1978). A. RICHOMME, *Marie Rivier* (Paris 1967). *Acta Apostolicae Sedis* 78 (1986): 707–710. *L'Osservatore Romano*, English edition, no. 24 (1982): 6–7.

[K. I. RABENSTEIN]

RIVIÈRE, JEAN

Theologian; b. Montcabrier, Tarn, Nov. 12, 1878; d. Bourg-Saint-Bernard, Haute Garonne, May 3, 1946. Jean, the son of a farmer, studied at the seminary of Lavaur, at the major seminary of Albi (1896–1901), and at the faculty of theology in Toulouse (1901–03), where he was a favorite disciple of the rector, P. Batiffol. He was ordained in 1901. He soon became professor of dogma at the seminary of Albi (1903–19). When the Holy Office censured Rivière's opinion on Christ's knowledge, the archbishop discreetly removed him from the seminary. With Batiffol's help Rivière was named by the French government to the chair of fundamental theology at the University of Strasbourg (1919–46). Through his writings he acquired a reputation as an authority in the history and theology of the dogma of Redemption. His principal works are: his doctoral dissertation, *Le Dogme de la Rédemption: Étude historique* (Paris 1905); *Le Dogme de la Rédemption: Etude théologique* (Paris 1914); *Le Problème de l'Église et de l'État au temps de Philippe le Bel* (Paris 1926); *Le Modernisme dans l'Église: Étude d'histoire religieuse contemporaine* (Paris 1929). His articles appeared especially in the *Bulletin de littérature ecclésiastique* (Toulouse) and the *Revue des sciences religieuses* (Strasbourg), and were compiled in a posthumous work, *Le Dogme de la Rédemption dans la théologie contemporaine* (Albi 1948).

Bibliography: R. BÄUMER, *Lexikon für Theologie und Kirche*, ed. J. HOFER and K. RAHNER, 10 v. (2d, new ed. Freiburg 1957–65) 8:1334. "In Memoriam Mgr Victor Martin et M. Jean Rivière,"

Revue des sciences religieuses 21 (1947) 5–16. *Jean Rivière, bibliographie et souvenirs* (Albi, France 1952).

[M. BÉCAMEL]

ROBERT, ANDRÉ

Old Testament exegete; b. Courseullessur-mer, France, Nov. 9, 1883; d. Paris, May 28, 1955. He was ordained on June 29, 1908, became a Sulpician in 1909, and subsequently received the doctorate in theology and the licentiate in sacred scripture at Rome (1911–12). Successively he taught fundamental and moral theology (1912), philosophy (1919), and Sacred Scripture (1922), at the seminary of Issy-les-Moulineaux. In 1928 he became Old Testament Professor at the Institut Catholique of Paris. Thereafter, he devoted himself to personal biblical research, assuming the management of the *Supplément au Dictionnaire de la Bible* (1940) and the partial editorship of the *Bible de Jerusalem* and the well-known biblical manual, *Initiation Biblique* (3d ed. Paris 1954–55). Besides substantial personal contributions to the above works, he published numerous articles on the Old Testament, especially in the field of literary genres. His *Le Cantique des Cantiques* (Paris 1963) was edited and supplemented by R. Tournay and A. Feuillet after his death.

Bibliography: *Mélanges bibliques rédigés en l'honneur de André Robert* (Paris 1957) 1–10.

[P. F. CHIRICO]

ROBERT BACON

First Dominican theologian at the University of Oxford and earliest Dominican writer; b. after 1150; d. Oxford, England, 1248. He studied probably at the University of Paris *c.* 1210 under John of Abbeville, became master of theology in 1219, and was exercising his functions as professor when he joined the Dominicans sometime before 1234. A close associate of St. EDMUND OF ABINGDON and RICHARD FISHACRE, he was active in Church, royal, civic, and university affairs. Most noteworthy was his public denunciation of PETER DES ROCHES before Henry III in his sermon before the Parliament of 1233. As a theologian Bacon was of the Augustinian tradition, conservative in content and method. Few of his works survive, but it is known that he composed a commentary on the Psalms, scriptural glosses, treatises in moral theology and in philosophy, sermons, and homilies. It was long believed he had composed an early life of St. Edmund, but this theory is now rejected.

Bibliography: B. SMALLEY, "Robert Bacon and the Early Dominican School at Oxford," *Transactions of the Royal Historical*

Society, 4th ser. 30 (1948) 1–19. W. A. HINNEBUSCH, *The Early English Friars Preachers* (Rome 1951) 360–363. A. B. EMDEN, *A Biographical Register of the University of Oxford to A.D. 1500* (Oxford 1957–59) 1:87.

[J. F. HINNEBUSCH]

ROBERT COWTON

English Franciscan theologian; fl. Oxford, 1300 to 1313. He was a FRANCISCAN at the Oxford friary in 1300 at a time when his fellow friars there included John DUNS SCOTUS, under whom he undoubtedly studied. He is known to have incepted in theology at the University of OXFORD by *c.* 1313. One of the foremost disciples of Scotus and his successor as lecturer on the Sentences (*see* SENTENCES AND SUMMAE) at Oxford, Cowton wrote a commentary on the Sentences, which was much in demand in England in the 14th and 15th centuries. The text shows that this commentary was based directly on Scotus's classes at Oxford between 1300 and 1302 and that it was written before Scotus drafted his final version of the *Opus oxoniense.* Cowton must have worked from Scotus's unedited notes or first draft, undoubtedly between 1303 and 1308. The commentary proves that Cowton was a SCOTIST of high order. Like Scotus, Cowton criticized HENRY OF GHENT, whose work he probably knew only through his teacher. Cowton has often been likened to his contemporary Franciscan, WILLIAM OF NOTINGHAM. About 1400 John Sharp and Richard Snetisham of Oxford made an abbreviated version of Cowton's commentary, which enjoyed a wide circulation, but the basic work remains unedited.

Bibliography: H. THEISSING, *Glaube und Theologie bei Robert Cowton OFM* (Aschendorff 1970). S. F. BROWN, ''Robert Cowton, O.F.M. and the Analogy of the Concept of Being,'' *Franciscan Studies* 31 (1971) 5–40. A. G. LITTLE, ''The Franciscan School at Oxford in the Thirteenth Century,'' *Archivum Franciscanum historicum* 19 (1926) 873–874. O. LOTTIN, *Etudes de morale histoire et doctrine* (Gembloux 1961) 27–46.

[M. J. HAMILTON]

ROBERT GROSSETESTE

English scholastic, translator, and bishop; b. Suffolk, *c.* 1168; d. Buckden, Huntingdonshire, Oct. 9, 1253. Although born of humble parentage, he studied at Oxford and most certainly at Paris, where he heard JACQUES DE VITRY, STEPHEN LANGTON, and ROBERT OF COURÇON. He became a master in arts between 1186 and 1191. While lecturing in arts, he wrote an *Introitus* to the study of the liberal arts, the treatise *De generatione sonorum,* and a commentary on Aristotle's *Sophistici elenchi* and *Posterior Analytics* (Venice 1494), in which he laid the foundation for all his later philosophical and scientific works. By 1214 he had become a master in theology either at Oxford or at Paris. Shortly after 1214 he was *magister scholarum* at Oxford, but the bishop of Lincoln would not allow him the title of chancellor. However, by 1221 this title was recognized at the Roman Curia; hence Grosseteste seems to have been the first chancellor of the University of Oxford (*see* OXFORD, UNIVERSITY OF). Of his lectures as regent master in theology there survive his commentary *In epistolam Pauli ad Galatas,* his *Moralitates super evangelia,* glosses on Psalms 1–100, and especially his *Hexaemeron,* which embodies materials from his lecture notes. He obtained several prebends, but after a grave illness he resigned all except a canonry at Lincoln in 1231. After the Franciscans enlarged their house in Oxford, they prevailed upon Grosseteste to lecture to them. This he did from *c.* 1232 until Lent 1235. Under him ''within a short time they made incalculable progress both in scholastic discussions and in the subtle moralities suitable for preaching'' [Eccleston, *De adventu fratrum minorum in Angliam,* ed. A. G. Little (Manchester 1951) 48]. Having great love for the order and sympathy with the Franciscan spirit, he profoundly influenced the Oxford Greyfriars through his theology and scholarship. While continental Franciscans disputed over the advantages of learning, the Oxford Greyfriars were firmly established in the tradition of learning. He was a teacher and intimate friend of ADAM MARSH, the first Franciscan regent master at Oxford, and he exerted considerable influence on later English Franciscans, notably on ROGER BACON. The majority of Grosseteste's scientific treatises were written after 1230. While he was still lecturing to the Franciscans, he began serious study of Greek, which bore fruit in later years in many translations into Latin from the Greek. He also began the study of Hebrew but never acquired the same proficiency.

Episcopal Career. He was elected bishop of Lincoln in Lent 1235, received royal assent on April 5, and was consecrated at Reading on June 3, 1235. Immediately he began a visitation of his diocese, the largest in England. Zealous and uncompromising in maintaining his ideal of the Church, he deposed many abbots and priors who were lax in their office. Their chief fault was neglecting to staff adequately the parish entrusted to them. In 1237 he witnessed the confirmation of MAGNA CARTA. From 1239 to 1245 he was at odds with the dean and chapter of his cathedral church, who claimed the right of exemption from episcopal visitation. This dispute, in which the dean was suspended and deprived of office, was settled by INNOCENT IV in a bull of Aug. 25, 1245, which gave the bishop full jurisdiction over the chapter. In 1245 he attended the Council of LYONS. During a visit to the papal court at

Lyons in 1250, he spoke *de coruptelis ecclesiae,* denouncing the custom of appointing Italians, ignorant of the language and country, to rich English benefices. Although deeply committed to the doctrine of the plenitude of papal power, he opposed papal taxation of the clergy on behalf of the king in 1251 and 1252, and the appointment of the pope's nephew to a canonry of Lincoln in 1253. As a bishop, zealous in the service of the Church, he denounced ignorance among the clergy and did everything in his power to improve the state of learning. He continued the study of Greek, employed the service of Greek scholars, and obtained numerous Greek manuscripts. He himself translated Aristotle's *Nicomachean Ethics, De lineis indivisibilibus,* a part of *De caelo* and *De virtute;* works of St. JOHN DAMASCENE and PSEUDO-DIONYSIUS; and the *scholia* of St. MAXIMUS THE CONFESSOR, the letters of St. IGNATIUS OF ANTIOCH, and the *Testamenta 12 patriarcharum.* Although other translations have been ascribed to him, their authenticity has not been firmly established. While he was bishop, he also commented on the four major works of Pseudo-Dionysius. His *Commentarius in octo libros Physicorum Aristotelis* (ed. R. C. Dales, Boulder, Colo. 1963) seems to have been written after 1230, while he was teaching the Franciscans or serving as bishop.

Many of his sermons are extant, at least in draft form. About 80 were collected by a student *c.* 1230 (Durham, Cath. Libr. MS A. III. 12); others belong to his episcopal period. Grosseteste often reworked his notes into a theological discourse. His *Dicta* were collected and arranged by himself from sermons and lectures; this work was highly popular in the 14th and 15th centuries. Passages from his Biblical commentaries were extensively quoted by Thomas Gascoigne in *Liber de veritatibus collectis* (Oxford, Bodl. Libr. Lincoln College MS 117–118).

Teaching and Influence. Grosseteste is important not only as an outstanding churchman, indefatigable in his service to the Church, but also as an independent thinker and scholar who influenced many generations of Englishmen. As a philosopher he was a pioneer in introducing the new Aristotelian learning to Oxford. However, he interpreted ARISTOTLE through AUGUSTINE and Arab Neoplatonists, taking over especially the Augustinian doctrine of LIGHT and ILLUMINATION. For him, light is a very subtle corporeal substance and the first form to be created in primary matter: "Formam primam corporalem, quam quidam corporeitatem vocant, lucem esse arbitror" (*De luce;* ed. Baur, 51). This first form of light multiplies its own likeness (*multiplicatio specierum*) in all directions, begetting corporeal dimensionality and specific powers (*virtutes*) according to determinable laws of mathematical proportionality. Grosseteste did not identify the first form called *lux* with visible light, which

is only one manifestation. Natural philosophy studies the propagation of species and powers, but not the essence of *lux* itself, the cause of propagation; this is reserved to metaphysics. Since the multiplication of species follows geometrical laws, the whole of natural philosophy is subalternated to mathematics. A clear example of this kind of subalternation is to be seen in optics, the science of visible light: experiments and experimental knowledge provide the facts (*quia*), but mathematics is required to provide the reason for the fact (*propter quid*). While mathematics as such abstracts from corporeal phenomena, natural philosophy, optics, and other mathematical-physical sciences must study corporeal phenomena with the aid of mathematics.

The human soul is a special manifestation of light, for it can study the nature of light itself. However, in all knowledge the soul needs to be illumined by God, the source of all light. Thus the existence of God is immediately knowable, even though His existence can also be demonstrated from motion. God, moreover, is the exemplary cause of all things, as well as the efficient and final cause. Grosseteste gave support to the Franciscan school in teaching the primacy of will over intellect and the primacy of divine omnipotence.

The basis for Grosseteste's metaphysics of light is found in Gn 1.1–3, where God is described as having first created primary matter (*materia prima*), then light (*lux*). Similarly, the doctrine of divine illumination is established in Jn 1.9: "It was the true light that enlightens every man who comes into the world." Thus the whole of philosophy is subalternated to revelation.

Several attempts to secure his canonization came to nothing. He has always been highly regarded in England. His body is buried in Lincoln Cathedral.

Bibliography: A. B. EMDEN, *A Biographical Register of the University of Oxford to A.D. 1500,* 3 v. (Oxford 1957–59) 2:830–833. D. A. CALLUS, ed., *Robert Grosseteste: Scholar and Bishop* (Oxford 1955); "The Oxford Career of Robert Grosseteste," *Oxoniensia* 10 (1945) 42–72. S. H. THOMSON, *The Writings of Robert Grosseteste* (New York 1940). L. BAUR, "Die philosophischen Werke des Robert Grosseteste, Bischofs von Lincoln," *Beiträge zur Geschichte der Philosophie und Theologie des Mittelalters* 9 (1912) 1–143. *Roberti Grosseteste episcopi quondam Lincolniensis epistolae,* ed. H. R. LUARD (*Rerum Britannicarum medii aevi scriptores* 25; 1861). A. TOGNOLO, *Enciclopedia filosofica* 4:170–172. F. L. CROSS, *The Oxford Dictionary of the Christian Church* (London 1957) 592–593. É. H. GILSON, *History of Christian Philosophy in the Middle Ages* (New York 1955). A. C. CROMBIE, *Robert Grosseteste and the Origins of Experimental Science* (Oxford 1953).

[J. A. WEISHEIPL]

ROBERT HOLCOT

English Dominican theologian; b. Holcot, Northamptonshire, *c.* 1290; d. Northampton, 1349. Known as *Doctor firmus et indefatigabilis,* he studied and taught at the University of Oxford from *c.* 1326 to *c.* 1334, becoming master in theology in 1332. An early version of his commentary on the *Sentences* of PETER LOMBARD was completed during his years as bachelor: this he revised and amplified in 1336, adding the *Sex articuli.* In his *Sermo finalis,* given at Oxford, he alluded to the disturbances that caused the secession of masters to Stamford in 1334. Possibly a regent master at Cambridge, he was one of the scholars encouraged and engaged by RICHARD OF BURY, Bishop of Durham. By 1343 he was assigned to Blackfriars, Northampton, and was licensed to hear confessions in the archdeaconry. He died during the Black Death and was buried in the church of his order at Northampton.

Works. The numerous manuscripts and early editions of his writings testify to his popularity both in England and on the Continent. He was particularly famous for his commentaries on Scripture that compensated for the excessive subtleties of decadent SCHOLASTICISM. His *Postilla super librum sapientiae,* which, according to two Paris MSS, was written at Cambridge, "made its author famous overnight and his fame held throughout the next two centuries" (Wey, 219). It brought together the traditional teaching of Scripture and a type of prehumanist study deriving from Richard of Bury and his circle. The same combination of learning was expressed in his commentaries on Proverbs (Paris 1510), Song of Songs (Venice 1509), and the Book of Sirach (Venice 1509), which ends abruptly at ch. 7, perhaps because of his death. For the use of preachers, he composed *Liber de moralizationibus* (Basel 1586) and a set of sermon outlines. This widely used collection of moralized *exempla* is notable for its classical allusions and for its technique of moral illustrations in stories. Most of his *Quodlibeta* are unedited. His *Quaestiones super libros Sententiarum* (Lyons 1497, 1505, 1518) enjoyed a popularity among nominalists.

Doctrine. As a Dominican, Holcot was bound to follow the doctrine of St. THOMAS AQUINAS, and he claimed to do so. But in fact he often disagreed with St. Thomas, adopting the new ideas of WILLIAM OF OCKHAM. Separating philosophy from theology, he insisted that theology has its own *logica fidei,* not conformable to the natural logic of Aristotle. He was skeptical about man's ability to know the existence and attributes of God through *logica naturalis.* Since all human knowledge comes through the senses, man cannot be certain of spiritual beings or form an idea of them. Man's knowledge of God and an-

gels comes from revelation. Admitting the utility of reasoning in theology to make faith more explicit, Holcot did not admit that this produced a scientific habit distinct from faith.

Stressing the absolute freedom and power of God, he distinguished God's absolute power (*potentia absoluta*) from His chosen power (*potentia ordinata*). Although God has chosen the present plan of salvation, He could dispense with grace, supernatural virtues, the moral code, and accept man's natural actions as meritorious for salvation. THOMAS BRADWARDINE criticized this view as a form of Pelagianism. Conceiving God and man as partial causes of human acts, Holcot held that God can be called the cause of man's sin but not its author. This doctrine was condemned at Paris in 1347. For him, the principle of causality (*A* is the cause of *B,* if *B* occurs every time it is preceded by *A*) is not self-evident, but, at best, only probable.

Bibliography: R. HOLCOT, "Utrum theologia sit scientia: A Quodlibet Question," ed. J. T. MUCKLE, *Mediaeval Studies* 20 (1958) 127–153. É. H. GILSON, *A History of Christian Philosophy in the Middle Ages* (New York 1955) 500–502. A. B. EMDEN, *A Biographical Register of the University of Oxford to A.D. 1500* (Oxford 1957–59) 2:946–947. J. C. WEY, "The *Sermo finalis* of Robert Holcot," *Mediaeval Studies* 11 (1949) 219–224.

[A. MAURER]

ROBERT KILWARDBY

Cardinal, Dominican theologian; b. Leicestershire, England, *c.* 1215; d. Viterbo, Italy, Sept. 10, 1279. As a student (*c.* 1231) and later a master in arts at Paris (*c.* 1237–*c.* 1245), just as the new Aristotelian learning invaded the university, Kilwardby gained a notable reputation as grammarian, logician, and author of philosophical commentaries. Before 1250 he became a Dominican, probably in England, and studied theology at Oxford. Asked to compose a summary of the origin, nature, and extent of all human sciences for beginners, he wrote *De ortu scientiarum,* which is extant in many manuscripts. Except for this philosophical work, he dedicated himself entirely to the sacred sciences. After lecturing on the *Sentences* (1252–54) and the Bible, he became master in theology in 1256, fulfilling his office as regent until 1261. To encourage serious study of patristic sources, he painstakingly composed alphabetical indices (*tabulae*), analytical indices (*concordantiae*), and chapter summaries (*intentiones*) of important patristic writings.

Administrative Positions. In 1261 he was elected provincial of the English Dominicans "because of his sanctity and observance of the rule." During his provincialate, he eschewed political involvements and devoted himself entirely to his order, establishing at least seven new priories. Having governed the province "most wisely" for 12 years, he was absolved from office by the general chapter of the order in 1272 with the request that he not be reelected immediately. However, his province did reelect him that same year at Northampton, but this term lasted only a few months. Appointed archbishop of Canterbury by Gregory X on Oct. 11, 1272, he was consecrated by William Button, Bishop of Bath and Wells, on Feb. 26, 1273, and enthroned on September 17. Even as archbishop he avoided politics, preferring to be a pastor of souls. In 1273 he called the first full diocesan synod to plan ecclesiastical reform. In 1274 he attended the Council of Lyons, and in his metropolitan visitations he conscientiously enforced its decrees of reform. In his first visitation of Oxford (1276), he issued beneficial injunctions for Merton College, founded two years before by his friend WALTER OF MERTON.

Condemnation of Thomism. The incident for which he is best known took place during his second visit to Oxford. On March 18, 1277, just 11 days after TEMPIER condemned 219 theses at Paris, he issued a condemnation of 30 propositions in grammar, logic, and natural science, some of which had been maintained by THOMAS AQUINAS. Defending his action against criticism of his confrere Peter of Conflans, archbishop of Corinth, he wrote that he did not intend to declare the propositions heretical, but only to prevent their being taught, because "some of them are philosophically at variance with truth, since some are close to intolerable error, and others patently iniquitous, being repugnant to the Catholic faith" [Denifle-Ehrle Arch 5 (1889) 614]. Of the 16 propositions in natural philosophy, five bear directly on the Thomistic doctrine of unicity of substantial form in natural bodies, and six presuppose or follow from it. To Kilwardby the new view was "fantastic," "false and impossible," and "repugnant to the Catholic faith." What he imagined to be consequences of the Thomistic doctrine were certainly contrary to faith; hence he aimed at suppressing the doctrine entirely.

On April 4, 1278, he was appointed cardinal bishop of Porto and Santa Rufina. By February 1279 he arrived in Rome, but on September 10 he died at Viterbo, where he was buried in the church of his Order. An outstanding theologian, he saw an incompatibility between certain fundamental views of pagan ARISTOTELIANISM and the Christian PLATONISM of the Fathers. Although he knew and taught the works of Aristotle, he interpreted them under the Platonizing influence of AVICENNA, AVICEBRON, and St. AUGUSTINE. Consequently he could view only with grave concern the innovations of ALBERT THE GREAT and Thomas Aquinas.

Bibliography: É. H. GILSON, *A History of Christian Philosophy in the Middle Ages* (New York 1955) 355—359, 703—705. J. QUÉTIF and J. ÉCHARD, *Scriptores ordinis praedicatorum* (New York 1959) 1.1:374—380. E. M. F. SOMMER-SECKENDORFF, *Studies in the Life of Robert Kilwardby, O.P.* (Rome 1937). A. B. EMDEN, *A Biographical Register of the University of Oxford to A.D. 1500* (Oxford 1957–59) 2:1051–52. R. SCHENK, "Christ, Christianity, and Non-Christian Religions" *Christ among the Medieval Dominicans*, ed. K. EMERY, JR. and J. P. WAWRYKOW (Notre Dame 1998).

[J. A. WEISHEIPL]

ROBERT OF ARBRISSEL, BL.

Founder of the Order of Fontevrault; b. Arbrissel, Brittany, France, *c.* 1055; d. Orsan, France, Feb. 25, 1117. He studied at Paris under ANSELM OF LAON, was archpriest of Rennes from 1085 to 1090, taught at Angers from 1090 to 1092, and then withdrew to the forest of Craon in Anjou to live as a hermit. Here he met BERNARD OF TIRON and VITALIS OF SAVIGNY, and attracted a number of disciples whom he formed into a community of canons regular at La Roë. In 1096 Pope URBAN II visited Angers and enjoined on Robert the work of itinerant public preaching, commending him as "second only to himself as a sower of the Word of God in men's hearts" (Mt 13.3–8). Robert resigned as abbot of La Roë and spent the rest of his life in preaching. He enjoyed a particular success with the poor, prostitutes, and lepers, and converted many men and women to the religious life. In *c.* 1100 he built a double monastery at FONTEVRAULT and later founded additional priories, until at the time of his death the congregation numbered about 3,000. In 1116 he drew up a constitution for the order and placed it under an abbess, Petronilla (d. 1150), in accordance with the gospel precept (Jn 19.26–27). Robert was buried at Fontevrault. He was praised by his contemporaries for his sanctity and for the apostolic simplicity of his life, and although many miracles were attributed to him, the efforts to bring about his CANONIZATION came to naught.

Feast: Feb. 25.

Bibliography: Writings ascribed to Bl. Robert, *Patrologia Latina* 162:1079–88 and *Bibliothèque de l'École des Chartes* 15 (1853–54) 209–235. Lives by Baldric of Dol and Andrew the Monk, in *Acta sanctorum* 3:608–613. S. HILPISCH, *Lexikon für Theologie und Kirche* 2 8:1335–36. L. A. PICARD, *Le Fondateur de l'Ordre de Fontevrault: Robert d'Arbrissel* (Saumur 1932). R. NIDERST, *Robert d'Arbrissel et les origines de l'ordre de Fontevrault* (Rodez 1952). *Histoire de l'ordre de Fontevrault, 1100–1908,* 3 v. (Auch 1911–15). A. M. ZIMMERMANN, *Kalendarium Benedictinum* 1:254–255. *Bibliographica hagiographica latina* 7259–60. B. M. KERR, *Religious Life for Women c. 1100–1350: Fontevraud in England* (Oxford 1999).

[B. HAMILTON]

ROBERT OF BRUGES, BL.

Abbot; b. Bruges, Belgium, end of 11th century; d. Clairvaux, France, April 29, 1157. He was teaching at LAON when BERNARD OF CLAIRVAUX, in the course of a journey to LIÈGE, convinced him to accept the monastic vocation. Together with about 30 companions, the so-called *captura leodiensis*, he followed the abbot and entered the CISTERCIAN Order at the Abbey of CLAIRVAUX in 1131. Bernard had a high regard for Robert, and in 1138 he installed him as first Cistercian abbot at LES DUNES, in Flanders, near his birthplace. On the death of Bernard in 1153, Robert succeeded him as second abbot of Clairvaux. Two letters are preserved that Bernard had written to his disciple before his death (*Patrologia Latina*, 182:530). He was early honored by the Cistercians, and he is mentioned in the martyrology of 1491, as well as in the Missal of 1526. He was buried at Clairvaux.

Feast: April 29.

Bibliography: *Acta Sanctorum* Oct. 13:91–96. BERNARD OF CLAIRVAUX, *Epistolae* 324, 325, *Patrologia Latina* 182:530. HERBERT, *De miraculis* 1.8, *Patrologia Latina* 185:1285–86, CONRAD OF EBERBACH, *Exordium magnum cisterciense* bk 1.21–23, ed. B. GRIESSER (Rome 1961) 118–123. *Biographie nationale de Belgique* 19:416–422. U. CHEVALIER, *Répertoire des sources historiques du moyen-âge. Biobibliographie*, 2 v. (2d. ed. Paris 1905–07) 2:3987. A. DIMIER, *Saint Bernard, pêcheur de Dieu* (Paris 1953) 57, 192. A. M. ZIMMERMANN, *Kalendarium Benedictinum: Die Heiligen und Seligen des Benediktinerordens und seiner Zweige*, 4 v. (Metten 1933–38) 2:123–127. W. BÖHNE, *Lexikon für Theologie und Kirche*, ed. J. HOFER and K. RAHNER, 10 v. (2d, new ed. Freiburg 1957–65) 8:1336. *Vita la S. Bernardi* 5.3, *Patrologia Latina* 185:361.

[M. STANDAERT]

ROBERT OF BURY SAINT EDMUNDS, ST.

Reputed martyr; b. 1171; d. 1181, Edmundsbury, England. Ten-year-old Robert is said to have been killed on Good Friday, a victim of ritual murder. Although he was never canonized, his cultus was strong. His relics were translated to the abbey church at Bury St. Edmunds. In his honor Jocelin of Brakelond wrote *Miracles of St. Robert*.

Bibliography: T. ARNOLD, ed., *Memorials of St. Edmund's Abbey, Rerum Britannicarum medii aevi scriptores* (London 1858–96; rpr. New York 1964) i, 223; iii, 6. WILLIAM OF WORCESTER, *Itineraries*, ed. J. H. HARVEY (1969), 163.

[K. I. RABENSTEIN]

ROBERT OF COURÇON

Theologian, cardinal; b. Keddleston?, England *c.* 1158–60; d. Damietta, Egypt, February 1219. Having been a student of arts in Paris from *c.* 1180 to 1190, Robert also studied theology there between 1190 and 1195 under PETER CANTOR. From 1204 to 1210 he taught theology in Paris, was a canon of Noyon (1204) and Paris (1209), and took part in the process against AMALRIC OF BÈNE and his followers. In 1212 Pope Innocent III raised him to the cardinalate, and on April 19, 1213, he was made legate to France; in this office he was often severe and not always prudent in his decisions. He reorganized studies at the University of Paris in 1215, and he drew up a set of statutes for the arts faculty and theologians, repeating, with additions, a previous prohibition against the teaching of Aristotle (*see* SCHOLASTICISM, 1). In February of 1216, he returned to Rome; then in August of 1218 he accompanied the Crusaders to Egypt, and died during the siege of Damietta. As a scholastic, Robert was a theologian of a primarily practical bent; his *Summa*, written between 1204 and 1208, contains many canonico-moral questions and medical cases. According to some catalogues, he also commented on parts of the *Sentences* of PETER LOMBARD.

Bibliography: M. and C. DICKSON, ''Le Cardinal Robert de Courson: Sa vie,'' *Archives d'histoire doctrinale et littéraire du moyen-âge* (1934): 53–142. M. GRABMANN, *I divieti ecclesiastici di Aristotele sotto Innocenzo III e Gregorio IX* (Rome 1941). A. B. EMDEN, *A Biographical Register of the University of Oxford to A.D. 1500*, 3 v. (Oxford 1957–59) 1:498–499. V. L. KENNEDY, ''Robert Courson on Penance,'' *Medieaval Studies* 7 (1945): 291–336.

[I. C. BRADY]

ROBERT OF FLAMBOROUGH

Canon penitentiary at the Abbey of SAINT-VICTOR, Paris, author of a Penitential that was forerunner of the *summae casuum* and so of later manuals of moral theology; b. probably Flamborough, Yorkshire, *c.* 1135–80; d. Paris, *c.* 1219–33. His Penitential, or *Liber poenitentialis*, completed between 1208 and 1213, is a small book of instruction for the confessor. The first two-thirds is a dialogue in which extensive use is made of commentaries on the *Decretum* of GRATIAN, especially that by HUGUCCIO, and of decretals of popes from ALEXANDER III to INNOCENT III. His uncritical use of these sources resulted in excessive legalism. The last third consists of old penitential canons copied from the Penitential of BARTHOLOMEW OF EXETER and from the *Decretum* of IVO OF CHARTRES. These canons, already obsolete in their literal application, were intended as a basis for the apportioning of penance. The author was criticized by his contemporaries for his reliance on these old canons; yet some continued to copy and annotate them for practical use even a century later.

Bibliography: ROBERT OF FLAMBOROUGH, *Summa de matrimonio et de usuris*, ed. J. F. SCHULTE (Giessen 1868), a partial ed.

of the *Penitential;* complete ed. is being prepared by F. FIRTH. P. MICHAUD-QUANTIN, "À propos des premières *Summae confessorum,*" *Recherches de théologie ancienne et médiévale* 26 (1959) 276–283, 292–296. S. KUTTNER, "Pierre de Roissy and Robert of Flamborough," *Traditio* 2 (1944) 492–499. F. FIRTH, "The *Poenitentiale* of Robert of Flamborough," *ibid.* 16 (1960) 541–556; 17 (1961) 531–532; *Lexikon für Theologie und Kirche,* ed. J. HOFER and K. RAHNER, 10 v. (2d, new ed. Freiburg 1957–65) 8:1338–39.

[F. FIRTH]

ROBERT OF MELUN (HEREFORD)

English theologian, bishop of Hereford from 1163; b. *c.* 1100; d. Feb. 27, 1167. Beginning in 1142 he taught theology in Melun, France, enjoying great renown as a teacher. He criticized the teachings of Peter ABELARD on original sin and Christ's person and of GILBERT DE LA PORRÉE on Trinitarian doctrines, and the claim of PETER LOMBARD that the power to sin was a true power coming from God. Robert's best theological elaboration is in his *Sentences* (1152–60), invaluable as a source of contemporary theological doctrines. In this work he criticized current theological teaching for superficiality, lack of synthesis, overuse of glosses, failure to search for truth, and excessive cult of literature. Though his exegesis was in the Platonic spirit of the school of Chartres, he also relied on St. Augustine. His writings were widespread, although they never became manuals as did the works of Peter Lombard. Nor, because of the excellence and popularity of Lombard's school and his own departure for England, did Robert ever become the head of a school. His is the glory of having made a notable advance in theological method. Of philosophical interest is his opposition to the NOMINALISM of ROSCELIN. He also followed the then-common interpretation of Boethius's distinction between *quod est* and *quo est,* or *esse.,* whereby the *quo est* is the form of the whole (*forma totius*).

Bibliography: *Oeuvres de Robert de Melun,* ed. R. M. MARTIN, *Spicilegium sacrum Lovaniense,* 3 v. in 4 (Louvain 1932–52) v. 1 *Quaestiones de divina pagina,* v. 2 *Quaestiones* (*theologice*) *de epistolis Pauli* (1938) v. 3: 1–2 *Sententie* (1947–52), ed. with R. M. GALLET. J. DE GHELLINCK, *Le Mouvement théologique du XIIe siècle* (Bruges 1948); *L'Essor de la littérature latine au XIIe siècle* (Brussels-Paris 1946). 1:55–57, with bibliog. F. ANDERS, ed., *Die Christologie des Robert von Melun* (Paderborn 1927). F. P. BLIEMETZRIEDER, "Robert de Melun und die Schule Anselms von Laon," *Zeitschrift für Kirchengeschichte* 53 (1934): 154–163. A. M. LANDGRAF, "Familienbildung bei Paulinenkommentaren des 12. Jahrhunderts: Robert von Melun und seine Schule," *Biblica* 13 (1932): 169–193. R. M. MARTIN, "Pro Petro Abaelardo: Un Plaidoyer de Robert de Melun contre s. Bernard," *Revue des sciences philosophiques et théologiques* 12 (1923): 308–333. P. W. NASH, "The Meaning of *Est* in the *Sentences* (1152–1160) of Robert of Melun," *Mediaeval Studies* 14 (1952): 129–142. U. HORST, *Die Trinitäts- und Gotteslehre des Robert von Melun* (Mainz 1964); *Gesetz und Evangelium: Das Alte Testament in der Theologie des Robert von Melun* (Munich 1971).

[P. W. NASH]

ROBERT OF MOLESME, ST.

Founder of CÎTEAUX; b. near Troyes in Champagne, France, *c.* 1027; d. Molesme, 1110. He was the Benedictine prior of Moutier-la-Celle, near Troyes, when he was elected abbot of Saint-Michel-de-Tonnerre, near Langres. Unable to effect the much-needed reform of discipline, he left. From 1072–73 he was prior of Saint-Ayoul in Provins. But a group of hermits at Collan, near Tonnerre, wanted him as their spiritual director, and with Pope ALEXANDER II's approval he took up residence with them. Their place of abode was most unhealthy so they moved to MOLESME in 1075. But Molesme, originally poor in wealth, but rich in regular observance of the BENEDICTINE RULE, in a short time became rich in property and correspondingly poor in its regular life. The community split and monks under the leadership of Robert who desired the strict monastic observance withdrew from the community. They went to HUGH OF DIE, the *legatus natus,* who was prominent in the GREGORIAN reform movement and thus welcomed Robert's request for the opportunity to live according to the strict interpretation of the Benedictine rule. In his letter confirming the demands made by Robert, Hugh mentions the laxity of observance at Molesme and the impossibility of Robert and his monks attaining their objectives there. Thus they were given permission to seek another place. Twenty-one monks joined Robert in the exodus from Molesme to Cîteaux, which was then a swamp. The bishop of Chalon-sur-Saône canonically installed Robert at Cîteaux, or, as it was called, "New Monastery" (1098). On Robert's departure the monks at Molesme elected Godfrey as their abbot, but he was uneasy about his status and journeyed to Rome. It was at his request that the pope directed Hugh of Die to see that Robert returned to Molesme. A provincial council was called, and it decided that Robert should return to his former abbey. Robert had been at Cîteaux only a year and a half. Henceforth the two abbeys remained peacefully independent. Thus, although Robert founded the abbey, it was Alberic, STEPHEN HARDING, and St. BERNARD who respectively built, organized, and propagated the CISTERCIANS. Robert was a part of the 11th-century movement that sought not only to reform but to renovate monasticism. This same century produced the Carthusians, Camaldolese, and Vallombrosans as well as such congregations as Tiron, Bec, and Savigny.

The basic document concerning Robert's place in the foundation of Cîteaux is the *Exordium parvum.*

Feast: April 29.

Bibliography: *Acta Sanctorum* April (Paris 1863–) 3:670–685. *Exordium parvum* in *Les Monuments primitifs de la règle cistercienne,* ed. P. GUIGNARD (Dijon 1878). U. BERLIÈRE, ''Les Origines de Cîteaux,'' *Revue d'histoire eccléstique* 1 (1900) 448–471; 2 (1901) 253–290. W. A. PARKER MASON, ''The Beginnings of the Cistercian Order,'' *Transactions of the Royal Historical Society,* NS 19 (1905) 169–207. J. LAURENT, *Cartulaires de l'abbaye de Molesme,* 2 v. (Paris 1907–19); ''Le Problème des commencements de Cîteaux,'' *Annales de Bourgogne* 6 (1934) 213–229; 12 (1940) 31–36. J. OTHON DUCOURNEAU, ''Les Origines cisterciennes,'' *Revue Mabillon* 23 (1933) 153–189. W. WILLIAMS, *Journal of Theological Studies* 37 (1936) 404–412. K. SPAHR, *Das Leben des hl. Robert von Molesme* (Fribourg 1947). S. LENSSEN, ''S. Robert, fondateur de Cîteaux,'' *Collectanea ordinis Cisterciensium Reformatorum* 4 (Rome-Westmalle 1937–38) 2–16, 81–96, 161–177, 241–253. F. DELAHAYE, ''Un Moine: S. Robert . . . ,'' *ibid.* 14 (1952) 83–106. J. A. LEFÈVRE, ''S. R. de Molesme dans l'opinion monastique . . . ,'' *Analecta Bollandiana* 74 (Brussels 1956) 50–83. N. KINSELLA, ''S. R.: A Monk in a Changing World,'' *ibid.* 24 (1962) 3–10. J. B. VAN DAMME, *Les trois fondateurs de Cîteaux* (Roybon 1966). M. RAYMOND, *Three Religious Rebels: The Forefathers of the Trappists* (Boston 1986).

[J. F. O'SULLIVAN]

ROBERT OF NEWMINSTER, ST.

Abbot; b. Yorkshire; d. Newminster, June 7, 1159. After studies in Paris he returned to England and was active as a secular priest, then as a Benedictine monk at the Abbey of WHITBY. In 1132 Robert joined the CISTERCIANS, participated in the foundation of the Abbey of FOUNTAINS, and in 1139 founded and became the first abbot of Newminster, near Morpeth, Northumberland. Under Robert, Newminster grew phenomenally, establishing three daughterhouses, Pipewell, Roche, and Sawley, in less than 10 years. Robert's tomb at Newminster became the scene of numerous miracles and was a popular pilgrimage shrine until the Reformation. He was never formally canonized, but in 1656 the Cistercian Order approved his cult.

Feast: June 7.

Bibliography: *Acta Sanctorum* June 2:46–49. J. D. DALGAIRNS, *The Cistercian Saints of England* (London 1844). G. MÜLLER, ''Der hl. Robert, Abt von Newminster,'' *Cistercienser-Chronik* 5 (1893) 321–328. S. LENSSEN, *Hagiologium cisterciense,* 2 v. (Tilburg 1948–49; suppl. 1951) 1:97–99.

[L. J. LEKAI]

ROBERT OF ORFORD (DE COLLETORTO)

English Dominican theologian; d. probably before 1300. Variations of his name include Tortocollo, Hereford, and Orphordius. Almost nothing is known of his life; it has been speculated that he may be a confusion of two scholars, or a Franciscan writer, or the Dominican WILLIAM MACCLESFELD. What is known of Robert is culled chiefly from his works, which show great depth; though written in defense of THOMISM, they are relatively mild in their polemic. Robert defended the teachings of St. THOMAS AQUINAS and his school in *Impugnatio Henrici de Gandavo,* aimed at the quodlibets of HENRY OF GHENT. He directed another work against GILES OF ROME, the *Reprobationes dictorum a fratre Aegidio in sententiarum libros.* Most likely he wrote the *Correctorium ''Sciendum''* against WILLIAM DE LA MARE. He also composed a commentary on the second book of the *Sentences,* a work on the unity of forms, and a commentary on Aristotle's *De somno et vigilia.*

Bibliography: D. A. CALLUS, *Lexikon für Theologie und Kirche,* ed. J. HOFER and K. RAHNER (Freiburg 1957–65) 8:1337. W. A. HINNEBUSCH, *The Early English Friars Preachers* (Rome 1951) 391–396. A. B. EMDEN, *A Biographical Register of the University of Oxford to A.D. 1500* (Oxford 1957–59) 2:1401. P. BAYERSCHMIDT, ''Robert von Colletorto, Verfasser des *Correctorium 'Sciendum','*'' *Divus Thomas* (Fribourg) 17 (1939) 311–326. P. GLORIEUX, ''Les Correctoires: Essai de mise au point,'' *Recherches de théologie ancienne et médiévale* 14 (1947) 287–304.

[J. F. HINNEBUSCH]

ROBERT OF SOLETO, BL.

Celestine monk (also known as Robert of Sala, Salle), b. Sala, Italy 1273; d. Morrone, July 18, 1341. He received the monastic habit from Peter of Morrone in 1289. When the latter was elected Pope CELESTINE V in 1294, Robert declined the cardinal's hat, for which PETRARCH commended him in his *De vita solitaria* (2.3, ch. 18). As prior and general procurator of the CELESTINES, Robert was the founder of monasteries and hospices for the sick and orphans. Contemporaries revered him for his mortification and devotion to the Sacred Passion.

Feast: July 18.

Bibliography: *Acta Sanctorum* July 4:498–509. A. M. ZIMMERMAN, *Kalendarium Benedictinum: Die Heiligen und Seligen des Benediktinerorderns und seiner Zweige,* 4 vol. (Metten 1933–38) 2:470–471, 473. J. L. BAUDOT and L. CHAUSSIN, *Vies des saints et des bienheureux selon l'ordre du calendrier avec l'historique des fêtes,* 12 vol. (Paris 1935–56) 7:408.

[V. GELLHAUS]

ROBERT OF TORIGNY

Known also as Robertus de Monte, abbot and chronicler; d. June 24, 1186. He was a BENEDICTINE at the Abbey of BEC from 1128 and became prior there (1154) and then the most celebrated abbot of MONT-SAINT-MICHEL, where he promoted monastic discipline, learning, and physical expansion. ALEXANDER III invited him to participate in the Synod of Tours in 1163. A man of high culture, he revised the *Gesta Normannorum ducum* of William of Jumièges, adding it as book eight of the *Historia Henrici I regis Anglorum;* his continuation of the chronicle of SIGEBERT OF GEMBLOUX is an important source of Anglo-French history. He was also interested in the history of the East, in the translation of the works of ARISTOTLE, and in the history of the episcopal sees of France, for which he drew up an important catalog.

Bibliography: *Chronica,* ed. L. DELISLE, 2 v. (Publication de la Société de l'histoire de normandie; Rouen 1872–73), also ed. L. C. BETHMANN, *Monumenta Germaniae Historica: Scriptores* (Berlin 1826–) 6:475–535; *Tractatus de immutationibus ordinis monachorum,* ed. L. DELISLE, *op. cit.* 2:184–206. M. MANITIUS, *Geschichte der lateinischen Literatur des Mittelalters,* 3 v. (Munich 1911–31) 3:346, 442–445. J. DE GHELLINCK, *L'Essor de la littérature latine au XIIe siècle,* 2 v. (Brussels-Paris 1946) 2:96–97. K. SCHNITH, *Lexikon für Theologie und Kirche,* ed. J. HOFER and K. RAHNER, 10 v. (2d, new ed. Freiburg 1957–65) 8:1343.

[O. J. BLUM]

ROBERT OF WINCHELSEA

Archbishop of Canterbury; b. probably Winchelsea, Sussex, England, *c.* 1240; d. Otford, Kent, May 11, 1313. He studied arts at Paris, possibly for a time under THOMAS AQUINAS, and became rector of the university in 1267. He then studied theology at Oxford, became a doctor of theology, and was chancellor by 1288. He delivered a series of *quaestiones* on the Trinity at St. Paul's Cathedral. Elected archbishop of CANTERBURY in 1293, he was forced by a vacancy in the papacy to wait 18 months before being consecrated at Aquila in 1294. He thus entered his office with enormous debts and was immediately faced with King Edward I's demands for clerical subsidies for the war with France. The archbishop struggled constantly to scale these down and was further embarrassed by the issue in 1296 of *CLERICIS LAICOS,* which he delayed publishing for a year. Upon refusing to make the king further grants, he and most of his clergy were punished by outlawry and the confiscation of their revenues. Robert had to live on charity for five months. Then, to ease his clergy's difficulties, he allowed each to follow his own conscience. A truce with France, invasion by the Scots, and the compromise offered by *Etsi de statu* allowed him to reach an accommodation with the king, but he continued to insist on all his other prerogatives. Pope BONIFACE VIII's death and the election of Edward I's vassal as CLEMENT V deprived Robert of any papal support, and in 1306 he was suspended from office and left En-

gland. After Edward I's death (1307), he was recalled by the new king but was soon at odds with him, particularly over Gaveston, whose banishment Robert supported in 1308. In 1310 he was chosen as one of the lords' ordainers to supervise Edward II's conduct of the government, and he was their guiding spirit until his death. Ascetic and generous, he also loved power; defending the Church against royal encroachments, he punctiliously upheld his own rights within the Church, conducting a prolonged feud with the archbishop of York and the royal treasurer, Bishop Walter Langton.

Bibliography: R. WINCHELSEY, *Registrum . . . ,* ed. R. GRAHAM (Canterbury and York Society, 123; London 1956). *The Dictionary of National Biography from the Earliest Times to 1900,* 63 v. (London 1885–1900) 21:626–632. A. B. EMDEN, *A Biographical Register of the University of Oxford to* A.D. *1500,* 3 v. (Oxford 1957–59) 3:2057–2059.

[B. S. SMITH]

ROBERT PULLEN

English theologian and cardinal (also Pullus, Pollanus, or Pulein); b. *c.* 1080; d. Viterbo, September 1146. He studied at Paris under WILLIAM OF CHAMPEAUX after 1103, according to F. Courtney. In 1133 he came from Exeter to Oxford and lectured for about five years on Scripture, ''which had fallen into neglect among the scholastics''; he also gained renown for his sermons. He was appointed archdeacon of Rochester in 1134. A letter of St. BERNARD OF CLAIRVAUX speaks of a journey to Rome by Robert before or during 1142, and mentions Bernard's advice that Pullen spend some time in Paris ''because of the sound doctrine he is acknowledged to possess'' (*Epistles* 205, *Patrologia Latina* 182:372–373). This marks the beginning of his teaching at Paris, a fact confirmed by JOHN OF SALISBURY (*Metalogicon* 2.10, *Patrologia Latina* 1:99:869). Pullen was called to Rome by Lucius II (1144–45) and made the first English cardinal. After the election of Eugene III, Bernard exhorted Pullen to counsel and support the new Cistercian pope (*Epistles* 362, *Patrologia Latina* 182:563–564). Pullen's death probably occurred at Viterbo, not Rome, before Sept. 18, 1146. His extant and known writings include a number of sermons and the *Sententiarum libri VIII* (*Patrologia Latina* 186:639–1010), written in Oxford, perhaps before 1142. While many questions parallel the *Sentences* of PETER LOMBARD, it appears to have had no influence on Lombard (*See* SCHOLASTICISM).

Bibliography: F. PELSTER, ''Einige Angaben über Leben und Schriften des Robertus Pullus,'' *Scholastik* 12 (1937): 239–247. F. COURTNEY, ''Cardinal Robert Pullen: An English Theologian of the 12th Century,'' *Analecta Gregoriana* 64 (Rome 1954).

[I. C. BRADY]

ROBERT WALDBY OF YORK

Augustinian opponent of Wyclif, archbishop; b. Yorkshire; d. Jan. 6, 1398. His elder brother or cousin was the celebrated Augustinian JOHN OF WALDBY. Robert was ordained at York in 1362. Studying first at the Oxford Convent, he earned his doctorate in theology at Toulouse, perhaps in the early 1370s. He had a long connection with Aquitaine; he was there probably with the Black Prince between 1363 and 1367, and was duchy chancellor in 1386 and bishop of Aire (1386–90). Prominent in the sermon and pamphlet war against John WYCLIF, he attended both the 1382 Black Friars synod of Archbishop William COURTENAY at London, and the 1392 council at Stamford that tried Henry CRUMPE and condemned Wyclif's teachings. Waldby is said to have written a work *Contra Wiclevistas*. As archbishop of Dublin (1390) he was a loyal supporter of King RICHARD II, holding the post of Irish chancellor in 1392. Richard obtained his translation to Chichester (1395) and, reputedly against the wishes of the monks, to the archbishopric of York (1396). The king had Robert's body buried in Westminster Abbey. He is reputed to have studied medicine as well as theology and to have been physician to Richard II.

Bibliography: J. TAIT, *The Dictionary of National Biography from the Earliest Times to 1900*, 63 v. (London 1885–1900) 20:469–470. A. O. GWYNN, *The English Austin Friars in the Time of Wyclif* (London 1940) 115–116, 270–272. A. B. EMDEN, *A Biographical Register of the University of Oxford to* A.D. *1500*, 3 v. (Oxford 1957–59) 3:1958.

[F. D. BLACKLEY]

ROBERTS, JOHN, ST.

Welsh Benedictine priest, martyr; b. Trawsynydd, Merionethshire (now Gwynedd), Wales, 1576 or 1577; hanged, drawn, and quartered at Tyburn (London), Dec. 10, 1610. Nothing is known of his parentage or his early education. On Feb. 26, 1593, he entered St. John's College, Oxford. Before taking his degree, he left the university to study at the Inns of Court, London. In 1598, while visiting Paris, he was received into the Church at Notre Dame. From Paris he went to Valladolid and there entered the English College on Sept. 15, 1598. Convinced that he had a vocation to the monastic life, he later joined the Benedictine monastery of S. Martino de Compostella, Valladolid. He was ordained in 1602; he left for England, reaching London (April 1603) where he became very famous among the English papists, and many resorted to him, some out of curiosity to see a Benedictine monk once again in England. Roberts was arrested and then released (1603), and exiled with Sigebert Buckley, a priest aged 86, a prisoner for 30 years and the last survivor of the pre-Reformation English Benedictine congregation. The same year Roberts was back in England ministering to the plague-stricken in London.

During the next seven years Roberts was arrested four times and banished at least twice; on one occasion he escaped from Gatehouse Prison, Westminster. His final arrest occurred on Dec. 2, 1610, the first Sunday of Advent, while he was finishing Mass at a house in Holborn. On Dec. 5, he was brought for trial before George Abbot, bishop of London, and Edward Coke, chief justice. He defended himself eloquently. When accused of being a "deceiver of the people," he turned on Bishop Abbot: "I do not deceive, but try to lead back to the right path those poor wandering souls whom you and your foolish ministers have led astray and infected with a thousand deceits and heresies"; then he told Abbot: "You had done much better, my Lord, to remain in your palace and in your church and chapter, reforming the dissolute conduct of your clergy than to come and sit on this bench, while matters of life and death are being decided." Roberts was found guilty. When three days later he was taken again before the bench to hear the sentence, he spoke nobly. On December 10 he was dragged from Newgate to Tyburn, where he was executed along with (Bl.) Thomas Somers, a Douai priest who had stood trial with him. He was beatified on Dec. 15, 1929, and canonized by Paul VI on Oct. 25, 1970 as one of the Forty Martyrs of England and Wales. Roberts is honored as the protomartyr of St. Gregory's Abbey, now Downside.

Feasts: December 10; October 25 (Feast of the 40 Martyrs of England and Wales); May 4 (Feast of the English Martyrs in England).

See Also: ENGLAND, SCOTLAND, AND WALES, MARTYRS OF.

Bibliography: W. PHILLIPSON, *Blessed John Roberts* (Postulation Pamphlet; London 1961). R. CHALLONER, *Memoirs of Missionary Priests*, ed. J. H. POLLEN (rev. ed. London 1924; repr. Farnborough 1969). B. CAMM, *A Benedictine Martyr in England: The Life and Times of Dom John Roberts* (London 1897). A. BUTLER, *The Lives of the Saints*, rev. ed. H. THURSTON and D. ATTWATER, 4 v. (New York 1956) 4:534–536. T. P. ELLIS, *Catholic Martyrs of Wales* (London 1933). J. GILLOW, *A Literary and Biographical History or Bibliographical Dictionary of English Catholics from 1534 to the Present Time*, 5 v. (London-New York 1885–1902; repr. New York 1961) 5:431–432.

[G. FITZHERBERT]

ROBERTS, THOMAS D'ESTERRE

Archbishop of Bombay (1937–50), outspoken defender of the importance of personal CONSCIENCE and intelligent obedience; b. March 7, 1893 in Le Havre, d. Feb. 28, 1976 in London. He was the son of a British consul descended from a line of French Huguenots. His father became a Catholic in 1900 and Thomas was educated at the Jesuit college in Liverpool. He entered the Society of Jesus Sept. 7, 1909 and was ordained to the priesthood Sept. 20, 1925. After teaching at Jesuit colleges at Preston and Beaumont, followed by a term as rector of St. Francis Xavier's College, Liverpool, he was appointed archbishop of Bombay in 1937, an appointment he first learned about from reading a local newspaper.

The See of Bombay at the time of his appointment had a long history of ecclesiastical divisions. The Portuguese, the original colonizers, had received from the Holy See the privileges of *padroado* protectorate, the government's right to approve ecclesiastical appointments. With Bombay under British rule, an agreement was reached that the archbishop would be alternately English and Portuguese. The sharp rivalries among the different factions within the archdiocese Abp. Roberts sought to overcome first, by personal diplomacy with the Portuguese government in Lisbon and then by reorganizing parish boundaries. He initiated a wide-ranging program of social services with particular emphasis on the needs of women, soldiers, and sailors. He also wrote a series of letters to children in the local newspaper that became an effective vehicle of instruction for young and old.

Above all, Abp. Roberts recognized that at a time of nationalistic aspirations for independence, the Church in Bombay should eventually be guided by an Indian archbishop. He pressed this view on the Holy See and, in 1946, an Indian, Valerian Gracias (later Cardinal), was appointed auxiliary. Bp. Gracias quickly assumed the day-to-day administration of the archdiocese as Abp. Roberts deliberately absented himself. When, in 1950, Bp. Gracias was officially named archbishop, Roberts returned to England.

In the next 25 years he became known as an unconventional churchman who labored indefatigably for such causes as disarmament and world peace, for a rethinking of Church teaching on artificial CONTRACEPTION, and for the rights of personal conscience. In 1954 he published *Black Popes—Authority: Its Uses and Abuses*, a small volume which attracted attention for its frank criticism of secular and ecclesiastical authoritarianism. He urged the need for "intelligent obedience," which he understood to be a characteristically Jesuit and Ignatian ideal. One of the most painful episodes in his life was his delation to Rome (1960) by the apostolic delegate for his views and public statements. Abp. Roberts, insisting that most of the charges were untrue, urged a full and impartial

hearing. Although Pope John XXIII promised such a hearing, it never was held. Roberts was not satisfied with assurances that he had been vindicated simply because the matter had not been pursued. Instead, he contrasted the standards of fairness found in English Common Law with the secrecy of ecclesiastical procedures, where there was never reparation of the damage done to personal reputation.

Through the years of VATICAN COUNCIL II (1962–65), Abp. Roberts called for reform of the Roman CURIA. Although he never did speak in the formal sessions of the council (despite his request to do so), he became a popular figure at the press briefings outside of the formal sessions. He sought to have the council issue a strong condemnation of all nuclear weapons, to support the rights of conscientious objectors to war, and urged reexamination of the teaching on artificial contraception, since he was convinced that the absolute ban on all contraception imposed heavy burdens on many Catholic families. The last issue brought him into conflict with members of the English hierarchy, in particular, Cardinal John Heenan, in 1964. Abp. Roberts had admitted publicly that he simply could not understand the rational arguments for the prohibition of all artificial contraception, Cardinal Heenan defended the traditional ban and lamented the fact that the faithful were being misled by some of their shepherds. The establishment of a special commission by Pope Paul VI to study the question was seen by some as a vindication of the questions raised by Roberts. The encyclical *HUMANAE VITAE*, issued in 1968, however, reiterated the traditional teaching.

Although considered by some to be a "maverick bishop," Abp. Roberts was a man with a rare sense of the ridiculous and the absurd, and his sense of humor appealed even to those who disagreed with him. He was also a pastor of extraordinary warmth and sensitivity to human suffering, and many who came in contact with him through retreats in England and the United States, and also through personal counseling at the Jesuit residence in Farm Street in London, found him a great source of faith. In addition to *Black Popes*, he wrote a foreword to *Nuclear Weapons and Christian Conscience* (1961) and contributions to *Problems of Authority* (1962), *Objections to Roman Catholicism* (1963) and *Contraception and Holiness* (1963). His last book was *The Diary of Bathsheba* (1970).

Bibliography: D. A. HURN, *Archbishop Roberts, SJ—His Life and Writings* (London 1966).

[J. A. O'HARE]

ROBERTSON, JAMES

Canadian Presbyterian leader; b. Dull, Perthshire, Scotland, April 24, 1839; d. Toronto, Canada, Jan. 4, 1902. His parents, James and Christina (McCallum) Robertson, immigrated to Canada with him in 1855. After education at the University of Toronto; Princeton University, N.J.; and Union Theological Seminary, New York City, he was ordained (1869) a minister of the Presbyterian Church in Canada. He served at Norwich, Ontario (1869–74), and was minister of Knox Church at Winnipeg (1874–81) before being appointed (1881) superintendent of the Presbyterian missions in western Canada. He held this post until his death, gaining a reputation for his ability to deal effectively with the problems of his farflung missions. In 1895 he was elected moderator of the Presbyterian Church in Canada, which in 1913 established the Robertson Memorial Lectureship, consisting of eight lectures to be given annually in the eight theological colleges of the United Church of Canada. One of the lectures must deal with some aspect of Dr. Robertson's life or with the territory in which he worked. He married (1869) Mary Anne Cowing; they had two daughters.

Bibliography: C. W. GORDON, *The Life of James Robertson, Missionary Superintendent in the Northwest Territories* (New York 1908). J. T. MCNEILL, *The Presbyterian Church in Canada, 1875–1925* (Toronto 1925).

[E. DELANEY]

ROBESPIERRE, MAXIMILIEN FRANÇOIS DE

French Revolutionary leader; b. Arras, May 6, 1758; d. Paris, July 28, 1794. Orphaned at nine, he studied law and became a judge in criminal cases. He was elected to the Estates-General (1789) and later to the National Convention. His rise to prominence during the FRENCH REVOLUTION was gradual. A champion of the rights of the people and of natural virtue, he espoused the reforms of Aug. 4, 1789, and advocated confiscation of ecclesiastical property and the death sentence for Louis XVI. When the revolution deteriorated toward extremism after June 1792, Robespierre upheld the constitution of 1791 and opposed war and military dictatorship. In the power struggle after the king's execution (Jan. 21, 1793), Robespierre conceived the Committee of Public Safety. Under his Jacobin leadership it prevented foreign invasion; established peace and prosperity; instituted republican government; and purged the Girondins, the radical Hebertists, and the conservative Dantonists, thereby placing the Jacobins in supreme control. Mounting problems necessitated stern legislative measures to further the dis-

tribution of state-appropriated lands and the expedition of justice; but these measures increased the savagery of this period of terror.

As a believer in natural religion and a follower of Jean Jacques ROUSSEAU, Robespierre instituted the Republic of Virtue (June 1794) and the cult of the SUPREME BEING as an alternative to Catholicism, atheism, and the cult of the goddess REASON; but popular enthusiasm was slight. Instead, the innovation precipitated a reaction and a conspiracy among the deputies that culminated in Robespierre's downfall and execution by guillotine.

Bibliography: *Oeuvres complètes,* ed. E. DÉPREZ et al. (Paris 1910–). L. E. HAMEL, *Histoire de Robespierre,* 3 v. (Paris 1865–67). A. MATHIEZ, *Études robespierristes,* 2 v. (Paris 1917–18); *The Fall of Robespierre, and Other Essays,* tr. from Fr. (New York 1927). J. M. THOMPSON, *Robespierre,* 2 v. (Oxford 1935); *Robespierre and the French Revolution* (New York 1953). G. WALTER, *Robespierre,* 2 v. (def. ed. Paris 1961). R. R. PALMER, *Twelve Who Ruled* (Princeton 1941). H. BELLOC, *Robespierre* (2d ed. London 1927). M. BOULOISEAU et al., eds., *Discours de Maximilien Robespierre,* 4 v. (Paris 1950–59).

[R. J. MARAS]

ROBINSON, CHRISTOPHER, BL.

Priest, martyr; b. at Woodside (near Carlisle), Cumberland, England; hanged, drawn, and quartered Aug. 19, 1598 at Carlisle. He studied at Rheims (1589–92), where he was ordained (1592) before entering the English Mission. In 1594, he witnessed the condemnation and execution of St. John BOSTE at Durham, of which he has left a graphic account (*Catholic Record Society's Publications,* v. 1, London 1905, 85–92). He labored primarily in Westmoreland and Cumberland until his arrest and imprisonment at Carlisle. During his confinement, the Protestant Bishop Robinson of Carlisle unsuccessfully engaged him in several disputations in an effort to persuade him to save his life by conforming to the new faith. He was beatified by Pope John Paul II on Nov. 22, 1987 with George Haydock and Companions.

Feast of the English Martyrs: May 4 (England).

See Also: ENGLAND, SCOTLAND, AND WALES, MARTYRS OF.

Bibliography: R. CHALLONER, *Memoirs of Missionary Priests,* ed. J. H. POLLEN (rev. ed. London 1924). J. H. POLLEN, *Acts of English Martyrs* (London 1891).

[K. I. RABENSTEIN]

ROBINSON, PASCHAL

Author and apostolic nuncio to Ireland; baptized Charles; b. Dublin, Ireland, April 26, 1870; d. Dublin,

Aug. 26, 1948. While Charles was still a boy, his family left Ireland for the U.S., where he entered the novitiate of the Order of Friars Minor in New York on Aug. 2, 1896. He received the name Paschal, pronounced his solemn vows in Rome, Oct. 4, 1900, and on December 21 of the following year was ordained. The next ten years were devoted to study, research, writing, and teaching. Paul Sabatier's book on St. Francis was the occasion for his own work, *The Real St. Francis* (1903). Other books followed in rapid succession: *Some Pages of Franciscan History* (1905), *The Writings of St. Francis* (1906), and *The Life of St. Clare* (1910). During this same period he was a contributor to many reviews and wrote a number of articles for the old *Catholic Encyclopedia*. In 1908, Paschal was appointed associate editor of the international Franciscan Review, the *Archivum Franciscanum Historicum*.

From 1913 to 1919, he taught medieval history at the Catholic University of America. In 1914 he was named a fellow of the Royal Historical Society of England. At the end of World War I, he was nominated by the U.S. government to assist its educational and economic commission at the Versailles Conference. There he presented a paper outlining the position and work of the Catholic Church and of the Franciscan Order in Palestine, which the British had received in the form of a mandate upon the dissolution of the Ottoman Empire. Subsequently he was employed by the Holy See in various missions to the Near East. He served as apostolic visitor to the Custody of the Holy Land in 1920; and five years later, to the Latin Patriarchate in Jerusalem and the Eastern Catholic Churches in Palestine, Transjordan, and Cyprus. In the meantime he had been appointed consultor to a number of Roman Congregations, including the Congregation of Propaganda (1925). In recognition of his work in behalf of the Holy See, he was created titular archbishop of Tyana, May 24, 1927.

After acting as mediator between the sacred and civil authorities on the island of Malta, where he once again earned the respect and gratitude of both the Holy See and the British government, Robinson was appointed papal nuncio to Ireland, Nov. 27, 1929, and served there until his death.

Bibliography: Archives of the New York Province, Order of Friars Minor.

[D. MCELRATH]

ROBLES HURTADO, JOSÉ MARÍA, ST.

Martyr, pastor, founder of the Victims of the Eucharistic Heart of Jesus; b. May 3, 1888, Mascota, Jalisco, Diocese of Tepic, Mexico; d. June 26, 1927, Jalisco, Diocese of Autlán. At age 12, he entered the seminary at Guadalajara, where he distinguished himself by his intelligence and dedication to both his studies and catechesis. While he was still in the seminary, the bishop of Tehuantepec invited him to work in his diocese. He ministered in various parishes after his ordination (1913), hearing confessions and caring for the sick. As pastor of Tecolotlán, Jalisco, he founded the *Victimas del Corazón Eucarística de Jesús*, now called the Sisters of the Sacred Heart of Jesus (*Religiosa Hermanas del Corazón de Jesús Sacramentado*). Because of his fervent love of the Sacred Heart, he wrote pamphlets to propagate the devotion. Robles hid himself during the persecution but did not abandon his flock. He was taken prisoner as he was preparing to celebrate Mass in a private home. He was hanged in the Quila mountain of Jalisco, Diocese of Autlán. Robles' mortal remains lie in the novitiate of the congregation he founded. He was both beatified (Nov. 22, 1992) and canonized (May 21, 2000) with Cristobal MAGALLANES [*see* GUADALAJARA (MEXICO), MARTYRS OF, SS.] by Pope John Paul II.

Feast: May 25 (Mexico).

Bibliography: J. CARDOSO, *Los mártires mexicanos* (Mexico City 1953). J. DÍAZ ESTRELLA, *El movimiento cristero: sociedad y conflicto en los Altos de Jalisco* (México, D.F. 1979).

[K. I. RABENSTEIN]

ROBOT, ISIDORE

Missionary, abbot; b. Tharoiseau, France, July 18, 1837; d. Dallas, Tex., Feb. 15, 1887. Robot entered the Benedictine monastery of Sainte-Marie, Pierre-qui-Vire, France, a recent foundation that emphasized Trappist-like discipline and foreign missions. He was ordained in 1862, and served as military chaplain in the Franco-Prussian War. Having left France (1873), accompanied by Brother Benedict Lambert, he was welcomed at New Orleans, La., by Abp. Napoleon Joseph Perche. While laboring briefly in northern Louisiana, Robot investigated the status of neglected native tribes. The Jesuits in Kansas informed him of the recent removal of Catholic natives, especially the Potawatomi Citizen Band, southward to Indian Territory. Bp. Edward Fitzgerald of Little Rock, Ark., authorized him to enter the territory, where no priest resided. On Oct. 12, 1875, Robot arrived at Atoka, Choctaw Nation. During early 1876 he explored the territory and held conferences with Choctaw and Potawatomi chiefs. In Sept. he received his appointment, dated July 9, 1876, as the first prefect apostolic of Indian Territory. Concluding an agreement with the Potawatomi, he selected as his headquarters the site of Sacred Heart Mission.

During 1877, with the arrival of recruits from France, a monastic community, with novitiate, began activities. A school for native boys was opened and upon the arrival of nuns, a girls' school (1880). Leo XIII conferred the abbatial dignity on Robot on Sept. 1, 1878. He attended the Third Plenary Council of Baltimore, Md., in 1884 and resigned his prefecture while visiting Rome in 1885. He had laid the groundwork for the later Vicariate and Diocese of Oklahoma.

Bibliography: Annals, Sacred Heart Mission, Okla.

[J. F. MURPHY]

ROCCA, ANGELO

Humanist and historian; b. Rocca Contrada, Italy, 1545; d. Rome, April 7, 1620. In 1552 he entered the Augustinians in Camerino, studied at Padua where he received his doctorate in 1577, and became in 1585 editor of the Vatican Press for the Bible, general councils, and Patristic works. In 1605 he was made titular bishop of Tagaste. With his excellent book collection he founded the first public library in Rome, the Biblioteca Angelica, named for him. In 1614 he placed it in the care of the convent of St. Agostino, which directed it until 1873 when the state assumed ownership. Rocca wrote more than 60 works and participated in the edition of the Vulgate under Sixtus V and Gregory XV. Many of his ascetical, liturgical, and historical writings were published in an incomplete *Opera omnia* (2 v. Rome 1719, 1745). He edited five volumes of works by Augustinians, wrote two volumes on St. Augustine and free will, and two volumes on the building activities of Sixtus V.

Bibliography: *Cenni biografici di Angelo Rocca* (Fabriano 1881). D. A. PERINI, *Bibliographia Augustiniana*, 4 v. (Florence 1929–38) 3:126–133.

[F. ROTH]

ROCCACASALE, MARIANO DA, BL.

Baptized Domenico, Franciscan lay brother; b. Jan. 14, 1778, Roccacasale (Aquila), Abruzzi, Italy; d. May 31, (Feast of Corpus Christi) 1866, Bellegra, Italy; beatified by John Paul II, Oct. 3, 1999.

Mariano's life was characterized by simplicity and poverty. He was one of six children of Gabriel de Nicolantonio and Santa de Arcángelo. In tending the family flocks in the Morrone mountains as a young boy, he grew to love silence and reflection. He entered Saint Nicholas Friary at Arischia, Abruzzi, took the name Mariano (Sept. 2, 1802) and pronounced his solemn vows the following

"*Saint Roch,*" *15th century painting by Giovanni Santi.* (©Archivo Iconografico, S.A./CORBIS)

year. For 12 years he engaged in prayer and work, as a carpenter, gardener, cook, and porter, at Arischia. In 1814, Mariano asked and received permission to transfer to the more austere Saint Francis Friary at Bellegra, where he served as porter for 40 years, welcoming pilgrims, other travelers, and the poor. Among those he greeted and inspired was Diego Oddi, who later became a Franciscan in the same friary. A miracle attributed to Blessed Mariano's intercession was approved by the pope, April 6, 1998, opening the way for his beatification.

Feast: May 30 (Franciscans).

Bibliography: *Acta Apostolicae Sedis* 19 (1999): 965. *L'Osservatore Romano*, Eng. ed. 40 (1999): 1–3; 41 (1999): 2.

[K. I. RABENSTEIN]

ROCH, ST.

Miracle-worker; b. Montpellier, France, *c.* 1350; d. Angera, Lombardy, *c.* 1378–79 (feast, August 16, 17, or

18). A historical figure, Roch is the unfortunate victim of incompetent biographers. The *Acta breviora,* sincere but poorly done, and the *Vita s. Rochi* by Francis Diedo (1478), more complete but chronologically impossible and of doubtful value, are today considered the best biographies available. Roch was the son of a rich Occitanian merchant and of a Lombard mother. In 1367, when Roch was about 17, Pope Urban V visited his home town. Since his parents were dead, he decided to go to Rome as a pilgrim. Roch became known for his love of poverty and for his charity toward the sick, and from these activities stemmed his gift of healing, which he began exercising first in Acquapendente and later in Cesena. In Rome he cured Cardinal Anglic, the Pope's brother. He left Rome in 1371 for Rimini, Novara, and Piacenza, where he remained for a time because of illness. He was arrested in Angera (*c.* 1374) on the shores of Lake Maggiore and imprisoned on charges of being a spy. He died there following a reunion with his maternal uncle. He was later honored (from *c.* 1410) in Montpellier because of his fame as a miracle-worker. His veneration in Italy is associated with the arrest of the plague in Ferrara in January 1439, attributed to his intercession. His relics were taken in 1485 to Venice where his most important shrine was erected. In 1629 his cult was approved for the many churches dedicated to him and in 1694 for the Franciscan Observants. Roch's membership in any religious order is doubtful. If he was a tertiary, it seems more likely that he was a member of the Third Order of St. Dominic.

Bibliography: A. FLICHE, "Le Problème de Saint Roch," *Analecta Bollandiana* 68 (Brussels 1950) 343–361. L. RÉAU, *Iconographie de l'art chrétien,* 6 v. (Paris 1955–59) 3.3:1155–61. J. OSWALD, *Lexikon für Theologie und Kirche,* ed. J. HOFER and K. RAHNER (Freiburg 1957–65); suppl., *Das Zweite Vatikanishe Konsil: Dokumente und Kommentare,* ed. H. S. BRECHTER et al. (1966) 8:1347–48.

[J. CAMBELL]

ROCHEFORT SHIPS, MARTYRS OF, BB.

Also known as Martyrs of La Rochelle, 64 priest martyrs of the French Revolution; d. 1794; beatified by John Paul II, Oct. 1, 1995.

In 1790 the authorities of the FRENCH REVOLUTION passed legislation requiring all priests to swear to the CIVIL CONSTITUTION OF THE CLERGY, which was intended to separate the Church of France from Rome. The following year the state considered as suspect those who would not take the oath, and began deporting them to French Guyana, South America (1792). A total of 827 priests and religious, who considered taking the oath an act of apostasy, were imprisoned to await deportation on hulk ships in the harbor of Rochefort (La Rochelle), particularly the *Deux-Associés* and the *Washington.* Departure was delayed by the British blockade of the French coast. Meanwhile conditions worsened aboard the hulks, which were previously used for storage or to house slaves, as more detainees were added. In addition to the physical hardships of hunger, thirst, and lack of sanitation was added the confiscation of all religious goods from the priests. The majority of the prisoners (542) died in captivity from maltreatment between April 11, 1794, and Feb. 7, 1795, and were buried in the sand of Île d'Aix (226) or the Île Madame (254). The survivors testified to the heroism of some of their fellows, including these beatified as martyrs for whom there was sufficient testimony as to their manner of death.

Feast: Aug. 18.

Adam, Louis-Armand-Joseph, OFMConv., Franciscan priest of Rouen; b. Dec. 19, 1741; d. July 13, 1794.

Ancel, Charles-Antoine-Nicolas, C.J.M., priest; b. Oct. 11, 1763; d. July 29, 1794.

Auriel, Antoine, pastor of Calviat, Diocese of Cahors; b. April 19, 1764; d. June 16, 1794.

Bannassat, Antoine, parish priest in Saint-Fiel, Diocese of Limoges; b. May 20, 1729; d. July 18, 1794.

Beguignot, Claude, O. Cart., Carthusian priest; b. Sept. 19, 1736; d. July 16, 1794.

Bourdon, Jean, OFMCap, Capuchin priest; b. April 3, 1747; d. Aug. 23, 1794.

Brigéat de Lambert, Scipion-Jérôme, deacon of the cathedral of Avranches (joined in 1854 to the Diocese of Coutances); b. June 9, 1733; d. Sept. 9, 1794.

Brulard, Michel-Louis, O.C.D., Discalced Carmelite priest; b. June 11, 1758; d. July 25, 1794.

Brunel, Gervaise-Protase, OCist, Cistercian priest and prior of the monastery at Mortagne; b. June 18, 1744; d. Aug. 20, 1794.

Charles, Paul-Jean, OCist, Cistercian priest, abbot of Sept-Fons Monastery, Diocese of Moulins; b. Dec. 29, 1750; d. Aug. 25, 1794.

Collas du Bignon, Charles-René, P.S.S., Sulpician priest, superior of the seminary in Bourges; b. Aug. 25, 1743; d. June 3, 1794.

Conte, Noël-Hilaires le, priest from the cathedral of Bourges; b. Oct. 3, 1765; d. Aug. 17, 1794.

CORDIER, Jean-Nicolas, SJ, Jesuit priest; professor of theology; b. Dec. 3, 1710, near Souilly, Lorraine, France; d. Sept. 30, 1794, Île Madame, La Rochelle, France.

Desgardin, Augustine-Joseph, OCist, Cistercian lay brother in Sept-Fons Monastery, Diocese of Moulins; b. Dec. 21, 1750; d. July 9, 1794.

Dumonet, Claude, priest, Diocese of Autun; b. Feb. 1, 1747; d. Sept. 13, 1794.

Dumontet de Cardaillac, Florent, vicar general of the Diocese of Castres (joined in 1922 to the Diocese of Albi); b. Feb. 8, 1749; d. Sept. 9, 1794.

Dupas, Jacques-Morellus, priest, Diocese of Poitiers; b. Nov. 10, 1754; d. June 21, 1794.

Duverneuil, Jean-Baptiste, O.C.D., Discalced Carmelite priest; b. 1737; d. July 1, 1794.

Faverge, Pierre-Sulpice-Christophe, F.S.C., in religion Brother Roger, Lasallian lay brother; b. July 25, 1745, Orléans, France; entered novitiate 1767; d. Sept. 12, 1794.

François François, OFMCap, Capuchin priest; b. Jan. 17, 1749; d. Aug. 10, 1794.

Gabilhaud, Pierre, parish priest in Saint-Christophe, Diocese of Limoges; b. July 26, 1747; d. Aug. 13, 1794.

Gagnot, Jacques, O.C.D., Discalced Carmelite priest; b. Feb. 9, 1753; d. Sept. 10, 1794.

Guillaume, Jean-Baptiste, F.S.C., in religion Brother Uldaric, Lasallian lay brother; b. Feb. 1, 1755, Fraisans, France; entered novitiate Oct. 16, 1785; d. Aug. 27, 1794.

Hanus, Charles-Arnaud, deacon and canon of Ligny cathedral; Diocese of Verdun; b. Oct. 19, 1723; d. Aug. 28, 1794.

Hunot, François, canon of Brienon, Archdiocese of Sens; b. Feb. 12, 1753; d. Oct. 8, 1794.

Hunot, Jean, canon and parish priest of Brienon, Archdiocese of Sens; b. Sept. 21, 1742; d. Oct. 9, 1794.

Hunot, Sebastian-Loup, canon of Brienon, Archdiocese of Sens; b. Aug. 7, 1745; d. Nov. 17, 1794. Brother of Bl. Jean Hunot.

Huppy, Louis Wulphy, from the Diocese of Limoges; b. April 1, 1767; d. Aug. 29, 1794.

Imbert, Joseph, SJ, Jesuit priest, apostolic vicar for the Diocese of Moulins; b. *c.* 1720; Marseille, France; d. June 9, 1794, on the *Deux-Associés.*

Jarrige, Barthélémy, from the Diocese of Limoges; b. March 18, 1753; d. July 13, 1794.

Jarrige, Jean-François, canon of Saint-Yrieix, Diocese of Limoges; b. Jan. 11, 1752; d. July 31, 1794.

Jarrige, Pierre, canon of Saint-Yrieix, Diocese of Limoges; b. April 19, 1737; d. Aug. 10, 1794.

Jean-Baptiste de Bruxelles, canon of Saint Leonard and pastor of St. Stefan's, Diocese of Limoges; b. Sept. 12, 1734; d. July 18, 1794.

Jouffret de Bonnefont, Claude-Joseph, parish priest in Saint-Sulpice; b. Dec. 23, 1752; d. Aug. 10, 1794.

Juge de Saint-Martin, Jean-Joseph, canon of the cathedral of Limoges; b. June 14, 1739; d. July 9, 1794.

Labiche de Reignefort, Marcel-Gaucher, priest of the *Societas Missionarium Lemovicensium;* b. Nov. 3, 1751; d. July 26, 1794.

Laborier du Vivier, Jean-Baptiste, deacon and cathedral canon of Mâcon (joined in 1853 to the Diocese of Autun); b. Sept. 19, 1734; d. Sept. 26 or 27, 1794.

Labrouche de Laborderie, Pierre-Yrieix, canon of Auvergne, Diocese of Limoges; b. May 24, 1756; d. July 1, 1794.

Laplace, Claude, parish priest in Saint-Bonnet, Diocese of Moulins; b. Nov. 15, 1725; d. Sept. 14, 1794.

Lebrun, Louis-François, O.S.B., priest of the French Benedictine Congregation of Saint-Maurus (*Mauristene*); b. April 9, 1744; d. Aug. 20, 1794.

Legroing de la Romagère, Pierre-Joseph, priest of the *Societas Navarrae* and vicar general of the Diocese of Bourges; b. June 28, 1752; d. July 26, 1794.

Leymarie de Laroche, Élie, prior of Saint-Jean, Diocese of Verdun; b. Jan. 8, 1758; d. Aug. 22, 1794.

Loir, Jean-Baptiste Jacques Louis Xavier, OFMCap, Capuchin priest; b. March 13, 1720; d. May 19, 1794.

Lombardie, Jacques, parish priest in St. Hilarius, Diocese of Limoges; b. Dec. 1, 1737; d. July 22, 1794.

Marchand, Michel-Bernard, pastor of Vaurouy, Archdiocese of Rouen; b. Sept. 28, 1749; d. July 15, 1794.

Marchandon, André-Joseph, parish priest in Marsac, Diocese of Limoges; b. Aug. 21, 1745; d. Sept. 22, 1794.

Mascloux, Claude-Barnabé de Laurent de, canon in Dorat, Diocese of Limoges; b. June 11, 1735; d. Sept. 7, 1794.

Mayaudon, François, vicar general in the Diocese of Soissons; b. May 4, 1739; d. Sept. 11, 1794.

Menestrel, Jean-Baptiste, canon of Remiremont, Diocese of Saint-Dié; b. Dec. 9, 1748; d. Aug. 16, 1794.

Mopinot, Jean, FSC, in religion Brother Léon, Lasallian lay brother; b. Sept. 12, 1724, Rheims, France; entered novitiate Jan. 14, 1744; d. May 21, 1794.

Noël, Pierre-Michel, associate pastor of Pavilly, Archdiocese of Rouen; b. Feb. 23, 1754; d. Aug. 9, 1794.

d'Oudinot de la Boissière, François, canon of Saint-Germain in Masseré, Diocese of Limoges; b. Sept. 3, 1746; d. Sept. 7, 1794.

Papon, Philippe, priest of Coutigny, Diocese of Moulins; b. Oct. 5, 1744; d. June 17, 1794.

Pergaud, Gabriel, OSA, Augustinian priest; b. Oct. 29, 1752, Saint-Priest-la-Plaine (Creuse), France; d. July 21, 1794.

Petiniaud de Jourgnac, Raymond, vicar general of the archdeacons of the Diocese of Limoges; b. Jan. 3, 1747; d. June 26, 1794.

Rehm, Jean-Georges, OP, Dominican priest; b. April 21, 1752; d. Aug. 27, 1794.

René, Georges Edme, canon of Vézelay, Archdiocese of Sens; b. Nov. 16, 1748; d. Oct. 1, 1794.

Retouret, Jacques, OCarm, Carmelite priest; b. Sept. 15, 1746, Limoges, France; d. Aug. 26, 1794, Île Madame, La Rochelle, France (age 47). Renowned as a preacher.

Richard, Claude, OSB, priest; b. May 19, 1741; d. Aug. 9, 1794.

Savouret, Nicolas, OFMConv., Franciscan priest and spiritual director for the Poor Clares of Moulins; b. Feb. 27, 1733; d. July 14, 1794.

Souzy, Jean-Baptiste, priest of the Diocese of La Rochelle; b. Nov. 19, 1734, La Rochelle, France; d. Aug. 27, 1794. He was named vicar general of the deported. He died after 10 months of abuse and was buried on Madame Island.

Tabouillot, Nicolas, parish priest of Méligny-le-Grand, Diocese of Verdun; b. Feb. 16, 1745; d. Feb. 23, 1795.

Tiersot, Lazare, OCist, Cistercian priest; b. March 29, 1739; d. Aug. 10, 1794.

Vernoy de Montjournal, Jean-Baptiste Ignace Pierre, canon of Notre-Dame in Moulins; b. Nov. 17, 1736; d. June 1, 1794.

Bibliography: I. GOBRY, *Les martyrs de la Révolution française* (Paris 1989). J. N. TYLENDA, *Jesuit Saints & Martyrs,* 2d ed. (Chicago 1998) 165–167. *Acta Apostolicae Sedis* (1995) 923–926. *L'Osservatore Romano,* no. 40 (1995) 3–5; *Documentation Catholique,* 19 (1995) 923–26.

[K. I. RABENSTEIN]

ROCHESTER, ANCIENT SEE OF

The smallest and least important of the medieval English dioceses, located in West Kent, England; its cathedral church is dedicated to St. Andrew. It is the oldest suffragan see of the province of CANTERBURY, founded by AUGUSTINE OF CANTERBURY, who consecrated its first bishop, JUSTUS (OF CANTERBURY), in 604. The cathedral chapter was composed of secular canons until the Norman Conquest. In 676 the original cathedral was severely damaged by marauding Mercians, and the incumbent bishop, Putta, fled from the diocese and never returned. It is indeed likely that he became the first bishop of HEREFORD. Most of the Anglo–Saxon bishops were undistinguished since the see was relatively poor and under the patronage, if not actual lordship, of the archbisbops of Canterbury. The last Saxon bishop, Siward (1058–75), unlike some of his kind, was allowed to remain in office until his death, when he was succeeded by Bishop Gundulf (1077–1108), who began the new (present) cathedral on the old Saxon foundation, and replaced the secular canons by BENEDICTINE monks, from whom a significant number of later bishops were drawn. The cathedral was consecrated in 1130, but was damaged by fire at the time. Ultimately in 1343 the choir was rebuilt and the central tower added, though the cathedral remains to this day largely Norman in appearance. Most of the post–Norman bishops except Arnulf of Beauvais (1115–24), a student of LANFRANC and historian of Rochester (*Patrologia Latina* v. 163), were undistinguished; the few who were outstanding, e.g., Bp. John ALCOCK (1472–76), were generally translated elsewhere. Most were regular clergy, primarily Benedictines or friars. In the 16th century the diocese had its most notable bishop and saint, John FISHER, who was both a scholar and a patron of scholars, a person of international reputation for piety and learning; in Holbein's drawing one sees a man of infinite human compassion and concern. He was executed under HENRY VIII in 1535. Henry re–founded Rochester as a diocese of the Church of England when he replaced the monastic chapter with a dean and secular canons.

Bibliography: A. I. PEARMAN, *Rochester* (Diocesan Histories; London 1897). R. C. FOWLER, in *The Victoria History of the County of Kent,* ed. W. PAGE, v. 2 (London 1926) 121–126. R. GARDINER, *The Story of Rochester Cathedral* (Blandford Forum, England 1978).

[H. S. REINMUTH, JR./EDS.]

ROCHESTER, JOHN, BL.

Carthusian priest, martyr; b. ca. 1498, Terling (?), Essex, England; hanged in chains at York, May 11, 1537. Cambridge-educated John Rochester, the third son of John Rochester of Terling and Grisold Writtle of Bobbingworth and brother to Sir Robert Rochester (1494–1557), joined the Carthusians of the London

Charterhouse as a choir monk. After his arrest for opposing the Act of Supremacy, he was placed under house arrest at the Hull Charterhouse, then moved to York where he was manacled with Bl. James Walworth. He was beatified by Pope Leo XIII on Dec. 9, 1886.

Feast of the English Martyrs: May 4 (England).

See Also: ENGLAND, SCOTLAND, AND WALES, MARTYRS OF.

Bibliography: R. CHALLONER, *Memoirs of Missionary Priests,* ed. J. H. POLLEN (rev. ed. London 1924; repr. Farnborough 1969). J. MORRIS, ed., *The Troubles of Our Catholic Forefathers Related by Themselves* (London 1872), I. J. H. POLLEN, *Acts of English Martyrs* (London 1891). E. M. THOMPSON, *The Carthusian Order in England* (New York 1930). W. WESTON, *Blessed Carthusian Martyrs* (London 1962).

[K. I. RABENSTEIN]

RODAT, ÉMILIE DE, ST.

Foundress of the Sisters of the HOLY FAMILY OF VILLEFRANCHE; b. Druelle, near Rodez (Aveyron), France, Sept. 6, 1787; d. Villefranche-de-Rouergue (Aveyron), Sept. 19, 1852. Émilie's parents, who belonged to the upper class, entrusted their daughter, at the age of 18 months, to the care of her maternal grandmother Mme. de Pomayrols, who lived in her chateau at Ginals. During the next 15 years, under her grandmother's direction, Émilie developed into a pious girl devoted to daily prayer and visits to the poor. In 1803 Mme. de Pomayrols retired to a house in Villefranche-de-Rouergue established by Mother Saint-Cyr, an Ursuline, for religious women who had been dispossessed during the FRENCH REVOLUTION. Émilie returned to Druelle until 1804 when she rejoined her grandmother at Villefranche. There she became acquainted with Abbé Antoine Marty (1757–1835), a former professor of philosophy in Paris who had suffered exile rather than subscribe to the CIVIL CONSTITUTION OF THE CLERGY. Under his spiritual guidance Émilie aided the poor and taught catechism classes. In 1809 she entered the novitiate of the Sisters of Charity and Christian Instruction of Nevers, but soon left.

In search of her vocation, she joined for a time the Picpus Sisters, then the Sisters of Mercy of Moissac. To satisfy the complaints of many persons who bemoaned the disappearance of the schools formerly run by the Ursulines, Émilie gathered three companions and in 1815 opened a school for poor children in Villefranche. From this humble beginning developed her religious congregation, whose purpose was the education of girls, the care of the sick, and other charitable works. Abbé Marty, who collaborated in the founding of the institute, composed the rule, modeled on that of St. Augustine, and approved by the bishop of Rodez (1832).

Émilie and her first companions pronounced perpetual vows in 1820. As superior general, Émilie was instrumental in the rapid growth of the congregation, which by 1852 had five cloistered convents, 32 houses connected with schools, and many orphanages. During these years Émilie was afflicted with many spiritual trials because of severe temptations to abandon faith and hope. She was beatified Jan. 9, 1940, and canonized April 23, 1950.

Feast: Sept. 19.

Bibliography: L. AUBINEAU, *Vie de la révérende Mère Émilie* (Paris 1855; 6th ed. Lyons 1891). É. BARTHE, *L'Ésprit de la révérende Mère Émilie de Rodat,* 2 v. (3d ed. Paris 1897). R. PLUS, *Sainte Émilie de Rodat* (Toulouse 1950). G. BERNOVILLE, *La Sainte de Rouergue: Émilie de Rodat* (Paris 1959). H. DELATTRE, *Dictionnaire de spiritualité et mystique. Doctrine et histoire,* ed. M. VILLER et al. (Paris 1932–) 4:610–614.

[V. A. LAPOMARDA]

RODRÍGUEZ, ALFONSO

Jesuit spiritual writer; b. Valladolid, April 1538; d. Seville, Feb. 21, 1616. After studying philosophy and arts at the University of Valladolid, and theology at Salamanca for two years, Rodríguez entered the Society of Jesus in Salamanca in July 1557. He was novice master in Salamanca in 1564, in Montilla from 1585 to 1597, and in Seville in 1607. He held also the posts of rector in Monterrey (1570–76) and moral professor and "resolver" of cases of conscience in Monterrey (1567–79) and in Valladolid (1579–85). From 1598 to 1607 he was in Córdoba engaged in the apostolic ministry. Rodríguez participated as a delegate for his province in the fifth general congregation at Rome. His contemporaries described him as a man of regular observance, mildness, and spiritual discretion, and, by nature, shy. His fame is due to his work the *Ejercicio de perfección y virtudes cristianas* (The Practice of Perfection and of Christian Virtues, Seville 1609). There are about 50 complete and 15 partial Spanish editions of this treatise. It was fully or partially translated into 23 languages. This work is a revision of the sermons he had given to the novices in Montilla [*see* I. Iparraguirre, *Répertoire de spiritualité* (Rome 1961) n.324]. In some places one can see the influence of the sermons of Gil González Dávila. The work is primarily a practical treatise, although it contains abundant spiritual doctrine, set forth with marvelous clarity through the use of Scripture and the Fathers, as well as medieval and contemporary authors. Emphasis is put upon the practice of the virtues and the specific means for acquiring them. The tone is that of a work intended for novices, with frequent illustrations and examples, of which many are historically inaccurate; however, they are always correct in style, and charming. The work lacks unity in its theological concepts.

Bibliography: C. SOMMERVOGEL, *Bibliothèque de la Compagnie de Jésus* 6:1946–63. J. DE GUIBERT, *La Spiritualité de la Compagnie de Jésus*, ed. E. LAMALLE (Rome 1953).

[I. IPARRAGUIRRE]

RODRÍGUEZ, ALPHONSUS, ST.

Jesuit lay brother and mystic; b. Segovia, Spain, July 25, 1532; d. Majorca, Oct. 31, 1617. This third son of the successful wool merchant Diego Rodríguez was instructed for his first Communion by Father Peter FABER during a mission in Segovia. When 14 years old, he was sent to the Jesuit college at Alcalá, but the death of his father prevented him from completing the first term. He returned home and assisted his mother in conducting the family trade, and in 1558 he married Maria Suarez, by whom he had a daughter, Maria, and two sons, Gaspar and Alonzo. His married life was content and devout, and he was impressed by the sermons of Jesuits passing through Segovia, especially Louis Santander and St. Francis Borgia. After financial failure and his great sorrow at the deaths of his daughter, his son Gaspar, his wife, and his mother in quick succession, he sold his business, and with his remaining son Antonio, retired to the house of his maiden sisters, Juliana and Antonia. There he learned habits of prayer and the practice of austerity. At the death of Antonio, he asked admittance into the Society of Jesus, but was refused because of his ill health, his age (he was nearly 40), and his insufficient education for the priesthood. Still hoping to become a priest, he tried to learn Latin, but without success, and for a time he considered the life of a hermit. On Jan. 31, 1571, against the advice of official Jesuit consultors, he was accepted as a lay brother, and after a six-month novitiate at Valencia, was sent to the college at Montesione on the island of Majorca. There he was house porter for 46 years, and is remembered particularly for his patience and humility in that office, his entire obedience to superiors, his mystical absorption in prayer, his welcome advice to the students, including St. Peter CLAVER, Apostle of the Negroes, and his devotion to the Mother of God. Though not the author of the Little Office of the Immaculate Conception, as has been wrongly alleged, he popularized its use. He was beatified on June 12, 1825, by Leo XII, and canonized on Jan. 15, 1888, by Leo XIII.

Feast: Oct. 30.

Bibliography: A. RODRÍGUEZ, *Obras espirituales*, ed. J. NONELL, 3 v. (Barcelona 1885–87); *Autobiography*, ed. W. YEOMANS (London 1965). P. DUDON, *Dictionnaire de spiritualité ascétique et mystique. Doctrine et histoire*, ed. M. VILLER et al. (Paris 1932–) 1:395–402. C. SOMMERVOGEL et al., *Bibliothéque de la Compagnie de Jésus*, 11 v. (Brussels-Paris 1890–1932; v. 12 suppl. 1960) 6:1943–46. A. BUTLER, *The Lives of the Saints*, rev. ed. H. THURSTON and D. ATTWATER, 4 v. (New York 1956) 4:225–227. M. DIETZ, *Zeitschrift für Aszese und Mystik* 30 (Würzburg 1957) 418–425. E. M. RIVIÈRE, *Dictionnaire d'histoire et de géographie ecclésiastiques*, ed. A. BAUDRILLART et al. (Paris 1912–) 2:751–752. L. KOCH, *Jesuiten-Lexikon: Die Gesellschaft Jesu einst und jetzt* (Paderborn 1934) 1552–53.

[E. D. MCSHANE]

RODRÍGUEZ DE MENDOZA, TORIBIO

Peruvian priest, educator, and politician; b. San Juan de la Frontera (Chachapoyas), April 15, 1750; d. Lima, June 10, 1825.

His early education was in his home with a tutor. He soon went to the seminary of San Carlos of Trujillo, and in 1766 he entered the seminary of Santo Toribio of Lima. He was a brilliant student, and on Sept. 22, 1770, he received the degree of doctor of theology in the Real y Pontificia Universidad de San Marcos. A year later, while still a student, he was named professor of philosophy and theology in the Colegio Mayor de San Carlos in Lima. On Feb. 5, 1773, he was made regent of the Cátedra del Maestro de las Sentencias. He was ordained on July 18, 1778 and became curate in Marcaval, a lowly town in the district of Huamachuco, where he carried out his duties as pastor and teacher of the indigenous peoples. On Feb. 3, 1785 he was named vice rector of the Convictorio de San Carlos in Lima; and on Aug. 16, 1786 he became rector, a position he held for 30 years.

Rodríguez de Mendoza is famous, first of all, in the field of education. He took a new approach to teaching, with the advice of Diego Cisneros and the help of Mariano Rivero and Juan Ignacio MORENO. They formed a triumvirate that transformed San Carlos by revising the curriculum. They did not make any substantial change in the courses of philosophy, rejecting the methodic doubt of Descartes and the analysis of Condillac as the definitive way for philosophical studies. Mathematics was added to the curriculum. Jurisprudence included natural law, international law, and constitutional law. The courses they settled on for the curriculum of the Convictorio were philosophy, theology, law, mathematics, and humanities. Rodríguez was to teach philosophy and theology; Rivero, natural law, international law, Newtonian physics, and Peruvian law; and Moreno, mathematics. The innovations brought a slow transformation in the education at San Carlos. Lecture halls were filled more and more, for not only the sons of the old conquistadores and the nobility of Lima and Peru came to study, but "from distant lands of all America students came to be instructed in literature, law, and to get new ideas." Rodríguez in later years said: "The Convictorio is a light that brightens the whole continent." It produced a galaxy of intellectual and patriotic leaders: Sánchez Carrión, Mariátegui, Pérez de Tudela, Olmedo, Muñoz, Pedemonte, Figuerola, Cuellar, Colmenares, Herrera, Oricaín, León, and Andueza.

[V. TRUJILLO MENA]

RODRÍGUEZ SANTIAGO, CARLOS MANUEL CECILIO, BL.

Lay founder of the Círculo de Cultura Cristiana (Circle of Christian Culture); b. Nov. 22, 1918, Caguas, Puerto Rico; d. there, July 13, 1963. Chali (Charlie), as he was known to his friends, was the second of the five children of Manuel Baudilio Rodríguez Rodríguez and Herminia Santiago Esteras. The home environment was indisputably pious: one sister became a Carmelite nun and his only brother a Benedictine monk and the first Puerto Rican abbot. He attended Catholic schools and earned a high school commercial diploma in 1939 despite frequent interruptions due to the chronic ulcerative colitis, which he suffered from age 13. In 1946, after working as an office clerk, he enrolled at the University of Puerto Rico, but continued illness forced him to leave school during his sophomore year. Nevertheless, he continued to study on his own, expanding his knowledge on a variety of topics.

While holding an administrative position at the Agricultural Experimental Station of the University of Puerto Rico at Río Piedras, he promoted his love of the Easter Vigil, the Paschal Mystery, and the liturgy within the Catholic University Center. There he founded the Circle of Christian Culture to enliven the faith of students and faculty, and the Te Deum Laudamus parochial choir in Caguas. Chali dedicated his salary to the poor, the funding of the circle, and publishing *Liturgy and Christian Culture* to promote understanding of the sacred liturgy.

During the last year of his life, while suffering rectal cancer, Chali experienced the "dark night of the soul"—a sense of abandonment by God; nevertheless, he clung to his faith in the Resurrection till the end. Uniquely his cause for beatification was initiated (Dec. 8, 1992) and propelled forward by the laity. Pope John Paul II declared him venerable (July 7, 1997), approved the miraculous cure of Deli Santana de Aguilóo's non-Hodgkins malignant lymphoma attributed to Charlie's intercession (Dec. 20, 1999), and beatified him (April 29, 2001). He is the first blessed from the Caribbean.

Bibliography: *L'Osservatore Romano*, Eng. Ed. 18 (2001), 1, 6–8; 19 (2001), 7, 10. Information from the Círculo Carlos M.

Rodríguez, Centro Universitario Católico, 10 Mariana Bracetti, San Juan, PR 00925-2201.

[K. I. RABENSTEIN]

RODRIGUEZ TÇUZU, JOÃO

Jesuit missionary, interpreter at the Japanese Court, and author; b. Cernancelhe, vicinity of Lamego, Portugal, *c.* 1562; d. Macau, Aug. 1, 1633. In 1577 Rodriguez (not to be confused with a contemporary Japanese missionary João Rodriguez Giram) came to Japan as a youth and entered the Society of Jesus, probably in 1580. There he studied the liberal arts, philosophy, and theology, and in 1594 he went to Macau to complete his theological course, was ordained, and returned to Japan (1596). Nagasaki, where he made his solemn profession on June 10, 1601, and was appointed province procurator, became his principal abode until 1610. Not only until the death of Toyotomi Hideyoshi (1598), but also during the reign of his successor, Tokugawa Iyeyasu, Rodriguez was official Portuguese interpreter at court; hence his name Tçuzu or Tçuxi (modern Tsuzu, Tsuji) or the Portuguese "O Interprete." He was therefore often at court, and at the wish of Iyeyasu he was for some years supervisor of the harbor of Nagasaki, which had been established by Christians (1571) and was in the possession of the Church (1580–87) until seized by Hideyoshi. Political pressure against the Jesuits forced Rodriguez's retirement to Macau in 1610. Between June 1613 and June 1615 he spent much time in the interior of China, and afterward many years at Macau. During this period Rodriguez sought the correct interpretation of the ancient Chinese name for God, and his study convinced him that the prevalent view was in error. Thus he was involved in a legitimate discussion of a question that later degenerated into the bitter CHINESE RITES CONTROVERSY. From 1628 onward he was again, with interruptions, in Inner China, accompanying Portuguese troops who were to support the Chinese Emperor against inroads of the Tartars.

The historical importance of João Rodriguez Tçuzu stems from his achievements as an influential interpreter and intermediary at the court of Japan, a philologist, and a historian and author. He is regarded as the best European authority on the Japanese language and culture in the 16th and 17th centuries. In place of M. de Couros, who was originally commissioned with this task, Rodriguez found time to write a history of the Church of Japan, *História da Igreja de Japam*. This enterprise was started *c.* 1620, and by 1628 a large part was finished. The work is significant for its descriptive chapters based on the personal experience of the author. In 1624 he added to the *História* an account of the bishops of Japan. João Rodriguez is believed to have taken part in compiling the *Vocabulário da Lingoa de Japam* (Nagasaki 1603–04). There also he printed the large *Arte da Lingoa de Japam* (1604–08), and in Macau, a smaller edition for beginners under the title *Arte breve da Lingoa japoa* (1620). His multivolume geographical work with its wealth of maps of the Far East is lost.

Bibliography: G. SCHURHAMMER, ''P. Johann Rodrigues Tçuzzu als Geschichtschreiber Japans,'' *Archivum historicum Societatis Jesu* 1 (1932) 23–40; repr. in his *Gesammelte Studien* (Rome 1962–65) 2:605–618. J. F. SCHÜTTE, ''A História inédita dos 'Bispos da Igreja do Japão' do Padre João Rodriguez Tçuzu, S.J,'' *Congresso Internacional de História dos Descobrimentos, Acta 5.1* (Lisbon 1961) 297–327. The *História da Igreja do Japão* has been pub. by J. DO AMARAL ABRANCHES PINTO (Macao 1954–56). T. DOI has pub. the large *Arte in Jap.* (Tokyo 1955) and is now preparing a Jap. ed. of the *História;* for helpful information on the tr. of the *Arte,* see the review in *Archivum historicum Societatis Jesu* 26 (1957) 315.

[J. F. SCHÜTTE]

RODRÍGUEZ ZORRILLA, JOSÉ SANTIAGO

Chilean bishop and politician; b. Santiago,1752; d. Madrid, 1832. He studied with the Jesuits in Santiago and at the universities of San Felipe in Santiago and San Marcos in Lima. He was ordained and received the doctorate in theology in 1775, and in 1802, the doctorate in both civil and canon law. He was a professor in the University of San Felipe and twice held the post of rector (1788–90, 1803–05). Before ordination he had accompanied Bishop Alday to the provincial council at Lima (1771–73); and since he kept the confidence of succeeding bishops, he held a number of ecclesiastical positions, being appointed vicar capitular in 1807. When he opposed the formation of the junta in 1810 and did not recognize the appointment of Bp. MARTÍNEZ DE ALDUNATE, his own appointment as vicar was not renewed. Rodríguez Zorrilla objected to the elimination of the word ''Roman'' in reference to the title of the Church in the constitution of 1812, and the government of Chile retaliated by refusing to recognize his designation as bishop-elect of Santiago, which had been made by the Spanish council of regency. Upon the restoration of Spanish power, he was consecrated in 1816. However, he took part in the persecution of the Chilean patriots (1814–17); and although he supported the peaceful entrance of the victorious Chileans into the capital in 1817, he was exiled until 1821. He returned to his see in 1822 and managed to hold it for two years, although the various governments were suspicious of his loyalty. He did not cooperate with the unsuccessful MUZI mission of 1824, and the civil authorities took over

the government of the see, exiling Rodríguez Zorrilla to Spain in 1825. He lived in Madrid, bereft of income, while the Holy See appointed an administrator for his diocese, leaving him his rights as bishop. Just before his death, he had obtained restoration of his income and his civil rights and was preparing to return to Chile. His remains were taken home in 1852. Because of his great involvement in politics, he had left the diocese practically without guidance for many years during a crucial period of Chilean history.

Bibliography: C. SILVA COTAPOS, *Don, José Santiago Rodríguez Zorrilla* (Santiago de Chile 1915). L. F. PRIETO DEL RÍO, *Diccionario biográfico del clero secular de Chile* (Santiago de Chile 1922).

[W. HANISCH]

ROE, ALBAN (BARTHOLOMEW), ST.

Benedictine martyr; b. Suffolk, 1583; executed at Tyburn, Jan. 21, 1642. As an undergraduate at Cambridge he was an ardent Protestant. A visit to a recusant named David in St. Alban's prison, ostensibly to convert him, instead unsettled Roe's own Protestant convictions; he returned to Cambridge very disturbed. After reading, and conferring with Catholic priests, he was received into the Church. In November 1607 Roe applied for admission to the English College at Douai; he was accepted in February 1608. The college was going through a difficult period, and perhaps there was still something of the conceited undergraduate about Roe. In any event, he was dismissed for insubordination in January 1611. Still determined to be a priest and armed with a testimonial from his fellow students, Roe arrived in 1613 at Dieulouard (later Ampleforth) to try his vocation as a Benedictine. He was professed in October 1614, taking the name Alban. The following year he was ordained, and the same year he left for Paris to help found the community of St. Edmund (Woolhampton).

By now Father Alban was no longer a brash undergraduate, and his superiors judged him ready for the English mission. He was caught in 1618, fairly soon after his arrival in England, and imprisoned. Roe was kept in New Prison, Maiden Lane, until 1623, when the Spanish ambassador procured his release. He was banished and warned that if he returned he would die as a traitor. Nevertheless, after a short stay at St. Gregory's, Douai (later Downside), he returned. Within two years he was again apprehended and, by a strange turn of fate, committed to jail in St. Albans, the same prison in which his encounter with the recusant had occurred. Friends succeeded in obtaining his transfer to the Fleet Prison in London. He then began a long prison apostolate. Charles I was a relatively lenient monarch, and the Fleet, a lax prison, so that Roe was able not only to minister to the Catholics inside the prison but to go out on parole. This arrangement ended at the time of the anti-Catholic Long Parliament. Roe was transferred to Newgate Prison and brought to trial on Jan. 19, 1642. After an initial refusal, Roe consented to be tried by a jury and was charged as a priest and seducer of the people. He was sentenced to be hanged, drawn, and quartered. On January 21 he said Mass before the other prisoners and made a short speech to them before his execution. He was beatified on Dec. 15, 1929 and canonized on Oct. 25, 1970, as one of the ENGLAND, SCOTLAND, AND WALES, MARTYRS OF.

Feast: May 4; Oct. 25.

Bibliography: B. CAMM, *Nine Martyr Monks . . .* (London 1931). R. CHALLONER, *Memoirs of Missionary Priests*, ed. J. H. POLLEN (rev. ed. London 1924). J. MCCANN and C. CARYELWES, eds., *Ampleforth and Its Origins* (London 1952). J. FORBES, *Blessed Alban Roe* (Postulation Pamphlet; London 1960). J. H. POLLEN, *Acts of English Martyrs* (London 1891).

[G. FITZHERBERT]

ROEMER, THEODORE

Historian; b. Appleton, Wis., Jan. 19, 1889; d. Mt. Calvary, Wis., Jan. 7, 1953. He attended St. Joseph School, Appleton, and the preparatory seminary, St. Lawrence College, Mt. Calvary, Wisconsin. Professed in the Capuchin Order in 1907 and ordained by Archbishop Sebastian G. Messmer on July 13, 1913, he began teaching at St. Lawrence College in 1915. From 1919 to 1921 he taught canon law at St. Anthony Seminary, Marathon, Wisconsin. After several years of pastoral activity in the Milwaukee archdiocese, he entered the Catholic University of America, Washington, D.C., where he specialized in American Catholic church history. Upon the completion of his master's thesis, *The Leopoldine Foundation and the Catholic Church in the United States (1829–1839)*, he devoted a year to study at the University of Louvain, Belgium, and to research in Germany and Italy. Returning to the Catholic University of America, he was awarded a doctorate in 1933. His doctoral study, *The Ludwig-Missionverein and the Church in the United States (1838–1918)*, traced the historical contribution made by the Ludwig Missionverein of Munich to the progress of the Catholic Church in the United States. From 1933 until his death, Roemer taught at St. Lawrence College. He was the author of *Pioneer Capuchin Letters* (1936), *Ten Decades of Alms* (1942), *St. Joseph in Appleton* (1943), *The Alumni, St. Lawrence College* (1946), and a textbook, *The Catholic Church in the United States* (1950).

[R. DUSICK]

ROGATION DAYS

By ancient tradition in the Roman rite, the historical days on which a procession of penance and supplication was held. Because the LITANY of the Saints was sung during the procession, the name for these days in ancient documents is *Major* or *Minor Litanies*.

The title Major Litany is not given in opposition to the Minor Litany, but because of the greater solemnity of the occasion, the feast of St. Mark, (April 25). Neither the origin nor the theme of the rogation observance has anything to do with St. Mark. Of strictly Roman origin, the Major Litany was instituted to supplant an already existing pagan ceremony called the Robigalia held on this day. The pagan Romans went in procession down the *via Flaminia* as far as the Milvian Bridge and there offered the entrails of a dog and a sheep to the god Robigus. The objective they sought was to protect the sprouting crops from blight caused by rust (*robigo*). Chanting the Litany of the Saints, Christians followed the same processional route but ended it at St. Peter's basilica. The name Major Litany appeared for the first time during the pontificate of Gregory the Great (d. 604).

The Minor Litanies were begun around 470 by Mamertus, bishop of Vienne, France. Several days of penitential procession were held to invoke divine protection against a recurrence of the earthquake that had recently wrought such havoc in the city. This custom soon spread to other French localities and even to Rome under Leo III (d. 816). These processions were held on each of the three days that immediately precede Ascension Thursday.

See Also: PROCESSIONS, RELIGIOUS.

Bibliography: A. ADAM, *The Liturgical Year: Its History and Meaning after the Reform of the Liturgy* (Collegeville 1981). A. NOCENT, *The Liturgical Year*, 4 v. (Collegeville 1977). T. J. TALLEY, *The Origins of the Liturgical Year*, rev. ed. (Collegeville 1992). I. H. DALMAIS, P. JOUNEL, and A. G. MARTIMORT, *The Liturgy and Time: The Church at Prayer* v. 4 (Collegeville 1992).

[J. H. MILLER/EDS.]

ROGER BACON

English Franciscan scholastic philosopher and experimentalist; b. Ilchester, Somerset, before 1220 (according to some, 1214); d. *c.* 1292.

Life. He came of minor nobility. Having learned the rudiments of grammar and logic, probably at Oxford, he received his degree in arts from the University of Paris by 1237. In Paris he lectured on the new Aristotelian learning ''longer than any other master,'' at least until

Roger Bacon. (Archive Photos)

1247. Most of his commentaries and lecture notes from this period have not survived, but to this period probably belong the published notes on the *Physics* and *Metaphysics* of ARISTOTLE, the *De plantis* and *De causis* of pseudo-Aristotle, and the *Summulae logicales* of JOHN XXI (*Opera hactenus inedita,* ed. R. Steele, Oxford 1905–40). In 1247 he relinquished his teaching position in Paris to devote considerable time and money to experiments, languages, "secret" books, instruments, and astronomical tables. For the next ten years (1247–57) he studied and promoted these branches of learning, which he felt were being neglected by contemporaries of greater influence and prestige. The intensity of his labors and the peculiarities of his own personality brought him near to a physical breakdown. He entered the Franciscan Order in England probably in 1257. In the order he did not have the prestige he had expected or the freedom he had desired to write and lecture. Finding it impossible to communicate, he gave up in despair (*Op. tert.* 13). Return of illness necessitated a two-year respite from all serious work. When his health improved, circumstances worsened, for he seems to have become an advocate of the eschatological views of Abbot JOACHIM OF FIORE.

Having made the acquaintance of Raymond of Laon, a cleric in the service of Cardinal Guy le Gos de Foulques, later CLEMENT IV, Bacon insisted that the whole of current education needed to be revised and intimated that the necessary revision could be found in his writings. These views were related to the cardinal, who, on becoming pope in February 1265, demanded to see these writings. Bacon had been misunderstood, for he spoke not about works already completed but about those he could write if he had the necessary freedom, leisure, and money. On June 22, 1266, Clement again wrote to Bacon commanding him to send without delay and as secretly as possible the writings previously requested, notwithstanding contrary commands of any prelate or constitutions of his order. Bacon was unable to clarify the situation either by direct letters or by his messenger, William of Bonecor. Clement was still under the impression that all that had to be done was to make a legible copy of an existing work, a major contribution to knowledge and to the welfare of the Church. Since secrecy was imposed and funds were unavailable, Bacon used various subterfuges to obtain funds to compose, single-handed and without knowledge of his superiors, an encyclopedia of all the sciences, called *Opus maius* (ed. J. H. Bridges, 3 v. Oxford 1897–1900), which he sent to Clement in 1267 through his favorite pupil, John (see Little, *Grey Friars* 211). The manuscript was in four separate packets, including multiple diagrams, a map of the world (now lost), and a concave lens made at great expense. The work was divided into seven parts: causes and remedies of human ignorance and error; the services that sane philosophy can render to theology; necessity and nature of languages, mathematics, optics, and experimental science; and a discussion of moral philosophy. This was followed, prior to November 1268, by the *Opus minus* and *Opus tertium* (ed. J. S. Brewer, London 1859), which are synopses and developments of various sections of the main work.

For Bacon, languages, mathematics, and experimental sciences were of far greater importance to theology and the Church than the four popular sciences of grammar, logic, natural philosophy, and metaphysics, cultivated by the "moderns." For him, nothing could be known without a knowledge of Greek, Hebrew, Arabic, and Chaldaean; many Latin words currently used could not be understood without a knowledge of Greek. In later years Bacon even wrote Greek and Hebrew grammars to overcome what he called an abysmal ignorance in the schools. Similarly, he considered mathematics a key to all the sciences and scorned all who failed to recognize this, even though Bacon himself was no mathematician. He made many suggestions concerning Biblical studies, chronology, reform of the calendar, geography, apologetics, ALCHEMY, and ASTROLOGY. Deeply influenced by the pseudo-Aristotelian treatise *Secretum secretorum,* he ardently defended alchemy and astrology. Although an ardent advocate of optics and the experimental sciences, his contribution to these sciences was negligible.

For many years Bacon idolized ROBERT GROSSE-TESTE and ALEXANDER OF HALES because the former cultivated mathematics and languages and the latter gave up all worldly possessions to become a Franciscan friar. Later he blamed both for bringing about a deterioration in theology. He was also severely critical of BONAVENTURE, minister general of the Franciscans. He was particularly resentful of ALBERT THE GREAT and THOMAS AQUINAS, who "presumed to investigate philosophy by themselves without a teacher" and became "masters in theology and philosophy before they were disciples." In his *Compendium philosophiae* (c. 1272) he returned to the treatment of his cherished languages, mathematics, optics, alchemy, and experimental sciences. The "moderns" with few exceptions, he wrote, especially the "boy" theologians of the Dominican and Franciscan Orders, despised and persecuted these sciences, for they entered religious life before the age of 20 without the benefit of a proper university training. At that time Bacon seems to have enjoyed considerable freedom to begin an encyclopedic work, only partially completed, comprising grammar, logic, mathematics, natural philosophy, metaphysics, and moral philosophy. The surviving sections, *Communia naturalia* and *Communia mathematica,* are the maturest expression of his thought.

Whatever freedom he did enjoy was brought to an end by Jerome of Ascoli (Pope NICHOLAS IV), minister general of the order (1274–79), who, prompted by many reports, condemned the teachings because they contained certain suspect novelties (*propter aliquas novitates suspectas*). These novelties were undoubtedly Joachite. Jerome even wrote to the Pope, Nicholas III, so that by his authority this dangerous doctrine (*illa doctrina periculosa*) might be completely extirpated. According to the *Chronicle of the 24 Generals* (*Archivum Franciscanum historicum* 3:360) Bacon himself was imprisoned, probably between 1277 and 1279. In the last of his writings, *Compendium studii theologiae* (1292), Bacon castigated the vices and defects of the whole of Christendom as well as the decline of theological studies in the schools of his day. A long tradition claims that he was buried in Oxford.

Teachings. Bacon was one of the earliest masters to teach the text of Aristotle in Paris. Like his Parisian master, ROBERT KILWARDBY, he interpreted Aristotle with the aid of Platonic sources, notably AVICENNA and AVICEBRON. Therefore Bacon never appreciated the true nature of Aristotelian philosophy (*see* ARISTOTELIANISM). Repeatedly insisting that "without mathematics no science can be had" (*Opus tertium,* ed. Brewer, 35, 64, 57), Bacon believed that the principles of natural science are

to be found in mathematics. He considered the study of mathematics second in importance only to that of languages (*Opus maius* 1:97–108; *Opus tertium* 105–120); he even called it *prima scientiarum*. His view of the hylomorphic composition of all creatures, spiritual and corporeal, by a succession of forms is identical to that of Kilwardby and other Platonizing Aristotelians of the 13th century (*see* SCHOLASTICISM, 1). Bacon identified the agent intellect with God and adapted the illumination theory of AUGUSTINE to his own view of Aristotle. While retaining the basic views of AUGUSTINIANISM, insisting on the dynamic and normative role of universal ideas (*virtus regitiva universi*), he emphasized more than most 13th-century schoolmen the primacy of the individual, the natural termination of knowledge. This led him to appreciate the importance of experimental science. Hence in Bacon's philosophy natural phenomena are to be studied sedulously with experimentation and the aid of mathematics. Mathematics itself leads to metaphysics and the study of God.

Although Bacon was not a theologian, he rightly denounced the use of Peter Lombard's *Sentences* by masters in theology. Instead of lecturing on the Bible, as had been the custom, Alexander of Hales and RICHARD FISHACRE began to lecture on the *Sentences*. Bacon rightly saw this as a deterioration of sacred science. Moreover, he encouraged the study of languages indispensable for understanding the sacred text.

Influence. Bacon had no disciples to continue his work either inside or outside the Franciscan Order. Immediate posterity all but forgot his name. However, with the origin of modern science in the 17th century and renewed pride at Oxford for medieval Mertonians, Bacon acquired new though unfounded fame as an inventor, experimentalist, and precursor of modern experimental science. Fantastic legends grew rapidly and were repeated by countless authors. For this reason it is difficult to separate fact from fiction in historical accounts of Bacon's life.

Bibliography: J. AERSTEN and A. SPEER, eds., *Raum and Raumvorsellungen im Mittelalter* (Berlin 1998). G. JEANMART, "La theorie baconnienne du language est-elle augustienne," *Revue des sciences philosophiques et theologiqes* 82 (1998) 415–30. J. HACKETT, "Roger Bacon," in *Individuation in Scholasticism* (Albany 1994) 117–139; "Averroes and Roger Bacon on the Harmony of Religion and Philosophy," in *A Straight Path: Studies in Medieval Philosophy and Culture* (Washington, D.C. 1988) 98–112. J. LONG, "Roger Bacon on the Nature and Place of Angels," *Vivarium* 5 (1997) 283–314. G. MOLLAND, "Roger Bacon and the Hermetic Tradition in Medieval Science," *Vivarium* 31 (1993) 140–60.

[J. A. WEISHEIPL]

ROGER DE PONT L'ÉVÊQUE

Archbishop of YORK and supporter of HENRY II in the great quarrel with Thomas BECKET; d. York, England, Nov. 21, 1181. Of Norman birth, Roger was a contemporary of Becket in the household of THEOBALD, archbishop of Canterbury. He became archdeacon of Canterbury (1148), and a royal chaplain entrusted with business on King STEPHEN's behalf at the papal Curia, before being consecrated archbishop of the northern province in 1154. Toward Becket, Roger was personally antipathetic, and his antagonism as archbishop led him to support King Henry II and to revive the claims of York as against CANTERBURY, notably in his coronation of the young King Henry in 1170. For this act Becket secured from Pope ALEXANDER III a bull suspending Roger from his office for infringing the prerogative of Canterbury. Following the murder of Becket, Roger was reinstated as archbishop after being absolved from complicity in the saint's death. A persistent champion of the rights of his see, Roger renewed the jurisdictional quarrel with the new archbishop, RICHARD OF CANTERBURY, and pressed, unsuccessfully, for recognition of the primacy of York over the Church in Scotland.

Bibliography: J. C. ROBERTSON, ed., *Materials for the History of Thomas Becket*, 7 v. in *Rerum Britannicarum medii aevi scriptores* (also called Rolls Series) 244 v. (London 1858–96) 1875–85, *passim*. W. H. HUTTON, *The Dictionary of National Biography from Earliest Times to 1900*, 63 v. (London 1885–1900) 17:109–111. D. KNOWLES, *The Episcopal Colleagues of Archbishop Thomas Becket* (Cambridge, Eng. 1951).

[R. S. HOYT]

ROGER LE FORT, BL.

Bishop and confessor; b. Ternes, Limousin; d. March 1, 1367 or 1368. He studied law at the University of Orléans. He became a canon at Rouen (1316), and was cathedral dean in Bourges (1317) and later professor of civil and canon law at Orléans. Successively bishop of Orléans (1321) and of Limoges (1328), he was finally appointed archbishop of Bourges in 1343. Zealous in the administration of his office and austere in his personal life, he established a hospital at Bourges and founded the Celestine priory at Ternes. He authorized the exhuming of the relics of ODILO OF CLUNY (1345). A benefactor of the poor, he ordered that his goods be distributed to them on his death. He is buried in Bourges cathedral. He is the author of sermons and juridical commentaries.

Feast: March 1.

Bibliography: *Acta Sanctorum* March 1:119–122. J. B. L. ROY-PIERREFITTE, *Études historiques sur les monastères du Limousin et de la Marche* (Guéret 1865) 67–80, 85–91. A. A. THOMAS, *Mélanges d'archéologie et d'histoire* 4 (1884) 31–34. J. L. BAUDOT and L. CHAUSSIN, *Vies des saints et des bienheureux selon l'ordre du calendrier avec l'historique des fêtes,* ed. by the Benedictines of Paris, 12 v. (Paris 1935–56) 3:26.

[D. ANDREINI]

ROGER MARSTON

Franciscan theologian; b. *c.* 1245; d. *c.* 1303. Marston studied at Paris under JOHN PECKHAM, probably between 1269 and 1272. There, *c.* 1270, he was present with THOMAS AQUINAS and Peckham at a vehement theological disputation presided over by GERARD OF ABBEVILLE at the inception of the precentor of Peronne. He was the 13th minister of the English Franciscan province, probably between 1292 and 1298. He was buried at Norwich.

Among his works are: (1) *Commentarius in Sententias,* date not yet identified; (2) *Quaestiones disputatae, c.* 1282–84; *De emanatione aeterna,* qq. 7; *De lapsu naturae humanae,* qq. 2; *De anima,* qq. 10 [ed. Quaracchi 1932; cf. *De humanae cognitionis ratione* (Quaracchi 1883) 197–220]; and (3) *Quodlibet 1–4, c.* 1282–86 (*see* Glorieux L, 2.264–269). Of these, *Quodl.* 3.25 (*De privilegiis O.P. et O.F.M. audiendi confessiones*) is edited by F. Delorme, *Studi Francescani* 31 (1934) 331–335; *Quodl.* 4.15–17 (*De dilectione, gaudiis et doloribus B. M. V.*), by A. Emmen, *Franziskanische Studien* 39 (1957) 210–214.

Marston's teachings are representative of English Augustinianism with borrowings from Arabic philosophers, principally from AVICENNA. He quotes Aristotle's *De anima* in the Arabic-Latin translation. Defending traditional Augustinian doctrines against the growing Aristotelianism, on almost all contested points he takes up an energetic, sometimes even reactionary, position against Aquinas. In his *Quodl.* 4.15–17, he shows a strong dependence on the *De excellentia B. V. M.* (*Patrologia Latina,* ed. J. P. Migne [Paris 1878–90] 159:557–580) of EADMER OF CANTERBURY, which he ascribes to ANSELM OF CANTERBURY. Though D. L. Douie is too severe in his judgment [*Archbishop Peckham* (Oxford 1952) 13, 284–285], the truth seems to be that Roger was conservative, somewhat small-minded, and somewhat unoriginal as a theologian; yet his doctrine is valuable in understanding many points of Duns Scotus's system.

Bibliography: A. PEREZ, *La Materia de Avicena a la Escuela Franciscana: Avicena, Averroes, Tomas de Aquino, Beunaventura, Pecham, Marston, Olivo, Mediavilla, Duns Escoto* (Maracaibo, Venezuela 1998) bibliography, 463–77. R. HISSETTE, "Esse–Essentia Chez Roger Marston," in *Sapientiae Doctrina; Melanges de Theologie et de Litterature Medievals Offerts a Dom Hildebrand* (Leuven 1980) 110–118. R. MARSTON, *Quodlibeta Quatour ad Fidem Codicum nunc Primum Edita Studio et Cura* (Rome 1968).

J.A. MERINO, *Historia de la Filosofia Franciscana* (Madrid 1993) 383–84.

[A. EMMEN]

ROGER OF ÉLAN, BL.

English Cistercian; d. Jan. 4, 1162–75. He joined the Cistercians at Lorroy-en-Berry, Diocese of Bourges, France, some time after 1129. In 1148 he was made first abbot of Élan, founded by Withier, Lord of Rethel, in the Diocese of Reims. His vita, written some time after his death, is based merely on tradition. It records that Abp. Henry of Reims (1162–75), brother of King Louis VII, not liking the bread offered to him on a visit to the abbey, granted as much land in Attigny as could be plowed by five yoke of oxen in a year to provide better grain. Miracles apart, no precise details of Roger's life or death are available. His relics, although partly dispersed during the French Revolution, are still the object of pilgrimage.

Feast: Jan. 4.

Bibliography: *Acta Sanctorum* Jan. 1:182–185. *Bibliotheca hagiographica latina antiquae et mediae aetatis,* 2 vol. (Brussels 1898–1901) 2:7288. *Cistercienser-Chronik* 27 (1915) 13. G. MÜLLER, *ibid.* 33 (1921) 161–164. J. L. BAUDOT and L. CHAUSSIN, *Vies des saints et des bienheureux selon l'ordre du calendrier avec l'historique des fêtes,* 12 vol. (Paris 1935–56) 1:73.

[C. H. TALBOT]

ROGER OF NOTINGHAM

Franciscan theologian; fl. 1343–58. A member of the Oxford friary, Roger was a bachelor in theology by 1343. Around the feast of SS. Peter and Paul (June 29) of that year, he completed a logical work on insoluble propositions, *Insolubilia* (Brit. Mus., MS Harley 3243, fol. 49–50v). According to him all true "insolubles" are false, although many propositions are only mistakenly considered to be "insolubles." While it is certain that he lectured on the *Sentences,* only an "introitus" or introduction to the second book is extant. Since he is not listed among the first 67 lectors of the Oxford friary, it is probable that he became master in theology after 1350. In 1358 he was one of the five FRANCISCANS of that friary licensed by SIMON ISLIP to preach in the Archdiocese of Canterbury. The extant theological fragment suggests that he followed the tradition of ROBERT GROSSETESTE, BONAVENTURE, RICHARD RUFUS, and DUNS SCOTUS.

Bibliography: A. B. EMDEN, *A Biographical Register of the University of Oxford to A. D. 1500* (Oxford 1957–59) 2:1377. E. A. SYNAN, "The 'Introitus ad sententias' of Roger Nottingham, O.F.M.," *Mediaeval Studies* 25 (1963) 259–279.

[J. A. WEISHEIPL]

ROGER OF SALISBURY

Bishop, chief minister and regent of Henry I and Stephen; d. Salisbury, England, December 1139. This obscure Norman clerk attached himself to the Conqueror's son, Henry, and administered his finances so well that the prince made him one of his principal advisers. After his coronation in 1100, HENRY I appointed Roger chancellor of England, then bishop of SALISBURY in 1101. Although Roger strengthened the landed endowment and educational facilities of his diocese and founded a number of priories, his tight control of other monasteries and his domination of the Canterbury archiepiscopal elections in 1114 and 1123 caused contemporary monastic chroniclers to hold him in low esteem. Yet his undoubted executive abilities pleased Henry, who designated him justiciar of all England. As justiciar, "second only to the King," he administered the legal and financial apparatus of the government and encouraged such innovations as the system of itinerant justices, the Board of Exchequer, the Pipe Rolls, and an improved coinage. After 1120 he also acted as regent during Henry's visits to Normandy. Roger swore in 1126 to support the Empress Matilda as heir to England's crown, but in 1135 he helped Stephen of Blois seize the throne. At first, King STEPHEN handsomely rewarded Roger, but finding himself badly in need of funds, he captured the aged prelate in June 1139 and confiscated his great castles and wealth. Roger, failing to obtain redress in a church council, returned to Sarum (Salisbury) shorn of his power and died there a broken man. He was one of the first of those ecclesiastical statesmen who, like Cardinals Wolsey and Richlieu, used their priestly position as a buttress for political power.

Bibliography: WILLIAM OF MALMESBURY, *The Historia novella,* tr. K. R. POTTER (New York 1955). C. L. KINGSFORD, *The Dictionary of National Biography from the Earliest Times to 1900* 17:103–106. E. J. KEALEY, *Roger, Bishop of Salisbury and Chief Justiciar of All England* (Doctoral diss. unpub. Johns Hopkins U. 1962). *Gesta Stephani: The Deeds of Stephen,* ed. and tr. K. R. POTTER (New York 1955).

[E. J. KEALEY]

ROGER OF SICILY

Roger I, Great Count of Sicily and Calabria from 1072 to June 22, 1101; b. 1031; d. Mileto (Calabria). He was the youngest son of the Norman TANCRED. Roger joined his brother Robert Guiscard in Apulia and took part in his expeditions against Arab Sicily. After the fall of Palermo (1072), he carried on alone and brought the conquest to a successful end (1091), becoming the true organizer of the new Sicilian state. When he returned Sicily to the Roman Church, Pope URBAN II granted him the apostolic legateship for Sicily, later called the *Monarchia sicula.* Roger introduced feudal landholding cautiously. He did not interfere with existing laws and customs. He granted religious freedom to Greek Christians, Jews, and Muslims. He enriched the treasury by making the export of grain to the Muslim state of North Africa a state monopoly.

Roger II, count, King of Sicily, 1101 to Feb. 26, 1154; b. 1095; d. Palermo. He was the son of Roger I and Adelaide. He effectively united Sicily with the Norman mainland possessions (1128). In the papal schism of 1130, he supported the antipope Anacletus II, who crowned him King of Sicily, Apulia, and Calabria on Christmas Day, 1130, at Palermo. He defeated the European coalitions against him and gained the recognition of Pope INNOCENT II (1139). Instead of participating in the second crusade, he raided Byzantium and founded a short-lived colonial empire in Tunisia. He introduced a new code of law (the Assizes of Ariano, 1140), centralized finances, and named agents of the central government for all districts of the mainland and island. His statesmanlike qualities, his rational approach to problems of government, and his genius for diplomacy and strategy marked him as "the first modern ruler." He is credited with that fusion of Western, Byzantine, and Arabic culture found in the Norman art of southern Italy and Sicily.

Bibliography: Sources. GAUFREDUS MALATERRA, *De rebus gestis Rogerii Calabriae et Siciliare comitis,* ed. E. PONTIERI. L. A. MURATORI, *Rerum italicarum scriptores, 500–1500* (Città di Castello 1900). ALEXANDER OF TELESE, *De rebus gestis Rogerii Siciliae regis,* in G. DEL RE, ed., *Cronisti e Scrittori,* 2 v. (Naples 1845–68) 1:85–146. M. AMARI, *Biblioteca Arabo-Sicula,* 2 v. (Turin & Rome 1880–81). **Literature.** For extensive bibliography see P. F. KEHR, *Regesta Pontificum Romanorum. Italia Pontificia,* 8 v. (Berlin 1906–35) 8:1–5 and H. WIERUSZOWSKI, "The Norman Kingdom of Sicily and the Crusades," *History of the Crusades,* ed. K. M. SETTON, 2 v. (Philadelphia 1962) v. 2.

[H. WIERUSZOWSKI]

ROGER OF SWYNESHED

English Benedictine, logician, and natural philosopher; d. Glastonbury Abbey, Somerset, shortly before May 12, 1365. He has been confused with the Merton mathematician, RICHARD OF SWYNESHED. Roger had no known connection with Merton College, but he attended Oxford early in the 1330s. He was probably a regent in arts (1330–35) and then became a master of theology, presumably of Oxford. Since it is not known when he became a Benedictine monk, he may have incepted as a secular master. He wrote *De obligationibus et insolubilibus,* two treatises on logic often found together, some time before 1335. These were used as textbooks at some Conti-

nental universities in the late Middle Ages (*see* LOGIC, HISTORY OF). Between 1328 and 1338 he wrote a work on physics, *De motibus naturalibus,* concerned in part with "the possible proportions of velocities in moving bodies," which had an importance in medieval science that is not yet fully appreciated. He is supposed to have written a work entitled *De consequentiis,* on the logic of consequences. If he wrote any works on theology they have not yet been identified. Friar Richard Trevytlam, in his defense of the mendicant friars against the monks, *De laude universitatis oxoniae* (*c.* 1367–70), upholds Roger, "subtilis Swynyshed" of good memory, as an ideal monk.

Bibliography: J. A. WEISHEIPL, "R. Swyneshed, O.S.B., Logician . . . ," *Oxford Studies Presented to Daniel Callus* (Oxford 1964) 231–252, differentiates between Richard, John, and Roger Swyneshed and corrects A. B. EMDEN, *A Biographical Register of the Scholars of the University of Oxford to A.D. 1500,* 3 v. (Oxford 1957–59) 3:1837.

[F. D. BLACKLEY]

ROGER OF TODI, BL.

Franciscan; b. Todi (Umbria), Italy; d. Jan. 5, 1237. Roger, one of the earliest companions of St. FRANCIS OF ASSISI, was received into the FRANCISCANS by Francis himself in 1216. He distinguished himself as one of the first Franciscans in Spain. Francis then assigned him as spiritual director of the convent in Rieti, Italy, where (Bl.) PHILIPPA MARERI and her companions established themselves under the rule of (St.) CLARE OF ASSISI. Roger was with Philippa when she died and he pronounced her eulogy. While Roger was still alive, his friend, Pope GREGORY IX, called him a saint; Gregory also approved Roger's cult for the city of Todi, where his remains were enshrined. Francis characterized Roger as an exemplar of charity (*Speculum perfectionis,* ch. 85); Thomas of Pavia, in his *Dialogus* written *c.* 1245, assigned 16 miracles to him. In 1751, Benedict XIV approved his feast for the Franciscan order though today it is celebrated only by the Franciscans in the province of Umbria.

Feast: Jan. 14.

Bibliography: *Acta Sanctorum* (Antwerp 1643– ; Venice 1734– ; Paris 1863–) March 1:415–417. B. MAZZARA, *Leggendario francescano,* 12 v. (Venice 1721–22) v.1. LÉON DE CLARY, *Lives of the Saints . . . of Saint Francis,* 4 v. (Taunton, Eng. 1885–87) 1:442–443. A. BUTLER, *The Lives of the Saints,* rev. ed. H. THURSTON and D. ATTWATER (New York, 1956) 1:88.

[J. J. SMITH]

ROGER OF WORCESTER

Bishop; b. *c.* 1133; d. Tours, France, Aug. 9, 1179. He was the son of Earl Robert of Gloucester (d. 1147) and grandson of HENRY I of England. He was educated at Bristol with his cousin (later HENRY II) and at Paris under ROBERT OF MELUN. Roger doubtless owed his swift promotion to his royal connections, but was Thomas BECKET's choice for the See of WORCESTER, and was consecrated by him at CANTERBURY on Aug. 23, 1164. The most spiritual, steadfast, and courageous of Becket's supporters, "the morning star which illuminates our sad story," he was uniquely loyal to his consecrator without entirely losing the favor of King Henry II. From 1167 he shared the archbishop's exile, and was absent from England in 1170 when Becket was murdered, returning only in 1172. Before and after Becket's martyrdom, he unswervingly upheld the principles for which the archbishop contended, but with moderation and concern for the authority of the king. His work as bishop and canonist was of outstanding importance, and he was an eminent judge-delegate who, with BARTHOLOMEW OF EXETER, was described by Pope ALEXANDER III as one of "the twin lights" illuminating the English Church. Roger left a striking record of his judicial activities in the primitive English DECRETAL collections from the mid-1170s, whereas his surviving *acta* throw light on his concern for his diocese. He was present at RICHARD OF CANTERBURY's synod at Westminster in 1175 and possibly at the Third LATERAN COUNCIL of 1179.

Bibliography: A. MOREY, *Bartholomew of Exeter: Bishop and Canonist* (Cambridge 1937). M. G. HALL (Mrs. M. Cheney), *Roger of Worcester: 1164–79* (B. Litt. diss. unpub. Oxford 1940). M. CHENEY, "The Compromise of Avranches of 1172 and the Spread of Canon Law in England," *English Historical Review* 56 (1941): 177–197. D. KNOWLES, *The Episcopal Colleagues of Archbishop Thomas Becket* (Cambridge, Eng. 1951). C. DUGGAN, *Twelfth-Century Decretal Collections and Their Importance in English History* (London 1963).

[C. DUGGAN]

ROGERS, MARY JOSEPH, MOTHER

Foundress of MARYKNOLL SISTERS of St. Dominic; b. Boston, Massachusetts, Oct. 27, 1882; d. New York City, Oct. 9, 1955. Mary Josephine Rogers ("Mollie"), the daughter of Abraham and Mary Josephine (Plummer) Rogers, grew up in a closely knit family of eight children. Following her public schooling in Boston, Massachusetts, she attended Smith College in Northampton, Massachusetts, graduating in 1905.

During her college years, she was struck by the missionary zeal of the Protestant students involved in the Student Volunteer Movement. After graduation, she returned to Smith College on a teaching fellowship in the college's biology department. A Protestant colleague urged Mollie to form a Bible Study Class for the Catholic students, and following the deeper yearnings of her own heart, she chose to do a Mission Study Class. Her search for mission materials led her to Fr. James A. Walsh at the Society for the Propagation of Faith Office in Boston, Massachusetts. She left her academic post at Smith in 1908 and began teaching in the Boston public schools. This enabled her to give all her spare time to collaborating with Walsh in the publication of the new mission magazine, *The Field Afar*.

In 1911, Walsh and Rev. Thomas Frederick Price founded the Catholic Foreign Mission Society of America (*see* MARYKNOLL FATHERS AND BROTHERS). Mollie organized a group of women who offered their services as secretaries to this new mission society in 1912. Mollie was chosen leader, and within a few years the number of women had grown. By 1920 they received canonical recognition as "The Foreign Mission Sisters of St. Dominic." A year later, the first group of sisters went to South China. As foundress of the community, Mollie, now known as Mother Mary Joseph (Rogers), became the first mother general of the congregation and remained in office until 1946.

Mission shaped every facet of life. In the early 1930s Rogers founded a teachers' college for her sisters at the motherhouse in Maryknoll, New York. A contemplative community was firmly established within the congregation; she held out the ideal that every Maryknoll Sister be a contemplative in the midst of an active mission life and encouraged the gifting of each sister. Cooperating with Bp. Francis X. FORD's plan of using sisters to carry the gospel message to the village women of Kaying, South China, she was also active in establishing centers to train indigenous personnel as catechists, nurses, teachers, and religious women. Impelled by her missionary spirit and charism, the congregation established international missions with a wide range of educational, medical, social and pastoral ministries. At the time of her death on Oct. 9, 1955, the congregation was actively serving the missions in nineteen countries in Africa, Asia, Latin America, the Central Pacific Islands, and the U.S.

Bibliography: C. KENNEDY, *To the Uttermost Parts of the Earth: The Spirit and Charism of Mary Josephine Rogers* (Maryknoll, NY 1980). P. LERNOUX, *Hearts on Fire: The Story of the Maryknoll Sisters* (Maryknoll, NY 1993). J. M. LYONS, *Maryknoll's First Lady: The Life of Mother Mary Joseph, Foundress of the Maryknoll Sisters* (Garden City, NY 1967). M. J. ROGERS, *Discourses of Mother Mary Joseph, Rogers, M.M., Foundress, Maryknoll Sisters*, compiled by Sr. Mary Coleman and staff, 4 vols.

(Maryknoll, NY 1982). J.-P. WIEST, *Maryknoll in China: A History, 1918–1955* (Armonk, NY 1988).

[J. M. LYONS/C. KENNEDY]

ROGUE, PIERRE RENÉ, BL.

Martyr; b. Vannes, northwestern France, June 11, 1758; d. there, March 1, 1796. After ordination (1782), he joined the VINCENTIANS (1786) and taught in their seminary in Vannes from 1788. During the FRENCH REVOLUTION he refused to take the oath supporting the CIVIL CONSTITUTION OF THE CLERGY. Although the government forbade him to exercise his priestly functions, he engaged secretly in apostolic work and rendered signal service during a typhus epidemic. While carrying the viaticum to the dying, Rogue was apprehended and imprisoned (Dec. 25, 1795). When offered an opportunity to flee, he refused to take it, and spent his days in prison helping fellow prisoners until he was guillotined. His remains are enshrined in the cathedral at Vannes. He was beatified by Pope Pius XI on April 29, 1934.

Feast: March 1.

Bibliography: L. BRÉTAUDEAU, *Un Martyr de la Révolution à Vannes: Pierre-René Rogue* (Paris 1908). J. L. BAUDOT and L. CHAUSSIN, *Vies des saints et des bienheureux selon l'ordre du calendrier avec l'historique des fêtes*, (Paris 1935–56) 13:114–119.

[M. LAWLOR]

ROHRBACHER, RENÉ FRANÇOIS

Ecclesiastical historian; b. Langatte (Moselle), France, Sept. 27, 1789; d. Paris, Jan. 17, 1856. After ordination in 1812, he served as chaplain at Insming and Lunéville, and in 1823 he became superior of the diocesan mission of Nancy. In 1826 he joined Hugues Félicité de LAMENNAIS at La Chesnaie and in 1828 entered the Congregation of St. Peter. From 1828 to 1835 he taught philosophy to the novices at Malestroit. He also collaborated on the publication of *L'Avenir*. When Lamennais, condemned by Rome, refused to submit, Rohrbacher broke with him (1835) and taught Church history and exegesis in the seminary at Nancy (1835–49). Partly in reaction against the views of Lamennais, Rohrbacher studied the relationship between faith and reason, the basis of certitude, and the place of the Catholic Church in the history of mankind. His most significant works, *Catéchisme du sens commun* (1825) and *Histoire universelle de l'Église catholique* (28 v. 1842–49; 9th ed. 1899–1903; Eng. tr.), attempted to rectify some ideas advanced by Lamennais. Hence the *Catéchisme* contended, with Louis de BONALD, that the first principles of knowledge and reason rest upon divine revelation. His *Histoire universelle* refuted the contention of Lamennais that the modern Catholic Church had become decadent. This work attacked the ecclesiastical history by Claude FLEURY, which was deeply imbued with GALLICANISM. Rohrbacher, an ultramontane, sought also to glorify the papacy's role in history, and he had considerable influence in the rapid growth of ULTRAMONTANISM among the French clergy. While Rohrbacher evidenced a commendable cosmic vision of the Catholic Church and an acquaintance with the vast literature on his subject, he relied solely on secondary sources, lacked critical sense, and was unduly polemical and apologetic. His works brought him both fame and opprobrium. His ultramontanism led to his dismissal from his professorship in 1849. He spent his last years in retirement as a guest of the Holy Ghost Fathers in Paris.

Bibliography: *Histoire universelle . . .* (9th ed. Paris 1899–1903) 1:1–138, biog. of the author. L. FINOT, *L'Abbé Rohrbacher* (Sainte-Marie-aux-Mines 1893). L. MARCHAL, *Dictionnaire de théologie catholique*, 15 v. (Paris 1903–50) 13.2:2767–2774. R. AUBERT, *Lexikon für Theologie und Kirche*, ed. J. HOFER and K. RAHNER (Freiburg 1957–65) 8:1363. *Biographie universelle*, ed. L. G. MICHAUD, 45 v. (Paris 1843–65) 36:347–348.

[M. H. QUINLAN]

ROJAS, JOSÉ RAMÓN

Franciscan missionary, defender of the rights of the Church, known as El Padre Guatemala; b. Quetzaltenango, Guatemala, Aug. 31, 1775; d. Ica, Peru, July 23, 1839. An older priest brother was his first teacher. In 1794 he entered the Franciscan Order at the Mission College of Cristo Crucificado of Guatemala, made famous by Father Margil. He was ordained there in 1798. The period from his ordination to about 1820 he spent for the most part in the missions of Costa Rica and Nicaragua, either as simple missionary or as superior. Two reports written in 1813 and 1814 attest his zeal and farsightedness. In 1819 he founded the Mission College of León in Nicaragua and there received into the Francisan Order Juan José de la Trinidad Reyes, later the founder of the present University of Honduras. Several villages begun by Rojas have grown into thriving centers. The emancipation of Central America brought with it the attempt of the new rulers to dominate the Church. Rojas, as official theological consultant to both the archbishop of Guatemala and the bishop of León, was quick to resist these efforts, especially the plan to intrude the priest José Matias Delgado as bishop of Honduras without the consent of Rome. For his resistance he was once sentenced to be shot and was twice exiled, the last time on April 15, 1831. Peru gave him refuge and Jorge Benavente, Archbishop of Lima, became his close friend. Rojas built the chapel of Guadalupe in Callao with an annexed hospital for sailors, and a retreat house in Ica. For his kindness and zeal he is still known in Peru, and each year the faithful gather to celebrate his memory.

Bibliography: E. D. TOVAR Y RAMÍREZ, *El apóstol de Ica, fray José Ramón Rojas, el Padre Guatemala* (Lima 1943). J. V. CORA, *Oración fúnebre* (Lima 1839).

[L. LAMADRID]

ROJAS, SIMON DE, ST.

Trinitarian priest, founder of the Congregation of the Servants of the Most Sweet Name of Mary (a secular institute); b. Oct. 20, 1552, Valladolid, Spain; d. Sept. 28, 1624, Madrid, Spain. The third of the four children of the noble Gregorio Ruiz de Navamanuel and Costanza de Rojas, Simon joined the Trinitarians at age twelve. He made his profession in Valladolid (1572) and was ordained priest upon completing his studies at Salamanca (1577). Thereafter he served the order in many capacities, including superior of the order; he became a famous preacher of missions; and, later in life, was appointed chaplain to the Spanish court of Philip III and tutor to the future King Philip IV (reigned 1621–65). He was offered, and declined, two bishoprics. His intense Marian devotion caused him to advocate for the liturgical inclusion of the feast of the Holy Name of Mary, promote the total consecration to the Blessed Mother throughout Germany and Spain, and found the Servants of the Most Sweet Name of Mary for the relief of the poor. When the priest affectionately known as ''Padre Ave Maria'' (''Father Hail Mary'') died, he was given royal honors. Although Simon was beatified in 1766, political turmoil delayed his canonization until July 3, 1988.

Feast: Sept. 28.

Bibliography: *Acta Apostolicae Sedis* (1988): 847. F. DE LA VEGA Y TORAYA, *Vida del venerable siervo de dios, y finissimo capellan de Maria santissima padre maestro fray Simòn de Roxas* (2d ed. Madrid 1760).

[K. I. RABENSTEIN]

ROLAND, NICOLAS, BL.

Priest and founder of the Sisters of the Child Jesus (Holy Child) (*Soeurs du Saint-Enfant Jésus de Reims*); b. Rheims, France, Dec. 8, 1642; d. Rheims, April 26 or 27, 1678. Roland was educated by the JESUITS in Rheims. When he discerned his priestly vocation, he went to Paris (1861) to study philosophy and theology. Upon returning to Rheims (1665), he was provided with a rich cathedral canonry. Roland was probably ordained in 1667 or 1668; the records were lost or destroyed during the French Revolution. Following his ordination, he went to Saint-Amand's in Rouen, where he lived in complete poverty.

Here Roland's life entwined with that of Nicolas Barré, who had established the Sisters of Providence in Rouen for the education of poor girls. When Roland returned to Rheims, he was entrusted with a poorly maintained orphanage that he transformed into a school. In 1670, Roland convinced Barré to send two women from Rouen, who were trained in his methods and acquainted with community life, to establish a similar foundation at Rheims. This became the Congregation of the Child Jesus that provides girls with free education designed to instill Christian values in both the children and their parents. The incipient congregation attracted criticism for teaching Christian doctrine, usually reserved to the ordained; however, Roland so convinced Archbishop Maurice Le Tellier of the efficacy of the approach that schools were opened throughout Rheims. Roland also served as spiritual director to, and encouraged the vocation of, Jean Baptiste de la Salle.

Roland died from a fever contracted while ministering to victims of an epidemic. Before his death, he charged de la Salle with executing his last will and testament: to seek approbation for the Sisters of the Child Jesus (given May 9, 1678) and ensure the growth of the congregation. The sisters took their first vows in 1684.

Nicolas Roland was beatified at Rome by Pope John Paul II on Oct. 16, 1994.

Feast: April 27 (LaSallian Brothers).

Bibliography: L. AROZ, *Nicolas Roland, John Baptist de la Salle and Sisters of the Child Jesus of Reims* (Rheims 1972); *The Succession of Nicolas Roland, Canon Théologal of the Notre Dame Church of Reims* (Rheims 1995). É. RIDEAU, *Nicolas Roland, 1642–1678: hier et aujourd'hui* (Paris 1976).

[K. I. RABENSTEIN]

ROLAND OF CREMONA

Philosopher and theologian; b. Cremona, toward the end of the 12th century; d. Bologna, 1259. In 1219, as professor of philosophy at the University of Bologna, he entered the Dominican Order. He founded the Dominican priory at Cremona in 1226. After receiving the doctorate in theology at the University of Paris in 1228, he remained there, and in 1229 was the first religious to occupy the chair of theology. He strenuously defended the rights of the Church against heretics, including the famous Ezzelino da Romano, even to the extent of placing his own life in jeopardy. His last years were devoted to teaching in the Dominican house of studies at Bologna.

His *Summa theologica,* which is the fruit of his teaching at Paris, is preserved as codex 795 in the Bibliothèque Mazarine of Paris. The third book of this *Summa,* once thought lost, is preserved in the Civic Library of Bergamo (Cod. Δ9, 13). A commentary on the Book of Job is also extant (Paris, Bibliothèque Nationale, Cod. Lat. 405). These works have great importance both for a knowledge of the author's character and scientific attitude and for the history of medieval thought.

Roland marked the transition from the old to the new scholasticism, of which THOMAS AQUINAS was the chief exponent. Not only did Roland know ARISTOTLE, who was for him "the great philosopher," but he showed his genuine Aristotelianism in his love for scientific research, spirit of observation, and logical rigor of argumentation. In addition to his knowledge of Scripture, Roland manifested a vast and sure store of information in philosophy and physical science, and spoke with competence in medicine, geography, astronomy, meteorology, magic, and witchcraft. Anything knowable was of interest to him, because he considered every science to lead to truth, and every truth to serve theology. Grammar, rhetoric, mathematics, and, in general, all the liberal arts, were necessary, in his judgment, for a serious study of theology. He was drawn more to an empirical study of phenomena than to pure conceptual speculation. Roland possessed an encyclopedic mind very much like that of ALBERT THE GREAT. He had a sharp critical sense, ready to condemn error and anyone fathering it—Augustine and his favorite philosopher not excluded.

Bibliography: G. DE FRACHET, *Vitae fratrum ordinis praedicatorum* (Louvain 1896) 26, 38, 168, 275. J. QUÉTIF and J. ÉCHARD, *Scriptores ordinis praedicatorum* (New York 1959) 1.1:125–127. F. EHRLE, "S. Domenico, le origini del primo studio generale del suo ordine a Parigi e la somma teologica del primo maestro Rolando da Cremona," *Miscellanea dominicana,* ed. I. TAURISANO (Rome 1923) 85–134. E. PRETO, "La posizione di Rolando da Cremona nel pensiero medioevale," *Rivista di filosofia neoscolastica* 23 (1931) 484–489; "Un testo inedito: la *Summa theologica* di Rolando da Cremona," *ibid.* 40 (1948) 45–72. E. FILTHAUT, *Roland von Cremona O.P. und die Anfänge der Scholastik im Predigerorden* (Vechta 1936). O. LOTTIN, "Roland de Crémone et Hughes de St-Cher," *Recherches de théologie ancienne et médiévale* 12 (1940) 136–143. A. DONDAINE, "Un Commentaire scripturaire de Roland de Crémone: 'Le Livre de Job'," *Archivum fratrum praedicatorum* 11 (1941) 109–137. A. D'AMATO, "L'origine dello Studio domenicano e l'Università di Bologna," *Sapienza* 2 (1949) 245–268.

[A. D'AMATO]

ROLDÁN LARA, DAVID, ST.

Martyr, lay youth; b. March 2, 1902, Chalchihuites, Zacatecas, Archdiocese of Durango, Mexico; d. Aug. 15, 1926, Puerto de Santa Teresa near Zacatecas. After the death of his father while David was still quite young, he became his mother's favorite and helped care for his siblings. Family poverty required Roldán, the eldest son, to leave the Durango Seminary. He was known as a joyful and generous companion, an understanding coworker, and an honorable employee of the mining company. In 1925 he was elected president of Catholic Action for Mexican Youth. At the beginning of the religious conflict, he was named vice-president of the National League and worked for the reversal of anti-ecclesial laws. Accused of plotting an armed revolt with (St.) Luis BATIZ SAINZ, he was arrested at home by General Ortiz. Although money was offered for their release, they were taken to a place near Zacatecas. He and his cousin (St.) Salvador LARA were shot after witnessing the execution of Batiz and Manuel MORALES. David was both beatified (Nov. 22, 1992) and canonized (May 21, 2000) with Cristobal MAGALLANES [*see* GUADALAJARA (MEXICO), MARTYRS OF, SS.] by Pope John Paul II.

Feast: May 25 (Mexico).

Bibliography: J. CARDOSO, *Los mártires mexicanos* (Mexico City 1953). V. GARCÍA JUÁREZ, *Los cristeros* (Fresnillo, Zac. 1990).

[K. I. RABENSTEIN]

ROLDUC, MONASTERY OF

Called also Kloosterrade, former abbey of CANONS REGULAR OF ST. AUGUSTINE in Rolduc, Limburg, the Netherlands; in the old diocese of Liège. Rolduc was founded in 1104 by Ailbert d'Antoing (d. 1122), a canon of Tournai and founder of Claire-Fontaine, who became its first abbot. The immunity granted it in 1108 was confirmed by Pope CALLISTUS II in 1122; after 1136 the abbey came under the protection of the counts of Limburg, who were buried there. Thirty-eight abbots, drawn for the most part from the aristocracy of Limburg, followed Ailbert. Abbot Wynand Lamberti saved Rolduc from suppression after the Peace of WESTPHALIA, but it was secularized in 1797. Repurchased by the exiled canons, it became a minor seminary for Liège in 1831 and then for the Diocese of Roermond, Netherlands, after 1843. From 1123 a flourishing school had existed in the monastery. Its book catalogue in *Chartularium Rodense* (*c.* 1230) lists more than 200 theological, philosophical, and classical works, ranking it among the largest of medieval monastic libraries. Deeply influenced by the school of Liège, it became AUGUSTINIAN in theology while showing a preference for allegory and mysticism. The crypt of the monastery church was built by Ailbert and consecrated in 1108. The church itself, dating from 1209, was restored in the 19th century and contains Ailbert's remains discovered at Sechten in 1771.

Bibliography: H. DUBRULLE, *Dictionnaire d'histoire et de géographie ecclésiastiques,* ed. A. BAUDRILLART (Paris 1912–) 1:1144. F. SASSEN,"L'Enseignement scolastique à l'Abbaye de Rolduc au XIIe siècle," *Revue néo-scholastique de philosophie* 36 (1934) 78–100. L. H. COTTINEAU, *Répertoire topobibliographique des abbayes et prieurés,* 2 v. (Mâcon 1935–39) 2:2496. A. F. MANNING, *Lexikon für Theologie und Kirche,* ed. J. HOFER and K. RAHNER, 10 v. (2d, new ed. Freiburg 1957–65) 6:350–351.

[G. E. GINGRAS]

ROLENDIS, ST.

Also known as Rollandis, virgin who lived in the seventh or eighth century. Her vita, composed probably in the 13th century, relates that Rolendis was the daughter of a Gallic king (J. Molanus and F. Zutman claim that she was a daughter of the Lombard King Desiderius; J. Roland identifies her as the princess divorced by CHARLEMAGNE). She was supposed to marry a Scottish prince. To escape this marriage she fled to the convent of St. Ursula in COLOGNE, but died en route in Villers-Poterie near Gerpinnes (Hainaut), Belgium. In 1103 her relics were exhumed by Bishop Othbert of LIÈGE. Her cult developed early in the Gerpinnes area around the relics contained in her eighth-century sarcophagus, rediscovered in 1951. Annually on Whitmonday a solemn procession is held, in which her relics, in an early 17th-century reliquary, are carried.

Feast: May 13.

Bibliography: *Acta Sanctorum* May 3:241–244. C. PARADIS, *La Vie de S. Rolandis* (Namur 1620). F. ZUTMAN, *La Princesse fugitive* (Liège 1667). J. L. ROLAND, *S. Rolende, vierge royale* (Namur 1933). M. COENS, "La *Vita Rolendis* dans sa recension gerpinnoise," *Analecta Bollandiana* 78 (1960) 309–335; *Lexikon für Theologie und Kirche,* ed. J. HOFER and K. RAHNER, 10 v. (2d, new ed. Freiburg 1957–65) 8:1367–68. J. MERTENS, *Bulletin de la Commission royale des monuments et des sites* 12 (1961) 1–72. É. LEMPEREUR, ed.,*Gerpinnes: bouquet de textes inspirés par Gerpinnes, sainte Rolende et sa "marche," depuis des siècles* (Loverval 1973).

[M. CSÁKY]

ROLEVINCK, WERNER

Carthusian author of more than 50 works on historical, biblical, and theological subjects; b. Laer bei Horstmar, Westphalia, 1425; d. Cologne, Aug. 26, 1502. He was a renowned figure in the celebrated Charterhouse of St. Barbara, Cologne, from 1447 until his death. He was highly esteemed by J. TRITHEMIUS and other scholars of the day for the sanctity of his life, his scholarship, and his gifts as a spiritual counselor. He died, a victim of charity, while ministering to seven of his brethren stricken by the plague. His most popular work was the *Fasciculus temporum* (Cologne 1470), a brief chronicle of world history from the coming of Christ to his own day, which went through 50 editions and was translated into numerous languages. Equally successful, and more lasting, was his *De laude veteris Saxoniae nunc Westphaliae dictae* (Cologne *c.* 1478; ed. H. Bücker, Münster 1953). It gives a lively and valuable account of the manners and customs of his homeland. His awareness of contemporary social problems is evident from the *De origine nobilitatis* (Cologne 1472), the *De regimine rusticorum* (Cologne *c.* 1427), and the *De contractibus* (Cologne *c.* 1475). Other works attest to his relation to the DEVOTIO MODERNA and his concern for monastic and clerical reform, for example, the *Quaestiones duodecim ss. theolegiae studiosis* (Cologne 1475). Most of his writings, which are chiefly biblical commentaries, still remain in manuscript form.

Bibliography: H. WOLFFGRAM, *Zeitschrift für vaterländische Geschichte und Altertumskunde* 48.1 (1890): 85–136; 50.1 (1892): 127–161.

[F. COURTNEY]

ROLL AND CODEX

Two distinct types of book format used in antiquity and during the Middle Ages.

Roll. The ancient papyrus roll (Gr. τόμος, τεῦχος Lat. *volumen;* also βύβλος, βίβλος prior to the appearance of the codex) or the epistolary and documentary roll (Gr. κύλινδρος, κυλιστός; medieval *rotulus*) has been known in some detail from the 3d century B.C. It is uncertain whether the stability it enjoyed as an institution was an Alexandrian tradition. Records were written along the length or width of the roll without columnization; in the older Ptolemaic, Byzantine, Coptic, and early Western medieval period the *charta transversa* (script parallel to the width) was popular. Books were written along the roll's length, which varied greatly, though a manageable size was favored. Pliny assumed rolls up to 20 sheets (about 5 meters) to be normal, but there were shorter and longer ones, often up to 10 meters in length. Birt's conjecture of "great rolls" for the older classical authors (e.g., Herodotus in one roll) is rejected today. The literary division, called the book, was not developed under the influence of the roll. Such divisions of larger works by the author was a Hellenistic practice.

The basic unit in the production of the book was not the individual sheet (Gr. σελίς, Lat. *pagina*), but rather the complete roll, onto which any desired number of additional sheets could be pasted. The roll was inscribed preferably on the inner side (*recto*), where the papyrus fibers run vertically to the sutures (Gr. κόλλημα), i.e., mostly horizontal for the copyist and so render unnecessary any ruling on the sheet. In earlier times, an obliquely cut rush or an unslit reed was used for writing; from the 3d century B.C. reeds were split and sharpened (Gr. κάλαμος Lat. *calamus, canna*), and a deep black India ink (Gr. μέλαν) was used. Ink was made of a mixture of gums, lampblack, and water and was washable. The text was arranged in columns, whose width (in harmony with the height of the roll) was determined by considerations of legibility; it amounted often to about 7.5 to 9 centimeters, the limit of length being that of the epic hexameter, which, like the iambic trimeter, filled the line. The columns of any given roll were of equal width; in the later lyric verse the lines were indented and adapted according to length. The length of the column depended on the height of the roll and was uniform throughout; it ran from less than 20 to as many as 70 lines (generally 20 to 30 lines). Between the individual columns was a blank space or intercolumniation (not identical with the suture), in which later marginal notes, commentaries, and glosses were often written.

The roll was not given a title, but was cited by its opening words, the *incipit;* from the 3d century B.C. it often carried a portrait of the author. The exact title came at the end of the work, on the blank tailpiece of the roll, the ἄγραφον. Only incomplete remnants of illustrated book rolls have been preserved. Originally (6th to 4th century B.C.) book rolls were stored in chests; the content of the roll was noted in the ἐπίγραμμα, a vertical external inscription written on a protective sheet of papyrus that reinforced the roll, or on a parchment strip, the πρωτόκολλον, pasted onto the first sheet of the roll. When the rolls were later (examples from Athens, 415 B.C.) kept in cupboards or bookcases, the upper edge of the rolls, which were arranged in a flat position, extended outward toward the viewer; a parchment streamer (σίλλυβος, σίττυβος, Lat. *index, titulus*) was attached, which hung down over the edge and gave the title of the work. This brought the ἄγραφον to the inside of the roll between the outer left edge and the beginning of the text. The original boxlike container (Gr. κιβώτιον, Lat. *capsa*) gradually assumed, in virtue of the use of the *tituli,* the shape of an elongated cylindrical receptacle into which the rolls were inserted. The rolls of any one work were numbered and were thus recorded in ancient library catalogues; from the time of the Alexandrians notations were added concerning origin, former owners, author, etc.

The roll was held in both hands by the reader and was read by unrolling it parallel to the length from the left, rolling it up again to the right, and usually rerolling it. Deluxe rolls appear to have been unrolled with the aid of a rolling rod (Gr. ὀμφαλός, Lat. *umbilicus*) that was usually placed loose inside the roll. The roll was held together by a band or cord (*lora*).

Unlike Egypt, the Near East preferred to use leather, which in Egypt was as old as papyrus but was rapidly supplanted. There is evidence of the use of leather rolls down to the Byzantine period. Rolls preferably of parchment were used in the Middle Ages. They are well exemplified by the south Italian Exsultet rolls, the English Pipe rolls, the Metz juridical rolls—trial records consisting of many individual pieces of parchment sewn together into rolls—necrology rolls, etc.; all comparable to the official documentary rolls (Gr. τόμος συγκολλήσιμος) and land registers of antiquity. Medieval rolls differed, however, in various ways from those of antiquity, especially in being unrolled parallel to the width (with the exception of the Torah scrolls).

Codex. The terms *codex* and *caudex* (tree trunk, piece of wood) were used by the Romans to designate by metonymy anything made out of several wooden boards, especially the writing tablet (δέλτος, δελτίον, δελτίδιον, Lat. *tabula, tabella;* waxed tablet, *tabula cerata;* tablet whitewashed with lime, *tabula cerussata*). The tablet had already been brought to the Greeks via the Phoenicians as early as the time of Homer and was early in general daily use in Rome. There the *tabulae*—since the time of Cato the Censor (d. 149 B.C.) synonymous with codex— were used also for official certificates and texts of laws, and it was customary to bind several tablets together into a notebook (*codex, codicillus, pugillaris, pugillare, pugillus*). In the stricter sense, *codex accepti et recepti* meant a debt register or cash book, and *codex rationum,* a levy book. By the 1st century B.C. at the latest, wood was replaced in notebooks by the thinner, finer, more pliable parchment (*membrana*) that was more suitable for longer texts, so that *membranae* and *codex* were practically synonymous with parchment notebook, as opposed to the Greek διφθέραι, Lat. *volumina in membrana* (parchment roll). The first reliable evidence of the publication of a literary work in codex format is found in a reference by Martial (*Epigr.* 14.184–192; 84–85 A.D.), who recommends the pocket-size parchment copybook (*pugillares membranei*) to the Romans for traveling. The earliest example of the use of *codex* as a book is in Commodian (*Carmen apologeticum* 11; 2d half of the 3d century A.D.). The early Christians were especially instrumental in developing the notebook into the codex book. The first disciples of Christ may well have noted down the words of the Lord just as the Jews inscribed their rabbinical writings on small tablets or leather leaves. In Rome during the 1st century they became acquainted with the *pugillares membranei,* i.e., the parchment notebook. In the further development of the parchment notebook into the codex, the Gospel of St. Mark, written in

Rome and very probably inscribed in codex format, and the *Acta s. Petri,* were decisive contributing factors, because of their authority, to the use of the codex format for later Biblical MSS. Further evidence for this view is attested by the Biblical MSS of the first 3 centuries of the Christian era, which almost exclusively use parchment and the codex format, and by the Coptic MSS from the mid-3d century. The genesis of the book in codex format in the West and the original use of parchment and not papyrus is evidenced by the Latin expressions, *codex* and *membranae,* which have no Greek equivalents, even in the 4th century σωμάτιον (body, *corpus*), πυκτίον (*tabula*), and κῶδιξ; by the predominance of parchment over papyrus in the oldest Biblical MSS found mostly in Egypt; and finally, by the technical perfection of even the earliest parchment codices in comparison with the bungling execution of the most recent papyrus codices. The codex format remained limited almost exclusively to the Bible in the first 3 centuries, whereas the Christian authors of the 2d and 3d centuries followed the Hellenistic-Roman custom in preferring the roll format for their works. Toward the end of the 3d and the beginning of the 4th century, the triumph of the codex over the roll was assured. A contributing influence was the publication in codex format of the great codes of laws having authoritative force, for example, the *Codex Gregorianus* and the *Codex Hermogenianus.* The decisive factor may have been the fact that, with the triumph of Christianity under Emperor CONSTANTINE I, the canon of the Bible, handed down in codex format, became the leading sacred book of the new society, the codex being virtually identified with the *Libri sancti.* This, and not the fact that the parchment codex was more durable and convenient to read, explains its ultimate supplanting of papyrus and roll. The codex replaced the customary book of the pagan world and became the accepted format of the Christian West. The result was an immense program of transcribing the writings of antiquity from roll to codex. This work accompanied the decline of ancient culture and preserved for the Christian world and for posterity the intellectual treasure of the pagan past.

Bibliography: T. BIRT, *Das antike Buchwesen in seinem Verhältnis zur Litteratur* (Berlin 1882); *Kritik und Hermeneutik nebst Abriss des antiken Buchwesens (Handbuch der Altertumswissenschaft* 1.3; 3d ed. Munich 1913). A. BÖMER, ''Träger der Schrift und Schreibgerät,'' *Handbuch der Bibliothekswissenschaft,* ed. F. MILKAU and G. LEYH, 3 v. in 4 (Leipzig 1931–40) 1:52–. A. BÖMER and A. MENN, *ibid.* (2d ed. Wiesbaden 1952–61) 1:100–105. H. BRESSLAU, *Handbuch der Urkundenlehre für Deutschland und Italien,* ed. H. W. KLEWITZ, v.2 (2d ed. Leipzig-Berlin 1931; repr. 1958). F. G. KENYON, *Books and Readers in Ancient Greece and Rome* (2d ed. Oxford 1951). H. LECLERCQ, *Dictionnaire d'archéologie chretienne et de liturgie* (Parix 1907–53) 9.2:1754–72; 13.1:1370–1520; 15.1:1027–35. J. MALLON, *Paléographie romaine* (Madrid 1952). H. I. MARROU, ''La Technique de l'edition à l'époque patristique,'' *Vigilae christianae* 3 (1949) 208–224. M. NORSA, *La scrittura letteraria dal secolo IV. a. C. all'VIII d.C.* (Florence 1939). R. A. PACK, *The Greek and Latin Literary Texts from Greco-Roman Egypt* (2d ed. Ann Arbor 1965). C. H. ROBERTS, ''The Christian Book and the Greek Papyri,'' *Journal of Theological Studies* 50 (1949) 155–168. W. SCHUBART, *Das Buch bei den Griechen und Römern* (3d ed. Heidelburg 1962); *Griechische Paläographie (Handbuch der Altertumswissenschaft* 1.4.1; Munich 1925). K. WEITZMANN, *Illustrations in Roll and Codex* (Princeton 1947). C. WENDEL, ''Geschichte der Bibliotheken im griechisch-römischen Altertum,'' *Handbuch der Bibliothekswissenschaft,* v.3 (Leipzig 1940). C. H. ROBERTS, ''The Codex,'' *Proceedings of the British Academy* 40 (1954) 169–204.

[A. BRUCKNER]

ROLLE DE HAMPOLE, RICHARD

English hermit, author of Latin and English devotional treatises and poetry; b. North Yorkshire, *c.* 1300; d. Hampole, Sept. 29, 1349. Richard, probably of humble stock, seems to have studied at Oxford, but not to have graduated. There is no indication that he received even minor orders, and he was certainly not ordained. While still a young man, he felt a vocation to the solitary, but not enclosed, life of a hermit.

Many of his early works are marred by a querulous, at times rancorous, resentment of his opponents, whom he is not slow to call persecutors. This appears clearly in the chief treatise of his youth, the *De Incendio Amoris,* which has little plan or nexus, but is a series of passionate rejoinders. The editor of *De Incendio Amoris,* Margaret Deanesly, has described it as ''the vindication of the life of the hermit or solitary, not merely from the charge of laziness or vagabondage, but of inferiority to the busy and active prelate or the devout monk.'' Yet if we set aside all the scornful and bitter railings against empty and unspiritual academic learning, against the worldliness and frivolity of those who wear the garb of humility and mortification, we can discern other more attractive traits; and this book contains evidence of his claim to be treated seriously as a contemplative and ecstatic.

He describes in detail the circumstances under which, after years of perseverance in solitary prayer, he first experienced those consolations that constituted both his perceptions of the divine nature and his assurance that he was divinely inspired. He calls them *canor,* the heavenly melodies of praise he had heard around the throne of God; *calor,* the sensations of heat in which he felt his heart consumed in love; and *dulcor,* the overwhelming sweetness with which his whole being was suffused. To experience these consolations, his own preparations—a complete renunciation of the world, a perfect purgation, a total love of God for Himself alone—were prerequisite: and these joys would follow. We shall know perfectly in

Title page of "Rycharde Rolle hermyte of Hampull in his Contemplacyons of the drede and loue of God, with other dyuerse tytles,"
woodcut, ca. 1529, by W. de Wrode.

Heaven; on earth we can only love, and it is love that makes us perfect and brings us to the heights of contemplative life. "Whoever receives this joy, and glories so in this world, is inspired by the Holy Spirit. He cannot err; let him do what he will, he is safe, for no mortal can give him the salutary counsel which he receives from Immortal God." The seeming arrogance of this is tempered in other places: he concedes that the favors he has gained, especially the *canor* he heard on one occasion, came not through his merits but through grace.

De Incendio Amoris shows how Richard's thought was permeated by the Psalms and the Pauline Epistles, as one would expect of a beginner in theology. As his career progressed, he evidently learned from other late, affective, popular writers, but evidence of much quickening or deepening of his first perceptions was lacking.

The later English writings, it is true, showed less of the introspection and self-absorption that characterized his early productions. Toward the end of his life he seemed to have seriously applied himself to systematizing his teachings for the instruction of others; and, doubtless under the same necessity, he abandoned the insufferable preciosity that made the *Melos* unreadable to write a simpler prose interspersed with his own poems of divine love. But even when we admit his superficial use of the categories of growth in contemplation that he found in Richard of Saint-Victor, his ideas still remain rudimentary, and his whole system is marked by a lack of intellectual perception and curiosity. He is as indifferent to the classical authorities in his own subject as he is impatient with every other form of restraint; and it is this impatience that made later writers, such as Walter Hilton and the author of *The Cloud of Unknowing,* distrustful of him. They thought him a guide who would be likely to lead astray those beginning their search for immediate perception of the divine nature; and they observed in his unwary followers superstitious veneration of self-induced "consolations" and a dangerous contempt for the counsel of authority.

Rolle's popularity and the best of his work, *Ego Dormio, The Commandment, The Form of Perfect Living,* and such independent lyrics as *A Song of the Love of Jesus,* point to his true achievement. This was not at all in the field where he himself claimed pre-eminence, but in writing songs of the love of the crucified Savior with a depth of sincerity and an artless fervor unequaled even in the great medieval English tradition. He was at his best when writing as a simple man for an unsophisticated audience.

Bibliography: R. ROLLE, *Incendium amoris,* ed. M. DEANESLY (New York 1915); *Melos amoris* (Oxford 1957). *The English Writings* (Classics of Western Spirituality; New York 1988). H. E. ALLEN, *Writings Ascribed to Richard Rolle* (New York 1927).

[E. COLLEDGE]

ROMAGNÉ, JAMES RENÉ

Missionary; b. Mayenne, France, July 10, 1762; d. Sacé, France, Nov. 19, 1836. During the French Revolution, Romagné refused to take the oath required by the Civil Constitution of the Clergy, and in August 1792 he fled to England, where he spent six years, partly on the Isle of Wight. Summoned to Boston in 1799 by Rev. John Cheverus, he devoted 18 years to serving the Abenaki people and Catholics of Maine.

As an Indian agent, he secured land from the Massachusetts legislature in 1801 for the tribes on Passamaquoddy Bay, and later he was granted $300 for a permanent church at Point Pleasant. Hoping to stabilize the Native American population, he taught the women to spin and weave, and the men to enclose fields for agriculture. In 1804, he completed a prayer book in tribal language for the Penobscot and Passamaquoddy tribes (*The Indian Prayer Book,* 1834). He also introduced vaccination among the Native Americans. In 1811 he and William Jenks headed a Massachusetts government commission to encourage the Penobscots to settle on and cultivate their lands. During the War of 1812, he persuaded the tribes to remain neutral and was treated considerately by the invading British.

In addition to his Native American missions, Romagné served the Catholics of Newcastle, Whitefield, Hallowell, Gardner, Bath, Waldoboro, Portland, and Boston. On Aug. 13, 1818, he exercised his ministry for the last time in Boston and sailed for France. Appointed parish priest of Sacé, France, he died there in 1836, leaving the church of Boston 4,000 francs.

Bibliography: Archives, Archdiocese of Baltimore, *Letters of James Romagné to Bishop John Carroll.* R. H. LORD et al., *History of the Archdiocese of Boston . . . 1604–1943,* 3 v. (New York 1944) v. 1. E. DE L'EPINE, *Bulletin de la Comm. Hist. . . . de la Mayenne,* 2e série, 10 (1895): 223.

[A. M. MELVILLE]

ROMAINMÔTIER, ABBEY OF

A former Benedictine monastery in the Diocese of Lausanne and the Canton of Vaud, Switzerland (Latin, *Monasterium ss. Petri et Pauli Romanense*). The monastery was founded by SS. ROMANUS (d. 463 or 464) and Lupicinus (d. 480) from the motherhouse of Condat *c.* 450. It was destroyed by the Alamanni in 610–611, but was restored by Duke Ramnelenus (646), who put it under the rule of St. COLUMBAN with Siagrus as abbot. It was visited by St. WANDRILLE sometime before 650 and by Pope STEPHEN II, who in 753 consecrated the abbey church to SS. Peter and Paul and granted it autono-

Romainmôtier Abbey. (©Josi F. Poblete/CORBIS)

my, directly dependent on the Holy See. Temporarily deserted, it became a royal abbey of the Kingdom of Burgundy in 888 and passed under the rule of CLUNY in 929 as a donation of Adelaide of Burgundy to Abbot ODO OF CLUNY. Its prosperity, begun under Abbot ODILO, continued down through the 15th century. When it was suppressed in 1536, the church was taken over by a CALVINIST congregation and the cloister buildings were secularized. Some monks withdrew to the Franche-Comté, where the community continued until the Revolution under a ''prior of Romainmôtier.'' The abbey church is from the 11th century with 13th-century additions and an ambo dates from the 7th century.

Bibliography: P. LADNER, *Lexikon für Theologie und Kirche,* ed. J. HOFER and K. RAHNER, 10 v. (2d, new ed. Freiburg 1957–65) 9:9. L. H. COTTINEAU, *Répertoire topobibliographique des abbayes et prieurés,* 2 v. (Mâcon 1935–39) 2:2497–98. H. LECLERCQ, *Dictionnaire d'archéologie chrétienne et de liturgie,* ed. F. CABROL, H. LECLERCQ and H. I. MARROU, 15 v. (Paris 1907–53) 5.2:2280 (fig. 4650), 2347 (fig. 4681); 6.2:2168–74. J. P. COTTIER, *L'Abbaye royale de Romainmôtier et le droit de sa terre* (Lausanne 1948).

[G. E. GINGRAS]

ROMAN CATHOLIC

This qualification of the name CATHOLIC seems to have been first introduced by those reformers who resented the Roman claim to any monopoly of CATHOLICITY. In England many of the reformers thought of themselves as catholic. So the term Roman Catholic became accepted as a useful designation of those who owed allegiance to the pope, and it passed into legal usage. English Catholics resented the appellation Roman insofar as it implied that they were but a part of the one true catholic church that also included the Anglo-Catholics and the Orthodox.

On the other hand, Roman is an apt designation of the true Church. Peter was given a PRIMACY in the Church by Christ; his successors continue this office; and as these successors are in fact the succeeding bishops of Rome, the Church of Christ is by this token Roman. Theologians discuss whether the connection with Rome is simply an accident of history or whether it was divinely intended from the beginning that Peter should set up his see in Rome, but all agree that there has been a special disposition of Providence that up to this moment has always connected the primacy with Rome, and so a condition of one's succeeding Peter is election to the See of Rome. This leaves open the question as to whether at some future date the pope himself could sever the connection with Rome. Up to now there has been an unbroken line since Peter. This connection with Rome does not necessarily involve actual residence in the city; it is sufficient that the pope should be bishop of Rome, but it is desirable that he should be in residence there.

There is a further aspect of the term Roman Catholic that needs consideration. The Roman Church can be used to refer, not to the Church universal insofar as it possesses a primate who is bishop of Rome, but to the local Church of Rome, which has the privilege of its bishop being also primate of the whole Church. This local Church has its own customs and rites; consequently one must not confuse these particularities with the practice of the universal Church. Historical circumstances have meant that the ROMAN RITE and law have won acceptance in many parts of the world, and this has been a potent factor in maintaining unity. Nevertheless one has to distinguish between the particular Roman elements that could be dispensed with, and the faith itself centered on the primacy, which is an essential element in the structure of the Church. There is always the danger that sufficient attention will not be paid to local cultures and the Church will become too closely bound up with western European thought. That is why Vatican Council II was anxious to decentralize on several matters and allow more scope to the local episcopate.

See Also: APOSTOLIC SEE; BRANCH THEORY OF THE CHURCH; CHURCH, ARTICLES ON.

Bibliography: C. JOURNET, *The Church of the Word Incarnate,* tr. A. A. C. DOWNES (New York 1955) 1:427–438. *Sacrae theologiae summa,* ed. Fathers of the Society of Jesus, Professors of the Theological Faculties in Spain (Madrid 1962), *Biblioteca de autores cristianos* 1.3:439–448. H. THURSTON, *The Catholic Encyclopedia* ed. C. G. HERBERMANN et al. (New York 1907–14) 13:121–123.

[M. E. WILLIAMS]

ROMAN EMPIRE

The greatest and most influential multicultural empire in world history to date. It is of particular importance for Christianity, because Christ was born under the reign of Augustus, and the early Church developed in the milieu of Greco-Roman civilization within the Roman Empire and was subject to its government. Indeed, the New Testament is an important source for the life of the common people in the first century of the Empire. In Late Antiquity, the Roman Empire collapsed in Western Europe, and the year 476, when the last emperor of Rome was dethroned, has become a date of convenience for the fall of the Roman Empire. In the eastern Mediterranean, however, the Roman Empire continued, developing seamlessly into the Byzantine Empire which lasted until Constantinople fell to the Ottoman Turks in 1453. Up into the nineteenth century, Greeks still called themselves '*Romaioi*' (Romans).

The Establishment of the Principate

Gaius Octavius, b. in Rome, Sept. 23, 63 B.C., was the son of Gaius Octavius, who was born into the equestrian order but who achieved senatorial rank, reaching the praetorship. His second wife, Atia, was the daughter of Julius Caesar's sister. Julius Caesar, who had no son of his own (he never acknowledged his son by Cleopatra, Caesarion, who would in any case have been illegitimate under Roman law) showed a marked liking for the young Octavius. He enrolled him among the patricians, and at the time of his assassination he was about to add Octavius to his staff for a campaign aimed first against the Dacians and then the Parthians. Julius Caesar's will left Octavius three-quarters of his estate and adopted him as his son, thereby giving him the name "Gaius Julius Caesar d(ivi) f(ilius) Octavianus."

It was, however, nearly a decade and a half before Octavian became master of the Roman world. Mark Antony and Cleopatra were defeated at the naval battle of Actium (31 B.C.) and the following year Octavian annexed Egypt. The royal treasury of Egypt made him rich enough to discharge the claims of his soldiers and veterans; 120,000 veterans were settled in colonies, each with a donative of 1,000 sesterces. Some two years after the victory at Actium, he returned to Italy and celebrated his triumph (Aug. 13, 29 B.C.). It now remained for him to regularize his position.

It is hardly correct to say, as many historians do, that he set about fulfilling a promise to restore the pre-Civil War "Roman Republic." In the first place, the term *res publica* he claimed to restore, which is translated as "Republic," does not have quite the same connotations as the English word, "republic." It is a more equivocal word, meaning something like "state" or "commonwealth." Second, the authority which Octavian possessed had two main bases. One was the charisma he enjoyed as the heir of Julius Caesar, reinforced by a personal oath of loyalty taken by the cities of Italy, Gaul, Spain, Africa, Sicily, and Sardinia to himself and his descendants (late 33 or early 32 B.C.). The other was the consulship; Octavian took up his third consulship (Jan. 1, 31 B.C.) in the year of Actium, and until his sixth consulship (28 B.C.) he had all 24 lictors attend himself, leaving none for his colleague. The symbolism was pointed. In Octavian's sixth consulship with his colleague the able general and his friend from his schooldays, Marcus Vipsanius Agrippa, the former custom of having 12 lictors to attend each consul was restored, but Octavian got the powers of a censor for himself and Agrippa. The census they conducted registered 4,063,000 citizens. He also tried to reduce the numbers in the Senate which had ballooned to over a thousand, and expelled some 150, but he failed to bring the number down to the Sullan figure of 600.

The following year (27 B.C.) Octavian, who had just begun his seventh consulship, again with Agrippa as colleague, met the Senate on the Ides of January (January 13) and resigned his extraordinary powers, placing his provinces at the Senate's disposal, though he remained consul with *imperium*: an office he continued to hold every year until 23 B.C. However the senate demurred; Octavian was promptly offered Spain (except Baetica), Syria, Cilicia, Cyprus and Gaul, and he accepted them with apparent reluctance. Egypt he also kept, and a prefect appointed by him administered it as a successor of the Ptolemaic kings. The Senate also voted him new honors, chief of them the appellation "Augustus" (the revered one). Octavian took a new name: "Imperator Caesar Augustus."

Halfway through his term as consul in 23 B.C., however, Augustus resigned the consulship and from this time on held the office only twice. He was granted, instead, tribunician power (*tribunicia potestas*), which henceforth became so important an element of imperial control that emperors dated their rule by the number of years they held it. The tribunician power gave him a tri-

Column of Trajan, marble sculpture, attributed to Apollodorus of Damascus, A.D. 113. (Alinari-Art Reference/Art Resource, NY.)

bune's right to convene the Senate and the popular assembly, submit proposals, as well as veto any item of public business or action of a magistrate, and the right to compel obedience to his demands. As well, he was granted proconsular *imperium maius* for life, valid even within the boundaries of the city of Rome, and superior to the *imperium* held by any other proconsul. This made up a bundle of powers which gave Augustus extraordinary authority, although at the same time the machinery of constitutional government did not cease to operate. Elections continued to be held; Rome continued to have consuls, praetors, tribunes, aediles, and quaestors. One could argue that the Augustan settlement was a façade: autocracy masked by precedents borrowed from the republican constitution as it had existed before the Civil Wars. Yet Augustus respected Roman traditions. He avoided any suggestion of monarchy where it might grate on Roman sensibilities, and preferred the informal title of *princeps* which had Roman precedents, whence the term ''principate'' which we apply to his constitutional settlement. In the East, however, which was accustomed to Hellenistic monarchy, he was called *autokrator* (autocrat).

In 12 B.C. Augustus was elected to another honor. After the assassination of Julius Caesar, who was *pontifex maximus*, the triumvir Marcus Aemilius Lepidus had acquired the office and held it until his death in 13 B.C. Augustus had made no move to shove Lepidus aside. Yet no doubt he wanted the office and now he acquired it. Emperors continued to hold the office of *pontifex maximus* until the emperor Gratian (375–383 A.D.), who declined it as unbecoming a Christian ruler.

There was an aura of ambiguity about the principate. Augustus was both *princeps* (first citizen) and *imperator* (generalissimo); the first title denoted prestige and influence within the customary constitution of Rome, and the second denoted military power. He enjoyed the confidence of the masses; when there were floods, a food shortage, and an epidemic in 22 B.C., they rioted to make him accept a dictatorship. The army was loyal. The commanders Augustus appointed were men whom he could trust; when he could, he chose members of the imperial family. The provinces were better governed, and had no reason to regret the passing of the old republic. The people accepted peace after a generation of civil war with relief and gratitude.

Military Reorganization

One of Augustus' most striking achievements was the organization of a professional military force which was efficient and economical. It was to last with little change for two centuries. The great army which had defeated Mark Antony was demobilized, and what Augus-

tus kept was a force of 28 legions of 6,000 men each, if at full strength, made up of Roman citizens, supplemented by *auxilia* of about the same number, and recruited from non-citizen provincials. In 9 A.D., three legions were destroyed in a disaster in Germany when Arminius, chief of a German tribe known as the Cherusci, ambushed the Roman commander Publius Quinctilius Varus in the Teutoburg Forest, and the legions remained at 25 until the end of the emperor Tiberius' reign (37 A.D.). Under the emperor Vespasian (69–79 A.D.) there were still only 29.

It was the 60 centurions in every legion who maintained discipline. The centurions were professional officers who rose through the ranks, and they might rise as high as centurion of the first rank (*primipilus*), but no higher. The higher officers belonged to the senatorial order. Legionary soldiers served for 20 years and received 225 denarii a year, from which rations and equipment were deducted. Until Septimius Severus (193–211), legal marriage was disallowed until discharge, when they received land grants in colonies in Italy or in the provinces. This was the general practice until 6 A.D., when Augustus established a bonus fund for the soldiers (*aerarium militare*) financed by an initial grant of 170 million from his personal fortune, and the revenue from a one percent sales tax (*centesima venalium*) and a five percent inheritance tax (*vicesima hereditatium*). Thereafter a veteran generally received a cash gratuity on discharge, set at 3,000 denarii, though veterans' colonies were still occasionally founded. Auxiliary troops were commanded by Roman citizens of the equestrian order; they served 25 years and were given Roman citizenship when they were discharged. A *diploma* (a certificate inscribed on bronze, of which a number have been found) was given to an auxiliary on discharge. It conferred citizenship on him, his children and descendants, and the wife he had at the time of discharge, or whom he might marry later, if he were single. Presumably auxiliaries also received a bonus but at a much more modest level than the legionaries received. The Romans relied on the auxiliaries for their cavalry and light infantry, and they provided specialties that the Roman arsenal lacked, such as archers, especially mounted archers.

In Italy, the only regular army corps was the Praetorian Guard of nine cohorts, each of 1,000 troops. It was an elite force commanded by two praetorian prefects and received special treatment: guardsmen served for only 16 years, their pay scale was triple that of the legionaries, and when they retired they received more generous gratuities. Augustus never allowed more than three praetorian cohorts to remain in Rome at one time, and even they lacked a permanent camp; the remainder he quartered in neighboring towns. It was Tiberius who established the Praetorian Camp (*Castra Praetoria*) on the Via Tiburtina, within a built-up part of the city, though outside the pomoerium, and thereafter the praetorian prefects came to exercise ominous authority in the imperial government.

The Administrative Corps of the Empire

The Senate. Augustus' accomplishment displays a nice balance between respect for senatorial traditions and eagerness to harness the abilities and loyalty of new blood. He chose his highest civil and military officers from among the senators, and three times (29/8, 18, 13 B.C.) he purged the rolls of the senate to rid it of undesirable members. For the first time he set a property qualification: either 800 thousand sesterces, according to Suetonius or 400 thousand (Cassius Dio) but he raised it periodically and at the start of Tiberius' reign it stood at one million. The republican magistrates continued to be elected. The consuls had little to do except preside over the Senate, but the consulship was still prestigious, and it opened the door for military commands and the governorship of senatorial provinces. Competition for the consulship was keen, and *c.* 5 B.C. the number chosen each year was doubled by introducing suffect consuls: the two consuls would resign office after six months and their places would be taken by two suffects. The praetors, eight until 23 B.C. then ten, and in Augustus' last years, 12, still had judicial duties; two of them became treasury officials after 23, managing the *aerarium*, and the next year they took over from the aediles the attractive duty of giving public games. The tribunes had nothing left to do, and the office became so unattractive to senators that in A.D. 12, Augustus opened it to the *equites*. Aediles had little to do except to repair streets and act as a small claims court in commercial cases, so there was, understandably, a dearth of candidates. The quaestorship gave admission to the Senate. Twenty quaestors were elected each year and about half served in the provinces. Elections in the Centuriate Assembly for the praetors and consuls were lively, and Augustus had to take steps to control corruption. He had another control as well: by virtue of his proconsular *imperium* he could reject nominees, and present his own preferred list of candidates for the consulship and the praetorship. Other consuls could also commend nominees, and Roman politicians regularly canvassed for their candidates, but when Augustus canvassed, his commendation carried particular weight. It would be too much to say that the elections in the Centuriate Assembly were entirely free. The emperor Tiberius abolished them, and henceforth magistrates were elected in the Senate.

The Equestrians

The term "equestrian order" (*ordo equestris*) is used in two senses. Strictly speaking, it was the 18 centuries of *equites equo publico* which once made up the cavalry of the Roman army, but their military function had been lost long ago and now they were only voting units in the Centuriate Assembly. Augustus tried to revitalize the *equites equo publico*, enlarging its number from 1,800 to 5,000 and reviving the annual march past, where the consuls inspected them. But in popular parlance and, in due time, officially as well, all freeborn citizens assessed at a minimum of 400,000 sesterces were *equites*, enjoying equestrian privileges such as the equestrian gold ring and the first 14 rows of seats in the theater. Augustus drew a number of his officials from their ranks. Augustus recruited his prefects from the *equites* with the exception of the urban prefect, the chief constable of Rome and commander of the three urban cohorts of security police, who was a senator and ex-consul. There were the two prefects of the Praetorian Guard, the prefect of Egypt, which Augustus ruled directly, the prefects of the Roman fleets, one based at Misenum on the Gulf of Naples and the other at Ravenna, the prefect of the night patrol (*vigiles*), and the prefect of the grain supply (*praefectus annonae*). Also recruited from the *equites* were Augustus' deputies, the *procuratores*, who might act as his private financial agents or govern small provinces. Small provinces in Alpine districts or Judaea were governed initially first by prefects but later by procurators. Pontius Pilate is designated a procurator in the Gospels, but in fact his title is proved to have been "prefect" by an inscription found in Jerusalem. It can hardly be true, however, that Augustus established a *cursus honorum* for the *equites* which paralleled that of the senators, for we can discern no regular path of promotion.

Beneath the equestrians in the Roman social hierarchy was the *plebs urbanus*, "the common people of city of Rome" who were entitled to a free distribution of grain every month until 2 B.C., when this privilege was restricted to a fixed group, the *plebs frumentaria* numbering eventually about 150,000. But beyond the city, the population of the empire was made up of freeborn citizens, freedmen, and provincials. All Italians were now citizens and increasing numbers of provincials were beginning to acquire it as well. Freedmen, that is, manumitted slaves who bore the family names of their former masters, were citizens with qualifications: they were, for instance, excluded from public office and military service. Augustus retained the disabilities for freedmen; yet the corps of 7,000 night watchmen (*vigiles*) which he instituted in A.D. 6 were all freedmen, and in the crises of Pannonian revolt of A.D. 6 and the disaster in the Teutoberg forest in A.D. 9, he recruited them into special cohorts in the army. But they did not become legionary soldiers. However, he allowed many Italian towns to institute the *seviri Augustales*, an annual board of six freedmen who looked after the cult of the *Lares Augusti*; contributions from them for public works and spectacles were expected in return. Later, under the emperor Claudius (81–54) freedmen were to capture positions of great power in the imperial bureaucracy, but under Claudius' successors, a shift in favor of *equestrians* began again, culminating with the emperor Hadrian.

Government in Italy and the Empire

1. Rome and Italy. In Rome, the three urban cohorts of 1,000 men each under the urban prefect's command kept law and order. The city was divided into 14 regions (*regiones*) which were subdivided into precincts (*vici*). There were 265 *vici*. Seven cohorts of *vigiles*, established in A.D. 6, combined the duties of a night watch and a fire brigade. Augustus also found that the people expected him to ensure adequate supplies of water and food and eventually he appointed a prefect of the grain supply.

Italy, which now included Cisalpine Gaul, was divided into 11 administrative regions, but these remained more important geographically than politically. Begun by Julius Caesar, the reform of the municipal constitutions—there were 474 municipalities in the peninsula—was completed by Augustus, and it set the model for new foundations and for incorporated towns in the provinces. The municipal governments were modeled roughly on Rome's; there were chief magistrates (*duoviri* or *quattuorviri*) and a senate (*curia*). A large number of young men of the leading families in the Italian municipalities were incorporated into the senatorial and equestrian orders at Rome and furnished a supply of new recruits for administrative careers. Augustus wanted Rome and Italy to enjoy a favored position in the empire, and unlike Caesar, he granted the franchise citizenship to provincials.

2. The Provinces. The agreement between Augustus and the Senate in 27 B.C. instituted a sort of dual governance for the provinces: some, generally those not threatened by enemies or internal disturbance, would be ruled by the senate, and Augustus governed the remainder, appointing legates to administer them. Governors of senatorial provinces would be chosen from the ranks of ex-consuls or ex-praetors; their term was one year, and they were accompanied by quaestors as financial officials. For the imperial provinces, Augustus chose his legates from senators who were ex-consuls or ex-praetors, and they held office at his pleasure. They could be moved from one province to another without any interruption in their career. Therefore, senatorial provinces were theoretically governed in the same way as they were in the Roman republic before the Civil Wars, and Augustus had republican precedent for this procedure as well. Although Pompey had become governor in Spain in 53 B.C., he re-

mained in Rome and ruled through legates in his provinces. However, Augustus could use his *maius imperium* to lay down rules in senatorial provinces if he wished. This is made dramatically clear by the Cyrene Edicts (*SEG* ix, 8). An inscription found in Cyrene in 1927 gives us four edicts of Augustus, (7/6 B.C.), which set forth regulations relating to friction between Greeks and Romans: the first specifically gives instructions to the provincial governor in the senatorial province of Crete and Cyrene and his successors.

The borders of the Augustan empire were not clearly marked, and beyond the provinces were the client states. In Germany beyond the Rhine, the Roman government manipulated the German tribes by tying friendly chiefs to them, rewarding them with Roman citizenship and subsidies, and fostering divisions where it was to Rome's advantage. Until the disaster of the Teutoberg Forest in A.D. 9, Rome intended to subdue the territory between the Rhine and the Elbe rivers, and after that objective had to be abandoned, Rome still sought to establish a control mechanism over the German chiefs. In the east, client kings were manipulated ruthlessly. Unsatisfactory kings were removed. Even generally satisfactory ones could fall at the whim of an emperor. Gaius Caligula (37–41) who was free-handed at bestowing kingdoms on his friends, deposed and executed Ptolemy of Mauretania, a descendant of Antony and Cleopatra, and annexed his kingdom. It is hard to discover a rational reason for his action. Client kingdoms had advantages: they masked the reality of the Roman yoke, and they conserved the army's manpower by relieving it of police duties in border areas. But the client-state system was in full decline by the end of the first century.

The Succession

Succession was to present the gravest problem for the well-being of the empire. How could one emperor succeed another peacefully? Augustus was in theory a magistrate and hence could not have a successor in a formal, dynastic sense. Nonetheless, it is clear that he wanted to transfer his charisma to a successor chosen by himself, and it was equally clear that he wanted an heir who would carry the genes of the Julian family. Though the principate was not a hereditary monarchy, still there was a certain ambivalence about it from the beginning. Augustus, like any Roman noble, took pride in his family and wanted to secure the position he had won for his descendants.

1. The Julio-Claudians. Augustus sired only one child, Julia, a daughter by his third wife, Scribonia, whom he had married for political advantage and divorced quickly. His last marriage was for love. Livia was a scion of one of the great Romans families, the Livii, and she had already been married once, to Tiberius Claudius Nero by whom she already had a son, and she was pregnant with another, Drusus, when she married Octavian in 38 B.C. They were to introduce the blood line of the Claudian *gens*, and hence the ruling family is labeled the Julio-Claudians in history books. But Livia had no more children. Augustus was left with Julia.

He married her to his nephew Marcellus, and, after Marcellus' death, to his right-hand man, Marcus Agrippa, whose military talent had served Augustus well in the Civil Wars. Agrippa sired five children in less than ten years, three of them sons, Gaius, Lucius, and finally Agrippa Postumus, born after his father's death and mentally unsound. But Gaius and Lucius died young, and Augustus was left with his stepson, Tiberius. In A.D. 4, Augustus adopted him and gave him tribunician power for a ten-year term, which was renewed when the term was up and the *imperium proconsulare* was added to it. But at the same time as Augustus adopted him, he made him adopt Germanicus, the grandson of Augustus' sister who was married to Julia's daughter, Agrippina. When Augustus died, it was clear that if Augustus was to have a successor, it would have to be Tiberius, a Claudian, but on his death the succession would revert to Augustus' own descendants.

In fact, it did, but not as Augustus intended. Germanicus died young, leaving three sons, and Tiberius' own son, Drusus, died not long afterwards. When Tiberius died in A.D. 37, it was Germanicus' youngest son, Gaius Caligula, who succeeded, and he was the great-grandson of Augustus. When Caligula was killed Jan. 24, 41, after four years of misrule, his uncle Claudius was found hiding behind an arras. Claudius had been considered feeble-minded and harmless, and his reputation had saved his life under Caligula. He was rushed off to the praetorian camp and proclaimed emperor, while the Senate was still deliberating the succession, and some spoke for "liberty," that is, government by the Senate without an emperor. But they reached no decision. The people demonstrated for Claudius, and the Senate had little choice but to accept him. He owed the imperial office to the praetorian guard, and acknowledged his debt by giving the guardsmen handsome gratuities: a prudent move under the circumstances, but it set a hurtful example that later emperors had to follow. It made brief reigns profitable. On Claudius' death, his successor was Nero (54–68). Whatever his failings, and they were many, he was a descendant of Julia though his mother, Agrippina the Younger, and the rank-and-file of the army was loyal. When Nero died, the Julio-Claudian family became extinct.

2. The Flavian. Who should succeed? The army decided. The year 68 was the year of the four emperors. The emperor who emerged victorious was Titus Flavius Vespasianus (69–79), the commander of the legions who were suppressing a Jewish revolt in Judea that had broken out in 66. With Vespasian, the family name of the Julio-Claudians, "Caesar," became an official title and was used as such by the emperors who followed him. Vespasian's ambitions were dynastic. He determined to found an imperial family, and the succession did pass smoothly to his two sons, first the elder, the much-liked Titus (79–81), and then Domitian (81–96), a truculent despot to the Senate, but admired by the soldiers, whose pay he raised by one-third, and whom he led personally on five campaigns on the Rhine and Danube. Domitian lost his life to a plot (Sept. 18, 96) by members of his household, including his wife, Domitia and one of the praetorian prefects. Having no candidate of their own, the assassins left the selection of a successor to the Senate. The Senate made a cautious choice: an elderly senator named Marcus Cocceius Nerva (96–98).

3. The Five Good Emperors (96–180) and Commodus (180–192). Within a year, Nerva found himself facing an insubordinate Praetorian Guard and swiftly adopted as his son and successor Marcus Ulpius Traianus (Trajan), an experienced soldier who was governor of Upper Germany. He became co-emperor immediately (October of 97), and on Nerva's death three months later he peacefully became emperor.

Nerva had found a method of peaceful succession. Trajan (98–117), who was adopted by Nerva, in turn adopted Hadrian (117–138) on his deathbed, and Hadrian adopted Antoninus Pius (138–161) and insisted at the same time that Antoninus adopt Marcus Aurelius (161–180) and Lucius Verus (161–169) as co-emperors. Marcus Aurelius, however, had a son, Commodus, and thus faced a dilemma. If he were to pass him over and adopt someone better qualified as his heir, the new emperor would regard Commodus as a threat and almost certainly put him to death. Thus he made Commodus co-emperor in 178, and in 180, when he died, Commodus (180–192) became sole emperor at the age of 18. His reign was disastrous.

The successful conspirators who murdered Commodus nominated Publius Helvius Pertinax, the urban prefect, as emperor, and he was taken to the Praetorian Camp where he received a half-hearted endorsement. But in less than three months, the praetorians killed him and auctioned the office to the man who gave the guardsmen the largest donative. The winner was a senator, Didius Julianus (March–June of 193). Rival candidates rapidly emerged: Decimus Clodius Albinus, put forward by the army in Britain, Gaius Pescennius Niger, backed by the Syrian legions, and Lucius Septimius Severus, supported by the legions on the Rhine and the Danube. Severus (193–211) reached Rome in early June of 193 and was confirmed as *princeps* by the Senate. In 193 and 194 he campaigned against Niger, who was defeated and killed. Albinus and Severus at first made a pact to cooperate, but after Severus disposed of Niger, he designated his own son to succeed him, thus making it clear that there would be no place for Albinus in his future plans. Albinus put up a fight, but Severus moved quickly against Albinus' forces, which were based in Lugdunum (Lyon) and defeated them in two battles. Albinus killed himself and Severus had his body thrown into the Rhine, his wife and children killed, and his supporters hunted down. With Severus the emperor emerges as autocrat. His power was rooted in the army's loyalty and he knew it: he increased the pay of the soldiers by half. When he died in 211, his last words to his sons Caracalla and Geta were ''Do not quarrel with each other, enrich the soldiers and scorn everyone else.''

Life under the *Pax Romana*

The expansion of the empire continued under Augustus though at a more measured pace than hitherto. The conquest of Spain, which had taken 200 years, was finally completed, the Balkan peninsula right up to the Danube was brought under Roman control, and by 9 B.C. Roman troops had reached as far as the Elbe River. Except for the unforeseen debacle of Varus in the Teutoberg Forest in A.D. 9, Augustus would have brought the region between the Rhine and the Elbe into the Empire. The accepted view is that he intended to make the Elbe and the Danube the imperial frontier, but an alternative view has been suggested recently that he was not thinking in terms of delimited frontiers, which, given the maps available, was not a concept that a contemporary Roman could easily grasp, but rather was pursuing the dream of world conquest. The idea of the ''frontier'' as a line to be defended arrived with Domitian. However, Tiberius abandoned the conquest of Germany, and except for the addition of Britain under the emperor Claudius and Dacia by Trajan, the great period of expansion was over.

The empire covered a vast area, and in the first two centuries, it was a generally peaceful and prosperous area. Pliny the Elder, who died in the eruption of Mt. Vesuvius in 79, coined the phrase: ''the immeasurable majesty of the Roman peace,'' and the ''Roman peace'' (*pax Romana*) became almost a cliché, but not an inaccurate one. There were military operations and rebellions, but the Roman army dealt with them efficiently and the even tenor of life was undisturbed. The pay scale of the legionary soldiers remained unchanged until the emperor Do-

mitian raised it by one-third, but even so the treasury found it a burden, and Nero started an evil practice of adulterating the silver *denarius* with ten percent base metal, thereby stretching the available silver bullion to cover the payroll. Yet emperors felt it necessary to spend lavishly on public buildings that affirmed the power and majesty of Rome and advertised their own magnanimity.

Various calculations have been made of the number of people living in Rome, Italy, or the empire in general, but most scholars still generally accept the estimates made by K. J. Beloch in 1886: between 750,000 and 1 million for the city of Rome in the early empire, between five and eight million for Italy, and between 50 and 60 million for the empire as a whole.

The Cities. The empire was made up of *civitates* (or, in the Greek-speaking east, *poleis*), that is, territories with their political and administrative centers in their chief town. In the east, Rome found *poleis* or ''city-states'' already well established with their own laws and customs, and Rome allowed these to continue. Life in the Hellenistic cities in the east continued with little change. Rome continued to foster cities as the Hellenistic kings had done before they were overtaken by Roman imperialism. In the west, cities and Romanization went hand in hand, and the Italian municipality provided the model for new city foundations. The city was responsible for administering its own territory. Egypt was the exception: except for Alexandria, the old capital of the Ptolemaic kingdom, cities were foreign to Egypt. The prefect ruled as the Ptolemaic kings had done before him until the Severan period, when municipalities were established there, too.

The members of the city councils (*curiae*) were chosen from the wealthy notables of the city, and during the great period of the *pax Romana* they considered it an honor to serve. The *curiae* were responsible for collecting the taxes, the *tributum soli*, a tax on land, and the *tributum capitis*, a poll tax. These were the empire's chief source of revenue, though in addition there were customs dues at the frontiers and at provincial boundaries as well as the *aurum coronarium*, which began as a voluntary offering of a gold crown by a city to an emperor on his accession and evolved into a supplementary tax that was demanded with increased frequency. Wealthy notables were also generous donors and paid for many of the public amenities out of their own pockets. The ruined cities of Roman Africa in particular bear mute witness to the euergetism of their citizens, who grew rich from the production of wheat and olive oil for export. However, most of the population lived in the countryside, in the territories belonging to the cities, and earned their livelihood from agriculture. The cities lived off the profits of the countryside. The great aqueducts that supplied the cities are indicative of the situation: they carried in water for baths and fountains from the countryside, where in many cases it might better have been used for farming.

It is convenient to classify farms as smallholdings, consisting of 10-80 *iugera* (a *iugerum* is a parcel 240' x 120'), medium-sized estates (80–500 *iugera*) and *latifundia* (over 500 *iugera*). Smallholdings were particularly common in central and south Italy in the fourth and third centuries B.C., and these small landholders had been the backbone of the Roman republican army. From the late Republican period on, *latifundia* grew in importance. They varied from ranches to large mixed farms. The small freeholder would probably work his own land with his family's help, but land was considered the best of all investments: hence the rise of large estates which might be worked by slaves with a slave overseer (*vilicus*), or by sharecropping, or by leasing to tenants (*coloni*) for a rent in cash. Sharecroppers on the large imperial estates in Africa in the second century A.D. normally paid one-third of their produce, but elsewhere the proportion might vary. Leasing to *coloni* for cash rent was the simplest method, and it lingered on in Italy until the sixth century A.D. But it involved problems, for in bad years a *colonus* might be unable to pay his rent, and if a landlord seized his goods in lieu of rent, the *colonus* would become even less able to pay in the future.

Commerce. Cities had markets on regular market days, and a farm close to a city (*fundus suburbanus*) would gear its production to the market. Timber, firewood, orchard fruit, dessert grapes, flowers, poultry and eggs were all in demand. Vineyards and olive orchards were profitable, and so was sheep ranching, which produced wool, hides, meat, and cheese. Cities were centers of small-scale manufacturing and service industries, and commerce was lively: we find shoemakers, weavers, fullers, silver workers who might combine their trade with some money-lending, millers, and bakers, and a whole host of other tradesmen, who generally passed on their trades from father to son. In the imperial period, however, we find that large estates would often set up their own workshops and produce their own jars, iron implements, cordage, tiles, and pots. This must have had an inhibiting effect on commerce in the cities.

Transport overland was slow and expensive. On sea it was cheap, but slow and risky in the winter. Yet bulky goods had to be carried by ship or riverboat, owned generally by a shipowner (*navicularius*) who sailed his own vessel, carrying cargoes of such goods as marble, timber, produce, firewood, or jars (*amphorae*) of wine or olive oil either on his own account or on consignment for others. Because the imperial government needed private shippers to carry supplies to Rome and to the army, the *collegia* of *navicularii* (leagues of shipowners) were the first trade alliances to be granted official recognition and privileges, for it was more efficient for the government to contract with them than with individual ship owners. *Collegia* of *navicularii* are first known in great numbers in the time of Hadrian, and they remained free agents until the third century, when they were brought under the aegis of the imperial service. The largest vessels belonged to the Alexandrian grain fleet, which brought wheat from Egypt to Rome. Lucian of Samosata (*The Ship* i-ix) describes one ship of between 1,200 and 1,300 tons that was blown off course and reached the harbor of Piraeus after 70 days at sea. Grain shipments had to be suspended in winter. St. Paul's voyage to Italy on a grain transport (Acts 27.1–28) illustrates vividly the danger of trying to sail too late in the sailing season on the Mediterranean.

Foreign trade was extensive. The Romans imported amber from the Baltic Sea, slaves, hides, timber for shipbuilding, hemp, wax and pitch from northern and eastern Black Sea ports, frankincense from Yemen, spices from India, and silk from China. Much of the silk was imported via India and followed a route from Indian ports up the Persian Gulf and from there by caravan to Mediterranean ports, but there was an alternative silk route from China to Black Sea ports in the Crimea. Roman mariners discovered the monsoons towards the end of the first century, and convoys of merchantmen began to sail directly from Red Sea ports to Sri Lanka and India. Fairs, both regional and local, assumed great importance in foreign trade, particularly in Late Antiquity, for merchants would come to these fairs, which were held periodically, to buy and sell their goods there. It has been argued that an unfavorable trade balance with the east drained the empire's gold supply, but the evidence is slight. Many Roman gold coins have been found in India; silver *denarii* up to the time of Nero have also been found, but after Nero debased the *denarius* it was no longer accepted in India.

The Importance of Slavery. Slaves were also an important item of trade. When the Romans captured a town, its inhabitants were considered part of the booty, and those unable to pay ransom would be sold to a slave dealer who would take them to market. A successful campaign could bring in a flood of slaves. After Vespasian's son, Titus, suppressed the revolt in Judea in A.D. 70, large numbers of Jewish slaves were brought to Rome, where they helped build the Flavian amphitheater (Colosseum). But as Rome's expansion ceased and the wars she fought became defensive, warfare provided the markets with fewer slaves. Piracy was another source of slavery, though the imperial fleet tried to keep it under control. Another source was unwanted children exposed by their parents. Slavers would pick them up, raise them, and then sell them as slaves. Slaves might also be bred: fertile slave women could be rewarded for bearing three or four children with exemption from work or freedom.

Slaves were an important item of foreign trade. The less civilized fringe regions of the empire sold surplus population to pay for merchandise from the empire. In particular, when Hadrian banned male castration within the empire, he created an import market for eunuchs, who were in demand particularly in the later period. Abasgia on the Black Sea became an important source of eunuchs until the emperor Justinian (527–56) put a stop to it; the king of Abasgia would seize handsome boys, castrate them and sell them to dealers.

Slaves were found in all areas of the Roman economy. They were used on farms, ranches, mines, and factories. Both the state and the imperial household owned slave crews to maintain the aqueducts. Slaves used in mining, which was an imperial monopoly, suffered terribly. Slaves had no rights; they could be flogged and subjected to physical or sexual abuse with impunity. If they ran away, they might be crucified if caught or sold to a producer of spectacles in the amphitheater where they would have to fight wild beasts. Household slaves generally got the best treatment, but even they were subject to harsh laws: if a slave killed his master, all the slaves in the house might be killed as punishment on the theory that protecting their master was their joint obligation and they had failed. The fear of slave revolt was always present, and harsh penalties were intended to enforce obedience.

One of the remarkable features of the Roman system of slavery was the frequency with which slaves were freed. It was not motivated simply by generosity. The prospect of freedom kept a slave docile and motivated him to serve his master faithfully. Manumission could also be profitable, for some owners would free their slaves only if they bought their freedom with their savings, thus allowing their owners to recoup the purchase price. A manumitted slave (*libertus*) was given a freedman's cap, a felt cap shaped like half an egg that fit close to the head, as a sign of freedom; the slave took the family name of his former master, who was now his patron, and became a Roman citizen. But a freed person was not free of obligations to his or her former master. The system was not without advantages for the *libertus*, who became a member of his former owner's *familia* and could be buried in the family plot. Moreover, he might go into business with his patron's backing and become wealthy. The *Satyricon* of Petronius describes a banquet offered by a freedman, Trimalchio, which is a vulgar display of new wealth, and freedmen like him cannot have been too uncommon.

Slavery thus fed the citizen body with new blood; it brought in new immigrants and assimilated them. They made a significant contribution to Roman culture: the poet Horace was the son of a freedman, and Phaedrus was a Thracian slave who lived in Rome as a freedman in the house of Augustus, where he wrote his collection of fables. By the end of the second century, the great majority of Roman citizens must have had at least one slave in their family tree.

Literature and Art. The reign of Augustus was the Golden Age of Latin literature. Gaius Maecenas, Augustus' chief diplomatic agent during the Civil War with Mark Antony and his *confidante* until his wife's brother was involved in a conspiracy (*c.* 22 B.C.), gathered about him a circle of poets, chief of them VERGIL (Publius Vergilius Maro, 70–17 B.C.). Vergil first published the *Eclogues*, a collection of pastoral poetry, and then the *Georgics*, four well-crafted books on farming, and finally his great epic, the *Aeneid*, which became the national epic of the empire. The chief archetypes of the *Aeneid* were the *Iliad* and the *Odyssey* attributed to Homer. The *Aeneid* told how Aeneas escaped the fall of Troy and wandered over the Mediterranean, visiting Carthage, where he had an ill-starred affair with the queen, Dido, and finally reaching Italy, where he had to fight to establish a settlement. It is a poem that celebrates Roman imperialism, but it is not without compassion for Rome's victims. HORACE was five years Vergil's junior and the son of a freedman. Vergil introduced him to Maecenas, who gave him his Sabine farm, which Horace made famous in his poetry. He wrote odes, epistles, satires and a didactic poem on the art of poetry, but he declined to try an epic. Tibullus (*c.* 54–19 B.C.) wrote graceful elegies on his love for Delia, as well as for peace and for country life. Propertius (*c.* 50–*c.* 16 B.C.) was a member of Maecenas' circle like Vergil, whom he admired, and Horace, whom he disliked. He left four books of elegies, whose chief theme is his love for Cynthia. Ovid (43 B.C. to *c.* A.D. 17) was an immensely talented and facile poet who wrote with wit and narrative skill and loved the fashionable society of Rome. His medley of myths of transformation called the *Metamorphoses* is his greatest work, but his *Art of Love* was his most notorious. For reasons that are unclear, in A.D. 8, Augustus banished him to Tomi on the Black Sea, where he spent the rest of his life. Livy (59 B.C.–A.D. 17) wrote an immense history of Rome which has partially survived. His style is mellifluent, but his accuracy is sometimes questionable.

The next generation produced authors such as Phaedrus (*c.* 15 B.C.–A.D. 50), who wrote a collection of fables in verse drawn from the Greek. Seneca the Younger (*c.* 4 B.C.–A.D. 65) was known chiefly as an essayist and playwright, Petronius (*c.* A.D. 20–66), the ''Arbiter'', so-called for having been the arbiter of taste for the emperor Nero, is the presumed author of a long picaresque novel, the *Satyricon*, which survives in fragments, the longest of which describes a banquet given by a rich freedman Trimalchio. Silius Italicus (A.D. 26–101) wrote an epic in the Vergilian style, the *Punica*, which is about the Second Punic War, the war with Hannibal. Lucan (39–65), was the nephew of Seneca the Younger, and his *Pharsalia* on the civil war between Julius Caesar and Pompey is the greatest Latin epic after the *Aeneid*. Persius (34–62) is the author of a slim volume of six satires that strike a high moral tone, but his Latin is the language of the streets. Statius (*c.* 45–*c.* 96) is the author of the *Thebaid*, an epic on the myths of Thebes, and the *Silvae*, occasional poems, which were much admired in the Middle Ages but are little read now. Martial (*c.* 40–*c.* 104) is the most famous of all writers of epigrams, and his friend Juvenal (*c.* 60–*c.* 140) is the author of satires that comment bitterly on Roman life, though it is noticeable that his attacks are on people who were dead by the time he wrote. A writer's life was not without perils; both Seneca and Lucan killed themselves at Nero's command, and Petronius did likewise in anticipation of Nero's order.

The same period produced a clutch of notable writers in Latin prose. Little is known about Vitruvius, but his *Ten Books on Architecture,* which were written about 27 B.C., served the Renaissance as an invaluable textbook. Pliny the Elder (24–79) was the prefect of the Roman fleet at Misenum when Mt. Vesuvius erupted, and he died investigating it. He was a prolific author but only one work survives: his *Natural History*, a great treasury of interesting information in thirty-seven books. His nephew Pliny the Younger (61–114) left a panegyric on the emperor Trajan and ten books of carefully crafted letters. Two from his tenth book are of great interest, for Pliny writes to Trajan from Bithynia, where Trajan sent him as *curator*, to ask for the correct legal procedures for the prosecution of a cell of Christians. Trajan assures him that Christianity is a capital crime, but he cautions against any witch-hunt. Tacitus (55–120) is the greatest of the Latin historians; he wrote *Annales*, covering the Julian-Claudian period, and *History*, covering the period to the death of Domitian in 96. He also wrote the *Agricola*, a laudatory biography of Julius Agricola, Tacitus' father-in-law, who had a successful career as governor of Roman Britain until he fell under Domitian's displeasure. Tacitus's *Germania* concerns the geography and ethnology of the Germans and was written, like the *Agricola*, in 98. His *Dialogue on Orators* was at one time considered Tacitus's earliest work, but now it is generally dated after the *Germania* and the *Agricola*. Of the *Annales*, the books dealing with Caligula's reign and the first six years of Claudius are lost, as well as the material dealing with the last two years of Nero's reign. The *History* breaks off in A.D. 70, and the remainder is lost. Tacitus claims in the proem of his *Annales* to be writing with neither bitterness nor partiality, but in fact he displays both. However, he consulted good sources and if his bias is separated from his evidence, he is a reliable historian. The rhetorician Quintilian (35–96), teacher of Pliny the Younger, Suetonius (75–150), and Apuleius (fl. 160) also deserve mention. The last wrote a novel, the *Metamorphoses*, popularly known as the *Golden Ass*, a ribald tale that turns out to have a pious intention: Lucius, who is turned by witchcraft into a donkey, is saved by the intervention of the goddess Isis and becomes a devotee. Suetonius' *Lives of the Twelve Caesars* is a gossipy source for the emperors of the first century.

During these first two centuries, Greek literature produced after the death of Augustus was more extensive than the Latin and included works on history, biography, geography, medicine, grammar, rhetoric, and philosophy. This was the period of the Second Sophistic when writers favored the Attic style, consciously taking as models the great authors of the classical period. Dionysius of Halicarnassus (fl. 30–8 B.C.) came to Rome in 30 B.C. and worked there for 22 years. He produced works on literary criticism and an *Ancient Roman History* (*Romaïke archaiologia*), published in 7 B.C., in twenty books, of which the first ten are completely preserved and there are fragments of the eleventh. He was an uncritical admirer of Roman *virtus*, a word which encompasses not only "virtue" but also hardihood. Flavius JOSEPHUS (37–*c.* 95) wrote a *History of the Jewish War against the Romans*, describing the revolt of Judea (66–70). He wrote it first in Aramaic and then translated it into Greek. His next work was the *Antiquities of the Jews*, a history from Adam down to the eve of the revolt of Judea. The first half, which reaches the Babylonian Captivity of 587 B.C., merely summarizes the Biblical account. His last work, known popularly as the *Contra Apionem*, is an impassioned defense of the Jews against anti-Semitic detractors. The "Apion" of the title was an anti-Semitic scholar in Alexandria a generation earlier whose calumnies Josephus refutes in the first half of Book Two of his work. Plutarch of Charonea (*c.* 46–*c.* 120), who wrote the *Parallel Lives*, biographies of famous Greeks each coupled with a life of a famous Roman, was immensely admired in the eighteenth century; his other writings, collected under the unfortunate title *Moralia*, represent a wide range of interests. About one-third of his writings have survived. Aelius Aristides (129–189) was the star orator of the second century, a period when public orators received the homage that great opera singers do nowadays. His *Roman Oration*, a panegyric on Rome, is the best witness to how an educated provincial viewed the

Empire in the second century. Appian of Alexandria, who was a lawyer in Rome under Hadrian and eventually secured the post of procurator, probably in Egypt, wrote a history of Rome in his old age, finishing it *c.* 160. Claudius Ptolemy (*c.* 100–178) produced a geocentric astronomy which was generally accepted until the Copernican system overthrew it; Galen (*c.* 129–199), who wrote on medicine, continued to be accepted as an authority until the Renaissance, and Lucian (*c.* 125–200) from Samosata on the upper Euphrates, a Syrian who learned Greek in school, made a reputation first as an orator and then turned to impudent dialogues and essays. Lucian laughs at human follies; popular philosophy and popular religion equally excited his amusement.

Flavius Arrianus of Nicomedea in Bithynia made his model Xenophon, who lived 500 years earlier. Like Xenophon he flirted with philosophy in his youth and associated with EPICTETUS. After Epictetus' death, Arrian published the notes he made: the *Diatribes* in eight books, of which four survive, and a summary of Epictetus' ethics (*Enchiridion*). They preserve all we know of Epictetus' philosophy. Then Arrian began a career in the imperial civil service and published works of a different kind: a *Periplus Ponti Euxini* (Mariner's Chart for the Voyage round the Black Sea), dedicated to the emperor Hadrian, a manual on tactics, and, after he retired to Athens, a treatise on hunting that was a commentary of sorts on Xenophon's essay on the same subject, and most important, his *Anabasis* of Alexander the Great, valuable because he relied on two reasonably reliable sources, now lost: Ptolemy *Soter*, who became king of Egypt, and Aristobulus, son of Aristobulus. Both men accompanied Alexander on his campaign.

Art and architecture flourished. In the Roman Republic, the patrons had been private individuals, politicians vying for popular esteem, but with the principate the emperors used art and architecture to advertise their virtues. Augustus claimed that he found Rome brick and left it marble. His two greatest projects, his temple of Apollo on the Palatine Hill and his great mausoleum, were planned before the Battle of Actium. Later emperors followed his example, and the cities of the first and second centuries were filled with public buildings in the classical style. Augustus borrowed the models he favored from the Greek Classical Period, and Hadrian, who was a fervent philhellene, sparked a second period of Classicism. Perhaps the most original Roman monument was the Column of Trajan, constructed A.D. 106–113, which presents 150 scenes from Trajan's Dacian War on a continuous scroll wound around the shaft of the column on top of which stood a statue of the emperor himself.

Religion and Public Morality. Religion was pervasive in Roman society. A visit to the remains of an an-

cient town like Pompeii makes us aware of it. At one end of the forum is the temple of Jupiter on its high podium, adjacent to west flank is the Temple of Apollo, and on the east side is the Temple of the Genius Augusti, the sanctuary of the imperial cult, which was built by the public priestess Mamia. Vitruvius recommends that a city should find an elevated site for the temple of the Divine Triad of Jupiter, Juno, and Minerva, a site in the forum or the market place for Mercury, Apollo, and Bacchus near the theater, Isis and Serapis in the market, Hercules at the gymnasium or amphitheater if the city has one, or otherwise at the circus, Mars and Venus outside the city, Mars at the trooping ground, and Venus by the harbor if the city is on the sea. In the houses of Pompeii we find small shrines to the Lares and the Penates, and the Genius of the household where the householder might make a small sacrifice of salted meal. Paganism was a religion of sacrifices, performed with rituals that adhered to rigid formulas and festivals that marked the yearly calendar.

The gods and goddesses were numerous, and there was always room for new imports. Immigrants, whether freemen or slaves, brought their native gods with them. Paganism was tolerant, but there were limits. Judaism was a *religio licita*, that is, an "approved religion" which had been accorded certain rights and privileges by Julius Caesar, but Rome punished the Jewish rebellion (66–70) by destroying the temple in Jerusalem and bringing the temple treasure as loot to Rome, where it remained until the Vandals looted it once again when they sacked Rome in 451. Yet Rome was to protect the rabbinical school at Jamnia and later at Tiberias, and its head, the *nasi*, would be given the status of an honorary prefect. Anti-Judaism was not imperial policy. Christianity was different: it was a crime. The Druids whom the Romans found in Gaul and Britain were exterminated. Rome also frowned on self-mutilation: by the second century it was unlawful to practice self-castration with flint knives that was once a feature of the "Day of Blood" in the Attis festival. The Roman sense of propriety should not be offended, but Rome had a marked respect for piety, which might be defined as honoring one's divinities according to ancestral custom.

Among the cults imported into the pantheon was a number of "MYSTERY RELIGIONS," so called because they admitted worshippers by an initiation ceremony where they were revealed a "mystery". Examples are the cult of Isis and Serapis from Egypt, Mithras with Iranian roots, Attis and the Great Mother from Asia Minor, Sol Invictus (the Unconquered Sun), Jupiter Dolichenus, and others. Mithraism centers on MITHRAS, a deity borrowed from Persian Zorastrinism, but in Iran there was no such cult, which seems to have developed towards the end of the first century A.D. within the Roman Empire itself. It may have begun as the royal cult of the client kingdom of Commagene where Mithras was identified with Sol Invictus, and moved to Rome when the last king, Antiochus IV, was deposed in A.D. 72, perhaps with a group of devotees. It became popular in the Roman army, but how universal it was is hard to say. Women were not admitted. Yet in the later third century the Sol Invictus/Mithras cult emerged as a rival for Christianity, counting among its devotees the emperor Aurelian (A.D. 270–275). Paganism had many facets. Dream interpretation, oracles, and theurgy fascinated growing numbers. Yet for most of the pagan cults, eternal salvation does not seem to have been the ultimate goal.

The reforms of Augustus extended to public morality. One receives the impression from Ovid, whose racy *Art of Love* depicts a society where sexual conquest was the chief aim of life, and from Juvenal, whose satires portray an amoral Rome and declare that the old-fashioned morality once found in Roman society had broken down, but we should take this evidence with a grain of salt. The erotic poetry of Horace, Tibullus, Propertius, and Ovid drew as much on literary convention as on real life situations. Still, Augustus attempted to regulate private life. To check the extravagance that was sapping the fortunes of the old Roman families, he passed a sumptuary law to limit the money spent on banquets, gold and silver plate, clothes, and the like. It failed. Roman law had always prescribed penalties for adultery, but it was not enforced; Augustus revised the law, making it less severe but trying to enforce compliance. He passed the *lex Iulia de maritandis ordinibus* to encourage marriage and the bearing of children. It mulcted the unmarried and the childless, whether male or female, by making them ineligible for legacies except from close relations and gave various privileges to persons with children. The inheritance restriction of this law was greatly disliked by the upper classes, and in A.D. 9 Augustus modified it with the *lex Papia Poppaea*. Augustus placed limits on the manumission of slaves and was chary of granting citizenship to provincials, because, Suetonius claims, he did not want the Roman people contaminated by foreign or servile blood. Later emperors were more tolerant and Roman citizenship was steadily extended: the emperor Claudius intervened personally with the Senate to admit men from the Gallic provinces to the citizenship (Tacitus, *Ann.* xi, 24), and an inscription found in Lyon in 1528 preserves part of the speech Claudius gave in the Senate on this occasion.

The Majesty of Rome

The legacy of Augustus was a period of general peace and prosperity that lasted two centuries. The period was not completely free of rebellion in the provinces.

There was a revolt in Pannonia in A.D. 6, which required the attention of Tiberius. There was the revolt in Judea at the end of Nero's reign, which is described by Josephus, and in 115–117 there was another Jewish revolt that started in Cyrene sparked by the appearance of a "Messiah." It spread to Egypt, Cyprus, and Mesopotamia and led to great loss of life. A third revolt, led by BAR KOKHBA, broke out in Judea in 132 that caused heavy losses to the Roman army and according to the historian Cassius Dio 580,000 Jews were slain. After the revolt was suppressed, Hadrian changed the name of the province from Judea to Syria Palaestina. There was a revolt in Roman Britain (60 A.D.) led by Queen Boudicca of the Iceni, which broke out when the Romans plundered the kingdom of the Iceni after its client king died and maltreated the queen and her two daughters. The northern regions of Roman Britain was a turbulent area in the Antonine period. There was also low-level resistance: brigands and robber bands, who fed on the discontent of the under classes, often made travel overland unsafe. Yet the revolts of Rome's subjects were relatively few. In general, we may agree with Edward Gibbon's appraisal in his *Decline and Fall of the Roman Empire* (ch. 2): "But the firm edifice of Roman power was raised and preserved by the wisdom of the ages. The obedient provinces of Trajan and the Antonines were united by laws and adorned by arts. They might occasionally suffer from the partial abuse of delegated authority, but the general principle of government was wise, simple, and beneficent." Gibbon goes on (ch. 3) to make a judgment which is much quoted: "If a man were called to fix the period in the history of the world, during which the condition of the human race was most happy and prosperous, he would, without hesitation, name that which elapsed from the death of Domitian to the accession of Commodus."

Trajan was the last great conqueror. He reduced Dacia to a province in two wars, ending in 106: an exploit that is commemorated by Trajan's column, which still stands in Rome. Dacia's importance was strategic: as a province it was not worth having, but it sustained Rome's control over the German and Sarmatian tribes across the Danube. Trajan's Parthian War (A.D. 114–117) conquered Mesopotamia, but the province was in revolt at his death. Hadrian withdrew and consolidated. The empire switched to a new strategy of defending fixed frontiers. Hadrian's Wall in Britain, built 122/3–c. 133 between the estuary in the east and the Solway Firth in the west, is mute evidence of this strategy. It was built to control traffic over the northern frontier of Roman Britain, and Hadrian's successor, Antoninus Pius, considered it necessary to secure the frontier even more by building another wall further from the Firth of Forth to the Clyde. In Germany and Pannonia, the Rhine-Danube line was the frontier, but in the region between the two rivers, where the Neckar valley and the Black Forest offered an invasion route, Domitian had already a chain of small forts and watchtowers. Under the Antonines this system of fortification was completed with walls or palisades linking the forts, towers, and auxiliary bases.

The army was stretched thin. Moreover, the civil war after Nero's death, which ended with Vespasian's accession (69 A.D.), had revealed the dark secret of the empire: the army could make or unmake an emperor, and troops fighting to install an emperor could not defend the frontiers at the same time. When Clodius Albinus took most of the Roman army from Britain for his ill-starred contest with Septimius Severus, the northern tribes invaded, breaking down Hadrian's Wall. Severus spent the last years of his life (208–211) campaigning there, and after he died at York, Caracalla conducted another successful campaign and then reestablished Hadrian's Wall as the frontier. Yet the army also played a role in the transformation of Roman society. Its corps of engineers provided a pool of expertise for building roads and bridges and even purely civilian projects like amphitheaters. Until Severus' principate, legionaries could not marry, but they did form alliances with women living near their camps, and they might wed them when they retired with their gratuities and savings and settle into civilian life with their families. Their sons not infrequently followed the example of their fathers and became soldiers. Auxiliary troops received citizenship when they retired. Thus the army was constantly feeding the citizenship roll.

It was not alone. Provincials might acquire citizenship through the generosity of emperors or patrons. Leading families in provincial cities might have citizenship conferred on them. The allure of citizenship, and the upward mobility it made possible, was one of the instruments that kept the provincials loyal. Finally, the emperor Caracalla brought the process to an end in 212 A.D. with the *Constitutio Antoniniana* which conferred citizenship on everyone in the empire except the *dediticii*: probably barbarians who were settled on deserted land in the empire. How large this group was at this point in time is not known.

Roman society became less Roman, if we can identify citizens by their origins. By the time of the Severi, the proportion of senators of known Italian ancestry is less than half, and there was only one senatorial family that could trace its family tree back to the pre-Augustan republic. The writers Lucan, Martial, and the Senecas were all Spaniards; so were the emperors Trajan and Hadrian. Africans become prominent in the senate from the time of Hadrian. Septimius Severus was born in Lepcis Magna in modern Libya and his unlucky rival, Clodius Albinus

was also an African. Severus' wife, Julia Domna, was a Syrian. By the second century's end, the legions were recruited almost entirely from the provinces. The city of Rome was still the heart of the empire, but Italy was no longer its heartland.

The Third Century: A Time of Troubles

Septimius Severus (193–211). The Empire reached a nadir in the third century and came close to breaking up. That it did not do so shows the extent to which the idea of a Roman Empire had been accepted by the peoples of the Mediterranean. Septimius Severus felt no great reverence for Augustan tradition and determined to found a dynasty. He assumed the persona of Marcus Aurelius' son, and made the Senate deify his "brother" Commodus. He deliberately excluded the Senate from active participation in the government, and for that matter downgraded the importance of Italy. The old praetorian guard which was still mostly Italian was disbanded and replaced with a new guard recruited from Septimius' own legions, and he appointed two new Praetorian Prefects, one of them an African. He raised three new legions after he had disposed of Albinus and put equestrian prefects in command of them, thus breaking with the Augustan tradition of choosing legates to head the legions from the ranks of the senate. Then, when he left Rome for the East to wage war on the Parthians (A.D. 195), he left one of his new legions behind, stationed a mere 20 miles from Rome. When Severus, having defeated Parthia, annexed Upper Mesopotamia and set up a new province, he put an equestrian governor in charge of it.

The office of Praetorian Prefect acquired increased importance. One prefect was commander of the armed forces in Italy, and the other was given jurisdiction in all criminal cases in Italy beyond the 100-mile radius of Rome and deputized for the *princeps* in hearing appeals from provincial courts. He took over the more important duties of the prefect of the grain supply (*praefectus annonae*) and chaired the *Consilium Principis* when the *princeps* was absent. Because of the judicial duties attached to the Praetorian Prefect's office, we find distinguished jurists like the great Papinian appointed to the prefecture, and after Papinian lost his life for criticizing Caracalla's murder of his brother Geta, Ulpian and Paul held the office successively. Once citizenship was made universal by the *Constitutio Antoniniana*, Roman law applied to everyone, but from the time of the Severi we find it recognizing a distinction between citizens of higher status (*honestiores*) and those of lower status (*inferiores*), with more severe penalties for the same offense imposed on the *inferiores*. The emperor became the source of law, not only in practice, for this had arguably been true earlier, but also in theory. Ulpian put it simply, "What the emperor decides is law."

Recruits for the army now came almost exclusively from the provinces. Poor administration by provincial governors, now called *praesides*, was sternly punished. Wars, the increased pay for the army, and the imperial building program all increased government outlays, and Severus depreciated the *denarius* by a further 20 percent. The ratio of silver to base metal in the silver *denarius* had been drifting downwards in the second century, but under the Severi the trend gathered pace. Severus also made sweeping confiscations of the property belonging to Albinus' supporters, which was assigned to a special treasury, the *res privata*.

Caracalla, Geta, Macrinus, Elagabulus and Severus Alexander. Septimius' sons, Geta (211–212) and Aurelius Antoninus, better known by his nickname "Caracalla," succeeded him, but their joint rule ended when Caracalla murdered his brother and obliterated his portraits and inscriptions. Edward Gibbon, influenced by the hostility to Caracalla of our main source, Cassius Dio, called him a "monster," and he may have deserved it. He gave the army generous donatives and increased pay, and he relaxed discipline in order to curry favor. While leading an offensive against Parthia, he was assassinated by his Praetorian Prefect, Opilius Macrinus, who became emperor himself to the dismay of the Senate, for he was only an equestrian. Macrinus recognized the need to relieve the stress on the economy, and though he did not dare revoke Caracalla's pay increases to the army, he recruited new soldiers on the old pay scale of Septimius Severus, which provoked discontent.

Meanwhile, Julia Maesa, the sister of Septimius' widow, Julia Domna, got the Syrian legions to support her grandson Varius Avitus Bassianus. He was a boy of 14, better known as Elagabal, for he was a priest and devotee of the sun god Elagabal that was worshipped at Emesa. Maesa launched a rumor that Bassianus had been sired by Caracalla, and he took the name Marcus Aurelius Antoninus. Macrinus marched out from his base at Antioch against the young pretender and was defeated. Elagabal, however, proved incapable and his devotion to his god, whose cult he tried to introduce into Rome, shocked Roman tradition so much that his grandmother transferred her support to another grandson, Marcus Aurelius Aurelianus Alexander, son of Julia Mamaea. Elagabal was killed and was succeeded by Alexander, who added "Severus" to his name.

Severus Alexander emerges dimly from the sources, but he appears an attractive figure. Julia Maesa soon died, so his mother, Julia Mamaea, acted as his advisor. But he was faced with a difficult situation. In the east, the Parthian dynasty, the Arsacids, was overthrown in 226 by Ardashir, founder of a new Iranian dynasty, the Sassanids, and Ardashir, taking the name Artaxerxes, was crowned king of a revived Persian Empire. In 230, Ardashir invaded Mesopotamia and threatened Syria. Alexander apparently mounted a successful defense. He returned to Rome and then on to the Rhine to meet a German threat. There he was murdered by his troops who were, it seems, disgusted when Alexander tried to defend the frontier by diplomacy and paying indemnities to the Germans. His successor, Maximinus the Thracian (235–238), was a great brute of massive size and barbarity, who visited neither Rome nor Italy during his three-year reign and introduced a half century of anarchy.

Anarchy and Recovery (235–284). There followed a rapid succession of emperors: Gordian I, the elderly governor of Africa and his son Gordian II, who lasted only a little longer than a month, two appointees of the senate, Pupienus Maximus and Balbinus (assassinated July 29, 238), Gordian III (238–244), a boy of thirteen who was the grandson of Gordian I, and Philip the Arab (244–249). Philip and his brother Priscus, who came from a village in Roman Arabia some 55 miles southsoutheast of Damascus, were praetorian prefects at Gordian's death, which Philip may have arranged, and he was proclaimed emperor by the army. He faced revolts in the East from Iotapianus, who claimed kinship with Severus Alexander, and on the Danube by Pacatianus. Both were suppressed, but when Philip sent Decius to restore order in the Danubian legions, they proclaimed him emperor. Once Decius defeated Philip, he had to face a massive invasion of the Goths, who crossed the Danube led by their king, Cniva, and lost his life in battle as he campaigned in modern Dobruja. Decius' successor, Trebonianus Gallus (251–253), negotiated the withdrawal of the Goths, who were allowed to take their loot with them. Valerian (253–260), who associated his son Gallienus (253–268) with him as co-emperor, was captured by Shapur I, *shahanshah* of Persia, outside was walls of Edessa. Valerian was the first emperor to be taken captive. His army decimated by plague, Valerian was trying to negotiate a peace when Shapur seized him and killed him. Gallienus ruled on alone until his murder in 268.

This was the nadir of the empire. In Syria, it was the sheik of the caravan city of Palmyra, Odenathus, who drove back the Persians and provided some law and order, and after his murder, his widow, Zenobia, continued to rule his empire independent of Rome. Spain and Gaul broke away under emperors of their own. In *c.* 263 A.D., a horde of Goths swept down from the Black Sea into Asia Minor as far south as Miletus, and the Milesians sought refuge behind the great walls of the Temple of Apollo at Didyma. Gallienus was left in secure control only of Italy, Africa, and Illyricum. The silver *denarius* was debased until it had only a trace of silver in it, and it appears that much of the economy was carried on by barter. The army had to be paid largely through requisitions in kind. German tribes invaded Gaul, and the GOTHS raided the Balkans and Asia Minor. In 267 a barbarian tribe known as the Herulians took advantage of a Gothic invasion of the Balkans to sack Athens. There followed a plague epidemic which caused serious loss of life. The nature of the illness is not known, though it was probably not bubonic plague. In the cities of the empire the burden of taxation fell heavily on the *curiae*. The town councils, which were staffed by the well-to-do citizens (*curiales*), who were responsible for collecting the taxes and serving on a council, which was once an honor, became something to be avoided by anyone who wanted to preserve his wealth. Pagan cults with expensive festivals could no longer rely on private euergetism. Private donors who had once built public buildings and kept them in repair became scarce. However, it is hard to generalize, since euergetism was largely a thing of the past in Britain, Gaul, and Italy by the end of the third century, though in Africa, which escaped the worst of the turmoil of the third century, it lasted to some degree up to the VANDAL conquest of the early fifth century.

Gallienus maintained control as best he could in the face of rebellion after rebellion. Senators were excluded from military commands, and an elite cavalry unit was created and based in Milan, under an equestrian commandant. Army generals could now rise from the ranks, and a cadre of new officers recruited in Illyricum emerged. After Gallienus was murdered in 268, they provided a series of able soldier-emperors. It is too easy to dismiss Gallienus as a failure. Without his tenacity in the face of disasters, the empire might have disintegrated.

Claudius Gothicus (268–270) was the first of the Illyrian emperors. He first defeated the Alamanni, who had invaded Italy. The Goths were again threatening the Balkans in spite of Gallienus' victories over them in 267, and Claudius moved against them with his general Aurelian and defeated them decisively at Naissus (268), whence his title "Gothicus." He died of plague at Sirmium, the only emperor in this period to die a natural death.

His successor, Aurelian, commander of the Balkan army, was a tough and able soldier who completed the restoration which Claudius had begun. His first challenge was an invasion of Italy by the Alemanni, who defeated Aurelian near Placentia, but Aurelian recovered to wipe out the Alemanni invaders. He then turned eastward, where Zenobia's empire extended over Syria, Egypt, and most of Asia Minor. He defeated the Palmyrene army in a pitched battle, took the city, and captured the queen, who had attempted flight. But news reached him as he left for Rome that the Palmyrenes had risen in his rear; he returned swiftly, recaptured Palmyra, and laid it waste. Zenobia was exhibited in Aurelian's triumph and ended her life in elegant detention in Rome. In the west, a brief campaign was enough to put an end to the "Gallic empire" under Tetricus and restore imperial rule in Gaul. It was a brilliant achievement. Yet two other actions of his are symptomatic of the times. He gave up the province of Dacia, which Trajan had conquered. Its defense was now too difficult. And he fortified the city of Rome with a circuit wall which still stands and is named after him: the "Aurelian Wall." Rome itself was no longer secure from attack.

Aurelian lost his life to a petty military plot. He was followed by the elderly Tacitus (275–276) and then by one of Aurelian's generals, Probus, who continued the work of restoration. His program included the settlement of large numbers of barbarians inside the frontiers and more extensive drafting of barbarian war captives into the Roman military forces. This policy, which later emperors also followed, was once considered a major cause of the Empire's decline, but barbarian recruits who were integrated into the army fought as well as recruits from the provinces, and the settlers were needed to bring land depopulated by pestilence and invasion back into production. Probus, a strict disciplinarian like Aurelian, was murdered by his troops. His successor, Carus (282–283), captured the Persian capital, Ctesiphon, but was killed ostensibly by a bolt of lightning, though conspiracy is not improbable. Carus' son, Numerian, led the retreat, but he died on the road under suspicious circumstances. In the rivalry for the imperial office that followed, Diocles was proclaimed emperor at Nicomedia by his soldiers (November of 284), and his first act was to slay the praetorian prefect, Aper, accusing him of murdering Numerian. He then took the name DIOCLETIAN. There followed a struggle with Carus' surviving son, Carinus (283–285), but after his defeat and death, Diocletian became undisputed emperor and undertook a major reorganization of the empire.

The Tetrarchy

Diocletian had risen from a modest background in Dalmatia to become commander of the *domestici*, the imperial guard. He was a competent soldier and a great organizer with an original mind, and in particular he was a dominant personality who knew how to assert his authority over his colleagues. He swept away what was left of the Augustan principate. He was no longer *princeps* (First Citizen) but *Dominus Noster* (our Lord and Master). The Senate had already been relegated to a minor role; Carus, for instance, had not bothered with the formality of having the Senate confer *imperium* on him. In Diocletian's reorganization, the Senate did not matter. Not that he excluded senators altogether from public administration: the evidence of inscriptions makes it clear that some senators were still to be found governing provinces, and they continued to be used as regional governors of Italy (*correctores*), but for a career in public service, senatorial status did not matter much under Diocletian. The trend towards absolute monarchy, which started as far back as Augustus, reached it final development with Diocletian.

In 285 Diocletian appointed a colleague, another Illyrian soldier named Maximian, as Caesar, then adopted him as his son, and then the next year named him Augustus. He was made responsible for the west, where Carausius had just had himself proclaimed Augustus in Britain, where he reigned six years (287–293) before his chief financial officer murdered him. Then in March of 293, Diocletian took a second step in the creation of the Tetrarchy. He gave Maximian and himself assistants with the title "Caesar": Constantius Chlorus became Caesar for Maximian and Galerius for himself. Diocletian took the divine title Iovius and Maximian the title Herculius. The symbolism was clear: Jupiter was king of the gods and Hercules his muscular assistant. The basis of their power was still military, but Diocletian was seeking to cloak it with pomp and circumstance.

The size of the army was increased. How much is hard to judge, for although Diocletian created new legions, they were much smaller than they once were. Typically they were made up of 1,000 men, compared with 6,000 in the first century if they were at full strength, which was never the case. Special detachments (*vexillationes*) would number about 500, give or take a few. The general consensus of scholars nowadays estimates the total size of the armed forces at not much more than 400,000. New forts were built on the frontiers; surviving examples look much the same, as if there was a standardized fort plan.

Diocletian's tax system did not represent a major break with the past. It was based as before on *capitatio*, that is, individual tax liability, and a land tax. However to calculate the land tax he introduced an elaborate system of tax units (*iuga*) as a basis of assessment. A *iugum* varied with the fertility of the land. It might vary from five *iugera* (1 *iugerum* = $5/8$th acre) of vineland in Syria, or as much as 40 *iugera* of poor quality land. Assessments were to be made by a regular census, organized by five-year periods known as indictions: the first was in 287 A.D., and indictions thereafter provided Late Antiquity with a gauge of chronology, with calendar years expressed as "Year *x*, Indiction *y*." Yet taxation consisted as before in *munera* (public services performed by the taxpayer for free) and payments in money or in kind. The collection of taxes continued to be a public service performed by the *civitates*, and the *curiales* (or *decuriones*) were held responsible for it. Tax collection became the chief function of the municipal councils (*curiae*); by the time of Constantine it was almost their only function, and personal liability for it was placed upon the *decaproti*, a council committee of the ten (sometimes twenty) wealthiest citizens. The burden became insupportable in the turmoil of the third century, and *curiales* attempted to escape it by any means possible. The imperial government tried to enforce fair distribution of the burdens but would not release the *curiales* from their duties. In the prosperous days of the early empire, the status of decurion had often been *de facto* hereditary; now in the grimmer economic climate of Late Antiquity, it was made hereditary by law.

The currency was in desperate need of reform, and in A.D. 296 Diocletian introduced new gold and silver coinage. It seems to have triggered a new wave of inflation, the root cause of which may have been the enormous government expenditures. Diocletian attempted to remedy the situation by setting price ceilings: he issued an Edict on Maximum Prices early in A.D. 301, which fixed price ceilings on a long list of merchandise and prescribed draconian penalties for noncompliance. The Edict was published throughout the empire; all of the numerous epigraphic fragments of it come from the East save one from Italy, but this does not necessarily mean that it was unevenly applied. However, it was a fruitless effort. Constantine was to reform the currency again with greater success.

Provinces were reduced in size, and they in turn were grouped into twelve dioceses, each headed by a deputy (*vicarius*) who represented the praetorian prefect. Thus, for example, Roman Britain now had four provinces making up one diocese; the diocese of Spain had six provinces. Within these new, smaller provinces, civil and military government were separated; the military commander was a "duke" (*dux*), and the *praeses* was in charge of civil affairs. The praetorian prefects, three in number for much of the fourth century and four after 395, were the emperor's second-in-command under Diocletian. They were in charge of administrative, financial, legislative, and military affairs, but under Constantine they were to lose their military duties to the "Masters of the Soldiers" (*magistri militum*) to whom the dukes in the provinces were made answerable. A new bureaucracy blossomed that was to develop under Diocletian's successors to become on of the strengths, and curses, of Roman government in Late Antiquity.

The new masters of the empire lived in style. Each tetrarch had his own court and staff of officials who moved with him as he went from one residence to another. A typical tetrarchic residence had an impressive audience hall and a hippodrome for chariot-racing where the Augustus or the Caesar might show himself to his subjects in the imperial loge. Diocletian built palaces at Nicomedia (Izmir) and Antioch; Galerius built palaces at Thessaloniki (the Rotunda that survives there was probably intended as his mausoleum), and Serdica (Sophia), Maximin's headquarters was Milan and Constantius Chlorus built a palace at Trier. Rome was not on their circuits. The great palace built by the emperor Domitian on the Palatine Hill stood empty, and the city itself was becoming more and more a magnificent museum of historical monuments.

In February of 303 Diocletian initiated the last great persecution of the Christians. Persecutions had lapsed since the end of the emperor Valerian's reign, and for 40 years Christianity had enjoyed unofficial toleration. Christian tradition called this period the "Peace of the Church." Christians began to construct church buildings unmolested. Two years before his abdication, Diocletian brought this tolerance to an end.

The Christian Persecutions. The first evidence we have that the Roman state took notice of Christianity is an ambiguous reference in SUETONIUS' *Life* of the emperor Claudius, which reports rioting in the Jewish community in Rome, the cause of which was "*Chrestos.*" But by the reign of NERO, Christians were clearly recognized as a sect separate from mainline Judaism, and after the Great Fire in Rome, Nero sought to deflect blame from himself by persecuting them. Some Romans suspected the Christians of setting the fire, and possibly some Christian millenarians were impolitic enough to rejoice at seeing Rome burn, thinking this was a sign of the Second Coming. The emperor Domitian executed a cousin, Flavius Clemens, for "atheism, for which offense a number of other also, who had been carried away into Jewish customs, were condemned . . . ." (Cassius Dio, 67.14), and historians have suspected that Clemens may have been a Christian. However, it was not until the reign of TRAJAN that Rome's official position was spelled out. PLINY THE YOUNGER addressed a letter (*Epist.* 10.96) to Trajan from Bithynia in 110 to report that he had found a cell of Christians in his province and asked what the proper legal procedure was. Specifically, he wanted to know if Christianity was a crime *per se*, or was it necessary to prove crimes attached to Christianity, for there were rumors of immoral rites practiced by Christian sects, but the worship Pliny unearthed was innocuous. Yet Trajan ruled that Christianity was a crime *per se*. But he would not sanction anonymous denunciations or witch-hunts.

It is difficult to understand why the Christians were persecuted. The charge commonly made against them was atheism, for they denied the pagan gods, and atheism did arouse dread in pagan society. It was feared that if the gods were disregarded, they would take offense and might visit revenge on the community, thereby harming pagan and Christian alike. Judaism also denied the pagan gods and yet it remained a *religio licita*: a "permitted religion" with certain legal rights. The difference seems to have been that Judaism was an ancient religion and the Romans respected it as such, whereas the Christians worshipped a provincial crucified for *maiestas* (treason), for that seems to have been the indictment against Jesus for which Pontius Pilate put him to death. The Christians were also intransigent in their refusal to take part in the cult of the emperor which was an integral part of Roman state religion. Jews would not say prayers *to* the emperor either, but they were willing to say prayers *for* him. Christians, it seems, would not even do that. Christianity was also universal: it assembled congregations of believers without regard for different ethnicities, thus destroying the barriers that separated different national religions. The authorities seem to have perceived Christianity as a mass movement and found it threatening. Pliny, in his letter to Trajan about the Christian congregation he found in Bithynia, terms it a "*hetaeria,*" that is, a political club.

Yet persecutions were sporadic, sparked often by local disasters, or even a shortage of criminals for the wild beast fights in the arena, until the time of the emperor DECIUS (249–251). The empire was in peril, the Goths were invading, and Decius believed it necessary to make peace with the gods. He required all Roman citizens across the empire to make sacrifice and get a certificate to prove they had done so. Christians were dismayed, and the persecution might have done real damage to the faith, except that Decius was killed in battle in 251. VALERIAN (253–260) renewed the persecution, but after Valerian's death, Gallienus addressed a rescript to the Christian bishops (261 A.D.) granting the Church liberty to perform its duties and ordered Christian places of worship and cemeteries left free for Christian use. In the "Peace of the Church" that followed, Christians openly erected purpose-built churches; hitherto they had worshipped in houses adapted for the purpose, an example of which has been excavated at Dura-Europos on the Euphrates. We find Christians serving on municipal councils. Christianity began to permeate all classes, including the Roman army. Then came the persecution of Diocletian.

Apparently there was an incident in 299 when diviners at an imperial sacrifice failed to find the right omens and blamed the presence of some Christians who, it was alleged, made the sign of the cross. The first step was a purge of Christians in the army. Then on Feb. 23, 303, as the emperor watched from his palace, the church at Nicomedia was destroyed by the praetorian prefect leading a group of officers. Then followed Diocletian's three edicts of increasing severity. The persecution was directed particularly against the clergy, though Christians in the imperial service were to be stripped of their rank and imperial freedmen would be reduced to slavery if they did not recant. But the decrees got uneven compliance. Maximian was a not unwilling persecutor, but he lacked enthusiasm for it, and Constantius gave nominal acquiescence. But Galerius was a convinced pagan, and after Diocletian abdicated in 305 he continued to persecute Christians until just before his own death in 311. His Caesar Severus administered the persecution in Italy and Africa until the revolt of Maxentius, and his other Caesar, Maximinus Daia, was particularly zealous. At last, in 311 Galerius, now seriously ill, issued an edict of toleration but restored no confiscated church property and imposed a rather vague limit of ''discipline'' on Christianity, by which he meant something like law and order.

The Empire of Constantine

The Struggle for Supremacy. Diocletian abdicated in 305, and Maximian followed suit, though with reluctance. In the east GALERIUS inherited Diocletian's position as senior Augustus, and in the west Constantius Chlorus took over Maximian's position and title. As Caesars, Galerius appointed his nephew Maximinus Daia in the east and Severus in the west. Maximian's son Maxentius was passed over. Constantius Chlorus' eldest son, Constantine, was with Diocletian and Galerius when the abdications took place, but he soon rejoined his father in Gaul. There is a tradition that Galerius did not want to let him go, and when Constantine finally did get leave, he left speedily and killed the post horses along the road to prevent pursuit. He joined his father who was on the point of crossing the Channel to Britain. When Constantius died at York in 306, his troops proclaimed his son Augustus, and though Galerius refused to accept him as Augustus, he did accept him as Caesar. But CONSTANTINE's elevation moved Maximian's son, Maxentius, to imitation. He revolted, and when Severus tried to suppress him, his troops deserted him rather than fight the son of old Maximian for whom they still felt residual loyalty. Galerius fared no better himself when he invaded Italy to avenge Severus' death. He was forced to retreat.

But rather than recognize Maxentius, he appointed Licinius in Severus' place. The Tetrarchy had broken down. Diocletian was persuaded to come out of retirement and chair a conference at Carnuntum, where Licinius was made Augustus, and old Maximian, who had attempted a comeback, was persuaded to retire again,

though only briefly (He died at Marseilles in May of 311, either by natural death or suicide forced on him by Constantine). On Galerius' death, Licinius and Maximinus Daia, who had been proclaimed Augustus by his troops, shared the eastern empire. In 312 Constantine decided it was time to strike. He moved swiftly into Italy, taking Turin, Milan, and Verona and marching south to Rome, where Maxentius met him outside the walls at the Milvian Bridge and was defeated and killed (October 28).

Constantine was now master of the west. In February of 313 he and Licinius met at Milan and made a pact, and Licinius sealed it by marrying Constantine's sister Constantia. They agreed on freedom for all religions. The so-called ''Edict of Milan'' (A.D. 313) that survives, which freed Christianity from persecution and restored confiscated Church property is, in fact, a rescript issued by Licinius from Nicomedia to a provincial governor, authorizing him to issue an edict of toleration in his province. But it expresses the agreement of both Augusti, and by convention it bears both their names. Licinius had to leave Milan quickly for word came that Maximinus Daia was making a power grab. But a few months later Daia was defeated and Licinius and Constantine shared the empire.

It was a fragile alliance. Constantine's ambitions were soon apparent. In 314–315 he wrested Pannonia from Licinius and moved his court to Sirmium and in 318 moved it again to Serdica. In 323 he defeated Licinius at Adrianople and forced him back to Byzantium, where Constantine's son, Crispus, defeated Licinius' fleet at the north entrance to the Hellespont. Licinius retreated to Asia Minor, where he was defeated again. In 324 Constantine was master of the Roman world, and though he granted clemency to his defeated rival whose wife, Constantia, pleaded for his life, he put him to death a few months later for reasons that are unknown.

Tradition has it that before the night before the Battle of the Milvian Bridge, Constantine had a vision that resulted in his conversion to Christianity. The earlier and simpler version comes from Lactantius, writing within four years of the event, but in Eusebius' *Life of Constantine*, published shortly after Constantine's death, there is a more elaborate version, which Eusebius claims to have heard from Constantine himself. His account relates that ''about noon, when the day was already beginning to decline, he saw with his eyes the trophy of a cross of light in the heavens, above the sun, and bearing the inscription, 'Conquer by This.''' (*Vita Const*. 1.28). That night, the figure of Christ bearing the same symbol visited him and told him to use it in the coming battle. Indeed Constantine may well have thought a divine power was guiding his fortune, for if Maxentius had stayed within the massive walls of Rome and forced Constantine to lay siege, the outcome of the contest could have been different. But Maxentius chose to do battle outside the walls. Constantine won, entered Rome a victor, and began a policy of generosity to the church. He gave Pope Melchiades the Lateran Palace, which had belonged to his wife, Fausta, and only a fortnight after the Battle at the Milvian Bridge, on November 9, we have the traditional dedication date of the first church he built in Rome, the Lateran Basilica. The Roman Senate, which was to be a stronghold of paganism until the century's end, dedicated an arch in Constantine's honor (315–316) and its attic bore an inscription attributing his victory neutrally to "*instinctu divinitatis*" (the prompting of divinity). By the same year, the basilica which Maxentius had been building for secular use, a massive fragment of which still stands in the Roman Forum, had been dedicated to Constantine and in it was a great statue of him holding a spear shaped like a cross. Constantine's Christianity can hardly be doubted, but he treated pagans with tact. The majority of the population was still pagan.

Constantine's Settlement. On May 11, 330, the Empire got a new capital city, CONSTANTINOPLE, now modern Istanbul. The inauguration ceremonies lasted 40 days. There was a city on the site before Constantine's new foundation, Byzantium, which was founded by the Greek city-state of Megara in 659 B.C. according to tradition. Unlike Rome, it had few monuments of its pagan past. There were temples to Artemis, Aphrodite, and the sun god Helios on its acropolis, which survived until the emperor Theodosius I turned them to secular uses, but Constantinople was to be a Christian city filled with churches. The Great Palace that Constantine began in the southeast section of the city was to grow into an immense complex of pavilions, churches—at least 20 of them—residential quarters and reception halls, and it was joined by a private passageway to the imperial loge in the Hippodrome that flanked the palace. In the middle of the Forum, oval-shaped and markedly different from the traditional rectangular forum of a Roman town with a temple of Jupiter at one end, stood a great porphyry column 100 feet high, bearing a statue of Constantine with the radiate crown usually associated with the Sun God: indeed, it may have been a recycled statue of Apollo. This new foundation was to be a worthy capital. The grain ships which had carried their cargoes from Egypt to Rome were diverted gradually to Constantinople, and Rome was left to get its grain from Africa and Sicily.

For the patriarch, Constantine built a noble patriarchal church, Hagia Eirene, and his son CONSTANTIUS II added a better one, HAGIA SOPHIA, served by the same clergy. The bishop of Byzantium had been only a suffragan bishop of the see of Heraclea Pontica, but now he be-

came the patriarch of Constantinople, with the prestige of the new capital behind him: the third canon of the Second Ecumenical Council of 381 which met at Constantinople was to state that the bishop possessed "prerogatives of honor after the Bishop of Rome, because Constantinople is New Rome." The pope in old Rome heard the news without pleasure and would not recognize the patriarch's claims. Nor did they sit well with the see of St. Mark in Alexandria which claimed second place itself.

A few pagan temples were closed. A temple of Aphrodite at Efge in Lebanon, where transvestites and women prostituted themselves, was razed. At Heliopolis (Ba'albek) where there were only women prostitutes, Constantine urged restraint on the people and built a church, but otherwise did not interfere. The town of Hispellum in Italy petitioned him towards the end of his life to allow the building of a temple dedicated to his family, and he consented with the proviso that there be no sacrifices (*C.I.L.* xi, 5265). He confiscated treasure from temples, some of which housed a wealth of dedications, no doubt to the success of his currency reform. He issued a gold coin, the *solidus*, which was valued at 72 to a pound of gold, and which was used until the fall of the Byzantine empire. He may have banned pagan sacrifices, though the law has not survived. His son Constantius II did pass such a ban (*Cod. Theod.* 16.10.2) and refers to one his father passed. Sacrifices were at the core of paganism and the pagan cults would be severely damaged if they were prohibited.

Constantine's personal life was not unblemished, but it was no worse than that of many later Christian monarchs. In 326, two years after his son Crispus had defeated Licinius' fleet at the Hellespont, Constantine put him to death, and shortly afterwards he put to death his wife, Fausta, who was Maxentius' sister. The reason why has eluded researchers, but the question has used up a great deal of scholarly ink. There is a harsh tone to his social legislation, particularly on marriage. If a husband is a murderer, his wife may divorce him and keep her dowry; otherwise not. A slave nurse who helps abduct a girl with a view towards marriage is to be killed by pouring molten lead down her throat. But slaves were not to be branded on the forehead for they, too, were made in God's image. The laws penalizing celibacy which went back to Augustus were repealed, which no doubt conduced Christian asceticism.

The church enjoyed favor. Most clergy supported themselves partly by farming or crafts, and Constantine ruled that they should be exempt from compulsory labor (*sordida munera*). (In 330, rabbis and heads of synagogues were also freed from compulsory public services involving physical labor). Constantius II extended the privileges of the clergy to their wives, children, and servants. But most of all Constantine shows his favor by building and endowing churches. In Rome his greatest church was St. Peter's, built over a necropolis where tradition had it that St. Peter was buried. In Jerusalem he built the church of the Holy Sepulchre, and Constantine's mother, St. HELENA, also built churches on the Mount of Olives and at Bethlehem. They set a pattern: in Late Antiquity private euergetism was to be directed towards building and endowing churches, and the secular public buildings it had once sustained were left to crumble.

Having accepted Christianity, Constantine found himself immersed without delay in the disputes of the Church. In Carthage, the Catholics were under attack by the followers of a certain DONATUS. In the persecution which had only recently ended, some clergy had surrendered the Scriptures, and the Donatists took a hard line, arguing that these *traditores* who had handed over sacred books should not be readmitted to he church. They appealed to Constantine, who referred the question to a caucus of bishops in Rome, and when the Donatists refused to accept its verdict, to a council with wider representation at Arles. The Donatist arguments failed again, whereupon the Donatists demanded to know what business the matter was of the emperor's. Constantine attempted a round of persecution to bring the Donatists to heel, but without success, and the Donatist schism endured well into the next century.

Once Constantine eliminated Licinius, he encountered a more serious contention centering on the doctrine of Arius, a presbyter in Alexandria who argued that in the Trinity the Son must be secondary to the Father. To solve this dispute, Constantine in A.D. 325 convened a council of bishops at NICAEA, the first of seven recognized ecumenical councils of the church. The minutes of this council have not survived, and we are dependent on the eyewitness account of EUSEBIUS OF CAESAREA in his *Life of Constantine* (3.7–14). Many of the bishops had experienced persecution less than a couple decades before, and it must have been a heady experience for them to meet with the emperor and have him defer to their opinions. Yet Constantine took an active role: he seems himself to have suggested the controversial nub of the Nicene Creed which emerges from the Council, that the Son was of *joint substance* (*homoousios*) with the Father.

In Late Antiquity it was common for Christians to postpone baptism as long as possible for it was believed that baptism wiped away all stain of sin, and a believer who was baptized on his deathbed would approach the Last Judgment spotless. In 337, Constantine, even as he was planning an expedition against Persia, felt death approaching and was baptized at Nicomedia by its bishop, Eusebius, and died, May 22, 337.

The Age of Transition: From the Sons of Constantine to Theodosius the Great

After the massacre of all male family rivals, except for Gallus and Julian, the three sons of Constantine succeeded their father. CONSTANTINE II attempted to eliminate his youngest brother, CONSTANS I, in 340 and died in battle in Italy. Constans himself was murdered ten years later by his troops in Gaul, who acclaimed a barbarian officer, Magnentius, as his successor. Constantius II eliminated Magnentius in a costly battle at Mursa in modern Croatia and became sole Augustus. But having no children of his own, he turned first to Gallus and them to Julian, the son of Constantine I's half-brother, made him Caesar, and sent him to Gaul, where he fought with success against the Franks. In 360 Constantius II, who was preparing for war against Persia, demanded reinforcements from Julian's army. The result was an insurrection, and Julian's soldiers acclaimed him Augustus. Constantius treated the action as a rebellion and marched westwards to suppress it, but at Tarsus he took ill and died.

JULIAN THE APOSTATE (361–363) was the last pagan emperor, and during his brief reign he attempted to breathe life into paganism. But the interrupted war against Persia called him to the eastern frontier, and Julian's strategic errors led to disaster. As he was retreating with his army, the Persians launched a sudden attack, and Julian was killed. The army chose a relative unknown, Jovian (363–364) to succeed him, and Jovian made a peace treaty with Persia by which he gave up Nisibis and Singara and agreed not to help the king of Armenia against any attack by Persia. In effect he negated the gains won by Galerius I in 297 while he was still Caesar. His victory was commemorated in the Arch of Galerius, a fragment of which still stands in Thessaloniki. Jovian headed back to Constantinople but died before he reached it.

The army chose a soldier from Pannonia, VALENTINIAN (364–375) as next emperor. He in turn chose his brother VALENS (364–378) as co-emperor to rule the east with his capital in Constantinople, while Valentinian ruled the west with his base in Milan. In 367 Valentinian made his seven-year-old son, GRATIAN, co-emperor, and when he died the army made Gratian's four-year-old half-brother, Valentinian II, co-emperor (375–392) as well. Gratian was 16 at his father's death, and he and his half-brother reigned on in the west until Gratian was overthrown and killed by a usurper, Maximus, Aug. 25, 383. In the east, however, Valens' reign ended in disaster. Visigoths, who had been driven out of the Russian steppe by the Huns, arrived at the Danube and sought new homes within the empire. Valens granted them entry, persuaded by the promise that they would supply recruits for the Roman auxiliaries. But local authorities in Thrace maltreated and robbed them, and in the summer of 377 they rose in rebellion. Valens went into battle without waiting for the reinforcements that Gratian was sending him and was crushed at Adrianople in August of 378: two-thirds of his army was destroyed and he himself was killed. It fell to Valens' widow, Domnica Augusta, to organize the defense of Constantinople and provide direction in the emergency.

Gratian turned to THEODOSIUS, who was living in retirement in his native Spain. His father, Count Theodosius, had been an able "Master of the Soldiers" in Britain, where he restored order after a concerted attack on the diocese (367) by the Picts, the Scots, and the Saxons, and rebuilt Hadrian's Wall for the third time. But he had fallen from favor for some reason and had been executed at Carthage (376). Theodosius I (379–395), whom Gratian proclaimed co-Augustus (January of 379), made Thessaloniki his headquarters while he restored order in Thrace. It was not until Nov. 24, 380, that he made a formal advent, or ceremonial entry (adventus) into Constantinople. Theodosius made peace with the VISIGOTHS (382), granting them land across the Danube in Moesia in return for service as auxiliaries under the command of their own leaders. They were to be foederati, translated misleadingly as "federate troops." They served under terms of a treaty that exempted them from taxation and gave them a yearly subsidy, but they did not have the right of intermarriage with Roman citizens. They were not to be assimilated. Taking recruits for the Roman armed forces from foreign sources was by no means new, but these "barbarian" soldiers had been integrated into the army, where they would become familiar with Roman culture and loyal to the empire. These new federate troops owed their loyalty first and foremost to their tribal chiefs. But the settlement served as a stop-gap during Theodosius' lifetime. It was after his death in 395 that problems arose with the emergence of an aggressive Visigothic leader, Alaric.

Life and Society in Late Antiquity

Social Structure. After the division of the empire between the sons of Theodosius, east and west increasingly went their own ways, though in law the empire was still one, and the consulship which conferred great social prestige if nothing else, was divided: one consul would hold office in Rome and the other in Constantinople. In the west, society came to be dominated by a small group of great land-owning aristocrats. Their great estates were worked by unfree coloni (tenants), tied to the land by a law of Constantine, and landowners were reluctant to supply them as recruits for the army. They liked lives of cultivated leisure, but they were also eager to hold the high offices of the empire, such as the praetorian prefecture, the urban prefecture, or the powerful post of "Master of the Offices," which brought status and wealth. A senator bore the title "illustris"; lesser grades of order which now did not imply senate seats were "spectabilis" (distinguished), and "clarissimus" (honorable). The title "Patrician" indicated immense prestige.

Free peasants survived better in the eastern empire. Constantius II founded a Senate in Constantinople in the 350s, and it expanded rapidly from barely 300 to 3,000 members before he died. The attraction was that achieving senatorial status made a man a citizen of the capital, and thus he could escape the curial duties of his own civitas. High offices in the bureaucracy were coveted for they were a road to prestige and wealth, and since a good classical education was necessary for entry to the civil militia, schools flourished, and though elementary education was left to private enterprise in both East and West, higher education was subsidized. Knowledge of Latin was necessary for the study of law, but in everything else, the language of culture in the East was Greek. The linguistic divide sharpened: the Greek-speaking East had never shown much interest in Latin except for professional reasons, but since Greek had been widely taught in the west, the ruling class in the early empire had been largely bilingual. Now the West was turning its back on Greek. At the same time Syriac in the patriarchate of Antioch and Coptic in the patriarchate of Alexandria were emerging as written languages with literatures of their own.

Literature and Art. There was an apparent dearth of literature in the third century, though it produced one Greek historian of note, Cassius Dio, a Greek from Bithynia who wrote a *Roman History* under the Severi. With the fourth century there comes a blossoming. The last great Latin historian is Ammianus Marcellinus, a Greek from Antioch, who served as a soldier before he turned to history. Although his *History* began where Tacitus left off, the first 13 books which are lost must have moved through the years swiftly, and he begins to write in detail in 353, when he joined the staff of Ursicinus, the Master of Soldiers in the East. He ends with the Battle of Adrianople. His great hero was the emperor Julian the Apostate, though he remains aloof as he witnesses the last struggles of paganism. But we cannot say with certainty that he was not a Christian. We can have no doubt about the paganism of Zosimus, who wrote in Greek under Anastasius, and whose *New History* attempted to show that Rome had declined because it had abandoned the faith of its founders. The traditions of classical literature lived on, and authors working within them take various stances towards the Christian faith. Claudian, a poet and panegyrist at the court of Honorius, who came from Egypt but wrote in Latin, ignored Christianity; he wrote about mythological subjects as if it did not exist. On the other hand, Rutilius Namatianus, a member of the old Gallo-Roman aristocracy who was urban prefect of Rome in 414, was bitter. His *On His Return*, which describes his journey from Rome back to Gaul in 416, is vituperative on the subject of Christian ascetics. Yet as time went on artifice took over. Procopius of Caesarea, historian and panegyrist under Justinian, wrote as if he were addressing Greek readers of the classical period, even in his *Anekdota* or *Secret History* which purports to relate the scandals he could not reveal in his published work. Yet he was a Christian.

Macrobius in the late fourth century gives us a picture of the pagan aristocracy of Rome in the eve of Alaric's sack of 410. In his *Saturnalia* he represents their leading members as spending the pagan festival of the Saturnalia together with learned discussions in the morning and lighter conversation at dinner. They are elegant connoisseurs of recondite knowledge, unconcerned by the growing crisis of the state. Chief among them was Symmachus, whose paganism was rooted in a love of the past. His friend, Ausonius, (*c.* 310–*c.* 395) the tutor of the emperor Gratian, belonged to the Indian summer of Gallo-Roman civilization in southern Gaul, before the Visigoths moved in a established a Visigothic kingdom. He wrote charming Latin poems in his old age at Bordeaux. One feels he wore his Christianity lightly. He cannot understand his old pupil Paulinus (*c.* 353–431), who after a brilliant civil career left to live the ascetic life at Nola in Spain. Paulinus, who wrote Christian poetry in classical forms, tried to explain, but the mentalities of the two men had grown apart.

It was in historiography that Christianity left its mark. EUSEBIUS OF CAESAREA, whose *Life* of Constantine is mentioned above, invented two new Christian genres: ecclesiastical history and chronicles. The subject of ecclesiastical history was the church. Whereas history written in the classical tradition avoided citing documents, and it invented speeches where the author could display his rhetorical skill, ecclesiastical history cited documents and excluded speeches. Eusebius' *History of the Church* was continued by Sokrates, who covered the years 309–439. He was followed by SOZOMEN, who covered 324–425, and Evagrius Scholasticus, who discussed the years 431–594. RUFINUS OF AQUILEIA introduced the genre into Latin; he wrote a digest of Eusebius and added two books to cover the years 324–395.

The World Chronicle was not a completely new invention: Eusebius looked back to the work of Sextus Julius Africanus (*c.* 160–*c.* 240). The motive behind the chronicle was the belief that the world would last 6,000 years and that Christ was born 5,500 years after Creation. St. Jerome took over Eusebius' chronicle, and it is through St. Jerome's translation that we know it. The genre continued past the year 500 A.D.; one of the most useful is the chronicle of JOHN MALALAS written under Justinian. For first centuries of Roman history it is evidence only of how indistinct early Rome had become, but for his own period, Malalas is valuable.

Late Antiquity is also the period when the submerged ethnic groups found a voice. Literature in Coptic and Syriac is available: mostly hymns and saint's lives, but also the works of one valuable ecclesiastical historian, John of Asia, who wrote *Lives of the Eastern Saints*, 58 chapters telling the stories of Monophysite ascetics in Syria and Mesopotamia, and a *Church History* in three parts which he wrote in prison at the end of his life. The third part survives almost in its entirety, as well as some of the second part, notably his description of the onslaught of bubonic plague in 542.

Art under the emperor Marcus Aurelius turned its back on the classicism of Hadrian. Marcus Aurelius' column imitates Trajan's, but the style of the sculpture is anti-classical Expressionism. War is shown as brutish and cruel, and the soldiers are degraded puppets. Gallienus favored classicism, but the portraits of the period fix their gaze in the distance, as if they seek something beyond the travails of the present. But with the Tetrarchy portrait sculpture is brutish, and figures in reliefs assume hieratic frontality. Classicism revives somewhat under Constantine, but the mood of the age devalued the human body and placed its emphasis on the life of the spirit.

The Last Days of Paganism. The pagans, known as the *Hellenes* in the Greek-speaking east and the *pagani* in the west, found themselves under increasing pressure. Constantius II outlawed pagan sacrifices (341), which his father may have done before him, and in 356 he ordered all temples closed and sacrifices to cease. In 359 he visited Rome for the first and last time, and while there removed the Altar of Victory from the Senate House. Julian the Apostate attempted a revival. He tried to give paganism a priestly hierarchy analogous to that of the Christian Church and to inject some theology taken from Neoplatonism, but his brand of paganism lacked popular appeal. Presumably he restored the Altar of Victory to the Roman Senate House for the emperor Gratian removed it again.

With Theodosius I paganism became an outlawed religion. Sacrifices and divination were forbidden again on pain of death (381), and Christians who converted to paganism were denied the right to make legal wills (383). A law of 392 again banned all sacrifices or even visiting a pagan temple. Yet paganism persisted into the reign of Justinian (527–565), and a few pockets survived even his vigorous effort to wipe it out. On the popular level, monks spearheaded the battle, and famous ascetics such as St. Symeon the Elder, who lived for 40 years (A.D. 419–459) on top of a pillar northeast of Antioch, were charismatic figures who attracted pilgrims by the thousands. The pagan gods lacked this popular appeal, once sacrifice was banned, and such festivals as remained were emasculated. Yet in rural areas there were still hallowed caves and sacred trees and springs that inspired religious awe. On the intellectual level as well, a modest revival took place: at the end of the fourth century the Neoplatonic Academy in Athens was re-founded as a kind of pagan monastery practicing theurgy, but at the same time continuing the intellectual heritage of Plato. It produced one brilliant philosopher, PROCLUS (412–485), who wrote commentaries on Plato's dialogues as well as treatises, notably *Platonic Theology* and *Elements of Theology*. Emperor Justinian finally closed the school in 529; at least we hear no more of it, although it has been argued that it continued to exist a little longer.

The Fall in the West and Survival in the East

Theodosius died at Milan (Jan. 17, 395) and left his ten-year-old son, Honorius (395–423), as ruler of the western empire with Stilicho, a Vandal, as his guardian and ''Master of the Soldiers,'' and his older brother, Arcadius (395–408), became emperor in Constantinople. The first threat was from Alaric, who rebelled (395) and ravaged Illyricum, where Stilicho's effort to mount a defense roused the hostility of Arcadius' court, which considered Illyricum under its jurisdiction. Alaric then invaded Greece and took Athens, where there is archaeological evidence for looting. There is evidence for the pillaging of Corinth as well. He was granted land in Epirus, but nonetheless invaded Italy (401–403) to then be expelled by Stilicho. On the last day of the year 406, a wave of Alans, Vandals, and Suevi under Vandal leadership crossed the frozen Rhine and ravaged Gaul for three years before moving to Spain. It was during this period of turmoil that the western court moved from Milan to Ravenna, which was easier to defend. Rome itself fell in 410. After Stilicho's death (408), Alaric and his Visigoths had Rome at his mercy. He sacked it in 410, and though Rome no longer had any military significance, the sack sent shock waves through the Empire. It was in the same year that the western emperor Honorius sent letters to the *civitates* of Roman Britain urging them to undertake their own defense, which marks the end of a Roman military presence in Britain.

Alaric died soon after the sack of Rome, and his brother Athaulf led the Visigoths into southern Gaul, tak-

ing with him Honorius' half-sister, Galla Placidia. A Visigothic kingdom lasted in southern France until it was overthrown by the king of the FRANKS, CLOVIS (486). In 414 the Visigoths invaded Spain and a Visigothic kingdom lasted there until it was overthrown by the Muslim Arabs.

The Vandals were to deal the western empire a mortal blow by capturing Africa. The Asding Vandals were not numerous, but they were led by a leader of genius, Gaiseric, who crossed over from Spain to Africa in 429 and began the conquest. Galla Placidia, who provided what direction there was for the western empire from Ravenna as regent for her young son, Valentinian III, failed to coordinate an adequate defense. Carthage fell in 439. Africa was one part of the western empire that had remained prosperous and its wheat fields fed Rome. Now Vandal conquerors displaced Roman landlords, and since the Vandals adhered to the Arian heresy, Catholics were deprived of their churches after 454 and persecuted. Italy had its own problems. Attila, who made himself leader of the Hunnic horde in 446, ravaged Gaul until the Master of the Soldiers, Aetius, met him in 451 with a combined Roman-barbarian force and worsted him at the Battle of the Catalaunian Fields (Châlons). Driven from Gaul, Attila invaded Italy the next year and reached Rome, but he withdrew after a meeting with Pope Leo the Great. He was to die on his wedding night in 453, and after his death his horde disintegrated. Yet Rome was to endure another sack. In 455 Gaiseric and his Vandals took the city, and the looting that followed lasted two weeks, compared to which Alaric's sack had been comparatively mild.

Between 455 and 472 there was a series of short-lived weak emperors who were made and unmade by the ''Patrician'' Ricimer, who was the power behind the throne until his death in 472. Yet one of Ricimer's choices, Majorian (457–461), was able enough to show that with vigorous leadership something might still have been saved. The last emperor was Romulus Augustulus, the young son of the Master of the Soldiers, Orestes, and he was dethroned by Odoacer, a warlord leading a mixed group of barbarians whom he settled in Italy, seizing one-third of the large estates of the landowners for the purpose. Odoacer sent the imperial insignia to Constantinople with the message that the empire needed only one emperor. But the emperor Zeno regarded Odoacer as an illegitimate ruler and encouraged THEODORIC the Ostrogoth to invade Italy in 488. After defeating and killing Odoacer, he established an Ostrogothic kingdom.

The year 476, when Romulus Augustulus was dethroned, is the conventional date for the fall of the Roman Empire. In fact little changed that year. The great landowners were still rich, though they had lost one-third of their estates, and there were still consuls and prefects. But in Constantinople, the last emperor of Theodosius' family, Theodosius II (408–450), though he was anything but vigorous, did provide continuity and stability. The east still had a good recruiting ground for the army in Asia Minor, and Leo I (457–474) rid himself of Aspar, the "First of the Patricians" by counterbalancing his followers with loyal recruits from Isauria. He married his daughter to an Isaurian chief, Tarasis, who became emperor and took the name Zeno (474–491). Thus the eastern empire passed through its time of crisis and survived.

The reign of Anastasius (491–518) was a period of growth and recovery. The Danube frontier was reestablished. Anastasius was followed by Justin I (518–527) and then by Justin's nephew, Justinian (527–565) under whom Africa and Italy were recaptured, as well as a foothold in Spain. Nonetheless the past could not be restored. Italy was left prostrate by Justinian's war, which destroyed the Ostrogothic kingdom. Moreover, bubonic plague visited Europe in the years following 542, when it first appeared in Constantinople, and it provides as good a date as any for the beginning of the so-called "Dark Ages."

Bibliography: C. WELLS, *The Roman Empire* (2nd ed. Cambridge 1992). E. A. JUDGE, "*Res Publica Restituta:* A Modern Illusion?" in J. A. S. EVANS, ed., *Polis and Imperium: Studies in Honour of Edward Togo Salmon* (Toronto 1974) 279–311. A. H. M. JONES, *Augustus* (London 1970). A. GARZETTI, trans. J. R. FOSTER, *From Tiberius to the Antonines. A History of the Roman Empire, A.D. 14–192* (London 1974). R. SYME, *The Roman Revolution*, rev. ed., (Oxford 1952); *The Augustan Aristocracy* (Oxford 1986). K. R. BRADLEY, *Discovering the Roman Family* (Oxford 1991). D. FISHWICK, *The Imperial Cult in the Latin West* (Leiden 1987). E. N. LUTTWAK, *The Grand Strategy of the Roman Empire* (Baltimore and London 1976). R. K. SHERK, *The Roman Empire: Augustus to Hadrian* (Cambridge 1988). M. HAMMOND, *The Antonine Monarchy* (Rome 1959). F. MILLAR, *The Roman Near East* (Cambridge 1993). J. E. LENDON, *Empire of Honour: The Art of Government in the Roman World* (Oxford 1997). F. MILLAR, *The Emperor in the Roman World (31 B.C.–A.D. 337)* (Ithaca 1977). C. ANDO, *Imperial Ideology and Provincial Loyalty in the Roman Empire* (Berkeley 2000). R. L. FOX, *Pagans and Christians* (New York 1989). A. WATSON, *Aurelian and the Third Century* (London 1999). P. HEATHER, *Goths and Romans 332–489* (Oxford 1991). G. FRIELL and S. WILLIAMS, *Theodosius: The Empire at Bay* (London 1994). A. K. BOWMAN, *Egypt after the Pharaohs 332 B.C.–A.D. 642* (Berkeley 1989). T. F. CARNEY, *Bureaucracy in Traditional Society* (Lawrence, Kansas 1971). A. LESKY, *A History of Greek Literature* trans. J. WILLIS and C. DE HEER (London 1966). A. CAMERON, *The Later Roman Empire* (Cambridge 1993); *The Mediterranean World in Late Antiquity, A.D. 395–600* (London/New York 1993). A. H. M. JONES, *The Later Roman Empire. A Social, Economic and Administrative Survey*, 2 vols., (Norman, Oklahoma 1964).

[J. A. S. EVANS]

ROMAN QUESTION

An expression referring to the politicoreligious conflict between the papacy and the Kingdom of Italy (1861–1929).

Origins. Italian political unification dates from the work of Mazzini and the foundation of Young Italy (1831, but the Roman Question arose when the Italian Chamber of Deputies proclaimed Rome as capital of the new kingdom, though the city was then part of the STATES OF THE CHURCH (March 27, 1861). Only then did the termination of the papal temporal power become an unavoidable and urgent question for European chanceries. The Austrian Empire confessed its inability to aid Pius IX (1846–78), and during the ministry of the Lutheran Count Friedrich von Beust (1867–71) pursued a friendly policy toward Italy. England, Russia, and Prussia favored Italy for religious and political motives. Pius IX's sole protector was NAPOLEON III, acting under pressure from French Catholics; but after France's defeat at Sedan (Sept. 1, 1870), the pope lacked all international help. This made it possible for Italy to resolve the problem in a radical and violent manner by invading and occupying the Eternal City (Sept. 20, 1870).

The peaceful solutions, favored by many moderate Italians, which would have continued papal temporal power on a more restricted scale, were always disdainfully rejected by Pius IX because he considered it impossible for him to dispose of territory belonging to the Church, of which he was merely the custodian. He also foresaw that concessions to the Italian state would inevitably stimulate further demands and spoliations and lead to the inglorious doom rather than to the salvation of his 1,000-year-old state. The final attempts at peaceful solution, implying Italian annexation of Rome except for the Leonine city, made by the government from Florence (September 1870) met the pope's adamant refusal. So did the proposal by GLADSTONE, supported by the Austrian chancellor Beust, of convoking a European congress, because Pius IX feared that this gathering might sanction spoliation while partially restoring his temporal power. Thereupon Pius IX issued the encyclical *Respicientes ea omnia,* excommunicating all who had ordered or executed the usurpation, but without specifically mentioning VICTOR EMMANUEL II (Nov. 1, 1870).

Law of Guarantees. Without delay the Italian government sought to reassure Catholics throughout the world of its intent to ensure free communication between the Holy See and the diplomatic corps, the hierarchy, and Catholics in general. Details of the manner in which this promise was to be kept appeared in the Law of GUARANTEES (May 13, 1871). This unilateral solution, which contained no permanent definition of papal rights, was solemnly declared unacceptable by Pius IX (May 15), who voluntarily became a prisoner in the Vatican, spurned the financial offer, and abstained from any act that might have implied, even indirectly, acceptance of the spoliation of his states. LEO XIII (1878–1903) maintained the same intransigent position and repelled all attempts at conciliation.

Progress toward Solution. Developments in France, notably the rupture of diplomatic relations with Rome, the abolition of the Concordat of 1801, and the passage of the law separating Church and State, along with mounting social problems and the growth of socialism, induced PIUS X (1903–14) to seek a *rapprochement* with Italy. This led to a softening of the NON EXPEDIT policy, thus authorizing Italian Catholics to participate in political elections (June 11, 1905), and to the Gentiloni pact (1913), which encouraged Catholics to support constitutional candidates favorable to conciliating the Church. World War I accentuated this trend, because of Catholic civil loyalty and the Holy See's scrupulous neutrality, which frustrated a tremendous German press campaign by declaring through Cardinal GASPARRI, Secretary of State to BENEDICT XV (1914–22), that it awaited "the appropriate settlement of its situation not by foreign arms but by the triumph of those sentiments of justice which fortunately spread ever more widely among the Italian populace in conformity with its true interests" (June 28, 1915).

After World War I, Msgr. Bonaventura Cerretti, Secretary of State for Extraordinary Ecclesiastical Affairs, discussed the Roman Question in Paris with Vittorio Orlando, the Italian Premier, and presented to him a solution composed by Cardinal Gasparri, that would have attributed to the enclosed Vatican the character of a sovereign state (May 1919). This led to a projected concordat, but the fall of Orlando's cabinet (June 1919) ended these discussions. In 1919 Italian Catholics founded under the leadership of Don Luigi STURZO the Popular party. Alfredo Rocco declared in Parliament: "It does not seem to me impossible to find a point of agreement which conciliates the teachings of the Holy See concerning complete independence with the domestic and international needs of the Italian state" (June 21, 1921). Official state mourning for a pope, decreed for the first time upon the death of Benedict XV, and the solemn blessing imparted by PIUS XI (1922–39) from the external loggia of the Vatican after his election symbolized the changed climate, which continued to improve.

The LATERAN PACTS (1929), which set up VATICAN CITY as a fully independent and sovereign state, concluded a concordat regulating Church-State relations, arranged a financial settlement, abrogated the Law of Guarantees, and definitively and irrevocably terminated the Roman Question, as stated in article 26 of the treaty.

Bibliography: Documents. H. BASTGEN, *Die römische Frage*, 3 v. (Freiburg 1917–19). P. PIRRI, ed., *Pio IX e Vittorio Emanuele dal loro carteggio privato*, 5 v. (Rome 1944–61). N. MIKO, *Das Ende des Kirchenstaates*, 2 v. (Vienna 1961–64). A. PIOLA, *La Questione Romana nella storia nel diritto* (Padua 1931). Literature. G. MOLLAT, *La Question romaine de Pie VI à Pie IX* (2d ed. Paris 1932); EncCatt 10:400–403. L. M. CASE, *Franco-Italian Relations (1860–1865): The Roman Question and the Convention of September* (Philadelphia 1932). S. JACINI, *La politica ecclesiastica italiana da Villafranca a Porta Pia* (Bari 1938). S. W. HALPERIN, *Italy and the Vatican at War* (Chicago 1939). Schmidlin v.2, 3, 4. A. C. JEMOLO, *La questione romana* (Milan 1938); *Church and State in Italy, 1850–1950*, tr. D. MOORE (Philadelphia 1960). V. DEL GIUDICE, *La Questione romans e i rapporti tra Stato e Chiesa fina alla Conciliazione* (Rome 1947). F. ENGEL-JANOSI, *Österreich und der Vatikan, 1846–1918*, 2 v. (Graz 1958–60). S. LENER, *La formazione dell' unità d'Italia e i cattolici* (Rome 1962). *The Roman Question: Extracts from the Despatches of Odo Russell from Rome, 1858–1870*, ed. N. BLAKISTON (London 1962). R. MORI, *La Questione romana 1861–65* (Florence 1963). R. AUBERT, *Le Pontificat de Pie IX* (Fliche-Martin 21; 2d ed. 1964).

[R. MORI]

ROMAN RELIGION

The history of Roman religion before the 5th century B.C. is obscure, and it is likewise complex, because Roman religion from an early stage exhibits a fusion of Italic and Etruscan elements with the Roman core proper. However, Roman religious institutions were remarkably conservative and persistent, and with the data furnished by Roman calendars, antiquarians, historians, archeology, and comparative religion, it is possible to get a reasonably clear and reliable idea of the basic religious concepts and institutions at least from the 6th century B.C. The Roman calendars, in particular, are of the greatest value in the reconstruction of early Roman religion. At the outset it may be stated that Roman religion was predominantly agrarian in character and that even the later calendars still stress the agrarian cycle of feasts and ritual.

Early Roman Religion (to 218 B.C.). The Latin word *religio* is best explained as meaning a "feeling of awe" or "anxiety" toward supernatural powers or forces (*numina*). These *numina* were regarded as dwelling in natural objects and in specific localities and as having a decisive role in every aspect of human life and activity. They were not thought of originally as personifications of natural forces but, primarily, as "spirits." This animistic character of early Roman religion helps to explain the striking fact that the Romans never created a mythology of their own. The primary concern of Roman religion was, by prayer, sacrifice, and scrupulous observance of

Caesar Augustus (Octavius).

ritual, to establish friendly relations with the *numina* governing the myriad activities of life, and thus to have reasonable assurance of their help and protection. Magic also played a very important role in Roman religion. It was regularly employed in both public and private life to discover the will of *numina* and to make certain of their help or, on the other hand, to obtain effective protection against the harmful actions of malevolent spirits.

Family Religion. Family worship was centered in the house, fields, and boundaries of the farmstead. A host of *numina* or spirits presided over the various parts of the house and the activities of house and farm. The *Penates* guarded the pantry; and *Janus,* the door. *Vesta,* the spirit of fire, was present in the hearth. The *pater familias* had an indwelling *Genius;* and the *mater familias,* an indwelling *Juno.* The *Lares* protected the fields. All these spirits were the object of cult, and the *pater familias* was the priest of the household—which included slaves as well as members of the family proper. A special festival, the *Terminalia,* was held in honor of the boundary stones, and in May the *Ambarvalia* was celebrated to insure the fertility of the fields. It included a solemn procession, prayers, and the sacrifice of a pig, sheep, and ox (*suovetaurilia*). Other feasts, likewise connected with agriculture, were celebrated throughout the year, and magic practices of various kinds were employed to ward off evil

spirits or diseases. The spirits of the dead, the *Di Manes,* were honored at the feast of the *Lemuria,* which was held in May. At first, the spirits of the dead were feared, and the rites were intended to propitiate them or drive them away. At the later feast of the *Parentalia,* however, relatives decorated the graves of their dead without fear and out of a feeling of duty and affection. Family religion in country areas remained at once relatively primitive and vital to the end of antiquity.

Religion of the State. According to Roman tradition King Numa established the Roman calendar with its cycle of feasts and its listing of days on which public business could or could not be conducted (*dies fasti et nefasti*). The king himself was chief priest. He was assisted primarily by two collegiate priesthoods, the College of Pontiffs, and the College of Augurs. After the establishment of the Republic (*c.* 509 B.C.), the two colleges mentioned became the two most important religious bodies in the state. The chief pontiff, the *Pontifex Maximus,* was the head of the state religion, with supervisory control over religion in general. A *rex sacrorum* continued, to some extent, the religious functions of the Roman kings. In the absence of a priestly caste, Roman magistrates served in these colleges and performed the priestly functions. The College of Pontiffs kept the calendar and were the guardians and interpreters of *ius divinum* and *ius humanum,* retaining a monopoly over the *legis actiones* or forms of pleading until the late 4th century B.C. The main business of the pontiffs was to maintain the *pax deorum,* the proper relations between the divine powers and the state. The College of Augurs, by observing the flights of birds and other phenomena, indicated whether the omens were favorable or unfavorable regarding a public action to be taken. In matters of grave concern the Romans made use of the *Etrusca disciplina,* or hepatoscopy. A priesthood, the *flamines,* performed certain rites in honor of Jupiter, Mars, and Quirinus; the Salian brotherhood were devoted to the worship of Mars; and the VESTAL VIRGINS spent the greater period of their lives in the cult of Vesta as symbolized in the sacred hearth fire of the state. A special college of priests, the *Fetiales,* carried out magicoreligious ceremonies connected with the declaration of war. The Roman TRIUMPH after victory was a solemn religious act of thanksgiving.

The Romans honored their divinities with sacrifices of animals, first fruits, libations, and prayers. The animals sacrificed were chiefly pigs, but sheep and oxen also were immolated. Every five years a solemn *lustratio* or purification of the city was held, consisting of a procession, sacrifices, and prayers. Of the early Roman temples, that erected to Jupiter Optimus Maximus on the Capitol was the most important. It should be noted also that the *ludi,* or public games of the Romans, were religious in origin and long maintained their religious character. The religious rites of the state had to be carried out with scrupulous exactness. They inculcated a spirit of discipline and order, but they had little emotional appeal.

Foreign Cults and Spread of Anthropomorphism. The Italic cults of Diana, Fortuna, Venus (a vegetation divinity), and Minerva (a goddess of weaving) were introduced very early. The worship of the triad, Jupiter, Juno, and Minerva, was probably of Etruscan origin. Greek influence came through the Etruscans or through increasing contacts with the Greek South. Among the Greek divinities introduced at Rome before the Second Punic War were Apollo, Hercules, Castor and Pollux, Ceres, Liber, and Libera (Greek Demeter, Dionysus, and Persephone), Mercury (Hermes), Neptune (Poseidon), and Aesculapius. A collection of the SIBYLLINE ORACLES was in use by the early 4th century B.C. and was entrusted to a special college, the *Decemviri sacris faciundis.* Greek divinities were worshiped with a ritual adapted from the Greek (*Graecus ritus*). The carrying of gods on couches (*lectisternia*) in procession, and processions of supplication (*supplicationes*) in times of grave crisis, were also of Greek origin. By the late 3d century, anthropomorphism had made great progress. The more important old Roman *numina* had acquired or were acquiring human form and were being assigned the attributes of their approximate Greek counterparts. Vesta, however, remained immune from anthropomorphism, and her temple contained no statue.

From the Second Punic War to the End of the Republic (218–231 B.C.). The long and terrible war with Hannibal caused an outburst of all kinds of superstition and led the state to resort to alien cults that seemed more effective. The *Ludi Magni* were celebrated with great pomp in 217; the *Ludi Apollinares* were instituted in 212; and the *Ludi Megalenses,* in 204. These games were intended primarily to honor the gods, but, by furnishing entertainment at the same time, they lessened anxiety and tension. After Cannae (216), the Romans buried alive two Gauls and two Greeks in the Forum Boarium to appease the angry gods. Later a *supplicatio* was decreed and a *lectisternium* in which 12 Greek and Roman gods were carried side by side, thus indicating that the Roman religion had really become Greco-Roman.

In 205, on the advice of the Sibylline Books, the cult of Cybele, the Great Mother of Asia Minor, was introduced at Rome, and her fetish, the black stone of Pessinus, was brought with all solemnity to Rome and placed in the Temple of Victory on the Palatine. Subsequently, the Romans restricted the cult of Cybele as much as possible, but it had come to stay. The orgiastic cult of DIONYSUS or Bacchus spread to Rome from South Italy, but in

Arch of Trajan, detail showing Hercules, Minerva, Bacchus, Jupiter, Ceres, Juno, and Mercury, Beneventum, A.D. 114–117. (Alinari-Art Reference/Art Resource, NY)

186 it was suppressed by the Roman Senate, whose stern decree, *Senatus consultum de Bacchanalibus,* is extant. On the other hand, from the early 3d century the state itself fostered the cults of abstract personifications, as that of Victory mentioned above. Thus *Libertas, Pietas, Concordia, Salus, Pax,* among others, were the object of cult. Caesar himself received divine honor indirectly by the erecting of a temple to his *Clementia.*

Vitality of Oriental Cults and Decline of the State Religion. Despite the vigilance of the state regarding the introduction of foreign cults and its refusal to give them full or even partial official recognition, the great influx of Greeks and Orientals into Rome in the 2d and 1st centuries led to the spread not only of new Greek cults but, especially, of Oriental cults that were highly emotional. They had elaborate liturgies and a professional priesthood, and promised an afterlife to their devotees. The Mysteries of ISIS AND OSIRIS, for example, came to Rome c. 100 B.C., a century after the introduction of the worship of the Great Mother of Asia Minor. Along with Oriental religions came astrology and other forms of magic and superstition.

The official cults of the state had lost all emotional appeal for the masses, but they continued to be main-

Egyptian priests celebrating the Mysteries of Isis, fresco, Pompeii, 1st century A.D.

tained—if in a neglected way—as a part of the governmental machinery by men who no longer held the old beliefs. They were even exploited by more or less unscrupulous candidates for high office, who used them merely to serve their political ambitions. Caesar, for example, although one of the confirmed agnostics of his age, sought and obtained, the office of *Pontifex Maximus,* the highest religious office in the state.

Impact of Greek Literature and Philosophy. The influence of Hellenism on Rome began in the 6th century B.C., but it became especially intense and all but overwhelming from the last half of the 3d century. A formal Latin literature was created under the direct influence of Greek models, and Latin antiquarians and poets connected Roman origins and Roman religion with Greek traditions and divinities as far as possible. Anthropomorphism now reached its full term, and Greek mythology was taken over by Latin writers and adapted to serve literary ends. The mythology of the Latin poets is simply Greek mythology in Latin dress. Aeneas the Trojan became the founder of Rome, and Caesar traced his ancestry back through Aeneas to Venus and Anchises. This religion of the poets reflects literary sophistication and convention rather than genuine belief, and it was so regarded by the small educated class for which it was written.

The rationalistic outlook of poets had its foundation in the rationalism of the Hellenistic Age as exemplified by Euhemerus, who was translated by Ennius, the father of Latin poetry. Under the impact of Hellenism, educated Romans became familiar not only with the older and con-

temporary Greek literature, but also with the various schools of Greek philosophy, especially with EPICUREANISM and STOICISM, which were the most influential. While Epicureanism led to the repudiation of traditional religion as superstition, Stoicism gave an allegorical interpretation of the old myths, and its religiophilosophical teachings offered intellectuals an attractive and meaningful way of life. However, through Posidonius especially, Stoicism found a place for astrology and astral religion in its system. The typical rationalistic attitude of the educated Roman is well exemplified in the pertinent writings of Cicero and Varro.

Under the Empire. Octavian began a systematic revival of the old state cults in the years before Actium (31), and then, as Augustus, founder of the Principate, he carried out this policy on a much wider scale. He instituted the *Ludi saeculares* in 17 B.C., and in 12 B.C., after the death of Lepidus, he assumed the office of Pontifex Maximus—held subsequently by all his successors until it was relinquished by Gratian, A.D. 382. He rebuilt temples throughout Rome, restored the old priesthoods, and required them to celebrate the rituals of their respective cults with the earlier regularity and pomp. He enlisted the help also of the great contemporary poets Horace, Vergil, and Ovid in his program of restoring the Old Roman cults and their celebration.

But the most important of his religious innovations was the imperial cult. It was in part Hellenistic, but the emphasis on the public worship of the *Genius* of the emperor, especially in Rome and Italy, gave it a Roman character as well. It was intended to serve as an effective symbol of unity in the universal empire of Rome and also to promote a deeper loyalty on the part of the army to its *imperator,* or commander in chief. Gradually, the imperial cult and its priesthoods lost much of their appeal, but they enjoyed a marked revival in the period from Aurelian to Diocletian. Under the influence of the central administration and the model set by Rome, the religious cults of the Roman provinces, despite local aspects, assumed more and more the Roman pattern, at least in external form.

Mystery Religions and the Spread of Superstition. The most vital forms of religion under the Empire were the Greco-Oriental MYSTERY RELIGIONS, especially the Mysteries of Isis, of Cybele (*Magna Mater Deorum*), and of MITHRAS. Their highly organized emotional cults and their promise of salvation and afterlife to their devotees appealed to all classes of society. The cult of Mithras was essentially a religion for men and was very popular in the legions; Mithraic shrines are found from Syria to Britain. Pagan religious credulity and superstition reached its high point under the Principate. Oracles, dreambooks, and other forms of divination had a wide vogue. Men like Apollonius of Tyana and Alexander of Abonoteichos acquired great celebrity as miracle workers, although the latter was a notorious charlatan.

Philosophy and Religion. With the exception of Epicureanism, which was in rapid decline in the 2d century A.D., philosophy in general became progressively more occupied with religion. Stoicism, Middle PLATONISM, and NEO-PYTHAGOREANISM were really religions, or at least religious philosophies. Astral religion, with its accompanying fatalism, had numerous adherents in this period also and, as already noted, had found a place within Stoicism. The supposed revelations of Hermes Trismegistus and other Gnostic teachings, derived from Oriental as well as Greek sources, combined philosophy, religion, and magic in more or less fantastic ways. Syncretism was a marked feature in all these philosophical religions. Furthermore, philosophy was regarded as a religious way of life. Hence there is frequent mention of "conversion," as in a strictly religious sense.

The last great philosophy of antiquity, NEOPLATONISM, founded by Plotinus (fl. 250–270), was a religion as well as a philosophy. With modifications by Porphyry (223–305) and Iamblichus (d. *c.* 330), Neoplatonism was able to include all pagan beliefs in its system. Thus, late paganism acquired a systematic theology, and in this form it became much more formidable to Christianity. Its refutation demanded the new kind of Christian philosophical and theological apologetic that is evident in St. Augustine's treatment of the major tenets of Porphyry in his *City of God.* Philosophical paganism was a conspicuous feature of Julian's attempted revival and of the circle of Macrobius. It had a continued life in the philosophical schools of Athens until their closing by Justinian in A.D. 529.

Persistence of Old Roman Religion. Despite the decay of the old Roman religion in Rome and other large urban centers in the West and the triumph of the mystery religions, and subsequently that of Christianity in these same centers, the old Roman agrarian cults and magic practices retained their vitality in the more remote municipalities and, above all, in country districts. The popular sermons of St. Augustine, Maximus of Turin, and other Christian preachers of the late 4th and early 5th centuries refer repeatedly to the continued observance of old pagan feasts and the resort to magic practices. Even as late as the 6th century MARTIN OF BRAGA and CAESARIUS OF ARLES found it necessary to condemn by name pagan superstitions and practices mentioned in the calendars of the late Republic and early Empire.

See Also: AFTERLIFE, 3; GREEK RELIGION; GREEK PHILOSOPHY (RELIGIOUS ASPECTS).

The theophany of Dionysus, Roman fresco, Pompeii or Herculaneum, before 79 A.D. (©Mimmo Jodice/CORBIS)

Bibliography: P. BILDE, "The Meaning of Roman Mithraism," in *Rethinking Religion* (Copenhagen 1989) 31–47. R. GORDON, "Religion in the Roman Empire: The Civic Compromise and Its Limits," in *Pagan Priests* (Ithaca, N.Y. 1990) 235–55. M. BARNETT and M. DIXON, *Gods and Myths of the Romans* (London 1996). H. CANCIK and J. RÜPKE, *Römische Reichsreligion und Provinzialreligion* (Tübingen 1997). J. SCHNEID, *La religion des Romains* (Paris 1998). J. CHAMPEAUX, *La religion romaine* (Paris 1998). E. BISPHAM, et al., eds., *Religion in Archaic and Republican Rome and Italy: Evidence and Experience* (Edinburgh 2000). J. A. NORTH *Roman Religion* (Oxford 2000). R. TURCAN, *The Gods of Ancient Rome* (Edinburgh 2000). J. RÜPKE, *Die Religion der Römer: eine Einführung* (Munich 2001). A. TRIPOLITIS, *Religions of the Hellenistic-Roman Age* (Grand Rapids, Mich. 2001).

[M. R. P. MCGUIRE/EDS.]

ROMAN RITE

The term Roman Rite, sometimes mistakenly called the Rite of St. Peter, is here taken to mean the entire complex of liturgical prayers and practices in the Mass, Office, and Sacraments, etc., which originated in, or were adopted by, the Diocese of Rome and later imposed on almost the entire (Western) Church. Here are discussed its history, its chief characteristics, and its main variants.

History. The beginnings of the Roman Rite in Latin from the Greek are obscure. Many scholars have ques-

Roman Catholic Archbishop of New York, Edward Michael Egan, holds up the chalice as he delivers Communion during the Mass of Installation at St. Patrick's Cathedral in New York City, June 2000. (©Reuters NewMedia Inc./CORBIS)

tioned the long-held assumptions about the date, origins, and authorship of the *Apostolic Tradition,* a church order that was traditionally associated with the Church of Rome by virtue of its supposed author, HIPPOLYTUS of Rome. The earliest extant manuscript evidence suggests that around 270 (parallel to the same occurence in northern Africa) the Greek liturgy of the Roman Rite was gradually translated into Latin.

One characteristic feature of the ancient Roman Rite was its solemn prayers—a series of prayers, each beginning with a bidding by priest or bishop, followed by silent prayer and ending with a concluding collect by the priest or bishop. Geoffrey Willis and Paul De Clerck have suggested that the biddings are older than the collects. During the season of Lent, the deacon would instruct the faithful to kneel (*flectamus genua*) for silent prayer, and rise (*levate*) for the concluding collect. The solemn prayers fell into disuse and survive only on Good Friday.

Another feature of the early Roman Rite was the litany known as the *Deprecatio Gelasii,* traditionally attributed to Pope GELASIUS (492–6). The Litanies are very similar to those in the Divine Liturgy of the Christian East, with the bidding of the deacon and the assembly's

responding "Lord have mercy" (*Kyrie eleison*). Over time, the Litanies disappeared. While older scholarship thought that the Litanies were abbreviated into the KYRIE ELEISON we know of today, many scholars now hold that they were simply dropped in favor of processional litanies.

The reforms carried out by several popes affected especially the prayer formulae, rituals, and chants. Under the Oriental influence of successive Eastern popes (from *c.* 640 to *c.* 750) certain texts (e.g., the *Agnus Dei,* inserted into the Roman Rite by Pope Sergius I, which was originally a *Confractorium*) and certain feasts (e.g., the Annunciation, "Dormition," and Nativity of the Blessed Virgin) were introduced.

The *Ordo Romanus Primus* gives us a detailed description of an 8th century papal mass at a stational church. By this time, the Solemn Prayers and the *Deprecatio Gelasii* had long disappeared. What was once a simple eucharist has evolved into an ornate and elaborate ritual complete with processions from the papal palace to the STATIONAL CHURCH.

Sometime after 754 the Roman Rite was officially introduced into Franco-German areas by the Carolingian monarchs, replacing the GALLICAN RITES. The Roman Rite succeeded in supplanting the liturgical forms of the old Frankish empire, not by abolishing them, but by assimilating them. Both Pepin (d. 768) and Charlemagne (d. 814) authoritatively introduced the liturgy of Rome into their realms; Alcuin, and later Amalarius, combined old Gallican elements with the Roman usage, thus achieving a new form which was practicable outside the city of the popes. It was this Gallicanized liturgy, embellished with new forms, that returned to Rome from the Rhineland (Cologne and Mainz) around 950. Important in this connection were the Germanic emperors and popes who brought back with them the Frankish Ordinals and especially the Romano-Germanic Pontifical of Mainz. After the year 1000 the smelting process began in Rome itself, especially under Gregory VII and Innocent III, who had service books made for the Roman Curia. These were used in turn by the Franciscans, who introduced them far and wide.

Between 1568 and 1614, Rome, at the behest of the Council of TRENT, created a uniform liturgy for almost the whole Latin Church, based principally on the Roman Curial books, themselves a mixture of Roman and Franco-Germanic elements. The books issued were the Roman Breviary (1568), Missal (1570), Pontifical (1598), Ceremonial of Bishops (1600), and Ritual (1614).

On Dec. 4, 1963, at the end of the second session of Vatican Council II, Paul VI approved and promulgated the conciliar *Constitution on the Sacred Liturgy* and implemented it with a special *motu proprio* on Jan. 25, 1964. The conciliar *Constitution on the Sacred Liturgy* crowned the reform work of the 20th-century popes beginning with Pius X, who gave the liturgical movement a decidedly pastoral orientation. The document contained not only many well-ordered pastoral admonitions, but pointed decrees for reform, the most important of which had to do with the translation of the Roman Rite into the vernacular, and adaptations to the genius of the diverse cultures throughout the world.

Though originally local in character and circumscribed in use, the Roman Rite became the most widespread in Christendom. It is found almost universally in western Europe and in every country evangelized by western Europe, including those that have native European liturgies.

Although the beginnings of a distinctly Roman liturgy are dim and uncertain, it seems to be an entirely native growth, though it was undoubtedly influenced by outside forces, particularly in its later development. No one any longer takes seriously the numerous conjectures of 19th- and early 20th-century scholars. The Roman Rite bears clear marks of its local origin: the Missal indicates the Roman stations, and the Canon of the Mass honors the Roman martyrs with special solemnity.

Chief Characteristics. The traits of the present Roman Rite are many and varied. But the sober, not to say somber, earnestness of the ancient Roman liturgy, with its clear, compact, and controlled style, is in strong contrast to the dramatic exuberance and prolixity of the Gallican liturgies and the poetry and volubility of the Oriental. However, the present Roman liturgical books contain an admixture of other styles, indicative of their long and complicated history. In fact, the Roman form was really incomplete as far as the development of many of the Sacraments and sacramentals was concerned, and the work of completion and enrichment was done in the Frankish realms and drawn from many sources, native and foreign.

Variants. The centuries before the Council of Trent were times of great liturgical diversification even within the framework of the Roman Rite. During the Middle Ages the rite developed a vast number of derived uses which were, for the most part, abolished by St. Pius V, in the bull *Quo primum*, July 14, 1570. Many dioceses and religious orders that had developed their own variants of the Romano-Frankish liturgy took advantage of a stipulation in the document *Quo primum*. Only Braga, Lyons, the CARMELITES, CARTHUSIANS, CISTERCIANS, DOMINICANS, and PREMONSTRATENSIANS have retained remnants of their own rite until the liturgical renewal of Vatican Council II.

See Also: BRAGAN RITE; LYONESE RITE; SARUM USE; CARMELITE RITE; CARTHUSIAN RITE; CISTERCIAN RITE; DOMINICAN RITE; PREMONSTRATENSIAN RITE.

Bibliography: A. A. KING, *Liturgy of the Roman Church* (Milwaukee 1957). J. A. JUNGMANN, *The Mass of the Roman Rite,* tr. F. A. BRUNNER, 2 v. (New York 1951–55); *The Early Liturgy to the Time of Gregory the Great,* tr. F. A. BRUNNER (South Bend, Ind. 1959). B. BOTTE, *La Tradition apostolique de saint Hippolyte: Essai de reconstitution* in *Liturgiegeschichtliche Quellen und Forschungen* (Münster 1909–40; 1957–) 39; (1963). S. J. P. VAN DIJK and J. H. WALKER, *The Origins of the Modern Roman Liturgy* (Westminster, Md. 1960). E. BISHOP, *Liturgica historica* (Oxford 1918; repr. 1962), T. KLAUSER, *The Western Liturgy and Its History: Some Reflections on Recent Studies,* tr. F. L. CROSS (New York 1952). G. G. WILLIS, *Essays in Early Roman Liturgy* (London 1964), and *Further Essays in Early Roman Liturgy* (London 1968). P. D. CLERCK, *La Prière Universelle dans les liturgies latines anciennes* (Münster 1977). G. P. JEANES, *The Origins of the Roman Rite* (Bramcote, Nottingham, Eng. 1991). P. F. BRADSHAW, ''Redating the *Apostolic Tradition*: Some Preliminary Steps,'' in *Rule of Prayer, Rule of Faith: Essays in Honor of Aidan Kavanagh, OSB,* eds. N. MITCHELL and J. F. BALDOVIN (Collegeville, Minn. 1996), 3–17. T. J. TALLEY, ''Roman Culture and Roman Liturgy,'' in *Rule of Prayer, Rule of Faith: Essays in Honor of Aidan Kavanagh, OSB,* eds. N. MITCHELL and J. F. BALDOVIN (Collegeville, Minn. 1996), 18–31.

[F. A. BRUNNER/EDS.]

ROMANIA, THE CATHOLIC CHURCH IN

Located in southeastern Europe, Romania (formerly ''Rumania'') is bordered on the north by Ukraine, on the east by Bessarabia and the Black Sea, on the south by the Danube River and Bulgaria, and on the west by Serbia and Hungary. While Romania contains portions of the Carpathian Mountains and the Transylvanian Alps, much of the country's landscape is characterized by rolling hills and fertile farmlands. Romania's natural resources include timber, natural gas, coal, iron and a declining reserve of petroleum. Occupied by a communist regime between 1947 and 1989, the nation's barren industrial base was in the process of regeneration by 2000, with the mining, timber and construction materials industries among the nation's major exporters.

Romania has its roots in the ancient Roman province of DACIA. Although a Latin people through the early influence of Bulgar invaders most Romanians adopted the Byzantine tradition that would ultimately evolve into the Romanian Orthodox Church. Meanwhile, Latin Catholicism developed strong roots in Transylvania while that area was under the domination of the Austro-Hungarian Hapsburgs, although many Transylvanian Catholics went on to convert to Protestantism under Turkish rule. The Turks also sent Greek princes to rule in Walachia and

Capital: Bucharest.
Size: 91,699 sq. miles.
Population: 22,411,121 in 2000.
Languages: Romanian, Hungarian, German.
Religions: 15,687,784 Romanian Orthodox (70%), 1,161,942 Romanian Greek-Catholics (5%), 1,344,667 Roman Catholics (6%), 1,433,500 Protestants and other denominations (6%), 2,783,228 without religious affiliation.
Ecclesiastical organizations: The Roman Catholic Church has an archdiocese in Bucharest, with dioceses in Iaşi, Oradea Mare, Satu Mare, and Timişoara.

Moldavia, establishing a Greek-Catholic presence through relations with monasteries in Greece. As a result of these diverse political influences, several churches evolved in Romania: the Latin or Roman Catholic Church, the Byzantine or Greek-Catholic Church, and the autocephalous Romanian Orthodox Church. The essay following this introductory section presents discussion of these churches within several historical epochs.

Early History to World War II

Christianity first came to the region in its Latin form and by the 3d century had penetrated the region near the Black Sea (modern Dobruja), which later formed the ecclesiastical province of Scythia, with Tomi (now Constanta) as metropolis. To the west, on the right side of the Danube, there existed the Diocese of Remesiana (near modern Palanka), whose bishop, St. NICETAS, a renowned Latin Christian writer, was venerated as the apostle of the Romanians. Christianity all but disappeared from these regions during the Bulgar invasions and the subsequent migration, which began in the 6th century and lasted for several centuries. During the Bulgarian rule that began in the 8th century, the Slavonic language spread and the BYZANTINE CHRISTIANITY became the predominant faith among the Romanians. Even after Bulgarian supremacy ceased, Slavonic remained the official language for the liturgy and also for the chanceries of Walachia and Moldavia.

Hungarians moved into the Transylvania region *c.* 1003. In the 14th century Walachia and Moldavia arose as independent principalities, but from the 16th to the 19th centuries they served as vassals to Turkish overlords while still retaining much of their autonomy. In 1859 these various principalities united under Prince Alexandru Ioan Cuza and in 1861 adopted the name Romania. After suffering a land shift during the Russo-Prussian War of 1877, Romania gained complete independence in 1878 and became a kingdom in 1881. At the start of World War II the country was ruled by Michael I, who remained king until his abdication in 1947.

Development of a Byzantine Tradition. During the 17th century the Romanian Church in Transylvania experienced pressure by Hungarian Protestant princes, especially those of the Rákóczy family. To resist this threat, a synod met in Iaşi in 1642 and condemned the Romanian catechism published by Prince George Rkóczy because it contained Calvinist doctrines. Union with the Catholic Church was also attempted at this time. In 1690 Austrian armies liberated Transylvania from Turkish domination and established Hapsburg rule. After negotiations with Romanian bishops Theophilus and Athanasius, a general synod of the Romanian clergy met in Alba Iulia (Oct. 7, 1698) and agreed to unite with the Catholic Church on the basis of the Ecumenical Council of Florence. While it was hoped that this union would include all the faithful of the Romanian rite, it did not turn out that way: a large part of the clergy and laity remained Orthodox. The Council of Florence marked the division of the region's Byzantine-rite Catholics into Romanian Orthodox and Greek-Catholics.

The Rise of the Romanian Orthodox Church. Because of the influence of the Bulgarian Church, Romanians had begun to embrace the Byzantine rite by the 10th century. They also imitated their Bulgarian rulers by adhering to the EASTERN SCHISM. When the Danubian principalities of Walachia and Moldavia were formed in the 14th century, the rulers requested the patriarch of Constantinople to erect a metropolis in their country. In 1359 Walachia received a metropolitan, who resided in Arges (later in Bucharest). Moldavia gained a metropolitan *c.* 1400; his residence was in Suceava (later in Iaşi). During the 15th century the Romanian principalities battled the Turks, and Pope Sixtus IV dubbed Prince Stephan the Great (1457–1504) an "athlete of Christ" for his valiant defense of Christianity during this period. While attempts were made to unite the Romanian Orthodox and the Latin-rite Church prior to the Ecumenical Council of FLORENCE they were ultimately unsuccessful.

Under the protection of the powerful Turkish princes of Walachia and Moldavia, Orthodox Christianity flourished during the 17th and 18th centuries. Rich gifts and foundations enabled monasteries at Tismana, Voditza, Neamt, Putna and elsewhere to become religious and cultural centers. From 1711 to 1821 the Turks sent Greek princes (phanariots) to rule Walachia and Moldavia; these men became generous benefactors of the Patriarchate of Constantinople and of the Greek monasteries at Mt. Athos, Mt. Sinai, Jerusalem and elsewhere. On the whole, Greek influence in the Romanian principalities increased under the phanariots, and by 1863 Greek monasteries possessed one-fifth of the land; their holdings were later secularized (*see* CONSTANTINOPLE, PATRIARCHATE OF; ORTHODOX CHURCH OF; ROMANIAN RITE).

In 1721 the Diocese of Făgăraş was erected for Romanian-rite Catholics. Its seat was transferred to Blaj in 1738, under Bishop Innocent Micu-Klein (1728–51), who also worked for the political and cultural emancipation of the Romanian people. He and his successors founded several schools that would become centers of the Romanian national renaissance. In 1777 the Diocese of Oradea Mare (which had been a ritual vicariate since 1748) was erected. In 1853 Pius IX created an ecclesiastical province for Catholics of the Romanian rite. FĂGĂRAŞ (with the addition of the historical name Alba Iulia) became the metropolitan see, with Oradea Mare, Gherla and Lugoj newly founded as suffragan sees.

The Romanian Orthodox Church declared itself autocephalous and independent of the Patriarchate of Constantinople in 1865, and this status was finally acknowledged in 1885. The metropolitan of Bucharest thenceforth held the title of primate. At that time Romanian-rite churches existed in Transylvania and Bukovina, which were part of Austria-Hungary. After the Kingdom of Romania was formed following World War I, the ecclesiastical union of the region quickly followed. On May 4, 1925 the Romanian patriarchate was erected, composed of five metropolitanates embracing 18 dioceses. The head of this autocephalous church was called archbishop of Bucharest, metropolitan of Ungrovalachia, and patriarch of Romania.

Latin Catholics. During the Middle Ages, following the slavonisation of the Bulgarian overlords, attempts were made to reintroduce the LATIN CHURCH into Romania. Franciscan and Dominican missionaries worked there from the 13th century. While several bishoprics

Roman Catholic Church of Jassy, Romania. (©Hulton-Deutsch Collection/CORBIS)

were established, including Milcovia (1228), Severin (1369), Sereth (1371), Arges (1380), Civitas Moldaviensis (Baia, 1420) and Bacău (1611), these sees were short-lived, and some never had resident bishops. In the 17th century care of the Latin Catholic minority residing in Moldavia was entrusted to Conventual Franciscans under a vicar apostolic, and care of those in Walachia, to Passionists. A Catholic bishop resided in Bucharest from 1792. In 1883, after emigration from Austria-Hungary, Italy and other countries had increased the numbers of Latin Catholics in Romania, the Archdiocese of Bucharest for Walachia and Dobruja and the Diocese of Iaşi for Moldavia were erected.

In Transylvania, which was part of Hungary after 1003, Latin Catholicism was solidly rooted. The region's Hungarians, Siculs (Székelyek) and other related ethnic groups were joined in the 13th century by Germans from Saxony. For these Latin Catholics the Diocese of Transylvania was erected in 1103 with its seat in Alba Iulia. When Transylvania became a vassal principality under

Turkish rule in the 16th century, most of Transylvania's Catholics embraced Protestantism: the Germans became Lutherans; the Hungarians, Calvinists; and the Siculs, Unitarians. In 1558 the Catholic bishop was exiled. In the provinces of Criana and Banat (in the southwestern part of modern Romania), Csanad became a diocese in 1035, and Oradea Mare, in 1077. The See of Satu Mare was erected in 1804.

The hierarchical structure for all Latin-rite dioceses was eventually reorganized according to the Romanian Concordat (1927) by the papal bull *Solemni conventione* (June 5, 1930). The Diocese of Timişoara was created for Romanian Banat. The Dioceses of Satu Mare and Oradea Mare were united, with the episcopal residence in the former city. Bucharest became a metropolitan see, with Alba Iulia, Iaşi, Satu Mare, Oradea Mare and Timişoara as suffragans.

World War I and After

During World War I Romania fought on the side of the Allies. Although suffering many human losses, a decision reached through regional assemblies (1918) and international treaties following the war (1919–20) gave Romania Transylvania, Bukovina, Bessarabia, southern Dobruja and eastern Banat. Pressured by political allies to join the Axis powers during World War II, Romania was invaded by the USSR in 1944, and withdrew from the war. The loss of Bessarabia, northern Bukovina and southern Dobruja preceded the country's adoption of a new constitution on Dec. 30, 1947 as the Communist People's Republic. In 1965 it became the Romanian Socialist Republic, with political power in the hands of Nicolae Ceauşescu as first secretary until he assumed the title of president in 1974.

Romania Suffers Communist Repression. Both through the new constitution of 1948 and subsequent laws, the special privileges enjoyed by the country's churches were abolished. The communist government ended all church control in schools, and mandated that all churches must secure statutory approval before being allowed to function. The Concordat with the Vatican (July 17, 1948) was unilaterally abrogated, and in 1949 all religious orders were suppressed. Even more dramatically, the government decreed that the Romanian Greek-Catholic Church was illegal; its membership was incorporated into the Romanian Orthodox Church and its property either destroyed, put under state control, or transferred to the ORTHODOX CHURCH.

Romania's Communist government continued its antireligious policies unabated until December of 1989, affecting each of the nation's churches in different ways. All churches, even those in favor with the state, were closely supervised by the Department of Cults and were subjected to the brutal methods of the dreaded *Securitate,* the Romanian secret police.

The Romanian Orthodox Church. On May 24, 1948 Justinian Marina (1901–77) became patriarch of the Romanian Orthodox Church. Well known for his socialist views and a personal friend of the first secretary of the Romanian Communist Party, Justinian guided the Orthodox Church through an initial period of vicious Stalinist persecution which saw the nationalization of church property, the imprisonment of thousands of clergy, a reduction of the number of Orthodox diocese to 12, and a reduction of the numbers of monks and nuns in the monasteries from over 7,000 in 1956 to 2,200 by 1975. Justinian later worked with communist leaders to establish a *modus vivendi* known as ''The Romanian Solution.''

Justinian accepted the narrow boundaries drawn around his church by the state in return for government toleration of a certain level of ecclesial activity. Even under a repressive political regime, he was able to oversee monastic reforms, improve the level of education of the clergy, and preserve many important historic churches, monasteries and other monuments.

Justinian led the Orthodox Church in a policy of accommodation during the Ceauşescu regime because Ceauşescu, who came to power in 1974, promoted a nationalist form of communism that included a role for the church in the life of the nation. Indeed, many Communist officials considered themselves Orthodox Christians.

Following Justinian's death in 1977, Justin Moisescu was elected patriarch of the Romanian Orthodox Church. More academician than politician, Justin was criticized for bowing to the government's decision to demolish some 24 churches and three monasteries in central Bucharest and for his handling of the defrocking and imprisonment of certain Orthodox priests opposed to the Ceauşescu regime. Even so, by 1985 the Romanian Orthodox was the most vigorous church in Eastern Europe, boasting 17,000,000 faithful (80 percent of the Romanian population). There were six seminaries and two theological institutes, one in Bucharest and one in Sibiu. High-quality theological journals were published, including three by the patriarchate itself and one by each of the five metropolitanates. In addition, the patriarchate was able to publish several volumes in a series of Romanian translations of the *Philokalia,* more than 30 in a projected series of 90 volumes of translations of patristic writings and an assortment of Bibles and other liturgical and theological works. In addition, the church published the theological contribution of Dumitru STĂNILOAE (1903–93), one of the most prominent Orthodox theologians of the 20th century.

Following Justin's death in 1986 Teoctist Arăpaşu, was elected patriarch. Teoctist had to contend with not only the destruction of more churches in Bucharest but even the government's desire to demolish the patriarchal complex in the capital and transfer the see to Iaşi. Teoctist was able to direct the republication of the 1688 Bucharest Bible, an event that illustrated the central role the church played in standardizing the Romanian language and influencing Romanian culture. Making several trips abroad, Teoctist became the first Romanian patriarch in history to visit a Roman pontiff when he met John Paul II in Rome on Jan. 5, 1989. (It was later revealed that the patriarch had acted against the wishes of the government in meeting with the pope.)

Latin Church Suffers under Communism. While the Orthodox Church managed to prosper under communism, such was not the case with the Latin Church. The declaration of the Communist People's Republic in Romania on Dec. 30, 1947 was quickly followed by repressive policies focused against all minority religions, among them the Latin Church. Stalinist policies included abrogating the Concordat of July 17, 1948, closing down all Latin dioceses but Alba Iulia and Iaşi, and engaging in a policy of religious persecution. Five of the six Latin bishops were immediately imprisoned, with the last sentenced to 18 months in prison in 1951; several would die while incarcerated. Priests refusing to convert to the Orthodox faith were first imprisoned, then freed and dispersed. By 1965 Alba Iulia would be the sole diocese with a Latin bishop, and many Romanian Catholics had fled abroad, 7,000 making their way to the United States. To provide pastoral care for these refugees, a titular bishop resident in Rome was appointed in 1960.

Although the government severely restricted its activity, it continued to tolerate the Latin Church because of Romania's need to maintain good relations with its communist neighbors, countries to which most Roman Catholics were ethnically linked. The diocese of Timişoara in the Banat comprised predominantly ethnic Germans, while dioceses in Transylvania (Alba Iulia, Oradea Mare and Satu Mare) were mostly Hungarian. The Latin Catholics in the Archdiocese of Bucharest and the Diocese of Iaşi were mostly ethnic Romanians or, according to some theories, Romanianized Hungarians called *Ceangai.*

The predominantly German diocese of Timişoara faced special problems because of the Ceauşescu government's decision to allow the emigration of ethnic Germans from Romania upon payment of a price by the West or East German government. Between 1977 and 1992 the number of ethnic Germans living in Romania fell from 359,000 to 119,000, drastically reducing the number of

Roman Catholics in the diocese. Of the 210 diocesan priests present in 1967 only 89 remained by 1992.

Many of the problems plaguing the Roman Catholic Church were related to the situation of the Hungarian minority in Transylvania: catechisms and prayer books in Hungarian were unavailable until 1976, and Bibles until 1980. In spite of Vatican II's sanction of the use of the vernacular in the liturgy, Mass in Romanian was forbidden by the government outside Moldavia and Bucharest until 1978.

In line with its efforts to persecute the Church, the government prevented Catholic bishops from leaving Romania to attend Vatican II, and banned access to the conciliar documents for many years. Limited contacts with the Holy See were resumed only after a 1967 visit to Romania by Cardinal König of Vienna. Still, Romania was the only Eastern bloc government to decline sending an official delegation to the installation of John Paul II in 1978.

During the four decades of communist rule, government-sponsored repression occasionally eased. Closed seminaries in Alba Iulia and Iaşi were reopened in 1952 and 1956 respectively, and by the mid-1970s they were allowed to receive as many students as they wished. However, such permissiveness was only temporary; in 1982 the government imposed a limit that required 20 of the 192 students at Alba Iulia to be expelled. In 1948 there were 1,180 Latin priests in Romania; by 1988 there were only 800, 60 percent of them over the age of 60. Besides three small, token communities that were not allowed to receive novices, religious orders were banned during the communist years.

After the repressive Ceauşescu regime took power in 1974, limited progress was made on the appointment of Latin bishops (Alba Iulia was the only Catholic diocese with an ordinary by 1965). In 1972 Antal Jakab was ordained coadjutor with right of succession to Bishop Aaron Marton of Alba Iulia; he succeeded in 1980. In 1981 Lajos Balint was appointed auxiliary; he became bishop after Jakab's retirement in 1991. In 1983 the Holy See was allowed to appoint priests as ordinaries *ad nutum Sanctae Sedis* of the dioceses of Timişoara and Oradea Mare, and later for Iaşi. In 1984 the pope was able to name a Latin bishop for Romania for the first time since 1950 when he appointed Bishop Ioan Robu as apostolic administrator of the Archdiocese of Bucharest.

Romanian Greek-Catholic Church Outlawed. The fate of the Byzantine-rite Greek-Catholic Church under Romania's Communist government was much worse than it was for the Latin Church. A mock Greek-Catholic synod was staged that abolished the Church's

union with Rome on Oct. 21, 1948. On Dec. 1, 1948 communists issued a decree formally dissolving the Greek-Catholic Church and confiscated all its property, turning most of its 2,588 churches within 1,794 parishes over to the Romanian Orthodox Church. All six Greek Catholic bishops were arrested on the night of Dec. 29–30 1948. Five of them died in prison; the sixth, Bishop Juliu Hossu of Cluj-Gherla, was released from prison in 1964, but placed under house arrest at Caldarusani Orthodox monastery near Bucharest, where he died in 1970. In 1973 Pope Paul VI announced that he had created Hossu a cardinal *in pectore* in 1969.

A Greek-Catholic hierarchy continued, however, in the underground. Before he was expelled from the country in 1950, the last papal representative, U.S. Archbishop Gerald Patrick O'Hara, secretly ordained five Greek-Catholic bishops. However, the communist Securitate broke into the nunciature, obtained a list of these bishops, and later imprisoned all of them. Some were released in 1964 and three were still alive in 1989.

Until 1989 Communist authorities maintained the position that the Greek-Catholic Church had freely and spontaneously asked for reunion with the Orthodox Church, and that it had simply ceased to exist. The Romanian Orthodox Church officially supported this position. In reality, the brutal suppression of the Greek-Catholic Church was strongly resisted and even occasioned heroic defiance of the regime.

Although a few Greek Catholics attended Latin liturgies, most continued to frequent their former parishes where, although they had officially become Orthodox, little had changed. There were also a few clandestine priests with secular jobs who met secretly with small groups to celebrate the sacraments, mostly in private homes, throughout the persecutions. The Securitate knew the existence of these groups, but as time went on they were tolerated as long as they stayed out of public view. The underground bishops even succeeded in training and ordaining a few men to the priesthood. Early in Ceauşescu's regime the surviving bishops made repeated requests for the reinstatement of their church, and in 1980 they even appealed to the Madrid Conference on Security and Cooperation in Europe.

The Fall of Communism. In December of 1989 Romania's communist government toppled, the political overthrow of Ceauşescu signaling the end of four decades of repressive rule. The new Romanian Constitution, adopted in December of 1991, guaranteed religious freedom. Article 29 prohibited any restriction of religious beliefs, guaranteed freedom of conscience and stated that "all religions shall be free and organized in accordance with their own statutes, under the terms laid down by law." It also forbade all forms of enmity among religions and declared that while religious cults are autonomous from the state, they also enjoy support from it, "including the facilitation of religious assistance in the army, in hospitals, prisons, homes and orphanages." The right of parents to provide for the religious education their children was also assured.

While communists would continue to hold political offices in Romania for several more years, their power was greatly diminished, and their increasingly liberal social policies ushered in a new era for Romania's churches, allowing them to function freely for the first time in decades. However, these new freedoms also led to interchurch conflicts, some of which would remain unresolved into the next century.

Orthodox Church Issues Apologies. The end of Ceauşescu's regime triggered a mixed response in the Romanian Orthodox Church. While the Church began the difficult task of rebuilding, it also had to deal with strong criticism over its public support of the Communist government. The Holy Synod met on Jan. 10, 1990, apologized for those "who did not always have the courage of the martyrs," and expressed regret that it had been "necessary to pay the tribute of obligatory and artificial praises addressed to the dictator" to ensure certain liberties. It also annulled all ecclesiastical sanctions it had been compelled to impose on members of the clergy for political reasons. In the face of harsh criticism for his collaboration with the Communist regime—it was even alleged that he oversaw an information exchange between confessional priests and the communist Securiate—Patriarch Teoctist resigned his office on Jan. 18, 1990. However, in early April Teoctist was asked to resume his duties by unanimous decision of the Holy Synod, which reasoned that his presence was valuable in maintaining continuity in the face of political change.

A few days after the fall of the Ceauşescu regime, a "Reflection Group for the Renewal of the Church" was established in Bucharest. Its seven clerical and lay members set out to interpret what they saw to be a growing desire among the Orthodox faithful for change and renewal in the life of the church, and to initiate a dialogue with the Church leadership to help it overcome the current "spiritual impasse." On June 7, 1990 a member of this group, 38-year-old auxiliary bishop of Timişoara, Daniel Ciobotea, was elected metropolitan archbishop of Iaşi, the second-ranking post in the Romanian Orthodox hierarchy. His election to the see from which all previous Romanian patriarchs had been taken was part of an effort to reform the Church and provide it with new and more vigorous leadership.

In September of 1990 the Holy Synod approved important modifications to the basic statutes of the Patri-archate. It removed those sections providing for state interference in the Church's affairs and declared the full autonomy of the Church from the State. At a meeting in January of 1993 it re-established two jurisdictions in areas that had been part of Romania before World War II: northern Bukovina (later in Ukraine) and Bessarabia (most of which became the independent republic of Moldova). This move sparked a confrontation with the Moscow patriarchate to which the Orthodox dioceses in those regions had belonged since World War II. Most Orthodox in those areas remained in newly established autonomous jurisdictions associated with the Russian Orthodox Church.

Communist Support Bolsters Demographics. In 1948, just prior to the country's communist takeover, Romanian Orthodox Catholics had numbered close to ten million; Greek-Catholics, as the country's second largest religion, 1,560,000; Latin Catholics 1,175,000; and Armenian Catholics 5,000. In 1992 a government census showed membership in the Romanian Orthodox Church at 19,802,389; Latin Catholics at 1,161,942, Greek-Catholics at 223,327, and Armenian Catholics at 2,023. By early 1993 the number of Orthodox seminaries in the country had risen to 18, while the theological institutes that had been allowed to function in Bucharest and Sibiu were reintegrated into their respective university faculties and ten other theology faculties were set up around the country. Monastic life once again thrived and, for the first time since 1948 churches began to engage in organized charitable activity, such as administering orphanages, hospitals and retirement homes. By the year 2000 1,628 parishes administered to Romania's Catholic faithful, while between the Byzantine and Latin Catholic Churches 1,590 priests, 180 brothers and 1,196 sisters served their faith.

Another result of the fall of Communism was the reactivation of banned Orthodox lay movements. Among the most important of these was the Oastea Domnului (Army of the Lord). Founded by Josif Trifa in 1923, this renewal movement emphasized evangelization, personal morality, an experiential relationship with God and Bible study. It grew quickly, and was absorbed into the structures of the Orthodox Church in the 1930s. During the Communist years the movement maintained a secret membership of perhaps as many as 500,000. While it again received the blessing of the Orthodox Church after resurfacing in 1990, some of its members had established connections with Protestant evangelical groups.

Latin Church Works to Rebuild. The downfall of the Ceauşescu regime affected the Latin-rite and Orthodox Churches differently. With sanctions against it now lifted, the Holy See acted quickly to provide a new hierarchy for the Latin Church in Romania. On March 14, 1990 the pope named bishops for all six dioceses in the country and a new auxiliary for Alba Iulia. On Sept. 29, 1991 the diocese of Alba Iulia was made an archdiocese immediately subject to the Holy See. Romania and the Holy See announced the re-establishment of diplomatic relations on May 15, 1992. Archbishop John Bukovsky was nominated apostolic nuncio on August 18, and the building of the apostolic nunciature was returned and officially re-opened three months later. The statutes for a Romanian Catholic Bishops' Conference that included Latins and Greeks were approved *ad experimentum* on March 16, 1991, and Greek-Catholic Metropolitan (later Cardinal) Alexandru Todea was elected its first president.

The new freedoms given the Roman Catholic Church in Romania allowed an increasing number of vocations to take place. Seminaries at Alba Iulia (for Hungarian- and German-speaking candidates) and Iaşi (for Romanian-speakers) experienced a major influx of students. The same was true for the various male and female religious orders that resumed activity in the country. As had been its tradition, the majority of Latin Catholics continued to be Romanians of Hungarian descent living in the Transylvania region.

Greek-Catholic Repression Ends. The repression endured by the Greek-Catholic Church finally came to an end after the downfall of the Ceauşescu regime. A few days after the revolt, on Jan. 2, 1990, the new Romanian government abrogated the 1948 decree that had outlawed the Greek-Catholic Church. The three surviving underground bishops, Ioan Ploscaru, Ioan Chertes and Alexandru Todea, emerged from hiding, and 540 priests also came forward, about 100 of them elderly.

On March 14, 1990 Pope John Paul II reconstituted the Greek-Catholic hierarchy by naming bishops to all five dioceses. Todea, named metropolitan archbishop of Făgăraş and Alba Iulia, would be created a cardinal in June of 1991. Ploscaru became Bishop of Lugoj, while Chertes, by now advanced in years, bore the personal title of archbishop until his death on Jan. 31, 1992. In official documents the Greek-Catholic Church became the "Romanian Church United with Rome." In 1997 the Church held a provisional council in which Greek-Catholic leaders worked to set up formal statutes, and worked to heed the Pope's call to all Eastern churches to "respond to the new needs of the faithful, who have finally been delivered from the hands of oppression, but now are assailed with new mirages and must answer new challenges."

In January of 1994 the Congregation for the Eastern Churches sponsored a meeting of the bishops and other representatives of the Romanian Greek-Catholic Church in Rome. A final document was adopted treating the orga-

nization of the eparchies, the formation of the clergy, the liturgy, catechetics, religious life and ecumenical relations. The participants unanimously called for the speedy canonization of those martyred for the faith during the persecutions. On July 20, 1994 Pope John Paul II accepted the resignation of 82-year-old Cardinal Todea and appointed Bishop Lucian Mureşan of Maramureş to succeed him as Greek-Catholic metropolitan.

Religious Rebirth Sparks Inter-Church Controversy. The resurgence of the Greek-Catholic Church in particular was accompanied by a confrontation with the Romanian Orthodox Church. Although the government had abolished the 1948 decree dissolving the Church and now promised to return all church property in state hands, it did not resolve the issue of ownership of churches that had been given to the Orthodox Church. In 1990 a joint Orthodox and Greek-Catholic committee was formed to oversee these property disputes.

The Greek-Catholic Church insisted that all 2,600 church properties confiscated in 1948 be returned as a matter of justice, a position they called *restitutio in integrum*. However, the Romanian Orthodox Church held that since the demographic situation had changed substantially since 1948, any redistribution of churches must allow for the pastoral needs of both communities, based on the results of a census and the deliberations of a joint commission. The hardening of positions created such an impasse that by March of 1993 the Greek-Catholic Church had regained only 66 of its former churches. The situation was complicated by the Greek-Catholic rejection of the results of the 1992 census, according to which only one percent of the population (228,377) belonged to this church. Statistics published in the 1993 *Annuario Pontificio* indicated a total of 1,842,486, while some Greek-Catholic sources claimed almost 3,000,000 members.

Although Greek Catholics later reduced their demands to under 300 properties, an atmosphere of mistrust and mutual recrimination grew between the two churches. The Orthodox portrayed Greek Catholics as less than fully patriotic and recalled the traditional identity between the Romanian people and the Orthodox Church. Some even drew a connection between the existence of the Greek-Catholic Church and a sinister effort to "magyarize" the Romanian population of Transylvania. For their part, Greek Catholics accused the Orthodox of willful collaboration with the Communists, of wholesale corruption and of perpetuating the Stalinist oppression of their church. The Greek-Catholic hierarchy also expressed fierce opposition to the work of the international commission for dialogue between the Catholic and Orthodox Churches that attempted to overcome the misunderstandings that arose in the wake of the re-emergence of the Greek/Byzantine Catholic Churches in Eastern Europe.

Romania Moves into New Millennium

In spite of the problems faced during its country's recovery from communist repression, the Romanian Orthodox Church was able to preserve the close links that traditionally existed between it and the majority of the Romanian people and remained the church chosen to preside over government ceremonies requiring prayer. Although its activity was hindered by the catastrophic economic conditions that followed the fall of Ceauşescu, the freedom of religion insured by Romania's new constitution enabled the Orthodox Church to reassert its prominent role in the country. While its spokesmen expressed concern over the "aggressive proselytism" of various minority Protestant faiths, the Romanian Orthodox Church has sought to establish the kind of relationship with the state, as well as with other churches, that would benefit a postcommunist and increasingly westernized nation.

Disputes over property continued to shadow Romania into the new millennium. Although by February of 1999 an agreement had been reached between competing church claimants that disputed buildings would be shared until the court resolved their ownership, fights and lock-outs continued sporadically. Not only Greek Catholics, but also Roman Catholics, Protestants and other faiths looked to the government for help in the restoration of church structures that had been closed by the former communist regime. By 2000 most of these sites, still in the hands of the government, had yet to be restored. In addition, secular structures that had been converted into schools, post offices and other public buildings under the previous government, remained in the hands of the government despite requests either for monetary compensation or for their return to church ownership.

By the mid-1990s Pope John Paul II had become an active supporter of the Catholic Church's efforts to regain confiscated property. On May 7, 1999 he visited Bucharest and called upon Catholic bishops to be "builders of communion" in an effort to rebuild Romanian society. The Pope's visit to Bucharest marked the first papal visit to a predominately Orthodox nation.

Anger toward the Romanian Orthodox Church for its collaboration with Communist oppressors gradually healed over time, in part due to the intervention of Pope John Paul II. In February of 2000 Patriarch Teoctist also made a public apology that acted to heal the breach between Orthodox and Greek Catholics, noting "I personally ask for forgiveness and I am doing it now because I didn't have enough courage before." The Romanian Greek-Catholic Church began to regain its footing. Seminaries appeared in Cluj, Baia Mare and Oradea, and Greek-Catholic theological institutes were established in Cluj, Oradea and at the historic center of the church at Blaj. The cathedral at Blaj, along with the episcopal residence and seminary complex, was regained in October of 1990. By 2000, 142 of the 300 churches requested to be returned from control of Orthodox congregations had reverted back to Greek-Catholic ownership.

Romanian Prime Minister Mugur Isarescu and the republican government in place in 2000 worked to maintain religious freedom within Romania, and also offered tangible support to minority churches in their efforts to restore their infrastructure. In 1999 over a million dollars in governmental grants were awarded to the country's Roman Catholic and Greek-Catholic Church to aid in church construction efforts. Although the government continued to support Romania's Catholic churches, many minority faiths continued to battle for recognition under the requirements imposed by the State Secretariat for Religious Cults.

See Also: EASTERN CHURCHES; ORTHODOX CHURCHES; CATHOLIC CHURCH (EASTERN CATHOLIC).

Bibliography: R. W. SETON-WATSON, *A History of the Romanians* (Cambridge, Eng. 1934). N. IORGA, *Histoire des Roumains et de la Romanité oriental,* 4 v. (Bucharest 1937); *Istoria bisericii romăneti,* 2 v. (2d ed. Bucharest 1929–32). J. ZEILLER, *Les Origines chrétiennes dans les provinces danubiennes* (Paris 1918). A. TĂUTU et al., *Biserica Română unită* (Madrid 1952). G. ROSU and M. VASILIU, comps., *Romania: Churches and Religion,* ed. V. GSOVSKI (*Mid-European Law Project,* New York 1955). F. POPAN and Č. S. DRAŠKOVIC, *Orthodoxie heute in Rumänien und Jugoslawien,* ed. K. RUDOLF (Vienna 1960). *Rom und die Patriarchate des Ostens,* eds., W. DE VRIES et al. (Freiburg 1963). T. BEESON, *Discretion and Valour: Religious Conditions in Russia and Eastern Europe* (London 1982). J. BROUN, "The Latin-rite Roman Catholic Church of Romania," in *Religion in Communist Lands,* 12 (1984) 168–184. V. GEORGESCU, *The Romanians: A History* (New York 1991). M. PACURARIU, *Istoria Bisericii Ortodoxe Române,* 3 v. (Bucharest 1980–81). A. SCARFE, "The Romanian Orthodox Church," in *Eastern Christianity and Politics in the Twentieth Century,* ed. P. RAMET, (Durham, NC 1988) 208–31. B. SPULER, *Die Religion in Geschichte und Gegenwart,* 7 v. (3d ed. Tübingen 1957–65) 5:1211–15. E. HERMANN and O. BÂRLEA, *Lexikon für Theologie und Kirche,* eds., J. HOFER and K. RAHNER, 10 v. (2d, new ed. Freiburg 1957–65) 9:95–99. *Bilan du Monde. Encyclopédie catholique du monde cherétien,* 2 v. (2d ed. Tournai 1956) 2:744–751.

[M. LACKO/R. G. ROBERSON/EDS.]

ROMANIAN CATHOLIC CHURCH (EASTERN CATHOLIC)

Officially known as "The Romanian Church United with Rome." Although there had been small but unstable unions of the Romanian Orthodox with the Church of Rome, such as the brief union brought about by Ioanitza Asan in 1204, a stable union between part of the Romanians and the See of Rome was realized only at the end of the 17th century, when the Romanians of Transylvania embraced the holy union together with their bishops, Theophilus (1697) and Athanasius (1698–1713). Various historical and social circumstances determined this union. After the withdrawal of the Turks from central-eastern Europe, Transylvania fell under the domination of Catholic Austria in 1688. The Jesuit Fathers, who had been expelled at the time of the Protestant supremacy, returned to their houses in Cluj and Alba Julia and thus approached the local Romanian bishop. The economic and social conditions of the Romanians of Transylvania were very poor. They were overburdened with taxes for war expenditures, deprived of civil and social rights while their Orthodox faith was spurned, and humiliated by Protestant proselytism. In order to avoid this situation, they saw no solution other than that of turning toward communion with the Apostolic See, hoping that, by the new union, they and especially the clergy would enjoy the rights and privileges that were reserved by the constitution of the Transylvanian principality to the four privileged religions (Catholic, Lutheran, Calvinist, and Unitarian). Emperor Leopold I, by a decree issued on April 14, 1698, promised that the privileges of the four religions would be granted to those who joined one of them. The outcome was that, in the general synods of 1697 under Bishop Theophilus and of 1698 under Bishop Athanasius, the clergy decided in favor of communion with the Roman Church. The synod of Sept. 5, 1700, in which about 2,000 members of the clergy and laity took part definitively, ratified the union and accepted the four dogmatic points of the Council of FLORENCE: primacy, unleavened bread as a legitimate matter for the Holy Eucharist, existence of purgatory, and the doctrine of the filioque. In liturgical and disciplinary areas they kept their own (Romanian) rite. In particular they were authorized to elect their own bishop-metropolitan as did the Romanian ORTHODOX CHURCH and to keep the Romanian vernacular as the liturgical language.

Opposition to the union came from the Transylvanian landlords who suffered heavy economic losses by the emancipation of the Orthodox priests and peasants. But the fiercest opposition came from the hierarchy of the Orthodox Church of Serbia, especially from the archbishop of Karlovitz, who wanted to keep the Romanian Orthodox Christians of Transylvania under his jurisdiction. Notwithstanding all these difficulties, the holy union did not perish but, thanks to the zeal and courageous activity of its bishops, became stronger.

Organization. The Catholic Romanians in 1700 numbered 200,000. To organize these faithful into an ecclesiastical diocese, Pope Innocent XIII in 1721 established the first Romanian Catholic Diocese of Fagaraş, which later was transferred to Blaj, where it is today. Bishop Innocent Micu-Klein (1728–51) strove heroically to gain for his people political, social, and cultural rights. He was forced to abandon his see and finally abdicated. Both he and his successor, Petru Pavel Aron (1752–64), raised the intellectual level of their people by opening secondary schools and a diocesan seminary and by maintaining a printing press that published liturgical, theological, and historical books. Thus the clergy and people were well organized through solid instruction received through schools and published literature. This fostered in the people a militant patriotism that yearned for the day of liberation from their Hungarian masters and complete reunion with their fellow Romanians. When the Austrian-Hungarian Empire was dissolved in 1918, the Romanians Catholics found themselves nationally united with the Romanian Orthodox but religiously a minority. Yet in spite of opposition from the Orthodox, the Romanian Catholic Church grew steadily.

Canonical Structure. The Romanian Catholic Church was once one of the most prosperous and well organized of the Eastern Catholic Churches. Its discipline and canonical structure are regulated by the decrees of three provincial councils held at Blaj in 1872, 1882, and 1900. The First Council of Blaj treated in ten chapters: the Catholic faith and the union that had as its basis the union of Florence (1439) and the unionistic synod at Alba Julia (1700); the Church, including the primacy of the Roman pontiff, the rights and duties of metropolitans, bishops, priests and cathedral chapters, rural deans, protopopes protopriests, and pastors; ecumenical, provincial, and diocesan synods; ecclesiastical benefices and their conferment; the Sacraments; divine worship and the liturgy; life and discipline of the clergy; the Order of Saint Basil; schools of various types; and ecclesiastical processes and tribunals. The Second Council of Blaj treated in six chapters: the Catholic faith, reproducing the formula prescribed by Urban VIII and Benedict XIV; statutes of the metropolitan chapter approved with the bull of erection of the province; religious orders of men and women; a detailed instruction on the procedure to be followed in matrimonial cases, as well as procedural norms for civil and penal processes; and norms on the administration of schools and ecclesiastical goods. The Third Council of Blaj reaffirmed the rights and integrity of the Province of Alba Julia and Făgăraş, considered as autonomous and independent, subject only to the Roman Apostolic See; the council also established norms concerning divine worship, insisting on the modern Romanian language as the approved liturgical language, and other norms regarding liturgical ceremonies, sacred buildings, and sacred vestments. The Holy See approved these enactments.

[L. TAUTU/R. ROBERSON/EDS.]

Romanian Catholic Church in the Communist and Post-Communist Years. The fate of the Romanian Byzantine Catholic Church in Romania under Communism was much worse than it was for the Romanian Latin Catholics. The government staged a mock Greek Catholic synod that abolished the union with Rome on Oct. 12, 1948. On Dec. 1, 1948, the government issued a decree that formally dissolved the Greek Catholic Church and confiscated all its property, turning most of its 2,588 churches within 1,794 parishes over to the Romanian Orthodox Church. All six Greek Catholic bishops were arrested on the night of Dec. 29 to 30, 1948. Five of them died in prison. The sixth, Bishop Juliu Hossu of Cluj-Gherla, was released from prison in 1964, but placed under house arrest at Caldarusani Orthodox monastery near Bucharest, where he died in 1970. In 1973 Pope Paul VI announced that he had created Hossu a cardinal *in pectore* in 1969.

A Greek Catholic hierarchy continued, however, in the underground. Before he was expelled from the country in 1950, the last papal representative, the American Archbishop Gerald Patrick O'Hara, had secretly ordained five Greek Catholic Bishops. However, the government Securitate broke into the nunciature, obtained a list of these bishops and later imprisoned all of them. Some were released in 1964 and three were still alive in 1989.

Until 1989 the Communist authorities held the absurd contention that the Greek Catholic Church had freely and spontaneously asked for reunion with the Orthodox Church, and that it had simply ceased to exist. The Romanian Orthodox Church officially supported this position. In fact, the brutal suppression of the Greek Catholic Church was strongly resisted and even occasioned heroic defiance of the regime.

Although a few Greek Catholics attended Latin liturgies, most of them continued to frequent their former parishes where, although they had officially become Orthodox, little had changed. However, there were a few clandestine priests with secular jobs who met secretly with small groups to celebrate the sacraments, mostly in private homes, throughout the persecutions. The existence of these groups was known to the Securitate, but in the later years they were tolerated as long as they stayed out of public view. The underground bishops even succeeded in training and ordaining a few men to the priesthood. In the late 1970s the surviving bishops made

repeated requests to President Ceauşescu for the reinstatement of their church, and in 1980 they even appealed to the Madrid Conference on Security and Cooperation in Europe.

This situation changed only after the downfall of the Ceauşescu regime. A few days after the revolt, on Jan. 2, 1990, the new Romanian government abrogated the 1948 decree that had outlawed the Greek Catholic Church. The three surviving underground bishops, Ioan Ploscaru, Ioan Chertes, and Alexandru Todea, emerged from hiding, and 540 priests also came forward, about 100 of them elderly.

On March 14, 1990, Pope John Paul II reconstituted the Greek Catholic hierarchy by naming bishops to all five dioceses. Todea was named metropolitan archbishop of Făgăraş and Alba Iulia (he was created a cardinal in June 1991), and Ploscaru Bishop of Lugoj. Chertes, an elderly man in retirement, was given the personal title of archbishop. He died on Jan. 31, 1992. In official documents the Greek Catholic Church now calls itself ''The Romanian Church United With Rome.''

The Congregation for the Eastern Churches sponsored a meeting of the bishops and other representatives of the Romanian Greek Catholic Church in Rome from Jan. 17 to 22, 1994. A final document was adopted treating the organization of the eparchies, the formation of the clergy, the liturgy, catechetics, religious life, and ecumenical relations. The participants unanimously called for the speedy canonization of those martyred for the faith during the persecutions. On July 20, 1994, Pope John Paul II accepted the resignation of 82-year-old Cardinal Todea and appointed Bishop Lucian Mureşan of Maramureş to succeed him as Greek Catholic metropolitan.

The rebirth of the Greek Catholic Church was accompanied by a confrontation with the Romanian Orthodox Church. This was due to the fact that although the government abolished the 1948 decree dissolving the church and promised to return its former property now in state hands, it did not resolve the issue of ownership of churches given to the Orthodox Church.

The Greek Catholic Church insisted that all the property confiscated in 1948 be returned as a matter of justice, a position they called *restitutio in integrum*. However, the Romanian Orthodox Church held that since the demographic situation had changed substantially since 1948, any redistribution of churches must allow for the pastoral needs of both communities, based on the results of a census and the deliberations of a joint commission. The hardening of positions created an impasse, such that by March 1993 the Greek Catholic Church had regained only 66 of its former churches. The situation was complicated by the Greek Catholic rejection of the results of the 1992 census, according to which only 1% of the population (228,377) belonged to this church. The 1948 figure had been 1,560,000. Statistics published in the 1993 *Annuario Pontificio* indicate a total of 1,842,486, while some Greek Catholic sources claim almost 3,000,000 members.

An atmosphere of mistrust and mutual recrimination exists between the two churches. The Orthodox portray the Greek Catholics as less than fully patriotic and recall the traditional identity between the Romanian people and the Orthodox Church. Some even draw a connection between the existence of the Greek Catholic Church and a sinister effort to "magyarize" the Romanian population of Transylvania. For their part, the Greek Catholics accuse the Orthodox of willful collaboration with the Communists, of wholesale corruption, and of perpetuating the Stalinist oppression of their church. The Greek Catholic hierarchy has also expressed fierce opposition to the work of the international commission for dialogue between the Catholic and Orthodox Churches that has attempted to overcome the misunderstandings that arose in the wake of the re-emergence of the Byzantine Catholic Churches in Eastern Europe.

Because of these tensions, the Catholic Church in Romania has been reluctant to engage in ecumenical projects that include the Orthodox. In late 1990, a Romanian Council of Churches was created, but neither the Latin nor Greek Catholic Churches took part in the initiative.

The Greek Catholic Church has set up seminaries in Cluj, Baia Mare, and Oradea, and there are now Greek Catholic theological institutes in Cluj, Oradea, and the historic center of the church at Blaj. The cathedral at Blaj along with the episcopal residence and seminary complex was regained in October 1990.

The Romanian Catholic Church suffered greatly under communist rule. It was forcibly dissolved in 1948, its bishops arrested and jailed, and its property handed over to the Orthodox Church of Romania. It survived underground, emerging only after the fall of the Ceauşescu regime. The 1948 dissolution of the Romanian Catholic Church was set aside on Jan. 2, 1980, and the underground church was able to emerge into public life. The hierarchy of the Romanian Catholic Church was reestablished on March 14, 1990. The 1990s was a period of conflict between the Romanian Catholic and Orthodox Churches over return of churches and other properties that were seized in 1948.

Bibliography: D. ATTWATER, *The Christian Churches of the East,* v.1 *Churches in Communion with Rome* (Milwaukee 1961). E. IVÁNKA, "Romanian Catholics of the Byzantine Rite," *The East-ern Churches Quarterly* 8 (1949–50) 153–62. I. RATIU, "The Communist Attack on the Catholic and Orthodox Churches in Romania," *ibid.* 163–97. R. ROBERTSON, *The Eastern Christian Churches: A Brief Survey,* (6th ed. Rome 1999).

[R. ROBERSON]

ROMANO OF ROME

Dominican theologian; d. before May 28, 1273. Born of the noble Orsini family, he was a younger brother of Cardinal Matthew, nephew of the future NICHOLAS III, and cousin of Latino Malabranca. He probably entered the order in Rome and was later sent to Paris in 1266 to complete his theological studies. One sermon of his is dated Feb. 6, 1267. He studied under THOMAS AQUINAS during the latter's second regency at Paris. He read the *Sentences* under Aquinas from 1270 to 1272, and succeeded him as master in 1272. From his unedited commentary on the *Sentences* it is evident that Romano was influenced by others besides St. Thomas, notably by St. BONAVENTURE, HANNIBALDUS DE HANNIBALDIS, and ROBERT KILWARDBY; he did not follow Aquinas, for example, in repudiating the Augustinian thesis of divine IL-LUMINATION. He in turn influenced GILES OF ROME and JOHN (QUIDORT) of Paris.

Bibliography: P. GLORIEUX, *Répertoire des maîtres en théologie de Paris au XIIIᵉ siècle* (Paris 1933–34) 1:129. J. QUÉTIF and ÉCHARD, *Scriptores Ordinis Praedicatorum,* 5 v. (Paris 1719–23); continued by R. COULON (Paris 1909–); repr. 2 v. in 4 (New York 1959) 1.1:263–264. G. SANTINELLO, *Enciclopedia filosofica,* 4 v. (Venice–Rome 1957) 4:186. J. BEUMER, "Romanus de Roma, O.P., und seine theologische Einleitungslehre," *Recherches de théologie ancienne et médiévale* 25 (Louvain 1958) 329–351.

[P. GLORIEUX]

ROMANS, EPISTLE TO THE

The longest and theologically most significant epistle of the Pauline corpus. This article will discuss the epistle's purpose and provenance, its authenticity and integrity, and its addressees; an outline and an analysis of its contents will then be given, followed by an explanation of its significance.

Purpose and provenance. The Epistle to the Romans is the least like a real letter of all the Pauline epistles because of its developed, treatise-like exposition of the gospel of Jesus Christ. It was written at the end of Paul's third missionary journey, probably during the winter of *c.* A.D. 57–58, just before he was about to return to Jerusalem with the collection for the poor of the Jerusalem mother church (Rom 15.25–26) taken up in various Gentile churches that he had founded (in Macedonia, Achaia, and Galatia). This return to Jerusalem was for Paul the end of missionary work in the eastern Mediterranean area (15.19–20,23). The gesture of help from the Gentile churches where his work had been successful was intended to convince the Jewish Christians of Judea of the solidarity of Gentile Christians in the same spiritual blessings that they enjoyed and of the Gentiles' recognition of the debt owed by them. Having desired for some time to evangelize the West, Paul turned his gaze toward Spain and hoped to visit Rome en route (15.23–24). After the journey to Jerusalem, his hopes were to be realized at last. Accordingly, he was emboldened to write this letter, from Corinth, to introduce himself to the already existing Christian community of Rome in view of his impending visit. As he wrote, he was aware that the Roman Church had already been founded by someone else (15.20). He hoped, nevertheless, that even a brief sojourn there would have some salutary effect among the Christians of the capital, even as it had had among heathens elsewhere (1.13). However, conscious of his apostolic commission, he fashioned his letter of introduction into an extended exposition of his understanding of the GOSPEL (1.16–17), which he was eager to preach to people in Rome too.

Romans is not a summary of Christian doctrine, or Paul's "last will and testament," or even a complete sketch of his teaching, because some of his characteristic teachings are significantly absent from it (Church, Eucharist, resurrection of the body, eschatology). It is rather a presentation of his missionary reflections on the historic possibility of salvation now offered in the gospel to all human beings. Through faith in Christ Jesus, whose death and resurrection are proclaimed as the means that opened up a new mode of salvation, people can now be justified in God's sight—by grace and without any concern for "deeds of the Law" (3.20–24). In Romans Paul presents the vast implications of the gospel that have dawned on him as a result of his recent missionary endeavors in that phase of his apostolate now coming to a close. Romans resembles Galatians (see GALATIANS, EPISTLE TO THE) in that it treats of justification and faith, of the relation of Christ to the Mosaic law (see LAW, MOSAIC), and of God's gracious and salvific uprightness. But while Galatians is a vehement letter, written in the heat of combat against a Judaizing error, Romans is an irenic, reflective presentation of much of the same doctrine with a slightly different emphasis and in a context devoid of polemics. Analogously, Galatians is to Romans as Colossians is to Ephesians.

Authenticity and integrity. Just as in antiquity, the Pauline authorship of Romans is almost universally admitted today. The few dissenting voices of the nineteenth century are no longer given serious consideration. Only in the case of the final doxology (16.25–27) is there a

Literary illustration, "Epistle to the Romans: Saint Paul Preaching," 1526. (©Archivo Iconografico, S.A./CORBIS)

problem today. Its authenticity has been questioned (1) because of the uncertain, varying position it has in several manuscripts of Romans [after 16.23 in the Hesychian tradition and mansucript D; after 14.23 in the Koine tradition; after 15.33 in P^{46} (oldest manuscript of Romans); after both 14.23 and 16.23 in manuscripts A, P; completely lacking in manuscript G and Marcion's text]; (2) because of its style—a long periodic sentence with vocabulary typical of liturgical hymns; (3) because of the mention of the divine "mystery" [see MYSTERY (IN THE BIBLE)] applied to the salvation of the Gentiles—an expression characteristic of later Pauline letters. Certainty in this matter is impossible; but one cannot exclude the possibility that the doxology is a later addition, added at the time of the formation of the Pauline corpus [J. Dupont, *Revue Bénédictine* 58 (1948) 3–22].

A more problematic part of Romans is 16.1 to 16.23 (16.24 is not in the best Greek manuscripts and only repeats a part of 16.20). While the Pauline authorship of verses 1 to 23 is not normally contested, the question is often raised whether it belonged to the original form of Romans, since Marcion's text omitted chapters 15 and 16, and the oldest manuscript of Romans (P^{46}) puts the final doxology after 15.33. Furthermore, 16.1 to 16, or at least 16.1 to 16.2, reads like a letter of recommendation that Paul wrote for Phoebe, a DEACON of the church at Cenchreae (port of Corinth); it resembles ancient letters of introduction preserved in Greek papyri that begin abruptly with "I recommend" [see A. Deissmann, *Light from the Ancient East* (London 1910) 226]. But are the greetings in 16.3 to 16.16 sent to the Roman community—or to the Ephesian church? According to a number of modern commentators (e.g. D. Schulz, R. Bultmann, E. Käsemann, G. Bornkamm, K. Lake, J. Moffatt), Rom 16.1 to 16.23 is really a fragment of a letter written by Paul to Ephesus, since Paul greets in it Prisca and Aquila, who had settled in Ephesus (Acts 18.18, 26; cf. 1 Cor 16.19; 2 Tm 4.19). He also salutes Epaenetus, "the first convert for Christ in Asia" (Rom 16.5), and at least 23 others by name. He is familiar with the groups that meet in various house-churches (16.5, 14, 15). Hence such commentators ask: Would Paul have known so many people in Rome and be so familiar with conditions there? Finally, the admonition in 16.17 to 16.20 is so different in tone from the rest of Romans that another group of people seems to be addressed here. None of these considerations, however, are strong enough to convince the majority of interpreters that Paul has written these verses with the Ephesian church in view. In particular, H. Gamble has shown that Romans would be a strange epistle in the Pauline corpus if 16.1 to 16.23 were not considered part of it (*The Textual History of the Letter to the Romans*, Studies and Documents 42; Grand Rapids, Mich. 1977).

Addressees. The problematic end of Romans (chap. 16) and the fact that the phrase "at Rome" (ἐν Ῥώμῃ, 1.7, 15) is missing in a few manuscripts (mainly G) have led some modern scholars to propose the view that Romans was really composed as a "circular letter" destined for more than one church [T. W. Manson, *Bulletin of the John Rylands Library* 31 (1948) 224–240; J. Munck, *Paul and the Salvation of Mankind* (London, 1959) 197–200]. Chapters 1 to 15 would have been sent only to Rome (with the doxology as in P[46]), but the form with chapter 16 would have been sent to Ephesus. However, the omission of ἐν Ῥώμῃ in relatively unimportant text-witnesses and the other reasons advanced for this hypothesis have not been generally accepted.

The character of the Roman church was once much discussed as an important element in the understanding of this letter. Was it predominantly Jewish-Christian (T. Zahn, F. Leenhardt) or predominantly Gentile-Christian (Sanday-Headlam, M. J. Lagrange, S. Lyonnet, O. Michel)? Much of this discussion is idle, once it is realized that Paul writes to introduce himself to a community that he does not know personally. The only specific problem of the Roman church that apparently has been reported to him is that of the "weak" and the "strong" in 14.1

to 15.13. Otherwise he is presenting his reflections on the gospel that have been derived from his recent missionary endeavors and conflicts in the East. He writes as "an apostle" (1.1), as one "commissioned to urge all heathens to the obedience of faith" (1.5), as the "apostle of the Gentiles" (11.13). Consequently, he considers the Roman addressees as Christians converted mainly from paganism (1.6, 11–15; 11.13, 16–32), although he is aware of the mixed character of the community (4.1, 12; 9.10).

Outline.

I. Introduction (1.1–15): Address and Greeting (1.1–7); Thanksgiving (1.8–9); Paul's desire to come to Rome (1.10–15).

II. Part I (1.16–11.36): Doctrinal Section: God's gospel of Jesus Christ Our Lord.
  A. Through the gospel God's uprightness is revealed, justifying people of faith (1.16–4.25).
    1. The theme announced (1.16–17): The gospel is the powerful source of salvation for all disclosing God's uprightness.
    2. The theme negatively explained (1.18–3.20): Without the gospel God's wrath is manifested against all people.
      a. Against heathens (1.18–32).
      b. Against Jews—indeed, against all human beings (2.1–3.20).
    3. The theme positively explained (3.21–31): God's uprightness toward all sinners is shown graciously through Christ and apprehended in faith.
    4. The theme illustrated in the Old Testament (4.1–25): Abraham was justified by faith, not by deeds.
  B. The love of God assures salvation to those justified through faith (5.1–8.39).
    1. The theme announced (5.1–11): The justified Christian is reconciled to God and will be saved, sharing, with hope, in the risen life of Christ.
    2. The theme explained (5.12–8.39): The new Christian life brings a threefold liberation.
      a. Freedom from sin and death (5.12–21).
      b. Freedom from sin and self through baptism and union with Christ (6.1–23).
      c. Freedom from the Law (7.1–25).
    3. The theme developed (8.1–39): Christian life is empowered by the Spirit.
  C. Justification and Salvation through faith do not contradict God's promises to Israel of old.
    1. Israel's failure is not contrary to God's control of human history (9.1–29).
    2. It comes from Israel's own culpable refusal (9.30–10.21).

3. It is partial and temporary (11.1–36).
III. Part II (12.1–15.13): Hortatory Section: The demands of upright life in Christ.
   A. Christian life must be a Spirit-guided worship paid to God (12.1–13.14).
   B. The duty of charity owed by the strong to the weak (14.1–15.13).
IV. Personal News (15.14–33): Paul's apostolate and plans. Final blessing (15.33).
V. Conclusion: Letter of Recommendation for Phoebe and greetings to various Roman Christians (16.1–23). [Doxology (16.25–27)]

Analysis of Contents. The opening formula, customary in a Pauline letter, incorporates phrases typical of the primitive KERYGMA (1.2–4) and key ideas of the letter itself (divine election, faith, gospel, salvation by Christ's death and resurrection). After invoking upon the Roman Christians his usual blessing of "grace and peace" (1.6–7), Paul apologizes in the "Thanksgiving" and prelude (1.8–15) for not having visited Rome earlier. He promises to come and preach God's gospel there too. Chapter 1.16 to 1.17 formulates Paul's main proposition: The gospel is God's power effecting the salvation of everyone who believes, Jew first and then Greek, for in it God's salvific uprightness is disclosed.

In the first part of the doctrinal section, the theme of the revelation of God's uprightness in the gospel is developed—at first antithetically. For those without the gospel, God's wrath is manifested against the universal impiety of human beings (1.18–3.20). Heathens, who have suppressed the truth about God and failed to honor and acknowledge Him who has made Himself perceptible in creation, incur this wrath inexcusably. They have been handed over consequently to the degrading pursuit of unnatural vice and indecent conduct (1.18–32). The Jew who listens to this indictment of heathen conduct may applaud, but he is really no better (2.1–3.9), for despite his possession and knowledge of the Mosaic law, he too incurs God's wrath for not observing it. God, indeed, shows no partiality. When at times pagans instinctively do some of the things that the Mosaic law prescribes, these are known to them, being written on their hearts. But then it would seem that the Jews are at a disadvantage despite their privileged heritage (3.1). Paul reassures them, but he quickly turns again to accuse them of infidelity, for "Jews and Greeks alike are under sin" (3.9), as Old Testament TESTIMONIA show. No one can boast, because in the sight of God no one becomes upright by observing the Mosaic law (3.20).

The first theme is now positively developed (3.21–28). God's uprightness has been disclosed quite independently of the Law—through faith in Christ. For though all people have sinned and are deprived of God's resplendent presence, God Himself has exposed Christ publicly as the means of expiating human sin [see EXPIATION (IN THE BIBLE)], and this justification takes place out of sheer benevolence [see GRACE (IN THE BIBLE)]. God did this to manifest His uprightness, to show that He was upright in making people of faith upright.

This theme is now illustrated from Scripture (4.1–25). A reflection on the Genesis story of Abraham, which differs from contemporary Jewish understanding of the patriarch's observance of the Mosaic law, explains how he became upright in God's sight through faith. He was justified, even before he was circumcised; and the promises God made to him were uttered long before the Mosaic law. So Abraham is the father of all those who come to justification through faith. The chapter ends with a significant proclamation of the role played by both the death and the resurrection of Christ in the justification of human beings.

A new theme is announced in 5.1 to 5.11: Justified Christians are reconciled to God and will be saved through the love of God made manifest in Christ. Through the Spirit poured into human hearts, the Christian is assured of the glory he or she will share. This theme is explained, first of all, in terms of a threefold freedom. As sin entered the world and affected all human beings through the transgression of one man (Adam), and death came in its wake, so through the obedience of one man (Christ, the Adam of the eschaton) came freedom from sin and death (5.12–21). In refuting an objection—that if this is so, then one should sin, so that God's grace might abound the more—Paul asserts the second freedom: freedom from sin and self through union with Christ Jesus (6.1–23). By Baptism the Christian has been identified with the death and resurrection of Christ. Risen now to a new life, the Christian cannot submit himself (his body, his flesh) to the reign of sin. The Christian's whole outlook is centered now on God alone. The third freedom is from the Mosaic law (7.1–25). Having died with Christ in Baptism, the Christian is one to whom the Mosaic law no longer applies. Despite its basic goodness, the Mosaic law never gave people the wherewithal to overcome the conflict that they sense within them. For while the mind acknowledges God's law, the ego, dominated by indwelling sin, does not follow its directives. So the Mosaic law only made people more conscious of their conduct as a formal transgression, thus aggravating the offense and serving as an instrument of sin. From this bondage to the Mosaic law, Christ has freed those who come to faith (7.25–8.2).

The positive development of the new theme follows (8.1–39): Christians live a life in union with God through the indwelling Spirit of God. The Spirit is the dynamic principle of the new life, making Christians adoptive children of God and co-heirs of Christ, destined to share his risen glory. To this status even the groaning material universe, Christian hope itself, and the Spirit testify. A hymn to the bounteous love of God manifested in Christ concludes the chapter.

How does Israel of old fit into this new mode of salvation based on faith? With the aid of Old Testament passages, Paul discusses the "rejection of Israel," that is, its failure to accept Christ. Paul is pained at the condition of his former coreligionists, privileged of old, but now excluded by their obstinacy from Christ (9.1–33). Israel's failure is not contrary to God's direction of human history, however, for it conforms to the pattern of divine ELECTION manifested in the Old Testament toward the patriarchs and even the pharaoh. "God's message has not failed" (9.6). However, physical descent from Abraham is not enough for salvation. Now that pagans through faith have attained the uprightness for which Israel was striving, they have been incorporated into Israel and are children of Abraham. If Israel has failed to accept Christ, this is not due to God, but only to itself (10.1–21). However, this rejection is only partial and temporary. God has not repudiated His people, for a remnant of it has come to faith. Yet because of the failure of many in Israel, salvation has been extended to pagans—a thing in itself providential. "So all Israel shall be saved" (11.26). Gentile Christians are not to look down on the Jews, for their salvation depends on the Jews. Gentile Christians are only a wild olive shoot grafted into the trunk of salvation history identified long ago with Israel's history; a place is still left on it for Israel to be grafted back in, into its own true place (11.1–36).

In the hortatory section Paul proposes various demands of the Christian life. Christian existence, as an act of Spirit-guided worship paid to God in the unity of the Body of Christ, must overcome evil with good (12.1–21). Civil rulers must be respected as ministers of God (13.1–7). For Christians, the epitome of the Mosaic law is, "Love your neighbor as yourself" (13.8–14). The weak (Jewish Christians of Rome) are to be helped by the strong (Roman Gentile Christians); neither is to judge the other, for both are members of God's household (14.1–15.13).

Paul appends personal news (15.14–33), explaining his apostolate, his journey to Jerusalem with the collection for the poor, and his desire to come to Rome en route to Spain. His farewell blessing is given in 15.33. Paul concludes with a letter of recommendation for Phoebe, in which he greets many Roman Christians (16:1–13) [Doxology (16.25–27].

Significance. Romans heads the Pauline corpus because of its length, but that primary place also reflects the renown it has enjoyed in the Christian Church, for its influence on Christian life and theology has been inestimable. Though addressed to a particular church and reflecting a specific conflict in Paul's ministry, the solution proposed in it lends itself easily to application to similar problems in the lives of all Christians. Romans influenced the composition of other New Testament books (1 Peter, Hebrews, James); it was widely quoted by Church Fathers (beginning with Clement of Rome); patristic commentaries on it abound (e.g., Origen, Chrysostom, Ambrosiaster). This letter played a large part in the controversies of Pelagius and Augustine and in the work of the Protestant reformers (Luther, Melanchthon, Calvin). Finally, many parts of it have provided the starting point for dogmatic development in the tradition of the Church (e.g., Original Sin, Grace and Justification, Trinity, Baptism).

Bibliography: Commentaries. O. KUSS (3 pts., chpts. 1–11; Regensburg 1957–1978). F. LEENHARDT, *Commentaire du Nouveau Testament 6* (2d. ed., Neuchâtel/Paris 1981). J. HUBY, *Verbum Salutis 10* (rev. S. Lyonnet; Paris 1957). C. E. B. CRANFIELD, *International Critical Commentary*, 2 v. (Edinburgh 1975, 1979). H. SCHLIER, *Herders theologischer Kommentar zum Neuen Testament 6* (Freiburg im B. 1977). J. A. FITZMYER, *Anchor Bible 33* (New York 1993), with extensive bibliog. D. J. MOO, (Grand Rapids, Mich. 1996). T. R. SCHREINER (Grand Rapids, Mich. 1998); B. BYRNE, *Sacra Pagina 6* (Collegeville, Minn. 1996). E. KÄSEMANN (Grand Rapids, Mich. 1980). U. WILCKENS, *Evangelisch-Katholischer Kommentar zum Neuen Testament 6/1–3* (Einsiedeln/Neukirchen-Vluyn 1978–1982). P. STUHLMACHER, *Das Neue Testament Deutsch 6* (14th ed. Göttingen 1989; English, Louisville 1994).

[J. A. FITZMYER]

ROMANTICISM, PHILOSOPHICAL

The process of conceptualizing the romantic intuition of man and being, and the doctrines resulting therefrom; also the movement, with its witnessing documents, in which this process transpired historically. Romanticism views man as pure, vital activity, generative of self and of the world, and as a finite principle open to an infinite revealing itself interiorly as the inexhaustible self-generative force of life, which is deployed through determinate expressive forms that can always be transcended. Romanticism views reality as the immanent determination of such activity. Historically, romanticism has been the expression of this vision in the complex culture succeeding to, and reacting against, the ENLIGHTENMENT and embracing all aspects of life: literary, artistic, political, social, religious, and scientific.

Characterization. Romanticism may be contrasted with classicism, which views man as possessing a determinate nature—defined as much by its limits as by its powers and achieving its perfection within these limits. It may be contrasted also with RATIONALISM, which, though conceiving man as open to the infinite, limits this openness to one power—reason or intellect. In romanticism, the integral, existing human principle is itself open, and it is open to an infinite that is not abstract but concrete.

The complex, expressive forms of romanticism give rise to the distinction between practical, or sentimental romanticism, and philosophical romanticism. The latter conceptualizes the basic intuitions of romanticism, whereas the former is characterized by its spontaneity and lyricism.

Philosophical romanticism may be characterized negatively as a reaction against the Enlightenment. Opposing the analytical method of the latter, it advocated the synthetic or speculative method. Against excessive intellectualism, it stood for a total reconstruction of human presence with renewed emphasis upon the positive power of the imagination, the senses, and the passions in attaining and witnessing to reality. Against mechanism, it stood for spontaneity and finality. Assigning limits to the natural sciences, it gave fresh vitality to history, the historical method, and the sciences depending on historical data.

The positive character of philosophical romanticism becomes apparent in its anthropology, whose basic note is integralism. The life-presence of man is a unity and totality, within which all powers conspire to a pure, transcendental consciousness. All dualisms, as between body and spirit, sense and reason, etc., are eliminated. The immediate, nonreflective operations of the human principle—passion, sense, imagination, will, and intuition—are recognized as positive elements of this synthesis. Integralism is extended also to the expressive forms. Art, as expression, is assigned the status of a principle of transcendental unity for consciousness. AESTHETICS, as the general theory of expression, becomes a fundamental discipline among the philosophical sciences. The social bond, earlier seen as contractual, becomes organic and historical; it rests upon spontaneous and affective processes as much as upon reflection and volition.

Historical Survey. Historically, philosophical romanticism is polarized between the figures of Giambattista VICO (1668–1744) and G. W. F. HEGEL (1770–1831). Its progress falls into three stages: protoromanticism, the critique of Kantianism, and the system of reason.

Protoromanticism. This movement is represented by Vico, whose *Scienza Nuova* (successive versions 1724–44) anticipates all the basic lineaments of philosophical romanticism. By the doctrine of "poetic consciousness," it achieves a total reconstruction of human presence; by the deployment of human presence through chronological time on the basis of ideal time (the latter determined by the constitutive modifications of the human mind), it establishes the order of history in the romantic sense; by the theory of "ideal and eternal history" informing every particular history, it establishes the openness of human history to the eternal and transcendent, in the manner of the romantic philosophy of history.

Critique of Kantianism. Although Kant is not included among the romantic philosophers, the speculative enterprise of philosophical romanticism takes form through criticism of the Kantian achievement. This formation exhibits two aspects: the dissolution of the thing-in-itself and the transformation of the synthetic a priori from a formal to a dynamic dialectical principle for the speculative construction of reality.

Numerous thinkers contributed to the process of the dissolution of the thing-in-itself. F. H. JACOBI (1743–1819) pointed out the dilemma in which this concept involved Kantian criticism, and J. F. Fries (1773–1843), advancing Jacobi's criticism, emphasized the unity of the noumenal world revealed in the *Critique of Practical Reason* as contrasted to the division of phenomenal and noumenal in the *Critique of Pure Reason.* K. L. Reinhold (1758–1823), a confirmed Kantian who wished to systematize his master's doctrine, substituted an order of objective consciousness for both the ego and the thing-in-itself. Both J. G. von HERDER (1744–1803) and J. G. HAMANN (1730–88) censured the Kantian division among the forms of cognition and sought some principle of unity for consciousness. They reintroduced the Leibnizian notion of a gradual transformation of sensibility into ideality, thus adumbrating both the system of reason and the phenomenology of spirit or mind. G. E. Schulze (1761–1833), in his *Aenesidemus,* offered a negative but important critique; Salomon Maimon (1754–1800) pointed out that the entire notion of the thing-in-itself demands a fresh analysis of consciousness; while J. S. Beck (1761–1840) drew the entire process to a focus by noting that it is the relation of thought and being that demands rethinking.

The process of dissolution, being negative, could not reveal adequately its own implications; these became clear, however, with the ideal construction of a unitary structure of intelligible existence through a dialectical interpretation of the synthetic a priori. This project corresponds completely with the principle of philosophical romanticism—that reality is a living process generating alike self and world, world-in-itself, self-in-the-world, and the complete in-and-for-itselfness of intelligible existence. The synthetic a priori, transformed from a formal to a dialectical principle, is the instrument of construction of the system of reason.

System of Reason. The construction of the system of reason is associated principally with J. G. FICHTE (1762–1814), F. W. J. von SCHELLING (1775–1854), F. D. E. SCHLEIERMACHER (1768–1834), and, principally, Hegel.

For Fichte, the structure of the system of reason rests upon the categorical imperative, the pure form of the rational will; the world becomes the matter of duty, the content of that imperative in sensuous form; the world is there (*dasein*) as the theater of human moral activity. The "ought" is the pure and ultimate form of reason and the ground of the world (subjective IDEALISM).

For Schelling, the system of reason rests on the ground of nature (objective idealism). The question thus arises: How does the self-conscious process of reason generate the order of objects in which it is (ostensibly) negated? That it *must* generate order follows from the previously established notion that rational activity is autonomous, i.e., it does not arise in the presence of a "given," as Kant had supposed, but generates even the "given" as a dimension of its own activity. Schelling replies: Nature, the order of objects, is the self-generative process of consciousness in its concreteness, in the process of becoming self-commensurate and wholly present to itself. Without the order of objects, nature would remain abstract and in alienation from itself.

Schleiermacher introduces a religious element into the system of reason. A tendency to make the ultimate unity of the noumenal and phenomenal orders the object of faith had long existed; Schleiermacher continued this into the construction of the system of reason. The faith of Schleiermacher resembles the activity that Kant discusses in the *Critique of Judgment;* it establishes an aesthetic relation between man and the world and manifests itself concretely as a feeling of dependence in man.

The construction of the system of reason culminates in Hegel, who judged the efforts of his predecessors negatively because they rested on partial principles of presence, namely, will, nature, etc. Logic alone can generate the system of reason by generating the Idea; in the Idea all the partial modes of presence are synthesized and transcended. This process is illustrated in the *Phenomenology of Spirit;* its principles are established in the *System of Logic* and elaborated in the *Encyclopedia of the Philosophical Sciences.* Through this process Hegel establishes in principle the totality of intelligible being and existence in its complex structure of being-in-itself,

being-for-another, and being-for-itself as the pure synthesis of being-in-and-for-itself.

Influence. The resonances of philosophical romanticism are widespread. They may be traced in TRADITIONALISM in France (though this has other sources as well); in the works of A. ROSMINI-SERBATI and V. GIOBERTI, as well as of others in Italy; and in TRANSCENDENTALISM in England and the United States. In its own right, the position that philosophical romanticism assumed has entered into the permanent philosophical heritage of the Western world.

Bibliography: V. MATHIEU, *Enciclopedia filosofica,* 4 v. (Venice-Rome 1957) 4:187–203. A. R. CAPONIGRI, *Time and Idea: The Theory of History in Giambattista Vico* (London 1953). J. G. ROBERTSON, *Studies in the Genesis of Romantic Theory in the Eighteenth Century* (Cambridge, Eng. 1923). H. I. C. GRIERSON, *Classical and Romantic* (Cambridge, Eng. 1923). G. BOAS, *French Philosophies of the Romantic Period* (Baltimore 1925). A. O. LOVEJOY, *The Great Chain of Being* (Cambridge, Mass. 1936). M. JOACHIMI, *Die Weltanschauung der deutschen Romantik* (Jena 1905). E. KIRCHER, *Philosophie der Romantik* (Jena 1906). O. F. WALZEL, *Deutsche Romantik* (Leipzig 1908). R. HAYM, *Die romantische Schule* (5th ed. Berlin 1928). W. SCHULZ, *Die Vollendung des deutschen Idealismus in der Spätphilosophie Schellings* (Stuttgart 1955).

[A. R. CAPONIGRI]

ROMANUS, POPE

Pontificate: July or August to November 897. A Roman priest of the Church of St. Peter in Chains, Romanus became pope amid the disorder following the assassination of Pope STEPHEN VI in 897 and held the see four months. The clergy and people of Rome were torn with strife between the parties who supported the "cadaveric" council held by Stephen in judgment on the corpse of Pope FORMOSUS and those who wished to rehabilitate the memory of the ill-fated pontiff. The body of Formosus was rescued from the Tiber and buried, but it was left for the successors of Romanus to restore the remains of the Pope to the tomb in St. Peter's and to revalidate the Orders conferred by him. The successor of Romanus, THEODORE II, was pope for only two weeks but in the subsequent pontificate JOHN IX nullified the acts of the council-of-the-corpse.

Bibliography: Liutprand, *Antapodosis, Monumenta Germaniae Historica: Scriptores rerum Germanicum* (Berlin 1826–) v.41. AUXILIUS OF NAPLES, "In defensionem sacrae ordinationis papae Formosae libellus," in *Auxilius und Vulgarius,* ed. E. L. DÜMMLER (Leipzig 1866). *Liber pontificalis,* ed. L. DUCHESNE (Paris 1886–92) 2:230. C. J. VON HEFELE, *Histoire des conciles d'après les documents originaux,* tr. and continued by H. LECLERCQ (Paris 1907–38) v.4. L. DUCHESNE, *Les Premiers temps de l'état pontifical* (2d ed. Paris 1904). H. K. MANN, *The Lives of the Popes in the Early Middle Ages from 590 to 1304* (London 1902–32)

4:86–87. A. FLICHE, *L'Europe occidentale de 888 à 1125* (Paris 1930). A. FLICHE and V. MARTIN, eds. *Histoire de l'église depuis les origines jusqu'à nos jours* (Paris 1935) 7:25–26. G. SCHWAIGER, *Lexikon des Mittelalters* 7 (Munich-Zurich 1994–95). J. N. D. KELLY, *Oxford Dictionary of Popes* (New York 1986) 116.

[P. J. MULLINS]

ROMANUS, SS.

The name of numerous saints in the ecclesiastical calendar, particularly in antiquity and the Middle Ages. The *acta* of St. LAWRENCE speak of a *Romanus Ostiarius* as a martyr at Rome on the Via Tiburtina (d. 258). EUSEBIUS OF CAESAREA mentions a deacon *Romanus of Caesarea* who was martyred at Antioch with a young boy named Barulas under Diocletian (*Historia ecclesiastica* 8.2); a sermon of JOHN CHRYSOSTOM at Antioch mentions this same Romanus as a martyr *c.* 303. GREGORY OF TOURS speaks of *Romanus of Le Mans* as a priest of Blaye in the Gironde (Gaul) and as a saint (d. 380). *Romanus the Hermit*, a native of Cilicia, is mentioned by THEODORET OF CYR because of his modesty and his charity; cures attributed to his prayers caused him to be named Thaumaturgus, or miracle–worker. The founder of the abbey of Condat in the Jura was also a Romanus, who lived first as a solitary under the direction of the abbot of Ainay (Lyon) before gaining the esteem of his contemporaries by his goodness (d. 463). The Roman MARTYROLOGY lists *Romanus of Subiaco* (d. *c.* 560) who was an early companion of St. BENEDICT. Also recorded as saints were Bishop *Romanus of Reims* (d. *c.* 535); Bishop *Romanus of Auxerre* (d. *c.* 550); Bishop *Romanus of Rouen* (d. *c.* 640). Pope BENEDICT XIII approved the celebration of the feast of the martyrs (d. 1010) SS. *Romanus (Boris) and David (Gleb)* for Russian Catholics. This Romanus, called Boris in Russian, is the patron of Moscow.

The lives of these saints were embellished by numerous legends. Some of them seem to have been the victims of duplication as in the case of the Roman priest of Mans, who is very similar to the one at Blaye. The existence of a Romanus, disciple of a certain Ptolemy, and bishop of Nepi, is recorded by a questionable vita. Many of these saints are honored with special feasts in particular localities.

Romanus Ostiarius's feast day: Aug. 9.

Romanus of Caesarea's feast day: Nov. 18.

Romanus of Le Mans's feast day: Nov. 24.

Romanus the Hermit's feast day: Feb. 9.

Romanus (founder of the abbey of Condat in the Jura) feast day: Feb. 28.

Romanus of Subiaco's feast day: May 22.

Bishop Romanus of Reims's feast day: Feb. 28.

Bishop Romanus of Auxerre's feast day: Oct. 6.

Bishop Romanus of Rouen's feast day: Oct. 23.

Romanus (Boris) of Moscow's feast day: July 24.

Bishop Romanus of Nepi's feast day: Aug. 24.

Bibliography: *Bibliotheca hagiographica latina antiquae et mediae aetatis*, 2 v. (Brussels 1898–1901; suppl. 1911), 7297–7321. J. L. BAUDOT and L. CHAUSSIN, *Vies des saints et des bienheureux selon l'ordre du calendrier avec l'historique des fêtes*, ed. BENEDICTINES OF PARIS, 12 v. (Paris 1935–56); v. 13, suppl. and table générale (1959). H. QUENTIN, *Les Martyrologes historiques du moyen âge* (Paris 1908). H. DELEHAYE, *S. Romain, martyr d'Antioche* (Brussels 1932). E. M. DUPEYRON and G. REICHER, *Une chronique chrétienne du IVme siècle; saint Romain d'Afrique et de Blaye* (Blaye 1946). R. AIGRAIN, *L'Hagiographie* (Paris 1953) 29, 226, 260, 265. *The Life of the Jura Fathers: The Life and Rule of the Holy Fathers Romanus, Lupicinus, and Eugendus*, tr. T. VIVIAN, K. VIVIAN, and J. B. RUSSELL (Kalamazoo, Mich. 1999).

[P. ROCHE]

ROMANUS I LECAPENUS, BYZANTINE EMPEROR

Reign: Dec. 17, 920, to Dec. 16, 944; b. Lakape, Armenia, *c.* 870; d. Prote, June 15, 948. He was the son of an Armenian peasant, Theophylactus Abastactus, who had become an officer by saving the Emperor Basil I's life. Romanus was befriended by Emperor Leo VI, who appointed him *strategos* of the naval theme of Samos in 911. Shortly afterward he was promoted, probably by Emperor Alexander, to *droungarios* (Admiral) of the Fleets. According to a hostile account (Theophanes Continuatus), Romanus failed to ferry Byzantine allies across the Danube, resulting in a resounding defeat by the Bulgarians at the river Acheloos in 917. In May 919, Romanus married his daughter Helen to the young Emperor CONSTANTINE VII PORPHYROGENITUS, in contravention of an arrangement brokered by Patriarch NICHOLAS I MYSTICUS with the Bulgarian Tsar Symeon. He took the *basileopator*; became caesar (September 24, 920); then, besting the general Leo Phocas, a rival candidate, became emperor (December 17, 920). To solidify his regime and marginalize the legitimate emperor, Romanus had his own son Christopher crowned *basileus*, i.e., given the imperial title (May 20, 921), and his two younger sons, Constantine and Stephen, later received the same dignity (Dec. 25, 924).

Romanus eventually achieved a peace with the Bulgarian King Symeon, reluctantly recognizing him as emperor of Bulgaria and spiritual brother (*pneumatikos adelphos*). Upon Symeon's death in 927, Romanus married his granddaughter, Maria, to the new Tsar Peter; Peter recognized Romanus as his spiritual father. Romanus restrained Arab depredations in southern Italy; entered an alliance with Caucasia and Armenia; deflected a Russian assault on Constantinople in 941; and through his general John Curcuas, forced Edessa to surrender the *hagion mandylion,* the picture of Christ supposedly painted for King ABGAR by the Savior himself. Romanus was the first emperor to legislate in favor of the poor (*penetes*): his novels were intended to defend small landholders against annexation of their lands by the powerful (*dynatoi*), and thus also strengthen imperial authority and the fisc in the face of aristocratic expansionism. Interventions in Church affairs saw Romanus issue a *Tomos* of Union in 920, and appoint his 16–year–old son Theophylactus Patriarch of Constantinople in 933.

Romanus's designated heir, Christopher, died in 931. On December 16, 944, his two other sons, Constantine and Stephen, rebelled and drove out their father; but they were in turn expelled by the Porphyrogenitus, who became sole emperor on Jan. 27, 945. Romanus was exiled to the island of Prote, where he died a penitent. Works produced under Constantine besmirched the deeds of the late usurper, but a sympathetic, almost hagiographical account of Romanus's reign is preserved in the chronicle of Symeon Logothete.

Bibliography: A. CAMERON, ''The History of the Image of Edessa: the Telling of a Story,''*Harvard Ukrainian Studies* 7 (1983) 80–94; *eadem,* ''The Mandylion of Edessa and Byzantine Iconoclasm,'' in *The Holy Face and the Paradox of Representation,* ed. H. L. KESSLER, G. WOLF (Bologna 1998) 33–54; R. JENKINS, ''The Peace with Bulgaria (927) Celebrated by Theodore Daphnopates,'' *Polychronion. Festschrift F. Dolger* (Heidelberg 1966) 287–303; R. MORRIS, ''The Powerful and the Poor in Tenth–century Byzantium: Law and Reality,'' *Past and Present* 73 (1976) 3–27. *New Cambridge Medieval History,* v.3. S. RUNCIMAN, *The Emperor Romanus Lecapenus* (Cambridge, Eng. 1929). *Théodore Daphnopates, Correspondance,* ed. & tr. J. DARROUZÈS, L. WESTERINK (Paris 1976). *Theophanes continuatus, Ioannes Caminiata, Symeon Magister, Georgius Monachus continuatus,* ed. I. BEKKER (Bonn 1825). M. WHITTOW, *The Making of Byzantium, 600–1025* (Berkeley 1996) 340–348.

[M. J. HIGGINS/P. STEPHENSON]

ROMANUS MELODUS, ST.

Preeminent religious poet of the Eastern Church; b. Emesa, Syria, *c.* 490; d. Constantinople, *c.* 560. Legendary evidence indicates that Romanus was of Jewish origin. He served as a deacon in Beirut, Lebanon, before arriving in Constantinople during the reign of ANASTASIUS I (491–518). According to hagiographic sources, the Virgin Mary appeared to him in a dream on Christmas Eve and, upon handing him a piece of paper, instructed him to swallow it. After awakening, Romanus mounted the pulpit in the Church of the Virgin Mother and sang his most famous work, *On the Nativity I.* Of the 1,000 poems that legend attributes to Romanus, only 85 have survived, and the authenticity of a number is doubtful. His possible authorship of the monumental AKATHISTOS hymn is an open question.

The verse form employed by Romanus is the *Kontakion,* a term derived from the staff around which the inscribed scroll was wrapped. Every Kontakion is organized in an intricate strophic system, most frequently consisting of 24 stanzas. Each stanza is a perfect structural imitation of the first. The metrical system, unlike classical quantitative patterns, is based on stress-accent, whose rhythmic arrangement was undoubtedly influenced by the melody to which the poem was originally sung. His honorific title, The Melodist, indicates that Romanus also composed the music, none of which survives.

A short prefatory stanza, the *koukoulion,* though metrically and melodically independent of the rest of the poem, introduced a refrain with which every stanza concludes, but it does not contribute to the initial-letter acrostic that signs the work. The language of Romanus is the standard literary koine, strongly influenced by the usages and vocabulary of scriptural Greek.

The Kontakion was sung after the reading of the Gospel in the morning Office, and its themes and techniques are characteristic of its liturgical function, that of a verse sermon. Most probably a preacher chanted the work, while the choir or the congregation sang the refrain. Themes suggested by the life and ministry of Christ, Old Testament events, and the deeds of martyrs and saints are woven together with flamboyant exegetical displays and elaborate antiheretical digressions to inspire and instruct the congregation. Romanus frequently dramatized his Biblical and patristic source material by exploiting suggestions of soliloquy, interior monologue, and dialogue and by paying careful attention to scene and plot arrangement and to adroit transition and climax.

There is no evidence that the Kontakia were ever theatrically produced. Rather, the poetically pregnant biblical phraseology and rhetorical figures, such as antithesis, parallelism, anaphora, paradox, and various types of wordplay, situate the Kontakion in the tradition of the great rhythmic prose homilies of the fifth and early sixth centuries. In this historical context the direct and indirect influence of Syriac literature, and especially of EPHREM THE SYRIAN, is considerable.

The sweeping grandeur of such Kontakia as the Nativity poem and some of the Passion–Resurrection cycle justifies the critical opinion that rates these works as mas-

Miniature detail of St. Romanus Melodus, 11th century, from "Menologian of Basil II."

terpieces of world literature and their author as perhaps the greatest religious poet of all time.

Feast Day: Oct. 1.

Bibliography: P. MAAS and C. A. TRYPANIS, eds., *Sancti Romani Melodi Cantica,* v.1, *Genuina* (Oxford 1963), v.2 *Dubia, Spuria et Fragmenta* (in press). H. G. BECK, *Kirche und theologische Literatur im byzantinischen Reich* (Munich 1959) 425–428. M. CARPENTER, *Speculum* 7 (1932) 3–22. L. PATON, *ibid.* 553–555. E. WELLESZ, *A History of Byzantine Music and Hymnography* (2d ed. Oxford 1961). J. GROSDIDIER DE MATONS, ed., *Romanos le Mélode,* 3 v. (Sources Chrétiennes, ed. H. DE LUBAC et al. (Paris 1941–) 99, 110, 114; 1964–65), v.1 *Hymnes I–VIII,* v.2 *Hymnes IX–XX,* v.3 *Hymnes XX–XXXI.* J. GROSDIDIER DE MATONS, *Romanos le Mélode et les origines de la poésie religieuse à Byzance* (Paris 1977). W. L. PETERSEN, *The Diatessaron and Ephrem Syrus as sources of Romanos the Melodist* (Louvain 1985). R. J. SCHORK, *Sacred Song from the Byzantine Pulpit: Romanos the Melodist* (Gainesville, Fl. 1995).

[R. J. SCHORK]

ROME

Ancient capital of the Roman state and empire, center of Christendom, episcopal see of the pope, and capital of modern Italy. The city is located on a series of hills that fortuitously surround a wide bend in the Tiber River not far from its entrance into the Mediterranean Sea, at an almost central point on the west coast of the Italian Peninsula. Rome's primitive history is dominated by legend, but archeological evidence and solid tradition point to village settlements by the Sabines and inhabitants of Latium that go back at least to the 10th century B.C. Ancient Roman historians differed in calculating the date of the city's legendary founding by Romulus, but M. Terentius Varro's estimate of 753 B.C. has become standard. In the course of five centuries B.C., the city of Rome became a great religious, economic, political, and cultural center, as is attested by archeological remains of its temples, cemeteries, monuments, and public buildings, as well as by its literature and art.

Rome is dealt with here as the center of Christendom in relation to: (1) early Christianity; (2) the Constantinian era; (3) papal rule in late antiquity and in the Middle Ages; (4) the Renaissance; (5) the post-Reformation period; and (6) modern and contemporary Rome.

EARLY CHRISTIANITY

Rome first entered directly into the history of Israel with a request for her aid against Syria made by the Mac-

Saint Peter's Church, St. Peter's Square, Vatican City. (©Reinhard Eisele/CORBIS)

cabees *c.* 161 B.C. After the conquest of Palestine by Pompey in 63 B.C., Rome dominated Jewish civil affairs; Christ was born under Roman rule (Lk 2.2) and put to death under Pontius Pilate, the Roman procurator of Judea (Lk 23.1–5, 13–25). While Rome is not mentioned directly in the Gospels, its presence is felt by the dominance of its emperors (Mk 12.13–17; Mt 22.15–22; Lk 20.20–26), and in certain New Testament writings the city receives explicit recognition. An edict of Claudius in A.D. 49 banishing the Jews from Rome is mentioned in Acts 18.2 as the occasion for the departure from Rome of Aquila and Priscilla and their meeting with St. Paul at Corinth.

Early Roman Christians. There is no evidence for the arrival of the first Christians in Rome, but a flourishing Christian community existed there in A.D. 58 when Paul wrote his Epistle to the Romans, and it is almost certain that SUETONIUS had this Christian settlement in mind when he stated that Claudius *Judeos impulsore Chresto*

tumultuantes Roma expulsit—"expelled the Jews from Rome as a result of a tumult caused by Chrestus," or Christ (*Claud.* 25.4). Paul arrived in Rome between A.D. 59 and 61 and was met outside the city at the *Forum Appii* and *ad Tres Tabernas* by a group of Christians (Acts 28.15). He remained there two years under guard in a private dwelling and was allowed to receive visitors and discuss the gospel with whoever came to him. It is possible that Luke wrote the Acts to the Apostles in Rome and that the Pauline Captivity Epistles originated there, as well as 1 Peter. Paul was brought to Rome a second time as a prisoner, probably after his arrest at Troas (cf. 2 Tm 1.16–17; 4.13), but there is no evidence as to the time of St. Peter's arrival. However, early tradition (1 Clem. 6) testifies that Peter and Paul were martyred in Rome during the Neronian persecution, recorded for the year 64 by Tacitus (*Annal.* 15.44), while Eusebius stated that they were put to death in 67 (*Hist. eccl.* 2.25.1–8). Nothing proves that they were not martyred in the same year.

Alongside a large Jewish settlement, the Christian colony grew during the reigns of Vespasian (69–79) and Titus (79–81). Despite persecution under Domitian (81–96), there is evidence that some patricians were Christians, including Flavia DOMITILLA (d. *c.* 100), granddaughter of Vespasian, wife of Titus Flavius Clemens, and a first cousin of Domitian. Clemens was put to death probably in the Domitian persecution against Christians and Jews (95–96), and Domitilla was banished to the island of Pandateria, while her property outside Rome on the Via Ardeatina seems to have been used in the 1st century as a Christian place of burial, later the cemetery or catacombs of Domitilla.

Second-century Popes. Despite minor discrepancies, the names of the early Roman bishops have been preserved in a reliable list (Liber pontificalis), but the first bishops of whom positive information exists are St. CLEMENT I (*c.* 88–97), who probably composed the *Epistle to the Church of Corinth;* the martyr St. TELESPHORUS (126–136); and St. PIUS I, brother of the author of the *Shepherd of HERMAS.* Evidence is supplied for the Christian importance of Rome by the *Epistle to the Romans* of IGNATIUS OF ANTIOCH (*c.* 110–117), who praised the charity of its Christians and begged them not to prevent his martyrdom through political influence (*Ad Rom.* 2). In the course of the 2d century, Rome was the object of visits from Christian leaders seeking confirmation of the unity of the Church, as is attested by the Epitaph of ABERCIUS, by HEGESIPPUS, and by heretics such as MARCION (fl. 135–160), the Gnostic VALENTINUS, and the Monarchian Theodore, who sought confirmation of their unorthodox teachings.

The description of the Church as a populous community, containing a segment of the rich and numerous poor, with a mixture of saints and sinners, provided by the *Shepherd of Hermas* (*Sim.* 8.4–11), probably refers to Rome (*c.* 150); it was, besides, a well-organized institution with bishops, priests, and deacons. JUSTIN MARTYR (*c.* 100–165) conducted a school of Christian philosophy in Rome, directed his *Apologiae* to the Roman authorities, and died a martyr there with some of his disciples in the persecution of Aurelian (161–180). POLYCARP OF SMYRNA visited Pope ANICETUS (*c.* 155–166), and IRENAEUS OF LYONS visited Pope ELEUTHERIUS (*c.* 177) to discuss the QUARTODECIMAN problem, which Pope VICTOR I IM (189–199), the first Latin-speaking pope, tried to settle in a Roman synod. Victor threatened to excommunicate Polycrates of Ephesus and the bishops of Asia Minor who followed the Jewish reckoning for the date of Easter. With Victor, who wrote several encyclical letters ordaining that synods be held by groups of bishops in other regions, the predominance of the Church at Rome was assured.

Central portion of the façade of the Church of San Marcello al Corso, Rome, designed by Carlo Fontana, built 1682–83. (Alinari-Art Reference/Art Resource, NY)

Title Churches. Roman Christians down to the late 2d century held their liturgical gatherings in the houses of richer members and used their burial places. Justin Martyr's evasive answers under imperial interrogation regarding Christian places of worship indicate that this practice was still in vogue *c.* 165 (*Acta Sanctorum* April 2:104–119). But archeological evidence and the tradition regarding Rome's title churches point to the existence in the late 2d century of edifices for Christian cult.

Excavations beneath the churches of St. Clement, St. Anastasia, and SS. John and Paul have unearthed foundations of the late 2d and early 3d century that had undergone great changes before the 4th century and indicate the enlargement and even the building over of the earlier edifices. Beneath the church of SS. Silvestri e Martino ai Monti Christian paintings have been discovered on the walls of a building that goes back to the Severian emperors (*c.* 195–235), and excavations beneath the churches of St. Sabina and St. Chrysogonus reveal similar early emplacements. Evidence exists also for pre–4th-century edifices on the sites of the churches of SS. Crescentia and Pudens (or Pudentiana), as well as of St. Cecilia and St. Callistus. The Basilica Apostolorum on the Via Appia seems to have been built in imitation of the mausoleum

Pantheon, c. 128–125 B.C., Rome. (©Michael Maslan Historic Photographs/CORBIS)

erected by Maxentius for his son Romulus, immediately after the emancipation granted by Galerius in 311. The construction of these churches reflects the basilica-type, large building common to Roman architecture of the age.

These pre-Constantinian churches seem to have been located close to the ancient wall of Servius Tullius within the city, except for St. Marcellus near the Campus Martius and S. Lorenzo in Lucina beside the obelisk of Augustus, close to the Via Flaminia in a quarter that had a Jewish colony (*Calcarenses*) housing the wine and marble merchants. The placement of these churches formed a crosslike pattern covering the poor, more populous parts of the city from the Quirinal Hill (SS. Susanna and Cyriacus) to Trastevere (SS. Chrysogonus, Cecilia, and Callistus), and as a transverse bar between the valley of the Viminal (St. Pudentiana), the Esquiline (St. Praxedes, SS. Silvestri e Martino ai Monti), the Caelian (St. Clement, SS. Peter and Marcellus, St. Sixtus, SS. Nereus and Achilleus, the Four Crowned Martyrs, and SS. John and

Paul), the Aventine (St. Prisca, St. Sabina), and, finally, the area near the *Forum Boarium* (St. Anastasia). Before the 4th century these churches were known only by the title of their emplacement or the donor of the property; only between the 4th and 6th centuries were they connected with the names of saints or early martyrs.

Catacombs and Persecutions. Some 40 distinct catacombs have been discovered outside the city on the main roads running northeast and south. Until the 4th century they were used primarily for burial, followed by the celebration of anniversaries that gradually assumed a liturgical form in honor of a martyr saint; but only some 25 such commemorations are recorded in the first Christian calendar in the mid-4th century. In the 4th and 5th centuries, the catacombs became regular places of assembly for Eucharistic cult. In them were likewise preserved the earliest examples of Christian art and symbolism, particularly in the stucco paintings on the walls and in designs on sarcophagi.

Fourth-century epitaph of the child Agathemerus, inscription contains the words "ANIMA TUA ΨΥΧΗ ΚΑΛΗ" Cemetery of Praetextatus, Rome.

As the persecutions were intermittent, followed by long periods of peace, Christians gradually acquired property, and, though they were not given legal recognition as religious corporations, they could occasionally vindicate their rights through judicial action, as in the case of an appeal to the Emperor Alexander Severus (222–235), who decided in favor of a Christian church near the Forum instead of a tavern (Lampridius, *Vita Alex. Sev.* 49.6—if this statement is reliable). Under the Severi, Pope CALLISTUS I (217–222) likewise attempted to regulate the ownership of church property and cemeteries, as is indicated by the attachment of his name to both the cemetery on the Appian Way and a sanctuary in Trastevere. St. Augustine reported having read that at the end of the persecutions, Pope Miltiades (d. 314) sent the deacon Strato to receive the ecclesiastical property restored to the Church by the prefect of Rome (*Brev. coll. Donat.* 18.34–35); and in the Constantinian peace of 313, it was ordered that "the places where Christians were accustomed to assemble should be given back to the corporate body or conventicle" (Lact., *De mortibus persec.* 48).

At the close of the Decian persecution, Pope Cornelius had held a synod of 60 bishops in Rome (251) to deal with the NOVATIAN schism; his own clergy consisted of 154 clerics, including 46 priests, seven deacons, and seven subdeacons. The number of Christians in Rome was thus considerable, justifying TERTULLIAN's statement at the end of the 2d century: "We Christians are but of yesterday; yet we fill your world and all that you have, cities, houses . . . , the palace, senate, forum. All we leave to you are the temples" (*Apol.* 37.4).

CONSTANTINIAN ERA

No statistics exist for the number of Christians in Rome immediately before the peace of the Church established by CONSTANTINE I and Licinius (313), nor is there a reliable estimate of the number of martyrs. What is significant, however, is the fact that on accepting the Christian faith Constantine erected three great churches within the city: the basilica close to the palace of Fausta at the Lateran (later named St. John's by Pope Hilary I in 461), which the emperor gave to the bishop of Rome as his residence near the imperial gardens; the nearby basilica of the Holy Cross in Jerusalem, one of the results of the dowager Empress Helena's benefactions; and the immense construction for the emplacement on the Vatican of the basilica anchored on the site venerated as the grave of St. Peter. Constantine built another church outside the walls on the Via Ostia, where tradition placed the burial of St. Paul.

These imperial benefactions were deliberately made on the periphery of the city in order not to awaken the hostility of the pagan Romans, who still predominated, and whose civic life was centered on the Senate and the Forum with its temples, markets, and administrative buildings. Constantine imitated the largesse of his predecessors by adorning the city with public monuments and baths before deciding to move his capital to the newly erected city of CONSTANTINOPLE on the Bosporus. By the beginning of the 4th century the population of Rome had reached its greatest density; it was provided with 11 major and 856 minor public baths, 27 libraries, some 1,352 fountains, eight athletic fields, five naumachiae for water spectacles, 11 large public fora, ten major basilicas, 19 aqueducts, 36 triumphal arches, three theaters, and eight bridges crossing the Tiber. The city had been enclosed within a wall by Aurelian in the 270s; it was 19 km in circumference, with 383 towers and 14 major and five minor gates.

Christian Asceticism. To accommodate the increase of Christian converts, Pope Julius I (337–352) built several churches, of which two within the city were at first known simply under his name but were later called the basilicas of the Twelve Apostles and of St. Mary in Trastevere. He is also credited with constructing basilicas at the catacombs of St. Felix, St. Valentinus, and Calepodius. Liberius (352–366) built St. Mary Major on the Esquiline; it was rebuilt by Pope Sixtus III (432–440). Both these popes were caught in the maelstrom of doctrinal disputes that disturbed the empire following the condemnation of Arianism at the Council of Nicaea in 325 and the rise of subsequent schisms and heresies that brought to Rome innumerable appeals from both orthodox and heretical prelates and occasioned the holding of Roman synods and visits by many of the parties concerned.

Athanasius of Alexandria stopped in Rome in the course of his exile to Treves (339–342) and gave further impulse to the ascetical movement that flourished under Pope Damasus (366–384) and his successors. Rufinus of Aquileia, Bonosus, and Jerome were students there in the early 360s. Jerome returned under Damasus, began his revision of the Latin Bible, and served as papal secretary and as spiritual director to a group of well-to-do ascetics on the Caelian and Aventine Hills, who included Paula, Eustochium, Blesilla, and the senator Pammachius. Augustine taught in Rome for a year before going to Milan and attested to the existence of a strong Manichaean faction.

Though the Western emperors resided at Milan rather than at Rome, they continued their benefactions, particularly toward the erection and decoration of churches. Damasus "discovered and gave honor to the bodies of many saints, decorating their burial places with verses" (Lib. pont. 1.212). He likewise erected a titular church of S. Lorenzo in Damaso close to the papal archive, giving impetus to the cult of the martyrs within the city by the inscriptions he composed and to the subsequent erection of new titular churches, such as that of the Apostles (later, St. Peter in Chains) on the Esquiline, situated between the baths of Titus and Trajan, and that of St. Eusebius near the Livian market.

Papal Authority. The authority of the popes gradually increased despite the exile of Liberius, the rise of the antipope Felix (355–365), and the strife that accompanied the elections of Damasus and Boniface (418–422). The canons of Sardica (343) recognized the traditional position of the bishop of Rome as a court of final appeal in doctrine and disciplinary matters, and this fact was embodied in the legislation of Gratian (375–383) and Theodosius I (379–395). Gratian removed the Altar of Victory from the Senate (382), and, despite the opposition of a strong faction led by Symmachus, Prefect of the city, Theodosius I and Honorius I (395–425) legislated against paganism.

In exercising their authority, the popes supported orthodoxy with an insistence on traditional beliefs, common sense, and a distrust of theological niceties, as is attested by the *Tractatus de gratia* produced under Pope Celestine. Pope Siricius issued the earliest known decretal: and Innocent I (401–417) condemned Pelagianism; Celestine (422–432), Nestorianism; and Leo I (440–461), Eutychianism with his famous *Tome,* whose explanation of the Incarnation prevailed at the Council of Chalcedon (451). During the 5th century, Rome frequently settled affairs of the Churches in Gaul, Spain, Africa, and the East; and it saw the coming and going of emissaries, prelates, heretics, and imperial officials. The city was sacked by Alaric the Goth (410), menaced by Attila and the Huns (452), and ravaged by Geiseric and the Vandals (455). As the imperial control of Italy declined, the provision and administration of the city, the protection of the poor and destitute, and the restoration of its churches became the function of the popes.

In the 3d and 4th centuries the work of the deacons had increased in importance as they cared for widows, orphans, the ill, and the aged. In the 5th and 6th centuries they managed the revenues from properties in Sicily and Italy, given to the bishops of Rome by imperial officials or inherited from rich benefactors. Leo I reorganized this papal patrimony, held yearly synods for the government of the Roman (Italian) patriarchate, and wrote frequently to regulate ecclesiastical affairs throughout the Church. During his pontificate also, the liturgical effectiveness of the Church was manifest in the spirited observance of the paschal and Christmas cycles, which he described with zest and classic propriety in his sermons. He bore witness to the assemblies of bishop, clergy, and people at stational or titular churches, particularly on a vigil or during Lent, for a Eucharistic celebration in honor of a sacred mystery or a saint, and he attempted to regularize Christian cult all over the empire.

Upon the abandonment of the pagan temples under the Christian emperors, they were pillaged of their decorations and materials for new constructions of both private and public buildings, despite decrees of Valentinian and Valens (376) and of Majorian (458) against such depredations. During the 5th century, however, the prefects of the city made heroic efforts to reconstruct and repair the buildings of the Fora, many of which had been destroyed by the fire that followed the city's capture by Alaric (410). After the earthquake of 442 the prefect Quadratianus repaired the Baths of Constantine, and in 450 Epitynchianus restored the Forum Esquilinum. Even under the Ostrogothic King Theodoric (475–526), orders were given to preserve the city's monuments. However, in the building of churches, these regulations were not always observed. Under Pope Simplicius (468–483), the churches of St. Bibiana and St. Stephen (Rotundo) were built, and the *schola domestica* of the Goth Theodobius was changed into an oratory honoring St. Andrew. Ricimer the Goth (459–470) built a church to St. Agatha for Arians in Rome.

Despite difficulties with Theodoric caused by the antipope Laurentius, Pope Symmachus (498–514) attached a church honoring St. Silvester to the old edifice of S. Martino ai Monti. Felix IV (526–530) invaded the Forum, building the basilica of SS. Cosmas and Damian on the Via Sacra and decorating its apse with a mosaic of Christ receiving a model of the church from the two saints. Near the palace of Caligula he reconstructed an old building and decorated it with frescoes as the church of Santa Maria Antica. While the art of the earlier period had been more or less impressionistic, by the close of the 6th century, the Byzantine style prevailed in the mosaics and other plastic representations in the churches.

PAPAL RULE IN LATE ANTIQUITY AND IN THE MIDDLE AGES

Between 536 and 555 Belisarius was entrusted with the Byzantine reconquest of Italy by Justinian I (527–565). The general entrenched his army in Rome, and in 536 Vitiges and his Goths besieged the city, cut its aqueducts, and by investing the port (Porto) near Ostia, prevented the provisioning of Rome with wheat from Sicily and Africa.

In 544 Totila attacked Rome; he finally took the city on Dec. 17, 546. Pope VIGILIUS (537–555), however, had been taken to Constantinople, and the Deacon Pelagius attempted to revive life there after the departure of the Goths. On becoming pope, PELAGIUS I (556–561) utilized the Pragmatic Sanction granted by Justinian on Aug. 13, 554, to restore the main churches and buildings, but his ecclesiastical difficulties with the churches in the West over the condemnation of the THREE CHAPTERS hampered his efforts.

In 568 Italy was invaded by the Lombards. They frequently menaced Rome, whose actual government was by then almost completely in the hands of the popes. In 554 Justinian had also agreed to continue the public provisioning of Rome from Sicily, and the governor of the island sent wheat to Rome in the fall each year. This *annona* was stored in the ancient granaries (*horrea Agrippina*) and in the old market places and was distributed by papal *horrearii*. When the Arab incursions interfered with Mediterranean shipping, Popes John V (685–686) and Conon (686–687), in reorganizing papal finances, obtained fiscal exemptions for the Church's patrimonies in Sicily, Calabria, Lucania, and Brutium (Lib. pont. 1:366, 369). Later Emperor Leo the Isaurian seized these properties to punish Roman opposition to ICONOCLASM under Gregory III (731–741). Pope Zachary (741–752) then organized nearby Latium and the Roman Campagna as districts to supply Rome with needed agricultural products.

Evidence for the division of Rome into seven ecclesiastical districts is supplied by the 7th-century Liber diurnus. Popes Agatho (678–681) and Leo II (682–683) are credited with distributing money to the Greek monasteries, whose establishment in Rome was encouraged by a series of popes, evidently of Byzantine origin, for the care of the poor. Pilgrims were housed in special hostels known as *scholae* founded by national groups such as the Saxons, Frisians, Franks, and Lombards. Inscriptions found in the churches of S. Maria in Cosmedin and St. Agnes, as well as the 8th-century *Itinerarium* or "Pilgrim's Book of Einsiedeln," indicate the main streets of Rome. They passed 18 *diaconiae* all located in connection with the main and titular churches: nine were on the Vicus Tuscus, Argiletum, and Clivus Suburanus; and another nine were in connection with the roads that led from the gate of St. Peter to that of St. Paul. A *diaconia* consisted of a church where the people of a district gathered to hear daily Mass; an administrative office in a rebuilt public building; and a monastery of monks, who controlled the distribution of food and alms. Four depots for wheat were located on the sites of ancient Rome's granaries or market places. Roman church building, confined mainly to the reconstruction of ancient edifices, continued despite the political difficulties: Pelagius II (579–590) rebuilt St. Lawrence, Honorius I (625–638), St. Agnes and the church of the Four Crowned Martyrs. With PASCHAL I (817–824) a new style was introduced in the rebuilding of the churches of St. Praxedes, S. Maria in Domnica, St. Cecilia, and St. Mark.

Carolingian Period. In 806, when Pope Leo III marked the 10th year of his pontificate upon his return from the court of Charlemagne at Treves, he decided on a special distribution of alms to the churches of Rome and had a record made of the 25 recipients in the Liber pontificalis. Beside almost each of the churches there was a monastery for the celebration of the Liturgy or the care of the *diaconia*. Leo's journey had been preceded by the Pope's coronation of Charlemagne as Roman emperor in St. Peter's on Christmas Day 800. This event had been prepared for in 753 when Stephen II (752–757) appealed to the Frankish King Pepin for support. In 773 Adrian I (772–795) called upon CHARLEMAGNE to destroy the Lombard power in Italy. Charlemagne gave the Exarchate of Ravenna and the Roman Duchy not to the Byzantine Emperor, but to the Pope as his estate.

During the 9th and 10th centuries the struggle between the leading families of Rome to control the papacy was marked by schisms, insurrections, imperial interventions, and synods. The Arabs sacked the city (846) and plundered the tombs of St. Peter and St. Paul, after which Pope Leo IV (847–855) built a wall to enclose the district surrounding St. Peter's, known since that time as the Leonine city. The election of Pope Benedict III (855–858) was disputed by ANASTASIUS THE LIBRARIAN, but the commissioners of Louis II of Germany decided ultimately in favor of Benedict. Because of his competence in Greek and his wide knowledge, Anastasius was selected papal librarian by Pope NICHOLAS I (858–867); he attended the last session of the Council of CONSTANTINOPLE IV and participated in the discussions involving Photius and his actions. Pope John VIII (872–882) chose Charles the Bald of France over Louis the German as the new Roman emperor and crowned him in Rome on Christmas Day 875. John also organized a fleet to contain the Arabic invasions and fortified St. Paul's against Saracen depredations from Naples, Gaeta, and the Campagna. He was murdered by his local enemies on Dec. 16, 882.

Lateran Councils. John IX (898–900) stemmed the local anarchy but only temporarily. For 60 years Rome was ruled by a single family who made and unmade popes at will. Under Prince Alberic (931–954), St. Odo of Cluny reformed the monasteries of Subiaco and Monte Cassino, founded a Cluniac monastery on the Aventine,

and began a religious revival in Rome. In 962 Otto I, King of Germany, was crowned emperor in Rome by the Pope. He deposed John XII (955–964) and eventually installed Leo VIII (963–965) as pope. Chaotic conditions prevailed, with a brief interval after the election of Silvester II (999–1003), until the archpriest of St. John's became pope as Gregory VI (1045–46) and brought the monk Hildebrand from the Benedictine monastery on the Aventine to be his secretary.

Pope Leo IX (1049–54) inaugurated a vast reform movement in Rome through LATERAN COUNCIL I (1049), which was followed by synods in Italy and northern Europe and prepared the way for Alexander II (1061–73) and Gregory VII (1073–85), who were elected in accord with a decree promulgated at Lateran Council II (April 1059). This decree established the right of the cardinals alone to elect the pope.

Under Alexander and Gregory, the bishop of Rome took a leading part in vitalizing the spiritual well-being of the city and of Christendom. Yet despite basic reforms and the attempt to destroy lay control of the Church in the INVESTITURE STRUGGLE, two families, the Pierleoni and the Frangipani, succeeded in violating the peace for another hundred years. Rome was invaded by the Normans, saw the rise of a republic that restored the Senate, reformed the "equestrian orders" (probably the lower nobility and higher citizens), elected a patrician, Arnold of Brescia, as consul with absolute power over the city, and witnessed the crowning of FREDERICK I BARBAROSSA (1152–89) as emperor by the English Pope ADRIAN IV (1154–59). Under Clement III in 1188 the Senate was brought under ecclesiastical control, following the struggle for political dominance between Barbarossa and Alexander III (1159–81). The republic experienced some success in expanding its territory and entering into commerce with the rising northern republics, but political tension with the popes and disagreements between the papacy and the emperors prohibited internal development. Despite the growth of economic power through minor industries, the continual visits of princes, clerics, and prelates on ecclesiastical affairs, and a swelling influx of pilgrims, little political stability was achieved.

Late Middle Ages. Innocent III (1198–1216) inaugurated the 13th century with a renovation of the politicocivic structure of the Church. However, between 1232 and 1235 a great civil rebellion began that had as its first objective the control of the territory outside the city. With the reestablishment of the republic, both ecclesiastics and laymen were placed under complete control of the law and were subjected to taxation but were promised free election of senators, the coinage of money, and even the payment of imposts by the pope. A two-year period, during which the Papal See was vacant (November 1241–June 1243), gave this movement further impetus and allowed the first families to take control. They summoned the senator Brancaleone degli Andalò from Bologna and gave him dictatorial powers, which he used judiciously to reorganize the city and restore public safety. Popes Innocent IV (1243–54) and Alexander IV (1254–61) had no choice but to concur. Both these popes established theological schools in the city, and, despite a great influx of students between 1263 and 1284 under Charles of Anjou, Rome enjoyed a true period of peace, strengthened by the French Pope Martin IV (1281–85).

Under Nicholas III (1277–80), the Orsini family had come to power, and under Nicholas IV (1288–92), the Colonna. Thereafter the two families vied to rule, with their sons as senators, cardinals, and popes. With Boniface VIII (1294–1303), the Caetani family from Anagni entered upon the Roman scene. Boniface presided over the Jubilee of 1300, which brought visitors from all over Christendom; he contributed to the embellishment of the Roman churches and founded the *Sapienza* as the university of Rome. Despite his exaggerated claims regarding papal supremacy and his final humiliation at Anagni by William of Nogaret, Philip of France's emissary, Boniface contributed much to the well-being of the city.

The Popes in Avignon. Under Clement V (1305–14) the papal residence was transferred to Avignon, and Rome lost much of its importance. For more than 70 years it was embroiled in the rivalries of the Colonna-Orsini houses, and experienced the rise of Cola di Rienzo (1313–54), whose attempt to restore order and the ancient splendor of Roman imperialism aborted. Rome returned to the rule of papal legates such as the rigid Cardinal Albornoz. Pope Urban V attempted to reestablish papal residence in Rome (October 1367–April 1370), but this was accomplished only by Gregory XI (Jan. 17, 1377). Boniface IX (1389–1404) fortified the Campidoglio, the ancient seat of the civil government, and renewed papal rule. He was followed by weak popes, however, and once more the city became prey to internecine rivalry, declining to the lowest ebb in 1415, when wolves roamed the cemetery of the Vatican.

Late Medieval Art. Roman devotion to building and the decorative arts was not neglected even during this disturbed period, and almost all the larger churches were provided with square bell-towers, thus evidencing a return to the architectural styles of both the 5th and the 8th centuries. The church of SS. John and Paul was furnished with an ornamental loggia outside the apse, and the basilicas of the Lateran and of St. Paul were provided with marble cloisters between the abbey and church, whose painstaking ornamentation was the work of the Vassallet-

to family. The polychrome sculpture and mosaics of the age took their name (cosmatesque) from the Cosmati artists. Gothic influence is shown by the church of Santa Maria sopra Minerva, built by the Sisto and Ristoro brothers of Florence. Arnolfo di Cambio ruled the world of sculpture from Rome for the last two decades of the 13th century with his monuments to Charles of Anjou on the Campidoglio, the ciboria in St. Paul and in St. Cecilia, and the crib in St. Mary Major. Giotto, Pietro Cavallini, and Jacopo Torriti dominated painting and mosaic with their popular and narrative scenes mainly of spiritual motivation.

THE RENAISSANCE

With the pontificate of the Colonna Pope, Martin V (1417–31), who was elected at the Council of CONSTANCE and entered Rome in 1420, the restoration of the city's churches and public buildings was begun in earnest. Aided by his family, he achieved political hegemony and turned his attention to world affairs, preparing the way for the temporary reunion with the Greeks accomplished by Eugene IV (1431–47) at the Council of Ferrara-Florence (1439–41).

Art and Scholarship. During the 15th and 16th centuries, Rome was the center on which descended the great artists of the period in ever-increasing numbers. Martin V had invited the painters Masolino, Masaccio, Gentile da Fabriano, and Pisanello, along with Donatello the sculptor, to assist in the decoration of his reconstructed churches, and Nicholas V (1447–55) called upon Fra Angelico to decorate the chapel of St. Lawrence in the Vatican. He celebrated the Jubilee of 1450 and followed this attempt at spiritual renewal in Rome with a series of decrees, against ecclesiastical and moral abuses, that were carried to Germany by Cardinal NICHOLAS OF CUSA and JOHN CAPISTRAN and to France by Cardinal d'Estoutville. In an attempt to pacify Bologna and tighten his control over the Papal States, Nicholas sent Cardinal BESSARION as his legate-governor and put down an insurrection under Porcaro (1453). He likewise proved to be a discriminating patron for the revival of Greek and Latin studies, commissioning the translation of both classic and patristic works and encouraging members of the Curia, such as POGGIO, as well as the Greek refugee scholars, in their search for ancient MSS.

This policy was followed with personal variations by his successors from Pius II (1458–64) to Leo X (1513–21) in the period that saw Rome as the center of European art and scholarship. The Papal Curia was infiltrated by foreigners, who helped bring a wider outlook on the Church's participation in world affairs, faced as it was particularly with the necessity of stemming the Muslim drive in the western Mediterranean. The leading

Roman families turned their attention from founding principates to amassing enormous wealth and prestige as cultivators of the arts.

Leo X brought to a close Lateran Council V (1512–17), whose reform decrees were issued as papal bulls. They dealt with preaching, with the laws of residence for cardinals in Rome and for bishops in their dioceses, and with simony and concubinage. If observed, these reforms might have done much to stave off the impending Protestant revolt. Instead, political and nationalistic considerations, as well as family ambition, entered into both the creation of cardinals and the election of popes. The local nobles built great palaces for protection as well as for ostentation: the Palazzo Venezia, by Pietro Barbo; the Palazzo dei SS. Apostoli, by Sisto and Raffaele Riario; the palace at the Governo Vecchio, by Stefano Nardini; the palace at the Penitenzieri, by Domenico della Rovere; the palace in the Borgo, by the Cesi; the palace of Andriano Castellesi; and especially the palace of the Farnesi. They were imitated by the Aldobrandini, Borghese, Barbarini, Altieri, Panfili, and Braschi families, who filled Rome with great buildings that still dominate parts of the city, and who built magnificent villas in the suburbs or the nearby Castelli Romani. The Medici, Spannocchi, and Chigi families became the papal financiers, and a class of papal ambassadors and representatives was formed among both the Romans and the foreigners who circled in and out of the Curia, employing the numerous lesser artisans whose presence in Rome rapidly increased its population.

Religious Life. On the strictly religious plane, Rome was the center of a new development in popular, religious art that sprang from the development of new devotions such as the Stations of the Cross and the Five Wounds. It witnessed also the multiplication of third orders and of guilds, whose corporate life was built around prayer, the Sacraments, and works of charity. The rich endowed colleges, schools, hospitals, and homes for the unfortunate, including the destitute and repentant prostitutes. The Bible was translated into Italian by the Camaldolese monk Nicolò Malerbi and collections of simple sermons and books of popular instructions, such as the *Libretto della dottrina cristiana,* vied with the learned translations of scholars for attention by printers and publishers. From the heart of the Curia under Julius II (1503–13) rose St. Cajetan, who founded the Order of the Theatines, provided Italy with a new episcopate, and helped to introduce to Rome (1519) the Oratory of Divine Love, a brotherhood of priests and laymen pledged to prayer and charity.

THE POST-REFORMATION

During the Renaissance period Rome, as a result of the upsurge of political, economic, artistic, and scholarly endeavors, had developed bifurcating mores that manifested themselves in great religious movements and at the same time in a return to the cultivation of man's natural interests, as well as in indulgence in vices of all kinds. Rome's worldly ostentation was denounced with mounting fury by the preachers, especially by monks such as SAVONAROLA in Florence and by the lower clergy. But lip service on the part of the majority of the higher clergy and a failure of the Renaissance popes to achieve a thorough reform, particularly in regard to financial administration, nepotism, and the teaching of theology, occasioned the outbreak in Germany of the Protestant Reformation, which quickly spread through northern Europe. Martin Luther (1483–1546) had defected soon after his return from Rome in 1511, where he had been scandalized by the extravagances and abuses rampant in the papal court, and he began to teach doctrines that were not in accord with Catholic theology. Rome's answer was slow in formulation but finally started with the reorganization of the University of Rome and the founding of the Collegio Romano by Ignatius Loyola. Out of Rome finally came the impetus for the Council of TRENT (1545–63), whose reforming decrees governed the Church's development down to the mid-20th century.

The Sack of Rome. Rome's security in an age of *bandetti* and *condottieri* had been the concern of Alexander VI (1492–1503), who fortified the Castel Sant' Angelo (the ancient tomb of Hadrian) by strengthening the wall connecting it with the Vatican palaces and building a tower to dominate the bridge of approach over the Tiber. Clement VII (1523–34) confided to Antonio da Sangallo the fortification of the city proper, since the old Aurelian wall no longer served as a defense against a possible European or Saracen siege. He built new towers on the Aventine and at the Porta Ardeatina and fortified the wall between the Vatican, the Janiculum Hill, and the bastion of the Belvedere. But these new edifices proved useless when Cardinal Pompeo Colonna joined forces with Emperor Charles V, entered Rome by stealth through the gate of St. John Lateran, and besieged the Vatican Palace on Sept. 20, 1526. Clement VII surrendered and signed a peace pact (September 22).

The following year, Rome was sacked by an unpaid band of imperial soldiers, despite the heroic resistance of the Pope and the local soldiery, and the city was held captive until 1528. Some 30,000 of its citizens lost their lives, and four-fifths of its houses were deserted. The Pope, who had escaped to Viterbo in 1528, on his return set about the rebuilding of the city, using its destruction as a warning and calling for reform ''in head and members'' of the Church and Christian society.

Under Paul IV (1555–59) Rome again suffered a setback when Emperor Charles V prepared to besiege the city. On the pope's death (Aug. 18, 1559) his enemies burned the palace of the Inquisition and destroyed the statue of the pope on the Campidoglio. Sixtus V (1585–90) displayed a strong hand in controlling the unruly elements of the city's population, and Urban VIII (1623–44) refortified the Castel Sant' Angelo as a center of local power. Great difficulty for the safety of the city was caused by the claims of foreign diplomats to immunity not only for their persons and palaces but for the piazzas and streets surrounding their residences, since their servants sheltered criminals and evil-doers of all types in the shadow of their masters' pennants. Innocent XI (1676–89) attempted to end this abuse by convincing the King of Spain to renounce the privileges (1677) claimed by his ambassador. Venice ceded in 1679; Spain, in 1682, and the cardinals, who had attempted to imitate this procedure, were forced to desist. After long opposition on the part of the French ambassadors, the Count of Lavardin finally submitted to a show of force by Alexander VIII (1689–91).

Urbanization. Julius II (1503–13) implemented the plans of Nicholas V for a complete renovation of the Vatican, and the execution of this great architectural and artistic work continued to the end of the 16th century. Julius also began the rearrangement of Rome's main streets with the Via Giulia, the Via Repetta, and the Via del Babuino as prongs of a trident off the Corso, running from the Piazza del Popolo to the center of the city. This work was brought to fruition by Domenico Fontana for Sixtus V (1585–90), when he arranged to have roads connecting S. Maria Maggiore with the Trinità dei Monti, with S. Giovanni Laterano, S. Croce in Gerusalemme, and S. Lorenzo, with the Forum of Trajan, and with S. Susanna in a starlike pattern. The pope also erected the obelisks in the piazzas of S. Maria Maggiore, S. Giovanni, S. Pietro, and the Piazza del Popolo as guidelines for further expansion of the inhabited area of the city, which was so cramped from the early Middle Ages in a great pocket of the Tiber in the shadow of the Vatican. Sixtus encouraged expansion by bringing aqueducts with water to other parts of the city, thus acknowledging the large population growth, which, from a few thousand in the late Middle Ages, rose to 130,000 during the Renaissance, and which, from less than 40,000 after the sack of Rome in 1527, had by the end of the 16th century reached 100,000 inhabitants.

In the 17th century an almost organic development saw the creation of the great piazzas, such as that fronting the Palazzo dei Barberini, the Piazza Navona, the Piazza S. Pietro, the Piazza di Spagna, and the reconstruction of the ancient Porto di Repetta by Clement XI (1700–21).

MODERN AND CONTEMPORARY ROME

After the first infiltration of baroque art into Rome during the 17th century, a classic reaction set in with the buildings of F. Duquesnoy and Alessandro Algardi and with the paintings of Nicolas Poussin, A. Sacchi, and C. Maratta supported by the theories of G. Bellori. In the 18th century the late baroque was represented by the Spanish Stairs, the Ripa Grande, the Trevi Fountain, the Piazza di S. Ignazio, and the facades of the Lateran (1735), S. Maria Maggiore, and S. Croce (1743) under Popes Clement XII (1730–40) and Benedict XIV (1740–58). The latter, a Bolognese and a learned canonist, as well as humanist, was elected in a conclave that lasted six months; he did much to recommend Rome to the Enlightenment, as well as to the courts of Europe, both Catholic and Protestant. The pope wrote definitive works on the process of canonization and the holding of synods and, in his letters, frequently discussed scientific subjects. He founded several academies of learning in Rome, thus attracting the erudite of many countries. Clement XIV (1769–74) introduced measures for the development of trade and industry in the Papal States, but his bad relations with the Roman nobility and with the Catholic states determined on suppressing the Jesuits, prevented his realization of projects for the betterment of the city itself.

French Revolution. Rome became a victim of the French Revolution, when on Dec. 28, 1797, Joseph Bonaparte intervened in its internal affairs and occupied Castel Sant' Angelo on Feb. 10, 1798. On the 15th he proclaimed the end of the papal power and the inauguration of the Roman Republic. The city suffered from internal disruption and was cut off from outside assistance for two years, until an army from Naples liberated it on Sept. 30, 1799. Pius VII (1800–23) was taken prisoner in 1809 by NAPOLEON I, and Rome was proclaimed an imperial city with whose restoration General de Tournon was charged. He began with a rearrangement of Monte Pincio, but met with considerable resistance on the part of the Roman nobility. Pius reentered the city on May 24, 1814, but had to flee a year later before the army of General Murat. He returned in June 1815 after the defeat of the Napoleonic forces at Tolentino (May 3–4).

In his efforts to revitalize Roman life, Gregory XVI (1831–46) encouraged an artistic and architectural resurgence and promoted the excavations of the Roman Forum, opening three museums to house the Etruscan, Egyptian, and ancient Roman discoveries (now located in the Lateran). In executing the urban renewal planned by Tournon, the Pope carried forward the realignment of the *borghi* or heavily populated sections of the city, ordered the creation of public parks, opened the cemetery of Verano, and proposed a revised approach to the Piazza del Popolo. New sections of the city opened to habitation included the *borgo* of Mastai and the region between S. Maria degli Angeli and the slope of the Quirinal Hill, now crossed by the Via Nazionale.

The Republic of 1849. The new spirit of the age in public affairs and the desire for a popular share in government prevailed on Pius IX (1846–78), soon after his election, to proclaim amnesty for political exiles and prisoners (July 16, 1848) and to create a municipal council with the right to elect nine magistrates and a senate for the city's public affairs. The attempt aborted upon the assassination of the papal prime minister, Pellegrino Rossi (Nov. 15, 1848). Ten days later the Pope fled to Gaeta. He prorogued the Senate and named Cardinal Castracane head of a new provisional government (Nov. 27 and Dec. 7, 1848).

On Feb. 9, 1849, a new republic was proclaimed that immediately repudiated the temporal power of the pope. It proceeded to confiscate ecclesiastical properties, take control of the schools, abolish the privilege of clerical immunity and the tribunal of the Holy Office, and cancel censorship of the press. But the ensuing financial crisis in particular made the new republic an easy target for the intervention of the French army under General Oudinot, dispatched to Rome by Louis Napoleon (III) at the request of Cardinal Antonelli, the pope's chancellor. After considerable fighting within the city itself, the French forces took full possession (July 3, 1849), and Pius returned to Rome on April 12, 1850.

The pope set about modernizing Rome, providing new administrative and social ordinances, introducing telegraph and railroad facilities, and encouraging new construction. Under French supervision the city enjoyed relative calm until 1867, when Garibaldi attempted to organize a revolution from outside, but he was defeated at Mentana (Nov. 3–4, 1867). The recall of the French troops for the Franco-Prussian War, however, left Rome defenseless, and on Sept. 20, 1870, the city was occupied by the Garibaldian troops. A truce was made by papal representatives, which included respect for the independence of the Vatican and the Leonine City. After a plebiscite on October 2, Rome was annexed by the Kingdom of Italy. In 1871 the Italian government transferred its capital from Florence to Rome and set about transforming the city into a modern metropolis.

Population and Urbanization. Between 1846 and 1870 the population of Rome had doubled to over 200,000 inhabitants, and it continued to increase, making a reordination of the city's inhabitable parts imperative. The plan published by P. Camporese and Alessandro Viviani in 1873, following the commission of General Cadorna, gradually made possible the spread of popula-

tion from the tight quarters of Trastevere. The destruction of landmarks such as the *ville principesche* in favor of new quarters on the Esquiline, Boncompagni Ludovisi, and the Salario, helped to inflame political differences but proved an absolute necessity. Likewise, the creation of a net of streets and avenues, such as the Via Nazionale, Corso Vittorio Emmanuele, Via Arenula, and Via Tritone, caused great resentment among conservative property owners and antiquarians. But in the end the city was provided with new architectural monuments, proper housing for its inhabitants, and hotels and conveniences for an ever-increasing stream of visitors, while historians and archeologists were given new insights into the city's ancient topography and buildings. Calderini's monument to Victor Emmanuel II on the Piazza Venezia (since 1921, the tomb of the unknown soldier) and the palace of justice by Sacconi were begun before 1890 and completed in 1911. They represented two types of architectural sentiment prevailing at the turn of the 20th century, almost totally alien to contemporary tastes.

Amid the feverish efforts at building and expansion, an anticlerical wave was created by political extremists and capped by the attempt to throw the body of Pius IX into the Tiber in the course of its removal from the Vatican to the cemetery of Verano (1882). The erection of a statue to Giordano Bruno in the Campo de' Fiori almost caused an insurrection on the part of the extreme clerical faction in 1887. However, with the accession of Victor Emmanuel II and the election of Pope LEO XIII (1878–1903), attempts were made to heal the political schism. The pope desired to make Rome an intellectual center for ecclesiastical studies; he prescribed the renewal of Thomistic philosophy and theology in the Roman seminaries and ecclesiastical colleges and encouraged the scientific pursuit of history and humane studies. But following the policy of Pius IX, he stayed strictly within the confines of the Vatican, refused to recognize the kingdom of Italy officially, and prohibited Catholics from participating in the civil government.

"Partito popolare" and Fascism. This policy was continued under St. Pius X (1903–14) and Benedict XV (1914–22), yet it proved impossible to implement, and gradually, with Vatican assent, Catholics entered administrative offices and participated in local Roman elections. In 1919 Luigi STURZO founded the *Partito popolare,* whose intent was to prepare the way for a government in which all the citizenry could be properly represented. While Italy's participation in World War I (1915–18) brought great hardships on the city, the efforts of Pope BENEDICT XV (1914–22) to put an end to hostilities and his charitable efforts in aiding the people of Rome did much to break down the last signs of enmity between the Vatican and the civil authorities.

At the beginning of his pontificate, Pius XI (1922–39) gave his blessing *Urbi et Orbi*—to the City and to the World—from the balustrade of St. Peter's, an ancient custom that had not been honored since 1870. Eight months later, the black-shirt army marched on Rome (October 1922) and brought Benito Mussolini's Fascist party into power, provoking a series of incidents that kept the city in turmoil for the next 20 years. Gradually the Fascist dictatorship destroyed popular liberties, persecuted the leaders and wrecked the centers of Catholic Action in Rome, dissolved the *Partito popolare,* and exiled Luigi Sturzo. Its one accomplishment was the signing of the LATERAN PACTS (Treaties) and Concordat on Feb. 11, 1929, whereby Vatican City was recognized as an independent state and the pope, as an independent sovereign ruler. The compensation made by the Italian government for the spoliation of the Papal States was made partly in monetary payments and partly in property, which the Vatican used to benefit the city of Rome as well as the Vatican State. Pontifical ecclesiastical institutes in Rome and other specified properties were given immunity as belonging directly to the Vatican, while transport, postal, and other Vatican necessities were assured safe passage through the city.

"Non abbiamo bisogna." Relations between the Vatican and Fascist Rome, despite the Concordat and pro-Fascist sympathies of certain ecclesiastical officials, were difficult. The Pope permitted the blessing of Italian troops during the Abyssinian War (1935–36) and spoke encouragingly to the Roman people, but he showed no sympathy for the regime's policies and insisted on the freedom of sale in Rome of *l'Osservatore Romano,* the Vatican paper. With the encyclical *Non abbiamo bisogna,* Pius condemned the racism and exaggerated nationalism of the Fascist political philosophy. Catholics in Rome, as well as statesmen and Jews, who were the objects of persecution, received shelter in the Vatican. When Hitler visited Rome, Pius pointedly left the city for his summer residence in Castelgandolfo.

World War II. The imminent approach of World War II brought Pius XII (1939–58) to the papacy, and during the war he exerted his energies in protecting the persecuted in the city and allaying the worst features of the Fascist defeat (July 25, 1943) and the German occupation (Sept. 10, 1943). Through his efforts Rome was considered an open city, and when the sectors of Tiburtino and Prenestino were bombed (July and August 1943), Pius hurried to the scene to condole with the people. The Pope made a great effort to provision the city and to prevent the deportation of its citizens, and he bewailed the massacres perpetrated in the Via Rasella and the Fosse Ardeatina (March 1944).

With the liberation of Rome by Allied troops on June 4, 1944, Rome became an official sight-seeing objective for millions of the military seeking an audience with the Holy Father, who had been hailed by the Romans as the *defensor civitatis,* or defender of the city. In the postwar period, Pius was an acknowledged world figure and received visits by heads of state and world leaders, as well as by pilgrims and learned societies of every persuasion, bringing to Rome millions of tourists each year. In 1950 Pius proclaimed a Holy Year, which was celebrated with great religious splendor, and the Pope left the Vatican on several occasions to participate in religious functions. His death and the subsequent papal election focused the eyes of the world on Rome and attracted over 1,000 radio and television reporters.

Modernization. The second half of the twentieth century brought enormous changes to the city of Rome. Pope John XXIII (1958–63) immediately gained Roman and world popularity by his joviality, simple religious faith, and frankness. Taking his office as bishop of Rome as a genuine pastoral responsibility, he frequently left the Vatican to visit infirm friends, institutions, and the various parishes of Rome, most especially those in the poorer quarters or on the periphery of the city. He held a Roman diocesan synod in his cathedral at the Lateran (1960) in preparation for Vatican Council II (1961–65). Pope John's convocation of the Council led to an increase of international attention on the city of Rome as witnessed by the arrival of many media personnel, as well as ecumenical and interfaith representatives. Catholics from around the world continued to arrive as pilgrims in large numbers and those at home followed the news from Rome eagerly during the Council. Following Pope John's beatification in 2000, his body was moved to the side altar dedicated to St. Jerome in St. Peter's Basilica and is displayed there for the veneration of the faithful. It is a popular shrine for Italian pilgrims as well as the many from afar who flock to the Eternal City.

Pope Paul VI (1963–78) built upon the work of his predecessor in the reform of the Church. Sadly, his reign coincided with a time of great turmoil within Italy. He was faced with political problems in secular affairs as well as the ecclesiastical realm. The Catholic governing body of Italy, the Christian Democratic Party, was the subject of numerous scandals and waning popularity. During the mid-1970s his close personal friend, Prime Minister Aldo Moro, was kidnapped by the Italian communist insurgent Red Brigade and assassinated despite personal pleas from the pope. The Mafia was also very active during this period, though their greatest civil disturbances were reserved for the 1990s. Despite the increased internationalism of the ecclesiastical institutions present in Rome, the dwindling numbers of religious vocations throughout much of the world greatly reduced the numbers of seminarians, priests, and religious in the city—often leaving them with enormous and half-empty buildings scattered throughout the historic center of Rome. This prompted further tension with the burgeoning population that demanded ''less churches and more houses'' as Rome struggled to put an ever-greater number of inhabitants and workers into a museum-like ancient city center. The Holy Year of 1975 provided an additional influx of pilgrims into the city and the realization of Rome's permanent status as annual host to millions of foreign visitors.

Pope John Paul I (1978) had a minimal impact on the city due to his short, month-long reign. He ventured from the boundaries of the Vatican City State into Rome only once as pope, but his winning smile endeared him to the people. A single red rose is often to be found on his tomb in the crypt of St. Peter's Basilica as a poignant sign of continuing affection.

Pope John Paul II (1978–) brought a new and international vigor to Rome. The Romans were skeptical of a non-Italian pope, especially since he was becoming the bishop of their city. He quickly allayed their fears as he initiated an ambitious plan to visit every parish in the diocese and actively sought to build new churches in suburban areas to accommodate population growth. His pastoral solicitude for his diocese reached a highpoint in the door-to-door campaign of evangelization and outreach that he personally inaugurated as a preparation for Rome's special role in the Great Jubilee. The pope's efforts are met by continued resistance in a city that regards the Church somewhat cynically and where Mass attendance has been estimated at ten percent of a population that is ostensibly Catholic in name and culture.

Pope John Paul II also had to deal with complications in Church-state relations caused by a wide-ranging financial scandal implicating Vatican-owned corporations and by the all-encompassing bribery and corruption probes, which led to the defeat and dissolution of the Christian Democratic Party, with its subsequent crisis of defining how Italian Catholics should best contribute to the political welfare of their nation. He became the outspoken leader of opposition to the Mafia in the face of murders of Italian priests and the bombing of his own cathedral of St. John Lateran and of the ancient church of St. George.

Pope John Paul II's success in international diplomacy led to the further prestige of Rome as a center of global politics. The peaceful end of the communist regimes of Eastern Europe, the resolution of Panamanian General Manuel Noriega's fate, and numerous other hidden initiatives occurred in this ancient capital due to papal skill in diplomacy. Continuing negotiations for peace in the Middle East often refer back to Rome, as witnessed by the frequent visits of Palestinian leader Yasser Arafat.

The international character of Rome continues to grow with many refugees and immigrants from the former Soviet-bloc and lesser-developed countries in Africa and Asia. As in the ancient world, Rome is truly a global crossroads. The pastoral challenges posed by this influx have been valiantly met by new Church outreaches to the poor such as the large Roman presence of Mother Teresa's MISSIONARIES OF CHARITY and the efforts of local lay movements such as the Community of SANT'EGIDIO. There has also been a general rise in the number of new religious orders and ecclesial movements from around the world that have established houses in Rome. An encouraging fruit of Vatican Council II is the increased number of international lay students of theology at the various pontifical universities.

Pope John Paul II's charisma and world travels have elicited great interest in Rome and increased the desire of people around the world to visit the Eternal City. His travels have also led to the posing of the previously unnecessary question: ''Is the Pope at home?'' The Wednesday general audiences with the pope draw thousands of pilgrims each week, and the record number of beatifications and canonizations have drawn further millions of the faithful to these special religious ceremonies in Rome. The apex of these visits was the Great Jubilee of 2000 that led to a wholesale refurbishing of the city and updating of its infrastructure. Vast public works projects achieved what has generally been acclaimed as the restoration of Rome to its baroque splendor while making it more ''user-friendly'' for modern, international visitors. The facades of nearly every important church and prominent building were meticulously cleaned and historic markers posted. Sadly, due to the terrible air pollution in Rome, some of the newly uncovered brilliant white travertine facades noticeably darkened soon afterward. The emergence of internet cafes and of fast-food restaurants also reflects the social changes, for better or worse, in the traditionally slow-paced life of Rome. The subway system (Metropolitana) was greatly extended and connected with an expanded and renovated Leonardo da Vinci airport—both projects meant to facilitate the movement of Jubilee pilgrims. The traffic patterns of Rome were reconfigured to ease tourist buses away from the congested narrow streets of the city center and new city bus lines between the major pilgrimage churches were added. An ambitious underground parking garage was built under the Janiculum hill adjacent to the Vatican and traffic tunnels and pedestrian zones added. The Great Jubilee completed an intense, half-century project to bring Rome into the modern world. Pope John Paul II used the

Great Jubilee as an opportunity for close and harmonious collaboration between the Vatican and the Italian government as they strove together to better the city and reconciled their inter-dependence with their independence

Bibliography: Istituto di studi romani, *Storia di Roma* (Bologna 1938–). F. GREGOROVIUS, *Geschichte der Stadt Rom im Mittelalter,* ed. W. KAMP, 5 v. (new ed. Basel 1953–57), Eng. tr. from 4th Ger. ed. *History of the City of Rome in the Middle Ages,* tr. A. HAMILTON, 8 v. in 13 (London 1894–1902). H. GRISAR, *History of Rome and the Popes in the Middle Ages,* ed. L. CAPPADELTA, 3 v. (London 1911–12). S. B. PLATNER, *A Topographical Dictionary of Ancient Rome,* cont. and rev. T. ASHBY (Oxford 1929). R. VIELLIARD, *Recherches sur les origines de la Rome chrétienne* (Mâcon 1941; repr. Rome 1959). R. KRAUTHEIMER, *Corpus Basilicarum Christianarum Romae* (Vatican City 1937–). M. ARMELLINI, *Le chiese di Roma dal secolo IV al XIX,* ed. C. CECCHELLI, 2 v. (new ed. Rome 1942). P. DUCATI, *L'Arte in Roma dalle origini al secolo VIII* (Bologna 1938). F. HERMANIN, *L'Arte in Roma dal secolo VIII al XIV* (Bologna 1945). E. HUTTON, *The Cosmati* (London 1950). J. KLACZKO, *Rome and the Renaissance,* tr. J. DENNIE (New York 1903). R. WITTKOWER, *Art and Architecture in Italy, 1600–1750* (Baltimore 1958). C. CESCHI, *Le chiese di Roma dagli inizi del Neoclassico al 1961* (Bologna 1963). P. HUGHES, *A History of the Church,* 3 v. (rev. ed. New York 1947–49). G. MOLLAT, *La Question romaine* (Paris 1932). S. DE GRADA, "Sviluppo demografico e topografico di Roma negli ultimo cento anni," *Rivista diocesana di Roma* (1961) 259–266, 327–333. *Prima romana synodus* (Vatican City 1960). E. CLARK, *Rome and a Villa* (2d ed. New York 1974). M. VASI and A. NIBBY, *Roma nell'Ottocento* (Rome 1976). G. BARACCONI, *I rioni di Roma* (Rome 1971). R. KAUTHEIMER, *Rome. Profile of a City, 312–1308* (Princeton 1980). G. MASSON, *The Companion Guide to Rome* (6th ed. Englewood Cliffs, NJ 1983). R. KRAUTHEIMER, *The Rome of Alexander VIII, 1655–1667* (Princeton 1985). C. D'ONOFRIO, *Visitiamo Roma nel Quattrocento: La città degli umanisti* (Rome 1989). D. J. BIRCH, *Pilgrimage to Rome in the Middle Ages: Continuity and Change* (Rochester, NY 1998). *Roma nell'alto Medioevo: 27 Aprile–1 Maggio 2000* (Spoleto 2001). I. DEGUTTRY, *Guide to Modern Rome: Architecture 1870-2000* (Rome 2001). R. M. SAN JUAN, *Rome: A City Out of Print* (Minneapolis 2001).

[F. X. MURPHY/J. JOHNSON]

ROME, LEGENDS OF CHRISTIAN

Originally, the passages in the lives and passions of the martyrs and confessors that were to be read (Latin *legenda*) for edification or as part of the liturgy. Only later did the word legend come to signify the stories and tales connected with poetic, religious, and folkloristic traditions. In Rome, with the rise of the veneration of martyrs and their relics, and particularly the ritualistic visitation of the catacombs and the translation of relics that began in the 4th century, embellishments were added to the original *Acta* or *Passiones* of the martyrs, and stories were created to explain the designations of localities or churches and to identify saints unknown but for their names.

A primary source of Roman Christian legends was the continuity between the Old and New Testaments based on Christ's words: "It is necessary that all things be fulfilled, that Moses and the prophets have written of me" (Lk 24.44). In the catacombs and earliest churches this was illustrated in the so-called Cycle of the Concordance of the Old and New Testaments; for example, Adam driven from paradise was replaced by the incident of the good thief; Joseph sold into Egypt, was paralleled in the incident of Christ sold by Judas; and Jonas escaping from the whale's belly, with Christ rising from the tomb. In the NT apocryphal literature details of the life of Christ not mentioned in the Gospels and the fate of the Apostles were supplied to illustrate theological beliefs or satisfy curiosity. Realism was achieved, e.g., by portraying the Magi as three kings carrying a crown of gold, globules of incense, and a phial of myrrh, even marked with the price in *denarii* (Roman currency). The lure of heresy is likewise depicted by adapting the story of Ulysses tied to the mast to avoid the sirens, to a Christian fastened to a cross that is the yardarm of a ship representing the Church. The Pseudo-Clementine literature attests the popularity of legends concerning SS. Peter and Paul with, in the beginning, considerable stress on the Prince of the Apostle's human weakness overcome by Christ's immediate assistance, as in the QUO VADIS story and in elaborations of the motif of the crowing of the cock after his denial of Christ (Mt 26.74–75).

In the acts of the martyrs realistic dialogue and scenes of heroic defiance, as well as humble submission to death, such as that of SS. LAWRENCE and CECILIA, seem to have been an early Roman contribution that is further illustrated by the stories connected with Rome's title churches. During the 5th century the original names of donors or locations of these churches were changed into saint's names and equipped with corresponding legends. This phenomenon was given impulse by the lives of the desert fathers, brought to the Eternal City; for example, St. ATHANASIUS (340) brought his *Life of St. Anthony* and PALLADIUS his *Historia Lausiaca* (420), which were quickly translated into Latin. Ancient myths and romances, Roman traditions, and Oriental tales were plagiarized for details and settings, and a specifically Christian type of legend came into being in Rome and grew to uncontrollable proportions during the Middle Ages.

Constantinian legends were connected with the emperor's vision of the cross and the words "*In hoc signo vinces*" (in this sign you will conquer); his Baptism by Pope SILVESTER I and his cure from leprosy; St. HELENA and the finding of the true cross; and the politically directed Constantinian DONATION. This series was continued with the CHARLEMAGNE legends of the Middle Ages. There were stories of divine intervention for the guidance of the popes from the appearance to Pope LIBERIUS of snow on August 5 to indicate the location for the basilica of St. Mary Major, the correction of the Tome of Pope LEO I laid on Peter's tomb, to Pope PASCHAL II'S discovery of the relics of St. AGNES, and the depiction of Sylvester II as a magician.

One of the most popular legends of the Middle Ages was supported by the displaying of Veronica's veil with the picture of the face of Christ on the way to Calvary. Another was the *Scala Sancta,* the staircase up which Christ was led for judgment before Pilate, that was said to have been brought to Rome from Jerusalem by St. Helena. In like manner, Vergil's *Fourth Eclogue* was considered a prophecy referring to the birth of Christ. With his preachment of *pietas* and propaganda in favor of virtue, VERGIL was considered a paragon of the ANIMA NATURALITER CHRISTIANA and used by DANTE as a guide in his *Divina Commedia,* a work that embodied a corpus of Roman Christian legend. A summation of the legends of the early Church had been contained in the *Gloria Martyrum* of GREGORY OF TOURS (538–594) and in the Dialogues of Pope GREGORY I (590–604). Those of the Middle Ages were embodied in the *Legenda Aurea* of JAMES OF VORAGINE and the *Vitae Patrum* of Rosweyde. During the Middle Ages every church and almost every ancient ruin, building, or statue had its legends, many of them a fantastic blending of Biblical stories with the lays of ancient Rome.

After a period of rejection during the Reformation; of complete cynicism during the Enlightenment; of an attempt to dechristianize the lives of the saints by tracing their origin and objectives to Celtic, Germanic, Oriental, and Buddhistic myths on the part of such scholars as P. Lucius, H. Usener, and R. Reitzenstein; modern investigation has returned to an appreciation of the value of Christian legends. They witness both to a kernel of historical fact regularly preserved in the legend and to the mentality and beliefs of the people among whom they were popularized. This reevaluation has been a contribution of the BOLLANDISTS in particular, with the *Acta Sanctorum;* but it has been due also to the increasing interest on the part of specialists in folklore, cultural anthropology, philology, and popular psychology.

Bibliography: H. LECLERCQ, *Dictionnaire d'archéologie chrétienne et de liturgie,* ed. F. CABROL, H. LECLERCQ, and H. I. MARROU, 15 v. (Paris 1907–53) 8.2:2309–2460. W. BÖHNE, *Lexikon für Theologie und Kirche,* ed. J. HOFER and K. RAHNER, 10 v. (2d, new ed. Freiburg 1957–65); suppl., *Das Zweite Vatikanische Konzil: Dokumente und Kommentare,* ed. H. S. BRECHTER et al., pt. 1 (1966) 6:876–878. H. DELEHAYE, *Cinq leçons sur la méthode hagiographique* (Brussels 1934); *Étude sur le légendier romain* (Brussels 1936). H. F. R. ROSENFELD, *Der hl. Christophorus* (Leipzig 1937). R. AIGRAIN, *L'Hagiographie* (Paris 1953). G. PARIS, *Poèmes et légendes du moyen-âge* (Paris 1900). H. THURSTON, *The Holy Year of Jubilee* (London 1900; repr. Westminster, Md. 1949).

P. LUCIUS, *Die Anfänge des Heiligenkults* (Tübingen 1904). E. MUSATTI, *Leggende popolari* (3d ed. Milan 1904). H. GÜNTER, *Legenden-Studien* (Cologne 1906); *Die christliche Legende des Abendlandes* (Heidelberg 1910); *Psychologie der Legende* (Freiburg 1949); *The Catholic Encyclopedia,* ed. C. G. HERBERMANN et al., 16 v. (New York 1907–14; suppl. 1922) 9:128–131. F. LANZONI, *Genesi, svolgimento e tramonto delle leggende storiche* (*Studi e Testi* 43; 1925). E. E. MALONE, *The Monk and the Martyr* (Washington 1950).

[F. X. MURPHY]

ROME, PATRIARCHATE OF

The division of the fourth-century Church into PATRIARCHATES for ecclesiastical government was the result of comparable divisions of the Roman Empire. The organization of individual patriarchates was subject to many local and historical factors, which accounts for the many differences among the patriarchates of Rome, CONSTANTINOPLE, ALEXANDRIA, ANTIOCH, and JERUSALEM.

The pope is the patriarch of Rome, or patriarch of the West as he is sometimes called, while at the same time holding other offices. He is the bishop of Rome and rules the See of Rome just as any other bishop rules his diocese. He is also the metropolitan who presides over the ecclesiastical Province of ROME and is primate of the bishops of Italy while exercising primacy and fullness of jurisdiction over the universal Church as POPE.

Division of the Empire. The lines for the future patriarchate of Rome were first drawn by Emperor Diocletian in 293 when he divided the Roman Empire into four prefectures: Gaul, Italy, Illyricum, and the Orient. After the death of Emperor Theodosius (395), a definitive division of the Empire into the Occident and the Orient was made. The Prefectures of Gaul and Italy constituted the Occidental Empire. Gaul was made up of three dioceses (a term originally used for civil administration): Spain, with seven provinces; Gaul, with seventeen; and Britain, with five. Italy was also made up of three dioceses: Africa, with seven provinces; Illyricum (Occidental), with seven; and Italy, with seventeen. In the Diocese of Italy there were seven provinces of the north dependent on the *vicarius* of Italy; the other ten were administered by the *vicarius* of Rome. This jurisdiction was divided and administered by the prefect of the city of Rome and the prefect of the suburban areas.

The ecclesiastical divisions coincided with the civil administrative divisions, thus, the pope of Rome enjoyed a gradually increased jurisdiction over the above-described area. The Council of Nicaea (325) gave the first hint of any ecclesiastical jurisdictional provinces in canon 6: "The ancient custom is to be observed throughout Egypt, Libya and Pentapolis wherein the bishop of Alexandria has power over all of these areas since he exercises a similar power as that exercised by the bishop of the city of Rome'' (J. D. Mansi, *Sacrorum Conciliorum nova et amplissima collectio* [Florence-Venice 1757–98] 2:670). Thus the extent, at least, of the pope's jurisdiction in his ecclesiastical area can be known from the civil division of administration.

As to the nature of the jurisdiction exercised, historical documents are not clear. The pope did not consecrate the bishops for Gaul, Spain, and Africa; neither did he call the synods for these churches. Latin Africa seemed to be highly centralized in Carthage, whereas Spain and Gaul gave no indication of any consistent centralization under the bishop of Rome. There are indications that the pope intervened occasionally (such as in the cases of Marcian of Arles and of two bishops in Spain, Merida, and Astorga), but the centralization of the well-defined future Roman patriarchate is not observable.

Under Pope St. Leo the Great in the fifth century, the Church of Rome made strides toward centralization. Emperor Valentinian III confirmed the pope's right to force bishops of all of the Italian provinces to appear before his tribunal. The greatest advance in papal centralization resulted from the expanding missionary activity emanating from Rome to Germany, the Frankish Empire, and England.

Legislation. Emperor Justinian (d. 565) codified in his civil and ecclesiastical laws the five chief patriarchates as the primary units of ecclesiastical administration: ''We decree therefore the most blessed archbishops and patriarchs, that is, of more venerable Rome, Constantinople, Alexandria, Antioch and Jerusalem . . . ''(*Corpus iuris civilis, Novellae* [Berlin] 126). In *Corpus iuris civilis, Novellae* 131 he fixed the order of precedence: ''The most holy Pope of ancient Rome, the first priest of all; the most blessed archbishop of Constantinople of New Rome has the second place.'' Thus, with Justinian's laws the Patriarchate of Rome and the four Oriental patriarchates became an officially recognized ecclesiastical organization with dignities, rights, duties, and areas of jurisdiction defined by law. It must be kept in mind, however, that the actual exercise of these jurisdictional rights within a given province varied because of factors peculiar to a given patriarchate.

The pope exercises his patriarchal jurisdiction over all of Western Europe, Africa west of Egypt, all other ''diaspora'' lands evangelized by missionaries from Europe—such as North and South America, Australia, and the major portion of India—and the Latin Christians in the Near and Far East of the Roman rite. He may call a patriarchal synod or simply choose by written decree to enact laws of discipline and liturgical usages applicable for the Roman or Western patriarchate only.

Bibliography: P. BATIFFOL, *La Paix constantinienne et le catholicisme* (2d ed. Paris 1914); *Le Siège apostolique, 359–451* (Paris 1924). L DUCHESNE, *Histoire ancienne de l'Église,* 3 v. (Paris 1906–10), v.1. H. BURN-MURDOCH, *The Development of the Papacy* (New York 1954). C. J. VON HEFELE, *Histoire des conciles d'après les documents originaux,* tr. and continued by H. LECLERCQ (Paris 1907–38) v.1. F. MAASSEN, *Der Primat des Bischofs von Rom und die alten Patriarchalkirchen* (Bonn 1853). Y.M.J. CONGAR, ''Le Pape comme patriarche d'Occident: approche d'une réalité trop négligée,'' *Istina* 28 (1983) 374–390.

[G. A. MALONEY/EDS.]

ROMERO, JUAN

Jesuit missionary and theologian; b. Marchena, Seville, 1559; d. Santiago, Chile, March 31, 1630. He entered the Jesuits in Montilla in 1580, and in 1589 went to Lima, where he completed his ecclesiastical studies. After ordination he was professor of theology in Lima. He received his training for the missions at Juli, Puno, Peru. From 1593 to 1598 he was superior of the Tucumán (Argentina) mission, did missionary work in Asunción, Salta, Jujuy, Córdoba, Santa Fé, and Corrientes. In 1597 he was the theologian for the diocesan synod of Santiago del Estero; in 1608, as reporter of his province to the Jesuit general, he went to Rome. He was superior of Buenos Aires, Santiago del Estero, Santiago de Chile, and Concepción. In 1625 he was the first vice provincial of Chile. His work was threefold: as missionary he worked in the areas of the Chaco-Santiagueno, Guaraní, Araucana, and Quechua native cultures; as superior he organized active missions and schools; as theologian and canonist he published a two-volume work, *De praedestinatione.* In 1610 as a result of his experience in Tucumán, he sent the Council of the Indies a memorial on future administrative policy for the port of Buenos Aires.

Bibliography: E. TORRES SALDAMANDO, *Los antiguos jesuitas del Perú* (Lima 1882).

[A. DE EGAÑA]

ROMERO, OSCAR A.

Archbishop of San Salvador, El Salvador (1977–80); b. Ciudad Barrios, Aug. 15, 1917; d. San Salvador, March 24, 1980. Romero is remembered for his courageous preaching and leadership of the San Salvador archdiocese. His efforts toward the creation of a more just society led to his assassination.

Ordained to the priesthood in 1942, Romero returned to his native El Salvador, where he served as pastor to a

Archbishop Oscar Romero. (Catholic News Service)

church in the city of San Miguel and earned a reputation as a radio preacher. In 1967 he was appointed secretary of the Salvadoran bishops' conference, and in 1970 he was made an auxiliary bishop of San Salvador. He became bishop of the rural diocese of Santiago de María in late 1974 and archbishop of San Salvador on Feb. 22, 1977.

At the time of his elevation to the rank of archbishop, wealthy landowners were attacking the Church's pastoral practice in the countryside. Peasants were forming small ecclesial communities in which they learned to discuss the gospel and apply it to the unjust social conditions that dominated their own lives. Many of them joined peasant organizations to seek social and political change. Controlling the mass media and the government, the oligarchy kept Romero under constant pressure and frequent attack. During his years as archbishop, six priests and numerous lay ministers were assassinated, but the archbishop was never intimidated. A compelling preacher, Romero reached large audiences through his use of the archdiocesan radio station, where he worked for the Church by defending the poor and calling for social justice.

Foreseeing his own assassination, he intensified his message in his final weeks. On March 23, 1980, he plead-ed with the government to stop the repression of dissent, calling on soldiers not to obey orders to murder peasants. The next day, an assassin's bullet felled him while he preached in the chapel of the cancer hospital that also served as his residence. He is widely venerated as a martyr, and his tomb in the San Salvador cathedral is a popular shrine.

Bibliography: O. A. ROMERO, *Mons. Oscar A. Romero: Su Pensamiento,* extant homilies in eight projected volumes (San Salvador 1980). *La Voz de los Sin Voz: La Palabra Viva de Monseñor Romero* (San Salvador 1980); English translation: *Voice of the Voiceless: The Four Pastoral Letters and Other Statements* (Maryknoll, N.Y. 1985). *The Church Is All of You,* ed. J. R. Brockman (Minneapolis 1984). J. R. BROCKMAN, *Romero: A Life* (New York 1990). J. SOBRINO, *Archbishop Romero: Memories and Reflections* (Maryknoll, N.Y. 1990).

[J. R. BROCKMAN]

ROMO GONZÁLEZ, TORIBIO, ST.

Martyr, priest; b. April 16, 1900, at Santa Ana de Guadalupe, near Jalostotitlán, Jalisco, Diocese of San Juan de los Lagos, Mexico; d. Feb. 25, 1928, Tequila, Jalisco, Archdiocese of Guadalajara. At thirteen he began studying at the minor seminary of San Juan de los Lagos. He participated in Catholic Action while attending Guadalajara's seminary (1920–22), and was ordained 1922. His ministry in various parishes (Sayula, Tuxpan, Yahualica, Cuquío, and Tequila) concentrated on preparing catechesis, assisting workers, and promoting Eucharistic devotion. Forced into hiding with St. Justino ORONA, he made his headquarters in an abandoned factory and conducted his ministry in Tequila at night. Soldiers broke in and shot him. In 1948, his body was enshrined in a chapel built for it at Jalostotitlán. Fr. Romo was both beatified (Nov. 22, 1992) and canonized (May 21, 2000) with Cristobal MAGALLANES [*see* GUADALAJARA (MEXICO), MARTYRS OF, SS.] by Pope John Paul II.

Feast: May 25 (Mexico).

Bibliography: J. CARDOSO, *Los mártires mexicanos* (Mexico City 1953). J. DÍAZ ESTRELLA, *El movimiento cristero: sociedad y conflicto en los Altos de Jalisco* (México, D.F. 1979).

[K. I. RABENSTEIN]

ROMUALD, ST.

Founder of the CAMALDOLESE; b. Ravenna, Italy, *c.* 952; d. hermitage at Val di Castro, near Fabriano, Italy, June 19, 1027. The son of a nobleman named Sergius, Romuald entered the monastery of San Apollinare in Classe when he was 20 years old to do penance on behalf of his father, who had killed a kinsman. He became a monk there after seeing St. Apollinaris in a vision. Three years later he went to the mainland near Venice in search of a more austere way of life and became the disciple of a hermit named Marinus. In *c.* 978 Romuald and Marinus, together with Guarin, abbot of the Abbey of CUXA in the Pyrenees, who was visiting Venice, persuaded the Doge PETER ORSEOLO to abdicate, and all three returned to Cuxa with Guarin. Romuald and Marinus lived an eremitical life there near the monastery. After ten years Romuald returned to Italy to strengthen the vocation of his father, who had become a monk, and he remained there for the rest of his life. Emperor OTTO III greatly revered Romuald for his sanctity of life, and in 998 appointed him abbot of San Apollinare in Classe, but at the end of a year Romuald resigned the office and went to live in a hermitage at Pereum in the nearby marshes. This became an important center for training clergy, e.g., BRUNO OF QUERFURT, for the Slavonic mission field. Romuald wanted to die a martyr's death and set out to preach to the Magyars, but was forced to abandon the journey on account of his age. He spent the rest of his life founding eremitical congregations in northern and central Italy, among them, VALLOMBROSA. But the most important of these was CAMALDOLI near Arezzo, founded in 1023–27, which later became the motherhouse of the Camaldolese Order. Romuald left no written rule for his monks. When his body was exhumed in 1466 it was found to be incorrupt. It was transferred to Fabriano in 1481.

Feast: June 19 and Feb. 7 (translation).

Bibliography: PETER DAMIAN, *Vita beati Romualdi,* ed. G. TABACCO (Fonti per la storia d'Italia 94; Rome 1957); *La Vie du bienheureux Romuald,* tr., L. A. LASSUS (Namur 1962). W. FRANKE, *Quellen und Chronologie zur Geschichte Romualds von Camaldoli* (Halle 1910); *Romuald von Camaldoli und seine Reformtätigkeit zur Zeit Ottos III* (Berlin 1913, 2d ed. Vaduz 1965). P. CIAMPELLI, *Vita di s. Romualdo abate, fondatore dei Camaldolesi* (Ravenna 1927). J. LECLERCQ, "Saint Romuald et le monachisme missionnaire," *Revue Bénédictine* 72 (1962) 307–323. G. TABACCO, "La data di fondazione di Camaldoli," *Rivista di storia della Chiesa iri Italia,* 16 (1962) 451–455. A. PAGNINI, *Vita di S. Romualdo abbate, fondature dei camaldolesi* (2d ed. Camaldoli 1967). T. MATUS, ed., *The Mystery of Romuald and the Five Brothers* (Trabuco Canyon, CA 1994). L. VIGILUCCI, *Camaldoli: A Journey into its History & Spirituality,* tr. P.–D. BELISLE (Trabuco Canyon, CA 1995).

[B. HAMILTON]

RONAN, ST.

Missionary bishop in Brittany *c.* seventh century. The legend that an Irish saint, called Ronan (Rumon or Ruan), labored and died in Brittany may have its origin in the cult of his relics there. He is possibly to be identi-

Stone carving of Saint Ronan, sculpture by Ken Thompson. (©Jacqui Hurst/CORBIS)

fied with one of the many saints of that name, about whom practically no historical details survive and who are mentioned in the Irish MARTYROLOGIES, e.g., Ronan of Lough Derg on the Shannon (January 13); Bishop Ronan of Lismore, County Waterford, whose obituary remains in doubt in spite of the effort of the *Annals of Inisfallen* to provide him with one at the year 763 (February 9); Ronan son of Fergus (April 8); Ronan of County Louth (April 30); Ronan of Lann Ronain in County Down (May 22); Ronan son of Máge (July 15); Ronan Find son of Berach of Druminiskin, County Louth (November 18); and Ronan Find son of Aíd of Achad Farcha in County Meath (December 23). The most famous of these was the Ronan son of Berach, who died 661 or 664, for his relics were carefully preserved in Ireland, and it is known also that his cult spread abroad, perhaps even as far as Brittany. The various feasts in Ireland and Brittany present a great but not insurmountable difficulty against identification, and it may well be asked what connection, if any, had these Ronans with the homonym venerated in Scotland under the form of the name Mo-Rónóc. The efforts of early glossators and some modern scholars at differentiating and identifying have been more ingenious than enlightening.

Feast: June 1.

Bibliography: Rónán of Druminiskin. *Vita,* ed. A. PONCELET in *Analecta Bollandiana* 17 (1898) 161–166, has little historical value but became the basis for the literary tradition of the saint. ''Fledh Dúin na nGéd,'' ed. C. MARSTRANDER, *Videnskabsselskabets skrifter,* II Hist-Filos. Klasse, 1909, No. 6 (Oslo 1910). J. G. O'KEEFE, ed., *Buile Šuibhne* (Dublin 1952), where he is identified with Rónán of Lann Rónáin. Rónán of Brittany. *Vita,* tr. into Fr. by F. PLAINE in *Bulletin de la Société archéologique de la Finistère* 16 (1889) 263–318, where he is also called Renan but this vita is fictitious. Rónán (or Rumon) of Tavistock in Devon. *Vita,* ed. P. GROSJEAN in *Analecta Bollandiana* 71 (1953) 359–375, based almost entirely on that of Rónán of Brittany. Literature. P. GROSJEAN, *op. cit.* L. GOUGAUD, *Les Saints irlandais hors d'lrlande étudiés dans le culte et dans la dévotion traditionnelle* (Louvain 1936) 159–166. A. P. FORBES, *Kalendars of Scottish Saints* (Edinburgh 1872) 441–442. J. GAMMACK, *A Dictionary of Christian Biography,* ed. W. SMITH and H. WACE, 4v. (London 1877–87) 4:554. L. BIELER, in *Lexikon für Theologie und Kirche,* ed. J. HOFER and K. RAHNER, 10 v. (2d new ed. Freiburg 1957–65) 9:38. R. E. DOISE, *Saint Ronan de Locronan* (Châteaulin 1973).

[C. MCGRATH]

RONCHAMP, NOTRE-DAME DU HAUT

Notre-Dame du Haut Ronchamp is a pilgrimage shrine chapel situated on the hill of Ronchamp (Haute-Saône) in eastern France, dedicated on June 25, 1955 and an important achievement in 20th-century church architecture.

The present structure was preceded by two churches: the first, probably a Romanesque structure dedicated to Our Lady of September (month of pilgrimages), was given an extension in the 19th century and was destroyed by fire in 1913; a second church (Neo–Gothic) was raised in its place, but in September 1944 the hill became a battlefront between French and German troops, and the church was reduced to crumbling walls.

Le Corbusier (Charles Édouard Jeanneret, architect, painter, writer), engaged by a diocesan committee animated by Canon Ledeur, drew plans for a new chapel that were approved by Archbishop Dubourg of Besançon on Jan. 20, 1951. Construction began in the spring of 1953 and ended in 1955.

The chapel has a human scale of modest dimension with the nave varying in height from about 15½ feet at its lowest to 33 feet at its highest over the main altar. The nave can accommodate about 200 people (seating designed for 48) and serves well for small groups or for individual worship. It houses also three side chapels. Utilizing the natural site of the hillside, an outdoor sanctuary with altar and pulpit is permanently installed to serve the exceptional crowds on pilgrimage days.

The east, north, and west walls and chapel towers are built of reclaimed stones, are curvatured for greater stability, and are covered with cement gun plaster (whitewashed gunite concrete); the south wall, mostly hollow, is a gunite shell structured with concrete posts and beams. The roof is composed of two thin concrete shells (about two inches thick) held apart by seven beams (each different) that rest on columns contained in the walls. The inner surface of the roof does not touch the walls, permitting a thin horizontal shaft of light to enter. The enameled panels of the main doors and the windows were all designed by Le Corbusier. Other elements are: pews, which have concrete supports with wooden backs, seats, and kneelers executed by Savina; communion table of cast iron; altar in dressed stone from Burgundy; floor paving of stone in the sacred places and concrete elsewhere.

The chapel derives its spatial order from the action of the liturgy giving each space its relative spiritual value. Thus the nave, walls, floor, and roof expand space toward the sanctuary with an easy orchestration of natural shapes. The inner space is animated with pure light, skillfully and precisely managed through many shafts that create a dimmer nave, lighten the concrete roof, and intensify the sanctuary spaces. The exterior curvatured walls reveal the shape of interior volumes; the whole structure derives strength from a sensitively designed correspondence with its natural setting.

Bibliography: E. N. ROGERS, ''Il metodo di Le Corbusier e la forma della 'Chapelle de Ronchamp,''' *Casabella continuita* No. 207 (1955) 2–6. C. E. JEANNERET–GRIS, *The Chapel at Ronchamp* (New York 1957); *Le Corbusier: Chapelle N.–D. du Haut à Ronchamp* (Paris 1957). J. PETIT, *Le Livre de Ronchamp, Le Corbusier* (*ibid.* 14; Paris 1961). P. MERKLE et al., *Ein Tag mit Ronchamp* (Einsiedeln 1958). J. PICHARD, *Modern Church Architecture,* tr. E. CALLMANN (New York 1962). G. MERCIER, *L'Art abstrait dans l'art sacré* (Paris 1964) 85–87. G. E. KIDDER SMITH, *The New Churches of Europe* (New York 1964) 86–97.

[A. TAVES]

RONGE, JOHANN

Founder of the ''German Catholics'' sect; b. Bischofswalde (Silesia), Oct. 16, 1813; d. Vienna, Oct. 26, 1887. Ronge, a man inclined to religious scrupulosity, studied theology at Breslau, was ordained (1840), and acted as curate in Grottkau. His bishop rebuked him privately for unpriestly behavior (Oct. 29, 1841) and sus-

Notre-Dame du Haut Ronchamp, built by Le Corbusier between 1950 and 1955. (©Marc Garanger/CORBIS)

pended him (Jan. 30, 1843) after he wrote an article in 1842 condemnatory of Rome. Ronge then became headmaster of a private school at Laurahütte. On Oct. 13, 1844, he issued a public letter vigorously attacking Bp. Wilhelm Arnoldi of TRIER for exhibiting (for the first time since 1810) the relic of the Holy Coat. The letter created a sensation, and Ronge was excommunicated and degraded from the priesthood. Protestants sympathized with Ronge and encouraged him to start a German Catholic movement that would draw together nationalistically inclined persons who were dissatisfied with the Church's position on dogmatic questions and on disciplinary matters, such as mixed marriages and celibacy. Ronge founded in Breslau a dissenting congregation that rejected most of the doctrines previously denounced by another ex-priest, Johann CZERSKI; however, Ronge's group was more rationalistic and nationalistic. To a council in Leipzig (1845) 15 autonomous congregations sent delegates. By 1847 the movement of *Deutschkatholizismus* reached its high point of 80,000 members. At a second council, held in Berlin (1847), 259 communities sent representatives, 88 of whom had formerly been priests. Despite intensive propaganda, directed to German Catholics even in the U.S., the movement declined after 1848. In 1850 the "German Catholics" joined the Protestant Free Con-

gregations, and in 1859 they united with the Friends of Light to form an anti-Christian sect. By 1900 there were scarcely 2,000 "German Catholics." In 1921 the remnant joined the antireligious *Volksbund für Geistesfreiheit.* Because of his active part in the revolution of 1848, Ronge had to seek asylum in London until 1861. Upon his return to Germany he dwelt in Breslau, Frankfurt am Main, and Darmstadt. He died a freethinker.

Bibliography: H. J. CHRISTIANI, *Johannes Ronges Werdegang bis zu seiner Exkommunikation* (Berlin 1924). W. LEESCH, *Die Geschichte des Deutschkatholizismus in Schlesien* (Breslau 1938). L. W. SILBERHORN, "Der Epilog eines religiösen Reformers," *Zeitschrift für Religions- und Geistes-geschichte* 6 (1954) 114–138. K. ALGERMISSEN, *Konfessionskunde* (4th ed. Hanover 1930) 181–221. K. ALGERMISSEN, *Lexikon für Theologie und Kirche*[2] 3:279; 9:38. G. MARON, *Die Religion in Geschichte und Gegenwart*[3] 2:112–113; 5:1181.

[V. CONZEMIUS]

ROOTHAAN, JOHANN PHILIPP

Superior general of the JESUITS; b. Amsterdam, Nov. 23, 1785; d. Rome, May 8, 1853. His parents were former Calvinists who had emigrated from Frankfort. After guidance from A. Beckers, a former Jesuit, classical studies under D. van Lennep, and serving as aide to his surgeon-father, at 18 he went to Dvinsk (Dunaburg) in White Russia, where in 1804 he joined the Jesuits who had survived the suppression. He taught classics there (1806–09). After studying philosophy and theology at Polotsk, he was ordained (1812). He was at Pusza when Pius VII restored the Society of Jesus throughout the world (Aug. 7, 1814). When Russia later expelled most Jesuits in 1820, Roothaan was sent from Orsza to Brig, Switzerland, where he taught rhetoric, preached missions, and aided the vice-provincial of Germany, Belgium, and Holland. Roothaan was founder and rector of a college at Turin (1823). Elected in 1829 superior general of the order, he was dismayed at the defiance confronting papal civil government and at the inadequate formation of the flood of post-restoration candidates (Ligthart, 71). He issued 11 letters to the Society to organize energetically, if sternly, worldwide Jesuit efforts to regain presuppression prestige and efficiency. He displayed courage in imposing a carefully studied but somewhat monolithic interpretation of IGNATIAN SPIRITUALITY, the RATIO STUDIORUM, and THOMISM. In his efforts to build the Church in the U.S., he appealed for volunteers to work there; made Maryland into a viable Jesuit province (89 members); and later detached the St. Louis province from it. He refused the offer of a college at Notre Dame, Ind., but sent Anton Anderledy, the later superior general, and other European Jesuits who were exiled in 1848, to found Marquette University in Milwaukee. During his term as superior general he saw the order double in numbers to 5,000.

Bibliography: J. P. ROOTHAAN, *Epistolae*, 5 v. (Rome 1935–40). C. J. LIGTHART, *The Return of the Jesuits: The Life of Jan Philip Roothaan*, tr. A. NAZE (London 1978). R. NORTH, *The General Who Rebuilt the Jesuits* (Milwaukee 1944).

[R. NORTH]

ROPER, WILLIAM

Biographer of St. Thomas MORE; b. *c.* 1495; d. Jan. 4, 1578. He was the eldest son of John Roper of Eltham, Kent, a prothonotary of the King's Bench and a friend of Sir John More, father of Sir Thomas.

William entered Lincoln's Inn in 1518 and came to live with the Mores in Bucklersbury. Three years later William married Margaret, the eldest and favorite daughter of Thomas More. About this time Roper became a Lutheran but later returned to the Catholic faith. When his father died in 1524, William succeeded him as prothonotary. He was called to the Bar in 1525. By then the Ropers had moved with the Mores to Chelsea. After More re-

signed as Lord Chancellor in 1532, he made a gift to the Ropers of a portion of his Chelsea estate known as Butclose. William and Margaret took the Oath to the Succession, but were not present at More's trial on July 1, 1535. William's account of the last meeting between Margaret and her father is so vivid that it suggests he was there. Margaret was present at her father's burial and she retrieved his head from London Bridge. The Council questioned her about her father's papers but took no further action.

A dispute in 1541 between Roper and Dame Alice More about Sir Thomas's lands in Battersea was settled by arbitration. His name is found in the reports of the opposition in Kent about 1542 to Cranmer but he escaped trouble. He was in the Tower for a period in 1543 for having aided an opponent of the supremacy, but he was released on paying a fine and resumed his position as prothonotary. Margaret died at Christmas 1544 and was buried at Chelsea. William did not marry again. He gave up Butclose in 1547 and with William RASTELL took the tenancy of Crosby Place in London.

During the reign of Edward VI Roper remained in England but sent his eldest son, Thomas, to Louvain University. After the accession of Mary Tudor, Roper became sheriff of Kent and a member of Parliament for Rochester in 1554. In the following year, he and William Rastell were made freemen of Canterbury, which they represented in Parliament in 1555 and 1558. While Rastell was editing the *English Works* of Thomas More, Roper helped financially with the publication in 1557. He also wrote down his recollections of More as an aid to Nicholas Harpsfield, who was writing a full biography. The small book by Roper is an imperishable portrait without which we should lack much of our knowledge of More as a person. It is also a tribute to Margaret Roper for she plays a leading part in the narrative. The book was first published with the title *The Mirrour of Vertue in Worldly Greatness;* it bore the imprint of Paris but was printed at the English College, St. Omer.

Among Roper's friends was Sir Thomas White who founded the College of St. John Baptist at Oxford in 1555; he appointed Roper one of the life visitors.

Roper was a generous man. He made an endowment for the relief of prisoners; he supported Nicholas Harpsfield during his 12 years in prison under Elizabeth; he contributed to the cost of publishing books by the Catholic exiles in defense of their religion; for this he was summoned before the Council in 1568 and was reprimanded. He also supported financially the English College founded at DOUAI in 1568. The first record of his recusancy is dated 1569 when he was reported for not attending his parish church, and a return of the Inns of Court in

1577 names him and his two sons for not receiving Communion. His official position no doubt protected him but he must have taken the oath to Elizabeth. In 1577 he attempted to relieve Bl. Thomas Sherwood in the Tower. He was a shrewd man of business for, at his death, he left property in six counties. His wish to be buried at Chelsea with his wife was not observed; he was buried in the Roper vault at St. Dunstan's, Canterbury, where the head of Thomas More rests.

Bibliography: W. ROPER, *Lyfe of Sir Thomas Moore, Knighte,* ed. E. V. HITCHCOCK (Early English Text Society 197; London 1935). E. E. REYNOLDS, *Margaret Roper* (New York 1960); *Saint Thomas More* (New York 1953); *Trial of St. Thomas More* (New York 1964). R. W. CHAMBERS, *Thomas More* (Westminster, MD 1949).

[E. E. REYNOLDS]

RORE, CIPRIANO DE

Renaissance composer famous for his madrigals; b. Low Countries (Mechlin or Antwerp), 1516; d. Parma, Italy, 1565. He studied with WILLAERT in Venice, and his early madrigals (1542–44) already show unusual talent. By 1546 he was maestro in Ferrara at the court of Ercole II, succeeding VICENTINO. In 1561 he joined the court of Ottavio Farnese in Parma, and he remained there until his death, except for a brief stay in Venice as Willaert's successor at St. Mark's. His Masses are in traditional style; the motets mediate between this and the madrigals. He relied for texts on Petrarch (e.g., the *Vergine bella*) but later turned to contemporary sonnet writers, such as Parabosco, Spira, and Molino. Despite the danger that such expressive poetry might dominate the music, compositional unity was artfully maintained. Stylistically he was influenced by Willaert; his own influence on Lasso, Monte, Palestrina, and even on Monteverdi was so great that he might safely be called the precursor of the *seconda prattica*.

Bibliography: *Opera omnia,* ed. B. MEIER, *Corpus mensurablis musicae,* ed. American Institute of Musicology v.14 (Rome 1959–). J. MUSIOL, *Cyprian de Rore* (Breslau 1932). A. EINSTEIN, *The Italian Madrigal,* tr. A. H. KRAPPE et al., 3 v. (Princeton 1949). A. PIRRO, *Histoire de la musique* (Paris 1940). A. H. JOHNSON, *Die Musik in Geschichte und Gegenwart,* ed. F. BLUME (Kassel-Basel 1949–) 11:897–901. "The Masses of Cipriano de Rore," *Journal of the American Musicological Society* 6 (Boston 1953) 227–239. G. REESE, *Music in the Renaissance* (rev. ed. New York 1959) 309, 329–. A. CAMBIER, "Hoe de herkomst van Cypriaan de rore ontrafeld werd," *Musica Antiqua* 5 (1988) 124–29. A. H. JOHNSON, *The New Grove Dictionary of Music and Musicians,* ed. S. SADIE (New York 1980). S. LAVIA, *Cipriano de Rore as Reader and as Read: A Literary-Musical Study of Madrigals from Rore's Later Collections (1557–1566)* (Ph.D. diss. Princeton University, 1991). A. J. LLOYD, *Modal Representation in the Early Madrigals of Cipriano de Rore* (Ph.D. diss. Royal Holloway College, University of

Cipriano de Rore, miniature painting by Hans Mülich, from a 16th-century Codex Monancensis.

London, 1996). J. OWENS, "The Milan Partbooks: Evidence of Cipriano de Rore's Compositional Process," *Journal of the American Musicological Society* 37 (1984) 270–98. D. M. RANDEL, ed., *The Harvard Biographical Dictionary of Music* (Cambridge, Massachusetts 1996). J. STEELE, "Marenzio: From Mannerist to Expressionist," *Miscellanea Musicologica* 11 (1980),129–131.

[F. J. SMITH]

ROSA Y FIGUEROA, FRANCISCO DE LA

Archivist and historian of the Franciscan province of the Holy Evangelist in New Spain; b. place unknown, 1697; d. probably Mexico City, end of the 18th century. He was of noble lineage, probably a Creole, and related to the Priego, Arcos, and Feria families. From 1717 to 1724, as a secular priest, he roamed through the episcopates of Michoacán, Puebla, and Oaxaca and mastered the Mexican language, on which he wrote *Arte de Artes* in 1752. In 1724 he entered the Franciscan order; he was curate of Santa María la Redonda, vicar in the convent of Nativitas, and minister coadjutor in Tepepan and Xochimilco. In 1735 he went to the convent of Cuernavaca. In 1772 he held the titles of preacher general, notary apostolic, and notary or censor of books for the Holy Office, and, from 1748, archivist of his Franciscan province. As archivist he classified and catalogued the very rich archives, publicizing the important documents: in 1756, on the first confraternity in New Spain; in 1772, on the will and the legacies of Hernán Cortés; in 1774, on the convent of Santa María la Redonda and the family of the Condes de Orizaba. Thus he corrected such famous chroniclers as Juan de TORQUEMADA and VETANCURT. In 1773 he wrote some *Discursos humildes* against a royal decree of Charles III, inspired by Bishop LORENZANA, to the effect that "the different languages in the dominions of his majesty should be outlawed, and only the Spanish tongue should be spoken." Rosa y Figueroa made an erudite and ardent defense of the native languages and stressed the necessity for teaching them.

Bibliography: F. OCARANZA, *Capítulos de la Historia Franciscana,* ser. 1. (Mexico City 1933).

[E. DEL HOYO]

ROSAL VÁSQUEZ, MARÍA VICENTE, BL.

Baptized Vicenta, known in religion as María Encarnación del Corazón Jesús (Mary of the Incarnation of the Heart of Jesus); reformer of the Institute of Bethlehemite Sisters; b. Quetzaltenango, Guatemala, Oct. 26, 1820; d. near Tulcán, Ecuador, Aug. 24, 1886. Vicenta recognized her religious vocation at age fifteen, as she reflected on the mystery of the Incarnation. On Jan. 1, 1837, she entered the BETHLEHEMITES, founded by Pedro de San José BETANCUR (1670). Distressed by the laxity of the Beatario de Belem—which drifted from its original charism—Vicenta (now Sister María Encarnación) migrated to the convent of the Catalinas. Finding that convent also unsatisfactory she returned to Belem resolved to reform it. She had her opportunity when she was elected prioress in 1855. She revised the constitutions; the older sisters, however, refused to accept them. After her continued attempts at disciplinary reform were resisted, she founded a new *beatario* in Quetzaltenango (1861). Her devotion to the Sacred Heart led to the tradition within the order of dedicating the twenty-fifth of each month to prayers of reparation. The Bethlehemites are now active in Africa, Costa Rica, Ecuador, El Salvador, Guatemala, India, Italy, Nicaragua, Panama, Spain, the United States, and Venezuela.

While endeavoring to reform her congregation, Mother María Encarnación founded two schools in Quetzaltenango (1855). When Justo Rufino Barrios expelled various religious orders from the country (1873–85), she continued her work of reformation of the order and evangelization abroad. Arriving in Costa Rica in 1877, María Encarnación established the first women's college in Cartago, about fourteen miles from San José. She was a refuge again in 1884 when the Costa Rican government unleashed a persecution against religious groups, but returned to found an orphanage in San José (1886). She continued to Pasto, Colombia, to start a home for abandoned children. Untiring in her travels, she established the Bethlehemites in Tulcán and Otavalo, Ecuador.

On a trip from Tulcán to Otavalo, Mother María Encarnación fell from her horse and died. Her incorrupt body was translated to Pasto, where it is enshrined. After her cause for beatification was introduced, April 23, 1976, María Encarnación was declared venerable on April 6, 1995. On Dec. 17, 1996, the decree was signed approving a miracle attributed to her intercession. When she was raised to the altars by John Paul II on May 4, 1997, Mother María Encarnación became the Guatemalan beata.

Feast: April 18.

Bibliography: *L'Osservatore Romano.* 18 (1997): 2–3, 21 (1997): 4. *Acta Apostolicae Sedis* 12 (1997): 599.

[K. I. RABENSTEIN]

ROSALES, ROMÁN ADAME, ST.

Martyr, priest; b. Feb. 27, 1859, Teocaltiche, Jalisco, Diocese of Aguascalientes, Mexico; d. Apr. 21, 1927, Yahualica, Guadalajara. After completing his seminary studies at Guadalajara, Román was ordained priest (Nov. 30, 1890) and assigned to various parishes. He concentrated his energies on catechesis, popular missions, the construction of chapels in the surrounding areas (and St. Joseph's Church), the care of the sick, and the education of children. He founded an association of the Daughters of Mary and encouraged nocturnal adoration of the Blessed Sacrament. As pastor of Nochistlán, Zacatecas, Archdiocese of Guadalajara, this profoundly humble priest secretly administered the sacraments during the persecution until his hiding place was betrayed. He was arrested at night and tortured. Later he was imprisoned at Yahualica, where he was deprived of food and water for several days. On the day of his execution, he was taken to the church cemetery, where a grave had already been opened for him, and shot. Román's body was exhumed and returned to Nochistlán. He was both beatified (Nov. 22, 1992) and canonized (May 21, 2000) with Cristobal MAGALLANES [see GUADALAJARA (MEXICO), MARTYRS OF, SS.] by Pope John Paul II.

Feast: May 25 (Mexico).

Bibliography: J. CARDOSO, *Los mártires mexicanos* (Mexico City 1953). J. DÍAZ ESTRELLA, *El movimiento cristero: sociedad y conflicto en los Altos de Jalisco* (México, D.F. 1979). V. GARCÍA JUÁREZ, *Los cristeros* (Fresnillo, Zac. 1990). Y. PADILLA RANGEL, *El Catolicismo social y el movimiento Cristero en Aguascalientes* (Aguascalientes 1992).

[K. I. RABENSTEIN]

ROSALIA, ST.

Patroness of Palermo, Italy; d. 1160. All information about her before 1624 is purely legendary. An inscription, seemingly composed by Rosalia herself, was not found until 40 days after her body was discovered and has no serious claim to authenticity. According to the inscription and legend, she was the daughter of Count Sinibaldi, lord of Quisquina and Rosa, in Sicily. Apparently she was a Basilian nun at first, then retired to live as a recluse on Monte Coschina and later in a grotto on Monte Pellegrino near Palermo. In the great plague of 1624, her body was discovered and brought in solemn procession to Palermo, and since then she has been venerated as the patroness of the city. Pope URBAN VIII placed her name in the Roman MARTYROLOGY in 1630. Her cult has had a wide diffusion in Sicily and Italy and has been carried overseas by Italian emigrants. The caves in which she lived have been transformed into chapels, and her body rests in a splendid chapel in the cathedral of Palermo. A rich folklore has developed around St. Rosalia.

Feast: Sept. 4 and July 15 (the finding of her body).

Bibliography: *Acta Sanctorum* Sept. 2:278–414. A. M. ZIMMERMANN, *Kalendarium Benedictinum: Die Heiligen und Seligen des Benediktinerorderns und seiner Zweige*, 4 v. (Metten 1933–38) 3:15. L. RÉAU, *Iconographie de l'art chrétien*, 6 v. (Paris 1955–59) 3.3:1170–71. C. CIVELLO, *Santa Rosalia* (Rome 1967). I. SUCATO, *Santa Rosalia, patrona di Palermo* (Palermo 1976). P. COLLURA, *Santa Rosalia nella storia e nell'arte* (Palermo 1977). J. BARGALLÓ VALLS and R. G. MINGUELLA, *La festa major de Torredembarra a la segona meitat del segle XIX* (Torredembarra, Spain 1988), cult. V. PETRARCA, *Di Santa Rosalia, vergine palermitana* (Palermo 1988).

[M. R. P. MC GUIRE]

ROSARY

The term usually refers to the so-called Dominican Rosary, a pious exercise composed of both vocal and mental prayer. It consists in the recitation of 15 decades of Hail Marys, each preceded by an Our Father, followed by a Glory be to the Father, and accompanied by a meditation, called a mystery. Its 15 mysteries, focusing atten-

A rosary. (©Zeva Oelbaum/CORBIS)

tion on the Incarnation, sufferings, and glorification of Christ are a compendium of the life of Jesus and Mary and a summary of the liturgical year. Like the liturgy, the Rosary presents Christian truth comprehensively and graphically, and possesses great power to sanctify those who pray it. A prayer to Jesus and His Mother, it leads through Mary to Jesus, the source of all grace.

The Rosary is begun and terminated in various ways. In the United States, it commences with the recitation of an Our Father, three Hail Marys, and a Glory Be to the Father, and ends with the recitation of the Hail Holy Queen and the prayer from the Feast of the Rosary. Dominicans start the Rosary with the verses that open Matins of the Divine Office. Neither these introductory and concluding prayers nor the Glory Be to the Father following the decades are integral parts of the Rosary. While he recites the vocal prayers, the worshipper does not direct his attention to them but dwells on the mystery assigned to the decade he is reciting. The meditation may be made immediately before or after the decade. It may take a general form or may consider a distinct point of each mystery at successive Hail Marys. The mysteries are divided into three sets of five, namely, the Joyful Mysteries—the Annunciation of Christ's Incarnation to Mary, her visit to Elizabeth, the birth of Christ, His presentation in the temple, His being found in the temple; the Sorrowful Myster-

"Institution of the Rosary," ceiling fresco by Giovanni Battista Tiepolo, Church of the Gesuati (Jesuits), Venice, 1738–39.

ies—the agony of Christ in the garden, His scourging, His crowning with thorns, the carrying of the cross, the crucifixion and death of Christ; the Glorious Mysteries—the Resurrection of Christ, His Ascension into heaven, the sending of the Holy Spirit, the Assumption of Mary into heaven, her coronation as Queen of Heaven. In public recitation of the Rosary, the leader of the prayer announces the mystery before beginning the decade. In German-speaking countries, however, the mystery is referred to in each Hail Mary after the phrase, "thy womb, Jesus." Thus, at that point throughout the fifth sorrowful mystery, the leader adds, "who was crucified for us."

Origin. The origin of the Rosary, especially St. Dominic's connection with it, has been the subject of much debate. According to pious tradition, Mary appeared to Dominic when he was working among the Albigenses, giving him the rosary and instructing him to preach it. She promised that much success would attend his apostolate, should he do so. This tradition has been current since the end of the 15th century and is traceable to ALAN DE LA ROCHE. It gained general acceptance owing to the widespread propagation of the Rosary Confraternity and to its insertion into papal bulls granting various indulgences for saying the Rosary.

Those who have favored the tradition have not succeeded in mustering convincing proofs to support it. All their evidence directly linking Dominic to the Rosary, when traced back, ends with Alan de la Roche. Their other arguments refer to the various elements that constitute the Rosary and prove only, as is generally admitted, that parts of the Rosary were practiced as independent devotions before or during the lifetime of Dominic. The most telling proof offered for the tradition is its inclusion by at least a dozen popes in bulls or encyclicals. However, the popes issued those documents to foster devotion, not to teach historical truth. They made no claim to have verified the tradition but cited it as piously believed. It was first mentioned in an indulgence bull granted to the Rosary Confraternity by Alexander VI, July 13, 1495. In preparing such bulls the papal chancery justified the grant of the indulgence by reviewing the reasons alleged by the petitioners. In the early Rosary bulls, the chancery inserted cautionary phrases such as, "it is piously believed" or "it is said," to indicate that it passed no judgment on the historicity of the material presented by the petitioners. Later chancery clerks failed to insert the cautionary phrases. Thus, papal documents seem to vouch for the veracity of the tradition.

It has also been alleged that the Rosary originated in Dominic's style of preaching. Inspired by Mary, he expounded the truths of the faith successively. To bring down grace upon his audience, he invited the listeners to recite the Lord's Prayer and the Hail Mary between his different expositions. This version of the Rosary's origin is unsupported by the sources. It reduces Dominic's share to the vanishing point and proves only that any great preacher who interlarded his sermons with prayer was the founder of the Rosary.

Militating against the tradition is the long silence about Dominic until the end of the 15th century. In his *Apology,* Alan de la Roche allegedly asserted that Dominic's connection with the Rosary is proved "both from tradition and from the testimony of writers," but justification for this broad claim has not been found. In all the sources where a reference to Dominic and the Rosary might be expected, there is absolute silence: in the acts of his canonization, in his early biographies, in sermons preached on his feast, in medieval art, notably his tomb and the paintings of Fra Angelico, in Dominican chronicles and collections of sermon materials, in the official records of the order, such as the Constitutions, the acts of general and provincial chapters, and letters of the masters general.

The most satisfying explanation of the Rosary's origin is that it developed gradually as various Christological and Marian devotions coalesced. The origins are traceable to the tender devotion to Jesus and Mary that arose in the 12th century, and to the desire to give the unlettered faithful closer participation in the liturgy. It appears that the recitation of 150 Our Fathers emerged as a substitute for the recitation of the psalms. The Our Fathers were often divided, as were the psalms of David, into sets of "three fifties." Strings of beads, called "paternosters," were used to count these prayers. Marian devotion followed a similar trend. Mary's clients celebrated her joys by saluting her with liturgical antiphons, especially the salutation of the Archangel Gabriel, believing that when they did so she relived the joy of the Annunciation. Hence they multiplied their Hail Marys, especially in "chaplets" of 50 (mystical crowns placed on Mary's brow), groups of 100, or psalters of 150. Because Mary experienced her joy in intimate association with Jesus, the words of Elizabeth, "Blessed art thou among women," were added to the Hail Mary in the early 12th century. During the next century the name of Jesus was added to the Hail Mary.

The development of the Rosary mysteries followed a parallel course. Psalters of Our Lord Jesus Christ or of the Blessed Virgin Mary, applying the psalms to Christ or His Mother, were formed by adding to each psalm a phrase that referred it to Jesus or Mary. In a later stage the psalms were omitted and the phrases evolved into brief lives of Jesus or Mary extending from the Annunciation to their glorification in heaven. Commemoration of Mary's joys also influenced the formation of the mysteries. At first only the Annunciation joy was recalled, but soon sets of 5, 10, 15, or 20 other joys, often in connection with the liturgical feasts, were fashioned, either by using liturgical antiphons or by composing brief phrases, often rhymed, recounting the joys. This devotion coalesced with the recitation of the Hail Mary. During the recitation of a chaplet of Hail Marys, the Annunciation joy would be considered. During a second or third 50, a second or third joy would be taken up. As devotion to Mary's sorrows arose during the 14th century, the second chaplet was dedicated to them. Logically, the third chaplet was set aside for her heavenly joys. Along with this development, chains of 50, 100, or 150 phrases, referring to as many joys, were composed or drawn from the lives of Jesus and Mary that had evolved from the Psalters of Jesus or Mary and were attached to the recitation of the Hail Marys, one phrase to each Hail Mary. The Carthusian DOMINIC OF PRUSSIA popularized this practice soon after 1409, when he linked 50 phrases referring to Jesus and Mary to 50 Hail Marys, undivided by the Lord's Prayer. Such a series of 50 points was called a *rosarium* (a rose garden), a common term used to designate a collection of similar material. In preempting this term, Mary's clients applied the rose, the symbol of joy, to

Mary. The name was later transferred to the recitation of 50 Hail Marys; "psalter" was reserved for 150 Hail Marys.

Meanwhile, the method of using the vocal prayers of the Rosary was evolving. First, the psalter of 150 Hail Marys was united with the psalter of 150 Our Fathers, a Hail Mary following each Our Father. Early in the 15th century, Henry Kalkar (d. 1408), Carthusian visitator on the Lower Rhine, bracketed the Hail Marys into decades by inserting 15 Our Fathers between them. It was a logical next step to separate chaplets of 50 Hail Marys by inserting five Our Fathers.

Thus, from the early 15th century, the Rosary was recognizable and its elements had amalgamated: Our Fathers, Hail Marys, and mysteries, though these latter, and the mode of attaching them to the vocal prayers, were still far from standardized.

So long as the Rosary meditations consisted of multiples of 50, the Rosary had to be a "read" prayer; the worshipper had to have a book before him listing the points. The Rosary could not become a universal devotion or a communal prayer until it was simplified. As early as 1480, Rosaries of 50 mysteries were reduced to five, one for each decade. In 1483, a Rosary book written by a Dominican, *Our Dear Lady's Psalter,* cut down the 150 points to 15, all of which, except the last two, corresponded to the present mysteries. The Coronation was combined with the Assumption and the Last Judgment was the 15th mystery. The Dominican Alberto da Castello, in 1521, in his book *The Rosary of the Glorious Virgin Mary,* united the old and the new form of the mysteries (a term he was the first to apply to the meditations). To each Our Father he attached a mystery, but kept the old series of 150 in connection with the Hail Marys. These became submysteries for the mystery of the Our Father. During the 16th century, the Rosary of 15 mysteries gradually prevailed.

The vocal prayers of the Rosary were completed during the same century with the addition of the Glory Be to the Father and the second half of the Hail Mary: "Holy Mary, Mother of God, etc." Since the apparitions of Our Lady of Fatima in 1917, the prayer taught by Mary to the children has often been added to each decade: "O my Jesus, forgive us our sins, save us from the fires of hell, lead all souls to heaven, especially those in greatest need."

A Rosary bull of Pius V, in 1569, and the introduction of the Feast of the Rosary in 1573, helped to standardize the Rosary by presenting it as a combined vocal and mental prayer and regarding the meditations as essential parts of the devotion.

Spread of the Rosary. Though the Carthusians had made significant contributions to the development of the Rosary, the Dominicans did most to propagate it and render it a general, community prayer. They accomplished this with their Rosary books, preaching, and promotion of the Rosary Confraternity. Other orders soon joined them, and great saints, notably Peter Canisius, Philip Neri, and Louis de Montfort became Rosary advocates. Beginning with Leo XIII, the ''Pope of the Rosary,'' the popes worked to maintain the Rosary as a traditional, popular prayer and to propagate it. The many indulgences that enrich its use, especially the plenary indulgence granted by Pius XI in 1938 for reciting it in the presence of the Blessed Sacrament, enhance its appeal to the faithful. Even while extolling the liturgy, Pius XII did not neglect to commend the Rosary and other venerable devotions.

Bibliography: F. M. WILLAM, *The Rosary: Its History and Meaning,* tr. E. KAISER (New York 1953). J. G. SHAW, *The Story of the Rosary* (Milwaukee 1954). M. WARD, *The Splendor of the Rosary* (New York 1945). H. THURSTON, ''The Rosary,'' *Month* 96 (1900) 403–18, 513–27, 620–37; 97 (1901) 67–79, 172–88, 286–304. A. DUVAL, ''Les Frères Prêcheurs et le rosaire,'' *Maria,* ed. H. DU MANOIR DE JUAYE (Paris 1949–) 2:768–82. M. MAHÉ, ''Aux Sources de nôtre rosaire,'' *La Vie spirituelle* Supplement 4 (1951) 100–20. Works favorable to the St. Dominic tradition. W. G. MOST, *Mary in Our Life* (3d ed. New York 1959) 228–33, 279–87. D. MÉZARD, *Étude sur les origines du rosaire* (Caluire, France 1912). M. M. GORCE, *Le Rosaire et ses antécédents historiques* (Paris 1931).

[W. A. HINNEBUSCH/EDS.]

ROSATI, JOSEPH

First bishop of St. Louis; b. Sora, Naples, Jan. 12, 1789; d. Rome, Italy, Sept. 25, 1843. At the age of nine, Rosati began his studies for the priesthood in his native village. He later entered the seminary of the Congregation of the Mission (Vincentian Fathers) at Monte Citorio in Rome where he was ordained Feb. 10, 1811. During the next four years he engaged in parish missions in the vicinity of Rome and Naples. In September of 1815, he accepted the invitation of his former theology professor, Felix de Andreis, CM, to go with him to the U.S. to assist Louis Dubourg, Apostolic Administrator of Upper and Lower Louisiana.

They arrived at Baltimore, Maryland, in July of 1816. A month later they moved to Bardstown, Kentucky, where they studied English and taught theology in St. Thomas Seminary. In 1818 they were summoned by Bishop Dubourg to Perryville, Missouri, to establish St. Mary's Seminary. Although Rosati was rector of the seminary, pastor of the parish, and superior of the Vincentian

Joseph Rosati.

Community, he found time to visit the missions throughout the state of Missouri. Dubourg requested that Rosati be named coadjutor bishop of New Orleans, in charge of the northern portion of the Louisiana Territory, and he was consecrated on March 25, 1824. Three years later, he was named the first bishop of St. Louis.

As bishop, Rosati erected a cathedral in St. Louis and devoted himself to the works of the missions from the Mississippi Valley to the territories of Texas and Oregon. He invited a number of religious communities to share in his missionary activities. The Jesuits came and established St. Louis University, and he brought the Sisters of St. Joseph from France to found the first of their many establishments in the U.S., at Carondelet, Missouri. The Sisters of the Visitation, at Georgetown in the District of Columbia, accepted his invitation to open a monastery at Kaskaskia, Illinois; the Daughters of Charity came from Emmitsburg, Maryland, to begin St. Louis Hospital. Prior to this he had assisted the Religious of the Sacred Heart in starting a school for native girls at Florissant, Missouri.

Rosati was a prominent member of the first four Councils of Baltimore, for which he wrote many of the major documents. Following the Fourth Provincial Council, he returned to Rome in the interest of his diocese. During the visit, Gregory XVI commissioned him apostolic delegate to the Republic of Haiti to reconcile Church–State difficulties in that country. In April 1842, after completing a concordat with the Haitian government, he returned to Rome. Illness prevented his return to St. Louis, and he died in Rome.

Bibliography: Archives, Kenrick Seminary, Webster Groves, Mo. F. J. EASTERLY, *The Life of Rt. Rev. Joseph Rosati* (Catholic University of America, Studies in American Church History 33; Washington 1942). J. ROTHENSTEINER, *History of the Archdiocese of St. Louis* (St. Louis 1928).

[F. J. EASTERLY]

ROSAZ, EDOARDO GIUSEPPE, BL.

Bishop, secular Franciscan, founder of the Secular Franciscan Missionary Sisters of Susa; b. Feb. 15, 1830, Susa (near Turin), Piedmont, Italy; d. there May 3, 1903. Edoardo's parents were hard working, devout refugees of the French Revolution. Because of his frailty, Edoardo was tutored at home until he was ten. He then attended the Gianotti di Saluzzo school in Turin from 1840 to 1845, until his family returned to Susa following the deaths of his father and brother. Edoardo entered the diocesan seminary in 1847, joined the Third Order of Saint Francis in 1853, and was ordained June 10, 1854. Thereafter, he dedicated himself to preaching, catechesis, social work, the ministry of reconciliation, and the spiritual direction of the Saint Joseph Sisters. His pastoral enthusiasm, which he shared with his friend (St.) John BOSCO, led to Rosaz's appointment as director of Susa's seminary in 1874. Three years later (Dec. 26, 1877) he was consecrated as bishop of Susa, a position he held until his death. Immediately upon assuming the cathedra Bishop Rosaz began to renew the spirituality of the diocese, to institute charitable programs, and to establish educational institutions for the young. He founded the Secular Franciscan Missionary Sisters of Susa to assist with these ministries. In addition to his works, Bishop Rosaz is remembered for his pastoral zeal, dedication to the good of his clergy, his self-mortifications, and love of the poor. Pope John Paul II beatified Rosaz in Susa, July 14, 1991.

Feast: May 3 (Franciscans).

Bibliography: *Acta Apostolicae Sedis* (1991), 814.

[K. I. RABENSTEIN]

ROSCELIN OF COMPIÈGNE

French dialectician and reputed founder of early medieval NOMINALISM; b. *c.* 1050; d. 1125. He studied at Soissons and Rheims, taught at Compiègne, Loches (where Abelard was his pupil), Besançon, and Tours. In 1092 at the synod of Soissons he was accused of tritheism. Although he denied holding tritheism, he nevertheless recanted. Nothing remains of his writings except an abusive letter to Abelard on the Trinity; our knowledge of his thought is derived almost entirely from his adversaries, St. Anselm and Abelard. In the controversy on UNIVERSALS, he appears as an extreme antirealist. In nature only the individual subsists; genera and species are not realities, but verbal expressions in general form (*voces, flatus vocis*). This may mean that universals have no kind of objective reality except a verbal one, or it may simply be an emphatic repudiation of the formal subsistence of universals, which does not exclude some form of conceptual universal. His theory was later described as that of the *nomina*, whence arose the term "nominalist." JOHN OF SALISBURY interpreted him as having held the crude form of nominalism (*sententia vocum*). Roscelin's tritheism is based partly on the Boethian definition of a person as *rationalis naturae individua substantia*, and partly on his nominalism. The three divine persons are three realities or substances (*res per se*), like three angels or souls. Were they but one reality, he argued, all three persons would have become incarnate. He concluded that, if usage permitted, they could well be called three gods. To save the dogma, Roscelin allowed that the divine persons were one in will and power.

Bibliography: Roscelin's letter to Abelard in J. REINERS', "Der Nominalismus in der Frühscholastik," *Beiträge zur Geschichte der Philosophie und Theologie des Mittelalters* 8.5 (1910) 62–80 (literature). PETER ABELARD, *Ep.*14, *Patrologia latina* 178:355–358; *Dialectica*, ed. L. M. DE RIJK, (Assen 1956) X, 554–555. ANSELM OF CANTERBURY, Epp. 128, 129, 136, 147 in *Opera omnia*, ed. F. S. SCHMITT, 6 v. (Edinburgh 1946–61) v.3; *Ep. de Incarnatione Verbi*, 1–2, *ibid.*, v.2. JOHN OF SALISBURY, *Metalogicon*, bk. 2.17, ed. C. C. J. WEBB (Oxford 1929), ed. and tr. D. D. MCGARRY (Berkeley 1955); *Policraticus*, ed. C. C. J. WEBB 2 v. (Oxford 1909). Literature. F. J. PICAVET, *Roscelin: Philosophe et théologien, d'après la légende et d'après l'histoire* (2d ed. Paris 1911). M. M. GORCE, *Dictionnaire de théologie catholique* 13.2:2911–15. M. M. C. DE WULF, *History of Mediaeval Philosophy*, tr. E. C. MESSENGER, 2 v. (3d ed. New York 1935–38) v.1. F. CORVINO, *Enciclopedia filosofica* 4:205–206.

[F. COURTNEY]

ROSCELLI, AGOSTINO, ST.

Founder of the Institute of Sisters of the Immaculata; b. July 27, 1818, Bargone di Casarza, Liguria, Italy; d. May 7, 1902, Genoa, Italy.

Agostino's family was poor, but the deep faith and peace that filled his home produced an introspective, contemplative soul open to the workings of God. He first felt called to the priesthood during a parish mission in 1835, but poverty made schooling difficult. With financial assistance, prayer, and hard work, he completed his seminary studies in Genoa and was ordained to the priesthood in 1846.

He began his parish work at St. Martin d'Albaro, then in 1854 he was assigned to the Church of Consolation. In addition to spending countless hours hearing confessions and providing spiritual counsel, Roscelli established residential centers to provide moral and educational support for young women.

In 1876, he founded the Institute of Sisters of the Immaculata to care for women at risk because of their poor circumstances. Beginning in 1874, he served 22 years as chaplain to the provincial orphanage, in addition to working with prisoners, especially those condemned to death.

Throughout his life Roscelli's contemplative spirit and mystical experiences spurred him to action for love of God. Pope John Paul II, who beatified Roscelli on May 7, 1995, cited Roscelli as a special model for pastors on the World Day of Prayer for Vocations. A second miracle was approved on July 1, 2000, opening the way for his canonization, June 10, 2001.

Feast: May 7.

Bibliography: *Acta Apostolicae Sedis* (1995): 564. *L'Osservatore Romano,* English edition, no. 19 (1995).

[K. I. RABENSTEIN]

ROSCREA, ABBEY OF

An Irish monastery located in County Tipperary, Ireland, Diocese of Killaloe. It was founded by St. Crónán (d. *c.* 665) on one of the ancient highways called the Slige Dála. By the beginning of the 9th century it had been given in COMMENDATION to a lay abbot. There was an abbot-bishop there in 918 and again in 1045, and some of its abbots held office also at the monastery of CLONMACNOIS in 839 and 1043. It was declared part of the Diocese of Killaloe in 1111, but was recognized as a separate diocese, suffragan of Cashel, in 1152. Around the end of the 12th century it was reduced to the status of a deanery of Killaloe. From its scriptorium came the *Book of Dimma,* which dates from the 8th century, the *Annals of Roscrea,* of which only one 17th-century fragmentary copy survives, and the *Rule of Échtgus Úa Cúanáin,* a tract on the Eucharist, from about the 12th century. The abbey's architectural remains are of various dates and include a round tower from *c.* the 9th century and the porch of the old church of Crónán in the Hiberno-Romanesque style from the middle of the 12th century.

Bibliography: A. GWYNN and D. F. GLEESON, *A History of the Diocese of Killaloe* (Dublin 1962) 60–78, 169. D. F. GLEESON, *Roscrea* (Dublin 1947) 5–17, 150–154. L. H. COTTINEAU, *Répertoire topobibliographique des abbayes et prieurés,* 2 v. (Mâcon 1935–39) 2:2535.

[C. MCGRATH]

ROSE OF LIMA, ST.

Patron of Peru; b. Lima, Peru, April 20, 1586; d. there, Aug. 24, 1617. She was the daughter of a conquistador from Puerto Rico, Gaspar de Flores, who had arrived in Peru in 1548, and the young María de Oliva. She was baptized Isabel de Flores, May 25, 1586, the Feast of Pentecost. The maid in the house, startled by the extraordinary beauty of the baby, exclaimed that she looked like a rose. The mother agreed and ordered that the child should be called Rose, despite the baptismal name. She was confirmed with this name by Abp. (St.) Toribio de MOGROVEJO when she was 14. Later, because of the special role the Virgin Mary played in her life, she took the name Rosa de Santa María.

Rose took as her model St. CATHERINE OF SIENA. While still a child she undertook fasts and other mortifications. She wished to enter a cloister, but denied this, she remained at home, contributing to the support of the family by selling the flowers she grew with such success. When she was 20, she found an answer to her desire for some solitude even within the family by joining the Third Order of St. Dominic. She chose to wear the habit from then on. Under the veil she wore a crown of thorns, but over it a crown of roses to please her mother. Rose lived a secluded life, spending as much time as she could in the hermitage she had built in the garden as a child. In one room of the house she set up a little infirmary where she cared for destitute children and infirm elderly people. This work was a beginning of social service in Peru. Her activities, secluded though they were, were brought to the attention of the Inquisition. Interrogators could only announce that she was directed by "impulses of grace." She had great mystical gifts, though she did not have the gift of writing about her experiences. The people of Lima believed that she saved them from pirates. She was widely known and beloved by rich and poor in Lima. At her death, which she had prophesied exactly, it was impossible to hold the funeral for several days because of the crowds, and finally the body was buried privately in the cloister of St. Dominic's Church as she had requested. The body was later moved into the church and is now buried under an altar in the crypt. The cause for her canonization was presented in Rome, July 1634. On March 12, 1668, CLEMENT IX decreed her beatification. She was canonized April 12, 1671, by CLEMENT X and proclaimed patron of Peru, all of America, the Indies, and the Philippines.

Ruins and doorway of Saint Cronan's Church, c. 1865–1869, Roscrea, County Tipperary, Ireland. (©Sean Sexton Collection/CORBIS)

Feast: Aug. 23.

Bibliography: R. VARGAS UGARTE, *Vida de Santa Rosa de Santa María* (2d ed. Lima 1951). F. P. KEYES, *The Rose and the Lily* (New York 1961). L. MILLONES, *Una partecita del cielo* (Lima 1993). J. F. ARAOZ et al., *Santa Rosa de Lima y su tiempo* (Lima 1995). L. M. GLAVE TESTINO, *De Rosa y espinas* (Lima 1998).

[J. M. VARGAS]

ROSE OF VITERBO, ST.

Third order FRANCISCAN; b. Viterbo, Italy, c. 1233; d. Viterbo, March 6, 1252. Although few details are extant regarding Rose's life, much can be gleaned from both the environment in which she lived and from the two separate, anonymous *vitae* written to initiate the process of her canonization. Shortly after Rose's birth, Viterbo found itself both socially and geographically central to the battles between the Ghibelline supporters of the Emperor Frederick II and the supporters of the papacy. Mendicant friars are credited with championing the latter cause and preaching loyalty to the papacy. To combat the Mendicant influences, the emperor supported and offered protection to the Waldensians and Humiliati. This debate made its way to the streets and piazzas of Viterbo

Vita I, written shortly after her death in 1253, is the most contemporary testimony to the magnitude of Rose's impact on her community. This hagiographical account reveals Rose as having a pious upbringing. Around the age of 11, she experienced a vision of the Virgin Mary somewhere outdoors, and thus felt called to praise Christ publicly and to wail mournfully through the streets. Because of her vision, Rose quickly gained followers and led processions through the streets of Viterbo, cross in hand, encouraging others to join her. Although unfinished, *Vita I* emphasizes the public nature of her preaching, her practice of virtuous living, and her talent for

Coronation of Saint Rose of Lima, 17th-century painting by Carlo Cignani. (©Archivo Iconografico, S.A./CORBIS)

drawing followers. She also demonstrated the ability to prophesy.

Vita II was written for the canonization process begun by Pope Calixtus III in 1457. This second *Vita* emphasizes the public nature of her apostolate, which was not the norm for women in this period in history. Her ability to preach Christ and the Good New daily to the people is emphasized. She also rages against the heretics supporting the emperor. While Rose was renowned for her miraculous cures and prophetic visions, she was followed because of her passionate preaching. *Vita II* also expands on her expulsion from Viterbo and hails her triumphant return from exile upon the fulfillment of her prophecy of the emperor's death. It is clear that Rose had a major role in defending the Church against the emperor.

Feast: Sept. 4.

Bibliography: D. PRYDS, "Proclaiming Sanctity: Rose of Viterbo," in *Women Preachers and Prophets through Two Millenia of Christian History* (Berkeley 1998) 159–72. A. VACCA, *La Menta

e la Croce* (Rome 1982). J. WEISENBECK and M. WEISENBECK, "Rose of Viterbo: Preacher and Reconciler," in *Clare of Assisi: A Medieval and Modern Woman*, Clare Centenary Series 8 (St. Bonaventure, N.Y. 1996) 145–55.

[R. D. HARSHMAN]

ROSELINE, ST.

Virgin, known also as Rossolina; b. Chateau d'Arcs (Fréjus), France, 1263; d. Celle-Roubaud (Provence), Jan. 17, 1329. Roseline, of the noble family De Villeneuve, entered the Carthusians in Bertrand about age 15–16 and was honored even during her lifetime for her severe penances and miracles. She became prioress in Celle-Roubaud *c.* 1300. When her coffin was opened in 1334, her body was found incorrupt. Her veneration was approved for Fréjus in 1851, for the whole of France in 1857. She is pictured in iconography as a Carthusian nun with maniple and stole.

Feast: Jan. 17; Oct. 16 (Carthusians); July 11 (translation of relics).

Bibliography: *Acta Sanctorum* June 2:484–498. J. E. STADLER and F. J. HEIM, *Vollständiges Heiligen-Lexikon*, 5 v. (Augsburg 1858–82) 5:147. L. LIOTARD, *Vie édifiante et populaire de Ste. Roseline de Villeneuve* (2d ed. Draguignan, France 1873). M. C. DE GANAY, *La Vie spirituelle* 19 (1928–29) 420–433. J. L. BAUDOT and L. CHAUSSIN, *Vies des saints et des bienheueux selon l'ordre du calendrier avec l'historique des fêtes*, ed. by The Benedictines of Paris, 12 v. (Paris 1935–56) 1:358. *The Book of Saints* (4th ed. New York 1947) 517. D. ATTWATER, *A Dictionary of Saints* (new ed. New York 1958). A. BUTLER, *The Lives of the Saints,* ed. H. THURSTON and D. ATTWATER, 4 v. (New York 1956) 1:112–113, G. SPAHR, *Lexikon für Theologie und Kirche,* ed. J. HOFER and K. RAHNER, 10 v. (2d, new ed. Freiburg 1957–65) 9:45.

[M. CSÁKY]

ROSELLI, SALVATORE MARIA

Dominican philosopher and theologian; b. Naples, date unknown; d. Rome, 1784. He taught at the College of St. Thomas at Rome (Minerva), and while there he furnished the basis for the Thomistic reconstruction of the 19th century. Personally reacting against the philosophy of DESCARTES, Roselli supported the directives of the masters general of the order to promote the philosophy of St. THOMAS. He wrote a *Summa philosophiae* (6 v. Rome 1777–83; Madrid 1788; 4 v. Bologna 1857), in which he presented authentic scholastic philosophy "ad mentem Angelici Doctoris." It was widely disseminated in Italy and Spain and frequently reprinted. A compendium of the work (3 v.) appeared at Rome in 1837. Roselli gave evidence of a comprehensive knowledge of ancient, medieval, and modern philosophy. In his *Summa* he offered, in the form of a dialogue, a comparison between the classical THOMISTIC philosophy and modern systems of empiricism, rationalism, Cambridge Platonism, and naturalism. He wisely substituted contemporary questions for the minutiae and subtleties characteristic of the medieval writers and their commentators. Because of the number of sources that Roselli employed in his *Summa*, some historians question his adherence to St. Thomas, suggesting that he might be better described as eclectic. In general, Roselli's work can be said to have marked the beginning of everything in the movement that goes by the name of neothomism.

Bibliography: H. HURTER, *Nomenclator literarius theologiae catholicae* (Innsbruck 1903–13) 5.1:259. I. E. NARCISO, ''Tomismo e filosofia moderna nella *Summa philosophiae* del Domenico Salvatore Roselli,'' *Aquinas* 7.2 (1964) 203–237. A. WALZ, *Dottrina e scuola* (Rome 1943) 11–12. A. MASNOVA, *Il neo-tomismo in Italia* (Milan 1923).

[F. J. ROENSCH]

ROSETTA STONE

The Rosetta Stone is a slab of black basalt, approximately 3 feet 9 inches long, 2 feet 4½ inches wide, and 11 inches thick, bearing a bilingual inscription in Egyptian and Greek. The top right- and left-hand corners and the right-hand bottom corner are missing. The stone was found in 1799 by a French officer named Boussard (sometimes given as Bouchard), near Rosetta (Rashid) in the Nile Delta. It passed into British possession when the French surrendered Egypt in 1801.

The inscription is divided into three sections, each in a different form of writing: Old Egyptian hieroglyphic, demotic (the ordinary Egyptian handwriting), and Greek. The first studies of the demotic text were those of Sylvestre de Sasy and J. D. Åkerbald in 1802. An Englishman, Thomas Young, demonstrated that the royal name ''Ptolemy'' occurring in the Greek text was found in the hieroglyphic version surrounded by an oval. This discovery provided Young with a clue to the phonetic values of the Egyptian symbols. In 1822, the alphabetic Egyptian characters provided by Young were corrected and enlarged by Jean François Champollion. This French scholar formulated a system of general deciphering that has been the foundation upon which all Egyptologists have worked. The deciphering of proper names provided the key to the Egyptian writing, but an understanding of the languages could not have been accomplished without the assistance of Coptic, the liturgical language of the Christian descendants of the ancient Egyptians.

The inscription is the decree of the Egyptian priests assembled at Memphis in 196 B.C. to celebrate the first

Rosetta Stone. (©Bettmann/CORBIS)

commemoration of the coronation of Ptolemy V. It proclaims the king's piety, his love of the Egyptians, the benefits he had conferred upon Egypt, and resolutions of gratitude to honor him. The stone is in the British Museum.

Bibliography: E. A. W. BUDGE, *The Rosetta Stone in the British Museum* (London 1929). H. HARTLEBEN, *Champollion: Sein Leben und sein Werk* (Berlin 1906).

[J. J. O'ROURKE]

ROSICRUCIANS

An occult sect of obscure origin that, according to one account, was organized in 1413 by Christian Rosencreuz, a German scholar. He is supposed to have visited (*c.* 1410) Cyprus, Damascus, Egypt, Fez, and Spain and to have garnered from the Muslim physicians and teachers of the different centers of learning a knowledge of medicine, philosophy, science, and religion beyond the understanding of the medieval West. On arriving in Austria (1413), he is alleged to have formed the Society of the Rose and Cross with three companions, who devoted themselves to study and acts of benevolence. These first Rosicrucians lived in common at a hospice called Domus Sancti Spiritus and went about curing the sick, free of charge. The Rosicrucian account goes on to relate that Rosencreuz composed a book, *Chymische Hochzeit* (1457), containing hermetic and occult secrets. He died, according to this version, in 1484, leaving instructions that his tomb was to be sealed for 120 years and then opened. Successive brethren of Rosicrucian fraternity kept the secret, and in 1604 the tomb was opened and a number of books important to the Rosicrucian movement were found within.

Seventeenth-century Developments. The more generally accepted version of the Rosicrucian genesis begins the story in 1610, when Johann Valentine Andrea (1586–1654) composed a work entitled *Fama fraternitatis.* This document, published at Cassel in 1614 and, in a slightly revised version, at Frankfurt am Main in 1615, was apparently an elaborate hoax, in which Andrea gave a lengthy history of the brotherhood formed by Christian Rosencreuz. The work ascribed to Rosencreuz himself, *Chymische Hochzeit,* first appeared at Strasbourg in 1616 and was acknowledged by Andrea as his own composition. If the entire concept of a brotherhood of Rosicrucians existing from 1413 to his own day, as Andrea claimed, was a pure fabrication, the intellectual climate of the early 17th century was nevertheless friendly to such an organization. In 1615 Julius Sperber issued a tract on the Brotherhood of the Rosy Cross at Danzig; and Michael Maier, a German physician, carried the idea to England. The fraternity of educated men interested in medicine, science, and occult lore that emerged was loosely organized; and in many cases, a knowledge of the promise of a universal reformation of the world through the Orden des Rosenkreuzes, promised in Andrea's book, may be presumed to have been their only link.

Robert Fludd (1574–1637) began to issue works similar to the original manifesto with his *Apologia compendaria* (Leyden 1616). His second work on Rosicrucianism appeared as *Tractatus apologeticus integritatem societatis de Rosea Cruce defendens* (Leyden 1617). A third apologetic work, addressed to King James I in behalf of the Rosicrucian brotherhood, *Declaratio brevis,* remained in manuscript. A copy in the British Museum includes a number of letters from Continental Rosicrucians; one composed by a Julius Helt insists that the brotherhood is not tainted by either Catholic or Lutheran doctrine, but asserts that "the theology of the Calvinists is the theosophy of the Fraternity." Some inkling of the purpose and intellectual outlook of the early Rosicrucians may be found in Fludd's writings, in which it is apparent that he regarded all true natural science as rooted in revelation. He opposed both Aristotelian science and Copernican astronomy, denying the diurnal revolution of the earth. His thought was Neoplatonic, viewing "all things as complicitly and ideally in God," with a marked pantheistic tendency. Other early adherents of the Rosicrucian idea shared Fludd's approach, using the language of alchemy, medicine, and the occult to transmit their philosophic speculations.

Sir Kenelm Digby (1603–65) may have taken part in the early Rosicrucian movement, but the evidence for Francis Bacon as a member, or even as the founder, of the brotherhood rests on a very dubious basis. The appearance of a Rosicrucian lodge, under the leadership of Elias Ashmole (1617–92), at London in 1646 is equally difficult to substantiate, but an English translation of the *Fama fraternitatis* was issued at London in 1652 and an English version of *The Chemical Wedding* at Cambridge in 1690. The subsequent history of this early Rosicrucian fraternity is equally vague, and it is improbable that it survived in any recognizable form after the late 17th century.

Nineteenth and Twentieth Centuries. Rosicrucianism, as it now exists, was organized by Robert Wentworth Little in 1866. *The General Statutes of the Order of Knights of the Red Cross of Rome and Constantine* was published at London in 1868. A somewhat revised version of *The General Statutes* now identifies the order as a branch of FREEMASONRY. Control of the *Societas Rosicruciana in Anglia* passed from Little to William Wynn Westcott, who published a history of the order in 1885. Rosicrucian colleges, as local units are designated, were formed in the United States and various parts of the British empire between 1875 and 1885. The system was extended to Continental Europe in 1890. The Ancient Mystical Order Rosae Crucis (AMORC) has U. S. headquarters at San Jose, Calif.; the Rosicrucian Brotherhood (Fraternitas Rosae Crucis), at Quakertown, Pa.; and the Society of Rosicrucians (Societas Rosicruciana in America), at New York City.

Bibliography: A. E. WAITE, *The Brotherhood of the Rosy Cross* (London 1924; repr. New Hyde Park, N.Y. 1961); *Emblematic Freemasonry* (London 1925); *Real History of the Rosicrucians* (London 1887); *The Secret Tradition in Freemasonry,* 2 v. (London 1937). W. W. WESTCOTT, *The Rosicrucians* (London 1885). C. MCINTOSH, *The Rose Cross and the Age of Reason: Eighteenth–century Rosicrucianism in Central Europe and its Relationship to the Enlightenment* (Leiden-New York 1992). S. ÅKERMAN, *Rose Cross over the Baltic: The Spread of Rosicrucianism in Northern Europe* (Leiden/Boston 1998).

[R. K. MACMASTER/EDS.]

ROSKOVÁNYI, AUGUSTUS

Bishop; b. Szenna, Hungary, Dec. 7, 1807; d. Feb. 24, 1892. He was ordained in 1831 after studies at the college of the Piarists at Kis-Szeben (1817–22), and at Eger (1822–24), and his theological studies at Pesth and the Augustineum in Vienna. In 1839 he received the Abbey of Saar as a benefice and in 1841 was appointed rector of the seminary at Eger. He was consecrated auxiliary bishop in 1847 and named bishop of Waitsen in 1851. In 1859 he was named bishop of Neutra. His works are noted for the documents they contain. Among his more notable works are *De primatu Romani Pontificis eiusque iuribus* (Augsburg 1839; 2d ed. Agram 1841); *De matrimoniis mixtis* (5 v. Funfkirchen 1842; Pesth 1854, 1870–71); *De matrimoniis in ecclesia Catholica* (2 v. Augsburg 1837–40); *Monumenta catholica pro independentia potestatis ecclesiasticae ab imperio civili* (14 v. Funfkirchen 1847; Pesth 1856, 1865, 1870–71); *Coelibatus, et breviarium: duo gravissima clericorum officia* . . . (11 v. Pesth 1861; Neutra 1877–81); *Romanus Pontifex tamquam primas ecclesiae* . . . (16 v. Neutra and Comaromii 1867, 1878); *Beata Virgo Maria in suo conceptu immaculata* (12 v. Budapest 1873–74; Neutra 1877).

Bibliography: J. SZINNYEI, *Magyar írók,* 14 v. (Budapest 1891–1914) 11:1188–90. J. VÁGNER, *Adatok a nyitra-városi plébániák történetéhez* (Nitra 1902).

[L. R. KOZLOWSKI]

Antonio Rosmini-Serbati.

ROSMINI-SERBATI, ANTONIO

Founder of the Institute of Charity, philosopher, theologian, and patriot; b. Rovereto, Trentino (then under Austrian domination, now part of Italy), 1797; d. Stresa (Lago Maggiore), 1855. Against the initial objections of his parents, he was ordained in 1821. His retired life until 1826 can be considered as a preparation for his work. During this period, his studies embraced mathematics, political theory, education, medicine, natural sciences, Oriental languages, and all branches of philosophy and theology. *The History of Love,* an early work of Rosmini on holy Scripture, bears witness to his intense application to the word of God and to his great talent for synthesis.

Rosmini's deliberate aim, in an age characterized by liberal ideas and revolt against established order, was to achieve a balance between old and new by showing how true development in every science depends upon growth from basic and unchangeable principles. On the advice of Pius VII he devoted himself to this task, principally in philosophy.

Rosmini's personal traits were defined and established in these early years. Prayer and devotion to the will of God became habitual with him; he grew familiar with practical affairs through the management of the large fortune inherited from his father; and his extraordinary capacity for lasting friendship with different types of men manifested itself (Manzoni, Tommasco, Capellari [later Gregory XVI], and Gustavo Cavour were among his many intimates). The plan of his Congregation, for which he had the active encouragement and advice of St. Maddalena di Canossa, was completed in 1828. His chief ecclesiastical work during this time, and what he called "nearly my only recreation," was the formation of a clerical circle at Rovereto to study the then too-much-disregarded St. Thomas Aquinas.

In 1826 Rosmini went to Milan to continue his research and to begin publishing the results of his philosophical studies. He was a writer of astounding fertility and originality. His complete works, many published posthumously, are at present (2001) being edited in a planned 80-volume critical edition (Rome-Stresa, 1966–). About 30 volumes have been produced to date. To these must be added 13 volumes, with some 700 pages per volume, of letters (Casale 1905). He treated thoroughly the problem of the origin of ideas and certitude, the nature of the human soul, ethics, civil society, the relationship between Church and State, human rights, metaphysics, grace, original sin, and the Sacraments in general. It is impossible to name a single school of thought to which he can be said to belong. Basing himself upon an encyclopedic reading of philosophers and ecclesiastical tradition, he endeavored to present principles that would interlock and serve as a basis of unity for all knowledge.

As the foundation of his system he placed the intuition of universal and undetermined being, which he was careful to distinguish from the concept of God. Although many of his adversaries (M. Liberatore, SJ, for example) later maintained that there could be no distinction between the two concepts and consequently accused Rosmini of ontologism and pantheism, this accusation is no longer accepted by scholars (see Congregation for the Doctrine of the Faith, *Note on the import of the doctrinal Decrees concerning the thought and works of the Priest Antonio Rosmini Serbati*, n. 6, Vatican, 1 July 2001). The ''idea of being'' is for Rosmini the objective and infallible light of reason, the source of man's dignity as a person, the font of moral obligation, the unshakable foundation of human rights, and the spring of the immortality of the soul. Man's moral goodness or badness depends upon the use or misuse of this innate light according to which he can either evaluate things in their objective order or attempt to place them in an order of his own creating.

Theological works published during Rosmini's lifetime concern the nature of original sin, which he maintained was more than a mere lack of sanctifying grace, the providence of God and what he called ''supernatural anthropology,'' a study of fallen human nature restored through the Sacraments.

His ascetical works are not numerous, but their content regards the fundamental issues of the Christian life. This is especially the case with *Maxims of Christian Perfection* (Rome 1830), in which he shows how all duties culminate in devotion to Christ's Church—a devotion that he himself manifested in submitting fully to the ecclesiastical prohibition of two of his works. *Maxims* form the basis of his *Constitutions of the Society of Charity*, synopsised in the Apostolic Letters *In Sublimi* (Gregory XVI, 1839) which approved the *Rule* of Rosmini's religious Institute.

From 1826 until his death, Rosmini's growing influence as a leader in the forces opposing the domination of sensism in European thought was subject to continual attack. He was looked upon with suspicion by Austria on account of a panegyric on Pius VII (Modena 1831), in which he condemned Josephinism. His *Treatise on Moral Conscience* (Milan 1839), which contained an attack on the use of probabilism as applied to the natural law, was repudiated especially by P. Ballerini, SJ, who wrote anonymously as *il prete bolognese*. Rosmini's teaching on original sin and the distinction he made between sin (*peccatum*) and fault (*culpa*) were also the source of bitter criticism. *The Five Wounds of the Church* (Lugano 1847), in which he treats of the dangers to the Church from within, and *A Constitution Based on Social Justice* (Milan 1848) were placed on the Index (1848) for unspecified reasons in the troubled days that followed the assassination of Pellegrino Rossi at Rome. At the same time, Rosmini, following Pius IX in his flight from Rome, fell from favor at Gaeta after expressing his views for a constitution and against Austrian domination.

In 1854, after a full examination of Rosmini's published writings, a papal commission, with Pius IX presiding at its final sitting, declared that the works under consideration were to be dismissed without censure. Posthumously, 40 propositions taken from all the works of Rosmini were condemned without any specific theological censure in 1887 under Leo XIII (*Enchiridion symbolorum*, 3201–41). Their contents cover practically every point of Catholic theology, but supporters of Rosmini have always denied that they express his genuine thought. Their position has been officially accepted today by the Magisterium in its examination of the 19th century doctrinal decrees concerning Rosmini's works (see Congregation for the Doctrine of the Faith, *Note on the import of the doctrinal Decrees concerning the thought and works of the Priest Antonio Rosmini Serbati*, n. 6, Vatican, July 1, 2001).

Rosmini exercises a growing influence through the philosophy of Christian spiritualism, and through his ascetical writings. John Paul II numbered him among modern thinkers in whom a fruitful meeting between philosophical knowledge and the Word of God has been realized (see Encyclical Letter *Fides et Ratio*, n. 74). He is also acknowledged as a man of great sanctity of life whose beatification process is currently (2001) with the Congregation for the Causes of Saints.

See Also: ROSMINIANS; SPIRITUALISM.

Bibliography: A. MICHEL, *Dictionnaire de théologie catholique*, ed. A. VACANT et al., (Paris 1903–50; Tables générales 1951–) 13.2:2917–52. A. HILCKMAN, *Lexikon für Theologie und Kirche*, ed. J. HOFER and K. RAHNER (Freiburg 1957–65); suppl., *Das Zweite Vatikanishe Konsil: Dokumente und Kommentare*, ed. H. S. BRECHTER et al. (1966) 9:53–55; *Die Religion in Geschichte und Gegenwart* (3d ed. Tübingen 1957–65) 5:1188–89. G. B. PAGANI, *Vita di Antonio Rosmini*, ed. G. ROSSI, 2 v. (rev. ed. Rovereto 1959). *Rivista Rosminiana* (Domodossola Stresa 1906–2001).

Sources in Eng. *Principles of Ethics*, tr. D. CLEARY, T. WATSON, C/W, (Leominster 1988); *Anthropology in Aid of Moral Science*, tr. C/W (Durham 1991); *The Philosophy of Right*, tr. C/W, 6 v. (Durham 1993); *The Philosophy of Politics*, tr. C/W, 2 v. (Durham 1994); *Conscience*, tr. C/W (Durham 1989); *Psychology*, tr. C/W, 4 v. (Durham 1999); *A New Essay concerning the Origin of Ideas*, 3 v, tr. R. MURPHY, D. CLEARY, T. WATSON (Durham 2001); *Maxims of Christian Perfection*, tr. W. A. JOHNSON (4th ed. London 1889; repr. 1963); *Theodicy*, tr. F. SIGNINI, 3 v. (London 1912); *The Five Wounds of the Church*, tr. D. CLEARY (Leominster 1987); *Constitutions of the Society of Charity*, tr. D. CLEARY (Durham 1992); *Counsels to Religious Superiors*, ed. and tr. C. LEETHAM (Westminster, Md. 1961); *Ascetical Letters* tr. J. MORRIS, 6 v. (Loughborough 1993–2000); *A Society of Love*, tr. D. CLEARY (Durham 2000). Studies: C. LEETHAM, *Rosmini, Priest and Philosopher* (New York 1982), complete chronological bibliog. of Rosmini's works. D. CLEARY, *The Principles of Rosmini's Moral Philosophy* (London 1961); *Antonio Rosmini: Introduction to His Life and Teaching* (Durham 1992).

[D. CLEARY]

ROSMINIANS

The Institute of Charity (IC, Official Catholic Directory #0300), as the Rosminians are officially entitled, was founded in 1828 at Calvario in Piedmont, Italy, by Rev. Antonio ROSMINI-SERBATI, at the instigation of St. Maddalena CANOSSA. The ascetic principles expressed in Rosmini's *Maxims of Christian Perfection* (1830) determined the nature of his religious institute, which was approved as a congregation of exempt religious by Gregory XVI in 1839.

In 1832 the congregation, which had spread in northern Italy, became associated with the Sisters of Providence, founded by one of Rosmini's disciples and given papal approval in 1946. In 1835 Rosmini sent three priests to England, where they were later joined by other recruits. Notable among them was Luigi Gentili, a zealous and ascetic Roman, who exercised an important influence on the Catholic community in England from 1842 to 1848. He spent three years evangelizing the newly developed industrial towns of England, preaching missions of two to three weeks duration. In 1848 he went to preach in Dublin, Ireland, where he died of cholera. Among the innovations brought to England and Ireland by the Rosminians were the introduction of the clerical (or Roman) collar, the wearing of the cassock and religious habit in public, the preaching of missions, the practice of the Forty Hours, May devotions, the use of the scapular, the celebration of novenas, public processions, and the blessing of throats on the feast of St. Blaise (February 3).

Members of the Institute of Charity profess the three religious vows. They carry out such ministries by the need of their neighbor or the invitation of the pope or bishops. No work is preferred and none refused; work once undertaken may not be abandoned for a more attractive apostolate. The institute has no distinctive habit, only the cassock.

The Rosminians first arrived in the U.S. in 1877. In the U.S., the congregation is principally involved in parish ministries. The U.S. headquarters is in Peoria, IL. The generalate is in Rome.

Bibliography: C. J. EMERY, *The Rosimians* (London 1960). C. R. LEETHAM, *Rosmini* (Baltimore 1958).

[C. R. LEETHAM/EDS.]

ROSS, JOHN ELLIOT

Priest, sociologist; b. March 14, 1884; d. Sept. 18, 1946, New York. Ross's family could trace its roots back through the colonial period to William the Conqueror. Among this lineage was George Ross who had signed the Declaration of Independence, as well as George's daughter-in-law, Betsy Ross. Ross grew up in Maryland, and after graduating from Loyola College in Baltimore he worked in the District of Columbia's Engineering Department while pursuing a master's degree at George Washington University. In September 1909, he joined the Paulist community at the Catholic University of America, where he began doctoral work in sociology under Monsignor William Kerby. He produced a dissertation that was later published as *Consumers and Wage Earners: The Ethics of Buying Cheap*. Two weeks prior to his graduation from CUA, on May 24, 1912, he was ordained to the priesthood at St. Paul the Apostle Church in New York.

After a brief period of studying in Rome, Ross was sent to a parish in Chicago, where he stayed for a year. In 1915, he was assigned to the University of Texas at Austin as chaplain to Catholic students. While in Austin, Ross wrote four books and was a mentor to the social historian Carlos Castañeda. During this period he began research into the effects on Catholics attending nonsectarian colleges for the United States bishops. The studies were never published. In 1923, when the Paulist general, Thomas Burke, sought to reassign Ross, the University administration asked the governor of Texas to intervene on Ross' behalf. In 1924, Ross was back in Washington teaching moral theology at the newly completed Saint Paul's College. The following year, he returned to chaplaincy work, this time in Columbia University's Newman House.

In 1929 Ross was given a long-awaited opportunity to join a non-sectarian faculty as a full professor. The University of Iowa had founded a School of Religious Studies, supported by private money, and sought out

Ross for its faculty. A conflict arose when his superiors denied him permission to move to an institution that had no contact with the Paulist Fathers and very few Catholics. With the prospect of becoming the first Catholic clergyman in the history of the United States to teach in a secular department of religion, he resigned from the Paulist congregation. The resignation was canonically mishandled and although eventually he would be reinstated, between 1929 and 1930 he was in ecclesiastical no-man's land. He left Iowa the following year, only to return to chaplaincy, this time at the University of Virginia. He would remain in Charlottesville from 1932 to 1943. While a resident there he suffered the first two of three strokes. His incapacitation forced him to return to the Paulist community at St. Paul's Church in New York where he died on Sept. 18, 1946, at the age of 62.

Ross was one of the leading Catholics attached to the former National Conference for Christians and Jews. Between 1929 and 1943, he was the principal Catholic consultant for NCCJ's projects, often detailing these in articles for *Commonweal* magazine. The most important project was a seven week, nation-wide "pilgrimage" to promote tolerance among Catholics, Protestants, and Jews—an effort that put Ross on the edges of ecclesiastical policy prohibiting Catholic involvement in "intercredal cooperation." The pilgrimage, which took place in 1933, consisted of a priest (Ross), a minister (Everett Clinchy, director of the NCCJ), and a rabbi (Morris Lazaron of Baltimore). The archdioceses of Cincinnati and Chicago refused to allow Catholic participation in this event, although Ross was permitted in every other see the trio visited. The group reached thousands, either through direct contact or radio broadcast, establishing local networks for improved relations between the monotheistic faiths.

Bibliography: Ross' papers are housed in the Paulist Fathers Archive, St. Paul's College, Washington, D. C. J. LYNCH, "A Conflict of Values, A Confusion of Laws," *The Jurist* 56 (1996) 182–199. P. ROBICHAUD, "J. Elliot Ross," *Paulist History*, v. 1:4 (1991) 4–15.

[P. J. HAYES]

ROSSELLO, MARIA GIUSEPPA, ST.

Foundress of the DAUGHTERS OF OUR LADY OF MERCY; b. Albissola Marina, Italy, May 27, 1811; d. Savana, Italy, Dec. 7, 1880. The daughter of Bartolomeo and Maria (Dedone) Rossello, she was baptized Benedetta. She became a Franciscan tertiary in 1827 and spent the next decade doing charitable works among the Savoyards. Then she, Pauline Barla, and the sisters Angela and Domenica Pescio offered themselves to the bishop of Savoy, Agostino de Mari, and thereby initiated a religious congregation to care for the abandoned girls of his diocese (Aug. 10, 1837). She received her habit (Oct. 22, 1837), and two years later pronounced her vows, taking the name in religion, Maria Giuseppa. Elected superior-general (1840), she directed her congregation for 40 years. During these decades the congregation grew with such rapidity that it was granted juridical status by the Italian government. Under Bp. Alessandro Riccardi, the successor of De Mari, the congregation was committed to the education of girls, especially orphans, and to the care of the sick. Upon the death of the foundress, the Daughters were established in nearly 70 houses throughout Italy and Latin America. She was beatified Nov. 6, 1938. At the time of her canonization, June 12, 1949, the congregation numbered some 3,000 members in 263 houses.

Feast: Dec. 7.

Bibliography: A. O. RICCARDI, *Lettere di un Vescovo* (Genoa 1971). G. GUZZO, *Santa M. G. Rossello* (Rome 1949). K. BURTON, *Wheat for This Planting* (Milwaukee 1960).

[V. A. LAPOMARDA]

ROSSETTI, CARLO

Cardinal and papal agent at the English court; b. Ferrara, 1614; d. Faenza, Nov. 23, 1681. This brilliant young noble of Ferrara attracted the notice of Cardinal Francesco Barberini (secretary of state to Urban VIII), who in 1639 sent him to succeed George CON as papal agent to Henrietta Maria, Queen of England. Rossetti, well received at Court, tried to ease the lot of English papists; and overoptimistic about the reunion with Rome, a topic then much discussed, he urged conversion on King Charles I. He also sought to further the Queen's desire for an English cardinal, and tried to negotiate a loan to aid the King against the Parliamentarians. All this drew on him the hostility of the Puritans, and in July 1641, Rossetti left for Flanders, where in September he was named titular archbishop of Tarsus and nuncio extraordinary to the Peace Conference at Cologne. In 1643 he was named bishop of Faenza and later cardinal deacon. His appointment as legate *a latere* to the Congresses of Münster and Osnabrück never took effect. Rossetti then devoted himself with great zeal to his diocese of Faenza, visiting, confirming, holding synods, opening hospitals, and caring for the poor. Promoted cardinal priest and then cardinal bishop, Rossetti was in 1680 chosen bishop of Porto by Innocent XI, but he died the following year. He is buried in Faenza cathedral. He wrote an account of his mission to England and commentaries on the *Summa* of Aquinas.

Bibliography: G. ALBION, *Charles I and the Court of Rome* (London 1935) 316–376. M. J. HAVRAN, *The Catholics in Caroline England* (Stanford 1962). G. MORONI, *Dizionario de erudizone storico-ecclesiastica,* 103 v. in 53 (Venice 1840–61); index, 6 v. (1878–79) 59:175–176.

[G. ALBION]

ROSSI, GIOVANNI BATTISTA DE

Founder of Christian archeology; b. Rome, Feb. 22, 1822; d. Castelgondolfo, Sept. 20, 1894. De Rossi studied law at the Collegio Romano (1838–40) and jurisprudence at the Sapienza (1840–44). After being introduced to the study of the catacombs by the Jesuit archeologist G. Marchi in 1841, he was appointed a scriptor in the Vatican Library. He followed A. Bosio in applying modern scientific method to his archeological explorations, utilizing, in particular, evidence available in the ancient Christian inscriptions, patristic writings, calendars, martyrologies, and the itineraries of the seventh and eighth centuries to identify his discoveries.

In the catacombs of St. Callistus he identified the tomb of Pope CORNELIUS (1852) and the crypt containing the remains of the third–century popes (1854), as well as the graves of St. CECILIA (1854) and St. Eusebius (1856). By a further systematic search of the debris and the already identified artifacts in the catacombs of Praetextatus (1863), Domitilla (1864), the basilica of Nereus and Achilleus (1873), the crypt of HIPPOLYTUS (1882) and FELICITAS (1883), and the Hypogeum or vault of Acilius, he eventually was able to describe the typography of the ancient Christian cemeteries of Rome. In this work he was assisted by geological information supplied by his brother, M. S. de Rossi (d. 1898), and was aided by the benevolence of Pope Pius IX. In his basic publication, *Roma sotterranea cristiana* (3 v. Rome 1864–77), De Rossi described the catacombs of St. Callistus and of St. Generosa and laid the foundations for the scientific study of Christian archeology. With his collaborators he founded and edited the *Bullettino di archeologia cristiana* (Rome 1864–), and took a special interest in classical and Christian EPIGRAPHY. He collaborated in the CIL (*Corpus Inscriptionum Latinarum*) and edited the first two volumes of the *Inscriptiones christianae urbis Romae septimo saeculo antiquiores* (Rome 1861–88). His contributions to learned journals on particular subjects of Christian archeology and epigraphy were enormous; they fill 32 volumes of a collection in the Vatican Library. He also published *Mosaici . . . delle chiese di Roma anteriori dal secolo XV* (25 fasc. 1872–96) and *Piante iconografiche e prospettiche di Roma ant. al sec. XVI* (Rome 1879). With L. Duchesne he edited the *MARTYROLOGY OF ST. JEROME* (*Acta Sanctorum* Nov. 2:1; 1894).

St. John Baptist Rossi.

Bibliography: P. M. BAUMGARTEN, *Giovanni Battista de Rossi* (Cologne 1892). G. GATTI, in *Albo dei sottoscrittori . . . del Comm. G. B. de Rossi* (Rome 1892). O. MARUCCHI, *Giovanni Battista de Rossi* (Rome 1903). E. KIRSCHBAUM, *Gregorianum* 21 (1940) 564–606. F. L. CROSS, *The Oxford Dictionary of the Christian Church* 390–391. U. M. FASOLA, *Lexikon für Theologie und Kirche* 2 9:58–59. H. LECLERCQ, *Dictionnaire d'archéologie chrétienne et de liturgie* 15.1:18–100.

[F. X. MURPHY]

ROSSI, JOHN BAPTIST, ST.

Patron of diocesan clergy; b. Voltaggio (Genoa), February 22, 1698; d. Rome, May 23, 1764. John Baptist came of an impoverished family and was educated with the assistance of benefactors; his cousin brought him to Rome to continue his education at the Jesuit college. Although stricken with epilepsy, probably from too rigorous mortification while a student of philosophy and theology with the Dominicans, he was ordained by special dispensation on March 8, 1721. He did not exercise the powers of confessor, however, until 1738, but from then until his death he was regarded as an outstanding and popular priest. Concern for both the temporal and spiritual welfare of the poorer classes marked his life. He preached to the people in marketplaces, hospitals, prisons, military barracks—any place where the poor and needy would congregate. By 1731 he had established a refuge for abandoned children and later a hospice for the homeless. After succeeding to the canonry of his cousin at St. Mary in Cosmedin in 1737, he spent the bulk of his benefices supporting his charities. On his death, he was buried at the altar of the Blessed Virgin in the church of Trinità de' Pellegrini. By 1781 his cause had been introduced. Pius IX beatified him in 1860 and LEO XIII raised him to the ranks of the saints on December 8, 1881. In 1965 his relics were translated to his new titular church in Rome.

Feast: May 23.

Bibliography: F. BAUMANN, *Lexikon für Theologie und Kirche,* ed. J. HOFER and K. RAHNER, 10 v. (2d, new ed. Freiburg 1957–65) 9:58. A. BUTLER, *The Lives of the Saints,* ed. H. THURSTON and D. ATTWATER, 4 v. (New York 1956) 2:379–381.

[P. D. SMITH]

ROSSI, LUIGI

Baroque composer of chamber cantatas, operas, and church music; b. Torremaggiore (Foggia), 1598; d. Rome, Feb. 19, 1653. Rossi first studied in Naples and then became attached to the household of Cardinal Marc'Antonio Borghese in Rome (*c.* 1620), organist at the church of San Luigi de' Francesi in 1633, and *virtuoso da camera* in the service of Cardinal Antonio Barberini in 1641. His first opera, *Il palazzo incantato,* was performed at the Barberini theater in 1642. After URBAN VIII (Maffeo Barberini) died, the remaining members of his family fled to France (*see* BARBERINI). From Paris they sent for Italian musicians, a group of whom (including Rossi) arrived there in 1646. Under the patronage of Cardinal MAZARIN, Rossi's second and last opera, *Orfeo,* received a lavish production in Paris. His church music includes the oratorios *Santa Caterina alla rota, Oratorio per la Settimana Santa,* and *Giuseppe figlio di Giacobbe.* Rossi's lyrical genius is most apparent in his more than 350 chamber cantatas. His skillful handling of recitatives and arias in these minature scene complexes influenced opera and church composers in his and in succeeding generations.

Bibliography: L. ROSSI, modern reprints in F. A. GEVAERT, ed., *Les Gloires de l'Italie,* 2 v. (Paris 1906). H. RIEMANN, ed. *Kantatenfrühling,* 2 v. (Leipzig 1912). F. VATIELLI, comp., *Antiche cantate d'amore* (Bologna 1916). Literature. A. GHISLANZONI, *Luigi Rossi* (Milan 1954). A. WOTQUENNE, *Étude bibliographique sur le compositeur napolitain Luigi Rossi* (Brussels 1909). W. C. HOLMES, *Die Musik in Geschichte und Gegenwart,* ed. F. BLUME (Kassel-Basel 1949–) 11:938–942. E. CALUORI, "The Cantatas of Luigi Rossi" (Ph.D. diss. Brandeis University, 1972); "Luigi Rossi" in *The New Grove Dictionary of Music and Musicians, vol. 16,* ed. S. SADIE (New York 1980) 217–221; *The Cantatas of Luigi Rossi: Analysis and Thematic Index* 2 vols. (Ann Arbor 1981). D. M. RANDEL, ed., *The Harvard Biographical Dictionary of Music* (Cambridge 1996) 764. P. RICCIARDELLI, *Repertorio bibliografico–storico delle composizioni del musicista Luigi Rossi* 2 vols. (Torremaggiore 1988). N. SLONIMSKY, ed. *Baker's Biographical Dictionary of Musicians, Eighth Edition* (New York 1992) 1544.

[W. C. HOLMES]

ROSSI, PELLEGRINO

Papal minister; b. Carrara, Italy, July 13, 1787; d. Rome, Nov. 15, 1848. Rossi became a professor of law in Naples, but was forced to flee the city after the downfall of Murat (1815). He then taught law at Geneva, and at the Collège de France, Paris, from 1833. In France Rossi became a close friend of GUIZOT, was appointed a member of the Chamber of Peers (1839), and ambassador to Rome (1846). His intellectual and personal qualities so impressed PIUS IX (1846–78) that he retained Rossi as an adviser after the 1848 revolution in France cost the ambassador his post. The pope named him chief minister (September 1848), hoping thereby to placate liberal bourgeois elements. The STATES OF THE CHURCH were facing pressing political, economic, and military problems. To avoid inflation Rossi had to arrange loans throughout Europe. He initiated reforms in finance and the civil service, and proposed building railroad and telegraph networks. His belief was that improved administration was more urgent than liberalization and democratization of government. He proved unable to satisfy any party, however, and was called a reactionary by some, a dictator by others. The clergy suspected him for his doctrinaire liberalism, his Protestant wife, and his intention to abolish some of their privileges. Vested interests disliked his economic solutions. Liberal nationalists disapproved of his favor shown to the plans of NEO-GUELFISM and a federated Italy under the presidency of the pope, and his opposition to papal involvement in war. Rossi was stabbed to death by a member of the revolutionary party as he prepared to present his reform program at the opening of the Chamber. The brutal crime incited an attack on the Quirinal Palace next day, and led to Pius IX's flight to Gaeta and subsequent change of attitude toward political reforms.

Bibliography: R. GIOVAGNOLI, *Rossi e la rivoluzione romana,* 3 v. (Rome 1898–1911). G. BRIGANTE COLONNA, *L'uccisione di P. Rossi* (Milan 1938). R. DE CESARE, *The Last Days of Papal Rome,* tr. H. ZIMMERN (London 1909). E. E. Y. HALES, *Pio Nono* (New York 1954). R. AUBERT, *Le Pontificat de Pie IX (Histoire de l'église depuis les origines jusqu'à nos jours* 21; 2d ed. 1964). C. A. BIGGINI, *Enciclopedia Italiana di scienzi, littere ed arti* 30:144–145.

[R. F. HARNEY]

ROSSINI, GIOACCHINO

Composer of operas and a few sacred works; b. Pesaro, Italy, Feb. 29, 1792 (christened Gioacchino Antonio); d. Passy (Paris), Nov. 13, 1868. His parents were theater musicians; at 13 he was a professional singer, horn player, and accompanist and at 15, was studying theory with Padre Mattei in Bologna. His first successful opera, *Tancredi* (1813), was followed by 29 more, of which the best known are *Otello* and *The Barber of Seville* (1816), *Semiramide* (1823), and *William Tell* (1829). With this climactic work he ceased opera composition, living thereafter in semiretirement, chiefly in Paris. His major religious works are the *Stabat Mater* (1832, revised and completed 1847), and the lengthy *Petite Messe Solennelle* (1863), neither of which is suitable for liturgical use. He reluctantly permitted the *Stabat Mater* to be published, and forbade public performance of the Mass during his lifetime. In a touching prayer on the final page of the Mass he asked, ''Is it sacred music [*musique sacrée*] or wretched music [*sacrée musique*] that I have just made?'' and admitted, ''I was born for *opera buffa*.'' Operatic influences permeate both works, but the Mass contains several impressive passages. His few motets (mostly early) generally favor solo singing.

Bibliography: G. RADICIOTTI, *Giaocchino Rossini*, 3 v. (Tivoli 1927–29). F. TOYE, *Rossini* (new ed. London 1955). *Baker's Biographical Dictionary of Musicians*, ed. N. SLONIMSKY (5th, rev. ed. New York 1958) 1373–76. M. DE STENDHAL, *Life of Rossini*, tr. R. N. COE (New York 1957). P. B. BRAUNER, ''The *Opera Omnia* of Gioacchino Rossini,'' *Journal of the Conductors' Guild* 14 (1993), 2–7. J. F. CROWLEY, ''The Pivotal Role of Rossini's *Otello* in the Evolution of Italian Dramatic Opera,'' *The Opera Journal* 26/3 (1993), 19–33. M. GRONDONA, *La perfetta illusione: 'Ermione' e l'opera seria rossiniana* (Lucca 1996). C. HENZEL, '''Du, Tell, du sollst der Führer sein . . .': Die Rossini-Bearbeitung von Julius Kapp und Robert Heger (1934),'' *Die Musikforschung* 52 (1999), 190–203. J. JOHNSON, ''Rossini in Bologna and Paris during the Early 1830s: New Letters,'' *Revue de Musicologie* 79 (1993), 63–81. W. KIRSCH, ''Gioacchino Rossinis *Stabat Mater*: Versuch einer exegese,'' *Kirchenmusikalisches Jahrbuch* 73 (1989), 71–96. A. L. BELLI, ''Hegel e Rossini. *Il cantar che nell' anima si sente*,'' *Die Belge de Musicologie* 49 (1995), 211–230. V. PAGÁN, ''Un italiano en Madrid: Gioacchino Rossini (estudio de iconografía),'' *Revista de Musicología* 18 (1995), 229–245. G. RUFFIN, ''Drammaturgia come auto-confutazione teatrale: aspetti metalinguistici alle origini della comicità nelle opere comiche di Rossini,'' *Recercare* 4 (1992), 125–163. P. SCHMID and D. WHITE, ''The Mysterious Case of *Ermione*,'' *The Opera Quarterly* 12/3 (1996), 7–15.

[R. M. LONGYEAR]

ROSWITHA OF GANDERSHEIM

German poet, canoness of the monastery of Gandersheim; b. *c.* 935; d. after 1000. Her education was fostered by Rikkardis and Gerberga, the niece of OTTO I;

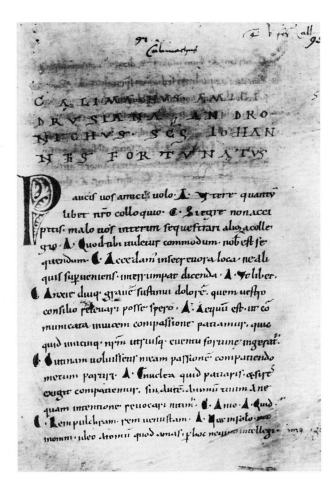

Manuscript page from ''Callimachus,'' 10th-century drama, by Roswitha of Gandersheim, marginal notes in handwriting of Conrad Celtis.

both were later abbesses at Gandersheim. The Latin works of Roswitha (Hrotsvitha, Hrosvitha), edited by Conrad Celtes in 1501, consisted of metrical legends, dramas, and historical problems and epics. Her works reveal something of her personality—she wrote in utter secrecy until she was finished, not confiding in anyone—and are evidence of an education surprisingly good in the 10th century. She was a product of her times, and yet had an unusual acquaintance with the writings of antiquity.

Roswitha's earliest works are eight legends in Leonine hexameters or elegiac distichs, dealing with the pagan-Christian conflict so recurrent in the monastic literature of the Middle Ages. In the *Theophilus* a compact with the devil forms the leading idea and is one of the earliest expressions of this now familiar Faustian theme. Her historic poems provide valuable source material for early German history.

The largest portion of Roswitha's works includes her six dramas or comedies. These are *Gallicanus, Dulcitius,*

Callimachus, Abraham, Paphnutius, and *Sapientia.* The plots of these plays are taken from ecclesiastical legends. The literary form of Roswitha's plays belongs to the ancient rather than the modern drama. As a self-acknowledged pupil of Terence she belongs to the classical world. She was an imitator, not an originator. In two important aspects, however, Roswitha did depart from classical precedent. She entirely disregarded the law of unities exemplified in Terence, and she admitted into her dramas a combination of the tragic and comic not to be found in the works of her prototype.

The works of Roswitha, primarily didactic and moralistic in tone, show little understanding of dramatic structure. For all the promise of further tuition from classical antiquity they displayed, her writings were apparently neglected in the Middle Ages, and were without influence before the Renaissance. In recent times her works have been translated and modern adaptations of her plays have received limited performance.

Bibliography: *Hrotsvithae opera,* ed. P. DE WINTERFELD, *Monumenta Germanica Scriptores rerum Germanicarum* (1902) v.59. *The Non-dramatic Works of Hrosvitha,* ed. and tr. M. G. WIEGAND (St. Louis 1936); *Hrosvithae Liber tertius,* ed. and tr. M. B. BERGMAN (Covington, Ky. 1943). F. J. E. RABY, *A History of Secular Latin Poetry in the Middle Ages* 1:277–278. *Geschichte der lateinischen Literatur des Mittelalters* 1:619–632. F. L. CROSS, *Oxford Dictionary of the Christian Church* 660–661.

[C. E. SHEEDY]

ROTH, HEINRICH

Missionary in India, Sanskrit scholar; b. Augsburg (Bavaria), Dec. 18, 1620; d. Agra, India, June 20, 1668. He had illustrious parents. He entered the Jesuits in 1639, was assigned to the Ethiopian mission, and in 1651 by the land route arrived in Goa; he was active in the nearby peninsula of Salsette. Then he was sent on an embassy to one of the native princes, and finally, in 1653, reached the Empire of the Great Mogul during the reign of Shâh Jahân (d. 1666). Roth was appointed rector of the Jesuit residence in Agra in 1659. He learned Urdu, Persian, and Sanskrit, and was the first European to compile a Sanskrit grammar. Roth was a friend of the explorer Francis Bernier, who admired his knowledge of Indian philosophy and religion. Roth spent 1664 in Rome and Germany but soon returned to India, where he died.

Bibliography: H. HOSTEN, *Jesuit Missionaries in Northern India, 1580–1803* (Calcutta 1906). E. MACLAGAN, *The Jesuits and the Great Mogul* (London 1932). B. ZIMMEL, *Die erste abendländische Sanskrit-Grammatik des P. H. Roth* (Vienna 1957). A. CAMPS, "Father Heinrich Roth, SJ, 1620–1668, and the History of His Sanskrit Manuscripts," in *Studies in Asian Mission History, 1956–1998* (Leiden 2000) 90–102. A. CAMPS and J. C. MULLER, *The Sanskrit Grammar and Manuscripts of Father Heinrich Roth, SJ (1620–1668)* (Leiden 1988).

[J. WICKI]

ROUGEMONT, ABBEY OF

Called also S. Mariade Rubeo Monte, a former convent of Benedictine sisters, in the Diocese of Dijon and the Department of Cote d'Or, France. It was founded by at least the 11th century for it is first mentioned in 1105 in a bull of PASCAL IV as being among the convents belonging to the Diocese of Langres. It was subject to the Benedictine abbot of Moutier-Saint-Jean and flourished during the 13th century when the abbey church was built. Abbess Catherine d'Arcy dissipated its wealth and secured transfer to the AUGUSTINIANS in the 15th century, occasioning a lawsuit and resulting in an order from Pope CALLISTUS III delegating the bishop of Chalon to reestablish the convent under the BENEDICTINE RULE. This was followed by a decline in spirituality in the 16th century when the abbesses were nominated by the Crown. Reform began again under Bishop Zamet despite resistance of the Abbess Lucrèce de Rochefort-Luçay (1621–66). To hasten reform, the crown in 1667 joined the convent to the priory of Saint-Julien-sur-Deheune, forming a single community renamed the Abbaye de Notre Dame et de S. Julien de Rougemont. The community was transferred to Dijon in 1673, and there the Abbess Mme. de Rouville built a new convent, St. Julien de Rougemont, in 1682.

Bibliography: J. LAURENT and F. CLAUDON in Beaunier, *Abbayes et prieurés de l'ancienne France,* v.12.3 (Paris 1941). L. H. COTTINEAU, *Répertoire topobibliographique des abbayes et prieurés,* 2 v. (Mâcon 1935–39) 2:2551.

[G. E. GINGRAS]

ROUGEMONT, FRANÇOIS

Jesuit missionary to China; b. Maastricht, April 2, 1624; d. T'ai Ts'ang, Nov. 4 or 9, 1676. He entered the Society of Jesus at Malines on Sept. 28, 1641, taught humanities and rhetoric for six years in Belgium, and made his priestly studies at Louvain. He left for China in 1656 and traveled through much of India on foot, arriving in China in 1659. Except for the years 1665 to 1671, when he was imprisoned and then exiled to Canton, he labored continuously in the missions around Shanghai. Aided by devoted and frequently highly educated catechists, he established and ministered several missions in the canal districts. He composed a series of pastoral books in Chinese, including catechisms for neophytes, refutations of paganism, the essentials for entering into the Church, and songbooks. His principal work is *Historia Tartaro-Sinica nova* (1660–66), written during exile in Canton. It relates the last phase of the Manchu takeover in China and the persecution by the four regents up until the expulsion of the missionaries (1660–68). In 1667 Rougemont addressed a memorial to Father Paul Oliva, General of the Jesuits, in favor of an indigenous Chinese clergy who would be permitted to read the Breviary and say Mass in Chinese. He also collaborated with the Jesuit Prospero INTORCETTA and others in a biography of Confucius and a tractate on his doctrines.

Bibliography: L. PFISTER, *Notices biographiques et bibliographiques sur les Jésuites de l'ancienne mission de Chine 1552–1773,* 2 v. (Shanghai 1932–34) 1:333–338.

[J. H. CAMPANA]

ROULEAU, FELIX RAYMOND MARIE

Cardinal archbishop of Québec, Canada; b. L'Île-Verte, Québec, April 6, 1866; d. Québec, May 31, 1931. His baptismal name was Felix; he studied at the minor seminary of Rimouski, at the Dominican novitiate of Saint–Hyacinthe, and then at their monastery in Corsica, where he was ordained Aug. 31, 1892. He served the order as professor at the Dominican Scholastic College in Ottawa, Canada, and became a master of theology (1909) and provincial (1919). He was consecrated as the second bishop of Valleyfield, Québec, in May 1923; transferred to the Archdiocese of Québec in 1926; and made a cardinal in 1927. The cardinal, a mystic and a great theologian, presided at the founding of the Canadian Academy of St. Thomas Aquinas at Laval University. He died suddenly in his palace on his way to celebrate a pontifical mass in the cathedral.

Bibliography: J. B. A. ALLAIRE, *Dictionnaire biographique du clergé canadien-français,* v. 5 (Montréal 1928) 190–191. L. A. PAQUET, *Annuaire de l'Université Laval (1931–32)* 261–267, éloge.

[H. PROVOST]

ROUQUETTE, ADRIEN EMMANUEL

Missionary, author; b. New Orleans, La., Feb. 13, 1813; d. New Orleans, July 15, 1887. He spent his boyhood at New Orleans and at St. Tammany Parish among the Choctaw. He attended the Collège d'Orléans, New Orleans, and Transylvania University, Lexington, Ky. After receiving instruction from a French schoolmaster named Value, he left to attend the Collège Royal in Nantes, France. On his return to New Orleans he studied law, but his early association with the native peoples and his growing interest in religion led him to other goals. He wanted to become a genuine "American" poet, and also wished to minister spiritually to the Choctaws. On July 2, 1845, he was ordained, becoming the first native priest since Louisiana's cession to the U.S. Rouquette; with his superior's permission, established mission chapels along the bayous in the woodland of St. Tammany Parish. The native peoples named him Chahta-Ima (like a Choctaw) and he became a recognized authority on Choctaw lore and language. Rouquette's books, written principally in French, reflected his personal beliefs while revealing many facets of a developing America. His principal works were: *Les Savanes, poésies américaines* (1841), *Wild Flowers* (1848), *La Thébaide en Amérique ou Apologie de la vie solitaire et contemplative* (1852), *La Question Américaine* (1855), *Catherine Tegahkwitha, the Saint of Caughnawaga* (1873), and *La Nouvelle Atala* (1879).

[D. R. LE BRETON]

ROUSSEAU, JEAN JACQUES

French writer and philosopher; b. Geneva, Switzerland, June 28, 1712; d. Ermenonville, near Paris, July 2, 1778. His mother died nine days after his birth, and he received a haphazard education from his father, a watchmaker. He left Geneva and his work as an apprentice engraver (1728), and was given hospitality in Annecy, France, by Mme. de Warens, a convert to Catholicism, whose influence was decisive on his life and thought. The same year Rousseau adjured Protestantism after a short stay in the Hospice of the Holy Spirit in Turin.

During the winter of 1738, spent at Les Charmettes, near Chambéry, Rousseau read widely in the French creative writers and philosophers. In 1742 he set out for Paris, hoping to win fame with a new system of musical notation. He was rejected by the Academy of Sciences, but he was received into the circle of the philosophers Diderot, Friedrich Grimm, and D' Alembert; he wrote an opera, *Les Muses Galantes,* and several articles on music for the *Encyclopédie* (see ENCYCLOPEDISTS). Around 1744 he took an ignorant servant girl, Thérèse Levasseur, as his common-law wife. They had five children whom they abandoned at a foundling asylum.

Literary Debut. In 1749 Rousseau decided to compete in the prize essay contest proposed by the Academy of Dijon on the subject "Whether the Sciences and the Arts have contributed to improve or to corrupt public morality." Rousseau opted for corruption, and his paper won the prize. He was thus projected into the limelight and was already a personage in the world of letters when,

Jean Jacques Rousseau. (AP/Wide World Photos)

in 1754, he competed in another contest organized by the same academy on the subject ''The origin of inequality among men.'' Rousseau's essay did not win because his ideas were too bold. At that time he took the title ''Citizen of Geneva'' and returned to Protestantism, the religion of his country. In 1756 he accepted the hospitality of Mme. d'Epinay at L'Ermitage. There he met Mme. d'Houdetot, sister-in-law of Mme. d'Epinay, and conceived for her a passionate if hopeless love that was to be reflected in many pages of *La Nouvelle Héloïse.*

Increasing Activity. During this period of intense activity, Rousseau worked on *La Nouvelle Héloïse, Émile,* and *Du Contrat Social;* but troubles with Mme. d'Epinay, Diderot, and Grimm forced him to move to Montmorency. In 1762, when *Émile* was condemned on publication by the French parliament, Rousseau fled to avoid arrest. Geneva, where *Émile* had also been condemned, offered him no asylum, and he traveled throughout Switzerland until David HUME invited him to England. He arrived there in January 1776, but his suspicious nature soon led him to believe that Hume was plotting against him. He left London secretly on May 22, 1777, and lived for a time in Grenoble before returning to Paris. He died on the estate of M. de Girardin at Ermenonville and was buried on an island in a lake on the the property. On Oct. 11, 1794, leaders of the Revolution paid solemn homage to Rousseau by transferring his ashes to the Panthéon.

The Two Discourses. Though badly composed, frequently rhetorical, and of a dubious logic, the *Discours sur les sciences et les arts,* his prize-winning essay of 1749 (known as the *First Discourse*), was published in 1750 and was immensely successful. Its fame was kept alive in part by the many refutations it evoked. By historical and philosophical arguments, Rousseau attempted to demonstrate that whenever sciences and arts flourish, public morals decline. Virtue resides essentially in simplicity of life and can be found only when man lives close to nature.

This idea of the natural goodness of man is presented more clearly and with more cogency in the *Discours sur l'origine de l'inégalité parmi les hommes* (1755), known as the *Second Discourse.* Originally, and by their very nature, runs the thesis, all men are equal, as are animals, and inequality is the result of the establishment of organized society. The natural man was more robust, more agile; his senses were more acute; he had fewer, more easily satisfied needs and was therefore happy. But when such a man decided to appropriate a piece of land to cultivate, society began with all its consequent evils. Laws were created to protect private property, and magistrates were appointed to enforce the laws. Thus was born despotism and the division of classes between rich and poor.

Castigation of the Theater. In 1758 Rousseau composed the *Lettre à d'Alembert sur les Spectacles* as an answer to the article ''Genève,'' which had just appeared in the seventh volume of the *Encyclopédie.* Its author, D'Alembert, back from a visit to Voltaire at Ferney and to Geneva, expressed regrets that the Protestant city forbade all theatrical performances. Rousseau, greatly perturbed, assembled all the arguments implicit in his two *Discourses,* adding others advanced by opponents of the theater, notably BOSSUET, to prove that the theater, as the highest expression of social organization, is also a result and a source of social corruption. In order to succeed, it must flatter the public and excite its passions. If a theater were installed in Geneva, it would surely result in laziness, new taxes, a love of luxury, and a weakening of civic virtue.

Solutions of the Social Problems. The three preceding works present the negative aspects of Rousseau's thought in regard to society; *La Nouvelle Héloïse* (1761), *Émile* (1762), and *Du Contrat Social* (1762) offer solutions to the problem raised; namely, since man cannot return to the state of nature and has to live in society, how can he correct the vices of society and be restored to his pristine virtue?

La Nouvelle Héloïse. Appearing under the guise of letters written by two lovers, *La Nouvelle Héloïse* relates the story of a love, which, though naturally good, is thwarted by social conventions and prejudices; Saint-Preux, the tutor, and Julie d'Etanges, his pupil, cannot marry because Saint-Preux is not of noble birth. To obey her parents, Julie then accepts as her husband the much older M. de Wolmar, whom she respects but does not love. In her household of Clarens she is the ideal wife and mother, living in the simplicity that Rousseau preached. Many letters in this novel express also Rousseau's ideas on other topics—the theater, education, the opera, religion, social life, fidelity in marriage, virtue triumphant over passion.

This sentimental, subjective work, in which Saint-Preux is an obvious personification of Rousseau, is the first manifestation of romanticism in France. It popularized the concept of a fatal, irresistible love, and of the beauty of nature as the consoler of man's afflictions. These new and bold ideas, couched in a lyrical style; these magnificent descriptions of nature; these appeals to virtue joined to voluptuous raptures: all explain the tremendous success of *La Nouvelle Héloïse,* the wide interest the work created and the many imitations it inspired.

Émile. In *Émile,* a treatise on education written also in the form of a novel, Rousseau proposes a system whereby man can be rehabilitated even in the social status to which he is condemned. Since society is evil and man is good, the sole aim of a carefully chosen tutor will be to preserve his charge from any contact with society. The child will be an orphan so that the tutor may assume full authority as early as possible. He will then merely assist Émile in developing his natural qualities, strengthening his body, educating his senses. Following MONTAIGNE and LOCKE, Rousseau advocates a system that will form the child's judgment rather than his intellect and will not load his memory with useless knowledge. Even at the age of 12, when Émile's formal education begins, he has read no book and knows nothing by rote. He possesses only those notions than can be acquired by sense experience: geography, astronomy, chemistry, physics, and agriculture. Aware of the instability of French society in the second half of the 18th century, and recognizing that today's rich may be tomorrow's poor, Rousseau insists that Émile learn a trade.

Not until Émile reaches the age of 15, when he is able to choose his own religion, will this subject be brought before him by an exponent, the vicar from Savoy, selected by the tutor. This unfrocked priest, addressing Émile in a scene of striking natural beauty destined to impart to the boy the idea of God's goodness, presents to him a natural religion, based on sentiment rather than on

reason, and excluding all revealed dogmas. Its precepts are few: belief in God, whose essence remains unknowable; in His law, which is written in one's conscience; in an immortal soul; in eternal life that rewards virtue but does not admit eternal punishment. All religions, except the Catholic religion, are good. In the fifth book of *Émile,* Rousseau writes an abridged tract on feminine education, for Émile must have a wife endowed like himself with all natural virtues. Sophie's education will not form a learned woman but a good wife and mother.

Du Contrat Social. Finally, in this, probably his best known work (1762), which was originally part of a never-published extensive treatise, *Institutions Politiques,* Rousseau undertakes to explain and to resolve his apparent contradiction: Man is born free, yet is everywhere a slave. Rousseau postulates a contract, either tacit or explicit, whereby man has voluntarily surrendered his liberty for the good of the community. He agrees to submit to the rules laid down by the general will that now regulates his actions as a member of society. Rousseau examines the various types of government and declares his preference for the republican regime, thus producing the first formal declaration of the new dogma of the sovereignty of the people to replace the divine rights of the king. In matters of religion, although he repeats that they are all good, Rousseau favors a state religion as more suitable to the stability and order of the government. But he specifically excludes the Catholic religion under the pretext that its members obey a foreign prince, and he banishes from his state all atheists, who may even be condemned to death. Five of Rousseau's works, including *Émile, Du Contrat Social,* and *La Nouvelle Héloïse,* are on the Index.

The Confessions. These were begun in 1765 and are an indispensable document on Rousseau's life and even on his thought, but they must be followed with utmost caution. Rousseau, often victim of delusions about himself, poses as a lover of virtue and of humanity who is persecuted for his very attachment to virtue. He boasts of his absolute sincerity and of having revealed in his *Confessions* dishonorable secrets unknown to his contemporaries. Yet many of his statements and even more of his judgments have been found erroneous.

The *Confessions* must be supplemented, for the years after 1765, by the *Dialogues: Rousseau juge de Jean-Jacques,* the ravings of a mind troubled by persecution mania, and by the *Rêveries du promeneur solitaire.* The latter are the soliloquies of an old and sick man, finding satisfaction in his walks through the countryside around Paris, reminiscing about his youth, his loves, at times almost delirious and on the verge of insanity, at other times seemingly resigned and at peace with the world. In the fifth *Rêverie* the word "romantic" is used for the first time in French literature, in a description of the shores of the Lake of Bienne in Switzerland, where Rousseau had spent some peaceful weeks in the difficult year of 1768.

His Influence. The lively and often bitter controversies Rousseau stirred up during his lifetime have not completely abated. He still has his fervent admirers and resolute opponents. Some of the latter are prone to make him responsible for most of the evils of the 19th and 20th centuries because he encouraged subjectivism, sentimentality, and sensualism, and he raised the individual above society and made him the sole judge of his actions. It cannot be denied that Rousseau's impact on literature and philosophy has been deep and lasting, notably in education, and in the fields of social and political ideas; but for the ideal of reason that had governed the classical age he substituted the reign of the heart and the autonomy of passion.

Bibliography: I. BABBITT, *Rousseau and Romanticism* (Boston 1919). J. MARITAIN, *Three Reformers: Luther, Descartes, Rousseau* (New York 1942). P. M. MASSON, *La Religion de Jean Jacques Rousseau* (Paris 1916). D. MORNET, *Rousseau: L'Homme et l'oeuvre* (Paris 1950). L. J. PROAL, *La Psychologie de Jean Jacques Rousseau* (Paris 1930). C. E. VAUGHAN, *Studies in the History of Political Philosophy before and after Rousseau*, ed. A. G. LITTLE, 2 v. (New York 1925). F. VIAL, *La Doctrine d'education de J. J. Rousseau* (Paris 1920).

[F. VIAL]

ROUSSEAU, SCUBILION, BL.

Baptized Jean-Bernard, catechist to slaves, Lasallian brother; b. Mar. 21, 1797, Anny-Côte, Burgundy, France; d. Apr. 13, 1867, Sainte-Marie, Isle de Réunion in the Indian Ocean.

Eldest of the four children of Bernard Rousseau, a stone cutter, and his wife Reine Pelletier, Jean-Bernard was born during the height of the French Revolution. He received his early education from his parents, his pastor, Father Petitier, and later a tutor. When the parish school reopened (1819) following the revolution, Jean-Bernard began teaching. His success in the field, combined with his sense of religious vocation, led him to the Brothers of the Christian Schools, who had just opened a school nearby. He entered their novitiate at Paris in 1822, where he became Brother Scubilion.

After teaching (1823–33) at Alençon, Poitiers, and Chinon, he was assigned (1833) with two other brothers to Bourbon (now Réunion). Here he initiated evening classes to teach slaves Christian doctrine and morality in preparation for receiving the sacraments. Following their emancipation (1848), he helped them to adapt to new freedom and responsibilities.

Brother Scubilion cared for the marginalized until his death 34 years after his arrival on the island. A constant stream of pilgrims visit his tomb on the island, where he was immediately venerated. He was beatified on Réunion by Pope John Paul II, May 2, 1989.

Feast: Sept. 27 (Lasallian Brothers); Dec. 20 (La Réunion, national holiday commemorating the abolition of slavery).

Bibliography: FRÈRE CONCORDE MARIE, *Le frère Scubilion* (St. Denis 1975). A. FERMET, *Jean-Bernard Rousseau, frère Scubilion* (Paris 1985). L. SALM, *Brother Scubilion Rousseau, FSC: Apostle of Freedom and Reconciliation* (Romeoville, Ill. 1986).

[K. I. RABENSTEIN]

ROUSSELOT, PIERRE

French philosopher, theologian, and apologist; b. Nantes, Dec. 29, 1878; d. in battle at Éparges, April 25, 1915. Rousselot entered the Jesuits in October 1895 and made his novitiate at Canterbury, England. In 1899 he returned to Nantes and completed the requirements for military service (1899–1900); he returned to Jersey for his scholasticate (1900–05) and was ordained in 1908. He received the doctorate from the Sorbonne, and from 1909 to 1914 he taught dogmatic theology at the Institut Catholique de Paris with an interruption of one year (1912–13), when he taught at Canterbury. On Aug. 2, 1914, he was recalled to military service.

Despite the brevity of his life, Rousselot exercised a profound influence on the revival of THOMISM and on the interpretation of the doctrine of St. THOMAS AQUINAS. His two doctoral theses gained for him an international reputation as an original commentator and expositor of Thomism. In his first and most important work, *L'Intellectualisme de saint Thomas* (Paris 1908), he established the objective validity of discursive knowledge on the intuitive apprehension of being, to which the human intellect is directed by its own nature. In his second thesis, *Pour l'Histoire du problème de l'amour au moyen âge* [*Beiträge zur Geschichte der Philosophie und Theologie des Mittelalters* 6.6 (1908)], he concerned himself with the relationship between love of self and love of God. He explored the natural love of man for God and the effects it may have suffered from original sin. He preferred the physical or the Greco-Thomistic conception of love, which reconciles the love of God and the love of self, to the ecstatic conception of love, which neglects man's natural inclinations and precludes the reciprocal causality of nature and grace. His position was predicated upon the Thomistic theory of PARTICIPATION, and it affirmed the hierarchical continuity between the perfections of God and those of creatures. As an apologist, Rousselot, in numerous scattered articles, scrutinized the traditional teaching of the act of faith and the judgments of credibility.

See Also: SCHOLASTICISM.

Bibliography: É. MARTY, *Le Témoignage de P. Rousselot* (Paris 1941). J. LEBRETON, *Dictionnaire de théologie catholique* 14: 134–138. M. COLPO, *Enciclopedia filosofica* 4: 236. *Encyclopedia universal ilustrada Europeo-Americana* 52:540. G. VAN RIET, *L'Épistémologie thomiste* (Louvain 1946) 301–313. J. DE WOLF, *La Justification de la foi chez St. Thomas d'Aquinas et P. Rousselot* (Paris 1946).

[F. J. ROENSCH]

ROVENIUS, PHILIPPUS

Archbishop of Philippi *in partibus,* second vicar apostolic of the Dutch mission; b. Deventer, Jan. 1, 1574; d. Utrecht, Oct. 10, 1651. After studies at Louvain, he was ordained (1599), became president of the Dutch seminary at Cologne (1602), and vicar-general of Deventer diocese (1606). On Oct. 11, 1614, Paul V appointed him to succeed Sasbout Vosmeer as vicar apostolic of the Dutch mission. Rovenius was nominated archbishop of Philippi on Aug. 17, 1620. His rule as vicar apostolic, important for the organization of the mission, brought him into conflict with the Jesuits and other regulars. He stimulated interest in the cult of national saints, such as Willibrord and Boniface, and published a catechism, a prayer book (*Het gulden wierookvat*), and books on the liturgy. Though friendly with Cornelius Jansenius, he himself was not a Jansenist. Because of the Spanish-Dutch war, Rovenius was condemned by a civil court on May 11, 1646, and banished. His major writings include the *Tractatus de Missionibus* (1626), *Institutionum christianae pietatis libri 4* (1635), and *Reipublicae christianae libri 2* (1648). The *Tractatus* establishes him as an eminent missiologist.

Bibliography: R. R. POST, ed., *Romeinsche bronnen* (The Hague 1941). L. J. ROGIER, *Geschiedenis van het katholicisme in Noord-Nederland,* 3 v. (Amsterdam 1945–47) 2:66–164.

[P. POLMAN]

ROWSHAM, STEPHEN, BL.

Priest, martyr; b. *c.* 1555 in Oxfordshire, England; hanged, drawn, and quartered March or April (?) 1587 at Gloucester. Upon completing his studies at Oriel College, Oxford, in 1572, he began a ministry in the Church of England. While serving at St. Mary's Church, Oxford, *c.* 1578, he became convinced of Catholicism. He made his way to Rheims in April of 1581, where he was ordained a Catholic priest (1582). He returned to England on April 30, 1582, but was recognized and arrested within days of his arrival. He spent half of the next three years confined to the "Little Ease" dungeon in the Tower of London, before being sent into exile. He stayed at Rheims from Oct. 8, 1585 to Feb. 7, 1586, then made his way back to his field of labor in the west of England. After a year's activity, he was apprehended in the home of the widow Strange at Gloucester, tried, and executed for his priesthood. He was beatified by Pope John Paul II on Nov. 22, 1987 with George Haydock and Companions.

Feast of the English Martyrs: May 4 (England).

See Also: ENGLAND, SCOTLAND, AND WALES, MARTYRS OF.

Bibliography: R. CHALLONER, *Memoirs of Missionary Priests,* ed. J. H. POLLEN (rev. ed. London 1924). J. H. POLLEN, *Acts of English Martyrs* (London 1891).

[K. I. RABENSTEIN]

ROY, MAURICE

Twenty-first bishop of Quebec City and Primate of Canada (Jan. 25, 1956 to March 20, 1981); cardinal; b. cathedral parish in Quebec City, Jan. 5, 1905; d.1985. He was a distinguished prelate whose quiet pastoral style and careful intellectual approach earned him both national and international respect.

Roy did his baccalaureate studies at the Petit Séminaire in Quebec, graduating in 1923. He was ordained a priest in 1927, the same year that he earned a doctorate in theology from Laval University. In 1929 he completed doctoral studies in philosophy at the Angelicum University in Rome. He then went for further studies in philosophy and literature at the Institut Catholique and the Sorbonne in Paris.

He returned to Quebec City in 1930 and for the next nine years variously taught dogmatic and sacramental theology at Level and apologetics at the Petit Séminaire. He also served as Secretary of the Faculty of Philosophy at Laval.

With the outbreak of war in 1939 he enlisted as a military chaplain with the Royal 22nd Regiment and served Canadian troops in Great Britain, Italy, Germany, France, Belgium, Holland, and Africa. He was mentioned in despatches, was awarded the Cross of the K.B.E., and rose to the rank of Honorary Colonel.

At the end of the war he resumed his teaching responsibilities at Laval and was named to the position of

Rector of the Grand Séminaire. However, within just a few months, on Feb. 22, 1946, he was named Bishop of Trois-Rivières, and assumed the role of military ordinary for the Canadian Armed Forces as well.

Upon the death in 1947 of Jean-Marie Rodrigue Villeneuve, Archbishop of Quebec, Roy was named the new Ordinary of Quebec, becoming Primate on Jan. 25, 1956. Pope Paul VI made him a cardinal in 1965. He was to serve as Archbishop of Quebec for 34 years, years of challenge, tumult, progress, and decline.

Role as Mediator. Roy was a consummate mediator. A personal friend of the controversial Union Nationale leader and Premier of Quebec, Maurice Duplessis, Roy played a pivotal role in laboring for a settlement of the disastrous Asbestos Strike of 1949. He was the principal mover behind the pastoral letter issued by the Quebec episcopate in 1959 on social and labor affairs. Roy exercised to a remarkable degree the pastoral function of reconciliation. This was especially important given the bitter struggles between the government of Duplessis, the Archbishop of Montreal, Joseph Charbonneau, and the fiery Dominican and social scientist, Georges-Henri Levesque.

In the 1960s Roy served on the Preparatory Commission on Church Doctrine for the Second Vatican Council and as President of two new post-conciliar dicasteries: the Pontifical Council for the Laity and the Pontifical Commission for Justice and Peace.

It was during his presidency of the Justice and Peace Commission that he issued his *Message on the Second Development Decade* (Nov. 19, 1970) to U Thant, Secretary-General of the United Nations, as well as his *Reflections on the Occassion of the Tenth Anniversary of the Encyclical "Pacem in terris" of Pope John XXIII* (April 11, 1973). It was also during his presidency of the Justice and Peace Commission that Pope Paul VI addressed to him his Apostolic Letter, *Octogesima adveniens* (1971).

During the "Quiet Revolution" in Quebec society in the 1960s Roy played, as Chairman of the Assemblée des évêques du Québec, a critical role in ensuring the pacific transfer into state hands of the public responsibility for schools, orphanages, hospitals, etc.

Cardinal Roy was a tireless worker and solicitous pastor, and yet during his long tenure as archbishop of Quebec he published only two pastoral letters: one on the Jubilee Year of 1950 and the other on fasting and abstinence in 1960. In his late years he manifested a post-conciliar penchant for delegating power.

See Also: CANADA, THE CATHOLIC CHURCH IN.

Bibliography: C. BLACK, *Duplessis* (Toronto 1977). K. J. KIRLEY, "Maurice Cardinal Roy: 1905–1985," *Canadian Catholic Review* (January 1986). J. RACINE, 'Le Cardinal Maurice Roy," *Relations* (December 1985).

[M. W. HIGGINS]

ROYAL DECLARATION

The Bill of Rights (1689), which prohibited the succession to the English throne of any Catholic or person married to a Catholic, required every monarch at his coronation or at the opening of his first Parliament, whichever occurred first, to "make subscribe and audibly repeate" the following declaration: "I . . . do solemnly and sincerely in the presence of God profess testify and declare that I do believe that in the sacrament of the Lord's Supper there is not any transubstantiation of the elements of bread and wine into the body and blood of Christ at or after the consecration thereof by any person whatsoever; and that the invocation or adoration of the Virgin Mary or any other saint, and the sacrifice of the mass as they are now used in the Church of Rome are superstitious and idolatrous, and I do solemnly in the presence of God profess testify and declare that I do make this declaration and every part thereof in the plain and ordinary sense of the words read unto me as they are commonly understood by English protestants without any evasion, equivocation or mental reservation whatsoever and without any dispensation already granted me for this purpose by the Pope or any other authority or person whatsoever, or without any hope of any such dispensation from any person or authority whatsoever or without thinking that I am or can be acquitted before God or man or absolved of this declaration or any part thereof although the Pope as any other person or persons or power whatsoever should dispense with or annul the same, or declare that it was null and void from the beginning."

This wording (used also to exclude Catholic peers from the House of Lords under the 1678 Test Act) is attributable to the circumstances under which it was originally drafted, viz, the "Popish Plot" frenzy of 1678; while its retention in 1689 accorded with the violent anti-Catholic feeling generated by the REVOLUTION OF 1688. More than a century later this declaration proved a barrier to Catholic Emancipation, for George III, although not personally ill-disposed toward Catholics, insisted that assent to Emancipation would violate both his coronation oath and the Bill of Rights in which the declaration was "expressly enacted and established 'to stand and remain and be the law of the land for ever.'" No change of wording followed the granting of Emancipation in 1829. By the end of the century pressure was mounting for the abolition of utterances objectionable to Catholics both in Britain and in the colonies, and in 1897 Lord Herries raised the matter, unsuccessfully, in the House of Lords. Four years later Edward VII, opening his first Parliament, showed his dislike of the offensive words by uttering them almost inaudibly, by insisting that his successors should not ''have to make such a declaration in such crude language,'' and by demanding a formula acceptable to Catholics, on whose behalf Cardinal Vaughan had protested. The government, however, so mishandled the business that it failed to pass the House of Lords. Lord Grey and the Duke of Norfolk were no more successful in 1903 and 1904 respectively. To these and other attempts in both Houses of Parliament were added representations from Canada and Australia and from Catholics in the colonies.

It was not until 1910, when George V refused otherwise to open Parliament, that a new declaration was devised, passing both Houses and receiving royal assent August 3 (1 Geo. V., c. 29). This accession declaration is as follows: ''I . . . , do solemnly and sincerely, in the presence of God, profess, testify and declare that I am a faithful Protestant, and that I will, according to the true intent of the enactments which secure the Protestant succession to the throne of my Realm, uphold and maintain the said enactments to the best of my powers according to law.''

Bibliography: C. G. ROBERTSON, ed., *Select Statutes, Cases and Documents to Illustrate English Constitutional History, 1660–1832* (London 1935). S. LEE, *King Edward VII* (New York 1925–27) v.2. H. NICOLSON, *King George the Fifth* (London 1952).

[J. A. WILLIAMS]

ROYCE, JOSIAH

One of the greatest American philosophers, leader of the idealist school; b. Grass Valley, Calif., Nov. 20, 1855; d. Cambridge, Mass., Sept. 14, 1916. His parents, Josiah and Sarah Royce, were English born, and went to California as ''forty-niners.'' Sarah Royce, a deeply religious woman, was a school teacher, and the beginnings of Josiah's education were in her school. In 1866 the family moved to San Francisco, where Josiah attended grammar and high school, and in 1871 he started college at the University of California in Berkeley. He was influenced there by his teachers, the Darwinian geologist J. LeConte and the poet E. R. Sill, and by the reading of J. S. MILL and Herbert SPENCER. Through Mill, Royce made contact with the British empirical tradition, which was to determine the empirical base of his own philosophy and to set for him (as for Kant) the special problematic about induction, truth and falsity, and extension of knowledge beyond the present moment. Royce the empiricist was to reject any rationalistic appeal to intuited self-evident

Josiah Royce. (©Bettmann/CORBIS)

principles. In 1875–76 Royce did graduate studies in Germany, first at Leipzig and then at Göttingen, studying under W. WUNDT, W. Windelband, and R. H. LOTZE and reading intensely in I. KANT, J. G. FICHTE, and A. SCHOPENHAUER. He was impressed by Fichte's transformation of Kant's unity of apperception from an instrument of method into a metaphysical reality and by Fichte's notion of immediate intuition of the subject's act and of noumenal principles unifying the categories. Although more influenced by Kant than any other thinker, Royce increasingly sought to go beyond him, abandoning the unknowable NOUMENA and seeking to ground Kant's forms in one absolute principle, some postulate of will.

In 1876 Royce accepted a two-year fellowship at the newly opened Johns Hopkins University, and it was there that his lifelong friendship with William JAMES began. Royce later testified that his own variety of absolute idealism was heavily indebted to James's *Will to Believe* and to James's view of an idea as a ''plan of action,'' a purpose seeking future realization. Royce's doctoral dissertation at Hopkins shows opposition to the sheer externality of realism (one of the four conceptions of being Royce was later to argue against powerfully in *The World and the Individual*). Existence is identified with consciousness, but individual consciousness in this early phase is considered but "shadowy" in comparison with the reality of the world.

After a four-year period of teaching in Berkeley, Royce, through the influence of James, was called to Harvard in 1882, where he was to remain for 33 years until his death. Already by 1882 Royce maintained that to admit finite error implies absolute truth. The problem of error was to be as central for Royce as for PLATO in the *Theaetetus.* An idea cannot be true or false to itself, but only to another idea, ad infinitum. Hence, if any thought is an error, there must be an infinite judge, an inclusive infinite thought. This Absolute is not the God of the churches, but it is "the religious aspect of philosophy." The unification of individual lives is not to be found in the world of description but in that of appreciation, of love.

In Royce's later development, the influence of C. S. PEIRCE became paramount, and the Absolute was transformed into a social community of interpretation. This constitutes Royce's final effort to surmount the limited empirical base from which he began.

See Also: IDEALISM.

Bibliography: Principal writings. *The Religious Aspect of Philosophy* (New York 1885); *The Spirit of Modern Philosophy* (New York 1892); *The Conception of God* (Berkeley, Calif. 1897); *The World and the Individual* (New York 1901); *The Philosophy of Loyalty* (New York 1908); *The Problem of Christianity* (New York 1913). Studies. G. DYKHUIZEN, *The Conception of God in the Philosophy of Josiah Royce* (Chicago 1936). J. E. SMITH, *Royce's Social Infinite* (New York 1950). J. H. COTTON, *Royce on the Human Self* (Cambridge, Mass. 1954). W. E. HOCKING et al., "In memoriam: J. R.," *Journal of Philosophy* 53.3 (1956) 57–139.

[L. J. ESLICK]

RUBATTO, MARIA FRANCESCA, BL.

Baptized Anna Maria, also known as Sister Mary Frances of Jesus; missionary of the Institute of Capuchin Sisters of Loano (of Mother Rubatto); b. Feb. 14, 1844, Carmagnola, Italy; d. Aug. 6, 1904, Montevideo, Uruguay.

After losing both her father (d. 1848) and mother (d. 1863) before she was twenty, Ana Maria Rubatto moved to Turin. Although she had little formal education, she was intellectually gifted. In the Piedmontese capital, she befriended noblewoman Marianna Scoffone, who soon became her patroness. Scoffone provided Ana Maria the time and means to teach children's catechism in several parishes, visit the sick in Cottolengo Hospital, and tend to the needs of the suffering.

Following Scoffone's death in 1882, Ana Maria discerned her true vocation. An act of charity for an injured worker brought Ana Maria to the attention of a newly forming community of women in Loano. They recognized her as the leader for whom they were praying. She joined the sisters in Loano in 1885, took the name Maria Francesca of Jesus, and, under the obedience to Bishop Filippo Allegro, became their superior. The congregation quickly expanded to Genoa (1888) and San Remo Italy, (1888), and Montevideo, Uruguay (1892). They also established missions in Argentina and deep within the Brazilian rainforest. Mother Rubatto crossed the Atlantic seven times in order to be with her daughters on both sides of the ocean, opening 18 houses in 20 years. She remained in America most of the last eight of her 39 years.

Mother Rubatto, known for her concrete love of the poor, was buried in Montevideo. She was beatified by John Paul II, Oct. 10, 1993.

Feast: Aug. 6.

[K. I. RABENSTEIN]

RUBEIS, LEONARDO DE (ROSSI)

Franciscan theologian; b. Giffoni, near Salerno, Italy; d. Avignon, after March 17, 1407. He became master of theology at Cambridge. As minister general of the FRANCISCANS, elected June 5, 1373, he was sympathetic to the Franciscan reform movement led by Paul Trinci. At the beginning of the WESTERN SCHISM, he was deposed as minister general by URBAN VI, from whom he refused the cardinalate. Instead, the antipope, CLEMENT VII at AVIGNON made him a cardinal, Dec. 16, 1378. But in 1381, the king of Sicily, Charles III of Durazzo, an ally of Urban, captured Leonardo in Naples and imprisoned him for five years. By 1387 he had returned to Avignon, where he was an inquisitor of the writings of the Dominican John of Monzon. Leonardo was also involved in the controversy concerning the condemnation of Raymond LULL (1395). In 1399, he severely criticized the antipope BENEDICT XIII for his hesitancy in attempting to heal the Schism, and by 1403 he was reunited with the pope. Leonardo's most important theological work is an unedited commentary of 143 chapters on the dogmatic and mystical theology of the *Canticle of Canticles.* In the main, it followed the Scotistic approach to the Incarnation. There are also many extant unedited sermons, a soliloquy written in prison, *Liber Solitoquiorum animae poenitentis ad Deum,* and two works on the Schism. A commentary on the *Four Books of Sentences* has been attributed to him.

Bibliography: E. LONGPRÉ, *Dictionnaire de théologie catholique,* ed. A. VACANT, 15 v. (Paris 1903–50; Tables générales 1951–) 9.1:396–397. C. SCHMITT, "La Position du cardinal Léonard de Giffoni. O.F.M., dans le conflit du grand schisme d'Occident,'' *Archivum Franciscanum historicum* 50 (1957) 273–331; 51 (1958) 25–72, 410–472.

[J. J. SMITH]

RUBINO, ANTONIO

Jesuit missionary and proponent of the Chinese rites; b. Strambino, Italy, March 1, 1578; d. Nagasaki, Japan, March 22, 1643. He entered the Society of Jesus in 1596, and in 1602 left for India, which was his missionary field for the next 36 years. Besides successfully catechizing and preaching, he left valuable descriptions of India in his letters to Christopher CLAVIUS and Christopher Grienberger, Jesuit mathematicians of the Roman College, descriptions that reveal a skill in cartography and mathematics. His *Catena evangelica* (seven volumes) became a useful exegetical guide for missionaries. As visitor for the province of Japan and the vice-province of China in 1638, he learned the native languages well enough to discuss theology with the bonzes. Rubino became impressed with the advantages in adapting some of the Roman ritual to that of the Far Eastern religions, and wrote a defense of his views, *Metodo della dottrina che i padri della Compagnia di Gesù insegnano ai neofiti nelle missioni della Cina con la risposta alle obiettioni di alcuni moderni che la impugnano* (1641). Rubino wrote originally in Portuguese; this Italian version by G. F. Marini, was placed on the Index in 1660. This identification with the cause of the CHINESE RITES followed him after death, when a calumnious book, *Difesa del giudizio formato dalla Santa Sede Apostolica* (Turin c. 1760), advocating an iconoclastic removal of crucifixes and other objects of the Roman rite from use in the East, was falsely ascribed to his authorship. In 1643 Rubino and his companions reached the Japanese island of Satauma, where they were seized; they were brought to Nagasaki, and after imprisonment, died.

Bibliography: C. SOMMERVOGEL, *Bibliotèque de la Compagnie de Jésus,* 11 v. (Brussels-Paris 1890–1932) 7:279–280. G. SAROGLIA, *Vita del P. Antonio Rubino da Strambino* (Trent 1894). S. DELACROIX, ed., *Histoire universelle des missions catholiques,* 4 v. (Paris 1956–59) 1:314; 2:61.

[E. D. MCSHANE]

RUBIO, ANTONIO

Mexican scholastic philosopher; b. Villa de Rueda, Spain, 1548; d. Alcalá, 1615. At 21 Rubio entered the JESUIT novitiate. He studied at Colegio Máximo de Alcalá de Henares under Cardinal Francis Toletus and succeeded Hortigosa as philosophy professor at Colegio Máximo de San Pedro y San Pablo in Mexico (1576–1601). In 1594 he was awarded a doctorate at the University of Mexico. He was highly esteemed for his learning by Mexican authorities, and became Jesuit procurator in Rome (1601). Thereafter he taught at Alcalá, where the university "ordered . . . all students to follow the same philosophical program" as that of its illustrious Mexican master. He wrote *Commentaria in universam Aristotelis Logicam* (1605), called *Lógica Mexicana* and adopted as a textbook at Alcalá; *Commentaria in libros Aristotelis de ortu et interitu* (1619); and *Commentaria in octo libros Aristotelis de physico auditu* (1605). Besides several previous editions these works were published in five volumes at Lyon in 1625. The Library of Congress, Washington, D.C., has a poetical work entitled *Poeticarum Institutionum liber variis ethicorum christianorumque exemplis illustratus* (Mexico 1605).

Rubio followed a sane THOMISM according to the Salamancan spirit of Dominic Soto and his teacher Toletus, especially on being and analogy and in physics. Though he concluded several works with the epilogue "to the praise and glory of . . . Blessed Thomas, whose teaching we follow," he was a personal thinker who maintained a rigorous philosophical attitude in weighing the reasons of the Angelic Doctor and who departed from him on several decisive points. Thus he denied the real distinction between essence and existence and the pure potency of matter. Actual existence is not a second act, ordered to the first act of the essence really distinct from it, but "is by nature in first act, an actual being *extra causas,* distinct by reason alone from . . . essence, and necessarily attributable to all real beings *extra causas.*" This divergence from traditional Thomism is heightened by giving partial subsistence to matter, which by nature exists as really distinct from form, as is clearly seen from the relation of matter to quantity. For his excellent grasp of Aristotle and his respectful commentaries on St. Thomas, Rubio deserves to be classed with his contemporaries Toletus, FONSECA, SUÁREZ, VALENCIA, and VÁSQUEZ.

Bibliography: F. J. ALEGRE, *Historia de la provincia de la Compañía de Jesús de Nueva España,* ed. E. J. BURRUS and F. ZUBILLAGA, 4 v. (new ed. Rome 1956–60).

[O. ROBLES]

RUBIO Y PERALTA, JOSÉ MARÍA, BL.

Jesuit priest; b. July 22, 1864, Dalías, Almeria, Andalusia, southern Spain; d. May 2, 1929, Aranjuez, Spain.

José María, the eldest of twelve children of farmers, began his studies for the priesthood in the minor seminary of Almería in 1876. He transferred to the seminary at Granada (1879), completed his training in Madrid, and was ordained in 1887.

Before teaching Latin, pastoral theology, and philosophy in the Madrid seminary for four years, he served as assistant pastor in Chinchón (1887–89) and pastor at Estremera (1889). In 1893, he became chaplain to Cistercian nuns in Madrid.

On Oct. 11, 1906, Fr. Rubio fulfilled a long held desire to become a Jesuit by entering the novitiate in Granada. Two years later he pronounced his vows and after a short time in Seville, returned to Madrid (1911), where he carried out his priestly ministry with distinction.

Fr. Rubio was known for his exceptional ability as a spiritual director, as a preacher—especially on the Blessed Sacrament and the Sacred Heart of Jesus—and, late in his life, as a miracle worker. He organized a group of over 6,000 women, called the Marys of the Tabernacles, who provided and cared for altarware, linens, and vestments, and lived ascetic lives. As part of his apostolate of charity, he directed the Honor Guard of the Sacred Heart of Jesus. Its 5,000 members, like their chaplain, were devoted to corporal and spiritual works of mercy.

Following his death from a heart attack while visiting the novitiate at Aranjuez, he was buried in its cemetery. In 1953, his remains were transferred to the Jesuit residence on the Calle Maldonado, Madrid. He was beatified on Oct. 6, 1985 by Pope John Paul II.

Feast: May 4 (Jesuits).

Bibliography: P. M. LAMET, *De Madrid al cielo* (Santander 1985). J. A. DE SOBRINO, *Tres que dijeron 'si'* (Madrid 1985). J. N. TYLENDA, *Jesuit Saints & Martyrs* (Chicago 1998): 123–5. *Acta Apostolicae Sedis* 78 (1986): 971–974. *L'Osservatore Romano,* English edition, no. 42 (1985): 6–7.

[K. I. RABENSTEIN]

RUBLËV, ANDREĬ

Russian icon painter and monk; b. *c.* 1360, origin and birthplace unknown; d. at Spasso-Andronikov monastery, Moscow, Jan. 29, 1430. Rublëv grew up during the wars of liberation against the Tartars and very early put himself under the spiritual direction of St. Nikon, successor to St. Sergius, at the monastery of the Holy Trinity near Moscow. Nothing is known of his artistic training, but it is recorded that he collaborated in 1405 on the Cathedral of the Annunciation, Moscow. In 1408, along with his fellow monk and painter Daniil Chernyĭ, he worked on the frescoes of the Uspenskiĭ cathedral, Vladimir. Later the same two collaborators worked at the Spas-

so-Andronikov monastery in Moscow and at the monastery of the Holy Trinity, where Rublëv executed his most famous painting, the ''Old Testament Trinity,'' now in the Tretiakov Gallery, Moscow.

All Rublëv's work bears the imprint of the spiritual heritage of St. Sergius; it is a direct expression of the Orthodox spiritual movement known as HESYCHASM. His exceptional artistic gifts combined with an extraordinary depth of spiritual insight to make him leader of a whole group of Russian icon-painters whose work represents the culmination of Orthodox church art in the 14th and 15th centuries. His work represents a vivid expression in Christian art of the principles of composition and the harmony inherent in classical art. It is characterized by a remarkable sense of proportion, a most striking harmony of colors, and a rhythmic suppleness of line. The simplicity and economy of his art serve to express the deep theological content of the image. His influence on the development of Russian icon painting through the 17th century was immense.

Bibliography: V. N. LAZAREV, ''Andrei Rublëv i ego shkola,'' Akademiia Nauk SSSR, Institut Istorii Iskusstv, *Istoriia russkogo iskusstva*, ed. J. E. GRABAR' (Moscow 1953–) 3:102–186. M. V. ALPATOV, *Andrei Rublëv* (Moscow 1959). G. H. HAMILTON, *The Art and Architecture of Russia* (Baltimore 1954) 86–88. E. VOORDEKKERS, ''Rublëv's *Old Testament Trinity*,'' *Eastern Church Quarterly* 14 (1961) 96–118, 166–176.

[L. OUSPENSKY]

RUDIGIER, FRANZ JOSEF, VEN.

Bishop; b. Parthenen (Vorarlberg), Austria, April 7, 1811; d. Linz, Nov. 29, 1884. After ordination (1835) he studied in Vienna, and taught ecclesiastical history, Canon Law, moral theology, and education at the seminary in Brixen. In 1845 he became director of the Frintaneum, an institute for advanced ecclesiastical studies; court chaplain; and tutor to Franz Josef and Maximilian, later emperors of Austria and Mexico respectively. In 1850 he became rector of the seminary and cathedral canon in Brixen, and in 1852, bishop of Linz. As bishop he was a zealous, farsighted pastor of souls; a strenuous defender of the rights of the Church; and a determined opponent of JOSEPHINISM and secular liberalism. He promoted Catholic associations, the Catholic press, and the Catholic social movement and defended confessional schools. Rudigier issued a pastoral letter attacking the regulations on marriage and education in the May Laws of 1868. As a result he was sentenced to 14 days' imprisonment (June 1869), but the emperor reversed the sentence the next day. In 1862 Rudigier started construction of a Gothic cathedral. Franz Doppelbauer, later Bishop of Linz, published several volumes of Rudigier's sermons, retreats, pastoral letters, and politico-ecclesiastical addresses and in 1905 introduced his cause for beatification.

Bibliography: K. MEINDL, *Leben und Wirken des Bischofs Rudigier,* 2 v. (Linz 1891). J. LENZENWEGER, *Lexikon für Theologie und Kirche,* ed. J. HOFER and K. RAHNER, 10 v. (2d, new ed. Freiburg 1957–65) 9:85.

[W. B. SLOTTMAN]

RUDOLF ACQUAVIVA AND COMPANIONS, BB.

Martyrs killed Monday, July 25, 1583 (Gregorian calendar), in the village of Conculim (Salsette, Goa, India); the group included Fathers Alfonso Pacheco, Peter Berno, Antonio Francisco, and Brother Francisco Aranha.

Rudolf Acquaviva; b. Atri old kingdom of Naples, Italy, Oct. 2, 1550. He was the fifth child of the duke of Atri and nephew of the future general of the Society of Jesus, Claudius ACQUAVIVA. His mother was a cousin of St. ALOYSIUS GONZAGA. He was admitted to the Society of Jesus April 2, 1568, in Rome and studied in Macerata and Rome. He was ordained and reached Goa, Sept. 13, 1578. Shortly after, he was selected as superior for the very important mission to the court of the Great Mogul Akbar, who in 1579 had sent an embassy to Goa with a request that two learned missionaries be sent to Fatehpur Sîkrî his favorite residence near Agra; Acquaviva arrived there at the end of February 1580. His zeal and austerity won the admiration of the Mogul and his court, who regretted his return to Goa in February 1583. At Goa, he was appointed superior of the Salsette mission, the post he held at his martyrdom.

Alfonso Pacheco; b. Minaya (Albacete) Spain, *c.* 1549. He entered the society on Sept. 8, 1567 in the Province of Toledo; in 1573 he studied theology in Alcalá. Before his ordination the following year, he sailed with A. Valignano for India, landing in Goa. His prudence and virtue influenced his being chosen in 1578 for an important European mission. He returned to India in 1581, and was made rector of Rachol (Salsette). He accompanied two punitive expeditions of the Portuguese to the village of Conculim, and was instrumental in destroying the pagodas there.

Peter Berno; b. Ascona (Locarno), Switzerland, *c.* 1552. He entered the society at Rome, July 2, 1577; two years later he left Lisbon for Goa. Soon he was appointed to Salsette. He, too, accompanied the punitive expeditions to Cuncolim and assisted in destroying the Hindu

temples; he overturned an anthill that was deemed very sacred, and killed a cow, thus deeply offending orthodox Hindus.

Antonio Francisco; b. Coimbra, Portugal, *c.* 1550–53. He was an impoverished student when he joined the society in Coimbra on Sept. 7, 1571, and accompanied Pacheco to India in 1581. Shortly afterward he was ordained in Goa. He was then sent to the Moluccas, but a storm impeded his voyage and he returned to Goa, where the superiors assigned him to the Church of Orlim (in Salsette).

Francisco Aranha; b. probably at Braga, Portugal, *c.* 1551. He was born of a wealthy and noble family and went to India with his uncle, the first archbishop of Goa, D. Gaspar de Leão (1560). There he joined the Society of Jesus as a brother on Nov. 1, 1571. He often accompanied the fathers in their apostolic work.

The five religious met in the Church of Orlim on July 25, 1583, and thence proceeded to Conculim in the southeast, accompanied by some native Christians, with the object of erecting a cross and selecting ground for a church. Hindus, aroused by this threat to their religious beliefs, decided to destroy them. The Hindus attacked the Jesuits and their followers, killing them and tossing their bodies into a well. A few days later, the bodies were recovered and solemnly buried in the Church of Our Lady of the Snows. In 1587 the remains were removed to the city of Goa, where they are still venerated.

A narrative describing their death, written in 1583 by Father Valignano, was reprinted and translated several times. The process of canonization began in 1600, but it was only in 1741 that BENEDICT XIV declared the martyrdom proved. On April 16, 1893, the solemn beatification of the five martyrs was celebrated in Rome, and in 1894, in Goa. The absence of miracles has delayed the process of canonization of the five as a group.

Feast: July 27; Feb. 4 (Jesuits).

Bibliography: D. BARTOLI, *Missione al Gran Mogor del P. Ridolfo Aquaviva . . .* (Venice 1851), a monograph on the five martyrs. N. ANGELINI and H. GRUBER, *Der selige Rudolf Acquaviva und seine Gefährten* (Regensburg 1894). E. D. MACLAGAN, *The Jesuits and the Great Mogul* (London 1932). J. N. TYLENDA, *Jesuit Saints & Martyrs* (Chicago 1998) 220–28.

[J. WICKI]

RUFFINI, ERNESTO

Archbishop, cardinal; b. San Benedetto Po, diocese of Mantua, Jan. 19, 1888; d. Palermo, June 11, 1968. Ruffini was ordained to the priesthood on July 10, 1910, and became one of the first students at the newly established Pontifical Biblical Institute in Rome. After his graduation and a trip to the Holy Land, he was appointed by his papal benefactor to the Lateran Seminary to teach Sacred Scripture. During his 35-year Roman residence he also taught at the Propaganda seminary, authored books and articles on Scripture, and served on a variety of curial congregations and commissions, including the Pontifical Biblical Commission and the congregations of Seminaries and Universities, of which he was fully in charge for several years.

Pope Pius XII appointed Ruffini as archbishop of Palermo in 1945 and a year later created him cardinal. Ruffini established a secular institute, a boys town with facilities to learn various industrial trades, a village bearing his name with new houses constructed for the poor, and similar works. He also wrote a book attacking Pierre TEILHARD DE CHARDIN (*The Theory of Evolution Judged by Reason and Faith* [Eng. ed., New York 1959]). During his visit to the United States in 1956 he was enthusiastically greeted by hundreds of his former students, including members of the hierarchy.

During Vatican Council II (1962–65) Ruffini was constantly studying council documents and avoided as far as possible purely social gatherings. Though his views were often criticized, some historians place Ruffini among the leading theologians of the council.

[J. E. STEINMUELLER]

RUFFO, FABRIZIO

Italian cardinal, leader of SANFEDISTS; b. S. Lucido (Cosenza), Sept. 16, 1744; d. Naples, Dec. 13, 1827. Of noble birth, he was placed early under the tutelage of Giovanni Braschi, the future Pope Pius VI. After completing his studies at the Collegio Clementino in Rome, he entered the service of the Roman Curia. In 1785 he became treasurer-general in the apostolic camera, where his devotion to needed economic and financial reforms in the STATES OF THE CHURCH roused so much hostility from vested aristocratic interests that he retired to the Kingdom of Naples after being made cardinal (1794). He received the deaconate in 1795. King Ferdinand IV appointed him superintendent of his utopian colony of silk manufacturers at San Leucio, near Caserta. After the royal family escaped the approaching French army by fleeing to Sicily on Admiral Nelson's British man-of-war ''Vanguard'' (December 1798), Ruffo joined the court at Palermo. After proposing a plan to recover Calabria and receiving royal authorization to act as the king's vicar, Ruffo returned to the mainland (Feb. 7, 1799), accompanied by

only eight companions and lacking funds or arms. The militant, audacious prelate, gifted with organizational talents, soon gathered from the civilian populace a sizable army, known as the Sanfedists. Ruffo aroused great enthusiasm by his understanding of the Calabrians and his desire to relieve them of oppressive feudal burdens, but he could not curb all the excesses of his motley troops. At the head of his army he proceeded to Naples, where he gained the capitulation of the French and Italian Jacobin forces of the Parthenopean Republic, after offering them mild terms, which Nelson and the restored Bourbons later disregarded by exacting bloody vengeance. Ruffo then fell into disgrace and left Naples for Rome (January 1800). During the Napoleonic era he tended to tolerate the emperor's religious policies. Upon his return to Rome in 1814, Pius VII appointed him to various posts. Ruffo regained favor with the Neapolitan Bourbons, and retired to Naples in his last years, which he devoted to study and writing on agricultural, economic, and military topics. Liberal historians have frequently reacted to Ruffo's counterrevolutionary activity by portraying his character in dark hues.

Bibliography: H. C. GUTTERIDGE, ed., *Nelson and the Neapolitan Jacobins: Documents . . . June 1799* (London 1903), biog. data and evaluation in introd. ix–cxii. H. M. ACTON, *The Bourbons of Naples (1734–1825)* (New York 1958). N. RODOLICO, *Enciclopedia Italiana di scienzi, littere ed arti* 30:221, with photo.

[M. L. SHAY]

RUFINA, SS.

There were several saints in the early Church by this name.

Rufina and Secunda are recorded as having been martyred in the Valerian persecution (*c.* 257) and buried on the Via Cornelia at the ninth milestone. A church was erected there, apparently by Pope DAMASUS; it became a basilica and was renovated by Pope ADRIAN I in the eighth century. This was the ancient See of Lorium, subsequently united with that of Porto, which became a suburbicarian see of Rome as Porto Santa Rufina, with a cardinal as its bishop. The Acta are legendary, and state that Rufina and Secunda were sisters, daughters of a Roman Senator Asterius, who were delated by their prospective fianceés and beheaded. In 1154 their relics were translated to the baptistery of the Lateran Basilica.

Feast: July 10.

Rufina and Justa are honored in Seville, Spain, as having been martyred in 287 upon refusing to sell their self-produced earthenware as vessels for pagan worship.

Feast: July 19.

Rufina of Caesarea, reputed mother of St. Mamas (d. c. 275), was said to have been martyred with her husband, St. Theodotus, and St. Ammia under Valerian. Nothing concrete is known of her life.

Feast: Aug. 31.

Rufina of Sirmium, Pannonia, led a group of eleven martyrs, who died probably in the fourth century.

Feast: April 6.

Bibliography: Rufina and Secunda. *Acta sanctorum* July 3:27–29. *Bibliographica hagiographica latina* 2:7359. L. BERRA, *Dizionario Ecclesiastico* 3:616. A. BUTLER, *The Lives of the Saints* 3:64. Rufina and Justa, and Rufina of Caesarea. F. G. ARQUÉS, *Sermón de las gloriosas santas vírgines y mártires, Iusta y Rufina*, ed. A. L. GALIANO PÉREZ (Valencia 1617, repr. Orihuela, Spain 1983). L. BERRA, *Dizionario Ecclesiastico* 3:616. H. QUENTIN, *Les Martyrologes historiques* (Paris 1908) 176–177. A. BUTLER, *The Lives of the Saints* 3:144–145.

[E. DAY]

RUFINUS

Archbishop, canonist, and theologian; b. central Italy, probably near Assisi, first half of the twelfth century; d. before 1192. Possibly he studied at Bologna, where certainly he taught after 1150. Sometime before 1179, when he gave the opening address at the Third Lateran Council, he became bishop of Assisi; between 1180 and 1186, at the instance of Peter II de Insulis, Abbot of Monte Cassino, he was translated to the archbishopric of Sorrento.

Writings. A man of vast cultural formation, Rufinus has left a number of writings: (1) *Summa Decretorum,* completed in 1160 [ed. H. Singer, *Die Summa decretorum des Magister Rufinus* (Paderborn 1902), with a valuable introduction]. (2) *De bono pacis,* written at the request of Abbot Peter between 1174 and 1180 (with a second recension between June 1180 and 1186) from rough notes (''sparsim vulgoque'') compiled earlier for Bishop Bernard of Sora [printed by B. Pez, *Biblioteca ascetica antiquo-nova* 9 (Ratisbon 1726) 1–110, whence *Patrologia Latina,* 217 v. (Paris 1878–90) 150: 1593–1638; both Pez and Migne, however, assigned the work to the late eleventh century]. (3) Sermons, including the discourse at the Third Lateran Council, discovered (Ambrosiana, Milan, manuscript 30 sup.) and discussed by G. Morin, ''Le discours d'oeuverture du concile générale de Lateran (1179) et l'oeuvre littéraire de maître Rufin, évêque d'Assise,'' *Atti della pontifica Accademia romana di archeologia* 3d series, Memorie 2 (Rome 1928), 113–133; discourse:116–120. (4) Some glosses on the *Decretum* are discussed by J. Juncker,

''Summen und Glossen,'' *Zeitschrift der Savigny-Stiftung f. Rechtsgeschichte Kan Abt.* 14 (1925): 427–462.

Technique and Teaching. The *Summa Decretorum* of Rufinus was the most influential Decretist writing until the appearance of the *Summa super Decretis* of HUGUCCIO (1188–1190). This was in no small measure due to a novel technique. Where the immediate successors of GRATIAN had been content to summarize or to provide an index of the *Decretum*, Rufinus introduced a systematic exposition of the text. Employing for the first time the analytical and exegetical techniques of the civil law schools, he glossed words and passages, noted cross-references, raised points not contained in the text, and, on occasion, disagreed with the master himself. Allied to these qualities was a wide range of sources outside the *Decretum:* the *collectio Dionysio-Hadriana* (*DIONYSIANA*), BURCHARD OF WORMS, the *De sacramentis* of HUGH OF SAINT-VICTOR, as well as Decretist writings such as the *Summa* of PAUCAPALEA (1140–48) and the *Stroma* (before 1148) of Roland Bandinelli (later ALEXANDER III). The result was an enormous stimulus to *Summa* literature and to the development of glossatorial techniques (*see* DECRETISTS). If Rufinus imitated the civilians, he had not, however, any great regard for civil law itself; the infiltration of civil law as such into ecclesiastical law came at a later stage of Decretist history. On the other hand, he belonged to the great canonico-theological tradition of Gratian and his school, although there were signs at the time that the marriage of law and theology was under some strain. Rufinus, in fact, is the first known author to use the *Summa Sententiarum* of PETER LOMBARD (1155–58); and he proves to be a source himself for some theologians later on, such as SIMON OF TOURNAI.

One of the more doctrinal contributions of Rufinus was a distinction (*ad Dist.* 23) between *auctoritas* and *administratio* in any ecclesiastical office other than that of pope. The pope alone had *auctoritas* and *administratio* from his very order (*potestas ordinis*), while all others had *administratio* by delegation or election. Applying the distinction cautiously to the emperor, Rufinus coined a formula *auctoritas papae-administratio imperatoris,* which became standard among moderate advocates of the emperor's submission to the pope. In time, however, other less temperate spirits stretched the formula to mean that the emperor as such had only an administrative capacity, that even in the temporal order he was only a sort of deputy of the pope.

In the *De bono pacis,* which is really an exposition of Augustine's *De civitate Dei,* Rufinus is completely in line with the doctrine of GELASIUS and Gratian of independent temporal and spiritual orders. Noting a possible ambiguity in Augustine's Jerusalem-Babylon division of Peace, Rufinus introduces a third Peace, that of Egypt (2:2–8). This is the spiritual society of the wicked, while Babylon (2:8–18) is the temporal order, where a peace rooted in justice (*aequitas;* a natural disposition) is the highest good, is common to Christian and Pagan, and is in harmony with the "Peace of the Church" (2:19–31).

Bibliography: J. F. VON SCHULTE, *Die Geschichte der Quellen und der Literatur des kanonischen Rechts,* 3 v. in 4 pts. (Stuttgart 1875–80; repr. Graz 1956) 1:121–130. S. KUTTNER, *Repertorium der Kanonistik* (Rome 1937) 131–133, 178–179. J. DE GHELLINCK, *Le Mouvement théologique du XIIᵉ siècle* (2d ed. Bruges 1948) 537, 538. A. M. STICKLER, "Imperator vicarius papae," *Mitteilungen des Instituts für österreichische Geschichtsforschung* 62 (1954): 165–212. Y. M. J. CONGAR, "Maître Rufin et son De bono pacis," *Revue des sciences philosophiques et théologiques* 41 (1957): 428–444. L. OTT, "Hat Magister Rufinus die Sentenzen des Petrus Lombardus benützt?" *Scholastik* 33 (1958): 234–247. R. L. BENSON, "From Election to Consecration: Studies in the Constitutional Status of an Electus in the High Middle Ages," *Dissertation Abstracts* 19 (1958–59): 2585–2586; *Dictionnaire de droit canonique,* ed. R. NAZ, 7 v. (Paris 1935–65) 7:779–784.

[L. E. BOYLE]

RUFINUS OF AQUILEIA

Fourth-century monk, translator, and ecclesiastical writer; b. Concordia, near Aquileia, 345; d. Messina, Sicily, 410. SIDONIUS APOLLINARIS called him Turranius Rufinus (*Epist.* 2.9.5), but JEROME named him Tyrannius (*Contra Ruf.* 1.1), obviously utilizing Acts 19.9 in a pejorative sense, just as Rufinus referred to Jerome's Hebrew teacher, Rabbi Bar-anina, as Barabbas (*Apol. contra Hier.* 2.15, 38). In the controversy between Jerome and Rufinus over the accusations of Origenism, history sided with Jerome, and it is only in recent times that the tarnish is being removed from the reputation of Rufinus.

Life. Rufinus made elementary studies in his native Concordia, and his parents, who were Christians, sent him, at age 15, to Rome, where he was associated with Jerome in school. He returned to Aquileia (*c.* 369), became a catechumen under the direction of Chromatius, future bishop of Aquileia, and was baptized *c.* 370 (*Apol. contra Hier.* 1.4). Jerome joined him and a group of ascetics in Aquileia under the guidance of the bishop until 372, when the circle dispersed for some unknown reason. Rufinus left for Egypt, met MELANIA THE ELDER, and suffered in the persecution that followed the death of ATHANASIUS (May 373). He settled in Alexandria for six years, and after an interval, for two years more; during this time he studied the Scriptures and the works of Origen under DIDYMUS THE BLIND and GREGORY OF NAZIANZUS and visited the desert fathers, such as Macarius, Isidore, and Pambo (Jer., *Epist.* 4.2; 5.2; *Ruf. Apol. contra Hier.* 2.15).

In 381 he was in Jerusalem where he founded a monastery on the Mount of Olives in association with Melania the Elder, was ordained a priest by Bishop John, and entered amicable relations with Jerome and Paula, who had settled at Bethlehem *c.* 386 (*Apol. contra Hier.* 2.11).

Quarrel over Origen. In 393 EPIPHANIUS OF SALAMIS sent an emissary named Atarbius to Palestine to induce the bishops to condemn Origenism. Badly received by Bp. JOHN OF JERUSALEM and Rufinus, Atarbius was welcomed at Bethlehem, and from a fervent admirer of ORIGEN, Jerome became an avid opponent of the Alexandrian's teaching. His attitude resulted in enmity between himself and both John of Jerusalem and Rufinus, and this quarrel was enlarged by a visit of Epiphanius. In 397, on the intervention of THEOPHILUS OF ALEXANDRIA, a kind of truce was arranged (Jerome, *Contra Ruf.* 3.33; *Epist.* 81.1), and Rufinus departed for the West with a collection of manuscripts of the Greek ecclesiastical writers.

Sojourn in Italy. Rufinus stopped for a time at the monastery of Pinetum near Terracina and translated a compilation of the rule of St. BASIL for the monks there. In Rome he was asked by a monk named Marcarius to translate the first book of the *Apolog ia* written by PAMPHILUS for Origen and Origen's *De principiis.* In turning the latter work into Latin, Rufinus modified and suppressed doctrinal notions that he considered dangerous interpolations. In his preface he claimed he was following the example and procedure of Jerome, who had translated some of Origen's homilies (*Pref. Periarchon*). Jerome was informed of this preface before the work itself was published and wrote a private letter of protest to Rufinus (*Epist. 81*), but Jerome's friends in Italy did not give it to Rufinus. Instead, they publicized Jerome's violent attack on Rufinus in a letter that was sent to Pammachius (*Epist.* 84).

Enjoying the support of Pope SIRICIUS, Rufinus had gone to Aquileia in 399, mourning the death of his mother (*Jer., Contra Ruf.* 2.2). He sent an *Apologia* to Pope Anastasius and replied to Jerome's attacks with his *Apologia contra Hieronymum.* Later, acceding to the counsel of Bp. CHROMATIUS OF AQUILEIA, he preserved silence on the issue despite the fact that until his death he was constantly the victim of Jerome's defamation.

He spent the last decade of his life in literary activities, particularly in translating Greek ecclesiastical works into Latin. In 407 he fled to Rome before the Gothic invasions, then to the monastery of Pinetum (Terracina), and finally, with MELANIA THE YOUNGER and Pinian, to Sicily, where he died in 410. Jerome's strictures prevented Rufinus from being considered a saint by posterity despite the excellent reputation he enjoyed with AUGUSTINE, GAUDENTIUS OF BRESCIA, PAULINUS OF NOLA, and

GENNADIUS (*De vir. illus.* 17). Le Nain de Tillemont controverted the poor opinion of Rufinus expressed by the 18th-century Bollandist J. Stilting, insisting that Rufinus gave evidence of an upright life and that, though not a great theologian, he was of inestimable service to the development of asceticism and theology in the West.

Writings. A translator rather than an original writer, Rufinus apparently began his literary career with his defense of the orthodoxy of Origen in *De adulteratione librorum Origenis,* adding as an appendix a translation of the *Apologia* of Pamphilus. He sustained the thesis that the unacceptable doctrinal passages in Origen were interpolations introduced by Origen's adversaries or by heretics. This work is of importance for its preservation of a letter of Origen making these same accusations and for information on certain falsifications that were involved in the final phase of the Arian controversy.

In 400 Rufinus sent an *Apologia ad Anastasium papam* from Aquileia, in which he defended himself against accusations brought to the pope by Jerome's friends. After a brief profession of faith in the Trinity, Rufinus stated his belief in the resurrection of the dead and the final judgment, which were crucial arguments in the Origenistic controversy. As for the origin of the soul, he submitted that the learned were still uncertain. He disclaimed either praise or blame for opinions of Origen, since his involvement was merely as a translator. Besides, in his translation he had tried to eliminate everything that might be considered contrary to the faith. In an apparent recognition of this writing, Pope Anastasius wrote to Bp. John of Jerusalem expressing disdain for Rufinus (*Epist. ad Joh. Hier.*).

Jerome and Origen. Rufinus used the same arguments concerning his translation of Origen in his *Apologia contra Hieronymum* in two books, written *c.* 401, in which he supplied a devastating confrontation of Jerome's assertions in his *Epistola* 84 with Jerome's previous writings. To justify himself as an anti-Origenist from the beginning, Jerome had referred to his own commentaries on Ecclesiastes and Ephesians as an indication of his true attitude with regard to Origen. Rufinus took him at his word and cited several passages from the Commentary on Ephesians to prove that Jerome had followed Origen even in his doctrine on the preexistence of souls and on the final restoration of all things. Jerome said he had praised Origen only a few times for his scriptural exegesis and not for his doctrine. Rufinus cited a dozen passages in which Jerome praised Origen without distinction and, following Eusebius, had attributed the campaign against Origen by Bishop Demetrius and other adversaries to envy. In several parts of his *Apologia* Rufinus extended his polemic to an attack on the person of Jerome,

accusing him of having translated the Scriptures directly from the Hebrew texts and of continuing to teach the pagan authors despite his promise several years earlier (Jer., *Epist.* 22.30) to abandon them completely. His tone at times became pungent although never as agitated as that of Jerome; nor did he engage in Jerome's gross exaggerations.

The Apostles' Creed. At the invitation of a Bishop Laurentius in 404, Rufinus wrote a commentary on the Creed (*Commentarius in symbolum Apostolorum*), which, according to Gennadius, achieved great popularity. The work was based on similar treatises by CYRIL OF JERUSALEM and GREGORY OF NYSSA and betrays ideas derived from Origen. In particular he held that the soul of Christ served as mediator between the Logos and His human body and conceived of Christ's redemptive action as a deception of the devil who had destroyed Christ's body, believing thus to be able to conquer him, but who was himself conquered through this action by the divinity of the Savior. Rufinus's work is important since it also contains the Latin text of the Roman Creed along with that of Aquileia and a canon of the Scriptures.

Exegesis. At the invitation of Paulinus of Nola, Rufinus, while staying at the monastery of Pinetum (Terracina) in 408 wrote a commentary on the Benedictions of the Patriarchs (*De benedictionibus patriarcharum;* cf. Genesis ch. 49). The first book contains a commentary on the Benediction of Juda (Gn 49.9–11), and the second is a commentary on the Benedictions of the other Patriarchs. Faithful to the Origenian canon, Rufinus gave a threefold explanation of each benediction: the literal, the typological, and the moral or psychological. In his typology he referred each Biblical passage to a happening in the life of Christ or the primitive Church; and in his moral exegesis he saw in each Biblical passage the war in the soul between good and bad.

In his typological interpretation Rufinus reflected an ancient exegetical tradition, which he could have taken from works on the same subject by Hippolytus and Ambrose, as well as from oral sources. For his moral considerations in which he described the slow ascent of the soul from the baseness of sin to the heights of sanctity, Rufinus was mainly dependent on material found in the homilies of Origen.

Among his original works is a continuation of Eusebius's *Ecclesiastical History,* covering events between 324 and 395; Rufinus's continuation was weak in information and system but was used widely by later historians.

Translator. It is in his translations that Rufinus contributed most to the theological formation of the West, particularly in his renderings of Origen's works. He translated the *Periarchon* in 398; four books of the Commentary on the Canticle of Canticles in 410; ten books of the commentary on Romans (*c.* 404); 16 homilies on Genesis, 13 on Exodus, 16 on Leviticus, 26 on Joshua, nine on Judges (403–404); 28 on Numbers (410); and nine on Psalms 36, 37, 38 (398).

Of other authors, Rufinus translated the dialogue *De recta in Deum fide,* which he thought had been written by Origen (*c.* 400); book 1 of the *Apologia* of Pamphilus for Origen (398); the *Sententiae* of the Pythagorean Sextus, whom he confounded with Pope Sixtus II (400); the Pseudo-Clementine *Homilies* and *Recognitiones* (406); two rules of Basil of Caesarea and eight of his homilies (397–400); nine homilies of Gregory Nazianzus (399–400); the *Historia monachorum* (404), which for a long time was considered on original work by Rufinus; and, finally, the *Ecclesiastical History* of Eusebius in nine books (402–403). It is uncertain whether he had also translated parts of Flavius Josephus; and the *Sententiae* of EVAGRIUS PONTICUS, which he may have translated, are lost.

Rufinus's work as a translator has been greatly criticized by modern philologists because of the excessive liberty in his renderings when they are compared with the Greek originals. But in antiquity, translation was considered a kind of paraphrase, leaving great liberty to the translator, while an absolutely literal translation was inconceivable. As regards his corrections of doctrine in the *Periarchon* and other works of Origen, Rufinus stated frankly that his desire was to make Origen known to the Latins in such fashion that he could be useful and not dangerous to their faith, as well as that a certain prudence was imposed upon him by controversy.

At a moment when knowledge of Greek was becoming rare in the West, the translations of Rufinus as well as those of Jerome had the great merit of familiarizing the Latins with certain great works of Greek Christianity, which would otherwise have remained unknown to them. The best sign of the usefulness of these translations is furnished by the popularity that they enjoyed in the Middle Ages.

Several works were falsely attributed to Rufinus; among them, a commentary on 75 Psalms of David, which is actually a medieval composition; commentaries on Osee, Joel, and Amos, which are works of JULIAN OF ECLANUM; a *Liber de fide,* probably by Rufinus the Syrian; and a *Libellus de fide,* a life of St. Eugenia, and *Dicta de fide.*

Bibliography: *Patrologia Latina,* ed. J. P. MIGNE, 217 v. (Paris 1878–90) v. 21; *Opera omnia,* ed. M. SIMONETTI (*Corpus Christianorum* 20; 1961), with bibliog; *Die griechischen christlic-hen Schriftsteller der ersten drei Jahrhunderte* 42, 51 (1953–), PseudoClementines; *A Commentary on the Apostles' Creed,* ed. and tr. J. N. D. KELLY (*Ancient Christian Writers* 20; 1955); *Apologia,* ed. and tr. M. SIMONETI (Alba 1957). H. CHADWICK, ed., *The Sentences of Sextus* (Cambridge, Eng. 1959); *Journal of Theological Studies* 10 (1959) 10–42. F. X. MURPHY, *Rufinus of Aquileia* (Washington 1945); *Revue des études augustiniennes* 2 (1956) 79–91, and Paulinus of Nola; *Lexikon für Theologie und Kirche,* ed. J. HOFER and K. RAHNER (Freiburg 1957–65) 9:91–92. H. LIETZMANN, *Paulys Realenzyklopädie der klassischen Altertumswissenschaft,* ed. G. WISSOWA et al. suppl. 1.1 (1914) 1193–96. M. VILLAIN, *Nouvelle revue théologique* 64 (1937) 5–33, 139–161, monk and student; *Revue des sciences religieuses* 32 (1944) 129–156, creed; 33 (1946) 164–210, Church history. M. SIMONETTI, *Rivista di cultura classica e medinevale* 4 (1962) 3–44, benedictions; "Note rufiniane," *ibid.* 2 (1960) 140–172, 307–325. H. HOPE, *Studi. . . P. Ubaldi* (Milan 1937) 133–150, tr. M. WAGNER, *Rufinus the Translator* (Catholic University of America, *Patristic Studies* 73; 1945). G. BARDY, *Recherches sur l'histoire du texte et des versiones latines du De principiis d'Origène* (Paris 1923); A. VACANT et al., ed. *Dictionnaire de théologie catholique* (Paris 1903–50) 14.1:153–160. F. CAVALLERA, *Saint Jérôme,* 2 v. (*Spicilegium sacrum Lovaniense* 1, 2; 1922).

[M. SIMONETTI]

RUGG, JOHN, BL.

Priest and martyr; hanged, drawn, and quartered at Reading, England, Nov. 15, 1539. John Rugg was a former fellow of the two St. Mary Winton colleges and the first holder of the Wykehamical prebend "Bursalis" at Chichester Cathedral. He had retired from active ministry to Reading Abbey in 1532. There he was arrested and tried for high treason for refusing to recognize Henry VIII's supremacy over the Church of England. He was executed with Bl. Hugh FARINGDON, abbot of Reading, and John Eynon (or Onyon), a priest of St. Giles's, Reading. They were beatified by Pope Leo XIII on May 13, 1895.

Feast of the English Martyrs: May 4 (England); Dec. 1 (Dioceses of Portsmouth and Westminster; English Benedictines).

See Also: ENGLAND, SCOTLAND, AND WALES, MARTYRS OF.

Bibliography: R. CHALLONER, *Memoirs of Missionary Priests,* ed. J. H. POLLEN (rev. ed. London 1924; repr. Farnborough 1969). J. H. POLLEN, *Acts of English Martyrs* (London 1891).

[K. I. RABENSTEIN]

RUINART, THIERRY

Benedictine scholar of the Congregation of Saint-Maur; b. Reims, June 10, 1657; d. Abbey of Hautvillers, Sept. 29, 1709. He entered the Abbey of SAINT-REMI in

1674, was professed in 1675 at Saint-Faron of Meaux, lived at CORBIE from 1677 to 1681, and in 1682 settled at Saint-Germain-des-Prés, where he became the favorite student of MABILLON. He died suddenly while on a scholarly trip. The first and most valuable of his works was the *Acta primorum martyrum sincera,* following his dissertation on the edition of the acts and the cult of the martyrs (Paris 1689; the Amsterdam edition of 1713 has Dom Massuet's life of Ruinart). This well-conceived work, several times republished and translated, does not fulfill the demands of modern criticism. Later, Ruinart wrote the *Historia persecutionis Vandalicae* (1694; *Patrologia Latina* 58); the first part consists of the works of VICTOR OF VITA, and the second, the history of the persecutions. Then came the *Gregorii Episcopi Turonensis opera* (1699; *Patrologia Latina* 71) with a preface on religion in Merovingian Gaul and on Gregory of Tour's manuscripts. After having published the *Acta O.S.B. saec. VI* (11th century) in 1701 with Mabillon, and while preparing volume 6 of the *Annales O.S.B.* (1739), Ruinart tried his hand at polemics with the *Apologie de la mission de saint Maur en France* (1702) and the *Ecclesia Parisiensis vindicata* (1706). Besides the *Histoire de Fr. Morosini* (*Mémoires de Trévoux,* Nov. 1703), he wrote the *Beati Urbani papae II vita, Dissertatio de pallio archiepiscopali* (in Thuillier, *Oeuvres posthumes de Mabillon,* 1724), and the *Abrégé de la vie de Dom J. Mabillon* (1709), whose *De re diplomatica* (1709) he reedited. The *Journal de dom Ruinart,* written daily in 1698 and 1699 at the height of the disputes between the JESUITS and MAURISTS, was published by Ingold, *Histoire de l'edition bénédictine de Saint Augustin* (1903). Ruinart's *Iter litterarium in Alsatiam et Lotharingiam* was published by Thuillier (*Oeuvres . . . Mabillon*). The Bibliothèque Nationale of Paris has preserved the correspondence of Dom Ruinart (MS Fr. 19665–66).

Bibliography: H. LECLERCQ, *Dictionnaire d'archéologie chrétienne et de liturgie* 15.1:163–182.

[J. DAOUST]

RUÍZ BLANCO, MATÍAS

Franciscan missionary in Venezuela; b. Estepa (province of Seville), Spain, 1645; d. *c.* 1708. Early in life he entered the First Order of St. Francis of Assisi, becoming affiliated to the Franciscan province of Andalusia. At 21 he was awarded the chair of arts at the Convent of Valle in Seville. In 1672 he volunteered to become a missionary in the Americas and joined other missionaries of his order who were leaving for the missions of Piritú in eastern Venezuela. Fray Ruíz Blanco remained a Piritú missionary for about 30 years. He was elected superior of the missions three times (1686, 1696, 1705). Twice, in 1683 and 1693, he led mission bands back to Piritú from Spain. Three times he journeyed to the court of Spain in the interests of the missions. Fray Ruíz Blanco, an author of note, wrote *Conversion en Piritú . . .* (Madrid 1690), *Manual para Catekizar . . .* (Burgos 1683), *Diccionario espanol cumanagoto* (Burgos 1683), and *Memorial de Fray Matías Ruíz Blanco al Rey* (n.p. 1701). He is remembered as a giant among the Franciscan missionaries of the Piritú missions; he was devoted to the welfare of the native peoples and was given the title of defender of the natives. His observations on the culture of the Piritú missions are of value today, and his endeavors to prepare grammars and dictionaries of the Cumanagoto language to serve as the common tongue of the various tribes in the Piritú area demonstrate his extraordinary ability as a linguist.

Bibliography: M. RUÍZ BLANCO, *Conversión en Piritú (Colombia) de Indios Cumanagotos y Palenques* (Madrid 1892). P. DE AGUADO, *Historia de Venezuela,* 2 v. (Madrid 1918–19).

[J. M. CASSESE]

RUIZ DE LOS PAÑOS Y ANGEL, PEDRO, AND EIGHT COMPANIONS, BB.

Martyrs, also known as Martyrs of the Diocesan Worker Priests; Ruiz de los Paños b. Sept. 18, 1881 at Mora, Toledo, Spain; d. July 23, 1936 at Toledo, Spain.

Pedro Ruiz de los Paños entered the seminary in Toledo at an early age. In 1904 he joined the Diocesan Worker Priests, a union of priests founded in 1883 by Blessed Manuel Domingo y Sol, mostly dedicated to the formation of future priests. That same year he was sent to the Seminary of Málaga as dean of students. On Apr. 9, 1905 he was ordained to the priesthood, and from 1905 to 1927 he served as dean of students in the seminaries of Málaga, Badajoz, and Seville. He published a number of books dealing with seminary education (including *El libro del seminarista, El estado sacerdotal,* and *La bondad educadora.*) In 1927 he was appointed rector of the Pontifical Spanish College in Rome, where he served until 1933. On July 31, 1933 he was chosen as the fourth general director of the Diocesan Worker Priests. He continued his work in the National Secretariat of Seminaries, published the journal *Vocaciones,* and authored *Idea de la Hermandad de Sacerdotes Operarios Diocesanos.* On July 16, 1936 he went to Toledo to found a community of sisters (Discípulas de Jesús) to vocational ministry. However, two days later the Spanish Civil War began and on the morning of July 23, he was arrested along with two other priests, and hours later they were killed on the streets of Toledo.

Eight other Diocesan Worker priests were also killed during the Spanish Civil War. José Sala Picó (b. June 24, 1889 at Pons, Lleida) was the rector of the Minor Seminary in Toledo when he was killed with Pedro Ruiz de los Paños. Guillermo Plaza Hernández (b. June 25, 1908 at Yuncos, Toledo) was killed on Aug. 10, 1936 at Argés, Toledo. Recaredo Centelles Abad (b. May 23, 1904 at Vall d'Uxo, Castellón) died in October 1936 after the militia men shot him twice. Martín Martinez Pascual (b. Nov. 11, 1910 at Valdealgorfa, Teruel) had only been a priest for 14 months when was martyred in his hometown on Aug. 18, 1936. Antonio Perulles Estivill (b. May 5, 1992 at Cornudella, Tarragona) served in different seminaries in Spain before being killed on Aug. 12, 1936 in Marsá. José Pascual Carda Saporta (b. Oct. 29, 1893 at Villareal, Castellón) dedicated his life to the formation of priests in Spain and Mexico; he was killed in Villareal on Sept. 4, 1936; Isidoro Bover Oliver (b. May 2, 1890 at Vinaros, Castellón) worked in Tortosa as the editor of *El Correo Josefino,* a magazine for seminaries, when he was killed on Oct. 2, 1936. José Maria Peris Polo, also a musical composer (b. Nov. 1, 1889 at Cinctorres, Castellón) died on Aug. 15, 1936 in Alzamora, Castellón.

The process of beatification began in 1958 in two different places: Toledo and Tortosa. In 1988 they were united in a single process. At their beatification, Oct. 1, 1995, Pope John Paul II remembered the urgency of vocational ministry.

Feast: July 23.

Bibliography: JUAN DE ANDRÉS, *Testigos de su sacerdocio* (Madrid 1990).

[RUTILIO J. DEL RIEGO]

RUÍZ DE MONTOYA, ANTONIO

Jesuit missionary in Paraguay; b. Lima, Nov. 11, 1583; d. there, April 11, 1653. After having led a not very pious life as a youth, he entered the Society of Jesus (Nov. 11, 1606). He made his novitiate in Córdoba, Argentina, and probably was ordained in 1610, for the following year he was in Paraguay beginning his missionary work. From 1623 to 1637, he was superior of the Paraguayan REDUCTIONS. During this period, the raids of the Paulistas made it necessary to move the missions. In 1637 he went to Spain to seek royal protection for them. In 1643 he returned to Peru, to whose viceroy fell the duty of carrying out the royal cedulas in favor of the Reductions. He was already on his way to Paraguay when he had to return to Lima to represent the province in the dispute with Bishop Cárdenas. After his death, in accordance with his wishes, his remains were taken to

Paraguay and buried in the church of the Reduction of Loreto. In addition to numerous letters and memorials, Ruíz de Montoya wrote four important works: *Conquista espiritual* (Madrid 1639; new edition, Bilbao 1892), *Tesoro de la lengua guaraní* (Madrid 1639), *Arte y vocabulario de la lengua guaraní* (Madrid 1640), and *Catecismo de la lengua guaraní* (Madrid 1640).

Bibliography: G. FURLONG, *Antonio Ruíz de Montoya y su carta a Comental (1645)* (Buenos Aires 1964).

[H. STORNI]

RUÍZ Y FLORES, LEOPOLDO

Mexican archbishop and apostolic delegate; b. Amealco, Querétaro, Nov. 13, 1865; d. Morelia, Dec. 12, 1941. After being reared in Temascalcingo, he was a student at the Clerical College of San Joaquín in Tacuba and later at the South American College in Rome. He received doctorates in philosophy, theology, and canon law in the Gregorian University. He taught philosophy in the archdiocesan seminary of Mexico City and was appointed successively pastor in Tacubaya, canon of Guadalupe, bishop of León (1900–07), archbishop of Linares-Monterrey (1907–11), and finally archbishop of Morelia (1912–41). He was apostolic delegate from 1929 to 1937. Archbishop Ruiz devoted a great deal of time to improving catechetical and general education in the Catholic schools. In León he founded the Instituto Sollano, the Instituto Teresiano, the school of the Sisters of the Adoration, the Instituto Guadalupe as well as the Marist school in Irapuato and later in Monterrey, and the schools of the Christian Brothers and the Sacred Heart Sisters. As archbishop he created many new parishes and the new Diocese of Tacámbaro. He stressed the social apostolate among industrial and agricultural workers. When the Madero rebellion broke out in 1911, Archbishop Ruiz, a long-time friend of Pres. Porfirio Díaz, felt bound to exhort his flock to remain loyal to the established government. As a result he was considered a reactionary by the victorious rebels and in 1914 was forced to take refuge in the U.S. During the religious persecution of 1925, in spite of his sympathy for conciliation movements, Ruiz y Flores was expelled by President Calles. Once more he sought hospitality in the U.S. Pope Pius XI named him apostolic delegate, and through the good offices of the ambassadors of the U.S. and Chile, he made a secret visit to Mexico in June 1929, accompanied by Bp. Pascual Díaz, to meet with Pres. Emilio Portes Gil. They agreed on a *modus vivendi* that would permit the restoration of worship in all the churches of the republic. When the Pope, in his encyclical *Acerba animi,* criticized the Mexican government for openly violating the agreement,

Archbishop Ruiz y Flores was again exiled. He lived in San Antonio, Tex., until 1937, when he returned after the dedication of the pontifical seminary in Montezuma. He devoted the few remaining years of his life to the Archdiocese of Morelia.

Bibliography: J. A. ROMERO, *Recuerdo de Recuerdos* (Mexico City 1942). E. VALVERDE TÉLLEZ, *Bio-bibliografía eclesiástica mexicana,* 3 v. (Mexico City 1949).

[D. OLMEDO]

RULE OF FAITH

St. Paul says that the just man lives by FAITH (Rom 1.17). This means that faith gives a direction to all his activity. His submission to the revealed word of God conditions the whole of his life and affects his attitude to things of this world and the next. In faith there is an immediate contact between God and the individual, and man submits totally to God's revelation.

But the commitment of the individual to God in faith does not mean that there is an interior intuition that determines a man's belief. This was the view of the Modernists (cf. *Pascendi;* H. Denzinger, *Enchiridion symbolorum,* 3484). Private religious experience is important, but revelation comes to man as a member of society. In the pastoral Epistles πίστις (faith) is used more in an objective sense, i.e., the faith that one believes, than in the subjective sense of that whereby one believes (1 Tm 4.1; 6.10; 2 Tm 3.8; Ti 1.13). The source of this faith, this rule of life, is to be found in the deeds and teaching of Christ, and just as originally the message was addressed to all men not in the privacy of their hearts alone but as members of society by the preaching of Christ, so it is today addressed to men in this capacity through the Church.

The Church has the task of preaching the gospel not by adding to it but by expounding it according to the needs of mankind and so bringing sanctification to those who hear the word and obey it. The teaching Church, then, is the rule of faith for all men. It tells them what they have to believe and do to be saved.

In the Early Church. In the first years of Christianity it was natural that there should be drawn up outlines and summaries of Christian belief as a help in the instruction of converts and to give the faithful a simple rule to guide their lives. These formularies varied and at first did not insist on an exact form or words; they were prior to the formulation of set CREEDS and were known as the ''canon of truth'' (Irenaeus) or the ''rule of faith'' (Tertullian). The canon of truth was constant not in the sense of a universally accepted creed or formula of words, but

in the sense that the doctrinal content did not vary wherever the Church was found. This was in contrast to the doctrine of the Gnostics, for whom there were several conflicting norms. In several places Irenaeus gave examples of this canon, which was much influenced by the text 1 Corinthians 8.6, belief in the one God the Father and one Lord Jesus Christ. Tertullian's rule of faith was very similar. It was the body of teaching handed on by the Church.

In the early apostolic Fathers there was expressed a primary concern to WITNESS to the traditional faith, and this was manifested in the instructions, preaching, and prayer of the Church. Only later did this rule or norm become a way of distinguishing true DOCTRINE from false. Later, too, a deeper reflection on this simple summary took place, and with men such as Origen one finds the first attempts to penetrate the content more profoundly and to explore its inner meaning. For this work human wisdom and reason guided by the Holy Spirit can be of great help. Such theology has to be guided by the rule of faith in another sense, viz, the preservation of that inner harmony that exists between one truth of faith and another. But important as this reflection may be in the history of Christian thought, the ordinary faithful were content with the rule of faith until the advent of serious HERESY meant that the simple rule had to give way to the exact formularies of the creeds.

Scripture and Tradition. The authentic faith is to be found in the teaching and preaching of the Church, which has continued unbroken from the time of the Apostles. Thus the proximate rule of faith suited to all men is this universal teaching of the Church, the living magisterium. But now a further question arises. How does the Church itself know what is revealed? It is under the protection of the Holy Spirit and so cannot err, and yet the decisions of the Church are not arbitrary; they must be reasonable. What precisely are the reasons?

In deciding what is the ultimate rule of faith, the inspired writings have an important and unique place. The Bible has been entrusted to the Church, and it draws nourishment by prayerful meditation on the word of God. The Church has always to be checking its message by the standard of the inspired word so that it can teach nothing at variance with the Scriptures. The very authority of the Church itself is proclaimed in the Bible.

This is not to fall into the error of maintaining that the Scriptures are the sole rule of faith. The Holy Spirit, who inspired the Scriptures, is also with the Church, and it is through the living tradition of the Church that the Scriptures reach man. The Church itself tells men they are inspired; it is the Church that draws men's attention to them and assures men of a right interpretation. Written and oral teaching are really inseparable. Oral preaching of the gospel preceded in time the New Testament writings, but even this oral teaching was focused on the Old Testament writings that found their fulfillment in the deeds of Christ. The New Testament itself appeals to the oral teaching (1 Cor 15.1–8; Gal ch. 1 and 2; Col 2.6; 2 Thes 2.15; 2 Jn 12; 3 Jn 13; 2 Pt 3.15–16).

When listening to the Scriptures in the liturgy or reading them privately at home the individual Christian can gain valuable insights into God's revelation, but these are not sufficient of themselves to constitute a rule of faith. The reformers very much minimized the part of the Church and overstressed the individual response to the Bible, but clearly this experience cannot be the final word, as one needs some authority to tell him what indeed are the inspired Scriptures and how they should be interpreted. Many of the reformers soon realized that the Bible cannot be left to individual interpretation and so soon began to allow for a further rule of faith such as the interpretation of the early Church (thus the convocation of 1571). The question of the canon of Scripture has always been a difficulty for this view.

On the other hand, Counter Reformation theology had to insist very much on the place of the Church and the importance of tradition; it tended to neglect the importance of the Bible. The ecumenical movement has meant there is a better appreciation by all Christians that both the Bible and the Church have their part to play in the rule of faith.

See Also: ANALOGY OF FAITH; ARTICLE OF FAITH; CONFESSION OF FAITH; DEPOSIT OF FAITH; DOGMA; REVELATION, THEOLOGY OF; TRADITION (IN THEOLOGY).

Bibliography: J. QUASTEN, *Lexikon für Theologie und Kirche,* ed. J. HOFER and K. RAHNER, 10 v. (2d, new ed. Freiburg 1957–65) 8:1102–03. J. N. D. KELLY, *Early Christian Creeds* (2d ed. New York 1960). *Early Christian Doctrines* (2d ed. New York 1960). G. H. TAVARD, *Holy Writ or Holy Church* (New York 1960).

[M. E. WILLIAMS]

RULES OF LAW (REGULAE IURIS)

The rules of law are collections of general legal principles which, when properly used, assist in the interpretation and application of canon law. Canonical collections of *regulae* do not have the force of law in themselves, but rather offer succinct statements, each of which is a summary principle derived from a number of legal situations or cases. As tools for interpretation, these rules require proper application so as not to be misused. Thus, for example, a specific rule is applied within the context of similar laws, general principles of law, canonical equity and praxis, and learned opinions by experts in the law. For texts of the *Regulae Iuris* in the *Liber Sextus* and the *Regulae Iuris* in the Decretals of Gregory IX, *see* Gauthier.

History. Pope Boniface VIII (1294–1303), to complement previous collections of legislation, ordered a new compilation that became known as the *Liber Sextus* and concluded with a collection of rules. He thus followed the example of Justinian who, in *Corpus iuris civilis, Digesta* 17 "de diversis regulis juris antiqui," collected no less than 2,025 rules.

Current scholarship holds that the famous jurist Dino Rosoni of Mugello (born in 1253, taught in Bologna and Rome and authored many works of law), while the author of the major commentary on the *regulae*, at the most only collaborated in their compilation (Stein). There are 88 rules, the number probably being symbolic; they cannot be classified into a systematic order, but rather give the impression of being mixed together. Many of them contain evident or almost evident principles and norms; some are of limited importance; quite a few, unless well interpreted, may lead to erroneous conclusions. Their main and most common source is Roman law, but some are exclusively from canon law and often of Scriptural origin. The following rules repeat the rules of the *Corpus iuris civilis, Digesta* almost to the letter: 17, 19, 24, 25, 26, 28, 30, 35, 36, 42, 45, 46, 48, 53, 59, 66, 74, 78, 80, 86.

Content. By dividing the rules according to subject, they may be classified into the following groups:

1. Rules with very general norms existing in some degree in any section of law
   a. On the total and the part: 35, 53, 80
   b. On possible and impossible things: 6, 41, 60, 66
   c. On accessory and principal matters: 39, 42, 81, 84
   d. On penalties and favors: the former to be mitigated—15, 22, 40; the latter to be restricted—28, 45, 74, 78
   e. On time and possession: 2, 18, 54
   f. On responsibility: 19, 27, 29, 48, 62, 76, 86
   g. On various subjects: 20, 31, 34, 37, 40, 55
2. Rules in which the personal element prevails
   a. On privileges: 6, 7, 16, 17, 28, 78
   b. On the qualities of persons, representation, succession: 9, 10, 14, 46, 67, 68, 72, 77, 79, 84
3. Rules regarding mostly things
   a. Possession: 1, 31, 36, 65
   b. Prescription: 2, 3
   c. Juridical acts in general: 21, 30, 33, 50, 57, 58, 59, 70, 73, 82, 83
4. Rules pertaining to trials and processes
   a. General duties of the judge: 12, 26, 31, 88
   b. Penal cases: 4, 5, 23, 24, 49

c. Treatment of the plaintiff and defendant: 11, 20, 32, 38, 63, 71

Many of the rules are criticized as useless because they appear obvious, as numbers 35, 53, and 80; or because they are too elastic as 43, 44, 47, and 50 (the first two, 43 and 44, are a sort of guessing game). Others are dangerous because they allow too many exceptions, e.g., 8, 13, 18, 21, 29, 54, and 64.

Given the nature of the rules as abstract principles and, in addition, the particular character of a rule (for example reiterating the obvious or capable of leading to diverse conclusions), they require careful application to avoid misunderstanding.

Bibliography: E. ROELKER, ''An Important Rule of Law,'' *Jurist* 17 (1957) 9–28; ''Succession and Delegation in the Rules of Law,'' *ibid.* 403–428; ''A Comparative Study of Ignorance in the Rules of Law and in the Code of Canon Law,'' *Jurist* 18 (1958) 128–148. A. REIFFENSTUEL, *Jus canonicum universium,* 7 v. (Paris 1864–70) v.7. V. BARTOCCETTI, *De regulis juris canonici* (Rome 1955). P. STEIN, *Regulae Iuris: From Juristic Rules to Legal Maxims* (Edinburgh 1966). A. GAUTHIER, *Roman Law and Its Contribution to the Development of Canon Law* (Ottawa 1996).

[V. BARTOCCETTI/R. J. KASLYN]

RUMMEL, JOSEPH FRANCIS

Ninth archbishop of New Orleans, La.; b. Steinmauern, Baden, Germany, Oct. 14, 1876; d. New Orleans, Nov. 8, 1964. At age six he immigrated to the United States with his parents, Gustav and Theresa (Bollweber) Rummel, becoming a naturalized American with them on Feb. 2, 1888. After attending Catholic schools in New York City and North East, Pa., he was trained at St. Anselm's College, Manchester, N.H. (B.A. 1896); St. Joseph's Seminary (Dunwoodie), Yonkers, N.Y.; and the North American College, Rome. Ordained in the Basilica of St. John Lateran by Cardinal Pietro Respighi on May 24, 1902, he earned a doctorate in sacred theology the following year.

Early Career. As priest of the Archdiocese of New York, he served as curate of St. Joseph's, Yorkville (1903–07); pastor of St. Peter's, Kingston (1907–15); vicar forane of Ulster and Sullivan counties (1912–15); pastor of St. Anthony of Padua, Bronx (1915–24); and pastor of St. Joseph of the Holy Family, Harlem (1924–28). He was appointed moderator of several Catholic groups, judge and vice-official on the archdiocesan matrimonial curia, and executive secretary (1923–24) of a national committee to raise funds and collect clothing for the destitute, especially children, of war-torn Germany. Pius XI named him a papal chamberlain on April 24, 1924 and bishop of Omaha on March 20, 1928. After consecration by Cardinal P. J. Hayes on May 29 in St. Patrick's Cathedral, New York, he was installed as ordinary on July 4, 1928, in St. Cecilia's Cathedral, Omaha.

Orderly and methodical by nature and training, Bishop Rummel soon introduced a standard system of accounting for the 135 parishes of the diocese. In 1930 he successfully launched the Confraternity of the Laity Campaign to raise funds for the expansion of St. James Orphanage and for work on the unfinished cathedral, as well as for expenses of the Sixth National Eucharistic Congress held in Omaha from Sept. 23 to 25, 1930. He convened a synod in June of 1934, the first in the diocese in more than 30 years. On March 9, 1935, Rummel was named successor to Archbishop John W. Shaw of New Orleans.

Archbishop. Rummel's reputation as a gifted orator and energetic administrator won him a warm welcome to New Orleans on May 14, 1935. He quickly sensed the challenge of reorganizing the archdiocese and invigorating lay groups. During the summer of 1935 he decreed that each parish was to form a Confraternity of Christian Doctrine, an organization that he vastly expanded and vigorously supported throughout his tenure. Several organizations for youth and professional groups emerged, and the programs of others already existing were enriched. Under his direction, hundreds of men and women became involved in the plans and preparations for the Eighth National Eucharistic Congress of Oct. 17 to 20, 1938, the first held in the South.

The Depression of the 1930s, unsettled conditions during World War II, and building material shortages in the mid-1940s, coupled with the archbishop's innate aversion for debt, permitted only a moderate increase in new parishes established and buildings erected during his first ten years in office. Between 1946 and 1961, however, he opened 40 parishes, making a total of 48 during his entire tenure. In the late 1940s, as the population of the Greater New Orleans and Baton Rouge areas burgeoned, he eased his policy, requiring that at least one-half of the funds needed for property acquisition or construction should be raised beforehand in cash or pledges. Within a ten-year period he launched two archdiocesan-wide financial campaigns that substantially exceeded their goals. The esteem of priests and people for the archbishop was demonstrated when St. Joseph Hall of Philosophy, Notre Dame Seminary, was erected in 1953 as a memorial to his silver jubilee as a bishop and the golden anniversary of his ordination.

The seventh diocesan synod, which he convened in June of 1949, gave the archbishop the opportunity to modernize the administration of the see, expand the curia, assign personnel to new commissions and offices, realign deaneries, and update regulations for the promotion of Catholic life. Until 1947, when the Holy See gave him as auxiliary Bishop L. Abel Caillouet, the archbishop alone handled all parochial and institutional visitations, confirmations, graduations, dedications, and other engagements. A facile writer, he was the author of pastoral letters and circulars that fill several thick binders. An eloquent speaker, he addressed all gatherings over which he presided, and he was often featured on programs of diocesan, regional, and national conventions. Throughout his career as a bishop and archbishop, he was active with the National Catholic Welfare Conference, serving on its administrative board and as episcopal chairman of the Catholic Committee for Refugees and of the Legal Department. He was a member of the Board of Trustees of The Catholic University of America, Washington, D.C., and of the National Catholic Community Service. Locally he was elected to numerous social welfare boards and civic committees. His readiness to aid the needy at home and abroad won for him both the acclaim of the community and honors from the governments of France, Italy, the Netherlands, and Haiti. Eight colleges and universities honored him with degrees, awards, and medals.

Integration Leader. For the last 15 years of his life, Archbishop Rummel was partially blind from glaucoma. This handicap kept him from officiating at ceremonies such as ordinations but did not curtail his other activities. While still recuperating from a fall in Baton Rouge on Oct. 9, 1960, he announced a crash program in the spring of 1961 for the erection of four new high schools in Jefferson Parish (county). To many observers this venture seemed particularly bold because of the sensitive social context of the times. Strong resistance to local public school desegregation in 1960 and open resentment to the archbishop's own clear denunciation of racial discrimination had manifested itself in the state legislature, mass meetings of the White Citizens' Councils, and activities of other segregationist groups. The archbishop's pastoral letter of March 15, 1953, entitled ''Blessed Are the Peacemakers,'' had apprised the faithful that segregation because of race would not be tolerated in Catholic churches and societies. On Feb. 11, 1956, he wrote another and more explicit pastoral on ''The Morality of Racial Segregation,'' in which he prepared the way for the eventual integration of Catholic schools. Finally, on March 27, 1962, he announced that, at the opening of the next term, all Catholic schools of the archdiocese would accept all qualified students at all levels. When opposition persisted from a vocal and organized minority, the archbishop warned seven, and eventually excommunicated three of the leaders.

Rummel announced his retirement on the 60th anniversary of his ordination; his coadjutor with right of suc-

cession, Archbishop John P. Cody, became apostolic administrator on June 1, 1962.

Bibliography: Archives, Archdiocese of New Orleans.

[H. C. BEZOU]

RUPERT OF DEUTZ

Abbot of Deutz, near Cologne, and exegetical theologian; b. probably Liège, *c.* 1075; d. Deutz, March 4, 1129. A series of visions in adolescence convinced him he had been granted true understanding of the Scriptures and he devoted his life to allegorical exegesis, particularly of the Apocalypse. An uncompromising Gregorian, he refused ordination until his simoniacal bishop had been reconciled to Rome (1106), and in 1116 he was forced to flee to Siegburg Abbey because of the hostility his attacks on simony had aroused. In 1117 he challenged ANSELM OF LAON's predestinarianism and debated with his pupils at Laon. He was appointed abbot of Deutz in 1119 or 1120. A defender of the Benedictine tradition, he opposed the introduction of logic into theology, rebutted the attacks on his order by the Canons Regular, was the first to interpret the Canticle of Canticles as Christ's love for the Virgin, and developed an Augustinian theology of history as the divinely ordained process of moral reeducation for mankind, divided into three ages under the guidance of the Trinity. Although Rupert was renowned during his lifetime for his literary style and knowledge of Scripture, he was given little attention after his death until the Reformation, when his imprecise language on the Eucharist caused him to be accused, falsely, of having preached impanation (*see* TRANSUBSTANTIATION).

See Also: ANSELM OF LAON.

Bibliography: *Opera Omnia, Patrologia Latina,* ed. J. P. MIGNE, 217 v. (Paris 1878–90) v. 167–170. M. MAGRASSI, *Teologia e storia nel pensiero di Ruperto di Deutz* (Rome 1959). R. HAACKE, ''Die Überlieferung der Schriften R. von D.,'' *Deutsches Archiv für Erforschung des Mittelalters* 16 (1960) 397–436. H. SILVESTRE, *Le ''Chronicon Sancti Laurentii Leodiensis'' dit de Rupert de Deutz* (Louvain 1952). M. BERNARDS, *Lexikon für Theologie und Kirche,* ed. J. HOFER and K. RAHNER, 10 v. (2d, new ed. Freiburg 1957–65) 9:104–106, excellent bibliog.

[B. S. SMITH]

RUPERT OF OTTOBEUREN, BL.

Abbot of the Benedictine monastery of OTTOBEUREN in Bavaria, Germany; d. Ottobeuren, 1145. Because of miracles attributed to prayer at his grave, Rupert (or Robert) was the object of great popular devotion. After being prior of St. George in the Black Forest, which had been founded by monks from HIRSAU, he became abbot of Ottobeuren in 1102. There he introduced reform in the Cluniac spirit by following the constitutions written in 1079 by Abbot WILLIAM OF HIRSAU, whose monastery had become a center of ecclesiastical reform in Germany and of opposition to Emperor HENRY IV.

Commemoration: Aug. 15.

Bibliography: *Monumenta Germaniae: Scriptores* (Berlin 1825–) 23:616–619. *Constitutiones Hirsaugienses, Patrologia Latina,* ed. J. P. MIGNE, 217 v. (Paris 1878–90) 150:923–1146. M. FISCHER, *Studien zur Entstehung der Hirsauer Konstitutionen* (Stuttgart 1910). R. BAUERREISS, "St. Georgen im Schwarzwald, ein Reformmittelpunkt Südostdeutschlands im beginnenden 12. Jahrhundert," *Studien und Mitteilungen aus dem Benediktiner-und dem Cistercienserorden* 51 (1933) 200. A. M. ZIMMERMANN, *Kalendarium Benedictinum: Die Heiligen und Seligen des Benediktinerorderns und seiner Zweige,* 4 v. (Metten 1933–38) 2:572–574.

[W. H. WALLAIK]

RUPERT OF SALZBURG, ST.

Founder and first bishop of Salzburg, patron of the church and region of Salzburg; d. March 27, *c.* 718. He was presumably a descendant of the Frankish MEROVINGIAN royal line. On mission territory entrusted to him by the Bavarian Duke Theodo (695–718), Rupert (Hrodbert or Robert) founded the monastery of SANKT PETER (*c.* 700) on the ruins of ancient *Juvavum* (Salzburg), with a community of Irish Celtic monks. He founded also the convent of NONNBERG, which he entrusted to his niece (St.) Erentrude (d. *c.* 718) as first superior. These communities, which were later to become Benedictine, are the oldest monasteries in Austria and Germany. Sankt Peter was headed by a monastic bishop, Rupert being its first abbot bishop. He and his monks not only evangelized the Salzburg people but contributed greatly to their culture. Rupert helped develop mining in the area. The founding of a church over the grave of St. Maximilian in Pongau (Bischofshofen) among the Rhaeto–Romanic peoples can be traced to Rupert. He went also into the region of Lorch on the Enns (the old Roman *Laureacum*), then moved to the south and built near Wallersee (today Seekirchen) a St. Peter's church. The main church in the city of Salzburg, built most likely on the site of the upper castle called Salzburg, was dedicated by Rupert to MARTIN OF TOURS, the Frankish Empire's patron saint and the protector of the Merovingians. It was later elevated to cathedral status with canons who lived according to the rule and constitutions of CHRODEGANG OF METZ. Rupert was buried in Sankt Peter's abbey church, but in 773 his remains were moved to the new cathedral of Abbot Bishop VIRGILIUS OF SALZBURG. A Frankish Sacramentary of the ninth century already recognized Rupert as a saint. He is

Dom St. Rupert, consecrated September 1628, Residenzplatz, Salzburg, Austria. (©Adam Woolfitt/CORBIS)

invoked in cases of erysipelas and children's convulsions. Often portrayed as a bishop with a barrel of salt, he is popularly venerated in Austria and in Bavaria, especially in the Rupertiwinkel between the Inn and Salzach Rivers. From 1701 to 1805 there was an Order of the Knights of St. Rupert composed of the Salzburg territorial nobility who bound themselves to celibacy and prayer.

Feast: March 27; September 24 (translation feast).

Bibliography: *Monumenta Germaniae Historica: Scriptores rerum Merovingicarum* 6:140–162. R. BAUERREISS, *Kirchengeschichte Bayerns* (St. Ottilein 1949–55; 2d ed. 1958–) v. 1. Wattenbach–Levison 1:143. A. BUTLER, *The Lives of the Saints,* rev. ed. H. THURSTON and D. ATTWATER, 4 v. (New York 1956) 1:700–701. I. ZIBERMAYR, "Die R. Legende," *Mitteilungen des Instituts für österreichische Geschichtsforschung* 62 (1954) 67–82. J. WODKA, *Lexikon für Theologie und Kirche,* ed. J. HOFER and K. RAHNER, 10 v. (2d, new ed. Freiburg 1957–65); suppl., *Das Zweite Vatikanische Konzil: Dokumente und Kommentare,* ed. H. S. BRECHTER et al., pt. 1 (1966)[2] 9:106–107. F. GRELL, *Der Salzbischof. St. Rupert* (Salz-

John Ruskin. (Archive Photos)

burg 1973). R. GRATZ and A. HAHNL, *Hl. Rupert von Salzburg*, eds. P. EDER and J. KRONBICHLER (Salzburg 1996).

[A. KRAUSE]

RUSKIN, JOHN

Art critic and social philosopher; b. London, Feb. 8, 1819; d. Coniston, Jan. 20, 1900. Only child of a wealthy wine merchant, Ruskin was raised in an Evangelical household whose strictness was somewhat lightened by his father's love of travel, literature, and painting. He matriculated at Christ Church, Oxford, in 1836, and took his B.A. in 1842 and his M.A. in 1843. He married Euphemia Gray in 1848, but the marriage was annulled in 1854.

The argument of his principal critical work, *Modern Painters* (1843–60), is rooted in the moral distinction between love and pride. An artist paints out of love for his subject, out of pride in his own virtuosity, or to minister to the pride of a patron. The first motive, love, is the root of all good art; the second motive, pride, is the source of all bad art. The development of this argument and its implications occupied Ruskin throughout his life.

To prove that the taste of Europe had been corrupted by the dazzling technique of the Renaissance masters, Ruskin turned, in *The Stones of Venice* (1851–53), to evaluate architecture, where individual genius is less evident and where he felt he could show that the RENAISSANCE had replaced something finer than itself. Ruskin's devotion to Gothic architecture should accordingly be understood as a tactic primarily in his defense of modern painters. Struck by the harmony that he saw between the medieval cathedrals and the culture from which they sprang, Ruskin turned to examine his own culture. He saw that industrial workers lived such miserable lives and were surrounded by so much ugliness that their taste for beauty must be impaired. He also believed that political liberalism and laissez-faire capitalism were creating a climate of anarchy, self-love, and competition in which art could not flourish. Hence, in *Unto This Last* (1862) and in *Fors Clavigera* (1871–84) he vigorously attacked the social system and spent his energy and his considerable fortune in futile efforts to change the direction of modern life. By 1860 he had perceived that he was dealing basically with the fallen nature of man; the last section of *Modern Painters* and *Sesame and Lilies* (1871) reflect this new awareness.

In 1869 Ruskin was elected the first professor of fine art at Oxford, holding the post from 1870 to 1878 and again from 1883 to 1885. In 1877 he had published his contempt for a picture by James A. M. Whistler. The painter successfully brought suit, and the case may be said to mark the end of Ruskin's active life; the principal work of his last years is *Praeterita* (1885–89), an autobiography noted more for its charm than for its accuracy. He was the most influential art critic of the 19th century, and has been shown to have influenced such diverse figures as Mohandas GANDHI, Frank Lloyd Wright, Henri BERGSON, Marcel Proust, and many of the early members of the British Labour Party.

The general identification of Gothic architecture with Roman Catholicism was a source of embarrassment to Ruskin and he vigorously dissociated himself from Augustus PUGIN and the Catholic Revival. He found difficulty in reconciling his Evangelical tradition with his love for Catholic art and architecture, and in his early works he zealously appended anti-Catholic notes to his works on these subjects. After 1858, when he had renounced his Evangelical heritage, he felt no need to attack Catholicism. On the contrary, he purged his early works of what he termed ''pieces of rabid and utterly false Protestantism.'' He tried by historical studies and by visiting monasteries to understand the culture that had built the great cathedrals. He was a cordial friend of Cardinal MANNING, and he once announced, for its shock effect, that he was a Catholic. His last Oxford lecture was a scandalous attack on Protestantism, which he had come to equate with the liberalism, competitive capitalism, and tastelessness of middle-class England. In spite of these episodes, he seems never to have considered actually becoming a Roman Catholic.

Bibliography: J. RUSKIN, *Works,* ed. E. T. COOK, and A. WEDDERBURN, 39 v. (London 1903–12); *The Diaries,* ed. J. EVANS and J. H. WHITEHOUSE, 3 v. (London 1956–59). J. D. ROSENBERG, *The Darkening Glass* (New York 1961). E. T. COOK, *The Life of John Ruskin,* 2 v. (London 1911). D. LEON, *Ruskin, The Great Victorian* (London 1949). F. G. TOWNSEND, *Ruskin and the Landscape Feeling* (Urbana, Ill. 1951). J. T. FAIN, *Ruskin and the Economists* (Nashville 1956).

[C. T. DOUGHERTY]

RUSSELL, BERTRAND

Third Earl, English philosopher, progressive thinker, and pioneer of symbolic logic; born in Trelleck on May 18, 1872; died Feb. 2, 1970, in Wales. Born into a great Whig family, champions of reform, he was brought up a Protestant. As a boy he tried in vain to find an acceptable rational basis for religion and became an agnostic. Educated privately and at Cambridge, he studied mathematics and philosophy. His life was principally that of a writer on philosophical, logical, and social questions, though he held teaching posts in England, the U.S., and China. Fellow of Trinity College at various periods, he was once put out for his pacifism. He stood for Parliament twice, once as a women's suffrage candidate, and was twice imprisoned, once in connection with pacifism and once with nuclear disarmament. At one time he conducted a school on educational principles of his own. He did not see this as a success and gave up the school in 1932. He received the Order of Merit and in 1950 the Nobel Prize for Literature. From the 1950s onward he increasingly turned from philosophy to international politics. He protested both the H-Bomb test on the Bikini Atoll, and the U. S. involvement in the Vietnam War, inciting people to mass civil disobedience. His views and his uncompromising implementation of them brought on him obloquy and even ostracism. As a brilliant writer and speaker with a mischievous wit, he knew and influenced many leading intellectual figures.

Logic and Mathematics. Partly under the influence of G. E. Moore, he soon abandoned his early idealism, being chiefly hostile to the doctrine that all relations are internal; since the he always believed in a plurality of objects standing in relations that leave their nature unaltered. After 1900 the writings of G. Peano inspired him to demonstrate that mathematics was not a set of synthetic a priori truths but was reducible to logic. Soon, however, he found a contradiction in the notion of a class, on which he had relied: for the class of all classes that are not members of themselves is a member of itself, if it is

not, and is not, if it is (*see* ANTINOMY). G. Frege felt shattered, but Russell eventually produced a solution, which he never quite relinquished, in his theory of types. The type, or range of significance, of a propositional function, $\varphi(x)$, is given by the range of constants that yield a meaningful proposition when substituted for x: it is not meaningful either to assert or to deny that the contradictious class mentioned above is a member of itself. (G. Ryle has since attributed many philosophical problems to informal type mistakes.) Russell and A. N. Whitehead set out their logicist account of mathematics in *Principia Mathematica* (3 v. Cambridge, Eng. 1910–13, 2d ed. 1925–27). Among philosophical objections to it are the unnaturalness of the theory of types and the non-self-evidence of certain axioms.

In his realist phase Russell thought that cardinal numbers, classes, and even objects of reference such as the golden mountain were real, but his theory of descriptions (1905) showed how propositions apparently involving reference to possibly nonexistent objects could be so rephrased that their meaningfulness did not involve the existence of those objects. "The King of France is bald" is meaningful even when there is no King of France, since it asserts merely that one and only one thing is the King of France and that that thing is bald. Such analyses facilitated Russell's increasingly frequent applications of Ockham's razor. Instances were now seen to be classes of events. Numbers, points, and physical objects were treated analogously.

Russell's program was to substitute logical constructions for inferred entities and to minimize the number of objects in which one had to believe. His logical atomism of 1914 to 1920 (which owed much to L. WITTGENSTEIN) consisted in using logical techniques to break down complex facts into their ultimate components. Every proposition ought to be explicable as equivalent to a truth function of basic propositions, in which each element stands for an object or universal with which one is acquainted. The most resistant propositions, those about mental facts, were given a behaviorist analysis (1921): consciousness succumbed to Ockham's razor, and (as in the neutral monism of W. JAMES) the propositions of science, when analyzed, were seen to refer only to elements that are in themselves neither mental nor physical.

Russell's concern was always with science, not with common sense or common usage (whose propositions might be incurably confused). He came to identify sense data with brain states and physical objects with the unknown but inferred causes of those states (1927). He departed from strict EMPIRICISM and sought the postulates required for the nondeductive inferences of science (1948).

Logical positivism and linguistic analysis alike have revealed difficulties in the analyses required by Russell. His fundamental assumption of the existence of particulars named by logically proper names has been criticized, notably by Wittgenstein, for embodying a primitive and partial conception of language.

Ethics and Religion. Russell's views on ethics, society, and politics, though influential and stimulating, are of little theoretical importance. He combined the conviction that assertions of value are groundless with a passionate attachment to certain values. He always repudiated humanism in its sense of awe before the human spirit: his nearest approach to religion is a sense of the infinite and a certain cosmic feeling. He rejected theology because he could see no validity in the traditional proofs. For him, a First Cause must itself have a cause, and necessity is an attribute of propositions; so there can be no "Necessary Being." Institutional religion is, perhaps inevitably, a source of evil.

Bibliography: Principal Works. *Principles of Mathematics* (Cambridge, Eng. 1903; 2d ed. New York 1938); *The Problems of Philosophy* (New York 1912); *Our Knowledge of the External World* (Chicago 1914); *Mysticism and Logic* (New York 1918); *Analysis of Mind* (New York 1921); *Analysis of Matter* (New York 1927); *Why I Am Not a Christian* (London 1927; ed. P. EDWARDS, New York 1957); *An Inquiry into Meaning and Truth* (New York 1940); *Human Knowledge* (New York 1948); *Logic and Knowledge,* ed. R. C. MARSH (New York 1956); *My Philosophical Development* (New York 1959). **Studies.** P. SCHILPP, ed., *The Philosophy of Bertrand Russell* (2d ed. Evanston, Ill. 1946). F. BARONE, *Enciclopedia filosofica* (Venice-Rome 1957) 4:251–256. R. MONK, *Bertrand Russell: The Ghost of Madness, 1921–1970* (New York; London 2001). J. DEJNOZKA, *Bertrand Russell on Modality and Logical Relevance* (Aldershot, Hants, England; Brookfield, Vt. 1999). A. C. GRAYLING, *Russell,* Past Masters series (Oxford 1996).

[B. F. MCGUINNESS]

RUSSELL, CHARLES TAZE

Founder of the movement known since 1931 as JEHOVAH'S WITNESSES; b. Pittsburgh, Pa., Feb. 16, 1852; d. Pampa, Texas, Oct. 31, 1916. He was baptized a Congregationalist, but his study of the Bible led him to deny the existence of hell and the doctrine of the Trinity and to express Arian views of the nature of Jesus Christ. Assuming the title of "Pastor," he left the haberdashery business and began to organize Bible study groups. He traveled on preaching missions throughout the U.S. and Europe, organizing his followers, called Russellites, Millennial Dawnists, or International Bible Students, in more than 1,200 congregations. Russell's Adventist views were expounded in the *Watch Tower and Herald of Christ's Presence,* which he founded in 1879. Between 1886 and 1904, he published a six–volume series, *Studies of the Scriptures,* elaborating his prediction of the second coming of Christ in 1914. He founded the Watch Tower Bible and Tract Society in 1884, moving its headquarters from Pittsburgh to Brooklyn, New York, in 1909. Russell's prestige among his flock was not appreciably affected by frequent scandals and legal difficulties, chiefly involving his divorce from Maria Frances Ackley in 1909.

[W. J. WHALEN]

RUSSELL, JOHN

Bishop, chancellor of England; b. Winchester, England; d. Lincolnshire, Dec. 30, 1494. Educated at Winchester and New College, Oxford, he became doctor of Canon Law in 1459. Before 1464 he entered the royal service and was rewarded with rapid ecclesiastical preferment, becoming archdeacon of Berkshire (1466) and eventually bishop of ROCHESTER (provided July 15, 1476). He was translated on July 7, 1480, to Lincoln, and held that see until his death. It seems, however, that secular rather than pastoral cares engaged him at least until 1486. For as an able and trusted councillor of Edward IV, he was much employed on diplomatic missions, and held office as keeper of the privy seal (May 1474 to April 1483). Chancellor of England from May 10, 1483, he was dismissed by Richard III in July 1485 on suspicion of disloyalty. Although Russell was sufficiently flexible politically to serve five kings, he was nevertheless esteemed by contemporaries, and Thomas MORE praised him as "a wyse manne and a good . . . one of the beste learned menne . . . Englande hadde in hys time." From 1483 to his death he was the first chancellor for life of OXFORD UNIVERSITY. His considerable library included many classical and humanist works, some of which he presented to New College.

Bibliography: *Calendars of Patent Rolls, 1461–85* (London 1897–1901). MS Register, Diocesan Record Office, Lincoln. S. B. CHRIMES, *English Constitutional Ideas in the Fifteenth Century* (Cambridge, England 1936) 167–191. A. B. EMDEN, *A Biographical Register of the Scholars of the University of Oxford to A.D. 1500,* 3 v. (Oxford 1957–59) 3:1609–11.

[C. D. ROSS]

RUSSELL, MARY BAPTIST, MOTHER

Foundress of the Sisters of Mercy in California; b. Killowen, Ireland, April 18, 1829; d. San Francisco, Calif., Aug. 6, 1898. After a private education, she entered the nascent Order of the Sisters of Mercy in Kinsale, Ireland. Following her profession, Aug. 2, 1851, she served in the schools and attended the poor and sick in an area slowly recovering from cholera and famine. When Abp. Joseph S. Alemany, OP, of San Francisco appealed to Kinsale for a Mercy foundation, she was appointed superior of the eight volunteers. The sisters arrived in San Francisco Dec. 8, 1854, and began their services of relief to victims of poverty, disease, and immorality in a decade of physical and moral disorder in the city. Negligent officials had failed to provide the overcrowded city with sanitary facilities; competent nursing care was unavailable; and when cholera struck in 1855, the city, gratefully accepting the sisters' experienced ministrations to the stricken, gave them complete charge of the county hospital. This institution was reopened by Mother Russell in 1857 as St. Mary's Hospital, providing the West Coast with its first Catholic hospital and furnishing a permanent social service center for the city's destitute. From these beginnings, a Magdalen Asylum for delinquent girls (1855) and a home for the aged (1872) were instituted. Foundations in Sacramento (1857) and Grass Valley (1863), and service in the city hospitals during the smallpox epidemic (1868) further absorbed the zeal of the foundress, preventing her from concentrating on the critical archdiocesan school problem until 1871. That year Mother Russell opened the first of the five schools she was to establish in the next 21 years. Her apostolate as foundress and social worker, builder and administrator, nurse and educator, lasted for 44 years.

Bibliography: M. A. MCARDLE, *California's Pioneer Sister of Mercy* (Fresno 1954). M. E. MORGAN, *Mercy, Generation to Generation* (San Francisco 1957).

[M. G. DAVIS]

RUSSELL, ODO

British diplomat; b. Florence, Italy, Feb. 20, 1829; d. Potsdam, Germany, Aug. 25, 1884. Unable to obtain parliamentary approval for a regular envoy to the Holy See, the British government used to send a member of the British legation in Florence or Naples to Rome as an unaccredited agent. In 1858 Russell succeeded Lord Lyons in this position. Although he was a Protestant and strongly favored the unification of Italy, Russell gained the affection of Pius IX. He was also on friendly terms with the papal secretary of state, Cardinal Giacomo ANTONELLI, and with Cardinal MANNING. Russell's mother was a Catholic, but his correspondence indicates that neither she nor Manning influenced his decision to remain neutral on the question of papal infallibility during VATICAN COUNCIL I. Russell believed that government intervention would only prejudice his influence in Rome and prevent him from dealing with the problem of Ireland. In 1871 Russell was appointed first British ambassador to the new

German empire; ten years later he was created first Baron Ampthill. In 1923 his son Odo was appointed British minister to the Holy See.

Bibliography: *The Roman Question: Extracts from the Despatches of Odo Russell, 1858–1870,* ed. N. BLAKISTON (London 1962). A. RANDALL, ''A British Agent at the Vatican,'' *Dublin Review* 233 (1959) 37–57. D. MCELRATH, *The Syllabus of Pius IX: Some Reactions in England* (Louvain 1964).

[A. RANDALL]

RUSSELL, RICHARD

Member of English Chapter and bishop; b. Berkshire, 1630; d. Vizeu, Portugal, Nov. 15, 1693. At an early age Richard (apparently of humble origins) went to Lisbon in the service of the English College there, and in 1647 he enrolled as a student for the priesthood. He finished his studies at Douai and Paris and was ordained in 1655. For the next 15 years his life was about equally divided between Portugal, where he served as the procurator of the English College at Lisbon (1657) and secretary to Queen Luisa (1660), and England, where he was chaplain to the Portuguese ambassador, Francisco de Mello, and made a canon of the English Chapter (1661). The Chapter, almost desperate after its long agitation to obtain a bishop with ordinary jurisdiction for England, saw in Russell's unique position a final hope—as a consecrated bishop of a Portuguese see, he could resign, return to England, and assume an episcopal leadership of the English clergy. Russell, resisting his old Chapter loyalties, saw the scheme as thinly disguised schism. He accepted the See of Portalegre in 1671 and remained there for ten years, relinquishing it only for another Portuguese see, that of Vizeu. There till his death, he was a worthy bishop, zealous and efficient for reform. In England, in the meanwhile, Philip Howard had been consecrated vicar apostolic, thus ending whatever danger of schism still remained.

Bibliography: J. GILLOW, *A Literary and Biographical History or Bibliographical Dictionary of the English Catholics from 1534 to the Present Time,* 5 v. (London-New York 1885–1902; repr. New York 1961) 5:455–457. W. M. BRADY, *Episcopal Succession in England, Scotland, and Ireland* (Rome 1876–77). W. CROFT, *Historical Account of Lisbon College* (Barnet, England 1902).

[R. I. BRADLEY]

RUSSELL, WILLIAM THOMAS

Fifth bishop of Charleston, S.C.; b. Baltimore, Md., Oct. 20, 1863; d. Charleston, March 18, 1927. He was the son of William T. and Rose (Patterson) Russell. After completing his high school and preparatory seminary studies at St. Charles College, Ellicott City, Md., he entered the North American College, Rome, in 1884. Poor health forced him to return home after he had completed his philosophy course, and he took his theology at St. Mary's Seminary, Baltimore. He was ordained June 21, 1889, and appointed pastor of St. Jerome's Church, Hyattsville, Md. When the army of unemployed being led in a march on Washington by Jacob S. Coxey settled in that area, Russell visited their camp at least twice a week to bring food and clothing to the destitute men. While pastor at Hyattsville, he also attended The Catholic University of America, Washington, D.C., and received the licentiate in theology.

In 1894 Russell was appointed assistant at the Baltimore cathedral and secretary to Cardinal James Gibbons. Fourteen years later he was made pastor of St. Patrick's Church, Washington, D.C., where he founded the League of the Good Shepherd; inaugurated the Pan-American Mass, which has continued to be offered annually on Thanksgiving day; and instituted the Field Mass said annually on the grounds near the Washington Monument. He also acted as the Washington representative of Cardinal Gibbons.

In 1911 Russell was made a domestic prelate, and subsequently his name was mentioned as a possible coadjutor to Abp. Patrick W. Riordan of San Francisco, Calif. Instead Russell was named bishop of Charleston on Dec. 7, 1916. Having been consecrated on March 15, 1917, by Cardinal Gibbons, he was installed on March 22. Upon the entry of the U.S. into World War I, the National Catholic War Council was formed to coordinate Catholic activities, and Russell was one of the four bishops named to the board. When the organization was continued after the war as the National Catholic Welfare Council (later Conference), he served as a member of the executive board and as episcopal chairman of the committee on publicity, press, and literature.

During Russell's episcopate, many new parishes were opened, the number of priests increased, and the Holy Ghost Fathers and the Oblate Sisters of Providence were introduced. He built a modern fireproof building for St. Francis Infirmary. Many of his sermons appeared in pamphlet form, and he published *Maryland, the Land of Sanctuary* in 1908. He also wrote for the old *Catholic Encyclopedia*. He was honored by St. Mary's Seminary, Baltimore, with a D.D. degree and by Mt. St. Mary's Seminary, Emmitsburg, Md., with an LL.D.

[R. C. MADDEN]

RUSSIA, THE CATHOLIC CHURCH IN

The largest country in the world, the Russian Federation is located in eastern Europe, and straddles the Ural mountains west into northern Asia. It is bordered on the north by the Arctic Ocean, on the east by the Chukchi Sea and the Bering Sea, on the south by China, Mongolia, Kazakstan, North Korea, Azerbaijan, Georgia and the Black Sea, and on the west by Ukraine, Belarus, Latvia, Estonia, Finland and Norway. The Kurli islands are also part of the region. Composed of 21 republics, the region has a diverse landscape, ranging from southern steppes to arctic tundra in the frozen northeast. Natural resources include petroleum and natural gas deposits, coal and other minerals, although the forbidding landscape and great distance prevented exploitation of many of these. Agricultural production, also limited by the lack of proper climate, included grain, sugar beets, sunflower seeds, fruits, vegetables and livestock and dairy farming. Much of Sibera is covered in permafrost. Several boundary disputes were ongoing into 2001.

The leader of a massive empire stretching over much of eastern Europe and northern Asia by 1900, Russia's defeat in World War I led to the fall of the czar and the rise of a communist government under Vladimir Lenin. In 1922 the USSR was formed, its constituent republics ruled over by a series of repressive regimes through the mid-1980s, after which a more open atmosphere fostered by Mikhail Gorbachev led to the demise of the communist union. In its decreased sphere of influence, the newly formed Russian Federation struggled to create a stable government, a viable market economy and a secure socio-cultural environment to replace the controlled communist system, while continuing to battle ethnic division into the 21st century.

Religious affiliation in Russia was traditionally linked with ethnic origin. All three branches of the East Slavic people—Great Russians, Ukrainians and Byelorussians—belonged mostly to the Russian Orthodox Church, although various other Orthodox denominations and the schismatic Old Believers retained a strong following. The Russian Orthodox Church also encompassed many Finno-Ugric groups such as the Komi, Mordvins, Mari and Udmurts or Turkic Chuvash, which were scattered throughout the northern and eastern parts of European Russia. After World War II the Soviet Union extended its boundaries to such areas as western Ukraine, comprising Galicia and the Transcarpathian *oblast,* that were inhabited by Catholics of the Eastern rite.

Eastern Slavs to 1917

Christianity of the Kievan Rus. The East Slavic tribes, which settled along the great waterway from the Baltic to the Black Sea, were welded into one political body by the Norsemen or Vikings. These adventurers, under the leadership of the semi-legendary Rurik, established themselves first in Novgorod; and then in the second half of the 9th century extended their control to Kiev on the lower Dnieper. They were called by the Finns Ruotsi, by the Slavs Rus, which became the name for the land they occupied, and for the people originating from the integration of foreign warriors with native settlers. The intervention of the Vikings or Varagians put the Slavs in contact with the BYZANTINE EMPIRE and northern Europe, and prevented them from falling under the spell of Islamic culture, as happened to the Volga Bulgarians and to some groups of the Khazars.

The first mention of Christianity in Kievan Rus dates from 867, when Patriarch PHOTIUS reported that the barbarian Rhos had received a bishop and a priest. A century later the Grand Princess Olga was baptized, probably during her visit to Constantinople in 957. Under her son Sviatoslav a pagan reaction followed, but her grandson St. VLADIMIR (979–1015) made Christianity the state religion, ordering the baptism of his retinue and people in 989. Church Slavonic became the vehicle of Christian culture and the liturgical language, facilitating the assimilation of foreign warriors to the Slavs, and creating a certain aloofness from Byzantium, a result welcome to Vladimir. Credit for the spread of Christianity is due to the missionaries from Bulgaria, where the work of Saints CYRIL and Methodius bore late fruit, and from Bohemia, which also transmitted to the Russian neophytes the veneration of the Czech national saints, Wenceslaus, Ludmila and Adalbert of Prague. Latin Christianity was well received also in Rus, and several Western canonical customs entered Russian ecclesiastical tradition. Missionary and cultural work was continued by the monasteries, some of which had been founded by princes after the Byzantine pattern, others by zealous ascetics. The most prominent of the second group was the monastery of the Caves near Kiev. The monasteries continued to profoundly influence the religious mentality of the faithful, and the monastic ethos remained a characteristic of Byzantine-Slav Christianity (*see* MONASTICISM).

The clergy first became acquainted with BYZANTINE literature of a religious type in translated form; but the disintegration of the Rus, the Mongol yoke and subsequent isolation hindered their access to all the treasures of classical antiquity. Byzantium was also less zealous in teaching its daughter churches than was Rome in educating the West. This cultural lag was evident until modern

---

Capital: Moscow.
Size: 6,592,800 sq. miles.
Population: 146,001,180 in 2000.
Languages: Russian; minority languages are spoken in various regions.
Religions: 354,000 Catholics (.2%), 18,980,140 Muslims (13%), 80,300,650 Orthodox (55%), 1,500,000 Jews (1%), 44,936,390 without religious affiliation.
Ecclesiastical organizations: Russia has Latin apostolic administrations in Moscow and in Irkutsk and Novosibirsk, Siberia. The Eastern Catholic Church has an apostolic exarchy in Moscow.

---

times among the Eastern Slavs, whereas classical formation was a constituent element of Western civilization. Byzantium was, however, very eager to control the Russian Church organization. The first known metropolitan of Kiev, Theopempt (1039), was a Greek, like most of his successors. All the metropolitans were confirmed and consecrated in Constantinople until mid-15th century (*see* CONSTANTINOPLE, ECUMENICAL PATRIARCHATE OF).

Kievan civilization reached its peak in the time of Yaroslav the Wise (1019–54). Desiring to make Kiev an imperial city, he constructed a church dedicated to the Divine Wisdom, founded schools, gathered a group of translators and drew up a collection of laws, known as Russian law, in which old Slavonic customs were ennobled by Christian principles.

Kievan Christians were in union with the universal Church even after the break between Rome and Byzantium in 1054. In 1075 Prince Iziaslav, looking for help against his rivals, successfully approached Pope Gregory VII. But estrangement from the West was growing. The people of Rus did not take part in the Crusades or other common enterprises of Medieval Latin Europe. Marriages among ruling families of the West and of Russia (Rurikides) became rare. Greek prelates taught Russians to distrust Latins. It was mainly Greek influence that drove the Rus out of the Christian Western commonwealth. But the West also was responsible for this estrangement. Alexander, Prince of Novgorod and, after 1252, also Prince of Vladimir on the Kliazma River, had to repulse Swedish invaders at the Neva River (1240). In 1242 he defeated the TEUTONIC KNIGHTS, who had established themselves in 1202 at the mouth of the Dvina for missionary work, and had made inroads into Slavic principalities. Victory over the Latins was made possible by Alexander's loyalty to the Mongol khans (*see* MONGOLS). By this time the turn toward the East and refusal to cooperate with the West was complete, though only the rejection of the Council of FLORENCE in 1441 constituted the explicit juridical act of separation (*see* EASTERN SCHISM; EASTERN CHURCHES).

Kiev Metropolitanate to 1450. The metropolitan of Kiev was the sole unifying agent amid the numerous principalities extending from Galicia in the west, northeast to the Upper Volga and Oka Rivers. Kiev kept losing prestige after the reign of Vladimir Monomakh (1113–25), and was destroyed by the Mongols in 1240. New local centers of gravitation came into existence: Halicz, Novgorod, Vladimir, later Moscow and Lithuania.

Halicz preserved Kiev's best traditions. Prince Daniel (1240–64), hoping to free his territories from Mongol control, promised obedience to the Holy See, and was crowned King by the papal legate at Dorohychyn (*c.* 1254). But negotiations between Rome and Halicz brought no tangible results. Attempts in 1303 and 1370 by the rulers of Halicz to form an independent metropolitan area brought only temporary success.

Novgorod, the most important city after Kiev, defended its democratic freedom stubbornly until its occupation by Moscow in 1478. It was a commercial city with a large hinterland, open to Western trade and ideas. Its bishops (after 1165, archbishops) enjoyed great authority even in purely political matters.

Rise of Moscow. In northern Russia MOSCOW was rising to power. Though it was only a small principality when it became the heritage of Daniel (1263–1303), youngest son of Alexander Nevsky, it grew stronger thanks to its geographical position, the consistent policy of its princes, the favor of the khans, and, significantly, the support of the Church. Metropolitan Maximus (1283–1305), without consulting the patriarch, left the devastated regions of the south and withdrew to the northeast. His successor Peter (1308–26) was from Volyn, but dwelt often in Moscow and died there. Theognost (1328–53), a Greek, lived in Moscow from the beginning of his office and excommunicated an enemy of that city, Alexander of Tver, and the city of Pskov that had given him hospitality. Alexis was even more zealous for the prestige of the upstart principality. He bestowed the Church's blessings and applied its sanctions to this purpose, and even identified Church policy with Moscow's power. Earlier, in 1274, Cyril II had summoned a synod of bishops to Vladimir on Kliazma in an attempt to consolidate the Church after the first 30 years of Tatar domination. Even then something new, independent of the rest of Christendom, was taking root: the merging of religious ideas with national traditions, producing a strictly ecclesiastical culture with an isolationist spirit that distrusted both the West and "Hellenistic wisdom." Byzantium nevertheless interfered effectively in the Church organization, mostly in favor of Moscow.

The 14th century was an era of ascetics for northern Russia, with a "new Thebaid" arising in its forests. Of all the monastic institutions that were centers of colonization and Christianization among the Finnish tribes, the most renowned was the Trinity monastery near Moscow founded by St. Sergius of Radonezh (d. 1392). The saint blessed Prince Dimitri before his battle with the Tatars at Kulikovo Pole (1380); where the reputedly invincible Mongols met defeat, although their domination persisted. The Mongol yoke was less burdensome for the clergy than for other classes, because the khans granted the Church privileges, especially freedom from taxes.

Lithuania. Although Moscow, home of the metropolitan of Kiev, became the spiritual heir of the ancient Rus, the Lithuanian princes in the 14th century inherited the political power of St. Vladimir. The marriage of the Lithuanian Jagailo with the Polish Queen Hedwig (1386) resulted in personal union with Poland, and the conversion of the Lithuanians to Latin Catholicism. This accentuated the estrangement of Lithuanian Slavs (almost nine-tenths of the inhabitants of the principality) from the other East Slavic populace, and directed Lithuania's policy Westward. The repeated attempt of Lithuanian princes to set up an independent metropolitan area for their Slavic territories, gained only temporary success because of opposition from Moscow and Constantinople. In 1436 the Patriarch of Constantinople Joseph II appointed ISIDORE OF KIEV, a Greek humanist favorable to the union, as metropolitan for the East Slavic metropolis. After the Council of Florence, Isidore found ready acceptance of union with Rome among the East Slavic population of Poland and Lithuania; but Basil II, the Great Prince of Moscow, rejected the union decreed at Florence and Isidore had to flee. In 1448 the Great Prince convoked a synod of Muscovite bishops. Ignoring the patriarch, he let the prelates elect as metropolitan the bishop of Riazan, Jonas, who was able to extend his jurisdiction to Lithuania by express consent of King Casimir (1451), and later even to Polish Halicz. In 1458 Pius II appointed Gregory, a friend of Isidore, metropolitan of the southern and western Russian territories that were controlled by the Polish King. The new metropolitan was accepted. Then in 1459 a synod of the Muscovite bishops declared Jonas and his successors legitimate metropolitans of Kiev and Russia, subject only to the approval of the Great Prince. Jonas was able to control also Tver and Novgorod. Thus was consummated the independence of the Muscovite Church from Byzantium,

Emperor Basil II (with saints and angels), manuscript illumination.

the final break from Rome, and the division of the Slavic Church of Eastern Europe into two metropolitan areas, Kiev and Moscow. Theodosius (1461–65), successor of Jonas, was the first to call himself metropolitan of Moscow.

Kiev Province, 1450–1805. After the death in 1362 of Romanos, metropolitan of western Russia, the bishoprics in Little Russia and Galicia returned to the jurisdiction of the Kiev metropolitan. Kiev remained part of Lithuania until 1569. During this interval Halicz was created a metropolitan see, with Cholm, Turov, Przemyśl and Vladimir, former suffragans to Kiev, as its suffragans. Novgorod and Lithuania stayed under the Kiev metropolis. Kiev metropolitans remained often in union with Rome after Isidore's efforts. Thus Gregory remained loyal to Rome until death (1472), but he was recognized also by the patriarch of Constantinople. Some of his successors during the next four decades were eager to remain in communion with Rome, although officially they depended on the patriarch of Constantinople. After 1517 there followed a series of Kiev metropolitans who renounced the union of Florence.

The Ruthenians (modern Ukrainians or Belarussians) living in Poland and Lithuania underwent a religious crisis in the 16th century. Unable to withstand the

Peter the Great.

onslaught of the Protestant REFORMATION, many Ruthenian nobles passed to CALVINISM. Dissident confraternities of gentry and burghers, particularly in LVOV and VILNA, set up schools. The Academy of Ostrog, established by the magnate Constantine Ostrozhski (d. 1608), provided higher education. The first complete Slavonic printed Bible was published in Ostrog (1581). But after 1555 the vigorous COUNTER REFORMATION, led by the JESUITS, strongly affected even dissident Ruthenians. The political union of Lublin (1569), welding the Polish and Lithuanian political units into one organism paved the way for a religious rapprochement. Ruthenian bishops hoped to regenerate their Church by renewing the union of Florence. Their representatives, the bishop of Vladimir, Hypatius Pociei, and the bishop of Lutsk, Cyril Terletski, went to Rome, where the whole ecclesiastical province of Kiev was received into the Catholic Church by Clement VIII (Dec. 23, 1595). The union was proclaimed at BREST in 1596, but some of the clergy and laity opposed it.

Succeeding the first reconciled metropolitan, Michael Ragosa, was the able, energetic Hypatius Pociei (1600–13), born of the high nobility and steeped in Eastern tradition. His successor, Velamyn Rutski (1614–37), tried with slight success to establish Ruthenian schools. Ruthenian nobles attended Jesuit colleges and usually

adopted the Latin rite, to the great detriment of the recently reconciled Church. Even the clergy had no seminaries of their own. The BASILIANS (BYZANTINE), reorganized by Rutski along Western lines, and a few of the diocesan clergy received their theological training in Olomouc, Prague, or Rome, far away from their people and their Eastern traditions. The situation of Ruthenian Catholicism deteriorated in 1620, when the patriarch of Jerusalem, Theophanes, under Cossack protection, reestablished the dissident Ruthenian hierarchy under a new metropolitan of Kiev, Job Boretski (1620–33), dependent on the patriarch of Constantinople. The attempts of the newly consecrated metropolitan to wrest bishoprics from legitimate Catholic prelates led to deplorable events. King Vladyslav's constitution of 1632 legally restored the dissident Church.

Catholic Ruthenians were harassed by their schismatic countrymen as traitors, yet received no help from Latin Catholics. Some Polish bishops behaved in an overbearing manner toward their Eastern brethren. Ruthenian prelates were excluded from the ecclesiastical class of the kingdom and consequently never obtained seats in the senate. The union was in danger of being completely destroyed during the uprising of Bogdan Khmelnitsky and the prolonged Cossack and Swedish wars. Thanks to the Ruthenian bishops and the Basilian monks, it survived and prospered during the reigns of Koribut Wiśniowetski (1669–73) and John Sobieski (1674–96). The Peace of Andrusovo (1667) ceded the whole eastern bank of the Dnieper to the Russian czar. The loss of this radically anti-Catholic territory brought some relief to Ruthenian Catholicism, which experienced a renaissance *c.* 1700, when the last three dissident ordinaries joined the Catholic Church.

Despite its numerical strength, the Eastern Catholic Church was too weak to create an autonomous Catholic Byzantine-Slavonic culture. Latin elements infiltrated its ecclesiastical life. The legislation of the Synod of Zamość (1720) was inspired by the Council of TRENT, not by traditional Eastern canonical norms or by the bull of Clement VIII approving the Byzantine-Slavonic rite and customs. Dissident Ruthenians profited from contact with Catholic Counter Reformation thought. This was due mainly to the outstanding metropolitan of Kiev, Peter Mogila (1633–47), who remodeled the school of Kiev on the pattern of a Jesuit college and drew abundantly from Western tradition for his theological writings and liturgical editions. The Orthodox metropolitan of Kiev lost his independence in 1685 when the patriarch of Moscow, without recourse to Constantinople, appointed Gedeon Chetvertinski metropolitan of Kiev, but complete assimilation to the Muscovite Church was achieved only later. The Catholic metropolitan of Kiev resided usually in

Novogrudek in Lithuania. After the division of Poland, the greater part of his ecclesiastical province was incorporated into Russia. With the death of Theodosius Rostotski (1805), the last Catholic metropolitan of Kiev disappeared.

Moscow, 1450–1700. The territory of Moscow as a metropolitanate and, after 1589, a patriarchate, was coextensive with the area controlled politically by Moscow's ruler. White Russia, Galicia and the city of Kiev belonged to Lithuania until 1569, and from then until 1680 to Poland. As colonization moved northward and eastward into Siberia, new dioceses suffragan to Moscow were created. When in 1685 the dissident metropolitan of Kiev lost his influence to the Moscow patriarch, the latter could claim all the territories inhabited by the Ruthenians.

The Third Rome. The Muscovite ruler was, in the eyes of his subjects, the savior of Orthodoxy, but the metropolitan attending the Council of Florence was considered its betrayer. Byzantium was said to have been punished in 1453 for its apostasy to Rome. Ivan III (1462–1505), by his marriage with Zoe (Sophia), niece of the last Byzantine emperor, inherited Byzantium's mission. He was successful in "reassembling the Russian lands," acquiring Tver in 1485 and crushing Novgorod in 1478. At the same time the last traces of Tatar sovereignty over Moscow disappeared. This development encouraged Metropolitan Zosima (1490–94) to proclaim Ivan III "the sovereign and autocrat of all Russia, new Tsar Constantine of the new city Constantinople-Moscow." To this reappraisal in the apocalyptic setting of the time, Philofei, monk of St. Eleazar monastery in Pskov, gave a classical formulation, when he declared that the first Rome became the prey of heresy; the second fell into the hands of the infidels; but the third Rome, Moscow, remains; and that after the present Muscovite era, there will descend the eternal kingdom of Christ. Thus the lofty theory of Moscow as the Third Rome was the creation of clerical intellectuals. It did not ennoble the rule of the princes, which proved as ruthless as that of the former Tatar khans, but it did inspire in the masses a naïve conceit and obscurantist hatred of the Latin West.

Heresy. A Judaizing heresy appeared in Novgorod *c.* 1470; it contained Judaic elements, but was basically a penetration of humanistic rationalism and Renaissance astrology into Russian backwardness. To counteract the claimed Biblical basis for the new doctrines, Gennadius, Archbishop of Novgorod (1485–1504), and the Croatian Dominican, Benjamin, translated with the help of the Vulgate those parts of the Bible not yet available in Slavonic. Joseph, Abbot of Volokolamsk (d. 1515), called for stern measures against the heretics. Other monks,

such as Nil Sorski (d. 1508), preferred persuasion to coercion. At the synod in 1504 the secular arm aligned with the Josephites to uproot the heresy.

Josephites. To attain the much-needed monastic reform, Nil Sorski and the Trans-Volga hermits urged the contemplative life in small semi-eremitical communities, free from involvement in ownership of villages and other worldly concerns. The Josephites believed the remedy lay in a strictly disciplined cenobitic life, with solemn liturgical services, strict obedience, and the retention of landed properties. They wished the monasteries to fulfill their social and ecclesiastical function insofar as was possible. The synod of 1503 supported the Josephites. Their ascendancy was complete by 1522, when the metropolitan see was given to one of them, Daniel. He in turn readily granted a divorce to Basil III, whose first wife was sterile. The Josephites had learned from the Byzantines to support the autocratic monarchy, and to cherish harmonious Church-State relations, merging both powers into one City of God. The end product of their efforts, however, was not a balanced "symphony," but an overriding State and a powerless Church.

Growing Importance. Metropolitan Macarius (1542–63), in the first part of the reign of Ivan IV, the Terrible (1533–84), consolidated the new ideology by his energetic reforms. He crowned the young Ivan and proclaimed him czar (1547). By collecting and revising annalistic and legendary records, he tried to assign to the God-chosen empire a unique place in salvation history. The synods of 1547 and 1549 canonized more than 40 saints. In 1551 a reform council published a collection of norms for ecclesiastical life in 100 chapters (Stoglav). The capture of the Tatar Kazan (1552) and the conquest of the Khanate of Astrakhan (1556) opened for the Church a new field of missionary activity, begun by the newly appointed archbishop of Kazan, Guri. A trend discernible for 150 years attained its goal in 1589, when the Russian government forced the visiting patriarch of Constantinople, Jeremiah II, to elevate Metropolitan Job of Moscow to the patriarchal dignity. The reorganized Muscovite Church now included four metropolitan sees: Novgorod, Kazan, Rostov and Krutitsy in the suburb of Moscow, but these were mere honorary titles, with no jurisdiction over the other sees.

Times of Troubles. The extinction of the Muscovite line of Rurikides and Ivan IV's cruelties prepared for the upheaval known as the "Times of Troubles" (1604–13), which started with the appearance on the Polish Muscovite border of a pretender who claimed to be Demetrius, son of Ivan IV, miraculously saved from death, and ended with the election of Michael Romanov as czar. Throughout these stormy years the Church showed itself to be the guardian of law and order. The only results of this unsuccessful attempt by Catholic Poland to gain control of all Eastern Europe were an awakening of the Russian national consciousness and an upsurge of anti-Catholicism. The restoration of order was due largely to Patriarch FILARET (1619–33), father of the czar, who had been forced by Boris Godunov to become a monk. As patriarch he shared with his son the title of ''Grand Sovereign,'' thereby introducing a kind of dyarchy.

Raskolniks. Filaret resumed the work of editing prayer books, a work started by Maxim the Greek (d. 1556) and completed by Patriarch NIKON (1652–67). The reform of the liturgical customs and texts was patterned on contemporary Greek usage. The ritual-minded Muscovites saw in it a threat to the centuries-old preeminence of the Third Rome. Opposition, headed by the archpriest AVVAKUM (d. 1682), was condemned by the Great Council of Russian bishops (1666–67), but brought about the schism of RASKOLNIKS (Old Believers).

Church-State Relations. The same Great Council, attended by two Greek patriarchs, solved an eight-year dispute between Czar Alexis I (1645–76) and Nikon by yielding to the czar and deposing the patriarch. This meant a declining role for the Church and amounted to setting up a new relationship between priesthood and kingship. The departure from traditional harmony was due to the subservience of the Greek patriarchs, and also to a new concept of the sovereign state, which entered Muscovy from the West. This secularizing and anticlerical spirit was evident in 1649, when the Code of Czar Alexis (*Ulozhenie*) erected a central office for administering Church property. The decree on Church property was temporarily suspended, but was renewed by Peter the Great in 1701.

From the 1640s onward, Ukrainian scholars, educated at Mogila Academy in Kiev, exerted the preponderant influence on Russian intellectual life. Among the pioneers were Epiphanius Slavinetski (d. 1675), representative of Greek-Slavonic culture; Simeon of Polotsk (d. 1680), familiar with Catholic theological thought; and his disciple Silvester Medvedev (d. 1691).

Synodal Period (1700–1917). PETER I, THE GREAT (1682–1725) transformed the Muscovite state into the modern Russian Empire. In the process he secularized Russian culture and removed the Church from a leading position in the nation's life by subordinating it to the civil power. After Patriarch Adrian's death in 1700, Peter named as patriarchal vicar STEFAN, Bishop of Riazan (d. 1722), a man educated in Kiev and conversant with Western Catholic thought. Church reorganization was arranged by Feofan PROKOPOVICH (d. 1736), who upheld a Lutheran concept of State-Church relations. The patri-

archate was replaced in 1721 by the HOLY SYNOD, a college of bishops and priests appointed by the government. It was subject to the czar, and direct control of it was entrusted to the chief procurator, a lay official. The aristocratic and governmental classes, much influenced by the French ENLIGHTENMENT, despised the Church. This secularization process continued under CATHERINE II (1762–96), who confiscated Church estates. The czarina regarded herself privately as ''head of the Russian Church,'' a title that her son Paul I (1796–1801) officially adopted.

ALEXANDER I (1801–25) envisioned a syncretistic and universal Christianity, which he claimed to rule, but he did not release the Church from its captivity. The emperors from NICHOLAS I (1825–55) to Nicholas II (1894–1917) strove to restore the Church-State harmony envisioned by the Josephites, but forgot that ecclesiastical freedom from state tyranny was a necessary preliminary. The destiny of Russian Christianity was no longer in the hands of the bishops, but in those of the chief procurators, the most influential of whom was POBEDONOSTSEV, who dominated Church-State affairs for 25 years after 1880. The tolerance edict of 1905 was, even for the Orthodox Church, a relief that aroused spirited interest in Church reform and in the reestablishment of the patriarchal dignity. It granted to all believers freedom of cult, but not practical religious rights.

Inner Life. A gap separated the laity from the clerical caste, made up of the cantors, deacons and priests, which together with its families numbered *c.* 500,000. Bishops were celibates recruited exclusively from the monks, and were considered primarily civil servants. They were transferred from one diocese to another at the chief procurator's whim, and often remained strangers to their flocks. The Westernized intelligentsia had no respect for the priesthood. To the upper class a priestly vocation was akin to degradation. The misery of the rural clergy was partly relieved in 1893 by the introduction of state stipends, although many did not receive them at all. The procurator's report in 1913 estimated membership in the Russian Orthodox Church at 98,534,000, but this total included many sectarians and Old Believers. There were also three metropolitans, 26 archbishops and 40 diocesan bishops. For other groups of clergy the 1914 statistics are incomplete, but those for 1908 listed 48,879 priests and 14,779 deacons. When Peter I died in 1725, Russia numbered perhaps 14 million people. Two centuries later, due to annexations and natural growth, the population was 12 times larger; the czarist empire was a multiracial and multiconfessional state, half of whose inhabitants belonged to the dominant Church. Pastoral work was greatly handicapped by the persistence of the Raskolniks. In the second half of the 18th century, a pseudoreligious revival spread among the masses, promoting the rise and spread of eccentric sects, such as the Khlysty, Skoptsy, DOUKHOBORS and Molokans. Estimates mention some 15 million Old Believers and sectarians before World War I.

The absorption of the Orthodox Church into the state machinery made her struggle with nihilism, materialism and Marxism very difficult. The Church was identified with absolute, oppressive autocracy. It did not denounce social injustices. Even the former custom of having the metropolitan intercede with the emperor (*pechalovanie*) had ceased to exist. In the policy of the pragmatic Peter the Great, monasteries had no place, and he had reduced their number and transformed their buildings into homes for veterans. Yet during that same period a renaissance of monasticism began from within, started by Paisi Velichkovski (d. 1794). With the removal of restrictive measures in the 19th century, monasteries once again increased in number. In 1914 there were 550 monasteries with 21,330 monks, and 475 convents with 73,300 nuns.

Ecclesiastical Education and Scholarship. The synodal period witnessed the development of an ecclesiastical school system. In the 18th century the Church conquered its fear that education would nurture heresy; in the 19th century it tried to balance the old ways, rich in folklore and liturgy, with an intellectual grasp of Christian faith. Seminaries, established in Peter the Great's time, offered the equivalent of a high school course, with emphasis on religion. At first they adopted the curricula of Jesuit colleges, but from the mid-18th century they borrowed heavily from Protestant educational systems. Latin remained the medium for teaching in seminaries until the early 19th century.

Only in the 1840s did an indigenous Russian theology come into existence, with both a traditional approach, exemplified by Filaret Drozdov (d. 1867) and Macarius BULGAKOV (d. 1882), and an independent approach influenced by SLAVOPHILISM. In 1914 the ecclesiastical academies at Moscow, Kiev, St. Petersburg and Kazan enrolled 995 students; and in addition 57 seminaries enrolled 22,734 seminarians. Students in these and other ecclesiastical schools were the children of the clergy, but only a minority of the graduates joined the ecclesiastical ranks. Although this school system had its merits, it estranged the clergy from an intelligentsia whose education was quite different from their own (*see* RUSSIAN THEOLOGY).

Mission Activity. Russia's expansion to central and eastern Asia intensified the Orthodox Church's activity. Missions among Muslims inside and outside Russia were organized in close cooperation with the government. Most successful was the Japanese mission, detached from political goals, organized by Nicholas Kasatkin (d. 1912,

as archbishop). In preaching and liturgy, Russian missionaries adopted the vernacular, copying the famous 14th-century missionary to the Zyrians (today the Komi), St. Stephan of Perm.

Roman Catholic Church. Despite the aftermath of the Council of Florence, Rome kept trying to resume contacts with Muscovy to attain religious reunion, and to forge a political alliance against the Turks. It exchanged diplomatic representatives, and sent Antonio POSSEVINO, SJ, as papal intermediary between Ivan IV and King Stephan BÁTHORY of Poland in 1582. But the hopes placed in these efforts proved illusory, as did those placed in Demetrius I (Pseudo-Demetrius, d. 1606), who became a Catholic of the Latin rite.

Moscow long opposed the erection of a Catholic Church for aliens. It was the Austrian embassy that gained government permission to open a Catholic Chapel in Moscow in 1683. Peter the Great's 1702 manifesto inviting foreigners into the empire decreed freedom of religion for "all Christian sects," but forbade proselytism. With the dismemberment of Poland (1772, 1793, 1795) large bodies of Latin and Eastern Catholics became subjects of the Russian Empire, whereas Catholic Ruthenians of Galicia came under Austrian rule. Emperor Francis I of Austria obtained from the Holy See the erection of the ecclesiastical province of Halicz with its seat in Lvov (1807).

The Russian government also tolerated Catholics, but only Latins, and those in ethnic groups that traditionally belonged to Catholic nations. Eastern Catholics were considered schismatic Orthodox and consequently not tolerated. The annulment of their union with Rome occurred during the reign of Nicholas I, whose motto "Orthodoxy, Russianism, absolutism" opposed the existence of Catholic Belarussians and Ukrainians. The plan to conscript Eastern Catholics into the Orthodox Church was prepared by Joseph Semashko, a priest who, like most of his colleagues of both rites, was educated in the seminary at Vilna, where he imbibed the principles of GALLICANISM. Several legislative measures, and the death of the metropolitan-delegate Josaphat Bulhak (1817–38), a man devoted to the Holy See but too weak to offer resistance, brought about the final blow. In 1839 the Union of Brest was declared nonexistent, and the Eastern Catholics were subjected to the Holy Synod of Moscow. Opposition met harsh suppression, and was the more easily subdued because many Ruthenian nobles had passed in earlier centuries to the Latin rite, and had aligned themselves with Poland, leaving the common people without leaders. In 1825 Eastern Catholics in Russia had one metropolitan, five bishops, 1,985 diocesan priests, 47 Basilian monasteries with 507 religious, and 1,427,000 faithful (*see* EASTERN CHURCHES).

After an unsuccessful rebellion in 1863, the kingdom of Poland became the Russian By-Visla Province; and the diocese of Chelm, together with the Eastern Catholics, suffered the same fate as had the Catholics of White Russia. The role formerly played by Semashko was reenacted by Marcel Popiel, appointed by Russia as administrator of the Chelm Diocese, who proclaimed its submission to the Orthodox Church in 1875, although the people remained secretly loyal to the Catholic Church. The Russian Ministry of Internal Affairs stated that between the issuance of the tolerance edict on April 17, 1905, and Jan. 1, 1910, 232,686 members of the State Church became Catholics. Most of these were former Catholic Ukrainians and Belarussians who had to adopt the Latin rite to remain Catholics.

Roman Rite. Roman Catholics in 19th-century Russia were all foreigners, and included Lithuanians, Latvians, Germans and French, but the majority were Poles; thus, Catholics were often identified with Poles. Catholics were strongest in the western provinces, but there was a Catholic diaspora throughout the empire, and every large city had a Catholic church. The government proceeded very arbitrarily in Church affairs, rarely consulted Rome and steadily refused to accept a permanent representative of the Holy See. Even the agreement of 1847 did not alter conditions. There were two metropolitan areas. One existed for the former Kingdom of Poland, with an archbishopric in Warsaw and six bishoprics. Catholics in Russia proper were subject to the metropolitan of Mogilev, residing in St. Petersburg (Leningrad), with bishoprics in Lutsk-Zhitomir, Samogitia (Kovno), Tiraspol (residence in Saratov) and Vilna. Catholic affairs were administered through the Roman Catholic Ecclesiastical College, a counterpart of the Holy Synod, erected in 1801 but never approved by the Holy See. The Catholic Ecclesiastical Academy of St. Petersburg was the higher theological institute, and had about 60 students, all priests or clerics in major orders. There were then some 4,600 priests serving 4,234 churches and 1,978 chapels, and around 15 million Catholics in the empire, almost six million of whom lived in the ecclesiastical province of Mogilev.

Converts. Despite strict prohibition, many Russians became Catholics during the 19th century. Some of these preferred to reside outside their native country, notably Anne Swetchine, Vladimir S. Pecherin (d. 1885), who became a Redemptorist, Gregory P. Shuvalov (d. 1859), who joined the Barnabites and Demetrius GALLITZIN (d. 1840), active as a parish priest in Loretto, Pennsylvania. Some Russian converts joined the Jesuits outside Russia. Catherine II did not allow the promulgation in her empire of the bull of Pope CLEMENT XIV that suppressed the Jesuits (1773). Because of her esteem for their schools, she permitted the order to carry on its activities, thereby saving it from extinction, but all candidates who joined the Society of Jesus during this period were non-Russians. In the 19th century converts who became Jesuits included the writer Ivan GAGARIN (d. 1882), the Bollandist Ivan Martynov (d. 1894) and the historian Paul Pierling (d. 1922).

Bibliography: A. M. AMMANN, *Storia della Chiesa russa* (Turin 1948), Get. tr. *Abriss der ostslawischen Kirchengeschichte* (Vienna 1950). E. E. GOLUBINSKI, *Istoriia russko tserkvi*, 2 v. (Moscow 1901–11). F. DVORNIK, *The Slavs: Their Early History and Civilization* (Boston 1956); *The Slavs in European History and Civilization* (New Brunswick, NJ 1962). I. SMOLITSCH, *Geschichte der russischen Kirche 1700–1917*, v.1 (Leiden 1964). G. V. FLOROVSKI, *Puti russkago bogosloviia* (Paris 1937). P. PIERLING, *La Russie et le Saint-Siège*, 5 v. (Paris 1896–1912). A. BOUDOU, *Le Saint-Siège et la Russie (1814–1883)*, 2 v. (Paris 1922–25). A. V. KARTASHEV, *Ocherki po istorii russko tserkvi*, 2 v. (Paris 1959). O. HALECKI, *From Florence to Brest (1439–1596)* (Rome 1958). E. AMBURGER, *Geschichte des Protestantismus in Russland* (Stuttgart 1961). T. WARE, *The Orthodox Church* (Baltimore, MD 1963). K. S. LATOURETTE, *A History of the Expansion of Christianity*, 7 v. (New York 1937–45). K. S. LATOURETTE, *Christianity in a Revolutionary Age: A History of Christianity in the Nineteenth and Twentieth Centuries*, 5 v. (New York 1958–62). N. ARSENIEW, *La Piété russe* (Neuchâtel 1963). D. SHAPIRO, *A Select Bibliography of Works in English on Russian History, 1801–1917* (Oxford 1962). G. VERNADSKY and M. KARPOVICH, *A History of Russia*, 4 v. (New Haven, CT 1943–59; rev. ed. pa. 1 v. 1961).

[J. KRAJCAR]

The Catholic Church since 1917

Sparked by massive oppression, poverty, and participation in a brutal world war, the Russian Revolution, which occurred in October of 1917, saw the government of Czar Nicholas II overthrown and the Bolskevik regime of Vladimir Lenin established in its place. The Revolution and the civil war that followed between 1918 and 1921, propelled many of the regions under the Russian empire to claim independence. This movement was quickly suppressed by the new communist government, and in 1922 the Union of Soviet Socialist Republics (USSR) was established, comprised of 15 soviet republics: Russia, Ukraine, Belarussia, Armenia, Georgia, Azerbaidzhan, Kazakhstan, Kirghiztan, Turkmenistan, Uzbekistan, Tadzhikstan, Estonia, Lithuania, Latvia and Moldavia. Despite communist efforts to destroy all religion within the ever-expanding Soviet sphere, Christian communities within these republics proved stronger and more resilient than was anticipated. Even though many churches were forced underground, Church attendance and religious observance by the 1960s compared favorably to Western Europe and in some instances, notably Poland, was unparalleled elsewhere on the Continent. While churches lost their pre-revolutionary or prewar wealth and institutional strength, they retained and developed their structure as Churches or denominations. Theological academies remained open and religious journals were published. The approach of the Soviet government to religion varied throughout the east European socialist community, their encounter with varied histories and cultures led to great diversity in religious patterns. Thus, in the German Democratic Republic, established in 1949, theological faculties remained, as in prewar times, a regular component in a number of state universities. Similarly in Czechoslovakia, which became a satellite of the USSR after World War II, and Hungary, which saw a liberalized communism after the mid-1950s, the state subsidized clerical support. However, feudally institutionalized Churches, particularly in Russia where they petrified over decades of operation underground, appeared anachronistic in the increasing light of the modern world. By the time of the fall of the Soviet Union in August of 1991, the churches in Russia were like tattered survivors of a famine, preservers of a Slavic culture and tradition that seemed out of step with a now-secularized society.

The Phasing-in of Communism. The introduction of communism was a process consisting of several phases. In the first phase, which lasted from the Revolution into the early 1920s, the state attempted to disrupt the established order, which meant undermining the Russian Orthodox Church, a powerful institution that was the foundation of Slavic culture in the vast region. To do this Bolsheviks encouraged the formation of sects, the growth of Protestant groups and the harassment, imprisonment and even murder of Orthodox priests. Orthodox churches were confiscated, monasteries looted and destroyed. By 1923, as Protestantism and smaller breakaway churches, such as Autocephalous Orthodox churches in Ukraine and Belarussia, gained a following, the state rescinded its support, and began to undermine their operations as well.

The next phase of communism promoted non-Slavic culture, a culture of the proletariat that extolled liberal values and promoted the restructuring of society through women in the workplace and a liberalized divorce law. The enemy became capitalism, and a strong propaganda campaign extended into the arts, literature and elsewhere. A schismatic Renovationist Church was established to fill the need for spiritual fulfillment, but this church, loyal to the state, was also gradually eliminated as oppression of the true religious and secularization of the culture increased. New secular holidays were established to replace holy days such as Easter and Christmas, and in 1929 a new religious law outlawed all religious propaganda, replacing it with a program of anti-religious advocacy. This period, known as "The Terror," saw a full assault on the church, as almost 100,000 religious of both Orthodox and Catholic faith were killed, and Muslim worship was almost totally eradicated. Hundreds of churches were demolished, priests were imprisoned and millions of Orthodox lost their lives within Russia.

World War II was pivotal in the formation of the next phase in the relationship between the churches and the State under communism. By the eve of that holocaust, organized religion had been all but eliminated. To be sure, the Orthodox Church, as the dominant Christian body in Old Russia, had already moved, by the late 1920s, through resistance to neutrality then to active support of the Revolution. That shift in policy by the Moscow leadership brought uncertain consequences, effected as it was by a *locum tenens* and the appointment by the State of the former Renovationist patriarch, Metropolitan Sergii Stragorodsky, as temporary leader of the Moscow patriarchate. After a brief imprisonment in 1927, Sergii made a declaration of loyalty to the Soviet State on behalf of all Orthodox. In June of 1941, with the Soviet government stunned by the sudden German invasion, Metropolitan Sergii moved quickly and publicly to rally the Russian people to the defense of the motherland. When some clerics wavered, notably in the western Ukraine, and welcomed the Germans as liberators, Sergii consolidated his patriotic commitment by rebuking such action in the strongest possible terms. Whether or not the metropolitan had so calculated, Soviet dictator Josef Stalin (1924–53), beleaguered by the invasion, sensed the importance of religious sentiment and support in the war effort and renegotiated a new understanding with the Orthodox hierarchy. The Holy Synod was permitted to meet and elect a Moscow patriarch, that office having been vacant since the death of Patriarch Tikhon in 1925. In exchange for patriotic support, worship was restored and many Orthodox churches reopened. The limitations of the original Leninist decrees, which limited religious expression to intramural cultic activity, were accepted by the Church.

The new *modus vivendi* between Church and State established as a response to World War II continued following the defeat of Germany, as the Soviet realm increased into eastern Europe. The enormous challenges confronting Soviet diplomacy in dealing with multiple ethnic and national groups were aided by its ability to provide a cohesive religious element as the phasing-in process occurred in Yugoslavia, Hungary, the German Democratic Republic, China and elsewhere. In all regions but China, the Churches could render important service, both in exerting influence and in improving the Soviet image abroad. Though the immediate postwar flux passed within a few years, the shift to a global scale in Khrushchev's "peaceful coexistence" campaign provided new challenges.

Despite its new attitude toward the Orthodox Church, the Soviet State continued its oppression of

Catholics, particularly those of Eastern Churches that had returned from Constantinople to Rome by way of various unions during the 16th and 17th centuries. By 1960 estimates held that of Soviet Catholics—which lived predominately in outlying regions such as Poland, Lithuania and Ukraine—over 12,500 priests and monks were killed, while another 32,000 were forced from the region. At least 50 bishops lost their lives in protest against Soviet tyranny, many due to their outspokenness over the treatment of Jews in Soviet nations that fell to German occupation between 1941 and 1944, while over two and a half million faithful also perished.

An Expanding Orthodoxy. In 1954, with the death of Stalin, the USSR came under the control of Nikita Khrushchev, whose first action was to lessen the government's harsh treatment of the Orthodox Church. Now with the support of the Soviet state, the Moscow Patriarchate moved actively among the ''family'' of Orthodox Churches existing in the increased Soviet sphere, taking control of many. These efforts brought Moscow increasingly into the modern era, and forced it to address modern concerns. A theological conversation begun in Prague in the late 1950s and oriented both to the past failures of the churches and the coming dangers of the nuclear age, quickly expanded in the 1960s into a global effort of the Soviet and other socialist-country Churches—the Christian Peace Conference. In a related move, the Russian Orthodox Church joined the World Council of Churches (WCC) in 1961 and sent observers to Vatican Council II. Both these conferences provided opportunities for the establishment of contacts with the Churches of the Third World, whose ecclesiastical ties otherwise were chiefly Western.

While the Orthodox church expanded its international profile in the 1960s, domestically it suffered increasing restrictions under Khruschev's increasing authoritarianism. At the same time that the Orthodox Patriarchate took up membership in the WCC the Synod, under the direction of the state Council for Russian Orthodox Church Affairs (CROCA), adopted a change in parish structure that weakened pastoral leadership and open parish management to interference by local political authorities. This change brought to a head, in various ''underground'' Churches, an issue that had long smoldered. Lenin's decrees and the Soviet Constitution declared a strict separation of Church and State and of the Church from education. At the same time, however, all religious property, including the objects needed for cult, were turned over to local civil authorities. These same authorities then entrusted these to duly registered religious groups (read Orthodox) for use. Thus both registration and administrative requirements involved the civil authorities in the life of the religious communities so directly that critics could view the arrangement as violating the law on the separation of Church and State.

The 50th anniversary of the formation of the Soviet Union saw marked changes in state toleration of the church. The mid-1970s witnessed a new wave of religious oppression, as the restoration of church properties ceased, atheism became a required subject in all Soviet schools and public censure was given to those openly participating in religious services such as weddings and baptisms. The implementation of the new regulations led to many irregularities at local levels in the removal of priests and the closing of churches. When parish members appealed to bishops and higher levels of the hierarchy, help was not forthcoming. The criticism mounted that Orthodox leaders had compromised or even betrayed the Churches. Indeed, much to the embarrassment of the hierarchies, and of the state, criticism reached both the World Council of Churches and the United Nations. Spokesmen of the Orthodox Church were accused of lying when confronted with the problem abroad. In the case of the Evangelical-Baptist AUCECB, *initsiativniki*, the dissidents, grew strong enough to set up a Council to replace the existing one. The result may have been a wholesome one, inasmuch as the AUCECB incorporated many of the reforms the dissidents demanded.

Religious dissent meanwhile became part of a wider current of dissent in the Soviet Union. Critics such as Alexander Solzhenitsyn regarded any improvements to society made during the 1960s and 1970s as merely tactical, and expressed the belief that harsh conditions might return. Others, including the Vatican, maintained that a process of historical change was under way, that in the longer perspective new possibilities were emerging. The Vatican developed a new *Ostpolitik* paralleling the bargaining relationship between the Russian Orthodox hierarchy and the Soviet party and government that climaxed in the 1977 reception of the First Secretary of the Hungarian Communist Party by Pope Paul VI. The assumptions of the Vatican and others that a change was occurring in the Soviet sphere would be proved accurate during the late 1980s, as a new wave of nationalism and dissatisfaction with communism washed over much of Russia and eastern Europe.

The Latin Church under Communism. Communist hostility to religion manifested itself also against Catholics, whether Latin or Eastern. This opposition was especially pronounced against the Roman Catholic Church as the main obstacle to the spread of Communist ideas. Communists utilized the historically conditioned anti-Catholic feelings of Orthodox Russians in this warfare. After 1917 the Soviet government viewed the papacy as Russia's worst enemy. The attack on the Catholic

Church was directed mainly against the hierarchy as the chief representative of the supranational spiritual power-blocking communism. The Catholic hierarchy, mostly Polish, endured persecution soon after 1917. Archbishop Edward von Ropp of Mogilev was long imprisoned and then banished. Several other bishops were driven from their posts. Archbishop CIEPLAK, Ropp's successor, was sentenced to death (1923), but was allowed to go to prison, and then to leave the country, due to the intervention of other governments. But his vicar-general, Budkiewicz, was executed on Good Friday, 1923. Many priests were also brought to court for supposed conspiracy and disobedience. This procedure seriously injured the Church administration, and made reorganization necessary.

Michael d' HERBIGNY, as chairman of a papal commission, came to Russia in 1926 with special powers to effect this, and set up nine administrative regions: Moscow, Mogilev-Minsk, Leningrad, Kharkov, Kazan-Samara-Simbirsk, Odessa, Saratov, the Caucasian region and Georgia, each headed by an apostolic administrator. Four of these were consecrated bishops. The new administrators were chosen from different nationalities. This reorganization would have strengthened the Catholic Church considerably, had it not been for continued governmental oppression, which led to the imprisonment of the apostolic administrators. Bishop Frison of Odessa, in the Ukraine, was later shot; the others were given lengthy prison terms, and then banished from the country. Hundreds of priests were jailed between 1929 and 1932, virtually destroying the Catholic Church organization.

During and after World War II, reestablishment of the Church was prohibited, despite the gradual weakening of persecution. Among those communities allowed to continue were Moscow's French church of St. Louis of France, in which a priest from the archdiocese of Riga delivered sermons in Russian through the 1950s, as well as a Catholic church in Leningrad, three in Lviv, Ukraine and one in Tiflis. Kisinev and Odessa had large Catholic communities that were sustained without a priest. The mass deportations ordered by the government during and after World War II caused unofficial underground Catholic communities to appear in remote parts of the USSR that were able to hold divine services secretly.

The Greek Church under Communism. While the treatment meted out to Roman Catholics under Soviet rule was oppressive, that extended to Eastern Catholics in countries such as Ukraine, Lithuania and Belarussia was often more prohibitive due to the dismal view held of these churches by the Moscow patriarchate. Seen as schismatic by Moscow, which refused to acknowledge the validity of the Union of Brest and other efforts toward communion with Rome, these churches faced legal hur-

dles that resulted in a total extinction and loss of property. Catholicism in Eastern garb met even less tolerance, and Russian converts to Catholicism usually joined the Latin Church. Russian philosopher SOLOV'EV was the first to supply the spiritual foundations for the erection of formal communities of a Byzantine-Slavonic rite, but conversions of the Orthodox to this rite were legally forbidden until April 17, 1905. Only after the ukase concerning religious liberty, and the manifesto, both in 1905, and after prolonged struggle, was it possible to obtain permission to establish officially one such community in St. Petersburg (1912), a permission that was revoked four months later. When religious freedom was openly proclaimed in 1917, Russian Eastern or Greek Catholics could for the first time organize properly. They created an exarchy under Metropolitan Andrei SHEPTYTS'KYI, which had only two parishes, one in Leningrad and one in Moscow. Sheptyts'kyi, with special powers from the pope, established this exarchate and named as exarch Leonid FEODOROV, who established many friendly relations with Orthodox priests. When persecution became very violent in 1922, his contacts with the Orthodox increased, but they were not allowed to continue. Soon the government abolished the exarchate itself. In 1923 Feodorov was brought to court in connection with the proceedings against Cieplak, and imprisoned until shortly before his death in 1935. During the German occupation of World War II, Sheptyts'ki was outspoken in his outrage over the treatment of Jews by Nazi troops, which outspokenness resulted in his arrest. Other priests who were attached to the exarchate also were imprisoned and later banished. The religious women who established a Catholic monastery in Moscow, directed by Catherine Abrikosova, were all sent to German concentration camps. Many laymen from parishes in the exarchate were imprisoned. While the Greek Church was forced to go underground after the return of communist control and was not officially restored in Russia, it was sustained in regions such as western Ukraine, quickly surfaced after the fall of communism, and by the late 1990s had resumed its strength as the second-largest church in that country.

The Church after Communism. The fall of the USSR in August of 1991 was precipitated by several years of increasing nationalist tensions, particularly in those nations incorporated into the Soviet Union following World War II. President Mikhail Gorbachev, attempting to ward off nationalist tendencies via an increasingly tolerant atmosphere embodied by *perestroika* (restructuring) and *glastnost* (openness), met with Pope Jon Paul II in the late 1980s and guaranteed the legalization of Eastern-rite churches and the return of religious freedom in the Soviet sphere. Only a few years later, on Dec. 26, 1991, months after a coup brought to power Boris Yeltsin, the Supreme Soviet met and voted to dissolve the USSR. Russia saw its size diminish drastically, as its former empire fragmented into 15 separate republics, the largest of which was the Russian Federation. A new constitution was promulgated in December of 1993. Efforts to preserve the region's economic structure resulted in the Commonwealth of Independent States, which included ten of the 15 newly independent republics. Unfortunately, the transition from a planned communist economy to a free market was a difficult one, and rising unemployment, inflation, high-level corruption and a series of ethnic insurrections during the 1990s resulted in the 2000 election of Vladimir Putin and a move toward a more centralized, less liberal political and economic environment.

In December of 1990 the Soviet government passed a law making all religions equal before the law. In response, in 1991 the Vatican established a new hierarchy in Russia, and in 1997 unveiled a Russian-language translation of the Catechism. Nineteen ninety-five marked the creation of the government-sponsored ecumenical Council for Cooperation with Religious Associations, which had representatives from all major denominations. Efforts by the region's churches to reacquire properties confiscated under communism were initiated, although objections from the Orthodox church caused such efforts to proceed slowly. The Catholic Church, which had 300 church buildings prior to the 1917 revolution, found itself with only two churches remaining by 1991, and the December 1999 reopening ceremony of Moscow's Cathedral of the Immaculate Conception, returned by the state in 1995, was a particularly symbolic occasion.

Under the new democratic government, the Russian Orthodox Church was able to expand its schools, rebuild important churches destroyed during the earlier decades, and gain an increasing foothold in Russian politics. In 1995 the Moscow patriarchate established a department to increase its interface with Russian armed forces, and during the civil war in Chechnya provided strong support to border forces in the region. Its development as an embodiment of Russian nationalism was in line with the many independent Orthodox churches that broke from it in countries formerly under Soviet control, some of which were granted self-governing status even before independence as a way to forestall a complete break with Moscow. Active in the battle against the legalization of abortion that was waging in Russia by the mid-1990s, the Orthodox Church also was proactive in the movement to canonize czar Nicholas II and his family as martyrs of the faith. In fact, the church's pro-Russia attitude was viewed by some observers as almost fascist in its zeal. In an increasingly democratic society, the Russian Orthodox Church remained authoritarian, and romantic in its notions of a pan-Slavic state.

Into the 21st Century. Despite the liberal attitude toward most religions in Russia immediately following independence, restrictions began to be put in place as the 1990s wore on. Under a controversial and somewhat contradictory 1997 religious law drafted with assistance from the Russian Orthodox Church, the governing Duma required religions desiring to register with the state prove their existence within the country for 15 years in order to gain legal property rights, provide religious education, or otherwise operate a religious community. While this law did not pose problems for the Latins, it affected both the Eastern Catholic Church, which was refused legal status, as well as the many foreign religious congregations that had flooded Russia by the mid-1990s, attempting to either help rebuild the existing churches in Russia or establish new faiths. While ostensibly targeting dangerous sects, the new law resulted in problems for the Jesuits, which had their initial application denied in 1999. Visa applications for foreign religious were restricted in 1998 to a three-month stay in Russia, thwarting efforts by many churches to bring in much-needed priests. In 2000 President Putin increased government control of religion by establishing seven districts, each of which was to review the new law and resolve conflicts with regional regulations.

By 2000 there were 280 Catholic parishes in Russia, half still without their own church. Priests numbered over 230, one third of them diocesan, while over 290 sisters were also active in rebuilding Catholic schools and hospitals in the region. The Russian Orthodox Church retained thousands of parishes throughout Eastern Europe as well as in Japan and China, although its power was expected to diminish outside of Russia proper, as it was viewed as a symbol of both communist oppression and centuries of czarist overlordship in an increasingly ethnically diverse and secularized society. Within Russia proper, despite the fact that most Orthodox did not attend church regularly, the Moscow patriarchate continued to dominate Orthodoxy, forcing the Eastern Catholic community in Moscow led by Andrei Udovenko to remain underground, its recognition by the government derailed by the Catholic archbishop in order to avoid reprisals to other Catholic denominations. Charges by the Russian Orthodox Church that Catholics were attempting to undermine its following by proselytization in Belarus, Russia, Kazakhstan and Ukraine, were made by Moscow Patriarch Aleksii II in June of 2000, and similar concerns caused the cancellation of a planned meeting between Aleksii and Pope John Paul II in 1997. The Russian Orthodox Church also withdrew from the WCC in January of 1999, citing increasing liberalism as the cause. Evangelical efforts among the Siberian natives, which were minimal throughout much of Russia's history, increased following the fall of communism in 1991, prompting an expansion of the Catholic hierarchy in 1993.

Bibliography: G. P. FEDOTOV, *The Russian Church since the Revolution* (New York 1928). J. S. CURTISS, *Church and State in Russia 1900–17* (New York 1940); *The Russian Church and the Soviet State 1917–50* (Boston 1953). P. B. ANDERSON, *People, State, and Church in Modern Russia* (New York 1944). M. SPINKA, *The Church and the Russian Revolution* (New York 1927); *The Church in Soviet Russia* (New York 1956). W. DE VRIES, *Kirche und Staat in der Sowjetunion* (Munich 1959). A. A. BOGOLEPOV, *Tserkov' pod vlast' kommunizma* (Munich 1958). *Church and State behind the Iron Curtain,* ed. V. GSOVSKI (*Mid-European Law Project;* New York). A. KISCHKOWSKY, *Die sowjetische Religionspolitik und die Russische Orthodoxe Kirche* (2nd ed. Munich 1960). *Religion in the USSR,* ed. B. IWANOV, tr. J. LARKIN (Munich 1960). W. KOLARZ, *Religion in the Soviet Union* (New York 1961). C. DE GRUNWALD, *The Churches and the Soviet Union,* tr. G. J. ROBINSON-PASKEVSKY (New York 1962). N. STRUVE, *Les Chrétiens en URSS* (Paris 1963). N. ZERNOV, *The Russians and Their Church* (New York 1945); *The Russian Religious Renaissance of the 20th Century* (New York 1963). J. CHRYSOSTOMUS, *Kirchengeschichte Russlands der neuesten Zeit,* v.1 *1917–25* (Munich 1965). L. J. GALLAGHER, *Edmund A. Walsh, S.J.* (New York 1962). S. W. BARON, *The Russian Jew under Tsars and Soviets* (New York 1964). *Bilan du Monde,* 2:872–892. *Religion and Atheism in the USSR and Eastern Europe,* eds., B. BOCIURKIW and J. W. STRONG (London 1975). M. BOURDEAUX, *Patriarch and Prophets* (New York 1970); *Religious Ferment in Russia* (London 1968). R. CONQUEST, *Religion in the USSR* (London 1968). D. J. DUNN, ''Papal-Communist Detente: Motivation,'' *Survey,* 22 (Spring 1976) 140–154. W. G. FLETCHER, *Religion and Soviet Foreign Policy 1945–70* (London 1973); *The Russian Church Underground 1917–1970* (London 1971). *Religion and the Soviet State: A Dilemma of Power,* eds., M. HAYWARD and W. C. FLETCHER (New York 1969). G. SIMON, *Church, State and Opposition in the USSR* (Los Angeles 1974). *Church within Socialism,* ed. E. WEINGÄARTNER (Rome 1976). *Eastern Christianity and Politics in the Twentieth Century,* ed. P. RAMET (Durham, NC 1988). S. P. RAMET, *Nihil Obstat: Religion, Politics, and Social Change in East-Central Europe and Russia* (Durham, NC 1998).

[J. CHRYSOSTOMUS BLASCHKEWITZ/P. PEACHEY/EDS.]

RUSSIAN CHANT

Historically, there were two types of church music in the Russian Orthodox Church, always unaccompanied: plainsong and figured music. The Byzantines first bequeathed to the Slavs their eight harmonic modes with varying intervals, but during centuries of foreign influence the simple Byzantine plainchant was replaced by diatonic modes with a penchant for figured music. The Kievian chant became a distinct form of Slav music after absorbing melodies originating in Greece, Bulgaria, Galicia, and Volhynia. Different chant brotherhoods of southwest Russia harmonized this plainchant at the end of the 16th and throughout the 17th century. It passed to Moscow and became the master-chant in all of Russia because of its simplicity and adaptability.

At about this same period a neo-Greek chant was imported to Russia by way of the Greek liturgical books and the general style of Greek usage favored by the Nikon reforms. It became the basic chant for the troparia, kontakia, and irmoi of Sundays, feast days, and occasions of solemnity.

The old form of simple chant in unison was discontinued and a harmonic chant (partesnoi penie) was introduced from southwest Russia. The Italian Renaissance was felt in all areas of Russian art and architecture, but especially in religious music. Giuseppe Sarti and Baldassare Galuppi were masters for generations of Russian composers who studied in Italy. Bortiniansky (d. 1825) is typical of the Russian composers who had studied in Italy and those whose polyphonic arrangements were imitated and copied during the greater part of the 19th century in Russia. However, toward the end of the 19th century a reaction against Italian influence began in Russian liturgical music, led by Tourtchaninov and Michael Glinka. Meanwhile, Balakirev and Rimsky-Korsakov continued the harmonization of the old sacred melodies that today are the most used in the Russian Church.

Bibliography: A. D. MCCREDIE, ''Some Aspects of Current Research into Russian Liturgical Chant,'' *Miscellanea Musicologica* 6 (1972) 55–152. V. MOROSAN, ''Penie and Musikiia: Aesthetic Changes in Russian Liturgical Singing during the Seventeenth Century,'' *St. Vladimir's Theological Quarterly* 23 (1979) 149–79. N. SCHIDLOVSKY, ''Sources of Russian Chant Theory,'' in *Russian Theoretical Thought in Music,* ed. G. D. MCQUERE (Ann Arbor, 1983) 83–108. D. E. CONOMOS, *The Late Byzantine and Slavonic Communion Cycle: Liturgy and Music* (Washington DC, 1985). J. VON GARDNER, *On the Synodal Chant Books of the Russian Church and their Usage in Today's Practice* (Glen Cove, NY, 1987). K. LEVY, ''The Slavic Reception of Byzantine Chant,'' in *Christianity and the Arts in Russia,* ed. W. C. BRUMFIELD and M. M. VELIMIROVIĘ (Cambridge, 1991) 46–51.

[G. A. MALONEY/EDS.]

RUSSIAN LITURGY

The first Typikon (book regulating all of the liturgical services in the Byzantine liturgy) brought from Constantinople to Kiev was that of Patriarch Alexis Studite of Constantinople; for the liturgy in the monasteries, the Typikon of St. Theodore Studite of the 9th century was the model. Various other Slavic liturgical books composed by Bulgarian and Serbian monks made their influence felt in Russia. In the 14th century a return to Greek usage was effected by the Russian Metropolitan Cyprian when he enforced the use of the Diataxis of Philotheus, Patriarch of Constantinople.

With the development of cultus to native Russian saints, the increase in liturgical influence from Serbia after the fall of Constantinople (1453), and the lack of centralization in Russia, varieties of usage developed, which the great Synod of Stoglav (1551) was unable to reform. Patriarch Nikon (1667) purified the Russian liturgical rite by taking as his model the Greek liturgical books, which were themselves based on the usages promulgated by the Patriarch of Jerusalem, Paisy, and supplemented by Andrew the Greek. His liturgical reforms were opposed by a section of the faithful, who broke away, calling themselves the Old Believers or Old Ritualists.

During the 17th and 18th centuries Latin influence was felt, especially in the Kievian theology and liturgical practices, and these were gradually accepted in the ritual books printed in Moscow. The Greek formula of absolution in the Sacrament of Penance, for example, was always deprecative (i.e., in the third person, ''May God forgive . . .''). Through Latin influence on Peter of Moghila, the indicative formula in the first person, ''I forgive . . .,'' was accepted in the 1677 edition of the Trebnik, or ritual book, for administration of the Sacraments. There was a weak protest in the centuries that followed, but by then the Russian rite customs had become a part of a standing tradition.

The liturgical books are numerous. The Service Book (Sluzhebnik) contains the fixed parts of the Liturgies of St. John Chrysostom, St. Basil the Great, parts of that of the Presanctified Gifts, along with the litanies and prayers for Vespers and Matins, and the Graduals and benedictions appropriate for all occasions. The Book of the Hours (Tchasoslov) corresponds to the Greek Horologion and contains, in addition to the Hours, those fixed portions of Vespers, Compline, Matins, Midnight Service, and so on, that are executed by the singers and readers. The Oktoikh contains the eight tones according to which various changeable parts in liturgical services are sung. Here are found the canons and hymns sung during Little and Great Vespers, Compline, Midnight Service, and Matins, the hymn for the day (Troparion), and the Collect hymn (Kondiakion). This book contains eight complete sets for each service for every day in the week, since each day of the week is sung in a different tone. The Mineya (i.e., monthly) is a collection of large books, one for each month, containing the order of services for all the fixed days of the liturgical year and giving a history of the saint or saints commemorated on each day. It includes the prayers in honor of each saint for Vespers and Matins with some special prayers for the Hours, liturgy, Compline, and the Midnight Service.

The Postnaya Triod (Fasting Triod) contains the changeable parts of the services for each day of the Great Fast of Lent. It is called Triod because the canons have

only three odes instead of the customary eight found in the Oktoikh. The Tzvyetnaya Triod (literally, the Flowery Triodion), also called the Pentikostarion, contains the order of services from Easter until Pentecost. The Tchinovnik is the pontificale containing those fixed portions of the liturgy that are celebrated by a bishop. The Apostol contains the Acts of the Apostles, the Epistles, Graduals, Introits, and Anthems for each day, and the feasts. The book chiefly appealed to when there is doubt concerning the intricate order of church services as found in the Russian rite is the Typikon, or Rule, which contains regulations for all possible contingencies. The Trebnik, or Book of Needs, contains all the Sacraments except Holy Orders and Holy Eucharist, along with various services such as the reception of converts and tonsure of monks. The Moliebny contains prayer services for different occasions and in honor of individual saints. Finally, the Irmologion contains the theme-songs of the canons along with the Akaphists or long services of song in honor of Our Lord, the Mother of God, St. Nicholas, and other honored saints.

Bibliography: H. WYBREW, *The Orthodox Liturgy* (London 1989). H. -J. SCHULZ, *The Byzantine Liturgy* (New York 1986). R. F. TAFT, *Liturgy of the Hours in East and West*, 2d. rev. ed. (Collegeville, Minn. 1993).

[G.A. MALONEY/EDS.]

RUSSIAN THEOLOGY

The theology of the ancient empire Rus' of Kiev, that of the Ukraine, that of the Moscovite Empire and Soviet Russia, and that of the recent Russian *émigrés*, covering a period from the 10th to the 20th century. It may be discussed in periods: (1) from the primitive stage to 1550; (2) from the establishment of the Patriarchate of Moscow to the reign of Peter the Great; (3) from Peter the Great to 1836; (4) from 1836 to the Communist revolution of 1917; (5) from the postrevolutionary period to the late 20th century.

The Primitive Stage to 1550. Ecclesiastical and theological literature first entered the empire of Kiev from Bulgaria, where the disciples of the Slavic apostles CYRIL AND METHODIUS had taken refuge, and later directly from Byzantium. The earliest Christian missionaries translated the works of the Greek Fathers, particularly of JOHN CHRYSOSTOM and JOHN DAMASCENE, into the Slavic language. Polemic against the Latins, fed particularly by the Byzantine bishops in Rus', began only at the end of the 11th century. There is an interesting, somewhat deferential answer made by the Greek metropolitan John II of Kiev (1080–89) to the antipope Clement III (1080–98). According to John, the Latins were not completely separated from the Church, but detached themselves by their teaching. The polemicists reproved the Latins with the reproaches made earlier by Photius and Cerularius. But there were also later ecclesiastical writers both at Novgorod and at Kiev who were not interested in polemics, such as the Metropolitan Clement of Smolensk toward the middle 12th century, the era also of the celebrated preacher CYRIL OF TURIV (1130–82). There followed a time of Mongol domination however (1237–1480) when ecclesiastical science reached its lowest level. Certain tracts were published against the Latins, this time reproving not the teaching of the FILIOQUE or the primacy of the pope but the presumed teaching that the Sacred Liturgy could be celebrated only in Hebrew, Greek, and Latin, and not in Slavic.

Strigolniki. The 14th and 15th centuries were marked by a move against internal heresy, such as that of the Strigolniki, who in their zeal against the simony of the clergy, rejected both the hierarchy and the Sacraments, the Liturgical Sacrifice, and the suffrages for the deceased. At the beginning of the 15th century at Novgorod the controversy over singing a double or a triple Alleluia during the Liturgy arose and was to assume considerable importance later on. Because of the use of a double Alleluia at Constantinople some zealots, such as the monk Euphrosinus, accused the Byzantines of apostasy from the true faith and a turning to the anti-Christ. Meanwhile, during the same period, several Byzantine theological works were translated, such as those of Gregory PALAMAS and Nilus CABASILAS.

Moscow, the Third Rome. After the fall of Constantinople to the Turks in 1453, the center of gravity of Orthodox theological study gradually shifted from the Greeks to the Slavs of Kiev and Moscow. Moscow, which became autocephalous in 1448, increased its suspicion against the Greeks, who had accepted union with the Latins at Florence in 1439. In monastic circles in Russia arose the theory of Moscow as the "third Rome" since it alone had remained orthodox after the fall into heresy of the first and the second. This theory was combated by the Greek monk Maximus (d. 1556), sent by the patriarch of Constantinople to Moscow to correct the Slavic liturgical books and to translate the Greek Fathers into Slavic. He arrived in Moscow in 1519 and wrote several tracts against the Latins, attacking indirectly the Roman primacy and directly the use of filioque in the Creed, the use of unleavened bread, and purgatory; but he was not successful in his battle against the independence of the Russian Church from that of Constantinople, to which the Church of Kiev in the second half of the 15th century had been directly subordinated.

Patriarchate of Moscow to Peter the Great. In 1589 Moscow became a patriarchate. A few years later (1595–96) the Union of BREST was signed, in which some of the Ukrainians and White Russians joined the Roman Church. This occasioned a war of tracts between Catholics and Orthodox. Among the more prominent writers were the Polish Jesuit Piotr SKARGA (1536–1612) and Benedict Herbestus (1531–93) on one side; and on the other, the anonymous Christopher Philalethos, who was answered by the also anonymous Arcudios, then by John Wishensky and Meletius Smotritsky. Smotritsky died as a Catholic in 1633.

School of Peter Moghila. Zachary Kopystensky (d. c. 1627) wrote against both the Catholics and the Protestants, as did the celebrated Peter MOGHILA, or Movila (1596–1646), Metropolitan of Kiev since 1633, a Rumanian by birth. His dealings with Pope Urban VIII in regard to reunion with the papacy were unsuccessful. While still an archimandrite of the Monastery of the Grottoes at Kiev in 1631, he founded a school that became an academy in 1633 and was the forerunner of the Ecclesiastical Academy inaugurated in 1701. Moghila's school was modeled on the Jesuit colleges, and became a center of Orthodox theology; it was frequented by Russians, Greeks, Rumanians, Serbs, and Bulgars. Philosophy and theology were taught there in Latin according to St. Thomas Aquinas and the scholastic method. Prescinding from the primacy of the pope, the doctrines were Latinized, and they reached a concordance in regard to the dogmas of purgatory, the Immaculate Conception of Mary, and the words of Christ as the form of the Eucharist. However, they were rather in disagreement as to the filioque. Moghila's most important writing was his Large Catechism, or Confession of Faith, which was intended to neutralize the Protestant influence of the Confession of the Patriarch of Constantinople Cyril Lucaris. It was written in both Latin and the vernacular but was published only in popular Greek (1667). The translator, Meletius Syrigus, however, in order to obtain the approbation of the four Orthodox patriarchs of the Near East, incorporated some corrections that were not in accord with the intention of the author, particularly regarding the state of souls after death and the form of the Eucharist. Later numerous editions and translations in different languages followed.

School of Kiev. Kiev produced many learned theologians, polemicists, and orators, such as Lasar Baranovich (1620–93), Innocentius Gisel' (d. c. 1683), Antonius Radivilovsky (d. 1688), and Yoanniky Galiatovsky (d. 1688). The influence of the Catholicizing school of Kiev extended as far as Moscow, where, however, toward the middle of the 17th century Greek influence began once more to make its presence felt. The clash between these two currents became violent with ample literary production on both sides, particularly regarding the moment of consecration of the Eucharist. The examination of these questions was intensified on the occasion of the reform of the Slavic liturgical books on the Greek model by the Patriarch Nikon in 1654, which caused the great schism, or *raskol*. Nikon had sanctioned the triple Alleluia against the *raskolniki*, who, in favor of the double Alleluia as well as the manner of making the sign of the cross, appealed to the Greek monk Maximus.

The more prominent Moscovite theologians of the period were from southern Russia. They were Epiphanius Slavinetsky (d. 1675), Simeon Petrovsky Sitnianovich, called Polotsky (1629–80), and his disciple Silvester Medvedev (1641–91), Innocent Monastyrsky, a friend of Silvester, and the saintly Bishop of Rostov, Demetrius Tuptalo (1651–1709). These theologians defended the Catholic doctrine concerning the moment of the Eucharistic consecration against the monk Euthemius and the Lichudy brothers. Since the Czar and the Metropolitan of Moscow Joachim III (1674–90) took the side of the Grecophile theologians against those favoring the Latins, under the influence of the Oriental patriarchs and particularly of Dositheus of Jerusalem, Greeks were thereafter engaged as professors. Among them were the brothers Joannes and Sophronius Lichudy, who arrived in Moscow in 1685 to teach in a projected Greek-Latin-Slavic school or academy. Another important theologian of this period was Adam Zernikavius, or Zoirnikabios, born a Lutheran in Prussia, who composed a polemic work on the procession of the Holy Spirit.

Peter the Great to 1836. With the ecclesiastical reform inaugurated by PETER THE GREAT, Russian theology became dependent on the czar, who entered into relations with the Protestants, Anglicans, and Gallicans. The Council of Moscow (1666–67) had decided that Catholics should not be rebaptized when coming over to Orthodoxy; this same decision was taken in regard to Calvinists and Lutherans by Peter the Great after consultation with the Patriarch Jeremia III of Constantinople in 1718. Peter's more influential adviser in the Protestantizing of the Russian Church was Feofan PROKOPOVICH (1681–1736), Bishop of Pskov and later Archbishop of Novgorod. From 1711 to 1716 he was rector of the Academy of Kiev, where he taught Lutheran opinions concerning Sacred Scriptures and tradition, the ecclesiastical magisterium, and justification by faith alone.

Ecclesiastical Academy of Moscow. The Lichudy brothers and the majority of professors at Kiev opposed this teaching of Prokopovich; they were supported by Theophylactus Lopatinsky, since 1706 rector of the Academy of Moscow and from 1723 Archbishop of Tver; also by Stephan Yavorsky (1658–1722), Bishop of Riazan and patriarchal Exarch after the death of the Patriarch

Adrian. He endowed the Greek-Latin-Slavic Academy of Moscow in 1701 on the model of that at Kiev. His principal work, *Petra fidei* (*Kamen very,* or Rock of Faith), could be published only in 1728, after the death of Peter the Great; though prohibited, it was reprinted in 1744.

Protestant Influence. Under the Empresses Anna (1730–40) and Catherine II (1762–86) Protestant influence predominated; it was notable, for example, in the works of Gabriel Petrov (d. 1801); Macarius Petrovich (d. 1766); Theophylactus Gorsky (d. 1788); Samuel Mislavsky (d. 1796), editor of various works of Prokopovich; and Silvester Lebedinsky (d. 1808). Of the same tendency were the Metropolitan of Moscow Plato Levshin (d. 1812), Methodius Smirnov (d. 1815), Ireneus Falkovsky (d. 1827), Filaret Amfitreatrov (d. 1857), and the celebrated Metropolitan of Moscow Filaret Drozdov (1782–1867). From the time of Prokopovich, and particularly through the influence of Filaret Drozdov, biblical studies were promoted. In 1812 the Russian Biblical Society was founded at St. Petersburg. During this period polemics were concerned mainly with the *raskol*.

Reform (1836–1917). A notable change in the direction of theology was produced in 1836 with the reform instituted by Nicholas Alessandrovich Protasov, lay procurator of the Holy Synod. Protasov was a student of the Jesuits. He ordered a return to the doctrine of the Confessions by Moghila and Dositheus, and of the *Petra fidei* by Yavorsky. At the same time patristic studies were pursued in the ecclesiastical academies in Russia, and many patristic monographs were produced. The Metropolitan Filaret Drozdov, as a preacher of Orthodox doctrine and as a theologian, even though inclined toward Protestantism, was constrained to cancel Protestant tendencies from his great Catechism. Instead of being written in Latin, the classical manuals of dogma of a new type were produced in Russian; and with the abolishment of Latin, the use of the speculative and scholastic method in theology began to decline. The main authors of these manuals, besides the priest Peter Ternovsky (editions of 1838, 1839, 1843), were bishops—Antonius Amfiteatrov (1815–79); Filaret Gumilevsky (1805–66); and of more recent date, Silvester Malevansky (1828–1908), who frequently cites the Fathers, and the Archpriest Nicholas Malinovsky (d. 1917).

Apologetic Writings. Beginning in 1884 a course of apologetics against the *raskol* and against the Western confessions was introduced into the ecclesiastical schools and academies. At the beginning of the 20th century the apologetic manuals of the Archimandrite Augustine and of I. Nikolin were widely diffused. Other writers who discussed the Catholic faith were A. M. Ivantsov-Platonov (d. 1894); N. J. Beliaev (1843–94); V. Guettée

(1816–92), who had been a Catholic priest; and particularly Alexander A. Lebedev (d. 1898), whose polemical writings attacked the Immaculate Conception, the cult of the Sacred Heart, and the papacy. Of greatest importance was the Slavophile theologian Alexius Stepanovich Khomiakov (1804–60), particularly in the ecclesiological sphere and in that of soteriology.

Khomiakov's Ecclesiology. Khomiakov describes the Church as one organism, free and charismatic, with unity, liberty, and charity of all the faithful. The philosophical foundation of his concept of the Church, which he and his friend Ivan Kireevsky elaborated, is based on the principle that a true understanding need not be abstract but concrete or integral, that is joined with all the other faculties of man; and for this reason the knowledge of the faith is not individual but depends on the union in love with all the other faithful. The infallibility of the Church is not possible in one isolated person, such as the pope, or in the hierarchy; hence to have value the decrees of ecumenical councils must be recognized by the whole ecclesiastical people.

With this doctrine that repudiated the charism of infallibility in the hierarchy, Khomiakov opposed traditional doctrine common to the Orthodox and Catholics. His opposition to Western Christianity was expressed in the formula that Catholicism is unity without liberty; Protestantism, liberty without unity; while in Orthodoxy is found a synthesis of unity with liberty in charity. He rejected the external authority of the Church and the concept of Catholicity in an extensive sense, basing his idea of Catholicity on an intensive idea of unity in multiplicity, or free unanimity expressed in the Slavic word *sobornyj* (from *sobor*, or collection, reunion, council), and thus he translated the word ''catholic'' in the creed. The ecclesiological conception of Khomiakov was thus described by his disciples as the *sobornost'*.

Khomiakov's ecclesiology, although at first opposed by the conservative theologians and censured by the Russian ruler, had penetrated into the official theology by the end of the 19th century. The priest Eugene P. Akvilonov (1861–1911) propagated his ecclesiology, while Pavel J. SVETLOV (1861–1942) championed his soteriology; and his thought has been diffused in modern times particularly among Slav and Russian theologians outside Russia. Another great layman and Russian theologian was Vladimir SOLOV'EV (1853–1900), with whom Russian religious philosophy attained its highest point. As philosopher-theologian, or Russian ''gnostic,'' Solov'ev became the proponent of modern *Sophiologia* (study of wisdom) and of a theandric direction in ecclesiology. In the first part of his book *Russia and the Universal Church* he wrote an apology for the Roman primacy and then at-

tempted to make a speculative deduction of the mystery of the Blessed Trinity. In his philosophy of religion, or fundamental theology, he did not accept the Catholic truth that man can know God with natural reason, but in accord with the majority of Russian apologetical theologians, he attempted to base a knowledge of God rather on mystical experience. Solov'ev can be considered a precursor of modern ecumenism.

Together with Khomiakov and Solov'ev, a group of theologians opposed the official theology; they included liberals who were anti-Catholic and sought the union of all Christians, distinguishing, among other things, the doctrines of the first seven ecumenical councils from the later theologumena, or theologizings, whose conclusions they considered free and discussible opinions. Among them were the theologians who after Vatican Council I sought union with the Old Catholics and the Anglicans in 1874 and 1875 and their successors: I. L. Yanyshev (1826–1900); the historian V. V. Bolotov (1854–1900), noted for his publications on ancient Church history and the controversy over the filioque; A. Lopuchin (d. 1904), editor of a theological encyclopedia, which was continued by N. N. GLUBOKOVSKIĬ (1863–1937) but remains incomplete because of the 1917 revolution; A. A. Kireev (1833–1910); and the Archpriest P. Svetlov, who between 1890 and the first decades of the 20th century gained a reputation as a speculative theologian, apologete, and soteriologist. Khomiakov inspired a new direction in Russian soteriology, which Svetlov developed in a moderate fashion while Sergius Stragorodsky (Patriarch of Moscow, 1943–44) and the Metropolitan ANTONIĬ KHRAPOVITSKIĬ pursued it radically. The latter sought to eliminate all trace of juridicism from the doctrine of the Redemption and ended by denying an objective Redemption, that is, the satisfaction and merits of Christ; they insisted exclusively on the subjective and moral significance of the work of the Redeemer. Antoniĭ, however, influenced, among others, by Dostoevsky, emphasized the spiritual rebirth of sinners brought about by the love of the Savior in the soul and the reform of man. Theological publications, particularly in the form of dissertations and articles, were augmented during the second half of the 19th century in the periodicals of the Ecclesiastical Academies of St. Petersburg, Moscow, Kiev, and Kazan'.

The Postrevolutionary Period. With the revolution of 1917 almost all theological activity came to an end in Russia. The representatives of theological learning were forced to emigrate and sought to found centers of study in various parts of the world. This new period was characterized by the absence of state censure outside the Iron Curtain and by immediate contact with both Catholic and Protestant theology. Some Russian theologians distinguished themselves by their activity in the ecumenical movement, particularly the professors at the Orthodox Theological Institute of St. Sergius in Paris, who established theological and liturgical conferences that were attended by Orthodox, Catholic, Anglican, and Protestant scholars from various countries.

St. Sergius Institute, Paris. In 1925, an institute was conducted by the Archpriest Sergeǐ BULGAKOV (1871–1944), the most original and fecund of the Russian theologians in exile. Bulgakov was famed as the representative of "wisdom theology," based on the idea of divine and human wisdom, and the theandrism inherited from Solov'ev. He was also distinguished as a Mariologist, the sole Russian theologian to have written a Marian monograph, and as an ecclesiologist in the footsteps of Khomiakov. With his doctrine on divine wisdom he provoked the "Sophianic" controversy and was condemned by two Russian hierarchies, that of Moscow and that of the former Karlovits of Yugoslavia.

Bulgakov's pupil and colleague at the Institute of St. Sergius, as well as his strenous defender, was L. Zander (d. 1964); and one of the better-known, influential professors was the Archpriest N. Afanasiev, who sought to reconstruct a genuine Orthodox ecclesiology based on the mystery of the Eucharist in the Eucharistic gathering of the local church presided over by the bishop. He believed that the local church contains in itself the fullness of ecclesial values and is therefore independent or autonomous of any superior juridical authority. He contrasted his Eucharistic ecclesiology with the universal ecclesiology in which individual churches are but part of the totalitarian organism. Afanasiev thus parted with the traditional ecclesiology of both Orthodox and Catholics. He admitted a hierarchy and even a primacy in the Church, but of love alone and not of law or power. Afanasiev wrote a monograph on the service of the laity in the church, insisting on their sacerdotal service in keeping with his Eucharistic ecclesiology.

One of the best-known of Russian theologians, the Archpriest George FLOROVSKY, first taught patrology at St. Sergius and later was professor of ancient church history at Harvard Divinity School and at the Grecoorthodox Seminary in Boston, as well as dean of St. Vladimir's Orthodox Theological Seminary. He sought to base his teaching on the doctrine of the Fathers of the Church, particularly the Greeks, and saw in the doctrine on God of the great Byzantine and Palamite theologians of the 14th century who were followers of Gregory Palamas (d. 1359) the continuation of the genuine patristic tradition, a tradition that he endeavored to restore.

Palamite Renaissance. The quintessence of the Palamite doctrine consists in three affirmations: that man can-

not know the essence of the transcendent God; that he can know the divine energies, or actions, operations, and attributes of God; and that therefore there must be in God a real distinction, although not a separation, between the unintelligible essence and the knowable energies. Among these energies it acknowledges divine grace and the light of Mt. Tabor seen by the three elect disciples on the mount of the Transfiguration. On the basis of Palamite doctrine the controversy over the divinity of the holy name of Jesus has become famous and involved the monks of the great Russian monastery of St. Panteleimon on Mt. Athos in 1912–13 and continued in Russia itself. These monks practiced, according to their ancient tradition, the invocation of the Savior with the noted prayer directed to Jesus (*see* JESUS PRAYER) and so exaggerated it that they called the invoked name of Jesus "God Himself."

Another propagator of Palamism was a monk of the Monastery of St. Panteleimon, Vasily Krivoshein, later the archbishop of the Patriarchate of Moscow for Western Europe. In 1936 he published a monograph on the ascetical and theological doctrine of St. Gregory Palamas, translated into German in 1939. He was also a student of the great Byzantine mystic SYMEON THE NEW THEOLOGIAN (fl. *c.* 1000) and editor of his works. J. Meyendorff was another renovator of the Palamite tradition and published, among other works, a large monograph in defense of the Hesychasts, or Palamites. Meyendorff, in an attempt to attenuate the doctrine of Gregory on the real distinction between the essence or nature of God and his attributes or energies, which is untenable because of the absolute simplicity of God, affirmed that the doctrine of Palamas is neither a philosophy nor a system and cannot be judged according to scholastic categories.

In this context another professor of St. Sergius deserves mention as being finely discriminatory in his judgment of Palamism, the Archimandrite Cyprian Kern (d. 1960), who wrote a vast exposition of the rich, patristic anthropology of Gregory Palamas. Another theologian of the same institute was the priest V. V. Zenkovsky (d. 1963), notable also as the author of a large History of Russian Philosophy.

Vladimir Lossky. Vladimir Lossky (d. 1958) wrote the famous *Essai sur la théologie mystique de l'Église d'Orient* (Paris 1944), translated (London 1957) into English. Son of a noted philosopher, Lossky was a professor in the Theological Institute of Saint-Denis at Paris, which was dependent on the Patriarchate of Moscow. In 1936 he wrote a treatise on the Sophian controversy controverting the position of Bulgakov. In his attitude toward mystical theology, which was completely patristic, not only did he propose, as a foundation of Orthodoxy, the theory that the Holy Spirit proceeds from the Father alone but also asserted that between the filioque and the ''from the Father alone,'' as in its roots, lay the profound difference between Oriental and Western spirituality.

Summary. Russian theology depended in the beginning on Constantinople, a dependence reinforced during the first half of the 16th century by the works of Maximus the Greek and in Moscow from the second half of the 17th century by the Patriarch Nikon and somewhat later by the Lichudy brothers. In the 17th century, however, the school of Kiev took prominence and showed the influence of Latin theology; and in the age of Peter the Great, there was a notable dependence on Protestant theology in official Russian doctrine. In the 20th century, most Russian theology was Khomiakovian, with the exception of a few teachers such as Vasily Vinogradov, former professor at the Ecclesiastical Academy of Moscow, who moved to Germany. The Metropolitan Antonius and the Archpriest Florovsky were inclined to repudiate as noncreative the official Russian theology of recent centuries.

New Directions. Florensky, Florovsky, Lossky, and others aspired to an original Orthodox theology based on the Greek Fathers and the Byzantine theologians and sought to emancipate themselves from the older dependence on the Catholic and Protestant West. Thus Florovsky announced in the theological Congress of Athens (1936) as his reforming program the attempt to surpass, by new creative activity, the results of the theological research of the West. He was in search of a synthesis of patristic-Byzantine tradition and the ecclesiology of Khomiakov, while other recent Russian theologians followed a more subjective or even Modernistic direction, such as that of Bulgakov.

The philosophy of N. Berdîâev reflects the ecclesiology of Khomiakov and the theandrism as well as the doctrine of ''all-in-unity'' taught of Solov'ev. Both Berdîâev and Bulgakov communicated the great vision of the mystery of the Church, although the Catholic influence of Solov'ev has not been accepted by the Russian theologians.

What was positive in the return to Palamism was the stress on the great mystery of the divinity. Also notable among the Russian theologians were the opinions on the dogmas defined by the Catholic Church after the separation. Finally, there were new attempts among Russian theologians to construct a living, intuitive, integral, and universal theology that would be at once Trinitarian and Christocentric by entering deeply in a theological anthropology. They aimed to communicate a universal Christian vision of the universe in God, and particularly in the Church of Christ, as in the *SOBORNOST*, that is, the unanimous community under the action of the Holy Spirit.

See Also: SCHNEEMAN, GEORGE; SCHMEMANN, ALEXANDER; MEYENDORFF, JOHN.

Bibliography: A. PALMIERI, *Theologia dogmatica orthodoxa*, 2 v. (Florence 1911–13). T. SPÁČIL, ''Doctrina theologiae orientis separati de revelatione fide dogmate,'' *Orientalia Christiana* 31.2 (1933) 145–391. M. GORDILLO, *Compendium theologiae orientalis* (3d ed. Rome 1950); *Mariologia orientalis* (Orientalia Christiana Analecta 141; 1954); *Theologia orientalium cum latinorum comparata* (*ibid.* 158; 1960). B. SCHULTZE, *Russische Denker* (Vienna 1950); in *Problemi e orientamenti di teologia dommatica*, v.1 (Milan 1957) 547–579, with bibliog., Eng. tr. by P. SHERWOOD in *The Unity of the Churches of God* (Baltimore 1963) 185–215, without bibliog.; ''Maria und Kirche in der russischen Sophia-Theologie,'' *Maria et ecclesia* 10 (1960) 51–141. B. SCHULTZE and JOHN CHRYSOSTOM, *Die Glaubenswelt der orthodoxen Kirche* (Salzburg 1961). Reviews and collections. *Unam Sanctam* (Paris 1946-), monograph ser. *Russie et chrétiené* (Boulogne-sur-Seine 1934–50), continued as *Istina* (1954-). *Irénikon. Das östliche Christentum* (Würzburg 1936-), monograph ser. *Ostkirchliche Studien* (Würzburg 1952-). *Orientalia Christiana* (1923-), divided since 1935 into *Orientalia Christiana Analecta* and *Orientalia Chritiana periodica*, pub. by the Pontificio Istituto Orientale in Rome. Orthodox. *Pravosl. bogoslovskaîa entsiklop,* ed. A. P. LOPUKHÎN and N. N. GLUBOKOVSKIÏ, 13 v. (St. Petersburg 1900–14), theol. encyc., incomplete. N. N. GLUBOKOVSKIÏ, *Ruskaîa bogoslovskaîa nauka v eë istoricheskom razvitii i noveĭišem sostoîa nii* (Warsaw 1928). S. ZANKOW, *Das orthodoxe Christentum des Ostens* (Berlin 1928). S. N. BULGAKOV, *The Orthodox Church,* tr. E. S. GRAM, ed. D. A. LEWIS (London 1935); *The Wisdom of God: A Brief Summary of Sophiology* (New York 1937). G. V. FLOROVSKIÏ, *Puti russkago bogoslovīa* (Paris 1937). H. S. ALIVISATOS, ed., *Procès-verbaux du Ier congrès de théologie orthodoxe à Athènes, 29 nov.–6 déc. 1936* (Athens 1939). P. EVDOKIMOFF, *L'Orthodoxie* (Paris 1959). N. AFANASIEV et al., *La Primauté de Pierre dans l'église orthodoxe* (Neuchâtel 1960), Eng. tr. *The Primacy of Peter* (London 1963). *Put': Organ russkoĭ religioznoĭ mysli* (Paris 1925-). *Pravoslavnaîa mysl'* (Paris 1928–40). *St. Vladimir's Seminary Quarterly* (New York 1952–56; NS 1957-). M. POMAZANSKY, *Orthodox Dogmatic Theology: A Concise Exposition,* tr. S. ROSE (2d ed. Platina, Calif. 1994).

[B. SCHULTZE/EDS.]

RUTH, BOOK OF

This charming idyll, named after the central character, is one of the Five Scrolls (*megillôt*) among the Writings (*ketûbîm*) of the Hebrew Bible [*see* BIBLE]. It follows the book of JUDGES in the Septuagint (LXX) and the Vulgate, probably because of the first verse. Since Talmudic times it has been the synagogal reading for Pentecost, the harvest festival.

Content. Because of famine, Elimelech of Bethlehem migrated to Moab with his wife Noemi and their two sons, who married MOABITE women, Ruth and Orpha. When her husband and sons died and the famine had ended, Noemi returned home with Ruth, who insisted on staying with her. During the barley harvest Ruth used the right of the poor to glean in the fields behind the harvesters. There she met Booz, a wealthy relative of Elimelech, who treated her kindly. At Noemi's suggestion Ruth went by night to Booz and requested that he marry her according to the LEVIRATE MARRIAGE law, which required a man to wed his dead brother's childless widow (Dt 25.5–10). He agreed after a closer relative ceded his rights; Booz purchased Elimelech's property and took Ruth as wife. From this union was born Obed, the grandfather of David.

Origins. The problems of dating and interpretation, for which scholars offer sharply conflicting solutions, are closely related. Suggestions for the composition of the book range from the time of Samuel, named in the Talmud as author (Baba Bathra 14b) and accepted as such for centuries by Christian writers, to the postexilic period because of supposed Aramaisms and intent to mitigate the law against marrying foreign women (Ezr 9.1–10.17; Neh 13.1–3). Both extremes are unlikely. The opening line implies the remoteness of the Judges' rule over Israel, and the explanatory note (Ru 4.7) presupposes unfamiliarity with ancient customs. The instances of Aramaisms are few and otherwise explainable. It is highly probable that the story had been widely circulated in oral form, put into writing by the 8th century, and that it underwent some redaction after the Exile. However, since the classical prose style, the delicate psychological portrayal of the characters, and the theological undercurrent of God's providence guiding the hearts of men bear a close resemblance to the brilliant court history of David (2 Samuel ch. 9–20) and to stories in the YAHWIST history, Ruth could well derive from the age of "Solomonic humanism."

In view of anti–Moabite sentiments and legislation (Dt 23.4), this tradition about David's Moabite origin (see also 1 Sm 22.3) must surely be historical. Therefore, the concluding statement and genealogy (Ru 4.17–22) would hardly be secondary additions. The artistic contrast in the characters and their roles, the highlighting of virtues, and possibly even the symbolism of the names indicate a literary embellishment that is delightful to popular imagination and common in short stories.

Interpretation. Doubtless the author intended to depict various virtues, such as family loyalty, charity, self-sacrifice, as well as the hidden, effective workings of divine providence in raising up an heir for Elimelech to save his "name" from extinction (Ru 4.5, 10–11; 2 Sm 7.9); but the book seems to have a deeper significance. Its total lack of polemic militates against the suggestion that the purpose was the mitigating of the legislation on foreign wives or revivifying the laws of levirate marriage (Dt 25.5–10). Nor is the theme of universalism particularly in evidence, although there may be a hint of attempted

rehabilitation for Moab (cf. Gn 19.35–38), still a part of the Davidic empire. The sevenfold repetition of "Ruth the Moabitess," who embraced Israel's God and destiny (1.16; 2.11–12), and the emphasis on her posterity (1.13; 4.5, 10–15) reveal the intent to underline Ruth's complete acceptance of and by the Israelite community. The lengthy legal transaction (ch. 4) manifests a similar object regarding the property (Lv 25.25–28). Thus, both David's ancestry and ancestral inheritance are portrayed as legitimated and incorporated into Israel's ancient structure. Moreover, there are parallels with several patriarchal motifs: famine (Gn 12.10; 26.1), childlessness of a future clan matriarch (Gn 16.1–18.15; 30.1–2), purchase of a field (Gn 23.1–20), and a link in prayer (Ru 4.11–12) with Rachel, Lia, and the ancestor Tamar (Gn 38). Just as the patriarchal history was conceived as divinely guided toward the Sinai Covenant and toward complete possession of the land, similarly the story of Ruth seems preparatory to God's special care in providing a ruling house for Israel whose eternal throne would be guaranteed in the Davidic Covenant.

Bibliography: A. CLAMER, *Dictionnaire de théologie catholique,* ed. A. VACANT et al., 15 v. (Paris 1903–50; Tables générales 1951–) 14:373–382. P. JOÜON, *Ruth: Commentaire philologique et exegetique* (Rome 1953). G. GERLEMAN, *Ruth* (Neukirchen 1960). H. H. ROWLEY, "The Marriage of Ruth," *Harvard Theological Review* 40 (1947) 77–99; repr. in *The Servant of the Lord, and other Essays on the O.T.* (London 1952) 163–186. J. M. MEYERS, *The Linguistic and Literary Form of the Book of Ruth* (Leiden 1955). G. S. GLANZMAN, "The Origin and Date of the Book of Ruth," *the Catholic Biblical Quarterly* 21 (1959) 201–207. O. LORETZ, "The Theme of the Ruth Story," *ibid.* 22 (1960) 391–399.

[P. J. CALDERONE]

RUTHERFORD, JOSEPH FRANKLIN

President of JEHOVAH'S WITNESSES; b. Morgan County, Mo., Nov. 8, 1869; d. San Diego, Calif., Jan. 8, 1942. Having practiced law in Missouri for 15 years, he became (1906) legal adviser of the Watch Tower Bible and Tract Society founded by Pastor Charles Taze RUSSELL. After Russell's death in 1916, Rutherford was elected president of the society. He and seven other officers were subsequently found guilty of violating the Espionage Law; after serving nine months in Atlanta penitentiary, they were released on bail and the charges were later dropped. In 1931 "Judge" Rutherford coined the name "Jehovah's Witnesses" for his movement. In 20 books and numerous pamphlets he attacked all Christian churches and was particularly critical of Roman Catholicism. At his death his followers numbered about 100,000.

[W. J. WHALEN]

RUYSBROECK, JAN VAN, BL.

Flemish mystic and mystical writer; b. Ruysbroeck, near Brussels, Belgium, 1293; d. Groenendael, Dec. 2, 1381. Of his father we know nothing. His mother was a devout woman who trained the child in ways of holiness. At 11 he left home and went to Brussels to live under the guidance of his uncle, John Hinckaert, a saintly priest and canon of St. Gudules. Closely associated with his uncle was a fellow canon, Francis van Coudenberg, also a man of great piety. Ruysbroeck's (also spelled Ruisbroeck, Rusbroek) studies were directed toward the priesthood, and in 1317 he was ordained. He continued to live, with the two canons, a life of retirement and austerity and probably also of study. Some later biographers have represented him as a simple, unlettered man, miraculously inspired in his writings, but this cannot have been true. His writings show a mastery of sacred science, and he must have enjoyed some reputation for learning as well as sanctity, for he was called upon to conduct a preaching mission against a notorious woman, Bloemardinne, the leader of a heretical sect in the city. She appears to have enjoyed a considerable influence and to have written works that contained false doctrine. From the little testimony that has survived, she and her followers seem to have been connected with the "Brethren of the Free Spirit." She preached a Manichaean dualism according to which it is possible for men in this life to achieve a state of grace in which they can no longer sin; they are "free in spirit" both from the body, which may be left free to do as it pleases, and from laws, which bind only the imperfect.

A desire for greater retirement and a more contemplative life led Ruysbroeck and the two canons to withdraw to a hermitage at Groenendael in the neighboring forest of Soignes. A number of disciples joined them there, and after a time it was decided that they should establish themselves formally as a religious institute. In March 1349 they became a community of canons regular. They adopted the rule of the Canons of Saint-Victor, without, however, surrendering their independent status. Francis van Coudenberg became the community's first provost, and Ruysbroeck was made prior. John Hinckaert did not make formal profession for fear the discipline of the community would suffer harm because of the many dispensations it would be necessary to grant him because of his infirmities and age. He continued to live at Groenendael, however, though he moved into a cell outside the cloister.

Writings. Ruysbroeck's literary career may have begun with pamphlets written in the vernacular and directed against the false doctrines of Bloemardinne. If so, none of these has been preserved. The earliest work of

Joseph Franklin Rutherford.

which we are certain is *The Spiritual Espousals,* which was his masterpiece. Among the more notable of his other writings are *The Kingdom of Lovers* and *The Tabernacle,* both of which are long and majestic treatises, written for those learned in spiritual science and already advanced in contemplation. His friends, the Carthusians at Herne, could not understand the *Kingdom,* and asked for parts of it to be explained. Ruysbroeck was perturbed to learn that they had seen a copy of it at all. It had been pirated for them by a scribe who had been forbidden by his master to circulate the book. Nevertheless, he sent the Herne Charterhouse the gloss for which they asked; and this, *The Little Book of Enlightenment,* is one of the best of his shorter treatises, and a categorical denial of the errors, notably quietist, that have since been groundlessly attributed to him. Another short work that may be especially commended for the clarity and devotional quality of its teaching on contemplation is that variously known as *The Book of the Sparkling Stone* or *The Treatise of Perfection of the Sons of God.* A work of quite different stamp, written with charm and simplicity and directed toward a more popular audience, is Ruysbroeck's *The Book of the Twelve Beguines.*

Doctrine. The age in which Ruysbroeck lived had seen much bitter conflict, especially in the Low Countries, between those of entrenched orthodoxy and those who were under suspicion, not always justly, of teaching heresy. Excess and error were often induced in the minds of simple men by an uncritical absorption with the ideas of *deificatio,* of how men become like God. Nevertheless, there were many faithful Catholics who felt themselves compelled, despite all ecclesiastical censure, to affirm that God asks of exalted souls nothing less than that they should become so like to Him as to be indistinguishable from Him.

It was given to Ruysbroeck to be able to see a way to the resolution of such conflicts. Their resolution, and the preaching of a true *deificatio,* is the essence of all his works. *The Spiritual Espousals* in particular reflects and was formed by his perception of the relations between truth and error, between the perversions taught by such heretics as "the Brethren" about deified man and what he himself had seen of man's true nature and how it reflects the being of God. It is the constant regard for the true nature of man that informs the *Espousals,* and, indeed, all his work. Absurd as it is to say that man can become God, still man's life "is nothing else than the image of God . . . in the noblest part of our souls, we are made as a living, eternal mirror of God" (*Mirror of Eternal Blessedness*); and in his inquiries into the life and nature of man, he was able to synthesize and develop the leads given to him, by St. Augustine and perhaps others, about man as a "created trinity." In the whole universe, and especially in man, he sees the similitude and image of the Trinity, so that "all his teaching is ultimately teaching about God."

In few works of mystical theology does one find surpassed the ordered lucidity with which the *Espousals* expounds its complex and profound ideas. Ruysbroeck tells of the anguish and contention in the soul striving against nature to cross the threshold of time into the eternity from which God calls to it, but coming to accept and welcome this agony as a precious gift from the Lord, as an indispensable stage in the soul's homeward journey. The total impression is of untroubled calm, spiritual and intellectual. Ruysbroeck's learning, his natural curiosity, and his literary gifts are all ordered and controlled, and the whole book breathes harmony and great peace.

The book is composed of three successive expositions of the text "See, the Bridegroom comes; go out to meet Him." He tells us in Book 1 how Christ the Bridegroom must be seen and met "according to common usage . . . in the active life . . . by all who wish to be saved." Book 2 describes that meeting as it may come about in "the interior, exalted, yearning life achieved by virtues and grace." In Book 3 we read of the extraordinary way along which some are called to travel toward Our Lord, "the supernatural life of the contemplation of God." It may be thought that there is nothing exceptional in such a plan, since writings abound that teach of an ascent to God out of activity, through purgation, into the vision of Him. But this is not at all what Ruysbroeck is telling us. Instead, he insists that quietism is wrong and dualism is false because these three lives must be led simultaneously: man must reflect in his nature that triune Godhead in whose image he was made. He must give to God and receive from Him, speak and be silent, act and suffer, if he is to find God as he ought. And the finding of Him will be nothing else than a flowing back again into that divine nature in which he has eternally existed.

The language and the metaphors that he employs to convey such thought are seldom original. The idea of a "flowing" between God and the soul, for instance, he had probably encountered in the Low German writings of his precursor, MECHTILD OF MAGDEBURG. But Ruysbroeck's thought is something new in the West. New spiritual insights enabled him to achieve a synthesis between Augustine's teaching on man's reflection of the divine nature, and what he had learned from Neoplatonism, notably from Dionysius, about *regiratio,* the eternal cycle through which the soul moves, out from God and back into Him. Just as the stars never falter in their silent march across the heavens, just as the sea never ceases to ebb and to flow, so is the soul called back again out of time into that unnameable abyss in which it will find God, where it left Him, and will take its delight in Him, and sink down into Him, and be one with Him.

But this deified soul will not be and will not do as heretics falsely teach. They think that such deification comes of their own effort and is an attribute of their own nature. Ruysbroeck teaches that this deification is of grace and, therefore, a supernatural gift. They say that they have become one with God in nature; he declares that this can never be. Though in the abyss the soul will lose all perception of difference, of difference between the Persons, of difference between Them and it, still that difference remains. The gift will be withdrawn, the soul will return to the body, and the cycle will have been completed and must be begun again. There is no false quietism in this; the soul does not rest in its cycle, for God's love "is so ravenous that it swallows and consumes in its own being everything which comes near it," and to approach and be so consumed is the soul's true work. Still less is there any hint of a complete passivity. God acts and the soul must act.

Souls whom God has called to this work must always live this threefold life of action and contemplation and union with Him; the means and the manner He has furnished for them in His Church. "God comes ceaselessly to dwell in us by means and without means; and He demands of us both that we take delight in Him and that we perform works, and that the one remain unhindered by the other, and indeed be ever strengthened by the other'' (*Espousals*). ''The contemplative must go out, living, in virtues, and go in, dying in God. In these two is set a perfect life, and these two are as closely united as are matter and form, soul and body'' (*The Little Book of Enlightenment*).

The chief means to resolve this apparent impossibility was, for Ruysbroeck, the sacramental life of grace. In an age in which it was possible for holy men to teach a life of contemplative prayer from which the Sacraments were wholly excluded, he insisted that without them man cannot live a life formed in God, and above all he was distinguished by his unending love for the Mass.

Feast: Dec. 2.

Bibliography: Standard Text. *Werken,* Naar het standaardhandschrift van Groenendaal uitg. door het Ruusbroec-Genootschap te Antwerpen, 4 v. (rev. ed. Tielt 1944–48). *Ons geestelijk erf* (Antwerp 1927–), a quarterly journal that contains many learned articles on Ruysbroeck. A. AMPE, *Kernproblem uit der leer van Ruusbroec,* 3 v. in 1 (Studien en tekstuitgaven van Ons geestelijk erf 11–13; Antwerp 1950–56) an exhaustive commentary. *The Spiritual Espousals,* tr. E. COLLEDGE (New York 1953). E. COLLEDGE and J. BAZIRE, eds., *The Chastising of God's Children* (Oxford 1957), contains versions from Latin translations made in England c. A.D. 1400 of *The Treatise of Perfection of the Sons of God* and parts of the *Espousals.* B. FRALING, *Der Mensch von dem Geheimnis Gottes. Untersuchungen zur christlichen Lehre des Jan van Ruusbroec* (Würzburg 1967); *Mystik und Geschichte* (Regensburg 1974). P. MOMMAERS, *The Land Within,* tr. D. N. SMITH (Chicago 1975); with J. VAN BRAGT, *Mysticism, Buddhist and Christian: Encounters with Jan van Ruusbroec* (New York 1995). M. MAETERLINCK, *On Emerson and Other Essays,* tr. M. J. MOSES (New York 1912, repr. Great Neck, N.Y. 1978); with N. DE PAEPE, eds., *Jan van Ruusbroec: The Sources, Content, and Sequels of His Mysticism* (Leuven, Belgium 1984). L. K. DUPRÉ, *The Common Life: The Origins of Trinitarian Mysticism and Its Development by Jan Ruusbroec* (New York 1984). P. VERDEYEN, *Ruusbroec l'admirable* (Paris 1990); *Ruusbroec and His Mysticism,* tr. A. LEFEVERE (Collegeville, Minn. 1994); *Jan van Ruusbroec* (2d ed. Leuven 1996). E. P. BOS and G. WARNAR, eds., *Een claer verlicht man* (Hilversum 1993). K. E. BRAS, *Mint de minne* (Kampen 1993). C. H. ROCQUET, *Ruysbroeck, l'admirable* (Paris 1998). R. VAN NIEUWENHOVE, ''Ruusbroec: Apophatic Theologian or Phenomenologist of the Mystical Experience,'' *Journal of Religion,* 80, no. 1 (Jan. 2000) 83–105. J. A. WISEMAN, ''The Birth of the Son in the Soul in the Mystical Theology of Jan van Ruusbroec,'' *Studia Mystica,* 14, no. 2–3 (1991) 30–44.

[E. COLLEDGE]

RWANDA, THE CATHOLIC CHURCH IN

A densely populated, landlocked nation located near the equator in east central AFRICA, the Rwandese Repub-

---

Capital: Kigali.
Size: 10,173 sq. miles.
Population: 7,229,130 in 2000.
Languages: Kinyarwanda, French, Swahili.
Religions: Catholics 4,120,605 (57%), 144,580 Muslims (2%), 1,734,990 Protestants (24%), 1,228,955 followed indigenous faiths.
Archdiocese: Kigali, with suffragans Butare (created 1963), Byumba, Cyangugu, Gikongoro, Kabbayi, Kibungo, Nyundo (1959), and Ruhengeri (1960).

---

lic is bordered on the west by Lake Kivu and the DEMOCRATIC REPUBLIC OF CONGO, on the north by UGANDA, on the east by TANZANIA and on the south by BURUNDI. The Nile-Congo divide runs through Rwanda, which is primarily an agricultural country of uplands, the volcanic Birunga mountains falling toward the east. Natural resources include gold, tin ore, tungsten and methane, while food crops consist of coffee, tea, pyrethrum, bananas, beans and potatoes.

A Tutsi kingdom was established in Rwanda in the 16th century, falling under military control of German East Africa from 1899–1916. The region was administered by Belgium as part of Rwanda-Urundi until independence was gained in 1962. In 1959 the Hutu majority overthrew the Nilotic Tutsi feudal hierarchy and drove 150,000 Tutsi out of the country. Civil war erupted in 1990, begun by exiled Tutsi, and in 1994 escalated to an ethnic war wherein 800,000 people were killed. The country's first national elections were held in 1999, despite the continued threat of violence from Hutu extremists and the government's support of rebel forces in the neighboring Democratic Republic of the Congo. One of the poorest nations in Africa, Rwanda also suffers from overpopulation, famine, diseases such as HIV/AIDS and drought. The life expectancy of an average Rwandan was 39.4 years in 2000.

History. The region was originally ruled by Tutsi kings who reigned over Bahutu farmers, its boundaries set in the 19th century. Germany incorporated it into German East Africa in 1890, and in 1900 White Fathers first arrived at Save. Following World War I, Belgium took control under a League of Nations mandate that was later transferred to the United Nations. The first Rwandan priests were ordained in 1917; in addition to native clergy, Belgian, Italian, Spanish, French and Swiss secular clergy began to assist European men's and women's congregations in missionary work, while German, Belgian and English Protestants also increased their evangelization efforts. In the 1930s and 1940s numerous conversions took place, primarily among the Tutsi; there were 300,000 Christians in 1940 and 358,000 in 1950. The Vi-

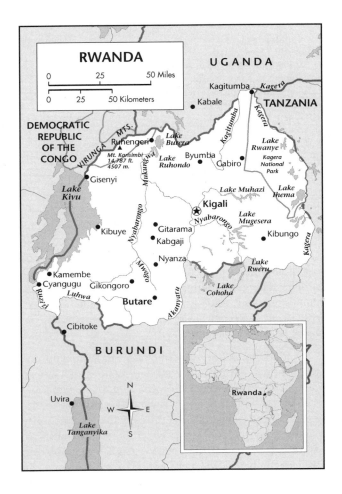

cariate Apostolic of Kivu (created in 1912) split into the vicariates of Burundi and Rwanda in 1922, and 30 years later Rwanda was divided into the vicariates of Nyundo and Kabgayi. When the hierarchy was established in 1959, Kabgayi became an archdiocese and the metropolitan see for Rwanda. The University of Butare opened in 1963 under Canadian Dominicans.

During World War II Church missions suffered from political troubles, made worse by a famine. During the 1950s the region also became involved in tribal conflicts between the Hutu majority (90 percent of the population) and the Tutsi elite. When civil war broke out in 1959, the Church was in the position of seeming to have to choose between Tutsi and Hutu. On July 1, 1962 Rwanda became independent, but the violence continued. In April of 1964 the presidents of both Rwanda and Burundi were killed in a plane crash that sparked a violent ethnic war, as Hutu guerillas murdered thousands of Tutsi, many of whom were Catholics. Among the victims were three bishops and a quarter of Rwanda's Catholic clergy; thousands more fled to neighboring African nations to await the outcome.

The election of Juvénal Habyarimana as president in 1973 brought stability to the region, and efforts were made to stabilize the economy under Habyarimana's one-party government. Tutsi rebels based in Uganda invaded the country in 1991, and following mediation a new constitution was adopted in June of 1991, and a coalition government formed. Habyarimana's assassination in 1994 and the subsequent installation of a new government precipitated another wave of violence by Hutus, during which thousands of Tutsi were massacred and reprisals begun, among them the murder of 17 ethnic Hutu students at a Catholic school near Butare in 1997. Many Hutus who fled the country in the wake of this violence had returned to live in government camps by 1997, although such refugee groups sometimes became the targets of Hutu extremists whose forced marches resulted in many deaths. A Tutsi government remained in place through 2000.

In January of 1997 the UN convened a war crimes tribunal for Rwanda, during which approximately 100,000, including many government officials and members of the clergy—particularly the White Fathers—were accused, jailed and put on trial. Pope John Paul II fully supported the punishment of all Church members who, in contravention of the Gospel, engaged in genocide during the struggle, but the Vatican donated $50,000 toward legal costs incurred by priests, religious and other Catholics as a means of ensuring fair trials. Unfortunately, questions regarding the impartiality of the legal system continued to be raised, as elimination of all Hutu clergy was suspected of being in the interest of the governing Tutsi. Following the 1999 arrest of Bishop Augustin Misago on genocide charges, the Vatican publicly denounced the Rwandan government for what it called a "defamatory campaign against the Catholic Church." While Misago was released in June of 2000 and avoided the firing squads that had claimed 116 others found guilty of crimes against humanity by 1998, charges against other priests continued to be leveled through 2000.

Into the 21st Century. By 2000 Rwanda had 132 parishes tended by 284 diocesan and 131 religious priests. Other religious included approximately 165 brothers and 1,100 sisters, some of whom ran the country's 1,032 primary and 102 secondary Catholic schools and tended to the humanitarian and medical needs of a nation of refugees from war or poverty. Although some missionary schools were nationalized in the mid-20th century, programs of religious or moral education continued to be offered. With government stability increasing under a military president, the advances in the economy shown in 2000 boded well for all Rwandans, who had been severely impoverished during years of civil war. Church leaders remained vocal in their objections to the distribution of abortifacients among Rwandese women by the UN and Red Cross begun in 1996. Tensions between the Church and the Rwandan government continued to exist, resulting from the government's plan to turn ten churches into genocide memorials. Church leaders expressed concern that such a use might cause identification of Catholicism with the minority Tutsi elite, thus sparking further ethnic violence.

Bibliography: J. R. CLÉMENT, *Essai de bibliographie du Ru* (Gayi 1961). *Ruanda-Burundi* (Bujumbura 1963–). *Bilan du anda-Urundi* (Usumbura 1959). L. DE LAGGER, *Ruanda* (Kabbayi 1967). *Monde* (1964) 2:767–771. *Annuario Pontificio* (1965) 204.

[J. PERRAUDIN/EDS.]

RYAN, ABRAM JOSEPH

Poet, journalist, lecturer; b. Hagerstown, Md., Feb. 5, 1838; d. Louisville, Ky., April 22, 1886. Son of Matthew and Mary (Coughlan) Ryan of County Tipperary, Ireland, he was educated at the Christian Brothers' Cathedral School, St. Louis, Mo.; St. Mary's Seminary, Perryville, Mo., where he joined the Congregation of the Mission; and at Our Lady of Angels Seminary, Niagara Falls, N.Y. He was ordained in St. Louis in 1860, preached parish missions and was professor at various Vincentian seminaries until September 1862, when he was appointed to St. Mary's parish, Peoria, Ill.

Ardently in sympathy with the Confederate cause, Ryan sought unsuccessfully to be commissioned a military chaplain. He was accepted by the Diocese of Nashville, in which he labored from 1864 to 1867. From time to time he interrupted his pastoral duties to serve as a free-lance chaplain with the armed forces of the South. Following Appomattox, he wrote in Knoxville, Tenn., "The Conquered Banner," which was sent by a friend to the New York *Freeman's Journal,* where it was published June 24, 1865, over the pen name of Moina. This poem, with "The Sword of Robert Lee" and others, soon earned him the epithet Poet of the Confederacy.

In March 1868, having transferred to the Diocese of Savannah, he became editor of the *Banner of the South* (Augusta, Ga.). Adopted by the Diocese of Mobile in June 1870, he was assistant at the cathedral until 1877, when he was appointed pastor of St. Mary's parish, Mobile. From 1871 he was a member of the editorial staff of the *Morning Star,* New Orleans, serving as editor in chief (1872–75) though residing in Mobile. For reasons of health and to find some literary leisure, he retired in October 1881, to Biloxi, Miss.

Ryan's spirited poetry, prose, and oratory embody one aspect of the glamor and nostalgia of the South—the

Mother feeding children outside church, Kigali, Rwanda. (©David and Peter Turnley/CORBIS)

Confederacy and its heroes. His most prominent works are *Father Ryan's Poems* (Mobile 1879); *Poems: Patriotic, Religious, Miscellaneous* (Baltimore 1880); *A Crown for Our Queen* (Baltimore 1882).

Bibliography: J. P. MCKEY, *History of Niagara University, Seminary of Our Lady of Angels, 1856–1931* (Niagara University 1931). I. DILLIARD, "Father Ryan, Poet-Priest of the Confederacy," *Missouri Historical Review* 36 (Oct. 1941) 61–66.

[E. A. EGAN]

RYAN, DERMOT

University professor, archbishop of Dublin; b. Dublin, June 27, 1924; d. Rome, Feb. 21, 1985. Ryan was ordained a priest in 1950. Among his academic degrees were the S.T.L. from the Gregorian University (1952), the S.S.L. from Rome's Pontifical Biblical Institute (1954), and the M.A. in Eastern languages from the National University of Ireland (1954). He served as professor of fundamental dogmatic theology at Clonliffe College, Dublin, from 1954 until 1957, at which time he was appointed Professor of Eastern Languages at University College, Dublin.

Ordained Archbishop of Dublin by Pope Paul VI, Ryan served in that capacity from 1972 to 1984. It was a time of unprecedented population growth, in which the number of parishes increased from 134 to 189. Ryan found it necessary to address the negative effects of rapid urbanization, namely, lack of housing, increase in drug abuse, sectarian conflict, materialism, and a declining sense of moral responsibility. Many of the initiatives taken by the Dublin archdiocese with regard the poor, the deprived, the illiterate and the unemployed were the result of his inspiration. Archbishop Ryan took an active part in the delicate negotiations between Church and State over health care and education, and had to face new challenges to the Church's teachings on marriage, sexuality, and unborn life. Ryan was also an active ecumenist and played a leading role in inter-church talks in Ireland.

In his capacity as vice-president of the Irish episcopal conference, Ryan attended the Synods of Bishops in Rome in 1974, 1977, 1980 and 1983, and served as chairman of the English language group at each session. On April 11, 1984, Ryan was appointed Pro-Prefect of the Sacred Congregation for the Evangelization of Peoples. He died suddenly a few months later at his residence in Rome.

[J. WILSON]

James Hugh Ryan.

RYAN, JAMES HUGH

Bishop, educator; b. Indianapolis, Ind., Dec. 15, 1886; d. Omaha, Nebr., Nov. 23, 1947. He was the son of John Marshall Ryan, of Indiana, and Brigid (Rogers) Ryan, a native of County Cavan, Ireland. After having finished high school in Indianapolis, he went to Holy Ghost College (later Duquesne University), Pittsburgh, Pa. He then attended Mt. St. Mary's Theological Seminary in Cincinnati, Ohio; North American College in Rome; Roman Academy (Ph.D. 1908); and the University of Propaganda (S.T.D. 1909). On June 5, 1909, he was ordained, by special dispensation because of his youth, at St. John Lateran in Rome. On his return to the U.S. he took up parish work but soon joined the faculty of St. Mary-of-the-Woods, Terre Haute, Ind., where he was professor of psychology from 1911 to 1921. Early in 1920 he became president of the college. Shortly afterward he left that post to become executive secretary of the Department of Education of the National Catholic Welfare Conference in Washington, D.C. In 1927 Ryan was made a domestic prelate, and on Nov. 14, 1928, he was installed as rector of The Catholic University of America, Washington, D.C. On Oct. 25, 1933, he was consecrated titular bishop of the See of Modra.

As rector of Catholic University, Ryan was chiefly concerned with academic reorganization. He found an in-

stitution that was patterned after the University of Louvain, Belgium, yet attempted to work with U.S. universities of quite different structure. He set policies intended to enhance the University's position in modern American scholarship. Despite strong opposition, he integrated the School of Sacred Sciences into the University and brought it under his authority. He decreed that only active scholars on the teaching staff should receive academic promotions. Indicative of his views was his early recognition of accrediting agencies, whose efforts to establish high academic standards were warmly supported by the University. Finances also constituted a major problem during Ryan's rectorship. He dropped the ambitious building program of his predecessor, Bp. Thomas SHA-HAN, and did much to put the University in sound financial condition before his departure in 1935.

Ryan was active as a public figure and a scholar. He was outspoken on controversial public subjects, opposing state medical services as "Hitlerized Medicine." He condemned too the American Medical Association's recognition of birth control, which he regarded as a counsel of gradual extinction. As an academician, he wrote on philosophy and medieval culture for leading periodicals and, in 1927, founded the *New Scholasticism,* which he edited for ten years. His publications include *A Directory of Catholic Colleges and Schools* (1921), *A Catechism of*

Catholic Education (1922), *An Introduction to Philosophy* (1924), and *The Encyclicals of Pius XI* (1927). Ryan was also a member of the American Philosophical Society, the National Catholic Educational Association, and the executive council of the Medieval Academy of America, of which he was a fellow.

Ryan remained at The Catholic University until Aug. 3, 1935, when he was appointed bishop of Omaha; he was formally installed Nov. 1, 1935, in St. Cecilia Cathedral. After ten years as bishop of the Diocese of Omaha, he was installed on Oct. 10, 1945, as Omaha's first metropolitan archbishop. Among the many honors he had received were: Knight Commander of the Crown of Italy, 1930; Grand Cordon of the Order of St. Sava, from the King of Yugoslavia, 1932; Chevalier of the Legion of Honor, 1934; Cavaliere Magistrale of the Order of Malta, 1935. The institutions of higher education that conferred honorary degrees upon him included Marquette University, Milwaukee, Wis.; National University of Ireland, Dublin; Manhattan College, New York; St. Bonaventure College (later University), St. Bonaventure, N.Y.; and The Catholic University of Milan.

[R. J. DEFERRARI]

John A. Ryan.

RYAN, JOHN AUGUSTINE

Pioneer American Catholic social philosopher; b. Dakota County, MN, May 25, 1869; d. Washington, DC, Sept. 16, 1945. Ryan grew up on a family farm in Vermillion, MN, the eldest son of 11 children of William and Mary Luby Ryan, Irish immigrants. He attended a local public school and the Christian Brothers' school in nearby St. Paul. In 1887 he entered St. Thomas Seminary (later St. Paul Seminary) and was ordained by Abp. John Ireland on June 4, 1898. Ryan then went to The Catholic University of America, Washington, DC, winning his licentiate in moral theology in 1900. He returned to St. Paul Seminary in the fall of 1902 as professor of moral theology and remained there for 13 years. In 1906, when The Catholic University awarded him his doctorate in sacred theology, his dissertation, *A Living Wage: Its Ethical and Economic Aspects*, won worldwide notice.

Ryan next became active with reforming groups such as the National Consumers League. He lectured frequently to labor unions, to Catholic fraternal groups, and at Catholic summer schools. He wrote many articles on moral and economic topics; his discussion of the moral aspects of labor unions in the *Catholic Encyclopedia* was standard and authoritative. In 1913 Ryan joined those who were working for minimum wage laws for women, especially in Wisconsin and Minnesota. Later that same year his debate with Morris Hillquit, a Socialist, became a minor classic, *Socialism: Promise or Menace?* (1914). Ryan joined the faculty at The Catholic University, where he first taught political science, then moral theology. In 1919 he was elected to his first of several terms as dean of the School of Sacred Theology. He also taught economics and later science at Trinity College, Washington, DC.

Distributive Justice, an analysis of the ethical obligation of all parties to modern industrial society, Ryan's most substantial work, appeared in 1916. He founded the *Catholic Charities Review* in 1917 and edited it for four years. In 1919 he wrote the advanced draft of the "Bishops' Program of Social Reconstruction," a progressive document embodying proposals for minimum wage legislation, unemployment, health and old-age insurance, etc., that have since become law but were then considered radical. The next year he became director of the Social Action Department of the National Catholic Welfare Council (later Conference), a post he held until his death. In 1921 he became lecturer in social ethics at the National Catholic School of Social Service. From his office at the NCWC, Ryan continued to lecture widely and to write frequently for magazines, principally, though not exclusively, for Catholic magazines. He helped to organize the Catholic Association for International Peace in 1927. He cooperated with his counterparts in the Federal Council of Churches of Christ in America and in the Central Conference of American Rabbis to promote social justice. Joining numerous secular groups, he frequently served as a member of their governing boards; the most controversial of these was the American Civil Liberties Union.

In the election campaign of 1928, Ryan figured as a combatant and also as an authority. A statement in his *The State and the Church* (1923) encouraged critics to think that once in power Catholics would deny religious freedom to non-Catholics. Ryan rejected this idea. Because Ryan owed his economic analysis mainly to John A. Hobson's underconsumption theory, he was immensely critical of Herbert Hoover's caution and comparably enthusiastic about the New Deal. Early in Franklin D. Roosevelt's first administration, Pope Pius XI appointed Ryan a domestic prelate; the formal investiture was on Dec. 8, 1933. A year later Ryan became a member of the Industrial Appeals Board of the National Recovery Administration. An enthusiastic New Dealer, he viewed the National Labor Relations Act as ''probably the most just, beneficial, and far-reaching piece of labor legislation ever enacted in the United States''; the Fair Labor Standards Act he considered the culmination of his life's work. Ryan supported Roosevelt in all four campaigns and gave the benediction at two inaugurations.

On social and economic questions, Ryan more than any other single person brought Catholics abreast of American progressive thought. His *Living Wage* laid the groundwork in theology and economics; his role as lobbyist, teacher, lecturer, and writer trained a generation of priests and laymen. He also helped to create a favorable image of the Catholic Church among non-Catholic reformers prone to see it as monolithic and conservative.

Bibliography: F. L. BRODERICK, *Right Reverend New Dealer: John A. Ryan* (New York 1963).

[F. L. BRODERICK]

RYAN, MARY PERKINS

Writer, editor, religious educator; b. Boston, Massachusetts, April 10, 1912; d. Goffstown, New Hampshire, Oct. 13, 1993. Her parents were Charles and Elizabeth (Ward) Perkins. In 1942 she wed John Julian Ryan and was the mother of five sons.

Shortly after earning a B.A. at Manhattanville College in 1933, Ryan joined the newly opened American branch of the publisher Sheed and Ward. Through her editorial work Ryan established herself as a leader in the liturgical movement, and was one of the speakers at the first Liturgical Week in Chicago in 1940. In 1954 the

Ryan family moved to South Bend, Indiana, where Ryan took a position in the Liturgical Institute founded at Notre Dame by Father Michael Mathis, CSC. It was also at Notre Dame that she met the Austrian Jesuit Johannes Hofinger, SJ, and helped him edit his classic *The Art of Teaching Christian Doctrine* (1957).

A total of 27 works carry her name as author, editor, or translator. Her first work, *At Ease in the Catholic Church* (1937) was written with the encouragement of Leonard Feeney, SJ. She translated works by Louis Bouyer and Jean Daniélou. Her best known book, *Are Parochial Schools the Answer?* (1964), focused on adult catechesis. Ryan edited *The Living Light,* an official publication of the United States Catholic Conference, from its inception in 1964 until 1972. Between 1973 and 1988, she edited *Professional Approaches for Christian Educators (PACE)* and worked as a freelance writer.

In her last years, Ryan suffered from the debilitating effects of Parkinson's disease and arthritis.

Bibliography: P. O'HARE, ''Mary Perkins Ryan (1912–1993): Mulier Fortis,'' *The Living Light* (spring 1994) 3–8. K. HUGHES, *How Firm a Foundation: Voices of the Early Liturgical Movement* (Collegeville 1990). M.C. BRYCE, ''Mary Perkins Ryan,'' *The Living Light* 12 (summer 1975) 276–281.

[B. L. MARTHALER]

RYAN, PATRICK JOHN

Second archbishop of the Philadelphia, Pa., archdiocese; b. Thurles, County Tipperary, Ireland, Feb. 20, 1831; d. Philadelphia, Feb. 11, 1911. After early education with the Christian Brothers in his native town and at the school of J. L. Naughton in Dublin, where he received a sound training in the Latin and Greek classics, he began his studies for the priesthood at St. Patrick's College, Carlow. Adopted for the Archdiocese of St. Louis by Abp. Peter Kenrick, he came to the U.S. in 1852 as a deacon. While still lacking priestly orders, he taught for a short time in the diocesan seminary at Carondelet, Mo., and preached often in the cathedral. The pulpit eloquence that would later rank him as the most outstanding ecclesiastical orator of his time was already evident. He was ordained by Kenrick on Sept. 8, 1853.

Early Career. Ryan held successively three pastorates at St. Louis: at the Cathedral of St. Louis, at the Church of the Annunciation (which he built), and at St. John's Church. At the Second Plenary Council of Baltimore in 1866 he was one of Kenrick's theologians, and was selected, with Abp. John Lancaster Spalding and Isaac Hecker, CSP, to preach the main sermons at the conclave. His reputation as an orator followed him to

Rome, where, on a visit in 1868, he gave the English Lenten course at the request of Pope Pius IX. He was vicar-general and administrator of the St. Louis archdiocese during Kenrick's attendance at VATICAN COUNCIL I (1869–70). On Feb. 14, 1872, Ryan was consecrated titular bishop of Tricomia, and coadjutor bishop of St. Louis with right of succession. Expert, tactful, and vigorous in handling the archdiocesan matters placed under his charge, he served in this post for 12 years, during which his work with converts also was notable.

Ordinary of Philadelphia. On Jan. 6, 1884, Ryan was appointed titular archbishop of Salamis; on June 8, he succeeded the deceased Abp. James F. Wood as head of the See of PHILADELPHIA. At the time Philadelphia was the second largest diocese in the nation. During his episcopacy in this key post, Ryan displayed an intense solicitude for the poor, an untiring zeal in building up archdiocesan educational facilities, and an unusual effectiveness in expounding to Catholics and Protestants alike the doctrines of the faith and in defining the attitude of the Church on current issues. He established the St. Francis Industrial School for Boys, the Philadelphia Protectory for Boys, the St. Joseph's Home for Working Boys, a foundling asylum and maternity hospital, and an additional home for the aged. St. Vincent's Home for orphan children was purchased with his golden jubilee fund of $200,000.

African Americans and Native Americans were always special objects of Ryan's charity, and Pres. Theodore Roosevelt appointed him to serve on the Federal government's Indian commission. With the archbishop's encouragement Mother Katharine DREXEL founded the Sisters of the Blessed Sacrament for Indians and Colored People. Two African American parishes were erected, and the Holy Ghost Fathers, devoted to serving black Catholics, were established at Cornwells, in suburban Philadelphia. Increased attention was given to the thousands of European immigrants who were flocking into the Philadelphia area and the up-country districts later included in the Diocese of Allentown. By 1912 more than 82 new parishes had been founded for the care of the various national groups in the archdiocese.

Interest in Education. In the field of parochial elementary and diocesan high school education, Ryan raised the Philadelphia archdiocese to a place of leadership. He opened the first diocesan high school for boys, the Roman Catholic High School, and Hallahan High School for girls. In several sections of the city, high school centers also were established for girls. The parochial schools already existing received constant attention, and in new parishes, the archbishop insisted on an adequate school before the erection of a fully satisfactory church building.

Ryan's style in the pulpit and on the lecture platform was in the best tradition of late 19th-century sonorous oratory. His wit and humor—evident too in his private intercourse—added spice to his performance. His sermons and lectures produced respect for and better understanding of the Church among Protestants. The honorary degree he received from the University of Pennsylvania was evidence of his success in breaking down the anti-Catholic feeling that had previously existed in Philadelphia. The love of learning that marked the best of Ryan's lectures led him to foster the *American Catholic Quarterly Review,* and to make it one of the leading exponents of Catholic thought. The memorial library that bears his name at the diocesan seminary at Overbrook appropriately symbolizes Ryan's use of scholarship for the spread of the faith.

Bibliography: J. L. J. KIRLIN, *Catholicity in Philadelphia* (Philadelphia 1909).

[J. T. DURKIN]

RYGGE, ROBERT

Chancellor of Oxford; d. Exeter, by April, 1410. He was a fellow of Exeter College (1361–65) and Merton, where he served as bursar (1371–74). He was also a secular priest and a doctor of theology (Oxford, 1379–80). Sudden notoriety came to him in 1382, when as chancellor of Oxford he invited two Wyclifites, Nicholas HEREFORD and Philip REPINGTON, to preach before the University. There is little reason to believe that Rygge was motivated by any sympathy for Wyclifite teachings; rather, he was asserting the independence of the university from outside pressure. Abp. William COURTENAY had ordered Oxford to publish a condemnation of 24 theses drawn from Wyclif's works; the chancellor's answer was to invite the two Wyclif followers to preach. But when he realized that his defiance of Courtenay could be interpreted as sympathy for suspected heretics, Rygge quickly threw himself on Courtenay's mercy. He agreed to publish the condemnation, to suspend John WYCLIF and four followers, and to ferret out all LOLLARDS. The Royal Council backed the archbishop and ordered Rygge to sue the secular power, if necessary. Henceforth, Rygge put aside all defiance. The rest of his life was uneventful. In 1395 he became a canon of Exeter; and in 1400, chancellor of Exeter cathedral.

Bibliography: C. L. KINGSFORD, *The Dictionary of National Biography from the Earliest Times to 1900,* 63 v. (London 1885–1900) 17:542–543. J. H. DAHMUS, *The Prosecution of John Wyclyf* (New Haven 1952). K. B. MCFARLANE, *John Wycliffe and the Beginnings of English Nonconformity* (New York 1953). A. B. EMDEN, *A Biographical Register of the Scholars of the University*

Brother Francis Xavier Ryken.

of Oxford to A.D. 1500, 3 v. (Oxford 1957–59) 3:1616–17. J. A. ROBSON, *Wycliff and the Oxford Schools* (Cambridge, Eng. 1961).

[J. E. HEALEY]

RYKEN, FRANCIS XAVIER, BROTHER

Founder of the Brothers of St. Francis Xavier; b. Elshout, Holland, Aug. 30, 1797; d. Bruges, Belgium, Nov. 26, 1871. Theodore James Ryken, a shoemaker by trade, felt called to the religious life. Since he was unable to enter a monastery because of the restrictions of the Dutch government, he began to teach catechism to the children of his village. In 1823 he entered a quasi-religious community founded by the Catholic convert and editor Jo-achim Le Sage ten Broek, but in 1826 left to attend the victims of an epidemic in northern Holland. In 1827–28 he visited Rome where he tried unsuccessfully to win papal approbation for a brotherhood dedicated to education. He then became a Trappist lay brother at the Abbey of Oelenberg in Alsace.

The Revolution of 1830 caused the monks to disperse, and Ryken journeyed to the U.S. to become a missionary. In 1832 he assisted Rev. Stephen Badin among the Potawatomi of southern Michigan, where he determined to devote himself to the Native American apostolate. Ryken returned to Bruges; there, with the aid of a Belgian priest, he hoped to found a brotherhood to aid the American mission. When the Belgian priest deserted the undertaking, Ryken attempted to carry on alone. With the sanction of Bp. Francis Boussen of Bruges, he returned to the U.S. to explain his plan to the American bishops, especially Bp. Joseph Rosati of St. Louis, Missouri. Rosati induced him to abandon his work with native peoples and devote himself to the instruction of American youth. He returned to Bruges with the testimonials of seven bishops and several prominent churchmen, and was permitted to organize the Xaverian Brothers in June of 1839.

Despite opposition and privations, the new community slowly grew. In 1843 four of the group took the habit, and in 1846 ten pronounced vows. Three schools were opened in Bruges, and the first branch house was established in England in 1848. Only in 1854, however, could Ryken and six brothers open their first American school at the invitation of Bp. Martin J. Spalding of Louisville, Kentucky. Six years later, because of financial and personal problems within the community, the bishop of Bruges requested the founder to resign in favor of a younger man. Until his death 11 years later, Ryken remained a simple subject, serving for a time as novice master. In 1964 the congregation he founded had provinces in Belgium, England, and the U.S., with missions in Africa and South America.

See Also: XAVERIAN BROTHERS.

Bibliography: J. J. DOWNEY, *March On! God Will Provide: The Life of Theodore James Ryken* (Boston 1961).

[D. SPALDING]

S

SA, MANOEL

Portuguese Jesuit theologian and exegete; b. Villa de Code (or Conde), diocese of Braga, 1530 (or 1528); d. Arona, near Milan, Dec. 30, 1596. Sa (Saa) entered the Society of Jesus April 7, 1545, and taught philosophy at Alcala and then at Gandia, where he also acted as tutor of Francis Borgia, duke of Gandia. In 1559 Sa's health broke down. He had been at the newly founded Roman College lecturing on the prophecies of Osee and the *Summa* (1a, 2ae) of St. Thomas Aquinas. While recuperating, Sa also acted as visitor to the colleges of Tuscany and Ancona. Upon his recovery he returned to the Roman College to fill the chair of exegesis. Because of the reputation he earned at the Roman College, he was appointed by Pius V to a commission in charge of revising the Vulgate. Afterward Gregory XIII appointed him to a commission in charge of publishing an authorized edition of the Septuagint. He devoted the last ten years of his life to a fruitful apostolate in northern Italy. There he continued in his renown as a preacher, a renown that he had from his earlier days at the Roman College. He also founded several houses of Jesuits in this part of Italy. He died at the novitiate of Arona in 1596. His exegetical works include *Scholia in Quatuor Evangèlia* (Antwerp 1596) and *Notationes in totam Scripturam Sacram* (Antwerp 1598). These works are brief but clear expositions of the literal meaning of Scripture. Sa's scholarship is evident; yet he was inaccurate in a few places and these inaccuracies did not go unnoticed by later critics. One of his works, *Aphorismi Confessariorum ex Doctorum sententiis collecti* (Venice 1595), was 40 years in preparation. This book was censured seven years after Sa's death, but with some corrections it was removed from the Roman Index in 1900. Sa wrote a life of John of Texeda, the Capuchin confessor of Francis Borgia, but this work has never been published.

Bibliography: P. A. FRANCO, *Ano santo da Companhia de Jesus em Portugal* (2d ed. Porto 1931). F. RODRIGUEZ, *História da Compania de Jesus na Assistência de Portugal* (Porto 1931–). C. SOMMERVOGEL et al., *Bibliothèque de la Compagnie de Jésus,* 11 v. (Brussels-Paris 1890–1932; v. 12, suppl. 1960) 7:354. H. HURTER, *Nomenclator literarius theologiae catholicae,* 5 v. in 6 (3d ed. Innsbruck 1903–13) 3:222–224.

[P. K. CLARK]

SA'ADIA BEN JOSEPH, GAON

Jewish philosopher, exegete, polemicist, and writer on religious topics; b. Dilaz in the Faijum region of Egypt, A.D. 882; d. Baghdad, 942.

Life. During his early years in Egypt, Sa'adia received a solid education in rabbinical studies and in Arabic literature and philosophy. Later he made higher Talmudic studies in the Jewish academies of Palestine. After teaching for a time in Egypt and becoming well known as a writer, he went c. A.D. 920 to Babylonia, the center of Jewish learning in the early Middle Ages, where he became a member of the faculty at the Academy of Sura (actually transferred to Baghdad by this time). This once-famous seat of Jewish scholarship was then already in its decline, and conditions were not much better at the Academy of Pumpedita, the other well-known Jewish school in Babylonia. The ardor of the high Talmudic period was dying, for the influence of Arabic culture and education had aroused other interests, and within Judaism itself disunion had increased as the result of the schism of Karaism (*See* JEWS, POST-BIBLICAL HISTORY OF THE).

Sa'adia used the weapons of his towering intellect in two fields. On the one hand, he fought against the Karaites in defense of rabbinical Judaism and thus prevented a further spread of the schism. On the other, he energetically opposed every movement that might bring division within the ranks of traditional Judaism. Thus, he rose up against the head of the Jewish school of Jerusalem, Gaon Ben Meir, who with his attempt at calendar reform was sowing discord and seeking to win scholarly supremacy for his own academy. The exilarch, David ben Zakkai, recognizing Sa'adia's merits, made him gaon, or head of the Academy of Sura in 928, even though he was not a native of Babylonia. Under Sa'adia's leadership, this seat of Jewish learning received a new lease on life. But because he refused to connive at certain illegalities in some of the exilarch's juridical acts, a bitter quarrel arose between the two. The exilarch pronounced the gaon deposed, and the gaon declared that the exilarch had forfeited his office. But Sa'adia got the worse of the dispute and had to spend some years in retirement at Baghdad. This, however, was really a blessing in disguise, for these were his most fruitful years in literary activity. In 937 the two were reconciled. Sa'adia was reinstalled in his position as head of the Sura academy and remained in this office for the last five years of his life.

Works. Sa'adia's genius lay in his many different intellectual interests, and these also found expression in his varied literary productions. Abraham ben Meïr IBN EZRA could say of him that he was "the highest authority in all fields." He is said to have written 100 works in Hebrew and 200 in Arabic, but only a fraction of these has been preserved.

His principal work is the *Kitāb al-Amanāt wal-I'tiqadāt,* preserved in the Hebrew translation *Emūnōt weDē'ōt* (Beliefs and Opinions, i.e., faith and knowledge), an exposition of the Jewish religion with the aid of philosophical principles in the manner of KALĀM in Muslim theology. This was the first attempt at such a synthesis in Judaism, and it inspired numerous subsequent religious-philosophical works. In his *Tasfir,* an Arabic translation of the Hebrew Bible, Sa'adia endeavored to produce a version that would be as faithful as possible to the original, although for the sake of clarity he was not adverse to the occasional paraphrase. His biblical commentary is also characterized by clarity and conciseness. A large part of Sa'adia's literary activity was taken up with anti-Karaite polemics. His "Refutation of Anan" was written during his early life in Egypt; his "Book of Distinctions," his "Refutation of Sakawaihi," and his "Refutation of an Arrogant Opponent" date from his Sura period. In the field of Hebrew linguistics, Sa'adia's *Agron* (Lexicon) is the first Hebrew dictionary, and his "Book on the Language" (written in Arabic) is the earliest-known Hebrew grammar. He also composed many Jewish RESPONSA, as well as a (now lost) methodological introduction to the TALMUD. Although devoted to rationalism, he wrote a sympathetic commentary on the cabalistic *Book of YEṢIRAH.* In addition to his Hebrew religious poetry (*baqqāšōt,* "prayers of petition"), he also published, under the title *Kitāb Jāmi'aṣ-Ṣalawāt wal-Tasābīḥ* (Collection of Prayers and Praises), an Arabic work on Jewish liturgy, which was the first scientific work of its kind.

Bibliography: H. MALTER, *Sa'adia Gaon: His Life and Works* (Philadelphia 1921). W. BACHER, *The Jewish Encyclopedia,* ed. J. SINGER, 13 v. (New York 1901–06) 10:579–586. R. GORDIS, *Universal Jewish Encyclopedia,* 10 v. (New York 1939–44) 9:289–291.

[K. HRUBY]

SABA (SHEBA)

Ancient country in South Arabia. Saba (Heb. *šᵉbā'* and *sᵉbā'*) and its inhabitants, the Sabaeans, are mentioned several times in the OT, where these people are portrayed as renowned traders, especially of gold and incense, and also as raiders. The best-known reference to them is in the account of the visit of the (unnamed) Queen of Saba to King Solomon (1 Kgs 10.1–13), which was primarily for a commercial purpose. Outside the Bible, the earliest certain mentions are to be found in the Assyrian annals in 738 B.C. and again *c.* 685 B.C. Four centuries later Greek writers refer to Saba and its population. The Assyrian and biblical sources prove the existence of rather large Sabaean colonies in the far north of the Arabian Desert, which depended on Saba in the south. Archeological discoveries in Palestine attest an early presence of south Arabian colonies.

The history of Saba with its capital city, Mârib, still remains very fragmentary, in spite of the addition of a recent information (especially from excavations by the American Foundation for the Study of Man). Its early stages (8th to 5th centuries B.C.) are characterized by the unification of small kingdoms around Mârib under the *mukarrib* (unifier). Rulers with this title subjugated the kingdom of Ma'in (to the northwest) before the end of the period. For reasons unknown to us, Karib'il Watar (*c.* 450 B.C.) changed his title of *mukarrib* to that of king and thus inaugurated the second major period, which is divided into four parts on the basis of the royal title. (1) The "King of Saba" period (*c.* 450–65 B.C.) may be characterized by a greater centralization of the royal power as well as by military efforts. (2) The "King of Saba and Raydân" period (*c.* 65 B.C. to A.D. 305) is best represented by the famous 'Ilšaraḥ Yaḥḍub, during whose reign the ill-fated expedition of Aelius Gallus (24 B.C.) took place. A long series of local wars gave these kings a much better hold over the surrounding countries. (3) The "King of Saba and Raydân and Ḥaḍramawt and Yamnat" period (*c.* A.D. 305–425) begins after the conquest of western Ḥaḍramawt and Yamnat (the South); toward the end of this period appear the first kings to embrace monotheism. (4) The "King of Saba and Raydân and Ḥaḍramawt and Yamnat and their Arabs in the high plateau and coast" period (*c.* A.D. 425–575) is characterized by conquests in the far north, by the anti-Christian persecution in Nejrân by King Yûsuf 'As'ar Yat'ar (Dû-Nuwâs), and by the Habašite (Ethiopian) and Persian occupations.

The social life of the Sabaeans, as of other Semitic populations, was based upon the clan unit. Polygamy doubtless existed from the beginning, but women enjoyed a rather high social autonomy. Thus a certain Gadan'amm was *mqtwyt* (high official) of her tribe Ḥazfarum. The so-called Queen of Sheba (Heb. *malkat-š ᵉbā'*) might have held a position similar to this. When traveling with her tribe (and Saba' is known also as a tribal name), she was the leader, and she could have been considered a queen by the Israelites, as the *mukarrib* Karib'il was considered a king by the Assyrians. Moreover, Makada or Makueda, the personal name of this queen in Ethiopian legend, might be interpreted as a popular rendering of the title of *mqtwyt*. (According to the Islamic tradition as represented by al-Hamdânî, the queen of Sheba was the daughter of 'Ilšraḥ Yaḥḍub.)

The economic situation of Saba was determined by wealth in precious stones and metals, and by fertile soil producing especially incense and tea with the aid of an irrigation system connected with the famous Mârib dam. Products were transported by caravans to the neighboring northern countries to be sold or exchanged. When this very successful caravan trade gradually became replaced by the ship trade, the Sabaeans could no longer sustain the cost of repairs for the Mârib dam, the ultimate collapse of which was the death-knell of their power.

See Also: ARABIA, 4.

Bibliography: A. JAMME, *La Paléographique sud-arabe de J. Pirenne* (Washington, D.C. 1957). R. L. BOWEN, JR., and F. P. AL-BRIGHT, eds., *Archaeological Discoveries in South Arabia* (Baltimore, Md. 1958). J. RYCKMANS, *L'Institution monarchique en Arabie méridionale avant l'Islam (Ma 'in et Saba)* (Louvain 1951); *La Persécution des chrétiens himyarites au sixième siècle* (Istanbul 1956). *Bulletin of American Schools of Oriental Research* 143 (1956) 6–10; 145 (1957) 25–30; 151 (1958) 9–16. *Encyclopedic Dictionary of the Bible* (New York 1963) 2067–70.

[A. JAMME]

SABAOTH

Sabaoth is a word used in the divine title, *yhwh ṣᵉbā'ôt* (usually translated as "the Lord of Hosts"); employed most frequently by the Prophets (247 times). This title is a contraction of the full form *yhwh 'ĕlōhê ṣᵉbā'ôt yiśrā'ēl,* "Yahweh, the God of the armies of Israel" (cf. Am 5.15; 1 Sm 17.45). Its first appearance in the Old Testament is in connection with the sanctuary at SILO (SHILOH), where the ARK of the covenant was housed (1 Sm 1.3, 4.3–5). The ark, the symbol of Yahweh's presence, was carried into battle as a sacred palladium. The name Yahweh Sabaoth would thus describe Israel's God as the supreme commander of its armies (Ex 7.4;12.41–42), a

Mar Saba Monastery, Kidron Valley, Israel. (©Richard T. Nowitz/CORBIS)

warrior who led the hosts of Israel into battle. The title, however, was later used by the Prophets in a more universal meaning to designate the Lord of the universe. Sabaoth is sometimes taken to mean the angels who serve at the throne of the Almighty (Jb 1.6); but the singular *ṣābā'* is used more frequently for this heavenly army (Jos 5.14; 1 Kgs 22.19; 2 Chr 18.18; etc.). Sabaoth may possibly refer also to the stars, which in their orderly sweep across the night sky suggest the movement of an army on the march (cf. Jgs 5.20); but, again, the army of the stars is usually the singular *ṣābā'* (Dt 4.19, 17.3; 2 Kgs 17.16; etc.). Since the Israelites were often warned against worshipping "the army of the heavens," i.e., the stars, as deities (Jer 8.2; So 1.5; etc.), the theological concept of the stars as Yahweh's creation may also have been intended by declaring Yahweh the God of (the heavenly) hosts. In any case, the term Yahweh Sabaoth expresses God's sovereignty over all things.

Bibliography: B. WAMBACQ, *L'Epithète divin Jahvé Sᵉbaôt* (Paris 1947).

[R. T. A. MURPHY]

SABAS, SS.

A monastic founder and two martyrs of the early Church.

Sabas of Palestine, monastic founder; b. Cappadocia, 439; d. Palestine, Dec. 5, 532. According to his biographer, CYRIL OF SCYTHOPOLIS, Sabas was born at Mutalaska in Cappadocia, and entered a monastery in his native province. In 457 he migrated to the monastery of Passarion in Jerusalem and met (St.) Euthymius, who because of Sabas' youth, sent him to (St.) Theoctistus in Wadi Mukelik, where he remained 17 years. In 478 he went to live in a grotto in Wadi en Nar and in 483 founded his famous laura there. After he was obliged by Sallustius, patriarch of Jerusalem (d. 494), to take sacred orders, he became director of all the anchorites who populated the lauras of Judea. Later he founded three other lauras, six monasteries, and four hospices, while his disciples in turn founded three lauras and two monasteries.

The four lauras of St. Sabas are: the Great Laura (today St. Sabas in the lower Cedron Valley) in 483; the New Laura (actually begun by rebel origenistic monks) in 507; the Laura Heptastomos in 512; the Laura of Jeremias in 531. The Great Laura had 150 monks and the New Laura 120.

Because of dissensions over Origenism (*see* ORIGEN AND ORIGENISM), many monks left the Great Laura and founded another; Sabas himself withdrew from the Great Laura to Nicopolis (Emawas), where he founded a monastery (503–8). Twice, in 512 and 531, he intervened with the imperial court for the abolition of the *crisorgirus* (an odious tax) and to defend the faith against the Monophysites (*see* MONOPHYSITISM). Cyril of Scythopolis salutes him and his monks as ''the strongest bulwark of the Catholic faith in Palestine.''

The *typikon* of St. Sabas, in its present state at least, dates only from the twelfth or thirteenth century. His influence was considerable on the organization of later monasteries. The original chapel tomb of the saint is in the monastery of St. Sabas, but his remains are in Venice. In Rome a church was erected in his honor on the Aventine in the ninth century. The body was returned to Palestine by Pope Paul VI in 1965.

Feast Day: December 5.

Sabas the Goth, fourth-century martyr; d. Cappadocia, April 12, 372. The persecution of King Athanaric (371) having broken out, Sabas supported his coreligionists in resisting an edict obliging them to eat meat sacrificed to the idols. For this he was exiled. He returned but was exiled again. While celebrating Easter of 372 with his friend Sansala, he was set upon by robbers; he was ill treated, tied to a beam, and ordered to eat the sacrificed meat. On refusing, he was drowned in the Musaeus River; he is one of 51 martyrs commemorated by the Greeks as having suffered in that nation. The Christian Goths wrote to St. BASIL regarding these events when the body was taken to Caesarea of Cappadocia by Julianus Soranus, duke of Scythia.

Feast Day: April 12; April 15 in Russia.

Sabas the Martyr is commemorated by the Latin and Greek martyrologies as a Roman who suffered under Aurelian; but otherwise he is unknown. He may be identical to St. Sabas the Goth.

Feast Day: April 24.

Bibliography: Sabas (of Palestine). E. SCHWARTZ, ed., *Kyrillos von Skythopolis* (Texte und untersuchungen zur Geschichte der altchristlichen Literatur 49.2; Berlin 1939). E. HOADE, *Guide to the Holy Land* (Jerusalem 1962). V. CORBO, ''L'Ambiente materiale della vita die monaci,'' *Orientalia Christiana Analecta* 153 (1958) 235–257. CYRIL OF SCYTHOPOLIS, *Vie de saint Sabas*, tr. A.–J. FESTUGIÈRE (Paris 1962). G. HEYDOCK, *Der Heilige Sabas und seine Reliquien* (Geisenheim, Germany 1970). J. PATRICH, *Nezirut Midbar Yehudah ba–tekufah ha–Bizantit* (Jerusalem 1995); *Sabas, Leader of Palestinian Monasticism* (Washington, D.C. 1995). Sabas the Goth. *Acta Sanctorum*, April 2:87–90. H. DELEHAYE ''Saints de Thrace et de Mésie,'' *Analecta Bollandiana*, 31 (1912) 213–221, 288–291.

[E. HOADE]

SABAS THE YOUNGER, ST.

Ascetic; b. Collesano, Sicily; d. Monastery of San Cesario, Rome, Feb. 6, 990. He entered monastic life at the Monastery of St. Philip of Agira, where he had been preceded by his father, Christopher. His mother Callí founded a monastery for women. The continuing advance of the Arabs into eastern Sicily and the famine of 940–941 obliged him to seek refuge in Calabria. At first, he stayed with relatives in Caronia; later, accompanied by his brother, Macarius the Younger, also a famous ascetic, he visited northern Calabria and Lucania. He traveled through the areas near the monastic eparchies of Mercurion and Latinianon, and near Lagonegro and Salerno, erecting small churches and monasteries. After a pilgrimage to Rome, he lived for a short while as a hermit in a cave near Amalfi. Sabas the Younger intervened to free the son of John, prince of Salerno, and the son of Mansone III, duke of Amalfi, who were being held as hostages at the court of the Holy Roman Emperor OTTO II.

Feast: Feb. 5.

Bibliography: G. COZZA-LUZI, *Historia et laudes SS. Sabae et Macarii* (Rome 1893). J. GAY, *L'Italie méridionale et l'Empire byzantin depuis l'avènement de Basile Ie . . .* (867–1071) (Paris 1904) 262, 264–266, 378–380. G. DA COSTA-LOUILLET, ''Saints de Sicile et d'Italie méridionale aux VIIIe, IXe, et Xe siècles,'' *Byzantion* 29–30 (1959–60) 130–139.

[M. PETTA]

SABATIER, LOUIS AUGUSTE

French Protestant theologian; b. Vailon (Ardèche), France, Oct. 22, 1839; d. Paris, April 12, 1901. Sabatier studied at the Protestant theological faculty of Montauban and at the universities of Tübingen and Heidelberg. He became professor of reformed theology at Strasbourg (1867) and later in the Protestant faculty at Paris (1877). Sabatier's religious theories continued the pattern originated by KANT and SCHLEIERMACHER, which eventually formed a liberal consensus concerning the nature of religion, revelation, and dogma. He assumed as self-evident the impossibility of analyzing religion except by reflecting on man's conscience and consciousness of God. Religion to him had its source in a feeling of uneasiness or anxiety, which rested on the discovery that, notwithstanding the loftiness of human insights and aspirations, man is frustrated by his inability to respond on his own to these noble inclinations. Consequently, he believed the primordial act of religion to be prayer, an act elicited from the soul in distress. From this interiorization of dependence on God arose revelation, which to Sabatier was the creation and progressive clarification of man's consciousness of God on both an individual and collective basis. The transcription of such subjective experiences into objective terms constituted dogma. By these principles the progressive evolution of dogma became axiomatic, and dogmatic formulas were treated as purely symbolic. Sabatier's thought has been variously called "symbolic fideism" and "critical symbolism." Of his works the most important was *Outlines of a Philosophy of Religion* (1897), in which he embodied much of his psychological and historical theories. Others of his works translated into English were *The Apostle Paul* (1891) and *Religions of Authority and the Religion of the Spirit* (1904). Sabatier's theories were close to those of LOISY and MODERNISM.

See Also: LIBERALISM, THEOLOGICAL.

Bibliography: E. MÉNÉGOZ, *Aperçu de la théologie d'A. Sabatier* (Paris 1901). K. SCHMITT, *Lexikon für Theologie und Kirche*[2] 9:187.

[M. B. SCHEPERS]

SABATIER, PAUL

Calvinist pastor and writer; b. Saint-Michel-de-Chabrillaneux, France, Aug. 3, 1858; d. Strasbourg, March 4, 1928. After studying at the Faculty of Theology in Paris under RENAN, Sabatier served as pastor in Strasbourg (1885–89). His bestselling *Vie de S. François d'Assise* (Paris 1894; éd. définitive, relatively unchanged, 1931; Eng. tr. London 1894) was marked by animus against the papacy and the veneration of saints. It was placed on the Index in 1894.

Despite Sabatier's impressive learning and a charming style, his subjective portrait of FRANCIS OF ASSISI, excluding the sacramental and the supernatural, was demonstrably unhistorical in attributing to the saint a hostile and grudging obedience to the Church. In 1908 Sabatier publicly admitted this error: "It would be absurd to make St. Francis of Assisi a rebel or an unconscious Protestant." Resigning his pastorate in 1894, he devoted himself to the study and publication of early Franciscan documents, for expamle, the *Actus Beati Francisci et Sociorum Ejus* (Paris 1902), the Latin original of the *FIORETTI;* and the *Speculum Perfectionis.* Sabatier's stubbornly maintained theory that the saint's secretary, Brother Leo (Leo of Assisi), wrote the latter in 1227 has been rejected by experts, who see in it a compilation made in 1318 of earlier texts, including some written by Leo in 1246 or later.

Between 1904 and 1914 Sabatier played an active part in Modernism, writing *An Open Letter to His Eminence Cardinal Gibbons* (Boston 1908) and delivering the Jowett Lectures on *Modernism* (London 1908). During World War I he substituted for drafted pastors, and defended the spiritual ideals of the Allied cause in *A Frenchman's Thoughts on the War* (London 1915). From 1919 until his death he taught at the University of Strasbourg. His (Franciscan) *Études inédites* (Paris 1932) reveal a marked intellectual evolution in his understanding of and sympathy for medieval spirituality. The stimulus and contributions that he made to Franciscan scholarship remain monumental.

Bibliography: C. BROOKE, "Paul Sabatier and St. Francis of Assisi," in *St. Francis of Assisi: Essays in Commemoration* (St. Bonaventure, N.Y. 1982) 41–58. P. SABATIER, "The Originality of St. Francis of Assisi," in *St. Francis of Assisi: Essays in Commemoration* (St. Bonaventure, N.Y. 1982) 25–40. T. VETRALI, ed., "Francesco d'Assis Attesa Dell'Ecumeniso: Paul Sabatier e la sua 'Vita di S Francesco' Cent'Anni Dopo," *Studi Ecumenici* 12 (Jl-S, 1994) 1–191. SOCIETA INTERNAZIONALE DI STUDI FRANCESCANI, *La Questione Francescana da Sabatier ad oggi: Atti del I Covegno Internazionale* (Assisi 1973).

[R. BROWN]

SABATIER, PIERRE

Biblical scholar renowned for his work on the Old Latin Version of the Bible; b. Poitiers, France, 1682; d. Reims, March 24, 1742. After his studies under T. RUINART at the Abbey of Saint-Germain-des-Prés, Paris, he became a Maurist Benedictine at Meaux (1700). From 1702 to 1709 he collaborated with Ruinart on the *Annales bénédictines,* but after Ruinart's death he devoted his energies to the study of the text of the Old Latin Version of the Bible. These labors were not interrupted by his transfer to the Abbey of Saint-Nicaisse, Reims, when, like many of his confreres, he was suspected of Jansenism after the publication of the bull *Unigenitus* (1713). For more than 30 years Sabatier gathered quotations taken from the Old Latin Version as found in the MSS and printed editions of the Church Fathers and liturgical documents. In 1735 he began preparing for the publication of the gigantic work, but he died shortly before it appeared under the title *Bibliorum sacrorum Latinae versiones antiquae, seu Vetus Italica* . . . (3 v. Reims 1743–49, Paris 1751). Although Sabatier labored under the false opinion that before St. Jerome's version there was only one Latin version of the Scriptures, which he called *Italica*, and despite certain other defects in his method, his work still remains of immense value for restoring the pre–Jerome Latin translations of the Bible. J. Denk (1849–1927) began work on a "New Sabatier," which since 1949 has been continued on a much more scientific basis by the Vetus Latina Institute of the Abbey of BEURON. *See* B. M. Peebles, *The Catholic Biblical Quarterly* 16 (1954) 210–225; 20 (1958) 105–108.

Bibliography: G. HEER, *Lexikon für Theologie und Kirche* [2] 9:188. E. MANGENOT, *Revue des sciences ecclésiastiques* 58 (1888) 97–132. J. DENK, "Sabatier, sein Itala-Sammelwerk und dessen Neubearbeitung," *Theologie und Glaube* 1 (1909) 787–791; *Der neue Sabatier* (Leipzig 1914).

[L. F. HARTMAN]

SABBATARIANISM

Sabbatarianism stems from two sources. The one, based upon the Mosaic Law, required, sometimes on pain of death, the rigid observance of the Sabbath (Saturday) as the Lord's day of rest. The Jews and Seventh-day Adventists follow the tradition of keeping Saturday as the Sabbath; there were also certain 16th-century Socinians and one or two now-extinct Baptist sects in the United States that kept this Sabbath. The other source is rooted in the Puritan reaction to pre-Reformation custom in holding the 7th day of the week, Sunday, as a day of recreation as well as worship. Sabbatarianism encompasses all those rigorists of several Protestant sects from the late 16th to the late 19th centuries (and, to a lesser extent, today) who scrupulously practiced and urged upon others the strict observance of Sunday as a day to be devoted solely to worship, and who would permit no work, travel, or any form of innocent exercise or entertainment on that day.

Although Elizabethan Puritans greatly advanced Sabbatarianism, the movement in the broadest sense did not originate entirely with them. Henry VIII forbade bowling and certain other recreations on Sundays, and Elizabethan Parliaments passed laws to suppress brutal sports such as bear-baiting among Lancashiremen in the 1580s. That these laws constrained largely Catholic recusants may have had something to do with the fervor with which the justices of the peace, Anglican clergy, and country gentry enforced them through fines, imprisonments, and social ostracism. By the late 1580s these Acts were extended throughout England among all sects. In the same decade the Puritans advocated the extension of these restrictions on Sabbath-keeping to more innocent activities. Puritan conferences in Cambridgeshire, Suffolk, Essex, Norfolk, and Middlesex discussed Sabbatarianism; Puritan clergy preached it at Oxford; and the leading Puritan spokesman, Thomas CARTWRIGHT, upheld it in his writings. By the 1590s the strict observance of the Sabbath was common among Puritans, as is evidenced by the widespread publication of Nicholas Bound's *True Doctrine of the Sabbath* (1595). The movement continued to spread until it burst into a storm of indignation over James I's *Book of Sports* (1618).

The occasion for the issuance of this book was the attempt by Lancashire magistrates in 1617 to suppress morris dances, May games, and other sports done on Sundays after church. When the crown legally recognized the innocence of such activities throughout England and required that a proclamation to that effect be read in all churches, the Puritans provoked a major controversy. The royal order notwithstanding, such pastimes were stringently proscribed in congregations controlled by Puritans. A similar Puritan Sabbatarianism occurred in Somersetshire, where, customarily, annual spring "wakes" featured drinking, dancing, and sporting, occasionally leading to rowdyism, promiscuity, and even homicide. An outburst of Puritan criticism ensued, but, out of fear that worse evils might result, neither the Anglican hierarchy nor a majority of the clergy in that county would suppress the festivities. Against this adverse criticism by Puritans, Charles I issued an amended *Book of Sports* (1633), Abp. W. LAUD attacked Sabbatarianism, and his protégé, P. Heylyn, publicized his convictions in *The History of the Sabbath* (1636). As one might have expected, the Parliamentarians of the Civil War and Interregnum periods gave legal force to Sabbatarianism by passing laws enforcing it in 1644, 1650, and 1655; and the Presbyterian Westminster Assembly (1644) supported Sabbatarianism also. Charles II, in order to appease dissenters, allowed certain restrictions on Sunday travel, and Queens Mary II and Anne gave some support to Sabbatarians' ideals. In 1711, for instance, the Anglican hierarchy in convocation caustically criticized the upper classes for Sabbath-breaking.

Sabbatarianism continued in England and Scotland during the 18th century as a result of Presbyterian and

Wesleyan Methodist pressure, although the first three Hanoverian kings, who regularly held council meetings, military reviews, and parties on Sundays, and the urban upper classes generally ignored it. Nevertheless, the movement had sufficient strength to restrict, and even to punish by fines, excommunication, and social ostracism some of those who broke the Sabbath by travel, recreation, or work. The Presbytery of Edinburgh in 1711 lamented the common practice of walking in the country after Sunday services, and in various parishes elders regularly roamed the streets searching for violators. Toward the end of the century the English reaction to the excesses of the French Revolution enhanced evangelicalism, which had already succeeded in having passed the Lord's Day Observance Act (1781), and various societies were formed for keeping a Puritan Sabbath. The spirit of this law is still alive in Scotland, England, Canada, and Australia, although 20th-century secularism is breaking it down. Today in England the Lord's Day Observance Society exerts considerable influence through pamphlets and the press.

Puritans carried Sabbatarianism to the American colonies in the 17th century when, in Massachusetts Bay Colony for instance, laws forbade all forms of work or exercise, even swimming. The movement declined in the 18th century, as it did in England, but during the 19th century, especially in the "burned-over district" of western New York, the rowdyism and drunkenness associated with the building of the Erie Canal provoked the Baptists into active opposition to the Continental Sunday of immigrant groups, as well as to Sunday travel. In New York City in 1828 Josiah Bissell organized the "General Union for promoting the observance of the Christian Sabbath in the United States," which enjoyed national membership.

Bibliography: R. COX, *The Literature of the Sabbath Question,* 2 v. (Edinburgh 1865). J. TAIT, "The Declaration of Sports for Lancashire (1617)," *English Historical Review* 32 (1917) 561–568. W. B. WHITAKER, *Sunday in Tudor and Stuart Times* (London 1933). G. DAVIES, *The Early Stuarts, 1603–1660* (2d ed. Oxford 1959). A. FRENCH, *Charles I and the Puritan Upheaval* (Boston 1955). W. R. CROSS, *The Burned-over District* (Ithaca 1950). U.S. Bureau of the Census, *Religious Bodies: 1926,* 2 v. (Washington 1929–30). A. M. MCCROSSEN, "Sabbatarianism: The Intersection of Church and State in the Orchestration of Everyday Life in Nineteenth-Century America," *Religious and Secular Reform in America,* ed. D. K. ADAMS and C. A. VAN MINNEN (New York 1999). B. W. BALL, *The Seventh-Day Men: Sabbatarians and Sabbatarianism in England and Wales, 1600-1800* (Oxford 1994). D. LIECHTY, *Sabbatarianism in the 16th Century: A Page in the History of the Radical Reformation* (Berrien Springs 1993).

[M. J. HAVRAN]

Four Orthodox Jewish men walk to Sabbath Services, Jerusalem, 1988. (©Paul A. Souders/CORBIS)

SABBATH

The seventh day of the week (Saturday) observed in Israel as a day sacred to Yahweh. This article considers the Biblical enunciation of the obligation to keep the Sabbath (Heb. *šabbāt*) holy, the evidence of its actual observance in ancient Israel, the derivation of the term, the natural-law kernel of the observance and its transfer to Sunday, and the question of the prohibition of so-called servile work on the day.

Biblical Enunciation of the Obligation. The first reference in the Bible to the Sabbath is in a verbal form in Gn 2.2–3: "And he [God] rested [literally "sabbathed," Heb. *wayyišbāt*] on the seventh day from all the work he had done. God blessed the seventh day and made it holy because on it he rested [Heb. *šābat*] from all his work of creation." This "seventh day" occurs here in a series possessing neither calendaric nor other concrete reality; it is a skillful artistic framework for the theological message of God's creative power and authority. The passage is typical of the strand of the Pentateuch attributed to the Pentateuchal PRIESTLY WRITERS (P) relatively late in origin (*c.* 500 B.C.). It is theoretical in ascribing to God from the very moment of creation the observance of a duty known much later to be incumbent upon His worshipers. The same theorizing appears in Ex 31.17 and in even more extreme degree in the Book of Jubilees, which, however, dates from *c.* 100 B.C. and is apocryphal.

The promulgation of the Sabbath as a genuine ritual law is found in Exodus three times, put in the mouth of Moses, or rather of God to Moses. Of these, the mention in Exodus (20.8) in the Decalogue (*see* COMMANDMENTS, TEN) forms part of what is justly regarded as the most original and specific contribution of the Sinai revelation (*c.* 1250 B.C.); on the divergences from Dt 5.14, see below. But the mention in Ex 23.12, forming part of the BOOK OF THE COVENANT, may well be regarded as stemming from long before the time of HAMMURABI (1700 B.C.), to whose laws it exhibits striking similarities that point to a stage of development in The Book of the Covenant that, though more retarded, was nobler.

Actually, before its promulgation in any of the legal passages of Exodus, the Sabbath is exhibited as being already observed in practice, in fact on the part of God even more than of men, through His apportioning of the MANNA (Ex 16.23). This passage is credibly ascribed to the YAHWIST or oldest strand of Mosaic tradition. But since here God's observance, rather than man's, is portrayed, it may seem warranted to consider the earliest concrete case to be rather in Nm 15.32. Here severe punishment is inflicted by the community itself for a Sabbath violation that consisted in gathering wood, commonly understood as firewood; and the passage is therefore parallel to Ex 35.3: "You shall not light a fire in any of your dwellings on the Sabbath day." In this perspective it turns out that the manna episode envisions the prevention of cooking, as shown by the Hebrew terms for "bake" and "boil" in Ex 16.23.

The conclusion may, therefore, be rightly drawn (despite E. Lohse) that the most primitive Sabbath observance consisted in a taboo on making fires. One need not here take issue on the further hypothesis (regarded tolerantly by R. de Vau) that such a taboo was suited to the tribe of smiths or Kenites (Gn 5.22) related in 1 Sm 15.6 to the Midianites, by whom Moses on Sinai was influenced (W. Schmidt), even cultically (Ex 18.12; 3.1). In such a tribe of nomads, whose livelihood depended on the forge, refraining from use of fire would be tantamount to that periodic rest from toil that nature itself requires. But in the Bible there is no such notion of repose attached to the Sabbath except in the accretion of Dt 5.14 discussed below.

There arose gradually within the Biblical revelation other prohibitions, not recognizably connected with fire-making: farming (Ex 34.10); carrying loads (Jer 17.21, allegedly interpolated); commerce (Am 8.5; Neh 13.15); eventually even traveling (Acts 1.12; but commended especially for the Sabbath in 2 Kgs 4.23, as was changing of the guard in 11.5); finally "no work at all" (Lv 23.3, of the P strand). Even so, there is no foundation in the Bible for Jerome's rendition of "servile work" (see below).

The obligation, though a peculiar token of the Israelite COVENANT (Ex 31.16; Ez 20.13; Is 56.6), was binding upon aliens and domestic animals (Ex 20.8) and even the earth itself (*see* SABBATH YEAR.) The variant, *šabbātôn*, occurs ten times, always in the P strand, seven times (Lv 16.31; 23.32; etc.) in solemn iteration of *šabbāt*, though the resemblance of this pairing to the Greek (σάββατα σαββάτων), like the Latin *sanctum sanctorum*, is fallacious. The word *šabbātôn* occurs alone only in Lv 23.39; 25.5, and before *šabbāt* only in Ex 16.23. Though *šabbātôn* is used also of the Day of ATONEMENT (Lv 16.31; 23.32), which may fall on any day of the week, it has of itself no penitential implications despite the fact that Greco-Roman annalists regarded the Sabbath itself as a fast day and as an isolating institution like circumcision.

The Sabbath was indeed a sort of fast from certain activities; but it was insistently called joyous (Is 58.13), and it was festive because of its cultic as well as its workban associations. Only a slight increase in liturgical observances was prescribed (Nm 28.9; Lv 24.8; Ez 46.1–5). But in Lv 23.3 the Sabbath is reckoned among "the festivals of the Lord" on which there was to be a holy assembly or convocation (Heb. *miqrā'*—in Neh 8.8 a public "reading"), and this, with 2 Kgs 4.23, may have given rise to the postexilic custom (of obscure origins: McKay) of gatherings in synagogue for instruction. Like any other day, the Sabbath began on what for us would be the preceding sunset; since the earlier part of that day was preempted for anticipating food cooking and similar needs, this was called the Preparation Day or Parasceve (Mt 27.62).

Evidence of Actual Observance There can be no doubt that the Sabbath had come to be observed among the Jews by a universal and rigorous abstinence from all activities resembling work (but with no implications of either servility or profit): Mt 12.2; 24.20; Mk 3.2; Lk 13.14; 4.6; Jn 5.10; Acts 1.12. This situation is reflected in the explicit and detailed supplement to the (variously called Third/Fourth) Commandment in both Ex 20.10 and Dt 5.14, which are identical up to the point where Deuteronomy inserts "Your male and female slave should rest as you do.'' This insertion then continues in Dt 5.15, ascribing the very origin of sabbath to an application of the Golden Rule: treat your slaves as you would have wished to be treated in the Egyptian slavery from which Yahweh's power liberated you. As against this, Ex 20.11 adds a wholly different reason: ''In six days the Lord made the heavens and the earth, the sea and all that is in them; but on the seventh day he rested. That is why the Lord has blessed the Sabbath Day and made it holy.'' This disparity is to some extent resolved by viewing both formulations as expressions of the covenant. Nevertheless, experts are agreed that the original form of all the ''Ten Words'' was the concise or lapidary ''Thou shalt (not) . . . .''

The Sabbath law is not negative, ''You shall not work on the sabbath,'' but rather, ''You shall keep holy the sabbath.'' No proof has ever yet been forthcoming that the word ''sabbath'' meant ''stoppage [of work or anything else],'' except as a denominative verb formed on the basis on an existing ritual practice. ''Its characteristic feature lies not in the regularity with which it recurs (*pace* Negretti's title; not all would accept his p. 26 & 87: social justice motivations secondary), nor in the cessation of work, nor in the various prohibitions which the cessation of work implies . . . . Its distinctive trait lies in the fact that it is a day made holy because of its relation to the God of the Covenant'' (De Vaux, 480; tacitly dissenting from Lohse).

It must be noted that the clearest and most numerous references both to the obligatoriness and to the meaning of the prohibitions against working on the Sabbath are in the Levitical or P strand of the Pentateuch. Even more recent are the (long assumed but recently combated single Ezra-Neh-Chr author) CHRONICLER's firm references in Neh 10.32 (while 2 Chr 23.4, 8 merely reechoes 2 Kgs 11.5, 7, 9) LPNY ŠBT on an ostracon found by J. Naveh at Yavneh Yam is taken as ''before Sabbath'' except by Robinson p. 91.

The Maccabees' fidelity to Sabbath rest even in wartime was recognized by themselves as self-defeating (1 Mc 2.40; 2 Mc 7.11; 15.1), and their compromise in 167 B.C. seems to have driven a wedge between them and their HASIDAEAN allies (1 Mc 2.42; 7.13), who in turn later split into the intensely Sabbatizing Pharisee and Essene (and/or) Qumran sects (CDC 11.4; 13.13; Josephus, *Bell. Jud.* 2.8.9). Nodet takes this very first indication of any scruple about defensive war on sabbath, despite frequency of the need in the early history of the biblical people, as point of departure for his sweeping claim that Sabbath itself was a Samaritan tradition, from the time of Joshua (24, at Shechem: ''covenant,'' ''ordinances'' apparently not mentioning Sabbath). Intriguing factual data are

claimed to support this view. The Shechemites in Josephus Ant 13.251–264 ask Alexander to sanction the Sabbath (which they admit having received from the Judahites, Nodet p. 378). There is nothing about sabbath taboos in ''Ezra's Torah'' (Neh 8.2), yet already Nehemiah (13.17) strongly forbids sabbath commerce. Nodet sees him relying on an interpretation newly established, though incorporated in the Torah only around 200 by Simon as in *Pirqe Abot* (Nodet p. 164, but his p. 12; 152; 386 really do not clarify at what *late* date the Sabbath was incorporated into the Samaritan Pentateuch and from there into the canonical Jewish Torah.

From a much earlier date, however, even before 750 B.C., the Prophets clearly assumed a widespread and conscientious ''observance'' (of something) linked with the Sabbath. This was sometimes lumped together with other purely external rituals in which the lack of requisite internal dispositions was deplored in Am 8.5; Hos 2.13; Is 1.13; 66.23. But in equally conspicuous cases Deutero-Isaiah himself (Is 56.2, 4, 6), Jeremiah (Jer 17.21–22, 24), and especially Ezekiel (Ez 20.12–13, 20; 22.26; 46.1–4) promoted existing Sabbath observance more formally than anything they had to say about sacrifice. To be examined later is the question how the Prophets stressed a link between the Sabbath and the moon that is otherwise not prominent in the Bible.

The actual practices attested in Nm 15.32 and Ex 35.3 show that Sabbath observance was taken seriously from a date even earlier than the Prophets and involved the omission of some workaday chores, but with no clarity as to whether they were prohibited because toilsome, or because of some taboo, such as fire; or because of the natural and social-justice requirement of an occasional off-work day. Emphasis on the Sabbath day as noteworthily subordinated to the SABBATH YEAR in the Book of the Covenant (Ex 23.10–12) shows that the usage was at the latest contemporary with Israel's early sedentarization in Canaan and, indeed, a great deal earlier, if one attaches due weight to the affinities with the Code of Hammurabi. Ultimately, the mention in the Book of the Covenant reflects the earliest situation recorded in the Bible and clearly imposes something as antithesis to work. Though the rendition as ''rest'' of a verb that means merely ''keep Sabbath'' is tendentious and premature, it is not without significance that the admirable *Lexicon* of Brown-Driver-Briggs from an enumeration of occurrences concludes firmly, ''originally observed simply by abstinence from labour ''even if this conclusion was doubtless dictated at least in part by the now unwarranted assumption that the verb *šābat* meant ''cease'' before it meant ''sabbatize.''

Derivation of the Term. The scholar De Vaux, himself a competent Assyriologist, rejects categorically any influence of Babylon on the Hebrew Sabbath, as did N. H. Tur-Sinai. De Vaux specifically disowns B. Landsberger's ''two-sevens'' etymology, which was favored in the point-for-point documentation of *Biblica* 36 (1955) 182–201. The clarity and force by which De Vaux's presentation undoubtedly excels are to some extent at the cost of simplifying or overstating facts that must reasonably be regarded as complex and ambiguous. These complexities are here analyzed.

As was insisted above, there is no evidence whatever that the verb *šābat* had an existence and meaning, either in Hebrew or in cognate languages, not dependent on the technical-ritual noun *šabbāt*. The likeliest cases (Is 24.8; Hos 7.4; Jb 32.1; Lam 5.14–15; Prv 22.10; Neh 6.3) are all vaguely cultic or at most involve a metaphor no bolder than when one speaks of an ''economic heresy.''

Though doubtless an ignorant overlooking of the final *'ayin* in *šeba'* (seven) led early Christian Fathers to equate seven (-day week) with Sabbath [see E. Vogt, *Biblica* 40 (1959) 1008, who disproves that *šabbāt* ever meant week] still the best grammarians now admit cases in which *'ayin* is in fact transmuted or lost. In the existing Syriac form *šabbā*, the loss of the final *t* is no less anomalous than that of the final *'ayin* would be.

Mystical or superstitious suggestiveness of the number seven has been so conspicuous from antiquity down to our own day that it may well have exerted some influence on the choice of the seventh as the day of either taboo or natural also correspond too closely with seventh-day recurrence to be ruled out of consideration on the ground of a disparity amounting to five percent (29.55- vs. 28-day period). Now the classic insistence on the ''New Moon'' occurring in the Bible 18 times, three more than ''sabbath'' though usually coupled with it, is McKay (p. 25–42, citing her summary in Eskenazi). She shows no interest in the link of the greatest feast of all, Passover, with the *full* moon. Andreasen p. 4 documents the brief heyday of Johann Meinhold's 1909 claim that sabbath was originally the full moon day, therefore *monthly* not weekly.

Traces of a primitive division of the year into seven 50-day periods, though doubtless overstated by J. and H. Lewy [*Hebrew Union College Annual* 17 (1942) 1–155], leave open a certain minimal possibility that seven-squared, loosely called 50, was the chiefly venerated number, of which the simple seven was a secondary application. This hypothesis is exemplified in the JUBILEE YEAR as seventh Sabbath year and finds some corroboration also in the apparent meaning of *šabbātôn* as ''big sabbath.''

Applicability of *šabbātôn* to a non-Saturday penitential day and the fact that Babylonian *šapattu* days were

unlucky rather than auspicious imply merely a sacredness (Latin *sacer* means accursed, too) that of its nature can involve simultaneously pleasurable and oppressive elements (*see* SACRED AND PROFANE).

However cultic or covenantal the Hebrew Sabbath may have been, it cannot reasonably be considered to have arisen devoid of any connection with the natural need of periodic festive repose from toil. This perspective tends to connect the Sabbath with a fire taboo of Kenite tinkers.

It would be imprudent to conclude categorically that any one of these factors is alone, or primarily, at the origin of the Hebrew Sabbath: week, the number 7, *šapattu*, new (and full) moon, the number 50, *šabbātôn*, natural repose, Kenites, fire-taboo. We now may even have to add from Eskenazi ''purification'' (S. Meier p. 6: seven days after menstruation Lv 12:2, 5, 7; or 14 after childbearing) and even ''the political'': American courts failing to uphold Adventist (M. Tyner p. 256) and Jewish (S. Rosenthal p. 261) rights against Sunday observance (on which see McCrossen). But even keeping all these ''possibilities'' in view does not warrant falling into a syncretism claiming to see features of all of these disparate practices finding their way little by little into the concept of the Sabbath. The present state of modern knowledge does not warrant deciding which, if any, of these factors were operative and to what extent. In De Vaux's words (480), ''If the Qenite hypothesis looks the least unlikely, this may be merely because we have no documents at all which contradict it. Obviously, the sabbath day may have originated outside Israel, but we cannot prove this.''

Natural-law Kernel and Transfer to Sunday. It is unmistakable that if one prescinds from the Sabbath precept, the Ten Commandments enunciate nothing other than the dictates of the NATURAL LAW. It might seem logical, therefore, to assume that Sabbath observance, too, is such a dictate. This can be defended in the sense that the commandment merely asserts the obligation of periodic festive rest on *some* (not necessarily the seventh) day that is therefore automatically called Sabbath, and for which Semitic cultures would tend to favor seventh or new moon, especially if the intervals at which it recurs involve the number seven. Some moralists, however, assert categorically that the OT Sabbath precept embodies no natural-law obligation whatever and that it is a purely positive precept. A middle group would claim that there is a basic natural obligation, but its linking with any specific day or interval is a purely arbitrary positive legislation. The exegete can live with any one of these moralist positions.

Recent discussions of the ''natural (law)'' demand of periodic festive repose from work have focused rather questions of social justice for the underprivileged. There are excellent reasons for maintaining that from its earliest (Ex 23.10) to its latest (Lv 25.2), the ''sabbath'' principle was ''so that the poor can have rest or food,'' and that *this* is the aspect of any sabbath-related biblical guidance which must be most urgently reinterpreted for our present day. Andreasen p. 126 focusing the ''socio-*economic* institution'' as possibly a *market-day* affording also cultic and recreational opportunities, strives (p. 126 & 255) to confront such views with the furious rejection of sabbath-marketing in Neh 13.17, 21.

Insofar as the sabbath precept would embody a natural-law obligation, there could be no question of Jesus' abrogating or belittling it. It is equally obvious that much of His polemic with the Pharisees seems to be deliberately provocative of their insistence on Sabbath. A second look suffices to show that in these cases Jesus is not downgrading the Sabbath itself but rather insisting that equally urgent obligations must not be lost sight of, exactly as in His echoing of the Prophets' so-called polemic against sacrifice (Mt 9.13; Jer 7.22; Am 5.25; Hos 6.6). Just as a man may in exceptional circumstances have to ''hate'' his mother in the sense of preferring another's claims over hers (Lk 14.26), so he could be said to ''hate'' even the Sabbath obligation in according precedence to a conflicting duty. This norm was fully admitted by the PHARISEES (*Yoma* 8.6; life can be saved on the Sabbath), as Jesus acknowledged when He made it the basis of His own counter argument (Lk 14.5; Mk 3.2). When Jesus declared in Mk 2.27, ''the Sabbath was made for man, not man for the Sabbath,'' He was in fact using the very words that would be handed down by a Pharisee rabbi in *Mekilta Exodus* 109b. One cannot prove or disprove that this rabbinical maxim either had a divergent import or was to some extent (re)formulated under Christian influence. Still, to glorify this maxim as ''Christian superiority over Pharisaism'' is unrealistic.

In some cases, indeed, such as Mt 12.8; Jn 5.8–10, 9.14, Jesus claimed the right to give to the Sabbath law an interpretation that would be henceforth more valid than that of the Pharisees; but this is a part of his more general claim not to destroy a single jot or tittle of the Law but to fulfill it (Mt 5.17–18). In principle Jesus had no quarrel with the Sabbath obligation itself or even with the Pharisees' interpretation of it, which for the most part was not unduly severe. Whereas the Essenes forbade even defecation (Josephus, *Bell. Jud.* 2.147), the Pharisees had no prohibition of the use of marriage on Sabbath; and though they commended timing to avoid the pangs of labor on a subsequent Sabbath, still in the case of a birth on the Sabbath the circumcision was to be performed on the octave (Jn 7.22). Jesus primarily remonstrated that men charged with imposing onerous obligations should lead by example and show that they would undergo privations imposed by their own juridicism (Mt 23.13).

Ultimately to assess with fairness the strictures on the Pharisees in Matthew ch. 23, one must take into account certain undeniable services that these zealous men had rendered both to God and to the poorer people. By conscientious casuistry, they had shown to many a way in which God's law could be observed with less discomfort than had been imagined. Thus, what they finally decided upon as an irreducible minimum enjoyed an authority destined to constitute an ultimate and insuperable barrier to the people's acceptance of Jesus' message. The Pharisees were excoriated therefore as a test case— not that they were any worse than other men, indeed, quite the contrary—because their very clinging to some fringes of what Jesus came to teach made their resistance more formidable.

Nothing in the comportment of Jesus gave the slightest hint that he would have considered it preferable to transfer the Sabbath observance to any other day.

Doubtless, as in the case of sacrifice, prayer, and fasting, it was at first taken for granted that the little Palestine Christian community ought to observe these regulations ''like the other Jews, only better.'' With the spread of Christianity to a Gentile milieu, especially by Paul, the problem had to be posed and decided: Christians were not bound by Jewish practices as such but only insofar as these embodied the natural law (Acts 15.28–29). When once Jewish devotions were acknowledged to be not binding, it became merely a question of prudence whether they might not nevertheless be profitable; and Paul required circumcision for Timothy though forbidding it for Titus (Acts 16.39; Gal 2.3). Similarly Paul declared exempt from Saturday observance the Christians to whom he wrote in Col 2.16; but in the case of Romans (Rom 14.5) he seems rather to have left the choice of day expressly to the local group or even to the individual. (Gal 4.10 may be rather an ironical comment against Pharisaism.)

Eventually the early Christians on a universal scale deliberately chose Wednesday and Friday as their fasting days simply because the Jews fasted on other days. As for the week's most solemn commemoration of the Lord's new Passover, the more suitable day for this would have been Friday or Thursday (or, in the light of the Qumran calendar, even Tuesday). Still, at this time there was never a question of making attendance at divine service obligatory once a week or connecting the weekly feast with the omission of work.

In the decision to celebrate the weekly festive day of rest on the LORD'S DAY (Sunday), it may even be that

Roman usages played a part, either as in the fixing of the Christmas festival, or in order not to be mixed in with historians' contempt for the Jews' "lazy" and isolating Saturday (McKay p.89f & 176f greatly enlarges customary access to relevant sources). Celebration of the Resurrection itself was not on a Sunday in the more primitive and oriental areas of Christianity but on the Passover fullmoon day itself (*see* QUARTODECIMAN.) Yet obviously the relevance and supremacy of the Easter event can never have been absent from the Christian mind in arriving at the eventual decision. That the transfer from Saturday to Sunday was an operation not of Jerusalem but of Rome is documented by Bacchiocchi (p.132–212; otherwise Callewaert).

Question of So-called Servile Work. The substitution of the first for the seventh day of the week as requiring cultic interruption of work for 24 hours is not even hinted at in Acts 20.7 or 1 Cor 16.2; the celebration of the EUCHARIST or AGAPE was not limited to that one day, especially when the minister was transient. (On the adaptation of the OT Decalogue Sabbath to NT morality by St. Augustine and later Christian writers, see F. Pettirsch.) Clarification of this transferred Sabbath obligation as prohibiting so-called servile work is a rather late tour-de-force of Cajetan (d. 1534). There is no more foundation for it in the Bible than for current efforts to invent a proof that gainful activity is the object of the prohibition [P. Delhaye, *Ami du Clergé* 68 (1958) 225–249].

The term "servile work" comes from St. Jerome's rendering of the Hebrew expression m^{el} e'ket 'ăbōdâ, which means simply "the doing of work," as *opus servile*. Both the Jewish 1963 *Torah* and the 2001 Oxford RSV[3] render the phrase in which the term occurs as "You shall not work at your occupations." Moreover, all the 11 passages of the P strand in which the term is found are concerned, not with the Sabbath, but with feast days other than the Sabbath (Lv 23.7–8, 21, 25, 35–36; Nm 28.18, 25–26; 29.1, 12, 35). The Septuagint translated it as ἔργον λατρευτάον, which the Greek Fathers applied to "a service of sin" (cf. Jn 8.34) or "idolatrous services" [see M. Zalba, *Periodica* 52 (1963) 134].

The truly Biblical observance would have to be a positive rather than a negative thing and to pervade the whole day rather than focus on a half hour of it. It would stress festivity and relaxation but also attention to the things of God and chiefly to the Scripture itself.

Bibliography: J. BRIEND, "Sabbat," *Dictionnaire de la Bible Supplément* 10 (1985) 1132–70. R. DE VAUX, *Ancient Israel, Its Life and Institutions,* tr. J. MCHUGH (New York 1961) 475–483, 550, bibliog. C. KÖRTING, et al., *Theologische Realenzyklopädie* 29 (1998) 518–533. G. HANEL, "Sabbath," *Anchor Bible Dictionary* 5 (1992) 849–856. W. SCHMIDT, *Exodus, Sinai und Mose*[3]: Erträge der Forschung 1994, p. 3 & 110–130; W. RORDORF, *Lexicon für*

Theologie und Kirche 8 (1999) 1401–5; *Sunday, the History of the Day of Rest and Worship in the Earliest Centuries of the Christian Church* (Philadelphia 1968). H. MCKAY, *Sabbath and Synagogue* (Leiden 1994). T. ESKENAZI et al., eds., *The Sabbath in Jewish and Christian Traditions* (New York 1991). S. BACCHIOCCHI, *From Sabbath to Sunday* (Diss., Rome 1977). E. NODET, "A Search for the Origins of Judaism, from Joshua to the Mishnah" (1993), tr. E. CROWLEY, *Journal for the Study of the Old Testament,* supp. 248 (Sheffield 1997). R. GOLDENBERG, "The Jewish Sabbath in the Roman World," *Aufstieg und Niedergang der Römischen Welt* 2.19.1 (Berlin 1979), 411–447. M. STRASSFELD, *Jewish Holidays* (New York 1985). D. CARSON, ed. & pp. 57–97, *From Sabbath to Lord's Day* (Grand Rapids 1982). N. NEGRETTI, *Il settimo giorno, Analecta biblica* 55 (Rome 1973). A. MCCROSSEN, *Holy Day, Holiday: The American Sunday* (Ithaca, N.Y. 2000). K. A. STRAND, ed., *The Sabbath in Scripture and History* (Washington, DC. 1982). N. ANDREASEN, *The OT Sabbath, a Tradition-Historical Investigation* (Diss. 1972). R. NORTH, "The Derivation of Sabbath," *Biblica* 36 (1955) 182–201, with copious bibliog. F. PETTIRSCH, "Das Verbot der *opera servilia* in der Heiligen Schrift und in der altkirchlichen Exegese," *Zeitschrift für katholische Theologie* 69. E. SPIER, "Sabbat:" Das Judentum 1 (Berlin 1989). M. GRUBER, "The Source of the Biblical Sabbath" [not Babylon], *Journal of the Ancient Near Eastern Society* 1, 2 (1969) 14–20. F. MATHYS, "Sabbatruhe und Sabbatfest," *Theologische Zeitschrift* 28 (1972) 241–262. H. CAZELLES, "Ex 34.21 traite-t-il du Sabbat?," *Catholic Biblical Quarterly* 23 (1961) 223–6. B. MALINA, *The Palestinian [Targum] Manna Tradition* (Leiden 1964). J. WEINGREEN, "The Case of the Woodgatherer (Nm 15,32–46)," *Vetus Testamentum* 16 (1966) 361–4 (19 [1969] 125–8 [A. PHILLIPS]). C. CALLEWAERT, "La Synaxe eucharistique de Jérusalem, berceau du Dimanche," *Ephemerides Theologicae Lovanienses* 15 (1938) 34–73.

[R. NORTH]

SABBATH YEAR

An Israelite religious-social institution whereby every seven years Hebrew slaves were set free, debts were canceled, farm-work was forbidden and spontaneous growth reserved to the poor.

The Book of the COVENANT (Ex 20.22–23.19), an ancient body of Israelite laws, contains legislation that, although not concerned with a regularly recurring period of seven years for the whole nation, shows the origin of the later legislation on such universally fixed periods. According to Ex 21.2–6, a Hebrew slave must be given his liberty in the seventh year of his service, unless he prefers to remain with his master for life. Since the text says that the slave must serve for six years, it is obvious that the seven-year period begins whenever he becomes a slave, and no fixed period for the whole nation is involved here.

According to Ex 23.10–11, every seven years a field, vineyard, or olive grove shall be "released and left alone" *tišm^ettennâ ûn^etaštāh,* (usually translated from the context as "let lie untilled and unharvested"), "that the poor among you may eat of it"; the primary purpose of this *š^emiṭṭâ* law (see below) is social justice for the poor and not a matter of taking a year off from work; moreover, it is not stated that the same seven-year period is fixed for all the people, although some exegetes see this implied here by the immediately following law (Ex 23.12) on the regularly recurring Sabbath day.

"Fallow" is the name commonly given to this aspect of the seventh year, which undoubtedly is described in terms akin to the needed agricultural practice. But Hopkins' recent research shows that farming need would require an interval closer to two than seven years. He admits that this need, not envisioned in the Bible, may have coexisted with a seven-year purely ritual "fallow"; such could more understandably have developed into the simultaneously universal cycle of the Jubilee law (Lv 25.1–7).

In Deuteronomy essentially the same law is given regarding the freeing of Hebrew slaves in their seventh year of servitude (Dt 15.12–18, quoted in Jer 34.14), and again obviously not on the basis of a fixed period for the whole nation, even though a general nonobservance of the law occasionally could call for a general emancipation (Heb. d^erôr; cf. Is 51.1) of all Hebrew slaves (Jer 34.8–11). However, in Dt 15.1–11 a period of seven years fixed for all the nation is prescribed for the š^emiṭṭâ that is here described as a relaxation of debts: at the end of every seven-year period Israelites must remit the debts that their fellow Israelites (but not gērîm, resident aliens) owe them. There may have been an older, unpreserved law canceling any debt seven years after it was incurred, but the law as it now stands in its seventh-century B.C. codification clearly prescribes a common š^emiṭṭâ year for all Israel. The same is true for the precept in Dt 31.9–13 prescribing the reading of the Mosaic Law at a general assembly of all Israel on the Feast of Booths "in the š^emiṭṭâ year that comes at the end of every seven-year period."

In Leviticus the term Sabbath year (Heb. š^enat šabbātôn, great Sabbath year) is first used and applied to every seventh year, fixed for all and reckoned as beginning with the seventh year after Israel's first occupation of the land of Canaan (Lv 25.1–7). Although this law, which at least in its present form is postexilic, still repeats the original ideal of letting the poor share in the growth of the seventh year. Essentially it is an extension to the seventh year of the law making the seventh day of the week, the Sabbath, a day of complete rest from farm labor: "during the seventh year the land shall have a complete rest [šabbat šabbātôn], a Sabbath for Yahweh, when you shall neither sow your field nor prune your vineyard" (25.4). To forestall the objection that a whole year without farm work would result in famine, it is stated in Lv 25.18–22 that God will miraculously double the crops of every sixth year. Nothing is said in Lv 25.1–7

about manumission of slaves or remission of debts in the Sabbath year; in Leviticus these obligations are postponed to every seventh Sabbath year, the JUBILEE YEAR (Lv 25.8–17, 23–55).

Actual observance of the idealistic legislation on the Sabbath year is not evidenced until the end of the OT period. In fact, it is expressly stated in 2 Chr 36.21; Lv 26.34 to 35, 43, that before the Exile the Israelites did not let their land have its Sabbath years.

The earliest evidence for the observance of the Sabbath year is in Greco-Roman times, where it is generally mentioned with the great religious fervor caused by some national crisis. A reference is made in 1 Mc 6.49, 53, to the lack of food in Judea on one occasion because it was the seventh year (exact date unknown). Some of the Murabba'āt documents (see DEAD SEA SCROLLS) written at the time of BAR KOKHBA's revolt imply a š^emiṭṭâ year for A.D. 133. Josephus refers to six Sabbath years at wide intervals, though open to queries detailed in Biblica 4 (1953) 501 to 515. According to the Talmud the year (A.D. 69) before the fall of Jerusalem was a Sabbath year. From such data, not always consistent, it is calculated that the year 1958 to 1959 would have been a Sabbath year. The matter is further complicated by the question whether the Sabbath year began with the spring or the fall equinox.

Jewish moralists have never agreed on the nature of the š^emiṭṭâ (whether a full remission or only a moratorium of debts) or on the legality of Hillel's prôsbûl (from the Greek πρὸς βουλῇ βουλευτῶν, at the council of the councillors), whereby a borrower could voluntarily renounce his š^emiṭṭâ rights. But they have always insisted on the Sabbath year as a realistic cultic obligation, legitimately bypassed by a theoretic sale of all lands to a non-Jew for the duration. The seven-year requirements of Exodus, Deuteronomy, and Leviticus show that what they have most in common is the rehabilitation of the bankrupt (Neh 5.1–13), or generically, an assertion of social justice, which is more valid for the present day than calendaric enigmas.

Bibliography: E. LOHSE, G. KITTEL, *Theologisches Wörterbuch zum Neuen Testament* (Stuttgart 1935–) 7:18–20. R. NORTH, *The Biblical Jubilee: After Fifty Years* (Rome 2000) 21–31; "Maccabean Sabbath Years," *Biblica* 34 (1953) 501–15; "Yâd in the Shemittah-Law," *Vetus Testamentum* 4 (1954) 196–99. C. WRIGHT, "What Happened Every Seven Years in Israel?," *Evangelical Quarterly* 56 (1984) 129–38, 193–201. N. LEMCHE, "The Manumission of Slaves The Fallow Year The Sabbatical Year The Jubilee Year," *Vetus Testamentum* 26 (1976) 38–59. D. HOPKINS, *The Highlands of Canaan; Agricultural Life in the Early Iron Age* (Sheffield 1985). L. NEWMAN, *The Sanctity of the Seventh Year*, Brown Judaic Studies 44 (Chico, Calif. 1983).

[R. NORTH]

SABELLIANISM

A trinitarian heresy, named after one of its proponents, the heretic Sabellius (fl. *c.* 220), and theologically defined by the terms MONARCHIANISM or MODALISM, the latter term devised by A. von Harnack. It consists in so emphasizing the unity of the Divine Being as to deny that the Son has a subsistence (or personality) distinct from that of the Father. Sabellianism gave rise to two series of discussions: one in the West, at the close of the 2d century; the other in the East, during the second half of the 3d century.

According to Tertullian (*Adv. Prax.* 1), the first teacher of this doctrine was an Asiatic called Praxeas, who came to Rome under the pontificate of Victor (189–198) (*see* PATRIPASSIANISM). HIPPOLYTUS, however, traces its origin to "a person named Noetus, of Smyrna" (*Philos.* 4.7), whose disciple Epigonos settled in Rome. Epigonos's pupil, Cleomenos, enjoyed the favor of Pope Zephyrinus. Possibly a native of Cyrenaica, Sabellius became a follower of Cleomenos; and if reports from 4th-century authors, notably ATHANASIUS and EPIPHANIUS OF SALAMIS, are accurate, he provided the doctrine with a metaphysical basis. Hippolytus relates further that Sabellius was at first favorably received by Callistus I, then excommunicated when Callistus became pope (217). Thereafter Sabellius may have gone back to his native country to propagate his doctrine, for a trinitarian controversy arose in Cyrenaica in 257 when some bishops hesitated to speak about Christ as the Son of God. Their metropolitan, DIONYSIUS OF ALEXANDRIA, a disciple of Origen, challenged their teaching, but some of the expressions he used in correcting them seemed in turn to be tainted with SUBORDINATIONISM. In answer to an appeal, Pope Dionysius (259–268) wrote against both the Sabellians and their subordinationist opponents and sent a personal letter to Dionysius of Alexandria, who answered with a *Refutation and Apology,* cited by Eusebius (*Praep. evang.* 7.9) and Athanasius (*Ep. de sent. Dion.*). His doctrinal explanations seem to have satisfied the pope.

Bibliography: A. VON HARNACK, *History of Dogma,* tr. N. BUCHANAN et al., ed. A. B. BRUCE, 7 v. (London 1896–99) 3:11–18. TERTULLIAN, *Treatise against Praxeas,* tr. and ed. E. EVANS (Society for Promoting Christian Knowledge, London; 1949) 6–15. J. DANIÉLOU and H. MARROU, *The First Six Hundred Years,* tr. V. CRONIN, v. 1 of *The Christian Centuries* (New York 1964–).

[P. LEBEAU]

SABETTI, LUIGI

Jesuit moral theologian; b. Roseto Valfortore, Two Sicilies, Jan. 3, 1839; d. Baltimore, Maryland, Nov. 26, 1898. Sabetti was the 15th child of Luigi Sabetti, who died three months before his birth, and of Maria Rosa Lapicola. He entered the Jesuit novitiate at La Conocchia in 1855 and was studying philosophy at Naples when the 1860 Garibaldian revolution drove him to France. He continued his studies there at Vals and later taught at the College of Sarlat. Assigned in 1865 to the Roman College, he soon returned to Vals and was ordained there on June 6, 1868.

He came to the U.S. in 1871 for work in the New Mexico missions, but was sent instead to teach at Woodstock College, Maryland. His students found him to be a clear, concise, and sympathetic professor of moral theology who adapted his subject to American conditions. In content and method he was a representative in the U.S. of the school of Hermann BUSENBAUM, Jean Pierre GURY, and Antonio BALLERINI. Cardinal James Gibbons of Baltimore consulted him frequently and followed his opinions in the matters of proposed condemnation of the Knights of Labor (1886) and of the Odd Fellows (1892) [J. T. Ellis, *The Life of James Cardinal Gibbons* 2 v. (Milwaukee 1952) 1:462, 497–498].

In 1884 Sabetti was a theologian of the Third Plenary Council of Baltimore, and in the same year brought out the first edition of *Compendium Theologiae Moralis,* for many years a standard and influential textbook in American seminaries. Thirteen editions were published in the author's lifetime. He also contributed regular articles on moral theology to the *American Ecclesiastical Review.* He is buried at Woodstock, where he had been a professor for 27 years.

Bibliography: R. BROUILLARD, *Dictionnaire de théologie catholique.* ed. A. VACANT et al., (Paris 1903–50) 14.1:438. H. HURTER, *Nomenclator literarius theologiae catholicae* (Innsbruck 1903–13) 5.2:2055–56. "Father Aloysius Sabetti: An Autobiography with Reminiscences," *Woodstock Letters* 29 (1900) 208–233.

[J. HENNESEY]

SABINA OF ROME, ST.

Early Christian martyr and patron of the title church of St. Sabina. Under Pope CELESTINE I (d. 432) the priest Peter of Illyria built a church on the Aventine hill in Rome that in the fifth century was referred to as the *titulus Sabinae* and became the *titulus sanctae Sabinae* in the sixth century. A legendary *passio,* also of the sixth century, describes a Sabina as a widow who together with a Christian Serapia of Antioch (feast: July 29) lived "in the town of the Vendinenses" and was martyred and buried there "ad arcum Faustini." As these locations are unknown to modern archeologists, there is a possibility of a text corruption. However, it is known that the original title of the Roman churches was frequently interpreted by later generations to signify a saint whom the Church honored, instead of the donor or the site of the original church. This confusion was perpetuated in the case of Sabina by the inclusion in the MARTYROLOGY OF ST. JEROME (475) of a virgin and martyr; thence the notice spread to the Capitulary of Würzburg, the St. Gall Sacramentary of Gelasius, and the Gregorian Sacramentary.

Feast: Aug. 29.

Bibliography: ALIPIO DA CELLE LIGURE, *S. Sabina di Samo* (Genoa 1971). A. AMORE, *Lexikon für Theologie und Kirche,* ed. J. HOFER and K. RAHNER, 10 v. (2d, new ed. Freiburg 1957–65) 9:195. *Acta Sanctorum* (Paris 1863–) August 6:496–504. *Bibliotheca hagiographica latina antiquae ct mediae aetatis,* 2 v. (Brussels 1898–1901; suppl. 1911) 7407. M. D. DARSY, *Dictionnaire d'archéologie chrétienneet de liturgie,* ed. F. CABROL, H. LECLERCQ and H. I. MARROU, 15 v. (Paris 1907–53) 15.1:218–238.

[E. HOADE]

SABINIAN, POPE

Pontificate: March 604 to Feb. 22, 606. As a Roman deacon of Tuscan origin, he was the *APOCRISIARIUS* of GREGORY THE GREAT to Constantinople under the Emperor MAURICE and the Patriarch JOHN IV the Faster. This post of papal ambassador at the Byzantine court was proof of Gregory's high esteem for him. But in the storm that arose over John's assumption of the title "ecumenical patriarch"—an act destructive of Christian unity under Rome, according to Gregory's view—Sabinian was too conciliatory and in 595 the Pope wrote: "I am amazed that he [John] has been able to trick you. . . . Fear no man. . . . Do with my total authority whatever must be done in this affair." In 597 Sabinian was recalled and succeeded by Anatolius, but by 602 the Emperor Phocas complained to the pope of the lack of a Roman *apocrisiarius* in Constantinople. Gregory replied that no Roman deacon had been willing to face the difficulties of the papal delegation at the imperial court. The position, despite its difficulties, was for Sabinian, as it had been for Gregory, a preparation for the papacy. Sabinian, elected pope after Gregory's death in March 604, was not consecrated until September 13 after the emperor's approval was received. Famine in central Italy and renewed attacks from the LOMBARDS troubled his short pontificate.

Bibliography: *Liber pontificalis,* ed. L. DUCHESNE (Paris 1886–92) 1:315. P. JAFFÉ, *Regesta pontificum romanorum ab condita ecclesia ad annum post Christum natum 1198,* ed. P. EWALD (repr. Graz 1956) 1:220. H. K. MANN, *The Lives of the Popes in the Early Middle Ages from 590 to 1304* (London 1902–32) 1.1:251–258. E. CASPAR, *Geschichte des Papsttums von den Anfängen bis zur Höhe der Weltherrschaft* (Tubingen 1930–33) v. 2. H. LECLERCQ, *Dictionnaire d'archéologie chrétienne et de liturgie,* ed.

St. Sabina of Rome, detail of a 6th-century mosaic in the basilica of Sant' Apollinare Nuovo, Ravenna, Italy.

F. CABROL, H. LECLERCQ, and H. I. MARROU (Paris 1907–53) 13.1:1227–28. A. FLICHE and V. MARTIN, eds., *Histoire de l'église depuis les origines jusqu'à nos jours* (Paris 1935) 5:391–393. E. KETTENHOFEN, *Biographisch–Bibliographisches Kirchenlexicon* 8 (Herzberg 1994). G. SCHWAIGER, *Lexikon des Mittelalters* 7 (Munich-Zurich 1994–95). J. N. D. KELLY, *Oxford Dictionary of Popes* (New York 1986) 68.

[P. J. MULLINS]

SABRAN, LOUIS DE

Jesuit preacher, chaplain to James II; b. Paris, 1652; d. Rome, 1732. He was the son of the Marquis de Sabran, French Ambassador in London in 1644, and he entered the Society of Jesus in 1670. In 1685 he was appointed royal chaplain to James II, during whose reign he was active as a preacher and controversialist. At the REVOLUTION OF 1688 he was seized at Rochester while trying to escape, but was released by the intervention of James II himself. In 1693 he was appointed procurator of the Jesuit College at Watten and in 1694 he tried to obtain support from German colleagues in Rome against the "probabiliorist" views of the Jesuit General Tirso González. In 1699 Sabran was installed by force of Protestant troops as president of the Episcopal Seminary at Liège, where certain professors had been accused of Jansenism. The archbishop of Malines was at this time conducting an anti-Jansenist campaign and urged the prince-bishop of Cologne (aged 24) to exercise his powers under the Tridentine decrees. As a result a group of English Jesuits from their nearby college, headed by Sabran, was forcibly installed as the staff of this secular clergy seminary. This episode, and Sabran's part in it, was attacked in print by Pasquier Quesnel. Sabran was an active anti-Jansenist, and in 1703 it was he who was responsible for taking some of Quesnel's voluminous archives, which had been seized at Malines, to Louis XIV. It was doubtless his activities in this field that disturbed the English secular clergy and that led to the accusation by Charles Dodd, the historian, that Sabran was guilty of stirring up trouble at the English secular seminary at Douai and that the Jesuits were planning to take it over. Sabran was vice provincial and visitor of the English province (1708–12), and rector of Saint Omer's (1712–15). He continued at Saint-Omer's for two years more as director of the sodality, and from 1717 till his death he was spiritual father at Rome.

Bibliography: H. FOLEY, ed., *Records of the English Province of the Society of Jesus,* 7 v. in 15 (London 1877–82). *A Literary and Biographical History or Bibliographical Dictionary of the English Catholics from 1534 to the Present Time* 5:460–63. H. CHADWICK, *St.-Omer's to Stonyhurst* (London 1962). *Annuaire d'histoire liégeoise* 3 (1947) 663–672. *Bulletin de l'institut historique beige de Rome* 29 (1955) 5–27. L. WILLAERT, *Bibliotheca Janseniana Belgica,* 3 v. (Brussels 1950).

[T. A. BIRRELL]

SACK, FRIARS OF THE

A mendicant order (*ordo penitencie Jesu Christi*) first established on the hill of Fenouillet, outside Hyères, in Provence, approved by INNOCENT IV in 1251, and confirmed by ALEXANDER IV in 1255. There were 13 convents by 1251, and by 1274 the number was well over 100—almost half of them in France, but several in Italy and the British Isles, and a few in Spain, Germany, and the Low Countries. This was the most important order forbidden to receive novices and new sites after the Second Council of Lyons in 1274; it disappeared rather quickly thereafter; the last trace was found in Marseilles in 1316. According to SALIMBENE, the order was founded under Franciscan inspiration; but its constitutions are distinctly Dominican in form. It was a typical mendicant group, clearly enjoying much popularity during its short

existence. By 1274 the order was organized into seven provinces: Provence, France, Spain, Italy, England, Germany, and the Holy Land. There seems no evidence for the existence of a second order of nuns attached to the order. Most of its sites passed to other orders after 1274, sometimes with surviving Sack Friars included in the transfer.

Bibliography: A. G. LITTLE, "The Friars of the Sack," *English Historical Review* 9 (1894) 121–127. R. W. EMERY, "The Friar of the Sack," *Speculum* 18 (1943) 323–334; 35 (1960) 591–595. I. BURNS, "The Friars of the Sack in Valencia," *ibid.,* 36 (1961) 435–438. G. GIACOMOZZI, *L'Ordine della Penitenza di Gesu Cristo* (Rome 1962); on which, cf. *Speculum* 37 (1962) 610.

[R. W. EMERY]

SACRA IAM SPLENDENT

The office hymn that was formerly sung at Matins on the feast of the Holy Family. The hymn has nine unrhymed stanzas, each containing three Sapphic verses and one Adonic. Pope LEO XIII composed the *Sacra iam splendent*—together with the hymns for Vespers, *O lux beam caelitum,* and for Lauds, *O gente felix hospita*—especially for the feast of the Holy Family. The classical form gives graceful expression to many thoughts from Leo's encyclicals.

Bibliography: U. CHEVALIER, *Repertorium hymnologicum* (Louvian-Brussels 1892–1921) 2:487. *Poems, Charades, Inscriptions of Pope Leo XIII,* ed. and tr. H. T. HENRY (New York 1902) 104–115, 282–284. M. BRITT, ed., *The Hymns of the Breviary and Missal* (new ed. New York 1948) 100–107. A. SCHWERD, ed., *Hymnen und Sequenzen* (Munich 1954) 69–70, 113–114. Connelly Hymns 68–71, text and tr.

[G. E. CONWAY]

SACRA VIRGINITAS

Sacra Virginitas is an encyclical of Pius XII (March 25, 1954) on holy virginity "to counteract the contemporary depreciation of the life of perfect chastity." The Holy Father expounds the teaching on consecrated virginity, calls for a true appreciation of its excellence, and defends it strongly against disparaging attacks.

The Christian idea of virginity was derived from the teachings of Christ (Mt 19.10–12). According to the Fathers, it is not a Christian virtue, unless embraced "for the Kingdom of Heaven." It is inspired by the love of Christ; its purpose is to "consecrate body and soul to Him," perpetually. Christian virginity is superior to marriage (Mt 19.10–11; 1 Cor 7.1, 7, 26, 38). It derives its excellence primarily from its higher aims (St. Thomas

Aquinas, *Summa theologiae,* 2a2ae, 152.3, 4). Perfect chastity renounces marriage love but chooses instead a "better one" that is ennobling and "the nearest approach to the love of the Word Incarnate."

In particular, the pope refutes those opinions that so exalt matrimony as to give it precedence over virginity. He shows clearly that those dedicated to Christ by vowing chastity do not stunt their personality; rather, they perfect it thereby. Objection is offered likewise to a type of counseling given to the young that discourages in them priestly and religious vocations.

Virginity is not necessary for Christian perfection; in the words of St. Ambrose, it is "not imposed but proposed" (*De Viduis,* 12.72). The Holy Father elaborates on the following means: vigilance and prayer (commended by Christ), the Sacraments, modesty, mortification, and devotion to Mary.

See Also: VIRGINITY.

Bibliography: PIUS XII, "Sacra virginitas," (Encyclical, March 25, 1954) *Acta Apostolicae Sedis,* 46 (1954) 161–191; Eng. tr. *Catholic Mind* 52 491–512. P. DE LETTER, "Sacra virginitas," *Clergy Monthly* 18 201–212.

[A. A. BIALAS]

SACRAMENTAL THEOLOGY

Sacramental theology is the systematic study of the sacraments based on reflection on the liturgical celebration of these rites throughout history and on the insights of theologians and other teachers in light of the magisterium. At given historical periods certain theological points came to be emphasized, sometimes for polemical reasons, and assertions of the magisterium clarified issues of conflict. The following overview is divided into historical periods. In each section attention is given to those aspects of the ritual enactment of the sacraments in that period that required particular theological reflection and to assertions of the magisterium, which assertions are best understood in their historical context. That the contemporary period is treated more fully reflects the disciplinary complexity and richness of sacramental theology today and the significant contributions made to the discipline since Vatican II. For more information on specific rites recourse should be made to articles on particular sacraments and to the historical evolution of the liturgy.

The Church's magisterium has never given a definition of the term "sacrament." In its teaching at the Councils of Trent and Vatican II there is insistence on certain essential characteristics of "sacraments" but no authen-

Orthodox priest administers sacrament to kneeling woman, Metropolitan Dabrobocanski Vladislav Orthodox Church, Sarajevo, Bosnia, Herzegovina, Yugoslavia. (©Dean Conger/ CORBIS)

tic binding definition. Succinctly put, sacraments are visible signs chosen by Christ and celebrated ritually in the community of the Church to draw the Church into an experience of Christ's paschal mystery by means of liturgical actions enacted through the power of the Holy Spirit under the agency of the Church's ordained ministers. The word "sacrament" is the English equivalent of the Latin *sacramentum,* which, in turn, is one of the renderings of the Greek word for "mystery." Thus an understanding of "sacrament" demands some appreciation of the significance of "mystery." beginning with the Scriptures.

Scriptural Data. The biblical authors have written about what have come to be called sacramental celebrations either directly in describing liturgical rites or indirectly when emphasizing aspects of the biblical experience of God. This follows from the very nature of revelation itself as the intervention of God in human history. In sum the fulfillment of the event of revelation is

"The Sacrament of the Last Supper," by Salvador Dali. (AP/Wide World Photos)

Christ, toward whom the Old Testament leads. Among others there are at least three essential aspects of the biblical witness that ground the Church's experience of this revelation in sacramental liturgy. (1) God spoke and acted among the chosen people of Israel. The repeated proclamation of God's word through the Scriptures characterizes every act of liturgy and sacrament. This derives from the biblical experience of God and the codification of God's revelation in the Scriptures. (2) The corporate nature of God's revelation to a chosen people and the corporate response of that people to God through conversion to biblical faith ritualized in liturgy and (what have come to be called) sacraments derives from the biblical witness. Israel's and the Church's nature as a corporate entity is an essential principle for understanding sacraments. (3) A further foundation for understanding liturgy and sacraments derives from the Hebrew notion of "memorial" wherein events of saving history, although accomplished once for all (*ephapa*), are perpetuated and thus experienced in the present which present experience leads to yearning for their fulfillment in the future (the time of their fulfillment). Corporate ritual acts of memorial, recalling God's intervention in saving history in the Scriptures (*mirabilia Dei*) are centered on the Exodus and Christ's dying and rising (i.e. his paschal mystery). The

contemporary rediscovery of the Jewish background to Christian liturgy in terms of "corporate person" and "memorial" (*anamnesis*) as well as the study of specific rites and texts in the Scriptures lead to a revitalized theology of sacraments as corporate actions and events of salvation.

Among the several senses in which "mystery" was used in the Old Testament two are especially important for our purpose: (1) the divine plan for the salvation of the human race and (2) the revelation of this plan to Israel. As used in the Gospel, "mystery" refers to the coming of the messianic kingdom in Christ. The gospel parables of the kingdom furnish some indications about what this divine reality is; in the writings of Paul the meaning of "mystery" is most fully developed. For him it includes: the divine plan of salvation in Christ; this plan hidden before creation; its manifestation by the Spirit through the Prophets and Apostles; Christ, who is the mystery manifested in His Incarnation and glorification; and Christ in us who receive salvation here and now, which salvation is to be completed at the end of time. The early writers of the Church both presumed and retained the various meanings of "mystery" found in Scripture.

In pagan writings *sacramentum* was applied to the rites of Christian initiation but by no means exclusively. Etymologically, *sacramentum* is derived from *sacrare*, meaning a person or thing constituted by divine right, a function reserved for public authority, the one who performed the consecration, the consecration itself, the person or thing consecrated, and the means used to effect it. The oath taken by soldiers was a *sacramentum* as they called upon the gods in binding themselves to service. This is an instance of an initiation with religious significance. *Sacramentum* was used also of the money placed in a sacred place by litigants. While the word "sacrament" had many meanings in Scripture and early ecclesiastical writings, the two concepts of a sacred secret and its manifestation are central.

Sacraments and the Paschal Mystery. From the moment of the Incarnation Christ the priest offered all He did in honor of His Father for the salvation of the human race. This priestly work was one of worship. All pointed to the "hour" of Christ, the hour to which reference is made throughout His life as not yet having come. This hour was the Pasch of Christ, His passing over from mortal life through death to resurrection and glory. It was the summit of His redeeming work.

Leo I once said, "What was visible in Christ has passed over into the Sacraments of the Church" (*Sermo* 74; *Patrologia Latina* 54:398). What was visible in Christ was His loving worship of His Father, in view of which the Father raised Him from the dead and in so doing brought into existence a race of which Christ, the second Adam, is Head. This is the Church, the community of the redeemed. The greatest evidence of Christ's loving worship is His Pasch. This event was the birth of the Church of the New Testament. From the time of Christ's Resurrection what had been accomplished in His mortal body continues in His Body, the Church. The visible Church is thus the sign of Christ in our day. What eyewitnesses saw in Him while on earth is now manifested in the Church. The dominant note of Christ's life was His worship of the Father. The dominant note of the Church is likewise the worship of the Father through the Son in the Holy Spirit. This worship is the summit and fount of all the Church does according to Vatican Council II (*Constitution on the Sacred Liturgy* 10). The Church's worship is centered in the Sacraments. In these acts Christ's redemptive work of worship continues to render salvation present.

Having been raised from the dead and seated at the right hand of the Father, Christ is the accepted sacrifice, the lamb, immolated and glorified, the heavenly sacrifice. Christ in heaven is ever making intercession for us. Since we must come in contact with this accomplished salvation if we are to be part of the race of the second Adam, this heavenly worship becomes visibly present in the Church through the Sacraments. They are the means by which people are drawn into the Pasch of Christ, once and for all accepted by the Father, operating among us through the power and work of the Holy Spirit. They are the means by which the Church brings to fulfillment the Redemption accomplished in Christ.

Patristic Period. The earliest ecclesiastical writers were guided by the needs of their times, principally people's preparation for the acceptance of Christ and the refutation of errors. Not surprisingly, the rites of Christian initiation (Baptism and Chrismation, later termed Confirmation) and its completion in the Eucharist were their main subject. The earliest of these writers include Justin, Irenaeus, the *Shepherd of Hermas*, and the author of the Didache. Some of these writings were principally apologetic, for example the defense of the Church's use of material creation in sacraments as opposed to those Gnostics or Manichees who shunned such usage and respect for created things. Tertullian wrote on Baptism and Penance, and the church order *The Apostolic Tradition* (traditionally attributed to HIPPOLYTUS) furnishes information regarding Christian practices, especially initiation and the Eucharist.

With the advent of the controversy on rebaptism of heretics came a considerable number of writings on this sacrament. The great catechetical works of SS. Gregory of Nyssa, Cyril of Jerusalem, and Ambrose are devoted mainly to initiation. Other writers do not present specialized or systematic works on the Sacraments but reflect contemporary teaching and practice. A chief exemplar of the kind of sacramental theology in the patristic era comes from St. AUGUSTINE. In his conflict with the Donatists he delineated aspects of baptismal theology that had not caught the attention of previous writers. For Augustine the term "sacrament" is used in a variety of ways and three classes of things are called sacraments: (1) religious rites of both Testaments and of paganism, (2) symbols or figures, and (3) revealed teachings of the Christian religion. These meanings are not mutually exclusive; the rites of the Old Testament are said to be symbols of those of the New. All Sacraments are related to the great sacrament-mystery, Christ and the Church. In connection with subsequent developments the following aspects of Augustine's teaching are significant: Sacraments are sacred signs; they bear a similitude to those things of which they are Sacraments; they are celebrations commemorating an event in such a way that what is signified is received. A different trend is seen in Isidore of Seville, who stressed the secret nature of the Sacraments as being concerned with hidden realities rather than the characteristics that Augustine noted and especially those that speak of them as signs.

One of the customary ways for the Church to speak of the sacramental rites (especially from the Middle Ages onward) is that they are comprised of two elements: matter and form. Attention is often drawn to scripture's reference to two elements in five of the Sacraments (Eph 5.26; Jn 3.5; Mt 28.19; Acts 8.14–17; Mt 26.26–28; Jas 5.14; Acts 6.6; 1 Tm 4.14). Reflecting on these passages and on the sacramental rites themselves, theologians have observed these as parallel realities in the visible rites. The early Fathers before Augustine distinguished these two elements as objects (*res,* such as water, oil, bread) and prayers that sanctified them. Later this distinction was expressed in the terms ''word'' (*verbum*) and ''element.'' Augustine furnished the formula that was the basis for later comment: ''The word comes to the element and a sacrament results'' (*In Ioh. hom.* 80.2; *Patrologia Latina* 35:1840). It should be noted that by *verbum* Augustine did not exclusively mean essential words such as the words of consecration. Studies indicate that the patristic understanding of *verbum* was very comprehensive (see Fransen).

Early Medieval Period. In the centuries immediately following Augustine there was little advance in the study of Sacraments in general. From the 9th through the 11th centuries attention on sacraments focused on Eucharistic controversies over how to describe the reality of the symbolic presence of Christ in the Eucharist. Important authors of this century were PASCHASIUS RADBERTUS, RATRAMNUS OF CORBIE, LANFRANC, and BERENGARIUS OF TOURS. In the 12th century the movement of synthesis began; the outstanding names are those of HUGH OF SAINT-VICTOR and PETER LOMBARD. It was Lonbard who introduced the term ''cause'' into treatises describing what sacraments accomplished. Lombard's summary of Catholic teaching, *Liber Sententiarum,* was the most widely followed in the commentaries of subsequent theologians. With regard to the Eucharist the terms of the debates in these centuries ultimately concerned the polarities of empty symbolism and crass realism. The patristic language that sustained a Eucharistic presence which was both real and symbolic was hard to sustain in succeeding centuries. (It remains the challenge for the Church in any age.)

The codifying of the theology of the Sacraments at this period was a masterful accomplishment. The teaching found in Scripture and in the treatment of the earlier periods was arranged in a system (e.g., Lombard's *Liber*). Questions that had not been posed previously began to suggest themselves. With the search for a definition of ''sacrament,'' notes common to all seven rites began to

be observed. It was only at this time that the tract ''sacraments in general'' came to be written. Matters that had been implicit in much that the Fathers, especially Augustine, had said were examined and explained at greater length. Thus the great *summae* were not merely compilations of familiar material but thrust ideas forward, especially in the area of speculative theology. Largely because the liturgy was celebrated in a language foreign to the people's vernacular and was done by clerics on behalf of a (largely passive) faithful the liturgy as a prime influence on the theology of sacraments was severely diminished.

Scholastic Period. With the systematic treatment of the 12th and 13th centuries the terms ''element'' and ''word'' were replaced with ''matter'' and ''form.'' These were borrowed from HYLOMORPHISM, in which material beings were spoken of as explainable according to an undetermined principle and one that specifies it.

St. Thomas explains the analogous use of these terms as follows. Words can be used in diverse ways to signify different mental concepts, and thus we express our thoughts more distinctly by words than in other ways. In sacramental signification the meaning of sensible objects used (matter) is determined by words (form) just as, according to hylomorphism, the undetermined element (matter) is determined by its form. The water in Baptism, for instance, can of itself signify ablution or cooling, but with the addition of the baptismal formula it becomes evident that this use of water signifies spiritual cleansing (see Aquinas, *Summa theologiae* 3a, 60.6). Together the two elements in Sacraments compose one sign.

The common use of this convenient terminology has often given the impression that the only part of the sacramental sign that is of real importance is that which composes the essential matter and form, that is, the minimum words absolutely required that the Sacrament be truly such. It is the more limited understanding of the term ''form'' as the absolutely essential words together with the presence of suitable ''matter'' that became the framework in which questions of the validity of Sacraments were judged. However this emphasis led to a lessening of appreciation for the whole sign, all that the Church does in her sacramental worship and the importance of the acts of the person involved in sacramental encounters. Happily, a corrective is afforded with the revival of a fuller understanding of the sacramental sign and the reflection of this renewal in the *Constitution on the Sacred Liturgy* of Vatican Council II.

Another influence of this era was the work done in the canonical field. In the collections of the 11th and 12th centuries, chief among them the *Decree of Gratian,* there is much that is theological and notably influential on the presentation of sacramental teaching. [*See* GRATIAN, DE-CRETUM OF (Concordantia Discordantium Canonum).]

The 13th century brought the greatest of the scholastic writers, St. THOMAS AQUINAS, disciple of St. ALBERT THE GREAT. The astounding influence of St. Thomas upon Catholic sacramental theology, even today, through his own writings and those of contemporary commentators on him (e.g., Karl Rahner, Edward Schillebeeckx and to an extent Louis-Marie Chauvet) can be explained only by his unusual combination of qualities (*see* THOMISM). Another school of theology arose about the same time and developed into a system called SCOTISM or the Franciscan school, the chief personalities of which were ALEXANDER OF HALES, St. BONAVENTURE, and John DUNS SCOTUS.

One of the most important issues to emerge from Lombard through the great Scholastics was how to describe that sacraments effect what they signify. Lombard is the first author to use the word "cause" to describe the effects of sacraments (*Summa Sententiarum* 1, IV). The Sacraments of the New Law are unique among signs because of their causal efficacy. To understand this causality properly it is necessary to remember that sacraments are signs, and they cause grace precisely in accord with their nature. They effect what they signify (*Summa theologiae* 3a, 62.1); they are signs that cause what they signify and cause by signifying.

Since the 13th century, at least, it has been common to express the unique efficacy of the Sacraments in the phrase *EX OPERE OPERATO*, an expression adopted by the Council of Trent (H. Denzinger, *Enchiridion symbolorum* 1608). Its meaning is that the grace given is the effect of the rite. What it highlights is the fact that grace is a gift of God, not the accomplishment of human effort on the part of the minister or the one who receives the Sacrament. It is meant as a corrective of the view that holds that the Sacraments are only external signs of grace received through faith. The Council of Trent defined the operation of the Sacraments by saying that they contain the grace they signify and confer it on those properly responsive (*ibid.* 1606).

It is commonly admitted that the phrase *ex opere operato* has often been misinterpreted in such a way as to make the Sacraments seem mechanistic means for obtaining grace rather than as encounters with Christ's saving action in the power of the Holy Spirit. A helpful insight has been afforded in the observation that the phrase is parallel to *ex opere Christi* (Fransen 17–22).

This doctrine was never meant to imply that the believing Church does not have an essential role to fulfill in his own sanctification. Without our response to Christ's saving actions (*ex opere operantis*) sacraments are not true to their nature as effective signs. But to say that the response of humans in sacraments is a requisite for grace is not the same as saying that the effect of the Sacraments is our work. Whatever grace we receive sacramentally is Christ's gift, but as in every gift, it must be willingly received; when one does not respond to Christ's action, there is no effect.

Theologians have long speculated on the manner in which the Sacraments confer (Trent *conferat*) or cause grace. This effort has resulted in many theories. It is common teaching today that any suggested explanation must present the Sacraments as more than mere occasions on which God gives grace, for this latter explanation does not seem to do justice to the evidence of Scripture, tradition, and the statements of the Church. The two main divisions of opinion from the Scholastic era are the theories of physical and moral causality. In addition, individual writers have proposed distinct explanations of their own [see L. Billot, *De Ecclesiae Sacramentis* (Rome 1931) 52–144; Van Roo 263–348].

Proponents of physical causality teach that the sacramental rite is directly involved in the infusion of grace in a manner analogous to that in which an instrument, such as a pen or a brush, is said to be the cause of an effect, the written page or picture. Adherents of this school of thought see St. Thomas as their model (*Summa theologiae* 3a, 62). Physical causality is divided into dispositive and perfective. The first considers the action of the sacramental rite as terminating in a physical disposition exigent of grace. The latter posits a physical influence in the rite that reaches efficiently to the grace itself.

Those who teach moral causality think of the Sacraments as effecting God's granting grace by reason of their inner worth as actions of Christ, in view of which grace is infallibly infused by God (B. Leeming 283–381).

With the *summae* of the 12th and 13th centuries the first systematic definitions appear. Chief among these is that of St. Thomas Aquinas, "A Sacrament is a sign of a sacred thing in as much as it sanctifies" (*Summa theologiae* 3a, 60.2).

St. Thomas speaks of the Sacraments as signs of three things: the Passion of Christ, grace, and glory (*ibid.* 3a, 60.3). In this teaching he shows himself to be in accord with the descriptions of the Sacraments in Scripture, where they appear as signs of Redemption. The clearest instance is Romans 6, in which Baptism is described as our burial and resurrection with Christ. In this and the other Sacraments Christ's work of redemption becomes ours sacramentally, that is, through the signs of that salvation; and by reason of this we are given God's life, grace. Again, since grace is the seed of glory and the ultimate effect of what Christ does sacramentally is our glorification, each Sacrament is a sign of this culmination of the Christian life. St. Thomas's teaching that the Sacraments are signs is obviously in keeping with the patristic descriptions (especially from St. Augustine) which speak of them as belonging to this genus. It is true that with the development of scholastic theology attention was drawn to the fact that these signs are causes of the grace they signify. However, in his treatment St. Thomas kept the proper balance, seeing them as signs that cause and that do so in accord with their nature as signs.

One of the contributions of scholastic reflection and the systematic presentation of sacramental doctrine during the 12th and 13th centuries has been the distinction of three elements in the Sacraments: (1) the sign that causes and is not itself caused, that is, the rite itself called *sacramentum tantum;* (2) the sacramental grace that is signified and caused but does not signify and cause, that is, the *res tantum;* (3) the element that is both signified and caused (by the *sacramentum tantum*) and itself signifies and causes the *res tantum* (in conjunction with the *sacramentum tantum*), that is, the *res et sacramentum,* or symbolic reality. The precise identification of this last in each individual Sacrament need not be introduced here; it is sufficient to mention that it is generally taught that such a ''middle term'' does exist in each of the seven. For Baptism, Confirmation, and Holy Orders the *res et sacramentum* is the sacramental character. While variously described, sacramental character refers to sacraments which cannot be repeated and to the fact that these sacraments configures one to Christ in a particular way (belonging, ministering).

The distinction among the three elements is helpful in speaking of the difference between a Sacrament that is merely validly received and one that actually imparts grace, or is fruitful. Whenever the minimum conditions on the part of the recipient are realized, presuming all else to be present on the part of the minister and the rite itself, the Sacrament is truly received; that is, the *res et sacramentum* is verified even if, through lack of disposition, grace is not infused.

For the valid and fruitful reception of Baptism in the case of an infant, no personal act is required since such is manifestly impossible. In adults there can never be a validly received Sacrament without a willingness to encounter God (at least an ''habitual'' intention) and, in all Sacraments other than Baptism, the previous reception of this initial Sacrament. For the Sacrament to attain its purpose, the infusion or increase of grace, there must be, in the Sacraments of Baptism and Penance, a true sorrow for sins and in the other five the life of grace. It is customary

in theological circles to speak of the absence of a requirement in the recipient as an obstacle (*obex*); one that prevents valid reception is an obstacle to the Sacrament and one that prevents fruitful reception is an obstacle to grace. In speaking of the Sacraments, it is ordinarily presumed that the conditions necessary for the reception of this grace are verified; only then does the sign fulfill its function of granting a share in God's life. There are, however, certain factors that give rise to exceptional circumstances in which the full effect is frustrated. To understand these it is necessary to speak of the distinction between valid and fruitful reception.

Theologians speak of the REVIVISCENCE of Sacraments. This refers to the situation in which a Sacrament, validly received, is unfruitful because of an obstacle to grace. In some instances the grace of the Sacrament is obtained subsequently when the defect of disposition is supplied (Schillebeeckx 147–152).

The Council of Florence in 1439 issued the *Decree for the Armenians*, containing a summary of sacramental teaching; it was an excerpt from the bull *Exsultate Deo* of Eugene IV. The decree is taken almost word for word from a work of St. Thomas, *De articulis fidei et ecclesiae sacramentis.* These decrees helped to frame assertions about sacraments in general which would result from the deliberations at the Council of Trent.

Reformation. It was not until the 16th century at the Council of Trent that the Church defined the truth that there are seven Sacraments of the New Law, no more or no less (H. Denzinger, *Enchiridion symbolorum* 1601). The reasons for this late official statement were mainly the gradual development of the term ''sacrament,'' which was for centuries applied to many things other than the seven saving rites of the New Law and the absence until this time of a challenge of the sacramentality of some of them.

The formula that there are seven and only seven Sacraments of the New Law was first set down in the 12th century as a result of the theological reflection and systematic presentation that commenced at that time. Before it had been determined what a Sacrament (in the sense limited to the seven saving rites of the New Law) consisted in, but it was impossible to enumerate those to which such a definition applied uniquely. There were from the beginning the seven saving rites, but they were not distinguished as ''Sacraments'' in our present sense of the word until a definition of this term was crafted. In the course of the development of sacramental theology it became evident that these seven rites, which had existed from the beginning, held a unique place in the economy of salvation. The delineation of the number *seven* began only with Peter Lombard. The number symbolism of seven (three plus four) is important. In some medieval authors "three" signified the Trinity, hence the divine part of the sacraments. "Four" delineated either the four directions (north, south, east, west) or the seasons (spring, summer, fall, and winter). Thus the divine and the cosmic were combined to reflect on the description and nature of "seven" sacraments. (Leeming 553–589).

That all the Sacraments of the New Law were instituted by Christ is a dogma of the Church (H. Denzinger, *Enchiridion symbolorum* 1601). Theologians differ about how to describe Christ's instituting the sacraments; commonly they distinguish between "explicit" and "implicit" or "immediate" and "mediate" institution. In these categories the New Testament evidence of baptism in water and sharing the eucharistic bread and cup are taken as evidence of "explicit," "immediate" institution. The other sacraments are deemed implicitly instituted by Christ; the Church was responsible for delineating how these sacred rites derived from Christ.

Modern Period. From the time of the great scholastic theologians there many definitions of sacrament have been suggested, but these have been in general reflections of the teachings of the masters. In the 1960s attempts were made at more comprehensive definitions in terms of Christ and the Church, e.g., those of K. Rahner and E. Schillebeeckx. This reexamination of the notion of Sacrament provides definitions that expressly mention elements such as personal encounter, the ecclesial dimension, and worship, which had not received proper attention in previous attempts to describe the sacramental mysteries. It is this new insight that is apparent in what Vatican Council II's *Constitution on the Sacred Liturgy* says: "The purpose of the Sacraments is to sanctify participants, to build up the body of Christ, and, finally, to give worship to God; because they are signs they also instruct. They not only presuppose faith, but by words and objects they also nourish, strengthen, and express it; that is why they are called 'Sacraments of faith.' They do indeed impart grace, but, in addition, the very act of celebrating them most effectively disposes the faithful to receive this grace in a fruitful manner, to worship God duly, and to practice charity" (59).

Though it is Christ who acts in the Sacraments to transform us into His Body, He does this through His Spirit. The New Testament clearly speaks of the Holy Spirit as guiding Christ throughout His mortal life. Through His passover from the flesh through death to glory, Christ made it possible for humans to be enlivened by this same Spirit. "For the Spirit had not yet been given, since Jesus had not yet been glorified" (Jn 7.39). The gift of the Spirit was as the soul of the Church. "After Christ's glorification on the cross, His Spirit is communicated to the Church in an outpouring, so that she and her individual members may become more and more like to our Savior" (Pius XII, *Mystici corporis* 56).

The liturgy is the exercise of the priestly work of Christ; that is, it is the exercise in the Church of those acts of worship by which salvation comes to us. This salvation is the work of the Spirit. In Biblical terms this means that the Redemption, which Christ accomplished for the entire human race, may be described as the gift of the Holy Spirit. Since the Sacraments are the chief acts of the liturgy, they are the principal means by which we are given the Spirit.

Because the Sacraments are the main actions by which Christ's priestly work of worship and salvation begun at the Incarnation continues in our times, Christ is the principal priest in every sacramental action, as Vatican Council II makes clear (*Constitution on the Sacred Liturgy* 7). Because the plan of Redemption is a sanctifying work in which humanity has an essential part, the sacramental system is constituted by human's sharing in Christ's powers in the Church. Christ alone can offer the saving worship that makes us one with the Father; since the Resurrection He offers it sacramentally through the willing cooperation of His Church.

Within that Body Christ consecrates certain members that they may bring into the midst of the congregation his saving acts of worship. Such are called ministers of the Sacraments. Their very name implies that they are Christ's agents for the benefit of the Church and, ultimately, of all people. There is no question that salvation could take place otherwise; but given God's plan, so considerate of our nature, the Church possesses his acts through the sharing by her members in his powers. This participation comes through Baptism and Confirmation, on the one hand, and by Holy Orders, on the other. Only those who share in Christ's priestly powers through sacramental characters can be the instruments by which Christ worships with his Church and thus sanctifies participants. For marriage Christ acts through the priesthood of the laity. For all others, save Baptism in exceptional cases, the minister is one who has received Holy Orders. Since every sacramental action is at once an act of Christ and his Church, those who perform these sacred rites are ministers of the Church as well as of Christ. Even in the case in which a non-Christian baptizes, there must be present the intention (at least implicit) of doing what the Church does.

It is God's plan that humans be saved through the divine-human Jesus Christ. In Sacraments God works through the human nature of Christ's ministers. This is not possible without the willingness of humans to serve in this way; ministers must exercise their powers by free choice. The Sacraments are not magic. In the course of theological history many distinctions have become accepted as guides to judging the presence of the requisite human freedom in ministers or what is called their intention. It is agreed that they must at least intend to perform the rite as a sacred action. This requirement is spoken of as the presence of internal intention. Anything less is insufficient (external intention). There are also distinctions regarding the intensity of intention: actual, elicited at the time; virtual, previously elicited by continuing to influence action; habitual, previously elicited but not consciously operating; interpretative, a supposition on the part of others regarding the mind of another. For the administration of Sacraments, it is said that actual or virtual intentions are required; for their reception a habitual intention suffices. The discussion regarding sufficient intention is obviously the result of a desire to set minimum guides to assure the essential conditions of sacramental acts; they were never meant as models of Christian response. The greater our openness to God, the closer we have Christ's mind in us, the nearer we are to a proper attitude.

Each of the Sacraments is meant to give, restore, or intensify the Christ-life in His members. Each does so in a particular way indicated in the sign that constitutes it. This sacramental grace is the immediate end of each sacramental encounter, and its ultimate end is the glory of which grace is the seed. (See GRACE, SACRAMENTAL for a scholastic presentation of this topic.)

Vatican II. The theological foment and liturgical movement prior to Vatican II helped to refocus attention on sacraments as the church's chief means ''to sanctify participants, to build up the body of Christ, and, finally, to give worship to God; because they are signs they also instruct. They not only presuppose faith, but by words and objects they also nourish, strengthen, and express it; that is why they are called 'Sacraments of faith.' They do indeed impart grace, but, in addition, the very act of celebrating them most effectively disposes the faithful to receive this grace in a fruitful manner, to worship God duly, and to practice charity'' (59).

The Church prolongs the priestly mission of Jesus Christ mainly by means of the sacred liturgy. Once Christ had passed over through death to the life of glory, His worship of the Father was definitively accepted. Nothing could be added to this perfect atonement. Yet everyone must be drawn into this worship if they are to live the new life. For us, then, the eternal worship, forever accepted by the Father in the Resurrection and Ascension, is made present on earth. This takes place in and through the Church; the acts of this worship are primarily the Sacraments, centered in the Eucharist. Since the Resurrection

true Christian worship (the saving worship of Christ) consists in the sacramentalizing of the heavenly worship that Christ is forever offering at the Father's right hand. This sacramental worship is made ours when Christ acts in and with His Church. As He worshiped the Father while on earth and thus saved all peoples, so He now offers this same worship in the Church.

The *Constitution on the Sacred Liturgy* ushered in a new era for the church's celebration of the liturgy and sacraments. Its first chapter offers both a synthesis if what the liturgy is and does (nn. 1–20) and general principles for the reform of the liturgy (nn. 21–46). Chapters 2 to 7 specify the areas where liturgical reform is necessary and offer general principles for this task. Clearly this Constitution, the other decrees from Vatican II and the theological preparations for the council mark a watershed in the church's self understanding in general and for liturgical-sacramental theology in particular.

Bibliography: J. AUER, *A General Treatise of the Sacraments and The Mystery of the Eucharist* (Washington 1995). L. BOUYER, *Liturgical Piety* (Notre Dame, Ind. 1955). A. CHUPUNGCO, *Sacraments and Sacramentals*, v. 4 (Handbook of Liturgical Studies; Collegeville, Minn. 2000). J. DANIÉLOU, *The Bible and the Liturgy* (Notre Dame, Ind. 1956). C. DAVIS, *Liturgy and Doctrine* (New York 1960). G. L. DIEKMANN, *Come, Let Us Worship* (Baltimore 1961). E. DORONZO, *Tractatus dogmaticus de sacramentis in genere* (Milwaukee 1946). R. DUFFY, ''Sacraments in General,'' in *Systematic Theology*, v. 2, eds. F. FIORENZA and J. GALVIN (Philadelphia 1991) 179–210. P. F. FRANSEN, *Faith and the Sacraments* (London 1958). J. FINKENZELLER, *Die Sakramente im allgemeinen. Band IV. Handbuch der Dogmengeschichte* (Wien 1982). B. LEEMING, *Principles of Sacramental Theology* (new ed. Westminster, Md. 1960). A. G. MARTIMORT, *The Church At Prayer* (Collegeville, Minn. 1986). J. H. MILLER, *Signs of Transformation in Christ* (Englewood Cliffs, N.J. 1963). K. RAHNER, *The Church and the Sacraments*, tr. W. J. O'HARA (New York 1963). A. M. ROGUET, *Christ Acts Through the Sacraments* (Collegeville, Minn. 1953). E. SCHILLEBEECKX, *Christ: The Sacrament of the Encounter with God* (New York 1963). C. S. SULLIVAN, ed., *Readings in Sacramental Theology* (Englewood Cliffs, N.J. 1964). C. VAGAGGINI, *Theological Dimensions of the Liturgy*, tr. L. J. DOYLE (Collegeville, Minn. 1959). W. A. VAN ROO, *De sacramentis in genere* (2d ed. Rome 1960). H. VORGRIMLER, *Sacramental Theology*, tr. L. MALONEY (Collegeville, Minn. 1992).

Contemporary Sacramental Theology. Contemporary sacramental theology continues to be influenced by the seminal works of E. Schillebeeckx and K. RAHNER who reinterpreted classical Catholic teaching on the seven Sacraments (particularly that of Thomas Aquinas) in terms of the important shift in systematic theology at the time, the turn to the subject. Here the seven Sacraments are appreciated as encounters with Christ as the basic sacrament (Schillebeeckx) in the context of the Church as foundational sacrament (Rahner). Their emphasis on symbolic causality and on the active engagement of participants in sacraments helped to overcome lingering quasi-magical understandings of *ex opere operato* causality.

More recently sacramental theologians have critiqued and moved beyond these approaches by giving new interpretations to classical Catholic sacramental teaching, thereby indicating that the context and method of modern Catholic systematic theology has moved significantly beyond preconciliar parameters. The following factors (among others) have fostered a significant reshaping of contemporary sacramental theology: the recontextualization of sacraments within a broad notion of sacramentality and ECCLESIOLOGY, the postconciliar liturgical renewal, increased ecumenical dialogue, and the influence of sacramental practice on sacramental theology (including the work of liberation theologians). Other voices from systematic theology which today influences sacramental theology are Hans Urs von BALTHASAR, Henri de LUBAC and Louis Bouyer. Von Balthasar emphasizes a soteriology focused on the cross as the manifestation of divine love and the bride/bridegroom imagery of salvation through Christ. Thus he finds the Church's form in complementarity of Mary's spirituality to the pastoral office, especially expressed in the office of Peter.

Sacramentality. Major advances have recently been made in recontextualizing the celebration of the seven Sacraments. Historical studies on patristic sacramental catecheses reveal a broad notion of sacramentality within which the rites of initiation were placed. The gestures, symbols and texts of the rites themselves were the basis of explanations of sacraments founded on the notion of creation and human life as disclosive of God's presence, which presence is particularly experienced through the sacramental use of symbols, gestures, and texts. Studies on the evolution of the term ''sacrament'' and the determination of the number seven have disclosed that prior to the mid-12th century the rites now designated as sacraments were often listed alongside other things such as the Paschal Mystery itself, liturgical seasons, rites for the dedication of a church, etc., all of which were called ''sacraments,'' thus indicating even here a wide notion of what was sacramental.

Basing themselves on an incarnational approach to theology in general, contemporary sacramental theologians have come to emphasize all of life as disclosive of God's presence. Where the linking of the human and the Christian life (or secular with the sacred) has been a hallmark of Rahner's theology in general (often pointing to Jesus as the paradigm of the one who fully realized this fusion), it clearly marks some of his essays in which liturgy and sacraments are understood as part of the continuum of the graced life experienced in all of life as well as

in sacraments specifically. This insight has led contemporary sacramental theologians to emphasize the life setting and life relation of sacraments in such a way that the experience and discovery of God's presence, as offered in human life, is established as the necessary setting for engagement in specific sacramental activity. Here liturgy and sacraments function as strong moments of encounter with God but they are not exclusive channels of grace. Similarly sacraments are seen as privileged but provisional experiences of God's presence which will be finally and fully realized only in the kingdom. They are regarded as unique but not the exclusive locus for communicating with God who is revealed in all life.

Closely allied with this is an appreciation of the role of creation in liturgy and sacraments as well as the sacramentality of creation itself as foundational for the very celebration of liturgy and sacraments. One particular contribution of the structure of Catholic sacramental engagement and living in contemporary theology is to a theology of creation itself and issues raised by ecology and environmental theology today. In addition the eschatological nature of sacraments and the pilgrim nature of the Church as emphasized since Vatican II has helped theologians to reemphasize how sacraments are intense experiences of the risen Christ and the kingdom while also serving to point believers beyond the present sacramental experience to a yearning for their full realization in God's kingdom. The former exclusive emphasis on seven Sacraments has thus been transcended in favor of appreciating sacraments as important for, but not the exclusive means of, experiencing God in the many signs and symbols of the divine in human life.

K. Osborne, among others, approaches sacraments from the perspective of the life contexts for sacraments and thus offers a kind of phenomenology of sacramental activity. In this perspective notions of initiation, dining, forgiving, and service are discussed as the setting for the Sacraments of Baptism, Confirmation, Eucharist, Penance and Holy Orders. In addition stress is placed on sacraments as interpersonal activities in which human subjects are engaged. (He relies on the important work of M. Heidegger, M. Merleau-Ponty and P. Ricoeur to establish the philosophical foundation for this dynamic notion of sacrament.) In addition, in Osborne's view Jesus is the revelation of God for humanity, and sacraments function as means of continuing to experience this revelation in the Church. Hence he sees a close connection between the humanity of Jesus and engaging in sacraments.

Bibliography: K. OSBORNE, *Sacramental Theology. A General Introduction* (New York 1988); *Christian Sacraments in a Postmodern World. A Theology for the Third Millennium* (New York 1999). K. W. IRWIN, ''The Sacramentality of Creation and the Role of Creation in Liturgy and Sacraments,'' in *Preserving the Creation*

(Washington 1994) 67–111. K. RAHNER, ''Considerations on the Active Role of the Person in the Sacramental Event,'' *Theological Investigations*, v. 14 (New York 1976) 161–184; ''On the Theology of Worship,'' *ibid.*, v. 19 (New York 1983) 36–76.

Ecclesiology. While Rahner has made a lasting contribution to contemporary sacramental theology through his understanding of the Church as at the heart of all sacramental activity, more recent sacramental theologians place less emphasis on Rahner's way of relating sacraments to the institutional Church in favor of placing stress on sacraments as the corporate engagement of local communities in expressions which are corporate and communal experiences of the presence of God. Here local church communities are the real locus of sacramental activity; the Church universal is understood as the communion of these local communities. Rahner's later comments on the world Church serve well as a way of speaking about the communion of local churches. Some have critiqued both Rahner and Schillebeeckx for overly optimistic appreciations of the world in which sacraments take place and for a notion of the way Church and sacrament relate that does not emphasize the Church's prophetic and active involvement in the world. Political theologians especially have moved beyond such passive notions of Church to those which are more politically attuned. Such influences are clear in contemporary sacramental theology, particularly in the work of liberation theologians.

Theologians such as E. KILMARTIN nuance the understanding of the Church as the continuation of the Incarnation (which understanding has found its way into sacramental writing that emphasizes Christ and Church as sacrament) and make a clear distinction between the Incarnate Logos and the Church, since the Church is the gathering of the new people of Christ in the Spirit. Most important here is the emphasis on the presence and role of the Spirit in the Church, which understanding has been notably absent or unemphasized in many Western ecclesiologies.

Bibliography: E. KILMARTIN, ''A Modern Approach to the Word of God and Sacraments of Christ,'' *The Sacraments: God's Love and Mercy Actualized*, ed. F. EIGO (Villanova 1979) 59–109. R. VAILLANCOURT, *Toward A Renewal of Sacramental Theology*, tr. M. O'CONNELL (Collegeville, Minn. 1979).

Liturgy and Sacramental Theology. For centuries, scholastic theological understanding that prevailed from the medieval period through the modern era separated liturgy from sacramental theology. Liturgy concerned the celebration (texts and rubrics) of the sacraments, and sacramental theology concerned the dogmatic meaning of sacraments. This separation was reflected in the post-Tridentine liturgical rituals and manuals of theology; the former were rubrically and textually precise (requiring strict conformity) while the latter were most often neo-

scholastic treatises largely devoted to issues that were controversial at the time of the Reformation and Trent (such as proving the number of seven sacraments from Scripture, the nature of causality, the right intention of the minister, etc.). In the present liturgical renewal where sacraments are celebrated in the vernacular by using rituals whose texts are readily comprehended and whose symbolic actions are readily entered into provides the opportunity to reunite liturgy and sacramental theology in such a way that the liturgy can once again become an important *locus theologicus*. The establishment of a proper hermeneutic to interpret the liturgy is crucial so that its orientation toward comprehension, participation, and symbolic expression is respected.

Significant attempts to recover the *lex orandi* were made by liturgists from the 1960s on, notably by A. SCHMEMANN, L. Bouyer and A. Kavanagh. Often these proposals resulted from serious historical scholarship on the evolution of the rites and prayers that comprised Christian sacraments. At the same time, however, this approach often limited the appreciation of liturgy only to the meaning of the texts of liturgical prayers, which content could then be used to help establish the theology of a particular sacrament. More recent work on the relationship of liturgy and sacramental theology emphasizes the context of liturgical celebration as an essential component for a proper interpretation of these texts. Recalling this context helps to respect the nature of such texts as oriented more toward evocation than information, toward poetic imagery than dogmatic precision, and toward metaphorical expression than theological accuracy. In this respect a combination of the kind of excellent historical research on liturgy and its meaning done by R. Taft and the theological reflection on sacraments from a theological and liturgical perspective by E. Kilmartin would exemplify the way liturgy is being restored as a proper *locus theologicus*.

The nature of the postconciliar liturgical reform, where variety and flexibility in the selection of the texts used as well as the option of adding freely composed comments during the liturgy (as well as the difference between what the rites say and what actually occurs in liturgy), makes the task of establishing the actual composition of the liturgy of the sacraments more difficult than it was before Vatican II. Even more pertinent is the emphasis given to greater communal involvement in symbol, gesture, and music as constitutive of sacramental liturgy. Thus it is imperative that a hermeneutic be developed which incorporates these liturgical factors.

In addition, where formerly the move was from liturgy to sacramental theology, contemporary liturgical theologians increasingly call for a reciprocal approach to liturgy and theology whereby advances in theology (e.g., grace, ecclesiology, Christology, Trinity) are incorporated into the liturgy. While some of this has already occurred in the revised rituals which contain many images for Christ and the Church which go beyond those found in the former rituals (precisely because of advances in Christology and ecclesiology), an ongoing assimilation into the liturgy of advances in areas of theology is possible because the present revision of liturgy is oriented toward ongoing INCULTURATION and indigenization (*Constitution on the Sacred Liturgy* nn. 37–40). Such an approach would also help to insure that elements of the former discipline of sacramental theology derived from doctrinal sources would continue to be operative in a liturgical-sacramental theology. Hence most contemporary sacramental theologians favor the collapse of the division between liturgy and sacramental theology with liturgy appreciated as a foundation for this theology. Along with the revival of interest in liturgy as a theological source has been the revival of interest in certain of its component elements among which are the word, symbol, ritual and the arts.

Bibliography: M. COLLINS, "Critical Questions for Liturgical Theology," *Worship* 53 (July 1977) 302–317. A. HOUSSIAU, "La liturgie, lieu privilegie de la theologie sacramentaire," *Questions liturgiques et paroissiales* 54 (1973) 7–12. "La redecouverte de la liturgie par la theologie sacramentaire (1950–1980)," *Maison Dieu* 149 (1982) 27–55. K. IRWIN, *Liturgical Theology: A Primer* (Collegeville 1990); "Context and Text," *Method in Liturgical Theology* (1994). A. KAVANAGH, *On Liturgical Theology* (New York 1984). G. LUKKEN, "La liturgie comme lieu theologique irremplacable," *Questions liturgiques et paroissiales* 56 (1975) 97–112. G. WAINWRIGHT, "Der Gottesdienst als 'Locus Theologicus,' oder: Der Gottesdienst als Quelle und Thema der Theologie," *Kerygma und Dogma* 28 (1982) 248–258. *Doxology* (New York 1980).

Word. Recent interest in the dynamism of the scriptural word (seen for example in narrative and story theology) parallels a renewed understanding of the way the scriptural word functions in sacramental liturgy. When communities gather for sacraments they gather to engage in acts of memory, which acts are specified in the recalling of the Church's common story and the ritual engagement in that story through symbol and blessing prayers. Thus the restoration of the liturgy of the word to all sacramental rituals has led theologians to develop a theology of sacraments based on the notion of engaging in acts of memory through word and symbol.

K. Rahner asserted that the word of God constitutes the basic essence of the sacrament and that with this as foundation, symbols used in sacraments have the secondary function of illustrating the significance of the word. Here the exhibitive and performative nature of the word is emphasized and sacraments can be said to effect what is signified in the proclaimed word (to adapt an adage

from conventional sacramental theology). Seen from this perspective the restoration of a liturgy of the word for each sacrament makes both a liturgical and theological statement about the primacy of the word and the nature of sacramental engagement as requiring that the word be seen as foundational to all liturgical-sacramental activity. In addition, such an appreciation of the operation of the word in sacraments requires that the act of preaching serve as an important link joining word and sacrament, otherwise the two parts of one sacramental act can remain separated in practice as well as in theory.

Closely allied with this understanding of Scripture in the liturgy is an appreciation of how language in general functions in sacraments. Exhibitive and performative understandings of sacramental language mark the work of L.-M. Chauvet and B. R. Brinkmann (among many others) and point to the creative and sustaining aspects of religious language. The evocative and effective aspects of sacramental words legitimately precedes but necessarily leads to consideration of liturgical symbols or actions. The differentiation of blessing prayers from orations, as well as comments and instructions from greetings and dismissal blessings helps not only in celebration by determining which texts to proclaim and which to speak, it also helps in an appreciation of the act of worship as involving many languages (including silence and singing) all of which converge in an act of worship where language functions to effect the reality of sacrament.

Bibliography: B. R. BRINKMANN, "On Sacramental Man," *Heythrop Journal* 13 (October 1972) 371–401; 14 (January 1973) 5–34; 14 (April 1973) 162–189; 14 (July 1973) 280–306; 14 (October 1973) 396–416; "Sacramental Man and Speech Acts Again," *Heythrop Journal* 16 (October 1975) 418–420. L.-M CHAUVET, *Du symbolique au symbole. Essai sur les sacrements* (Paris 1979), tr., *Symbol and Sacrament* (Collegeville, Minn. 1991–95). K. RAHNER, "What is a Sacrament?," *Theological Investigations,* v. 14 (New York 1976) 135–148.

Symbol and Aesthetics. Concomitant with an emphasis on symbol in theological discourse in general has been a reemphasis on the essentially symbolic nature of the liturgy as reflected in the writings of such sacramental theologians as W. Van Roo and D. Power (who rely on the works of S. Langer, C. Geertz, P. Ricoeur, L. Gilkey and A. Vergote). Central to this recovery is the characteristically Catholic view of creation that sees the mediation of the divine through created matter and human interaction, which elements are essential aspects of sacramental activity. (Here Schillebeeckx's work on an incarnational and christological approach to sacraments should be recalled.) In sacramental discussions in particular symbols are understood less as objects (the unfortunate legacy of the late medieval and Tridentine approach to efficacy and presence) and more as elements of creation or human productivity that are used in stylized symbolic gestures in liturgical rites to mediate and actualize God's presence in the gathered community. Power maintains that an appreciation of symbol in sacramental activity helps to emphasize meaning over objects, human values over utilitarianism, the inner world over the external, and imagination over images alone. Such symbolic actions involve the inherent polyvalent meanings involved in symbols, which meanings affect participants in a variety of conscious and unconscious ways. Hence to engage in symbolic activity is to unleash a power that cannot be reduced to a single meaning.

The use of water, for example, evokes images of washing, cleansing, refreshment, purification, and an end of thirst (hence the continuance of life), as well as images of the uncontrollable force of storms, torrents, the realm of demons, and the place of drowning (hence the loss of life). Even though the sacramental use of water is accompanied by a blessing prayer which recalls scriptural (mostly positive) images of its use in salvation history, which are all brought to bear at this sacramental moment, nonetheless, contradictory meanings will be disclosed when water is used because such meanings are inherent in the use of this symbol.

Louis Marie Chauvet has used the category of the *symbolic* to revivify sacramental theology by emphasizing how Christian existence itself can be view from a sacramental perspective. He critiques traditional emphases on causality in sacraments and prefers a language reflective of the way sacraments and all of life are gifts of God to us. This work stands in line with other postmodern critiques of the Western metaphysical tradition. It also offers fresh ways to understand sacramental theology and the sacramental nature of the Christian life. Another postmodern critic, Jean-Luc Marion offers a sacramental theology relying heavily on openness to the iconic (as opposed to the idol, which for him is some Western preoccupation with metaphysical systems). He emphasizes God's acts in sacraments as gifts to us, especially as they express the supreme act of self donation and gift to us, the cross of Christ.

Bibliography: L. BOFF, *Os Sacramentos da Vida e a Vida dos Sacramentos. Enscio do Theologia Narrativa* (Pietropolis 1975). G. DURAND, *L'Imagination Symbolique* (Paris 1968). H.-G, GADAMER, *Truth and Method* (New York 1982). S. LANGER, *Philosophy in a New Key. A Study in the Symbolism of Reason, Rite and Art* (Cambridge 1978). J.-L. MARION, *God without Being* (Chicago 1991). D. POWER, *Unsearchable Riches* (New York 1984); *Sacrament. The Language of God's Self Giving* (New York 1999). W. VAN ROO, *Man the Symbolizer* (Rome 1981).

Ritual. Recent crosscultural and interreligious studies on ritual have produced an increasing body of literature that emphasizes its nature as stylized, repetitious, and familiar communal activity. Authors such as R.

Grimes emphasize the inescapably biological and natural roots of ritual as a rhythmic response to the patternings and events which precede and define human persons and communities. In this perspective Christian sacramental activity is seen to be essential since it mediates Christian identity far more traditionally and clearly than does intellectual assent to theological truths. The effect of Christian sacramental involvement is communal and social cohesion and a reaffirmation of personal and communal identification with Christ.

Sociological studies of initiation rituals, for example, demonstrate the enduring power of religious ritual, the importance of tactility and symbols in ritual, and the deep impact which certain rituals at events such as marriage and funerals continue to have on participants. Not unlike the use of symbols in worship, however, religious ceremonies are often conflict laden because ritual involves power (its use or misuse), and ritual action involves acknowledging who controls and who is controlled through ritual. Sometimes this power serves the function of getting things accomplished; sometimes it can paralyze because of the way it manipulates. Some feminist theologians critique sacramental structures and sacramental activity precisely because of the lack of shared power in the leadership position of presiding.

Christian ritual is the means of reenacting or representing (but not redoing or repeating) the saving event of Christ's paschal mystery. As such it takes an event of the definitive past and makes it operative in a way that involves and incorporates people in the present. Sacraments do this specifically in ways that help to articulate times of the liturgical year and transition times in a person's life such as birth, marriage, and death. Here the writings of A. van Gennep and Victor TURNER on rites of passage has been somewhat influential on sacramental theologians, chiefly in appreciating the social and crosscultural foundation of much sacramental ritual. Particularly helpful has been the drawing of important parallels between rites of passage and adult initiation. For further discussion, *see* RITUAL STUDIES.

Bibliography: R. GRAINGER, *The Language of the Rite* (London 1974). S. HAPPEL, ''Speaking from Experience: Worship and the Social Sciences,'' *Alternative Futures for Worship*, v.2, *Baptism and Confirmation*, M. SEARLE (Collegeville 1987) 171–188. ed. S. ROSS, *Extravagant Affections. A Feminist Sacramental Theology* (rev. ed. New York 2001). V. TURNER, *The Ritual Process: Structure and Anti-Structure* (London 1969).

Ecumenical Sacramental Conversations. Since Vatican II the proliferation and depth of ecumenical dialogue and agreed statements on the sacraments has provided participating churches with significant avenues to explore for sacramental hospitality and eventual reunion. Methodologically these efforts have resulted in moving participants beyond the narrowness of individual confessional explanations of sacraments to the use of terminology and concepts about sacraments taken from those used by other churches either in the past or at present. Most significant has been the movement in the FAITH AND ORDER COMMISSION of the WORLD COUNCIL OF CHURCHES that has resulted in the publication of the multilateral agreed statement *Baptism, Eucharist and Ministry* (*see* LIMA TEXT).

The Catholic Church has participated in a number of bilateral and multilateral conversations the progress and results of which have been very influential on Catholic sacramental thinking especially on questions of method and language. Initially, impressive results came from international and national bilateral conversations that offered great hope and stimulus toward reunion (e.g., the international and American Lutheran/Roman Catholic dialogues on Baptism and Eucharist as sacrifice, and Eucharist and Ministry) largely because the dialogue enabled participants to differentiate actual from apparent areas of disagreement. However, more recent assessment of this work reveals that some bilateral agreements reflect positions held in common by participating churches, which agreed upon positions are actually inadequate formulations of the theology of the sacrament under discussion. For example, the fact that Lutherans and Roman Catholics can formulate an agreement on eucharistic presence and sacrifice betrays the fact that both churches held similar but inadequate positions on the Eucharist precisely because each found itself preoccupied with these two elements of eucharistic theology exclusive of the wide variety of notions of Eucharist that went unexplored at the time of the Reformation. Some have even remained relatively unexplored in present ecumenical conversation.

Examples of such underexplored categories include the Eucharist and eschatology, Eucharist as the epiphany of the church and Eucharist as the work of the Holy Spirit (which itself would move the discussion away from a Christocentrism in eucharistic theology). Furthermore, more recent work in bilateral conversations has been devoted to issues related to agreements on sacramental theology; examples include the American Lutheran-Roman Catholic statement on JUSTIFICATION and the dialogue undertaken by this group on veneration of the saints and intercession on behalf of the present church. The particularly thorny question of how to deal with human mediation in sacraments still remains unresolved between Catholics and Protestants despite the fact that agreed statements on sacraments have been published.

In addition participation in multilateral dialogue and a number of bilateral dialogues has helped participants derive challenge and insight from a variety of churches whose experience and theology has helped to move each from tried and true ways of dealing with differences. For example, ecumenical dialogue on ministry has challenged Catholics to move beyond the terms *in persona Christi* and *in persona ecclesiae* in a way that serves to reunite them as complementary and not separate, and in a way that recontextualizes the discussion of the ordained ministry in terms of the ministry of all the baptized. At the same time some recent ecumenical initiatives on sacraments, e.g., American Lutherans and Episcopalians regarding intercelebration and mutual recognition of sacraments, have caused theologians across denominational lines to assess notions of apostolic succession and the role of succession in the enactment of sacraments.

Bibliography: M. FAHEY, *Catholic Perspectives on Baptism, Eucharist and Ministry* (Lanham, Md. 1986). Faith and Order Paper 111, *Baptism, Eucharist and Ministry* (Geneva 1982). F. J. VAN BEECK, *Grounded in Love. Sacramental Theology in an Ecumenical Perspective* (Washington 1981).

Sacramental Practice and Liberation Theology. The recent attention given to sacramental practice and its influence on the shape of sacramental theology often arises out of pastoral questions about the value of sacraments, the relationship of evangelization and sacraments, the relationship between faith and sacrament, and the question of how to deal with the baptized who no longer profess or practice the faith. The work of the following authors exemplifies the way that such issues of sacramental practice are addressed in contemporary sacramental theology. Most often these authors utilize some form of social science method to deal with sacramental practice which use reflects the attention being paid by sacramental theologians about how to incorporate creatively and constructively the valuable methods of social science research into sacramental theology.

Among the most poignant critiques of the value of sacraments in general has come from liberation theologians, for example J. Segundo and L. Boff. Writing from a Latin American context, Segundo maintains that the practice of the faith is often not commensurate with the value still placed on engagement in sacraments. Part of Segundo's critique centers around a lack of true evangelization and a sacramental crisis that is part of a broader crisis in ecclesial life itself. He argues that a certain magical understanding of sacraments still perdures, which understanding comes from the conventional understanding of sacramental causality. He argues forcefully for a sacramental practice that links ritual with human experience and for sacramental activity that reflects concern for one another through ecclesial structures such as base communities (*see* BASIC CHRISTIAN COMMUNITIES). Segundo asserts that sacraments function as expressions of evangelization for the world, then as celebrations for the Church. Clearly he prefers the witness of sacraments for the world in order to avoid a self-consciousness that dulls the challenge inherent in sacraments. However to understand sacraments as also for the Church can offer as real a challenge so that sacramental celebration leads to sacramental living. In addition, part of the critique by liberation theologians concerns how sacraments and justice as well as worship and mission are (or should be) correlative.

While Segundo offers observations based on a sociological approach to sacramental activity, some have criticized his lack of appreciation that a sociological approach would also affirm the performative character of a ritual, since participants in ritual are themselves changed by a well executed event itself. While not wanting to eliminate or derogate from programs of proper preparation for sacraments and follow up that are thoroughly evangelical and appropriately challenging in terms of living what is celebrated (as seen in the Rite of Christian Initiation for Adults), such programs function most effectively when they derive from and uphold the priority of human engagement in ritual for confirmation and renewal of Christian identity. In addition, some have observed that his emphasis on the liberative and justice aspects of sacraments could be more adequately presented if linked clearly with the eschatological nature of sacraments. Thus the temptation to turn the liberation aspects of sacraments into an ideology would be avoided; sacraments would be seen as both countercultural and as experiences that lead to the fullness of the coming Kingdom.

Writing somewhat later than Segundo, Boff articulates the sacramentality intrinsic to sacraments and what might be called a sacramental ecclesiology. For him sacraments are basic constituents of human life and as such (to use his term) should be viewed *sub specie humanitatis* (from the perspective of humanity). His sacramental ecclesiology is closely linked with Segundo's emphasis on basic Christian communities; his anthropology of sacraments is reminiscent of foundational insights from both Rahner and Schillebeeckx.

A particularly insightful and creative contribution to a synthesis of sacramental theology for today's Latin American context is found in the work of Antonio Gonzaez Dorado. His intention is to summarize traditional categories of Catholic sacramental theology and to recontextualize them for a church in need of what he term "liberating evangelization." The result is a comprehensive "manual" that transcends the negative aspects of the manual genre as it uses it to offer important insights about what sacraments can offer regarding a re-evangelization of Latin America. His use of important theologians from the tradition, principally Tertullian and SS. Augustine and Thomas Aquinas, helps to ground his thesis in the Catholic tradition. At the same time his insights about these authors, principally their time and place in the church's life (e.g. Tertullian in a time of martyrdom, Augustine in a time of theological and ecclesial difficulties and Aquinas in a time of theological synthesis) help to respect what they say and why they said it in their particular contexts. Such an approach helps to avoid uncritical or overly simplistic summaries of their teachings.

Writing from the perspective of the contemporary church in France, R. Didier addresses a very different phenomenon from these liberation theologians. He addresses the question of people asking the radical questions of what is the value of sacraments for a "post-Christian" constituency which sees little value in rite but which values authenticity in human living. In addressing these issues Didier argues from an anthropological perspective that roots sacramental action in human ritual in general (as noted above). In paralleling sacraments with rituals such as holiday traditions, the ritual of family dining, rites of fall/spring, courtship and marriage, etc., he sees an important anthropological foundation for Christian sacraments where the latter are seen as intrinsic to human nature and hence need to be retained. The conserving and integrating function of ritual is also emphasized. Didier admits, however, that a major factor militating against this conserving function in community is the individualism and privatization that marks many areas of contemporary life. In attempting to address the question of "why sacraments" Didier relies on the insights of other contemporary theologians about the enduring power of symbol, the ecclesial dimension of sacraments, and the importance of balancing Christian sacramental activity with a wide appreciation of sacramentality. In addition, just as a compartmentalization of sacraments from life is inappropriate, so is a notion of sacraments that does not emphasize the mission and justice components of liturgy.

In an American context the sociologist-pastoral theologian P. Murnion has offered a unique way of approaching the question of sacramental theology that returns us to the remarks made at the beginning of this article about sacramentality and ecclesiology. In the present American culture, Murnion argues, there are some "fundamental faults" which the Catholic understanding of sacramentality and ecclesiology can help to address. Part of the importance of this approach is to see sacramental activity in a wide perspective. The faults Murnion delineates are a radical individualism, utilitarianism, materialism, separation of private from the public spheres of action and increased polarizing of classes. His proposed new order to deal with such faults includes a new communitarianism, a new measure of the common good (based on the conviction about the quality of all human life), new emphasis on the integral development of the whole person (intimately tied to the depth and endurance of human relationships), a new symbiosis of private and public life in terms of consistent virtues, and a new sense of unity among all peoples. These, he maintains, can be articulated and upheld most fully by a Catholic vision and a sacramental approach to life. While some have critiqued his approach as not being sufficiently reflective of the variety of peoples in America today (specifically whether these faults exist in Hispanic, black, or other ethnic groupings), at base it offers one way of dealing with the important relationship between practice (in church and in society) and sacramental theology. Murnion's thoroughly incarnational approach to sacramentality provides a new perspective on the christological and phenomenological approach to sacramental theology emphasized by E. Schillebeeckx in the early 1960s.

Conclusion. The complexity of contemporary sacramental theology is evident in the variety of approaches reflected in this modest synthesis. That additional work is needed both on areas reviewed here as well as on correlative areas such as theological anthropology, religious sociology, and liturgy (e.g., relating sacraments to the liturgical year) is clear. The retrieval of the principle that liturgy and sacramental theology are intrinsically connected is a foundational insight for the integrity of any study of the sacraments today. That so much has been accomplished in the past four decades to revive sacramental practice and theology in churches attests to the centrality of liturgy and sacraments in the life of the church. That more needs to be done in a variety of areas attests to the perennial challenge for Catholic theology in any age.

Bibliography: L. BOFF, *Iglesia: Charisma e poder.* (Pietropolis 1981, Eng. trans. New York 1985). H. BURGEOIS, "Theologie Sacramentaire," *Recherches de science religieuse* 72 (1984) 291–318. H. DENIS, *Des sacrements et des hommes. Dix ans apres Vatican II* (Lyon 1975); *Sacrements sources de vie. Etudes de theologie sacramentaire* (Paris 1982). A. G. DORADDO, *Los Sacramentos del Evangelio: Sacramentologia fundamental y organica* (Santa Fe de Bogota 1991). E. KILMARTIN, "Theology of the Sacraments: Toward a New Understanding of the Chief Rites of the Church of Jesus Christ," R. DUFFY, ed., *Alternative Futures For Worship,* v. 1. *General Introduction* (Collegeville, Minn. 1987) 123–175. P. MURNION, "A Sacramental Church in the Modern World," *Origins* 14 (June 21, 1984) 81–90. A. SCHMEID, "Perspektiv und Akzente heutiger Sakramenttheologie," *Wissenschaft und Weisheit* 44 (1981) 17–45. J. SEGUNDO, *The Sacraments Today,* tr. J. DRURY (Maryknoll 1974). F. TILLMANS, "The Sacraments as Symbolical Reality of Faith," H. J. AUF DER MAUR, et al., eds., *Fides Sacramenti Sacramentum Fidei* (Assen 1981) 253–276.

[K. W. IRWIN]

SACRAMENTALS

Prior to the definition of the term "sacrament" in the 12th and 13th centuries, it was used of rites, prayers, and objects other than the seven Sacraments as well as of these institutions of Christ. With the refinement of the term "sacrament" by scholastic theology, the term "sacramental" became the designation for those actions that the Church herself instituted. Until Vatican Council II the definition of the 1917 Code of Canon Law was often taken as a guide: "Sacramentals are things or actions that the Church is accustomed to use, in imitation of the Sacraments, in order to obtain through her intercession certain effects, especially spiritual ones" (see, e.g., 1917 *Codex Iuris Canonicis* c.1144). This has been superseded by that contained in Vatican Council II's *Constitution on the Sacred Liturgy:* "These are sacred signs which bear a resemblance to the Sacraments: they signify effects, particularly of a spiritual kind, which are obtained through the Church's intercession. By them all are disposed to receive the chief effect of the Sacraments, and various occasions in life are rendered holy" (60).

Sacramentals are part of the sign language of the liturgy. Their resemblance to the Sacraments consists in the fact that they are signs and that their effect does not come about primarily because of the prayers of individuals, but because of the Church's priestly prayer. They differ from the Sacraments in that they have been instituted by the Church and give grace by reason of her intercession.

Signs. Precisely because sacramentals are signs, they must be understood. For this reason Vatican Council II calls for an updating of sacramentals. "With the passage of time, however, there have crept into the rites of the Sacraments and sacramentals certain features that have rendered their nature and purpose far from clear to the people of today; hence some changes have become necessary to adapt them to the needs of our times" (62). Since they are part of the public worship of the Church there must be opportunity for participation by the faithful. This is one of the norms on which the Council insists in ordering alterations in her sacramentals. "The sacramentals are to undergo a revision which takes into account the primary principle of enabling the faithful to participate intelligently, actively, and easily; the circumstances of our own days must be considered. When rituals are revised . . . new sacramentals may also be added as the need for these becomes apparent" (79).

Effects. The sacramentals include a wide variety of rites, and consequently their effects are fairly numerous. Chiefly, however, these are spiritual. Like the Sacraments, they are for the good of all peoples. While it is true that through sacramental we are sometimes aided in our temporal needs; their first purpose is our sanctification, for they are signs of the paschal mystery. Thus among the sacramentals are prayers for health, rain, and good harvests. Through them, in their own way, come graces, remission of sin and temporal punishment, freedom from demonic influence, and the blessing of persons and objects.

Efficacy. It is through the Church's intercession that these effects of the sacramentals are obtained. The rites and prayers that she designates to be such are her petition and have an efficacy that surpasses that of nonofficial prayers, whether offered by individual Christians or in common. On the other hand, this intercession is different from the causality of the Sacraments (*ex opere operato*). It has become customary to refer to this efficacy of the Church's prayer in the sacramentals as *ex opere operantis Ecclesiae.* By the term it is understood that as the spouse of Christ, using Christ's power of priesthood, the Church offers a uniquely holy prayer always pleasing to God. This quality is not characteristic of those petitions prompted by the simultaneous devotion of members of the Church in exactly the same way. (For a discussion of the relation of other common prayer to the sacramentals see Vagaggini 64–67; Dalmais 83–87.)

The chief reason for the value of sacramentals is the Church's intercession, of which they are signs. This is not meant to imply that the holiness of the minister and subject are unimportant. If these dispositions are essential for the effectiveness of Sacraments they are certainly so also for the effectiveness of sacramentals. As in the Sacraments, however, the sanctification that is effected is not the work of the individual participants; it is the prayer of the Church in which members join and from which they profit according to their generosity. Because they are ecclesial in this sense, the sacramentals sometimes have effectiveness infallibly, even in the absence of dispositions. The Divine Office as the prayer of the Church is always such when recited in circumstances designated by the Church, regardless of the moral qualities of those who celebrate it. Blessings are effective as such even when the minister or subject is not properly disposed to receive their sanctifying gifts of grace. (For the minister of sacramentals *see* BLESSINGS, LITURGICAL.)

Which Signs Are Sacramentals? The exact determination of what should be understood by "sacramentals" has been the subject of some debate. This has centered mainly on two points: whether the term applies to objects blessed by the Church and whether those ceremonies that form part of the celebration of Mass and other Sacraments beyond the actions performed *in persona Christi* are to be considered as sacramentals (see Michel 465–476).

Primary Meaning. In view of the manner in which the sacramentals have their efficacy, as impetrations of

the Church, there is much weight to that opinion that maintains that sacramentals are primarily some form of blessing and that only secondarily can objects that have been blessed be included under this name. While the 1917 Code of Canon Law (c.1144) included "things" as well as actions in its definition of sacramentals, the *Constitution on the Sacred Liturgy* (60) omits any reference to blessed objects as such. Hence there is even greater force to the position of J. H. Miller: "Sacramentals consist immediately and primarily in the Church's prayer of impetration, and only in second place and mediately (through this impetratory prayer) in the sanctification of an object. In the most proper sense, a sacramental would be the immediate object of the Church's impetratory power, namely, the *blessing* or similar *action* actively using the Church's prayer; the thing blessed, became of this blessing, increases our reverence for divine worship or helps to elevate the tenor of our daily lives. The private use of such blessed objects is not, therefore, liturgical in the strict sense of the word, but rather brings to us and our lives the aid of the Church's liturgical prayer'' (Miller 429–430).

Sacramentals and the Sacraments. The first of the two functions of sacramentals specified by Vatican Council II is that of disposing all men and women to receive the chief effect of the Sacraments. This highlights the central place of the Sacrifice and Sacraments in the plan of salvation and depicts the sacramentals as aids to our deeper sharing in the paschal mystery. It would also seem to lend considerable weight to the view of modern theologians that the ceremonies with which the Church has surrounded the actual rites of the Sacraments themselves are to be considered as sacramentals (Michel 465–475; Miller 428–429).

Sacramentals could only have been instituted by the Church in service of the Sacraments, of which they are imitations. From the viewpoint of their connection with Sacraments, it becomes easy to indicate various classes of sacramentals. Connected with Baptism are the following: the blessing of baptismal water at the Easter Vigil, the blessing of holy water; the ceremonies of BAPTISM and the CATECHUMENATE (exorcisms, signs of the cross, anointings, impositions of hands, the giving of the white garment and candle), religious profession, the consecration of virgins (for the last two see Miller 448–450). The chief sacramental connected with Penance is the blessing and distribution of ashes on Ash Wednesday.

That all sacramentals, as everything else in the Church, are related to the Eucharist is emphasized by provision in the *Constitution on the Sacred Liturgy* for their more manifest connection with the Mass. What has been evident for the blessing of the holy oils on Holy Thursday, the blessing and procession of palms, Candlemas, the Easter Vigil, will be true of some other celebrations. Among the provisions of Vatican Council II in this regard is the order that religious profession should preferably be made within the Mass (80).

Sacramentals related to Holy Orders include the consecration of the holy oils, the blessings of abbots, and the dedication of churches (see Miller 495–500). Among the chief sacramentals connected with Matrimony are the blessing of the home and the various blessings of women. Most closely associated is the nuptial blessing itself, which is now to be given even when marriage takes place apart from Mass (*Constitution on the Sacred Liturgy* 78). Connected with the Anointing of the Sick are the sacramentals of blessings for members of the Church at various stages of illness, the commendation of the departing soul, and the burial rites (see Miller 472–475).

The second function of the sacramentals specified by the *Constitution on the Sacred Liturgy* is the sanctification of various occasions in life. For the Christian, brought into a new order through his death to sin and resurrection to Christ's life in Baptism, everything is a proper subject for inclusion into this way of life. The many circumstances of human activity are specifically consecrated through prayers that the Church makes available to her members. Her activity has as its center Christ's Sacrifice and the other Sacraments, but it is obviously not limited to this. The living out of the commitment made and renewed in sacramental encounter is the proof of our sincerity in worship. To teach this lesson and to enable us to put it into practice the Church gives us sacred signs by which she begs God's blessing on all manner of human situations that we may meet them with a truly Christian spirit. "Through the sacramentals the Church brings all created things into the orbit of God's blessing, in reality touches everything with the grace of the redemption, making so many material things and persons instruments and channels of the grace of God" (O'Shea 533).

Sacramentals are an extension of the central work of the Church, her worship of God with her Head in His Sacrifice and other saving actions. Very accurately, they may be called "little sacraments" [M. B. Hellriegel, *The Holy Sacrifice of the Mass* (St. Louis 1944) 15]. For they too are sacred corporate signs of sanctification in which the Church in union with Christ teaches redemption and draws all men and women more intimately into a share of new life in Christ. Their first function is to extend the sign language of the acts of Christ himself and to prepare us for the most fruitful possible participation in these. Beyond this, they remind us that all life's activities have a Christian dimension and bless these. A proper apprecia-

tion of the sacramentals rests on the realization of their place in the ecclesial plan of salvation: they may be less than the Sacraments but more powerful than purely private prayer. Such an attitude removes any danger of exaggerating sacramentals at the expense of Sacraments or of overlooking their significant place in Christian living.

Bibliography: I. H. DALMAIS, *Introduction to the Liturgy*, tr. R. CAPEL (Baltimore 1961). A. G. MARTIMORT, ed., *L'Église en prière* (Tournai 1961). A. MICHEL, *Dictionnaire de théologie catholique*, ed. A. VACANT et al., 15 v. (Paris 1903–50; Tables générales 1951–) 14.1:465–482. J. H. MILLER, *Fundamentals of the Liturgy* (Notre Dame, Ind. 1960) 427–433. J. H. MILLER, *Signs of Transformation in Christ* (Englewood Cliffs, N.J. 1963). W. J. O'SHEA, *The Worship of the Church* (Westminster, Md. 1957). C. VAGAGGINI, *Theological Dimensions of the Liturgy*, tr. L. J. DOYLE (Collegeville, Minn. 1959).

[J. R. QUINN/EDS.]

SACRAMENTARIANS

Certain Reformers who denied the Real Presence of the body and blood of Christ in the Eucharist. Among the Sacramentarians (name given them by Martin Luther) were Huldrych ZWINGLI, Johannes OECOLAMPADIUS, and Andreas KARLSTADT. Martin BUCER adopted a mediating position, and John CALVIN could do no better than to imitate Bucer's syncretism. That Sacramentarianism did not appear until the mid-1520s shows that it had no intrinsic connection with the principal Reformation doctrine of justification by faith. Rather, it was the fruit of the rejection of the teaching authority of the Church. In its day the controversy was sharp. At the Marburg Colloquium (1529) Luther and Zwingl met at the behest of Bucer, but did little more than exchange mutual recriminations. A compromise statement was framed in the Wittenberg Concord (1536), but the issue lived on in the churches of the Reformation. The controversy occasioned the development of UBIQUITARIANISM among the Lutherans.

Bibliography: L. CHRISTIANI, *Dictionnaire de théologie catholique* (Paris 1903–50) 14.1:441–465. K. ALGERMISSEN, *Lexikon für Theologie und Kirche*, ed. J. HOFER and K. RAHNER (Freiburg 1957–65) 9:243–244.

[M. B. SCHEPERS]

SACRAMENTARIES, I: HISTORICAL

The name *Liber Sacramentorum* or *Sacramentarium* denotes in the Western Church the liturgical book used by the celebrant at Mass, from the end of the 4th century to the 13th, when it was replaced by the Missal. Besides the Mass prayer formularies, it originally contained ordination formularies, various blessings, and other prayers that the bishop or priest required from time to time. In fact, much of the present-day Pontifical was found within its pages.

In this article, the history and development of the Sacramentary is traced from its earliest origins, toward the end of the 4th century, until it attained its official form, in the middle of the 9th century, as the authentic Carolingian service book. This period of almost 500 years was a time of immense activity in the compilation of liturgical books throughout the West. Its history is a complex one, with many ramifications.

Historical Background. As Christianity moved from its apostolic roots through the period of early persecutions and into the time of imperial toleration and patronage, its liturgy also passed through stages of development and elaboration. Early documents known as church orders, dating from the third and fourth centuries, often contained general directions and certain texts to be used as models for the celebration of various liturgical celebrations, especially for the eucharist, along with other types of guidelines for the orderly structuring of the life of a local church community. However, the development of specific books to be used only for the celebration of the public liturgies of the Church was a somewhat later series of complex processes that took several centuries. Some books were used only at the celebration of the Divine Office (e.g. the collectar); others would be used for the eucharist and other sacramental celebrations. For example, the lector would use the epistle-lectionary; the cantor would use an *antiphonale* or a *graduale*. Chief among these books was the sacramentary, the book used by the priest- or bishop-presider for the celebration of the Eucharist. The developmental period of the sacramentary stretched from the late sixth through the early ninth centuries. The full missal, or *missale*, containing all of the material necessary to celebrate the Eucharist (including readings and music), was a later development dating from the 12th century.

The *Veronense* (Leonine) Sacramentary. The earliest form of a eucharistic liturgical book was not a book at all, but more like a booklet or missalette: a *libellus* or "little book." Each of these *libelli* would contain the presider's prayers for the Mass of one particular Sunday or feast day. In the Roman rite, these prayers would include a series of proper collects for the day, generally the *oratio* (opening prayer); *secreta* (offertory prayer), and the *post communio* (prayer after communion). This basic set of prayers is called a *Mass formulary*. The earliest protosacramentary still extant dates from the late sixth century, and is basically a private collection of several of these libelli, bound together into a single, incomplete, volume. Since it was originally thought that the collection had

been made by Pope Leo I, the book was first called the Leonine Sacramentary. Research by 20th century scholars showed that the collection was compiled after the death of Pope Leo I, although a case might be made for a Leonine composition of some of its prayer formularies. Authorship of this collection has not been conclusively established, although scholars do agree that it was assembled together outside Rome. Many scholars have begun referring to this collection as the Veronense or the Verona Sacramentary, after the city in which it was discovered.

Roman Sacramentaries. Later Roman sacramentaries can be roughly divided into two groups: the Gregorian, prepared for the use of the pope at eucharistic liturgies, and the Gelasian, used by other presiding presbyters in other Roman churches (*tituli*). Both the papal sacramentary and the presbyteral sacramentary migrated north of the Alps in the eighth century to the Franks, where both sacramentary traditions were adapted for use in this area, incorporating elements from the Gallican Rite then prevalent.

The Gelasian Sacramentary Tradition. Copies of the Gelasian sacramentary made their way to Frankish lands in the seventh century. The earliest exemplar is the *Gelasianum Vetus* or "Old Gelasian" (MS Vat. Reg. Lat. 316) which already shows signs of Gallican influence. The original Roman text was later adapted in many places to accommodate liturgical structures and prayer texts common to Gallican, not Roman, practice. As a group, these books are referred to as the *Eighth-Century Gelasian Sacramentaries*. Perhaps the most important example of this type of sacramentary is the Sacramentary of Gellone (circa 790–800).

The Gregorian Sacramentary Tradition. One form of the papal sacramentary, the *Hadrianum*, was sent to Charlemagne in the last decades of the eighth century by Pope Hadrian. Dating perhaps to the pontificate of Honorius (mid-seventh century), this sacramentary reflected the presiding patterns of the pope, not the surrounding *tituli*. Partly as a result of this, the sacramentary was incomplete, and had to be expanded for general use by the addition of a Supplement. This Supplement, originally thought to have been composed by Alcuin of York but now known to be the work of Benedict of Aniane, was connected to the main book by a preface, the *Hucusque*. Eventually, the preface was dropped, and the contents of the Supplement were directly merged with the *Hadrianum* itself. Two other forms of the Gregorian tradition should also be noted: the Sacramentary of Padua (*Paduense*), a Roman adaptation of the papal sacramentary to wider presbyteral use; and the Sacramentary of Trent, a witness to pre-*Hadrianum* Gregorian practice.

Structure. In addition to the prayer texts of various mass formularies, other material was needed for the full celebration of the Mass. The sacramentaries contained only prayer texts and their titles. Directions for liturgical ministers, including step-by-step directions on how the rituals were to be performed (the *ordo*), were also originally recorded in *libelli*. Many of the most important were eventually collected as the *ordines romani* (OR) (*see* ORDO, ROMAN).

The outline of the structure of the mass itself, the *ordo missae* (OM), could also be found in separate *libelli* into the eleventh century. Often, the text of the Roman canon was included in this outline, along with several variable sections of the prayer to be used on certain feasts or other occasions. In many areas, this outline was elaborated by the addition of numerous private penitential prayers for the presider to recite at points in the service when other liturgical ministers were active (e.g. the chanting of the Gloria, the offertory). The number of these prayers was reduced by the liturgical reforms of Gregory VII (1073–85) and the OM was eventually incorporated into the body of the sacramentary itself.

Since the texts for the celebration of mass were ordered in part according to the liturgical year, *calendars* were also eventually incorporated into the sacramentary books. Mass formularies could be generally grouped in two sections: those which followed the *temporal* cycle (i.e. the liturgical seasons), and those which followed the *sanctoral* cycle (i.e. the feasts of the martyrs and saints). The Gelasian sacramentaries generally separated these two cycles, placing the temporal cycle in the first section of the volume, and the sanctoral cycle in the second section. The Gregorian tradition blended these two cycles in one chronological structure.

Both sacramentary traditions incorporated a third section of mass formularies, the votive masses. Some of these were for use in certain situations, e.g. in time of war or plague. However, early sacramentaries could also contain a great deal of other liturgical material. While they were primarily used for the celebration of mass, sacramentaries were often used for other ritual occasions, and included eucharistic texts for these as well, e.g. the nuptial mass. A sacramentary intended for the use of a bishop might include prayers for baptism, confirmation, ordination, or for an official visit to a monastery. Presbyteral sacramentaries could also include other more common parochial liturgical celebrations, for instance, baptismal liturgies, or the services for the churching of women, or for funerals. Slowly, a separate book, the *Rituale* (*see* RITUAL, ROMAN) evolved; this book contained the texts for most or all non-eucharistic liturgical services. At the same time another liturgical book, the *Pontificale* (*see* PONTIFICAL, ROMAN) was also in the process of development; this book would contain liturgical material for all rituals presided over by the bishop, e.g. confirmation and ordinations. Texts for the blessing of various objects (e.g. bells) or persons (e.g. pilgrims) were also frequently included in sacramentaries. Therefore, for several centuries, liturgical services could be found in a number of "mixed" liturgical books, e.g. a sacramentary-ritual, or a sacramentary-pontifical.

Non-Roman Sacramentaries. So far this entry has covered the Roman and Roman-Frankish sacramentary traditions, which would eventually give rise to the Roman Missal. However, several other western Christian rites were in use in late antiquity and the early medieval period, and a few of these early sacramantaries or sacramentary-type books still survive. The Gallican Rite, for example, was used in parts of Gaul; exemplars include the *Missale Gothicum*, the *Missale Gallicanum Vetus*, and the Bobbio Missal. In Spain, one would find the Mozarabic Rite, as evidenced in the *Liber Ordinum* and *Liber Mozarabicus sacramentorum*. The Ambrosian Rite, named in honor of Saint Ambrose, was in use in Milan and parts of Italy; see for example the *Sacramentarium Bergomense*. And finally the Celtic Rite was the dominant liturgical form in Britain and Ireland; one important text is the Stowe Missal.

By the end of the 11th century, the sacramentary genre began to give way to the *missalis plenaries* in which the texts found in the epistolary, evangelary, and antiphonary gradually were incorporated and variously arranged into sacramentaries.

Bibliography: E. PALAZZO, *A History of Liturgical Books: from the Beginning to the Thirteenth Century*, trans M. BEAUMONT (Collegeville MN 1998). C. VOGEL, *Medieval Liturgy: An Introduction to the Sources*, trans and rev W. G. STOREY and N. K. RASMUSSEN, O.P. (Washington, D.C. 1986). G. AUSTIN, O.P. "Sources, Liturgical," in P. FINK, S.J., ed., *The New Dictionary of Sacramental Worship* (Collegeville, MN 1990) 1213–20. J. M. PIERCE, "The Evolution of the *ordo missae* in the Early Middle Ages," in L. LARSON-MILLER, ed. *Medieval Liturgy: A Book of Essays* (New York, London 1997) 3–24.

[H. ASHWORTH/J. M. PIERCE]

SACRAMENTARIES, II: CONTEMPORARY

In the current usage of the Roman Rite, the Sacramentary has again become the principal liturgical book for the celebration of the Eucharist, together with the Lectionary for Mass, (*see* LECTIONARIES, II: CONTEMPORARY ROMAN CATHOLIC) and the *Graduale Romanum* for music. The retrieval of the Sacramentary flows from one of the main intuitions of Vatican II's Constitution on the Sacred Liturgy, which requires that all participants in the liturgy, whether clergy or laity, who have an active role in the liturgy, should not do all, but only those parts which pertain to their office by the nature of the right (*Sacrosanctum Concilium*, 28). As a result, specific books pertain to specific functions of the liturgy. The English-speaking world adopted the title "Sacramentary" to the liturgical book in English translation that contains the parts of the *Missale Romanum* (*editio typicae* 1969, revised 1975, *editio typicae altera* 2001) pertinent to the priest-celebrant.

[J. SULLIVAN/EDS.]

SACRAMENTINE NUNS

(OSS, Official Catholic Directory, #3490); officially known as the Religious of the Order of the Blessed Sacrament and of Our Lady, probably the first community established specifically for the perpetual adoration of the Blessed Sacrament. It is a cloistered, contemplative order whose members take solemn vows and have papal enclosure. The order was begun at Marseilles, France, in 1639 by Antoine Le Quieu, OP (1601–76), but not officially established until 1659 when it was canonically erected by the bishop of Marseilles. Papal approbation was granted in 1693 by Innocent XII. Each monastery is autonomous.

During the French Revolution, 13 Sacramentines of the Bollène monastery were guillotined at Orange. They were beatified in 1925 (*see* ORANGE, MARTYRS OF). When the anticlerical laws of 1901 forced the nuns to leave their monastery at Bernay, France, they found refuge in Belgium. Some of the exiled religious came to the U.S. in 1912 and were accepted into the Archdiocese of New York, where they founded a monastery in Yonkers. In 1951 a second monastery was established in Conway, MI, by seven religious from Yonkers. The Yonkers community moved to Scarsdale, NY, in 1998.

[M. M. BROGAN/EDS.]

SACRAMENTINE SISTERS OF BERGAMO

Also known as Suore Sacramentine di Bergamo, a congregation with papal approbation (1908), founded at Bergamo, Italy, in 1882 by Geltrude Catarina COMENSOLI (1847–1903). The sisters have as their special purposes daily eucharistic adoration and the education of youth. Catarina, who became known in religion as Mother Gertrude of the Blessed Sacrament, gathered her first companions in 1882, and received the religious habit in 1884. From Bergamo, where they had started their activity, the

sisters had to move to Lodi, Italy, where they received episcopal approval in 1891. The foundress died in 1903. The congregation has expanded to Europe, Africa, and South America.

Bibliography: C. COMENSOLI, *Un'anima eucaristica, madre Gertrude Comensoli* (Monza 1936). *La Suora Sacramentina alla scuola della Serva di Dio Madre Gertrude Comensoli* (Bergamo 1960).

[F. SOTTOCORNOLA/EDS.]

SACRAMENTS, ARTICLES ON

The principal entry on the history and theology of Sacraments is SACRAMENTAL THEOLOGY, and the related entry SACRAMENTALS. The sacramental principle is further treated under SYMBOLISM, THEOLOGICAL. The general efficacy and effects of Sacraments are treated in GRACE, SACRAMENTAL; REVIVISCENCE, SACRAMENTAL; EX OPERE OPERANTO; EX OPERE OPERANTIS; and SACRAMENTS, CONDITIONAL ADMINISTRATION OF.

The Sacraments of healing are treated under PENANCE, SACRAMENT OF; EXOMOLOGESIS; CONFESSION, AURICULAR; and ANOINTING OF THE SICK, I (THEOLOGY OF).

The Sacraments of initiation are covered under BAPTISM, SACRAMENT OF; BAPTISM OF INFANTS; LIMBO; CONFIRMATION; IMPOSITION OF HANDS; EUCHARIST IN CONTEMPORARY CATHOLIC THEOLOGY; SACRIFICE IV (IN CHRISTIAN THEOLOGY); TRANSUBSTANTIATION; and COMMUNION, FIRST.

The Sacraments of vocation are discussed under MATRIMONY, SACRAMENT OF; HOLY ORDERS; PRIESTHOOD IN CHRISTIAN TRADITION; BISHOP (SACRAMENTAL THEOLOGY OF); and DEACON. Controversial issues in the sacrament of holy orders are discussed under ANGLICAN ORDERS; APOSTOLICAE CURAE; and REORDINATION.

[J. Y. TAN]

SACRAMENTS, CONDITIONAL ADMINISTRATION OF

The minister of the Sacraments may be obligated at times, especially with regard to Baptism, Penance, and the Anointing of the Sick, to administer a Sacrament conditionally. Were he to do otherwise, he might be guilty either of irreverence for these sacred symbols, because the recipient lacks the requisites to receive them, or of depriving unjustly someone who needs them. He should not, for example, give the Anointing of the Sick absolutely to someone who is declared dead, lest the sacramental rite be administered disrespectfully and without effect, and yet he should not deprive the person, who may be only in deep coma, of the Sacrament. By giving the Anointing of the Sick under the condition, ''If you are capable'' (of receiving it), he provides for the reception of the Sacrament, which will cause grace either then and there, if the recipient is properly disposed, or at reviviscence, if the recipient later disposes himself for the reception of grace. The intention of the minister must be to do as the Church does, namely, as Christ intended when He instituted the Sacraments as means of grace for those capable of being sanctified by them. The minister as a person has no power to administer Sacraments except so far as he conforms his intention to that of the Church. The Sacraments are Sacraments of the Church, of Christ and His Mystical Body (see SACRAMENTS, THEOLOGY OF).

Bibliography: H. DAVIS, *Moral and Pastoral Theology,* 4 v. (rev. ed. New York 1958) v.3.

[P. L. HANLEY]

SACRAMENTS, ICONOGRAPHY OF

The representation of the Sacraments as rites performed by the clergy appeared first in the 14th century. Earlier representation was typological. Few examples of representation of rites can be noted before that time, though there is the instance in Carolingian ivories of the school of Metz. The iconographic representation of Sacraments may thus be considered under two manifestations: those representations based on the typology of the Sacraments and those descriptive of the liturgical rite itself.

Typological Representation. Since the origin of Christian art, sacramental connotations have underlain many aspects of symbolism, whether under the veil of the *testimonia* of the Old Testament or the veil of the *mysteria* of the New Testament. The typology of the Sacraments has to be considered as a branch of typology in general (J. Daniélou, *Bible et Liturgie,* Paris 1958), since testamentary images or types may signify or symbolize a sacramental content. For a millennium the typology of the Sacraments remained, in Christian art as in its theological prototypes, immersed, as it were, in typology at large. For instance, the Last Supper carved on the doorways of Romanesque churches in Burgundy, Provence, and Languedoc has a twofold meaning. On the one hand, the Last Supper is the memorial of the institution of the Eucharist by Christ. Yet on the lintels of the doorways of Saint-Julien at Jonzy, Vandeins, Bellenaves, Savigny, Saint-Pons at Thomières, and Saint-Gilles-du-Gard, the Eucharist is associated also with Baptism and Penance. These two Sacraments are ''typified'' by Christ's wash-

ing of the feet of the Apostles. On the traditional connection of the washing of the feet with Baptism and Penance, there is the testimony of Walafrid Strabo (*Glossa ordinaria, Evangelium secundum Johannem,* 13.8). The example of a double illumination painted *c.* 1085 in the Vyšehrad (Coronation) Gospelbook (National and University Library, Prague MS 14, A13) presents the Last Supper with the inscription *Panem sanctificat Christus quo secula pascat.* Underneath the Last Supper, the washing of the feet bears the inscription *Abluit exterius sordes qui cor lavat intus.* On the other hand, an eschatological implication accompanies the Romanesque doorways cited above because, over the lintel carved with the ''figures'' of Eucharist, Baptism, and Penance, the *Majestas Domini* was set in the tympanum to recall that, through the union of Christ and His Church in His Sacraments, the soul is invited to the mystical banquet.

Types of Sacraments exist in figures of the Old Testament and in mysteries of the New Testament. Examples signifying the Eucharist are: the sacrifice of Isaac; Melchisedec bringing out to Abram bread and wine; the fall of manna; and the multiplication of the loaves of bread and of the two fish. The multiplication of the loaves and the fish, quite frequent in early Christian art and second in importance only to the Last Supper, was gradually replaced by the miracle at Cana. On the Romanesque doorway at Charlieu, the miracle at Cana, a New Testament type of the Eucharist manifested *sub gratia,* is carved on the tympanum above its Old Testament symbolical anticipation *sub lege.* The Old Testament type is a liturgical sacrifice in the Temple of Jerusalem. Both scenes at Charlieu symbolize the blood shed on Mt. Calvary and the lamb sacrificed on the altar by the consecrating priest.

Until late Gothic art sacramental symbolism remained focused primarily on Baptism and the Eucharist. As early as the end of the 2d century, frescoes in the Cappella Greca (Roman catacomb of Priscilla) symbolized Baptism by the figures of the Ark of Noah and the water struck from the rock of Horeb, and by the miracle of Christ healing the cripple at the pool of Bethsaida.

During the typological period of the iconography of the Sacraments, some figures from the Old Testament and miracles in the New Testament kept an ambiguous symbolism and could be interpreted in terms of either Baptism or the Eucharist. The bronze baptismal font in the cathedral of Hildesheim (*c.* 1208) summed up the traditional typology of Baptism; the Baptism of Christ was cast on the vat, and on the lid, an additional commentary of the sacramental effect of Baptism (*significando causat*), the remission of sins. This is shown as the forgiveness obtained by the sinful woman who anointed Jesus' feet. The crossing of the Jordan by Israel, an Old Testament type of Baptism cast on the vat, was explained on the lid by the allegorical figure of *misericordia*. Thus *misericordia* is the pity of God opening the promised land to his Church through the channel of the Sacraments. A second crossing, of the Red Sea, was cast on the vat and duplicated on the lid by a New Testament figure: the massacre of the Innocents, intimating the innocence of Christ the slaughtered Lamb.

Transition to Liturgical Character. In an earlier baptismal font cast *c.* 1117 by Renier of Huy for the baptistery of the cathedral of Liège (today in St. Bartholomew, Liège), the stress was laid for the first time on the liturgical character of the rite, through the double baptism—by both immersion and aspersion—of the centurion Cornelius by St. Peter (Acts, ch. 10) and, according to apocryphal tradition, of the philosopher Crato by St. John at Ephesus. The neo-Hellenic elegance of the figures modeled by Renier of Huy announced the idealism of Gothic art. At the same time the iconographic program of the Liège font ushered in a decisive shift in the representation of the Sacraments.

The seven Sacraments illustrated as a sequence and in the realistic vein of liturgical enactments appear for the first time in the Passionary of Cunegonde, daughter of Ottakar II and abbess of the monastery of St. George in the castle of Prague (Prague, National and University Library MS 14, A17). Possibly, the program was dictated by the Dominican who wrote a treatise incorporated in the Passionary; the decoration of the book was not finished at the time of Cunegonde's death (1321). Although the seven vignettes representing the Sacraments are only pen drawn and tinged, they are imbued with a sense of atmosphere and corporeity that indicates Italian models. Italy must have inspired also the seven Sacraments with which, as "bas de pages," Jean Pucelle decorated the Dominican Breviary written *c.* 1325 for Jeanne de Belleville (Paris, Bibliothèque Nationale, ms. lat. 10483–84). Each Sacrament is bracketed between an allegory of a vice and an allegory of the contrary virtue, so that the reader is confronted with a systematic representation of seven Sacraments and seven virtues and vices (*see* VIRTUES AND VICES, ICONOGRAPHY OF). Unfortunately, in the Belleville Breviary an illumination is missing that was intended to take place between the calendar and the Psalter in order to illustrate the concept developed in the iconography of Sacraments. It is described, however, in the *"exposition des ymages des figures qui sunt ou Kalendier et ou Sautier"* as Christ crucified, the cross erected in the middle of the Garden of Delights, His blood watering the garden through seven rivulets symbolizing the seven Sacraments of the Church. The iconography of the Sacraments in the Belleville Breviary was reproduced in the Breviary of Charles V (Paris, Bibliothèque Nationale, ms. lat. 1052).

The idea of connecting the seven Sacraments with other "septenaries," e.g., the virtues and vices, the gifts of the Holy Spirit or the works of mercy, betrays a scholastic arrangement. Not before scholastic theology undertook to define the Sacraments and to fix their number was it possible for the time-honored quaternity of the Rivers of Paradise to steer a septuple course.

A more intimate relationship between Christ crucified and the Sacraments was materialized by the linking of streams of blood. This is found in the triptych (*c.* 1400) of Bonifacio Ferrer, a work of the school of Valencia, Spain. This painting (Fine Arts Museum, Valencia), which belongs to the International style and possibly reflects the influence of the Florentine Gherardo Starnina, was executed for the chapel of the Cross in the Carthusian Church of Porta Coeli, near Sagunto. The sacramental crucifixion, represented on the central panel, is accompanied on the proper left by the conversion of St. Paul; and on the proper right, by the Baptism of Christ. The tripartite program follows the teaching of St. John that there are three that bear witness on earth: "the Spirit, and the water, and the blood; and these three are one" (1 Jn 5.7–8).

Sacraments as the Church. The concept that the "Sacraments out of which the church is built" (St. Augustine, *In Psalm.* 126.7), associated with the flowing of His blood and the water when one of the soldiers speared the side of Christ crucified (Jn 19.34–37), was developed by the commentators on St. John's text (e.g., St. Augustine, *In evang.* 120; St. John Chrysostom, *Hom. in Ioh.* 84). The notion that the Sacraments derive their efficacy from the Passion of Christ was asserted by prescholastic theologians (Peter Lombard, *Sententiae* 4.1, *De sacramentis*) and by the scholastics (St. Thomas Aquinas, Summa theologiae 3a, 17.1). St. Bonaventure wrote on "Christ crucified . . . the Tree of Life set in the center of Paradise, that is the Church, and, through the channel of the Sacraments, rushing life into the other members of the *Corpus Mysticum.*" These terms are analogous to those used by the Dominican author of the iconographical program of the Belleville Breviary. It has to be recalled at this point that the expression *Corpus Mysticum* until the middle of the 12th century referred to the Eucharist, whereas *Corpus Christi* was applied to the Church. However, a curious reversal of meaning, or *chassé-croisé*, permuting the terms, occurred *c.* 1150 [H. de Lubac, *Corpus Mysticum* (Paris 1949) 88]. This explains why in late Gothic art Christ crucified amid the Sacraments symbolized the Eucharist. On both sides of the cross, the Sacraments that issued out with the blood and the water from the wounded side of Christ were represented enframed within the visible structure of a church, thus giving an architectural embodiment to the *Corpus Mysticum.*

The painting ''The Seven Sacraments,'' executed toward 1450 in the workshop of Roger van der Weyden (Museum of Fine Arts, Antwerp), is the accomplished exponent of the mystical and material link between the sacrifice of Christ and the Sacraments within the framework of the Church. Van der Weyden designed, if he did not actually execute, this nonfolding triptych as the cross section of a church. The huge cross, soaring up to the main vault, is set up at the location reserved since Carolingian religious architecture for the altar of the cross, at the symbolical heart of the church, identified with the eastern part of the nave. In the axis of the crucifixion, at the entrance to the choir, the Host is elevated. The six other rites are performed in the northern and southern aisles. Angels hover above the seven Sacraments, clad in liturgical or symbolical colors: green (Eucharist), white (Baptism), yellow (Confession), red (Penance), violet (Holy Orders), blue (Matrimony), and dark purple (Anointing of the Sick). The angels hold scrolls that are inscribed with texts relating to the symbolism of the Sacraments. The scroll proffered by the angel of Matrimony presents a peculiar interest, because it mentions the betrothal consummated in blood when Sephora, the foreign wife of Moses, circumcised her son with a stone (Ex 4.24–26). This Old Testament type alludes to the marriage of Christ with the Church made of the reunion of the church of the Nations and the church of the Circumcision. In the Antwerp painting timelessness and transiency, liturgy and realism, mystery and rite are fused into a unified composition. The Confirmation is administered by Jean Chevrot, Bishop of Tournai, who commissioned the painting. The hands of the two betrothed are wrapped up in the stole of the ministering priest (in 14th- and 15th-century illuminations the two betrothed were sometimes represented with their heads covered by a single veil).

There is from the workshop of Van der Weyden a second composition representing the Sacraments in the manner of the Antwerp triptych. It is the so-called Cambrai altar (Prado Museum, Madrid). The Sacraments are represented there as carvings painted in *trompe-l'oeil* and set in jambs of a Gothic portal opening on a Crucifixion. The episodes of the Passion are painted, also in *trompe-l'oeil,* in the archivolt of the portal. This was probably the work of Vrancke van der Stockt, an assistant of Van der Weyden. Drawings by Vrancke, similar to the *trompe-l'oeil* carvings of the Prado panel, are kept in the Ashmolean Museum, Oxford. They were copied on the orphreys of a cope commissioned by Jacques de Savoie, Count of Romont, for the cathedral of Lausanne and now in the Historical Museum, Bern. The central motif represents the Eucharist as the Consecration of the Host and the Communion of the faithful; and, between, appears the Trinity with the corpse of Christ lying on the lap of the Father, flanked by the Virgin and St. John entreating God. In a Netherlandish drawing of the end of the 15th century, which condenses the same Weydian composition, the cross is set immediately and symbolically under the keystone of the Gothic vault of a church choir (Musée Condé, Chantilly).

Sacraments Related to Crucifixion. The relationship between the Crucifixion and the Sacraments also was a theme carved on a number of stone fonts in Norfolk and Suffolk (late 15th, early 16th century). These fonts have an octagonal vat set on a pedestal, the number eight connoting, as it did in the octagonal early Christian baptisteries, salvation after death in the light of Christ resurrected and, therefore, the first day of a new creation. On these fonts of East Anglia the Confirmation is depicted as administered to infants (according to a decision of the Synod of Exeter, 1287) and Penance as a flagellation scene (cf. also a fresco in the Incoronata church, Naples). A Mosan enameled cross (see illustration), presents an early scheme of the relationship between the cross and the Sacraments of Eucharist (*Innocentia* and Lamb) and Baptism (*Fides* and baptismal vat). Each one is personified by an angelic allegory at the extremities of the cross bar. A contemporary Mosan enameled plaque typified baptism in the figure of Naaman the Syrian, who was cured of his leprosy after having bathed seven times in the Jordan by order of Eliseus (British Museum). The Sacraments appear in stained-glass windows of the second half of the 15th century in western and northwestern England. They are connected with Christ crucified or with an image of the Savior crowned with thorns and robed in a purple mantle, by seven streams of blood branching from the five wounds.

The canopy of the pulpit in the cathedral of Vienna (1514–15), in which are set reliefs representing the Sacraments, is octagonal, like a baptismal font. The resemblance to a vat is again suggested by the double representation of Baptism: the Baptism of Christ and the liturgical rite. The bust portraits of the Fathers of the Latin Church on the four panels of this pulpit recall the authority delegated by Christ to the Church to administer the Sacraments. These figures, masterpieces of expressionist portraiture, were carved by Anton Pilgram, whereas the reliefs of the Sacraments were left to an assistant.

Representation of Sacramental Rites. Italian influence suggested to the painter of Cunegonde's Passionary and to Pucelle the representation of the Sacraments as contemporary liturgical rites. The Sacraments were painted as genre ''stories'' completed by an allegory of the triumph of the Church by a Sienese artist on a ribbed vault of S. Maria Incoronata (Naples, *c.* 1335). They were carved with the same straightforward picturesqueness (*c.*

1350, probably by Alberto Arnoldi) on the campanile of the cathedral of Florence. There the sculptures are set above reliefs of Genesis and the founders of the liberal arts, executed after models by Giotto or by the hand of Andrea Pisano. The Sacraments appear in an allegorical and cosmological context, side by side with representations of the virtues and of the planets. Their figures present a smooth and elongated compactness that, in keeping with their stern sobriety, indicates the influence of Orcagna.

In 1533 the sculptor of Charles V, Jean Mone, carved the Sacraments as rites in seven roundels decorating the alabaster main altar of Notre Dame at Huy. The roundels are framed by eight statuettes carved in the round—the four Evangelists and the four Fathers of the Latin Church—and the composition is topped by a symbol of the Crucifixion: the Pelican in her piety. Penance was treated by Mone as an allegory: the Church absolving the sinner situated between figures of contrition and sanctification.

Poussin painted two series of Sacraments. One (1634–42) was for Cassiano dal Pozzo; five paintings are in the collection of the Duke of Rutland, Belvoir Castle; one, Baptism, is in the National Gallery, Washington, DC; Penance, destroyed, is known through an engraving. The other series (1644–48), for Chantelou, is in the Earl of Ellesmere collection on loan at the National Gallery of Scotland. These paintings echo the definition of the Council of Trent that Christ instituted the Sacraments. Poussin's Baptism, Eucharist, Penance, and Holy Orders are based directly on the life of Christ as told in the Gospel "in such a manner that no interpreter is needed, with the proviso that the Gospel has been read" (Poussin's letter to Chantelou, June 3, 1647). In the Eucharist, Christ and the Apostles are lying on couches around a three-sided table set in a reconstituted Roman triclinium. Such an archeological approach was in line with certain recommendations of the fathers who gathered at Trent. This approach was first attempted in Ciacconius's *De Triclinio* (1588). The main source of inspiration for Poussin's Sacraments was the work of the Jesuit Louis Richeome (*Tableaux sacrés des figures mystiques du très auguste sacrifice et sacrement de l'Eucharistie,* 1601). The ambition of Richeome had been to provide an iconographical pattern book for the use of Christian artists similar to the *Imagines* of Philostratus. Poussin cast his stories of the Sacraments in the most disciplined classical mold when he came to paint the second series, which, compositionally, is based on Raphael, but which, by its austere aura and heroical spirit, announces the spirit of David's painting. The triclinium was used also in the depiction of Penance as the episode of the sinful woman anointing the feet of Jesus. In the Holy Orders painting Poussin exalted the primacy given to the Roman Catholic Church in the person of St. Peter receiving the keys. The Confirmation is based on an episode of the persecution suffered by the Christians of Lyons in 177, and the Anointing of the Sick, in spite of its impersonal atmosphere resulting from the antique costumes and a mood of stoic restraint, alluded to the death of Louis XIII, so that the series was pervaded by a discreet spirit of Gallicanism. It should be pointed out that Poussin's Sacraments were inspired partly, as one may infer, by frescoes painted in the refectory of the novitiate of the Jesuits at S. Andrea al Quirinale, Rome (destroyed 1658), and that consequently, they reflect an important Jesuitic aspect in the art of the Counter Reformation.

Bibliography: E. P. BAKER, "The Sacraments and the Passion in Medieval Art," *The Burlington Magazine* 66 (1935) 81–89. L. BECHERUCCI, "I relievi dei sacramenti nel campanile del duomo di Firenze," *Arte* 30 (1927) 214–223. A. C. FRYER, "On Fonts with Representations of the Seven Sacraments," *The Archaeological Journal* 59 (1902) 17–66. A. LOUIS, *L'Église Notre-Dame de Hal (Saint-Martin)* (Brussels 1936). R. DE MARIGNAN, "'Les Sept Sacrements 'convertis en sept autres histoires' par Nicolas Poussin," *Revue des questions historiques* 63 (November 1935) 73–99. K. MORAND, *Jean Pucelle* (Oxford 1962), cf. M. R. JAMES, *Descriptive Catalogue of the Second Series of 50 manuscripts in the Collection of Henry Yates Thompson* (Cambridge, England 1902) 365–368. J. NEWWIRTH, "Zur Geschichte der Miniature-Malerei in Böhmen," *Mittheilungen der Kaiserlichen und Königlichen Centralcommission,* NS 11 (1885) 17–33. P. ROLLAND, "Het drieluik der Zeven Sacramenten van Rogier van der Weyden," *Annuaire du Musée Royal des Beaux-Arts d'Anvers* (1942–47) 95ff, cf. E. PANOFSKY, *Early Netherlandish Painting,* 2 v. (Cambridge, MA 1953) 282–285, and P. WESCHER, "The Drawings of Vrancke van der Stoct (The Master of the Cambrai Altar)," *Old Master Drawings* 13 (1938) 1–5. G. M. RUSHFORTH, "Seven Sacraments Compositions in English Mediaeval Art," *Antiquaries Journal* 9 (1929) 83–100. I. SCHLOSSER, *Die Kanzel und der Orgelfuss zu St. Stefan in Wien* (Vienna 1925). J. VANUXEM, "Les Tableaux sacrés de Richeome et l'iconographie de l'Eucharistie chez Poussin," *Colloque Nicolas Poussin* (Paris 1960) 151–162. A. VENTURI, *Storia dell' arte Italiana,* v.5 (Milan 1907) 638–649. P. VERDIER, "Un Monument inédit de l'art mosan du XIIe siècle, la Crucifixion symbolique de Walters Art Gallery," *Revue Belge d'archéologie et d'histoire de l'art* 30 (1961) 115–175. J. WILPERT, *Fractio Panis. La Plus ancienne représentation du sacrifice eucharistique à la Capella Greca découverte et expliquée* (Paris 1896), also in a German edition.

[P. VERDIER]

SACRED AND PROFANE

The distinction between the sacred and the profane is of prime importance in all religions. Here the nature of these two concepts will be considered, first from the viewpoint of comparative religion, and then as understood in the Bible.

In Comparative Religion. The sacred may be defined most easily as the opposite of the profane, but it must be kept in mind that this distinction is not applicable in the same way in all cultures and stages of culture. Yet even when all necessary attention has been given to cultural elements special to time and place, it is still evident that man, in respect to the phenomenon of religion, exhibits a kind of psychic reaction that is ambivalent. He feels himself drawn to the sacred and, at the same time, he regards the sacred as awe-inspiring or frightening mystery (cf., e.g., Ex 3.5; Lk 5.8). Accordingly, since R. Otto, the sacred has been called a *mysterium fascinans* and *mysterium tremendum*. The rites in the various religions recognize this ambivalence, since they are at once expressions of awe and precautionary measures. Encounter with the sacred is dangerous, and the mingling of the sacred and the profane is avoided everywhere.

Religion as the oldest and most universal phenomenon of mankind is intelligible and explicable only if it is conceived as a reaction of man to a call of the sacred previously made to him. The sacred in the full sense of the word is God. Man understands the sacred as the "wholly Other," and therefore he recognizes himself as a creature dependent and prepared for subjection. At the same time, on the basis of his consciousness of his personality, he feels himself impelled to domination and to initiative action. Man is aware of the sacred, because it manifests itself, appearing in various objects (hierophany), e.g., the firmament, stars, water, trees, vegetation, and stones. These objects are never worshiped in themselves, but always because the sacred reveals itself in them. The sacred stone remains a stone, but through a hierophany it is changed into a supernatural reality for the *homo religiosus*.

The experience of the sacred is independent of the nature of the object in which it manifests itself, because this experience does not signify a subjective disposition through which the sacred is projected into the objects concerned. The sacred space or area is designated by a hierophany or a theophany (Jgs 6.24–26; 2 Sm 24.16–25) and must be separated from amorphous profane space (Gn 28.17; Ez 42.20). Sacred time is homogeneous, and profane time, heterogeneous. Accordingly, religious feasts can be repeated at any time and frequently, and their mystery can always be represented again or reenacted. The liturgy of Good Friday, for example, makes possible a participation in the event of the first Good Friday. Christianity differs from all other religions in its evaluation of the sacred. For the Christian there are close connections between sacred and good, religion and morality, God and love. He knows no ambivalent attitude toward the sacred. Vacillation between fear and love has its source only in the conscience of the individual; the fear of God signifies reverence exclusively, and not an existential anxiety.

The sacred has a thoroughly personal character, for the sacredness of objects, places, and actions is constituted by their concrete relation to sacred persons, and ultimately, always to God.

Bibliography: R. OTTO, *The Idea of the Holy,* tr. J. W. HARVEY (2d ed. New York 1958). M. ELIADE, *The Sacred and the Profane,* tr. W. R. TRASK (New York 1959); *Patterns in Comparative Religion,* tr. R. SHEED (New York 1958) 1–37. R. CAILLOIS, *L'Homme et le Sacré* (2d ed. Paris 1953). B. HÄRING, *Das Heilige und das Gute* (Freiburg 1950). O. SCHILLING, *Das Heilige und Gute im A.T.* (Leipzig 1956). J. DILLERSBERGER, *Das Heilige im N.T.* (Kufstein 1926).

[W. J. KORNFELD]

In the Bible. The original Hebrew word expressed by holy or sacred is *qādôš* (holy; *qōdeš,* holiness), with the general meaning of separated or removed from the profane or unclean and destined for God's service. Profane (*ḥōl*) is derived from a root that means permissible for ordinary use. Thus the profane is accessible to all, whereas the sacred is removed from common use.

According to Lv 10.10, priests are to distinguish between sacred and profane, clean and unclean. A person or thing is sacred according to its proximity to Yahweh Himself. Unlike other religions, the OT religion proposes Yahweh as "the holy One of Israel." He is the entirely Other, superior to all, inaccessible to the created world (1 Sm 6.20). The angels are the holy ones of God's court, reserved for His service. Priests who serve His sanctuary are holy (Lv ch. 21).

To be sacred is, in an active sense, to keep oneself free from impurities, and passively, to be set apart as something to be revered. The priest's clothing is sacred (Ex 28.43; Nm 8.7; Ex 29.29; 31.10). The priest's offering is sacred (Lv 6.10–11). Such sacredness is a "state" or "condition" from which men emerge to reenter normal life.

Israel as a nation is holy (Ex 19.5) because Yahweh has chosen it to be "His own" (Lv 20.26; Dt 7.6; Jer 2.3). The land of Israel is holy because it is Yahweh's abode (Hos 8.1; 9.15; 4 Kgs 5.17; Zec 2.16; 2 Mc 1.7); Jerusalem and the Temple are holy (Is 52.1; 3 Kgs 9.3); the dwelling is approachable only by Levites (Nm 1.51); and the ark is untouchable (Lv 16.1–2). To approach the sanctuary or altar in an unclean state is to profane things sacred to Yahweh (Lv 21.23). Times also are sacred. Working on the Sabbath desecrates it (Ex 31.14; Ez 20.13).

The distinction between sacred and profane reaches God Himself. Yahweh is profaned when something sacred to Him or His holy name is profaned (Lv 22.2; Mal 1.12). His name is profaned by the sacrificing of children to Moloch (Lv 18.21) and by idolatry (Ez 20.40). Yahweh is depicted as profaning His heritage (Is 48.6), His sanctuary (Ez 24.21), and His holy gates (Is 43.28). Profane is used as synonymous with and parallel to unclean (Ez 22.26; Lv 10.10).

In the NT the ritualistic distinction between the profane and the sacred is abolished (Mk 7.15; Acts 10.15, 28; Rom 14.14). Christ (Mt 15.11–20) and His Spirit (Acts ch. 10–11) convinced the Apostles that what profanes man is moral impurity.

See Also: HOLINESS (IN THE BIBLE); PURE AND IMPURE; SIN (IN THE BIBLE).

Bibliography: *Encyclopedic Dictionary of the Bible*, tr. and adap. by L. HARTMAN (New York 1963), from A. VAN DEN BORN, *Bijbels Woordenboek* 1012–18; 1927–28. J. MUILENBURG, G. A. BUTTRICK, ed., *The Interpreters' Dictionary of the Bible*, 4 v. (Nashville 1962) 2:616–625. L. E. TOOMBS, *ibid.* 3:893.

[J. LACHOWSKI]

SACRED HEART (BERGAMO), DAUGHTERS OF THE

(*Congregatio Filiarum Sacri, Cordis Jesu*, FSCJ); founded in 1831 at Bergamo, Italy, by Teresa Verzeri and Canon Giuseppe Benaglio (1767–1836). This religious congregation began during a period of great political, social, and religious unrest, and aimed to revive faith and reduce social conflicts by means of the education of women and girls. Misunderstood by the local bishop, the Daughters withdrew to the adjoining Diocese of Brecia two months after receiving papal approbation (1841). Pius IX approved the constitutions (1847). During the disturbances of 1848, blamed on the Jesuits who were advisers to the foundress, the civil power threatened to suppress the congregation. After this followed peaceful progress, slow but constant. Since 1919 there has been no distinction of grades among the religious. The generalate is in Rome.

Bibliography: *Annali della Congregazione* (Rome 1902). D. T. DONADONI, *Teresa Verzeri* (Turin 1964).

[D. T. DONADONI/EDS.]

SACRED HEART, DEVOTION TO

A special form of devotion to the Word Incarnate that focuses attention on the physical heart of Jesus Christ as the symbol of His threefold redemptive love. In the devotion to the Sacred Heart the special object is Jesus' physical heart of flesh as the true natural symbol of His threefold love: the human love, sensible and spiritual (in-

fused supernatural charity), and the divine love of the Word Incarnate. In and through adoration of the physical heart the threefold love is adored and ultimately the Person of the Word.

To the adoration of this redemptive love are added acts of interior and exterior devotion that spring from the character of this special object: imitation of the virtues of Christ's Heart, especially His redemptive love; consecration as dedication to Christ or the gift of self in response to Christ's love; and apostolic REPARATION for sin as sharing in Christ's redeeming sacrifice of atonement. Historically, the more popular forms of the devotion included celebration of the feast on the Friday following the Sunday after Trinity Sunday; observance of the monthly First Friday with HOLY HOUR or votive Mass of the Sacred Heart, consecration of families to the Sacred Heart, and enthronement of the Sacred Heart in the home (*see* SACRED HEART, ENTHRONEMENT OF).

History. At one time it was customary to set the beginning of this devotion at about the year 1000, since the devotion as a distinctive form of cult to the Heart of the God-Man as symbol of His love appeared only in the early Middle Ages. Since 1928, however, as the result of scholarly studies and encouragement by Pius XII's encyclical *Haurietis aquas*, theologians are seeking out the Biblical, patristic, and liturgical sources of the devotion as the perennial worship rendered to the pierced Heart of Jesus, streaming forth living waters of grace upon the Church.

Scriptural Foundation. Pius XII stated that ''nowhere in the Sacred Scriptures is there clear mention of any veneration or love for the physical heart of the Word Incarnate, considered precisely as the symbol of His ardent charity.'' However, the basic elements of the ecclesiastical devotion are found there in the true humanity assumed by the Word in hypostatic union and in the unfolding history of salvation as the story of God's everlasting love for men, seen especially in the covenant, described by the Prophets (Hosea, Isaiah, Jeremiah) in terms of a father's love for his children or a husband's love for his wife, and prefiguring the Messiah's sacrificial love in the new covenant.

A remote foundation of the devotion may be seen in the Biblical use of ''heart'' and similar words (Heb. *lēb, lēbāb, beten;* Gr. καρδία, κοιλία, σπλάγχνα; Lat. *cor, venter, viscera*) as the seat of the whole inner life of man, both natural and supernatural: his rational, emotional, volitional, moral, and religious life. References to the human heart of the Messiah are thus found in the Psalms (15.9; 21.15; 39.7–9; 68.21) and in Jeremiah (30.21–24).

In the New Testament Christ Himself on the feast of Tabernacles, commemorating the miracle of the Exodus when Moses had saved the people by making water flow from a rock, promised a fountain of living waters from His heart (Jn 7.37–39), thus referring to the messianic promise of living waters (Is 12.3; Ez 47.1–12; Zec 13.1) that the new Moses would strike from the rock of His body. For John the living water is the Holy Spirit, whom the risen Christ will send upon His Church. This prediction was fulfilled at Christ's death, the hour of His glorification, in the piercing of His side (Jn 19.33–37). From the first Pentecost on, the waters of salvation (the Spirit) have flowed from the pierced heart of the Messiah (Jl 2.28; Is 44.3; Acts 2.17).

Patristic Teaching. The teaching of the Fathers begins with the interpretation of Jn 7.37–39, which has come down in two different textual versions and consequently in two different interpretations. The more widely known but less probable (Alexandrian) reading sees the streams of living water flowing from the heart of the believer (Origen, Ambrose, Jerome, Augustine). The other (Ephesian) reading, the original punctuation and the interpretation of which were adopted by Pius XII, considers the living water streaming from the heart of Christ (Hippolytus, Irenaeus, Justin, Apollinaris of Hierapolis, Cyprian, Tertullian). This passage, joined to Jn 19.33–37, forms the early Christian picture of the Sacred Heart as the fountain that dispenses the Spirit from the Savior's wounded side. From this came the idea of the Church born from the pierced Heart of Christ as the new Eve from the new Adam.

The Middle Ages. Although much historical research remains to be done on the question, there seems to have been no sudden discovery of this devotion in the early Middle Ages (1100–1250), but rather a gradual transition from the patristic theology of the wound in Jesus' side as the source of grace to the medieval preaching of the Heart of Jesus as the express object of a particular, more personal devotion (St. Anselm, St. Bernard, and the Benedictine monks). In the period of the great mystics (1250–1350), the patristic heritage merged completely into the more subjective piety of the Middle Ages due to the strong emphasis on the Passion, special veneration of St. John, and numerous commentaries on the SONG OF SONGS. To this period belong the Franciscans, especially St. Bonaventure and the *Vitis Mystica* (long ascribed to him); the three Cistercians of Helfta: the two MECHTHILDS and St. GERTRUDE THE GREAT, for whom the devotion was a deeper penetration into the mystery of Christ living in His Church through the liturgy; and the Dominicans (St. Albert the Great and St. Catherine of Siena). In the last period (extending to 1700), following a period of decline, the devotion, preached chiefly by the Carthusians and supported by the *Devotio Moderna,* became widespread among the laity. Through the Benedic-

tine Francis Louis BLOSIUS, the tradition passed to St. FRANCIS DE SALES (1567–1622), who imbued his Order of the Visitation with it. The newly founded Society of Jesus numbered ardent advocates of the devotion among its members and ascetical writers. These two orders were to work together to obtain a place for the devotion in the public life of the Church.

Official Public Cult. St. John EUDES (1601–80), although mainly concerned with veneration of the Immaculate Heart of Mary, also worked zealously to promote devotion to the heart of Jesus, especially by the establishment of a Mass and Office, for which Pius X called him the initiator, teacher, and apostle of the liturgical cult of the Sacred Heart. But the last phase of the history of the devotion is dominated by the name of the Visitandine St. Margaret Mary ALACOQUE (1647–90). The private revelations made to her by Our Lord at Paray-le-Monial (1673–75), while not the source of the official public cult, gave a great impetus to publicizing the devotion and shaping its practices. Prominent features were the establishment of a universal liturgical feast and the offering of reparation for the outrages committed against divine Love, especially in the Blessed Sacrament. St. Margaret Mary was assisted in her task by three Jesuits: her spiritual director, Bl. Claude La Colombière, Jean Crosiet, author of the first theological treatise on the devotion, and Joseph François de GALLIFET, promoter of the cause in Rome.

Ecclesiastical Approbation. In his bull *Auctorem fidei* Pius VI had authoritatively vindicated the devotion against the objections of the Jansenists. But early efforts at introducing a liturgical feast met with failure in Rome, chiefly because the devotion was presented as based upon the heart as principle and organ of love. The petition of 1765, which omitted the objectionable explanation, was granted by Clement XIII to the bishops of Poland and the Roman Archconfraternity of the Sacred Heart. In 1856 Pius IX extended the feast to the universal Church; later Leo XIII raised its rank. During the second half of the 19th century, mainly through the efforts of Henri Ramière and the APOSTLESHIP OF PRAYER, first approved by Pius IX in 1854, groups, families, communities, and states consecrated themselves to the Sacred Heart. In 1899 Leo XIII, by his encyclical *Annum sacrum,* decreed the consecration of the world to the Sacred Heart, which Pius X ordered to be renewed annually and Pius XI, 25 years later, transferred to the newly established feast of Christ the King. In 1928 Pius XI issued his encyclical *Miserentissimus Redemptor* on reparation to the Sacred Heart, complemented in 1932 by the encyclical *Caritate Christi compulsi.* To commemorate the centenary of the extension of the Feast of the Sacred Heart to the entire world, Pius XII in 1956 published his encyclical *Haurie-*

tis aquas on the nature of the devotion to the Sacred Heart. Unlike the two earlier encyclicals, Leo XIII's *Annum sacrum* on consecration and Pius XI's *Miserentissimus Redemptor* on reparation, the approach in *Haurietis aquas* is strictly theological, showing the dogmatic foundation of the devotion in Scripture and tradition.

Theology. The scriptural and patristic sources of the devotion (outlined above) found concrete expression in the liturgy over the centuries preceding and during the Middle Ages. After a period of experimentation with many different Masses of the Sacred Heart, the definitive Mass prescribed by Pius XI represents a return to the more traditional sources of the devotion.

Controversies have arisen over the precise object of the officially approved devotion, whether "heart" was to be understood as physical, metaphorical, or symbolic, and whether the love was human or divine. It is now generally admitted, following Pius XII, that both the physical heart and the total love of Christ are included in the object of the cult. Without the physical heart the public devotion authoritatively approved and prescribed for all Catholics by the Church is not realized. Although every part of Christ's sacred humanity is worthy of the strict adoration due to God alone, the heart is singled out for a special devotion because of its inherent symbolism. Pius XII calls the physical heart of Christ a natural symbol of His threefold love. While neither Scripture nor the Fathers expressly refer to the physical heart as the symbol of Christ's love, they do explicitly declare that Christ has a true and integral human nature and hence a heart upon which His entire affective life exercises a real physical influence. This real connection between the physical heart and the affective life provides the basis for the natural symbolism of the heart in respect to love. The Heart of Christ is the symbol of the total love of His person, more directly of the sensible love and affections, but also of the twofold spiritual love, human and divine. Through and beyond the human heart one goes to the total love of the Word Incarnate and also to that love by which the Father and the Holy Spirit love sinful mankind. Since the love of Christ is redemptive on each of these three levels, the pierced Heart of Christ hanging on the cross perfectly epitomizes the whole paschal mystery of our Redemption.

Excellence. Leo XIII called devotion to the Sacred Heart the most excellent form of religion; Pius XI, the synthesis of our whole religion and the norm of a more perfect life; Pius XII, the most perfect expression of the Christian religion and of strict obligation for all the faithful. Although objections have been raised against the devotion in the course of its history, many of them stem from psychological forms and sentimental accretions that have obscured the true devotion based on Scripture, interpreted by the Fathers, expressed in the liturgy, and authoritatively explained by the magisterium. The genuine form of the devotion as the worship the Church renders to the pierced Heart of Jesus, streaming forth living waters of grace upon His Church, has been restored in the definitive Mass of Pius XI and in the magisterial exposition of Pius XII.

Bibliography: A. HAMON, *Dictionnaire de spiritualité ascétique et mystique. Doctrine et histoire,* M. VILLER et al. 2.1:1023–46. J. STIERLI and A. VAN RIJEN, *Lexikon für Theologie und Kirche,* ed. J. HOFER and K. RAHNER, 10 v. (2d, new ed. Freiburg 1957–65) 5:289–294. E. AGOSTINI, *Il Cuore di Gesù* (Bologna 1950). J. BAINVEL, *Devotion to the Sacred Heart,* ed. G. O'NEILL, tr. E. LEAHY (London 1924). A. BEA et al., eds, *Cor Jesu,* 2 v. (Rome 1959). A. J. DACHAUER, *The Sacred Heart* (Milwaukee 1959). A. FEUILLET, "Le Nouveau Testament et le Coeur du Christ," *Ami du Clergé* 74 (1964) 321–333. A. HAMON, *Histoire de la dévotion au Sacré-Coeur,* 5 v. (Paris 1923–41). H. MARÍN, ed., *El Sagrado Corazón de Jesús* (Bilbao 1961), papal documents. J. STIERLI, ed., *Heart of the Saviour,* tr. P. ANDREWS (New York 1957).

[C. J. MOELL/EDS.]

SACRED HEART, ENTHRONEMENT OF THE

As a ceremony, the Enthronement of the Sacred Heart is public recognition and acceptance of the rule of the Sacred Heart of Jesus over the family. This is outwardly and permanently expressed by the solemn installation of the image of the Sacred Heart in a prominent place in the home and by an act of consecration to the Sacred Heart. As a permanent state, it means a way of life, in which love is fostered by the sharing of family interests with Christ and Mary through frequent renewal of the consecration to the Sacred Heart in union with the Immaculate Heart of Mary, and by fuller liturgical life at home and in church. It is not limited to the home, but can be carried out in any institution.

As an organized social crusade, it began at Parayle-Monial, France, in the chapel of apparitions in August 1907. Encouraged by four popes from St. Pius X to Pius XII, Mateo CRAWLEY-BOEVEY, SSCC, its founder, preached his crusade in all parts of the world. The Enthronement Crusade was inspired by the requests and promises of the Sacred Heart, especially these: "I will reign through My Heart" and "I will bless every place where the image of My Heart is singularly honored." The Enthronement combines these two requests by installing prominently the image of the Sacred Heart as a sign of the acceptance of the reign of the Sacred Heart in the home.

The Enthronement of the Sacred Heart is derived from the recognition of the merciful love of God as manifested in the Old and New Testaments, teachings on Christ regarding the primacy of love and of His Kingship, and from realization of the dignity and importance of the family. It is a practical application, to the home, of the liturgy of the Feasts of the Sacred Heart, Christ the King, Corpus Christi, and the Holy Family. It is based on the four Sacred Heart encyclicals, *Annum sacrum, Miserentissimus Redemptor, Quas primas,* and *Haurietis aquas.* In a private letter to Father Mateo in 1917, Benedict XV gave formal approval to the Enthronement; this was renewed by Pius XII in 1948.

Bibliography: M. CRAWLEY-BOEVEY, *Jesus: King of Love* (5th ed. Pulaski, Wis. 1963); *Father Mateo Speaks to Priests on Priestly Perfection,* tr. F. LARKIN (Westminster, Md. 1960). F. LARKIN, *Enthronement of the Sacred Heart* (2d ed. New York 1960).

[F. LARKIN/EDS.]

SACRED HEART, ICONOGRAPHY OF

The iconography of the Sacred Heart, properly speaking, does not appear in Christian art until the end of the 17th century following the apparition to St. Margaret Mary ALACOQUE. The Heart was popularly depicted with a wound, encircled by a crown of thorns, and a small cross above, the whole radiating light. The Sacred Heart was first depicted alone, separate from a figure of Christ. Popular images were already made *c.* 1685 at Paray and were worn or carried close to the heart following the example of Margaret Mary. Representation of the Sacred Heart on the breast of the Person of Christ developed more slowly. In 1780 the Italian artist Pompeo Batoni painted an image of the Sacred Heart of Jesus for the Queen of Portugal. In this painting Christ holds in His left hand an enflamed heart topped with a little cross and encircled with a crown of thorns. The Congregation of Rites (directive in 1878) did not approve this form of representation as suitable for gaining granted indulgences; the visible figure of the Heart was required to be represented externally on the breast of Our Lord. A further clarification (1891) permitted images of the Heart without the rest of the body for private devotion, but these were not to be exposed on the altar for public veneration.

Statues and paintings of disputable taste, often of vulgar sentiment repulsive to educated sensibilities, proliferated from the beginning of the 19th century. Occasional efforts have been made in reaction to these depictions of the Sacred Heart, but they have not effected a widespread and deeply meaningful image. The interest of the French painter George Desvallières led him to execute his celebrated ''Sacred Heart'' (1905), which depicts the Christ crowned with thorns tearing at His heart.

More recently Lambert Rucki has carved a figure of Christ showing his five wounds. In the church of the Sacred Heart, Audincourt, France, in the stained glass designed by LÉGER (1950–52) behind the high altar, the five wounds are shown shining as five suns, recalling the vision of Margaret Mary.

Bibliography: A. L. DELATTRE, *La représentation du Coeur de Jésus dans l'art chrétien* (Tunis 1927). H. J. GRIMOUARD DE SAINT LAURENT, *Les images du Sacré Coeur au point de vue de l'histoire et de l'art* (Paris 1880). K. KÜNSTLE, *Ikonograhpie der christlichen Kunst,* 2 v. (Freiburg 1926–28) 1:615–618. L. RÉAU, *Iconographie de l'art chrétien,* 6 v. (Paris 1955–59) 2:47–49.

[J. U. MORRIS]

SACRED HEART, SISTERS OF THE SOCIETY DEVOTED TO THE

A religious congregation of women of diocesan right (SDSH; Official Catholic Directory #4050) founded in Hungary and Czechoslovakia in 1941. The work of the society is directed especially to those who are not easily reached by other apostolic groups. In the U.S., the sisters are engaged in religious education in public and parochial schools, catechist formation, camps for children and youth, retreats and spiritual direction, catechetical programs for immigrants, and foreign missions. As a result of the rise to power of communism in Eastern Europe, the sisters moved their motherhouse from Hungary to California in 1957, under the leadership of Sister Ida Peterfy, the superior general. In addition to their houses in California, the sisters have overseas foundations in Taiwan and Hungary.

[I. PETERFY/EDS.]

SACRED HEART, SOCIETY OF THE

(RSCJ, Official Catholic Directory #4070); an institute of religious women devoted to the work of education. Rev. Léonor de Tournely first planned the society to meet the need for Christian education after the French Revolution. At his death Rev. Joseph VARIN D'AINVILLE chose Madeleine Sophie BARAT of Joigny (1779–1865), France, as its foundress. In Paris on Nov. 21, 1800, the first members consecrated themselves to the Sacred Heart; a number of other foundations followed the establishment of the first convent at Amiens. In 1806 Mother Barat was elected superior general. Constitutions based on those of the Society of Jesus and centered on devotion to the Sacred Heart were adopted in 1815. That year the first motherhouse was established in Paris. On Dec. 26, 1826, Leo XII formally approved the society.

During the lifetime of the foundress, 111 houses were opened in Europe, Algeria, Chile, and North America, where the society was brought (1818) by Rose Philippine DUCHESNE. From her pioneer convent in St. Charles, MO, the society spread through the U.S., Canada, and the Antilles, largely through the zeal of Mother Aloysia HARDEY. In Europe, Mother Barat traveled widely and governed with wisdom and energy until her death in Paris on May 25, 1865.

From Europe and the Americas the society was extended successively to: New Zealand, Australia, Egypt, Japan, China, the Congo, India, Korea, and Taiwan. Native vocations came from all these countries. The society suffered attacks and lost convents during revolutions in Italy and Switzerland, during the Kulturkampf in Germany, and under the Third French Republic (which closed 47 houses). Anticlericalism in Mexico, Communist aggression in Spain, China, Hungary, and Cuba closed other houses. New houses were opened for those lost.

In the U.S., the society is engaged in the ministry of academic education at all levels, catechetics, adult education, healthcare, parish ministries, and social outreach. The U.S. provincialate is in St Louis, MO. The generate is in Rome.

Bibliography: L. CALLAN, *The Society of the Sacred Heart in North America* (New York 1937).

[M. WILLIAMS/EDS.]

SACRED HEART BROTHERS

(SC, Official Catholic Directory #1100); a religious congregation of men founded near Lyons, France, Sept. 30, 1821, by Rev. André Coindre, for the care of abandoned or homeless boys. Their principal ministry is education.

To the original group of ten members, Coindre gave the rule of St. AUGUSTINE and the constitutions of St. Ignatius, intending to provide at a later date a detailed rule of life suited to their particular work. A novitiate was set up at Monistrol, France, and by 1826 the brothers had opened five schools. Coindre died suddenly in 1826, and the work continued under the direction of his brother, Rev. Vincent Coindre, until 1841, when he resigned as superior. The brothers, in a general chapter held in September of that year, unanimously elected Brother Polycarp as superior general. Since that time the brothers have always chosen their superior from their own ranks. The set of rules and statutes composed by Brother Polycarp was approved by the general chapter of 1846. Final approbation of the rules and constitutions was granted by the Holy See in 1927.

In 1847 five brothers were sent from France to the U.S. to take charge of a home for orphans at Mobile, AL.

Within the next two decades the congregation extended its work to other cities in the South. St. Stanislaus School at Bay in St. Louis, MS, was opened in 1854; an orphanage at Natchez, MS, in 1865; and St. Aloysius School in New Orleans, LA, in 1869. In 1870 a novitiate was established in Indianapolis, IN. The congregation made its first foundation in the New England states with the opening of a school in Manchester, NH (1889). In 1872 the brothers extended their work to Canada, establishing a school at Arthabaskaville in the Province of Quebec.

The Brothers of the Sacred Heart also established their presence in other parts of the world: Madagascar and Uruguay (1928), Argentina and Syria (1930), Italy (1931), Basutoland, South Africa (1937); the Egyptian Sudan (1929); Uganda, Africa (1931); Haiti (1943); Brazil (1945); Kenya (1948); the Cameroons (1953); Holland and New Caledonia (1954); England and French Guiana (1955); Colombia and Northern Rhodesia (1956); the Ivory Coast (1957); and the Philippines (1958).

The first general headquarters of the congregation was at Paradis, near Le Puy, France. Later the general council took up residence in Renteria, Spain, and in 1950 headquarters were transferred to Rome, Italy. In the U.S., there are three provinces: New Orleans Province (estab. 1947 and headquartered in New Orleans, LA), New England Province (estab. 1945 and headquartered in Pascoag, RI), and the New York Province (estab. 1960 and headquartered in South Ozone Park, NY).

[B. DOWNEY/EDS.]

SACRED HEART MISSIONARIES

(MSC, Official Catholic Directory #1110); a congregation of priests and brothers founded in Issoudun (Indre), France, by Rev. Jules CHEVALIER to renew the faith of France through devotion to the Sacred Heart. Chevalier, a young assistant pastor in the Issoudun parish, had formulated plans for his new organization while still a seminarian in Bourges. In 1854 he made a novena to the Blessed Virgin in preparation for her feast of December 8; this day is considered the founding date of the new community, which was granted status as a diocesan congregation on Sept. 9, 1855. The congregation was recognized by the Holy See in 1869.

The first MSC apostolic school (minor seminary) was opened on Oct. 2, 1867, at Chezal-Benoît, France. During the French anticlericalism of the 1880s, the members of the society were dispersed; they opened similar schools in other countries, thus making the congregation international in character early in its history. MSC members expanded their work further when Leo XIII requested them to undertake the difficult island missions of Micronesia and Melanesia in the South Pacific. Despite limited resources and his knowledge of previous missionary failure there, Chevalier accepted the assignment and three priests and two brothers embarked from Barcelona, Spain, Sept. 1, 1881. Although not originally founded as a foreign mission congregation (members must volunteer for mission assignment), the society considered this work very appropriate to the fulfillment of its motto: May the Sacred Heart of Jesus be loved everywhere!

The U.S. province is headquartered in Aurora, IL. This province developed from the work of a few priests under the leadership of Joseph Stettner, MSC; in 1910 they left the German province to assist in the Diocese of La Crosse, WI, where they established a mission house at Sparta. The MSC opened another mission house in Reading, PA, and accepted the responsibility of the parishes in Nazareth and in Haycock Run, PA. In 1924, under Father Bernard Greifenberg, they formed an MSC community in Aurora, IL (which later became the provincial headquarters), and in January 1926 began classes in the minor seminary in nearby Geneva. In 1927 the congregation officially organized all these communities as the American district under Father Stettner and in 1935 inaugurated a major seminary at Shelby, OH. On July 22, 1939, the various MSC communities in the U.S. (excluding those of the Canadian province) were granted independent status as the U.S. province, with Joseph Averbeck, MSC, as first provincial. The generalate is in Rome.

Bibliography: A. DUPEYRAT, *Papouasie: Histoire de la mission, 1885–1935* (Paris 1936). H. VERMIN, *Le Père Jules Chevalier* (Rome 1957). *The Missionaries of the Sacred Heart: 1854–1954* (Berwyn, IL 1954).

[L. F. PETIT/EDS.]

SACRED HEART OF JESUS, APOSTLES OF THE

(ASCJ; Official Catholic Directory #0310) Originally known as the Missionary Zelatrices of the Sacred Heart (MZSH); a congregation of women religious with papal approbation, founded at Viareggio, Italy, in 1894, by Mother Clelia Merloni. During the early years, when the sisters were engaged in the education of youth and the care of orphans and the aged, financial ruin threatened the community. Bp. Giovanni Battista SCALABRINI befriended the sisters and suggested that they extend their work to the centers of Italian immigration in the New World. Accordingly, in 1900 the congregation established its first foundation in the Americas with a school in Brazil.

In 1902 the work of the U.S. province began with a hospital in Boston, Mass. After some difficulties in Bos-

ton, the congregation took root in the Archdiocese of Hartford. The provincial house, originally established in New Haven, Conn., was moved to Mount Sacred Heart, Hamden, Conn., in 1954. The generalate is in Rome. In the U.S., the sisters are engaged in education at all levels, catechetics, parish ministries, healthcare, and social outreach.

[M. T. MARZULLO/EDS.]

SACRED HEART OF JESUS, DAUGHTERS OF THE CHARITY OF THE

(FCSCJ; Official Catholic Directory #0750); a congregation of women religious with pontifical approbation whose motherhouse is in La Salle-de-Vihiers, in the Diocese of Angers, France. The community came into existence early in the 19th century when the pastor of La Salle-de-Vihiers, Jean Maurice Catroux, unable to obtain religious teachers for the children of his parish, decided to found a new congregation. One of his parishioners, Rose Giet, became the first sister in 1823.

The congregation continued to grow in France until, at the end of the 19th century, anticlerical laws closed religious schools and forced the sisters to seek new fields of labor. In 1905 four sisters came to the U.S. and opened a school in Newport, VT. In 1906 they extended their work to Champlain, NY, and in 1908, to Canada. In the U.S., the sisters are engaged in academic education at all levels, catechetics, pastoral ministries and counseling. The U.S. headquarters is in Littleton, NH; the generalate is in La Salle de Vihiers, France.

[S. L. GRANDPRÉ/EDS.]

SACRED HEART OF JESUS, PRIESTS OF

A clerical religious institute of pontifical status (SCJ; Official Catholic Directory #1130) founded at Saint-Quentin, France, in 1878 by Rev. Léon G. DEHON.

Dehon had been ordained nine years, possessed doctorates in theology, civil and Canon law, and philosophy, and had been made honorary canon of the cathedral of Soissons when he founded the congregation in 1878. Ten years later, Leo XIII granted the decree of praise to the congregation, which in this same year undertook its first missionary work in Ecuador. It also spread throughout Europe, rapidly developing in size and in activity. Missionaries were sent to Brazil in 1893 and to the Congo in 1897. Two years after Pius X granted the congregation the decree of approbation (1906), mission work began in Finland, and in 1912, in Cameroon. In 1923 missions were established in the Union of South Africa and Indonesia, and a foundation was made in the U.S. at the Indian mission of Lower Brule, South Dakota. The same year the constitutions of the congregation received final approbation from the Holy See. In the U.S., the work initiated by Father Matthias Fohrman and his companions from the German province, expanded so rapidly that in 1933 the North American province was formally erected.

In the U.S., the congregation are engaged in parish administration, chaplaincies, catechetics, mission work at home and abroad, retreats, spiritual direction, counseling, pastoral ministries, social outreach and education. The U.S. provincialate is in Hales Corner, WI. The generalate is in Rome.

[J. T. O'CONNOR]

SACRED HEART OF JESUS, SOCIETY OF THE

Religious institute established May 8, 1794, in the former Jesuit residence at Eegenhoven near Louvain, Belgium, which followed the rule of the JESUITS. Its main purpose was to effect the restoration of the Society of Jesus, suppressed since 1773. Members promised to seek admission into this order upon its restoration. The founder and first superior was Éléonor de TOURNÉLY, aided by Charles de Broglie, a nobleman whose brother was Bp. Maurice de BROGLIE. Both were French priests, *émigrés* from the French Revolution, and former seminarians at St. Sulpice, Paris, as were the other two original members. Joseph VARIN, superior (1797–99) after Tournély's death, soon joined them. Advancing armies of the French Revolution forced the group to flee to Cologne, then to Augsburg where the nine members pronounced vows (Nov. 15, 1794) similar to those of St. IGNATIUS OF LOYOLA and his first companions at Montmartre, Paris, in 1534. They sought admission about this time into the remnant of the Jesuits existing in White Russia; but acceptance of their petition was deferred. After moving to the neighborhood of Vienna to escape the French (August 1796), the Society established its headquarters in Hagenbrunn (April 1797), in a house donated by the Abbey of KLOSTERNEUBURG. Two years later its 50 members were well organized, influential, and possessed of considerable material resources. About half were priests, most being from distinguished backgrounds and well educated. Upon the recommendation of Pius VI, who noted the nearly identical rule and aims of the two organizations, the Society united with the PACCANARISTS (April 18, 1799); ac-

cepted Paccanari, who initiated the negotiations, as superior; and exchanged its own title for that of the Society of the Faith of Jesus, official name of the Paccanarists. Its subsequent brief history is that of the Paccanarists.

Bibliography: F. SPEIL, *P. Léonor Franz v. Tournély u. die Gesellschaft des heiligsten Herzens Jesu* (Breslau 1874). O. PFÜLF, *Die Anfänge der deutschen Provinz der neu entstandenen Gesellschaft Jesu* (Freiburg 1922). A. GUIDÉE, *Vie du R. P. Joseph Varin* (Paris, 2d ed. 1860). J. BURNICHON, *La Compagnie de Jésus en France 1814–1914* v.1 (Paris 1914). L. KOCH, *Jesuiten-Lexikon: Die Gesellschaft Jesu einst und jetzt* (Paderborn 1934); photoduplicated with rev. and suppl., 2 v. (Louvain-Heverlee 1962)1763–64.

[J. F. BRODERICK]

SACRED HEART OF MARY, RELIGIOUS OF THE

The Religious of the Sacred Heart of Mary (RSHM; Official Catholic Directory #3465), a pontifical institute of women religious, was founded in Béziers, France on Feb. 24, 1849 by a diocesan priest, Pierre Jean Gailhac (1802–1890), and Appollonie Cure Pelissier (1809–1869). Although marked for ecclesiastical advancement, Gailhac elected to devote his energies to education and to the needy. In collaboration with Appollonie Cure Pelissier, a widow who was for some years under his spiritual direction, he saw an opportunity to establish an institute for various works. Together, they shaped the vision of the institute— that all might have life through knowledge and love of God—and oversaw the works of the congregation and the formation of its members.

As Mother St. Jean, Appollonie Cure became first superior general. Her death occurred as the first foundations outside France were being organized in Ireland. With her successor, Mother St. Croix Vidal, Gailhac pioneered the institute's first schools in northern Ireland (1870), Portugal (1871), England (1872), and the United States (1877) where the first foundation was in Sag Harbor, N.Y. Gailhac shared with Mother St. Felix Maymard, the succeeding general superior, the satisfaction of seeing the congregation's constitutions approved by Pope Leo XIII. When Gailhac died in 1890, he bequeathed to his community many decades of successful apostolic works and a number of spiritual writings. Mother St. Constance Farret, elected general superior in 1905, further advanced those works by establishing foundations in Spain and Brazil.

In the U.S., a period of rapid expansion began under Irish-born Mother Marie Joseph Butler, who arrived in Long Island City, N.Y. in 1903. This expansion broadened when in 1926 she was elected general superior. With the founding of Marymount Colleges, begun in Tarrytown, N.Y., in 1907, she inaugurated a network of educational institutions that her closest collaborator and successor, (in 1946) Mother Marie Gerard Phelan, extended worldwide. Mother Gerard carried the founder's cause for beatification to near completion and initiated that of Mother Butler as well.

The RSHM sisters engage in educational, pastoral and social ministries on three continents: Europe (France, Ireland, Italy, Portugal, England, Wales and Scotland); the Americas (United States, Brazil, Mexico); and Africa (Mali, Mozambique, Zambia and Zimbabwe). In the U.S., the congregation has two provinces: Eastern American Province with headquarters in Tarrytown, New York, and Western American Province with headquarters in Montebello, California. The generalate is in Rome.

Bibliography: *A Journey in Faith and Time: A History of the Religious of the Sacred Heart of Mary,* (1990–93), 2v.

[F. S. BORAN/M. MILLIGAN]

SACRED HEARTS, SISTERS OF THE

Also known as the Sisters of the Sacred Hearts of Jesus and Mary, or simply, the Sacred Hearts Sisters (SS. CC.; Official Catholic Directory #3690). The Congregation of the Sacred Hearts of Jesus and Mary and Adoration (SS.CC.), was founded in 1797 at Poitiers, France, by P. M. Joseph COUDRIN and Henriette AYMER DE LA CHEVALERIE. For a fuller treatment of the congregation's history, *see* SACRED HEARTS, FATHERS OF THE. Like the Sacred Hearts Fathers, the Sacred Hearts Sisters were also popularly called the Picpus Sisters, after Rue Picpus in Paris, the location of the motherhouse until it moved to Rome in 1966. The rule is based on the BENEDICTINE RULE and combines the contemplative and active lives. Papal approval of the original institute came in 1817, and of the revised one in 1922. Sisters take simple, perpetual vows. Historically, they wore a white tunic with a badge of the Sacred Hearts on their scapular, and a red mantle during adoration. The congregation's ministries include devotion to the Sacred Hearts; Perpetual Adoration; schools and education; pastoral work in parishes and among the poor and underprivileged; counseling and retreats; and foreign missions. In 1834 there were 18 houses, all in France. The first overseas foundation in Chile opened in 1838. In the U.S., the congregation founded a house in Hawai'i in 1859 after ten sisters died during an unsuccessful attempt in 1842. In 1908 a community was established in the continental U.S., in Fairhaven, MA. In the U.S., the congregation has one province (Pacific Province, headquartered in Honolulu, HI) and a region (East Coast Region, headquartered in Fairhaven, MA). The generalate is in Rome.

Bibliography: *Mère Henriette and Her Work,* adapted from Fr. ed. (St. Louis 1926).

[M. G. CREACH/EDS.]

SACRED HEARTS OF JESUS AND MARY, CONGREGATION OF THE

(SS.CC., Official Catholic Directory #1140); a religious congregation of priests, brothers, and sisters, founded to continue the work of the communities suppressed by the French Revolution but with a new motivation: reparative love for the Sacred Hearts of Jesus and Mary. Its founders were Rev. Pierre Marie Joseph COUDRIN, newly ordained priest of the Diocese of Poitiers, France, and Countess Henriette de la Chevalerie, a young aristocrat who had been imprisoned and condemned to death. After her release, she joined a small group of women known as the Association of the Sacred Heart, who were secretly keeping perpetual adoration of the Blessed Sacrament. Coudrin was named director of the association in 1792, and two years later the priest and the countess established the Congregation of the Sacred Hearts of Jesus and Mary and of Perpetual Adoration of the Most Blessed Sacrament of the Altar. In its early days, the congregation was popularly known as the Picpus Fathers, from the Rue de Picpus, Paris, where its first house was founded and where the Picpus cemetery, containing 1,700 victims of the guillotine and the body of the Marquis de Lafayette, is located.

Pius VII approved the new congregation in 1817. In 1825 Leo XII requested missionaries for Oceania, and priests and brothers went to Hawaii in 1827, the Marquesas Islands and Tahiti in 1833, Easter Island in 1837, and the Gambier and Tuamotu Islands in 1838. The twentieth century witnessed the congregation establishing missions in Japan, China, Southeast Asia, Africa, Norway, South America, and the South Seas.

Because of Protestant opposition, two of the priests sent to Hawaii in 1827 were exiled to California in 1832. During the next ten years, French-born Alexis Bachelot became the first resident pastor in Los Angeles while Irish-born Patrick Short founded the first school near Monterey. In 1845, a group of these fathers arrived from Valparaiso, Chile, to found a college but were assigned instead to staff the vacant California missions from San Francisco to San Diego. Later they withdrew after having opened a school in San Francisco. In 1835, Bp. Benedict J. Fenwick of Boston, MA, asked for missionaries to evangelize the Passamaquody natives in Maine. Fathers Edmund Demillier and Amabilis Petithomme labored there and in Massachusetts, New Hampshire, and Vermont, and even as far north as Nova Scotia. Demillier wrote the first grammar and catechism in the native language. In 1905, Bp. William Stang of Fall River, MA, invited the society to establish a residence in his diocese at Fairhaven.

The congregation has three provinces in the U.S.: Eastern Province (estab. 1946 and headquartered in Fair Haven, MA); Western Province (estab. 1970 and headquartered in La Verne, CA); and Hawaii Province (headquartered in Kaneohe, Oahu, HI). The generalate is in Rome. Renowned members of the congregation include Father Damien (Joseph de VEUSTER), well-loved missionary to Hawaii who is remembered for his care of those afflicted with Hansen's disease.

Bibliography: V. JOURDAN, *La Congrégation des Pères des Sacrés Coeurs* (Paris 1928).

[F. LARKIN/EDS.]

SACRED HEARTS OF JESUS AND MARY, SISTERS OF THE

(SHJM, Official Catholic Directory #3680); originally known as the Chigwell Nuns in England, they stem from the Servantes du Sacré-Coeur de Jésus, a congregation founded in France in 1866 by Father Victor Braun (1825–82). In 1870, during the Franco-Prussian War, a group of sisters established the first English foundation at Stratford. The English community separated from France in 1903 and received papal approbation in 1924. The motherhouse (estab. 1896) is located at Chigwell, Essex, near London, in the Diocese of Brentwood. The work of the congregation includes education, healthcare, pastoral ministries, and counseling. The U.S. headquarters is in Oakland, CA.

Bibliography: D. DEVAS, *Chigwell* (London 1928). F. FRODL, *Le Père Victor Braun* (Paris 1937).

[A. SAVAGE/EDS.]

SACRED HUMANITY, DEVOTION TO THE

Devotion to the God-Man, Christ, has two basic forms. First, those devotions whose particular focus of attention (which theologians call the proximate material object) is on the mysteries of the life of Christ, i.e., the contemplation of Christ the Incarnate Word in the mystery of His birth, infancy, Passion, etc. Second, those devotions that focus immediately on the human nature of Christ, on the physical body of Christ as the instrument

of our redemption and guarantee of His love, e.g., devotion to the Five Wounds of Christ, to His Precious Blood, the Holy Face, the Sacred Heart. This second form is devotion to the sacred humanity strictly speaking. Neither form, obviously, is totally independent of the other, but they are not the same, and between them a wide spectrum of practices and attitudes is possible. The tendency and tone of any Christological devotion is determined by how directly the humanity of Christ is being stressed, on how sharply Christ's ''humanness'' or His divinity is being brought into the focus of attention.

Historical Development. Christ in the mysteries of His Incarnation and Redemption is the theme of the New Testament. In the Synoptic Gospels there is emphasis on the humanity of Christ; in Saint John, an underlining of the divinity. In the Epistles of Saint Paul there is explication of the meaning of the Crucifixion, death, and Resurrection of Christ. The Fathers of the Church deal with these same mysteries and, specifically, with the wounds of Christ, especially, the wounded side of Christ, which is seen as pouring forth His grace, giving birth, as it were, to the Church. The Fathers' point of stress is not the suffering of the Lord, but the Lord who triumphed over suffering and death. The focus is on the victorious and glorious Christ. Thus the early Church's consideration of the Passion and death of Christ has an altogether different tone than that developed in the early Middle Ages. The difference can be seen in their way of considering the cross as a Christian symbol and the historical evolution of the crucifix. The cross is found early in Christian art, most often in various disguises to avoid the ridicule of the pagans of the empire who could see the cross only as punishment and degradation. (This is not the only cause of obscurity, however; other problems, both religious and artistic, were involved for the Christian community itself in presenting Christ crucified without irreverence, shock, or offense.) With Christianity's new status in the empire after Constantine and after the finding of the cross by Saint Helena, there was in the 5th century an open presentation of the cross, yet still without the figure of Christ. In the 6th century there was a presentation of Christ on the cross, but He is not represented as dead or in agony. About the 8th century the scene of the crucifixion had the figures of the Passion as reported in the Gospels—soldiers, the two thieves, Saint John, and Our Lady. But Mary was not yet the sorrowful mother of the *Stabat Mater*. Realism in a grimmer mode appeared in the 10th century, and Christ was depicted crowned with thorns, with blood flowing from the wounds of the nails, and with His body contorted with pain. Whereas the triumphant Christ held the attention of the early Church, the image of the suffering, humiliated Christ came to be preferred in the Middle Ages. This development, which occurred in and was confined to the West, marks a certain difference in outlook between the Eastern and Western Church. The Church of the East generally continued to maintain the first point of view. Byzantine art in its unearthly formalism and hieratic symbolism captured the majesty and otherworldliness of the great Lord Jesus who sits at the right hand of the Father and rules the universe in regal glory.

In the West the shift continued, and with Saint Bernard (1090–1153), it shaped a distinctive approach in Christian spirituality. The convert barbarians of the West were not attuned to Greek speculations and apophatic theology. The concrete image of God become man in Bethlehem, teaching, suffering, dying for them, was better calculated to hold and motivate them. Bernard took the Christian conviction that Jesus is the pattern men must follow in being refashioned in the image of God and pointed out that this was to be done by man's imitation of the human life of Christ. In his treatment of the Christian life there was a new emphasis on meditation on the details of Christ's human life to draw from it implications for one's spiritual life. Christ's life from the poverty of Bethlehem to the starkness of Calvary pointed the way. In a special way the wounds of Jesus speak of His love. However, Bernard continued, this devotion to the sacred humanity of Christ is not the termination of the devotion. The Christian is to go on into the inner life of Christ and mount to His divinity. The devotion to the sacred humanity is a means of arousing an emotional response to the love of Christ—and this is psychologically sound, for men do not grasp love in the abstract—but the Christian is to move beyond the emotional response and reach to mystical union with Christ.

Saint Francis of Assisi (1182–1226) exerted a powerful influence at least as great as that of Bernard in focusing attention on Christ's having become vulnerable for us through love, the motive of the Incarnation. In the turbulence of the age, Francis, preaching the gospel of peace, made visible the meaning of Christ made man.

> The Crib, the stigmata, the preachings to the beasts, St. Francis's whole life of dedication to his bride, Lady Poverty, were all messages addressed to those great powers who in this fateful hour were struggling in Italy and Europe for the possession of mankind. To the Cathars the message ran: God is not only ''pure spirit'' but also wholly man, vulnerable, helpless, bleeding flesh, and the blood of His brother men is too precious to be shed in warfare of any kind. To Byzantium and the Eastern Church it said: even in his Transfiguration, Christ still appears to us poor men in His crucified body (Francis's vision on Mount La Verna). To Rome, the Church which claimed to rule the emperors and kings of this world, it said: Christ came to earth to be the servant of His own. The war-mad Italian towns, standing for embattled Christendom as a whole, were reminded that Christians were called to be peacemakers. [Heer, 223, 224]

Devotion to the Five Sacred Wounds and to the Passion of Christ became a theme of meditation for the medieval mystics, and developed later into such forms as devotion to the Precious Blood of Christ and the Stations of the Cross. Gradually one of the wounds was singled out, and the devout began to concentrate on the side of Christ pierced by the lance of the soldier (John 19.33–34). From the open side to the heart exposed by the lance and thence to the love that brought Christ to the cross there was a natural and inevitable progression. Saints Gertrude (d. 1298) and Mechtilde (d. 1303), the Benedictine mystics, were granted visions of the Heart of Jesus beating with love for men. This was the early shaping and development of devotion to the Sacred Heart, which has come to hold the major place among all the devotions to the sacred humanity of Christ. From the 13th to the 15th centuries the devotion was spread among religious of the Benedictine, Cistercian, Carthusian, Franciscan, and Dominican Orders. Little by little devotion to the Sacred Heart of Jesus became something fully distinct from the devotion to the Five Sacred Wounds. Saint John Eudes (1601–80) was the author of the liturgical cult of the Sacred Hearts of Jesus and Mary. His piety, trained in the spirituality of Bérulle, drove him into the core of things, into the depths of the Redeemer. He distinguished three hearts: the physical heart, the spiritual heart, and the divine heart—all united in the person of Christ. Although not in definitive form, this contained the basic elements of devotion to the Sacred Heart. John Eudes was a link in the chain that continued with a nun of the Visitation, Saint Margaret Mary Alacoque (1647–90) who was the great apostle of the Sacred Heart and helped as no other to make the devotion a common possession of all the faithful. She gave the devotion the particular shape familiar to modern times. From her time the devotion was articulated distinctly: Christ's physical heart is the material object of the devotion; it is the symbol of His human and divine love. Devotion to the Sacred Heart for Saint Margaret Mary consisted in recognizing and returning the love of Jesus for men, best symbolized by His heart. In her presentation there was a new note, that of reparation, for she saw Christ's heart, His love, ignored, wounded, ridiculed, sinned against in ingratitude. The saint's mission was fulfilled, but not in her lifetime, nor yet for a good many years after her death. There was much opposition; some of it well taken, because not all zealous presentations of a good thing are necessarily well done; some of it well intentioned but mistaken; some, malicious. In presenting the heart of Christ as an object of worship certain theological issues basic to any devotion to the sacred humanity of Christ were necessarily involved. When the dust had settled the Church had condemned certain propositions of the Synod of Pistoia that denied the legitimacy of adoration of the humanity of Christ in general and devotion to the Sacred Heart in particular (H. Denzinger, *Enchiridion symbolorum* 1661–62). The devotion spread far and wide thereafter to the point where Pierre Pourrat in his monumental history of Christian spirituality could call devotion to the Sacred Heart the contemporary form of devotion to Our Lord. The devotion has indeed spread widely, though not always in depth. Pope Pius XII in *Haurietis aquas* (May 15, 1956) called for an examination and rooting of the devotion in its sources in Scripture and theology that it might bring forth in full measure the fruits of holiness it contains for the whole Church.

Theology. Devotion to the sacred humanity, which, unlike any form of devotion to the Blessed Virgin Mary or to the saints, includes worship in the strict sense, is justified theologically on the basis of the hypostatic union, that is, the fact that to the one person, Jesus Christ (who shares the divine nature with the Father and Holy Spirit), is united a true human nature (which He does not share with the Father and Holy Spirit). Since there is need for precise understanding of the point, it is worth the trouble of stating the matter in technical language.

> On Account of the hypostatic union of Christ's humanity with the Logos, it too is to be reverenced with *latria,* the adoration due to God, *in itself, though not for its own sake.* The object of worship in this case is not the God-man as a whole, but His humanity alone, but then only in its connection with the Logos. To understand this proposition correctly, we must not forget that this Church dogma would not have Christ's humanity worshipped for its own sake (*propter se*) but in itself (*in se*), in its hypostatic bond with the Logos. His human nature is simply the object of worship (*objectum materiale*), but not the motive or, in Scholastic usage, the formal object (*objectum formale*) of worship. The motive and formal object is exclusively the Logos, the Godhead. It would be sheer idolatry to offer *latria* to Christ's humanity for its own sake. [K. Adam, 240–41]

The particular value of devotion to the sacred humanity consists in this: it anchors a Christian in the reality of the Incarnation, and the mystery of the Incarnation is the pivot point of his faith. He does not go to God in just any way, but only in Christ and through Christ, since Christ is the revelation of God's plan to bring men to Himself (cf. Eph 3.1–6). It is an appreciation of the reality of the humanity of Christ that makes one aware of Christ as priest and mediator in the liturgy, for Christ is mediator or priest precisely because He took on human

nature. Further, the fact that He whom the heavens and the earth could not contain was carried in the womb of the Blessed Virgin Mary contributes to an appreciation of human nature, which is no small thing in view of the havoc that pessimistic evaluations of man's humanity have wrought in history. The Church has encouraged devotion to the sacred humanity of Our Lord because of these values and because of the benefits that the faithful have reaped in holiness from such devotions. Recognizing the needs of men, she offers in addition to her official liturgy the help of private and popular devotions to aid the Christian in the appreciation and practice of his faith and to help him penetrate more deeply into the saving mysteries of the faith. Such is the function and true value of devotions to the sacred humanity of Christ.

On this point Pope Pius XII wrote in his encyclical on the sacred liturgy, ''No conflict exists between public prayer and prayers in private, between morality and contemplation, between the ascetical life and devotion to the liturgy'' (*Mediator Dei* 36). While this is certainly true, it must be noted that the ideal balance between public and private or popular devotions has not always been achieved in the history of spirituality. Whenever there is an imbalance it must be put back in proper equilibrium again, for devotion to the sacred humanity of Christ, or any devotion, achieves its true value only when it is integrated with the totality of the mystery of salvation through Christ [cf. *Constitution on the Sacred Liturgy* (Dec. 4, 1963) 13].

Bibliography: P. POURRAT, *Christian Spirituality,* tr. W. H. MITCHELL et al., 4 v. (London-Westminster, Md. 1922–55). M. A. WILLIAMS, *The Sacred Heart in the Life of the Church* (New York 1957). F. HEER, *The Medieval World,* tr. J. SONDHEIMER (Cleveland 1962). K. ADAM, *The Christ of Faith,* tr. J. CRICK (New York 1957).

[J. P. BRUNI]

SACRED SPACE

Sacred space is distinguished from other spaces by the use to which it is put or by the religious memories, reverence and awe commonly associated with a particular place.

Historically sacred space encompasses various kinds of places, including those that are erected as religious shrines, such as churches and temples, as well as geographical entities that are religiously interpreted, such as mountains, deserts, caves and rivers. The 1983 Code of CANON LAW (cc. 1205–1243) defines sacred places as those which have been designated for divine worship or for the burial of the faithful through a dedication or blessing prescribed by the liturgical books. Included in this category are not only churches, but also oratories and private chapels, shrines, altars and cemeteries. New in the 1983 Code is the special recognition of shrines; a shrine is defined as a church or other sacred place to which the faithful make pilgrimages. Canon law restricts the use of these places to activities that serve the purpose of worship, piety, and religion. Although the ordinary can permit profane uses in individual cases, activities that are contrary to the holiness of the place are forbidden.

A place may be sacred and non-sacred at the same time, depending on the interpretation that one gives to it. Since it is not a space of wholly human choice or construction, a sacred space is different from other spaces. Its significance is grounded in the fact that the divine has intervened or continues to intervene in a particular way at such a place. Hence a sacred space is a symbol of divine presence. Although the motif of the "holy place" (*maqom qadhosh*, in Hebrew; *hieros topos*, in Greek) is common to most religions, this article concentrates chiefly on sacred space in the Biblical and Catholic tradition.

Forms and Functions of Sacred Space. A space is sacred because it fulfills a religious role, not because it has special aesthetic or physical qualities. It is customary to identify three functions of sacred space. A sacred space is first a place of communion with the divine. Jewish, Christian and Islamic traditions abound with stories of "theophanies," visions and auditory experiences wherein the divine presence makes itself felt. Hence a sacred space is often marked by a special symbol such as an altar, a statue, a mandala or a pillar, which represents the presence of the divine in an intense way. Secondly, it is a special place where divine power manifests itself. The effect that the power of divine presence has on human life varies from one religion to another. In some traditions, the transformation is described as salvation, in others as healing. Sacred places have often been the locations of miraculous cures. Thirdly, a sacred place is often regarded as a mirror of what the human world should look like as it relates to the divine. It provides an orientation for human life and focuses attention on what is thought to be significant for human transformation. In some religious traditions, sacred places face in a certain direction. The axis of Jewish synagogues is traditionally oriented toward Jerusalem, and that of mosques toward Mecca. Among Hindus, sacred places sometimes face north because it is the opposite of the south, the direction where the dead are thought to dwell. Early Christians faced eastward when they prayed, the direction of the rising sun— "the morning star"—symbolic of the resurrected Christ. Later their church edifices were also oriented toward the east for the same reason.

The Christian Tradition. The distinctive Christian understanding of sacred space is rooted in the Bible. The Acts of the Apostles recounts how Stephen spoke of the prophesies concerning the destruction of the Jerusalem temple, which was superseded by the spiritual temple of Christ's body. He said, "The Most High does not dwell in houses made with hands" (7:48). Later, Paul proclaimed the same teaching at Athens: "The God who made the world and everything in it, being Lord of heaven and earth, does not dwell in shrines that our hands have made" (17:24). These accounts touch on one of the fundamental truths of Christianity. The practice of religion as taught by Christ is not confined to an edifice built by human hands. Paul and Stephen affirmed the universal character of Christianity. God is present everywhere, hence God can be found wherever people in fact search for God. Nonetheless, Christians have never considered the teaching in the Acts of the Apostles as an absolute prohibition against regarding certain places, buildings and spaces within buildings with a sense of reverence and piety. The truth proclaimed by Stephen and Paul, properly understood in light of the Old and New Testament teaching on the presence and worship of God, makes it clear that no one place of pilgrimage, no one temple, no one sanctuary within a temple, circumscribes the divine presence in the world.

Old Testament. During the period of the patriarchs, there were many stories of epiphanic visitations of Yahweh to Abraham, Isaac, and Jacob. Genesis tells that in various places Abraham built an altar to the Lord and there invoked God's name (Gn 12:6–8; 13:4–5; 13:18). Etiological traditions kept alive the tales of how the ancestors built altars to commemorate and sacralize the places where they encountered the presence of the divine. In the time of the Judges and the Kings, toward the end of the second millennium B.C., these places became the chief sanctuaries of Israel—Shechem, Mamre, Beersheba, Bethel, Penuel.

The covenant proclaimed by Moses was inextricably linked with the religion of the patriarchs, but with important developments. The Mosaic tradition kept alive the memory of numerous theophanies, but they do not tell of Moses establishing a fixed shrine or altar. They are all associated with the "mountain of God" so that Mt. Sinai and its immediate vicinity (Horeb in the Elhoist tradition) represents forever sacred space. Although the site never came to be regarded as a sanctuary, the story of the burning bush, remembered in the context of a cultic ceremonial, prescribed how a mere human behaves in the presence of the divine. Moses was told, "Come no nearer! Remove the sandals from your feet, for the place where you stand is holy ground" (Ex 3:5). In the Mosaic covenant God placed greater emphasis on the mediatorial role of particular individuals, rites and objects. With Moses there was the appearance of a priesthood (Ex 28, 29; Lv 8–10), a ritual of sacrifice (Ex 25:23–30; Lv 28; 10:1), and above all the ark of the covenant and the sacred appurtenances that accompanied it (Ex 25–29). Since people need visible symbols to relate to the invisible, the ark became the principal symbol of God's presence for the Israelites. God's presence, however, was not confined to a determined place. The ark was housed in a tent; easily portable, it accompanied and focused the wanderings of the Israelites. They did not regard the ark as the dwelling place of God but rather a symbol of the divine presence in their midst. God was present to the Israelites wherever they sojourned: in Egypt, on Mt. Sinai, in the wilderness and in Canaan. Thus divine nomadism lasted from the time of Moses until the time of David who triumphantly carried the ark into Jerusalem (2 Sm 6).

Beginning with the accession of David, little by little in the course of two centuries, the center of Yahwism moved from Israel (the northern tribes) to Judah. Bringing the ark from Kiriath-Jearim to Jerusalem, David turned the ancient fortress of Jebus into the Holy City, the place of authentic worship, and symbol of God's presence. It was left to his son Solomon to build the temple as a special earthly dwelling place by a manifestation analogous to that of the Exodus. After affirming God's special presence in the temple, Solomon exclaimed in his dedicatory prayer: "Folly it were to think that God has a dwelling place on earth. If the very heavens and the heavens that are above the heavens cannot contain you, what welcome can it offer you, this house that I have built" (1 Kgs 8:27). From this prayer it is clear that God did not actually dwell in the temple because he could not be enclosed in the confines of any sanctuary. The temple, nonetheless, was the place of sacrifice, a privileged place of prayer, the special meeting place of God and the people. (Today the Dome of the Rock, popularly known as the Mosque of Omar, stands on the site of Solomon's temple. The remains of the western wall of the temple courtyard still stands, the "Wailing Wall," still sacred to Jews the world over.)

The temple signaled a change in the way that the Israelites imaged their relationship to Yahweh. God no longer appeared as a nomad among nomads but rather as a king in a palace, a sovereign dwelling in the privacy of his apartment available to no one but his special servants. Within the temple, the place where the ark was housed was called the "holy of holies," to which only the priests had access. For ten centuries the temple played an important role in Israel's history. It was the great place for prayer; it was there that the people assembled just as of old they assembled around the ark; it was a source of great blessing for Israel.

Because the Israelites tended to lose the interior spirit of true worship and set up false idols in their lives while continuing to practice the required temple rituals, God raised up the prophets who denounced their hardened hearts and their formal ritualism and who prophesied the destruction of the temple. In 587 B.C. Jerusalem was captured by Nebuchadnezzar, the temple was razed and the Judahites were driven into exile far from their own land. God, however, did not abandon the people but was with those who suffered and continued to trust in the covenant. While the Jews were far from the promised land, God was "for them a sanctuary" (Ez 11:16). During the exile, God prepared a holy people who were purified, who loved God and were animated by the spirit of love which they had shared with one another. When the Jews returned to Jerusalem after the exile, they reconstructed the temple—the Temple of Zerubbabel—and dedicated it in 515 B.C. It stood until 19 B.C. when Herod undertook to build a new, more magnificent temple, a project that took 46 years (see Jn 2:20).

The Synagogue. In Jewish tradition the synagogue represents another kind of sacred space. At first they were places for private gatherings in private dwellings that began during the period of the exile. By New Testament times the synagogue was an established and essential part of Jewish life and cult, and was found in every Palestinian town of any size and in cities outside Palestine where there was a sizeable community of Jews. Although it had a different function than the temple, the synagogue was still regarded as sacred place because it was a house of prayer and a place for the study of the law.

New Testament. The synagogue played a major role in the origins and growth of the early Church, but it never gained the symbolic importance that the temple had for Jews and even for non-Jewish Christians. In his first letter to the Corinthians he wrote: "Do you not know that you are the temple of God and that the Spirit of God dwells in you? . . . The temple of God is holy and you are this temple" (3:16–17). The theme is also developed in the letter to the Ephesians (2:20–22). The terms used—house of God, building, holy temple—call to mind the temple at Jerusalem, but the temple Paul wrote of is not built of inert stones nor is it built only of people of good will but rather of those who are members of Christ through Baptism.

The first letter of Peter also spoke of the community of the faithful as a temple: "Be yourselves as living stones, built into a spiritual house, a holy priesthood, to offer spiritual sacrifices acceptable to God through Jesus Christ" (2:4–5). The author spoke of the Christian people as living stones grafted on to the living cornerstone which is Christ.

The destruction of the temple at Jerusalem in A.D. 70, foretold by Christ, marked the end of an epoch. It disappeared just as the Church was beginning to spread throughout the world. And like the Jews of old, the Christians, too, had a need to assemble, above all to listen to the Word of God and to share in the Eucharist. For the early Christians, the actual place of assembly was not of great importance, for they knew that God dwelt not within the walls of a building but within the assembly of the faithful. Motivated by a practical need for a place of assembly, the early Christians used private dwellings, especially those of the wealthier Christians. These were the so-called house churches. The earliest known Christian church, a third century edifice at Dura-Europos, is an example of a private house converted to religious use.

It was not until the fourth century under Constantine that Christians began to develop a distinctive architecture. They adapted the style of the Roman business hall, the basilica, to church use. Designed for its interior spaces where the faithful assembled for worship, it was rectangular in shape along an east-west axis. Simple barriers marked off in functional fashion the areas dedicated to the liturgy of the word and reserved for the celebration of the Eucharist. As the basilicas became larger and more ornate, with vaults and coffered ceilings, Christians regarded them as symbolic of divine creation. Eusebius of Caesarea found their splendor to reflect the image of "the great temple which the Word, the great Creator of the universe, built throughout the whole world beneath the sun, forming again the spiritual image on earth of those vaults beyond the vaults of heaven" (*Ecclesiastical History* 10.4.69).

The term "church" designates both the assembly of the faithful and the building where they gather, just as the term "synagogue" designates the community of Jews and their place for worship. Church buildings are essentially functional; they are meant to help the community embrace the divine revelation that human persons are the special dwelling place of God. God lives in them but also transcends the limitations of human persons. Although Christians, like all other people, may find God everywhere and always, they believe that God's presence is symbolized for them in a special way when they assemble as a community to hear the Word of God proclaimed in the Scriptures and broken in the homily, when they celebrate the Sacraments, especially the Eucharist, and when they pray and sing and minister to one another in God's name. For Christians, churches are sacred spaces because they are constructed to help people place themselves in the presence of God and in communion with their brothers and sisters who are the children of God in Christ through the power of the Holy Spirit.

Environment and Art. An effective statement on the meaning of sacred space for Christians was issued in November 1977 when the Bishops' Committee on the Liturgy of the United States National Conference of Catholic Bishops (NCCB) published a detailed document on *Environment and Art in Catholic Worship.* It was the result of a cooperative effort on the part of the Federation of Diocesan Liturgical Commissions and the Bishops' Committee to provide principles for those involved in building or renovating liturgical spaces for the worship of the Christian assembly. Probably more than any other post-conciliar document this text provided an inspiring vision of liturgy as embodied prayer. It drew special attention to the non-verbal elements of Christian worship and emphasized that in the liturgy as well as its actions, gestures and rites communicate meaning to persons and communities on deep religious levels. The document did not confine its attention to a treatment of the altar, ambo, baptistery, place of eucharistic reservation and images but rather began with a carefully nuanced statement on the worship of God and its requirements. It then moved to a discussion of the assembly gathered for celebration, commented on the body language and other artistic expressions of those who celebrate, and only then discussed the furnishings and objects used in the liturgy. Such a statement of priorities is most important for it reaffirms the primacy of persons over things, acknowledges that people have access to the transcendence of God because of the divine immanence in and through the Incarnation of the Logos, and asserts that liturgy is primarily designed to transform persons and communities rather than to satisfy God's need.

A number of statements from the document deserve special commendation: "Liturgy flourishes in a climate of hospitality: a situation in which people are comfortable with one another, either knowing or being introduced to one another . . ." (n. 11). "The experience of mystery which liturgy offers is found in its God-consciousness and God-centeredness. A simple and attractive beauty in everything that is used or done in liturgy is the most effective invitation to this kind of experience" (n. 12). "The norm for designing liturgical space is the assembly and its liturgies. The building or cover enclosing the architectural space is a shelter or 'skin' for a liturgical action . . ." (n. 42). "Because the Sunday eucharistic assembly is the most fundamental ecclesial symbol, the requirements of that celebration will have the strongest claim in the provision of furnishings for liturgy" (n. 63)."The altar is holy and sacred to this assembly's action and sharing, so it is never used as a table of convenience or as a resting place for papers, notes, cruets, or anything else" (n. 71). "New baptismal fonts should be constructed to allow for the immersion of infants, at least, and to allow for the pouring of water over the entire body of a child or adult" (n. 76). "The purpose of reservation (of the Eucharist) is to bring Communion to the sick and to be the object of private devotion. Most appropriately, this reservation should be designated in a space designed for individual devotion. A room or chapel specifically designed and separate from the major space is important so that no confusion can take place between the celebration of Eucharist and reservation . . .'' (n. 78).

Of special value is the attention which the document gives to expertise in the building and renovation of churches, and the importance of educational effort in order to restore respect for competence in the arts. ''This means winning back to the service of the Church professional people whose places have long since been taken by 'commercial' producers, or volunteers who do not have the appropriate qualifications. Both sensitivity to the arts and willingness to budget resources for these are the conditions of progress so that quality and appropriateness can be real'' (n. 26). Objections are sometimes raised when money is spent on liturgical spaces that could have been given to the poor. Certainly crass ostentation is always out of place in the liturgy, but so is ugliness. It is not a part of Christian poverty to assess everything economically by materialist standards or to override aesthetic or other values for the sake of cheapness or squalor. Such a mentality narrows the human spirit and even creates those very evils accompanying destitution which all Christians must try to banish from the earth. The creation of a simple but beautiful sacred space for worship has the same goal as well-intentioned poverty programs, namely, the humanization of God's people so they might be fully restored to the image of God.

Bibliography: K. C. BLOOMER and C. W. MOORE, *Body, Memory and Architecture* (New Haven, CT 1977). R. L. COHN, *The Shape of Sacred Space* (Chico, CA 1981). Y. CONGAR, *The Mystery of the Temple* (Westminster, MA 1962). M. ELIADE, *The Sacred and the Profane: The Nature of Religion* (New York 1959). C. NORBERG-SCHULTZ, *Genius Loci: Towards a Phenomenology of Architecture* (New York 1980). M. T. ROONEY, *A Theology for Architecture: An Analysis of the Theological Principles Applicable to Church Building in the Postconciliar Renewal* (Rome 1977). R. DE VAUX, *Ancient Israel. Its Life and Institutions* (New York 1961). A. J. CHUPUNGCO, ed., *Liturgical Time and Space* (Collegeville, MN 2000).

[R. K. SEASOLTZ]

SACRED TIME

Time and space are the two most basic categories regularly used to analyze culture, for they tend to be the fundamental perceptions in which people cast and interpret reality. Calendars organize time in categories of days, months and years according to lunar and solar cycles. History counts time in relation to significant events.

These secular categories, reflected in language, speak of a past, present and future. Sacred time introduces the category of the eternal, a notion that transcends the temporal as it is ordinarily understood and makes past and future coterminous with the present. Sacred time is organized according to rituals and seasons that celebrate eternal mystery. The liturgical calendar of the Christian churches measures time in terms of seasonal cycles, feast days and days of penitence, and other special occasions that commemorate the principle events in salvation history and the life of Jesus. The liturgy makes these saving events eternally present to all who believe. The principal seasons and cycles have been described in previous volumes under the headings of ADVENT; LENT; EASTER AND ITS CYCLE; and, more generally, LITURGICAL YEAR IN ROMAN RITE. This article makes some generalizations about sacred time in the context of world religions and the Biblical world view, and then describes some of the more significant changes in the liturgical calendar of the Roman rite.

World Religions and the Biblical Worldview. In terms of time, culture manifests an internal dynamic, an historical movement, and various stages of development. Time is both the context and to some extent the content of reality; it is the eternal, unchanging context of being and its momentary, always-changing mode of expression. Time then is both timeless and timely. Human involvement in time is so inescapable and so complete that it is difficult to analyze the nature of time. Augustine lamented this in his *Confessions* ''What is time? If nobody asks me, I know, but if I want to explain it to someone, then I do not know'' (11.14.17). Time is often considered abstractly as the measure of change or the principle of duration, but it is likewise considered the cause of change and duration.

World religions try to understand both the stages of relative time and the link between the timely and the eternal. Some think of time as linear, as a sequence of moments that are related to the whole of eternity. Some see these moments as progressive, others as circular, and still others as degenerative. There are world religions which conceive of time as infinite and hence conclude that it is uncaused; there are others which think of time as finite and caused but they naturally wonder what existed before time began and what will exist after time ends.

The role played by time is one of the most basic characteristics of Biblical revelation. The Bible speaks of time and history as progressive. Designed by God at the beginning of creation as the medium for both the full realization of being and for the salvation of the human race, time is meaningful. It progresses purposefully from its beginning at creation by God to its fulfillment by God at the end. Throughout this progression, the Bible affirms that God is continually intervening in creation according to the covenant made with the people. God then both transcends time and is immanently involved in it. Time manifests God's will but human freedom often acts contrary to that will, resulting in disharmony within creation. Nevertheless Judaism affirms that at the end of time, God will bring the purpose of creation to fulfillment and the evil in creation caused by human sinfulness will be overcome. Although the Bible is realistic about the evil of human sinfulness, it maintains an optimistic view of history because it views both creation and sinfulness against the background of the covenant God made with the people and the promise of a redeemer. However, with the coming of the Christian era, Judaism increasingly placed less emphasis on the future expectation of a messiah and more stress on the presence of the divine in human history. Hence the focus shifted from God's eternal transcendence to divine immanence in present time. Some contemporary Jewish scholars argue that each moment of time is open to God's fulfilling presence.

Christianity and Eschatology. Like Judaism, Christianity also affirms that time is grounded in eternity. It asserts God's ongoing involvement in human history. But whereas Judaism calculates history from the presumed date of creation, Christianity dates events from the birth of Christ. Christians structure all of history before and after what they consider to be God's extraordinary manifestation in Jesus Christ whom they affirm to be the very Incarnation of God. As Oscar Cullman has written, "The specifically 'Christian kernel', as we derive it from all the Primitive Christian sources, really stands or falls with the redemptive history." For Christians divine revelation takes place primarily through historical events, above all through the life, death and Resurrection of Jesus Christ. Irenaeus and other Fathers of the Church, writing in the gospel tradition, tried to show that in the Incarnation Christ "recapitulates" the whole history of salvation and reveals the meaning of that salvation.

For the Israelites linear time had three principal stages: time before creation, the period between creation and the final "Day of the Lord," and the "last times" following the "Day of the Lord." Time as a whole was punctuated by two major events: the creation by God and the final coming of the Lord on the last day. The time in between these two events was also marked by divine interventions such as the theophanies to Noah, Abraham and Moses. Christians also see time as divided into three main periods but they calculate the periods differently; they speak of the time before, during and after Christ. For Christians the birth of Christ radically altered the Israelite conception of time. They believe the divine Incarnation was a decisive event whereby the transcendence of God became so immanent in creation as to be one with humanity. In Christ God took on a human history. According to John's Gospel, the eternal, absolute reality that is God came into time in Jesus who identified Himself as the beginning, end and centerpiece of time (8:58; 13:19). In affirming "I am who am" Jesus asserted that absolute reality is eternal and therefore omnipresent. Christians believe that those who identify with Jesus in faith through the power of the Holy Spirit are able to transcend the limits of time and share in eternal life.

Through His passion, death and Resurrection Jesus Christ was constituted Lord of all creation in His humanity, a status He had in His divinity from the first moment of creation. With Christ's Resurrection and the outpouring of the Holy Spirit on all of creation at Pentecost, the Day of the Lord was brought forward from the end of time to the present time. Jesus Christ is the fulfillment of all that went before Him in time; He is also the interpretation of all that follows His Incarnation in time. Christ conquered sin and death and became Lord of all creation. Since the Resurrection, cosmic time continues on its course, apparently unchanged, but historical time is in fact given a new direction, for with the establishment of Christ as Lord of creation, a time of fulfillment has been realized. He is the hope of the world, giving us a preview of the end and an assurance that the world itself is being called into the future to share with Christ in His victory over everything that is evil, including sin and death. Eternal life is something that is initiated in history; it is not something that comes at the end of this life. Nevertheless Christian hope in the future is not simply optimism about an evolution of the present time in a progressive line of development. Eternal life is not simply the continuation of this life but is something that is radically new. There is continuity between the historical humanity of Jesus and His resurrected humanity. Christians believe that God did not disregard the earthly body of Jesus but mysteriously raised it from the dead and transfigured it so as to reveal what is in store for human beings and their world. Christian salvation then does not consist in escaping from the world and its history; it consists rather in an extraordinary transformation of the world and its history.

The new time that has been realized in Jesus Christ and which is to some extent here and now shared with us through the power of the Holy Spirit is the time of the Church, the time in which all creation is recapitulated or taken up into the life of the Risen Christ. This time is the time of the Holy Spirit who makes the new creation and prepares for the final coming of Jesus Christ. The time of the Church is a mystery which will come to an end in the revelation of the presence of the Lord who directs the course of the Church's life through the Holy Spirit. Until that final revelation, the Spirit is given only as "first fruits'' (Rom 8:23) or as a pledge (2 Cor 1:22). While Christ reigns as Lord over all creation, that reign is not yet fully manifested. However the first fruits of the Spirit make the time of the Church radically new even now. The Spirit is the Paraclete really and personally present in time in the world, though in a hidden way, just as Jesus Christ was present in time in the world through the Incarnation. That presence of the Holy Spirit is made manifest through those special gifts which build up the Church as the Body of Christ. In the celebration of the liturgy Christians pray especially in the epiclesis that the Spirit may descend upon the community and reveal the reign of God in Christ.

Only at the parousia when Christ comes again in glory will he deliver ''the kingdom to God the Father after destroying every rule and every authority and power . . . that God may be everything to every one'' (1 Cor 15:24, 28). In the meantime the Lord is present in the Church—present in the liturgical assembly, in special ministers, in bread, wine, oil and water, in prayer and song and in word, all of which prolong the life of the Incarnate Lord who is risen from the dead but wants to live in the members of the Church as his Body. In a sense then the Lord is both present and absent in the Church. He is present above all in the liturgy through the power of the Holy Spirit but he is also absent since he is seated at the right hand of the Father, whence he shall come again to judge the living and the dead. He is also absent in that he does not reign fully in His Church because of human sinfulness. The time of the Church is eschatological time but it is neither a futurist nor a realized eschatology. It is an initiated eschatology, for what is already fully realized in Christ is not yet fully realized in the Church. Hence the time of the Church is also historical time, during which the Church itself and all in the Church must strive to make a full response to God's self-gift in Christ through the power of the Holy Spirit.

For Christians, sacred time is oriented toward the past, the present and the future. They live in the past through anamnesis. They remember the great deeds that God has done for creation in Christ and they appropriate those deeds and make them their own. Their response to the past is one of wonder and gratitude for God's goodness, but it is also one of penitence as they remember their frequent failures to allow God to be God in their lives and in the world. In their failures, however, they remember that God has sent a Savior into the world to free humanity from its sinfulness; they remember that their sins are forgiven. Mindful of their weakness, they are penitent but they do not despair.

Christians also live in the present through affirmation. They affirm the goodness of God operative here and now in the world through the power of the Holy Spirit and they commit themselves to build up the Body of Christ in the world and to transform creation by their efforts to cooperate with the Holy Spirit in the establishment of a reign of justice and peace. Finally, Christians live in the future as people of hope. Their hope, however, is different from what we mean by mere expectation which is usually the projection into the future of what we know at present. Expectation usually envisages the possibilities of the future either in terms of what one has known in the past or of what one knows is possible in the present. In contrast Christian hope is rooted in the endlessly creative power of God to generate something entirely new, to draw life out of death, and to create a future that is utterly different from our own programs and plans. Christians can remember the past as past and commit themselves to the present as present because they know there will be a glorious future. They are called then not to indulge in nostalgia or in daydreaming but to engage in the hard work of cooperating with the establishment of God's reign in the world here and now.

Bibliography: S. G. F. BRANDON, *History, Time and Deity* (Manchester 1963). O. CULLMANN, *Christ and Time*, tr. F. V. FILSON (rev. ed. Philadelphia 1964). I. H. DALMAIS, ''Le Temps de l'Eglise,'' *L'Eglise et les Eglises* (Chevetogne 1954). M. ELIADE, *Cosmos and History: The Myth of the Eternal Return* (New York 1954). A. HAYES, *What Are They Saying About the End of the World?* (New York 1983). A. G. MARTIMORT, ed., *The Liturgy of Time* (Collegeville, MN 1986). J. NEUSER, *Between Time and Eternity* (Encino 1975). A. VAN DER WALLE, *From Darkness to Dawn* (London 1984). A. F. AVENI, *Empires of Time: Calendars, Clocks, and Culture* (New York 1989). A. J. CHUPUNGCO, ed., *Liturgical Time and Space* (Collegeville, MN 2000).

[R. K. SEASOLTZ]

SACRIFICE, I (HUMAN)

The term is employed to designate all cultic killing of human beings, including self-inflicted death, even if the strictest sense of offering or sacrifice—the full surrender of one's own life in view of a debt to be paid or an atonement to be made—is not adverted to, but magical considerations prevail. The magical is a significant factor much in evidence in human sacrifice, and it was certainly present from the outset; human sacrifice was introduced only after killing as such became a cultic act, as it did in the early stage of the food-producing cultures. In the myth of the primitive being who was put to death, and from whose members cultivated plants sprang forth, the ideological foundation for human sacrifice is clearly established. Hence bloody sacrifice, with the division and distribution of the parts of the victim, including those of a human victim, and their consumption in a cultic meal, is pushed back nearly to the very beginning of this kind of bloody offerings.

Toltec relief sculpture, 12th century, depicting human sacrifice, El Tajin, Mexico. (©Charles & Josette Lenars/CORBIS)

To a later date are to be assigned the origins of two other forms of offering in which human sacrifice dominated, namely, the foundation sacrifice and the joint-burial of wife and followers with the dead husband. The first practice presupposed permanent domiciles, and the second the development of governmental structures or lordship. Primitive hunters and food-gatherers were not familiar with ritual killing. It was certainly an innovation far removed from the age of human origins.

Headhunting stands in rather close relation with the earliest bloody human sacrifices. This practice developed under the influence of the concept of lunar mythology. The skull was thought to have a connection with the moon, and the moon, some connection with the mystery of life and death. There is question here of a phenomenon exhibiting several strata in its development, for bloodless forms of killing, such as strangling women (in Peru), sacrifice by drowning or submersion, especially in deep wells (*zenote*) among the Maya, and burial alive, cannot

be included in a single category. This is even more true of the rich and magnificent grave offerings noted first in ancient Mesopotamia and often at the end of the Neolithic Age, in the Bronze Age in Europe, and in the Shang period in China.

Man, as the superior living thing, became the object of cultic sacrifice. Even where, as in Peru, chiefly thieves and robbers were formerly used as victims, the death penalty is still evaluated as a sacrificial action, and the sacrifice of prisoners, as that of gladiators, receives its dignity from the high value placed on the warrior's profession. In Mexico war was prosecuted solely to secure victims for the numerous and gruesome human sacrifices demanded by Aztec religion. The victim selected especially for sacrifice to the god Tezcatlipoca was given the same honors as the god himself. He served as his representative; in him the god died and was restored to life. Great importance was attached to the fact that the prisoner accepted his fate willingly; or at least the fiction was adopted that this was the case. Clear examples are known of voluntary sacrifice on the part of individuals themselves, and these not only the leaders; but it would be going too far to imagine, in a romantic vein, that this was the rule. In the great majority of cases men were slaughtered as victims, and on rare occasions women were also.

In addition to its occurrence among the Celts, the sacrifice of women is found also among the Maya; but with the latter, it took the form of drowning. The Pawnee sacrificed a maiden as an arrow-offering to the morning star. The Phoenicians in an early phase of their history sacrificed children; the practice was followed also among the Canari in northern Ecuador. On a mountain in this area 100 children were once killed in a solemn feast in honor of the Maize-God.

The practices of prophesying from the blood of sacrificed prisoners (among the Cimbri and Celts), and the tearing out of the heart (among the Aztecs in Mexico), as well as the twirling of new fire in its place, are frequently attested. They are to be explained on the basis of the magic value attached to blood.

Bibliography: J. HAEKEL, *Lexikon für Theologie und Kirche*, ed. J. HOFER and K. RAHNER (Freiberg 1957–65) 7:294–296. F. HAMPL et al., F. KÖNIG, ed., *Religionswissenschaftliches Wörterbuch* (Freiburg 1956) 533–535. A. CLOSS, *ibid.* 915–916; "Opfer in Ost und West," *Kairos* 3 (1961) 153–161. F. SCHWENN, *Paulys Realenzyklopädie der klassischen Altertumswissenschaft*, ed. G. WISSOWA et al. (Stuttgart 1893–) 15.1 (1931) 948–956. M. ELIADE, *Patterns of Comparative Religion*, tr. R. SHEED (New York 1958) 341–346. G. HOGG, *Cannibalism and Human Sacrifice* (London 1958). A. E. JENSEN, "Über das Töten als kulturgeschichtliche Erscheinung," *Paedeuma* 4 (1950) 23–38. J. MARINGER, "Menschenopfer im Bestattungsbrauch Alteuropas," *Anthropos* 37–40 (1942–45) 1–112.

[A. CLOSS]

SACRIFICE, II (GRECO-ROMAN)

The most complete descriptions of sacrifices in ancient Greece, and the earliest preserved, are found in the Homeric poems. In fact, the rites, as found established in Homer, are maintained almost without change during more than ten centuries.

Sacrifice in Homer. As there are Olympian or celestial gods (o'ὑράνιοι) and infernal or chthonic divinities (χθόνιοι), the ritual of sacrifice can be Olympian or chthonian.

Olympian Sacrifice. In the Olympian ritual, the sacrifice (θυσία) is a meal offered to the gods and one in which men participate. It can be propitiatory, as the hecatomb to Apollo to atone for the abduction of Chryseis, which is described in Book 1 of the *Iliad;* more often it

is one of petition, as the supplication of the Trojan women in Book 6, or Nestor's appeal to Athena in Book 3 of the *Odyssey.*

Propitiatory Sacrifice. In order to atone for the offense committed against Apollo, in the person of his priest Chryses, Odysseus brings a hecatomb to Chryses, which the Achaeans arrange about the altar.

> They washed their hands, and took up the barley grains. Then Chryses, with hands extended to heaven, prayed for them in a loud voice: "Hear me, thou of the silver bow, who protectest Chryses and holy Cilla . . . do thou now fulfill my desire: ward thou off the loathsome plague from the Danaans." So he spake in prayer, and Phoebus Apollo heard him. Then, when they had prayed, and had sprinkled the barley grains, they first drew back the victims' heads, and cut their throats, and flayed them, and cut out the thigh-pieces, and covered them with a twofold layer of fat, and laid raw flesh upon them. And the old man burned them on a pile of firewood and poured a libation of flaming wine over them, and beside him young men held in their hands five-pronged forks. But when the thigh-pieces were completely burned, and they had tasted the inner parts, they cut up the rest and put it on spits, and roasted it carefully, and drew all the pieces from the spits. Then, when they had ceased from their labor and had prepared the meal, they feasted, nor did their hearts lack any part of the equal feast. [*Iliad* 1.447–468]

The barley grains undoubtedly had the same purifying virtue as lustral water with which the victim was also sprinkled before being sacrificed. In *Iliad* 3, in a sacrifice with an oath (269–301), the barley grains are replaced by hair cut from the forehead of lambs. The purpose of the hecatomb is explained by Odysseus: "We wish to appease the god" (*Iliad* 1.444).

Sacrifice of Supplication. The best example is found in *Iliad* 6, when, in the name of the aged wives of Troy, the priestess Theano supplicates Athena: "that we may now sacrifice to thee in thy temple twelve sleek heifers that have not felt the goad, if thou wilt take pity on Troy and the wives of the Trojans and their little children" (305–310). The prayer of the aged wives is accompanied by the ritual cry (ὀλολυγή), which was later replaced by flute-playing.

As J. Rudhart has observed (*Notions fondamentales,* 289–290): "sacrifice is essentially the act of a community . . . and comprises three fundamental actions. These are: (1) the putting to death of a living being; (2) the removal from the body of the victim of some parts that are regarded as essential; (3) the use of these choice portions."

Chthonian Sacrifice. Homer furnishes several examples. Thus in *Odyssey* 10.516–528, Circe gives Odysseus the following instructions. He must dig a square pit, and around it pour three libations to all the dead, first of milk and honey, then of sweet wine, and thirdly of water. He must then sprinkle the hole with white barley meal. Finally, after invoking the dead, he must sacrifice to them a ram and a black ewe, turning their heads toward Erebus. In this ''aversion'' ritual, the sacrifice is made at night, without an altar or upon a low altar (ἐσχάρα). The victim, usually black in color, is not eaten, but ordinarily is consumed entirely by the fire.

Sacrifice of the Kings of Atlantis. Plato's interest in old rites led him to describe a very archaic ritual, namely, the sacrifice of the kings of Atlantis in his unfinished dialogue, *Critias* or *Atlantis* (119D–120C). The ritual comprises four principal stages: (1) The sacrifice of the god, for the bull selected by lot incarnates and represents Poseidon, the father of the kings of Atlantis; (2) the communion sacrifice uniting the kings and the god; (3) the administering of the oath; (4) the examination and atonement for ritual faults. The mythical age imagined appears to be the reign of Minos. The customs of the kings of Atlantis decorate the walls of the palace at Cnossus, being especially evident in the bull-leaping and in the priestly gestures of the fleur-de-lis king. There are traces of the Creto-Mycenaean or Aegean period in Homer, but the problem is to identify them precisely. The inscriptions such as that of Cyrene, e.g., which reproduce a ''Founders' oath,'' always, as in the case of the kings of Atlantis, make provision for the punishment of subsequent transgressors. The narrative of the *Critias* indicates familiarity with anathemas engraved on stone (119E) and a nocturnal judgment (120C). Through the blood with which the kings of Atlantis sprinkle themselves, a pact is made between the god and his worshippers. Each of these, in order to attach himself as closely as possible to the god, dips a golden cup in the crater which receives the blood of the immolated bull. This act identifies the kings with their father Poseidon. They put on his dark blue robe and sit on the ground in the ashes of the sacrifice, which, being now filled with the god's power, remain sacred. By this contact, they bind themselves to the bull, offered in holocaust and representing the god, in order that they may be able to render perfect justice.

Perhaps in all this there is a survival of the primitive ideas found among the hunters of the Arctic and the herdsmen of Central Asia. However, the holocaust was not common in Olympian sacrifices; rather a form of simulation was adopted in which only thighs of the victims and bones of their other members were reserved for the gods. But all was covered with fat and represented the entire victim. This procedure recalled the deceit of Prometheus as related by Hesiod (*Theog.* 533–557; cf. *Works* 48 and 337).

Roman domestic sacrifice, fresco from the House of Livig on the Palatine Hill in Rome.

Sacrifices in Popular Religion. Already in Homer, the people offer sacrifice. The sacrifice offered by the swineherd Eumaeus in Book 14 of the *Odyssey* (418–436) imitates or perhaps parodies that of Nestor in Book 3, except that the cutting of the bristles from the boar's head replaces the sprinkling of the barley grains, instead of accompanying it. Some information, although rather scanty, can be gleaned from inscriptions or from the tragic and comic poets. Thus, Aristophanes mentions the sausages offered at the feast of the Apaturia (*Acharnians* 146), the slaughter of the steer at the Dipolia (*Clouds* 984–985), and the celebration of the *Panathenia* (*ibid.* 386); his parodies of sacrifices in the *Clouds* (426), and in the *Birds* (848 and 862), are also helpful. Information becomes more copious in the Hellenistic Age, e.g., in the *Idylls* of Theocritus and the *Mimes* of Herondas. In the latter's *Women Worshippers* (at the temple of Asclepius at Cos) a cock is offered to the god, and the priest has a right to keep one leg of the fowl. There are many references to sacrifices, too, in the *Palatine Anthology.* Animals of all kinds were sacrificed, but reference is made also to offerings of vegetables, fruits, honey, and cheese. There are sacrifices, or offerings, of expiation, supplication, or thanksgiving, and the worshippers belong to all classes of society, even the most humble.

Judgment of the Philosophers. Sacrifice, like prayer, was so essential that its suppression would have destroyed religion. Accordingly, the philosophers are not so much against sacrifice itself as against the abuses which it authorizes. Too often sacrifice was made for mere form's sake to justify a crime committed or to be committed, or to get the gods on one's own side. The idea that the gods allowed themselves to be seduced by the fat and smoke of sacrifices seems to Plato the worst of impieties (cf. *Rep.* 2.365E; *Laws* 10.885B, 888C, 906B-E), and he considers Homer particularly blameworthy on this score. But the dying Socrates reminds his disciples that he had promised a cock to Asclepius (*Phaedo* 118A), and Plato has the Athenian say in the *Laws* (4.716D): "to sacrifice to the gods and to be continually in communion with them by prayers, and offerings, and every form of divine worship, is, for the good man, most noble and good, and helpful towards the happy life, and fitting also to the highest degree."

Roman Sacrifice. Roman religion exhibits the principal sacrificial rites of the Greeks and reflects the same basic ideas: a circuit of power which goes from the human gift to the god and returns to man, and a meal offered to the gods in which men participate. In the process of sacrificing, there is question of strengthening the god (*mactare*), as in forcing a spring by throwing into it flowers because of their vegetative power. There were bloody and unbloody sacrifices, the usual victims being the pig, sheep, bull (the animals of the *suovetaurilia*), and, more rarely, the female or male goat. Originally, fowls were offered only to Greek divinities. The victims (*hostiae*) were called *consultatoriae* when their entrails were examined. At Rome the art of the *haruspices,* or diviners, enjoyed a widespread development.

Bibliography: S. EITREM, *Oxford Classical Dictionary,* ed. M. CARY et al. (Oxford 1949) 787–788. L. R. FARNELL, J. HASTINGS, ed. *Encyclopedia of Religion and Ethics,* 13 v. (Edinburgh 1908–27) 11:12–18. P. E. LEGRAND and J. TOUTAIN in *Dictionnaire des antiquités grecques et romaines d'après les textes et les monuments,* ed. C. DAREMBERG and E. SAGLIO, 5 v. (Paris 1877–1919) 4.2:956–980. L. ZIEHEN, *Paulys Realenzyklopädie der klassischen Altertumswissenschaft,* ed. G. WISSOWA et al. (Stuttgart 1893–) 18.1:579–627. R. K. YERKES, *Sacrifice in Greek and Roman Religions and Early Judaism* (New York 1952). M. P. NILSSON, *Geschichte der griechischen Religion,* 2 v. (2nd ed. Munich 1955–61) 1.2:121–146. J. RUDHART, *Notions fondamentales de la pensée religieuse et actes constitutifs du culte dans la Grèce classique* (Geneva 1958).

[E. DES PLACES]

SACRIFICE, III (IN ISRAEL)

The study of Israelite sacrifice brings one into contact with a principal element of the cult of YAHWEH. Although the OT did not give either a definition or a theology of sacrifice, whenever Israel "came before the Lord" to worship Him, praise Him, thank Him, petition His aid, or ask His forgiveness, it did so through its sacrificial rites.

Israel did not initiate its various rites; studies of the surrounding cultures (e.g., the findings at UGARIT) indicate that the Israelites used the same basic rites as their Canaanite neighbors. Israel's sacrifice, however, was not simply an exact imitation of the traditional Semitic rites; it had its own distinctive character. Yahweh was not the same as other gods and was not to be worshiped as they were.

Israel's sacrificial rites were sacred. A specific place was set aside for sacrifice (various sanctuaries, the Temple of Jerusalem); holy objects were employed (the ALTAR); the rite was performed under the leadership of holy men (the priests). In addition, ritual practices, fixed holy days, and seasons were established (*see* FEASTS, RELIGIOUS).

The exact meaning of Israelite sacrifice is not clear, but it is generally admitted that gift giving, gratitude, petition, expiation, and communion with God were connoted by each sacrificial act. Exegetes usually define Israelite sacrifice as an exteriorization of Yahwistic prayer by means of characteristic symbolic rites.

The present study treats Israel's sacrifice under the headings of terminology and liturgical calendar, the various kinds of sacrifices, and the evolution of the notion of sacrifice.

Terminology and Liturgical Calendar. Before describing the various types of Israelite sacrifices it will be helpful to examine the nomenclature of Israelite sacrifice and the liturgical calendar.

Terminology. The oldest generic term in the OT for sacrifice is *minḥâ,* meaning a gift or tribute. This tribute could be paid either to men (Gn 32.14; 33.10) or to God (Gn 4.3; Jgs 13.19; 1 Sm 2.17; 26.19; Is 1.13; Am 5.25). The use of *minḥâ* as a generic term appears confined to an early period, in which it represented both bloody and unbloody offerings. In the tradition of the Pentateuchal PRIESTLY WRITERS and in later prophetic writings, *minḥâ* was used as a specific term meaning cereal offering (Lv 2.1–13). Other generic terms for sacrifice were *qorbān* (CORBAN, literally "the thing brought near": Lv 1.2–9; Ez 20.28; 40.43) and *zebaḥ* (a sacred "slaughtering": Gn 31.54; Ex 10.25; 12.27). The latter was the word most

"Abraham Offering up His Son Isaac." (©Historical Picture Archive/CORBIS)

commonly used for a communion sacrifice. Its influence can be seen in the word *mizbēaḥ,* a place of sacred slaughtering, i.e., an altar. Normally, however, in referring to sacrifice, OT writers indicated a specific type of sacrifice, as for example HOLOCAUST (*'ōlâ*) or a communion sacrifice to complete a vow (*zebaḥ šᵉlāmîm*).

Israelite Liturgical Calendar. Israel celebrated three major feasts in its cultic year (Lv 23.1–44). A commentary on the cultic calendar along with a schedule of victims to be offered on various feasts is found in Nm 28.9–29.39. These documents contain part of the tradition of the Pentateuchal priestly writers and consequently represent, for the most part, the liturgical practice in the Temple in the postexilic period.

In Lv 6.2–6 (see also Ex 29.38–42; Nm 28.2–8) mention is made of daily morning and evening sacrifices. Each sacrifice consisted of one lamb as a holocaust, flour kneaded with oil, and a libation of wine. In Ezr 3.5 and Neh 10.34 this is called the ''perpetual sacrifice'' (*'olat tāmîd*). In Dn 8.11–13, however, it is indicated that the daily sacrifices were interrupted during the persecution of ANTIOCHUS IV EPIPHANES. They were reestablished by Judas Machabee. (*See* MACCABEES, HISTORY OF THE.)

The sacrifices offered on the SABBATH (Lv 23.2; Nm 28.9–10) doubled the number of victims offered at the daily sacrifices. Presumably the Sabbath sacrifices were offered at the same hour of the day as the daily offerings.

On the first day of each new lunar month a holocaust was offered (called the sacrifice of the New-Moon Feast) consisting of two bulls, one ram, seven lambs, cereal offerings, a libation, and a goat as an offering for sin (Nm 28.11–15). In many ways this sacrifice was typical of the sacrifices offered on the major feasts of the year. Although the motives prompting the celebration of the feasts varied, the victims remained numerically and specifically constant. The sacrifices offered on the following feasts were the same, generally, as those on the Hebrew NEW-MOON FEAST: the Feast of PASSOVER (Lv 23.4; Nm 28.16–25), the Hebrew Feast of PENTECOST (Nm 28.26–31), and the Hebrew Feast of the New Year (Lv 23.23; Nm 29.1–6). On the Day of ATONEMENT (Yom Kippur: Lv 23.26–32; Nm 29.7–11) only one bullock was offered, while the accompanying victims were as usual. The primacy of the Feast of BOOTHS (Tabernacles: Lv 23.33–43; Nm 29.12–38) was indicated by its octave of sacrifices. Each day of the octave had its specific offering, fewer victims being offered as the eight-day celebration drew to a close.

Various Kinds of Sacrifice. The richness of Israelite ritual allowed for many different classes and modes of sacrifice, depending upon the sacrificer, the things offered, and the way in which the sacrifice was performed.

Public and Private Sacrifices. Public sacrifices were offered for the community as a whole. In Lv 4.13–21 a young bull was to be offered as a sin offering for an inadvertent fault of the people. Sacrifices offered for the alleviation of a plague (2 Sm 24.21–25; 1 Chr 21.22–27), for the sin of a priest having social consequences (Lv 4.3; 16.11), sacrifices at the consecration of an altar, at the ordination of a priest (Lv 8.1–36), at the installation of a king (1 Sm 10.8; 11.15), and at the outset or end of a battle (1 Sm 7.9; 13.9) were all public sacrifices.

Private sacrifices were offered on behalf of individuals. In this category there were some of the SIN OFFERINGS and guilt offerings. The sacrifice for sin had a graduated system of expiatory victims depending on the rank and public character of the offender (Lv 4). Other descriptions of guilt offerings are found in Lv 5.14–26; 7.1–6. VOTIVE OFFERINGS (Lv 7.16–17), PEACE OFFERINGS (Lv 7.11–21), free-will offerings (Ex 35.20–29), communion sacrifices and sacred meals (Jos 22.21–29; Jgs 20.26), and holocausts, or wholly burnt offerings (Gn 8.20; Ps 50[51].21; 2 Kgs 16.13), all served as private sacrifices. In addition, to celebrate certain personal events, offerings were made on behalf of individuals, such as the sacrifices offered after childbirth (Lv 12.6–7), and at the consecration of NAZIRITES (1 Sm 1.24–28).

Victims. The predominant objects of sacrifice were the products of the herd, the flocks, and the fields. Catalogs of sacrificial victims are found in Lv 1.1–7.38; Nm 7.1–88; 18.8–32; 31.1–54. Like their neighbors, the Israelites sacrificed those things on which their daily life most depended. Although certain specific sacrificial victims were varied as Israel changed from a seminomadic status to an agrarian one, nevertheless the most common victims remained constant.

The products of the field that were offered were mostly cereals mixed with frankincense, oil, and/or salt (Lv 2.1–13). Of the animals, any beast ''without blemish'' could be offered (Lv 1.2–3, 10), such as cattle (Gn 15.9; 1 Sm 6.14; 2 Sm 24.22–25), sheep (Gn 22.7, 13; 1 Sm 7.9), and goats (1 Sm 10.3). In the case of free-will offerings the victim did not have to be ''without blemish,'' but male animals were preferred (Lv 1.3; 1 Sm 1.24).

Although cereals could be offered only in the form of parched grain (Lv 2.14–16; 6.7–16), most cereal offerings were concomitant to other sacrifices (Nm 28–29). The bread was unleavened, since leaven induced putrefaction and therefore uncleanness.

Human sacrifice was sometimes offered in Israel (Ps 105[106].37–38), but at no time was it considered a part of orthodox Yahwism, for the practice was vigorously condemned (2 Kgs 16.3; 21.6; Jer 7.31; 32.35; Ez 16.20; 23.37–39). The accounts of Abraham's intended sacrifice of Isaac in Gn 22 and Jephte's sacrifice of his daughter in Jgs 11.29–40 were, possibly, polemical stories aimed at stamping out the custom of human sacrifice.

Ways of Israelite Oblation. Israelite sacrifice was offered in four different ways. When the offering was an inanimate object, e.g., money or the Temple tax (2 Kgs 12.4–5), it was simply surrendered to the proper authority. The offering of the first fruits of the soil in thanksgiving did not entail any destruction but provided for a sacred meal, while tithe offerings were surrendered for the use of the priests and the poor (Dt 26.1–15). Other sacrifices were partially consumed by fire, the remainder being eaten by the offerer and the priests or by the priests alone, as was the case with sin offerings and guilt offerings. Finally, in another common type of sacrifice, the offerer brought the victim to the altar, placed his hands upon it, killed it by himself or through the priest's ministry, and had the priest collect the blood and sprinkle it on the base of the altar. The animal was then skinned and quartered, the offerer washing the inner organs and hind quarters. The priest then burned the entire victim on the altar until it was completely consumed (Lv 1.9).

In the latter ritual the symbolic significance of the imposition of hands admits of no easy explanation. Some interpret it as a transferral of sin to the animals, as in the ritual of the SCAPEGOAT (Lv 16.20–22). This explanation is unlikely, since the scapegoat was driven from the community as unclean because of the sin imposed upon it, whereas Leviticus demands an unblemished animal for a holocaust (Lv 1.3–9). It is more probable that the gesture proclaimed the union between the victim and the offerer. What was about to take place in the victim's body expressed what was taking place in the offerer's mind, namely, his regret for past sins, his total surrender to God, and his desire to ascend and be united with God like the smoke rising from the altar. Perhaps the best explanation, because of its simplicity, is that the gesture signified that the victim came from this individual donor as an offering in his name and that the benefits of the sacrifice should accrue to him (see R. De Vaux, *Ancient Israel, Its Life and Institutions,* tr. J. McHugh [New York 1961] 416).

The complete or partial destruction of the offering was not absolutely necessary, but it was commonly regarded as the best way to assure God's favorable reception. Perhaps in the minds of the Israelites such destruction rendered the victim useless and the gift irrevocable (see R. De Vaux, *Ancient Israel, Its Life and Institutions,* 416). Also, such destruction transferred the victim into the realm of the invisible. The use of an official sacrificer, i.e., a priest, was not essential to the sacrifice, since, even in the case of a wholly burnt offering, it was not always the priest who slaughtered the victim, but the donor himself sometimes performed this rite (Lv 1.5).

The sprinkling of the victim's blood on the sides of the altar evolved from the Semitic concepts of blood and altar. For Israel and its neighbors blood was the symbol of life, indeed it was life itself (Gn 9.4; Lv 3.17), while the altar represented the deity and was a symbol of God's presence, the place of mediation between God and man. By sprinkling against the altar the blood that he had been given by God, a man acknowledged the gift and returned it to God. (*See* BLOOD, RELIGIOUS SIGNIFICANCE OF.)

Sacrifice as a Gift. The earliest generic term for sacrifice was *minḥâ*, a gift or tribute. Yahweh commanded Israel, ''No one shall appear before me empty-handed'' (Ex 23.15; 34.20). In bringing their gifts to the Lord the Israelites chose the animals and vegetables that were needed for their sustenance. The gifts were thus part of themselves. The ritual used for giving the gifts was, consequently, made up of symbolic gestures expressing the offerer's disposition. Since all things already belonged to God (Ps 49[50].7–15), however, the gift aspect of Israelite sacrifice must be interpreted accordingly. In the culture of the Near East the giving of a gift to a superior was an expression of tribute (2 Kgs 5.5; Jgs 3.17; Mal 1.8). A notion of tribute was thus involved in the gift aspect of Israelite sacrifice, a conclusion supported by the Canaanite culture, which viewed its gods as giving life to all things that grew in the soil. As a tribute to their fertilizing role, the deities were entitled to a share of the procedure. This sentiment is echoed in the prayer of 1 Chr 29.12–16 and in Hos 2.10–11.

The giving of the first fruits of the barley and wheat harvest manifested this gift-tribute aspect. The Israelite joyfully brought before the Lord the first fruits as a tribute of thanksgiving (Lv 23.10–11; Dt 26.1–11). The firstborn son and the firstborn male domestic animals were likewise brought before the Lord (Ex 13.1–2) to acknowledge God's dominion over His creatures. The father of a firstborn son bought him back through the payment of a ransom (Nm 3.44–51) and recalled thereby God's merciful redemption of Israel from Egypt (Ex 13.11–16).

Communion Sacrifices. In the early cult of Israel, communion sacrifice, in which the sacrificer and his family ate at least part of the roasted or boiled animal, was perhaps the most common. The practice may have developed from a form of TOTEMISM in which union with the god was thought to be achieved by eating a portion of the totemic animal. Tribal gods of the Canaanite milieu were thought to be related by kinship to the tribal members. The life of the god circulated in a special animal (totem) sacred to him. In the sacrificial meal in which this animal was eaten the tribal members hoped to be united with their god and in some way share his divine life. Another theory about the origin of communion sacrifice holds that in the sacrificial ritual the imposition of hands and the sprinkling of blood played a central role. At the imposition of hands the person's sins and life principle were transferred to the animal and took up residence in the animal's blood. By the slaughtering of the animal the person's sins were carried away, and the life principle was released along with the blood. The blood was then taken and sprinkled on the altar or a representation of the deity, thereby establishing a union between god and man. There is insufficient evidence that either of these attitudes was the foundation for Israelite communion sacrifices.

The general characteristics of communion sacrifice were the immolation of the victim and a subsequent sharing of the victim by God, the priests, and the offerer. The ritual for communion sacrifice is found in Lv 3.1–17; 7.11–38; 10.12–15; 22.17–25.

Although communion sacrifice exemplified their quest for union with God, the Israelites had no idea of being physically united with God, either by eating a victim delivered by death to God or by transferring into the divine realm a victim with which man identified himself. The portion set aside for Yahweh was presented to Him on the altar; the offerer with his friends and relatives then ate the remaining portion at a communal religious meal. Just as the Semites concluded a contract by sharing a meal (Gn 26.28–30; 31.44–54), so too the covenant, the personal fellowship between Yahweh and His people, was symbolically renewed by this sacrificial meal (Ps 49[50].5; 80[81]).

The Israelite communion sacrifice, then, was not necessarily a meal taken with God, although Canaanite thinking very likely influenced the attitude of the common man so that he thought he was sharing a meal with God. Orthodoxy in this matter is found in Ps 49(50).12–13. The texts mentioning the table and the food of Yahweh (Ez 44.7, 16; Mal 1.7, 12) are rather late (i.e., exilic and postexilic) and therefore from a period when Israel could not possibly have thought God to be in need of food. These passages must have retained formalized phrases of a more primitive mentality and were used, not in their literal meaning, but for their symbolic value alone.

The communion sacrifice had three modes of expression: the thanksgiving sacrifice (Lv 7.12–15; 22.29), the voluntary sacrifice (Ex 35.29; Lv 22.18–23) offered spontaneously out of devotion rather than by legal prescription, and the votive sacrifice (Gn 28.20–22; Nm 21.2–3) offered by one who had obliged himself by a vow.

The ritual for communion sacrifice is described in ch. 3 of Leviticus. The victims were the same as for the holocaust with the exception of birds. The portions belonging to Yahweh, which were placed on the altar, consisted of the kidneys, liver, and fat around the intestine. The fat, like the blood, was considered a life-giving part. The priest received two portions: the breast that was "waved" before the Lord and the right leg that was "raised" before the Lord. The remaining portions went to the offerer. Usually there were concomitant cereal offerings of which Yahweh and the priests received a share.

Evolution of Israelite Sacrifice. The OT contains many warnings that urged the Israelite worshiper to purer interior dispositions and a greater obedience to the Lord than was occasioned by bloody sacrifices (1 Sm 15.22; Prv 21.27; Sir 34.18–19). Especially in the Prophets is this true. By their criticism of hypocritical, external worship, they paved the way for NT concepts of sacrifice.

The Prophets and Sacrifice. The Prophets' criticism of Israelite sacrifices was so severe that many scholars have questioned whether they attacked sacrifice itself as an institution or merely the ritual abuses that they observed. Recently the common opinion among Catholic, Protestant, and Jewish exegetes is that the prophetic condemnations were directed at hypocritical ritualism and not at the institution as such.

In their zeal for the orthodox religion, the Prophets, of course, attacked sacrifices offered to pagan gods, to idols (Hos 11.2; Jer 11.12), or to sacred animals (Ez 8.7–15), as well as human sacrifice (Ez 20.31). In their zeal for a more holy worship of Yahweh they inveighed against the number and costliness of the sacrificial rites performed in His honor (Is 1.11–17; Am 4.4–5; 5.4–5, 21–25; Mi 6.6–8) and the intemperance that at times accompanied the cult (Hos 4.4–19; Am 2.7–8). They labeled the sacrifices of the immoral as abominations and useless. The essence of the Prophets' attack was the condemnation of the formalistic, mechanical performance of the sacrificial rites. In their demand for a more spiritual religion they stressed obedience to the Lord's word (Jer 7.21–23), moral goodness, and justice (Is 1.16–20, 26–27).

Along with their sharp criticism of the cult, however, the Prophets did exhibit respect for sacrifice (Is 19.19–21). They spoke respectfully of the Temple and the Temple liturgy (Jer 7.5–11; 26.2; 33.11; Is 30.29). Hosea considered the cessation of sacrifice a punishment for the nation (3.4; 9.4–5). The school of Jeremiah envisioned a place for sacrifice in the purified worship of the future (Jer 17.26; 33.18). Finally, despite their call for a more moral and interior religion, the Prophets often performed symbolic religious acts (Is 20.2–6; Jer 27.2).

Their attacks on sacrifice, then, were part of their general criticism of a decadent and impious society.

Sacrifice in the New Testament. The Israelite concept of sacrifice is found again in the Epistle to the Hebrews. (For a treatment of the specifically Christian notion of sacrifice, *see* SACRIFICE, IV.)

Of all the NT writings, Hebrews most elaborately amplified the ancient-Israelite theme of sacrifice. The author of Hebrews was concerned with contrasting the Levitical sacrifices with the sacrifice of Christ. He depicted God as the initiator of the sacrifices of the Old Covenant, but he also maintained that these were merely foreshadowings of Christ, in which He was both High Priest and victim (Heb 7.1–10.18). He argued that the sacrifices of the Old Law were temporary, whereas Christ's was eternal and unique (8.1–2; 9.25–26; 10.11–14; 12.2). The holocausts of Israel (10.5–10), the covenant sacrifices (9.15–28), the offerings for sin (10.1–10), and the atonement sacrifices (9.1–14) had all been replaced by the unique efficacious and eternal sacrifice of Christ on the cross.

The mortal and sinful priests of Israel had been replaced by Christ, the Son of God who was without sin (7.11–8.6). Nine times in Hebrews Christ is called our High Priest. The author had in mind the Feast of the Atonement when the High Priest offered the annual sacrifice for his own and the people's sins (Lv 16.1–34). Now it was Christ who had assumed this priestly function. He was the one who had expiated the sins of the people. He had once and for all destroyed sin by His sacrifice. The blood of goats and calves had been replaced by the blood of Christ.

See Also: HIGH PRIEST; SACRED AND PROFANE; SHOWBREAD; WORSHIP (IN THE BIBLE).

Bibliography: A. MÉDEBIELLE, *Dictionnaire de la Bible,* suppl. ed. L. PIROT et al. (Paris 1928–) 3:1–262. *Encyclopedic Dictionary of the Bible,* tr. and adap. by L. HARTMAN (New York 1963), from A. VAN DEN BORN, *Bijbels Woordenboek* 2082–90. R. DE VAUX, *Ancient Israel, Its Life and Institutions,* tr. J. MCHUGH (New York 1961) 406–474; *Les Sacrifices de l'Ancien Testament* (Paris 1964). A. J. HESCHEL, *The Prophets* (New York 1962). B. VAWTER, *The Conscience of Israel* (New York 1961). J. PEDERSEN, *Israel, Its Life and Culture,* tr. A. MØLLER and A. I. FAUSBØLL, 2 v. (New York 1926–40; rev. ed. 1959), v. 2. L. SABOURIN, *Rédemption sacrificielle* (Bruges 1961). W. EICHRODT, *Theology of the O. T.,* tr. J. A. BAKER (Philadelphia 1961–), v. 1. G. VON RAD, *O.T. Theology,* tr. D. STALKER (New York 1962–). H. RINGGREN, *Sacrifice in the Bible* (pa. New York 1963). P. VAN IMSCHOOT, *Théologie de l'Ancien Testament,* 2 v. (Tournai 1954–56), v. 2. W. J. O'ROURKE, "Israelite Sacrifice," *American Ecclesiastical Review* 149 (1963) 259–274. H. H. ROWLEY, "The Religious Value of Sacrifice," *Expository Times* 58 (1946–47) 69–71; "The Prophets and Sacrifice," *ibid.* 305–307; "The Meaning of Sacrifice in the O.T.," *Bulletin of the John Rylands Library* 33 (1950–51) 74–110.

[J. S. HOMLISH]

SACRIFICE, IV (IN CHRISTIAN THEOLOGY)

While Old Testament revelation transformed the meaning of sacrificial ritual by means of a series of salvation events and gradually laid stress on the role of interior dispositions, in more profound fashion, the Incarnation provided a new dimension to sacrifice.

The New Testament. Even apart from the Epistle to the Hebrews, whose central theme is the superiority of Christ's sacrifice over that of the Old Law, the literature of the New Testament gives rich evidence of the insight of the early Church's faith into Christ's act of Sacrifice and into Christian participation in that Sacrifice. Understandably, primitive Christian reflection on sacrifice focused on the unique event of Christ's Passover. However, the entire earthly career of Jesus was viewed as the expression of his inner self-offering to the Father. This can be seen from the baptism scene at the Jordan, which introduces and interprets Christ's public life. In accepting baptism from John, Jesus publicly dedicated himself to human redemption and thereby glorified his Father. All the actions of the public life translate Christ's continuing attitude of self-oblation; these come to climax in the Supper-Calvary-Easter event. That a similar extension of the idea of sacrifice applied to the Christian community itself is clear from the baptismal catechesis contained in the Petrine Epistles (1 Pt 2.5).

Probably the most important Synoptic teaching on sacrifice is contained in the description of the Last Supper. Reflecting an already established liturgy, the account of the institution of the Eucharist clearly shows Christ's act to parallel the sacrificial establishment of the covenant at Sinai. His blood poured out for men is the New Covenant; it is the reconciliation of men to God. Sacred covenant meal, fulfillment of the Old Testament Passover, the supper as described in the Gospels is Christ's ritual offering of Himself to His Father.

In this context, introduced by the scene of the Supper, the death of Christ as narrated in the Gospels is clearly sacrificial. Particularly in Luke, the Passion and death of Christ are closely linked with the rejection and ultimate destruction of the Old Testament place of sacrifice, Jerusalem. As a symbol of this, the Temple veil is rent at the moment of Christ's death (Lk 23.45). John's Gospel complements the Synoptics on this point by connecting Christ's death on Calvary with the slaying of the paschal victims in the Temple (Jn 19.14, 36).

Essentially the same point of view is found in the letters of Paul, although he speaks more explicitly about the reconciling effect of Christ's shedding of blood (Eph 2.13). Like the Synoptics, he relates the Supper to Sinai

(1 Cor 11.25) and describes communing in the body of Christ as participating in a sacrificial repast (*ibid.* 10.14–18). Divine acceptance of Jesus' willing victimhood comes in His glorification, the transforming act of the Father in raising Him from the dead.

From the first decades of the Church's existence, the early Christian communities connected the celebration of the Eucharistic meal with Christ's death as well as with the Last Supper. Gathered together for the "breaking of the bread," they were aware that they fulfilled Christ's command, "Do this in remembrance of me" (*ibid.* 11.24). They were aware that these community gatherings, although simple in their ritual structure, proclaimed "the death of the Lord until he come" (*ibid.* 11.36). They seemed aware, too, of the presence of the risen Christ with them as they assembled to commune in His body and blood (Mt 18.20).

How soon the early Christians, especially the Jerusalem community, saw the continuing Eucharistic act as replacing and rendering unnecessary the Temple sacrifices of Israel is difficult to say. Certainly the point is established by the time of the compositions of the Gospels, although the Judaizing tendencies of some within the Christian community may have tended to obscure the matter in the early years. It may well be, too, that the primitive Christian Church did not immediately recognize the sacrificial import of Christ's death and Resurrection; but this was a consciously grasped element of faith by the time Paul wrote his early Epistles.

So, too, the understanding that Christian life is sacrificial emerged very early. Prepared by Old Testament prophetic teaching that stressed the "sacrifice of the heart" (Hos 6.6), and especially by Malachi's reference to a "pure offering" (Mal 1.10–11), Christian faith immediately grasped the wider meaning of sacrifice. Paul's exhortation to the Romans that they offer themselves "a living victim" (Rom 12.1) characterizes his moral catechesis to the early communities. All the various responsibilities and activities of life are linked to this Christian dedication, which should be characterized by constant thanksgiving (Eph 5.19–20).

Patristic Period. One can scarcely say that the early Christians had a theology of sacrifice; yet the primitive catechesis as reflected in New Testament literature was clearer and more explicit about the sacrificial character of Christianity than was the writing of the early decades of the second century. With the apologetic writings of Justin, however, we find clear and purposeful explanation of the Christian Eucharist as sacrifice. In fulfillment of the prophecy of Malachi, the Eucharist replaced Old Testament sacrifices as effective worship. Being communion in the real body and blood of Christ, it commemorates the

Supper, Calvary, and the Resurrection; and it gives the Father worthy thanks for these events of redemption (*Dialogus cum Tryphone* 41; *Patrologia Graeca*, ed. J. P. Migne [Paris 1857–66] 6:564). Irenaeus, too, describes the Eucharist as the true, spiritual offering of which Malachia spoke, the body and blood of the risen Christ that feed men unto risen life (*Adv. haer.* 4.17.5; *Patrologia Graeca* 7:1023–24); but he applies the notion of sacrifice to Christian life as well, stressing the importance of the community's sincere self-offering to the Father and its profession of faith in the final resurrection (*ibid.* 4.18.5; *Patrologia Graeca* 7:1028–29).

Throughout the patristic period, among both Latin and Greek Fathers, the statements are clear and explicit that the Eucharistic action is the sacrifice of both Christ and the Church and that it is linked both with the Last Supper and with Calvary. However, for the most part there is no lengthy development of the sacrificial nature of the Eucharist or, consequently, of Christian life as sacrifice. A notable exception is the tenth book of St. Augustine's *De civitate dei*. Contrasting Christian sacrifice with pagan cult, Augustine insists on the personal self-giving to God. "It is only by shedding our blood in fighting for His truth that we offer Him bloody victims. We burn the sweetest incense in His sight when we are aflame with holy piety and love" (10.3; *Corpus Christtianorum. Series Latinum* 47:275). Sacrifice, whether it be this internal homage or its expression in external rite, can be directed toward God alone (10.4; *ibid.* 276). God wants external sacrifice only as the sign of the inner disposition, for "mercy is the true sacrifice" (10.5; *ibid.* 277–278). All divine precepts of sacrifice refer really to love of God and neighbor (10.5; *ibid.* 278).

Augustine states, then, his famous definition of sacrifice: "every work that unites us in holy communion with God, every work that is directed to that final good in which alone we find true beatitude" (10.6; *ibid.* 278). Every work of mercy toward others or ourselves, if it be directed to God, is truly sacrifice. Every person consecrated to God is a sacrifice. Christians, sharing this dedication, bound together in one body in Christ, are the sacrifice that the Church celebrates in the Sacrament of the altar. "The Church herself is offered in the very offering she makes to God" (10.6; *ibid.* 279).

Thomas Aquinas. When one comes to the scholasticism of the Middle Ages, one finds little development of the idea of sacrifice. Although the elements for a developed treatise on sacrifice exist in scattered form in the writings of men such as Thomas Aquinas, discussion of the structure and efficacy of the Eucharist as Sacrament and the controversies concerning the Real Presence of Christ occupied theologians' attention. St. Augustine's treatment of sacrifice continues to have wide influence, particularly his emphasis on the inner human act of conscious conformity to the divine will (cf., e.g., Thomas Aquinas, *Summa theologiae* 3a, 48.3).

Actually, Thomas Aquinas's fullest treatment of sacrifice occurs (*Summa theologiae* 2a2ae, 85–86) as part of the discussion of the virtue of religion. This location of the topic as part of Aquinas's moral theology results in a concentration upon the obligation of offering sacrifice rather than upon an analysis of the nature of sacrifice. However, several elements regarding the nature of sacrifice are mentioned.

First among these is the primacy of interior sacrifice, the offering of self to God (*Summa theologiae* 2a2ae, 85.4). Such interior recognition of the sovereignty of God is an obligation flowing from the law of nature (85.1) and can be given only to God (85.2). The form of external sacrifice will, however, depend upon the historical situation in which one finds oneself (85.4).

Second, the element of offering is frequently mentioned as basic to the action of sacrifice; it is applied both to the interior and to the exterior aspects. Yet external sacrifice in the most proper sense requires that something be done to make the offering sacred: animals must be burned, bread must be broken and eaten and blessed (85.3 ad 3).

Third, referring to St. Augustine's definition of sacrifice, "every work done in order to achieve unity with God in holy communion," Aquinas accepts this wider range of meaning for sacrifice. The very desire to reach such unity is itself an act of reverence of God, and so any act of virtue shares in the notion of sacrifice (85.3 ad 1). Later in the *Summa theologiae,* when treating of the manner in which Christ's passion is sacrificial, St. Thomas again draws from the Augustinian definition. The suffering of Christ is a sacrifice precisely because it is the expression of his love for men and his Father (3a, 48.3).

Modern Period. With the Protestant Reformation's questioning of the validity of the Mass as truly efficacious sacrifice, and the Council of Trent's lengthy defense of the Catholic position (H. Denzinger, *Enchiridion symbolorum*, ed. A. Schönmetzer [Freiburg 1963] 1738–1743), an era of more developed discussion about the nature of sacrifice began. At stake was the relationship between the Mass and the death of Christ on Calvary, the Protestants insisting that Calvary was the all-sufficient and unique sacrifice that rendered further sacrificial acts useless, the Catholics insisting that the Mass was the same sacrifice of Calvary. Directed in their thinking by this Counter-Reformation atmosphere, Catholic theologians until well into the 20th century discussed

the Mass as sacrifice almost totally in terms of its link with Christ's Passion and death. As a result, in their theorizings about the nature of sacrifice, the death of a victim received an emphasis it had not previously had. A shift in understanding of the broader notion of sacrifice is observable in the centuries after Thomas Aquinas's analysis of sacrifice as a virtue. While the earlier centuries had stressed the element of "making sacred," later developments gradually underscored the aspect of "giving up something."

Contemporary Period. In the years that followed World War I, a reaction set in that led to a number of new approaches to the theology of sacrifice, and more specifically to theological explanation of the Eucharist as sacrifice. A number of pioneering theological studies (those of De la Taille, Casel, Masure) began to reorientate thinking by insisting on the aspects of offering, mystery, and transformation. Less direct but not less radical was the impact of Biblical studies. Reflection upon the texts that deal with Old Testament sacrificial ritual did much to force a reconsideration of the role of immolation in sacrifice. Rediscovery of the profound continuity between the two covenants brought the action of the Cenacle into clearer light, and a closer scrutiny of New Testament literature drew attention to the early Church's emphasis on the link between Eucharist and Last Supper, as well as to the link between Eucharist and Resurrection.

Perhaps contemporary Catholic theology of sacrifice is seen best as part of the wider development of soteriology. One of the things that characterizes this present-day reflection upon Christ's saving act is the growing tendency to see all the various acts of Christ as a integrated whole. This is particularly true of the event that stretches from the Last Supper to Pentecost; Cenacle, Calvary, Resurrection, Ascension, and Pentecost are seen more as stages in the redeeming act than as discrete events; the whole is the mystery of Christ's passage to the Father, the mystery of His conquest of evil, the mystery of His self-gift to mankind.

Considerable attention has been paid to the role of Christ's risen state in the positive redemptive reconstitution of man; but there has been an important deepening also in the study of human death, and specifically of the death of Christ, in the work of salvation. In this context, Christ's act of sacrifice is seen as an acceptance of the death that may free Him from limited life and set Him aside for the fuller risen life in which He can exercise full life-giving power in human history. Death and risen life form one inseparable mystery of redeeming love, two moments in Christ's Passover, and therefore the sacrificing presence of Christ in the Christian Eucharist involves somehow both aspects of this mystery.

Central to the integration of these facets of the redemptive act is the human decision of Christ: it is this inner act of choice that governs all the elements of the unfolding external action; that imparts redeeming power to the rest; that is the heart of the Eucharist as sacrifice, for the risen Christ who acts in Eucharist does so by retaining this attitude of self-oblation. Christian Eucharist deserves the name sacrifice only because it is Christ in the midst of the Christian community who continues His human decision to give Himself for the sake of His brethren, thus rendering glory to the Father. There are not two sacrificial actions, the one taking place at the Last Supper and Calvary and the other taking place in the Mass. There is one continuing act on Christ's part, and it is this that is the heart of the Eucharistic action.

Contemporary theology also lays stress on the fact that Christ is present in the Eucharistic action as the life-giving Word of God. Communication of the Word is not incidental to the Mass; it forms an integral element of the Christian sacrifice, as ch. 6 of John's Gospel indicates. Christ gives Himself as the object of faith but also as life, for he is creative Word; faith and life are effected sacramentally in the Eucharist; faith and life both enter into the Church's sacrificial response. On Christ's part, this vivifying gift of Himself is the implementing of the inner decision of sacrifice; for this is precisely the task that His Father sends Him to accomplish.

Although the Eucharist is the sacrifice of Christ, it is also truly the sacrifice of the Church; Christ continues to offer sacrifice in and through the sacrificial act of the Christian community, for it is this act that gives expression in space and time to His enduring sacrificial attitude. Nor is it simply a matter of the Church's acting as medium to express Christ; the gestures and words of the Mass speak the Church's own sacrificial mentality. With Christ in its midst—and this is what gives its own act unique significance and effectiveness—the community of the faithful offers itself and Christ to the Father. This it is able to do only because it shares in Christ's own priestly role and power. There are not, then, two sacrifices occurring simultaneously and in intimate relationship; there is one single act of sacrifice, that of Christ in which the Church shares.

In the Eucharistic act the Church expresses supremely her faith and life; but this act is not divorced from the rest of her being and activity. Rather, it serves as the ritual symbolic expression of her willingness to enter into the redemption of human history. The Mass is the solemn dedication of the entire social function of changing the patterns of human life to conform to the principles of Christ. Genuine acceptance in the action of the Mass of Christ's word of wisdom implies the implementation of this wisdom in the manifold circumstances of man's daily life. Living in the midst of men, Christians are dedicated to transforming human society into the new man in Christ; that is what they say solemnly in offering sacrifice.

Bibliography: O. CASEL, *The Mystery of Christian Worship,* ed. B. NEUNHEUSER, tr. I. T. HALE (Westminster, Md. 1962). F. CLARK, *Eucharistic Sacrifice and the Reformation* (Westminster, Md. 1960). B. COOKE, ''Synoptic Presentation of the Eucharist as Covenant Sacrifice,'' *Theological Studies* 21 (1960) 1–44. F. X. DURRWELL, *The Resurrection: A Biblical Study,* tr. R. SHEED (New York 1960) 59–77, 319–329. E. MASURE, *The Sacrifice of the Mystical Body,* tr. A. THOROLD (London 1954). J. H. MILLER, *Signs of Transformation in Christ* (Englewood Cliffs, N.J. 1963); ''Until He Comes: The Eucharist and the Resurrection,'' *Proceedings of the North American Liturgical Week* 23 (1962) 39–44 R. J. DALY, *The Origins of the Christian Doctrine of Sacrifice* (Philadelphia 1978)

[B. J. COOKE]

SACRIFICE OF THE CROSS

The sacrifice of the cross and the glorious RESURRECTION OF CHRIST converge into one paschal mystery, which is the central event in human history (Thomas Aquinas, *Summa theologiae* 3a, 62.5 ad 3). All SALVATION HISTORY anterior to Calvary has been but a shadowy prelude to the great paschal mystery inaugurated there and complemented by the empty tomb of Easter. All subsequent development of the mystic Christ looks back to this paschal mystery as the font of life and strength. The sacrifice of the cross is humanity's perfectly worshipful homage to the God of all history, and the Resurrection of Christ is the living testimony to God's acceptance of mankind's spotless sacrifice.

In the paschal mystery (1) Jesus, humanity's high priest, offered Himself to God as an immolated victim. Thereby (2) He fulfilled all the sacrificial foreshadowings of Calvary established by God's old covenant with men. (3) He reconciled sinners to God by a lasting reconciliation and formed a new people cleansed by His redemptive blood. (4) His sacrifice on Calvary inaugurated the rite of the Christian cult and (5) aptly set forth its spirit sacramentally on the cross.

Jesus, Priest and Victim. The man Jesus, His humanity personally united to the uncreated Word of God, is the natural mediator between God and sinful men (1 Tm 2.5). He is the one substantially holy priest that the human race can claim for itself (Heb 7.26–28). He came among men primarily to be the perfect adorer of God. By the intensity of His interior devotion, animated by obedient love, Christ was endowed with power to offer perfectly worshipful praise to the ever-blessed Trinity. His sacrificial love was a priestly service.

All actions of Jesus, as humanity's high priest, were empowered by measureless efficacy for reconciling mankind with God. But acts anterior to Calvary lacked the specifically sacrificial meaning of the sacrifice of the cross. Sacrifice is an act of external WORSHIP; in it the interior act of RELIGION, through which a creature pays homage to God and is united with Him, must be set forth under a recognizable symbol of visible oblation. Calvary did not evoke new charity or new devotion from the priestly soul of Christ (*Summa theologiae* 3a, 48.1 ad 3). It simply made Him a victim actually set forth as such by His voluntary surrender to the cross (ibid. 3a, 22.2 ad 2).

From His public identification by the Baptist (Jn 1.29) until His final solemnization of the paschal meal (Lk 22.14–20), Jesus progressively revealed Himself as a victim-messiah, the true LAMB OF GOD. He came to be "sanctified" (Jn 17.19). He is an immolated lamb (1 Pt 1.19), who expiates men's sins by His victimhood (Rom 3.25). In the heavenly liturgy He receives grateful testimony from the elect of God (Rv 5.5–14), and in His glorified humanity the Lamb of God leads His people to the perfection of glory (Rv 7.17).

Fulfillment of Old Covenant. The oblation of the true lamb, Christ, was the consummation of all the sacrifices established at the command of God Himself (Heb. 9.114). Calvary fulfilled all the sacrificial foreshadowings of itself proper to the old covenant (*Summa theologiae* 3a, 22.2). Holocausts, sacrifices for sin, and peace offerings were all sensible signs of the invisible spirit of worship demanded by the Prophets of Israel (Am 5.24; Hos 6.6; Mi 6.8). Such sacrifices dramatized the creature's duty of total surrender to God, the need of ATONEMENT FOR SIN, and the yearning for communion with God in peace. But Calvary alone expressed all this in a way worthy of God's acceptance (Heb 10.1–7).

In consummating His sacrifice on the cross Christ in one perfect gesture of devotion fulfilled all the moral, ceremonial, and juridical precepts of the Old Testament worship: all moral precepts because they were all reducible to the commandment of love, and Jesus suffered for love (Jn 14.31); all ceremonial precepts because they were all ordered to the sacrificial worship of God, and Jesus offered the one true sacrifice by dying for men (cf. Col 2.16–18); all juridical precepts because they were all ordered to make amends for injuries inflicted on others, and Jesus died to ransom men from their unjust sinfulness (Mk 10.45; *Summa theologiae* 3a, 47.2 ad 1). And this high priest who saved all by His satisfactory sacrifice merited the glory of His own Resurrection by the undeviating intensity of His own devotion (ibid. 3a, 22.4 ad 2).

Reconciliation and New Alliance. The precious blood of Christ "as of a lamb without blemish and without spot" redeemed the old Israel from "the vain manner of life" handed down by its forefathers (1 Pt 1.19). Chosen race though it was, Israel, like a faithless spouse, needed to be reconciled anew by the redemptive sacrifice of the cross—God's gratuitous assurance of His own love for men (Rom 5.8). The Prophets promised a new alliance between God and His people (Jer 31.31–34; Ez 37.26). Unlike the old covenant the new alliance would reach out and sweep all nations into its blessed mercies. Those who were at one time "aliens from the community of Israel, and strangers to the covenants of the promise" were no longer to be "strangers and foreigners" but "citizens with the saints and members of God's household" (Eph 2.12, 19).

The cross became the barrier-breaker (Eph 2.14) and the meeting place for the old Israel and the new chosen race—"a royal priesthood, a holy nation, a purchased people" (1 Pt 2.9). Constructed into a "temple of the living God" who will dwell among them and be their God forever (2 Cor 6.16), the reconciled people of God has been called to walk in love and imitate the crucified love of Christ so as to become in turn "an offering and a sacrifice to God to ascend in fragrant odor" (Eph 5.2).

On the night before He died Christ made it clear that His redemptive blood was blood of a new alliance (Mk 14.24). His passage out of the world by death and His glorious return to the Father in power was the new paschal mystery. Christ Himself, victim for sin and powerful conqueror of death; is man's passover (1 Cor 5.7). Consequently, God's new people must ever "keep festival" not with the "leaven of malice and wickedness, but with the unleavened bread of sincerity and truth" (1 Cor 5.8).

Inauguration of Christian Worship. On the cross Christ through His Passion initiated the rite of Christian religion by offering Himself voluntarily as a sacrifice to God. As perfect adorer of God on the cross Christ, whose power to bring salvation is the hope of the world, committed all who would ever belong to Him to a similar service of God (2 Cor 5.14–15). "Thus by Baptism men are plunged into the paschal mystery of Christ: they die with Him, are buried with Him, and rise with Him . . . . In like manner, as often as they eat the supper of the Lord they proclaim the death of the Lord until He comes" [Vatican II, *Constitution on the Sacred Liturgy* 6, *Acta Apostolicae Sedis* 56 (1964) 100].

By instituting the sacramental renewal of the redemptive mystery under the appearances of bread and wine, Christ left mankind a sacrifice by which the already accomplished bloody sacrifice of Calvary would be set forth sacramentally, in keeping with man's daily needs, and the memory of it endure until the end of time (H. Denzinger, *Enchiridion symbolorum* 1740). For having celebrated the old passover in memory of the Exodus from Egypt, Christ instituted a new pasch wherein He would Himself be immolated through His priests by visible signs in memory of His transition from this world to His Father, when He redeemed men through the outpouring of His blood, snatched men from the powers of darkness, and transferred them to His own kingdom (ibid. 1741). In Christian worship as often as the commemoration of this paschal mystery is enacted sacramentally ''the victory and triumph of His death are again made present'' (ibid. 1644) and ''the work of our Redemption is made effective'' (Secret, 9th Sunday after Pentecost).

This power to bring salvation— *virtus salutifera*—is in Christ's sacred humanity and extended to the Sacraments. The Sacraments are gifts of the crucified and triumphant Christ. They operate by the power of His presence within them. This power perfects the soul for all that pertains to Christian cult (*Summa theologiae* 3a, 62.5).

Sacramental Significance of the Cross. The spirit of Christian worship was aptly dramatized in a sacramental way by the cross itself. By its very structure the cross is a sign of cosmic Redemption; it is a summons to all-embracing unity; it is the Christian's personal call to mystic crucifixion; it is a realistic portrayal of the demands of salutary charity.

Early writers and Fathers of the Church, notably Irenaeus, Hippolytus, Gregory of Nyssa, Athanasius, and Augustine, have seen a sacramental significance in the cross, as suggested by St. Paul's prayer that his converts might be able to comprehend ''the breadth and length and height and depth'' and know the love of Christ which surpasses all understanding (Eph 3.18,19). These mysterious dimensions are seen as the limitless dimensions of God's far-reaching power and providence, Christ's all-pervasive love of man and his cosmos, and the Christian's uncalculating response to the overtures of God's love as manifested on the cross.

The cross, with its universal embrace of all reality, assures men that the whole universe has been transfigured by the power of the Crucified; brooks and vineyards and wheat fields and olive groves have all received new dignity under the touch of God's redemptive grace; and all creation awaits its full and final deliverance at ''the revelation of the sons of God'' (Rom 8.19).

The cross, with Christ fixed at the very heart of it, proclaims the shattering truth that there can be no barriers between ''Gentile and Jew,'' ''Barbarian and Scythian,'' ''slave and freeman,'' for Christ is all things and in all (Col 3.11). All threats to unity He has swallowed up in victory so that ''he might create in himself one new man,

and make peace . . . having slain the enmity in himself'' (Eph 2.15, 16).

The cross, upholding a victim Christ, who ''emptied himself'' (Phil 2.7), is a sign of man's interior conflict, which must be accepted, endured, transfigured, and sanctified by sacrificial love. The cross proclaims the cost of discipleship. The Christian who is challenged by the crucified Christ to deny himself, take up his own cross, and come follow his Leader must deny his own flesh with its passions and desires (Gal 5.24) and be mystically crucified with Christ (Gal 2.19, 20).

The cross, instrument of self revelation for the model human lover (Jn 8.28), is a symbol of salutary love. Its dimensions set forth the universality, the perseverance, the unearthliness, and the humility of Christian charity, which emerges from the heart of man by the gratuity of God's grace (*Summa theologiae* 3a, 46.4). God's love for man made manifest on the cross evokes a human response of salutary love ''in which the perfection of human salvation consists'' (ibid. 3a, 46.3). He is the God of Abraham, the God of Isaac, the God of Jacob, and the God of every unique product of His workmanship (Eph 2.10). The cross tells the world that only God sets the limits of each man's sacrificial love.

See Also: CRUCIFIXION, THEOLOGICAL SIGNIFICANCE OF; EXPIATION (IN THEOLOGY); PASSION OF CHRIST; PRECIOUS BLOOD, I (IN THE BIBLE); PRECIOUS BLOOD, II (THEOLOGY OF); REDEMPTION; SACRIFICE, III (IN ISRAEL); SACRIFICE, IV (IN CHRISTIAN THEOLOGY), SATISFACTION OF CHRIST.

Bibliography: A. GAUDEL, *Dictionnaire de théologie catholique,* ed. A. VACANT et al., 15 v. (Paris 1903–50; Tables générales 1951–) 14.1:662–692. J. RIVIÈRE, ibid. 13.2:1912–2004. P. CLAUDEL, ibid. 2: 2598–2639. M. OLPHE-GALLIARD, *Dictionnaire de spiritualité ascétique et mystique. Doctrine et histoire,* M. VILLER et al. 2.2:2607–23. F. X. DURRWELL, *The Resurrection: A Biblical Study,* tr. R. SHEED (New York 1960). C. V. HÉRIS, *The Mystery of Christ,* tr. D. FAHEY (Westminster, Md 1950). R. GARRIGOU-LAGRANGE, *Christ the Savior,* tr. B. ROSE (St. Louis 1950). W. J. MCGARRY, *Paul and the Crucified* (New York 1939). L. RICHARD, *Le Mystère de la Rédemption* (Tournai 1959). L. SABOURIN, *Rédemption sacrificielle* (Bruges 1961).

[A. P. HENNESSY]

SACRILEGE

In a wide sense, sacrilege is any sin against the virtue of RELIGION; more strictly, it is the abuse or violation of a sacred person, place, or thing (respectively, a personal, local, or real sacrilege). The sacredness of the object of sacrilege arises, not from private decision, but from public dedication to divine worship, by either divine or ecclesiastical law. All sacrilege is against the virtue of religion, but it is commonly admitted that not all offenses against the virtue of religion are sacrilegious. True sacrilege is not simple irreverence for an object, but for an object precisely as sacred. Anything dedicated to the service of God by proper authority acquires a new dignity; it is stamped, so to speak, with the seal of God. Because it enters, in a sense, into the sphere of the divine, irreverence to it is an irreverence to God Himself (*see* St. Thomas, *Summa theologicae*, 2a2ae 99.1).

Personal sacrilege is the physical mistreatment of a person whom dedication to the service of God has made sacred. To strike, wrongfully imprison, or bring to a public court—without approval, implicit or explicit, of competent authority—a cleric or a member of a religious community, even a novice, would be personal sacrilege. Also any external action of impurity involving the person of one with a public VOW of chastity, whether performed by the person under vow or by another, is sacrilegious. (Not all authors agree that sins against chastity involving those with a private vow have a sacrilegious effect.) Double sacrilege is certainly involved in any impurity between two persons, both of whom are bound by public vows of chastity.

Local sacrilege is the violation of a sacred place, such as a church, a public oratory, or a cemetery, whether these have been blessed or consecrated. Theft of a holy object from a church, for example, is sacrilegious, whereas to pick the pocket of a fellow churchgoer would not be. To use a sacred place for a profane purpose, for example, to use a church as a dance hall or bar–room, would involve sacrilege. Any external act of impurity or the shedding of blood to the point of mortal guilt, if committed in a sacred place, is sacrilegious.

Real sacrilege is the misuse of sacred things, that is, of things that have been formally dedicated to the service of God, or things that of their nature pertain to divine service. To administer the Sacraments, for example, or to receive Holy Communion while in the state of mortal sin, would be a real sacrilege.

Sacrilege is commonly admitted to be a mortal sin of its nature (*ex genere*), because it is seriously opposed to the virtue of religion. But a sacrilege may be a venial sin from the slightness of the matter with which it is concerned. Slightness of matter, for example, makes the thoughtless use of holy water a venial fault. Diverse degrees of gravity in sacrilege depend upon the relative sacredness of the thing profaned. To profane the Holy Eucharist is thus more grave than to steal a chalice. Practically, to estimate the gravity of a sacrilege, one must take into account the degree of sacredness of the person, place, or thing involved, the sinful action itself as viewed by prudent people, and the intention of the one who performs the action.

Bibliography: J. ABBO and J. HANNAN, *The Sacred Canons*, 2 v. (St. Louis 1960). L. G. FANFANI, *Manuale theoricopracticum theologiae moralis* (Rome 1950–) 3:175–182. B. HÄRING, *The Law of Christ: Moral Theology for Priests and Laity*, tr. E. G. KAISER (Westminster, Md. 1961–) 2:209–214. L. BENDER, in F. ROBERTI et al., *Dictionary of Moral Theology*, ed. P. PALAZZINI et al., tr. H. J. YANNONE et al. from 2d Ital. ed. (Westminster, Md. 1962) 1087.

[M. HERRON]

SACRIS SOLEMNIIS

Office hymn that was traditionally sung at Matins on the feast of CORPUS CHRISTI, as well as during the procession of that day. It was composed by THOMAS AQUINAS at the request of Pope Urban IV for the feast of Corpus Christi, which was instituted in 1264 by the bull *Transiturus de hoc mundo ad Patrem*. Each of its seven strophes (including the doxology) consists of three Asclepiadic lines, with the caesura occurring regularly after the sixth syllable, and one Glyconic. There is perfect *incisio* throughout the hymn. The same rhythmic pattern is to be found in Horace, but the meter of the *Sacris solemniis* is accentual, not quantitative, and may, therefore, except for the last line, conveniently be read as dactylic tetrameter acatalectic. From a purely technical standpoint, the most outstanding characteristic of the hymn is the intricate rhyme-scheme (ababcbc), which is best apparent when the Asclepiadic lines are divided at the caesura, where rhyme also occurs:

> Sacris solemniis / juncta sint gaudia,
> Et ex praecordiis / sonent praeconia;
> Recedant vetera, / nova sint omnia,
> Corda, voces, et opera.

Despite objections to its theological implications [Delaporte, ''Les Hymnes de bréviaire romain,'' *Rassegna Gregoriana*, (Nov.-Dec. 1907) 501], the phrase *Te trina Deitas* has been retained in the doxology of this hymn although in the version that was formerly sung at first and second Vespers in the Common of the Martyrs, *Sanctorum meritis*, the phrase was revised to *Te summa O Deitas*. Like all the hymns of Thomas Aquinas, the *Sacris solemniis* is remarkable for its combination of precise dogma, deep piety, and majestic style.

Bibliography: *Analecta hymnica* 50:587–588. J. JULIAN, ed., *A Dictionary of Hymnology* (New York 1957) 2:986, MSS and trs. M. BRITT, ed., *The Hymns of the Breviary and Missal* (new ed. New York 1948) 182–185. F. J. E. RABY, *A History of Christian-Latin Poetry from the Beginnings to the Close of the Middle Ages* (Oxford 1953) 402–410. J. CONNELLY, *Hymns of the Roman Liturgy* (Westminster MD 1957).

[M. F. MCCARTHY]

Sacristan standing next to Virgin's Veil, Chartres Cathedral, Chartres, France. (©Dean Conger/CORBIS)

Bibliography: G. T. RYAN, *The Sacristy Manual* (Chicago 1993). T. V. MCDONALD, *The Sacristan in the Catholic Church: A Practical Guide* (Stowmarket, England 1999). S. A. STAUFFER, *Altar Guild and Sacristy Handbook* (Minneapolis 2000).

[J. A. ABBO/EDS.]

SACRISTY

Part of every church where the clergy vest for sacred functions and where the vestments, books and vessels for use in liturgical services are kept. In early centuries (at first in Syria about 400) the diaconicon and prothesis, the chambers joined to the sides of the apse, were used for this purpose. This is generally true in the Orthodox Church even today. In churches of the West such rooms were built as "side apses." Gradually special rooms were destined for canons, altar boys, and others. In smaller churches a compartment either beside or behind the altar sufficed. The sacristy strictly so-called did not make its appearance until the 16th century. The size and importance of the church determines the size and number of sacristy areas. The main sacristy should be near the sanctuary and accessible from the sanctuary and the nave as well as from the outside.

Bibliography: J. A. ABBO, "The Sacristy and its Requirements," *Catholic Property Administration* 27 (1963) 40–43, 80–82. J. B. O'CONNELL, *Church Building and Furnishing* (Notre Dame, IN 1955) 116–121. G. T. RYAN, *The Sacristy Manual* (Chicago 1993). T. V. MCDONALD, *The Sacristan in the Catholic Church: A Practical Guide* (Stowmarket, England 1999). S. A. STAUFFER, *Altar Guild and Sacristy Handbook* (Minneapolis 2000).

[J. A. ABBO/EDS.]

SACRISTAN

The person charged with the care of a church and its sacristy, as well as preparation for all its liturgical celebrations. Some of the sacristan's duties were first performed by the *janitor* or *aedituus* (house custodian), then by an ordained cleric, the *ostiarius* or porter (in Rome by the *mansionarius*). When the sacristan's office had become a distinct one with peculiar rights and duties, it was entrusted to a cleric, preferably to a priest. In his *Regula* (ch.19), St. Isidore (570–636) states: "The custodian of the sacristy is entrusted with the care of the church . . . of the sacred veils and vestments, vessels, books and all appurtenances, of the oils, candles and lights." The *Decretals* of Gregory IX speak of both the office of sacristan and of the "custodian," or sacristan's helper (*Corpus iuris canonici*, ed. E. Friedberg X 1.26.1, 27.1–2). The Council of Trent urged that all sacristans be clerics. This proved impractical, such that by the 19th century, the functions of the sacristan came to be carried out by qualified laypersons.

SADDUCEES

Members of a Jewish sect of the priestly class that flourished prior to and at the time of Christ. The name most likely derived ultimately from Zadok, the high priest under Solomon (2 Sm 8.17; 1 Kgs 1.8;1 Chr 24.3).

Origin and History. The sect was formed, according to the most probable opinion, during the Maccabean period, after the PHARISEES had separated from the priestly Hasmonaean dynasty during the reign of John Hyrcanus. Many priests formed a party to maintain the priestly powers and to preserve the older Israelite views in opposition to the more liberal-minded Pharisees, and they took as their patron the great high priest Sadoc of Solomon's time, from whom they claimed descent. During the Roman occupation the Sadducees had control of the Temple and its worship. Exercising great power in the government, they were never popular with the common people. They were swept away by the catastrophe of A.D. 70, when Titus and the Roman Legions destroyed Jerusalem.

Interior sacristy of Church of Sao Salvadore, Horta, Azores, Portugal. (©Tony Arruza/CORBIS)

The Sadducees were entrenched in conservatism. They rejected all dogmatic developments based upon oral traditions, preserving the older Israelite doctrines. Accordingly, they denied the immortality of the soul, the resurrection of the body, and the existence of angels (see Acts 4.1–2; 23.6–9). Their moral teaching was one of strict legalism, according to the written Law without the mitigations of the oral interpretations. Their chief concern was with the maintenance of external worship.

Politically they accommodated themselves to Herod the Great and later to the Roman domination. Under the leadership of the house of Annas, which maintained itself in the high priesthood for many years, they preferred to preserve the status quo rather than venture into unknown areas of insurrection and revolt.

The QUMRAN community was not allied to the Sadducees' party, despite the fact that its leaders were known as $b^e n\hat{e}$ $\d{s}\bar{a}d\bar{o}q$ (sons of Sadoc). There was little in common between the two, except that both were priestly movements.

In the New Testament. There are but a few direct references to the Sadducees in the NT. The SYNOPTIC GOSPELS agree in assigning them to the role of protagonist in the dispute over the resurrection of the body (Mk 12.18; Lk 20.27; Mt 22.23). Matthew joins them to the Pharisees as participants in another controversy (Mt 16.1–10). John does not mention them specifically.

St. Luke gives more information about them in Acts 4.1–2; 5.17–33; 23.6–9. He writes that they denied the resurrection of the body, belonged to the party of the chief priests, and were the most opposed to the Christian movement. Ordinarily the Sadducees were opposed to the Pharisees, but in the case of Jesus and His followers the two sects came to some agreement to cooperate in crushing the movement. The Sadducean high priests, under Annas especially, feared that Jesus and his followers would upset their domination. The statement of CAIPHAS (Jn 11.49–51) makes this clear.

While a man of Annas's ill repute could well have been motivated by selfish political gains, it would be unfair to conclude that all Sadducees were inspired by similar base motives in their opposition to Jesus. From what is known of their religious views it appears that many Sadducees were opposed to Jesus' teaching, which must have appeared to them to be more revolutionary and heretical than that of the Pharisees. Some Sadducees, therefore, opposed Jesus and His followers sincerely because of their religious views.

Bibliography: M. SIMON, *Les Sectes juives au temps de Jésus* (Paris 1960). G. STEMBERGER, *Jewish Contemporaries of Jesus: Pharisees, Sadducees, Essenes* (Minneapolis 1995). A.J. SALDARINI, *Pharisees, Scribes, and Sadducees in Palestinian Society: A Sociological Approach*, new ed. (Grand Rapids, Mich. 2001). J. WELLHAUSEN, *The Pharisees and the Sadducees: An Examination of Internal Jewish History* (Macon, Ga. 2001).

[R. MERCURIO/EDS.]

SADLIER

A family of publishers. Brothers Denis and James Sadlier, who founded the firm of D. & J. Sadlier, were born in Cashel, Co. Tipperary, Ireland (Denis in December 1816 and James in September 1821). They came to New York City in 1830 with their widowed mother, their father having died in Liverpool enroute to the U.S. They began publishing in New York City in the 1830s with a monthly serial edition of Butler's *Lives of the Saints*, followed in 1838 by a similar series on the Bible from plates of the 1829 Devereux edition (Utica, N.Y.). By the 1840s the firm was well enough established in New York to consider expanding its reach. James Sadlier established a branch in Montreal, and in 1846 was married there to Mary Anne Madden, born in County Cavan, Ireland, who became a well-known and prolific author, writing under the name Mrs. J. Sadlier.

The company continued to grow through the 1850 as the Catholic population of the U.S. and Canada increased through immigration. In 1853 the publisher and bookseller John Doyle left for California, and the Sadliers purchased his stock and rights. In 1857 the firm acquired the *American Celt*, a weekly newspaper founded by Thomas d'Arcy McGee, and changed the name to the *New York Tablet*. Many of Mrs. J. Sadlier's novels were serialized in the *Tablet*. Other writers who contributed were McGee himself and Orestes Brownson, after his *Review* ceased publication in 1864. James and Mary Anne Sadlier returned to New York from Montreal in 1860 to assist Denis, possibly because the *Tablet* needed their talents

and energies. In addition to being noted for its editions of the Scriptures and for publishing translations of devotional works by leading figures of the church in Europe such as Orsini, the firm also began a line of Catholic school texts, including the *Metropolitan Readers*. In all, from the 1830s to the late 1890s, a total of 652 D. & J. Sadlier imprints appeared, the best known being the *Catholic Directory*, *Almanac*, and *Ordo*.

After James Sadlier's death in 1869, Mary Anne Sadlier wrote very little. Since her works had been a mainstay of the company's publishing list, this was a blow to the company's fortunes. Turbulent economic times in the country at large did not help. Although Denis and James each had a daughter who carried on the family's literary tradition, writing biographies and stories, several of their sons died fairly young, or else were not interested in the business. Denis died in 1885, and by the 1890s there was not much activity at the firm. The one bright moment in this decade came in 1895 when Mary Anne Madden Sadlier was awarded the Laetare Medal by the University of Notre Dame for her contributions to Catholic literature. Mary Anne Sadlier died in Montreal in 1903. Some of the remaining rights of D. & J. Sadlier, including the rights over the *Catholic Directory*, were sold to P. J. Kenedy in 1912.

Management of the Sadlier publishing business was taken over by William H. Sadlier, a nephew of Denis and James Sadlier, who was born in New York in 1846. William joined D. & J. Sadlier around 1860, and became a "traveling agent" for the firm. In 1874 he decided to start his own textbook publishing company. When he died very suddenly in 1877 at the age of 31, his young widow, Annie Cassidy Sadlier, resolved to carry on the company. Frank X. Sadlier, son of Annie and William, took over from his mother as president of the firm in 1909. At his death in 1939, Frank X. Sadlier, who had no children, was succeeded by his nephew, F. Sadlier Dinger, son of his sister, Rose Sadlier Dinger. He continued the family's catechetical and educational heritage, publishing numerou titles and programs to serve the needs of Catholic school children and children from public schools enrolled in parish catechetical programs. His suggestion of workbooks for teaching religion resulted in the *Baltimore Catechism with Study Lessons* by Dr. Ellamay Horan, and was followed by the groundbreaking *On Our Way* Series, written by Sr. Maria de la Cruz Aymes, S.H. The firm expanded into the public school arena with the 1972 acquisition of Oxford Book Company, Inc.

[E. P. WILLGING/G. F. BAUMBACH]

SADNESS

A state of dejection of soul caused by great afflic-
tion; a languor of spirit and a discouragement engendered
by the knowledge that one is afflicted by some evil. Sadness has many degrees and expresses itself in many ways.
As an affective movement of the sensitive APPETITE, it is
the emotional reaction to an evil recognized as present
and no longer avoidable. This apprehension of evil (or the
loss of a good, which is felt as an evil) may arise from
the senses, the imagination or memory, or the intellect.
Although it is not itself a privation, it results from awareness of a privation—a positive act that arises from contact
with evil. Sadness then has its source in love and desire
of a good that is lost or is absent, or in the presence of
an evil that is hated and for which one has aversion.

In addition to the sadness experienced over one's
own evil, there is also pity, which is sadness over another's evil; envy, which is sorrow over another's good; anxiety, which one experiences when escape from sadness
seems impossible; and torpor, which is the mental anguish that makes movement virtually impossible.

Psychology. As an emotion, sadness is psychosomatic. Sadness is even evident in one's physiognomy—
dull eyes, drooped lips, grave expression of duress. The
internal bodily changes accompanying sadness are the
slowing down of respiration and heartbeat and the consequent loss of bodily strength. In sadness, the only organ
significantly activated is the gall bladder; the increased
flow of bile may back up into the stomach, thus causing
loss of appetite or nausea. The passive motor functions
are stopped or suppressed; the active motor functions
react defensively—crying, contortions, or convulsions.
Of all the passions, sadness, especially when prolonged,
is the most harmful to the body. Physical activity performed in a state of sadness is seldom performed well.

Psychologically, the effects of sadness are listless-
ness and lack of vital energy. Just as joy dilates the heart,
sadness constricts it. As sadness becomes more intense
or extreme, there is increasing absorption in one's pain
or suffering, leading to depression and at times to stupor.

Some causes of sadness are inherent in human nature; others are peculiar to the individual. All men are
subject to sickness and physical suffering, fatigue and ex-
haustion, and infirmities that are the sad precursor of
death. The moral suffering, deceptions, fears, remorse,
apprehension about the future, discouragement about the
present, etc.—the sources of suffering for each individual—differ greatly. Often one can be sad without being
able to find a precise cause. Loss or lack of possessions,
friends, honor, reputation, respect, etc., as well as unfulfilled or conflicting desires, are legitimate causes of sadness for human persons. The true psychological cause of
all sadness is the feeling of one's inability or powerless-
ness to cope with present evil or the loss or absence of
a good.

The remedies for sadness are pleasurable experiences, crying (a normal outlet), sympathy of friends, the
contemplation of truth (in proportion to one's appreciation of the search for truth), sleep, bathing, and exercise.
Since one of the greatest causes of sadness is unfulfilled
desire, or conflict of desires, one of the simplest remedies
is the limitation of one's desires.

One's tendency to sadness is closely related to TEM-
PERAMENT. The sanguine person tends to pass with extreme facility from joy to sadness or vice versa, neither
being very intense or lasting. Sadness in the sanguine
tends to express itself in speech. Choleric and melancholic persons experience no emotion by halves—every impression penetrates and endures. Sadness in persons of
these temperaments is more likely to be manifested by silence.

Age and sex also seem to play a related role in the
experience of sadness. In children, sadness (unlike anger)
is not present, for they are not yet aware of the labor, the
dangers, and the miseries of human existence. Because
of their keener sensitivity, women seem to experience
sadness more easily than men; and they more readily suffer or are sad because of conflict, loss, frustration, or failure in the sphere of human love.

Morality. In its nature as an emotion, sadness is
morally neutral; but in the totality of a human experience,
it is good when moderated, and lacking in goodness when
it completely exceeds reasonable limits either in its object, or duration, or intensity. Sadness is not necessarily
in disaccord with reason; it need not be avoided as
shameful or useless, but must be integrated into harmonious living. No human life passes without suffering—
physical and moral—and therefore sadness must be accepted under the control of reason.

See Also: PASSION.

Bibliography: M. L. FALORNI, *Enciclopedia filosofica* (Venice-Rome 1957) 4:1318–19. THOMAS AQUINAS, *Summa theologiae*
1a2ae, 35–39. J. MAISONNEUVE, *Les Sentiments* (3d ed. Paris 1954).
G. DUMAS, *Nouveau traité de psychologie* (Paris 1930) v. 2.

[M. W. HOLLENBACH]

SADOLETO, JACOPO

Cardinal, bishop of Carpentras, distinguished for his
classical scholarship and his participation in the early
Catholic Reformation; b. Modena, July 12, 1477; d.

Jacopo Sadoleto.

Church—a profoundly sincere though sometimes quixotic agent of reunion and reconciliation. His overtures to Philip Melanchthon (1537) and Jakob Sturm (1538), like his letters "To the Princes and People of Germany" (1538) and "To the Council and People of Geneva" (1539), provoked bitter attacks in Catholic and Protestant circles alike. But Sadoleto continued to oppose the use of force in the suppression of heresy and remained a partisan of peace, the council, and internal reform to the end of his life, standing far closer to the position of Contarini and Reginald POLE, than to that of Girolamo ALEANDRO or Bartolomeo Guidiccioni.

Bibliography: *Opera quae extant omnia*, 4 v. (Verona 1737–38); *Epistolae quotauot extant proprio nomine scriptae*, ed. V. A. COSTANZI, 3 v. (Rome 1760–64); *Lettere del Card. Jacopo Sadoleto e di suo nipote*, ed. A. RONCHINI (Modena 1871); *Epistolae Leonis X, Clementis VII, Pauli III, nomine scriptae*, ed. V. A. COSTANZI (Rome 1759). A. JOLY, *Étude sur Jacques Sadolet, 1477–1547* (Caen 1856). S. RITTER, *Un umanista teologo: Jacopo Sadoleto* (Rome 1912). G. VON SCHULTHESSRECHBERG, *Der Kardinal Jacopo Sadoleto: Ein Beitrag zür Geschichte des Humanismus* (Zurich 1909). G. MÜLLER, *Die Religion in Geschichte und Gegenwart*, 7 v. (3d ed. Tübingen 1957–65)[3] 5:1278–79. R. M. DOUGLAS, *Jacopo Sadoleto, 1477–1547: Humanist and Reformer* (Cambridge, Mass. 1959), bibliog.

[R. M. DOUGLAS]

Rome, Oct. 18, 1547. Although Giovanni Sadoleto expected his son to prepare for a career of public service in the regime of the Este in Ferrara, Jacopo went to Rome in 1498 to pursue classical studies in the household of Cardinal Oliviero Caraffa. There he was soon recognized as a minor poet, an accomplished Latinist, and a prominent figure in the Roman Academy. He was ordained in 1511. Leo X appointed him, with Pietro Bembo, to the Apostolic Secretariate in 1513. Three years later Sadoleto was invested with a diocese in the Comtat VENAISSIN, where he lived as a devoted and often militant bishop in the interludes (1523–24, 1527–36, 1538–42, 1543–45) between assignments to the Curia. During his service to CLEMENT VII (1524–27), Sadoleto emerged as an exegete and ecclesiastical reformer. In 1527 Sadoleto left the Vatican for Carpentras and turned the next nine years to the greatest literary output of his career, producing both his most ambitious work as a humanist, the Neoplatonist *De laudibus philosophiae* (1538); and his most controversial work as a theologian, the neo-Pelagian *In Pauli Epistolam ad Romanos Commentariorum libritres* (1535). In 1535 he was recalled to Rome by Paul III to join Gasparo CONTARINI's commission on reform and in December 1536 he was named cardinal. Although consistently unwilling to compromise with the Protestants on matters of dogma, Sadoleto vigorously argued for the reform of the

SAFAVIDS

A dynasty of Shiïte Muslim shahs of Iran between 1502 and 1736; it took its name from Shaykh Ṣafī-al-Dīn Ishāq (1252–1334), from whom the founder of the dynasty, Ismāʿīl Shah, was descended. The family appears to have originated in Ardebīl as the hereditary leaders of a powerful Sūfī fraternity of a type that had come to replace ordinary political authority on the Turkoman frontier (*see* SUFISM). As the dynasty expanded its military organization in Gīlān, it developed strong Iranian nationalist feelings and championed the cause of the SHIÏTES. Ismāʿīl Ṣafāvī assumed the title of shah when he captured Tabriz in 1502. He went on to secure his power in northwestern Iran and then defeated the Uzbek forces at Merv in Khorasan. His successes aroused the Ottoman Sultan Selim to action, and in 1514 the OTTOMAN TURKS occupied Kurdistan and Diyarbekr, withdrawing later from Tabriz and Georgia. Ismāʿīl Shāh made Shiïsm a state religion, recognizing in it a means for uniting the Persians against the Ottomans and Uzbeks, who were SUNNITES. He also enlisted the staunch and much-needed military support of seven Shiïte Turkish tribes known as the *Kizilbash* ("redheads"). He died in 1524 and was succeeded by his ten-year-old son Ṭahmāsp, who ruled until 1576. During Ṭahmāsp's reign the twin frontiers of Safavid warfare were clearly distinguished: the Uzbeks in the north, whom Ṭahmāsp successfully expelled from Khorasan, and the Ottomans in the west, who managed to keep the upper hand but concluded a peace treaty in 1555. At this point Safavid Iran began to attract the attention of the European powers as a possible permanent second front against the Ottoman Turks. Ṭahmāsp's fourth son Ismāʿīl II proved to be an ineffectual ruler, who allowed the Safavid empire to suffer from factionalism and invasion.

Shāh ʿAbbās I, known as "the Great," succeeded his father in 1587 and ruled the Safavid empire until 1628. When he inherited the title, the Uzbeks and the Ottomans had invaded his provinces and his tribal chieftains were in revolt. ʿAbbās immediately sued for peace with the invaders at disadvantageous terms in order to consolidate his position. In 1598 the Sherley brothers, Anthony and Robert, arrived from England and began a reorganization of the Safavid army at ʿAbbās' request. They equipped it with better artillery and instituted the *tufangchis* (riflemen) to match the Ottoman Janissaries and the *Shah Savan* (friends of the Shah) to offset the power of the *Kizilbash*. ʿAbbās also renovated communications within Iran and stamped out brigandage. He sent Sir Anthony Sherley to Europe as his ambassador and began a long series of victorious campaigns on the Ottoman frontier. One important outcome of Sherley's journey was the arrival of a papal mission in Persia entrusted to the Discalced Carmelite friars. Although forbidden to proselytize among Moslems, the friars worked with success among the dissident Armenians at New Julfa outside the Safavid capital of Isfahan and represented the Holy See with distinction, though with varying fortunes, for a century and a half. They also filled the bishoprics of Baghdad and Isfahan. Shāh ʿAbbās proved less friendly toward the end of his reign, however, when the European powers were not aiding him sufficiently and had turned on one another, as, for example, in the British attack on the Portuguese at Hormuz in 1622.

ʿAbbās' grandson Ṣafī I reigned tyrannically for 14 years (1628–42) and lost territory to the MUGHALS. The Ottomans recovered Baghdad and even, for a time, Tabriz. During the reign of ʿAbbās II (1642–66), the eastern frontiers were secured and relations with the Ottomans improved. This state of affairs continued during the 29-year reign of his son Sulaymān Shāh. In 1694 Sulaymān's son Ḥusayn became shah, but he permitted the Shiïte clerics to dictate policy; at this, the Sunnite Afghans, who held the eastern frontier, declared their independence under Mīr Wais in 1709. In 1722 Mīr Wais' son Maḥmūd invaded Persia and captured Isfahan. Shāh Ḥusayn was deposed and Ṭahmāsp II was placed on the throne by the emergent Afghan leader Nādir Qūli, who, however, soon deposed the shah in favor of his infant son ʿAbbās III. The child died soon afterwards and Nādir

himself assumed the title of shah in 1736, putting an end to the Safavid dynasty.

See Also: PERSIA.

Bibliography: P. SYKES, *A History of Persia* (3d ed. London 1951) 2:158–255. *A Chronicle of the Carmelites in Persia*, 2 v. (London 1939). *Tadhkirat al-Mulûk*, tr. V. MINORSKY (London 1943). L. LOCKHART, *The Fall of the Safavid Dynasty and the Afghan Occupation of Persia* (Cambridge, Eng. 1958).

[J. KRITZECK]

SAGHEDDU, MARIA GABRIELLA, BL.

Also called Maria Gabriella of Unity; Trappistine nun; b. Mar. 17, 1914, Dorgali, Sardinia, Italy; d. Apr. 23, 1939, in Grottaferrata, Frascati. After the death of her sister, Maria Gabriella became a young woman of prayer and charity, enrolling in Catholic Action, teaching catechism, and tending the aged. At 21, she entered the monastery of Grottaferrata, then headed by Mother Pia Gullini. After her profession (1937) her life was marked by gratitude for her calling to religious life and a desire to submit completely to God's will. When the community was asked to pray for Christian unity, Maria Gabriella immediately undertook the task and offered her life as an oblation. After three and one-half years of religious life, she died with tuberculosis. Her body rests in the monastery chapel of Vitorchiano (Viterbo), to which the community of Grottaferrata was transferred. The beatification of Sister Maria Gabriella by John Paul II on June 25, 1983 ended the Week of Prayers for Christian unity (1983) and was attended by representatives of the Anglican, Lutheran, and Orthodox churches.

Feast: April 22.

Bibliography: *L'Osservatore Romano*, English ed. 5 (1983): 5–6. P. CUSACK, *Blessed Gabriella of Unity: A Patron for the Ecumenical Movement* (Portland, OR 1995). M. DRISCOLL, *A Silent Herald of Unity* (Kalamazoo, MI 1990). M. KERVINGANT, *Le monachisme, lieu oecuménique* (Paris 1983). B. MARTELET, *La petite soeur de l'Unité* (Paris 1984). P. B. QUATTROCCHI, *A Life for Unity: Sr. Maria Gabriella*, tr. M. JEREMIAH (Brooklyn, NY 1990).

[K. I. RABENSTEIN]

SAGRA DI SAN MICHELE, ABBEY OF

Or San Michele della Chiusa, former Benedictine abbey, present-day monastery of the ROSMINIANS, near Susa, Piedmont, Italy, Diocese of Turin. The Benedictine abbey founded by St. JOHN VINCENTIUS (d. 1012), a disciple of St. ROMUALD, was picturesquely and strategically located on a rocky abutment that commanded the valley of the Mt. Cenis Pass. Its very location made it important, and under the protection of the Savoy family it acquired immense political importance. It gradually gained vast holdings in Italy, France, and even Spain, provoking hostility on the part of secular powers and even the clergy and other monasteries. Conversely with the rise of the abbey's temporal power, its monastic life disintegrated, and in 1256 papal visitors excommunicated the entire community. Subsequent visitations and attempts at reform proved unsuccessful; the abbey's vassals meantime were becoming independent through continuous rebellions. Despite a brief revival under Abbot William of Savoy (1310–26) and his successor, Rudolph (1326–59), the monastery again lapsed into dissoluteness under simoniacal abbots. In 1375 the monks were again excommunicated and Abbot Peter di Forgeret was deposed; shortly afterward the abbey was given in perpetual COMMENDATION to the House of Savoy. However, this did not succeed in arresting the decline of the monastery; in 1586 Pope Sixtus V forbade the abbey to accept new postulants, and in 1622 the abbey was suppressed by Gregory XV, who entrusted it to the secular clergy of nearby Giaveno. Meanwhile the buildings, erected partly on the rock and partly on an enormous artificial pylon, were gradually disintegrating, including the old abbey church, started in the 12th century and completed much later. In 1836, by the initiative of King Charles Albert, the Rosminians came to occupy the old monastery. The buildings were restored at the beginning of the 20th century. Portions of the scattered Benedictine library and archives are preserved in Giaveno and Turin.

Bibliography: L. H. COTTINEAU, *Répertoire topobibliographique des abbayes et prieurés,* 2 v. (Mâcon 1935–39) 1:775–776. A. MELLANA, *L'Abbazia di San Michele della Chiusa dalle origini sino al secolo XIV* (Rome 1940), with bibliog. G. BORGHEZIO, *Enciclopedia Italiana de scienzi, littere ed arti,* 36 v. (Rome 1929–39; suppl. 1938–) 30:437–438.

[I. DE PICCOLI]

SAHAGÚN, BERNARDINO DE

Franciscan historian, linguist, and ethnologist, considered the precursor of modern cultural anthropology and father of American ethnology; b. Sahagún de Campos, León, Spain, 1499; d. Mexico City, 1590. Nothing is known of Sahagún's life in Spain, not even his correct name, except that like so many other outstanding missionaries, *letrados,* and functionaries in Spanish America, he studied at the University of Salamanca. In Salamanca Sahagún entered the Franciscan Order. In 1529 he sailed from Cádiz for Mexico. Sahagún found Mexico still suffering from the tremendous shock of the Spanish conquest and of the fall of the powerful Aztec empire. Four years before his arrival, the first group of Franciscan missionaries, under the leadership of Fray Martín de VALENCIA, had landed and begun the work of evangelization. To this effort, Fray Bernardino brought a profound knowledge of the Nahuatl language and culture, a deep love for the defeated Native Americans, and a strict scientific attitude.

His first years in Mexico (1530–35) were spent in that part of the valley of Mexico famous for the *chinampas* (floating gardens), doing evangelical work in the convents of Tlamanalco and Xochimilco. There he learned the Mexican (Nahuatl) language and was fascinated by the native culture, still well preserved despite the trauma of the conquest. He noted the superficiality of many of the rapid conversions to Christianity and the powerful influence of the ancient native beliefs. There Sahagún formed the attitudes that he maintained for the rest of his life: the native culture was estimable and in certain aspects superior to that being imposed upon the natives; it was necessary to study and to know this culture thoroughly, not only to be able to combat the pagan beliefs successfully, but also to be able to preserve it and to integrate it into the common heritage that he foresaw would be the national culture of Mexico.

Innovations in Education. About 1536 Sahagún was transferred to Tlaltelolco, the twin city of Tenochtitlán, and together with it, the site of the modern Mexico City. The College of Santa Cruz had just been founded there for the sons of the caciques and principal native nobility. This school was a result of the policy of Fray Martín de Valencia of beginning a school for Native Americans in every convent, and it continued the work of the first school begun by Pedro de GANTE. Not only were the humanities and letters taught, but also the arts and trades.

Sahagún taught there for about five years and left a deep imprint on the school. For example, he introduced regulations for the native boarding students based on the traditional organization of native schools for young men, and he placed the study and proficiency in Nahuatl on a par with Spanish and Latin. Sahagún insisted that the work of evangelization required an understanding of the native languages and the use of textbooks prepared especially in those tongues and not merely translated from Latin or Spanish. The years 1540 to 1545 he spent in the convents of Huejotzingo and Cholula near Mexico City. In 1545, he returned to the college at Tlaltelolco where he began a daring reform: Sahagún decided to entrust most of the teaching and administration of the college to its native graduates.

Studies. At this same time Sahagún began the systematic collection of information that later enabled him to write his monumental work *Historia general de las cosas de Nueva España.* On this work is based his reputation as father of American ethnography and creator of its methodology. The *Historia general* is made up of 12 books written in Nahuatl. It deals partly with the history and the language, but principally with the material and spiritual culture of the Mexican people (religion, social and political organization, technology, etc.). It is an ethnographical study in the strict sense of that term and one that has remained the principal source for the study of Mexican culture at the time of the conquest.

To gather the needed information, Sahagún prepared a detailed questionnaire that he submitted to older natives who were well informed concerning the ancient customs of the peoples of Tepepulco, Tlaltelolco, and Mexico in general. He also made it a habit to talk constantly with his native informants in their own language. From these conversations he took notes in Nahuatl that he used to check against the information he had already received or had gained through the questionnaire. He also used the native professors and students of the college as an added means of control. An ethnologist of today, even the most demanding, could not readily find a better method.

The work of Sahagún unleashed a violent storm of opposition from those who thought that he was going to contribute to the survival of the pagan beliefs and to render the work of complete Christianization more difficult. For many of the adversaries of Sahagún, Christianization meant ''Hispanization,'' without restriction. To this Sahagún was opposed, for he wanted to preserve the most valuable elements of Mexican culture. The dispute made his work more difficult, but it did not prevent it altogether; nor did it stop the preparation in Spanish of a somewhat shortened and modified version of his *Historia general.* Nor did it render impossible the preparation of a large number of shorter works, such as *El calendario mexicano, El arte adivinatoria,* a grammar and vocabulary in Mexican, and sermons and hymns in Nahuatl. In 1578, when he was about 80 years old, Sahagún received the cruel blow of a royal decree confiscating all the texts and documents of his 50 years of labor. As a result, science and the world were deprived of the knowledge of his work until the 19th century.

Extent of Influence. The influence of Sahagún and of his work as an evangelizer and as a man of science were not destroyed by the long delay in the publication of his *Historia general.* His intellectual influence was wielded above all and in a very deep and lasting way with the professors and students of the college of Tlaltelolco; with his fellow Franciscans in Mexico, even those who did not completely agree with his point of view; and with the religious and civil authorities of the viceroyalty. The

work and the attitude of Sahagún were continued through the centuries, at times by disciples who hardly even knew his name, and reached down to modern times to influence the attitude and the activity of anthropologists, indigenists, and rulers of modern Mexico.

Bibliography: J. DE ALVA, H. NICHOLSON, and E. KEBER, *The Work of Bernardino de Sahagun, Pioneer Ethnographer of Sixteenth-Century Aztec Mexico* (Albany, N.Y. 1988). L. D'OLWER, *Fray Bernardino de Sahagun, 1499–1590,* tr. M. MIXCO (Salt Lake City 1987).

[A. PALERM]

SAHAGÚN, JOHN OF, ST.

Augustinian preacher and reformer, patron of city and Diocese of Salamanca; b. John González, at Sahagún (formerly San Facundo), Asturias, Spain, 1429; d. Salamanca, Spain, June 11, 1479. John was educated by the BENEDICTINES of Sahagún Abbey, patronized by Bp. Alfonso of Burgos, and ordained in 1445; he soon renounced his plural benefices, studied Canon Law four years at Salamanca University, and devoted himself to parish work at Burgos. Nine years later, as the result of a vow he made before an operation, he entered the AUGUSTINIANS at Salamanca (1463). Novice master, prior (1471–73, 1477–79), wonder-worker, and visionary, John had special gifts as preacher, as penetrating confessor, and in those feud-torn times as peacemaker. Almost single-handedly he reformed Salamanca. But his denunciation of vice and of oppression by landlords against their tenantry brought assassination attempts by the Duke of Alba and others. He died probably of poisoning. Beatified in 1609, he was canonized in 1690. Iconography shows him holding a chalice.

Feast: June 12.

Bibliography: JOHN OF SEVILLE, *Vita, Acta Sanctorum* June 3:115–125. ALFONSO OF OROZCO, *Vida* (1570), repr. in M. VIDAL, *Agustinos de Salamanca* (Salamanca 1751) v.1. T. CÁMARA Y CASTRO, *Vida de San Juan de Sahagún . . .* (Salamanca 1891; El Escorial 1925). G. DE SANTIAGO VELA, *Ensayo de una biblioteca iberoamericana de la orden de San Agustín,* 7 v. in 8 (Madrid 1913–31) 7:7–24. A. BUTLER, *The Lives of the Saints,* ed. H. THURSTON and D. ATTWATER, 4 v. (New York 1956) 2:526–527. P. LUNA, *San Juan de Sahagun, Angel de la paz* (Madrid 1998).

[R. I. BURNS]

ṢAIFI, EUTHYMIOS

Founder of the Basilian Salvatorians and inaugurator of reunion of the Syrian Melchites with the Holy See; b. Damascus, *c.* 1648; d. there, Oct. 16, 1723. After receiving an extensive education at the patriarchal school in Damascus, he was ordained in 1666. In 1682 he was consecrated metropolitan to the Sees of Sur (Tyre) and Saida (Sidon). Having been influenced toward Catholicism by the Jesuits in Damascus, he sent his profession of faith to Rome on Jan. 20, 1683. In the same year he began to organize a new religious group of young men as missionaries for the Catholic apostolate in the Melchite patriarchate; these were later formed into a religious order following the rule of St. Basil and called Salvatorians after the name of the Monastery of the Holy Savior (Deir al-Muḥalliṣ), which he had founded near Sidon in 1685. His appointment by the Holy See in 1701 as apostolic administrator of all the Melchites in the Near East allowed him to extend his missionary zeal throughout Palestine, Syria, Lebanon, and North Arabia. The hostility of the Orthodox brought him excommunication from the patriarch of Constantinople, with persecution and imprisonment in his native land. His famous book, *Kitāb ad-dalāla al-lāmi'a* (Bright Guidance), was composed in Arabic for the benefit of his disciples. This work, which discusses successively the marks of the Catholic Church, the primacy of the pope, the filioque, purgatory, and many lesser divergencies between the East and the West, cites Biblical, liturgical, and patristic texts in the original languages and cites all the sources.

Bibliography: A. SCHALL, *Lexikon für Theologie und Kirche*, ed. J. HOFER and K. RAHNER, 10 v. (2d, new ed. Freiburg 1957–65) 3:1211–12. G. GRAF, *Geschichte der christlichen arabischen Literatur*, 5 v. (Vatican City 1944-53); *Studi e Testi* (Rome 1900–) 118, 133, 146, 147, 172. 3:179–184. C. BACHA, *Tarīḫ Ṭāifa ar-Rum al-Malakīya*, 2 v. (Deir al-Muḥalliṣ 1938).

[L. MALOUF]

SAILER, JOHANN MICHAEL

Theologian, bishop of Regensburg; b. Aresing, Upper Bavaria, Nov. 17, 1751; d. Regensburg, May 20, 1832. He attended the Jesuit gymnasium in Munich and entered the Society of Jesus in 1770. He began his philosophical studies at the University of Ingolstadt; and after the suppression of the society, he continued his studies there and was ordained a secular priest in 1775. He was appointed professor of dogmatic theology at Ingolstadt in 1780 but the following year lost this position when the faculty was taken from the secular clergy. In 1784 he was made professor of ethics and pastoral theology at the University of Dillingen in Bavaria. After he had spent ten years at successful teaching, envious colleagues, suspecting him of rationalism, secured his dismissal. For a time he traveled extensively and busied himself with writing. In 1799 he was appointed professor of pastoral theology at the University of Ingolstadt and the following year he moved with the University to Landshut, Bavaria. Again

he enjoyed great success as a teacher, but as before he was attacked by his own colleagues, who were supported this time by (St.) Clement HOFBAUER. In consequence of this attack he lived under a cloud of suspicion until 1821. In 1819 he was nominated bishop of Augsburg, but enough question about him remained to cause Rome to reject the nomination. Crown Prince (later King) Louis of Bavaria was active in helping to clear his name. Sailer was appointed a cathedral canon at Regensburg in 1821, auxiliary bishop and coadjutor with the right of succession in 1822, and cathedral provost in 1825; finally in 1829 he became bishop of Regensburg.

Not only did Sailer possess a broad learning, especially in philosophy and theology, but he was also remarkable for his literary activity. His complete works number 41 volumes. He was extraordinarily effective as a teacher and exercised a profound influence upon those who studied under him, many of whom achieved considerable prominence in scholarly and public life. He was important as a leader in religious thought during the revival of Catholic life after the Enlightenment and the confusion of the Napoleonic period. The Enlightenment had questioned the fundamental dogmas of Christianity, and various ills beset the Church; ''externalism, contempt for Christian mysticism, worldliness of the clergy, degradation of the pulpit by the treatment of secular topics, relaxation of ecclesiastical discipline, denial of the primacy of papal jurisdiction, efforts of the State to gain control of the Church, turbulent reforms within the Church, and a one-sided training of the mind in education'' (R. Stölzle, *The Catholic Encyclopedia*, ed. C. G. Herbermann et al., 16 v. [New York 1907–14; suppl. 1922] 13.328). Against these evils Sailer strove mightily and with good effect. He had no leaning toward scholasticism or toward the philosophy of antiquity, preferring to draw upon the Fathers, Fénelon, and the philosophers of the 17th and 18th centuries. Because of the circumstances in which he wrote and the range of subjects that engaged his attention, Sailer is regarded as a pioneer in the fields of modern pedagogy, catechetics, homiletics, and pastoral theology. Indeed, he is looked upon by many as the founder of the science of pastoral theology. In pedagogy and catechetics his principal contribution consisted in breaking down the then current idea that education was simply a matter of intellectual formation. He stressed the importance of a parallel development of the emotions.

Sailer is remembered also for the good relationships he cultivated with orthodox Protestants. He was a friend of the distinguished German legal scholar, Friedrich Karl von Savigny. He avoided polemics against Protestants and thought it much more important to seek to bring about the cooperation of the different Christian bodies against the negations of infidelity. Without sacrificing any point in his strict adherence to Catholic doctrine, he managed nevertheless to make a significant contribution to both Catholic and Protestant piety.

Bibliography: *Sämtliche Werke*, ed. J. WIDMER, 41 v. (Sulzbach 1830–45). F. W. BODEMANN, *Johann Michael von Sailer* (Gotha 1856). G. AICHINGER, *Johann Michael Sailer* (Freiburg 1865). P. FUNK, *Von der Aufklärung zur Romantik* (Munich 1925). W. SCHLAGS, *Johann Michael Sailer, der Heilige einer Zeitwende* (Wiesbaden 1932). B. LANG, *Bischof Sailer und seine Zeitgenossen* (Regensburg 1932). M. GRABMANN, *Die Geschichte der katholische Theologie seit dem Ausgang der Väterzeit* (Freiburg 1933). P. HADROSSEK, *Die Bedeutung des Systemgedankens für die Moraltheologie in Deutschland seit der Thomas-Renaissance* (Munich 1950). P. KLOTZ, *Johann Michael Sailer als Moralphilosoph* (Paderborn 1909). L. RADLMAIER, *Johann Michael Sailer als Pädagog* (Berlin 1909). J. BRÖGGER, *Johann Michael Sailer als Homilet* (Paderborn 1932); ''Dem Andenken Johann Michael Sailers zum hundertsten Todestage,'' *Theologie und Glaube* 24 (1932) 273–287.

[J. F. GRONER]

ST. AGNES, CONGREGATION OF SISTERS OF

(CSA, Official Catholic Directory #3710); established in 1858 at Barton, Wisconsin. The congregation owes its origin to Casper Rehrl, a missionary from Austria, who in 1845 offered his services to Bp. John Martin Henni of Milwaukee, Wisconsin. After establishing parishes throughout the state, Rehrl determined to found a religious society of women to teach Christian doctrine to the young during his absence on visits to his numerous parishes. With the permission of Pius IX, he began the congregation with a nucleus of three young ladies from the vicinity of Barton. On July 3, 1864, Sister M. Agnes (Anna Mary Hazotte) was elected first superior by the five sisters who then comprised the community. Then only 17 years old, she guided the congregation until her death on March 6, 1905.

In 1870 the congregation moved from Barton to a more favorable location at Fond du Lac, Wisconsin. Rules and constitutions, written for the sisters by Rev. Francis Haas, OFM, were declared praiseworthy by the Holy See in 1875. Five years later, after a few revisions in the rule, the congregation became a papal institute. The rules were derived from those of St. Augustine commonly followed by religious women who combine the active and contemplative life. Initially the Sisters of St. Agnes confined themselves to teaching in Catholic and public elementary schools in Wisconsin, whence they spread to other sates. In 1896 they entered the nursing field by opening St. Agnes Hospital in Ford du Lac.

The sisters are engaged in the field of academic education at all levels, catechetics, hospitals, healthcare, care

Johann Michael Sailer, painting by August Graf von Seinsheim, 1826.

facilities for the aged, parish ministries, social outreach services, and pastoral ministries. They have established overseas communities in Honduras, Nicaragua and Russia. The generalate is in Fond du Lac, Wisconsin.

Bibliography: M. V. NABER, *With All Devotedness: Chronicles of the Sisters of St. Agnes, Fond du Lac, Wisconsin* (New York 1959).

[M. V. NABER]

SAINT ALBANS, ABBEY OF

Former English Benedictine MONASTERY, at present-day Saint Albans (the ancient *Verulamium*), Hertfordshire, England, about 20 miles northwest of London. There had been a church at the reputed site of the martyrdom of St. ALBAN since the time of BEDE, but the Benedictine abbey was founded there only *c.* 794 by King Offa of Mercia in expiation for his murder of King ETHELBERT OF EAST ANGLIA. After the turmoil of the 9th and early 10th centuries, the monastic foundation at Saint Albans had to be refounded in 969(?). A century later, the first Norman abbot there, Paul of Caen, a nephew of Archbishop LANFRANC, rebuilt both the monastic buildings and the still-extant abbey church (1077–88). The abbey's

St. Albans Abbey. (©Niall MacLeod/CORBIS)

subsequent progress under a long line of distinguished abbots motivated the only English Pope, ADRIAN IV, to grant Saint Albans episcopal EXEMPTION and to give it precedence over all English abbeys. For the next three centuries the abbey was one of the artistic and literary centers of England. Especially notable was its "school" of chroniclers, Roger of Wendover, MATTHEW PARIS, William Rishanger, and Thomas WALSINGHAM, who were responsible for a continuous account of the history of the abbey, its abbots, and, in a sense, England. Abbot John Whethamstede (d. 1465) was one of the early English humanists. Saint Albans suffered much during the 15th-century War of the Roses. It was given in COMMENDATION to Cardinal Thomas Wolsey in 1521. In 1539 the abbey was suppressed under King HENRY VIII. The above-mentioned abbey church escaped destruction and became a local parish church. When the Anglican See of Saint Albans was constituted in 1877, the abbey church became the cathedral, which it remains today.

Bibliography: W. DUGDALE, *Monasticon Anglicanum* (London 1655–73); best ed. by J. CALEY et al., 6 v. (1817–30) 2:178–255. *The Victoria History of the County of Hertford,* ed. W. PAGE, 4 v. (Westminster, England 1902–14) 4:367–416. L. F. R. WILLIAMS, *History of the Abbey of Saint Albans* (London 1917). V. H. GALBRAITH, ed., *The Saint Albans Chronicle, 1406–1420* (Oxford 1937). R. VAUGHAN, *Matthew Paris* (Cambridge, England 1958). D. KNOWLES and R. N. HADCOCK, *Medieval Religious Houses: England and Wales* (New York 1953) 75. D. KNOWLES, *The Monastic Order in England, 943–1216* (2nd ed. Cambridge, England 1962), *passim.* D. KNOWLES, *The Religious Orders in England,* 3 v. (Cambridge, England 1948–60) v.1, 2, 3 *passim.*

[M. J. HAMILTON]

SAINT ALEXANDER OF OROSH (OROSHI), ABBEY OF

Or Shën Llezhri i Oroshit, an abbey *nullius* (*see* Abbot Nullius) directly under the jurisdiction of the Holy See, situated in the village of Orosh, or Oroshi, 4,690 feet above sea level, among the mountains of Mirditë in the interior of northern Albania. In ancient times it was an abbey of Basilian monks (or, as some assert, of Benedictines) dedicated to St. Alexander the Martyr. After the Turkish occupation of Albania (*c.* 15th century) the abbey disappeared and its territory was divided between the parishes of Orosh and Saint Nicholas of Spaci as part of the Diocese of Lesh. Because of difficulties of communication the Congregation for the PROPAGATION OF THE FAITH by a decree of Oct. 5, 1888, detached the abbey *nullius* from the diocese and joined five parishes to it, adding three more in 1890, and then two from the Diocese of Säpë (decree of July 2, 1906). The ordinary has the title of abbot and is elected from among the Albanian secular clergy. The first bishop was J. Gjonali; the last, Francis Gjini, was killed by the communist regime in Albania in 1947. In 1996, the abbey came under the jurisdiction of the newly created See of Rrëshen.

Bibliography: F. CORDIGNANO, "Antichi monasteri benedettini in Albania, nella tradizione e nelle leggende popolari," *La civiltà cattolica* 80 (1929) 3:26–28, 4:507–515; *L'Albania a traverso l'opera e gli scritti di un grande missionario italiano, il P. Domenico Pasi* (Rome 1933–) v.3. *Le missioni cattoliche: Storia, geografia, statistica* (Rome 1950) 72–73. *Revue Bénédictine* (1893) 226.

[S. OLIVIERI]

SAINT-AMAND-LES-EAUX, ABBEY OF

Former Benedictine abbey in Saint-Amand (Nord), France, 20 miles southeast of Lille; formerly known as Elnone. It was founded by St. AMANDUS before 639 and may be the oldest abbey in Flanders. It was richly endowed by the Merovingian kings, but experienced difficult times during the Carolingian era as a result of SECULARIZATION OF CHURCH PROPERTY and the NORMAN invasions (881, 884). Prosperity increased from the 11th through the 13th century. This was followed by an era of economic crisis prolonged by the Hundred Years' War and extravagant spending by unworthy abbots during the 15th century. In the 16th century, the abbey, and the whole area generally, suffered from religious uprisings (1566–76). During the 17th century Abbot Nicolas Dubois (1621–73) planned and carried out an integrated reconstruction of the abbey, making it a showplace of the Low Countries. During the 18th century it was often ruled by commendatory abbots of the high nobility; it was suppressed during the French Revolution. Only the interesting church tower and entrance lodge remain today. The abbey had been an intellectual center; during the 9th century it produced the theologians, Milo and HUCBALD; during the 12th century, painters of miniatures; of these Sawalo was the most famous.

Bibliography: H. PLATELLE, *Le Temporel de l' abbaye de Saint-Amand* (Paris 1963); *La Justice seigneuriale de l'abbaye de Saint-Amand* (Louvain 1965).

[H. PLATELLE]

SAINT-ANDRÉ-LEZ-BRUGES, ABBEY OF

The Benedictine *Sancti Andreae de Zevenkerken* in St. Andries, west Flanders, Belgium; Diocese of Bruges. It was founded with monks from AFFLIGEM *c.* 1100 by Robert II of Flanders to fulfill a vow made during the siege of Antioch in 1098. Made an abbey in 1188, it was sacked by Calvinists in the 16th century and suppressed by the French in 1796. In 1899 Gérard van Caloen of Matredsous, in charge of the restoration of Benedictines in Brazil, opened in St. Andries the *procura* that Leo XIII made an abbey in 1901 (inaugurated in 1902).

The abbey church (1907–27), which is composed of ''seven churches'' in one, modeled after S. Stefano, Bologna, was consecrated by Cardinal Ildefonse SCHUSTER in 1935. In 1919 the abbey withdrew from the Brazilian congregation to form a Belgian congregation with Maredsous and Mont-César (Louvain). The first abbot, Theodore Nève (1912–58; d. March 27, 1963), was succeeded by Theodore II Ghesquière. From Saint-André, a missionary abbey, has radiated the influence of the Church and monasticism. In 1910 it undertook to evangelize Haut-Katanga in the Congo. The priory of Si-shan (1927) in Sichuan, China, was moved to Chengdu in 1947; after being suppressed by the Communists in 1952, it reopened in Valyermo, Calif., in 1955. In 1950 Saint-André founded the first Benedictine monastery in India at Siluvaigiri (now in Asirvanam, Bangalore). In 1939 Polish monks from Saint-André restored the archabbey of Tyniec in Poland. The monks played a prominent role in the LITURGICAL MOVEMENT between World Wars I and II, producing, e.g., the Missals of Gaspar Lefebvre. The preparatory school (founded 1910) has 150 students. Besides the series *Assemblées du Seigneur* (since 1962), the monks publish the periodicals *Paroisse et liturgie, Rythmes du Monde,* and *Art d'Église.*

Bibliography: U. BERLIÈRE, *Monasticon belge* (Bruges 1890–) 3:86–129. *La Belgique monastique* (Brussels 1958) 29–33.

V. FIALA, *Lexikon für Theologie und Kirche,* ed. J. HOFER and K. RAHNER, 10 v. (2d, new ed. Freiburg 1957–65) 9:130–131.

[N. N. HUYGHEBAERT]

SAINT ANDREWS, PRIORY OF

Former monastery of CANONS REGULAR OF ST. AUGUSTINE, attached to the former cathedral of Saint Andrews, East Fife, Scotland (Latin, *Prioratus Sanctiandree in Scotia*). It was founded in 1144 from Nostell Priory, Yorkshire, by Bp. Robert of Saint Andrews, an Austin Canon, with the collaboration of King DAVID I. It was intended to replace the virtually laicized Celtic community of CULDEES, established there perhaps as early as King Angus I (731–761). In 1147, Pope Eugene III confirmed the canons' exclusive right to elect the bishops.

The ''Culdees,'' probably losing all that was monastic and Celtic, survived as a juridical body, becoming a collegiate church of secular canons (St. Mary's on the Rock, *c.* 1250); they intervened in elections up to 1255, being excluded definitively by Pope Boniface VIII in 1298 or 1299. The priory soon became the leading house of Austin Canons in SCOTLAND, where the order enjoyed a prestige it achieved nowhere else in Europe. However, the priory suffered from civil disorder, from the side effects of the WESTERN SCHISM, from disputed elections and curial interference in the 15th century, from the imposition of unworthy priors by royal nomination after 1483, and finally from the practice of COMMENDATION imposed in 1538.

Yet throughout, Saint Andrews retained remarkable vigor and influence, attaining a period of real greatness under Priors James Bisset and John Haldenston (1393–1443), and was admired by historians Walter Bower (in the 1440s) and Hector Boece (in the 1520s). It had a grammar and a song school in the 15th century. Prior James Bisset was one of the founding fathers of St. Andrews University in 1414, and the priory remained closely connected with university affairs, especially in the theology faculty. Prior John Hepburn (1483–1522) founded St. Leonard's College on the model of Standonck's Montaigu. Andrew of Wyntoun (d. *c. 1420*), author of *De Orygnale Cronykil of Scotland,* and W. Bower (d. 1449), continuator of J. de Fordun's *Scotichronicon,* were both canons of the priory.

During the REFORMATION, Saint Andrews became a focal point of both Catholic and Protestant reforming ideas. G. Logic, the Lutheranizing principal of St. Leonard's College, although not a canon, trained many of the community, and in the 1550s the influence of both Zurich and Geneva was evident there. James Stewart, illegitimate son of King James V of Scotland, was made commendator in 1538; he later became the political leader of the Protestant party, 1558–70. In 1560 the priory ceased to be a religious community, but the legal fiction of a body of canons was continued until 1592 when it was made a temporal lordship. In 1560 the names of 28 canons can be recognized; the Subprior John Winram (d. 1582) became an ambiguous leading figure in the new Reformed Church in which 12 or more of the canons took service, but others are recorded as remaining true to the old faith. In June of 1559 the cathedral, at least, had been ''purged'' by the Reformers under John KNOX; the extent of the damage done is disputed, but the buildings rapidly became ruins. The meager remains are today a public monument.

Saint Andrews Priory made no new foundations but annexed three earlier priories: Portmoak, or Loch Leven, an ex-Culdee house (1152–53); Monymusk, another ex-Culdee house (before 1245); and Pittenweem, or Isle of May, formerly Benedictine (before 1318).

Bibliography: *Liber Cartarum Prioratus Sancti Andree in Scotia,* ed. T. THOMSON (Edinburgh 1841). J. HALDENSTONE, *Copiale Prioratus Sanctiandree,* ed. J. H. BAXTER (Oxford 1930). *Early Records of the University of St. Andrews,* ed. J. M. ANDERSON (Edinburgh 1926). *Calendar of Entries in the Papal Registers,* ed. W. H. BLISS et al. (London 1893–). *Acts of the Lords of Council in Public Affairs, 1501–1554,* ed. R. H. HANNAY (Edinburgh 1932). JOHANNIS DE FORDUN, *Scotichronicon cum supplementis et continuatione Walteri Boweri,* ed. W. GOODALL, 2 v. (Edinburgh 1759) 367–376. G. MARTINE, *Reliquiae Divi Andreae* (St. Andrews 1797) 160–201. Hist. Mon. Comm., . . . *Fife* . . . (Edinburgh 1933) 228–250. S. CRUDEN, *The Cathedral of St. Andrews* (Edinburgh 1950). G. W. S. BARROW, ''The Cathedral Chapter of S. A. and the Culdees,'' *The Journal of Ecclesiastical History* 3 (1952) 23–39. D. E. EASSON, *Medieval Religious Houses: Scotland* (London 1957) 78–80, 82, 191.

[J. O'DEA]

ST. ANNE, SISTERS OF

(SSA, Official Catholic Directory #3720); a congregation founded at Vaudreuil, P.Q., Canada, in 1850 by Marie Esther Sureau-Blondin (Mother Marie Anne) during the episcopacy of Ignace BOURGET. Miss Blondin, educated in her village school but enriched by 15 years of teaching experience, sought to establish rural schools for the neglected children of the Canadian countryside and to tend the sick poor. She opened her schools to boys as well as girls, to Protestants as well as Catholics, and free of national bias, she taught English to her French-speaking students. All these were exceptional procedures in her day. Her educational aim was one of service to both the Church and the nation. The spirit of the rule, modeled on that of St. Ignatius and approved by Rome in 1903,

requires the Sisters of St. Anne to emulate the holy women of the Gospel particularly in the service they had rendered the nascent Church. In time the sisters came to serve in schools (elementary through college), hospitals, homes for the aged, dispensaries, and foreign missions.

In 1858 four sisters made an arduous two-month trip to establish a missionary outpost on Vancouver Island in western Canada. Their primitive log cabin was the beginning of the hospitals, Indian residential schools, boarding schools, and sanitariums for the aged and destitute that later developed in British Columbia, Alaska, and the Yukon Territory. In 1880 the community began answering the invitations of the pastors of Franco-American parishes and gradually took over bilingual schools in New York, Massachusetts, Rhode Island, and Maine. A Japanese mission was opened in 1934. In Omuta, in the Diocese of Fukuoka, six sisters conducted a commercial high school and a kindergarten. In October 1942 they were interned in a concentration camp, but were repatriated the following autumn. The closing of that mission coincided with the opening of a new field of service in the Diocese of Les Cayes, Haiti, where the sisters conduct one secondary and four elementary schools, three dispensaries, and a novitiate for native candidates.

In the U.S., the sisters are engaged in academic education, catechetics, campus ministry, chaplaincies, retreats, spiritual direction, counseling, pastoral ministry, nursing, and the care of the aged. The generalate is in Lachine, Quebec, Canada. The U.S. provincialate is in Marlboro, MA.

[M. J. CHAUVIN/EDS.]

ST. ANSELM PRIORY (TOKYO)

A postwar foundation from ST. JOHN'S ABBEY, Collegeville, MN, serves a parish that was established on November 28, 1947, by Abp. Peter Totsuo Doi of Tokyo. Beginning with a congregation of nine it developed, under the pastor and prior Hildebrand Yaiser, OSB, to a congregation of 1,250 within a decade. Located on a minimal plot of land between an elevated railroad and a busy street, the compound is economically planned for maximum use of space without giving the sense of congestion. With architectural force the structure fuses 20th-century Japan with a vital Christian liturgy. In 1956 the church was consecrated, and the kindergarten, library, and assembly hall were completed. A few years later the rectory (St. Anselm Priory) was added.

The architect Antonin Raymond not only designed the complex but was able to oversee construction, plan interior design, and, with his wife Noèmi Pernessin Raymond, design and execute the altar, crucifix, tabernacle, candlesticks, and stations of the cross. Raymond, a disciple of Frank Lloyd Wright, planned the church as central to the rectory-priory and the school building. The open court to the rectory side is a traditional Japanese garden while the court on the school side serves as playground and outdoor parish meeting area.

The church, of reinforced concrete and rectangular plan, seats 500. The baptistery juts out toward the street and is surmounted by a large cross on the exterior. The concrete, poured in thin sheets, is interrupted along the nave by thin slits of glazing extending from ceiling to floor. The unsurfaced concrete has been polychromed in panels with earthy colors such as ochre, indian red, and gray-green. The communion rail, lecterns, and baldachino are all of concrete. The graceful baldachino, covered with gold leaf, and the altar candelabra suggest the rhythmic flow of the Japanese flower arrangements, which originated as a part of temple worship. Behind the altar the concrete wall has been painted white with circular patterns inscribed on the surface, suggesting the Japanese shoji walls. A simple granite altar, of Sendai Ishi, dominates the sanctuary from a platform of Japanese sandstone. The tabernacle of wrought iron has an outer shape echoing the arches of Shinto shrines. The Stations are simple designs in metal, comprised principally of expressive hands, placed directly on the concrete panels between the nave windows. A fine 13th-century Byzantine Virgin icon is enthroned in a simple enshrined area. Besides being well-planned religious architecture, St. Anselm is a living center for the culture and faith it represents and serves.

Bibliography: J. PICHARD, *Les Églises nouvelles à travers le monde* (Paris 1960). C. J. BARRY, *Worship and Work* (Collegeville 1956) 319–320.

[J. BECKER]

ST. ANSGAR'S SCANDINAVIAN CATHOLIC LEAGUE

St. Ansgar's Scandinavian Catholic League was founded in New York (1910) for Catholics of Scandinavian background and Americans interested in the renaissance of the Catholic faith in Denmark, Norway, Sweden, Finland, and Iceland. In addition to offering prayers daily, the members contribute an annual donation to the Scandinavian bishops. In 1950, a Mass stipend program was set up, under which all intentions and funds were sent to the Scandinavian bishops. The league's publications include pamphlets, leaflets, and an annual magazine giving the historical background of the Scandinavian

countries, as well as a yearly report on the Catholic Church in each of these countries. The league's headquarters are located at 28 West 25th Street, New York City.

[V. F. E. RAMBUSCH/V. B. RAMBUSCH]

SAINT-ANTOINE-DE-VIENNOIS, ABBEY OF

Former central house of the Hospital Brothers of St. Anthony, Department of Isère, France, Diocese of Grenoble, formerly Archdiocese of Vienne. The foundation originated as the church of Saint-Antoine-de-la-Mothe, built to receive relics of St. ANTHONY OF EGYPT brought back from Constantinople by Geilen or Jocelin (1070–95). The abbey, entrusted to the Benedictines of MONTMAJOUR (*c.* 1083), was erected into a Benedictine priory (1101) and consecrated (1119) by Pope Callistus II. But repeated conflicts between the Benedictines and the Antonine HOSPITALLERS, who had been founded by Gaston de Dauphiné at Saint-Antoine *c.* 1095, led Pope Boniface VIII in 1297 to erect a church, detached from Montmajour, into an abbey with the Antonines' Grand Master, Aymon de Montagny, as first abbot (1273–1316), constituting them CANONS REGULAR under the Rule of St. AUGUSTINE. Numerous dependent commanderies were founded in Europe; Saint-Antoine became a center of pilgrimage (14th–15th centuries). Pillaged five times by the Huguenots (1562–90), the abbey declined, despite reforms under Brunel de Grammont (d. 1634), until Pius VI joined it to the KNIGHTS OF MALTA (1776–77). The abbey was suppressed during the French Revolution. The abbey church (13th–15th century) now serves as a parish church; the cloister, under canons regular of the Immaculate Conception until 1901, is now occupied by a minor seminary, municipal offices, and a distillery.

Bibliography: H. DIJON, *L'Église abbatiale de Saint-Antoine en Dauphiné* (Grenoble 1902). L. MAILLET-GUY, ''Les Commanderies de l'ordre de St. Antoine en Dauphiné,'' *Revue Mabillon* 16 (1926) 1–26; 17 (1927) 218–236, 352–378; 18 (1928) 1–23, 81–95. L. H. COTTINEAU, *Répertoire topobibliographique des abbayes et prieurés,* 2 v. (Mâcon 1935–39) 2:2593–95. J. DAVID, *Dictionnaire d'histoire et de géographie ecclésiastiques,* ed. A. BAUDRILLART (Paris 1912–) 3:733–734. A. MISCHLEWSKI, *Lexikon für Theologie und Kirche,* ed. J. HOFER and K. RAHNER, 10 v. (2d, new ed. Freiburg 1957–65) 9:133.

[G. E. GINGRAS]

SAINT ASAPH, ANCIENT SEE OF

One of the four ancient dioceses of WALES, said to have been founded by St. KENTIGERN, Celtic bishop of

Glasgow, who *c.* 560 founded a monastery in the present-day cathedral village-city of Saint Asaph, or Llanelwy (English name not being used until 12th century), in Flintshire, northern Wales. The diocese, which took its name from Kentigern's favorite disciple, St. Asaph, covered the Kingdom of Powys and the Middle Country. Its medieval bishops included GEOFFREY OF MONMOUTH (d. 1155) and Reginald Pecock (1444–1450). King Edward I confirmed the liberties of the diocese in 1275 and with the support of Bishop Anian vainly begged the Pope in 1281 to permit the transfer of the cathedral from its exposed and solitary site to the new town of Rhuddlan where it would be protected by the new castle; the bishop's position was necessarily precarious since his flock included dissident Welsh and English, his diocese being partly in the English Marches and partly in Wales.

The early wooden cathedral was burned by the English in 1247 and 1282, and Owain Glyndêr (*c.* 1402) almost demolished the one built by Bishop Anian (completed *c.* 1291). Bishop Richard Redman's building (*c.* 1480) was completed only when the choir was built, *c.* 1770. The 19th century saw considerable restoration. The church, plain cruciform with a square tower, is generally decorated. It shows the influence of Early English architectural style. It is the smallest cathedral in Great Britain. In the episcopal library are preserved various early charters relating to the diocese, and the Red Book of Saint Asaph, which includes a 14th-century fragmentary life of the saint.

Although Saint Asaph was part of the Church of England after the REFORMATION, in 1920 its bishop was enthroned in his cathedral as the first archbishop of the Church of Wales. Bishop William Morgan (1601–04) translated the Bible into Welsh. At present the diocese includes the counties of Flint and Denbigh and parts of four others.

Bibliography: D. R. THOMAS, *St. Asaph* (New York 1888); *History of the Diocese of St. Asaph* (London 1874). F. M. POWICKE, *The Thirteenth Century* (2d ed. Oxford 1962). G. WILLIAMS, *The Welsh Church from Conquest to Reformation* (Cardiff 1962). P.B.I. BAX, *The Cathedral Church of Saint Asaph: A Description of the Building and a Short History of the See* (London 1904). T.R.K. GOULSTONE, *St. Asaph Cathedral: Yesterday and Today; 560–1999* (St. Asaph 1999).

[N. DENHOLM–YOUNG/EDS.]

SAINT AUGUSTINE, ABBEY OF

The Abbey of Saint Augustine was first known English monastery, at Canterbury. When AUGUSTINE OF CANTERBURY persuaded King ETHELBERT OF KENT to accept Baptism, the king promised to found a monastery in which the kings of Kent and the archbishops of Canterbury might be buried. When this abbey was consecrated by Augustine's successor, Abp. LAWRENCE OF CANTERBURY, it was dedicated to SS. Peter and Paul, a dedication that bears witness to Augustine's Roman origins and papal commission. In the course of time the association of the abbey with the Apostle of the English led to the popular dedication of the abbey to St. Augustine himself. It is not now thought that the abbey was originally a Benedictine monastery, as there is no reason to believe that either Pope GREGORY THE GREAT or Augustine himself was Benedictine. It cannot be proved that the BENEDICTINE RULE was introduced into the abbey until the accession of Abbot Sigeric *c.* 980. Early in the history of Canterbury the cathedral clergy was formed into a monastic chapter. In the middle of the 8th century this chapter successfully secured the right to bury their archbishop in the cathedral rather than the abbey. The monks of Saint Augustine's lamented their loss of prestige, and the two communities became bitter rivals. Even when abbots of Saint Augustine's became archbishops of Canterbury and, as in the 12th century, cathedral monks became abbots of Saint Augustine's, relations between the communities were never good.

In the 12th century the abbey initiated a lawsuit that dragged on throughout the Middle Ages, for the abbey claimed that from its foundation it had been exempted by the pope from the diocesan authority of the archbishop of Canterbury. The monks produced a long series of forged charters and papal bulls to justify this claim, and it is still not clear whether all the documents were totally fabricated or whether some genuine base may underlie them. Pope ALEXANDER III actually granted Saint Augustine's exemption from the oath of obedience normally given by a newly elected abbot to the diocesan, but the monks strove to interpret this so widely that the abbey and all the parishes it served would be exempt from diocesan authority of any kind. Claims were constantly taken to Rome, but a series of popes avoided giving definite sentences, thus leaving the way open for a series of negotiated compromises, which seldom lasted longer than a generation. And so, when the abbey was dissolved in 1538 under King HENRY VIII, it became apparent that the extensive literary efforts of the monks of this first monastery of the Anglo-Saxon Church amounted to little more than a voluminous history of the abbey's lawsuits.

Bibliography: THOMAS OF ELMHAM, *Historia monasterii S. Augustini cantauriensis,* ed. C. HARDWICK (*Rerum Britannicarum medii aevi scriptores* 8; 1858). W. LEVISON, *England and the Continent in the 8th Century* (Oxford 1946). F. L. CROSS, *The Oxford Dictionary of the Christian Church* (London 1957) 232. E. JOHN, "The Litigation of an Exempt House, St. Augustine's, Canterbury, 1182–1237," *The Bulletin of the John Rylands Library* 39 (1947) 390–415. D. KNOWLES and R. N. HADCOCK, *Medieval Religious*

Houses: England and Wales (New York 1953). D. KNOWLES, *The Monastic Order in England, 943–1216* (2d ed. Cambridge, Eng. 1962), *passim.*

[E. JOHN]

ST. AUGUSTINE, SISTERS OF CHARITY OF

(CSA, Official Catholic Directory #0580); a congregation founded in the Diocese of Cleveland, Ohio. On September 24, 1851, in response to the appeal of Amadeus Rappe, first bishop of Cleveland, Mother M. Bernardine Cabaret and Sister M. Françoise Guillement, Augustinian Sisters of St. Louis Hospital, Boulogne-sur-Mer, France, accompanied by two postulants, came to the U.S. They spent the winter of 1851 visiting the sick and the poor in their homes. Within a year after their arrival they opened Cleveland's first general hospital.

When two of the sisters returned to France, Bishop Rappe appointed Mother M. Ursula Bissonnette, a native of Ohio, superior of the new community. In 1853 Mother Ursula provided a small home for dependent boys, a work which later developed into ''Parmadale,'' the Children's Village of St. Vincent de Paul. When increasing population and the return of soldiers wounded in the Civil War called for a larger hospital, Bishop Rappe purchased property and broke ground for St. Vincent Charity Hospital on June 23, 1863. This hospital, greatly expanded, serves the needs of downtown Cleveland. Mother M. Joseph Muselet, with the approval of Bp. Richard Gilmour, opened St. Ann's Hospital and Infant Home on March 17, 1873. This has developed into two separate institutions, St. Ann Hospital and the De Paul Maternity and Infant Home, the latter providing care for unwed mothers and infants.

The Sisters of Charity of St. Augustine (CSA) serve in the Dioceses of Cleveland and Youngstown, Ohio; and Charleston, South Carolina. They operate hospitals and care facilities, and provide all types of healthcare services. Mount Augustine, the motherhouse is located at West Richfield, about 20 miles south of Cleveland. The congregation follows the Rule of St. Augustine and has as its motto: In all things charity.

[M. S. WEINHEIMER]

ST. BARTHOLOMEW'S DAY, MASSACRE OF

The Massacre of St. Bartholomew's Day was a slaughter of Huguenots begun in Paris on Aug. 24, 1572.

Huguenot leader Gaspard de Coligny.

Although there had been others in 1562—at Vassy (March 1), at Sens (April 12), and at Orléans (April 21)—this is the most widely known massacre of the Huguenots in France. It was not a premeditated measure, but was prompted by the ''logic of events,'' which had both political and religious causes and was largely shaped by the policy of expediency pursued by CATHERINE DE MÉDICIS. It was not the result of a deep-laid plan inspired by religious hatred, even though many individual killings were caused by the spirit of intolerance and a desire for revenge. Despite rumors that the plan was hatched by Catherine and the Spanish Duke of Alva already at Bayonne in 1565, the decision seems to have been the result of circumstances. Catherine's tactical moves immediately before the massacre reflect the degree to which her internal and foreign policies were interlinked with the whole Huguenot question.

Huguenot Power and the French Crown. At first little seemed to augur the events of August 1572. The third war of religion had ended with the Peace of Saint–Germain (Aug. 8, 1570)—on terms very favorable to the Huguenots. Catherine reversed her policy toward the latter. Seeing a positive role for them in keeping the other parties in check, she worked on a rapprochement between the Huguenot and the Catholic camps. Gaspard de Coligny, the Huguenot leader, received an influential position as member of the Council, came to the court, and soon joined with King Charles IX in planning a campaign against Spain in the Low Countries to support the rising of William of Orange. But the preparations for war ended in a rift between the Queen Mother and the Huguenot leader; whereas Catherine was apprehensive of Spanish military power and was reluctant to engage in open conflict with Philip II of Spain (her son-in-law), Coligny pressed strongly for an all-out war. He also gained the support of Charles IX, who, without Catherine's knowledge, allowed a Huguenot army to march to the relief of Mons, besieged by Alva. The army was easily defeated by the Spaniards. Catherine stopped further preparations for the campaign from an uneasiness that France might have to wage war singlehandedly—neutrality at best was expected from England—and from her jealousy of Coligny's gaining power through his influence over the young king. She then thought of destroying Coligny—an idea that had occurred to her during the previous war. Although she was aware that his murder would reverse her policy of conciliation, she accepted the fact but did not yet conceive the plan of sweeping off the Huguenots by a single blow.

The Massacre and Its Sequel. On August 22, three days after the marriage of Catherine's daughter Marguerite to Henry of Navarre (the nominal Huguenot leader), Coligny was wounded by two shots fired from an arquebus. The inquiry ordered by the king revealed that the house from which shots were fired belonged to the former preceptor of Henry, Duke of Guise; Henry's uncle the Duke of Aumale had introduced the assassin Maurevel (Maurevert) to the household. Fearful that her role in the plot would soon be discovered and that as a result the wars of religion would start anew, Catherine impressed on Charles IX the idea that a major Huguenot conspiracy was being aimed at the arrest of the royal family and the establishment of a republican government. She overcame his objections by referring to recent threats by the Huguenot nobles, who were demanding justice after the wounding of Coligny. The king in terror acquiesced to a mass slaughter, exclaiming that they should all be slain ("Qu'on les rue tous"). The order was given on August 23 for the following midnight. The Huguenots, assembled in Paris for the festivities connected with the recent wedding of Henry de Navarre, were an easy target. Henry de Guise supervised the murder of Coligny and of a number of other Huguenot leaders. Charles IX watched the killing from the royal palace. The citizens of Paris hunted the Huguenots for several days; many provincial towns followed their example. Thousands were killed. Estimates of the number of victims in Paris vary; the available figures are not reliable. The highest figure (10,468) is quoted in the *Martyrologie* of Jean Crespin. The most

frequently quoted estimate is 3,000 to 4,000. Among the more illustrious victims were the Count de la Rochefoucauld, the Marquis de Reynel, M. de Guerchy, J. Groslot, the philosopher P. RAMUS, and the historian P. de la Place. The only Huguenot nobles to escape the slaughter were the young princes of the blood, Henry de Navarre and the Prince of Condé (who renounced their faith), Caumont-la-Force, Count de Montmorency, and Vidame de Chartres.

Internally, the immediate sequel to the massacre was the fifth war of religion; the long range result was an even deeper cleavage between the Huguenot minority and the Catholic majority. Externally, France clearly dissociated herself from the rebellion led by William of Orange, whom she had planned to support against Spain; but she managed to maintain good relations with the Protestant countries despite their indignation over the massacre.

Bibliography: P. ERLANGER, *St. Bartholomew's Night . . . ,* tr. P. O'BRIAN (New York 1962). H. NOGUÈRES, *La Saint–Barthélemy* (Paris 1959). L. ROMIER, "La Saint–Barthélemy, les événements de Rome et la préméditation du massacre," *Revue du XVIe siècle* (1913) 529–560. H. BORDIER, *La Saint–Barthélemy et la critique moderne* (Geneva 1879). C. C. M. H. ARTAUD DE LA FERRIÈRE, *La Saint–Barthélemy: La veille, le jour, le lendemain* (Paris 1892). H. HELLO, *Catholiques et protestants au XVIe siècle: La Saint–Barthélemy* (Paris 1899).

[W. J. STANKIEWICZ]

ST. BENEDICT'S ABBEY

Founded in Atchison, KS, in 1856 from ST. VINCENT ARCHABBEY, Latrobe, PA, by Henry LEMKE; became an independent priory, in 1858 and an abbey in 1876.

The purpose of the foundation, and its chief work throughout the 19th century, was to care for the spiritual needs of settlers flooding into the West. The principal mission field of the community was northeastern Kansas, southeastern Nebraska, and parts of Iowa. A number of parishes, mostly in Kansas, are still served by monks from the abbey. A mission in Mineiros, Brazil, was begun in 1961.

In 1859, the monks opened a school primarily to educate priests but also to provide better educational facilities for children of Catholic settlers. The curriculum was enlarged and modernized at the beginning of the 20th century, particularly under the guidance of Sylvester Schmitz, OSB; St. Benedict's College (Atchison, KS) was accredited by the North Central Association in 1927. By 1963, it had 19 major departments and about 700 students. The high school was moved to a separate campus south of Atchison in 1919. Called Maur Hill, it had an enrollment of 280 by the mid-20th century.

Louis Mary (Michael) FINK was prior from 1868 to 1871, when he was appointed coadjutor to the vicar apostolic of Kansas. The abbots of the community have been Innocent Wolf, who was born in Schmidheim, Rhenish Prussia, April 13, 1843, elected Sept. 29, 1876, and died Oct. 14, 1922; Martin Veth, born in Dettelbach, Bavaria, Sept. 25, 1874, elected Nov. 10, 1921, and died Dec. 12, 1944; Cuthbert McDonald, born in Dublin, Ireland, July 6, 1894, and elected July 6, 1943; and Thomas Hartmann, born in Wathena, KS, June 24, 1910, and elected June 7, 1962. The community in 1963 numbered 128 priests, 18 clerics, and 27 brothers.

Bibliography: P. BECKMAN, *Kansas Monks: A History of St. Benedict's Abbey* (1957).

[P. BECKMAN]

SAINT-BENOÎT-SUR-LOIRE, ABBEY OF

The Abbey of Saint-Benoît-Sur-Loire is under the Benedictines of the Congregation of Subiaco, in the Diocese of Orléans, central France; also called Fleury (Roman *Floriacum*). At the point of the bend in the Loire River, the place was probably a Druid shrine. A monastic foundation (*c.* 650), perhaps a mission, became a pilgrimage shrine under Abbot Mummulus with the translation of relics of St. Benedict from Monte Cassino (672–674). The debatable authenticity of the relics, now under study, does not lessen their importance in the history of the abbey which gave up the patronage of St. Peter for that of St. Benedict while the land came to be called Saint-Benoît-sur-Loire. The abbey then became one of the most powerful in the Middle Ages, reaching a peak between the 10th and the 13th centuries, with learned abbots, such as THEODULF OF ORLÉANS (d. 826) and ABBO (d. 1004), with HUGH (d. 1120), and with a scriptorium of scribes that gave it one of the richest libraries in Christendom (Latin classics, Fathers of the Church, several unique manuscripts of St. Augustine's sermons). Most of the library was lost when Huguenots plundered the abbey in 1562. Fleury became a center of the Cluniac reform after 930, its influence extending to England, thanks to St. OSWALD OF YORK (d. 992), a monk of Fleury. After 1072 the abbots, who supported the Capetians, claimed primacy among abbots of Gaul. Gauzlin, son of Hugh Capet, became abbot in 1005, and Philip I was buried there in 1108. The abbey slowly declined during the Hundred Years' War and became commendatory in 1485. In 1627 Richelieu, commendatory abbot, introduced the MAURIST reform. Suppressed in 1790 by the French Revolution, the monastery was demolished and the church turned to parish use. In 1865 Bishop F. DUPANLOUP of Orleans gave the parish and the relics of St. Benedict to monks of Pierre-Qui-Vire (founded in 1850 in the Diocese of Sons). But French law exiled religious in 1900, and it was only in 1944 that the abbot of Pierre-Qui-Vire, where monks had returned in 1922, could send a community to restore Fleury. Today 50 Benedictines lead a contemplative life in new and unfinished buildings and care for a parish of 1,500 souls.

Abbot Gauzelin (1005–30) began the era of building by raising "a tower to serve as a model for all Gaul." The 296.5-foot Basilica of St. Benedict, one of the largest Romanesque churches, and best lighted, has unusual harmony. The eye is immediately drawn to the choir where the main altar is placed on a pavement of antique marble between two rows of five columns. The 15th-century stalls, where the monks chant their office, have just been returned to their old place at the corner of the transept. The Romanesque nave, with a Gothic vault completed in 1218, makes a monumental porch for Gauzelin's tower, which it adjoins. Under the apse is the half-circle crypt, a forest of cylindrical supports around a central pillar where the relics of St. Benedict repose.

Bibliography: J. N. M. ROCHER, *Histoire de l'abbaye royale de Saint-Benoît-sur-Loire* (Orléans 1865). H. LECLERCQ, *Dictionnaire d'archéologie chrétienne et de liturgie,* ed. F. CABROL, H. LECLERCQ, and H. I. MARROU, 15 v. (Paris 1907–53) 5.2:1709–60. M. AUBERT in *Congrès archéologique de France* 93, (Orléans 1930) 569–656. G. CHENESSEAU, *L'Abbaye de Fleury à Saint-Benoît-sur-Loire* (Paris 1931). A. VIDIER, *L'Historiographie à St.-Benoît-sur-Loire et les miracles de St. Benoît* (Paris 1964). L. COTTINEAU, *Répertoire topobibliographique des abbayes et prieurés,* 2 v. (Mâcon 1935–39) 2:2610–13. O. L. KAPSNER, *A Benedictine Bibliography: An Author-Subject Union List,* 2 v. (Collegeville, Minn. 1962) 2:254–257.

[A. DAVRIL]

SAINT-BERTIN, ABBEY OF

The Abbey of Saint-Bertin is the former Benedictine monastery, Saint-Omer, France (modern Diocese of Arras). When St. OMER became bishop of Thérouanne, he sent to LUXEUIL for three Columban monks, whom he established in a cella, or small monastery, on the River Aa, under the direction of Mommelinus. When the latter became bishop of Noyon-Tournai, St. Omer gave the monks a new monastic site a league upstream, the island of Sithiu, which was formed by a meander in the river. St. BERTINUS was the first abbot of this monastery dedicated to SS. Peter and Paul. On a neighboring hill was Omer's chapel of Sainte-Marie, which he gave to the monks (663) with a privilege of immunity on condition that he be buried nearby. The abbey prospered, but after a century it needed reform. Abbot Fridogisius, imitating

CHRODEGANG OF METZ, dismissed any monks lacking do-cility, restored the rule of the monks on the island, and made the monks of Sainte-Marie canons regular under his authority. The area between these two monasteries be-came the city of Saint-Omer, France (1127).

The monastery of Sithiu, which became completely Benedictine under the name of Saint-Bertin, prospered for 11 centuries, under 83 abbots, until the French Revo-lution (1791). It survived pillaging by the NORMANS (860, 878), fires, wars, and epidemics. It was reformed by GE-RARD OF BROGNE (944), and Richard of Saint-Vanne (1201). From the time of Abbot LAMBERT OF SAINT-BERTIN (1095) until 1139 it was part of the CLUNIAC RE-FORM. This affiliation was resumed in 1776. In order to have ''regular visitors'' as recommended by the Council of Trent, the abbey joined the ''Congregation of the Ex-empt of Flanders'' in 1569. It usually had 60 monks, but at one time as many as 150. Thanks to gifts, purchases and exchanges of property, and the good administration of its abbots, Saint-Bertin was one of the great French ab-beys. It also had extensive properties in England and the Rhineland.

The abbey was a famous cultural center. From the earliest times, the monks had a school at the abbey, and later in every parish under their patronage. In the 16th century Abbot Gerard d'Haméricourt founded a school for the poor of Saint-Bertin (1561), which drew an intel-lectual elite from the lower classes. He also founded a college at the University of LOUVAIN. The scriptorium of Saint-Bertin was famous, the illuminated manuscripts of Abbot Odbertus being especially noteworthy. It was con-stantly producing, buying, and exchanging manuscripts. Consequently, by the 12th century Saint-Bertin's library possessed more than 400 manuscripts, one of the richest collections in France. The abbey's chroniclers and histo-rians such as FOLCWIN OF LOBBES, LAMBERT OF SAINT-OMER, and Abbot John V of Ypres (1365–83) were fa-mous. It was there that two chapters of the Golden Fleece were held. It was also the scene of princely weddings, great receptions, and tournaments. Its third abbey church (1365–83) was especially grand and superbly decorated.

Bibliography: H. DE LAPLANE, *Les Abbés de Saint-Bertin*, 2 v. (Saint-Omer 1854–55), old but accurate. H. LECLERCQ, *Diction-naire d'archéologie chrétienne et de liturgie*, ed. F. CABROL, H. LE-CLERCQ, and H. I. MARROU, 15 v. (Paris 1907–53) 15.1:1499–1501. V. REDLICH, *Lexikon für Theologie und Kirche*[2], ed. J. HOFER and K. RAHNER (Freiburg 1957–65) 2:269–270. R. RAU, ed., *Jahrbücher von St. Bertin*, v. 2 of *Quellen zur karolingischen Reichsgeschichte* (Berlin 1956–).

[G. COOLEN]

ST. BONAVENTURE UNIVERSITY

A Catholic university in the 750-year-old Franciscan tradition of learning, administered by the Franciscan Fri-ars of the Province of the most Holy Name of Jesus of the Order of Friars Minor. It is located on a 500-acre cam-pus in western New York State.

Historical Background. In 1854, Nicholas Dever-eux (1791–1855) and Bishop John Timon of Buffalo (1797–1867) traveled to Rome and at the suggestion of Pope Pius IX requested Venantius Celano, minister gen-eral of the Friars Minor, to establish a Franciscan mission and educational center in the southern tier of the Diocese of Buffalo. The Friars Minor provided priests and broth-ers for the mission, and Devereux supplied land and fi-nancial aid for the school that was to become St. Bonaventure University.

Bishop Timon laid the cornerstone for the college in 1856. Pamphilus de Magliano, O.F.M., was appointed first superior and president of St. Bonaventure College in 1859, overseeing a freshman class of 15 students. The college, which then focused on seminary studies and lib-eral arts, granted its first B.A. degree in 1876 and was of-ficially charted by the state of New York in 1883. In 1901 the Province of the Immaculate Conception transferred the title and administrative control to the Province of the Holy Name.

Thomas Plassmann, O.F.M., president of the college from 1920 to 1949, greatly expanded the college. When three campus buildings were destroyed by fire, Plass-mann oversaw an extensive rebuilding program. Women first entered the college as summer session students in 1922 and as full-time day students in 1942. The first M.A. in education was conferred in 1925 and the first Ph.D. in 1930. Reserve Officers' Training Corps (ROTC) came to the campus in 1936. In 1950, Plassmann was succeeded by Juvenal Lalor, O.F.M., the same year that the state of New York granted the college university status, and it of-ficially became St. Bonaventure University.

Since that time, the university has added a substan-tial number of buildings to the campus, including class-rooms, administrative offices, and athletic facilities. Christ the King Seminary was established in 1952 and re-mained until 1974 when it moved off campus. The Spe-cial Collections of the University Archives contains manuscript material by the Trappist monk and sometime instructor at St. Bonaventure University, Thomas MER-TON, the poet Robert Lax, the writer and journalist Jim Bishop, and the broadcast journalist Douglas Edwards.

In 1998 the Clare College core curriculum was insti-tuted at St. Bonaventure, the most radical and compre-hensive curricular change since the university came into existence. The core takes an interdisciplinary approach to learning, but one which is firmly grounded in the Franciscan tradition, in general, and the learned tradition of St. Bonaventure, in particular. The core draws support from all divisions within the university and has attracted national attention. In addition to the Master of Arts, the School of Franciscan Studies offers an Advanced Certificate in Franciscan Studies.

Five St. Bonaventure graduates have been awarded the Pulitzer Prize. The university expanded its mission to serve with the opening of the Franciscan Center for Social Concern in 1999. The Warming House, a Bonaventure facility, is the oldest soup kitchen run by students in the United States.

Franciscan Institute. Established in 1940 as a teaching and research unit within St. Bonaventure University, the Franciscan Institute gained a worldwide reputation as a scholarly research center for Franciscan Studies under the leadership of its first director, the eminent German medievalist Philotheus BOEHNER. Boehner initiated the research and preparation of the critical edition (1967–85) of the writings of William of Ockham, a project that involved other prominent medievalists such as Eligius Buytaert, O.F.M., Innocent Dahm, O.F.M., Gaudens Mohan, O.F.M. and Ernest A. Moody. In 1984, the institute initiated the preparation of the critical edition of the works of John Duns Scotus and Adam de Wodeham. The Institute has published over 80 volumes of Franciscana research under the imprint of "Franciscan Institute Publications." The Franciscan Institute library contains more than 16,000 volumes, the largest collection of Franciscana in the western hemisphere.

Bibliography: W. HAMMON, *The First Bonaventure Men* (St. Bonaventure, New York, 1958). M. V. ANGELO, *The History of St. Bonaventure University* (St. Bonaventure, New York 1964). P. J. SPAETH, "St. Bonaventure University," *The Encyclopedia of American Catholic History*, ed. M. GLAZIER and T. J. SHELLEY (Collegeville, MN 1997) 1236. M. V. T. WALLACE, *And They Were Giants: The St. Bonaventure Football Book* (St. Bonaventure, New York 1989); *Bonaventure Fact Book 2000–2001* (St. Bonaventure, New York 2001); *4 Year Colleges 2001* (Lawrenceville, NJ 2001).

[J. MULRYAN]

SAINT-CALAIS, ABBEY OF

Former BENEDICTINE abbey in the Diocese of Le Mans, Sarthe, France. It was first mentioned by GREGORY OF TOURS (576), who called it Anninsola or Anille. It was founded supposedly by Carileffus (or Calais) and his companions Daumerus and Gall (c. 515–542) and renamed Saint-Calais some time after 752 in honor of Carileffus, whose body reputedly rested there. Its first known abbots were Sigiramnus and St. Siviard (d. 683) who obtained territorial rights from King Thierry III. The controversy with Bp. Robert of Le Mans over the abbey's autonomy was resolved in the abbey's favor by the Council of Verberie (863) with the acquiescence of Pope Nicholas I. Although abandoned and destroyed during the late 9th-century NORMAN invasions, the abbey was rebuilt during the 10th and 11th centuries. Though allied with the English during the Hundred Years' War, the abbey was burned (c. 1424–29) by the Duke of Bedford. Its greatest medieval abbot was Jean Tibergeau (d. 1415). In 1562 the Calvinists pillaged it. Following vain efforts at reform, particularly under Samuel de Courianne (d. 1614), the MAURISTS took possession in 1659. A portion of the relics of St. Carileffus, transferred to Blois in the 9th century, were returned in 1663; the remainder was restored by Bp. H. B. GRÉGOIRE, Constitutional Bishop of Blois. When the monastery was suppressed during the French Revolution, the church (dating from 1360) became a parish church and the cloister a municipal building.

Bibliography: É. LESNE, "Nicolas I et les libertés des monastères des Gaules," *Moyen-âge* 24 (1911) 277–306. L. H. COTTINEAU, *Répertoire topobibliographique des abbayes et prieurés,* 2 v. (Mâcon 1935–39) 2:2625. P. SCHMITZ, *Dictionnaire d'histoire et de géographie ecclésiastiques,* ed. A. BAUDRILLART (Paris 1912–) 11:333–334. H. LECLERCQ, *Dictionnaire d'archéologie chrétienne et de liturgie,* ed. F. CABROL, H. LECLERCQ et H. I. MARROU, 15 v. (Paris 1907–53) 15.1:482–498. L. RENARD, *Saint-Calais: Des Origines à la Révolution française* (Saint-Calais 1945).

[G. E. GINGRAS]

ST. CASIMIR, SISTERS OF

(SSC, Official Catholic Directory #3740); a congregation with papal approbation established in 1907 to instruct the children of Lithuanian immigrants, most of them refugees from the czarist persecution of the late 19th century. A group of priests, led by Bishop John W. Shanahan of Harrisburg, Pennsylvania, obtained permission from Rome to found the congregation in 1906 and put Reverend Anthony Staniukynas in charge of the project. Casimira Kaupas, a novice at Holy Cross convent in Ingenbohl, Switzerland, since 1902, was being prepared to lead the new community. She arrived in New York in 1905 with two companions. At Mount St. Mary's, Scranton, Pennsylvania, the Sisters of the Immaculate Heart of Mary prepared them for their work in American schools. In August 1907 these three sisters pronounced simple vows, and in October they opened their first convent at Mt. Carmel in the Harrisburg diocese.

Archbishop James E. Quigley of Chicago, Illinois, invited the sisters to work in his archdiocese and dedicated their motherhouse there in 1911. Casimira Kaupas, as Mother Maria, continued to direct the community until her death in 1940. The sisters established a branch of their congregation in the Republic of Lithuania in 1920 and opened missions in Argentina in 1941.

In the United States, the sisters are engaged in the field of academic education, pastoral ministry, hospitals and care facilities for the aged. The generalate is in Chicago, Illinois. In addition to their houses in the United States, the congregation also maintains a presence in Argentina.

Bibliography: K. BURTON, *Lily and Sword and Crown* (Milwaukee 1958).

[A. M. RAKAUSKAS/EDS.]

SAINT-CLAUDE, ABBEY OF

Former BENEDICTINE MONASTERY, forerunner of the present Diocese of Saint-Claude, suffragan of Besançon, in the department of Jura, France. The monastery was founded by SS. ROMANUS and Lupicinus as the Abbey of Condat *c.* 425–450, and was later known as Saint-Oyen-de-Joux [*S. Eugendi* (or *Augendi*) *Jurensis*] after its third abbot, EUGENDUS (OYEND) OF CONDAT. It was renamed Saint Claude *c.* 1213 when the relics of the 12th abbot, CLAUDIUS OF CONDAT, were interred there. It was the motherhouse of Lauçonne, La Balme, and ROMAINMÔTIER. It developed, *c.* 510, its own rule, which was adopted by Agaune, but Saint-Claude subsequently adopted the BENEDICTINE RULE. As a pilgrimage center (14th–16th centuries), it was visited by Anne of Brittany, wife of King Louis XII. An autonomous territory of the Holy Roman Empire, it became part of France only in 1674. Subsequently religious life grew lax under commendatory abbots, e.g., Cardinal d'Estrées (1681–1742). Pope Benedict XIV erected the abbey into the bishopric of Saint-Claude (1742), suffragan of Lyons, and the count-bishop inherited abbot's rights, with the cathedral chapter holding the abbey's dependencies until the French Revolution. It was this abbey that was central in the controversy over MORTMAIN involving Voltaire. Only the cathedral of St. Peter, built between the 14th and the 18th centuries, remains standing.

Bibliography: P. BENOIT, *Histoire de l'abbaye . . . de Saint-Claude,* 2 v. (Montreuil-sur-Mer 1890–92). L. H. COTTINEAU, *Répertoire topobibliographique des abbayes et prieurés,* 2 v. (Mâcon 1935–39) 2:2635. R. VAN DOREN, *Dictionnaire d'histoire et de géographie ecclésiastiques,* ed. A. BAUDRILLART (Paris 1912–) 12:1072. G. BARDY, *Catholicisme* 2:1171–72.

[G. E. GINGRAS]

ST. CLOUD, DIOCESE OF

Located in central Minnesota and covering an area of 12,251 sq. miles, the diocese of St. Cloud (S. Clodoaldi), suffragan of the metropolitan See of St. Paul-Minneapolis, was erected by Leo XIII on Sept. 22, 1889, with the see city in densely Catholic Stearns County.

Though a Winnebago mission was served by Canon Francis de Vivaldi at Long Prairie in 1851, the acknowledged founder of the Church in the area was Rev. Francis PIERZ, a Slovenian missionary who at the age of 67 arrived in central Minnesota in 1852 to work among the Native Americans. When his enthusiastic letters, reports, and advertising attracted German settlers by the thousands, his ministry was extended to Sauk Rapids, Belle Prairie, St. Joseph, Jacob's Prairie, St. Augusta, and St. Cloud. Pierz appealed to Bp. Joseph Crétin in St. Paul, who in turn contacted Abbot Boniface Wimmer of St. Vincent's, Latrobe, Pennsylvania. In the spring of 1856 four Benedictines arrived to minister to the new settlers. The monks settled in St. Cloud, founding ST. JOHN's Abbey; soon their influence spread throughout Stearns County. The next year Benedictine nuns from Pennsylvania (founded from Eichstatt, Bavaria) came to help. Revs. Joseph Buh and Ignatius Tomazin joined Pierz in serving the native population. In 1873 Mother Mary Ignatius nee Elizabeth Hayes, founded the Franciscan sisters at Belle Prairie.

When the Vicariate of Northern Minnesota was formed in 1875, Abbot Rupert Seidenbusch (1830–95), first abbot of St. John's, was consecrated vicar with residence in St. Cloud. The continuing stream of immigrants—Germans, Irish, Poles, and Slovenes—swelled the ranks of the faithful. In 1888, when Seidenbusch resigned, there were 65 churches, a number of schools, and a hospital serving the Catholic population.

Erected in 1889, the diocese was headed by Bishop Otto Zardetti, who was consecrated Oct. 20, 1889. A diocesan monthly was published during his episcopate, the Franciscan sisters at Little Falls were organized into a community, and the Catholic school system was promoted. When Zardetti was named archbishop of Bucharest, Romania in 1894, he was succeeded by Martin MARTY, OSB, the bishop of Sioux Falls. Marty's brief episcopate in St. Cloud ended with his death on Sept. 19, 1896. The third bishop, James Trobec (1838–1921), pastor at St. Agnes in St. Paul, was consecrated Sept. 21, 1897. When Trobec resigned April 15, 1914, the number of parishes had increased to 123, and schools to 25.

Joseph F. Busch (1866–1953) was installed as St. Cloud's fourth ordinary on March 19, 1915. Director of the St. Paul Diocesan Mission Band, he had been consecrated in 1910 for the See of Lead, South Dakota (now Rapid City), where he had been a pioneer in supporting the cause of social justice and social action. A number of parishes were established shortly after World War I, as well as a model orphanage and a monastery for the Poor Clares. A diocesan paper, the *St. Cloud Register*, later the *St. Cloud Visitor*, was successfully founded. In 1937 St. Mary's in St. Cloud was designated the cathedral church.

In 1942, Busch received Peter W. Bartholome (1893–1982), pastor at St. John's, Rochester, Minnesota, as his coadjutor. After World War II extensive building to erect or replace churches, schools, rectories, convents, and old folks homes took place. In addition St. John's Seminary was built at Collegeville and administered by diocesan priests with a Benedictine faculty.

On May 31, 1953, at Busch's death, Bartholome succeeded as fifth ordinary. He fostered and guided the Rural Life and Family Life movements in his diocese and in the nation. Catholic Charities was reorganized, vocation work emphasized, diocesan units of the National Council of Catholic Men and the National Council of Catholic Women were established, and a marriage counseling board set up.

Bishop George H. Speltz (1912–), auxiliary bishop of Winona, came to St. Cloud in June, 1966, as coadjutor, and succeeded Bartholome when he retired in 1968. The new structures resulting from Vatican II were implemented in parish councils, the diocesan pastoral council, the presbyteral council, which diminished the role of the diocesan consultors and deans. The Pro-Life Movement started in 1970 to educate on abortion and euthanasia. After the Vietnam War Catholic Charities sponsored refugees to resettle in central Minnesota, and expanded its role in low-income public housing, "meals on wheels" for the home-bound, and various kinds of counseling, with the support of public monies.

When Speltz resigned on Jan. 13, 1987, he was succeeded by Abbot Jerome Hanus, OSB, of Conception Abbey in Missouri, who became seventh bishop of the diocese. On Aug. 23, 1994, Hanus was appointed coadjutor archbishop of Dubuque. His successor was John F. Kinney (1937–), bishop of Bismarck, who was installed as eighth bishop on July 5, 1995.

The decline of priestly vocations since 1966 left a dearth of priests. Many parishes were twinned under one pastor, and projections were made for facing future shortages. Permanent deacons were assigned for parish duties. The number of seminarians remains low, that of permanent deacons is rising.

Although the geographical area of the diocese remained constant, there were notable shifts in population at the end of the century. The western counties lost population because of the decline in family farms. Several parishes were closed. The eastern counties grew rapidly with people from the Twin Cities moving into suburban communities. Because of the population shifts the Catholic image and influence has diminished.

In the year 2000 religious communities in the diocese were the Benedictine Fathers of St. John's Abbey at Collegeville and the Crosier Fathers of Holy Cross Monastery in Onamia; the Benedictine Sisters of St. Benedict Priory in St. Joseph, the Franciscan Sisters in Little Falls, and the Poor Clare Monastery in Sauk Rapids.

Bibliography: Archives, Diocese of St. Cloud. C. J. BARRY, *Worship and Work: St. John's Abbey and University, 1856–1956* (Collegeville, MN 1956). W. P. FURLAN, *In Charity Unfeigned: The Life of Francis Xavier Pierz* (Paterson 1952). V. A.YZERMANS, *The Spirit in Central Minnesota* (St. Cloud, MN 1989).

[P. ZYLLA]

ST. COLUMBAN, MISSIONARY SISTERS OF

(SSC, Official Catholic Directory #2880); also known as Columban Sisters, a pontifical institute founded in Ireland by Reverend John Blowick in 1922, and engaged in educational, medical, catechetical, and social services in overseas missions. Originally organized for work in China, the Columban Sisters maintained schools and hospitals there for 25 years before being expelled by the communist authorities. In 1930, the sisters established their first foundation in the United States, followed by the Philippines in 1939 and Myitkyina, Upper Burma in 1947. After their expulsion from China in 1952, the congregation established new foundations in Hong Kong and South Korea. The generalate is in Wicklow, Ireland. The United States headquarters is in Brighton, Massachusetts.

[M. V. DOYLE/EDS.]

SAINT DAVIDS, ANCIENT SEE OF

The Ancient See of Saint Davids is one of four ancient dioceses of WALES. The cathedral, in the present village of Saint Davids, is situated on the Alun, a small stream, two miles from the north shore of St. Bride's Bay and 16 miles from Fishguard, Pembrokeshire, Wales. It owes its isolated position to the fact that it preceded the diocese. Though legend says that St. Patrick founded a missionary college, Ty Gwyn, there, it is certain that some time after 530 DAVID, the patron of Wales, who was trained by St. ILLTUD, made the site of the present cathedral the site of his monastery. It was here that the historian GILDAS was a monk *c.* 589. The monastery grew into a diocesan church, or cathedral, with the principality of Dyfed (i.e., Pembrokeshire and the adjacent parts of Carmarthenshire and Cardiganshire) as its area. Despite its secluded location, Saint Davids became the chief seat of the British church in Wales. It retained this preeminance in south Wales all through the Middle Ages, and its bishops exercised metropolitan rights over that area until ANSELM OF CANTERBURY appointed a Norman monk, Bernard, as bishop in 1115 and made Saint Davids a suffragan see of Canterbury. GIRALDUS CAMBRENSIS (d. 1223) strove vainly to regain for the cathedral chapter the power to elect its own bishops without reference to the English king or primate. Bishop Thomas Bek (1280–93) refused to recognize in Wales the metropolitan rights of Abp. John Peckham of Canterbury but was the last to insist on the independence of the Welsh Church.

Saint Davids was a port for pilgrim traffic from Ireland and Wales to SANTIAGO DE COMPOSTELA in Spain. Two pilgrimages to the shrine of St. David were popularly thought to equal one to Rome.

The present cathedral, which is mainly transitional Norman, with an oak roof, was begun by Bp. Peter de Leia (1176–98). Bishop Henry Gower (1328–47) built the fine rood screen, as well as the magnificent episcopal palace (now ruined) across the Alun. Other bishops included Henry CHICHELE. Under Bp. William BARLOW (1536–48) Saint Davids became a diocese of the Church of England. It is now one of the six dioceses of the Church of Wales.

Bibliography: Gt. Brit. Royal Commission on the Ancient and Historical Monuments and Constructions in Wales and Monmouthshire, *An Inventory of the Ancient Monuments in Wales and Monmouthshire* (London 1911–), v.7 *County of Pembroke* (1925). W. L. BEVAN, *St. David's* (London 1888). J. C. DAVIES, ed., *Episcopal Acts and Cognate Documents Relating to Welsh Dioceses, 1066–1272* (Cardiff 1946–). G. WILLIAMS, *The Welsh Church from Conquest to Reformation* (Cardiff 1962). A. A. SAMPSON, *St. David's* (St. David's, Wales 1974).

[N. DENHOLM–YOUNG]

SAINT-DENIS-EN-FRANCE, ABBEY OF

One of the oldest of the Parisian abbeys, located a short distance from the city of Paris, especially noted as the repository of the tombs of French monarchs. The basilica was erected on the site where, according to tradition, the body of the martyred Bishop St. DENIS was buried (*c.* 273). The Abbot HILDUIN (819) gave currency to the erroneous identification of the Parisian martyr with PSEUDO-DIONYSIUS the Areopagite. Hilduin also reformed the abbey and is thought to have visualized Saint-Denis as a second Rome. Some have seen in this the beginnings of GALLICANISM. It was again reformed by ODILO OF CLUNY in 1008. The Benedictines took over the abbey in 656 and remained there until 1792.

The history of the abbey is inextricably bound up with that of the French kings, its greatest benefactors. King Dagobert I (d. 639) endowed it and aided in the reconstruction of the church. He and his successors were buried there. PEPIN the Short (d. 768) also began the rebuilding of parts of the structure that was completed under CHARLEMAGNE. The Capetians similarly maintained close ties with the abbey. LOUIS VI (d. 1137) adopted its standard, the *Oriflamme*, as the banner of the kings of France, and he chose as his principal adviser Abbot SUGER, who served also as administrator of the kingdom in the succeeding reign, while LOUIS VII was absent on the Second CRUSADE (1147–49). Under Abbot Suger, reconstruction of the basilica was begun June 9, 1140; it was he who collected and continued the chronicles of the abbey. In the 13th-century reconstruction under its architect, Pierre de Montereau, the abbey took on the characteristic features of the Gothic style, for which it became noted. LOUIS IX (d. 1270) treasured the abbey for this reason as one of the most precious of French monuments.

The later history of the abbey is a record of additions, demolition, reconstruction, and decline. During the Hundred Years' War, ramparts and towers were added; and the abbey was successively captured and recaptured by Armagnacs, English, and Burgundians. During this time, many of its monuments and possessions disappeared, including several royal tombs. The church was further pillaged during the civil and religious wars of the 16th and 17th centuries. During this time some of the 13th-century buildings were demolished and replaced by others inspired by classical models. In 1528 Saint-Denis became a commendatory abbey; in 1691 the title and office of abbot were suppressed and were replaced by that of prior. However, the abbey suffered the greatest destruction and desecration in the 18th century. In 1700 demolition of the claustral building was begun, and in 1771 the western façade was enlarged. In 1781 a black and white pavement was added to cover up the 12th-century pavement. The church was pillaged between 1792 and 1794, following the overthrow of the monarchy. Equally damaging to the early church were the well-intended efforts at restoration made by NAPOLEON I and his successors. Between 1847 and 1879 Viollet-le-Duc carried on the work of reconstruction. The abbey suffered further damage in the bombardment of Paris in 1871 and in the 20th-century wars.

Bibliography: Source. SUGER, *Abbot Suger on the Abbey Church of St. Denis and Its Art Treasures*, ed. and tr. E. PANOFSKY

(Princeton 1946). Literature. H. LECLERCQ, *Dictionnaire d'archéologie chrétienne et de liturgie* (Paris 1907–53) 4.1:588–642. L. H. COTTINEAU, *Répertoire topobibliographique des abbayes et prieurés* (Mâcon 1935–39) 2:2650–57. S. M. CROSBY, *The Abbey of St. Denis, 475–1122* (New Haven 1942); *L'Abbaye royale de Saint-Denis: Cent trente photos de Pierre Devinoy* (Paris 1953). J. FORMIGÉ, *L'Abbaye royale de Saint-Denis: Recherches nouvelles* (Paris 1960). A. LAPEYRE, *Des Façades occidentales de Saint-Denis et de Chartres* (Paris 1960).

[P. KIBRE]

ST. EDMUND, SOCIETY OF

(SSE, Official Catholic Directory #0440); a religious congregation of priests and brothers founded at Pontigny, France, in 1843 by Jean Baptiste MUARD, under the patronage of St. Edmund Rich, Archbishop of Canterbury, who died in exile at Pontigny in 1240. It had become a pontifical institute in 1876 and had received full canonical approval in 1911.

The society, known originally as Prêtres Auxiliaires, Missionaires de St. Edmund, conducted missions and retreats in an effort to offset the effects of Jansenism, and gave assistance to the diocesan clergy whenever needed. In 1867 a house was opened at Mont-Saint-Michel and public devotion and honor to St. Michael, patron of France, was renewed and increased under the society's direction. The society, adding education to its other works, undertook the direction of the College of the Immaculate Conception, Laval, France (1879), and the college at Château Gontier, Brittany (1893). In 1895 it founded St. Edmund's school at Sens.

In 1891 two Edmundite fathers went to Montreal, Canada, to establish a house in North America. They were directed to Burlington, VT, and for a time conducted a mission at Keeler's Bay, South Hero, VT. In 1895, Bp. Louis de Goesbriand of Burlington gave them the parish of Swanton where they opened a juniorate in 1898. When the French law of association of 1901 brought an end to the work of the society in France, a number of the members exiled in England established a mission at Hitchen, Hertfordshire. Others went to the U.S. in 1902 and began their scholasticate at Winooski, VT. The scholasticate was moved to Swanton in 1904 and St. Michael's College for men was built in Winooski.

From 1913 to 1925 the society had missions in Montana where remarkable results were achieved among the Cheyenne Indians at St. Labre. In 1925 the mission at Hitchen was given back to the diocese, and a year later the fathers there returned to Pontigny. In 1934, another mission was opened in England, at Whitton. Three years later, the society began work among African Americans, opening its first mission at Selma, AL. In 1938 a mission was opened at Greenfield Park, Canada.

The U.S. general motherhouse is located in Colchester, VT.

[G. E. DUPONT/EDS.]

ST. ELMO'S FIRE

A natural phenomenon interpreted by Mediterranean seamen as a sign of St. ELMO's protection, or as a portent of bad weather. Legends about fire reveal the spirit of each age. St. Elmo's relation to fire is an illustration of a medieval tendency to honor saints more for what they were supposed to have done for their devotees than for the sanctity of their lives. The incidents connected with fire in the legendary life of St. Elmo or St. Erasmus supposedly occurred during the DIOCLETIAN PERSECUTION. He was rolled in pitch, which was then ignited; he was tortured with an iron chain and a red-hot cuirass. An angel brought him to Formiae (Italy). Such a favored person would be ideal as a heavenly protector from disturbances in nature.

Neapolitan seamen, who noticed the blue lights at the mastheads before and after storms, gradually interpreted the flashes as signs of their patron's protection. These blue, luminous flashes, called St. Elmo's Fire, occur when the atmosphere becomes charged and an electrical potential, strong enough to cause a discharge, is created between an object and the air around it. Because the saint was honored as the patron of mariners, it was believed that he manifested his protection in this manner after the storm had passed. Later Portuguese sailors adopted St. PETER GONZÁLEZ as their patron, and to them St. Elmo's Fire became Peter's lights.

Bibliography: *Bibliotheca hagiographica latina antiquae et mediae aetatis* (Brussels 1898–1901; 1:2578–85. *Acta Sanctorum* June 1:206–214. A. BUTLER, *The Lives of the Saints*, rev. ed. H. THURSTON and D. ATTWATER (New York 1956) 2:453–454. W. WATSON, *Early Fire-Making Methods and Devices* (privately pr. Fairfax, Va. 1939).

[L. L. RUMMEL]

SAINT-ÉVROULT-D'OUCHE, ABBEY OF

Former BENEDICTINE MONASTERY, in the Forest of Ouche, Ferté-Fresnel, Orne, France, formerly Diocese of Lisieux, present-day Séez. It was originally founded by (St.) ÉVROUL (EBRULF), who died 596; he was a Merovingian courtier who led a group of hermits into the Forest of Ouche. This foundation was ravaged in the 9th-century invasions of the Vikings, and the site was reoccupied only in the mid-11th century, when William, son of Giroie, became a monk at BEC and granted the site to the monks. Later his nephews, Hugh and Robert de Grand-mesnil, founded there an independent monastery that was generously endowed by many leading Norman lords and enjoyed royal patronage in the 13th century. It remained prosperous till the Hundred Years' War. The writer ORDERICUS VITALIS was a monk here, and his *Ecclesiastical History* is the most important single source of information about this and other monasteries in Normandy until 1141. The MAURISTS undertook to reform the house in 1628, but in 1790 the monks were dispersed. Only unimportant ruins of the buildings survive.

Bibliography: ORDERICUS VITALIS, *Historia ecclesiastica,* ed. LE PRÉVOST and L. V. DELISLE, 5 v. (Paris 1838–55); tr. T. FORESTER, 4 v. (London 1853–56). *Gallia Christiana,* v.1–13 (Paris 1715–85), v.14–16 (Paris 1856–65) 11:813–830. L. H. COTTINEAU, *Répertoire topobibliographique des abbayes et prieurés,* 2 v. (Mâcon 1935–39) 2:2669–71.

[D. J. A. MATTHEW]

SAINT-FLORENT-LE-VIEIL, ABBEY OF

Former Benedictine monastery near Cholet, Maine et Loire, France, in the Diocese of Angers. The abbey was founded at Mont-Glonne, where Florentius, a disciple of MARTIN OF TOURS, had retired (*c.* 390); it was first mentioned in a charter (718). It was under Abbot Albaud (779–810) that the original anchorites were organized into a community of monks and Saint-Florent became the model of reform for the abbeys of Aquitaine. Charlemagne reputedly rebuilt and adorned it. Partly burned by the NORMANS *c.* 847 and pillaged by the Breton chief Nominoe, it was repaired by Charles II the Bald, who exempted it from episcopal jurisdiction. When it was pillaged anew by Normans (905), its monks fled, taking the relics of St. Florentius to Tournus, Burgundy. The religious split into two groups in the 10th century, the larger congregation founding SAINT-FLORENT-LÈS-SAUMUR; the original abbey, rebuilt by Guallo (1030), was reduced to PRIORY status, dependent on the newer foundation, but retained the title ''abbey'' because of antiquity. King Louis XIII gave the abbey to Charles Bouvard, who introduced MAURISTS (1637–39); it was suppressed and destroyed in the French Revolution (1791).

Bibliography: F. UZUREAU, *Dictionnaire d'histoire et de géographie ecclésiastiques,* ed. A. BAUDRILLART (Paris 1912–) 1:1386. L. H. COTTINEAU, *Répertoire topobibliographique des abbayes et prieurés,* 2 v. (Mâcon 1935–39) 2:2675. G. JACQUEMET, *Catholicisme* 4:1357. G. BÖING, *Lexikon für Theologie und Kirche,* ed. J. HOFER and K. RAHNER, 10 v. (2d, new ed. Freiburg 1957–65) 4:171.

[G. E. GINGRAS]

SAINT-FLORENT-LÈS-SAUMUR, ABBEY OF

Former BENEDICTINE MONASTERY near Saumur, Maine-et-Loire, France, in the Diocese of Angers. It grew up originally around the tomb of the hermit Florent at Mont-Glonne-sur-Loire (now SAINT-FLORENT-LE-VIEIL) in the 5th century. A common rule of life was imposed on the hermits; this rule led to regular monastic life in the 8th century. Forced to flee out of fear of the Vikings, the monks traveled as far as Burgundy before they were recalled to the Loire Valley by the Count of Blois, Theobald ''Le Tricheur,'' who installed them in the castle of Saumur in 950. After the castle was taken by the Angevins in 1025, the monks were moved to their final home, now known as Saint-Florent-lès-Saumur. The new abbey church was consecrated in 1041. From this time the monastery extended its endowment throughout western France, and was by no means weaker for the loss of its secular patrons. Its possessions were found in every part of the later Plantagenet empire and it had more than a dozen churches in the Diocese of Paris. These possessions gave rise to the establishment of many priories. The influence of the monastery was therefore more notable outside its own diocese. From the 16th century it was held *in commendam* (*see* COMMENDATION), but the MAURISTS undertook reform in 1637. It was dissolved in 1790; of all its buildings only the 12th-century porch of the church remains. A great number of its archives survive at Angers.

Bibliography: P. MARCHEGAY, *Chroniques des églises d'Anjou* (Paris 1869). *Gallia Christiania* 14:620–640. H. L. COTTINEAU, *Répertoire topobibliographique des abbays et prieurés,* 2v. (Mâcon 1935–39) 2:2677–79.

[D. J. A. MATTHEW]

ST. FRANCIS, BROTHERS OF THE POOR OF

(CFP, Official Catholic Directory, #0460); originally called the Poor Brothers of St. Francis Seraph. It is a pontifical society of lay brothers originally founded to minister to the spiritual and educational needs of underprivileged boys. The congregation was founded Christmas Eve 1857, at Aix-la-Chapelle, Germany, by Johannes Hoever (1816–64). When Bismarck, in 1875, expelled religious from Prussian territory, the young community reestablished its motherhouse at Bleyerheide, Holland. After 1888 the brothers were allowed to return to Prussia, where several foundations were made. In July 1868, at the invitation of John Baptist Purcell, Archbishop of Cincinnati, OH, the brothers opened St. Anthony

Home for poor boys in Cincinnati. On Sept. 17, 1871, they inaugurated a U.S. province, dedicated to St. Joseph, with headquarters at Mt. Alverno on the Ohio River beyond the western limits of Cincinnati. Here, too, was opened a Protectory for Boys, an institution where needy, orphaned, and delinquent boys were given a grade school education and trained in various trades. Later, the brothers assumed the direction of similar institutions for boys in Cold Springs, KY; Columbus, OH; Detroit, MI; and Danville, NJ. Lack of vocations and of endowment forced the brothers to relinquish many of these institutions. Since 1921 the brothers have directed the Morris School, a boarding school for boys in Searcy, AR.

In the U.S., the brothers are principally engaged in academic education at all levels, the care of and education of neglected youth, AIDS ministry, prison ministry, counseling, youth ministry, group homes, and residential facilities for the aged and retired clergy. The U.S. provincialate (Province of St. Joseph) is located in Burlington, IA; the generalate is in Aachen, Germany.

Bibliography: H. SCHIFFERS, *Johannes Höver* (Freiburg 1930).

[H. BLOCKER]

ST. GEORGE, ORDERS OF

In the Middle Ages St. GEORGE was the patron of all knights, chiefly of those created by pope, emperor, or king (*milites aurati*). The Knights of St. George formed organizations at times modeled on crusading MILITARY ORDERS; others were companies or collar orders; later, orders of merit were named for St. George. The following groups may be distinguished. (1) The Constantinian Order of St. George is traditionally the oldest. That it derived from a company of exiled guard officers from Constantinople, evolving from the Labarum Guard of CONSTANTINE THE GREAT, is legendary. It dates back, however, to Isaac II Angelus (1191), survived the fall of the Byzantine Empire, and in 1699 came under the hereditary grand master of the house of Farnese. Charles of Naples, the heir of the last Farnese princess, transferred the seat of the order to his capital in 1734. Under the grand mastership of the house of Bourbon in Sicily, the order was engaged in pious and charitable activities. Its members were to be Catholics, with precedence given to noblemen. The Cross of Merit can be conferred on other Christians. Its badge is the cipher XP on a red cross flory. A branch of the order existed in Parma from 1816 to 1907. (2) In 1316 JAMES II OF ARAGON reorganized the TEMPLARS of his realm into the new Order of St. George, later known as the KNIGHTS OF MONTESA. The order relinquished celibacy in 1572; in 1578 its administration

was united to the crown of Spain by the Pope. (3) In 1326 Charles I of Hungary founded a short-lived Order of St. George. (4) EDWARD III of England (1348) founded the Order of the Garter in honor of St. George. (5) In the County of Burgundy the Company of St. George survived among the nobility from 1366 to the French Revolution. (6) In Germany the Frankish Company of St. George (1375) was integrated (1422) with the Swabian Company of the Shield of St. George, founded in 1392. In 1488 it became the law enforcement union of Swabian nobility, surviving until 1805. (7) In 1468 Frederick III founded the Order of St. George at Millstatt (Carinthia) to oppose the Turkish invasions. It decayed during the Reformation and was abolished in 1598. (8) In 1534 PAUL III founded the short-lived Order of St. George at Ravenna, also to fight the Turks. For the next generations, however, the Reformation prevented the growth of such organizations.

Other orders honoring St. George were founded in the 18th and 19th centuries: one by the Emperor Charles VII (1729) was suppressed by Hitler, but exists today as a pious charitable corporation of Catholic noblemen; the Order of the Four Emperors, by the Count of Limburg (1768); one established by Catherine II of Russia (1769); another by Ferdinand I of the Sicilies (1819); one by Ernest August of Hanover (1839); and the Order of SS. George and Constantine, by George II of Greece (1937).

Bibliography: E. VON DESTOUCHES, *Geschichte des königlich bayerischen Haus-Ritter-Ordens vom Heiligen Georg* (Bamberg 1890). G. BASCAPÉ, *Il sacro militare ordine costantiniano di s. Giorgio* (Milan 1940), older literature. R. HINDRINGER, *Lexikon für Theologie und Kirche*, ed. J. HOFER and K. RAHNER, 10 v. (2d new ed. Freiburg 1957–65) 4:692–693. B. HEYDENREICH, *Ritterorden und Rittergesellschaften* (Würzburg 1960).

[K. SCHWARZENBERG]

SAINT-GERMAIN-DES-PRÉS, ABBEY OF

Saint-Germain-Des-Prés is the former BENEDICTINE ABBEY in Paris, France. The monastery was founded by King Childebert I (*c.* 543) with St. Droctoveus from Autun, under the Basilian Rule. It was originally dedicated to the Holy Cross, St. Vincent (whose relics were brought from Spain by Childebert), and St. Symphorianus. Childebert I, Chilperic, and their families were buried there, as was St. GERMAIN, early bishop of Paris (d. 576), who gave his name to the monastery's new church when his reliquary was exalted (754) by the first Carolingian monarch PEPIN III. The CAROLINGIAN RENAISSANCE was a magnificent period for the abbey: by 815 there were 212 monks living there under the BENEDICTINE RULE (adopted before the end of the 7th century). Their intensive literary activity resulted in the *Polypticus* (of Abbot Irmino), several annals, their famous obituary, the martyrology of USUARD, the *Liber miraculorum,* and the later *De bellis Parisiacae urbis* by Abbo. The abbey's estate was immense. But decay came quickly: the NORMANS burned the buildings, and the dukes of Paris became secular abbots retaining only a small *mensa* (income) for the few monks; many of the abbey's villae were alienated. The Capetians and a regular abbot, WILLIAM OF SAINT-BÉNIGNE OF DIJON (c. 1025), sparked a revival. The estate was partly recovered; the *burgus S. Germani* (1159) outside the walls of Paris was organized according to municipal law and grew rich through its periodic fairs. In 1107 the abbey was placed *sub tutela sancti Petri* with episcopal EXEMPTION and with local jurisdiction. A new Romanesque church, which is still partially standing, was built, and Pope Alexander III consecrated it (1163). The scriptorium produced fine illuminated manuscripts such as the *Commentary on Leviticus* (Paris, Bib. Nat. Lat. 11564); historical works such as the *Historia regum Francorum ab origine gentis ad annum 1214* were written. Saint-Germain, like most religious houses, underwent a great spiritual and temporal decline in the later Middle Ages. The abbey was reformed according to the statutes of CHEZAL-BENOÎT in 1514 but, practically speaking, found a new life only with the MAURISTS (1630). Saint-Germain became the seat of the superior general and the center of Maurist studies. Thus, the revival was not only spiritual (despite some JANSENISM) but intellectual. MABILLON, E. Martène, U. Durand, RUINART, among others, worked there. The monastery was suppressed in the French Revolution. The superior general and 40 monks were massacred in the abbey with many other bishops and priests (Sept. 2, 1792), some of whom are now beatified as martyrs.

Bibliography: *Gallia Christiana,* v. 1–13 (Paris 1715–85), v. 14–16 (Paris 1856–65) 7:416–490. L. COTTINEAU, *Répertoire topobibliographique des abbayes et prieurés,* 2 v. (Mâcon 1935–39) 2:2207–11. H. LECLERCQ, *Dictionnaire d'archéologie chrétienne et de liturgie,* ed. F. CABROL, H. LECLERCQ, and H. I. MARROU, 15 v. (Paris 1907–53) 6.1:1102–50. P. SCHMITZ, *Histoire de l'Ordre de Saint-Benoît,* 7 v. (Maredsous, Bel. 1942–56). F. LEHOUX, *Le Bourg Saint-Germain-des-Prés* (Paris 1951). F. RIBADEAU DUMAS, *Histoire de St-Germain-des-Prés* (Paris 1958).

[P. DELHAYE]

SAINT-GILDAS-DE-RHUYS, ABBEY OF

Former BENEDICTINE monastery in the Diocese and *arrondissement* of Vannes, Commune Sarzeau (Morbihan), France (Lat. *S. Gildasius, Ruyense,* or *S. Gustanus de Revisio*). The abbey, founded in the 6th century by (St.) GILDAS THE "WISE," the first abbot, was destroyed during the NORMAN invasions, and the reliquary of St. Gildas, according to tradition, was transferred to Bourg-Dieu-sur-l'Indre c. 919. In 1008 the Abbey of Rhuys was restored by FLEURY, and c. 1032 its church was consecrated. ABELARD was made abbot there in 1125, but had to renounce the office in 1129. Rhuys was at that time a fairly important monastery on which depended the priories of Auray, Gâvre, Taupont, Locminé, Locmaria, Saint-Sauveur de Châteauroux, Arz, Quiberon, Argenton-sur-Creuse (Diocese of Bourges), etc. By 1625, however, the abbey was in a deplorable condition; in 1649 it was incorporated into the Congregation of Saint-Maur (see MAURISTS). In 1768 only nine religious were left at the abbey. In 1772 the abbey's revenues were united to the bishopric of Vannes. There were only four monks left when the abbey was suppressed during the French Revolution. The abbey church became a parish church of Sarzeau, and the cloister buildings became the motherhouse of the Sisters of Charity of Saint-Louis.

Bibliography: Archives of Morbihan has ten registers and 42 files on the abbey. *Gallia Christiana,* v.1–13 (Paris 1715–85), v.14–16 (Paris 1856–65) 14:958–965. *Chronicon Ruyense, 1008–1291* in G. A. LOBINEAU, *Histoire de Bretagne,* 2 v. (Paris 1707) v.2. J. L. BAUDOT and L. CHAUSSIN, *Vies des saints et des bienheueux selon l'ordre du calendrier avec l'historique des fêtes,* ed. by The Benedictines of Paris, 12 v. (Paris 1935–56) 1:583–585. J. FONSSAGRIVES, "Saint-Gildas-de-Rhuys," *Congrès archéologique de France* 81 (1914) 356–378. L. H. COTTINEAU, *Répertoire topobibliographique des abbayes et prieurés,* 2 v. (Mâcon 1935–39) 2:2713–15.

[J. DE LA C. BOUTON]

SAINT-GILLES

Former Benedictine abbey and pilgrimage center at the mouth of the Rhone River, in the Diocese of NÎMES, France. The origins are legendary, the tenth-century vita of St. Giles being only a legend. In fact, a monastery dedicated to St. GILES, whose relics were there, was founded in the nineth century in place of an old oratory dedicated to SS. Peter and Paul. Pilgrimages, organized at the time of foundation, reached a peak in the 12th century; Saint-Gilles was on the road to SANTIAGO DE COMPOSTELA for pilgrimages coming by the Rhone. The abbey became exempt under Benedict VIII (1022–24). Gregory VII had it enter the congregation of CLUNY in 1066, but left the election of the abbot free. Urban II (1095, 1096), Gelasius II (1118), and Innocent II (1130) visited it as pilgrims. Clement IV (1265–68), a monk of Saint-Gilles, gave it privileges.

The abbey, which had been richly endowed by the counts of Toulouse, found itself involved in the struggle between the Church and these counts during the ALBI-GENSIAN war. In 1143 the heretic PETER OF BRUYS was burned there; and in 1208 the papal legate PETER OF CAS-TELNAU, a Cistercian abbot, was murdered on leaving the town by a follower of the Count of Toulouse, the event that started the war. In 1209 Raymond VI of Toulouse was forced to make amends in the abbey church, whipped by the papal legate Milo as he entered the church naked. The abbey came under the King of France in 1226 and thrived in the 13th century. The town of nine parishes around the abbey was a prosperous port of embarkation for the CRUSADES. Commendatory in 1472, the abbey was made collegiate in 1538. In 1562, after a battle be-tween Protestants and Catholics, the abbey was looted and the monastery burned. The Protestants returned in 1574 and occupied the town until 1622, when they tore down the bell tower. The French Revolution, which sup-pressed the abbey, brought more ruin.

One visits Saint-Gilles for the beautiful 12th-century façade of the abbey church, modeled after St. Trophime in ARLES (same date). The façade has a close marriage of motifs of classical architecture and Romanesque motifs. A school of artists from Toulouse did the main portal (Christ in majesty, Passion scenes, Cain and Abel). Sculptors from the Ile-de-France did the side portals, the most beautiful (Adoration of the Magi and Christ's entry into Jerusalem to the left; and to the right the Crucifixion, Mary Magdalen at the feet of Jesus, the holy women going to buy perfumes and at the tomb, and Christ resur-rected). A third school, local, did the *avant-corps*. É. MÂLE thinks this iconography comes from the illumina-tions of Byzantine MSS.

Bibliography: A. FLICHE, *Aigues-Mortes et Saint-Gilles* (Paris 1950). E. LAMBERT, *Études médiévales,* 4 v. (Toulouse 1958). É. MÂLE, *L'Art religieux au XIIᵉ siècle en France* (1st ed. Paris 1922). L. H. COTTINEAU, *Répertoire topobibliographique des ab-bayes et prievrés* (Macon 1935–39) 2:2716–17.

[E. JARRY]

SAINT-GUILEHM-DU-DÉSERT, ABBEY OF

Former BENEDICTINE monastery in the Diocese of Lodève, present-day Diocese of Montpellier, France, known originally as Gellone (*monasterium Gellonense*), from the valley northwest of Montpellier where it was lo-cated. The eponymous designation *S. Guillelmus de De-serto* superseded the old usage. Duke WILLIAM OF AQUITAINE (d. 812) founded the monastery *c.* 804; it was affiliated with ANIANE, and immediately flourished as a Benedictine house under royal patronage and through the ardor of its first abbot, BENEDICT OF ANIANE. Despite a

jurisdictional dispute with Aniane, Saint-Guilhem-du-Désert attained its apogee in the 11th and 12th centuries. From this period dates the surviving church, with its fine altar. The repute of the founder (honored as a saint proba-bly from the 10th century) as a warrior against the Span-ish infidel, and the possession of a relic of the True Cross (Charlemagne's gift), rendered the abbey a pilgrim shrine. Saint-Guilhem declined during the later Middle Ages, but managed to survive under nonresident abbots, often neighboring bishops, until the French Revolution, when the few remaining monks were dispersed and the properties sold.

Bibliography: L. H. COTTINEAU, *Répertoire topobiblio-graphique des abbayes et prieurés,* 2 v. (Mâcon 1935–39) 2:2723–24. P. ALAUS et al., eds., *Cartulaires des Abbayes d'Aniane et de Gellone,* 2 v. (Montpellier 1898–1910). P. MARRES et al., eds., *Saint-Guilhem-du-Désert* (le milieu et l'homme) (Montpellier 1956).

[T. N. BISSON]

SAINT-HUBERT, ABBEY OF

Monastery in the Ardennes in Belgian Luxembourg (originally *Andagium*). It was founded *c.* 704 by St. Beregis, the chaplain of Pepin of Heristal, as an abbey of Augustinian canons, and was reformed by Bishop Wal-caud of Liège (d. 836), who introduced Benedictine monks and brought the body of St. HUBERT OF MAAS-TRICHT to the abbey. It was reformed by Bishop Richar in 942. The abbey was brought into the INVESTITURE STRUGGLE by Bishop Otbert, then reformed in 1618 by the Congregation of St. Vanne (*see* VERDUN-SUR-MEUSE, ABBEY OF), and suppressed in 1796. The present late-Gothic abbey church was built between 1525 and 1564. The heavy, baroque façade was added in 1700. It was raised to the rank of minor basilica in 1927, and is today a parish church visited by many pilgrims because of the tomb of St. Hubert. The abbey buildings, rebuilt after 1729, are now occupied by a state-supported school.

Bibliography: *Chronicon sancti Huberti Andaginensis usque ad a. 1106,* ed. L. C. BETHMANN and W. WATTENBACH, *Monumenta Germaniae Scriptores* (Berlin 1826–) 8:565–630. *Chartes de l'Abbaye de Saint-Hubert en Ardenne,* ed. G. KURTH (Brussels 1903–). P. CLEMEN, ed., *Belgische Kunstdenkmäter,* 2 v. (Munich 1923). L. H. COTTINEAU, *Répertoire topobibliographique des ab-bayes et prieurés,* 2 v. (Mâcon 1935–39) 2:2731–32. É. POUMON, *Abbayes de Belgique* (Brussels 1954).

[J. C. MOORE]

SAINT HUBERT, ORDER OF

The name given to several knightly or hunting orders since the 15th century. One, the highest order of Bavaria, was founded in 1444 by Gerard V, Duke of Jülich and Berg, in memory of a battle won on the feast day of St. HUBERT OF MAASTRICHT. Rules were formulated in 1476 by Gerard's son, William. The badge of the order was the image of St. Hubert, worn by the noble members on a collar of hunting horns. The order went into abeyance at the time of the Reformation but was restored in 1708 by the Catholic, John William, Elector Palatine and Duke of Jülich-Cleve-Berg. The new badge was a maltese cross, white strewn with flames, with rays at the angles, and St. Hubert's image in the center. It was worn either on a collar that alternated the Saint's image with the initials TV, or on a ribbon purple, fimbriated green. The motto was *In traw vast*. When the Elector Palatine succeeded in 1777 to the throne of Bavaria, the Order of St. Hubert took precedence over other Bavarian orders. It acquired new rules in 1808 as the great order of the Bavarian royal house. It was conferred on princes and titled statesmen and was retained by the royal house after the 1918 revolution. (For an illuminated 15th-century armorial of the order, see *Beiträge zur Geschichte der Heraldik*, Berlin 1939.)

Another order of the same name was instituted in 1416 by the principal lords of the Duchy of Bar in an attempt to end the perpetual conflicts between the Duchy of Bar and the Duchy of Lorraine. When these two duchies became part of France, King Louis XV confirmed the members in their ancient privileges. The order was ended by the revolution of 1830. The badge of the order was a cross with St. Hubert and a stag on one side and the insignia of the Duchy of Bar on the other.

Bibliography: H. LAHRKAMP, *Lexikon für Theologie und Kirche*, ed. J. HOFER and K. RAHNER (Freiburg 1957–65) 5:503.

[K. SCHWARZENBERG]

SAINT-JEAN-D'ANGÉLY, ABBEY OF

Former French Benedictine abbey, on the banks of the Boutonne River in the department of Charente-Maritime, former province of Saintonage. It is in the Diocese of La Rochelle, the former Diocese of Saintes (Latin, *S. Joannis Baptistae Angeriacensis*). Founded *c.* 800 and endowed by Pepin of Aquitaine in 838, it was destroyed by the Normans in 867. After its restoration in the 10th century by Ratgarius, it enjoyed continuous existence as an abbey throughout the Middle Ages, flourishing particularly in the 11th and 13th centuries. Although it was pillaged and suppressed by the Huguenots in 1569, it was again restored as a house of the Benedictine Congregation of Saint-Maur (*see* MAURISTS) in 1623, so continuing until its secularization during the French Revolution. The claustral buildings erected during the Maurist period are now occupied by a college. The present parish church, reconstructed in 1899, incorporates some elements of 13th-century construction. The monumental façade of a church begun in 1755 and never completed is also extant.

Bibliography: L. H. COTTINEAU, *Répertoire topobibliographique des abbayes et prieurés*, 2 v. (Mâcon 1935–39) 2:2738–39. P. VICAIRE, ''Les Monuments religieux du XIe siècle en Saintonge,'' *Bulletin de la Société des antiquaires de l'Ouest*, 4th ser., 1 (1949) 3–40. E. BONAZZI, *Saint-Jean d'Angély de 1372–1453. Son histoire, ses institutions* (Thesis École Nationale des Chartes: see *Positions des thèses;* Paris 1948).

[A. TEGELS]

ST. JOAN'S INTERNATIONAL ALLIANCE

Also known as *Alliance Internationale Jeanne d'Arc*, Saint Joan's International Alliance is a Catholic association of men and women working for the implementation of the principle of equality of the sexes in society and in the Church. Founded in 1911 in London by Gabrielle Jeffery, May Kendall, and Beatrice Gadsby as the Catholic Women's Suffrage Society, the organization recruited members in other countries and extended its activities to all aspects of women's rights. In 1924, under the name of St. Joan's Social and Political Alliance, it became a founding member of the Liaison Committee of Women's International Organizations. A French section was established in 1931, the U.S. section was formed in 1965. At the beginning of the 21st century, the society had sections and members in 15 countries.

The Alliance has worked with the League of Nations and the United Nations for the abolition of forced marriages, child marriages, female slavery, and other forms of economic servitude, trafficking of women for sexual exploitation, and the sexual mutilation of women. It has campaigned for equal opportunities for women in education, employment, and leadership positions; equal pay between the sexes for the same jobs; and the right of married women to employment.

Promoting equality for women in the Catholic Church was an important concern for the Alliance. During the 1950s and 1960s, the Alliance maintained cordial relations with Pius XII, John XXIII, and Paul VI. In 1961, when Pope John XXIII invited the laity to express their opinions before the approaching Vatican Council II, six members of the Alliance (a lawyer and five theologians) published in Zürich an eloquent plea for the admission of women to the ministerial priesthood entitled *Wir schweigen nicht länger*. The Alliance presented petitions for the opening of the restored diaconate to women (1961), for the presence of laity as observers at the Council

(1963), for the admission of women to the priesthood (1963),and for the revision of Canon Law (1965). In the wake of Vatican Council II, membership was opened to men. The Alliance focused its efforts in the Church and removed ''Political and Social'' from its name. It joined the Conference of International Catholic Organizations. In 1967, at the insistence of the Alliance's president, the World Congress of the Laity in Rome interceded, with near total unanimity, for the rights of women in the Church. In 1971, following the intervention of the Alliance's Canadian section, the Canadian Catholic Bishops made an unprecedented plea at the Synod of Bishops for the ministerial ordination of women.

The promulgation of the *Declaration on the Admission of Women to the Ministerial Priesthood* in 1976, followed by subsequent documents prohibiting further discussion of this issue changed the landscape. Many members, dispirited and discouraged, left the Alliance and the Catholic Church. In the social arena, the Alliance has made full use of its unique position as the only feminist NGO officially accredited to both the United Nations and the Vatican to work for better conditions for women all over the world. Before the Synods of African Bishops and Asian bishops, it submitted recommendations on the widespread victimization of women in Africa and Asia.

The Alliance's official journal, *The Catholic Citizen,* has appeared uninterrupted since 1915. In 1977, a second journal, *L'Alliance,* appeared in French, replaced in 1993 by a quarterly published in Belgium entitled *Terre des Femmes Sociétés Religions Nouvelles Internationales.*

Bibliography: G. HEINZELMANN, ed. *Wir schweigen nicht länger. Frauen äussern sich zum II. Vatikanischen Konzil* (Zürich 1964). M. DALY, *The Church and the Second Sex* (New York 1968) 85–6. P. and W. PROCTOR, *Women in the Pulpit: Is God an Equal–Opportunity Employer?* (New York 1976) 157–158.

[A.–M. PELZER]

ST. JOHN OF GOD, SISTERS OF

Also known as S.S.J.G., founded in 1871 at Wexford, Ireland, by Thomas FURLONG, Bishop of Wexford, and Mother Visitation Bridget Clancy as a diocesan congregation of sisters to teach, nurse in hospitals, and visit the sick poor in their homes. Since 1931, the congregation has been a pontifical institute having simple perpetual vows. In 1895, on the invitation of Bishop Matthey Gibney of Perth, eight sisters went to Australia to care for the victims of the typhoid epidemic that was spreading through the gold mines. The Australian mission has grown to include hospitals, schools, hospices, nursing homes and retreat facilities. Mission work in Africa began in the 1960s, where the sisters ran bush clinics,

hospitals, colleges, and schools. The Sisters of St. John of God have communities in Australia, Ireland, England, Wales, Pakistan, and Cameroon. The generalate is located in Wexford, Ireland.

[P. J. CORISH/EDS.]

ST. JOHN THE BAPTIST, SISTERS OF

(CSJB, Official Catholic Directory #3820); a congregation that began in Angri, southern Italy, when Canon Alfonso Maria Fusco (d. 1910) organized a group of women to take care of orphaned and abandoned children. Maddalena Caputo, a young woman who desired to consecrate herself to God in religion, and at the same time devote her life to the care of the needy and the poor, joined with Fusco in his project. On Sept. 25, 1878, Maddalena and three companions began their work. The rapid growth of the congregation resulted in the opening of houses throughout Italy. On Aug. 2, 1888, the bishop of Nocera, where the motherhouse was then located, approved the community. The final approbation of the Holy See in 1927 placed the congregation under pontifical jurisdiction. Mother Bernardino d'Auria brought the sisters to the United States in 1906, when she came with five companions to assume the direction of St. Lucy's parish school and orphanage in Newark, New Jersey. The community has since extended its work to education, healthcare, care of the elderly and children. In 1939 four members of the United States community went to assist their sisters from Italy to establish a foundation in Brazil. The following year sisters from the United States opened a mission in Chile, another in Rhodesia (modern Zimbabwe) in 1947, and in Canada in 1962. The generalate is in Rome; the United States provincialate is in Bronx, New York.

[A. GALLO/EDS.]

ST. JOHN'S ABBEY AND UNIVERSITY

St. John's Abbey and University is the oldest Catholic institution of higher education in Minnesota and the oldest institution of higher education in continuous existence in the state. Located in Collegeville, Minn., 80 miles north of Minneapolis, St. John's embraces a campus of 2,000 acres of wooded land with two lakes. This school was chartered by the Territory of Minnesota in 1857, one year after the monks of St. Benedict had come to the area surrounding the headwaters of the Mississippi River.

Early Development. At the request of Rev. Franz Xavier PIERZ, missionary, Bp. Joseph Cretin, first bishop of St. Paul, had invited the Benedictines to establish a monastery in his expansive frontier diocese to care for the rapidly increasing German immigrant families and to bring permanent spiritual assistance to the Chippewa and Sioux tribes of the region. Cretin had written to Abbot Boniface WIMMER, OSB, founder of the American Benedictines, at St. Vincent Abbey, Latrobe, Pa.; and on April 5, 1856, one priest, two clerics, and two brothers departed for Minnesota via the Ohio and Mississippi Rivers (*see* ST. VINCENT ARCHABBEY).

This first foundation effort of St. Vincent Abbey was under the charge of Prior Demetrius di Marogna, OSB. Shortly after their arrival in St. Paul, Cretin ordained the clerics, Cornelius Wittmann, OSB, and Bruno Riess, OSB; and the small party moved to St. Cloud in central Minnesota, where more than 200 German immigrants had already staked claims. On Feb. 17, 1857, the territorial legislature of Minnesota authorized by charter the establishment of St. John's Seminary. This school was to be founded as "a scientific, educational and ecclesiastical institution" in order "that the youths of this new but flourishing Territory be not only instructed in the elementary sciences, but, moreover, be educated in sound moral principles." Although St. John's Seminary was its legal title, it was known from the beginning as St. John's College. In 1869 it was authorized to confer academic degrees, and in 1883 its legal title was changed to St. John's University.

St. John's Abbey was originally known as the Abbey of St. Louis on the Lake, in memory of King Ludwig I of Bavaria, patron of the 19th-century Benedictine revival and major supporter of Abbot Boniface Wimmer's endeavors in America. After several initial efforts to establish a monastery, the Minnesota Benedictines in 1866 settled in the "Indianbush" ten miles north of St. Cloud, and in 1881 the names of the abbey and university were fixed under the missionary patronage of John the Baptist.

St. John's developed rapidly with steady support from surrounding Catholic immigrant families who sent their sons to the frontier school. Many of these first-generation Americans joined the original European members of the monastery (raised to the status of an abbey in 1866). The first abbot, Rupert Seidenbusch (1830–95), had been the prior of St. Vincent Abbey. He served as abbot of St. John's from Dec. 12, 1866, until his appointment as vicar apostolic of northern Minnesota on Feb. 12, 1875.

Bishop Seidenbusch's successor was Abbot Alexius Edelbrock, OSB (1843–1908), son of a pioneer St. Cloud family. During the years of St. John's second abbot's administration the institution made major educational and missionary advances in the upper Middle West, and the physical facilities at Collegeville, a name he gave to the institution, were developed on the grand scale typical of American 19th century "brick and mortar" Catholicism. For 14 years he worked at a feverish pace and with an industry that overcame most obstacles. Beginning with a religious community of 52 members, by 1889 he was directing the far-flung activities of 57 priests, ten clerics, 37 brothers, and 32 scholastics. Enrollment in the school had increased from 183 to 350. The monastery was caring for 45 missions, of which he had inaugurated 35. During the first century (1856–1956) of St. John's history, 113 parishes, 146 missions, and 102 stations were developed and served by monks of the abbey. The number of different congregations attended from St. John's totaled 361.

Later Development. Members of the St. John's community became divided over the excessive external activity of the monk missionaries. This division of opinion, together with ecclesiastical political moves under the leadership of Bp. John IRELAND of St. Paul, who directed the establishment of the Province of St. Paul, combined to bring about the resignations of both Seidenbusch and Edelbrock from their respective offices. During the last years of the 19th and early years of the 20th centuries the development of St. John's was then gradually concentrated more on internal monastic affairs under Abbot Bernard Locnikar, OSB (1848–1894), and on educational matters under Abbot Peter Engel, OSB (1856–1921), In 1891 the monks of St. John's undertook the spiritual care of the Catholics in the Bahama Islands, an apostolate that they continue to exercise to the present time (1965). New abbeys were established as St. Peter's, Muenster, Saskatchewan, Canada (1892), and St. Martin's, Olympia, Wash. (1895).

The advent in 1922 of Abbot Alcuin Deutsch, OSB (1877–1951), to the abbatial office at St. John's began a new era in the maturing of the largest Benedictine religious house in the world. The liturgical movement that had begun in Europe during the 19th century was brought to America by Virgil MICHEL, OSB (1890–1938), and developed at St. John's through the publications of the Liturgical Press, as well as *Orate Fratres* (now *Worship*) magazine, *Sponsa Regis* magazine for the sisterhoods, the *Bible Today* and the *American Benedictine Review*. During the first two quarters of the 20th century Collegeville became a national focus of publications for the liturgical apostolate in the U.S. Educational, social action, and rural life institutes were held regularly; summer institutes in Scripture, seminars on the relation of religion and mental health, and ecumenical dialogues were inaugurated. Under the direction of Marcel Breuer a centennial architectural program was begun in 1954. By 1965 seven buildings had been constructed, including the abbey and university church, consecrated in 1961.

In 1951, Abbot Baldwin Dworschak, OSB, became the sixth abbot of St. John's. He directed the spiritual and temporal activities of a Benedictine community numbering 400 members, and fostered the development of monastic foundations in Nassau, Bahamas; Tokyo, Japan; Mexico City, Mexico; and Humacao, Puerto Rico. Under his direction about 40 parishes and missions continued to be staffed by St. John's monks (1965). St. Maur's Priory, an interracial monastery in South Union, Ky., became an independent priory in 1963.

Following Vatican II, Abbot Dworschak sought to implement the recommendations of the Council by introducing the use of the vernacular into the liturgy, by making changes in the monastic formation program, by integrating the lay brothers more effectively into the community, by modifying lines of authority in the abbey, and by directing individual monks toward the acceptance of greater personal responsibility. Upon the resignation of Abbot Dworschak in 1971, the community elected Father John Eidenschink as his successor. During his eight-year term, the dependent priory in Puerto Rico became an independent abbey and renewed interest was shown in the community's apostolate in Japan.

After Abbot John completed his term in 1979, Father Jerome Theisen was elected abbot. His leadership resulted in marked growth in theological scholarship. In the School of Theology a monastic studies program was inaugurated along with a renewed commitment to the continuing education of diocesan, monastic, and lay pastoral ministers. Abbot Jerome also fostered the development of the Episcopal House of Prayer in 1989 on five acres of abbey land leased to the Episcopal Diocese of Minnesota.

When Abbot Jerome was elected Abbot Primate of the Benedictine Confederation in 1992, whereupon he took up residence at the International Sant' Anselmo Benedictine College in Rome, and the Saint John's community elected Father Timothy Kelly as its ninth abbot. He strongly promoted the East-West monastic dialogue and the education of Chinese seminarians in the School of Theology. He also addressed the problem of sexual abuse in American society by establishing the Inter-Faith Sexual Trauma Institute on campus.

Upon the completion of his eight-year term of office in November 2000, the community elected Father John Klassen on Nov. 24, 2000. He leads a community of 196 Benedictine monks who sponsor and work at Saint John's Preparatory School, Saint John's University, and The Liturgical Press, as well as in parishes, hospital chaplain-cies, and dependent priories in Nassau, Bahamas and Fujimi, Japan. Both the preparatory school and university are flourishing institutions. The latter collaborates closely with the College of Saint Benedict in Saint Joseph, Minnesota. A number of impressive buildings have recently been added to both campuses; together the institutions educate about 3,800 hundred men and women.

The Liturgical Press celebrated it 75th anniversary in April 2001. Staffed by around 60 monks and lay people, each year it publishes approximately 100 new titles on the liturgy, theology, monastic studies, and Scripture.

Bibliography: C. BARRY, O.S.B., *Worship and Work: Saint John's Abbey and University, 1856–1992* (Collegeville, Minn. 1992). V. TEGEDER, O.S.B., ''Saint John's Abbey, Collegeville, Minnesota'' and ''Saint John's University, Collegeville, Minn.,'' *The Encyclopedia of American Catholic History*, ed. M. GLAZIER and T. SHELLEY (Collegeville, Minn. 1992).

[C. BARRY/V. TEGEDER]

ST. JOSEPH, CONGREGATION OF (TURIN)

Congregatio Sancti Joseph (CSJ, Official Catholic Directory #1150); a society of priests and brothers with definitive papal approval (1904), founded in Turin, Italy, in 1873 by Bl. Leonardo MURIALDO (1828–1900). The principal mission of the congregation is the education of youth, especially the poor. Members, known also as *Giuseppini*, take St. Joseph as their model. During the founder's lifetime the congregation spread through northern Italy. Later it expanded to Libya (1904), Brazil (1915), Ecuador (1922), Argentina and Chile (1935), the U.S. (1949), and Spain (1961). In the U.S., the congregation operates schools, centers for troubled youth and parishes. Members are engaged in teaching, counseling, retreat and spiritual direction, youth ministries and parish administration. The U.S. provincialate is in San Pedro, CA. The generalate is in Rome.

Bibliography: E. REFFO, *Il fine della Pia Società di S. Giuseppe* (Pinerolo 1961). E. REFFO and G. REALE, *Cronistoria della Pia Società Torinese di S. Giuseppe dalla fondazione* (Rome 1950).

[G. MILONE/EDS.]

ST. JOSEPH (GERONA), DAUGHTERS OF

(FSJ; Official Catholic Directory #0930); or *Josefinas*, a religious congregation founded in Spain in 1875 by Francisco Butiño, SJ (1834–99), and Isabel de Maranges (1850–1922). A group of young women—

including the noble-born Isabel de Maranges—who lived together in Calella de la Costa, a town in the Barcelona province, and led a retired life of prayer and work under the spiritual direction of Father Butiño, formed the nucleus of the Servants of St. Joseph (*Siervas de San José*). Their first house opened in 1875 with the local bishop's authorization and received the privilege of a private oratory in 1876. Butiño helped form the spirit of the institute until his death, by which time the sisters had spread throughout Spain. Mother Isabel acted as superior-general until December 1912. Papal approval (*decretum laudis*) came in 1900, when the name was changed to its present one of *Congregacion de Religiosas Hijas de San José*. The papal decree approving the institute appeared in 1902, and the definitive decree approving the constitutions in 1935. In carrying out their triple ideal of promoting the glory of God, the good of souls, and devotion to St. Joseph, the sisters aid the infirm and operate schools, colleges, orphanages, hospitals, clinics, and homes for the aged. The generalate is in Madrid, Spain. The United States headquarters is in Los Angeles, California.

[E. MENDÍA/EDS.]

ST. JOSEPH, SISTERS OF

The titles Sisters of Saint Joseph (SSJ) and Congregation of Saint Joseph (CSJ) embrace numerous religious congregations of women, either of pontifical or diocesan jurisdiction, who follow the rule and adhere to the spirit of the foundation made in 1650 at Le Puy-en-Velay, France, by Jean-Pierre Médaille, SJ (1610–1669), who associated with John Francis Regis (1597–1640), a great champion of social causes, and Noël Chabanel (1613–1649), one of the North American martyrs. The first congregation was canonically erected by Bishop Henri de Maupas (1606–1680), bishop of Le Puy. Their institute executed the original plan of St. Francis de Sales (1567–1622) for the Visitation nuns. It combined apostolic works of charity in the active life with the interior spirit of contemplation.

European Origins and Development. In drawing up the Constitutions for his newly formed society, Médaille followed the Ignatian rule and ideals. He chose St. Joseph as the patron for his *Little Design*, a society of widows and young girls unable to enter the cloister, who would imitate the saint by their devotion to others as Joseph served Jesus and Mary. The original Constitutions provided a general guide for a life of perfection based on the love of God and neighbor as expressed in works appropriate for the time and place. Their model was to be Christ as hidden in the Eucharist, and they professed a special Trinitarian orientation. Médaille described their

union with God, with one another, and with "the dear neighbor" as "a total double union." Their spirituality was Ignatian, tempered by Salesian gentleness.

The first six Sisters of St. Joseph under the leadership of Françoise Eyraud cared for homeless children in the disintegrating district of Montferrand. The other five were: Claudia Chastel, Marguerite Burdier, Anna Chalayer, Anna Vey, and Anna Brun. Tradition gives the date of Oct. 15, 1650, for their reception of the habit, although at that time, they dressed in the style of widows. Their religious names are not known. On March 10, 1651, Bishop de Maupas received their vows and canonically erected them as a religious congregation through *lettres patentes*. Their early work was limited to caring for orphans and the sick, and visiting hospitals, because only one of the original members could read and write. Father Médaille called the sisters to "all the works of charity of which women are capable," and it was not long before they became teachers and opened schools.

Médaille worked as a missionary in the region of the Massif Central. He also wrote religious texts for the early sisters. *The Eucharistic Letter*, believed to predate the official foundation in 1650, cites Christ hidden in the Eucharist as a model for the early community. The *Règlements* (*Rules*), also predating 1650, seem to be addressed to small rural communities, one of which is known to have existed in Dunières in 1649. The *Maxims of Perfection*, a longer and more developed version of the *Maxims of the Little Institute*, use a literary form common in the seventeenth century to help the illiterate memorize directives for a virtuous life. In addition, thirteen manuscript forms of the *Constitutions*, five of them complete, have been preserved. The first text was printed in Vienne in 1694. These early documents formed the basis of the *Holy Rule of the Sisters of St. Joseph* until Vatican II, and have influenced the spirit of revised Constitutions since that time.

The congregation soon spread to other parts of Velay, Vivarais, Auvergne, Dauphiné, and Languedoc, all located in southeast and south central France. Each house was independent, elected its own superior, and formed its postulants and novices. If a rural house was very small, it worked in unison with a larger city house. Usually dependent on the local clergy, the sisters responded to the needs of the parish. Hospitals and schools were established with the aid of local authorities, and the sisters continued to visit the sick poor in their homes, and to work especially with women and young girls. By the time of the French Revolution in 1789, there were about 150 houses located in southern France.

Like other religious women and men, the Sisters of St. Joseph suffered greatly during the Revolution. Almost all their houses were closed, communities were forced to disband, and some members faced the guillotine. On June 17, 1794, two sisters were executed in Le Puy at the Place du Martouret: Anne-Marie Garnier and Jeanne-Marie Aubert. On Aug. 5, 1794, three sisters mounted the guillotine at Privas, in Ardèche: Sisters Sainte-Croix Vincent, Toussaint Dumoulin, and Madeleine Senovert. Mother Saint John Fontbonne, originally from Bas-en-Basset, and superior of the community of Monistrol, was imprisoned along with some other members of her group at Montfranc (St-Didier-en-Velay). Their execution was halted by the fall of Robespierre on July 27, 1794.

After the Revolution, Mother Saint John Fontbonne, along with other Sisters of St. Joseph, returned discretely to their work. In 1807, Father Claude Cholleton, Vicar General of Joseph Cardinal Fesch of Lyon, called her to direct a group of religious in Saint-Etienne, known as the "Black Daughters." She instructed them according to the Rule and spirit of Médaille, and on July 14, 1808, received them as Sisters of St. Joseph, thus restoring the Congregation. In 1816 the motherhouse was transferred from Saint-Etienne to Lyon. Mother Saint John supervised the reopening of many houses, founded others, and by the time of her death in 1843 left 240 houses and over 3,000 Sisters of St. Joseph. Unlike the pre-revolutionary structure, central motherhouses were established, usually according to diocesan boundaries. Throughout the 19th century, missionaries went to many countries. They established foundations in Denmark, Norway, Sweden, Russia, Iceland, Brazil, Argentina, India, Algeria, North America, Italy, the United Kingdom, Ireland, Switzerland, and Belgium. Twentieth-century missions include many African, South and Central American, and Asian countries.

U.S. Foundations. Around 1834, Bishop Joseph Rosati, the first bishop of St. Louis, Missouri, advertised for sisters in his enormous diocese. A wealthy woman of Lyon, Countess de la Rochejacquelin, a friend of Mother St. John Fontbonne, offered to pay all the expenses for the sisters who would go to America. Six, among them Sisters Fébronie and Delphine, both of whom were nieces of Mother St. John Fontbonne, arrived in St. Louis on March 25, 1836. Two others, trained in education of the deaf and dumb, Sisters Celestine Pommerel and St. John Fournier, arrived shortly after. Their first missions were in Carondelet and Cahokia, near St. Louis. Education was the principal work of the first sisters in the U.S., although health care and social work were also important. New houses, primarily with American recruits, developed quickly in the St. Louis diocese, under the leadership of Mother Celestine Pommerel.

Most of the American foundations stem from Lyon through St. Louis (Carondelet). Because of distance and other factors, each of them remained independent, with the exception of the four provinces of the Carondelet congregation. Mother St. John Fournier founded the Philadelphia group in 1847, which in turn sent sisters to Brentwood NY (1856) and Toronto, Ontario (1851). The five other Anglophone Canadian foundations developed from Toronto. Francophone Sisters of St. Joseph came to Québec from Saint-Vallier in 1903. From Brentwood sisters went to Rutland, VT, and Boston, MA (1873), to Baden, PA (1869) and Springfield, MA (1883). Other foundations directly from Carondelet include Wheeling, WV (1853), Rochester and Buffalo, NY (1854), Watertown, NY (1880), Erie, PA (1860), and Cleveland, OH (1872). These motherhouses in turn founded other congregations: Tipton, IN (1888), Columbus, OH (1966), Nazareth, MI (1889), Concordia, KS (1883), Wichita, KS (1888), La Grange, IL (1899), Superior, WI (1907), and Orange, CA (1912).

Two foundations stem directly from Le Puy: St. Augustine, FL (1866) independent since 1899, and Fall River, MA (1902), which merged with Springfield, MA, in 1974. The Sisters of West Hartford CT, came from Chambéry in 1812, and are still united with the French motherhouse. The three foundations from Bourg: New Orleans, LA (1855), Cincinnati, OH (1962), and Crookston, MN (1905) merged in 1977 to form the Médaille Congregation. The Sisters of Winslow, ME (1906) remain attached directly to the Lyon motherhouse.

In the nineteenth and early twentieth centuries, education and health care were the primary works of all Sisters of St. Joseph. They established hospitals, academies, elementary and high schools, and many opened colleges for women. The sisters participated actively in parochial schools. Since Vatican II, the work of the Sisters of St. Joseph has become much more diversified, in keeping with the spirit of the founder, the mandates of the Church, and a greater awareness of social justice. Twelve colleges sponsored by the Sisters of St. Joseph have formed a consortium permitting a student registered in any one to attend any other for the same fees. Many congregations have missions in the third world, often staffed by Sisters of St. Joseph from various provincial houses.

Federation of the Sisters of St. Joseph. Like religious of other congregations, following Vatican II, and the call of *Perfectae Caritatis*, the Sisters of St. Joseph began a search for their roots and a revitalization of their identity. This has led them to develop the Federation, a collaborative movement among congregations claiming the same founder and spirit. The French Sisters of St. Joseph moved in this direction as early as 1951, and in 1971 officially formed a Federation of thirteen congregations. Mergers and other unions have reduced the number to seven. The American Federation was officially formed in 1966 with the membership of twenty-three congregations. Among the activities in which they have participated are: the writing of the *Core Constitutions*, National Events, summer Institutes, Intercongregational Novitiate, programs, workshops, and publications. While maintaining their traditional autonomy, congregations in the Federation work together to achieve common goals. In 1974, the members clarified the Federation as "a dynamic union of Sisters of St. Joseph, which moves us to a greater consciousness of our kinship of grace and calls us to fidelity to that grace." Other Federations of Sisters of St. Joseph are the Italian (1966), Canadian (1966), and Argentinian (1971). By the end of the 20th century, the Sisters of St. Joseph numbered about 16,000 worldwide. About one-half of this number were in North America. They were one of the largest religious congregations in the world.

The motherhouses of the Sisters of St. Joseph (SSJ, or CSJ) in the United States and members of the American Federation are: CSJ of Boston, MA, [Cath Dir 3830–01]; CSJ of La Grange, IL [3830–02]; CSJ of Orange, CA [3830–03]; CSJ of Brentwood, NY [3830–05]; SSJ of Buffalo, NY [3830–06]; CSJ of Cleveland, OH [3830–08]; SSJ of Erie [3830–09]; CSJ of Tipton, IN [3830–10]; SSJ of Nazareth, MI [3830–11]; SSJ of Watertown, NY [3830–12]; CSJ of Baden, PA [3830–13]; SSJ of Rochester, NY [3830–14]; CSJ of Concordia, KS [3830–15]; SSJ of Springfield, MA (with whom Rutland VT merged in 2001) [3830–16]; SSJ of Wheeling, WV [3830–17]; CSJ of Wichita, KS [3830–18]; CSJ of Carondelet, MO [3840], with provinces of St. Louis, MO, St. Paul, MN (with whom Superior WI merged in 1985), Albany, NY, Los Angeles, CA, and Vice-Province of Hawaii; Provincial House of Chambéry, France: CSJ of West Hartford, CT [3850]; Provincial House of Lyon, France: CSJ of Winslow, ME [3870]; CSJ of Medaille (Cincinnati, OH) [3880]; SSJ of Chestnut Hill, Philadelphia, PA [3893]; and SSJ of St. Augustine, FL [3900].

Bibliography: Archives of the American Federation of the Sisters of St. Joseph. C. A. BOIS, *Les Sœurs de Saint-Joseph, Filles du Petit Dessin* (Lyon 1950). C. COBURN, and M. SMITH, *Spirited Lives* (Chapel Hill, NC 1999). F. GOUIT, *Les Sœurs de Saint-Joseph du Puy-en-Velay, 1648–1915* (Le Puy 1930). M. E. KRAFT, and Sisters of St. Joseph, *Eyes Open on a World* (St. Cloud 2001). SISTER M. K. LOGUE, *Sisters of St. Joseph of Philadelphia* (Westminster, MD 1950–). M. NEPPER, *Aux origines des Filles de Saint-Joseph* (Sarl Solaro, 1969). SISTER M. L. LUCIDA, *The Congregation of Saint Joseph of Carondelet* (St. Louis 1923). Sœurs de Saint-Joseph, Fédération Française. *Par-delà toutes frontières* (Strasbourg 1998). Sœurs de Saint Joseph. *Textes primitifs* (Clermont-Ferrand 1981). M. VACHER, SSJ, *Des régulières dans le siècle* (Clermont-Ferrand 1991).

[M. H. KASHUBA]

ST. JOSEPH OF PEACE, SISTERS OF

This pontifical congregation (CSJP; Official Catholic Directory #3890) originated from the order of Poor Clares (now Sisters of St. Clare) and was founded by Sr. Mary Francis Clare (Margaret Anna Cusack), also known as Mother Clare or the Nun of Kenmare. In December 1883, after an unsuccessful attempt to found a convent of her order at Knock, Co. Mayo, Ireland, Mother Clare was welcomed into the diocese of Nottingham, England by its bishop, Edward G. Bagshawe, who encouraged the foundation of a new congregation. Bishop Bagshawe approved the Rule and Constitutions of the institute which was then variously known as Sisters of Peace, Sisters of St. Joseph of Peace, and St. Joseph Sisters of Peace of the Immaculate Conception. The first house of the new congregation was opened in Grimsby, in the diocese of Nottingham, January 1884.

This congregation had its origin in the Founder's response to the social concerns and needs of the time. Attracted by this commitment, Honoria Gaffney, later named Mother Evangelista, together with a few other women, joined the community. From the beginning the Sisters were involved in ministries of social service, education and health care; they worked directly with the poor and sick in their own homes, provided housing and care for women, orphans, blind children and adults, and as need arose, established schools and hospitals.

After Margaret Anna Cusack left the congregation in 1888, Mother Evangelista Gaffney was elected Mother General. The Congregation received a Decree of Praise as a pontifical religious institute in 1895 and its constitutions were approved in 1929 for seven years. In that year also the name of the congregation was changed to Sisters of St. Joseph of Newark because its principal house was then in the diocese of Newark, New Jersey. On June 16, 1936, the Constitutions of the Sisters of St. Joseph of Newark were granted definitive approval. In the process of renewal called for by Vatican Council II, the congregation returned to its original title "of Peace." A renewed constitution was approved by Rome on March 19, 1994. This constitution also welcomed women and men who lived their spirit and mission as associates of the congregation.

The Congregation comprises three provinces: Sacred Heart Province (England, Scotland, and Ireland), St. Joseph Province (Eastern U.S.) and Our Lady Province (Western U.S.). The Congregation Office is located in Washington, D.C. Each province sponsored a variety of ministries in accordance with the needs of the locale and the charism and mission of the congregation.

[C. O'CONNOR]

SAINT-JOUIN-DE-MARNES, ABBEY OF

Former Benedictine monastery in the Diocese of Poitiers, west central France. *S. Jovinus Ansionense* or *Enixionse,* as the abbey was called before the 10th century, was founded by St. Jouin (Jovinus) in the late 4th century; at the time of its suppression in 1790, it was one of the oldest monasteries in France. After 9th-century Viking raids it prospered from the 10th to the 12th century with many donations from the nobles of Poitou and Anjou; in 1179 there were 130 benefices. The destruction of the Hundred Years' War ushered in a decline that the MAURIST reform checked briefly in 1655. The 12th-century abbey church, known for its façade and capitals, is one of the best examples of Romanesque art in west France.

Bibliography: Sources. L. H. COTTINEAU, *Répertoire topo-bibliographique des abbayes et prieurés,* 2 v. (Mâcon 1935–39) 2:2747–48. C. L. DE GRANDMAISON, ed., *Chartularium sancti Jovini* (Niort 1854). Literature. B. LEDAIN, *Notice historique et archéologique sur l'abbaye de Saint-Jouin-de-Marnes* (Poitiers 1884). A. LEROSEY, "L'Abbaye d'Ension ou de Saint-Jouin-de-Marnes," *Mémoires de la société historique et scientifique des Deux-Sèvres* 11 (1915) 3–195; 13 (1917–18) 197–517.

[G. T. BEECH]

SAINT-JURE, JEAN BAPTISTE

Jesuit spiritual director and writer; b. Metz, France, Feb. 19, 1588; d. Paris, April 30, 1657. Saint-Jure entered the Society of Jesus on Sept. 4, 1604, and taught grammar and philosophy for a time. In 1645 and 1646 he was spiritual director at the College of Clermont. He served as rector of Amiens, Alençon, and Orleans and later was in charge of the professed house at Paris. He spent some time in England during the reign of Charles I. Many mystics came to him throughout his life for spiritual direction—among them the Baron of Renty and Mother Jeanne of the Angels. He also acted as spiritual director for the cloistered Dominican nuns of Paris, an exceptional position for a Jesuit. The superior of the convent, Mother Elizabeth of the Child Jesus, wrote in glowing terms of his inspirational guidance in bringing her Dominicans safely through the storm of Jansenism.

Saint–Jure had immediate success as a writer and exercised a profound influence upon the Christian piety of 17th-century France. His book on the life of the Baron of Renty went through seven editions by 1654, three years after its initial publication. His other published works include a treatise on the knowledge and love of Jesus (1634); meditations on the important truths of the faith, and on the purgative, illuminative, and unitive ways to perfection (1637); a treatise on the means for the main actions of the Christian life (1644); considerations on the crucified Savior (1643); a treatise in two volumes on the spiritual life (1646); meditations on the principal mysteries of Christ's life, also in two volumes (1653); a consideration of Christ's instructions to men (1649); a treatise on faith, hope, and charity (1646); and a treatise on the vows of religious life and the qualities necessary for living the community life of a religious (1658).

Bibliography: H. BRÉMOND, *Histoire littéraire du sentiment réligieux en France depuis la fin des fuerres de religion jusqu'à nos jours* (Paris 1911–36) 3:258–279. M. M. DE MAUROY, *La Vie de la vénérable mère Élizabeth de l'Enfant Jésus* (Paris 1680). C. SOMMERVOGEL et al., *Bibliothéque de la Compagnie de Jésus* (Brussels–Paris 1890–1932) 7:416–429.

[P. K. CLARK]

SAINT LAUMER OF BLOIS, ABBEY OF

In Blois, central France. Benedictines from the monastery of Corbion, founded near Chartres *c.* 575 by St. Laumer (d. *c.* 590), fled with the relics of their founder to Blois at the time of the Norman invasions (*c.* 874). Under the castle of Count Thibault in 924 they built the new Abbey of St. Laumer, which flourished in the Middle Ages. Commendatory in the early 16th century and pillaged by HUGUENOTS in 1568, the abbey joined the MAURISTS in 1627 and revived. In 1697, however, Louis XIV gave the abbot's monastic revenue (some 8,000 livres) to the new Diocese of Blois; and benefices for the cathedral chapter were carved out of other abbatial properties. The abbey was greatly reduced in membership and wealth when it was suppressed by the French Revolution in 1791. The 13th-century Romanesque church, with noteworthy sculpture, was modified several times since and became a parish church; other buildings served as a hospital.

Bibliography: U. CHEVALIER, *Répertoire des sources historiques du moyen–âge. Topobiobibliographie,* 2 v. (Paris 1894–1903) 2:2720. L. H. COTTINEAU, *Répertoire topobibliographique des abbayes et prieurés,* 2 v. (Mâcon 1935–39) 1:397–398, 871. M. VINET, *Le Royal monastère bénédictin de Saint-Laumer de Blois* (La Roche-sur-Yon 1960).

[L. J. LEKAI]

SAINT-LÉONARD-LE-NOBLAT, MONASTERY OF

An abbey founded near Limoges, France, in the forest of Pauvain, by St. LEONARD of Noblat in the 6th century. Its origins are legendary, going back possibly to the days of King CLOVIS or his immediate successors, who granted Leonard a piece of land in gratitude for his intercession. The house later developed into a collegiate church in the commune of Saint-Léonard-le-Noblat. The lower parts of the structure, the nave, apsidal chapels, and the base of the tower are in Romanesque style, dating from the 11th century. The west portal is of the 13th century. The interior décor includes carved choir stalls from the 15th century and an alabaster bas-relief in the chapel of St. Joseph, which possibly antedates that period. The church became famous as a pilgrimage spot honoring the saint whose name it bears.

Bibliography: L. H. COTTINEAU, *Répertoire topobibliographique des abbayes et prieurés*, 2 v. (Mâcon 1935–39) 2:2764–65. L. RÉAU, *Iconographie de l'art chrétien*, 6 v. (Paris 1955–59) 3.2:799–802. *Acta Sanctorum* Nov. 3:139–209. A. M. ZIMMERMANN, *Lexikon für Theologie und Kirche*, ed. J. HOFER and K. RAHNER, 10 v. (2d, new ed. Freiburg 1957–65) 6:965–966.

[O. J. BLUM]

SAINT-LÔ, MONASTERY OF

Former abbey of CANONS REGULAR OF ST. AUGUSTINE, in Saint-Lô, Manche, France, in the diocese of Coutances. A college of canons had existed on this site in Normandy in the 9th century; the religious foundation was resurrected by Bishop Hugh in 990, as part of the process of reviving the diocese. Hugh transferred some canons there from the priory of Saint-Lô at Rouen. Then in 1132 Bishop Algar brought the Augustinian canons from Sainte-Barbe-en-Auge and provided an ample endowment. The canons served several churches in the town of Saint-Lô and in the rest of the diocese. Two abbots of the 16th century were coadjutor bishops. In the 17th century stricter discipline was reintroduced by an uncle and nephew, both called André Merlet, who introduced canons from the Congregation of SAINTE-GENEVIÈVE in 1659. In 1790 the canons were dispersed, and the abbey church, dedicated in 1202, was destroyed.

Bibliography: R. TOUSTAIN DE BILLY, *Histoire ecclésiastique du diocèse de Coutances*, ed. F. DOLBET and A. HÉRON, 3 v. (Rouen 1874–86). *Gallia Christiana*, v.1–13 (Paris 1715–85), v.14–16 (Paris 1856–65) 11:935–940. L. H. COTTINEAU, *Répertoire topobibliographique des abbayes et prieurés*, 2 v. (Mâcon 1935–39) 2:2768–69.

[D. J. A. MATTHEW]

ST. LOUIS, ARCHDIOCESE OF

Metropolitan see, comprising 5,968 square miles in the east central part of Missouri. The diocese (*S. Ludovici*) was established July 14, 1826; the archdiocese, July 20, 1847. The suffragan sees include the dioceses of Jefferson City, Kansas City-St. Joseph, and Springfield-Cape Girardeau, all in Missouri. In 2001 the archdiocese numbered 555,000 Catholics in a total population of 2,064,548.

Early History. The Missouri bank of the Mississippi River was probably first seen by Catholics in 1683. Forming the eastern boundary of the Archdiocese of St. Louis, as it did of the diocese when erected in 1826, this perimeter of the present state was passed by Jacques MARQUETTE and Louis Joliet on the Frenchmen's voyage of discovery. More than a century before, Coronado's expedition had penetrated into the territory originally in the diocese. The Spaniards made no permanent settlement there; one of their number, the Franciscan Juan de PADILLA, later became the protomartyr of the U.S. French fur traders, and settlers along the Mississippi were accompanied by missionaries whose evangelization of the Native Americans followed a sequence that proved to be a pattern before and after the erection of the diocese. Initial gratifying success gradually gave way to discouraging disappointment as the Native Americans fell victim to the diseases of the Europeans or the more devastating plague of hard liquor. Rich deposits of lead in the state attracted also miners, and Jesuits from across the river at Kaskaskia probably attended to their spiritual needs from the very beginning, although the first sacramental record extant is for 1749. However, with the suppression of the Society of Jesus in 1763, the area was left with only a few Franciscans.

That same year Pierre Laclède Liguest, partner in a New Orleans, La., trading firm, selected a site for a trading post near the confluence of the Missouri and Mississippi Rivers. The following Feb. 15, 1764, young Auguste Chouteau made the actual foundation, which Laclède named St. Louis after the patron of the reigning French monarch. The first baptism recorded in St. Louis was in 1766 by Sébastian MEURIN, a former Jesuit who was then the only priest in the area. Two years later assistance came in the person of the newly ordained Pierre GIBAULT, who blessed a log cabin as the first church in St. Louis in 1770. The Capuchin Bernard de Limpach became the first resident pastor of St. Louis in 1776 and remained until 1789. A month before his arrival a palisaded church replaced the log cabin, and the following year a stone rectory was completed. After the transfer of Friar Bernard, settlements on both sides of the river in upper Louisiana were dependent upon itinerant members of religious orders. Gibault, who had moved to the Spanish or Missouri side of the river, was joined in 1796 by a Spanish-trained Irish priest, James Maxwell. Maxwell was assigned to Ste. Genevieve by the first bishop of Louisiana and the Floridas, Luis PEÑALVER Y CÁRDENAS. However, when the United States acquired the Louisiana Territory, Peñalver was sent to Guatemala and not replaced. With the hoisting of the stars and stripes in St. Louis in 1804, an influx of Americans served to weaken and then to replace the French predominance. Among the newcomers in that year were Irish-born John Mullanphy and his family, whose wealth (he became Missouri's first millionaire) and strong religious influence benefited the Church.

Diocese. Shortly after the outbreak of the War of 1812, Abp. John Carroll of Baltimore, Md., dispatched the Sulpician Louis William Valentin DUBOURG to the Louisiana Territory as administrator. Dubourg, finding there only a few priests, and some of them reluctant to acknowledge his authority, left for Rome in 1815, determined either to secure assistance or to resign from the administration of the diocese. Plus VII's response was to name Dubourg bishop of Louisiana and to assign the Congregation of the Mission (Vincentians) to help him.

Dubourg (1815–26). While in France, Dubourg encouraged the foundation of the Society for the PROPAGATION OF THE FAITH, and was promised nuns of the Society of the Sacred Heart for his frontier diocese. After returning to Baltimore in September 1817, he journeyed over the mountains to Bardstown, Ky., where his first European recruits awaited him. On Jan. 5, 1818, accompanied by Benedict Joseph FLAGET, the first bishop of that Kentucky see, Dubourg entered St. Louis. In the first year he supervised a number of enterprises. South of St. Louis, at the Barrens, a seminary was founded under the direction of Rev. Joseph ROSATI, who with his fellow Italian Vincentian, Felix de Andreis, had volunteered for the U.S. mission. A brick cathedral was started in St. Louis. Five religious of the Sacred Heart, led by Philippine DUCHESNE, opened the first Catholic girls' school in Missouri at St. Charles. Dubourg started St. Louis Academy for boys, which later developed into ST. LOUIS UNIVERSITY. Although episcopal help was needed for a diocese covering half a continent, Dubourg's own indecision delayed the appointment of a coadjutor. Finally, however, Rosati was named coadjutor to Dubourg, and consecrated by him March 25, 1824. But two years later, discouraged by the opposition to him that persisted in New Orleans, Dubourg left for Europe, where he resigned from the Diocese of Louisiana and later, in 1826, was appointed ordinary of Montauban, France.

Rosati (1827–43). When the Diocese of Louisiana was divided in 1826, Rosati was reluctant to assume responsibility for the See of New Orleans because of his greater familiarity with the northern part of the territory. In 1827, therefore, he was named first bishop of the Diocese of St. Louis, although he continued to administer New Orleans for a time. His jurisdiction extended from the southern boundary of Arkansas to the Great Lakes, and from the Mississippi River to the Rocky Mountains. Moreover, the diocese became even larger before it began to contract, for in 1834 approximately half of the state of Illinois was annexed to St. Louis and remained part of it until Chicago was erected as a diocese ten years later. Under Rosati, a hospital was founded in St. Louis in 1828 by the Sisters of Charity from Emmitsburg, Md.; the hospital was the recipient of liberal benefactions from John Mullanphy, and later from his daughter Ann Biddle. Dubourg's cathedral had never been completed—primarily because of the lack of funds—so another was started in 1831 and formally dedicated Oct. 26, 1834.

Although conversion of the Native American populations had been almost universally the intention of the early missionaries, only sporadic attempts had been possible because of shortage of personnel. In 1840 Rosati authorized the Jesuit Pierre Jean DE SMET to embark on the mission that eventually made him one of the most famous of missionaries. In 1841 Rosati, while visiting Philadelphia, Pa., consecrated Peter Richard KENRICK his coadjutor; Kenrick succeeded to the see following Rosati's death in Rome, Sept. 25, 1843.

Kenrick (1843–95). Almost immediately after his consecration, Kenrick set out for Missouri, arriving Dec. 28, 1841, in St. Louis, his residence for the next 55 years. The two principal problems confronting the second ordinary involved finances and nationalities. The accumulated debt was surmounted by Kenrick's energetic methods, help from Europe, and successful appeals to the wealthy. Dissension between Irish and German immigrants was quieted if not silenced, as Kenrick directed the Americanization of the many Catholics of diverse nationalities that immigration had brought to his diocese, even acting as banker for many of the newcomers, to their profit and the benefit of the Church.

Archdiocese. When St. Louis was elevated to an archbishopric on July 20, 1847, Kenrick became its first archbishop. Three years later the extent of his jurisdiction was contracted to the state of Missouri. Before his death in 1896, some 16 new sees had been erected out of the original Diocese of St. Louis. Kenrick's long episcopate was beset by many hardships, including a disastrous fire on the riverfront and a severe cholera epidemic late in the 1840s. During the Civil War, Kenrick, although sympathetic to the South, prudently refrained from direct comment. When radical Republicans in control of the state after the war sought to impose a censorship on all clergymen, the archbishop quietly but adamantly refused to conform. Several priests were arrested for failing to take the so-called test oath of the Drake constitution. Although rebuffed in the local and state supreme tribunals, Kenrick carried the case to the U.S. Supreme Court, where the constitution was declared null and void.

In 1866, the archbishop took a prominent part in the Second Plenary Council of Baltimore. At Vatican Council I (1869–70), he opposed the definition of papal infallibility, publishing his views in his famous *Concio*. Once the council had been prorogued, Kenrick returned to St. Louis and gave his acceptance of the doctrine of infallibility. Thereafter the archbishop went into virtual seclusion, refraining from public appearances and sermons, while his coadjutor John Patrick Ryan handled the external affairs of the archdiocese for more than a decade until he was named archbishop of Philadelphia in 1884. Despite his age Kenrick then resumed all the episcopal functions of the archdiocese, and in 1891 was honored as the first to complete 50 years as a bishop in the United States. After his jubilee, however, he declined rapidly and in 1893, Bp. John Joseph Kain of Wheeling, W. Va., was named his coadjutor. In December of the same year Kain became administrator of the archdiocese and succeeded to the see when Kenrick died on March 4, 1896.

Kain (1895–1903). Although Kain's tenure was the briefest thus far for the archdiocese, a major accomplishment of his administration was the reactivation of the archdiocesan seminary. Called Kenrick Seminary, it was entrusted to the priests of the Congregation of the Mission, who continued to direct it in its several locations. Kain also selected the site for a new cathedral, established the parish, and began the collection of funds. Recognizing that his health was failing, he requested a coadjutor, and on April 27, 1903, John Joseph GLENNON, whom he had consecrated coadjutor of Kansas City, Mo., in 1896, was appointed. Soon after Glennon's arrival in St. Louis, the archbishop departed for Baltimore, where he died Oct. 13, 1903.

Glennon (1903–46). Glennon's first major project was the erection of the new cathedral. In 1908 the cornerstone was laid by Diomede Falconio, then apostolic delegate to the United States. Six years later the first Mass was offered in the edifice, which was finally completed in 1926 and consecrated at a ceremony attended by four cardinals and most of the bishops and archbishops of the United States. Under Glennon's direction two Catholic colleges for women were added to the archdiocese's educational system, and quality teaching was ensured by the archbishop's insistence on full academic training for the sisters conducting them. St. Louis University, a comparatively small institution at the beginning of the twentieth century, developed and expanded under his episcopal encouragement. The parochial school system was strengthened and diocesan high schools, inaugurated before

World War I, were increased in number, five new ones being provided in 1944. During World Wars I and II many priests of the archdiocese entered service as chaplains. The archbishop himself was a founder of the National Catholic War Council, predecessor of the National Catholic Welfare Conference.

During the pioneer era help from Europe had come to the Diocese of St. Louis from European organizations designed to assist foreign missions of that time. Inspired by Dubourg, the Society for the Propagation of the Faith from its foundation in 1822 manifested a lively interest in this diocese. In 1926 a reversal of contributions commenced from the Archdiocese of St. Louis, and under the active encouragement of the respective ordinaries, the donations steadily increased. Reports for 1960 listed St. Louis as first in the nation in per capita contributions, outranked only by the more populous centers of Brooklyn, N.Y., and Chicago, Ill., in the aggregate amount given. Early in Glennon's regime two priests were trained at The Catholic University of America, Washington, D.C., to form a preachers' institute, which did excellent work in and outside the diocese. During the first quarter of the twentieth century, new national groups were constantly added to the mixture of peoples in the Church, and Glennon was successful in directing their assimilation. To give the German-speaking Catholics a voice unimpeded by language barriers, Kenrick provided a separate vicar-general for them, but under Glennon the two offices again became one without protest.

Glennon carried out all episcopal functions by himself until 1933, when he consecrated Christian H. Winkelmann first auxiliary bishop of the archdiocese. Upon Winkelmann's transfer to Wichita, Kans., in 1940, Glennon consecrated his last bishop and his second auxiliary in the person of George J. Donnelly. In 1946, shortly after he had received the cardinalitial honor, Glennon died in the presidential palace of Eire; his remains were interred in a crypt in the Cathedral of St. Louis, beside those of the first bishop of St. Louis, Joseph Rosati.

Ritter (1946–67). On July 20, 1946, the Holy See announced the choice of Joseph E. RITTER, first archbishop of Indianapolis, Ind., as St. Louis's fourth archbishop. Ritter had been ordained in 1917; consecrated March 28, 1933; and had served as auxiliary and then ordinary of Indianapolis, until his transfer to St. Louis. Under him, diocesan synods were held regularly at the intervals prescribed by Canon Law. St. Louis, already blessed with a high percentage of priests for its Catholic population, experienced an increase in vocations under the new ordinary, and a third seminary was added to the two constructed during the previous episcopacy. Not long after his arrival, Ritter announced that the archdiocesan schools would be fully integrated. Although this was some years before segregation was discontinued in the public schools, opposition was comparatively minor. As the proportion of African Americans in the total population increased, expanded efforts were made to care for the Catholics among them and to attract others to the Church.

In 1956 the archdiocesan boundaries were again adjusted, leaving only the ten counties surrounding the city of St. Louis within the archdiocese's territory. At the same time, the diocesan boundaries were completely realigned, with the third suffragan see of Jefferson City added in the state of Missouri. The same year Pius XII named Ritter assistant at the pontifical throne, and St. Louis became the first U.S. archdiocese to undertake a mission in another country when the archbishop dispatched three volunteer priests to the Archdiocese of La Paz in Bolivia. Although the priests remained incardinated in the Archdiocese of St. Louis, which supplied financial support for them and their mission, their work was subject to the local ordinary. Additions were made periodically to the clerical personnel, with consequent amplification of operations. Since the first hospital west of the Mississippi River was a Catholic institution in St. Louis, it is not surprising that the Church's interest in the sick was expanded. An excellent medical school developed at St. Louis University; and Catholic hospitals continually increased their bed capacity, even in the decade after the mid-century when there was a general decline elsewhere in this respect.

After Ritter's advent, there was an average of one new high school constructed each year, as well as an increase of four new parishes annually after 1950. Most of these achievements were facets of the increased participation by the laity in the operation of the archdiocese, mainly through the archdiocesan Councils of Catholic Men and Catholic Women. Each spring laymen directed and conducted a campaign for capital and operational funds beyond those of the individual parish units. Each fall the lay people invited their non-Catholic friends to learn the truth about the Catholic Church through information forums and other means. When, on Jan. 16, 1961, Ritter was elevated to the College of Cardinals, non-Catholics joined enthusiastically in celebrating the event.

Carberry (1968-79). Paul VI named John Joseph Carberry, bishop of Columbus, as archbishop of St. Louis on Feb. 17, 1968. Born in Brooklyn, N.Y., Carberry was ordained to the priesthood in 1929 and served as bishop of Lafayette in Indiana from 1957 to 1965, in which capacity he attended the Second Vatican Council. He was created cardinal in 1969, and participated in both conclaves of 1978. Carberry continued the high school and parish expansion programs begun by Ritter. After the Su-

preme Court's rulings on abortion in 1973, Carberry established an archdiocesan pro-life committee, the first such in the United States. He was influential in the founding of several organizations concerned with the state of the Church in the United States after the council, including the Institute on Religious Life and the Fellowship of Catholic Scholars. He retired in 1979, at the age of 75, and died on June 17, 1998.

May (1980-92). John L. May, bishop of Mobile since 1969, was appointed archbishop of St. Louis on Jan. 24, 1980. He was born in Evanston, Illinois, on Mar. 31, 1922. He was ordained to the priesthood on May 3, 1947, and appointed auxiliary bishop of Chicago in 1967. Like Carberry, he gained a reputation as a national leader, and served from 1986 to 1989 as president of the National Conference of Catholic Bishops. As archbishop, he advocated the restoration of an archdiocesan pastoral council and the formation of deanery and parish councils. He also called for expansions in the ministries of Catholic Charities and the pro-life office. In 1987, the undergraduate program of Cardinal Glennon College was combined with Kenrick Seminary to form Kenrick-Glennon Seminary. May resigned in 1992 and died two years later.

Rigali (1994–). Justin Francis Rigali, a native of Los Angeles, was appointed archbishop on Jan. 25, 1994. Ordained a priest in 1961 and consecrated a bishop in 1985, he served in a number of positions in the Roman Curia from 1985 till his appointment to St. Louis. From the beginning of his tenure Rigali emphasized the need for youth ministry, making major changes to the programs available in the archdiocese. Part of this effort was a campaign for the relocation and construction of Cardinal Ritter College Prep High School, a move meant to serve the needs of the inner-city African-American community. In 1999, Pope John Paul II visited St. Louis after issuing his post-synodal apostolic exhortation *Ecclesia in America* in Mexico City, the only time the pontiff visited a single U.S. city in his travels. While in St. Louis, the pope asked the governor of Missouri for clemency for a convicted murderer who was scheduled to be executed a few weeks later. The governor granted the pope's request. The event sparked a renewed attention on the part of Catholics in the archdiocese and throughout the U.S. to the pope's reiterated appeals for an end to the death penalty.

Bibliography: Archives, Archdiocese of St. Louis. Archives, University of Notre Dame. R. BAUDIER, *The Catholic Church in Louisiana* (New Orleans 1939). R. BAYARD, *Lone-Star Vanguard: The Catholic Reoccupation of Texas, 1838–1848* (St. Louis 1945). G. J. GARRAGHAN, *Catholic Beginnings in Kansas City, Missouri* (Chicago 1920). J. E. ROTHENSTEINER, *History of the Archdiocese of St. Louis*, 2 v. (St. Louis 1928). P. C. SCHULTE, *The Catholic Heritage of Saint Louis: A History of the Old Cathedral Parish* (St. Louis 1934). F. G. WALKER, *The Catholic Church in the Meeting of Two Frontiers: The Southern Illinois Country, 1763–1793* (Catholic University of America Studies in American Church History 19; Washington 1935).

[P. J. RAHILL/EDS.]

ST. LOUIS, SISTERS OF

A congregation of teaching religious (SSL, Official Catholic Directory #3935) with papal approbation. They were originally founded in 1842 at Juilly, France, by the priest-philosopher Louis BAUTAIN, but did not prosper under his direction. The subsequent development of the congregation centered around the motherhouse founded in Ireland in 1859. In that year Mother Genevieve Beale established a convent of the Sisters of St. Louis in Louisville, Monaghan, under the auspices of the bishop of Clogher. Nearly a century later, in 1949, the community came to the U.S. and established itself in California. The generalate is in Louisville, Monaghan, Ireland; the U.S. headquarters is in Woodland Hills, CA. In the U.S., the sisters are engaged in education, pastoral ministries, and social outreach.

[M. B. EATON/EDS.]

ST. LOUIS UNIVERSITY

Founded in 1818, a coeducational institution in midtown St. Louis, Mo. operated by the Society of Jesus (*see* JESUITS), the first university west of the Mississippi River and the second oldest Jesuit university in the United States.

History. The university's beginnings date from 1818, three years before Missouri became a state, and when St. Louis was a pioneer settlement of some 3,000 people. At this time Louis William DUBOURG, Bishop of Louisiana, opened St. Louis Academy under the direction of the Rev. Francis Niel and three other diocesan priests on the St. Louis Cathedral staff.

The academy began with French-speaking classes in a one-story stone house, which later became St. Louis College. It held its first classes in the fall of 1820 in a new two-story brick building beside the cathedral. The growing school soon overtaxed the secular clergy's limited time for ministerial duties, and steps were taken to transfer the administration to the Society of Jesus.

In 1823 at the suggestion of John C. Calhoun, Secretary of War, DuBourg offered the society a farm near Florissant, Mo., for a school for Native Americans, and additional property in the city for the building of a college. Although unable to furnish a college faculty, the Maryland provincial authorized a band of two Belgian Jesuits, seven scholastics, and three lay brothers to set out for Missouri in April 1823.

The group, under the leadership of Charles Felix VAN QUICKENBORNE, included Peter J. VERHAEGEN, who later became the first president of Saint Louis University, and Pierre Jean DE SMET, the first treasurer of the university. They arrived in late spring at the farm 17 miles northwest of St. Louis, and there opened their school for native boys the following year. While negotiations continued for the society's adoption of St. Louis College, a teacher shortage forced the institution to suspend operations at the end of the 1826–27 session. For want of better schools, prominent St. Louis families enrolled their sons in the Jesuits' "Indian seminary" at Florissant. Among these students was Charles Pierre Chouteau, great grandson of Pierre Laclède, the founder of St. Louis. When the Jesuits agreed to staff the college, ground was broken in the autumn of 1828 for a three-story building on a city lot donated for a Catholic college. During construction, classes were conducted at Florissant. On Nov. 2, 1829, the college was formally reopened in St. Louis. Within a few weeks enrollment numbered 150 students. On Dec. 28, 1832, the institution became St. Louis University when Gov. Daniel Dunklin signed the charter granted by the general assembly of Missouri. That year also marked the founding of the graduate school. Degrees were first conferred by the university at commencement ceremonies two years later.

Shortly after the opening of the school of divinity in 1834, Verhaegen and a committee from the St. Louis Medical Society discussed the establishment of a medical school at the university. A medical faculty was appointed in 1836 and classes were started in 1842. Among the first professors were Daniel Brainard, later founder of Rush Medical College, Chicago; Moses L. Linton, founder of the nation's first medical monthly publication, the *St. Louis Medical and Surgical Journal;* and Dr. Charles Alexander Pope, later president of the American Medical Association. Although the medical school's reputation brought in students from cities throughout the West, the Know-Nothing movement in 1854 posed a threat to the school (*see* KNOW-NOTHINGISM). University authorities and the medical school faculty agreed in 1855 to sever their connection as a matter of prudence. In addition to Know-Nothing persecution, the university suffered through war and pestilence during its first 50 years. Among the crises it weathered was the city's raging cholera epidemic of 1849, which left the student body and faculty unharmed. The student sodality subsequently placed a silver crown on a statue of the Virgin as they had vowed to do if protected from the plague.

Problems created by the Civil War included the state and Federal draft laws, from which all the Jesuits were exempted, and the Drake Constitution of 1865, which required a "no-Southern sympathies" oath of clergymen and teachers, and a heavy tax on schools. The Supreme Court declared the oath null and void in 1867 and the city remitted the tax, which had amounted to an annual $10,000 for the university. In 1888 the University moved to its present midtown site, which had been purchased in 1867.

A hundred years later, in 1967, the university moved toward adopting and implementing a lay board of trustees, the first Catholic institution to do so. Paul C. REINERT, S.J., the university's 27th president, was a driving force behind this movement. He believed that lay boards were necessary for U.S. Catholic colleges and universities to survive and flourish in the contemporary world, a position that was later accepted in U.S. Catholic academic circles.

In 1987, Lawrence Biondi became president of St. Louis University. Under his leadership, the university experienced unprecedented growth. Biondi upgraded and modernized the university buildings and revitalized the surrounding campus environment. He committed vast resources to academics, student scholarships and financial aid, faculty research and technology. Financial exigencies however necessitated the sale of the university hospital to Tenet Healthcare in 1997, a decision that generated controversy between the university and the archdiocese.

Schools. Expansion of the university's academic programs continued at the turn of the century. In 1889, the school of philosophy was founded. Ten years later, the school of divinity, closed since 1860, was reopened. The school of divinity became a pontifical institute with the right to grant canonical degrees in 1934. In 1903, acquisition of the Marion-Sims-Beaumont College of Medicine, with its St. Louis College of Dentistry, brought medical education back to the university and marked the beginning of the university's school of dentistry. Five years later, law studies were added to the university's curriculum. In 1910, the university's school of commerce and finance (later renamed the John Cook School of Business) became one of the first collegiate schools of business in the West. Radio station WEW, which subsequently became a commercial station, received the second broadcasting station license in the U.S. in 1912, and became the first university station in the world.

Geophysics was pioneered by the university with the establishment of the department in 1925, under the direction of James B. MACELWANE, SJ. The department, which grew out of a geophysics laboratory set up in 1909, was the forerunner of the Institute of Technology, founded in 1944. In 1928, the school of nursing and health services was established, followed by the school of social service in 1933 and the Institute of Social Order in 1944. Parks College of Aeronautical Technology, founded in 1927 as the first federally approved aviation school in the country, became part of the university since 1946.

Libraries. Established in 1959, the Pius XII Memorial Library houses the university archives and the Vatican Film Library, which made Vatican documents available on microfilm for the first time in the western hemisphere. Official permission for the microfilm undertaking was granted by the Holy See on Oct. 23, 1950 with work beginning in 1951. The Vatican collection has been a primary source of information on the history of Western thought since Pope NICHOLAS V founded the library in the 15th century. Manuscripts range in age from the 5th to the 19th centuries and many are copies of earlier works.

Other important collections housed in the library include a rare-book section especially rich in early Western Americana, the archives of the Missouri province of the Society of Jesus, the St. Louis archdiocesan archives, and the Jesuitica Americana with more than 1,000,000 microfilmed pages dealing with the work of the Jesuits in the New World. Largely as a result of the latter, a branch of the Jesuit Historical Institute outside of Rome was established at the university. The university's Omer Poos Law Library, is one of the few law school libraries in the United States to be part of the Library of Congress National Cooperative Cataloging Project. In 2001, the university's libraries held more than 1.7 million volumes and more than 14,72 total journals.

Academics. The university boasts several firsts. It was the first to award medical and doctoral degrees west of the Mississippi (1839 and 1883 respectively), and it trained the first African-American surgeons in St. Louis (1919). It also developed the first department of geophysics in the western hemisphere (1925). Parks College of Engineering and Aviation was the first federally licensed school of aviation (1927). Alphonse Schwitalla, S.J, dean of the school of medicine from 1927 to 1948, was the first Catholic priest to serve as president of the North Central Association of Colleges and Universities. In 1944, the university admitted five African Americans to become America's first integrated school of any level in the South. The university was the site for the first human heart transplant in Missouri (1972), and it established Missouri's first medical helicopter (1979) and the state's first school of public health (1991). Faculty members have won various distinctions and awards. Among the most outstanding was the 1944 Nobel Prize in medicine given to Dr. Edward A. Doisy, director of the biochemistry department, for his work in isolating vitamin K.

St. Louis University was among the earliest American colleges and universities to offer its students an opportunity to study abroad when it expanded its ''campus'' across the Atlantic Ocean by opening a college program in Madrid, Spain, in 1969. This program initially was offered in conjunction with the Jesuit university of Comillas, Spain. When the Jesuit university moved in 1972 to a new suburban location, the St. Louis University program became independent and remained in Madrid near the University of Madrid campus. Spain's higher education authority has recognized the university in Madrid as an official foreign university, the first U.S. institution ever so recognized.

[P. C. REINERT/C. WALDVOGEL]

SAINT-MAIXENT, ABBEY OF

Former Benedictine abbey, in the town of Saint-Maixent, Deux-Sèvres, France, Diocese of Poitiers. In addition to being one of the most renowned BENEDICTINE monasteries in medieval France, Saint-Maixent was a favorite shrine for French pilgrims in the early Middle Ages due to the fame of its first abbot, Maxentius (d. *c.* 515), and that of the 7th-century abbot St. Leger, who became bishop of Autun. By the reign of Charlemagne pious donations had made Saint-Maixent one of the richest houses in France, a position which was weakened by Viking attacks in the 9th century and by the feudalization of its domains in the 10th and 11th centuries. Expansion ceased in the 13th century, and deterioration set in during the Hundred Years' War. This was climaxed by the destruction of the abbey church in 1568 during the WARS OF RELIGION. The MAURIST reform movement of the early 17th century arrested the decline until the suppression of the monastery in 1791 during the French Revolution, when the medieval church dedicated to Leger was transformed into a Protestant church. In 1879 the crumbling edifice was restored as a national monument.

Bibliography: A. RICHARD, ed., *Chartes et documents pour servir à l'histoire de l'Abbaye de Saint-Maixent,* 3 v. (Poitiers 1887). ''Chronicon abbatiae S. Maxentii Pictavensis,'' *Chroniques des églises d'Anjou,* ed. P. MARCHEGAY and É. MABILLE (Paris 1869) 349–433. H. RAVAN, *Essai historique sur l'Abbaye de Saint-Maixent et sur ses abbés depuis l'année 459 jusqu'en 1791* (Niort, France 1864). L. H. COTTINEAU, *Répertoire topobibliographique des abbayes et prieurés,* 2 v. (Mâcon 1935–39) 2:2775–77. H. LECLERCQ, *Dictionnaire d'archéologie chrétienne et de liturgie,* ed. F. CABROL, H. LECLERCQ and H. I. MARROU, 15 v. (Paris 1907–53) 15.1:508–511. P. HELIOT, *Les Églises abbatiales de Saint-Maixent* (Poitiers 1955).

[G. T. BEECH]

SAINT MARK'S (VENICE)

To Western eyes the most ''Oriental'' church in Italy, the appearance of Saint Mark's derives from both Byzantine workmanship and native imitation. The first structure on the site was erected to house the relics of St. Mark taken from Alexandria in the early 9th century. Doge Giovanni Partecipazio (826–837) brought from Constantinople the concept of a church modeled on the Byzantine *Apostoleion,* a cross plan with arms of equal length and its elevation topped by domes creating two lofty, intersecting halls in the interior. Alterations by Doge Domenico Contarini (*c.* 1070) and further decoration in the 13th century raised the domes, making them visible from the piazza that acts as the church's atrium.

The sacking of CONSTANTINOPLE (1204) and the Venetian claim to a portion of the Byzantine Empire produced the four bronze horses, the marble slabs that now encase the church, and a mosaic program designed to reinforce the historical validity of the claim. The appearance of Contarini's church, however, survives in an older mosaic on the Porta Sant'Alippio.

The aesthetic effectiveness of the exterior derives from defiance of both Byzantine practice and architectural good sense. The domes rise from behind a façade of ogival pinnacles and a colonnade gallery running around the structure. This, in turn, depends on an essentially Romanesque first story.

The highly variegated exterior, superb in the color contrast of its porphyry columns and green marble jambs, is matched by the diversity inside. As in a middle Byzantine church, the four central piers are penetrated by arched openings that correspond to the arcades in the nave and transepts. As at St. Sophia, the church is lit by windows in the domes that rise from barrel vaults springing from the piers.

The mosaic sheathing of the doors and walls incorporates Eastern Christian elements (Christ Immanuel and the Virgin Orans, the Ascension and the Pentecost) distributed however in a fashion that is quite un-Byzantine. Greek iconography is so far adapted as to substitute St. Mark for St. John Baptist in the Deësis mosaic. The narthex decoration consists of the lives of Joseph and Moses and a presentation of Genesis derived from an early Christian *rotulus.* In the baptistery, the Crucifixion includes a kneeling Doge Andrea Dandolo (1343–54) below Latin and Greek inscriptions. The story of the Baptist exemplifies the Gothic conquest of Venetian mosaic: Herod appears in the guise of a medieval Western monarch. Renaissance adornments include mosaics by TINTORETTO, but the essential form of the structure is determined by its function as state church of the Venetian empire. Political religiosity made of St. Mark's a heterogeneous but aesthetically triumphant anomaly in the history of architecture.

See Also: CHURCH ARCHITECTURE, HISTORY OF, 2. EARLY CHRISTIAN; BYZANTINE.

Bibliography: O. DEMUS, *The Church of San Marco in Venice: History, Architecture, Sculpture* (Washington 1960); *Die Mosaiken von San Marco in Venedig, 1100–1300* (Baden 1935); ''A Renascence of Early Christian Art in 13th Century Venice,'' *Late Classical and Med. Studies in Honor of A. M. Friend, Jr.,* ed. K. WEITZMANN et al. (Princeton 1955). P. TOESCA, *Storia dell'arte italiana nel medioevo,* 2 v. (Turin 1927). P. TOESCA and F. FORLATI, *Mosaics of St. Mark's* (Greenwich, Conn. 1958).

[A. CUTLER]

SAINT-MARTIN OF TOURNAI, ABBEY

Former BENEDICTINE monastery in Tournai, Belgium. It was founded in 1092 by Odo of Cambrai and several of his disciples as a monastery of CANONS REGULAR OF ST. AUGUSTINE, but it soon adopted the Benedictine customs of CLUNY. The abbey was renowned during the Middle Ages for the activity of its SCRIPTORIUM. Famous men of the abbey besides Odo included Heriman, author of a very important *Liber de restauratione* (*c.* 1142–47), and Abbot Giles Li Muisis, chronicler and poet (1272–1352). The abbey was suppressed during the French Revolution, and today its remains house Tournai's city hall and form a city park.

Bibliography: U. BERLIÈRE, *Monasticon belge* (Bruges 1890–) v.1. A. D'HERBOMEZ, *Chartes de l'abbaye de Saint-Martin de Tournai,* 2 v. (Brussels 1898–1901). A. D'HAENENS, *L'Abbaye Saint-Martin de Tournai 1290 à 1350: Origines, évolution et dénouement d'une crise* (Louvain 1961); *Un Prélat bourgeois: Gilles Li Muisis, abbé de St-Martin de Tournai, chroniqueur et poète* (Brussels 1966); ed., *Comptes et documents de l'abbaye de Saint-Martin de Tournai sous l'administration des gardiens royaux, 1312–1355* (Brussels 1962).

[A. D'HAENENS]

ST. MARY OF NAMUR, SISTERS OF

(SSMN, Official Catholic Directory #3950); a pontifical institute of teaching sisters founded at Namur, Belgium. In 1819, with the help of Josephine Sand and Elisabeth Berger, Nicolas Joseph Minsart, a Cistercian who was secularized during the French Revolution, opened sewing classes in St. Loup parish, where he was endeavoring to restore Christian family life. In 1834 the members of his parish group were permitted by the bishop to form a religious society and to consecrate their lives to God through Mary by the vows of religion. The Christian education of youth is the primary purpose of the congregation; a period of nine years of spiritual and scholastic training precedes the taking of perpetual vows. In 1863, Pierre Jean DE SMET arranged with Bishop John Timon of Buffalo, New York, to establish a convent of the sisters in that diocese. Mother Emelie, with four companions, opened a school in Lockport, New York. From there the sisters spread throughout the United States and Canada. The United States provincial houses are located in Buffalo, New York (Eastern Province) and Fort Worth, Texas (Western Province); the generalate is in Namur, Belgium. In the United States, the sisters are engaged in academic education at all levels, catechetics, diocesan administration, pastoral ministries, social services, healthcare, and refugee and migrant assistance.

[M. L. CORCORAN/EDS.]

ST. MARY OF OREGON, SISTERS OF

(SSMO, Official Catholic Directory #3960); a congregation with papal approbation, founded in Sublimity, Ore., by William H. GROSS, Archbishop of Portland, in 1886. The constitutions of the congregation were approved by Pius XI in 1934 Gross, with less than 30 priests and few religious teachers, was concerned about providing for the education of children. After testing the sincerity of seven young ladies who desired to consecrate their lives to God and to the services of the Church, he decided to establish his own community of sisters. These young women began their religious training and preparation for the work of teaching under the guidance of two religious brought to Oregon for this purpose from O'Fallon, Missouri. In 1891 the sisters were placed in charge of an orphanage at Beaverton, Oregon. The motherhouse at Sublimity, because of its remoteness from railroad facilities, was transferred to Beaverton about this time. A tract of land was purchased, a new motherhouse built, and in a short time the sisters opened an academy for both resident and day students. The generalate is in Beaverton, Oregon. The principal ministry of the sisters is teaching. In addition, the sisters engage in parish ministries, social outreach and nursing homes.

[M. X. MCHUGH/EDS.]

ST. MARY'S SCHOOL (PHILADELPHIA, PA.)

The mother school of Catholic parochial education in the American colonies, St. Mary's School was officially founded in 1782, although tradition, for which there is no documentary evidence, points to an earlier date, 1763. St. Mary's was not the first school of its kind; records of earlier foundations go as far back as the 17th century in New Mexico, Florida, and Maryland. The circumstances of St. Mary's foundation, however, the organization and characteristics of the school, and the special work of its founders combined to effect great influence on American Catholic educational patterns.

Despite penal laws, Catholics in Pennsylvania, by reason of their numbers, were allowed to build churches and schools by the middle of the 18th century. By 1763 the original Catholic parish of St. Joseph in Philadelphia had become too small to accommodate the city's Catholics and a new parish, St. Mary's, was formed.

Much of the progress of St. Mary's church and school is attributable to two zealous Jesuits, Ferdinand Steinmeyer and Robert MOLYNEUX, who contributed their services to the Catholic population of Philadelphia from 1758 through the Revolution. Steinmeyer, a German by birth, later took the name of Farmer because of his association with the German immigrants, most of whom were farmers (*see* FARMER, FERDINAND).

The church and priests' residence served as a school until 1782 when a two-story building was erected. There were two divisions: an upper school for the younger students, and a lower school for those who could ''read and cypher.'' Instruction was given in religion and in the common branches of learning in keeping with established standards of excellence, and cash premiums were offered each month to students with the best records. Under the direction of Molyneux, Catholic textbooks were designed in reading, spelling, catechism, and the elementary subjects. St. Mary's also pioneered in evening school for those students who could not attend day sessions.

Although the school was first intended to be tuition-free, for financial reasons, and also because of the stigma still attached to the ''free school,'' the original plan had to be modified and most students paid tuition of 20s. annually in the lower school and 17s. 6d. in the upper school. In 1783 the church board decided that each teacher would give free instruction to six students a year. The tuition scheme was later abandoned in favor of school revenues obtained through collections and gifts from private benefactors.

The school had two teachers, one for the upper and one for the lower school. A third was later added for students who could not afford tuition. The teacher supply problem, however, was acute, and salaries were soon a major issue. The decision to separate boys from girls and to employ a woman teacher for the latter helped solve some difficulties.

After Farmer's death in 1785 the German Catholics petitioned for a separate national church. A new school, similar to St. Mary's, however, began immediately; a

third parish soon followed suit, and by 1800 Catholic parochial education had been established.

St. Mary's parish seemed to have solved the problem of Catholic education for its time and, although torn by factional dispute after 1785, the school continued to serve the cause of Catholic education.

Bibliography: J. A. BURNS, *The Catholic School System in the United States* (New York 1908). J. A. BURNS and B. J. KOHLBRENNER, *A History of Catholic Education in the United States* (New York 1937). J. D. G. SHEA, *A History of the Catholic Church Within the Limits of the United States,* 4 v. (New York 1886–92) v.2.

[R. M. MANGINI]

SAINT-MAUR-DES-FOSSÉS, ABBEY OF

Former royal BENEDICTINE monastery, canton of Saint-Maur-des-Fossés, Seine, France, a suburb of Paris; modern Diocese of Paris (Latin, *Fossatum, S. Petrus Fossatensis*). It was founded in 638 under King Clovis II and Bp. Aubert, by Bildegisilus, archdeacon of Paris. The first abbot was St. Babolinus. The original monastery was only a *coenobiolum;* in the 9th century, it had to be rebuilt and a new church constructed. The monastery withstood an attack by the NORMANS in 861, On April 7, 868, at the request of CHARLES THE BALD, the relics of St. Maur (*see* MAURUS OF SUBIACO) were transferred from the cathedral in Paris to the abbey, where it was easier to protect them against the Normans. Bishop Aeneas of Paris carried the body to the monastery himself and ordered a triennial procession in commemoration of this translation, a custom that was observed for several centuries. Furthermore, he gave the abbey a prebend in the cathedral. In the 11th century the abbey participated in the CLUNIAC REFORM. The abbey enjoyed great prosperity in the Middle Ages thanks to pilgrimages to its holy relics—pilgrimages which, however, did not always occur without serious disorder. At the request of King Francis I *c.* 1534, Pope Clement VII transformed the abbey into a secular chapter of CANONS with the abbot as dean, the deanery being united to the Diocese of Paris. The chapter consisted of a chanter and eight canons, appointed by the bishop, each with yearly incomes of from £1,500 to £1,600; four perpetual vicars; one school-teacher; and four choirboys. In 1749 the chapter was incorporated into the chapter of Saint-Louis of the Louvre. By 1786 hardly any of the abbey buildings were still standing.

Bibliography: Beaunier, *La France monastique,* v.1 of *Abbayes et prieurés de l'ancienne France,* ed. J. M. L. BESSE, 12 v. (Paris 1905–41). L. H. COTTINEAU, *Répertoire topobibliographique des abbayes et prieurés,* 2 v. (Mâcon 1935–39) 2:2800–02.

[H. TARDIF]

SAINT-MAUR-SUR-LOIRE, ABBEY OF

Or Glanfeuil Abbey, former Benedictine monastery in the arrondissement of Saumur, canton of Gennes, commune of Saint-Georges-le-Thoureil (Maine-et-Loire) France, Diocese of Angers (Latin, *S. Maurus supra Ligerum* or *Glanafoliense*). It was founded in the 6th century by a certain Maurus, whom an unlikely tradition has identified with MAURUS OF SUBIACO. After being plundered, it was restored in 831 by the monks of Saint-Pierre-des-Fossés near Paris, but was abandoned again during the Norman invasions (862), to be restored at the beginning of the 11th century. The abbey church was consecrated in 1036. By 1096 the house had 30 monks and in 1098 it was restored to abbey status. The abbey was sacked during both the Hundred Years' War and the Wars of Religion. In 1668 it was admitted into the Congregation of Saint-Maur (*see* MAURISTS) but by 1768 only seven monks remained. The abbey was suppressed and the abbey church destroyed during the French Revolution. In 1890 the monks of SOLESMES reestablished monastic life there, but in 1910 the community finally settled at CLERVAUX, Luxembourg. Today the Saint-Maur buildings house a seminary of the ASSUMPTIONISTS.

Bibliography: Sources. Archives of Maine-et-Loire. Chartulary in P. A. Marchegay, ed., *Archives d'Anjou*, 2 v. (Angers 1843–53) v.1. ODO OF GLANFEUIL, *De miraculis S. Mauri, Monumenta Germaniae Scriptores* (Berlin 1826–) 15.1: 460–472. Literature. *Gallia Christiana*, v.1–13 (Paris 1715–85), v.14–16 (Paris 1856–65) 14:681–693. H. LECLBRCQ, *Dictionnaire d'archéologie chrétienne et de liturgie*, ed. F. CABROL, H. LECLERCQ and H. I. MARROU, 15 v. (Paris 1907–53) 6.1:1283–1319. L. H. COTTINEAU, *Répertoire topobibliographique des abbayes et prieurés,* 2 v. (Mâcon 1935–39) 2:280–203. R. GAZEAU, *Catholicisme* 5:44–46.

[J. DE LA C. BOUTON]

SAINT-MAURICE, ABBEY OF

Belonging to CANONS REGULAR OF ST. AUGUSTINE, in Valais canton, Switzerland, on the Rhone River. It is an abbey *nullius dioceseos* with 3,980 Catholics, six parishes, 112 religious priests, 135 monks in one abbey and 79 women in seven convents (1964); and occupies 37 square miles. As *Acaunum* (French Agaune), capital of the *Nantuates,* Saint-Maurice became important when the relics of St. Maurice and the other martyrs of the THEBAN LEGION were translated to a basilica built by St. Theodore (380–391), first bishop of Valais in *Octodurus* (Martigny). In honor of the martyrs, King St. SIGISMUND OF BURGUNDY in 515 founded an abbey that replaced secular clergy who had been there from the 4th century, richly endowing it with lands from Lyons to Aosta. As a pilgrimage center known for its perpetual psalmody (*Laus perennis*) and located on the road over the Great St. Bernard Alpine pass, Saint-Maurice gained some fame. The monks became secular canons *c.* 830, and the abbots began to serve as bishops of Sion. Rudolph I of Burgundy, who was crowned at Saint-Maurice in 888, disposed of the lands; but Rudolph III restored the abbey to secular canons in 1018, and the Salian Conrad I bestowed it on the Savoyan dynasty in 1034. Count Amadeus III (d. 1148) reformed the cloister, giving it to Augustinian canons in 1128 and restoring its goods in 1147 while the House of Savoy filled the office of provost. In 1196 the abbots gained pontificalia rights, and from 1150 to 1798 they were lords of the wine-growing area in the neighborhood. In 1782 the king of Sardinia made them counts. The Helvetic government secularized the abbey after the Napoleonic invasion, but the art treasures, with Carolingian items, were safeguarded and restored to the abbey when it reopened in 1814. In 1840 the abbot became titular bishop of Bethlehem. Saint-Maurice's territorial dispute with the bishops of Sion was settled in 1933. The abbey church, built in 1627, was made a minor basilica and restored in 1948. The abbey school dates from 1806.

Bibliography: M. BESSON, *Monasterium Acaunense* (Fribourg 1913). L. H. COTTINEAU, *Répertoire topobibliographique des abbayes et prieurés,* 2 v. (Mâcon 1935–39) 2:2805–06. L. DUPONT-LACHENAL, *Les Abbés de St-Maurice* (St-Maurice 1929); in *Dictionnaire biographique et historique de la Suisse,* 8 v. (Neuchâtel 1921–34) 5:679–682, with list of abbots 515–1914. J. M. THEURILLAT, *Lexikon für Theologie und Kirche,* ed. J. HOFER and K. RAHNER, 10 v. (2d, new ed. Freiburg 1957–65) 9:163–164. *Annuario Pontificio* (1964) 730.

[A. MAISSEN]

SAINT-MAXIMIN, ABBEY OF

Now the basilica and priory of St. Mary Magdalene, in the village of Saint Maximin-la-Baume, Department of Var, France, a pilgrimage shrine founded to house the relics of St. Mary Magdalene. The abbey is a monument of Gothic architecture, begun in 1295 and finished about 1500. At the Holy Grotto (St.-Baume) on Mount St. Cassian, monks from the 5th century and later on Benedictines guarded the relics in nearby St. Maximin's Church. King Charles II of Naples, Count of Anjou, replaced the Benedictines with Dominicans (1295), and began a new church. Charles III gave it a rich manuscript library. King René of Naples, Duke of Anjou, founded its college (1476); SIXTUS IV confirmed it (1477). The relics were encased in increasingly precious reliquaries until desecrated during the FRENCH REVOLUTION. Partially saved, they were restored on Jan. 3, 1804. The church and priory were declared national monuments and were returned to the Dominicans.

Bibliography: L. ROSTAN, *Notice sur l'église de Saint-Maximin* (3d ed. Brignoles, France 1886). J. H. ALBANÈS, *Le Cou-*

vent royal de Saint-Maximin en Provence (Marseilles 1880). M. H. LAURENT, ''La Bibliothèque du couvent de Saint-Maximin . . . ,'' *Archivum Fratrum Praedicatorum* 1 (1931) 350–364.

[B. CAVANAUGH]

ST. MEINRAD ARCHABBEY

A Benedictine abbey of the Swiss American Congregation, located in Spencer County, Indiana, in the Archdiocese of Indianapolis. It was founded in 1854 by the Swiss abbey of Maria Einsiedeln in answer to Rev. Josef Kundek's request for German speaking priests to serve his Catholic colony centered around St. Ferdinand, Indiana. Facing curtailment of their work in Switzerland as a result of the 1847 Sonderbund War, Abbot Heinrich IV Schmid sent Ulrich Christen and Bede O'Connor to investigate making a foundation in America. In 1854, an agreement was reached with the bishop of Vincennes, Maurice de St. Palais, and a German speaking district was placed into the monk's care centered around their priory dedicated to St. Meinrad. After several years of struggle, order and financial security were brought to the monastery in 1860 with the arrival of Martin Marty, who started a successful school to train a native clergy while also taking on greater pastoral responsibilites throughout the diocese. In 1870, St. Meinrad was made an independent abbey, with Marty appointed its first abbot by Pope Pius IX.

In addition to parish work and education, Marty expanded the abbey's scope of activities to include missionary work among Native Americans in the Dakotas and contributed to the founding of Subiaco Abbey, Arkansas (1878). Abbot Fintan Mundwiler (1880-1898), became the first president of the Swiss-American Congregation with the erection of Conception Abbey in 1881, and consulted with Abbot Frowin Conrad, a devotee of Beuron, to establish the observances and customs of the new congregation. Continuing the work of monastic expansion, Mundwiler instigated the foundation of St. Joseph Abbey, Louisiana (1889), but failed in his attempt to create a permanent mission house in Uruguay.

Under its next two abbots, Athanasius Schmitt (1898–1930), and Ignatius Esser (1930–1955), the size of the seminary grew along with the prestiege of the monastery, which began to participate in the LITURGICAL MOVEMENT. Starting in the late 1920s and continuing through the 1960s, publications of the monastery's Abbey Press, such as *The Grail* and later, *Marriage*, sought to promote the apostolate of the Christian family and had subscribers nationwide. During this time new monastic foundations were made at Marmion Abbey in Illinois (1933) and as a result of previous missionary activity on the northern

plains, Blue Cloud, South Dakota (1952). On the occasion of its centenary in 1954, Pope Pius XII raised St. Meinrad to the rank of an archabbey.

Monks were sent to California in 1958 to create what would later become Prince of Peace Abbey during the tenure of Archabbot Bonaventure Knaebel (1955–1966), and to answer the call of Pope John XXIII, in 1962 a mission house was established in Huaraz, Peru (closed in 1985). After the Second Vatican Council, and under the leadership of archabbots Gabriel Verkamp (1966–1978) and Timothy Sweeney (1978–1995), St. Meinrad became involved in the ecumenical movement, and continued making contributions to the liturgy through helping to provide translations of the Scriptures and adaptations of Gregorian chant to English. It was also at this time that the college and school of theology gained a reputation for the emphasis placed on pastoral formation and for the implementation of liturgical reforms. More recently, two years after Lambert Reilly's election as archabbot in 1995, the undergraduate school was closed due to declining enrollment and changing patterns in education for ministry. The monastery carries on its tradition of seminary education through the St. Meinrad School of Theology, which enrolls students from a number of dioceses throughout the U.S.

The community of 130 monks continues to serve in parishes, is active in retreat and mission work, supports the Archabbey Library which possesses a substantial collection of historical and theological works, and maintains its outreach to Christian families through the publications and products of Abbey Press.

Bibliography: Archives, St. Meinrad Archabbey and daughter-houses. *St. Meinrad's Raben* (1888), later incorporated in *St. Benedikts-Panier* (1889), which became *Paradiesesfrüchte* (1895), all published by St. Meinrad. A. KLEBER, *History of St. Meinrad Archabbey, 1854–1954* (St. Meinrad, IN, 1954). J. RIPPINGER, *The Benedictine Order in the United States* (Collegeville, MN, 1990). P. YOCK, *The Role of St. Meinrad Abbey in the Formation of Catholic Identity in the Diocese of Vincennes 1853–1898* (Ph.D. diss. Pontifical Gregorian University, Evansville, IN, 2000).

[P. YORK]

SAINT-MIHIEL, ABBEY OF

A former Benedictine monastery in the diocese of Verdun, which according to a probably false tradition, is said to have been founded by Count Vulfoad, a powerful 8th-century Austrasian lord. In the same century it seems also to have been a dependency of SAINT-DENIS. About 815 the abbey was transferred to its present site on the bank of the Meuse by SMARAGDUS, the author of many theological and ascetical works, who was abbot, from *c.*

809 until his death sometime after 825. Favored by the Carolingian and German sovereigns in the 9th and 10th centuries, the abbey remained prosperous throughout the Middle Ages and retained regular observance until the end of the 15th century, when it passed under a commendatory abbot (*see* COMMENDATION).

The church was completely rebuilt in about the middle of the 11th century according to a vast Ottonian plan still recognizable in the present edifice, built between 1700 and 1710. In 1606 the abbey was affiliated with the Lorraine congregation of Saint-Vanne and Saint-Hidulphe. In the 17th century it became an important center for the diffusion of JANSENISM, particularly through M. PETIT-DIDIER, the author of an *Apologie des ''Lettres provinciales'' de Louis de Montalte* (1696–97) and Dom Monnier, who wrote the famous *Problème ecclésiastique* (1698). The abbey was suppressed in 1791.

Bibliography: J. DE L'ISLE, *Histoire de la célèbre abbaye de Saint-Mihiel* (Nancy 1757). A. LESORT, ed., *Chronique et chartes de l'abbaye de Saint-Michiel*, 4 fasc. (Paris 1909–12). C. ALMOND, *Les Nécrologes de l'abbaye de Saint-Mihiel* (Bar-le-Duc 1923). R. TAVENEUX, *Le Jansénisme en Lorraine, 1640–1789* (Paris 1960).

[J. CHOUX]

ST. OMER, COLLEGE OF

The College of St. Omer, also known under the anglicized form, St. Omers, was founded in Saint-Omer, France, by Robert Persons, SJ, in 1593. It represented a reaction to a proposal to make even harsher the already stringent laws against Catholic education in England. Philip II of Spain acceded to Persons' request to aid in the establishment of an English college in Flanders, then under Spanish rule. He promised an annual subsidy and chose the site of the proposed college, which formally opened in a rented house in Saint-Omer in November 1593.

In its early years the College was simply a residence for English boys who followed the classes in the local Jesuit school. It was considerably hindered by financial difficulties, by opposition from municipal officials, and by the restriction of its enrollment to 16 scholars. Most of these difficulties, however, were overcome by Giles Schoondonch, SJ, who became rector in 1601. Before he died in office in 1617, he had transferred the College to a new and permanent location and had provided it with a public church and its own faculty. The number of students had risen to 130.

The curriculum and regime at St. Omers were very much like those of other Jesuit schools. Boys entered at about age 12 and proceeded through the six classes of fig-

ures, rudiments, grammar, syntax, poetry, and rhetoric. The staple of instruction was Latin and Greek with great emphasis on eloquence in the classical languages and on debating ability. Of the four features that distinguished the College, the first two, special emphasis on Greek and a marked enthusiasm for music and drama, are attributed to Schoondonch. In his time the splendor of the theatrical presentations at St. Omers was recognized throughout Europe. The last two, a mild disciplinary regime suited to the English temperament, and a great missionary spirit, were introduced and fostered by the first English rector, William Baldwin, SJ (1621–32).

During the first half of the 17th century the College press, under the direction of John Wilson, SJ, was the most important source of the proscribed Catholic literature that nourished the piety and loyalty of English recusants. In 1635 the number of scholars rose to 200, but in 1651 the English Civil War reduced enrollment to 110. It hovered around that figure throughout the 17th and 18th centuries. The fortunes of the College, moreover, reflected the tribulations of the English Catholic body in the homeland. St. Omers consequently suffered hardships during the OATES PLOT and the bitter repressions following the Jacobite uprisings of 1715 and 1745.

Although the College was originally destined for the education of the laity as well as of future priests, the latter were generally in the majority. By the middle of the 17th century more than half of the new English province of the Society of Jesus were alumni of St. Omers. Among the earliest were Bl. Thomas GARNET (d. 1608), the college's protomartyr, and Andrew WHITE, the apostle of Maryland. St. Omers was also an important source of recruits for the seminaries of the secular clergy in Rome and Spain.

Many boys came from Maryland in the 18th century, among them Charles CARROLL of Carrollton and John CARROLL, first Archbishop of Baltimore. The latter, on the completion of his studies at St. Omers, entered the Jesuit novitiate at nearby Watten in 1753. He later returned to teach at his Alma Mater in 1758 and went into exile with the whole school when the Jesuits were expelled from France in 1762.

The Jesuit school continued its corporate existence first in Bruges, Belgium (1762–73), and then, after the suppression of the Jesuits, in Liège, Belgium (1773–94). Driven out of that principality by the French Revolution, they returned to England. There, one of their alumni, Thomas Weld, gave them refuge at Stonyhurst in Lancashire, the present home of the College, which claims continuity with that founded by Persons in 1593.

After the suppression of the Jesuits in 1773, the buildings at St. Omers were taken over by the English secular clergy who conducted a school there until driven out by the French Revolution in 1793. Some of the scholars and teachers took refuge in England at the new college of St. Edmunds at Old Hall.

Bibliography: H. CHADWICK, *St. Omers to Stonyhurst* (London 1962). B. N. WARD, *The Dawn of the Catholic Revival in England, 1781–1803,* 2 v. (London 1909). T. A. HUGHES, *The History of the Society of Jesus in North America: Colonial and Federal,* 4 v. (London 1907–17) v.2.

[T. H. CLANCY]

SAINT-OUEN, ABBEY OF

Former Benedictine monastery in the city of ROUEN, France. Originally dedicated to St. Peter by Bishop Filleul (533–542), it was later known as Saint-Ouen from the relics of Bp. OUEN OF ROUEN (d. 684), who was buried there. After the Viking raids of 841 monastic life was suspended until the early 11th century. This abbey played an important part in the revival of Norman MONASTICISM, and several monks went from there as abbots to other houses. It remained an influential intellectual center, having papal approval of its theology school in the 13th century. In the 15th century it maintained a grammar school. Pope Alexander IV made it a mitered abbey in 1256, and it enjoyed special privileges in both spiritual and secular Norman assemblies. After 1462 a number of distinguished prelates held it in COMMENDATION, and in 1562 the Calvinists pillaged it. Conventual life was resumed only under the MAURISTS (1660). New buildings were begun in 1753, but the work was interrupted by the French Revolution when the abbey was suppressed (1790). The monks' lodging became the Town Hall of Rouen. The extant abbey church, one of the finest in France, was begun in 1319 after a succession of disastrous fires. It was completed (except for the façade added in the 19th century) only at the end of the 15th century.

Bibliography: F. POMMERAYE, *Histoire de l'Abbaye royale de Saint Ouen de Rouen* (Rouen 1662). *Gallia Christiana,* v.1–13 (Paris 1715–85), v.14–16 (Paris 1856–65) 11:135–155. L. H. COTTINEAU, *Répertoire topobibliographique des abbayes et prieurés,* 2 v. (Mâcon 1935–39) 2:2547–50. A. MASSON, *L'Abbaye de Saint-Ouen de Rouen* (Rouen 1930).

[D. J. A. MATTHEW]

ST. PATRICK'S MISSIONARY SOCIETY

(SPS, Official Catholic Directory #1170); also known as St. Patrick Fathers, canonically established on March 17, 1932, with headquarters at Kiltegan, County Wicklow, Ireland. The founder and first superior general was Monsignor P. J. Whitney. It is a pontifical society of secular priests devoted entirely to the missionary needs of the Church. The society was a development of a movement initiated in 1920 among the Irish diocesan clergy. In response to an appeal made in that year at the national seminary, Maynooth, diocesan priests volunteered to work for a period in southern Nigeria. With the development of their work there, the need was felt for a permanent organization that would ensure a steady and increasing supply of priests. Even after the establishment of the society, volunteer priests from Irish dioceses and, later, from England, Scotland, and elsewhere, continued to assist the regular members in the mission work. In 1950 the society established its first foundation in the United States at Camden, New Jersey. The generalate is in Wicklow, Ireland.

[T. LUCEY/EDS.]

ST. PAUL, PIOUS SOCIETY OF DAUGHTERS OF

A religious congregation (DSP; Official Catholic Directory #0950) with papal approbation (1953), founded in Alba, Italy, in 1915 by the Rev. Giacomo Alberione (1884–1971), assisted by Teresa Merlo (1894–1964), who, as Mother Thecla, was to serve as superior general for 49 years. Both Fr. Alberione and Mother Thecla have been declared venerable. The congregation's purpose is evangelization through the media of mass communication. The Daughters of St. Paul, also known as Paulines, write, edit, and produce Catholic publications, radio programs, videos, and other contemporary media. They distribute religious and cultural books and media through Pauline centers in 50 nations, including the United States and Canada.

The sisters arrived in New York in 1932. Difficult beginnings and gradual expansion took place under the leadership of Sr. Paula Cordero (1908–1991). Since 1956 the provincialate and publishing house (now known as Pauline Books & Media) have been located in Boston. The generalate is located in Rome.

Bibliography: Web site: http://www.pauline.org.

[A. E. HEFFEMAN]

ST. PAUL (CHARTRES), SISTERS OF

A congregation (Official Catholic Directory #3980) founded in 1696 by Louis Chauvet, parish priest of Levesville-la-Chenard, France, and dedicated to works of

Façade of former Abbey Church of Saint-Ouen in Rouen. (©Vanni Archive/CORBIS)

charity. The *Soeurs de Saint Paul de Chartres* (SPDC) became a diocesan congregation when Paul Godet des Marais, Bishop of Chartres, established the sisters in his diocese in 1708. Early in their history the sisters took up the mission apostolate when they went to French Guyana in 1722. After the French Revolution the community was reorganized and obtained the approval of Pius IX in 1861. By the time that final papal approbation was granted (1949), the sisters were well established in Vietnam, China, Japan, Korea, Thailand, Laos, the Philippines, and Africa, as well as in France, Belgium, Switzerland, Italy, England, the West Indies, and Canada. In the United States, the sisters' ministries include education, health, social work, and pastoral ministries. The motherhouse is in Chartres, the residence of the superior general is in Rome, and the district superior for the United States resides in the diocese of Marquette, Michigan.

Bibliography: R. GOBILLOT, *The Sisters of St. Paul de Chartres* (Manila 1956). J. VAUDON, *Histoire générale de la communauté des Filles de Saint-Paul de Chartres*, 4 v. (Paris 1922–31).

[M. P. DE LOS REYES/EDS.]

ST. PAUL AND MINNEAPOLIS, ARCHDIOCESE OF

The diocese of St. Paul was established on July 19, 1850. Initially, the diocese was bounded by Iowa on the south, Canada on the north, Wisconsin on the east and the Missouri and White Earth Rivers in the Dakotas on the west. It became an archdiocese in 1888, and in 1966, Pope Paul VI redesignated it as the Archdiocese of St. Paul and Minneapolis (*Archiodioecesis Paulopolitana et Minneapolitana*. The other dioceses in Minnesota as well as the diocese of North and South Dakota are its suffragan sees.

The city of St. Paul grew up around and was named after the log chapel that Father Lucien Galtier dedicated to St. Paul in 1841, and wherein French-born Joseph CRETIN was installed as the first bishop of the diocese on July 2, 1851. He immediately set about constructing a new cathedral. Cretin had served in the Diocese of Dubuque before coming to St. Paul. Arriving with with two priests and three seminarians, he opened a mission for the Native Americans at Blue Earth and established a parish near the Falls of St. Anthony, thus opening the first Catholic church and parish school in what would become Minneapolis. Conversions of Chippewa and Sioux natives in northern parts of the diocese were helped by Jesuits around Grand Portage and the veteran missionary Francis Pierz, who came to the diocese in 1852, establishing a mission near Brainerd.

Cretin ceded the original log chapel to the Sisters of St. Joseph, whom he had invited into the region to teach young girls. This chapel became the original St. Joseph's Academy and also served as the original St. Joseph's Hospital when the sisters were called on to minister to the sick during the cholera epidemic of 1855. Cretin authorized new churches to be built in Wabasha, Chaska, Hastings, Maryburg, Credit River, New Prague, Winona, Lake City, and Derrynane. By the end of Cretin's administration, there were 29 churches and 35 stations with about 20 priests attending a Catholic population of about 50,000. The diocese had a Catholic Temperance Society, a St. Vincent de Paul Society, a Society of the Living Rosary, and a Confraternity of the Sacred Heart of Mary. Bishop Cretin died on Feb. 22, 1857 and was buried in Calvary Cemetery, which he had blessed in 1856. Augustin Ravoux, the vicar general, administered the diocese until a new bishop was appointed two years later. Ravoux served as vicar general of the diocese until 1892 when poor health demanded retirement. He died in 1906, and is remembered for the services he rendered to the condemned 38 Sioux after the infamous Sioux Uprising in 1862.

Thomas Langdon Grace, OP, a native of South Carolina known for his administrative skills and his commitment to Catholic education, was named the second bishop of St. Paul on July 29, 1859. He devised a constitution for the diocese, stipulating directives for the celebration of the Eucharist, the erection of parish buildings, the teaching to children the rudiments of Catholicism, and the keeping of parish records. The mettle of Grace was tested during the Civil War (1861–1865), when, because of his Southern roots, his loyalty was questioned. He sent the young Father John Ireland to serve as chaplain for the Northern forces in battles fought on Southern soil. Upon his return to the diocese, Ireland became Grace's secretary. The Sioux Uprising of 1862 further tested his diplomatic skills. His correspondence with the Bureau of Indian Affairs in Washington fell upon deaf ears.

Grace championed Catholic education, inviting various groups of teaching religious to address this need. He established many new ethnic parishes, and in an attempt to ward off the slander against the Catholic Church by the Know-Nothing Party, was an advocate of the Catholic press, making *The Northwestern Chronicle* the official organ of the diocese. He is also credited with organizing deaneries in the diocese in an attempt to implement the directives of the Second Council of Baltimore. Grace resigned in 1884 and died in 1897, leaving a legacy of brilliant intellectual attainments. He had been a staunch advocate of establishing The Catholic University of America, founded in 1889. He had advocated for a major seminary in the diocese, and this was finally realized when St. Thomas Seminary was opened in 1886 where the University of St. Thomas now stands. During his capable administration, the Catholic population of the state rose to about 130,000 with a presbyterate of 147: 119 diocesan and 28 regular clergy. There were 195 churches and 51 stations, 29 seminarians, six religious communities of men, 14 religious communities of women, two hospitals, five asylums, and ten academies and boarding schools for young women. The diocese boasted seven St. Vincent de Paul Conferences, Total Abstinence Societies in many communities, and rosary societies, sodalities, and confraternities of the Sacred Heart in most parishes.

John IRELAND, a native of Ireland and immigrant to Minnesota, had been sent to France to study for the priesthood by Bishop Cretin. He was ordained in 1861, served briefly as a curate in the cathedral parish, and then as a military chaplain. After the war he was appointed rector of the cathedral, and was made Cretin's representative at Vatican Council I, which the ordinary of St. Paul did not attend. Originally designated vicar apostolic of Nebraska, Cretin succeeded in having the nomination revoked, and in Ireland's being named his own coadjutor, with right of succession, in 1875. Ireland was a vigorous proponent of the Catholic Total Abstinence Society and became a nationally known speaker in its cause. He also was notable as the Catholic prelate most identified with support of the American public school system, and he sought to accommodate Catholic immigrant sensibilities with the Protestant dominated educational system. His experiments at Stillwater and Faribault, MN, of cooperation with local school boards in the administration of parochial schools drew international attention and the ire of his ecclesiastical opponents, both in the United States and in Rome. The attempts at accommodation, however, soon failed to satisfy the school boards as well, and were ended by the civic authorities.

These and other public stances firmly identified Ireland with the ''Americanist'' cause during the years of that controversy. Together with Cardinal James GIBBONS, and Bishops Denis O'CONNELL, John J. KEANE, and others, Ireland strongly identified himself and attempted to identify the Catholic Church in the United States with patriotic and democratic sensibilities. These later proved useful to Leo XIII, who in 1892 sent Ireland as his envoy to France in order to bolster support for the pontiff's new policy of *ralliement* to the Republic. Ireland opposed the efforts of the German lay leader Peter Paul Cahensly to establish special ecclesiastical jurisdictions and appointments for German, Italian, and other immigrants in the United States. Ireland is often faulted with causing the alienation of thousands of Eastern Rite Catholics to the Orthodox Churches because of his ''Americanizing'' convictions and his unwillingness to recognize the juris-

diction and validity of their immigrant priests. Closely associated with many major political figures, both local and national, Ireland was often seen as a supporter of and influential figure within Republican Party politics. He was unable, however, to deter the course toward war with Spain in 1898, the diplomatic mission the Holy See had entrusted to him. He was more successful in his efforts to negotiate a settlement between the Holy See and the United States with regard to friars' lands in the Philippine Islands in the wake of the war.

Ireland was a strong advocate for the establishment of The Catholic University of America in Washington, D.C., and he remained a supporter of the institution throughout his life. He opened St. Paul Seminary in 1894 and was often personally involved in its development and in the formation of its seminarians. Notwithstanding his political involvements, Ireland was also a supporter of the Knights of Labor and endorsed Gibbons' efforts to prevent a papal condemnation of the Knights of Labor. He was also an outstanding leader in the fight against racial discrimination within the Church and society.

St. Paul was made an archiepiscopal see in 1888, and Ireland was its first archbishop. His influence within the newly created province and throughout the region, and his strong personality, caused him to be known as ''The Patriarch of the West,'' as well as ''the consecrated blizzard of the northwest.'' It was often rumored that he would be created a cardinal, but the appointment to the Sacred College was never made, despite the efforts of his friends. He died on Sept. 25, 1918.

Ireland's successor in office, Austin DOWLING, a native of New York City, was ordained for the Diocese of Providence, RI, in 1891, following studies at The Catholic University of America. He taught church history at St. John's Seminary in Brighton, MA, served as editor of the *Providence Visitor,* and was named rector of the cathedral church. He was consecrated the first bishop of Des Moines, IA, in 1912, and was translated to St. Paul in 1919. He was instrumental in the establishment of the National Catholic Welfare Conference and was elected to its first administrative board. Locally, he firmly established offices of Catholic Charities in the archdiocese and advanced the cause of Catholic education through fund raising and the establishment of educational institutions, including a diocesan teachers college for sisters and lay teachers (1925). Dowling published scholarly works and lectured throughout his episcopacy. He died in 1930.

John Gregory Murray, former auxiliary bishop of Hartford and bishop of Portland (Maine), was installed as third Archbishop of St. Paul, Jan. 27, 1931. In marked contrast to the style of his predecessor, Murray was often seen riding the trolleys or walking in the downtown area of the capital city. His concern for the downtrodden prompted him to organize a crusade of charitable giving to support those in need regardless of creed or color. In November of 1935, he opened the Catholic Labor School for members of labor unions. The school offered classes in Catholic social teaching, economics, parliamentary procedures, and labor law. Priest-teachers became well acquainted with labor leaders and were frequently called on as arbitrators in industrial disputes in the region.

Murray encouraged the certification of teaching sisters at the diocesan teachers' college. He organized the Confraternity of Christian Doctrine and study clubs to train teachers for instructing Catholic youth attending public schools during the "release periods" permitted by law. The Confraternity of Christian Doctrine also sponsored the formation of The Catholic Choral Club under Rev. Francis A. Missia and the opening of Catholic Youth Centers in St. Paul and Minneapolis.

Murray attacked the prevalent evils of socialism, communism, anarchy, eugenics, and birth control, forbidding Catholics to become members of societies supporting birth control and sterilization. Murray was committed to a hierarchical image of the Church. When The National Conference of Catholic Charities met in St. Paul in 1937, problems of families, youth, and social concerns were addressed, but attendance did not include the laity. Yet, when Cardinal Eugenio Pacelli (later Pope PIUS XII) arrived in St. Paul in 1936 on an unofficial visit to the United States, he encountered a flourishing parochial life within the archdiocese. Moreover, when the ninth National Eucharistic Congress was held in the Twin Cities, on June 22–26, 1941, there were hundreds of thousands of participants. During World War II, when many priests and laity were called into armed services abroad, and women were called to replace men in defense plants, family life became strained. To meet the crisis, Murray formed the Diocesan Bureau of Charities, the Family Guild, and began an Archdiocesan Prayer Front for Peace.

In response to regional immigration, Murray opened a new parochial school for black Catholics in St. Peter Claver parish. In the years following World War II, 59 new parishes were established in the Twin Cities and suburbs to meet the needs of the growing Catholic population. Enrollment in grade schools increased, and additional Catholic high schools were in demand. The SCHOOL SISTERS OF NOTRE DAME opened St. Agnes Parish High School and the Sisters of Charity of the Blessed Virgin Mary staffed Our Lady of Peace Academy. Several small parish high schools were also opened in rural areas. Enrollment in the two Catholic colleges in the Twin Cities tripled, and seminary enrollment grew. The

Newman Center and chapel near the University of Minnesota in Minneapolis was erected in 1953. Murray also oversaw the establishment of four retreat houses, two homes for the aged, and a home for incurable cancer patients. He authorized an independent priory of the Sisters of St. Benedict to be erected in St. Paul (1948) and the establishment of a major seminary of the Conventual Franciscan Fathers in Chaska (1951). James J. Byrne was appointed auxiliary bishop in 1947. When Byrne became bishop of Boise, Idaho, in 1956, Bishop William O. Brady of Sioux Falls, SD, was appointed coadjutor archbishop, with right of succession. Archbishop Murray died on Oct. 11, 1956, and was buried in Resurrection Cemetery in Mendota Heights.

Archbishop Brady oversaw 17 counties in Minnesota, which numbered over 434,000 Catholics. In 1957 the Diocese of New Ulm was carved from this territory and Alphonse Schladweiler appointed its first bishop. At the same time, Leonard Cowley was named an auxiliary bishop to assist Brady. Brady was a vibrant and forward-looking decision maker. When freeway construction displaced many in his cathedral parish, he worked with the St. Paul Housing Redevelopment Authority to assist in family relocation. During the Cold War he made the archdiocese an active participant in civil defense functions. The birth of baby boomers, suburban sprawl, the debate over birth control, and the drug culture were all addressed in the revised *Catholic Bulletin*. Brady also encouraged the expansion of the *Catholic Digest* into Europe. This periodical, published in St. Paul under the leadership of Rev. Louis Gales, reached a circulation of almost 900,000 in 1958. Brady furthered the work of women's groups and promoted the extension of lay volunteers for the Home Missions and Papal Volunteers for Latin America (PAVLA). He encouraged the organization of parish-based cells of Young Christian Workers. He also seized the opportunity of more affluent times to undertake the major completion of the interior of the dome of the cathedral, to erect a new chancery office, and to launch a campaign for the building of needed Catholic high schools.

Brady had a pariticular interest in the liturgy. His leadership encouraged the implementation of the new ritual of Holy Week approved by Pope Pius XII throughout the archdiocese. As a member of a special liturgical committee of the Conference of United States Bishops, he championed the use of the vernacular in the administration of the sacraments and in all liturgical rites. During a flight to Rome while working on a pre-conciliar liturgical commission, Archbishop Brady suffered a heart attack and died in Rome on Oct. 1, 1961.

Leo Binz, archbishop of Dubuque, became archbishop of St. Paul in 1962. He attended the sessions of the

Second Vatican Council and was challenged with implementing its decrees. The most immediate changes were liturgical, But Binz's policy was to withhold formal approbation of any changes until Rome and the National Council of Catholic Bishops had spoken. The *Minneapolis Tribune* persisted in challenging the Catholic Church to respond to questions arising from contemporary social issues, but satisfying answers were slow to come. Despite Binz's hesitancy, auxiliary bishop James Shannon strove to get priests and laity to become actively involved in ecumenical affairs.

Binz authorized the first Cursillo in the archdiocese in 1968, continued the May Day Rosary processions, and strove unsuccessfully to elevate the rosary to a place alongside the Divine Office as an official prayer of the Church. The Holy Year (1975) was a special year of reconciliation and renewal, calling for lay discussion groups within the parishes. A new role, director of religious education, appeared on many parish staffs; new architecture for parish complexes emerged; the cost of Catholic secondary education skyrocketed; and some schools closed because of low enrollment. Yet, the commitment to Catholic education remained a top priority within the archdiocese. Prompted by the growth of the Twin Cities metropolitan area, the archdiocese was redesignated the Archdiocese of St. Paul and Minneapolis in 1966.

Catholic Charities expanded during the 1960s, addressing the needs of the marginalized. The Christian Family Movement and the Rural Life Conference addressed the family life problems in rural areas of the archdiocese. Concerns for the rights of the working class in the state were championed by clergy of the archdiocese, especially by Monsignor Francis J. Gilligan, who spoke for the archdiocese at religion and labor meetings and who often acted as arbiter in settling many local labor-management disputes. Minnesota Citizens Concerned for Life was a strong citizen lobby against abortion legislation and abortion clinics in the state. Care for retarded children, long given in Faribault, saw new programs in the metropolitan Catholic hospitals and a new facility in St. Paul. The Catholic Interracial Council provided grants for minorities to attend Catholic schools. Parishes through the Black Catholics Concerned program worked to obliterate discrimination, and the archdiocese supported the St. Paul NAACP in its struggle for equal justice for African Americans in Minnesota. The work of Sister Giovanni, SSND, with the Hispanic community on St. Paul's West Side, kept the needs of that minority before the attention of the archdiocese as well as the state. In 1967 the archdiocese sponsored four PAVLA volunteers for work in Latin America. Eventually, large numbers of refugees from Vietnam and Laos in the Twin Cities necessitated new ministries.

Leo C. Byrne became coadjutor bishop of St. Paul and Minneapolis in 1967, and ordinary in 1975, when Binz retired because of poor health. A champion of the Second Vatican Council, Byrne was an advocate of a married deacons program for the archdiocese, collaborated with the Joint Religious Legislative Coalition in its work for social justice, and established the Board of Investment Ethics to review the portfolio of the archdiocese. The code drawn up by this board was the most comprehensive of any U.S. diocese. Byrne also encouraged workers to organize their own unions. He supported St. Mary's Hospital treatment center for alcoholics and established a policy for addressing the issue of alcohol and drug abuse among clergy and religious. An advocate of the aged, he also planned a retirement home for archdiocesan priests. In order to involve laity more directly in local church affairs, he set up the Archdiocesan Pastoral Council in 1972 to act as an advisory group. When the American Indian Movement moved its headquarters to Minneapolis and a flood of new immigrants added to the homeless poor in the urban areas, the Priests' Senate, with Byrne's approval, organized an Inner-City Urban Ministry to help with housing concerns in the Twin Cities. In 1971 Raymond Lucker and John Roach were consecrated auxiliary bishops for the archdiocese.

Though he called for the Church to study the issue of women in ministry as a justice issue, Byrne nevertheless was slow to address women's issues in his own archdiocese. The papal encyclical *Humanae Vitae* caused the greatest controversy of Byrne's episcopacy. When more than 70 priests of the archdiocese publicly dissented from the encyclical, he demanded obedience of his priests in support of the Church's teaching. Although *Humanae Vitae* received strong support in many quarters of the archdiocese, notably the Council of Catholic Men and the Council of Catholic Women, the encyclical prompted some to leave the priesthood and religious life, including Auxiliary Bishop James Shannon. During this same period the great number of religious men and women leaving religious congregations created personnel problems for Catholic parishes and service institutions under archdiocesan auspices.

When the U.S. Supreme Court issued the *Roe vs. Wade* decision, a natural family planning program was established as one means of counteracting the massive influx of birth control and pro-abortion literature that flooded the area.

Archbishop Byrne organized an Ecumenical Commission, which included clergy, laity, and men and women religious. Byrne worked with leaders of other faiths and brought closer ties with Jewish leaders in the area. Many groups within the state were working hard for ecumenism, but he was hesitant to join the Minnesota Council of Churches, fearing their aggressive approach. When Archbishop Byrne died suddenly on Oct. 21, 1974 he left behind a reputation for commitment to social justice, reconciliation, and valuing human life. Archbishop Binz returned to St. Paul from his retirement to administer the archdiocese until a new archbishop could be appointed.

In 1975, John Roach was the second native son to become archbishop. As rector of the preparatory seminary, Nazareth Hall, he oversaw its closing and the establishment of St. John Vianney Seminary at the College of St. Thomas. Regarding the Second Vatican Council as the most significant event in the 20th century, he approached renewal and revitalization of the Church in his archdiocese with optimism and vision. As president of the United States Bishops' Conference, he supported collegiality and mutuality within all structures of the Church. He supported the Detroit Call to Action program of 1976. A believer in delegating authority, Roach called on clergy and laity within the local Church to address issues through various archdiocesan commissions. He championed the cause of ecumenism at the local and national levels. He appointed a special Commission on Women, and named many women to serve on archdiocesan boards and commissions. New religious groups, such as the Brothers of Peace, were welcomed into the archdiocese. The growing demands of episcopal leadership in the archdiocese prompted Roach to ask for auxiliary bishops. Bishops Paul Dudley; John Kinney; Richard Hamm, MM; William Bullock; Robert Carlson; Joseph Charron, CPPS; and Lawrence Welsh were all consecrated during Roach's episcopacy. All but Bishop Welsh, who died in 1999, were called to serve as ordinaries of other dioceses.

New immigrant groups moved into the archdiocese in the 1970s and 1980s. Hmong were notably served at St. Mary's in Lowertown St. Paul, and Vietnamese in north Minneapolis, making St. Joseph's Church their parish church. By 1978 Hispanics were scattered throughout the archdiocese. Roach called for lay and religious leaders to help these newcomers assimilate into American culture. Roach strove for better relations between Catholics and Jews in the archdiocese and throughout the universal Church. In August of 1987, he represented the NCCB at a meeting in Rome to establish a commission whose purpose was to draw up an official Catholic statement on the Holocaust. During his administration the Catholic Education Center influenced the passage of a Minnesota State law in 1978 that mandated public service to handicapped children within non-public schools within the state. Ministry to gays and lesbians in the local church became an important issue when the question of hiring homosexual teachers in parochial schools arose. Roach

acceded to the urging of many priests, religious, and laity in establishing an AIDS ministry in the archdiocese. During the Roach years, Catholic Charities grew into the largest non-governmental social service agency in the metropolitan area. Through the 35-year leadership of Monsignor Jerome Boxleitner, this agency put faces on those in need and upheld their dignity as persons. To address the growing needs of the aging, Catholic Elder Care was opened in northeast Minneapolis, with archdiocesan support. Roach led the archdiocese in a campaign of prayer to fight the atrocities against human rights committed abroad, especially the killing of religious and lay missionaries in Latin America and Africa. He used his influence as president of the NCCB to draw the attention of Congress to these matters. Prodded by lay leaders in the archdiocese, Roach supported the establishment of the Minnesota Center for Medical and Legal Aspects of Torture to provide services for victims of human rights violations seeking asylum in the United States. The Archdiocesan Urban Affairs Commission endorsed the Nuclear Freeze Campaign, urging Congress to press for negotiations between the United States and the U.S.S.R. for nuclear arms reduction. When the problems of farmers escalated during the 1980s, Roach, as leader of the National Catholic Rural Life Conference, lobbied Congress for just laws protecting farmers.

The press put pressures on the archbishop to address local problems of sexual abuse by archdiocesan clergy. Roach adopted a policy that included sexual awareness training for all archdiocesan personnel in all ministries. The Newman Center at the University of Minnesota was authorized to set up a chapter of Dignity for gay Catholics, and asked that all its members sign a statement of support of the Church's teaching on HOMOSEXUALITY. Dignity members refused and a difficult public separation between the archbishop and area homosexuals followed. Roach tried to reinforce Catholic teaching on sexual morality through the Catholic Education Center.

On Feb. 22, 1994 Archbishop Harry J. Flynn of Lafayette, Louisiana, was appointed coadjutor archbishop of St. Paul and Minneapolis. He assumed full responsibilities in 1995, upon Roach's retirement. Flynn's new see covered 12 counties, and included 222 parishes and more than 40 archdiocesan agencies serving a variety of ministries. His weekly column in the official organ of the archdiocese, which he renamed *The Catholic Spirit,* emphasized the on-going presence of Christ in the work of His Church. A staunch supporter of the Pro-Life Movement, he also spoke out against capital punishment. When he came to St. Paul, problems of domestic violence, racial discrimination, fair wages, full employment, health care needs, and welfare reform abounded. Flynn had to address two immediate problems: just financial compensation and financing on-going education for those in Church ministry. He strongly encouraged an active role for the laity. Because of the shortage of priests and the shifting areas of population growth in the metropolitan area, Flynn called on his flock to support the merging of some parishes and the founding of others.

The year 2000 marked the sesquicentennial of the Archdiocese of St. Paul and Minneapolis with many special celebrations. At that time, the Catholic population of the archdiocese numbered 759,662 in a total population of 2,792,064. There were 342 diocesan priests, 158 religious priests, 171 permanent deacons, 50 brothers, 1094 sisters, and 563 lay ministers. There were 222 parishes, three Catholic hospitals, four homes for the aged, five centers for social services, three colleges and universities, nine Catholic high schools, and 89 Catholic elementary schools. The schools were staffed mainly by laity. The shortage of priests continues to be a major problem in the archdiocese. In early 1999 auxiliary bishop Lawrence Welsh died after a long illness. That same year, Fr. Frederic Campbell was consecrated an auxiliary bishop for the archdiocese, and in 2001 Richard Pates was appointed auxiliary as well.

Bibliography: *Archives of the Archdiocese of St. Paul and Minneapolis,* St. Paul, MN. P. H. AHERN, ed., *Catholic Heritage in Minnesota, North Dakota, South Dakota* (St. Paul 1964). A. RAUCHE and A. M BIERMAIER, *They Came to Teach: The Story of Sisters Who Taught in Parochial Schools and Their Contributions to Elementary Education in Minnesota* (St. Cloud, Minn. 1994). J. M. REARDON, *The Catholic Church in the Diocese of St. Paul* (St. Paul 1952). J. C. WOLKERSTORFER, *You Shall Be My People: A History of the Archdiocese of St. Paul and Minneapolis* (France 1999). M. R. O'CONNELL, *John Ireland and the American Catholic Church* (St. Paul 1988).

[J. C. WOLKERSTORFER]

SAINT PAUL-OUTSIDE-THE-WALLS, ABBEY OF

Benedictine abbey *nullius* adjacent to the basilica of St. Paul-Outside-the-Walls, Rome, Italy. The first mention of a monastic community near the tomb of St. Paul the Apostle, just beyond the city walls of ancient ROME, was in the 6th century. Later, the Monastery of S. Cesario—the original nucleus of Saint Paul's—is mentioned in the *LIBER DIURNUS* of Pope GREGORY II (d. 731). Pope Gregory III (d. 741) ordered the monks to celebrate five daily Masses at five different altars in the nearby basilica over St. Paul's tomb. Such activity served to identify the monks more and more closely with the basilica. Then in the 9th century the Saracens destroyed the monastery when they destroyed the tomb of St. Paul. The CLUNIAC REFORM by St. ODO OF CLUNY (942) and by St.

MAJOLUS (994) restored the dignity and prestige of the community for nearly a century, but by the 11th century the monastery had again fallen into spiritual and material depths. Pope LEO IX chose Hildebrand (the future Pope GREGORY VII) to revive it, giving him the title of "Abbas et Rector" of Saint Paul. Under him, both abbey and basilica were restored and the monastery grew spiritually and materially until it became a strong ecclesiastic feudal domain. Hildebrand is still memorialized in the abbey's bronze Byzantine door and a Carolingian Bible in its library. During the AVIGNON PAPACY the abbey was distinguished both by its general prestige and by its loyalty to the pope. In the 15th century, however, the general decadence of Rome affected both the economic and the spiritual life of the monastery. The reform of St. Justina of Padua, promoted by L. Barbo (d. 1443), gave new spiritual life to the abbey and saved it from economic disaster. From the 15th to the 18th century Saint Paul's was a center for many saintly and learned men; its economy was based on a great landed estate. However, the Napoleonic and later Italian suppressions divested it of all its possessions and seriously compromised its monastic life. Its religious and economic revival in the late 19th century has resulted in the present-day monastery, which is marked by austere regular observance and serious study.

Bibliography: L. H. COTTINEAU, *Répertoire topobibliographique des abbayes et prieurés,* 2 v. (Mâcon 1935–39) 2:2521. I. SCHUSTER, *L'Abbazia di S. Paolo* (Rome 1929). G. FERRARI, *Early Roman Monasteries* (Rome 1957). G. PENCO, *Storia del monachesimo in Italia* (Rome 1961).

[S. BAIOCCHI]

ST. PAUL'S CATHEDRAL (LONDON)

Most important baroque church in England and Sir Christopher Wren's masterpiece. An early church on Ludgate Hill, London, was removed *c.* 1080 and Old St. Paul's Cathedral was finished by the end of the 13th century. Following 17th-century repairs by Inigo Jones and the Great Fire of 1666 that almost destroyed the structure, Wren was called upon for further repairs. At first he thought to rebuild the Gothic church, but the walls proved insecure, and in 1668 Wren began work on a fresh plan. His initial plan called for a Greek cross with a dome over the intersection after the manner of S. Maria della Salute in Venice. For the sake of the liturgy, this plan was dropped in favor of a medieval arrangement with extended choir and nave of equal lengths and short transept arms. Though Wren believed that Paris was "the best school of architecture in Europe," the cathedral has many Roman features. The dome, like Michelangelo's dome on St. Peter's, spans the width of both nave and aisles, a diameter of 100 feet, and its exterior profile is clearly dependent on Bramante's Tempietto of St. Pietro in Montorio. The space suggested is not that of the known, as in the Pantheon, nor the mystical unknowable space of the medieval conception, but the knowable, yet unknown, space of the Renaissance experience. The clock towers of the façade, moreover, are reminiscent of Borromini's S. Agnese in Piazza Navona, Rome. Yet the whole church, dominated by the dome from whatever angle it is viewed and encircled by a two-storied facing on all sides, makes for an impressive unity.

Bibliography: *Publications of the Wren Society,* ed. A. T. BOLTON and H. D. HENDRY, 20 v. (London 1924–43) v.13–16. S. B. HAMILTON, ''The Place of Sir Christopher Wren in the History of Structural Engineering,'' *Transactions of the New-comen, Society . . . , London* 14 (1933–34) 27–42. R. DUTTON, *The Age of Wren* (New York 1951). J. N. SUMMERSON, *Architecture in Britain, 1530–1830* (4th ed. *Pelican History of Art* Z3; 1963). S.A. WARNER, *St. Paul's Cathedral* (London 1923). W.R. MATTHEWS and W.M. ATKINS, eds., *A History of St. Paul's Cathedral and the Men Associated with It* (London 1964). D.F. EWIN, *St. Paul's Cathedral* (London 1976).

[W. S. RUSK/EDS.]

ST. PETER OF MUENSTER, ABBEY OF

Founded in 1903 in central Saskatchewan, Canada, by the members of the Benedictine priory of Cluny, Ill., augmented by several Benedictines from St. John's Abbey, Collegeville, MN, to provide spiritual care for the pioneer Catholic homesteaders. The priory became St. Peter's Abbey in 1911, and in 1921 an abbey *nullius* with territory detached from the Diocese of Prince Albert. The Benedictines serve in the parishes of the abbacy, conduct a high school (1921), and (since 1926) St. Peter's Junior College. A German weekly was published from 1904 to 1947; an English weekly began in 1922. Alfred Mayer was the prior of the original foundation. He was succeeded by Bruno Doerfler (1906), who was appointed first abbot (1911–19); Michael Ott (1919–26), who became the first abbot ordinary; Severin Gertken (1926–60); Jerome Weber (1960–96); and Peter Novecosky (1996–). In 2001, the abbey was home to 33 monks.

Bibliography: *Fifty Golden Years* (Münster, Sask. 1953).

[J. WEBER]

ST. PETER'S BASILICA

The architectural history of the basilica of St. Peter falls into four main phases: (1) the small memorial set up to mark the Apostle's grave after his martyrdom under Nero (54–68); (2) the great basilica, Old St. Peter's, initiated by Constantine *c.* 324 and apparently completed by his son Constantius *c.* 354; (3) the transitional stage, 1506 to 1546, when construction of the new basilica was in a state of flux; and (4) the present building, begun by Michelangelo in the 16th century and completed by Bernini in the late 17th century.

Old St. Peter's. Recent excavations under the basilica have shown that both the Old and the New St. Peter's were centered with great care on a particular grave, although this involved very great technical difficulties. This is presumably the ''Trophy'' of St. Peter mentioned *c.* 200 by Gaius; certainly it was believed to be the tomb of Peter by Emperor Constantine (d. 337), under whom the first great basilica was begun. Old St. Peter's, with the Lateran, was one of the first great churches erected for the newly liberated Christians; its architectural features, still preserved in essentials in the Lateran, were fundamental for future church building. Old St. Peter's consisted of an enormous nave and four aisles for the congregation, joined to the *confessio,* the tomb of the Martyr, which was set at the junction of nave, transepts, and presbytery. The plan drawn by Alpharanus (engraved 1590), together with several drawings and paintings, gives a good idea of the appearance of Old St. Peter's.

During the papacy of Nicholas V (1447–55) it became evident that the building, then more than 1,000 years old, would have to be replaced, Nicholas and his architectural adviser L. B. Alberti apparently began fresh foundations for a choir at the southwest angle, under the direction of Bernardo Rossellino. It is not known how much progress was made, since construction was discontinued soon afterward; but a serious start had been made, judging from Bramante's early designs, which take account of this work.

New St. Peter's. The history of New St. Peter's began soon after the election of Julius II (1503) and before the laying of the foundation stone on April 18, 1506. Julius seems to have decided very early in his pontificate that a real start had to be made on a new building and that he had an adequate architect in Bramante. Perhaps the lack of an architect of Bramante's ambition and experience was responsible for the long delay between Nicholas V and Julius II. The early stages of the planning are very obscure, since no definitive program seems to have been prepared and the medal struck in 1506 to commemorate the laying of the foundation stone seems to represent a Bramante project rather than a specific program. Only one drawing by Bramante himself can be attached to this first project—a large plan on parchment, which may represent half of a symmetrical Greek-cross plan or may be

Exterior view of dome of Saint Peter's Basilica, designed by Michelangelo, middle of the 16th century. Photograph by Peter Wilson. (Corbis)

no more than a design for transepts and choir, to be added to the existing nave. It appears that Bramante experimented for many years with different designs, some in the form of a Greek cross, others closer to the traditional Latin cross of Old St. Peter's. The principal idea was to replan the new building around the tomb, which *ipso facto* ruled out plans that could not be fitted to the site. There is a large collection of drawings in the Uffizi, Florence, of projects for the new building, but most of them seem to be no more than design exercises by Bramante's pupils and assistants. From these drawings, the medal of 1506, and a group of small centrally planned churches (all built after *c.* 1508), one may deduce that Bramante's principal project was for a large Greek-cross building with apsidal projections on each side and crowned with an enormous dome, imitating the Pantheon. There is serious doubt whether such a dome would have stood on the four piers that were the basis of the plan. One of these piers was established in 1506 and another was begun before Bramante's death, so that the existing basilica was conditioned by the space between these two piers and the great arch that joins them and, hence, the space of the crossing and the dome over it. This, however, was practically all that Bramante contributed to the present build-

ing. After the death of Julius II in 1513, followed by that of Bramante in 1514, comparatively little was done, although the superintending architects were Raphael and Peruzzi, both of whom had worked with Bramante. All building was brought to a stop by the sack of Rome in 1527, and for many years the basilica looked like one of the ruins of Rome, as may be seen from drawings made in the 1530s.

A fresh start was made when Antonio da Sangallo the Younger was called in; he modified the plan considerably. He prepared an elaborate model (1539–46), with many variations from the original designs. The first great change was to abandon the central plan in favor of a long nave, better suited for large crowds. Bramante himself had experimented with a long-nave plan, and Sangallo's model was an awkward compromise consisting of a centrally planned shape, based on one of Bramante's designs, linked by a huge bridge to an elaborate nave with two great towers and a Benediction Loggia in the façade. Sangallo, who was an experienced engineer, also tackled the problem of the dome, redesigning it to spread the weight more effectively and, at the same time, greatly enlarging the supporting piers. Nevertheless, his design was ugly; Sangallo was totally unable to cope with the prob-

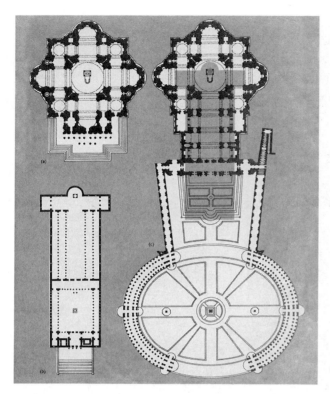

Three architectural drawings of St. Peter's Basilica by Michelangelo based on 1569 engraving by Duperac, old basilica plan, and completed piazza and colonnade.

lems of colossal scale. He died in 1546, before much work had been done on the actual building.

Design of Michelangelo. Sangallo was succeeded by MICHELANGELO, who at once redesigned the whole building, claiming that he was returning to the basic principles laid down by Bramante—at the same time making caustic remarks on Sangallo's work. Michelangelo's appointment began on Jan. 1, 1547, by which date he had already prepared a rough model; at his death on Feb. 18, 1564, more work had been accomplished than under all his predecessors. Michelangelo's design returned to a central plan with a great dome over it; but unlike Bramante's central plan, one side was emphasized as the entrance side and marked by a portico. Engravings made shortly after Michelangelo's death give a good idea of his plan, which differs from the executed building in the dome, nave, and entrance.

The existing dome, built between 1585 and 1590 by Giacomo della Porta and Domenico Fontana, was probably given its present pointed shape because this helped to spread the load, while the hemispherical dome shown in the engravings after Michelangelo might have proved impractical. The other major difference between the existing building and Michelangelo's project was the reversion once more to a Latin-cross plan. There seems no doubt that Michelangelo, following Bramante, preferred the Greek-cross shape as more symmetrical and more suited to the character of the church. Nevertheless, the Constantinian church had been basilican in plan with an enormous nave, and practical considerations determined the rejection of the Greek-cross in favor of a longer nave. This was achieved very skillfully by Carlo Maderno, who added a long nave to Michelangelo's entrance façade. By this means he also secured large chapels at each side, usable as sacristies until the present sacristy was built in the 18th century. The change from Greek- to Latin-cross involved considerable problems with the façade, since the dome was no longer clearly visible from the front, and the arms of the transepts projected rather awkwardly until they were masked by extending the façade at each side. Maderno's façade is treated like Michelangelo's designs for secular palaces, so that the forms themselves are Michelangelesque, although there is a curiously secular flavor about the façade as a whole. The Benediction Loggia was placed by Maderno over the main door. The two ends were to have had towers added, which would have been a reversion to the original Bramante plan; but when they were begun in 1637, under BERNINI, the foundations proved inadequate and they had to be demolished.

The piazza outside the church was very successfully incorporated into the design by Bernini when he added an enormous Doric colonnade with semicircular ends, so that the whole of the piazza together with the façade forms a single architectural unit. Originally the colonnade was closed off by a block at the end of the present Via della Conciliazione, so that the visitor saw nothing until he entered the piazza, when the whole design became visible at once. This effect of surprise was ruined by Mussolini, who demolished the central block to give a "vista" from the river bank.

The interior is almost entirely 17th century, although the painting of the dome and the rich mosaics were begun about 1590. Bernini's work was completed by the enormous bronze baldacchino of 1633, followed, as viewed down the nave, by the equally enormous Cathedra Petri, completed in 1666. The whole interior decoration is thus of baroque design. However, the mosaic of "Peter's Barque," originally designed by Giotto, and the bronze doors by Filarete have survived from Old St. Peter's.

See Also: VATICAN

Bibliography: No full modern bibliography has been published; two most useful works on the whole history of the building are S. SCHÜLLER-PIROLI, *2000 Jahre Sankt Peter* (Olten, Switz. 1950) and C. GALASSI PALUZZI, *San Pietro in Vaticano,* 3 v. (Le Chiese di Roma illustrate; Rome 1965); both have extensive literary references. For the problem of the Apostle's tomb there are, in English, E. KIRSCHBAUM, *Tombs of St. Peter and St. Paul,* tr. J.

St. Peter's Basilica and the piazza surrounded by the colonnade, aerial view. (Alinari–Art Reference/Art Resource, NY)

MURRAY (New York 1959) and J. M. TOYNBEE and J. W. PERKINS, *The Shrine of St. Peter* (New York 1956). For Old St. Peter's the principal authority is T. ALFARANO, *De Basilicae Vaticanae antiquissima et nova structura,* ed. M. CERRATI (Studi e Testi 26; 1914). Many of the drawings and plans for New St. Peter's are reproduced in P. LETAROUILLY, *Le Vatican et la Basilique de S. Pierre,* 2 v. (Paris 1882; repr. London 1953). The principal sources are still H. VON GEYMÜLLER, ed., *Die ursprünglichen Entwürfe für Sanct Peter in Rom,* 2 v. (Vienna 1875–80) and D. FREY, *Bramantes S. Peter: Entwurf und seine Apokryphen* (Vienna 1915).

[P. MURRAY]

SAINT-PIERRE-SUR-DIVES, ABBEY OF

Former BENEDICTINE monastery of Notre Dame, Séez diocese, France. It was founded first for nuns, then for monks, by Countess Lescelina of Eu. To secure self-sufficiency and complete independence for the house, she recruited the first monks and their abbot from Saint-Trinité, Rouen (*c.* 1046). This Abbot Aynard was a noted religious poet. In the mid-12th century the rebuilding of the church was the occasion of several remarkable acts of devotion. The monastery flourished until the 14th century and was fortified during the Hundred Years' War without suffering important damage. At this time it was known as Notre Dame d'Espinay.

The abbey was burned and pillaged by the Calvinists in 1562. It continued to languish under commendatory abbots and recovered only when the MAURISTS were installed in 1668. It was dissolved in 1790 during the French Revolution. The abbey church (13th and 14th century) now serves as the parish church; the chapter house and some claustral buildings survive.

Bibliography: *Gallia Christiana,* v.1–13 (Paris 1715–85), v.14–16 (Paris 1856–65) 11:728–735. L. H. COTTINEAU, *Répertoire* *topobibliographique des abbayes et prieurés,* 2 v. (Mâcon 1935–39) 2:2851–52.

[D. J. A. MATTHEW]

SAINT-QUENTIN, MONASTERY OF

Former foundation of Canons Regular in Vermandois, city of Saint-Quentin, Aisne, France (Latin, *S. Quintinus Veromanduensis*). A small building erected over the tomb of the martyr St. Quentin in 355 seems to have been destroyed *c.* 362 under Emperor Julian the Apostate and then rebuilt in 497 after the baptism of CLOVIS. When ELIGIUS, Bishop of Noyon, rediscovered the relics of Quentin (650), he founded a monastery whose first abbot was Ebertran, a German from Constance and former monk of LUXEUIL. Abbot Fulrad, who was succeeded by Hugh, a son of Charlemagne, restored the basilica between 814 and 824, but the NORMANS burned it in 883. In the 10th century CANONS REGULAR OF ST. AUGUSTINE replaced the monks, their superiors for some time retaining the title of "abbot." One of the deans was Dudo of Saint-Quentin (first half of the 11th century) who wrote the *Historia Normanorum* in three books. At this time, the monastery's income was divided into individual prebends and the community suffered a corresponding weakening of discipline. Eventually in 1214, Robert of Courtonne, Cardinal and Legate of the Holy See, divided the area, which had previously comprised one parish for Saint-Quentin, into nine parishes. In 1257 the relics of SS. Quentin, Victricius, and Cassian were transferred to the church choir in the presence of King Louis IX. Numerous conflicts from the 13th to the 18th century erupted between the dean and chapter, or between the canons and bishop of Noyon. The French Revolution abolished the abbey. The collegiate church with one of the most magnificent naves in France survives, having been restored after World War I bombing. The architecture is 13th- and 14th-century Gothic with surviving traces of the 1114 edifice. It is 315 feet long and 175 feet high; it has two transepts separated by a double ambulatory with four bays, and 110 windows, those of the choir being 13th- and 14th-century stained glass. The crypt (13th century) houses the tomb of St. Quentin.

Bibliography: O. HACHET, *La Basilique de St. Quentin* (Saint-Quentin 1909). H. LECLERCQ, *Dictionnaire d'archéologie chrétienneet de liturgie,* ed. F. CABROL, H. LECLERCQ and H. I. MARROU, 15 v. (Paris 1907–53) 14.2:2025.

[J. DAOUST]

ST. RAPHAEL'S SOCIETY

St. Raphael's Society was founded at the Catholic Congress in Mainz, Germany (1871), by Peter Paul CA-HENSLY, an outstanding Catholic layman, merchant, and member of the Prussian Diet. Its purpose was to advise prospective emigrants, to protect them while they were in transit from the port of embarkation, and to help them upon their arrival in the country of their choice. The society had its representatives in every major port of Europe, North and South America, and Africa. During the 1880s and 1890s it was criticized for its alleged exclusive interest in German nationals. Strong opposition developed to its advocacy of settling immigrants in colonies to preserve their language and faith and its insistence on obtaining pastors of the same nationality as the colonists. To make its real scope better known the society broadened its base of operation and organized daughter societies, the first of which was in the U.S. (1883) with Bp. Winand M. WIGGER of Newark, N.J., as first president. Similar organizations were established in Austria (1889), Italy (1889), and Spain (1913). World War I interrupted emigration and the work of the society; after the war only the American and German societies resumed operations. In New York, Leo House, a hospice for immigrants established earlier, moved to a new location nearer the piers. In Germany, George Timpe, SAC, began a reorganization of the society and served as its secretary general until 1930. After World War II the work of reorganizing was continued by the new secretary general, Friedrich Fröhling, SAC.

Under Church auspices, the society is now guided by a board of directors, made up of clerical and lay members, the president of which is a member of the hierarchy. The president of the German society is always the bishop of Osnabrück in whose diocese the headquarters at Hamburg are located. The president of the American society is always the archbishop of New York. Information offices in all the major cities of Europe and the U.S. carry on the advisory work of the society. In 1964 more than 18,000 persons received help and advice from these offices. In the course of time the society's work shifted from the countries of immigration to those of emigration. It is supported by free-will offerings and contributions from the hierarchy and international funds.

The society was instrumental in improving conditions on the ships carrying immigrants and it helped to preserve the faith of many Catholic immigrants. In the mid-20th century its purpose was to remain an effective instrument in the hands of the Church for carrying out papal suggestions concerning immigration.

Bibliography: C. J. BARRY, *The Catholic Church and German Americans* (Milwaukee 1953). G. TIMPE, *Raphaelshandbuch* (Hamburg 1921).

[O. A. BOENKI]

SAINT-REMI, ABBEY OF

Former BENEDICTINE Abbey in Reims, France (Latin, *S. Remigius Remensis*). As early as 550 the funeral chapel of St. REMIGIUS OF REIMS in the Christian cemetery on the outskirts of Reims was served by a community of clerics under the jurisdiction of the bishop. Archbishop Tilpin introduced Benedictine observance (790), and he and his successors titled themselves abbots. Then in 945 Abp. Hugh of Vermandois had the monks reformed by the abbot of Fleury (SAINT-BENOÎT-SUR-LOIRE). Saint-Remi became autonomous and had an abbot of its own, the abbot's and the monastery's revenues being kept separate; the archbishops became the protectors of the abbey. Its original wealth was constantly augmented by royal and seigneurial gifts (e.g., priories such as Corbény, Hesdin in Artois, Saint-Rémy in Provence, and numerous villages). Saint-Remi was the primatial abbey of REIMS, and its monks were on a par with the canons of the cathedral chapter until the 13th century. Then a conflict arose with the archbishops, who wanted to end the abbey's episcopal EXEMPTION. As a result, the abbey placed itself under royal protection. Several kings were crowned in the abbey church and are buried there. In 1627, Saint-Remi was affiliated with the MAURIST congregation. It was suppressed in the French Revolution, but the abbey church (built 1005–1170) is extant, and the conventual buildings are now a museum.

Its library, the best in Reims, had at least 600 manuscripts, most of which were lost in the fire of 1774. In the 9th and 10th centuries the abbey school produced HUCBALD OF SAINT-AMAND, REMIGIUS OF AUXERRE, and FLODOARD; in the 12th century, Odo, author of *Miracula s. Remigii,* and PETER OF CELLE; in the 17th and 18th centuries, the Maurist scholars William Marlot (the historian of Reims), Denis de Sainte-Marthe, MABILLON, and Edmond Martène.

Bibliography: B. GUÉRARD, ed., *Polyptique de l'abbaye de Saint-Remi. . . IXème siècle* (Paris 1853). L. DEMAISON, "L'Église Saint-Remi," *Congrès archéologique de France . . . à Reims en 1911,* 2 v. (Paris 1912) 1:57–106. J. HOURLIER, "Le Monastère de St-Remi . . .," *Mémoires de la société d'agriculture, commerce, sciences et arts du département de la Marne* 75 (1960) 37–56. N. HUMANN, "Les Constructions médiévales à St-Remi . . .," *ibid.* 74 (1959) 34–87; 75 (1960) 57–69.

[P. COUSIN]

SAINT-RIQUIER, ABBEY OF

Former Benedictine abbey, near Abbeville (Somme), northern France (Diocese of Amiens). It was named after St. Riquier (Ricarius), who lived in the *vicus* of Centule in Ponthieu, France, and who was converted to Christian-

Saint-Remi Abbey. (©Sandro Vannini/CORBIS)

ity during the reign of Dagobert (628–638). Having become a priest, he dedicated himself to preaching, spending his last years in a hermitage known as *cella Forestis (Forestmoutiers)*, in the forest of Crécy. He was buried there, but shortly afterward his body was transferred to Centule, where a Benedictine abbey, which soon received his name, was founded over his grave. Thus, the abbey was not founded by Riquier himself—in fact, little is known about the precise circumstances of its foundation. Under the CAROLINGIANS the community numbered up to 400 monks; the cloister buildings were completely rebuilt and enlarged, and three churches were built. There is an interesting 11th-century drawing, known now only through copies, that shows these churches and cloister in their triangular arrangement. ANGILBERT, one of the most remarkable men of the CAROLINGIAN RENAISSANCE, was abbot. This abbey, like so many others, was ruined by the NORMANS, but was later restored by GERARD OF BROGNE. In 1659 the abbey became part of the congregation of Saint-Maur (*see* MAURISTS); it disappeared in the French Revolution. The main abbey church remains today, a superb building in flamboyant style, the earlier Romanesque church there having been the predecessor of the six-towered Romanesque cathedral (e.g., Mainz, Speyer).

Bibliography: J. HÉNOCQUE, *Histoire de l'abbaye et de la ville de Saint-Riquier,* 3 v. (Amiens 1880–88). HARIULPHE, *Chronique de l'abbaye de Saint-Riquier,* ed. F. LOT (Paris 1894). L. H. COTTINEAU, *Répertoire topobibliographique des abbayes et prieurés,* 2 v. (Mâcon 1935–39) 2:2868–69. G. DURAND, *L'Église de Saint-Riquier* (2d ed. Paris 1960).

[H. PLATELLE]

SAINT-ROBERT-DE-CORNILLON, PRIORY OF

Former BENEDICTINE monastery of the commune Saint-Egrève, Diocese and *arrondissement* of Grenoble, Isère, France (Latin, *S. Robertus de Cornilione*). The priory was founded between 1073 and 1077 by Count Guigo II the Fat and his son Guigo III and given to the Abbey of CHAISE-DIEU. Its dependencies included Notre-Dame des Vignes, in Côtes de Sassenage (1328) and the priory of Les Plantées, both of the Diocese and arrondissement of Grenoble. Saint-Robert was never very important. It was united to the Congregation of Saint-Maur (*see* MAURISTS), and conventual life continued there until the French Revolution. Today only some ruins remain. The insane asylum of Saint-Robert has now been built on the site.

Bibliography: Archives of Isère, B, 4289 (1209–1782), H, 72 (1209–18th cent.). E. PILOT DE THOREY, *Prieuré de St. Robert: Notes et documents* (Bibliothèque, Grenoble, MS R 7906). A. AUVERGNE, ed., *Le cartulaire de Saint-Robert . . .* (Grenoble 1865). E. DUFOURD, *Notice sur . . . le prieuré de S. R.* (Annecy 1871). L. H. COTTINEAU, *Répertoire topobibliographique des abbayes et prieurés,* 2 v. (Mâcon 1935–39) 2:2870.

[J. DE LA C. BOUTON]

SAINT-SAËNS, CAMILLE

Romanticist composer, pianist, organist, critic; b. Paris, Oct. 9, 1835 (christened Charles Camille); d. Algiers, Dec. 16, 1921. After sound musical preparation under his great-aunt Charlotte Masson, he studied at the Paris Conservatory and later was organist at the church of Saint-Merry (1853–57) and the Madeleine (1858–77). Thereafter he devoted himself exclusively to composition and worldwide concert tours (including the U.S., and at 81, South America). He composed prolifically in all forms and for virtually all media. He is best known for his symphonic poems, especially *Danse macabre* and the witty *Carnival of the Animals,* third symphony (with organ obbligato), opera *Samson and Dalila,* and A-minor cello concerto. Although an excellent organist, Saint-

Saëns left few organ works, and they have been overshadowed by those of such successors as FRANCK and Guilmant. His intimate *Christmas Oratorio* (1863) is popular with amateur choirs, and *Le Déluge* (1876) contains effective choral writing. Because of its lack of dramatic action and the powerful choruses in acts 1 and 3, *Samson and Dalila* might be more effective as a semistaged oratorio. Saint-Saëns' significance is not primarily as a church composer, but rather as a founder of 19th-century French instrumental music, friend of French musical nationalism (he was a founder of the Societé Nationale de Musique, 1871), roving ambassador for French music, and editor of music by GLUCK, RAMEAU, and MOZART. In his critical writings he strongly opposed WAGNER, D' INDY, and DEBUSSY. His music is characterized by impeccable (if "academic") craftsmanship and spirited idiomatic scoring for voices and instruments.

Bibliography: J. CHANTAVOINE, *Camille Saint-Saëns* (Paris 1947). M. COOPER, *French Music* (London 1951). P. C. R. LANDORMY, *La Musique française de Franck à Debussy* (Paris 1943). M. D. CALVOCORESSI, *Grove's Dictionary of Music and Musicians,* ed. E. BLOM 9 v. (5th ed. London 1954) 7:365–370. *Baker's Biographical Dictionary of Musicians,* ed. N. SLONIMSKY (5th, rev. ed. New York 1958) 1400–02. J. HARDING, "*Samson et Dalila* [*Samson and Delilah*]" in *International Dictionary of Opera* 2 vols., ed. C. S. LARUE (Detroit 1993) 1176. J. HARDING and D. M. FALLON, "(Charles) Camille Saint-Saëns" in *The New Grove Dictionary of Music and Musicians,* vol. 16, ed. S. SADIE, (New York 1980) 400–407. E. R. HARKINS, "The Chamber Music of Camille Saint-Saëns" (Ph.D. diss. New York University, 1976). R. SMITH, *Saint-Saëns and the Organ* (Hillsboro 1992). M. STEBEMANN, *Camille Saint-Saëns and the French Solo Concerto from 1850 to 1920,* trans. A. C. SHERWIN (Portland 1991). R. STEVENSON, "Saint-Saëns's Views on the Performance of Early Music," *Performance Practice Review* 2 (1989), 126–132. S. STUDD, *Saint-Saëns: a Critical Biography* (London 1999).

[R. M. LONGYEAR]

SAINT-SAVIN-DE-BIGORRE, ABBEY OF

Former Benedictine abbey located in the Diocese of Tarbes, department of the Upper Pyrenees, *arrondissement* and canton of Argelès. Its origins date back probably to the reign of CHARLEMAGNE and to the convent of Saint-Martin (-de-Bencer), where the body of St. Savinus had been transported (d. *c.* 794). His relics were the object of veneration by the pilgrims of Compostela. (*See* SANTIAGO DE COMPOSTELA.) The abbey was affiliated with SAINT-VICTOR IN MARSEILLES in 1080 and was reformed by the congregation of Saint-Maur in 1625. The old abbey church is still admired for its austere but beautiful architecture.

Bibliography: *Archives départementales des Basses-Pyrénées* H 147–158. *Archives départementales des Haules-*

Pyrénées H 95–117. A. MEILLON, *Histoire de la vallée de Cauterets,* 2 v. (Cauterets 1920–36), v.1 *Les Origines: Le Cartulaire de l'abbaye de Saint-Savin-en-Lavedan,* v.2 *L'Abbaye de Saint-Savin-en-Lavedan.* L. H. COTTINEAU, *Répertoire topobibliographique des abbayes et prieurés,* 2 v. (Mâcon 1935–39) 2:2882–83.

[J. TRÉMENBERT-LE BRAZ]

SAINT-SAVIN-SUR-GARTEMPE, ABBEY OF

Former Benedictine monastery, department of Vienne, France, Diocese of Poitiers (Latin, *S. Savinus ad Wartimpam*). Founded *c.* 800 by the count abbot Badilon of Marmoutier, it was named for the 5th-century martyr St. Savinus, originally interred nearby. His relics were transferred to the abbey when it was enlarged by Louis the Pious, who reputedly entrusted it to BENEDICT OF ANIANE. It was a center of monastic reform from the 9th through the 11th centuries, and its religious reestablished regular observance of the BENEDICTINE RULE in other houses. From here, Hugh of Anzy (d. *c.* 930) became the reforming abbot of Saint-Martin-d'Autun, and Gombaud reformed Charroux (1023). Prosperity declined during the Hundred Years' War. Pillaged repeatedly during the WARS OF RELIGION (1562–85), it fell into decay under simoniacal abbots. MAURISTS were introduced in 1642–43; it was suppressed during the French Revolution. The 11th-century abbey church, renowned for its Romanesque frescoes (11th–12th centuries) of the Apocalypse, Redemption, and Genesis, serves as parish church; the monastic buildings house municipal offices.

Bibliography: É. MAILLARD, *L'Église de Saint-Savin sur Gartempe* (Paris 1926). I. YOSNIKAWA, *L'Apocalypse de Saint Savin* (Paris 1939). L. H. COTTINEAU, *Répertoire topobibliographique des abbayes et prieurés,* 2 v. (Mâcon 1935–39) 2:2881.

[G. E. GINGRAS]

SAINT-SEVER, ABBEYS OF

The SS. Severus are mostly shrouded in legend. Severus, bishop of Barcelona (feast, Nov. 6), was martyred in 302 under DIOCLETIAN; his relics were discovered in 1079, taken to the monastery of San Cugat del Vallés, and translated to Barcelona in 1405. Severus, 12th bishop of Naples, 363 to 409 (feast, April 29 or 30), received a letter from St. AMBROSE in 393 (*Patrologia Latina,* ed. J. P. Migne, 217 v., 16:1232–33); a book of his miracles was written *c.* 1046. Severus, 12th bishop of Ravenna (feast, Feb. 1), patron of weavers, since weaving was his own profession originally, and patron of spinners and police, attended the Council of Sardica in 343. A basilica was dedicated to him *c.* 580 in Ravenna; his relics, and those of his wife and daughter were translated to Mainz and Erfurt in 836; his vita was composed in Mainz soon after 586; in 1871 his relics were discovered in a 5th-century reliquary in Grado. Severus (d. *c.* 500), a Syrian monk, founded the flourishing abbey of Saint-André in Agde, which in 1064 came under SAINT-VICTOR IN MARSEILLES; his relics are in the abbey of Saint-Sever in Agde, known in the 9th century, of which the bishops of Agde were for many years abbot and which became part of the chapter endowment in 1158. The shepherd Severus, bishop of Avranches, whose relics were venerated in Rouen, founded *c.* 523 a monastery in the Diocese of Coutances that Normans ruined and Benedictines restored in the 11th century.

The abbey of Saint-Sever (Gascony) in the Diocese of Aire has obscure origins. There was a Benedictine monastery (*c.* 700) near the tomb of a martyr on one of the roads to SANTIAGO DE COMPOSTELA in the place where one of the oldest Romanesque churches of southwest France now stands. Count William Sancho of Gascony began the abbey church *c.* 1000. In 1028 the abbey was attached to CLUNY and put under Abbot Gregory of Montaner (d. 1072), for whom was illuminated a famous MS of the Apocalypse (Paris BN Lat. 8878). It was restored by the MAURISTS in 1645, and lasted until the French Revolution.

Bibliography: Archives, Department of Landes, H, 1–130, 237–238, L. H. COTTINEAU, *Répertoire topobibliographique des abbayes et prieurés,* 2 v. (Mâcon 1935–39) 2:2888–89. J. L. BAUDOT and L. CHAUSSIN, *Vies des saints et des bienheueux selon l'ordre du calendrier avec l'historique des fêtes,* ed. by The Benedictines of Paris, 12 v. (Paris 1935–56) 11:10–11. A. RASTOUL, *Dictionnaire d'histoire et de géographie ecclésiastiques,* ed. A. BAUDRILLART (Paris 1912–) 1:929. G. GORDINI and G. LUCCHESI, *Lexikon für Theologie und Kirche,* ed. J. HOFER and K. RAHNER, 10 v. (2d, new ed. Freiburg 1957–65) 9:704.

[J. TRÉMENBERT-LE BRAZ]

SAINT-SEVER-DE-RUSTAN, ABBEY OF

Former BENEDICTINE monastery in Rabastens, Hautes-Pyrénées, France, Diocese of Tarbes (Latin, *S. Severus de Rustano* or *de Albiciaco*). Reputedly founded as a monastery *c.* 500 but destroyed by the Saracens *c.* 732, it was refounded under the Benedictine rule in the 10th century. A charter, restoring this abbey near the tomb of St. Severus, was granted by Count William Sancius, and the first known abbot was Arscinus. To restore discipline, Count Centullus of Bigorre made it dependent on SAINT-VICTOR IN MARSEILLES in 1087; the grant was confirmed by Pope Urban II in 1089. It suffered heavily

Claude Henri De Rouvroy Saint-Simon.

during the WARS OF RELIGION of the 16th century, being sacked in 1573. It came under the MAURISTS between 1646 and 1650; it was suppressed during the French Revolution. The abbey church, dating in part from the 11th century, now serves as a parish church. The cloisters (14th century) have been transported to the museum of Tarbes.

Bibliography: *Acta Sanctorum* Nov. 1:238–240. *Gallia Christiana,* v.1–13 (Paris 1715–85), v.14–16 (Paris 1856–65) 1:1243–46. L. H. COTTINEAU, *Répertoire topobibliographique des abbayes et prieurés,* 2 v. (Mâcon 1935–39) 2:2889.

[G. E. GINGRAS]

SAINT-SIMON, CLAUDE HENRI DE ROUVROY

Social philosopher and reformer; b. Paris, Oct. 17, 1760; d. Paris, May 13, 1825. He is said to have been educated by D'Alembert. He visited America, fought at Yorktown, suggested a linking of the Atlantic and Pacific oceans through Nicaragua, was during his later life in France rich and poor in turn, and attempted suicide in 1823 because he had failed to impress the men in power with his schemes of social reconstruction.

Saint-Simon's thought, which was not without fluctuations, was based on belief in a general law of history and the conviction that society, which in the past had been organized for war, would in the future be organized for production and peace. He saw his own day as a period of transition, mankind's "crisis of puberty." The feudal nobility had steadily declined; the industrial class had progressively developed and was ready to assume the responsibility of the state and society. Defining the industrial class as including both employers and workers, Saint-Simon understated the distinction, soon to be emphasized by Marx, between the propertied and the propertyless strata. He saw all engaged in industry (including agriculture) as bound together by a common interest in technical progress and rising standards of living. Thus he was not, properly speaking, a socialist. Rather, he envisioned a society led by a managerial élite.

In its detail, Saint-Simon's system was characterized by many ideas of the age, notably egalitarianism, representative government, liberalism, and utilitarianism. In domestic politics Saint-Simon expected "domination over men" to be replaced by a noncontentious "administration of things"; in international affairs he recommended supranational parliaments to look after common concerns. In philosophy of science, he started as a near-rationalist, seeing the laws of physics as the model of all true scientific insights, but he changed after 1814 to a more romantic position and tended increasingly to set biology up as the master science. Finding "critical" periods, such as the 18th century, lacking an inner principle of spiritual coherence, he advocated a nondogmatic and moralistic *Nouveau Christianisme* to do for the coming "organic" period of industrialism what Catholicism had done for the Middle Ages.

Owing to the presence of disparate strains in his thought, Saint-Simon fathered at least three dissimilar movements. One, developed by Barthélemy Prosper Enfantin and Saint-Amand Bazard, was quasi-religious, producing a sect and a cult that went beyond Saint-Simon's own position. The second brought out the more scientific implications of Saint-Simon's thought; Auguste COMTE based his attempt to create a positivist (i.e., unmetaphysical) social science on the inspirations of his master. Finally, Saint-Simon influenced men of action such as Ferdinand de Lesseps, creator of the Suez Canal, and the brothers Jacob Émile and Isaac Péreire, founders of the Crédit Mobilier. The fervor with which they pursued their projects owed much to Saint-Simon's messianic belief that concentration on the task of production, in a humanitarian spirit, would remove most of the evils from which humanity was suffering.

Bibliography: M. LEROY, *La Vie véritable du Comte Henri de Saint-Simon (1760–1825)* (Paris 1925). H. G. GOUHIER, *La Jeunesse* d'Auguste Comte et la formation du positivisme, 3 v. (Paris 1933–41), esp. v. 2. F. E. MANUEL, *The New World of Henri Saint-Simon* (Cambridge, Mass. 1956). M. M. DONDO, *The French Faust: Henri de Saint-Simon* (New York 1955). *The Doctrine of Saint-Simon: An Exposition,* tr. G. G. IGGERS (Boston 1958), a course of lectures given in Paris in 1828–29 by the Enfantin-Bazard circle.

[W. STARK]

ST. TERESA OF JESUS, SOCIETY OF

Also called Teresian Sisters (STJ; Official Catholic Directory #4020); a religious congregation founded in Spain in 1876 by Enrique de Ossó y Cervelló (1840–96), a priest and seminary professor, for the education of girls. The Holy See issued a *decretum laudis* and temporary approval of the constitutions in 1888. Definitive approval came in 1908. The Teresians first came to the U.S. in 1910. In the U.S., the sisters are engaged in education at all levels and ministries to the youth. The motherhouse is in Rome. The U.S. provincialate is in Covington, LA.

[J. F. BRODERICK/EDS.]

ST. THOMAS OF VILLANOVA, SISTERS OF

(SSTV, Official Catholic Directory #4030); religious congregation founded in 1661 at Lumballe, Brittany, by Pierre LeProust (1624–97), an Augustinian priest. In 1670 the members began to take vows, wear religious garb, and adopt their own constitutions modeled on the third rule of St. Augustine. Originally established to restore hospitals and care for the sick in them, the institute broadened its work during the founder's lifetime to aid in all forms of spiritual as well as material need. The congregation spread quickly through France but almost disappeared during the French Revolution. Napoleon I in 1801 aided its renewal, led by Pauline de Pinczon. In 1860 came the papal *decretum laudis;* and in 1873, papal approval of the institute and constitutions. Besides work in hospitals, orphanages, and schools, the sisters also aided the sick poor, principally in Brittany, Normandy, and Île de France. The congregation established their first foundation in the United States in 1948. The generalate is in Neuilly-sur-Seine, France. The United States provincialate is in Norwalk, Connecticut.

Bibliography: G. BERNOVILLE, *Les Religieuses de Saint Thomas de Villeneuve* (Paris 1953).

[J. F. BRODERICK/EDS.]

SAINT-TROND, ABBEY OF

Or the Flemish Sint-Truijen; former BENEDICTINE monastery in Limburg, Belgium (Lat. *Trudonense*). It was founded in 662 on a site called *Sacrinium* or *Sarchinium* by St. TRUDO (or Trond) of Brabant, and was dedicated (664) to St. Quentin and to St. REMIGIUS of Reims by Bp. Theodard of Maastricht. Trudo ruled his monastery with the simple title of superior; Grimo, his second successor, became first ''abbot'' there even though the abbey depended on St. Stephen's of Metz until the bishop of Liège became its protector (1227). Bp. EUCHERIUS OF ORLÉANS, who was exiled by Charles Martel, died at Saint-Trond in 742; Libertus was martyred there by the NORMANS who destroyed the monastery in 884. Adalbert I, Bishop of Metz, and abbot of Saint-Trond (944–964) revived the monastery. In the 11th century, under Abbots Gontran (1034–55) and Adalard II (1055–82), the monastery prospered, and the BENEDICTINE RULE was regularly observed. Abbot Thierry (d. 1107), who wrote a life of St. BAVO and *De vita et miraculis sancti Trudonis,* introduced the CLUNIAC REFORM. His successor Rudolph (d. 1138) composed a chronicle of the monastery and seven books against simoniacs; also, he had the abbey church consecrated by Otbert, Bishop of Liège (1117). The decline of the abbey was rapid in the 15th century; in 1520 Abbot William IV of Brussels, who was later to develop the Louvain Library (1525), invited monks from GEMBLOUX to renew Benedictine observance at Saint-Trond. In 1603 the monastery was attached to the BURSFELD Congregation; it was suppressed in 1796 and partially destroyed in 1798. Remains include a church tower with an 11th-century base, and a spire that dates from the 17th century.

Bibliography: C. PIOT, ed., *Cartulaire de l'abbaye de Saint-Trond,* 2 v. (Brussels 1870–74). *Gesta, Monumenta Germaniae Scriptores* (Berlin 1826–) 10:227–448. G. SIMENON, *L'Organisation économique de l'abbaye de Saint-Trond* (Brussels 1912). L. H. COTTINEAU, *Répertoire topobibliographique des abbayes et prieurés,* 2 v. (Mâcon 1935–39) 2:2905–06. M. COENS, ''Les Saints particulièrement honorés à l'abbaye de Saint-Trond,'' *Analecta Bollandiana* 72 (1954) 85–133, 397–426; 73 (1955) 140–192. É. BROUETTE, *Lexikon für Theologie und Kirche,* ed. J. HOFER and K. RAHNER, 10 v. (2d, new ed. Freiburg 1957–65) 9:176.

[J. DAOUST]

ST. URSULA, SOCIETY OF

(SU, Official Catholic Directory #4040); a congregation founded in 1606 in Dole, France, by Ven. Anne de XAINCTONGE. From the beginning it was a noncloistered community, one of the first female congregations to combine a contemplative life of prayer with an active life in the work of teaching. Inspired by the Jesuits' educational apostolate, the foundress based her community's constitutions on the Rule of St. Ignatius of Loyola. By 1621 the society of St. Ursula had established itself in eastern France, Switzerland, and Germany. The French Revolution closed the convents in France, but when Napoleon I permitted the reestablishment of religious orders, the society reopened at Dole and at Tours in 1814. Exiled by French anticlerical law in the beginning of the 20th century, the sisters from the motherhouse at Tours established themselves in Belgium, the United States (1902), and Italy. In the United States the sisters are engaged in education, parish ministries and social outreach. The generalate is in St. Cyr-Loire, France. The United States provincialate is in Rhinebeck, New York.

[M. T. BRESLIN/EDS.]

SAINT-VAAST (ARRAS), ABBEY OF

Former Benedictine abbey in the town and Diocese of Arras, France (Latin, *S. Vedastus Atrebatensis*). Founded in 667 by Bishop Aubert to serve the funeral chapel of St. VEDAST, it received large donations from King Thierry III, who also made it a royal abbey exempt from episcopal jurisdiction. This wealthy abbey's rapid growth during the 8th century was responsible for the bourg that grew up opposite the bishop's Gallo-Roman city of Arras. About 800 the abbey church was repaired and the sanctuary redecorated. During the NORMAN invasions, the monks fled to Beauvais, where they lost all the abbey's documents in a fire (886). Abbot Richard of Verdun (1009–1020) restored the monastery under the observance of VERDUN-SUR-MEUSE. Under Abbot Leduin (1020–40) the CLUNIAC REFORM was adopted and the abbey church rebuilt; Abbot Martin I (1155–84) strengthened the abbey temporally and spiritually.

During the 12th and 13th centuries the abbey had numerous conflicts over jurisdiction with the bishop, the Count of Artois, and the bailiffs. At this time more than 3,000 poor and sick were cared for annually by the abbey. Both the town and the monastery were devastated by occupying German troops during the war between France and the Hapsburgs (1479–92). In the 16th century Jean Sarrasin, the future archbishop of Cambrai, was abbot (1578–98). He was succeeded by Philip Caverel (1598–1636), founder of the college of DOUAI and author of the Latin chronicle of Saint-Vaast, the miracles of St. Vedast, and the history of the monasteries of Flanders. From 1569 to 1768 Saint-Vaast was part of the Exempt Congregation of Flanders, but then returned to the Cluniac observance. When the abbey was suppressed during the French Revolution, there were 74 monks. Today the convent buildings are a museum, a library, and

general treasury. The abbey church, which was rebuilt between 1755 and 1833, is now the cathedral.

Bibliography: A. H. GUESNON, ed., *Un Cartulaire de l'abbaye de Saint-Vaast d'Arras* (Paris 1896). L. BROU, ed., *The Monastic Ordinale of St. Vedast's Abbey, Arras,* 2 v. (Henry Bradshaw Society 86, 87; London 1957). A. DE CARDEVACQUE and A. TERNINCK, *L'Abbaye de Saint-Vaast . . . ,* 3 v. (Arras 1865–68). P. GRIERSON, ''La Bibliothèque de St-Vaast d'Arras au XIIᵉ siècle,'' *Revue Bénédictine* 52 (1940) 117–140. G. BESNIER, ''Le Cartulaire de Guiman d'Arras, ses transcriptions. Les Autres cartulaires de SaintVaast,'' *Moyen-âge* 62 (1956) 453–478.

[P. COUSIN]

SAINT-VALERY-SUR-SOMME, ABBEY OF

Former BENEDICTINE monastery at the mouth of the Somme River, arrondissement of Abbeville, Somme, France. The monastic foundation dates back to the time of St. WALARICH (VALÉRY), a disciple of COLUMBAN, who settled there in 611 on land donated by King Clothair II. The monastery took its original title from the contemporary name of that area, Legonacum. It suffered much from the NORMANS in the 9th century and much from secular abbots in the 10th century who replaced the monks with secular clerics. The abbey was restored in 981 by Hugh Capet before he ascended the French throne. He reinstated there Benedictine monks from Saint-Lucien in Beauvais and returned the body of St. Valéry from Sithiu (SAINT-BERTIN). Henceforth, the abbey was called Saint-Valéry. It suffered during the late Middle Ages from the Hundred Years' War and from the ravages of the Calvinists. The abbey was affiliated with the MAURIST congregation in 1644; it was destroyed during the French Revolution.

Bibliography: *Gallia Christiana,* v.1–13 (Paris 1715–85), v.14–16 (Paris 1856–65) 10:1231–41. L. H. COTTINEAU, *Répertoire topobibliographique des abbayes et prieurés,* 2 v. (Mâcon 1935–39) 2:2911–12.

[H. PLATELLE]

SAINT-VALLIER, JEAN BAPTISTE DE LA CROIX CHEVRIÈRES DE

Second bishop of Quebec, Canada; b. Grenoble, France, Nov. 14, 1653; d. Quebec, Dec. 26, 1727. He was the son of Jean de la Croix, Lord of Chevrières, Count of Saint-Vallier, and of Marie de Sayne. He studied at home and in the seminary of his native city. He became a doctor at the Sorbonne in Paris (1672), a priest (1675), and ordinary almoner of the king (1676). He founded a hospital and a community of Sisters of St. Joseph at Saint-Vallier-sur-Rhône. Well-liked by the king, he was offered important bishoprics in France; instead he went to Canada (1685) to serve as vicar-general of Bishop F. de M. Laval of Quebec, and subsequently published an optimistic narrative entitled: *Estat présent de l'église et de la colonie française de la Nouvelle-France* (Paris 1688, repr. 1856). In January 1688 he was consecrated Laval's successor in Quebec, and he administered affairs there for the next 40 years. He enlarged the cathedral; erected a bishop's house and a chapel of ease in the lower city; founded (1693) and endowed with his revenues l'Hôpital-Général of Quebec; presided at the establishment of many religious groups of men and women throughout Canada; stimulated the missions, especially in Acadia and in the Mississippi area; improved the organization of the diocese; and founded several parishes. Under him four diocesan synods were convoked and their mandates and ordinances promulgated; a catechism and ritual were published. He made three trips to Europe; during his last one (1702) he saw Clement XI and was, thus, the first North American bishop to make his *ad limina* visit. On his way back to Canada in 1704 he fell into English hands and was imprisoned; he did not reach Quebec until 1713. That year the Capuchin, Louis François de Mornay, was appointed coadjutor; but since he never left France, Saint-Vallier continued to administer the diocese without help until his death. His long and brilliant career was somewhat overshadowed by his instability, irritability, stubbornness, absolutism, and harshness, which frequently resulted in quarrels with both civil and religious elements in the colony.

Bibliography: *Mgr. de Saint-Vallier et l'Hôpital-Général de Québec* (Quebec 1882). H. TÊTU, *Les Évêques de Québec* (Quebec 1889). A. H. GOSSELIN, *L'Église du Canada depuis Mgr. de Laval jusqu'à la conquête,* 3 v. (Quebec 1911–14) v.1; *Mgr. de Saint-Vallier et son temps* (Évreux 1899). A. RAMBAUD, ''La Vie orageuse et douloureuse de Mgr. de Saint-Vallier,'' *Revue de l'Université Laval* 9 (Oct. 1959) 90–108. F. PORTER, *L'Institution catéchistique au Canada français 1633–1833* (CUA Washington 1949).

[H. PROVOST]

SAINT-VICTOR, MONASTERY OF

A Paris community of canons regular founded by WILLIAM OF CHAMPEAUX in 1108. Since its foundation, it has had a twofold orientation. The first tendency was expressed in an attempt to reform the diocesan clergy by imposing on them the obligations of the religious life, especially community of property. In fact the founder, who was its first superior, was a PRIOR, not an ABBOT; however, one of the early Victorines, Thomas, was archdeacon

of Paris. The monastery school was open to all, as were other canons' schools; it was to this school that HUGH OF SAINT-VICTOR brought great fame. Victorines served also as pastors in country churches. The Diocese of Paris granted prebends to the Victorine canons in the hope that some day all canons of the diocese would accept the regular life rather than the secular. But although this Victorine reform was successful in the provinces, e.g., at Séez, it met strong opposition in Paris. The archdeacon was assassinated; the prebends were contested. Little by little the Victorine canons withdrew to themselves, giving in to the second tendency: imitation of real monastic life, especially that of the CISTERCIAN (William of Champeaux, who had become bishop of Chalons, was a close friend of BERNARD OF CLAIRVAUX). Elements of the BENEDICTINE RULE were admitted into the *Liber ordinis.* The superior became an abbot (although he did not enjoy exemption and the use of *pontificalia*). The school was closed to nonreligious; RICHARD OF SAINT-VICTOR gave it a mystical orientation; and WALTER OF SAINT-VICTOR championed this emphasis against GODFREY OF SAINT-VICTOR, who wanted to continue the humanism of Hugh. Meanwhile Saint-Victor became an abbey separated from the world like other abbeys, with only a few outside activities. It became the head of a powerful congregation of canons regular, which stretched from England, to Denmark, to the Kingdom of Naples.

Late Middle Ages. Early in the 13th century Abbot John the Teuton, originally from Trier, definitively organized the abbey. He placed emphasis on liturgical life: Saint-Victor had its own rite (imitated by the TRINITARIANS), which survived to the 17th century. Victorine parishes far from Paris became priories, each having at least four religious, bound to chant the Office solemnly. The University of PARIS recognized the *studium* of the abbey as a college with resident instruction leading to degrees. This recognition required that there be at least four students provided with special financial resources. A census of Saint-Victor was taken, and this dragged the abbey into interminable litigation. The 14th century saw the appearance of the first historian of Saint-Victor, John of Paris. Unfortunately, it was somewhat late to recapture the beginnings of the abbey, and thus its history is encumbered with an unusually large number of legends and bits of false information regarding its origins. The reforms imposed by Pope BENEDICT XII on all religious had their effect also on Saint-Victor. The abbey was able to retain only a few of its privileges within the federation of canons of the province of Reims and Sens, to which it was annexed. Abbots were to participate fully in the community life and not to consider themselves grand seigneurs. They had to take an oath to this effect when elected. Later, abbots were obligated to an *AD LIMINA* VISIT every two years, at which time they paid heavy revenues to the Apostolic Camera. The poems of André Húays of Saint-Victor suggest that in his day (d. 1471) religious life at Saint-Victor had been deteriorating for some time.

Modern Era. At the end of the 15th century, reform was attempted through the incorporation of Saint-Victor into the congregation of Windesheim, a congregation of Dutch BRETHREN OF THE COMMON LIFE, apostles of the DEVOTIO MODERNA. The attempt failed because of the canons' nationalism, love of the past, and desire to preserve their own way of life. Jean Mauburne, the author of this attempt, succeeded at Ligny, where he became abbot, and at about ten other French abbeys. In 1505 these abbeys formed the Congregation of France, to which Saint-Victor finally attached itself in 1513. This Congregation held annual meetings of the general chapter at Saint-Victor, but the elected general was usually chosen from another monastery. The first (and only) regular abbot elected according to this reform was Jean Bordier (d. 1543), who rebuilt the abbey church and part of the convent of Saint-Victor. He reorganized the abbey library with the help of Claude de Grandrue, and in the abbey reactivated life according to the rule. His successor, Anthony Caracciolo, even though a Victorine, had the court name him commendatory abbot. He later became bishop of Troyes and there solemnly became a Calvinist. Later the community was directed by prior-vicars. Once again, the monastery had fervent religious and good students, worthy of the abbey's past; their work resulted in the excellent library, part of which is in the Bibliothèque Nationale of Paris. A few of the canons were Pierre Grenier, Pierre Janus, Jean Picard, and Jean de Thoulouze. In general, the religious advocated a conservative theology, which exposed them to the mockery of Rabelais and the humanists.

Excessive attachment to the glories of the past prevented Saint-Victor from accepting necessary reforms and changes. As a result, the canons regular of France did not group themselves around Saint-Victor but around SAINTE-GENEVIÈVE. When the abbey was forced to enter the Congregation of Sainte-Geneviève, it did so with reluctance. Most of the canons had come from important bourgeois families of Paris. They brought to the monastery (along with the 1,000 livres expected from them) a certain haughtiness and often a Jansenistic tendency. They had every intention of keeping their independence, and each deacon was free to spend his prebend as he wished. When the Assembly abolished monastic vows during the French Revolution, only one religious (an old man of 81) desired to remain at Saint-Victor; the abbey church was demolished in 1798. The buildings were transformed into a wine market, the *Halle aux vins,* which

was later replaced by the new Faculty of Sciences of the University of Paris.

Bibliography: F. BONNARD, *Histoire de l'abbaye royale et de l'ordre. . .St-Victor de Paris,* 2 v. (Paris 1904–08). L. H. COTTINEAU, *Répertoire topobibliographique des abbayes et prieurés,* 2 v. (Mâcon 1935–39) 2:2221–22. P. DELHAYE, ed., *Le Microcosmus de Godefroy de St-Victor: Étude théologique* (Lille 1951). J. C. DICKINSON, *The Origins of the Austin Canons* (London 1950). *Gallia Christiana,* v.1–13 (Paris 1715–85) 7:656–99. P. HÉLYOT, *Histoire des ordres monastiques. . . ,* 8 v. (Paris 1714–19) 2:149–56. A. L. A. FRANKLIN, *Histoire de la bibliothèque de l'abbaye de Saint-Victor à Paris* (Paris 1865).

[P. DELHAYE]

SAINT-VICTOR IN MARSEILLES, ABBEY OF

Former monastery of Benedictine monks, subsequently secular canons, in Marseilles, France. About 410, after his long trip to the Near East, John CASSIAN established a church and a monastery over the cemetery close to the port of Marseilles where the martyr VICTOR (*c.* 290) and his companions had been buried. This monastery, immediately dependent on the bishop and managed by one of his priests, mixed the eremitic and the COMMON LIFE in a pattern Cassian had observed in Egypt and Palestine. His rule, *De coenobiorum institutis,* of which the first four books were most important, was later abridged as the *Regula Cassiani.* Saracen and Norman attacks on the monastery in the 9th and 10th centuries were especially destructive. In 1040, the monastery was revived on a new basis: it adopted the BENEDICTINE RULE and became directly dependent on Rome. At the time of GREGORY VII it was *juris s. Petri* and a papal instrument of power. A number of monasteries were incorporated into an "order" under Saint-Victor, and the order soon spread throughout southern France, Spain, and northern Italy. The abbey's estate grew extraordinarily; it also had its own port and a fleet (the future papal fleet of the Avignon popes). A new church was built (1200–09). Popes Innocent III and Benedict XII tightened the discipline of the order through new statutes and by appointing papal visitors. The abbey gained special luster through Abbot Guillaume de Grimoard, the later URBAN V, who is buried in the still existing church. He founded the abbey's house of studies at Montpellier University. With the Western Schism and the Renaissance, monastic discipline declined: the abbey was given *in commendam* (1480); the monks abandoned the religious habit for clerical garb; the monastic Breviary was abandoned for the *Pianum* (1568). The monks became secular canons (1751), and the abbey was suppressed in the French Revolution.

Bibliography: BEAUNIER, *Abbayes et prieurés de l'ancienne France,* ed. J. M. L. BESSE, 12 v. (Paris 1905–41) v.2. L. H. COT-

TINEAU, *Répertoire topobibliographique des abbayes et prieurés*, 2 v. (Mâcon 1935–39) 2:2916. H. LECLERCQ, *Dictionnaire d'archéologie chrétienneet de liturgie*, ed. F. CABROL, H. LECLERCQ and H. I. MARROU, 15 v. (Paris 1907–53) 15.1:545–557. L. F. M. LAURIN, *Notice sur l'antique abbaye de Saint-Victor de Marseille* (6th ed. Marseilles 1952).

[P. DELHAYE]

ST. VINCENT ARCHABBEY

The first Benedictine monastery in the U.S.; founded at Latrobe, PA, in 1846 by Boniface WIMMER, monk of St. Michael Abbey in Metten, Bavaria. Concern for the spiritual needs of German immigrants in the U.S. led Wimmer, with four candidates for the priesthood and 14 for the brotherhood, to initiate the monastic, educational, and missionary activities that have remained characteristic of his foundation. Bishop Michael O'Connor of Pittsburgh, PA, donated the chapel and farm at St. Vincent parish to the young community, and on Oct. 24, 1846, Wimmer invested his candidates with the Benedictine habit. The superior assumed charge of the local parish and ministered to the Catholics of Westmoreland County and other parts of Pennsylvania.

The monastery became St. Vincent Priory in 1852; it was raised to an abbey three years later, with Wimmer as abbot of the growing community of 150 members. By 1900, beginning with a foundation in Minnesota in 1856 (now ST. JOHN'S ABBEY, Collegeville, MN), small bands of St. Vincent monks had founded priories in 15 states. After the Holy See established the American Cassinese Congregation of the Benedictine Order (1855), Wimmer was named its first president.

For 41 years Wimmer guided the community at St. Vincent and directed the national expansion of the order. At Latrobe his monks increased their parish activities and developed a major and minor seminary for the education of diocesan and Benedictine priests. Rome honored this pioneer of American Benedictinism with the personal title of archabbot and the privilege of wearing the *cappa magna.*

Since Wimmer's death (Dec. 8, 1887), St. Vincent Archabbey has consolidated and expanded its work in education and the parish missionary apostolate. The second archabbot, Andrew Hintenach (1844–1927), resigned his office in 1892. Leander Schnerr (1836–1920), who ruled for 25 years, coordinated the parish apostolate and improved the major seminary. Archabbot Aurelius Stehle (1877–1930), educator and author, developed St. Vincent College as a department separate from the seminary and led the American Cassinese Congregation in founding the Catholic University of Beijing, China (now the Fu Jen Catholic University of Taipei, Nationalist China). Archabbot Alfred Koch (1879–1950) directed the monastery for two decades, expanded the college department, and advanced the graduate training program for faculty members. After his election as coadjutor archabbot in 1949, Rt. Rev. Denis Strittmatter began a complete abbey renovation and building program, extended parochial activity, and broadened the scope of graduate studies for priest faculty members. As president of the American Cassinese Congregation Strittmatter was a voting member of Vatican Council II.

In 1963, a devastating fire destroyed a quadrangle of buildings which included the historic St. Vincent parish chapel (built in 1836), the abbey choir chapel, and a major part of the monks' cells. In the decades that followed, new buildings were erected. Expansion of the archabbey outside of the United States have led to the foundation of the Wimmer Priory of St. Boniface, at Taipei, Taiwan. and the adoption of St. Benedict Priory in Vinhedo, near São Paulo, Brazil.

Bibliography: O. MOOSMÜLLER, *St. Vincenz in Pennsylvanien* (New York 1873). F. FELLNER, *Abbot Boniface and His Monks* (privately published and available only at St. Vincent Archabbey).

[R. J. MURTHA/EDS.]

ST. VINCENT DE PAUL, SOCIETY OF

An international association of Catholic laity devoted to the service of the poor; the first conference was formed in Paris in 1833 by Antoine Frédéric Ozanam and his associates.

Origins. At the initial meeting, over which Vincent BAILLY presided as first president and which Sorbonne students Ozanam, Felix Clare, François Lallier, Paul Lamache, Auguste Le Taillandier, and Jules Devaux attended as charter members, the name Conference of Charity was adopted and the principal objective stated as the sanctification of members and of society through good works. By 1834 there were more than 100 members of the Conference of St. Vincent de Paul, as the organization was retitled. July 19 was chosen as the society's principal feast, and at Ozanam's suggestion, the conference was placed under the protection of the Blessed Virgin and the feast of the Immaculate Conception was chosen as the day to pay her special honor. A rule, based on the writings of St. VINCENT DE PAUL, was ratified at the general meeting held on Dec. 8, 1835. It was published ten years later and, with revisions, has continued to be used.

Growth. During the first five years the membership increased to more than 2,000 in 15 centers throughout France, of which the one at Nîmes was the first estab-

The high altar of the basilica at St. Vincent Archabbey, Latrobe, Pennsylvania.

lished outside Paris. Although the society was still composed primarily of students, by 1838 Ozanam counted among the participants ''a peer of France, a chancellor of state, several generals, and distinguished writers.'' In 1845 the Vincentians had increased to 9,000. Moreover, the society spread to other countries: Italy (1842); Belgium, Scotland, and Ireland (1843); England (1844); Germany, Holland, Greece, and Turkey (1846); Switzerland (1847); and Austria and Spain (1850). Shortly after Ozanam's death in 1853, the president general of the society reported to Pius IX that more than 1,532 conferences had been established throughout Europe, Africa, Asia Minor, and North America. By 1855 more than 2,900 conferences existed, including 1,360 in France and its colonies, 14 in Austria, 208 in the German states, four in Luxembourg, 374 in Belgium, 229 in Spain, 137 in Great Britain and Ireland, 374 in Italy, 105 in the Netherlands, 31 in Switzerland, and one each in Denmark, Turkey, and Greece. There were three in Asia outside Turkey, 17 in Africa, and 72 in the Americas. By 1860 worldwide membership exceeded 50,000.

The 1860s were difficult for the society in France and Spain. In October 1861 the French government suppressed the central and provincial councils of the society; there followed nine years of struggle between the government and the society during which a centralized authority and international unity survived only by delegating the powers of the president general to the superior councils of Brussels (Belgium), Cologne (Germany), and The Hague (Netherlands). Eventually the original position of a council general was restored, but by then France had lost almost half its conferences. Moreover, from 1870 on the society's growth was very slight. The 1913 report recorded 8,000 conferences with 133,000 members, and an annual expenditure of 15 million francs for the alleviation of human distress. Although World War I affected recruitment, a notable experiment was the formation of conferences in prisoner of war camps. At the society's centennial in 1933, the number of conferences had risen to 13,000, with an active membership exceeding 200,000. Organizations developed in China, Taiwan, Japan, Malaysia, Singapore, Indochina, Burma, India, Sri Lanka, Madagascar, and East Africa.

Lay Character. The conferences began and developed as lay organizations, and the approbation of ecclesiastical authority was not sought, nor were conferences erected by act of ecclesiastical superiors. In 1845 Gregory XVI formally approved the lay character of the society. Other pontiffs, including Pius IX, also desired that the society retain its character as a lay or non-ecclesiastical society.

In the period of rapid growth between 1845 and 1850, opposition to the authority of the council general

revealed itself both within the society and in its relationships with ecclesiastical authority. Prevention of schism and dissolution became the concern of Adolphe Baudon, the third president general of the society. Although no historical precedent existed for the appointment of a cardinal protector to a lay organization, Baudon's petition led Pius IX to name Cardinal Nicolò Fornari for the post, and each succeeding pope has followed this practice. A decree of Nov. 13, 1920, further clarified the legal status of the society as an association that does not take its existence from the Church and ''so neither is it governed and ruled by the ecclesiastical authority, but by the laity designated in its own statutes.'' However, the society itself has interpreted the term ''lay'' to connote faithfulness rather than independence, and new conferences are formed and work undertaken only with ecclesiastical approval. Moreover, conferences and councils are presided over by the ordinary and parish priests as honorary presidents and members, and cordial relations with the Holy See and the local hierarchy and clergy are manifested in various ways.

Structure and Activities. Catholic women and men who desire to unite in prayer and perform works of charity are eligible for active membership and participate personally in the charitable works and regular life of the society. Corresponding members, former active members residing where no conference exists, continue membership by performing as far as possible the usual Vincentian conference practices. Honorary members ordinarily do not participate in active work or weekly meetings of the conference but do attend general religious festivals and meetings, and contribute a fixed yearly sum for the support of conference works. In addition to members, the rule enumerates subscribers, persons of either sex including non-Catholics, who are benefactors of the society. Although the first article of the Vincentian statutes refers to Catholic young men as members, the emphasis on youth is not interpreted literally.

The conference, the basic unit of Vincentian organization, is nearly always associated with the parish, from which it derives its name. Conferences obtain their official status in the society by aggregation, which entails approbation by the council general, following a probationary period. Each conference enjoys autonomy in functioning, provided it adheres to the general rule of the society. The parish conference, with its weekly meeting and visitation of families under care, holds the most honored place within the society. It is in immediate relationship with members who serve the poor and the poor who are served by them. As in Ozanam's time, under the leadership of the president or spiritual director, the meeting opens with prescribed Vincentian prayers and spiritual reading. Then follow the reports of conference visitors on family care, discussion of works of charity to be undertaken, an accounting of conference funds, and the secret collection from the participating members to sustain charitable activities. The rule prescribes also the celebration of the quarterly feasts of the organization and other meetings associated with them.

Purpose. The fundamental work of the society is the visitation of the poor in their own homes. Other activities of councils and conferences include hospital and institutional visitation on a regular basis, ministry to immigrants and refugees, social outreach to the homeless, summer camps for needy children, guidance programs for young men, work with delinquent youth, visitation of prisoners and work with probationers, maintenance of hospices, operation of Catholic centers for seamen, employment services, providing of clothing and furniture for needy families, operation of thrift stores, and catechetical instruction for children and adults

Development in the U.S. On Nov. 20, 1845, the first conference in the U.S. was organized at the old cathedral parish in St. Louis, Mo., after the Vincentian John TIMON had interested Bp. Peter Kenrick in the project. With Rev. Ambrose Heim, assistant priest at the cathedral, as spiritual guide, Dr. Moses L. Linton as president and Judge Bryan Mullanphy, vice president, the Cathedral Conference was formally aggregated by action of the council general, Feb. 2, 1846. Thereafter the society established itself in New York City, 1847; Buffalo, N.Y., 1847; Milwaukee, Wis., 1849; Philadelphia, Pa., 1851; Pittsburgh, Pa., 1852; Louisville, Ky., 1853; Brooklyn, N.Y., 1855; St. Paul, Minn., 1856; Chicago, Ill., and Washington, D.C., 1857; New Orleans, La., 1858; Dubuque, Iowa, 1859; San Francisco, Calif., 1860; Boston, Mass., 1861; Baltimore, Md., 1864; Cincinnati, Ohio, and Portland, Ore., 1869; and San Antonio, Tex., 1871. The Particular Council of New York was instituted in March 1857 and the Superior Council of New York in February 1860. By 1915 there were seven major independent jurisdictions in the U.S.: the Superior Councils of New York, St. Louis, New Orleans, and Chicago; the Metropolitan Central Councils of Boston and Philadelphia, and the Particular Council of Brooklyn. The first general assembly of the society in the U.S. was held in New York City in 1864; the first printed report of the Superior Council of New York was published the same year. The value of national unity was periodically discussed and on June 7, 1915, the Council General in Paris instituted the Superior Council of the U.S. The first national president, Thomas M. MULRY, known as the American Ozanam, was inaugurated at formal ceremonies held at The Catholic University of America, Washington, D.C., on Nov. 21, 1915.

The society's early years in the U.S. were limited to relief efforts on the parish level. After 1860 a larger program included religious instruction to Catholic children in almshouses and in parishes. Solicitude for the immigrant impelled Vincentians to investigate and to change conditions in public life and institutions prejudicial to the faith of Catholics. The society founded or helped to establish the Catholic Protectory in New York City, the Industrial School for Boys in Chicago, St. Vincent's Home for Destitute Boys in New Orleans, and St. Vincent's Lodging House for Boys, which became the Mission of the Immaculate Virgin at Mount Loretto in New York. Foster home programs under Catholic auspices were pioneered by Vincentians. They established Catholic boys' clubs, libraries, recreational and cultural programs, and home-finding bureaus and worked to modify existing practices of incarcerating boys for slight infractions of the law. The first central office of the society was set up in Baltimore and was soon followed by a similar bureau in Chicago, with others following for all large Vincentian centers.

The national meetings of the society helped to prepare for the formation of the National Conference of Catholic Charities (1910), and cooperation between the two organizations continued. The society has also established cooperative arrangements with Catholic Relief Services. Despite the vast involvement of government in social security and public relief programs, which characterize 20th-century and 21st-century U.S., the society continues to perform a significant role in alleviating the misery of material want.

Bibliography: C. K. MURPHY, *The Spirit of the Society of St. Vincent de Paul* (New York 1940). A. P. SCHIMBERG, *The Great Friend: Frederick Ozanam* (Milwaukee 1946). E. O'CONNOR, *The Secret of Frederic Ozanam* (Dublin 1953). D. T. MCCOLGAN, *A Century of Charity,* 2 v. (Milwaukee 1951). *Manual of the Society of St. Vincent de Paul,* tr. from Fr. by the Superior Council of Ireland (21st ed. Dublin 1958). *The Ozanam News* (New York 1956–). *Bulletin de la Societé de Saint-Vincent de Paul* (Paris 1848–).

[D. BAKER/EDS.]

SAINTE ANNE DE BEAUPRÉ, SHRINE OF

A Canadian sanctuary dedicated to the mother of the Blessed Virgin Mary. The devotion was brought to Canada by the first French colonists, most of whom came from the east of France, where the cult had recently been revived at the Shrines of Sainte-Anne d'Auray and Sainte-Anne du Carrefour (St. Anne of the Crossroads). On March 8, 1658, Étienne de Lessard, of the Beaupré coast, donated a piece of land ''on condition that, within the present year, the inhabitants of the place begin and continue without surcease the building of a church or chapel.'' Gabriel Queylus, then parish priest of Quebec, wished it to be dedicated to St. ANNE. According to the *Jesuit Diary,* March 13, 1658, ''Father Vignard, delegate of Father [Queylus] blessed the site of the church of Petit Cap. My Lord the Governor [D'Ailleboust] laid the first stone.'' Miracles were described by the priest in charge, Thomas Morel, in the *Jesuit Relations;* in 1662 three boatmen whose skiff was wrecked off Cape Tourmente were said to be miraculously saved by St. Anne and cast up on shore close by the chapel. This event seems to have attracted pilgrims to the shrine, which became known as the Sailors' Chapel. Since then the pilgrimage movement has increased steadily. By mid-20th century about two million visitors and pilgrims, roughly half of whom are from the U.S., visit the Basilica of St. Anne yearly. In 1992, the first Basilica was destroyed by fire. The new Basilica was consecrated on July 4, 1976.

Bibliography: Archives, Basilica of Sainte Anne de Beaupré, contain thousands of MSS dating back to 1658. Archives, Seminary of Quebec, contain documents on the Confraternity of Ste. Anne and on the origins of the Shrine. Archives, Judicial, Quebec, contain all the original notarial acts, particularly those concerning land grants. G. BÉLANGER, *Royal House of Beaupré* (Ste. Anne de Beaupré 1946). E. LEFEBVRE, *A Land of Miracles for Three Hundred Years* (Ste. Anne de Beaupré 1958). G.-U. GAGNON, *St-Anne-de-Beaupré: Past and Present Churches* (Quebec 1994).

[L. E. GAGNÉ/EDS.]

A shrine to Sainte Anne de Beaupré, known as the Lourdes of North America, church of Saint Anne de Beaupré, Quebec. (©Robert Estall/CORBIS)

STE. CHRÉTIENNE, SISTERS OF (SSCH)

(Official Catholic Directory #3750); a congregation with papal approbation (1899) whose official title is Sisters of the Holy Childhood of Jesus and Mary of Ste. Chrétienne, and whose motherhouse is in Metz, France. The community was founded in 1807 by Anne Victoire de Méjanès, née Tailleur (d. 1837), under the direction of Bp. André Jauffret of Metz (d. 1823). The purpose of the congregation was the education of children and the care of the sick poor. When the sisters were forced into exile by the hostile French government in 1903, 15 of them came to the United States, where they founded a central house in Salem, Mass. The U.S. provincialate is in Waltham, Mass.

[A. J. ENNIS/EDS.]

SAINTE-GENEVIÈVE-DE-PARIS, MONASTERY OF

The Monastery of Sainte-Geneviève-De-Paris, former monastery of Victorine canons, then canons of Sain-

te-Geneviève, the present day Panthéon on the Left Bank in Paris. It began as a Merovingian foundation of CLOVIS I and CLOTILDE, who, on the suggestion of St. GENEVIÈVE, built a church dedicated to St. Peter and the other Apostles in the neighborhood of Paris (*c.* 506). Since Geneviève's relics were in the crypt of the church, it gradually became known as St. Geneviève's rather than St. Peter's. The clergy, or canons regular, of the church lived a common life under an abbot. Under the Carolingians Sainte-Geneviève lost its preeminence to SAINT-DENIS-EN-FRANCE. In the 9th century the NORMANS burned the monastery, but the canons escaped with the relics of St. Geneviève. In the next centuries, the canons were secularized under a *decanus* or superior who held the political prerogatives of lord of the faubourg Sainte-Geneviève along the Left Bank, exercising justice and enjoying episcopal exemption. The chancellor at the School of Sainte-Geneviève granted the *licentia docendi,* and before the end of the 11th century founded the ''Latin quarter'' for liberal arts schools; during the next century, however, this school was eclipsed by the nascent University of Paris. In 1148 Victorine canons were introduced into Sainte-Geneviève; the ensuing revival resulted in a new Scandinavian foundation (*see* WILLIAM OF AEBEL-HOLT, ST.) and in the rebuilding and reformation of Sainte-Geneviève itself under STEPHEN OF TOURNAI. The monastery, however, always remained secondary to nearby SAINT-VICTOR.

A new reliquary for St. Geneviève was made in 1242; the forged reliquary of 1614 was later destroyed in the French Revolution. The 13th-century poem honoring St. Geneviève, written by the Canon Renaut, proved one of the most popular pieces of medieval French vernacular verse. In the 14th century, the young canons within the monastery were trained according to the rules of BENEDICT XII. To students outside the monastery but within the jurisdiction of Sainte-Geneviève, the abbey's chancellor, with the help of four professors chosen by him, could grant the *licentia* (in competition with the University of Paris). Once again, in 1619, the Abbey was reformed, this time by Cardinal François de LA ROCHEFOUCAULD, with the help of Canon Faure and several religious of Senlis. It became the head of the Canonical Congregation of France, including the monasteries of VAL-DES-ECOLIERS, the Chancelade, and Saint-Victor itself. Superiors in this order were appointed for only three years, and the regulations of the Council of TRENT were observed. A large library (which still exists) was provided for the young canons, whose training included two years of arts, two of philosophy, and three of theology. Many canons of the order of Sainte-Geneviève attended lectures at the universities and are known in literary history. In 1757 Sainte-Geneviève began construction of a new church alongside the old; it was not yet completed when the French Revolution confiscated it and transformed it into the Panthéon. The old church was destroyed and a part of the monastery became the present Lyceum Henry IV.

Bibliography: *Gallia Christiana,* v. 1–13 (Paris 1715–85), (Paris 1856–65) 7:699–815. P. FERET, *L'Abbaye de Sainte-Geneviève et la congrégation de France,* 2 v. (Paris 1883). H. LECLERCQ, *Dictionnaire d'archéologie chrétienne et de liturgie,* ed. F. CABROL, H. LECLERCQ, and H. I. MARROU, 15 v. (Paris 1907–53) 13.2:1875–77. L. H. COTTINEAU, *Répertoire topobibliographique des abbayes et prieurés,* 2 v. (Mâcon 1935–39) 2:2206. P. BROUTIN, *La Réforme pastorale en France au XVIIᵉ siècle,* 2 v. (Tournai 1956).

[P. DELHAYE]

SAINTS, DEVOTION TO THE

The paying of honor on the basis of recognition of the supernatural excellence of those members of Christ declared by the Church to be now in heaven and, consequently, constituted as intercessors with God for the living and for souls in purgatory is devotion to the saints. In the fullness of Catholic practice it takes the form of praise and imitation of the saints's virtues and of invocation, both private and public, addressed directly to the saints in order to win their intercession.

Early History. Identified in its origins with cult of the MARTYRS, devotion first took the form of praise and imitation; but by the 3rd century the efficacy of intercession of the saints was clearly recognized [Origen, *In Lib. Iesu Nave,* 16.5; *Patrologia Graeca,* ed. J. P. Migne, 161 v. (Paris 1857–66) 12:909] and reference is found to their invocation [Origen, *De orat.,* 14; *Patrologia Graeca,* ed. J. P. Migne, 161 v. (Paris 1857–66) 11: 464].

The 4th and 5th centuries saw the extension of cult from martyrs in the strict sense to those whose ascetic life could be considered equivalent to martyrdom: first in the East (Gregory Thaumaturge, d. *c.* 270), then in the West (Sylvester I, d. 335; Martin of Tours, d. 397; Ambrose, d. 397; Augustine, d. 430). (*See* CONFESSOR.) Like the martyrs, the new saints were honored on their anniversaries, their lives were publicized, and churches were placed under their patronage (in Rome by 500). In the 5th and 6th centuries antiphons in honor of the saints were introduced into the Mass. First in the East (from the 5th century), later in the West (from 8th century), antiphons and readings from the "Lives" were included in the night office. Veneration of images developed primarily in the East; that of relics, in the West (*see* IMAGES, VENERATION OF; RELICS).

Though the early theologians carefully distinguished between honor of the saints and adoration of God, there were at first no suitable terms to express the distinction. St. Augustine successfully suggested adoption of the Greek term *latreia* for adoration of God [*Civ.* 10.1; *Corpus scriptorum ecclesiasticorum latinorum* (Vienna 1866–) 47:272]; but confusion could still be caused in the West by the terminology of the Second Council of Nicaea, 787 [H. Denzinger, *Enchiridion symbolorum,* ed. A. Schönmetzer (32d ed. Freiburg 1963) 601]. The term *dulia* for honor of the saints dates from the Carolingian period.

The Middle Ages produced in the West a flowering of popular devotion to the saints, with pilgrimages, increasing honor of relics, extensive naming of patrons (*see* PATRON SAINTS), and feasts developing into civic festivals. Demand for information led (from the 9th century) to a multiplication of "Lives," very many of them stereotyped and "edifying" rather than factual (*see* SAINTS, LEGENDS OF THE). Exaggerated practices in this popular devotion frequently brought protests from the Church (e.g., Council of Avignon, 1209; Fourth Lateran Council, 1215). The first formal canonization, that of Ulrich (d. 973), took place in 993 (H. Denzinger, *ibid.,* 675).

Reformation Period. The Cathari and Waldenses (13th century) already denied the intercession of the saints and their knowledge of men's prayers. The Confession of Augsburg (1530), approved by Luther, while acknowledging the example of the saints, denied as prejudicial to Christ's unique mediatorship their role as intercessors. The Defense of the Confession (1530), however, conceded that the saints pray for the universal Church, while it maintained the condemnation of invocation. Zwingli and Calvin rejected the doctrine of intercession.

The Council of Trent, session 25 (December 1563), appealing to apostolic tradition and to the teaching of the Fathers and Councils, directed that the faithful should be instructed that the saints intercede for men and that it is ''good and useful'' to invoke them to obtain for men benefits from God through Christ, the sole Redeemer (H. Denzinger, *ibid.*, 1821).

Synthesizing the work of Catholic controversialists, St. Robert Bellarmine laid down the principal lines of present Catholic teaching.

The task of revising the lives of the saints, begun by Lipomani, Surius, and Baronius, was based on critical method by Bolland (*Acta Sanctorum*).

At present devotion to the saints is regulated by 1917 *Codex iuris canonici* cc.1255–56, 1276–78. Clearly distinguished are: divine worship (*latria*), honor of Mary (*hyperdulia*), and honor of the saints and angels (*dulia;* 1917 *Codex iuris canonici* c.1255.1). The teaching of the Council of Trent is repeated; devotion to Mary is perhaps of precept (1917 *Codex iuris canonici* c.1276). For other regulations, *see* CANONIZATION OF SAINTS (HISTORY AND PROCEDURE). Private devotions should conform to the decree of Holy Office of May 26, 1937 [*Acta Apostolicae Sedis* 29 (1937) 304–305]. For John XXIII's statement on abuses, *see Acta Apostolicae Sedis* 52 (1960) 969. See also VATICAN COUNCIL II, *Constitution on Liturgy,* 104; *Dogmatic Constitution on the Church,* ch. 7. Among Protestants, although invocation of the saints is still rejected, attempts are being made to increase awareness of their role in the communion of the saints.

Scripture. The hesitation of Jewish thought on the fate of the dead long precluded invocation, but an example is found in the 2nd century B.C. (2 Mc 15.12–16). Any account of the New Testament doctrine must be based on a clear affirmation of the unique and all-sufficient mediation of Christ (Heb 7.25; Rom 8.34; 1 Tm 2.5; etc.). Devotion to the saints then finds its justification in the scriptural teaching on the MYSTICAL BODY OF CHRIST and Communion of Saints, as interpreted in the practice of the Church. Indications supporting this living interpretation are found in St. Paul's confidence in the prayers of the living (Rom 15.30–32; Eph 6.18–19; etc.), the relations between the Church on earth and in heaven (Eph 2.19), and the honor paid the ''cloud of witnesses'' (Heb 12; cf.

Bell tower of the Cathedral of Saints Peter and Paul, designed by Domenico Trezzini, (1712–1732), Saint Petersburg, Russia. (©Paul Almasy/CORBIS)

13.7). See also 1 Cor 12 (cooperation within the Body); Rv 2.26–27; 5.8; 6.9–10. The Catholic doctrine should be seen as an example of the ''praise of the glory of [the Father's] grace'' (Eph 1.6, 12, 14).

Theology. As an aspect of the life of the Mystical Body, devotion to the saints, involving not only imitation but also invocation, far from detracting from the prerogatives of Christ, serves to glorify His redemption, for the earthly merits and heavenly prayers of the saints derive their efficacy from His saving mysteries. This implies no essential addition to His mediation but rather a realization of its potential and a subordinate cooperation of His members in the application of the fruits of His redemption (see Aquinas, *Summa theologiae,* 3a, 25.6; 26.1).

Latria is an act of the virtue of religion by which honor is paid the Supreme Lord of creation. Supernatural *dulia,* the honor paid the saints, pertains to the virtue of reverence (*observantia*). It honors that excellence of virtue and intercession which is given the saints by grace (Acquinas, *Summa theologiae,* 2a2ae, 103; 121.1 ad 3). Concretely, invocation of the saints, since it seeks their intercession for blessings which only God can give, involves the activity of both religion and reverence under direction of the theological virtues.

Bibliography: P. MOLINARI, *I santi e il loro culto* (Rome 1962). H. DELEHAYE, *Sanctus: Essai sur le culte des saints dans l'antiquité* (Brussels 1927; repr. 1954). J. B. WALZ, *Die Fürbitte der Heiligen* (Freiburg 1927). M. LACKMANN, *Verehrung der Heiligen:*

"Female Saint," 12th century fresco painting by Cimabue, Basilica of San Francesco, Assisi, Italy. (©Elio Ciol/CORBIS)

Versuch einer lutheranischen Lehre von den Heiligen (Stuttgart 1958).

[C. O'NEILL]

SAINTS, ICONOGRAPHY OF

Determining the correct identification, location, and execution date of representations of saints is the proper concern of their iconographical study. Cult, legends, and attributes of saints (as well as changing aesthetic ideals) have developed in the evolution of saint imagery a complex but rich deposit of iconography in both the Western and Eastern churches. Although systematic accounts of the lives of the saints (*see* HAGIOGRAPHY) had been inaugurated early in the 17th century by the BOLLANDISTS, it was not until the first half of the 19th century, with a revived interest in the Middle Ages and the work of men such as Seroux d'Agincourt, that the science of iconography originated. (*See* ICONOLOGY AND ICONOGRAPHY.) This article treats the iconographic classification of saint images and the general development of their representation. (For the problems of devotion to images and their cult, *see* IMAGES, VENERATION OF; ICONOCLASM.) The iconography of Jesus Christ and of Mary (Blessed Virgin) are treated under their respective titles; see also specific saints.

1. Classifications

The development of saint images and statues in Christianity had its origins in the veneration of martyrs and their relics; popular piety had a tendency to substitute images and icons for the actual relics of martyrs for devotional purposes; they became kinds of anthropomorphic reliquaries. Images without relics were less desirable than relics; yet the remains of the saints (relics) alone held a weak attraction in themselves, which seems to explain why reliquaries were made (toward the end of the Merovingian era) in such forms as foot, arm, finger, and hand. The intercessory power attributed to saints and the efficacy of prayer through devotion to their relics influenced the making of saint images and the evolution of their iconography.

Personal characteristics and attributes. Methods of representing the saints gradually evolved into an elaborate system by the time of the Renaissance. Representations of holy persons became a kind of language, which, when correctly understood, might reveal much about the life, attributes, and devotion of the depicted subject; further interpretation might reveal the spiritual posture and theological orientation of its makers, as well. The iconography of specific saints has evolved around two distinct elements that are sometimes confused: personal characteristics and attributes. Personal characteristics are those elements of the physical appearance or clothing proper to the saint and identified with him, such as the baldness of St. Paul, the corpulence of St. Thomas Aquinas, or the woven-palm tunic of Paul the Hermit. An attribute is a sign added to the person to identify him. This might be an emblematic object (key of St. Peter), an animal accompanying him (lion of St. Mark, lamb of St. John the Baptist), or an instrument of martyrdom (stones for the stoning of St. Stephen). These may be distinguished further as being either real (the cross of bishops and abbots) or symbolic (palm of martyrs, key of St. Peter). In the absence of physical description, attributes sometimes serve to identify the subject, though several may be necessary to distinguish him; thus some popular saints (e.g., St. Anthony) have come to be distinguished by as many as seven or eight attributes. Attributes have become superfluous to characterize modern saints, since there are portraits or photographs by which they can easily be known.

The Nimbus. The most common attribute, applied to all saints, is the nimbus (cloud), a luminous defined shape surrounding the head of the saint. Its origins are pre-Christian, and examples are found in Hellenistic art of pagan inspiration; the halo was used, as evidenced in mosaics and coins, for demigods and divinities such as Neptune, Jupiter, Bacchus, and in particular Apollo (god of the sun). This solar emblem, also struck on the coins of the Roman emperors, was transformed by Christianity into a sign of sanctity, though it was not reserved exclusively for saints since it was employed honorifically for Christian emperors. More commonly, the halo is found in the form of a disk or circle; the less common square or rectangular nimbus was used to honor persons who were still living when the representation was made. The square nimbus symbolizes the earthly vault or place on earth, whereas the circular one, considered perfect in form, symbolizes the celestial vault or heavenly place. John the Deacon in his life of Pope Gregory the Great explained that Gregory preferred to be represented with the square nimbus, which was the sign of the living (*insigne viventis*), and not the crown (*Patrologia Latina* [Paris 1878–90] 75:461). Its usage can be traced to encaustic portrait images painted on Egyptian mummies (see H. Leclercq, *Dictionnaire d'archéologie chrétienne et de liturgie* [Paris 1907–53] 11:1744–52; 12:1272–1312). The circular nimbus was adopted by Christian art in the 4th century, when it seems to have been reserved for Christ alone; it first appears on a saint in the mid-5th century and by the 6th century appears uniformly on the saints in the mosaics of S. Apollinare (Ravenna). To avoid confusion with the saints, the nimbus of Christ was inscribed with a cross, forming the cross-nimbus proper to Him; as another type of distinction, the figure of Christ came to be surrounded with the almond shaped aura (called *mandorla,* or aureole), which was sometimes given as well to the Virgin. The nimbus evolved from a flat opaque disk to a three-dimensional mobility (following the direction of the head) with the introduction by Giotto of painting the figure in a believable three-dimensional space. During the Renaissance it assumed various kinds of transparency or became simply a circular contour or filigree ring. With Rembrandt the strict nimbus was replaced with a luminous atmosphere surrounding a part of the figure. Although originally the gold nimbus was used only for Christ, it came to be applied to all the saints after the introduction of the cross-nimbus (*see* HALO).

Other Attributes. Attributes have also emerged that are applicable to categories of saints such as martyrs, bishops, and apostles. The widest, yet not universal, categorical attribute is the scroll or the book, which might be either open or closed. Thus it might be used with Christ as teacher, the Evangelists, popes, bishops, founders of orders, and great teachers. With a specific inscription, it becomes an individual attribute (e.g., Holy Rule for St. Benedict). There are numerous categorical notes of identification: armor for warrior saints; miter for bishops; dalmatic for deacons; tiara for popes (conical up to the 14th century, then a triple crown); and the garb proper to the order of various religious and monks. Founders of churches and abbeys may be pictured holding a model of their building; the chaste of either sex may receive the lily branch (St. Joseph, St. Catherine of Siena); martyrs bear the palm and receive the crown; decapitated martyrs (*cephalophores*) hold their heads in their hands; the dove

"Joan of Arc," painting by Albert Lynch. (Corbis)

may appear with all those inspired by the Holy Spirit, notably, the Evangelists and the Doctors of the Church.

Individual attributes became more frequent toward the end of the Middle Ages; these were rare and nearly unknown in the Eastern Church. In the West, however, a multiplication of individual attributes from the 13th century on created an involved saint iconography that reached its greatest complexity in the saint images of the 15th century. Individual attributes were initiated to identify more specifically the represented saint. These might come from the name itself, such as Christopher (*Christopheros,* Christ bearer), which originally meant one who carried Christ in his heart; both legends and iconography surrounding St. Christopher grew from this name; whence he was pictured in older monuments literally bearing the full-grown bearded Christ in Majesty on his shoulders in a huge frontal position. By the beginning of the 14th century, he was more commonly depicted as fording a river on foot, bearing the Infant Christ on his shoulders. Other individual attributes might be borrowed from the trade of the subject, such as the carpenter tools for St. Joseph. Popular stories, legends, and accounts of the saints' lives are another source of individual attributes. The bread basket, rope, and broken bell are attributed to St. Romanus, who was said to have fed Benedict in the mountainous cave by lowering a basket of food with a rope and ringing a bell (Dialogues of St. Gregory, bk. 2; *Patrologia Latina* [Paris 1878–90] 66:128–130). For martyrs, the instruments of their death are frequently employed as a proper attribute. Thus the oblique cross in the form of an ''X'' (*crux decussata*) is an attribute of St. Andrew, who suffered death on such a cross. Finally allusions to patronage or cult can also be their source. Toward the end of the 15th century St. Cecilia (Roman martyr of the late 2d century) was adopted as patron of music, which gave rise then to her individual attribute, the musical instrument. Because of reciprocal influences and the interplay of legend, patronage, and iconography, it is difficult at times to discover whether the attribute led to the patronage (or even legend) or vice versa.

Changes in type. The identification of a saint image alone does not necessarily reveal much of the content of the work, since the work itself generally incorporates the aesthetic ideals and religious tendencies of its makers. For example, one can find two different types of St. Francis. The pre-Reformation St. Francis bears a human warmth presented with picturesque Italian charm and implies that joy in simple earthly things is a virtue. L. Réau labels this type Giottesque (*Iconographie de l'art chrétien* [Paris 1955–59] 3:519), an exclusively Italian type, particularly of the 14th century. The Counter Reformation type, however (El Greco, Zurbarán, Ribera), is an emaciated and wan St. Francis, drained of joy (sometimes given the additional attribute of a skull), dramatically elevating a spirit of penitence. Thus El Greco charged his St. Francis paintings (and paintings of other saints) with the mystic ardor of an ascetic engaged with intense inner experience. This shift in representation suggests how transformations occur in saint imagery and how different attributes may be added (such as the skull for St. Francis) to suit the particular religious tendencies of a period or a generation.

[R. J. VEROSTKO]

2. Historical Evolution

The evolution of pictorial representations of saints has produced a great variety of types through the centuries, revealing shifting spiritual approaches in devotion.

Early Christian to Renaissance. At first, in the catacombs of Rome, Naples, Arles, and other places, where honor was early rendered to the heroism of the martyrs, a Greco-Roman naturalism was used to depict allegorical subjects. By the side of Christ as the Good Shepherd and elsewhere there was portrayed the ORANS, a standing praying figure with arms stretched out forming a cross; these praying figures have been explained variously as the soul in paradise, as a symbol of the Church, or as one in heaven praying for those on earth. Occasionally there is an obvious attempt at portraiture, with some indication of activity on earth.

Preserved well are the high-relief sculptured marble sarcophagi (*see* SARCOPHAGUS), which present biblical scenes with sacramental interpretation. The Apostles are shown in Roman togas, in a realistic fashion, though sometimes they are presented symbolically as sheep. On the cross in the mosaic of the apse of St. Clement, the Twelve appear as doves.

Following the fall of Rome in the 5th century and the rise of Byzantium, there was a shift in the manner of portraying saints. In the East the classical Greek ideal of the human form was transformed into a highly stylized art with hieratic figures and Persian decorative elements.

The saints were not represented as they were on earth, but now as in heaven, dressed in garments of the Byzantine court, symbol of the kingdom of God. On the nave walls of the church of S. Apollinare Nuovo, there are two lines of saints, men on one side, women on the other, all dressed alike and facing the apse, offering the crowns of their martyrdom together with Christ's sacrifice, on the altar. The names written above are the only distinction of one saint from the other. The pictures recall the presence of the saints of the Church Triumphant, with whom all the faithful on earth pray in unity with Christ to God the Father.

The change in the representation of the saints was not simply a matter of aesthetics. It resulted from the development of theological expression obtained through visual art as much as through verbal means. The book found by Didron on Mt. Athos, though written at a late date, does give instructions handed down from early times regarding the way subjects should be painted in churches according to Greek tradition. Every part of the church is important in a complete iconographic scheme. The Prophets of the Old Testament and the saints of the New Covenant all have their proper locality in the basilica. ST. MARK'S in Venice gives some idea of how richly and carefully worked out an iconographic scheme could be.

The outbreak of the iconoclastic controversy (*see* ICONOCLASM) in the East, which raged longer than 100 years during the 8th and 9th centuries, though successfully overcome, had the effect of keeping some restraint on pictorial representations.

In the East images remained flat, without any attempt being made to create an illusion of the figure in the round. In the West, where sculpture was used with less fear of idolatry, a kind of representation developed that was quite distinct from that of the East. It emerged too with a hieratic quality but had undergone transformations through the influence of Celtic art and that of the barbarian tribes. During the 11th and 12th centuries, Romanesque art had achieved its richest realizations in its churches. Architecture and sculpture were blended into a rhythmic whole, expressing vast theological and biblical themes. Holy personages of the OT, the Evangelists, and the elect or damned in general received their respective places in the grand tympanum themes (Autun, Vézelay, etc.).

The rise of the Cistercians under St. Bernard of Clairvaux created a kind of puritanical movement long before the Reformation. The gaunt style of architecture, expounded in St. Bernard's *Apologia,* flourished particularly in 12th-century Cistercian churches. In order to avoid distractions from prayer and meditation in monastic churches (and as protest to the luxury of Cluny churches), paintings and sculpture were renounced; walls were all white and the architecture itself served to lift the soul to prayer.

Cistercian art did not prevail universally but was limited, for the most part, to the monastic centers of the order. Beginning in the 12th century, a saint image in sculpture and STAINED GLASS emerged with Gothic architecture as an "elegant" type of saint reflecting the prestige of the royal court. The St. Theodore on the south portal jamb of Chartres, approaching high Gothic, has an easy courtly elegance suggesting the ideal Christian soldier who has achieved a peaceful and elevated life. In the 13th century in Italy, there was an awakening of a humble humanism following the spirituality of St. Francis. Saints began to appear in a more believable space with an earthly familiarity, combating the difficulties of life on earth. The saint image was injected with human sentiment and participated in the newly discovered delights of nature.

Renaissance to the present day. With the return to classical humanism during the Renaissance, the Gothic fragility disappeared and the saint image emerged with an elevated intelligence and the prestige of learning. The saint was presented in a rationalized three-dimensional space with learned correctness arrived at through the laws of perspective (both linear and spatial) and the study of anatomy. The cult of the nude derived from studies of anatomy and an interest in classical ideals. Thus the blessed (and the damned) were presented in the nude in Luca Signorelli's frescos in the S. Brixio chapel of the Orvieto cathedral; the nude saint achieved brilliant strength from the hand of Michelangelo in the Sistine Chapel. The saint was often presented with some learned association, deliberately conscious of himself as an individual and appropriately "posed" within the frame of the picture. Good examples may be seen in paintings by Mantegna and Bellini of the Madonna enthroned with saints, a popular subject by the end of the 15th century.

The exaltation of noble families and rich patrons through humanistic vainglory occurred as donors themselves were often included in the painting with the holy personages. This, along with the rising popularity of mythological subjects, produced a less believable saint image. Meanwhile, reformers in the North, fearful of idolatry and wishing to emphasize the importance of preaching the Word, initiated a new iconoclasm; they destroyed statues and paintings of Christ, Mary, and the saints.

The Council of Trent (H. Denzinger, *Enchiridion symbolorum* [Freiburg 1963] 1821–25) took measures to check abuses in the representation of religious subjects and reaffirmed the position on the veneration of images that was asserted by the Council of Nicaea II (*ibid.* 600) and the Council of Constantinople IV (*ibid.* 653, 656). After the Council of Trent the saint image began to assume a new posture; the classical pose of the Renaissance was replaced with the theatrical flare of the baroque, and the saint became engaged with expressions of intense inner experience and ecstatic gesture. It was present in Bernini's *The Ecstasy of St. Theresa* and spread to the North as exemplified by Rubens and in Spain by El Greco and Zurbarán.

In England, the vigorous illuminations of the Saxon and Norman centuries, of the antiphonaries and psalters of the Westminster School, and of the later Gothic period, which demonstrate a deep religious life, were to be abandoned for landscape and portraiture because of Puritanical pressure. Later, when the pre-Raphaelites tried to recapture medieval spirituality, they were unable to do so, since they were imprisoned by a naturalistic art, which, when rendered in a romantic light, was fictive and unconvincing. William Blake alone stood out, creating his own symbolism against a tide of realism.

By the 19th century, religious art was at a very low ebb. After the industrial revolution, when personal creative work was replaced by standardized industrial production, a cheap plaster image emerged along with lithographed and engraved saint reproductions. These images, often with little intelligent iconography and bearing more sentiment than authentic spiritual content, have been labeled from their greatest centers of distribution such as La Place Saint-Sulpice ("Sulpician Art").

In the later 19th century and early 20th century, various efforts were made to restore the integrity of the religious image. In Beuron through Father LENZ a hieratic neo-Byzantine effort known as BEURONESE ART was introduced; in France, Maurice Denis and George Desvallières attacked false religiosity in images; Alexandre Cingria with a group of six Swiss artists, backed by Bishop Besson, tried to counteract the decadence of their period; in England Stanley Spencer forcefully put modern man into his pictures (Burghclere Chapel), and Eric Gill tried to restore integrity through expert and sensitive craftsmanship (Stations of the Cross, Westminster Cathedral).

Although a great painter such as Georges Rouault produced a saint image of true religious spirit, which touched the 20th-century sensibility, it did not have an organic force sufficient to culminate in a unified, widespread Christian image. Organized efforts through the Liturgical Arts Society and the Liturgical Press at Collegeville, Minn., and the work and publications of the Dominicans in France accomplished much in raising consciousness to the problem of the saint image. However, after World War II and the continued growth of abstract art, the use of the image for devotional purposes began to be replaced with a sometimes barren aniconic religious art.

In order to avoid the unauthentic and unconvincing saint image, modern church architecture has tried to achieve devotional ends through the use of space and very limited imagery (much like the Cistercian ideal under St. Bernard). The attempt of Henri Matisse at the chapel of VENCE to achieve a work of art with a complete and unified iconographic scheme, though masterful in itself, stands isolated and has not led Christianity to discover the authentic saint image of the 20th century. The earlier effort at ASSY achieved individual pieces of strength (Rouault's *Veronica*) but, because of the variety of talent employed, failed to point convincingly in any direction. The recent saint photograph reproductions of the New Image Editions in France are notable, since they attempt to rise above the impersonal portrait photograph and present a personal, living encounter with a believable holy person.

In the East, tradition has been maintained with some variations but not with any real change of outlook. The Russian Orthodox have developed the Byzantine style and are famous for their icons. Other national branches of the Eastern churches have continued their own specific variation of a similar style, untouched by the violent changes in the West. The Syrians and Copts, Armenians, and Ethiopians have left many miniatures manifesting their devotion to the saints, in the Eastern style, which they continued much later than the Celts, whose somewhat related art was arrested early by the Romanized West.

Bibliography: C. CAHIER, *Caractéristiques des saints dans l'art populaire enumerées et expliquées. . . ,* 2 v. (Paris 1867). F. C. HUSENBETH, *Emblems of Saints: By Which They Are Distinguished in Works of Art . . .* (3d ed. Norwich 1882). A. N. DIDRON, *Christian Iconography,* tr. E. J. MILLINGTON, completed by M. STOKES, 2 v. (London 1886). C. ROHAULT DE FLEURY, *Archéologie chrétienne: Les Saints de la messe et leurs monuments. . . ,* 10 v. (Paris 1893–1900). A. B. JAMESON, *Sacred and Legendary Art,* ed. E. M. HURLL, 2 v. (New York 1896). M. E. TABOR, *The Saints in Art, with Their Attributes and Symbols Alphabetically Arranged . . .* (London 1908). E. E. GOLDSMITH, *Sacred Symbols in Art* (2d ed. New York 1912). ARTHUR DE BLES, *How to Distinguish the Saints in Art by Their Costumes, Symbols and Attributes . . .* (New York 1925). W. MOLSDORF, *Christliche Symbolik der mittelalterlichen Kunst . . .* (Leipzig 1926). L. BRÉHIER, *L'Art chrétien, son développement iconographique des origines à nos jours* (2d ed. Paris 1928). K. KÜNSTLE, *Ikonographie der christlichen Kunst,* 2 v. (Freiburg 1926–28). E. RICCI, *Mille santi nell'arte* (Milan 1931). J. BRAUN, *Tracht und Attribute der Heiligen in der deutschen Kunst* (Stuttgart 1943). A. GRABAR, *Martyrium: Recherches sur le culte des reliques et l'art chrétien antique,* 3 v. (Paris 1943–46) v. 2. É. MÂLE, *L'Art religieux de la fin du XVIe siècle, du XVIIe siècle et du XVIIIe siècle: Étude sur l'iconographie après le concile de Trente, Italie, France, Espagne, Flandres* (2d ed. Paris 1951). G. KAFTAL, *Iconography of the Saints in Tuscan Painting* (Florence 1952). G. W. FERGUSON, *Signs and Symbols in Christian Art* (New York 1959). H. ROEDER, *Saints and Their Attributes* (London 1955). W. SCHAMONI, *Le Vrai visage des saints,* tr. L. POUCRAULT (Bruges 1955). J. PICHARD, *L'Art sacré moderne* (Paris 1953). W. RUBIN, *Modern Sacred Art and the Church of Assy* (New York 1961). P. RÉGAMEY, *Religious Art in the Twentieth Century* (New York 1963). G. MERCIER, *L'Art abstrait dans l'art sacré* (Paris 1964).

[J. U. MORRIS]

SAINTS, INTERCESSION OF

Omitting the complex history of the term *sanctus* (see Delehaye, *Sanctus: Essai sur le culte,* 24–59), and stating in advance that the Church has never authentically proposed a complete definition, one may offer the following theological description: A canonized saint is a member of the Roman Catholic Church who hearing and unconditionally responding to God's call has led a life of ever-increasing union and conformity with Christ through the practice of CHARITY and of all the other Christian virtues, and who, because of this virtuous life, confirmed by subsequent miracles, has been proclaimed by the infallible teaching authority of the Church as being a person particularly pleasing to God. In fact, God through miracles has made known His will that the saint be counted by the other members of the Mystical Body of Christ as mediator and intercessor *per Christum, cum ipso, et in ipso* for all those who have not yet reached the end of their journey toward the full glorification of God in heavenly blessedness, as worthy of the religious cult of *dulia,* as visible proof of His providential action in the Church, and therefore the norm and example of a life typically and truly Christian (see Molinari, *I santi e il loro culto,* 25–26).

In Catholic Theology. Three elements may be distinguished in this description: (1) the constituent qualities of a saint; (2) the act of ecclesiastical authority by which a person is declared a saint; (3) the reasons why God raises up saints in the Church and wishes them to be recognized as such. [For (2) *see* CANONIZATION OF SAINTS (HISTORY AND PROCEDURE); here (1) is principally discussed, but (3) also receives some consideration.]

When one says that a saint is a person who has attained an eminent degree of union and conformity with Christ, one means that his greatness derives from and is founded primarily and wholly on Christ, who by means of grace has invited the person to follow Him, has elevated him to share in His life, and has sustained him in all his actions (*see* ELEVATION OF MAN). However, at the same time one must point out that grace, by elevating the liberty of the human person, has rendered it capable of freely responding to God's love and of surrendering itself entirely to Christ in order to live in Him. The saint, consequently, is the masterpiece of God's grace, but precisely as such, he is at the same time the model of a free person.

Contrary to what people sometimes believe, neither extraordinary deeds, nor the graces of the mystical life, nor the accidental phenomena that can accompany it (*see* MYSTICISM) are what constitute a saint, but rather the fact that united to Christ he has lived in the practice of the virtues of his state (and particularly the love of God and neighbor) after a manner truly Christoform, that is, faithful, constant, ready, to the point of heroism (*see* VIRTUE, HEROIC; HOLINESS).

Faithful to the promptings of GRACE and sharing with ever-increasing intensity in the life of the Incarnate Word (*see* INDWELLING, DIVINE), the saints continue to develop and with special efficacy to diffuse the redemptive activity of Christ in the midst of and for the greater good of His Mystical Body. By the example of their lives they irradiate the lovableness of Christ, thus drawing souls to Him and teaching them to lead a truly Christian life in the most varied situations and circumstances. Above all, however, in virtue of the fundamental law of intercommunion among its members, the whole Mystical Body benefits from the heroic life of labor, the prayers, and the sacrifices of saints (*see* CHURCH, ARTICLES ON; MYSTICAL BODY OF CHRIST; COMMUNION OF SAINTS), that is, insofar as by God's will the distribution of divine grace has been made at least partly dependent on the contribution that the members make to the Head, and hence on their MERITS and on the prayers they offer for others. This will not seem surprising once the true meaning of justification, grace, and INCORPORATION IN CHRIST is understood. For the members of the Mystical Body through the gift of themselves to Christ, enable Him, dwelling within them, to avail Himself of the unique riches of their personal existence, to overcome the limitations of His individual human nature (hypostatically assumed by the Word and most perfect, but, nevertheless, created and therefore limited), and to complete in this way qualitatively and quantitatively the work of Incarnation and Redemption.

Invocation and Intercession. The foregoing statements help to clarify the true meaning of the invocation and intercession of the saints. If, in virtue of the principles given above, Christ, availing Himself of the free contribution of His members, completes in them His life and activity and applies at least in part—through this very gift—the fruit of His life and activity, it is obvious that the members who receive the benefits that derive from this contribution ought to feel particularly obliged and grateful to those who have freely given it in Christ. But since the life and activity of the members of the Mystical Body of Christ do not cease with life on earth, but, on the contrary, are ennobled by their entrance into life eternal with Christ, where they enjoy more intimate participation in the glorious life of Christ Himself, who "lives always to make intercession" (Heb 7.25), the saint's ardent concern for the spread of God's kingdom in souls is intensified when, in the light of celestial glory, he understands with greater clarity the spiritual needs of those on earth, and with love inflamed by the beatific vision longs to see Him glorified by these who are still on the road to eternal happiness. *See* BEATIFIC VISION; HEAVEN (THEOLOGY OF). Prompted by this disinterested love, the saint offers in Christ and with Christ his merits and prayers for wayfarers, becoming their advocate and protector; that is to say, he intercedes for them with Christ and through Him with the Father. Those on earth, for their part, respond to the saint's intercession not only by expressions of gratitude and by the acknowledgement of his supernatural excellence, but also by the invocation of his efficacious assistance in their own spiritual and material needs (*see* CULT; DULIA). Thus between saint and those on earth there is established a bond of confident intimacy, like that existing between older and younger brothers, a bond that, far from detracting from the relationship with Christ and with God, enriches and deepens it, just as does every act of truly supernatural love among the members of the Mystical Body of Christ.

Considering the saints, then, in this theological perspective, one understands how they, more than other Christians, contribute to the building up of the whole Christ, Head and members, and at the same time to the glorification of the Most Holy Trinity intended and willed by God in this historic order as the praise offered by all creation recapitulated in Christ and lived by, with, and in Him (*see* RECAPITULATION IN CHRIST).

The keen awareness that all men are called to union with Christ, and through Him to union with one another, obviously has some profound repercussions on all human activity but finds its most noble expression in the liturgical cult that by its very nature is social and communitary (*see* LITURGY). For this precise reason the liturgy of the Church not only promotes but gives life to the union with those members of the Mystical Body who, having terminated their earthly existence, are now unfailingly incorporated in Christ and constitute in heavenly glory the richest part of the people of God. And if in virtue of these considerations one ought actively to live in union with all his heavenly brothers, it is none the less clear that this contact ought to take place first of all with canonized saints, that is, with those whom one knows with infallible certainty—based on the declaration of the supreme teaching authority—to be actually in heaven, particularly united to Christ and who—in virtue of miracles—are individually indicated by Him as especially worthy and qualified to be friends and intercessors.

Historical Perspective. If Holy Scripture does not speak explicitly of the intercession and invocation of saints, it offers a complete basis, especially in the clear Pauline teaching on the Mystical Body. In addition to this, in the Old and New Testaments frequent mention is made of impetratory and satisfactory intercession of the living for the living (Gn 18.22–32; 20.7; Ex 32.11–014; Nm 14.13–20; Job 42.8; Acts 7.60; 12.5; Rom 15.30; Eph 1.15–19; 6.18–20; 1 Tm 2.1–4; Jas 5.16–18). Scripture also speaks of the intercession of the angels for men (Zec 1.12; Job 33.23–24; cf. Tb 12.12; 5.8; 8.3). In regard to the intercession of the dead for the living—about which no mention is made in the most ancient books of the Old Testament, in which is found, as is well known, a very imperfect knowledge of the lot of the dead—one has the familiar text of 2 Maccabees 15.11–16. If in the New Testament writings—set down, one must remember, not as formal treatises but rather as casual pieces—nothing on the subject is explicitly mentioned, one still has in the practice of the early Church an abundant harvest of evidence that demonstrates faith and conviction in the intercessory power of those who had "died in Christ." Such evidence (which is clearly of very great value since it reflects the mind of the early Christians, who lived entirely in the apostolic tradition and preaching) is seen in the many epitaphs, anaphorae, litanies, liturgical documents, acts of the martyrs, and in the frequent allusions encountered in Oriental, Greek, and Latin patristic literature. For example, there is the following inscription on a tomb: "Gentianus fidelis in pace, qui vixit annis XXI mens(e)s VIII dies XVI, et in orationi(bu)s tuis roges pro nobis, quia scimus te in Christo" (see Delehaye, *Les Origines*, ch. 4).

In the same source (100–140) there are also many passages chosen from patristic literature on the invoca-

tion and intercession of the saints, and in first place one finds the classical texts of Hippolytus of Rome, Origen, Cyprian, Eusebius, Basil, Gregory of Nazianzus, Cyril of Jerusalem, Ambrose, John Chrysostom, Augustine, Jerome, and many others. After the great Roman persecutions, the cult originally reserved to those who had sacrificed their lives or suffered for Christ was gradually extended to include those who had consecrated themselves entirely to Christ as virgins, hermits, or cenobites, and at last to anyone who had led a life of heroic virtue.

The invocation of the saints as intercessors reached its greatest intensity in the Middle Ages, particularly in the veneration of patron saints that gave rise to local feast days and confraternities and affected customs and folklore. In the 16th century the heads of the Protestant reform rose in violent revolt against the Catholic doctrine concerning the intercession of the saints and their invocation. If these attacks were occasioned also by the exaggerations and abuses existing in this sector, it must be said that the true motive of these attacks is found in the Protestant concepts of the Incarnation, Redemption, justification, merit, and the Church, insofar as they are opposed to Catholic teaching. To counteract the wrong interpretations of the Protestants, the Council of Trent (H. Denzinger, *Enchiridion symbolorum*, ed. A. Schönmetzer, 1744, 1755, 1821–24, 1867) solemnly reaffirmed Catholic doctrine, pointing out its Christocentric nature. To avoid any misunderstanding or prejudice, it is therefore most important in ecumenical dialogue to explain, in ways ever more positive and in the light of what has been said, what the effects of incorporation in the Church are, for only then shall one contribute to making others understand that the authentic Catholic concept of saints, far from dimming the greatness of Christ, the fount of all grace and merit and sole mediator (*see* MEDIATION), greatly contributes to its splendor, and that the invocation of the saints not only does not diminish but actually increases the WORSHIP (*latria*) of God. This aspect has been brought out very clearly by Vatican Council II. Chapter 7 of the *Dogmatic Constitution on the Church* contains a complete systematic exposition of Catholic teaching on the saints [*Acta Apostolicae Sedis* 57 (1965) 53–58].

See Also: INTERCESSION

Bibliography: P. SÉJOURNÉ, *Dictionnaire de théologie catholique*, ed. A. VACANT et al., 15 v. (Paris 1903–50) 14.1:870–978. A. P. FRUTAZ, *Lexikon für Theologie und Kirche*, ed. J. HOFER and K. RAHNER, 10 v. (2d, new ed. Freiburg 1957–65) 7:127–32. H. DELEHAYE, *Les Origines du culte des martyrs* (2d ed. Brussels 1933); *Sanctus: Essai sur le culte des saints dans l'antiquité* (Brussels 1927). R. LANSEMANN, *Die Heiligentage, besonders die Marien-, Apostel- und Engeltage in der Reformationszeit* (Göttingen 1939). P. MOLINARI, *I santi e il loro culto* (Rome 1962). K. RAHNER, "Die Kirche der Heiligen," *Schriften zur Theologie* (Einsiedeln 1954–) 3:111–26. J. B. WALZ, *Die Fürbitte*

Reliquary with depiction of saints. (©Archivo Iconografico, S.A./CORBIS)

der Heiligen (Freiburg 1927). A. EBNETER, "Der Heilige im Protestantismus," *Orientierung* 25 (1961) 216–20; "Fürsprache und Anrufung," *ibid.* 27 (1963) 222–26. J. PASCHER, "Die *communio sanctorum* als Grundefüge der katholischen Heiligenverehrung," *Münchener theologische Zeitschrift* 1 (1950) 1–11.

[P. MOLINARI]

SAINTS, LEGENDS OF THE

The term legend (from the Latin *legenda,* something to be read) originally meant the lesson (*lectio*) or reading of selected portions of the lives and passions (sufferings) of the martyrs and confessors, intended for spiritual edification. By extension it came to mean a collection of legends, or a legendary, in which the acts of the saints were recorded month by month, as for example in the Golden Legend of JAMES OF VORAGINE (*c.* 1265). Thus the primary significance of the word legend had no relation to a judgment of the historical or fictitious character of the events narrated. This was to be determined according to the regular criteria of history.

In modern languages, the term legend tends to have a pejorative meaning because of the bad reputation that the legends of the saints have among historians; thus it has come to mean a popular or poetic recitation in which historic reality has little part and which is based on fantasy or fiction.

Literary Genres. The literary type or genre represented by the legend of a saint has its origin in the Biblical MIDRASH and developed early in primitive Christianity. Examples of legends from the 1st century are available in the apocryphal Gospels and Acts of the Apostles, in the reworking of the Acts of the Martyrs, in the recitation of the finding and translation of relics. In the 4th century, these were extended to the biographies of the monks, and later pervaded the amplification and embellishment of the martyrologies and synaxaries, finally entering the lives of the saints. Here appear certain elements adapted from the myths and romances of antiquity, Oriental, Buddhistic and Indian stories (e.g., BARLAAM AND JOASAPH), Celtic and German legends (e.g., the Grail). But these borrowings should not be exaggerated, although the material covers a large expanse of human interest from the combat of dragons and the intervention of animals (horses, doves, bees, stags) to incest; these are minimal beside the properly Christian elements, particularly the miracles attributed to the Eucharist and to the saints and their relics.

The authors of the legends retell the lives of the saints not with the intention of recounting history in a strict sense but to give edification to the reader, to encourage him to imitate the Christian hero, and to strengthen him in the faith. They sometimes explain the name of a place or village (onomatologic legend), the origin or significance of a saint's image or statue (iconographic legend), or advance the reasons for building a church or inaugurating a pilgrimage. In these instances they do not hesitate to exalt their saint beyond measure, and to the detriment of rival saints. Hence there is nothing astonishing in the fact that they transform and deform historic facts, confound them with incidents in the lives of older saints, or sometimes retell them in the same terms. In the eyes of the author, the end he has in view justifies such plagiarism. What interests him above all else is the miracle as a proof that his hero enjoyed divine favor and exemplified great sanctity.

In the light of these summary observations, it is easy to see why the critical historian finds that legends are a difficult subject. He has to inquire of each one what it transmits that is factually useful and, by weighing the mentality of the author, the purpose he had in mind, and the materials at his disposal, to draw out of apparently valueless recitals, information that is useful from a point of view other than that intended by the composer of the legend.

History of the Legends. It has often been repeated on the authority of the Liber pontificalis that Pope Saint CLEMENT I had appointed Roman regional notaries to collect the ACTS OF THE MARTYRS, and that Pope ANTERUS and Pope FABIAN later perfected the system. As a matter of fact no such notaries ever existed, no more than did a Roman corpus of the passions of all Christian martyrs. However, we do have a certain number of documents relating to the early martyrs: the official verbal processes in proconsular acts; the passions of certain martyrs such as those of PERPETUA AND FELICITY; letters, such as the Letter of the Church at Smyrna to that at Philomelium on the martyrdom of Saint POLYCARP; and biographies, including that of Saint CYPRIAN OF CARTHAGE by the Deacon Pontius. These texts are known to us through the mention that EUSEBIUS OF CAESAREA makes of them in his *Ecclesiastical History,* fragments of his *Acts of the Martyrs,* and his *History of the Martyrs of Palestine.*

In the Orient Saint ATHANASIUS of Alexandria composed a life of Saint Anthony *c.* 360 that served as a model for the *History of the Monks of Egypt (see* RUFINUS OF AQUILEIA), PALLADIUS's *Lausiac History,* and even for Syrian and Asiatic hagiographers, for example, John Moschus's (d. 619) *Pratum spirituale.* Of note also are the SYNAXARIES, for example, those of Symeon Metaphrastes and Gregory PALAMAS.

In the West this genre was begun by Saint JEROME who wrote lives of Paul of Thebes, Hilarion, and Malchus in the form of historical romances. His fundamental work, the *De viris illustribus* on a more historical basis, was imitated by GENNADIUS OF MARSEILLES (*c.* 450), ISIDORE OF SEVILLE (616–18), and ILDEFONSUS OF TOLEDO.

In Gaul the most important work at this time was the life of Saint Martin of Tours by SULPICIUS SEVERUS. Biographies of this type were written by Paulinus of Milan (Saint Ambrose), Possidius (Saint Augustine), and Eugippius (Saint Severin of Noricum). Saint GREGORY I gathered the miracles of the Fathers of Italy in his *Dialogues.* GREGORY OF TOURS (d. 594) somewhat credulously, but conscientiously and in good faith, supplied unique details of Gallo-Roman and Merovingian hagiography in his *History of the Franks, Virtues of St. Martin of Tours, Miracles of St. Julian, Glory of the Martyrs, Glory of the Confessors,* and the *Lives of the Fathers.*

In Africa VICTOR OF VITA wrote a history of the African persecution (*c.* 486) and Fulgentius Ferrandus, a life of Saint FULGENTIUS OF RUSPE (d. 533). From Spain have come the useful *Lives of the Fathers of Mérida* by the deacon Paul of Merida (d. 672) and EULOGIUS OF CÓRDOBA's *Memoriale Sanctorum* (d. 859), an account of the Moslem persecutions. In the Celtic and Anglo-Saxon lands, along with the *Ecclesiastical History* of BEDE (d. 735), there are lives of the Irish and English abbots and missionary saints.

Medieval Legends. During the Carolingian period many of the earlier lives were rewritten with more care for literary style but with little concern for historical criticism. During this time HILDUIN identified PSEUDO-DIONYSIUS with Saint Denis of Paris in his *Areopagitica,* and biographers attempted to prove the Apostolic origin of the Frankish churches by means of invented or falsified lives. During the 8th and 9th centuries the Germanic lands also furnished numerous lives of their early bishops, such as Saint WILLIBALD OF EICHSTÄTT, Corbinian of Freising, and Lambert of Liège, along with biographies of the monastic founders.

In the 10th century hagiographic activity was notable in France with the work of Hucbald of Saint-Amand, Adso of Montier-en-der, and others. ODO OF CLUNY wrote the life of Gerard of Aurillac; FLODOARD (d. 966), the hagiographer of Rheims, celebrated the saints of Palestine, Antioch, and Italy in his poems on *The Triumphs of Christ.*

In the 12th century there was a continuation of this tradition. EADMER OF CANTERBURY wrote a life of Saint Anselm; Paul of Bernried, a life of Saint GREGORY VII; Saint BERNARD OF CLAIRVAUX, the life of Saint Malachy; and William of Saint-Thierry, Arnaud of Bonneval, and Geoffrey of Auxerre each wrote a life of St. Bernard. In the 13th century with the rise of the mendicant orders hagiography received a new stimulus. JORDAN OF SAXONY (d. 1237) wrote the life of Saint Dominic; Gerald of Frachet (d. 1271), the *Vitae fratrum ordinis Predicatorum* (Dominicans); and lives of Saints Francis of Assisi, Bonaventure, and Anthony of Padua appeared, each full of legendary material. Besides the hagiographers among these new orders, biographers such as CAESARIUS OF HEISTERBACH produced lives of Saint Engelbert and Saint Elizabeth of Hungary; THOMAS OF CANTIMPRÉ compiled a legend-filled *Bonum universale de Apibus;* and Joinville composed his *Book of the Holy Sayings and Good Deeds of St. Louis of France* (1305).

In the 14th century the lives of the saints multiplied, with the confessor, chaplain, or friends recording the doings of such outstanding saints as MARGARET OF CORTONA and CATHERINE OF SIENA. The Dominican William of Tocco wrote the first life of Saint Thomas Aquinas. Continuing this tradition in the 15th century, Philip of Mézières, counselor to Charles I, wrote a life of Saint Peter Thomas; John Mattioti wrote the life of his penitent Saint FRANCES OF ROME (d. 1440); and Pierre de Vaux, of his penitent Saint Colette.

In the West as well as in the Orient compendia of saints' lives were put together; they were the LIBER PONTIFICALIS at Rome, the *Gesta* of the bishops of Auxerre, Le Mans, Verdun, etc.; the deeds of abbots (e.g., *Gesta abbatum Fontanellensium*), enriched with biographical notices; and martyrologies, legendaries, and passions of the saints. In the 13th century, more popular compilations appeared, such as the *Sanctoral* of Roderick of Cerrat, the *Legenda de sanctis* of Peter Calo de Chioggia, the *Abregé of the Life and Miracles of the Saints* by Jean de Mailly, the *Golden Legend* of James of Voragine, the *Speculum historiale* of VINCENT OF BEAUVAIS, the *Speculum sanctorale* of Bernard of Gui, and the Venetian Peter de Natalibus's *Catalogus sanctorum et gestorum eorum,* which contained 1,500 notices. All these compilations were made with great piety but with little critical sense.

The Protestant Reformation. Beginning in the 16th century, the refusal of Protestants to venerate saints diminished to a certain degree this luxuriant flowering of legends. The literary interest of John Milton (d. 1674), Abram of Santa Clara (d. 1709), and Martin von Cochen (d. 1712) helped to keep them alive. But in the 18th century the Enlightenment in Germany and Voltaire and the Encyclopedists in France covered them with a massive disdain, thus reinforcing the rationalist and hypercritical attitude of the Protestant reform. These challenges incited both Catholics and Protestants to begin a scientific study of the legends.

HAGIOGRAPHY on a historical basis was begun in the 16th century, and was developed in the 17th, particularly by the BOLLANDISTS, who took their name from their founder Jean Bollandus, SJ (1596–1665); they influenced many of the writers and compilers of the legends of the saints in the 19th and 20th centuries.

Bibliography: H. DELEHAYE, *Les Légendes grecques des saints militaires* (Paris 1909); *Cinq leçons sur la méthode hagiographique* (Brussels 1934); *Étude sur le légendier romain* (Brussels 1936). A. VAN GENNEP, *La Formation des légendes* (Paris 1910). H. QUENTIN, *Essais de critique textuelle* (Paris 1926). R. AIGRAIN, *L'Hagiographie* (Paris 1953). H. GÜNTER, *Psychologie de la légende,* tr. J. GOFFINET (Paris 1954). J. MARILIER, *Catholicisme. Hier, aujourd'hui et demain,* ed. G. JACQUEMET (Paris 1947–) 5:485–92. W. BÖHNE, *Lexikon für Theologie und Kirche,* ed. J. HOFER and K. RAHNER, 10 v. (2d, new ed. Freiburg 1957–65) 6:876–78.

[J. LE BRUN]

SAINTS AND BEATI

The veneration of saints, beginning with the cult of martyrs, has been a hallmark of the Catholic tradition from the earliest days of the Church. Between the sixth and tenth centuries, the number of deceased who received honor as saints notably increased. A reputation for a holy life, a great spirit of charity, and especially a report of miracles were the only requirements for sainthood in those early days. New names were added to the calendars and martyrologies; the number of feasts rapidly grew; and lives of the saints, often legendary, were written.

In the early medieval period popular fame or the *vox populi* proved to be an inadequate criterion for sanctity. Abuses crept in, and ecclesiastical authorities gradually introduced more formal procedures, first by local bishops, later by Roman pontiffs. The first papal canonization for which there is documentary evidence was that of St. Udairicus in 973. Pope Gregory IX formulated procedural norms (1234) that guided inquiries into a person's reputation for sanctity. In the sixteenth century when Pope Sixtus V reorganized the Roman curia with the constitu-

St. John the Evangelist from Sculptural Program of the Cathedral of Notre Dame, Paris. (©Stefano Bianchetti/CORBIS)

tion *Immensa aeterni Dei* (1588), he entrusted the task of overseeing the canonization process to the Congregation of Rites. The congregation developed procedures and norms that lasted into the pontificate of Pope Urban VIII. In 1642 Pope Urban codified the decrees governing the canonization of saints in a single volume under the title *Urbani VIII Pont. O.M. decreta servanda in canonizatione et beatificatione sanctorum.* In the following century Pope Benedict XIV wrote a masterful treatise that set the norms for centuries to come. *De Servorum Dei beatificatione et Beatorum canonizatione* explained in a clear and definitive manner the principles and methods governing the processes of beatification and canonization and clarified the fundamental concept of the heroic degree of virtue.

The 1918 Code of Canon Law summarized the juridical and administrative procedures in the beatification and canonization of saints (cc. 1999–2141). The 1983 Code says simply, "The causes of the canonization of the servants of God are regulated by special pontifical law" (c. 1403). Pope Paul VI issued two documents on the subject. *Sanctitas clarior* (1969) was a step in implementing Vatican II's constitution *Lumen gentium* (nos. 40, 47, 50). It clarified the competencies and procedures of bishops with regard to the introduction of causes of servants

of God for beatification. *Sacra rituum congregatio* divided the Congregation of Rites into two congregations, one for Divine Worship and the other for the Causes of Saints. The new Congregation for the Causes of Saints included an office with historiographic and hagiographic functions.

Pope John Paul II's apostolic constitution *Divinus perfectionis magister* (Jan. 25, 1983) and the respective *Normae servandae in inquisitionibus ab episcopis faciendis in causis sanctorum* (Feb. 7, 1983) reformed the procedures for promoting the cause of a saint and restructured the congregation. The constitution enlarged the role of local ordinaries in saints' causes by giving them the right to initiate investigations into the lives, virtues, martyrdom, veneration, and asserted miracles for the candidate. It also assigned to the congregation a college of relators whose task is to assist with the drafting of the *Positiones super vita et virtutibus (o super martyrio)* of the servant of God.

John Paul II has called on the Church "to foster the recognition of the heroic virtues of men and women who have lived their Christian vocation in marriage" and to honor Christ by acknowledging his "presence through the fruits of faith, hope and charity present in men and women of many different tongues and races who have followed Christ in various forms of Christian vocation" (*Tertio millennio adveniente,* no. 37). The new saints and blesseds represent all walks of life from peasant to royalty; laity, religious, and the ordained; artists, children, farmers, founders, scientists, scholars—in short, the whole gamut of human experience.

Announcing the Jubilee 2000, John Paul II placed special emphasis on the person of the martyr, noting that at the end of the second millennium, "The Church has once again become a Church of the martyrs" (*ibid.*). The majority of those raised to the altars are martyrs who died primarily in the twentieth century during periods of civil unrest and religious persecution, including World War II, the Spanish Civil War, and the Mexican Revolution. The increased number of beatification and canonizations in the last century manifests the vitality of the local Churches (ibid.). The pope sees these canonizations and beatifications as an instrument for the evangelization of local churches and as a sign of the universal call to salvation and holiness.

See Also: BEATIFICATION; CANONIZATION OF SAINTS (HISTORY AND PROCEDURES).

[K. I. RABENSTEIN/EDS.]

"St. Lawrence Giustiniani with Other Saints" by Giovanni Antonio de Sacchis, called Il Pordenone, 1532, Venice, Italy.

SS. CYRIL AND METHODIUS, SISTERS OF

(SS.C.M., Official Catholic Directory #3780); an American congregation of religious women of papal jurisdiction founded by Matthew Jankola, priest of the Diocese of Scranton, Pennsylvania, for the care and education of Slovak children. In November 1903, with the approbation of his bishop, M. J. Hoban, Jankola placed several young women with the Sisters of the Immaculate Heart of Mary to be prepared for this mission. Six years later, after the Sisters of Saints Cyril and Methodius had received papal approval, the first group professed simple temporary vows. Their constitutions, based on the rule of St. ALPHONUS LIGUORI, were formulated and approved in 1912, revised in 1930, and received final approbation in 1946.

The sisters opened their first school at Sacred Heart parish, Wilkes-Barre, Pennsylvania (1908), and took over the care of the new Middletown, Pennsylvania, orphan-age (1914) sponsored by the First Catholic Slovak Union, which turned over some adjoining property to the congregation for a temporary motherhouse and novitiate. A permanent motherhouse, Sacred Heart Villa, was established five years later in Danville, Pennsylvania. In 1922 an academy, chartered as the First Catholic Slovak Girls High School but later titled St. Cyril Academy, was opened at the motherhouse. The sisters are engaged in academic education, catechetics, parish ministry, retreats, spiritual direction, counseling, chaplaincy, prison ministry, and care of the aged and retired.

[M. E. PETRASEK/EDS.]

SALA, MARIA ANNA, BL.

Religious of the Congregation of St. Marcellina; b. Apr. 21, 1829, Brivio, Italy; d. Nov. 24, 1891, Milan, Lombardy, Italy. Maria Anna's parents, Giovanni and Giovannina Sala, sent her to school with Marcelline Sisters at Vimercate. However, she returned home to assist her ailing mother. At age 21, circumstances enabled Sala to join the Marcellines, who staff hospitals, conduct social work, and engage in missionary activities. Following her novitiate and profession in 1852, she dedicated her life to teaching at Cernusco, Chambéry, Genoa, and Milan. Diagnosed with malignant throat cancer in 1883, Sister Maria Anna continued forming young girls into women of character, commitment, and obedience until her death. During her beatification (Oct. 26, 1980), Pope John Paul II praised Sala for silent suffering in union with that of Christ.

Feast: Nov. 24.

Bibliography: M. FERRAGATTA, *Visse per le anime, vita della serva di Dio suor Maria Anna Sala* (Milan 1963). *Acta Apostolicae Sedis* 73 (1981): 532–534. *L'Osservatore Romano,* English edition, no. 44 (1980): 10–11.

[K. I. RABENSTEIN]

SALADIN

The European name for Ṣalāḥ al-Dīn ibn Ayyūb, founder of the Ayyubid dynasty, Kurdish officer, who brought to an end the Fāṭimid anticaliphate of Cairo, reconquered Jerusalem from the Crusaders, and successfully contained Europe's counteroffensive, the Third Crusade; b. Tikrit, Mesopotamia, 1138; d. Damascus, Syria, March 4, 1193.

He was the son of Ayyūb, a Kurdish vassal of Nūr al-Dīn, the militantly anticrusading Zangid Atabeg of Damascus. Ṣalāḥ al-Dīn was sent at the age of 27 with forces to bolster the fading power of the Ṣhī'i Fatimid regime, threatened by the attacks of Amaury of Jerusalem. By 1171 he was the real master of Egypt, which he returned to orthodox Sunni allegiance under the 'Abbāsid caliph at Baghdad (*see* 'ABBĀSIDS). To the consternation of the Franks, Egypt's wealth and resources were now devoted to the anti-Crusade. When Nūr al-Dīn died in 1174, the Turkish Zangids of Syria were apprehensive of his powerful vassal, and became openly hostile to the upstart Kurd, who soon felt compelled to seize control of Damascus. But since there could be no all-out war against the Crusaders as long as he had to fear the plots of the Zangids of Aleppo and Mosul, from 1179 to 1185 Ṣalāḥ al-Dīn was occupied with the unification of Muslim Syria. In this he was careful to secure legality by caliphal investiture and to cancel all taxes not prescribed by Muslim law. He furthered the SUNNITES by founding religious academies, and he fortified Cairo with its great citadel. In Syria his strict observance of his word and his reckless generosity disarmed his enemies and produced devoted followers. To isolate the Syrian Franks he gave trading concessions to the fleets of the Italian merchant-cities and signed a treaty with Byzantium, hard pressed by the SELJUKS and increasingly fearful of Crusader greed. At the same time, to gain a free hand in North Syria, he signed and scrupulously observed a truce with the Crusaders, until it was broken in 1187 by the Seigneur of Kerak. He then invaded Palestine where the rashness of Guy of Lusignan, king of Jerusalem and Cyprus, gained Ṣalāḥ al-Dīn a decisive victory at the Horns of Hattin, in Galilee. Jerusalem and the cities of the interior soon fell, and the Third Crusade sent from Europe found the Franks blockaded in coastal Tyre, Tripoli, Antioch, and a handful of fortresses.

Ṣalāḥ al-Dīn's moral authority over his own people kept his tired feudal armies in the field for three years, and despite intense efforts, the combined forces of England, France, and Germany were unable to break out of the coastal plain. The only real Crusader gain was the capture in 1191 of Syria's best port, the fortified city of Acre, which for the next century was the capital-in-exile of the Kingdom of Jerusalem.

While fanatical against Christian political power in Syria, Ṣalāḥ al-Dīn behaved honorably to Christians as individuals, this in sad contrast to Crusader behavior. He died shortly after the war, leaving almost no personal possessions. He has been remembered by Muslims as a great hero of their faith and by Christians as a noble and magnanimous enemy. His family, the Ayyubids, confined their wars with Crusaders to self-defense when attacked. They partitioned Syria and Egypt among themselves and ruled there until replaced by the Mamelukes.

Bibliography: H. A. R. GIBB, "The Career of Nur-ad-Din," and "The Rise of Saladin, 1169–1189," *The First Hundred Years,* ed. M. W. BALDWIN, v.1 of *A History of the Crusades,* ed. K. M. SETTON (Philadelphia 1955–). BAHĀ ED-DĪN, *The Life of Saladin* (London 1897). S. LANE-POOLE, *Saladin* (New York 1898). P. K. HITTI, *History of Syria, Including Lebanon and Palestine* (2d ed. New York 1957). C. CAHEN, *Encyclopedia of Islam,* ed. B. LEWIS et al. (2d ed. Leiden 1954–), 1:796–807.

[J. A. WILLIAMS]

SALAMANCA, UNIVERSITY OF

A state institution of higher learning that originated in a 13th-century center of Spanish culture.

Early History Like all Spanish universities founded before the 14th century, Salamanca was created by royal decree and not by papal bull, although academic degrees were conferred in the name of both pope and king in a ceremony held in the cathedral. Like many early European universities, however, it had its origin in a cathedral school (*see* CATHEDRAL AND EPISCOPAL SCHOOLS) directed by a *magister scholarum,* although, unlike its French counterpart, the University of PARIS, its emphasis was not so much on theology as on law.

Founded by Alfonso IX of Leon (*c.* 1227) shortly before his death (1230), Salamanca had no foundation charter and did not take root as an institution of higher learning until FERDINAND III, King of Castille, issued a charter on April 6, 1243, confirming the privileges that his father had granted the students when he established higher schools or universities properly so-called (*studia generalia*) and lower schools or colleges (*studia*). The university's academic equilibrium, however, continued unsettled until 1254 when Ferdinand's scholarly son, Alfonso X, the Wise (1221–84), issued his "magna charta" that launched the institution on a long period of prosperity and intellectual progress with the establishment of three chairs in Canon and civil law, and one each in grammar, arts (including the organon and logic), and physics.

Despite the university's organization by royal decree as a *studium generale,* its schools retained the constitutional features of cathedral schools, which were sponsored by the bishop, and directed by a *magister scholarum* or *scholasticus* who, as Rashdall points out, played a more important role in Spanish universities than the grand chancellor at the University of Paris or BOLOGNA. Even the term *claustro* (cloister), commonly used throughout Spain to indicate the university building or academic staff, emphasizes the close affiliation that existed between universities and cathedrals.

At Alfonso's request, in April 1255 Pope Alexander IV issued a bull recognizing the existing *studium gener-*

ale at Salamanca and conferring on it extensive privileges of ecclesiastical exemption applicable to the university as a corporate body, to administrative officers, and to students. To graduates he granted the *licentia docendi* at all *studia generalia* except Paris and Bologna. Pope John XX in 1333 lifted this restriction on the *jus ubique docendi.*

In 1263, Alfonso the Wise issued the *Siete Partidas,* containing the first educational code of its kind in Europe, and in which, according to D'Irsay, Title II deals extensively with universities. In this code, Alfonso (1) clarified the meaning of *studium* (school) and *studium generale* (university); (2) recognized the union of masters and students as a *universitas,* and the university as an autonomous organization empowered to elect its own rector; (3) provided a modest endowment to pay professors' salaries and other expenses; (4) gave particular emphasis to the study of law; and (5) introduced music into the curriculum, making Salamanca apparently the first European university to offer music degrees.

Decline and Revival. Toward the end of the century, however, when Alfonso's son Sancho IV (1257–95) neglected to pay the meager endowment stipulated by his father, the unpaid professors went on strike and the *studium* was suspended. In 1300, Ferdinand IV (1285–1312), Sancho's son and successor, in an endeavor to restore the university to its earlier vigor, decided to transfer the ecclesiastical tithes from the churches to the university and in 1301 Pope Boniface VII approved the plan. In 1306, however, Pope Clement V ordered the tithes restored to the churches, which, deprived of financial support, had fallen into disrepair. The university was then again suspended until 1313 when Clement, in an attempt to solve the complex problem, allotted a third of the tithes to remunerate the professors of civil and Canon law, logic, grammar, music, and medicine. In fact, medicine, which had flourished in the 13th century in the universities of Salerno and Montpellier and then declined, was revived at Salamanca by professors who had translated the works of Avicenna and Averroës from the Arabic. Also during this period, notably sterile in literary pursuits, Salamanca together with Paris, Bologna, and OXFORD was ordered by the council of Vienne (1311–12) to introduce the study of Arabic and other Eastern languages. Theology was introduced into the *studium* in 1355 but did not gain prominence until 1416 when the antipope BENEDICT XIII (Pedro de Luna) gave the university a constitution similar to that of Bologna and established chairs in theology. In 1422 Pope Martin V drew up definitive constitutions, reestablished the chairs of theology, and numbered Salamanca among the four greatest universities of the world (Paris, Bologna, Oxford, Salamanca). By the 16th century Salamanca had become a theological center to which the

popes could turn for champions of the faith, a position that it held throughout the 17th century.

During the reign of Charles V (1500–58) and Philip II (1527–98) new statutes were added to Martin V's constitutions, the curriculum was reorganized, and Salamanca reached the highest peak of its development. By the 1560s the university had 11 chairs in philosophy and logic; ten in Canon Law; seven each in medicine and in theology; four in Greek; two in Hebrew and Chaldaean; one each in music and in astronomy; and 17 in grammar and rhetoric. The Faculty of Theology was divided into Prime and Vespers (according to the canonical hours), with chairs in the Bible, St. Thomas Aquinas, Duns Scotus, and the nominalists. The Bible included both the Old and the New Testament offered in alternate years. Peter Lombard's *Sententiae* were studied in both Prime and Vespers. In 1526 F. de VITORIA introduced Thomas Aquinas's *Summa theologiae* as a textbook into Prime, and in the 1530s D. de Soto used it as a text in Vespers.

Although in the 16th century the university was one of the largest in Europe, ranking with Oxford and Paris as a center of learning, in the early years enrollment at Salamanca was small. In fact, in 1335 the century-old university had only 439 students, including masters, licentiates, bachelors, and scholars in the various faculties. The numbers gradually increased, however, in the 15th and through the 16th centuries until in 1552 they totaled 6,328; and in 1584, 6,778, the highest in its history. In the 17th century numbers began a steady decrease with 4,000 in 1601; 3,908 in 1641; 2,000 in 1701; 1,500 in 1750; 1,000 in the early 19th century; 412 in 1822; and 391 in 1875, its nadir.

Colleges and Schools. For almost 175 years, however, Salamanca had no colleges or schools. The first of the four famous major colleges, the College of St. Bartholomé, later the Old College, was founded in 1401 by Diego de Anaya Maldonado, Archbishop of Seville, for poor students, to include ten canonists and five theologians. Other major colleges were Cuenca, founded in 1500; Monte Olivete, in 1517; and Fonseca, also known as the Archbishop's College, in 1521. A number of minor colleges also developed in rapid succession in the 16th century: St. Thomas of Canterbury (1510), sponsored by the English hierarchy for the training of priests; St. Millan (1517); Santa Maria (in 1528 renamed Juan de Burgos); Santa Cruz of Canizares (*c.* 1534); Santa Magdalena, sponsored by the Order of Knights; Santa Susanna (Norbertines, 1570); Guadalupe (Brethren of the Common Life, 1572); St. Pelayo (1546), St. Elias (Discalced Carmelites, 1581); and four military colleges.

In 1592 under the sponsorship of Philip III and at the request of Thomas White, SJ, an Irish College, El Real

Colegio de Nobles Irlandeses, was founded at Salamanca. It was open to students from all Irish provinces, although it was contended at the time that White had refused to receive students from Ulster and Connaught or the exiled chiefs, O'Neil and O'Donnell. The college was the training ground for many eminent Irish clergymen and members of the hierarchy. It was administered by Spanish Jesuits with an Irish Jesuit as vice rector, until 1767 when the Jesuits were expelled from Spain and the college, later known as St. Patrick's, was entrusted to the secular clergy. The college was closed after World War II and the library holdings were transferred to St. Patrick's College (Maynooth).

In 1600 the Discalced Carmelites at the university founded a school of philosophy called Salamina. A group of its teachers, the Salmanticenses, were the authors of the *Cursus Theologicus Summam d. Thomae Complectens,* an encyclopedic commentary on the *Summa* of St. Thomas Aquinas, designed to provide a solid theological basis for the friars of the Teresian reform which took 70 years to complete.

Pontifical University of Salamanca. In the late 18th century the liberals suppressed the major colleges under the pretext of decadence, without, however, replacing them; and in the early 19th century they closed the minor colleges. The laws of 1845 finally dissolved the last remnant of the medieval university, replacing it with a secular institution under government control. The Faculty of Theology was discontinued in 1868.

To replace the ecclesiastical faculties, the Spanish episcopate founded the Pontifical University of Salamanca in September 1940. The university is under the jurisdiction of an episcopal commission, the president of which is the cardinal archbishop of Toledo, primate of Spain. The bishop of Salamanca is the secretary general of the commission and grand chancellor of the university. The university opened with the faculties of theology, Canon Law, and philosophy, and expanded into the other humanities and sciences, offering bachelor, licentiate, and doctoral degrees.

Bibliography: H. RASHDALL, *The Universities of Europe in the Middle Ages,* ed. F. M. POWICKE and A. B. EMDEN, 3 v. (new ed. Oxford 1936). S. D'IRSAY, *Histoire des universités françaises et étrangères des origines à nos jours,* 2 v. (Paris 1933–35). C. POZO, *Lexikon für Theologie und Kirche,* ed. J. HOFER and K. RAHNER (Freiburg 1957–65) 9:256–258; *Fuentes para la historia del metodo teológico en la Escuela de Salamanca* (Granada 1962) v.1. F. MARTÍN HERNANDEZ, *La Formación clerical en los colegios universitarios españoles* (Vitoria 1961). P. URBANO GONZÁLEZ DE LA CALLE and A. HUARTE Y ECHENIQUE, *Constituciones de la Universidad de Salamanca, 1422* (Madrid 1927). L. SALA BALUST, ed., *Constituciones, estatutos y ceremonias de los antiquos colegios seculares de la Universidad de Salamanca* (Madrid 1962–63) v.1–2.

[M. B. MURPHY/EDS.]

SALAS, JUAN DE

Jesuit theologian; b. Gumiel de Iban, in the province of Burgos, Spain, Dec. 3,1553; d. Salamanca, Sept. 20, 1612. He entered the society in 1569, and taught philosophy at Segovia and theology at Compostela, Barcelona, Salamanca, Valladolid, and Rome. In Rome Salas was employed by C. Acquaviva, general of the society, as censor of books and theological adviser, and he was given a place among those appointed to represent the Jesuits at the *CONGREGATIO DE AUXILIIS.* He was a man of broad learning and an authority of considerable repute, especially in the field of moral theology. During his lifetime Salas published three volumes of commentary on the *Prima secundae* of the *Summa theologiae* of St. Thomas Aquinas (Barcelona 1607, 1609; Lyons 1611). After his death his commentary on the portion of the *Secunda secundae* dealing with contracts was published by D. Muñoz (Lyons 1617). He is also credited by Sommervogel with a *De gratia et auxiliis* that was not published because of the Holy See's prohibition of further works on the subject. Salas's treatment of contracts is of historical, as well as theological, importance because of its discussion of the business practices of the time and especially of the problem of interest taking.

Bibliography: C. SOMMERVOGEL et al., *Bibliothèque de la Compagnie de Jésus,* 11 v. (Brussels-Paris 1890–1932; v. 12, suppl. 1960) 7:448–449. H. HURTER, *Nomenclator literarius theologiae catholicae,* 5 v. in 6 (3d ed. Innsbruck 1903–13) 3:589. R. BROUILLARD, *Dictionnaire de théologie catholique,* ed. A. VACANT et al., 15 v. (Paris 1903–50; Tables générales 1951–) 14.1:1032. *Enciclopedia de la Religión Católica,* ed. R. D. FERRERES et al., 7 v. (Barcelona 1950–56) 6:948.

[P. K. MEAGHER]

SALAT, HANS

Swiss Catholic historian, poet, and pamphleteer; b. Sursee (Lucerne), 1498; d. Sursee, Oct. 20, 1561. A ropemaker and later a surgeon, he served as a French mercenary in Italy (1522–27). In 1529 he fought in the First Kappel War and gained citizenship in Lucerne. In October 1531 he became city historian. After the Second Kappel War (1531), he produced satirical poems against the Protestants. His ferocious satire against H. ZWINGLI, *Triumphus Herculis helvetici* (1532), compared the Reformation to a witches' Sabbath. Meanwhile he was writing his *Chronicka und Beschrybung von Anfang des nüwen Ungloubens* (1536). This highly partisan work, which regards the Reformation as divine punishment, covers the period 1517 to 1534. Salat wrote also military histories, political pamphlets, and at least one drama. Personal and political causes drove him from Lucerne in 1540. He soldiered again, taught school at Fribourg until dismissed (1547), and spent his final years as a surgeon. In 1552 he returned to Sursee.

Bibliography: H. SALAT, *Chronicka,* in *Archiv für die schweizerische Reformationsgeschichte,* 3 v. (Freiburg 1869–75) 1:1–396; ''Memorial der Regierung von Unterwalden über den bewaffneten Zug der Abwaldner in das Haslithal wider die Berner und über die daherigen Verhandlungen und Folgen von Anno 1527 bis Anno 1531,'' *ibid.,* 2:99–151. J. BAECHTOLD, ed., *Hans Salat: Ein schweizerischer Chronist und Dichter aus der ersten Hälfte des XVI. Jahrhunderts: Sein Leben und seine Schriften* (Basel 1876). E. F. J. MÜLLER, *Lexikon für Theologie und Kirche,* ed. M. BUCHBERGER, 10 v. (Freiburg 1930–38) 9:110–111.

[C. G. NAUERT JR.]

SALAWA, ANIELA, BL.

Domestic servant, Franciscan tertiary; b. Sept. 9, 1881, Siepraw (near Krakow), Poland; d. Mar. 12, 1922, Krakow, Poland. Raised in a family of modest means, Aniela Salawa entered domestic service in Krakow at age sixteen (1897). Following the death of her sister Teresa (1899), Aniela was moved to dedicate her life to God. Thereafter she exercised an active apostolate among other servants in the city and fed her spiritual life through prayer, while never neglecting her duty to her employers. She joined the Third Order of Saint Francis in 1912, following the deaths of her mother and her mistress in 1911. During World War I, Aniela comforted wounded soldiers in Krakow's hospitals during her free time. After falling seriously ill in 1917, Aniela was forced into retirement. In the five years before her death at age forty, she offered her continual pain to God in expiation of sins and for the conversion of sinners. Pope John Paul II beatified Aniela, Aug. 13, 1991, in the Market Square at Krakow.

Feast: March 12.

Bibliography: I. BORKIEWICZ, *Aniela Salawa: opowiadania o zyciu* (Warsaw 1987). J. STABINSKA, *Charyzmat sluzby: zycie Anieli Salawy* (Warsaw 1988); *Z nadmiaru milosci: zycie wewnetrzne Anieli Salawy* (Warsaw 1987). A. WOJTCZAK, *Aniela Salawa* (Warsaw 1983).

[K. I. RABENSTEIN]

SALAZAR, DOMINGO DE

First bishop of Manila; b. Labastida (Rioja), Ebro, Spain, *c.* 1512; d. Madrid, Spain, Dec. 4, 1594. He was professed as a Dominican at Salamanca (1546), and studied there under Francisco de VITORIA. Although originally assigned to missions in Venezuela, in 1548 he was transferred to Mexico, where he did missionary work among the Guajaca people. From 1558 to 1561 he accom-

panied Tristan de Arellano on an ill-fated mission to Florida. After his return to Mexico (1562), Salazar served as prior at Oaxaca and Puebla. Following his return to Spain in 1576 as provincial procurator, he was nominated by Philip II as first bishop of Manila (1579). In 1581 he set out for the Philippines with 20 Augustinians, one Dominican, five Franciscans, three Jesuits, and six secular priests. There he erected a cathedral and hospital and summoned a diocesan synod (1582). He engaged in controversies with religious orders exempted from his episcopal jurisdiction, particularly the Augustinians. Salazar also fought against the greed and cruel policies of the civil authorities, especially Gov. Ronquillo of Manila. As a student of Bartolomé de LAS CASAS, Salazar condemned encomienda and other Spanish practices used to subjugate the natives. On the advice of a number of theologians, he later modified his views and opposition. Salazar also favored Spanish military action against China as the necessary means by which Christianity would overcome Chinese opposition and resistance to the Gospel. In 1587 the Dominicans entered the Philippines at his invitation. His disagreements with the civic authorities, especially Gov. Gómez Pérez Dasmariñas, led Salazar to Spain (1591), where he obtained relief for the natives, reestablished the *audiencia,* and secured the creation of more bishoprics, thus leading to the erection of the autonomous ecclesiastical province of the Philippines (1595).

Bibliography: H. M. OCIO Y VIANA, *Reseña biográfica de los religiosos de la prov. del SSmo. Rosario de Filipinas* (Manila 1891) pt. 1, 38–49. L. HANKE, ed., *Cuerpo de documentos del siglo XVI* (Mexico City 1943). V. F. O'DANIEL, *Dominicans in Early Florida* (New York 1930).

[B. M. BIERMANN]

SALESIAN SISTERS

Officially designated as Daughters of Mary Help of Christians (FMA, Official Catholic Directory #0850), one of the largest religious congregations of women in the world. They were founded by (St.) John BOSCO in 1872 at Mornese, Italy, for the Christian education of youth, especially the less privileged. In a small group of sodalists of Mornese, John Bosco found the nucleus of this new congregation, which, with the help of (St.) Maria MAZZARELLO, he established and named in honor of Our Lady. Rome approved the institute temporarily in 1911 and finally in 1921. Foundations multiplied rapidly. In 1877 the first missionary group left for South America. The sisters opened houses in the Middle and Far East, in Africa, and in many parts of Europe.

The Salesian Sisters came to the United States in 1908, establishing their first center in Paterson, N.J. The sisters are principally involved in educational work in private and parochial elementary and secondary schools. The sisters give social assistance and catechetical instruction to Puerto Rican immigrants in the Paterson-Passaic area of New Jersey. In many parts of the world Salesian sisters staff boarding and day schools, kindergartens, teacher-training colleges, elementary and secondary schools, commercial and professional schools, orphanages, residences for working girls, summer camps, leper colonies, hospitals in mission posts, sodalities, alumnae organizations, retreats for teenage girls, and organized clubs.

[R. DUNN/EDS.]

SALESIANS

(SDB, Official Catholic Directory #1190); the Society of St. FRANCIS DE SALES (Societas Sancti Francisci Salesii), popularly known as the Salesians, or Salesians of Don Bosco (SDB), is a religious congregation devoted to the Christian education of youth. It was founded in 1859 by (St.) John BOSCO; its members include priests, clerics, and lay members called coadjutors. Since Vatican II a secular institute of consecrated women, the Volunteers of Don Bosco has been formally approved. Salesian youth work is developed in oratories (recreational and cultural organizations concentrating their activities at an oratory or chapel), in technical high schools, schools of arts and trades, preparatory schools, grade schools, parishes, and foreign missions; and by the spread of good books through graphic-arts schools and editorial guilds.

Origins. Don Bosco was 26 years old when in 1841 he began his great work by befriending and instructing an orphaned child-laborer in the church of St. Francis of Assisi in Turin, Italy. Five years later he located his first oratory in a shed in the Valdocco section of Turin where the motherhouse now stands. As his boys increased in number, Don Bosco decided to prepare the best among them to assist him and to continue his work. In 1859, with 17 members, he founded the Salesian Society, which received the *decretum laudis* of Pius IX on July 23, 1864, and papal approbation on March 1, 1868. The constitutions were approved on April 3, 1874. Official recognition stimulated expansion outside Italy, to France, Latin America, and Spain. In 1875 the first missionaries left for Argentina, led by the Reverend Giovanni Cagliero, who later became the first Salesian bishop and cardinal. At the death of the founder (Jan. 31, 1888) there were 1,039 Salesians in 57 foundations in Italy, Spain, France, England, Argentina, Uruguay, and Brazil. Don Bosco was beatified in 1929 and canonized on April 1, 1939.

Growth. The society continued to develop rapidly under Don Bosco's successors: Michael Rua (1888–1910), Paul Albera (d. 1921), Philip Rinaldi (d. 1931), Peter Ricaldone (d. 1951), and Renato Ziggiotti (d. 1983). This development has not ceased in the postconciliar period, under the leadership of Luigi Ricceri (d. 1989), Egidio Viganò (d. 1995) and Juan Vecchi. In 2001 there were more than 18,000 Salesians in 1,800 houses spread through 116 countries.

Don Bosco also founded the Institute of the Daughters of Mary Help of Christians (1872), popularly known as SALESIAN SISTERS. This institute has the same end and applies the same educational methods in the apostolate for girls, as does its male counterpart in the education of boys. Its cofounder was Mother Maria Domenica MAZZARELLO (1837–81), canonized by Pius XII in 1951. Don Bosco's third Salesian family, the Cooperators, is similar to the older third orders, with the difference that, whereas these latter seek Christian perfection principally through practices of piety and penance, the Salesian Cooperators seek it through the exercise of charity toward needy youth, according to the spirit of their founder. They are canonically associated in a pious union approved by Pius IX on May 9, 1876. The secular institute of consecrated women, the Volunteers of Don Bosco, was granted diocesan recognition in 1971, and is of pontifical rite since 1978. The *Salesian Bulletin*, published in 32 editions, is the official organ of the Cooperators. In 1909 the Salesian alumni movement, which goes back to the time of Don Bosco, was organized and later formed national federations and a worldwide confederation, with hundreds of thousands of members.

Activities. Following Don Bosco's norms, Salesian education is based upon reason, religion, and love. Its method is to evaluate and employ all that is humanly useful in character formation—study, work, associative organization, and sports. At the heart of the system is Don Bosco's notion of "the preventive system." Young people are to be accompanied and guided in growth, rather than educated in any repressive way. The earlier Salesian mission fields in Brazil, Ecuador, Paraguay, Venezuela, India, China, Thailand, and the Congo have exploded in the postconciliar period. Following the society's first postconciliar general chapter in 1978, the then rector major, Viganò, launched "project Africa." This new missionary outreach reached further, especially into Asia and the Pacific. There are Salesians in Angola, Benin, Cambodia, Cameroon, the Ivory Coast, Egypt, Eritrea, Ethiopia, the Philippines, Fiji, Gabon, Ghana, Japan, Indonesia, Kenya, Lesotho, Nigeria, Madagascar, Malawi, Mali, Mozambique, Nigeria, Papua New Guinea, Samoa, Senegal, Sierra Leone, Tanzania, East Timor, Togo, Tunisia, Uganda, Vietnam, and Zambia.

Like most religious congregations, the Salesians undertook a large-scale renewal of their self-identity and mission in the postconciliar period. Four general chapters (1978, 1984, 1990, 1996) attended to the renewal of the constitutions and the Salesian way of life (1978 [provisional constitutions], 1984 [definitive constitutions]) and the Salesian apostolate among the young (1990 [educating contemporary young people to the faith], 1996 [the association of the lay people with the Salesian mission]). In the chapter of 2002, the issue of the administrative structure and coordination of this vast society was scrutinized. All postconciliar leaders of the Salesians have increasingly drawn the Salesians into the question of the radical change of culture that highlights the present era.

Following the lead of Don Bosco, who in 1853 began the publication of the monthly *Catholic Readings,* the Salesians continue a worldwide involvement in publications and mass media. Works edited by Salesian publishing guilds are literary, scientific, technical, fictional, and religious. Of particular distinction are the International Publishing Society (the Societè Editrice Internazionale, or the SEI) of Turin, Madrid, and Buenos Aires, and the guilds of Tokyo and São Paulo, Brazil. A significant international contribution is made to catechetics and religious education (a major concern of the Salesians, and their university in Rome) by the publishing house LDC (Elle di Ci) in Turin. Many rich Salesian resources can also be found on the Internet, where Salesians all over the world participate in the increasingly important cyber technology.

Notable members of the society include (St.) Dominic SAVIO, a pupil of Don Bosco's oratory, Bishop Aloisius Versiglia and Father Callisto Caravario, martyred in China in 1948 and canonized in 2000, and 99 Spanish martyrs beatified in 2001. The society also boasts of a tradition of scholarship, exemplified by G. B. Lemoyne, A. Caviglia, E. Ceria, Jules Cambier, Francis Desramaut, and a number of contemporary Salesians who direct Salesian universities in many parts of the world, and who play leading roles on the faculty of other international Catholic universities. Other significant figures have been the explorer A. M. De Agostini, the musician G. Pagella, and theologians L. Piscetta and A. Gennaro. Closely associated with the name of Father Gennaro is the Salesian Pontifical University in Rome, Italy, an ecclesiastical university with schools of theology, philosophy, education, and canon law. The Salesians have also given to the Church numerous cardinals, bishops, and archbishops.

In 2001 Salesians served in 116 countries and were divided into 71 provinces. In the United States they began work in San Francisco, California, in 1897 at the request of Archbishop Patrick Riordan and ministered to the Italian immigrants of the parishes of SS. Peter and Paul, and Corpus Christi. In 1898 the Italian immigrants of New

York came under the society's care when Archbishop Michael Corrigan of New York entrusted to them the parish of St. Bridget. After 1940 the work of Don Bosco spread more rapidly into many other states. By 2001 there were 41 Salesian houses in the United States, divided into two provinces, with more than 400 confrere.

Bibliography: ST. JOHN BOSCO, *Memoirs of the Oratory: The Autobiography of Saint John Bosco* (Paramus, N.J. 1988). M. WIRTH, *Don Bosco and the Salesians* (Paramus, N.J. 1982). P. BRAIDO, *Don Bosco Educatore. Scritti e testimonianze* (3d. ed. Rome 1996).

[W. KELLEY/F. J. MOLONEY]

SALIMBENE

Franciscan chronicler, Balien Adam, called Ognibene by his relatives and Salimbene by his confrères; b. Parma, Italy, Oct. 9, 1221; d. after 1288. He left his bourgeois family to enter the Franciscan Order in Parma, Feb. 4, 1238. After completing his novitiate at Iesi, he studied at Lucca, Siena (subdeacon), Pisa (deacon, December, 1246), Cremona, and Parma (1247). When FREDERICK II laid siege to his native city, Salimbene was sent to France to study. In Lyons he had an audience with INNOCENT IV. After All Saints Day, 1247, he left for Troyes; he was in Provins in December and spent eight days in Paris (February 1248). Taken ill in Sens, Salimbene spent the spring in Auxerre. He returned to Sens in time for the June chapter meeting, and there saw LOUIS IX, whom he accompanied to Vézelay. At the end of June he was in Arles, and from there went to Hyères to join HUGH OF DIGNE. He spent the winter in Genoa, where he was ordained December 1248. He took a short trip to Lyons in 1249, and, from there, his provincial, Friar Rufinus, sent him back to Italy. Remaining in Ferrara for seven years until 1256, he attended the solemn profession (1254) of Beatrice d'Este, who founded the POOR CLARES in that city. Subsequently, Salimbene lived in many of the friaries of his province. He finished his *Chronicle* between 1283 and 1288 at Reggio and at the friary near Montefalco. Nothing is known of Salimbene's career after June 1288.

Salimbene's *Chronicle* (a similar work by him is lost), composed over a period of several years, beginning *c.* 1262, is incompletely preserved in MS Vat. lat. 7260. Surprisingly, in view of some of its racy narratives, he dedicated the work to his niece, Sister Agnes, a Poor Clare nun. His autobiography reveals its author as clearly a pious friar of honest character, curious and loquacious. However, he is also seen as somewhat of a braggart and, at times, even a scandal-monger. In spite of its verbosity and long digressions, the text is pleasant reading because of its lively accounts, lifelike portraits, vivid descriptions, and lucid language. Many of its details, such as the accounts of John of Parma, Hugh of Digne, and JOHN DA PIAN DEL CARPINE, are of interest to the historian. Although Salimbene was hostile toward ELIAS OF CORTONA, his minor errors may be forgiven as he clearly loved his order and defended it against calumny. A prudent man, Salimbene was able, in time, to free himself (c. 1250) of his attachment to the illusions of JOACHIM OF FIORE.

Bibliography: J. PAUL, *Salimbene da Parma: Testimone e Cronista* (Roma 1992), M. D'ALATRI, ''La Riligiosita Poplare nella Cronaca di Fra Salimbene,'' in *Melanges Berube: Études de Philosophie et Théologie Médievales Offertes a Camille Berube, OFM-Cap.* (Rome 1991), 185–200. SALIMBENE, *The Chronicle of Salimbene de Adam*, ed. J. E. BAIRD et al. (Binghamton 1986). D. WEST, ''The Present State of Salimbene Studies—with a Bibliographic Appendix of the Major Works,'' *Franciscan Studies* 32 (St. Bonaventure, N.Y. 1972), 225–241.

[J. CAMBELL]

SALINAS Y CÓRDOVA, BUENAVENTURA DE

Franciscan Peruvian author; b. Lima, 1592; d. Cuernavaca, Mexico, Nov. 15, 1653. Buenaventura was the younger brother of Fray Diego Córdova y Salinas, but his personality was very different. He became the first great voice of Peruvian Creoles; Fray Diego remained aloof from such questions. Buenaventura served as page for three viceroys (1601–16) and *secretario mayor* for the Marqués de Montesclaros (1615–16). He was educated in the Jesuit Colegio de San Martiín and joined the Franciscan Order in 1616.

From 1621 to 1635 Buenaventura was engaged primarily in teaching in various Franciscan schools in Peru, but his early experiences at the viceregal court had awakened an interest in social, economic, and political affairs that could not be confined to the classroom. His brother, Fray Diego, requested him to write a foreword for his life of Francis SOLANO, but the effort resulted in a volume of almost 400 pages in which praise for the virtues and achievements of the Peruvians, especially in Lima, alternated with many examples of several abuses that Buenaventura had witnessed. The foreword became a book (*Memorial de las historias del Nuevo Mundo,* Lima 1630 and 1957). In 1635 a sermon in the cathedral of Cuzco on the same general theme caused the bishop, Diego de Vera, to denounce Buenaventura to the Crown.

Although the viceroy cleared Buenaventura, at the bishop's unwise insistence Buenaventura was sent to Spain for a hearing; he took with him such honorable commissions as delegate of the archbishop of Lima to

make his *ad limina* visit to the Holy See, representative of the Franciscan province of Lima in the general chapter (Rome 1639), and procurator for the cause of Francis Solano. In Spain, Buenaventura was quickly cleared; he then went to Italy, where he remained until 1644, to fulfill his numerous commissions. While there, he helped defend the work of his old friend Solórzano Pereira (*De jure indiarum*) against the censures of the Roman Inquisition and Lelius. Even though his efforts did not completely free the work from censure, Buenaventura's learning and eloquence won favorable comments from the pope. To these Buenaventura replied: ''Your Holiness, my teachers remain in Peru.''

Although appointed regent of studies at Santa Maria la Nova of Naples, Buenaventura found time to become so involved in the Catalan and Portuguese separatist movements that in Rome he was considered a spy for the king, and in Madrid, a spy for the pope. He was recalled to Spain in November of 1643, and subsequently his friend, José Maldonado, Commissary General of the Indies, had him appointed commissary general of New Spain, an office that he filled with great distinction and efficiency (1646–53). He was noted in particular for his interest in studies and in the missions. At the same time, his personal prestige enabled him to act as a mediator in the difficulties between Bishop PALAFOX and the viceroy of New Spain.

Bibliography: W. COOK, ''Fray Buenaventura de Salinas y Córdova: Su vida y su obra,'' in B. DE SALINAS Y CÓRDOVA, *Memorial de las historias del nuevo mundo Pirú* (Lima 1957) xxixlxxiii; *Revista del Museo Nacional* 24 (Lima 1955) 19–49. M. C. KIEMEN, ''A Document concerning the Franciscan Custody of Rio Verde, 1648,'' *Américas* 11 (1954–55) 295–328.

[L. G. CANEDO]

SALISBURY, ANCIENT SEE OF

The medieval Diocese of Salisbury (Latin, *Saresberiensis*) comprised the counties of Dorset, Wiltshire, and Berkshire, England. In 705 ALDHELM became the first bishop of the new See of SHERBORNE, which covered the greater part of Wiltshire and those parts of Dorset and Somerset—and later of Devon—which were under the control of the kings of Wessex. In 909 the see was partitioned: Somerset came under the new bishopric of Wells; Devon, under that of Crediton; and Wiltshire, together with Berkshire (taken from WINCHESTER diocese), under that of Ramsbury; leaving only Dorset to Sherborne.

In 1058 Herman, bishop of Ramsbury, was translated to Sherborne, and the two sees were reunited. In 1075 Herman moved his seat from Sherborne to the ancient fortress of Old Sarum, where he began the building of a

The historic Old Sarum site north of Salisbury. The 56 acre site consists of earthworks, the ruins of Norman fortifications and the inner walls and foundations of the ancient cathedrals on the site. Photograph by Colin Garratt. (©Milepost 92 ½/CORBIS)

cathedral. The cathedral was completed in 1092 but five days after its consecration it was partially destroyed by lightning. It was rebuilt and enlarged from *c.* 1125 to 1138 during the administration of Bishop ROGER (LE POER) OF SALISBURY.

Diocesan organization. At Sherborne the cathedral had originally been served by secular canons but was converted to a monastic house *c.* 993. In 1091 Bishop OSMUND (1078–99) formally constituted a cathedral chapter at Sarum, which, according to a 15th-century document, consisted of a dean, chanter, chancellor, treasurer, subdean, succentor, four archdeacons, and 32 prebendaries. It is certain that the late-medieval chapter included a dean, subdean, precentor, chancellor, treasurer, four archdeacons, and 52 secular prebendaries. The foundation charter, the *Institutio Osmundi,* laid down the rules of residence and defined the privileges and jurisdiction granted to the dean and chapter. The original chapter of officials

and 32 prebendaries were supported by property given by Osmund. This property was more than doubled through later endowments by kings, magnates, bishops, and lesser men, particularly in the 12th and 13th centuries. Its endowment was at its most lavish during the reign of King HENRY I, due largely, it may be surmised, to the influence of Bishop Roger of Salisbury.

By the middle of the 13th century, Salisbury diocesan organization was complete. There were the four archdeaconries created in 1091, which were probably territorial jurisdictions from the beginning. Those of Dorset and Berkshire were coterminous with the counties; Wiltshire was divided between two archdeaconries, the Wiltshire archdeaconry being the northern, and Salisbury archdeaconry the southern, part of the county. Dorset was the first of the archdeaconries to appear (1097). Hervey, archdeacon of Salisbury, was so named in 1149; Roger, archdeacon of Wiltshire (under the title of Ramsbury) officiated in 1157; and Geoffrey, archdeacon of Berkshire, officiated *c.* 1175.

The archdeaconries were divided into rural deaneries; Salisbury had five (Potterne, Wilton, Wylye, Amesbury, and Chalke); Wiltshire had four (Avebury, Malmesbury, Marlborough, and Cricklade); Berkshire had four (Abingdon, Newbury, Reading, and Wallingford); and Dorset had five (Bridport, Dorchester, Pimperne, Shaftesbury, and Whitchurch).

New Sarum or Salisbury. Old Sarum proved to have a number of disadvantages as the site of a cathedral. The hilltop fortress was a superb defensive position, but it was restricted, exposed, and treeless, much subject to gale and storm, and water was scarce, difficult, and expensive to obtain. What made the site intolerable to the cathedral chapter, however, was none of these things but rather the friction between the castle garrison and the cathedral clergy, the castle and cathedral being only yards apart.

Consequently, *c.* 1200 the decision to move was made. Royal permission was granted, the land was obtained beside the River Avon in the valley below Sarum. In 1219 papal permission was gained, and the foundation stone of the new cathedral was laid in 1220. The east end was consecrated by Abp. STEPHEN LANGTON in 1225; the whole building was consecrated in 1258. The structure was completed with lead roofing in 1266. The chapter house and cloisters were added (*c.* 1260–80); the central tower was raised, and the great spire added at the end of the 13th and beginning of the 14th centuries. The whole of this unified and harmonious building was framed from the beginning by a close of unusual size, so that to this day Salisbury is not only one of the most beautiful but also one of the most beautifully situated cathedrals in the world. During the reign of Henry VIII, Salisbury became part of the Church of England.

See Also: SARUM USE; SIMON DE GHENT.

Bibliography: W. H. R. JONES, *Fasti ecclesiae Sarisberiensis* (Salisbury 1879). *Sarum Charters and Documents,* ed. W. H. R. JONES and W. D. MACRAY in *Rerum Britannicarum medii aevi scriptores* v. 97 (London 1891). *The Register of St. Osmund,* ed. W. H. R. JONES, 2 v., *ibid.* v. 78 (London 1883). D. BURNETT, *Salisbury: The History of an English Cathedral City* (Tisbury, Eng. 1978). K. EDWARDS, *Salisbury Cathedral: An Ecclesiastical History* (Trowbridge, Eng. 1986). T. COCKE and P. KIDSON, *Salisbury Cathedral: Perspectives on the Architectural History* (London 1993). P. BRIMACOMBE, *A Tale of Two Cathedrals: Old Sarum, New Salisbury* (London 1997).

[J. L. GRASSI/EDS.]

SALLÉS Y BARANGUERAS, MARÍA DEL CARMEN, BL.

Baptized Carmen Francisca Rosa, known in religion as Mary of Mount Carmel, foundress of the Conceptionist Missionary Teaching Sisters (*Concepcionistas Misioneras de la Enseñanza*); b. Apr. 9, 1848, Vich near Barcelona, Catalonia, Spain; d. July 25, 1911, Madrid, Spain. Daughter of José Sallés and Francisca Rosa Barangueras, Carmen studied pedagogy at *La Enseñanaza* school run by the Company of Mary and began teaching young woman following her graduation. Combining the Dominican ideals of contemplation and action, she founded the Missionary Teaching Sisters of the Immaculate Conception (1892) to witness to the Blessed Mother in the secular world and form young Christians. Before her death, the congregation operated thirteen schools, including one in Brazil (opened in 1911). The Conceptionist Missionaries have since expanded to 12 countries. María del Carmen was declared venerable Dec. 17, 1996, a miracle attributed to her intercession was approved on Dec. 18, 1997, and she was beatified by John Paul II, March 15, 1998.

Bibliography: *Acta Apostolicae Sedis* 8 (1998): 399.

[K. I. RABENSTEIN]

SALMANTICENSES

Name designating the authors, Discalced Carmelites of the College of St. Elias in Salamanca, Spain, of two important theological treatises published in the 17th and 18th centuries. The first of these, the *Cursus theologicus,* by far the more important, is considered along with its authors, nature, and method; and a brief appraisal of the second work is given.

The Cursus Theologicus. This monumental treatise is mainly the work of three theologians. Antonio de la Madre de Dios (b. León, 1583; d. Salamanca, 1637) outlined its general plan, basing it on St. Thomas Aquinas's *Summa theologiae,* and wrote the first two volumes (*De Deo Uno; De Deo Trino, de angelis*), which appeared in 1631 and 1637. His successor, Domíngo de Santa Teresa [called *Doctor consummatus;* b. La Alberca (Salamanca), 1604; d. Madrid, 1660] contributed two more volumes (*De ultimo fine, De Beatitudine, De Voluntario . . .; De vitiis et peccatis*). The work was then brought to near completion by Juan de la Anunciación (b. Oviedo, 1633; d. Salamanca, 1701), who in 15 years (1679–94) published seven more copious volumes (*De gratia; De iustificatione et merito; De virtutibus theologicis; De statu religioso; De Incarnatione; De sacramentis in com.; De*

Eucharistia) and helped prepare the final volume (*De Poenitentia*). This last had been first undertaken by Antonio de San Juan Bautista [b. Lloreda (Santan.), 1641; d. Salamanca,1699] and finished by Ildefonso de los Angeles [b. Zeclavin (Cáceres), 1663; d. Salamanca, 1737]. Over 80 years were needed to publish the entire *Cursus* (1631–1712). However, even before it had begun to appear, a course of Thomistic philosophy had emanated from the Discalced Carmelite school of philosophy in Alcalá de Henares (*Complutum* in Latin; hence the name *Complutenses* given its authors), composed by a group of professors, which included Antonio de la Madre de Dios and Juan de la Anunciación, already mentioned. Much material that appeared therein was presupposed, and simply referred to, by the *Cursus theologicus.*

The *Cursus* adheres strictly to the scholastic method, which seeks a deeper grasp of revealed truth by maximum use of speculative reasoning, as opposed to the dogmatic method, which attempts to defend this same truth against error, and the historical method, which evaluates historical fact and studies the evolution of Christian belief. Although first intended solely as a manual for Carmelite theological students, the *Cursus* quickly developed into a scholastic treatise of unusual proportions (see, e.g., the *De vitiis et peccatis*). Its many tracts were, however, always based on lectures first given in the classroom, where the subject matter was freely discussed with the students. When especially difficult questions arose, the lector would seek the advice of other theologians, many of whom were members of different religious families and taught at the renowned University of Salamanca. When the faculty at the College of St. Elias could not agree on a point, a vote was taken and the more common view was integrated into the final draft. Thus, after ample revision, the material was presented to the order's censors for approval and then finally published. This method evidently made rapid progress impossible, but it won the *Cursus* unusual prestige, because the published work presented the views not of a single author but of a whole group of respected theologians. No less significant is the Salmanticenses' commitment to adhere constantly to the doctrine of St. Thomas, something they did with untiring devotion. Because they lacked proper historical perspective and were sometimes unduly influenced by other currents of thought, the authors of the *Cursus* did not in fact always faithfully reflect the teaching of the Angelic Doctor. Still, it must be remembered that this work is not a commentary on the *Summa theologiae* in the strict sense (as is, e.g., the commentary of Cajetan); it follows its general outline, but it does not comprise all of its parts and even introduces problems and developments not found in the *Summa.* The Salmanticenses make frequent use also of other sources, especially the major commentaries on the *Summa:* after Cajetan, very often quoted, the 16th-century Dominican school of Salamanca (BAÑEZ) notably seems most strongly to have influenced their views. Contemporary Jesuit theologians, such as Gabriel VAZQUEZ and Francisco SUÁREZ, received considerable attention but, more often than not, only to be severely criticized. Neither Biblical nor patristic sources were exploited to any extent, though fairly often quoted; this is undoubtedly because of the somewhat exclusively speculative method of the *Cursus.* Judged within its own scope, this treatise must be rated with the best of its genre. Nevertheless, it received little attention after the first decades of the 18th century. Only late in the 19th century did it regain some favor, through the publication of a new 20-volume edition (Paris, 1870–83) and the support of noted scholars such as M. SCHEEBEN. Even in mid-20th century, however, this major work was getting far less attention than it deserved.

The Cursus Theologiae Moralis. Published between 1665 and 1724, this six-volume work completed the *Cursus theologicus* in that it treated *ex professo* of moral questions, most of which had been intentionally omitted in the earlier work. Its express aim was to prepare students for the ministry of the confessional. Though the authors also of this treatise are referred to as the Salmanticenses, they did not remain anonymous as had the writers of the other *Cursus.* Their names are Francisco de Jesús Maria (d. 1677); Andrés de la Madre de Dios (d. 1674); Sebastian de San Joaquin (d. 1714); and Ildefonso de los Angeles, who finished the *Cursus theologicus.* While generally reliable, this moral treatise falls far short of the high standards set by its predecessor. At times it leans unduly toward laxist solutions and too often quotes sources inaccurately. Despite these limitations, however, it remains a landmark in the history of Catholic moral theology.

Bibliography: T. DEMAN, *Dictionnaire de théologie catholique*, ed. A. VACANT et al., 15 v. (Paris 1903–50; Tables Générales 1951–) 14.1:1017–31; *Divus Thomas*, v.1-6 (Piacenza 1880–1900); 2d series, v.1-6 (Piacenza 1900–05); 3d series (Piacenza 1924–) 27 (1949) 342–351, a review of O. MERL, *Theologia salmanticensis* (Regensburg 1947). E. DEL SAGRADO CORAZÓN, *Los Salmanticenses: Su vida y su obra* (Madrid 1955); "Los Salmanticenses y la Immaculada: Su tesis sobre la redención y el débito de la Virgen," *Salmanticensis* 2 (1955) 265–298. M. DE STE. MARIE, "La Doctrine des Salmanticenses sur l'Immaculée Conception," *Ephemerides Carmeliticae* 7 (1956) 149–228. C. JOURNET ET AL., *Le Péché de l'ange* (Paris 1961). R. A. COUTURE, *L'Imputabilité morale des premiers mouvements de sensualité de Saint Thomas aux Salmanticenses* (Rome 1962) 156–167, 188–190.

[R. A. COUTURE]

SALMASIUS, CLAUDIUS

Or Claude de Saumaise, French Huguenot scholar; b. Semur in Burgundy, April 15, 1588; d. Spa, Belgium, Sept. 3, 1653. As a youth, under the direction of his father, he began to study Greek and Latin. At the age of 16 he went to Paris for further studies and was greatly influenced by I. Casaubon, who was in turn impressed by the youth's erudition. In 1606 Salmasius went to Heidelberg, where his diligent work in the Palatine library led to the discovery of the anthology compiled by Cephalas under Constantine VII, from which he transcribed some epigrams for J. J. Scaliger. In deference to his father's wishes he returned home and served for a time as counselor to the parliament of Dijon. In 1632 he went to the university of Leyden as Scaliger's successor. As a scholar Salmasius is known chiefly as the editor of classical texts and the author of treatises with theological, canonical, and political implications.

In Greek and Latin studies his most important works are an annotated edition of the *Historia Augusta,* which established Salmasius' reputation as a learned commentator, and his impressive *Plinianae exercitationes,* a work still useful, which explains the excerpts from Pliny that Gaius Julius Solinus incorporated in his *Collectanea rerum memorabilium.* Of his numerous treatises the following are examples of their wide range: *De usuris* and *De modo usurarum* defend the licitness of interest taking for both clergy and laity. In 1645 he published *De primatu papae,* to which he added those writings of Nilus CABASILAS and BARLAAM OF CALABRIA attacking papal primacy that he had published earlier at Heidelberg in his student days. This work stirred up opposition and controversy in France. The *Defensio regia pro Carolo I,* written at the request of CHARLES II, then in exile, aims to vindicate Charles I and the claims of absolute monarchy. This treatise is known for the feud it started rather than for the quality of its contents. John Milton replied with his *Pro populo anglicano defensio,* which refers to the "outlandish rhetorician's wanton lies" and takes Salmasius to task for poor latinity. The *Ad Miltonern responsio* levels similar charges at Milton. While Salmasius' learning was indeed encyclopedic, his writings show a lack of critical revision and his numerous controversies betray his penchant for invective.

Bibliography: J. T. FOISSET in *Biographie universelle,* ed. L. G. MICHAUD, 45 v. (Paris 1843–65) 38:51–53. J. E. SANDYS, *History of Classical Scholarship,* 3 v. (Cambridge, Eng.) v. 1 (3d ed. 1921), v. 2, 3 (2d ed. 1906–08); repr. (New York 1958) 2:285–286. G. COHEN, *Écrivains français en Hollande* (Paris 1920). E. DE WAELE and D. NAUTA, *De Katholieke Encyclopaedie,* ed. P. E. VAN DER MEER et al., 25 v. (Amsterdam 1949–55) 21:418. H. R. GUGGISBERG, *Die Religion in Geschichte und Gegenwart* 7 v. (3d ed. Tübingen 1975–65) 5:1335–36. J. H. ZEDLER, *Grosses vollständiges Universal-Lexikon,* 68 v. (Leipzig 1732–54; repr. Graz 1961) 33:99.7–1000.

[H. DRESSLER]

SALMERÓN, ALFONSO

Preacher, theologian, and exegete; b. Toledo, Sept. 8, 1515; d. Naples, Feb.13, 1585. A member of the first small group at Paris of the first religious companions of IGNATIUS OF LOYOLA (1536), Salmerón played an important role throughout his life in the early history of the Society of Jesus. As a theologian, he had influence on the formulation of several of the dogmatic decrees issued by the Council of Trent. His principal publication was a 16–volume commentary on the New Testament: 11 volumes on the Gospels, one volume on the Acts, and four volumes on the Pauline Epistles (Madrid 1598–1601; Brescia 1601; Cologne 1602–04 and 1612–15; only the Cologne editions together contain all 11 Gospel volumes). These diffuse commentaries are based on Salmerón's sermons and lectures as revised with help from Bellarmine. Although very popular in their time, they are now of but little more than historical interest, showing how an erudite scholar could interpret scripture in defense of Catholic doctrine as defined by the Council of Trent.

Bibliography: C. SOMMERVOGEL et al., *Bibliothèque de la Compagnie de Jésus* (Brussels-Paris 1890–1932) 7:478–483. H. HURTER, *Nomenclator literarius theologiae catholicae,* 5 v. (3rd ed. Innsbruck 1903–13) 3:224–227. G. BOERO, *Vita del servo di Dio, padre Alfonso Salmerón* (Florence 1880); Span. tr. I. TORRES (Barcelona 1887). F. DE LANVERSION, *Dictionnaire de théologie catholique,* ed. A. VACANT et al. (Paris 1903–50) 14.1:1040–47.

[L. F. HARTMAN]

SALUTARY ACTS

Those human actions that positively lead to man's true goal: eternal life, or SALVATION. The term is not synonomous with the expressions good acts or meritorious acts. The term "good acts" is more extensive, for one may conceive of an act that is morally or ethically good, but that—since it is of the NATURAL ORDER—does not lead one to his SUPERNATURAL goal. Every act that is salutary is not meritorious. Those acts of a person not yet justified that are done under the influence of actual GRACE and are dispositive for JUSTIFICATION are salutary but not meritorious, for habitual grace and CHARITY are lacking in the one acting (*see* MERIT). Theologians, therefore, distinguish between such merely salutary acts (*actus mere vel simpliciter salutares*) and salutary acts that are also meritorious (*actus salutares et meritorii*). One may clarify the characteristics of these acts and indicate their relation to God's grace by considering briefly various stages in the presentation of this doctrine.

Sacred Scripture and the Fathers. The Old Testament writers recognized their need of God's loving action for the removal of their sinfulness and for their salvation [Psalm 50(51); Jer 31.18–40]. In the New Testament this recognition is repeated, the notion of salvation is expanded, and its dependence on Christ proposed very explicitly (e.g., Jn 6.44; 15.5). Indeed, throughout Sacred Scripture one constantly reads of the need that man has for divine help in order to be freed from his sins and to come to union with God. The prayers of the early Christian community and the writings of the Fathers of the Church express this same dependence on God's loving care. St. Clement of Rome (*1 Cor.* 60, 64), St. Irenaeus (*Adv. haer.* 3.17.2), St. Cyprian (*De oratione dominica* 14), and Tertullian (*De anima* 21) might be cited from this early period. Writers of the 4th century more explicitly teach that even the beginning of man's salutary action is from God. Thus St. Ambrose writes: "You see, indeed, that the power of the Lord works everywhere along with human efforts so that no one can build without the Lord, none can protect without the Lord, indeed no one can begin without the Lord" (*In Luc.* 2.84). St. John Chrysostom (*In Gen. homil.* 25.7) and St. Gregory of Nazianzus (*Orat.* 37.13) among others reflect this same teaching.

Pelagianism. At the beginning of the 5th century Pelagianism denied the absolute necessity of supernatural grace for salvation. This heresy, so opposed to Catholic teaching about the nature of salvation and the role of Christ and His Sacraments, found a strenuous opponent in St. Augustine. Many of his works are concerned with this problem. Perhaps his most famous dictum relative to the heresy is found in his commentary on the allegory of the vine and branches: "Lest someone think that the branch can bear some small fruit of itself . . . , He [Christ] does not say that without me you can do little, but 'without me you can do nothing.' Whether great or small, then, without Him it cannot be done, without whom nothing can be done" (*In evang. Ioh.* 81.3). A local council at Carthage in 418 (*see* H. Denzinger, *Enchiridion symbolorum,* ed. A. Schönmetzer 222–230), confirmed at least in part by Pope Zosimus, condemned Pelagianism, but the error was proposed again in mitigated form during the next century. This later version, known as Semi-Pelagianism, admitted the necessity of divine grace for acts meritorious of eternal life, but taught that the beginning of salvation (i.e., merely salutary acts) were possible without supernatural assistance. A local council at Orange, France, in 529 (*ibid.* 370–397), relying heavily on the words of St. Augustine and St. Prosper of Aquitaine, condemned this milder version of Pelagian-

ism. Although this council was only local, its acts were approved by Pope Boniface II (*ibid.* 398–400) and are an authoritative expression of Catholic doctrine. The beginning of FAITH—indeed, every work pertaining to salvation—depends on divine grace. Without the aid of the Holy Spirit one cannot believe, will, or act as he ought. (*See* PELAGIUS AND PELAGIANISM.) The Fathers of the Church and ecclesiastical documents, echoing scriptural terms, speak of salutary acts as those in which one acts as he ought, *sicut oportet, ut expedit* (cf. Rom 8.26; *Enchiridion symbolorum* 376, 377, 1553, 3010).

Late Medieval Developments. The scholastics of the 13th century clearly taught the necessity of grace for salutary acts, arguing theologically from the supernaturality of the object of these acts. In the 14th and 15th centuries, however, divergences from their teaching appear among Catholic thinkers. For Duns Scotus and his followers grace did not seem to be something supernatural essentially, but only modally, i.e., by reason of its efficient cause [see Scotus, *In 1 sent.,* prol., 1.1.34 (ed. Balič 15:14–15)]. For Scotus and many theologians of the nominalist school, an act of natural love and of meritorious love seemed to be essentially the same, differing only in their acceptance by God. Some nominalist theologians carried this tendency to EXTRINSICISM even further, asserting that by God's absolute power, natural acts—even sinful acts—could be salutary by reason of God's acceptance of them. A tendency toward Semi-Pelagianism is evident in some theologians belonging to the nominalist school (*see* NOMINALISM).

Reformers and Catholic Response. Early in the 16th century Martin Luther proposed his radically new doctrine. Although it included a strong reaction to the tendency of some nominalists toward Semi-Pelagianism, it carried to its ultimate term the nominalist tendency toward extrinsicism with regard to grace. He taught the absolute corruption of man's nature by sin and justification as a merely extrinsic imputing of Christ's merits to man without any inward transformation of the one with grace. Pelagianism had taught that man could perform salutary works without grace. Luther, at the opposite extreme, denied that man—even with grace—was capable of any act proportioned to eternal life, because of the essential corruption of nature, even of a man who was justified. (*See* IMPUTATION OF JUSTICE AND MERIT.)

A similar doctrine, although milder in form, was presented later in the century by M. Baius (1513–89), a Louvain professor (*see* BAIUS AND BAIANISM). Like Luther, he taught the corruption of man's nature by sin, but his chief error seemed to be in the confusion of the natural and supernatural orders. The Catholic teaching concerning these points is found in the decrees of the Council of Trent (1545–63). This council carefully excluded both the tendency to Semi-Pelagianism that occasioned Luther's strong reaction and the extrinsicism that would consider God's love as ineffective in transforming man. The primacy of the divine initiative and the free response of man in justification were clearly taught. Similarly, the council stressed both man's dependence on grace in order to merit and the fact that his actions coming from grace have a proportion to his supernatural goal.

One further dogmatic teaching should be noted. In opposition to the teaching of the semirationalistic theologian G. Hermes (1775–1831) the Vatican Council I defined that faith—even without charity—is a gift of God and as an act pertaining to salvation requires grace (*Enchiridion symbolorum* 3010; *see* HERMESIANISM).

Summary. Catholic theologians commonly teach, therefore, that actual grace is necessary for all acts leading to salvation, whether they precede or follow justification or the reception of habitual or sanctifying grace. Their common theological argument is based on the necessity of a proportion between man's goal and the acts that lead to it. Since both justification and the BEATIFIC VISION, or the attainment of God in glory, are essentially supernatural, the acts that lead to this must also be supernatural, i.e., caused in man through grace.

See Also: GOOD WORKS; INDIFFERENT ACTS; JUSTIFICATION.

Bibliography: THOMAS AQUINAS, *Summa Theologiae* 1a2ae, 109, 114, and the commentators on these places. J. VAN DER MEERSCH, *Dictionnaire de théologie catholique,* ed. A. VACANT, 15 v. (Paris 1903–50) 6.2: 1554–1687. R. HEDDE and É. AMANN, *ibid.* 12.1:675–715. K. JÜSSEN, *Lexikon für Theologie und Kirche,* ed. J. HOFER and K. RAHNER, 10 v. (2d, new ed. Freiburg 1957–65) 5:145–146. E. DAVID, *De obiecto formali actus salutaris* (Bonn 1913).

[J. HENNESSEY]

SALUTATI, COLUCCIO

Chancellor of Florence, chiefly responsible for forming the Florentine humanistic circle; b. Stignano, Italy, Feb. 16, 1331; d. Florence, May 4, 1406. His Guelf father fled to Bologna after a Ghibelline victory. There Salutati was educated as a notary. After returning to Stignano in 1350, he practiced in that region. From 1368 to 1370 he assisted a papal secretary in the Curia. In 1375 he became chancellor of Florence, an office whose importance was greatly enhanced during his 31 years' tenure. His Latin letters to other states were so effective that the Milanese tyrant said 1,000 Florentine horsemen were less damaging than Salutati's epistles. Most important of Salutati's writings were his private letters, dealing with philosophi-

cal matters, literary and textual criticism, etc. Particularly well known were four letters in which he tried to end the WESTERN SCHISM. He wrote also *De laboribus Herculis, De seculo et religione, De fato,* and other works. Salutati's greatest contribution was to arouse an interest in the new HUMANISM. He influenced numerous disciples, men who made Florence the center of humanism in the 15th century: POGGIO, L. Bruni, Niccoli, VERGERIO, Angeli, Rossi, Loschi, and others. He played a major role in bringing the Greek teacher Manuel Chrysoloras to Florence in 1396, thus initiating the serious study of Greek in Italy. Part of Salutati's large library passed to St. Mark's, Florence.

Bibliography: C. SALUTATI, *Epistolario,* ed. F. NOVATI, 4 v. in 5 (Rome 1891–1911); *De nobilitate legum et medicinae. De verecundia,* ed. E. GARIN (Florence 1947); *De laboribus Herculis,* ed. B. L. ULLMAN, 2 v. (Zurich 1951); *De seculo et religione,* ed. B. L. ULLMAN (Florence 1957). B. L. ULLMAN, *The Humanism of Coluccio Salutati* (Padua 1963). A. PETRUCCI, *Il protocollo notarile di Coluccio Salutati* (Milan 1963). C. TRINKAUS, *In Our Image and Likeness* (Chicago, 1970). R.G. WITT, *Coluccio Salutati and his Public Letters* (Geneva 1976). C. TRINKAUS, *In the Footsteps of the Ancients* (Leiden 2000).

[B. L. ULLMAN]

SALVADOR, VICENTE DO

The religious name of Vicente Rodrigues Palha, first Brazilian historian; b. near Salvador, Bahia, c. 1564; d. before 1639. Salvador was educated by the Jesuits in Bahia and then went to Coimbra, Portugal, where he graduated in Canon Law. On his return to Brazil, he was ordained in Salvador and was soon a canon of the cathedral and vicar-general. He entered the Franciscan Order in Brazil on Jan. 27, 1599. He was the first superior of the Convento de San Antonio in Rio de Janeiro (1607) and in 1612 was elected custos of the Franciscans. During the following decade he traveled extensively in northeastern Brazil and was called to Lisbon. On his return (1624), he was captured by the Dutch, who were then occupying Bahia, and imprisoned on board a ship for six months. By 1630, he was again superior of the friary of Bahia, as he had been in 1612. Of his subsequent life, very little is known except that he was a missionary among the native peoples in Parahiba, that he was still alive in 1636, and that he had died by 1639.

Salvador's claim to fame is based on his *História do Brasil,* which he completed in 1627. He gave the manuscript to his friend, Severim de Faria, to have it published, but for some unknown reason it was not published at that time. The manuscript was discovered in the Torre do Tombo in Lisbon in the second half of the 19th century and was then published for the first time. In a felicitous style, Salvador tells the history of Brazil from its discovery in 1500 to 1627 with witty observations and prudent judgments. He was also the author of a history of the Franciscan custody in Brazil, but this work was not published and the manuscript has not yet been located. Salvador, despite his education and the high positions that he held, was a man of simplicity and humility, who enjoyed the esteem of his contemporaries for his wisdom, pastoral zeal, and personal virtues.

Bibliography: VICENTE DO SALVADOR, *Historia do Brasil,* rev. ed. Capistrano de Abreu (São Paulo 1918).

[T. BEAL]

SALVATIERRA, JUAN MARÍA

Jesuit missionary in New Spain and founder of the missions of Lower California; b. Milan, Nov. 15, 1644; d. Guadalajara, Mexico, July 17, 1717. Salvatierra entered the Society of Jesus at Genoa in 1688. He arrived in New Spain (Mexico) in 1675, and there finished his theological studies and was ordained. His first mission assignment was to the Sierra de Chínipas. After a decade there he was sent north as *visitador* to report on conditions in the new mission of Pimería Alta; here he became acquainted with the great Padre KINO, from whom he received the inspiration to attempt to reopen the mission field on the California peninsula. When permission was finally granted for this Lower California enterprise, the Jesuits had to undertake the financing of the mission with very little royal aid. Salvatierra and Juan de Ugarte, through their personal begging, began what developed into the later famous PIOUS FUND. In 1697 the Lower California mission field was reopened. In 1704 Salvatierra was called back to the mainland to become provincial superior, but in 1707 he returned to the peninsula, where he remained until his health failed in 1717. Death overtook him at the Jesuit college at Guadalajara as he was on his way back to the capital. The California mission went on, through periods of success and reverses, until 1767, when the Jesuits were expelled. Franciscans, who were soon to push the mission frontier into Alta California, took over the peninsula missions.

Bibliography: M. VENEGAS, *Juan María de Salvatierra of the Company of Jesus,* tr. and ed. M. E. WILBUR (Cleveland 1929). P. M. DUNNE, *Black Robes in Lower California* (Berkeley 1952). F. J. ALEGRE, *Historia de la provincia de la Compañía de Jesús de Nueva España,* ed. E. J. BURRUS and F. ZUBILLAGA, 4 v. (new ed. Rome 1956–60).

[J. F. BANNON]

SALVATION

The most generic term used to describe the divine action of restoring mankind to the state from which it had fallen by the sin of Adam. (For the main article on this topic *see* REDEMPTION [THEOLOGY OF].) Since the experiences of suffering and guilt are universal, the hope for salvation by some act of the deity is a prominent element in many religions.

The Judeo-Christian religion is gospel, good news, because it announces how God out of love and mercy saved mankind. After promising salvation (Gn 3.15), God prepared men for their SAVIOR by choosing the Hebrews as the people of God. Repeated political captivity whetted their longing for a savior. By rescuing His people, e.g., from Egypt under Moses, God, ever faithful to His promise, gave them the conviction that He alone saves [1 Sm 14.39; Ps 67(68).20; Jer 3.23] by raising up a human leader (Jgs 6.36; Dt 18.15–18). In the course of time elements were added to the concept of Savior: He would be a king of David's line [Mi 5.1; Ps 109(110).1], who would save a faithful remnant of the people (Is 10.20–22) through suffering (Is 52.13–53.12), yet be a mysterious SON OF MAN come from heaven with miraculous power (Dn 7.13; Is 35.4), the Wisdom of God descended to earth to recreate it (the Book of Proverbs; the book of Wisdom).

God the Son became man and saved mankind by His teaching and miracles, by the example of His life, by His death, Resurrection, and Ascension, and by establishing the Church and sending to it His Holy Spirit.

The core of the apostolic preaching was that Jesus alone saves (Acts 4.9–12; Lk 4.17–21). Men were lost, the Good Shepherd leads them (Jn 10.11); men were sick, the Good Samaritan heals them (Lk 10.34); He works miracles to show that the Healer of souls and bodies has come (Lk 7.18–23). Men were defiled, His blood washes them (Rv 7.14); men were sinners, i.e., guilty of crimes against God and sentenced to death; their Advocate nullifies the conviction by abolishing their guilt and bearing their debt of punishment (1 Jn 2.1; 3.5; Col 2.14; Mt 8.17; Acts 5.31; 1 Pt 2.22–25). Men were confused by the darkness of error, He is the light of the world (Jn 8.12). Men were enslaved by the dread of death, by their passions, by the corrupt powers of this world and of Satan; Jesus is the victorious liberator, the second Moses, who by His death and Resurrection conquers death, the world, and Satan, thus freeing mankind (Acts 26.18; Romans ch. 5–8; 1 Jn 3.8; Col 1.13). Christ restores men in essentials to their original state. From the state of being enemies, men are reconciled to God by the one Mediator (*Enchiridion symbolorum* 1513: 1 Tm 2.5; Rom 5.10); from spiritual death and disinheritance men are reborn as children of God and heirs of heaven (Rom 8.17); from captivity men are redeemed, purchased by His blood, and by a new title become the people of God (Ti 2.14; 1 Pt 1.18; 1 Cor 6.20); from exile and dispersion men are reunited to God in Christ (Jn 17.20–23); out of spiritual chaos, men are recreated in the IMAGE OF GOD by the creative Word of God (Col 3.10; Gal 6.15; Rv 21.5).

See Also: BEATIFIC VISION; DESIRE TO SEE GOD, NATURAL; DESTINY, SUPERNATURAL; ELEVATION OF MAN; HAPPINESS; HOPE OF SALVATION (IN THE BIBLE); INCORPORATION IN CHRIST; JUSTIFICATION; REBIRTH (IN THE BIBLE); REDEMPTION; SALUTARY ACTS; SALVATION, NECESSITY OF THE CHURCH FOR; SUPERNATURAL.

Bibliography: T. G. PINCHES et al., J. HASTINGS, ed., *Encyclopedia of Religion & Ethics,* 13 v. (Edinburgh 1908–27) 11:109–151. *Encyclopedic Dictionary of the Bible,* tr. and adap. by L. HARTMAN (New York 1963) 2101–07. X. LÉON-DUFOUR, ed., *Vocabulaire de théologie biblique* (Paris 1962) 988–994. M. É. BOISMARD, *St. John's Prologue,* tr. Carisbrooke Dominicans (Westminster, MD 1957). L. CERFAUX, *Christ in the Theology of St. Paul,* tr. G. WEBB and A. WALKER (New York 1959). J. DANIÉLOU, *Christ and Us,* tr. W. ROBERTS (New York 1961). F. X. DURRWELL, *The Resurrection: A Biblical Study,* tr. R. SHEED (New York 1960). A. GÉLIN et al., *Son and Saviour,* tr. A. WHEATON (rev. ed. Baltimore 1962). S. LYONNET, *De peccato et redemptione* (Rome 1957—), 4 v. planned. D. M. STANLEY, *Christ's Resurrection in Pauline Soteriology* (*Analecta Biblica* 13; Rome 1961); ''The Conception of Salvation in Primitive Christian Preaching,'' *The Catholic Biblical Quarterly* 18 231–254; ''The Conception of Salvation in the Synoptic Gospels,'' *ibid.* 345–363. A. STOCK, *Lamb of God* (New York 1963).

[W. G. TOPMOELLER]

SALVATION, NECESSITY OF THE CHURCH FOR

Christianity is essentially a soteriology. The gospel is a message of SALVATION. The KINGDOM OF GOD is destined to assume the dimensions of the entire world: all men are called to supernatural destiny (*see* DESTINY, SUPERNATURAL). But to enter the kingdom certain conditions are laid down. God's call to the kingdom does not reach man through reason alone, but through definite manifestations of God in history, through a positive historical body vested with divine authority. Man must come into contact with this divine economy in order to be saved. And this contact is established through supernatural faith, without which ''it is impossible to please God'' (Heb 11.6), and through the Catholic Church, which is the MYSTICAL BODY OF CHRIST, outside of which there is no salvation [*See* CHURCH, II (THEOLOGY OF)].

This article considers the historical development of the doctrine; its proofs; and the ways of belonging to the Church.

Historical Development. The Fathers of the first four centuries were impressed by the fact that the light of the gospel had shone on the world relatively late. How could the many millions of pagans who lived before Christ attain salvation? The explanation they offered was based on the Pauline text: ''For since the creation of the world his invisible attributes are clearly seen . . . being understood through the things that are made'' (Rom 1.20). The chosen people, therefore, were not the only beneficiaries of God's divine plan of salvation. The same argument was used by the apologists in regard to the pagans who lived after Christ.

The controversies on grace in the 5th century forced theologians to look more closely into the doctrine of salvation. Against the Pelagians, AUGUSTINE defended the gratuitousness of faith and grace, which are dispensed by the Church, and the absolute necessity of both for salvation; against SEMI-PELAGIANISM, PROSPER OF AQUITAINE maintained that God truly wills the salvation of all men.

In the Middle Ages the doctrine on the necessity of the Church for salvation made further progress, until it reached a balanced synthesis. In the present dispensation the Sacrament of BAPTISM, by which a person becomes a member of the Church, is necessary for salvation; it was, however, already generally held at this time that Baptism of desire (*in voto*) could supply for the Sacrament (*in re*) in case of the impossibility of receiving the Sacrament or invincible ignorance. These sacramental concepts were later transferred to ecclesiology and applied with regard to ways of belonging to the Church. Like his contemporaries, St. THOMAS AQUINAS taught that at least the echo of the gospel had reached the farthest limits of the earth in his time, and if by any chance there should yet be any person still invincibly ignorant of the truths that are necessary for salvation, God would send him a missionary to teach him these truths (*De ver.* 14.11 ad 1).

With the discovery of America, the whole problem of salvation through the Church once more confronted theologians in its concrete reality. If outside the Christian faith there is no salvation, what had been the fate of the peoples living in the western hemisphere? The positions taken by the reformers and Catholic theologians in this regard were diametrically opposed. The attitude of the reformers was one of pessimism. LUTHER held that explicit faith in Christ was absolutely necessary for salvation, and that therefore all pagans who had been excluded from the benefit of the Church's preaching were the object of God's reprobation and predestined to hell. The Catholic position was more optimistic. Some theologians, for lack of a better solution, suggested that the doctrine on LIMBO might be applied to adults who had lived all their lives according to the precepts of natural law and died invincibly ignorant of the Church.

The official position in this regard, however, was elaborated in the Council of TRENT. Defining the doctrine on grace, the council insisted on its necessity and priority in the order of JUSTIFICATION and salvation; but it asserted that the infidel, under the influence of actual grace, can make a progressive preparation for faith and thus God will eventually lead him to justification and salvation. A question, however, still remained to be answered: how can an infidel, even with the help of grace, make an act of faith if he is ignorant of revelation and has not been reached by the preaching of the Church? Here SUÁREZ's opinion became generally accepted, stating that implicit faith (*fides in voto*) in Christ and the Trinity would suffice wherever the gospel has not yet been divulged.

After VATICAN COUNCIL I, which dealt with some important aspects of the Church, theologians preferred to consider the problem of salvation from an ecclesiological standpoint. If those who are not members of the Church can be saved, what is their relationship to the Church outside of which there is no salvation? Much light was thrown on this problem by the encyclical *MYSTICI CORPORIS* of PIUS XII, which appeared in 1943. While Vatican Council I had emphasized the juridical aspect of the Church, the encyclical stressed the spiritual aspect and explained the doctrine of the Church as the Mystical Body of Christ, which, while being visible by nature, exerts an invisible influence that reaches the souls of all men of good will. The same concept was taken up again and developed in VATICAN COUNCIL II, as can be seen from its *Dogmatic Constitution on the Church.*

Proofs. Scripture, tradition, and the teaching authority of the Church offer a solid basis and proof of the doctrine.

Scripture. The main object of the gospel's message was the Redemption performed by Jesus Christ, to whose will and teaching all men must adhere in order to be saved. Christ instituted the Church on earth and entrusted it to His Apostles; furthermore, He communicated to it His own mission and endowed it with His own authority to carry on His message of salvation and to apply the fruits of His Redemption: "He who believes and is baptized shall be saved, but he who does not believe shall be condemned" (Mk 16.16). The Apostles were sent by Him to the ends of the earth as His own representatives; what is more, He identified Himself with them: "He who hears you, hears me; and he who rejects you, rejects me" (Lk 10.16). He also identified Himself with the Church, which is the kingdom set up by Him to continue His presence on earth; just as there can be no salvation without Christ, so there can be no salvation without the Church.

In the Epistles of St. Paul, the Church appears as the Mystical Body of Christ (Eph 1.22; 4.4; 5.23; 1 Cor 12.27): whoever is separated from this living Body cannot have divine life in him. According to St. Paul, the Church is also the Spouse of Christ (2 Cor 11.2; Eph 5.26): for her sanctification and salvation Christ laid down His life, and he who is excluded from her is also excluded from Christ.

Tradition. The necessity of the Church for salvation is illustrated in the Fathers by means of Biblical figures, such as that of the ark in the deluge. IRENAEUS declares that wherever there is the Church, there is the Holy Spirit; and wherever there is the Holy Spirit, there is also the Church and all grace (*Enchiridion patristicum*, ed. M. J. Rouët Dejournel [21st ed. Freiburgim Breisgau 1960] 226). ORIGEN is the first to formulate the dogmatic axiom *EXTRA ECCLESIAM NULLA SALUS* (*ibid.* 537); and CYPRIAN writes that one cannot have God as one's Father unless one also has the Church as one's mother (*ibid.* 557). The same notions were repeated by the Latin Fathers, especially by JEROME and Augustine.

The Magisterium. The necessity of the Church for salvation is explicitly defined by the Church as a revealed truth. It is contained in the pseudo-Athanasian Symbol (H. Denzinger, *Enchiridion symbolorum,* 75–76) and has remained one of the most basic points of her teaching throughout the centuries. Thus, Boniface VIII asserts in his bull *Unam sanctam* that outside the Church of Christ there can be neither salvation nor remission of sins (*Enchiridion symbolorum* 870–875); and Pius IX, in his allocution *Singulari quadam,* clearly states that this doctrine must be held as a matter of faith (*Enchiridion symbolorum* 2865, introd.). In the encyclical *Mystici Corporis* of Pius XII, the Catholic Church is identified with the Mystical Body of Christ. The already defined doctrine of the necessity of the Church for salvation is declared again in the *Dogmatic Constitution on the Church* of Vatican Council II [*Lumen gentium* 14; *Acta Apostolicae Sedis* 57 (1965) 18–19]; in this important document the Church is again identified here on earth with the Mystical Body of Christ (8; *ibid.* 11–12) and described as the people of God, i.e., the gathering of those who acknowledge God in truth and serve Him in holiness of life (9; *ibid.* 12–14). The *Catechism of the Catholic Church* emphasizes the positive formulation of this doctrine: "all salvation comes from Christ the Head through the Church which is his Body" (*CCC* 846), including those means, known only to God, by which he leads those who are ignorant of the gospel to faith.

Ways of Belonging to the Church. If the Catholic Church is necessary for salvation, it follows that no one can be saved unless one belongs to the Church in some way or other. One can therefore distinguish the following categories:

1. Potential members of the Church are all human beings, since all are destined to a supernatural end and since God wants all men to be saved (1 Tm 2.4).

2. Actual members of the Church are those who are recognized as such by the Church herself, namely, all Catholics. These are fully members of the Church, because they are formally incorporated into her and in them are verified all the conditions laid down by the Church as a juridical society, namely, sacramental Baptism, profession of the true faith, and obedience to the legitimate authority (cf. Pius XII *MysCorp*). These formal members can be perfect or imperfect, depending on whether or not they are in the state of sanctifying grace.

3. Radically joined to the Church are all validly baptized non-Catholics. Although these lack formal recognition by the Church, still they have baptismal character which gives them a proximate intrinsic exigency for incorporation into the Church (cf. 1917 *Codex iuris canonici* c. 87); if, besides, they have faith and sanctifying grace and are in good faith, they really belong to her without knowing it.

4. Belonging to the Church by intention and desire are all non-Christians in the state of grace. Those who, without fault of their own, have never heard of Christ as their only Savior and who at the same time, helped by grace, follow the dictates of their conscience, can be saved. And if they are actually saved, it is through the Church that they are saved, for there is no salvation except by her mediation. These are not members of the Church, but belong to her and are sufficiently joined to her to receive divine life and salvation through her. Their link with the visible Church is invisible, and hence they are sometimes called invisible or spiritual members; this terminology, however, is not to be adopted, for they are nowhere called members in Church documents. Their implicit desire or intention, which is called *votum* by theologians, must of course be accompanied by supernatural faith and informed by perfect charity. [Concerning the above categories see *Lumen gentium* 13–16; *Acta Apostolicae Sedis* 57 (1965) 17–20.]

According to some theologians, especially before *Mystici Corporis,* justified non-Christians as well as baptized non-Catholics living in the state of grace can be said to belong to the SOUL OF THE CHURCH, rather than to her body, because they actually receive the life of grace from the Holy Spirit, who is the Soul of the Church. This explanation, however, is theologically inaccurate and misleading. It is inaccurate because the Church, being the Mystical Body of Christ, is one living organism; it is the whole Church, Body and Soul, that is necessary for salvation; and if one is related at all to the Church, this relation must be not only to the Soul but also to the Body animated by the Soul. It is misleading because it suggests a split in the reality of the Church into a spiritual organization and a social institution, into an invisible Church and a visible one. Both *Mystici Corporis* and *Humani generis* emphatically declare that the Mystical Body here on earth is not only identified with but is coextensive with the Roman Catholic Church, and both encyclicals warn theologians against the danger of admitting a double economy of salvation.

See Also: INFIDEL; NECESSITY OF MEANS; NECESSITY OF PRECEPT; VOTUM; SOCIETY (THEOLOGY OF); FAITHFUL.

Bibliography: K. RAHNER, *Theological Investigations,* v.2, tr. K. H. KRUGER (Baltimore 1964) 1–88. J. C. FENTON, *The Catholic Church and Salvation* (Westminster, Md. 1958). M. EMINYAN, *The Theology of Salvation* (Boston 1960). L. CAFÉRAN, *Le Problème du salut des infidèles* (Toulouse 1934). J. BEUMER, *Lexikon für Theologie und Kirche,* ed. J. HOFER and K. RAHNER (Freiburg 1957–65) 1:343–345; *ibid.* 3:1320–21. *Dictionnaire de théologie catholique,* ed. A. VACANT et al. (Paris 1903–50; Tables générales 1951–) Tables générales 1:1118–21. F. MCSHANE, ''America, Theological Significance of,'' *A Catholic Dictionary of Theology,* ed. H. F. DAVIS et al. (London 1962) 1:69–70.

[M. EMINYAN/EDS.]

SALVATION ARMY

A non-denominational religious organization founded in London, England (1865), by William BOOTH (1829–1912). It was known as The Christian Mission until 1878, when the name was changed to Salvation Army. Booth underwent a profound religious experience at the age of 15; he became a regular preacher in the Methodist Church, but separated from it (1861) in order to work among the poor of the London slums. Although personally satisfied with the existing churches, he was forced to establish his own when his poor found themselves unwelcome in the class-conscious congregations. Convinced that the masses of poor needed a unique form of evangelism, he founded his church on the pattern of the British Army, with uniforms, brass bands, titles, marching orders, furloughs, and knee drills. At first scorned, the Army soon won the admiration of the English people and later the esteem of the world for its vast system of social services ranging from the rehabilitation of alcoholics to the operation of maternity homes, welfare bureaus, employment centers, and stores selling a variety of used items.

In general the doctrines of the Salvation Army follow those of the Methodist Church. No great emphasis is placed upon theology, although the Bible is acknowledged as the source of God's revelation. Conversion consists of an inner experience that leads to trust in Jesus Christ, the divine Son of God. The sinfulness of the human race is stressed along with the need for complete confidence in Christ's vicarious atonement for sin. Emphasis is on the preaching of the gospel to all and the practice of Christian service to one's neighbor.

Churches are not used. The religious services, held in halls, are evangelical, with free prayer, hymn singing, testimony, preaching, and Bible reading.

International headquarters are in London, and commanders are in charge of clearly defined territories in almost every country throughout the world. Each territory is organized into divisions commanded by colonels or majors. These divisions are subdivided into corps (similar to parishes) under a captain or lieutenant. Converts are expected to become soldiers, but those not wishing to don the uniform and to devote their lives to the salvation of sinners are free to join other churches. Officers are recruited from the ranks of soldiers, and no distinction is made because of sex.

Two schisms occurred in the Salvation Army ranks at the close of the 19th century. The first (1882) resulted in the foundation of the American Rescue Workers, while the second brought into existence the Volunteers of America.

Bibliography: F. S. MEAD, S. S. HILL and C. D. ATWOOD, eds., *Handbook of Denominations in the United States*, 11th ed (Nashville 2001).

[E. DELANEY/EDS.]

SALVATION HISTORY (HEILSGESCHICHTE)

The view of history as found in the Bible is called salvation history because the events that are recounted in the Bible are regarded in it as God's acts for the salvation of the world. Since the fact that history in the eyes of the inspired writers of the Scriptures is basically religious history was primarily recognized by German Biblical scholars, the German term for salvation history, *Heilsgeschichte,* was adopted and became the technical term even among English-speaking scholars. After considering the strictly Biblical aspects of salvation history, this article will discuss its import from a viewpoint both of dogmatic and of moral theology.

IN THE BIBLE

The ancient Israelites were interested in history, not so much for the sake of the events themselves that took

Salvation Army meeting, 1930. (©Hulton-Deutsch Collection/ CORBIS)

place as for their why and wherefore. Their thinking, however, was entirely colored by their religion, so that for them there was no merely profane history; for them all history was religious history. They therefore saw the hand of God in the historical events that affected Israel throughout the OT period, and they thus prepared the way for the full revelation of man's salvation as wrought by God in the NT period.

In the Old Testament. The notion of salvation history is rooted in the experience of the Mosaic period. Israel remembered the Exodus as Yahweh's great saving act (Ex 15.1–18; Dt 5.15; Jos 24.17; Am 9.7; Os 13.4; Mi 6.4; and many Psalms). If Yahweh led His people out of Egypt, it was to make His COVENANT with them (Ex 19.1–6) and to bring them to the land promised to the Patriarchs (Dt 4.1). As Israel contemplated these events, it recalled its ancient traditions and realized that even its prehistory unfolded under Yahweh's guiding hand. Yahweh had called Abraham, Isaac, and Jacob, made a covenant with them and promised them land and posterity (Gn 12–50). Creation and man's earliest experiences of guilt and GRACE were the prelude to Yahweh's call of Abraham (Gn 1–11).

The DEUTERONOMISTS and the Biblical CHRONICLER tell how God permitted the establishment of a monarchy and made a covenant with the Davidic dynasty (2 Sm 7; 1 Chr 17). When the kings failed Him, God punished His people with exile and loss of national independence. He restored them when they were purified.

The Prophets upheld belief in the divine guidance of history. But more important is their eschatology [*see* ES-CHATOLOGY (IN THE BIBLE)]. They look beyond earthly history to the climax of salvation history: the old covenant will be fulfilled in a new eternal covenant (Jer 31.31–34; Ez 37.26–28); David's kingdom will be reestablished by the MESSIAH (Is 9.5–6; 11.1–5; Am 9.11–15; Hos 3.5; *see* MESSIANISM); the Mosaic period of salvation will be renewed (Hos 2.16–17; Is 11.11–16; 52.11–12; Jer 31.2–6; Ez 20.33–38); paradise will return (Hos 2.20; Am 9.13; Jl 4.18; Is 11.6–9; Ez 34.25–29). But only a remnant will be saved (Is 6.13; Jer 23.3). Salvation will come by way of vicarious suffering (Is 52.13–53.12; *see* SUFFERING SERVANT, SONG OF).

Beginning with the prophetic books and continuing through Daniel and apocryphal writings, apocalyptic literature develops the eschatological viewpoint and introduces new elements. The tendency to divide history into fixed periods (Dn 2.37–45; 7.1–14), to present a detailed picture of the end of the present evil AEON (Ez 38–39; Dn 12.1), and to calculate the end of the world (Dn 9.24–27; 12.7) are typical. Belief in resurrection (*see* RESURRECTION OF THE DEAD, 1) gives a strong impulse to the hope of salvation [Dn 12.2–3; *see* HOPE OF SALVATION (IN THE BIBLE)].

In the New Testament. Jesus sees His work as the fulfillment of the prophecies (Mt 11.4–15) and of the whole hope of salvation (Mt 13.16–17). He places Himself at the end of OT salvation history (Mt 23.37–38) and announces that the eschatological KINGDOM OF GOD is near (Mk 1.15), and is in fact present in His activity (Mt 12.28). Still, salvation history awaits its final completion in the PAROUSIA, resurrection, and judgment. Meanwhile Jesus summons men to repentance and total commitment.

This is precisely the way the early Church understood its Lord: for it, too, salvation has already come in Jesus (Heb 1.2; Jn 5.25), yet remains in the future (Acts 3.21); the present evil aeon still exists, but is, to the extent that Christ rules, compenetrated by the coming aeon (Gal 1.4; 1 Cor 7.26–31).

A basic conception of the originally single work of Luke and Acts seems to be that Jesus' earthly activity stands between the time of Israel and the time of the Church. Luke foresees a period of time for spreading the gospel (Lk 24.47; Acts 1.8) and a later Parousia (Lk 21.24; Acts 1.11). He clearly delineates epochs of salvation history (Lk 16.16; Acts 10.36–43). His concept,

however, is essentially that of the early Church and other Synoptics.

For St. Paul, to be "in Christ" is eschatological existence (Gal 2.20; 6.15; 2 Cor 5.17) in the "now" of the hour of salvation (2 Cor 6.2; Rom 3.21; Eph 2.13), obliging to an eschatological "unworldly" conduct in this passing world (1 Thes 5.4–10; 1 Cor 7.29–35; Rom 12.2; Col 3.5–11) in order to attain the eschatological goal (Rom 6.22; 1 Cor 1.8; Phil 3.12–14). From the viewpoint of Christianity, all previous history was a time without salvation, but now Christ, as the new Adam, has redeemed humanity (Rom 5.12–21; 8.29; 1 Cor 15.22, 45–49). Nevertheless, Abraham shows to advantage as the prototype and spiritual father of believers (Rom 4), the one who received the promises fulfilled in Christ (Gal 3). Moses is mediator of the Law, which brings an increase of transgressions (Gal 3.19) and greater recognition of sin (Rom 3.21), though even in this the divine plan of salvation is forwarded (Rom 5.20–21; Gal 3.22, 24). In the new era of salvation, the unbelief of most of Israel does not nullify God's fidelity; rather, God's fidelity inspires hope for the future conversion of all Israel (Rom 9–11). God has called all, Jews and Gentiles, to be united in Christ (Eph 2.11–22).

In the Gospel of St. John the earthly life of Jesus is the time of eschatological revelation and salvation (6.47; 8.51), but history will reach its goal only in the resurrection and final judgment (6.39–40, 44).

The book of Revelations teaches that even in the messianic era there will be fearful tribulations, but finally there will come the cosmic revelation of eschatological salvation, the destruction of the forces of evil (Rv 19–20) and the establishment of God's rule in a new world (Rv 21).

Bibliography: R. SCHNACKENBURG, *Lexikon für Theologie und Kirche,* ed. J. HOFER and K. RAHNER (Freiburg 1957–65) 5:148–153; *God's Rule and Kingdom,* tr. J. MURRAY (New York 1963). G. E. WRIGHT and R. H. FULLER, *The Book of the Acts of God* (Garden City, N.Y. 1957). E. BEAUCAMP, *The Bible and the Universe,* tr. D. BALHATCHET (Westminster, Md. 1963). C. H. DODD, *History and the Gospel* (London 1938).

[H. KISTNER]

IN DOGMATIC THEOLOGY

The term salvation history became established in theology chiefly through the influence of J. C. von Hofmann, a German Protestant Biblical theologian of the 19th century. Salvation history designates both a principle of scriptural interpretation and a theological affirmation.

As a principle of interpretation, salvation history asserts the fact that God has made a progressive revelation of Himself and His will in Scripture. The interpreter, therefore, must expect an organic growth in the deposit of Biblical faith. The principle expresses the axiom of St. Augustine, "Distinguish the times and you will harmonize Scripture."

As a theological affirmation, salvation history proposes two interrelated theological conceptions. Since language is the sign of understanding, the two nouns in the term signify a unity in conception of two realities: SALVATION and history. Salvation is the divine act, revealed and accomplished by God, which delivers man from evil and reunites him in grace with God. When the purpose only of deliverance from evil is considered explicitly in the divine act, the noun REDEMPTION, or the adjective redemptive is adjoined to make "Redemption history" or "redemptive history." History refers both to the actual course of human events and to the interpretative memory and record of what happened in the past. Salvation history, as a theological conception, affirms that salvation is historic and that history is salvific.

The historicity of salvation includes three assertions. (1) The salvific act of God is directed toward the course of human events so that salvation begins in time through the actual happenings wrought by God in mankind. (2) God's salvific act begun in time is brought to completion within the historic processes of human activity. (3) The saving act of God, as performed in time, has past, present, and future realizations.

Wrought by God. God's saving activity is retained within the context of the act of creation, which brings man and his history into existence. God made man right and his world good. Man, by the abuse of his freedom, introduced evil into his person, into his world, and consequently into his history. The fundamental revelation of Scripture is God's purpose to save man from this evil.

Within the context of the universal creative act, God's saving activity appears as a new creation, as a creation-saving. Just as from the first creational act there issued the very course of human events, so in the salvific act there issue real events. God interrupts the course of evil in mankind and intervenes to restore what man lost through sin.

Salvation is historic both because the salvific act is directed to the restoration of the historic condition of mankind and because this saving activity is productive of such events in time and place as will issue in the deliverance from evil and reunion with God.

In Human Activity. These saving events done at given times, in particular places, and in the lives of various persons pass to other times, places, and persons by means of the historic processes of human activity. These processes are fourfold. There is the process of continuity as the past becomes the matrix of the present. There is the process of causality as the past becomes the condition of possibility for the present. There is the process of immanence as the past becomes a determinant of the present. There is the process of transcendence as the present makes its unique contributions to what is given from the past. God's work, once done in mankind, both initiates these processes and is assumed into these processes and thereby becomes extended in time, expanded in place, and multiplied in the lives of persons.

Realizations. The salvific work, however, is not done only once. God's interventions are repeated, each deposited in the course of human affairs and taken up into the historic processes. Each creative-saving "Word" of God is sent to the world and produces its effects. The New Testament marks the "fullness of time" when God intervenes decisively and definitely by sending the Word made flesh to dwell among men (Jn 1.1–18).

For the New Testament writers, God's sending His Son is the Present, the Now. God's previous interventions are the Past. The Future is the fulfillment through the processes of human history of that saving event begun in and through Christ.

Theology also affirms that history is salvific. This means that the events wrought by God and the processes initiated by these events issue in a deliverance from evil and a reunion in grace. But this also means that the very memory and the record of these events are salvific.

The memory and the record (concretely, the Scriptures and the teaching of the Church) are salvific because the faithful, hearing in faith the recital of the remembered past experiences of God's saving acts, are led to understand in Christ the God who saves and their need of His salvation; and, inspired by the Spirit, they respond by accepting the salvation God offers (*see* BIBLICAL THEOLOGY; KERYGMA; KERYGMATIC THEOLOGY; SOTERIOLOGY).

Bibliography: A. DARLAPP, *Lexikon für Theologie und Kirche,* ed. J. HOFER and K. RAHNER (Freiburg 1957–65) 5:153–156. H. OTT, *Die Religion in Geschichte und Gegenwart* (3d ed. Tübingen 1957–65) 3:187–189. P. BLÄSER and A. DARLAPP, *Handbuch theologischer Grundbegriffe,* ed. H. FRIES (Munich 1962–63) 1:662–680. J. BAILLIE, *The Idea of Revelation in Recent Thought* (New York 1956). O. CULLMANN, *Christ and Time,* tr. F. V. FILSON (rev. ed. Philadelphia 1964). R. LATOURELLE, *Théologie de la révélation* (Bruges 1963). J. MOUROUX, *The Mystery of Time,* tr. J. DRURY (New York 1964). E. H. SCHILLEBEECKX, *Christ: The Sacrament of the Encounter with God,* tr. P. BARRETT (New York 1963). G. E. WRIGHT, *God Who Acts* (Studies in Biblical Theology 8; Chicago 1952).

[E. L. PETERMAN]

IN CATECHESIS

There is no substitute for the forthright proclamation that in Christianity God's plan for the universe's perfection has been revealed and is being worked out. If all man's history from his food-gathering stage to the nuclear space age has full meaning only in Christ, His cross and exaltation, as Christians believe, then this must be proclaimed as the most important truth known to man. Peace and war, poverty and overpopulation, life and death, and anything else have only *ad hoc* meanings apart from the truth that the whole creation is groaning for "the glory to come that will be revealed" in the complete freedom that is enjoyed by God's sons through Christ (Rom 8.18–22).

Though the doctrine bears with it its own urgency, only witnesses who are utterly convinced of its value as the ultimate historico-human reality can transmit it properly. Mere humans are incapable of such witnessing; but the missionary or catechist is no mere human. He transmits Christ's message through the authority and enlightenment of the Holy Spirit, whom Jesus sent to continue His teaching mission (Jn 14.15–17, 26;15.26–27; 16.7–14). He must then be familiar with salvation history as it has been divinely recorded in the Bible, and yet he must not neglect that the Church in its own history, its theological growth, and its liturgical and sacramental life has continued and is now continuing to apply to mankind the fruits of God's salvation in Christ (*see* WITNESS, CHRISTIAN).

Salvation is of the past; yet by its perdurance in the Body of Christ, the Church, it makes all the past vitally relevant to mankind at the present moment.

Bibliography: J. A. JUNGMANN, *The Good News Yesterday and Today,* tr. W. A. HUESMAN (New York 1962). M. C. BOYS, *Biblical Interpretation in Religious Education: A Study of the Kerygmatic Era* (Birmingham, AL 1980).

[J. E. FALLON]

SALVATOR OF HORTA, ST.

Franciscan lay brother; b. Santa Coloma de Farnés, Catalonia, Spain, 1520; d. Cagliari, Sardinia, Italy, March 18, 1567. At the age of 21, Salvatore, of humble origin, became a lay brother in the Franciscan convent near Barcelona. Besides personal sanctity, his religious life was marked by a gift of working miracles, a power exercised especially for the sick and infirm. Because of the crowds that besieged the convents where he was assigned, his residence was repeatedly changed by the superiors on the plea that religious tranquility was being disturbed. Twice, on account of his wonder-working, he was denounced to the Inquisition. Salvatore acquired the appendage to his name from the remote convent of Horta, where he remained the longest and whence his fame spread throughout Spain. He was finally transferred in 1565 to Cagliari, where he died two years later. His widespread cult received official approbation by CLEMENT XI, Jan. 29, 1711; he was canonized by PIUS XI, April 17, 1938.

Feast: March 18.

Bibliography: *Acta Canonizationum quibus . . . Pius papa xi . . . BB. Andreae Boboli M., Ioanni Leonardi C. atque Salvatori ab Horta C. sanctorum caelitum honores decrevit . . . collecta,* ed. A. CARINCI (Iles de Lérins 1941). J. FOQUET, *El taumaturgo catalán beato Salvador de Horta* (Vich, Spain 1927). F. GAMISSANS, *Salvador d'Horta* (Barcelona 1967). E. ZARAGOZA PASCUAL, *Vida de San Salvador de Horta* (Barcelona 1967). A. BUTLER, *The Lives of the Saints,* rev. ed. H. THURSTON and D. ATTWATER, 4v. (New York 1956) 1:630.

[J. B. WUEST]

SALVATORIANS

The Society of the Divine Savior (SDS, Official Catholic Directory #1200) was founded in Rome, Italy, on Dec. 8, 1881, by Father Franziskus Maria of the Cross JORDAN. Its members, popularly known as Salvatorians, are priests and coadjutor brothers who, in addition to the vows of poverty, chastity, and obedience, are bound by the "promise of the apostolate," which is made at the time of profession and constitutes a fourth vow. The zeal for souls that this promise symbolizes prompted the founder to place the society under the special protection of the Blessed Virgin Mary and the Apostles. The specific purpose of the society is the preservation and spread of the faith through the sacred ministry, the education of youth, retreats, and missionary work among non-Catholics.

Father Jordan originally intended to form a congregation of priests and laity who, while working in the world, would be united by vows and a common purpose. It was first entitled the Apostolic Teaching Society and it received enthusiastic support among some of the hierarchy and the blessing of Leo XIII. Thus encouraged, Jordan pursued his goal vigorously, finding strong support in his first follower, Father Bonaventure Luethen, a noted author.

Jordan's plan, however, proved to be too radical for his times; thus his group finally settled into a more conventional pattern. After overcoming further difficulties, the society was recognized as a religious congregation in 1883 and received its present name in 1894. The first papal approval was granted in 1905 and final approbation in 1911. Jordan remained superior general until 1915. Before his death in 1917, he was instrumental in founding two congregations of women, the Sisters of the Sorrowful Mother and the Sisters of the DIVINE SAVIOR (1888).

In 1889, with only six priests and 17 brothers, Jordan applied to the Holy See for a foreign mission. Soon after, two fathers and two brothers established the society's first mission in the newly erected Prefecture Apostolic of Assam, India. Unfortunately, World War I reduced the effectiveness of this mission and the Salvatorians were later sent to China. After China fell to the Communists, the missionaries began work in Taiwan. In 1955 the society established foundations in Africa. As membership increased, the society spread to other areas of the world. The society's work generally centered in parishes, seminaries, and schools.

In the U.S. the Salvatorians were introduced in 1896 at St. Nazianz, Wis., by Jordan himself. This mission was regarded as the original U.S. foundation, since a previous mission in Oregon had been short-lived. The Fathers assumed the spiritual care of the Oschwald Association and later opened a seminary and a publishing department that has since become the Salvatorian center for publications, promotion, and public relations. The principal work of the society in the U.S. is the education of youth. Salvatorians in the U.S. also staff parishes and conduct retreats. The provincial residence is in Milwaukee, Wis. The generalate is in Rome.

Bibliography: P. PFEIFFER, *Father Francis Mary of the Cross Jordan,* tr. W. HERBST (St. Nazianz, Wis. 1936).

[R. MOLLEN/EDS.]

SALVE MUNDI SALUTARE

A hymn of seven cantos, each dedicated to one of the suffering members of Christ's crucified body. Each canto has five stanzas of ten lines, all in trochaic dimeter except the fifth and tenth lines, which are iambic dimeter. The rhyme scheme is *aaaabccddb.* The authorship, still uncertain, is attributed to BERNARD OF CLAIRVAUX (d. 1153). Daniel ascribes to Bernard the first two cantos, *Ad pedes* and *Ad genua,* but holds that the others were written by different authors at later times when devotion to the Passion was becoming stronger. Since the manuscripts present such a varied arrangement of titles and stanzas, Julian considers it difficult to determine which parts, if any, were actually written by Bernard. The last and most beautiful canto, *Salve caput cruentatum,* has frequently been attributed to Arnulf of Louvain, Abbot of Villers (d. 1250).

Bibliography: H. A. DANIEL, *Thesaurus hymnologicus,* 5 v. (Halle-Leipzig 1841–56) v.1, 2, 4. R. C. TRENCH, *Sacred Latin Poetry* (3d ed. London 1886) 138–143. F. A. MARCH, ed., *Latin Hymns* (New York 1874; repr. 1898) 114–119, 277. J. JULIAN, ed., *A Dictionary of Hymnology* (New York 1957) 989–991. A. SCHWERD, *Hymnen und Sequenzen* (Munich 1954) 67–69, 111–112. U. CHEVALIER, *Repertorium hymnologicum* (Louvain-Brussels1892–1921) 2:515.

[G. E. CONWAY]

SALVE REGINA

The MARIAN antiphon that was traditionally sung at Compline beginning from Trinity Sunday through Friday before the first Sunday of Advent. The text of the antiphon (the familiar prayer "Hail, Holy Queen") has been attributed to several writers, such as St. BERNARD OF CLAIRVAUX, Adhemar of Puy, Bishop Peter of Compostela (*c.* 952–1002), and Hermanus Contractus of Reichenau. Stylistic features of the text, and the fact that it was troped as early as the late 11th century, point to Hermanus as probable author.

Liturgical History. One of the earliest liturgical uses of the *Salve Regina* was as processional chant at Cluny, *c.* 1135, but it may have been in use elsewhere in the preceding century, since it seems to have inspired a *Benedicamus Domino* trope in the 11th-century Karlsruhe MS Aug. LV. That it was used also in the 12th century as the Magnificat antiphon for the feast of the Annunciation is clear from its insertion at that time into earlier MSS, such as St. Gall 390. The Cistercian Order sang it as a daily processional chant from 1218 and after daily Compline from 1251. The Dominicans had the same practice from 1230, including it also as a prayer for the dying; the Franciscans added it to daily Compline no later than 1249; and in the Carmelite rite at one time it replaced the Last Gospel of the Mass. Pope Gregory IX (1227–41) ordered its chanting after Compline on all Fridays, and from the 14th century on it was generally sung after Compline in all Latin rites until the Breviary of Pius V (1568) extended its use to the other hours. From 1884 to 1964 it was one of the prayers prescribed by Leo XIII for recitation after every public and private recited Mass of the Roman rite.

Musical Settings. Current liturgical chant books give two different monophonic settings. The first, in mode I, assigned to more solemn feasts, is essentially the melody originally associated with the text and was probably composed by the author of the text. (For three late medieval versions of this melody, see Wagner.) The simpler melody, in mode V, was probably composed by Henri du Mont (d. 1684). A large number of polyphonic versions were composed during the Renaissance and baroque periods. These were usually intended, not for the

Office, but for the various paraliturgical services held daily or weekly in Marian chapels or at the Marian altar found in all principal churches. The *Salve Regina* was also the source for several German lieder of the 16th century, and one of them, *Bist grüsst maget reine,* a translation of Heinrich von Laufenberg (*c.* 1390–1460) set to a new melody, found its way into almost all German Catholic songbooks of the 16th and 17th centuries.

Bibliography: J. MAIER, *Studien zur Geschichte der Marienantiphon ''Salve Regina''* (Regensburg 1939). K. S. MEISTER and W. BÄUMKER, *Das katholische deutsche Kirchenlied,* 2 v. (Freiburg 1958) v.2. J. M. CANAL, *Salve Regina misericordiae* (Rome 1963). P. WAGNER, ''Das Salve Regina,'' *Gregorianische Rundschau* 2 (1903) 87–90. H. LECLERCQ, *Dictionnaire d'archéologie chrétienne et de liturgie,* ed. F. CABROL, H. LECLERCQ, and H. I. MARROU (Paris 1907–53) 15.1:714–724. W. IRTENKAUF, *Lexikon für Theologie und Kirche,* ed. J. HOFER and K. RAHNER (Freiburg 1957–65) 9:281–282. F. L. HARRISON, *Music in Medieval Britain* (New York 1958). G. REESE, *Music in the Middle Ages* (New York 1940); *Music in the Renaissance* (New York 1959). W. APEL, *Gregorian Chant* (Bloomington IN 1958).

[R. J. SNOW]

SALVETE CHRISTI VULNERA

The office hymn that was historically sung at Lauds on the former feast of the PRECIOUS BLOOD. It is composed of nine stanzas in iambic dimeter. The hymn is of unknown authorship, and dates probably from the 17th century.

Bibliography: U. CHEVALIER, *Repertorium hymnologicum* (Louvain-Brussels 1892–1921) 2:530. J. JULIAN, ed., *A Dictionary of Hymnology* (New York 1957) 992. M. BRITT, *The Hymns of the Breviary and Missal* (new ed. New York 1948) 256–258. J. CONNELLY, *Hymns of the Roman Liturgy* (Westminster MD 1957) 206–209.

[G. E. CONWAY]

SALVI, LORENZO MARIA, BL.

Known in religion as Lorenzo Maria of Saint Francis Xavier, Passionist priest; b. Oct. 30, 1782, Rome, Italy; d. June 12, 1856, Capranica (near Viterbo), Italy. The son of Antonio Salvi, steward to the counts of Carpegna, and Marianna Biondi, Lorenzo was raised in the faith. Salvi studied at the Jesuit Pontifical Gregorian University. After professing his vows as a Passionist (1802) and being ordained (1805), he participated in the governance of communities and the province. Salvi was a popular preacher and spiritual advisor and promoted devotion to the Infant Jesus by word and example. Dominic BARBIERI, who had lived with Salvi, sought the superior general's permission to send Salvi to England because of the strength of his preaching and his leadership ability within the Passionist community. Permission was denied. Following his death Salvi was enshrined at Sant'Angelo di Vetralla. Pope John Paul II beatified Salvi on Oct. 1, 1989.

Feast: June 12.

Bibliography: A. LIPPI, *Il beato Lorenzo Salvi: apostolo di Gesù bambino,* 2d ed., (Torino 1989). *Acta Apostolicae Sedis* (1989): 1030.

[K. I. RABENSTEIN]

SALVIAN OF MARSEILLES

Ecclesiastical writer; b. *c.* A.D. 400; d. after 480. Salvian, probably a native of the Trier-Cologne area (*De Gubernatione Dei* 6.13.72; *Epistolarum lib.* 1.5), married Palladia, whom he converted to Christianity. They had a daughter Auspiciola, and later entered a pact of continence when the family lived at a distance from Palladia's birthplace (*Epistolarum lib.* 4), apparently in Southern Gaul (*De Gubernatione Dei* 7.2.8). It seems that Salvian embraced monasticism at Lérins, where he served as a priest prior to 431 (Hilary of Arles, *Sermo* 19) and later, as a tutor (*Epistolarum lib.* 9). Gennadius writing *c.* 480 describes Salvian as a priest of Marseilles, an instructor of bishops, and gives as a list of his writings: *De Virginitatis bono lib. III, Adversus Avaritiam lib. IV, De Praesenti judicio lib. V, Ad Salonium lib. I, Expositio libri Ecclesiastici, Epistolarum lib. I,* a verse *De Genesi lib. I,* Homilies for the use of bishops, and Sacramentaries or Missals (*De Viris inlust.* 68).

Nine Epistles are extant: (1) without title but seemingly addressed to the monks of Lérins; (2) and (8) to Bp. Eucherius of Lyons; (3) to Bp. Agrycius of Sens or Antibes; (4) to Hypatius and Quieta, parents of Palladia; (5) to Cattura; (6) to Limenius; (7) to Aper and Verus; and (9) to Bp. Salonius of Geneva. The homilies, in whole or in part, may possibly appear in the collection called the Gallican Eusebius in the *Maxima Bibliotheca Veterum Patrum* [(Lyons 1677) 6:618–686; 8:823–825; ed. J. Leroy, *L'oeuvre oratoire de s. Fauste de Riez* (Strasbourg thesis 1954) 2], while the Gallican Missal edited by A. Dold, *Das Sakramentar im Schabcodex M 12 Sup. der Bibl. Ambrosiana* (Beuron 1952), may be one of Salvian's Sacramentaries, though K. Gamber (1959) feels that it is the work of Musaeus of Marseilles (d. 461). Two other works mentioned by Gennadius can be identified: the *Adversus Avaritiam* is the extant *Ad Ecclesiam lib. IV* [*Corpus scriptorum ecclesiasticorum latinorum* (Vienna 1866–) 8:224–316; variants, *Revue Bénédictine* 43 (1931) 194–206] and the *De Praesenti judicio* is the *De*

Gubernatione Dei lib. VIII (*Corpus scriptorum ecclesiasticorum latinorum* (Vienna 1866–) 8:3–200), with its preface to Salonius, which may be the *Ad Salonium.*

Ad Ecclesiam, addressed to the universal Church under the penname of Timothy (cf. *Epistolarum lib.* 9), seems to date from 435 to 439. It inveighs against avarice, which it sees as widespread among Christians. It stresses both the duty and the advantages of almsgiving and urges that all, the childless especially, bequeath their possessions to the poor (3.2.9–11). A striking phrase points to humility instead of pride as the proper attitude in beneficence: *non offerat quasi praesumptione donantis sed quasi humilitate solventis* (1.10.54).

De Gubernatione Dei or On the Governance of God is subsequent to 439 and is Salvian's chief work; it ranks with Orosius's *Historiae adversus paganos* as a documentary of the miseries known during the 4th- to the 5th-century migration of nations. Rhetorical and at times vapid, it expounds the thesis that God executes judgment in the present world (2.4.15), thus supplying a title to the five books Gennadius knew. It is a theology of history that views calamities as the means whereby Divine Providence brings unfaithful Christians to their knees. Although too severe on the failings of the faithful (3.9.44–49; 6), too flattering in its depiction of the barbarians (7.22.94–100) to be taken at its word, *De Gubernatione Dei* nonetheless must be said to stand as a classic work in justifying the ways of God with man.

Bibliography: *Opera omnia,* ed. F. PAULY (*Corpus scriptorum ecclesiasticorum latinorum* 8; 1883); Eng. tr. J. F. O'SULLIVAN (*The Fathers of the Church: A New Translation,* ed. R. J. DEFERRARI et al. [New York 1947]). *Clavis Patrum latinorum,* ed. E. DEKKERS (2d ed. Streenbrugge 1961) 485–487. M. PELLEGRINO, *Vigiliae christianea* 6 (1952) 99–108; *Salviano di Marsiglia* (Rome 1940). M. IANNELLI, *La caduta d'un impero nel capolavoro di Salviano* (Naples 1948). G. VECCHI, *Studi Salvianei* (Bologna 1951). M. SCHANZ, C. HOSIUS, and G. KRÜGER, *Geschichte der römischen Literatur,* 4 v. in 5 (Munich 1914–35) 4.2:523–528. O. BARDENHEWER, *Geschichte der altkirchlichen Literatur,* 5 v. (Freiburg 1913–32) 4:573–579. B. ALTANER, *Patrology,* tr. H. GRAEF from 5th German ed. (New York 1960) 542–544. C. FAVEZ, "La Gaule et les Gallo-Romains," *Latomus* 16 (1957) 77–83. K. GAMBER, "Das Lektionar und Sakramentar des Musäus von Massilia," *Revue Bénédictine* 69 (1959) 198–215.

[H. G. J. BECK]

SALZMANN, JOSEPH

Educator, editor; b. Münzbach, Austria, Aug. 17, 1819; d. St. Francis, Wis., Jan. 17, 1874. He attended schools at Münzbach, Linz, and Vienna, where he earned a doctorate in theology. After ordination Aug. 8, 1842, at Linz, he was influenced by Bp. J. M. HENNI to work on the American mission, and he arrived Oct. 7, 1847, at Milwaukee, Wisconsin. In addition to pastoral work, he served as editor of *Der Seebote* (1851) and *Die Columbia* (1871), both of Milwaukee. He was organizer of St. Francis Seminary (1856), Milwaukee, for which he collected $100,000 in the East, South, and Middle West; this institution proved a vital factor in the progress of the Church. He used the press and other means to counter the attacks of anticlericals and the pulpit to inform his people about political issues. Throughout the U.S. Civil War he criticized President Abraham Lincoln, the draft, and Yankees. As a member of the faculty and rector of the seminary, he taught history. He was a Germanophile and dreamed of a German Catholic university for the U.S. A direct consequence of his normal school, Holy Family in St. Francis, Wisconsin, which graduated over 500 organists and teachers, was his founding of the American branch of the Caecilian society for the reform of Church music. Although the society had a membership of 5,000 in the U.S. by 1920, it had abandoned its original purpose out of deference for the motu proprio on Church music (1903).

Bibliography: J. RAINER, *A Noble Priest: Joseph Salzmann,* tr. J. W. BERG (Milwaukee 1903).

[P. L. JOHNSON]

SAMARITANS

A religious group in Palestine related to the Jews. They were known up to the time of the early Islamic writers (7th and 8th centuries). Thereafter silence fell until the 16th century, when the first scholarly contacts were established (J. J. Scaliger, Pietro della Valle). The Samaritans reserve for themselves the name Israel, allow the name Samerim only as an equivalent to the Hebrew Shomerim, "those who observe (the Law)," and have done so since pre-Christian times. The name derives from the place name Samaria, which was extended to the entire territory only after the Assyrian conquest of Galilee and part of Transjordan. Today Samaria signifies what was originally the highlands of EPHRAIM. The modern Samaritans, however, are associated with only a small part of this area, modern Nablus, between Mt. Garizim (Gerizim) and Mt. Ebal; this area has been their center since Hellenistic times.

Before New Testament Times. Reconstruction of their early history is disputed; the main generally accepted conclusions follow. The people are largely the descendants of the Ten Tribes of Israel that broke away from Juda at the death of Solomon. Jewish contentions that they were merely descendants of imported Babylonians (hence their use of the name Kuthim; see 2 Kgs 17.24) are exaggerated and polemical. The Assyrians had indeed colonized Ephraim with captives, but the peasant population remained, and was definitely Israelite (see 2 Chr 34.9; Jer 41.5). The newcomers adopted the religion of the land; SHECHEM became their national shrine. Between this new hybrid people and the Judaites only religion subsisted as a link. When the Jewish exiles returned from Babylon, the Samaritans made at least one attempt to join them, perhaps demanding that the Temple be built in Shechem (Ezr 4.1–5). The Jews naturally refused. The split was increased by the ruthlessness with which Ezra prevented intermarriage and even destroyed already existing marriages. The Samaritans opposed the rebuilding of the walls of Jerusalem (Ezr 4.7–23) and actually stopped the work by decree of Artaxerxes until Nehemiah intervened (Neh 2.1–8). With the completion of the walls (despite the opposition of the Samaritan governor Sanaballat), the prohibition of intermarriage, and doctrinal differences (Jerusalem vs. Garizim; Samaritan rejection of the prophetic books), the rift widened continually. By the time of Christ, for a Jew to call someone a Samaritan was an insult (Jn 8.48). In Jewish noncanonical writings there are few references to Samaritans, all disparaging. The Samaritans, as well as the Jews, were persecuted by ANTIOCHUS IV EPIPHANES (2 Mc 5.23; 6.2). After a brief respite John Hyrcanus again captured their shrine and destroyed it (c. 128 B.C.).

In New Testament Times. Jesus encountered both courtesy and discourtesy at the hands of the Samaritans (Jn 4.39–42; Lk 9.51–56). One of the 10 lepers healed by Jesus was a Samaritan, and all were told to show themselves to the Jewish priests in accordance with what we know of their division of religious jurisdiction (Lk 17.11–19). In His answer to the question "Who is my neighbor" Jesus pointedly chose the despised Samaritan (Lk 10.25–37), but to a Samaritan He was careful to point out that "salvation is of the Jews" (Jn 4.22). In restricting the first mission of the Apostles He also distinguished the Samaritans from pagans (Mt 10.5; cf. Acts 1.8). There are indications in Acts 8.5; 9.31; 15.3 of a flourishing Christian community at Samaria. The Fathers of the Church regarded the Samaritans as a branch of the chosen people.

After New Testament Times. Under the Romans, a Council of Elders governed the Samaritans and they possessed a native militia. Their religion was *religio licita* within the imperial framework. Vespasian built a new city a short distance from ancient Shechem and renamed it Flavia Neapolis, which is modern Nablus. TRAJAN's Declaration hit Christian and Samaritan alike. Only their book of the Law and their priestly succession survived the destruction of A.D. 135 (*see* BAR KOKHBA, SIMON). Christian influence on Constantine introduced a

period of repression, and life was not easier under Islam until Harun ar-Rashid (Caliph 786–809). The Samaritans emerged under Turkish rule as a small, self-contained religious community. Accounts of the intervening centuries by Arabic historians and Samaritan chroniclers still await comprehensive study. In 1623–24 the priestly succession (supposedly from Aaron) failed, and now Levitical priests of the house of Uzziel officiate. The Samaritans are now pitifully reduced. Since the 1970s, their number has hovered around the 500s.

Samaritan Religion. The Samaritans have only the Pentateuch (in Hebrew and in an Aramaic Targum) as their Sacred Scripture. The five constituents of their belief are: faith in Yahweh, in Moses, in the Holy Law (the Pentateuch and it alone), in Mt. Garizim-Bethel-Luza, and in the Day of Vengeance and Recompense (showing some Islamic influence). Salvation history is divided into uneven periods of *Rahuta* (divine favor) and *Fanuta* (divine disfavor). The first *Rahuta* ended with the sin of Adam; a second began with Moses and ended with the apostasy of Eli. Only with the coming of the *thb* (variously pronounced, but generally explained as "He Who Shall Return"), the Samaritan Messiah, will the definitive *Rahuta* be inaugurated.

The Samaritans have a rather developed angelology. Creation was the single act of God alone; the giving of the Law was a second creation through Moses, who holds much the same position as Muḥammad in Islam, and no other prophet is allowed on equal footing with him. Patriarchs and other OT heroes are the Guiltless, the Meritorious Ones. Using Dt 27.4 (reading Garizim for Ebal) they maintain that Mt. Garizim was the site of the first altar of God, and the real Bethel of patriarchal history. Before the time of Marqah (4th Christian century) it seems they held the normal OT (Sadducean) doctrine on SHEOL. Thereafter the doctrine of the resurrection of the body appears. They await an eschatological battle against the forces of evil. The Messiah will be a man specially instructed by Yahweh. After the millennium, the wrath of God will be loosed on the Day of Vengeance; then the good will pass on to the Garden of Eden forever, the bad down into the fire.

Bibliography: L. FINKELSTEIN, *The Pharisees: The Sociological Background of Their Faith,* 2 v. (3d ed. rev. Philadelphia 1962). J. BOWMAN, *The Samaritan Problem: Studies in the Relationships of Samaritanism, Judaism, and Early Christianity* (Pittsburgh 1975). R. J. COGGINS, *Samaritans and Jews: The Origins of Samaritanism Reconsidered* (Atlanta 1975). R. PUMMER, *The Samaritans* (Leiden 1987). A. D. CROWN, *The Samaritans* (Tübingen 1989). N. SCHUR, *History of the Samaritans,* (2d rev. and enl. ed. New York 1992). I. HJELM, *The Samaritans and Early Judaism: A Literary Analysis* (Sheffield, England, 2000). R. T. ANDERSON, *The Keepers: An Introduction to the History and Culture of the Samaritans* (Peabody, Mass. 2002).

[T. A. CALDWELL/EDS.]

SAMOSATA

An important Christian center in the early Church and still a titular see (Samosatensis), is identical with modern Samsat in Turkey. The capital of the ancient Seleucid kingdom of Commagene, it was added to the Roman province of Syria in 17 B.C. as a garrison town. The pagan philosopher Lucian, who exhibits some knowledge of early Christian literature, probably wrote his satire *De Morte Peregrini* there *c.* A.D. 170, and the names of seven 3d-century martyrs—Philotheus, Hyperechius, Abibus, Julianus, Romanus, Jacobus, and Paregorius—are connected with Samosata. Its first-known bishop was Peperius, who was present at the Council of Nicaea (325). Among its earlier churchmen were St. LUCIAN OF SAMOSATA (b. *c.* 250), who founded the School of ANTIOCH and was a teacher of Arius, and Paul (*see* PAUL OF SAMOSATA), the contemporary governor under Queen Zenobia of Palmyra, who became bishop of Antioch in 260 and was later condemned as a heretic (268) for his erroneous teachings on Christology and the Trinity. Samosata was a center of the Arian disturbances; one of its bishops, Eusebius, was assassinated and another, Andrew, supported JOHN OF ANTIOCH at EPHESUS (431), in opposing St. CYRIL OF ALEXANDRIA. The city is mentioned as joined to the See of Amida in the Photian Council of Constantinople (879). It was conquered by the Muslims in 1150. Traces of an ancient wall (probably from the 1st century), remains of another wall, and an artificial hill on which a fortress was erected are the scarce archeological particulars of Samosata.

Bibliography: *Paulys Realenzyklopädie der klassischen Altertumswissenschaft,* ed. G. WISSOWA, et al. (Stuttgart 1893–) 1A.2 (1920) 2220–24. M. LE QUIEN, *Oriens Christianus,* 3 v. (Graz 1958) 2:934–936. A. VON HARNACK, *The Mission and Expansion of Christianity in the First Three Centuries,* tr. and ed. J. MOFFAT, 2 v. (2d ed. New York 1908) v. 2. ''Samosata,'' *Lexikon für Theologie und Kirche,* ed. J. HOFER and K. RAHNER, 10 v. (2d, new ed. Freiburg 1957–65); suppl., *Das ZweiteVatikanische Konzil: Dokumente und kommentare,* ed. H. S. BRECHTER et al., pt. 1 (1966) 9:301.

[J. VAN PAASSEN]

SAMSON

Last of the major JUDGES and hero of popular Israelite saga. His story is told in Judges, ch. 13 to 16. He lived in the region of Beth-Sameš (Beth-Shemesh), which was seriously threatened by the advance of the PHILISTINES. There are but few scholars who would still see in the Samson story a ''sun myth'' (because of his Hebrew name, *šimšôn,* ''little sun'') or who would deny the existence of a Danite peasant of extraordinary strength who led a private war against the Philistines.

Literary Form. A proper understanding of these chapters requires an appreciation of their literary form.

The saga of Samson is a type of heroic epic. The function of such a narrative is to capture the ''great moment'' of a given age and preserve it. The nature of the great moment depends on the scheme of values in contemporary society. A knowledge, then, of the world and the *Sitz im Leben* out of which the Samson cycle grew is necessary.

The age was one of great upheaval, of invasions and migrations. The Israelites had only an insecure foothold on the hill country of the Promised Land and were surrounded by hostile peoples, the strongest of whom were the Philistines, who alone in Palestine possessed iron weapons. Confronted by the strength of iron, the politically disunited Israelites faced the threat of extinction. Their only hope was in religious unity and the help of Yahweh, who kept sending liberators to them when they returned to Him from idolatry. Samson was one of these warriors of Yahweh who fought, with godlike strength, a private war against the major menace. After he died, his great moment was talked about around the campfire and at various sanctuaries and became a stirring example in Israelite folklore.

Religious Meaning. The religious sense of the Samson stories lies, then, not so much in the episodes themselves as in the context in which they were placed by the inspired editor. Such a context is found at the beginning of chapter thirteen: a balanced series of episodes, gathered around the ''heroes'' of premonarchic times, retold to an audience of a later age to inculcate a religious lesson.

The key to the episodes lies in Samson's consecration. He was one of the NAZIRITES who were forbidden to take strong drink, to have their hair shaved, or to have contact with a dead body. Each episode in the Samson saga involved a violation of this vow and consequent disaster. The first violation came in his contact with the dead lion; the second, in the feast he made for the marriage; the third and fatal one, in the revelation of his dedication. This led to the cutting off of his hair by Dalila and to his death. Thus, the breach of the vow led to sin and, through sin, to death. Nevertheless, Samson was used by Yahweh as a liberator of his people even in his death. This was his great moment.

See Also: JUDGES, BOOK OF.

Bibliography: *Encyclopedic Dictionary of the Bible,* tr. and adap. by L. HARTMAN (New York 1963), from A. VAN DEN BORN, *Bijbels Wǫordenboek,* 2116–17. H. CAZELLES, *Dictionnaire de la Bible,* suppl. ed. L. PIROT, et al. (Paris 1928–) 4:1405–06. J. GAMBERONI, in *Lexikon für Theologie und Kirche,* ed. J. HOFER and K. RAHNER, 10 v. (2d new ed. Freiburg 1957–65) 9:301–302.

[J. MORIARITY]

SAMSON OF BURY-ST.-EDMUNDS

English abbot; b. Tottington, Norfolk, *c.* 1135; d. BURY-ST.EDMUNDS, 1212. Though always proud of being a Norfolk man, Samson studied in the schools of Paris through the good offices of a chaplain who financed his studies with money from the sale of holy water. While still a layman, Samson journeyed to Rome *c.* 1160 on the business of the Abbey of Bury, to whose patron, St. Edmund, he showed lifelong devotion. He joined this monastery five years later and by virtue of his managerial ability rose through the offices of subsacrist and third prior to become abbot, an office he held from 1182 until his death. As abbot he reformed the abbey's finances and carried out an extensive rebuilding program. He helped the town of Bury gain a charter and granted it extensive market rights. Samson, a staunch defender of the rights of his abbey, came into conflict with kings HENRY II, Richard I (especially over the abbey's contribution to Richard's military activity), and John. As a member of the Royal Council, he frustrated the efforts of William de Longchamp to curtail the rights of the BENEDICTINES in England. Thomas Carlyle included an essay on Samson in *Past and Present*.

Bibliography: *The Chronicle of Jocelin of Brakelond,* tr. and ed. H. E. BUTLER (London 1949). A. L. POOLE, *From Domesday Book to Magna Carta* (2d ed. Oxford 1955). D. KNOWLES, *The Monastic Order in England, 943–1216* (2d ed. Cambridge, England 1962).

[D. NICHOLL]

SAMUEL

An Old Testament figure whose story is recounted essentially in 1 Sm 1–16. His birth and early life are covered in 1 Sm 1–7; his involvement with Saul is told in 1 Sm 8–12 (Saul's anointment as king) and 1 Sm 13–15 (Saul's rejection); his involvement with David is limited to David's anointment (1 Sm 16) and a brief story of David, in flight from Saul, taking refuge with Samuel (19:18–24). Subsequent mentions recount his death (25:1), and Saul's desperate attempt to seek counsel from Samuel's ghost (28:3–25). Samuel is an important personage, but transitional: he represents the best of the old order of judgeship, which proved itself incapable of adequately governing Yahweh's people, and points forward to the new order of monarchy by anointing Saul and David, the first kings of Israel.

Narratively, the character of Samuel is complex. The account of his birth and early life culminates in his assumption of all the standard leadership offices in ancient Israel: he is a Nazirite (1:11); a prophet (3:19–4:1); a priest (7:9–10, 17), despite not being from the priestly tribe of Levi; and a judge (7:15–17). He, or Israelite forces under his leadership, subdue the Philistines (7:10–14, but contrast 13:5–15), but he cannot control his own sons (8:1–3). He is reluctant to anoint a king until Yahweh approves (8:4–9); he warns the people about royal abuses (8:11–18), then gives the king *carte blanche* (10:7); he condemns Saul when he takes decisions Samuel deems disobedient (13:8–14), and yet grieves when Yahweh rejects Saul from the kingship (15:35–16:1). He embodies the conflict of Israelite enthusiasm and hesitation before the irrevocable step of political transformation to autocracy, the ambivalence of cultic and charismatic leaders toward a dynast who will relieve them of both civil power and military responsibility, and even the obliquity of a deity whose motives are not always entirely clear (compare 1 Sm 10:23–24 with 16:7–8).

Historically, we can say unfortunately little about Samuel. With no external evidence about him from archaeology or non-biblical documents, we are restricted to conjectures based on the biblical text. That a transition from tribal confederacy to monarchy took place is virtually certain; that one or more individuals were pivotal in that transition is highly probable. That the artistically constructed narrative of those events has inherited and preserved, through several centuries of oral tradition and written elaboration and editing, authentic memories of one of those individuals is not impossible. But contemporary scholars' growing hesitation about the historical reliability of the biblical accounts of Israel's earliest days, and our increasing appreciation of the depth, richness, and sophistication of ancient Israel's genius for literary creativity, together urge caution about moving too readily from narrative characterization to historical reconstruction.

The Chronicler mentions ''The Chronicles of Samuel the Seer'' as one of several sources for the life of David (1 Chr 29:29), but no such book has come down to us. That remark may be the source of the later Jewish legend that gave the Books of Samuel their name and attributed them to his authorship, but the legend is certainly without historical foundation.

Bibliography: L. M. ESLINGER, *Kingship of God in Crisis* (Bible and Literature; Sheffield: 1985). G. W. RAMSEY, ''Samuel,'' in *The Anchor Bible Dictionary* (New York 1992); 5:954–57. See also the commentaries on 1 Samuel under ''Samuel, Book(s) of.''

[J. T. WALSH]

SAMUEL, BOOK(S) OF

Name and Division. The Hebrew Bible contains a single book called ''Samuel'' followed by a single book called "Kings." The translators of the Septuagint (LXX), an ancient Greek translation of the Hebrew Bible, divided each of these books into two and called the resulting four books "1–4 Kingdoms." When Jerome translated the Bible into Latin (the Vulgate) in the fourth Christian century, he kept the LXX's divisions but called the books "1–4 Kings" instead of "1–4 Kingdoms." After the Reformation, the Protestant tradition drew closer to Hebrew usage by naming the first two books "1–2 Samuel" and the last two "1–2 Kings." Roman Catholic Bibles, however, continued to follow the Vulgate until Pope Pius XII's encyclical *Divino Afflante Spiritu* (1943), which urged Catholic biblical scholars to use the original language texts in their translations and commentaries. Since that time, Roman Catholic Bibles, like Protestant ones, use the titles 1–2 Samuel and 1–2 Kings.

The division between 1 and 2 Samuel occurs at a natural point, the death of King Saul. The continuity of the books is clear, however, in that 2 Samuel 1 is the natural sequel to Saul's death: a runner brings the news to David, who sings his famous lament over Saul and over Jonathan, Saul's son and David's bosom companion. The division and continuity between 2 Samuel and 1 Kings are also manifest in the text: 2 Samuel focuses on the successes and failures of David's rule; 1 Kings begins with the necessity of assuring the succession to the now aged and moribund David.

Content and Organization. The Books of Samuel constitute the second part of what scholars call the "Deuteronomistic History," that is, the books of Joshua, Judges, 1–2 Samuel, and 1–2 Kings, composed during the late monarchic and early exilic periods by writers inspired by the theology of the book of Deuteronomy—hence, "Deuteronomistic." (Although in the Christian Old Testament the book of Ruth appears between Judges and 1 Samuel, it is not part of the Deuteronomistic writers' opus. It was put there by later tradition because of its chronology: "In the days when the judges were judging . . ." [Ru 1.1].)

The first part of the Deuteronomistic History, Joshua and Judges, tells of the Israelites' arrival in the "Promised Land" and the history of their loosely organized tribal confederacy during their first centuries in Canaan. It bemoans the fact that the looseness of their political structure eventually resulted in their subjection to Philistine military superiority and in intertribal chaos among the Israelites themselves: "In those days, there was no king in Israel; everyone did what was right in his own eyes" (Jgs 21.25). The second part of the History, 1–2 Samuel, recounts the emergence of monarchy in Israel. The last judge (Samuel), with some hesitation, inaugurates kingship in Israel by anointing first Saul, then, when Saul proves unsatisfactory as a king, David. It then fol-

lows the vicissitudes of David's career. The third part of the History, 1–2 Kings, tells of the tragic failure of the monarchic experiment, and the eventual dispersion of the people in the Assyrian and Babylonian exiles.

The Books of Samuel are organized around principal characters and their destinies:

1. Samuel (1 Sm 1–7)
2. Saul (1 Sm 8–15)
   a. inauguration of Saul's kingship (1 Sm 8–12)
   b. rejection of Saul's kingship (1 Sm 13–15)
3. David (1 Sm 16–2; 24)
   c. David and Saul
      i. David at Saul's court (1 Sm 16–20)
      ii. David flees from Saul (1 Sm 21–26)
      iii. The death of Saul (1 Sm 27–2 Sm 1)
   d. David established as king (2 Sm 2-8)
   e. David's troubles
      i. Sins against the family (2 Sm 9–14)
      ii. Crimes against the kingdom (2 Sm 15–20)
   f. Additional material about David (2 Sm 21–24)

History of the Text. The Deuteronomistic History took the form in which we have it today during the Babylonian Exile. It is generally held, however, that the work had at least one earlier edition, either during the reign of Josiah (c. 640–609 B.C.) or perhaps of Hezekiah (c. 715–687 B.C.). Since elsewhere the Deuteronomistic Historian directs the reader to older works that we may presume to have been used in writing the History (e.g., Jos 10:13; 1 Kgs 11:41; 14:19; 15:23), there is no reason to doubt that such sources were used in 1–2 Samuel as well, although only one is explicitly named there (2 Sm 1.18). Many commentators believe that the impressive literary quality and strong narrative coherence of 2 Sm 9–20 points to an earlier written "Court History of King David"—not indeed an official record (which would be unlikely to depict David's sins of adultery and murder so frankly), but a powerfully conceived account of the uncertainties surrounding the succession to David's throne. (Since that suspense is not resolved until 1 Kgs 1–2, scholars often reckon those two chapters part of the "Court History" as well.) Others would also see a source concerned with the history of the Ark of the Covenant behind 1 Sm 4–6 and perhaps other passages, e.g., 2 Sm 6. The incorporation of oral traditions is evidenced by tensions and disagreements that remain unresolved in the text (e.g., whether or not Samuel succeeded in subduing the Philistines [compare 1 Sm 7.13 with 13:5–15], or who killed Goliath [compare 1 Sm 17 with 2 Sm 21.19]).

Samuel as History. It is difficult to reach any firm conclusion regarding the historical reliability of the information contained in the Books of Samuel. The text as we have it is several centuries removed from the events it purports to recount and reconstruction of earlier written or oral traditions is fraught with conjecture and uncertainty. Moreover, other ancient sources offer no help. Neither Samuel nor Saul nor David is mentioned in contemporary or near-contemporary historical records; indeed, "Israel" as a nation is not named in ancient Near Eastern texts before the time of the divided monarchy in the ninth century B.C. All historical judgments, then, must be based on internal evidence from the Books of Samuel itself. In the past, many biblical scholars were inclined to treat the Court History as the work of an eyewitness and essentially historical, but a growing appreciation of the sophistication of the biblical authors' creativity is presently leading to a resurgence of the view that the Court History is a novel (as proposed long ago by Gressman, Eissfeldt, and others).

The large sweep of the story is politically and economically plausible. Archaeology confirms the presence and technological capabilities of the Philistines on the south Palestinian coast. Samuel tells how their monopoly of ironworking and their military organization gave them the upper hand over Israel's poorly organized and poorly armed peasantry. In such a situation, the transformation of Israel from loose tribal confederacy to the centralized, monarchical state is understandable and almost inevitable. It is entirely possible that the stresses of such a transition could destroy a vulnerable personality like Saul's and require the military and political genius of a David to surmount them.

On the other hand, the portraits of the three principal characters are drawn so strongly that they resemble heroes of legend more than makers of history. After the Book of Judges has recounted the degeneration of judgeship in Israel from the glory of Deborah to the bathos of Samson, Samuel appears as one who sums up in himself all that is best in Israel—prophecy (3.19–4.1), priesthood (7.9–10), and judgeship (7.15–17). Yet, despite his apparent victories (7.10–14), he cannot stop the downward spiral (8.1–3). Under pressure from the people, and with the resentful approbation of God (8.7–9), Samuel anoints Saul as king. Saul, however, proves to be a disaster. In a tragedy worthy of Sophocles, Saul is undone by jealousy, drives away David, his closest and most gifted military champion, and ultimately, bereft of David's prowess, falls in battle. In the aftermath, David succeeds where Saul failed: he unites the divided tribes of north and south, throws off the Philistine yoke, and establishes Israelite hegemony over a far-flung empire. At the height of his successes, however, he succumbs to temptation. His adultery with a married woman and subsequent murder of her husband unleash forces that tear his family apart and nearly destroy his kingship. His first-born and heir, Amnon, rapes his half-sister Tamar and dies at the hands

of her brother, Absalom. Absalom in turn, after apparent reconciliation with his father, rises up in rebellion against him. The rebellion is crushed, Absalom dies in battle, and David regains the throne; but the familial disintegration points up the political dilemma that will remain unresolved at the end of 2 Samuel: who shall reign after David?

Samuel as Theology. The fundamental theological issue in 1–2 Samuel is the problem of reconciling two apparently contradictory theological absolutes: Yahweh is the only true King of Israel, yet the line of Davidic kings is chosen by Yahweh himself. The dynamism of the narrative leads inexorably to David. Samuel supersedes Eli, but proves to be a transitional figure himself. Saul the king supersedes Samuel the judge, and the new order is born. David in turn supersedes the flawed first king and establishes a dynasty that will reign virtually unbroken for over four centuries.

Yahweh's role in all this is ambiguous, to say the least. After an initial angry reaction, God seems to approve the inauguration of a human king (1 Sm 8.7–9). Yet there are indications that God may have knowingly chosen a weak vessel (compare 1 Sm 10.23–24 with 16.6–7) and foreseen, if not intended, his failure. God refuses Saul a second chance, despite his abject repentance (15.24–29), a decision about which Samuel apparently has reservations (15.30–31, 35; 16.1). Saul's madness is due to "an evil spirit from Yahweh" (16.14). There is no ambiguity in David's case, however. God's choice is unforced (16.1, 12–13), David's victories are from Yahweh (18.14), and Yahweh makes an eternal covenant with David and his dynastic line (2 Sm 7). That covenant does not fail, despite the sins and crimes of David and his sons (2 Sm 9–20, the "Court History").

The Deuteronomistic Historian, writing during the Babylonian Exile after the failure of the monarchic experiment in Israel, is aware of both the glories and the abominations of the kings. In view of their realized potential for obedience as well as for malfeasance, the Historian's attitude toward kingship cannot but be ambivalent, and it is entirely reasonable that the Deuteronomist's God share that attitude. For the Historian's audience of Jewish exiles in Babylon, that very ambivalence could be, paradoxically, a source of hope. If the Exile is the due punishment for sins of Judah's kings and people (2 Kgs 17.19–20), yet even this was foreseen (1 Kgs 8.46–53); and the release of Jehoiachin from prison (2 Kgs 25.27–30) can fuel the desperate longing of the exiles for restoration of the promised eternal kingdom (2 Sm 7.16).

Reading Samuel Today. The reader today, in a world plagued by human evil on every level from international injustice to personal sin, needs the same hope. There is good in the world as well as evil, and likewise on every level. The Christian reader believes that the promises to David have been kept, not in the human political realm, but transformed and universalized in the reign of the Son of David, the Messiah, and in the opening of the Kingdom of God to all peoples. The slow but, as faith believes and hopes, inevitable establishment of peace and justice in this world is but the outward manifestation of the burgeoning of that Kingdom wherein not only sin, but even the death that sin earns, have been overcome forever.

Bibliography: H. GRESSMANN, et al., *Narrative and Novella I Samuel* (reprint; Sheffield 1991). L. ROST, *The Succession to the Throne of David* (reprint of 1926 edition; Sheffield 1982). H. W. HERTZBERG, *I & II Samuel* (OTL; London 1964). R. N. WHYBRAY, *The Succession Narrative* (London 1968). D. M. GUNN, *The Story of King David* (Journal for the Study of the Old Testament Supplement Series; Sheffield 1978). D. M. GUNN, *The Fate of King Saul* (Journal for the Study of the Old Testament Supplement Series; Sheffield 1980). P. K. MCCARTER, JR., *I Samuel* (Garden City 1980). J. P. FOKKELMAN, *Narrative Art and Poetry in the Books of Samuel* 4 v. (Assen 1981–1993). R. W. KLEIN, *1 Samuel* (Waco 1983). P. K. MCCARTER, JR., *II Samuel* (Anchor Bible; Garden City 1984). L. M. ESLINGER, *Kingship of God in Crisis* (Bible and Literature; Sheffield 1985). P. D. MISCALL, *1 Samuel: A Literary Reading* (Bloomington 1986). J. ROSENBERG, *King and Kin* (Bloomington 1986). A. A. ANDERSON, *2 Samuel* (WBC; Waco 1989). J. ROSENBERG, "1 and 2 Samuel," in *The Literary Guide to the Bible*, ed. by R. ALTER and F. KERMODE (Cambridge, Mass. 1987) 122–45. V. PHILIPS LONG, *The Reign and Rejection of King Saul* (Society of Biblical Literature Sources for Bible Study; Atlanta 1989). A. F. CAMPBELL and J. W. FLANAGAN, "1–2 Samuel," in *The New Jerome Biblical Commentary* (Englewood Cliffs 1990) §9. W. BRUEGGEMANN, "Samuel, Book of 1–2," in *The Anchor Bible Dictionary* (New York 1992); 5:957–73. R. POLZIN, *Samuel and the Deuteronomist* (Bloomington 1993). R. POLZIN, *David and the Deuteronomist* (Bloomington 1993). A. BRENNER, *A Feminist Companion to Samuel and Kings* (Sheffield 1994). D. JOBLING, *1 Samuel* (Berit Olam; Collegeville 1998). R. ALTER, *The David Story* (New York 1999). M. J. EVANS, *1 and 2 Samuel* (NIBCOT; Peabody, Mass. 2000). C. MORRISON, *2 Samuel* (Berit Olam; Collegeville 2000).

[J. T. WALSH]

SAN ALBERTO, JOSÉ ANTONIO DE

Carmelite bishop; b. El Frasno, Aragon, Feb. 17, 1727; d. Chuquisaca, Bolivia, March 25, 1804. He entered the Discalced Carmelites of Aragon at an early age, taught for many years in Huesca and Calatayud, and filled a number of administrative positions in the order. Made bishop of Córdoba in Tucumán, he took charge of his diocese in 1778; in 1786 he was in charge of the Archdiocese of La Plata (now Sucre, in Bolivia). His letters, printed in *Colección de instrucciones pastorales* (Madrid 1786), indicate his pastoral knowledge. The letter written to the pastors of Córdoba in 1778 began with an explana-

tion of the biblical and historical ecclesiastical origins of the parish ministry, emphasizing its dignity and its duties. He warned the faithful against mere ritualism and urged them toward inner sanctity. Another pastoral referred to the orphanages founded in Córdoba, insisting upon catechetical instruction in them. In a pastoral to the pastors of La Plata, he preached their obligation to reside in their parishes and warned them against avarice. San Alberto also played a role in bringing about the enlightened reform of the curriculum in the University of Córdoba. The best known of his works is the *Catecismo real* (Madrid 1786) on the obligations of vassals to the king, written in the form of questions and answers. This formulation of the Gallican doctrine of the divine right of kings, following the model of Bossuet, affirms the total independence of the kings in the temporal sphere: responsibility only before God, absolute power limited only by the moral law, right of patronage, the illicitness of all resistance on the part of the vassals, the duty of not only external but also internal obedience. It is one of the most important works enunciating the Gallican doctrine of royal power in Hispanic America, a doctrine that dominated the second half of the 18th century and the first decade of the 19th.

Bibliography: J. A. DE SAN ALBERTO, *Catecismo real* (Madrid 1786). J. C. ZURETTI, *Historia eclesiástica argentina* (Buenos Aires 1945).

[M. GÓNGORA]

SAN ANTONIO, ARCHDIOCESE OF

(*Sancti Antonii*) Metropolitan see embracing 23,180 square miles in the state of Texas. The diocese was established Sept. 8, 1874; the archdiocese, Aug. 3, 1926. The suffragans include all the dioceses of Texas: Amarillo, Austin, Beaumont, Brownsville, Corpus Christi, Dallas, El Paso, Fort Worth, Galveston-Houston, Laredo, Lubbock, San Angelo, Tyler and Victoria. In 2001, Catholics in the archdiocese numbered 679,712, about one-third of the total population of 1,949,506.

Early History. San Antonio was a little-known village in 1691, when the chaplain of a Spanish expedition, Damian Massenet, OFM, camped on that site and gave it the name of the day's saint, Anthony of Padua. The first settlement was made and the first mission founded, "San Antonio de Valero" (the Alamo), in 1718, and by 1745 the Franciscans had established four other missions in the vicinity: La Purisima Concepción, San Juan Capistrano, San Francisco de la Espada, and San José; this last was made illustrious by the ministry of Fray Antonio MARGIL. The small settlement was increased by 15 Canary Island families, and organized the first city government in Texas

Exterior of Mission San Antonio, arched portico along building front, Jolon, California. (©David Muench/CORBIS)

in 1731. The colonists immediately provided for the building of a church and the support of a parish priest. Under Spanish rule there was a very clear distinction between a mission and a parish church. The mission was devoted entirely to the care of the Native Americans, while the Spanish colonists were organized into regular parishes. Thus, the first parish in Texas, and for many years the only one, was the old San Fernando Church of San Antonio, founded in 1738. The original dome and sanctuary form part of the present cathedral, while the rest has been rebuilt and replaced several times. The grandiose plan of the mission churches never really worked out in San Antonio, and after a few years was almost entirely abandoned as the Native Americans moved away. San Fernando likewise suffered as, in turn, Mexico waged war against the mother country and Texas revolted against Mexico.

During these years of revolution, the Texas and San Antonio Catholics were practically abandoned. The achievement of Texas Independence (1836) left them nominally under the jurisdiction of the bishop of Monterey, who had no English-speaking clergy to serve the American settlers. It was the Catholics of San Antonio, represented by John McMullen, who petitioned the closest (600 miles) American bishop, Anthony Blanc of New Orleans, for priests to keep the scattered flock together. The Holy See had already been apprised of the plight of the faithful in Texas and had also asked Blanc to investigate. In 1838, at Blanc's request, John TIMON, provincial of the Vincentians, made a reconnaissance tour of the young republic. There he estimated the population at 1,500 with 50 American Catholics attended carelessly by two clerics of the old regime. The first Vincentians arrived in the spring of 1839, and later that year when Timon was appointed prefect apostolic of Texas, he sent John Mary ODIN, CM, as vice prefect. Odin landed at Port Lavaca, July 12, 1840, and immediately proceeded to San Antonio where he formally appointed his Spanish companion Miguel Calvo, CM, pastor of San Fernando. Gradually the haphazard conditions of the Church in San Antonio were improved, as instanced by Odin's decree that church bells would be rung henceforth only to summon the faithful to services instead of the former practice of ringing them to announce horse races, cockfights, public dances, and the burial of non-Catholics. In late September, Odin visited the old missions and made plans to establish clear title to them for the Church. Three months later, with the help of the French chargé d'affaires, Alphonse de Saligny, he obtained from the legislature the restoration to the "chief pastor and his successors" of all former Spanish and Mexican Church property, including that of the Alamo and all other San Antonio missions.

Odin was named vicar apostolic of Texas on July 16, 1841, and consecrated in New Orleans on March 6, 1842. On May 4, 1847, on the recommendation of the Sixth Provincial Council of Baltimore (1846), Rome raised the vicariate to the Diocese of Galveston, and appointed Odin the first ordinary and suffragan of New Orleans. At that time there were ten churches in actual use, served by six Vincentians and four secular priests. In 1847 he was able to appoint resident pastors for St. Louis in Castroville and for the German settlements of Fredericksburg (1848) and New Braunfels (1849). Ursuline Academy was opened in 1851, and the next year the Brothers of Mary started a school for boys in the city. When San Fernando became too small for the growing population, St. Mary's was opened in early 1857 and remained a landmark in the heart of the city until 1923, when it was torn down and rebuilt after a disastrous flood. Claude Dubuis, who was in charge of both congregations when Odin was promoted to New Orleans (1860), succeeded his compatriot as second bishop of Galveston and was consecrated by Odin in their home diocese of Lyons, France.

In 1868 Dubuis blessed the new St. Michael's Church (Polish) in San Antonio and laid the cornerstone of St. Joseph's (German). The Poles and the Czechs meanwhile had built churches and even schools in many of their settlements south and east of the city. The closing years of the 1860s were notable for the arrival of religious communities destined to play an important role in the fields of education and charity in San Antonio.

Among them were the Sisters of Divine Providence, who arrived at Castroville in 1868, and the Sisters of Charity of the Incarnate Word, at San Antonio in 1869. Both congregations have provided higher education for women and both have staffed many elementary and secondary schools and hospitals. The second diocesan synod met in December 1868 for the purpose of reorganizing the constantly expanding diocese. Although the synod was held in two sections, Galveston for the East, San An-

tonio for the West and South, busy pastors of scattered communities could not absent themselves for long, so only half of Dubuis's 80 secular and religious priests were in attendance. Four chancellors were named for Galveston, San Antonio, Brownsville and Laredo, foreshadowing the impending partition of the huge diocese.

Diocese. When in 1874 the Holy See created the Diocese of San Antonio and the vicariate apostolic of Brownsville, later dioceses of Corpus Christi and Brownsville, Anthony D. Pellicer, a native of Florida, was consecrated Dec. 8, 1874, for San Antonio, where he found about 12,000 Catholics in the city and 40,000 in the diocese. St. Mary's became the episcopal residence and chancery office for Pellicer, whose jurisdiction covered all counties between the Colorado and Nueces Rivers and extended as far west as El Paso and New Mexico, about 90,000 square miles (this remained without significant change until the creation of the Diocese of EL PASO in 1914). Frequent long journeys over the vast area, not reached by railroads until 1877, and the hardships of pioneer life undermined the health of the bishop, who died on April 14, 1880. At that time there were 47,000 Catholics in the diocese, served by 45 priests and 50 churches. From 1876 to 1880, the Mexican Jesuits had accepted students for the priesthood in their short-lived Guadalupe College at Seguin.

The next two ordinaries, John Claude Neraz (1881–94) and John Anthony Forest (1895–1911) had spent all their priestly lives in the diocese. Neraz was pastor of San Fernando, and Forest had had a long and distinguished missionary career at Hallettsville, Lavaca County. They were the last representatives of the French secular priests who came to the United States in the 19th century, and who laid the foundation of the Church in Texas. They seldom exercised their ministry among their own countrymen, but learned English and tried to master the language of the Mexicans and even those of the various other European immigrants to the area. In 1884 Neraz invited the Oblates of Mary Immaculate to take over St. Mary's parish and the mission district of the western part of the diocese. From 1884 to 1890 he accepted the additional burden of administering the affairs of the vicariate apostolic of Brownsville. By 1894, the Brothers of Mary had completed the first building of St. Louis College in the western outskirts of the city, later the main campus of St. Mary's University.

Under Bishop Forest the Catholic population increased from 66,000 to almost 100,000, and many missions and stations developed into self-sustaining parishes, some of them even able to build and maintain parochial schools. Forest laid the cornerstone of the new motherhouse of the Sisters of Divine Providence at Our Lady of the Lake (1895) and that of the Sisters of Charity of the Incarnate Word at Brackenridge Park (1899). In 1903 he blessed the new St. Anthony's Theological Seminary, operated by the Oblate fathers, and sent some of his own seminarians there during the following decade. The death of Forest marked the end of the missionary period in the greater part of the diocese. He was succeeded in 1911 by his coadjutor, John William Shaw, who in turn was promoted to New Orleans in January 1918. Both Shaw and his successor, Arthur Jerome Drossaerts (1918–40), sponsored charitable works on behalf of refugees from Mexico, especially members of the hierarchy. They successfully met the challenge of a growing population with many new churches and schools. Shaw founded the first diocesan seminary (1915) in the former episcopal residence and chancery on Dwyer Avenue. Bishop Drossaerts later moved it to a more suitable location next to Mission Concepción (1920). Closely associated with Shaw was his chancellor, William W. Hume, who served as first rector of the seminary and began the restoration of the four famous missions south of San Antonio.

Archdiocese. On Aug. 3, 1926, when San Antonio was raised to metropolitan rank, Drossaerts became the first archbishop. The new province included all of Texas and the state of Oklahoma, with the exception of the Diocese of El Paso. Its suffragans were Galveston, Dallas, Corpus Christi, Oklahoma City and Amarillo, to which Austin was added in 1947, and San Angelo in 1961. Although by 1908 the United States as a whole had ceased to be a frontier mission, outside aid was still vital to the preservation and spread of the faith in many sections of the South and West. The archdiocese was unable to raise enough priests for its own needs, and was indebted to the Irish and other clergy. In addition, the original Diocese of Galveston received from the Lyons Council of the Propagation of the Faith a total of $309,646 between 1846 and 1901, a sum larger than was granted to any other diocese in the United States. Between 1874 and 1918, San Antonio itself received $34,000 from the same source. The help extended by the Catholic Church Extension Society enabled the dioceses of Texas to care for the thousands of Spanish-speaking Catholics who came from Mexico during the troubled years of the Mexican persecution. By 1950 it had contributed to the Archdiocese of San Antonio alone the sum of $392,388 (not counting $138,446 in Mass stipends) for buildings, furnishings, and priests' support. Also, the AMERICAN BOARD OF CATHOLIC MISSIONS gave the archdiocese $307,925 from 1925 to 1951, and the Commission for Catholic Missions Among the Colored and Indians contributed $156,750 during the period from 1887 to 1951.

Growth and New Developments. Under the leadership of Archbishop Robert E. Lucey, who succeeded to the see in 1941, a CCD program was instituted in all the parishes of the archdiocese. A Catholic Welfare bureau was established as the church agency to coordinate Catholic social work; a Catholic Action Office was organized and extensive restoration of the Old Spanish Missions was begun. Although the *Southern Messenger* had been published for more than 50 years by the Menger family and was the official paper of the diocese, Lucey founded the *Alamo Register* as the official Catholic paper. The *Messenger* remained as the official paper for other dioceses in Texas. In 1957 the *Messenger,* merged with the *Register* to form the *Alamo Messenger* and its companion in Spanish, *La Voz.*

The archdiocese also provided permanent headquarters for the Bishop's Committee for the Spanish Speaking to promote social justice among Spanish-speaking peoples in the Southwest and among the migratory farm workers in the North. Lucey combined a social liberalism with an ecclesiastical conservatism. He led the state in a sucessful racial integration of parochial schools in 1954, three years before the federally mandated integration of the public schools. With social activists such as Fr. Sherrill Smith, he was able to spotlight farmworker problems in Texas. In 1966 Lucey brought three federally funded poverty programs to San Antonio.

Lucey took part in Vatican II and began implementing some of the council's recommended liturgical changes, but he refused to resign after reaching the age of 75, as prescribed by Vatican II rules. In 1968, some 51 diocesan priests petitioned Pope Paul VI for Lucey's retirement. The resulting conflict between Lucey and his clergy resulted in the departure of about one-third of the clergy and most of the seminarians. Rome intervened and appointed Bishop Francis Furey of San Diego as his successor. Furey actively promoted the lay movement with the use of the extraordinary ministers of the Eucharist, and led the country in the promotion of the permanent diaconate. He picked as his auxillary, Patrick F. Flores, the first Mexican-American to become a bishop (and the third to become archbishop). He began a pension plan for the priests and lay finance boards. The diocesan paper was reorganized under the name *Today's Catholic.*

In 1972, with Fr. Virgil Elizondo and Bishop Flores, Furey oversaw the establishment of the Mexican American Cultural Center on the campus of Assumption Seminary. His achievements were many: the establishment of 11 new parishes, maintenance and promotion of a strong anti-abortion stance, active promotion of labor rights, support of the Citizens Organized for Political Service (COPS) program, strong leadership of his growing Hispanic flock.

A year after the death of Archbishop Furey (April 23, 1979), Bishop Patrick Flores of El Paso became the fourth archbisop of San Antonio. Archbishop Flores lost no time in getting to work. In June 1981, he laid out his vision for the archdiocese in a document called *A New Pentecost,* calling for action in five areas: (1) A call to ministry, stressing the role of the lay ministry; (2) Parish development, focusing on office parish development to educate leaders and work along with COPS; (3) preference for persons with special needs, developing new programs for the poor, elderly and handicapped; (4) reorganization of diocesan structures to focus on service and increased attention to the needs of the rural areas of the diocese; and (5) the development of the Emmaus program for priestly development.

An important highlight of the episcopate of Archbishop Flores was the visit of Pope John Paul II to San Antonio on Sept. 13, 1987. The pope spent 22 hours in the city and made three major speeches.

Other significant developments include the convocation of a synod in 1994 to plan for the future direction of the archdiocese; the introduction of new programs for the spiritual needs of prison inmates, pregnant adolescents, homeless, abused children and battered women; the encouragement of lay participation through programs such as RENEW; the establishment of a diocesan television station (the only diocesan-operated station in the United States), providing 24-hour broadcasting; and the erection of new dioceses. The Victoria diocese was formed from nine eastern counties of the archdiocese and counties from Corpus Christi and Galveston-Houston. Bishop Grahmann became the first bishop. In 2000, four western counties were detached from the archdiocese and added to some from Corpus Christi to form the new diocese of Laredo.

The NEWMAN APOSTOLATE expanded to all the non-Catholic colleges and universities in the archdiocese. Boys Town of Nebraska established two facilities in the archdiocese to care for runaway and abandoned youth and to provide family counseling. In 1982 the Catholic Consultation center was established to provide psychological screening for seminarians and religious as well as mental health programs. This subsequently expanded to include laity of all faiths. The Catholic Youth Organization provides recreation and sports for hundreds of thousands of youth throughout the archdiocese as well as an annual youth congress and other youth programs. A Marian congress is held each year at the Municipal Auditorium in San Antonio.

Bibliography: *Archdiocese of San Antonio, Diamond Jubilee, 1874–1949* (privately printed; San Antonio 1948), although a commemorative album, this is a better than average illustrated record of the foundation and growth of all the parishes and institutions of the archdiocese. Archives (Catholic), Austin, Texas. Archives, University of Notre Dame. R. BAYARD, *Lone-Star Vanguard: The Catholic Reoccupation of Texas, 1838–1848* (St. Louis 1945). C. E. CASTAÑDA, *Our Catholic Heritage in Texas, 1519–1936,* 7 v. (Austin 1936–58). M. A. FITZMORRIS, *Four Decades of Catholicism in Texas, 1820–1860* (Washington 1926). L. V. JACKS, *Claude Dubuis: Bishop of Galveston* (St. Louis 1947). P. F. PARISOT and C. F. SMITH, *History of the Catholic Church in the Diocese of San Antonio* (San Antonio 1897). BONY, *Vie de Mgr. Jean-Marie Odin: Missionaire lazariste, archevêque de la Nouvelle-Orléans* (Paris 1896). S. E. BRONDER, *Social Justice and Church Authority. The Public Life of Archbishop Robert E. Lucey* (Philadelphia 1982). S. A. PRIVETT, *Robert E. Lucey: Evangelization and Catechesis Among Hispanic Catholics* (Ann Arbor, MI 1985). M. MCMURTREY, *Mariachi Bishop: The Life Story of Patrick Flores* (San Antonio 1987).

[B. DOYON/E. LOCH]

SAN BENEDETTO DI POLIRONE, ABBEY OF

Benedictine monastery, Diocese of Mantua in Lombardy, northern Italy. It was founded in 1003 by Theobald of Canossa at the junction of the Po and Lirone Rivers, whence its name, and it soon numbered two saints among its monks: Simeon (d. 1016) and ANSELM OF LUCCA, who in 1077 put the house under CLUNY. It developed rapidly under MATILDA OF TUSCANY, who founded the library, donating a famous gospel book; at her death she was buried in the monastery, where her body remained until 1633, when it was transferred to Rome. Because of the monastery's devotion to the cause of the papacy, it was sacked for the first time by the Emperor HENRY IV. The abbey's flourishing economy coincided with imposing schemes of reclamation and farm organization that made the monastery a center of agriculture and communal collectivism. Already in decline by 1419, the abbey was given *in commendam* (COMMENDATION) to the Gonzagas of Mantua, who the next year affiliated it with the Congregation of St. Justina of Padua. The next century saw an increase in internal strife, clashes with dependent farmers, and struggles with the lords of Mantua, all of which undermined the material and spiritual foundations of the abbey. Frequent floodings of the Po, epidemics, depredations, and molestations on the part of French, Spanish, and German armies—all combined to hasten the end. When the monastery was suppressed in 1797, parts of the library were transferred to Mantua and Milan. Of the buildings, only the church remains. It was first built about 1070, restored and further adorned by Giulio Romano in the 16th century and restored recently, and it contains fragments of mosaics from the 12th century.

Bibliography: L. H. COTTINEAU, *Répertoire topobibliographique des abbayes et prieurés,* 2 v. (Mâcon 1935–39) 2:2314–15. A. VAN DIJK, "The Customary of St. Benedict at Polirone," in *Miscellanea liturgica in honorem L. Cuniberti Mohlberg,* 2 v. (Rome 1948–49) 2:451–465. T. LECCISOTTI, "Un esempio di

Interior of Kendrick Hall Rotunda, University of San Francisco.

gestione agricola monastica nel secolo XVII: S. Benedetto di Polirone," *Benedictina* 13 (1959) 215–234.

[I. DE PICCOLI]

SAN FRANCISCO, ARCHDIOCESE OF

Metropolitan see, established July 29, 1853, the Archdiocese of San Francisco (*Sancti Francisci*) embraces the California counties of San Francisco, Marin, and San Mateo, an area of 1,012 square miles. In 2001 the archdiocese numbered some 422,500 Catholics in a total population of 1,760,000, about 24 percent. The ecclesiastic Province of San Francisco includes northern California, and the states of Nevada, Utah, and Hawaii. Its suffragan sees are the Dioceses of Sacramento (established May 28, 1886), Oakland (Feb. 21, 1962), Santa Rosa (Feb. 21, 1962), Stockton (Feb. 21, 1962), and San Jose (Jan. 27, 1981) in California; Salt Lake City in Utah (Jan. 27, 1891); Reno (March 27, 1931) and Las Vegas (March 21, 1995) in Nevada; and Honolulu, Hawaii (Sept. 10, 1941).

Early History. Explorers such as Juan Rodriguez Cabrillo (1542), Sir Francis Drake (1572), and Sebastian Vizcaino (1602–03) visited what is now northern California but actual colonization did not begin until late in the 18th century. In 1769 Gaspar de Portola's party began the actual Spanish penetration of modern California; his soldiers and the Franciscans under Junípero SERRA founded San Diego. Almost immediately Portola, Father Juan Crespi, and a detachment of soldiers marched north in an effort to find the Monterey Bay described by Cabrillo and Vizcaino. Crespi's diary gives an excellent account of this exploration in which the party, failing to recognize the open roadstead of Monterey as Cabrillo's sheltered port, continued on to discover San Francisco Bay. On Nov. 1, 1769, the expedition's scout, Sgt. José de Ortega, became the first white man to see this almost landlocked bay that Crespi described as ". . . a very large and fine harbor, such that not only all the navy of our Most Catholic Majesty, but those of all Europe could take shelter in it." From November 6 to 11 the explorers made their base of operations beneath a giant redwood (the *palo alto*) that has given its name to the adjacent university city and that can be seen from nearby St. Patrick's Archdiocesan Seminary, Menlo Park.

In 1770, when the Dominicans took over the missions in Baja California of modern Mexico, Father Francisco PALÓU, later the founder of the Mission Dolores in San Francisco, was released to join his fellow Mallorcans, Serra and Crespi, in the new Franciscan mission field of Alta California. In 1772 Crespi and Lt. Pedro Fages returned north, exploring along the east shore, or *contra costa,* of San Francisco Bay. They were the first white men to pass through the area where the large population centers of Hayward, San Leandro, Oakland, Berkeley, Richmond, Martinez, and central Contra Costa County later developed. From Mt. Diablo they discovered the great Central Valley and its rivers.

In 1774 hopes for the extensive colonization of Alta California soared when Juan Bautista Anza of Mexico opened up a land route from Sonora in Mexico to San Gabriel Mission near modern Los Angeles. It was along this new route that San Francisco's first colonists traveled. On Aug. 1, 1775, Juan Manuel Ayala successsfully brought the galleon *San Carlos* through the mile-wide entrance into San Francisco Bay; on September 29 Anza and the Franciscan Pedro Font, a Catalan, led the original San Francisco colonists from their homes in Sonora and Sinoloa on the first stage of a 1,600-mile trek to the new site at the Bay of St. Francis. The contingent began with 240 persons and reached San Gabriel on Jan. 4, 1776, with 244. At Monterey, Anza and Font left the colonists behind while they pushed on to pick the actual sites for the mission and presidio on San Francisco Bay.

In 1774 Palóu, while exploring with Rivera, had recommended establishing a mission near modern Palo Alto on San Francisquito Creek. But Anza and Font chose sites on the tip of the peninsula, with the presidio near the harbor entrance and the mission beneath the shelter of the Twin Peaks. When, on March 29, 1776, both agreed on the new mission site, they called it *Arroyo de los Dolores* because it was the Friday of Sorrows. They also recommended the establishment of a future mission in San Mateo. The actual foundation of the colony in San Francisco was made by Lt. José Joaquin Moraga, Anza's aide, and by Father Palóu, while Anza and Font left for Sonora, never to return to California.

Under their new leaders Palóu and Moraga, the San Francisco colonists reached the *Arroyo de los Dolores* on June 29, 1776. Mass was celebrated in the presidio for the first time on July 28. The presidio was formally dedicated on September 17, and the new mission chapel was blessed on October 3. Other Franciscan missions within the present limits of the archdiocese include Santa Clara and San Rafael; the first Mass at Santa Clara was celebrated by Father Tomes de la Pena on Jan. 12, 1777. Later that year California's first town, as distinguished from missions and military installations, was established by colonists from San Francisco and named San José, but the proximity of that pueblo to the mission was not a source of consolation to the missionaries of Santa Clara.

On June 11, 1797, Father Fermin Francisco de Lasuen, Serra's successor, founded Mission San José de Guadalupe, the first church in Alameda County (now the Diocese of Oakland). The first Mass at the *asistencia* of San Rafael Arcangel, which was to serve as a branch of Mission Dolores, was celebrated on Dec. 14, 1817. Subsequently San Rafael became a mission, but this first foundation north of San Francisco Bay was established too late in California's mission period to prosper. The only California mission opened during the Mexican period was Mission San Francisco Solano, founded on July 4, 1823, in Sonoma (now the Diocese of Santa Rosa). This northernmost of the missions was hampered from the start in that unsettled time of revolution and secularization.

When, on July 17, 1781, Yuma tribespeople wiped out the Spanish settlements along the Sonora border, the plan to colonize California by land expeditions was abandoned, leaving Alta California with the prospect of inadequate manpower. By 1820 there were only 3,270 non-Native Americans in all that territory. In 1811 all aid from Spain to the California establishments ceased because of the revolutionary situation in Mexico; from then until 1834 the missions sustained both their own works and that of the civil authority. In April 1822, California recognized the new regime in Mexico, and on November 22 Luis Argüello, a native Californian, was appointed governor of the territory north to Oregon and east to the Rocky Mountains. On Jan. 7, 1824, news reached Monterey that the new empire of Mexico had become a republic, and on March 26, 1825, California was officially declared a territory of the Mexican Republic. Eight years later the Mexican government decreed that the friars

should be replaced with secular priests and their possessions put under civil control. On Aug. 9, 1834, the California assembly published the law of secularization of the missions; a year later 15 of the 21 missions had been secularized as regards property. In 1836, the Mexican government recommended that a diocese of the two Californias be formed; it agreed to contribute for its support $6,000 annually, plus the right to administer the PIOUS FUND. Unfortunately, however, when the diocese was formed in 1840 this support was not given. Meanwhile, the native Californians began to resist the Mexican government, and their policies toward the missions eventually led to the complete breakdown of the system so carefully prepared by the Franciscans.

First Bishop. California's first bishop, the Zacatecan friar, Francisco Garcia Diego y Moreno, was consecrated on Oct. 4, 1840, for a see to be established at San Diego. However, when he found that town too small to support him, he moved to Santa Barbara on June 10, 1842. On June 29 he ordained Miguel Gomez there; this was the first ordination ceremony in California. Father Gonzales Rubio, who played an important role after Diego's death, moved down from Mission San José to be his secretary. At that same time President Santa Anna of Mexico took over the Pious Fund to finance his new regime, with the promise that he would pay the diocese six per cent annually on the capital. Meanwhile the new bishop was without support. Although he founded a seminary at Santa Inés Mission in 1844, the shortage of clergy remained acute. The Mission Dolores in San Francisco was without a priest from 1839 to 1846, while Gen. Mariano Vallejo in Sonoma studiously insulted the bishop and any priest who attempted to serve that area. Diego died on April 30, 1846. Four days later Pio Pico, leader of the Spanish-speaking Californians, in disregard of the restrictions of the Mexican government, began to sell the last mission properties.

American Period. A new force entered the field when war broke out between the U.S. and Mexico on May 13, 1846, and a group of Americans ran up the Bear flag in Sonoma (June 14) in revolt against the Mexican government and started the short-lived Republic of California. On July 7 the American flag was flown in Monterey and two days later it was raised in San Francisco. In 1847 the Church in California was saved from complete extinction after Gen. Stephen W. Kearney assumed charge of the state's civil government and made Monterey his capital. On March 22 he issued a proclamation that the missions of Santa Clara, San José, Santa Cruz, and Santa Ines were to remain in the hands of the priests until such time as a proper tribunal could study the cases. This strong action held off both California despoilers and Yankee squatters and paved the way for the 1854 decision of the government land commission that confirmed Abp. Joseph Alemany's claim to parts of the mission property. Kearney's military successors, Col. Richard Mason and Gen. Bennett Riley, maintained this same position and even removed Yankee squatters from mission buildings.

On Jan. 30, 1847, the name San Francisco was given to the little town then numbering 375 whites, 34 Native Americans, 40 Sandwich Islanders, and ten African Americans. In addition there was a young Spanish-speaking secular priest, Prudencio Santillan, newly appointed to the Mission Dolores. With the conclusion of the Mexican War in 1848, California was ceded to the U.S. and steps were taken to set up a constitutional government there. In November 1849 Peter Burnett, a Catholic convert from Tennessee, was elected the first civilian American governor, and San José was chosen as the first capital. During this same year over 80,000 gold seekers came into a California that had but 15,000 white inhabitants a year earlier. On Feb. 18, 1850, the new legislature created the 27 original counties of the state, and on September 9 California officially became a state.

During this period of transition the affairs of the Church in California were in the hands of the Zacatecan Franciscan, José María Gonzales Rubio, who had been named administrator of the see of the two Californias after Diego's death. He protested the rapacity of the native Californians, obtained the protection of the American military governors, kept the small seminary in Santa Ines open, assigned his few priests as effectively as he could, and sought clerical assistance from other areas. His appeal to the Congregation of the Sacred Hearts (Picpus Fathers) brought help from their missions in the Sandwich Islands and in Valparaiso, Chile. In December 1848 Father John Baptist BROUILLET, a French Canadian then serving as vicar-general of the Diocese of Walla-Walla in the Oregon Territory, arrived in San Francisco to visit those who had left the North for California's gold fields. Moved by San Francisco's grave need, he built the first Catholic church in the old Yankee settlement of Yerba Buena and named it St. Francis. With Rubio's encouragement, he wrote to Oregon for help.

Brouillet was able to remain only a year in the new settlement, but was joined by another French Canadian, Anthony Langlois, who arrived on July 19, 1849, en route to Missouri, and remained to work at St. Francis during this critical time. After Brouillet returned to his Oregon post in December 1849, he was replaced by the Jesuits Michael ACCOLTI and John NOBILI, who had come from that territory in response to Brouillet's letter. These two recruits were to play a notable role in the ecclesiastical development of northern California, including the estab-

lishment of Santa Clara University and the University of San Francisco. In 1850 Santillan left the Mission Dolores to return to Mexico, but in midyear James Croke, an Irish priest on his way from Paris to the Oregon missions, reached San Francisco just when cholera broke out. He stayed to help and was the only English-speaking priest there when Alemany, the new bishop, arrived on December 6. Subsequently Croke went on to Oregon but returned later to become the pastor of the first Catholic church in Oakland, vicar-general, founder of St. Mary's College (then in San Francisco), and manager of St. Vincent's orphanage, San Rafael.

Alemany. In May 1849, the Seventh Provincial Council of Baltimore submitted three names to Rome for bishop of the Californias, and Charles Pius Montgomery, OP, of Zanesville, Ohio, was chosen by Pius IX in November of that year. When Montgomery's refusal of this assignment reached Rome in the spring of 1850, the pope appointed Joseph Sadoc ALEMANY, U.S. provincial of the Dominicans, who was then in Rome to attend a chapter meeting. Alemany was consecrated in Rome on June 30 and returned to the U.S. with Francis VILARRASA, OP, who established the Dominican Order in California, and the Belgian Sister M. Goemare, OP, the first Catholic sister for the new state. In New York Alemany accepted for service in his new diocese John Maginnis, who had been ordained in 1823 and who subsequently became the first pastor of St. Patrick's Church, San Francisco, founder of the first parochial school in the city, and director of the orphan asylum that the Daughters of Charity staffed in 1852.

When Bishop Alemany arrived in San Francisco by ship on Dec. 6, 1850, and offered Mass in St. Francis of Assisi Church, there were an estimated 20,000 people in San Francisco. The entire state had only 24 churches open, and 22 of these were either old mission or pueblo churches. The other two were St. Francis, San Francisco, and St. Rose, Sacramento. The latter was built in 1850 by Peter Augustine Anderson, OP, who had served with the new bishop in the eastern field, but who died of cholera just before Alemany arrived in California. Anderson was succeeded shortly after his death by John Ingoldsby of Chicago, Ill., who was probably the first priest to penetrate into northern California's active mining region. For all California Alemany had 12 diocesan priests, seven aging Franciscans left from the earlier period, seven French Picpus priests from the missions of Valparaiso and the Sandwich Islands, a Dominican who had transferred from Baja California to Monterey, and a Jesuit (Accolti had returned to Oregon to become provincial). This shortage was further complicated by the fact that Alemany's jurisdiction included, until Dec. 21, 1851, Baja

California, although protests of the Mexican government made this responsibility a purely technical one.

On Feb. 4, 1851, Alemany transferred his residence from Santa Barbara to Monterey, where the royal chapel of the presidio served as his cathedral. There also Vilarrasa and Mother Goemare established their Dominican communities. Concepción Argüello received the Dominican habit from the bishop on April 11, 1851, becoming the first native Californian to enter a religious community for women. In that same year the Sisters of Notre Dame de Namur entered the state and on August 14 opened in San José the first foundation of religious women within the present confines of the Archdiocese of San Francisco. In December John Nobili established at the Santa Clara mission a school that later became the University of Santa Clara. During the year Eugene O'Connell, later bishop of Grass Valley (Sacramento after 1886), came from All Hallows in Ireland to direct the struggling diocesan seminary at Santa Ines.

On March 19, 1852, Alemany held the first synod of his new diocese; it treated of the rights of the Church to the mission properties, parish and diocesan support, and the laws of Christian marriage. Shortly thereafter Alemany left for the First Plenary Council of Baltimore. While in the East he was successful in persuading the Daughters of Charity of St. Vincent de Paul at Emmitsburg, Md., to accept a mission in San Francisco. Two of the pioneer band died of fever while crossing the Isthmus of Panama en route to California, but the remaining sisters succeeded in establishing the first convent in San Francisco. They not only took over the orphans whom Father Maginnis of St. Patrick's Church was sheltering, but also taught in the parish school there. Another recruit for the California mission was Father Hugh Gallagher, who had served as theologian to Bp. Michael O'Connor of Pittsburgh, Pa., at the council. Gallagher volunteered to work for a year in the West, but remained there for the rest of his life and played a major role in bringing the Presentation Nuns and the Sisters of Mercy to San Francisco in 1854. On Nov. 21, 1852, Eugene O'Connell was assigned to Mission Dolores, where the diocesan seminary was reestablished. On December 26 John Quinn, a seminarian from St. Patrick's, Carlow, Ireland, was ordained at St. Francis Church in the first ordination ceremony in San Francisco.

Archdiocese. On July 29, 1853, Alemany became archbishop of San Francisco, a see that included all of California from the southern boundary of the Pueblo of San José to the Oregon border, together with all the territory north of the Colorado River and west of the Rocky Mountains. At the same time Bp. Thaddeus AMAT, CM, was appointed to the Diocese of Monterey, with resi-

dence in Santa Barbara. When the archdiocese was formed it had 22 priests, 25 churches, and approximately 50,000 Catholics. Outside of San Francisco only 13 churches had resident pastors, and ten of these were in the mining regions of northern California. The three non-mining-area churches outside the see city were St. Joseph, San José; St. Rose, Sacramento; and St. Mary, Stockton. While St. Mary's Cathedral was being built for its dedication in 1854, St. Francis Church served as a temporary cathedral.

The struggling archdiocese received new help with the arrival in 1854 of five Presentation Nuns on November 13 and eight Sisters of Mercy on December 8. With the earlier arrivals, these sisters established schools, hospitals, and works of charity—despite the violence that led to the formation of the Vigilantes, the regular cholera outbreaks, the disappointments, the bigotry of the Know-Nothings, who carried the 1856 elections, and dire financial need. In 1868 the Holy Names Sisters arrived to open the first Catholic school in Oakland, and the Dominican Sisters from Holy Cross Convent, Brooklyn, N.Y., followed in 1876. In distant Utah, still part of the archdiocese in 1875, the Holy Cross Sisters reached Salt Lake City. During Alemany's episcopacy the Ursuline sisters established their school in Santa Rosa in 1880, and the Sisters of St. Joseph of Carondelet established theirs in Oakland in 1883. The first brothers arrived in 1868 when the devoted sons of St. John Baptist de la Salle took over St. Mary's College, which had been operated by diocesan priests since 1863. In 1884 the Brothers of Mary reached Stockton.

The sprawling archdiocese was first divided when the Vicariate of Marysville was formed in 1861 to include all of California north of the 39th parallel. Although the Diocese of Sacramento eventually developed from the Marysville vicariate, the archdiocese retained Sacramento, Yolo, El Dorado, Amador, Calaveras, Tuolumne, Alpine, Mono, and Mariposa counties until 1886. Alemany strengthened Church administration through the diocesan synod of 1862 and the provincial councils of 1874 and 1882. In 1877 the *Monitor,* which had been founded in 1858, was made the official paper of all the dioceses in the Province of San Francisco. In 1872, under the direction of Msgr. John J. Prendergast, vicar-general of the archdiocese between 1874 and 1914, Elizabeth Armer, foundress of the Holy Family Sisters, began her work with neglected children. In 1878, in response to Alemany's request, Bp. William Elder of Natchez, Miss., was appointed to aid Alemany, but an outbreak of yellow fever in Mississippi forced him to ask for a delay. In 1880 he was sent as coadjutor to Cincinnati, Ohio, and a disappointed Alemany renewed his appeal for assistance. In 1883 Patrick W. RIORDAN of St. James Church, Chicago, was named coadjutor of the San Francisco archdiocese; he was consecrated on September 16.

Riordan. Leo XIII accepted Alemany's resignation on March 27, 1884, but the act did not become effective until December 28. In the interval the archbishop attended the Third Plenary Council of Baltimore, where he served as chairman of the commission of bishops to report on the expediency of a uniform catechism (the famous Baltimore Catechism). When, on Dec. 28, 1884, Riordan succeeded to the see, there was a Catholic population of 120,000, served by 156 priests in 133 churches and chapels. Two years later the next territorial change in the Archdiocese of San Francisco took place when the Diocese of Grass Valley, formerly the Vicariate of Marysville, was changed to the Diocese of Sacramento. At this time certain counties south of the 39th parallel, including Sacramento and Yolo, were transferred to the new see. Another change took place when the Vicariate Apostolic of Utah was formed on Jan, 25, 1887.

During Riordan's episcopacy, the solid foundations of he archdiocese were further strengthened despite the impact of the Spanish-American War and the tragic 1906 earthquake and fire. More religious communities of men and women arrived to share in the work of the pioneers. The new St. Mary's Cathedral was solemnly dedicated on Jan. 11, 1891. In 1892 the *Monitor* was taken over by the archdiocese as owner and publisher. On Sept. 20, 1898, St. Patrick's Seminary, Menlo Park, was opened with the Sulpician priests in charge. Encouraged by the Council of Baltimore, parochial schools began to increase rapidly. Prior to this period all but a handful of schools had been academies or community operated, but toward the end of the 19th century the parish school became dominant. Riordan established a board of diocesan education and in 1894 introduced the annual convention of teaching orders. Father Peter C. YORKE (1864–1925) was active at this time not only in arranging programs but also in writing his widely used textbooks of religion (1896). In 1899 John J. Cantwell, later archbishop of Los Angeles, began the Newman Club for Catholic students at the University of California at Berkeley.

Public matters also claimed the attention of Archbishop Riordan. In 1894 he named Yorke as editor of the *Monitor,* with a commission to combat the wave of bigotry stirred up by the AMERICAN PROTECTIVE ASSOCIATION. In 1900 Riordan led a successful campaign to free the churches in California from the burden of state taxation, and two years later he represented the hierarchy of California before the International Court at The Hague in their successful prosecution of justice in the Pious Fund case. By 1903, when the archdiocese was celebrating its 50th year, there were 250,000 Catholics, in contrast to the

40,000 throughout all northern California in 1853. They were served by 271 priests in 148 churches and missions. Riordan's request for a coadjutor was answered on March 27, 1903, when George Montgomery, Bishop of Monterey-Los Angeles, was appointed titular archbishop of Osimo and coadjutor with right of succession.

On April 18, 1906, while Riordan was in the East, northern California was struck by a severe earthquake that was followed in San Francisco by a calamitous fire. Twelve parishes, with all their facilities, were wiped out by the fire, along with St. Mary's and Mary's Help Hospitals, two colleges and three academies, three day homes for children, the home for the aged poor, and the Youths' Directory for homeless boys. In the unburned part of the city, two other churches were destroyed and three were damaged, while elsewhere in the diocese a number of buildings, including the new St. Patrick's Seminary, were severely shaken. During this disaster over 300,000 people left the city. Oakland, which had about 66,000 people in 1900, grew to more than 276,000 in 1907. Although San Francisco rapidly rebuilt after this tragedy, the strain was too much for Montgomery, who died on Jan. 10, 1907, and Riordan again petitioned Rome for a coadjutor. Rome did not believe that the time was opportune for a coadjutor but on Dec. 24, 1908, named Denis J. O'Connell, former rector of the North American College in Rome and of The Catholic University of America, Washington, D.C., as auxiliary to Riordan. When, on Jan. 16, 1912, O'Connell was transferred to the Diocese of Richmond, Va., the archbishop again appealed for a coadjutor; on Oct. 22, 1912, Edward J. HANNA of Rochester, N.Y., was appointed titular bishop of Titopolis and auxiliary of San Francisco.

Hanna. Riordan's death on Dec. 27, 1914, ended his 31-year episcopacy and Hanna succeeded to the see. He was installed on July 28, 1915, as third ordinary by Abp. John Bonzano, apostolic delegate. He gave immediate attention to diocesan administration, appointing John J. Cantwell as his vicar-general; establishing a matrimonial court under the direction of the eminent canonist Henri Ayrinhac, SS; and strengthening Catholic education by the appointment of Rev. Ralph Hunt as first superintendent of diocesan schools (1915). The archbishop also directed the formation of a teachers' scholastic council to advise about texts and courses of study (1916) and of a teachers' institute (1916); he appealed for, and received, city health services in the schools (1916). Moreover, he sponsored a one-week summer school (1916), the first four-week summer school in the archdiocese (1918), the national convention of the Catholic Education Association (1918), and the opening of new schools on all levels.

Hanna's prominent role in the National Catholic War Council of the bishops during World War I resulted in his election as the first chairman of the administrative council of the postwar National Catholic Welfare Conference. He also took a leading part in the effort to lift the burden of taxation from orphanages (1920), cemeteries (1926), and nonprofit elementary and secondary schools (1933). Through Hanna's civic activities the Church achieved a position in public life that did much to offset the unfortunate efforts of the Ku Klux Klan and other misguided groups of the post-World War I period. During this era of war, boom, and depression, the main chapel of St. Patrick's Seminary was completed (1918); St. Joseph's College, Mountain View, the archdiocesan minor seminary, was opened (1924); the College of Notre Dame was transferred from San José to Belmont (1923); St. Mary's College moved its site from Oakland to Contra Costa County (1928); San Francisco College for Women opened at the Lone Mountain location (1930); the Convent of the Good Shepherd came into being (1932); and the Catholic Youth Organization was established (1933). Interest in the foreign-born resulted in the formation of the Italian Catholic Federation (1924), St. Mary's Chinese School (1921), and Morning Star Japanese School (1930). In 1922 the creation of the Diocese of Monterey-Fresno slightly altered the southern boundary of the archdiocese; the new line followed existing counties.

Mitty. To assist him in meeting the demands of the growing archdiocese, Hanna received as his coadjutor, on Jan. 29, 1932, John J. MITTY, who had been appointed bishop of Salt Lake City, Utah, on June 21, 1926, while serving as pastor of St. Luke's Church, New York City. Hanna resigned on March 2, 1935, and died in Rome on July 10, 1944. Mitty, after succeeding to the see on March 2, 1935, presided over the second diocesan synod (1936), which produced a complete set of statutes governing the activities of the various departments in the archdiocese. In June 1936 Los Angeles, a suffragan of San Francisco, was raised to an archdiocese, and California became the first state with two distinct ecclesiastical provinces. During World War II, when San Francisco became the major port of embarkation to the Pacific theater of war, the resources of the archdiocese were generously used to assist military personnel and their dependents; 35 diocesan priests and 54 religious from the archdiocese served in the chaplain corps.

In the postwar period the spectacular growth of the Far West was reflected in the increase of population in the archdiocese. It led to an extension of social services, youth activities, the Confraternity of Christian Doctrine (CCD), and specialized Catholic Action to an unprecedented degree. New elementary schools and new high schools were opened, and each of the seven Catholic four-year colleges in the archdiocese expanded both in buildings and in program. In 1952 and 1958 campaigns

to free private, nonprofit schools from the burden of taxation were vigorously and successfully prosecuted in the archdiocese. In 1955 a new chancery building, housing the archbishop's office, the diocesan curia, the *Monitor,* the department of education, and the Confraternity of Christian Doctrine, was constructed adjacent to the Mission Dolores. Wider participation in Catholic Action characterized these years, making possible the Family Rosary Crusade, which culminated in a public rally attended by an estimated 500,000 people in the polo field of Golden Gate Park on Oct. 7, 1961. Eight days after this great public prayer, Archbishop Mitty died at St. Patrick's Seminary, Menlo Park.

McGucken. On Feb. 19, 1962, Joseph T. McGucken, Bishop of Sacramento, was appointed fifth archbishop of San Francisco, and his solemn installation in St. Mary's Cathedral took place on April 3, 1962. McGucken, born in Los Angeles and a former student at St. Patrick's Seminary, Menlo Park, and at the North American College, Rome, was the first native Californian to be named to the see. With his appointment Rome announced also the formation of the three dioceses of Oakland, Santa Rosa, and Stockton thus downsizing the territory, population, and the number of institutions in the San Francisco Archdiocese. The destruction of St. Mary's Cathedral by fire, Sept. 7, 1962, marred the first year of McGucken's episcopacy. The loss spurred a generous response when the archbishop launched a successful building drive to replace the cathedral despite some protests, construct new high schools and a home for the aged, and expand the archdiocesan seminary. McGucken played an active role in Vatican Council II, particularly as episcopal moderator of the American press panel. Even while Vatican II was still in session, he established social action committees in every parish, and took steps to encourage the renewal called for by the council. In 1972, priests of the archdiocese threatened a strike in the face of McGucken's opposition, and successfully agitated for a priest association.

When McGucken retired in 1977, the Most Reverend John R. Quinn, Archbishop of Oklahoma City was transferred to San Francisco as his successor. Quinn's tenure oversaw the increasing ethnic-cultural diversification of the archdiocese, with huge influxes of Mexican migrant laborers and their families, Vietnamese refugees and other Asian immigrants. A high point of his episcopacy was Pope John Paul II's visit to San Francisco in 1987. At the same time, Quinn had to grapple with worsening archdiocesan finances. In response, he proposed a new archdiocesan pastoral plan, reorganized archdiocesan structures, initiated opportunities for lay ministries, established innovative youth and other service and outreach programs, and set up a school for training laity for leadership and ministry roles. His attempts to reign in the growing archdiocesan deficit generated much controversy when he attempted to close ten inner-city parishes and consolidate their dwindling congregations, including the city's oldest parish church, St. Francis.

When Quinn submitted his resignation in 1995, he was succeeded by the Most Reverend William J. Levada. Levada was Archbishop of Portland, Oregon from 1983 to 1995, when he was transferred to San Francisco as Co-adjutor Archbishop to Quinn.

Catholic higher institutions of learning in the Archdiocese of San Francisco include the Jesuit-run University of San Francisco, the College of Notre Dame in Belmont (sponsored by the Sisters of Notre Dame de Namur), and the Dominican College of San Rafael (sponsored by the Dominican Sisters). Of these, the University of San Francisco is the oldest and largest, established 1855 as St. Ignatius College for men. Upon attaining university status in 1930, it was renamed University of San Francisco. It became coeducational in 1964.

Bibliography: Archdiocesan Archives, San Francisco, including the diary of Bishop Diego y Moreno, continued by Archbishop Alemany. Archives, University of Santa Clara, including the diary of Father Langlois. Spanish and Mexican archives in the University of California. The California Historical Society papers. Dominicana (St. Dominic's Priory, San Francisco) files. J. A. BERGER, *The Franciscan Missions of California* (Garden City, N.Y. 1948). J. CRESPI, *Fray Juan Crespi, Missionary Explorer on the Pacific Coast, 1769–1774,* ed. H. E. BOLTON (Berkeley 1927). P. FONT, *Font's Complete Diary: A Chronicle of the Founding of San Francisco,* tr. and ed. H. E. BOLTON (Berkeley 1933). B. C. CRONIN, *Father Yorke and the Labor Movement in San Francisco, 1900–1910* (Washington 1944). F. PALÓU, *Life of Fray Junípero Serra,* tr. and annot. M. J. GEIGER (Washington 1955). M. J. GEIGER, *The Life and Times of Fray Junípero Serra,* 2 v. (Washington 1959). F. J. WEBER, *A Biographical Sketch of the Right Reverend Francisco Garcia Diego y Moreno* (Los Angeles 1961); J. BURNS *A History of the Archdiocese of San Francisco* 3 v. (Strasbourg, N.D.); J. B. MCGLOIN *California's First Archbishop: The Life of Joseph Sadoc Alemany, O.P.* (New York 1966); H. L. WALSH *Hallowed Were the Gold Dust Trails: The Story of Pioneer Priests of Northern California* (Santa Clara 1946); J. B. MCGLOIN *Jesuits by the Golden Gate* (San Francisco, 1972); J. P. GAFFEY *Citizen of No Mean City, Archbishop Patrick Riordan of San Francisco, 1841–1914* (Consortium 1976); J. BRUSHER *Consecrated Thunderbolt: A Life of Father Peter C. Yorke of San Francisco* (Hawthorne, N.J. 1973); R. GRIBBLE *Catholicism and the San Francisco Labor Movement 1896–1921* (San Francisco 1993); A. BACCARI et al, *Saints Peter and Paul Church: The Chronicles of the 'Italian Cathedral of the West'* (San Francisco 1985); *San Francisco Monitor* Special Centennial Issue, (September 1953); J. P. GAFFEY *Men of Menlo: Transformation of an American Seminary* (Washington, D.C. 1992); P. T. CONMY and J. M. BURNS "The Mexican Catholic Community in California," in J. DOLAN and G. HINOJOSA, eds., *Mexican Americans and the Catholic Church, 1900–1965* (Notre Dame 1994).

[J. T. FOUDY/EDS.]

SAN FRUTTUOSO (CAPODIMONTE), ABBEY OF

Ancient BENEDICTINE monastery in the picturesque village of Capodimonte, five miles from Camogli in the province and Archdiocese of Genoa, Italy; it lies in a deep, narrow inlet on the southwest coast of Portofino promontory (Latin, *S. Fructuosi*). It was founded at the end of the 10th century and enriched with benefices by the empress, (St.) Adelaide of Burgundy, Queen of Italy. After a period of splendor in the 13th century it later decayed; and in 1550 Pope Julius III converted it into a secular abbey, giving its patronage to the Doria family, in whose possession it still remains. The abbey church with its three aisles is in the pure Lombard style but shows touches of Byzantine and some Provençal influence. The façade and part of the church were carried away by a flood in 1928. There are Roman marble remains in the cloister. Members of the Doria family were buried under the monastery from 1275 to 1305. The adjoining 13th-century palace was restored in 1934.

Bibliography: P. F. KEHR, *Regesta Pontificum Romanorum. Italia Pontificia,* 8 v. (Berlin 1906–35) 6.2:346–347. A. BUSIRI, *Abbadia di S. Fruttuoso nella Liguria . . .* (Genoa 1886). "L'abbazia di S. Fruttuoso di Capodimonte," *Rivista storica benedettina* 10 (1915) 475–476.

[A. OLIVIERI]

SAN GALGANO, ABBEY OF

Former Cistercian abbey on Monte Siepi, near Siena, in Tuscany, Italy. CISTERCIAN monks from Casamari built a small church and hermitage there at the site of the tomb of St. Galgano (d. *c.* 1181) in 1185. In 1206 a group of Cistercians arrived from CLAIRVAUX, and Pope Innocent III confirmed the abbey. Between 1224 and 1288 the monks constructed a large church and abbey at the foot of the hills. Under episcopal, aristocratic, and civil patronage it grew rapidly in wealth and influence. During the 13th century SIENA sought and received aid from these Cistercians in financial and architectural affairs. Signs of decay were apparent in the 14th century, and the abbey lands were plundered by the Company of Adventurers. The 15th century was a period of revival, but the old splendor never returned. In 1509 Pope Julius II gave the abbey in COMMENDATION. Urban VIII reduced its status as an abbey in 1632, and it was secularized in 1652 when the Cistercians withdrew. The ruins show the style of French Cistercian architecture.

Bibliography: A. CANESTRELLI, *L'Abbazia di San Galgano* (Florence 1896). F. SCHEVILL, "San Galgano—A Cistercian Abbey," *American Historical Review* 14 (1908–09) 22–30. P. TOESCA, *Storia dell'arte italiana nel medioevo,* 2 v. (Turin 1927).

[M. B. MORRIS]

SAN GIOVANNI IN FIORE, ABBEY OF

Referred to also as Flore or La Fioreale, former Florian monastery on the eastern slopes of the Sila not far from Cosenza, the capital of Calabria, Italy. It was founded in 1189 by JOACHIM OF FIORE, a Cistercian mystic and a native of Celico near Cosenza, who drew up its constitutions, which were then approved by Pope Celestine III (1196). The monks were called FLORIANS and were an independent order, not affiliated with CITEAUX. In 1470 the regular abbots were replaced by commendatory abbots (*see* COMMENDATION), and the order showed signs of decline. In 1505 the abbey of Fiore and many of its affiliated monasteries were united to the CISTERCIANS. The monastery was suppressed in 1806. Today only meager ruins remain.

Bibliography: L. JANAUSCHEK, *Origines Cistercienses,* v.1 (Vienna 1877). P. FOURNIER, "Joachim de Flore et le *Liber de vera philosophia,*" *Revue d'histoire et de littérature religieuses* 4 (1899) 37–66. F. RUSSO, *Gioacchino da Fiore e le fondazioni florensi in Calabria* (Naples 1959). G. PENCO, *Storia del monachesimo in Italia* (Rome 1961).

[M. B. MORRIS]

SAN JOSÉ DE LA PAZ, MARÍA ANTONIA

The "Beata de los Ejercicios" who founded Argentine retreat houses based on the Jesuit Spiritual Exercises; b. Santiago del Estero, Argentina, 1730; d. Buenos Aires, March 7, 1799. Nothing is known of her early life except that she lived as a *beata* in her native city and under the spiritual care of the Jesuits came to appreciate the closed retreat as a means of personal sanctification. Even though she was of a retiring, shy disposition and the circumstances of the times did not favor any work so intimately identified with the Jesuits, after their expulsion in 1767 María Antonia felt impelled to propagate this idea. At first the authorities, both ecclesiastical and lay, were hostile to her plans and the people called her a witch, probably because she wore as an outer garment a Jesuit mantle given her by one of the departing fathers. Her tact and firmness finally won over even such antagonists as Bp. Sebastian Malvar of Buenos Aires and Viceroy Vértiz. In time she founded houses for closed retreats in Santiago del Estero, Salta, Jujuy, Córdoba, Montevideo, and finally in 1779 in Buenos Aires. In the last house from 1779 to 1784 more than 30,000 people, including the former viceroy of Peru, Manuel de Guirior, and his wife, made the ten-day retreat. These were not endowed retreat houses in the colonial pattern. Maria Antonia administered them, contacted the priests to give the retreats, and supported them from alms and offerings of the retreatants. Her work survived her death and the numerous revolutions of the early 19th century.

Bibliography: P. LETURIA, "Ejercicios cerrados en la América Española," *Manresa* 6 (1930) 272–283.

[A. S. TIBESAR]

SAN JUAN, CATARINA DE

"La china poblana "; b. a native of the kingdom of Mogor in China, *c.* 1613; d. Puebla, Mexico, Jan. 5, 1688. Beautiful and from a well-to-do family, she was called Mirra among her own people. Corsairs captured her to sell as a slave and brought her to Mexico around 1625. In Puebla she was adopted by Don Miguel de Sosa and Doña Margarita de Chávez, a pious couple who had no children. Here she acquired the name "la china poblana." She lived with them, devoted to housework, until they died. She then went to the household of a worthy priest, Pedro Suárez. After this she entered into a strange marriage with a Chinese named Domingo Suárez, only to take care of him; she retained her virginity. When she was widowed, she went to live in the poorest room of a neighboring house; there she died at the age of about 75. She was buried in the sanctuary of the Jesuit church. Because of her great charity, her simplicity, and modesty, she earned the reputation of a saint. According to her two biographers, who were also her confessors, she had frequent trances and visions in which she spoke with God. The term "china poblana," which was very fitting for Catarina de San Juan, has taken on a quite different meaning with the passage of time: now it refers to the typical, showy costume of the partner of the Mexican cowboy in one of Mexico's best known folk dances, the "jarabe tapatío."

Bibliography: A. RAMOS, *Prodigios de la omnipotencia y milagros de la gracia en la vida de la venerable sierva de Dios Catarina de San Juan* (3 v. Puebla 1689; Mexico City 1960, 1962). J. DEL CASTILLO GRAJEDA, *Compendio de la vida y virtudes de la venerable Catarina de San Juan* (Puebla 1692; 2d ed. Mexico City 1946).

[A. JUNCO]

SAN MARCOS, MAIN NATIONAL UNIVERSITY OF

An autonomous institution of higher learning in Lima, Peru, that traces its origin to the 16th century.

Early Development. Founded by royal decree issued in Valladolid, Spain, by Charles V in 1551, San Marcos is considered the oldest University in the New

World, although this primacy, contested by the University of Mexico, also founded in 1551, has often been an interesting topic of inter-American debate. This is understandable since the establishment of an institution of higher learning in Spanish colonial America usually involved three acts: the sanction of the Church, the granting of a royal charter, and the actual inauguration of studies, any one of which could be considered the founding date. The University of San Marcos bases its claim to priority on the royal decree's date of issuance, May 12, 1551, in comparison with that of Mexico's royal decree, September 21, 1551 [*Recopilacion de las Leyes de Indias* (Madrid 1756) Ley I, 110].

To reinforce its claim, the university points to a center of learning established in Cuzco in 1548 by Dominicans, whose provincial, Fra Tomás de SAN MARTÍN, in 1549 went to Spain to petition the Spanish crown for permission to establish in Lima a similar center of learning to be modeled on the University of Salamanca. Appointed first bishop of Charcas, Spain, Fra Tomás did not return to Peru but sent back the royal cedula to Lima, where the university had opened at the Dominican convent of San Rosario in 1553. Fra Tomás died in 1554 leaving his Dominican confreres to continue the work he had initiated.

The university's early years under Dominican administration were marked by hardship and poverty for want of sufficient financial aid from the viceroy of Peru, the Marqués del Canete, who in 1557 had allotted the university the meager sum of 400 pesos for its upkeep. From 1553 to 1571, known as the monastic period, emphasis was placed on theology, arts, and grammar. The bull of Pius V, issued in July 1571, terminated this period and confirmed the 1553 royal decree that granted the university the same privileges and immunities enjoyed by the University of Salamanca. On December 30 of the same year, however, Philip II ordered the suspension of Dominican control and the secularization of the institution. The viceroy, Don Francisco de TOLEDO, acting on the unusual powers granted him by the king, proceeded to execute the orders, taking immediate steps to elect a lay rector before the king had signed the decree.

Development. Since classes continued to function within the monastery, the change of administration to lay control gave rise to internal strife and unrest, and in 1574 the professors and students withdrew to a new and independent center. That same year saw the establishment of the Faculty of Law and the adoption by vote of the institution's official title: The Royal and Pontifical University of San Marcos of Lima.

From then on the university began a new era of progress, financially assisted by the viceroy, who not only provided funds and created endowments that enabled the institution to establish Faculties of Arts, Theology, Sacred Scripture, Canon Law, and Medicine, and to attract cultured and learned professors to chair them, but also drew up constitutions that remained in force throughout the colonial period until the first years of the republic (1821).

During the colonial period, San Marcos, although a state institution, enjoyed considerable autonomy and carefully guarded its privilege to elect the rector and hold public examinations for the appointment of professors by staff vote to vacant chairs. The university also exerted direct influence on the establishment of other institutions of higher learning in Latin America: the University of Guatemala (1562), founded by a San Marcos alumnus; the College of St. Rose of Lima, which later became the University of Venezuela (1696); the University of Cordoba, Argentina (1613); and St. Francis Xavier of Chuquisaca, Bolivia (1621).

The early years of San Marcos were strongly influenced by the traditional scholasticism; in the late 18th century it fell under the spell of the ENLIGHTENMENT, and in the first decades of the 19th century, stirred by the pervading spirit of freedom, the university allied itself with the movement for independence. On July 30, 1822, shortly after José de San Martín had proclaimed Peru's independence, professors and students at San Marcos pledged their loyalty to the new political regime and on Jan. 18, 1822, received San Martín at the university. A few years later, on June 3, 1826, San Marcos solemnly received Simón Bolívar, the Liberator.

Bibliography: M. V. VILLARÁN, *La universidad de San Marcos: Los orígenes* (Lima 1938). D. RUBIO, ed., *La universidad de San Marcos durante la colonización española* (Madrid 1933). J. T. LANNING, *Academic Culture in the Spanish Colonies* (New York 1940). *International Handbook of Universities,* ed. H. M. R. KEYES (2d ed. Paris 1962) 484.

[M. B. MURPHY]

SAN MARINO, THE CATHOLIC CHURCH IN

The Republic of San Marino, independent since the 9th century at least, is one of the smallest and oldest sovereign states in the world. It forms a mountainous enclave entirely surrounded by Italy, and is located near the Adriatic Sea between Emilia and the Marches. Building stone is the country's major natural resource; agricultural products include wheat, grapes, corn, olives and livestock.

Politics and culture in San Marino are closely aligned with those of Italy. Governing power is in the

Capital: San Marino.
Size: 24 sq. miles.
Population: 26,940 in 2000.
Languages: Italian.
Religions: 25,945 Catholics (96%), 300 Muslims (1%), 600 Protestants (2%), 95 Baha'i (.3%).
Diocese: San Marino, suffragan to Ravenna-Cervia, Italy. While the region maintains a minister plenipotentiary at the Holy See, there is no official papal diplomatic representative in San Marino.

hands of two Capitani reggenti, elected for six-month terms, and a Congresso di Stato. Legislative authority resides in the Consiglio Grande e Generale with 60 elected members. Administratively the country is divided into nine *castelli,* or towns. The state has its own coinage and postal system, maintains diplomatic relations with the principal nations and has treaties of friendship and economic agreements with Italy. Agriculture, cattle raising and tourism are the main industries of the Sammarinese, while the sale of postage stamps provides the government's main income. About one-fifth of the inhabitants dwell in the capital, San Marino, located near the summit of Mt. Titano, the region's highest point.

History. According to a 9th- and 10th-century legend, the republic owes its origin to St. Marinus, a Christian stonecutter from the island of Arbe who went there with some companions during Diocletian's persecution, seeking refuge and a place of prayer, after being given Mt. Titano by Felicitas, a wealthy lady from Rimini whom he had converted. Marinus, it is said, received the diaconate from the bishop of Rimini and erected a small monastery, which formed the nucleus of the country's capital. Its official date· of inception was celebrated as Sept. 3, 301. St. Marinus was supposed to have bequeathed this territory to his ''faithful followers'' with the understanding that it remain independent of all outside civil and ecclesiastical authorities. Its inaccessibility and poverty preserved its independence during the barbarian invasions. There is mention of a Castellum Marini as early as 755. San Marino became, sometime after the 11th century, a medieval commune, like northern Italian cities. Its oldest preserved statutes date from 1263. The Pope recognized its independence in 1291. From the 14th to the 16th centuries San Marino became involved in the turbulent political life of the peninsula, but resisted all efforts to incorporate it into the STATES OF THE CHURCH. The region promulgated its first constitution in October of 1600, and when URBAN VIII annexed the Duchy of Urbino in 1631, he solemnly reconfirmed San Marino's independence. Succeeding popes frequently defended this liberty. Cardinal Giulio ALBERONI, legate to Romangna,

occupied the republic in 1739, but the citizenry's stout resistance and diplomatic efforts led Clement XII soon to withdraw his claims and sign a treaty of perpetual friendship.

Italy guaranteed San Marino's independence and signed a treaty of friendship with the enclave in 1862; these agreements were reaffirmed in 1948. Throughout the 20th century San Marino's political course mirrored that of Italy: It had a fascist government in the 1930s that was replaced in 1943 by Communists and left-wing Socialist coalition. By 1960 Christian and Social Democrats had gained control. While the republic did not possess its own civil code of laws, in 1878 it promulgated a penal code. All other basic laws continued to derive from its 16th-century constitution, which was based on Roman and canon law. Canon law regulated almost all relations between Church and State, including matrimonial questions, until the 1930s when secularizing influences appeared. A 1939 treaty with Italy permitted Italians to obtain marriage annulments in San Marino that were considered valid in Italy. Civil marriages were recognized beginning in 1952. In 1999, in response to charges that it violated Article 9 of the European Convention, San Marino's Parliamentary oath was altered to exclude reference to the Holy Gospels. However, the traditional oath remained for other offices not under the sway of the European Court. While the Catholic Church was not proclaimed the state religion, it received an allocation of income tax monies. Although there were no Catholic schools, Catholic instruction was provided in all state schools.

San Marino's only remaining medieval monument is the 13th-century church of St. Francis, which underwent several alterations over the centuries, including a transformation of its interior in the 18th century. A much larger basilica in neoclassical style, completed in 1838, replaced the ancient church in the highest part of the town, dedicated to St. Marinus. The small nearby chapel of St. Peter, erected by St. Marinus himself according to tradition, was completely transformed. By 2000 there were 13 parishes tended by 9 diocesan and 19 religious priests. Other religious included approximately two brothers and 23 sisters.

Bibliography: O. GUERRIERI, *La Repubblica di San Marino* (Florence 1939). P. AEBISCHER, *Essai sur l'histoire de St. Marin des origines à l'an mille* (San Marino 1962).

[F. SOTTOCORNOLA/EDS.]

SAN MARTÍN, TOMÁS DE

Spanish Dominican, considered the founder of the oldest university in America; b. Palencia (or Córdoba), Spain, March 7, 1482; d. Lima, Peru, March 1554. He was professed in the convent of San Pablo at Córdoba in 1498 and graduated in arts and theology from Santo Tomás in Seville. He went to America in 1525 and returned to Spain four years later. Once again, in 1538, he visited the New World, this time participating in the important events of the establishment and early development of the Peruvian viceroyalty. He contributed toward the pacification of the country during the conqueror's struggles; and in order to favor the Indians, whom he strongly defended, he opposed the perpetuation of the *encomiendas*. He corresponded with B. de LAS CASAS about moral problems of the conquest and provided information on the situation of the Peruvian Indians. San Martín was the first provincial of the Dominican Order in Peru and promoted the rapid expansion of the order there. He founded numerous *doctrinas* and schools for the Indians that were operated by the members of his order. In 1548, in the Dominican convent in Lima, he started a curriculum that shortly afterward developed into a university. To obtain the charter for its foundation, he was commissioned by the cabildo of Lima to go to Germany. He also negotiated with the Council of the Indies the establishment of schools for Creoles, mestizos, and Indians in the principal cities of the viceroyalty. In 1552 he was appointed first bishop of Charcas. He was consecrated in Spain but died before he could occupy his see.

Bibliography: L. A. EGUIGUREN, *El fundador de la Universidad de San Marcos* (Lima 1911), with bibliog. and portrait.

[E. T. BARTRA]

SAN MARTINO AL MONTE CIMINO, ABBEY OF

An abbey *nullius* founded in the 13th century, four miles from Viterbo, Italy, in a fine position 1,840 feet above sea level on the northwest slopes of the Cimini mountains. Around the abbey grew a village of the same name. A church dedicated to St. Martin, a dependency of the Abbey of FARFA, is known to have existed on the spot from 838. About 1045 BENEDICTINES from Farfa rebuilt the church; a century later, however, the monastery had so decayed that Pope Eugene III assigned it to the CISTERCIANS of Saint-Sulpice near Belley (Savoy). As even this measure had not succeeded in restoring it to prosperity, Pope Innocent III ordered it transferred to the Cistercians of PONTIGNY, whose rule was stricter, and at the same time granted them special privileges (1207). To this latter period belongs the present church, built under Abbot Pietro and consecrated *c.* 1230. After a period of splendor the Abbey was placed *in commendam* (*see* COMMENDATION) in 1378, and in 1645 was given by Pope Innocent X to the patronage of the Pamphili family, who built a baronial residence beside the church, demolishing and transforming a large part of the monastic buildings and overlaying the church with baroque ornamentation. Restoration work between 1911 and 1915 removed the baroque additions, revealing the original structure. Since May 2, 1936, the bishop of Viterbo has held the joint title of abbot of San Martino al Monte Cimino.

Bibliography: P. EGIDI, "L'abbazia di S. Martino sul Monte Cimino," *Rivista storica benedettina* 1 (1906) 579–590; 2 (1907) 161–199, 481–552. A. MUÑOZ, "Monumenti di architettura gotica nel Lazio," *Vita d'arte* (September 1911) 75–103. P. TOESCA, *Storia dell'arte italiana nel medioevo*, 2 v. (Turin 1927). L. H. COTTINEAU, *Répertoire topobibliographique des abbayes et prieurés*, 2 v. (Mâcon 1935–39) 2:2798.

[S. OLIVIERI]

SAN MIGUEL, ANDRÉS DE

Carmelite architect; b. Medinasidonia, Spain, 1577; d. Salvatierra, 1644. He studied mathematics in Seville.

In 1594 he sailed for the Indies. When he was shipwrecked near Florida, he promised to become a Carmelite religious if he was saved. He kept his promise and entered the order as a lay brother in Puebla in 1598. He specialized in architecture and built the first and most important monasteries of his order in New Spain: Puebla (the chapels were later added to the church); Desierto de los Leones (which was completely rebuilt in 1722); Salvatierra (now changed); Querétaro; Morelia; and San Angel, near Mexico City. He also built a bridge over the Lerma River between Mexico and Toluca. San Miguel established the style of Carmelite architecture: long, narrow churches completed by an apse; reliquary chapels at the sides; belfries instead of towers; a small cloister next to the church; and closed courtyards for the cells. In the library at Austin, Texas, is preserved his manuscript on mathematics and architecture, which contains interesting drawings of wood floors and ceilings in the Mudejar style, in which he was an expert. He worked also on the drainage of the valley of Mexico and was correct in his criticisms of the drainage system devised by Enrico Martínez.

[F. DE LA MAZA]

SAN PIETRO IN BREME, ABBEY OF

A Benedictine foundation in the Diocese of Pavia, between the Po and Ticino Rivers in Lombardy, northern Italy. After the destruction of the Abbey of Novalesa at the beginning of the 10th century, the dispersed community was offered refuge at Breme in Lomellina by Adalbert, Marquis of Ivrea. The monastery established there was thenceforth considered the heir of Novalesa, and it was in the Abbey of San Pietro that the famous *Chronicon Novaliciense* was written. Breme had holdings in Montferrat, in Piedmont, and in Lombardy but had to wage a protracted campaign to maintain independence. In 950 it had been put under the dominion of Arduin of Susa; in 1026 the Emperor CONRAD II deposed Abbot Odilo and gave the monastery to Alberic, Bishop of Como. In 1093 it became a dependency of Pavia; in 1164, a dependency of the Marquess of Montferrat; and finally, in 1210 it attained independence. In 1530 the abbey, by then in a state of frightful decay, was entrusted to the bishop of Vigevano, and 13 years later the remaining monks were removed and the monastery ceded to the Olivetan monks of Milan, who held it until its suppression and the confiscation of its possessions decreed by Victor Emmanuel I in 1785; by then the number of monks had been reduced to only seven. Finally, under NAPOLEON I the church was destroyed and the other buildings alienated. Apart from the anonymous author of the above-

mentioned *Chronicon,* mention should be made of one other distinguished monk of this abbey, the abbot Adraldus, a friend of PETER DAMIAN, who went on to become bishop of CHARTRES from 1070 to 1075.

Bibliography: L. H. COTTINEAU, *Répertoire topobibliographique des abbayes et prieurés,* 2 v. (Mâcon 1935–39) 1:485–486. L. C. BOLLEA, *Cartario della Abbazia* (Biblioteca della Società storica subalpina 127; Turin 1933). A. CLERVAL, *Dictionnaire d'histoire et de géographie ecclésiastiques,* ed. A. BAUDRILLART (Paris 1912–) 1:594. M. MANITIUS, *Geschichte der lateinischen Literatur des Mittelalters,* 3 v. (Munich 1911–31) 2:294–99.

[I. DE PICCOLI]

SAN SALVATORE (MAGGIORE), ABBEY OF

Former Benedictine monastery in the Diocese of Rieti, about 35 miles north of Rome in central Italy. Its foundation goes back to 735, and during the high Middle Ages the abbey was an important monastic center of great moral repute. In the first part of the 9th century, because of its strict monastic observance and its numerous dependencies, the abbey reached its zenith in both material and spiritual grandeur. There are, however, no descriptions of the buildings or of its church. CHARLEMAGNE raised it to the rank of imperial abbey, and PASCHAL I enriched it with liturgical vestments and the relics of the martyr St. HIPPOLYTUS. The abbey had its own musical style, different from the Gregorian chant, a fact lamented by LEO IV. On Pentecost, 872, Abbot Anastasius and his monks met the Emperor Louis the German at Farfa, obtaining from him confirmation of imperial privileges. Destroyed by the Saracens in 891, the abbey was rebuilt in 974. Its three-naved Romanesque church was decorated with paintings in the 11th century, and still later with cosmatesque works. However, the new abbey's discipline was far from vigorous, and during the INVESTITURE STRUGGLE it remained in the background. Nevertheless, the abbey contributed to the development of literary and artistic studies in the Duchy of Rome. The last abbot worthy of mention, Adinolfo (d. 1144), later made a cardinal, gave some luster to the abbey in the 12th century. In 1264 URBAN IV made it a *diocesis nullius*. Attacked by its vassals during the 14th century, the abbey was impoverished, and its economy collapsed. In the 15th century the popes annexed San Salvatore in COMMENDATION to the Abbey of FARFA, but the patrimony of the abbey continued to diminish and monastic discipline slowly disappeared. URBAN VIII suppressed it in 1629 and in 1632 used its possessions for the endowment of collegiate churches in the Marches. Today the abbey lies desolate, but its ruins continue to show unmistakable traces of its former glory.

Bibliography: L. H. COTTINEAU, *Répertoire topobibliographique des abbayes et prieurés*, 2 v. (Mâcon 1935–39) 2:2875. I. SCHUSTER, *Il monastero imperiale del Salvatore* (Rome 1914). GREGORIO DI CATINO, *Il Regesto di Farfa*, ed. I. GIORGI and U. BALZANI, 4 v. (Rome 1879–92). *Patrologia Latina,* ed. J. P. MIGNE, 217 v. (Paris 1878–90) 100:173–174. *Liber pontificalis,* ed. L. DUCHESNE (Paris 1886–1958) 2:59. G. SILVESTRELLI, *Città, castelli e terre della regione romana* (Città di Castello 1914).

[S. BAIOCCHI]

SAN SALVATORE DI MESSINA, MONASTERY

The largest and most important Basilian monastery in southern Italy. Between 1122 and 1132, ROGER II of Sicily built the abbey near the lighthouse tower at the tip of the isthmus. The Emperor CHARLES V demolished it in the 16th century to make room for a castle, and it was rebuilt elsewhere in Messina. BARTHOLOMEW OF SIMERI (d. 1130) helped to found it, but in 1131 Roger II entrusted the direction of San Salvatore to his disciple (St.) Luke (d. 1149).

The monastery was organized as an archimandria, i.e., it became the head of a monastic confederation with jurisdiction over 41 monasteries located in the vicinity of Messina and Reggio (Calabria), and was declared exempt from any ecclesiastical or lay jurisdiction. Archimandrite Luke codified its statutes in the *Typikon* promulgated in 1133. The appointment of an archimandrite and the reforms introduced by Luke were new features in the Byzantine monastic arrangement in Italy which had followed until then the Studite tradition (*see* STUDION [STUIU]). Privileges and donations made the archimandrite an important ecclesiastical and political personage in Sicily. The library of San Salvatore contained many splendid Greek codices, 175 of which may be found in the university. Decline, which became more pronounced under Angevin rule, was checked by Cardinal BESSARION. In the 17th and 18th centuries the Basilian Congregation of Italy was established with happy results. San Salvatore was, however, suppressed by the Italian government in 1883, and its territory was incorporated into Messina.

Bibliography: Important documents on this monastery in MS Rome, Vat. Lat. 8201. R. PIRRI, *Sicilia sacra*, ed. A. MONGITORE, 2 v. (3d ed. Palermo 1733). F. MATRANGA, "Il monastero dei Greci del S. Salvatore dell'acroterio di Messina . . ." *Rendiconti dell'Accademia Peloritana* (Messina 1887). G. COZZA-LUZI, *De typico sacro messanensis monasterii archimandritalis* in *Nova Patrum bibliotheca,* ed. A. MAI and G. COZZA-LUZI, 10 v. (Rome 1852–1905) 10.2:117–137. A. MANCINI, *Codices graeci monasteri messanensis S. Salvatoris* (Messina 1907). M. SCADUTO, *Il monachismo basiliano nella Sicilia medievale* (Rome 1947).

[M. PETTA]

SAN VINCENZO AL VOLTURNO, ABBEY OF

A Benedictine foundation in the ancient Diocese of Isernia in central Italy. The monastery rose on a spot near the source of the Volturno at FARFA; there in 703 three noblemen of Benevento—(St.) Paldo, who became the first abbot, Tato, and Taso—retired to live a monastic life. It grew rapidly in importance, extending its rule over an extensive area so as to form a virtual monastic duchy. CHARLEMAGNE recognized its immunity, but in 882 the Saracen invasion resulted in massacre of the monks living there and the devastation of the buildings. The remainder, who fled to Capua, returned after a few decades and rebuilt the monastery. It was always intimately linked with MONTE CASSINO and vied with it in the study of the humanities, history, and theology, as well as in its artistic and agricultural achievements. Its famous names bear witness to this: e.g., the theologian Ambrose AUTPERT (8th century) and the monk John, compiler of the famous *Chronicon Vulturnense.* The *Chronicon* has made possible a reconstruction not only of various events in San Vincenzo and in several of the nearby monasteries, but also of the historical and political events of central Italy, down to *c.* 1070. During the 11th century, the abbey experienced a period of decline. Nevertheless, plans were made, in view of the huge holdings of the monastery and the inaccessibility of the abbey itself, located in the mountain fastness of the Apennines, to erect a *pro-casa,* or official residence, in Capua, where the abbot spent a large part of his time. About 1160, the local feudal lords began to invade the abbatial lands and incorporate them into their own domains, and the later practice of COMMENDATION hastened the decline in numbers among the monks and the ruin of the monastic buildings. A frescoed crypt dating from the days of Abbot Epiphanius (first half of 9th century) has been preserved and slightly restored. Around it are other buildings of more recent date.

Bibliography: *Chronicon Vulturnense,* L. A. MURATORI, *Rerum italicarum scriptores, 500–1500,* 25 v. in 28 (Milan 1723–51) 1:319–523; ed. V. FEDERICI 3 v. (Rome 1925–38). V. FEDERICI, "Ricerche per l'edizione del *Chronicon Vulturnense* del monaco Giovanni," *Bullettino dell'Istituto storico italiano . . . e archivio muratoriano* 53 (1939) 147–236; 57 (1943) 71–114; "L'origine del Monastero di San Vincenzo al Volturno," in *Studi di storia e diritto in onore di Carlo Calisse,* 3 v. (Milan 1940) 3:3–13. L. H. COTTINEAU, *Répertoire topobibliographique des abbayes et prieurés,* 2 v. (Mâcon 1935–39) 2:2918–19. M. DEL TREPPO, "Longobardi, Franchi e papato in due secoli di storia vulturnese," *Archivio storico per le provincie napoletane* NS 34 (1954) 37–59; "La vita economica e sociale in una grande abbazia del Mezzogiorno: San Vincenzo al Volturno nell'alto medioevo," *ibid.* NS 35 (1955) 31–110.

[I. DE PICCOLI]

SAN VITORES, DIEGO LUIS DE, BL.

Jesuit missionary priest, martyr; b. Nov. 12, 1627, Burgos, Spain; d. April 2, 1672, at Tomhon Beach, Agana, Guam.

Born into the Spanish nobility, Diego attended the Imperial College, Madrid, and was raised in the royal court. From age eleven, Diego wanted to join the Society of Jesus and become a missionary despite his parents' hope that he would aspire to a political career.

He entered the novitiate of the JESUITS at Villarejo de Fuentes in 1640, completed his studies at Huete and Alcalá de Henares, and was ordained in 1651. Thereafter he taught at Oropesa, Madrid, and Alcalá de Henares (1655), where he also undertook a ministry to the sick and gave parish missions.

Given permission to go to the Philippines, Diego sailed via Mexico, where he landed at Veracruz (July 28, 1660). Unable to secure passage to the Orient, he conducted missions and evangelized in the streets of Mexico City. After finally reaching Manila (July 10, 1662), he studied Tagalog while serving as university dean and master of novices. In his spare time he engaged in missionary work in the interior of Luzon and on Mindoro Island.

With the permission of King Philip IV of Spain (reigned 1621–65), Diego sailed back to Mexico City to obtain permission and funds for a mission to the Ladrones Islands, renamed in 1668 to Marianas Islands in honor of the regent Mariana of Asturia. The missionaries left Acapulco, Mexico, on March 23, 1668, and arrived at the archipelago on June 15, 1668. There they learned and adopted local customs, and converted some 50,000 people on Saipan, Tinian, and Guam, including High Chief Quipuha (Kepuha), whose clan provided the land for the basilica built in 1669. Diego also compiled a grammar and vocabulary of the *lingua Mariana*, opened two seminaries, and erected eight churches before the mission was beset with problems.

Prompted by false rumors spread about Christianity, some of the new converts abandoned the faith and others became hostile. These heightened suspicions and societal changes led to the martrydom of Diego and his catechist Bl. Pedro CALUNGSOD. Influenced by this hostile climate, Chief Matapang did not consent to the baptism of his infant daughter—requested by his wife who did not otherwise need his permission—and became irate at Diego and Calungsod. With his companion, Hirao, Matapang brutally attacked the priest and the catechist and threw them into the ocean tied to rocks. A memorial now stands on the site of their martyrdom.

San Vitores was beatified by John Paul II, Oct. 6, 1985.

Feast: Oct. 6 (Jesuits).

Bibliography: *L'Osservatore Romano*, Eng. ed. 42 (1985): 6–7. *Father San Vitores, His Life, Times, and Martyrdom*, ed. E. G. JOHNSTON (Agana, Guam 1979). F. GARCÍA, *Sanvitores in the Marianas*, tr. F. PLAZA (Mangilao, Guam 1980). A. DEL LEDESMA, *Mission in the Marianas: An Account of Father Diego Luis de Sanvítores and His Companions, 1669–1670*, tr. WARD BARRETT of *Noticia de los progressos de nuestra Santa Fe, en las Islas Marianas . . . desde 15 de mayo de 1669* (Minneapolis 1975). P. MURILLO VELARDE, *The "Reducción" of the Islands of the Ladrones, the Discovery of the Islands of the Palaos, and Other Happenings*, tr. F. E. PLAZA (Mangilao, Guam 1987). F. PLAZA, *Sanvitores, bibliografía de las materias existentes en el Micronesian Area Research Center* (Agana, Guam 1975). A. RISCO, *The Apostle of the Marianas: The Life, Labors, and Martyrdom of Ven. Diego Luis de San Vitores*, tr. J. M. H. LEDESMA, ed. O. L. CALVO (Agana, Guam 1970). J. A. DE SOBRINO, *Tres que dijeron 'si'* (Madrid 1985). J. N. TYLENDA, *Jesuit Saints & Martyrs* (Chicago 1998): 337–339.

[K. I. RABENSTEIN]

SANCHES, FRANCISCO (SÁNCHEZ)

Philosopher and physician; b. 1550 or 1552, Braga, Portugal, or Tuy, Spain; d. Toulouse, November 1623; son of a Jewish New Christian physician, who fled to Bordeaux. Like his distant cousin M. E. de MONTAIGNE, Sanches probably studied at the Collège de Guyenne then in Rome; he went from there to Montpellier. He subsequently became professor of philosophy and later of medicine at Toulouse. He wrote *Quod nihil scitur* (Lyons 1581); a letter to the mathematician, Clavius (1574–75); and medical works and tracts against Renaissance pseudosciences.

Sanches developed a skeptical and nominalistic attack against ARISTOTELIANISM, challenging the possibility of gaining knowledge of reality through definitions, syllogisms, and causes. He argued also against mathematical knowledge. Science, Sanches claimed, is perfect and complete knowledge of individual objects. This cannot be attained because of the nature of things and man's limitations. Instead Sanches recommended careful empirical study of objects as all that man can accomplish. He is probably the first to use the term "scientific method," and to develop a constructive skepticism, i.e., a positivistic-pragmatic view of science, independent of any metaphysics. Sanches may have influenced Descartes, Gassendi, Mersenne, and Leibniz.

See Also: SKEPTICISM.

Bibliography: *Opera philosophica* (new ed. Coimbra 1955). J. MOREAU, "Doute et savoir chez Francisco Sanches," *Aufsätze zur Portugiesischen Kulturgeschichte*, 24–50, v. 1 of *Portugiesische Forschungen der Görresgesellschaft* (Münster 1960–). R. H. POPKIN, *The History of Scepticism from Erasmus to Descartes* (Assen 1960).

[R. H. POPKIN]

SÁNCHEZ, JUAN

Moral theologian; b. Avila, Spain, date unknown; d. c. 1624. He was an exponent of LAXISM, and one of the propositions condemned by the Holy Office, March 2, 1679, was his (Denz 2104). As did other laxists, Sanchez maintained that an opinion enjoying speculative probability was also practically probable, and that all probable opinions were equally safe in practice. One of his works, *Selectae et practicae disputationes de rebus in administratione sacramentorum* (Madrid 1642), was put on the Index *donec corrigatur* (i.e., pending its correction) because of the many lax opinions it contained.

Bibliography: H. HURTER, *Nomenclator literarius theologiae catholicae*, 5 vol. (3rd ed. Innsbruck 1903–13) 3:592–594.

[P. K. MEAGHER]

SANCHEZ, THOMAS

Jesuit moralist and canonist; b, Córdoba, 1550; d. Granada, May 19, 1610. He entered the novitiate of the Society of Jesus in 1567. An impediment in his speech at first prevented his acceptance into that order, but upon imploring delivery from it before a highly venerated picture of Our Lady at Córdoba, he was so freed from the infirmity that only a slight trace of it remained. Sanchez was for a long time master of novices at Granada; he was a confessor for many colleges, especially at Córdoba, and for many years was a professor of moral theology and Canon Law. The remainder of his life he devoted to the composition of his works.

The contemporaries of Sanchez bear testimony to the energy and perseverance with which he labored toward self-perfection from his novitiate until his death. His penitential zeal rivaled that of the early anchorites, and, according to his spiritual director, he carried his baptismal innocence to the grave. He was likewise a man of remarkable learning. The penetration of his insights in offering solutions to the most difficult cases of conscience won him considerable renown. The work that brought him the greatest acclaim was his *De Sancto Matrimonii Sacramento* (3 v. Madrid 1605). Clement VIII proclaimed that up to his time, there was no greater authority who treated the most difficult problems of matrimony than Sanchez. Jurists and theologians from every country came to consult him.

But this work, which brought him his greatest fame brought him some of his greatest abuse. Some of the editions of his third volume were placed on the Index on Feb. 4, 1627, on the grounds that, at the instigation of the government of the Venetian Republic, they omitted San-chez's doctrine that the pope had the right to legitimize illegitimate children independently of any intervention of the civil authority. With the revision of the Index in 1900, Sanchez's name was removed.

The mode of expression and the detailed treatment of every possible point in the work brought further criticism upon the author, with charges even of immorality. It was thought that he analyzed the most delicate matters too completely, but it should be remembered that this work was published for the use of confessors. They must necessarily be able to distinguish in matters of right and wrong, just as doctors and lawyers should be able to make every medical and legal distinction.

According to Wernz (*Jus decretalium*, 4.20), San-chez's work, *De Matrimonio*, is still considered by the Roman Curia as among the classical works on marriage.

Bibliography: J. E. NIEREMBERG, *Varones ilustres de la compañia de Jesús,* cont'd. A. DE ANDRADE and J. CASSINI, 9 v. (2d ed. Bilbao 1887–92) v.7. C. SOMMERVOGEL, *Bibliothéque de la Compagnie de Jésus* 7:537–538. E. DE GUILHERMY, *Ménologe de la Compagnie de Jésus*, ed. J. TERRIEN, 13 v. (Paris 1867–1902). H. HURTER, *Nomenclator literarius theologiae catholicae* 3:592–594. R. BROUILLARD, *Dictionnaire de théologie catholique* 14.1:1075–85.

[L. L. GOOLEY]

SÁNCHEZ DE TEJADA, IGNACIO

Colombian diplomat who obtained recognition of the independence of New Granada from the Vatican; b. El Socorro, Colombia, 1764; d. Rome, 1837. As an official of the viceroyalty in his early years, he allied himself with the Comuneros and was exiled to Spain. There he was pro-French, approving even Napoleon's designs in the Cortes of Bayonne in 1809. As a consequence, he had no real contact with the Creole independence movement, even when he began to see its probable success. The victorious Bolívar tried to establish contact with Rome and, after two fruitless missions, appointed to the task Sánchez de Tejada, who was waiting out the persecution of the Restoration in London. The Holy See, encumbered with the obligations to Spain as a result of royal patronage, ignored the Colombian envoy. His government, disappointed at the delay, threatened measures that might lead to schism. Sánchez de Tejada settled all the difficulties and through his logical arguments persuaded the Vatican to name the first bishops for Colombia (1827) in spite of Spain's wrath. On the dissolution of the first Colombian state, New Granada retained him as its representative in Rome. Evidence of his success in the position was the recognition of the independence of the nation by the Holy See in November 1835. He was unable to prevent the appointment of Gaetano BALUFFI as internuncio to Bogotá. In spite of his predilection to regalism, Sánchez de Tejada showed himself a Catholic zealous in achieving the aim of his work, which was to bring together the Holy See in Rome and a nation that had arisen from the revolution. He was the most experienced and skillful emissary of the Hispano–American nations accredited to the Vatican during the period.

Bibliography: J. L. MECHAM, *Church and State in Latin America* (Chapel Hill 1934). P. LETURIA, *Relaciones entre la Santa Sede e hispanoamérica*, 3 v. *La internunciatura de Mons, Cayetano Baluffi en Bogotá, primera en hispanoamérica 1837–1842* (Rome 1953).

[A. M. PINILLA COTE]

SÁNCHEZ DELGADILLO, JENARO, ST.

Martyr, priest; b. Sept. 19, 1876, at Zapopán, Jalisco, Archdiocese of Guadalajara, Mexico; d. Jan. 17, 1927, Tecolotlán. Guadalajara. He completed seminary studies at Guadalajara, was ordained (1911), and zealously exercised his priesthood as an associate in various parishes. When the government closed the churches, Sánchez furtively continued his sacramental duties. He was captured by soldiers while walking in a field with some friends. Although his companions were freed, he was tortured and hanged. Initially buried in the church at Tecolotlán, his body was translated (1934) to that of Cocula. Fr. Sánchez was both beatified (Nov. 22, 1992) and canonized (May 21, 2000) with Cristobal MAGALLANES by Pope John Paul II.

Feast: May 25 (Mexico).

Bibliography: J. CARDOSO, *Los mártires mexicanos* (Mexico City 1953). J. DÍAZ ESTRELLA, *El movimiento cristero: sociedad y conflicto en los Altos de Jalisco* (México, D.F. 1979).

[K. I. RABENSTEIN]

SANCHO DE GUERRA, MARÍA JOSEFA DEL CORAZÓN DE JESÚS, ST.

Professed religious and co-foundress of the Servants of Jesus of Charity; b. Vitoria, Spain, Sept. 7, 1842; d. Bilbao, Spain, March 20, 1912. María's poor, pious family provided her with a Christian education and contributed to the recognition of her religious vocation. She was the eldest daughter of the chair-maker, Bernabe Sancho, who died when María was seven, and his wife, Petra de Guerra. While studying in Madrid she discerned her calling to a religious life.

She attempted to join the contemplative Conceptionists at Aranjuez in 1860, but fell ill with typhus. Upon her recovery, she understood that God was calling her to a more active order. She entered the Servants of Mary in 1864 and worked in the poorest districts of Madrid. In 1865 she helped plague victims without consideration for her own health and safety. With the spiritual counsel of Abp. (St.) Anthony Mary CLARET and St. María Soledad TORRES ACOSTA, the foundress of the Servants of Mary, she left the order prior to her profession to start another.

She was accompanied by several other sisters to Bilbao, Spain, where they founded (July 25, 1871) a new congregation—the Servants of Jesus of Charity—to serve the indigent and sick in hospitals, clinics, sanitariums, retirement homes, and daycare centers. At the time of her death—after 42 years as superior—the congregation had expanded to 42 houses in Spain and one in Chile. Today there are 1,100 sisters ministering in Argentina, Chile, Colombia, the Dominican Republic, Ecuador, France, Italy, Mexico, Peru, the Philippines, Portugal, and Spain.

Mother María Josefa was buried in the city cemetery of Bilboa until the translation of her relics to the chapel of the motherhouse in 1926. The informative process for her cause opened May 31, 1951 and was accepted in Rome on Jan. 7, 1972. Pope John Paul II declared Mother María Josefa venerable (Sept. 7, 1989), beatified her (Sept. 27, 1992), and approved a second miracle attributed to her intercession (June 28, 1999). She was the first native Basque to be canonized (Oct. 1, 2000).

Feast: May 18.

Bibliography: P. BILBAO ARÍSTEGUI, *La Beata María Josefa Sancho de Guerra: una vida al servicio de los enfermos* (Vitoria, Spain 1992). *Acta Apostolicae Sedis* (1992), 919.

[K. I. RABENSTEIN]

SANCIA, ST.

Cistercian nun; b. Coimbra, *c.* 1180; d. Cellas, March 13, 1229. Sancia, daughter of King Sancho I (1185–1211) of Portugal, after refusing several marriage proposals, dedicated herself entirely to works of piety. She sponsored the first Franciscan and Dominican settlements in Portugal and in 1216 founded Sta. Maria de Cellas, a convent for Cistercian nuns. She herself entered there in 1223. After six years spent in the practice of heroic asceticism she died among her nuns, but her body was taken for burial to the convent of Lorvão, where her sister, St. Theresa, lived as a nun. The immemorial cult of both sisters in Portugal was approved by Pope Clement XI in 1705.

Feast: March 17 (formerly March 13).

Bibliography: *Acta Sanctorum* June 4:385–435. M. GLONING, ''Zwei selige Cistercienserinnen aus königlichem Hause,'' *Cistercienser-Chronik* 19 (1907). S. LENSSEN, *Hagiologium cisterciense* 1:143–144.

[L. J. LEKAI]

SANCTION

Sanction is here understood as the act of legislative authority that secures a measure of inviolability for a law by providing either reward (premial sanction) for its observance or punishment (penal sanction) for its transgression; or as the reward or punishment so prescribed. In human experience effective legislation requires sanctions, which are commonly penal rather than immediately premial in kind, to provide motives to induce those subject to laws to conform to their requirements. A lawmaker neglecting to provide a sufficient motive to enforce the keeping of a law would be acting foolishly in making the law at all, for without such a motive the effect intended would no more probably be achieved with the law than without it, and the law itself would be useless. Moreover, it is necessary to verify the order that is reasonably held to exist between good action and happiness, and between evil action and the loss of happiness. But the faithful performance of duty often entails sacrifice and self-denial, while the neglect of it brings unmerited gratification. Unless something exists to balance the scales and restore the order between good action and happiness when this is disturbed, the reasonable expectation of men is defeated, and the difference between what is good and what is not is obscured, if indeed any appreciable difference is left.

Natural and moral as well as positive law requires a sanction. Concretely many different rewards and punishments serve as sanctions for moral law. Some of these affect an individual in himself, such as approval or remorse of conscience, interior peace and tranquillity or the want of it. Others affect the individual in his relation to others—for example, the enjoyment of the esteem, respect and affection of his fellows, or his subjection to their contempt. For the Christian still others affect the individual in his relation to God—for example, friendship with God, or the loss of it, and especially the final attainment of, or separation from, God.

The proponents of naturalistic ethics tend to regard the natural consequences of vicious action that recoil on the evildoer as adequate sanction for morality and sufficient in themselves to ensure right conduct. While it may be admitted that the virtuous, even in their earthly lives, enjoy a greater measure of happiness than the wicked and that the way of the transgressor is often a hard one, it cannot be seriously maintained that virtuous living invari-

ably results in happiness so far as the present life is concerned or that vice and crime always meet an adequate measure of retribution. Human experience too obviously affirms the contrary. To provide a motive capable of inducing a man to live virtuously, it is reasonable that the rewards held out for the observance of the moral law should exceed the sacrifice and self-denial entailed in its observance. But commonly enough in ordinary life, and especially where virtue makes demands that approach the heroic, earthly reward and punishment seldom provide a sufficiently impelling incentive. Any idea of a sanction for moral law that leaves out of account man's relationship to God must be, for the generality of men at least, partial and inadequate.

See Also: PUNISHMENT.

Bibliography: M. CRONIN, *The Science of Ethics,* 2 v. (Dublin 1939). O. LOTTIN, *Principles de morale,* 2 v. (Louvain 1947). R. POUND, *Social Control through Law* (New Haven 1942). A. MICHEL, *Dictionnaire de théologie catholique,* ed. A. VACANT et al., 15 v. (Paris 1903–50; Tables générales 1951–) 15.2:2621–22.

[P. K. MEAGHER]

SANCTION, DIVINE

The term divine SANCTION is used to convey the idea that man is ultimately answerable to God for his actions here on earth. This belief is fundamental to a religious view of the world. It implies that man is not autonomous but is under God and yet at the same time a free agent and not the victim of fate (*see* FATE AND FATALISM). It means that events in this life have effects far transcending the purely temporal order.

The concept of reward and PUNISHMENT found among non-Christian peoples expresses this truth only very inadequately. The doctrine of METEMPSYCHOSIS in its various forms is widespread and owes its popularity to the difficulty man experiences in imagining a sanction that is final and irreversible. A succession of lives, as propounded by many Asian religions and various forms of THEOSOPHY, allows for some sort of reward or punishment but does not take into account the continued existence of the human person. The true idea of expiation is destroyed if man does not know for what he is atoning.

It is to revelation that one must turn for a full treatment of divine sanction that preserves the freedom and responsibility of man. In the earlier writings of the Old Testament there is a firm conviction that any transgression of the law brings unhappiness in this life. Plague, famine, war are taken as indications of God's displeasure with His people (e.g., in 1 Kgs 9.9). Only later, when the problem arises of the suffering of the just (Book of Job), is it recognized that the only true explanation is to be sought in a reward and punishment after death. It is in the later wisdom literature that the immortality of the soul and the nature of the afterlife are more fully worked out. The New Testament stresses the fact that this sanction will be in the next life. Christ does speak of compensation in this life (Lk 18.29–30), but the impact of His affirmations is that the real reward or punishment is reserved for afterward and this is of a spiritual nature and not to be compared with the joys and sorrows of this life.

Man's nature is such that the appeal to a final sanction will always be necessary; the Stoic and Kantian ideal of virtue for virtue's sake does not take into account man in his present fallen situation. But Stoicism does well to react against a servile worship of God whose only motive is fear of punishment or hope of reward (*see* STOICISM; KANTIANISM). The belief in God as rewarder and punisher is to instill in man a sense of dependence on God and responsibility in his actions. God's sanction is not an arbitrary decision imposed with no intrinsic connection with what man does. Rather, it is the manifestation of how his activities stand in reality. If his life is God-directed, he will reap the reward and obtain God; if it is not directed to Him, he will not attain Him.

See Also: FIRE OF JUDGMENT; JUDGMENT, DIVINE (IN THE BIBLE); JUDGMENT, DIVINE (IN THEOLOGY); MERIT; ESCHATOLOGY, ARTICLES ON.

Bibliography: *Dictionnaire de théologie catholique,* ed. A. VACANT, 15 v. (Paris 1903–50; Tables générales 1951–), Tables générales 2:2705–19. W. PESCH, H. FRIES, ed., *Handbuch theologischer Grundbegriffe,* 2 v. (Munich 1962–63) 2:748–751.

[M. E. WILLIAMS]

SANCTIS, DIONISIO DE

Dominican bishop in 16th-century New Granada, active in the education of the indigenous peoples; b. Palma del Rio, Spain, *c.* 1507; d. Cartagena, New Granada (now Colombia), 1577. He was professed in Santo Domingo convent of Jerez de la Frontera on Nov. 1, 1523. Hence he was called "de Sanctis" or "de los Santos." He was ordained before 1530 and then continued further studies at the College of San Gregorio in Valladolid. He received the Praesentatus in 1551 and the master of theology degree in 1561. He served as prior in Murcia, Osuna, Palma del Rio, Granada, and San Lucar de Barrameda before being elected provincial of the province of Andalucía in 1565. In 1574 he was named bishop of Cartagena. In the New World he found the native population of his diocese poorly trained; they had forgotten their instruction and prayers. To facilitate their reeducation he compiled a cat-echism, the *Doctrina cristiana para los Indios,* and a primer for teaching reading, *Cartilla para enseñar a leer a los Indios.*

Bibliography: H. SANCHO DE SOPRANIS, "Un Obispo doctrinero de Indios, Fr. Dionisio de Sanctis, O.P.," *Missionalia Hispánica* 8 (1951) 317–373.

[A. B. NIESER]

SANCTORAL CYCLE

In her liturgy, the Church celebrates the mysteries of Christ every Sunday and on all the feasts of the temporal cycle. Almost every day a feast of a saint is celebrated. Such feasts, spread throughout the year, make up a sanctoral cycle.

History

There were two characteristics of the cult of saints in the Church's beginning. One was that it was directed only to martyrs, confessors, and bishops. The other was that it was strictly local; each church venerated only those martyrs whose tombs were in the locality and only those bishops who had exercised their functions in the city.

Martyrs. Martyrs were the first chosen to be the objects of the Church's cult, such veneration being but a more solemn form of the honor paid to the dead, for members of the Christian community assembled each year at the tombs of the dead on their anniversaries. The East venerated its martyrs long before the West. The oldest witness concerns St. Polycarp, martyred between 155 and 177; the Christians of Smyrna gathered each year at his tomb with joy and gladness to celebrate the anniversary of his martyrdom (*Martyrdom of Polycarp* 18; *The Fathers of the Church: A New Translation,* ed. R. J. Deferrari et al. [New York 1947–60; Washington 1960–] 1:160). In the West the earliest information comes from Cyprian, who attests to the regularity of such anniversary celebrations at Carthage (*c.* 250); he indicates that the Eucharist was a part of the celebration (*Epist.* 12.2, 39.3; *Corpus scriptorum ecclesiasticorum latinorum* [Vienna 1866–] 3:503, 583). Rome does not seem to have given any particular cult to martyrs before the middle of the 3d century; the persecution of 258, which took the life of Sixtus II and seven of his deacons, probably led the Church of Rome to begin liturgical celebrations in honor of her martyrs.

Confessors. In the course of the fourth century, another category of Christians became the object of liturgical cult, those who had not shed their blood for the faith, but who had nonetheless given extraordinary testimony of their attachment to Christ. The first such group consists of those who during persecution suffered exile, imprisonment, or torture. They are generally called confessors, but sometimes they are given the name martyr, for example, Popes Pontian (d. 235), Cornelius (d. 253), and Eusebius (d. 309), all of whom died in exile; and Bishops Paulinus of Trier (d. 358), Dionysius of Milan (d. 359), Eusebius of Vercelli (d. 370), and Athanasius of Alexandria (d. 373), all of whom were likened to martyrs because resistance to Arianism led to exile.

Another group is made up of those monks who, the moment the persecutions ended, fled to the desert to engage in asceticism. They were the successors of the martyrs in their renunciation of the world, their attachment to Christ, and their struggle against the powers of evil; they also soon succeeded the martyrs in popular veneration. Immediately after their deaths, for example, St. Anthony (d. 356) and St. Hilarion (d. 372) became the object of a cult that manifested itself in the construction of a sanctuary and a solemn celebration of their anniversaries [Jerome, *Vita Hilarionis* 31 (*Patrologia Latina*, ed. J. P. Migne [Paris 1878–90] 23:45); Sozomen, *Hist. Eccl.* 3.14 (*Patrologia Graeca*. ed J. P. Migne [Paris 1857–66] 67: 1078)]. It is to be noted that the ascetics who received liturgical honors were all men; until the fourth century, only women who were martyrs received such cult.

Bishops. Toward the end of the fourth century, Christian communities began to celebrate the anniversaries (*depositio*) of their more illustrious bishops. As Irenaeus asserts (*Adv. haer.* 3.3.1; *Patrologia Graeca* 7:848), every church kept a list of its bishops. Soon the custom arose of reading these lists during the Mass at the time when the commemorations were made; little by little these lists of deceased bishops who were commemorated became lists of bishop saints who were given a liturgical cult. The first bishops to be inscribed in the calendar were SS. Gregory the Wonderworker (d. *c.* 270) and Basil of Caesarea (d. 379) in the East, and SS. Silvester (d. 335) and Martin (d. *c.* 397) in the West. Subsequently, every episcopal city celebrated the anniversary of its principal bishops.

Diffusion of Saints' Feasts. During the fifth and sixth centuries (the fourth in a few exceptional cases), local calendars were broadened to include some saints from other churches and those of interest to all Christendom. This extension, at once geographical and theological, led to the elaboration of a universal sanctoral cycle.

In the Roman calendar of 354 there appeared the names of three martyrs of Carthage and a few from towns near Rome. At the end of the fourth century, Constantinople celebrated the feasts of SS. Athanasius and Cyprian. St. Augustine states that in his day St. Vincent, a deacon of Saragossa martyred in 304, was venerated in the whole world (*Sermo* 276.4; *Patrologia Latina* 38: 1257).

Perhaps theological reasons helped favor the acceptance of foreign saints; there was a desire to manifest the unity of the Church. However, the really determining factor was without doubt the transfer of saints' bodies and distribution of relics. This process began in 350, at least in the East. Possession of an illustrious martyr's relics was looked upon as a pledge of protection for a given community, and the transfer of such relics almost always brought with it the institution of an annual feast.

In the same epoch, calendars began to carry the names of saints who belonged, not to any particular community, but to the entire Church. Sometime before 380, Caesarea of Cappadocia observed the feast of St. Stephen on December 26, those of SS. Peter, James, and John on the 27th, and that of St. Paul on the 28th. A Syrian martyrology of 411 also mentions these feasts, and a Carthaginian calendar from the beginning of the sixth century has the feasts of John the Baptist (June 24), Peter and Paul (June 29), the Maccabees (Aug. 1), Luke (Oct. 13), Andrew (Nov. 29), Stephen (Dec. 26), John and James (Dec. 27), and the Holy Innocents (Dec. 28). By describing these Apostles and early witnesses of Christ in their calendars, the Christians of these times showed they recognized that the honors they paid to martyrs and bishops were due also to those who played an essential role in the birth and propagation of the universal Church. This is a fact of capital importance for the history of the sanctoral cycle: the cult of the saints emerged from the veneration of the dead.

Later Evolution. Reflection on the role of the saints became more systematic in the Middle Ages. The question was posed: Which saints had so important a function in the Church that an official cult not only may, but should be paid them? Thus at the beginning of the ninth century, Frankish liturgists inserted into the Roman sanctoral cycle a series of feasts for Apostles and evangelists; in the 11th century Gregory VII, desirous of restoring the prestige of the Holy See, decided that all pope martyrs would have the right to a universal cult.

At the end of the 12th century a very important step was taken; no longer were the saints of the past alone to be feted, but, also and above all, those of the present. Thus the sanctoral cycle became a reflection of the Church's life. The first modern saint to be inscribed in the Roman calendar was St. Thomas Becket, Archbishop of Canterbury, martyred in 1170; his feast appears in a Lateran Basilica Missal from the end of the 12th century. Almost all the other saints who were inserted into the sanctoral cycle during this period were members of the religious orders recently founded, at first Franciscans and Dominicans, later Jesuits and those of younger congregations. This invasion of the calendar on the part of religious was due, not only to the vitality of the new orders, but also to the fact that, in a world that seemed to become more and more unchristian, it was thought that sanctity flourished only in the cloisters.

Theology

The history of the sanctoral cycle shows that the cult of the saints is directed to persons more remarkable for their functions in the Church than for their personal sanctity. From the very beginning, the Church has classified her saints in the liturgy according to categories: martyrs, bishops, Apostles, virgins, confessors, abbots—each corresponding to a role in the Church. The establishment of a Common of Doctors and a Common of Popes has further accentuated the functional aspect of this cult. The greater attention given in the 20th century to the role of the laity in the life of the Church, especially by Pope John Paul II have resulted in the canonization and veneration of those laity who live out their faith in their daily lives.

In this perspective saints' feasts appear as a celebration of the mystery of the Church, an immense feast of the Church spread throughout the year and recapitulated in the Feast of All Saints. In observing these feasts of the saints, the Church celebrates the success of Christ's redemptive work in human hearts. The cult of the saints, in other words, does not stop with them, but goes beyond and through them to God whose glory they reflect, the "God who is admirable in all the saints."

If one looks upon the saints' feasts as a celebration of the mystery of the Church, completing the celebration of the mysteries of Christmas, Easter, and Pentecost, one will avoid the pitfall of opposing or separating the sanctoral and temporal cycles or of allowing saints' feasts to take precedence over the feasts of the temporal cycle (Vatican Council II, *Constitution on the Sacred Liturgy* 106). The veneration of saints is one aspect and moment in the liturgical celebration of the mystery of salvation. Moreover, if one takes the time, one can discover the intimate connection between certain sanctoral and temporal feasts.

If martyrs alone were venerated in Christian antiquity, it was because only they had fully lived the paschal mystery; having followed Christ through His Passion and death, they joined Him in glory. It is very significant that the Christians of the first three centuries who feted no other saints but martyrs knew no other temporal feast but Easter. The Common of Martyrs in Paschal Time still evidences the special association between the martyr and the paschal mystery.

The Apostles' feasts too have a paschal character, for Apostles were, above all else, witnesses to the Resurrec-tion of Christ. A special Common of Apostles in Paschal time is also provided by the liturgy. If, in the older calendars, feasts of the Apostles had been fixed for the days after Christmas, it was because they were venerated as companions of Christ before they were feted as actors in the drama of salvation.

The oldest MARIAN FEASTS are Mary, Mother of God, January 1, at Rome, and the Dormition of Our Lady, August 15, in the Christian East. St. Joseph's feast, which some Byzantine churches had celebrated on December 25 or 26, was introduced into the West in the tenth century and fixed by Sixtus IV for March 19, the date of an older Roman popular celebration for laborers. The liturgical cult of SS. Anne and Joachim, of Eastern origin, was introduced in the West by the Crusaders and reached its high point in the 14th and 15th centuries. In 1584 Gregory XIII extended the feast of St. Anne (July 26) to the universal Church. St. Joachim's feast, fixed at first on March 20 by Julius II, was suppressed by Pius V, then transferred to the Sunday within the octave of the Assumption, placed on August 16 by Pius X, and finally combined with the feast of St. Anne (July 26) in the 1969 revision of the liturgical calendar.

Many saints' feasts are linked, by object and date, to the mystery of the Incarnation. Since the beginning of the sixth century, the feast of St. John the Baptist has been observed on June 24, six months before Christmas. And the Holy Innocents have always been feted on December 28 as the first martyrs.

The second Vatican Council's *Constitution on the Sacred Liturgy* spelled out the norms for the revision of the sanctoral cycle of the Roman Calendar. In paragraph 111 it stated: "Lest the feasts of the saints should take precedence over the feasts which commemorate the very mysteries of salvation, many of them should be left to be celebrated by a particular Church or nation or family of religious; only those should be extended to the universal Church which commemorates saints who are truly of universal importance."

The Roman Calendar was revised with the guiding norm of universality in mind. Universality was desired not only in importance, but also with regard to class (martyrs, bishops, etc.), date of birth, and geographical origin. The 1960 Calendar served as the working basis for the general revision.

The saints were divided into three categories: popes, non-Roman martyrs, and saints who were not martyrs.

The 1960 Calendar included 38 popes, of which 26 were honored as martyrs of the first centuries. Few of the 26 appear in the early Roman sacramentaries since their cult developed only in later ages. In the 1969 revised Calendar, 15 popes are included.

In the 1960 Calendar many non-Roman martyrs were included. The revised Calendar has representatives of three classes of martyrs: those of early antiquity (e.g., Polycarp, Cyprian), those whose cults were especially popular in Rome and elsewhere (e.g., Vincent, George), and those who represent the medieval and modern ages (e.g., Stanislaus, Paul Miki and companions).

It is also fitting that a universal Calendar honor saints from various geographical areas, most of whom would not be martyrs. The desire for such a geographical universality caused some 30 saints to be removed from the former general Calendar, many of whom were of Italian origin. Saints from other regions were in turn inserted into the revised Calendar (e.g., Isaac Jogues and companions—Canada, U.S.A.; Charles Lwanga and companions—Africa).

As the Roman Calendar was reformed, the particular or local calendars took on greater importance. In the establishment of the particular calendars of countries, dioceses, and religious communities, local and patron feasts are to be given proper consideration.

While recent calendar reforms reaffirm the centrality of the Christological mysteries in the celebration of the liturgical year, the traditional respect for the memory of the martyrs and other saints is maintained. The Constitution on the Sacred Liturgy provides the rationale: "For the feasts of the saints proclaim the wonderful works of Christ in his servants, and display to the faithful examples for their imitation" (111).

Bibliography: H. DELEHAYE, *Sanctus: Essai sur le culte des saints dans l'antiquité* (Brussels 1927; repr. 1954); *Les Origines du culte des martyrs* (2d ed. Brussels 1933). P. ROUILLARD, "Le Culte des saints au temps des pères," *Assemblées du Seigneur* 89 (1963) 72–85; "Le Recrutement des saints," *La Vie spirituelle* 109 (1963) 342–360. P. MOLINARI, *I santi e il loro culto* (Rome 1962). United States Catholic Conference, *Roman Calendar*, rev. by decree of Vatican Council II and pub. by authority of Paul VI (Washington, D.C. 1970); *Lectionary for Mass*, the Roman Missal rev. by decree of Vatican Council II and pub. by authority of Paul VI (Washington, D.C. 1969). *Missale Romanum*, Ex decreto Sacrosancti Oecumenici Concilii Vaticani II instauratum auctoritate Pauli PP. VI promulgatum (Typis Polyglottis Vaticanis 1970). A. ADAM, *The Liturgical Year: Its History & its Meaning after the Reform of the Liturgy* (New York 1981). A.J. MARTIMORT, ed. *The Church at Prayer IV: The Liturgy and Time* (Collegeville 1986). T.J. TALLEY, *The Origins of the Liturgical Year* (Collegeville, 1991).

[P. ROUILLARD/T. KROSNICKI/EDS.]

SANCTORUM MERITIS

The office hymn that was formerly prescribed for Vespers of the Common of Many Martyrs outside Paschal time. It has six unrhymed stanzas of four verses each

(three Asclepiadean and one glyconic). It appeared anonymously in manuscripts of the 9th century. Dreves includes it in a group of hymns he attributes to RABANUS MAURUS, Abbot of Fulda and later Archbishop of Mainz (d. 856). But other scholars, such as Raby, feel that this austere, simple, albeit learned, monk did not possess such creative poetic ability. HINCMAR OF REIMS (d. 882), who did not know the author of this hymn, took exception to one of the phrases in the doxology, *Te trina Deitas,* which he considered blasphemous. Yet the phrase remained until the revision of hymns by Pope URBAN VIII, when it was changed to the present *Te summa o Deitas.* The original, *Te trina Deitas,* may be found at the end of Thomas Aquinas's *SACRIS SOLEMNIIS.*

Bibliography: F. J. E. RABY, *A History of Christian-Latin Poetry from the Beginnings to the Close of the Middle Ages* (Oxford 1953) 182–183. U. CHEVALIER, *Repertorium hymnologicum* (Louvain-Brussels 1892–1921) 2:548–549. *Analecta hymnica* 50:180–209. G. M. DREVES, *Hymnologische Studien zu Venantius Fortunatus und Rabanus Maurus* (Munich 1908). J. JULIAN, ed., *A Dictionary of Hymnology* (New York 1957) 1:645; 2:993–994. M. BRITT, ed., *The Hymns of the Breviary and Missal* (new ed. New York 1948) 361–364. J. CONNELLY, *Hymns of the Roman Liturgy* (Westminster MD 1957) 142–145. J. SZÖVÉRFFY, *Die Annalen der lateinischen Hymnendichtung* (Berlin 1964–65) 1:214, 222, 226.

[G. E. CONWAY]

SANCTUS

An acclamation of praise within the eucharistic prayer immediately following the preface, beginning *Sanctus, Sanctus, Sanctus* (Holy, holy, holy). The first part of the acclamation is an adaptation of Isaiah 6:3 "Holy, holy, holy is the Lord of hosts [creatures]! . . . All the earth is filled with his glory!" To the *Sanctus* there was added quite early the *Benedictus* ("Blessed is he who comes in the name of the Lord . . .") with which the crowds greeted Christ at his triumphal entry into Jerusalem (Mt 21:9). The ancient Christian liturgy conceived the *Sanctus* as the song of the people; later it became customary to accompany it with instruments.

Origin and history. Clement of Rome (d. *c.* 96) remarked that the Christians of his day sang this hymn in common, but he did not indicate whether the hymn was a part of the Mass (*Letter to the Corinthians* c.34). There is no *Sanctus* in the Eucharistic Prayer of the *Apostolic Tradition*, the oldest complete anaphora in existence. The *Sanctus* is found in the liturgy of the Papyrus Dêr Balyzeh (J. Quasten *Monumenta eucharista et liturgica vetustissima* 41) of the 3rd century and in the *Euchologion* of Serapion (*ibid.* 61) of the 4th. According to the *Apostolic Constitutions* of the 4th century (8.1227; F. X. Funk, ed. *Didascalia et constitutiones apostolorum* 1:507), the people sang the *Sanctus*. In the Roman Rite of the Mass, the *Sanctus* is to be found already in the Gelasian Sacramentary (*Cod. Vat. Reg. lat.* 316; ed. Mohlberg, 1243). The *Sanctus* is an integral part also of the Gallican, Mozarabic, and Milanese rites in the West. Insistence on the people's role can be found as late as Hildebert of Lavardin (d. 1134) and Honorius of Autun (d. *c.* 1156). The last evidence for the singing of the *Sanctus* by priest and people is found in the 11th century; at about that time the *Sanctus* seems to have gradually been taken over by the choir.

Music. The plainchant MS tradition of *Sanctus* melodies goes back to the 10th century. P. J. Thannabaur has indexed a total of 231 *Sanctus* melodies from MSS of the 11th to the 16th centuries. *Sanctus* melody XVIII of the Vatican edition, hitherto regarded as the oldest of all, can be traced only to the 11th century. Thannabaur's belief is that it is a later version of an originally more elaborate melody now lost. The richest period of monophonic *Sanctus* composition was in the 11th and 12th centuries. Most of the melodies were used in relatively small areas; the only ones to achieve wide currency were II, IV, VIII, XI, XII, XV, XVII, and XVIII of the Vatican edition. The *Sanctus* melodies have little in common stylistically with the basic repertory of GREGORIAN CHANT.

Bibliography: J. A. JUNGMANN, *The Mass of the Roman Rite,* tr. F. A. BRUNNER, 2 v. (New York 1951–55). M. HUGLO, ''La tradition occidentale des mélodies byzantines du Sanctus,'' *Der kultische Gesang*, ed. F. TACK (Cologne 1950) 40–46. P. J. THANNABAUR, *Das einstimmige Sanctus der römischen Messe in der handschriftlichen Überlieferung des 11. bis 16. Jahrhunderts* (Munich 1962). B. D. SPINKS, *The Sanctus in the Eucharistic Prayer* (Cambridge 1991). R. F. TAFT, ''The Interpolation of the Sanctus into the Anaphora: When and Where? A Review of the Dossier,'' *Orientalia Christiana Periodica* 57 (1991) 281–308. G. WINKLER, ''Nochmals zu den Anfängen der Epiklese und des Sanctus im Eucharistischen Hochgebet,'' *Theologische Quartalschrift* 174, no. 3 (1994) 214–231.

[E. J. GRATSCH/H. HUCKE/EDS.]

SANDAY, WILLIAM

Anglican scripture scholar who fostered New Testament studies in England; b. Nottinghamshire, England, Aug. 1, 1843; d. Oxford, Sept. 16, 1920. He was educated at Repton School and Oxford, and became a fellow of Trinity College, Oxford, in 1866. He was the principal of Hatfield Hall, Durham; then, recalled to Oxford, he became Dean Ireland Professor (1882), and then Lady Margaret Professor (1895–1920). His never–attained goal was to write a life of Christ based on the new German critical methods. He passed from a conservative position in *The Fourth Gospel* (1872) to a skeptical modernist view in *Form and Content in the Christian Tradition* (1916) and *The Position of Liberal Theology* (1920). Notable works were a commentary on Romans written in conjunction with A. C. Headlam (1895) and *The Life of Christ in Recent Research* (1907). In *Personality in Christ and in Ourselves* (1911), he employed psychological speculations to explain the union of two natures in Christ. A cautious, trusted, yet unoriginal scholar, he inspired many by his works.

Bibliography: *The Dictionary of National Biography from the Earliest Times to 1900,* (London 1912–21) 482–484.

[R. L. ZELL]

SANDER, NICHOLAS (SANDERS)

Controversialist, historian, Catholic agent; b. Charlwood, Surrey, *c.* 1530; d. Ireland, 1581. An Oxford graduate and promising scholar, he left England shortly after the accession of Elizabeth (1559); went to Rome, where he acquired a doctor of divinity degree; and was ordained by Thomas Goldwell, Bishop of St. Asaph. In 1561 he accompanied Cardinal Stanislaus HOSIUS to the Council of Trent and on subsequent missions to Prussia, Poland, and Lithuania. From 1565 to 1572 he was a member of the theological faculty of the University of Louvain. In this period Sander was authorized by the papacy to grant to priests in England faculties for absolving cases of heresy and schism and to prohibit Catholic attendance at Anglican services. He did not return to England to carry out the papal mandate. Instead, in 1573, Sander visited Madrid, where he received a pension from Philip II. He tried to stimulate a strong resistance to Elizabeth's government and he was commissioned by the papacy to go to Ireland for the purpose of inciting the Irish chieftains to rebellion. This latter effort failed, and as a fugitive Sander is alleged to have died of hunger and cold in the Irish hills.

Sander was very popular with English exiles and militant in his opposition to the Elizabethan persecution of Catholics, advocating the excommunication and deposition of the Sovereign and ''the stout assailing'' of the kingdom. This prolific writer's most notable work, *De visibili monarchia ecclesiae* (1571), is important for its list of names of those who suffered various penalties for recusancy. He left in Spain the manuscript *De clave David* (1588), a reply to attacks on his *De monarchia*. He left also an unfinished manuscript. *De origine ac progressu schismatis anglicani* (Cologne 1585), which became the source material for many Catholic accounts of the English Reformation. Although intemperate in expression, it is generally conceded to be historically accurate.

Bibliography: R. BAGWELL, *Ireland under the Tudors*, 3 v. (London 1885–90). N. SANDERS, *Rise and Growth of the Anglican*

Schism, ed. E. RISHTON, tr. D. LEWIS (London 1877). P. HUGHES, *The Reformation in England.* T. M. VEECH, *Dr. Nicholas Sanders and the English Reformation* 1530–1581 (Louvain 1935). *A Literary and Biographical History or Bibliographical Dictionary of the English Catholics from 1534 to the Present Time* 5:476–479. É. AMANN, *Dictionnaire de théologie catholique* 14.1:1090–93. T. G. LAW, *The Dictionary of National Biography from the Earliest Times to 1900,* 17:748–751. *Nomenclator literarius theologiae catholicae* 3:167–170.

[J. J. O'CONNOR]

SANDYS, JOHN, BL.

Priest, martyr; b. in the Diocese of Chester or Lancashire, England; hanged, drawn, and quartered Aug. 11, 1586 at Gloucester. He studied at Oxford and Rheims (1583–84), where he was ordained priest (1584) by Cardinal Louis de Guise. On October 2 that year, he was sent to Gloucestershire, where he labored until his arrest and conviction as an unlawful priest. He was beatified by Pope John Paul II on Nov. 22, 1987 with George Haydock and Companions.

Feast of the English Martyrs: May 4 (England).

See Also: ENGLAND, SCOTLAND, AND WALES, MARTYRS OF.

Bibliography: R. CHALLONER, *Memoirs of Missionary Priests,* ed. J. H. POLLEN (rev. ed. London 1924); *Acts of English Martyrs* (London 1891). YEPES, *Historia Particular de la persecucion de Inglaterra* (Madrid, 1599). STAPLETON, *Post-Reformation Catholic Missions in Oxfordshire* (London, 1906).

[K. I. RABENSTEIN]

SANFEDISTS

Term first used in southern Italy in 1799 and applied during the following two decades to Catholics who, as defenders of their holy faith (*Santa Fede*), joined in popular, spontaneous armed insurrections, to overthrow the republics set up by French and Italian Jacobins and to abolish the religious, political, and social innovations introduced under the influence of the FRENCH REVOLUTION. They were similar in cause and character to the French uprisings in Vendée (1793–96), and occurred in Piedmont, Venice, Modena, Toscany, and the States of the Church. Most famous was the army of several thousand Sanfedists organized and led by Cardinal Fabrizio RUFFO in the Kingdom of Naples: in 1799 it destroyed the short-lived Parthenopean Republic, which had proved very hostile to the Church, and restored the Bourbon monarchs who had fled to Sicily. In the process the heterogeneous collection of recently organized and ill-disciplined troops of peasants, mixed with some criminal elements, committed atrocities as savage as those of their opponents, against the will of the cardinal. Once King Ferdinand IV regained power, he refused to honor the mild capitulation terms offered by Ruffo to the defeated Jacobins in Naples and was responsible for the cruel vengeance wreaked on them. Unworthy of credence is the so-called Sanfedist oath to have no pity on young or old, to shed every drop of blood of the abhorred liberals, and to hate undyingly all enemies of the faith. Liberal historians, opposed to the counterrevolutionary movement and to the Sanfedist type of patriotism, local rather than national, have severely but unreasonably condemned Ruffo and the Sanfedists in Naples and elsewhere by ascribing the excesses of a few to the entire mass.

After 1815 reactionary groups in the STATES OF THE CHURCH and other Italian states that opposed the CARBONARI were also called Sanfedists, as were those in the States of the Church after 1859 who were unfavorable to annexation to the new Italian kingdom. Liberal polemic extended the meaning of Sanfedist in a pejorative sense to include all supporters of the union of throne and altar; but after the mid-19th century, it preferred to substitute the term "clerical" for Sanfedist.

Bibliography: H. ACTON, *The Bourbons of Naples (1734–1825)* (London 1956). E. E. Y. HALES, *Revolution and Papacy, 1769–1846* (Garden City, NY 1960). V. CUOCO, *Saggio storico sulla rivoluzione napoletana del 1799,* ed. N. CORTESE (Florence 1926). W. MATURI, *Encyclopedia Italiana di scienzi, littere ed arti,* 36 v. (Rome 1929–39) 30:639.

[M. L. SHAY]

SANGNIER, MARC

Pioneer of Christian Democracy in France, founder of the Sillon movement condemned by PIUS X; b. Paris, Apr. 3, 1873; d. Paris, May 28, 1950. Sangnier was born into an upper middle-class family and manifested the literary talent of his great-grandfather, Jacques Aucelot, a member of the Académie Française, and the oratorical fluency of his maternal grandfather, the well-known lawyer Charles Lachaud. He accompanied his father, also a lawyer, on travels in Europe and North Africa. The influence of an intelligent and devout mother left an indelible mark on him. At the Collège Stanislas, where the Society of Mary inculcated in the pupils a solid faith rare among men of the time, Sangnier studied under Paul Desjardins and Maurice BLONDEL and won first place in philosophy in a national competition. In 1895 he entered the École Polytechnique to prepare for a military career that he later abandoned for the cause of social education. Between 1914 and 1918, however, he resumed his post as an officer and in 1916 was in charge of a Red Cross mission to Rome. He was elected a deputy to Parliament in 1919, 1945, and 1946.

Origins of Le Sillon. The French Republic of Sangnier's youth was anticlerical, and the masses were rejecting Christianity in spite of Leo XIII's RERUM NOVARUM (1891) and pronouncement on the RALLIEMENT (1892). Sangnier founded the monthly *Le Sillon* (1894–1910) to show that one could be a Christian and a republican at the same time and that a workman could be a Christian without renouncing his fellows. He confided his project to a few companions at the Collège whom he brought together in a kind of cave (la Crypte), telling them, "The truth must be sought with all one's soul," and "Love is stronger than hate." These aphorisms became watchwords of the Sillon movement. The young men took as their models OZANAM, LACORDAIRE, and GRATRY. Archbishop John IRELAND, stopping in Paris in 1892, praised their work.

Beginning in 1899 this group founded first in Paris, then throughout France, study circles for the social education of youth. All social classes were mingled, all members averred, "We have a common soul." In 1901 the Instituts Populaires were founded to make it possible for workmen to continue their education. When the anticlerical minister J. Combes expelled the religious from France in 1902 and prepared the way for the separation of Church and State that was accomplished in 1905, the Sillonists organized protest meetings. To maintain order in the rallies of miners, Sangnier organized a courageous Jeune Garde, several members of which were seriously wounded by anticlerical demonstrators on May 23, 1903. The Sillonists were outstanding for amity, purity of life, and respect for prayer and the Sacraments. Impressed by the good that they accomplished, Pius X encouraged them on their pilgrimages to Rome in 1903 and 1904.

Democracy. Beginning in 1905, Sangnier concentrated his efforts on democratic doctrine and action. He defined democracy as "a social organization that tends toward the maximum development of individual conscience and civic responsibility." To him the best incentive for the sense of responsibility and the love of others implied in democracy was the moral strength implanted in Christian hearts by the grace of God. This grace he thought the Sillonists should devote to the development of democracy in order to restore Christ to a society that believed it could expel Him by anticlerical laws. The Sillonists founded a weekly, the *Eveil démocratique* (1905–1910). Sangnier met leading socialists, anarchists, trade unionists, and representatives of cooperative movements. His group established several successful cooperatives. Its members interested themselves in rural democratic movements, and Sangnier declared before one of these that he was proud to be a Catholic but wished to engage in dialogue with all men of good will.

Each year the Sillonists met in a monastic retreat, where prayer and study were alternated. They also held annual national congresses to determine lines of conduct. At Orléans in 1907 they decided to gather around themselves (while not admitting to membership) non-Catholics attracted by their moral ideals. This new group was called "the greater Sillon." At the Paris congress in 1908 Sangnier announced that the Sillon would establish a new political party, the République démocratique, which would weaken the position of the traditional parties and prove that it was not necessary to be anticlerical in order to adhere to the Republic and to maintain a strong social policy. On two occasions in 1909 and 1910 he ran unsuccessfully in party and parliamentary elections. His campaigns called attention to the new party and its principles. By 1910 the Sillonists had their own daily, *La Démocratie,* for which they raised the capital themselves, partly by doing without even the necessities of life.

Letter of Pius X. On Aug. 25, 1910, a public letter of Pius X called for the dissolution of the Sillon. The organization was accused of avoiding episcopal direction, of placing so much emphasis upon the human origins of authority as to detract from the divine, of attenuating the divine character of Christ by exaggerating His humanity, of preferring tolerance to truth in giving the impression that men could be united in a religion more universal than the Catholic Church. Sangnier's loyalty to the Church had never faltered, but in order to win over his anticlerical adversaries he had at times been conciliatory to the point of imprudence. He and his disciples submitted immediately to the Holy See and the pope was deeply moved by this proof of their loyalty.

Effort for International Peace. After World War I Sangnier was one of the first leaders in Europe to work toward the reconciliation of peoples, especially toward Franco-German understanding, by means of congresses and other international meetings.

Bibliography: M. SANGNIER, *Discours,* 5 v. (Paris 1910–25); *L'Education sociale du peuple* (Paris 1899); *L'Esprit démocratique* (Paris 1905); *Le Plus grand Sillon* (Paris 1908); *La Lutte pour la démocratie* (Paris 1908); *La Paix par la jeunesse* (Paris 1926). A. DARRICAU, *Marc Sangnier* (Paris 1958). J. G. DE FABREGUES, *Le Sillon de Marc Sangnier* (Paris 1964). S. and H. GALLIOT, *Marc Sangnier, 1873–1950* (Paris 1960). The Amitiés Marc Sangnier pub. a bulletin *L'Âme commune.*

[J. CARON]

SANKT BLASIEN, ABBEY OF

The abbey of Sankt Blasien is the former BENEDICTINE monastery, today housing a Jesuit Gymnasium, in the Black Forest, Baden, Germany, in the former Diocese of Constance. The origins of the abbey are obscure. The relationship of a *cella Alba* (with relics of St. BLAISE), which belonged to RHEINAU after 858, and the hermitage of Reginbert (founder of the *cella S. Blasii* according to tradition) is not clear, but the latter must have come into existence in the late 10th century. It is not certain that Werner, who signed himself "abbot" in 1064, bore that title rightfully or that Henry IV's privilege of immunity of 1065 is authentic. Beside the bishop of Basel and Henry IV, Rudolf of Rheinfelden, Duke of Swabia, later antiking, also assured the prosperity of the emerging monastery. He brought the monks into contact with Empress Agnes and through her, with the great CLUNIAC reform center of FRUTTUARIA (c. 1072) whose customs Sankt Blasien accepted, becoming in turn a reform center for southern Germany. It not only founded the priories of Wiblingen and Ochsenhausen but under Abbots Giselbert (1068–85), Uto (1086–1100), and their successors, reformed MURI (1082), GÖTTWEIG (1094), Garsten (1107), SEITENSTETTEN (1112), Ensheim (1123), and Engelberg (1143). In the INVESTITURE STRUGGLE the abbey adopted the program of the papal party under King Rudolf; and BERNOLD OF CONSTANCE, a monk of Sankt Blasien 1085, took a strong stand against the emperor in his chronicle. Otto of Sankt Blasien (d. 1223) continued the chronicle of OTTO OF FREISING. The office of advocate, first held by the bishops of Basel, then by the Dukes of Zähringen (1125–1218), came into the hands of the HAPSBURGS in 1254 and with it eventually the abbey's territory. In 1746, however, the abbot was made prince-abbot. In the 18th century Sankt Blasien once again became a center of learning, especially of historiography; several of its monks were trained by the MAURISTS in France. Abbot Martin II GERBERT VON HORNAU (1764–93) began the publication of the *Germania sacra,* a monumental Church history of Germany by dioceses. In 1807 the abbey was dissolved by Baden and the community settled at SANKT PAUL in Carinthia (1809). The abbey church built under Martin II (1768–83) is an outstanding example of neoclassical architecture. Since 1934 Jesuits have occupied the baroque buildings.

Bibliography: T. RASCHL, *Lexikon für Theologie und Kirche,* ed. M. BUCHBERGER, 10 v. (Freiburg 1930–38) 2:390–391, map of territory, 1612–1803. H. OTT, *Lexikon für Theologie und Kirche,* ed. J. HOFER and K. RAHNER, 10 v. (2d, new ed. Freiburg 1957–65) 9:135–136. W. WATTENBACH, *Deutschlands Geschichtsquellen im Mittelalter. Deutsche Kaiserzeit,* ed. R. HOLTZMANN, v. 1.1–4 (3d ed. Tübingen 1948; repr. of 2d ed. 1938–43) 3:521–528. H. RÖSSLER and G. FRANZ, eds., *Sachwörterbuch zur deutschen Geschichte* (Munich 1958) 1111. J. WOLLASCH, "Muri und St. Blasien, Perspektiven schwäbischen Mönchtums in der Reform," *Deutsches Archiv für Erforschung des Mittelalters* 17 (1961) 420–446.

[A. A. SCHACHER]

SANKT EMMERAM, ABBEY OF

Former BENEDICTINE MONASTERY in Regensburg, Germany. Having been founded in the early 8th century, over the tomb of St. EMMERAM, the abbey was a great religious and cultural center, especially after the German CAROLINGIANS had made Regensburg their main residence. Bishop WOLFGANG OF REGENSBURG separated the office of abbot from his own and summoned Ramwold of Saint-Maximin in Trier to reform the abbey. Abbot Ramwold (975–1000) introduced the customs of GORZE and helped to spread them throughout Bavaria. The reinvigorated abbey emerged as an outstanding school of book illumination, e.g., the "Gospel Book of Uta." The abbey was never greater than in the 11th century when it produced such authors as Hartwich, Arnold, and OTHLO, or such religious leaders as Gerard, later cardinal bishop of Ostia, ULRIC OF ZELL, and WILLIAM OF HIRSAU. Sankt Emmeram was made a free imperial abbey soon after 1295 and an exempt abbey (*see* EXEMPTION) in 1326. In 1451–52, it joined the reform congregation of KASTL. Its abbot became a prince-abbot in 1732. The late 17th and 18th centuries saw a great flowering of scholarship in the abbey. In 1802 Prince-Primate K. T. DALBERG was granted Sankt Emmeram together with the imperial city of Regensberg; in 1810 the abbey was transferred to Bavaria, which dissolved it in 1812. Its manuscripts went to Munich; the abbey church, medieval in structure, with baroque decorations, became a parish church; the other buildings went to the princes of Thurn und Taxis.

Bibliography: B. BISCHOFF, *Die südostdeutschen Schreibschulen und Bibliotheken in der Karolingerzeit,* v.1 (Leipzig 1940) 171–183. W. WATTENBACH, *Deutschlands Geschichtsquellen im Mittelalter. Deutsche Kaiserzeit,* ed. R. HOLTZMANN, v.1.1–4 (3d ed. Tübingen 1948; repr. of 2d ed. 1938–43) 2:26–30, 268. R. BAUERREISS, *Kirchengeschichte Bayerns,* v.1 (2d ed. St. Ottilien 1958). M. PIENDL, *Lexikon für Theologie und Kirche,* ed. J. HOFER and K. RAHNER, 10 v. (2d, new ed. Freiburg 1957–65) 9:141–142.

[A. A. SCHACHER]

SANKT FLORIAN, MONASTERY OF

In the Diocese of Linz, upper Austria. At the tomb of the martyr St. Florian (d. 304) arose a popular shrine that was a Benedictine cell at the time of Charlemagne. In 1071 Bp. St. ALTMAN OF PASSAU granted it to Augustinian canons, under whose provosts it has flourished to the present. The abbey soon had a famous school and was a center of learning and of the GREGORIAN REFORM. Until the 15th century there was a women's cloister adjoining. In 1686 Provost David Fuhrmann started the present magnificent abbey, a masterpiece of the baroque style by the architects C. A. Carlone and J. Prandtauer, completed in 1745, and known for its refectory, prelature, and a marble hall. In the majestic church with its famous organ, the largest in Austria, A. Bruckner was organist from 1845 to 1855. Noted for its scholarship in the 19th century, Sankt Florian has a library of 120,000 volumes, 800 precious MSS, and more than 800 incunabula, besides rich collections of medieval art and numismatics. The abbey was suppressed (1941–45).

Bibliography: J. STÜLZ, *Geschichte des Chorherrnstiftes St. Florian* (Linz 1835). F. LINNINGER, *Reichgottesarbeit in der Heimat* (St. Florian 1954); *Führer durch das Chorherrnstift St. Florian* (4th ed. Linz 1960). G. SCHMIDT, *Die Malerschule von St. Florian* (Graz 1962). J. ZAUNER, *Lexikon für Theologie und Kirche,* ed. J. HOFER and K. RAHNER, 10 v. (2d, new ed. Freiburg 1957–65) 9:143–144.

[N. BACKMUND]

SANKT GALLEN, ABBEY OF

Former Benedictine monastery lying south of Lake Constance, on the upper Steinach River, in the city of Sankt Gallen, Switzerland, Diocese of Sankt Gallen. Founded in 612 by the Irish hermit St. GALL, it was given its present appearance by Prince-Abbot Celestine II, Gugger von Staudach, who had the extant late baroque abbey church and library built in 1760 according to the plan of the Vorarlberg architect Peter Thumb. The predecessor of this baroque church was a large Carolingian basilica with transept, square choir, apse, and crypt; it was erected after 830 at the direction of Abbot Gozbert (816–837). Abbot Ulric VIII Rosch (1463–91) had the basilica decorated with a late Gothic choir portico (completed in 1483).

Most of the monks in the original monastic settlement—under the diocese of Chur—came from Raetia, but King Dagobert I (628–638) put the monastery under the rule of the Alemanns, and subsequently, the monastery was repeatedly destroyed in the struggles between Alemanns and Franks at the turn of the century. Only under the Alemann OTHMAR, who became abbot of Sankt Gallen in 720, did the monastery become historically important. Holdings steadily increased: reports under Abbot Gozbert spoke of holdings stretching into northern Switzerland, extending from Swabia to north of the Danube, and in Breisgau. Abbot Othmar founded the hospital and scriptorium; he introduced true cenobitic life at Sankt Gallen in 720 and the BENEDICTINE RULE in 747 or 748. To preserve the free status of the abbey, Othmar resisted Frankish rule, which was established over the monastery in 741. For this he was arrested by the Frankish Count and died in prison in 759. Upon his death, the bishop of Constance, embodying a personal union of offices, was made abbot of Sankt Gallen, but the abbey begged Louis

the Pious for aid, and in 818 he granted it immunity and raised it to the status of an imperial abbey. This marked the beginning of the abbey's intensive cultural development.

The most important MSS produced in the Sankt Gallen SCRIPTORIUM belong to the 100-year period under Abbots Gozbert; Grimald (841–872), who was simultaneously archchancellor of Louis the German; Hartmut (872–883); and Solomon (890–920), who was also bishop of Constance. The blueprint of Sankt Gallen was drawn *c.* 820, probably as an ideal blueprint for a rich, populous monastery. The sketch, with its exhaustive explanations, gives an excellent picture of a Carolingian monastic plant. In planimetric outline, it shows completely and in detail the arrangement of work rooms, living quarters, and outbuildings around church and cloister (*see* MONASTERY). The MS illuminations produced at the abbey during that century are marked by imaginative ornamentation, influenced by Irish 9th-century illuminations, examples of which reached Sankt Gallen through the Irish monks on pilgrimage to the tomb of St. Gall. (Irish miniature work is still to be found in the monastery library.) Through the 11th century Sankt Gallen produced important poets and scholars such as Tutilo, NOTKER BALBALUS, NOTKER LABEO, and the four EKKEHARDS. Their individual works are still preserved in the large monastery library and archives, which contain an exhaustive collection of medieval Biblical and liturgical writings, as well as works on Latin philology, history of literature, art, law, and medicine.

In the INVESTITURE STRUGGLE, Sankt Gallen, under Abbot Ulric of Eppenstein (1077–1121), later patriarch of AQUILEIA, became involved in clashes deleterious to the abbey by siding with the imperial party. Schismatic elections of abbots and the attendant party strife among the monks led to the cultural decline of the monastery. FREDERICK BARBAROSSA tried unsuccessfully to stem this decline by granting the abbey once again a special legal status as a newly privileged imperial monastery. But revival began only about the mid-15th century, especially under Prince Abbot Ulric VIII, an energetic organizer, who established the monastic domain of Sankt Gallen as an associate state of the Swiss Confederation; the city of Sankt Gallen became independent of the monastery in 1455. In 1525 the city joined the Protestant cause in the Reformation; the abbey remained Catholic. One result of this was the destruction of the entire stock of medieval works of art held by the monastery. In 1805 the monastery was suppressed. Politically, the monastic state was dissolved, and the city of Sankt Gallen became the capital of the canton of the same name. The area formerly belonging to the monastery was placed under the spiritual jurisdiction of the Diocese of Constance until 1814. Then for a short time there was a dual Diocese of Chur-Sankt Gallen; in 1847 an independent Diocese of Sankt Gallen was erected.

See Also: BLARER; SFONDRATI.

Bibliography: J. M. CLARK, *The Abbey of St. Gall as a Centre of Literature and Art* (Cambridge, Eng. 1926). A. FÄH, *Die Schicksale der Kathedrale St. Gallen seit ihrer Erbauung* (Einsiedeln 1928). W. EHRENZELLER, *St. Gallische Geschichte im Spätmittelalter und in der Reformationszeit,* 2 v. (St. Gallen 1931–38). A. BRUCKNER, ed., *Scriptoria medii aevi Helvetica* (Geneva 1935–) v.2, 3. T. MAYER, ''Konstanz und St. Gallen in der Frühzeit,'' *Schweizerische Zeitschrift für Geschichte* 2 (1952) 473–524. *Urkundenbuch der Abtei St. Gallen,* ed. H. WARTMANN et al., 6 v. (Zurich-St. Gallen 1863–1950). E. A. LOWE, *Codices latini antiquiores* (Oxford 1934) 7:893–997. K. GRUBER, ''Der karolingische Klosterplan von St. Gallen. Neue Forschungsergebnisse,'' *Bodenseebuch* 37 (1960). *Die Kunstdenkmäler des Kantons St. Gallen,* v.3.2 *Das Stift,* ed. E. POESCHEL (Basel 1961). J. DUFT, *Lexikon für Theologie und Kirche,* ed. J. HOFER and K. RAHNER (Freiberg 1957–65) 9:144–147.

[W. GRAPE]

SANKT LAMBRECHT, ABBEY OF

In the Diocese of Graz-Seckau, Styria, Austria, belonging to the Austrian congregation of Benedictines. The Bavarian Count Markward of Carinthia *c.* 1076 began the foundation which his son Duke Henry III completed in 1092, the rich endowment of lands on the right bank of the Isar River being jointly administered with the bishops of Regensburg. (St. EMMERAM's martyrdom is depicted on an altar in Sankt Lambrecht.) The abbey, under papal protection after 1109, contested its quasiepiscopal rights with the bishops of Salzburg and was represented in Rome in 1226 by the famous lawyer Albert the Bohemian. It was in charge of missions in western Austria (1652–1786) and had a famous philosophical-theological school (1684–1783) before its suppression by Joseph II (1787). It was restored (1802) and again suppressed (1939–47). The early Romanesque church, now richly baroque, collapsed in 1328, was restored in 1430 as a Gothic hall church, and in 1644 was enlarged. In the Middle Ages the abbey was strongly fortified. The famous pilgrimage center Mariazell (12th century) is a foundation of Sankt Lambrecht. Scholars from the abbey taught in Salzburg and Graz. There was a boys' choir school (1838–1932).

Bibliography: Mansdorf Chronicle and Peter Weichsler's Chronicle, *Beiträge zur Kunde steiermärkischer Geschichtsquellen,* 32 v. (1864–1902), v.1 and 10. L. H. COTTINEAU, *Répertoire topobibliographique des abbayes et prieurés,* 2 v. (Mâcon 1935–39) 2:2755–56. O. WONISCH, *Lexikon für Theologie und Kirche,* ed. M. BUCHBERGER, 10 v. (Freiburg 1930–38) 6:353–354. J. PLONER, *Lexikon für Theologie und Kirche,* ed. J. HOFER and K. RAHNER, 10 v. (2d, new ed. Freiburg 1957–65) 9:155.

[W. FINK]

SANKT PAUL, ABBEY OF (CARINTHIA)

In Lavantal (Wolfsberg), Diocese of Klagenfurt, belonging to the Austrian congregation of BENEDICTINES. Count Siegfried of Spanheim, before he died on a pilgrimage, left instructions to found the monastery, which his son Engelbert settled with 12 monks from HIRSAU after 1090. The Palatinate Spanheimers came to Bavaria by marriage with the Aribonen, counts of the Chiemgau. Choir and crypt were consecrated in 1093 by Bl. THIEMO of Salzburg. Abbots Peregrinus and Ulrich built the present beautiful Romanesque basilica (three naves, three apses, and transept) with massive walls (*c.* 1200). After a fire in 1367 Gothic vaulting was added with fantasy paintings by M. and F. PACHER (1470–80). Baroque additions were made in the monastery (1618–83 and in 1744). The abbey was suppressed (1782–87) by JOSEPH II, but given in 1809 to refugee monks from SANKT BLASIEN, who brought MSS and treasures with them and reopened the school. In 1828 Sankt Paul helped establish the gymnasium and school of philosophy in the new abbey of St. Stephan in AUGSBURG. Its members have included Latinists and scholars, one of whom was Beda Schroll, noted for his research in Carinthian history.

Bibliography: J. PLONER, *Lexikon für Theologie und Kirche,* ed. J. HOFER and K. RAHNER, 10 v. (2d, new ed. Freiburg 1957–65) 9:166.

[W. FINK]

SANKT PETER, ABBEY OF

Benedictine house, founded by St. RUPERT OF SALZBURG, *c.* 700; it is the oldest monastery north of the Alps, and the basis for the town and Diocese of Salzburg. Under the Abbot-bishop John, St. BONIFACE it introduced the BENEDICTINE RULE, whereas, previously, a rule of Columbanian provenance had been in use. Preaching and the assarting of woodland were the chief occupations of the monastery. Under CHARLEMAGNE, Salzburg became an archdiocese (798) and Abbot-bishop Arno its first archbishop. In 987 Archbishop Frederick separated the abbey from the archiepiscopal administration and gave Sankt Peter its own abbot. Nevertheless, later archbishops often considered Sankt Peter as a proprietary monastery.

The first church built by St. Rupert, together with the monastery, was destroyed by fire in 847. Following a second fire in 1127, the present collegiate church was built between 1130 and 1143, and despite baroque renovations, its old Romanesque nave is still recognizable. The rococo style of the interior ornamentation is in peculiar contrast to the heavy Romanesque style of the achitecture. The vestibule and the main entrance, both masterpieces of Romanesque, were done in 1244 and 1245. The monastic buildings as well as the present form of the famous cemetery of Sankt Peter, the oldest burial grounds of Salzburg, date from the 17th century.

According to tradition, the catacombs that interlace the "Mönchsberg" (monks' mountain) are of early Christian origin. In the 8th and 9th centuries, Sankt Peter housed a famous SCRIPTORIUM; its oldest extant work is the *Liber vitae* (the *Verbrüderungsbuch,* written under the direction of the Abbot-bishop VIRGILIUS OF SALZBURG). Between the 11th and 13th centuries, outstanding works of book illumination were produced in the abbey. Sankt Peter played an important role in the founding of the Benedictine University in Salzburg (1622). Before its suspension in 1810, many of its monks, such as the theologian Paul Metzger and the historian Joseph Metzger, were professors. In 1925 Sankt Peter became an archabbey, and Archabbot Petrus Klotz built the college for Benedictine scholastics. The monastery was suppressed in 1941, but was reestablished in 1945.

Bibliography: J. METZGER, *Historia Salisburgensis* (Salzburg 1692). B. SEEAUER, *Novissimum chronicon antiqui monasterii ad S. Petrum Salisburgi* (Augsburg 1772). P. BERHANDTSKY, *Anszug aus der neuesten Chronik des alten Benediktinerklosters zu St. Peter in Salzburg,* 2 v. (Salzburg 1783). H. WIDMANN, *Geschichte Salzburgs,* 3 v. (Gotha 1907–14). H. TIETZE, ed. *Die Denkmale des Benediktinerstiftes St. Peter in Salzburg* (Österreichische Kunsttopographie 12; Vienna 1913). F. MARTIN, *Salzburg,* ed. I. WEGLEITER (Dehio-Handbuch. *Die Kunstdenkmäler Österreichs;* 4th ed. Vienna 1954). K. FORSTNER, "Die Karolingischen Handschriften in den Salzburger Bibliotheken," *Mitteilungen der Gesellschaft für Salzburger Landeskunde,* suppl. 3 (Salzburg 1962). F. HERMANN, *St. Peter, Salzburg* (Christliche Kunststätten Österreichs 1; Salzburg 1962).

[M. M. ZYKAN]

SANKT ULRICH VON AUGSBURG, ABBEY OF

Former imperial BENEDICTINE monastery in AUGSBURG, Germany, founded in 1012 by Bp. Bruno over the tomb of SS. ULRIC and AFRA, replacing an earlier monastery of canons. It was settled by monks from TEGERNSEE under Abbot Reginbald from SANKT GALLEN, who was bishop of Speyer at his death in 1039. During the INVESTITURE STRUGGLE, the abbey supported the pope, while the bishop sided with the emperor. In the 12th century it was considered a model monastery; after 1440 it was the center of the Melk Reform in Swabia. During the Renaissance the abbey was the center for humanist artists of Augsburg. Although the monks were banished during the

Reformation (1537–48), for most of the 16th century the abbey remained an exemplary Benedictine institution. Abbot Bernhard Hertfelder (1632–42) was considered the savior of Catholicism Augsburg. Scholarship and art reached a high level during the first half of the 18th century; but under Abbot Josef Maria von Langenmantel (1753–90) the abbey declined financially and Abbots Benedikt Maria Angehrn of Neresheim and Robert Kolb of Elchingen were installed as administrators by the emperor and the Bavarian elector. Good discipline was restored under Abbot Wikterp Grundner (d. 1795). The abbey was secularized in 1802, but the monks continued to lead a community life until an epidemic struck in 1806. Efforts to reestablish the abbey in 1828 and 1883 were unsuccessful. The abbey church, famous for its three altars (*c.* 68 feet high) and for its treasury, became a Catholic parish church, and in 1937 it was declared a minor BASILICA.

Bibliography: S. DREXEL, *Reichsstift und Reichsstadt* (*Studien u. Mitteilungen zur Geschichte des Benediktiner-Ordens* . . . , Ergänzungsheft 14; Munich 1938). B. SCHROEDER, *Die Aufhebung des Benediktiner-Reichsstiftes St. Ulrich und Afra in Augsburg, 1802–1806* (*ibid.* 3; 1929). H. SCHNELL, "St. Ulrich und Afra in Augsburg," *Jubiläumsjahrbuch* (Augsburg 1955). H. RINN, ed., *Augusta, 955–1955* (Munich 1955). N. LIEB, *Augsburg, St. Ulrich und Afra* (2d ed. Munich 1955).

[G. SPAHR]

SANSEVERINO, GAETANO

Neoscholastic philosopher; b. Naples, Aug. 7, 1811; d. Naples, Nov. 16, 1865. After ordination for the archdiocese of Naples in 1834, he studied at the University of Naples and was appointed to the Royal Library. In 1840 he founded the series *Biblioteca Cattolica,* intended to include all major Catholic works, and the periodical *Scienza e Fede,* in which he published many important articles. From 1846 until his death he taught philosophy in the diocesan Liceo in Naples; in 1846 he also founded an academy of Thomistic philosophy that became in 1874 the Academy of St. Thomas Aquinas. Having made the transition from CARTESIANISM to THOMISM, he became a zealous promoter of Thomistic thought as the only sound means of solving current problems. Through his efforts the Neapolitan school became one of the principal centers of the Thomistic revival, promoted by such disciples as N. Signorello, G. Prisco, and S. Talamo. Among his major works are *Institutiones logicae* (Naples 1854) and *Philosophia Christiana cum antiqua et nova comparata,* planned for 15 volumes, of which the first five were published by him (Naples 1862), volumes 6 and 7 being published posthumously (Naples 1866, 1878) by Signorello, who also compiled a widely used summary, *Elementa philosophiae Christianae* (3 v. Naples 1864, 1865, 1870).

See Also: SCHOLASTICISM.

Bibliography: A. MASNOVO, *Il neo-tomismo in Italia* (Milan 1923). P. NADDEO, *Le origini del neo-tomismo e la scuola napoletana di G. Sanseverino* (Salerno 1940). P. DEZZA, *Alle origini del neo-tomismo* (Milan 1940). D. LANNA, "La scuola tomistica di Napoli," *Rivista di filosofia neoscolastica* 17 (1925) 385–395.

[R. M. PIZZORNI]

SANT' ANTIMO, ABBEY OF

Former Benedictine monastery in the Diocese of Chiusi in the Orcia Valley, near Siena, Italy. Its origins can probably be traced to a grant of CHARLEMAGNE who endowed the house in gratitude for the passing of an epidemic that had ravaged his army in the Val d'Orcia. The abbey housed the relics of SS. ANTHIMUS and SEBASTIAN, acquired from ADRIAN I by Charlemagne, at whose death (814) his son Louis I the Pious endowed the monastery with Montalcino and its supporting territory. The abbey church, begun *c.* 1118, is representative of Italian Romanesque architecture; the crypt, dating from 813, with its vault supported by four small columns, is an important pre-Romanesque monument. Within the church a semicircular *deambulatorium,* showing the influence of CLUNIAC ARCHITECTURE, demonstrates a feature rarely found in Italian construction. As the abbots lost their feudal jurisdiction with the rise of Siena, the house declined in wealth and discipline; it was suppressed by PIUS II in 1462.

Bibliography: A. CANESTRELLI, *L'abbazia di S. Antimo* (Siena 1910). L. H. COTTINEAU, *Répertoire topobibliographique des abbayes et prieurés,* 2 v. (Mâcon 1935–39) 2:2593. G. PENCO, *Storia del monachesimo in Italia* (Rome 1961) 121, 541–542, 563.

[O. J. BLUM]

SANT' EGIDIO, COMMUNITY OF

The Community of Sant' Egidio is a public association of lay people dedicated to evangelization and charity in more than 35 countries around the world. The community has as its center the Roman Church of Sant' Egidio, from which the community takes its name. The community began in Rome in 1968 in the period following the Second Vatican Council at the initiative of Andrea Riccardi, a young man who was then less than twenty. Riccardi gathered a group of high-school students to listen to and to put the Gospel into practice. The first Christian communities of the Acts of the Apostles and Francis of Assisi served as reference points. Thus, the small group

of women and men began visiting the crowded slums on the outskirts of Rome and started an afternoon school (*Scuola Popolare* ["People's School"]; now known as "Schools of Peace") providing tutoring for drop-out children.

From its very beginnings, the community has maintained a continuous presence of prayer and welcome for the poor and for pilgrims in the area of Trastevere and in Rome as it spread throughout the world. The different communities share the following principles: prayer, evangelization, solidarity with the poor, ecumenism and dialogue. The first work of the community is prayer, which is an essential part of the life of the community in Rome and communities throughout the world and central to the overall direction of the community's search for a more authentic Christian living. The communities gather frequently to pray together, and in many cities there is a common prayer open to everybody. The second pillar is communicating the Gospel. The members take personal responsibility to communicate the Good News to others, leading them to a "missionary fraternity" in many parts of the world.

The third fundamental and daily commitment typical of Sant' Egidio that flows from this commitment to the Gospel is the service to the poor, lived as friendship. This friendship widened to other poor people—the physically and mentally disabled, homeless, immigrants, the terminally ill—and to different situations: prisons, homes for the elderly, gypsy camps, and refugee camps. The communities' love for the poor has become work for peace and reconciliation, taking the view that war is the greated of all poverties. Through prayer, meetings, dialogues, and stress on common humanity, the community tries to resolve conflicts and facilitate humanitarian aid to the civil populations who most suffer from war.

The evangelically rooted commitment to work with poor people is at the base of other humanitarian initiatives, addressed to all people of good will, with no regard to their religious belief. These include a campaign against anti-personnel mines; aid to refugees, war, and famine victims; and working against slavery and capital punishment. These activities, rooted in the struggle to affirm the value of life without exceptions, involves the members of Sant' Egidio all over the world.

The community is also committed to serving ecumenical and interfaith dialogue. Since 1987 Sant'Egidio has been committed both at the grassroots and international level to host meetings and prayer gatherings in the spirit of the 1986 World Day of Prayer for Peace in Assisi. In 1998 the community promoted the 12th International meeting *Uomini e Religioni*, which brought together representative of all the major religions in Bucharest to pray and work together for peace. As Pope John Paul II said in Sant' Egidio on its 25th anniversary in 1993 they have no other limit "but charity."

Bibliography: COMUNITÀ DI SANT' EGIDIO, *Stranieri nostri fratelli; verso una società multirazziale* (Brescia 1989). A. MONTONATI, *Il sapore dell'utopia: la comunità di Sant' Egidio* (Rome 1999). A. RICCARDI, *Sant'Egidio, Roma e il Mondo* (Rome 1997).

[EDS]

SANT' EUTIZIO DI NORCIA, ABBEY OF

Originally a convent, then a Benedictine monastery after 536, in the Diocese of Spoleto, six miles from Norcia, in the Italian Campania. It was founded, according to tradition, by an Abbot Spes, who is mentioned by St. GREGORY in the *Dialogues* (3.38), on a site in the Castoriana valley, near the birthplace of St. BENEDICT. Its second abbot and cofounder was (St.) Eutychius, a former hermit who, legend says, had come from Syria and had been a companion of (St.) Lawrence, the founder of the Abbey of FARFA, an establishment with which the monastery of Sant' Eutizio always maintained close relations. The monastery came under CLUNIAC influence in the 11th century, the period of its greatest splendor and achievement. The abbey was at this time a cultural center with an important SCRIPTORIUM and library, holdings extending to the Adriatic and a monumental complex of buildings, among them the church restored by Abbots Teodino I and Teodino II in the late 12th and early 13th centuries. On abolition of the abbey's property holdings by INNOCENT IV in 1257 a period of decline set in. In 1327, after bitter clashes and the use of armed force, JOHN XXII put it under the Duke of Spoleto and later, the Curia. After an attempt at reform by Abbot Anastasius (1448–49), the abbey was put under COMMENDATION, beginning in 1449. Thenceforth, despite the efforts of the commendatories, the process of disintegration was inexorable. In 1820 Pope PIUS VII in recreating the Diocese of Norcia made the bishop abbot *in commendam* of Sant' Eutizio. Of the library and archives, there remains only a very small portion that was, fortunately, given to BARONIUS in 1595. Of the buildings there remains the ancient and remarkable Romanesque church, restored and reopened in 1956.

Bibliography: L. H. COTTINEAU, *Répertoire topobibliographique des abbayes et prieurés,* 2 v. (Mâcon 1935–39) 2:2669. P. PIRRI, *L'Abbazia di Sant' Eutizio in Val Castoriana (Studia anselmiana* 45; 1960).

[I. DE PICCOLI]

SANTA CRUZ (COIMBRA), MONASTERY OF

Former monastery of CANONS REGULAR OF ST. AUGUSTINE, at Coimbra, Portugal. The monastery, one of the glories of medieval Portugal, was founded by Tello, archdeacon and member of the cathedral chapter of that city. The cornerstone was laid on June 28, 1131; soon after the canonical customs of Saint-Ruf near Avignon were adopted for the governance of the monastery. Jurisdictional conflicts with the Diocese of Coimbra prompted Tello to seek papal exemptions from episcopal control. After the founder's death in 1136 the history of Santa Cruz was intimately associated with THEOTONIUS, the first prior (1132–52). Through Portugal's first king, Afonso Henriques, it became an institution of considerable wealth. It became a religious center of widespread influence, but by 1527 it was badly in need of reform. The Hieronymite, Blaise of Braga, laid down new rigorous statutes for the monastery, and it reached the height of its renown in this century. The congregation of Santa Cruz included 19 monasteries. The monastery remained in existence until the decree of secularization in 1833. The church in Manueline style is now used by the parish. The monastic buildings serve diverse purposes.

Bibliography: *Livro Santo,* an unpublished 140-folio cartulary found in the Arquivo Nacional da Torre do Tombo. *Vita Tellonis archidiaconi* in *Portugaliae monumenta historica, Scriptores* 1:64–75. C. ERDMANN, *Papsturkunden in Portugal* (Berlin 1927). E. A. O'MALLEY, *Tello and Theotonio: The Twelfth-Century Founders of the Monastery of Santa Cruz in Coimbra* (Washington 1954). L. H. COTTINEAU, *Répertoire topobibliographique des abbayes et prieurés,* 2 v. (Mâcon 1935–39) 1:830.

[A. O'MALLEY]

SANTA FE, ARCHDIOCESE OF

Metropolitan see comprising an area of 61,142 square miles in the state of New Mexico, the Archdiocese of Santa Fe (*Sanctae Fidei*) was established as a vicariate apostolic in 1850, a diocese in 1853, and an archdiocese in 1875. Originally it covered New Mexico, Arizona, and Colorado, but after the creation of the Vicariates of Arizona and Colorado in 1868, it was confined to New Mexico, minus the southernmost counties bordering on Texas and Mexico; these counties, as part of the Gadsden Purchase, were first in the Arizona vicariate (later the Diocese of Tucson), then in the Diocese of El Paso, Tex., created in 1914. With the erection of the Diocese of Gallup in 1939 and the Diocese of Las Cruces in 1982, the archdiocese was further restricted to the eastern and north central part of the state. The suffragan sees are Tucson and Phoenix in Arizona, and Gallup and Las Cruces in

Loretto Chapel, Santa Fe, New Mexico. (©Danny Lehman/CORBIS)

New Mexico. In 2001, the Catholic population of the Archdiocese of Santa Fe numbered approximately 30 percent of the total population, distributed among 92 parishes and 217 active missions.

Early Period. The area's early history is associated entirely with Catholicism. Discovered by Fray Marcos de NIZA in 1539, it was explored by the Coronado expedition of 1540 with the double purpose of extending the Spanish Empire and propagating the faith. No ''golden cities'' were found to justify immediate colonization, but two Franciscans did remain to start a rudimentary mission; subsequently Fray Juan de PADILLA was killed by Native Americans on the Great Plains, while Fray Luis de Ubeda, a lay brother left at the pueblo of Pecos, was slain by his charges. Some 40 years later, three friars, Agustin Rodriguez, Francisco LÓPEZ, and Juan de Santa Maria, were sent by the viceroy on another exploratory mission; unscrupulous soldiers accompanying them foiled their purposes and the trio was killed by Tigua tribes people

of the middle Rio Grande Valley. But in 1598 a permanent colony was established at last under Gov. Juan de Oñate, while a sizable missionary band began ministering to the pueblos.

By 1610, the Villa of Santa Fe (*Holy Faith*) was founded as a permanent capital, the only Spanish town in that century. Like other Santa Fe's in Spanish America, it was named after the royal military camp near Granada, where Ferdinand and Isabella dealt the final blow to the Moors in Spain. The original patronal title of the parish church was Our Lady of the Assumption, which in the next decade became that of the Conception. Enshrined in it was a statue of the Assumption, brought by Fray Alonso de BENAVIDES in 1625; it began gathering lasting fame as *La Conquistadora,* the Queen of the Kingdom of New Mexico and its Villa of Santa Fe. There also was the chapel of San Miguel for the indigenous Mexicans brought along by the Spaniards. The mission enterprise, called the Custody of the Conversion of St. Paul, began most auspiciously, having within a short time more than 30 churches, ranging from the northernmost pueblo of Taos near the present Colorado border down to the pueblo of Guadalupe del Paso, now the city of Juárez in Mexico. Several of these missions lay well east of the Rio Grande basin, touching on the Great Plains, while as many more stretched westward to the Hopi pueblos in what is now northeastern Arizona. Each of these great mission establishments was built by the Native Americans under the guidance of a lone Franciscan.

However, grave opposition developed among the ruling medicine men, particularly when it was deemed necessary to destroy their idolatrous ceremonial chambers and suppress their immoral secret dances; this and the interference of certain Spanish officials brought on troubles that ended in a giant holocaust. Posing for years as the spokesman for the Great Spirit *Po-he-yemu,* a mulatto former slave hiding in Taos cleverly united the various pueblo leaders into inciting the great Pueblo Revolt of 1680, which produced 21 Franciscan martyrs in a single day. Santa Fe was sacked, Our Lady's church destroyed completely, and San Miguel chapel partially. The colonists managed to fight their way out, fleeing south to Guadalupe del Paso where they remained exiled for 13 years. Late in December 1693, they and the missionaries returned in what is called the DeVargas reconquest. They had saved *La Conquistadora* from destruction and kept up her cult during exile and the reconquest of Santa Fe. For about a year Mass was celebrated in the palace of the governors, until Governor DeVargas built a temporary church of St. Francis in 1695. Further political troubles and by Native Americans campaigns prevented the rebuilding of the original parish and shrine of Our Lady as the governor had publicly vowed; these were finally built on the site of the old parish (1714–17), but the title of the temporary church was carried over to the new structure, thus making St. Francis of Assisi the permanent parish and town patron.

Gradually most of the missions were reestablished, while the Spanish people began spreading out in new towns with their own chapels. However, the new century proved disastrous to both the colonists and their Pueblo neighbors, for by 1800 long periods of drought and continual invasions had seriously impoverished the people. Spain, a rapidly waning power, had been unable to help. Nor could Mexico do much, even after its separation from Spain in 1821, due to the hundreds of miles of arid wilderness that separated New Mexico from the rest of Spanish America. Life there was not only precarious, but also devoid of educational opportunities and even material necessities when, in 1846, the U.S. took over New Mexico and the surrounding Southwest.

Ecclesiastical Jurisdiction. Although jurisdiction was claimed by the bishops of Mexico, Guadalajara, and Durango, the Franciscan Custody had acted as an independent mission for more than a century. In 1730 Bp. Benito Crespo of Durango began exercising effective jurisdiction, when he appointed a secular priest Santiago Roybal, who had been born in Santa Fe in 1694 or 1695, as his vicar in Santa Fe. The Franciscans continued in charge of all mission and parish work but in a steady decline, due to economic circumstances and conflict with Native Americans as well as a dearth of missionary replacements from their motherhouse in Mexico City. In 1798 the bishop of Durango secularized the parishes of Santa Fe and other large towns, but few of the diocesan priests sent up stayed for long. Several native New Mexicans were ordained after 1800, but these and the last few aging friars were unable to meet the demands of so vast and impoverished a region. Mexico's independence from Spain in 1821 aggravated the situation by removing Spanish-born missionaries. By the time the U.S. took over, the Church in New Mexico was in a sorry state. The ancient Franciscan missions were crumbling fast; the descendants of the Spanish colonists, for the most part illiterate, had kept the faith ardently alive but sadly marred by ignorance; and the Pueblo peoples, never fully Christianized, had merely covered their pagan beliefs with the outward signs of Catholicity.

Soon after New Mexico's annexation by the U.S. in 1846, the American hierarchy petitioned the Holy See for a bishop in the Great Southwest. Historic Santa Fe was selected as the see city and John Baptist LAMY was named bishop, arriving in Santa Fe late in 1851.

Lamy. The new bishop chose St. Francis as patron of the diocese and the old parish church of St. Francis became the cathedral. Finding a mere handful of priests, some of whom resented him as an intruder, Lamy not only brought numbers of French clergy to serve his vast territory but soon ordained some worthy native candidates, and founded a seminary. Priests were also sent to the faraway populated areas of Tucson and Denver. The lack of educational facilities was remedied by the introduction of religious teachers. In 1853 the Kentucky Sisters of Loretto founded Our Lady of Light Academy in Santa Fe, later opening schools at Taos, Mora, Las Vegas, Albuquerque, Bernalillo, Socorro, and Las Cruces; in 1859 the French Christian Brothers founded St. Michael's in Santa Fe, subsequently opening other schools at Las Vegas, Mora, and Bernalillo. By 1865 the Cincinnati Sisters of Charity had founded St. Vincent's Hospital and Orphanage in the capital, and followed with an academy and two parish schools in Albuquerque. In 1867 the bishop welcomed a group of Neapolitan Jesuits who, through their printing of *La Revista Catolica* in Las

Vegas and by their mission preaching all over the Territory, helped to save the faithful from the many Protestant proselytizers who poured in with the coming of the railroad. In 1869 a new stone cathedral replaced the old adobe church—keeping intact, however, the ancient Conquistadora shrine as its Lady Chapel. In 1875 Santa Fe was erected a metropolitan with Tucson and Denver as suffragan dioceses. Lamy resigned in 1885 and died three years later.

Salpointe, Chapelle, Bourgade. John Baptist Salpointe, coadjutor since 1884, succeeded to the see on July 18, 1885, and devoted much of his time and effort in behalf of education for the Native Americans. St. Catherine's Indian School, under the direction of the Sisters of the Blessed Sacrament for Indians and Colored People, was opened in Santa Fe. Salpointe's term was marked also by difficulties with the *Penitentes,* a flagellant society, which flared up in opposition to diocesan regulations. He resigned on Jan. 7, 1894, and retired to Banning, Calif., where he wrote his *Soldiers of the Cross,* a source history of the pioneer American Church in the Great Southwest. His successor was Placide Louis CHAPELLE, coadjutor since 1891, who became third archbishop of Santa Fe on Jan. 7, 1894, but was transferred to New Orleans in 1897. During his brief term the Leavenworth Sisters of Charity founded St. Anthony's Hospital at Las Vegas. His successor was Peter Bourgade, who had served as vicar apostolic of Arizona and, since 1897, as first bishop of Tucson, before his transfer to Santa Fe on Jan. 7, 1899.

As bishop of Tucson, Bourgade had induced the Cincinnati Franciscans to open missions among the Navahos; as archbishop he reintroduced them to some of the ancient Pueblo missions of New Mexico and to the whole northwest section of the state, which eventually passed into the Gallup diocese. The Franciscans founded the first parishes in the opposite southeast part of New Mexico. Bourgade also took a leading part in founding the Catholic Church Extension Society. The Lafayette Franciscan sisters opened mission schools in areas served by the Franciscan fathers. The Charity sisters from Santa Fe founded St. Joseph Hospital and a school of nursing in Albuquerque, while the Sisters of the Sorrowful Mother established St. Mary's Hospital in Roswell. By 1908 there were 45 parishes with 340 mission chapels in the archdiocese, denoting a marked increase in the population as well as a definite economic progress. This progress, however, had not caught up with that of other parts of the nation where large industry and extensive agriculture helped dioceses to develop much more rapidly.

Later Archbishops. Bourgade died in 1908 and on Jan. 3, 1909, was succeeded by John Baptist Pitaval, who

had been his auxiliary since 1902. Pitaval introduced the Oblate Fathers of Texas to the extensive Springer parish, while the Franciscan sisters founded St. Anthony's Orphanage for boys in Albuquerque. New Mexico became a state in 1912; three years later Pitaval dedicated a fine bronze statue of Archbishop Lamy in front of the cathedral, the first state governor and other major officials taking part in the ceremonies. Resigning in February 1918 because of ill health, Pitaval was succeeded by Albert T. Daeger, OFM, who was consecrated on May 7, 1919, thus marking the end of a continuous line of French archbishops. Since the recruiting of clergy from France had ceased during the war, the new archbishop faced a serious dearth of priests. Lamy's original seminary had closed with his death; Daeger tried to remedy the situation by starting one at Las Vegas, but this one also was short-lived. Meanwhile, the Holy Family fathers from Spain took over the large Santa Cruz area, while the Servite fathers from Chicago were given that of Belen. The Franciscans returned to the cathedral after a century, at the urging of Msgr. A. Fourchegu, vicar-general since 1895, who personally financed the cathedral debt and purchased the major furnishings. Archbishop Daeger also received the vows of the first Missionary Catechists of Our Lady of Victory, founded in Indiana for work in his archdiocese. He died on Dec. 2, 1932, and was succeeded the following summer by Rudolph Aloysius Gerken, first bishop of Amarillo.

After his installation in Santa Fe on Aug. 23, 1933, Gerken was able to organize archdiocesan ministration along more modern lines. A seminary was established in Albuquerque, new parishes and schools were opened throughout the state, and new religious communities introduced. The archbishop personally supervised the preparation of the historic Montezuma Hotel near Las Vegas as a major seminary, which the U.S. and Mexican hierarchy founded in 1937 for seminarians from persecuted Mexico. The very first Presidium of the Legion of Mary in America was established at Raton. The Franciscan sisters in Albuquerque opened a teachers' college, while the Dominican sisters established Nazareth Sanatorium at Alameda, and Holy Family sisters took over a new hospital in Taos. Archbishop Gerken died on March 2, 1943, and was succeeded by Edwin Vincent Byrne, who had served as first bishop of Ponce, Puerto Rico, and then bishop of San Juan there, before his transfer to Santa Fe on June 15, 1943.

The war and its aftermath brought enormous changes to New Mexico as a consequence of the permanent military and atomic installations there, which spurred other industries and brought in many new Catholic families to swell the increasing native population. The need for more parishes with schools was successfully met as these increased from five to 21 in Albuquerque alone. The diocesan seminary, transferred to Santa Fe under the title of the Immaculate Heart of Mary, grew steadily in students and facilities and warranted the addition of a philosophy department in 1962; as a result, native ordinations also increased steadily. Old St. Michael's in Santa Fe was established (1947) as a four-year liberal arts college, as was also the College of St. Joseph on the Rio Grande in Albuquerque. One of the best-equipped Newman Centers in the nation was established at the University of New Mexico under the Dominican fathers; two branch universities at Las Vegas and Portales also have active Newman Centers. Two local foundations, which in a few years spread far beyond the archdiocese, were the Servants of the Holy Paraclete (1952) and the Little Brothers of the Good Shepherd (1951).

When Byrne died on July 25, 1963, his successor was Abp. James Peter Davis, who was transferred from San Juan, Puerto Rico and installed in Santa Fe, Feb. 25, 1964. Archbishop Davis had attended sessions of Vatican Council II and led the archdiocese through the early changes and renewal programs promulgated by the council. To conform to the new liturgical norms, he began renovations at St. Francis Cathedral beginning with the sanctuary. Parts of earlier church structures from 1717, 1806 and 1895 were razed in order to accommodate the changes in the cathedral including the addition of a new Blessed Sacrament chapel. Many of the changes and renovations were criticized because they did not complement the soft Romanesque look of Archbishop Lamy's original building. More recent renovations that include the addition of New Mexico–style *santero* art under the direction of Archbishop Sanchez and Archbishop Sheehan made it more conformable in style with New Mexico's long Catholic tradition. In 2001, a full immersion baptismal font was added in the central portion of the nave.

Archbishop Davis restored the diaconate and ordained the first deacons for the archdiocese in 1972. The Archdiocese of Santa Fe joined the inter-denominational Council of Churches that led to the establishment of the archdiocesan Office of Ecumenical Affairs in 1979. Davis relocated the archdiocesan administrative offices from the see city to the larger, and more centrally located, city of Albuquerque in 1967.

One of the most lasting programs of Archbishop Davis is the institution of official pilgrimages in the archdiocese that led to the establishment of the historic Santuario de CHIMAYO as the official archdiocesan pilgrimage site in 1979. This site has been known since prehistoric times as a place of spiritual and physical healing. Regular pilgrimage to the Santuario began after WW II when survivors of the Bataan Death March made a pilgrimage in thanksgiving for their safe return to New Mexico.

Archbishop Davis retired in 1974 and passed away in Albuquerque, March 4, 1988. Prior to his retirement, Archbishop Davis, other priests and lay people from New Mexico had recommended that the next Archbishop of Santa Fe be someone from among the native born Hispanic priests in the archdiocese. One of those recommended was Father Robert Fortune Sanchez, born and raised in Socorro, New Mexico, and a priest of the archdiocese since his ordination in 1959. Father Sanchez had served as teacher and assistant principal at St. Pius High School as well as assistant pastor of Annunciation Parish in Albuquerque. He also attended Catholic University of America in Washington, D.C., for special studies in Canon Law. When he returned from Washington, he was appointed pastor of the combined parishes of St. Joseph/Holy Family in the remote northeastern portion of the state. In 1971 he was appointed pastor of the historic parish of San Felipe de Neri in Albuquerque and Archbishop Davis appointed him vicar general of the archdiocese on May 1, 1974. He was serving the archdiocese in these positions when he was named the tenth Archbishop of Santa Fe in 1974.

Archbishop Sanchez's installation brought great joy to the people of the archdiocese, not only because he was a native New Mexican but because of his strong dedication and pastoral leadership. He established formal programs to assist and meet the pastoral needs of Hispanic, Native Americans and those immigrating to the U.S. Among these is the archdiocesan newspaper, the *People of God*, established in 1982 and distributed by parishes to thousands of Catholics in the archdiocese and the weekly televised Mass seen at one of the local TV channels that reaches many home bound Catholics. Efforts to increase Native American spirituality and participation in liturgy were advanced in 1974 when the archbishop celebrated the first Native American liturgy in the Cathedral of St. Francis. Native rituals such as prayers, blessings and ceremonial dances were for the first time held in the cathedral.

The archbishop's love for New Mexico, its people and history—especially the role the church has played in this history—led him to establish the Archbishop's Commission for the Preservation of Historic New Mexico Churches in 1987. The commission developed guidelines for any renovations or preservation efforts that were being planned by parishes and missions. During this period many New Mexico churches, including the Santuario de Chimayo, San Jose de Gracia in Las Trampas and San Francisco de Assisi in Ranchos de Taos were designated as National Historic Landmarks and listed on the State

Register of Cultural Properties and the National Register of Historic Places.

Another institution in the archdiocese, Via Coeli ("Heaven's Way"), that gained a reputation for its ministry to priests troubled by addictions and other problems became the focus of much criticism and notoriety in the 1980s. The therapeutic program at the center sponsored by the SERVANTS OF THE PARACLETE was one of the first to offer specialized treatment for the clergy. Dioceses and religious orders from across the country sent priests to the center located at Jemez Springs for treatment of addictions and problems of various kinds, including pedophilia. A number of priests were rehabilitated and returned to the active ministry in their home dioceses; some stayed to work in New Mexico; and some relapsed. It was this last group that created serious problems for the archdiocese and the archbishops of Santa Fe. The allegations, the legal costs, and the monetary compensations paid to the victims and their families damaged the morale of the archdiocese and brought it to the brink of bankruptcy. These problems along with charges of sexual misconduct with women brought against the archbishop himself led to the resignation of Archbishop Sanchez in 1993. Subsequently, the Servants of the Paraclete closed the therapeutic program at Jemez Springs, concentrating instead on retreats and spiritual renewal.

On April 6, 1993, the Most Reverend Michael J. Sheehan, who was serving as the first bishop of Lubbock at that time, was named as apostolic administrator of the Archdiocese of Santa Fe. He was appointed the 11th Archbishop of Santa Fe on August 17 and installed on Sept. 21, 1993. His leadership and pastoral guidance helped the archdiocese and its people through this most difficult period. His immediate concern and love for the Archdiocese of Santa Fe and its people was evident by his involvement in programs and the long traditions of the church of New Mexico. Archbishop Sheehan brought a new sense of trust to the archdiocese by committing himself to working closely with clergy, religious, and lay people. Ministries and programs of the archdiocese were given a new sense of hope for the future by his promise to serve the people of the archdiocese with all his energy and with all his heart. During the first years of his episcopate, Archbishop Sheehan visited many parishes and missions of the archdiocese including a visit to the Native American parishes and missions. He had a processional cross with stand, depicting a Native American Christ, made and presented them as gifts to each of the Pueblo parishes and missions. He also involved the native peoples in church plans for the commemoration of the 400th anniversary of the formal establishment of New Mexico in 1998. Church events during this yearlong observance were considered by all who participated extremely suc-

cessful because of their sensitive and accurate interpretation of historic events involving Native American peoples and their culture and traditions. The archbishop's command of the Spanish language and its inclusion in liturgy as well as his love for and participation in long standing Hispanic and Native American traditions truly symbolize his commitment to the people of the Archdiocese of Santa Fe.

Administratively, offices of the archdiocese were given a greater sense of their role in the pastoral ministry of the church and were brought up to more professional standards. The archdiocesan museum, a dream of Archbishop Sanchez, was completed, opened and blessed by Archbishop Sheehan in October of 1993. The success of the Catholic Foundation, established in 1991 was made a priority and by 2001 the foundation had assets totaling close to $20 million. The Annual Catholic Appeal Foundation, founded as Faith in Action in 1983 as an annual archdiocesan-wide appeal to support the pastoral, educational, evangelical and developmental needs of the archdiocese as well as the universal church, donated nearly $35 million to support the mission of the archdiocese. Through the rebate feature of the ACA, all the parishes of the archdiocese shared in nearly $8 million returned for local use. The Office of Lay Personnel Services, later Human Resources, is responsible for seeing that rights and benefits are provided for all employees of the archdiocese. The finance division of the archdiocese is responsible for all financial dealings and the profits from the sale of land previously occupied by St. Pius High School made it possible for the Archdiocese of Santa Fe to be debt free.

Pastoral ministries of the archdiocese including offices of Evangelization, Family Life, Formation for Christian Service, and Pastoral Outreach are directed by committed individuals who initiate and plan programs. The youth office promotes its ministry through the yearly Youth Conference, established in 1979, where the youth of the archdiocese are invited to come together for prayer, reflection and discussion of youth-related issues. The Catholic schools of the archdiocese are also of great importance to Archbishop Sheehan and the Archdiocese of Santa Fe. The Archbishop's School Fund Dinner, established in 1978, provides much-needed funds for school programs and scholarships for students who are not able to afford the tuition.

Archbishop Sheehan successfully led the archdiocese through the RENEW program, a spiritual process that nourishes spiritual growth of Catholics. Its goals were the teaching and witness to the word of God, the building of a vibrant faith community and the promotion of justice. He was also very committed to the commemoration of the anniversary of Christ's birth, the Jubilee Year, beginning on Christmas Eve 1999. Catholics were encouraged to visit Jubilee churches of the archdiocese and to attend the Eucharistic Congress held during the Jubilee Year on Sept. 23, 2000, planned and sponsored by the archdiocesan office of worship.

Bibliography: J. B. SALPOINTE, *Soldiers of the Cross* (Banning, Calif. 1898). A. CHAVEZ, *Archives of the Archdiocese of Santa Fe, 1678–1900* (Washington 1957); *The Old Faith and Old Glory: Story of the Church in New Mexico since the American Occupation, 1846–1946* (Santa Fe 1946). F. A. DOMINGUEZ, *The Missions of New Mexico, 1776,* tr. E. B. ADAMS and A. CHAVEZ (Albuquerque 1956). *Lamy Memorial: Centenary of the Archdiocese of Santa Fe, 1850–1950* (Santa Fe 1950). ARCHDIOCESE OF SANTA FE, *Four Hundred Hears of Faith (1598–1998) — Seeds of Struggle-Harvest of Faith* (Santa Fe 1998).

[A. CHAVEZ/M. OCHOA]

SANTA MARIA D'ARABONA, ABBEY OF

Former CISTERCIAN MONASTERY near Chieti, in Abruzzi, Italy. Founded on the spot where a temple dedicated to the goddess Orbona had once stood, this Cistercian abbey was a daughterhouse of the Abbey of TRE FONTANE near Rome, whose monks had originally come from CLAIRVAUX. It was founded in 1208 by St. Aldemaro, who was its first abbot. In 1257 Pope Alexander III added the monastery of Santo Stefano to its possessions, and in a short time it achieved great splendor. However, by 1330 it showed signs of decline. In 1587 Pope Sixtus V gave it in COMMENDATION to the Franciscans of the Institute of Saint Bonaventure in Rome, who held it until 1818. The ancient monastery, now private property, contains an interesting chapter room. The abbey church of Santa Maria d'Arabona was restored in 1951.

Bibliography: V. BINDI, *Monumenti storici ed artistici degli Abruzzi* (Naples 1889). L. H. COTTINEAU, *Répertoire topobibliographique des abbayes et prieurés,* 2 v. (Mâcon 1935–39) 2:2395–96. P. TOESCA, *Il Trecento* (Turin 1951) 691.

[M. B. MORRIS]

SANTA MARIA DI FINALPIA, ABBEY OF

A Benedictine monastery established in the 15th century by Olivetan Benedictines (*see* BENEDICTINES; BENEDICTINES, OLIVETAN); situated in the commune of Finale Ligure on the Italian Riviera, 16 miles from Savona, Italy, on the main Genoa-Ventimiglia railroad, in the province and Diocese of Savona. It was founded by Marchese Biagio Galeoto del Carretto in 1477, near the shrine in which was venerated an ancient painting on wood of Our Lady (*Maria di Pia*); and except during the period of suppression under Napoleon (1799–1819), it remained continuously in possession of the Olivetan monks until 1844, when, at the request of King Charles Albert, it passed to the Benedictine Cassinese Congregation. In 1855 it was again suppressed, and it was not until 1905 that the Benedictine monks were able to return. As a center of the liturgical movement, it started publication in 1914 of the *Rivista Liturgica,* which has been and is still the leading advocate for liturgical renewal in Italy.

The abbey church was remodeled in 1724 by the architect G. Veneziano (*Il Fontanetta*) but still retains traces of its earlier Gothic structure. The only remains of the ancient shrine is the fine 12th-century Romanesque bell tower. There are terra-cotta figures by Della Robbia and carvings by Fra Antonio da Venezia in the abbey and the sacristy.

Bibliography: G. SALVI, *Il santuamario di Nostra Signora in Finalpia, su documenti inediti* (Subiaco 1910). L. H. COTTINEAU, *Répertoire topobibliographique des abbayes et prieurés,* 2 v. (Mâcon 1935–39) 1:1143. G. PENCO, *L'abbazia di Finalpia nella storia e nell'arte* (Finalpia 1955).

[S. OLIVIERI]

SANTA MARIA DI POLSI, ABBEY OF

A Basilian monastery on the Butrano River, in the Calabrian Apennines, altitude 2,500 feet, present Diocese of Gerace-Locri in Calabria, south Italy. The origin and life of this monastery, situated in a solitary mountainous region, is shrouded in mystery and legend. Tradition assigns its foundation to Count Roger I in the last half of the 11th century. It was inhabited by BASILIAN monks who later abandoned it during the crisis of Greco-Italian monasticism. It appears, however, that hermits continued to live in the neighborhood while the cult of Our Lady was developing there and the locality became a place of pilgrimage for the whole of Calabria, Lucania, Apulia, and as far off as Sicily. In the 16th century the church was restored and a hostel for pilgrims was built. The present church dates from the 19th century and is still frequented by pious pilgrims who come to pray before the Madonna of Polsi. The title of commendatory abbot of Polsi is still retained by the bishops of Gerace-Locri.

Bibliography: D. FERA, *Memorie sul Santuario di Polsi* (Reggio Calabria 1895). G. B. MOSCATO in *Rivista storica Calabrese* 10 (1907) 215–225. F. PANGOLLO, *Memorie del Santuario di Polsi* (Polistena 1933).

[I. DE PICCOLI]

SANTAMARIA, GRIMOALDO OF THE PURIFICATION, BL.

Baptized Ferdinando, Passionist seminarian; b. Pontecorvo, Frosinone, Italy, May 4, 1883; d. Santa Maria di Corniano Abbey near Cecceano, Frosinone, Italy, November 18, 1902. Ferdinando, the eldest of five, demonstrated his attraction to spiritual matters from an early age. At eight, he was serving regularly at Mass; the following year he joined in the religious exercises of the Congregation of the Immaculata; at twelve, he was catechizing his peers. He joined the Passionists at Pugliano, March 5, 1899, after attending retreats directed by the fathers. In 1900, he was professed with the name Grimoaldo, patron of his hometown, and began his seminary studies at Santa Maria di Corniano near Cecceano. The youth, known for his joy, died of acute meningitis before ordination. On July 2, 1994, a miracle attributed to Grimoaldo's intercession was approved, leading the way to his beatification by John Paul II, January 29, 1995.

Feast: November 18.

Bibliography: PASSIONIST MISSIONARIES, *Curved Bridge to Calvary* (Union City, N.J. 1996). *Acta Apostolicae Sedis,* no. 5 (1995): 249. *L'Osservatore Romano,* English edition, no. 6 (1995): 3.

[K. I. RABENSTEIN]

SANTARELLI, ANTON

Jesuit moralist; b. Atri, Teramo Province, Italy, 1569; d. Rome, Dec. 5, 1649. His work *Tractatus de haeresi, schismate, apostasia, sollicitatione in sacramento paenitentiae, et de potestatae romani pontificis in his delictis puniendis* (Rome, 1625), created a furor at the University of Paris because of its remarks on the power of popes over kings. Cardinal Richelieu eventually became involved in the dispute. Pope Urban VIII and Jesuit General Vitelleschi considered the book regrettable, but refused to condemn it.

Bibliography: R. BROUILLARD, *Dictionnaire de théologie catholique,* ed. A. VACANT et al., 15 vol. (Paris 1903–50) 14.1:1102–1103. H. FOUQUERAY, *Histoire de la Compagnie de Jésus en France,* 5 v. (Paris 1910–25) v.4.

[W. J. FULCO]

SANTAS CREUS, ABBEY OF

Cistercian monastery in Tarragona province, Spain—with Poblet, the Escorial of Catalonia. Several Catalan families, including the Moncada, contributed to its foundation in 1158 with monks from Valldaura. In 1160, while it was being built, Alexander III placed it under papal jurisdiction. The severe and elegant ogival church (1174–1211), completed under Abbot Bernard de Ager and his 45 monks, still remains, as do the old and new (1313–41) cloister and the royal palaces of PETER II and James II of Aragon, both buried in the abbey. Abbot Bernard Calvó (1226–33) was bishop of Vich and councilor of James I of Aragon. In 1296, under James II, the abbots became chaplains-in-chief of the kings of Aragon. The first prior of the KNIGHTS OF MONTESA, founded in 1317, was named by the Abbot of Santas Creus. The abbey's prosperity came to an end with the sacking and looting during the Napoleonic Wars and the Revolution of 1820. It was suppressed in 1834. After more lootings, restoration began in 1884, and the Cistercians have returned.

Bibliography: B. HERNÁNDEZ SANAHUJA, *El monasterio de Santa Creus* (Tarragona 1886). *Enciclopedia universal illustrada Europeo–Americana,* 70 v. (Barcelona 1908–30; suppl. 1934–) 54:227–240.

[J. PÉREZ DE URBEL]

SANTAYANA, GEORGE

Spanish-American poet, essayist, philosopher; b. Madrid, Spain, Dec. 16, 1863; d. Rome, Italy, Sept. 26, 1952. He was the only child of a second marriage of his widowed mother, Josefina Borras Sturgis, to Don Augustín Ruiz de Santayana, and spent his early years in Avila, Spain. He, his mother, a half–brother, and two half-sisters moved to Boston, Mass., shortly before George's ninth birthday. He retained his Spanish nationality throughout his life. He attended Boston Latin School and Harvard University, graduating *summa cum laude* in 1866. After a period at the University of Berlin, he returned to Harvard to complete graduate studies and remained as a professor of philosophy from 1889 to 1912. The enthusiastic reception of his first book, *The Sense of Beauty* (1896), ensured literary success and financial independence. From 1912 he lived abroad, mainly on the Continent. His health began to fail in 1940, and he settled in Calvary Hospital, Rome, until his death. At his own request he was buried in ''neutral'' (unblessed) ground in Rome's Catholic cemetery, Campo Verano.

Santayana wrote 22 works in 29 volumes, and numerous articles in journals, but his real excellence is clear mainly in his purely literary works; the best known and most acclaimed were *The Sense of Beauty* (1896), *Interpretations of Poetry and Religion* (1900), *Poems* (1922), *Soliloquies in England* (1922), *The Last Puritan*, a novel (1935), *Persons and Places* (1944), *The Middle Span* (1947), and *My Host the World* (1953). His essential philosophy is contained in *Scepticism and Animal Faith* (1923) and *Realms of Being* (1942).

Santayana had been a student of William JAMES and Josiah ROYCE at Harvard and was himself acclaimed a dominant figure in the neorealistic school of philosophy. His critics insist, however (and he himself acknowledged), that his philosophical synthesis was a personal accommodation of thought rather than a public proposal of a system. Though he claimed to be a realist, he was in the Kantian tradition of idealism, proposing a theory of intuited essences as the only possible object of knowledge. He was a materialist as to the origin of things, yet extolled the superiority of the human spirit.

Santayana was a baptized Catholic, but never received another sacrament or adhered to the church's ritual or moral discipline. He was a professed agnostic. Yet, because of his sentimental attachment to the external beauty of the church and the internal consistency of its logic (recurring themes in his writing), he was considered ''Catholic'' by many critics.

Bibliography: R. BUTLER, *The Mind of Santayana* (Chicago 1955); *The Life and World of George Santayana* (Chicago 1960). D. CORY, *Santayana: The Later Years* (New York 1963). T. N. MUNSON, *The Essential Wisdom of George Santayana* (New York 1962).

[R. BUTLER]

George Santayana.

SANTIAGO DE COMPOSTELA

Pilgrimage shrine and metropolitan see (*Compostellanus*) since 1120 in Galicia, northwest SPAIN. The discovery of relics of the Apostle St. JAMES (SON OF ZEBEDEE), caused the Roman-Visigothic See of Iria to be moved to Santiago.

Shrine. The oldest certain document for the tradition that the Apostle St. James the Greater preached in Spain is the *Breviarium apostolorum,* a 6th–7th century Latin translation of debatable historical value. Earlier, DIDYMUS THE BLIND (*Patrologia Latina,* ed. J. P. Migne, 271 v., indexes 4 v. [Paris 1878–90] 39:488) and THEODORET OF CYR (*Patrologia Graeca,* ed. J. P. Migne, 161 v. [Paris 1857–66] 83:1010) spoke of an Apostle who reached Spain but did not say who he was. Other testimonies, certainly based on the *Breviarium,* are from ALDHELM of Malmesbury in 709 (*Patrologia Latina* 89:187) and from an interpolated recension of the *De obitu patrum* of ISIDORE OF SEVILLE (*Historisches Jahrbuch* 77 [1958] 467–472). Modern scholars are divided on the credibility of the tradition, inasmuch as there is no mention of it in Spanish Christian literature before the 8th century.

Relics of St. James were found in Libredón (later Compostela) near the See of Iria under Bishop Th-

eodemir (847), who concluded from the *Breviarium* text that disciples of the Apostle had brought his body there from Jerusalem. The event was of major importance in the later history and culture of Europe and the world, as St. James became the battle cry and patron of the reconquest of Spain from the Moors. Recently, however, endless interpretations, theories, hypotheses, and controversies have arisen about the tradition, including a claim that the cult of the saint is a continuation of that of the pagan gods Castor and Pollux (*Ciencia Tomista* 88 [1961] 417–474, 559–590). Some scholars deny that the Apostle ever came to Spain. The best explanation seems to be that the relics discovered in the 9th century were relics of the Apostle, of greater or lesser importance, brought to Galicia in antiquity. The nature of the relics and the date of their arrival are debated. They have been identified as those mentioned in a 7th century inscription as being in the basilica of Santa Maria in Mérida, perhaps brought north with Christian refugees from the Arab invasion of 711. But cultural ties between Galicia and the Holy Land go back at least to the time of the *Peregrinatio Aetheriae* (*c.* 400), and the relics may have come to Santiago even earlier. Recent excavations beneath the basilica in Santiago have uncovered remains that date from the 1st to the 12th century, but the earliest ones may not be Christian.

Church of Santiago de Compostela, photograph by Xurxo S. Lobato. (©Voz Noticias/CORBIS)

At any rate, from the 9th century people began to believe that St. James had come to Spain and was buried in Santiago. King Alfonso II of the Asturias (791–842) built a church over the tomb to which pilgrims came. After Iria was sacked by Northmen (*c.* 850), and the bishops moved to Compostela, Alfonso III (866–910) built a larger church, consecrated in 899, which became a national shrine for the new kingdom of León; Bermudo II was crowned there in 982. In 997 al-Mansur of CÓRDOBA destroyed Compostela, except for the tomb, and a new church was consecrated in 1003. Bishop Diego Peláez of Iria (1070–88) began a new church (*c.* 1075), but work was halted in 1087 when he was imprisoned by Alfonso VI for treason. Individual and group PILGRIMAGES began early, from Spain, Europe, and the whole Christian world: the French bishop of Le Puy came in 950, Hugh of Vermandois (of Reims) in 961, the hermit Simon of Armenia in 983–984, the bishops of Lyons and Mainz and Count Raymond of Burgundy in the 11th century; in the 12th came Matilda, widow of Emperor HENRY V, William of Aquitaine, Louis VII of France; and later, St. DOMINIC, St. FRANCIS OF ASSISI, St. Isabella of Portugal, and others. A group of German pilgrims came from the Rheingau in 1203, and crusaders to the Holy Land (Dutch and Germans in 1217) came first to Santiago, which ranked with Jerusalem and Rome as a pilgrimage center. A pilgrimage to Santiago was frequently imposed as a sacramental penance or as a punishment by judges. SHRINES and brotherhoods dedicated to the Apostle were established in France, Flanders, England, Germany, Russia, and even in the East. In 1195 the KNIGHTS OF ST. JAMES had their statutes approved by the pope.

Jubilee years were held when the feast of St. James (July 25) fell on a Sunday. Kings issued general safe-conducts for foreigners; and certain routes, the Road to Santiago, were accorded special protection. From north central France, three roads from the monasteries of Le Puy, Vézelay, and Orléans joined in Saint-Jean Pied du Port and via Cise-Roncevalles entered Spain. In Puente la Reina this route joined the southern route from ARLES via Toulouse, Col de Somport, and Jaca. From Puente la Reina to Santiago took ten days via Estella, Nájera, Burgos, Frómista, Sahagún, León, Rabanal, Villafrance, and Triacastela. Large guest houses and hospitals cared for the pilgrims en route. In Roncevalles 30,000 meals a year were served; in Burgos 2,000 pilgrims could be accommodated it seems. Some of these buildings still survive in Roncevalles, Villarente, Orbigo, Santo Domingo de la Calzada, San Marcos de León, and Santiago itself. SS John Ortega and DOMINGO DE LA CALZADA built bridges and repaired roads on the pilgrimage route. Documents and pilgrims' accounts mention abuses by innkeepers, the barbarity of the Basques, and robbery by thieves disguised as pilgrims, but kings and local authorities punished the abuses severely. A whole literature developed, for pilgrim guides and for edification, including the famous *Liber sancti Iacobi* and the Guide of the Pilgrim of Picaud in France (12th century), a 14th-century English work published by Samuel Purchas in 1625, a rhymed German account and a work by von Harf (15th century), several 16th-century French itineraries, and a 17th-century Italian one by the Dominican de Laffi. The spread of Romanesque art in Europe owes much to ties that began with the pilgrimages.

Archdiocese. Known bishops of Iria date from the 6th century. Andrew (561–72) had seven or eight successors under the Visigoths and another seven under the Moors before Bishop Theodemir in 847. SS. Rosendus (968–77) and Peter Mesonzo (985–1003) were known for the pastoral care of their flock and of the many pilgrims who had begun to arrive. After the consecration of the cathedral in 1003, the bishops began to regard themselves as primates of Spain. In 1049 Pope Leo IX censured Cresconius for calling himself "bishop of the apostolic see"; in 1060 and 1063 Cresconius held synods to restore discipline. Urban II in 1088 revived the Visigothic primacy of Toledo, whose bishop became papal legate in 1095, the year in which Urban transferred the See of Iria to Santiago under Bishop Dalmatius (1094–95) and exempted it from the metropolitan authority of Braga. In 1120 Santiago became a metropolitan see with a dozen suffragans.

Archbishop Diego Gelmírez (1100–40), man of letters, warrior, politician, builder of churches and monasteries, and pastor, gained the good will of kings and popes, hoping to have Santiago replace TOLEDO in primacy. Pascal II confirmed Santiago's exemption in 1101 and granted Gelmírez the pallium in 1104. Callistus II in 1120 transferred to Santiago the metropolitan dignity of Mérida, which with its former suffragans were to become suffragan to Santiago after their reconquest. He also made Gelmírez papal legate in the province of Braga and Santiago. But the prelates of Toledo and Braga, whose territory separated Santiago from its suffragans, hindered the exercise of metropolitan authority by Gelmírez, whose legatine powers were not renewed by Honorius II or Innocent II. In 1127 Alfonso VII made the metropolitan of Santiago chancellor of the Kingdom of León. Gelmírez convoked provincial synods and reorganized his cathedral chapter with 72 canons, 7 of whom Pascal II allowed to call themselves cardinals in 1101 and to use the miter in 1105.

French, especially CLUNIAC, influence was strong in Galicia under Gelmírez, who sent clerics to study in France and obtained masters from France and Italy for his reorganized cathedral school. In time Santiago annexed the Portuguese Sees of Coimbra, Lisbon, Évora, Lamego, Viseu, and Idanha, and the Spanish Sees of Ávila, Salamanca, Ciudad Rodrigo, Zamora, and Coria, despite the protests of Toledo. The *Historia Compostelana,* an enthusiastic chronicle written to glorify the see, is of great interest for ecclesiastical history from the 9th to the 12th century. Bp. Rodrigo del Padrón (1307–16) stands out in the next two centuries of splendor enjoyed by the bishops of Santiago, who were among the richest and most powerful magnates of Galicia with their vast lands, vassals, strongholds, a navy, and a mint. The moral decline of the 14th century ended in the WESTERN SCHISM. In 1393 Santiago lost its Portuguese suffragans to Lisbon but gained Lugo, Orense, and Mondoñedo from Braga.

The 16th century saw a renaissance in the archdiocese. Pope Clement VII approved the statutes of the university in 1526. Brotherhoods of the Blessed Sacrament appeared in all the parishes, and devotion to Mary increased, thanks to zealous prelates such as the learned humanist Alfonso III de Fonseca (1506–24), Gaspar de Abalos (1542–45), Cardinal Juan Álvarez de Toledo (d. 1557), and Gaspar de Zúñiga (1558–69), who promulgated the decrees of the Council of TRENT. Protestantism made dangerous inroads through the pilgrimages, as did the ENLIGHTENMENT in the 18th century and Liberalism in the 19th. The abuses of French Napoleonic troops continued under liberal governments that suppressed the *voto de Santiago* (a contribution of wheat and bread from certain Spanish workers) as well as the national offering, and suppressed monasteries, exiled bishops, and confiscated ecclesiastical goods. This caused a scarcity of clerics, who in turn became lax. Alfonso XII restored the national offering in 1877. After excavations of 1878–79 beneath the basilica, Pope Leo XIII in 1884 recognized the legitimacy of the relics and the tomb of St. James. A provincial synod of 1887 promulgated the decrees of VATICAN COUNCIL I, and in 1891 a synod applied the decisions of the Council of Compostela.

The cathedral, a Romanesque masterpiece modeled after St. Sernin in Toulouse, was begun in 1075 and completed and consecrated in 1211 by Abp. Peter Muñoz. The original three naves and wide transept were elaborately buried under plateresque and BAROQUE façades and towers in the 16th and 17th centuries; and the cathedral is surrounded by the grandiose episcopal palace, the cloister, and the library. The famous Portal de la Gloria (1168–83) of the architect-sculptor Maestro Mateo fills a side façade with Christian, Jewish, and pagan symbolic imagery. A statue of St. James is covered with gold and silver leaf, and the huge Botafumeiro censer almost five feet high, which swings from the roof of the transept, was gold and silver in the 18th century but now is brass. The Monastery of Antealtares was once a pantheon of bishops and abbots. The grandiose 17th-century Benedictine monastery of San Martín Pinario is now a conciliar seminary. The Romanesque churches of Santa Susana, Santa Salomé, and Santa Maria la Real de Sar date from the 12th century. The Franciscan and Dominican convents, the palace of Diego Gelmírez, and the Gran Hospital Real (with a rich façade) built as a hospice for pilgrims by Ferdinand and Isabella are noteworthy monuments. Many parish churches in the archdiocese were once monastery churches.

University. The university, built in plateresque style, was founded in 1501 by Abp. Alfonso III de Fonseca with Fonseca College (1506–1841) and the College of San Jerónimo for 24 poor students (16th–19th centuries, in classical style); it has included the College of San Clemente for boys (1602–19th century), the Seminary of Confessors (1750–72), and the college for acolytes and choir boys (1589). From the beginning, the university offered degrees in theology, arts, and law; and from 1769, theology, canon and civil law, medicine, and philosophy. In 1845 it became a state university that now has faculties of philosophy and letters, law, medicine, sciences, and pharmacy. The conciliar seminary founded in 1825 was a pontifical university from 1897 to 1932.

The cathedral archives have documents dating back to 1136. The archives of Diocesan Notaries (15th century), of the Secretariat of the Chamber (from the 12th century), of the Benedictines of San Pelayo (from the 10th century), the chapter library (16th–19th centuries), and the rich library of the seminary are important, as are the museum of the cathedral and the museum of music.

Bibliography: J. GUERRA, ''Notas críticas sobre el origen del culto sepulcral a Santiago en Compostela,'' *Ciencia Tomista* 88 (1961) 417–474, 559–590. A. LÓPEZ FERREIRO, *Historia de la Santa A.M. Iglesia de Compostela,* 11 v. (Santiago 1898–1911). L. VÁZQUEZ DE PARGA et al., *Las peregrinaciones a Santiago,* 3 v. (Madrid 1948–49). L. HUIDOBRO Y SERNA, *Las peregrinaciones jacobeas,* 3 v. (Burgos 1950). G. G. KING, *The Way of Saint James,* 3 v. (New York 1920). A. G. BIGGS, *Diego Gelmírez, First Archbishop of Compostela* (Washington 1949). D. GELMÍREZ, *Historia Compostelana,* Span. tr. F. M. SUÁREZ (Santiago 1950). A. F. G. BELL, *Spanish Galicia* (London 1922). K. J. CONANT, *The Early Architectural History of the Cathedral of Santiago de Compostela* (Cambridge, Mass. 1926). W. M. WHITEHILL, *Spanish Romanesque Architecture of the Eleventh Century* (Oxford 1941). S. CABEZA DE LEÓN, *Historia de la Universidad de Santiago de Compostela,* ed. E. FERNÁNDEZ VILLAMIL, 3 v. (Santiago 1945–47). J. FILGUEIRA VALVERDE, *Santiago de Compostela: Guía de sus monumentos e itinerarios* (La Coruña 1950). A. CHAMOSO LAMAS, *Santiago de Compostela* (Barcelona 1961). Z. GARCÍA VILLADA, *Historia eclesiástica de España,* 3 v. in 5 (Madrid 1929–36) 1.1:27–379. T. D. KENDRICK, *St. James in Spain* (London 1960). Y. BOTTINEAU, *Les Chemins de Saint-Jacques* (Paris 1964). *Annuario Pontificio* (1964) 400–401, 1417.

[A. G. BIGGS/M. RIOS/J. VIVES]

SANTO

A term of Spanish origin adopted into English to designate religious images made in Spanish colonies, particularly in the southwestern U.S. A *santo* may be a statue (*bulto*), or a flat image painted on wood, canvas, metal, paper, or leather (*retablo*). One who makes *santos* is called a *santero*. A *bulto* was made of smoothed sections of dried cottonwood root, pegged together and coated with gesso, then painted with water-soluble native pigments. The New Mexico *santero* carved a figure in the round, but drew within a two-dimensional plane when painting a *retablo,* where emphasis was on symbolism rather than on realism and perspective.

Santos developed in frontier NEW MEXICO Franciscan headquarters for the conversion of Pueblo (village-dwelling) peoples. Lacking academic works of art for visual instruction of Pueblo pupils, resourceful if impoverished Franciscans painted fundamental subjects with available dyestuffs on tanned buffalo hides. These *santos* hung in all New Mexican missions, until they were discarded by bishops from the Diocese of Durango, Mexico (1820–51). Well-known carvers of wooden *santos* were Fray Andres Garcia, who served in New Mexico (1747–79), and Bernardo Miera y Pacheco (d. 1785), a military engineer who was also the first to map New Mexico from personal surveys.

By 1800 Spanish power had collapsed and Franciscan missionaries were withdrawn from New Mexico, but semiliterate laymen continued to make *santos,* sometimes continuing an imagery that was considered heretical or had lost favor elsewhere, such as that of the Holy Trinity represented as three identical persons. Interpreting the Council of Trent (Session 25, on sacred images, H. Denzinger, *Enchiridion symolorum,* ed. A. Schönmetzer 1821–25) foreign clergy condemned *santos* for unorthodox symbolism during the 19th century, but New Mexicans still cherished them. New Mexican *santeros* of record are: Molleno (probably the ''Chili painter'') José Aragon, José Rafael Aragon, Miguel Herrera, Juan Ramon Velasquez, and José Benito Ortega, last of the great ''saintmakers'' (1858–1907).

Santos are recognized today as the most original body of folk art produced within the territorial U.S. since the arrival of Europeans. Without formal training or rich materials, but with purity of color and direct, if sometimes naïve, composition, the *santero* expressed the intense piety of the Spanish New Mexicans.

Bibliography: E. BOYD, *Saints and Saint Makers of New Mexico* (Santa Fe 1946); ''Literature of Santos,'' *Southwest Review* 35 (1950) 128–140. A. CARRILLO Y GARIEL, *Imaginería popular novoespañola* (Mexico City 1950). J. E. ESPINOSA, *Saints in the Valleys* (Albuquerque 1960). M. MAURON, *Santos of Provence* (New York 1959). M. A. WILDER and E. BREITENBACH, *Santos: The Religious Folk Art of New Mexico* (Colorado Springs 1943). F. ZOBEL DE AYALA, ''Philippine Colonial Sculpture: A Short Survey,'' *Philippine Studies* 6 (1958) 249–294; *Philippine Religious Imagery* (Manila 1963). G. KUBLER, *The Religious Architecture of New Mexico* (Colorado Springs 1940; repr. Chicago 1962).

[E. BOYD]

SANTO DOMINGO (1992)

Santo Domingo in the Dominican Republic was the site of the Fourth General Meeting of the CONSEJO EPISCOPAL LATINOAMERICANO or Latin American Bishops' Conference held October 12–28, 1992. Nine years previously, at a gathering of bishops in Haiti, Pope John Paul II announced that the topic for CELAM IV would be New Evangelization and that its opening would coincide with the five hundredth anniversary of the landing of Columbus in the Western hemisphere, Oct. 12, 1492, and the beginning of the first evangelization.

CELAM IV brought together Catholic bishops from twenty-two nations in South and Central America. It was chaired by the Vatican secretary of state, Angelo Cardinal Sodano. Much of the preparatory work for the meeting, including the drafting of the ''working document,'' was in the hands of the secretary general of CELAM, Bishop Raymundo Damasceno Assis, who also served as co-secretary general of the meeting. The other co-secretary, Bishop Jorge Medina Estévez, was appointed by the Holy See. In addition to a number of lay observers, there were also five Protestant observers from traditional Protestant groups (but no representatives of newer Pentecostal movements).

Preparations. During the nine years between the pope's speech and the CELAM conference, an enormous amount of time and energy was devoted throughout Latin America to meetings, study and research, discussions with laity, and working drafts (that soon became good-sized books). The most important of the drafts was a document entitled *Secunda Relatio* (''Second Report''), which provided an excellent synthesis of the ideas of all the national bishops' conferences of Latin America, thus providing a panorama of the Church in the entire continent. This *relatio* was not accepted, however, by conservative leaders of the conference. Another document, the *Documento de Trabajo* (''Working Document''), was also rejected on the very first day of the conference. The proceedings then were entrusted to small working groups, thirty in all, which were not open to plenary sessions. They discussed and produced drafts on a wide range of topics and issues that were synthesized by a powerful drafting committee and then presented for discussion and voting in the plenary sessions.

Up to the last few days of the meeting in Santo Domingo, there were serious forebodings that the seventeen-day meeting would not be able to produce a final document. In the end, however, a staff under the direction of Archbishop Luciano Mendes de Almeida of Brazil, working around the clock, was able to produce a final document during the last frantic days of the conference. In places it displays signs of haste and poor organization and has been criticized because of its lack of prophetic vision. Although there were serious differences of opinion among the bishops, the document was approved by 201 of the 206 voting delegates, with five abstentions and no opposing votes.

Results of the Conference. Pope John Paul II inaugurated the meeting with a lengthy "Opening Address" to the bishops. The general interpretation of the speech is that it did not open new avenues, but neither did it close any doors. The pope's outline included (1) a "new evangelization," with Jesus as the model; (2) "human development," which appeared to be a euphemism for the struggle for justice and liberation; and (3) "Christian culture," that is, the inculturation of evangelization and social justice in the nations of Latin America and the Caribbean. These three chapters became the major building blocks of the final documents.

Chapter One was concerned largely with the diverse ministries and charisms for the new evangelization, including approbation of the base ecclesial communities and the crucial role of all lay persons, especially women and the young. Evangelization was envisioned not only as essential catechesis (a huge task), but also as a vigorous outreach to lapsed and indifferent Catholics and as dialogue with non-Christian religions, non-believers, and members of Christian "fundamentalist" sects.

The subject of women was treated in seven carefully crafted paragraphs (nos. 104–111) of Chapter One. This is the most substantive and profound statement on women to be found in the writings of the Latin American bishops. A less successful statement, however, is to be found in the ecumenical arena (nos. 139–146). The first sentence on this topic does not bode well for authentic dialogue: "The problem of the sects has reached dramatic proportions and has become truly worrisome, particularly due to increasing proselytism."

In Chapter Two, the bishops achieved a consensus regarding nine "new signs of the times." Each sign was elaborated by a brief social analysis, followed by pastoral reflections and plans for action. These signs for Latin America are (1) human rights, (2) ecology, (3) the earth as God's gift, (4) impoverishment, (5) human labor, unemployment, and underemployment, (6) migration, (7) democracy, (8) foreign debt, and (9) the integration of Latin American economies.

Chapter Three, on "Christian culture," is the shortest part of the document and appears to have taken approaches and concepts from both of the previous chapters, resulting in a kind of mélange. From the beginning a great deal of attention is devoted to inculturation toward the indigenous or Amerindians, the African Americans, and the *mestizos,* i.e., those of mixed blood. (The new interest in ethnicity and women's issues was dramatically highlighted by the presence at the meeting of Rigoberta Menchú, a Guatemalan Indian woman who had been awarded the Nobel Prize for Peace.)

Santo Domingo also emphasized the culture of the city. Everywhere on the continent there is a "passage from rural culture to urban culture, which is the location and driving force of the new universal civilization" (no. 155). On the other hand, the bishops showed themselves quite aware of the belts of poverty and misery that surround the cities. Finally, the Santo Domingo documents make a strong appeal for Catholic education, from the lowest grades to the universities, and plea for much more expertise in the use of the social media of communication.

Bibliography: A. T. HENNELLY, ed., *Santo Domingo and Beyond: Documents and Commentaries from the Fourth General Conference of Latin American Bishops* (Maryknoll, N.Y. 1993).

[A. T. HENNELLY]

SANTOS, JOÃO DOS

Dominican missionary; b. Evora, Portugal, date unknown; d. Goa, India, 1622. He joined the Dominicans and left Lisbon for India in 1586 in response to Bp. Ribeiro Gayo's request for missionaries to Malacca. On his way, Santos stopped at Mozambique and was assigned to Sofala (1586–90). Subsequent assignments in other parts of Mozambique detained him from going to the Far East. Finally, in 1597, he arrived in India where he worked, except for study in Portugal (1606–17) until his death. He labored chiefly in Goa and Cochin. His principal book, *Ethiopia Oriental,* is a major account of the Portuguese expansion in Africa during the 16th century. It contains a perceptive account of native customs, the fauna, the Portuguese conquest, and Dominican missionary activity in East Africa.

Bibliography: G. M. THEAL, *History and Ethnography of Africa South of the Zambesi from the Settlement of the Portuguese at Sofala,* 3 v. (3d rev. ed. London 1916–22) v.1. *Enciclopedia de la Religión Católica,* ed. R. D. FERRERES et al., 7 v. (Barcelona 1950–56), 6:1077.

[B. M. BIERMANN]

SANZ Y JORDÁ, PEDRO MÁRTIR, ST.

Dominican bishop martyr, baptized Joseph; b. Sept. 22, 1680, Asco (Tortosa), Tarragona, Catalonia, Spain; d. May 26, 1747, Fukien (Fuzou), Tunkien, China. Upon entering the Dominican convent at Lerida at age 18, Sanz changed his name to Peter Martyr. There he was ordained on Sept. 24, 1704. After volunteering for the Chinese mission, he was sent to the Philippines for two years to study the language (1713–1715). For the next 31 years he labored furtively under extremely difficult conditions among the Chinese. In 1730 he was named vicar apostolic of Tunkien and consecrated bishop of Mauricastra in Guangdong. When he learned that others had been arrested and were being tortured in an effort to find him, he surrendered himself to authorities. Just before being beheaded, he turned to his executioner and said: ''Rejoice with me, my friend; I am going to heaven!'' And as his head lay on the block: ''If you want to save your soul, my friend, you must obey the law of God!'' Because his sanctity was recognized by his contemporaries, his relics, which would not burn, were collected. He was beatified by Pope Leo XIII (May 14, 1893) and canonized (Oct. 1, 2000) by Pope John Paul II with Augustine Zhao Rong and companions.

Feast: June 5.

Bibliography: M. J. SAVIGNOL, *Les Martyrs dominicains de la Chine au XVIIIᵉ siècle* (Paris 1893). H. I. IWEINS, *Le Bx Pierre Sanz et ses quatre compagnons* (Ostende 1893). J. M. GONZÁLEZ, *Misiones dominicanas en China, 1700–1750* (Madrid 1952). M. J. DORCY, *Saint Dominic's Family* (Dubuq, Iowa 1963), 484–87.

[K. I. RABENSTEIN]

SÃO TOMÉ AND PRINCIPE, THE CATHOLIC CHURCH IN

The Democratic Republic of São Tomé and Principe are volcanic islands located in the Gulf of Guinea, west of Gabon, off the coast of Africa. The former, 319 square miles in area, lies on the equator; the latter, occupying 52 square miles, is 100 miles to the north. Mountainous, the region has a tropical climate with a rainy season from October through May. Natural resources consist of fish and hydropower, while agricultural products include cocoa, coconuts, cinnamon, pepper, coffee and bananas. Most plantations on the large island were carved from the jungle during the 16th century.

Held by the Portuguese since the late 15th century, the region changed its political status to that of overseas territory in 1951. Slavery was abolished in the islands in the early 20th century, and in 1975 the region became politically independent. The first free elections were held in

Capital: São Tomé.
Size: 371 sq. miles.
Population: 159,880 in 2000.
Languages: Portuguese.
Religions: 142,290 Catholics (89%), 1,500 Protestants (1%), 8,000 practice indigenous faiths (5%), 8,090 without religious affiliation.
Diocese: São Tomé and Principe (formerly suffragan of Luanda in Angola), immediately subject to the Holy See.

1991. The permanent population on both islands is largely rural and attached to the plantations. The majority are Africans descended from slaves brought from the African mainland, while small minorities of Europeans and Creoles also exist. Although contract laborers from Angola, Mozambique and the Cape Verde islands frequently lived on the islands without permanent residency status, by 2000 an economic decline had resulted in a 50 percent unemployment rate in the region.

Originally uninhabited, the islands were discovered by Portuguese explorers *c.* 1471, and settlers and missionaries quickly colonized the region. The introduction of slave labor allowed the region to become a major sugar cane producer within a century. In 1534 São Tomé became a diocese with jurisdiction extending to the Congo and Angola. By 1597 São Tomé had a cathedral and seven parishes; and Principe a single church. In addition to the growth of the cocoa and coffee plantations, the islands quickly became a major transportation center for African slaves, creating a difficult environment for the Church. Foreign aggression, the exodus of many inhabitants, and the erection of separate ecclesiastical jurisdictions on the mainland caused the Church to decline in importance throughout the next several centuries, and the last resident bishop, Bartolomeu dos Mártires, died in 1816. Despite the dwindling of the slave trade by the mid-1700s, the few priests sent from Portugal could not stem the decline, which continued through the 19th century. Finally, in 1927 the CLARETIAN FATHERS were entrusted with the two islands.

Although São Tomé was the world's largest cocoa producer by the turn of the 20th century, the inhuman treatment of its plantation workers prompted an international boycott by major chocolate manufacturers in 1909. The seeds of a nationalist movement were sown in 1953 following the deaths of hundreds of African workers during labor riots. As a result of the Portuguese revolution in 1974, on July 12, 1975 the region declared political independence, although a stable government did not take power until the election of Miguel Torvoada as the region's first president in 1991. During the 1990s the economy suffered as drought reduced the relied-upon cocoa

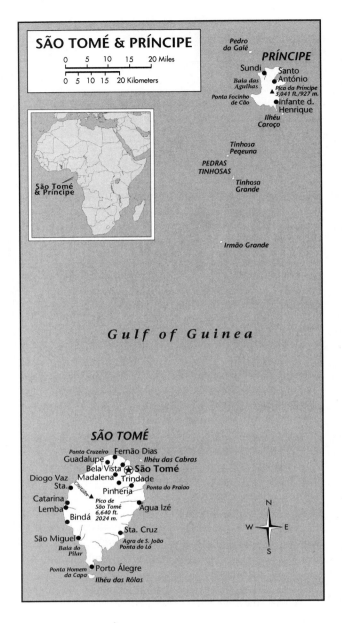

exports. Increased poverty and a dependence on foreign aid were the result. Government corruption did not aid in the region's stability, but the state remained optimistic that exploration of its off-shore areas would result in the discovery of petroleum deposits in the early 21st century. A new government, elected in 1998, also boded well for economic reforms.

By 2000 there were 12 parishes tended by 12 Claretian priests, assisted in their ministrations by three brothers and approximately 40 sisters. During a 1992 visit to the region, Pope John Paul II recalled São Tomé's past in addressing the institution of slavery as a ''cruel offense'' to the dignity of the African people. In response

to the poverty of the region, which had resulted in a foreign debt equaling 283 percent of the islands's Gross National Product, in 1999 the Italian Bishops's Conference donated money to both ease the debt and reinvest in São Tomé's economy.

[R. PATTEE/EDS.]

SAPIEHA, ADAM STEFAN

Cardinal, archbishop of Kraków, Poland; b. May 14, 1867, in Krasiczyn near Przemysl, Poland (then in Austrian Galicia), d. July 27, 1951, in Kraków; buried in the Wawel Cathedral in Krakow.

Adam Sapieha was born into an Polish-Lithuanian aristocratic family, and from an early age was taught the values of patiotism an public service. He took a degree in law from the Jagiellonian University in Kraków (1890), in theology from the University of Innsbruck (1894), and finally a doctorate in law from the Gregorian University in Rome (1896), in addition to which he received training in diplomacy. He was ordained a priest of the diocese of Lwow (L'viv) Oct. 1, 1893.

After his ordination, he quickly distinguished himself in pastoral work, most notably in his service to the sick during a cholera epidemic. He served as vice-rector of the Metropolitan Seminary in Lwów in the years 1897 to 1901. In 1906 he was made chamberlain to Pope PIUS X, and had considerable influence on his policies toward the church in historically Polish lands.

He was named Bishop of Kraków in 1911 and was consecrated by Pius on December 17 of that year, taking up his diocese March 3, 1912. In 1925 he was made the first archbishop-metropolitan of Kraków. His interests and activities as a bishop were many, ranging from a strong concern for the intellectual and moral formation of the clergy, to education, to youth ministry, to the charitable activities which were so especially needed in the wake of the two world wars, their aftermath, the Great Depression of the 1930s.

Sapieha was always a strong proponent of Poland's independence, and during the Nazi occupation (1939–45), his support for the Polish underground in the face of Nazi attempts to liquidate all vestiges of Polish nationhood and national leadership (including many members of the clergy) was notable and courageous. He also encouraged the provision of baptismal papers to Jews to save them from extermination.

On Feb. 18, 1946, he was named Cardinal Presbyter of Sancta Maria Nova by Pius XII. Cardinal Sapieha spent the last years of his life rebuilding and stabilizing the church in his archdiocese after the cataclysm of the Second World War. From 1945 he was head of Caritas in Poland, until the Communist authorities put it under state control in 1950. He ordained Karol Wojtyła (the future JOHN PAUL II), and acted as his mentor both when Wojtyła was a seminarian and when he was a young priest.

Bibliography: *Ksiega sapieżynska,* vols. 1–2, J. WOLNY, ed. Kraków: 1982–1986. J. CZAJKOWSKI, *Kardynał Adam Stefan Sapieha,* Wrocław: Ossolineum, 1997.

[P. RADZILOWSKI]

SAPIENTIA CHRISTIANA

An apostolic constitution issued by Pope JOHN PAUL II on April 15, 1979. *Sapientia Christiana* is the canonical, academic law governing "ecclesiastical" postsecondary education.

Sapientia Christiana has two major parts: a discursive proemium or introduction in six brief sections, followed by a total of 94 normative articles, including a few transitional norms for putting the constitution into effect. The articles are both general norms for all ecclesiastical universities, faculties, and institutes and special norms for particular faculties, especially theology, philosophy, and canon law. This second main section concludes with an enumeration of the other kinds of faculties already authorized as ecclesiastical: Christian archeology, Biblical studies and ancient Christian studies, Church history, Christian and classical literature, liturgy, missiology, sacred (liturgical) music, psychology, educational science or pedagogy, religious science, social sciences, Arabic and Islamic studies, medieval studies, oriental ecclesiastical studies, *utriusque iuris* (both canon and civil law).

The general norms of the apostolic constitution (nos. 1–64) are divided into 10 sections: nature and purpose of ecclesiastical universities and faculties; the academic community and its government; teachers; students; officials and staff assistants; program of studies; academic degrees; matters relating to teaching; economic matters; and planning and cooperation of faculties. These sections are closely paralleled in the norms of application, and the same is true of the series of special norms in both documents (nos. 65–87 of *Sapientia Christiana*) concerning the particular kinds of faculties.

In dealing with the governance of ecclesiastical faculties, the constitution introduces the distinction between personal governance (by academic administrators) and collegial governance (by the teachers in their councils, committees, and the like); there is concern as well for a role for students to take part in the academic community

"in those aspects which can contribute to the common good of the faculty or university." In the respective sections dealing with teachers and students, it is required that the statutes safeguard rights—of the individuals, of the institution, of the ecclesial community.

The role and authority of the chancellor or *magnus cancellarius* is spelled out: he is "the ordinary prelate on whom the university or faculty legally [i.e., canonically] depends, representing the Holy See to the university or faculty and equally the university or faculty to the Holy See." Commonly but not necessarily, the diocesan bishop or other local ordinary is the chancellor, except in the case of the ecclesiastical faculties of religious institutes.

An important section deals with the appointment and dismissal of teachers, with emphasis upon the kinds of academic credentials expected in a particular region and upon the probity of life and integrity of doctrine of teachers. They are to carry out their work "in full communion with the authoritative magisterium of the Church, above all, with that of the Bishop of Rome." Those who teach disciplines concerning faith and morals require a canonical mission from the chancellor "for they do not teach on their own authority but by virtue of a mission they have received from the Church." Teachers in other disciplines (and teachers who are not Catholics) require a permission to teach (*venia docendi*), again from the chancellor. Prior to permanent appointment (that is, with continuous tenure) and/or prior to promotion to the highest academic rank of ordinary or full professor, a teacher must also have a declaration or clearance from the Holy See, the *nihil obstat*.

Corresponding to these requirements for appointment or tenure, the norms of application spell out the steps to be taken before the suspension or dismissal of a teacher, but require that the internal statutes of each faculty determine the precise procedure. In the section treating the program of studies, the constitution attempts to define a balanced ACADEMIC FREEDOM (no. 39).

The pastoral concern of the constitution, and of the norms for application, is evident in the sections on planning and cooperation of ecclesiastical faculties. Methods of affiliation, aggregation, and broad cooperation among institutions are proposed, with special mention of the need to study the distribution of ecclesiastical faculties, a responsibility also attributed to the conferences of bishops. For the rest, the documents deal with specific requirements of persons and programs, of criteria for admission and the conferral of degrees, of support and facilities. In almost every case it is expected that the universal norms of the Roman documents are to be made effective through more detailed statutory norms enacted by the respective faculties.

As a whole *Sapientia Christiana* and the supplementary *ordinationes* may be described as a combination of principles and binding requirements, and the question of their specificity is a matter of degree. It went into effect at the beginning of the 1980–81 academic year or of the 1981 academic year, depending on the calendar in use in various places.

[F. R. MCMANUS]

SAPIENTIAL BOOKS

Sapiential Books, the biblical books of PROVERBS, JOB, ECCLESIASTES, SIRACH (or ECCLESIASTICUS), and WISDOM, which are the five key books of Old Testament wisdom literature. The Church has traditionally associated with them the Book of PSALMS and the SONG OF SONGS. However, only a few of the Psalms (1, 36, etc.) are properly sapiential, and the Song of Songs is a collection of love lyrics that may have been preserved for a didactic purpose. In addition, there are many influences of wisdom literature discernible in the works of the PROPHETS (*see* J. Lindblom in *Vetus Testamentum* [Leiden 1951–] Suppl 3 1955 192–204), and in books like BARUCH (3.9–4.4) and TOBIT (4.3–21; 12.6–13). In the New Testament, the epistle of JAMES is sapiential in tone, and many sayings of Jesus are couched in the style proper to the books of wisdom. [For details and bibliography *see* WISDOM (IN THE BIBLE).]

[R. E. MURPHY]

SARACENI, MAURUS

Theologian, exegete, missionary; b. Fossombrone, Italy, 1540; d. Vilna, Lithuania, Oct. 22, 1588. In 1553 he joined the Conventual Franciscans, and after a brilliant student career, taught in university colleges of the order in Florence, Urbino, Naples, Milan, Padua, and Bologna. He was elected procurator general of his order (1578) and was later visitator general in Sicily and then in France. In 1583 he was appointed to the chair of Hebrew at the Sorbonne. Besides being proficient in theology and exegesis, Saraceni was well versed in many European and Oriental languages, in physics, astronomy, mathematics, and music. In 1586 he left Paris and went as a missionary to Vilna. There he established a public school to strengthen Catholics in their faith and to obtain the conversion of heretics. He died of the plague, to whose victims he had been ministering. His school, however, continued to produce good results for many years. His works, almost all unpublished, cover the whole of theology and a good part of scripture, physics, and philosophy.

Bibliography: J. FRANCHINI, *Bibliosofia e memorie letterarie di scrittori francescani conventuali* (Modena 1693) 455–497. J. H. SBARALEA, *Supplementum et castigatio ad scriptores trium ordinum S. Francisci a Waddingo,* 2 vol. (Rome 1806) 2:244. A. TEETAERT, *Dictionnaire de théologie catholique,* ed. A. VACANT et al., 15 vol. (Paris 1903–50) 14.1:1108–09.

[P. D. FEHLNER]

SARCOPHAGUS

A coffin, usually of limestone, that was considered by the ancients as consuming the flesh (σάρξ, flesh, and φαγεῖν, to eat) of the corpses laid in it. The best of this particular type of limestone was quarried at Assos in the Troad.

History. The use of a coffin, whether of wood, lead, or stone, came from the ancient East and was intimately connected with veneration for the dead. Traces of prehistoric sarcophagi have been found among the Egyptians and Cretans, who used wood, earthenware, and stone, and fitted the vessel with a cover. From Egypt in the 5th century B.C. the anthropoid type of sarcophagus spread. This coffin was shaped like a human being and usually crowned with a mask. The Greeks created the artistic sarcophagus, decorating one or several of its sides with figures and ornamentation. Etruscan sarcophagi of stone or terra cotta frequently had covers made in the form of a bed or couch with a representation of the deceased stretched out in various poses.

In Rome with the spread of rites for inhumation instead of urn burial of the ashes (2d century A.D.) the construction of artistic marble coffins utilized the experience of the Greeks and Etruscans. The quadrangular type dominated, exhibiting the sculptured face of the deceased, but otherwise with top and sides plain. Sometimes the front was extended above the top of the coffin and sculptured with a fresque. In the age of Hadrian myths and Amazonian battle scenes were frequent depictions. In more simple types there was a central slab in front with a likeness of the deceased, while the rest of the frontispiece was decorated with wavy lines. Frequently this frontispiece contained mythological or biographical representations, e.g., husband and wife, often in a tragic attitude capable of inciting pity, scenes of battles between Romans and barbarians, or lion-hunting scenes. In the age of Gallienus the philosopher figure became usual (253–268), and this was included on the first Christian sarcophagi.

The Christians from the beginning buried their dead in the ground or in surface coffins or mausoleums, following Hebrew practices. Along with the early cemeteries, the sarcophagi constitute the richest documentation for the history of art in the late empire as well as for the illustration of Christian ideas. Rome was the chief center of production and influenced communities in North Africa, southern Italy, southern Gaul, and Spain. The influence of RAVENNA and Salonika on sarcophagi came later.

The style of the figures followed variations in the artistic current of the period from pictorial representation rich in classical reminiscences, as in the Sarcophagus of Jonas (Lateran Museum), to expressionism as on that of Adam and Eve (Lateran Museum) and the abstract art of Ravenna. It is possible to establish certain art styles and trace their influences and to characterize them as Severian, Gallienic, Tetrarchian, Constantinian, and post-Constantinian. The earliest Christian types have been difficult to date precisely (end of 1st century down to *c.* 225). Furthermore, sarcophagi were frequently reused by later generations.

The repertory of Christian sarcophagal art reveals certain popular traditional styles as well as cycles. While Christian funerary representation had as its purpose the demonstration of particular beliefs relative to death and the future life, the types changed. In earlier times symbolic and allegorical themes predominated: the myth of Amor and Psyche for the status of the soul; Orpheus playing to the beasts for Christ attracting sinners; Prometheus for Creation, more particularly in an idealistic representation of the Garden of Eden, enriched with the well-known figures of the Good Shepherd, the Orans, Christ as the Fisher, etc., as on the Sarcophagus of the Rams (Lateran Museum) or in the church of S. Maria Antiqua.

Under the tetrarchy (284–312) the influence of popular art is evident in scenes of rural and animal life. In the early 4th century appear passages from the Old and New Testaments about Jonah, Noah and the ark, Daniel among the lions, the sin of Adam and Eve, Baptism, resurrection of Lazarus, entrance into Jerusalem. The Constantinian period is rich in fresco decorations, representing the miracle cycle of Christ as a youth, a Peter cycle, Old Testament scenes. The so-called Trinity Sarcophagus (Lateran Museum) is from the Arch of Constantine. After 313 appeared frontispieces and side walls separated into sections by columns and decorated with scenes of the Passion of Christ, or of Peter and Paul, or of the Presentation of the Law (*c.* 330–350). This type seems to derive from Sidamara in Asia and is best represented by the sarcophagus of Junius Bassus (d. 359).

In the Theodosian period a series of costly single pieces betray Eastern influences with elaborately developed Biblical scenes (St. Sebastian Sarcophagus); it ushers in a new type of composition in the *Traditio legis,* acclamation, and the crown-bearing Apostle. The Miracle and Passion scenes recur, but seem to disappear *c.* 420. In Gaul there is a rich flowering of Roman-inspired sarcophagi; toward the end of the century ornamental

motives predominate, as in the sarcophagus of the Good Shepherd (Lateran Museum) or that of St. Constance.

Ravenna. The influence of Asia Minor and Constantinople is prevalent in theme and style on the sarcophagi at Ravenna (columned sarcophagi in the church of S. Francesco). Figured scenes are depicted amid open spaces in rigid and symmetrical patterns, e.g., the Sarcophagus of Rinaldo in the cathedral. This anti-illustrative taste, based on abstract symbolism, led to the substitution of symbols for human figures, particularly in the age of THEODORIC THE GREAT: the lamb on the hill between two sheep; the goat at the mystical fount; the palms of paradise (Sarcophagus of Galla Placidia). From the end of the 6th century these figurations become more ornate, as on the Sarcophagus of Bishop Theodore, until they become pure ornamentation. This development reaches a climax in the simple representation of the cross or monogram of Christ, dating immediately before the full barbarian occupation, as on the Sarcophagus of Theodora (d. 720) in the Museo Civico of Pavia.

Bibliography: M. LAWRENCE, *The Sarcophagi of Ravenna* (New York 1945). F. GERKE, *Die christlichen Sarkophage der Ukorkonstantinischen Zeit* (Berlin 1940); *Christus in der spätantiken Plastik* (3d ed. Mainz 1948). J. BAYET, *Mélanges d'archéologie et d'histoire* 74 (1962) 171–213. G. BOVINI, *I sarcofagi paleocristiana* (Vatican City 1949); ''Sarcofagi costantinopolitani dei secoli IV, V e VI d. C.,'' in *Corso di cultura sull'arte ravennate e bizantina,* v.9 (Ravenna 1962); ''Principale bibliografia su Ravenna romana, paleocristiana e paleobizantina,'' *ibid.* v.8 (1961) 7–37. R. FARIOLI, ''I sarcofagi paleocristiani e paleobizantini della Sicilia,'' *ibid.* v.9 (1962) 241–67. P. VERZONE, ''La scultura decorativa dell'Alto Medio Evo in Oriente e in Occidente,'' *ibid.* v.10 (1963) 371–88. E. LE BLANT, *Les Sarcophages chrétiens de la Gaule* (Paris 1886). G. M. GABRIELLI, *I sarcofagi paleocristiani e altomedioevali delle Marche* (Ravenna 1961). A. OVADIAH, ''A Jewish sarcophagus at Tiberias,'' *Israel Exploration Journal* 22:4 (1972) 229–32. L. M. MARTÍNEZ-FAZIO, ''Eucaristía, banquete y sacrificio, en la iconografía paleocristiana,'' *Gregorianum* 57:3 (1976) 459–519. J. M.C. TOYNBEE, ''The Religious Background of Some Roman Sarcophagi of North Italy and Dalmatia,'' *Jahrbuch für Antike und Christentum, Jahrgang* 18 (1975) 5–18. R. TURCAN, ''Les sarcophages romains et le problème du symbolisme funéraire,'' *Principat 16/2; Heidentum* (Berlin 1978) 1700–35. N. A. SILBERMAN, ''Coffins in a Human Shape: A Short History of Anthropoid Sarcophagi,'' *Biblical Archaeology Review* 16:4 (1990) 52–54. J. HUSKINSON, ''The Decoration of Early Christian Children's Sarcophagi,'' *Studia patristica* 24 (1993) 114–18. J. MARTÍ I AIXALÀ, ''La escena pro tribunali, Jesus ante Pilatos, en los sarcófagos de pasión,'' *Historiam pictura refert* (Rome 1994) 1–14. J. P. PETTORELLI, ''Péché originel ou amour conjugal: note sur le sens des images d'Adam et Ève sur les sarcophages chrétiens de l'antiquité tardive,'' *Recherches Augustiniennes* 30 (1997) 279–334.

[V. RICCI/EDS.]

SARDICA, COUNCIL OF

Convoked by the Emperors CONSTANS I and CONSTANTIUS II at the request of Pope JULIUS I, the Council of Sardica (modern Sofia) was held in the year 342 according to E. Schwartz, who disputes the date 344, given by Mansi. Its task was to reexamine the case of Athanasius of Alexandria, Marcellus of Ancyra and Asclepiades of Gaza, who had been deposed at the Council of Tyre in 335 by the Semiarian Eusebians. Athanasius had fled from Alexandria in 340, expelled by the intruder Gregory and appealed to Pope Julius in Rome. In 341 or 342 Marcellus had also appealed to Rome by letter. All had found refuge in Rome with Julius, including Paul of Constantinople, who was likewise expelled by the Eusebians. The latter held a Synod at Antioch in 341 and sent flattering letters to Julius but announced that they would accept the Roman settlement only if it agreed with the decision taken at Tyre.

The Council of Sardica was presided over by Hosius of Córdoba with the Roman legates Archedamius and Philoxenus. It was attended by Athanasius, Marcellus and Asclepiades together with six Oriental bishops in communion with some 100 Western bishops. Some 80 Eusebian bishops were also on hand, among whom the leaders were Acacius of Caesarea in Palestine, BASIL OF ANCYRA, Maris of Chalcedon and the Western bishops Ursacius of Singidunum and Valens of Mursa. When the Eusebians saw that the Western bishops favored Athanasius and his companions, they refused to sit in council with them and betook themselves to Philippopolis, where they excommunicated Pope Julius, Hosius and the others, and promulgated a new formula of faith that was in agreement with the fourth formula Synod of Antioch (341).

Meanwhile, the Council of Sardica confirmed the orthodoxy and legitimate consecration of Athanasius, Asclepiades and Marcellus, but failed to recognize that the doctrine of Marcellus, although violently anti-Arian, savored of SABELLIANISM. The Council condemned as Arians and deposed Gregory, Acacius of Caesarea, Theodore of Heraclea, Basil of Ancyra, Ursacius and Valens. It also promulgated a formula of faith preserved by Theodoret of Cyr (*Hist. Eccl.* 2.6) in which it declared that the hypostasis of the Father and the Son was one, taking the word hypostasis in the sense of nature or substance. But this terminology was not clear, since at the end of the fifth century the word hypostasis was interpreted as person. Hosius supported the new formula; but it was rejected by Athanasius, who claimed that the formula of Nicaea (325) was sufficient; hence the synod made no dogmatic declaration. It set the date of Easter for the following 50 years and promulgated 20 canons that were handed down in all the Greek collections and were frequently attributed to the Council of Nicaea.

Canons 3, 4 and 5 describe the right of appeal for bishops, particularly the appeal to Rome. Canon 3, proposed by Hosius, forbade bishops to transfer from one province to another; in a dispute between bishops a judge might not be brought in from another province; and it was illegitimate to visit or seek the assistance of the secular court (canons 7–9). Canon 4 stated that a deposed bishop who appealed to Rome should not be replaced until judgment was passed; canon 5 acknowledged the right of the bishop of Rome to receive and judge an appeal, to send the case to be adjudicated by neighboring bishops, or to send or designate the judge. This had already been done in the case of Athanasius and Marcellus.

The Council sent an encyclical letter to all the churches describing its decisions. It wrote to the Church of Egypt and to Pope Julius upholding the innocence and orthodoxy of Athanasius and declaring the propriety of the provinces in keeping in touch with "the head, that is the See of Peter the Apostle."

The Council of Sardica was not a great success. It did not convince the Semiarians to accept the judgment favoring Athanasius against the condemnation at Tyre. The synodal canons, though recognized in the West as regulating relations between metropolitan sees, were not accepted in the Eastern churches. But the fundamental differences between Western and Oriental thinking on theological and disciplinary matters received its first open expression.

Bibliography: C. J. VON HEFELE, *Histoire des conciles d'après les documents originaux,* tr. and continued by H. LECLERCQ, 10 v. in 19 (Paris 1907–38) 1.2:737–823. *Histoire de l'église depuis les origines jusqu'à nos jours,* eds., A. FLICHE and V. MARTIN (Paris 1935–) 3:123–130. H. HESS, *The Canons of the Council of Sardica, A.D. 343* (Oxford 1958). P. JOANNOU, *Discipline générale antique (II*e*–IX*e*s.)* (Sacra Congregazione Orientale, *Codificazione orientale, Fonti,* 1962–) 1.2:156–189. S. G. HALL, "The Creed of Sardica," *Studia Patristica,* 19 (1989): 173–184. L. W. BARNARD, *The Council of Sardica, 343 AD* (Sophia 1983).

[I. ORTIZ DE URBINA]

SARDINHA, PEDRO FERNANDES

First bishop of Brazil; b. Evora or Setubal, Portugal, *c.* 1496; d. Alagoas, Brazil, June 1556. Sardinha was a fellow student of Ignatius Loyola at the University of Paris in 1525. In 1529 he was named chaplain of St. Sebastian Church on Madeira Island. Later he was appointed a chaplain in Lisbon, and finally royal preacher in Oporto. In 1545 he was sent to Goa as dean of the cathedral under the famous governor, João de Castro. Shortly thereafter he was vicar-general of the diocese, noted for his interest in the colony but especially for his strict control of his clergy and for his warm friendship with the Jesuits. When the governor died (1548), Sardinha returned to Portugal, where he resumed his studies in Canon Law at the University of Coimbra.

Brazil had been under the jurisdiction of the Order of Christ until 1514, and then under the bishop of Madeira until 1551, when the Holy See by the bull *Super specula militantis ecclesiae* of Feb. 25, 1551, erected the Diocese of Salvador (Bahia). Sardinha was appointed the first bishop with actual jurisdiction over the entire colony. He arrived in Salvador on June 22, 1552, only to find himself disappointed and disgusted by the low morality of its 1,000 inhabitants, the poor conditions of life, and the smallness of his see city. Soon he was in trouble with the governor and with the Jesuits. In general, the root of the trouble was the contrast of the spirit of the Renaissance with that of the Counter Reformation. He disliked the adaptation system of the Jesuits and demanded that the Indians should have at least a façade of European culture before they were baptized. This is not to say that Sardinha did not fulfill his episcopal duties, as he understood them. He was zealous in his visitations of his church and stubborn in his condemnation of evil conduct even in the son of the governor, Alvaro da Costa. He had trouble, however, with his cathedral chapter. This matter reached its climax when he wounded two clerics who had disobeyed him and when he excommunicated the civil authorities who had sided with his chapter against him. He had built an episcopal residence and begun the construction of a cathedral when the King in 1555 named a vicar-general for the diocese and called Sardinha home. In June 1556 he set out; but his ship was wrecked near Alagoas, and the bishop and some 30 companions were captured by the Caeté, who were cannibals. Sardinha, reserved for the last, died heroically, encouraging and comforting his companions. Sardinha was a zealous pastor and an excellent preacher, and he loved liturgical pomp. He began the first primitive seminary in Brazil and wrote the first ''regimento'' for the clergy of his diocese.

Bibliography: O. VAN DER VAT, *Princípios da Igreja no Brasil* (Rio de Janeiro 1952). M. DE AZEVEDO, ''O primeiro Bispo do Brasil,'' *Revista do Instituto Histórico e Geográfico da Baía* 11 (1904) 83–97. G. SCHURHAMMER, ''Novos documentos sôbre M. Pedro Fernandes Sardinha, primeiro Bispo do Brasil,'' *Revista de philologia e de historia* 2 (Rio de Janeiro 1932) 317–322.

[T. BEAL]

SARKANDER, JAN, ST.

Martyr of the seal of confession; b. Skoczów (Skotschau), Austrian Silesia, December 20, 1576; d. Olomouc (Olmütz), Moravia, March 17, 1620. He attended Jesuit schools at Olmütz and Prague where he completed his course of philosophy (1603). In 1606 he interrupted his course in theology to marry Anna Platska, a Lutheran, but his wife's death the following year strengthened his resolve to become a priest. Following his ordination (1609) he undertook pastoral ministry in the diocese of Olmütz.

After Baron Ladislaus Lobkovič (Lobkowitz) bought the estates of Holešov (Holleschau), Moravia, previously in the control of the Bohemian Brethren, he returned the church to the Catholics. Cardinal Franz von Dietrichstein appointed Sarkander pastor in 1616. Lobkovič also established a Jesuit College, formerly occupied by the Bohemian Brethren. The many converts made by Sarkander and the Jesuits increased the rivalry between the baron and his anti-Catholic neighbors, especially Bitovsky of Bystrzyca (Bystritz).

At the beginning of the THIRTY YEARS' WAR (1618–1648) the Protestants seized power in Moravia. Sarkander made a pilgrimage to the Polish shrine of Our Lady of Częstochowa and remained in Cracow for some months before returning to his parish.

In 1620 Sigismund III, King of Poland, sent Cossacks into Moravia to support Emperor Ferdinand II in his struggle with the Protestant Estates. They pillaged Protestant lands, but spared Holešov when they met Sarkander carrying the Blessed Sacrament. Bitovsky accused him of conspiracy with the Poles, and imprisoned him while awaiting questioning.

At his trial Sarkander denied any treasonable acts and defied his judges, who, in an attempt to implicate Lobkovič, demanded that he reveal confessional secrets. Sarkander was tortured for several days and a month later he died in prison. Sarkander was venerated as a martyr immediately afterward.

The Silesian bishops opened his cause for sainthood under Benedict XIV, and Pius IX beatified him on May 6, 1860. Sarkander's relics are in an altar dedicated to his name in the cathedral of Olomouc. On May 21, 1995, during his sixty-fourth international pastoral visit, John Paul II canonized at Olomouc's airport Zdislava Berka and Jan Sarkander. He is the patron of Moravia and Silesia.

Feast: March 17.

Bibliography: BIRKOWSKY, *Positio super martyrio.* . . . (Rome 1825). F. LIVERANI, *Della vita e della passione del ven. servo di Dio, Giovanni Sarcander* (Rome 1855). F. SEIBT, ''Sarkander, Johannes,'' *Lexikon für Theologie und Kirche,* 2d. ed. 9: 330.

[F. J. LADOWICZ]

SARNELLI, GENNARO MARIA, BL.

Januarius; lawyer, ascetical writer, Redemptorist priest; b. Sept. 12, 1702, Naples, Italy; d. there, June 30, 1744.

The fourth son of Baron Angelo Sarnelli of Ciorani, Gennaro was inspired at age 14 by the beatification of John Francis REGIS to become a Jesuit himself. His father persuaded him instead to study canon and civil law, in which he earned a doctorate (1722). He succeeded admirably in the legal profession, while daily Mass, visits to the Blessed Sacrament, and attendance on the sick in the hospital of incurables filled his free time.

He abandoned the bar at age 26, entered the seminary in 1728, and was assigned to catechize children at St. Anne di Palazzo parish. In 1730 he entered the novitiate in the Congregation of the Apostolic Missions, a society of secular missionary preachers. Throughout his seminary training he continued his catechetical work with children, visited the elderly in the Hospice of San Gennaro, and ministered to sick sailors. During this period he and Alphonsus LIGOURI became friends and together organized the Evening Chapels (*cappelle serotine*), an association of workers and artisans formed for the purpose of mutual assistance, religious instruction, and works of apostolic zeal.

After his ordination in 1732, he served as director of religious education at a poor parish in the Spanish quarter of Naples, where he found employment for poor women to keep them out of prostitution. The year after Alphonsus's founding of the Congregation of the Most Holy Redeemer (Nov. 9, 1732), Sarnelli defended his friend against unjust criticism and in June of that year joined him in Salerno. They gave missions together along the coast of Amalfi until Sarnelli's health failed. In April 1736, he officially entered the Redemptorists in Naples. Once his health improved he began a successful written crusade in defense of young girls in danger, again undertook missions, and promoted meditation in common among the laity until his precarious health forced him into retirement in April 1744.

Sarnelli composed 30 major works on various legal, pedagogical, and theological topics, including *Il Mondo santificato*, 2 v. (Naples 1738); *Il Mondo riformato* (Naples 1739); *Le glorie e grandezze della divina Madre* (Naples 1739); *Il Cristiano santificato* (Naples 1739); *L'Anima illuminata*, 3 v. (Naples 1740); *L'Anima desolata* (Naples 1740); *Discrezione degli spiriti* (Naples 1741); *L'Ecclesiastico santificato* (Naples 1741). In his spiritual works he insists that meditation is essential for perseverance and within reach of all Christians. His writings in this area occasioned Benedict XIV's granting an indulgence for meditation (Dec. 16, 1746).

Sarnelli died at age 42 in the presence of his friend St. Alphonsus Ligouri, who reported that Sarnelli's body exuded the odor of sanctity that "remained in the room long after his interment." An urn containing his relics can be found in the Redemptorist church at Ciorani, S. Antonio a Tarsia. Sarnelli was beatified, May 12, 1996, by Pope John Paul II.

Feast: June 30 (Redemptorists).

Bibliography: *Riproduzione di tutte le opere*, 14 v. (Naples 1848–55). A. M. DE' LIGUORI, *Compendio della vita del servo di Dio G. M. S.* (Naples 1752). *Neapolit. beatificationis et canonizationis p. J. M. S. positio* (Rome 1889). *Acta Apostolicae Sedis*, no.12 (1996): 551–53. *L'Osservatore Romano*, English edition, no. 11 (1996): 1–2. R. GIOVINE, *Vita del gran servo di Dio p. G. M. S.* (Naples 1858). F. DUMORTIER, *Le vénérable serviteur de Dieu, le p. J. M. S.* (Paris 1886). M. DE MEULEMEESTER, *Bibliographie générale des écrivains rédemptoristes*, v. 2 (Löwen 1935), 373–377; v. 3 (Löwen 1939), 379. G. SPARANO, *Memorie istoriche per illustrare . . . gli atti della Congregazione delle Apostoliche Missioni* (Naples 1768), 2:345ff. H. F.G. SWANSTON, *Saint Alphonsus and His Brothers: A Study of the Lives and Works of Seven Redemptorists* (Liguori, Missouri 2000).

[K. I. RABENSTEIN]

SARPI, PAOLO

Brilliant and controversial scholar; b. Venice, Aug. 14, 1552; d. Venice, Jan. 14, 1623. Expert in theology, philosophy, law, politics, and natural sciences, the author of many works, he had a mortal enmity for the Roman Curia and the Jesuits. He had Protestant leanings and associations and probably died outside the Church. In his early life he was a close friend of St. Charles BORROMEO and St. Robert BELLARMINE. Although he was a Servite in 1565, priest in 1574, and rose to provincial (of Venice) in 1579, procurator general in 1585, and vicar-general 1599 to 1604, he failed to secure Rome's confirmation as bishop on several occasions. In 1606, as official theologian, jurist, and canonist of Venice, he maintained resolutely that the interdict of Paul V against that city was invalid. Summoned to Rome, he refused to leave the protection of Venice and was excommunicated. He blamed an attack on his life in 1607 on the Roman Curia. Until 1622 he served the Republic of Venice with his vast learning. Almost all of his writings, including many letters, were published posthumously (1st ed. of complete works 1677). His *Istoria del concilio Tridentino*, however, was published in London in 1619 by the apostate archbishop De Dominis (perhaps without Sarpi's consent, and under an anagram of his name. The work, based chiefly on the Archives of Venice, was placed on the Index immediately but went through several editions and five translations in ten years. In replying, S. Pallavicino wrote his own history of the council (1656–57) using the Vatican archives.

Sarpi's champions make him a learned saint who knew the hypocrisy and corruption of many persons in the Church. For his enemies, he may have been learned but he was not a saint. In almost 1,000 decisions, as official theologian of Venice, he exhibited a Machiavellian understanding of political affairs, and championed the state and councils at the expense of the papacy. He was anti-Aristotelian, and was influenced by Scotus and Ockham, and by Renaissance Stoicism and naturalism. Galileo thought no one in Europe could surpass Sarpi in mathematics, and he has been credited with the discovery of the circulation of the blood before W. Harvey.

Bibliography: G. ABETTI, *Amici e nemici di Galileo* (Milan 1945). H. JEDIN, *History of the Council of Trent.* A. MERCATI and D. PELZER, *Dizionario ecclesiastico* 3:721–723. H. WOLTER, *Die Religion in Geschichte und Gegenwart* ³ 5:1371–72.

[G. ABETTI]

SARTRE, JEAN-PAUL

Existentialist philosopher; b. Paris, June 21, 1905; d. April 15, 1980. He received his degree in philosophy from the École Normale Supérieur in 1929, and taught at various Lycées from 1931 to 1944. In 1933 he went to Germany for a year to study the philosophy of E. HUSSERL and M. HEIDEGGER. Returning to France he taught philosophy until 1939, at which time he was drafted into the French army; there he remained until the downfall of France, when he became a prisoner of war. After his release in 1941 he taught philosophy at the Lycée Condorcet. In 1944 he gave up teaching and devoted himself to writing. Sartre wrote novels and plays in defense of individual freedom, human dignity, and social responsibility. He had a great concern for the poor and the working class. Following the war, he became an admirer of the Soviet Union until the Hungarian revolution was crushed in 1956, though he continued to see Marxism as the only philosophy for the modern era. In 1964 he was awarded the Nobel Prize for Literature for *Les Mots*, but he refused to accept. In 1971 he moved away from writing and became a street activist for left-wing causes, advocating "the revolution." The following year he returned to writing, which he continued until his death.

Thought. Sartre in his philosophy is both a phenomenologist and an existentialist. He is an existentialist in that his main concern is with the problems experienced by the existing human individual as he lives his particular, concrete situation; he is a phenomenologist in that the methodology he employs in his analysis of this existence is the descriptive method developed by Husserl and Heidegger.

God and Man. Sartre insists that modern man must face up to the fact that God does not exist. Far from being

Paolo Sarpi.

the creatures of a loving and beneficent Father, the world and the beings in it are things that exist without any reason. There is no reason for their being the kinds of things they are; nor is there any reason for their existence, they just are. Because there is no reason for their being, Sartre calls them the Absurd. This absolute contingency, total gratuity, and sheer facticity of the world engenders in man the feeling of nausea. Possessed of consciousness and freedom, man alone can give himself a reason for existence by consciously making himself to be the kind of man he has freely decided to be. By choosing his morality, by actively fulfilling his decision, man makes his own essence, he creates himself. Hence Sartre calls man being-for-itself, whereas all other beings are being-in-itself.

Man's freedom in Sartre's view is so absolute that there can be in him no nature anterior to his own making, for any determination would destroy his freedom. In freely creating his own essence, each man is striving to become the absolutely self-caused, the *Causa Sui;* and since for Sartre, *Causa Sui* is the traditional definition of God,

Jean-Paul Sartre. (AP/WideWorld Photos)

he describes man as striving to become God. Because the project is doomed to failure, he maintains that human life is a useless passion.

Freedom and Anguish. Man's freedom is not only the foundation of his own essence; it is also the reason why there are values, ends, and objects in the world. By his freely chosen projects man puts order into the things of the world; he makes the world a universe, and he alone gives meaning to being.

This absolute freedom of man brings with it the anguish of total responsibility. Since there is no God to establish values nor any objective standards to guide him in his decision, each man is "on his own," he is abandoned to his own judgment, and he is responsible for all that he does. Although man did not give himself responsibility, he must carry it as a burden so long as he is. Hence Sartre's statement that each is responsible for everything except for the fact of being responsible. Man can always

get away from the obligation by suicide, but so long as he does not use this release, he is freely choosing to live his life with all the concrete and varied conditions that will envelop it. He is freely accepting responsibility for all that occurs. Thus, there are no accidents in a man's life; wars, famines, catastrophes exist for a man because he freely chose to continue to exist.

Because anguish, abandonment, and responsibility are, for Sartre, the very quality of human existence, these notes are predominant in all his works. His novels and plays are centered on the drama of people trying to avoid responsibility for the situation in which they find themselves, or of people having neither the courage nor the good faith freely to choose to become what they would like to be.

Being and Nothingness. Freedom and consciousness are intimately connected with another Sartrean theme, viz, negation, negativity, or nothingness. Thus, a man can desire an object only because he does not now possess it. He sees the deficiency in himself because he views his present status in relation to an ideal situation that does not yet exist. By projecting himself toward this object or end, the individual is not only turning himself toward a new man to be created by his future actions, but he is also turning away from or negating the present man that he now is. Freedom is thus defined by Sartre as a nihilating rupture with the present.

Consciousness is oftentimes depicted by him as a negation, in the sense that consciousness is always consciousness of something, viz, of an object that is not the knowing consciousness precisely as knowing. In its questioning concerning the problem of being, consciousness again indicates its radical negativity. There is, first of all, the very questioning itself, which shows an ignorance or an "is not" on the part of consciousness itself; secondly, the search may terminate in negative as well as affirmative replies; and thirdly, the questioner expects an objective answer so that he can say: it is thus and not otherwise. Hence "nothing," "nobody," and "never" are objective possibilities when consciousness is asking about being. Consciousness soon discovers that it is encompassed by nothingness; that nonbeing is a component of the real. This does not mean, according to Sartre, that BEING and NONBEING are on the same plane; rather, nonbeing, negation, is always subsequent to being in that it denies being in some way or other. Nothingness has its ground in being, depends on being, and can be known only by being; for nothingness is nonidentity between things, or an absence of a thing, or a destruction of a thing, and the like.

Works. A prolific author, Sartre published philosophical studies of various lengths, essays devoted to literary criticism, novels and plays, besides founding and editing a journal, *Les Temps Modernes.* A partial listing of his works that have been translated into English would include (1) the philosophical studies: *Psychology and Imagination, The Transcendence of the Ego, Being and Nothingness, Existentialism and Humanism* and *The Problem of Method;* (2) the novels: *Nausea* and the trilogy, *Roads to Freedom;* (3) the plays: *The Flies, No Exit, The Respectful Prostitute, Dirty Hands, The Devil and the Good Lord,* and *The Condemned of Altona;* and (4) the critical essays: *What Is Literature?, Literary and Philosophical Essays,* and *Saint Genet.*

See Also: EXISTENTIALISM; ATHEISM.

Bibliography: H. E. BARNES, *The Literature of Possibility* (Lincoln, Nebr. 1959). W. DESAN, *The Tragic Finale* (Cambridge, Mass. 1954). F. JEANSON, *Le Problème moral et la pensée de Sartre* (Paris 1947); *Sartre par lui-même* (Paris 1955). E. KERN, ed., *Sartre* (Englewood Cliffs, N.J. 1962). I. MURDOCH, *Sartre: Romantic Rationalist* (New Haven 1959). P. THODY, *Jean-Paul Sartre* (New York 1960). R. D. LAING and D. G. COOPER, *Reason and Violence: A Decade of Sartre's Philosophy, 1950–1960* (New York 1964). W. DESAN, *The Marxism of Jean-Paul Sartre* (New York 1965). P. R. WOOD, *Understanding Jean-Paul Sartre* (Columbia, S.C. 1990). C. HOWELLS, *Sartre: The Necessity of Freedom* (Cambridge [Cambridgeshire] 1988).

[V. M. MARTIN/EDS.]

SARUM USE

The liturgical customs, rites, chants and calendar associated with the medieval cathedral of Salisbury, whose liturgical books were widely copied and whose liturgy became the closest of any to constituting a uniquely English liturgy during the Middle Ages. The term "Sarum" derives from *Sarisburia,* the Latin form of "Salisbury." The origins of the Sarum Use are shrouded in obscurity. It is not an independent liturgical rite as such, but rather, an English adaptation of the Roman Rite that incorporated extensive Norman, French and Gallican influences. This accounts for similarities between the Sarum Use and those of the Dominican, Carmelite, and other medieval orders (*see* DOMINICAN RITE and CARMELITE RITE).

The final form of Sarum melodies showed economy of range, balance of cadence, advanced sense of musical form, and some transposition for effect or contrast. Much of the Gradual remained closer to Gregorian than did the Antiphonal. Alleluia verses and hymns varied most, new melodies being written continuously until 1500. The hymns, especially, yielded to the sort of variation that was found in the transmission of folk songs. As on the Continent, a great variety of sequences continued to be used until the 16th century. In the early Norman period, tropes were used extensively.

From the 13th century onwards, the Sarum Use was increasingly adopted by other cathedral, parochial and collegiate foundations. Its impact was also felt in Portugal, in the Use of Braga. By the 16th century, almost every English diocese had accepted the Salisbury Use in full or in part. The only holdout was York, which consistently retained its own independent Use. In 1542, the Convocation of the Province of Canterbury imposed the Sarum Use on the entire province. This achievement was short-lived. In 1549, Archbishop Thomas Cranmer suppressed the Sarum Use, replacing it with the reformed English liturgy of the Book of Common Prayer. The ascendency of Catholic Queen Mary resulted in its brief respite, but the Elizabethan settlement of 1559 sealed its final fate, when it was permanently suppressed. The 19th century Oxford Movement gave it a new lease of life when its members promoted the revival of pre-Reformation liturgical ceremonies and chants. Old Sarum chants and melodies were adapted to English texts.

Bibliography: N. SANDON, ed., *The Use of Salisbury, I: The Ordinary of the Mass* (Newton Abbot 1984, 2/1990); *2: The Proper of the Mass from Advent to Septuagesima* (Newton Abbot 1986, 2/2000); *3: The Proper of the Mass from Septuagesima to Palm Sunday* (Newton Abbot 1991); *4: The Masses and Ceremonies of Holy Week* (Newton Abbot 1996); *5: The Proper of the Mass from Easter to Trinity* (Newton Abbot 1998); *6: The Proper of the Mass from Trinity to Advent* (Newton Abbot 1999). W. H. FRERE, ed., *Graduale Sarisburiense* (London 1894); *Antiphonale Sarisburiense* (London 1901–25). G. R. RASTALL, ed., *Processionale ad usum Sarum 1502* (Clarabricken 1980). *The Sarum Missal* (London 1989). T. BAILEY, *The Processions of Sarum and the Western Church* (Toronto 1971). E. DUFFY, *The Stripping of the Altars: Traditional Religion in England c. 1400–1580* (London 1992).

[L. ELLINWOOD/EDS]

SASSERATH, RAINER

Franciscan Conventual moral theologian; b. Holtzheim, near Neuss in the Rhineland, Aug. 20, 1696; d. Cologne, February 1771. In 1712 Sasserath became a Friar Minor Conventual at Cologne, where he took his doctorate at the university in 1744 and taught moral theology for many years. He defended PROBABILISM in theory but was cautious, even hesitant, about applying it to the solution of practical cases. He introduced, or at least adopted, a division of moral theology that subsequently came into common use. His work *Cursus theologiae moralis tripartitus . . .* (Cologne 1753) is divided into three parts that treat respectively the following topics: (1) human acts, laws, conscience, sins, censures, and the theological virtues; (2) the virtue of religion and the sins opposed to it, right and justice, and contracts; and (3) the Sacraments, in general and particular, and indulgences. The *Cursus theologiae moralis* went through many editions before and after Sasserath's death and exercised a broad influence on moral theology in the 18th century. Its indirect influence was important also, for Jean Pierre GURY, SJ, whose *Compendium theologiae moralis* was so widely used in the 19th and early 20th centuries, owed much to Sasserath.

Bibliography: H. HURTER, *Nomenclator literarius theologiae catholicae* (Innsbruck 1926) 5.1:232–233. A. TEETAERT, *Dictionnaire de théologie catholique*, ed. A. VACANT et al., (Paris 1903—50) 14.1:1128–29. D. SPARACIO, *Frammenti bio-bibliografici discrittori ed autori minori conventuali . . .* (Assisi 1931) 169–170.

[P. K. MEAGHER]

SATAN

The Hebrew term *satan* referred to an accuser in the court of law, but most often in the Bible it is used in a metaphorical sense to refer to an adversary of one kind or another. In the Old Testament it appears except in one case (1 Chr 21.1) with a definite article, thus "the satan." The Septuagint translation of the Old Testament term is often *diabolus* (the basis of the English "devil" and "diabolic"), "accuser" or "slanderer," and in the New Testament the Greek words *satanas, satan,* and *diabolos* are used indifferently.

Judeo-Christian concepts about the DEVIL had a long evolution, the stages of which are outlined in the Old Testament, in the writings and tradition of the intertestamental period, in the New Testament, and in Christian tradition and art.

In the Old Testament. The Hebrew verb *śāṭan* (to oppose, harass someone, especially by accusing him) is the root whence comes the substantive *śāṭān,* used of the angel who hindered BALAAM (Nm 22.22) and, in a legal sense, of any accuser or prosecutor [Ps 108(109).6; Zec 3.1–2]. Among the SONS OF GOD in Jb 1.6–12, *haśśaṭan,* the accuser or adversary, apparently had the task of testing and accusing men as a function on behalf of God. His tempting of Job failed, and his prediction of Job's unfaithfulness (Jb 2.4–5) proved incorrect. In 1 Chr 21.1 Satan was much more than the overseer patrolling the earth, charged with reporting man's sins to God; he was the tempter and allurer of man into sin and the adversary of Israel and God. No mention of such a role is found in the more ancient account of this episode in 2 Samuel ch. 24. Satan's evil function in 1 Chr 21.1, then, shows that the Chronicler was aware of a personal principle of evil that warred against God and enticed man to rebel against Him. One may safely assume that the lying spirit of 1 Kgs 22.19–23 would have been identified with Satan by a Jew of the Chronicler's period, whereas in the text itself the lying spirit was a personification of the prophetic spirit that Yahweh used to deceive Ahab, or an angel carrying out Yahweh's intentions to punish Ahab. The serpent in Genesis ch. 3 who deceived Eve was eventually identified with the devil through whose envy death entered the world (Wis 2.24). The text of Sir 21.27 (Greek) seems to warn against blaming one's evil tendencies on Satan as if he were the cause of all evil, although the adversary here might have meant simply any enemy of the godless man. It was only very late, then, that Hebrew thought began to identify Satan with an evil force, personal and superhuman, who opposed God by enticing man to sin, although the idea was as ancient as the Yahwistic account of man's primitive rebellion against God (Gn ch. 3).

In the Intertestamental Period. In the traditions handed down by the Jewish rabbis and in the Jewish apocrypha, Satan was described as the arch opponent of Israel and was given such evil-sounding names as Belial (worthlessness) and Sammael (perhaps, God's poison).

As the avenger, the tempter, and the troublemaker, he disturbed Israel's covenant relationship with God by tempting man to sin and by trying to frustrate God's benevolent providence. As in Wis 2.24, he was identified with the serpent of Genesis in both the Targums and the MIDRASHIC LITERATURE. Contact with Persian demonology probably influenced Judaism to solidify its concept of Satan; human life and history with their conflicts became the battleground between good and evil, between God and Satan. A transcendental dualism was thereby introduced into Judaism for the first time.

In the New Testament. The earliest Christian writers almost always transliterated Satan into Greek with the definite article, thereby signifying the adversary of God in a very special sense. The Greek translation of Satan, ὁ διάβολος, whence came the word devil, had the connotation of a slanderous accuser. The devil was called also BEELZEBUL (Mt 5.37) and Beliar, or Belial (2 Cor 6.15). Other characteristic appellations were the evil one (Mt 5.37), the accuser (Rv 12.10), the adversary (1 Pt 5.8), and the enemy (Mt 13.39). In Lk 10.18 he is characterized as the leader of the devils who were subject to Christ and His Disciples. He was the tempter of Christ, a murderer, a liar, and the father of murderers and liars (Jn 8.39–44). He was the strong man whom Christ was defeating (Mt 12.29), the prince of the world to be cast out by Jesus' sacrifice (Jn 12.31; 14.30; 16.11), and the instigator of Judas Iscariot (Jn 13.2, 27). He and his evil spirits were doomed to everlasting fire (Mt 25.41). The dragon of Revelation ch. 12, the devil, had two beasts in his service, the symbols of the pagans who persecuted the Church (Revelation ch. 13). His final defeat, already determined in heaven (Rv 12.10–12), would be accomplished by Christ at His return from heaven, His PAROUSIA (2 Thes 2.1–12). The idea of a personal, superhuman power of evil was, therefore, a constant and integral part of NT thought. Christ's use of the term satan for Peter, who was opposing the divine plan of the Cross, was a return to the more ancient concept of a satan as a hindrance or obstacle (Nm 22.22).

In Christian Tradition and Art. The Fathers echoed the New Testament in calling Satan the adversary, the accuser, and the evil one. The catechumen had to renounce him in the traditional liturgy of Baptism. His power was destroyed by the celebration of the Eucharist, for, in Christian theology, Christ had redeemed men from his power by paying a just ransom.

The devil was first depicted in Christian art in the 6th century, appearing as an angelic figure in miniatures and frescoes. The art of the Middle Ages, however, portrayed him as an ugly and horrifying monster.

In morality plays he was presented as the deceiver of men and adversary of Christ; he could always be rec-

ognized, despite his disguise, by the limp (a result of his fall from heaven) that his portrayer affected.

See Also: DEMON (IN THE BIBLE).

Bibliography: J. GUILLET, *Themes of the Bible,* tr. A. J. LAMOTHE (Notre Dame, IN 1960) 137–170. *Encyclopedic Dictionary of the Bible,* translated and adapted by L. HARTMAN (New York, 1963) 2134–37. W. FOERSTER and G. VON RAD, G. KITTEL, *Theologisches Wörterbuch zum Neuen Testament* (Stuttgart 1935) 2:69–80. H. L. STRACK and P. BILLERBECK, *Kommentar zum Neuen Testament,* 4 v. (Munich 1922–23) 1:136–149. H. VORGRIMLER, *Lexikon für Theologie und Kirche,* ed. J. HOFER and K. RAHNER, 10 v. (2d, new ed. Freiburg 1957–65) 9:341.

[W. F. BARNETT/EDS.]

SATANISM

This term is here understood to signify the cult honoring Satan with quasi-religious ceremonies in mockery of Christian rites, and with the performance of other works tending to promote the cause of Satan's dominion in this world. That such a cult exists appears clearly established, but no reliable information is available regarding the extent of its diffusion. For an explanation of the sources and rationale of this curious phenomenon, as well as for a judgment of its morality, *see* DEVIL WORSHIP.

[M. D. GRIFFIN]

SATELLICO, ELISABETTA MARIA, BL.

Known in religion as Maria Crucifixa (Mary Crucified), Poor Clare abbess; b. Dec. 31, 1706, Venice, Italy; d. Nov. 8, 1745, at Ostra Vetere, Italy. Elisabetta and her parents, Piero Satellico and Lucia Mander, lived with her maternal uncle, a priest who early encouraged her gifts for music and prayer. She studied under the Poor Clares at Ostra Vetere, where she sang and played the organ. In 1726, she received the religious habit there and took the name Maria Crucifixa. She undertook penances in order to become more like Jesus Crucified. She was elected abbess and employed her mystical gifts for the benefit of the community. Upon her death at age 39, she was buried in Santa Lucia, Ostra Vetere. The cause for her canonization was opened shortly after her death, and she was beatified at Rome by John Paul II, Oct. 10, 1993.

Feast: Nov. 8 (Franciscans).

Bibliography: G. B. SCARAMELLI, *Vita di Suor Maria Crocifissa Satellico monaca Francescana nel monastero di Monte Nuovo,* 5th ed. (Rome 1819). This work was originally published in Venice in 1750.

[K. I. RABENSTEIN]

SATIS COGNITUM

Encyclical of Pope LEO XIII, dated June 20, 1896, formulating the pope's teaching on the unity and unicity of the Church. The first lines express Leo's concern for the return to the "fold" of "sheep that have strayed," the fold being "under the guardianship of Jesus Christ, the chief Pastor of souls." The encyclical understands unity as the oneness of the Catholic Church with Jesus Christ, and therefore reunion as the return of all Christians to the Catholic Church.

The encyclical has no internal divisions, though paragraphs have been numbered by most translators (16 in Claudia Carlen, *The Papal Encyclicals*). The text is easily divided into five parts, with an introduction and a conclusion: the visibility of the Church (3–5), the unity of the Church (6–7), the Magisterium (8–9), the divine society (10–12), the Roman Pontiff and the bishops (13–15). Parts one and two give a strongly Christocentric picture of the visible Church, which is based on the doctrines of the Incarnation and Redemption. The documentation is Scriptural, chiefly Pauline, and, more abundantly, patristic. Parts three and four explain the Catholic understanding of the patristic doctrine as it had developed through the Middle Ages and the Counter-Reformation, with a strong emphasis on the task and responsibility of the bishops and popes to teach the true doctrine and the corresponding duty of all believers to accept all the doctrines without exception. That the Church is thus constituted as a "divine society" was a popular notion in the ultramontane party in its arguments with Gallicanism before and after Vatican Council I. Part five draws the logical conclusions regarding the necessity and the divine authority of papal and episcopal government, though evidently without the nuances that were to be brought in by Vatican II with its emphasis on the collegiality of the episcopate. In n.15 Pope Leo teaches that bishops who "deliberately secede from Peter and his successors" thereby lose all jurisdiction, thus indirectly and presumably unintentionally throwing doubt on the ecclesiality of the Orthodox Churches. He goes on to assert that the pope's "power over the episcopal college" is "clearly set forth in Holy Writ." The conclusion is an appeal to all those who believe in Christ to "obey" the pope's "paternal charity."

The doctrine of *Satis cognitum*, commonly labelled "unionism," in contrast with the ecumenism of Vatican Council II, took no account of the theological insights of the school of Tübingen or of the thought of Cardinal John Henry Newman. Nonetheless, it inspired and encouraged devotion to the unity of the Church and the reunion of the Churches. Unionism began to be abandoned with the start of the ECUMENICAL MOVEMENT at the Missionary Con-

ference of Edinburgh in 1910, by the formation of the World Council of Churches in 1948, and by the subsequent commitment of the Catholic Church to the restoration of Christian unity as explained in the conciliar decree *Unitatis redintegratio* of Vatican II, and in the encyclical *Ut unum sint* of John Paul II (May 25, 1995).

Bibliography: Latin text: *Acta Sanctae Sedis* 28, 708–739. English text: C. CARLEN, ed., *The Papal Encyclicals 1878–1903* (Ann Arbor, Mich. 1990) 387–404.

[G. H. TAVARD]

SATISFACTION OF CHRIST

The mode of operation proper to Christ's satisfaction for sin is not a matter of divine and Catholic faith. The theological principle underlying it was first enunciated by Saint ANSELM OF CANTERBURY in his *Cur Deus homo*. Although the term satisfaction was current before Anselm's time and was even applied to the work of Redemption in the Mozarabic liturgy, the great archbishop of Canterbury was the first theologian to analyze the idea of satisfaction thoroughly and to stress its primary importance in the theology of Redemption. As developed by Saint Thomas Aquinas, the principle is stated thus: "He properly atones for an offense who offers something which the offended one loves as well as or even more than he detests the offense. But by suffering out of love and obedience, Christ gave more to God than was required to compensate for the offense of the whole human race" (*Summa theologiae* 3a, 48.2). Still further study, particularly from the viewpoint of BIBLICAL THEOLOGY, has made it clear that a theological explanation cannot be given without advertence to the following points.

Divine Initiative in Establishing the Mystery of Christ. The Man Jesus sums up in Himself the whole mystery of God's redemptive love (H. Denzinger, *Enchiridion symbolorum*, ed. A. Schönmetzer, 624). This mystery "hidden for ages and generations, but now . . . clearly shown to his saints" (Col 1.26) identifies God's incarnate Son with the cause of sinful humanity. He has so steeped Himself in man's history that all men of all time make one body with Him. He and they together make "one mystic person" before the heavenly Father (*Summa theologiae* 3a, 48.2 ad 1). Consequently, the works of Christ are related both to Himself and to men, His members, in the same way another man's works are related to himself alone (*Summa theologiae* 3a, 48.1).

The purpose of the redemptive INCARNATION of God's Son is to achieve this oneness with a needy human race. "In this has the love of God been shown in our case, that God has sent his only-begotten Son into the world

"Deposition from the Cross," oil on canvas painting by Caravaggio.

that we may live through him'' (1 Jn 4.9). Satisfaction is unintelligible unless there is a social significance to Christ's life and death (*Enchiridion symbolorum* 261). It must be meaningful for all who dwell in Him as in one mystic person. This is the mystery that ''God foreordained before the world unto our glory'' (1 Cor 2.7). God's love for mankind established a solidarity of men in Christ in such a way that mankind's offense was offset by God's own gift (*Enchiridion symbolorum* 623). ''But not like the offense is the gift. For if by the offense of the one many died, much more has the grace of God, and the gift in the grace of one man, Jesus Christ, abounded unto the many'' (Rom 5.15).

''Severity of God'' as a More Bountiful Mercy. The Biblical notion of God's justice is not identical with the attitude of an angry father nor with the zeal of a righteous judge. The introduction of a dolorous Passion into Christ's work of satisfaction is not a punitive measure of God. Christ, our Savior, could never take the full punishment of sin upon Himself. He, the innocent, well-beloved Son of God, could never really be punished by His Father, not even as a substitute for all the brethren who would make one body with Him (*C. gent.* 4.55 ad 20).

The Prophets and the Psalmist appeal to the JUSTICE OF GOD when yearning for deliverance. Goodness, mercy, fidelity, constancy—all these are aspects of the Biblical notion of God's justice. When Saint Thomas speaks of ''the severity of God'' that was ''unwilling to forgive sin without punishment,'' he rightly couples this immediately with ''His goodness'' in giving mankind one who could adequately satisfy in behalf of all those who deserved punishment (*Summa theologiae* 3a, 47.3 ad 1).

The satisfaction of Christ is called vicarious not because Jesus became a scapegoat actually enduring the punishment for mankind's sins (*Summa theologiae* 3a, 13.3 ad 2). In giving His own Son as a propitiation for man's sins God was lovingly safeguarding the dignity of even fallen man (*Summa theologiae* 3a, 46.1 ad 3; 46.3). Man's own Brother made atonement for him (*Enchiridion symbolorum* 801). Thus the Apostle can say: ''But now he has reconciled you in his body of flesh through his death, to present you holy and undefiled and irreproachable before him'' (Col 1.22).

Father's Role in Delivering His Son to the Cross. It was this loving justice of God that delivered Jesus to the cross. It was the Father who planned the dolorous Passion of mankind's Savior; it was the Father who inspired the human will of Jesus to surrender lovingly to a sacrificial death; it was the Father who allowed Christ's enemies to have their way with Him when, as Jesus Himself assured Peter, He might have sent 12 legions of angels to deliver His beloved Son (*Summa theologiae* 3a,

47.3). He did all this so that men might be ''justified freely by his grace through the redemption which is in Christ Jesus, whom God has set forth as a propitiation by his blood through faith, to manifest his justice'' (Rom 3.25).

The word propitiation reminds one that Christ's suffering and death were an expiation for an offense or an appeasement of an offended God. Though God's loving justice was not punishing His innocent Son, He did so plan the redemptive Passion as to enable Jesus to express His filial love through experiences that came to mankind historically as punishments for sin, namely, suffering and death (*Summa theologiae* 3a, 14.3 ad 2). In this respect there is a penal element in Our Lord's work of satisfaction (*Collectio Lacensis: Acta et decreta sacrorum conciliorum recentiorum*, ed. Jesuits of Maria Laach, 7.543.3). But it is inseparable from the moral value of Christ's love that made that encounter with pain fruitful for all mankind (*Summa theologiae* 3a, 47.3 ad 3). In Christ all the afflictions in the life of man, when imbued with love, become works of satisfaction (*Summa theologiae* 3a Supplement, 15.2–3; *Enchiridion symbolorum* 1690), ''for God has not destined us unto wrath, but to gain salvation through Our Lord Jesus Christ, who died for us in order that, whether we wake or sleep, we should live together with him'' (1 Thes 5.9).

Son's Filial Obedience Prompted by Love. In His sacred Passion Jesus referred to His sufferings as a chalice given to Him by His Father (Jn 18.11). To drink it to its last bitter dregs was a costly experience. ''For Jesus in the days of his earthly life, with a loud cry and tears, offered up prayers and supplications to him who was able to save him from death, and was heard because of his reverent submission'' (Heb 5.7). He has knowledge of the costliness of obedience, even when prompted by filial love. ''And he, Son though he was, learned obedience from the things that he suffered; and when perfected, he became to all who obey him the cause of eternal salvation . . .'' (Heb 5.10).

The formal or constitutive element in Christ's satisfaction for sin is this obedience prompted by love (*Summa theologiae* 3a, 48.2). This is what makes penal realities, like pain and death, become sacrificial. Without His interior love and obedience Our Lord's sufferings would have been merely a feat of endurance, unworthy of God's acceptance as a redemptive sacrifice (*Enchiridion symbolorum* 1529).

Obedience is fittingly the dynamic behind Christ's satisfaction. By it mankind's justification is achieved through a reversal of tactics by one representative Man. ''For just as by the disobedience of the one man the many were constituted sinners, so also by the obedience of one many will be constituted just'' (Rom 5.19).

This obedience reconciled man to God and delivered man from all the punitive aftermath of the first disobedience—enslavement to sin, Satan, the law, and death itself (*Enchiridion symbolorum* 1347). In inspiring His Son to die for man from obedient love, God remade a new people enriched by His love. ''He who has spared not even his own Son but has delivered him for us all, how can he fail to grant us also all things together with him?'' (Rom 8.32)

Penal Element as a Price of Deliverance. The Scriptural image of innocent bloodshedding as a price or ransom for deliverance (1 Pt 1.19) accentuates the penal element in the work of satisfaction. The external bodily pain and the internal anguish of Jesus, while in no sense accompanied by a consciousness of rejection, contrition, or self-rebuke, are nonetheless the dolorous offspring of sin. There is no suffering in humanity's history that is not originally a punishment for sin (*Summa theologiae* 3a, 14.1). Christ took these historically punitive evils, associated them with His loving obedience, and converted them into the raw material for sacrificial love (*Enchiridion symbolorum* 1025–1027).

His sorrow, as a loving work of satisfaction, was the greatest ever endured in the history of mankind. Whether Christ's Passion is considered in the causes of His bodily and mental suffering, or in His exquisite sensitivity to pain, or in the unassuaged purity of His grief, or in the earnestness of His desire for self-emptying, always His sorrow is unmitigated (*Summa theologiae* 3a, 46.6). This accumulation of sorrow, costly in human endurance, is the ''great price'' (1 Cor 6.20) of man's deliverance; by it man who was once afar off has been brought near through the blood of Christ (see Eph 2.13).

Price of Deliverance a Superabundant Satisfaction. A rigorously juridical concept of satisfaction can suggest an exchange governed by commutative justice. Excessive humanization of the Creator-creature relationship can effect the theological discussion of whether or not Christ's payment of satisfaction in mankind's name was in the strictest sense a work of justice.

Theologians, generally, observe that a strictly just exchange between a debtor and a recipient of payment must involve goods that are (1) completely the debtor's own, (2) in no way due under another title, and (3) offered so compellingly that the creditor cannot refuse them.

Christ, as Man-God, became a voluntary debtor acting in mankind's name. The same Divine Person who made satisfaction in His humanity accepted it in His divinity. Accordingly, human notions involved in justice transactions do not have unqualified application to the di-

vine-human relationship in Christ's satisfaction. Jesus, man's Savior, was preeminently the perfect religious Man.

Rightly, however, and incontestably His ATONEMENT is called superabundant. This is so for three reasons: (1) the dignity of His life, which He laid down for man—the human life of God, (2) the greatness of His charity with its unchanging capacity for merit, and (3) the extensiveness of His suffering, so apt to remove all obstacles, ontological and psychological, preventing man's complete surrender to God (*Summa theologiae* 3a, 48.2).

Total Victory as the Goal of the Work. Paul the Apostle voiced the instinctive yearning of every Christian in the presence of Christ's work of satisfaction. He yearned to ''know him and the power of his resurrection and the fellowship of his sufferings'' (Phil 3.10). Sacrificial love in Christ is always moving toward total deliverance from humiliation and pain. In Christ men's own satisfaction for sin becomes a progressive march toward total victory (*Enchiridion symbolorum* 1691). Men's fellowship with Him both in suffering and in triumph is a prelude to final glorification with Him.

This fellowship graces men with His entire gospel of sanctified pain (1 Pt 4.12). It enriches men with the total assets of His glorified existence in men's behalf (1 Cor 3.22). In Him men are already pledged to multiple sharings in His victory, both in time and in eternity (Eph 2.4–8). Even now gladness is men's birthright (Col 1.13, 14). Satan is stamped under men's feet with dispatch (Rom 16.20). The burden of the Law has yielded to the sweet yoke of Christ (Rom 7.4–7). Death itself is but a final immolation of love for the sake of full consummation of union with the risen Christ (2 Cor 5.4–5). Men are called to be the happy, holy, victorious people of God (1 Pt 2.5–9).

See Also: JESUS CHRIST, ARTICLES ON; PASSION OF CHRIST, I, II; REPARATION, THEOLOGY OF; EXPIATION (IN THEOLOGY)

Bibliography: ANSELM OF CANTERBURY, *Cur Deus homo* in *Opera omnia*, ed. F. S. SCHMITT, 6 v. (Edinburgh 1938–61) 2:37–133. S. LYONNET, ''De 'Justitia Dei' in Ep. ad Rom.,'' *Verbum Domini* 25 (1947) 23–34, 118–21, 129–44, 193–203, 257–63. J. RIVIÈRE, *Dictionnaire de théologie catholique*, ed. A. VACANT et al., 15 v. (Paris 1903–50) 13:2:1912–2004. A. D'ALÈS, *Dictionnaire apologétique de la foi catholique*, ed. A. D'ALÈS, 4 v. (Paris 1911–22) 4:541–82. L. HÖDL, *Lexikon für Theologie und Kirche*, ed. J. HOFER and K. RAHNER, 10 v. (2d, new ed. Freiburg 1957–65) 4:683–85. ''Satisfaktionstheorien,'' *Lexikon für Theologie und Kirche*, v.9. PHILIPPE DE LA TRINITÉ, *What Is Redemption?*, tr. A. ARMSTRONG (New York 1961). B. M. AHERN, *New Horizons: Studies in Biblical Theology*, ed. C. STUHLMUELLER (Notre Dame, Ind. 1963), J. S. WHAEL, *Victor and Victim* (Cambridge, Eng. 1960). A. VONIER, *The Victory of Christ* (London 1934). A. SCHLITZER, *Redemptive Incarnation* (Notre Dame, Ind. 1962).

[A. P. HENNESSY]

Francesco Satolli.

SATOLLI, FRANCESCO

Cardinal, first apostolic delegate to the U.S.; b. Marsciano, near Perugia, Italy, July 21, 1839; d. Rome, Jan. 8, 1910. After ordination (1862), he received a doctorate at the Sapienza University, Rome; went to teach in the seminary at Perugia (1864); became pastor in his native town (1870); and joined the Benedictines at MONTE CASSINO (1872–74). He was professor of theology in Rome at the College of Propaganda (1880–92), and also at the Roman Seminary (1882–86). He became rector of the Greek College in Rome (1884), and president of the Pontifical Academy of Noble Ecclesiastics (1886–92), where he also lectured on Canon Law. He played an important part in the development of NEOSCHOLASTICISM and THOMISM promoted by Leo XIII, both in the classroom and as the author of several once-influential theological works. In 1888 he became titular archbishop of Lepanto. Satolli came to the U.S. in 1889 as papal ablegate for the centenary celebration in Baltimore of the establishment of the hierarchy in the U.S. and he also delivered an address at the inauguration of The CATHOLIC UNIVERSITY OF AMERICA. On his second visit, in 1892, he represented the Pope at the World's Columbian Exposition in Chicago, acted as ablegate to settle educational problems with the hierarchy, and lectured on philosophy at The Catholic University. When the permanent APOSTOLIC DELEGATION

IN THE U.S. was created (January 1893), he was given the post and held it until October 1896, when he returned to Rome as archpriest of the Lateran Basilica (1896) and prefect of the Congregation of Studies (1897). On the occasion of the St. Louis Exposition (1904) he made his final visit to the U.S. His addresses in the U.S. were collected and published in *Loyalty to Church and State* (1895).

Bibliography: J. T. ELLIS, *The Life of James Cardinal Gibbons,* 2 v. (Milwaukee 1952).

[A. RANDALL]

SATOR AREPO

A cryptogram called the "magic square," whose date, origin, and interpretation are the subject of great uncertainty. A possible transliteration is: *sator,* the sower; *arepo,* with his plow; *tenet,* holds; *opera,* with purpose; *rotas,* the wheels. The five words can be read consecutively either horizontally or perpendicularly; and while the disposition of the words varied in both East and West during the Middle Ages, the device was traced to the 4th century A.D. and considered of Christian origin.

The affinity of the word *arepo* with the Celtic *arepennis,* which means acre (French, *arpent*) and can signify a plow led J. Carcopino to place its origin in Gaul. The fact that *tenet* in both the horizontal and vertical reading forms a cross seemed to give further assurance that it was a Christian symbol. However, a possible connection with Ezechiel (9.6) seemed to argue for a Jewish source. The discovery of four copies of the cryptogram at DURA-EUROPOS in 1932 pushed back its dating to the 3d century, for that city had been lost to sight since 256. Since it was associated with the A and O (Alpha and Omega), Grosser deciphered it as an anagram of the Pater Noster arranged between A and O, referring to the Apocalypse's symbolism of God as the Beginning and the End.

Its presence at Pompeii, discovered in 1937, threw doubt on its Christian origin since Pompeii was destroyed A.D. 79. More recently I. Daniélou has indicated a possible knowledge of the cryptogram on the part of IRENAEUS OF LYONS, who spoke of Him "Who joined the beginning with the end, and is the Lord of both, and has shown forth the plough at the end" (*Adv. haer.* 4.34, 4). Irenaeus was refuting the Gnostics who interpreted John 4.37, "One sows, another reaps," as an opposition between the Demiurge, who created, and Christ, who redeemed. He maintained that the creator and redeemer are one, and the passage refers to the cross, symbolized by the plow, which was shown forth at the beginning or seed time, and in the end at the final weeding. Despite intensive study, nothing certain is known of the origin or planning of this anagram. H. Leclercq traces it to folklore and doubts its connection with Hebraic or Christian SYMBOLISM.

Bibliography: G. DE JERPHANION, *La voix des monuments: Études d'archéologie,* NS (Rome 1938) 38–94. J. CARCOPINO, *Études d'histoire chrétienne. Les Fouilles de St. Pierre et la tradition. Le Christianisme secret du carré magique* (2d ed. Paris 1963). M. DELLA CORTE, *Rendiconti della R. Acc. di Arch. Lett. e belle Arti di Napoli* 19 (1939). A. FERRUA, *La civiltà cattolica* (Rome 1850–) (1937) 3:130–135. M. SIMON, *Verus Israel* (Paris 1948). H. LECLERCQ, *Dictionnaire d'archéologie chrétienne et de liturgie,* ed. F. CABROL, H. LECLERCQ and H. I. MARROU, 15 v. (Paris 1907–53) 15.1:913–915. J. DANIÉLOU, *Primitive Christian Symbols,* tr. D. ATTWATER (Baltimore 1964) 99–101.

[V. RICCI]

SATURNALIA

A very old pagan Roman festival, probably of agrarian origin. Its beginnings are obscure. Macrobius (*Saturn.* 1.7) notes that various explanations were given. He states that it was celebrated originally on December 17, but in his time lasted for seven days, December 17–23. On the 17th a sacrifice was offered to Saturn in the Forum. The next few days were marked by festivities—gifts, feasting, and license for the slaves, who were served by their masters. The custom of drawing lots for a king of the feast is mentioned by Tacitus (*Ann.* 13.15.2) and is found also in the *Acts* of St. Dasius. Dasius, a Roman soldier elected to be king of the Saturnalia, refused because he was a Christian. He was put to death on November 20, 303 [cf. F. Cumont, "The Acts of St. Dasius," *Analecta Bollandiana* 16 (1897) 5–16]. This recital, the gist of which appears authentic, gives some hitherto unknown details on the celebration of the Saturnalia by the Roman army outside Rome (in this case at Durostonum in Maesia), but it contains a serious error in saying that the king must finally be offered in sacrifice.

St. Epiphanius (*Adv. haer.* 51.22:5) confuses the Saturnalia with the festival of the winter solstice: "This day [of the solstice] called Saturnalia among the Romans, Kronia among the Egyptians, and Kikellia among the Alexandrians, was celebrated by the Greeks [i.e., the idol worshippers] on the 8th day before the calends of January" (December 25). He was mistaken on the date, for the Saturnalia ended December 23. Since celebrations of the *Natalis invicti* began on the night of December 24–25, Epiphanius thought that they were concerned with the one festival. However, the Saturnalia had nothing to do with the solstice festival, nor with the cult of the sun. Accordingly, the Saturnalia had no influence on the institution of the feast of Christmas.

An attempt was made to connect the practice of choosing a king at the feast of the Epiphany with what was done in the case of the Saturnalia. But this custom was of Greek origin and did not properly belong to the Roman festival.

Bibliography: H. J. ROSE, *The Oxford Classical Dictionary,* ed. M. CARY (Oxford 1949). 797. W. H. ROSCHER, ed., *Ausfürliches Lexikon der griechischen und röischen Mythologie,* 6 v. (Leipzig 1884–1937) 4:427–444. M. NILSSON, *Paulys Realenzyklopädie der klassischen Altertumswissenschaft,* ed. G. WISSOWA, et al. 2A.1 (Stuttgart 1921) 201–211.

[B. BOTTE]

SATYRUS OF MILAN, ST.

Younger brother of St. AMBROSE of Milan; b. Trier, Germany, *ca.* A.D. 340; d. Milan, Italy, A.D. 375. Uranius Satyrus, following the death of his father, was brought to Rome, along with Ambrose and their sister (St.) Marcellina, by his mother, and was educated there. Although he never enjoyed robust health, he entered, and rose rapidly in, the imperial service. But after the election of Ambrose as bishop of Milan, Satyrus resigned his post in order to administer the family property and free his brother from the temporal cares of his episcopal household and diocese. He suffered shipwreck and exposure on a return voyage from Africa, whither he had gone on family business, and died shortly afterward. Before leaping into the sea, he had received a particle of the Holy Eucharist from a fellow voyager and wrapped it in a scarf about his neck. Although a man of the highest integrity and blameless life, he was still a catechumen at this time and was baptized only after his return to Milan.

The chief source for the career and character of Satyrus is the first oration of St. Ambrose, *On the Death of His Brother.* The second oration is less personal, and is rather a treatise of consolation based on faith and the Resurrection.

Feast: Sept. 17.

Bibliography: *Acta Sanctorum* Sept. 5:496–505. AMBROSE, *De excessu fratris 1–2,* ed. O. FALLER, *Corpus scriptorum ecclesiasticorum latinorum* 73 (1955) 207–325. L. P. MCCAULEY et al., trs, *Funeral Orations by Saint Gregory Nazianzen and Saint Ambrose* (Fathers of the Church; New York 1953) 157–254. F. H. DUDDEN, *The Life and Times of St. Ambrose,* 2 v. (Oxford 1935), esp. 1:177–184.

[M. R. P. MCGUIRE]

SAUDI ARABIA, THE CATHOLIC CHURCH IN

Saudi Arabia is located on the Arabian peninsula connecting Asia and Africa. It is bordered on the north

Capital: Riyadh.
Size: 865,000 sq. miles.
Population: 22,023,500 in 2000.
Languages: Arabic.
Religions: 21,423,500 Muslim (97%), 600,000 Christian (3%).
Apostolic vicariate: Arabia.

by Jordan, Iraq and Kuwait, on the northeast by Qatar, on the east by the Persian Gulf, the United Arab Emirates and Oman, on the south by Yemen and on the west by the Red Sea. The al-Sarah mountains run parallel to the western coastline, with plateaus along their eastern slopes. Most of the region is covered by two deserts, the Great Nufud and the Empty Quarter (*ar-Rub' al-Khâlï*), the latter constituting the largest continuous body of sand in the world. Bisected by the Tropic of Cancer, the region is temperate, the lowlands semitropical. Sandstorms occur inland, with monsoons to the east. Rainfall is scarce—in the deserts no rain may fall for up to ten years—and a few small rivers flow along the southern and eastern coasts. Human life is possible in much of the region only because of the presence of oases, some of which are large enough to support several villages. Agricultural products, limited due to the harsh conditions, include dates, wheat, barley, alfalfa, coffee, grapes and peaches. Natural resources include vast petroleum reserves in al-Ahsâ, near the Persian Gulf, as well as iron ore gold, copper and natural gas.

Saudi Arabia was founded in 1932 by Abdul 'Aszîz Ibn al Sa'ûd (1880–1953). Most Arabians are descended from southern Qahtan and northern Adnan tribes. Abdul 'Aszîz effectively started the *reconquista* by retaking Riyadh in January of 1902; the unification of what is known as the kingdom of Saudi Arabia was completed in 1934. Controlling one-fourth of the world's oil reserves, the region is dominated economically by the state-run ARAMCO company, which extracts crude oil. Fahd bin Abdul 'Aszîz ibn al Sa'ûd ruled as king and prime minister beginning in 1982.

What follows is a history of the modern state of Saudi Arabia (for a history of the Arabian peninsula, *see* ARABIA).

History. Saudi Arabia is a modern state created from the territories conquered by the Saud family, strict followers of the branch of Sunni Islam called Wahabism, founded by the 18th-century religious reformer Muhammad Ibn Abd al-Wahab. In 1916 a British-backed revolt led by Hussein ibn Ali, sharif of Mecca, freed the Arabian Peninsula from Ottoman rule. Following World War I Hussein claimed the title of king of Arabia, but foreign interests recognized only his sovereignty over the Hejaz

region, the cradle of Islam that contained both Mecca and Medina. Hussein and his son, who became king in 1924 were soon at war with the Saud tribal confederacy under Abdul 'Aszîz ibn al Sa'ûd, sultan of Najd. Ibn al Sa'ûd, who had captured Riyadh as early as 1902, defeated Hussein, conquered the Hejaz and proclaimed himself king in 1926, and proceeded to unify the peninsula under his own rule. In 1932 he assumed the title of king of Saudi Arabia.

The region's economy relied upon the pilgrim trade through Mecca and Medina until the discovery of enormous deposits of oil in the eastern part of the country in the 1930s. The exploitation of these oil deposits, first by the U.S. Standard Oil Company in 1938, markedly changed the fortunes of the region. In 1944 the government reorganized the oil company as the Arabian American Oil Company (ARAMCO), which brought it increasingly into world affairs.

Despite its international business dealings, Saudi Arabia remained a Sunni Muslim state, denying freedom of religion and declaring the Qu'ran and the Sunna of Muhammad to be the constitution. Religion and government remained wholly interconnected. The public practice of other Muslim orders, of Christianity, or of any other religion was strictly forbidden. Private practice of Christian faiths was tolerated for diplomats and other authorized foreigners. Despite the region's wealth, the government remained concerned about limited supplies of drinking water, a growing population and the region's dependence on a finite supply of oil.

By 2000 there were six priests and under 20 religious tending to the spiritual needs of the foreign Catholics living in the country on worker's visas. Christians—Catholics, Copts, and Protestants— were predominately from the Philippines, India or African countries. However, by the late 1990s the future of even foreign Christians in the country appeared questionable, as reports surfaced of Christians arrested for possession of Bibles, or for meeting for clandestine prayer groups and Bible study. The punishment for practicing a non-Sunni Muslim faith was on the order of two to six months' imprisonment, forced conversion to Islam or deportation. The punishment for proselytization was torture and the death penalty, although a 1995 case involving a foreigner charged with conversion ended with the prisoner's 1997 release following an international outcry. The government appeared to be making a concerted effort to seek out and remove all practicing Christians, whether citizens or not, as part of the planned "Saudiization" effort that would replace foreign workers with Saudi citizens.

Bibliography: R. H. SANGER, *The Arabian Peninsula* (Ithaca, NY 1954). H. ST. J. B. PHILBY, *Saudi Arabia* (London 1955). P. K.

HITTI, *History of the Arabs* (6th ed. New York 1956). K. S. TWITCH-ELL, *Saudi Arabia* (3d ed. Princeton 1958). G. A. LIPSKY et al., *Saudi Arabia* (New Haven 1959).

[J. A. DEVENNY/EDS.]

SAUDREAU, AUGUSTE

Writer on the ascetical and mystical life; b. St. Lambert du Latay, near Angers, France, Jan. 17, 1859; d. Angers, Nov. 20, 1946.

Auguste Saudreau was ordained for the Diocese of Angers in 1883. He was parish priest in Saumur until 1895, when he was appointed chaplain at the mother-house of the Good Shepherd Sisters, at Angers, where he remained until his death. When he became chaplain, Saudreau began to write on spiritual theology. He was a prolific writer and soon acquired an international reputation as a spiritual director through his books and his articles in periodicals. Many of his books were translated into several languages.

Saudreau followed the doctrines of St. Thomas Aquinas and St. John of the Cross on the structure of the spiritual life and the growth of the soul in grace. He taught that the mystical state embraced infused contemplation, which proceeds from faith illumined by the gifts of knowledge, understanding, and wisdom, and also an infused love, the fruit of a special, operating grace, to which the gift of piety renders the soul increasingly docile. The mystical life thus described is not an extraordinary phenomenon, but the normal development of the virtues and the gifts.

His principal books were: *Les Degrés de la vie spirituelle* (Angers 1896; 6th ed. 1935); *La Vie de l'union à Dieu et les moyens d'y arriver, d'après les grands mîitres de la spiritualité* (Paris 1900; 3d ed. 1921); *L'État mystique, sa nature, ses causes* (Paris 1903; 2d ed. 1921); *La Voie qui mène à Dieu* (Paris 1904; 3d ed. 1920); *Les Faits extraordinaires de la vie spirituelle* (Paris 1908); *Manuel de spiritualité* (Paris 1908; 3d ed. 1920); *L'Idéal de l'âme fervente* (Paris 1920; 2d ed. 1923); *La Piété à travers les âges* (Paris 1927); *La Pratique de l'oraison* (Paris 1932); and *La Spiritualité moderne* (Paris 1940). Among the numerous articles he contributed to reviews of spiritual theology, two are especially significant: ''L'Oraison d'après Ste. Jeanne de Chantal,'' in *La Vie Spirituelle* 13:199–234, 302–320; and ''L'Oraison d'après S. François de Sales,'' in *La Vie Spirituelle, Supplément* 17:1–31.

Bibliography: C. BAUMGARTNER, *Dictionnaire de spiritualité ascétique et mystique* 2:2159–71. *Revue d'ascétique et de mystique* 23 (1947) 97. R. GARRIGOU-LAGRANGE, *Vie Spirituelle* 76 (1947) 458–462, I. NOYE, *Lexikon für Theologie und Kirche* 2 9:346–347.

[P. MULHERN]

SAULI, ALEXANDER, ST.

General of the BARNABITES and bishop of Aleria and Pavia; b. Milan, Italy, Feb. 15, 1534; d. Calosso (Asti), Italy, Oct. 11, 1592. He was of a noble Genoese family; and after humanistic study at Pavia, he came to Milan as a page of Emperor Charles V. At 17 he was accepted by the recently founded order of Barnabites, after undergoing the trial imposed on the feast of Pentecost 1551, of walking through the crowded streets of Milan, dressed as a page and carrying a heavy cross, and then preaching in the Piazza dei Mercanti. Following studies in philosophy and theology at Pavia, he was ordained (1556) and began a ministry among the students of the university, organizing them into an academy, the precursor of such associations in modern universities. At 33 he was elected general of the order. In this office he continued his work with the formation of youth, donated his rich library to the college [see G. Boffito, *Biblioteca Barnabitica* (Florence 1934) 3:412–440)], and fostered the growth of the order in Pied-

mont, Venice, and Rome, although he resisted a suggested union with the HUMILIATI, who at this time were very rich and in spiritual decline. He was elected bishop of Aleria in Corsica in 1570 and was consecrated by Cardinal Charles BORROMEO, whose confessor and collaborator in the reform at Milan he had been. Conditions in Aleria were alarming; there had been no bishop for 70 years, the clergy was ignorant, and the people were poor and barbaric. He constructed a seminary, a cathedral, and an episcopal residence; reformed his clergy; and in three synods introduced the decrees of the Council of Trent. During the pestilence of 1580 he showed heroism similar to that of Charles Borromeo at Milan. He is credited with miraculous cures, the calming of storms at sea, successful resistance of the raids from the corsairs from the Barbary Coast, and prophecies. In spite of his physical frailty, he worked in this mission for 20 years. He had refused translation to the Diocese of Tortona and Genoa, but in obedience to Gregory XIV he accepted, in 1591, the important Diocese of Pavia, where he died after a year. He was canonized by Pius X in 1904; his body is venerated in the cathedral at Pavia.

Feast: Oct. 11.

Bibliography: G. A. GABUZLO, *Vita . . .* (Milan 1748), reproduced in *Acta Sanctorum* Oct. 5:806–834. G. S. GERDIL, *Vie du bienheureux Alexandre Sauli* (Rome 1805). F. T. MOLTEDO, *Vita di S. Alessandro Sauli* (Naples 1904).

[U. M. FASOLA]

SAUVECANNE (SILVACANE), ABBEY OF

Former French Cistercian abbey, Archdiocese of Aix. It was founded by the CISTERCIANS of MORIMOND in 1147 at the request of Abp. Pons de Lubières (1132–57) of Aix. After two centuries of prosperity, it lost its independence and under the administration of commendatory abbots, declined rapidly. A bull of Pope Eugene IV (1443) suppressed the abbey and transferred its goods and revenues to the cathedral chapter of Aix. The surviving church, constructed between 1175 and 1230, is a fine example of Cistercian Gothic. Much of the monastery, once a structure of remarkable beauty, is in ruins.

Bibliography: E. DE SAINT-JEAN, ed., *Histoire del'abbaye cistercienne de Silvacane en Provence* (Aix 1891). U. CHEVALIER, *Répertoire des sources historiques du moyen-âge. Topobiobibliographie,* 2 v. (Paris 1894–1903) 2:2963–64. L. H. COTTINEAU, *Répertoire topobibliographique des abbayes et prieurés,* 2 v. (Mâcon 1935–39) 2:3037–38.

[L. J. LEKAI]

SAVANNAH, DIOCESE OF

The Diocese of Savannah (*Savannensis*), suffragan of the metropolitan See of Atlanta, covers 60 percent of Georgia and accounts for about one-third of the Catholics in the state. The original diocese, created in 1850, included the states of Georgia and Florida. In 1937 the name was changed to Savannah-Atlanta and remained so until Nov. 8, 1956, when, with the erection of Atlanta as a separate jurisdiction, the original title was resumed. In the year 2000 the diocese had seven vicariates forane or deaneries: Albany, Augusta, Columbus, Macon, Savannah, Statesboro, and Valdosta-Brunswick.

Although Spanish Catholics met with considerable success in evangelizing the Guale people in the area, the founding of the British colony of Georgia in 1733 and General James Oglethorpe's victory over the Spanish at the Battle of the Bloody Marsh (1742) ensured the ascendancy of Protestantism in the 13th British colony. Until the end of the Revolutionary War, Catholicism was officially proscribed in Georgia; religious toleration for Catholics became a reality only with American independence.

About 1790, a group of Catholics from Maryland settled in Locust Grove, near Washington, Georgia. Father Jean le Moyne, a refugee from the French and Haitian Revolutions, became their pastor, with responsibility for Catholics in the entire state. The first entry (1796) in the baptismal register of the Congrégation de St. Jean le Baptiste in Savannah records Father Olivier le Mercier blessing Le Moyne's grave. Le Mercier served the needs of a Catholic population that included many French refugees like himself. On May 30, 1799, the Mayor and Aldermen of Savannah passed a resolution reserving half a trust lot for the congregation's use. One year later, on May 30, 1800, Le Mercier laid the cornerstone for the small frame Church of St. John the Baptist. On May 30, 1801, the Legislature of Georgia incorporated the "Roman Catholic Church of Savannah"; Governor Josiah Tattnall, Jr., signed the act on Nov. 30, 1801. The total number of Catholics in the city of Savannah was approximately 100. In December 1803, Father Antoine Carles arrived in Savannah and remained in Georgia for over 16 years.

When John England became the first Bishop of Charleston in 1820, his new diocese included Georgia as well as both the Carolinas. The Sisters of Charity of Our Lady of Mercy, founded by England in 1829, came to Savannah to establish St. Vincent's Academy in 1845.

In 1850, Pope Pius IX established the Diocese of Savannah, with Francis X. Gartland as its first bishop. The diocese included both Georgia and Florida, until 1857, when the Vicariate Apostolic of Florida was established. The brick Church of St. John the Baptist, on Drayton Street, the seat of the only parish in Savannah, was designated the cathedral. With the opening of a parish at St. Mary's, Georgia, there were now six parishes in the state. In 1854, Gartland died while ministering to his people during a yellow fever epidemic, shortly after the death of his friend, the missionary Bishop Edward BARRON, who had come to Savannah to assist him. In 1857, Bishop John BARRY, who had been the pastor in Augusta, took over the leadership of the diocese, but died in Paris in 1859, while raising funds.

Augustine VEROT, Vicar Apostolic of Florida, became the third Bishop of Savannah in 1861, while remaining in charge of the church in Florida. Despite the disruptions caused by the Civil War, the "Rebel Bishop" established a second parish in Savannah, St. Patrick's, for the influx of Irish immigrants. With Verot's permission, Father Peter Whelan, captured when Fort Pulaski fell to the Union, served as chaplain in the famous prisoner of war camp at Andersonville where he ministered to Union soldiers as well as to Confederates. At Verot's request, the Sisters of St. Joseph came from his native Le Puy, France, to minister to Georgia's freed slaves in 1866.

In 1870, during the First Vatican Council, Verot was transferred to the new diocese of St. Augustine, Florida, and the Capuchin missionary Bishop Ignatius PERSICO took his place in Savannah. Persico founded churches in Brunswick and Darien, and made the preliminary plans for building a new Cathedral of St. John the Baptist on Lafayette Square. In 1871, Benedictines from St. Vincent Abbey in Latrobe, Pennsylvania arrived to work among the newly freed slaves. Their monastery and school at Skidaway Island failed, but they founded two successful parishes and schools (St. Benedict's and Sacred Heart) in Savannah.

Redemptorist Bishop William GROSS succeeded Persico, who resigned for reasons of health in 1873. During his tenure, the new cathedral was built in Savannah. Gross published a diocesan newspaper, *The Southern Cross*, 1875–1877. A Jesuit seminary was established in Macon and the Brothers of the Sacred Heart came to teach in Augusta. Mother Mary Ignatius of Jesus (Elizabeth Hayes), foundress of the Missionary Franciscan Sisters of the Immaculate Conception, came to Georgia in 1878, "to work solely and entirely for the poor colored people." Gross was promoted to Archbishop of Oregon City (now Portland), Oregon, in 1885.

Bishop Thomas A. BECKER of Wilmington, Del., was transferred to Savannah as the diocese's sixth bishop. He invited the Marist Fathers to work in Brunswick (1897); they remained for nine decades. During Becker's time, the Little Sisters of the Poor opened their home for the elderly in Savannah, and the Jesuits opened St. Joseph Church in Macon. Although Becker petitioned Rome to transfer the see to faster-growing Atlanta in 1896, his petition was denied. He completed the Cathedral by adding two spires and building the adjacent bishop's house (now the rectory), only to witness the cathedral's destruction by fire on February 6, 1898. He died in 1899, before the cathedral could be rebuilt. In 1900, Becker's vicar general, Benjamin Keiley who took over the leadership of the diocese, continued the effort to reach out to the African Americans in the community He brought Father Ignatius Lissner, SMA, to establish parishes and schools for them in Savannah, Macon and Augusta. Mother Katherine DREXEL provided financial support for building an orphanage. A group of Poor Claire nuns, at the urging of the bishop, operated a school and orphanage for black girls. When they departed the diocese, a remarkable black woman from Louisiana, Mother Mathilda BEASLEY, who had settled in Savannah, continued their work. By this time, Marist Brothers were teaching boys in Savannah and Augusta.

Marist Father Michael J. Keyes became Georgia's eighth bishop in 1922, following Keiley's resignation for reasons of health. Keyes led his people through the years following World War I and the difficult days of the Depression. Despite financial difficulties, new churches were built in Valdosta and St. Simons Island, as well as in Macon and Savannah.

Savannah-Atlanta. Gerald P. O'Hara, auxiliary of Philadelphia, was transferred to Savannah late in 1935, after Bishop Keyes' retirement. O'Hara expanded the range of the missionary endeavors into the rural areas. New religious orders, the Franciscan Fathers and Oblates of Mary Immaculate, came to south Georgia. In the summer, children from rural parishes gathered at Camp Villa Marie for religious instruction. With the growth of the Catholic population in the northern part of the state, the diocese gained a new name in 1937: "Savannah-Atlanta." World War II brought An influx of Catholic families during World War II caused new parishes to be established in a number of places. At the end of the war, O'Hara was posted to Romania as Regent of the Apostolic Nunciature in Bucharest. Expelled by the Communists, he returned briefly to Savannah. Named an archbishop, he became papal nuncio to Ireland and then apostolic delegate to Great Britain, while remaining bishop of Savannah until 1959.

Savannah-Atlanta was divided into two dioceses, Savannah and Atlanta, on Nov. 8, 1956. O'Hara's auxiliary, Bishop Francis X. Hyland, became the first Bishop of Atlanta, and Bishop Thomas J. McDonough, auxiliary in St.

Augustine, was transferred to Savannah in 1957. After O'Hara resigned in 1959, McDonough was appointed 10th Bishop of Savannah in 1960. He brought the Glenmary Fathers and Sisters to Georgia to build up the church in rural areas. In 1963 McDonough established a diocesan newspaper for Savannah and naming it *The Southern Cross,* after the short-lived publication of the 1870s. He attended the Second Vatican Council (1962–65), and returned to implement its provisions in the diocese. He also integrated the Catholic schools. McDonough founded a minor seminary on the Isle of Hope and arranged with the bishop of Cork, Ireland, for newly-ordained Irish priests to come to the diocese help meet the increased need for clergy occasioned by the expanding rural missions.

On McDonough's promotion to archbishop of Louisville (1967), Gerard L. Frey became Savannah's 11th bishop, presiding over the diocese as it adjusted to the post-Vatican II changes and struggled with issues that followed the passage of the Civil Rights Act of 1964. He faced difficult questions, such as the merger of three parishes in Augusta (two white and one black) and the closure of a home for the aged and the minor seminary.

After Frey was transferred to Lafayette, Louisiana, he was succeeded by Raymond W. Lessard in 1973. Lessard took charge at a time of unprecedented growth and change. He was responsible for the establishment of the permanent diaconate in the diocese. His tenure saw the Catholic population of the diocese almost double, from approximately 35,000 to nearly 70,000. He presided over the diocese during a period of expansion in rural areas as well as in the cities of south Georgia. During his episcopate, missions to Vietnamese refuges in Savannah and to Spanish-speaking migrant workers in the rural areas were established.

When Lessard resigned for reasons of health in 1995, J. Kevin Boland, a native of Cork, Ireland, who had served in parishes in Savannah and Columbus and as vicar general, was named 13th Bishop of Savannah. Boland commissioned feasibility studies of the Savannah deanery parishes and schools, with the goal of a more efficient allocation of resources and personnel. Under his leadership, a major restoration of the Cathedral, timed to coincide with the Jubilee Year and the Sesquicentennial of the diocese, was undertaken, as was an increased outreach to the Spanish-speaking.

Bibliography: M. V. GANNON, *Rebel Bishop: The Life and Era of Augustine Verot* (Milwaukee 1964). T. J. PETERMAN, *The Cutting Edge: The Life of Thomas A. Becker, First Catholic Bishop of Wilmington and Sixth Bishop of Savannah* (Devon, Pa. 1982). G. W. MCDONAGH, *Black and White in Savannah, Georgia* (Knoxville

1993). M. J. BEVARD, ed., *One Faith . . . One Family: The Diocese of Savannah 1850–2000* (Syracuse NY 2000).

[D. K. CLARK]

SAVARIC OF BATH

Bishop of BATH and Glastonbury; date and place of birth unknown; d. Civita Vecchia, 1205. He was a conjoint archdeacon of Canterbury (1175–80), then treasurer of Sarum (Salisbury) and archdeacon of Northampton. While on the crusade with King Richard I he obtained, through his influence with the king, the bishopric of Bath, and was consecrated at Rome in 1192, after having first been ordained. He negotiated with Emperor Henry VI the release of King Richard from captivity and used his position to obtain the king's permission for the annexation of the Abbey of GLASTONBURY to the bishopric of Bath. The monks of Glastonbury resisted Savaric for seven years but failed to obtain a reversal of papal decrees uniting Glastonbury and Bath as one cathedral church. Savaric died while on a visit to Rome in 1205.

Bibliography: W. HUNT, *The Dictionary of National Biography from the Earliest Times to 1900*, 63 vol. (London 1885–1900) 17:840–843. Glastonbury Abbey, *The Great Chartulary of Glastonbury*, ed. A. WATKIN 3 v. (Frome, Eng. 1947–57). D. KNOWLES, *The Religious Orders in England*, 3 vol. (Cambridge, Eng. 1948–60) v.1–2.

[F. COURTNEY]

SAVELLI

One of the oldest, and from the late 12th century until it became extinct in 1712, one of the four most important noble families in ROME. Outstanding members included Pope HONORIUS III whose father, *Aimerico*, was the first known Savelli; Pope HONORIUS IV; and seven cardinals. The family built an early palace on the Aventine hill. In 1368 it acquired the theater of Marcellus and built there a palace that was replaced (1523–27) by a more splendid one. One of the Savelli villages, CASTEL GANDOLFO, was sold to the papacy in 1596. In the GUELF-GHIBELLINE struggle, the Savelli were sometimes Guelfs, but generally they supported the COLONNA against the papacy. Until the Savelli court was disbanded (1655), it could try cases for minor offenses. As a reward for Savelli support, Pope PAUL III made the office of custodian of the conclave hereditary in the family. The seven cardinals, with dates of creation and death, were: *Cencio*, 1191–1218; *Giovanni Battista*, 1480–98; *Giacomo*, 1539–87; *Silvio*, 1596–99; *Giulio*, 1615–44; *Fabrizio*, 1647–59, nephew of Giulio; and *Paolo*, 1664–85. Giovanni Battista served as legate in Perugia and envoy in

Geneva before he was a hostage (1482–83) in the Colonna–papacy conflict during the pontificate of SIXTUS IV. Later, he was legate in Ancona, Spoleto, and Bologna. Giacomo had 20 years' experience in various dioceses. As vicar-general of Rome he effected there some of the reforms specified by the Council of TRENT. He was one of the learned and able cardinals of his day. The last of the line was a brother of Paolo, *Giulio* (d. 1712).

Bibliography: G. MORONI, *Dizionario de erudizione storico-ecclesiastica* 61:294–308. L. CÀLLARI, *I palazzi di Roma* (3d ed. Rome 1944).

[M. L. SHAY]

SAVIGNY, ABBEY OF

Former French abbey, head of a monastic congregation, Diocese of Avranches. In 1105, Savigny was founded as a hermitage in the forests between Brittany and Normandy by VITALIS OF SAVIGNY (d. 1122), a follower of Robert of Arbrissel. Between 1112 and 1115 the growing number of disciples necessitated the construction of an abbey. The new foundation was privileged by Pascal II, and in 1119 was taken under papal protection by Calixtus II. Abbot Vitalis adopted the Benedictine Rule, with emphasis on poverty, simplicity, and manual labor, virtues that had been much neglected within the powerful congregation of Cluny. Savigny proved to be so successful that under the second abbot Godfrey (1122–39), 32 affiliated houses were founded in France, England, and Scotland. Expansion in England was promoted by Henry I. Following the example of CÎTEAUX, Savigny tried to ensure uniformity by annual chapters attended by all abbots and by an effective system of mutual visitation. The similarities between Savigny and Cîteaux induced the third abbot, Serlon (1139–58), to negotiate the fusion of the two monastic orders, which was approved by the Cistercian General Chapter of 1147. Henceforth the whole congregation of Savigny shared the fate of the Cistercians. The 13th century was the era of greatest prosperity. The new Gothic church of Savigny was consecrated in 1220. The 100 Years' War brought much destruction. Savigny came under the rule of commendatory abbots in 1517, and the civil and religious wars of the 16th century aggravated the desolation. Gradual recovery began in the 17th century, while moral recovery followed the introduction of the Cistercian Strict Observance in 1676. In 1768 the abbey numbered 18 monks; it was suppressed by the French Revolution in 1791. Church and cloister fell into disrepair; but the church was rebuilt in the 19th century and continues to serve the local parish.

Bibliography: H. SAUVAGE, *Saint-Vital et l'abbaye de Savigny* (Mortain 1895). C. AUVRY and A. LAVEILLE, *Histoire de la*

congrégation de Savigny, 3 v. (Paris 1896–98). U. CHEVALIER, Répertoire des sources historiques du moyen-âge. Topobiobibliographie, 2 v. (Paris 1894–1903) 2:2871. L. GUILLOREAU, "Les Fondations anglaises de l'abbaye de Savigny," Revue Mabillon 5 (1909) 290–335. J. BUHOT, "L'Abbaye normande de Savigny," Moyen-âge 46 (1936) 1–19. L. H. COTTINEAU, Répertoire topobibliographique des abbayes et prieurés, 2 v. (Mâcon 1935–39) 2:2965–67.

[L. J. LEKAI]

SAVIO, DOMINIC, ST.

Lay youth; b. Riva, near Turin, Piedmont, Italy, April 2, 1842; d. Mandonio (Asti), March 9, 1857. He was one of ten children of a blacksmith, Carlo, and a seamstress, Birgitta Savio. Domenico (Dominic) was introduced to Don (later St.) John BOSCO and in 1854 entered the latter's famous school at Turin, the Oratory of St. Francis de Sales. Under Don Bosco's guidance, Dominic developed a spirituality mature beyond his years, characterized by exact observance of discipline, marked friendliness to all, wisdom in counseling others, and intense love of purity and the Eucharist. Especially striking was his cheerfulness in manner and approach. His failing health, due perhaps to tuberculosis, occasioned his departure to his parents from the Oratory (March 1, 1857). Soon after his death, Don Bosco composed a biography recording his disciple's sanctity. Dominic was beatified (March 5, 1950), and canonized (June 12, 1954).

Feast: March 9.

Bibliography: P. ARONICA, God's Teenager (New Rochelle, N.Y. 1950). D. HIGGINS, The Challenge (New Rochelle, N.Y. 1954). J. BOSCO, The Life of St. Dominic Savio, tr. P. ARONICA (New Rochelle, N.Y. 1955). L. LAURAND, Un enfant de lumière (Brussels 1969). G. TOMASELLI, Il giglio di Mondonio (Messina 1969).

[E. F. FARDELLONE]

SAVIOR

The concept savior is here treated first as it is found in non-Biblical contexts, then in the Bible, and finally in theological synthesis.

In Non-Biblical Contexts. The title σωτήρ (savior) was frequently applied to pagan gods who intervened in times of need, such as sickness, shipwreck, or war, to rescue their clients. Asclepius received the title because he was the god of healing; Zeus, because he was a helper in daily necessities; and the gods of the mystery religions, because they freed from death and matter and dispensed life. Later the title was given to various Hellenistic kings, such as Ptolemy I, since the divinized ruler was a symbol of peace and order. In the 1st century B.C. Roman emperors appropriated the title. Augustus became the "world savior" because in his reign men saw the fulfillment of their desire for peace.

In the Bible. In the Septuagint the Greek verb σώζω (save) translates various Hebrew verbs, such as yš', nṣl, and plṭ, but especially yš' when God's activity is described. The basic meaning of yš' is to be broad or spacious, and the causative form means to take one out of straits. Positively, the notion involves an exercise of strength that gains victory; negatively, it connotes liberation from danger, misfortune, hostile powers, and above all, from death and Sheol. The Greek word σωτήρ always translates some form of yš' (yᵉšû'â, yēša', môšîa'). Yahweh is frequently called the savior of His people (Dt 32.15; Is 12.2; 25.9; 45.15, 21–22; 62.11; passim in the Psalms) and even of the pagans (Is 45.24). The salvation He brings becomes more individual, more spiritual and eschatological as revelation progresses. In the beginning, the sacred writers speak of deliverance from merely temporal evils (1 Sm 10.19; 11.9), then of the deliverance of the chosen people from Egypt (Ex 14.13) and from the Babylonian Exile (Is 45.17). Gradually, as the Prophets look forward to messianic times, salvation comes to mean deliverance from sin (Is 33.22–23; Ez 36.28–29) and the conferring of all God's gifts (Is 45.17; 49.6).

In the New Testament the words σωτήρ and σώζω are used of both God the Father and Christ. As Yahweh saved His people in the Old Testament, so now in the New Testament God the Father is viewed as the initiator of salvation: He "saves" (1 Cor 1.21; Ti 3.5; 2 Tm 1.9) or is a savior (1 Tm 1.1; 2.3; 4.10; Ti 1.3; 2.10; 3.4; Lk 1.47) of all who believe. Frequently the verb is used in the accounts of Christ's miracles; in healing the Samaritan leper (Lk 17.19), the woman suffering from hemorrhage (Mk 5.34), and the blind Bartimeus (Mk 10.52), as well as in forgiving the penitent woman (Lk 7.50), Christ says: "Thy faith has saved thee." It is also used of Christ's work of delivering from sin and eternal death and conferring messianic salvation (Mt 18.11; 1 Tm 1.15; 2 Tm 4.18; Heb 7.25; Jn 12.47). Christ is, therefore, called "the Savior" from the earliest preaching (Acts 5.31) to the later apostolic catechesis (Eph 5.23; Ti 1.4; 2.13; 3.6; 2 Tm 1.10; Lk 2.11; Jn 4.42). From all these texts it is apparent that the New Testament develops and brings to perfection the Old Testament notion of Yahweh as savior. God the Father Himself is the initiator of salvation. Christ carries out this work of salvation on both a temporal and a spiritual level. His miracles of healing are a deliverance from temporal evils; but they belong also to the spiritual sphere insofar as they are a sign and a kind of inauguration of spiritual salvation (Acts 4.9–12). Both God the Father and Christ are called savior principally because they deliver men from sin and confer eternal life. This is essentially an eschatological reality (Acts 5.31; Phil 3.20), but it already begins on earth (Ti 3.5; 2 Tm 1.9). A synthesis of this twofold aspect of salvation is found in Ti 3.4–7. Finally, it becomes clear that God the Father and Christ are saviors in a much more profound and comprehensive sense than the saviors of the pagans. It may easily be that Paul used the title as a polemic against the cult of the emperors.

See Also: HOPE OF SALVATION (IN THE BIBLE); MESSIANISM; REDEMPTION (IN THE BIBLE); SALVATION HISTORY (HEILSGESCHICHTE).

Bibliography: P. WENDLAND, ''Σωτήρ,'' *Zeitschrift für die neutestamentliche Wissenschaft und die Kunde der älteren Kirche* 5 (1904) 335–353. W. WAGNER, ''Über σῴζειν und seine Derivate im N.T.,'' *ibid.* 6 (1905) 205–235. D. M. STANLEY, ''The Conception of Salvation in Primitive Christian Preaching,'' *The Catholic Biblical Quarterly* 18 (1956) 231–254; ''The Conception of Salvation in the Synoptic Gospels,'' *ibid.* 345–363. C. SPICQ, *Saint Paul: Les Épîtres pastorales* (Études bibliques 1947). S. LYONNET, ''De notione salutis in N.T.,'' *Verbum Domini* 36 (1958) 3–15.

[H. KISTNER]

Theology. Jesus Christ, the GOD-MAN, is the Savior sent into the world. ''. . . and thou shalt call his name Jesus; for he shall save his people from their sins'' (Mt 1.21). SALVATION includes a liberation of mankind from sin, a gracious deliverance of man by God in the Person of His Son, Jesus. However, this is not the whole truth; St. Paul completes the description of this reality when he says Christ ''was delivered up for our sins, and rose again for our justification'' (Rom 4.25). Justification adds to the notion of salvation the positive blessings of GRACE, i.e., a sharing in the divine life of the risen Christ, which brings man back into living union with God the Father.

Simply speaking then, salvation means the return of humanity to God in Jesus Christ, who died and rose again. This is the culminating point of God's intervention in the history of man to bring mankind back to Himself. Salvation then is something that God has been bringing about since the Fall of Adam; it is something that He is accomplishing now and will continue to accomplish until Christ comes in judgment. Christ is the Savior promised to Adam (Gn 3.15), prefigured in Moses, prophesied elsewhere in the Old Testament (especially Jeremiah and the Songs of SUFFERING SERVANT of Isaiah), and definitively realized in His passage from this world to the Father. This transition of Christ in His human nature from this world to the new order of glorified creation is a transformation by which His manhood is taken up into manifest eternal union with the Trinity.

In history, God's action, bringing man back to Himself, has taken a variety of forms, yet there exists a certain continuity and similarity that is more than analogical. Between these realities, there is a living unity, that progresses but is constant, can to effect change without itself changing, and can operate on different levels without losing its unifying dynamism. For example, in the call of mankind to salvation in Abraham, Moses, and Christ there is a liberation initiated by God, for a sacrificial act of worship that transforms man's living relationship to God and promises a glorious destiny with God's faithful protection. In Abraham a single individual is called to salvation. Abraham's faith liberates or separates him from his pagan relatives to worship the one true God (he would even have sacrificed his own son Isaac). In view of his faith and love he is given a promise that in his seed all nations shall be blessed. In Moses the whole nation of the Jews is liberated from slavery in Egypt in order to become the people of God by the sacrificial covenant sealed in blood (symbolic of a mingling of their life with God's), and it receives a promise to become a great nation in its new land. In Christ, salvation is extended to all men; the types and figures above receive in Him their complete fulfillment. Through Christ all men are liberated from slavery to sin, to become one family with Christ in the New Covenant sacrifice sealed in His own blood (the real mingling of men's life with God in Christ), and they receive the promise of eternal life with God in a new and glorious resurrection.

Traditional theology has tended to consider salvation in terms of an act of merit, of a satisfaction of divine justice capable of repaying man's debt, and of a sacrifice of Christ's life for the remission of man's sin. Recent Biblical scholars (e.g., F. X. Durrwell, L. Cerfaux, S. Lyonnet) have focused on the importance of the RESURRECTION OF CHRIST as a necessary and essential aspect of man's salvation. A restricted view of the saving action of Christ is giving way to a more dynamic view of salvation as a rebirth of mankind from the death of sin to a new life in Jesus Christ the Risen Savior. [*See* REBIRTH (IN THE BIBLE).] Transformed by his new life man is now motivated interiorly, with his hope of victory firmly rooted in the victory of Christ over sin and its consequences, to act in the service of God and his fellowmen in charity.

Bibliography: A. MICHEL, *Dictionnaire de théologie catholique*, ed. A. VACANT et al., (Paris 1903—50) 8.1: 1227–46. C. DAVIS, *Theology for Today* (New York 1962). H. F. DAVIS et al., *A Catholic Dictionary of Theology* (London 1962–) 1:189–198. F. X. DURRWELL, *The Resurrection: A Biblical Study,* tr. R. SHEED (New York 1960). S. LYONNET, ''Redemptive Value of the Resurrection,'' *Theology Digest* 8 (1960) 89–93. K. O'SULLIVAN and J. T. NELIS, *Encyclopedic Dictionary of the Bible*, tr. and adap. by L. HARTMAN (New York 1963) 2101–07.

[J. C. MURRAY]

SAVONAROLA, GIROLAMO

Dominican reformer; b. Ferrara, Italy, Sept. 21, 1452; d. Florence, May 23, 1498.

Career to 1495. The Savonarolas came from Padua, whence Girolamo's grandfather, a distinguished and pious physician, had migrated to Ferrara in 1440. Girolamo, the third of seven children, was intended for the medical profession and received a good education, studying Aristotle and Aquinas and becoming familiar with the Bible. His growing sense of a religious vocation was accompanied by deep distress at the prevalent moral corruption both in the world and in the Church. In April 1475 he suddenly, without warning his parents, entered the DOMINICAN novitiate at Bologna. In 1479 his studies brought him back to Ferrara, a circumstance that led to his friendship with the celebrated humanist PICO DELLA MIRANDOLA. In 1482 he was assigned, as *lector* in theology, to the priory of San Marco, FLORENCE. During the next four years the characteristic "prophetical" note began to sound in his sermons: the Church, he declared, would soon be terribly chastised and then renewed. An interval of preaching in northern Italy preceded his recall to Florence in 1490 at the instance of the city's ruler, Lorenzo de' MEDICI, and in July 1491 he became prior of San Marco. During the same year he delivered his first sermons to ever-increasing audiences in the Duomo, combining violent onslaughts on vice with criticisms of the Medici government.

For the next three years Savonarola's influence in Florence grew steadily; by mid-1495 he virtually ruled the city from his pulpit. It was, however, a moral ascendancy facilitated by political events, by the fall of the Medici government, and by the Italian expedition of the French King, Charles VIII, in 1494. Lorenzo had died in 1492. The account that Savonarola had refused him absolution at the end is groundless. In fact the friar was at first on good terms with Lorenzo's son and successor, Piero, who, for political reasons, supported Savonarola's plan to set up a reformed Dominican congregation in Tuscany, independent of the Lombard congregation, to which San Marco actually belonged. In May 1493 a papal brief was obtained placing San Marco directly under the jurisdiction of the Dominican master general. This was the first step to the establishment of a new congregation including, with San Marco, priories at Fiesole, Prato, and Pisa, and ruled by Savonarola as vicar-general.

In autumn 1494 the French invaded Italy and were soon at the gates of Florence. Piero de' Medici fled, and the whole city turned for guidance to Savonarola. For his part, the friar saw in this invasion a fulfillment of his prophecies of a divine chastisement that was to come upon Italy: Charles VIII was the *gladius Domini,* the

"new Cyrus." This identification was to have fatal consequences for Savonarola. Since *c.* 1490 he had formed the conviction (due in part to his predilection for the prophetical books of the Bible) that he was a prophet inspired to announce God's judgments on Italy and the Church. It was not this claim as such, however, but his support of the French invader that brought him into conflict with the reigning pope. Already in 1493 ALEXANDER VI had formed an alliance with Milan and Naples against the French, and in 1495 the league included Venice, Spain, and the Emperor Maximilian I. Florence, kept faithful to Charles by Savonarola, was an obstacle to the pope's plans. It was inevitable, even apart from the moral issues involved, that Alexander should come to regard Savonarola as a political nuisance and should attempt either to silence him or to remove him from Florence.

Meanwhile this city's internal affairs also were developing in a way to make it ever more difficult for Savonarola (given his temperament) to avoid an eventual clash with the pope. Through 1495 his influence in Florence was supreme. The new "popular" regime was inspired by his ideals. The city was swept by a campaign of rigorous moral reform, in which children were incited—imprudently—to take a large part. The Duomo could not contain the crowds that came to hear their prophet. San Marco swarmed with young recruits to the Dominican Order. And all this was only part of a wider program: from Florence, "the watchtower of Italy," the light of reform was to shine out on Italy and thence over Christendom. But this grand design became increasingly dangerous, spiritually as well as politically, as Savonarola grew convinced that its success depended on his own presence and preaching in Florence and on the maintenance, in the form he had given it, of the new San Marco congregation; for these were matters he could not legitimately withdraw from papal control.

Savonarola and Alexander VI. The inevitable duel between Savonarola and Alexander VI began on July 21, 1495, when the pope, in courteous terms, summoned the friar to Rome to explain the revelations he claimed to have received from God. Savonarola replied (July 31) that he could not, for the present, obey: he was too ill to travel; he might be murdered on the road; in any case he was badly needed at Florence: "So it is not God's will that I leave just now." As for the revelations, he would send Alexander a book he had recently composed (*Compendium revelationum*), which would give the pope all necessary information. To this letter Alexander did not reply directly. But on September 8, perhaps feeling his hand strengthened by the French army's retreat to northern Italy in the summer, he issued a brief vehemently condemning Savonarola's claim to divine inspiration and suspending him from preaching, pending the examination of his case by (Bl.) Sebastian Maggi (d. 1496), vicar-general of the Lombard congregation, to which San Marco was to be reunited. Savonarola's answer was a long letter (September 29) reducible to five main points: (1) he submits to the Holy See; (2) he has never claimed to be an inspired prophet; (3) but if he had done so, this would not imply unorthodoxy; (4) he vehemently protests against the reunion of San Marco with the Lombard congregation; and (5) he objects to the appointment of the Lombard vicar-general as his judge. In the meantime an inquiry into the whole case had been held at Bologna, and it seems to have reported favorably to the pope, to judge from the mildness of his next brief, *Licet uberius* (October 16). Savonarola was again ordered not to preach, but the reunion of San Marco with the Lombard congregation was temporarily suspended.

Through the winter 1495–96 Savonarola did not in fact preach; but he began to do so again on Feb. 16, 1496, and continued throughout Lent, using increasingly violent language against the Roman Curia. Incidentally, he made it clear that it was not out of obedience to the pope that he had desisted from preaching, but only to examine his conscience as to his motives and manner of preaching. He hinted, however, that he did in fact have Alexander's permission. The truth seems to be that in March or April Alexander had let it be known that he would tolerate Savonarola's preaching so long as he moderated his language and kept off the subject of politics. It is not likely that the pope thought these conditions would be realized, but he was loath to offend the Florentine Signory (which through the winter had continually begged him to lift the suspension), and he probably reckoned that—owing to the political isolation of Florence—the friar's fortunes would soon decline in any case—in short, that the pope could afford to bide his time. A period of calm ensued.

Florentine affairs were not going well, either politically or economically, but the opposition to Savonarola was not yet strong enough to challenge his power openly. It was Alexander who took the next step, this time attacking Savonarola indirectly through his position in the Dominican Order. A papal brief (Nov. 7, 1496) set up a new Tuscan-Roman congregation, in which San Marco and its dependent houses were included. The San Marco community, undoubtedly with the approval of their prior, protested at once to the pope. Later they published a manifesto against the brief, with a preface by Savonarola, declaring themselves not bound to obey the pope in this matter since his order was against the interests of religion. And in fact the brief remained, rather strangely, a dead letter for the time being. Savonarola continued, irregularly, as vicar-general, just as he went on preaching though officially suspended. Alexander for his part pursued his aim of getting Florence into his league with the other Italian states; but it would be rash to conclude that this political motive alone was decisive in bringing him to the point of at last excommunicating Savonarola with the brief *Cum saepenumero* (May 13, 1497). Sinner though he was, Alexander had a sense of the respect due his office, and there is no reason to doubt that a proper desire to uphold the authority of the Holy See played its part in convincing him to excommunicate one whose words and actions must have seemed plainly subversive of that authority.

The excommunication was published in Florence on June 18, and Savonarola immediately published a letter, addressed "to all Christians," denying its validity. However, he did not preach again in 1497. A plague prevented all preaching in Florence during the summer, and later that year his restraint was probably due to a wish not to impede the efforts that the Florentine government—still friendly to Savonarola—was making at Rome to have the censure removed. On October 13 he wrote to Alexander asking for pardon but without declaring his submission on any specific point. The pope did not reply. Savonarola then pushed his defiance to the point of saying Mass publicly on Christmas Day and of recommencing his preaching in the Duomo (February 11), declaring in his first sermon that whoever accepted his excommunication as valid was a heretic. On March 17, however, the Signory, fearing that Alexander was about to lay an interdict on the city, begged Savonarola to stop preaching; and he did. But he took the further and fatal step of drafting letters to the sovereigns of Europe, calling on them to summon a council to reform the Church and to depose Alexander. Meanwhile his disciple Domenico da Pescia had foolishly accepted a challenge from a Franciscan of S. Croce to an ordeal by fire that would, by a miracle, decide the issue between Savonarola and his enemies. The ordeal (April 7) proved a fiasco and touched off a popular reaction against Savonarola, who surrendered to the Signory after the mob had stormed San Marco.

Evaluation. Savonarola's trial, which, with the pope's permission, involved torture, was begun before lay judges but concluded before two papal commissioners sent from Rome. The official records of his confessions made under torture were falsified, but one thing stands out clearly enough: from the canonical point of view the most serious charge against Savonarola, and the one that justified (if anything could) his condemnation for heresy, schism, and contempt of the Holy See, was that he had invoked the civil power to call a council and depose the pope. Sentenced to death with two companions, Savonarola was hanged and then burned in the Piazza della Signoria at Florence. Savonarola was a great Christian and, in some sense, certainly a martyr. His subjective position regarding Alexander VI is beyond question; and only the matter of his objective guilt, depending on the legal judgment of his day, awaits further investigation. Indeed, as early as 1499, Savonarola was locally venerated as a saint.

Bibliography: R. RIDOLFI, *Cronologia e bibliografia delle prediche* (Florence 1939); *Studi Savonaroliani,* 2 v. (Florence 1935); *Life of Girolamo Savonarola,* tr. C. GRAYSON (New York 1959). M. FERRARA, *Bibliografia savonaroliana* (Florence 1958). *Edizione nazionale delle opere di Girolamo Savonarola* (Rome 1955-), to be completed in 20 v. L. PASTOR, *The History of the Popes From the Close of the Middle Ages* 4, 5, 6. J. SCHNITZER, *Savonarola: Ein Kulturbild aus der Zeit der Renaissance,* 2 v. (Munich 1924). G. SORANZO, *Il tempo di Alessandro VI papa e di Fra G. Savonarola* (Milan 1960). G. GIERATHS, ed. and tr., *S. Ketzer oder Heiliger?* (Freiburg 1961); *Lexikon für Theologie und Kirche*[2] 9:353–355.

[K. FOSTER]

SAWLES WARD

A 12th-century homily, very freely adapted from the *De Anima* (4.13–15) of HUGH OF SAINT-VICTOR. The same passage was translated by Dan Michel of Northgate as part of his *Azenbite of Inwyt,* but *Sawles Ward* (Guardian of the Soul) is a far more accomplished piece, in a much livelier and more evocative style. The homiletic narrative, based on Mt 24.43, presents man's body as a house, with Wit (Conscience) as its master and Will as its mistress, containing the soul as its treasure, guarded by the cardinal virtues. Two speeches, by Fear on the pains of hell and by Love of Life on the bliss of heaven, constitute the major part of the homily. *Sawles Ward* is one of the "Catherine Group" (*see* ANCRENE RIWLE) of 12th-century devotional pieces noteworthy for their identical Middle English dialect, giving evidence for the first "school" of English prose writers known to us.

Bibliography: *Sawles Ward: An Early English Homily,* ed. R. M. WILSON (Leeds 1938). R. M. WILSON, *Early Middle English Literature* (London 1939). R. W. CHAMBERS, *On the Continuity of English Prose from Alfred to More and His School* (Early English Text Society 191A; London 1957).

[N. D. HINTON]

SAYER, ROBERT GREGORY (SEARE)

Benedictine moral theologian; b. Redgrave (Suffolk), 1560; d. Venice, October 30, 1602. Other variant forms of his family name occur; he is sometimes called Sayr or Saire, or in Latin Sarius or Sayrus, and in Italian Sario or Sairo. Robert was his baptismal name, Gregory his name in religion. He studied at Caius College, Cambridge, but was denied his degree because of his papist tendencies. Leaving Cambridge in 1582 he went to the

English College of Douai, then located at Reims, and later the same year went on to the English College in Rome. He was ordained in 1585 and became a Benedictine at Monte Cassino in 1588. He taught moral theology at Monte Cassino until 1595, when he was sent to the Monastery of St. George in Venice where he remained until his death. In spite of the relatively short span of his teaching career he produced a number of important theological works that enjoyed a considerable success and earned him a place among the leading moralists of his time. Among them were: *De sacramentis in communi* (Venice 1599), *Thesaurus casuum conscientiae* (Venice 1601); *Clavis regia sacerdotum casuum conscientiae sive theologiae moralis thesauri,* etc. (Venice 1605). He was a probabilist, though he cannot be classified as such without some qualification. His works show the influence of Bartolomé de MEDINA and Martin ASPILCUETA. It would be inaccurate to infer from the titles of some of his works that he was chiefly a casuist, for he used casuistry simply as a means of clarifying and expounding moral principles.

Bibliography: J. MERCIER *Dictionnaire de théologie catholique,* ed. A. VACANT, 15 v. (Paris 1903–50; Tables générales 1951–) 14.1:1241–42. J. GILLOW, *A Literary and Biographical History or Bibliographical Dictionary of the English Catholics from 1534 to the Present Time,* 5 v. (London-New York 1885–1902; repr. New York 1961) 5:481–482. E. J. MAHONEY, *The Theological Position of Gregory Sayrus, O.S.B.* (doctoral diss. Fribourg 1922); "Gregory Sayers, O.S.B.: A Forgotten English Moral Theologian," *American Catholic Historical Review* 5 (1925) 29–37.

[P. K. MEAGHER]

SAYERS, DOROTHY LEIGH

Novelist and playwright; b. Oxford, England, June 13, 1893; d. London, Dec. 18, 1957. As the daughter of an Anglican parson, she was educated privately and at Somerville College, Oxford. In 1926 she married Capt. Atherton Fleming (d. 1950). Her early and solid reputation rested on a series of highly successful detective stories, the first of which was *Whose Body?* (1923); the last, *Busman's Honeymoon* (1937). Although they are straight stories of mystery and detection, several of them indicate her strong interest in ecclesiastical matters (e.g., *The Nine Tailors,* 1934). With the outbreak of World War II, a marked religious development took place in her writing. In 1941 she published *Begin Here,* a study of the moral issues facing her country; a similar book in 1947 was entitled *Creed or Chaos?* Her most effective religious work was the series of radio plays entitled *The Man Born to Be King* (1942). These vivid and realistic studies of the life of Christ manifested both detailed scholarship and deep religious insight. When published (1943), they became one of her most popular books. Other plays of deep Christian import are *The Zeal of Thy House* (1937) and *The Just Vengeance* (1946). An even deeper indication of her interest in religion and its relation to literature is clear in her work on Dante. She published a translation of the *Inferno* (1940) and a volume of essays, *Introductory Papers on Dante* (1954). *The Mind of the Maker* (1941) is a fascinating study of the process of creative writing seen as a rough analogue of the relationships within the Trinity. Her religious position was very close to the central Catholic tradition, although she never joined the Church of Rome. On practically every point of theology her orthodoxy was unimpeachable, and she made no secret of her personal commitment to Christianity. She was one of that small group of Anglicans (the best known, perhaps, was C. S. LEWIS) who have had a lasting influence on Christian thinking in the English-speaking world.

[T. CORBISHLEY]

SBARAGLIA, GIOVANNI GIACINTO, (SBARALEA)

Historian, Franciscan Conventual; b. near Forlì, Italy, March 13, 1687; d. Rome, June 2, 1764. His most important historical contribution was his posthumously published 734-page *Supplementum* to Luke WADDING's *Scriptores*. It lists 3,583 Franciscan authors as opposed to Wadding's list of 1,919. Those authors covered by Sbaraglia but not by Wadding are distinguished by Arabic numerals in the *Supplementum*. The numerous corrections and additions made by Sbaraglia are more difficult to distinguish. Before its publication, the *Supplementum* was corrected and edited by other Franciscan Conventuals, William Della Valle, Anthony Contarini, Stephen Rinaldi, and finally Nicholas PAPINI TARTAGNI under the title *Supplementum et castigatio ad scriptores Trium Ordinum S. Francisci a Waddingo aliisque descriptos* (3 v. Rome 1806; 2d ed. Rome 1908–36). Sbaraglia edited the *Bullarium Franciscanum* for the years 1218 to 1304 (4 v. Rome 1759–68). His many unpublished manuscripts include the *Chronotaxis Romanorum Pontificum*, the *Opus miscellaneum*, *Critica Pagii in Annales Baronii*, and *Supplementum ad "Italiam Sacram" Ughelli*.

Bibliography: D. SPARACIO, "Gli studi di storia e i Minori Conventuali," *Miscellanea Francescana* 20 (1919) 113–123, with a complete bibliog, H. LEMAY, "History of Franciscan Bibliography," *Franciscan Educational Conference* 16 (1934) 149–174. A. TEETAERT *Dictionnaire de théologie catholique*, ed. A. VACANT, 15 v. (Paris 1903–50; Tables générales 1951–) 14.1:1242–46.

[J. J. SMITH]

Bl. Giovanni Battista Scalabrini.

SCALABRINI, GIOVANNI BATTISTA, BL.

Bishop of Piacenza, "father of migrants," founder of the Congregation of the Missionaries of Saint Charles (Scalabrinians) and the Missionary Sisters of St. Charles Borromeo; b. July 8, 1839, at Fino Mornasco (near Como), northern Italy; d. June 1, 1905, at Piacenza, Italy.

On the Feast of the Dedication of St. John Lateran (November 9) 1997, the pope's cathedral church, John Paul II beatified Scalabrini and recalled his repeated saying: "Would that I could sanctify myself and all the souls entrusted to me!"

He was the third of the eight sons of Luigi Scalabrini, a wine merchant, and his wife, Colomba Trombetta, a religious couple of modest means. After ordination (May 30, 1863) he was a professor of History and Greek at St. Abundius Seminary in Como (where he had studied), and then rector (1867–70).

As pastor of one of the largest parishes in Como (San Bartolomeo) he was distinguished for his solicitude for the working class as well as for his forward thinking on political, social, and economic matters. His published conferences on Vatican Council I brought him to the attention of Pius IX, who named him bishop of Piacenza

(1875). As bishop he distinguished himself by frequent visitations of all 365 parishes and diocesan synods. In his eagerness to reorganize catechetical teaching throughout Italy, he instituted the first National Catechetical Congress at Piacenza. Pius IX referred to him as the "Apostle of the Catechism."

Unlike many churchmen, he was open-minded on the ROMAN QUESTION, which dominated the relations between church and state in Italy in the last part of the nineteenth and early twentieth century. It asked: "should the lands of central Italy remain under the political control of the Church as they had since the Middle Ages, or should they become part of a united Italy?" At Leo XIII's request he outlined possible approaches and solutions to the Roman Question in a memorandum which labeled as ruinous the policy of urging Catholics to refrain from participating in secular politics in protest against the Italian government's confiscation of the papal states.

To assist the huge number of Italians emigrating to various parts of the world, he founded the Scalabrinians (Nov. 28, 1887) with Fr. Joseph and Mother Assunta Marchetti, and promoted the work of the congregation by journeying in 1901 and 1904 to North and South America. With the same aim, he convinced St. Frances Xavier CABRINI to travel to America (1889), founded (Oct. 25, 1895) the Missionary Sisters of St. Charles Borromeo, and co-founded the Missionary Zelatrices of the Sacred Heart. To provide material and social aid to emigrants he established (1889) the lay Society of St. Raphael. Among his other charitable activities, he founded an institute to help mutual aid societies, rural banks, cooperatives and women who were hearing and speech impaired.

He encouraged frequent Communion and Perpetual Adoration. He also had a deep devotion to the Blessed Mother that he expressed in homilies and Marian pilgrimages. His heroic charity was demonstrated during a cholera epidemic and the fact that he sold everything he had, including his horse and pectoral cross to care for the poor.

He died on the Solemnity of the Ascension saying: "Lord, I am ready. Let us go." His mortal remains are venerated in the cathedral of Piacenza. Scalabrini's cause for beatification was introduced by Bishop Menzani at Piacenza in June 1936. On March 16, 1987, Pope John Paul II promulgated a decree recognizing him as venerable, the first step to sainthood. The required miracle was approved July 7, 1997, permitting the Nov. 9, 1997 beatification.

Feast: June 1.

Bibliography: Sources for the study of Blessed John Baptist Scalabrini: *For the Love of Immigrants: Migration Writings and Letters of Bishop John Baptist Scalabrini,* ed. by S. M. TOMASI (New York 1999). *La Societá italiana di fronte alle prime migrazioni di massa* (New York 1975). Records of the Congregation of the Missionaries of St. Charles (Scalabrians), v. 8 of *A Guide to the Archives,* ed. N. FALCO (New York 1988). Literature about Blessed John Baptist Scalabrini: *L'Osservatore Romano,* English edition, no. 46 (1997): 1–3. M. CALIARO and M. FRANCESCONI, *John Baptist Scalabrini, Apostle to Emigrants,* tr. A. I. ZIZZAMIA (New York 1977). I. FELICI, *Father to the Immigrants, the Servant of God,* tr. C. DELLA CHIESO (New York 1955). M. FRANCESCONI, *Giovanni Battista Scalabrini, vescovo di Piacenza e degli emigrati* (Rome 1985); *Giovanni Battista Scalabrini. Spiritualità d'incarnazione* (Rome 1989). F. GREGORI, *La vita e l'opera di un grande vescovo, Giovanni Battista Scalabrini* (Turin 1934). G. LANDI, *Un vescovo e la legge sull'emigrazione* (Milan 1986). T. DE ROSA, *Bishop John Baptist Scalabrini, Father to the Migrants* (Darien, Conn. 1987). G. SARAGGI, *Giovanni Battista Scalabrini. Vescovo insigne e padre degli emigrati* (Cinisello Balsamo 1986). L. M. SIGNOR, *John Baptist Scalabrini and Italian Migration: A Socio-Pastoral Project* (New York 1994).

[L. SABATINI]

SCALABRINIANS

(CS, Official Catholic Directory #1210); officially known as the the Missionaries of St. Charles, and popularly as the Scalabrini Fathers, was founded on Nov. 28, 1887, in Piacenza, Italy. Its purpose, besides the personal sanctification of its members, is the spiritual and, whenever possible, the pastoral care of Italian emigrants, many thousands of whom have left their native land to settle in new homes, especially in the New World. Scalabrini was a pioneering apostle in many fields. While zealously and effectively caring for a vast diocese, he labored to meet the difficulties confronting the Church in Italy at the turn of the century. Toward the solution of the problems of Italian emigration, not only did he found the society of the Missionaries of St. Charles, but he established the Missionary Sisters of St. Charles, cofounded the Apostles of the SACRED HEART OF JESUS on March 19, 1889, and bestowed on (St.) Francis CABRINI and her six missionary sisters the missionary cross, on the occasion of Mother Cabrini's first apostolic venture on behalf of Italian emigrants.

Among his writings Bishop Scalabrini left several treatises on Italian emigration, and contributions on other problems current in his day. He took a special interest in both the reform of clerical studies and the development of improved methods of teaching Christian doctrine. In the very controversial question of church-state relationships following the Italian Risorgimento he opposed the position of the "intransigents" and favored some kind of compromise with the new Italian state. Scalabrini also was the author of a work titled *Il Concilio Vaticano* (Como 1873).

Through the work of his missionary congregation, Bishop Scalabrini became familiar with the U.S. and foresaw a happy future for the Church there. The members of his congregation are today established in various parts of both the Old and New Worlds, where they labor in parishes, schools, centers for immigrants and refugees, and homes for the aged. In the U.S., the congregation has two provinces: the Province of St. Charles Borromeo (estab. 1888 and headquartered in New York City), and the Province of St. John Baptist (estab. 1903 and headquartered in Oak Park, IL).

Bibliography: F. GREGORI, *La vita e l'opera di un grande vescovo, Giovanni Battista Scalabrini* (Turin 1934). I. FELICI, *Father to the Immigrants: The Servant of God, John Baptist Scalabrini . . .* , tr. C. DELLA CHIESA (New York 1955).

[G. TESSAROLO/EDS.]

SCANDAL

From the Greek σκάνδαλον, in the sense of "offense, downfall, or a stumbling against something"; in popular use scandal signifies an objective act, person, or thing that gives offense or shocks the moral feelings of people. Thus it might be said that the slum section of a large city is a "scandal." Often it is used in a subjective sense to signify the reaction in people to the knowledge or report of something shameful or discreditable. In this case the word is used to refer not so much to the person or act that causes the shame, but to the reaction itself. In this sense a decent citizen might be said to take "scandal" at the sight of notorious slums.

In moral theology, however, scandal signifies not so much something shameful and therefore likely to cause a reaction of indignation and outrage, but something that provides occasion and incitement to the sin of another. It is not necessary that sin be actually committed in consequence of it; it is enough that the evil act or word provides incitement to wrongdoing, and it is precisely in this that the sin of scandal consists. If charity obliges us to assist our neighbor in his spiritual and temporal necessities, it obliges us still more strongly not to cause him spiritual loss or ruin.

The word "scandal" occurs a number of times in Sacred Scripture and appears to be used in various senses. Christ says to the followers of St. John the Baptist: "Blessed is he who is not scandalized in me" (Mt 11.6). He told Peter, who had suggested that He evade the cross: "Get thee behind me, satan, thou art a scandal to me!" (Mt 16.23). After His promise of the Eucharist He said: "Does this scandalize you?" (Jn 6.62). In these instances He used the word in the sense of offense or shock to the recipient's moral feeling. In a well-known passage Christ used the word very clearly in the sense of leading some-

one into sin: "It is impossible that scandals should not come; but woe to him through whom they come! It were better for him if a millstone were hung about his neck and he were thrown into the sea, than that he should cause one of these little ones to sin" (Lk 17.1, 2).

Theologians make certain distinctions in treating of scandal. The incitement to the sin of another by word or deed may be indirect or direct. It is indirect if the sin is not intended, although it may be foreseen as inevitable or at least likely. The scandal is direct if the sin of another person is intended as a direct consequence of one's word or action. If the giver of scandal has the specific intention of expressing his own hatred of God by inciting another to sin, he is said to be guilty of diabolical scandal, because quite clearly he is doing the devil's work by his evil action.

Scandal may be understood either in an active or a passive sense: active scandal is that of a person who incites another to sin; passive scandal is found in the person who is the victim of the incitement. The immediate effect of scandal can be only the temptation to sin, not sin itself. No one sins except willingly.

Moral Evaluation. What is the malice of scandal giving? In the case in which the sin of another is directly willed, or, although not directly willed, is foreseen by the scandal giver as likely to follow upon his evil example, one must acknowledge that serious guilt can be involved. In both cases there is a sin against charity. Direct scandal (and, according to some, indirect scandal as well) involves also an offense against the virtue or commandment that the scandal giver incites his victim to violate. Thus, to persuade another person to commit an act of theft would be, for the scandal giver, a sin against both charity and justice.

Direct scandal is serious sin unless there is a lack of sufficient deliberation, or unless the sin to which occasion is given is of its nature venial, or unless circumstances make it clear that no one is likely to be much influenced by the scandal giver.

Pharisaical Scandal. Scandal is not infrequently taken unreasonably. Pharisaical scandal is the morose reaction of those who, like the Pharisees in the time of Christ, wrest the words and actions of a good man to their own hurt by a perverse misconstruction. Thus, when Christ healed the sick upon the Sabbath, they professed to be scandalized (Lk 13.14). It should be clear that no guilt devolves upon the one whose conduct is maliciously misconstrued in this way.

Scandal of the Weak. There is, however, some obligation incumbent upon all of taking reasonable steps to avoid scandal of the weak and the ignorant, even when the particular actions involved are in themselves good or at least indifferent. If we perceive that scandal is the likely result of a certain act, we should refrain from that act, if this can easily be done, while making it clear at the same time that we are not refraining from it because we regard it as wrong. St. Paul, after making it clear to the Corinthians that they were permitted to eat food even though it had been sacrificed to idols, nevertheless went on to advise them: "Still, take care lest perhaps this right of yours become a stumbling block to the weak . . . if food scandalizes my brother, I will eat flesh no more forever, lest I scandalize my brother" (1 Cor 8.9, 13).

It should be added that the fulfillment of positive precepts, whether divine or human, if necessary for salvation, may never be omitted in order to avoid scandal. Much less would it be permissible to do something essentially evil, such as lying, stealing, or blaspheming, for the purpose of preventing the sin of another. There may even be circumstances in which one is bound to continue on a good course of action even though, through ignorance, the weak are scandalized; for it would not be right, for the sake of avoiding scandal, to inflict serious harm or loss on oneself or the community.

Reparation for Scandal. As to the duty of making reparation for having given scandal, it would seem clear that if, by his words or actions, one has led others into serious temptation or sin, he should do what he can to undo the wrong. At the very least, he should offset the bad example previously given by the good example that he now strives to offer. Generally, indeed, the reparation that is demonstrated by a visible and outward change of life will be the best way to make reparation. It is fitting that one who has given public scandal, and especially one of some standing in the community, should in some way publicly acknowledge his wrongdoing and his sincere intention to better his life.

Bibliography: THOMAS AQUINAS, *Summa Theologiae* 2a2ae, 43. H. DAVIS, *Moral and Pastoral Theology,* 4 v. (rev. ed. New York 1958) 1:333–340. A. VERMEERSCH, *Theologiae moralis: Principia, responsa, consilia,* 4 v. (3d ed. Rome 1944–48) v. 2.

[L. G. MILLER]

SCANLAN, LAWRENCE

Missionary, first bishop of Salt Lake City, Utah; b. Ballytarsha, County Tipperary, Ireland, Sept. 29, 1843; d. Salt Lake City, May 10, 1915. He was the son of Patrick and Catherine (Ryan) Scanlan; his brother Daniel was a priest in Cashel, Ireland. After attending St. Patrick's College, Thurles, Ireland, and the seminary of All Hallow's, Dublin, Ireland, he was ordained in Dublin on June 24, 1868. Abp. Joseph Alemany of San Francisco, Calif., adopted him when priests were needed to serve the increasing numbers of Irish parishioners in California. Scanlan became assistant pastor of St. Patrick's Church (1868–70) and St. Mary's Cathedral (1870–71) in San Francisco. After three months as pastor in Woodland, Calif., he served in a mining camp at Pioche, Nev. (1871–72), before going to Petaluma, Calif. His concern for the unfortunate won him the support of railroad laborers, miners, and cattlemen, who despite their distaste for preaching and moral crusades, helped him to build a church and a hospital at Pioche. In 1873 he was sent to Utah, a territory that had been served by a handful of missionary priests. Alone, he administered the 85,000 square miles embraced by his parish until the arrival of a small band of priests, among whom was Denis Kiely, later his vicar-general. Scanlan laid the foundation for almost every parish in the diocese, built more than 30 churches, and won the respect of the Mormons, who let him use their tabernacles. His assistant, Pierre Jean DE SMET, SJ, established friendly and lasting relations with Brigham Young, the Mormon leader.

Scanlan was responsible for the establishment of All Hallows College, Salt Lake City (1855), operated by the Marist fathers; and academies in Salt Lake City, Ogden, Park City, and Silver Reef, Utah, staffed by the Holy Cross sisters. In 1875 Holy Cross Hospital in Salt Lake City was built, and three years later, St. John's Hospital in Silver Reef. St. Ann's Orphanage and Mary Judge Memorial Home for miners were founded also under his supervision. Despite his many duties, he took an interest in civic affairs and was especially concerned with immigration. He was consecrated titular bishop of Larandum and vicar apostolic of Utah on June 29, 1887, and named first bishop of the newly created Diocese of Salt Lake City on Jan. 30, 1891. He worked until his death to create a sound basis for the church in Utah. He was buried in the crypt of St. Mary Magdalene, the cathedral he had built in Salt Lake City and that Cardinal James Gibbons had dedicated in 1909.

Bibliography: W. R. HARRIS, *The Catholic Church in Utah* (Salt Lake City 1909). R. J. PURCELL, *Dictionary of American Biography,* ed. A. JOHNSON and D. MALONE, 20 v. (New York 1928–36; index 1937; 1st suppl. 1944; 2d suppl. 1958), 16:408–409.

[J. L. MORRISON]

SCAPEGOAT

The goat, chosen by lot, upon whom the sins of the people, deliberate and indeliberate, were transferred by the high priest on the Day of Atonement. Bearing the sins of the people, it was led into the desert, into the domain of the demon Azazel [Lv 16.5, 7–10, 20–22; *see* ATONE-MENT, DAY OF (YOM KIPPUR)].

The English term, scapegoat, connoting in general usage the idea of a substitute victim, is actually derived from a faulty translation of the Hebrew phrase "for Azazel" in Leviticus (16.8, 10, 26). The Latin Vulgate version, following the erroneous Greek translation in the Septuagint, rendered this expression *caper emissarius* (emissary goat), which became in English the "escaping goat" or scapegoat.

The notion of transmitting evil arising from sin, disease, or even demons to animals is an ancient practice and was fairly widespread among primitive peoples. Relics of this practice are found in some cultures to the present day. Significant parallels in the ancient Orient have been found in Babylonian and Hittite sources. An analogous case in the Bible itself is that of the bird liberated at the time of the leper's purification (Lv 14.7). The extra-Biblical evidence is sufficient to see that the Israelite rite was a purified adaptation of prevailing pagan custom. In Israel the act was not demon worship; the animal was not sacrificed to Azazel but, becoming impure, was rendered unfit for any future use. The rite was, moreover, divested of any magical connotation; God Himself prescribed and alone effected the sin transfer through the priestly action. In the expiation ritual [*see* EXPIATION (IN THE BIBLE)], the blood of the sacrificial goat, sprinkled on the propitiatory (the top of the ark), purified from sin (see Lyonnet, 35–36); the scapegoat was not a sacrifice. Since sin was conceived of as an almost tangible reality, a symbolic assurance of its removal and proper consignment was realized in the scapegoat rite.

Because the scapegoat was never viewed as an offering to God, this concept received no development in New Testament soteriology. The reference to Christ's "becoming sin for us" (2 Cor 5.21) in describing His atoning action means that He became a SIN offering for man, i.e., a sacrifice that atones for sin; the New Testament word ἁμαρτία, following the Hebrew *ḥaṭṭā't,* can mean either "sin" or "sin offering," depending on context. It is to be noted that the scapegoat was not sacrificed; its blood was not shed; it was not a sin offering. To interpret Christ's role as analogous to that of the scapegoat on the basis of His having "suffered outside the gate" (Heb 13.12–13) is contrary to the inspired author's intention (see Lyonnet, 37). As the passage itself indicates, the analogy is between Christ and those Old Testament sacrificial offerings that required the transfer of the victim's remains to a place outside the camp, the present reference suggested to the author of Hebrews by the parallel found in Christ's death outside of Jerusalem.

Bibliography: S. LYONNET, "De munere sacrificali sanguinis" with appendix "De ritu capri emissarii," *Verbum Domini* (Rome 1921–) 39 (1961) 18–38. C. L. FEINBERG, "The Scapegoat of Lev 16," *Bibliotheca Sacra* 115 (1958) 320–333. S. LANDERSDORFER, "Keilinschriftliche Parallelen zum biblischen Sündenbock," *Biblische Zeitschrift* 19 (1931) 20–28. J. G. FRAZER, *The Golden Bough* (abr. ed. New York 1952) 651–675. R. DE VAUX, *Ancient Israel, Its Life and Institutions,* tr. J. MCHUGH (New York 1961) 508–509.

[R. J. FALEY]

Lawrence Scanlan.

SCAPULARS

A scapular is a part of some RELIGIOUS HABITS that consists in a length of cloth worn over the shoulders. It developed from a kind of apron worn by monks during manual labor, and the *Rule of St. Benedict* prescribed its use *propter opera* (ch. 15). It was a straight piece of cloth, generally from 14 to 18 inches in width, with a hole in the middle so that it could pass over the head and hang down from the shoulders before and behind.

Some earlier forms of the scapular appear to have been shorter, but later they came down to the knees or even to the ankles. Sometimes a hood was fitted to the opening for the head to protect the wearer from the cold or from rain or snow. The front and back portions of the scapular were often fastened together under the wearer's arms by straps or bands, and these transverse fastenings, joined with the vertical lengths of cloth made it possible to see the form of a cross in the scapular.

In the course of time a symbolic meaning was attached to the garment. It was considered a kind of cross carried on the shoulders, and it naturally suggested the yoke of Christ: "If anyone wishes to come after me, let him . . . take up his cross daily and follow me" (Lk 9.23). To become a monk meant to follow Christ, and that in turn meant taking up one's cross as the yoke of Christ. The scapular thus became the symbol of the working monk as well as of a life of penance and austerity.

The scapular was not at first a part of the monastic dress worn in choir, nor does investment with it appear to have been part of the ceremony of clothing or profession in earlier times. As early, perhaps, as the end of the 11th century the scapular was considered part of the habit of some orders. With the Benedictines it became a part of the complete habit. The Cistercians adopted it, as did also the Premonstratensians and other canons regular, the Dominicans, Carmelites, Servites, Mercedarians, Trinitarians, Camaldolese, Olivetans, and the religious of various later congregations.

The Third Order Scapulars. It was common in the 13th century for devout lay people, living in the world but desiring some corporate form of religious life, to associate themselves under the direction of the monks or friars of a nearby religious house, whose spirit they would imitate by various practices of prayer and austerity and even by the taking of such vows as were compatible with their state of life. St. Francis of Assisi introduced a confraternity or order of penance for the purpose of providing a regular way of life for people of this kind; and when those who followed this rule became too numerous, the Church ordered them to divide into groups according to the religious communities in whose churches they performed their devotions, and to refrain from intercommunication. Thus there arose third orders of penance for the different religious orders then existing, e.g., the Augustinian, Franciscan, Dominican, and Servite. It became customary for the religious of these orders to give such people a part of the religious habit, or something to signify the habit—a cord, a mantle, or very often a scapular of the same color as the habit—as a token of their affiliation with the order and their participation in its spirit, its activities, and its merit before God. When this symbol took the form of a scapular it generally consisted of two pieces of cloth, one of which was worn on the chest and the other on the back, and the two were connected by strings or tapes over the wearer's shoulders.

The Small Scapular. From the beginning of the 16th century a reduced form of the third order scapular came into use and was known as the small scapular. The

pieces of cloth were generally smaller than two inches square. Sometimes the small scapular consisted of two pieces like the third order scapular and sometimes of a single piece that was hung around the neck by a string. While the third order scapular was generally plain, the small scapular was frequently embroidered and had upon it the picture of Our Lady, or of a saint in whose honor it was worn, or of the object of devotion it signified, for example, the Sacred Heart or the Passion. These small scapulars were given to lay people who wished to associate themselves with a religious order, but less closely than as tertiaries because they were not prepared to attempt the full observance of a third order rule, yet were willing to undertake certain prayers or other practices of piety.

Originally these scapulars belonged to religious orders, but other scapulars became emblematic of separate confraternities. Since Dec. 16, 1910, the Holy See has permitted the wearing of a medal instead of one or more small scapulars, provided the medal represents the Sacred Heart on one side and Our Lady on the other, and is blessed as the scapular [*Acta Apostolicae Sedis* 3 (1911) 22–23].

The Value of the Scapular. In addition to the symbolic value of the scapular as representative of Christ's cross and yoke, the scapular with the rest of the habit of which it is a part, keeps before the mind of the individual religious what his order represents—its ideals, traditions, and the holiness of life achieved by many, perhaps, who have been clothed in the same uniform. As part of a uniform it is also a sign of a special bond of charity that unites those who wear and have worn it. The smaller scapular given to tertiaries or oblates is the sign of their admission into a kind of fellowship with the religious of an order and is meant to encourage their participation in the prayer, activities, and spirit of the order. Moreover, it is a pledge of some measure of participation in the merits of the order. It rests upon the doctrine of the Communion of Saints, and the practice of wearing scapulars has been approved and indulgenced by the Church.

Certain claims regarding the spiritual benefits to be gained through the wearing of religious habits or scapulars have been the subject of controversy. In the 14th century John WYCLIF (c. 1328–84) reproached friars for claiming that those who wore their habit would never go to hell. Apparently there were friars who made such a claim, or at least claims that lent themselves to distortion into that form, and these were transferred to the small scapular when this began to be used in the 16th century. Although friars of other religious orders may have made similar claims, attention has focused more strongly upon the privileges claimed for the Carmelite scapular. According to Carmelite legend, Our Lady appeared to St. Simon Stock in Cambridge in 1251 and, showing him a brown scapular, declared that whoever wore it until death would be preserved from hell and on the first Saturday after his death would be taken by her to heaven. It is beyond the scope of the present article to go into the disputed question of whether this vision (or even the scapular, for that matter) was known to Carmelite friars of the mid-13th century, or whether the legend was an invention of later times. Whatever the truth of the origin of the legend, the promises contained in it deserve attention.

With regard to either of the two promises, it should be noted that they cannot be reasonably represented as requiring merely the material fact of wearing the scapular without respect to the interior dispositions with which it is worn. To do so would be to attribute a magical efficacy to the scapular and make it out to be a more potent channel of grace than the Sacraments. Against the hypocrisy and formalism of the Pharisees, Our Lord taught that to be pleasing to God, worship must be an expression of the dispositions of the heart. External acts have no value in God's sight unless they are the expression of a right mind and a sincere will. The wearing of the scapular must therefore be understood to include the right and salutary interior dispositions with which it is worn; it is primarily through these, and only remotely and instrumentally through the actual carrying of the scapular, that salvation is secured.

With regard to the promise of preservation from hell—or, and this comes to the same thing, the grace of final PERSEVERANCE, or the grace of a good death—this must always be understood in conformity with the teaching of the Church regarding the uncertainty of salvation. At most, the wearing of the scapular cannot be more than a fallible sign of pre-destination, of its nature no more certain than many others, and valid only in conjunction with the right interior dispositions.

With regard to the promise of deliverance from purgatory on the first Saturday after death, this was claimed on the basis of the supposed bull *Sacratissimo uti culmine* of John XXII. This bull, however, is now universally regarded by scholars as spurious [B. Zimmerman, *Monumenta Hist. Carmelit.* 1 (Lerins 1907) 356–63]. Christians are, however, permitted to hold as a matter of pious belief that the Blessed Virgin will extend her maternal help to the souls who were, while on earth, her faithful servants, and even that her beneficence in this respect may be exercised in a special way on Saturdays, for the seventh day of the week is dedicated to her cult.

Bibliography: F. BÉRINGER, *Les Indulgences: Leur nature et leur usage,* tr. P. MAZAYER, 2 v. (4th ed. Paris 1925), with good bibliography and list of small scapulars. C. P. CEROKE, "The Credibili-ty of the Scapular Promise," *Carmelus* 11 (1964) 81–123. B. M. XIBERTA Y ROQUETA, *De visione sancti Simonis Stock* (Rome 1950). L. OOSTERLAAN, "The Significance and Use of the Scapular," *The Irish Ecclesiastical Record* 10 (1901) 311–29. B. ZIMMERMAN, "The Origin of the Scapular," *ibid.* 15 (1904) 142–53, 206–234, 331–51. H. THURSTON, "Scapular Tradition and Its Defenders," *ibid.* 29 (1911) 492–506. D. DE BRUYNE, "Note sur le costume bénédictin primitif," *Revue Bénédictine* 33 (1921) 58–61. R. COPSEY, "Simon Stock and the Scapular Vision," *Journal of Ecclesiastical History* 50 (1999) 652–83.

[P. N. ZAMMIT/EDS.]

SCARAB

A beetle and its conventionalized representation that was widely used as a talisman and seal in ancient Egypt. The *scarabaeus sacer,* a large black beetle, became almost a personification of ancient Egypt, so common was its association with Egyptian culture. This beetle owed its prominence to the fact that it was connected with the Egyptian sun-god RA (RE), though the reasons for such a connection remain obscure. One explanation is that the sun rolling across the sky suggested the practice of some beetles of rolling balls of dung. Another is that the beetle was venerated as a symbol of life after death, since the offspring seemed to emerge from decaying matter; only in a later time was the identification made with Ra. Still another is that there is merely a verbal connection between Khopri, one of Ra's appellations, and Khopirru, the Egyptian name for the scarab.

The image of this beetle and related species was used in such abundance on amulets and signet rings by the Egyptians that Egyptian influence can be detected in any country where these artifacts are found. The beetle's image when used as an amulet was regarded as having some prophylactic power. In rings, one side of the image was often used as a SEAL. The engraved portion carried a design and personal name. Some scarab rings bear the name of the pharaoh or local officials and thus provide a *terminus a quo* for dating purposes. The shape of the image also is a dating aid, since it changed in the course of centuries. Such scarab seals provide, in addition, useful information on the art and religious practices of Egypt. Caution, however, must be exercised in interpreting the data. Scarabs were often copied and mass-produced by men who in their ignorance or lack of skill distorted the originals.

Bibliography: *Encyclopedic Dictionary of the Bible,* translated and adapted by L. HARTMAN (New York, 1963) 2140–41. J. BECKERATH, *Lexikon für Theologie und Kirche,* ed. J. HOFER and K. RAHNER, 10 v. (2d, new ed. Freiburg 1957–65); suppl., *Das ZweiteVatikanische Konzil: Dokumente und kommentare,* ed. H. S. BRECHTER et al., pt. 1 (1966) 9:816. M. PIEPER, *Paulys Realenzyklo-pädie der klassischen Altertumswissenschaft,* ed. G. WISSOWA, et al.

3A.1 (Stuttgart 1927) 3A.1 (1927) 447–459. F. BODENHEIMER, *Animal and Man in Bible Lands* (Leiden 1960) 80–81.

[T. H. WEBER]

SCARAMELLI, GIOVANNI BATTISTA

Jesuit spiritual writer; b. Rome, Nov. 23, 1687; d. Macerata, Jan. 11, 1752. He entered the Jesuits in 1706 and was ordained in 1717. He spent the greater part of his priestly life as a home missionary. As a sacred orator he reflected the temper of the 18th century. A strong and rather severe character, Scaramelli conducted his missions with a theatricalism that attracted great crowds to hear him. He is chiefly remembered, however, for his ascetical and mystical writings, of which he composed six: *Vita di Suor Maria Crocifissa Satellico* (Venice 1750), *Discernimento degli Spiriti* (Venice 1753), *Direttorio Ascetico* (Venice 1754), *Direttorio Mistico* (Venice 1754), *La dottrina de San Giovanni della Croce* (Venice 1815), and *Vita della serra di Dio Angelica Cospari* (unpub.).

The *Vita di Suor Maria Crocifissa* was put on the Index in 1769 probably because the author affirmed too categorically the sanctity of the religious before an ecclesiastical decision had been given. The *Discernimento degli Spiriti* ran through 11 editions in Italian, three each in Spanish and French, and two in German. The *Direttorio Ascetico,* which treats of Christian perfection and the virtues, had 29 editions in Italian, 21 in French, five in German, four in Spanish, three in Latin, and eight in English (the earliest, London 1868–70). *La dottrina di San Giovanni* was an early composition of Scaramelli and has been reprinted three times. The unpublished work was discovered recently.

The *Direttorio Mistico,* the most important and original of Scaramelli's works, treats of contemplation and its degrees and of passive purification of the senses and spirit. This work became a classic in this difficult field, went through 15 editions in Italian before 1900, and was translated into Spanish, German, French, Latin, and Polish. In 1913 an English abridgment by the Anglican D. H. Nicholson was published. Scaramelli's object in this work was practical: to aid directors in their conduct of souls. Consequently, he is not satisfied with a simple exposition of doctrinal principles. Almost every chapter has advice for directors as well as answers to objections. As a writer Scaramelli shows strong convictions, while he relies on an abundance of arguments rather than on subtle logic. He is always the missionary, a composer of Lenten discourses rather than the professor of mystical theology. He was, however, an influential mystical writer and expounded traditional Catholic doctrine with precision and rare breadth of judgment.

Bibliography: L. A. HOGUE, *Dictionnaire de théologie catholique*, ed. A. VACANT et al., 15 v. (Paris 1903–50; Tables Générales 1951–) 14.1:1259–63; ''The *Direttorio Mistico* of J. B. Scaramelli, SJ,'' *Archivum historicum Societatis Jesu* 9 (1940) 1–39.

[E. A. RYAN]

SCARAMPI, PIER FRANCESCO

Papal envoy to the Irish Catholic Confederacy (1643–45); b. Monferrato, Piedmont, 1596; d. Rome, Oct. 14, 1656. As the son of a noble family of the duchy of Monferrato, he first followed a military career, but at the age of forty, he joined the Roman Oratory. On April 18, 1643, Urban VIII named him special envoy to the Irish Catholics, who in the previous year had formed an armed confederacy to defend their religious and political rights and had sought help from the papacy and the Catholic European powers.

He arrived in Ireland in July and was immediately faced with a serious problem. Certain leaders of the Catholic Confederacy, in a search for political agreement with the Marquis of Ormond, King Charles I's Lord-Lieutenant in Ireland, were prepared to content themselves with an assurance that the King would permit them to practice their religion in private. Scarampi insisted that the right to free and public exercise of religion must be part of any political agreement, but in spite of his opposition, agreement was finally reached with the Marquis of Glamorgan, a special envoy from Charles I, in the late summer of 1645. This agreement conceded the demand for free and public exercise of religion, but the concession was to be kept secret. Scarampi opposed this compromise also.

Meanwhile, the new Pope, INNOCENT X, decided to accredit a nuncio to the Confederates, and chose Giovanni Battista RINUCCINI, Archbishop of Fermo, who arrived in Ireland on Oct. 22, 1645. Scarampi was ordered to remain as his adviser. A crisis developed in the early summer of 1646 when the Supreme Council of the Confederation made public an agreement with Ormond that gave no guarantee of the public exercise of religion.

Rinuccini, supported by Scarampi, decided to use ecclesiastical authority to the full to have this peace rejected. They succeeded in their efforts, but over the next year differences of opinion developed between them. They were agreed that a guarantee of the public exercise of religion had to be part of any settlement between the Irish Catholics and Charles I, but Scarampi seems to have felt that Rinuccini's tactics were tending to identify the interests of the Church with the ''Old Irish'' political group, thereby forcing moderates of the other group, the Anglo-

Irish or "Old English," to identify themselves with the faction willing to reach agreement with the King without satisfactory guarantees for the Catholic religion.

After repeated requests, Scarampi was allowed to return to Rome, where he arrived on May 15, 1647, bringing with him five Irish seminarians, among them Oliver PLUNKETT, the future martyr-archbishop of Armagh. Scarampi became superior of the Roman Oratory, and died while tending the sick in the pestilence that ravaged Rome in 1656.

Bibliography: M. J. HYNES, *The Mission of Rinuccini* (Dublin 1932). S. KAVANAGH, ed., *Commentarius Rinuccinianus*, 6 v. (Dublin 1932–49). P. ARINGHI, *Memorie storiche della vita del . . . P. F. Scarampi* (Rome 1744). G. ALBION, *Charles 1 and the Court of Rome* (London 1935).

[P. J. CORISH]

SCARLATTI, ALESSANDRO

Important composer of the baroque period; b. Palermo, May 2, 1660 (christened Pietro Alessandro Gasparo); d. Naples, Oct. 24, 1725. As a boy of 12 he became a student of CARISSIMI in Rome, where his first known opera was produced in 1679 and where he was for a time in charge of music for Queen Christina of Sweden. He was again in Rome (1703–09) as *maestro di cappella* at St. Mary Major. In 1710 he was appointed *maestro* to the royal court at Naples, a post he held for life. Scarlatti wrote more than 115 operas (50 of which are extant) and more than 500 chamber cantatas for one or two voices and harpsichord. He founded the so-called Neapolitan school of opera, whose chief stylistic characteristics are florid and elegant melodic lines, extensive use of the *da capo* aria form, and rapid, staccato recitatives. He also influenced the development of the Italian overture (fast section, slow section, fast section). Most, though not all, of his church music is inferior to his operas and cantatas. It is set in either of two styles: the "old style" in imitation of Palestrinian counterpoint; or the prevalent operatic style of Scarlatti's day. Research by Beekman C. Cannon of Yale University indicates that Scarlatti was apparently the first composer to set the complete, unaltered text of the St. John Passion. Because he composed in great haste his music is of uneven quality, but his best works rank among the baroque masterpieces.

Bibliography: E. J. DENT, *Alessandro Scarlatti*, ed. F. WALKER (rev. ed. London 1960). E. HANLEY, *Die Musik in Geschichte und Gegenwart*, ed. F. BLUME (Kassel-Basel 1949–) 11:1482–1506. F. A. D'ACCONE, *The History of a Baroque Opera: Alessandro Scarlatti's 'Gli equivoci nel sembiante'* (Hillsboro 1985). L. DAMUTH, "Interrelationships between the Operas and Datable Cantatas of Alessandro Scarlatti" (Ph.D. diss. Columbia University, 1993). U. D'ARPA, "La famiglia Scarlatti: nuovi documenti biografici," *Re-cercare* 2 (1990), 243–248. D. J. GROUT, E. HANLEY, and M. BOYD, "(Pietro) Alessandro (Gaspare) Scarlatti" in *The New Grove Dictionary of Music and Musicians, vol. 16,* ed. S. SADIE (New York 1980) 549–567. G. G. JONES, "Alessandro Scarlattis *Il Ciro,*" *Hamburger Jahrbuch für Musikwissenschaft* 1 (1978), 225–237. D. POULTNEY, "Alessandro Scarlatti" in *International Dictionary of Opera* 2 vols. ed. C. S. LARUE (Detroit 1993) 1184–1187. D. SWALE, "The *Judith* Oratorios of Alessandro Scarlatti," *Miscellanea Musicologica* 9 (1977), 145–155.

[W. C. HOLMES]

SCARLATTI, DOMENICO

Baroque composer and harpsichord virtuoso; b. Naples, Oct. 26, 1685; d. Madrid, July 23, 1757. He studied first with his father, Alessandro SCARLATTI, and later in Venice with Gasparini; at age 16 he was organist at the royal chapel in Naples. In Rome (1709) he engaged in his famous contest with HANDEL, in which Handel was judged the better organist, and Scarlatti the better harpsichordist. He was *maestro di cappella* at the Vatican from 1714 to 1719, but resigned to go first to Portugal and then to Spain (1729), where he became tutor to Princess Maria Barbara and *maestro de cámara* when she became queen. In Spain he composed more than 600 harpsichord "sonatas" and created a Spanish instrumental school. Considered the founder of modern keyboard technique, Scarlatti was the first composer to utilize such typical keyboard devices as the crossing of hands, fast repeated notes, and passages in parallel thirds and sixths. He also wrote much church music, most of which was unpublished. His last work was a *Salve Regina* for soprano and strings (1756).

Bibliography: *Opere complete per clavicembalo,* ed. A. LONGO, 10 v. and suppl. (Milan 1906); *Sixty sonatas,* ed. R. KIRKPATRICK, 2 v. (New York 1953). R. KIRKPATRICK, *Domenico Scarlatti* (Princeton 1953); *Die Musik in Geschichte und Gegenwart,* ed. F. BLUME (Kassel-Basel 1949–) 11:1506–18. P. BARCABA, "Domenico Scarlatti oder Die Geburtsstunde der klassischen Sonate," *Österreichische Musik Zeitschrift* 45 (1990), 382–390. M. BOYD, "Die kirchenmusik von Domenico Scarlatti," *Kirchenmusikalisches Jahrbuch* 72 (1988), 117–125. J. V. GONZÁLEZ VALLE, "Fondos de música de tecla de Domenico Scarlatti conservados en el Archivo Capitular de Zaragoza," *Anuario Musical* 45 (1990), 103–116. M. S. KASTNER, "Repensando Domenico Scarlatti," *Anuario Musical* 44 (1989), 137–154. M. MARX-WEBER, "Domenico Scarlattis *Stabat Mater,*" *Kirchenmusikalisches Jahrbuch* 71 (1987), 13–22. Á. PEDRERO-ENCABO, "Los *30 essercizi* de Domenico Scarlatti y las 30 tocatas de Vicente Rodríguez: Paralelismos y divergencias," *Revista de Musicología* 20 (1997), 373–391. D. SUTHERLAND, "Domenico Scarlatti and the Florentine piano," *Early Music* 22 (1995), 243–256. MA. TERESA FERNÁNDEZ TALAYA, "Memoria con las últimas voluntades de Domenico Scarlatti, músico de cámara de la reina María Bárbara de Braganza," *Revista de Musicología* 21 (1998), 155–168. A. RUIZ TARAZONA, "Fuente Scarlattiana en un manuscrito olvidado," *Revista de Musicología* 22 (1999), 261–266. J. H. VAN DER MEER, "The Keyboard String Instruments at the Disposal of Domenico Scarlatti,'' *The Galpin Journal* 50 (1997), 136–160.

[W. C. HOLMES]

SCAVINI, PIETRO

Moral theologian; b. Intra, Italy, Oct. 22, 1791; d. Novara, Nov. 17, 1869. He taught at the seminary of Novara and was a canon of the cathedral of that city. His *Theologia moralis universa ad mentem S. Alphonsi* (4 v. Novara 1841) enjoyed a considerable popularity and went through 16 editions, the last being that of Milan, 1901. Scavini engaged in a controversy with his friend A. ROSMINI on the validity of the REFLEX PRINCIPLE *Lex dubia non obligat*. In the course of the debate, in which others also had part, Scavini's interpretation of the mind of St. Alphonsus and of PROBABILISM in general was vigorously criticized and defended.

Bibliography: H. HURTER, *Nomenclator literarius theologiae catholicae*, 5 vol. (3rd ed. Innsbruck 1903–13) 5.2:1795–96. G. CAVIGIOLI, *Il teologo Mons. Pietro Scavini* (Pallanza 1920).

[P. K. MEAGHER]

SCHAAF, VALENTINE THEODORE

Franciscan minister general, canon lawyer; b. Cincinnati, Ohio, March 18, 1883; d. Rome, Italy, Dec. 1, 1946. Theodore, one of 17 children, attended St. Francis Preparatory High School, Cincinnati. As a candidate for priesthood in the Order of Friars Minor of the Province of St. John the Baptist, Cincinnati, he was ordained July 29, 1909. He was lector of languages and mathematics at St. Francis Preparatory High School for nine years. He then studied at the Catholic University of America, Washington, D.C., receiving the J.C.D. degree (1921) and joining the canon law faculty (1923). From 1933 to 1936 he served as dean of that faculty and as definitor for his Franciscan province. In 1939 he became general definitor for English–speaking Franciscans at Rome, and a year later was appointed consultor of the Congregation of the Sacraments. He also served as extraordinary professor of canon law at the Atheneum Antonianum, Franciscan international house of studies in Rome. On July 4, 1945, he was designated minister general of the order by Pius XII. He was the first American to occupy the highest Franciscan office.

[D. MCELRATH]

SCHAFF, PHILIP

Church historian and theologian; b. Chur, Switzerland, July 1, 1819; d. New York City, Oct. 25, 1893.

Schaff was the son of a poor village carpenter and obtained his education through scholarships, first at Chur and later at Korntal Academy and the Stuttgart Gymnasium in Germany. In 1837 he entered Tübingen University, studying under Ferdinand Christian BAUR. Two years later he transferred to Halle and, in 1840, to Berlin, where he was profoundly influenced by F. A. G. Tholuck, E. W. Hengstenberg, and J. A. W. Neander.

His theories of history and the development of the Christian Church are drawn from Neander, a debt he acknowledged in his biographical study of Neander. As a *Privatdocent* in the theological department at the University of Berlin in 1843, Schaff was invited to accept a professorship at the Reformed Seminary, Mercersburg, Pa. His inaugural address, *The Principle of Protestantism* (Chambersburg 1844; new ed. Philadelphia 1964) linked him with his colleague John Williamson NEVIN in its theory of doctrinal development and its stress on the Catholic and Reformation heritage as the dynamic force in Protestantism, opposed to rationalism and sectarianism. Although favorably reviewed by theologians as diverse as Charles HODGE and Francis P. KENRICK, the address led to his trial (1845) before the Reformed Synod on charges of Puseyism; he and Nevin were vindicated. Their joint efforts developed a tradition of liturgical renewal, ecumenism, and a return to Reformation theology that became known as the Mercersburg movement (*see* MERCERSBURG THEOLOGY).

Besides his contributions to the *Mercersburg Review,* Schaff founded and edited (1848–54) *Der Kirchenfreund* to popularize these views. Visiting Europe in 1854, he lectured on church unity and on American democracy; the latter was published as *America* (New York 1855; new ed. Cambridge, Mass. 1961). His chief work began with the publication of *The History of the Apostolic Church* (New York 1857). Although he moved to New York in 1864, he did not sever his connection with Mercersburg until 1867. He held a lectureship at Hartford Seminary, Conn. (1868–71), and accepted a call to Union Theological Seminary, New York City (1870) where he taught until 1893.

Beginning in 1866, his ecumenical efforts were concentrated on the EVANGELICAL ALLIANCE. Holding that reunion was only possible on a firm doctrinal basis, he issued *The Creeds of Christendom* and *A Harmony of the Reformed Confessions* (New York 1877). His historical studies generally were intended ''to remove ignorance and prejudice and bring Christians closer together.'' His *History of the Christian Church to 600 A.D.* (New York 1858) was enlarged and revised in 1882. He organized the American Society of Church History, contributed to its publication series (from 1889), and edited the pioneering series of American denominational histories (begun in 1891). He made the writings of the patristic age available in English translation through the *Select Library* series. From 1870 to 1885 he was closely engaged in the revision of the English Bible. His own scriptural studies include *A Companion to the Greek Testament* (New York 1883) and *A Commentary on the New Testament* (New York 1881). He served as general editor of the *Schaff-Herzog Encyclopedia of Religious Knowledge*. His last effort, an address on *The Reunion of Christendom* (Chicago 1893), was written on his deathbed.

Bibliography: D. S. SCHAFF, *The Life of Philip Schaff* (New York 1897). J. H. NICHOLS, *Romanticism in American Theology* (Chicago 1961).

[R. K. MACMASTER]

SCHÄFFER, ANNA, BL.

Lay mystic; Franciscan tertiary; b. Mindelstetten (between Regensburg and Ingolstadt), Bavaria, Germany, Feb. 18, 1882; d. Mindelstetten, Oct. 5, 1925. Anna Schäffer was one of many children of a carpenter. Offering her life to God for the welfare of others, she began working in Regensburg to help support her family, although she had hoped to become a missionary sister. Following the death of her father (1896), she worked in Landshut, then in the laundry at Stammham, where on Feb. 4, 1901 an industrial accident left nineteen-year-old Anna immersed in a tub of boiling bleach. After a year in the hospital, she was discharged (May 1902) because the specialists were unable to heal her wounds. She was virtually bedridden for the next 25 years. With disability came poverty.

In time her anger turned to understanding that her suffering could be united with that of the Crucified Christ and offered as a sacrifice for others. Her confessor, Father Karl Rieger, said that he never heard Anna Schäffer complain during the twenty-five years he brought Communion to her daily.

From spring 1910 she had many mystical experiences. She related that God gave her three keys with which she opened heaven's gates: her suffering, her sewing needle, and a pen. In her beautiful embroidery for churches, Anna would illustrate the Sacred Heart with the flames bent inward like a head of wheat. She used this symbol often on the letters she wrote to those seeking her prayers or counsel in Austria, Switzerland, and America.

Anna suffered greatly in her last days. Soon after her death, her tomb in the churchyard at Mindelstetten became a popular pilgrimage destination. After her relics were identified and transferred into the church (July 26,

Philip Schaff, engraving by J. J. Cade. (Archive Photos)

1972), the diocesan process for her beatification was opened (1973). She was declared venerable in 1995. Pope John Paul II noted during Anna's beatification (March 7, 1999) that ''between atrocious pains she became aware of the responsibility every Christian has for the salvation of his neighbor. . . . Her bedside became the cradle of a wide apostolate through correspondence.''

Feast: Oct. 5.

Bibliography: *Acta Apostolicae Sedis* (1999): 310–12. *L'Osservatore Romano,* no. 10 (1999): 1–2. *L'Osservatore Romano,* English edition, no. 29 (1995): 5.

[K. I. RABENSTEIN]

SCHALL VON BELL, JOHANN ADAM

Missionary in China and astronomer; b. Cologne, May 1, 1591; d. Beijing, Aug. 15, 1666. After studying at the Germanicum in Rome, he entered the Society of Jesus on Oct. 20, 1611. Following his ordination, he left Lisbon for the China mission on April 16, 1618, landing in Macau in 1619, and arriving in Beijing on Jan. 25, 1623. Except for a three-year interlude in Xi'an, Shaanxi (1627–30), Beijing remained the center of his activities until his death.

The reform of the Chinese calendar had long been a matter of grave concern to the government. Hsü Kuangch'i, leading Chinese Catholic, had repeatedly urged that Jesuit astronomers be employed in the task. In 1629 his efforts bore fruit. The emperor ordered the establishment of a calendrical bureau to undertake the scientific reform of the calendar, putting Hsü Kuangch'i in charge and, in an edict of Sept. 27, 1629, approved the employment of Jesuits. The brilliant Johann Terrenz Schreck died a few months after having been assigned to the task, and Schall, together with Giacomo Rho, was appointed to take his place. The two men performed brilliantly. By 1635 they had completed a series of translations on astronomical subjects comprising 137 *chüan.* Official adoption of the reformed calendar, blocked by adherents of the old schools, had, however, to await the advent of a new dynasty in 1644.

Schall had enjoyed considerable prestige during the last years of the Ming dynasty, but it was under the Ch'ing dynasty that he attained a preeminent position in the empire.

Influence at Court. His relations with the precocious young Shun-chih emperor were close; the emperor always called him ''Ma-Fa'' (grandfather). In 1644 Dorgon, the regent, named Schall director of the bureau of astronomy. As such he was ex officio an official of the fifth grade, first division, of the mandarinal hierarchy that consisted of nine grades, each of two divisions. On Feb. 2, 1658, he reached the pinnacle of the hierarchy when he was made a mandarin of the first class, first division. A year earlier a member of a Dutch embassy reported: ''Father Adam Schall is in such great favor with this prince that he has access to him at any hour.'' In 1661 his younger associate, Ferdinand Verbiest, wrote: ''Schall has more influence upon the emperor than any viceroy, or than the most respected prince, and the name of Father Adam is better known in China than the name of any famous man is in Europe.'' In 1650 Francesco Brancato, writing from Shanghai, had said: ''All of us who are in this mission bask by divine favor in the aura of Father Adam.'' Schall, however, made enemies as well as friends, among them some of his fellow Jesuits. One of these, Gabriel de Magalhães, mounted a campaign against him that lasted for 17 years and ended only with Schall's death. First, he attempted to have Schall expelled from the Society of Jesus on personal charges that were characterized by Verbiest as ''calumnies and lies.'' Thorough investigation cleared Schall. De Magalhães then urged that he be removed as head of the astronomical bureau upon the ground that the office was incompatible with his vow against accepting proferred dignities and that its functions involved him in superstition. Both questions were ultimately resolved by Rome in Schall's favor,

but when word of final vindication reached Beijing, Schall was already dead.

Last Years. Schall's last years were shadowed with tragedy. The Shun-chih emperor died in 1661. Under the influence of Yang Kuang-hsien, a notorious anti-Christian crusader, Oboi, the most powerful of the four regents, removed Schall from his office, stripped him of his titles, and on Nov. 12, 1664, committed him, together with the other three Jesuits then in Beijing, one of whom was De Magalhães, to prison. Schall had suffered a stroke and, partially paralyzed, could not speak. His assistant, Verbiest, conducted his defense. In January of 1665, Schall was sentenced to death by strangulation, changed by Oboi in April to the terrible penalty of death by dismemberment. The anger of the empress dowager and the protest of Schall's admirers and friends forced Oboi to retreat. Although five of his Christian scholar-colleagues had been executed, Schall and the other Jesuits were released. Complete vindication came after his death at the age of 75. In 1668 the K'ang-hsi emperor dissolved the regency. The following year, Oboi was imprisoned for treason and tyranny. Yang Kuang-hsien was exiled. Verbiest was made director of the bureau of astronomy. All of Schall's titles and ranks were restored, as were those of the five Christian astronomers executed in 1665, and Schall was honored with an official funeral.

Schall was a man of exceptional attainments. Science was his specialty, but he was a typical Renaissance man in the universality of his knowledge. Besides his native German, he had a perfect mastery of Portuguese, as well as of both literary and vernacular Chinese. He was at home in Italian, had a fair knowledge of Spanish, and easily understood Dutch. In his old age he still wrote beautiful Latin. In practical skills, he manufactured cannons, drew plans for the fortifications of Beijing, planned and built a baroque church, constructed astronomical instruments, rebuilt a spinet, built a sailing boat for the emperor, and wrote a treatise on mining.

The distinguished sinologist, Paul Pelliot, wrote of him: ''Man of the Church, man of science, man of action, man capable of irony and anger, a many faceted figure, attractive and intriguing. Schall would have made an impact anywhere.''

Bibliography: A. SCHALL, *Historica relatio de ortu et progessu fidei orthodoxae in regno Chinensi* (Regensburg 1672); *Lettres et mémoires d'Adam Schall, S.J.,* ed. H. BERNARD, tr. P. BORNET (Tientsin 1942). D. BARTOLI, *Istoria della compagnia di Gesù: La Cina, terza parte dell'Asia,* 8 v. in 5 (Naples 1859). C. R. BOXER, *Fidalgos in the Far East 1550–1770: Fact and Fancy in the History of Macao* (The Hague 1948). G. H. DUNNE, *Generation of Giants: The Story of the Jesuits in China in the Last Decades of the Ming Dynasty* (Notre Dame, Ind. 1962). L. PFISTER, *Notices biographiques et bibliographiques sur les Jésuites de l'ancienne mis-*

sion de Chine, 1552–1773, 2 v. (Shanghai 1932–34). A. VÄTH, *Johann Adam Schall von Bell* (Cologne 1933). R. ATTWATER, *Adam Schall: A Jesuit at the Court of China, 1592–1666* (New York 1963). *Archivum Societatis Iesu* (The Jesuit archives in Rome contain a great deal of unpub. material).

[G. H. DUNNE]

SCHANZ, PAUL

Theologian; b. Horb, Germany, March 4, 1841; d. Tübingen, June 1, 1905. He studied philosophy and theology at the University of Tübingen (1861–65). In 1866 he was ordained and became a doctor of philosophy. He was professor of mathematics and natural sciences in Rottweil in 1872, and in 1876 he was professor of the exegesis of the New Testament in Tübingen. In 1883 he succeeded his teacher, J. KUHN, as professor of dogma and apologetics. Schanz's commentary on the fourth Gospel (1879–85) is written in a philological and historical-critical method. He does not penetrate the theological and dogmatic content of Holy Scripture. His apologetics and dogmatics are determined by the positivism of exegesis and the history of dogma. The proof of each dogma is brought from Scripture and tradition, and its historical development is shown. His sacramentology (1893), too, follows this method. Numerous essays in the *Theologische Quartalschrift* are devoted to sacramentology. In his life he demonstrated an independence of understanding and judgment and a reserve in giving his views that sprang from his irenic nature. His chief works were *Die Lehre von den heiligen Sakramenten der katholischen Kirche* (Freiburg 1893) and the three-volume *Apologie des Christentums* (Freiburg 1887–88).

Bibliography: W. KOCH, *Lexikon für Theologie und Kirche,* ed. M. BUCHBERGER, 10 v. (Freiburg 1930–38) 9:218–219. H. HURTER, *Nomenclator literarius theologiae catholicae,* 5 v. in 6 (3d ed. Innsbruck 1903–1913); v.1 (4th ed. 1926) 5.2:1896–97.

[J. R. GEISELMANN]

SCHARPER, PHILIP J.

Editor, author, educator, lecturer, ecumenist; b. Baltimore, Md., Sept. 15, 1919; d. North Tarrytown, N.Y., May 5, 1985. For almost 11 years (1937–48) he was a member of the Maryland Province of the Society of Jesus, during which time he received a B.A. (1943), Ph.L. (1944), and M.A. in education (1945) from Georgetown University, and an M.A. in English (1947) from Fordham University. Subsequently he was assistant professor of English at Xavier University, Cincinnati (1948–50) and Fordham (1951–55).

From 1955–57 he was associate editor of *COMMONWEAL,* and from 1957–70 editor-in-chief of Sheed and Ward, Inc., New York, where he introduced North Americans to the writings of such prominent theologians as Karl RAHNER, Hans Küng, Edward Schillebeeckx, John Courtney MURRAY, and Robert McAfee Brown. During this period, he was the first Catholic president and chairman of the board of the Religious Education Association of the U.S. and Canada. In 1964, he was a special consultant to the commission of the Second Vatican Council responsible for drafting Schema XIII which was later incorporated into *Gaudium et spes,* the Pastoral Constitution on the Church in the modern world. He served in a similar capacity in 1967 for the Vatican Secretariat for Promoting Christian Unity. As national Catholic co-chairman for Clergy and Laity Concerned about Vietnam, he helped persuade Dr. Martin Luther King, Jr., to publicly oppose U.S. involvement in Vietnam.

In 1970 Scharper was invited by the MARYKNOLL FATHERS to be the founding editor of ORBIS BOOKS. Under his leadership, Orbis brought LIBERATION THEOLOGY and the spiritual experience of the Third World to the attention of the First World. Among the authors he introduced are Gustavo Gutiérrez, Leonardo Boff, and Juan Luis Segundo.

Married in 1949, he and his wife, Sarah Jane Moormann, had six children. Together they wrote over 30 television scripts for religious programming, for which they received over 20 awards, including two Emmys. In addition to numerous articles, he wrote *Meet the American Catholic* (1968) and edited and contributed to 16 books.

He was recognized internationally as a compassionate, courtly, and articulate advocate of a more just and humane world.

Bibliography: P. SCHARPER, ed., *American Catholics: A Protestant-Jewish View* (New York 1959); *Torah and Gospel: Jewish and Catholic Theology in Dialogue* (New York 1966). P. and S. SCHARPER, eds., *The Gospel in Art by the Peasants of Solentiname* (Maryknoll, N.Y. 1984). M. GLAZIER, ed., *Where We Are: American Catholics in the 1980s—A Celebration for Philip Scharper* (Wilmington, Del. 1985).

[S. B. SCHARPER]

SCHATZGEYER, KASPAR

Franciscan friar and opponent of Lutheranism in Bavaria; b. Landshut, 1463 or 1464; d. Munich, Sept. 18, 1527. Schatzgeyer (or Sasgerus) studied at Inglostadt in 1480, and after entering the Franciscan order, he lectured in theology from 1487 to 1513. He was then appointed guardian of Inglostadt, Munich, and Nuremberg. In 1517 he wrote the *Status de observantia,* advocating a compromise course in the disputes raised by the French Franciscan provincial, Boniface à Ceva, over the interpretation of the Rule of St. Francis. In that year Schatzgeyer became provincial of the Strassburg province, and began his preaching and polemical writings against Andreas OSIANDER, Johann von STAUPITZ, and Johann von Schwarzenberg. He wrote more than 23 books on grace, the Mass, the Sacraments, and monasticism, which won praise from Luther's foremost opponent, Johann ECK, and which were published by Eck in Inglostadt in 1543.

Bibliography: N. PAULUS, *Kaspar Schatzgeyer: Ein Vorkämpfer der katholischen Kirche gegen Luther in Süddeutschland* (St. Louis 1898). H. HURTER, *Nomenclator literarius theologie catholicae,* 5 vol. (3rd ed. Innsbruck 1903–13) 2:1253–54. E. ISERLOH, *Lexikon für Theologie und Kirche,* ed. J. HOFER and K. RAHNER, 10 vol. (2nd ed. Freiberg 1957–65) 9:371–372.

[E. D. MCSHANE]

SCHÄZLER, KONSTANTIN VON

Theologian; b. Regensburg, Germany, May 7, 1827; d. Interlaken, Switzerland, Sept. 19, 1880. He studied law at Munich and Heidelberg, and after serving as an officer in the Bavarian army took his doctorate in law at Erlangen and entered practice. He became a convert in 1850 and entered the Society of Jesus in 1851, while studying theology at Louvain. After his ordination in 1856, he left the Jesuits and took a doctorate in theology at Munich in 1859. While a tutor at the Osnabrück seminary in 1861, he entered the Dominican novitiate but did not make profession. From 1862 until 1873 he taught the history of dogma at Freiburg im Breisgau; in 1866 he was appointed archiepiscopal councilor. During Vatican Council I he was Bp. J. Fessler's theologian. He took up residence in Rome in 1873 and was made a domestic prelate in 1874. Until he reentered the Jesuits in 1878, he served as a consultor to numerous Roman Congregations.

He was a rigidly Thomistic theologian and made a significant contribution to the neoscholastic movement of the 19th century. His writing was devoted to exposing the doctrine of St. Thomas Aquinas and to defending it in controversy especially with J. KUHN of Tübingen. While his works are not of great value at the present time, his presentation of Thomistic teaching concerning grace, the supernatural, and the Sacraments was competent and served a good purpose in his day. That his understanding of the spirit and thought of St. Thomas was not as deep as it might have been is evidenced by his unsuccessful attempt to oppose it to the liberalism of his time in a work entitled, *Divus Thomas Doctor angelicus contra Liberalismum invictus veritatis catholicae assertor* (Rome 1874). His doctoral dissertation was entitled *Die Lehre von der Wirksamkeit der Sakramente ex opere operato in ihrer Entwicklung innerhalb der Scholastik und ihrer Bedeutung für die christliche Heilslehre dargestellt* (Munich 1860).

Bibliography: *Nomenclator literarius theologiae catholicae* 5.2:1505–06. J. F. KNÖPFLER, *Allgemeine deutsche Biographie* 30:649–651. G. M. HÄFELE, "Constantin von Schäzler: Zu seinem hundertsten Geburtstag," *Divus Thomas* 5 (1927) 411–448. J. P. GRAUSEM, *Dictionnaire de théologie catholique* 14.1:1270.

[A. ROCK]

SCHEEBEN, MATTHIAS JOSEPH

Theologian; b. Meckenheim (near Bonn) March 1, 1835; d. Cologne, July 21, 1888. Having studied at the Gregorian University in Rome (1852–59), he was ordained on Dec. 18, 1858. He first served as director and teacher for the Ursulines in Münstereifel. From 1860 to 1888 he taught theology in the seminary at Cologne. Scheeben's great contribution was in speculative theology. He was influenced by Cardinal N. P. WISEMAN's methodology, and demonstrated exceptional mastery of the Fathers (especially the Greeks), the scholastics, and his own contemporaries. Moreover, anticipating by 100 years the concept of theology for the laity, he aimed at an audience beyond the trained theologian. He cherished the deep conviction that speculative theology is of supreme importance for the truest and highest formation of mind and heart.

Scheeben's works are the means and measure of his success. His first article, "Die Lehre von dem Übernatürlichen" [*Der Katholik* 3 (1860) 280–299; 4 (1860) 657–674], was a daring attempt to establish a new methodology for teaching theology. *Natur und Gnade* (Mainz 1861) was his first speculative work. A series of articles in *Der Katholik* [5 (1861) 257–283, 567–591; 6 (1861) 65–90, 257–281; 7 (1862) 41–75, 528–549; 8 (1862) 276–298, 513–540, 641–674] prepared Scheeben for the greatest work of his earlier period, *Die Mysterien des Christentums* (Freiburg 1865). *Die Herrlichkeiten der göttlichen Gnade* (Freiburg 1863) was directed toward a lay audience. His devotional works include a Marian anthology, short lives of contemporary saints, popular articles, and a prayerbook.

Scheeben defended (1870–82) papal infallibility against J. J. I. DÖLLINGER's (d. 1890) attacks. His last great work was the *Handbuch der katholischen Dogmatik,* (3 v., Freiburg 1873–82). By June of 1888 Scheeben had almost completed a new edition of *Die Mysterien des Christentums,* but he died before it was finished. His notes for the new edition were used inadequately or not at all until Josef Höfer's 1941 edition scrupulously reproduced all Scheeben's revisions. C. Vollert faithfully translated this 1941 edition into English as *The Mysteries of Christianity* (St. Louis 1951). This second edition represents the work of Scheeben's best scholarship and the apogee of his theological development.

Bibliography: J. HÖFER, *Lexikon für Theologie und Kirche,* ed. J. HOFER and K. RAHNER, 10 v. (2d, new ed. Freiburg 1957–65) 9:376–379. G. FRITZ, *Dictionnaire de théologie catholique,* ed. A. VACANT et al., 15 v. (Paris 1903–50; Tables Générales 1951–) 14.1:1270–74. E. HOCEDEZ, *Histoire de la théologie au XIXᵉ siècle,* 3 v. (Brussels-Paris 1947) 3:377–384.

[C. M. AHERNE]

SCHELER, MAX

Philosopher, early proponent of PHENOMENOLOGY; b. Munich, Aug. 22, 1874; d. Frankfurt am Main, May 19, 1928. Scheler's father was Protestant, his mother Jewish. At age 14 he was baptized into the Catholic Church, but there was little direct religious influence upon his formative years. He studied in turn at the universities of Munich, Berlin, Heidelberg, and Jena. At the university in Berlin he was influenced by W. DILTHEY in the history of philosophy and the philosophy of vitalism, by Carl Stumpf in descriptive psychology, and by Georg Simmel (1858–1918) in the study of social forms. At Jena, Scheler studied Kant under Otto Liebmann (1840–1912), and there he met his most influential teacher, Rudolf Eucken (1846–1926). Eucken introduced Scheler to St. Augustine and Pascal and to "the philosophy of the spirit."

Teaching. Scheler's Jena dissertation of 1897, published in 1899, upheld the thesis that logic and ethics were irreducible to each other. Also in 1889 he submitted as his *Habilitationsschrift* the work entitled *Die transzendentale und die psychologische Methode,* in which he attempted to move away from Kant and psychology to a "study of spirit." Then, in 1901, he met Edmund HUSSERL for the first time at Halle. They immediately formed a close and fruitful intellectual bond. Upon returning to the University of Munich in 1907, Scheler joined the so-called Munich Circle of phenomenologists; later, forced to leave Munich, he went to Göttingen to be near Husserl and the members of Göttingen Circle. While in Göttingen, Scheler delivered occasional lectures on problems of ethics and began a number of independent phenomenological investigations (published posthumously in 1933) on death, shame, freedom, the idea of God, and epistemology.

At this time Husserl and Scheler worked together in founding and editing the *Jahrbuch für Philosophie und phänomenologische Forschung.* Volume 1, part 2, of the Jahrbuch was Scheler's major work, *Der Formalismus in der Ethik und die materiale Wertethik* (1913–16). This is both a summa of much of Scheler's thought and a concrete application of his method of phenomenology to discredit the formalistic ethics of Kant, to describe the given hierarchical scale of values, and to define and describe the ethical meaning of person.

During World War I Scheler served in the German Foreign Office and published a series of books on the war experience. In 1916 he was received back into the Church and for the next six years, his "Catholic period," his writings strongly reflected his Catholic faith. *Vom Ewigen im Menschen* (Leipzig 1921), the fruit and climax of his Catholic years, was his major work in the philosophy of religion.

In 1919 Scheler accepted the chair of philosophy and sociology at the University of Cologne, where he remained until 1928. By 1922 he began to give public evidence of a rather radical shift in metaphysics that led to a public repudiation of his Catholic faith. His final detailed statement in sociology, as well as his influential theories on the sociology of knowledge, appeared in *Die Wissensformen und die Gesellschaft* (Leipzig 1926). *Die Stellung des Menschen im Kosmos* (Darmstadt 1928) was Scheler's last exposition of his philosophical anthropology and his later views on the incomplete, evolving deity being realized in the spiritual acts of man. Five of his last short works were gathered together in *Philosophische Weltanschauung* (Bonn 1929). In the spring of 1928, he accepted a position at the University of Frankfurt am Main, where he died suddenly of a coronary stroke at the age of 54.

Critique. The personality of Scheler has usually been interjected into his thought. Though his thought is vigorous, rich, and seminal, it is described as unsystematic, changing, and contradictory—as fits his personality. However, there are strong lines of unity and inner consistency in Scheler's spirit and method of phenomenological philosophy as applied to man and metaphysics. For Scheler, the attributes of being itself are the metaphysical principles of life *(Drang)* and spirit *(Geist).* These principles come to climactic tensions in man, to the extreme degree that man becomes the very locus for the actual realization of God. Scheler's brand of phenomenology was in time publicly rejected by Husserl. Yet much of the early vitality of the phenomenological movement—in its studies of values, emotions, ethics, sociology, and religion—received its impetus from Max Scheler.

Bibliography: Works. *Gesammelte Werke,* ed. MARIA SCHELER (Bern 1954—); *The Nature of Sympathy,* tr. P. HEATH (New Haven 1954); *Ressentiment,* ed. L. A. COSER, tr. W. W. HOLDHEIM (New York 1961); *On the Eternal in Man,* tr. B. NOBLE (New York 1961); *Man's Place in Nature,* tr. H. MEYERHOFF (Boston 1961); *Philosophical Perspectives,* tr. O. A. HAAC (Boston 1958).

Literature. M. DUPUY, *La Philosophie de Max Scheler* (Paris 1959); *La Philosophie de la religion chez Max Scheler* (Paris 1959). J. HESSEN, *Max Scheler* (Essen 1948). Q. LAUER, *The Triumph of Subjectivity* (New York 1958). P. MULLER, *De la psychologie à l'anthropologie, à travers l'oeuvre de Max Scheler* (Neuchâtel 1946). H. SPIEGELBERG, *The Phenomenological Movement,* 2 v. (The Hague 1960).

[E. W. RANLY]

SCHELL, HERMANN

Theologian; b. Freiburg im Breisgau, Feb. 28, 1850; d. Würzburg, May 31, 1906. After ordination in 1873, he dedicated a few years to parochial work. From 1879 to 1881 he studied theology at Rome, and in 1884 began teaching apologetics and the history of Christian art at the University of Würzburg. He served as rector of the University from 1896 to 1897.

Schell left an immense amount of theological work: *Der Katholizismus als Prinzip des Fortschrittes* (Würzburg 1897); *Die neue Zeit und der alte Glaube* (Paderborn 1898); *Das Wirken des dreieinigen Gottes* (Mainz 1885); *Katholische Dogmatik* (4 v. Paderborn 1889–93); *Apologie des Christentums,* 1: *Religion und Offenbarung* (Mainz 1901), 2: *Jahwe und Christus* (Mainz 1905); *Christus, das Evangelium in seiner weltgeschichtlichen Bedeutung* (Mainz 1903); *Schells kleinere Schriften,* C. Hennemann, ed. (Paderborn 1908).

In these writings he sought to open Biblical revelation in a new way to his contemporaries conditioned by monism and the natural sciences. To this end, following the method of IMMANENCE APOLOGETICS, he first showed the force, light, life, and universality of the Christian faith; only afterward did he refute errors. His special concern was to analyze the faith as the salt of the earth and light of the world, and to overcome the inferiority complex of Catholics before modern culture. Although he decidedly used immanence apologetics to give new impulse and life to traditional apologetics, he avoided its extreme forms.

In the content of his theology he tried to present the faith in a new way that would be both intelligible to and formative of the times, while he respected the demands of tradition; in this he was influenced especially by O. Sengler and F. BRENTANO. He believed that a moderate actualism was in order. He sought a middle course between the Aristotelian-Thomistic metaphysics of being and the Scotistic metaphysics based on the will.

At the center of his theology stood an actualistic Trinitarian concept of God. Instead of following other theologians in calling God *ratio sui,* Schell characterized Him as *causa sui,* under the influence of G. W. F. HEGEL. Later he abandoned this misleading notion in favor of the expression "God's self-realization." He attributed a quasi-sacramental efficacy to man's suffering and death decreed by God. According to him, the only sin that merits hell is hatred of God.

Schell suffered greatly because of the estrangement between the Church and the world, and tried to show how modern culture and the Church could encounter each other. He believed that, although the Church possessed an immutable element, she nonetheless could, and had to, renew herself continually. He emphasized the fact that progress was not unreligious, and that the Church could allow herself to enter into dialogue with the times without betraying her nature.

It was precisely his teaching on the compatibility of Church and modern culture, together with his assertion that God is the cause of Himself and his explanation of hell, that led to his principal works being put on the Index (1898). In his letter of submission (March 1, 1899) and in later declarations he stressed his loyalty to the Church, and years later Piux XII acknowledged the integrity of his sentiments. Nevertheless, he had to endure a galling struggle with his theological opponents (E. Commer, O. Braun, and J. Stufler) who persecuted him with inconceivable reproaches and calumnies. Despite the dated character of his books, modern theologians recognize the theological significance of his work and draw from it valuable insights.

Bibliography: N. PALMARINI, A. MERCATI and A. PELZER, *Dizionario ecclesiastico,* 3 v. (Turin 1954–58) 3:741. J. HASENFUSS, *Herman Schell als existentieller Denker und Theologe* (Würzburg 1956). G. MARON, *Die Religion in Geschichte und Gegenwart,* 7 v. (3d ed. Tübingen 1957–65) 5:1395–96.

[M. SCHMAUS]

SCHELLING, FRIEDRICH WILHELM JOSEPH VON

German philosopher of the romantic school; b. Leonberg (Württemberg), Jan. 27, 1775; d. Ragaz, Switzerland, Aug. 20, 1854.

Life and Works. As a student at Tübingen his promise won him the patronage of the luminaries of the romantic movement, J. W. von GOETHE, J. G. FICHTE, Novalis (1772–1801), and F. SCHLEGEL. On Goethe's nomination he was made extraordinary professor at Jena. His earliest writings constitute a defense of Fichte, whose influence is apparent in Schelling's *Erster Entwurf eines Systems der Naturphilosophie* (Jena-Leipzig 1799).

The chief document from this phase of his thought quickly followed: *System des tranzendentalen Idealismus*

(Tübingen 1800). When accused of atheism, he left Jena for Würzburg, entering a new phase of philosophical activity inspired by an interest in B. SPINOZA. At Würzburg he produced two important works: *Darstellung meines Systems* (1801) and *Vorlesungen über die Methode des akademischen Studiums* (1803), the latter containing the most rigorous presentation of his doctrine of the Absolute as the undifferentiated unity of opposites—the concept whose derisive criticism in the *Phenomenology of Mind* caused his alienation from G. W. F. HEGEL. The influence of the mystic J. BÖHME initiated a third phase of his thought and inspired the last document of his early activity: *Philosophische Untersuchungen über das Wesen der menschlichen Freiheit* (Landshut 1809). He left teaching, and a long decline in his work followed. In 1841, at the suggestion of Schlegel, he was called to the chair at Berlin; there he delivered the lectures published posthumously as *Philosophie der Mythologie* and *Philosophie der Offenbarung.*

The romantic philosophers were divided, from the point of view of method, between the intuitive and the dialectical. Schelling adhered to the former, the essential note of which was the postulation of some immediacy at the basis of every speculative construction. In his case, the immediacy was that of the Absolute; for him, the constructive work of philosophy must proceed within the ambit of this intuition, which remains unmediated. (Hegel, by contrast, espoused the dialectical method of total mediation, in which all immediacies and presuppositions are resolved in the creation of a system of reason.) The development of Schelling's thought may conveniently be treated under three periods: the philosophy of nature and transcendental idealism, the philosophy of identity, and the philosophy of freedom and existence.

Nature and Transcendentalism. The philosophy of nature represents the fusion of the romantic sentiment of nature and Schelling's scientific interests. Its problem is to integrate the philosophy of the pure object with that of the pure subject, which had appeared opposed in the thought of Fichte. Schelling achieves this integration by suggesting that the absolute principle of the real is the absolute unity of subject and object. Nature, the objective pole, represents the unconscious product and action of this principle and deploys itself in three powers, the first of which appears in gravity; the second, in light, magnetism, and chemical processes; and the last, in organic life. In sensibility, the unity of the principle is revealed as spirit stirring in nature. The history of nature and the unconscious is succeeded by the history of self-consciousness in its three powers of knowledge, action, and aesthetic intuition.

The "System of Transcendental Idealism" takes up this theme at a more sophisticated level. The unity of the

Friedrich Wilhelm Joseph von Schelling.

principle of spirit and nature—subject and object, interiority and exteriority—and the processes by which these are first differentiated and then synthesized in the transcendental self, first stated dogmatically, are here subjected to direct analysis. The point of departure is a seeming contradiction between an objective world to which man's representations correspond and representations rising freely within man that effectively pass over into nature. Schelling suggests as a first resolution a preestablished harmony, and then seeks to account for this. An accounting can be made, in his view, only if the activity by which the objective world is produced is the same as that manifested in the interior movements of life: representation and will—unconscious in the former, but free and conscious in the latter. This unity of principle is the SELF. The demonstration embraces two aspects, the "how" of this production, and the "why" or logical necessity. It advances significantly by the discovery within consciousness of a moment, the aesthetic, in which conscious and unconscious interpenetrate. Art thus becomes the universal organon of philosophy in constructing the system of reason. On the pattern of aesthetic activity, philosophical analysis of the self reveals its passage—by the dialectic of finite and infinite, unlimited and act of limitation—to the positing of the Absolute, God. In God all differences are resolved in a fundamental unity that is not a vacuum but a plenum including all differences within itself.

Identity. The high point of Schelling's speculative achievement is the philosophy of identity. Taking its point of departure in the Absolute established by transcendental idealism, it proceeds in an opposite direction and seeks to establish the reason and the process by which the Absolute gives origin to the differentiated realms of spirit and nature. The philosophy of identity has been called the biography of God, in which is revealed the process and necessity of His generation of the world. Its first question—Why does the system of differences arise from the basic lack of differentiation in the Absolute—is answered by a principle already available in the philosophy of idealism: the infinite can establish its infinity in a self-conscious mode only by positing itself as its own opposite, as a limit. Since the Absolute is no vacuum of indifference, but rather an indifference that is compacted of all differences when brought to their unity of principle, it can be seen as Absolute only if such differences are explicated in relation to their synthesis. But the principle of difference is the other, the limit; hence the process of reality as a system of reason must be the self-limitation and differentiation of the Absolute. The "how" of this question is answered in the doctrine of powers; these are the paradigms on which the Absolute proceeds in its own self-realization through the dialectic of limitation and transcendence of limits. Since the Absolute is a plenum, the first of the powers is affirmation, in which it grasps itself as affirming, as the affirmed, and as their unity; to these correspond, in turn, the real, the ideal, and their unity; and to these, in turn, thought, action, and their unity. Finally, to these moments of the divine life correspond the ideas of the true, the good, and the beautiful. Philosophy is the pure mode of the self-conscious of the Absolute, consciousness that is pure unity in and through the total explication of all limits and differences.

Freedom and Existence. The life of the Absolute as so depicted is still abstract, removed from the concrete texture of existence as it is experienced in nature and in history. It remains to be shown how it is precisely in these existential processes that the great dialectical processes speculatively depicted transpire. This is the task that Schelling now undertakes. Man experiences life under two supreme rubrics that are inseparable: freedom and evil. Schelling spurns any mode of unification that relegates these wholly to the realm of the finite, for then the reconciliation at the level of the Absolute is an empty one; it is of such a unification that he accuses Hegel. Reconciliation can be effected only by showing that the struggle and burden of existence and of freedom and evil are aspects of the intimate life of the Absolute. The principle on which this is established is that the Absolute, to find realization as Absolute, must raise itself to the status of personal consciousness. This it does immanently in man, who in his personal existence, with its tensions, etc., thus constitutes a precise moment in the life of the Absolute, the moment in which the Absolute achieves concrete personal consciousness and existence. Therefore, in his experience of existence, of freedom and its perils, and of evil, man does not discover his alienation from the Absolute, but rather precisely the principle and the form of his unity with and in the Absolute. The term of this process of existence is transcendence: the emergence of God as personality. In this transcendence, the consciousness of man, wherein the struggle of freedom and evil takes place, is negated, only to be taken up in the order of revelation at a higher level. It is in revelation, the process that most clearly reveals the unity of man and the Absolute, that the tensions of freedom, the irrational, and evil are resolved. Reason and revelation are thus united according to the most exacting demands that are made by each.

See Also: IDEALISM; ROMANTICISM, PHILOSOPHICAL.

Bibliography: Works. *Sämmtliche Werke,* ed. K. F. A. SCHELLING, 14 v. (Stuttgart 1856–58); *The Ages of the World,* tr. F. DE W. BOLMAN (New York 1942); *Of Human Freedom,* tr. and ed. J. GUTMANN (Chicago 1936). Studies. W. WIELAND, *Schellings Lehre von der Zeit* (Heidelberg 1956). W. SCHULZ, *Die Vollendung des deutschen Idealismus* (Stuttgart 1955). H. FUHRMANS, *Schellings Philosophie der Weltalter* (Düsseldorf 1954). S. DRAGO DEL BOCA, *La filosofia di Schelling* (Florence 1933). R. GRAY-SMITH, *God in the Philosophy of Schelling* (Philadelphia 1933).

[A. R. CAPONIGRI]

SCHERER, MARIA THERESIA, BL.

Baptized Anna Maria Katharina; co-foundress of the Sisters of Mercy of the Holy Cross; b. Meggen (near Lucerne), Switzerland, October 31, 1825; d. Ingenbohl, Switzerland, June 16, 1888. Maria Theresia Scherer was seven years old when her father died, and she was placed in the care of two uncles who provided her with a Christian education. A conscientious child, she began working in hospitals at age sixteen.

Following a pilgrimage to Einsiedeln, she recognized her vocation and joined the Teaching Sisters of the Holy Cross, or Menzingen Sisters, an order founded in 1844 by Theodosius Florentini (1808–65). After teaching in three different parochial schools, and in an industrial school, she became superior of the congregation's first hospital (1852). Out of this institute developed the Sisters of Mercy of the Holy Cross, or Ingenbohl Sisters, founded in 1856 by Florentini to care for the poor, aged, and sick in their homes or in hospitals, and to train children who were mentally or physically handicapped. Maria Theresia, generally considered as cofoundress, was one of the first members. As the first superior general (1857–88), she was noted for her energy, sacrifice of self, and ability as organizer and administrator.

Despite many material difficulties, she established and directed houses in her native land, in Germanic and Austrian-Hungarian territories, and in Rome. Throughout the growth of the Ingenbohl Sisters, she retained her motto: ''No work of Christian love of neighbor may be considered beyond the scope of this institute.'' At the time of her death (1888) following a prolonged, painful illness, her order had become one of the largest religious congregations. She was beatified, October 29, 1995, by Pope John Paul II.

Feast: June 16.

Bibliography: V. GADIENT, *Die Dienerin Gottes, Mutter M. Theresia Scherer* (Basel 1954). W. HEIM, *Briefe zum Himmel. Die Grabbriefe an Mutter M. Theresia Scherer in Ingenbohl* (Basel 1961). E. MARTIRE, *Madre M. Teresa Scherer* (Rome 1947). C. RUT-ISHAUSER, *Mutter Maria Theresia Scherer: Leben und Werk* (Ingenbohl, Switz. 1959), Fr. tr. R. M. MERMOD (Paris 1964). M. G. SECCHI, *Suor Maria Teresa Scherer e i suoi tempi* (Milan 1959).

[A. KUNZ]

SCHERVIER, FRANZISKA, BL.

Foundress of the Franciscan Sisters of the Poor; b. Aachen, Germany, Jan. 3, 1819; d. there, Dec. 14, 1876. Franziska, daughter of Johann, a prominent businessman, and Marie (Migeon) Schervier, a Frenchwoman, was distinguished from her earliest years by concern for the poor and active charity. Drawn first to the contemplative life of the Trappistines, she served the poor as a laywoman and then founded, with four companions, a religious institute dedicated to caring for the poor and infirm (Oct. 3, 1845). The foundress and her young community were almost immediately tested during a cholera epidemic and later during the wars of 1866 and 1869–70, in which they rendered invaluable service nursing wounded soldiers. Such was the devotion of Franziska to the poor and afflicted that she was affectionately known as ''Mother Frances.'' By 1876 the congregation had grown under her direction to 31 foundations in Europe and ten in America. Franziska also gave encouragement and financial aid to Johannes Höver, founder of the Poor Brothers of St. Francis. Her cause was introduced in 1934, leading to her beatification by Paul VI on April 28, 1974.

Bibliography: E. HÖNINGS, A. FRINGS, and H.-G. SOQUAT, *Franziska Schervier, Mutter der Armen, 1819–1876* (Aachen 1992). I. JEILER, *Venerable Mother Frances Schervier,* tr. B. HAMMER (St. Louis 1895). E. KOCK, *Franziska Schervier: Zeugin e. dienenden Kirche* (Mainz 1976). T. MAYNARD, *Through My Gift: The Life of Frances Schervier* (New York 1951).

[M. V. SCHREINER]

SCHEYERN, ABBEY OF

Benedictine house in Bavaria, Germany. It was founded *c.* 1050 by hermits in Margaretenzell (today Bayrischzell) and after their death settled by monks from HIRSAU Abbey *c.* 1077 at the request of Haziga (d. 1103), widow of Count of the Palatinate Otto II yon Scheyern. It moved to Fischbachau before 1087, to Petersberg near Dachau before 1104, and *c.* 1119 to the family castle, Schyren, donated by Haziga's descendants who had built a castle at Wittelsbach, near Aichach. Scheyern continued as a burial place and family cloister for the Wittelsbachs until 1253. With the remains of Conrad III, last Count of Dachau (d. 1180 or 1183) and a Schyren descendant, there came to Scheyern a large relic of the Holy Cross, which the counts of Dachau had wrongfully obtained and brought home from the First Crusade and which numerous pilgrims still venerate. I. G. Herkomer of Augsburg made a famed monstrance for the cross (1738). Fischbachau, Petersberg, and Scheyern (which has been altered many times through the centuries) were all built in the style of Hirsau. The work of Scheyern's famous miniaturists (1200–1500), e.g., the *codex matutinalis,* went to the state library in Munich after the secularization of the abbey (1803). After the introduction of the MELK reform in 1452 (*Consuetudines Schyrenses*), Scheyern flourished in discipline, administration, and scholarship almost continuously until *c.* 1700, despite the THIRTY YEARS' WAR. Simon Fürbass (d. 1641), the canonist Ägidius Ranbeck (1608–92), and Gregor Kimpfler (abbot 1658–93) taught in Salzburg University. Under Kimpfler, Scheyern became a noted monastery in the Bavarian congregation founded in 1684 and, despite afflictions within and without in the 1700s, was healthy when secularized in 1803. In 1838 the Wittelsbach Louis I King of Bavaria (1825–48) restored the family cloister with Benedictines from METTEN. Since then, Scheyern has resumed its tradition of pastoral care, education, and scholarship. Prior Peter Lechner, with Boniface WIMMER of Metten, was active in the founding of ST. VINCENT ARCHABBEY in Pennsylvania (1847–51). Abbot Rupert III Metzenleitner and Baron Theodore von Cramer-Klett restored the monasteries of Ettal (1900, abbey 1907) and Plankstetten (1904, abbey 1917). Scheyern cares for widespread parishes and maintains a liberal arts school

The Benedictine Abbey of Scheyern.

(Gymnasium), a seminary, and a Byzantine institute founded in 1939 for research in Eastern theology.

Bibliography: L. H. COTTINEAU, *Répertoire topobibliographique des abbayes et prieurés,* 2 v. (Mâcon 1935–39) 2:2977–78. O. L. KAPSNER, *A Benedictine Bibliography: An Author-Subject Union List,* 2 v. (2d ed. Collegeville, MN 1962): v.1 author part; v.2, subject part; 2:277. S. KAINZ, *Lexikon für Theologie und Kirche,* ed. M. BUCHBERGER, 10 v. (Freiburg 1930–38)¹ 9:246–247. I. KREUZER, *Lexikon für Theologie und Kirche,* ed. J. HOFER and K. RAHNER, 10 v (2d, new ed. Freiburg 1957–65) 9.395; "Die Wiedererrichtung der Benediktinerabtei Scheyern," *Studien und Mitteilungen aus dem Benediktiner-und Zisterzienserorden* 71 (1960) 189–234; 72 (1961) 69–146.

[I. KREUZER]

SCHINER, MATTHÄUS

Bishop of Sion (Sitten), cardinal and papal legate, commander of Swiss forces fighting the French (1510–15); b. Mühlbach, Switzerland, between 1465 and 1470; d. Rome, Oct. 2, 1522. He studied classics and theology at Sion, Zurich, and Como, and was ordained in 1489. He supported Jorg auf der Fluh (Supersax) against Jost von Sillenen, Bishop of Sion, who favored French influence in the Canton of Valais. His uncle, Nicholas Schiner, became bishop of Sion in 1496 and Matthäus was given a parish and then made canon and dean of the cathedral. When his uncle resigned, Matthäus became bishop of Sion and suzerain lord of Valais (September 1499). He helped Ludovico SFORZA regain Milan in January 1500, but the Swiss there turned Sforza over to the French in April. The French in return ceded Bellinzona to the Swiss. Between 1503 and 1510 the Swiss were at peace with France. But Schiner, who may secretly have been made a cardinal in 1508, was in Rome between December 1509 and March 1510 and helped persuade the Swiss to join the Holy League. He was made bishop of Novara, and notice of his elevation to the cardinalate was given on March 10, 1511. When the French defeated the Holy League at Ravenna in April 1512, with Swiss troops Schiner advanced out of Verona, entered Cremona and Pavia, and in January 1512 received the surrender of Milan, which was turned over to Maximilian Sforza. In return Sforza ceded Locarno, Val Maggia, Mendrisio, and Lugano to the Swiss. In 1513 Schiner participated in the election of Leo X, after which he helped promote another alliance between the Pope and the Swiss. When the French tried to return to Lombardy, they were routed by the Swiss at Novara, June 6, 1513. Schiner continued to oppose the French, even after their victory at Marignano. He supported the election of Charles V in 1519 and in 1521 led a Swiss army in the Spanish conquest of Milan. In his zeal for reform he associated briefly with Zwingli, but he was a strong opponent of Luther at the Diet of Worms in 1521. He left a large and scattered correspondence.

Bibliography: A. BÜCHI, *Kardinal Matthäus Schiner* (Zurich 1923-). W. OECHSLI, *History of Switzerland, 1499–1914,* tr. E. and C. PAUL (Cambridge, Eng. 1922). E. MÜLLER, *Lexikon für Theologie und Kirche*[1] 9:252–253. B. MOELLER, *Die Religion in Geschichte und Gegenwart*[3] 5:1417.

[D. R. CAMPBELL]

SCHININA, MARIA OF THE SACRED HEART, BL.

Cofoundress of the Sisters of the Sacred Heart of Jesus; b. Apr. 10, 1844, Ragusa, Sicily, Italy; d. there June 11, 1910. Born into the nobility of Sicily, Maria received a good education and Christian upbringing from her parents. In 1860, Maria shocked her peers by recruiting several companions to work with her to relieve the suffering of prisoners of war and the peasantry tormented by the *Risorgimento*. With the approval of the bishop of Syracuse, Maria and five companions formed (1885) the Sisters of the Sacred Heart of Jesus to serve a variety of apostolates among orphaned girls, the elderly, the infirm, and prisoners. She also aided other religious institutes, such as the Ladies of Charity and the Carmelites, by providing a home when they were forced from their convents due to political unrest, financed seminaries, and sponsored educational programs. All in need received help from the Sacred Heart sisters.

According to the Pope John Paul II, Maria of the Sacred Heart responded to God's love by emphasizing "contemplation, adoration, and reparation" (beatification homily, Nov. 4, 1990).

Bibliography: *Acta Apostolicae Sedis* (1990): 1091.

[K. I. RABENSTEIN]

Matthäus Schiner.

SCHISM

St. Paul uses the term schism (σχίσμα, literally, a split, crack, or tear) metaphorically to designate the coteries and factions plaguing the Church at Corinth (1 Cor 1.10; 11.18; 12.25). These rival parties, arising from personality cults within the community (1 Cor 1.12), menaced the Church's unity but did not fracture it. Hence the Pauline use of schism, while providing the remote background for the later introduction of the term into the Christian vocabulary, does not yet bear a specifically Christian sense.

Fathers of the Church. Insofar as the Fathers distinguish schism from HERESY, schism means any sinful splitting off of a group from the Catholic Church without, however, manifest heterodoxy as yet worsening the division. Schism is a sinful breach of Church Communion, at once orthodox and collective. St. Isidore of Seville passed on to the Middle Ages this understanding of schism, which he in turn had quarried from St. Augustine. "For together with the same worship and rites schism has the same faith as the rest; what it delights in is simply the division of the congregation" (*Etymologiae* 8.3.5; *Patrologia Latina* 82:297). Isidore noted that the practical posture of schism is often a puritan or rigorist separatism, embraced to escape the contagion of the unclean. For this general view of schism, see Augustine, *Fid. et symb.* 10.21, *Corpus scriptorum ecclesiasticorum* 41:27; *C. Gaud.* 2.9.10, *Corpus scriptorum ecclesiasticorum* 53:267.

St. Jerome held that schism, begun as an orthodox breach of communion, is so unstable that it will, if continued, wind up in heresy. "There is no schism," he wrote, "which does not invent some heresy for itself in order to justify its departure from the Church" (*In Titum* 3.10–11; *Patrologia Latina* 26:598). Augustine shared Jerome's viewpoint; indeed, he would seemingly go farther than Jerome in this direction and reduce the difference between schism and heresy to a question of degree and not of kind. Arguing against the Donatist Cresconius, Augustine held that some kind of wrongheadedness or error is at the root of schism (*C. Cresc.* 2.7.9, *Corpus scriptorum ecclesiasticorum* 52:367). Donatists, so Augustine reasoned, split off from the Church because they interpreted the Scriptures wrongly, not entering into the true sense of the prophecies bearing on the nature of Christ's Church. This attitude, which sees error either at the root of schism, or else quickly supervening, may explain in part why the Fathers were often incurious about distinguishing schism and heresy.

To the Fathers the great malice of schism was the abandonment of the one Body of Christ in defiance of the one Spirit of Christ, with the setting up of a rival altar and a rival Eucharist, focusing another assembly of believers which could be only a counterfeit communion.

Scholastic Theology. St. Thomas Aquinas, treating schism from the viewpoint of a moralist, defined it as a gravely sinful act directly and essentially opposed "to the unity of ecclesiastical charity" (*Summa theologiae* 2a2ae, 39.1 ad 3), a charity that "unites the whole Church in the unity of the Spirit" (*ibid.* corp.). Schism by its nature aims at violating "the fraternal grace by which the members of the Church are united" (*Summa theologiae* 2a2aë, 14.2 ad 4). St. Thomas considered the unity of communion that schism outrages in two integrated factors: (1) the communion of the members, one with another, in the interdependence of common life and (2) the dependence of the members on the Head—i.e, Christ invisibly, and the hierarchy visibly and vicariously—as regulating the common life of the members (*Summa theologiae* 2a2ae, 39.1). St. Thomas also noted that schism tends to form a countercommunion, a church apart, challenging the unique role of the Catholic Church:"schismatics . . . wish to form by themselves a particular church" (*In 4 sent.* 13.2.1).

Cajetan, commenting on *Summa theologiae* 2a2ae, 39.1, emphasized that the Holy Spirit moves all members of the Body to "act as parts of the one whole" and to act "for the good of the one whole and in accord with the one whole." One becomes a schismatic in rebelliously flouting the precise union that the Holy Spirit brings into being by inspiring all the members to act in love as parts of the one Body. A schismatic who "refuses to act as a part of the Church" becomes a pseudo-whole, a "kind of a whole apart," over against the true whole that is the Catholic Church.

Schism is then a rebellious defiance of the brotherly love in the Christian community that the NT calls *philadelphia* (ἡ φιλαδελφία). The Eucharist, "the Sacrament of ecclesiastical unity" (St. Thomas, *Summa theologiae* 3a, 80.5 ad 2), is the sign-reality in which each member is fully made a part and fully acts as a part of the whole Body. The unity of communion in love, from which schism segregates itself, is in its central focus and reality a unity of Eucharistic Communion, hierarchically directed and dispensed.

The *Code of Canon Law* defines schism as "the refusal of submission to the Supreme Pontiff or of communion with the members of the Church subject to him" (*Codex iuris canonici* 751). In light of Vatican Council II, it is evident that the term is applied canonically only to those baptized or later received into the Catholic Church. It does not apply to persons born and baptized into communions that are separated from the Catholic Church (*Unitatis redintegratio* 3).

See Also: APOSTASY; BRANCH THEORY OF THE CHURCH; COMMUNION OF SAINTS; MYSTICAL BODY OF CHRIST; SOUL OF THE CHURCH; UNICITY OF THE CHURCH; UNITY OF FAITH; UNITY OF THE CHURCH.

Bibliography: Y. M. J. CONGAR, *Dictionnaire de théologie catholique,* ed. A. VACANT et al. (Paris 1903–50) 14.2:1286–1312. C. MAURER, in G. KITTEL, *Theoligisches Wörterbuch zum Neuen Testament* 7:959–965. M. MEINERTZ, "Σχίσμα und αἵρεσις im Neuen Testament," *Biblische Zeitschrift* 1 (1957) 114–118. S. L. GREENSLADE, *Schism in the Early Church* (New York 1953). J. DUPONT, "Le Schisme d'après Saint Paul," in L. BEAUDUIN, *L'Église et les églises, 1054–1954,* 2 v. (Chevetogne 1954–55) 1: 111–127. M. PONTET, "La Notion de schisme d'après Saint Augustin," *ibid.,* 1:163–180.

[F. X. LAWLOR/EDS.]

SCHLARMAN, JOSEPH HENRY

Archbishop; b. Breese Township, Ill., Feb. 23, 1879; d. Peoria, Ill., Nov. 10, 1951. He was the tenth child of Bernard Joseph and Philomena (Keyser) Schlarman of Clinton County, Illinois. He attended St. Francis Solanus College (now Quincy College), Quincy, Illinois; the University of Innsbruck, Austria; and the Gregorian University, Rome, where he earned doctorates in philosophy and canon law in 1907. He was ordained in the cathedral of Brixen in the Tyrol, June 29, 1904, for the diocese of Belleville, Illinois, and was named (1907) diocesan chancellor and assistant pastor of St. Peter's Cathedral. Later he became vicar-general in *matrimonialibus,* diocesan consultor, member of two curias, and, in September 1921, domestic prelate. On June 17, 1930, Schlarman was consecrated as bishop of Peoria. During his episcopate he established the Clergyman's Aid Society in his diocese, remodeled the cathedral, commissioned a diocesan edition of the *Register,* and developed the liturgical and catechetical apostolates. He prepared the constitution for the National Catholic Rural Life Conference (NCRLC), of which he was president from 1943 to 1945. He was a founder and director of the rural life institutes established at Montezuma Seminary, New Mexico, to assist in the training of Mexican seminarians. In addition to translating the ritual for rural blessings, Schlarman published a pamphlet, *Why Prisons?* (1938), based on his experience on the Illinois Commission for the Study of Prison Problems. He also wrote a pamphlet on mixed marriage, *Why Six Instructions?* (1938); a history of French-American exploration, *From Quebec to New Orleans* (1929); and *Mexico, a Land of Volcanoes* (1949). In 1950 he was given the NCRLC award for distinguished service and was named assistant at the pontifical throne by Pius XII. He was made archbishop *ad personam* in June 1951.

Bibliography: M. B. HELLRIEGEL, "He Loved the Church," *Worship* 26 (1952) 82–83. *American Catholic Historical Review* 37 (1952) 486.

[J. J. SWANER]

SCHLATTER, ADOLF

Swiss Protestant theologian; b. Saint Gall, Switzerland, Aug. 16, 1852; d. Tübingen, Germany, May 19, 1938. Although the son of a Baptist minister who was drawn to PIETISM, Schlatter belonged, like his mother, to the Swiss Reformed Church. After theological studies at Basel and Tübingen, he held pastoral charges at Zürich and Kasswill-Uttwill, where his colleagues were supporters of theological LIBERALISM and RATIONALISM. He first taught New Testament at Bern (1880) and later, systematic theology at Griefswald (1888). In 1893 he was awarded the chair of theology at Berlin, where he became the friend and collaborator of Adolf von HARNACK. He transferred to Tübingen in 1898 as professor of New Testament, but he incorporated much theology and ethics in his courses. Schlatter presented his theology as a middle way between the Christomonism of late 19th-century Protestantism, especially as exemplified in the thought of Albrecht RITSCHL, and what he understood to be the Hellenic Christianity of Catholicism. Much of his scholarship was devoted to studying Hebraic ways of thought as they influenced Christianity, but he ultimately espoused a syncretism that embraced as valid all forms of Christianity. His thought and writings were very influential in the early years of the ECUMENICAL MOVEMENT, and anticipated Barthianism.

Bibliography: H. SCHLIER, *Lexikon für Theologie und Kirche,* ed. J. HOFER and K. RAHNER, 10 v. (2d, new ed. Freiburg 1957–65) 9:410. U. LUCK, *Die Religion in Geschichte und Gegenwart,* 7 v. (3rd ed. Tübingen 1957–65) 6:1420–21.

[M. B. SCHEPERS]

SCHLATTER, MICHAEL

German Reformed minister; b. St. Gall, Switzerland, July 14, 1716; d. Chestnut Hill, PA, Oct. 31, 1790. He was educated in his native city and was ordained in Holland in 1745. In 1746 the Synods of North and South Holland sent him to Pennsylvania, where he visited German settlements and organized Reformed churches. In 1747, with the aid of John Philip BOEHM, he formed the Synod of Pennsylvania. Schlatter returned to Europe in 1750 to recruit ministers and raise money for the new congregations. From 1754 to 1756 he was general superintendent of schools for the Reformed Church in Pennsylvania. He served as chaplain of the 60th Royal American Regiment during the French and Indian War, but suffered for his attachment to the patriot cause in the American Revolution.

Bibliography: H. HARBAUGH, *The Life of Rev. Michael Schlatter* (Philadelphia 1857).

[R. K. MACMASTER]

SCHLEIERMACHER, FRIEDRICH DANIEL ERNST

Protestant theologian, philosopher, educator; b. Breslau, Nov. 21, 1768; d. Berlin, Feb. 12, 1834. Schleiermacher has been called the "father of modern theology" (i.e., of nineteenth- and early twentieth-century Protestant liberal theology). He came from a Moravian background. After attending a Moravian seminary for two years, he left the Moravians and studied theology at the University of Halle, where he made extensive studies of Plato, Spinoza, and Kant. After brief periods as tutor to the family of Count Dohna, as preacher at an orphanage in Berlin, and as pastor of a church in Landsberg, he became chaplain to those of the Reformed faith at the Charité Hospital, Berlin. Between 1796 and 1802, in Berlin, he was attracted to ROMANTICISM through a circle of friends that included Karl Schlegel. Under the stimulus of these associations, he published *Über die Religion* (1799, Eng. tr. *On Religion: Speeches to Its Cultured De-*

Friedrich Daniel Ernst Schleiermacher.

spisers, 1893, repr. 1958). In 1800 appeared *Monologen* (Eng. tr. *Soliloquies,* 1926). Following further brief engagements as court preacher in Stolpe and professor and chaplain in Halle, he returned to Berlin as pastor of Trinity church and took up his final post as head of the theological faculty in the new University of Berlin (1810–34). In addition to his chief theological work, *Die Christliche Glaube* (1821, 2d ed. 1830, Eng. tr. *The Christian Faith,* 1928, repr. 1963), he produced a German translation of Plato and works on exegesis, on philosophical and theological ethics, and on hermeneutics. The 30 volumes of his collected works include 10 volumes of sermons.

In Schleiermacher's thought, faith always issues in knowing (doctrine) and doing (ethical action), but it is first of all a kind of "feeling" or intuition, the "feeling (consciousness) of absolute dependence." He used this notion apologetically when he suggested to the "cultured despisers" of religion that when they rejected traditional dogmas, they were not necessarily rejecting the faith that lay behind the dogmas. To him religion, properly understood, was intrinsic to human nature, the highest expres-

sion of self-consciousness, which at its best is also God-consciousness. Although faith, in his view, belongs primarily to "immediate" self-consciousness, it is also linked with a second level, the "sensible" self-consciousness, the level on which the self is related to the world. "World" includes nature and society. Religion is thereby connected with culture and history. God is not "objectively presented" in immediate self-consciousness, but knowledge of Him is to be inferred from the contents of self-consciousness in conjunction with our experience of the world.

The disadvantage of Schleiermacher's view is that he spoke about God in terms of human experience; and this threatened to supplant revelation with a human norm. But God is the active source or ground of our religious responses; and Schleiermacher can be construed more positively as a historical thinker who understood that God reveals Himself in and through historical events or processes.

In *The Christian Faith,* Schleiermacher's thinking was more churchly and Christocentric than in his earlier works. In this book he held that piety always has a communal as well as an individual dimension, and that religious affections are always formed in particular ways within religious communities or churches. Christianity, he wrote, derives its distinctive pattern from its founder; it is "a monotheistic faith, belonging to the teleological (i.e., ethical) type, [in which] everything is related to the redemption accomplished by Jesus of Nazareth." Redemption is necessary because man is subject to sin, that is, he has an interrupted, unsteady God-consciousness. This is the result of man's becoming too much immersed in and too preoccupied with the world, the finite and sensory, so that his sense of the Infinite is obscured. Consequently man's life becomes fragmented and disoriented. Redemption is the reorienting of life in all its elements, individual and social, in proper relation to God. Christianity is unique and universally valid because it is the only religion to make redemption central. Christ is unique because He had a perfect, uninterrupted God-consciousness, and because He had no need of redemption Himself (which distinguishes Him from other founders of religions). Rather he was the initiator and mediator of man's redemption. We receive the effects of His life and work through participation in the life of the Spirit in the church, the redemptive community. Redemption means the fulfillment of true humanity as intended by God, and men are so constituted that no individual can be completely fulfilled until all are brought into harmonious and loving relationship with each other in the kingdom of God.

See Also: LIBERALISM, THEOLOGICAL.

Bibliography: *Sämtliche Werke*, 30 v. (Berlin 1835–64). W. DILTHEY, *Das Leben Schleiermachers*, 2d ed. H. MULERT (Berlin 1922). H. E. BRUNNER, *Die Mystik und das Wort* (2d ed. Tübingen 1928). R. B. BRANDT, *The Philosophy of Schleiermacher* (New York 1941). F. FLÜCKIGER, *Philosophie and Theologie bei Schleiermacher* (Zollikon-Zurich 1947). K. BARTH, *Protestant Thought from Rousseau to Ritschl*, tr. B. COZENS (New York 1959). P. H. JØRGENSEN, *Die Ethik Schleiermachers* (Munich 1959). R. R. NIEBUHR, *Schleiermacher on Christ and Religion* (New York 1964). W. A. JOHNSON, *On Religion: A Study of Theological Method in Schleiermacher and Nygren* (Leiden 1964). L. CRISTIANI, *Dictionnaire de théologie catholique*, 15 v. (Paris 1903–50) 14.1:1495–1508. F. L. CROSS, *The Oxford Dictionary of the Christian Church* (London 1957) 1223–1224. H. G. FRITZSCHE, *Evangelisches Kirchenlexicon: Kirchlich-theologisches Handwörterbuch*, 4 v. (Göttingen 1956–61) 3:801–805. P. HERMANN and E. WENIGER, *Die Religion in Geschichte und Gegenwart*, 7 v. (3d ed. Tübingen 1957–65) 5:1422–1436. P. MEINHOLD, *Lexikon für Theologie und Kirche*, 10 v. (2d new ed. Freiburg 1957–65) 9:413–416.

[W. E. WIEST]

SCHMALKALDIC LEAGUE

A military organization of German Protestants that originated in 1531 in reaction to CHARLES V's announced policy of suppressing the Lutheran movement by force. Named after the little town on the boundaries of Saxony and Hesse where its assemblies often took place, it was initiated by John of Saxony and Ernest of Brunswick. It included at its origin Philip of Hesse, Wolfgang von Anhalt, the Counts Gerhardt and Albert of Mansfeld, and representatives of 11 towns. It continued to expand and eventually included even the Catholic Dukes of Bavaria who joined it out of hostility to the Hapsburgs. Distracted by the menacing Turks, Charles signed a truce with the league, the Peace of Nuremberg (1532), which guaranteed peace until a general council could be held within a year. Charles's hopes for a council failed to materialize, however, and the Protestant movement continued to spread. When Pope PAUL III finally issued a bull summoning the council to meet at Mantua in May of 1537, the Schmalkaldic League rejected an invitation to attend. The emperor then attempted to solve the problem within the empire itself by conferences of Lutheran and Catholic theologians from 1539 to 1541 (*see* INTERIMS). As the differences proved irreconcilable, and as the Protestants refused to attend the opening of the Council at TRENT (1545), Charles decided again in favor of war. The position of the league had been weakened by Philip of Hesse's treaty with Charles, which broke off all alliances of the league with non-Germans. In addition, Charles made treaties with several German Protestant princes, including the powerful Maurice of Saxony and Joachim II of Brandenberg. Charles gained a decisive victory at Mühlberg on April 24, 1547, and captured John Frederick

of Saxony and Philip of Hesse. A theological settlement, however, was as remote as ever when Maurice of Saxony reopened the political question by rebelling. The Second Schmalkaldic War that ensued necessitated political recognition of the Protestants. Charles resigned in favor of his brother Ferdinand, who negotiated with the Protestants the Peace of AUGSBURG (1555).

Bibliography: ST. SKALWEIT, *Lexikon für Theologie und Kirche*, ed. J. HOFER and K. RAHNER, 10 v. (2d, new ed. Freiburg 1957–65); suppl., *Das Zweite Vatikanische Konzil: Dokumente und kommentare*, ed. H. S. BRECHTER et al., pt. 1 (1966) 9:426–427. W. MAURER, *Die Religion in Geschichte und Gegenwart*, 7 v. (3d ed. Tübingen 1957–65) 5:1455–56. H. HOLBORN, *A History of Modern Germany*, 3 v. (New York 1959–) v.1. *New Cambridge Modern History* (2d ed. London–New York 1957–) 2:162–183.

[T. S. BOKENKOTTER]

SCHMALZGRUEBER, FRANZ

Jesuit canonist; b. Griesbach, Oct. 9, 1663; d. Dillingen, Nov. 7, 1735; entered the Society of Jesus in 1679. Having obtained the doctorate in theology and Canon Law at Ingolstadt, he taught humanities, philosophy, and dogmatic theology at various universities. From 1703 to 1716, except for a two-year period when he was professor of moral theology, he taught Canon Law at Dillingen and Ingolstadt. Twice chancellor of the University of Dillingen, he spent two years in Rome as censor of books for the Jesuits and two years as prefect of studies at Munich. He was noted for his sound judgment and clearness in handling matters of ecclesiastical jurisprudence. On the occasion of the annual disputations from 1712 to 1718, he published a series of legal tracts, uniting these, in 1719, into his most famous work, the *Jus ecclesiasticum universum*. The work, utilizing the lecture notes taken in his class by his students, was summarized and published at Augsburg in 1747 as the *Succincta sacrorum canonum doctrina, seu compendium iuris ecclesiastici*. Very complete for its time, this work was held in high esteem by the Roman Curia and is still of great value. His other canonical writings include the *Judicium ecclesiasticum, Clerus saecularis et regularis, Sponsalia et Matrimonia, Crimen fori ecclesiastici*, and *Consilia seu responsa iuris*. All of these appeared at Augsburg between 1712 and 1722, ample proof of his position as one of the classic authors of the canonical renaissance of his day.

Bibliography: A. DELCHARD, *Dictionnaire de théologie catholique*, ed. A. VACANT, 15 v. (Paris 1903–50; Tables générales 1951–) 14.1:1509–10. C. SOMMERVOGEL, *Bibliotèque de la Compagnie de Jésus*, 11 v. (Brussels-Paris 1890–1932) 7:795–798.

[D. W. BONNER]

SCHMEMANN, ALEXANDER

Russian Orthodox theologian, *protopresbyter*, ecumenist, and defender of religious freedom; b. Revel, Estonia, Sept. 13, 1921; d. Yonkers, USA, Dec. 13, 1983. Son of a Russian émigré family with Baltic German ancestry on his paternal side, Schmemann moved to Paris at the age of seven. In France, he attended a Russian military school in Versailles, and transferred to the Lycée (high school). From 1940 to 1945, he studied at the St. Sergius Orthodox Theological Institute in Paris, completing a candidate's (MDiv) thesis on Byzantine theocracy. After graduating from St. Sergius, Schmemann taught there as an instructor in church history. In 1946 he was ordained to the priesthood.

In 1951, Schmemann emigrated to the United States with his wife, Juliana, and joined the faculty of St. Vladimir's Theological Seminary, where he taught liturgical theology. At St. Vladimir's Seminary, he collaborated closely with his colleague, George FLOROVSKY, who had directed the faculty since 1949.

In 1959 Schmemann obtained his doctorate from St. Sergius. In 1962, when St. Vladimir's Seminary moved to its present campus at Crestwood, N.Y., he assumed the post of dean, which he held until his death. In addition to teaching at St. Vladimir's, he held adjunct professorships at Columbia University, New York University, Union Theological Seminary, and General Theological Seminary in New York. From the latter he received an honorary of Doctor of Sacred Theology degree. He was similarly honored by Butler University, Lafayette College, Iona College, and Holy Cross Greek Orthodox School of Theology.

Schmemann's ecumenical involvement began in France, when he became vice-chairman of the Youth Department of the World Council of Churches (WCC). He served as an Orthodox observer for the Second Vatican Council of the Roman Catholic Church from 1962 to 1965. He also served as a member of the WCC's influential Commission on Faith and Order. In 1970, he played an important role in the establishment of the autocephalous ORTHODOX CHURCH IN AMERICA (OCA), which he believed would unify the various ethnic jurisdictions representing Eastern Orthodoxy in America. A supporter of Christian unity, he was also a fervent preacher for religious freedom. For 30 years He delivered sermons which were broadcast in Russian on "Radio Liberty" and which gained him a wide following across the former Soviet Union.

Schmemann wrote on a variety of subjects, but the Church itself was always the primary focus of his intellectual interests and commitments. Influenced by his teachers A. V. Kartashev, Cyprian Kern, and N. Afanassieff, he strove to bring the intellectual and cultural traditions of Russian emigrant theology to the New World. Although the "eucharistic ecclesiology" developed by Afanasieff provided the direction for Schmemann's further development as atheologian, his theological worldview, as distinguished by its "eucharistic" approach, was shaped during his Paris years under the influence of the Liturgical Movement. The seminal ideas of the key thinkers of the Liturgical Movement, notably Odo CASEL, Lambert BEAUDUIN, Jean DANIÉLOU, Louis BOUYER, Josef JUNGMANN, and Romano GUARDINI, contributed to shaping Schmemann's mind and propelling his quest for rediscovering the deeper meaning of the Paschal Mystery.

Schmemann's theology focused on the meaning of worship and the sacramental life of the Church by stressing the eschatological dimension of the Church and its Liturgy. He saw the Church as the mystery of the Kingdom and as its primary point of reference. The image of the Trinity as an embodiment of divine love is essential for a comprehensive understanding of Schmemann's teachings about the Eucharist. Christ, whose life is a sacrifice of love to God, is mysteriously present in the Eucharist through the priestly proclamation. By contrasting the Orthodox doctrine of the EPICLESIS from the Western doctrine of ANAMNESIS, he emphasized that the priestly word of the Church is transformed and sacramentally identified with the word of Christ. The Christ who is proclaimed and made present by the Eucharist is the Jesus who died, the resurrected Christ who yet lives as the Lord who will return in glory. Schmemann published numerous books and articles which enjoyed wide circulation. His principal area of interest was liturgical theology, although his first publication (1954) in the United States, which introduced his name as a scholar, was historical. Entitled *Historical Path of Eastern Orthodoxy*, this work originated in Paris under Kartashev's influence and offered thereader a general outline of the historical Orthodoxy. Other significant studies include *Sacraments and Orthodoxy* (1965, its revised and expanded edition, titled *For the Life of the World: Sacraments and Orthodoxy*, was republished in 1973 and 1982, and translated into eleven languages); *Ultimate Questions: An Anthology of Modern Russian Religious Thought* (1965); *Introduction to Liturgical Theology* (1966); *Of Water and The Spirit: A Liturgical Study of Baptism* (1974); *Church, World, Mission: Reflections on Orthodoxy in the West* (1979); *Eucharist: Sacrament of the Kingdom* (1988); *Liturgy and Tradition: Theological Reflections of Alexander Schmemann* (1990).

Bibliography: *The Journals of Father Alexander Schmemann, 1973–1983*, tr. J. SCHMEMANN, (Crestwood, New York

2000). J. MEYENDORFF, "A Life Worth Living." *St. Vladimir's Theological Quarterly* 28, no. 1, (1984) 3–10. P. SCORER, "Protopresbyter Alexander Schmemann," *Sobornost* 6, no. 2) 1984 (64–68.)

[M. YOUROUKOV]

SCHMID, CHRISTOPH VON

Educator and a leader in the modern reform of catechetical methods; b. Dinkelsbühl, Bavaria, Aug. 15, 1768; d. Augsburg, Sept. 3, 1854. After studying theology at Dillingen he was ordained in 1791 and served as assistant in several parishes until 1796, when he became the head of a large school in Thannhausen on the Mindel. During this time he also taught pedagogy and aesthetics at Dillingen, served as a school inspector for the district of Mindel, and generally played an important role in the reform of the Bavarian education system. He was pastor at Oberstadion in Württemberg from 1816 until 1826, when he was appointed a canon of the Augsburg cathedral. In 1841 he began to publish his scattered writings in an edition that, when completed, amounted to 24 volumes. A number of these works were eventually translated not only into most European languages, but also into such mid-Oriental and Oriental languages as Arabian, Turkish, Japanese, and Chinese.

Schmid had long recognized that the clergy in their sermons, instructions, and counsels had been gradually losing contact with the laity. From the beginning of his Thannhausen assignment, he began to apply the pedagogical ideas of J. M. SAILER by using fables, stories, and legends in the catechetical instruction of the children under his care. In his desire to free sacred history from the abstractions that made it difficult for children to grasp, he produced in 1801 the first Bible history as a simplified account of the history of salvation illustrated by sketches and paintings. He wrote in simple language and used examples that appealed to the minds and the hearts of the young. Although this Bible history, as well as the collections of fables, stories, and legends, may be of little use today, Schmid's position in the development of catechetics, and, more generally, of child education, is a very important one, acknowledged by Catholics and Protestants alike. For his own time, he helped to stem the spread of idealism in the German universities by providing a more or less completely rounded foundation for the development of faith among the persons who came under his influence; and his reassertion of the importance of fables, stories, and legends in the education of children was a noteworthy contribution to the improvement of catechetical methods.

Bibliography: R. ADAMSKI, *Lexikon für Theologie und Kirche*2 9:432–433. E. REINHARD, *Lexikon der Pädagogik* 4:15–16.

F. ECKERT, *Christoph von Schmid's Lebenserinnerungen,* 2 v. (Saarlouis 1920).

[F. C. LEHNER]

SCHMID, FRANZ

Theologian; b. Terenten, Oct. 5, 1844; d. Brixen (now Bressanone, Italian Tyrol), Sept. 18, 1922. From 1866 to 1873, he studied at the German College in Rome, where he heard the lectures of J. KLEUTGEN (d. 1883), J. FRANZELIN (d. 1886), and D. PALMIERI (d. 1909). He was ordained in 1872 at Rome, and then did pastoral work for six years at Stilfes (in the diocese of Brixen). He was spiritual director as well as professor of church history at the seminary in Brixen from 1879 to 1882, and professor of dogmatic theology from 1882 to 1908. In 1894 he was named a canon, and in 1905, domestic prelate. From 1908 to 1916, he was rector of the seminary; and from 1916 to 1918, vicar-general of the diocese. Besides his most famous work, *Die ausserordentlichen Heilswege für die gefallene Menschheit* (Brixen 1899), he contributed many others to the development of theology; the most important are *Quaestiones selectae ex theologia dogmatica* (Paderborn 1891), *Christus als Prophet* (Brixen 1892), *Die Wirksamkeit des Bittgebetes* (Brixen 1895), and *Die Sakramentalien der katholischen Kirche* (Brixen 1896). His favorite writers were St. Augustine, St. Thomas Aquinas, and Suárez. His works excel in clarity, discretion, faithfulness to the Church, and objective investigation of facts.

[J. BAUR]

SCHMIDLIN, JOSEPH

Missiologist; b. Klein-Landau (Alsace), March 29, 1876; d. Struthof bei Schirmeck (Breuschtal), Jan. 10, 1944. Shortly after Schmidlin was ordained, he turned to the study of history at the University of Freiburg where, in 1901, he took his degree. L. von Pastor invited Schmidlin to Rome to work with him for four years on his *History of the Popes.* In 1906 he became academic lecturer in the Catholic theological faculty at the University of Strasbourg. A year later he was called to Münster to be the university lecturer on medieval and modern Church history. There he became the father and founder of Catholic missiology. By 1910 he had already been appointed professor of mission science. Subsequently in 1911 he founded the *Zeitschrift für Missionswissenschaft.* Then in 1914 he became the first ordinary professor of missiology at Münster. Beginning in 1911 he was also the director of the scientific commission of the International Institute for Missiological Research. His *Einführung in die Missionswissenschaft* (2d ed. Münster 1925) appeared in 1917. This work was followed by *Katholische Missionslehre im Grundriss* (Catholic Mission Theory, tr. M. Braun, SVD, Techny 1931) in 1919 and *Katholische Missionsgeschichte* (Catholic Mission History, tr. M. Braun, SVD, Techny 1933) in 1925. All three works are basic and have lost none of their significance. Besides his scientific work, Schmidlin directed the extraordinarily fruitful and effective Catholic Mission Organization that he founded in Germany. A man of outstanding intelligence, brilliant creativity, and unbounded idealism, Schmidlin had all the qualities necessary to become the pioneer in the new field of missiology. His intense spirit led him, to be sure, into much discussion and even controversy both within and outside of the Catholic Church. The national socialist era led to his forced pensioning in 1934, soon to be followed by repeated arrests and imprisonments. Later he was interned in an asylum, and finally he suffered a violent death in the concentration camp at Struthof bei Schirmeck.

Bibliography: His autobiography in *Die Religionswissenschaft der Gegenwart in Selbstdarstellungen,* v. 3 (Leipzig. 1927) 167–191. K. MÜLLER, ''Joseph Schmidlin: Leben und Werk'' in *50 Jahre Katholische Missionswissenschaft in Münster, 1911–1961,* ed. J. GLAZIK (Münster 1961) 22–33.

[K. MÜLLER]

SCHMIDT, WILHELM

Anthropologist; b. Hoerde, Westphalia, Germany, Feb. 16, 1868; d. Fribourg, Switzerland, Feb. 10, 1954. Early in life Schmidt resolved to become himself a foreign missionary, and he joined the Society of the Divine Word, studying at the Gymnasium in Steyl, Holland, and at St. Gabriel Mission Seminary, Mödling, near Vienna. After ordination in 1892, he studied linguistics in Berlin and then taught languages and ethnology at St. Gabriel. There, in 1906, he founded the Anthropos-Institut and the journal *Anthropos,* which continues to give preference to manuscripts submitted by missionaries. In 1918 he was appointed professor of ethnology and the science of religion at the University of Vienna. Escaping arrest by the Nazi police in June of 1938, he received a friendly welcome in Switzerland and lectured at the University of Fribourg until shortly before his death.

Schmidt was a successful organizer. At the invitation of Pope Pius XI, he built up between 1924 and 1927 the Vatican mission exhibit, which became the Pontificio Museo Missionario-Ethnologico in the Lateran Palace. He was appointed the first director and continued as director *ad honorem* until his death. He organized several conferences, especially for missionaries to discuss the religion and ethics of non-Christian peoples, and was frequently in charge of congresses and meetings of ethnologists and linguists. His efforts brought about the founding of the Museum of Ethnology in Vienna.

Concerned that native cultures should be thoroughly and systematically studied, Schmidt organized several expeditions to Pygmy and pygmoid peoples; the natives of Tierra del Fuego; the African bushmen; the indigenous peoples of Brazil, India, Tibet, New Guinea, among other places. In linguistics, his first and greatest love, his major accomplishment was the discovery of the ''austric linguistic stock,'' which prevails over almost two-thirds of the earth's inhabited area. In 1952 he published a magnificent study of the long-dead languages of Tasmania. His monumental 12-volume *Ursprung der Gottesidee* (Münster 1912–54) was the most significant of his many works, a complete bibliography of which was published in *Anthropos* 49 (1954): 713–718.

Schmidt's contributions to ethnology and the study of primitive religion can be fully appreciated only when it is recalled that at the end of the nineteenth century, the ascendant evolutionary theory portrayed man and civilization as products of a unilinear, step-by-step rise from a primitive state. Developing the theories of F. Ratzel and F. Graebner, Schmidt formulated the ''culture-historical method'' in which ethnology was regarded as a branch of cultural history depicting the existence, growth, and activity of primitive peoples as fully human types. This school's search for archaic culture types and the classifications resulting therefrom never gained recognition among English-speaking anthropologists, but it had considerable influence on both field research and theory on the Continent, especially through the reports of missionaries published in *Anthropos.*

Bibliography: F. BORNEMANN, ''Verzeichnis der Schriften von P. W. Schmidt (1868–1954),'' *Anthropos* 49 (1954): 384–432. A. BURGMANN, ''P. W. Schmidt als Linguist,'' *ibid.* 627–658.

[M. GUSINDE]

SCHMUCKER, SAMUEL SIMON

Lutheran educator and pioneer advocate of church union; b. Hagerstown, Md., Feb. 28, 1799; d. Gettysburg, Penn., Aug. 26, 1873. He was the son of a Lutheran clergyman and was educated in the University of Pennsylvania, Philadelphia; and Princeton Theological Seminary, N.J.; as well as under private tutors. From 1820 to 1826 Schmucker was pastor of five small congregations in and near New Market, Va. Largely in response to his urging, the Lutheran Theological Seminary was established in

Gettysburg in 1826 and Gettysburg College, in 1832. He served as a professor and administrative head of the seminary from its founding to his retirement in 1864. At a time when Lutherans in America, chiefly cut off from sister churches in Europe, were floundering theologically and ecclesiastically, Schmucker gave them vigorous leadership. He provided them with an articulate, though deficient, theology in his *Elements of Popular Theology* (1834). He framed synodical and other constitutions, collaborated in the preparation of a hymnal and catechism, organized missionary societies, and wrote extensively for the church press on social and political questions of his day. By the middle of the 19th century the Lutheran Church, strengthened by large new immigrations from Germany and the Scandinavian countries, moved beyond Schmucker, criticized his LATITUDINARIANISM, and finally repudiated his leadership. He was remembered, however, not only for his organizational talent and his contributions to Lutheran institutions, but also for his tireless promotion of Church union. Notable in this respect was his *Fraternal Appeal to the American Churches, with a Plan for Catholic Union* (1838).

Bibliography: V. FERM, *The Crisis in American Lutheran Theology* (New York 1926). A. R. WENTZ, *History of the Gettysburg Theological Seminary* (Philadelphia 1927).

[T. G. TAPPERT]

SCHNEEMANN, GERHARD

Theologian; b. Wesel, Westphalia, Germany, Feb. 12, 1829; d. Kerkrade (Limburg), Netherlands, Nov. 20, 1885. At Bonn he studied law (1845–47) and theology (1847–49). He then entered the seminary in Münster, completed his studies in Rome (1850), joined the Jesuits (1851), and was ordained (1856). After pastoral work in Cologne, he taught philosophy in Aachen and Bonn (1860–62), and Church history and Canon Law at the Jesuit scholasticate of Maria Laach (1863–69). Released from teaching, he devoted himself thereafter to scholarly research. His first literary attempts were on apologetic subjects, including pamphlets against the presentation by DÖLLINGER of Pope HONORIUS I in the *Fables of the Popes* (1864) and in support of the SYLLABUS OF ERRORS (1865). These writings displayed the intellectual and historical orientation that made him an indefatigable defender of papal infallibility. Other writings of his, published anonymously, kept him in controversy during the KULTURKAMPF. He was a cofounder and, from 1879, editor of the Jesuit periodical *Stimmen aus Maria Laach,* which carried many of his own articles. Schneemann's main scholarly contribution was in the field of modern conciliar history. He inaugurated and edited the first six volumes

Arnold Schoenberg.

of the *Acta et decreta s. conciliorum recentiorum,* known as the *Collectio Lacensis,* 7 v., (1870–90), comprising mainly the provincial councils of the Church since 1682 (v. 7, containing documents on VATICAN COUNCIL I, was edited by Granderath). This monumental collection is an indispensable source work.

Bibliography: J. FÄH, *Stimmen aus Maria Laach* 30 (1886) 167–189. C. SOMMERVOGEL, *Bibliotèque de la Compagnie de Jésus,* 11 v. (Brussels-Paris 1890–1932) 7:822–826. *Allgemeine deutsche Biographie* 32:97–99. J. DE BLIC, *Dictionnaire de théologie catholique,* ed. A. VACANT, 15 v. (Paris 1903–50; Tables générales 1951–) 14.1:1513–16.

[V. CONZEMIUS]

SCHOENBERG, ARNOLD

A pivotal figure in the development of 20th-century music; b. Vienna, Sept. 13, 1874; d. Los Angeles, Calif., July 13, 1951. A long process of evolution (rather than revolution, as is sometimes claimed) led him from the intensely chromatic tonal language of postromanticism, through so-called atonality (a term of which he disapproved), to dodecaphony, or serialism. First fully formulated by him in 1923, this last system remained the structural basis for his most significant succeeding works, although he returned to tonality occasionally toward the end of his life. His profound influence on succeeding generations was immediately felt through his pupils Berg and WEBERN. Even Stravinsky, long antipodal to him in outlook and technique, eventually embraced his 12-tone procedures. It is often said, incorrectly, that Schoenberg was a convert to Catholicism. As an exile from impending Nazism he had, it is true, publicly reaffirmed his adherence to Judaism (in Paris 1933); but according to his widow, Gertrud Schoenberg, "he was never a Catholic by Baptism" (letter to the author, Feb. 24, 1964). In any case, as he was quoted in the *New York Times*, composing was for him primarily "a sharing of spiritual goods, resembling the religious experience," rather than a means of merely diverting an audience or expressing "himself and his own feelings,"

Bibliography: J. RUFER, *The Works of Arnold Schoenberg: A Catalogue of His Compositions, Writings and Paintings*, tr. D. NEWLIN (Glencoe, Ill. 1963). K. H. WÖRNER, *Schoenberg's 'Moses and Aaron'*, tr. P. HAMBURGER (New York 1963), complete libretto in Germ. and Eng. H. H. STUCKENSCHMIDT, *Arnold Schoenberg*, tr. E. T. ROBERTS and H. SEARLE (New York 1960); *Die Musik in Geschichte und Gegenwart*, ed. F. BLUME (Kassel-Basel 1949–) 12:18–26. P. YATES, "Arnold Schoenberg: Apostle of Atonality," *New York Times Magazine* (Sept. 11, 1949) 19:74–77. *Baker's Biographical Dictionary of Musicians*, ed. N. SLONIMSKY (5th, rev. ed. New York 1958) 1454–57. A. SCHOENBERG, *Letters*, ed. E. STEIN, tr. E. WILKINS and E. KAISER (New York 1965). M. BENSON, "Schoenberg's Private Program for the String Quartet in D Minor, Op. 7," *The Journal of Musicology* 11 (1993) 374–395. S. FEISST, "Arnold Schoenberg and the Cinematic Art," *The Musical Quarterly* 83 (1999) 93–113. P. GRADENWITZ, *Arnold Schönberg und seine Meisterschüler: Berlin 1925–1933* (Munich 1998). E. HAIMO, "Developing Variation and Schoenberg's Twelve-Note Music," *Music Analysis* 15 (1997) 349–65. T. L. JACKSON, "*Your Songs Proclaim God's Return:* Arnold Schoenberg, the Composer and His Jewish Faith," *International Journal of Musicology* 6 (1997) 281–317. R. S. PARKS, "A Viennese Arrangement of Debussy's *Prélude à l'après-midi d'un faune:* Orchestration and Musical Structure," *Music and Letters* 80 (1999) 50–53. M. C. STRASSER, "*A Survivor from Warsaw* as Personal Parable," *Music and Letters* 76 (1995) 52–63.

[F. J. BURKLEY]

SCHOLA CANTORUM

The introduction of the CHOIR into Christian religious music is related to the practice of antiphonal singing between a group of precentors and the congregation. In earliest times choirs were composed of boys, of young women, of lectors, of clerics, or of other groupings. A special type of choir is found in monastic communities. Their choir and congregation are one. After the 5th century there is testimony that monastic communities were entrusted with the Office (and ecclesiastical chant) in important churches (basilican monasteries). As the *cho-rus monachorum* or the *chorus clericorum* took over responsibility for chants formerly sung by the congregation, the need arose to establish within it, or in addition to it, a specialized group of singers; and it was suggested that in doing so they might make use of lectors and cantors and of boys preparing for the priesthood. That priests excelled from youth on *in divinis scripturis et cantilena* is learned from papal epitaphs of the 7th century.

The first documentary evidence of a separate group of singers in Rome is found in the *Vita* of Pope Sergius I (687–701) in the Liber pontificalis. It is said there that he came to Rome during the reign of Pope Adeodatus II (672–676) and was taken into the Roman clergy. "Studiosus erat et capaux in officio cantilenae, prior cantorum pro doctrina est traditus." In the Liber diurnus (end of the 7th century) there is mention of an *ordo cantorum,* which is probably the same institution that is later encountered under the designation *schola cantorum*. Its responsibility was to provide the music for papal Masses. Since the *schola cantorum* of the 9th century traced its founding to Pope St. Gregory the Great, it may well have been on of the products of his reorganization of the stational Mass (*see* STATIONAL CHURCH). Gregorian chant grew up in the Roman *schola cantorum* of the 7th and 8th centuries; the Gradual was referred to as "libellum musicae artis scolae cantorum." As the Roman liturgy and Gregorian chant spread in the West, *scholae cantorum* were established, according to the Roman model, at important churches. With the introduction of secular musicians into church music in the later Middle Ages, the *schola cantorum* fell into a decline. In the Renaissance it was incorporated into the *chorus musicorum.*

Bibliography: K. MEYER, *Der chorische Gesang der Frauen* (Leipzig 1917). J. QUASTEN, *Musik und Gesang in den Kulten der heidnischen Antike und christlichen Frühzeit* (Münster 1930). J. HANDSCHIN, *Musikgeschichte im Überblick* (Lucerne 1948). H. HUCKE, "Die Entwicklung des christlichen Kultgesangs zum Gregorianischen Gesang," *Römische Quartalschrift für christliche Altertumskunde und für Kirchengeschichte* 48 (1953) 147–194. "Zu einigen Problemen der Choralforschung," *Die Musikforschung* 11 (1958) 385–414. J. SMITS VAN WAESBERGHE, "Neues über die Schola cantorum zu Rom," *Internationaler Kongress für katholische Kirchenmusik*, v. 2 (Vienna 1954) 111–119. F. L. HARRISON, *Music in Medieval Britain* (New York 1958). S. CORBIN, *L'Église à la conquête de sa musique* (Paris 1960). S. J. P. VAN DIJK, "Papal Schola 'Versus' Charlemagne," *Organicae voces: Festschrift Joseph Smits van Waesberghe angeboten anlässlich seines 60. Geburtstag*, ed. P. Fischer (Amsterdam, 1963) 21–30. J. DYER, "The Schola Cantorum and its Roman Milieu in the Early Middle Ages," *De musica et cantu: Helmut Hucke zum 60. Geburtstag*, ed. P. CAHN and A.-K. HEIMER (Hildesheim 1993) 19–40.

[H. HUCKE/EDS.]

SCHOLASTIC METHOD

Derived literally from *methodus* (μέθοδος, manner or way) and *scholastica* (pertaining to the schools), the common method of teaching and learning in the schools of the Middle Ages after 1200 (*see* EDUCATION, SCHOLASTIC). From this method is derived the term SCHOLASTICISM, which is sometimes mistaken for a definite body of doctrines or a unique harmony of faith and reason. The scholastic method was essentially a rational investigation of every relevant problem in LIBERAL ARTS, PHILOSOPHY, THEOLOGY, medicine, and law, examined from opposing points of view, in order to reach an intelligent, scientific solution that would be consistent with accepted authorities, known facts, human reason, and Christian faith. Its ultimate goal was science (*scientia*), although frequently schoolmen had to be content with probable opinions and dialectical solutions (*see* DIALECTICS; DIALECTICS IN THE MIDDLE AGES). Its highest form, developed in the 13th century, was a positive contribution to education and research (*see* SCHOLASTICISM, 1). In the 16th century the medieval method assumed the form of theses, proofs, and answers to objections to meet catechetical and apologetic exigencies (*see* SCHOLASTICISM, 2). This modern scholastic method reached new prominence with the revival of THOMISM in the 19th century (*see* SCHOLASTICISM, 3).

Medieval Scholastic Method

Convinced that the best way to learn established truths was to duplicate the original process of discovery, schoolmen of the 12th and 13th century taught that the method of teaching (*modus docendi*) ought to follow the pattern of discovery (*modus inveniendi*). Therefore the order of instruction (*ordo doctrinae*) followed as closely as possible the order of discovery (*ordo inventionis*). This pedagogical conviction existed in early scholasticism prior to the introduction of the "new Aristotle" into the Latin West. From its earliest, obscure beginnings there were two essential features of scholastic method: exposition (*lectio*) and disputation (*disputatio*). Disputation was undoubtedly the more original and characteristic feature, but exposition was its foundation: *Lectio autem est quasi fundamentum et substratorium sequentium* (Peter Cantor, *Verbum abbreviatum,* 1; *Patrologia Latina,* ed. J. P. Migne, 205:25). Both features employed three essential methods of scientific knowledge (*modi sciendi*): DEFINITION, DIVISION, and REASONING. Gerbert, later Pope SYLVESTER II, had already emphasized the importance of definition and classification in his *De rationali et de ratione uti.* Employing Latin grammarians and Aristotelian logic preserved by BOETHIUS, and inspired by dialecticians of an earlier period, 12th-century masters in cathedral schools, such as Laon, Chartres, and Paris, gradually developed the basic elements of the scholastic method.

Exposition of the Text. The basis of all medieval teaching was the master's lecture (*lectio*), or commentary on the text accepted as an *auctoritas.* For theology the Bible alone was the official text to be expounded by the "master of the sacred page." In the liberal arts leading to theology and other advanced studies, Cicero was the "authority" in RHETORIC; Priscian and Donatus, in grammar; and Aristotle, in LOGIC; in the 13th century Aristotle's philosophical works were recognized texts in the "three philosophies." Collections of ecclesiastical law were the official text for the study of Canon Law. The schoolmen were convinced that students should learn from the great books of antiquity, difficult as they were to understand. The master's exposition was not simply an exegesis, but an intellectual grappling with real problems examined by the author. To understand a particular problem, words, ideas, and realities had to be clearly defined, distinguished, and examined from all sides. Recognition of a problem meant appreciation of all arguments *sic et non,* i.e., for and against, a specific question. Such questions could arise from the text, conflicting interpretations, doubtful solutions, or new insights; these gave rise to the disputation.

Disputation of a Question. The scholastic *quaestio disputata* seems to have arisen at Laon in the early 12th century from conflicting patristic interpretations of Scripture. Authorities *pro* and *contra* were disputed, noted in the margin of the text, and a tentative solution proposed. By the middle of the 12th century these occasional digressions became extremely numerous and elaborate. Collections of *sic* and *non* authorities were made not only in theology, but also in law, grammar, and logic. Doctors of canon and civil law collected conflicting legislation and interpretations of law for the purpose of establishing general principles and consistent solutions to problems. The well-known collection of *Sic et non* attributed to ABELARD and his school is merely one example of a growing interest in *quaestiones disputatae* in the schools.

With the evolution of the *quaestio* the disputation became a special feature in scholastic method, conducted at a distinct time of the academic day. Generally, the lecture on a text was given in the morning, and the disputation on some significant point was held in the afternoon as a kind of seminar. The question was posed by the master; a senior student, later called a bachelor, was appointed to respond to closely argued objections (*videtur quod non*) proposed by other students. In conclusion the master summarized the state of the question, methodically presented his own solution called a *determinatio,* and resolved major objections, usually reshaping the response of his bachelor.

The protocol of disputations in every discipline was formalized to ensure proper conduct; logic was the universal instrument of debate, but each discipline had its own principles, sources, and method. Originally the order of questions proposed followed the order of the text. The Bible, however, offered no order that could be called systematic. By the middle of the 12th century, theological questions were organized to conform with articles of the CREED. From this arose the SENTENCES AND *SUMMAE* of theology.

During the 13th century two types of disputation emerged, at least in the faculty of theology: the ordinary *quaestio disputata* and the *quodlibet.* Ordinary disputations, already highly systematic, sophisticated and subtle, were on a specific subject, such as *De potentia Dei, De veritate,* and *De virtutibus,* chosen by the master and divided into logically distinct points, with each point (*quaestio*) subdivided into a logically ordered series of scientific problems (*articuli*). Quodlibetal disputations, on the other hand, were conducted only by outstanding masters in theology during Advent and Lent on any question proposed by anyone present (*de quolibet ad voluntatem cuiuslibet*).

Influence of Aristotle. Aristotle's *Posterior Analytics,* dealing with scientific method, exercised an important and valuable influence on the scholastic method, once it was understood. Although it was translated from Arabic and Greek around the middle of the 12th century, its nuances and significance could not be appreciated until scholastics saw how Aristotle applied his scientific method in the real sciences. Basically this method consists in raising the right question at the right time and in the logical way of finding an answer. Scientific questions fall into four categories: does it exist (*an sit*), what is it (*quid sit*), does it have a given characteristic (*quia sit*), and why (*propter quid*). One of the first scholastics to appreciate fully the scientific method of Aristotle was ALBERT THE GREAT. Saint THOMAS AQUINAS applied this method in all of its subtlety in his *quaestiones disputatae.* Undoubtedly the most outstanding example of medieval scholastic method is the *Summa theologiae* of Aquinas.

Modern Scholastic Method

Humanist denunciations of the scholastic method were directed mainly against an extreme penchant for subtle questions, principally *de sophismatibus,* barbarous Latinity, and a disregard for sources, particularly the Bible. After the Reformation a new effort was made in ''second scholasticism'' to restore established doctrines and defend them against attack.

Rationalist Revisions. Modern manuals generally replaced ancient texts and the preliminary dialectic in disputation was eliminated. The new form of disputation started with a thesis to be defended, followed by an ex-

planation of terms, a list of contrary opinions, a proof of the thesis, and finally answers to opponents. This form of scholastic disputation, exemplified in 17th-century manuals, suited the needs of seminaries and resembled the deductive, geometric reasoning popularized by R. DESCARTES. In this methodology the *ordo inventionis* was recognized as distinct and preliminary to the order of doctrinal presentation, which was deductive and synthetic.

Descartes's *Discours de la méthode* exercised considerable influence on scholastic thinkers, who came to require recognition of first principles and deduction of necessary conclusions both in philosophy and in theology. Following their contemporaries, scholastic philosophers distinguished two types of method: analytic, which proceeds from effect or composite to elements and causes, and synthetic, which proceeds from causes and elements to effect or composite. Scholastic manuals invariably identified the analytic method with the *ordo inventionis* and the synthetic with the *ordo doctrinae* or *disciplinae.*

Neoscholastic View. With the revival of scholasticism in the 19th century scholastic method was thought to consist primarily in a synthetic and deductive explanation of all things. For D. MERCIER philosophy ''has for its object, not the discovery of any new objects of knowledge by way of analysis whether direct or indirect, but the synthetic explanation of the results already reached by analysis'' [*Ontologie* (Louvain 1903) 18]. Similarly, for M. DE WULF philosophy ''becomes the science par excellence, because it seeks a synthetic and deductive explanation of things'' [*Scholasticism Old and New* (Dublin 1907) 82]. In this view, investigation, dialectics, and analysis are considered inferior and foreign to scholastic philosophy.

Some neoscholastics, such as J. S. Hickey, praised scholastic method as the happy combination of analysis and synthesis; thus NEOSCHOLASTICISM differs from POSITIVISM, which neglects synthesis, and from IDEALISM, which neglects analysis [*Summula phil. schol.* (Dublin 1915) 1:128]. Neoscholastics commonly identified scholastic method with epistemological REALISM and discussed it as such in an appendix to logic. Some manualists, as S. TONGIORGI, E. HUGON, S. Reinstadler, J. GREDT, C. Boyer, and Hickey added another appendix on the correct form of the ''syllogistic'' or ''scholastic disputation.''

Neoscholastic identification of scholastic method either with deduction (synthesis), epistemological realism, or modern scholastic disputations has led to misunderstanding concerning the original significance of the term.

See Also: METHODOLOGY (PHILOSOPHY); ANALYSIS AND SYNTHESIS; SCHOLASTIC PHILOSOPHY.

Bibliography: J. A. WEISHEIPL, ''The Evolution of Scientific Method,'' *The Logic of Science,* ed. V. E. SMITH (New York 1964) 59–96; ''Curriculum of the Faculty of Arts at Oxford in the early 14th century,'' *Mediaeval Studies* (Toronto-London 1938–) 26 (1964) 143–85. S. CARAMELLA, *Enciclopedia filosofica,* 4 v. (Venice-Rome 1957) 3:565. M. GRABMANN, *Die Geschichte der scholastischen Methode,* 2 v. (Freiburg 1909–11). A. LANDGRAF, ''Zum Begriff der Scholastik,'' *Collectanea Franciscana* (Rome 1931–) 11 (1941) 487–90. M. D. CHENU, *Toward Understanding St. Thomas,* tr. A. M. LANDRY and D. HUGHES (Chicago 1964) 58–69, 77–99.

[J. A. WEISHEIPL]

SCHOLASTIC PHILOSOPHY

The system of philosophical thought traditionally taught within the Christian schools. This article treats of the notion of scholastic philosophy, various misconceptions concerning it, and the manuals and schools in which it is taught.

Notion. Scholastic philosophy is characterized by its emphasis on system. It is a synthesis that attempts to organize all the questions philosophy asks and to present the answers in a strictly logical format. This systematization most frequently uses the Aristotelian concept of SCIENCE (*scientia*) as its internal principle of organization. The scholastic philosopher attempts to explain things in terms of their causes with the aid of DEFINITION, DIVISION, and DEMONSTRATION.

The content of scholastic philosophy comprises several sciences: LOGIC, PHILOSOPHY OF NATURE (including PSYCHOLOGY), ETHICS, and METAPHYSICS (a part of which is natural THEOLOGY). It explains human knowledge by a system of moderate REALISM, teaching that outside the mind there exist real things possessing a common nature to which man's universal ideas correspond. All knowledge begins with sense data, but the intellectual knowledge developed from such data differs essentially from simple sense knowledge. This doctrine separates scholastic philosophy from most modern and contemporary philosophies.

Perhaps the most striking characteristic of scholastic philosophy is its method—basically the logic of ARISTOTLE as augmented and refined by later scholastic philosophers. The method, when abused, results in a rigid formalism, insisting upon the mechanics of science rather than on an intellectual grasp of reality. Properly used as a technique of organization for either teaching or research, scholastic method has often produced splendid results. (*See* SCHOLASTIC METHOD.)

Misconceptions. The popular misconceptions about scholastic philosophy have arisen out of its character as the philosophy of the Christian schools. In common usage ''scholastic philosophy'' connotes an arid verbalism, a closed system of thought perpetuated by rote memorization. Yet the technical vocabulary of scholastic philosophy is a necessary instrument of its precision. Behind this abstract terminology lies an intense effort to gain insight into the nature of reality by induction from the facts of experience. While the system is traditional, it is subject to constant criticism and reevaluation, and is open to new development in all directions.

Scholastic philosophy has been identified with medieval philosophy. This is warranted only in the sense that it reached maturity during the 13th century, when the great scholastic syntheses were achieved. But the philosophical origins of scholastic philosophy go back to Plato, Aristotle, the Neoplatonists, and St. Augustine, as well as to Arabian and Jewish thinkers. Scholastic philosophy has been continually developed since the Middle Ages, even within Protestant circles, though it has generally suffered from the isolation of Catholic thought since the Reformation. In fact, scholastic philosophy claims to represent the tradition of Western philosophy, preserving what is best in every age.

Confusion of scholastic philosophy and Catholic theology has resulted in the recurring criticism that scholastic philosophy uses AUTHORITY as its first criterion and is no more than a method for rationalizing predetermined conclusions dictated by ecclesiastical authority. Such is not the spirit, at least, of scholastic philosophy. Its basic commitment is to the facts of reality, objectively observed. Its attitude is that, in philosophy, reason must be convinced by EVIDENCE. This is expressed in St. Thomas Aquinas's famous dictum that, in philosophy, authority is the weakest of arguments.

Since the Reformation, scholastic philosophy has flourished mostly in Catholic seminaries, where emphasis has been on the philosophical notions necessary for scientific theology, giving a pragmatic cast to scholastic philosophy and obscuring its proper function of exploring the concrete realities of the universe. The tendency to separate scholastic philosophy clearly from theology, and to respect it as an autonomous discipline, is growing.

Manuals and Schools. Any system of philosophy taught in schools produces capsule formulations of its entire doctrine for the use of students. Such are the scholastic manuals, which have, like all manuals, the advantage of conciseness and the disadvantage that the student may study words and not realities. Intended to cover a vast amount of material economically, manuals condense the matter into little more than a logical outline. Moreover, if the authors use similar books as their sources, the result is a condensation of other condensations. For the student to acquire true philosophical insights from such an arid presentation requires a teacher of genius. Nonetheless, if readings in original source materials are introduced into the course in scholastic philosophy, manuals can provide a framework for the organization of the student's knowledge.

Various schools of thought have grown up within scholastic philosophy. Although these share many common doctrines and methods, they differ somewhat in content (*see* THOMISM; SCOTISM; SUAREZIANISM; AUGUSTINIANISM; OCKHAMISM). For the history of scholastic philosophy, see SCHOLASTICISM.

See Also: CHRISTIAN PHILOSOPHY.

Bibliography: Manuals. R. P. PHILLIPS, *Modern Thomistic Philosophy,* 2 v. (New York 1934–35). H. GRENIER, *Thomistic Philosophy,* tr. J. P. O'HANLEY, 3 v. (Charlottetown, Canada 1948–49). D. J. MERCIER, *A Manual of Modern Scholastic Philosophy,* tr. T. L. and S. A. PARKER, 2 v. (St. Louis 1928). Literature. J. COLLINS, "The Problem of the Philosophia Perennis," *Thought* 28 (1953–54) 571–597. J. F. ANDERSON, "Is Scholastic Philosophy Philosophical?" *Philosophy and Phenomenological Research* 10 (1949–50) 251–259; G. W. CUNNINGHAM'S reply, *ibid.* 260–261; remarks, 262. G. F. MCLEAN, ed., *Teaching Thomism Today* (Washington 1964). *American Catholic Philosophical Association. Proceedings of the Annual Meeting* 32 (1958); 30 (1956); 12 (1936).

[W. H. CRILLY]

SCHOLASTIC TERMS AND AXIOMS

Like other philosophical systems, SCHOLASTICISM has developed its own terminology. Some medieval scholastic expressions were simply Latin versions of Aristotle's dicta, e.g., *abstrahentium non est mendacium* and *propter quod unumquodque tale et illud magis.* Other axioms, such as *actiones sunt suppositorum,* came from the scholastics themselves. The majority of the resulting distinctions and principles stubbornly resist translation and have been left in their Latin original. However, since Latin has faded from the family of living languages, the need for translation and explanation is imperative if scholasticism is to exercise influence outside its rather limited circles.

In the following listing, terms and expressions have been grouped before axioms, and separate alphabetization has been used in each category.

Terms and Expressions

For the most part, the fundamental Aristotelian-Thomistic meanings are presented here. One must realize that even within scholasticism, many shades of meaning are attached to these terms. The present listing is neither extensive nor exhaustive, but is intended merely as a handy reference to the best known expressions.

Actu exercito (*obliquely, indirectly*), **actu signato** (*expressly, directly*). In general, something is done *actu signato* when it comes about through the direct, express intention of the one acting; on the other hand, when the agent only indirectly or obliquely intends the effect, then the result is said to be brought about *actu exercito.* This distinction has application in several diverse areas, and in each of these respective areas its meaning undergoes a different refinement. In logic, for example, it is used to clarify the way in which the human intellect forms a universal CONCEPT. The mind does not know "universality" as such and then attribute it to the concept that it has formed (*actu signato*); rather, it recognizes the concept as pertaining to many individuals, and thus becomes aware of its universality indirectly (*actu exercito*). In the moral order, a person is said to indicate his intention *actu signato* when he expressly manifests it in words, but *actu exercito* when he shows it equivalently by his deeds. This distinction thus underlies the popular adage, "Actions speak louder than words." (*See* ACT.)

Adequatio rei et intellectus (*the adequation of the thing and the intellect*). In this way does St. THOMAS AQUINAS define TRUTH, after giving definitions by Augustine, Hilary, and Anselm (cf. *Summa theologiae* 1a, 16.1). "When the mind is the rule or measure of things, truth consists in the equation of the thing to the mind just as the work of the artist is said to be true when it is in accordance with his art" (*Summa theologiae* 1a, 21.2). However, for the most part REALITY is the measure of the INTELLECT, and truth consists in the mind's apprehending things as they are. Yet "truth principally is in the intellect, secondarily in things, insofar as things are compared in the intellect as to a principle" (*Summa theologiae* 1a, 16.1; cf. Aristotle *Meta.* 1027b 18–29).

A posteriori (*from what comes afterward, from effect to cause*), **a priori** (*from what comes before, from cause to effect*). These terms are often used to indicate relations of cause and effect (*see* CAUSALITY). In scholastic logic, *a posteriori* would refer to the inductive process of immediate EXPERIENCE necessary for arriving at a universal proposition; this proposition, in turn, is used in a SYLLOGISM as an *a priori* premise to a new conclusion. Both processes take place in common knowledge. From the sight of smoke we conclude that there is a fire (*a posteriori*); knowing the quality of fire, we warn that it will burn one's hand (*a priori*). *See* INDUCTION; DEDUCTION.

De facto (*in fact*), **de iure** (*by right*). *De facto* expresses what the situation actually is; *de iure* indicates what it ought to be. A military clique rules the country *de facto,* although a civilian has been legally elected *de iure.*

Ens actu (*actual being, being in act*), **ens potentia** (*potential being, being in potency*). A monumental contribution to philosophy is the distinction between POTEN-CY and ACT introduced by Aristotle. Found throughout his works, the distinction is first made when he is analyzing the meaning of nature (*Phys.* 192b 10), and has undergone further development and refinement by the scholastics. Actual being refers to any BEING—whether substantial or accidental, natural or artificial—that is here and now exercising actuality, such as seeing by an eye, the living of a man, or the existence of a tree or a painting. Any kind of EXISTENCE can be included under actual being, including even that of logical beings, which exist only in the mind. Potential being refers to a real capacity on the part of any being to be something more, to do something, or to become something. The eye closed but healthy is in potency to see, the tree bare of leaves is in potency to blossom, the seed can become the flower, and propositions in the mind can be united to make a syllogism. St. Thomas puts the whole distinction briefly: ''Now a thing is said to be a being in two ways: first, simply, i.e., whatever is being in act; secondly, relatively, i.e., whatever is a being in potentiality'' (*Summa theologiae* 3a, 10.3). *See* POTENCY AND ACT.

Ens rationis (*being of reason*), **ens reale** (*real being*). ''Being is twofold, namely, being of reason and being of nature. A being of reason is properly called one of those intentions which the mind discovers in the things considered, such as the notion of genus, species, and the like which indeed are not found in reality but follow upon the consideration of the mind. Of this kind, namely, being of reason, is properly the subject of logic.'' (St. Thomas, *In 4 meta.* 4.574.) Real being is that which exists independently of the human mind, and is known as ontological being. Hence, all objective reality is embraced under real being. (*See* INTENTIONALITY.)

Formaliter (*formally, present according to the intrinsic form*), **virtualiter** (*virtually, present according to the intrinsic power*), **eminenter** (*eminently, present according to a more excellent mode*). These three terms indicate the different ways in which one thing is contained in another. A quality is formally in something if it is actually present in the very definition of the thing, e.g., reason is formally in man because we must refer to reason in order to define man. A quality is virtually in something if it can be produced by that thing, as every effect is virtually in its cause. A quality is eminently in another when contained in a more excellent way, as the human soul in man can do whatever vegetative and sensitive souls do in plants and animals, and more besides (*see* DISTINCTION, KINDS OF; SOUL, HUMAN).

In fieri (*becoming, in the process of being made*), **in facto esse** (*made, in real and complete existence*). These terms are used by Aristotle to help explain the reality of

change. Using an example from art, he writes: ''Take for instance the buildable as buildable. The actuality of the buildable as buildable is the process of building. For the actuality of the buildable must be either this or the house. But when there is a house, the buildable is no longer buildable'' (*Phys.* 201b 9–14). Whatever has not attained its end, terminus, or perfection but is moving towards it, whether in nature or in art, is described as BECOMING, or ''in the process of being made'' what it is meant to be. The goal of the becoming is the completed being. Once this goal is attained, then the thing is; it has reached its completion in its line of existence.

As used by Aristotle in his works on nature, these terms refer primarily to generation and growth. However, the terms have been adapted to many other aspects of philosophy; they appear also in theology, where philosophical principles are often used to facilitate doctrinal explanations. Thus St. Thomas applies the distinction when writing on the change in the Eucharist: ''In instantaneous changes a thing is in becoming (*in fieri*), and is in being (*factum esse*) simultaneously, just as becoming illuminated and to be actually illuminated are simultaneous. In such cases, a thing is said to be in being (*factum esse*) according as it now is; but to be in becoming (*in fieri*) according as it was not before'' (*Summa theologiae* 3a, 75.7 ad 2).

Medium quod (*the means which*), **medium quo** (*the means by which*), **medium a quo** (*the means from which*), **medium sub quo** (*the means under which*). These terms are employed to assist in understanding the theory of KNOWLEDGE. The so-called *medium quod* is not really a medium or means in the strict sense; it refers rather to the OBJECT itself that is to be seen or known. The remaining three terms indicate true means of knowing, as is evident from the following: ''In any seeing a threefold medium can be considered. One is the medium under which (*sub quo*) it is seen; another is that by which (*quo*) it is seen, which is the species of the thing seen; another, from which (*a quo*) the knowledge of the seen thing is taken. Thus, in bodily seeing the medium under which (*sub quo*) it is seen is the light by which something is made actually visible and the sight is perfected for seeing. The medium by which (*quo*) it is seen is the very species itself of the sensible thing existing in the eye which, as the form of the one seeing inasmuch as he is seeing, is the principle of visual operation. The medium from which (*a quo*) knowledge of the seen thing is taken is as a mirror from which, meanwhile, the species of any visible thing, as a stone, is made in the eye, not immediately from the stone itself'' (St. Thomas, *De ver,* 18.1 ad 1). *See* SPECIES, INTENTIONAL; CONCEPT.

Natura naturans and **natura naturata.** Neither term is translatable and neither had extensive use among scholastic philosophers. The following gives some idea of the distinction. *Natura naturans:* (1) is used to refer to God as the author, preserver, and ruler of nature; or (2) signifies nature taken universally as constituting the essence of particular things. *Natura naturata:* (1) is used to express the totality of created reality; or (2) indicates the universal nature particularized in the singular thing. [See H. A. Lucks, ''Natura Naturans—Natura Naturata,'' *The New Scholasticism* 9 (1935) 1–24.]

Numerus numerans (*number counting*), **numerus numeratus** (*number enumerated*). ''Number is said two-foldly. In one way, as that which actually is numbered or which can be numbered, as when we say ten men or ten horses. This is called a number enumerated because the number is applied to the things counted. In another way number is said as that by which we number, that is, the number itself taken strictly, as two, three, four'' (St. Thomas, *In 4 phys.* 17.11). The latter exists in the mind only, while the former is considered as existing outside the mind since it refers to the reality that is counted or numbered.

Obiectum formale (*formal object*), **obiectum materiale** (*material object*). The formal object is that definite, precise characteristic of a complex whole that engages a vital power, that is, the special, primary, immediate aspect considered or sought in a material or total object. Thus, for example, color is the formal object of sight.

The material object is the total object or the thing in all its reality, and not merely the particular feature falling under the action of a power, habit, or act. It is the general or common subject matter, rather than the specialized feature of study or the limited point of view under which the subject is attained. Thus, all colored physical things are the material object of sight. (*See* CONCEPT; KNOWLEDGE.)

Ordo intentionis (*the order of intention*), **ordo executionis** (*the order of execution or accomplishment*). Used conjointly, these terms refer to the final cause along with the means used for attaining an END. Before attempting to achieve an end, the mind ascertains whether the end is possible and attainable. Then the mind works on the means for obtaining the end, as a sculptor conceives the figure he intends to make and then gathers the material and instruments for making the product. The correlation of these two terms gives rise to the expression: What is first in intention is last in execution. Thus, the artist first conceives what he wishes to make, and this conception of the end product is prior to the operations that he performs to bring it into being; but in the order of reality the finished product is ultimate, the last thing achieved. In the moral order, the happy coordination between the

orders of intention and execution constitutes the virtue of prudence.

Per se (*through itself, directly, essentially*), **per accidens** (*through another, indirectly, accidentally*). These terms are used extensively in philosophy and theology. St. Thomas writes: ''Whatever are in another thing through themselves (*per se*) either are of its essence or follow upon essential principles. . . . Everything present to another thing accidentally (*per accidens*), since it is extraneous to its nature, must pertain to it from some exterior cause'' (*De pot.* 10.4). Such is the basic distinction, and its applications to CAUSALITY, natural and artificial objects, modes of composition, methods of speaking, etc., are almost without limit. A few illustrations will show the wide variety of ways in which the terms are employed. A room is illumined directly by the sun, and accidentally by the person who pulls up the shade so that the sun can shine in. The doctor cures as doctor (*per se*), and indirectly by reason of his race or religion. Rationality belongs to man essentially (*per se*); his nationality belongs to him accidentally. (*See* PREDICABLES.)

Pons asinorum (*asses' bridge*). Although of earlier origin, in philosophy this term was applied to the diagram that Peter Tartaretus constructed to assist the student of logic in the discovery of the middle term of a SYLLOGISM. The expression suggests that getting students of logic to find the middle term of a syllogism was as difficult as getting asses to cross a bridge.

Propter quid (*on account of which*), **quia** (*because, the fact that*). These terms refer to different types of logical DEMONSTRATION. When the proper cause is given for establishing a conclusion, the demonstration is termed *propter quid.* Thus, from the truth that man is a composite being, we can establish by a *propter quid* demonstration that he is also a mortal being. In such logical demonstrations, which proceed from proper and immediate causes, the predicate is a property of the subject and the middle term of the syllogism is a definition of the subject. When the proper cause is not known, an effect (or in some instances even a remote cause) is sought as a basis for establishing the validity of the conclusion. This is demonstration *quia,* or demonstration simply of the fact; the proofs for the existence of GOD are demonstrations of this sort. Demonstrations from the proper or remote causes are also known as *a priori,* while those demonstrations from effect to cause are *a posteriori.*

Quo est (*that by which a thing is; existence*), **Quod est** (*that which is; essence*). These terms have a wide variety of usage, and their full implications have been the subject of one of the most intense debates within scholasticism. The problem concerns the real distinction between ESSENCE and EXISTENCE. Essence refers to the thing that exists; hence it is "that which is." Existence is the act that places the essence in the realm of existing beings; thus, it is "that by which" the essence or thing exists. All scholastics admit some kind of distinction between essence and existence, and consequently recognize these terms as valid. There is much dispute, however, as to the kind of distinction. (*See* ESSENCE AND EXISTENCE; DISTINCTION, KINDS OF.)

Regressus in infinitum (*infinite regress*). This expression is especially canonized by reason of the first three proofs for the existence of God as set forth by St. Thomas (*see* GOD, PROOFS FOR THE EXISTENCE OF). An infinite regress refers to an endless series of causes in which no beginning is postulated. The infinite regress cannot explain the evident fact of motion, the order of efficient causes in sensible things, or the contingency in nature. An infinite regress would deny the real distinction between potency and act that is clearly involved in motion, efficient causality in the sensible order, and contingency. The infinite regress is impossible among things essentially related as cause and effect; in other words, the effects here and now realized are still essentially dependent upon a first mover, first efficient cause, and necessary being. However, it is possible to have an infinite regress where an accidental line of causality is involved, i.e., one wherein the present effect has no real dependence for its existence upon the previous causes; thus, a man once generated can continue to live even though his parents die.

Sic et non (*yes and no; this way and that; for and against*). Peter ABELARD used these words as the title of a work in which he gathered genuine and apparently opposing opinions from the early Church writers on doctrinal and moral points, leaving the conflicts unresolved. Examples of Abelard's technique to arouse DOUBT, then inquiry, and finally to attain the truth are such propositions as: "No one can be saved without baptism of water; one can be saved without baptism of water." "At times we sin unwillingly; we always sin willingly." This method was later adopted, with modifications, into the Summas of such writers as PETER LOMBARD and St. Thomas Aquinas. (*See* SCHOLASTIC METHOD.)

Simpliciter (*simply, strictly, absolutely, under every aspect*), **secundum quid** (*after a fashion, in some way, partially, relatively*). These terms have wide application, as is evident from a few citations. "The superiority of one thing over another can be considered in two ways, strictly (*simpliciter*) and relatively (*secundum quid*)" (*Summa theologiae* 1a, 82.3). Then follows a comparison of the intellect and will. Again: "The expression simply (*simpliciter*) can be taken in two senses. [In one sense it means] the same as absolutely. . . . In another way, sim-

ply is the same as altogether or totally" (*Summa theologiae* 3a, 50.5). *Simpliciter* and *per se* are frequently used interchangeably, as are *secundum quid* and *per accidens*. Thus, we speak most rigidly and strictly when we talk *per se* and *simpliciter,* while we are less formal and exact when we speak *per accidens* and *secundum quid.*

A few illustrations will make evident the value of this distinction. God is simply eternal; that is, He is without succession of past, present, and future. Such is the strictest significance of eternal. Man's soul, on the other hand, is relatively eternal; that is, it will never cease to be, but never does it embrace its complete existence in an eternal NOW. Again, a rose that has all that pertains to its perfection is good simply; one that lacks a due perfection, e.g., a pleasant fragrance, is only relatively good. St. Thomas employs a more subtle use of the distinction when he points out that by reason of substantial existence a thing is strictly a being, but good only after a fashion, that is, only by reason of its being. Yet, when the thing has its ultimate perfection it is said to be a being after a fashion and good strictly or absolutely (*Summa theologiae* 1a, 5.1 ad 1).

Species impressa (*impressed species*), **species expressa** (*expressed species*). These terms are employed for explaining details of the process of ideation. Man's intellect somehow attains universal knowledge of the particular objects perceived by his senses. In order to explain how this is achieved, Aristotle postulated an active intellect that abstracted and dematerialized the sensible species formed by the imagination, and a possible intellect that received this dematerialized species and thus formed the idea by which man knows. The form produced by the active intellect is the impressed species; that produced by the possible intellect, i.e., the idea, is the expressed species.

These terms are also employed in reference to the sensible order. Here, the impressed species is the result of the external stimuli of the object upon the sense organ; the expressed species is a phantasm formed by the imagination as a result of the stimuli communicated to it from the external sense organs. (*See* SPECIES, INTENTIONAL; IDEA.)

Sui generis (*unique, of its own kind, in a class by itself*). This expression comes from the logical device known as the PREDICABLES. A GENUS is a universal that normally is said of many SPECIES, as animal is said of man, dog, cat, etc. When a thing is such that it is the only one of its kind, so that its nature cannot be predicated of anything other than itself, it is called unique or *sui generis.*

Scholastic Axioms

As in the case of terms, here again an attempt has been made to list the axioms most frequently employed by the scholastics in the elaboration of their syntheses, with stress on the interpretation given to Aristotle's thought by St. Thomas Aquinas.

Ab esse ad posse valet illatio (*From actual existence, the possibility of existence is validly inferred*). From the fact that something is known actually to be, we rightly judge that it is possible for it to be. We know that eclipses of the sun and earthquakes are possible, even though they are not normal occurrences, because in fact they do sometimes happen. This axiom has wide application in philosophy, especially in natural philosophy and metaphysics, and it is also of great importance in Catholic apologetics. For example, the most effective proof that MIRACLES are possible is the fact that they have been known to take place.

Abstrahentium non est mendacium (*The work of abstracting is not a lie*). When one leaves aside certain real and concrete characteristics of an object in order to study one aspect more perfectly, as the mathematician does with lines and number, no deception or falsehood is involved provided that the fact of leaving out the other traits is never denied. Aristotle makes this point when discussing how the mathematician considers physical reality: ''Now the mathematician, though he too treats of these things, nevertheless, does not treat them as the limits of a physical body . . . that is why he separates them; for in thought they are separable from motion, and it makes no difference, nor does any falsity result, if they are separated'' (*Phys.* 193b 34). The very truth of universal KNOWLEDGE and of SCIENCE depends on the validity of this axiom. (*See* ABSTRACTION.)

Actiones sunt suppositorum (*Actions are of the individual*). The subject of an action is not the part, as the hand, or an organ, as the eye, or even the form, as the soul, but the individual substance. For example, a man strikes another not immediately through his substance, but mediately through the action or operation of his hand; the act of striking, however, is attributed properly to the man rather than to his hand (cf. St. Thomas, (*Summa theologiae* 2a2ae, 58.2). The individual is the incommunicable substance, and when that is a man it is called a PERSON. This axiom is important in treating of Christ, who is the God-man having the divine and human natures. His actions are of His Person, which is divine and not human, and hence they have infinite value; for the dignity and worth of an action is taken from its subject, which is the individual.

Actus est prior potentia (*Act is prior to potency*). Aristotle develops this axiom in his *Metaphysics* (1049b 4–1050a 29). The expression can be understood in a number of ways: (1) Act is prior to potency conceptually. This means that ACT by its definition is prior to POTENCY, because potency can be defined only through act. Thus, we define a singer as one able to sing, i.e., one in potency to perform the act of singing. (2) Act is prior to potency naturally. What is completed or perfect is superior to what is only in potency. Hence, the adult is more perfect than the child. (3) Act is prior to potency temporally, although there is a sense in which act is temporally posterior to potency. In the order of generation, what is less perfect precedes what is more perfect, as the seed precedes the flower. Thus, potency is prior to act in the sense of the potential advancing to greater perfection. Nevertheless, act is prior to potency in the sense that nothing can be reduced from potency to act except by something already in act; thus, nature is actually moving the seed toward its perfection as a flower (cf. St. Thomas, (*Summa theologiae* 1a, 85.3 ad 1). *See* POTENCY AND ACT.

Actus limitatur per potentiam (*Act is limited through potency*). Act is perfection, and, precisely as perfection, cannot contain any limitation. Hence, any limitation of ACT must come from an extrinsic principle, namely, POTENCY, which is the real capacity to receive act. Thus, the human soul is a life-giving principle, but each soul is restricted in its act to the body that it vivifies. From this principle it also follows that act, in the material order, is multiplied through potency; thus, we have many men because many bodies receive the many human souls. (*See* INDIVIDUATION.)

Agere sequitur esse (*Acting depends on being*). This axiom confirms the essential correlation between existence and operation, between the being and the activity of a thing. One understanding of the principle is that just as a being is, so does it operate. Thus fire, being hot, generates heat and not cold. Another meaning intended is that being has priority in nature to acting, although not necessarily in time. Striking a match results in flame and, simultaneously, in the heating and illuminating that result from the flame. (Cf. St. Thomas, *C. gent.* 3.69; *Summa theologiae* 3a, 34.2 ad 1.)

Bonum est diffusivum sui (*Good is diffusive of itself*). Good adds to BEING the notion of desirability. Then, acting in the mode of a final cause, GOOD attracts, elicits, and moves the efficient cause. In this way, good is said to be diffusive of itself or to communicate its goodness. Thus a good person by his very example of virtue inspires others and influences them to be good. However, PSEUDO-DIONYSIUS in *De divinis nominibus* employs the expression in relation to God, comparing God to the sun, which spreads its light everywhere. God is the total cause of all that is good, and is both the efficient and final cause of goodness. "Good as substantial good extends goodness to all existing things" (4.1.95). *See* NEOPLATONISM; EMANATIONISM.

Bonum ex integra causa (*Good results from integral totality*). What is perfect is good, but nothing is perfect that lacks what belongs to it; a blind man is imperfect because he is deprived of sight, a perfection due to him. Perfect health would require the complete harmony of the whole body; the presence of even a single defect (such as the lack of sight) results in the physical EVIL of sickness. Thus, as Pseudo-Dionysius states, "Good is from one total cause; evil is from many particular defects" (*De divin. nom.* 4.30.237). This axiom has great importance in the moral order, where the goodness of an act must be determined from its object, end, and circumstances; a defect in any one of these results in an evil act. Thus, the pride that motivates the giving of alms vitiates what otherwise would be a good deed. (*See* MORALITY.)

Causa cessante cessat effectus (*The cause ceasing, the effect ceases*). This is true only in those effects that depend on their causes both for their becoming and their being. A book depends on the hand supporting it against gravity in order both to be where it is and to remain there. St. Thomas explains the principle at length when treating of God's conserving power in creatures ((*Summa theologiae* 1a, 104.1). *See* CAUSALITY; CONSERVATION, DIVINE.

Ens et unum convertuntur (*Being and one are convertible*). Being and one are TRANSCENDENTALS, extending themselves to everything. Whatever is, is being, because being is the subject of existence. Being and one are subjectively the same, but one signifies the notion of indivision or undividedness. One, thus understood, must not be confused with homogeneity. Man, though heterogeneous in his many parts, is one; that is, he is undivided in himself since he is a human being, and not many beings by reason of his parts. The principle means that whatever is, is one in this transcendental sense. Hence we can say that whatever is, is one, and whatever is one, is. (Cf. St. Thomas, *In 10 meta.* 3.1974–80.) *See* UNITY.

Ex nihilo nihil fit (*From nothing, nothing comes*). When the "from" refers to the material cause, then truly nothing can result from nothing. However, when the "from" refers to the order of events—as in CREATION, first there was nothing and then something—then the axiom is not valid. The formulation of the axiom is from the Eleatic school of philosophy. (*See* GREEK PHILOSOPHY.)

Generatio fit in instanti (*Generation is instantaneous*). Acceptance of this axiom presupposes the HYLOMORPHISM of Aristotle. Fundamentally and ultimately, each material thing is composed of prime matter and a substantial form (*see* MATTER AND FORM). The substantial form determines what the thing is. No substance, therefore, can have more than one substantial form at any given moment. Were not substantial change or generation instantaneous, however, a substance would have two specifying forms at the same time, and thus it would be two different things simultaneously. (*See* SUBSTANTIAL CHANGE; INSTANT.)

Generatio unius est corruptio alterius (*The generation of one thing is the corruption of another*). The fact that NATURE perpetuates itself is evident. How these changes are explained has puzzled men of every age. Aristotle has summarized his doctrine in the dictum: The generation of one thing means the corruption of another, and the corruption of this means the generation of that (*Gen. et cor.* 318a 25–27). It is evident enough that when wood is burned, ashes remain. The more profound problem is with such living changes as the development of the seed into the plant. The seed perishes, giving way to a higher form of life; the passing of the plant, in turn, means the disintegration of the power (the form) that maintained its inner harmony of parts. Obviously the principle is not meant so literally as to suggest that the corruption of this plant means the generation immediately of a new one; rather, the plant during its own existence produces seeds that will develop into new life. As with the preceding axiom, the acceptance of hylomorphism makes the principle more understandable. Prime matter is never without a substantial form. Consequently, when a change takes place in any substance, its loss of one form immediately calls forth the form of another. (*See* MATTER AND FORM; GENERATION-CORRUPTION.)

Individuum est incommunicabile (*The individual is incommunicable*). The individual is undivided in itself, but is divided from everything else by reason of its ultimate completing element. Understood in this way, the term individual refers to the concrete, particular SUBSTANCE that is complete in its own line of essence and existence. In other words, unlike the universal or genus, an individual cannot be predicated of inferiors; that is, it cannot have species under it. Furthermore, the individual cannot communicate its nature to another in the sense of constituting another's essence out of its own. The axiom does not refer to efficient causality, let alone deny it. Thus flame does communicate its heat as well as increase itself when burning new material; man does generate man, as well as communicate his ideas to others. Yet, in these cases the individual as such is not associated with its effects or products in such a way as to constitute their essence; rather, its powers are exercised in bringing about a change in other individuals. (*See* INDIVIDUALITY; INDIVIDUATION.)

Intellectus fit omnia (*The intellect becomes all things*). Not physically but conceptually, man's mind becomes everything he knows. The existential order outside man's INTELLECT is impressed upon his senses and eventually abstracted and universalized. Thus, after this intentional mode, the intellect is made what it knows. (*See* ABSTRACTION; UNIVERSALS.)

Nemo dat quod non habet (*No one gives what he does not have*). The proper nature of CAUSALITY shows that the cause cannot produce an effect with qualities superior to the cause itself. This axiom is expressed in many popular sayings, such as "You can't make a silk purse out of a sow's ear."

Nihil est causa sui ipsius (*Nothing is the cause of itself*). To be its own cause in the order of substantial being, a thing would have to be and not-be at the same time. The thing would have to not-be, for if it already were, it would not have to be caused. Yet, it would also have to be, since CAUSALITY is an action or operation, and act follows upon being. Hence, the notion of something's causing itself is self-contradictory. (*See* CAUSALITY, PRINCIPLE OF.)

Nihil est in intellectu quod prius non fuerit in sensu (*Nothing is in the intellect that was not first in the sense*). Man is composed of body and soul, operating according to the demands of his composite nature. Although the INTELLECT is immaterial, while united to the body it depends on phantasms that were gathered by the various senses. Man's normal acquisition of KNOWLEDGE is not intuitive, but is an abstracting process beginning in the external SENSES.

Omne agens agit propter finem (*Every agent acts for an end*). This axiom is a statement of the principle of finality and means that every active or efficient cause tends toward that which is good or agreeable to it, whether without knowledge, as in purely natural movements, or with knowledge, as in those of the sense appetite or under the command of reason. (*See* FINALITY, PRINCIPLE OF.)

Omne quod movetur ab alio movetur (*Everything moved is moved by another*). The movable is in potency even while in MOTION, for it is in potency to that toward which it is being moved. Since nothing can reduce itself from potency to act, but depends on a being already in act, it follows that the mover and the moved are distinct, just as are potency and act, and that act absolutely considered is prior to the actualization of the potency. (*See* MOTION, FIRST CAUSE OF.)

Potentia et actus dividunt omne ens (*Potency and act divide all being*). Whatever is, either is pure act or is intrinsically composed, in its ultimate metaphysical re-

finement, of POTENCY and ACT. This principle is at the pinnacle of scholastic thought and upon its validity stands the perennial philosophy. God alone is pure act; all beings other than God are in some way potential as well as being in act. The source of the distinction is natural philosophy; act and potency primarily pertain to the mobile order, since this order depends upon them. Yet, the mobile order and the order of being as such, i.e., the metaphysical order, are materially the same in extension. Consequently, all being, materially speaking, is either potency or act. Indeed, even formally being is either one or the other, for potency and act verify in themselves the formality of BEING, and are therefore coextensive with being (cf. St. Thomas, *Summa theologiae* 1a, 77.1).

Potentiae specificantur per actus et obiecta (*Potencies are specified through their acts and objects*). Every POTENCY is of its very nature ordered to some ACT, but act on its part must be about some OBJECT. Thus, the powers of the eye and ear are ordered respectively to seeing and hearing, which in their turn must be immediately and properly related to some objects, namely, color and sound. Accidental differences in the colored or sounding objects do not so specify as to require a new potency for each act of seeing or hearing. (*See* FACULTIES OF THE SOUL.)

Propter quod unumquodque tale et illud magis (*Whatever makes a thing to be in a certain way, is that and more so*). Whatever is the cause of any formality or perfection in other things, itself possesses that formality or perfection in a greater, more eminent degree. If water is made hot by a fire, then the fire possesses heat more perfectly than the water, let alone the other things made hot by means of the hot water. The axiom is found in Aristotle: "A thing has a quality in a higher degree than other things if in virtue of it the similar quality belongs to the other things as well" (*Meta.* 993b 24). *See* PARTICIPATION.

Quidquid recipitur ad modum recipientis recipitur (*Whatever is received is received after the mode of the one receiving*). A proportion exists between the receiver and the received, as between potency and act. The receiving subject has a certain capacity and disposition, determined by its nature, for receiving some act. It is according to the greater or lesser capacity of the receiver that something is received, as, in teaching, the pupils receive the imparted knowledge according to their respective intellectual capacities. *See* EDUCATION, PHILOSOPHY OF.

Verum et bonum convertuntur (*Truth and good are convertible*). Everything true is good and everything good is true. True and good are TRANSCENDENTALS, each adding to being merely a new relation. TRUTH is being related to the intellect; GOOD is being related to the appetite. The principle refers to the ontological good and true, and hence, does not refer directly to the moral order.

Virtus consistit in medio (*Virtue is found in the mean*). Aristotle's basic principle of good moral action is to place VIRTUE between two extremes that are called vices. Virtue is the good habit whose act avoids the extremes and maintains the mean of honest living. Aristotle puts it in this way: "Virtue, then, is a state of character concerned with choice, lying in a mean, i.e., the mean relative to us, this being determined by a rational principle, and by that principle by which the man of practical wisdom would determine it" (*Eth. Nic.* 1107a 1–3).

Bibliography: R. J. DEFERRARI et al., *A Latin-English Dictionary of St. Thomas Aquinas Based on the Summa Theologica and Selected Passages of His Other Works,* 5 fasc. (Washington 1948–53). T. W. WILSON, *An Index to Aristotle in English Translation* (Princeton, N.J. 1949). D. D. RUNES, ed., *Dictionary of Philosophy* (Ames, Iowa 1955). *Enciclopedia filosofica* 4.1859–62. N. SIGNORIELLO, *Lexicon peripateticum philosophico-theologicum* . . . (Naples 1906; Rome 1931). PETRI DE BERGOMO, *Tabula aurea* (Photocopy from Thomas Aquinas's *Opera Omnia,* Editiones Paulinae; Rome 1960).

[R. SMITH]

SCHOLASTICISM

First used in a derogatory sense by humanists and early histories of philosophy in the 16th century, scholasticism has come to mean either a historical movement or a system of thought that was bequeathed by that movement.

In the historical sense described in this article, it is an intellectual movement in the history of the Church that can be divided into three periods: medieval, modern, and contemporary. Medieval scholasticism arose gradually in the 12th century from the use of Aristotelian DIALECTICS in theology, philosophy, and Canon Law; it matured in the 13th with the assimilation of new philosophical literature and consequent concentration on metaphysics; it declined in the succeeding period; and it passed into desuetude with the RENAISSANCE. Modern (or middle) scholasticism, extending from 1530 to the early 19th century, witnessed a revival of metaphysics in the 16th century, a multiplicity of eclectic schools in the 17th, and an abandonment of ancient sources and method in the 18th. Contemporary scholasticism began with the rediscovery of the works of St. Thomas Aquinas in mid-19th century, spread throughout the Catholic world under the aegis of Leo XIII, and flourished in the 20th century, particularly in Continental Europe and in North and South America.

As a system, scholasticism has sometimes been unjustly described as "one of the greatest plagues of the human mind" (Diderot), or as "philosophy brought into slavery to papist theology" (C. A. Heumann), and curtly dismissed as not meriting attention. At the other extreme, some seem to consider it a homogeneous body of doctrine providing answers to all possible problems. The truth lies between these two extremes (*see* SCHOLASTIC METHOD; SCHOLASTIC PHILOSOPHY).

1. MEDIEVAL SCHOLASTICISM

It is customary to trace the roots of scholasticism to the Carolingian age and to divide medieval scholasticism into four periods: prescholasticism (*c.* 800–1050), early scholasticism (1050–1200), high scholasticism (1200–1300 or 1350), and late scholasticism (1350–1500).

Prescholasticism. The learning of the Middle Ages has its origins in the enactments of CHARLEMAGNE and in the vision of ALCUIN that brought about the establishment of episcopal and monastic schools and the gradual revival of the trivium and quadrivium. In this early period, dialectics occupied a relatively small place in the trivium and relied mainly on *De nuptiis Mercurii et Philologiae* of Martianus Capella, the *Institutiones* of CASSIODORUS, a few chapters of the *Etymologiae* of ISIDORE OF SEVILLE, the *Dialectica* of Alcuin, and perhaps some treatises of BOETHIUS. What came to be called the old logic (*logica vetus*), i.e., Aristotle's *Categories* and *Perihermenias* and Porphyry's *Isagoge,* was not popularly known or used [J. Isaac, *Le Peri Hermeneias en occident de Boèce à saint Thomas* (Paris 1953) 38–42].

The "new Athens" that Alcuin sought to build in France [*Epist.* 86; *Patrologia Latina,* ed. J. P. Migne, 217 V., indexes 4 v. (Paris 1878–90) 100:282] was not marked by any great philosophical revival. Alcuin himself was content to duplicate the culture of the past; RABANUS MAURUS was primarily a compiler who brought Alcuin's program to Germany; Fredegisus (d. 834), disciple and successor of Alcuin, showed perhaps a wider interest, since his *De nihilo et tenebris* contains some original thought; while the *Dicta* of CANDIDUS OF FULDA offers the first medieval proof of the existence of God based on dialectics. The court of Charles II the Bald witnessed a discussion on the nature of the soul, its origin and relation to the body, involving HINCMAR OF REIMS, RATRAMNUS OF CORBIE, and PASCHASIUS RADBERTUS. Above all, the court was famous as the home of the one truly original thinker of this period, JOHN SCOTUS ERIUGENA, whose *De divisione naturae* (*c.* 866) is a synthesis of theology based on Neoplatonic principles. In theology proper, the Carolingian period was marked by controversies on predestination and the Real Presence, initiated by GOTTSCHALK OF ORBAIS. Neither controversy seems to have resulted from the use of dialectics.

Early Scholasticism. The Carolingian renaissance was of short duration. The dismemberment of the Empire, the coming of the Normans, frequent wars, and general political disorder were hardly favorable to intellectual pursuits. Yet the 10th century was not wholly devoid of intellectual life in some monasteries and cathedrals; one need only consider the learning of Gerbert of Aurillac, who became Pope SYLVESTER II, and his disciple FULBERT OF CHARTRES. Such men prepared for the revival of learning in the 11th century that centered largely on the question of dialectics. As *scholasticus* at Reims (973–982) Gerbert had provided a full course on the old logic (J. Isaac, *op. cit.* 44).

Less than a century later St. PETER DAMIAN complained of the Aristotelian subtlety that had spread through the schools and of those who forgot it was but a handmaid and not the queen (*Patrologia Latina,* 145:603). He may have had in mind his contemporary, BERENGARIUS OF TOURS, who had urged recourse to dialectics on all questions, since reason was the gift of God. Applying this science to the Eucharist, Berengarius concluded that since reason proclaims that accidents cannot exist apart from substance, the bread and wine must remain after the Consecration. The effect of the Consecration is but to add another form to the bread, that of the ''intellectual body'' of Christ: an allegorical, spiritual, and symbolic rather than a real, physical presence is the result. Berengarius remained throughout the 12th century an example of reason and logic intruding where it had no place. Yet, while some reacted strongly against dialectics, others were quick to recognize its value if used with restraint. ''For those who examine the matter carefully, dialectics does not undermine the mysteries of God'' (Lanfranc of Bec, *In 1 Corinthians* 1.11; *Patrologia Latina,* 150:157), and what St. Paul reproves is not the art of disputing but the perverse use some make of it (*In Colossians* 2.3; *Patrologia Latina,* 150:323). In this approach LANFRANC prepared the way for the daring but sound metaphysical meditations on dogma of St. Anselm.

Anselm of Canterbury. The *Monologium* of ANSELM OF CANTERBURY is a profound prayerful study of the existence and nature of God, yet professedly is based on reason and not on the authority of Scripture. In it, Anselm clearly affirmed that faith is his starting point; yet through reason he will seek to understand what he believes. ''Faith seeking understanding'' (*Fides quaerens intellectum*) was, in fact, the original title of his second great work, the *Proslogion*. Conscious of the novelty of his position—he had been reproved by Lanfranc for his daring—Anselm himself recommended prudence in the spread of his writings (*Epist.* 1.74; *Patrologia Latina,* 158:1144).

The dialectic that Anselm fostered among his pupils at Bec led to the systematic *Sententiae* and *Summae* of the 12th century. The first steps were taken by ANSELM OF LAON, pupil of St. Anselm, who for some 30 years taught in the episcopal school of Laon. Though his teaching was primarily on Scripture, he did apparently organize the material of older theology in more systematic fashion. His school attracted a host of pupils who were to become famous in 12th-century theology: GILBERT DE LA PORRÉE, and ROBERT OF MELUN (HEREFORD), Alberic of Reims, Lotulphus of Novara, and WILLIAM OF CHAMPEAUX.

Peter Abelard. Of much more importance for the systematization of theology was the work of Peter ABELARD. The *Sic et Non* produced by his school is a vast repertoire of Biblical, patristic, and canonical material for and against specific points of doctrine. Its prologue, the work of a master dialectician, sets forth principles for the reconciliation of opposing texts through the analysis of words, authentication of texts, or noting changes of opinion on the part of an author. Perhaps the most influential Abelardian principle was that ''one can often solve a controversy by showing that the same words are used in different senses by different authors'' (*Patrologia Latina,* 178:1344D). The dialectical method of Abelard was utilized by both canonists and theologians, reaching notable heights in the *Decretum* of Gratian, originally known as the *Concordantia discordantium canonum,* and the *Libri sententiarum* of PETER LOMBARD (*see* SENTENCES AND SUMMAE; GRATIAN, DECRETUM OF).

Abelard is perhaps best known for his role in the controversy concerning UNIVERSALS, ''which is always the most important question for those engaged in dialectics'' (*Historia calamitatum* 1.2). Disputing the solutions of his teachers, ROSCELIN and William of Champeaux, Abelard attributed universality to names, not things. This position, sometimes called NOMINALISM, was vastly different from the nominalism of the 14th century. The 11th-century controversy centered on grammar and logic without the aid of Aristotle's metaphysics and psychology.

School of Chartres. During the first half of the 12th century the most eminent center of learning was the cathedral school in Chartres. Inspired by a deep feeling for ancient culture, masters such as BERNARD OF CHARTRES, THIERRY OF CHARTRES, Gilbert de la Porrée, and CLARENBAUD OF ARRAS cultivated an integral humanism that was literary as well as theological. Perhaps JOHN OF SALISBURY, later Bishop of Chartres, was the most eloquent spokesman of the literary humanism typical of this school. WILLIAM OF CONCHES, HONORIUS OF AUTUN, and BERNARD SILVESTRIS developed a Platonic cosmology out of earlier sources. Acquainted only with Platonic sources, apart from the *Organon* of Aristotle, the philosophy taught at Chartres was mainly an eclectic Platonism, centered on questions of God and the world, EXEMPLARISM, creation, the sciences, as well as the Latin classics and the LIBERAL ARTS. ADELARD OF BATH and other alumni became well known translators of scientific works from Arabic into Latin.

Mysticism. At Paris the Abbey of Saint-Victor, founded in 1108 by William of Champeaux for the CANONS REGULAR OF ST. AUGUSTINE, became a flourishing school of theology and mysticism under HUGH OF SAINT-VICTOR and RICHARD OF SAINT-VICTOR. To his contemporaries, Hugh was the "new Augustine, the agent of the Holy Spirit," a learned theologian famous for his theological summa *On the Sacraments of the Christian Faith* (tr. R. J. Deferrari, Cambridge, Mass. 1951), his program for Christian schools, the *Didascalicon* (tr. J. Taylor, New York 1961), and his ability to use all knowledge as paths to union with God. Richard was the outstanding mystical writer of this school; his works were appreciated and used especially by St. Bonaventure and St. Thomas Aquinas.

Cistercian mysticism, stemming from St. BERNARD OF CLAIRVAUX, was marked by its psychological approach. Almost every writer of this school of mysticism produced a treatise on the soul as a preface and key to his spiritual doctrine (*see* SOUL, HUMAN, 2; ISAAC OF STELLA; ALCHER OF CLAIRVAUX; WILLIAM OF SAINT-THIERRY). One exception to this was ALAN OF LILLE, who had taught at Paris and Montpellier before entering monastic life. He is known mainly for his theological works against the heretics of his day and for his attempt to reduce theology to a more exact science.

High Scholasticism. History can never be divided by centuries. Yet mid-13th-century Paris, with St. ALBERT THE GREAT, ROGER BACON, St. BONAVENTURE, and St. THOMAS AQUINAS, was a far different "city of letters" from the mid-12th-century Paris of Peter Lombard. The 12th and preceding centuries had been essentially patristic in content, largely dominated by the doctrine and spirit of St. AUGUSTINE.

Introduction of Aristotle. Apart from his logic, Aristotle was known only through secondary sources; and the West little suspected that he had written anything else. In the 13th century scholastics were caught up in a ferment of thought as their cultural horizon was suddenly broadened and their allegiance to the past was deeply challenged through the influx of a vast philosophical and scientific literature translated from the Greek and Arabic. For the first time they came face to face with a world-system, a *Weltanschauung,* which relied completely on reason and appeared almost entirely at variance with the Christian faith. They were faced with doctrines such as the Prime Mover, eternal motion, denial of creation and providence, uncertainty on the immortality and spirituality of the soul, and a morality based on reason alone. Such theories seemed almost like a new revelation, or, for many, like intruders from an alien world. "The Christian people," said WILLIAM OF AUVERGNE, "is plunged in astonishment by theories hitherto entirely unknown to it" [*De universo* 1.3.31 (Paris 1674) 1:805b]. The first reaction on the part of traditionalists was one of distrust: the synod at Paris in 1210 forbade the use of Aristotle's writings on natural philosophy or commentaries on them in the schools; the University of Paris statutes of 1215 extended this prohibition to the "metaphysics and natural philosophy, *summae* on them, or books on the doctrine of DAVID OF DINANT, AMALRIC OF BÈNE, or Maurice of Spain." Yet such prohibitions, renewed in 1231 by Gregory IX, did not exclude private study or use of such works, or prevent their growing popularity. In 1255 the new statutes for the faculty of arts officially included all the known works of Aristotle in the texts assigned for public lectures. As the profundity and novelty of Aristotle's thought was further complicated by the crudity and literalness of the translations, scholastics were inclined to turn to AVICENNA and, after 1230, to AVERROËS as guides in understanding the Philosopher (*see* ARABIAN PHILOSOPHY). Unfortunately, Avicenna's interpretation was largely Neoplatonic, especially on the origin of things from God by necessary emanation, and on the nature of the soul (*see* EMANATIONISM). The acceptance of Averroës as the Commentator gave rise eventually to a crisis at Paris.

Universities. This influx of literature clearly could not have produced its far-reaching effects had it not been for the formation and organization after 1200 of a new scholastic milieu, in the founding of the University of PARIS, and those of OXFORD, Cambridge, Toulouse, BOLOGNA, and others. Usually divided into four faculties of theology, medicine, law, and arts, the universities are remembered mostly for the work achieved in theology and in arts, which quickly became primarily a school of philosophy. In the theological faculty, while the older traditions were maintained, new methods, inspired partly by the "new logic" of Aristotle (the *Analytics, Topics,* and *Sophistical Refutations,* translated about 1128 by James of Venice), produced a new type of scientific theology in contrast to the scriptural studies (*sacra pagina*) of the 12th century. Roger Bacon complained bitterly of the displacement of the Bible as the heart of theology by the *Sentences* of Peter Lombard. He blamed ALEXANDER OF HALES, who as dean of the school had made the first public gloss on the *Sentences* (c. 1230). For better or for worse, Alexander was making use of a procedure already in vogue in the arts faculty, of using the work of some "authority" (e.g., Aristotle, Porphyry, Donatus) as the basis of scholastic lectures. In arts at Paris, Roger Bacon himself seems to have been the first to undertake such courses on the newly discovered writings of Aristotle.

English Scholars. The Englishman Roger Bacon was a product of the University of Paris, where he lectured in arts longer than any other master. Bacon traced his own preference for mathematics and mathematical methods to ROBERT GROSSETESTE, one of the most original and versatile minds of the century. Conversant with the works of Aristotle, some of which he had translated, Grosseteste was by inclination more Neoplatonist and Augustinian. Influenced likewise by optics and perspective, he attempted to deduce from the nature of light a complete cosmological system, wherein the dynamic energy of light produced the finite world and the multiplication of individual beings. Such scientific ideals, especially his faith in mathematical reason, reappeared in Bacon, who set as his ideal the renewal of contemporary thought through a reassessment and reorganization of Christian wisdom. On the other hand, in ADAM OF BUCKFIELD one finds a proof that Aristotle's writings were by no means neglected at Oxford. Yet both Dominicans, such as RICHARD FISHACRE and ROBERT KILWARDBY, and Franciscans, such as THOMAS OF YORK, ROGER MARSTON, and JOHN PECKHAM, were inclined to an eclectic type of Aristotelianism and to resist the complete acceptance of the Philosopher in Christian schools. The trends implanted by Grosseteste retained their vitality even in the 14th century, with a renewed interest in mathematics and physics on the part of THOMAS BRADWARDINE and the Merton College group of physicists (*see* JOHN OF DUMBLETON; RICHARD OF SWYNESHED; WILLIAM OF HEYTESBURY).

Parisian Scholars. For the medieval schoolman, as for the modern historian, scholasticism meant primarily the University of Paris, the *studium* of the Church, "the city of books and learning" (Gregory IX). The long tradition of schools at Notre Dame, Sainte-Geneviève, Saint-Victor, gave rise about 1200 to a guild (*universitas*) of masters and scholars, which under royal patronage and papal direction soon became the most famous and important seat of learning in the Western world. At first, most of the masters in theology, guided by the directives of Pope Gregory IX (1228 and 1231), continued the conservative, so-called Augustinian, traditions of the 12th century. At the same time, the Aristotelian ideal of a science gradually made clear the distinction between philosophy and theology, and indeed the further distinction between theology as exegesis and theology as an organized body of knowledge (M. D. Chenu, *La théologie comme science au xiiie siècle*, Paris 1957).

Franciscan School. Alexander of Hales, who joined the Franciscan Order in Paris after a long and fruitful theological career, showed very little tendency to use the works of Aristotle; at most, he cited well-known axioms and principles. In contrast, his associate, JOHN OF LA ROCHELLE, depended closely on Avicenna in his *Summa de anima;* otherwise he remained close to traditional theology.

A much greater knowledge of the philosophers was manifested by St. Bonaventure, likely because when he had studied in the arts faculty Aristotle was given more prominence. Nonetheless, though he spoke the language of Aristotle, considered him "the more excellent among the philosophers," and made great use of his works, Bonaventure can hardly be called an Aristotelian. Primarily the theologian whose only master was Christ, Bonaventure regarded philosophy as a help in understanding the faith: "As the children of Israel carried away the treasures of Egypt [Ex 3,22; 12, 35], so theologians make their own the teachings of philosophy" [*Opera omnia* (Quaracchi 1882–1902) 8:335b], "taking from philosophical knowledge on the nature of things what they need to build" the structure of theology and reach an understanding of the things of God (*ibid.* 5:205a). Yet a close examination of the philosophy thus incorporated into the synthesis of Christian wisdom shows relatively little acceptance of Aristotle. In later years, faced by the Averroist crisis, Bonaventure became vehemently critical of Aristotelianism and of any attempt to philosophize independently of the safeguards of faith. Though his disciples, John Peckham and MATTHEW OF AQUASPARTA, made more use of the Philosopher, they were close to Bonaventure in outlook and spirit.

Dominican School. A marked contrast to the Franciscan and early Dominican school is found in St. Albert the Great and St. Thomas Aquinas. Among the scholastics Albert was the first to see what riches the Greco-Arabic science and philosophy contained for Christian thought. He was inclined to emphasize the practical separation of philosophy and theology, since philosophical problems should be handled by philosophical methods, and to establish a new hierarchy of authority: "In matters of faith and morals Augustine is to be believed rather than the philosophers, if they are not in agreement. But if one speaks of medicine, I should rather believe Galen or Hippocrates; or if of the nature of things, I believe Aristotle or some other who is expert in the nature of things" (*In 2 sent.* 13.2). If Albert did not succeed in building a true philosophical synthesis from such an overwhelming wealth of material, he did make possible the work of St. Thomas, providing as well inspiration for a school of his own among the German Dominicans, who emphasized the Neoplatonism inherent in his thought (*see* THEODORIC

OF FREIBERG; ULRIC OF STRASSBURG; ECKHART, MEISTER).

For Thomas Aquinas, the basic problem was to discover how as a Christian scholar he could order anew the whole structure of Christian wisdom in such a way that pagan philosophy would be made tributary to the Christian faith. For Thomas there was no need to reject or despise whatever pagan reason had discovered of the truth; just as grace does not destroy nature but perfects it, so sacred doctrine presupposes, uses, and perfects natural knowledge (*Summa theologiae* 1a, 1.8 ad 2). Some truths about God exceed the ability of reason. But there are other truths that the natural reason of man is able to reach (*C. gent.* 1.3). Both come under theology because God has seen fit to reveal both and propose them to man for belief (1.4), even though the second group is properly of the philosophical order. Both kinds of truth are incorporated into the *Summa contra gentiles* and the *Summa theologiae*.

Many contemporaries took scandal at the synthesis Thomas achieved, complaining that he had brought Aristotelian naturalism and metaphysics into the heart of theology in speaking of the being of God and creatures, the POTENCY of MATTER (to the abandonment of Augustine's SEMINAL REASONS), the definition of soul as FORM, and the rejection of any theory of ILLUMINATION in knowledge. Yet they apparently failed to see that the Aristotle of St. Thomas was not simply the Aristotle of Athens in Latin dress, but an Aristotle brought into captivity to Christ, whose principles found interpretations and applications in problems he himself had never faced. Above all, the synthesis of St. Thomas is *his* synthesis; Thomism is not the mere evolution of Aristotelianism, but a revolution born of St. Thomas's own great intellect.

Averroist Crisis. The Angelic Doctor's knowledge of Aristotle and Averroës helped him meet in adequate fashion the crisis that had developed in Paris after 1255 (*see* AVERROISM, LATIN; INTELLECT, UNITY OF). With the introduction of the unfamiliar corpus of Aristotle into the arts curriculum, many masters turned for aid and enlightenment to the commentaries of Averroës. Under the latter's influence some came to seek a philosophy free from theological control. When their teachings contradicted the faith, they were careful to propose them merely as the conclusions of reason and philosophy. To philosophize, as SIGER OF BRABANT said, was to expound as faithfully as possible the thought of Aristotle, in methodical abstraction from the faith. The theologians were quick to react. In 1267 and 1268 Bonaventure publicly rebuked and condemned errors current in the university that ''arose from the unbridled use of philosophical investigation.'' Yet only with the return of St. Thomas to Paris

were such brash philosophers met on their own level. Attacked by innumerable theologians, the Averroist movement was formally condemned on Dec. 10, 1270, by the bishop of Paris, Étienne TEMPIER. The 13 propositions condemned embodied the essential tenets of Latin AVERROISM. This condemnation seems to have had little effect; the conferences *In Hexaemeron* of Bonaventure in 1273 witness the bitterness of his opposition to Aristotle and Averroists. After the death of Thomas Aquinas and Bonaventure in 1274, there was no theologian great enough to stem the Averroist tide in Paris. In the eyes of many, notably John Peckham and Robert Kilwardby, the Aristotelianism of Aquinas was dangerously close to that of the Averroists.

Condemnation of 1277. When the Parisian unrest was felt at the Papal Curia, Pope JOHN XXI wrote to Bishop Tempier on Jan. 18, 1277, directing him to ascertain where and by whom the errors in question had been taught or written, and to transmit to him, as soon as possible, all pertinent information [*Chartularium universitatis Parisiensis,* ed. H. Denfile and E. Chatelain, 4 v. (Paris 1889–97) 1:541]. Apparently without reply or further consultation with the Curia, Bishop Tempier issued a motu proprio and a condemnation of 219 propositions on March 7, 1277, the third anniversary of the death of Aquinas. In the prefatory letter, Tempier explicitly named Siger of Brabant and BOETHIUS OF SWEDEN as propagators of the errors condemned, and warned against the pretext of teaching a proposition as true according to reason, while it may be false according to faith (*ibid.* 1:543; *see* DOUBLE TRUTH, THEORY OF). The propositions condemned by Tempier included Averroist doctrines already condemned, multiplicity of worlds, each and every limitation of God's absolute freedom of action, individuation by matter, and certain crucial teachings of St. Thomas (*ibid.* 1:544–555). However, no proposition touched the specific Thomistic doctrine of the unicity of substantial form, so violently attacked by Peckham and other Augustinians. Consequently, Robert Kilwardby, Archbishop of Canterbury, proceeded at Oxford on his own authority to condemn 16 additional propositions, including 6 that touched the unicity of form, on March 18 (*ibid.* 1:558–559). The Paris condemnation, confirmed by the Pope on April 28, was an overwhelming victory for traditional Augustinianism.

In the light of the condemnation of 1277, WILLIAM DE LA MARE tried to preserve orthodox Franciscan teaching by drawing up a *Correctorium* of individual passages in the writing of Aquinas. This *Correctorium* was officially adopted by the Franciscan Chapter of Strasbourg in 1283; only notably intelligent lectors were allowed to read the works of Aquinas, and then only with the *Correctorium* as a guide. Spontaneously, early supporters of

THOMISM, particularly at Oxford and Paris, where controversy was most intense, replied with CORRECTORIA to William de la Mare's "Corruptorium" [see RICHARD KNAPWELL; THOMAS OF SUTTON; JOHN (QUIDORT) OF PARIS].

Early 14th Century. Another reaction was the numerous controversies that occupied the scholastic world well into the 14th century concerning ESSENCE AND EXISTENCE, the unicity and plurality of FORMS, ILLUMINATION, the soul and its powers, and the like, that involved GILES OF ROME, HENRY OF GHENT, PETER THOMAE, WALTER OF CHATTON, and others. In the midst of this intellectual turmoil, faced with the skepticism of theologians on the one hand and the audacity of philosophers on the other, John DUNS SCOTUS sought to create a new synthesis. In a critical yet positive spirit, he undertook to examine anew the limits of reason contrasted to faith, the whole problem of knowledge (mainly against Henry of Ghent), the object of metaphysics, and the doctrine of being, giving greater emphasis to divine liberty and metaphysical proofs for God's existence. Whether Scotus was successful in weaving all these elements into a true synthesis is not altogether evident, but SCOTISM became a thriving school of thought in later periods of scholasticism.

The last of the great scholastics of this period was WILLIAM OF OCKHAM, who epitomized the spirit of criticism that pervaded the early 14th century. His contemporaries called his nominalist position the "modern way" (*via moderna*) in contrast to the "old way" (*via antiqua*) of Thomas and Scotus. His NOMINALISM also played a significant role in the later development of scholasticism (*see* OCHKAMISM).

Late Scholasticism. After 1350 scholastic thought quickly moved away from the metaphysics utilized so fruitfully by the great theologians of the 13th century and was beginning to examine new questions. To this extent it did not immediately lose its vitality. One evidence of this change was the 14th-century interest in speculative grammar, that is, the philosophical analysis of language, in which metaphysics became the foundation of grammar. Parallel to this was the growth of logic after the *Summulae logicales* of Peter of Spain (JOHN XXI); WILLIAM OF SHERWOOD is an example of the close bond between logic and metaphysics. Late scholasticism also witnessed the beginnings of modern physics and scientific methodology. At Oxford physicists began to apply mathematics to the study of nature, and to construct new theories on space and motion. At Paris, JOHN BURIDAN, ALBERT OF SAXONY, and NICHOLAS ORESME anticipated, by their teachings on IMPETUS, gravitation, and the universe, many later discoveries in physics and astronomy;

their doctrines implied radical departure from the physics of Aristotle.

While such new ideas occupied the professors of the arts faculty, the theologians appear to have advanced little beyond the giants of the preceding period. Instead, they manifested the tendency to crystallize into schools. THOMISM, which had become the official doctrine of the Dominican Order, was championed by HARVEY NEDELLEC, JOHN OF NAPLES, John CAPREOLUS, and later by Tomasso de Vio CAJETAN. Since Scotism was not official among the Franciscans, more originality and independence was found in such scholastics as ANTONIUS ANDREAS, Francis of Meyronnes, HUGH OF NEWCASTLE, Peter Thomae, and WILLIAM OF ALNWICK. Among the Augustinians, the doctrines of Giles of Rome were made official even within his lifetime.

With this, Paris unfortunately became a city of conflict and confusion. Religious-minded scholars revolted against it, while the growing number of humanists sought means to restore the classical concept of the liberal arts and return to the prescholastic type of culture. Since the University of Paris failed to achieve a synthesis of all these elements, old and new, one might take the founding of the Collège de France (1530), for the study of classics not provided at the university, as a sign that scholasticism was at an end. In Germany, the vitriolic attacks of Martin LUTHER on the schoolmen and on philosophy, and the ravages of the Reformation, destroyed whatever scholasticism was in that country. There had been little scholasticism, as such, in Italy, and it gave way before the humanists. Only in Spain did it show new life with the rise of middle scholasticism.

Bibliography: E. GILSON, *History of Christian Philosophy* (New York 1955). A. A. MAURER, *Medieval Philosophy,* v. 2 of *A History of Philosophy,* ed. É. H. GILSON, 4 v. (New York 1962–). F. C. COPLESTONE, *History of Philosophy* (Westminster, Md. 1946–) v. 2–3. D. KNOWLES, *The Evolution of Medieval Thought* (Baltimore 1962). J. PIEPER, *Scholasticism,* tr. R. and C. WINSTON (New York 1960). P. VIGNAUX, *Philosophy in the Middle Ages,* tr. E. C. HALL from 3d French ed. (New York 1959). P. DELHAYE *Medieval Christian Philosophy,* tr. S. J. TESTER (New York 1960). F. UEBERWEG, *Grundriss der Geschichte der Philosophie,* ed. K. PRAECHTER et al., 5 v. (11th, 12th ed. Berlin 1923–28) v. 3. A. FOREST et al., *Le Mouvement doctrinal du XIe au XIVe siècle (Histoire de l'église depuis les origines jusqu'à nos jours,* eds., A. FLICHE and V. MARTIN, 13; 1951). J. DE GHELLINCK *Le Mouvement théologique du XIIe siècle (2d ed. Bruges 1948)* B. BAZÀN, J. WIPPEL, G. FRANSEN and D. JACQUART, *Les questions disputées et les questions quodlibétiques dans les facultés de theologie, de droit et de médecine* (Turnhout 1985). L. BOYLE, *Facing History: A Different Thomas Aquinas* (Louvain 2000). L. BIANCHI and E. RANDI, *Vérités dissonantes: Aristote . . . la fin du Moyen Age* (Fribourg 1990). J. WIPPEL, *The Metaphysical Thought of Thomas Aquinas: From Finite Being to Uncreated Being* (Washington 2000).

[I. C. BRADY]

2. MODERN OR MIDDLE SCHOLASTICISM

Modern or middle scholasticism extends roughly from 1530 to 1830. It may be conveniently divided into three periods: second scholasticism (1530–1650), reaction and adjustment (1650–1750), and crossroads and transition (1750–1830),

General Characteristics. As a system and method of speculative and practical thought modern scholasticism exhibited seven general characteristics that resulted from a peculiar combination of traditionalism and modernity in both philosophy and theology: (1) continuity with the past; (2) orientation of philosophy to the Word of God; (3) systematic realism; (4) rational method; (5) adjustment to contemporary science and modern philosophy; (6) concern with ideology; and (7) developments characteristic of different religious orders and of Protestant scholasticism. At times many of these positive characteristics were excessive; they were frequently ridiculed and misinterpreted by nonscholastics who, using the term scholasticism in a pejorative sense, revealed some of the negative characteristics of the system such as its antiquarian character and reliance on authorities in philosophy to the detriment of legitimate speculation.

The leaders of this movement were predominantly, though not exclusively, Catholic priests and Protestant clergymen. Among members of religious orders DOMINICANS, FRANCISCANS, and JESUITS predominated, although the diocesan clergy, BENEDICTINES, CARMELITES, AUGUSTINIANS, and members of other orders also made substantial contributions.

The transition to modern or middle scholasticism was necessitated by the humanists of the Renaissance whose use of, as well as expressed contempt for, scholasticism exemplified its unique characteristics; those who tried to change or destroy it were themselves shaped by it, and they adapted the results of this development to their own problems and times. Most significant were the invention of printing (c. 1440), the fall of Constantinople (1453), the discovery of America (1490–92), and the Protestant REFORMATION. These world events changed radically the cultural milieu of early modern scholasticism with powerful consequences for its evolution during subsequent centuries. Thus modern scholasticism began in the turmoil of the Reformation and terminated in the confusion of the French Revolution, the dissolution of monasteries, the suppression of religious orders, and the diminution of scholastic writers who were forced into practical apologetics.

Geographically, modern scholasticism flourished in Belgium, Great Britain (including Ireland and Scotland), France, Germany (together with Austria and the Netherlands), Hungary, Italy, Portugal, Poland, and Spain, usually in the shelter of Catholic or Protestant universities and in religious houses of study. Scholasticism was also transplanted to the New World with the establishment of religious orders and the founding of institutions of higher learning in North and South America and the Philippines. American colleges, such as Harvard, Yale, and William and Mary, reflected the scholasticism current in Protestant universities of the 16th century, especially Cambridge and Oxford, Edinburgh, Glasgow, and institutions in Germany and the Lowlands.

Second Scholasticism. The ''second scholasticism'' of the late 16th and early 17th centuries was a period of renewed activity after the chaos of the 14th century. Generally by 1500 the various theological schools were free to hold distinctive philosophical positions and to make consequent theological interpretations of revelation and church doctrine that became characteristic of the great religious orders. Despite these variations within schools, the following core of scholastic philosophical doctrine may be noted as common to all: (1) Thinkers agreed that the world is apprehended immediately as other than the individual knowing mind and that sense and intellect are two different modes of knowing. (2) Natural philosophy and psychology were characterized by an advocacy of pluralism (as opposed to monism), of a teleological dynamism operative within the world of nature, and of freedom and responsibility in man, who was regarded as having an immortal soul. (3) The possibility of metaphysics was recognized, as well as that of a normative and not merely descriptive ethics, not autonomous in the rationalist's sense but dependent on law and on a lawgiver knowable to man without benefit of revelation. (4) The existence of one God, infinite in being and power, a free Creator who conserves the universe by His all-powerful will, was regarded as demonstrable. (5) Knowledge was divided in a way that kept the philosophical and theological orders formally distinct, yet considered Christian revelation an indispensable auxiliary to reason and to moral integrity.

Three famous schools were well established at the beginning of the modern period: the Thomist (whose various interpretations are sometimes styled Thomistic to distinguish them from the original doctrine of St. Thomas), the Scotist (and similarly, Scotistic), and the nominalist. After 1600 the teaching of F. Suárez and his school (Suarezianism) was added to the traditional three. Common to all scholastic and nonscholastic thinkers within the Church was the powerful Augustinian movement of long standing in Christianity. Among the scholastics the resulting variety and doctrinal differences were jealously guarded; at times the various religious orders exploited their chosen masters with a loyalty that might have been expressed: ''my order, right or wrong.'' Yet, out of this welter also proceeded many outstanding scholastic works.

Dominicans. Among the Dominicans, John CA-PREOLUS, Tommaso de Vio CAJETAN, and Francis Sylvester FERRARIENSIS, together with JOHN OF ST. THOMAS, constituted a classical commentator tradition that sought a positive rather than an apologetical understanding of St. Thomas. At the University of Salamanca, Francisco de VITORIA instituted a new pattern of achievement in scholasticism on the eve of the Reformation when he took the actual text of the *Summa theologiae* of St. Thomas as a text in theology in place of the *Sentences* of Peter Lombard. His successor, Melchior CANO, was famous for his treatise on sources, in which he also presented a scheme for the reform of theology and philosophy. Among Cano's pupils were the Dominicans, Bartolomé de MEDINA and Domingo BÁÑEZ, and the Augustinian, Fray Luis de LEÓN. The Jesuit J. MALDONATUS had been, with Cano, a pupil of Vitoria. Báñez and others at the end of the 16th century engaged in a prolonged debate with the Jesuits over theological explanations concerning human freedom and divine grace (*see* THOMISM).

Franciscans. Franciscan scholastics of the period, like Dominican and Augustinian thinkers, were rooted in the systematic achievements of their medieval predecessors. St. Bonaventure or John Duns Scotus, for some, and William of Ockham, for others, constituted the sources of speculative guidance. Franciscans were free of official pressure to follow one master exclusively. Scotus was declared their doctor in 1593, although in 1550 the Capuchins had been forbidden to follow him and were encouraged to return to St. Bonaventure. Neither St. Thomas, declared a Doctor of the Church by Pius V in 1567, nor St. Augustine was excluded, and Aristotle appeared often in a Scotistic context.

Outstanding interpretations of the Franciscan tradition appeared early in the 16th century in works of M. O'FIHELY and Francesco Licheto (Lychetus, d. 1520), whose commentary on Lombard's *Sentences* was reissued in 1639 by Cardinal Sarnan. Other 16th-century authors were A. TROMBETTA and the Capuchin theologian Peter Trigosus (Pedro Trigoso de Calatayud).

Seventeenth-century Franciscan scholastics useful in interpreting Scotus include Hugh Cavellus (MacCaughnwell, 1571–1626), Johannes Bosco, a Belgian recollect, and B. MASTRIUS. The Italian, L. BRANCATI, with Andrew Rochmarius, a Pole (d. 1626), and Alphonsus Bricero (d. 1667), called a second Duns Scotus when teaching in Lima, Peru, exemplify the international spread of 17th-century Scotism. John Ponce of Cork assisted L. WADDING in editing the works of Scotus and wrote his own manuals, *Integrum philosophiae cursum*

ad mentem Scoti, together with a complete course in theology according to the mind of Scotus. He is also credited with introducing, in the 17th century, the actual formula often attributed to Ockham, *Entia non sunt multiplicanda praeter necessitatem* (Entities are not to be multiplied unnecessarily).

William van Sichem (d. 1691) produced a clear, easy-to-teach *Cursus philosophicus* harmonizing Scotus, St. Thomas, and Bonaventure. Mattheus Ferchius (1583–1669) and Gaudentius Bontempi (1612–72) exemplify commentators on St. Bonaventure's work.

An important and scholarly presentation of the theology of Duns Scotus came from the pen of C. Frassen, a doctor at the Sorbonne in 1662, whose *Scotus academicus* and *Cursus philosophiae* embody noteworthy simplicity of style, clearness of method, and subtlety of thought; both volumes went through numerous editions until late in the next century. By the middle of the 18th century, however, Franciscan philosophy and theology had suffered the general decline of modern scholasticism. In many writers of this period the original basic accord between Scotus and Thomas had been transposed into an irreconcilable opposition (*see* SCOTISM).

Augustinians. By 1530, the Augustinians (Hermits of St. Augustine) had a commitment to an earlier scholastic tradition that fitted in with their special claim on St. Augustine. In 1287 a general chapter of Florence commanded members of the order to accept and defend the position of GILES OF ROME, one of their members who had been a pupil of St. Thomas Aquinas, himself declared a second doctor of their order in 1560. This new synthesis avoided some disadvantages associated with the Platonic elements in Augustinianism, especially its theory of knowledge and its absence of a dialectical method and of an ordered system. The school flourished into the 18th century, with the teaching of Augustinian philosophy and theology at Salamanca, Coimbra, Alcalá, Padua, Pisa, Naples, Oxford, Paris, Vienna, Prague, Würzburg, Erfurt, Heidelberg, Willenberg, and other centers of learning.

Bartholomaeus ARNOLDI taught Luther during his monastic days and later was his theological opponent. Both Arnoldi and J. Altenstaig were *moderni* or nominalists in their philosophy. In the 16th-century disputes about grace, Augustinian scholastics generally accepted an efficacy of grace *ab intrinseco,* as opposed to the Molinist doctrine *ab extrinseco.* Cardinal H. NORIS, a Louvain theologian, and Cardinal G. L. BERTI, invited by the general of his order, Schiaffinati, to write a methodic exposition of Augustinian theology, were involved in the dispute over grace. They confronted the "primitive" Augustinianism of BAIUS and his followers, C. O. JANSEN, and J. DUVERGIER DE HAURANNE.

Earlier in the 16th century Raffaelo Bonherba (d.1681) examined the principal controversies between St. Thomas and Duns Scotus in the light of the doctrine of Giles of Rome, as did Fulgentius Schautheet about 1660. Federico Nicola Gavardi (1640–1715) was one of Giles's most important interpreters. In the works of Jordan Simon (1710–76) there is a curious eclectic philosophy built on a foundation derived from Raymond LULL. (*See* AUGUSTINIANISM.)

Oratorians. In the 17th century, with the physics of Aristotle in ruins and that of Galileo in triumph, there came a joining of Augustinianism and CARTESIANISM through the influence of the Congregation of the Oratory, founded in 1661 by Cardinal P. de BÉRULLE. Among the ORATORIANS, the cause of Augustinianism, as a vehement protest against the alleged paganization of Christianity by Thomism, was advanced by THOMASSIN, R. SIMON, B. LAMY, J. B. DU HAMEL and especially N. MALEBRANCHE, of whom J. B. BOUSSUET said that his doctrine was *"pulchra, nova, falsa."*

Benedictines. The Order of St. Benedict bore many attacks against Catholicism but managed to produce some of the classic works of scholarship in the modern period and, as with other religious orders, less distinguished manuals and compendia. Many Benedictine authors took St. Thomas as their guide, but some looked to St. Anselm of Canterbury as an intellectual father. Andreas de la Moneda (d. 1672), a Spaniard, wrote a course in scholastic and moral theology "according to the mind of Anselm and Thomas." Probably the best work on dogmatic theology produced by a German Benedictine was *Theologia scholastica secundum viam et doctrinam divi Thomae Aquinatis* (Augsburg 1695, 1719) by Paul Mezger (1637–1702). The *Philosophia Thomistica Salisburgensis* (Augsburg 1706) of Ludwig Babenstuber (1660–1726) was in the old peripatetic tradition. Celestin Pley (d. 1710) offered a synthesis of rationalism, Thomism, and Benedictinism in his *Theoremata theologiae angelicae Beneditino-Thomistica* (Salzburg 1711). Nor was the Franciscan Doctor, Scotus, neglected, as the works of A. C. Hermann (*c.* 1720) and Marianus Brockie (1687–1757), written "according to Scotus," indicate.

Carmelites. Carmelite professors at Alcalá and Salamanca early in the 17th century published their lectures in a series of manuals of Thomistic scholastic philosophy and theology. Authors of the philosophy manuals were designated as COMPLUTENSES (the old Roman name of Alcalá was Complutum) and those of the theology series as SALMANTICENSES. The works exhibited a high degree of consistency in doctrine because of the discussions that influenced the final form of each work. Disputes were settled by vote.

Later in the 17th century, attempts were made by some to elevate to the rank of a theological school the doctrine of John Baconthorp, a Carmelite Averroist. St. JOHN OF THE CROSS, the classic writer on "empirical mysticism," was intimately acquainted with the *Summa theologiae* of St. Thomas from his higher studies at Salamanca. Carmelites engaged also in polemic writings against QUIETISM, JANSENISM, GALLICANISM, Cartesianism in philosophy, and RATIONALISM in Scripture and history.

Servites. Founded in 1233 at Florence, the Order of SERVITES originally followed Scotus. Later they turned from him to Henry of Ghent, actually a secular master but mistakenly thought to be a Servite. His Augustinian philosophy of a Neoplatonic character was made obligatory during the 1600s. H. A. Borghi, at Pisa in 1627, wrote a text for students based on Henry of Ghent, as did Jerome Scarpari (d. 1650) and Calistus Lodigeri (d. 1710); the last named was said to have advocated Henry's doctrine so strongly as almost to bring the man himself back from the grave. But Gerard Baldi (d. 1660) followed St. Thomas in his *Catholica monarchia Christi,* a theological treatise, and Marc Struggl (d. 1760) followed Molinism. At the beginning of the 19th century, Constantine Battini (d. 1830) contributed to the restoration of theological studies in Italy that later fructified in the works of the Servite cardinal, A. LÉPICIER.

Jesuits. Founded in 1540, some five years before the beginning of the Council of Trent, suppressed in Europe in 1773 and restored in 1814, the Society of Jesus came into the stream of modern scholasticism in time to contribute with the Dominicans to the flowering of Spanish scholasticism. St. IGNATIUS OF LOYOLA personally and in the official documents of the Society rooted Jesuit philosophical and theological speculation in Aristotle and St. Thomas, a directive reiterated in the RATIO STUDIORUM.

The guidance given by St. Thomas was not taken as strictly as among the Dominicans, however, and a certain liberty of thought independent of established masters soon characterized Jesuit theology and philosophy. This appeared to some as eclecticism and to others as laxism—e.g., the teaching of PROBABILISM in problems affecting conscience. Many early Jesuits broke away from the physics of Aristotle in favor of new scientific movements. Later, some Jesuit textbook writers departed completely from metaphysics and the Thomistic synthesis, some adopting a Cartesian orientation, others the methodology and format of C. WOLFF or modifications of the sensism of É. B. de CONDILLAC and J. LOCKE. Yet some of the pioneers of the return to St. Thomas in the 19th century were members of the Society of Jesus.

Francisco de TOLEDO, first Jesuit cardinal and "father of scholastic philosophy in the Society of Jesus," had held the chair of philosophy at the University of Salamanca before becoming a Jesuit and had studied under the Dominican Domingo de SOTO. During Bellarmine's time at the Roman College practically all the professors were Spaniards, e.g., Gabriel VÁZQUEZ and his rival, F. SUÁREZ. M. SA was a Portuguese from Coimbra. C. ALAMANNI, born at Milan, studied under both Vázquez and Suárez and wrote a *Summa totius philosophiae e divini Thomae Aquinatis doctrina* (Padua 1618–23), which follows the form of St. Thomas's *Summa theologiae.* Later, following the style of the new manuals stimulated by Suárez, he published a *Summa philosophica D. Thomae ex variis eius libris in ordinem cursus philosophici accomodata* (Paris 1639), which F. EHRLE reedited at Paris in 1894. GREGORY OF VALENCIA, J. de LUGO, and L. LESSIUS were also at the Roman College at some time during their careers.

Peter da FONSECA, called the "Portuguese Aristotle," was provincial when the work of the Coimbricenses was undertaken by the Jesuit professors of the University of COIMBRA. Somewhat like the project of the Carmelites at Alcalá and Salamanca, this famous course was later published at the direction of the Jesuit general, C. ACQUAVIVA. Fonseca may also be the father of the doctrine on *SCIENTIA MEDIA* made famous by his pupil, L. de MOLINA, in his *Concordia . . .* (Lisbon 1588). (*See* SUAREZIANISM; MOLINISM.)

Council of Trent. In its totality scholasticism embraces exegesis of Scripture, patrology, and Church history, as well as systematic theology and its related philosophy. In all areas, but particularly in philosophy and theology, scholastics contributed to the formulation of conciliar decrees at Trent (1545–63), clarifying and making precise the concepts and definitions expressing the imputation of guilt, the causal influence and effects of supernatural grace, the reality of infused virtues, the analogy of matter and form in the Sacraments, and the sacramental character. These decrees also exemplify the masterful use by the Church of the contributions made by various orders and schools through their delegates at the council.

Later, in turn, scholastic philosophy was influenced by Trent in such matters as the distinction of three degrees of CERTITUDE that appears in the manuals after 1563. The discussion of certitude in the theological context of the Lutheran teaching on justification by faith alone and the Christian's personal certitude of his own state of justification shifted the emphasis from the objective to the subjective order. To be certain meant to be secure, although certitude had reference also to the truth of things. In the manuals it went through curious forms that bear little resemblance to the teaching of the great medieval scholastics [S. Harent, *Dictionnaire de théologie catholique,* ed. A. Vacant et al., 15 v. (Paris 1903–50) 6:211–215].

Sociopolitical and Moral Theory. Diego LAÍNEZ, a Jesuit delegate to Trent, had held the doctrine that the power to govern was delegated by the people to the sovereign, who was responsible to them for just rule. Another Jesuit, St. Robert BELLARMINE, for whom the Dominicans, Pedro de SOTO and Domingo de SOTO, were favorite authorities, carried on a famous controversy with James I, King of England, and his apologist, Filmore, over the political theory on the divine right of kings. Suárez gave powerful expression to the scholastic position on the origin and nature of civil power in his *Tractatus de legibus* (Coimbra 1612). The Dominican Vitoria shared with three other Spanish theologians, Domingo de Soto, Molina, and Suárez, the creation of a body of classic political theory attending to natural law and its implications.

Vitoria, Soto, and Suárez may be grouped also with Cajetan, Toletus, Bellarmine, and Gregory of Valentia in their brilliant reworking of the scholastic position on warfare. More the legalist, Suárez was interested in the source of lawmaking and took the existence of a plurality of individual states, each enjoying its own sovereignty as a perfect society, as a practical datum of 16th-century life. But Vitoria maintained that the good of the world as a whole (*bonum orbis*) was the care and concern of all, and he seems to have been the last scholastic internationalist until the 19th-century Jesuit, L. TAPARELLI D'AZEGLIO.

Generally in Europe, economic expansion raised questions in moral theology concerning just prices, monetary standards, and usury. Another development centered around the rights of penitents and practical standards or rules of confessors to make equitable moral judgments. St. Alphonsus LIGUORI, who had founded the Redemptorists at Scala in 1732, published his *Annotationes* (1744) to a classic work in moral theology by the Jesuit H. BUSENBAUM. Reissued in 1753 as *Theologia moralis,* after being recast in Liguori's own classic style, it was the source of many compendia of moral theology. By 1750 CASUISTRY, or the practice of formulating cases and solving them to illustrate the right or wrong involved, had become a synonym for moral laxity; but not before the Dominicans had forbidden the use of probabilism to their confessors and the Jesuits had developed a considerable doctrine and practice of the same. The Redemptorists sought a balance in EQUIPROBABILISM.

Reaction and Adjustment. From 1650 to 1750 the multiplicity of schools, writings, changes in format, and attempts to combine the traditional with the modern found a type of unity with the rise of the new manuals, first under the influence of Suárez and then later with Leibnizian-Wolffian developments. Allied with this was the growth of Protestant scholasticism and scholasticism's continuing confrontation with the new science and with modern reforms in philosophy.

New Manuals. Under the pressure of a widespread polemic and reflecting contemporary change in method, the four areas in which scholastics were trained became increasingly specialized. Theologians, despite the work of such scholars as the Benedictines of Saint-Maur, made a dialectical rather than a historical use of Scripture and the Fathers. Texts were excerpted for the specific defense of decrees of the Church or to "prove" scholastic theses in theology. As a result of this, there appeared autonomous manuals and compendia in dogmatic and moral theology that were harmful to an integral understanding and practice of the faith.

Further, attacked as philosophers, scholastic teachers and writers attempted to counterattack as philosophers and had little time for the ponderous tomes of previous eras. Concurrently there arose a variety of courses, manuals, and systematic disputations designed to simplify the teaching of basic matter and attempting to incorporate what was useful in the new sciences. In some of these may be detected the beginning of a more radical enterprise, that of exploring and explaining revelation in terms of philosophies lacking roots in Greek thought. While textbook commentaries declined, works that gave an entire course in philosophy or theology or an integral part of theology became more numerous. In physical appearance these manuals were reduced in size from the folio to the quarto or smaller format.

One landmark terminating this process of change was Suárez's *Disputationes metaphysicae* (Salamanca 1597). Without manifesting a commitment to any one of the classical scholastic traditions, Suárez nevertheless stayed within the boundaries sketched by Thomas, Scotus, and Ockham, while incorporating his own reactions to the philosophical concerns and achievements of nonscholastics. Among these concerns was the subject of metaphysics, now considered in the context of new problems, one of which was the quest for an ontological principle from which everything else could be derived. According to some interpreters, Suárez's inclusion of the possible in the meaning of BEING (defined as "whatever is or can be") meant that metaphysics could be turned into an ontology and the way opened to working out a *mathesis universalis* along lines proposed by G. W. LEIBNIZ and C. WOLFF.

Soon shorter manuals appeared, displacing those of Fonseca (an excellent commentary on Aristotle) and To-

ledo. Most influential were works by the Jesuits, Pedro Hurtado de Mendoza (1578–1615), R. de ARRIAGA, and F. de Oviedo. The last named's *Cursus philosophicus* (Antwerp 1632–39), with its notable stress on principles, perhaps foreshadowed later developments when philosophy would be defined as the "science of principles." J. E. Mora sees Arriaga, very influential during his teaching years at Prague, as representing the link with the scholasticism of Leibniz and Wolff that influenced Kant through his teacher, Martin Knutzen (1713–51).

Dominicans who adopted the manual method and format include A. GOUDIN, A. PINY, and Nicholaus Arnu (1629–92). The Carmelite PHILLIP OF THE BLESSED TRINITY, the Benedictines, A. Reding and Joseph Saenz d'Aguirre (1630–68), and the Theatine Z. Pascualigo, followed a similar method and doctrine.

A curious combination of theology and philosophy appeared in the works of prominent scholastic theologians between 1650 and 1750 who used both the Fathers and ancient pagan author to provide historical evidence for their non-Thomistic view that "God exists" is a self-evident proposition. This trend is illustrated by the Oratorian THOMASSIN, the Portuguese Jesuit Antonio Cordeyro (1640–1722), the Sorbonne scholar H. de TOURNELY, the Minim Antoine Boucat (d. 1730), the Capuchin Thomas of Charmes (1703–65), and the Augustinian cardinal G. L. BERTI. These authors presaged positivistic practices that were to appear later and may also have originated the modern argument for the existence of God *ex consensu gentium*.

Protestant Scholasticism. Luther's personal contempt for Aristotle and the schoolmen was bound up with his doctrine on the nature and effects of faith. Other factors were his nominalist background in philosophy and the influence of the Devotio Moderna exemplified in THOMAS À KEMPIS and the Brothers of the Common Life at Deventer, itself a reaction to the confusions of late medieval scholasticism. But MELANCHTHON undertook to construct a Protestant theological system and introduced among Lutherans a humanistic ARISTOTELIANISM set to the service of religion. Also in the background of all the Reformers was the scholasticism of Peter RAMUS, whose *Dialecticae institutiones* (1543) was an attempt to substitute for the logic of the schoolmen a more simple type composed ostensibly from Plato, Cicero, and Quintilian. In this sense Ramus was the first "scholastic" Protestant. But with the growing appreciation of metaphysics for establishing the meanings at issue in the Christian dialogue, Ramus's antimetaphysical logic was forbidden in the Protestant universities—at Leyden in 1591, at Helmstedt in 1597, and at Wittenberg in 1603.

Since humanistic Ramism and philosophical skepticism were as unsatisfactory to Dutch, German, and Bohemian Protestants as they were to Catholics, the scholastic teacher of Protestant theology in Central Europe began to rely on the work already cloned by Spanish and Portuguese scholastic philosophers. Of the compendia, Suárez's *Disputationes metaphysicae* outranked all Catholic scholastic literature and served as a textbook in philosophy for many German universities in the 17th and part of the 18th centuries. Soon Protestant authors began to produce their own manuals. Cornelius Martini (1568–1621) at Helmstedt, who, with Johannes Caselius (1535–1613), worked in the Italian Aristotelian tradition pioneered among Protestants by Jakob Schegk (1511–87), wrote an early work using quotations from St. Thomas and Cajetan. In 1604, after making acquaintance with the Spanish scholastics, he printed his *Metaphysicae commentatio.* Jakob Martini (1570–1649) published a *Theoremata metaphysicorum* (Wittenberg 1603–04) showing the influence of Suárez's *Disputationes,* which had appeared in the Mainz edition several years earlier.

By 1617 Christoph Scheibler (1589–1653), author of an *Opus metaphysicum,* was known as the Protestant Suárez. F. P. Burgersdijck (1590–1635), author of an *Institutiones logicae* (Leyden 1626), used his own composition of a kind of Suarezian compendium published posthumously in 1640. Burgersdijck's pupil and successor at Leyden, Adrianus Heereboort (1614–61) also wrote a logic and metaphysics based on his teacher's work. He taught many academic philosophers of the 17th century in the Netherlands, among whom were two of Leibniz's teachers, Jakob Tomasius (1622–84) and J. A. Scherzer (1628–83), both also influenced by Daniel Strahl. B. SPINOZA, who mentions Heereboort, also shared the debt to Spanish scholasticism and took Burgersdijck's division of the causes into his own systematic organization of philosophy. Other prominent Protestant authors were Bartholomew Keckermann (1571–1608); Polanus von Polansdorf (1561–1610); William Ames (1576–1633), under Ramist influence but essentially scholastic; and Johann Heinrich Alsted (Alstedius; 1588–1638), a Protestant encyclopedist.

Across the Atlantic, the records of the Boston Book Market together with the curricular offerings and public dissertations at Harvard show this same scholastic influence in the New World. John Harvard (1607–38) left to the college library his copy of a popular compendium, that of the French Cistercian, Eustachius a S. Paolo, whose *Summa philosophiae* (preface dated 1608) was mentioned favorably by Spinoza.

In England, the Oxford of John LOCKE likewise reflected these manual developments. The Puritans' concern for scriptural preaching alienated them from the use of scholastic matter, and yet John WESLEY and Richard HOOKER are known for their scholastic borrowings. Works by J. Ray, W. Derham, and C. Mach and the famous *Natural Theology* of William Paley, so disappointing to Darwin, echoed as late as 1836 a scholasticism long since strained thin and mixed with innumerable other elements. As with the Roman Catholics, Protestant scholastics experimented with the Cartesian contribution to modern philosophy. An obdurate Aristotelian among Protestants was Georgius Agricola, who objected in 1665 to the Copernican geocentric system, claiming that if the earth were a star men would all be in heaven!

Modern Science and Philosophy. In the light of subsequent history, the new science of mathematical physics evolving at the hands of G. GALILEI and I. Newton was of utmost importance. B. PASCAL confessed his inability to decide between the Ptolemaic, Copernican, and Tychonean systems, a decision involving further complex options concerning matters in Aristotle's *Physics.* But this was only one of a number of areas that engaged the attention of modern scholastics. At a time when the advance of knowledge with new methods and theories called for quiet scholarship and balanced evaluation, the scholastic world generally was much concerned with the polemic and ideological issues it judged crucial for human welfare in general.

For some, occultism helped to compensate for the decreasing interest in philosophy and theology and was a factor in the terrible witch trials in Europe. The nonphysical atmosphere of predictive ASTROLOGY seemed to provide a way of contending with a mechanical interpretation of reality that appeared to menace human values. In the 18th century this materialistic threat had become a powerful ideology at the hands of the ENCYCLOPEDISTS, who threatened institutions and societies in conflict with their ideas and seemed to have the destruction of Christianity as one of their avowed aims.

Moreover, polemic concern with the Reformation distracted competent minds. Controversial theology, a preliminary form of the more developed discipline of APOLOGETICS, began to grow. But putting the old physics or the new science to work for the sake of securing an advantage over skeptics, atheists, and impious materialists did not make clear what the new physics was about in its method and conclusions. Nor did Isaac Newton's famous affirmation of THEISM in the General Scholion appended to the 2d edition (1713) of his *Mathematical Principles of Natural Theology* help the situation.

Despite a few scholastics who were interested in science during the modern period, such as the Jesuit R. G. Boscovich and the Cistercian Juan CARAMUEL LOBKOWITZ, the majority showed little evidence of scientific knowledge in their works. With Galileo's defeat in his battle for freedom from theological control, and with Copernicus also on the Index from 1616 to the turn of the 19th century, it seemed safer to scholastic philosophers to adopt a watch-and-wait attitude that inhibited scholarly examination and evaluation of the new ideas. Preachers and casuists gained prominence and writers of manuals in philosophy and theology worked almost always with the aim of apologetics in mind.

Crossroads and Transition. The last period of modern or middle scholasticism, roughly between 1750 and 1830, may be characterized as one of crossroads and of transition. Noteworthy in this period were the development of Wolffian manuals preceding the revival of Thomism, the concern for ideology, and the Cartesian influence within the scholastic tradition.

Wolffian Manuals. In 1720, Christian WOLFF began producing at the Protestant University of Halle, first in German and then in Latin, some 40 volumes of philosophy according to a new method and format. Using Euclid and his geometric method as a model, he aimed to present philosophy systematically by reducing it to its principles. He first proposed a new division of philosophy based on the distinction between experience and reason—a distinction later to widen into the divergent streams of EMPIRICISM and RATIONALISM and never to be closed in scholastic works of Wolffian origin. For Wolff, philosophy belongs to the realm of reason, as distinct from that of experience, and its theoretical or speculative part is metaphysics. Using a systematic breakdown into genus and species, he divides metaphysics into general metaphysics or ONTOLOGY and special metaphysics, and the latter in turn into three parts: COSMOLOGY, PSYCHOLOGY, and THEODICY (*see* SCIENCES, CLASSIFICATION OF). Wolff's definition of philosophy as *cognitio rationis eorum quae sunt vel fiunt* then sets the tone for its later development, which makes special use of the principles of CONTRADICTION and of SUFFICIENT REASON. Because sensation is radically distinct from rational knowledge and since existence is systematically meaningless in this conception, a philosophy understood as a science of reasons or *rationes* must be a science of essences. But the essence is the possible, and the possible is ultimately the noncontradictory. Thus the primacy of essence for the Wolffian system is practically equivalent to the primacy of logic.

For the most part, scholastic imitators of Wolff maintained a kind of static tension between the extremes of experience (empiricism) and reason (rationalism). Many continued, as did Wolff, one of the less commendable characteristics of postmedieval scholasticism, viz, a rationalistic attitude toward reality that segregates and exalts the speculative power of man's reason while de-

preciating his other powers. Others, however, expressed reservations over the new philosophy. Among Protestant theologians at Wolff's own Halle and in the Berlin Academy there was criticism of his system, especially on the point of sufficient reason. This principle took on an ideological dimension in that, if reason were understood as a determining reason, difficulties were created over the freedom of the will and a point made in favor of fatalism. Mansuetus a S. Felice, (d. 1775), an Augustinian professor of moral theology, wrote several philosophical-theological dissertations on the principle of sufficient reason in connection with liberty, a best possible world, and the various aspects of grace and predestination (Cremona 1775). Cardinal Hyacinthus Sigismond Gerdil of the Barnabites (1718–1802) wrote a short essay on the *Mémoires* of N. de Béguelin (1714–89) that illustrated how the problem of determinism in the moral order brought its metaphysical aspect to the foreground. Earlier, the Benedictine Anselm Desing (1699–1772) wrote *Diatriba circa methodum Wolfianum* (1752), using diatribe in its original Greek meaning of a study or discussion. This purported to show that Wolff's approach was neither a method nor scientific, especially for establishing the principles of natural law.

Scholastic Imitators. Scholastic imitation of Wolff's method and format began about 1750. German Jesuits principally in Austria and Franciscan manual writers in Germany and Italy produced a body of philosophical compendia that, in the next two centuries, was to be mistakenly regarded as an embodiment of the scholastic tradition. Often, too, the Kantian critique of Leibnizian scholasticism in its Wolffian form would be taken as a competent demolition of genuine scholastic doctrines.

The Jesuits Joseph Redlhamer (1713–61) and Berthold Hauser (1713–62) were among the early scholastic imitators of Wolff. Two other prominent Jesuit Wolffians were Benedict Stattler (1728–97) and S. von STORCHENAU. Stattler made use of the principle of sufficient reason almost to the saturation point in his *Philosophia methodo scientiis propria explanata* (Augsburg 1769–72), granting the principle an eminence that rivals its use in Wolff and that probably was not equaled in any subsequent scholastic work. Storchenau had taught philosophy at Vienna for ten years when the Jesuits were suppressed in 1773. His *Institutiones logicae* (Vienna 1769) and his *Institutiones metaphyxicae* (Vienna 1772), with its division into metaphysics, cosmology, psychology, and natural theology, went through numerous editions until as late as 1833. Both Storchenau and Stattler are related to Suárez in certain features of their philosophy. Stattler's cosmology, already without any doctrine of matter and form to give it substance, is more of an outline of the apologetics of miracles and a remote preparation for "proving" the existence of God from the fact of law in nature. The Austrian government in 1752 had forbidden the teaching of Aristotelian doctrine on matter and form, and the same prohibition was requested also in Germany. Generally HYLOMORPHISM was held in complete disrepute among these philosophers.

Franciscan manual-writers who reflected the current of the times were Herman Osterrieder (d. 1783) and Laurentius Altieri. The former taught philosophy to Franciscan students in Ratisbon and his *Metaphysica vetus et nova* (Augsburg 1761) was adapted to their needs. It combined basic Scotistic notions with the Wolffian order of ontology, placing the principle of sufficient reason in its accustomed place after the principle of contradiction before treating "the concept of being and its attributes in general." Giuseppe Tamagna (1747–98) published his *Institutiones philosophicae* (Rome 1778), with a second edition in 1780 under the patronage of the minister general of the Franciscans. In his logic he showed concern for the practical aspects of criteriology and commented on Wolff's mistake of confusing the existence of sufficient reason with the ability to assign a sufficient reason. He also tried to break out of the Wolffian logic of essences into the assertion of existential reality independent of deduction.

In face of the chaotic condition of textbooks, the minister general of the Friars Minor proposed for uniform adoption a *Philosophiae universae institutiones;* this appeared anonymously in 1843 or 1844 but had the author's name, Dionysius of St. John in Galdo, displayed on the second edition (Rome 1846).

Concern for Ideology. The Jesuits, Ignace Monteiro (1724–1812), *Philosophia rationalis electica* (Venice 1770), Antonio Eximeno y Pujader (1729–1808), and Juan Andrés (1740–1817), attempted to assimilate atomistic and sensualist philosophies in Spain and were ardent defenders of doctrines proposed by Locke in England and Condillac in France, while repeating the strictures of Antonio Genovesi (1713–69) and L. A. Verney (1713–92) against Aristotelian philosophy. Locke's sensism was taught at the Vincentian college in Piacenza for a time. Vincenzo Buzzetti (1777–1824) was influenced while studying theology by an exiled Spanish Jesuit, Baltasar Mesdeu (1741–1820), who helped him abandon Locke. He taught the three Sordi brothers, who later entered the Society of Jesus (restored in 1814) and worked for the restoration of scholastic and particularly Thomistic philosophy in their order.

The Celestine, Appiano Buonafede (1716–93), a distinguished philosopher, was imbued with doctrines of Condillac. J. BALMES in Spain and the Jesuit J. KLEUTGEN in Germany were not writers of textbooks, but they worked with an eclectic method of drawing useful matter from St. Thomas and opposed sensism in scholastic writers.

At an opposite pole of the reaction against rationalism were the powerful tendencies already at work in Cartesian and Leibnizian philosophies toward various forms of IDEALISM. In these the world of matter and the experience of sense knowledge, if not denied, had no systematic relevance. Three famous scholastic theologians who launched positive attacks against "scholastics" and attempted a synthesis with the genuine values of critical and idealistic philosophy were G. HERMES, A. GÜNTHER, and J. FROHSCHAMMER. Kleutgen's defense in Germany against their attacks on scholasticism did not always identify the sources and nature of the scholasticism at issue. A contemporary, J. B. Hauréau, in *De la philosophie scolastique* reduced everything to the problem of UNIVERSALS. The crucial questions at issue in the attempts of these three theologians to assimilate the new philosophy centered around the relation between being and knowledge in the context of faith.

Less successful in confronting the new while maintaining what was valid in the old were apologists such as the Spanish Benedictine B. J. Feijóo y Montenegro (1676–1764). Feijóo admired F. BACON and Newton for their work in the order of experimental truth and eulogized Descartes as a genius. His *Teatro critico universal sopra los erroes communes* (Madrid 1726–40) was not lacking in critical sharpness, unlike the work of another Benedictine, François LAMY, whose refutation of Spinoza, *Le nouvel athéisme renversé,* did not touch the issues very profoundly.

The Benedictine Maternus Reuss in Germany exalted Kant's philosophy and sought permission to visit the great German philosopher to profit from conversations with him. Other Benedictines teaching Kantian philosophy about this time (*c.* 1788) were Placidus Muth (1753–182) and Augustinus Schelle (1742–1805). P. ZIMMER followed J. G. FICHTE, while both Zimmer and Marianus Dobmayer (1753–1805) showed evidence of assimilating doctrine from F. W. J. SCHELLING.

J. M. SAILER, Cajetan von Weiller (1762–1826) and Jacob Salat (1766–1851) attempted to use insights from the fideism of F. H. JACOBI and J. G. HAMANN. In France the Abbé Jean Marie de Prades (1720–82) was close enough to the philosophy of the ENLIGHTENMENT to contribute the article on "Certitude" to the famous *Encyclopédie.*

Cartesian Influences. Finally, one of the most powerful influences within modern scholasticism in its later period was that of Cartesian Catholic philosophy. Descartes had led the way in adapting his system to scholastic needs when, in the vain hope of having it adopted as a Jesuit textbook at his Alma Mater, he cast his metaphysical masterpiece, *Meditations on First Philosophy* (1641), into scholastic form in *Principles of Philosophy* (1644). (*See* CARTESIANISM.) Toward the end of the 17th century, however, Catholic philosophers were teaching a brand of philosophy that was committed to Cartesian starting points and methods—sometimes combined with traditional scholasticism, sometimes generating systematic opposition and tensions. Antoine Le Grand (d. 1699), a Franciscan professor at Douai, the Benedictine Robert Desgabets (1620–78), the Minim Emmanuel Maignan (1601–76), and Andreas Pissini found difficulty squaring their Cartesian philosophy with the truths of faith. The Jesuit Honoré Fabri (1607–88) attempted to construct a system based on Aristotle that ended up not very different from the atomism of P. GASSENDI. P. D. HUET began as a partisan of Cartesian philosophy but, coming to regard it as a danger to the faith, wrote *Censure philosophiae cartesianae* (Paris 1680), which was severe in its strictures and of great influence among Catholic philosophers and theologians.

Some 18th-century Cartesians whose manuals went into the following century include the Jesuit C. BUFFIER, whose *Traité des premières veritez* was edited by Lamennais in 1822 and influenced the Scottish philosopher, T. REID; Jean Cochet (d. 1771), who combined the Cartesian *Cogito* with the Wolffian division and method; L'Abbé Para du Phanjas (1724–97); Michael Kalus (d. 1792); and J. V. de Decker. Claude Mey (1712–96) and Antoine Migeot (1730–94) also wrote in this tradition, all of them seeing in Descartes the savior of philosophy after its peripatetic decadence. Migeot was also a good witness to a widespread conception that SCHOLASTIC METHOD was identical with that of Wolff and the geometrical ideal in general.

One of the masterpieces of Cartesian manual writing—which G. VENTURA DI RAULICA, a former Jesuit, onetime general of the Theatines, and a moderate traditionalist in philosophy called "*le cours classique du cartésianisme*"—was the *Institutiones philosophicae auctoritate D.D. Archiepiscopi Lugdunensis.* Written by a Father Joseph Valla (d. 1790), whose name does not always appear on the title page of later editions, it was first used in the Diocese of Lyons and became generally known as *Philosophie de Lyon.* Valla, as well as G. C. Ubaghs (1800–75), Belgian traditionalist, drew considerable inspiration from Malebranche. Emphasizing the importance of a philosophy that conceives man as a soul temporarily confined in a body, Valla warned against philosophical theories that detract from the excellence and spirituality of the mind of man. He urged a doctrine

of innate ideas, emphasizing that the philosopher must not conceive man's mind as so dependent upon the organs of the sense as to derive its ideas from them.

Among the Sulpicians, manuals by Valla (purged of Jansenism), and L. Bailly, *Theologia dogmatica et moralis ad usum seminariorum* (Dijon 1789; 2d ed. Lyons 1804), remained in use until the middle of the 19th century. But French predominated as the language of instruction and Saint-Sulpice was characterized by the general absence of dogma in favor of apologetics and morals, the latter quite juridical and on the rigorous side. Pierre Denis Boyer (1766–1842), one of the more original professors, developed his course on religion and the Church under the inspiration of Bishop Jean Baptiste Duvoisin (1744–1813), a professor at the Sorbonne before the French revolution. But aware of the change from 18th-century hostility to 19th-century indifferentism, Boyer introduced a thesis to show that indifferentism was "contrary to reason, harmful to God, opposed to man's nature, temerarius or opposed to prudence, and contrary to the welfare of society."

Bibliography: General works. F. C. COPLESTONE, *History of Philosophy* (Westminster, Md. 1946–) v.3, 4, 6. G. FITZ and A. MICHEL, *Dictionnaire de théologie catholique,* ed. A. VACANT et al., 15 v. (Paris 1903–50) 14.2:1691–1728. H. S. LUCAS, *The Renaissance and the Reformation* (2d ed. New York 1960). È. H. GILSON, *The Unity of Philosophical Experience* (New York 1937). J. QUÉTIF and J. ÉCHARD, *Scriptores Ordinis Praedicatorum,* 5 v. (Paris 1719–23). C. SOMMERVOGEL et al., *Bibliothèque de la Compagnie de Jésus,* 11 v. (Brussels–Paris 1890–1932). H. HURTER, *Nomenclator literarius theologiae catholicae³,* 5 v. in 6 (3d ed. Innsbruck 1903–13). Second scholasticism. C. GIACON, *La seconda scolastica,* 3 v. (Milan 1944–50). F. ROTH, *History of the English Austin Friars, 1249–1538,* 2 v. (New York 1961). *A Catalogue of Renaissance Philosophers, 1350–1650,* ed. J. O. RIEDL, (Milwaukee 1940). L. THORNDIKE, *A History of Magic and Experimental Science,* 8 v. (New York 1923–58) v.5, 6. B. HAMILTON, *Political Thought in Sixteenth Century Spain* (New York 1964). Later developments. J. E. GURR, *The Principle of Sufficient Reason in Some Scholastic Systems, 1750–1900* (Milwaukee 1959). M. GRABMANN, "Die *Disputationes metaphysicae* des Franz Suarez in ihrer methodischen Eigenart und Fortwirkung," *Mittelalterliches Geistesleben,* 3 v. (Munich 1926–56) 1:525–560. J. F. MORA, "Suárez and Modern Philosophy," *Journal of the History of Ideas,* 14 (1953) 528–547. É. H. GILSON, *Études sur le rôle de la pensée médiévale dans la formation du systeme cartésien* (Paris 1930); *Index scolasticocartésien* (Paris 1913). G. SORTAIS, "Le Cartésianisme chez les jésuites français au XVIIᵉ et au XVIIIᵉ siècle," *Archives de Philosophie,* 6.3 (1928) 1–93. W. J. ONG, *Ramus: Method, and the Decay of Dialogue* (Cambridge, Mass 1958). W. T. COSTELLO, *The Scholastic Curriculum at Early Seventeenth Century Cambridge* (Cambridge, Mass. 1958). S. E. MORISON, *Harvard College in the Seventeenth Century* (Cambridge, Mass. 1936). M. WUNDT, *Die deutsche Schulphilosophie im Zeitalter der Aufklärung* (Tübingen 1945). P. DIBON, *La Philosophie néerlandaise au siècle d'or* (New York 1954–) v.1. E. A. BURTT, *The Metaphysical Foundations of Modern Physical Science* (rev. ed. New York 1950). J. DILLENBERGER, *Protestant Thought and Natural Science: An Historical Interpretation* (Garden City, N.Y. 1960). R. CESSAIO, *Le Thomisme et* *les Thomistes* (Paris 1999). *Jean Capreolus en son temps: Colloque de Rodez,* eds., G. BEDOUELLE, R. CESSARIO and K. WHITE (Paris 1997). J. F. COURTINE, *Suarez et le systéme de la métaphysique* (Paris 1990).

[J. E. GURR]

3. CONTEMPORARY SCHOLASTICISM

Contemporary scholasticism is predominantly a rediscovery of the thought of St. THOMAS AQUINAS that began early in the 19th century, developed slowly in Catholic countries of Europe, gained momentum through the efforts of Leo XIII, spread to most countries of the world, and survives today in various forms. Beginning as an ideological discovery by Catholic philosophers confronted with contemporary problems, it was supported by serious historical studies of the Middle Ages and of scholastic authors previously neglected. These historical and doctrinal studies led to a clearer distinction between NEOSCHOLASTICISM AND NEOTHOMISM. Although contemporary scholasticism includes revived SCOTISM, SUAREZIANISM, and a variety of eclectic adaptations, it is predominantly an attempt to return to the vital thought of St. Thomas in a way that is relevant to contemporary man.

Origins of the Revival. The study of St. Thomas never entirely died out in the Dominican Order, although the general chapter of 1748 had to emphasize ancient obligations. In 1757 the Master General, J. T. Boxadors, reviewed the ancient legislation and insisted that all Dominicans return immediately to the solid teaching of the Angelic Doctor. His long letter was included in the acts of the general chapter that met in Rome in 1777 [*Monumenta Ordinis Fratrum Praedicatorum historica,* ed. B. M. Reichert (Rome-Stuttgart-Paris 1896–) 14:344–350]. That year Salvatore ROSELLI, professor at the College of St. Thomas in Rome (Minerva), published a scholarly six-volume *Summa philosophica* dedicated to Cardinal Boxadors. Intended to renew Thomism in the order, the *Summa* directly influenced all leaders of the Thomistic revival in Italy, Spain, and France. Three editions of this work (Rome 1777, 1783; Bologna 1857–59) and a four-volume compendium (Rome 1837) were quickly exhausted.

Italy. The prevailing philosophy in Italy was ONTOLOGISM, promulgated principally by A. ROSMINI-SERBARI and V. GIOBERTI. The earliest pioneer of the Neothomistic movement in Piacenza was Canon Vincenzo Buzzetti (1777–1824). Taught the philosophy of J. LOCKE and É. B. de CONDILLAC by the Vincentian Fathers of Collegio Alberoni, he abandoned Locke's sensism under the influence of Baltasar Masdeu (1741–1820), an exiled Spanish Jesuit. Buzzetti discovered St. Thomas by reading Roselli and a smaller, simpler text by the

French Dominican Antoine GOUDIN. As professor of philosophy in the diocesan seminary (1804–08), Buzzetti wrote *Institutiones sanae philosophiae iuxta divi Thomae atque Aristotelis inconcussa dogmata* [*Enciclopedia filosofica,* 4 v. (Venics–Rome 1957) 1:845–846]. Basically Thomistic, this work suffered from the influence of Christian WOLFF and an insufficient understanding of St. Thomas. Among Buzzetti's disciples were two Sordi brothers, who later became Jesuits, and Giuseppe Pecci, brother of the future Leo XIII.

Serafino Sordi (1793–1865), the younger brother, entered the Society of Jesus (restored in 1814) and tried desperately to revive Thomism. The general was dissuaded from assigning him to the Roman College (Gregorianum) as professor of logic because of faculty opposition: "so strong are the prejudices against Fr. Sordi because he is a Thomist" (letter of the provincial, Oct. 2, 1827; Dezza 33). Domenico Sordi (1790–1880) followed his brother into the Society and was assigned to teach, even though he had many enemies. Among his disciples was the Jesuit Luigi TAPARELLI D' AZEGLIO, author of several Thomistic essays on natural law, who, on becoming provincial of the Naples province, secured the services of Domenico Sordi in 1831 and procured Goudin's *Philosophia* for the Jesuit College in Naples. Sordi, wishing to revive Thomism, formed a private philosophical society that was discovered and disbanded by a Roman visitor in 1833; Sordi was prevented from teaching and Taparelli was sent to Palermo to teach French. In 1834 Matteo LIBERATORE, a Jesuit who had not been a member of the disbanded group, was appointed professor in the college. The first edition of Liberatore's *Institutiones philosophiae* (Naples 1840) was entirely eclectic, influenced mainly by V. COUSIN. By 1853 Liberatore became convinced of Thomism, largely through association with *Civiltà Cattolica,* founded in Naples in 1850 by Carlo Maria Curci and Taparelli. This journal strongly promoted the Catholic cause and restoration of the Christian philosophy of St. Thomas. Giuseppe Cornoldi (1822–92), confrere and close friend of Liberatore, wrote manuals of Thomistic philosophy and many works attacking Rosminianism, ontologism, pantheism, and scientism.

Most zealous for the revival of Thomism in Italy was Gaetano SANSEVERINO, a diocesan priest of Naples. Originally a Cartesian in philosophy, he was influenced about 1840 by Roselli's *Summa.* With assistance from Taparelli and Liberatore, he began publishing and writing articles for *La Scienza e la Fede,* a journal that systematically criticized current rationalism, idealism, ontologism, and liberalism. When he wrote *Philosophia Christiana* (5 v. Naples 1853), refuting D. HUME, T. REID, I KANT, F. W. J. SCHELLING, H. F. R. de LAMENNAIS, and Gioberti, he was a thoroughly convinced Thomist. Reviewing this work in 1865, the Spanish Dominican Ceferino GONZÁLEZ Y DÍAZ TUÑÓN criticized it for being too Thomistic and contemptuous of modern thought. Sanseverino's work was continued in Naples by Nunzio Signoriello (1831–89) and by many disciples who began publishing major works of St. Thomas, neglected for almost a century. Between 1850 and 1860 the *Summa theologiae* was published also in Parma, Bologna, and Paris. The Parma edition of the *Opera omnia* was published by Fiaccadori (1852–73) in 25 folio volumes.

In Rome the center of Thomistic revival was the Dominican College of St. Thomas (Minerva), where the *Summa theologiae* was used as a textbook. Among the eminent theologians there were Vincenzo Gatti (1811–82), author of *Institutiones apologeticae* (1866), Francisco Xarrié (d. 1866), author of *Theologia Thomistica* and coauthor with Narciso Puig (d. 1865) of *Institutiones theologicae ad mentem D. Thomae* (1861–63), and the philosopher Tommaso ZIGLIARA. Zigliara, regent of the college from 1870 to 1879, wrote an influential *Summa philosophica* that ran through 17 editions and many Italian treatises against traditionalism and ontologism. In 1879 Leo XIII acknowledged his contribution to the Thomistic revival by creating him cardinal and appointing him director of the Leonine Commission entrusted with editing the critical text of St. Thomas.

Spain. The influential philosopher J. L. BALMES openly professed to follow the Christian philosophy of St. Thomas in his *Filosofia fundamental* (1846) and *Curso de filosofia elemental* (1847) when Thomism was still unpopular. His friend J. D. Cortés (1809–61) utilized St. Thomas in an attempt to develop Christian political theory. In Spanish seminaries, according to a student plan adopted in 1824 and decreed in 1868 by the board of education, the *Summa theologiae* of St. Thomas was adopted as the basis of theological studies. Enthusiasm for Thomistic theology was renewed at Salamanca by the Dominican Pascual (d. 1816), at Cervera by Francisco Xarrié, and by other Dominicans at colleges in Coria and Ocaña. As early as 1820 the Dominicans Felipe Puigserver and Antonio Sendil vehemently opposed philosophical errors of the day and tried to restore the whole of medieval scholasticism, even its Aristotelian cosmology. In the University of Madrid J. M. Orti y Lara (1826–1904), professor of metaphysics and a layman, openly taught St. Thomas and attacked the prevailing Kantian philosophy of Karl Krause and his Spanish disciples.

The most important and influential representative of the Thomistic revival was Ceferino González y Díaz Tuñón, Dominican professor of philosophy in Manila and Ocaña, later bishop (1874) and cardinal (1884). His *Estudios sobre la filosofia de S. Tomás* (Manila 1864), *Philosophia elementaris* (3 v. Madrid 1868), and *Historia de la filosofia* (6 v. Madrid 1879–85) were translated into many languages and became standard textbooks of Neothomism throughout the world.

France. With the restoration of the monarchy in 1814 French Catholics, such as F. R. de CHATEAUBRIAND, J. M. de MAISTRE, L. G. A. de BONALD, and H. F. R. de Lamennais, fought prevailing rationalism with historical and Christian apologetics. They proposed TRADITIONALISM as historical proof of divine revelation of both natural and supernatural truths. Historical researches of V. Cousin aroused curiosity concerning 12th-century thought and the problem of universals. Catholic seminaries, however, continued to teach eclectic CARTESIANISM exemplified by the *Philosophia Lugdunensis* of Joseph Valla. In 1850 the Dominican Order was reestablished in France by J. B. H. LACORDAIRE, and interest in Thomism was renewed even outside the Dominican Order. Pierre Roux-Lavergne (1802–74), professor in the diocesan seminary in Nîmes, wrote two philosophical textbooks ''according to the doctrine of St. Thomas'' (Paris 1850–59; 1856) and revised the celebrated *Philosophia* of Goudin (4 v. Paris 1850–51; 4th ed. 1886). A conscientious attempt to return to the philosophy of St. Thomas was made in 1851 by G. VENTURA DI RAULICA, former Jesuit and onetime general of the THEATINES. Ventura, a moderate traditionalist, invoked St. Thomas and attempted to develop a Christian philosophy that required revelation for clear and distinct knowledge of God's existence, the spirituality of the soul, and moral obligations. Although works of St. Thomas were published in Paris prior to the Vivès edition of the *Opera omnia* (1871–82), the revival of Thomism was impeded by traditionalism on the one hand and ontologism on the other; both philosophies fused natural and supernatural orders of truth.

Germany and Austria. Instead of combating prevailing idealism, Catholic thinkers tried to reconcile Catholicism with Kant and G. W. F. HEGEL. Georg HERMES, distinguished and influential rector of the Catholic University of Bonn, developed a Kantian rationalism demonstrating supernatural truths that was condemned in 1835. Anton GÜNTHER, rejecting scholasticism completely, elaborated a Christian Hegelianism to prove truths of revelation. By the middle of the 19th century Günther's Catholic Hegelianism was taught in major universities of Austria and southern Germany, even after it was condemned in 1857.

Foremost leaders in the scholastic revival in Germany were Clemens, Werner, Stöckl, Kleutgen, and Commer. Franz Jacob Clemens (1815–62), professor at Münster, wrote on the relation of philosophy to theology from the scholastic point of view (1856) against Günther. Karl Werner (1821–88), professor at Vienna and one-time follower of Günther, wrote a pioneer study *Der hl. Thomas v. Aquin* (3 v. Ratisbon 1858–59), containing the earliest history of Thomism and numerous historical studies of late scholastic philosophers. Albert Stöckl (1825–95), professor at Münster, wrote the first German textbook of scholastic philosophy, *Lehrbuch der Philosophie* (3 v. Mainz 1868), and the first strictly Catholic history of medieval philosophy, *Geschichte der Philosophie des Mittelalters* (3 v. Mainz 1864–66). Hermann Plassmann (1817–64), professor of theology at Paderborn, wrote a less satisfactory, though influential, summary of Thomistic philosophy, *Die Schule des hl. Thomas* (5 v. Soest 1858–61), based on Goudin's *Philosophia*. Franz Morgott, theologian of Eichstätt, was among the most zealous and prolific proponents of Thomism. Morgott, through extensive reading and continual correspondence with Liberatore, Cornoldi, González, and other foreigners, was sufficiently informed to write extensively on the Neothomistic revival in Europe.

The most outstanding German Thomist was the Jesuit Joseph KLEUTGEN (1811–83) called *Thomas redivivus* by M. SCHEEBEN and *princeps philosophorum* by Leo XIII. Through various editions of his *Theologie der Vorzeit* (1st ed. 1853–60), he strenuously opposed Hermesianism, Güntherianism, and the pseudo-Thomistic traditionalism of Ventura. In *Philosophie der Vorzeit* (1860) he attempted to give an accurate account of Thomistic philosophy for his day. Although Kleutgen was professor in Rome for 40 years, he earned a wide reputation in Germany as well as in Rome. It is said that he wrote the first draft of *Aeterni Patris*.

Aeterni Patris and Legislation. The first encyclical issued by LEO XIII (*Quod apostolici muneris,* 1878) concerned socialism and the general need of a sound Christian philosophy. This was followed by AETERNI PATRIS (Aug. 4, 1879), in which he called for the restoration of Christian philosophy and exhorted bishops to "restore the golden wisdom of Thomas and to spread it far and wide for the defense and beauty of the Catholic faith, for the good of society, and for the advantage of all the sciences" [*Acta Sanctae Sedis,* 11 (1879) 114]. Leo XIII exemplified this restoration through numerous subsequent encyclicals concerning social problems, government, human liberty, the religious question, Sacred Scripture, Catholic Action, marriage, and education. The first draft of *RERUM NOVARUM* was written by an eminent Thomist, Cardinal Zigliara. To implement the restoration of scholasticism, Leo XIII founded the Roman Academy of St. Thomas (Oct. 13, 1879); established a commission for editing the critical text of St. Thomas; ordered in 1880 that an Institut Supérieur de Philosophie be established in Louvain as "a center of studies for promulgating the doctrines of St. Thomas"; and made St. Thomas patron of all Catholic universities, academies, colleges, and schools throughout the world (Aug. 4, 1890). The Catholic University of Fribourg, Switzerland, was founded in 1890, the theological faculty being entrusted to Dominicans.

Journals. Although CIVILTÀ CATTOLICA zealously promoted the restoration of Thomistic philosophy, other journals occasionally published articles of scholastic interest. The first scientific journal devoted to Thomistic studies was *Divus Thomas* (1880–), published in Latin by the Collegio Alberoni, Piacenza. Ernst COMMER, doctor in theology from the Dominican College of St. Thomas in Rome (1880), founded and edited *Jahrbuch für Philosophie und spekulative Theologie* (1887–). Thomistic and neoscholastic journals multiplied rapidly: *St. Thomas-blätter* (1888–), edited by Ceslaus Schneider of Regensburg; *Philosophisches Jahrbuch* (1888–) by professors of the diocesan seminary in Fulda; *Revue Thomiste* (1893–) by French Dominicans; *Revue néoscolastique de philosophie* (1894–) by Louvain; *Rivista Italiana di filosofia neoscolastica* (1909–) founded by the Franciscan Agostino GEMELLI and edited by professors of the Catholic University of Milan; and *La Ciencia Tomista* (1910–) by Spanish Dominicans.

Effect of Modernism. During the pontificate of Leo XIII the reestablishment of scholasticism had six goals: (1) to edit critically the text of scholastic authors, particularly St. Thomas; (2) to study the historical origins and evolution of scholastic philosophy; (3) to expound the solid doctrine (*philosophia perennis*) of scholastic philosophy for a modern age, discarding useless and false views; (4) to study and refute errors of recent and contemporary philosophers; (5) to study the physical sciences and examine their relevance to philosophy; and (6) to construct a new scholastic synthesis of all philosophy consistent with the progress of modern science. Since this program could not be accomplished by one man or one group, it was hoped that cooperation of all Catholic intellectuals could be counted on. This was impossible in the crisis of MODERNISM that broke out after the death of Leo XIII in 1903.

One of the principal causes of Modernism in Italy and France was lack of philosophical and theological training among those who felt the impact of German historicism and higher Biblical criticism. Unable or unwilling to return to the principles of St. Thomas, they felt that scholasticism was not "modern enough" for modern needs. The Holy Office decree *LAMENTABILI* (July 3,

1907) condemned 65 errors of Modernism, many of them directly contrary to the ideals and teaching of neoscholasticism. St. PIUS X noted in his encyclical *PASCENDI* (Sept. 8, 1907) that the Modernists "deride and heedlessly despise scholastic philosophy and theology" [*Acta Sanctae Sedis,* 40 (1907) 636].

Efforts of Later Pontiffs. There was no universal acceptance of the Thomistic revival proposed by Leo XIII. Some institutions were willing to teach an eclectic scholasticism; others made no attempt whatever to return either to St. Thomas or to scholasticism. Disturbed by various attempts to evade the directive of his predecessor and being aware of the dangers of Modernism, Pius X insisted that by "scholasticism" he meant "the principal teachings of St. Thomas Aquinas." In *Doctoris Angelici* (June 29, 1914) he left no room for doubt, declaring solemnly "that those who in their interpretations misrepresent or affect to despise the principles and major theses of his philosophy are not only not following St. Thomas, but are even far astray from the saintly Doctor." Acknowledging commendations of other saints and doctors by the Holy See, Pius X maintained that their doctrine was commended "to the extent that it agreed with the principles of Aquinas or was in no way opposed to them" [*Acta Apostolicae Sedis,* 6 (1914) 338]. He went on to insist that all institutions granting pontifical degrees had to use the *Summa theologiae* as a textbook in theology; failure to comply within three years was to result in withdrawal of pontifical status. The question immediately raised was the meaning of "major theses" of Thomistic philosophy. For clarification the Congregation of Studies on July 27, 1914, issued a list of 24 theses, compiled by the Jesuit Guido Mattiussi (1852–1925) as the *principia et pronuntiata maiora* of St. Thomas [ActApS 6 (1914) 383–386]. In reply to queries, the Congregation of Seminaries and Universities stated on March 7, 1916, that the *Summa* was to be used at least as a major reference work for speculative theology and that the 24 theses were to be taught in all schools as fundamental theses in philosophy.

The 24 theses, of which 23 were contrary to the teaching of F. SUÁREZ, posed a problem in conscience for many Jesuits who could not accept them. On Jan. 18, 1917, Wladimir LEDÓCHOWSKI, General of the Society, submitted a letter, intended for Jesuits, to BENEDICT XV for approval or revision. Emphasizing the traditional place of St. Thomas in the Society, the letter stated that although the essentials of Thomistic philosophy are contained in the 24 theses, the prescriptions of Pius X are "sufficiently satisfied, even though not all the theses are held, as long as they are proposed as safe directive norms" [*Zeitschrift für katholische Theologie,* 42 (1918) 234]. This interpretation was approved by Benedict XV on March 19, 1917.

The Code of Canon Law issued under Benedict XV in 1917 required all professors of philosophy and theology to hold and to teach the method, doctrine, and principles of the Angelic Doctor (1917 CIC c.1366.2).

PIUS XI reiterated the mind of his predecessors concerning St. Thomas in *Studiorum ducem* (June 29, 1923), saying that "the Church has adopted his philosophy for her very own" [*Acta Apostolicae Sedis,* 15 (1923) 314]. The apostolic constitution *DEUS SCIENTIARUM DOMINUS* (May 24, 1931) imposed with the fullest apostolic authority a detailed curriculum of studies for all seminaries.

The "New Theology." Ecclesiastical legislation during and following the Modernist crisis failed to achieve the broad goals of Leo XIII. A narrow legalized Thomism, out of touch with modern movements after World War II, created resentment and a "new theology" that found inspiration in EVOLUTIONISM, PHENOMENOLOGY, and the teachings of P. TEILHARD DE CHARDIN. PIUS XII, an ardent advocate of modernity, found it necessary to condemn dangerously extreme views of the *théologie nouvelle* in HUMANI GENERIS (Aug. 12, 1950). After reviewing the importance of solid philosophical formation in the light of St. Thomas, he lamented, "How deplorable it is then that this philosophy, received and honored by the Church, is scorned by some who shamelessly call it outmoded in form and rationalistic, as they say, in its method of thought" [*Acta Apostolicae Sedis,* 42 (1950) 573].

The new spirit of JOHN XXIII made it possible for theologians well trained in Thomistic principles to study modern problems in the light of history, revelation, and scholastic theology. Deeper research into the true meaning of St. Thomas and the breadth of medieval concerns likewise made possible a new, less rigid, and less legalistic scholasticism.

Philosophers and Problems. At the beginning of the Leonine revival, the principal centers of scholasticism were Rome and Louvain; but by 1930 there were strong centers in every country. The main concern of philosophers was to expound the ARISTOTELIANISM of St. Thomas's philosophy, drawn largely from his theological writings.

Textbooks. Early textbooks of Neothomistic philosophy were influenced by the Wolffian division of the sciences: logic, ontology, cosmology, psychology, theodicy, and sometimes ethics. This order was followed notably in the influential textbooks of Zigliara, J. J. URRÁBURU, Vincent Remer (d. 1910), Michaele de Maria (1836–1913), Pius de Mandato (1850–1914), and Sebastian Reinstadler of Metz. Ethics and natural theology, when discussed at all, were extracted from the *Summa theologiae* of St. Thomas. Problems of EPISTEMOLOGY were discussed in major logic, and the scholastic method was thought to be a deductive and syllogistic defense of theses (*see* SCHOLASTIC METHOD). This conception of scholastic philosophy was made familiar to beginners by the Jesuit Stonyhurst series (R. F. Clarke, John Rickaby, Joseph RICKABY, Michael Maher, and Bernard Boedder) and the simple *Summula* (Dublin 1903) by the Irish Cistercian J. S. Hickey (1865–1933). The *Cursus philosophicus* of JOHN OF ST. THOMAS was the basis for better texts by Edouard HUGON, Josef GREDT, F. X. Maquart, and Jacques MARITAIN. A highly influential text was Gredt's *Elementa philosophiae Aristotelico-Thomisticae* (2 v. 1st ed. Rome 1899–1901; 12th ed. 1958). Gredt, a German Benedictine of San Anselmo, seriously faced problems of modern science, but followed the theological order of the *Summa* for psychology, natural theology, and ethics.

A complete course in the philosophy of St. Thomas was given in Louvain by Cardinal D. J. MERCIER between 1882 and 1889. As president of the Institut Supérieur (1889–1905), he and his assistants, Simon Deploige (1868–1927), Maurice DE WULF, Désiré Nys (1859–1927), and Armand Thiéry (1868–1955), developed all branches of a *philosophia perennis* based on Aristotle and St. Thomas, integrating all modern science and mathematics. Mercier, Nys, and De Wulf prepared a *Cours de philosophie* that became influential in many countries through various translations (Eng. tr. 1916). The precise meaning of *philosophia perennis* raised problems for later neoscholastics.

Medieval studies at Louvain were led by Maurice De Wulf, who published the first edition of *Histoire de la philosophie médiévale* in 1900. Believing ''scholasticism'' to be a single body of doctrine, he inevitably limited the content of *philosophia perennis* as well as the number of true ''scholastics'' in the Middle Ages. In 1901 he launched the collection ''Les Philosophes Beiges,'' containing texts of medieval Belgian philosophers.

The neoscholastic revival at Louvain exerted great influence through its numerous publications and long line of distinguished professors, notably Leon Noël (1878–1955), Auguste Mansion, Jacques Leclercq, Fernand Van Steenberghen, Georges Van Riet, Albert Michotte, Louis De Raymaeker, Albert Dondeyne, Alphonse De Waelhens, Gérard Verbeke, and Fernand Renoirte.

New Interests. During the first two decades of the 20th century Thomist philosophers emphasized the primacy of POTENCY AND ACT in Thomism (N. del Prado, G. Mattusi, E. Hugon, and G. Manser). In the 1920s the importance of ANALOGY was seen to be the key to Tho-

mistic metaphysics (N. Balthasar, M. T. L. Penido, and S. Ramirez). In the middle 1930s the doctrine of PARTICIPATION and the recognition of Platonic elements in St. Thomas was considered the basis for a deeper appreciation (L. B. Geiger, C. Fabro, A. Little). In the 1940s the existential character of Thomistic metaphysics was emphasized, and some philosophers considered EXISTENCE (*esse*) to be the deepest and truest characteristic of Thomistic metaphysics (J. Maritain, É. GILSON, C. Fabro, and G. B. PHELAN). After the middle of the century other scholastics sought to synthesize St. Thomas with M. Heiddeger or E. HUSSERL, leaving the older controversies behind.

Between 1925 and 1950 the principal philosophical controversy concerned the meaning of CHRISTIAN PHILOSOPHY. After a review by P. MANDONNET of Gilson's *Philosophy of St. Bonaventure* (Paris 1924), the mounting controversy involving all leading Thomists of the period centered on the relation between revelation and philosophy. Some maintained the autonomy of reason in philosophical discourse and only an extrinsic normative influence of revelation on Christian philosophers (Mandonnet, Ramirez, and Van Steenberghen). Others, arguing from various points of view, maintained a direct, intrinsic influence of revelation on Christians who philosophize (Gilson, Maritain, and M. D. Chenu). This fundamentally theological question was argued mainly by philosophers and historians.

Historians and Historiography. The revival and development of neoscholasticism profited much from the work of medievalists of the 19th and 20th centuries. German historiography, establishment of the École des Chartres (1829), the work of V. Cousin and J. B. Hauréau, and a new curiosity about the Middle Ages made possible the edition of critical texts and a critical study of scholastic authors. The pioneering work of Catholic historians—Pietro Uccelli, H. S. DENIFLE, Franz EHRLE, Clemens Baeumker, Georg von Hertling, and M. Baumgartner—was continued by Mandonnet, Franz Pelster, August Pelzer, Konstanty Michalski, Martin GRABMANN, Chenu, Gilson, and many others.

The critical edition of the *Opera omnia* of St. Thomas, begun in 1882, continued under eminent Dominican scholars. A center for editing works of St. Bonaventure and other Franciscan scholastics was established at Quarrachi, near Florence, in 1877; the edition of Bonaventure (1882–1902) was followed by work on Alexander of Hales and other Franciscan authors. A separate Scotus Commission was established in Rome (1938) under the direction of C. Balić to publish the *Opera omnia* of Duns Scotus (1950–). The Comissió Lulliana undertook the edition of Ramon Lull's *Opera omnia* (1906–50). The

Benedictines of Solesmes assumed responsibility for publishing a new edition of John of St. Thomas's *Cursus theologicus* (1931–), and the Albertus Magnus Institut, founded in Cologne in 1931, began publishing the *Opera omnia* of Albert the Great in 1951.

Widespread use of photoelectric reproduction after World War II made old editions of scholastic authors easily accessible to scholars in America. Two institutes of medieval studies were established in North America, one in Toronto in 1929 by Gilson, the other in Ottawa in 1930 under the inspiration of Chenu, which transferred to Montreal in 1942.

Results of these medieval studies were better understanding of St. Thomas, appreciation of different currents in medieval thought, and recognition of pluralism in medieval scholasticism (*see* PLURALISM, PHILOSOPHICAL).

Theologians and Renewal. The last two regents of the College of St. Thomas in Rome (Minerva) were Alberto LEPIDI and Enrico Buonpensiere, who expounded the *Summa* in the tradition of older commentators. In 1909 the college was organized into the Pontifical Athenaeum ''Angelicum,'' which received university status together with the Lateran in 1963.

In the first half of the 20th century Thomistic theologians concentrated on apologetics, developing specialized treatises *De ecclesia* and *De revelatione* as outlined by VATICAN COUNCIL I. Notable among these apologists were J. V. De Groot (1848–1927), A. M. WEISS, Reginald Schultes, Ambroise GARDEIL, Antonin SERTILLANGES, Christian PESCH, and Reginald GARRIGOU-LAGRANGE. (*See* APOLOGETICS (HISTORY OF).)

Revival of Thomism also renewed ancient controversies concerning grace in the writings of G. SCHNEEMANN, A. M. Dummermuth (1841–1918), J. B. Stufler (1865–1952), Norbert del Prado, Francisco MARÍN-SOLÁ, Charles Boyer, B. M. Xiberta, and numerous Spanish Jesuits and Dominicans. (*See* THEOLOGY, HISTORY OF.)

Mystical theology was developed in a way that was notably different from 19th-century asceticism in the writings of A. A. TANQUEREY, J. G. ARINTERO, Bartholomé Froget, and Garrigou-Lagrange. Moral theology was continued somewhat in the older tradition by Hieronymus NOLDIN, Dominikus PRÜMMER, and B. H. MERKELBACH. (*See* MORAL THEOLOGY, HISTORY OF.)

With World War II a new spirit entered scholastic theology in the extensive writings of Dom Odo Cassel, Romano Guardini, Yves Congar, Chenu, Karl Rahner, Hans Küng, and Edward Schillebeeckx. Leaving aside older controversies, they approached current problems in the light of vital scholastic principles. This renewal of scholastic theology supported by Biblical, historical, and liturgical studies, led to the general renewal in the Church effected by VATICAN COUNCIL II.

Scholasticism in the U.S. Prior to the Leonine directive, Jesuits taught a form of scholasticism in their universities; Dominicans taught St. Thomas in *studia* and colleges; and Orestes A. BROWNSON expressed hope for a scholastic revival, although he knew little of St. Thomas. American bishops, Catholic schools and seminaries, and The CATHOLIC UNIVERSITY OF AMERICA responded obediently to the directives of the Holy See regarding scholasticism and the subsequent fear of Modernism. The principal influences on Catholic teaching in the U.S. were Rome and Louvain. Notable pioneers of American neoscholasticism were the Jesuits Nicholas Russo (1845–1902) and Biagio Schiffini, both of Georgetown University. Russo's *Summa philosophica iuxta scholasticorum principia* (2 v. Boston 1885) and Schiffini's *Institutiones philosophicae ad mentem Aquinatis* (Turin 1889) were used for many years in some seminaries. The Dutch Dominican E. L. Van Becelaere (d. 1946) did much to make Thomism respectable among American philosophers outside the Church, notably Josiah ROYCE, who wrote an introduction to Van Becelaere's *La philosophie en Amérique depuis lea origines jusqu' à nos jours* (New York 1904). The Bavarian priest John Gmeiner (1847–1913) taught Thomistic philosophy for seven years at St. Francis Seminary in Milwaukee and later at St. Thomas Seminary in St. Paul, Minn. Textbooks generally used in seminaries and religious houses were European. Some English texts were written for college students by Msgr. Paul Glen, Celestine Bittle, Henri Renard, and others. In 1927 the American Catholic Philosophical Association was formed by Msgr. E. A. PACE of Catholic University, who was its first president. The *New Scholasticism,* official journal of the association, was founded and edited by Pace and James H. RYAN in 1927. In 1990 the *New Scholasticism* changed its name to *American Catholic Philosophical Quarterly,* reflecting a diminished interest in scholastic philosophy among many members of the Association. On the other hand, the Association's annually elected presidents and the recipients of its annually conferred Aquinas Medal continue, for the most part, to be distinguished philosophers who are interested in maintaining and developing the scholastic tradition.

Recent Developments. During the past three decades the study of scholasticism and scholastic philosophy has developed in several directions. New critical editions of medieval scholastic texts by both major and minor authors have continued to appear. Between 1881 and 1965, the Leonine Commission had produced 15 of the projected 50 volumes of its edition of Aquinas's *opera omnia*;

since 1965 another 13 new volumes have appeared, one of the earlier volumes has been revised, and preparation of several more volumes has begun. An important complement to the Leonine edition has been provided to Thomistic scholars by R. Busa's *Index Thomisticus* (1974–80; CD-ROM, 2nd rev. ed. 1993). The critical edition of Scotus's *opera omnia* is now being produced in two academic centers: in Rome the Commissio Scotistica is continuing to work on Scotus's revised Oxford lectures (the *Ordinatio*); working now at The Catholic University of America, the Scotus Project has produced three volumes of the *opera philosophica*, and two more volumes are soon to be published.

As these recent critical editions attest, historical knowledge of the methods, language, and writings of medieval scholastic authors has become ever more precise and minute. Further evidence of this development is provided by a collection of studies of the disputed question (1985), by a monograph by J. Wippel on the metaphysics of Aquinas (1999), and by a collection of papers on Aquinas by L. Boyle (2000). The publications and quinquennial conferences of the *Société Internationale pour l'étude de la philosophie médiévale*, which serve to coordinate the work of medievalists on an international level, have also contributed to this growing historical knowledge. Scholastic philosophy continues to be studied seriously both in Europe (for example at the Universities of Cologne and Paris) and in the U.S. [for example at The Catholic University of America, The Center for Thomistic Studies at the University of St. Thomas (Houston), and Boston College]. The Pontifical Institute of Medieval Studies (Toronto) continues to publish monographs, translations, and the journal *Mediaeval Studies*. On balance it might be said that exact historical knowledge of the scholastic tradition has come to predominate in academic work in the field, while the kind of original philosophizing from within the scholastic tradition exemplified in an earlier generation by Maritain and Gilson has declined.

This last observation might be thought to be countered by the emergence of "analytic Thomism" and more generally "analytic medieval philosophy," exemplified by the work of B. Davies, N. Kretzmann, and J. Haldane, by *The Cambridge Guide to Later Medieval Philosophy*, and by the journal *Medieval Philosophy and Theology* (1991–). But although this school seems to have discovered new ways of reading and reflecting on medieval scholastic thought that speak to at least some contemporary philosophers, its critics suggest that it tends to disregard the literary and historical contexts of medieval works and to value medieval philosophy only for points of convergence with the interests and perspectives of analytic philosophy. Still, it is a vigorous move-

ment, producing numerous monographs, collections of studies, and translations.

Pope John Paul II's encyclical *FIDES ET RATIO* (1998), in its defense of both faith and reason, reiterated recommendations of earlier papal documents that the writings of Aquinas and other scholastics be used in the search for timeless truth.

See Also: THOMISM; NEOSCHOLASTICISM AND NEOTHOMISM.

Bibliography: H. HURTER, *Nomenclator literarius theologiae catholicae*³, 5 v. in 6 (3d ed. Innsbruck 1903–13) 5 v. P. WYSER, *Der Thomismus* (Bibliog. Einführungen in des Studium der Philosophie 15–16; Bern 1951). J. L. PERRIER, *The Revival of Scholastic Philosophy in the Nineteenth Century* (New York 1909). F. KLIMKE, *Institutiones historiae philosophiae*, 2 v. (Rome 1923) 2:230–335. J. A. WEISHEIPL, "The Revival of Thomism: An Historical Survey," *Programmata scholarum et status personalis* (River Forest, Ill. 1962). R. VILLENEUVE, "Le Thomisme avant et après l'encyclique *Aeterni Patris*," *Revue Dominicaine*, 26 (1929) 273–282, 339–354, 479–496. A. M. WALZ, *Compendium historiae ordinia praedicatorum* (2d ed. Rome 1948). M. GRABMANN, *Die Geschichte der katholischen Theologie seit dem Ausgang der Väterzeit* (Freiburg 1933); "Der Anteil des Dominikanerordens an der Entstehung und Entwicklung der Neuscholastik im 19. Jahrhundert," *Neue Ordnung*, 1 (1948) 98–112. S. M. RAMIREZ, "The Authority of St. Thomas Aquinas," *Thomist*, 15 (1952) 1–109. A. MASNOVO, *Il neotomismo in Italia* (Milan 1923). P. DEZZA, *Alle origini del neotomismo* (Milan 1940); *I neotomisti italiani del secolo XIX*, 2 v. (Milan 1942). G. SAITTA, *Le origini del neotomismo nel secolo XIX* (Bari 1912). G. E. ROSSI, *La filosofia del Collegio Alberoni ed il neotomismo* (Piacenza 1959). A. FERMI, *Origine del tomismo piacentino nel primo ottocento* (Piacenza 1959). B. M. BONANSEA, "Pioneers of the 19th-Century Scholastic Revival in Italy," *The New Scholasticism*, 28 (1954) 1–37. I. NARCISO, "Alle fonti del neotomismo," *Sapienza*, 13 (1960) 124–147; "Il movimento neotomista," *ibid.* 14 (1961) 441–458; "La concezione dell'essere nella filosofia razionalistica e nel neotomismo," *ibid.* 15 (1962) 86–107; "La dialettica del conoscere nel neotomismo," *ibid.* 419–447; "I *Tesari* domenicani del 1751 e l'inizio del neotomismo," *ibid.* 277–301; "Neotomismo e scolastica eclettica," *ibid.* 16 (1963) 417–453; "La manualistica domenicana," *ibid.* 17 (1964) 120–128. M. BATLLORI, *Baltasar Masdeu y el neoscolasticismo italiano* (Barcelona 1944), also in *Analecta Sacra Tarraconensia*, 15 (1942) 171–202; 16 (1943) 241–294. L. FOUCHER, *La Philosophie catholique en France au XIXᵉ siècle avant la renaissance thomiste et dans son rapport avec elle, 1800–1880* (Paris 1955). J. BELLAMY, *La Théologie catholique au XIXᵉ siècle* (Paris 1904). D. J. MERCIER, *Le Christianisme dans la vie moderne*, ed. L. Noël (Paris 1918). L. DE RAEYMAEKER, *Le Cardinal Mercier et l'Institut Supérieur de Philosophie de Louvain* (Louvain 1952). J. A. MANN, "Neo-Scholastic Philosophy in the United States of America in the 19th Century," *American Catholic Philosophical Association. Proceedings of the annual Meeting*, 33 (1959) 127–136. *Teaching Thomism Today*, ed. G. F. MCLEAN (Washington 1964). *One Hundred Years of Thomism*, ed. V. BREZIK (Houston 1981). J. HALDANE, "Thomism and the Future of Catholic Philosophy," *New Blackfriars,* 80 (1999). G. MCCOOL, "The Tradition of Saint Thomas in North America: At 50 Years," *The Modern Schoolman*, 65 (1988): 185–206; *From Unity to Pluralism: The Internal Evolution of Thomism* (New York 1989). *The Cambridge History of Later Medieval Philosophy,* eds., N. KRETZMANN, A. KENNY and J. PINBORG (Cambridge, 1982). T. NOONE, ''Medieval Scholarship and Philosophy in the Last One Hundred Years,'' in *One Hundred Years of Philosophy,* ed. B. SHANLEY (Washington 2001) 111–32. B. SHANLEY, ''Analytical Thomism,'' *The Thomist,* 63 (1999): 125–37; *Handbook for the Contemporary Philosophy of Religion: The Thomist Tradition* (Dordrecht 2002).

[J. A. WEISHEIPL/EDS.]

SCHOLASTICUS

Magister scholarum, maistreescoles, cancellarius, or master of schools, originally a functionary attached to the cathedral chapter who exercised control of schools (*regimen scholarum, jus scholarum, jus in regendis scholis*) throughout the area under the jurisdiction of the chapter. (In other places, jurisdiction over schools was exercised by certain other ecclesiastical bodies, usually a monastery, a priory, etc.) Before and even during the 12th century, when the great medieval universities were forming, schools of an area continued to have only one *scholasticus* or *magister,* some member of the cathedral chapter. He was the sole ruler of the schools in the cathedral's jurisdiction but had the right to appoint assistants or substitutes. With the increase in the demand for teachers, he granted the *licentia docendi,* or the permission to teach, to persons he judged suitable. No competent teacher could be refused this *licentia,* and it had to be granted freely, without payment of fee, to avoid suspicion of simony (though there were abuses). In Paris the schools (even the university itself) continued to be ruled by the chancellor of the cathedral church, on whom the duties of the *scholasticus* fell. At Salamanca the *scholasticus,* or as he was now called, the chancellor of the university (as opposed to rector), had the right to imprison scholars (a right that he shared with the bishop from 1254 onward), since he was held to be the *iudex ordinarius* of students.

Bibliography: É. LESNE, *Histoire de la propriété ecclésiastique en France,* v. 5, *Les Écoles . . .* (Lille 1910–43) 453–512. H. RASHDALL, *The Universities of Europe in the Middle Ages,* ed. F. M. POWICKE and A. B. EMDEN, 3 v. (new ed. Oxford 1936) 1:279–282; 2:84–88, 144–146, 155–158. H. JEDIN, ''Domschule und Kolleg,'' *Trierer Theologische Zeitschrift* 67 (1958) 210–223.

[T. C. CROWLEY]

SCHOLIUM

A biblical scholium may be defined as a brief exegetical explanation of a passage that is difficult on account of variant readings, obscure historical or geographical allusions, grammatical difficulties, and the like. Scholia are usually found in the margin of the text, less frequently at the foot of the page. The author as well as the collector of scholia is called a scholiast.

While this definition agrees with the usage of contemporary authors, it requires certain qualifications. As worded, it is intended to distinguish a scholium from a gloss and from a commentary. Unfortunately all Christian biblical literature does not justify quite so clear-cut a definition of the term. The works to which it has been applied range from a scholium as just defined (Origen) to a full-fledged commentary (Arethas of Caesarea on Revelation).

Once the term's meaning is understood to roam about in this way, we may claim the remains of numerous biblical scholia. Perhaps the earliest are those of Clement of Alexandria in his Hypotyposis of which only fragments survive. Others, to list a few, are those of Origen, Hippolytus, Gregory Nazianzen, Jerome, Hesychius of Jerusalem, Procopius of Gaza, and Arethas of Caesarea.

To consult these and all others, the exegete is obliged to call on the patrologist to help him locate the most accurate available editions. Still a desideratum is a corpus of biblical scholia in the sense defined above.

Bibliography: J. SCHMID, *Lexikon für Theologie und Kirche,* ed. J. HOFER and K. RAHNER, 10 v. (2d, new ed. Freiburg 1957–65) 9:448–449. A. GUDEMAN, *Paulys Realenzyklopädie der klassischen Altertumswissenschaft,* ed. G. WISSOWA, et al. 2A.1 (Stuttgart) (1921) 625–705. G. ZUNTZ, ''Die Aristophanes-Scholien der Papyri,'' *Byzantion* 14 (1939) 547–594.

[C. O'C. SLOANE]

SCHOLLINER, HERMANN

Benedictine theologian; b. Freising (Bavaria), Jan. 15, 1722; d. Welchenberg, July 16, 1795. He entered the Abbey of Oberaltaich in 1738. After his philosophical and theological studies at Erfurt and Salzburg, he was appointed director of the house of studies of the Bavarian Benedictines (1752–57), and then taught dogmatic theology at Salzburg (1759–66). He became prior at Oberaltaich (1772), and after the suppression of the Jesuits, taught at Ingolstadt (1776–80). As a member of the Bavarian Academy of Sciences he wrote *Monumenta Niederaltacensia* and *Monumenta Oberalticensia, Elisabethcellencia et Oosterhofensia,* which are parts of the master collection *Monumenta Boica,* guided by Scholliner in 1768. Among his other works are *De magistratum ecclesiasticorum origine et creatione* (Salzburg 1751–52), *De disciplinae arcani antiquitate et usu* (Tegernsee 1755), *Ecclesiae orientalis et occidentalis concordia in transubstantiatione* (Regensburg 1756), *De hierarchia ecclesiae catholica* (Regensburg 1757), *Historia theologiae christiani saeculi primi* (Salzburg 1761), and *Praelectiones theologicae ad usum studii communis congregationis Benedictino-Bavaricae* (12 v. Augsburg 1769).

Bibliography: P. A. LINDNER, *Schriftsteller des Benediktiner Ordens in Bayern, 1750–1880,* 2 v. (Regensburg 1880). O. L. KAPSNER, *A Benedictine Bibliography: An Author-Subject Union List,* 2 v. (2d ed. Collegeville, Minn. 1962): v.1, author part; v.2, subject part. 1: 535.

[N. R. SKVARLA]

SCHÖNBORN

The name of a famous Catholic German noble family from the Rhineland that rose to renown in the 17th century. Many members were prelates of the church.

Lothar Franz, archbishop of Mainz; b. Bavaria, Oct. 4, 1655; d. Mainz, Jan. 30, 1729. He entered the clerical state at an early age and filled church positions in Bamberg, Würzburg, and Mainz and was entrusted with numerous governmental duties as well. On Nov. 16, 1693, he was elected bishop of Bamberg; on Sept. 3, 1694, he became coadjutor to Anselm Franz, the ailing archbishop of Mainz. After Franz's death in March 1695, Lothar Franz succeeded as archbishop. He was well known for his appreciation and interest in art and learning.

Johann Philipp, prince bishop of Würzburg; b. Würzburg, Feb. 5, 1673; d. near Löffelsterz, Aug. 18, 1724. He was the nephew of Lothar Franz and the eldest son of Melchior Friedrich, who held the hereditary office of Elector of Mainz. He obtained his higher education at the German College in Rome. His outstanding intellectual gifts, his skill in oratory, plus the connections with so renowned a family won him recognition in the episcopal service and a number of highly regarded church benefices in Mainz, Bamberg, Würzburg, and Frankfurt on the Main. Johann Philipp was also active in diplomatic service at the papal, imperial, and royal courts. On Sept. 18, 1719, he was unanimously elected to the office of prince bishop of Würzburg. He contributed significantly to the family interest and promotion of education, culture, and the welfare of Würzburg as the Schönborn Chapel, the magnificent Schönborn mausoleum, and the splendid palace. Johann Philipp died suddenly while returning from a visit to the Grand Master of the German Order of Knights in Mergentheim.

Friedrich Karl, also prince bishop of Würzburg; b. Mainz, March 3, 1674; d. Würzburg, July 25, 1746. He was a younger brother and second successor of Johann Philipp. In 1729, after a notable episcopal career in Mainz and Bamberg, Friedrich succeeded to Würzburg. Diplomatic missions to Polish, Prussian, Saxon, Lorraine, and Roman courts made Friedrich Karl the most distinguished politically among the Schönborns. During the 17 years that he headed the dioceses of Bamberg and Würzburg, foreign affairs demanded his attention and he gave valuable service to the Hapsburgs. In both dioceses he effected great reforms in higher education, was patron of the arts, built churches and palaces, founded many institutions, and was responsible for worthwhile economic measures.

Damien Hugo, cardinal, prince bishop of Speyer and Constance; b. Mainz, Sept. 19, 1676; d. Bruchsal, Aug. 17, 1743. He became a cardinal in 1713 and coadjutor of Speyer in 1716. He was prince bishop of Speyer (1719–43) and of Constance (1740–43). Bruchsal Castle is a lasting monument to this exemplary churchman.

Franz Georg, prince bishop of Worms; b. Mainz, June 15, 1682; d. Mainz, Jan. 18, 1756. He was the brother of Damien Hugo. He became archbishop and electoral prince of Trier in 1729 and in 1732 succeeded to Worms and became provost of Ellwangen. He was an ardent supporter of the Hapsburgs, and was praised by Frederick the Great and Maria Theresa as an excellent ruler.

Franz, cardinal, archbishop of Prague; b. near Prague, Jan. 24, 1844; d. near Falkenau bei Eger, June 25, 1899. He was a member of the Prague branch of the Schönborn family. He took part in the War of 1866 as an Austrian officer. In 1873 he was ordained; he became vice rector of the Prague Seminary in 1879 and rector in 1882. He became bishop of Budweis in 1883 and prince archbishop of Prague and primate of Bohemia in 1885. Four years later he received the cardinalate.

Bibliography: H. HANTSCH, *Lexikon für Theologie und Kirche* 1 9:310–313. T. HENNER and K. G. BOCKENHEIMER, *Allgemeine deutsche Biographie* 32:268–280. *Der grosse Brockhaus,* 12 v. (16th ed. Wiesbaden 1952–57) 10:460.

[M. V. SCHULLER]

SCHOOL SISTERS OF NOTRE DAME

(SSND, Official Catholic Directory #2970) A religious congregation founded in Bavaria in 1833 by Bp. George Michael Wittmann and Karolina Gerhardinger. The congregation, dedicated to the work of education, was one of many religious communities that arose in 19th-century Europe after long secularization of religious schools. Wittmann, canon of the Cathedral of Ratisbon, conceived the plan of establishing a congregation of teaching sisters to continue the work of the suppressed canonesses of St. Augustine de Notre Dame, the French community founded by Peter FOURIER and Alix Le Clerc in Lorraine in 1597. This congregation had had over 2,000 members in Western and Central Europe when secularization closed many convents in France and all of those in Germany. The last Bavarian house at Stadtamhof was suppressed in 1809. Wittmann, aware of the serious consequences that would follow from the loss of religious teachers to the Church, initiated preparations for the foundation of a new religious community of women dedicated to the education of young girls.

Foundation. In 1812 Wittmann selected three young girls as the nucleus for his work. Karolina Gerhardinger, the youngest of the three and the only one to persevere, was but 12 years of age when the project was begun. During the three years of training in a Bavarian normal school and ten years of teaching in a public school, they received instructions in the spiritual life under the guidance of the bishop. In 1825, encouraged by the cessation of anti-religious hostility and by the generosity of King Louis I of Bavaria, Karolina, supported by Wittmann, petitioned the Bavarian ministry for permission to form a religious society to teach in Stadtamhof. The sanction for this religious foundation was granted, but the authorities of the city refused to allow them to use the confiscated cloister school because of the revenue it afforded the town. Karolina and her companions continued to teach in public schools until the opportunity to form a community presented itself. Eight years later in 1833, through Wittmann's friend, Sebastian Job, chaplain of the Imperial Court of Austria, a suitable house was obtained in Job's native city, Neunburg vorm Wald. Although the founding of the first house of the congregation and its pioneer development took over 20 years, this new community called Poor School Sisters of Notre Dame had, within a few decades, as many members as the congregation founded by Fourier.

Rule. For the guidance of the sisters, Wittmann wrote a preliminary draft of a rule and constitutions based on that of Fourier. Although Wittmann did not live to finish the work, Job completed the statutes which he called the ''Spirit of the Constitutions of the Poor School Sisters of Notre Dame.'' However, the rule was intended to serve the congregation only until experience should provide the guidance needed for a rule more suited to the times. The new congregation received episcopal recognition on March 26, 1834, as a distinct, self-sustaining religious society. As such, it cannot be considered a branch of the 16th-century French order. Karolina Gerhardinger, now Mother Teresa of Jesus, was appointed superior general and foundress. Unfortunately, Wittmann and Job, the two most instrumental in the foundation of the congregation, did not live to see their work receive episcopal or papal recognition. The rule written by Mother Teresa was submitted to the Holy See in 1852. It was approved tentatively in 1859 and permanently in 1865.

Mother Teresa's rule differed fundamentally from Fourier's; it required a stricter observance of poverty, provided for smaller communities to staff country schools for the poor, and established a strong centralized government to safeguard the unity of the congregation. This latter point was novel for communities of religious women, which had customarily been placed under the authority of the local bishop; but Mother Teresa's long struggle with well-meaning opponents finally ended, and in 1859 this point was incorporated into the rule: that branch houses be subject to the provincial motherhouse and all houses be under obedience to the superior general. Since Neunburg vorm Wald was a small, inaccessible town in 1843, Mother Teresa transferred the motherhouse to the city of Munich where it remained until 1957 when the generalate of the congregation was moved to Rome.

Growth. Within 14 years Mother Teresa was governing 125 sisters teaching in 16 schools, and the demand for their services was increasing. Large numbers of young girls continued to request admission to the thriving congregation. Thus, from 1847 to 1854, when the influx of German immigrants into the U.S. reached its height, the School Sisters of Notre Dame in Germany were among the first religious teachers called upon to help solve the grave problem facing the American bishops, namely, the preservation of the faith of German Catholics in the U.S.

With the encouragement of the archbishop of Munich and the help of King Louis I of Bavaria and the LUDWIG MISSIONSVEREIN, Mother Teresa arrived in the U.S. in 1847 with five sisters. Although she had been promised St. Mary's near Harrisburg, Pa., as the site for a motherhouse, the location proved so disappointing that she and her companions sought out the Redemptorist provincial, Bp. John Neumann of Philadelphia, Pa., for further direction. Although he could give them little help financially, he did offer them a house in Baltimore, Md., adjoining St. James's Church. This became the first American motherhouse. In 1850 Bp. John Martin Henni of Milwaukee, Wis., persuaded Mother Teresa to transfer the motherhouse to his episcopal city. Mother Mary Caroline Friess, although only 26 years of age, was appointed superior of the motherhouse in Milwaukee and vicar-general of the American branch of the congregation. Between 1847 and 1850, even before the new motherhouse was finished, schools were opened in Buffalo, N.Y., and Pittsburgh and Philadelphia, Pa.

While her original plan had been to staff parochial schools for the children of German immigrants, Mother Caroline decided to open her classrooms to children of all races and nationalities. At her death in July 1892 the congregation in the U.S. had three provinces, numbered 2,000 sisters, with 200 schools in 30 dioceses, and served 70,000 children and 1,500 orphans. During the first 130 years of its existence, the congregation made a vital contribution to the growth of the parochial school system. In 1963 there were 384,418 children under the sisters' care. Of this number nearly 296,490 were in the U.S. and Canada.

The School Sisters of Notre Dame are devoted exclusively to education on every level—kindergarten, elementary, high school, and college—and are established on four continents and in 19 countries. They conduct special schools in the U.S. for the handicapped (deaf, emotionally disturbed, retarded), catechetical centers, day nurseries, prevocational schools, and orphanages. Under a mother general in Rome, there are 20 provincial superiors exercising authority over 12,000 sisters, 327 novices, 652 candidates, and 872 aspirants. At present there are 937 houses in Canada, the U.S., Honduras, Guatemala, Brazil, Argentina, Bolivia, Japan, England, Germany, Sweden, Switzerland, Italy, Austria, Poland, Hungary, Rumania, and Czechoslovakia. There are seven North American provinces: Western—Mequon, Wis. (1850); Eastern—Baltimore, Md. (1876); Southern—St. Louis, Mo. (1895); Northwestern—Mankato, Minn. (1912); Canadian—Waterdown, Ontario, Canada (1927); Northeastern—Wilton, Conn. (1957); South Central—Dallas, Texas (1961). Five of the American provinces have missionary fields: the West, in Guam; the Northwest, in Guatemala; the East, in the southeast U.S.; the South, in Japan, Okinawa, Ryukyu Islands, and Honduras; Canada, in Bolivia with a vicariate in England; and the Northeast, in Puerto Rico. The English, Argentinians, Japanese, Brazilians, and Guamanian missions have novitiates for their native populations. The sisters conduct six colleges within the U.S. and Canada; the College of Notre Dame of Maryland, established in 1896, was the first Catholic college for women in the U.S.

The growth of the congregation peaked in the 1960s with a total of more than 12,000 members, approximately half of whom were ministering in the United States. In the last 50 years, School Sisters from the United States have traveled to Sierra Leone, Ghana, Nigeria, Kenya, Japan, Guam, Yap, Ebeye, Chunk, Mexico, Guatemala, Honduras, Bolivia, Peru, Chile, Paraguay, El Salvador, Pakistan and Nepal to minister with the people. After the Maryknoll Sisters, SSND is the largest group of women religious missionaries in the Church.

Post-Vatican II Developments. Following the directives of Vatican II, the congregation studied its charism and heritage and rewrote its rule. *You Are Sent*, the title based on the words of Jesus to go forth and teach all nations, is the revised constitution which guides more than three thousand School Sisters of Notre Dame today. Teaching on the elementary, secondary, and university levels remains a strong ministry. The sisters also serve the poor wherever there is a need, in the heart of large cities or in Appalachia, within the U.S. borders and beyond. Their ministry extends to shelters for homeless women, classes for illiterate adults, aid to agricultural workers, and programs for disadvantaged children, among others.

In 1986, as a service to the wider community, 678 School Sisters of Notre Dame, ranging in age from 75 to 106, volunteered to be part of a study on aging. University of Kentucky scientist David A. Snowdon led the ongoing research project to learn more about Alzheimer's disease. By allowing their personal and medical histories to be examined and by donating their brains for autopsy, the older sisters, who were eager to help others learn about the causes, treatment and prevention of the disease, also found a renewed sense of mission. "There is great promise in old age," concluded Dr. Snowdon in the Bantam book *Aging With Grace: What the Nun Study Teaches Us About Leading Healthier and More Meaningful Lives*, published in 2001.

The *Mandate for Action*, the resulting document of the Twentieth General Chapter, called the sisters to live out a sense of global responsibility, to reverence all of creation, to prefer and seek solidarity with persons who are poor, and to work to change unjust structures. Responding to the mandate, the international congregation applied for and received nongovernmental status at the United Nations in 1993.

Bibliography: M. D. CAMERON, "School Sisters of Notre Dame," *Catholic World* 165 (May 1947) 163–166. F. FRIESS, *Life of Reverend Mother Mary Teresa of Jesus Gerhardinger* (Baltimore 1907). M. T. FLYNN, *Mother Caroline and the School Sisters of Notre Dame in North America*, 2 v. (St. Louis 1928). M. L. ZIEGLER, *Mutter Theresia von Jesu Gerhardinger* (Munich 1950); *Die armen Schulschwestern von Unserer Lieben Frau* (Munich 1935). M. E. KAWA, *Mutter and Magd: Mutter Maria Theresia von Jesu Gerhardinger* (Augsburg 1958).

[M. V. GEIGER/D. TUREK]

SCHOONENBERG, PIET

Theologian; Dutch JESUIT; b. Amsterdam, Oct. 1, 1911; d. Nijmegen, Sept. 21, 1999. Schoonenberg entered the Dutch province of the Society of Jesus in 1930 and was ordained to the priesthood in 1939. He studied philosophy, theology, and exegesis in Nijmegen, Maastricht, and the Pontifical Biblical Institute in Rome. In 1948 he received the doctorate in theology at Maastricht with a dissertation on theology as interpretation of faith according to recent French literature (*la nouvelle théologie* and its critics). After teaching for several years at Maastricht and Amsterdam, he became associated with the Higher Catechetical Institute at Nijmegen in 1957. In 1964 he was appointed ordinary professor of dogmatic theology at the Catholic University of Nijmegen, where he became professor emeritus in 1976. A prolific and at times controversial author, Schoonenberg is best known for his contributions to contemporary Catholic rethinking of the doctrine of sin, Christology, and trinitarian theology. He was also significantly involved in the preparation of the *De nieuwe katechismus* (1966), a widely translated and much-discussed adult catechism commissioned by the Dutch Catholic bishops and prepared at the Higher Catechetical Institute.

Theology. Schoonenberg's writings on the theology of sin seek primarily to expand the idea of original sin to encompass the broader notion of the sin of the world (cf. John 1:29). Instead of understanding original sin as a misdeed at the dawn of human history that results in an inherited privation of sanctifying grace on the part of later generations, he describes original sin as a negative situation effected by the cumulative force of all human sin. Placed in this sinful situation from birth, all human beings are intrinsically and adversely influenced in the subsequent exercise of their personal freedom. While initial explorations in this vein envision original sin as definitively present in the world only since the rejection of Christ, against whom all sin is ultimately directed, this specification is absent from Schoonenberg's later treatments of the issue. Schoonenberg's proposal, while widely credited with stimulating a needed reexamination of the doctrine of sin, is often judged deficient in expressing the intrinsic effect of past sin on human freedom.

Schoonenberg also contributed significantly to contemporary theology in the area of Christology. The publication in 1966 in the *Tijdschrift voor theologie* of three essays on Christology by Schoonenberg, Ansfridus Hulsbosch, and Edward Schillebeeckx attracted international attention to Christological thought in the Netherlands. Schoonenberg's own position was developed further in *The Christ* (Dutch original: 1969) and in several subsequent essays that nuanced and clarified his thought. A resolute advocate of a "Christology from below," he strongly emphasized the integral humanity of Christ and proposed speaking of Christ as a human person (in a modern sense of that term, i.e., as a conscious and free subject) in whom God was totally and definitively present (cf. 2 Cor. 5:19); in this sense, the Word of God becomes a person only in and through the Incarnation. This departure from terminology deriving from the Council of Chalcedon (one person [divine]; two natures [divine and human]) occasioned considerable theological discussion and raised questions about the orthodoxy of Schoonenberg's thought. In response to such developments, the Congregation for the Doctrine of the Faith defended tra-

ditional christological doctrine in its declaration *Mysterium Filii Dei* [*AAS* 64 (1972) 237–241].

Schoonenberg's contribution to trinitarian theology is similarly both stimulating and controversial. Pursuing trinitarian issues more thematically than in his earlier writings on christology, Schoonenberg proposed in 1973 a set of 36 theses on trinitarian theology in which he maintained that human knowledge of the divine nature is too limited to permit us to conclude from the experience of God as triune in the history, or economy, of salvation ("economic Trinity") to an eternal triune existence of God ("immanent Trinity"). While sharply criticized in many quarters and modified in subsequent writings, Schoonenberg's treatment of the mystery of God's triune existence has proven influential in the intensive recent discussion of the relationship of the economic Trinity and the imminent Trinity.

Bibliography: Bibliography (to 1971): *Tijdschrift voor theologie* 11 (1971): 351–372. For bibliography from 1945–1991: "Bibliografie van Piet Schoonenberg 1945–1991," in *De Geest, het Woord en de Zoon* (Averbode and Kampen 1991) 219–252. P. SCHOONENBERG, *Man and Sin* (London 1965); *The Christ* (New York 1971); "Trinity—The Consummated Covenant," *Studies in Religion* 5 (1975–76) 111–116; *Auf Gott hin denken* (Vienna 1986); *De Geest, het Woord en de Zoon: Theologische overdenkingen over Geest-christologie, Logos-christologie en drieëenheidsleer* (Averbode and Kampen 1991). R. NORTH, *In Search of the Human Jesus* (New York 1969). S. PUJDAK, *Christological Statements: Fact and Interpretation. A Study in the Christology of Piet Schoonenberg* (Ann Arbor 1975). A. KAISER, *Möglichkeit und Grenzen einer Christologie "von unten:" Der christologische Neuansatz "von unten" bei Piet Schoonenberg und dessen Weiter- führung mit Blick auf Nikolaus von Kues* (Munster 1992).

[J. P. GALVIN]

SCHOPENHAUER, ARTHUR

German philosopher, proponent of an atheistic and pessimistic metaphysics of self-redemption based on the epistemological TRANSCENDENTALISM of I. KANT; b. Danzig, Feb. 22, 1788; d. Frankfurt am Main, Sept. 21, 1860.

Life. As a boy, he traveled with his father, a wealthy patrician merchant, through most of Europe. When his father committed suicide, his mother, Johanna, a selfish society woman and a mediocre novelist, moved to Weimar, then the center of German culture. Schopenhauer acquired proficiency in Greek and Latin at the Gymnasium at Gotha and Weimar. He attended the universities of Göttingen and Berlin (1809–13), studying first medicine and then philosophy. A voracious reader, he familiarized himself with Buddhist-Indian philosophy and mysticism, with the German mysticism of Meister ECKHART, with

Arthur Schopenhauer. (Archive Photos)

the theosophy of Jakob BÖHME, and with the thinkers of the RENAISSANCE, the BAROQUE (especially Francisco SUÁREZ), and the French, English, and German ENLIGHT-ENMENT. In Berlin he attended the lectures of J. G. FICH-TE and F. D. E. SCHLEIERMACHER. He subsequently attacked the philosophy of German IDEALISM—"the professorial philosophy of the philosophy professors"—and in particular the "system" of G. W. F. HEGEL, whom he called a quack, a charlatan, and a sycophant of the Prussian government. For a short time he lectured at the university in Berlin as *Privatdozent* but, with Hegel's fame at its apogee, he found no response. The cholera epidemic of 1831, which claimed Hegel's life, caused Schopenhauer to move to Frankfurt.

Thought. At Rudolstadt in the Thuringian forest, Schopenhauer wrote his doctoral dissertation on the fourfold root of the principle of SUFFICIENT REASON, *Über die vierfache Wurzel des Satzes vom zureichenden Grunde* (1813; publ. Berlin 1913). The principle states that "nothing is without reason why it is, rather than is not." It was for Schopenhauer, as it was for G. W. LEIBNIZ, the

integrating factor of cognition, the a priori condition of "objective" knowledge. But "being-objective" meant for him "being-object-for-a-subject." Corresponding to the four different classes of objects that present themselves to cognitive consciousness, there are four types of sufficient reason. The "fourfold root," then, contains the principles of becoming, being, knowing, and acting (*fiendi, essendi, cognoscendi, et agendi*). And since the fourfold root begets four kinds of consequents, there are four kinds of necessity: mathematical, physical, moral, and logical.

Schopenhauer regarded himself as the legitimate heir of Kant. His two-volume masterpiece, *Die Welt als Wille und Vorstellung,* was written in Dresden (1814–18) and first published at Leipzig in 1819. It contains the quintessence of his metaphysics and ethics. Epistemologically, it espouses pure PHENOMENALISM. The world is nothing but the "ideal mental representation" (*Vorstellung*) of the subject. The intellect's innate forms of space, time, and causality work upon matter, producing a regulated corporeal world. Space and time as such are formal expressions of the principle of sufficient reason. With Kant, Schopenhauer holds that the noumenal *Ding an sich* (thing in itself) cannot be known by means of reason, but it can be experienced in introspective inner perception. It is essentially WILL, the "will-to-live," a dark and blind urge that is alive as a cosmic principle in all being but becomes intelligible only on the level of human existence. This cosmic will is primary; intellectual cognition is secondary and merely auxiliary. The universal "world will," itself aimless and purposeless, causes desire, disease, suffering, and death, thus forging an endless chain of transmigrations occurring within the cycle of birth, death, and rebirth.

While in his metaphysics Schopenhauer shows only the influence of Buddhism, in his ethics Buddhist and Christian motifs fuse. Sympathy with all suffering, asceticism, and the resolute negation of the cosmic will can break the vicious circle and liberate from pain and suffering in the eternal quiescence of nirvana. Schopenhauer discusses two other attempts to overcome the cosmic will that are either futile or inadequate: suicide destroys only the individual (phenomenal) but not the universal (noumenal) will; aesthetic contemplation, owing to the fact that works of art (especially music) are "objectivations" of Platonic Ideas, offers man only a temporary release from the cosmic will.

Schopenhauer further elaborated his philosophy in a collection of essays titled *Über den Willen in der Natur* (Frankfurt 1836) and in two prize-winning essays submitted to the Societies of Science of Norway and Denmark, dealing respectively with the freedom of the will and the foundation of morality (publ. jointly under the title *Die beiden Grundprobleme der Ethik,* Frankfurt 1841). The treatises titled *Parerga und Paralipomena* (2 v. Berlin 1851) discuss the philosophy of history, academic philosophy (*Universitätsphilosophie*), and the theory of colors, wherein Schopenhauer sustains the theses of Goethe's *Farbenlehre* against Newton.

While for G. W. Leibniz the created universe was "the best of all possible worlds," Schopenhauer called it "the worst of all possible worlds," "a business whose profits do not cover its expenses." Schopenhauer's misanthropy, his conviction of the prevalence of evil, and his demand of total renunciation of desire did not prevent him from enjoying the pleasures of life. He had a highly developed aesthetic sense and an unusual command of ancient and modern languages; he was also a master stylist. The ATHEISM, pessimism, and voluntarism of his philosophy are incompatible with Christianity, but his thinking exerted great influence on Eduard von HARTMANN, Richard WAGNER, the early F. NIETZSCHE, Henri BERGSON, and others.

See Also: PESSIMISM; VOLUNTARISM.

Bibliography: Works. *Sämtliche Werke,* ed. P. DEUSSEN and A. HÜBSCHER, 16 v. (Munich 1911–42); *"On the Fourfold Root of the Principle of Sufficient Reason,"* and *"On the Will in Nature,"* tr. K. HILLEBRAND (rev. ed. London 1907); *The World As Will and Idea,* tr. R. B. HALDANE and J. KEMP, 3 v. (6th ed. London 1907–09); *The Basis of Mortality,* ed. and tr. A. B. BULLOCK (London 1915); *Selected Essays,* tr. E. B. BAX (London 1891), from *Parerga und Paralipomena.* Literature. F. COPLESTON, *Arthur Schopenhauer: Philosopher of Pessimism* (London 1946). V. J. MCGILL, *Schopenhauer: Pessimist and Pagan* (New York 1931). H. ZIMMERN, *Arthur Schopenhauer: His Life and His Philosophy* (rev. ed. New York 1932).

[K. F. REINHARDT]

SCHORSCH, DOLORES

Author and teacher; b. Morris, Ill., June 16, 1896; d. June 17, 1984. Alma Francis was the eighth of twelve children of Anton and Maria Czagany Schorsch. She entered the Benedictine Order at St. Scholastica Priory, Chicago, Illinois, Feb. 12, 1922, making perpetual profession Aug. 18, 1926. Sr. Dolores' first teaching assignment was at the Academy of St. Scholastica in Canon City, Colorado; later she taught history and served as principal at St. Scholastica High School in Chicago, during which time she was appointed community school supervisor, a position she held until her retirement in 1968.

At the request of the Reverend Daniel F. Cunningham, superintendent of schools of the Chicago archdiocese, and with the collaboration of her brother the

Reverend Alexander Schorsch, C.M., she wrote and edited *A Course in Religion for Elementary Schools* (1935), later renamed the *Jesu-Maria Course in Religion,* based on the method developed by H. C. Morrison of the University of Chicago. The series, complete with detailed lesson plans for teachers, was intended for use in all eight grades of the elementary school. It was innovative in that it was designed to meet the needs and talents of children at their own grade level. The lessons included poetry, stories of the lives of the saints, and Church history. It also introduced children to many of the great hymns of the Church.

The entire series of books was continuously revised, the latest revision being done in the mid-1960s. It was used not only in the archdiocese of Chicago, but in many other dioceses throughout the United States, and in England, Australia, New Zealand, Canada, and the British West Indies. An adaptation of these materials was also made in China.

Schorsch's collected papers and correspondence are in the archives of St. Scholastica Priory, Chicago.

[A. M. MONGOVEN]

SCHOTT, ANSELM

Liturgist; b. Staufeneck, near Göppingen (Württemberg), Sept. 5, 1843; d. Maria Laach, April 23, 1896. He studied theology at Tübingen and Munich and was ordained in 1867 at Rottenburg-on-the-Neckar. In 1868 Schott became a Benedictine at Beuron; he made his profession June 6, 1870. At first he was active as lecturer in Beuron's school of theology. After the expulsion of the monks during Bismarck's Kulturkampf, he spent the years 1876 to 1881 in Beuron's Belgian foundation at Maredsous, working on the editing of monastic-liturgical books for the *Missel des fidèles* (ed. Dom Gerard VAN CALOEN), which stimulated Schott to edit *Das Messbuch der hl. Kirche* (Freiburg 1884) when he returned to Beuron in 1882. Subsequently, millions of copies of the various editions of the *Schott Messbuch* appeared, and it became an essential foundation for the liturgical renewal in German-speaking areas. The *Vesperbuch lateinisch und deutsch* (Freiburg 1893) did not enjoy such success. In 1892 Schott was sent to the newly founded Abbey of Maria Laach.

Bibliography: D. ZÄHRINGER, "Der Beitrag Beurons zur liturgischen Erneuerung," *Beuron* 1863–1963 (1963) 337–357. R. BERON, *Lexikon für Theologie und Kirche,* ed. J. HOFER and K. RAHNER, 10 v. (2d, new ed. Freiburg 1957–65) 9:477. S. MAYER, *Beuroner Bibliographie, 1863–1963* (Beuron 1963) 132–135.

[V. FIALA]

SCHRADER, KLEMENS

Theologian; b. Hanover, Nov. 22, 1820; d. Poitiers, Feb. 23, 1875. He studied at the German College in Rome and was ordained in 1846. Two years later he entered the Society of Jesus and in 1850 returned to the German College as prefect of studies. In 1851 he was appointed to the faculty of the Roman College. He shared with C. PASSAGLIA an interest in the Fathers of the Church and collaborated with Passaglia's work on the Immaculate Conception, *De immaculata Deiparae semper virginis conceptu* (3 v. Rome 1854). Though scholastic in method, he sought to incorporate into his teaching the best of positive theology. He learned several oriental languages to assist his study of ancient Christian sources. He taught dogmatic theology at Vienna from 1857 until he was forced to resign ten years later rather than take the oath of fidelity to the constitution of 1867. His somewhat narrow devotion to the papacy gave rise to his most competent work, *De unitate Romana*, (2 v. Freiburg im Breisgau 1862; Vienna 1868), and to his part in the editing of the periodical *Der Papst und die modernen Ideen* (Vienna 1864–67). He considered Pius IX's SYLLABUS OF ERRORS a series of definitions, and he interpreted it so strictly as to equate freedom of conscience with indifferentism and liberal with atheistic.

He was on the planning commission for VATICAN COUNCIL I and in 1872 became director of studies for the new theological faculty at Poitiers to which he brought great renown. His almost unintelligible literary style lessened his influence perhaps even more than his extreme dogmatic position; yet he had and deserved the respect of his contemporaries for his learning and his devotion to principle that led him to stand the walls of Rome in 1870 ministering to the spiritual needs of the defenders of the papacy.

Bibliography: A. FERRETTI, ''De vita et scriptis R. P. Clementis Schrader,'' in C. Schrader, *De theologico testium fonte* (Paris 1878). H. HURTER, *Nomenclator literarius theologiae catholicae* 5.2:1527–29. J. DE BLIC, *Dictionnaire de théologie catholique* 14.2: 1576–79.

[A. ROCK]

SCHREMBS, JOSEPH

First bishop of Toledo, Ohio and archbishop bishop of Cleveland, Ohio; b. Wurzelhofen (Regensburg), Bavaria, March 12, 1866; d. Cleveland, Nov. 2, 1945. The 15th of 16 children of George and Mary (Gess) Schrembs, Joseph became a member of the celebrated Regensburg Boys' Choir. When he was 11 years old, he came to the U.S. to enter the scholasticate at St. Vincent Archabbey, Latrobe, Pennsylvania, where his older brother Ignatius was already a priest. At 16 he was teaching at St. Martin's parish school in Louisville, Kentucky, and two years later was accepted for the Diocese of Grand Rapids, Michigan.

After attending Laval University, Quebec, he finished his training at the Grand Séminaire, Montreal, developing his native oratorical powers there. He was ordained on June 29, 1889, by Bp. Henry J. Richter of Grand Rapids and appointed curate to St. Mary's in Saginaw, Michigan. He was next stationed at St. Mary's in Bay City, Michigan., first as curate, then as pastor. In 1900 he became pastor of St. Mary's, a German parish in Grand Rapids. In 1903 he was appointed vicar-general of Grand Rapids, and in 1906, a domestic prelate. On Jan. 8, 1911, he was appointed titular bishop of Sophene and auxiliary to Richter, who consecrated him Feb. 22, 1911. On August 11 of that year he was made first bishop of Toledo, taking possession of his see on October 4. After a decade of creative organizational work in Toledo, he was appointed fifth bishop of Cleveland on June 16, 1921, and installed there on September 8.

As parish priest and founding bishop, Schrembs had revealed great capacity for leadership; in Cleveland this talent developed to the fullest. The chancery offices, set up in the days of Bp. Richard Gilmour, were reestablished under his direction, and in 1938 he initiated a thorough reorganization of all diocesan agencies. Remembered for his zeal on behalf of diocesan charitable and social institutions, he was also deeply committed to education. He founded several primary and secondary schools, authorized the Ursuline Nuns and Sisters of Notre Dame to establish colleges, and erected a new diocesan seminary. Never forsaking his early love for sacred music, he composed several hymns, helped produce manuals of Gregorian chant and Catholic editions of elementary music text books. In 1915 he revealed a plan for Church music reform that would begin with young children.

He was one of four bishops on the Catholic War Council during World War I, and it was largely through his efforts, personally pursued in Rome, that the National Catholic Welfare Conference received papal approval as a permanent peacetime agency. As chairman of the NCWC Department of Lay Organizations, he was chiefly responsible for the creation of the NATIONAL COUNCIL OF CATHOLIC MEN and the NATIONAL COUNCIL OF CATHOLIC WOMEN, both in 1920. In 1939, the golden jubilee of his ordination, he received the title of archbishop as a personal honor. In 1942 he was joined by Bp. Edward F. Hoban of the Rockford (Illinois) Diocese as coadjutor.

Bibliography: M. J. HYNES, *History of the Diocese of Cleveland* (Cleveland 1953). W. G. ROSE, *Cleveland: The Making of a*

City (Cleveland 1950). "The Death of Archbishop Schrembs," *Catholic World* 162 (Dec. 1954) 274.

[W. A JURGENS]

SCHRIJVERS, JOSEPH

Redemptorist ascetical writer; b. Zutendel (Limburg) Belgium, Dec. 19, 1876; d. Rome, March 4, 1945. He completed his secondary studies at the College of St. Joseph, Hasselt. After joining the Redemptorists in 1894 and completing his novitiate at Saint-Trond, he made final vows in 1895. He was ordained Oct. 2, 1900, after completing his philosophy and theology at Beauplateau, Belgium. Here he later was professor of philosophy and spiritual prefect of the scholastics (1902–13). In 1913 at Uniw in Ukrainian Galicia, which was then Russian territory, he established the first Redemptorist house of the Ukrainian rite. He remained in the Ukraine until 1933 as vice provincial of the province of Lvov. During this time, he was also engaged in the direction of two institutes of religious sisters and was apostolic visitor for sisters of the oriental rite in the Ukraine, Canada, the United States, and, in 1932, Brazil. In 1933 he was appointed provincial of the Belgian Redemptorists and in 1936, consultor general to the rector major. Schrijvers' writings were for the most part works on ascetical subjects: *Les Principes de la vie spirituelle* (1912), *La Bonne volonté* (1913), *Le Don de soi* (1918), *Le Divin ami* (1922), *Ma mère* (1925), *Les Âmes confiantes* (1930), *Le Message de Jésus à son Prêtre* (1932), and *Notre Père qui êtes aux cieux* (1942). Translated into ten languages, including English, his works counted 150 editions, 600,000 copies. The spirituality of Schijvers is based upon God's fatherhood. He placed great stress upon abandonment to the divine will, but there is no foundation for the accusation of quietism leveled against his works. Schrijvers closely approached the Little Flower's Little Way of spiritual childhood.

Bibliography: M. DE MEULEMEESTER et al., *Bibliographie générale des écrivains rédemptoristes*, 3 v. (Louvain 1933–39) 2:391–394; 3:383–384. *La Voix du Rédempteur* 54 (1947) 45–51. *Vita cristiana* 16 (1947) 54–63. *Analecta C.SS.R.* 20 (1948) 34–38.

[L. VEREECKE]

SCHROEDER, PETER JOSEPH

Theologian; b. Beek, near Geilenkirchen in the Rhineland, April 26, 1849; d. Wuppertal, Germany, May 3, 1903. He studied at the Gregorian University and was ordained in Rome in 1873. During the KULTURKAMPF, he left Germany to teach in the diocese of Liège, Belgium, first as professor in the minor seminary in St. Trond

(1875–87) and then for a short time in the major seminary at Liège (1887). He was appointed (1888) to the seminary in Cologne, Germany, by Abp. Philip Krementz, who wished him to succeed Matthias J. SCHEEBEN, who died that year. He had taught at Cologne only one year when Bp. John J. KEANE, newly appointed rector of the Catholic University of America, Washington, D.C., invited him to occupy the chair of dogmatic theology there. As a member (1889–98) of the first faculty of Catholic University, Schroeder took an active interest in the German-American Catholic community and its problems. In the school controversy he was uncompromising in his opposition to his colleague T. J. Bouquillon and to Bps. Keane and John IRELAND (*see* BOUQUILLON CONTROVERSY). On resigning from Catholic University, he joined the theological faculty at Münster, Germany. When Münster was raised to university status (1902), he was appointed its first rector, serving in that capacity until shortly before his death. Among his writings are *Sur la tolérance de l'Église* (1879), *Der Liberalismus in Theologie und Geschichte* (1881), and *Church and Republic* (1891).

Bibliography: E. HEGEL, *Lexikon für Theologie und Kirche*, ed. J. HOFER and K. RAHNER, 10 v. (2d, new ed. Freiburg 1957–65) 9:497. *Chronik der Universität Münster* 18 (1904 series). C. G. HERBERMANN, "The Faculty of the Catholic University," *American Catholic Quarterly Review* 14 (1889) 701–715. H. HECKER, *Chronik der Regenten, Dozenten und Ökonomen im Priesterseminar des Erzbistums Köln 1615–1950* (Cologne 1952).

[J. P. WHALEN]

SCHUBERT, FRANZ

Eminent composer of the classical school and master of the German lied; b. Vienna, Jan. 31, 1797; d. Vienna, Nov. 14, 1828. He was the 12th child of Franz, a suburban schoolteacher, and Elizabeth (Vitz) Schubert. His father was devoted to music, and gave the gifted boy the best possible instruction. At 12 young Franz entered the Imperial Chapel Royal choir and the Stadt-convict, where the then-famous composer Salieri was his principal teacher and where he created his first important works. For three years after finishing there he taught in his father's school, but at 20 ventured on a career as free-lance composer. He occasionally accompanied his lieder but otherwise neither conducted nor performed in public nor taught regularly; he lived entirely on the earnings from his published songs, which his large circle of personal friends helped to popularize. For years he was depressed and intermittently ailing; he died of typhoid fever shortly after a special Schubert concert without ever having heard his major works performed. While he shared the anticlericalism of his day, he died a Catholic; his body was buried next to that of BEETHOVEN in the Währing District cemetery.

Franz Schubert.

Although he had composed music of high distinction for piano and for choral, chamber, and symphonic combinations, his fame rested on his lieder until attention was drawn to his other works by BRAHMS, who anonymously edited the last Mass and piano music; by Sir George Grove, who wrote the first comprehensive Schubert essay; and by others who assessed his true importance. Today he is recognized as the last of the Viennese classicists. He mastered the classical language as a child and used it creatively without revolutionizing it. His leaning toward long movements, however, anticipates the future as does the use of ''cyclic'' motifs. Unlike that of Beethoven, Schubert's music rarely conveys one prevailing mood. His oscillation between major and minor is characteristic, as is his use of Viennese folk music and dance patterns.

Of the six completed Masses, four belong among his masterworks: the G major (D.167), written when he was 18; C major (D.452), with a *Benedictus* recomposed in 1828 (D.961); A-flat major (D.678); and E-flat major (D.950). Their serene beauty, heightened by occasional passages of almost mystical inspiration, rules out prominent vocal solos and orchestral dramatics. As he stated in a letter of July 25, 1825, with reference to his celebrated *Ave Maria,* ''I have never forced devotion in myself and never compose hymns or prayers. . . unless it over-

comes me unawares; but then it is usually the right and true devotion.'' In all his Masses he omitted certain words (not always the same ones) from the text, but there is no evidence that this was caused by more than negligence. Their use in Catholic worship would require completion of the text, as well as the admissibility of orchestral accompaniment. Of his other spiritual works, the *German Requiem* (D.621), the completed portion of his Easter cantata, *Lazarus* (D.689), the Offertorio *Intende Voci* (D.963), the *Ave Maria* and other devotional songs are of the greatest beauty.

Bibliography: *Franz Schuberts Werke: Kritisch durchgesehene Gesammtausgabe,* ed. J. BRAHMS et al., 43 v. in 41 (Leipzig 1884–97). O. E. DEUTSCH, *Schubert: Thematic Catalogue* (London 1951); *Schubert, A Documentary Biography,* tr. E. BLOM (London 1947). A. EINSTEIN, *Schubert: A Musical Portrait,* tr. D. ASCOLI (New York 1951). M. J. E. BROWN, *Schubert* (London 1958). M. J. E. BROWN et al., *Die Musik in Geschichte und Gegenwart,* ed. F. BLUME (Kassel-Basel 1949–) 12:106–185, extensive bibliog. O. WISSIG, *Franz Schuberts Messen* (Leipzig 1909). L. BLACK, ''Schubert and *Fierrabras:* A Mind in Ferment,'' *The Opera Quarterly* 14/4 (1998) 17–39. R. BOCKHOLDT, ''Die Kunst, heim zu finden: Über Schlüsse und Anschüsse in Schuberts Instrumentalmusik,'' *Musiktheorie* 13 (1998) 145–56. K. HAID, ''The Sad Story Behind Schubert's Variations,'' *Flute Talk* 20/2 (2000) 22–23. R. KRAMER, *Distant Cycles: Schubert and the Conceiving of Song* (Chicago 1994). A. LINDMAYR-BRANDL, ''Johannes Brahms und Schuberts *Drei Klavierstücke* D. 946: Entstehungsgeschichte, Kompositionsprozess und Werkverständnis,'' *Die Musikforschung* 53 (2000) 134–44. D. MONTGOMERY, ''Modern Schubert Interpretation in the Light of the Pedagogical Sources of His Day,'' *Early Music* 25 (1997) 100–118. R. STEBLIN, ''The Peacock's Tale: Schubert's Sexuality Reconsidered,'' *19th Century Music* 17 (1993) 5–33. M. WESSEL, ''Die Zyklusgestaltung in Franz Schuberts Instrumentalwerk: Eine Skizze zu Anlange und Ästhetik der Finalsätze,'' *Die Musikforschung* 49 (1996) 19–35. S. YOUENS, *Schubert, Müller, and 'Die schöne Müllerin'* (Cambridge 1997).

[K. WOLFF]

SCHULTE, AUGUSTINE JOSEPH

Educator; b. Philadelphia, Penn., May 5, 1856; d. Philadelphia, May 23, 1937. He was the son of August and Louise (Bille) Schulte and attended St. Charles Seminary, Overbrook, Pennsylvania (1874–79), and the North American College, Rome (1879–83), He was ordained in Rome on June 3, 1882, receiving his S.T.L. from the Urban College. Having served as vice-rector of the NORTH AMERICAN COLLEGE (1883–84), he was, after the death of the rector, Msgr. Louis E. Hostlot, pro-rector from February 1884 to June 1885. When he learned in March 1884 that the Italian government proposed to confiscate the buildings of the college, his quick report to the American bishops enabled them to petition the U.S. government for immediate and effective action. He also promoted the canonical establishment of the College

(Leo XIII, brief *Ubi primum*, Oct. 25, 1884). In 1885 Denis J. O'Connell was chosen rector and Schulte returned to the Archdiocese of Philadelphia, where he was assigned to the staff of St. Charles Seminary. He spent the rest of his career there as professor of liturgy and modern languages, and in disciplinary and administrative capacities. He wrote several articles on rubrical subjects for the old *Catholic Encyclopedia* and (over the initials S.L.E. and S.L.T.) for the *American Ecclesiastical Review*. His two books, *Benedicenda* (1907) and *Consecranda* (1907, 1956), were useful manuals for the blessings and consecrations of the Latin rite.

Bibliography: R. F. MCNAMARA, *American College in Rome, 1855–1955* (Rochester 1956).

[R. F. MCNAMARA]

SCHUMANN, ROBERT

Romanticist composer of vocal and instrumental music; b. Zwickau (Saxony), Germany, June 8, 1810 (christened Robert Alexander); d. Endenich (near Bonn), July 29, 1856. The fifth child of a bookseller and publisher, he early displayed both musical and literary talents. Apart from the musical tuition received at school, he had no guidance in composition. In 1828–29 he studied pianoforte with Friedrich Wieck, but an attempt to strengthen his fingers by a mechanical device so disabled one finger that a virtuoso career became impossible. From age 18 on he composed prolifically and was active also as a musical journalist, founding in 1834 the *Neue Leipziger Zeitschrift für Musik* to promote new ideas and composers. In 1840 he married Clara Wieck, one of the leading pianists of the day. Throughout his life he suffered from mental disturbances (possibly similar to dementia praecox) that culminated in complete insanity two years before his death.

In common with that of most German romanticist composers, his religion was sincere, but doctrinally vague and tending toward pantheism. He wrote little religious music in the strict sense, though many of his songs and shorter choral pieces are imbued with religious feeling. The so-called oratorio *Das Paradies und die Peri* (Op. 50; 1841–43) is based on a tale from Hindu mythology. A *Missa Sacra* (Op. 147) and *Requiem* (Op. 148) for chorus and orchestra (1852) have unenterprising texture: the choral writing is largely homophonic in four-square phrasing and repeated rhythms that at times become monotonous. Like most 19th-century Masses they have little or no relevance to the liturgy; if they are to be revived, their place is in the concert hall. His lasting fame rests on his secular works, in which shapeliness of form combines with a personal, expressive lyricism.

Robert Schumann. (Archive Photos)

Bibliography: R. SCHUMANN, *Gesammelte Schriften über Musik und Musiker,* 4 v. (Leipzig 1854), tr. F. R. RITTER, 2 v. (8th ed. London 1880), selections ed. by K. WOLFF, tr. P. ROSENFELD (New York 1946); *Jugendbriefe* (Leipzig 1885), tr. M. HERBERT (London 1888); *The Letters of Robert Schumann.* ed. K. STORCK, tr. H. BRYANT (London 1907). E. SCHUMANN, *The Schumanns and Johannes Brahms,* tr. M. BUSCH (New York 1927). G. ABRAHAM, ed., *Schumann: A Symposium* (New York 1952); *Grove's Dictionary of Music and Musicians,* ed. E. BLOM 9 v. (5th ed. London 1954) 7:603–640. M. BEAUFILS, *Schumann* (Paris 1932). J. CHISSELL, *Schumann* (The Master Musicians, NS; London 1948). R. H. SCHAUFFLER, *Florestan: The Life and Work of Robert Schumann* (New York 1945). E. A. LIPPMAN, *Die Musik in Geschichte und Gegenwart,* ed. F. BLUME (Kassel-Basel 1949–) 12:272–325. *Baker's Biographical Dictionary of Musicians,* ed. N. SLONIMSKY (5th, rev. ed. New York 1958) 1474–78. J. BELLMAN, "Aus alten Märchen: The Chivalric Style of Schumann and Brahms," *The Journal of Musicology* 13 (1995) 117–35. D. EHRHARDT, "Les *Études symphoniques* de Robert Schumann: projet d'intégration des variations posthumes," *Revue de Musicologie* 78 (1992) 289–306. J. W. FINSON, "Schumann's Mature Style and the *Album of Songs for the Young,*" *The Journal of Musicology* 8 (1990) 227–50. C. GOLDBERG, "Going into the Woods: Space, Time, and Movement in Schumann's *Waldszenen* op. 82," *International Journal of Musicology* 3 (1994) 151–74. R. HALLMARK, "The Rückert Lieder of Robert and Clara Schumann," *19th Century Music* 14 (1990) 3–30. K. KÜSTER, "Schumanns neuer Zugang zum Kunstlied: Das Liederjahr 1840 in kompositorischer Hinsicht," *Die Musikforschung* 51 (1998) 1–14. S. MEYER, "The Trope of the Double in Schumann's *Genoveva,*" *The Opera Journal* 27/1 (1994) 4–22. G. SCHNITZLER, "Heine und Schumann: *Im wunderschönen Monat Mai,*" *International Journal of Musicology* 7 (1998) 167–184. M.

STOCCO, ''Variation der Variation der Variation. . .; Einheit als Chaos: Analytische Beobachtungen über die *Papillons* op. 2 von Robert Schumann,'' *Musiktheorie* 11 (1996) 139–58.

[A. MILNER]

SCHUSTER, ALFREDO ILDEFONSO, BL.

Cardinal archbishop of Milan, Cassinese Benedictine, liturgist; b. Jan. 18, 1880, Rome, Italy; d. Aug. 30, 1954, at Venegono Seminary near Milan, Italy.

Although his father, Johannes (d. 1888), a tailor in Rome, was born in Bavaria, and his pious mother, Anna Maria (Tutzer), came from Bolzano in the Austrian South Tyrol, Alfredo Ludovico Schuster grew up a thorough Roman. He was accepted as a Benedictine monk by the Roman Abbey of St. Paul-outside-the-Walls at the age of 11 in 1891, and given the name Ildefonso; he made his monastic profession on Nov. 13, 1899. After priestly studies at Sant'Anselmo, Rome, he was ordained on March 19, 1904. He then developed into a model religious, thanks in large measure to the counsel of his saintly confrère (Bl.) Placido RICCARDI, O.S.B. Schuster served his abbey as master of novices (1904–16) and as prior (1916–18). From 1914 to 1929 he was procurator-general of the Benedictine Cassinese Congregation. On April 6, 1918, he was elected abbot-ordinary of the abbey *nullius* of St. Paul-outside-the-Walls.

Recognizing his talents, the popes gave him various assignments, including consultorships on the Congregation of Rites (Liturgy, Causes of Saints) and the Congregation for the Oriental Church. Additionally, he was censor of the Academy of Sacred Liturgy, president of the Commission for Sacred Art and Apostolic Visitator for Italian seminaries. Pius XI named him archbishop of Milan on June 26, 1929, created him cardinal priest of SS. Silvestro e Martino ai Monti on July 15, 1929, and personally consecrated him on July 21, 1929. The frail ascetic, with a spirit worthy of a successor of St. Charles Borromeo and St. Ambrose, embarked upon a tireless episcopal career notable for both its liturgical emphasis and its contemporary pastoral awareness. He emphasized catechetics and promoted the role of the laity in parishes and in Catholic Action. During the German military occupation of Lombardy (1943–45), the cardinal gave his flock strong and provident guidance, and the advice to surrender that he gave to the German commandant in 1945 had a decisive influence.

From 1938 on Schuster had stood firm against the racist views and other ''Germanizations'' of Italian Fascism. Prior to that, however, he had shown public benev-olence toward the Fascist regime, to the particular chagrin of many Catholics in other lands. Whether rightly or wrongly—and he was content to let history judge—he had chosen this course for pastoral, not political, reasons. He also interpreted strictly the pledge of loyalty that he, before his consecration, had made to the king, pursuant to art. 20 of the Lateran Concordat of 1929. He was the first Italian prelate to be affected by that rule. Had he not maintained his punctilious personal concern for Mussolini, he might never have had that last interview of April 25, 1945, at which he urged the dictator to make peace with God and man. Unfortunately, Mussolini spurned the admonition, to his own quick disaster.

Although his spirituality is best characterized by his intense prayer life; his opposition to racism was simply a manifestation of his egalitarian spirit: He believed that the goal of all Christians is holiness. He worked toward this ideal by seeking justice during and after World War II and founding the Institute of Ambrosian Chant and Sacred Music to inspire the faithful through beautiful liturgy. Schuster also won great esteem as a liturgical and monastic historian. During his lifetime he wrote many scholarly articles and several books. Among the books were *Storia di San Benedetto e dei suoi tempi* (Viboldone 1943), which was translated into English as *St. Benedict and His Times* (St. Louis 1951), and the classic *Liber Sacramentorum* (9 v. Turin 1919–29). The latter, a most influential work, has been translated into several languages [Eng. ed., *The Sacramentary: Historical and Liturgical Notes on the Roman Missal* (5 v. New York 1925–31)].

Having tended his flock through nine turbulent post-war years, Schuster died in 1954 with a reputation for high sanctity. He was entombed in the metropolitan cathedral of Milan. The diocesan process for his canonization was initiated in 1957 by his successor, Giovanni Battista Montini, who became Pope Paul VI. A miracle attributed to his intercession was approved on July 11, 1995.

During Schuster's beatification on May 12, 1996, Pope John Paul II observed: ''Schuster's pastoral ministry was motivated by the spirit of prayer and contemplation proper to the Benedictine tradition. His monastic spirituality, nourished by daily meditation on Sacred Scripture, thus expanded into active collaboration with the Holy See and into his generous service to the Ambrosian community, edified and consoled by him until the very end by the regular, devoted celebration of the sacred mysteries and by the example of a clear and consistent life'' (Ambrosian Missal, Preface of the Memorial).

Feast: Aug. 30.

See Also: LATERAN PACTS.

Alfredo Ildefonso Cardinal Schuster presiding over ground-breaking ceremony of the new Church of St. Rita, Milan, 1940.
(©Bettmann/CORBIS)

Heinrich Schütz. (Archive Photos)

Bibliography: *L'Osservatore Romano,* English edition. no. 29: 5. *L'epistolario card. Schuster-don Calabria,* ed. A. MAJO and L. PIOVAN (Milan 1989). *Scritti del Cardinale A. Ildefonso Schuster,* ed. G. OGGIONI (Varese 1959); *Gli ultimi tempi di un regime,* 2d ed. (Milan 1946). *Ildefonso Schuster: Cenni biografici* (Viboldone 1958). G. BASADONNA, *Cardinal Schuster. Un monaco vescovo nella dinamica Milano* (Milan 1996). D. A. BINCHY, *Church and State in Fascist Italy* (New York 1941). A. M. BOZZONE, "Schuster, A.I.," in A. MERCATI and A. PELZER, *Dizionario ecclesiastico,* 3 v. (Turin 1954–58) 3:756. E. CAVATERRA, *Salvate Milano! La mediazione del cardinale Schuster nel 1945* (Milan 1995). G. JUDICA CORDIGLIA, *Il mio Cardinale* (Milan 1955); *Così sorrideva il Cardinale Schuster* (Milan 1957). A. M. FORTUNA, *Incontro all'Archivescovado* (Florence 1971). A. MAJO, *Gli anni difficili dell'episcopato del card. A. I. Schuster* (Milan 1978); *Schuster: una vita per Milano* (Milan 1994); with G. RUMI, *Il cardinal Schuster e il suo tempo* (Milan 1979).

[R. F. MCNAMARA]

SCHÜTZ, HEINRICH

Composer whose work established baroque on German soil; b. Köstritz (Saxony), Germany, Oct. 4, 1585; d. Dresden, Nov. 6, 1672. Apart from an early book of madrigals and an opera whose score is lost, Schütz devoted his long life to church music, originally for Protestant use. As a youth he sang in the chapel choir of Landgrave Moritz of Hesse-Kassel, who sent him to Venice in 1609 to study with Giovanni GABRIELI. The effect of this contact with a leading exponent of the new baroque *concertato* style became immediately evident in Schütz's first published church music, the *Psalmen Davids* of 1619. After returning to Germany, he entered the service of the Elector of Saxony at Dresden and proceeded to Italianize the musicians as well as the music. He paid a second visit to Italy in 1628 to study with MONTEVERDI, whose more intimate religious music clearly influenced the *Symphoniae sacrae* of 1629. These were Latin motets for solo voices and instruments, whereas two later sets with a similar title consisted of German motets. In the *Kleine geistliche Concerte* (two sets, 1636 and 1639) he provides a *basso continuo* for vocal solos and ensembles, again with German texts. His four Passion settings employ a style of monodic narrative deriving from the simpler kind of plainsong. His Christmas and Easter oratorios, and the *Seven Last Words,* are of considerable importance in the development of church music in the 17th century.

Bibliography: *Sämtliche Werke,* ed. P. SPITTA, (Leipzig 1885–1927); *Neue Ausgabe sämtlicher Werke,* ed. F. SCHÖNEICH et al. (Kassel 1955–). H. J. MOSER, *Heinrich Schütz: His Life and Work,* tr. C. F. PFATTEICHER from 2d rev. Ger. ed. (St. Louis 1959). M. F. BUKOFZER, *Music in the Baroque Era* (New York 1947). P. H. LÁNG, *Music in Western Civilization* (New York 1941). H. EICHORN, "Heinrich Schütz: Geistliche Chor-Music, Neue Darstellungsaspekte aus alten Quellen," *Musik und Kirche* 70 (2000) 97–108. H. KRONES, "Heinrich Schütz und der Tod," *Studien zur Musikwissenschaft* 42 (1993) 53–75. M. LINDLEY, "Heinrich Schütz: intonazione della scala e struttura tonale," *Recercare* (1989) 41–96. E. LINFIELD, "Modulatory Techniques in Seventeenth-Century Music: Schütz, a Case in Point," *Music Analysis* 12 (1993) 197–214. U. WEIDINGER, "Die Weihnachtshistorie von Heinrich Schütz—ein *modernes* Werk? Sein *Beschluß* unter dem Aspekt der Moduslehre analysiert," *Österreichische Musik Zeitschrift* 51 (1996) 520–530.

[D. STEVENS]

SCHWANE, JOSEPH

Theologian; b. Dorsten, Westphalia, April 2, 1824; d. Münster, June 6, 1892. He was ordained in 1849, became *Privatdocent* in the theological faculty at Münster in 1853, assistant professor of moral theology and history of dogma in 1859, and professor of the same in 1867. In 1881 he was given the chair of dogmatic theology, which he retained until his death. Schwane was the first German theologian to produce a major work on the whole history of dogma. His *Dogmengeschichte* (4 v., v.1, 2 Münster, 1862–69; v.3, 4, Freiburg 1882–90) is still considered a respectable work in its field as Schwane conceived this to be. Each volume covers a given period—pre-Nicene, late patristic, scholastic, and modern—and is divided according to the division of dogmatic topics commonly used in manuals of dogmatic theology in Schwane's time. However, the work as a whole is notably more dogmatic than historical in character, and it amounts in fact to an exposition of dogma in the light of history. For that reason it is not quite a history of dogma in the sense in which the term later came to be understood. Schwane also published two systematic works on moral theology, *Spezielle Moraltheologie* (3 v. Freiburg 1873–78) and *Allgemeine Moraltheologie* (Freiburg 1885), and some monographs of importance, among which were *Controversia de valore baptismi haereticorum* (Münster 1860), *De operibus supererogatoriis et consiliis evangelicis* (Münster 1868), *Die theologische Lehre über die Verträge* (Münster 1871), and *Die eucharistische Opferhandlung* (Freiburg 1889).

Bibliography: G. FRITZ, *Dictionnaire de théologie catholique,* ed. A. VACANT, 15 v. (Paris 1903–50; Tables générales 1951–) 14.1:1583. E. HEGEL, *Lexikon für Theologie und Kirche,* ed. J. HOFER and K. RAHNER, 10 v. (2d, new ed. Freiburg 1957–65) 9:531. M. OTT, *The Catholic Encyclopedia,* ed. C. G. HERBERMANN, 16 v. (New York 1907–14; suppl. 1922) 13:592.

[P. K. MEAGHER]

SCHWARTZ, ANTON MARIA, BL.

Piarist priest, founder of the Catholic Association of Apprentices *Katholischer Lehringsverein* and the Congregation of Christian Workers of St. Joseph Calasanz (*Kalasantiners*), apostle to working men; b. Baden (near Vienna), Austria, Feb. 28, 1852; d. Vienna, Sept. 15, 1929. The ministry of Anton Schwartz was shaped by his early life growing up in a large, working-class family. He was the fourth of thirteen children of a theater musician. While attending secondary school in Vienna, Anton sang at the Heiligenkreuz. He joined the Piarists at Krems (1869), but left when the prevailing *Kulturkampf* threatened the suppression of religious orders. After completing his studies in philosophy and theology at the diocesan seminary in Vienna, he was ordained (1875).

His first assignment was as chaplain in Marchegg (1875–79). Thereafter he was appointed chaplain at the Daughters of Charity hospital at Vienna-Sechshaus, where he witnessed the suffering of young workers.

In 1882, Schwartz became the "apostle of social justice" for working men decades before Pope LEO XIII issued the encyclical *RERUM NOVARUM*. Recognizing that no organization within the Church focused on the problems experienced by apprentices and young workers, Schwartz established an association in Vienna to educate them and advocate for their rights.

With four confreres he founded the Kalasantiners (November 24, 1889) to serve working-class men just

days after the consecration of the first church built by Schwartz for workers (November 17, 1889). The order of priests and brothers follows a modified Piarist Rule. They teach religion and practical skills, operate oratories, offer social services for workers, and diffuse literature, including Father Schwartz's prayer book for workers, biographies, and the monthly *Saint Calasanctius-Blätter* (since 1888). The order's constitutions were approved by the Vatican in 1939.

Schwartz fought against exploitation by appealing to Christian ethics, advocated for compensation for overtime and free time on Sundays for worship, and defended the right to organize. In 1908, he withdrew from all public controversy, but continued his quiet assistance.

Anton Maria Schwartz was declared venerable by John Paul II (April 6, 1995). That pope beatified him in Vienna's Heldenplatz on June 21, 1998.

Bibliography: J. BRUCKNER, *Der Wiener Arbeiterapostel P. A. M. S.* (Vienna 1934). A. INNERKOFLER, *Anton Maria Schwartz* (Vienna 1931). F. ZIMMERMANN, *Die ersten 25 Jahre der Calasantiner-Congregation* (Vienna 1914). *Acta Apostolicae Sedis* (1998): 690.

[K. I. RABENSTEIN]

SCHWARTZ, EDUARD

Eminent Protestant church historian and philologist; b. Kiel, Aug. 22, 1858; d. Munich, Feb. 13, 1940. After studying philology under H. Usener and U. Wilamowitz-Moellendorff, he taught at Rostock (1888), Giessen (1893), Strassburg (1897), Göttingen (1912), and Munich (1919–40). His chief interest was early Church history, to which he turned definitely in 1903 with his preparation of the edition of Eusebius's *Histoire ecclesiastique* for the Berlin Corpus (*Die griechischen christlichen Schriftsteller der ersten drei Jahrhunderte,* 3 v. 1903–09) and his plan for the edition of the *Acta Conciliorum Oecumenicorum;* he completed the volumes on the councils of EPHESUS (431) and CHALCEDON (451). In his preparation for these two monumental works he entered into an analysis of many of the perplexing historical problems of the first six centuries. His competence in dealing with the sources and institutions of Oriental tradition, chronology, geography, juridical concepts, and theology enabled him to publish numerous separate monographs shedding light on the growth of the Church from its Judeo-Christian beginnings to the Monophysite struggles. He composed monographs on the Easter Tables of the Early Church, the Pseudo-Apostolic Church Order, St. Athanasius, and on the schism and heresies of the fourth, fifth, and sixth centuries, always integrating the history of the Church with that of the Empire. His genius enabled him to make vivid

Friedrich Joseph Von Schwarzenberg.

the men and deeds of the past after the manner of the great MAURISTS as an editor, and of Theodor Mommsen as an historian (Altendorf).

Bibliography: *Gesammelte Schriften,* ed. H. D. ALTENDORF, 5 v. (Berlin 1938–62). H. D. ALTENDORF, *Die Religion in Geschichte und Gegenwart,* 7 v. (3rd ed. Tübingen 1957–65) 5:1589–90. W. OTTO, *Historische Zeitschrift* 162 (1940) 442–444.

[P. JOANNOU]

SCHWARZENBERG, FRIEDRICH JOSEPH VON

Austrian cardinal; b. Vienna, April 6, 1809; d. Vienna, March 27, 1885. A talented, pious, and idealistic descendant of a wealthy Bohemian family, he studied law for a short time, but the influence of the philosopher Anton GÜNTHER and other priestly teachers led him to transfer to the theology faculty at Salzburg. Augustin Gruber, Archbishop of Salzburg (1823–35), who proved a fatherly friend, appointed him a cathedral canon (1830). While in Vienna preparing his doctorate in theology, he was ordained (1833). Upon Gruber's death he succeeded to the see of Salzburg (1835) and became a cardinal

(1842). The affable young prince of the Church proved an outstanding bishop who safeguarded the Church's rights capably and courageously during the 1848 revolution. In 1848 he summoned the bishops of his province to a synod, and also played an important part in the gathering of German bishops in Würzburg. He presided at the episcopal meeting in Vienna (1849), whose proposals for Austrian Church-State relations were later incorporated in the concordat of 1855. It had been to his advantage that his brother Felix (d. 1852) was Austrian prime minister. Schwarzenberg transferred to the See of Prague (1850) because the Emperor recognized his popularity with both sections of the population, and hoped that he could ease the religious, political, and nationalistic tensions there. As bishop he sought to utilize the newly won ecclesiastical liberty to better the Church and its clergy. In the *Landtag* and in the upper chamber he supported the policies of the Bohemian nobles against liberalism and centralization. He was entrusted with the official visitation of Austrian religious houses (1852–59). In 1860 he held a provincial synod, and in 1863 a diocesan synod for carrying out the provisions of the concordat. He was friendly to the ideas of Günther but opposed to the SYLLABUS OF ERRORS. At VATICAN COUNCIL I he opposed the definition of papal primacy and infallibility, but later accepted it. Schwarzenberg was one of the last and best of the type of eminent, aristocratic ecclesiastical princes of the old Austria.

Bibliography: C. WOLFSGRUBER, *Friedrich Kardinal Schwarzenberg,* 3 v. (Vienna 1906–17). C. BUTLER, *The Vatican Council,* 2 v. (New York 1930). K. ZU SCHWARZENBERG, *Geschichte des reichsständigen Hauses Schwarzenberg, Teil 2* (Neustadt-Aisch 1964).

[J. WODKA]

SCHWENCKFELDER CHURCH

Named after Caspar Schwenckfeld; b. Ossig, principality of Liegnitz, Silesia, Germany, 1489; d. Ulm, Dec. 10, 1561. He was of noble rank, studied at various universities, experienced the influence of Martin LUTHER in 1518, and entered the service of Friedrich II of Liegnitz, persuading him to launch an evangelical movement in Silesia. He was thrice a visitor in Wittenburg, but was rejected by Luther because of his peculiar view of the Lord's Supper. He moved closer to the more radical reformers and sacramentarians and became a chiefexponent of evangelical spiritualism. Advising the suspension of the outward Eucharist (1526) and emphasizing an inward feeding on the celestial flesh of Christ, he developed his own theological views regarding the Lord's Supper, Baptism, Christology, the Church, and other doctrines. Since he favored a "standstill" with regard to the use of the Sacraments, waiting for the time when a general agreement could be reached, he did not become an organizer of another evangelical church. Expelled from Silesia, he spent some time in Strassburg, Ulm, and other places in southern Germany. In Strassburg he met Melchior HOFFMAN and Pilgram MARBECK. With the latter he entered into a considerable literary exchange of views.

Schwenckfeld was a prolific writer. His writings were read by his followers in reading circles, which was the primary reason that the group survived despite its small numbers. He had followers in Silesia and in southern Germany. Promoters of his views were Adam Reusner and Daniel Sudermann. In southern Germany, followers of Schwenckfeld were found up to 1660. In Silesia they underwent severe persecution. Between 1725 and 1736 more than 500 Schwenckfelders fled, finding refuge on the estate of Nikolaus ZINZENDORF, in Saxony. With the help of some Dutch and German MENNONITES, some 212 of them migrated to southeastern Pennsylvania in 1734 and settled in Philadelphia, Montgomery, Berks, and Lehigh counties.

The first minister was George Weiss, and the first meetinghouse was built in 1789. In 1909 the group incorporated as the Schwenckfelder Church with a congregational church polity. Since 1877 the Lord's Supper and (adult) baptism, which were discouraged by Schwenckfeld, have been observed. The Schwenckfelder Board of Missions was organized in 1895 and the Board of Publication in 1898. The Schwenckfelder Library at Pennsburg, Pa., and the Perkiomen School (1891) belong to the church.

Bibliography: G. MARON, *Individualismus und Gemeinschaft bei Caspar von Schwenckfeld* (Stuttgart 1961). H. W. KRIEBEL, *The Schwenckfelders in Pennsylvania* (Lancaster, Pa. 1904). P. L. MAIER, *Caspar Schwenckfeld on the Person and Work of Christ* (Assen, Neth. 1959). S. G. SCHULTZ, *Caspar Schwenckfeld von Ossig* (Norristown, Pa. 1946). G. H. WILLIAMS, *The Radical Reformation* (Philadelphia 1962). F. S. MEAD, S. S. HILL and C. D. ATWOOD, eds., *Handbook of Denominations in the United States* (Nashville 2001).

[C. KRAHN]

SCHWETZ, JOHANN BAPTIST

Theologian; b. Bosan, Moravia, 1803; d. Vienna, 1890. He taught dogmatic theology first at Olmütz and then at the University of Vienna. In 1863 he was named head of the canons of the cathedral chapter of Vienna and director of St. Augustine Seminary. In 1861 he had published his *Theologia dogmatica catholica,* a work remarkable for its precision, clarity, and erudition. Because of its opposition to the errors of JOSEPHINISM and A. GÜN-

Caspar Schwenckfeld.

THER, it was prescribed by civil and ecclesiastical authority as the textbook in dogmatic theology for use throughout the Austro-Hungarian Empire for some years. Schwetz took part in Vatican Council I by preparing a schema against the errors of Günther.

Bibliography: H. HURTER, *Nomenclator literarius theologiae catholicae,* 5 vol. (3rd ed. Innsbruck 1903–13) 5.2:1514–16. E. HOCEDEZ, *Histoire de la théologie au XIX siècle,* 3 vol. (Brussels-Paris 1952) 2:56, 343.

[C. MEYER]

SCIENCE (SCIENTIA)

A term much used in the Aristotelian-Thomistic tradition to designate a type of perfect knowing (*scire simpliciter*). According to Aristotle, one obtains such knowledge of any object when he knows its cause, when he knows that that cause is what makes the object be what it is, and when he therefore knows that the object could not be otherwise than it is (*Anal. post.* 71b 8–12). For St. THOMAS AQUINAS, science is KNOWLEDGE of something through its proper cause (*C. gent.* 1.94). He locates it in the category of intellectual knowledge, as opposed to sense knowledge; and within this category he characterizes it as mediate intellectual knowledge, as opposed to immediate knowledge of concepts and FIRST PRINCIPLES, insofar as it is acquired through the prior knowledge of principles or causes. As a type of knowledge it can be further considered as the ACT itself by which such knowledge is acquired or the habit of mind resulting from one or more such acts (*ibid.* 2.60). And apart from the act and the habit, the body of knowledge that is known by one possessing the habit—the body of truths and conclusions attained—also is said to constitute the science (*ibid.* 1.48, 56).

Apart from this strict notion of science, Aristotle allowed application of the term to a less perfect type of knowledge: thus he spoke of more or less perfect explanations and those that merely ''save the appearances,'' somewhat akin to the explanations of modern science. This broader usage was countenanced by the scholastics and figured prominently in the evolution of the concept of science that dominated the modern period. In contemporary thought there is no full agreement on the definition of science; yet there is, for the most part, agreement that some intellectual knowledge is scientific and some nonscientific and that the scientific enterprise is an effort to find the order of things and to assign reasons for this order. Science has thus become an analogical term legitimately but diversely applicable to many differing disciplines in a set wherein perfectly demonstrated knowledge ranks as the prime analogate.

This article considers first the stricter notion of science in discussing its object and subject, its kinds, and its status as a habit, and then describes the evolution of the broader notion with the rise of modern science.

Object and Subject. When a psychological analysis of any act of knowing is made, the act itself is said to be specified by its object, because this is what confronts the mind, or is ''thrown against'' (*ob-iectum*) the mind, when something is actually known. In this object, St. Thomas Aquinas makes the distinction between what is formal and what is material: the former is the aspect under which the object is related to the knowing faculty, whereas the latter is that which underlies this aspect (*De carit.* 4). In the classical example of the faculty of sight, the formal object is thus said to be color or the colored, whereas the material object is said to be the body in which the color is seen. And the formal object is further distinguished into two aspects: that which is attained by the knowing faculty, or the *obiectum formale quod*, and that by which it is attained, or the *obiectum formale quo* (Capreolus). Again in the example of sight, the formal object *quod* is said to be color, as that which is seen as such, whereas the formal object *quo* is said to be light, as that by which color is made visible, and therefore able to be attained by the sense of sight (*De ver.* 14.8 ad 4).

Applying this terminology to the act of knowing that is characteristic of science, the object of a science is that at which the act of scientific knowing terminates, which, in turn, is the result of the DEMONSTRATION that is proper to the science. The terminating object is ultimately some singular thing that exists in extramental reality; but since the knowing act itself is a JUDGMENT, even though a mediate one, the knowledge attained is expressed by the mind as a complex entity composed of subject and predicate. The latter complex entity is the matter that is known, and it can be spoken of as the material object of the science; the formal aspect under which it is known is the middle term of the demonstration that produces the assent to the conclusion (*De carit.* 13 ad 6; *Summa theologiae* 2a2ae, 1.1). The formal object *quod* of the science is, then, what is attained by the particular formality (*ratio formalis*) under which the object is viewed, while the formal object *quo* is the particular intellectual light by which it is attained, after the analogy of visual knowledge already mentioned (*see* ABSTRACTION).

The expression ''object of a science'' is thus proper whenever one is talking about the knowledge act involved in scientific knowing and, consequently, about the intellectual habit produced by one or more such acts. When, by way of contrast, attention is focused on the knowledge that is the result of such acts, or what is known in the science that results when such objects are attained, then it is more proper to speak of the subject of the science. This view is more logical than psychological: it considers the object confronting the mind as the subject of various operations in the order of demonstration. Thus the subject of a science is that about which the scientist seeks to learn, or that to which predicates are applied in the science through mediate judgments, or that about which there is demonstration that is proper to the science.

Kinds of Science. Although sciences can be classified in various ways, one of the most basic divisions is that into speculative science, which is concerned primarily with knowing and not with doing, and practical science, which is concerned with knowing as ordered to doing.

Speculative Science. The subject of any speculative human science must fulfill two conditions: it must be something that has prior principles, known as the principles of the subject; and it must have parts and passions that belong to it *per se*. Yet the distinction of the sciences does not arise precisely from a diversity of subjects, but rather from a diversity of principles or of formal considerations that can be found in a subject. Thus, for the unity of a science, it is necessary to have one subject genus that is viewed under one formal light or way of considering, whereas for the distinction of sciences it suffices to have a diversity of principles (*In 1 anal. post.* 41.10).

All human sciences have their origin in sense knowledge, and all therefore commence with the same material objects. The differentiation of the sciences comes about from the different ways of demonstrating properties of these objects, and this in turn is traceable to the different middle terms or definitions that are employed. Careful examination of the various possibilities shows that there can be but three distinct speculative sciences—natural science, mathematics, and metaphysics—each with its own subject and its own proper principles (*see* SCIENCES, CLASSIFICATION OF). Should the principles proper to one subject be applicable to another subject, however, it is possible to generate a hybrid science, known technically as a *scientia media*. Thus mathematical physics can be seen as a *scientia media* intermediate between mathematics and natural science, insofar as it takes the same subject for its consideration as does natural science but considers it under the light of mathematical principles. This possibility gives rise to what is known as the subalternation of speculative sciences, when, for example, mathematical physics is subalternated to mathematics and natural science is subalternated to mathematical physics.

Apart from the human sciences, it is possible also for man to possess a divine science known as sacred theology. This can happen only when the human intellect is illumined by a special light that enables it to understand divine being, and thus it requires a revelation or manifestation of truths that exceed the natural capabilities of the human mind. Granted such a revelation and its acceptance through FAITH, man can develop a theological science that takes divine things, as they are in themselves, as its proper subject (*In Boeth. de Trin.* 5.4). This science, although divided into DOGMATIC THEOLOGY and MORAL THEOLOGY as integral parts, is formally only one science (*see* THEOLOGY).

Practical Science. Just as speculative knowledge is distinct from practical knowledge, so also is speculative science distinct from practical science. As sciences, both speculative science and practical science seek knowledge through causes; what distinguishes them is that speculative science seeks causal knowledge of what man can only know, viz, universals, whereas practical science seeks causal knowledge of what man can do or make, viz, singular operables. To the extent that a practical science engages in causal analysis, it can speculate and use analytical procedures similar to those of the speculative sciences. But whereas a speculative science seeks demonstrative knowledge of its subject, a practical science seeks actually to construct or produce its subject, and needs scientific knowledge in order to do so. This operational requirement demands of practical science an even more detailed knowledge of its subject than is found

in speculative science. It does not suffice in practical science, for instance, merely to know the cause of an effect; the perfection of the science requires knowledge of all the movements and operations necessary to assure that such an effect will actually follow from that cause in the order of execution.

Among the practical sciences may be listed the moral sciences, the medical sciences, and the architectural and engineering sciences. Moral sciences are concerned with human action and with the direction of such action to its proper end as human; they employ an analytical or resolutive procedure similar to that of philosophical anthropology or psychology and a compositive procedure that is peculiarly their own. They do not attain the singular operable, i.e., the HUMAN ACT, directly, but must be complemented by the art of PRUDENCE, which has as its proper concern the individual human act in its particular concrete circumstances. The medical sciences are concerned with health and with all the means necessary to restore health to those who do not possess it; they employ an analytical procedure similar to that of biology and their own proper compositive procedures such as are found in doctoring, nursing, and the administrations of medical technicians. The architectural and engineering sciences are concerned with buildings and other products of man's mechanical abilities; they employ analytical procedures similar to those of the physical sciences and their own proper constructional methods and procedures.

None of the practical sciences is concerned with truth or certitude for its own sake. They do attain a type of practical truth and practical certitude, however, which is determined by their conformity or adherence to the norms or rules that determine sound practice. It is difficult to draw a sharp line of demarcation between any practical science and the art or arts with which it is associated, because both practical science and art are judged by their conformity to rules. *See* ART (PHILOSOPHY). It can be said, however, that art is more properly concerned with the actual construction of the singular object or operable and that its truth is more judged by freedom from errors in execution, whereas practical science is more concerned with causal analysis that will lead to proper construction of the object or operable and is judged true more on the basis of its ability to provide sound norms for such execution. (*See* COGNITION SPECULATIVE-PRACTICAL.)

Habit of Science. St. Thomas, following Aristotle, taught that science is a habit of the INTELLECT, or an intellectual VIRTUE, and as such is distinct from the other intellectual virtues, UNDERSTANDING (*INTELLECTUS*) and WISDOM (*Summa theologiae* 1a2ae, 50.4). As a habit, it disposes one to reason accurately and with ease in a particular subject matter, i.e., to arrive at truths that can be expressed as conclusions reached by syllogistic reasoning from self-evident premises. To grasp the difference between the habit of science and that of understanding, one should note that some propositions have only to be understood in order to command assent; an example is the principle of CONTRADICTION. The ability to grasp and exercise such propositions or principles is the fundamental endowment of the intellect and is known as understanding. The human intellect has also the power to deduce conclusions in the light of these self-evident principles by seeking proper definitions in various subject matters and discoursing from these to predicate new attributes to appropriate subjects. This ability is referred to as the reasoning faculty of the intellect; it is perfected by the habit of science. Science, as such, is concerned with causes, because the knowledge of proper causes is what enables the intellect to discourse accurately and predicate new attributes. It is distinguished from the habit of wisdom in that it is concerned with all causes, whereas wisdom is concerned only with the highest causes (*Meta.* 981b 28, 982b 9). As St. Thomas states, ''Wisdom is a science, insofar as it has that which is common to all the sciences: viz, to demonstrate conclusions from principles. But since it has something proper to itself above the other sciences, inasmuch as it judges of them all, not only as to their conclusions, but also as to their first principles, therefore it is a more perfect virtue than science'' (*Summa theologiae* 1a2ae, 57.2 ad 1).

The knowledge of many conclusions pertaining to a single science counts as a single habit. A geometer who learns a new theorem extends the scope of his knowledge of geometry but does not acquire a new habit. As a habit, science comes into being and is increased or diminished in strength or perfection just as are other habits. It is generated by a single act of demonstration in the appropriate subject matter; this demonstration, of course, must be seen and understood by the one who is said to acquire the habit. It grows, or is perfected, as more conclusions are demonstrated or grasped with greater certitude, whereas it diminishes through disuse or through persistence in erroneous reasoning. (*See* HABIT.)

Evolution of the Concept. The concept of science described above is that accepted in Greek and scholastic philosophy and is not to be identified completely with the concept of modern science. There can be no doubt, however, that the medieval precursors of modern science subscribed to the Aristotelian ideal of strict demonstrative knowledge and, in complying with that ideal, prepared the way for the 17th-century development. Thus ROBERT GROSSETESTE initiated a current of thought at Oxford University that strongly influenced ROGER BACON and others in their early attempts at experimental science (see

Crombie). Similarly, THEODORIC OF FREIBERG performed exhaustive experimental and theoretical researches on the rainbow and related optical phenomena in the framework of a strict Aristotelian procedure (see Wallace). As science passed from the medieval to the modern era, however, the rigorous Aristotelian ideal was gradually relinquished, to be replaced by a looser and broader conception of the nature of scientific knowledge.

In the initial stages of this evolution, it appears that most thinkers thought of science as capable of achieving complete certainty concerning its subject matter. Renaissance scientists such as Leonardo da Vinci and Luiz Coronel were clearly of this conviction. Francis BACON thought of science as a search for causes, but had special views concerning the role of forms and of final causality in scientific explanation. Galileo GALILEI and Rene DESCARTES were insistent on developing all science along mathematical lines and prepared the way for the acceptance of RATIONALISM and MECHANISM as the dominant philosophy behind scientific investigation. It has been argued, somewhat unconvincingly, that such 17th-century thinkers had a conception of the interplay between theory and experiment that characterizes 20th-century science (see Blake). It seems more accurate to think of these thinkers as motivated by the Aristotelian ideal in their search for truth and certitude, but as placing more faith in mathematical insight than in the search for causes in the traditional Aristotelian mode. (For a fuller discussion of these and later thinkers, *see* PHILOSOPHY AND SCIENCE.)

The 20th-century conception of science differs from the Aristotelian-Thomistic notion mainly in its insistence that science is not concerned exclusively with a search for causes and in its conviction that science can never attain to knowledge that is absolutely certain and not subject to further revision. Associated with these is the rejection, by most philosophers of science, of Aristotle's requirement that the premises of scientific reasoning be better known than the conclusion arrived at. Thus, ''Aristotle's requirement that the explanatory premises be better known than the explicandum is entirely irrelevant as a condition for anything that would today be regarded as an adequate scientific explanation'' (Nagel, 45). Although it is in accord with the logical positivist ideal of science, this characterization leaves unexplained the substantial contributions made by scientists to man's knowledge of the universe and reduces all of science to the status of DIALECTICS. A more accurate characterization seems to be that science can attain to *some* truth and certitude, even though this is frequently buried in the great mass of theories and hypothetical constructions with which contemporary scientists must surround their work. To the extent that TRUTH or CERTITUDE is attained, it may be accounted for by an implicit following of the Aristotelian canons, granted that these are not explicitly acknowledged by the practicing scientist.

See Also: SCHOLASTIC METHOD; METHODOLOGY (PHILOSOPHY).

Bibliography: THOMAS AQUINAS, *Summa theologiae* 1a2ae, 49–58, tr. A. KENNY (New York 1964–) v.22. J. CAPREOLUS, *Defensiones theologiae divi Thomae Aquinatis,* ed. C. PABAN and T. PÈGUES, 7 v. (Tours 1900–08). M. J. ADLER, ed., *The Great Ideas: A Syntopicon of Great Books of the Western World,* 2 v. (Chicago 1952) 2:682–705. A. C. CROMBIE, *Robert Grosseteste and the Origins of Experimental Science* (Oxford 1953). W. A. WALLACE, *The Scientific Methodology of Theodoric of Freiberg* (Studia Friburgensia NS 26; Fribourg 1959). R. M. BLAKE, C. J. DUCASSE, and E. H. MADDEN, *Theories of Scientific Method: The Renaissance Through the 19th Century* (Seattle 1960). E. NAGEL, *The Structure of Science* (New York 1961).

[W. A. WALLACE]

SCIENCE (IN ANTIQUITY)

Though science is often used in a broader sense, it is here taken to mean the conscious search for regularities in nature. To describe the first instances of such activity is impossible. This article reviews certain aspects of the search that have been ancestral to Western culture; they took place in Egypt, Babylonia, the Greek cities, and the Roman Empire. For the sake of continuity of ideas, the physical sciences and biological sciences will be treated separately.

Physical Sciences

The oldest scientific activity that scholars are acquainted with is that of Egypt, whose people used a calendar established prior to 2500 B.C. However—apart, perhaps, from the admiration of Egyptian accomplishment expressed in the writings of Herodotus and other Greeks—there are no indications that native Egyptian science ever rose to any considerable level. Astronomical observation was used for timekeeping. It gave rise not only to the concept of the four cardinal directions but also to their accurate determination; the Great Pyramid of Khufu (or Cheops), built about 2500 B.C., had a base aligned on true north within less than one-tenth of a degree. This sort of activity, taken together with the engineering skill manifested in so many ways—most strikingly in the fabrication, transportation, and upending the giant obelisks—might seem like a beginning from which a growth of science must follow. In fact, it did not follow; surviving papyri show that medicine, after an auspicious start, developed hardly at all during the succeeding 1,000 years, and that when the late Egyptians learned astronomy, they learned it not from their ancestors but from the Chaldeans and the Greeks.

The Chaldeans. The Chaldeans, or Babylonians, were intellectual heirs of the Old Babylonians, whose clay tablets dating from 1800 to 1600 B.C. show a highly developed arithmetic far surpassing that of the Egyptians. For example, one Old Babylonian tablet evaluates √2 to within one part in a million. If the Old Babylonians had an astronomy, little or nothing is known of it. Political and social upheaval submerged them and their Semitic conquerors; after 1600 B.C., there are but few tablets from Babylonia until the Seleucid period, which began in 312 B.C. From the four centuries that followed there is a wealth of recovered tablets, of which many hundreds contain astronomical texts or tables.

Cuneiform tablets dealing with astronomy were first deciphered by J. Epping, who worked from texts laboriously transcribed from clay tablets in the British Museum by J. N. Strassmaier [Strassmaier and Epping, "Zur Entzifferung der Astronomischen Tafeln der Chaldäer," *Stimmen aus Maria Laach* 21 (1881) 277–92]; their initial work was followed by the significant contributions of F. X. Kugler. Many other tablets have been translated in more recent years, notably by O. Neugebauer and his co-workers.

Though the Seleucid period followed the conquest of Babylon by Alexander, its culture was Babylonian, not Greek; the astronomers continued the development begun by their predecessors. Unlike the Greek methods, which were based on geometrical models, the Chaldean astronomical techniques were essentially arithmetical. Nevertheless, they were highly successful.

Development of the Calendar. The Chaldean astronomical techniques can be discerned in broad outline by considering the Chaldean calendar, whose fundamental units were the day and the month. The month was the period between successive new moons; a new day began at sunset, and a new month began on the first day at whose beginning the moon's new crescent was visible. This system generated two important problems of an astronomical kind. One was that some months had 29 days, whereas others had 30; it was desirable to know in advance how many days a given month would have. The other major problem was that a 12-month year would not stay in step with the sun; rigid adherence to a 12-month year would mean that a given month would not correspond to any particular season.

At first the authorities solved the second problem simply by inserting a 13th month in any year in which they deemed it beneficial. By about 400 B.C. astronomical progress permitted the establishment of a fixed system of intercalation. A lunation, the time between new moons, averages 29.5306 days as presently calculated, whereas the time between vernal equinoxes is 365.242 days. The latter figure multiplied by 19 is 6,939.60 days, and the former one multiplied by 235 is 6,939.69 days. Therefore 19 (tropical) years comprise almost exactly 235 lunations; and if a lunar calendar is contrived so that seven years in every 19 contain 13 months, the calendar keeps in step with the seasons moderately well, since (7 × 13) + (12 × 12) = 235. The period of 6,940 days is known as the Metonic cycle, because the relation just described was recognized (not later than 432 B.C.) by Meton of Athens; it has long been the basis of the ecclesiastical calendar.

The other problem, the prediction of the length of a month, was more complex. The first appearance of the moon, after conjunction with the sun, depends on a number of factors: the time interval between conjunction and sunset; the rate of motion of the moon with respect to the sun, which may be as little as 10° per day, or as much as 14°; the angle between the sun's path (the ecliptic) and the horizon, which at Babylon varies from less than 34° to nearly 81°, depending on the time of year; the departure of the moon's path from the ecliptic. The Chaldean method of taking all these effects into account was to approximate each time-varying element by means of a periodic and linear zigzag function, calculating the situation from day to day by increments based on arithmetic progressions, and then to sum the functions. To the modern mind, the method resembles Fourier analysis, but the functions added are linear zigzags instead of sinusoids, and their periods need not be simply related to one another. Sometimes step-functions took the place of the zigzags.

Museums contain many tablets of lunar ephemerides; these are simply tables of numbers, in which for each day the zigzags are added to find the relative positions of sun and moon and to indicate the day on which these would be such that a new month should begin. Each row gives the linearly approximated values of the variables for that day. For one method there are 18 columns of variables. An interesting by-product is the indication of whether or not the moon is new (or full) when it is on the ecliptic. If it is, then an eclipse of the sun (or moon) is possible. Even as late as the birth of Our Lord, there is no indication that the Chaldeans could be sure whether an eclipse of the sun would be visible or not.

Locating the Planets. The same technique of finding periods and appropriate zigzag or step-function approximations, and from these forming arithmetical progressions for the relevant variables, was applied to the planets. The goal was to predict the dates of visibility and invisibility of the planets, and also the dates of the "stationary points" mentioned below. The first and last appearances occur near the horizon, where refraction is a source of error, and the stationary points are not sharply defined. The attribution of great accuracy to the Chaldean observers is therefore no longer taken seriously. There is a little evidence that the astronomers were priests and that their interest was in the casting of horoscopes for the guidance of the government. Nowhere do the known tablets hint at geometrical models or at what would now be called a physical theory of the planets. In 1900, when scientists were thoroughly habituated to thinking in terms of models, many of them would doubtless have questioned whether Chaldean astronomy deserved to be called science, since it employed no models. (Quite probably it had an oral tradition along with the tablets, and the content of that tradition can only be guessed at.) In a view to which many scientists now subscribe, however, a scientist's task is merely to make systematically correct predictions of observable phenomena; a model is not a necessity, and it may be a hindrance. By this standard, the astronomy of the Chaldean tablets, when stripped of its astrological associations, must be regarded not only as science, but even as science operating by an exceptionally clean method.

The School of Miletos. Science as presently understood was developed by the Greeks. The first of these people associated with science were citizens of Miletos, a highly prosperous city on the west coast of what is now Turkey. Thales, the oldest of these men, was a successful businessman, active in politics. In Greek literature, he was regarded as the first natural philosopher, or physicist. The writers credit him with many accomplishments: recognition of electrification and of magnetism, the broadening of geometrical facts learned in Egypt into general propositions about similar triangles, the prediction of an eclipse of the sun (presumably in 585 B.C.) as a result of his contacts with Babylonian learning, and a belief that the moon shines by reflected light. Anaximander (*fl.* 570 B.C.), a slightly younger Milesian, made a systematic study of the shadows cast by an upright post (a gnomon) and therefrom drew conclusions about the motion of the sun. He stated that man evolved, through animals, from fishes. For him, the world was cylindrical, like a stone in a column, and unsupported; he made a map of it. Anaximenes (6th century B.C.), also of Miletos, stated that the stars are like nails fixed in a vault that rotates around the earth, and that a rainbow is made by the reflection of the sun's rays from a dense cloud. He put forward, too, the concept of man as the microcosmic parallel of the great cosmos.

Along with many valid conclusions, of which some of those just quoted are representative, the Milesian philosophers reached many that are not valid. Present-day knowledge of their thought, and even of the thought of most Greek scientists who lived later, is pitifully fragmentary. Typically, all that is preserved of their writings is a few quotations written down by other writers, perhaps centuries later, in books that happened to survive. Even the dates when important men lived are often uncertain.

Thales (*fl.* 590 B.C.) is a shadowy figure, from whom no writing survives. Certainly the story about his prediction of an eclipse is implausible, because all the evidence indicates that even hundreds of years later the Chaldean astronomers could predict only when an eclipse of the sun *might* be visible. With respect to Anaximander a bit more is known, because he wrote a book that survived until after 150 B.C.

The details of attribution to particular persons are uncertain and not really important. What matters is that Ionians of this period—or very little later—sought to explain the world in material terms, without resort to myth. Though their writings are lost except for a few brief quotations, one can probably catch something of their rationalist spirit in the writings of Herodotus, an Ionian who lived only about a century later, the text of whose history is well preserved. His weighing of plausibility of the various explanations of the Nile flood (Herodotus 2.19–29) makes firm contact with the mind of a modern scientist, whose methodology is so much the same.

Pythagoras. A quite different line of development stems from Pythagoras (*fl.* 530 B.C.), later than Thales but equally lost in the shadows. The extant accounts of Pythagoras as a person were written by uncritical biographers after A.D. 200, but it is fairly certain that he existed, that he was born an Ionian on the island of Samos, and that he established some kind of a brotherhood at Croton in the south of Italy. Though ascribing any particular advance in thought to Pythagoras himself is so risky as to be unjustifiable, some early and insistent traditions about the Pythagoreans are worth repeating. They are said to have been interested in geometry and also in number theory. That they knew the Pythagorean theorem, relating the square of the hypotenuse of a triangle to the sum of the squares of the other two sides, is plausible, but it is no great credit to them; the Old Babylonians knew and used the relation more than a millennium earlier. The contrast between Greek mathematics and Babylonian mathematics is nicely illustrated by their respective findings about $\sqrt{2}$. The Babylonians calculated it with great accuracy; the Greeks—very likely the Pythagoreans—proved that it is irrational.

The Pythagoreans developed a notable cosmology. Its outlines can now be perceived but vaguely, because it is known only from documents written long afterward and because at various times certain members of the group modified the system. There may also be the handicap of a tradition of secrecy in the brotherhood. Almost certainly, the Pythagoreans (or some of them) believed the earth to be a sphere. To Philolaus (*fl.* 430 B.C.), who was one of them, is ascribed the teaching that the universe is spherical too, but that the earth is not at its center. At the center he placed a Central Fire, and he had the earth revolve around it, along with the moon, the sun, the other planets, and the sphere of fixed stars. The distances of these bodies from the Central Fire were different; they probably increased in the order just given.

The Pythagorean universe is distinguished by a counterearth (ἀντίχθων). For the introduction of this body, two motives are given by Aristotle. One of them (*Cael.* 293b 24) is that the counterearth can account for the fact that eclipses of the moon are more frequent than those of the sun. The other reason (*Meta.* 986a 12) was to bring the number of the celestial bodies up to ten, since that was a sacred number. The sphere of the fixed stars counted as one body, the counterearth and earth as two more; the sun, the moon, and five other planets raised the total to ten. The counterearth may have moved about the Central Fire on the opposite side of it from the earth and in an orbit of the same size, or it may have had a slightly smaller orbit and stayed between the Central Fire and the earth, thus shielding the ANTIPODES from the fire.

The striking thing about this whole theory, of course, is that it ascribes motion to the earth and locates that body elsewhere than at the center of the universe. The earth traverses its orbit once every 24 hours, keeping its uninhabited or antipodal side toward the Central Fire. Its motion with respect to the sun causes day and night; the motion of the sun, in an orbit inclined to that of the earth, produces the seasons. Circular motions of the moon and the five remaining planets accounted for the major phenomena associated with these bodies. The inhabitants of Greece and neighboring countries had no direct view of the Central Fire, but the suggestion was made that the ashen light on the moon (now called earthshine and ascribed to sunlight reflected from the earth) was caused by rays from the Central Fire. To move in its orbit while keeping one side turned away from the fire, the earth would have to rotate, though this consideration is not mentioned in the accounts of the theory that have survived.

The importance attached to having ten bodies circling the Central Fire may seem bizarre now, but it illustrates perhaps the most characteristic trait of Pythagoreanism, which is an emphasis on number. Legend attributes to Pythagoras himself a discovery that two strings sounding one of the musical intervals (an octave, for example, or a fifth) have lengths in the ratio of small integers. Aristotle (*Meta.* 985b 23–986a 3) says that in part because of this discovery, the Pythagoreans supposed numbers to be the basis of all things and the heavens to be numerical and musical. The type of reasoning is exhibited in Plato's argument that the number of elements needed in the universe is four (*Tim.* 31B–32B). Though such arguments now seem like free flights of fancy, it is worth noting that the association of numbers with the musical intervals must have been based on experiment—or, at the very least, on quantitative observation of a real phenomenon.

Except perhaps for some of the Pythagoreans, the Greeks whose scientific opinions have been discussed thus far were all Ionians, from the coast of Asia Minor or the islands nearby. The last important representative of this tradition was Anaxagoras of Clazomenae (*fl.* 460 B.C.), and he was the first of them to take up residence in Athens, where he became a friend of Pericles. Of his writings there has been preserved an exceptionally large remnant—more than a dozen fragments, comprising in all about three pages of a modern book. From these one learns that he ascribed the brightness of the moon to light from the sun, and the rainbow to the reflection of sunlight by clouds. He believed in a plurality of worlds, the other worlds than the earth having their men, their animals and cultivated fields, and "a sun and a moon and the rest as with us." Later Greek commentators state that Anaxagoras considered the earth to be flat and the stars to pass under it; that he considered the sun to be a fiery stone larger than the Peloponnesos, and the moon to be closer than the sun and of the same material as the earth; also that he was the first to explain correctly the origin of the moon's light and the relations of sun, moon, and earth during eclipses. Though he may well have understood the origin of the moon's light and the nature of eclipses, it is not really likely that he was the first to do so. In 467 B.C. a sizable meteorite (the elder Pliny says it was the size of a wagonload) fell at Aegospotami, on the Gallipoli Peninsula; Anaxagoras maintained that it had fallen from the sun. Perhaps it was this event which caused him to assert that the sun is a hot stone and that the moon is earth-like. These views were too much for the Athenians, and Anaxagoras was tried for impiety in about 432. Perhaps the real motive for the trial was political and related to his friendship with Pericles. Whatever the motive, it is interesting that Anaxagoras's opinions on cosmology could be used as a reason or a pretext for driving him out of Athens.

The Nature of Matter. Along with their concern for cosmology, these Ionian philosophers pondered the nature of matter. The early ones all adopted a species of monism, a belief that there is just one ultimate substance. Thales thought it to be water. Water was the natural choice, since Thales knew it not only as the lifegiving liquid but also as rigid ice and aerial steam.

Later Ionians differed from Thales in their choice of the primordial material. His fellow citizen Anaximander concluded that no substance known to the senses will serve, so he postulated a fundamental stuff, which he called ἄπειρον, the "unlimited," or "indefinite." In the next generation Anaximenes of Miletos held that the primary substance is air; when rarefied, it is fire, whereas in successive states of compaction it is water, earth, and rock.

Parmenides (*fl.* 470 B.C.) gave Greek thought a new direction by insistence on rigor in reasoning. His logic led him to distinguish between the evidence of the senses and the dictates of reason. Reason, he argued, forbids the ascription of different forms to the One. Yet reason recommends monism, though the senses demand recognition of change, which implies pluralism.

The ideas of Parmenides were applied and enlarged by Empedocles (*fl.* 450 B.C.), who, however, accepted sense perception as a guide to inquiry. To explain the changes that matter undergoes, he posited the existence of four root substances (ῥιζώματα) and two agents of change, φιλότης and νεῖκος, commonly translated as Love and Strife but having physical manifestations corresponding approximately to attraction and repulsion. The four Empedoclean elements, fire, air, water, and earth, held an important place in European thought for the next 2,000 years. By observing the behavior of what amounted to an inverted funnel dipped into water while its upper orifice was alternately shut and open, Empedocles demonstrated that air is corporeal.

Probably influenced by the strictures of Parmenides, Anaxagoras offered a combination of monism and pluralism. His unitary and unmixed element was νοῦς, for which the customary translation is Mind. It is the cause of motion, or change, in all things. All things were in the beginning thoroughly mixed, but under the action of whirls or vortices caused by νοῦς, they have become partially separated, so that they are experienced in states approximating purity. Only νοῦς is completely separated from any other entity; Anaxagoras wrote that "there is a portion of everything in everything," asking "How can hair be made of what is not hair, or flesh of what is not flesh?" He urged that what appears as "coming into being" or "passing away" is merely the mingling or separation of things that *are,* thus formulating (perhaps not for the first time) the principle that matter is conserved; however, he believed not in atoms but in the unlimited divisibility of matter, saying that what is cannot cease to be, by being cut.

Leucippus, probably of Miletos, took a different view, which was elaborated by his disciple Democritus of Abdera (*fl.* 420 B.C.). They introduced the concept of atom (ἄτομος, uncuttable) and coupled with it the concept of vacuum. The atoms were invisibly small, infinite in number, alike in substance but different in shape. The differences in things arose from differences in the shapes, positions, and arrangement of the atoms, which were in motion in the vacuum. Coming into being was the aggregation of atoms, and passing away was their dispersal; the atoms themselves were indestructible. The theory thus reconciled stability with endless change. Aristotle rejected this escape from monism, but it was adopted by Epicurus (*fl.* 301 B.C.) and his many followers, and was described at length in the didactic poem *De rerum natura* by Lucretius about 60 B.C. The atomic hypothesis became a part of the learned tradition and was a basis for the thought of Boyle, Newton, and others during the rebirth of science in the 17th century.

Though the foregoing paragraphs describe many hypotheses that have proved fruitful, the Greek record thus far was not one of continuous advance. A major reason is that the key to progress in science—heavy reliance on propositions that can be tested by interrogating Nature—had not yet been found. The next century, roughly 425 to 325 B.C., belongs to Socrates (*fl.* 430 B.C.), his pupil Plato (*fl.* 387 B.C.), and Aristotle (*fl.* 344 B.C.), pupil of Plato and tutor of Alexander the Great. It began with an upsurge of interest in moral, rather than natural, philosophy; but it ended with science reestablished on a new and far firmer base.

Early Planetary Systems. Though he belittled science, Socrates contributed to its improvement by his strictures on unsound reasoning. Plato's primary concern was with moral questions; however, he valued mathematics and fostered not only its development but also its application in science, particularly in astronomy and geography. One of the great mathematicians of all time, Eudoxus of Cnidos (*fl.* 368 B.C.) was associated briefly with Plato's Academy. Along with basic work in mathematics, Eudoxus accounted for the appearance of the stars and the planets by means of combinations of uniform circular motions. His universe consisted of 27 spheres homocentric (i.e., concentric) with the earth. The outermost sphere carried the fixed stars and rotated once per day, westerly. The innermost sphere carried the moon and rotated westerly with a period of 27 days; its axis was carried by a sphere that rotated easterly and made one revolution in 223 lunations, and this in turn was carried by a larger sphere that moved in the same way as that of the fixed stars. By assigning appropriate directions to the axes of these three motions, Eudoxus was able to account quite well for the rather complicated course of the moon's

position, expressing it as the resultant of three uniform circular motions. Similarly, he assigned three spheres to move the sun, and four each to Mercury, Venus, Mars, Jupiter, and Saturn. The system did not account well for the motion of Venus, and for Mars it failed miserably, but it accounted well for the then-known appearances of the other bodies. The progression of ideas from Thales to Eudoxus took only two centuries.

The system of Eudoxus was a work of genius. It brought order to the seemingly irregular motions of the planets, and did so with great economy of means; present-day heliocentric theory employs six adjustable constants for each planet, but Eudoxus's earth-centered system used only three. More important, the theory could be tested by comparing it quantitatively with the world of experience, and its shortcomings could be alleviated by making better choices of the constants and by employing additional spheres when they were needed, as for Venus and Mars and for newly discovered details of the motions.

Eudoxus had the first recorded observatory in Greece. Very likely his theory stimulated observation, and certainly it was elaborated and better fitted to the data by his follower Callippus (*fl.* 330 B.C.). This establishment of an interplay between theory and observation is a momentous event—perhaps the major event—in the history of Greek astronomy.

Very soon after Eudoxus, Heracleides of Pontos (*fl.* 350 B.C.) made two stupendous proposals whose adoption would further simplify the scheme of the universe. The first was that what rotates in one day is not the heavens, but the earth. The second—based, almost certainly, on the fact that Mercury and Venus are seen always in directions close to that of the sun—was that these two planets revolve not around the earth, but around the sun. A few decades later Aristarchus of Samos (*fl.* 270 B.C.) went all the way and taught that only the moon circles the earth, which is a planet that circles the sun along with all the other planets—an anticipation of the Copernican hypothesis. The earth rotates, while the sun and the stars are at rest. In a treatise that has survived, Aristarchus deduced from observation that the diameter of the earth is about three times that of the moon, and that the sun is very much larger than the earth. He reached this conclusion when he was yet young, and very likely it was the basis of his heliocentric hypothesis, since to assume that a large body revolves around a smaller one is dynamically unattractive. The heliocentric hypothesis, though preserved in the literature, won few converts.

Aristotle. Aristotle transmitted to Christendom a qualitative and cumbersome adaptation of the system of Eudoxus. It was cumbersome because Aristotle, who did not believe in the existence of empty space, made the spheres into material bodies with no space between them, so that the movement of one influenced all the others. To compensate for the undesired motions thus induced, Aristotle had to introduce additional spheres rotating in reverse. Thus, instead of working with at most five coupled spheres, as Callippus did, the users of Aristotle's system had to work with 56. The change was ruinous. Though Greek astronomy passed Aristotle by, the scholarly world held to his books while it all but lost those of the working astronomers.

Denying the possibility of empty space, Aristotle had to reject atomism. He accepted the Empedoclean elements; but in order to provide for a continuum of properties and for the conversion of one element into another (e.g., when water by boiling changes into air), he associated with each element two qualities from the contraries hot and cold, fluid and dry. Thus, earth is dry and cold, air is hot and fluid, and so on. (Concerning the transformation of element into element, see *Gen. et cor.* bk. 2.) These elements move naturally in straight lines—earth and water toward the center of the universe, but air and fire away from the center. To the unchanging heavens and their natural circular motion, Aristotle assigned a fifth and unchanging element, the ether.

Aristotle's physics is notorious. How could such a great genius go so far wrong? The popular idea that he disregarded experience is merely folklore; in Aristotle's scientific treatises, appeals to observed phenomena are frequent. It has been suggested that the physical treatises were composed early, while Aristotle was still under the Pythagorean influence of Plato, and that the biological treatises, which are brilliant in their observations and insights, were composed in later years, when Aristotle had learned to do valid research. An objection to this view is that the treatises were used by Aristotle in his teaching at Athens near the end of his life and that presumably they, like any other teacher's lecture notes, would be revised as his thinking changed. Perhaps the fact is that Aristotle thought in terms of form and function and that such analysis has been successful in biology but not in physics, where progress has come from mathematical analysis of idealized ''models.'' However this may be, what actually put Aristotelian physics into bad repute was the parroting of it by the schoolmen of Europe nearly 2,000 years after he died. He should not be blamed for their failure, since their method was very non-Aristotelian.

The Alexandrian School. The golden age of Greek science occurred during the Hellenistic period, which began nearly coincidentally with the death of Aristotle. Its center was not Athens but Alexandria, where the Museum, with its great library, played much of the role of a modern university. Of the giants in mathematics and the physical sciences who did some of their work there, this article can mention only a few: Euclid (*fl.* 300 B.C.), Archimedes (*fl.* 247 B.C.), Eratosthenes (*fl.* 235 B.C.), Hipparchus of Nicaea (*fl.* 150 B.C.), and PTOLEMY (*fl.* A.D. 150).

Euclid, in his *Elements* (στοιχεῖα), systematized the geometry of his time so admirably that no improvement was made in the next 2,000 years. G. Sarton has said that ''Euclid created a monument that is as marvelous in its symmetry, inner beauty and clearness as the Parthenon, but incomparably more complex and more durable.'' It deals not only with what is now considered geometry but also with the theory of numbers. He also wrote on optics. Archimedes, who worked mainly in Syracuse, was also primarily a mathematician—an even greater one than Euclid, and one of the greatest of all time. Among his accomplishments were calculations of the volumes and surface areas of solids with curved surfaces, tasks now performed by means of integral calculus. In mechanics, he established statics and hydrostatics as mathematical sciences, quite unlike Aristotelian physics; he also won lasting fame as an inventor of actual devices. Eratosthenes is remembered chiefly for his work in geodesy. The Pythagorean belief that the earth is a sphere had been adopted by Plato and Eudoxus and endorsed by Aristotle, who not only cites several observations that support it but gives an estimate of its size, correct in general order of magnitude (*Cael.* 297a 9–298a 20). Eratosthenes, by means of the noon shadows of vertical posts, measured the difference in latitude between two points, Aswan and Alexandria, nearly on the same meridian and a known distance (about 500 statute miles) apart. His result was 252,000 stades; the length of his stade is uncertain, but a statement by Pliny (*Naturalis Historia* 12.53) leads to the inference that Eratosthenes's stade was 600 Egyptian cubits, so that his value for the polar circumference of the earth was 24,700 miles, in quite good accord with the modern value, 24,818 miles. It is fashionable to ascribe this accuracy to mere luck; but since his method has come down only in a secondhand and perhaps oversimplified account, composed several centuries later, the judgment may be too harsh.

Late Planetary Systems. Hipparchus, too, worked on mathematical geography, but he is rememberd chiefly as one of the truly great astronomers. None of his own major treatises has survived; his work is known mainly through the writings of Ptolemy, and the contributions made by Hipparchus cannot be known with certainty. However, it is generally agreed that he discovered the precession of the equinoxes, estimated well the distance and size of the moon, underestimated the distance and size of the sun (by about a factor ten), made a catalogue of the positions and magnitudes of some 850 stars, and brought to a state of high development the description of the planetary motions. Though his elder contemporary Seleucus the Babylonian had accepted the heliocentric model put forward by Aristarchus, Hipparchus was a principal contributor to the system that came to be called Ptolemaic. By this time Greek and Chaldean astronomy had come into close contact. The extent to which Hipparchus was influenced by Chaldean methods is uncertain, but it seems that at the very least he profited from the long records of observations that were kept in Babylonia.

Even though he knew that the sun is much larger than the earth, the rejection of the Aristarchian system by Hipparchus is not surprising. All other considerations apart, the Aristarchian system did not agree with the phenomena of the skies, since it employed circular orbits where elliptical ones meet the facts. Consider, for example, the apparent motion of the sun along the ecliptic. If the earth moved about the sun in a circular orbit, the sun would seem to move from vernal equinox to autumnal equinox in just half of 365 ¼ days, which is a little less than 183 days, and it would continue along to the vernal equinox in a like period. Actually, passage from the vernal equinox to the autumnal one takes 186 ½ days, and return to the vernal equinox occurs in the remaining 178 ¾ days. An earth-centered astronomy can account for this difference by assuming that the sun travels at a steady rate along a circle whose center is displaced from the center of the universe, the earth. Such an orbit is called an eccentric.

The apparent motions of the planets are more complex. Although their general tendency is to move eastward, as the sun does, with respect to the fixed stars, the planets sometimes move westward. To account for the retrograde motions, the Hellenistic astronomers developed the theory of epicycles. The planet moves uniformly around the epicycle, of which the center moves around the deferent circle. If the deferent is centered at the earth and if the center of the epicycle moves uniformly around it, then the resulting motion of the planet with respect to the earth is exactly equivalent to what would result if the earth and the planet moved around the sun in circular orbits, the orbits being in a single plane. Since the orbits with respect to the sun are in truth not circles and do not lie in a common plane, the deferent and epicycle just described cannot represent any planet's motion exactly; but they do take into account the gross aspects of a planet's motion as viewed from the earth.

It has well been remarked that the importance of a scientific treatise can be gauged by the number of earlier works that it renders superfluous. By this measure, two treatises that rank supremely high are Euclid's *Elements* and Ptolemy's *Almagest* (ἡ μαθηματικὴ σύνταξις); in their respective fields, both books supplanted the earlier treatises so completely as nearly to wipe out the evidence on which a history might now be based. Ptolemy left the planetary theory in highly developed form, in which the epicyclic principle is elaborated in a number of ways that permit better adjustment of the theory to the observed data. For example, he lets the deferent be not centered on the earth (i.e., it is an eccentric), and he lets the center of the epicycle revolve uniformly with respect to a point (the equant point) that is not even at the center of the deferent. This is a far cry from uniform circular motion around the earth. However, it seems certain that Ptolemy did not regard his system as a description of physical reality, but only as a computational analogue.

Ptolemy wrote also an influential and enduring treatise on geography, and one on astrology (the *Tetrabiblos*) that bears his name is probably his. In the three centuries that separated Ptolemy from Hipparchus, progress in astronomy had been slow; after Ptolemy, it effectively ceased. By this time Egypt had been ruled directly by Rome for more than 100 years, and science was foreign to the Roman mind.

Philoponus. The last memorable Hellenistic contributor to science, JOHN PHILOPONUS, worked in Alexandria as late as A.D. 525. Noteworthy parts of his voluminous output are his treatise on the plane astrolabe and his prolix but vigorous commentaries on numerous works of Aristotle. Though his ideas on falling bodies were not free from error, they were much in advance of Aristotle's; Philoponus states, for example, that if one weight is several times as heavy as another, the two will fall through equal distances in nearly equal times. In his discussion of the motion of an arrow, he rejected the Aristotelian formulation and put forward—indistinctly, to be sure—the idea of inertia. He also rejected Aristotle's distinction between sublunar and celestial matter, arguing that terrestrial and heavenly matter are the same in kind and have the same physics. He based his case partly on the conflict between Aristotle's ideas and the observable world; for example, Aristotle's fifth element, whose natural motion was a circling centered on the earth as the center of the universe, was not consistent with the epicyclic theory or with the sensory evidence that the planets are not at unvarying distances from the earth. Philoponus's belief in the physical unity of heaven and earth was supported, or perhaps inspired, by his monotheism and his belief that all matter was created by God.

Philoponus was a Christian (a Monophysite and perhaps a convert), though adherence to the scientific tradition usually implied loyalty to Greek ideals and therefore to paganism. He was the last of the Hellenistic physicists. The end of the Museum had come a century earlier, in A.D. 415, with the murder of its learned head, Hypatia. However, the Museum and the associated library had both seen their best days before the rise of Christianity and indeed even before Christ was born. As the Greek society that supported it became submerged, science slowly disappeared. The death of Archimedes at the hands of a Roman solider in 212 B.C. was a starkly symbolic event.

It is hardly too strong a statement to say that Rome had no native science. There was some effort by Romans to learn about Greek science, but this was only a scholarly activity, resulting in mere compilations in Latin of Greek lore and opinion. The sources were, for the most part, encyclopedic treatments of science by Greek popularizers; rarely were they the works of the scientists themselves.

The Biological Sciences

The scientific study of living things undoubtedly commenced as the study of sick or injured man. Surviving Egyptian medical treatises date from at least as early as 1500 B.C., and they derive from works very much older. Disease was believed to be caused by an invasion of the body by a deity, an enemy, or a dead person. The appropriate remedy was likely to be a prayer to Isis or to nine other beneficent dieties. The medical papyri give the proper incantations for various ailments; nevertheless, they do describe medicines and their mode of application. At least in part, the goal of the medicines seems to have been to make things unpleasant for the alien spirit that was causing the illness. Excrements from a whole ark of animals, from the fly to the hippopotamus, played prominent roles. Other animal, vegetable, and mineral products were also recommended, however, and some of the prescriptions may have had some degree of efficacy as sources of vitamins or other helpful compounds. At any rate, the pharmacopoeia of the Egyptian medical papyri is hardly more startling than that of England 30 centuries later. In the papyri that deal with bone surgery, there is no resort to magic; the tone is so rational that it can fairly be called scientific, though it does not go beyond the empirical.

Hippocrates and Aristotle. In Greece the scientific approach to medicine developed at Cos, an island near the coast of Asia Minor. The dominant figure was HIPPOCRATES (*fl.* 420 B.C.). From the school, which endured for generations, there survives a considerable body of writing, the Hippocratic Corpus; it is pragmatic, rational, clinical, devoid of superstition. Hippocratic medicine centered its effort on assisting the body to restore itself to health.

In zoology the greatest of the Greeks was Aristotle, son of a physician. He was a patient and acute observer, with a strong interest in marine animals and in embryology. A few of the phenomena that he described were not rediscovered until the 19th century. He made a strong start on the classification of animals; on the basis of blood, he separated the vertebrates from the invertebrates; he noted the distinction between bony and cartilaginous fishes; he classed whales not with fishes but with men and horses. Taking a strongly teleological view of the world, he rejected the idea of evolution by random trial, which had been put forward by Empedocles.

Aristotle's successor as head of the school that he had founded (the Lyceum) was his pupil and colleague Theophrastus (*fl.* 330 B.C.), who wrote the earliest systematic account of botany that has survived—one that was not surpassed until the 16th century. In Alexandria, Herophilus (*fl.* 300 B.C.) greatly advanced the knowledge of human anatomy by dissection of cadavers, a procedure that was rarely practiced during classical antiquity. Tradition says that he examined the internal organs of living criminals condemned to death; in an age when scourging and crucifixion were standard practice, it is a wonder that this was not one more often. Herophilus made many anatomical discoveries; among them was the recognition of the nerves. Aristotle had taken intelligence to be associated with the heart, but Herophilus returned to the earlier view that the seat of intelligence is the brain. His younger contemporary Erasistratus (*fl.* 260 B.C.) also made advances in anatomy, though he is more celebrated as a physiologist. He too dissected cadavers and, perhaps, living men. He distinguished between motor and sensory nerves, and he inferred the existence of capillaries connecting the arteries with the veins. Though his physiology invoked the idea of atoms, it depended heavily on varieties of vapor, πνεῦμα (Latin *pneuma*), that were supposed to permeate the organism. One kind was carried by the arteries and another by the nerves, while blood flowed through the veins. He thought disease to be caused chiefly by excess of blood. Nevertheless, he discouraged bloodletting, which physicians of that time used habitually; he preferred to reduce the supply of blood by attention to diet.

Galen. In medicine, progress at Alexandria slowed earlier than it did in the physical and mathematical sciences. However, the last great figure, Galen (*fl.* A.D. 170), was a contemporary of the astronomer Ptolemy. Like Ptolemy, Galen was at once a contributor to his science and a codifier of the work of his predecessors, and his work dominated its field for about 1,500 years.

Born in Pergamon, Galen studied in Asia Minor and at Alexandria. In A.D. 162 he went to Rome, where he was spectacularly successful, becoming physician to the Emperor, Marcus Aurelius. His clear and forceful writings reflect a high regard for the Hippocratic school, but he was himself an able investigator. For dissections he depended mostly—perhaps entirely—on animals, especially monkeys. He made advances in the description of the muscles and of the functions of the spinal cord. He showed by experiment that the arteries, during life, carry blood. However, he was not aware that the blood circulates; he thought rather that it was consumed in the tissues. Galen did not establish a school, and when he died in A.D. 199 progress in medicine as a rational science came to a halt that, in the Christian world, lasted for more than 1,000 years.

Bibliography: The whole period. R. TATON, ed., *A History of Science,* v.1 *Ancient and Medieval Science,* tr. A. J. POMERANS (New York 1963). M. R. COHEN and I. E. DRABKIN, *A Source Book in Greek Science* (New York 1948; repr. Cambridge, Massachusetts 1959), Period before Christ. G. SARTON, *A History of Science,* 2 v. (Cambridge, Massachusetts 1952–59). Mathematics and astronomy, especially in Egypt and Mesopotamia. O. NEUGEBAUER, *The Exact Sciences in Antiquity* (2d ed. Providence 1957). Early Greeks. J. BURNET, *Early Greek Philosophy* (4th ed. London 1930; repr. pa. New York 1957). G. S. KIRK and J. E. RAVEN, *The Presocratic Philosophers* (Cambridge, England 1957). K. FREEMAN, tr., *Ancilla to the Pre-Socratic Philosophers* (Cambridge, Massachusetts 1948; repr. 1957). W. K. C. GUTHRIE, *A History of Greek Philosophy* (Cambridge, England 1962–). Later Greeks and their successors. M. CLAGETT, *Greek Science in Antiquity* (New York 1955). W. D. ROSS, *Aristotle* (5th ed. New York 1953). Greek astronomy. T. L. HEATH, *Aristarchus of Samos* (Oxford 1913; repr. 1959). J. L. E. DREYER, *A History of Astronomy from Thales to Kepler* (2d ed. New York 1953). Roman science. W. H. STAHL, *Roman Science* (Madison 1962).

[J. J. G. MCCUE]

SCIENCE (IN THE MIDDLE AGES)

The term "Middle Ages" will be taken, somewhat arbitrarily and for convenience, to extend over the period A.D. 500 to 1500, and to embrace the science of three different, but more or less intimately related, centers of civilization: Byzantine (Eastern Roman) Empire, Islam, and West Europe. China and India, while important, are outside the scope of this article.

Introduction

Greek theoretical science had always lacked popular appeal, for it was the work of a relatively few gifted individuals. To satisfy curiosity about the physical world, a tradition of popular science emerged in the form of handbooks, the purpose of which was to communicate the results of the more technical, theoretical treatises. The Romans enthusiastically adopted the handbook form—translating, paraphrasing, plagiarizing, and diluting Greek treatises. As W. H. Stahl puts it, "[A]t Rome there was only one level of scientific knowledge—the handbook level" [*Roman Science* (Madison 1962) 71].

From this tradition handbooks were produced in the Roman Empire period that were to be enormously influential throughout the Latin Middle Ages (e.g., those of Seneca, Pliny the Elder, Solinus), especially in the period from A.D. 500 to 1150, when they constituted the major source of scientific knowledge. Neoplatonic cosmography and interpretations were transmitted to the Middle Ages by three Latin encyclopedists: Chalcidius (fl. A.D. 4th century), who translated into Latin and commented upon a large portion of Plato's *Timaeus;* MACROBIUS (fl. A.D. 400), author of the commentary *In somnium Scipionis;* and Martianus Capella (5th century A.D.), who wrote the famous allegory *De nuptiis Mercurii et Philologiae,* which fixed the number of liberal arts at seven.

Christian Encyclopedists. Of the previously mentioned encyclopedists none is known with certainty to have been a Christian, but a number of Christian encyclopedists were to follow in their footsteps, of whom BOETHIUS (c. 480–524), CASSIODORUS (fl. c. 540), ISIDORE OF SEVILLE (c. 570–636), and the Venerable BEDE (673–735) deserve mention. Of these, Boethius was the most significant since his knowledge of Greek enabled him to comprehend, utilize, and translate Greek treatises. Two of the most comprehensive scientific works that were available prior to the 12th century were provided by Boethius. His *Arithmetica,* a free translation and slight rearrangement of Nicomachus of Gerasa's (fl. c. A.D. 100) *Introductio arithmetica,* served as the basic textbook of theoretical arithmetic throughout the Middle Ages; his work *De Institutione musica,* based on earlier Greek treatises, was fundamental. Boethius is said to have translated Euclid into Latin (no extant translation exists; a pseudo-Boethian geometry, *Ars geometriae,* is not by him and is illustrative of the decline of mathematical thought) as well as Archimedes and Ptolemy (Cassiodorus, *Lib. Var.* 1.15), but no translations have been found. Of great importance were his commentaries on and translations of Aristotelian logical treatises, which rank him as the most significant of the Latin authors who shaped the scientific and intellectual tradition of the early Middle Ages.

The other three authors mentioned above utilized science as an aid to Christian life and a better understanding of Scripture. Indeed, Bede's principal scientific treatises, *De temporibus* and a later expanded version *De temporum ratione,* were each essentially a *computus*—i.e., a work on calendar reckoning, which explained how to calculate the variable date of Easter and frequently had tables associated with it. Bede used a 19-year cycle—the best available—and provided a lucid and well thought out explanation. He also observed that the tides were constant for a given port (''the establishment of the port'')—i.e., the time interval between the meridian passage of the moon and subsequent high tide is approximately constant. This time interval, Bede observed, differed for different ports along the coast.

Decline of Science. Bede, however, must be set down as an exception, for in western Europe the period from 500 to *c.* 1150 was a period of scientific decline. This is borne out, for example, by the level of understanding of Greek mathematics. In his *Etymologies,* Isidore of Seville devotes to geometry a scant two pages, consisting largely of confused definitions and concepts. Similar confusions are found in Cassiodorus's account of the quadrivium. The meagerness of geometrical knowledge and understanding is illustrated in a treatise written about 1050 by Franco of Liège called *De quadratura circuli.* Squaring the circle was one of the three classical problems in Greek geometry whose solution had to be achieved by ruler and compass. In this insoluble problem the objective was to equate the area of a quadrilateral figure, usually a square, with that of a circle. Franco ''solves'' it by employing a rule formulated by Roman surveyors that the area of a circle equals 11 d^2/14, where *d* is the diameter of the circle. Assuming that *d* is 14 feet, Franco calculates the area of the circle as 154 square feet and then ''squares the circle'' by constructing a rectangle whose sides are 14 and 11 feet, respectively. Actually, most of his treatise is devoted to finding a square equal to a rectangle of 154 square feet. His solution is hopeless, since he does not utilize, and probably did not know, the Euclidean proposition for constructing a mean proportional line between two given straight lines (*Elements,* 6.13). However, Franco was convinced that he had solved the problem.

At best, the Latin encyclopedists preserved some scientific knowledge, usually a pale reflection of what once was. Incompatible concepts were often included without the compiler's awareness. A typical illustration is found in Macrobius's *Commentarium in somnium Scipionis.* Macrobius accepts a fixed order of the planets and yet speaks of Venus and Mercury as sometimes above and sometimes below the planets, thus destroying the fixed order.

Medicine and *materia medica* were at a higher level, largely as the result of translations into Latin (5th to 9th centuries) of certain treatises by GALEN, HIPPOCRATES, Dioscorides, and some of the late Greek medical writers. Practical considerations—the need to cure the sick—no

doubt lent impetus to this translating activity. The literature available was adequate to permit the development of the Italian medical school of Salerno in the 9th century.

Byzantine Empire

In the Byzantine (Eastern Roman) Empire, where Greek was the common language, commentaries on available Greek scientific classics played a significant role. For example, Eutocius (fl. *c.* 520) revised and commented upon the text of the first four books of the *Conics* of Apollonius of Perga (fl. *c.* 250 B.C.), one of the greatest geometrical works of antiquity. He commented also upon at least three treatises of Archimedes and reawakened an interest in Archimedian manuscripts. But for his efforts, these works might have been lost.

Philoponus. Among Aristotelian commentators, JOHN PHILOPONUS, a Christian, and Simplicius, a pagan (fl. early 6th century), were especially significant for later centuries. In his commentary on Aristotle's *Physics,* Philoponus repudiated Aristotle's law of MOTION, which is sometimes represented as $V \propto S/T \propto F/R$, where *V* is velocity, *S* distance, *T* time, *F* motive force, and *R* resistance of a medium or object, or both. Aristotle had insisted that local motion required a force capable of moving an object through a medium, and denied the existence of void space. Philoponus insisted that motion in a vacuum was possible and would occur in a certain original time; however, the same motion of that same object in a medium would be of greater duration because of the resistance of the medium. Philoponus held that in a vacuum the ratio of weights is inversely proportional to their times of fall, i.e., $W_2/W_1 = T_1/T_2$ when $S_2 = S_1$ and *W* is the weight of a body. In a medium, additional time must be added, which is taken as proportional to the resistance of the medium. Philoponus also appealed to experience, insisting that two unequal weights dropped from a height would reach the ground in almost equal times. Not only does this refute Aristotle, but it is also incompatible with Philoponus's emended version of that law. It is noteworthy that the dropping of unequal weights to refute Aristotle was done long before by Simon Stevin (1548–1620) and Galileo GALILEI (1564–1642).

In the same *Physics* commentary, Philoponus repudiates Aristotle's explanation that air is a continually acting motive force that maintains the motion of a projectile no longer in contact with its initial mover (for Aristotle, a motion would automatically cease if contact was broken between motive force and moving body). Rejecting the role of a medium producing motion, Philoponus assumed that an incorporeal motive force is imparted from the projector to the projectile. Thus motion in a vacuum would be possible since the medium is not required as a moving force. This interpretation was widely adopted by Arab and Latin authors. Simplicius, in his commentary on Aristotle's *De caelo,* which was later translated into Arabic and Latin, cited three different explanations of the acceleration of falling bodies. These were to form part of the medieval discussion of this problem.

In an exclusively Christian framework, commentaries on the account in Genesis of the first six days of CREATION (*In Hexaemeron*) dealt with concepts of matter, astronomy, cosmology, and zoology as they bore upon creation. Drawing upon Greek science, St. BASIL of Caesarea (329–379) produced one of the most influential of these works, which was translated into Latin in the 5th century.

Alchemy and Astrology. The pseudosciences of ALCHEMY and ASTROLOGY developed markedly in late antiquity as an intermingling of Greek science, mysticism, and superstition. Alchemy was a fusion of the Aristotelian theory of transmutation of elements, practical metallurgy, and allegorical mysticism. But in this vain quest, several chemical discoveries were made, along with a steady development of apparatus and technique. In his *Tetrabiblos,* PTOLEMY bequeathed to the Middle Ages its greatest astrological treatise. His contention that the celestial bodies could determine human behavior was opposed by the Church, but the influence of celestial bodies on natural phenomena (e.g., drought, flood, tides) was accepted by many Christians even during the Middle Ages.

Arab Science

A fair portion of the Greek scientific corpus found its way eastward through the intermediary of Syriac-speaking Christians who, beginning in the 4th century, translated Greek logical and scientific treatises—especially medical works—for use in their schools.

The Arabs were beneficiaries of this rich legacy. But for approximately 150 years after the death of Muḥammad they displayed little direct interest in science. During the 9th century, however, there was unparalleled translating activity, and works from Syriac and Greek were translated into Arabic. By the 10th century the Arab world had almost all the extant Greek scientific corpus for study and assimilation. Although they wrote in the Arabic language, the contributors to Arab science included Muslims, Jews, Christians, and pagans who resided in lands governed by Muslim rulers.

Mathematics. In mathematics, the Arabs made significant contributions. Although algebra, which was wholly rhetorical, was established independently of geometry, geometrical proofs were often added for numerical problems solved algebraically. The geometrical proof

was deemed more causal and fundamental. Equations were classified by the number of their terms rather than by powers of the unknown. Equations with only two terms were classified as binomials (e.g., $ax^2 = c$); those with three terms were trinomials (e.g., $ax^2 + bx = c$). Later, Omar Khayyām (*c.* 1038–1124) extended algebraic equations to four terms (tetranomials) by adding the cube of the unknown. In Arabian algebra negative roots were ignored as unintelligible (Bhāskara, a Hindu of the 12th century, first clearly asserted that a positive quantity had both a positive and a negative root; in Europe negative roots were finally acknowledged in the 16th century by Cardano in his *Ars magna* of 1545).

The Arabs developed the six trigonometric functions in conjunction with their astronomy. Arab geometers followed the best of Greek geometry and dealt with problems such as the trisection of an angle, finding two mean proportionals, and construction of regular polygons. Omar Khayyām solved cubic equations by means of conic sections and in so doing was conscious of his originality.

Astronomy. Astronomy was held in high esteem, since it permitted the Arabs to calculate the time of religious observances. Observatories were built and excellent instruments constructed (al-BĪRŪNĪ, 973–1048, mentions a sextant with a radius of 40 cubits) to gather more accurate observations for improving astronomical tables and correcting some of Ptolemy's results. Both al-Battānī (d. 928) and al-Bīrūnī revealed discrepancies in the data concerning the longitude of the solar apogee, which pointed to a special motion of the solar apogee itself. This important discovery of the motion of the line of apsides was unknown to Ptolemy. Arab astronomers also redetermined with greater accuracy the value of precession of the equinoxes, and in lieu of Ptolemy's 1° in 100 years Thabit ibn Qurra (*c.* 826–901) and al-Battānī offered 1° in 66 years, and al-Bīrūnī, 1° in 68 years and 11 months. In the reign of Caliph al-Mamun (813–833), a degree of latitude was paced off north and south of a chosen position and averaged out to 56 2/3 Arabian miles. The Arabs also engaged in a controversy that had echoes in the Latin West in the 13th century. Was the function of astronomy to represent real motions and true cosmology, or merely to save the appearances? Could the epicycles and eccentrics used in Ptolemaic astronomy have actual counterparts in the heavens, or were they mere computational devices?

Mechanics. In physics the Arabs were interested in both theory and experiment. Apparently following Philoponus, a number of Arabs challenged Aristotle's account of projectile motion. The concept of an impressed force, called *mail* (*inclinatio* or IMPETUS in Latin), was clearly expounded by AVICENNA (980–1037) and ABŪ AL-BARAKĀT (d. *c.* 1164). Both authors accepted a natural inclination (*mail tabi'i*) in natural upward motion (for fire and air) and downward motion (for earth and water) and an unnatural inclination (*mail qasrī*) in motion away from natural place—i.e., in violent motion. Avicenna insisted that the *mail* imparted to the projectile by the motive force was a permanent entity but destructible by the resistance of the medium through which any body moved. Void space was impossible because all motions were terminated by resistant media. Abū al-Barakāt favored a naturally self-expending non-permanent *mail* and argued that projectile motion in a void was conceivable because any motion would terminate upon the total disappearance of the impressed force. In the natural downward accelerated motion of heavy bodies, both authors accounted for the acceleration by assuming that the gravity, or heaviness, of the body continually produced additional natural *mail,* which increased the speed accordingly. For Abū al-Barakāt an additional factor was the continually lessening resistance of violent *mail* (he assumed its coexistence with natural *mail*) to the successively produced natural *mail.* Scholastic commentators in the Latin West were to consider independently many of the same viewpoints in their discussion of impetus theory.

A number of other views appeared that did violence to the accepted interpretation of Aristotle. Thabit ibn Qurra rejected Aristotle's doctrine of natural place. He enunciated a qualitative theory of gravitation based on the concept that like attracts like. When a piece of earth is displaced from the earth itself, it is attracted back to the earth. Of two separate quantities of earth in void space, the greater quantity would attract the lesser; if they were equal in magnitude, they would meet at the midpoint. Nasr ibn Khosraw (*c.* 1003–89) rejected the notion that bodies are absolutely light or heavy and opted for relative weight. There were also atomists who defended their position by theological arguments and some who used arguments more akin to those of Greek ATOMISM.

The Arabs determined specific gravities of liquids and solids and used such data to detect fraud and to distinguish alloyed from unalloyed metals. Al-Khāzinī (fl. A.D. 1100), in his elaborate *Book of the Balance of Wisdom,* gives specific gravities for numerous substances (e.g., gold, mercury, and silver). It was recognized also that ice had a larger volume than the same weight of water; its specific gravity was put at 0.965. The "Balance of Wisdom" was a hydrostatic balance utilizing Archimedian hydrostatic principles and the concept of center of gravity.

Optics. In optics the foremost Arabian author was Ibn al-Haitham (*c.* 965–1039), known to the Latins as Al-

hazen. His treatise on optics, which was translated into Latin in the late 12th or early 13th century, surpassed anything that has survived in Greek science. He demonstrated conclusively that light rays come to the eye from luminous objects (Avicenna also adopted this position) rather than emanate from the eye to the object, as Euclid and Ptolemy had assumed. Among a number of arguments, he observed that when one looks into a mirror reflecting solar light, the dazzling light compels one to close his eyes. This was best explained on the assumption that light comes to the eye. Using the *camera obscura,* he showed that light and colors are not mixed in air. Al-Haitham manufactured his own plane and parabolic mirrors, discovered spherical aberration, and determined the point of reflection of a concave spherical mirror when the positions of the eye and observer were known. To explain refraction he concluded that light rays travel more slowly in denser media (Newton incorrectly insisted that the velocity of light was greater in a denser medium), and he analyzed both incident and resultant rays into two components, one parallel, the other perpendicular, to the surface separating the two media. The velocity was made dependent on the parallel component, which was retarded in a denser medium.

Alchemy. Alchemy was pursued with vigor. A large collection of treatises written by the Brethren of Purity in the 10th century was ascribed to Jābir ibn Hayyān (fl. *c.* A.D. 760). These works classified substances as (1) spirits or volatile bodies (e.g., mercury, sulphur, arsenic); (2) metallic bodies, embracing all metals except mercury; (3) bodies, or all substances omitted from the first two categories. The formation of metals resulted from a compounding of pure mercury and sulfur. By altering their proportions and purity one could theoretically change one metal to another and, hopefully, base metals to gold.

Al-Rāzī (Rhazès), *c.* 825–925, a Persian, was a practical chemist who possessed apparatus to carry out the processes of distillation, calcination, solution, evaporation, crystallization, sublimation, filtration, amalgamation, and ceration. The Arabs discovered how to prepare ammoniac, sal ammoniac, mineral acids, and borax. Mention of mineral acids occurs in the Latin West in the 13th century in a collection of alchemical works ascribed to "Geber" (the Latin name for Jābir) and based on Arabic sources.

Medicine. Arab medicine was hampered by prohibitions against human dissection; anatomy had to be learned from books. But the Arabs achieved a high level of excellence in clinical medicine. Al-Rāzī, their greatest clinical physician, was a true Hippocratic who distinguished between measles and smallpox in his *Liber de pestiliencia.* His *Liber continens* was a great influence in

Europe. Scholastic medicine received its greatest organization from Avicenna's *Canon of Medicine,* which attempted to coordinate systematically the medical doctrines of Hippocrates and Galen with the biological concepts of Aristotle. The breadth of learning and authoritative tone made it the most widely used medical book in Islam; in Europe it was used until the 17th century. It was in a *Commentary on the Anatomy in the Canon of Ibn Sina* (i.e., Avicenna) that Ibn al-Nafis (d. 1288) enunciated his theory of the lesser circulation. He rejected Galen's view that blood flowed from the right ventricle to the left through pores in the ventricular septum. He insisted that blood flowed from the right ventricle to the lung via the pulmonary artery and, after mixing with air in the lungs, through the pulmonary artery to the left ventricle. This was an important step leading to the correct theory of the circulation of the blood.

The Arabs introduced many drugs, vegetables, and chemicals into their medicines and dispensed drugs in pharmacies, some of which were associated with excellent hospitals that had special wards for women, for eye diseases, and for fevers.

By the middle of the 12th century Arab science was in decline. In 1258 the Mongol sack of Baghdad and the concomitant destruction of numerous books dealt a great blow to science.

Latin West 1100 to 1500

By the 12th century western Europe was in close contact with the Muslims at a number of points. As Europeans became aware of the superior scientific knowledge possessed by the Arabs, they sought eagerly to make it their own. Translations from Arabic and Greek into Latin during the 12th and 13th centuries produced a true renaissance of Greek science. By the close of the 13th century there were available a significant portion of Greek science (though not as much as the Arabs had acquired in the 9th and 10th centuries) and many treatises by Arab authors. The new science engulfed the old handbook tradition, which, nevertheless, continued. Whereas previously Plato had been more influential than Aristotle, the latter now became the dominant influence in shaping medieval physical, biological, and logical thought.

Great universities began to develop, first at Paris and Bologna, and subsequently at Oxford, Cambridge, and many other places. Science was essentially a university enterprise embodied in special forms of literature. Commentaries on the works of Aristotle and others were commonplace. More important was the *questio* form in which problems of special interest were thoroughly discussed. Of particular significance were *Questiones* on individual Aristotelian works. In such treatises it was customary to present at the outset the arguments against one's own position, followed by arguments in support of it. Even doubts about one's own position were raised and then resolved. At the end of each question the contra arguments mentioned at the beginning were disposed of in order of presentation. Emphasis was on logical consistency. Appeals to experience or experiment, though sometimes included, were usually of secondary importance. (*See* EDUCATION, SCHOLASTIC; SCHOLASTIC METHOD.)

Until the latter part of the 13th century scholastics adhered rather closely to Aristotelian physical and philosophical concepts, convinced that most of his principles and demonstrations were necessarily true. Alarmed at a trend that seemed to restrict God's absolute power to have done things differently, Étienne TEMPIER, Bishop of Paris, condemned (March 7, 1277) 219 articles, many of which were deterministic or claimed to be necessarily true. The effects of this action were to inhibit claims that Aristotle's principles and demonstrations were necessarily true—at best they were to be considered only probable—and to encourage the formulation of possible alternative explanations, many of which were in direct conflict with Aristotle. Aristotle's influence was undermined further because some of his arguments were found to be inconsistent and unsatisfying. Finally, where Aristotle had been vague, scholastics interpreted him as they saw fit—often in novel ways. Thus in the 14th century many non-Aristotelian positions became quite respectable, and a lively interplay of scientific ideas developed.

Motion. The Aristotelian law of motion, $V \propto F/R$, was abandoned by many because its critics noted that by repeatedly doubling R, it could be made greater than F; when R was greater than F, no velocity could result, but this was not what the formula expressed. To obviate this defect, THOMAS BRADWARDINE proposed a new exponential law of motion that is usually represented as $F_2/R_2 = (F_1/R_1)^{V_2/V_1}$. Therefore if $F_2/R_2 = 8/1$ and $F_1/R_1 = 2/1$, then the ratio, or exponent, $V_2/V_1 = 3/1$, and F_2 moves R_2 with a speed three times that with which F_1 moves R_1. This function was widely adopted and designated a *ratio of ratios* (*proportio proportionum*). In his *De proportionibus proportionum,* NICHOLAS ORESME provided an elaborate mathematical foundation for this function, and even considered exponents, or ratios of velocities, that were irrational (the concept of an irrational exponent may have originated with Oresme).

Existence of Void Space. The possible existence of void space and motion in such a space was widely discussed. St. THOMAS AQUINAS and many subsequent authors held that if void space existed—almost all authors, including Thomas but excepting NICHOLAS OF AUTRECOURT, denied its existence—motion through it would be of finite duration, not instantaneous as Aristotle held. Thomas insisted that void space would be a magnitude; and like any extended magnitude, its parts could be traversed successively so that motion would occur in some definite time interval. Although void space within the Aristotelian cosmos was denied by almost all scholastics, Bradwardine and Oresme asserted that beyond the cosmos there extended an infinite, dimensionless, indivisible void space. The attributes of this space were associated with God, who is infinite, dimensionless, and indivisible. Oresme said that ''this space . . . is infinite and indivisible and is the immensity of God and is God himself.'' The relationship between God's immensity and an infinite void space was a hotly debated problem in the 17th and early 18th centuries, involving Isaac Newton through the famous Clarke-Leibniz correspondence of 1715–16.

The existence of other worlds beyond our cosmos—Aristotle had rejected this—was made a moot point by article 34 of the condemnations of 1277, which, in effect, asserted that God could create more than one world. Almost all scholastics accepted the uniqueness of our cosmos, but some began to examine the conditions that might obtain if a plurality of worlds did exist. Oresme maintained that the elements of every world would behave just as those of our world—i.e., heavy matter would tend toward the center of its own world and light matter toward the circumference. This was a repudiation of Aristotle's doctrine of natural place, in which the natural places of the four elements were unique; now each world had its own set of natural places.

Many abandoned Aristotle's explanation of projectile motion in favor of the impetus theory (its possible connections with the Arab *mail* theory have yet to be established). Francis of Marchia was the first Latin scholastic to propose the theory of impetus in his explanation of sacramental causality when commenting on the *Sentences* at Paris (1319–20). The most important exposition of the theory was given at the University of Paris by JOHN BURIDAN, who measured the impetus of a body by its quantity of matter (analogous to mass) and the velocity imparted to it. From this standpoint impetus is analogous to Newton's momentum (mv). However, unlike momentum, impetus also acted as a force that maintains a body's motion. Like the Arabs earlier, some (e.g., Buridan) thought of the impressed force as a permanent quality that is always destroyed by the external resistance of the medium, while others (e.g., Oresme; Galileo in his youth) held that it was self-expending. Buridan even suggested that the continuous circular motion of celestial bodies was a result of the action of impetus that God had implanted in them at the creation. The impetus remained constant since no form of resistance to motion existed in the heavens.

Acceleration of freely falling bodies also was explained in terms of impetus. Buridan assumed that the natural gravity of a body, which moves it downward, also produces impetus during the fall that causes the acceleration.

The Merton Theorem. In the 1300s at Merton College, Oxford, the mean speed theorem was formulated by WILLIAM OF HEYTESBURY, RICHARD OF SWYNESHED, and JOHN OF DUMBLETON. Here, apparently for the first time, a definition of uniform acceleration was enunciated: the acquisition of equal increments of velocity in equal time periods (i.e., $v \propto t$). In the mean speed theorem this definition was utilized to demonstrate that a distance traversed by a uniformly accelerated motion was equivalent to the distance traversed in the same time by a body moving with a velocity equal to the velocity at the middle instant of the time of acceleration. The Merton theorem can be expressed as (1) $S = 1/2\ V_f\ t$, for acceleration from rest, where S is the distance traversed, V_f is the final velocity, and t is the time of acceleration; or as (2) $S = [(V_o + 1/2)(V_f - V_o)]\ t$, for acceleration from some velocity V_o. Since, in the first case, $V_f = at$ (a being the acceleration), (1) can be reduced to the familiar formula $S = 1/2\ at^2$. In the second case $V_f - V_o = at$. And thus (2) reduces to $S = V_o t + 1/2\ at^2$. The context from which this theorem developed was the ''intension and remission of forms,'' or ''latitude of forms,'' a subject that considered how forms, including qualities, increased or decreased in intensity. Without operational justification, most qualities were treated in a purely quantitative manner involving addition and subtraction of quantitative parts of qualities. Motion was treated as just another quality capable of such treatment. At Oxford proofs of the Merton theorem were arithmetical, while later at Paris they were geometrical. The high point of this development was Oresme's *De configurationibus qualitatum,* in which uniformly and nonuniformly varying qualities were represented by geometric figures. In his demonstration of the mean speed theorem, Oresme assumes that the altitude of rectangle *AFGB* is equal to line *DE,* the mean velocity of the uniformly accelerated motion represented by triangle *ABC.* He then shows that the area of rectangle *AFGB* equals the area of triangle *ABC,* so that the distances traversed are equal since the two figures represent the total distances traversed. In his *Two New Sciences* (1638) Galileo proves the mean speed theorem (Third Day, theorem 1, prop. 1) in a manner similar to Oresme's geometric method; although Galileo inverts the coordinates, his diagram is like Oresme's. There is little doubt that Galileo is following the medieval tradition. Application of the theorem to falling bodies was made by Domingo de SOTO in 1555. Thus the widely accepted medieval view that the velocity of a falling body is proportional to distance (i.e., $v \propto s$) was now corrected, since the Merton mean speed theorem made velocity directly proportional to time (i.e., $v \propto t$). Galileo, who also believed that bodies fell in a manner described by this theorem, made very significant use of it in helping to formulate modern mechanics.

Statics. Acquainted with the Greek and Arabic statical treatises, Jordanus de Nemore composed a series of original works that made notable contributions to statics. In proofs of the laws of the lever, inclined plane (this had eluded the Greeks), and bent lever (proved correctly for the first time), he utilized the principle of virtual work. M. Clagett summarizes the proof of the law of the lever as follows: ''(1) Either a lever with weights inversely proportional to the lever arms is in equilibrium or it is not. (2) If it is assumed that it is not, then one weight or the other descends. (3) But if one of the weights descends, it would perform the same action (i.e. work) as if it lifted a weight equal to itself and placed at an equal distance from the fulcrum through a distance equal to the distance it descended. But equal weights at equal distances are in equilibrium. Thus a weight does not have the force sufficient to lift its equal weight the same distance it descends. It, therefore, does not have the force to perform the same action—namely, to lift a proportionally smaller weight a proportionally longer distance'' (*Science of Mechanics* 77–78). Jordan also utilized the concept of a component of force in what he called *positional gravity* (*gravitas secundum situm*). This is equivalent to the assertion that $F = W \sin a$, where F is the force along the oblique path, W is the weight, and a the angle of inclination of the oblique path. Medieval statics influenced such later authors as Leonardo da Vinci, N. Tartaglia, and perhaps Galileo.

Optics. Optics dealt with the anatomy of the eye and the nature of light. Greek and Arabic sources (especially the *Optics* of Alhazen) were fundamental. The behavior of light (reflection and refraction) was considered geometrically, but consideration was given also to the physical nature of light. Under Neoplatonic and Augustinian influence, light was taken as a fundamental universal entity (it was the basis of matter and corporeality for ROBERT GROSSETESTE), and its study was expected to reveal basic knowledge about the world. The transmission of light was held to be a special case of the transmission of effects through a medium (known as the ''multiplication of species'').

The law of reflection was well known, but no law of refraction was enunciated until Grosseteste proclaimed a quantitative, though false, law in which the angle of refraction equaled half the angle of incidence. The greatest triumph of medieval optics was THEODORIC OF FREIBERG's (d. *c.* 1311) correct qualitative explanation of the formation of primary and secondary rainbows. Previous accounts relied on either reflection or refraction in clouds until WITELO (b. *c.* 1230) emphasized both reflection and refraction in individual raindrops. ROGER BACON gave the correct maximum altitude of the primary bow as 42° and properly noted that each observer sees a different bow that moves with him. But it was Theodoric who explained that the primary bow is formed when light falling on raindrops is refracted upon entering, then reflected at the inner concave surface and refracted out again. For the secondary bow, whose colors are in reverse order, a second internal reflection occurs before the second refraction. Centuries later, DESCARTES gave essentially the same explanation buttressed by a superior geometrical description. Of the colors of the rainbow, Theodoric could offer no adequate explanation, and none appeared until Newton's classic experiments.

The first systematic description of magnetism is found in the *Letter on the Magnet* (1269) by Peter of Maricourt (Peregrinus). Although some of its properties were known in antiquity (e.g., attraction and repulsion), Peter advances far beyond by distinguishing the north and south poles and explaining how to locate them on a spherical lodestone (this may be the first extant account of an artificial magnet). He also records the repulsion of like poles and the attraction of unlike, as well as the fact that each part of a broken magnet is itself a complete magnet with north and south poles. Peter includes what may be the first description of a dry pivoted magnetic compass with a graduated circle on which were marked the cardinal points.

Astronomy and Mathematics. Although no striking innovations or improvements were made in medieval technical astronomy, a conflict developed between Aristotelian cosmology and Ptolemaic astronomy. The former, with the earth in the exact center and only one motion permitted for each sphere, could not save the astronomical phenomena, while the latter could do so only by violating these generally accepted cosmological principles. In the end most accepted both—Ptolemaic astronomy for computational purposes and Aristotelian cosmology as representative of physical reality. Some, however, such as Bernard of Verdun (fl. *c.* 1300), acting on the belief that the system that best saved the phenomena must be physically true, tried to construct a universe in terms of physical epicycles and eccentrics.

The possible diurnal rotation of the earth was considered long before Copernicus asserted its reality. Buridan and Oresme, and Aquinas less explicitly, argued that if the earth had a diurnal rotation while the sphere of the fixed stars remained immobile, the same astronomical phenomena would be saved equally well. On other grounds, however, both acquiesced in the traditional Aristotelian view of an immobile earth. But some of their arguments were to appear later in Copernicus's revolutionary treatise.

Except for the work of Leonardo Fibonacci (*c.* 1170–*c.* 1240), mathematics did not attain the high level reached by the Greeks and Arabs. This may be explained partly by the absence (except for fragments) of the *Conics* of Apollonius and because the works of Archimedes, translated by WILLIAM OF MOERBEKE in 1269, were but little used. Fibonacci, however, had studied the best Greek and Arab authors. In a series of important treatises he systematically expounded the Hindu (or Arabic) numerals, used the Fibonacci series (named after him) where each term is equal to the sum of the two preceding terms, and handled difficult algebraic problems, as well as extracting approximative square and cubic roots. He included indeterminate problems of the first and second degree. He was also a capable geometer. No subsequent mathematician before 1500 equaled him in ability. There was, however, a great interest in mathematics; and scholastics argued about its foundations, as, for example, whether lines, planes, and solids were composed of indivisibles or of continuously divisible magnitudes. Infinite convergent and divergent series were widely discussed, and many such series were formulated in both physical and mathematical contexts. For example, Oresme shows the convergence of the series $a/n + a/n (1 - 1/n) + a/n (1 - 1/n)^2 + \cdots + a/n (1 - 1/n)^m + \cdots = a;$ and the divergence of the harmonic series $1 + 1/2 + 1/3 + 1/4 + \cdots + 1/n + 1/n + 1 \cdots.$

Medicine and Biology. Medicine received its academic formalization in the medieval universities of western Europe. Galen, Hippocrates, Avicenna, and Rhazès formed the foundation of the medical curriculum. Physicians from the first Western medical school at Salerno helped spread medical learning and influenced developments. A measure of advance is seen in the fact that, while animals only were dissected at Salerno, human dissection, an outgrowth of postmortems, was a regular feature at the University of Bologna from the late 13th century. Human dissection, which had been prohibited since the days of the Roman Empire, focused attention once again on the human body. Bologna became the leading medical school, where, in contrast to Paris, surgery was taught along with medicine. The greatest medieval anatomist was Mondino de' Luzzi, who personally performed dissections and wrote the most widely used anatomical text, the *Anathomia*. In the 15th century the Branca family of Sicily performed plastic surgery, replacing and repairing noses, lips, and ears. The flesh was taken at first from the face and then from the arm to prevent facial deformity. Of clinical interest were the *con-*

silia begun by Taddeo Alderotti (1223-*c.* 1300) and continued into the 17th century. A *consilium* was a prominent physician's case history, usually incomplete because it preceded rather than followed treatment. It had a formal basic structure, listing, in order, the ailment and its symptoms, regimen, and prescriptions for drugs and medicines. The many plagues that swept Europe in the 14th and 15th centuries compelled many cities to establish quarantines and other sanitary measures. A great body of literature emerged concerning the plague and its effects.

In biology some excellent descriptive works appeared in zoology and botany. Emperor FREDERICK II composed a remarkable treatise on falconry, *De arte venandi cum avibus,* with brilliant anatomical descriptions of birds. ALBERT THE GREAT described animals and plants with considerable accuracy and rejected fanciful stories about certain animals (e.g., the beaver and salamander). Albert also repeated Aristotle's experiment on hen's eggs, tracing the development of the embryo by opening a collection of eggs at various intervals. Albert was perhaps the greatest natural scientist of the 13th century. He is remarkable for the reliance he placed on observation and experiment, and this alone is enough to set him above his contemporaries and many who followed him. More naturalistic representation of plants and animals are found in medieval manuscripts, although the difficulty of reproducing naturalistic drawings prior to the invention of printing prevented widespread standardization of illustrations and hindered the advance of biology. Biological classification schemes tended to follow the general principles laid down by Aristotle.

Bibliography: G. SARTON, *Introduction to the History of Science* (Baltimore, Md. 1927–48). L. THORNDIKE. *A History of Magic and Experimental Science* (New York 1923–58). P. M. M. DUHEM, *Le Système du monde,* 10 v. (Paris 1913–17; repr. 1954–59); *Études sur Léonard de Vinci,* 3 v. (Paris 1906–13; repr. 1955). M. CLAGETT, *The Science of Mechanics in the Middle Ages* (Madison, Wis. 1959); *Archimedes in the Middle Ages* (Madison, Wis. 1964). A. C. CROMBIE, *Medieval and Early Modern Science,* 2 v. (2d ed. Cambridge, Mass. 1961); *Robert Grosseteste and the Origins of Experimental Science* (Oxford 1953). E. J. DIJKSTERHUIS, *The Mechanization of the World Picture,* tr. C. DIKSHOORN (Oxford 1961). J. A. WEISHEIPL, *The Development of Physical Theory in the Middle Ages* (New York 1960). A. MAIER, *Studien zur Naturphilosophie der Spätscholastik,* 5 v. (Rome 1949–58). C. H. HASKINS, *Studies in the History of Medieval Science* (2d ed. Cambridge, Mass. 1927). R. TATON, ed., *A History of Science,* v. 1 *Ancient and Medieval Science,* tr. A. J. POMERANS (New York 1963). L. LECLERC, *Histoire de la médicine arabe,* 2 v. (Paris 1876; New York 1961). A. CASTIGLIONI, *History of Medicine,* tr. and ed. E. B. KRUMBHAAR (2d ed. New York 1947). K. SUDHOFF, *Kurzes Handbuch der Geschichte der Medizin* (Berlin 1922), 3d and 4th ed. of J. L. PAGEL, *Einführung in die Geschichte der Medizin,* 3 v. (Jena 1901–05). F. STURNZ, *Geschichte der Naturwissenschaften im Mit-*

telalter (Stuttgart 1910). J. NEEDHAM, *A History of Embryology* (2d ed. New York 1959).

[E. GRANT]

SCIENCE (IN THE RENAISSANCE)

The story of science in the RENAISSANCE is essentially that of science in the 16th century. The limits, necessarily arbitrary, may be set as early as 1450, since the discovery of printing and the reproduction of numerous, identical copies of scientific books is an important Renaissance phenomenon. To extend much beyond 1600, however, would necessitate the inclusion of Galileo GALILEI, and while he represents a culmination of Renaissance thought, he is best considered as ushering in the modern era rather than bringing the Renaissance to a close.

This article discusses science in the Renaissance rather than the renaissance of science. During this period many of the concepts and the methods that paved the way for modern science began to emerge, but there was no "rebirth" in the sense of the return to the classics that characterized the literary renaissance. It was a period of questioning, of probing, of tentative steps forward, of confused viewpoints. Tycho Brahe placed observational astronomy on a firm foundation without abandoning astrological predictions, and KEPLER continued to cast horoscopes while enunciating his three laws; Paracelsus issued diatribes against current medical practice and urged the application of chemistry to medicine, but the chemistry he wished to apply contained some of the worst forms of alchemy; Leonardo produced some of the finest anatomical drawings known, yet he not only "saw" but drew the "invisible" pores in the heart, which made possible what Galen considered back and forth surging of the blood. There was assuredly a greater questioning of Aristotle, of Galen, of PTOLEMY, but most of the scientists who emerged in this period were not ready to abandon them completely; there was indeed a much greater reliance on observation and experiment so long as this did not conflict too drastically with existing notions.

The Renaissance abounds in great names, and in a summary such as this some of them will merely be catalogued. Most of them are the subjects of individual biographical articles elsewhere in the *Encyclopedia*. To these the reader is referred in order to fill out the picture.

One of the events that not only stirred the imagination of the people but encouraged scientific investigation was the discovery of the earth. The great voyages of discovery opened to man a new earth: there were new lands and new peoples, new plants and new animals—all for

men to see and study. This pointed out the need for aids to navigation—instruments to plot one's course and adequate maps on which to locate one's position. It spurred interest in terrestrial magnetism, a knowledge of which would make the compass an effective instrument for long journeys.

Mathematics. The flurry of publication of mathematical books that characterized the period included not only Greek and Latin versions of Euclid, Archimedes, Appolinias, and Pappros but many original works of first importance. The *De triangulis omnimodis libri quinti* (1533) of Regiomontanus is the foundation of modern trigonometry. This was preceded by the work of G. Purbach and followed by the development by G. Rheticus (1514 to 1567) and B. Pitiscus (1561 to 1613) of accurate tables; these were to become almost useless after 1620, when the first set of logarithmic tables was published.

In algebra the cubic equation was solved by N. Tartaglia, and the solution was published and generalized by G. Cardano, in his *Ars Magna* (1545). L. Ferrari (1525 to 1565) then found the general solution of the quartic. Considering the cumbersome notation of the 16th century, these are outstanding achievements. Work on the theory of equations was continued by R. Bombelli in Italy and François Viète (1540 to 1603), the greatest French mathematician of the Renaissance. They not only systematized the existing knowledge but expanded it considerably.

The international character of this development is emphasized in the person of Simon Stevin of Bruges, who clarified the treatment of negative roots, but whose greatest achievement was his vindication of decimal fractions in 1585.

Astronomy. The publication (1543) of the *De revolutionibus orbium coelestium* of COPERNICUS stands as the most significant astronomical event of the Renaissance. Though Copernicus's conception of the universe was neither original (Aristarchus had certainly expressed much the same ideas) nor correct, the restatement of the heliocentric theory coupled with the diurnal rotation of the earth was a bold step forward.

Tycho Brahe rejected the ideas of Copernicus both because the Copernican system disagreed with some of Brahe's observations and because he still could not understand the movement of the "sluggish" earth. Instead he substituted a system in which the sun revolved about the earth and the other planets revolved about the sun. Only when Kepler, using Brahe's data, abandoned the idea of circles and used ellipses instead was the heliocentric system placed in a form close to that accepted today. But Tycho Brahe was the greatest of pretelescopic observational astronomers. Two of his observations were of immediate importance. In 1572 he observed a new star in Cassiopeia and followed its gradual changes in magnitude until its disappearance 16 months later. By the absence of parallax he proved it was indeed among the fixed stars—and to an Aristotelean who held a doctrine of the immutable heavens, this was indeed a startling revelation. He also carefully observed the comet of 1577, showed that it was not in the sublunar region, where Aristotle had placed comets, and cast doubt on the "spheres" that carried the planets since the comet seemed to pass readily through these. Without Brahe's accurate observations, Kepler could not have arrived at his theory and the three laws that bear his name. And as Brahe paved the way for Kepler, so did Kepler pave the way for Newton and the scientific revolution that he fathered.

Physics. The work of Stevin on statics (1586) is a book solidly in the Archimedean tradition. Among other things Stevin expounded the law of equilibrium for an inclined plane and stated the hydrostatic paradox usually associated with Pascal. The use of gunpowder and cannon promoted the study of dynamics, since there was little use in possessing cannon unless the laws that governed the motion of a projectile were known. A noteworthy contribution was made by Tartaglia, who pointed out that a projectile fired horizontally did not move in a horizontal line and then suddenly fall vertically under the influence of gravity but rather that its path was curved since gravity was continually acting.

Little information is available concerning the status of mechanics in the 16th century, although writers during this period were responsible for transmitting the 14th-century development of mechanics and its terminology to such innovators as Galileo [see M. Clagett, *The Science of Mechanics in the Middle Ages* (Madison, Wisconsin 1959) for details]. Possibly the most original contribution in this period was that of the Spanish Dominican Domingo de SOTO, who had studied at Paris and was acquainted with the work of the Mertonians THOMAS BRADWARDINE and WILLIAM OF HEYTESBURY, and the Parisian nominalist ALBERT OF SAXONY. Soto is the first writer known to have applied the Mertonian rule for determining distance in a uniformly accelerated motion to the motion of freely falling bodies, thereby anticipating Galileo's famous law of falling bodies by more than 50 years (*ibid.* 658; cf. 555). His *Quaestiones super octo libros physicorum Aristotelis* (Salamanca 1545) went through ten editions and served as an important textbook in physics until the beginning of the 17th century.

One of the classics of science to appear in the Renaissance was the *De magnete* (1600) of William Gilbert of Colchester. Though he was a physician, Gilbert's fame

rests on this book, to which he had devoted his leisure for 17 years, much of this time being devoted to careful experimentation. Gilbert studied the poles of elongated lodestones, broke them and detected the poles of the fragments, and found that he could increase the attractive power of a magnet by placing iron caps over its ends. Most significant of all he studied a spherical lodestone and concluded that the earth behaved as a huge magnet. This explained not only why a compass pointed north but also the declination and inclination of the needle. Unfortunately he identified the magnetic pole with the geographic pole and was unable therefore to give an adequate explanation of declination. In this work also, Gilbert posed the existence of a magnetic *field* and made the first clear distinction between magnetism and electricity.

Chemistry. Though the Renaissance witnessed an increase in chemical techniques and apparatus as well as the preparation of new compounds, the science of chemistry was still shackled by alchemical ideas. Despite the application of chemistry to medicine (iatrochemistry), which Paracelsus championed, and which certainly was a notable advance, Paracelsus not only adhered to the ideas of the four elements, four qualities, and four humors but also popularized the concept of the "three principles" (Sulfur, Mercury, and Salt) that were the embodiment of certain properties in various forms of matter. What was perhaps the most significant textbook of chemistry during this period still bore the title *Alchemia* (1597). The author, Libavius (Andreas Liban, *c.* 1540 to 1616), defended the traditional alchemical thesis of the possibility of the transmutation of base metals into gold. What advances there were during this period were in chemistry as a practical art; little was done to advance theoretical chemistry, and Lavoisier was still almost two centuries away.

Biology. Considerable interest in biological sciences developed in the 16th century, stimulated by a return to careful examination of both flora and fauna. In botany this was the period of the herbals, books giving careful descriptions and precise illustrations of plants with medicinal properties, real or supposed. In succeeding publications the authors included additional plants, even though they possessed no known medicinal value, and then initiated attempts at the classification of the specimens to remove some of the confusion resulting from unorganized presentation of species.

Most of the advances in animal biology developed in the medical schools, where the emphasis was on the exact description of human anatomy. In this premicroscope period, the main interest was in gross structure, but the careful dissections by men like Vesalius made possible the great discoveries of Harvey and Malpighi.

Botany. This discussion must begin with the "German fathers of botany." As naturalists began to realize the need for illustrations made directly from nature, they found at hand both artists and woodcut makers capable of transferring information to the printed page. Many of the drawings were both accurate and beautiful, and the herbals that this kind of collaboration produced are among the finest books of the period.

The first herbal was the work of Otto Brunfels of Mainz (d. 1534), with drawings by Hans Weiditz. Brunfels accompanied the illustrations of German plants with descriptions of plants of the Near East given by Dioscorides. Many of the resulting discrepancies were removed in the work of Jerome Bock (Tragus 1498 to 1544), where the plants were actually described from nature. The best herbal before 1550, however, was the *De historia stirpium* (1542) of Leonhard Fuchs (1501 to 1566), in which more than 500 plants were accurately described and illustrated. These and other Germans reawakened interest in botany, but with the growing curiosity about the plants and animals found in newly discovered lands, men of other countries produced popular works. Outstanding among these was the work of the Italian P. A. Mottiali (1500 to 1577), the various editions of which sold more than 30,000 copies. As herbals continued to appear, each was a bit better than its predecessors in scope, in completeness, in description, and in the quality of the illustrations. Three Flemings deserve mention in this connection: Dodonaeus (Rembert Dodoens, 1516 to 1585), Clusius (Charles de l'Écluse, 1526 to 1609), and Lobelius (Matthias de Lobel, 1538 to 1616). The last-named is particularly important since in his work (1570 to 1571) is found one of the first attempts at scientific classification of plants. Lobelius based his classification on characteristics of leaves and was thus able to indicate the distinction between dicotyledons and monocotyledons. The botanical interest of the period is indicated also by the foundation of numerous botanical gardens and the initiation of the practice of collecting dried plant specimens into herbaria.

Physiology. Two outstanding works of the Renaissance were the natural histories of Conrad Gesner (1516 to 1565) and Ulisse Aldrovandi. They were monumental works, and each was completed after the death of the originator. Gesner's *Historia animalium* (1551 to 1587) appeared in five folio volumes; Aldrovandi's (1599 to 1668) ran to 13 volumes, only four of which appeared during his lifetime. Much of the material in these books was legendary, but they contained accurate descriptions and drawings of many fish, birds, and animals, of both the Old and New World.

Anatomy and Medicine. Throughout history the dissection of human bodies was periodically forbidden,

and always rare. Though never completely abandoned, dissections were seldom performed on the human corpse because of a superstitious fear of the dead or out of respect for the body precisely as human. Galen had dissected monkeys, and the medieval anatomical school at Salerno had dissected pigs—not because they were interested in either monkeys or pigs but in order to learn about the human body, which was similar. Many professors of anatomy considered themselves above the mundane task of dissection, preferring to gain their knowledge from books (Galen or Avicenna); and when experience contradicted the book, it must have been due to some deformity in the body under examination. The two great anatomists of this period were Leonardo da Vinci and the Fleming Andreas Vesalius, who worked at Padua. The bodies dissected were often those of executed criminals, and executions of several men condemned at the same time were often spaced to satisfy the needs of the medical school.

Vesalius. The *De humani corporis fabrica* of Vesalius appeared in 1543, the same year as the publication of the *De revolutionibus* of Copernicus. The *Fabrica* is a landmark in scientific history; here for the first time were accurate descriptions of the human body accompanied by admirable woodcuts to illustrate the text. Vesalius was a skilled dissector, and while he was not able to break away from the authority of Galen completely, his work struck the spark that kindled the anatomical interest, and led to the discoveries, of the next century.

Leonardo da Vinci. The man who perhaps best epitomizes the good qualities of the Renaissance is the Florentine Leonardo da Vinci. Artist, humanist, philosopher, scientist—Leonardo was all these and more; but his importance in the history of science is not what it should have been, for he published nothing. Therefore his influence was limited to the few who might have seen his notebooks. But this cannot diminish his personal glory, even as a scientist. His drawings of parts of the body, made during dissections he performed himself, are still among the best available. He also left behind sketches of animals, plants, rocks, and shells. He gave the first rational explanation of fossils. His fertile mind was constantly concocting new ideas, many that simply failed to mature, for he too soon turned his attention to something else. In him art and science met as perhaps they never have or never will again.

Others. Medicine had consisted of the study of botany and anatomy until Paracelsus added chemistry to these and asserted that the aim of alchemy was not to make gold but to prepare medicines. He introduced chemicals of nonvegetable origin into the treatment of disease. While not the founder of iatrochemistry, he was its chief exponent. There is much of what is superstitious combined with what is good in Paracelsus. If he was not a great discoverer, he was a tireless experimenter and an exciting person who could not be ignored. He shook the very foundations of Galenic medicine and helped establish a climate favorable to future discoveries. The discovery by SERVETUS of the lesser or pulmonary circulation was another blow to the Galenic medicine since it did away finally with the invisible pores in the septum of the heart. Two more doctors deserve mention: Jean Fernel (1497 to 1558) and Ambroise Paré; the first, the founder of physiology; the second, of a new surgery. Fernel's *Opera* went through 34 editions before 1681. His physiology was the study of the body's normal functioning, and he divided his texts into circulation, respiration, digestion, muscular function, etc. He made no great discovery—many of these had to await the microscope, but he was a careful observer and a good physician who stimulated further research. Paré was a military surgeon who promoted the humane treatment of gunshot wounds, and his worth was such that he was surgeon to three kings.

Conclusion. This brief survey has tried only to indicate a few trends and to place some of the great Renaissance scientists in their historical context. The bibliography cites only general works; for material on particular scientists, see the bibliographies at the end of their respective biographies.

See Also: BIOLOGY I (HISTORY OF).

Bibliography: G. A. L. SARTON, *Six Wings: Men of Science in the Renaissance* (Bloomington, Indiana 1957); *The Appreciation of Ancient and Medieval Science during the Renaissance* (Philadelphia 1955). W. P. D. WIGHTMAN, *Science and the Renaissance* (Toronto 1962). A. R. HALL, *The Scientific Revolution, 1500–1800* (Boston 1954). A. C. CROMBIE, *Medieval and Early Modern Science,* 2 v. (2d ed. Cambridge, Massachusetts 1961); ed., *Scientific Change* (New York 1963). W. C. DAMPIER, *A History of Science* (4th ed. New York 1949). H. BUTTERFIELD, *The Origins of Modern Science, 1300–1800* (New York 1960).

[N. SCHEEL]

SCIENCES, CLASSIFICATION OF

SCIENCE (*scientia*) is an analogical term legitimately but diversely applicable to many differing disciplines in a set in which demonstrated knowledge ranks as prime analogate (*see* DEMONSTRATION). This article considers the division of science, understood in this analogously general sense, into its types. There are as many legitimate divisions as there are formally diverse relevant principles of differentiation. To illustrate the various possibilities, several different ways in which the sciences can be classified are first considered. Then the different ways in which the sciences have been classified by certain key figures in the history of thought are sketched, with emphasis upon the classification proposed by St. Thomas Aquinas.

Principles of Differentiation

Sciences can be distinguished on the basis of relevant differences in OBJECT (i.e., subject matter), END (i.e., intention or purpose), or method. We say "relevant" because there are some differences that touch sciences only accidentally, and these suggest divisions that are noetically trivial at best, e.g., the intention of the scientist as a man (*finis scientis*) as contrasted with the intention of the science as such (*finis scientiae*).

Difference in Object. LOGIC can be distinguished from the other sciences on the basis of a difference in subject matter. Logic studies second intentions, the non-real relationships that accrue to things *as known* and that set the demands for discursive procedures. The other sciences confront the things themselves. Only the object of logic is second intentional; the object of every other science is first intentional; and logic can be seen to differ from these other sciences on the basis of a difference in object. It will be seen later that the other sciences can themselves be distinguished one from another on the basis of a further difference in object.

Difference in End. Some sciences in themselves intend nothing beyond truth in knowledge; others intend some activity beyond knowing. The former are said to be theoretical or speculative sciences, while the latter are practical (*see* COGNITION SPECULATIVE-PRACTICAL). This is a distinction based upon a difference in end. METAPHYSICS consists in a knowledge of being, whereas medicine consists in a knowledge of the curable body. Being is worth knowing about only for the sake of the very knowledge of being. The end of metaphysics is truth about being: it is a speculative discipline. On the other hand, the curable body as curable is worth knowing about not primarily for the knowledge of the curable but for the curing of the curable. The end of medicine is action: it is a practical discipline.

Difference in Method. Sciences can also be distinguished by differences in method. For example, one type of science, namely, sacred theology, resolves its conclusions into divinely revealed truths. The ultimate criterion according to which a proposition in sacred theology is to be judged is the authority of God revealing. No other science depends for its ultimate illumination upon the word of any authority. The others depend upon the natural light of reason; they resolve their conclusions into premises seen by the scientist himself to be true. A difference in method can be seen to distinguish a science such as Euclidean geometry from a science such as contemporary physics. The geometer attempts to establish theorems by resolving them ultimately into self-evident premises. If he is successful, his theorems are certainly seen to be necessarily true. The method of geometry is strictly demonstrative. The physicist, on the other hand, attempts to "verify" his hypotheses by showing that true conclusions (observed to be true in experiments suggested by the hypotheses) follow from them. Since a true conclusion *can* come from a false antecedent, the physicist can never ascertain the truth of his hypotheses. The best he can do, as his hypotheses are seen repeatedly to lead to true consequents, is to establish their probability. His method is dialectical, not demonstrative.

Interrelations. Though some sciences have been distinguished on the basis of a difference in object, others on the basis of a difference in end, and still others on the basis of a difference in method, it would be a mistake to suppose that there can be but one type of difference in force at any one time. Speculative sciences intend truth in function of an object that is nonoperable; and practical sciences intend action in function of an object that is operable. Further, the method of the speculative sciences, in virtue of their object and end, is characteristically resolutive, whereas the method of the practical sciences, in virtue of their object and end, is characteristically compositive. However, it would also be a mistake to suppose that object, end, and method are always identically proportioned to one another. For example, though an operable is worth knowing about primarily so that it can be produced (and, under this formality, the end of the science in question is action and its method is compositive), an operable can be approached simply for the knowledge it affords (and then the end of the science is truth and its method is resolutive). Science of an operable with action as its end that is achieved in a compositive mode is wholly practical, while science of an operable with truth as its end that is achieved in a resolutive mode is partly practical and partly speculative.

Classifications in the History of Thought

The key figures in the history of thought who have proposed distinctive classifications of the sciences include Aristotle, Boethius, St. Thomas Aquinas, and Christian Wolff; more recent developments include the classifications proposed by the positivists and contemporary Thomists.

Aristotle. Aristotle divides the sciences into the theoretical, the practical, and the productive. The theoretical is knowledge for the sake of knowledge; the practical, for the sake of conduct; and the productive, for the sake of useful or beautiful artifacts. The theoretical sciences, which are more excellent than the others, are further divided into physics (whose object is inseparable but not immovable), mathematics (whose object is immovable but not separate), and theology, i.e., first philosophy or metaphysics (whose object is separate and immovable).

The object of mathematics is known by way of an abstraction that consists in a subtraction of matter rendering the now separated form of quantity present to the mind of the mathematician. The object of physics, on the other hand, is known by way of an addition, for the forms of natural things must be known *with* matter if they are to stand present to the mind of the physicist as subject to motion. The object of first philosophy, which is being *qua* being, is known neither as conditioned by a subtraction nor with an addition. Logic is not classified with the sciences but is spoken of as a discipline demanded of any cultured mind prior to any serious approach to the sciences.

Boethius. BOETHIUS divides science into two kinds: theoretical, which is knowledge for its own sake, and practical, which is knowledge ordered to action. Though he classifies theoretical sciences differently on different occasions, in the *De Trinitate* he follows the lead of Aristotle, listing them as natural science, mathematics, and theology. These three are distinguished by differences in their objects, depending upon whether these are forms more or less separated from matter.

Thomas Aquinas. St. THOMAS AQUINAS gives his most significant treatment on the classification of the sciences in questions 5 and 6 of his commentary on the *De Trinitate* of Boethius. Three of the most significant articles in these questions are articles 1 and 3 of question 5 and article 1 of question 6. In these articles St. Thomas distinguishes between sciences on the basis of differences in object, end, and method. The following are brief summaries.

In Boeth. de Trin. 5.1. The practical sciences have operables as objects and operation as end, while the speculative sciences have nonoperables as object and knowledge of these as end. The speculative sciences are in turn distinguished one from another by differences in their objects precisely in reference to what makes them objects of scientific speculation. An object is speculable insofar as it is immaterial, for the INTELLECT is an immaterial power; and it is scientific insofar as it is immobile, for science is of the necessary. Objects of speculative science are thus differently objects, and so objects of different sciences, insofar as they are differently related to matter and motion. One object of speculation depends on matter both to be and to be known: this is the object of physics or natural science. Another depends on matter to be but not to be known: the object of mathematics. Still another depends on matter neither to be nor to be known: the object of metaphysics. Logic is not included under speculative science as a principal part but remains outside these sciences as a tool for them.

In Boeth. de Trin. 5.3. The intellect can consider one thing without considering another (even though the first cannot exist without the other) so long as the meaning of the first does not depend on the other. This is a way of abstracting spoken of strictly as ABSTRACTION (*abstractio, proprie loquendo*). The intellect can think one thing to be without another so long as the first does not depend upon the other for its existence. This is a way of abstracting spoken of strictly as separation (*separatio, proprie loquendo*). The objects of natural science or physics and mathematics are known by an abstraction: for physics, an abstraction of the whole essence of the natural thing from its nonessential characteristics (*abstractio totius*); for mathematics, an abstraction of the form of quantity from sensible matter (*abstractio formae*). The object of metaphysics is known by a separation of being from all matter (*separatio*).

In Boeth. de Trin. 6.1. It is especially characteristic of natural science or physics to proceed according to the mode of reason (*rationabiliter*), of mathematics to proceed according to the mode of learning (*disciplinabiliter*), and of metaphysics to proceed according to the mode of intellect (*intellectualiter*). The mode of reason involves moving from things more knowable to man but less knowable in themselves, and from one thing to another thing. The mode of learning is one that most easily assures certainty in its conclusions. The mode of intellect involves a unified vision of all things in the light of the most universal of principles.

Other Teaching on Abstraction. Elsewhere Aquinas adds to what is found in these articles (*In 1 phys.* 1.1–3; *In 3 anim.* 8.707–717; *Summa theologiae* 1a, 85.1 ad 2). Abstraction of the natural species (*abstractio totius* of 5.3) is described as an abstraction from individual sensible matter but not from common sensible matter. The abstraction of the mathematical species (the *abstractio formae* of 5.3) is described as an abstraction from all sensible matter and from individual intelligible matter but not from common intelligible matter. The abstraction of such things as being (the *separatio* of 5.3) is explained as an abstraction from all matter.

These three abstractions (which can be correlated with the three degrees of formal abstraction of CAJETAN and JOHN OF ST. THOMAS, namely, with physical, mathematical, and metaphysical abstraction) yield formally different scientific objects that, precisely as different, constitute diverse genera of speculative science. Each genus of speculative science is, at least theoretically, open to specific differentiation. For example, mathematics is a genus of science that divides specifically into arithmetic and geometry. John of St. Thomas shows that arithmetic and geometry are in the same genus of science insofar as they share, apropos of abstraction, the same *terminus a quo*. The object of each abstracts from all sensible matter and from individual intelligible matter. Yet they differ in the *terminus ad quem* of the abstraction appropriate to each. Discrete quantity, which is the object of arithmetic, is known without reference to position. It is thus attained on a higher level of abstraction than is continuous quantity, the object of geometry, which, including a reference to position, is less immaterial than discrete quantity.

Unity and Diversification. St. Thomas, following Aristotle, teaches that the unity of a given science depends on the unity of its characteristic subject and that the diversification of different sciences depends upon a diversification in the principles from which they proceed. Effectively this reduces to the same thing, for a subject is subject in a given science in virtue of the peculiar mode of its abstraction from matter, and the middle term of any scientific demonstration (which is *the* principle of demonstration) is a principle in a given science precisely insofar as it represents, as a DEFINITION, a mode of defining involving a peculiar degree of abstraction from matter.

Relationships between Sciences. In addition to showing how sciences are one in themselves and yet different from other sciences, St. Thomas shows how sciences, though different, can be interrelated. For example, a given science can be different from another and yet be included under it as subalternated to it. This is the case when one (higher and subalternating) science supplies the reason for the fact established in another (lower and subalternated) science. In natural philosophy, for example, reasons are given for things that are seen to be facts in medicine, and in arithmetic reasons are given for things that are seen to be facts in music. St. Thomas also recognizes the existence of sciences that are noetically mixed, that is, sciences that are formally mathematical and materially physical. These sciences, e.g., astronomy, are mathematical in their mode of demonstrating, but the subjects investigated in them are physical. Contemporary physics, which is spoken of by many as *the* science, is an example of one of these mixed sciences; much of its content is aptly described as mathematical physics.

Wolff. Christian WOLFF proposed a classification of the sciences considerably different from that of St. Thomas. Yet his classification has made its influence felt on many supposedly Thomistic manuals in philosophy. Wolff distinguishes between logic, which comes before all the other disciplines, and philosophy proper. Philosophy is subdivided into the speculative and the practical. Practical philosophy includes ethics, economics, and politics, while speculative philosophy is identified with metaphysics. Metaphysics, in turn, includes ONTOLOGY, rational psychology, COSMOLOGY, and THEODICY. Ontology is general metaphysics, while the latter three represent different types of special metaphysics.

Positivists. The classification of Wolff, who is a rationalist, can be contrasted with that of the positivists, whose influence is significant in contemporary philosophy. Auguste COMTE, the founder of POSITIVISM, rejected all sciences except the positive sciences, listing the six major positive sciences, in a hierarchical order going from the most abstract and independent to the most concrete and dependent, as mathematics, astronomy, physics, chemistry, biology, and sociology. Philosophy at best is a generalized theory of the several positive sciences.

Recent positivism is distinguished from the earlier positivism by reason of the emphasis more lately placed upon the logical analysis of language (*see* LOGICAL POSITIVISM). Contemporary logical positivists of the school of linguistic analysis set philosophy off against science. The aim of science is the discovery and use of laws. The aim of philosophy is simply the elucidation of concepts. Science is divided into logic (which includes pure mathematics), wherein resolution is finally into analytic statements or pure tautologies, and empirical science, wherein resolution is finally into experience. The empirical sciences include physics, chemistry, biology, and even ethics and aesthetics. Philosophy is essentially a method of elucidation, involving for the most part the analysis of the concepts, methods, and presuppositions of the sciences. It includes, in metalogic, the analysis of logical concepts; in the philosophy of science, the analysis of concepts common to all the sciences; and in the philosophy of physics, or of chemistry, etc., the analysis of concepts appropriate to the science in question. Metaphysics, as thought to deal with synthetic a priori statements, is rejected as a meaningless enterprise.

Recent Thomists. The Louvain school has been a major influence in scholastic philosophy in the 20th century, and the classification of the sciences of Cardinal D. MERCIER has made its mark on the teaching of philosophy, especially in Catholic schools. Mercier distinguishes between the particular sciences of observation (physics, chemistry, biology, and the like), philosophy, and mathematics. Philosophy is further divided into the speculative and the practical. Speculative philosophy is subdivided into general physics (which includes cosmology, rational psychology, natural theology, and even epistemology) and general metaphysics or ontology. Practical philosophy includes logic, moral philosophy, and aesthetics. In general the order of learning requires that the particular sciences come first, to be followed by general physics, which is the philosophical complement of these sciences. This is followed by mathematics, then ontology, and finally logic.

This manner of dividing and arranging the sciences owes something to Aquinas, but it represents a revision of St. Thomas's scheme in the face of contemporary demands. Other Thomists of this century, though intent upon keeping philosophically up-to-date, see no need for revising St. Thomas's scheme of the sciences though they may build from it. This is true of the Laval school (C. De Koninck), the River Forest school (Albertus Magnus Lyceum), and the Maritain school—though these schools do differ in their explanation of the way in which the philosophy of nature is related to the contemporary physical sciences (*see* PHILOSOPHY AND SCIENCE; SCHOLASTICISM, 3).

Bibliography: THOMAS AQUINAS, *The Division and Methods of the Sciences,* q. 5–6 of *Commentary on the ''De Trinitate'' of Boethius,* ed. and tr. A. MAURER (Toronto 1953). JOHN OF ST. THOMAS, *The Material Logic,* tr. Y. R. SIMON et al. (Chicago 1955). V. E. SMITH, *The General Science of Nature* (Milwaukee 1958). F. G. CONNOLLY, *Science versus Philosophy* (New York 1957). C. DE KONINCK, ''Abstraction from Matter,'' *Laval Théologique et Philosophique* 13 (1957) 133–96; 16 (1960) 53–69, 169–88. E. D. SIMMONS, ''The Thomistic Doctrine of the Three Degrees of Formal Abstraction,'' *The Thomist* 22 (1959) 37–67. W. H. KANE, ''Abstraction and the Distinction of the Sciences,'' *The Thomist* 17 (1954) 43–68. J. MARITAIN, *The Degrees of Knowledge,* tr. G. B. PHELAN et al. (New York 1959); *Philosophy of Nature,* tr. I. C. BYRNE (New York 1951).

[E. D. SIMMONS]

SCIENTIA MEDIA

According to Molinists, *scientia media,* middle knowledge, is that knowledge by which God, prior to any absolute decree, but not without the supposition that He would decree, infallibly perceives free FUTURIBLE acts of creatures. He knows what a man would do in any circumstances if He would decree to concur in them, before He makes any absolute decree establishing the situation.

Free futuribles are known by God prior to any absolute decree existing in Him; for, being only conditional existents, they presuppose only conditionally existing causes, a subjectively conditional decree in God, and conditionally existing human cooperation.

God's knowledge of futuribles had long been recognized, but the name *scientia media* applied to it first occurs explicitly in theological literature of the 16th century. Peter da FONSECA (1528–99) in his commentaries on the *Metaphysics* of Aristotle speaks of *scientia mista.* Independent of Fonseca, who was never his teacher, Luis de MOLINA made middle knowledge famous in his solution of problems connected with human freedom, on the one hand, and, on the other, God's foreknowledge and efficacious GRACE, proposed in his *Concordia* (1588).

Middle knowledge gets its name because it partakes partly of the nature of two extreme kinds of divine knowledge, while partly differing from them.

There is God's natural or necessary knowledge (called *mere naturalis* by Molina), prior to every decree, and inconceivable as absent from God (His knowledge of Himself); there is also His free, contingent knowledge (which Molina called *mere libera*), presupposing an absolute decree, and conceivable as absent from God (His knowledge of human history). Because it is prior to every absolute decree, between these two is middle knowledge. It is like God's natural knowledge, being prior to any absolute decree, but unlike it, in being conceivably absent from God; it concerns contingent being. It is also like God's free knowledge, since both can be absent from God; but unlike it, because God's free knowledge presupposes an absolute decree that something be. Molina speaks of middle knowledge only in this sense.

There is also God's knowledge of simple intelligence, which represents things, but not as existing (possibles), and His knowledge of vision, which represents things as absolutely existing. Because its object is the free futurible, between these two is middle knowledge. It is like the former, since neither represents an object as absolutely existing, but unlike it, because knowledge of a futurible represents a conditionally existing thing. Also it is like knowledge of vision, since neither represents its object as merely possible; but unlike it, for vision represents its object as absolutely, not conditionally, existing.

This article has dealt with God's direct middle knowledge, by which He knows, prior to any absolute decree, what a free creature would do in any contingency. There is also God's reflex middle knowledge, by which He knows what He Himself would do in any circumstances. Such circumstances may depend upon God alone: "if I would create another universe, I would create so many angels"—God as it were reflects upon His own conditional action, "if I would create"; or circumstances may depend upon God and a creature: "if I would see Adam obeying, I would still send Christ"—here God reflects upon an object of His own direct middle knowledge, namely Adam obeying.

Direct middle knowledge is held by all Molinists, but not all admit reflex middle knowledge. Molinists also hold God's middle knowledge, together with that of simple intelligence, to be the cause of things only as directive of divine action.

See Also: GRACE, CONTROVERSIES ON; MOLINISM; FREE WILL AND GRACE; OMNISCIENCE; BÁÑEZ AND BAÑEZIANISM.

Bibliography: E. VANSTEENBERGHE, *Dictionnaire de théologie catholique,* ed. A. VACANT, 15 v. (Paris 1903–50; Tables générales 1951–) 10.2:2094–2187. A. MICHEL, *ibid.* 14.2:1598–1620. "Scientia Media," *Lexikon für Theologie und Kirche,* ed. J. HOFER and K. RAHNER, 10 v. (2d, new ed. Freiburg 1957–65); v. 9. A. WHITACRE, J. HASTINGS, ed., *Encyclopedia of Religion & Ethics,* 13 v. (Edinburgh 1908–27) 8:774–777. T. DE DIEGO DÍEZ, *Theologia Naturalis* (Santander 1955). J. HELLÍN, *Theologia Naturalis: Tractatus Metaphysicus* (Madrid 1950). R. MARTÍNEZ DEL CAMPO, *Theologia Naturalis* (Mexico City 1943). S. GONZÁLEZ and I. SAGÜÉS, *Sacrae theologiae summa,* ed. Fathers of the Society of Jesus, Professors of the Theological Faculties in Spain, 4 v. (Madrid 1962) 3.3:264–328.

[F. L. SHEERIN]

SCIENTISM

Scientism is a system of thought or attitude of mind holding that science constitutes the only valid knowledge and is alone capable of solving all human problems. Science is here understood in the sense of a systematized body of knowledge obtained from empirical procedures, entailing objectivity in the measurement of phenomena and the reduction of particular laws to a small number of principles. Observation of phenomena, description, classification, explanation, and verification are the techniques it employs. Scientism asserts that truth can be arrived at solely through such techniques, and hence regards philosophy and religion as purely subjective in character.

Contemporary scientism is the outgrowth of the rapidity of developments in the physical sciences, mathematics, and technology. Philosophically, its roots lie in the mathematicism of R. DESCARTES; in the empiricism of J. LOCKE, D. HUME, and J. S. MILL; in the physicalism of I. KANT; and in 19th-century POSITIVISM and pragmatism. Throughout the history of thought it has frequently manifested itself as MATERIALISM. Its chief proponents in the 1960s are the schools of LOGICAL POSITIVISM and scientific EMPIRICISM—the latter seeking to unify all sciences into a science of sciences through the analysis of language.

Scientism, like much of science itself, is wedded to formalism and axiomatic method, conceptualization through signs, univocity of concepts, and the transcendence of mind over reality. Such an approach to reality results in knowledge of a purely univocal nature. Yet man's knowledge is not restricted to univocal knowledge alone. Analogical concepts acquired through the natural light of reason are valid, as is the knowledge of God, man, and the world acquired through the supernatural light of faith. Moreover, love, affectivity, beauty, personality, and a host of other realities are by their very nature inaccessible to empirical methods.

Science, philosophy, and theology can lay equal claim to validity when dealing with their own subject matter and according to their proper methods and principles. Scientism, by restricting valid knowledge to the level of science, overgeneralizes the scientific method and overrestricts reality to the confines of matter alone.

See Also: LOGICISM; METAPHYSICS, VALIDITY OF.

Bibliography: J. ABELE, *Christianity and Science,* tr. R. F. TREVETT (New York 1961) 113–121. J. C. MONSMA, ed., *Science and Religion* (New York 1962). E. Q. FRANZ, "Philosophy and the Unity of Knowledge," *American Catholic Philosophical Association. Proceedings of the Annual Meeting* 27 (1953) 16–31. C. E. M. JOAD, *A Critique of Logical Positivism* (Chicago 1950).

[E. Q. FRANZ]

SCIENTOLOGY

A quasi-scientific and religious movement founded by L. Ron Hubbard, an American science fiction author. Hubbard's book, *Dianetics: The Modern Science of Mental Health* (New York 1950), became an international best seller and led, in 1952, to the incorporation of an international organization which later evolved into Scientology. Dianetics initially claimed to be "a science of mental health," but with the creation of the Founding Church of Scientology (offices in Wash., D.C., and in New York, N.Y.) in 1955, the organization took a religious turn. The church has followers in English speaking countries throughout the world, as well as in Denmark, France, and Sweden, and has claimed up to several million adherents.

Although formal religious services play no part in the activities of the organization, Scientology does possess a highly structured system of beliefs and identifies itself as a church. It accepts a doctrine of reincarnation that claims the human being is a *thetan,* a preexistent spiritual being. In this life human beings possess a body and mind that enable them to travel through the physical universe, called MEST (matter, energy, space, time). Mental functioning is guided by the quest for survival, the fundamental drive of human existence, which divides the mind into "analytic," or conscious, and "reactive," or subconscious functions. Every experience in one's life is said to be recorded as a mental image. Painful experiences, called "engrams," are not immediately available to the analytic mind, but are recorded in the reactive. They may be exceedingly difficult to detect, some tracing their origins back to prenatal injuries in the womb. When stimulated later, Scientology claims, they may lead to irrational behavior.

Therapy proceeds with the help of an "E-meter," similar to a skin galvanometer or lie detector, which identifies emotionally charged words. An "auditor" reviews one's past to help reduce the power of engrams or to convert them into conscious memories. Through long discipline in this procedure, a novice or "preclear" becomes a "clear" and is able to become an auditor to others or a minister of the church.

The church has been criticized for its scientific and religious claims, and for the financial demands it makes on its members. Psychotherapists deny that the unconscious mind can be neutralized by the procedures Hubbard proposed. Although the literature of Scientology and E-meters now carry medical disclaimers, the church has been plagued from its inception by lawsuits filed both by various governments and by disaffected members.

For its part, the church has filed scores of lawsuits against governmental agencies, asserting that it has been a victim of religious persecution. When L. Ron Hubbard died Jan. 28, 1986, at the age of 74, the church was still under investigation by the U.S. Internal Revenue Service. The church suffered its most serious blow in 1984 when the IRS successfully argued that the church's tax-exeempt status should be revoked.

Bibliography: L. R. HUBBARD, *Dianetics: The Modern Science of Mental Health* (Los Angeles 1968); *The Problems of Work: How to Solve Them and Succeed* (Los Angeles 1983). P. ROWLEY, *New Gods in America* (New York 1971).

[E. J. FURTON/EDS.]

SCIOPPIUS, KASPAR

Philologist, polemicist, and diplomat; b. Neumarkt (Upper Palatinate), May 27, 1576; d. Padua, Italy, Nov. 19, 1649. After studies in philology in Heidelberg, Altdorf, and Ingolstadt, Scioppius (Schoppe) published the first of his many scientific works, *Verisimilium libri quatuor* (1595), suggesting improvements in the writings of Plautus, Symmachus, and Cornelius Nepos. He became a convert to Catholicism in 1598, writing about it in *De migratione sua ad Catholicos* (1599). He moved to Rome, where he displayed his antagonism to Protestantism by a prodigious writing campaign that included *Pro auctoritate ecclesiae* (1598) and *De variis fidei controversiis* (1600). His uncompromising Catholicism won favor and admiration from the popes, Prince Ferdinand, and the Dukes Wilhelm and Maximilian of Bavaria. His successful polemics made him the protagonist for the Catholic cause during the THIRTY YEARS' WAR (1618–48). In the *Classicum belli sacri* (1619) he challenged the use of arms against heretics. Though he had always showed reserve toward the Jesuits with the *Actio perduellionis in Jesuitas* (1632) he opened a sharp attack that startled his patrons and friends. His antagonism increased and he wrote 17 polemics against the Jesuits, including *Flagellum Jesuiticum* (1632), *Arcana Societatis Jesu* (1635), and *De strategematis et sophismatis politicis Societatis Jesu* (1641). He died in solitude and hostility to the world.

Bibliography: H. KOWALLEK, ''Über G. Scioppius,'' *Forschungen zur deutschen Geschichte* 11 (1871) 403–483, full bibliog. M. RITTER, *Deutsche Geschichte im Zeitalter der Gegenreformation . . .*, 3 v. (Stuttgart 1889–1908) 3:435ff. R. HOCHE, *Allgemeine deutsche Biographie* 33:479–484. R. BÄUMER, *Lexikon für Theologie und Kirche,* ed. J. HOFER and K. RAHNER, 10 v. (2d, new ed. Freiburg 1957–65) 9:552. J. MERCIER, *Dictionnaire de théologie catholique,* ed. A. VACANT, 15 v. (Paris 1903–50; Tables générales 1951–) 14.2:1571–74.

[J. KRASENBRINK]

SCOFIELD, CYRUS INGERSON

Author of *The Scofield Reference Bible* and influential disseminator of dispensational theology in America; b. Aug. 19, 1843, Michigan; d. July 24, 1921, Long Island, N.Y. Scofield's early career was plagued by legal problems and scandals. Converted in 1879, he was greatly influenced by a prominent dispensationalist pastor in St. Louis, James H. Brookes. In 1882 Scofield moved to Dallas and became pastor of the First Congregational Church. In 1909 he published his famous reference Bible. Using the King James Version as its translation, *The Scofield Reference Bible* interprets the biblical text through the lens of dispensational theology. The centerpiece of the reference Bible is the division of all history into seven dispensations or time periods from creation to the millennium. Each dispensation represents a specific form of revelation given by God to humanity with a corresponding covenant: Scofield's seven dispensations are: Innocence (Edenic Covenant), Moral Responsibility (Adamic Covenant), Human Government (Noahic Covenant), Promise (Abrahamic Covenant), Law (Sinaitic Covenant), the Church (Covenant of Grace), and the Millennium (Christ's 1,000 year reign on Earth). Its attractive format, copious notes, and ample cross-referencing made *The Scofield Reference Bible* an immediate success. Revised once by Scofield himself in 1917 and several times since by other dispensationalists, *The Scofield Reference Bible* continues to be a best-seller among fundamentalists and dispensationalists in America.

Bibliography: J. M. CANFIELD, *The Incredible Scofield and His Book* (Vallecito, Calif. 1988). C. G. TRUMBULL, *The Life Story of C. I. Scofield* (New York 1920).

[W. T. STANCIL]

SCOTISM

One of the major movements in scholastic thought, Scotism consists in the assimilation, application, and development of the basic doctrines of John DUNS SCOTUS in the centuries following his death. Although fostered principally by Franciscan philosophers and theologians, Scotism exercised considerable influence beyond the order, particularly on the secular clergy and on philosophers outside the Catholic Church.

As a doctrine, Scotism is characterized by fundamental doctrines derived from the Subtle Doctor. Foremost among these is the univocity of the metaphysical concept of being that is the proper object of the human intellect. In terms of this abstract univocal concept, God and creatures are two distinct modes of being: Infinite and finite. As the metaphysical concept of being is the proper object of the mind, metaphysics is the highest and most connatural study for mankind. In natural theology, emphasis is placed on the supremacy of God's freedom and love, while in moral philosophy, man's ultimate happiness and freedom are found in love of God above all things. In psychology, Scotism recognizes only a formal distinction *a parte rei* between the soul and its faculties and between the faculties themselves. In natural philosophy, Scotism recognizes a plurality of formal perfections, or *formalitates,* and *haecceitas* as the principle of individuation.

Scotism also reinterprets the Aristotelian doctrine of matter and form, denying the pure potentiality of primary matter. In Christology, Scotists assign God's love for man as the primary motive of the Incarnation and stress the need for man to respond to Christ's redemptive suffering through love of Him. In Scotism, human natural actions are meritorious of eternal life *de congruo* because of God's infinite love in creating man and in predestining him to eternal happiness from all eternity. Most notable in the history of Scotism is the doctrine of Mary's IMMACULATE CONCEPTION and her intimate role in the economy of salvation.

As a movement, Scotism can be divided into four unequal periods of development: (1) early Scotism, from the death of Duns Scotus to about 1500; (2) resurgent Scotism, from 1500 to the General Chapter of Toledo in 1633; (3) universal Scotism in the Franciscan Order, from 1633 to the decline of SCHOLASTICISM and of religious life generally in the second half of the eighteenth century; and (4) the revival of Scotistic studies in the twentieth century.

Early Scotism. During his own lifetime, Duns Scotus attempted to synthesize the traditional AUGUSTINIANISM of the Franciscan school with ARISTOTELIANISM. St.

THOMAS AQUINAS had already created a new Aristotelianism that was espoused by the Dominicans, even though some of the basic theses, such as the unicity of substantial form, individuation by matter, and the pure potentiality of primary matter, had been condemned in Oxford and Paris in 1277 (*see* THOMISM; SCHOLASTICISM, 1). Despite the efforts of WILLIAM DE LA MARE and the Franciscan General Chapter of Strasbourg (1283) to safeguard the traditional Augustinianism of St. BONAVENTURE through the *Correctorium fratris Thomae,* the Franciscans had no doctrinal synthesis on par with Thomism. Duns Scotus created such a synthesis in his commentaries on the *Sentences.* The way was prepared, not only by the older tradition of Bonaventure, but by the more proximate efforts of JOHN PECKHAM, ROGER MARSTON, RICHARD OF MIDDLETON, VITAL DU FOUR, GONSALVUS HISPANUS, and WILLIAM OF WARE. The impact of Scotus's subtle arguments was considerable in Oxford and Paris. THOMAS OF WILTON, a junior contemporary of Scotus, gave a very vivid account of the theological disputations in the hall (*aula*) at Oxford involving "Doctor Scotus," bachelors in theology, and those who *scotizant,* that is, followed Scotus in method and doctrine (Manuscript Vat. Borgh. 36, fol. 85vb).

Disciples. Although Duns Scotus was only 42 years old when he died and left few finished works, his teachings stimulated a strong following among the new generation in Oxford and Paris. In Oxford, WILLIAM OF ALNWICK and ROBERT COWTON showed great sympathy for Scotist doctrine, particularly in questions of grace and divine foreknowledge. Scotus, however, left his strongest mark on Paris, where his doctrines were immediately developed by his disciples ANTONIUS ANDREAS, ANFREDUS GONTERI, James of Ascoli, and especially Francis of Meyronnes, who is the author of Scotism in the sense of a developing movement. Faithful to the univocity of being and to the formal distinction, Francis interpreted in his own way the notion of existence as an intrinsic mode of essence, even in God. On two important points, Francis abandoned the teaching of Scotus, as WILLIAM OF VAUROUILLON pointed out in the fifteenth century, namely, the distinction between divine Ideas and the divine nature, and the nature of the divine Idea as a simple "secondary object" of divine knowledge.

The essential features of Scotism were defended by John of Bassolis (d. 1347), who upheld the reality of genera and species in the sense Duns Scotus meant it, namely, not as universals constructed by the mind but as distinct formalities constitutive of essences. Similar views were held by Alfred Gontier (fl. 1322–25), HUGH OF NEWCASTLE, Gerard of Odone (d. 1348), Landolph CARACCIOLO, and Francis of Marchia.

Opposition. The teaching of Scotus did not find universal acceptance in the Franciscan Order; there were still many who preferred the older simplicity of St. Bonaventure. Strongest opposition within the order came from WILLIAM OF OCKHAM, who, in the name of a truer Aristotelianism, attacked the objective nature of UNIVERSALS defended in Scotism. The enormous success of Ockham's NOMINALISM prevented the consolidation of Scotism in the Franciscan Order in the early period. In the philosophical and theological controversies that flourished throughout the following centuries, three principal schools emerged: Scotism, Thomism, and nominalism. Within the Franciscan Order there were not only Scotists and Ockhamists, but also those who defended the older Augustinianism of Bonaventure. In Paris, PETER AUREOLI carried on a relentless attack on Scotism, while the influential JOHN OF RIPA criticized both Ockham and Aureoli without ever fully following Duns Scotus. At Oxford, WALTER OF CHATTON and the secular WALTER BURLEY criticized both Scotus and Ockham without committing themselves to any particular school of scholasticism. In Italy, however, Peter of Aquila, commonly known as Scotellus, remained faithful to the thought of his master.

Characteristics. The chief characteristic of early Scotism is the use of Scotistic doctrine in independent commentaries on the *Sentences* of Peter Lombard, and the composition of treatises *De formalitatibus.* The outstanding exception to this general characteristic was the controversy over the Immaculate Conception, in which Dominicans, bound to maintain the doctrine of St. Thomas, denied the Scotist position, which had become almost universal. In 1439 at the Council of Basel the doctrine was declared to be consonant with Catholic faith (J. D. Mansi, *Sacrorum Conciliorum nova et amplissima collectio,* [Florence-Venice 1757–98] 39:182). The council, however, was not an ecumenical one at that time, and the doctrine was opposed by two Dominican referees, John of SEGOVIA and Juan de TORQUEMADA. Only after silence was imposed on the disputants in the seventeenth century was the doctrine able to develop and become known as a doctrine of defined faith.

Resurgent Scotism. After the invention of printing, there appeared a number of editions of Scotus's *Opus Oxoniense* and *Quodlibeta.* Following the example of the Dominicans, who had replaced the *Sentences* of Peter Lombard with the *Summa Theologiae* of St. Thomas, Franciscan studia introduced the text of Duns Scotus as the basic authority. The efforts of the Irish Franciscan Maurice O'FIHELY, in Italy, and the Italians Antonio Trombetta and Francesco Licheto (d. 1520) initiated the second period of Scotism. Throughout the sixteenth century, Scotists, both Franciscan and non-Franciscan, published innumerable commentaries on the works of Duns

Scotus, and re-edited the text of the Subtle Doctor and of early Scotists. This led to the writing of manuals, such as the *Parvus Scotus* of Le Bret (*c.* 1527), the Scotus lexicon of Antonius de Fantes (1530), the *Monotesseron formalitatum* of John Dovetus (1579), and the *Flores theologiae* of the moralist Bishop Joseph Angles (d. 1587). Although the Capuchins forbade their friars in 1550 to follow Scotus and returned to Bonaventure, who was declared a doctor of the universal Church in 1588, the Franciscans declared Scotus their doctor in 1593. By the end of the century, Scotism was a vital force at the universities of Salamanca, Alcalá, Coimbra, Rome, Padua, Paris, Louvain, Budapest, and Cracow. This resurgence led to the official formation of the Scotist school by legislation.

Early in the seventeenth century, the Irish Franciscan Luke WADDING gave the following description of the resurgence of Scotism:

> The Angelic Doctor has his own private professors and disciples; so too has the Subtle Doctor. From one chair the teachings of St. Thomas are expounded, and from another those of Scotus. I went to three of the most notable universities in Spain, Coimbra, Salamanca, and Alcalá, and at each I saw a chair appointed for the masters who taught the views of Scotus; also at the academy in Paris, Padua, and even Rome itself, the very capital of the world, Scotus acquired a chair. Furthermore in the University of Salamanca, no professor [in that chair] could expound any doctrine other than that of Scotus, and in doing so, he was supposed to explain his text and clarify the ideas at great length, and not merely summarize, or mention them by way of conclusion [Wadding, *Annales Minorum,* ad an. 1308, n. 51 (Quaracchi 1931) 6:143–144].

Universal Scotism for Franciscans. The general chapter of the Franciscan Order, meeting in Toledo in 1633, directed four lectors to write a manual of Scotist philosophy for the entire order; once this was written, all lectors in philosophy were obliged to teach from this course under pain of irremissible removal from office. Meanwhile, courses in Scotistic philosophy were to be organized in the major countries of Europe with a view to an international unified course [*Annales Minorum, continuati,* ed. A. Chiappini (Quaracchi 1941) 28:36]. The same chapter commissioned a new edition of the works of Duns Scotus to be published as soon as possible in folio and in sufficient numbers for every library of the order. This task was undertaken by Luke Wadding with the assistance of other Irish Franciscans from the College of St. Isidore in Rome. The *Opera omnia* was published in Lyons in 12 volumes in 1639 and contained commentaries by Francesco Pitigiani of Arezzo (d. 1616), Hugh

MacCaughwell (d. 1626), O'Fihely, Licheto, John Ponce of Cork (d. 1670), Anthony Hickey (d. 1641), and Wadding.

As a result of the directive of the general chapter and the new edition of Scotus's works, the seventeenth century abounded with manuals of philosophy and theology *ad mentem Scoti.* The Irishman John Ponce himself wrote an *Integrum philosophiae cursum ad mentem Scoti* and a complete course in theology. The Belgian Franciscan William van Sichem (d. 1691) produced a clear, easy-to-teach *Cursus philosophicus* at the request of his superiors, ''harmonizing'' Scotus, St. Thomas, and St. Bonaventure. One of the most important and influential presentations of Scotism in manual form came from the pen of Claude Frassen, a doctor of the Sorbonne in 1662; his theological *Scotus academicus* (4 v. Paris 1672–77; 12 v. Rome 1900–02) and *Philosophia academica* exemplify a simplicity of style, clearness of method, and subtlety of thought that emphasized the difference between Scotism and Thomism. To bring out more clearly the Scotist answer to Thomism, Jerome of Montefortino published in 1728 a *Summa theologica* compiled from the works of Scotus and arranged in the order of the *Summa* of St. Thomas Aquinas.

In the early eighteenth century, the influence of Duns Scotus and Scotism was strongly felt outside of the Franciscan Order. Particularly noteworthy is the influence of Scotism on the philosophy of Christian WOLFF; consciously or unconsciously, Wolff adopted the Scotist concept of being.

By the middle of the eighteenth century, Scotism and other scholastic systems were on the decline, being replaced gradually by the philosophy of John LOCKE and E. CONDILLAC, the science of Isaac Newton, and theological manuals that were too often eclectic, sterile, and apologetic. The Kantian critique of Leibniz and Wolff was taken as a refutation of scholasticism in general. Although Scotist manuals continued to be written by Franciscans, such as B. Sarmentero (d. 1775), P. Mayer (d. 1781), and S. Lypnica (d. 1794), they were insignificant and uninfluential. The decline of scholastic studies was due, in large measure, to the French Revolution, the suppression of religious houses, and the Napoleonic wars.

Revival of Scotistic Studies. Renewed interest in Duns Scotus was shown more outside the Franciscan Order than within during the nineteenth century. Early in the nineteenth century, the Lutheran theologian L. Baumgarten-Crusius published *De theologia Scoti* (Iena 1826). Even during the Thomistic revival in Italy, Spain, France, and Germany, Scotus attracted the attention of non-Franciscan historians and philosophers. In 1859 Aloys Schmid published *Die Thomistische und Scotistische*

Gewissheitslehre (Dilligen), and even after AETERNI PATRIS, non-Franciscan scholars, such as Karl Werner, J. Müller, R. Seeberg, A. Vacant, É. H. Gilson, and C. Harris, published historical studies on the philosophy and theology of Duns Scotus, often in comparison with St. Thomas, or in relation to some contemporary problem. In the United States, C. S. PEIRCE was also interested in Scotus.

The revival of Thomism under Leo XIII and the rise of historical scholarship led to renewed interest in Franciscan scholastic authors. The principal author to benefit from this revival was St. Bonaventure, whose works were published in a critical edition by the international center of Franciscan studies at Quaracchi, near Florence. While other authors received respectful attention, a wave of prejudice engulfed the figure of Duns Scotus, who was accused of being a forerunner of all erroneous doctrines that have existed since the fourteenth century, including Protestantism, Kantianism, and modernism. In 1903 the Syrian Franciscan Gregory Dev Oglu vindicated Scotus of ONTOLOGISM. From 1905 until his death in 1926, Parthenius Minges devoted his energy to defending Scotus from the charges of Pelagianism, Lutheranism, indeterminism, fideism, and other misconceptions.

Many articles on Duns Scotus and Scotism appeared in Franciscan journals begun in the early twentieth century: *Études Franciscaines* (Paris 1899—), *Archivum Franciscanum Historicum* (Quaracchi 1909—), *Franziskanische Studien* (Münster 1914—), *Studi Francescani* (Arezzo 1914—), and *Franciscan Studies* (St. Bonaventure, N.Y. 1940—). These early studies contributed greatly to a more balanced appreciation of the Subtle Doctor and the Scotistic school of scholasticism [E. Bettoni, *Vent' anni di studi scotisti* (Milan 1943)] This prompted the Franciscan Order to establish an international Scotist Commission with headquarters in Rome to prepare a critical edition of the works of Duns Scotus. The first volume was published by the Vatican press in 1950. More recently, American scholars have begun a critical edition of the philosophical works of Duns Scotus, working first at the Franciscan Institute and then at the Catholic University of America. By the year 2001, 11 volumes had appeared in the Vatican edition of Scotus's Oxford theological writings, along with three volumes of his *Opera philosophica*, edited by the American team of scholars. The writings of early Scotists, such as William of Alnwick and James of Ascoli, have appeared gradually in article form.

Appreciation. Throughout its long history, Scotism has always been contrasted with Thomism on the one hand, and with nominalism on the other. While metaphysical principles of Duns Scotus differ radically from those of St. Thomas, they are not on that account unscholastic, or incompatible with Catholic doctrine. Scotism is an authentic scholastic view, and it was developed within the context of the Catholic faith. Some Scotists, such as Francis Macedo (d. 1681) and John of Rada (d. 1606), and some Thomists, such as CAPREOLUS and Tommaso de Vio CAJETAN, emphasized in the course of their works the various points of disagreement between the Subtle Doctor and the Angelic Doctor. Some Scotists, such as Jerome Lorte y Escartin (d. 1724) and Fulgence Stella, compiled lists of the basic differences between the two schoolmen, as though they had nothing in common. At the other extreme, some authors have maintained that the disagreement is merely verbal and not real. One such author was the Conventual Franciscan Constantius Sarnano, whose *Conciliatio dilucida* of all the controversies between the two theologians, tried to persuade men of good will that *verbis non autem rebus tantos viros dissensisse.*

While differences between Scotus and Thomas should not be overemphasized or underestimated, they should be recognized as two different approaches, primarily to theological understanding. The point of departure for Duns Scotus, as É. Gilson pointed out, was Avicenna, while Thomas Aquinas took Aristotle for his point of departure. Both schoolmen, however, used philosophical principles to understand divine revelation better; in so doing, they created two Christian philosophies compatible with Christian revelation.

Cardinal F. EHRLE expressed the mind of the Church when he wrote:

> The Church, for all the esteem it has for the *Doctor Communis,* still refuses to lay such emphasis on the teaching of this saint as to condemn, or even to disapprove, the views of other important schools. She knows too well the importance, for the pursuit of truth, of a free exchange of ideas that alone makes the clarification of a problem possible, even though thinkers start from different points of view. Provided that faith and charity are preserved, truth can only profit from such an exchange. Thus she allows a proper freedom to all teachers, students, and seekers for truth. If a particular thinker, religious order, or institute should wish to follow more closely St. Thomas, or any other master, they have every right and perfect freedom to do so [*La Scolastica e i suoi compiti odierni* (Turin 1932) 92].

Bibliography: É. H. GILSON, *History of Christian Philosophy in the Middle Ages* (New York 1955) 454–471. D. DE CAYLUS, ''Merveilleux épanouissement de l'école au XVIIᵉ siècle,'' *Études Franciscaines* 24 (1910) 5–21, 493–502; 25 (1911) 35–47, 306–317, 627–645; 26 (1912) 276–288. H. J. STORFF, ''De schola et doctrina Franciscana B. Joannis Duns Scoti,'' *Acta Ordinis*

Fratrum Minorum 51 (1932) 36–42. D. SCARAMUZZI, *Il pensiero di Giovanni Duns Scoto nel Mezzogiorno d'Italia* (Rome 1927). A. BERTONI, *Le Bienheureux Jean Duns Scot: Sa vie, sa doctrine, ses disciples* (Levanto 1917). V. COMTE–LIME, "Le Mouvement scotiste de 1900 à 1914 d'après les publications de langue française," in *Congrès des lecteurs franciscains* (Lyons 1934) 147–189. C. PIANA, "Gli inizi e lo sviluppo dello Scotismo a Bologna e nella regione romagnolo-flaminia (saec. XIV–XVI)," *Archivum Franciscanum historicum* 40 (1947) 49–80. C. BALIĆ, "Skotistična škola u prošlosti i sodašnjosti," *Collectanea Franciscana Slavica* 1 (1937) 3–54. M. GRAJEWSKI, "Scotistic Bibliography of the Last Decade (1929–1939)," *Franciscan Studies* 22 (1941) 73–78, 55–72, 71–76; 23 (1942) 61–71. S. DUMONT, "The Univocity of the Concept of Being in the Fourteenth Century: John Duns Scotus and Willia of Alnwick," *Mediaeval Studies* 49 (1987) 1–75; "The Univocity of the Concept of Being in the Fourteenth Century: II, the De ente of Petrus Thomae," *Mediaeval Studies* 50 (1988) 186–256; "Transcendental Being: Scotus and Scotists," *Topoi* 11 (1992) 135–148. T. B. NOONE, "Alnwick on the Origin, Nature, and Function of the Formal Distinction," *Franciscan Studies* 53 (1993) 231–261.

[C. BALIĆ/J. A. WEISHEIPL/T. B. NOONE]

SCOTLAND, CHURCH OF

The origins of the Church of Scotland are not to be found in 1560, but much earlier, if not with the Scottish Lollards, at least shortly after Martin Luther's Theses of 1517. The passionate treatise on the Word by Patrick Hamilton (burned for heresy Feb. 29, 1529) and the more irenic works of Alexander Alane (1500–65, renamed Alesius by Melanchthon), were influenced by contact with Marburg and Wittenberg. With George WISHART's translation of the Swiss Confession of Faith can be seen the beginnings of that influence from Zurich and Geneva, later so pervasive (*see* CONFESSIONS OF FAITH, PROTESTANT). The name of Alesius was associated with Philipp MELANCHTHON and the AUGSBURG CONFESSION [and therefore with John Macalpine (Machabaeus, d. 1557), later to be one of the panel of translators of the Danish Bible] and at the same time with the English Service Book. There was a period in 1543 when it looked as though an English version of the Reform might have been adopted by the Regent James Hamilton, Earl of Arran (d. 1575), well-suited to the role of "godly prince" in the place of the See of Rome. After Luther's death, the leadership of the Reform having passed over to John Calvin, this, plus traditional Scottish associations with an old ally, helped to reinforce French intellectual influence at a time when, under Mary of Lorraine, French political influence was being resisted. The Lords of the Congregation, who banded together under John Knox's inspiration in 1557, accepted the theological leadership of Geneva without a precise idea of what it might mean, and the first underground "privy" kirks used the English Prayer Book. It is quite clear that the Catholic catechism of 1552 did not appreciate how rapidly the position was changing.

Role of the "Godly Prince." Even the men who drew up the First Book of Discipline of 1560, though trained abroad, were not all necessarily enthusiasts for a single church order. Knox himself underlined the diversity of current opinion; of his collaborators, John Row (1525?–80) had long been an agent in the Roman Curia, John Douglas a medical graduate of Paris, and John Willock (d. 1585) a correspondent of Heinrich BULLINGER. Hence it would not be correct to envisage PRESBYTERIANISM as existing from the date of the 1560 Reformation Parliament that abolished papal jurisdiction or to deduce that the removal of the medieval Mass meant the removal of all medieval practices and habits of thought. The Scottish Reformers, Knox among them, still hoped for a "godly prince" or a "godly magistrate" (more applicable to the self-contained municipalities of Geneva or Strassburg than to the contemporary Scottish burgh) to preside at their General Assemblies. The new superintendents were like the old bishops "writ small"; as a matter of fact, one of the superintendents had the title archbishop of Athens before seceding from Rome.

Mary Queen of Scots continued to adhere to Rome, however, and could not function as "godly prince." The Lords were slow to digest Genevan ideas, and the First Book of Discipline's idealistic projects for social and educational service remained as yet paper projects. Policy, if not theology, suggested that conformity to England was preferable to conformity to Geneva. After Mary's deposition, her Protestant half brother, James Stewart, Earl of Moray (d. 1570), settled the succession and the Establishment and strengthened the lay patrons, failing to make adequate provision for traditional Church responsibilities, such as the hospital services. The General Assemblies, originally to be councils of the people of God investigating His will for the nation, were not permitted to acquire that role either by the regents or by James VI, Mary's son and successor. As a result, the Kirk drifted into the next century uncertain about the relation of the higher secular powers and its main assembly.

The Two Kirk Parties. The Presbyterianizing process was accelerated by the arrival from Geneva after Knox's death of Andrew MELVILLE. Replacing the notion of the king as prince with that of the king as vassal in the Kirk, in his Second Book of Discipline he devised a new constitution in which superintendent, bishop, and minister were titles of the same pastoral office. In addition to the local kirk with its Kirk Session court, the ministry was to be strengthened with the new court of the Presbytery (at first a sort of "deanery" gathering for the spiritual "exercise"). Melville had the support of the younger ministry, collaborating to secure their stipends and their role as welfare officers, but also embracing a program of political agitation. The principle of conformity with England, which Moray and later James Douglas, Earl of Morton (d. 1581), had sponsored and which it became increasingly King James's policy to foster, was overthrown, and the claim of the middle and lower classes stressed, in the face of that of the nobles, the bishops, and the Crown. Thus were formed the two Kirk parties and later the two Kirks, episcopalian and presbyterian.

Struggles of the Presbytery. In all this conflict over ministerial parity, even after James VI became King of England as well (as James I, 1603–25), the actual worshipers were little involved, until the Perth Assembly of 1618, under royal pressure, attempted to enforce a more English type of liturgy, an attempt taken up again by Charles I (1625–49) in the so-called Laud's Liturgy. The result was the 1638 National Covenant, whereby signatories from all citizen categories, while emphasizing their loyalty, rejected bishops and episcopal worship. Soon, however, by the Solemn League and Covenant of 1643, they were involved in asserting "the Crown Rights of the Redeemer" in the rest of the United Kingdom, becoming apostles of intolerance of any spiritual kingdom except a Presbyterian one. The Westminster Confession (1648), a subordinate standard of faith, was a product of this league. After the Cromwellian Union (1654), the Stuart kings continued their exercise of divine right in conjunction with episcopal divine right. They were opposed by the COVENANTERS, the Bible-dominated and Bible-inspired mystics who were persecuted with a harshness the memory of which is hard to obliterate. With the arrival in 1688 of William of Orange and the ejection of the Episcopalian "curates," William Carstares (1649–1715) arranged a marriage of convenience whereby the leaders of the Presbyterian rebels became courtly adherents of the Crown Establishment, and as such were in time to breed their own dissenting families.

Question of Patronage. In Queen Anne's reign (1702–14), the problem of lay patronage raised problems in a pro-Hanoverian kirk, that time was slow to solve. The Moderates, an enlightened, but somewhat cold, remote, and ineffectual group, had the task of persuading the passionate religious rebels to put their trust in princes. They made the Establishment culturally respectable at the cost of alienating popular religion, so that an "associate" presbytery and "secession" and "relief" kirks mushroomed up beside the Establishment. The French Revolution and industrial change aggravated such problems as pluralities, antiquated parochial divisions, and seat rents (the synod, which still exists, is based on medieval divisions); and Thomas Chalmers (1780–1847) led the agitation against patronage generally, which led to the exodus from the 1843 Assembly of over one-third of the ministry, impoverishing both Kirk and university. Some goodwill returned when the Patronage Act three decades later

restored power to the congregations. Problems of extension, of the "voluntary principle" as against state control, and of reunion were to occupy the new century; and in 1900 the Free Church (except for a remnant called "Wee Frees") joined with the United Presbyterians to form the United Free Church, which in 1929 (except for the inevitable remnant) reunited with the Church of Scotland.

Twentieth-Century Trends. The post–World War II period saw the release of the controversial "Bishops Report" regarding which, as in Knox's day, there were diverse opinions. Although many would have deplored the attempt to identify the Church with its institutional structure or were more interested in the newer theological approaches, for others the Kirk was growing from the grass roots upward, and the Presbytery was the nucleus of ecclesiastical authority, the final court of decision. There was a new stress on: (1) the Cup as well as the Book that rejoins Calvin rather than 17th-century Eucharistic practice; (2) a new search for dignified worship, and not only on the part of the Iona Community; this was founded in 1938 by George Macleod (b. 1895) to rebuild the ancient abbey of IONA; and (3) a departure from the narrow moralism and windy rhetoric of the earlier days. Many of the original threads of incipient Presbyterianism were still recognizably there and make of the modern Church of Scotland a more complex structure than ecclesiastical polemics have generally allowed.

Bibliography: D. MCROBERTS, ed., *Essays on the Scottish Reformation, 1513–1625* (Glasgow 1962). J. T. COX, ed., *Practice and Procedure in the Church of Scotland* (2d ed. Edinburgh 1939). J. KNOX, *History of the Reformation in Scotland*, ed. W. C. DICKINSON, 2 v. (New York 1949). J. H. S. BURLEIGH, *A Church History of Scotland* (New York 1960). A. R. MACEWEN, *A History of the Church in Scotland, 396–1560*, 2 v. (London 1913–18). W. D. MAXWELL, *A History of Worship in the Church of Scotland* (New York 1955). G. D. HENDERSON, *The Claims of the Church of Scotland* (London 1951). G. DONALDSON, *The Scottish Reformation* (Cambridge, Eng. 1960). D. SHAW, *The General Assemblies of the Church of Scotland, 1560–1600* (Edinburgh 1964). G. DONALDSON, *The Making of the Scottish Prayer Book of 1637* (Edinburgh 1954). H. J. WOTHERSPOON and J. M. KIRKPATRICK, *A Manual of Church Doctrine*, ed. T. F. TORRANCE and R. S. WRIGHT (2d ed. New York 1960). M. B. MACGREGOR, *The Sources and Literature of Scottish Church History* (Glasgow 1934), standard work. R. S. LOUDEN, *The True Face of the Kirk* (London 1963).

[J. DURKAN/EDS.]

SCOTLAND, THE CATHOLIC CHURCH IN

Located in the North Atlantic Ocean and part of the United Kingdom of Great Britain and Northern Ireland, Scotland covers the northern portion of the Island of

> **Capital:** Edinburgh.
> **Size:** 29,797 sq. miles.
> **Population:** 5,114,600 in 2000.
> **Languages:** English, Gaelic.
> **Religions:** 767,190 Catholics (15%), 3,580,220 Protestants
> (70%), 153,438 other (3%), 613,752 without religious
> affiliation.
> **Metropolitan sees:** Saint Andrews and Edinburgh, with suf-
> fragans Aberdeen, Argyll and the Isles, Dunkeld, and Gal-
> loway; and Glasgow with suffragans Motherwell and Paisley.
> There are two major seminaries, one in each province.

Great Britain. Scotland is bound by the Atlantic Ocean to the north and west, the North Sea to the East, and by England and the Irish Sea to the south. The region is divided into the southern uplands bordering England, the central lowlands through which run the Clyde, Tay and Forth rivers, and the Highlands, a rugged, mountainous region that covers most of Scotland. Scotland also encompasses three groups of smaller islands: the Shetland Islands, the Orkney Islands, and the Hebrides. Oil deposits discovered in the North Sea during the mid-20th century boosted the region's traditionally weak economy. In addition to agricultural products such as wheat, barley, oats, potatoes, and livestock, Scotland is noted for its fishing and shipbuilding industries and its export of textiles and whisky. Another export, the game of golf, originated in Scotland.

Consistently fighting with England for political independence, Scotland was made a part of Great Britain by the Parliamentary Act of 1707, and the parliaments of the two countries joined. A nationalist movement gained increasing strength during the 1980s and 1990s, and a 1997 vote awarded the region a local parliament with limited autonomy. Elections to the resurrected Scottish Parliament were held in 1999. Despite its incorporation with Great Britain, Scotland retained its own legal system.

The history of the Catholic Church in Scotland is divided into the following four parts: the Celtic Church, 400 to 1070; the medieval period, 1070 to 1560; the Reformation through the restoration of the hierarchy, 1560 to 1878; and the modern Church.

The Celtic Church: 400–1070

Originally occupied by the Picts (from the Latin *picti*, or "painted people"), Scotland was unsuccessfully invaded from the south by the Romans beginning *c.* A.D. 80. St. Columba would be much more successful, converting the Highland Picts to Christianity in the 6th century. Although the early church in Scotland retained an individualistic Celtic character, with the coming of the

Normans *c.* 1070, it joined the mainstream of Western Christendom.

Early Christianity. Christianity was established in the region by the early 5th century. Its first recorded bishop, St. NINIAN, or Nynia, was a native Briton who had studied in Rome and then returned to establish his see at WHITHORN or Candida Casa, Galloway. He was succeeded in southwest Scotland (eventually part of the Anglian kingdom of Strathclyde) by St. KENTIGERN (MUNGO), founder of the Church at GLASGOW between 543 and 560, and his friend St. Serf. A new era of evangelization began following the arrival of St. COLUMBA from Ireland in 563. Establishing his monastery at IONA, he and his companions traversed the lochs and islands to the north, and sought out the Pictish King Brude, whose highland kingdom centered on Inverness. By the end of the century the Gospel had reached the more remote parts of the country.

Ninian and Columba defined the Celtic Church, which was tribal and monastic in organization, placing it in communion with Rome despite its geographical isolation. There were practices in Scotland that differed from those current in Rome, such as its mode of clerical dress and tonsure and, more significantly, its less accurate method of calculating Easter. When Rome's mission to the English (597) reached Scotland, friction was inevitable. In an early effort to resolve these differences, King Oswiu of Northumbria decided, at the synod of WHITBY (664), to adopt the Roman usages then common to the Western Church. After considerable debate, the community at Iona began to conform. Further progress occurred under ADAMNAN, Abbot of Iona (d. 704), but final settlement waited until 710, when the Pictish King Nechtan decreed Celtic conformity with Roman practices throughout his kingdom and encouraged the development of episcopal sees at Abernethy and elsewhere.

Scandinavian Invasion. During the 8th century, Scotland was far from politically unified. The Pictish kings, whose territory extended from the Firth of Forth north to the river Spey, attempted to impose their suzerainty over the Scottish kings of Dalriada in the west, while the presence of the Strathclyde Britons in the southwest and the Northumbrian Angles in the east prevented any kind of political hegemony. It would be the Scandinavian invasions of the late 8th and 9th centuries that united Picts and Scots into the kingdom of Alban to prevent their complete subjugation. Meanwhile, the Scottish Church suffered severely from the Vikings. Christian settlements in the Shetlands and Orkneys, the western Isles and Iona were sacked and destroyed, their clergy exiled or killed. Some inkling of conditions may be inferred from the remarkable discovery in 1958 of an exquisite sil-

ver hoard of Celtic sacred vessels of the period, which had been hastily secreted, buried in a box under the altar of the church at St. Ninian's Isle, Shetland, prior to one such raid. In consequence of these raids, the primatial see was moved from Iona inland to Dunkeld, whose abbot was the chief bishop (*primepscop*) of Alban. About 900 the ecclesiastical capital was thought to have moved to SAINT ANDREWS, perhaps for political reasons.

While no record remained of the pattern of Church government in Alban during the 9th and 10th centuries, some kind of territorial organization with bishops and secular clergy on the English or Roman pattern likely existed. Yet the old Celtic structure had by no means disintegrated. At Dunkeld, Brechin, and Saint Andrews communities of clergy leading a monastic or eremitical life and known as CULDEES (*Keledei,* friends of God) had charge of parish churches, and such groups likely existed

Mary Stuart.

elsewhere. It is reasonable to infer also that as Scotland's political center moved east and south, so did its ecclesiastical one, since the interests of both were bound with England and the Continent. Most importantly, the Viking invasions isolated the Scottish Church from the monastic and secular reforms invigorating the Western Church throughout the 11th century.

Medieval Period: 1070–1560

St. MARGARET, Queen of Scotland, who married Malcolm III (*c.* 1070), was responsible for initiating the ecclesiastical changes needed to make the Scottish Church once more an integral part of Western Christendom.

Normanization. By persuading her friend LANFRANC, Archbishop of Canterbury, to send a small colony of monks from Christ Church, CANTERBURY, to form the nucleus of her new foundation of Holy Trinity at DUNFERMLINE, Margaret introduced the latest Benedictine reforms into Scotland. These monastic reforms were not only constitutional, but were closely linked with a renaissance in architecture, art and classical education. A series of judicious ecclesiastical appointments, such as that of her confessor Thurgot to the bishopric of Saint Andrews, ensured the wide dissemination of these reforms, which

were accomplished with a proper regard for Celtic traditions. Characteristically Margaret generously supported Culdee establishments, while encouraging them to abandon liturgical or doctrinal irregularities. Kings Edgar, Alexander I and DAVID I, her sons, continued to implement this policy; David I, particularly, founded many Benedictine, Tironian, Cistercian and Augustinian abbeys, reestablished sees, and reorganized diocesan and parish life on the Roman pattern. At David's death in 1153, the Scottish Church had turned away from its Celtic past and assumed the new direction and character it would retain for the next four centuries. This had disadvantages.

Anglo-Scottish Relations. The increasingly complex political relationship between the Scottish kings and the Norman kings of England encouraged the archbishops of York, and then of Canterbury, to claim metropolitan jurisdiction over the Scottish Church, which lacked a METROPOLITAN. Being governed instead by a provincial synod weakened its plea for independence at the papal Curia. It was not until 1192, when Pope Celestine III, in the bull *Cum universi,* made the Sees of Aberdeen, Argyll, Brechin, Caithness, Dunblane, Dunkeld, Glasgow, Moray, Ross and Saint Andrews subject directly to Rome, that the matter was settled. The Sees of Orkney and the Isles were made suffragan to the Norwegian archbishopric of TRONDHEIM at this time, and Whithorn alone was suffragan to York. Having won their ecclesiastical freedom from the jurisdiction of the two English provinces, during the next two centuries the Scottish hierarchy almost invariably supported the Scottish crown in its struggle for political independence against England. Thus when King Edward I resolved to conquer Scotland after 1296, his most determined opposition came from the Scottish bishops. Their approval, though not their seals, can be seen in the Scottish declaration of independence addressed to Pope JOHN XXII (1320). Not until the 15th century did astute Scottish clerics fully recognize the futility of fratricidal conflict and seek a lasting peace between the two countries. Indeed, the more important embassies to England in the later Middle Ages were led by bishops such as William ELPHINSTONE, whose political maturity was often far superior to that of the Scottish baronage, and even to that of the crown. The higher clergy was important in the political formation of Scotland as a nation; it would be again in the country's downfall.

Religious Orders. The rapid expansion of the religious orders in 12th-century Scotland ended within a century. By 1300 almost all the great orders were represented and were actively engaged in the nation's spiritual, cultural and economic life. The MENDICANT ORDERS, particularly, made a distinct contribution to Scottish spiritual and intellectual life. The DOMINICANS came first, in 1230, at the invitation of King Alexander II, who founded eight

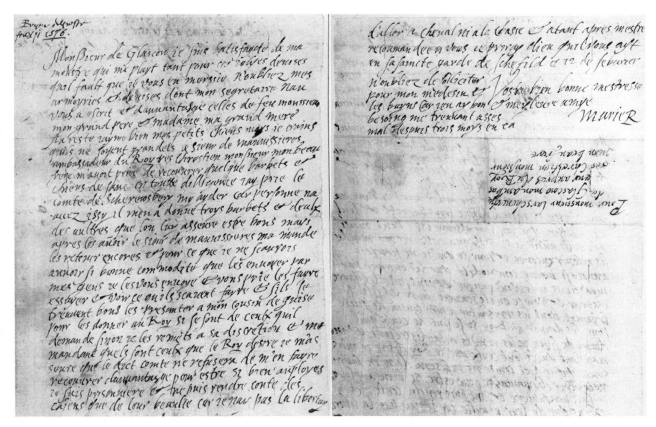

Holograph letter from Mary, Queen of Scots, to Archbishop James Beaton of Glasgow, written in French from Sheffield, dated February 12, 1576.

of their 17 houses. The FRANCISCANS arrived in 1231 and had five of their eight friaries established before 1300. The CARMELITES and AUGUSTINIANS entered later, the former establishing 11 houses, the latter one, located at Berwick. The Knights TEMPLARS had two Scottish houses before their suppression in 1309, and the Knights HOSPITALLERS maintained a house at Torphichen. Convents of Cistercian, then Franciscan and Dominican nuns were also established. A new type of nonmonastic foundation also developed in late medieval Scotland: colleges of secular clergy, either parochial or nonparochial, with their own dignitaries similar in pattern to cathedral clergy. Over 40 such establishments existed by the 16th century, most serving parishes, but two with academic foundations: St. Salvator's College, at Saint Andrews (1450) and St. Mary's (later King's) College, at Aberdeen (1505). Two of Scotland's 13 cathedrals were staffed not by secular canons, but by religious orders, the CANONS REGULAR OF ST. AUGUSTINE serving St. Andrews and the PREMONSTRATENSIANS serving Whithorn or Candida Casa.

Defects. Despite the country's many religious houses, hospitals, and corporations, the late medieval Scottish Church displayed several disturbing weaknesses. For some of these the clergy alone were not responsible; the Hundred Years' War and the 14th-century rebellions against English rule often isolated religious communities, cutting them off from their motherhouses on the Continent and considerably impoverished them. The BLACK DEATH, which depleted the secular clergy more than the laity, also weakened the parish structure and left gaps that could not rapidly be filled. Moreover, the WESTERN SCHISM resulted in widespread demoralization and confusion. For a time Scottish and English clergies gave allegiance to different papal claimants.

However, the Scottish clergy and crown were responsible for some of these deficiencies. To fund overly ambitious building programs, several religious orders and secular corporations began appropriating parish revenues and staffed churches with clergy whose stipends were inadequate to meet rising living costs. As a result, as cathedrals, abbeys and colleges became more opulent, parishes became poorer. While much of this may have been the result of natural economic development in the country, by the 16th century more than half the parish churches had been treated thus. Meanwhile parish priests and university clerks often contested among themselves to hold simultaneously several benefices. More seriously, an indult of Pope Innocent VIII to King James III in 1487 enabling the Scottish crown to choose bishops and abbots allowed the later Stuart kings to indulge in nepotism and other kinds of political and economic opportunism, often to the grave detriment of the Scottish Church. Thus in 1497 James IV secured the Saint Andrews archbishopric for his brother, a layman; and after his brother's death, for his illegitimate son, aged 11. In 1533 James V petitioned Pope Clement VII to fill this metropolitan see and two others with three of his illegitimate children. While some bishops of this period seriously attempted to fulfill their obligations, for the most part the hierarchy lacked theological training and interest in ecclesiastical reform.

It also suffered from rivalries that worked against the unity so urgently needed. When Saint Andrews was raised to archiepiscopal and metropolitan rank (1472), opposition to its primacy was so strong that Innocent VIII thought it prudent to give Glasgow a similar status (1492). The gradual secularization of many religious houses occurred even before their dissolution, while the practice of appointing abbots in COMMENDATION meant that many abbots never resided in their monasteries. Frequently the abbot was a layman who, while receiving most of the abbey's income, appointed others to supervise internal monastic affairs. In general, the social gap between prelates and the rank and file of the clergy and religious kept widening. On the other hand the Church still provided most of the nation's culture and education, and its Canon Law often afforded protection when civil law did not. Moreover, a serious attempt to revitalize the Church from within had already begun. The liturgical and pastoral reforms initiated by Elphinstone at Aberdeen were part of a wider effort to restore parish life throughout the country. The humanist interests of an increasing number of secular and religious clergy reflected the intellectual renaissance taking place throughout the Western Church at the time. Unfortunately Scotland's reform program was inadequate and started too late.

The Reformation to the Restoration of the Hierarchy: 1560–1878

The causes of the Scottish Reformation were complex, involving vital political, dynastic and religious issues in close interrelation. James IV had fallen to the English at the Battle of Flodden Field in 1513, leaving his infant son James V on the throne and the allegiance of the Scottish baronage and hierarchy divided. Some support went to the proposed regency of the Duke of Albany, a Scot educated entirely in France and therefore tied to the "auld alliance"; others respected the wishes of the dead king in supporting his widow, Margaret Tudor, sister of HENRY VIII OF ENGLAND.

French Sympathies. When after several years of political anarchy James V assumed control, his political sympathies lay with France rather than England. His marriage to the French princess Madeleine (1537), and after her death to Mary of Guise (1538), incurred the political hostility of Henry VIII, then implacably opposed to France. Henry had rejected papal authority in England in 1533. After the premature death of James in 1542, Henry shrewdly encouraged political disaffection among those of the Scottish nobility who were attracted to the new Protestant beliefs and who feared their leaderless country might soon be dominated by Catholic France. These fears were intensified by the political activities of Mary of Guise, who governed Scotland as regent during the minority and absence in France of her daughter MARY, Queen of Scots. The Scottish hierarchy, led first by James BEATON and later by the able but ill-fated Cardinal David Beaton, lent its full support to the pro-French policies of the regent while at the same time strongly opposing the tide of heresy flooding across the border. In one of its purges it caused noted Scottish Lutheran George WISHART to be burned at the stake.

With the death of Henry VIII and the accession of his Catholic daughter, MARY TUDOR, in 1553, the situation steadily deteriorated. Mary's persecution of heretics drove a number of influential English lords northward, while the pro-French policy of Mary of Guise was unpopular with Catholic and Protestant Scottish nobles alike, neither of whom had any desire to attack England at the bidding of either the French king or Pope Paul IV. The already-considerable social unrest throughout Scotland was inflamed further by the sermons and pamphlets of John KNOX, and events moved rapidly to a climax following Elizabeth I's accession to the English throne in 1558. For political and dynastic reasons, it was vitally important that Elizabeth defeat the French party in Scotland, especially after the death of Henry II of France made his widow, Mary, Queen of Scots, also Queen of France in 1560. It was equally urgent for Elizabeth to encourage the Protestant cause in Scotland. When the Scotch Protestant nobility, known as the lords of the Congregation, appealed for English aid in 1559, she supplied it. The following spring a combined force of English troops and the army of the Congregation entered Edinburgh. In August 1560, shortly after the death of Mary of Guise, an act of the Scottish Parliament abrogated papal authority and ended, after more than 11 centuries, the old Scottish Church.

The return of Mary, Queen of Scots, from France in 1561 and the vicissitudes of her later tempestuous career were an epilogue of the Scottish Reformation. Young, constitutionally isolated from her subjects, and often in considerable danger, she was incapable of reversing the tide of affairs throughout the remainder of her tragic reign. Upon her abdication in 1567 Scotland finally committed to the Protestant cause, but while papal authority was abrogated by an act of Parliament, a means of uniting dissident forces proved elusive. For a long time the reformers were unable to provide a stable system of church government. At first a form of episcopacy existed alongside a Presbyterian organization dominated by Calvinist theology; but in time each party sought a compromise that would satisfy Presbyterians but allow some kind of episcopal or royal control over the Church. Meanwhile Catholicism was proscribed and the old hierarchy disbanded or worse. While most of its members abjured their faith, John Hamilton, Archbishop of Saint Andrews, was executed in 1571; James Beaton, Archbishop of Glasgow, fled to France and was declared an outlaw by the Privy Council in 1574. Some in the secular clergy and religious orders defected; others were pensioned, or settled abroad. There was considerable vandalism and destruction of church buildings and furnishings, in which a notable proportion of the nation's artistic heritage perished. In 1587 the crown annexed all lands and revenues owned by bishoprics and abbeys, most of which were erected into temporal lordships for the Scottish nobility. The universities at Saint Andrews, Glasgow, and Aberdeen were reformed and reorganized, and a fourth was endowed at Edinburgh in 1582 with funds appropriated from the sale of Church lands (*see* REFORMATION, PROTESTANT, IN THE BRITISH ISLES.)

Scottish Mission. From the first, the Counter Reformation made little headway in Scotland. While a small number of Scottish secular priests, trained at Paris or Douai, returned as missionaries and with the help of a few Jesuits succeeded in winning back several powerful nobles in the north, the movement was essentially an underground one with little chance of large-scale success. The crown's attitude toward Catholicism after Elizabeth's death in 1603, was ambivalent. Although sympathetic to Catholics, James VI, as king of both Scotland and England, had good cause to fear a Catholic insurrection, especially after the Spanish threat to England. At the same time the Protestant nobility in both countries watched vigilantly for the slightest sign of royal support for Catholics. James's reign saw much religious uncertainty and anarchy, and several periods of persecution occurred, during one of which the Jesuit priest John OGILVIE was hanged in Glasgow (1615). The popes lacked reliable information about Scotland, were preoccupied with France, Spain, Germany, and the Netherlands, and were in any event unable to supply positive assistance.

The establishment of the Congregation for the PROPAGATION OF THE FAITH (Propaganda) in 1622 resulted in a more enlightened and realistic Roman policy toward countries severed from Catholic unity. Missionaries were now expected to concentrate solely on pastoral work and to avoid all political activity; Propaganda would assume responsibility for their financial support. When the Scottish Catholic secular clergy incorporated in 1653 as a missionary body, with William Ballantyne as prefect apostolic, a new era began. Now properly organized, the Scots colleges in Rome and Madrid (later transferred to Valladolid) were able to add their quota of seminary priests to those trained in Paris and Douai. Irish Franciscans began working in the Gaelic-speaking islands and Highlands with some success, despite physical difficulties and irregular financial assistance. Jesuits and Benedictines also labored throughout the country. The progress made by this quiet conversion became evident when in 1694 the prefecture was raised to a vicariate apostolic, with Bishop Thomas Nicholson as the first vicar. In 1731 the country was divided into two ecclesiastical districts, the highland, or Gaelic-speaking, area in the west and north, and the lowland, or non-Gaelic, area east of the highland line.

Development of Seminaries. While the need for a Catholic seminary in each district was now imperative, the project was considered hazardous because the struggle between Episcopalianism and Presbyterianism had been resolved. When Charles I (1625–49) attempted to introduce into Scotland a new prayer book and liturgy more closely conforming with Anglican doctrines, it brought a sharp reaction from Presbyterians and united them with the English Puritans under Cromwell. Both Catholicism and Episcopalianism were proscribed, and the Scottish penal laws were harshly enforced, particularly after the Scottish Parliament ratified the Presbyterian system of church government (1690). Moreover, the REVOLUTION OF 1688 that prompted the abdication of James VII (II of England) because of his Catholic sympathies, resulted in a government alert to the possibility of a Catholic uprising. Revolts materialized in 1715 and 1745, when many Catholics allied themselves to the Stuart cause. It was essential, then, to locate the seminaries in remote spots that, while providing basic training to Scottish missionaries, could also serve as bases or retreats for the vicars apostolic.

Not until 1717, after an abortive attempt in Loch Morar in western Inverness-shire, did Bishop James Gordon found a lowland seminary at Scalan, in a small, dry stone, turfed hut. There the first of the many "heather" priests were trained and ordained. In 1738, when the number of students had increased to ten, Bishop Gordon replaced this building with a larger and more permanent one nearby. When he died in 1746, his seminary seemed firmly established, but within a year, following the disastrous failure of Prince Charles's uprising (1745), Scalan was reduced to a burnt-out ruin. Within four years the students were in residence again.

Meanwhile, Bishop Hugh Macdonald of the highland district had founded a seminary in remote Arisaig— later moved to Glenfinnan, thence to Buorblach, to Samalaman and finally to Lismore. As in Scalan, the course of study included Latin and Greek, some history, and a good grounding in philosophy and theology. A meager supply of books came mostly from the Continent, as opportunity permitted.

Ironically, it was the final defeat of the Stuart cause that brought relief to the hard-pressed vicars apostolic, and freedom from molestation for the seminaries. From 1759 the bishops of the highland and lowland districts worked confidently toward Catholic emancipation from penal laws, the first phase of which came with the passing of the Catholic Relief Bill in 1793. The French Revolution brought further toleration, as after 1793 the British government offered domicile to priests, nuns and others exiled from France. The closing of the Scots colleges at Douai and Paris also increased the need for a larger Scottish native seminary. The students from Scalan were transferred to Aquhorties in 1797, and then to Blairs College, Aberdeen, in 1829, where the highland students from Lismore joined them. The closing of Scalan and Lismore ended an era. In the course of eight decades they had contributed to the training of over 100 priests. While the concurrent isolated missionary labors of Benedictines, Jesuits, and other religious had been useful, the contribution of the heather priests far surpassed these.

Catholic Growth. Great social and economic changes occurred in Scotland and Ireland from the late 18th to the mid-19th century that reversed the trend of a steadily declining Catholic population and radically altered the demographic pattern of the Scottish Church. Mass immigrations of Catholics to Canada occurred before 1800 as a result of the failure of the Jacobite rebellions and the Highland clearances—the large-scale evictions of rural crofters, ostensibly for economic reasons—both of which principally affected Catholics. On the other hand, the collapse of the Irish rebellion in 1798 sparked a large migration of Irish Catholics to southwestern Scotland, particularly to the Glasgow area. In 1800 Scotland had an estimated 30,000 Catholics; by 1827, the year three vicariates for the eastern, western, and northern districts were created, it had 70,000, of whom 25,000 lived in the Glasgow region. Another sharp increase would follow the Irish famine, and in 1851 Catholics totaled 145,860, or five percent, of the entire population of Scotland. By the late 1870s that figure had more than doubled.

Restoration of the Hierarchy. Inevitably problems and frictions accompanied such rapid Catholic expansion. Led by their own priests during the early wave of immigration, the Irish formed, at least for a time, an enclave that was not readily absorbed into Scottish Catholic life. In addition to religious differences, poverty, and overcrowding, the resultant outbreaks of cholera and typhoid created a stressful situation. New churches and schools were needed and funds required to raise them. Religious intolerance and outbursts of sectarian violence were not uncommon. By 1861 a thorough ecclesiastical reorganization became imperative to accommodate the greatly enlarged Catholic population and the shift in its strength from the northeast and the Enzie to the southwest. Leo XIII restored the hierarchy in his letter *Ex supremo apostolatus apice* (March 4, 1878), making Saint Andrews and Edinburgh again a metropolitan see, with four suffragans. The Archdiocese of Glasgow was subjected directly to the Holy See; in 1947 it would become Scotland's second metropolitan see, with two suffragans.

Bibliography: P. D. HANCOCK, *A Bibliography of Works Relating to Scotland, 1915–1950,* 2 v. (Edinburgh 1959–60). *Bibliography of British History: Tudor Period,* ed. C. READ (2d ed. New York 1959). *Bibliography of British History, Stuart Period,* ed. G. DAVIES (Oxford 1928). *Bibliography of British History, 1714–89,* eds., S. M. PARGELLIS and D. J. MEDLEY (Oxford 1951). Sources, Celtic. *Early Sources of Scottish History, A.D. 500–1286,* ed. and tr., A. O. ANDERSON, 2 v. (Edinburgh 1922). *A Source Book of Scottish History,* ed. W. C. DICKINSON et al., 3 v. (2d ed. London 1958–61). BEDE, *Eccl. Hist.* Medieval. A. THEINER, *Vetera Monumenta Hibernorum et Scotorum historiam illustrantia* (Rome 1864). *Calendar of Documents Relating to Scotland 1108–1509,* ed. J. BAIN 4 v. (Edinburgh 1881–88). D. PATRICK, *Statutes of the Scottish Church, 1225–1559* (Edinburgh 1907). *The Apostolic Camera and Scottish Benefices, 1418–1488,* ed. A. I. CAMERON (New York 1934). D. E. R. WATT, *Fasti Ecclesiae Scoticanae mediiaevi* (St. Andrews 1959). Reformation. *Papal Negotiations with Mary Queen of Scots,* ed. J. H. POLLEN (Edinburgh 1901). W. C. DICKINSON, ed., *John Knox's History of the Reformation in Scotland,* 2 v. (Edinburgh 1949). ''Narratives of the Scottish Reformation,'' *Innes Review,* ed. W. J. ANDERSON, 7 (1956) 27–59, 112–121; 8 (1957) 39–66, 99–129. *Irish Franciscan Mission to Scotland, 1619–1646,* ed. C. GIBLIN (Dublin 1964). Literature. Scottish Church History in general. G. GRUB, *An Ecclesiastical History of Scotland,* 4 v. (Edinburgh 1861). A. BELLESHEIM, *History of the Catholic Church of Scotland,* tr. D. O. HUNTER-BLAIR, 4 v. (Edinburgh 1887–90). A. R. MACEWEN, *A History of the Church in Scotland,* 2 v. (London 1913–18). H. SCOTT, *Fasti Ecclesiae Scoticanae,* 8 v. (2d ed. Edinburgh 1915–50). J. H. S. BURLEIGH, *A Church History of Scotland* (New York 1960). G. DONALDSON, *Scotland: Church and Nation through 16 Centuries* (Naperville, IL 1960). W. C. DICKINSON and G. S. PRYDE, *A New History of Scotland,* 2 v. (New York 1962). *A Short History of Scotland,* ed. R. L. MACKIE (rev. ed. New York 1963). Celtic Church. W. F. SKENE, *Celtic Scotland,* 3 v. (2d ed. Edinburgh 1886–90). J. A. DUKE, *The Columban Church* (London 1932). N. K. CHADWICK, *The Age of the Saints in the Early Celtic Church* (New York 1961). J. BULLOCH, *The Life* *of the Celtic Church* (Edinburgh 1963). Medieval Church. J. LESLEY, *The History of Scotland . . . 1436–1561,* ed. T. THOMSON (Edinburgh 1830). F. MICHEL, *Les Écossais en France, Les Français en Écosse,* 2 v. (London 1862). D. MACGIBBON and T. ROSS, *The Ecclesiastical Architecture of Scotland,* 3 v. (Edinburgh 1896–97). *Early Scottish Charters,* ed. A. C. LAWRIE (Glasgow 1905). J. DOWDEN, *The Medieval Church in Scotland* (Glasgow 1910); *The Bishops of Scotland* (Glasgow 1912). H. LECLERCQ, *Dictionnaire d'archéologie chrétienne et de liturgie,* eds., F. CABROL, H. LECLERCQ and H. I. MARROU, 15 v. (Paris 1907–53) 4.2:1889–1921. R. K. HANNAY, *The Scottish Crown and the Papacy, 1424–1560* (Edinburgh 1931); "The Universities of Scotland," in H. RASHDALL, *The Universities in Europe in the Middle Ages,* ed. F. M. POWICKE and A. B. EMDEN, v.2. (new ed. Oxford 1936). K. S. LATOURETTE, *A History of the Expansion of Christianity,* 7 v. (New York 1937–45) v.1, 2. R. N. HADCOCK, *Map of Monastic Britain; Scotland* (Chessington, Eng. 1950). A. I. DUNLOP, *The Life and Times of James Kennedy* (Edinburgh 1950). J. DURKAN, "William Turnbull, Bishop of Glasgow 1447–1454," *Innes Review,* 2 (1951) 5–61. J. BURNS, "The Scotland of John Major," *ibid.* 65–76. J. DURKAN, "The Beginnings of Humanism in Scotland," *ibid.* 4 (1953) 5–24. N. BACKMUND, "The Premonstratensian Order in Scotland," *ibid.* 25–41. G. W. S. BARROW, "From Queen Margaret to David I: Benedictines and Tironians," *ibid.* 11 (1960) 22–38; *The Acts of Malcolm IV, King of Scots, 1153–1165* (Edinburgh 1960). J. DURKAN and A. ROSS, *Early Scottish Libraries* (Glasgow 1961). L. J. MACFARLANE, "William Elphinstone, Founder of the University of Aberdeen," *Aberdeen University Review,* 39 (196–162) 1–18. J. H. BURNS, *Scottish Churchmen and the Council of Basle* (Glasgow 1962). Reformation. G. DONALDSON, *The Scottish Reformation* (Cambridge, Eng. 1960). *Essays on the Scottish Reformation, 1513–1625,* ed. D. MCROBERTS (Glasgow 1962). Modern. A. M. DAWSON, *The Catholics of Scotland* (London 1890). W. FORBES-LEITH, *Memoirs of Scottish Catholics during the 17th and 18th Centuries* (New York 1909). M. V. HAY, *A Chain of Error in Scottish History* (London 1927); *The Blairs Papers, 1603–1660* (London 1929). F. GOLDIE, *A Short History of the Episcopal Church in Scotland* (London 1951). G. D. HENDERSON, *The Claims of the Church of Scotland* (London 1951). W. D. MAXWELL, *A History of Worship in the Church of Scotland* (London 1955). W. R. FOSTER, *Bishop and Presbytery* (London 1958). J. HIGHET, *The Scottish Churches* (London 1960). P. F. ANSON, *The Catholic Church in Modern Scotland, 1560–1937* (London 1937); "Catholic Church Building in Scotland . . . 1560–1914," *Innes Review,* 5 (1954) 125–140. J. DARRAGH, "The Catholic Population of Scotland since the Year 1680," *ibid.* 4 (1953) 49–59. W. J. ANDERSON, "Abbé Paul Macpherson's History of the Scots College, Rome," *ibid.* 12 (1961) 3–171; "The College for the Lowland District of Scotland at Scalan and Aquhorties," *ibid.* 14 (1963) 89–212. W. A. MCNEILL, "Documents Illustrative of the History of the Scots College, Paris," *ibid.* 15 (1964) 66–85. K. S. LATOURETTE, *Christianity in a Revolutionary Age: A History of Christianity in the Nineteenth and Twentieth Centuries,* 5 v. (New York 1958–62) v. 1,2,4. Reference. A. H. DUNBAR, *Scottish Kings* (2d ed. Edinburgh 1906). *Handbook of British Chronology,* ed. F. M. POWICKE and E. B. FRYDE (2d ed. London 1961).

[L. MACFARLANE/EDS.]

The Modern Church

Following the Reformation, Catholicism became a minority religion in Scotland, and often a proscribed one as well. Presbyterians eventually came to regard Catholicism as a foreign importation, leaving many Scottish Catholics defensive about their faith. However, the experience of World War II in particular, which brought many Catholic refugees and prisoners of war to Scotland; the all-pervasive influence of radio and television; the greatly increased opportunities for foreign travel; and above all, the nation's higher educational level eventually widened the religious horizons of most Scots, lowered sectarian barriers, and decreased public manifestations of religious bigotry. Following the pontificate of John XXIII, relations among the Catholic Church, the Church of Scotland, and other religious bodies became more amicable, and cooperation in matters of social welfare increased. The laity, too, displayed evidence of solid devotion, an increased interest in liturgical developments, and a critical awareness of events throughout the Church and the world. Still, allegations of discrimination against Catholics surfaced as late as 2000, prompting the Scottish Parliament to form an "equalities unit" to investigate such claims. While the Church of Scotland professed anti-Catholic bigotry among Protestants to be a thing of the past, its own efforts to require Presbyterian rather than more broadly Christian invocations be used to opening the nation's parliament in 1999 echoed the historic relationship between these two faiths.

Catholic Education. Unlike the public schools that were open to all and maintained by local and national governments, Catholic schools were supported entirely by the voluntary contributions of the faithful until 1918, when the Scottish Education Act provided that local education authorities accept full financial responsibility for all voluntary schools in their area. The Act was a landmark in the development of the Catholic community in Scotland because it secured the freedom of religious education while bringing Catholic schools within the state system of education without incurring financial burdens. Somewhat ironically, by 2000 one negative aftershock from the Act was felt as Scotland's teacher's union cited discrimination in initiating a legal battle to end the Catholic school tradition of employing only Catholic teachers. However, from the late 1960s the government policy of comprehensive education that sought to offer every student a similar quality of education, combined with the raising of the school-leaving age from 15 to 16 years in 1972, allowed Catholics to participate fully in the country's educational renaissance, opening many public schools on the primary and secondary levels, and a number of excellent colleges run by religious orders, all supported by local and national public funds. Private Catholic schools charging tuition also existed, adding to the increasing number of Catholic university graduates that went on to participate in Scottish public life and letters during the 20th century. The success of Catholic schools played a crucial role in building a Catholic middle class and integrating Catholicism into the cultural life of Scotland.

Religious orders contributed significantly to the Church's involvement in the life of the nation by their commitment to education in private schools and secondary schools, in chaplaincies at Scottish universities, and in colleges for educating teachers. However, during the late 20th century, as schools throughout Scotland faced rising costs of building, staffing, and maintaining their campuses, the presence of religious in secondary education diminished dramatically, leaving only one Catholic college of education in Scotland, St. Andrew's College in Glasgow. It was funded by the state to prepare all Catholic teachers for Catholic schools in Scotland, a substantial responsibility given the large number of Catholic primary and secondary schools.

Intellectual Life. Among the journals and newspapers devoted to Catholicism was the *Innes Review,* a journal named after Thomas Innes (1662–1744) that was published semi-annually by the Scottish Catholic Historical Committee. The *Scottish Catholic Observer,* a newspaper, focused on more parochial concerns. Library resources included collections on Catholicism at St. Andrew's College of Education and at the national seminary in Glasgow, as well as historical resources in Edinburgh at the Scottish Catholic Archives, Columba House, and in the National Library of Scotland. Extensive divinity collections were also housed at libraries of the universities of Aberdeen, Edinburgh, Glasgow, and St. Andrew's.

A significant phenomenon in the life of the Church in Scotland after Vatican II was the translation of the Sunday liturgies and lectionary readings into Scots Gaelic. This accomplishment brought significant cultural enhancement to the celebration of weekly worship, especially in the parishes of Argyll and the Isles.

Governance. The Scottish Bishop's Conference had its roots in the principle of collegiality that permeated Vatican II. Of the conference's various agencies, the work of the Glasgow-based Scottish Catholic Tribunal achieved the most significant growth, dealing as it did with requests for the dissolution of the bond of marriage and declarations of nullity. The collegiality of the Bishops' Conference also inspired many pastoral letters, some receiving international recognition. After Pope Paul VI's encyclical *Humanae vitae* in July of 1968, the Scottish bishops published a letter in support of the encyclical, confirming the papal teaching and insisting that papal authority on artificial contraception could not be overridden by the primacy of individual conscience. In 1982 the conference published the pastoral letter *Disarmament and Peace.* Considered among their most important, the letter condemned nuclear war and nuclear deterrence as im-

moral. While their stance was acclaimed widely within Great Britain, it received a lukewarm reception at a meeting of bishops called by the Vatican. It was the first time in modern history that Scottish bishops ventured beyond Rome's teaching with regard to a controversial moral concern. In 1990, the Scottish Bishops' Conference published the pastoral letter *A Challenge for the '90s,* implementing Pope John Paul II's call for a decade of evangelization.

Ecumenism. Catholicism remained a minority religion in Scotland, where the Protestant majority was divided between the Church of Scotland (Presbyterian), Anglican, Episcopalian and other denominations. After the Vatican published the *Ecumenical Directory, Part I* in 1967, the National Ecumenical Commission was established in Scotland, and was renamed the Commission for Christian Unity in 1977. In 1969 two official Catholic "observers" attended meetings of the Scottish Churches' Council, and after 1966 similar participation was made in the British Council of Churches. In 1968 the Church of Scotland invited the Catholic hierarchy to send a visitor, the first attending in 1969 with the status changed to delegate in 1991. In 1968 the Catholic Church and the Episcopal Church began an ongoing dialogue, generating such reports as *The Nature of Baptism and Its Place in the Life of the Church* (1969), *The Ecclesial Nature of the Eucharist* (1973), and *Priesthood and the Eucharist* (1979). In 1974 the Joint Commission on Christian Marriage was set up between the Church of Scotland and the Catholic Church, marking the first official talks between them since the Reformation, and by the following year a joint (but not agreed) statement on the doctrine and discipline of marriage was completed. A Joint Commission on Doctrine was also organized. In 1990 an ecumenical breakthrough occurred when the Catholic Church agreed to became a full member of two national ecumenical bodies: the Council of Churches for Britain and Ireland (CCBI) and the Action of Churches Together in Scotland (ACTS). ACTS was launched echoing the words of Pope John Paul II on his 1982 visit to Scotland: "We are strangers no longer but pilgrims together on the way to Christ's Kingdom." Replacing the Scottish Churches' Council, ACTS consisted of nine churches committed to working together.

Religious Life. While corporate religious life ended following the Reformation, by the restoration of the hierarchy in 1878 there were 15 houses for men's orders and 24 houses for women's orders, with considerable expansion thereafter. Despite the improved standing of the Church within Scottish society, there was a statistical decline in many aspects of Catholic religious life during the late 20th century. Between 1965 and 2000 the number of major seminarians declined from 159 to 56. Because of the substantial decline in vocations in Scotland, in the 1990s seminaries and other centers of learning were forced to either consolidate or close. Between 1965 and 2000, the number of diocesan priests decreased by more than a third, from 1,021 to 677 (including religious, the total number of priests declined from 1,309 to 847). Although the Catholic population also decreased slightly—from 826,000 to approximately 760,000—Catholic baptisms and marriages more or less halved in number. Because of changing demographics, the number of parishes increased from 421 to 459, but fiscal management necessitated the closure and amalgamation of many. Similar ratios of decline occurred in the other denominations in Scotland.

Voice of Moral Leadership. In 1994 Glasgow Archbishop Thomas Joseph Winning (1925–2001) became the third Scottish cardinal since the Reformation. Winning remained an outspoken, and even controversial, advocate of traditional Catholic values, and he was tireless in keeping alive public debate on such social issues as declining moral values, abortion, human cloning, sex education in the schools, and institutional racism. By the 1990s Scotland had the highest rate of teen pregnancy in the United Kingdom, a situation prompting the Scottish Health Ministry to dispense more birth control. Winning responded by noting that ''Family life in Scotland is under attack from many quarters,'' and that ''government should be attempting to support it, not undermine it with . . . clinics which effectively promote immorality.'' Pressure also mounted to liberalize abortion laws. In response to this movement, which culminated in the opening of the first abortion clinic in Scotland in 2000, Winning began a pro-life initiative that offered financial and emotional support for pregnant women. And in March of 2001 he achieved a significant victory when his advocacy of teaching core values in the schools resulted in the passage of a law ordering all Scottish schools to instruct students in the vital role marriage and parenthood play within the family. The law was passed at the end of a heated debate over the repeal of Section 28, a law banning the promotion of homosexuality in schools, during which Winning fought tirelessly for preserving the ban. In support of Winning's position on this issue, Scotland's bishops issued a message stating: ''We pray we can build a Scotland of justice for all, free of bigotry and intolerance but ever mindful of God's law and morality.''

Bibliography: B. ASPINALL, ''The Formation of the Catholic Community in the West of Scotland,'' *Innes Review* 33 (1982) 44–57. *Dictionary of Scottish Church History and Theology,* ed. N. M. DE S. CAMERON (Edinburgh 1993). *Catholic Directory for Scotland* (Glasgow 1829–). J. DARRAGH, *The Catholic Hierarchy in Scotland. A Biographical List, 1653–1985* (Glasgow 1985). M. DILWORTH, ''Roman Catholic Worship,'' in *Studies in the History of Worship in Scotland,* ed. D. B. FORRESTER and D. M. MURRAY (Edinburgh 1984) 113–31. G. DONALDSON, ''Into a Secular Age?,'' in *The Faith of the Scots* (London 1990), 138–147. T. GALLAGHER, *Glasgow: The Uneasy Peace. Religious Tensions in Modern Scotland* (Manchester 1987); *Edinburgh Divided* (Edinburgh 1987). C. JOHNSON, *Scottish Catholic Secular Clergy 1879–1989* (Edinburgh 1991). *Modern Scottish Catholicism,* ed. D. MCROBERTS (Glasgow 1979). M. T. R. B. TURNBULL, *Cardinal Gordon Joseph Gray. A Biography* (Edinburgh 1994). *Annuario Pontificio* has latest data annually on all dioceses.

[G. MAGILL/EDS.]

SCOTT, MONTFORD, BL.

Priest, martyr; sometimes spelled Monford Scot; b. c. 1550 at Hawkestead, diocese of Norwich, England; hanged, drawn, and quartered July 1, 1591 in Fleet Street, London. He was one of the earliest theology students at the English College of Douai, having arrived there in 1574. In 1575, while still a subdeacon, he accompanied Dominic Vaughan to England, where they fell into the hands of the authorities in December 1576. Vaughan betrayed the names of Catholics in London and Essex. Released, Scott returned to Douai for presbyteral ordination at Brussels in 1577 then set out for the English Mission in a ship that was attacked by pirates. He worked primarily in East Anglia and is mentioned as having labored in Kent (1580), Norfolk, Suffolk (1583), Lincolnshire, and Yorkshire (1584). In 1584, he was arrested at York with his cousin, Bl. Brian Lacey (beatified 1929), who served as his assistant and whose brother had betrayed them. He was taken to London and imprisoned for seven years until his release was secured by a monetary payment on the condition that he leave the country. Before going into exile, Fr. Scott paid a visit to the prisoners at Wisbeach Castle, where he was again apprehended. Scott was brought to trial (June 30, 1591) at Newgate in the company of Bl. George BEESLEY, condemned for being in the country illegally, and executed the following day. He was beatified by Pope John Paul II on Nov. 22, 1987 with George Haydock and Companions.

Feast of the English Martyrs: May 4 (England).

See Also: ENGLAND, SCOTLAND, AND WALES, MARTYRS OF.

Bibliography: R. CHALLONER, *Memoirs of Missionary Priests,* ed. J. H. POLLEN (rev. ed. London 1924). J. H. POLLEN, *Acts of English Martyrs* (London 1891).

[K. I. RABENSTEIN]

SCOTTISH SCHOOL OF COMMON SENSE

A philosophical school founded by Thomas REID, who held that common sense should not be formed by philosophy, but the latter by the former. "The most immediate conclusions which reason draws from perception constitute common sense" or that body of data according to which men govern themselves in the ordinary affairs of life; the most remote conclusions constitute science. Science and common sense are closely knit "that we cannot say precisely where the former begins and the latter ends." Man's knowledge of nature "can be compared with a tree having its roots, its trunk, and its branches. Perception is the root, common sense the trunk, science the branches" (*An Inquiry into the Human Mind,* 6.20).

Characteristics. Opposed especially to the EMPIRICISM of Locke and Hume, and on many points, to the RATIONALISM of Descartes and Leibniz, the Scottish School has four characteristics: (1) the careful and detailed analysis of the faculties of the mind; thus, according to some of his critics, Reid is convinced that there is a science of observation having the human mind as its object and the internal senses as its means, its result being the determination of its laws; (2) the claim that the reality of things and minds depends upon a "primitive belief," the evidence of which cannot be doubted without opposing common sense; (3) the conclusion that, since man's knowledge is limited to phenomena, he cannot know substance; and (4) since perception is immediate, ideas are excluded as intermediaries, inasmuch as they are deemed to be the source of skepticism and fictitious entities that obstruct the true knowledge of reality.

The last point is the most original aspect in Reid's theory of knowledge as well as that which offers the greatest difficulty. For Reid, perception is different not only from sensation but also from reason. The assent it inspires results from instinct alone; conclusions are thus distinct from what it simply perceives. Perception being the sole basis for reasoning, Cartesian rationalism is overturned and reason is subordinated to what is grasped immediately. Here Reid opposes the mechanistic rationalism of the Cartesians and in preference to the fixed and eternal laws of the intellect, reasserts the spontaneity of human nature by assigning it a prior validity over the rules of reason. Reason comes only later to draw its conclusions: both the immediate conclusions that form common sense and the remote conclusions that constitute science. As an immediate datum, then, perception is the root from which common sense and science spring, both being a part of a whole that is in immediate relation with reason and in mediated relation with perception.

Reid unifies common sense and science, instinct and reason, in opposition to abstract analysis and in support of the validity of the mind's immediate activity. The immediacy of perception is always such without the intervention of reason; yet Reid also assigns a decisive value to reason itself. His perception, moreover, is not the synthetic a priori of Kant. Herein lies the real difficulty in Reid's theory of knowledge. Perception is not synthesis; it contains the two elements of knowledge, independent in themselves, yet related in a way that is inexplicable and impossible to comprehend.

Dugald Stewart. The continuator of Reid's philosophy was his Edinburgh disciple Dugald Stewart (1753–1828), who taught in the university of his native city as well as in that of Glasgow. In his most important works, all published in Edinburgh [*Elements of the Philosophy of the Human Mind,* 3 v. (1792–1827); *Outlines of the Moral Philosophy* (1793); *Philosophical Essays* (1810); *Dissertation Exhibiting the Progress of Metaphysics . . .* 2 v. (1815–22); *Philosophy of the Active and Moral Powers of Man,* 2 v. (1828)], he expounds what he himself calls the teaching about the "fundamental laws of belief." According to this doctrine, there are in man innate primitive and elementary laws that make him believe, with irresistible persuasion, in the existence of the external world (things perceived) and of men (sentient and thinking subjects), in the uniformity of the laws of nature, in the continuity of man's personal identity, etc.

Others in Britain. Even while Reid was still living, he was succeeded at Aberdeen by James Beattie (1735–1803), author of various works of poetry, as well as of the *Essay on the Nature and Immutability of Truth* (1770). At the same time, James Oswald (1715–69) applied the principles of the Scottish School to the problem of religion in his *Appeal to Common Sense in Behalf of Religion* (2 v. Edinburgh 1766–72); denying the validity of metaphysics, he upheld the validity of common sense in reference to the defense of Christian truths. Meanwhile Thomas Brown (1778–1820) succeeded to the chair of moral philosophy at Edinburgh. This chair passed from Brown to H. Colverwood and then to Thomas S. Baynes, who introduced the Scottish School into St. Andrew's University.

During the same era W. HAMILTON (1788–1856) obtained the chair of logic and metaphysics at Edinburgh; the principal edition of Reid's works (1846; 6th ed. 1863) is due to him. When they were reprinted, they contained some works by Hamilton himself that represent one phase of his thought. However, there is a strong influence of Kantian criticism in Hamilton, which thereby became engrafted to the philosophy of common sense. Hamilton extended his agnosticism to time, space and causality. He reproduced the unknown aspects and mysteries in Reid's philosophy, and counterbalanced the idealistic theories of Coleridge and Carlyle. Through this continuator, Reid's philosophy, formulated in such a way as to remedy the skeptical consequences in Hume's thought, was now employed against the audacities of "trancendental philosophy" and assumed a new role in the history of English thought. However, Hamilton, who worked in a cultural climate different from that of Reid, accentuated agnosticism and made the philosophy of common sense similar to that of skeptical PHENOMENALISM, to which the former had been opposed.

Hamilton's disciple was H. L. Mansel (1820–71), who made his teacher's agnosticism even more rigid in his works *The Limits of Religious Thought* (London 1858) and *Philosophy of the Conditioned* (London 1866). Here the inconceivability of the Absolute is expressly taught: "The Absolute cannot be conceived as either conscious or unconscious, complex or simple . . . . It cannot be identified with the universe nor can it be distinguished from it." Nevertheless, the construction of man's mind forces him to believe in the existence of an absolute and infinite Being (a belief based also upon revelation). Driven to this point, agnosticism is mere skepticism and fideism.

Influence Elsewhere. In France, the works of Reid and Stewart were translated by M. Jouffroy (4 v., Paris 1836), with a critical introduction by Jouffroy himself and a life of Reid by Stewart. The psychology of the Scottish School especially became an object of study. Introduced by P. P. Royer-Collard (1763–1843), it spread from the Sorbonne into intellectual circles and influenced Condillacism; its mysterious elements served to unveil the pretenses of Cabanis's materialism. It influenced MAINE DE BIRAN, whose "effort" psychology clarified and amended the teaching of Condillac's followers regarding the passivity of the mind. Excluding the analogy between matter and mind, Reid's psychology of analysis and of interior observation was crystallized, although with vigorous tones and despite the influence of Maine de Biran, in the speculation of T. S. Jouffroy (1796–1842). Finally, although combined without any originality, Reid's motives are present in the ECLECTICISM of V. COUSIN, who preserved as the foundation of his own system, immediate apprehension in the sense of the Scottish School.

The teaching of this school was widely diffused also in Italy, especially in the kingdom of Naples. It was espoused and criticized in relation to Kant's philosophy, notably by P. GALLUPPI, A. ROSMINI-SERBATI and V. GIOBERTI.

The American James McCosh (1811–94), who studied at Edinburgh, introduced the "common sense" doctrine to America, but other Hamilton successors departed from this teaching. The tradition continued at Glasgow until the end of the 19th century, when the school broke

up as the teachings of Berkeley and Hume were revived and post-Kantian idealism exercised its influence.

Bibliography: F. C. COPLESTON, *History of Philosophy* (Westminster, Md 1946–) 5:364–394. M. M. ROSSI, *Enciclopedia filosofica*, 4 v. (Venice-Rome 1957) 4:479–480. M. F. SCIACCA, *Reid* (Milan 1945). F. HARRISON, *The Philosophy of Common Sense* (London 1907). H. LAURIE, *Scottish Philosophy in Its National Development* (Glasgow 1902). J. H. FAUROT, "Common Sense in the Philosophy of Thomas Reid," *The Modern Schoolman,* 33 (1956) 182–189. W. P. KROLIKOWSKI, "The Starting Point in Scottish Common-Sense Realism," *ibid.,* 139–152.

[M. F. SCIACCA]

SCRIBES (IN THE BIBLE)

A group of Jewish leaders who flourished from the time of the Exile until the destruction of the Jewish state by Titus (70 A.D.). Originally their name (Heb. *sōperêm,* writers) was used merely of clerks whose function was to copy royal and sacred manuscripts. Later, the title signified the official post of one who was learned in the Law of Moses (Ezr 7.6, 11; Neh 8.1, 4). The people admired the scribes' erudition and their interpretations of precedents and tradition. Sirach extols the work of the scribe (Sir 38.24–39.11).

At the time of Christ many of the scribes adhered to the teachings of the PHARISEES and shared their casuistry, legalism, and externalism. With the CHIEF PRIESTS, SADDUCEES, and Pharisees, the scribes composed the Jewish aristocracy of the time; and many were members of the SANHEDRIN.

The scribes are mentioned frequently by the Evangelists as being opposed to Jesus and His teaching (Mk 2.6–7, 16; 11.27–28; Lk 5.21, 30; 6.7; 20.1–2, 19–23). They are also associated with the chief priests and ELDERS in causing Jesus' death (Mk 14.43, 53; 15.1, 31; Lk 22.66; 23.10). In Jesus' denunciations of the Jewish leaders Matthew includes the scribes as well as the Pharisees (Mt 23.2–36). The lawyers condemned in Lk 11.45–52 for their hypocrisy are also to be identified with the scribes. Their spiritual descendants were the RABBIS whose teachings are recorded in the TALMUD.

Bibliography: *Encyclopedic Dictionary of the Bible,* tr. and adap. by L. HARTMAN (New York 1963) 2143–44. S. LÉGASSE, "Scribes et disciples de Jésus," *Revue biblique* 68 (1961) 321–345, 481–505. A. F. J. KLIJN, "Scribes, Pharisees, High Priests and Elders in the N.T.," *Novum Testamentum* 3 (1959) 259–267.

[R. MERCURIO]

SCRIPTORIUM

Prior to the invention of the art of printing, books were made and written exclusively by hand (*see* BOOK, THE

Miniature depicting scriptorium activity at Michelberg Cloister, Bamberg, from manuscript by St. Ambrose, first quarter of 12th century.

MEDIEVAL). The Middle Ages differ from antiquity (*see* BOOK, THE ANCIENT) when bookmaking was a commercial enterprise, aimed at selling the published material. In the Middle Ages, during the period that extends to the 12th or 13th century, MSS were as a rule produced with no intention of selling them but primarily for the personal use of the producers, i.e., the monasteries. This was the golden age of the scriptoria. In subsequent centuries (from the 13th to the 16th) it was practically only the CARTHUSIANS who continued, indeed almost more intensively than before, to occupy themselves with producing books for their own libraries as a work pleasing to God, whereas the BRETHREN OF THE COMMON LIFE pursued bookmaking as a trade by which to support themselves. Neither the studios of the Carthusians nor those of the Brethren, however, can be classed with the earlier scriptoria; still less can the MS production of the *stationarii,* of the MENDICANT ORDERS, or of the many private copying establishments that produced most of the books at the end of the Middle Ages, be linked with the monastic scriptorium.

The scriptorium (Du Cange s.v.) was the workroom in the monastery where books were written; it was early made a separate room and was often beside the library, which the scriptorium often needed. By metonymy, scriptorium came to designate the center of the artistic, calligraphic, literary, and scholarly activity of the monastery. The organization of the medieval scriptorium can be quite accurately deduced from numerous reports and from the MSS themselves. The plan of SANKT GALLEN (820–830) presents a diagram that is not a mere idealization, but most probably corresponds to reality. The scriptorium is located under the library; it has six windows and seven writing tables set against the walls, at which the monks wrote sitting down. In the middle of the room is a large table, but it is not known how it was used.

An *armarius* often directed the scriptorium. He had charge of the writing materials, distributed them to the copyists under him (in convents to the nuns), gave them the required instructions, and organized the writing, art work, and collating. He was ultimately responsible for the general management of the scriptorium and was also in charge of the library. Often he was a great writer himself and not infrequently the head of the school, and engaged in scholarly work. By far the most important work in the scriptorium was copying. Independent literary or scholarly production occupied only a relatively small place in the early period of the scriptoria. Whether this latter activity went on in the cell of the scholar or poet in question or in the scriptorium itself must remain in most cases an open question.

Methods of Work. The copying of available texts, which were obtained by exchange with other monasteries or which came from the monastery's own library or were acquired in some other way, did not follow a unified and standardized plan; this at least can be established in the cases where a sufficiently large number of MSS originating from the same scriptorium is available. The possibility existed (and this can often be documented) that a single copyist would reproduce an entire codex. But more often, several copyists were engaged simultaneously in copying one original, which in this case was divided and distributed among them; another possibility was that several copyists successively worked on the original. A third method of procedure was for the main work to be done by a single copyist with others collaborating on a page now and then, i.e., substituting for the main copyist when he had to be absent for some reason or other. These variations in the work can be established quite exactly by means of PALEOGRAPHY. On occasion all these methods are encountered simultaneously in the same scriptorium. Sometimes there is fairly detailed information on the method of distributing the work; occasionally the codex will even contain the names of the copyists, written in another hand, perhaps that of the *armarius.* From an exact paleographic analysis of the individual codices of a scriptorium, the number of copyists simultaneously working on a manuscript can be ascertained. In the same way the method of organizing the work can be discovered. At times detailed information on the original from which the copyists were working is available.

Development of Styles. It is a peculiarity of the scriptoria that in many monasteries obvious idiosyncrasies developed in the script, in abbreviations, in the punctuation and reference marks, and in ornamentation and cover decoration, so that it is possible to speak of specific schools of copyists and of their peculiar scripts. Such schools persisted for varying periods. Often a scriptorium came into being at the beginning of a monastic foundation so that its first copyists were monks who had come from the founding abbey, and their scripts reveal a relation to the MS production of the house from which they came. During the great period of monastic growth, scriptoria were the intellectual centers of the monasteries. In some cases they did not last more than one generation; in others they lasted many decades, even more than a century. The scriptorium revealed the intellectual capacity of its monastery. Of many scriptoria nothing more is known than the names. Many MSS cannot be assigned to any scriptorium for want of decisive local coloration. Even though a school of copyists had distinctive peculiarities of style, as mentioned above, and can in this way be distinguished from other schools, still, besides the "local" manuscripts, one may find manuscripts copied by monks from other houses who, though working in the scriptorium, were unfamiliar with its writing habits. Thus, on the one hand, the appearance of such MSS often shows a remarkable dependence upon other schools or scriptoria. On the other hand, one may also encounter the idiosyncrasies of a given scriptorium in some other scriptorium, so that it must be concluded that either a member of the former scriptorium or someone trained there was the copyist of the MS in question. This is also proof that connections with other places existed, except that here one can recognize an extension of a scriptorium's influence into other regions rather than the transfer of an individual monk. Paleography devotes itself to the investigation of this sort of problem; it contributes to the recognition and clarification of important relationships in intellectual history. Of course, there were many scriptoria that never developed such individualized scripts, but one is not therefore justified in denying them the status of scriptoria.

Stages in the Production of a Manuscript. The individual copyist had a threefold assignment. First, he produced the book-block using the parchment and certain tools given him. The manner of executing this work provides at once the necessary clues by which to ascertain whether the scriptorium was in its beginnings or at the height of its productive activity. The more artistically and carefully the book-block was executed in all its details, the clearer evidence there is that it was done in a model writing room. After completing this work, an important preliminary for the next phase, the scribe began the actual copying. The copyist was provided by the *armarius* with the necessary originals; copying from dictation was rare. A simple codex without richly elaborated initials or illuminations was most often produced by a single copyist (or, as mentioned above, by division of labor); this single copyist would then execute not only the text but also the rubrication. On the basis of much MS material it can be convincingly maintained that, at least in the age of the scriptoria, the red capital letters, decorations, and the like were usually executed by the copyist and not by the *rubricator,* even in the instances in which a blank space was left for the capitals but never filled in. The copyist either executed the rubrication simultaneously with the writing of the text, or he left space for the capitals, etc., and then inserted them after finishing the entire codex, or his part of the work, where it was done piecemeal. Capital letters might naturally be forgotten in this process. If there were entire sentences to be written in red, the copyist often wrote them in tiny minuscule in the margin; but even in such cases the rubrication is very often the copyist's rather than anyone else's. It was a favorite practice of the copyist to add a final wish after the completion of his work: his thanks to God on completing the work, a curse on any person daring to steal the book, a request to the reader to remember the copyist in his prayers, etc.

Identification of Copyists. Much less frequent in centuries before the 14th is the appearance of the copyist's name, the *subscriptio* or colophon; moreover it must be remembered that on occasion the copyist transcribed the colophon of the original, a fact that can lead to errors in interpretation and dating. The colophon of the original can be distinguished easily enough from that of the copy. A MS dated by the scribe is very rare in this period, in contrast to the 14th and 15th centuries when colophons, dating, and entries on place of origin are much more frequent. Pictures of the copyist are equally rare; dedications are more frequent, often in rhymed verse or blank verse; these are important for a relative dating of the codex if the personage named in the dedication can be identified.

Illumination. In the case of illuminated MSS, the sections or the entire codex were handed over, after completion of the calligraphic work, to the *miniator,* who now had the important assignment of executing the illuminated initials, the miniatures, the decorative work, the magnificent titles, *incipit's* and *explicit's,* etc. These were often sketched first on the parchment and then painted. Very seldom did the painters sign their names. Most illuminators are unknown to us. Only very rarely would the calligrapher decorate and illuminate the codex, as did the Engelberg master (*c.* 1200).

Corrections. The third stage of the copyist's work consisted in the collation and correction of the copy. This task was done frequently by the copyist himself, although older, experienced monks were often enlisted to execute this very responsible operation. Corrections made at this stage must be distinguished from the marks on many MSS made considerably later by scholars whose reactions while reading are expressed in corrections, changes in spelling and punctuation, and by marginal and interlinear notes. These notations prove that work and study still went on in the scriptorium for centuries. One of the most important goals of paleographic research is to investigate systematically the medieval scriptoria and to discover their historical environment, as was previously done for such traditional sources as annals, chronicles, profession and confraternity books, necrologies, deeds, etc. For the history of scriptoria, however, MSS that were certainly produced and used in a given scriptorium are the chief source and these must be studied paleographically. The distinguishing features of a scriptorium can be detected in many cases only by meticulous work, by comparison of a script in question with that of MSS positively identified, and by consulting medieval book catalogues; for only in rare cases is the copyist known by name and monastery, or by his individual handwriting.

Bibliography: B. BISCHOFF, *Die südostdeutschen Schreibschulen und Bibliotheken in der Karolingerzeit,* v. 1 *Die bayrischen Diözesen* (Leipzig 1940; 2d ed. Wiesbaden 1960). B. BISCHOFF and

J. HOFMANN, *Libri Sancti Kyliani: Die Würzburger Schreibschule und die Dombibliothek im 8. und 9. Jh.* (Würzburg 1952). C. BONACINI, *Bibliografia delle arti scrittorie e della calligrafia* (Florence 1953). A. BRUCKNER, ed., *Scriptoria medii aevi helvetica* (Geneva 1935–); "Scriptorium," *Historisch-biographisches Lexikon der Schweiz*, ed. H. TÜRLER et al., 7 v. and suppl. (Neuenburg 1921–34) suppl. 156ff. F. M. CAREY, "The Scriptorium of Reims during the Archbishopric of Hincmar (845–888)," in *Classical and Mediaeval Studies in Honor of E. K. Rand*, ed. L. W. JONES (New York 1938). M. L. GIULIANO, *Coltura e attività calligrafica nel sec. XII a Verona* (Padua 1933). I. HAJNAL, *L'Enseignement de l'écriture aux universités médiévales* (Budapest 1954; 2d ed. 1959). L. W. JONES, *The Script of Cologne, from Hildebald to Hermann* (Cambridge, Mass. 1932); "The Script of Tours in the 10th Century," *Speculum. A Journal of Mediaeval Studies* 14 (1939) 179–198; "The Art of Writing at Tours from 1000 to 1200 A.D.," *ibid.* 15 (1940) 286–298; "The Scriptorium at Corbie . . .," *ibid.* 22 (1947) 191–204, 375–394. *Der Karolingische Klosterplan von St. Gallen* (Schweiz). *The Carolingian Plan of St. Gall Abbey* (Switzerland). *Facsimile-Wiedergabe in acht Farben, mit einer Monographie: Der St. Galler Klosterplan, von Hans Reinhardt* (St. Gallen 1952). *Die Kultur der Abtei Reichenau*, 2 v. (Munich 1925). V. LAZZARINI, *Scritti di paleografia e diplomatica* (Venice 1938). É. LESNE, *Histoire de la propriété ecclésiastique en France*, 6 v. (Lille 1910–43); v. 4 *Les Livres, scriptoria et bibliothèques . . .* (Lille 1938); v. 5 *Les Écoles de la fin du VIIIe siècle à la fin du XIIe* (Lille 1940). W. M. LINDSAY, "The Bobbio Scriptorium," *Zentralblatt für Bibliothekswesen* 26 (1909) 293–306; "Breton Scriptoria: Their Latin Abbreviation-Symbols," *ibid.* 29 (1912) 264–272; "The (Early) Lorsch Scriptorium," *Palaeographia Latina*, ed. W. M. LINDSAY, 6 pts. in 1 v. (Oxford 1922–29) 3:5–48. S. TAFEL, "The Lyons Scriptorium," *ibid.* 2:66–73; 4:40–70. W. M. LINDSAY and P. LEHMANN, "The (Early) Mayence Scriptorium," *ibid.* 4:15–39. K. LOEFFLER, "Zur Frage einer Konstanzer Schreibschule in karolingischer Zeit," *ibid.* 5:5–27; "Die Sankt Galler Schreibschule in der 2. Hälfte des 8. Jhs.," *ibid.* 6:5–66; "Die St. Galler Schreibschule in der 1. Hälfte des 9. Jhs.," *Neue Heidelberger Jahrbücher* (Heidelberg 1937) 28ff. J. LOUBIER, "Die Herstellung der mittelalterlichen Bücher nach einer Miniatur des 12. Jhs.," *Zeitschrift für Bücherfreunde* 12 (1908/09) 409ff. E. A. LOWE, *The Beneventan Script* (Oxford 1914). E. A. LOWE, *Codices latini antiquiores. A Palaeographical Guide to Latin Manuscripts prior to the Ninth Century* (Oxford 1934–). H. MARTIN, "Notes sur les écrivains au travail," *Mélanges offerts à M. Émile Chatelain* (Paris 1910) 535–544. H. NELIS, *L'Écriture et les scribes* (Brussels 1918). G. ONGARO, *Coltura e schola calligrafica veronese del sec. 10* (Venice 1925). G. PRAGA, *Lo "scriptorium" dell'abbazia benedettina di San Crisogomo in Zara* (Rome 1930). J. PROCHNO, *Das Schreiber- und Dedikationsbild in der deutschen Buchmalerei*, v. 1.2 (Leipzig-Berlin 1929). E. K. RAND, *A Survey of the Manuscripts of Tours*, 2 v. (Cambridge, Mass. 1929). E. K. RAND and L. W. JONES, *The Earliest Book of Tours . . .* (Cambridge, Mass. 1934). J. VON SCHLOSSER, *Die abendländische Klosteranlage des früheren Mittelalters* (Vienna 1889). *Scriptorium* (Antwerp 1946–47). M. VENTURINI, *Vita ed attività dello scriptorium veronese nel secolo XI* (Verona 1930). W. WATTENBACH, *Das Schriftwesen im Mittelalter* (3d ed. Leipzig 1896; 4th ed. repr. Graz 1958).

[A. BRUCKNER]

SCROLL

Modern readers take for granted the codex form of books in use today. In ancient times, however, the familiar form was that of a scroll (Heb. mᵉgillâ; Gr. χαρτίον βιβλίου in the Bible, also κύλινδρος elsewhere, Lat. *volumen*). Papyrus, leather, or parchment sheets were glued together to form a long strip. The usual dimensions were from nine to 11 inches high and 20 to 30 feet in length, although some scrolls were only five inches high, while others reached 15 inches. The length varied according to the work's length or the type of writing. Thus, a scroll of Romans would have been about 11 ½ feet long; scrolls of Luke and Acts, each 31 or 32 feet, necessitating the two "books" of Luke (Acts 1.1). The DEAD SEA SCROLL of Isaiah (Dsia) ran 35 feet. The books of Samuel, Kings, and Chronicles required three scrolls in the Hebrew originals; but when they were translated into Greek, their length was doubled, and two scrolls were needed for each book. This fact explains the books' modern division into 1 and 2 Samuel, etc. The Pentateuch was written on five scrolls, which were deposited in their containers (τεῦχος) when not in use, and thus came to be called the Pentateuch or "five-container" work.

At times several works were written on one scroll. Thus the 12 MINOR PROPHETS constituted "The Twelve," one scroll (Sir 49.10). Song of Songs, Ruth, Lamentations, Ecclesiastes, and Esther were also usually included on one scroll. By the 6th century A.D. the latter books were known as "the scrolls" (*hammᵉgillôt*).

Normally scrolls were written on only one side, though there were examples of writing on both sides. The exceptional practice is attested to in the Bible (Ez 2.10; Rv 5.1). The text appeared usually in columns four to six inches wide, so that the reader could unroll the scroll to the length of three or four columns as he read (Jer 36.23). The columns were frequently close together with not much room allowed for marginal notes. The scribe cared little about correlating the columns with the glued seams, and as a result the writing often extended over the juncture point.

The scroll was normally read by holding its bulk in the left hand, unrolling it with the right, and reading the columns from right to left. At times, the scroll was attached to wooden rollers, but this was exceptional, and in use only with deluxe editions. The usual practice was to reinforce the beginning and end of the scroll with narrow strips of the writing material in use. In reading only a section of a work, as was required in the synagogue service, a person unrolled the scroll until he came to the desired section, read, and then rolled up the scroll again. An example of this practice is found in Lk 4.17, 20. The scrolls were stored in containers, which at times were simply pottery jars, as is evidenced at Qumran. Since the biblical books for the most part were written on separate scrolls, it is clear that little attention would have been paid to the order of various books in the Bible.

The scroll form was used all through the Old Testament period and during the first centuries of the New Testament. Though the codex, or book form, was known in the 1st Christian century, it was the 2d or 3d century before the scroll form fell into disuse.

See Also: BOOK, THE ANCIENT; ROLL AND CODEX.

Bibliography: *Encyclopedic Dictionary of the Bible,* translated and adapted by L. HARTMAN (New York, 1963) 2144–46. H. GERSTINGER, *Lexikon für Theologie und Kirche,* ed. J. HOFER and K. RAHNER, 10 v. (2d, new ed. Freiburg 1957–65) (1966) 2:748–749. L. KOEP, *Reallexikon der Assyriologie,* ed. E. EBELING and B. MEISSNER (Berlin 1928–) 64–669.

[T. H. WEBER]

SCROPE, RICHARD

Archbishop of York; b. *c.* 1346; d. York, England, June 8, 1405. Born of a noble Yorkshire family, he is said to have studied arts at Oxford and law at Cambridge. He was doctor of both laws by 1379 and was chancellor of Cambridge University (1378–79). He was elected bishop of CHICHESTER in 1385, but King Richard II quashed the election. However, he did become bishop of COVENTRY and Lichfield in 1386 and was made archbishop of YORK in 1398 through Richard's influence. He served Richard as emissary to Scotland and in Rome (where he petitioned unsuccessfully for Edward II's canonization), but was in the deputation that received Richard's resignation; he joined Thomas ARUNDEL, Archbishop of Canterbury, in enthroning King Henry IV (1399). Although closely associated with the rebel Henry Percy, Earl of Northumberland, Scrope was not openly opposed to the government until 1404, when he and Arundel protested parliamentary proposals to confiscate church property. In 1405 Scrope circulated a manifesto charging the King with injustice and demanding reforms. Northern insurgents met the royal army on Shipton Moor, where Scrope and others were captured by trickery. Henry appointed a trial commission headed by Chief Justice Sir William Gascoigne; but he, knowing the law, refused to try a prelate and was replaced. Arundel arrived to protest, but Scrope was summarily convicted of treason and executed, dying with exceptional courage. Pope INNOCENT VII prepared a bull of excommunication against Scrope's murderers; but since England's support was needed against Avignon (*see* WESTERN SCHISM), it remained unpublished. Scrope's tomb in York Minster became a center of pilgrimage, and Northerners called him saint and martyr. Contemporary chroniclers attest to his sanctity. His archiepiscopate saw completion of the rebuilding of York Minster choir.

Bibliography: J. H. WYLIE, *History of England under Henry the Fourth,* 4 v. (London 1884–98) v.2, for relevant chronicle sources. J. TAIT, *The Dictionary of National Biography From the Earliest Times to 1900,* 17:1082–85. A. B. EMDEN, *Biographical Register of the University of Oxford to A.D. 1500,* 2:1659–60. A. B. EMDEN, *Biographical Register of the Scholars of the University of Cambridge before 1500,* 513–514.

[R. W. HAYS]

SCROSOPPI, LUIGI, ST.

Also called Luigi (Aloysius or Louis) of Udine; Oratorian (St. Philip Neri Oratory) priest and founder of the Sisters of Divine Providence (*Suore della Provvidenza*); b. Udine, Italy, Aug. 4, 1804; d. Udine, April 3, 1884. Following Luigi's ordination in 1827, he immediately began an apostolate to tend the poor and abandoned by establishing the *Casa delle Derelitte.* Additionally, he founded the *Casa Provedimento* for the formation of young women and the *Opere* for deaf-mute girls. He formed the women who assisted him in his charitable work into the Sisters of Divine Providence, and placed them under the patronage of Saint CAJETAN. The sisters continue to educate young girls in Argentina (since 1929), Bolivia (1980), Brazil (1927), India (1977), Italy (1837), Ivory Coast (1973), Romania (1992), Togo (1985), and Uruguay (1929). Scrosoppi, known for his exceptional charity and prayer life, gave his family fortune to the poor and joined the Oratorians before he died at the venerable age of eighty. He was both beatified (October 4, 1981) and canonized (June 10, 2001) by Pope John Paul II. The miracle required for canonization (approved July 1, 2000) involved the complete and instantaneous healing in 1996 of a Zambian Oratorian seminarian with advanced AIDS.

Feast: April 3 (formerly October 5).

Bibliography: *Acta Apostolicae Sedis* (1982): 534–37. *L'Osservatore Romano,* Eng. ed. 41 (1981): 1, 12. G. BIASUTTI, *Tutto di Gesù!* (Udine, Italy 1968).

[K. I. RABENSTEIN]

SCRUPULOSITY

Deriving from the Latin *scrupus,* whose diminutive form *scrupulus* means a small sharp stone, scrupulosity signifies habitual and unreasonable hesitation, doubt, coupled with anxiety of mind, in connection with the making of moral judgments.

Description of the Condition. The scrupulous person's life journey has been aptly likened to that of a traveler whose pebble-filled shoes make every step painful and hesitant. Scruples render one incapable of making with finality the daily decisions of life. This psychic impotence, providing a steady source of anxiety and indecisiveness, is especially prevalent in ethical or pseudomoral areas. It causes ordinary, everyday questions to be viewed as impenetrable and insoluble. Decisions require a disproportionate amount of time and energy, and are always accompanied by feelings of guilt and doubt. Never at peace, the mind compulsively reexamines and reevaluates every aspect of a matter about which scruples center. With increasing doubts and mounting fear the mind is so blinded and confused that volitional activity becomes difficult or impossible. The will is unable to act without immediately reacting against its previous decision. There is a more or less constant, unreasonable, and morbid fear of sin, error, and guilt. The mind demands mathematical certitude in moral matters, and when this is not forthcoming, there is a fear reaction that is both unreasonable and unholy.

Scruples occur in varying degrees of severity. They may be temporary or chronic, mild or severe, limited or almost boundless in extent. The temporary attack of scruples is not uncommon, but tends to confine itself to a particular area, and this, most frequently, is sexual in nature. In the young it is often due, partially at least, to faulty information and immature moral development. Chronic scrupulosity tends to be diffusive of itself, showing both stimulus and object generalization.

View Taken by Earlier Moralists and Spiritual Writers. The teaching of moralists and spiritual writers of the past regarding the detection, identification, and treatment of the scrupulous conscience is still valuable as it was based on much accumulated observation and experience, and it should not be discarded as naïve or outmoded simply because emphasis has shifted to a more psychologically sophisticated approach to the problem.

Characteristics. Among the features of the malady that attracted the attention of these writers was that it is often accompanied by a remarkable indifference or laxity of behavior with respect to matters about which the victim is not scrupulous. This, coupled with the fact that the scrupulous person's emotional distress and vacillation of judgment are generally based on slight grounds or none at all, suggested a displacement of anxiety. Moreover, as they observed, the anxiety about sin tends to be self-centered and to involve little real concern about the offense given to God and neighbor. Confessors were cautioned to expect numerous questions, repetitious in form and content, and to be prepared to find their advice habitually ignored, misinterpreted, or challenged. It was observed that under an appearance of docility, obstinacy, doubt, suspicion, and even open hostility can often be detected. Presentation of the victim's excessively complex problems commonly brings all circumstances into sharp

focus, the relevant and irrelevant ones receiving equal emphasis. The tendency of the scrupulous to substitute an exaggerated precision in minor matters for the accomplishment in major ones of which they are—or at least feel themselves—incapable, was noted, as was the intensity of their introspective activity and self-concern. Although they readily seek relief in going to confession, absolution provides them only with reason to doubt their sincerity and the validity of the Sacrament.

Causes. Moralists and spiritual writers have thought that in a negative sense God is a cause of scruples, not that He is the author of the interior suffering, the anxiety, and the bad judgments of the afflicted person, but because He withholds the enlightenment of mind that would dispel the victim's illusion and would enable him to see clearly what is right and what is wrong. God withholds this enlightenment either in punishment for sin or for the purpose of promoting the victim's spiritual development by providing an occasion for the exercise of patience and humility and trust in God. It cannot be supposed, however, that God wishes the scrupulous state to continue if it leads, as often it does, to moral evil such as despair, discouragement, distaste for God's service, and the neglect of prayer.

The positive cause of scruples could be either Satan, whose object is to impede or to destroy the victim's spiritual health, or some physical or psychological condition in the victim himself. Some early writers blamed scruples on keen and overactive imaginations, especially when accompanied by a poor capacity for judgment, or a melancholic or phlegmatic temperament inclining one to suspicion, obstinacy, timidity, or despondency. Other causes were felt to be natural nervousness or association with the scrupulous or faulty training received from scrupulous parents, teachers, or confessors.

Treatment. While admitting the generally apparent futility of proposing remedies to victims of serious scruples, moralists and spiritual directors nevertheless offered directions that seemed to hold promise of bringing relief if only the victim could be brought to follow them, and these no doubt proved helpful to some, especially to those in whom the malady appeared in milder form or was treated in its incipient stages. The scrupulous person was to be convinced that he was really scrupulous, and that his judgment in the matter with which his scruples were concerned was unreliable. He was urged to seek the direction of one good confessor, whose direction he was to follow with humble obedience, and he was not to take his troubles to other confessors. He was not to concern himself with the possibility of being led astray, because even if the confessor or director erred, he (the penitent) would not be held accountable. His examinations of conscience were to be brief; he should never seek peace of mind by giving way and acting as his scruples prompted. The hope of finding peace in that way was bound ultimately to prove illusory, and the scrupulous condition would only be aggravated by yielding to it and so lead to greater anxiety in the future. The penitent was to act without question upon the confessor's judgment that doubtful sin was not certain sin, and that he need not confess doubts but only certainties. If disturbed about the possibility of having consented to evil thoughts, he was to assume that there was no consent; if troubled about his past confessions, he must assume that they were good.

In spite of the effectiveness of this method of treatment in some cases, it often failed because it dealt with the disturbance too exclusively on the superficial level of symptoms. It was open to criticism also on the grounds that it tended to make the scrupulous person, already lacking in normal maturity and self-reliance, too dependent on his confessor. This danger was recognized, however, and some authors tried to provide against it by recommending that the penitent, after gaining some victories over his condition, should be led little by little to rely more upon his own judgment.

Contemporary Thought. More recent moralists and spiritual writers show the influence of modern psychological theory and tend to see in scruples a disorder involving the deeper levels of personality dynamics and development. The malady is viewed as a form of neurosis, an obsessive-compulsive reaction characterized by unavoidable thoughts, always unpleasant, and frequently accompanied by compulsive behavior. About 1900 Pierre Janet classified it as a psychasthenia, an obsolete term indicating a kind of psychic weakness that disturbs the delicate balance of psychic energy, tipping it in the wrong direction. He noted that the "fixed ideas" of hysterics were amenable to suggestive therapy, whereas those of the scrupulous were not. Cure could be achieved, he thought, by discovering the source of disequilibrium and restoring balance through reeducation.

The psychoanalytic movement retained the notion of psychic energy but gave emphasis to conflicts in the unconscious realm of personality. New concepts were evolved to describe the symptoms. The reality-testing ego is the battleground for the conflicting demands of the animal-like id and angel-like superego. The superego makes excessively high demands on the ego by imposing impossible standards of conduct. Simultaneously pulled into the dirt by the id and lifted up to the heavens by the superego, the conscious ego is torn apart. It is unable to form practical judgments and attempts to effect a compromise in the form of various defense mechanisms. Some view scruples as an infantile attempt to avoid responsibility and think, therefore, that a confessor who exacts unquestioning obedience merely increases this futile dependency.

Those who take the view that scrupulosity is more an emotional sickness than a moral one think that in severe cases at any rate the priest should give way to the physician. The scrupulous do not confess their sins but rather their unconsciously motivated anxiety. For them confession is primarily an obsessional purification rite and only secondarily a Sacrament. They seek alleviation not through moral perfection but in achieving infallible precision in details. Since the malady is essentially unconscious and emotional, therapy directed at the intellectual components will naturally be ineffective.

Evidence of a scientific and statistical nature is still rare because of the inherent difficulties of the matter. On the basis of tests scruples have been estimated to occur in varying degrees of severity in 20 to 30 percent of adolescents. Equally distributed as to sex, it seems more related to the age variable, with puberty the peak period. If transitory, adolescent scruples may last for varying periods up to three years. Frequently faulty knowledge retards the proper development of conscience and this appears to contribute to the incidence of scruples. The more severe and chronic cases may indicate graver pathology and possibly a psychotic condition. While knowledge of scruples has grown and the appreciation of their complexity has increased, the precise cause or causes are still a matter of theory. As a consequence, the most effective methods of therapy still await either refinement or invention.

Bibliography: ALPHONSUS LIGUORI, *Theologia moralis,* ed. L. GAUDÉ, 4 v. (new ed. Rome 1905–12) 1.11–19. A. GEMELLI, *De scrupulis* (2d ed. Florence 1921). F. V. RAYMOND, *Le Guide des nerveux et des scrupuleux* (Paris 1926). J. L. DUFFNER, *Pour consoler et guérir les âmes scrupuleuses et craintives* (Tournai 1938). *Proceedings of the Institute for the Clergy on Problems in Pastoral Theology* (New York 1958–). A. SNOECK, *Confession and Pastoral Psychology,* tr. T. ZUYDWIJK (Westminster, Md. 1961). A. TANQUEREY, *The Spiritual Life,* tr. H. BRANDERIS (2d ed. Tournai 1930; repr. Westminster, Md. 1945). N. IUNG, *Dictionnaire de théologie catholique,* ed. A. VACANT et al., 15 v. (Paris 1903–50; Tables générales 1951–) 14.2:1735–45. O. FENICHEL, *The Psychoanalytic Theory of Neurosis* (New York 1945).

[C. HARNEY]

SCUPOLI, LORENZO

Theatine spiritual writer (name in the world, Francesco); b. Otranto, Italy, *c.* 1530; d. Naples, Nov. 28, 1610. Nothing is known of his early life. In 1569, when he was about 40, Scupoli entered the Theatines at the convent of S. Paolo Maggiore in Naples. There he made his novitiate under St. Andrew AVELLINO. He pronounced his solemn vows in 1571 and was ordained in Piacenza at Christmastide 1577. In 1578 he began his ministry at Milan, whence he was transferred to Genoa and, in 1588, to Venice. From 1589 to 1591, he was at Padua, where it is said he met Francis de Sales, then a student at the university. In 1585, the general chapter of the Theatines ordered that Scupoli be reduced to the lay state, for some reason that has never been revealed. He himself offered no defense, and he spent his remaining 25 years in retirement in Theutine houses.

Scupoli is generally credited with the authorship of the *Spiritual Combat*, although it has, at times, been ascribed, in whole or in part, to other authors. The work first appeared anonymously in 1589, the year the young Francis de Sales received a copy of it from a Theatine in Padua. The first edition to bear Scupoli's name was published in Bologna in 1610, the year of his death. It is agreed by historians that the basic chapters, at least, were produced by Scupoli and may have been added to by others. Many editions of the book have been published, and it has been translated into all the modern languages. It is considered to be a spiritual work of great value.

Other works are ascribed to Scupoli, notably *Del Modo di consolare ed aiutare gli infermi a ben morire* and *Il modo di recitare la Corona della Madonna*. The *Della pace interiore*, or *Sentiero del Paradiso*, and *Dolori mentali de Cristo*, long considered Scupoli's work and sometimes published with the *Spiritual Combat*, are now thought the writings of others.

Bibliography: H. BRÉMOND, *Histoire littéraire du sentiment réligieux en France depuis la fin des guerres de religion jusqu'a nos jours* 7:52–57. P. POURRAT, *Christian Spirituality*, v.3 (New York 1927; repr. Westminster, Md. 1953). FRANCESCO ANDREU, *The Catholic Encyclopedia* 11:203–204.

[P. MULHERN]

SEABURY, SAMUEL

First Protestant Episcopal bishop of Connecticut; b. Groton, Conn., Nov. 30, 1729; d. New London, Conn., Feb. 25, 1796. He was the son of an Anglican missionary. After graduating from Yale College (now University) in 1748, he studied medicine at the University of Edinburgh, Scotland. Having decided on the ministry, he was ordained in 1753 and served parishes in Jamaica, L.I., and Westchester (now Bronx), N.Y. When he published a series of pamphlets against the Continental Congress, using the pseudonym *A Westchester Farmer,* he was imprisoned in 1775 by the American authorities. Following his release, he joined the British army as a chaplain in 1776. Seabury, elected bishop of Connecticut, was consecrated in 1784 by the bishops of the Scottish Episcopal Church at Aberdeen. As bishop, he published *The Order for Holy Communion, with Private Devotions* (1786), which was adopted in the American *Prayer Book* of 1789. In the same year, he united the autonomous church in Connecticut with the Protestant Episcopal Church in the other states. He also secured restoration of the Nicene and Athanasian Creeds, and clearer recognition of the episcopate, priestly orders, and Sacrament of Baptism.

Bibliography: E. E. BEARDSLEY, *Life and Correspondence of the Right Reverend Samuel Seabury* (Boston 1881). W. THOM, *Samuel Seabury* (Greenwich, Conn. 1962).

[R. K. MACMASTER]

SEAL

Ancient seal devices were frequently used throughout the ancient Near East. The Israelites were acquainted with the usage of seals by other peoples (Gn 41.42; Est 3.12; Dn 6.17), but they also used them from earliest times, the first recorded incident being preserved in the clan saga of Judah where the patriarch surrendered his signet and cord, probably a cylinder seal, to Tamar (Gn 38.18). Probably every free citizen owned a seal bearing his name and emblem.

The seal was used to authenticate or ratify legal, commercial, or official documents. In an age when the art of writing was in the hands of a special class of scribes, such documents had to be certified. The seal established rights and fixed responsibility. A Mesopotamian could simply roll his cylinder seal across a clay tablet, thereby authenticating its contents. If his seal depicted his gods, he would also be placing the document under their protection. In areas where papyrus or leather was used as writing material, the owner could impress his stamp seal into the lump of clay that had been pressed on the string holding the rolled or folded document, or he could use ink and stamp the document itself. Thus Jezebel "wrote letters in Ahab's name and sealed them with his ring" (1 Kgs 21.8), Jeremiah sealed the deed for the field he bought from Hanamel (Jer 32.10, 44), and Isaiah had a cylinder seal made for his future son (Is 8.1–2).

Besides authenticating a document, the seal often was used as a means of security. Thus sealed documents could be opened only by authorized persons. Closed doors were sealed by stretching a rope over the stone blocking the entrance and then impressing a seal into the lump of wax or clay affixed to the rope. Isaiah, for example, entrusted a sealed oracle to his disciples (Is 8.16). Only the proper person might open the scroll sealed with seven seals in Rv 5.2, 5, 9. The lion's den was sealed shut

Cylinder seal of Darius I "The Great" (hunting lions). (The Granger Collection, New York)

to keep unauthorized persons out in Dn 6.17, and the tomb of Christ was sealed to prevent the disciples from stealing the body (Mt 27.66).

Finally, in some areas, seals, especially scarab seals, lost all significance and were worn by women and children as decorative amulets. On the other hand, the mere possession of a seal could be regarded as a badge of delegated authority. Examples are found in Gn 41.42; Est 3.10; and 1 Mc 6.15. The word for seal was used frequently in the Bible in a metaphorical sense, the general signification being that of authentication, ratification, or security (Sg 8.6; Dt 32.34; Rom 4.11).

Bibliography: *Encyclopedic Dictionary of the Bible,* translated and adapted by L. HARTMAN (New York, 1963) 2147–51. J. HASTINGS and J. A. SELBIA, eds., *Dictionary of the Bible,* 5 v. (Edinburgh 1963) 892–893. O. TUFNELL, *Interpreters' Dictionary of the Bible,* 4 v. (Nashville 1962) 4:254–259. A. G. BARROIS, *Manuel d'archéologie biblique* v.2 (Paris 1953). D. DIRINGER, *Le iscrizioni antico-ebraiche palestinesi* (Florence 1934); "The Royal Jar-Handle Stamps of Ancient Judah," *The Biblical Archaeologist* (New Haven 1938) 12 (1949) 70–86. P. W. LAPP, "Late Royal Seals from Judah," *The Bulletin of the American Schools of Oriental Research* 158 (1960) 11–22.

[T. H. WEBER]

SEATTLE, ARCHDIOCESE OF

Metropolitan see in the state of Washington, bounded by the Canadian border on the north, the Columbia River on the south, and extending from the crest of the Cascades on the east to the Pacific Ocean, an area of 24,834 square miles. In 2001 there were 525,040 Catholics in a total population of 4,526,200. It was erected May 31, 1850, as the Diocese of Nesqually, but was renamed the Diocese of Seattle (*Seattlensis*) on Sept. 11, 1907; it became an archdiocese June 23, 1951 and the metropolitan see of the Seattle Province, with dioceses of Spokane and Yakima as its suffragan sees.

First Missionaries. The area's Catholic history began with the arrival at Fort Vancouver on Nov. 24, 1838, of two missionary priests, Francis Norbert BLANCHET and Modeste Demers, who had been sent from the Diocese of Quebec, Canada, in answer to the repeated requests of the Canadian and Iroquois employees of the Hudson's Bay Company. There Mass was celebrated for the first time by Blanchet, vicar-general of the new mission, which numbered 26 Catholics, Canadian and Iroquois. Within a short time, Demers learned the Chinook language, began to instruct the native residents, translated the most important prayers, and composed hymns. From

Vancouver, Blanchet visited the Catholics at Cowlitz, where several delegations of Native Americans came to hear and see the Blackgown. To instruct the native peoples, Blanchet hit upon a singularly effective device called the Catholic ladder. Taking a flat board, he drew 40 marks to represent the 40 centuries before Christ. With 33 points, he indicated the 33 years of Christ's life. A cross recalled the Redemption. Eighteen marks and 39 points represented the years since the birth of Christ. At either side of this symbolic outline of Church history, the missionary graphically represented important Christian doctrines. The use of the Catholic ladder spread widely and rapidly.

Demers followed the route of the hunters and trappers, visiting settlements and stopping at Nesqually, Walla Walla, and Colville. Within a few years, the company's chief factor, James Douglas, permitted the missionaries to make foundations south of the Columbia. In 1842 Pierre Jean DE SMET, SJ, arrived at Vancouver from the northeast section of the Oregon Territory, where he had been sent by the bishop of St. Louis, Mo., to work among the native peoples. At a conference of the missionaries, it was decided that De Smet would try to enlist additional workers in St. Louis and Belgium and also bring to the attention of ecclesiastical authorities the need for a bishop in the Oregon Country. His mission succeeded: De Smet returned to Oregon with more helpers and on Dec. 1, 1843, the Oregon mission was made a vicariate apostolic with Blanchet as vicar apostolic.

After his consecration in Montreal, Canada, on July 25, 1845, Blanchet sailed for Europe to enlist assistance for his vicariate and to lay its needs before the Holy See. On July 24, 1846, Plus IX named him archbishop of the new Province of Oregon City; his brother Augustine Magloire Alexander Blanchet was appointed bishop of the newly established Diocese of Walla Walla; and Father Demers was named bishop of Vancouver Island.

Augustine Blanchet. The first and only bishop of Walla Walla, who in 1850 became the first bishop of Nesqually, was born near St. Pierre Riviere du Sud, Canada. He was ordained on June 3, 1821, became a canon of the Cathedral of St. James in Montreal, and was consecrated bishop of Walla Walla on Sept. 27, 1846. When he left Canada, he had with him only one priest for his new jurisdiction, John BROUILLET; but four others, Oblates of Mary Immaculate, joined him later. In the northeastern part of the diocese five Jesuits worked among the native populations. Shortly after Blanchet's arrival in his diocese—which included eastern Washington and eastern Oregon, the state of Idaho, that portion of Montana west of the Rockies, and the northwest corner of Wyoming—the Protestant missionary Dr. Marcus Whitman was mur-

St. James's Cathedral, Seattle, Washington.

dered on Nov. 29, 1847. Because of the hostilities resulting from this crime and its punishment, the presence of non-natives at Walla Walla and its vicinity was forbidden, so the bishop established his headquarters at the Dalles.

In 1850, after the bishop had petitioned the Holy See to move his headquarters to Ft. Nesqually near Vancouver, Rome officially made the territory of Nesqually a diocese. This region, until 1850 subject to the Archdiocese of Oregon City, included the territory west of the Cascade Mountains and north of the Columbia. When appointed bishop of Nesqually, Blanchet decided to establish his cathedral at Vancouver, where it remained until 1907. Among those who worked under him for the welfare of the diocese were Fathers John Brouillet, Charles Marie Pandosy, and Eugene Casimer Chirouse, and the Sisters of Charity of Providence. The first Mass was said in the city of Seattle in 1852 by Bishop Demers. In 1853 the Diocese of Walla Walla was suppressed and Nesqually acquired that part of its territory west of the Rockies, north of the Columbia and the 46th degree of latitude. In 1868 the creation of the Vicariate Apostolic of Idaho further reduced the area of the diocese, confining it to the limits of the state of Washington. When Blanchet resigned in 1879 he was named titular bishop of Ibara; he died Feb. 25, 1887.

Junger and O'Dea. Blanchet's successor, Aegidius Junger, who had served the diocese since ordination, was consecrated on Oct. 28, 1879. An earnest worker, fluent in English, French, and German, the new bishop directed the diocese well during a period when Washington became a state and the Catholic population increased from 12,000 to 30,000. To care for parishes and missions, the bishop sought the help of Jesuits, Redemptorists, and Benedictines. The Sisters of the Holy Names, Dominicans, Good Shepherd, and Franciscan Sisters undertook the direction of new schools in various parts of the diocese. The Brothers of Our Lady of Lourdes staffed a school in Seattle. Under Junger 60 new churches, including a cathedral, were built, and 15 parish schools, two schools for Native Americans, and three colleges begun.

Junger died on Dec. 26, 1895, and Edward John O'Dea was consecrated at Vancouver, Wash., on Sept. 8, 1896. The problems facing the young bishop were enormous; among these were heavy debts on the cathedral and diocese, and a great financial depression throughout the country. The pastors and their people generously cooperated with the bishop to meet the financial problem. In response to the bishop's appeal to other dioceses throughout the country and in Europe for priests for his ever-increasing flock, volunteers arrived, many of them from Ireland.

When the first years of the 20th century brought a change in the center of state activities to Seattle, Bishop O'Dea found it increasingly difficult to administer the diocese from Vancouver. Accordingly, he made Seattle the cathedral city, built St. James Cathedral, and dedicated it on Dec. 22, 1907, announcing the official change in title of the diocese from Nesqually to Seattle. A few years later, the increasing population of eastern Washington impelled O'Dea to recommend to Rome the establishment of a new diocese in that part of the state and on Dec. 17, 1913, the Diocese of Spokane was created. The line of division, north and south, nearly coincided with the 120th meridian and the north and south course of the Columbia River. In 1928 the bishop decided to establish a seminary in Seattle under the Sulpicians, a project the bishops of the province had approved in 1917. The first students were admitted to the new St. Edward's Seminary on Sept. 15, 1931. O'Dea survived the completion of his work only a year, dying Dec. 25, 1932. During his tenure the number of Catholics in the diocese had increased from about 42,000 to 100,000, diocesan priests from 40 to 113, the regular clergy from 29 to 123, and churches from 42 to 90.

Shaughnessy and Connolly. On July 1, 1933, Pius XI appointed Gerald SHAUGHNESSY, SM, bishop of Seattle. Without delay, he set about strengthening the finan-cial structure of the diocese. He also sought and obtained priests from other sections of the country and from Europe, and founded the SERRA INTERNATIONAL for help in recruiting and supporting seminarians. The years of Shaughnessy's administration were important for the consolidation and organization of diocesan affairs rather than for the multiplication of buildings. He suffered a serious cerebral hemorrhage in 1945 and, after several years of enforced inactivity, died on May 18, 1950.

In February 1948, upon Shaughnessy's petition, Rome had appointed Bp. Thomas A. Connolly, auxiliary of San Francisco, as coadjutor bishop of Seattle with the right of succession. Connolly, once chancellor of the archdiocese of San Francisco and pastor of the historic Mission Dolores parish there, had been consecrated in San Francisco on Aug. 24, 1939. Soon after his arrival in Seattle, he began to make plans for celebrating the centenary of the diocese. Missions were preached in all parishes as part of the spiritual program, and work on the renovation of the cathedral was begun. A pilgrimage, led by Bishop Connolly, journeyed to Rome to unite the jubilee of Seattle with that of the Universal Church. On Sept. 14, 1950, Amleto Cicognani, then apostolic delegate to the U.S., celebrated the centennial Mass of thanksgiving in the presence of the largest gathering of the hierarchy the Pacific Northwest had yet seen.

The next year, Pope Pius XII created a new ecclesiastical province in the Northwest (June 23, 1951); Seattle became the metropolitan see of the new province and Connolly the first archbishop. At the same time Pius XII created the Diocese of Yakima from parts of Spokane and of Seattle and appointed the Most Reverend Joseph P. Dougherty, chancellor in Seattle, as ordinary of the new suffragan see. During the next few years, it became more and more difficult for Archbishop Connolly to perform all episcopal functions and attend to the multiplying details of administration. In 1956 Rome appointed Thomas E. Gill, rector of St. James Cathedral and archdiocesan director of Catholic Charities, as auxiliary bishop of Seattle.

To provide the laity with retreat facilities all year round, Connolly undertook the construction of two retreat houses. Numerous educational institutions of the archdiocese were established also under Connolly's direction, among them Blanchet High School, Seattle (1955), and the major seminary of St. Thomas the Apostle, Kenmore (1958). The first, a coinstructional school for 1,500 students, is directed by priests of the archdiocese, assisted by sisters of various communities and by lay teachers. The new seminary' building was dedicated on April 14, 1959, by Cardinal James McIntyre of Los Angeles, Calif., the first students having been received the preceding September. Connolly's record of accomplishment included the establishment of 26 parishes, 30 schools, and an extensive building program.

Connolly retired because of age and on Feb. 25, 1975, Raymond G. Hunthausen (1975–91) became the second archbishop of Seattle. As bishop of Great Falls, Mont., Hunthausen was the youngest bishop in attendance at the Second Vatican Council. Inspired by the ecclesiology of Vatican II he moved to instill in the archdiocese a vision of the local church as a communion of communions (parishes). He promoted formation of the laity, engaged extensively in ecumenical conversation, and participated in tax resistance as a protest against nuclear weapons. His commitment to peace, including nuclear disarmament, garnered international attention. It inspired many inside and outside the church, and evoked opposition in a state with a heavy military presence. In the 1980s, the Holy See investigated allegations of liturgical and doctrinal irregularities in the archdiocese. Chicago-born Thomas J. Murphy, who had been bishop of Great Falls since 1978, was appointed coadjutor archbishop in 1987 and became third archbishop of Seattle when Archbishop Hunthausen retired in 1991.

After Archbishop Murphy died of leukemia in June 1997, Bishop Alexander J. Brunett, since 1994 the bishop of Helena, was installed as his successor. Archbishop Brunett committed himself to the participative leadership style of his two predecessors and to fostering collaboration among the parishes and other agencies of the archdioceses.

Bibliography: D. BUERGE and J. ROCHESTER, *Roots and Branches* (Seattle 1988). P. O'CONNELL KILLEN, "The Geography of a Minority Religion: Roman Catholicism in the Pacific Northwest," *U.S. Catholic Historian* 18/3 (Summer 2000): 51–72. W. SCHOENBERG, *A History of the Catholic Church in the Pacific Northwest, 1743–1983* (Washington, D.C. 1987). C. A. SCHWANTES, *The Pacific Northwest: An Interpretive History* (Lincoln 1996). C. TAYLOR, ed., *Abundance of Grace: A History of the Archdiocese of Seattle 1850–2000* (Strasbourg, France 2000).

[J. MCCORKLE/EDS.]

SEBASTIAN, ST.

Early Christian martyr. Sebastian is commemorated in the *Depositio Martyrum* (c. 350) as buried in the cemetery *in catacumbas,* and is mentioned in other martyrologies, for his cult spread rapidly. St. Ambrose says that he was a native of Milan and suffered during the persecution of Diocletian between 297 and 305. This seems to be confirmed by the place of his tomb *in catacumbas,* which cannot be older than the second half of the third century.

The *Passio S. Sebastiani,* a romance compiled c. 450, was probably the work of a monk of the monastery that Pope SIXTUS III erected *in catacumbas* to expand the cult. According to it, Sebastian was an army officer condemned for the faith to be pierced with arrows by his fellow soldiers; he was buried by the matron Lucina *in catacumbas in initio cryptae iuxta vestigia Apostolorum.* The Romans credited him with the cessation of the plague in 680; they had invoked him mainly because the arrows were likened to nails, which were always looked upon in Rome as a sacred-magical means "to nail down ill luck."

Under the Renaissance he was represented as an old soldier; then, as a young man with strong delicate limbs or as a heroic soldier before the archers. In art he is most important, and there is a vast iconography. In the earliest representations he is depicted as a bearded Roman warrior, later as a cleanshaven younger man. The scene of his first "martyrdom" with arrows is the most popular episode of his life seen in painting and sculpture. According to legend he recovered and was later beaten to death. This event and the scene with St. Irene nursing his wounds are rare. He is frequently depicted in altar paintings merely standing and holding an arrow, or as punctured with arrows.

Feast: Jan. 20.

Bibliography: *Acta Sanctorum* Jan. 2:621–660. G. MANCINI and B. PESCI, *San Sebastiano fuori le mura* (Rome 1959). B. PESCI, "Il culto di S. Sebastiano a Roma," *Miscellanea historica Oliger* (Rome 1945) 177–200. V. KRAEHLING, *Saint Sébastian dans l'Art* (Paris 1938).

[E. HOADE]

SECKAU, ABBEY OF

Benedictine, in the Diocese of Graz-Seckau, Styria, Austria, founded with Augustinian canons from SALZBURG cathedral in 1140; a double monastery until c. 1500. It came under an elected provost with the creation of the See of Seckau in 1218 by Abp. Eberhard II of Salzburg. In 1782 JOSEPH II suppressed it, but Benedictines from BEURON resettled it in 1883. Abbot Ildefonse Schober (1887–1908) rebuilt church and abbey. Under Abbot L. Zeller, Seckau restored the abbey of St. Matthias (Trier) in 1922. After 1926 Abbot Benedict Reetz established a secondary school (gymnasium) and printing press and made Seckau a center of the liturgical movement, notably by publishing the Seckau popular Breviary. The abbey was restored in 1945 after suppression in 1940. The Romanesque basilica (three naves, three apses, no transept, flat roof) was built in Saxon style (1143–64). The tomb of Archduke Charles II (c. 1600) is late Renaissance, and the huge monastery is 17th-century Renaissance. In 1963 H. Boeckl completed frescoes of the Apocalypse in the Angel Chapel, and a crucifixion group

"Martyrdom of Saint Sebastian," painting by Il Sodoma, Galleria Palatina, Palazzo Pitti, Florence. (©Archivo Iconografico, S.A./
CORBIS)

was raised over the new main altar in 1964. Gold work is done in the abbey today. Seckau's MSS are in the University of Graz. Since 1932 the abbey has published *Seckauer Hefte* and *Seckauer geschichtlichen Studien*.

Bibliography: B. ROTH, *Seckauer Apokalypse und ihre Deutung* (Vienna 1961); *Seckau: Geschichte und Kultur* (Vienna 1964). V. REDLICH, *Lexikon für Theologie und Kirche,* ed. J. HOFER and K. RAHNER, 10 v. (2d, new ed. Freiburg 1957–65) 9:560–561.

[V. REDLICH]

SECOND SOPHISTIC

"New, or Second Sophistic" is a term used in the third century A.D. by Philostratus in his *Lives of the Sophists* in reference to Greek rhetoric and oratory after Isocrates (436–338). Today the first century is used as the boundary between the "New Sophistic" and the "Old," and with a modern sense of the unity of Greco-Roman civilization, "Second (New) Sophistic" now includes both late-Greek models and derivative Latin rhetoric, pagan writings and their Christian counterparts. Philostratus finds the essentials of the New Sophistic already elaborated in the Old; but the Old had, in its earlier stages, a far more comprehensive aim than the production of oratory. Even in its oratorical achievements the Old Rhetoric was far superior in style and content to the theatrics of its successor. For in the turbulent decades from Pericles to Alexander, as in the last century of the Roman Republic, the Old Sophistic was self-transcendent. Moreover, it constantly competed with philosophy after Socrates. The Second Sophistic, as oratory, had no rival until Christianity adopted its devices. Apart from its chronological function, the term also denotes the aesthetic decline and pervasive extravagances in oratory and other literary genres, both pagan and Christian, from A.D. 100 to 500.

Rhetoric as Precursor. The Old Sophistic began in the fifth century B.C. as a method of educating men capable of solving the complex political problems of the new democratic city-state after the Persian Wars. In the sixth century poetry had still been the educational medium of leadership, instilling a sense of hereditary nobility in a simple, aristocratic society. In the fourth century, Plato, carrying on the polemic for reform initiated by Socrates, sought to replace poetry by philosophy in this office. Instead, the Sophistic prevailed in education from the fifth century onward, despite the poverty in theory of which the philosophers justly accused it. It lasted not only because it served to awaken the intellectual powers required for leadership, as did poetry and philosophy, but also because it invented an instrument for quickly mastering the growing individualism of the citizens by winning votes,

and later, for furnishing this individualism with opportunities for identification, escape and entertainment to fill the void left by the failure of democracy. This instrument, rhetoric, is comparable in many respects to modern liberal education in its aims, prerequisites and curriculums. Although it was the pioneer for Western prose of ordered discourse and those stylistic adornments hitherto the monopoly of poetry, it was at the same time the precursor of the aesthetic excess that later characterized the absurdities of the Second Sophistic. Gorgias, who brought the Sicilian rhetoric into Athens in 427 B.C., called rhetoric "the artificer of persuasion." In other words, it was the key to power (and to ultimate self-corruption) not only in the legislature and courtroom but also in public assembly where suffrage was limited to applauding or jeering the performer and his performance.

Dominance of Epideixis. The obscure beginnings of rhetoric in fifth-century Athens are embodied in the remains of the deliberative oratory used in legislative gatherings and in the forensic oratory of the courts, and are preserved in Greek from Antiphon through Aeschines. However, a third type, epideixis or display oratory, anticipating the essentials of the Second Sophistic, is found in remnants of Gorgias. The subject matter for Gorgias was incidental to oratorical and histrionic technique. Gorgias' mindless confection in praise of Helen of Troy, for example, is a euphonious, calculated outpouring of strange words, audacious metaphors, parallelisms of structure and sound, sense and no-sense substituted for substance. It is a demonstration of what the orator could effect without conveying a message. Isocrates in the fourth century, reacting to the anti-oratical polemic of Plato, tried to give solidity to the epideixis by introducing Panhellenic and patriotic ideals, but failed. The reliance of Sicilian rhetoric on probability rather than proof, as well as the philosophical relativism of leading sophists, hindered the Isocratic reform. The decline of integrity resulting from the Peloponnesian War, the cloistral character of the schools even in politically active periods, and the tendency of oratory to pervert values led to further decline in rhetorical responsibility. With the collapse of Isocrates' Panhellenism and the last illusions about Greek liberty, unabashed epideixis prevailed as a symbol of the general contemporary flight from reality, and in its long reign over rhetoric and oratory left its impress on other literary forms until the end of antiquity.

Fusion of Asianism and Atticism. In Athens, after the death of Alexander, epideixis was confined mostly to the schools, but it found a public outlet in the cities of Asia Minor where departures from the best Attic standards paralleled the soft ways of the people. There the short, choppy sentences of Gorgias with their heavy cadences, meaningless metaphors, elaborate circumlocutions, outlandish themes and specious loftiness could flourish uninhibited by recollections of Isocrates and his Attic predecessors. These new extravagances spread over the Mediterranean basin, to win the pejorative shibboleth "Asianism" as early as 300 B.C. About a century later, in reaction to the excesses of Asianism, "Atticism" arose, with its equally excessive adherence to classic Attic style. Out of the commingling of these two archaistic escapes from the present came, c. A.D. 100, the Second Sophistic. This may be described as the epideictic oratory of Asia Minor tempered by the influence of Alexandrian scholarship.

Influence of the Second Sophistic. Despite the dominance of the Second Sophistic from c. the second to sixth century many writers by intention, taste, or indifference refrained from its extravagances. Among these were Epictetus and Plutarch, as well as Lucian, Arrian, Appian, Ptolemy and Cassius Dio. Marcus Aurelius also was impervious to it, as were most of the earliest Christian writers. The Christian apologists retained traces of their sophistic training despite themselves. But the Neoplatonist Plotinus was concerned with thought, not style, while Clement of Alexandria purposely did not "write well," and ORIGEN was allergic to false rhetoric. Only with St. GREGORY THAUMATURGUS among Christians does preoccupation with style become conspicuous. Christianity in its final struggles with paganism, in the fourth century, helped to save orators from the worst of the standard sophistic excesses. Such pagans as Libanius and Himerius and the great Christian orators, Basil, Gregory Nazianzen and John Chrysostom—although excessive at times, even in the denouncing of sophistic devices—nevertheless rose above their training. With the settling of the Trinitarian controversies, the banning of public pagan worship, Augustine's adapting of the best pagan techniques to Christian rhetoric (*Doctr. christ.*) and the spread of asceticism and mysticism, the Second Sophistic had almost disappeared by the early sixth century. It had been the most conspicuous surviving symptom of the malaise of the age and a classic example of the failure of an art form to transcend itself.

Bibliography: G. LEHNERT, "Griechisch-römische Rhetorik 1915–1925," *Jahresbericht über die Fortschritte der Klassischen Altertumswissenschaft*, 285 (1944–55) 5–11; for a digest of literature from 1874 to 1914 and complete coverage of the literature from 1915 to 1925. J. M. CAMPBELL, *The Influence of the Second Sophistic on the Style of the Sermons of St. Basil the Great* (Catholic University of America Patristic Stud. 2; Washington 1922). C. S. BALDWIN, *Medieval Rhetoric and Poetic to 1400* (New York 1928). W. KROLL, *Paulys Realenzyklopädie der klassischen Altertumswissenschaft*, ed. G. WISSOWA et al., (Stuttgart 1893–) Suppl. 7:1039–1138. K. GERTH, *ibid.,* Suppl. 8:719–782.

[J. M. CAMPBELL]

SECRET, DISCIPLINE OF THE

Latin, *disciplina arcani.* A custom prevalent in the early Church, particularly from the 3d to the 5th century, forbidding the divulgence of information concerning the sacred rites and truths.

The term discipline of the secret was first used by the Protestant theologian Jean DAILLÉ in a work on the writings of PSEUDO-DIONYSIUS (Geneva 1666) and evoked a violent controversy between Canon Emmanuel van Schelstrate and the Protestant W. Ernest Tentzel. In the 19th century it was thought that this custom was prevalent in the primitive Church and was modeled on the pagan mystery religions whose rites and secrets could be shared only with the initiated. But other than a prudential circumspection, no secrecy was imposed; this practice actually began only later with the formal organization of the CATECHUMENATE.

The earliest martyrs publicly proclaimed the truths of the faith and the practices of their cult (Pliny, *Epist.* 10.96); the 3d-century pagan polemicist CELSUS was extremely well informed with regard to Christian beliefs and practices; and JUSTIN MARTYR unhesitatingly gave details of the Baptismal and Eucharistic Liturgy (*Apol.* 1.61–67). It was in the 4th century that the ceremonies of Baptism were surrounded with an aura of secrecy; this liturgical development grew out of the fact that the Christian rites and beliefs were only gradually revealed to prospective converts. In the homilies of St. Athanasius, CYRIL OF JERUSALEM, JOHN CHRYSOSTOM, THEODORET OF CYR, EPIPHANIUS OF SALAMIS, BASIL, and GREGORY OF NAZIANZUS, frequent mention is made of this secrecy that is found in the West with AMBROSE, ZENO OF VERONA, AUGUSTINE, PETER CHRYSOLOGUS, and Pope INNOCENT I. They insisted upon the mysteries of the Christian faith, which do not pertain directly to this world. This discipline was extended to (1) Baptism and Confirmation, the Baptismal Symbol, and the Our Father, and other teachings that were to be communicated to the catechumens only gradually; (2) the rites and formularies of the Eucharist; (3) the sacred Scriptures; (4) the church, for during the ceremonies, the doors of the edifice were kept closed and non-Christians were excluded; and (5) the time, for the solemn initiatory ceremonies were performed during the night.

This practice was surrounded with a casuistry that increased the sensibility of the Church in exercising prudence in the communication of its beliefs and mysteries; but no law is known that enforced this silence on the neophytes, nor is there any indication of an oath or promise of secrecy exacted from the catechumens. After the 5th century only a rapid, perfunctory reference was made by the Fathers to secrecy or silence concerning the truths of faith.

The liturgy retains traces of this custom. In the Divine Liturgy of the Eastern churches, the deacon admonishes the catechumens to leave the church before the Offertory. In the West, this practice was reintroduced in the restored CATECHUMENATE.

Bibliography: H. GRAVEL, *Die Arcandisciplin* (Lingen 1902). P. BATIFFOL, *Études d'histoire et de théologie positive. Deuxième serie, L'Eucharistie* (9th ed. Paris 1930) 1–41. O. PERLER, *Reallexikon für Antike und Christentum*, ed. T. KLAUSER [Stuttgart 1941 (1950–)] 1:667–76. A. ZEOLI, *Storia della chiesa* (Brescia 1959–) 1:49–50. H. I. MARROU, ed. and tr., *À Diognète* (*Sources Chrétiennes*, ed. H. DE LUBAC et al. (Paris 1941–) 33; 1951.

[G. FERRARI/EDS.]

SECRET SOCIETIES, CHURCH POLICY ON

Since the early 18th century, secret societies have existed in the United States. Their membership and influence reached a peak in the late 19th century, probably as a result of the social and economic insecurity of the period and the attraction of their mysterious rituals. Many U.S. Catholics gave their allegiance to secret societies that had originated in Ireland because of English oppression; others became involved in those of Continental and English origin, i.e., Masons, Odd Fellows, Knights of Pythias, and United Workmen. The last group, deist in their philosophical outlook, emphasized fraternal benevolence and maintained insurance systems that provided a measure of economic security not easily available elsewhere. Although their spokesmen insisted that the societies' teachings were moral rather than religious, the organizations developed cults of their own. The extent of Catholic membership among them cannot be ascertained, but it was sufficient throughout the century to occasion anxiety among the bishops, who objected particularly to the oath-bound secrecy of these associations, the blind obedience exacted from their members, and their tendency to undermine revealed religion by emphasizing a purely natural morality as the one requirement for human perfection.

In condemnation of secret societies, Pope Clement XII issued *In Eminenti,* in 1738; Benedict XIV, *Providas,* in 1751; Pius VII, *Ecclesiam,* in 1821; and Leo XII, *Graviora,* in 1825. These bulls named as reasons for censure the oath-bound secrecy of the societies and their conspiracies against Church and State. U.S. bishops found it difficult to decide whether the bans applied to groups, such as the Odd Fellows and Sons of Temperance, that, although secret, were not conspiratorial. The fact that 19th-century labor unions had to be secret if they were to survive further complicated the issue. Naturally the secrecy of the groups made it difficult for the bishops to gain information about them or to be sure of the accuracy of such information as they could obtain.

From 1794 when John Carroll first mentioned the matter until 1895 when it was finally settled, there was recurrent controversy that was intensified after 1880 because of the alarming growth of these groups. Seventy-eight fraternal societies had been established in the United States by 1880, and 124 new ones had developed by 1890. Five years later, 136 additional groups had emerged, while in the next six years 230 more established themselves. By the end of the century their combined rosters carried about 6,000,000 names. Large cities contained more lodges than churches, and these centers of growth for secret societies were also centers of Catholic population.

Decisive action on the part of individual bishops was restrained by a decree of the second Plenary Council of Baltimore (1866), which declared: "We do not wish that anyone in these Provinces, in any ecclesiastical dignity, whatever, should from now on condemn by name any society, unless it certainly and beyond all doubt is clearly one of those comprehended in the Pontifical Constitutions, insofar as they were interpreted by the Sacred Congregation of the Inquisition."

This directive effectively prevented the condemnation of individual societies for a generation. At the third Plenary Council of Baltimore (1884), the fathers agreed that condemnation of any society should be reserved to a committee consisting of all the archbishops. Should they fail to reach unanimity in any given case, the matter would go to the Holy See for decision. The most significant aspect of this policy was that even the nonsubversive secret societies, so numerous in the United States, could be condemned if the archbishops reached unanimity. Debate was focused largely on the Ancient Order of Hibernians, a large, influential society whose rosters included many practicing Catholics, and which was suspect in ecclesiastical circles because of its reputed ties with the subversive Clan-na-gael and Board of Erin fraternities, and with the Molly Maguires, Pennsylvania coal miners who protested the inhuman conditions of their employment with acts of violence.

Meanwhile, the question of the Knights of Labor arose when Cardinal Elzear Taschereau of Quebec condemned the union as a secret society. In 1886 at a meeting in Philadelphia ten out of 12 U.S. archbishops voted against any condemnation of the Knights (*see* KNIGHTS OF LABOR). At their meeting in 1892 the archbishops considered the Odd Fellows, Sons of Temperance, and Knights of Pythias, and, failing to reach unanimity, referred the matter to the Holy See. In 1894 the Holy Office notified the U.S. hierarchy through Abp. Francesco Satolli, the apostolic delegate, that the faithful should be kept from these orders. However, Leo XIII left the execution of the decree to the prudence of the archbishops. As the condemnation was finally interpreted, Catholic members of these societies could keep passive membership for the purpose of protecting their insurance payments, should this be necessary.

Bibliography: F. MACDONALD, *The Catholic Church and the Secret Societies in the United States,* ed. T. J. MACMAHON (U.S. Catholic Historical Society 22; New York 1946). H. J. BROWNE, *The Catholic Church and the Knights of Labor* (Catholic University of American Studies in American Church History 38; Washington 1949).

[J. BLAND]

SECRETARIAT FOR NON-BELIEVERS

The Secretariat was established by Pope PAUL VI in April 1965; and Franz Cardinal Koenig, Archbishop of Vienna, was named as its first president. The seed for its creation was sown by Pope JOHN XXIII when he addressed his 1963 encyclical letter *PACEM IN TERRIS* to "all men of good will" as well as to believers. The Pope realized that a new world order of peace and justice could not be achieved unless there was cooperation between Catholics, other Christians, and "men of no Christian faith whatever, but who are endowed with reason and with a natural uprightness of conduct."

Pope Paul VI developed this understanding further in his first papal encyclical, *Ecclesiam Suam* (1964), when he wrote that it is not the right course for the Church "to isolate itself from dealings with secular society" or to limit itself to "pointing out the evils that can be found in secular society, condemning them and declaring crusades against them" or "to strive to exert a preponderant influence on it or even to exercise a theocratic power over it." Rather, the path for the Church to follow in its dealings with the world "can better be represented in a dialogue . . . conceiving the relationships between the sacred and the secular in terms of the transforming dynamism of modern society, in terms of the pluralism of its manifestations, likewise in terms of the maturity of man, be he religious or not, enabled through secular education to think, to speak and to act through the dignity of dialogue."

VATICAN COUNCIL II also contributed to this perspective, especially in two documents published on Dec. 7, 1965. In its Declaration on Religious Freedom it indicated dialogue as one way in which truth can come to be known freely and without coercion, in accord with the dignity of the human person (1, 3). The Constitution on the Church and the Modern World, addressed to "the whole of humanity" indicated that the existence of atheism constituted a problem that was in need of understanding and of resolution through dialogue on matters of basic concern to all peoples.

There were two prominent dimensions of the Secretariat's activity. One was the development of a fuller understanding of dialogue both as a method and in practice. Its document on "The Dialogue with Non-Believers" (March 8, 1967) stressed the importance of dialogue: "The dignity and value of human persons are always better recognized by our contemporaries within the framework of the general evolution of culture and society. In fact the intensification of social relations has helped man to realize that pluralism is a characteristic dimension of society. But true pluralism is possible only if men, communities and cultures hold dialogue." In pursuit of this goal the Secretariat recommended and offered support to such dialogues and the structures necessary to support them in various nations and locales.

A second dimension of its activity was stressed by Cardinal Koenig when the Secretariat was opened—that is, the task of carrying on and encouraging scientific research with regard to the bases of atheism and conveying the results of that research to Catholics, in its periodical *Ateismo e Dinlogo.*

At its peak, the Secretariat comprised some 30 bishops from around the world, assisted by over 50 consultants and experts. In 1988, it was reorganized under Pope John Paul II's apostolic constitution *Pastor Bonus* (1988), and renamed the Pontifical Council for Dialogue with Non-Believers. In 1993, its functions were subsumed into the newly formed Pontifical Council for Culture.

[J. F. HOTCHKIN/EDS.]

SECRETARIAT FOR NON-CHRISTIANS

This secretariat was inaugurated by Pope PAUL VI on Pentecost Sunday 1964 with Cardinal Paolo Marella as its first president. The basis of its work was further established in *ECCLESIAM SUAM,* the first encyclical letter of Pope Paul, dated Aug. 6, 1964. In it he set forth the necessity and extent of the dialogue with others in which the Church must engage as an indispensable feature of its life in the face of religious pluralism. This need was further stated in *Nostra Aetate* (Oct. 28, 1965), the declaration of VATICAN COUNCIL II on the non-Christian religions.

The secretariat was given a permanent role in the Roman Curia in the 1967 reform of the Church's central administration (*Regimini Ecclesiae Universae*).

From its inception, the secretariat sought to initiate contact and dialogue with all other major religions (except for Judaism, which came under the purview of the secretariat for promoting Christian unity). Over the years, the secretariat had shown itself to be both innovative and productive. Documents issued under its auspices reflect the expertise of its permanent staff and worldwide consultors. In addition to its *Bulletin,* published three times a year, the secretariat issued both general and specific guidelines for engaging in dialogue with various religious groups, a brief presentation of the Catholic faith for use by non-Christians, and in-depth studies of the religious experience itself. The secretariat sought to engage experts from other religious traditions directly in its own meetings. In 1988 the secretariat was reorganized under Pope John Paul II's apostolic constitution *Pastor Bonus* (1988), and renamed the PONTIFICAL COUNCIL FOR INTER-RELIGIOUS DIALOGUE.

[J. F. HOTCHKIN/EDS.]

SECRETS

In ordinary usage a secret (*secretum,* from *secernere,* to set apart) means some hidden knowledge, something that is known only to one person, or to a very few. The question of secrets enters the moral sphere because a person has a right of ownership to his secrets. There is a moral obligation to respect this right. And the protection of the right is necessary in the interest of the individual and for the welfare of the community. Thus the obligation to respect the right of secrecy arises basically from the virtue of justice—from commutative justice primarily but also from social justice.

Since a person owns his secrets, others may not seek to acquire them unjustly, and if they do acquire them, justly or unjustly, they may not lawfully use them or further divulge them in any way contrary to the reasonable will of the owner. So long as secrets remain intact—that is, in the exclusive possession of their owner —they pose no general moral problems. Particular circumstances, however, could arise in which the owner of the secret would be bound to divulge the hidden knowledge if this divulgation were really necessary to prevent serious loss or injury to the public good or to innocent persons, and if it could be made without disproportionate loss to the owner.

The moral obligations and problems arise more immediately when the secrets have somehow passed from the owner and have come into the possession of another or of some few others. Traditionally moral theology begins its discussion of secrets at this point, and a secret is briefly defined as "the possession of some hidden knowledge belonging to another that may not be divulged."

Division. There are three kinds of secrets: natural, promised, and entrusted. This is a broad division and various subdivisions might be introduced under each class. But these subdivisions have no particular moral relevance except under the third class of entrusted secrets.

The Natural Secret. This secret is hidden knowledge concerning another that may not be divulged because its divulgence would cause pain, offense, or loss to the owner of the secret. The obligation to honor such a secret arises from the nature of things and thus derives immediately from the natural law. Violation of this obligation is a sin against justice and also against charity. It does not matter how the secret knowledge was acquired—whether by chance or by fraud. The sin committed by the violation is objectively grave if serious pain, offense, or injury results to the owner.

The Promised Secret. A secret of this kind is so called because its specific obligation arises from a promise made, after the acquiring of the hidden knowledge, not to divulge it. The content of the promised secret may have been freely revealed by the owner or may have become known by chance or even by fraud. The obligation that arises from a promised secret *qua tale* is one of fidelity to the promised word, which generally binds under pain of venial sin. Exceptionally, however, the person giving the promise might freely intend to bind himself in justice and *sub gravi,* and in these exceptional circumstances, violation of a promised secret would be a grave sin if the matter in issue were of grave consequence. It may happen also, indeed it will often happen, that a promised secret, by reason of its content, will also be a natural secret, and when this is so the principles governing violation of natural secrets apply.

The Entrusted Secret. A secret is of this kind when it is revealed by the owner to another on trust. That is to say, when the owner reveals it under a prior agreement or understanding—which may be express or implied—that the recipient will not divulge it to others. Thus an agreement to preserve the secret is a condition on which it is shared. The condition may be expressly stipulated—that is formally asked for and accepted; or it may be implicit—that is, implied in the relationship that exists between the parties concerned. The secret is shared on the accepted understanding that it will be conserved by the recipient because this person is in a position or office of trust vis-à-vis the owner of the secret. Consequently the implicitly entrusted secret is often identified with the official or professional secret. While this identification is not entirely complete, the professional secret is the most important, as well as the most usual, type of implicitly entrusted secret. This secret arises for instance, between a client and his legal adviser; between a patient and his doctor; between a priest and those who seek his advice confidentially *extra tribunal,* and at the highest level—indeed at a unique level—between the penitent and the confessor.

From the entrusted secret, by reason of the onerous contract or quasi contract involved in it, there arises an obligation of strict justice—a grave obligation *exgenere suo.* This obligation is additional to that which derives from the secret *qua* natural. Moreover, the preservation of professional secrets is necessary for the common good—to ensure free and confident access to the various levels of professional advice and, therefore, violation of these secrets is also an offense against social or legal justice. Professional secrecy is safeguarded in the provisions of Canon Law. Civil codes also generally grant privilege to at least some kinds of professional secrets.

Exceptions to Moral Inviolability. Leaving aside the question of the sacramental seal, which entails a unique inviolability, the obligation that flows from other secrets is not absolute. In general the obligation to observe the secret remains so long as the owner retains his right over it. He may voluntarily forgo this right—provided that doing so does not disproportionately injure others. It is often said that it may be presumed the owner of a secret forgoes his right to it whenever its observance would entail injury or loss to himself. This is certainly a reasonable presumption in regard to natural and promised secrets but it may not always be readily applied in the case of professional secrets because in these there is a nonpersonal factor to be considered, namely, the public good. A person may lose his right to have his secrets conserved. In estimating the cause that involves this loss of right and justifies revelation of a secret, account must be taken of the type of secret in question. The more serious its nature and its content, the more grave must be the cause required to justify its revelation. As a general guiding principle it can be said that the advantage gained from the revelation must always outweigh the loss sustained, with all relevant factors taken into account. This particular type of judgment always demands a delicate assessment of all the values involved.

The assessment is particularly difficult in the case of professional secrets, which, in addition to their contractual element, have a great social importance. Yet these secrets are not inviolable. The commonly accepted teaching of moralists is that it is lawful, even obligatory sometimes, to reveal a professional secret if its observance en-

tails grave injury to the common good, to an innocent third party, to the professional person to whom the secret has been entrusted, or to the owner of the secret. But great caution must be exercised in applying these excusing causes. Professional secrecy must be jealously guarded as a feature of civilized living. In the exposition of the excusing causes it would be preferable, and indeed more accurate, to say that the professional secret must be sedulously observed unless its revelation is really necessary to prevent a disproportionately grave injury to the common good, to an innocent third party, to the recipient, or to the owner of the secret. The qualification "disproportionately" is very important, however difficult it may be to apply it, when some imponderable elements are in the issue. The professional secret is in possession, so to speak. It must, therefore, be evident after a careful balancing of all the factors that, as a result of the violation of the professional secret, the benefit accruing to the common good or to the individuals mentioned clearly outweighs the injury done to the personal and social values inherent in this type of secret. In fine, the revelation of a professional secret (apart of course, from the case of the free and justifiable permission of the owner) is lawful only as a last resort, that is, when the revelation is the only available means to prevent serious and imminent injury to the common good or to innocent individuals.

Bibliography: THOMAS AQUINAS, *Summa Theologiae* 2a2ae, 70.1. ALPHONSUS LIGUORI, *Theologia moralis* 3:970–972. B. H. MERKELBACH, *Summa theologiae moralis,* 3 v. (8th ed. Paris 1949) 2:852–856. T. A. IORIO, *Theologia moralis,* 3 v. (4th ed. Naples 1953–54) 2:276–283. H. DAVIS, *Moral and Pastoral Theology,* revised and enlarged by L. W. GEDDES (New York 1958) 2:422–425. R. E. REGAN, *The Moral Principles Governing Professional Secrecy with an Inquiry into Some of the More Important Professional Secrets* (Washington 1941) 20–25, 95–112. N. IUNG, *Dictionnaire de théologie catholique,* ed. A. VACANT, 15 v. (Paris 1903–50; Tables générales 1951–) 14.2: 1756–64.

[J. L. MCCARTHY]

SECT

Historically, the term "sect" applied to religious movements within the Christian tradition that deviated from official (i.e., Catholic) doctrines and/or conflicted with Church authority. Modern usage of the term is less theologically oriented and is derived, instead, from the sociological theorizing of Max WEBER (1864–1920) and Ernst TROELTSCH (1865–1923). Troeltsch, in particular, was the first to develop an extensive typology contrasting sect with church-type social organizations.

According to Troeltsch, structural and ideological differences in "church" and "sect" orientations were dialectical developments inherent in the tension within

Christianity between accommodation with, and protest against, "the world." The sect tended to be smaller, more intimate and exclusivistic, egalitarian, lower-class, and a more ethically austere and demanding religious group. The sect was also voluntaristic, stressed personal achievement, and held that the locus of spirit or charisma lay within the individual rather than the ecclesiastical institution or office. The church, in contrast, was universalistic, inclusivistic, instrumental of objective grace, hierarchical, and sacramental. Unlike the ascribed nature of church membership, sect membership was voluntary.

H. Richard NIEBUHR (1894–1962) applied the church/sect distinction to Christianity in the United States. Niebuhr saw division in the Church stemming primarily from Christianity's inability to transcend social and economic realities rather than from theological factors, as did Troeltsch. Niebuhr also asserted that sects, as voluntaristic organizations, were valid for only one generation. With few exceptions, sects inevitably became more accommodationist toward their cultural milieu, thereby forming a new social structure called a "denomination." Denominations tended to be more middle-class, had differentiated lay/ministerial roles, and espoused more of a world-accommodating ethos than that associated with sects.

Because of the structural differentiation of religion in modern society and the fact that correlates associated with the concept "sect" have not always held up with consistency in the face of empirical research, efforts have been made to move discussion of the term away from Troeltsch's "ideal type" scheme. One approach has been to assert that the key to sectarianism lies in the concept of tension; sects are religious movements that hold deviant beliefs from cultural norms and standards. Sects also devalue nonmember attributes and remain separatist. Another approach focuses on types of sects (viz., conversionist, introversionist, revolutionist, utopian, manipulationist, thaumaturgical, reformist) in relationship to how religious groups answer the key question of "what shall be done to attain salvation?"

More recent scholarship has defined a sect as a religious movement seeking to cause or prevent change in a system of beliefs, values, symbols, and practices concerned with ultimate reality. What distinguishes a sect from other types of religious movements (i.e., a "cult") is the fact that a sect has a prior tie with another religious organization. To be a sect, a religious movement must be schismatic in nature, although the sect need not break entirely from a church; sects sometimes break off from other sects. Because sects are schismatic groups, they typically present themselves as something old and uncorrupted, as the authentic, pure, and/or a refurbished ver-

sion of the faith from which they separate. CULTS, by contrast, are more syncretistic and do not have a prior tie with another religious body in the society in which they exist.

Considerable research has also been devoted to the developmental dynamics of sectarian movements, particularly the tendency on the part of sects to assume a more accommodating posture over time. This tendency has generally been associated with changes in the class composition of sects, the difficulties of maintaining separation and isolation, and the weakening of admission standards and ethical requirements.

It has also been observed that "sectarian" tendencies can be maintained within a church or denominational structure. Catholic religious orders with their voluntaristic nature, requirements of celibacy, high levels of personal commitment, special dress, and rules for expulsion illustrate these dynamics.

Bibliography: E. TROELTSCH, *The Social Teachings of the Christian Churches* (London 1931). L. VON WIESE and H. BECKER, *Systematic Sociology* (New York 1932). H. R. NIEBUHR, *The Social Sources of Denominationalism* (New York 1929). A. EISTER, "Toward a Radical Critique of Church-Sect Typologizing," *Journal for the Scientific Study of Religion* 6, 1 (1967) 69–77. B. JOHNSON, "On Church and Sect," *American Sociological Review* 28 (1963) 539–549. B. WILSON, *Religious Sects* (New York 1970). R. STARK and W. S. BAINBRIDGE, *The Future of Religion: Secularization and Cult Formation* (Berkeley, Calif. 1985).

[W. D. DINGES]

SECULAR ARM

The theory and practice on the part of the Church of turning to the State for carrying out the punishment for grave crimes committed by clerics, and in particular for the punishment of persistent heresy in the case of laymen as well as clerics. The use of the secular arm in such cases had largely disappeared by the end of the 18th century.

See Also: HERESY; INQUISITION; CHURCH AND STATE.

Bibliography: R. NAZ, *Dictionnaire de droit canonique*, ed. R. NAZ, 7 v. (Paris 1935–65) 2:980–981. R. LAPRAT, *ibid.* 981–1060. J. LECLER, *Catholicisme. Hier, aujourd'hui et demain*, ed. G. JACQUEMET (Paris 1947–) 2:232–234. C. JOURNET, *The Church of the Word Incarnate*, tr. A. H. C. DOWNES, v.1 (New York 1955).

[M. M. O'CALLAGHAN]

SECULAR INSTITUTES

With the apostolic constitution, *Provida Mater Ecclesia*, dated Feb. 2, 1947, Pope Pius XII formally recognized secular institutes as a specific and unique form of total consecration to God and others, lived out in the secular state. Historically, secular institutes had precedents in the ministry of St. Angela Merici (*c.* 1474–1549), whose followers remained in their homes while consecrating themselves to God and carrying out charitable works. In various parts of Europe, as persecution, anticlericalism, and social and cultural secularism threatened the foundations of the faith and placed increasing obstacles in the way of priests and religious, initiatives were undertaken to bring the Gospel into the fabric of society in more discreet ways. An early clerical institute, Priests of the Sacred Heart, was founded in the eighteenth century by Père Pierre-Joseph Picot di Clorivière (1735–1820) following the suppression of the Jesuits in France. In Poland, Bl. Onorato Kosminski, OFM Cap. (1829–1916) founded numerous institutes. In Italy, Agostino Gemelli OFM (1875–1959) wrote a *Pro Memoria* (1939) defending the possibility of lay persons consecrated to God in the world, and with Armida Barelli, he founded the Missionaries of the Kingship of Christ.

Foundational Documents.. The apostolic constitution *Provida Mater Ecclesia* recognized secular institutes as a true and complete "state of perfection." Before its publication, the state of perfection, or consecrated life, had been considered synonymous with religious life. The apostolic constitution also provided the particular legal norms (*lex peculiaris*) needed for the institutes since there was no reference to them in the 1917 Code of Canon Law. In the *lex peculiaris* secular institutes were distinguished from all other associations by the fact that their members "make profession of the evangelical counsels, living in a secular condition for the purpose of Christian perfection and full apostolate" (Art. I). Members were permitted to use a vow, oath, or consecration binding in conscience for celibacy, and vows or promises for poverty and obedience (Art. III).

On the first anniversary of *Provida Mater Ecclesia*, Pope Pius XII's *motu proprio* entitled *Primo feliciter* complemented the earlier document, using terminology that continues to be echoed in ecclesial texts. Secular institute members must be light, salt, and leaven in the contemporary world (Intro.). They live a full profession of Christian perfection "in the world," adapted to secular life (II-a). The whole consecrated life of the members must "become an apostolate" in the world and growing out of the world (II-b).

A third foundational document was an instruction from the Sacred Congregation for Religious, *Cum sanctissimus* (March 19, 1948). It provided additional guidelines to help distinguish secular institutes both from associations that did not have the characteristic of a total-

ly consecrated life, and from religious institutes whose lifestyle and law they were not to follow (n. 7-d; n. 8). The distinction between members in the strict sense, and others associated with them, flowed from the stable assumption of the evangelical counsels (n. 7-a).

Vatican II. In *Perfectae caritatis*, the Decree on the Renewal of Religious Life (1965), the Second Vatican Council reaffirmed that secular institutes are not religious institutes, although they involve "a true and full profession of the evangelical counsels in the world" (n. 11). The institutes, whether of men or women, clerics or laity, are identified by their secular character, carrying on an effective apostolate everywhere in and, as it were, from the world. They are to be leaven for the strengthening and growth of the Body of Christ. The original inspiration of a transforming presence in the midst of temporal realities was greatly enriched by Vatican II's ecclesiology and its emphasis on the role of the laity in the Church and the world. The identification of the laity's secular character for permeating temporal affairs with the spirit of the Gospel (*Lumen gentium* n. 31) coincided with the role assigned to secular institutes. *Apostolicam actuositatem* (1965) on the apostolate of the laity provided further validation of lay members' lives which, through consecration, were to become apostolate. The Pastoral Constitution on the Church in the Modern World, *Gaudium et spes* (1965), articulated the Church's radical redefinition of its own locus within the modern world, reflecting on such issues as culture, economics, social life, politics, human solidarity, and peace. Pope Paul VI, saw the charism of the secular institutes as a realization of that reality and referred to them as "experimental laboratories" in which the Church could test her relations with the world. He frequently described the life of the members with synthetic terms, such as "secular consecration" and "consecrated secularity."

Canonical Norms. The 1983 Code of Canon Law for the Latin Church replaced the *lex peculiaris* of *Provida Mater Ecclesia*. As institutes of consecrated life, secular institutes are regulated by the norms common to all such institutes (cc. 573–606) and by those specific to secular institutes (cc. 710–730). Their particular identity in continuity with the earlier documents is preserved in the canons. The members' role of contributing to the sanctification of the world from within (c. 710) is carried out without a change in their canonical status as lay persons or clerics (c. 711). While their whole consecrated life is to become apostolate (c. 722 §2), their particular apostolic activities will follow from their particular state. Laity share the Church's evangelizing task in and of the world, through the witness of their lives and their efforts to inform the temporal with the power of the Gospel (c. 713 §2). Clerics work for the sanctification of the world through witness within the presbyterate and through sacred ministry (c. 713 §3). The gospel image of leaven characterizes the apostolic approach of secular institutes and their members (c. 713 §1). Typically, lay members work individually in any form of secular profession or labor, although some institutes have certain corporate works.

The assumption of the evangelical counsels in secular institutes continues to allow for the use of diverse sacred bonds. These bonds and the obligations flowing from them must be defined in the constitutions of each institute. A life of permanent celibate chastity is integral to membership in secular institutes. The life of evangelical poverty and the obligations of obedience will be defined in constitutions, preserving the distinctive secularity of the institute (c. 721). Normally members contribute from their earnings to the financial needs of the institute, but do not place their goods in common or depend on the institute for their material needs or future retirement. Because clerical members are usually incardinated in a diocese, they depend on the diocesan bishop except in matters specific to their consecrated life in the institute (c. 715 §1). In keeping with the secular character of the institutes, members live in the "ordinary conditions of the world," alone, with family, or with others of their institute (c. 714). They are to maintain an intense spiritual life of personal, liturgical, and sacramental prayer; retreats; and spiritual direction (c. 719).

Provida Mater Ecclesia provided for secular institutes to follow, with adaptation, the model of religious and of societies for structuring offices and organs of governance (IX). There are moderators with councils at various levels, and delegate assemblies through which members participate in the animation and governance of the institute. Moderators are to foster the unity of spirit of the institute and encourage active participation of members (c. 717 §3). Initial formation in secular institutes is longer than that of religious, respecting the particular nature of the vocation. First probation prior to undertaking sacred bonds must be a minimum of two years (c. 722 §3) while first incorporation must be for a minimum of five years (c. 723 §2).

Institutes are clerical or lay (c. 588); pontifical or diocesan (cc. 589, 594, 595). Each has its own spiritual patrimony and enjoys a rightful autonomy of life and governance in order to live and preserve it (c. 586 §1). The initial erection of an institute and approval of its constitutions, are in the hands of the diocesan bishop in consultation with the Apostolic See (c. 579). Competency rests with the Congregation for Institutes of Consecrated Life and Societies of Apostolic Life, or with the Congregation for the Oriental Churches. Parallel norms for Eastern rite secular institutes are found in the Code of Canons for the Eastern Churches (cc. 563–569).

The World Conference of Secular Institutes (CMIS) holds international assemblies every four years and publishes a quarterly, *Dialogue,* in various languages. National Conferences of Secular Institutes exist in a number of countries as expressions of collaboration and ecclesial communion. Commenting on the role of secular institutes in the Church, the post-synodal apostolic exhortation *Vita Consecrata* reiterated: "Through their own specific blending of presence in the world and consecration, they seek to make present in society the newness and power of Christ's kingdom, striving to transfigure the world from within by the power of the Beatitudes" (n. 10-b).

Statistics for 2000 from the Congregation for Institutes of Consecrated Life and Societies of Apostolic Life indicate 71 secular institutes of pontifical right and 135 of diocesan right. At the end of 1998, the estimated number of members was 38,665, of whom 33,125 were women, 4,794 clerics, and 746 lay men.

Bibliography: *Annuario Pontificio*, published annually. J. BEYER (ed.) *Etudes sur les Instituts Séculiers*, 3 v. (Bruges 1963, 1964, 1966). *Commentarium pro Religiosis et Missionariis* 78 (1997) 191–346. Issue dedicated to Secular Institutes on the 50th Anniversary of their Constitution. CRIS. "Secular Institutes—Informative Documents," *CLD* 11, 109–131. S. HOLLAND, "Secular Institutes: Can They Be Both Clerical and Lay?" *CLSA Proceedings* 49 (1987) 135–145. JOHN PAUL II, "Bearing Witness to Christ in Secular Life," *L'Osservatore Romano,* Eng. (February 12, 1997) 5. B. M. OTTINGER and A. S. FISCHER, eds., *Secular Institutes in the 1983 Code* (Westminster, Md. 1988). *Secular Institutes, Documents* (3d ed. Rome 1998). G. SOMMARUGA, "Les Instituts Séculiers en route vers l'an 2000," *Vie Consacrée* 59 (1987) 247–252.

[S. HOLLAND]

SECULARISM

A form of humanism that limits true value to those temporal qualities that contribute to man's natural perfection, both individual and social, to the actual exclusion of the SUPERNATURAL. More than abstract theory, secularism, a generic term for the forms it assumes, is a philosophy of life, a movement of thought, and in the broad sense of the word a religion. Secularistic ethics is founded upon the principles of a purely naturalistic morality that is independent of revealed religion or supernaturalism. As a movement, it pervades government, economic theory, education, and family. In the sense that secularistic theories are concerned with ultimate truths, they may be considered as religious or sacral convictions. Secularism may be described as "a view of life that limits itself not to the material in exclusion of the spiritual, but to the human here and now in exclusion of man's relation to God here and hereafter'' (U.S. Bishops' Statement, 1947).

Historical Development. Secularization of man's thought and action developed with the historical framework of modern Western civilization; its origins can be traced to significant economic, political, and religious changes within Christian culture itself. Common to each of these changes is greater separation of the temporal order from its religious influence by transferring various functions from religious to secular authority.

Early Indications. The 14th-century revival of commerce and the emergence of the merchant class within feudal society provided at least two indications of a forthcoming secularistic economic trend: first, the notion of ''useful'' freedom from external restraint, an acquired right granted by the free cities and distinct from the natural right inherent in land ownership; second, the attempted reconciliation of business practice with the religious prescriptions denouncing the profit motive. This personal liberty of the merchant class to follow business according to the dictates of their own self-interest became, in fact, the forerunner of 18th- and 19th-century laissez-faire individualism. Furthermore, the Church's attitude toward the change from the established ''natural'' economy to the rising ''money'' economy stigmatized the merchant as socially inferior and ethically questionable. Resisting the established authority, the rising middle class justified the change by structuring a juridically recognized society and by fostering revised theological opinion on such things as just price and usury.

The trend of thought in the 15th-century Italian RENAISSANCE was homocentric, glorifying the natural and emphasizing the human. The alliance of the papacy and the humanists was one of the dominant features of this culture (Dawson). Nonetheless, the advancement of the arts and empirical sciences, the rise of individualism and the decline of social responsibility (Neill), the failure of the conciliar movement for ecclesiastical reform and the personal failure of the papacy (Hughes), the ascendency of power and nationalism in the sociopolitical sphere (e.g., Machiavellian theory), and the need of secular education for expanding financial and commercial enterprises—these were the factors precipitating a crisis between secular preoccupations and religious inspirations within a society that remained basically Christian.

Reformers. Reacting against the abuses of Italian humanism and striving to return Christianity to its primitive purity, Martin Luther insisted upon an ''invisible'' Church, thereby separating religion from its cultural accretions. After the Peasants' War of 1524, the secular state, with its autonomous authority, became the new guarantor of the social order. John Calvin, on the con-

trary, established an autonomous ''visible'' church that claimed theocratic authority: collaborating with the state while at the same time controlling it from above. Assimilating current intellectual, economic, and political trends, while at the same time rejecting French Renaissance culture, Calvin offered a doctrine that appealed to the middle class: good works in the form of thrift, diligence, sobriety, and frugality are indispensable as a proof that salvation has been attained. Although neither the humanists nor the Reformers dreamt of the destruction of Christendom, the chief cause of the secularization of Western culture was, according to Dawson, the loss of Christian unity in the 16th century.

Rational Approaches. Scientific discovery (e.g., by Galileo, Isaac Newton) shattering medieval cosmology, discovery of ancient religions (e.g., Buddhism), and competition among Christian sects (notwithstanding the attempted religious tolerance of the Politiques) occasioned the search of intellectuals, starting with the 17th century, for a rational approach to faith in the study of nature itself: René Descartes in the reorganization of knowledge according to abstract principles; John Locke in his atomistic view of society, his political philosophy (preservation of property), and his reduction of faith to reason and charity to natural duty; Voltaire and the *philosophes* in their concept of society as a collection of individualistic interests and in their religion of DEISM, which acknowledged only the existence of God, virtuous living, and eternal reward. Deism, signifying the excision of supernatural revelation and institutional religion (in its revealed aspects) from the center of human life, was also followed by Ethan Allen, Thomas Paine, and Thomas Jefferson of the American Revolution. Economic theory absorbed the laissez-faire of Adam Smith and the economic liberty of the Physiocrats. God and state were thus reduced to the role of safeguarding individual rights so that Reason, Nature, and Humanity might progress uninhibited to produce a harmony of enlightened self-interest and social welfare. Underlying these theories was the Cartesian principle of strict rational criticism.

Final Separation. But spiritual values, religious truths, and moral absolutes were finally separated from the public forum in the 19th-century application of Jeremy Bentham's utilitarianism, in Thomas Malthus's doctrine of population, David Ricardo's classical economic theory (iron law of wages), and Herbert Spencer's politico-economic application of the scientific law of natural selection and individual freedom within representative government. Furthermore, Charles Darwin's theory of evolution had the effect of making God's relation with the world extremely remote and impersonal; the process of growth and decay seemed to rule out from the scientific point of view any conclusion about God. A distinct philosophy called secularism developed in the mid-19th century by George Holyoake and Charles Bradlaugh of England postulated: principles of natural morality independent of all revelation and supernatural orientation; absolute freedom of opinion on all matters, including morality; natural improvement in this life; absolute separation of Church and State. (These same tenets are currently proposed by the American Humanist Association and the ethical culture societies.) The Constitution of the United States contained the freedoms of liberalism; the theories of Spencer, however, were not widely adopted until the last two decades of the 19th century. Unlike some European ideologies (laicism, communism), American democracy is pluralistic, with nonconfessional politics, but affording protection to religion.

The 20th century was characterized by its many forms of POSITIVISM, which applied the empirical basis of science to all intellectual investigation, social theories, and religious beliefs. Industrialized, technical civilization governed predominantly by economic values produced a mind closed to transcendent values, to metaphysics, and to theology; positivism reflected that mentality (Frederick Copleston). Besides LOGICAL POSITIVISM and analytical philosophy, the pragmatism of William JAMES and the instrumentalism of John Dewey flourished in the democratic climate and pluralistic society of the United States. A form of secular HUMANISM, it contains all the requirements for the development of a secular society.

In the late 20th century secularism appeared with nuanced meanings in three distinctive settings: Vatican Council II documents; the secular city process; the evangelical and the charismatic movements.

(1) *The Dogmatic Constitution on the Church* placed a positive emphasis on the vocation of the laity to work within secular affairs to which they bring a Christian dimension; nonetheless, "that ominous doctrine must rightly be rejected which attempts to build a society with no regard whatever for religion" (*Lumen gentium* 36). The text did not contain the term "secularism" so as to avoid confusion with "laicism" (sometimes called laicization), which suggests either a positive role in the Church for the laity or the negative meaning (found in English and German) of freeing the laity from ecclesiastical control.

(2) Not to be confused with secularism is the notion of the Secular City (H. Cox), a process of desacralization through emancipation: aware of his potentialities and responsibilities, man must make life possible in the world, which becomes his city under the care of his providence. Within this framework, the social sciences, especially sociology, become a principal source for the development of theology. Reaction included accusations of: establish-ing a Christian elite without concern for the typical layperson; ignoring further developments in which Christians are not supposed to despise the world but rather lift it up, consecrate it, and fulfill it. Less apparent but more critical in this process is the parallel growth of rationalism (in the strict sense) wherein internal consistency, rather than authority and faith, increasingly becomes the principal criterion for personal and social values and thus eliminates any religious dimension in the evaluating procedure.

(3) Supplanting institutional values (both ecclesiastical and nonreligious) with personal values based on an identification with diverse public and private interest groups, causes, communities, and movements frequently occasioned the juxtaposition (if not interpenetration) of secular and religious values within the same social setting. In addition, the lack of adequate criteria for evaluating seems to have contributed to two subsequent changes: the "reappropriation" of distinctive Catholic values among certain theologians (e.g., Rahner); and a turning toward a fundamentalist view of Scripture in some Christian assemblies and in charismatic groups within the more structured Churches. The fundamentalists or evangelicals and the charismatics pursued the distinction between "the world" (as evil) and "the born again" through the Spirit (as saved). The secular, whether personal, institutional, or social, thus became synonymous with secularism (irreligious) and was therefore rejected as a value for the "born again" Christian, who has Christ as his personal Savior and sole criterion of value.

Systematic Presentation. Although secularism is neither theistic nor atheistic, 20th-century American secular humanism generally appeared to be antitheistic. Negatively, the secular humanism of Dewey removed all dualism between the natural and the supernatural. Differing from the deists who did not deny truths about the existence of God and the immortality of the soul, later secularists considered the distinction between God and nature to be antagonistic; it is impossible to accept both the eternal and the temporal. This position is similar to Friedrich Nietzsche's contention that one who is loyal to the earth is a sworn enemy to the transcendent God. Furthermore, an immaterial principle is totally irreconcilable with the unity of human nature (against Cartesian depreciation of bodily values). Contrary to the Kantian notion of a faith that does not employ the scientific method, secularism maintains that whatever is real is also natural, both in the sense of not being supernatural and in the sense of being available in principle to scientific knowledge. New qualitative developments in nature and human experience cannot, however, break the biological continuity of life or place modes of being beyond the competence of scientific inquiry (e.g., the existence of God or an immaterial principle in man), since nature is ultimately defined by secularist thinkers in terms of what falls within the scope of the scientific method. Secularism also retains the pragmatic emphasis upon discernible consequences: man the knower is involved essentially in a process of adjustment to his environment and employs knowledge as a practical means of satisfying his needs and desires. In the social order, adjustment refers to both a technical control of nature and a social control of man.

Although antitheistic, secularism is not necessarily antireligious, especially in light of a religious feeling for the welfare of the secularist social ideal. Institutionalized religions, however, are divisive in that they attempt to mold personal and social conduct in conformity with norms derived from divine wisdom and law. Consequently, secularists seek absolute separation of CHURCH AND STATE. Moral judgments can be determined only with respect to specific and developing situations; there cannot exist, therefore, universal norms of conduct, nor do human values have absolute or permanent significance. But an individual or society, in choosing a certain value as important, will establish a useful relation between an action and a goal; the actual attributed value, however, is relative to the current situation and is not dependent upon fixed, eternal ends. But social adequacy does provide a working criterion for choice: those actions are morally good that tend to extend the naturalistic outlook. Unhampered intellectual freedom, broadening opportunities for education, work, and cultural experience, and development of social agencies are social goods having moral overtones. Law is also a pragmatic instrument, used to satisfy the needs of all groups joined in the wider community. The doctrine of secular idealism, which on the one hand transforms nature, does not, therefore, transcend the temporal—coextensive with the material—to the spiritual and the supernatural.

Critical Evaluation. Inasmuch as secularism is centrally concerned with human destiny, it can be conceived as a form of humanism. In Christian humanism, man's destiny is both eschatological and incarnational: in the present order the last end of man transcends any end that man himself might propose; at the same time, however, man finds perfection of his nature as man—natural, human, terrestrial. Secular humanism, on the other hand, postulates nature as the self-sufficing totality of being; appraising man's ordination toward eternal life as a degradation of his nature, it tends to emphasize current human values to the exclusion of man's relation to God and His divine providence. Therefore, inasmuch as secularism rejects end and purpose to human life, it is antiteleological; preoccupied with the efficient causality of the present in the evolutionary process of creating its own

ends as it progresses, it practically excludes final and exemplary causality.

Secularism's narrow conception of knowledge, apart from its denial of essence, logically excludes any knowledge of God and the spiritual world. Human morality cannot thus be adequately explained. Although certain values (e.g., social progress) are desirable, they cannot be shown to be either ultimate or even obligatory: even though science might not need justification beyond its progress, science and morality are not coextensive. Furthermore, the denial of universal moral principles among secularists who treat separately fact and interpretation of anthropological discoveries according to evolutionary process can be questioned by historical investigation of the generalizations on which the assumptions of evolution as empirical hypothesis and as a universal philosophical principle of explanation are formulated.

See Also: AGNOSTICISM; ATHEISM; ENLIGHTENMENT, PHILOSOPHY OF; FREETHINKERS; RATIONALISM; TEMPORAL VALUES, THEOLOGY OF; THEISM.

Bibliography: "On Secularism," *Catholic Mind* 46 (January 1948) 1–8, annual statement of the hierarchy of the U.S., Nov. 16, 1947. J. COLLINS, "Marxist & Secular Humanism," *Social Order* 3 (1953) 207–232. C. H. DAWSON, *The Judgment of the Nations* (New York 1942); *The Movement of World Revolution* (New York 1959). B. DE VAULX, *History of the Missions,* tr. R. F. TREVETT (New York 1961). G. J. HOLYOAKE, *The Principles of Secularism* (London 1859). E. J. HUGHES, *The Church and the Liberal Society* (Princeton 1944). T. P. NEILL, *The Rise and Decline of Liberalism* (Milwaukee 1953). H. PIRENNE, *Economic and Social History of Medieval Europe,* tr. I. E. CLEGG (New York 1937). A. RADEMACHER, *Religion and Life* (Westminster, Md. 1962). A. J. TOYNBEE, *The World and the West* (New York 1953). D. CALLAHAN, ed., *The Secular City Debate* (New York 1966). Y. CONGAR, *Christians Active in the World* (New York 1968); "The Role of The Church in the Modern World," *Commentary on the Documents of Vatican* II, 5v., H. Vorgrimler et al., eds. (New York 1967–69) 5:202–223. H. COX, *The Secular City* (New York 1965). C. GEFFRÉ, ed., *Humanism and Christianity. Concilium* 86 (New York 1973). F. KLOSTERMANN, "The Laity," *Commentary on the Documents of Vatican* II, 5v., H. Vorgrimler et al., eds. (New York 1967–69) 1:231–259.

[T. F. MCMAHON]

SECULARITY

Many Christian theologians use the term "secularity" to signify the mentality that regards the effects of secularization as compatible with and even conducive to contemporary man's authentic religious experience. In the context of its impact upon religion and theology, secularization is the historical process that results in the relative independence of worldly or temporal realities from any ties with religious structures. The various aspects of the secular dimension in human existence, as culture, the arts and sciences, the institutions of society, etc., have thereby assumed a meaning and value in their own right. In a secularized world, nature, ideas, customs, social forms, etc., are understood in their immanence and not only as signs of man's transcendent destiny. Christian secularity considers such a society as the normal development of the implications in the Gospel message itself. The incarnation implies that the closer God becomes present to a creature, as in the case of Christ's perfect humanity, the more completely is its own nature fulfilled. In Jesus Christ God entered our history without ceasing to be divine, and man was elevated to the most intimate union with divinity in the person of the Word without ceasing to be human. Furthermore, Christian secularity infers that the saving presence of God in the world summons a more authentic response from man in his freedom when society is not sacralized since his motives for believing in Jesus Christ are more likely to be genuinely religious than social or political.

In Christian theology secularity is carefully distinguished from secularism or the ideology that interprets the effects of secularization as meaning the absolute autonomy of the world. There are varying degrees of the secularistic outlook on life, but all basically reduce reality and human knowledge to the confines of the cosmos. According to secularity, whenever this ideology makes itself a quasi-religion by absolutizing an earthly value that demands a man's total dedication, secularity runs counter to secularization. Another sacred or religious sphere, set over against the ground of Being itself, would be established within the world. On the other hand, Christianity is not to be viewed as a religion that regards the holy to be a special sphere separated from the secular order. Rather the healing and elevating grace of Christ is offered man to sanctify his experiences of temporal objects without sacralizing them, i.e., removing them from their worldly setting. Vatican II endorses in principle a mentality of Christian secularity when it asserts that the relative autonomy of creatures "is not merely required by modern man, but harmonizes also with the will of the Creator" (*The Church in the Modern World* No. 36).

In the history of philosophical and theological reflection, the Western process of secularization has extended the horizon of man's rational understanding, which has set the stage culturally for a new concept of God as the absolute future of man (E. Schillebeeckx, *God the Future of Man*). Progress in science and technology has given humanity a great control over its destiny in this world and so contemporary man does not look to God as a problem-solver. Christian secularity, however, reveals the need for us to accept divine grace lest we become more and more dehumanized as slaves to a utopian future. Christian faith does not impose limits upon God's plan of salvation. He ever reveals himself anew enabling man to cooperate in the shaping of a terrestrial future. A theology of secularity teaches that the contemporary Christian is called to change secular history into saving history in the human project of working toward a better world, without losing his roots in the unique Christ event of the past, and without losing sight of his need for the sacred symbols of the liturgy to experience the transcendent God in faith.

Bibliography: J. B. METZ, *Theology of the World* (New York 1969). E. SCHILLEBEECKX, *God the Future of Man* (New York 1968). Y. CONGAR *Laity, Church and World* (Baltimore 1960). H. COX, *The Secular City* (New York 1965). D. BONHOEFFER, *Letters and Papers from Prison* (New York 1965). C. DAVIS, *God's Grace in History* (New York 1966). J. MACQUARRIE, *God and Secularity* (Philadelphia 1967). E. MASCALL, *The Secularization of Christianity* (New York 1966). R. L. RICHARD, *Secularization Theology* (New York 1967). P. TILLICH, *The Religious Situation* (New York 1964). L. GILKEY, *Naming the Whirlwind: The Renewal of God-Language* (New York 1969). L. DUPRÉ, *The Other Dimension* (Garden City, NY 1972). M. J. TAYLOR, ed., *The Sacred and the Secular* (Englewood Cliffs, NJ 1968), K. T. HARGROVE, ed., *The Paradox of Religious Secularitry* (Englewood Cliffs, NJ 1968). A. SCHLITZER, ed., *The Spirit and Power of Christian Secularity* (Notre Dame 1969). C. DUQUOC, ed., *Secularization and Spirituality*, v. 49 of *Concilium* (New York 1969). *The Christian and the World: Readings in Theology Compiled at the Canisianum, Innsbruck* (New York 1965).

[F. M. JELLY]

SECULARIZATION

A social and cultural process by which nonreligious beliefs, practices, and institutions replace religious ones in certain spheres of life. As such it is an aspect of a general trend toward structural differentiation in a society, a trend that is manifested in the increasing emergence of specific institutions to solve the functional problems of maintenance or survival. Secularization, therefore, is not to be equated with SECULARISM, which is an antireligious ideology. The historical link between the two phenomena in Western Christianity suggests that there is a causal relationship between secularization and secularism; in actuality, however, secularism is a countertendency, a reaction to secularization. Moreover, secularization assumes various historical forms and is not limited to Western or to contemporary societies. Many sociologists consider it an integral component of inevitable social change.

Nature of the Process. In the process of secularization the loss of the secular functions of the religious order parallels the loss of the religious functions of secular institutions. Accepting Émile DURKHEIM's basic distinction between the sacred and the profane, Bronislaw Malinowski, in his studies of primitive society, showed that although the two orders are intimately connected they are not reducible to one another, since each has its own distinctive components, the sacred dealing with the mysterious, the unknown, and the supernatural, and the profane with the empirical. Although specifically religious groupings are sometimes found among primitives, the groups encountered are usually pluralities in which religious and social ties are identical. [*See* RELIGION (IN PRIMITIVE CULTURE).] This identification of religious and other social structures creates problems when society becomes more complex, as in the ancient Hebrew, Egyptian, Babylonian, Assyrian, Hittite, Persian, Greek, Roman, Chinese, Japanese, Mexican, and Peruvian nations informed by their national religions. Not only does numerical growth lead to division and subdivision, with increasing differences in occupation and social rank that encourage variations in religious thought and organization, not only does progress in human knowledge repulse the frontiers of the unknown and the mysterious, but the religious experience itself follows its own particular development, seen, for example, in an increasing emphasis on universal brotherhood transcending natural ties. Inevitably there arise the problems of defining the respective competences of the sacred and secular orders and the establishment of the temporal and spiritual authorities. The tensions generated exist both within individuals and within the social complex; they become intensified in the relations of CHURCH AND STATE.

Historical Examples. With the founding and growth of a universal religion these tensions become especially acute. Historically, solutions have ranged from mutual rejection through indifference to mutual adoption with either Church or State enjoying primacy. In the early days of Christianity its relation with imperial Rome ran the gamut of possibilities and culminated, on the one hand, in Byzantium, in Justinian's ruling the Church and extending the *jus publicum* to contain the *jus sacrum,* and on the other, in the West, in the Church's developing a *jus ecclesiasticum* that regulated and defined the Christian secular order. Domination of either Church or State by the other has not proved stable, especially when societies have become complex. This is true with respect to Christianity and to the other major religions in the world as well. India, for example, having experienced with the rest of the Orient the various possibilities, has entered a phase of secularization; and it is doubtful whether HINDUISM, in spite of its traditional and paradoxical capacity to incorporate many systems of thought, can reestablish itself as the main integrating force in Indian society.

In the West there were dramatic struggles between the empire and the papacy. With the advent of nation-states, the Renaissance, the Reformation, humanism, and concern with empirical science that made possible in-

creasing control of the forces of nature, there developed a plurality of conceptions of Christian society. Religious unity was shattered and a plurality of disciplines claimed competence in many areas of life. Through a series of actions and reactions, conflicts between the traditional order and the new developments were aggravated to the point where the process of secularization became identified with secularism, i.e., the dogmatic rejection of the competence of religion in any area of life and the exclusive acceptance of secular disciplines and principles (leading to the sorrowful statement of F. Nietzche's madman, "God is dead"). But just as it has been impossible for Christianity to recreate the medieval synthesis, so secularism's attempt to forge a new unity has proved futile. The religious and secular components of society, though mutually influencing each other, remain relatively autonomous. This suggests movement toward a new level of unity prefigured in certain provisions of the Constitution of the U.S. and in the implications of religious encounter and witness.

Implications. Any such unity requires redefinition of the relative areas of competence of the sacred and secular orders. In effect this need arises from the general evolutionary tendency enabling men, though biologically and culturally differentiated, increasingly to adapt and control their physical and social environment. Many sociologists hold that this trend—what Max WEBER and Talcott Parsons have called the increasing institutionalization of rationality—is inevitable; its only limit has been formulated by Wilbert Moore as a question: "Can an intelligent species that has achieved the reliable capacity for its own destruction avoid using it?" Rationality in this context implies division of labor, structural differentiation, and the growth of "new authorities" that challenge "old authorities," all precluding the unity of a monolith and the stability of a feudal order. Change itself becomes institutionalized and requires constant redefinition of what is sacred. When religion refuses to participate in the process, on the pretext that some of its principles are unchanging, the rise of secularism is encouraged.

In contrast with the situation in Europe, where reactions to secularization led to the formation of religious and secularistic political parties, the relations between religion and secular society in the U.S. were redefined and a new mode of institutionalization accepted. The political arm of the state refrains from encouraging religion but guarantees religious freedom. In a sense religion thus becomes a private concern; and its influence on the secular order is, in principle at least, not direct but maintained through the actions of believers and citizens.

Certainly structural differentiation and secularization have inflicted losses on religion in America, but they have also produced gains. Religion has lost the right to claim the support of the state, to define secular intellectual culture, and to govern exclusively the kingdom of God on earth. It has gained increasing personal commitment free from the subtlest political compulsion, a situation in which, according to modern theologians, the gospel thrives vigorously; and it has gained proportionately the largest church-attending membership in the world.

Bibliography: H. U. VON BALTHASAR, *Science, Religion and Christianity,* tr. H. GRAEF (Westminster, Md. 1958). C. DAWSON, *America and the Secularization of Modern Culture* (Houston 1960). W. E. MOORE, *Social Change* (Englewood Cliffs, N.J. 1963). D. L. MUNBY, *The Idea of a Secular Society and its Significance for Christians* (New York 1963). T. PARSONS, *Structure and Process in Modern Societies* (Glencoe, Ill. 1960).

[R. H. POTVIN]

SECULARIZATION OF CHURCH PROPERTY

The term secularization refers to the seizure by laymen or by the state of all or part of the permanent endowment of ecclesiastical institutions. The word was apparently first used in this sense in the negotiations concerning the Peace of WESTPHALIA (1648), though such confiscations formed a major part of the history of Church property since the early Middle Ages. This article will consider secularizations in three major phases: (1) the Church in the Roman Empire (to *c.* 500); (2) the Middle Ages (*c.* 500 to *c.* 1500); (3) the modern world (*c.* 1500 to the present).

The Church in the Roman Empire. From *c.* 200, the Christian churches acquired both an endowment in real property and a recognized juridical capacity to hold it (*see* CHURCH PROPERTY). As all landlords, they therefore enjoyed the technical right of disposing of it or alienating it as they wished. However, Canon Law early imposed severe restrictions upon the alienation of property once given to a church. The roots of this canonical opposition were several. Roman law itself had distinguished sharply between profane and sacred property. The possessions of the gods or their temples were considered sanctified by their religious function and were not to be restored to secular purposes (Gaius, *Inst.* 2.2–2.9). Christian tradition also maintained a strict distinction between profane and sacred property, which Christ's treatment of the money changers in the temple had amply sanctioned (Mt 21.12). Moreover, the possessions of the churches were from earliest times considered the patrimony of the poor; the bishops and their subordinate officials, while exercising administrative control over the endowment, were in no sense its true owners and were strictly ac-

countable before God for their stewardship. Alienating Church property for anything less than the most grave causes was equated with robbery of the poor. Furthermore, responsibility to the donors, through whose pious generosity the endowment of the churches grew, helped establish this principle of inalienability. The donors had made over their property with the expressed or implied understanding that it would help support the Church's work of intercession, for their own souls and the souls of all Christians. To turn it to other uses seemed to mean the silencing of a prayer and the betrayal of a trust.

Grave distrust of alienations was thus ingrained in the moral sense of the early churches, though not until the 4th century did the first explicit prohibitions appear. The earliest of them was the 15th canon of the Council of Ancyra (314), which forbade alienations of Church property during vacancies of the episcopal see. The Council of Antioch (332 to 341) gave the provincial synod of bishops the right to judge a bishop accused of appropriating Church property for his private interests. In 447 Pope LEO I (*Ep.* 17) forbade the bishops of Sicily to alienate property, except for the good of their churches and with the consent of the clergy. In 502 Pope Symmachus applied a like prohibition to the Church in Rome. In Gaul the Council of Agde (506) required for alienations the consent of at least three neighboring bishops, and other Gallican councils in 517 and 533 insisted that the agreement of the metropolitan or of the provincial synod of bishops were to be first obtained.

The question of alienations was abundantly treated also in the constitutions of the Christian emperors. In 470 Emperor Leo I forbade all alienations of the properties of the church of Constantinople (*Corpus iuris civilis, Digesta,* ed. T. Mommsen and P. Krueger, 1.2.14). In a constitution dated between 491 and 517, Emperor Anastasius extended the prohibition to all churches in the patriarchate of Constantinople, but allowed alienations for reasonable causes (*ibid.* 1.2.17.1). Justinian forbade alienations throughout the empire (*ibid.* 1.2.24; *Corpus iuris civilis, Novellae,* ed. R. Schoell and G. Kroll, 7, A.D. 535). He did, however, permit them for the sake of paying debts and tax arrears (Nov 46, A.D. 537), for the church's evident utility (Nov 40, A.D. 536) and for charitable purposes such as the redemption of captives and the alleviation of famine (Nov 7, A.D. 535).

The repeated prohibitions show that loss of Church property through episcopal malfeasance must have been a fairly common phenomenon. St. CYPRIAN (*De lapsis* 6) had already castigated bishops who used their churches' holdings in their private interest. The *Canons of the Apostles* (*see* APOSTOLIC CONSTITUTIONS), reflecting conditions in the Eastern churches in the late 4th century, had to prohibit bishops from turning over Church property to their poor relatives. As stated in a Roman synod of 499, even candidates for the papal see had been known to cultivate support for their candidacy through promises of Church property. The chief abuse seems not to have been outright alienations but the granting of ecclesiastical property under easy leases (perpetual *emphyteusis, beneficium, precarium, ius colonarium*). Laymen thereby acquired the use of and profit from the land, while the Church retained a distant and shadowy ownership over it. But in an increasingly tumultuous period, that ownership was easily forgotten.

It is, however, impossible to evaluate precisely the extent of these private secularizations. While common, they evidently did not prevent the churches from building up, in the period of the late empire, a rich patrimony, which, in subsequent centuries, attracted the greed not only of private individuals but of the state itself.

Middle Ages. The first extensive secularizations of Church property by the state occurred almost simultaneously in the Eastern and Western churches in the 8th century.

Byzantium. In the Byzantine Empire, the controversy over ICONOCLASM, precipitated by the banning of images in the churches by Emperor LEO III in 727, included an attack upon the extensive land holdings of the Greek monasteries. The reign of Leo's successor, CONSTANTINE V Copronymos (741 to 775), was marked by open persecution of the monks, the suppression of many monasteries, and the confiscation of their properties. The monasteries were great centers of image worship, and the strong iconoclastic convictions of the Isaurian emperors partially explain these persecutions and suppressions. But the emperors were attempting also to reorganize and strengthen the Byzantine state and army. Monastic wealth, for them as for many later rulers, offered a rich and easily appropriated resource for the fulfillment of their policies.

The West. In the Latin West, CHARLES MARTEL, the great Frankish mayor of the palace, initiated a similar policy of secularization in the interest of military reorganization. Threatened by the Arabs from beyond the Pyrenees, apparently engaged in changing the basis of the Frankish army from foot soldiers to cavalry, and needing estates to support the mounted fighters, Charles found the land of the churches essential for his task. Much obscurity surrounds this earliest Western example of extensive state secularizations. No contemporary writer refers to it. The oldest reference—and even this is doubtful—dates from shortly after Charles's death, in an interpolation preserved in the letters of St. BONIFACE and probably attributable to the English Bishop EGBERT OF YORK. Charles's

reputation as a secularizer was not really established until the publication by HINCMAR OF REIMS in 858 of the "Dream of Saint Eucherius." EUCHERIUS, Bishop of Orléans, reputedly saw in a vision Charles's body devoured by a dragon because he had dispersed the lands of the churches.

With few and late sources, it is difficult to fix the responsibility of Charles Martel in initiating or pursuing these secularizations. But there is no doubt that both Charles and his successors in the Carolingian line pursued fiscal policies that resulted in whole or partial secularizations of Church property. Their motivation was, to be sure, exclusively financial. There is no suggestion, as in later attacks upon Church property, of opposition to ecclesiastical wealth on moral or doctrinal grounds.

The Carolingians. Secularizations took three principal forms under the Carolingian rulers. The crudest was the appointing of laymen as administrators over vacant dioceses or as lay abbots over monasteries. This recourse enabled the Frankish mayors and kings to support their retainers without technically secularizing the ecclesiastical endowment. So widespread did this practice become that by the early 9th century churches and monasteries had to set aside special portions of their revenues, called *mensae,* for the support of the clergy and monks. The Frankish rulers also forced bishops or abbots to grant land under favorable terms to laymen. This benefice (*precarium*) "by order of the king" (*precarium verbo regis*) again diverted ecclesiastical revenues to the support of lay ministers or fighters, without technically secularizing Church lands. Finally, the Carolingians imposed heavy military levies and taxes upon ecclesiastical and particularly upon monastic estates. Even the "immunities" that the Frankish rulers granted liberally to churches and monasteries involved no true exemption from fiscal burdens, but only the privilege of themselves arranging for tax collections and recruitment.

Carolingian policy toward Church properties seems only rarely to have involved outright confiscations. The Carolingians preferred to use the administrative skill of the churches in managing the large estates. With royal favor, Church property seems even to have grown considerably after Charles Martel, constituting about a third of the cultivated land under his Grandson CHARLEMAGNE. But the Carolingians did divert a substantial portion of the ecclesiastical revenues to the support of their army, while usually leaving title to the land and even the administrative responsibility for it to the churches. This shrewd exploitation of ecclesiastical wealth, utilizing the skills as well as the lands of churchmen, undoubtedly helped make possible the Empire's impressive expansion and considerable military success.

Post-Carolingian Period. In the late 9th and the 10th century, the renewed invasions by Northmen, Saracens, and Magyars and incessant internal strife led to the disintegration of the Carolingian state. The prevailing chaos also made possible a massive attack upon the ecclesiastical endowment that one historian (A. Pöschl) called "the great secularizations." The chief culprits were initially the feudal magnates. Lords such as Arnulf of Bavaria (d. 937) seized the monastic lands for the support of their knights, and all over Europe the need and greed of the undisciplined petty nobility took a toll from the largely undefended churches. The emergence in Germany of a more effective state under the Saxon (919 to 1024) and Salian (1024 to 1125) kings and emperors helped curtail the more flagrant robberies. But the revived Empire itself, as the Carolingian state before it, still relied greatly upon the income from Church lands for the support of its administration and army.

This pillaging of the ecclesiastical endowment and diversion of ecclesiastical revenues to secular ends directly contributed to the spread of moral and spiritual abuses in the 10th-century Church. Deprived of adequate means of support, clerics were sorely tempted to use their spiritual powers for material profit. SIMONY, rather than representing an occasional moral failing among the 10th-century clergy, seems to have served for many of them as an essential means of support. Understandably, the GREGORIAN REFORM of the 11th century sought with some success to reconstitute the ecclesiastical endowment, and councils and popes from that time on tried energetically to defend it from all further encroachments. Thus, in 1123 the First LATERAN COUNCIL, first of the ecumenical councils to be held in the West, reiterated the traditional condemnation of alienations (ch. 22) and prohibited all lay control of ecclesiastical appointments (ch. 18). In 1139 the Second Lateran Council forbade lay ownership of churches, altars, or tithes. In a strong reaffirmation of the Church's claim to tax immunity, the Third Lateran Council in 1179 permitted taxation of Church property only with the consent of the bishop and clergy. In 1274 at Lyons, Pope Gregory IX required papal approval for alienations, and in 1296 in the bull *CLERICIS LAICOS* Boniface VIII allowed taxation of the clergy only with papal approval.

Later Middle Ages. From the 12th century to the end of the Middle Ages, the Church remained strong enough to protect its endowment against major losses. However, the same period was marked also by the appearance of the first extensive attacks upon the Church's right to hold property. In the 12th century, the ALBIGENSES, WALDENSES, and other heretics violently condemned ecclesiastical wealth and called for a return to the apostolic poverty of the first Christians (*see* POVERTY MOVEMENT). At the

same time, satirists such as GIRALDUS CAMBRENSIS and WALTER MAP were ridiculing the alleged avarice and high living of the monks and the fiscal machinations of the Roman Curia. The chorus of criticism was swelled in the 13th century by the protracted debate concerning the Franciscan rule and the degree of poverty imposed by it (*see* POVERTY CONTROVERSY). Radical segments of the Franciscan community, the *zelanti* and the Franciscan SPIRITUALS, castigated propertied monks and friars and declared absolute poverty to be the *sine qua non* of true spiritual living.

In the 14th century, three great rebels against the medieval ecclesiastical order— WILLIAM OF OCKHAM, MARSILIUS OF PADUA, and John WYCLIF—gave these criticisms their most systematic and forceful expression. Starting from quite different premises, all three agreed in conceding to the state supreme dominion over Church property. In his *Defensor Pacis* (1324), Marsilius declared that Church property not needed for worships, for the support of the clergy, or for the helpless poor could be used by the "human legislator," or state, for the common welfare and defense. John Wyclif (d. 1384) was considerably more radical. Advancing the theory that grace alone conveyed rights of dominion and of ownership, Wyclif categorically denied to the papacy, monks, friars, and other "sects" as he called them, any claim to power or property. The lay magistrate was God's vicegerent and alone could exercise true dominion. Moreover, the lay magistrate had the positive responsibility of supervising the Church, assuming control over its endowment, and correcting the terrible abuses that the sects were perpetrating.

Some few efforts were made in the late Middle Ages to realize these proposals. In 1371 the English parliament heard with some sympathy the proposition that the Church's property could be legitimately used for the defense of the kingdom, but it avoided direct secularizations. In 1376 the commune of Florence, then at war with the papacy, actually set about confiscating and selling Church property to finance the war, but with the restoration of peace they abandoned the policy. There were also a few suppressions of poor or decayed religious houses, and the transference of their endowment to other, stronger houses or to new establishments such as university colleges. Such suppressions were permitted by Canon Law, and flagrant violations were avoided. The relative stability of the ecclesiastical endowment in the later Middle Ages stands in surprising contrast to the frequent and extreme theoretical attacks upon it. Virtually all the criticisms, policies, and proposals that the Protestant reformers advanced in regard to Church property had been anticipated by the rebellious thinkers of the closing Middle Ages.

Modern World. Confiscations of ecclesiastical property accompanied the Protestant REFORMATION from its origins. LUTHER himself, in his *To the Christian Nobility of the German Nation* (1520), denied all temporal dominion to the priesthood, denounced the fiscal abuses of the Roman Curia, and impassionately summoned emperor and nobles to protect the German people from Roman extortions. The theme was taken up with singular violence by Ulrich von Hutten and helped inspire the Knights' War of 1522, a direct, though ultimately unsuccessful, attack by the impoverished knights of the middle Rhine upon the ecclesiastical principalities. Denials of the Church's right to property were implicit also in the radical social movements of the early Reformation, the PEASANTS' WAR (1524 to 1525) and the ANABAPTIST revolt at Münster (1534 to 1535).

Reformation. Meanwhile, the Protestant reformers and princes were proceeding to a more systematic and permanent spoliation of the older churches and monasteries. In 1523 the town of Leisnig, on Luther's advice, required that all ecclesiastical possessions be joined together in a "common chest" to be administered by an elected board of ten laymen. Zurich, under ZWINGLI's influence, dissolved all religious houses and directed that their properties be given over to the support of education and the relief of the poor (Dec. 5, 1524). In 1523 and 1524, numerous German towns (Frankfurt am Main, Schwäbisch-Hall, Magdeburg, Ulm, Strassburg, Bremen, Nünberg) took similar measures.

The princes quickly followed. In 1525 ALBRECHT OF BRANDENBURG-ANSBACH, Grand Master of the Teutonic Order, renounced his vows, secularized the order's extensive territories in East Prussia, delivered them to King Sigismund I of Poland, and received them back as a hereditary fief. By the late 1520s, most German Protestant princes within the Empire were adopting policies characterized by the entire suppression of religious orders and confiscation of their lands, the secularization also of episcopal properties considered superfluous, and the imposition of a strict lay supervision over the remaining endowment of the Church.

Against this mounting flood, the Catholics were able to take little effective action. At the Peace of AUGSBURG (1555), Emperor CHARLES V implicitly recognized all secularizations accomplished before the earlier Peace of Passau (1552). He also included in the treaty, over Protestant objections, the provision that if any Catholic priest after 1552 abandoned the old religion, he must also give up all benefices or territories he may have held by virtue of his ecclesiastical office. This was the famous "ecclesiastical reservation." It became almost at once a source of friction between the Catholic and Protestant parties

within the Empire and was a major issue in that climactic event of the German Reformation, the THIRTY YEARS' WAR (1618 to 1648). The Treaty of Westphalia that closed the war sanctioned all secularizations up to Jan. 1, 1624, but reaffirmed the ecclesiastical reservation for all later apostasies from the old faith.

Outside the Empire, in Denmark, Frederick I (1523 to 1533) permitted nobles to reclaim property given by their ancestors to the churches, and under his successor, Christian III (1534 to 1558), the work of secularization was carried to completion. In Sweden, the Riksdag (Diet) of Västeras (1527) decreed that the "surplus revenues" of the bishops, chapters, and monasteries should be transferred to the crown, and that the nobles could reclaim all land given to religious houses since 1454. In England, even before the formal break with Rome (1534), Cardinal WOLSEY, the minister of HENRY VIII, between 1524 and his fall in 1529 secured the canonical suppression of 29 religious houses. Henry, after breaking with Rome, embarked on the suppression of all the English monasteries (1535 to 1539). In 1535 "visitors" were appointed to investigate the monastic houses of England, and they claimed to have discovered rampant vice. In 1536 smaller houses with annual net income of less than £200 were dissolved, and in 1538 and 1539 the larger houses were similarly suppressed. The former monks were given small pensions and the properties sold for benefit of the royal treasury. This secularization proved final. Even during the Catholic restoration under MARY TUDOR, no effort was made to recover the monastic properties. In the bull *Praeclara* (June 20, 1555), Pope Julius III allowed the purchasers of the formerly monastic lands to retain them in peace. [*See* REFORMATION, PROTESTANT (IN THE BRITISH ISLES)].

The Protestants, however, were not alone in associating religious reform and secularizations. In 1537 a commission of nine high ecclesiastics, including four cardinals, presented a report to Pope Paul III, the *Consilium de emendanda ecclesia,* which proposed a quite radical program of reforms, including the suppression of all houses of the conventual friars. Even in Russia, a group of reformers known as the Trans-Volga elders and led by Nil Sorsky tried to persuade Tsar Ivan III (1462 to 1505) to secularize Church lands. Ivan did secularize the monastic lands of the territory of Novgorod, which he had conquered in 1478, but he left Church lands elsewhere in Russia intact.

The Enlightenment. In Catholic countries, attacks upon Church property gained momentum during the age of absolutism and then of enlightened despotism (*c.* 1648 to 1789). The high notions of royal power characteristic of the absolutist age freely conceded to the king ultimate dominion over Church property, and in this the defenders of the ''Gallican liberties'' of the French church concurred (*see* GALLICANISM). LOUIS XIV (1643 to 1715) intervened at will in Church affairs, dominated appointments, and diverted revenues; his finance minister, J. B. Colbert, seems to have contemplated a systematic secularization. By the 18th century, the progress of the ENLIGHTENMENT and of physiocratic and liberal economic thought associated with it engendered a new wave of criticism of Church property and new demands for its confiscation. The principle of MORTMAIN (the inalienability of Church property) was anathema to the liberal economists, since it prevented the reorganization of agricultural production in the interest of greater efficiency and in response to the forces of a free market.

Imbued by such liberal ideas, the enlightened despots of the 18th century initiated policies of systematic expropriations. In Austria, Emperor JOSEPH II set out in 1782 to suppress monasteries and by 1786 had dissolved no fewer than 783 of them; his brother Leopold II, Grand Duke of Tuscany (1765 to 1790), pursued a similar program of JOSEPHINISM. Polish monastic properties were confiscated as a result of the second and third partitions (1793 and 1795). In 1764 CATHERINE II the Great secularized the monastic lands of Russia. A major victim of these enlightened secularizations was the Jesuit Order. In connection with its missionary activities, the order had achieved some commercial prominence in the colonial trade and reputedly owned secret caches of great wealth. The JESUITS were expelled from Portugal in 1759, from France in 1762, and from Spain in 1767; and their property, which proved disappointingly small, was seized. In 1773 in the brief *Dominus ac redemptor noster,* CLEMENT XIV sanctioned these highhanded policies and suppressed the order in the entire Church.

Revolution and Aftermath. The FRENCH REVOLUTION added new force to this policy of secularization. The National Constituent Assembly on Nov. 2, 1789, declared that all Church property belonged to the nation. In the Concordat of 1801 with NAPOLEON I, PIUS VII had no choice but implicitly to accept the loss. The advance of the Revolutionary armies spread this policy of secularization to other European areas. In the Empire, the treaty of Lunéville (1801) gave the left bank of the Rhine to France, but the dispossessed German nobles were to be compensated by the ecclesiastical principalities on the Rhine's right bank. In 1803 the recess of the Diet of Regensburg secularized the lands of four archbishoprics (Mainz, Trier, Cologne, and Salzburg) and 18 bishoprics; and 16 Catholic universities, numerous collegiate churches, and abbeys were suppressed. Much of the surviving endowment of Lutheran churches was also taken. This spoliation again proved permanent. The Congress of Vi-

enna (1814 to 1815) took no action to restore the ecclesiastical principalities or to compensate the dispossessed churchmen.

The coming of peace and the restoration of the old ruling houses in Europe brought only a short-lived pause in the attack upon ecclesiastical property. After 1830 the more liberal regimes, particularly in Latin Europe, were again closing down monasteries and taking their lands: Spain (1835 to 1837), Portugal in 1833, Switzerland in 1834 and 1841. The kingdom of Piedmont-Sardinia suppressed religious corporations in 1855. Newly unified Italy similarly suppressed religious houses in 1866 and seized and sold all Church lands in 1867. In 1870 Rome itself was taken. The French Third Republic, in its passionate crusade against CLERICALISM, suppressed all unauthorized religious corporations in 1901 and in 1905 vested control of Church lands in congregational assemblies (*associations cultuelles*). The Communist Revolution in Russia (1917) resulted in a complete confiscation of Church property.

After World War I, however, this attack upon the Church and its property abated considerably in most areas of Europe, reflecting new and more favorable attitudes towards religion and the successful diplomacy of PIUS XI. Pius was able to secure the reestablishment of religious orders and freedom for the churches to acquire and administer property through numerous treaties, concordats, and agreements: with Italy, 1929; the Third Reich, 1933; Latvia, 1922; Poland, 1925; Romania, 1927; Lithuania, 1927; Czechoslovakia, 1928; and Portugal, 1928. These agreements helped stabilize relations between CHURCH AND STATE and bring a new and welcome era of relative peace. But the Church still had to suffer renewed depredations under the many Communist regimes established after World War II.

Conclusion. Perhaps the most striking feature of the history of secularizations since the Middle Ages is the continuity of this policy under regimes of such contrasting political coloration. Protestant, absolutistic, liberal, and Communist governments have all feasted upon the spoils of the ecclesiastical endowment. It might of course be argued, although with some cynicism, that fiscal need and greed, rather than any considerations of political philosophy, social welfare, or religions reform, have been the principal reason for confiscations. Certainly Church property many times has offered to hard-pressed regimes a fiscal resource through which the government could be strengthened and the loyalty of subjects purchased. But these secularizations must also be considered a reflection of the low moral prestige of the Church over much of the modern period, which allowed many persons to believe that its spoliation was an act of progress. The ultimate justification for, and the ultimate defense of, ecclesiastical property is the quality with which the Church fulfills its mission of worship, charity, and education.

Bibliography: G. LECARPENTIER, *La Vente des biens ecclésiastiques pendant la Révolution Française* (Paris 1908). B. J. KIDD, ed., *Documents Illustrative of the Continental Reformation* (Oxford 1911). G. KALLEN, ''Der Säkularisationsgedanke in seiner Auswirkung auf die Entwicklung der mittelalterlichen Kirchenverfassung,'' *Historisches Jahrbuch der Görres-Gesellschaft* 44 (1924) 197–210. A. COULY, *Dictionnaire de droit canonique*, ed. R. NAZ, 7 v. (Paris 1935–65) 1:403–15. D. KNOWLES, *The Monastic Order in England, 943–1216* (2d ed. Cambridge, England 1962). D. KNOWLES, *The Religious Orders in England*, 3 v. (Cambridge, England 1948–60). A. LATREILLE et al., *Histoire du catholicisme en France,* 3 v. (Paris 1957–62). E. E. Y. HALES, *Revolution and Papacy, 1769–1846* (Garden City, New York 1960). G. D'AMELIO, *Stato e Chiesa: La legislazione ecclesiastics fino al 1867* (Milan 1961). A. DRU, *The Church in the Nineteenth Century: Germany 1800–1918* (London 1963).

[D. HERLIHY]

SEDELLA, ANTONIO DE

Missionary in colonial Louisiana; b. Granada, Spain, Nov. 18, 1748; d. New Orleans, La., Jan. 19, 1829. He was the son of Pedro Mareno and Ana of Arze. He was ordained in the Capuchin convent in Granada, on Dec. 21, 1771. Ten years later, Sedella went to the Louisiana mission where, except for five years of exile, he remained until his death a half century later. At various times he received appointments as assistant vicar for Louisiana-West Florida, ecclesiastical judge, commissary of the Inquisition, and pastor of St. Louis parish (later cathedral) in New Orleans. The motif of his public life was conflict with authority, and his influence, for good and for evil, has remained a subject of controversy.

Sedella clashed with the auxiliary of Havana, Cuba, Bishop Cyril de Barcelona, when the latter visited the Louisiana missions in the late 1780s and accused the friar of ignoring his episcopal authority, submitting incomplete financial statements, and endangering colonial stability by threatening to establish a tribunal of the INQUISITION. Having concluded that Sedella's presence in New Orleans was inimical to the mission's general welfare, Cyril asked Governor Estevan Miró to send the pastor to Spain. In April of 1790 the friar was quickly and secretly deported to Cadiz, Spain. There, through the services of a lawyer provided by friends from New Orleans, Sedella appealed to the crown; Charles IV used the PATRONATO REAL and ordered the Capuchin restored to his office as pastor of St. Louis parish. In July of 1795 Sedella returned to New Orleans in the company of the first ordinary of that see, Luis Peñalver y Cardenas.

Ten years later, as a result of the transfer of Peñalver to Guatemala and the purchase of the Louisiana Territory by the new republic of the United States, the lines of ecclesiastical jurisdiction became tangled. Taking advantage of the hazy situation, Sedella (known at this stage of his career and in subsequent literature as Père Antoine) challenged the authority of Patrick Walsh, the acting vicar-general. When Walsh suspended Antoine, a public meeting was called, and the people demanded Père Antoine as their pastor. Walsh immediately wrote to Rome, where the Congregation for the Propagation of the Faith settled the jurisdictional question by making New Orleans the responsibility of Bishop John Carroll of Baltimore, Md. When Carroll named Reverend John Olivier vicar-general for Louisiana, Antoine was reluctant to acknowledge the new appointed, but he finally did so after the dispute reached the newspaper. However, five years later Louis William Dubourg as apostolic administrator failed to control Père Antoine and eventually was forced to suspend the priest and place the cathedral under interdict. In his official correspondence, Dubourg denounced the Capuchin as a dangerous man and reported, after his consecration as ordinary of New Orleans, that he feared to reside in his see city as long as Père Antoine held sway there. Relying on these reports, the historian John G. Shea judged that Antoine was the ''scourge of religion in Louisiana,'' while Roger Baudier made him responsible for the afflictions of Catholicism in the early history of New Orleans.

At first Dubourg administered his vast territory from St. Louis, Mo. For a brief period the bizarre idea of appointing Père Antoine as his auxiliary to mollify the people of New Orleans appealed to him. Putting aside this idea, Dubourg finally went south in 1820, where Antoine and the people received him with genuine affection. The Capuchin continued as rector of the cathedral until his death, earning the love of his flock through personal detachment, charity to the poor, and pastoral care during epidemics. His funeral in 1829 was the most remarkable the city had seen; government officials attended as a body and the greatest possible honors were paid his remains.

Appraisals of Sedella's role in the history of New Orleans have been extreme and frequently prejudiced, either indicting him for criminal behavior or proposing him for canonization. Many of his actions or postures—service as a secret agent for Spain, fractious attitude toward authorities, lax conscience relative to canonical regulations for funerals and marriages, association with Masons and rebellious trustees—cannot be written off as simple idiosyncracies. On the other hand, responsibility for the irreligion of the day cannot justly be assigned to Père Antoine. Any objective judgment of the influence of his pastorate must consider the environment of New Orleans as a rough frontier port city and the acute shortage of religious personnel there.

Bibliography: M. J. CURLEY, *Church and State in the Spanish Floridas, 1783–1822* (Catholic University of America, *Studies in American Church History* 30; Washington 1940). R. BAUDIER, *The Catholic Church in Louisiana* (New Orleans 1939). C. W. BISHPAM, ''Fray Antonio de Sedella: An Appreciation,'' *Louisiana Historical Quarterly* 2 (1919): 24–37; ''Contest for Ecclesiastical Supremacy in the Mississippi Valley,'' *ibid.,* 1 (1918). F. M. KIRSCH, *Dictionary of American Biography,* 20 v. (New York 1928–36) 1:321–322.

[E. F. NIEHAUS]

SEEBERG, REINHOLD

German Lutheran theologian and historian of dogma; b. Pörrafer, Estonia, April 5, 1859; d. Ahrenshoop, Germany, Oct. 23, 1935. He studied theology at Dorpat (later Tartu) in Estonia and at Erlangen, Germany, and taught at Dorpat (1884–89), Erlangen (1889–98), and Berlin (1898–1927). Seeberg's numerous works were concerned with the history of dogma and stressed the theory of the development of doctrine. Believing that the fundamental truths of Christianity persisted in different but increasingly more precise forms, he wrote *Die Grundwahrheiten der Christlichen Religion* (1902; tr. *Fundamental Truths of the Christian Religion,* 1908). to refute HARNACK's *Wesen des Christentums* (1901). Seeberg's most important work on the history of dogma was *Lehrbuch der Dogmengeschichte* (1895–98; 5th ed., 4 v. 1954; tr. as *Text-Book of the Doctrines,* 1905). He wrote also *Grundriss der Dogmengeschichte* (1901; 7th ed. 1936). In addition, he published works on social ethics and systematic theology. His *System der Ethik* (1911) interpreted Christian morality as a dedication to God based on principles formed within a Christian framework but realized under concrete circumstances and possibilities. Although he regarded morality as primarily personal, he insisted that it must extend to social, political, and national problems. Seeberg's *Christliche Dogmatik* (2 v. 1924–25) described Christianity as a life-process between the infinite spirit of God and the finite spirit of man.

Bibliography: R. SEEBERG in *Die Religionswissenschaft der Gegenwart in Selbstdarstellungen,* ed. E. STANGE (Leipzig 1925) 173–206, autobiog. sketch, H. LAMMERS, *Reinhold Seeberg Bibliographie* (Stuttgart 1939). H. BEINTKER, *Evangelisches Kirchenlexikon: Kirchlich- theologisches Handwörterbuch,* ed. H. BRUNOTTE and O. WEBER, 4 v. (Göttingen 1956–61) 3:895. E. SCHOTT, *Die Religion in Geschichte und Gegenwart,* 7 v. (3rd ed. Tübingen 1957–65) 5:1632–33. A. DEISSMANN, *Lexikon für Theologie und Kirche,* ed. J. HOFER and K. RAHNER, 10 v. (2d, new ed. Freiburg 1957–65); 9:564–565.

[L. J. SWIDLER]

SEEKERS

A minor nonconformist group of left-wing Puritan societies in early 17th-century England, living principally in Cumberland, Westmorland, and Yorkshire, who represented, along with the Dutch ''Collegiants,'' the culmination of continental pietistic religion. They were closely allied to the Society of FRIENDS, which most of them had joined by 1652. Although different in views and practice from the Ranters and Fifth Monarchy Men, the Seekers likewise exhibited Antinomian and Millenarian ideas and were identified with the Independents of the Civil War and Interregnum periods. (*See* MILLENARIANISM.) The Seekers, finding neither truth nor spiritual satisfaction in any formal, ritualistic church, formed small communities of worshippers who were seeking and waiting for God's manifestation of the true church through new prophets and miraculous revelations. Their emphasis on a vital inner faith unfettered by reliance on the Scriptures, the Sacraments, preaching, and dogma was based on the principles of 16th-century German and Dutch spiritual reformers, including Kaspar Schwenckfeld of Silesia, Sebastian Franck of Schwabia, and Dirck Coornhert of Holland. Schwenckfeld held that the visible church had forsaken its authority and power, and Franck expected God, in the fullness of His plan, to restore the church to the purity and evangelical power of Apostolic Christian times. The term ''Seeker'' allegedly first appeared in England in J. Morton's tract, *Truth's Champion* (1617), but the Seeker Bartholomew Legate suffered martyrdom at Smithfield in 1612.

Although the unceremonious Seekers eschewed precise doctrinal definition, they generally agreed that all churches that had a visible organization and an ordained ministry, relied on the Bible as a source of faith, and administered Sacraments had fallen into apostasy because the infallible Divine Will had abandoned them. Since Seekers had questioned the efficacy of the Sacraments, even Baptism, and renounced Scripture as a sure means of salvation because of the loss of the true texts, although some Seekers studied it, Seeker services consisted of silent gatherings of families in homes and austere chapels wherein men would speak only when divine inspiration aroused them. Occasionally one among them would lead the meetings. The Seekers were among the first Englishmen to advocate absolute religious freedom for all. Seeker views were so similar to those of the Quakers that George FOX made hundreds of converts among them, including such prominent leaders as Francis Howgill, Thomas Taylor, and John Audland, during a trip into the North Country in the early 1650s. John Saltmarsh, the Antinomian divine of the Parliamentary army, O. Cromwell's daughter, Claypole, and Roger Williams of Rhode Island professed Seeker ideas. Seekers authored numerous tracts until the Restoration, by which time their communities had generally dispersed.

Bibliography: R. M. JONES, *Studies in Mystical Religion* (London 1909); *Spiritual Reformers in the 16th and 17th Centuries* (Boston 1914; pa. reprint 1959). J. HASTINGS, ed., *Encyclopedia of Religion & Ethics,* 13 v. (Edinburgh 1908–27) 11:350–351. W. C. BRATTWAITE, *The Beginnings of Quakerism* (2d ed. Cambridge, England 1955). G. FOX, *Journal,* ed. J. L. NICKALLS (rev. ed. Cambridge, England 1952). D. MASSON, *The Life of John Milton,* 7 v. (London 1859–94; reprint Gloucester, MA 1962) v. 3, 5.

[M. J. HAVRAN]

SEELOS, FRANCIS XAVIER, BL.

Redemptorist missionary priest; b. Jan. 11, 1819, Füssen, Bavaria, Germany; d. Oct. 4, 1867, New Orleans, Louisiana, U.S.A.

The sixth of the twelve children of Mang Seelos, weaver and parish sacristan, and his wife Frances Schwarzenbach, Seelos spent six years at St. Stephen's Gymnasium, Augsburg, and three more at the University of Munich, Germany.

Having immigrated to America to join the Redemptorists in April 1843, he was professed May 10, 1844, ordained Dec. 22, 1844, and he served at St. James, in Baltimore, MD, until August 1845. He was transferred then to St. Philomena's, in Pittsburgh, PA, where he shared the rectory with St. John NEUMANN, his spiritual director, whom he succeeded as pastor (1851). During nine years there, as subject, master of novices, and rector, he won the highest praise from people, priests, and bishop.

After three years as rector of St. Alphonsus, Baltimore, he became prefect of students and rector of the Redemptorist seminary at Cumberland, MD. (1857). When Bp. Michael O'Connor of Pittsburgh sought to have him named as his successor (1860), Seelos himself wrote to PIUS IX to discourage the appointment.

In 1862 the Civil War forced the seminary to move to Annapolis, MD, where Seelos cared for military and civilian victims of the conflict. From 1863 to 1865 he was superior of the Redemptorist missionary band, laboring with them from New England to Illinois.

In September 1866, after nine months as an assistant at Old St. Mary's in Detroit, MI, he went to New Orleans, where he died a year later of yellow fever contracted while making sick calls.

He was enshrined in the sanctuary of St. Mary's Assumption, New Orleans, next to Brother Wenceslaus Neumann, St. John Neumann's brother. He was beatified by John Paul II, Apr. 9, 2000, in St. Peter's Square, Rome.

Feast: Oct. 5 (Redemptorists).

Bibliography: B. BECK, *Goldenes Jubiläum des Wirkens der Redemptoristenväter an der St. Philomena Kirche in Pittsburg und Umgegend* (Ilchester, MD 1889): 158–159, 192–211. M. J. CURLEY, *Cheerful Ascetic: The Life of Francis Xavier Seelos, C.SS.R* (New Orleans 1969); ''The Nomination of Francis X. Seelos for the See of Pittsburgh,'' *Spicilegium Historicum Congregationis SSmi Redemptoris* 11 (1963): 166–181. W. GRANGELL, *Seelos and Sanctity. The 12 Monthly Virtues* (New Orleans 1968–69). C. W. HOEGERL and A. VON STAMWITZ, *A Life of Blessed Francis Xavier Seelos, Redemptorist* (Liguori, MO 2000). J. SCHLEINKOFER, *Leben des ehrw. Dieners Gottes P. Franz Seelos aus der Congregation des allerheiligsten Erlösers* (Innsbruck 1901). A. VON STAMWITZ and C. W. HOEGERL, *Blessed Francis Xavier Seelos, Redemptorist* (Liguori, MO 2000). P. ZIMMER, *Leben und Wirken des Hochwürdigen P. Franz Xaver Seelos* (New York 1887).

[M. J. CURLEY/EDS.]

SEGESSER, PHILIPP

Missionary in Pimería Alta; b. Lucerne, Switzerland, Sept. 1, 1687; d. Ures, Mexico, Sept. 28, 1761. The third of 17 children of Heinrich Ludwig Segesser and Maria Katharine Ruscone, he entered the Society of Jesus at Landsberg, Bavaria, in 1708, studied theology at Jesuit University of Ingolstadt (1719–22), and was ordained in 1721. In 1731 he arrived in New Spain (Mexico), with several other Jesuits from the Germanies. (After 1675, Spain had allowed non-Spanish missionaries into her Indies.) In that same year he was sent north to the Pimería Alta mission, then in a period of revival and expansion. After Segesser had studied the Indian languages at San Ignacio, the elder Capt. Juan Bautista de Anza, father of a more famous son, took him to the outpost station, earlier served by KINO, where the San Javier del Bac mission (near the modern Tucson) was formally established. Later he was in charge at Guévavi, and for a time was superior in the Pimería. During this time Segesser wrote a very valuable and penetrating account, *Una relación,* describing life on that far frontier. He, Keller, Sedelmayr, Stiger, and others were the great figures there in the mid-18th century.

Bibliography: P. SEGESSER, ''The Relation of Philipp Segesser,'' ed. and tr. T. TREUTLEIN, *Mid-America* 27 (1945) 139–187, 257–260.

[J. F. BANNON]

SEGHERS, CHARLES JOHN

Archbishop, founder of the Alaska missions; b. Ghent, Belgium, Dec. 26, 1839; d. Nulato, Alaska, Nov. 27 or 28, 1886. His parents, Charles Francis and Pauline Seghers, died when he was still a child. Desiring a missionary career, he attended the diocesan seminary in Ghent, completed studies at the American College of the University of Louvain, Belgium, and was ordained May 31, 1863. In November 1863, he went to Vancouver Island, Canada, to work with Bp. Modeste Demers, whom he succeeded on June 29, 1873. As bishop, Seghers promoted apostolic work on Vancouver and made five journeys into the Territory (now state) of Alaska. On his second trip he covered the western Yukon River system, concentrating on the region near Nulato, and on his third he stationed John Althoff at Wrangell as first resident missionary in Alaska.

On Dec. 10, 1878, he was appointed coadjutor to Abp. Francis N. Blanchet of Oregon City, and succeeded him on Dec. 20, 1880. As archbishop, Segher traveled extensively through Idaho, Montana, and Oregon, evangelizing both settlers and Native Americans and interrupting his program only for preparatory work in Rome on the Third Plenary Council of Baltimore (1884). In Rome, Seghers successfully petitioned Leo XIII to reappoint him to the See of Vancouver Island when Bp. John B. Brondel was transferred to the new Diocese of Helena, Mont. He returned to Vancouver in April 1885, but left later that year to explore southeastern Alaska and establish permanent missions at Juneau and Sitka. Seghers, intent upon opening the Alaskan interior, obtained help from Joseph Cataldo, Jesuit superior of the Rocky Mountain region. In midsummer 1886 Seghers left Victoria, accompanied by the Jesuits Pascal Tosi and Louis Robaut, and by a former lay employee at De Smet Mission in Idaho, Francis Fuller. The group traveled north to the confluence of the Stewart and Yukon rivers, where Seghers went ahead down the Yukon to forestall Protestant evangelizing in the area. Near Nulato, Seghers was mysteriously shot to death by Fuller, who suffered from delusions of persecution brought on by the rigors of travel and the promptings of an American trader offended at the presence of the Jesuits.

Bibliography: M. DE BAETS, *The Apostle of Alaska,* tr. M. MILDRED (Paterson 1943). J. CRIMONT, *Sketch of the Martyrdom of Archbishop Charles John Segher* (Victoria, Canada 1943). Archives, Oregon Province of the Society of Jesus.

[G. G. STECKLER]

SEGNERI, PAOLO

Jesuit preacher and ascetical writer, commonly considered Italy's greatest orator after Bernardine of Siena and Savonarola; b. Nettuno, Province of Rome, Italy, March 20, 1624; d. Rome, Dec. 9, 1694.

Before his entrance into the Society of Jesus in 1637, Segneri studied at the Roman College under Sforza Pal-

Paolo Segneri.

lavicino and was strongly influenced by Pallavicino's interest in sacred oratory. Concentrated studies in the Scriptures, and the Fathers' and Cicero's oratorical works rounded out Segneri's background for his preaching ministry, which began soon after his ordination in 1653.

He began his career preaching from cathedral pulpits, but from 1661 to 1692 he gave himself mostly to Lenten sermons and popular missions. His preaching, which was often accompanied by self-flagellation in the pulpit and penitential processions, quickly achieved wide recognition in Italy, especially in the Papal States and Tuscany where he concentrated his work. Not only crowds of common people flocked to his sermons, but also many prominent figures, notably the Grand Duke Cosimo III and his family. Antonio Pignatelli read and admired his Lenten sermons and, as Innocent XII, summoned Segneri to Rome in 1692 to be his preacher, and made him a theologian of the Sacred Penitentiary.

Despite occasional lapses into figures of questionable taste and misuse of secular erudition, both of which were characteristics of 17th-century Italian literature and oratory, Segneri succeeded in almost totally reforming the art of pulpit oratory. In the *Quaresimale,* Lenten sermons (Florence 1679, with many later editions), in the *Prediche* (Rome 1694), and in the *Panegirici sacri* (Bologna 1664), Segneri manifests a tremendous command of figures and imagery, indomitable vigor and zeal, and a multiplicity of converging proofs and arguments in the manner of Bourdaloue, although the latter lacked Segneri's rich imagination. His style was in the best classical tradition; his delivery rapid, fiery, and impetuous.

Segneri added to his renown as a preacher a certain eminence as a theologian. He opposed the publication of *Fundamentum theologiae moralis,* a work of Thyrsus González, SJ, which advocated PROBABILIORISM. When the book was published despite Segneri's defense of PROBABILISM, Segneri continued his opposition with the *Lettere sulla materia del probabile* (first published Cologne 1732). Against Quietism he wrote the *Concordia tra la Fatica e la Quiete nell'Orazione* (Florence 1680). His adversaries denounced the work to the Inquisition and it was condemned. He was allowed to reprint it in 1691 with certain changes.

Bibliography: *Opere complete,* 4 v. (Turin 1855).

[W. J. FULCO]

SEGNERI, PAOLO, THE YOUNGER

Jesuit preacher, nephew of the renowned ascetical writer and orator; b. Rome, Oct. 18, 1673; d. Sinagaglia, June 25, 1713. After studies at the Roman College, he joined the Society of Jesus in 1689; like his uncle, Paolo Segneri, he dedicated himself to mission and retreat work. His preaching throughout central and northern Italy was marked by astonishing conversions, and he soon acquired a widespread reputation. He was a writer of considerable merit, composing and translating treatises dealing with mission preaching and the spiritual exercises. *Dell' amore di Dio e de' mezzi per acquistarlo* appeared in 1707 at Lucca and underwent many editions; a translation into Italian of F. Nepveu's *De l'amour de Jesus* appeared the same year, followed by the *Instruzione sopra la converzioni moderne* in 1711 in Florence.

Bibliography: L. A. MURATORI, *La Vita del padre Paolo Segneri Juniore* (Modena 1720), includes several of Segneri's shorter works. P. PIRRI, ''Ludovico Antonio Muratori e Paolo Segneri juniore. Una amicizia santa,'' *Rivista di storia della Chiesa iri Italia* 4 (1950) 5–69, with letters and documents.

[W. J. FULCO]

SEGOVIA, JOHN OF

Spanish theologian, exponent of conciliarism; b. Segovia?, late 14th century; d. Aiton?, Savoy, after 1456. Nothing is known of him before 1432, when he was canon of Toledo, archdeacon of Villaviciosa, and professor of theology at SALAMANCA. On Nov. 4, 1433, he joined the Council of BASEL as a representative of his university and of John II of Castile. He soon distinguished himself with pamphlets in which he expounded conciliarist views, arguing that the Church is the community of all believers and that it, and not the pope or a general council, is infallible. In 1434 he argued that the council should not accept the cardinals sent by EUGENE IV to preside over it. After an unsuccessful attempt to reconcile the Pope and the Council (1434–36), John returned to Basel to discuss and write on Hussite usages and reunion with the Orthodox, and in favor of the Immaculate Conception (1437). He played a leading part in the Council's deposition of Eugene IV, which he tried to justify in pamphlets, and in the election of the antipope FELIX V (Nov. 5, 1439). Felix made him a cardinal (Oct. 12, 1440) and sent him on an unsuccessful mission to seek recognition of Felix by France and Germany (1440–42). When Felix renounced his claim to the papacy, John lost his cardinalate, but was compensated in turn with the bishoprics of Saint-Paul-Trois-Châteaux (1449), Maurienne (1450), and the titular archbishopric of Caesarea. He retired to Aiton, where he wrote his *Historia gestorum generalis synodi Basiliensis* (2 v. Vienna 1873–96), which reaches the year 1444; defended the authority of bishops against clerical democracy; and translated the Qur'ān into Latin and Spanish.

See Also: CONCILIARISM (HISTORY OF).

Bibliography: J. HALLER et al., eds., *Concilium Basiliense,* 8 v. (Basel 1896–1936). É. AMANN, *Dictionnaire de théologie catholique* 8.1:816–819. J. GONZÁLEZ, *El maestro Juan de Segovia y su biblioteca* (Madrid 1944). D. CABANELAS RODRÍGUEZ, *Juan de Segovia y el problema islámico* (Madrid 1952). U. FROMHERZ, *Johannes von Segovia als Geschichtsschreiber des Konzils von Basel* (Basel 1960). J. VINCKE, *Lexikon für Theologie und Kirche* [2] 5:1081–82.

[D. W. LOMAX]

SÉGUR, LOUIS GASTON DE

Priest, spiritual writer; b. Paris, April 15, 1820; d. Paris, June 9, 1881. He was the son of Countess Sophie de Ségur, writer of well-known works for children, and the grandson of Count Rostopchine, governor of Moscow in 1813. After studying law, he became attached to the French embassy in Rome (1842–43) but soon renounced a diplomatic career for the seminary of St. Sulpice in Paris and was ordained (1847). Thence he devoted himself to a popular apostolate and founded a short-lived priestly community animated with the same spirit. He worked in Rome as auditor in the Roman Rota (1852–56) and was named prothonotary apostolic (1856), but blindness caused him to relinquish his post and return to Paris. Named canon of Saint-Denis, he also acted as chaplain at the College of Stanislas, where until his death he devoted himself to the direction of souls as a preacher and as confessor of various religious communities.

Ségur was a widely read spiritual and apologetic writer of some 60 works, mostly brief devotional tracts. Some were translated into English and other languages. His theological outlook was that of BÉRULLE and others of the 17th-century French school of spirituality, combined with that of St. FRANCIS DE SALES. His writings promoted the imitation of Christ, frequentation of the Sacraments, the practice of charitable works, devotion to the Blessed Virgin, ardent love of the Church and the pope, and Eucharistic pilgrimages (forerunners of EUCHARISTIC CONGRESSES). As a militant ultramontane, he wrote several books on the pope and papal infallibility. To counteract Protestant polemics, especially when the writings of Marnix de Sainte-Aldegonde were reedited, he published *Les Causeries sur le protestantisme* (1869). *La Piété enseignée aux enfants* remains charming and useful. He wrote an eight-volume work, *La Piété et la Vie intérieure* (1864), one volume of which, subtitled *Jesus vivant en nous,* was placed on the Index (1869) because of possible pantheistic and quietistic interpretations. Later the author revised the text, submitted it to Pius IX, and published it under a new title, *La Grâce et l'Amour de Jésus.*

Bibliography: M. EVEN, *Mgr. Gaston de Ségur* (Paris 1937). M. DE HÉDOUVILLE, *Mgr. de Ségur* (Paris 1957). J. RIVET, *Dictionnaire de théologie catholique* 14.2:1781–83. For a list of his works and their various eds. see the catalog of the Bibliothèque National 169:963–995.

[J. DAOUST]

SEGURA LÓPEZ, MANUEL, BL.

Martyr, priest of the Order of Poor Clerics Regular of the Mother of God of the Pious Schools (Piarists); b. Jan. 22, 1881, Almonacid de la Sierra, Saragossa Province, Spain; d. July 28, 1936. Fr. Segura was ordained in 1907. He was serving as novice master in Peralta at the outbreak of anti-religious sentiment. He was shot along with David Carlos MARAÑÓN for being a religious during the Spanish Civil War. Manuel was beatified on Oct. 1, 1995 by Pope John Paul II together with 12 other Piarists.

Feast: Sept. 22.

See Also: PAMPLONA, DIONISIO AND COMPANIONS, BB.

Pedro Segura Y Sáenz.

Bibliography: ''Decreto Super Martyrio,'' *Acta Apostolicae Sedis* (1995): 651 656. *La Documentation Catholique* 2125 (November 5, 1995): 924.

[L. GENDERNALIK/EDS.]

SEGURA Y SÁENZ, PEDRO

Cardinal, archbishop of Toledo and of Seville; b. Carazo, Burgos, Spain, Dec. 4, 1880; d. Madrid, April 8, 1957. After studying at the seminary in Burgos and at the Pontifical University in Comillas, he obtained doctorates in philosophy, theology, and Canon Law. Ordained (Nov. 9, 1906), he became a doctoral canon of the cathedral of Valladolid, professor of Canon Law at the Pontifical University of Valladolid, secretary to the archbishop of Valladolid, and in 1916 auxiliary bishop of that see. He was named bishop of Coria-Cáceres (1920), archbishop of BURGOS (February 1927), archbishop of TOLEDO, primate of Spain, and cardinal (Dec. 18, 1927). He revived an ancient practice of holding councils at Toledo. A man of austere character, he was wont in his pastoral letters to criticize severely modern paganism and impiety. As a convinced monarchist, Segura denounced the Second Republic and lauded King Alfonso XIII in a pastoral letter (April 1931). This caused his expulsion from Spain by the Republican government. After resigning his primatial see (Sept. 26, 1931), Segura was appointed to curial offices in the Vatican. In 1937 he returned to Spain and was given the See of Seville. His relations with the Franco government were never cordial. He particularly opposed the Falange and refused to admit any memorials to the Falangist José Antonio Primo de Rivera (d. 1939) in his churches. He was reputed to be a very influential opponent of collaboration with Nazi Germany during World War II. He was distressed that the Spanish Concordat of 1953 conceded too much liberty to Protestants, and he feared lest the influence of the U.S., growing out of military aid agreements, encourage the spread of Protestantism (*see* SPAIN).

[I. BASTARRIKA]

SEIPEL, IGNAZ

Austrian priest, statesman; b. Vienna, July 19, 1876; d. Pernitz, Lower Austria, Aug. 2, 1932. After ordination (1899) he gained a doctorate in theology (1903) and became professor of moral theology in Salzburg (1909) and Vienna (1917). A student and disciple of the social theorist and moral theologian Franz Schindler, he served as minister for social welfare in the last imperial cabinet, that of Heinrich Lammasch (1918), and as a member of the constitutional convention (1919). As leader of the Christian Social party from 1921, he was chancellor five times (1922–24, 1926–29). After the monarchy's downfall (November 1918) Seipel played a decisive role in creating a new state without bloodshed or strife and prevented a split of the Christian Social party into monarchial and republican wings. Along with Cardinal Piffl, Archbishop of Vienna (1913–32), Seipel was the outstanding Catholic opponent of Austrian Marxism's antireligious propaganda. As head of the *Bürgerblock*, a coalition regime of all the non-Socialist parties, he led a heroic battle to win foreign acceptance of his country. By stabilizing the currency he preserved his nation's vitality and independence. In the July revolt (1927) his decisive action averted civil war and Communist seizure of power. The unbridled leftist agitation against Seipel's person and priesthood led to an assassination attempt (1924) and gave rise to a strong movement of separation from the Church. Political opposition and failing health caused Seipel to retire from governmental affairs (April 1929), save for a short term as foreign minister (1930).

Seipel was the father of the 1929 Austrian constitution. His last years were preoccupied with questions of the social order, advanced in Pius XI's encyclical *QUADRAGESIMO ANNO* (1931). During a very critical period he was a statesman of European stature, who esteemed

the common welfare above party politics and based his policies on fundamental principles of Christian outlook and morality. To him the "restoration of souls" ranked higher than economic and financial health. He was a man broad in vision, clear in concepts, and practical in handling problems. Friend and foe esteemed his democratic disposition and personal unpretentiousness. His diaries reveal a lofty character, ascetic, priestly, self-sacrificing, and self-controlled. Although a prelate and prothonotary apostolic who delighted in ecclesiastical functions, he declined higher Church offices, including the archbishopric of Salzburg, because he believed his lifework lay in striving by political rather than purely religious means for the welfare and upbuilding of a Christian Austria. His publications include scholarly works, as well as his diary and speeches.

Bibliography: Works. *Reden in Österreich und anderwärts*, ed. J. GESSL (Vienna 1926); *Mensch, Christ, Priester in seinem Tagebuch*, ed. R. BLÜML (2d ed. Vienna 1934); *Die wirtschaftsethischen Lehren der Kirchenväter* (Vienna 1907); *Nation und Staat* (Vienna 1916); *Die geistigen Grundlagen der Minderheitenfrage* (Vienna 1925); *Der Kampf um die österreichische Verfassung* (Vienna-Leipzig 1930). Literature. B. BIRK, *Dr. Ignaz Seipel* (Regensburg 1932). W. THORMANN, *Ignaz Seipel, Der europäische Staatsmann* (Frankfurt a. M. 1932). H. BENEDIKT, ed., *Geschichte der Republik Österreich* (Munich 1954). A. M. KNOLL, *Neue österreichische Biographie*, v.9 (Vienna 1956) 113–129. A. DIAMANT, *Austrian Catholics and the First Republic* (Princeton 1960). A. WANDRUSZKA, *Staatslexikon*, ed. Görres-Gesellschaft, 8 v. (6th, new and enl. ed. Freiburg 1957–63) 7:23–24, J. A. TZÖBL, in *Gestalter der Geschicke Österreichs*, ed. H. HANTSCH (Innsbruck 1962) 579–609.

[J. WODKA]

SEITENSTETTEN, ABBEY OF

Benedictine monastery of the Blessed Virgin, Diocese of Sankt Pölten, Lower Austria. It was founded in 1109 by Udalschalk of Stille and Heft for Augustinian canons, was given to BENEDICTINES from GÖTTWEIG ABBEY in 1112, and became an abbey in 1114. Bishops Ulrich of Passau and Wichmann of Magdeburg endowed it with land. Most of its 14 parishes, with 22,100 parishioners in 1964, had been incorporated in the 12th century, when the abbey began its agricultural development. The oldest register of land dates from the end of the 13th century. The Gothic church (1254–1300) was made baroque in the 17th century, when the abbey recovered from a decline it had suffered during the Reformation. In 1814 the centuries-old abbey school became a public Gymnasium. The famous shrine of the Holy Trinity at Sonntagberg with its baroque church (1706–29) by Jacob Prandtauer belongs to Seitenstetten. The present monastic buildings, erected between 1719 and 1749, contain many paintings

Abbey of Seitenstetten from the northeast.

by B. Altomonte, P. Troger, J. M. Schmidt, and J. I. Mildorfer, and a library of 55,000 volumes, 270 MSS, and 230 incunabula.

Bibliography: L. H. COTTINEAU, *Répertoire topobibliographique des abbayes et prieurés,* 2 v. (Mâcon 1935–39) 2:2995–96. P. ORTMAYR, *Lexikon für Theologie und Kirche,* ed. M. BUCHBERGER, 10 v. (Freiburg 1930–38)[1] 9:433–434; *Das Benediktinerstift Seitenstetten* (Wels 1955).

[A. KURZWERNHART]

SEIXAS, ROMUALDO ANTÔNIO DE

Church leader in Imperial Brazil; b. Camutá, Pará, Feb. 7, 1787; d. Salvador, Bahia, Dec. 29, 1860. Born into a poor but respected family, he began his studies in Pará under the direction of his uncle, Romualdo de Sousa Coelho, later bishop of Pará. He continued his studies in Lisbon at the Oratorian Seminary, where he had the famous Theodoro de Almeida as teacher. He returned to Pará when he was 19 and became a teacher of rhetoric and philosophy at the episcopal seminary. He was ordained (1810) at the age of 23. He was nominated bishop of Bahia Oct. 12, 1826, consecrated Oct. 28, 1827; he took possession of his see on Nov. 26, 1828. There he remained until his death. In 1841 he was named archbishop and primate of Brazil.

For many years Seixas was active in politics, and it was here that he made his greatest contribution. He was an elected deputy to the Brazilian General Assembly, twice from Pará and twice from Bahia. In 1838 the bishop was nominated minister and secretary of state, but he refused the honor, preferring to remain in his diocese. In the General Assembly his help was urgently needed to defend the rights of the Church. Although a moderate regalist in politics, he refused to go along with extravagant attacks on the Church and its doctrines; and often his was one of the few voices raised in the Assembly against the radical proposals. Among his published works are many sermons and various representations he made to the General Assembly, e.g., on the privilege of ecclesiastical forum (Bahia 1832) and on marriage impediments and matrimonial law procedures (Bahia 1832). He also published articles in newspapers on questions of the day, such as clerical celibacy, sundering ties with the Holy See, and destroying male and female religious orders. His was always a voice of moderation. As a reward for his service, Pedro II conferred on him the titles of Conde and afterward Marques de Santa Cruz.

Bibliography: *Collecção de obras . . .* , 5 v. (Pernambuco 1839–57); *Memorias do Marquez de Santa Cruz, arcebispo da Bahia, d. Romualdo Antônio de Seixas, metropolitano e primaz do Brasil . . .* (Rio de Janeiro 1861). A. V. A. SACRAMENTO BLAKE, *Diccionario bibliographico brazileiro,* 7 v. (Rio de Janeiro 1883–1902; Index, 1937) 7:154–159.

[M. C. KIEMEN]

SELF, THE

The notion of self as employed in both philosophy and psychology has different referents, but the common element in all uses of the term is that it applies only to human beings. It is closely connected with CONSCIOUS-NESS and arises from a dialectical consideration of the nonself. Before Descartes, the term was rarely used. As the concept of self developed in philosophy, a two-fold aspect became evident—that of the self as knower or SUBJECT and that of the self as thing known or OBJECT. This article traces the history of the concept of self from implicit references to it in Greek philosophy to its explicit use in modern psychology, and then explores the relationship of the term self to other concepts of philosophy and psychology.

Pre-Cartesian Notions. The development of the concept of the self among the Greeks parallels the gradual awareness of the self by the child. The child becomes itself by seeing itself as distinct from them world and other objects. Each denial, "This is not me," strengthens the idea of "me." In Homer there is no dialogue of the soul with itself. HERACLITUS is aware of a self that can develop itself by itself. The lyric poets had a more precise appreciation of the self and its distinctive qualities; thus Archilocheus reckoned his life (his self) more than his shield. When Sappho showed that the greatest value is that embraced by her own soul, the notion of self as subject and greater than the world was ready for SOCRATES and PLATO. In his imagery of the charioteer, Plato emphasized the self as subject, choosing his own character.

With Aristotle and medieval thinkers, the problem of the knowledge of the self was raised more explicitly. Through an analysis of self-consciousness, St. AUGUSTINE testified to the reality, autonomy, and persistence of the self or ego. Memory, in his view, is nothing more than the mind's knowledge of itself; thus mind is inseparable from self-knowledge. His "Si enim fallor, sum" anticipated Descartes's *Cogito* by a millennium and revealed the ego as separate from its actions and independent of change. If the soul looks for itself, it sees itself dimly through the veil of sensations; this hides its true nature, for by nature it is knowledge and life even though it forgets this. St. THOMAS AQUINAS, too, refers to the self primarily when discussing how man can know himself. He recognized the inferential character of this knowledge, for one does not apprehend his essence directly but only the existence of his soul or self. Thus the self is inferred as the principle of knowledge both of itself and of the sense world.

Cartesian Philosophy. It is with R. DESCARTES that the word self as it is currently used was introduced into philosophy. Descartes saw the self as a spiritual substance; thus, in the *Cogito,* though aware only of his thinking, he assumes that thinking requires a thinker. Subsequent philosophers felt that this, too, should be submitted to doubt. But for Descartes the absolute first principle of philosophy is the indubitable knowledge of the thinking self. It was not long before the self, as confined only to thinking, was replaced by the mind and, in reaction, philosophers such as F. MAINE DE BIRAN and B. PASCAL tried to identify self with all deliberate striving—including motor and conative activity, willing and feeling, and knowing. OCCASIONALISM, too, expanded Descartes's theory of substance to the limits of monism. The self is only the mind; the ego is the pure occasion for God's all-embracing causality.

Empiricism and Rationalism. The English empiricists continued to question the reality of man's experience of substance and applied this doubt to the substantial nature of the self. J. LOCKE disagreed with Descartes, doubting whether the self is substantial or that it always thinks. Self, to Locke, is the PERSON as he sees himself and person is the self as seen from outside. "I am a self only for myself and a person for others." Locke could have chosen either or both of the traditional senses of the concept of SUBSTANCE: that of a thing subsisting in itself or that of a support for accidents. He chose the second aspect and thereby changed substance (and self as substance) into a meaningless and unknowable point of reference for qualities. G. BERKELEY showed the uselessness of this concept in the realm of matter, and D. HUME demonstrated its nonexistence and uselessness in the realm of spirit. For Locke himself, the existence of the self depends on the consciousness of oneself continuing the same as in the past. Here the continued self is the seat of personal identity and is distinct from the soul or spiritual substance, which is regarded as something over and above psychical continuity.

Hume continued to challenge the substantial nature of the soul or self by an analysis of consciousness. He found it impossible to intuit a permanent self. His intuition was always of himself with a perception, and thus he could neither deny nor prove a thread of permanent self. There is only subjective validity in the inference of the self. Yet Hume was dissatisfied with this atomistic view of the self as a "congeries of perceptions": his own experience implied a knowledge of the substantial unity and causal power of the self, which his principles, denying the existence of both substance and causality, would not allow. He had to admit that the experience of self is far less than the self at any given time.

Rationalist philosophers chose the other view of substance as something subsisting in itself. Since only God has complete subsistence, B. SPINOZA, instead of denying the substantial nature of the self, proceeded to identify the self with the world and God as aspects of one substance. G. W. LEIBNIZ tried to extend the view of self as a mere thinking substance by pointing out the underground area of little perceptions, later to be clarified by J. F. Herbart, and perhaps akin to the unconscious posited by Freud.

Kantianism. I. Kant pointed out the complexities of regarding the self both as known and knower. The phenomenal self is known by man; the noumenal self may be there, but man cannot know it. There are three aspects of self in Kant: the self insofar as it has power of intuition, i.e., of receiving impressions; the self insofar as it has the power of pure thought; and the self insofar as it is known. The last has the status of mere appearance; it is an object of knowledge like all other PHENOMENA. The intelligent self at the root of perceptual experience does not stand for any reality at all, whether sensible or nonsensible. The only status applicable to it is that of a basic condition involved in knowledge or thought in general. The self revealed to man in knowledge is a phenomenal self from which one can draw no metaphysical conclusions.

Yet, antimetaphysical as Kant appears to be, his ethical self seems to have metaphysical existence. This is not a static reality to be cognized by the intellect, but it is observable through man's conduct. When the intelligent self and moral self are treated as equivalents, the supersensible self should not be regarded as an actual entity to be found in a realm inaccessible to empirical observation. Selfhood does not mean a self-subsistent reality existing in its own right, but something that man is called upon to realize and bring into existence. Unlike the transcendental ego, the functions of the moral self can be known. In the consciousness of duty and freedom, the true self comes to know itself.

Idealism. J. G. FICHTE developed the idea of a self growing in opposition to the nonself and laid the foundation for the dialectic of Hegel and Marx. In final form Fichte held that the subject or self or ego of the world is fashioned after God, the Absolute Ego, who becomes conscious of Himself by emptying Himself into finite egos. The reality of the self consists in its action of self-positing. The nonego is opposed to the intuited self, a

process ungrounded in anything else. The nonego is an instrument for the realization of self-consciousness. The intelligence then synthesizes self and nonself in a new function of mutual limitation. Fichte then reified these logical functions into the absolute subject, the finite ego, and the finite nonego. Thus the ego is the unconditioned absolute principle that, by its unity, guarantees the unity of the antithetical principles of existence.

G. W. F. HEGEL further developed Fichte's implicit dialectic. No nature can be conceived without generating its opposite. The self must become external to itself, it must become alienated in order to reach self-consciousness. Through the agency of man, spirit completes its growth from being-in-itself (thesis), to being-external-to-itself (antithesis), to being-in-and-for-itself (synthesis). Mature selfhood thus reveals itself as a self-alienating process in which it divides itself into the self and the other-than-self in order to discover its own presence in the object thus posited.

Subsequent idealists begin with the self or content of the mind and become aware of outside objects as the nonself, the reverse of the process used by Greek and medieval philosophers. F. H. BRADLEY denied that the self has any metaphysical reality. It is mere appearance because it cannot maintain itself against external relations. It is a bundle of discrepancies, a construct based on and transcending immediate experience. He distinguished between self and soul, maintaining that some selves are too fleeting to be called souls while some souls cannot properly be called selves.

Dialectical Materialism. Alienation and encounter with the other, the I-Thou relationship, are two ideas developed by L. FEUERBACH and K. MARX. Religion to the former was the means by which man was alienated from himself because he externalized his real self in an image of God. To him, the most real being is not the ego of Kant and Fichte or the absolute mind of Hegel. It is man, or man's essence as found in the unity of man with man, of the I and Thou, which unity is God. Alienation to Marx meant the externalizing of aspects of one's self through the sale of one's labor. It is the exploitative social relationship created by the economic system.

American Philosophy. J. ROYCE distinguished between the phenomenal self, a group of ideas, and the metaphysical self, a group of aims and ideals to be contrasted with the rest of the world. Each human self is the Absolute or God, but men retain their individuality and distinction from one another insofar as their life plans are mutually contrasting and include recognition of other life plans as different.

W. JAMES described self in the broadest terms as the sum total of all that man can call his. Consciousness of self reveals an "I," a stream of thought, and the "me," consisting of many selves. The nucleus of "me" is the bodily existence or the material self; the other constituents are the social self or selves (the recognition man gets from others), the spiritual self, and the pure ego. There can be as many social selves in one man as there are individuals or groups who know him. All progress in the social self is in the substitution of higher groups for lower groups. The spiritual self is a man's inner subjective being taken concretely; it is not the bare principle of personal unity or pure ego. The "I" cannot be an aggregate, nor need it be—for psychological purposes—unchanging, such as soul or pure ego viewed out of time. The "I" is a pure thought appropriative of the previous minute and including all the past, a stream of consciousness. The thought is the thinker. James conceded that there may be another nonphenomenal thinker but that this postulate is not needed to express the facts. To explain the facts, to ask who that knower or thinker is, would become a metaphysical problem. The natural science of psychology must stop with the mere functional formula. Only if one were to deny that he has any direct knowledge of thought would he have to postulate a thinker.

G. H. Mead (1863 to 1931) employed a strictly genetic method of deriving mind and self from the biosocial process. The self arises in the process of conversation when the individual takes the roles of the others and acts toward himself, now the generalized other, as others do. The generalized other was, for Mead, a regulative and functional concept—the generalization of the process of role—taken within a common social activity. Like the self of James, this self has two aspects—the "I," initiating the responses, and the "me," the set of attitudes of others that the individual assumes. The "me" is a man's reply to his own talk. Though all selves are constituted by or in social process, especially language, there is implied a fictitious "I" always out of sight of himself.

Phenomenology. The view of self of E. HUSSERL is bound up with his phenomenological method—his plea to return to things as they are, to make philosophy a rigorous science. The epoche, or suspension of belief, includes not only the empirical self and other natural existents but the entire view of the world. Reflection must be centered on a transcendentally purified ego, or consciousness, upon that which alone remains immediately valued after the entire belief in a world has been bracketed. This ego constitutes the meaning of the world. Perhaps, in the end, Husserl, like the idealists, made the self constitute itself and the world. Aware of the danger of SOLIPSISM and of complete subjectivity, however, he tried to show how the transcendental ego constitutes other egos as equal partners in an intersubjective community that in turn forms the foundation for the objective or intersubjective world.

M. MERLEAU-PONTY rejected the *Cogito* of both Descartes and Husserl because of its extreme dualism. A true *Cogito* is being-present-in-the-world. The body as subject is a self-transcending movement. The body is a self (*soi*) that belongs to the world and is distant from it.

Existentialism. S. A. Kierkegaard developed the idea of alienation, but he was the first to place man's relation to God at the heart of his selfhood. True selfhood lies in being rightly related to God. Despair lies in estranging oneself from God, either by not willing to be oneself or by despair at willing to be oneself. Despair also results in not being conscious of having a self. Man is a self-constituting being, not a self-creating one. The self is a dynamic relation to itself, derived from its relation to God. The self must constitute itself by freely choosing and accepting its dependence on the transcendent. Instead of Descartes's "Cogito, ergo sum" as a description of the origin of the self, a better formula, according to Kierkegaard, is "Pugno, ergo sum." This indicates the primacy of the will whereby one breaks out of the aesthetic and ethical levels into the religious or authentic level of selfhood.

J. P. Sartre denies the notion of person, the existence of a permanent and underlying entity that allows one to say "I am," for he feels that only an empty for-itself can understand that which is. His prereflexive *Cogito* reveals no ego, for in his ontology, the ego must be excluded. Only the in-itself has ontological value; the for-itself is the void of the in-itself, existing only for the object, a subjectivity without a subject. Sartre explains the feeling of identity by the notion of transversal transmissions of the past to the present.

For G. Marcel the self is incarnate consciousness. To be a man is to be a bodily incarnate being, not so much a container as a subject who carriers a container with him. Selfhood can be compromised by greater concern with the order of having than with that of being. The self, thus, is also transformed into an object. The regaining of the sense of one's self is by recollection, wherein one recognizes the source of the personal self.

Both Marcel and K. Jaspers stress the necessity of treating others as selves and the increase and growth of selfhood as dependent upon involvement with other selves. Jaspers, however, admits the ambiguity of the word self. He proposes the notion of self as an original power, or a will, or a decision that has its echo in the individual historical decisions of one's own existence. The absolute will to communication is the very act of achieving selfhood. The positive and deficient modes of communicative life are on the four levels of existence: (1) *Dasein;* (2) consciousness as such; (3) spirit in the medium and order of ideas; and (4) existence in the realization of the self. While Kierkegaard had said that the measure of the self is God, Jaspers says that the depth of the self has its measure in the transcendence before which man stands. All selves are separate except for the unity of transcendence by which they are encompassed. Love, in communication among men who have become selves, is the highest possibility there is within this life. Existential truth is alive in the triadic relation—existence, coexistence, and transcendence; truth is the realization and manifestation of the individual self. The self is openness to itself; the evil man is enclosed. Intersubjectivity, for Jaspers, seems impossible because two staring subjects, in interaction, make each other objects.

M. Heidegger discusses conscience in its role as the means of distinguishing between authentic and unauthentic self. Self is neither a thing nor an ''I'' but a way to exist. The *Dasein* declines because it clings to the self of the common man in its ''throwness'' and not to its own self. Conscience calls man from the common self to authentic selfhood. Genuine selfhood and freedom are constituted only when man stands open to being. Only then is there ''ex-sistence,'' the free response of man to the call of being, *Dasein's* independence from and presence to things that are.

M. Buber regards the self as a self-other system rather than as a mind. Speech or dialogue is the chief mechanism constituting selfhood. It is an achievement rather than a birthright. While Mead's dialogue is merely horizontal, between man and man, Buber's self stands in a triadic pattern of relations to nature, to other men, and to God, the Eternal Thou.

Relationships to Other Concepts. The term self does not supplant the older concept of SOUL, nor is it the same as ego, mind, or person. It is a concept used to designate functions that philosophers felt were not included in soul—which, for them, was no longer the substantial form of Aristotle; i.e., the source of life, of dynamic specific activity, and of growth in man. Soul had become for them a term designating the static thinking substance revealed by the *Cogito* of Descartes. As this term was rejected with the rejection of substance, mind was substituted for it and the mind-body problem replaced the problem of the relationship of the soul to the body (*see* SOUL-BODY RELATIONSHIP). With the advent of the philosophers of the will, mind became inadequate to represent the human person in his dynamic growth and development. PERSON referred to the individual substance of a rational nature—a definition that emphasized the common givenness of all men and seemed to ignore the concrete individual developing in the world; it regarded man more as an object of classification than as a subject of free decisions. Self then began to be used to suggest

all those aspects of man thought to be left out by the terms soul, mind, person, and NATURE—and to designate the unifying, purposeful, growing, and interacting aspect of man's activities. It included also the notions of alienation and of encounter.

In many respects the term self refers to functions included in the Thomistic concept of soul, except for the view of the soul as the principle of life and as source of a common nature. In contemporary thought, the term also includes the view of self by the self, which view confirms the aspect of historicity implicit in the notion. Thus the concept self can be divided into the self one can know as reflected from others, and the self that knows, a division Kant was the first to propose.

See Also: PERSONALITY; SOUL, HUMAN, 4

Bibliography: F. C. COPLESTON, *History of Philosophy* (Westminster, Maryland 1946–). J. D. COLLINS, *A History of Modern European Philosophy* (Milwaukee 1954). H. J. TALLON, *The Concept of Self in British and American Idealism* (Washington 1939). R. C. WYLIE, *The Self Concept* (Lincoln, Nebraska 1961). H. SPIEGELBERG, *The Phenomenological Movement*, 2 v. (The Hague 1960). C. MOUSTAKAS, ed., *The Self* (New York 1956). P. E. PFUETZE, *The Social Self* (New York 1954), reprinted as *Self, Society, Existence* (Torchbks 1961). R. FRONDIZI, *The Nature of the Self* (New Haven 1953). B. SNELL, *The Discovery of the Mind: The Greek Origins of European Thought*, tr. T. G. ROSENMEYER (Cambridge, Massachusetts 1953).

[M. GORMAN]

SELF-ABANDONMENT, SPIRITUAL

The English term used in referring to ABANDONMENT understood in its active sense, that is, the surrender of oneself to divine providence. Self-abandonment, then, signifies a conformity to the divine good pleasure, a conformity that arises from love.

Christ is the supreme model of self-abandonment, especially in the Garden of Gethsemane: ''Yet not my will but thine be done'' (Lk 22.42); ''yet not as I will, but as thou willest'' (Mt 26.39). The practice of self-abandonment has been stressed particularly by French spiritual writers. St. Francis de Sales has been called the doctor of self-abandonment. Other French writers noted for their teaching on abandonment are: Bossuet, A. Piny, J. P. de Caussade, J. N. Grou, H. Ramière, C. L. Gay, and V. Lehodey. But St. Thérèse of Lisieux, with her little way of spiritual childhood, has contributed most to the spread of interest in the practice of abandonment.

Self-abandonment requires the practice of the theological virtues and of detachment. In the act of abandonment there is a dynamic mingling of faith, hope, and love that unites the soul to God and to His action. This union in turn involves detachment from oneself, one's own will and interests, as well as concern for nothing but God's will. Abandonment is above all an expression of love that leads to the perfection of love. To love God a person must abandon himself to God; to abandon himself to God he must love. Self-abandonment is thus the most integral expression of perfect love.

Like providence, the practice of abandonment reaches out to all things: to the past, the present, and the future; to the body and its various conditions; to the soul, with all its good and bad qualities; to the malice in men as well as to their good will; to the changes and disturbances of the material world and to the revolts of the moral world; to time and to eternity. However, since abandonment embodies conformity to the divine will, it does not excuse one from any positive duty. The absolute sacrifice of one's salvation would lack an essential element of abandonment, for the will to be damned is not conformable to the divine will. If in the folly of their intense love, some saints seem to have renounced even salvation in order to be more abandoned to God, they did not make this sacrifice absolutely but conditionally, with the realization that God wills their salvation.

Finally, since man's sanctification calls for his free cooperation as well as for the work of grace, self-abandonment does not excuse one from effort, as the quietists maintained, nor does it eliminate repugnances or always free a man from inner struggle.

See Also: ABANDONMENT, SPIRITUAL; QUIETISM.

Bibliography: J. P. DE CAUSSADE, *Self-Abandonment to Divine Providence,* ed. J. JOYCE, tr. A. THOROLD (London 1959). P. POURRAT, *Christian Spirituality,* tr. W. H. MITCHELL et al., 4 v. (Westminster, MD 1953–55) v. 4. F. JAMART, *Complete Spiritual Doctrine of Saint Thérèse of Lisieux,* tr. V. VAN DE PUTTE (New York 1961). M. VILLER, *Dictionnaire de spiritualité ascétique et mystique. Doctrine et histoire,* ed., M. VILLER et al. (Paris 1932) 1:2–25.

[K. KAVANAUGH]

SELF-DENIAL

In common Christian usage, the depriving of self of certain pleasures and satisfactions when the privation is undertaken for the purpose of self-discipline, mortification, or sharing more intimately in the cross of Christ. In its New Testament foundation, however, the term appears to have a more profound meaning. Jesus said: "If anyone wishes to come after me, let him deny himself . . ." (Mt 16.24). This is not simply a denying of some gratification *to* oneself, but a denying *of* oneself. It is, in a sense, a refusal to recognize one's own personal self, and a man who denies himself in this way says in effect, "I do not

know myself." The same Greek verb ἀπαρνέομαι, is used here that is employed in connection with Peter's denial of Christ, when he said that he did not know Him. To deny oneself in this sense amounts to giving up, in a way, one's own personality and to emptying one's self completely in order to live in the unselfish manner of Christ. This sense of the term includes the refusal to gratify one's own inclinations at certain times and in certain matters, but it reaches beyond this to include the total unselfishness toward which particular exercises of self-denial should aim.

Self-denial is necessary because of the effects of original sin. Because of his inheritance from Adam (Eph 4.21–24), man is from birth inclined to evil, disposed to error, attracted to unreasonable pleasures. These effects of original sin remain in the baptized, and self-denial helps to nullify them and makes the soul more disposed to God's action. To obey the Commandments requires in some measure this denial of self, and a man without such power cannot do even what is necessary for salvation.

Many examples of the practice of self-denial are to be found in the lives of the saints, and in some cases self-denial was carried to an extreme because their love of God was such that they were not satisfied with half measures. In some instances these extremes might have been exaggerated by pious hagiographers, who sometimes emphasized the extraordinary so strongly that it cannot be seen in proper perspective. Moreover, not all the extremes even in the lives of the saints are defensible, and some of the saints themselves acknowledged that they had been imprudent, as, for example, St. Francis of Assisi, who declared toward the end of his life that he had been somewhat too hard on Brother Ass. In any case, most authorities on the spiritual life caution against undertaking extraordinary measures of self-denial or mortification without the approval of a prudent confessor or director.

All moralists teach that some self-denial is required for all Christians and that greater self-denial is necessary for a life of extraordinary sanctity. The teaching of Molinos, who counseled against self-denial, was condemned, as were the teachings of the Jansenists, who overemphasized its importance.

Bibliography: R. GARRIGOU-LAGRANGE, *The Three Ages of the Interior Life,* tr. M. T. DOYLE, 2 v. (St. Louis 1947–48) 1:275–298. A. TANQUEREY, *The Spiritual Life,* tr. H. BRANDERIS (2d ed. Tournai 1930; repr. Westminster, MD 1945) 362–391. A. ROYO, *the Theology of Christian Perfection,* ed. and tr. J. AUMANN (Dubuque 1962) 217–317. J. LEBRETON, "La Doctrine de renoncement dans le NT," *Nouvelle Revue Théologique* (1938) 65 385–412.

[P. MULHERN]

SELF-KNOWLEDGE

In the Christian spiritual life, self-knowledge is the realization that one is nothing apart from God's creative love, and that one is, in God's hands, a unique, unrepeatable value manifesting His beauty in a way that no one else does; each individual is a person toward whom He has a unique love and through whom He expresses a unique power to be used toward the fulfillment of His providential plan. It is, moreover, an understanding of the personal needs and challenges in an individual's life that lend themselves to the full flowering of one's individual, God-given potential—the gifts that God uses to guide each person in his spiritual role.

In the Old Testament, the theme of self-knowledge is found in Ps 50.4–5 and Ps 118.59; it is prominent in the Wisdom literature. The interiorization of religion that marks the preaching of Jesus made self-knowledge mandatory for spiritual progress.

The Fathers of the Church echo this concern of the Gospel, although they seldom make it the express theme of their preaching, as St. Basil did (Homily on the *Attende tibi ipsi, Patrologia Graeca* ed. J. P. Migne 31:197–). It is most prominent, perhaps in St. Augustine (e.g., *Conf.; Trin.* 9). In the Middle Ages St. Bernard takes up the theme repeatedly in his *Sermons* and in the *De gradibus humilitatis* [*Select Treatises*, ed. B. Mills (Cambridge 1926)], and St. Bonaventure treats it in the *Itinerarium mentis ad Deum* [*Omnia Opera*, v.5 (Quaracchi 1941), or *Mystical Opuscula*, tr. J. De Vinck (Paterson, N.J. 1960)]. The patristic and scholastic treatment is marked especially by concern for the essential human condition of dependence on God rather than by concern for the differences in individual temperaments that specify the nature of this dependence in one's own life. It is a metaphysical rather than a psychological treatment.

The spiritual writers of the Renaissance, St. Ignatius (*The Spiritual Exercises*), St. John of the Cross (*The Dark Night of the Soul*), and St. Francis de Sales (*Introduction to a Devout Life*), tend toward a more psychological emphasis. Their psychology, however, is expressed in the terminology of their day, and is of dubious value now.

Self-knowledge ought to be sought apart from the context of neighbor, nor should it concentrate excessively on the accumulation of virtues or consist in progressive disenchantment. Christian growth is a response to the divine initiative of grace.

Bibliography: E. A. STRECKER and K. E. APPEL, *Discovering Ourselves* (New York 1958). J. NUTTIN, *Psychoanalysis and Personality,* tr. G. LAMB (New York 1953). J. H. VAN DER VELDT and R. P. ODENWALD, *Psychiatry and Catholicism* (2d ed. New York 1957). J. GOLDBRUNNER, *Holiness is Wholeness,* tr. S. GODMAN (New York 1955); *Cure of Mind and Cure of Soul,* tr. S. GODMAN (New York 1958). M. ORAISON, *Love or Constraint?,* tr. U. MORRISSY (New York 1959).

[J. B. WALL]

SELF-LOVE

A term that designates a disordered love of self, having as its object, therefore, one's own personal or private good without that good's being put, according to right reason, in subordination to the divine good. A somewhat equivalent term is egoism, which puts into relief the tendency to be habitually wrapped up in oneself and on that account to seek one's own advantage.

St. Augustine used strong language in describing the effect of man's penchant to love himself in this way: *amor sui usque ad contemptum Dei facit civitatem Babylonis* (*Civ.* 24.28). It is obvious, moreover, that in a general sense this dichotomy is always verified: man will be operating either for his own advantage (out of self-love, ultimately) or for the glory of God. Therefore, although spiritual writers have designated various remedies for it, such as mortification, humility, and obedience, the most direct antidote is charity itself, which effectively causes man to leave himself and, through Jesus, to be in God.

Gospel references to "loving one's own life" and the Pauline statement about charity's "not seeking its own advantage" are the basis for the spiritual tradition on this matter. Among the early ecclesiastical writers, however, self-love was most often treated with the monastic life in mind. For example, St. Basil wrote of self-love (φιλαυτία) as an intention to be autonomous and independent of authority, an attitude directly opposed to the cenobitic life he advocated. In the same vein, St. John Climacus viewed obedience as the instrument whereby self-love is most effectively destroyed. St. Maximus the Confessor seems to have been the first writer to introduce the idea that self-love involves inordinate love for one's own body. In his mind, therefore, it is opposed to both charity and continence.

Among medieval writers, St. Bernard of Clairvaux was in the Basilian tradition and viewed self-love as the fruit of the drive to be autonomous [see *Serm. in temp. Resurrection* n. 3 (ML 183, 289)]. St. Thomas Aquinas appears to have been aware of the complexity of the tradition since he observed: "[S]elf-love, insofar as it designates the appetite for all things as ordered to oneself, is the common principle of all sins. Insofar, however, as a person in a peculiar fashion desires for himself carnal pleasures, self-love is said to be a daughter of lust"

(*Summa Theologiae* 2a2ae, 153.5 ad 3; 1a2ae, 77.4; 84.2 ad 3;109.3; *In II Sent.* 42.2.1). Medieval mystics such as St. Catherine of Siena saw clearly that self-love prevents perfect union with God.

Among the spiritual writers of modern times a distinction can be made between those in whom a trace of optimism is manifest (e.g., St. Francis de Sales) and those whose view of the matter is quite dismal. The bishop of Geneva pointed out that there exists a legitimate love of self, which, however, tends quite con-naturally (i.e., according to man's present condition) to get out of hand. St. Vincent de Paul also expressed himself in this way. Among the writers of the Bérullian school of spirituality, however, such observations are not to be found; and the absolute opposition between love of God and love of self (obviously in the pejorative sense) is emphasized almost exclusively. Writers of the Ignatian school, moreover, make much of the practice of abandonment to divine providence; and one may view this as a sort of first sketch of St. Thérèse of Lisieux's resolution of the problem of self-love in the present age. For her the solution consisted in a moment-by-moment lending of one's will to God as an instrument of His mercy.

Finally, it must be observed that the problem of self-love entered into the controversies surrounding the errors of the Jansenists and the quietists. The Jansenists tended to be altogether despairing of the possibility of man's overcoming self-love in any effective way, while the quietists looked upon the pure love of God as something quite normal, without the exercise of that cooperation with the grace of God demanded by St. Thérèse.

Bibliography: R. DAESCHLER, *Dictionnaire de spiritualité ascétique et mystique. Doctrine et histoire,* ed., M. VILLER et al. (Paris 1932) 1:533–544. C. ANTOINE, *Dictionnaire de théologie catholique,* ed. A. VACANT, 15 v. (Paris 1903–50; Tables générales 1951–) 4.2:2224–30.

[M. B. SCHEPERS]

SELF-OBLATION

Is the application to self of the sacrificial idea expressed by the term "oblation"—an extension of the thought that readily suggests itself to one who bears in mind the symbolism of the sacrificial act. The oblation of an external victim represents the inner offering that one makes of himself to God (St. Thomas Aquinas, *Summa Theologiae* 2a2ae, 85.2). This oblation in Christian practice is generally made in union with Christ's offering of Himself upon the cross. It is a way of following Christ, who said: "If anyone wishes to come after me, let him deny himself and take up his cross and follow me" (Mt 16.24; Mk 8.34; in Lk 14.27 ". . . take up his cross

daily . . ."). In these passages Jesus was speaking directly and primarily of persecution, but the words may be understood to include not only external persecution but also the inner denying of oneself in order to live only for God (*see* SELF-DENIAL). This same thought, coupled with the association of the sacrifice with that of Christ, is contained in St. Paul's graphic words about being nailed to the cross with Christ (Gal 2.16–20). Inspired by these words, many Christians throughout the centuries have made an explicit offering of themselves to God through Christ in a life of prayer and sacrifice. It is such a desire, indeed, that has led to the establishment of the many religious communities in which men and women consecrate their lives to the service of God. Nevertheless, self-oblation as an act of the virtue of religion is not confined to those who take public vows and live according to the rule of a religious community. SS. Peter and Paul urged all Christians to present themselves as an oblation to God (1 Pt 2.4; Rom 12.1). The Church, especially through the devotion to the humanity of Christ and to the Sacred Heart of Jesus, has continued to promote self-oblation as a practice for devout Christians in all walks of life. Pius XII, for example, invited every Christian, through the Mass especially, to "assume to some extent the character of a victim . . . so that we can apply to ourselves the words of St. Paul, 'With Christ I am nailed to the Cross'" (*Mediator Dei* 37). The Church, in the indulgences with which it has enriched private prayers, like the morning offerings of the APOSTLESHIP OF PRAYER, the act of consecration to the Sacred Heart, and the act of consecration of St. Louis Marie GRIGNION DE MONTFORT, continues to encourage self-oblation as an act of devotion.

Bibliography: PIUS XII, *Mediator Dei.* A. TANQUEREY, *The Spiritual Life,* tr. H. BRANDERIS (2d ed. Tournai 1930; repr. Westminster, MD 1945) 270–276. *Raccolta* (New York 1952) 155–159.

[P. MULHERN]

SELJUKS

A Turkic people of Central Asian origin who in the 11th and 12th centuries played a major role in south Central Asia, Iran, and Asia Minor. The name (also spelled Saljuk, Salchuk, Selchuk) is that of an *Oghuz* (*Ghuz*) chieftain who in the second half of the 10th century moved with his tribe into the region of Lake Aral and thence to Bukhara, where he and his people embraced Sunnite Islam. Seljuk mercenaries served anyone willing to hire them. In 1025 Mahmud of Ghazna settled some of them in Khorasan, which these nomads "devoured as if it were food laid out for hunting falcons." By 1040 the Seljuks were so powerful that, at the battle of Dandanqan, Seljuk's grandsons Tughril and Chagri were able to annihilate the Ghaznavid army of Sultan Mas'ūd. In 1055 Tughril made a triumphant entry into Baghdad, where he was greeted by the caliph as a liberator from Buwayhid servitude. Tughril's son and successor, Alp Arslan (1063–72), advanced further west and wrested Jerusalem from the Fatimids in 1070. The following year near Manzikert in Armenia he inflicted a crushing defeat on the Byzantine armies of Romanus III Diogenes.

The Seljuk impact on Asia Minor can be considered the catalyst of the Crusades. Control of the access to the Christian shrines came into the hands of a new ethnic group, unfamiliar with established custom, unknown to the Western world. Malik shah (1072–94) and his powerful and erudite minister, Nizām al-Mulk, were unaware of and disinterested in the possibilities offered by westward expansion. While Samarkand and distant Kashghar were incorporated into the Seljuk Empire, the affairs of Asia Minor were delegated to Malik's cousin Suleyman, who in 1081 set up residence in Nicaea. This was the first capital, followed by Iconium, of the so-called Seljuk Sultanat of Rum, which survived until 1302, and was an important factor in the history of Asia Minor. The so-called Great Seljuks of Persia maintained their rule over a predominantly Iranian population until 1157.

Bibliography: Sources. A listing of these will be found in C. CAHEN, *La Syrie du nord à l'époque des croisades et la principauté franque d'Antioche* (Paris 1940). H. W. DUDA, *Die Seltschukengeschichte des Ibn Bībī* (Copenhagen 1959). **Literature.** C. CAHEN, "The Turkish Invasion: The Selchükids," in *A History of the Crusades,* ed. K. M. SETTON (Philadelphia 1955–) 1:135–176, best introduction. V. A. GORDLEVSKIJ, *Gosudarstvo Sel'džukidov Maloj Azii* (Moscow 1941), the major monograph. P. WITTEK, "Deux chapitres de l'histoire des Turcs de Roum," *Byzantion* 11 (1936) 285–319. C. CAHEN, "Le Malik-nâmeh et l'histoire des origines seljukides," *Oriens* 2 (1949) 31–65; "Le Problème ethnique en Anatolie," *Cahiers d'histoire mondiale* 2 (1954) 347–362. O. TURAN, *Türkiye Selçuklulari hakkinda resmî vesikalar* (Ankara 1958). T. T. RICE, *The Seljuks in Asia Minor* (New York 1961), on Seljuk art. C. E. BOSWORTH, *The Ghaznavids* (Edinburgh 1963), on the early Seljuks.

[D. SINOR/EDS.]

SEMANTICS

The term "semantics" came into general use in many disciplines during the 20th century. The word was first coined and used by Michael Bréal in 1883 to designate the study of the laws that govern changes in meaning. It is popularly used to mean a study designed to improve human relations by an understanding of the ways in which words can mean different things to different persons because of their various emotional and experiential backgrounds. This is called general semantics by the followers of Alfred Korzybski (d. 1950) and pragmatics by Charles Morris.

According to Morris, semantics is one of the three branches of semiotics, the science of signs, which consists of syntactics, semantics, and pragmatics. Each of these branches can be theoretical or empirical. Linguistic semantics is descriptive and empirical, attempting to discover from history and from social science the laws that govern changes in the meaning and structure of words. Pure semantics, as a branch of logic, discusses relationships between expressions and the objects they denote with special emphasis on the problems of truth, denotation, and meaning. It is derived from the Vienna Circle and developed in Cambridge, England, thence going to America with Rudolph Carnap and Alfred Tarski, its chief exponents (*see* LOGICAL POSITIVISM). Bertrand RUSSELL, while one of the originators, has since disavowed its extreme theories. Willard V. O. Quine and P. F. Strawson are interested in the denotation of words, but they have not developed the formalized system of Tarski and Carnap. John G. Kemeny is associated with semantics through his interest in symbolic logic (*see* LOGIC, SYMBOLIC). Linguistic analysis, while related to semantics in its neopositivist assumptions and in its insistence that all problems in philosophy are due to confusion over terms, does not attempt a formalized language but prefers to discuss the meaning of words as used in ordinary language.

This article deals with pure semantics, discussing its origins; its chief concepts, such as antinomy, metalanguage, truth, description, and meaning; and its relation to traditional logic.

Antinomy and Metalanguage. The relationship between language and the objects denoted by it has been studied as far back as the time of Aristotle. As a separate discipline, however, pure semantics can be said to have begun only in the late 19th century when Russell, in a letter to Gottlob Frege, formulated his antinomy of the class of classes. Other antinomies, both linguistic and mathematical, were soon pointed out; these showed weaknesses in a natural language, such as English, when it is used to discuss itself. Accordingly language came to be intensively studied not merely as an instrument for other disciplines, but as itself an object of research. This led to the invention of formalized languages. In order to talk about a natural or object language, a stronger language is needed, a metalanguage, which in turn can be discussed only by a still stronger metalanguage. An adequately formed system of semantics therefore requires a hierarchy of formalized languages. For example, English could be the metalanguage of a simple calculus language, or object language, in which one designates capital letters to represent adjectives and small letters to represent nouns; French could then be the metalanguage of English, or a stronger formalized language could be developed.

When it was seen that metaphysical difficulties arise from the improper use of words or from an inadequate understanding of their use, interest centered in syntax. Logical syntax, as understood by Carnap, abstracts from both the object denoted and the thinking subject and lays down rules for the formation and transformation of linguistic entities. It soon became evident, however, that such matters as truth, denotation, and meaning cannot be discussed in a science of syntax that abstracts from objects.

Truth, Denotation, and Connotation. Tarski, maintaining that TRUTH as such can be considered without involvement in contradictions, based his notion of truth on denotation and satisfaction. A meaning of a WORD can be either the objects denoted by the word or the notion or IDEA given by the word. The denotative or extensional meaning of the word "man" is all the men who have ever lived. This is called *Bedeutung* by Frege, denotation by J. S. Mill, extension in traditional logic, and reference by Max Black. The idea of man is given as rational animal and this is called *Sinn* (sense) by Frege, connotation by Mill, comprehension in traditional logic, and sense by Black. Current usage distinguishes between "essence" (e.g., rational animal) and "connotation," the essence plus emotions usually associated with the word used to designate it. An extensional definition of the word "horse" would be the listing of all horses ever existing; an intensional definition would be the notion or meaning of the concept of horse, and would be declared nonexistent by neopositivists. Two words can have the same denotation, while the comprehension or intensional meaning may vary. For example, morning star and evening star have the same denotation, Venus, but the connotation varies slightly.

Tarski uses the semantic concepts of denotation, satisfaction, and definition when attempting to formulate the conditions under which a sentence may be said to be true. Thus, "the author of *Waverley*" *denotes* Scott and "Scott" *satisfies* the sentential function "X is the author of *Waverley*." To *define,* for Tarski, means to uniquely determine; thus, the equation $2x = 1$ uniquely determines the number 1/2. The word "true" does not apply to such relations, but rather expresses a property of certain expressions, especially of sentences.

Tarski says that he uses "true" in the sense of Aristotelian metaphysics: "To say of what is that it is not or of what is not that it is, is false, while to say of what is that it is or of what is not that it is not is true." In realist terms this would be: "The truth of a sentence consists in its agreement with (or correspondence to) reality." As a condition for the term "true" to be adequate, he adds that all the equivalences of the form, "X is true, if and only if *P*," must logically follow and be able to be asserted. When one fills in values for "X" and "P," one gets a definition of the truth of one sentence; the general definition would then be a union of all partial truths, and would constitute the semantic concept of truth. For example, the sentence, "snow is white" is true if, and only if, snow is white. The first sentence, "snow is white," is the name (or *suppositio formalis* in traditional logic) of the sentence following the conditional, which asserts a matter of fact (*suppositio materialis* in traditional logic). Therefore, Tarski's definition of truth is simply this: a sentence is true if it is satisfied by all objects; otherwise it is false.

Analytical Truth. While the semantic concept of truth is based on denotation, satisfaction, and extension, the concept of analytical truth is based on connotation, intension, and meaning. According to Immanuel Kant, a sentence whose predicate is contained in the meaning of the subject, and is noncontradictory, is analytically true. The sentences, "Bachelors are unmarried men," and "Man is a rational animal," are analytically true. Synthetic propositions, also called propositions of fact, are different from this in that they depend on information from the physical world. An example would be: "It is raining." Negation of this sentence, if it *is* raining, is synthetically false.

A sentence valid in all models (negative, disjunctive, and universal) is analytically true; a sentence valid in no model is analytically false or self-contradictory. By the principle of the EXCLUDED MIDDLE, a sentence is either analytically true or not analytically true, but not necessarily analytically false. It could be synthetically true or synthetically false, since this is valid in some but not in all models.

There has been much discussion of the concept of analytical truth, especially by Quine. He questions the existence of any analytic sentences and maintains that all sentences are synthetic or that the differences between the two types are minimal. For example, "The earth is a flat surface" could have been considered an analytically true sentence in 1450, while after 1492 it came to be considered as analytically false.

Ambiguity and Description. Two minor problems associated with denotation concern AMBIGUITY and description. An ambiguous term can be clearly true of one object and clearly false of others. Ambiguity causes variation in the truth value of a sentence due to variation in the circumstances of its utterance.

The denotation of a description presents a different problem. According to Russell, descriptions do not function as names nor do they require a name. A description is true only if there is but one denoted object. Descriptions, however, may denote the same object while being factually different. For example, Paul VI is denoted by the two descriptions: "the successor of Pope John XXIII" and "the Archbishop of Milan in 1960." Both of these must be factually ascertained.

Russell maintains that a description such as "Franklin Delano Roosevelt was the 32nd President of the United States" is really an abbreviation of: "There was one and only one man who was the thirty-second president of the United States, and Franklin Delano Roosevelt was this man." The first part in this sentence would be false if there were no man, or more than one man, satisfying the denotation. Alonso Church, on the other hand, holds that a description is about two concepts, not about the object to which they refer. Thus, in the example above, the two concepts about Pope Paul VI are related to each other rather than to the person of this pope. All are agreed that descriptions can never be analytically true but must be factually verified, and, therefore, can be only synthetically true.

Meaning of Meaning. Another problem discussed by semanticists is that of the meaning of meaning. Carnap seems to hold that language, like mathematics, can be arbitrarily imposed; thus, for him, words have meanings and objects have names (therefore meanings) that are decreed by men. In this view, there is no meaning except by convention. Others have formulated alternative explanations, as summarized in the following list:

1. Meaning is the object of which the sign is name denotative.
2. Meaning is an intrinsic property of objects, e.g., Mill's connotation.
3. Meaning is an ideal object, as for PLATO, or, as Edmund HUSSERL puts it, an ideal entity manifesting itself in intentional acts owing to a direct eidetic intuition of the essence of the thing.
4. Meaning is the relation between words, e.g., the lexical meaning obtained by getting a synonym of the word.
5. Meaning consists in the reaction to the word. William JAMES called it practical consequences of a thing in our future experience. For Ivan Pavlov, meaning is a reflex conditioning of the human organism to the sign or signal. According to C. S. S. Peirce, "to develop its [the word's] meaning, we have . . . simply to determine what habit it produces."
6. Meaning is the set of operations man can perform with the object, as in P. W. Bridgman's OPERATIONALISM.
7. Meaning is the total personal reaction to a thing. This is somewhat like 5 but stresses the *personal* reaction. It is the theory of the general semanticists,

who hold, as does B. L. Whorf, that language molds the worldview of a people rather than vice versa.

8. A direct relationship exists between thought and object; and an indirect relationship between word and object. Only when a thinker makes use of words do they stand for anything or have meaning. Therefore words have the meanings of the persons who use them. This is the theory of C. K. Ogden and I. A. Richards.

Traditional scholastic logic does not discuss meaning as such, but its detailed treatment of first and second intentions is quite relevant to modern discussions of the problem of meaning (*see* CONCEPT; INTENTIONALITY). In fact, the medieval problem of UNIVERSALS seems once again to be revived by semanticists. Since for the most part they eliminate cognitive elements and favor a behavioristic interpretation of language, they seem to join medieval nominalists in holding that words are mere sounds, or *flatus voces* (*see* NOMINALISM). Yet some object to such a characterization, since semanticists do recognize a kind of personal meaning.

Evaluation. Pure semantics is an effort to solve philosophical problems by making language more precise. It is a modern form of nominalism to the extent that it regards language as arbitrary and erects its theory of metalanguage on this base. For most semanticists, names have no intrinsic relation to the objects they denote. While seeing quite correctly that *many* philosophical difficulties arise over meanings of words, these thinkers universalize the diagnosis and conclude that *all* philosophical problems can be solved by establishing a formalized language. Problems that cannot be so solved they regard as pseudo-problems.

Despite this narrowness of viewpoint, semanticists have made important contributions in the field of analytical philosophy, and in those areas of philosophical thought related to modern science and its methodology. Their sentential calculi and formalized languages have been particularly valuable in research involving digital computers, and in setting up computations for decision making (*see* CYBERNETICS).

The problem of truth and that of the relationship existing between words and objects and between objects and thought, however, remain perennial problems in philosophy. The semantic movement, Anglo-Saxon in origin and positivist in inspiration, has attempted to bring scientific accuracy to their solution. Philosophers from other lands and with other orientations question, with good reason, whether rigorous language or vocabulary can of themselves provide lasting solutions to these problems.

Bibliography: R. CARNAP, *Introduction to Semantics* (Cambridge 1942); *Meaning and Necessity: A Study in Semantics and Modal Logic* (2d ed. Chicago 1956). H. FEIGL and W. SELLARS, eds., *Readings in Philosophical Analysis* (New York 1949). L. LINSKY, ed., *Semantics and the Philosophy of Language* (Urbana, Ill. 1952). C. W. MORRIS, *Foundations of the Theory of Signs* (Chicago 1938); *Signs, Language and Behavior* (New York 1946). C. K. OGDEN and I. A. RICHARDS, *The Meaning of Meaning: A Study of the Influence of Language upon Thought and of the Science of Symbolism* (New York 1949). C. S. S. PEIRCE, ''Logic as Semiotic; The Theory of Signs,'' *The Philosophical Writings of Peirce,* ed. J. BUCHLER (New York 1955) 98–119; *Values in a Universe of Chance,* ed. P. P. WIENER (Stanford 1958). W. V. O. QUINE, *From a Logical Point of View* (Cambridge, Mass. 1953); *Word and Object* (Cambridge 1960). B. RUSSELL, *An Inquiry into Meaning and Truth* (London 1940). A. TARSKI, *Logic, Semantics, Metamathematics: Papers from 1923 to 1938,* tr. J. H. WOODGER (Oxford 1956). S. ULLMANN, *The Principles of Semantics* (Glasgow 1951). M. W. HESS, ''The Semantic Question,'' *New Scholasticism* 23 (1949) 186–206. J. A. OESTERLE, ''The Problem of Meaning,'' *Thomist* 6 (July 1943) 180–229; ''Another Approach to the Problem of Meaning,'' *ibid.* 7 (April 1944) 233–263.

[M. GORMAN]

SEMINAL REASONS

Invisible principles inserted by God in the world during creation, which develop in time into all the plants, trees, birds, fishes, animals, and human bodies that will ever exist. Of Stoic origin, the notion passed from the Neoplatonists to St. AUGUSTINE, who used it to explain certain scriptural passages. In medieval thought these reasons became instrumental powers for St. THOMAS AQUINAS and principles and terms of material souls for St. BONAVENTURE. Since Augustine was the first to incorporate these reasons into Christian thought, his theory is detailed and criticized.

Augustine's Theory. By seminal reasons Augustine explains the OT stories of creation, of the instant change of Aaron's rod into a snake, and of the production of spotted sheep in Jacob's flocks. According to the first chapter of Genesis, God created plants and trees on the 3d day, fishes and birds on the 5th day, and animals and the human body on the 6th day. The second chapter relates how God created these same living things on these days. Why this repetition of the creation story? Augustine answers that the account in the first chapter means that God placed in the elements the invisible seminal reasons of all living beings below man and of all human bodies that would ever exist except the body of Christ. The second chapter then describes how God caused the seminal reasons of these living beings to develop into visible things. Similarly, Augustine explains that Aaron's rod turned into a snake because, in conformity with God's will, angels arranged the elements in the rod so that a seminal reason would suddenly change into a snake. Again, Jacob was able to increase the number of spotted sheep over what his father-in-law had promised to give him by a like application: the seminal powers of the offspring were modified when the pregnant sheep looked at the white and green sticks Jacob placed in the water trough.

In his literal commentary on Genesis Augustine envisions the eternal reasons as causes of the seminal reasons, the seedlike powers themselves as principles of the living being, and creatures as conditions of the development of these seminal qualities. For him, there is an eternal reason for every creature and for the seminal principles, and this reason is the exemplary cause of the seminal power. Thus, on the 3d day, when God created the seminal virtues of plants and trees in the earth, He made the unformed creature imitate the form of the Word. Likewise, on the 5th day the eternal reasons produced the seminal virtues of birds and fishes in the water. Again, on the 6th day God placed the seedlike qualities of animals and human bodies in the earth. In the time following creation these eternal reasons then conserve the seminal powers and cause them to effect the birth, growth, and death of the particular being.

Is the seminal principle itself a cause? The seminal reason is like a secondary efficient cause in the sense that it changes elements into a developed being. The seminal power of a tree changes the surrounding earth and water into distinctive characteristics, such as branches, leaves, and fruit (*Gen. ad litt.* 5.23; *Patrologia Latina* 34: 337). The seminal potency is also a kind of formal cause, for it is due to the seminal cause that one type of living thing develops and not another; under its influence, for example, a grain of wheat produces wheat and not beans (*ibid.* 9.17; *Patrologia Latina* 34:406). Obviously there can be no evolution of species in this explanation. Seminal principles develop at one time rather than at another only because a creature acts as a CONDITION for the unfolding of the seminal cause. Conditioned on rainfall and the warmth of the sun, the seminal reason of a tree begins to evolve; but creatures themselves do not exert causality by educing a form from matter (*see* MATTER AND FORM).

Critique. This theory has certain shortcomings. Although seminal reasons may account for the appearance of some things in the universe, they account neither for inorganic and organic change, nor for evolution. There is also no explanation of what happens to the seminal reason when the body carrying it dies. Because of such limitations, Augustine's theory has been relinquished by most scholastics in favor of Aquinas's doctrine on CAUSALITY.

See Also: EXEMPLARISM.

Bibliography: É. H. GILSON, *The Christian Philosophy of Saint Augustine*, tr L. E. M. LYNCH (New York 1960) 197–209. A. A. MAURER, *Medieval Philosophy* (New York 1962) 15–16. E. PORTALIÉ, *A Guide to the Thought of Saint Augustine* (Chicago 1960) 136–151. J. M. BRADY, ''St. Augustine's Theory of Seminal Reasons,'' *The New Scholasticism* 38 (1964) 141–158.

[J. M. BRADY]

SEMINARY EDUCATION

In ecclesiastical writings ''seminary'' designates a special type of school dedicated to the spiritual, moral, and intellectual formation of the clergy. It is derived from the Latin word *seminarium,* which was commonly used to describe a place where young seedlings were prepared for eventual transplantation. The first official use of this word to describe institutions for clerical training dates back to the Council of TRENT (Sess. 23, c.18), which did not invent the term as such but accepted it from some of the writings of the period, by men such as Cardinal Reginald POLE, St. John FISHER, and St. IGNATIUS OF LOYOLA.

Tridentine Discipline. The Council made it obligatory for every diocese to erect a seminary for the purpose of educating the local clergy. Whenever possible, this institution was to be built near the cathedral church so that the young aspirants to the priesthood might serve a sort of apprenticeship there by participating, each according to his rank, in the divine offices presided over by the local bishop. If an individual diocese was too small or lacked the necessary funds, it could join with other dioceses for the construction of a provincial or interdiocesan seminary. Those to be admitted had to be born of lawful wedlock and had to be at least 12 years of age. They were obliged to possess certain minimal educational requirements and to have a sincere desire to dedicate themselves wholeheartedly to the service of the Church. Special preference was to be given to the children of the poor; the children of the rich, however, were not to be excluded if they paid for their training. The young men were to study letters, humanities, chant, liturgy, Sacred Scripture, and dogmatic, moral, and pastoral theology. Their spiritual formation required daily assistance at the Eucharistic Sacrifice even though, according to the practice of the time, they were permitted to communicate only on the days indicated by their spiritual directors. Their moral development was also to be supervised to the extent that the disorderly and incorrigible were to be punished and, if necessary, expelled. Special priests were to be chosen by the local bishop himself as instructors and spiritual guides for the young candidates. The courses also were to be determined by the decision of the bishop, who was the primary judge as to what would be necessary for the particular circumstances of his diocese. The seminary was to receive its support from an intricate system of benefices in addition to taxes imposed on the revenues of bishops and other ecclesiastical dignitaries and institutions. The chief administrator of the school was to be the local bishop himself, who would be aided by two administrative boards, one to assist him in disciplinary and spiritual matters, and the other to help him with temporalities.

Origins of the Tridentine Decree. The Council's legislation *de seminariis* was not a new creation. It presented, rather, a restoration and renovation of the traditional manner in which young clerics received their formation. Fundamentally, it presented a return to the concept of the cathedral school, where from the earliest times in the Church, young men were prepared for the priesthood. With the breakdown of feudalism and the rise of the universities, this ancient system of clerical formation became either impoverished or generally abandoned. As a result, a large segment of the late medieval and pre-Reformation clergy received inadequate training and were very often ordained for an office they were not sufficiently equipped to exercise. Even though the question of clerical formation had been mentioned by the preparatory commission and had come to the fore not only in the discussions on the teaching of Sacred Scripture but also in the work of the fathers at Bologna, it was not until the 23d session of the Council that the problem was given a sound and practical solution.

It is commonly admitted that the immediate source of the Tridentine seminary legislation was canon 11 of the synodal legislation promulgated for England in 1556 by Cardinal Pole. This is quite evident from the first draft of Trent's decree, which closely parallels the corresponding section in Pole's *Reformatio Angliae.* As early as 1562 the entire text of the English cardinal's legatine synod was available at Trent and so, when the members of the commission studying abuses in the administration of the Sacrament of Orders took up the problem of seeking a means whereby the intellectual and moral training of the clergy might be assured, their attention focused easily upon the late cardinal's solution: the erection of seminaries at every cathedral church. The fathers of the council leaned upon Pole's solution to the problem, and the first draft of their own legislation *de seminariis erigendis* presents a striking similarity to it. Even though the final ratification of the decree promulgated in the 23d session differs considerably from the 11th canon of Pole's synodal legislation, the essence of his program was largely preserved.

Several proximate sources of the Tridentine seminary decree may be enumerated also. First of all, there were some documents presented to the Council in 1563 that highlighted certain abuses and remedies in connection with the administration of the Sacrament of Orders. Mention might be made of the *Memoriale de quibusdam abusibus in ecclesia corrigendis* submitted by Louis Beccadelli, Archbishop of Ragusa, who suggested that a *seminarium clericorum* be established; the *Articuli super reformatione sacramenti ordinis* presented by the archbishop of Reims, who advised the establishment of special schools attached to cathedral churches; and the petitions of Emperor Ferdinand, who urged the erection of special *collegia* for the clergy near the universities. Secondly, there was the influence of the Jesuits as illustrated by the work of Claude Le Jay in Germany and by the establishment of the *Germanicum* in Rome. During his mission to Germany (1542 to 1545) Le Jay constantly insisted upon the necessity of providing adequate means for clerical formation. He spoke of this urgent need to bishops, to civil rulers, and to the Council fathers themselves. He insisted that special schools be established with the express purpose of preparing young men for the ministry. Through the instigation of Cardinal John Morone, Le Jay's ideas found fruition, at least in Rome, in the *Germanicum,* established there in 1552. This institution was not a seminary in the Tridentine sense, but rather a *collegium,* in which the students lived under a determined rule while they attended classes at the Roman College. Finally, other proximate sources were the contemporary attempts to restore the cathedral schools as places of clerical formation. It suffices here to cite the work of three men: Gian Matteo GIBERTI, Bishop of Verona, who restored and improved the already well-known Acolyte School of Verona; Johannes GEILER VON KAYSERSBERG, the renowned German preacher, who in vain urged his bishop, Albert of Bavaria, to open a theological school in connection with the cathedral church; and, of particular ecumenical interest, Thomas CRANMER (1489 to 1556), Archbishop of Canterbury, who supervised the revision of the cathedral school of Canterbury and legislated for improved clerical formation by means of the section *de scholis habendis in ecclesiis cathedralibus,* a considerable portion of his famous *Reformatio legum,* which was completed in 1553.

Remote sources of Trent's seminary legislation included not only particular and general councils of the Church but also the pastoral concern of certain popes. As early as 826 Pope EUGENE II, in a council held at Rome, legislated that next to every cathedral church a dwelling should be erected in which young clerics would be formed in ecclesiastical discipline. In 1179 the Third Lateran Council laid down the general injunction that every cathedral in the universal Church was to establish a benefice for the support of a schoolmaster who would be charged with teaching the clerics attached to the church. Almost 40 years later, in 1215, the Fourth Lateran Coun-

cil once again formulated legislation regarding this matter and added that every metropolitan church was to employ a theologian who would be entrusted with the instruction of priests in Sacred Scripture and pastoral theology. As good examples of papal concern for the betterment of clerical education, mention should be made of the *Super specula* of HONORIUS III (d. 1183) and the *Cum ex eo* of Boniface VIII (d. 1298). Even though the above constitutions did not themselves envision the establishment of institutions of learning, nevertheless they did adapt the residence laws in such a way that many clerics were released from their obligations of living in their benefices while pursuing higher studies. They also gave added impetus to the desire of setting up a permanent, workable solution to the problem of inadequate clerical formation.

Implementation of the Tridentine Decree. Almost immediately after its promulgation, plans were made for the law's implementation. In 1565 Pope PIUS IV erected a seminary for the Diocese of Rome, and sections *de seminariis erigendis* were incorporated into the canons of many provincial councils. One of the most outstanding proponents of the seminary decree was St. Charles BORROMEO, Archbishop of Milan. He opened a major seminary under the patronage of St. JOHN THE BAPTIST with facilities for 150 students. Also, recognizing that all candidates for the priesthood did not have the intellectual capacity to be admitted to this institution, he established "La Canonica" for about 60 students who would be prepared for the care of souls by classes in Sacred Scripture, case studies, and the fundamentals of the faith as laid down in the Tridentine Catechism. In various parts of his archdiocese he also founded three preparatory seminaries: one for older students, another for adolescents, and a third for younger boys. From these institutions the candidates would pass either to the major seminary or to "La Canonica." In the beginning Borromeo staffed his seminaries with Jesuits, but later on he placed them under the direction of the Oblates of St. Ambrose, an order that he founded himself. His *Institutiones ad universum Seminarii regimen pertinentes* are valuable amplifications of the Tridentine decree.

In France the cardinal of Lorraine who was archbishop of Reims took the first steps to implement the seminary legislation. The Wars of Religion occasioned such a turmoil, however, that very little of a constructive nature was done before the beginning of the 17th century. St. VINCENT DE PAUL, John J. Olier, and St. JOHN EUDES were the most outstanding contributors to the establishment of seminaries in France, institutions that were to have considerable influence later on in the erection of similar houses of study in the British Isles, Canada, and the United States. Vincent de Paul's work in this field had its origins in a series of spiritual conferences and instructions he was accustomed to give to young men about to be ordained to the priesthood. At first these lasted only for a period of ten days, but later on they developed into a two- or three-year course given between the completion of philosophical studies and actual ordination to the priesthood. In 1635 he established a seminary at the Collège des Bons-Enfants for students of theology; later on he founded Saint-Lazare for young candidates who were studying the humanities; and in 1642 he erected a junior seminary, which he dedicated to St. Charles Borromeo. Prior to the FRENCH REVOLUTION, his congregation directed one-third of all the French seminaries; 53 of them were major, and nine were minor.

Olier, the founder of the SULPICIANS, began his contribution to the seminary system by establishing such an institution in 1642 within the boundaries of the parish of St. Sulpice. It was his intention that this should serve as a national seminary, and within two years there were representatives in attendance from 20 dioceses in France. In 1651 the rules for this seminary were adopted by many of the other institutions that were being constructed throughout France, even though it was not his original intention to found a congregation for the direction of seminaries. His intention had been merely to lend his priests to help in their establishment. A great number of requests from bishops led him to modify his plans to the extent that he finally accepted the task of staffing seminaries permanently.

St. John Eudes, a member of the Oratory and later the founder of the Society of the Sacred Hearts, played a significant role in the establishment of seminaries. In 1663 he erected his first seminary at Caen, and by the 18th century his priests staffed 40 seminaries.

The upheavals of the 18th century—the French Revolution, JOSEPHINISM, and the ENLIGHTENMENT—had disastrous effects upon the seminary system of western Europe. Many were closed and others were entirely suppressed. The 19th century, however, saw the reestablishment of many seminaries and the construction of countless others. In Ireland, Maynooth was erected in 1795 and All Hallows, in 1842; England witnessed the opening of St. Edmund's, Ushaw, and Oscott; and in the United States, St. Mary's Seminary was opened at Baltimore in 1791.

In the United States

Historical Development. The origin of seminaries in the United States can be traced to Baltimore in the 1780s, where Bishop John CARROLL, seeing the isolation of American Catholics from Europe after the American Revolution and the need for priests, made plans to develop a native American clergy. His efforts resulted in the establishment of Georgetown Academy in 1789, and in an offer by the Society of St. Sulpice to begin a seminary in the new diocese of Baltimore. Carroll intended Georgetown Academy (later GEORGETOWN UNIVERSITY) as a preparatory school to educate Catholic laymen and provide candidates for seminary study.

The arrival of four Sulpician priests with five seminarians in 1791 to open St. Mary's Seminary in Baltimore marked the formal beginning of Catholic seminary education in the United States. From 1799 to 1852 the Sulpicians conducted a lay college affiliated with the seminary that provided institutional support to maintain the small seminary program. In 1808 the Sulpicians opened Mount Saint Mary's College at Emmitsburg, Maryland. The small enrollment of young aspirants to the priesthood, however, soon led them to open the school to boys who did not intend to become priests in order to bring in more revenue and sustain the college. In 1826 the Sulpicians ceded control of Mt. St. Mary's to a corporation of diocesan priests under the direction of the Reverend John DUBOIS. It was an example of a "mixed" seminary, that is, one in which a theologate for seminarians stood side by side with a college for laymen.

In 1848 the Society of St. Sulpice opened St. Charles College in Catonsville, Maryland, and four years later closed the lay college that they had run in connection with the seminary in Baltimore. Thus St. Mary's Seminary became the American prototype of a "freestanding" seminary, that is, one in which the seminarians and clerical faculty devoted themselves exclusively to the task of clerical formation in an environment separated from other activities. Similarly St. Charles Seminary was the country's first freestanding minor seminary.

Diocesan Seminaries. There were 22 dioceses in the United States in 1845. Some bishops sent seminarians to Baltimore and Emmitsburg for training, but most were eager to start their own diocesan seminaries. By 1843 there were 22 seminaries in the country with a combined enrollment of 277 or an average of 13 students per seminary. Most of these local seminaries collapsed during the 1840s and 1850s for one or more reasons: a lack of local youth attracted to the priesthood, the uneven supply of immigrant seminarians, the lack of clerical personnel to conduct them, and the lack of regular funding to sustain their operation.

As dioceses were promoted to the rank of archdiocese with neighboring dioceses grouped around them to form ecclesiastical provinces, efforts were made to form a regional seminary in each province. Thus the Cincinnati archdiocese opened Mount Saint Mary's Seminary of the

West at Cincinnati in 1851; the New York archdiocese opened St. Joseph Seminary at Troy, New York, in 1864. St. Francis Seminary, established by the archdiocese of Milwaukee in 1856, became a regional center for clerical formation especially for German-speaking Catholics. Philadelphia had its local St. Charles Seminary since the 1830s, and in 1871 relocated it in a spacious and costly building in the suburb of Overbrook. These seminaries were what social historians of 19th-century life label ''total institutions'' whose internal life is ordered for one specific purpose: in the case of seminaries, the training of priests.

Religious orders of priests also sponsored and staffed diocesan seminaries. The VINCENTIANS, established a seminary for the St. Louis archdiocese in 1818, and conducted diocesan programs at their colleges for laymen at St. Vincent's College, Cape Girardeau, Missouri (1858), and at Niagara College, Niagara Falls, New York (1857). Likewise, Benedictine monks from German-speaking Europe came to the United States to serve German communities. In connection with their monasteries they operated schools for laymen, and educated diocesan and monastic seminarians for the priestly ministry. This was the case in St. Vincent's Archabbey and Seminary established in 1846, near Latrobe, Pennsylvania, St. John's Abbey and Seminary, Collegeville, Minnesota established in 1857, and St. Meinrad Archabbey and Seminary established in 1854. Italian Franciscans were invited to western New York in 1863 where they started a lay college and seminary that became ST. BONAVENTURE UNIVERSITY.

The dependence of the American Catholic Church on Europe led to various proposals for establishing seminaries in Europe near the sources of funding and students. In 1857 an American College was established in the shadow of the Catholic University at Louvain, Belgium. During the first half century of the college's history, it trained many Europeans, especially Germans, for the American missions. In 1859 Pope PIUS IX ordered the opening of an American College in Rome exclusively for American seminarians.

Religious Orders. Religious orders experienced a parallel development. As early as 1834, the Dominicans founded their first *studium generale* in the United States at Somerset, Ohio. About 1860 they established a similar institution on the West Coast at Monterey, later transferred to Benicia, where it remained until 1932. By 1820 the Vincentians had begun a log rectory-seminary at Perryville, Mo., that continued until about 1868 when St. Vincent's Seminary was opened at Germantown, Pennsylvania.

The REDEMPTORISTS opened their first house of studies in 1849 in New York City. It moved two years

later to Cumberland, Maryland, and in 1907 to a farm at Esopus, New York. The origins of the Franciscan School of Theology now at Berkeley, California, can be traced back to rudimentary beginnings in 1854.

In 1823 the JESUITS established a novitiate at Florissant, Missouri, outside St. Louis, where they taught philosophy and theology. By 1837 Jesuit scholastics were studying at St. Louis University. In the East, Jesuit scholastics studied at Georgetown which had received in 1833, from the Sacred Congregation for the Propagation of the Faith, the power to grant ecclesiastical degrees in philosophy and theology. In 1869, however, the Jesuits unified their seminary program in a single national free-standing seminary, the College of the Sacred Heart, at Woodstock, Maryland, near Baltimore. Woodstock College, as it was known, remained the Jesuits' national seminary until the early 20th century.

Until more information is assembled and analyzed, we may assume that the above patterns were somewhat typical for religious orders through much of the nineteenth century. The growing number of religious seminarians kept pace with the increase of diocesan seminarians. By 1900 there were some 76 seminaries, minor and major, diocesan and religious, enrolling 3,395 seminarians. Religious orders and congregations continued to establish free-standing seminaries into the era of Vatican Council II. These houses of study remained ''total institutions,'' fully staffed with their own professors and with a student body made up entirely of members of the order or congregation. There seem to have been many such foundations that lasted only a few years before they were moved or closed.

Program Content and Duration. The vision of ministry in the developing American Catholic Church influenced the kind and length of all seminary programs. The urgent need for priests to minister the Sacraments to the rapidly growing Catholic immigrant population required quick training. Dogmatic and moral theology ''tracts'' or short articles on theological topics bound together in ''manuals'' were the basis of instruction with other subjects secondary or not offered. There was no Church legislation governing the length of the program. Moreover, the volume of seminary activities, substantial though it appears by the 1870s, did not produce the priests needed for the growing Catholic population. To resolve this and other pressing issues in the American Catholic community, the American bishops convened for their Third Plenary Council of Baltimore in 1884.

The Council's seminary decrees were aimed to improve the content and length of seminary training by requiring a six year course for minor and major seminaries. The major seminary decree listed and described the courses of the curriculum giving unprecedented attention to formerly neglected subjects such as Biblical studies, homiletics, and Church history. The minor seminary decree aimed to prepare students for the major seminary with an education that was firmly grounded in the humanities, classical languages, and the rudiments of clerical spirituality and culture. Diocesan seminary educators now had the guidance of a curricular program for a prescribed number of years, though it would be years before all seminaries complied fully with the six-year requirement for the major seminary.

The Third Plenary Council initiated action that led to the establishment of a national university in Washington, D.C. The CATHOLIC UNIVERSITY OF AMERICA opened in 1889. Although the Catholic University was originally intended for priests doing graduate study, it acted as a magnet attracting seminarians to the city. The Paulists and other religious orders established residences and houses of study near the university so that their members could take advantage of the university's philosophy and theology programs. In 1905 the DOMINICANS opened their own house of studies as a free-standing seminary across the street from the university where their seminarians could pursue the Order's distinctive theological program and pontifical decrees without recourse to the university.

The training offered in seminaries in the 20th century continued the methods of spiritual formation of the kind pursued since the 17th. Moreover, the separation of seminary communities from lay culture was more complete within the self-contained world of the free-standing seminary and under the more rigorous standards decreed by Church authority. The methods of formal learning in most diocesan seminaries and in many seminaries of religious orders were similar. Dogmatic and moral theology dominated the subjects of study.

Preconciliar Period. By the 1950s seminary educators began to develop among themselves a sense of common concerns. The initiative was taken by various religious orders engaged in educational activities, either through their own seminaries or through seminary education for dioceses. They discussed the need for reform and for common educational policies. It was, however, the seminary department of the NATIONAL CATHOLIC EDUCATIONAL ASSOCIATION (NCEA) that provided the national forum for seminary educators. The annual convention offered an occasion for the discussion of seminary concerns and the exchange of ideas.

In 1958 the NCEA appointed a full-time executive for the seminary department, Reverend J. Cyril Dukehart. Father Dukehart was a persistent advocate of ways to bring the seminary out of its isolation from the rest of the

educational world that often regarded the Catholic seminary as inferior. He targeted three major areas for seminary reform: first, the importance of accreditation so that unordained former seminary students and clerical alumni would have academic records and degrees that would be recognized in the educational world; second, the formation of an American Association of Catholic Theological Seminaries as a means to improve the standards of seminaries and to establish a professional degree for seminaries; and third, the acute problem of the weakness of over 100 minor and major seminaries having fewer than 50 students.

In 1959 the seminary department of the NCEA reported that there were 381 seminaries, major and minor, diocesan and religious, in the United States, representing a 28 percent increase during the decade. By 1961, the total number of all seminarians, diocesan and religious, was 42,349 in 402 seminaries and houses of religious formation. These institutions ranged in size from great free-standing seminaries of large dioceses and large religious orders, many of them having been established after 1900, to programs of small religious orders training a handful of seminarians. The high enrollments were tributes to the attractiveness of the priesthood to youth born and raised in American Catholic culture. Many seminary educators believed that the growth would continue indefinitely and the need for improvement of seminaries was therefore urgent.

By 1962, the year of the opening of the Second Vatican Council, the main lines of an agenda of seminary reform in the United States had been determined. The following decade saw the implementation of most reforms that were designed to end the isolation of the seminary and to enlarge its educational purposes. These changes were accompanied by both the theological renewal brought by the Second Vatican Council that would alter the content of seminary learning, and the rapid cultural changes taking place within the American Catholic community that would change the attitude of young men toward entering the seminary.

Normative Documents. The immediate impetus for change in seminary curriculum and style of life came from the documents of Vatican II that in one way or another related to priesthood and priestly formation, especially *Presbyterorum ordinis* and *Optatam totius*. *Optatam totius*, the decree that dealt specifically with priestly formation, posited three fundamental principles: first, along with the decree on the priesthood, *Presbyterorum ordinis*, it stated clearly a doctrine of "the unity of the Catholic priesthood." Second, it affirmed, seemingly as a corollary to the foregoing, that the same "priestly formation is required for all priests—secular, religious and of every rite.'' Third, it assumed that the diocesan priesthood with its parochial ministries is the analogue according to which the appropriateness of all priestly training is measured.

Optatam totius and *Presbyterorum ordinis* were the bases of the *Ratio fundamentalis* for priestly formation issued January 1970 by the Congregation for Catholic Education. The *Ratio* uses the term "seminary" in the general sense of "institutions organized for the formation of priests" (n. 1). This usage is symptomatic of the erosion of the older distinction between *seminarium,* the diocesan institution, and the *studiorum domus* (house of studies) of religious orders, a distinction that has also disappeared from the new Code of CANON LAW.

When the first edition of *The Program of Priestly Formation* (PPF) was published by the National Conference of Catholic Bishops in 1971 in accordance with the provisions of the *Ratio fundamentalis* of the previous year, it contained a special section on "The Religious Priest's Formation.'' The preface to the document noted:

> The Conference of Major Religious Superiors of Men . . . agreed to accept the *Program* as the recommended program for religious priests' formation, if there were added to the *Program* a short section prepared by them on religious life (Part Four). The National Conference approved the *Program* as the one program for all seminarians, diocesan and religious, and the addition of Part Four (pp. xii–xiii).

Thus, within the short period between the publication of the *Ratio* and the publications of the first edition of the PPF, "seminaries" of the orders and congregations found that their training, for the first time in history, seemed to require episcopal approval.

The second edition (1976) of the *Program* contained the same Part Four unchanged. The third edition (1981), however, dropped this section on religious priests because, according to the "Statement from the Conference of Major Superiors of Men,''

> Religious and diocesan priests share an increasingly pluriform priesthood; their needs for priestly formation as such do not differ. . . . Thus the Conference of Major Superiors of Men adopts the program of priestly formation as the one program for all United States religious seminarians (p. 3).

All three editions of *The Program of Priestly Formation* (1971, 1976, 1981) were the result of collaboration among the bishops of the United States, personnel involved in priestly formation programs, and other knowledgeable individuals. This document, approved in the name of the HOLY SEE by the Sacred Congregation for Catholic Education, concerns itself with all aspects of formation at the theologate, college, and high school level. According to the PPF, the three principal components of formation are: "spiritual and personal formation through community life and worship and personal spiritual guidance; academic preparation through humanistic and theoretical studies; and pastoral training through supervised practical experience'' (n. 39).

Besides the omission of the special section on the formation of religious priests, the 1981 edition made several major changes: new emphasis is given to safeguarding the distinctive training and life style of priests (n. 19); formation for celibacy (n. 22); acceptance of older candidates (nn. 24–25); and preparation for social justice (nn. 26–28). Finally, a section on the significance of the seminary for the life of the Church is added (nn. 29–33).

The 1983 Code of Canon Law embodies legislation for seminaries in 33 canons (nn. 232–264), substantially longer than the 19 canons governing the establishment and direction of seminaries in the 1917 Code (cc. 1352–1371). The revised code emphasizes the entire process of preparing a person to be a cleric rather than on the seminary as an institution. Unlike the 1917 code which treated seminaries in the section dealing with the ecclesiastical magisterium, the 1983 code places the section, "The Formation of Clerics,'' in Book II of the code which treats "The People of God.'' This new placement reflects the fact that seminary training is broader than doctrinal education.

Significant points in the 1983 Code include the recognition of candidates of a more mature age and the need of programs to assist them; an extensive summary of Vatican II teachings on the spiritual formation of a priest; and the need of pastoral training which includes ministerial field experience. It reiterates the need of four full years of theological studies with distinct professors for all the major disciplines. Only faculty who have a doctorate or licentiate from a university or faculty recognized by the Holy See are to be appointed by bishops to teach in the major disciplines. The latter is stricter than previous legislation. Canon 242 calls for the episcopal conference of each nation to prepare a program of priestly formation adapted to the pastoral needs of their region. While restating the norm of the earlier code that each diocese should have a major seminary, the 1983 code recognizes that this is not always possible and collaborative efforts on the part of several dioceses may be necessary. It supports minor seminaries, but it no longer requires them of dioceses.

The *Ratio fundamentalis* for priestly formation was revised in 1985 to bring it into closer conformity with the 1983 Code of Canon Law. The new version contains very few emendations to the original edition: it highlights the study of Thomistic philosophy, and notes the need of background in the ''economic questions'' of parochial administration.

Post Vatican II. It is against this general background, and especially against the impact of Vatican Council II, that the dramatic series of relocations and reorganizations of seminaries and houses of study that took place in the post-conciliar years must be viewed. Between 1966 and 1970 a large number of theologates related themselves in a variety of formal and informal ways to other religious bodies and institutions of learning. Some of the major changes included the formation of the Catholic Theological Union at Chicago, which originated in 1967 from the joint sponsorship of provinces of several religious orders. A somewhat similar arrangement came into force at the Washington Theological Union, which was incorporated in 1969 as the Washington Theological Coalition. In Berkeley, Calif., Franciscan, Dominican, and Jesuit theologates associated themselves with the Graduate Theological Union and the University of California in the late 1960s. Several diocesan seminaries closed during this period, but most retained their freestanding status. All of the formal clusters or unions and most of the individual schools soon became affiliated with the Association of Theological Schools and accredited by it. The first such affiliations took place in 1968.

Bibliography: *Seminaria ecclesiae catholicae* (Vatican City 1963), a detailed and carefully documented history of seminary development, with extensive bibliog. *Enchiridion clericorum* (Rome 1938). M. BARBERA, ''L'Origine dei seminari a norma del Concilio di Trento,'' *La civiltà cattolica* 91.3 (1940) 215–21. G. CULKIN, ''The English Seminaries,'' *Clergy Review* 35 (1951) 73–88. A. DEGERT, *Histoire des séminaires français jusqu'à la Révolution,* 2 v. (Paris 1912). M. F. DINNEEN, ''St. Mary's Seminary of St. Sulpice, Baltimore,'' *American Ecclesiastical Review* 16 (1897) 225–41. H. JEDIN, ''Domschule und Kolleg,'' *Trierer theologische Zeitschrift* 67 (1958) 210–23. L. MCDONALD, *The Seminary Movement in the United States (1784–1833)* (Washington 1927). W. S. MORRIS, *The Seminary Movement in the United States (1833–1866)* (Washington 1932). A. MULDERS, ''Het Trentsche Seminarie-decreet,'' *Nederlandsche katholieke stemmen* 28 (1928) 226–39. J. A. O'DONOHOE, *Tridentine Seminary Legislation: Its Sources and Its Formation* (Louvain 1957). B. POÜAN, *De seminario clericorum* (Louvain 1874).

[J. A. O'DONOHOE/W. BAUMGAERTNER/K. SCHUTH]

SEMI-PELAGIANISM

Semi-Pelagianism is a doctrine concerning divine GRACE that while repudiating PELAGIANISM, nevertheless assigns a greater role to man's will than to God's grace in an individual's conversion to a religious way of life leading to salvation. The term itself was first applied to Molina's system of grace (*see* MOLINISM), but usually it is restricted to the doctrine in the period between 427 and 529 of theologians in Africa and especially in southern Gaul who opposed AUGUSTINE's final teaching on grace. Augustine's doctrine may be summarized as follows: Mankind shared in Adam's sin and therefore has become a *massa damnationis* from which no one can be extricated save by a special gift of divine grace that cannot be merited; but God in His inscrutable wisdom chooses some to be saved, and grants the graces that will infallibly but freely lead them to salvation. The number of the elect is set and can be neither increased nor decreased.

But Vitalis of Carthage and a community of monks at Hadrumetum, Africa (*c.* 427), found fault with these principles, asserting that they destroyed freedom of the will and all moral responsibility since wrongdoers could allege that they lacked God's grace. Augustine's reply to Vitalis (Letter 217) and to the monks in his *De gratia et libero arbitrio* and *De correptione et gratia* contains an excellent résumé of his arguments against the Semi-Pelagians: The grace of God is universally necessary for all, even for infants; it precedes and does not depend on human merits, and no act can be supernaturally meritorious without it; even the initial act of faith is itself a grace of God; the freedom to sin is actually slavery, for the will is efficaciously good and free only when vivified by grace; the predestination of some to glory is a gratuitous gift of God, for which He does not have to render an account; and finally, He is not guilty of injustice toward those who remain in the *massa damnationis.*

John Cassian. This explanation satisfied Vitalis and the community at Hadrumetum, but was opposed by the monks of Marseilles under John CASSIAN (*Collationes* 3.5 and especially 13) and by HILARY OF ARLES. Their teaching, brought to Augustine's attention by two lay theologians, PROSPER OF AQUITAINE and Hilary of Africa in 428–429, was as follows: The beginning of faith or the impulse to do good sometimes comes from man's will, unaided by grace; for, in spite of original sin, the will is still capable of performing good and salutary acts. Supernatural grace is necessary for salvation, but no special help from God is needed to persevere to the end; a fixed number of the elect is contrary to the universal salvific will of God; infants who died without Baptism were punished because God foresaw what sins they would have committed if they had lived longer.

Augustine answered them kindly in *De praedestinatione sanctorum* and *De dono perseverantiae,* for he himself had once held the same opinion about the initial act of faith, but had abandoned it after more careful study. The very nature of grace—its gratuitousness—leads logically to his teaching about final perseverance and predestination, which he defines as ''the foreknowledge and preparation of those gifts whereby whoever are liberated (from sin), are most certainly liberated'' (*De dono perseverantiae* 14); last of all he pointed out how absurd it was to punish children for something they might have done.

Prosper of Aquitaine. His critics were not convinced and the struggle continued after his death (430), when Prosper of Aquitaine appealed to the Roman See in behalf of his revered master. In 431 CELESTINE I, in a letter to the bishops of southern Gaul, extolled Augustine's learning, sanctity, and loyalty to the Apostolic See, but gave no specific approval to his system of grace and predestination. Hence the Semi-Pelagians continued to circulate anti-Augustinian writings including the *Praedestinatus* of ARNOBIUS THE YOUNGER and the *Commonitorium* of VINCENT OF LERINS. The latter, in *Objectiones Vincentianae*, accused Augustine of teaching that God had created the greater part of mankind for eternal reprobation and was the cause of man's sins. Anonymous treatises were likewise distributed, the most important of which was the *Capitula objectionum Gallorum.* Prosper wrote spirited replies against John Cassian, Vincent, and the critics in Gaul.

Faustus of Riez. A period of relative quiet followed the death of John Cassian (435), but ended with the emergence of FAUSTUS, Abbot of Lerins, who became bishop of Riez *c.* 462. A priest named Lucidus was then teaching that all unbaptized infants, sinners, and pagans were sent indiscriminately to hell; Christ did not die for all mankind; original sin had completely destroyed freedom of the will. Faustus forced Lucidus to retract these errors at a council of Arles *c.* 473, and at the request of his fellow bishops wrote *De gratia Dei et libero arbitrio.* He explicitly condemns the heresy of Pelagius. However, he declares that Adam's sin caused man's bodily, but not his spiritual death; he cites examples of the ancient patriarchs and pagans to show that man by himself can take the first step toward sanctification and also avoid sin; predestination is therefore merely God's foreknowledge of what man himself has freely decided. Thus man's ultimate fate depends more upon his own efforts than upon God's grace. Faustus's reputation for learning and holiness seems to have stilled all opposition to his doctrine, and Semi-Pelagianism prevailed in the theological circles of southern Gaul.

A reaction began with a letter of Pope GELASIUS I on Nov. 1, 493, in which he reproached certain bishops for tolerating attacks of the Semi-Pelagians against JEROME and Augustine. In 520 Pope HORMISDAS was asked by Possessor, an African bishop residing in Constantinople, to give his opinion about the orthodoxy of Faustus. The pope replied that Faustus enjoyed no authority in the Church; this was an allusion to the so-called Gelasian decree that had placed the bishop of Riez's writings with those of heretics and persons under suspicion. Hormisdas added that the mind of the Holy See on questions concerning grace and free will was best expressed in the writings of Augustine, especially in those addressed to Prosper and Hilary of Arles, namely, *De praedestinatione sanctorum* and *De dono perseverantiae.* In 523, 12 African bishops, expelled by the Vandals and living in Sardinia, held a synod in which they adhered without reserve to Augustine's teaching on grace and free will. Their most learned member, FULGENTIUS OF RUSPE, wrote *Contra Faustum,* which is no longer extant. But the most important opponent of the Semi-Pelagians was St. CAESARIUS OF ARLES.

Caesarius of Arles. Although trained at Lerins, Caesarius became an admirer of Augustine, and as archbishop of Arles (503), he labored to win over the members of the hierarchy to his way of thinking. Twelve bishops accepted his invitation to the second Council of Orange in 529, whose purpose was to settle the disputes about grace, free will, and predestination that had been troubling southern Gaul for more than a century. Before the sessions began, Caesarius had consulted the Holy See, and FELIX IV had sent him 24 propositions taken in their entirety from the works of Augustine and the *Sententiae* of Prosper. They were unanimously approved by the council, which added only one of its own. Its most important decisions were the following: Man's body and soul have been changed for the worse by Adam's sin (c. 1); sin, the death of the soul, has passed from Adam to the whole human race (c. 2); even those who are reborn and holy must always call upon God in order to persevere (c. 10); the beginning of faith and the desire to believe is itself a gift of God (c. 5); had man's nature retained its original integrity it would still be totally incapable of performing a salutary act without the grace of God (c. 19); and works performed under the action of grace can acquire a claim to a supernatural reward (c. 18). The only reference to predestination comes in the profession of faith that follows the canons. ''We not only refuse to believe that some are predestined by divine power to evil, but if there are any willing to believe so horrible a thing, in all detestation we anathematize them'' [H. Denzinger, *Enchiridion symbolorum,* ed. A. Schönmetzer (Freiburg 1963) 371–397].

The acts of this Council of Orange were approved by BONIFACE II Jan. 25, 531. This gave it an ecumenical authority and it was later cited by the Council of TRENT. Semi-Pelagianism gradually died out; later theological disputes where this term occurs do not consider the pivotal problem of Semi-Pelagianism—the priority of the human will over the grace of God in beginning the work of salvation.

Bibliography: L. DUCHESNE, *L'Église au VIe siècle* (Paris 1925). R. GARRIGOU-LAGRANGE, *Predestination,* tr. B. ROSE (St. Louis 1939). E. PORTALIÉ, *A Guide to the Life and Thought of Saint Augustine* (Chicago 1960). É. AMANN, *Dictionnaire de théologie catholique,* ed. A. VACANT et al., 15 v. (Paris 1903–50; Tables générales 1951) 14.2:1796–1850. PROSPER OF AQUITAINE, *Defense of St. Augustine,* tr. P. DE LETTER in *Ancient Christian Writers,* ed. J. QUASTEN et al. (Westminster, Md.-London 1946–) 32, 1963. G. DE PLINVAL, A. FLICHE and V. MARTIN, eds., *Histoire de léglise depuis les origines jusqua'à nos jours* (Paris 1935–) 4:397–419. R. H. WEAVER, *Divine Grace and Human Agency: A Study of the Semi-Pelagian Controversy* (Macon, Ga. 1996). B. R. REES, *Pelagius, a Reluctant Heretic* (Woodbridge 1988).

[S. J. MCKENNA]

SEMIRATIONALISM

Semirationalism was a theological point of view that exaggerated the ability of human reason to demonstrate and explain the mysteries of Christian revelation without being guilty of all the errors of pure RATIONALISM. The principal theologians who fell victims to semirationalism wrote and taught, for the most part, in the century prior to Vatican Council I (1869–70), which put an end to the error. Semirationalists were to be found especially in German-speaking lands. Often, though not in every case, they remained submissive to the Church. In general, they were dissatisfied with the results of SCHOLASTIC PHILOSOPHY and SCHOLASTIC THEOLOGY, and they had recourse to the philosophies of their time to explain and defend the dogmas of faith.

Benedikt Stattler, SJ (1728–97), a professor at Ingolstadt in southern Germany, was a student of Christian WOLFF's philosophy. He attempted to prove [in his *Demonstratio catholica* (1775), for example] that the dogmas of faith were consistent with reason. His attempt was unorthodox, and some of his works were placed on the Index.

Georg HERMES (1775–1831) wished to defend Catholic dogma by employing Kantian principles. He began his theological investigations by doubting really and positively even the dogmas of faith. Such a procedure he recommended to others. He escaped from his doubt by accepting as certain and true what the speculative reason affirmed as such, without being able to act otherwise, and what the practical reason found consistent with human dignity. He maintained that one must accept Christian revelation because it enables one to realize his human dignity to the highest degree. FAITH is nothing more than the state of certitude that man acquires through the speculative and practical reasons (*see* HERMESIANISM).

Anton GÜNTHER (1783–1863) wished to correct the errors of both scholastic and contemporary philosophy. In doing so, he hoped to lay a new foundation for Christian revelation and to prove ultimately that God created the world and redeemed man through Christ. Günther's starting point was psychological CONSCIOUSNESS: an analysis of one's own ego enables him to know himself. Through knowledge of himself, man comes to know the reality and nature of other things. For example, being certain about the reality and contingency of his own being, man is compelled to assert the existence of God. Günther's procedure in this respect is reminiscent of that of DESCARTES, who deduced all from the principle *cogito ergo sum*. In the Trinity, Günther recognized three egos, or Persons, whose existence he accounted for by an explanation suggesting HEGEL'S thesis, antithesis, and synthesis. Moreover, contemplating and affirming Himself, God necessarily contemplated and affirmed that which was not God; thus, God created the universe by necessity. God did not create the world for His own glory, as the scholastics maintained, for such a purpose would be intolerable egoism; rather, He created the universe to procure the happiness of the intelligent creature. Creation resulted in a trinity of elements consisting of spirit, nature, and man. In man there is another trinity of elements, namely, body, psychic principle, and spirit. (One notes in Günther a harmonizing tendency; for example, to reduce all to the number three.) Man was created with grace; unfortunately, he sinned, but he was redeemed by Jesus Christ. For Günther, the mysteries of faith are SUPERNATURAL only because they were made known by Jesus. Now that these mysteries have been revealed, philosophy is capable of explaining the "why" and "how" of them. Günther maintained that only the languishing state of philosophy prevented this explanation. A number of Günther's more prominent disciples became OLD CATHOLICS; for example, J. B. Baltzer of Breslau, and F. P. Knoodt of Bonn. Knoodt was Günther's biographer. J. E. Veith remained in the Church.

Jakob FROHSCHAMMER (1821–93), professor at the University of Munich, was, like Hermes and Günther, a Catholic priest. Among his works are *Einleitung in die Philosophie* (1858) and *Über die Freiheit der Wissenschaft* (1861); he founded a periodical, *Athenäum,* to defend his views. After an examination, these works and others characterized as erroneous and opposed to Catholic doctrine were placed on the Index. While Hermes and Günther died as members of the Church, Frohschammer died unreconciled. In his letter *Gravissimas inter* (Denz 2850–61) to the archbishop of Munich (Dec. 11, 1862) Pius IX described the two chief errors of Frohschammer. First of all, Frohschammer ascribed to human reason capabilities that it does not possess. Thus he maintained that human reason could perceive and understand even those Christian dogmas that are the chief object of faith. Frohschammer taught, for example, that once God has revealed the mystery of the INCARNATION, human reason is able to arrive at a scientific knowledge of this mystery in virtue of its own principles and powers. Therefore, the chief dogmas of faith cease to be mysteries according to this erroneous conception. Commenting upon this error, Pius IX noted that reason is capable of demonstrating certain truths that faith also presents, such as the existence of God and His nature and attributes. However, the Pope wrote, there are certain Christian dogmas that remain obscure even after they have been revealed. Frohschammer's second chief error was that he granted to philosophy a freedom that amounted to license. He taught that a philosopher has an obligation in certain circumstances to submit to authority, but that philosophy itself has no obligation whatsoever to submit to any authority. Commenting upon this second error, Pius IX wrote that philosophy is legitimately free to use its own principles, methods, and conclusions, and even not to accept anything beyond its scope and not acquired on its own terms. On the other hand, in contradiction to Frohschammer's view, philosophy is not free to speak against divine revelation, to question a revealed truth that it does not understand, or to reject a decision of the Church about a philosophical conclusion connected with revelation.

See Also: FAITH AND REASON; METHODOLOGY (THEOLOGY); REVELATION, THEOLOGY OF.

Bibliography: G. FRITZ, *Dictionnaire de théologie catholique*, ed. A. VACANT et al., 15 v. (Paris 1903–50; Tables Générales 1951–) 14.2:1850–54. J. BERNARD, *Dictionnaire de théologie catholique*, ed. A. VACANT et al., 15 v. (Paris 1903–50; Tables Générales 1951–) 14.2:2567–79. A. THOUVENIN, *ibid.* 6.2:2288–2303. A. FORTESCUE, "Hermesianism," J. HASTINGS, ed., *Encyclopedia of Religion and Ethics*, 13 v. (Edinburgh 1908–27) 6:625–626. P. GODET, *Dictionnaire de théologie catholique*, ed. A. VACANT et al., 15 v. (Paris 1903–50; Tables Générales 1951–) 6.2:1992–93. H. THURSTON, "Guntherianism," J. HASTINGS, ed., *Encyclopedia of Religion and Ethics*, 13 v. (Edinburgh 1908–27) 6:455–456. A. W. ZIEGLER, *Dictionnaire de théologie catholique*, ed. A. VACANT et al., 15 v. (Paris 1903–50; Tables Générales 1951–), Tables générales 1:1753–54. "Semirationalismus," *Lexikon für Theologie und Kirche*, ed. J. HOFER and K. RAHNER, 10 v. (2d, new ed. Freiburg 1957–65) v.9.

[E. J. GRATSCH]

SENAN, ST.

Founder of a monastery on Scattery Island (Inis Cathaigh) in the Shannon estuary, Ireland, with a *paruchia* of island churches; b. near Kilrush, Co. Clare, Ireland; d. *ca.* 544(?). He is not mentioned in the Irish annals, but in his *Lives* he is made contemporary with peo-

ple who lived in the 4th, 5th, 6th, and 7th centuries. It seems, however, that his biographers had principally the 6th century in mind. He appears in the legends of SS. PATRICK and BRIGID, but only in the legends' more developed (later) forms. These place him at the beginning or end of the 6th century. The Life of Ciaran of Clonmacnois mentions him in the mid-6th century. However, neither this nor the mythological associations of his name and legend disprove his historicity. Irish genealogies distinguish several saints of this name.

Feast: March 8.

Bibliography: S. BARING-GOULD and J. FISHER, *The Lives of the British Saints*, 4 v. (London 1907–13) v.4. *Bethu Phátraic,* ed. with tr. K. MULCHRONE (Dublin 1939) 124, places S. 120 years after Patrick. *Vita anonyma* of Brigid (see *Bibliotheca hagiographica latina antiquae et mediae aetatis*, 2 v. (Brussels 1898–1901; suppl. 1911) 1:1455–56, 1460), makes him her contemporary. "Vita sancti Ciarani de Cluain," in C. PLUMMER, comp., *Vitae sanctorum Hiberniae*, 2 v. (Oxford 1910) 1:200–216, a contemporary of Ciaran. J. F. KENNEY, *The Sources for the Early History of Ireland:* v. 1, *Ecclesiastical* (New York 1929) 364–366. A. BUTLER, *The Lives of the Saints,* rev. ed. H. THURSTON and D. ATTWATER, 4 v. (New York 1956) 1:522–523. P. GROSJEAN, "Trois pièces sur S. Senán," *Analecta Bollandiana* 66 (Brussels 1948) 199–230; 47 (1929) 164–165; 79 (1961) 230–231, on supposed cult in Cornwall and Brittany. D. F. GLEESON and A. GWYNN, *A History of the Diocese of Killaloe*, v.1 (Dublin 1962) 15–23.

[C. MCGRATH]

SENECA, LUCIUS ANNAEUS

Stoic philosopher, who exercised considerable influence on Christian writers; b. Córdoba, Spain, 4 B.C., into a rich equestrian family; committed suicide near Rome, A.D. 65, at the command of Nero, who suspected him of conspiracy. St. Paul came into contact with Seneca's brother Gallio, governor of Achaea (Acts 18.12–17). Seneca's writings, both those in verse and those in prose, are of so high an ethical and religious standard that they have been deemed worthy of a Christian author.

Correspondence of Seneca and St. Paul. In the fourth century St. Jerome judged that he should place Seneca, "very much master of himself (*continentissimae vitae*), in the catalogue of the saints" by virtue of the letters "of Seneca to Paul and Paul to Seneca" (*Vir. ill.* 12; Aug. *Epist.* 153.14). In the Middle Ages PETER THE VENERABLE and Peter ABELARD were of the same mind (*Patrologia Latina* 189:737; *Patrologia Latina* 178:535–536, 1033–34, 1164). Many medieval MSS, 300 for the period 1200 to 1500 alone, contain the letters, eight by Seneca and six by Paul, often with Jerome's words. Later writers, especially in the 17th century (J. P. Camus, Georges d'Amiens, Guez de Balzac), doubted that the letters were authentic, although they granted that Seneca could have known St. Paul. In the 19th century the form of the letters was submitted to critical study, the content not being significant. The letters may actually go back to the fourth century, but today no one regards them as authentic or believes that Seneca was Christian. The kinship between Seneca's philosophy and Christianity is quite superficial and owes its explanation to the community of philosophical ideas.

Seneca in the Patristic Era. His influence was little. Tertullian, who calls him "our Seneca," cites him as an authority but twice (*Anim.* 20.1; *Apol.* 50.14) and attacks him elsewhere (*Anim.* 42.2; *Carn.* 1, 3). The only relationship between the two appears in their moral diatribes on marriage, and is due perhaps to the subject matter. Most of the parallels pointed out by H. Koch and F. X. Bürger between Seneca and the Christians CYPRIAN and MINUCIUS FELIX can be similarly accounted for. Seneca's dialogue *De providentia*, however, surely guided the pens of the two Christians at times—especially *Dial.* 1.3.10 and 4.5 on Cyprian's *Ad Donat.* 12, and *Mort.* 12; and *Dial.* 1.3.1 and 6.6, 4.12, 6 on Minucius 37.3 and 36.5, 8. Lactantius, who does not hesitate to refer to Seneca as "the most subtle of the Stoics" (*Inst.* 2.8.23) and who quotes him more than 15 times; only once with reserve, does not believe he was Christian but only that he deserved to be (6.24.14). Jerome, who would make him Christian, uses him freely but on one point only (*Adv. Iovin.* 1.41–49), where he quotes 18 fragments from a lost dialogue on marriage. The austerity pleased Jerome. Ambrose in his *De officiis* comes close to the Roman moralist Seneca but there is no definite contact. Augustine rarely borrows from Seneca (*Epist.* 153.14; *C. Faust.* 20.9; especially *Civ.* 5.8 and 6.10–11). MARTIN OF BRAGA, however, took whole passages from him. Three of his works are almost all from Seneca: *Formula vitae honestae*, part of a lost work of the Stoic; *De ira*, a résumé of Seneca's work of the same name; and *De paupertate*, assorted excerpts from Seneca. Canon 14 of the second Council of Tours in 567 even cites Martin's *Libellus de moribus* as Seneca's work.

Seneca in the Middle Ages. At a time when Stoicism was not in vogue his works could be found in many abbeys. The Premonstratensians may have been the source of this wide diffusion, but the Cistercians were Seneca's most fervent apostles. In the ninth century Sedulius Scotus, Paschasius Radbertus, and others made use of Seneca; in the tenth, EUGENIUS VULGARIUS annotated the tragedies; in the 11th, OTHLO OF SANKT EMMERAM, sought to model the form and the content of his own *Proverbia* after those attributed to Seneca (*Patrologia Latina* 146:299–300). In the 12th century Seneca gained more disciples: RUPERT OF DEUTZ

(*Patrologia Latina* 170:521); ALAN OF LILLE, who calls him *venerabilis* (*Patrologia Latina* 210:931); JOHN OF SALISBURY, who mentions him 28 times in the *Polycraticus* alone; Abelard; and others. WILLIAM OF SAINT-THIERRY in his *Epistola ad fratres de Monte Dei* (*Patrologia Latina* 184:307–354) owes more to Seneca than to any Church Father. GODFREY OF SAINT-VICTOR admired him and said that Seneca's words were worth almost as much as the Gospel [*Microcosmus* 1.58 (ed. Delhaye, 75); *Fons philosophie*, 103]. Seneca then was a basic source for the traditional moralists, who continued to be pragmatic in the face of the new moralists, more philosophical and inspired by Aristotle. And so he figured prominently in FLORILEGIA, such as those of Oxford, Brussels, Kilmacduagh, and the Gallican; and in ethical treatises, which had just about ceased to be original: WILLIAM OF MALMESBURY's *De dictis et factis memorabilibus philosophorum*, PETER CANTOR's *Verbum abbreviatum*, and especially the *Moralium dogma philosophorum*, very likely by WILLIAM OF CONCHES, who also made free use of Seneca's *Quaestiones naturales* in his *De philosophia mundi*. Seneca's popularity continued in the 13th century with VINCENT OF BEAUVAIS (*Speculum doctrinale*) and William Peraldus (*Summa de vitiis et virtutibus*). In the 15th century *The Imitation of Christ* (1.20.2) made use of Seneca's letter to Lucilius (7.3) (*see* IMITATION OF CHRIST).

Neostoicism. Seneca was the center of the Neostoicism of the Renaissance, a Western Latin phenomenon. In the 16th century countless editions, translations, and commentaries sprang up. Even religious writers used him: Petrus Crinitus (P. Ricci), Augustine Steucho, Josse Clichtove, Lawrence of Paris, and Martín Del Río who annotated the tragedies for Christian readers. LOUIS OF GRANADA, OP, used him in sermons and in the most spiritual of his writings—at least five times in the *Guia de pecadores* (1556) and much more in his *Introducción al simbolo de la fey* (1582). His *Collectanea moralis philosophiae* (1582) is a collection of excerpts from Seneca for preachers. Louis illustrates the strong mark that Seneca made on Spanish spirituality in the 16th and 17th centuries. Following the popularity of Justus LIPSIUS and Pierre CHARRON in the 17th century, Seneca was used by every religious author who made use of Stoicism: especially by Sebastian of Senlis (166 quotations in *Entretiens du sage*, 107 in *Maximes du sage*, and 143 in *Flambeau du juste*) and J. F. Senault (151 of 370 quotations in *De l'usage des passions* are from Seneca).

Conclusion. Sometimes people borrow from Seneca more for literary reasons than for philosophical. He has been a source of moral precepts and examples, and especially of psychological descriptions on a higher level—in particular for Yves of Paris, Sebastian of Senlis, Senault,

Julian Hayneufve, and Nicholas CAUSSIN. Some of his works have been used more than others, in this order: Letters to Lucilius, *De beneficiis, De providentia, Quaestiones naturales, De ira, De vita beata, Consolationes.* . . . The tragedies have been used much less, except by Castori. After the 17th century Seneca's popularity waned. The great Roman Stoic left the stage along with the great French moralists.

Bibliography: *Patrologia cursus completus, series latina*, suppl., ed. A. HAMMAN 1:673–678. A. MOMIGLIANO, ''Note sulla leggenda del cristianesimo di Seneca,'' *Rivista Storica Italiana* 62 (1950) 325–344. A. KURFESS, ''Zu dem apokryphen Briefwechsel zwischen dem Philosophen Seneca und dem Apostel Paulus,'' *Aevum* 26 (1952) 42–48. P. BENOIT, ''Sénèque et saint Paul,'' *Revue biblique* 53 (1946) 7–35. J. N. SEVENSTER, *Paul and Seneca* (Leiden 1961). J. M. DÉCHANET, ''Seneca Noster: Des lettres à Lucilius à la lettre auz frères du Mont-Dieu,'' *Mélanges Joseph de Ghellinck, S. J.,* 2 v. (Gembloux 1951) 2:753–766. M. J. GONZÁLEZ-HABA, ''Séneca en la espiritualidad española de los siglos XVI y XVII,'' *Revista de filosofía* 11 (1952) 287–302. K. D. NOTHDURFT, *Studien zum Einfluss Senecas auf die Philosophie und Theologie des 12. Jahrhunderts* (Leiden 1963).

[M. SPANNEUT]

SENEGAL, THE CATHOLIC CHURCH IN

Located in West Africa, the Republic of Senegal borders the North Atlantic Ocean on the west, Mauritania on the north and northeast, Mali on the east and Guinea and Guinea-Bissau on the south. The Republic of the Gambia forms an enclave extending into central Senegal from the Atlantic coast. The region's low plains rise to rolling hills in the southeast, and the tropical climate is characterized by a rainy season from May to November, balanced by a dry season during which hot harmattan winds are common. Natural resources include iron ore, phosphates and fish from the Atlantic; agricultural products consist of peanuts, millet, corn, sorghum rice cotton, vegetables and the raising of livestock.

An independent republic since 1960, Senegal was a French territory for 300 years. In 1895 the region was incorporated into French West Africa, and in 1958 became an autonomous republic within the French community. Joined to the Federation of Mali from 1959 to 1960, under the leadership of Léopold Sédar Senghor it gained independence on April 4, 1960, with Senghor as president. The ill-fated union with the Gambia as Senegambia lasted from 1982 to 1989; intermittent separatist violence from the southwestern Casamance region continued into 2000 following the dissolution of that union. Economic reform was instituted in 1994 with the help of international funds, although unemployment, increasing drug use, illegal drug trafficking and petty crime among the nation's youth remained problematic.

Capital: Dakar.
Size: 197,161 sq. miles.
Population: 9,987,495 in 2000.
Languages: French; Wolof, Pulaar, Joal, and Mandinka are spoken in various regions.
Religions: 299,650 Catholics (3%), 9,388,240 Muslims (94%), 99,880 Protestant (1%), 199,725 follow indigenous beliefs.
Archdiocese: Dakar, with suffragans Kaolack, Kolda, St-Louis du Sénégal, Tambacounda, Thiès, and Ziguinchor.

History. Encompassed by a succession of ancient empires, Senegal became predominately Muslim in the 11th century as a result of the Moorish influence upon the Tukulor tribe. Islam developed slowly until the 18th century, during which it spread more rapidly. Senegal's first contact with Christianity came soon after the Portuguese discovered the Cape Verde Islands *c.* 1460. Senegalese chief Bohemoi was baptized in Lisbon (*c.* 1486–90), helping to promote the faith. During the 16th and 17th centuries occasional apostolic visits to Senegal were made by Jesuits and Capuchins from Portugal or São Tomé and also by French naval chaplains, who acted as pastors at Saint-Louis and at Gorée.

In 1779 the Prefecture Apostolic of Saint-Louis was created, and Senegal was entrusted to the HOLY GHOST FATHERS. In 1819 there arrived the St. Joseph Sisters of Cluny, whose foundress Blessed Anna JAVOUHEY dwelt there (1822–24). Due to her care the first three Senegalese were prepared for their ordination in 1840. In 1845 the Society of the Holy Heart of Mary, founded by the Venerable François LIBERMANN, sent its first missionaries to Senegal. One of them, Monsignor Truffet, became vicar apostolic of the Two Guineas and resided at Dakar until his death a year later. Truffet's successor, Bishop Kobès, was the real organizer of the mission of Senegambia, which became a distinct vicariate in 1863. After the establishment of the hierarchy in 1955, the diocese of Ziguinchor and Saint-Louis were entrusted to the Holy Ghost Fathers and Kaolack to the SACRED HEART MISSIONARIES.

Into the 21st Century. Under the Senegalese constitution revised in 1991, freedom of religion was guaranteed, and despite its Muslim majority the country was proclaimed a secular state. The government provided financial aid for certain religious functions, and supported the 135 primary and 41 secondary schools run by the Catholic Church, which were considered among the best in the nation. Interfaith dialogue between the Church and Senegal's Islamic leaders in the late 20th century was greatly facilitated by the Church-sponsored Brottier Center in Dakar.

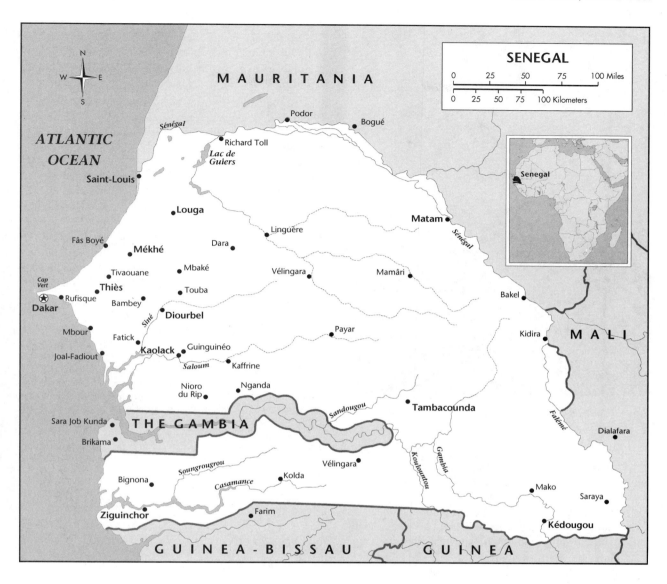

SENEGAL

By 2000 there were 86 parishes tended by 200 diocesan and 148 religious priests. Other religious included approximately 150 brothers and 660 sisters, whose efforts in the area of health care and education prompted the praise of Pope John Paul II during his 1992 trip to the region. The region, which suffered increasingly from the spread of the Sahara to its west, was aided by the private papal charity Cor Unum, which began to donate funds to combat the increasing famine in the region in 1996. In 2001 Church leaders expressed hope that the continuing violence sparked by a Casamance-based separatist group were at an end following a peace agreement and the election of a new legislative assembly. The Casamance movement was represented by Father Augustine Diamancoune Senghor, a relative of Senegal's former president. Previous cease fires in 1991, 1993 and 1995, had not been successful in ending the violence, which began in 1982 and resulted in the displacement of over 60,000 Senegalese.

Bibliography: *Le missioni cattoliche: Storia, geographia, statistica* (Rome 1950) 107–108. *Bilan du Monde. Encyclopédie catholique du monde chrétien*, 2 v. (2d ed. Tournai 1964) 2:783–788. *Annuario Pontificio* has information on all diocese. For additional bibliog., *see* AFRICA.

[J. BOUCHAUD/EDS.]

SENESTREY, IGNAZ VON

German archbishop, theologian; b. Bärnau, Upper Palatinate, July 13, 1818; d. Regensburg, Bavaria, Aug. 16, 1906. After studies at the German College in Rome, he was ordained (1842), became a lecturer on philosophy

Bishop Ignaz von Senestrey.

at Eichstätt (1843), a curate in Munich (1845), a pastor at Kühbach (1847), a cathedral canon at Eichstätt (1853), and bishop of Regensburg (1858). He proved a strong-willed and energetic bishop who showed special concern for liturgical renewal; he completed construction of his cathedral by 1869. He also established two minor seminaries, supervised carefully the spiritual training of his clergy, and sought to strengthen Catholic life in the diaspora of Upper Franconia. He vigorously defended papal temporal power. At VATICAN COUNCIL I he was a member of the commission on faith, and, along with MANNING, one of the most prominent members of the group striving for the definition of papal infallibility; he was one of the few German bishops who wanted this doctrine defined. In furtherance of his concepts of religious freedom and legitimate ecclesiastical spheres of influence he was sometimes unnecessarily sharp, and became involved in numerous controversies with the government, especially on educational matters and during the KULTURKAMPF in Bavaria. Pius IX termed him *"vir fortissimus,"* and Leo XIII granted him the archbishop's pallium (1892).

Bibliography: C. BUTLER, *The Vatican Council,* 2 v. (New York 1930). L. HAMMERMAYER, *Lexikon für Theologie und Kirche,* ed. J. HOFER and K. RAHNER, 10 v. (2d, new ed. Freiburg 1957–65) 9:665–666.

[V. CONZEMIUS]

SENFL, LUDWIG

Outstanding church composer of Renaissance Germany; b. Zürich, Switzerland, *c.* 1490; d. Munich, before or during 1556. He was Heinrich ISAAK's pupil and assistant at Augsburg, and he sang in the court chapel of Maximilian I. After Isaak died in 1517, Senfl succeeded him as chamber composer, remaining at Augsburg after Maximilian's death in 1519. From 1523 until the 1540s he was associated with the Bavarian court in Munich. While there his fame grew so rapidly that one writer referred to him as the prince of all German music, and in a letter to him on Oct. 4, 1530, Martin Luther praised him highly. When Isaak left his monumental work *Choralis Constantinus* unfinished at his death, Senfl completed the St. Ursula sequence, and then supervised the editing and copying of the entire collection. His own works include seven Masses, motets, Magnificats, and numerous lieder.

Bibliography: *Sämtliche Werke,* 7 v. (Wolfenbüttel, Ger. 1949–62). H. ISAAK, *Choralis Constantinus: Book III,* ed. L. CUYLER (Ann Arbor 1950) 15–23. G. REESE, *Music in the Renaissance* (rev. ed. New York 1959). A. GEERING, *Die Musik in Geschichte und Gegenwart,* ed. F. BLUME (Kassel-Basel 1949–) 12:498–516. M. BENTE, *Neue Wege der Quellenkritik und die Biographie Ludwig Senfls: Ein Beitrag zur Musikgeschichte des Reformationszeitalters* (Ph.D. diss. Tübingen, 1968); *The New Grove Dictionary of Music and Musicians,* ed. S. SADIE (New York 1980). J. C. GRIESHEIMER, *The Antiphon-, Responsory-, and Psalm-Motets of Ludwig Senfl* (Ph.D. diss. Indiana University, 1990). D. M. RANDEL, ed., *The Harvard Biographical Dictionary of Music* (Cambridge 1996). N. SLONIMSKY, ed., *Baker's Biographical Dictionary of Musicians* (New York 1992).

[L. J. WAGNER]

SENSATION

Sensation may be described as the most elementary cognitive reaction of an organism to its environment. The awareness of green, of warm, of sharp—when not accompanied by the awareness of something green, warm, or sharp—is a simple sensation; the awareness of a particular green leaf, on the other hand, is not a sensation but a PERCEPTION. Pure perceptions occur in animals, e.g., a dog perceives a cat. But in man every perception is integrated into a more complex totality, involving the CONCEPT and the JUDGMENT. When someone sees a cat and makes the statement: "That is a cat," he expresses a judgment containing an affirmation, a concept (cat), a perception (being here and now aware of this cat), and a certain number of sensations (e.g., gray, soft, purring). Much of what is traditionally said about sensation, it should be noted, does not strictly apply to simple sensation but rather to sense knowledge or to perception.

This article outlines a philosophical view of sensation, based mainly on the teaching of St. THOMAS AQUI-

NAS, and considered in the totality of cognitional EXPERIENCE.

The Thomistic teaching on sensation defies simple, brief presentation. When simplified it is easily misunderstood, and when presented in its totality, it is difficult and calls for considerable insight. It is best explained, therefore, by first giving a rough outline that can serve as an approximation, and then correcting this on points of specific detail.

Act of Sensation. Several stages may be distinguished in the act of sensation. In the physical stage, an outside stimulus (e.g., electromagnetic or sound waves) originating from some object impinges upon a sense organ. This is followed by a physiological stage, wherein a modification is produced by the stimulus in the sense organ. Since the organ is living and animated, its physiological modification is accompanied by another, or psychic modification, whose production constitutes the psychological stage. The result produced is called the impressed species or the impressed intentional form (*see* SPECIES, INTENTIONAL). It is a substitute for the outside object within the sense power, by means of which the object becomes known. Up to this point the sense power can be regarded as passive or receptive. But knowledge is an activity. Hence there is a last stage, the active psychological stage, in which the sense power turns, as it were, toward the object, grasps it, and knows it. Only when this occurs is there real KNOWLEDGE.

This elementary explanation of sense knowledge raises a number of questions that must now be considered.

Impressed Species and Object. Why do the senses know the object itself, and not simply its substitute, the impressed species? One answer is: because the species is a formal, not an objective, SIGN. Objective signs must be known first in themselves, before the thing they signify can be known; examples would be a photograph, a traffic light. Formal signs, on the other hand, are not known in themselves, but become the means whereby the signified object is known. An example of a formal sign is the retinal image, or picture of a perceived object on the retina of the eye; man never sees the image itself, but through it he sees the object.

In sensation, therefore, man knows the object itself, and not simply the impression made by the object. If he knew only the impression, he would forever be cut off from reality. He would not know that any impression was a faithful reproduction of the outside world, since, in that hypothesis, he could never be in contact with the outside world. He could not even be certain that there is a reality "outside" of himself. If man knew only impressions pro-

Ludwig Senfl. (Archive Photos)

duced on his senses, he would arrive at knowledge of reality only by inference, by reasoning that this impression must be the effect of some external cause and thus applying the principle of CAUSALITY. To claim that the sense powers reason to the existence of an outside world in this way, however, is quite implausible.

What man knows, therefore, is not simply impressions made upon him by things, but things themselves. The problem of the passage from an outside world to an inner world is thus a pseudoproblem. There is no real passage—these two worlds unite in man. Through his body, he is part of the outside world, a material object among other material objects and continually influenced by them. The human SOUL, man's inner world, animates his body. Together body and soul constitute not a union, but a unity, the animated body.

Cartesian Dualism. To admit a passage from outer to inner world is to fall into the DUALISM of René DESCARTES. Every time the body is affected, so is the soul, because what is affected is the animated or besouled body. Man's awareness of objects is neither merely subjective nor merely objective. He is aware neither of the impression alone, nor of the object alone; but of the object as it affects him, or of himself as affected by the object. External sensation may thus be described as the zone of consciousness that occurs at the common boundary of outside objects and animated corporeity.

The physicist and the psychologist are, of course, free to consider electromagnetic or sound waves as causes of sensation. But philosophers cannot be content with this type of explanation alone, lest it lead them into insuperable difficulties. To explain sensation by means of light or sound waves, themselves knowable to philosophers only through sensation, is to become involved in a vicious circle. Psychologists may be content to explain sensation by the stimulation of sense organs, nerves, and brain. Should philosophers do the same, they could fall into Cartesian dualism. For example, they might say that the stimulus coming from outside affects the organ, travels through the nerves, and is led into the brain center. But this explanation would tacitly assume that the soul is at the end of this circuit supposedly dwelling inside the body to listen, receive the message, and interpret it. Such a view is Cartesian. The organs, the nerves, and the brain center do not lead up to man, they *are* man. They are animated, besouled organs; as soon as they are affected, the human soul is affected.

These observations, inspired by Gabriel Marcel, explain why external sensation or perception does not require an image or substitute for the object. Thomists therefore deny the need of an expressed species in external sense knowledge; in their analysis, perception puts man directly in contact with reality, and not merely with some substitute for it.

Powers of Sensation. A distinction is usually made between external and internal sense faculties (*see* FACULTIES OF THE SOUL). External sense faculties, the five senses commonly referred to, put man directly in contact with the outside world. Through the intermediary of the external senses, the internal senses also attain reality. Thus IMAGINATION is the internal faculty that provides representations of singular, material objects, in the absence of such objects. Memory also furnishes such representations, but further recognizes objects as formerly perceived. The two remaining internal senses are the central sense and the estimative power.

The CENTRAL SENSE, or common sense, makes man aware of the objects and operations of the external senses. When a person sees a dog, he is aware of the dog and of seeing that dog. Such awareness is not an act of seeing, nor is it an intellectual operation. It stands between external sensation and thought, and is attributed to the central or common sense, which may be considered as the seat of sense CONSCIOUSNESS.

The ESTIMATIVE POWER corresponds roughly to the cognitive aspect of INSTINCT. Animals perceive not only colors and sounds, but also the usefulness or danger of things in their environment. Since this awareness cannot be attributed to reasoning, nor to the operation of the external senses, it is explained as the effect of a special internal sense. In animals this power is a lower analogate of prudence, through which animals know, with knowledge previous to any experience, that a particular thing is useful or harmful. In man the estimative power takes on new functions because of its connection with intelligence, and is called the COGITATIVE POWER. It serves as a transition between the intellect with its universal ideas and the senses with their individual perceptions, and is the point of contact between sense and intellectual knowledge.

Functioning of the Sense Powers. Although it is useful to distinguish between external and internal senses, these powers are not completely independent of each other. True, the internal senses may operate without the actual cooperation of the external senses; but the opposite is not true. Whenever the external senses act, the internal senses act with them. One would be unable to hear a sentence or a melody, unless, at the end of that sentence or that melody, he somehow remembered the first words or the first bars. When the eyes take in a landscape or a large painting, they scan what is present before them; one sees the painting only if, throughout the whole process of perception, he keeps remembering what was perceived before.

Expressed Species. Imagination and memory know objects that are not actually exerting influence from the outside. Physiologically this supposes the reactivating of the traces of a previous action of such objects upon the brain. On the conscious level, one speaks of images of these objects; Thomists identify such images as expressed species. The expressed species is that ''in which'' one knows, imagines, or remembers an object. It differs from the impressed species in three ways: (1) man is conscious of the expressed species, whereas he is not conscious of the impressed species; (2) the expressed species is that ''in which'' he knows the object, while the impressed species that ''by means of which'' he knows the object; and (3) the production of the former is the act of knowing, whereas the production of the latter precedes knowledge.

Validity of Sensation. It has already been shown that sensation is not purely subjective. Man does not know the impression objects make, but rather the objects themselves. On the other hand, sense knowledge is not as objective as intellectual knowledge; through sensation one does not know things as they are in themselves. This explains why color-blind people perceive some objects differently than those with normal vision. The state of the sense organ affects the sensations, and renders sense knowledge to some extent relative. Man knows objects as they affect him, as they appear to him. To use a Kantian terminology, the senses give a phenomenal, not a noumenal knowledge of reality (*see* NOUMENA; PHENOMENA). It should be remembered, in this connection, that man never experiences pure sense knowledge. Human sensations are always accompanied by concepts and judgments, which assure an objective knowledge of reality.

Organic Bases of Sensation. Sensation is rooted in the animated body. Whereas the body is only a necessary CONDITION of thinking, it is, together with the soul, a cause of sensation. This organic causality is exercised by specialized parts of the body, known as SENSES or sense organs. Traditionally five of these senses are mentioned: sight, hearing, smell, taste, and touch.

Modern psychology calls the fifth sense the somesthetic sense, and distinguishes within it four cutaneous and three intraorganic senses. The cutaneous senses are those of pressure, cold, warmth, and pain. They are considered distinct senses, because they consist of specialized nerve endings that, as a rule, react only to their specific stimuli. The senses of sight, hearing, smell, taste, pressure, cold, warmth, and pain are called exteroceptive senses. They give information about the exterior world.

The intraorganic senses inform man about his own body. These are divided into the proprioceptive and the interoceptive senses. Proprioceptive sensations are known also as kinesthetic sensations. Through them man is aware of the movements of his limbs in relation to each other (e.g., flexing the arm, stretching the leg), and of the resistance met by such movements. The organs of this sense are in the muscles and the tendons. The two interoceptive senses are the static and the visceral sense. The static sense, whose organ is located in the inner ear, tells man about the position of his body as a whole; it is the sense of balance and of equilibrium. Movement of the body as a whole, when nonuniform, may also be perceived by this sense. Visceral or organic sensations provide information about the state of the inner organs. Under this heading come such sensations as hunger, thirst, satiety, fatigue, and nausea. Such sensations gradually fade into feeling and drives. The general bodily feeling constituted by the totality of the visceral sensations is sometimes called coenesthesis. It is important for man's affective life, as an underlying basis of his moods, and seems to function also in his perception of TIME.

See Also: KNOWLEDGE, PROCESS OF; SENSE KNOWLEDGE; SENSIBLES.

Bibliography: THOMAS AQUINAS, *Summa theologiae* 1a, 78.3–4; 85.1. J. F. DONCEEL, *Philosophical Psychology* (2d ed. rev. and enl. New York 1961). G. P. KLUBERTANZ, *The Discursive Power* (St. Louis 1952); *Philosophy of Human Nature* (New York 1953). J. E. ROYCE, *Man and His Nature* (New York 1961). R. E. BRENNAN, *General Psychology* (rev. ed. New York 1952); *Thomistic Psychology* (New York 1941).

[J. F. DONCEEL]

SENSE KNOWLEDGE

The component of KNOWLEDGE that is directly traceable to the operation of the SENSES. Since man's intellectual and verbal abilities add new dimensions to his knowledge even at the level of SENSATION, ''pure'' sense knowledge is only a hypothetical entity. As commonly understood, sensing is the ability to respond to certain stimuli on an automatic or preconscious level; as such it makes knowledge possible, although in itself it ''knows'' nothing. Yet, granted the existential unity of man's sensory and intellectual activities, one can still make an epistemological study of the role of the senses in knowledge. This article outlines such a study, explaining the generation of sense knowledge, its validity, its relation to intellectual knowledge as conceived by St. THOMAS AQUINAS, and its evaluation by other philosophers.

Generation. Sensation is proper to the animated organism, i.e., to a psychosomatic unity. Highly specialized cells or receptors receive various kinds of stimuli and transform these into neural impulses. Each receptor is sensitive to a particular form of physical energy. Because of the relational character of sensation, the two facets of this phenomenon cannot be grasped as one—thus the tendency to reduce sensation either to a purely psychic activity or to a purely physical modification.

Thomists regard sensation as the operation of a psychical power or faculty through a corporeal organ (*see* FACULTIES OF THE SOUL). One aspect is the act of the form functioning as a formal cause and specifying the power; the other is the act of the sense that apprehends the sensible and formally constitutes sensation. The formal object of the sense is the aspect of the material object that is capable of becoming the intrinsic form of the power when activated. The sensible causality of the object precedes the intelligible causality in generation, although in the order of finality the intelligible principle is the source of sensory activity.

The extramental reality or object, in this explanation, must have characteristics that enable the particular receptor or sense organ to react toward it. In this very proportionality lies the possibility of some aspect of the object becoming the sense power's intrinsic form. In other words, only beings or objects that can have a causal relation to the cognitive sense powers are sensibly knowable.

When this condition is satisfied, the psychical capabilities of the sense powers can be actuated by material or physical phenomena. The INTELLECT then assimilates the essential nature (form) of its object, changing only the object's mode of existence.

Validity. A psychosomatic unity, man perceives as an epistemological unit; his bodily senses serve this unit as a bridge between his mind and the external world. They must be considered a trustworthy source of knowledge because they testify to the existence of man's own body and of other bodies. The evidence they themselves provide is confirmed by an intellectual analysis of the facts of sense PERCEPTION.

The intellect in judging may be in error in its interpretation of the phenomena that stimulate sensation, but sensation as such cannot be false. To test the validity of a sense reaction, a normal state of organism must be assumed as a standard. When such a standard is established, errors are traceable to defective senses, to improper media, or to some disproportion existing between the sense and the object. The most frequent source of error, however, lies not in the sense but in the intellect's precipitancy in judging.

The actual impinging of the object on the senses is the objective grounding of all human knowledge. Only in experience can intellectual knowledge be resolved, and since the external senses are ultimate among the cognitive powers, either man contacts reality through them or he never contacts it at all. Sensation is the only intuitive knowing accessible to him. Experience everywhere confirms it and abstract knowledge demands it. The intellect would be powerless to infer the existence and attributes of beings without the data of sense.

Relation to Intellect. Phenomena act upon the human senses and alter them during the process. A formal, sensible likeness is produced; in the Aristotelian-Thomistic tradition this is termed the impressed species (*see* SPECIES, INTENTIONAL). The sense power becomes its object intentionally on the level of sensation. The act of external sensation in turn initiates the act of internal sensation or perception, which integrates, synthesizes, stores, and evaluates external sense impressions. Perception itself terminates in a highly refined sensorial image called the PHANTASM.

St. Thomas recognized in human intelligence a dual power, the ability to abstract, which characterizes the agent intellect, and the ability to understand, which characterizes the possible intellect. The datum of sense is presented to the agent intellect by way of the phantasm. The agent intellect illuminates the phantasm, abstracts from its individuating characteristics, and discerns the

nature underlying these. This product of the agent intellect is termed the impressed intelligible species. By virtue of its immaterial action upon the possible intellect the latter is enabled to generate the CONCEPT or IDEA.

The intelligible species or disengaged form is the vehicle whereby the intellect is actualized to know the object or phenomenon, "becoming" that object in an intentional way. The species is the prolongation of the phenomenon's action upon the knowing power. It bears within itself a relation to the phenomenon as existing and at the same time represents the formal nature of the object that acts. When impressed with the species, the intellect is informed by a formal and existential prolongation of the objective phenomenon. Since the intelligible species lacks individuated matter, the intellect grasps the existence of the thing whose species activates it only by reflecting back upon the phantasm that represents the object concretely. The intellect knows the form, but in order to know that it has existence in an object, it must restore the form to the thing, must recapture its individuality, and in and through this, its existence. The phenomenon itself causes this reflexive process. In producing the species and thus causing its "re-presence" within the intellect, its being-before-a-knower, it moves the intellect to operate. The act in which the intellect knows the phenomenon is the act of JUDGMENT, which is the culmination of human knowledge.

Various Theories. J. LOCKE considered secondary qualities (color, sound, taste, smell, and tactile qualities) as occurring only in the experience of the sentient organism and as having no objective reality in the sensible object. He derived all simple ideas from external experience and held that ideas are transfigured sensations. In making ideas the immediate object of human knowledge, Locke, followed by G. BERKELEY and D. HUME, rendered it logically impossible to know whether or not these conform to reality. Hume, an empiricist, held that the mind knows only its own subjective sense impressions and that beyond these nothing is knowable. All perceptions, for him, fall into the two categories of impressions and ideas, which are distinguishable only by their force or vivacity.

The sensists, in the tradition of DEMOCRITUS and LUCRETIUS, explained all cognitional states in terms of a mechanical, passive transformation of external sensations. Thought they reduced to the level of sense perception and regarded quantified matter as adequately explaining the phenomenon of knowing. This theory recurred in the thought of T. Hobbes, E. B. de CONDILLAC, Hume, Alexander Bain, James MILL, T. REID, and H. SPENCER.

The rebirth of empirical philosophy in the 20th century was due mainly to the work of G. E. Moore and B.

RUSSELL. The new realism of Moore and Russell views human ideas, both of common sense and of the sciences, as logical or linguistic constructions of sense data. In the early stages of LOGICAL POSITIVISM it was assumed that the data of the senses were the only possible objects of direct observation; a proposition must either be given a meaning in terms of sense data or be discarded as meaningless. From a Cartesian starting point, Moore found himself in the dilemma of attempting to resolve how a self aware only of sense data could transcend these data. By holding that the objects of self are simply the specific sense qualities, Moore denied himself the material to work out a conclusive theory of perception. His appeal to sense phenomena inevitably led him back to the position of Hume.

Critique. The limitation of experience to singular sense experiences, however, results in the inability to provide an adequate foundation for universal ideas or for scientific knowledge. Mere phenomenal similarity or the imaginative association of ideas is not adequate to uphold necessity or universality. On the other hand, to limit human experience to sensibly verifiable phenomena is to fail to be sufficiently empirical, for a thoroughgoing empiricism demands that all factors of human experience be acknowledged and explained.

Although there is intimate involvement between intellectual acts and sense representations, moderate or critical realists recognize a real distinction between sense images and intellectual concepts. The latter represent natures or essences of things abstracted from sensible qualities, e.g., ''life,'' ''truth,'' ''humanity,'' and ''existence.'' Even the concepts of sensible qualities are abstract and universal, e.g., ''color'' and ''redness.'' This abstract and universal character of concepts is never experienced in any sensation or image, for these always represent existing and concrete phenomena.

See Also: CERTITUDE; EPISTEMOLOGY; KNOWLEDGE, PROCESS OF; KNOWLEDGE, THEORIES OF; PHENOMENALISM; SENSIBLES; SENSISM.

Bibliography: M. J. ADLER, ed., *The Great Ideas: A Syntopicon of Great Books of the Western World*, 2 v. (Chicago 1952); v. 2, 3 of *Great Books of the Western World* 2:706–729. L. M. RÉGIS, *Epistemology*, tr. I. C. BYRNE (New York 1959). G. VAN RIET, *Problèmes d'épistémologie* (Louvain 1960). F. A. GELDARD, *The Human Senses* (New York 1953). W. SELLARS, *Science, Perception and Reality* (London 1963). D. W. HAMLYN, *Sensation and Perception* (New York 1961). D. M. ARMSTRONG, *Perception and the Physical World* (New York 1961). K. T. GALLAGHER, ''Recent Anglo-American Views on Perception,'' *International Philosophical Quarterly*, 4 (1964) 122–141.

[M. M. BACH]

Humorous illustration of ''The Five Senses.'' (©Historical Picture Archive/CORBIS)

SENSES

The senses are the immediate principles of sensation. They have an organic structure that is scientifically observable and are energized by an operative power or faculty of the soul, a fundamental source of vital energy. Organic structure and vital energy or power are intrinsically linked to make a unique reality, namely, sense.

The existence of the external senses is obvious; ordinary experience recognizes most of them, and scientific observation confirms and completes its findings. As will be seen, the existence and nature of the internal senses is problematic. The organic structure of the external senses must be sought in the peripheral and central nervous systems. Sensory receptors that are anatomically and functionally discernible and are specifically affected by different typical stimuli are generally distinguished. The peripheral organ's stimulation unleashes in the connector nerve fibers afferent influxes that rise to the brain along complex routes, intersected by synaptic relays. In the brain these influxes terminate in different zones. It is in these zones that attempts are made to pinpoint specific centers for each sensation. The internal senses, without peripheral organs, are all found in the brain or at its base.

External Senses

Five senses are traditionally noted: sight, hearing, smell, taste, and touch. Aristotle considered these sufficient for knowing all sensible qualities, although he recognized that touch is a complex sense (*Anim.* 424b 22–425a 13). St. THOMAS AQUINAS followed Aristotle's lead seeking to make the distinction of the senses more precise: he classified them according as (1) the modification needed for sensation is made (*a*) by direct contact with the sensible (touch and taste), or (*b*) through an intermediary, and then (i) with an alteration of the sensible (smell), or (ii) by local movement (hearing), or finally (2) without any modification either of the sensible or of the organ—sight—a position that is no longer tenable (*In 3 de anim.* 1.583).

Principle of Classification. Even if the experimental criteria of the ancients and the scholastics were scientifically imperfect, the functional principle they used to classify the senses was and is valid. Since the senses are passive powers, they are distinguished from each other in terms of the external SENSIBLES that are capable of affecting them. This principle is still applied in experimental psychology, but with greater precision owing to developments in physics, physiology, neurology, etc., all of which give better understanding of the stimulus-object and the receptor-subject.

A stimulus is defined as an energy pattern that arouses a sensory receptor. Sensory receptors, reacting to specifically distinct stimuli, constitute as many different senses. Beginning with this fundamental distinction made with respect to stimuli, a difference can be noted among receptors by considering the proper organs, the nerves linking these organs to the brain, and the zones of the brain where the nerves terminate. In this way sight and hearing are very clearly distinguished. Smell and taste are similarly dissociated, despite the close chemical interdependence between them. The criteria for distinction applied to touch can be physiological (e.g., epicritic and protopathic sensibility), functional (e.g., kinesthesis), qualitative (e.g., heat and cold), or perceptual (e.g., hunger and nausea). These criteria serve as cross-checks upon each other. For all practical purposes, distinctions can be made among (1) tactile or cutaneous sensitivity that selectively perceives pressure, pain, warmth, and cold; (2) deep organic sensitivity, namely, kinesthesis or proprioception for muscular sensation, and deep touch for the viscera and internal organs; and (3) vestibular function, localized in the semicircular canals, for the positioning and movement of the body in equilibrium, a function that works in harmony with kinesthesis and deep touch.

Seat of External Senses. Common experience has always recognized organs adapted to the various senses.

It was also known that somewhere in the organism there must be a central reference point or some kind of principle for external sensation, but this was long unidentified. While attributing some role to the brain in sensation, Aristotle, followed almost unanimously by his commentators, made the heart the main organ or *sensorium* for all the external senses (*Somn. vig.* 454a 4–6; *Sensu* 439a 1). Advances in the biological and physiological sciences have shown the importance of the nervous system in their structure and functioning.

Problems concerning the seat of the external senses may refer to their peripheral organ, or to the ascending nerve fibers, or finally, to the brain. Although enough is known about the superior senses as regards the structure of the peripheral organ, many questions arise concerning touch. Histological and electro-physiological techniques are used in attempts to localize the sensitive points of the skin, to study the different subcutaneous nerve endings, and to determine their respective roles in the reception of tactile impressions, such as pain and temperature. The question of the transmission of sensation through nerve fibers has been dominated, for more than a century, by the theory of specificity of nervous energy of Johann Müller, elaborated to include in the same explanation often disconcerting phenomena (e.g., the production of different sensory impressions while the same stimulus, electricity for example, is applied to various receptors). According to Müller, specificity could reside in the nerve itself; its central portion would conduct this type of influx, thus transmitting this type of stimulus. It could also be localized in the region of the brain where the various sensory nerves terminate. The discovery of an almost constant identity of neural excitation in the various nerves at first led to the belief that it was at the level of the cerebral endings that specificity of sensations had to be sought. But if it has been possible to localize with sufficient precision the subcortical structures serving as relays to sensory impressions, as well as their cortical projections, it has also been recognized that the brain too exercises a universal influence. What counts is not so much the cortical centers as such, but rather their functional integration in a total pattern of reaction within the nervous system. There is reason to distinguish structurally between a peripheral organ and a central organ of the external sense, but functionally each must be considered as inseparably bound in the production of sensation.

Objects of the External Senses. Noting that the senses know only when they are moved by external things, Aristotle preceded his study of the objects of the various external senses by reflections of a general nature on the object of all senses considered together (*Anim.* 416b 33–418a 25). The external senses' object is called a sensible because it can modify the sense. It appears as a complex ensemble that acts upon the senses in many ways. There are, first of all, qualities capable of specifically stimulating this or that sense, to which they belong as their own immediate sensibles (*sensibilia per se propria*). These qualities, however, exist as properties of quantified material realities; thus they are located in space and time, and are subject to movement. They therefore affect also the senses in a way that is related to these quantitative aspects. Because these can act simultaneously upon many senses and are common to all of them, they are designated as common sensibles (*sensibilia per se communia*). Finally, these quantitatively conditioned qualities manifest the natures of material realities, as well as their functional value for the knowing subject. Perception of these natures and of these values is made possible by the activity of the senses, but immediately surpasses simple sensation and requires other principles of knowing (e.g., the COGITATIVE POWER and the INTELLECT), whose proper operation it constitutes. Considered from this angle, such realities can be seen as mediate proper sensibles (*sensibilia per accidens*).

Internal Senses

Apart from the external senses, whose knowing activity does not explain all the riches of sensible experience, the existence of other principles of knowledge must also be recognized. These are the internal senses, so called because they contact external reality only through the intermediary of the external senses.

Principle of Classification. To identify these principles of knowledge, whose nature and distinction are not revealed with the same evidence as is available for the external senses, one must investigate functions of sense knowledge that are irreducible to the external senses. These functions must be grouped around specific objects; whatever functions cannot be referred to the same object must then require distinct principles of operation. Such is the methodological principle given by St. Thomas, who thus arrives at the following four internal senses (*Summa theologiae* 1a, 78.4).

Central Sense. The CENTRAL SENSE (*sensus communis*) is necessary for consciousness of sensation, which is impossible for the external senses because their organic structure prohibits reflection on themselves. It is also needed to explain comparisons between sensations of the various senses, comparisons that no sense can make since it does not know the objects of the other senses.

Imagination. The IMAGINATION registers the impressions unified by the central sense to reproduce these subsequently, sometimes with fanciful elaborations. According to St. Thomas, the organic structure of the central sense does not permit it to retain its own impres-

sions. Moreover, functioning in synergy with the external senses, the central sense knows reality only when this actually affects the senses, whereas the imagination brings back the image of these realities known in their absence.

Cogitative Power. Through data arriving from the external senses, the central sense, and the imagination, the cogitative power (*vis cogitativa*) detects values whose perception escapes these inferior powers (*intentiones insensatae*). These include the functional meaning of reality for the subject and the existence of this reality as concrete, individual, and reducible to a general category (*individuum existens sub natura communi*).

Memory. The memory stores up these experiences and recalls them later, under the stimulus of analogous experiences, to situate them in a type of temporal continuity that is measured by the projection of perception toward the past. This assures the continuity of experiences lived by the subject and is indispensable for organizing his personality.

Seat of Internal Senses. Since the internal senses are organic cognitive powers, they occupy a definite, experimentally identifiable place in the nervous system. Faced with the complexity of the problems of cerebral localization, one must be indulgent here with the scholastics, whose imperfect knowledge of anatomy and physiology led them to very conjectural formulations. In modern times there is agreement in recognizing that complex psychic functions are isolated with difficulty and that their unfolding involves activities of the entire brain.

According to M. B. Arnold, the central sense must be sought in the sensory cortex needed for various sensations (visual, auditory, etc.) as well as in the connector areas and the associative fibers. The preservation of images probably takes place by the cortex's registering impressions that come from the various external senses. Contrary to what St. Thomas believed on this matter, Arnold wonders if it is not physiologically necessary to link the preservation of these images to the central sense and assign their reproduction specifically to the imagination. Be this as it may, the activity of the imagination seems to require the concurrence of the associative cortical areas as well as of numerous subcortical structures: hippocampus, amygdaloid nuclei, fornix, and sensory hypothalamic and thalamic nuclei. All these regions seem to be selectively reactivated according to demands for the simple recall of images or for the formation of fanciful images. The cogitative power would use certain nerve endings linked to the medial thalamus and to the limbic cortical areas, together with specific activation of the mammillary bodies and the hippocampus. Memory would set in motion the associative cortex, the limbic areas, the hippocampus, and the fornix up to the anterior thalamic nuclei. W. Pensfield has shown how the ganglia at the base of the brain cooperate in registering lived experience.

Modern Problems. Are the internal senses distinct cognitive powers or simply various functions of one and the same knowing power? While Aristotle considered imagination and memory simply as activities of the central sense (*Anim.* 429a 1–2; *Memor.* 450a 11–12), his commentators came to attribute functions of superior sensible knowledge that were irreducible to one operative principle to as many distinct powers. The progress of the science of man, especially of experimental psychology and neurophysiology, should eventually produce an answer to this question. The matter of identifying the organ for these functions is of prime importance, although contemporary scholastic philosophers have shown little interest in the problem. Yet various investigations begun by Arnold and J. A. Gasson, W. W. Meissner, M. Ubeda Purkiss, and others promise fruitful results. In general they seem to confirm the intuitions of the scholastics who, centuries ago, laid a foundation for classifying the superior psychic functions of sensibility with their theory of the internal senses.

See Also: SENSATION; SENSE KNOWLEDGE

Bibliography: E. G. BORING, *Sensation and Perception in the History of Experimental Psychology* (New York 1942). R. S. WOODWORTH and H. SCHLOSBERG, *Experimental Psychology* (rev. ed. New York 1954). H. A. WOLFSON, ''The Internal Senses in Latin, Arabic, and Hebrew Philosophic Texts,'' *Harvard Theological Review* 28 (1935) 69–133. A. SUÁREZ, ''Los sentidos internos en los Textos y en la sistemática tomista,'' *Salmanticensis* 6 (1959) 401–475. M. B. ARNOLD, ''The Internal Senses: Functions or Powers?'' *Thomist* 26 (1963) 15–34. J. A. GASSON, ''The Internal Senses: Functions or Powers?'' *ibid.* 1–14. W. W. MEISSNER, ''Neurological Aspects of the Sense Powers of Man,'' *ibid.* 35–66. M. UBEDA PURKISS and F. SORIA, ''Introduccion,'' 577–626, in THOMAS AQUINAS, *Tratado de las pasiónes* (*Summa theologiae* 1a2ae, 23–48), (Biblioteca de autores cristianos 126; Madrid 1954). W. PENFIELD, ''The Permanent Record of the Stream of Consciousness,'' *Acta Psychologica* 11 (1955) 47–69.

[A. M. PERREAULT]

SENSIBLES

Those features or aspects of reality that can be perceived by the SENSES; in scholastic terminology, the proper objects of the various senses. Aristotle and the scholastics distinguish between the ''proper'' and the ''common'' sensibles, whereas most modern thinkers since the time of J. LOCKE regard the sensibles as ''primary'' and ''secondary'' qualities. Sense qualities that can be perceived by a single external sense, such as color, sound, taste, smell and tactile sensations, are the proper sensibles or secondary qualities, while qualities that are perceived by more than one sense, such as extended surface, shape, volume, number, rest and motion, are the common sensibles or primary qualities.

Perception. The common sensibles are not apprehended in the abstract by any joint action of the senses. The individual, concrete data from which the INTELLECT abstracts such thought objects as magnitude or three-dimensional extension are complex data gleaned from more than one external sense. These composite sense data do not contain any sense element beyond the proper sensibles contributed by the separate senses in cooperation. Thus the perception of a common sensible involves the conscious coordination of the proper objects of vision and of tactile, muscular and motor sensations. Yet common sensibles are real objects of sense awareness, *sensibilia per se,* unified by the integrating internal sense faculty known as the CENTRAL SENSE, the *sensus communis* of the Aristotelian-Thomistic tradition. Both the common and the proper sensibles, being direct data of sense perception, are percepts, not concepts. While the senses reveal the concrete complex of perceived qualities, the intellect apprehends the knowable object as a real substance having a specific nature or essence as determined by the perceived qualities.

The sensory and intellectual activities involved in perceptual and conceptual processes cannot be isolated as though sense perception in the human adult were prior to and independent of intellection in any simple and unqualified sense. The mind as a principle of intelligence possesses the tendency to form sensory data into some kind of perceptual whole or pattern, to render the extramental environment intelligible. The distinction between primary and secondary qualities should therefore not be pushed to excess, as though any sensible quality can be perceived independently of all relations to the senses. However, to attain a philosophical analysis of these relations, one must strive for some knowledge of the absolute terms that are related.

Objectivity. Thinkers in the Aristotelian-Thomistic tradition consider both primary and secondary qualities to have objective existence in extramental reality. GALILEO, Locke and many modern critical realists, on the other hand, hold that primary qualities have objective existence but that secondary qualities do not.

To the realist, the resistance one directly encounters from external objects is something proper to the objects themselves. Granted that vibrations of an atmospheric medium may be quite unlike the sensations of sight and hearing, it is nonetheless by the senses that the vibrations are discovered. The senses do not judge, they merely report the presence of certain sense impressions. Reason judges whether anything objective in nature corresponds to the sensations and perceptions. Sense knowledge is thus not intended as an objective report on the constitution of material reality. Its function is to offer an awareness of reality, a stimulus to intellection.

Phenomena or appearances presuppose that which appears. Thus they constitute the object of the external senses as a reality, a being, regardless of what kind; if they did not, one would be forced to conclude that perception terminates in absolutely nothing. One can know the sense object as a reality, a being, whether its *esse* is its *percipi* or not, whether it is internal or external, whether the one perceiving has caused it or not.

The material object of every sense is a being; by every sense man knows being, even though not precisely as being. By sight he knows a being as colored, by hearing as sounding. What man sees is a colored being. Thus the object of the external senses has absolute epistemological value for the intellect under the aspect of being.

All forms of PHENOMENALISM deny that the object has any epistemological value whatever. Objective or immediate realism attributes absolute value to the object, because of itself the object satisfies man's desire to know the real-as-it-is. Critical or mediate realism holds that the object has only relative epistemological value as a means by which one may know the real-as-it-is, though of itself it cannot satisfy this appetite.

Critical Realism. Is the object that appears red to the human knower "really" red? If by red is meant the quality exactly as it is perceived, critical realists would answer in the negative. If by "red" is meant that quality really in an object whose very nature it is to be seen as red by a human being in the condition of conscious awareness, the answer would be in the affirmative. The red that is sensed does not exist apart from the human knower exactly as he senses it. Independently of his perception, however, it exists materially—inseparably combined with the light energy of which it is only a distinguishable aspect. Thus it is not true that red exists only in the knower, with no objective quality of redness in the lighted object. In the very atomic-molecular structure of the object is the quality of objective color, such that, when illuminated and perceived by a sensing subject, the object can be said to be colored.

Several basic objective aspects are revealed in all incidents of general perceptual response. For example, such a response presupposes an interaction of the end organ and its immediate environment that involves an exchange of energy. The specific reaction occurring in the end organ is not initiated by any and every energy influence in the environment, but only by those within a rather well defined range of energies. Each of the different possible energies falling within this range can be said to possess the common property of being able to interact with the sensory organ in question. These factors, it would seem, are sufficient to ground the objectivity of external sensation.

According to critical realists, the sensation "red" is the same as the red appropriate to material things but in a derivative sense. The sensation "red" is analogous to what the physicist calls objective red. Although red exists in the human perceiver in a different way from that in which it is found in a red flower, there is a real resemblance—the experience red has an objective foundation. There is an analogous relationship between the flower's redness and the redness in the human perceiver. Reality is thus neither a univocal cause nor an equivocal cause; it is an analogous cause of human sensation. Objective color, sound, tactile, olfactory and gustatory qualities are translated into perceptual experiences so that intellect, the human power of generalizing thought, may possess knowledge of the nature of reality. Sensation is objective in that it attains, contacts and presents objectively existing reality; its "presentation," in turn, serves as an analogous cause of intellectual knowledge.

Only in EXPERIENCE can man's intellectual knowledge be resolved. The external senses are ultimate among his cognitive powers, and as such, are his only source of experiential knowledge; either he contacts real beings through them or he can never contact them at all. This resolution to things themselves is the unique source of CERTITUDE in the human order of knowing.

Quality. St. THOMAS AQUINAS ascribes to the physical cause of sensation a formal and qualitative aspect rather than a quantitative one; he does this on the basis of his metaphysics, not on the basis of an outmoded science. Only FORM or QUALITY is act, and only act causes. Consequently, all the physical realities capable of stimulating human cognitive powers are referred to as sensible qualities. QUANTITY conditions this causality but does not constitute it. Aquinas considers the common sensibles to be reducible to quantity, but he holds that the proper sensibles first affect the senses since they are the qualities that cause alteration. Since physical qualities exist only in quantified bodies, quantity conditions the efficacy of the qualities through such modifications as those of dimensions, space, motion and rest. Existing reality is always the cause of knowledge, but its causality is exerted through such quantitative modifications, and these in turn reveal the inner nature of reality in its dynamic and formal aspect.

The physical union of the human knower with the physical object through the instrumentality of quantified qualities is therefore the initial step in sense knowledge. Subject and object here become in some way identified and this even before the immanent act of sensing takes place.

See Also: SENSATION; SENSE KNOWLEDGE; KNOWLEDGE; PERCEPTION.

Bibliography: L. M. RÉGIS, *Epistemology,* tr. I. C. BYRNE (New York 1959). R. F. O'NEILL, *Theories of Knowledge* (Englewood Cliffs, N.J. 1960). D. M. ARMSTRONG, *Perception and the Physical World* (New York 1961). D. W. HAMLYN, *Sensation and Perception* (New York 1961). W. F. SELLARS, *Science, Perception and Reality* (London 1963). W. VON BUDDENBROCK, *The Senses,* tr. F. GAYNOR (Ann Arbor 1958). F. A. GELDARD, *The Human Senses* (New York 1953).

[M. M. BACH]

SENSISM

A theory of knowledge holding that whatever is intelligible is also sensible. Sensists make sense perception the primary function of the cognitive process, and regard memory, imagination, and reasoning as activities of the same faculty that receives external sense perceptions. They tend to regard man as differing from other sentient beings only in degree. Representative thinkers in this tradition include DEMOCRITUS, LUCRETIUS, T. HOBBES, J. LOCKE, D. HUME, A. COMTE, A. Bain, James MILL, T. REID, and H. SPENCER. Many contemporary schools of psychology also teach an implicit sensism. Examples would be the structuralist school, which equates ideas with images; the behaviorist, which identifies thought with tacit vocalization; the Gestalt, which views all intellectual acts as self-regulating cortical patterns; and the Freudian, which considers all human activities as emerging from instinct. G. E. Moore, B. RUSSELL, and logical positivists also implicitly hold a sensist theory of knowledge.

Most realists, taking into account the full spectrum of phenomena given to human experience, acknowledge that knowing involves an immaterial principle. They affirm a functional relationship between SENSATION and REASONING, but maintain also that a distinct faculty is necessary for the ABSTRACTION of UNIVERSALS from particulars. Thus they make a real distinction between the image of sense and the universal CONCEPT or IDEA. An abstract and universal character is not found in sensations or images, for these always represent particular concrete objects. The eye does not see color as such, abstracted; it sees this particular colored object existentially present. The common image of Locke and J. F. Herbart is an insufficient explanation of the universal idea, for conscious experience affirms that the image remains in some way

concrete, possessing sense qualities. If the imagination represents an angle, it is a certain kind of angle, obtuse, right, or acute, whereas the concept of angle prescinds from every size and kind.

If man is regarded as a psychosomatic unity, his sense knowledge is merely a primary source of KNOWLEDGE. Moreover, his INTELLECT has a dynamic orientation to possess intelligible being, which is realized in its intentional possession of the forms of material realities.

See Also: PHENOMENALISM; SENSE KNOWLEDGE; KNOWLEDGE, THEORIES OF.

Bibliography: M. J. ADLER, ed., *The Great Ideas: A Syntopicon of Great Books of the Western World,* 2 v. (Chicago 1952); v. 2, 3 of *Great Books of the Western World* 2:706–729. R. F. O'NEILL, *Theories of Knowledge* (Englewood Cliffs, NJ 1960. P. COFFEY, *Epistemology,* 2 v. (New York 1917; repr. Gloucester, MA 1958). F. VAN STEENBERGHEN, *Epistemology,* tr. M. J. FLYNN (New York 1949). R. E. BRENNAN, *Thomistic Psychology* (New York 1956).

[M. M. BACH]

SENSUS FIDELIUM

Two theological terms have come to express the understanding that all believers participate in elaborating Christian truth: *sensus fidei* and *sensus fidelium.* The first refers to the Christian's possession of the fundamental truth of his faith. The second refers to his role in actively defending and elaborating that faith. Though the Second Vatican Council employed both terms (*sensus fidelium*: GS 52; *sensus fidei*: LG 12, 35; PO 9; see also John Paul II, *Christifideles laici* 14 and *Ut unum sint* 80) writers since the council have generally preferred the more active-subjective term, that is, *sensus fidelium.*

Historical Considerations. Historically, the common teaching in the Church saw an active role of all the faithful in determining Christian belief. The whole community attested to the apostolicity of the faith. Though the bishops increasingly taught with authority and defined the emerging orthodox synthesis at synods and general councils, the concrete life of the community was always considered and the faithful were routinely consulted. Chapters 6 and 15 of the Acts of the Apostles give us a glimpse of the inclusiveness of the whole community's participation. In the first five centuries, the characterization of a local church as "apostolic" pointed to its whole life: its Scriptures, sacraments and liturgy, authorized leaders, moral norms, ecclesiastical discipline and polity, interaction with pagan culture, socialization of its members, and its explicit beliefs. The belief of the faithful proved decisive in determining the canon of Scripture, the full and unquestioned divinity of Christ, Mary's virginity and her title of Mother of God, baptismal theory and practice, the necessity of grace, the veneration of the saints, etc. The faithful played no minor role in helping to decide doctrines as well as matters of *praxis*.

Though the influence of the faithful was somewhat diminished in the Latin Church after the fall of the Roman empire in the West, it continued to exercise an active role in the Church's life. However, the struggle to eradicate the practice of lay investiture, the reforms of Gregory VII, and a general tendency toward viewing social reality in more juridical categories and to impose more institutional forms on the life in the Church resulted in a depreciation of the gifts and contributions of the laity. Martin Luther's reassertion of the teaching of the priesthood of all the faithful led to the restriction of its use in the Latin Church, because that teaching was understood as a dimension of his attack on the rightful use of authority by the hierarchy. A few influential theologians, such as Melchior Cano (1509–60) and C. R. Billuart (1685–1757), made room for the contributions of the faithful. Gradually, the language of the certitude of propositions of belief, or a propositional view of revelation, replaced the earlier view of the whole Church's witnessing to God's revelation as always active and present. The ancient *communio* ecclesiology that had supported the earlier view was superseded by the ascendant juridical categories of the second millennium. It was only a matter of time till a theologian like J. B. Franzelin (1816–86) would distinguish between the faithful as constituting a passive *ecclesia discens* from the hierarchy as the active *ecclesia docens*.

Vatican II. The council's focus on what the Church itself was and how it related to the larger world necessarily involved a deeper appreciation of all believers in the Church. The laity in particular needed to be reminded of their inherent dignity and of their contribution to the building up of God's kingdom. The council spoke of all the faithful participating in the offices of Christ as prophet, priest, and king. Baptism into Christ means that each believer can claim to exercise these offices. The council also spoke of the Holy Spirit imparting the gift of faith and bestowing charisms on each Christian. A positive, active, and dynamic understanding of the believer emerged. The teaching of the *sensus fidelium* in particular helped clarify the prophetic duty of the believer to proclaim the word of God. The laity were challenged to deepen their understanding of the faith by prayer, study, discussion, and committed action. The ambit of their intellectual penetration is not restricted solely to secular matters, though there obviously the laity have an especial contribution to make and in such matters they speak with particular authority. On matters of faith and morals, too,

they are called to fulfil their prophetic task in communion with their leaders.

Postconciliar Reflection. Shortly after the council a number of theologians began to argue for retiring the distinction of two categories of members in the Church, the "teaching Church" and the "learning Church." Others related the council's reflections to the broader questions of the nature of revelation and the response of faith. More recently a number of commentators have paid special attention to the nature of truth and the hermeneutics of faith-statements. The postmodern questioning of the whole category of truth and the growing influence of the "hermeneutics of suspicion" and its attendant ideology critique have become a focus of reflection on the *sensus fidelium*. Recent studies point to the problems surrounding human knowledge and the search for truth, the phenomenon of the ever-increasing pluralism of positions, and the growing sense of the person's lostness in a decentered world. They find in the conciliar and immediately postconciliar discussions a certain naiveté that could prove impotent in the face of the increasingly urgent questions of late modernity.

In practical terms, the postconciliar period saw calls for reducing the degree of centralization in the Church and for greater participation by all in the teaching activity of the Church. Likewise, claims were made that some officials in the Church were impeding efforts to fully acquaint the faithful with their ecclesial responsibilities. Some commentators pointed out, for instance, that the Code of Canon Law of 1983 failed to give juridical expression to the Council's teaching on the participation of the laity also in the teaching activity of the Church and in decision making. There is a growing realization that at some point the *sensus fidelium* must lead to some form of *consensus fidelium*. The proper means of communicating effectively in the Church, e.g., greater use of synods, demand implementation for consensus to emerge. "Consensus" is now emerging as a major focal point of the discussion.

The scope of the *sensus fidelium* includes the whole range of ecclesial questions: morality, sacraments, the social doctrine of the Church, Church practice and polity, the Church-world relationship, etc. Yet the term has no commonly agreed meaning among theologians. Some point to such categories as a sure instinct for the supernatural or knowing by connaturality (M. Löhrer and W. M. Thompson), a *conspiratio* of faithful, theologians, and the magisterium in understanding Christian truth (J. M. R. Tillard), a precognitive and comprehensive "grasp" (*Vorgriff*) of reality (K. Rahner), an interior predisposition for and an internal adhering to the whole of revelation (M. Seybold), a true criterion of the faith and one of the indispensable "synchronic" communities of revealed truth (W. Beinert), a genuine *locus theologicus* (M. Löhrer and W. Beinert), a "being attuned to" Christian revelation especially in the ordinary experiences of lived faith (H. Wagner), an expression of the *communio* of all believers that comes to expression in Christian witness to the Apostolic faith in preaching, education, theological scholarship, formation of individuals and communities, etc. (J. M. R. Tillard), and an underlying structured synthesis of lived reality understood in the light of the Gospel (Z. Alszeghy).

Bibliography: Z. ALSZEGHY, "The *Sensus Fidei* and the Development of Dogma," *Vatican II: Assessment and Perspectives Twenty-Five Years after (1962–1987),* 3 v., ed. R. LATOURELLE (New York 1988) 1:138–56. J. J. BURKHARD, "*Sensus fidei*: Meaning, Role and Future of a Teaching of Vatican II," *Louvain Studies* 17 (1992) 18–34; "*Sensus fidei*: Theological Reflection since Vatican II," *Heythrop Journal* 34 (1993) 41–59, 123–34. G. KOCH, ed., *Mitsprache im Glauben? Vom Glaubenssinn der Gläubigen* (Würzburg 1993). M. LÖHRER, *Mysterium Salutis: Grundriss heilsgeschichtlicher Dogmatik,* 5 v., ed. J. FEINER and M. LÖHRER (Einsiedeln 1965) 1:545–55. J. B. METZ and E. SCHILLEBEECKX, eds., *The Teaching Authority of Believers,* Concilium 180 (Edinburgh 1985). M. SEYBOLD, "Kirchliches Lehramt und allgemeiner Glaubenssinn. Ein Reformatorisches Anliegen aus der Sicht des I. und II. Vatikanischen Konzils," *Theologie und Glaube* 65 (1975) 266–77. W. M. THOMPSON, "*Sensus Fidelium* and Infallibility," *American Ecclesiastical Review* 167 (1973) 450–86. J. M. R. TILLARD, "*Sensus Fidelium,*" *One in Christ* 11 (1975) 9–40; "Authorité et mémoire dans l'Église," *Irénikon* 61 (1988) 336–46, 481–84. H. WAGNER, "Glaubensinn, Glaubenszustimmung und Glaubenskonsens," *Theologie und Glaube* 69 (1979) 263–71. S. WIEDENHOFER, "Sensus fidelium—Demokratiesierung der Kirche?," in J. ERNST and S. LEIMGRUBER, eds., *Surrexit dominus vere. Die Gegenwart des Auferstandenen in seiner Kirche.* FS J. J. DEGENHARDT (Paderborn 1995) 457–71. D. WIEDERKEHR, ed., *Der Glaubenssinn des Gottesvolkes – Konkurrent oder Partner des Lehramts?* QD 151 (Freiburg 1994).

[J. J. BURKHARD]

SENTENCES AND SUMMAE

Since theology is based essentially on authority, being affirmations of Scripture or tradition examined by reason, it was natural that its earliest elaboration should take the form of collections of Sentences borrowed from the Fathers and early Christian writers. As theological thought progressed, it was marked by a growing use of reason and by a more orderly presentation of material.

Sentences. The collections referred to were called *Sententiae* or *Summa sententiarum.* The term "Sentences" indicates either citations and excerpts from works by the Fathers (such as the ancient FLORILEGIA, *Flores patrum, excerpta,* and *catenae*), or simply their doctrinal positions. The latter meaning was generally preferred. The Sentences thus became something more than

a series of selections from one book or one author. For example, the teaching of AUGUSTINE appeared in the work of PROSPER OF AQUITAINE, that of GREGORY I, in Paterius, and many florilegia of the 8th and 10th centuries. The materials were methodically chosen and carefully ordered.

Doctrinal Sentences in canonical, historical, or ascetical anthologies, as well as Sentences of grammar or logic, centered around one or more points of dogma or morals, and soon even around the totality of doctrine. Each author, choosing the order he preferred, built his synthesis around an idea that seemed fruitful or valid. Thus these collections were diversified and more or less complete and coherent.

The doctrinal type of Sentences appearing at the beginning of the 12th century developed rapidly, especially at the time of ANSELM OF LAON. His Biblical commentaries, enriched with many *quaestiones,* gave rise to collections named after the place of origin of their manuscripts, such as the *Sententiae Attrebatenses, Berolinenses,* and *Varsavienses;* or by their first words, such as the *Summa Principium et causa, Deus de cujus principio,* and *Prima rerum origo;* or simply the *Sententiae divinae paginae.*

Gradually the genre developed method and originality. ABELARD's *Introductio ad theologiam* (1125), and *Sic et non* show selection of patristic texts expressing pros and cons on the principal questions of theology. PETER LOMBARD although proceeding somewhat in the same manner, took an independent stand. To the school of Abelard belong the Sentences of Master OMNIBONUS, the *Sententiae Florianenses,* and the *Sententiae Parisienses.* About 1139 HUGH OF SAINT-VICTOR published his *De sacramentis christianae fidei.* There followed the *Summa sententiarum,* and the *Sententiae divinitatis,* both of unknown authorship; the Sentences of ROBERT OF MELUN (1152–60); and of Gandolph of Bologna. Roland Bandinelli (*see* ALEXANDER III, POPE) wrote his Sentences *c.* 1149; ALAN OF LILLE, his *Summa Quoniam homines c.* 1160. Peter Lombard had published his *Libri IV sententiarum c.* 1155 to 1157. About 1167 to 1170 PETER OF POITIERS produced his *Sententiarum libri quinque;* SIMON OF TOURNAI's work appeared *c.* 1170, as did PETER COMESTOR's *Sententiae de sacramentis.* These are the important but by no means the only collections.

The Sentences vary in plan, presentation of problems, and method. Thus the six treatises that make up the *Sententiae divinitatis* examine in succession: the creation of the world; the creation of man with free will; original sin; the Incarnation; the Sacraments; and finally, God and the Trinity. Robert of Melun, on the other hand, first treats of what he calls the "sacraments" of the Old Law

(God, the angels, and man), then of the ''sacraments'' of the New Testament (the Incarnation, the Sacraments, the virtues, and eschatology). The plan of Alan of Lille provides for three books on the Creator, creation, and re-creation. Peter Lombard discusses God in His unity and Trinity; Creation, including man and original sin; the Incarnation; and lastly the Sacraments.

Commentaries on the Sentences. Of all these, the *Sentences* of Peter Lombard won official acceptance despite the violent opposition they occasionally encountered, e.g., from WALTER OF SAINT-VICTOR in his *Contra quatuor labyrinthos Franciane* (1178). The explicit approbation given in 1215 to the Master's doctrine by the Fourth LATERAN COUNCIL confirmed the position he had already attained. His *Sentences* became the textbook for students and candidates for the degree of master of theology, on a par with the works of Priscian, Aristotle, Justinian, Gratian, Galen, and Hippocrates, in the faculties of the arts, law, and medicine.

It was as an auditor that the student came into contact with various theological problems. Then by ''lecture'' (reading) and his coherent commentary on these problems, the bachelor was introduced to theological teaching. Starting with the literal reading, which he explained, and following the identical order of distinctions and articles adopted by the Master of the Sentences, he took whatever position he pleased on all the problems raised. He was free to sift, complement, and develop as he chose. Moreover, it was on positions thus taken, on their value and on the arguments advanced by him, that he would be judged. On the basis of this his licentiate would be granted or refused.

Thus the commentary on the *Sentences* required the student to examine the totality of theological problems, providing a framework within which teaching must necessarily be given. However, it gave each one an opportunity to prove his capacity for original thinking by delving more deeply into the questions, presenting new aspects or new problems, and advancing new arguments, some of which might express his disagreement with an outworn solution. Thus, from their first contacts with theology, the future bachelors began to prepare themselves for the commentary that would be required of them. It was therefore not a work of improvisation, but the product of mature reflection. Besides, no one could become a bachelor of the Sentences until he was 29 years old, or a master before he was 35.

The commentaries on the *Sentences* preserved in manuscripts are the literary product of the bachelors' studies. They were, therefore, the works of beginners that in some cases were later revised and published by the author after he had become a master. Stegmüller, who has prepared the most complete catalogue of these commentaries, lists 1,407 titles. And these are only a fraction of the total production. Many have undoubtedly been lost; many more consisted merely of *reportata* or notes taken in class by students but not revised into final form by the author. Finally, many were never put down in writing.

The study of the commentaries is of great value for what they reveal about an author and his doctrinal positions. Moreover, the variety of questions he had to answer, the arguments he presented, and the authorities on which he relied, quickly reveal the author's intellectual quality and his doctrinal filiation. Finally, because of the many terms of comparison the documents provide and because they can usually be dated with accuracy, these commentaries are valuable for a study of the progress and evolution of theology. It is possible to follow the trends within various schools, the rise and development of polemics, changes in problematic emphasis, and the furtherance or decline of certain doctrines.

Summae. The bachelor commenting on the *Sentences* enjoyed real latitude with regard to the positions he adopted, the choice of questions he would treat, and the importance he would give them. However, certain more original minds were hardly satisfied with merely doing a work so highly dependent upon a text. Lombard's plan hampered them. They conceived both presentation and interrelationships differently and adopted other systems dependent upon other theories. Such was the origin of the theological *Summae* properly so called. They were distinguished by their freedom from dependence on Lombard's text, and by an individual approach to the whole field of theology. They were works of masters, written especially in the 13th century; in the century that followed, the genre quickly disappeared.

The *Summa* was not bound by any strict rules. Some of them encompassed the whole of theology; others were incomplete. ROBERT OF COURÇON, for example, dealt particularly with morals; Guy de l'Aumône, with the law and the Commandments; Guy of Orchelles, with the Sacraments. Certain *Summae* had previously provided subjects of oral instruction as *Quaestiones disputatae*. Such was undoubtedly the case with the works of ALEXANDER OF HALES, PETER JOHN OLIVI, and HENRY OF GHENT. Other *Summae* included several treatises published separately, such as WILLIAM OF AUVERGNE's *Magisterium divinale;* ALBERT THE GREAT's *Summa de creaturis,* containing five *Summae: De quatuor coaevis, De homine, De bono et virtutibus, De sacramentis, De Incarnatione et resurrectione.* However, Albert the Great's *Summa theologiae,* written toward the end of his life, was an independent work, complete in itself. The same is true of most of the other *Summae,* of which the best known by far is the

Summa theologiae of THOMAS AQUINAS. This *Summa* was to become in its turn a textbook, on a par with the *Sentences* of Peter Lombard.

Each of the *Summae* should be studied individually. Some have not yet been edited, e.g., the *Speculum universale* of Ralph Ardent (*c.* 1179); the *Summae* of Martin of Fougàres, Robert of Courçon, Prepositinus of Cremona (1190–94), Godfrey of Poitiers (1210–15), Ardengus, and Hubert of Auxerre (*c.* 1230–34), the last depending upon the *Summa aurea* of WILLIAM OF AUXERRE (1215–20); the *Sententiae* of ROLAND OF CREMONA; PHILIP THE CHANCELLOR's *Summa de bono* (1230–36), whose importance cannot be exaggerated; the *Summae* of Guy de l'Aumône, of an anonymous author of Basel (B.IX.18) *c.* 1240 to 1250; Ulrich of Strasbourg's *Summa de bono;* and those of Gerard of Bologna, NICHOLAS OF STRASSBURG, and of the author of MS Vat. lat. 4305.

The study of the *Summae,* even more than that of the commentaries on the *Sentences,* offers rich insight into the character and originality of an author, who has allowed himself greater freedom of thought and expression than would have been possible in commenting on a specific text. The *Summae* reveal the underlying tendencies of their authors, the influences exerted on them, their reactions, and their progress. They also unfold the history of doctrine. For these reasons they may be considered one of the most precious legacies we possess.

Bibliography: P. GLORIEUX, *Dictionnaire de théologie catholique,* ed. A. VACANT et al., 15 v. (Paris 1903–50) 14.2:1860–84, 2341–64. F. STEGMÜLLER, *Repertorium commentariorum in Sententias Petri Lombardi,* 2 v. (Würzburg 1947). J. DE GHELLINCKM, *Le Mouvement théologique du XII e siècle* (2d ed. Bruges 1948). O. LOTTIN, *Problèmes d'histoire littéraire: L'École d'Anselme de Laon et de Guillaume de Champeaux,* v. 5 of *Psychologie et morale aux XII e et XIIIe siècles,* 6 v. in 8 (Louvain 1942–60).

[P. GLORIEUX]

SEPT-FONS (-FONDS), ABBEY OF

CISTERCIAN abbey, Bourbonnais, France, in the former Diocese of Autun (present-day Moulins diocese). It was founded in 1132 under the name of Notre-Dame de Saint-Lieu Sept-Fons as a daughter-abbey of Fontenay, of the filiation of CLAIRVAUX. After the troubles and disasters of a century of war, Abbot Jean de Ramilly (1487–1512) reestablished the regular monastic life there; Abbot Eustache de Beaufort (1663–1700) reformed the monastery and revived the ancient customs; and Abbot Dorothée Jalloutz (1757–78) rebuilt the buildings. In 1759, the priory of Val-des-Choux, in the Diocese of Langres, was united to Sept-Fons. After the

French Revolution, the abbey church was demolished except for the 18th-century façade. In 1845 the abbey was restored by TRAPPISTS from the Abbey of Le Gard under the direction of Abbot Stanislas Lapierre. Today the abbey has four daughter abbeys.

Bibliography: L. JANAUSCHEK, *Origines Cistercienses,* v.1 (Vienna 1877). L. H. COTTINEAU, *Répertoire topobibliographique des abbayes et prieurés,* 2 v. (Mâcon 1935–39) 2:3010–11. F. LAMY and E. BEAUMONT, *Histoire de N. -D. de Saint-Lieu Sept-Fons,* 2 v. (Moulins 1937–38).

[M. A. DIMIER]

SEPTUAGINT

The accepted name for the earliest translation of the Old Testament into Greek. Based on Latin *septuaginta,* 70, it reflects the legend given in the Letter of ARISTEAS according to which the Greek translation of the Hebrew Pentateuch was the work of 70 (or rather, 72) translators sent from Jerusalem to Alexandria during the reign of Ptolemy II Philadelphus, from 285 to 246 B.C.. The time and place thus given for the compilation of the Greek Pentateuch are in keeping with what is otherwise known of Hellenistic Judaism (*see* DIASPORA, JEWISH) and its literature, and can be taken as fact. The extension of the name Septuagint or "Seventy," abbreviated LXX, to the Greek Old Testament as a whole became established usage among Christian writers by the fourth century; and the name is applied today to the printed text of the Old Testament in Greek and to its manuscript witnesses, even for those books either composed in Greek, or based on a Semitic original now wholly or partly lost, and excluding only the identifiable work of revisers and translators subsequent to the first Christian century, such as Aquila, Symmachus, and (though the case is confused) Theodotion. Together with the original Greek books of the New Testament, the Septuagint is still the official Bible of both the Greek Orthodox Church and the Byzantine Catholic Churches.

Formative period. The assembling of this corpus of Old Testament texts was the work of fully 400 years, from the early third century B.C. to the early second Christian century (Ecclesiastes). The prologue to Sirach (Ecclesiasticus), written about 116 B.C. by its Greek translator, grandson of the author, admits of the inference that the Jews of Alexandria had, by that date, translations of the Mosaic law and of substantial portions of the historical books and the writing Prophets, as well as at least some of the "other books," that is, the wisdom literature and the Psalms. An occasional note, such as the vague one attached to the end of the Greek Esther, points in the same direction (see 2 Mc 1.9). Also, internal evidence of the type of Hebrew text actually translated, of the time of origin in Greek of the deuterocanonical books and of the *Letter of Aristeas,* and of the use in Wisdom and 1 Maccabees especially of existing LXX materials helps to establish that by the end of the second century B.C. the repertory of Old Testament materials in Greek was nearing completion in substantially the form in which it is now known.

Question of Unity of the LXX. In the period 1941 to 1960, vigorous controversy was waged, especially in England, on the subject of LXX origins. P. E. Kahle was the protagonist for a theory that denied that the materials transmitted as the one ''Septuagint'' for most Old Testament books actually represent one single, pre-Christian, accepted Jewish rendering. He proposed instead that the earliest Greek renderings were oral and fluid, like the Palestinian targums, and that in the midst of a number of fluctuating partial translations no standardized Greek Old Testament came into being until the early fourth Christian century, when the Greek biblical text became fixed by the authoritative decision of the hierarchy of the Christian Church. This position is historically untenable; but it was based on real difficulties in the actual texts and early citations (in Philo, the New Testament, Josephus, Justin, etc.). The difficulties could not be resolved as long as it was presumed that the first serious critical work on the LXX text dated from the days of ORIGEN (d. A.D. 254) and his Hexapla. The opposite standpoint to that of Kahle, maintained by P. Katz in England and H. Orlinsky in America, harked back to the 100-year-old enterprise of P. A. de Lagarde, directed toward identifying in the extant manuscripts recognizable families that can be used as avenues of approach to the single underlying rendering posited for pre-Christian times. This view governed the comprehensive editorial projects (see below) centered in Cambridge and in Göttingen. The latter, in the Prophets especially, through the efforts of Monsignor Joseph Ziegler, yielded very satisfactory results during the same period in which the theoretical discussions were taking place.

New Evidence of Continuity. Evidence in the form of actual text fragments in Greek of pre-Christian and first-Christian-century date has been accumulating in recent years both from Egyptian sources and as a result of the DEAD SEA SCROLLS discoveries at Khirbet Qumran and in the Wadi Khabra in Palestine. From Egypt have come two fragmentary manuscripts of Deuteronomy: P. Rylands Gr. 458 of the mid-second century B.C., and P. Fuad inv. 266 of a slightly later date. From Qumran are an Exodus fragment (7Q1), bits of Leviticus on leather (4QLXX Lev[a]) and on papyrus (4QLXX Lev[b]), of Numbers on parchment (4 QLXX Num), and of the ''Letter of Jeremia'' on papyrus (7Q2); the oldest of these is 4Q

LXX Lev[a], about 100 B.C., the youngest 4Q LXX Num, about the turn of the era. From the Wadi Khabra comes a fragmentary scroll of the Minor Prophets of the first Christian century, which has been studied by D. Barthélemy, OP. None of these gives any warrant for the hypothesis of a lack of continuity between the pre-Christian Jewish texts and the medieval manuscripts; quite the contrary. Later witnesses, but illustrating the character of the text before Origen, are the papyrus codices and fragments of many Old Testament books from the second and third Christian centuries (see below). Between these and the witness of the early Coptic and Old Latin secondary versions, the evidence for a continuity of transmission of one same written LXX text for most of the books of the Old Testament is overwhelming.

Expansions, recensions, and supplements. To the unity of the LXX certain qualifications are necessary, however, and these are of major importance. Added to the collection were not only certain books that had been composed wholly in Greek (Wisdom, 2 Maccabees), but also others that were translated from Semitic texts now no longer extant, in whole or in part (Tobit, Judith, Sirach, Baruch, 1 Maccabees). Still other LXX texts show a recension of a Semitic book differing from that in the Masoretic Text and including some purely Greek additions (Daniel, Esther). For some books the LXX offers an expanded text in all manuscripts (Proverbs) or in some (Sirach) that are based on copious reworkings and double renderings with an eye to the original. Finally there are books that show in the LXX manuscripts two strikingly different recensions (Judges) or even three (Tobit); in which an existing Alexandrian rendering is generally ignored (Daniel, 3 Esdras) in favor of a later, more labored but less erratic translation; or in which a primitively short LXX text, whether bad (Job) or good (Jeremiah), has been filled out at a different time in a different style by another hand.

Proto-Theodotion. Barthélemy's study of the Wadi Khabra fragments of the Minor Prophets has disclosed that they represent a recension made in the first Christian century of the earlier LXX on the basis of a Hebrew text; that it is this same recension that supplied the seventh column, or *quinta editio,* of Origen's Hexapla for these books; that it also accounts for approximations to the Hebrew text in the Sahidic Coptic and in the Freer codex in Greek; that it is the recension that Justin Martyr quoted in the mid-second century; that it is identical in technique with the valid evidence at hand for the so-called Theodotion; and that it forms the actual substratum for the work of Aquila. Extending his study to other putative work of Theodotion, he is able to establish that the recension in question is Palestinian in origin and that its witnesses include the supplements to Job and Jeremiah in the LXX, the "Septuagint" renderings of Lamentations and (probably) Ruth, the so-called Theodotion text of Daniel, the *quinta* form of the Psalms, and the text of 2 Sm 11.2 to 3 Kgs 2.11 [2 Sm 11.2 to 1 Kgs 2.11] in the LXX column of the Hexapla. The same recension again stands as "Septuagint" for Origen in 3 Kgs [1 Kgs] 22.1 to 22.54 with all of 4 Kgs [2 Kgs]. As a corollary to all this, Barthélemy reaffirms what has long been suspected, that the "Septuagint" of Ecclesiastes is in fact the work of Aquila.

Other Recensional Activities. In the perspectives thus opened up, it becomes possible to find other evidences of early recensional activity in the LXX. Since the secondary recension of Sir 12.1 is quoted in the Didache 1.6, the expanded form of Sirach in codex 248 and the Old Latin dates back to at least the first Christian century. Since the variant form of Prv 2.21 is quoted in Clement of Rome (*1 Clem.* 14.4), the reworking of the first nine chapters of the LXX of that book may be dated in the same first century at the latest. In Ezekiel, Ziegler has shown that pap. 967 (the Beatty-Scheide manuscript) displays a pre-Origen, first-century recensional treatment of the text. The reworked and harmonizing character of Deuteronomy and Isaia in the Greek tradition reflects, not only tendencies of that sort in Greek translators or revisers in pre-Christian times, but, in Isaia at least, a harmonizing, expansionist technique in the Hebrew text from which the Greek was prepared.

Proto-Lucian. For the Pentateuch and Samuel, a further step has been made possible to F. M. Cross by the evidence of Hebrew manuscripts from Qumran cave 4. The recension of the LXX associated with the name of St. LUCIAN OF ANTIOCH (d. 312) has long presented problems equally thorny to those in the "Theodotion" material, typified most strikingly by the fact that Josephus Flavius at the end of the first Christian century employed a characteristically "Lucianic" text. For Exodus through Deuteronomy, it has been possible to establish that a "proto-Lucianic" form of the LXX was the type of text circulating from pre-Christian times in Palestine and Syria and cited by the Fathers of the "School of Antioch"; it was this text and a similar text in Samuel and Kings that were available to Josephus. The manuscript 4Q LXX Num is of this type, though it seems already to have "Theodotionic" features also. A "Lucianic" text is identified by Barthélemy as having been displaced from the LXX column of the Hexapla for 1 Kgs 11.2 to 3 Kgs 2.11 [1 Sm 11.2 to 1 Kgs 2.11] and for 3 Kgs [1 Kgs] ch 22 plus 4 Kgs [2 Kgs] by a later, "Theodotionic" reworking (see above); the displaced text found room in the adjoining sixth column of the Hexapla, where it appears related to the "Lucianic" material of the minuscule manuscripts b, o, c^2, e^2. On the basis of three Hebrew

manuscripts of Samuel, that is, 4Q Sam^{a,b,c}, Cross is able to affirm that this "proto-Lucianic" text is not the primitive LXX subject to incidental corruption, but it is part of a deliberate recension carried out in the second or first century B.C. to bring the Greek rendering from Egypt into better harmony with the Hebrew manuscripts then current in Palestine. He applies the same interpretation to the Pentateuch evidence, where he sees again a deliberate harmonizing of the older LXX text from Egypt with the evolved Palestinian Hebrew manuscripts of the second or first century B.C. For the portions of Samuel and Kings in which the "Theodotionic" recension has made inroads into the main stream of LXX transmission, the proto-Lucianic stage is the first one available because, according to Cross, a primitive LXX from Egypt is not extant in these sections.

From this it can be seen that the forthcoming period of LXX criticism will be aided by a chronology, both relative and absolute, for the known text types, one that will clear up many existing anomalies in their evaluation. This will be accompanied by a fuller appreciation of the nature and extent of the recensions described above; and it will be backed up by a generous sampling of Hebrew texts of pre-Christian date and varied text types from Qumran, which will illustrate the prototypes available for consultation at different stages of the evolution of the LXX. The realization that Aquila (*c.* A.D. 130) builds on "Theodotion," and that "Theodotion" builds on "Lucian," which in turn revises the primitive LXX, and that Symmachus late in the second century and Origen before 245 stand rather toward the end than toward the beginning of an intensive reworking of the LXX text lays the foundation for a much more effective use of the successive Greek recensions to penetrate to the underlying Hebrew originals in the period before the definitive fixing of the Hebrew consonantal text *c.* A.D. 100.

Manuscripts of the LXX. Apart from the eight fragmentary witnesses described above (fragments of early scrolls), the manuscripts of the LXX are almost all in codex (book) form: either on papyrus, or on vellum in uncial (rounded capital) script, or on vellum or paper in a cursive minuscule hand.

Papyri of the LXX. These provide our oldest extensive texts. In the Chester Beatty collection, now in London, there are portions of Numbers, Deuteronomy, and Jeremiah of the second Christian century; of similar date are fragments of the Psalms in London and Oxford. In the same group of manuscripts from the Egyptian Fayyûm, purchased in part by C. Beatty and in part by J. H. Scheide, there are third-century texts of portions of varying size of Genesis, Isaiah, Ezekiel, Daniel, and Esther. Of a third-century manuscript of the Minor Prophets, 33 leaves are in the Freer collection in Washington, and further fragments of third-century date representing Genesis, Psalms, Proverbs, Wisdom, and Sirach are in Oxford, Geneva, and London. With the fourth century, papyrus witnesses begin to multiply; some 200 may be counted through the seventh century.

Uncial Codices. The great uncial codices on vellum of the fourth to the tenth century were, until the 1900s, not only the most careful and the most complete, but also the oldest available witnesses to the LXX. They are usually pandects, or complete Bibles, including also the New Testament. The most significant for the LXX are the following.

The *Codex Vaticanus* (known as B), Vat. Gr. 1209, of the mid-fourth century, lacking only Gn 1.1 to 46.8 at the beginning, some verses of 2 Samuel ch. 2, and about 30 Psalms; 1 and 2 Maccabees were never contained in it. For a number of Old Testament books this codex is in a class by itself as the best single witness to the earliest form of the LXX text.

The *Codex Sinaiticus* (S or *Aleph*), also of the fourth century, is presently in the British Museum, except for 43 leaves in Leipzig and some sizable lacunae. Careless though it is in its orthography, it is witness to a very early text tradition often related to that of B. In Tobit it is the unique Greek witness to the longer and more nearly original form of the text. With 1 Maccabees is joined 4 Maccabees; 2 and 3 Maccabees were never in the manuscript.

The *Codex Alexandrinus* (A), also in the British Museum, fifth century, with slight Old Testament lacunae in Genesis and 1 Samuel, and again missing about 30 Psalms. It is often at variance with B, strikingly so in Judges; in general, it shows proto-Lucianic and also hexaplaric tendencies. It includes 3 and 4 Maccabees in addition to the canonical books.

The *Codex Marchalianus* (Q), Vat. Gr. 2125, sixth century, containing Prophets only. It is notable for the copious citations of Aquila, Symmachus, and Theodotion in its margins.

Minuscule Codices. Of cursive manuscripts between the ninth century and the spread of printing in the sixteenth, some 1,500 contain the LXX text. Nearly 300 were collated, with varying degrees of accuracy, early in the nineteenth century for the edition of R. Holmes and J. Parsons [*Vetus Testamentum Graecum cum variis lectionibus,* 5 v. (Oxford 1798–1827)].

Printed editions. The LXX of the Complutensian Polyglot, published in 1521 (*see* POLYGLOT BIBLES) offers, from the minuscule manuscript *b* (Holmes and Parsons, 108), a text of ''Lucianic'' type, mingled with

portions and eclectic readings from other minuscules, notably cod. 248. The Aldine Greek Bible of 1518 based its LXX text on minuscule manuscripts in Venice. The Sixtine edition of 1587, an outgrowth of the Council of Trent, had great influence on subsequent editions; as it was based largely on codex B, it offered a good foundation for critical study. J. E. Grabe's edition based on codex A (Oxford 1707–20) is noteworthy. The extensive collations undertaken by Holmes and Parsons drew on 20 uncials, nearly 300 minuscules, and evidence from several daughter versions of the LXX and from patristic citations. K. von Tischendorf produced a good manual edition of the LXX, several times revised from 1850; the 1887 edition, overseen and supplemented by E. Nestle, attained a high degree of accuracy; it offered a revised Sixtine text with an apparatus from the great uncials. Manual editions in current use are those of H. B. Swete, *The Old Testament in Greek* (3 v. Cambridge, Eng.; several editions since 1894), and A. Rahlfs, *Septuaginta* (Stuttgart 1935, 6th ed. 1959). Both offer a collation from the great uncials, Rahlfs under an eclectic text, Swete under that of B where it is extant (in Genesis, that of A; the Psalms lacuna from S); useful for ready reference though they are, neither is now an adequate critical instrument. Of a projected Lucianic edition by P. de Lagarde, volume 1 appeared in 1883; though Lagarde was a great scholar, this edition was not really successful, and it is now antiquated. The full-scale undertaking, to include all pertinent evidence for text, secondary versions, and citations of LXX, directed by A. E. Brooke, N. McLean, and H. St. John Thackeray at Cambridge has yielded editions of all the historical books from Genesis (1906) to 1 and 2 Chronicles; Esther, Judith, and Tobit are included (1940). The continuous text reproduces an uncial (B when available); the user is left largely to his own devices in disentangling from the apparatus the jumble of recensions described above. The Göttingen Academy of Sciences sponsors a parallel endeavor that has so far published in full the LXX Prophets (Isaiah, Jeremiah with Lamentations and Baruch, Ezekiel, Daniel, and the Twelve, ed. J. Ziegler, between 1939 and 1954); 1, 2, and 3 Maccabees (W. Kappler and R. Hanhart, 1936, 1959–60); Psalms (Rahlfs, 1931); Wisdom (Ziegler, 1962); Sirach (also Ziegler, *Sapientia Jesu filii Sirach,* 1965). In this series, the editor establishes the running text and presents his collations, by family groups when possible, against that base. Outside these series, M. Margolis published (Paris 1931–38) a separate edition of most of Jostle, and the Göttingen undertaking offered sample editions of Genesis (1926) and Ruth (1922).

Significance of the LXX: Its use in textual criticism. The LXX is especially noteworthy as having provided a cultural milieu and a literary vehicle for the preaching of earliest Christianity. This providential role for it, combined with its not infrequent shortcomings and liberties in dealing with the Hebrew, and its notable divergence from the more narrowly based and rigid standard of the Hebrew consonantal text of about A.D. 100, made it increasingly distasteful to the Jews, who replaced it with Aquila for the most part.

For the use of the LXX in textual criticism, the primary rule is that each book of the Old Testament in Greek had its own history and must be studied on its own terms: competence and idiosyncrasies of its translator(s), possible recensions, time of its original rendering and its successive modifications, and only then at last the force of its individual readings in their relation to a presumed Hebrew prototype that may or may not coincide with the received Hebrew text or with variants on it known from elsewhere. It is often our earliest witness, and is sometimes the best; but any sweeping general statement about the value of the LXX as a whole, whether for praise or for blame, is the fruit of ignorance.

Bibliography: E. HATCH and H. REDPATH, *A Concordance to the Septuagint and the Other Greek Versions of the Old Testament,* 2 v. (Oxford 1892–97; suppl. 1900–06; repr. Graz 1954). H. B. SWETE, *An Introduction to the Old Testament in Greek* (rev. ed. Cambridge, Eng. 1914). A. RAHLFS, *Verzeichnis der griechischen Handschriften des Alte Testament* (Berlin 1914). F. G. KENYON, *Our Bible and the Ancient Manuscripts,* rev. A. W. ADAMS (5th ed. New York 1958) 97–134. R. DEVREESSE, *Introduction à l'étude des manuscrits grecs* (Paris 1954). P. E. KAHLE, *The Cairo Geniza* (2d ed. New York 1960). P. KATZ, ''Septuagint Studies in the Mid-Century,'' *The Background of the New Testament and Its Eschatology,* ed. W. D. DAVIES and D. DAUBE (Cambridge, Eng. 1956) 176–208. J. ZIEGLER, *Die Septuaginta: Erbe und Auftrag* (Würzburg 1962); *Lexikon für Theologie und Kirche,* 10 v. (Freiburg 1957–65) 2:375–380. H. M. ORLINSKY, ''The Textual Criticism of the Old Testament,'' in *The Bible and the Ancient Near East,* ed. G. E. WRIGHT (New York 1961) 113–132. D. BARTHÉLEMY, *Les Devanciers d'Aquila* (Vetus Testamentum suppl. 10; 1963). F. M. CROSS, ''The History of the Biblical Text in the Light of Discoveries in the Judaean Desert,'' *Harvard Theological Review* 57 (1964) 281–299. O. EISSFELDT, *Einleitung in das Alte Testament* (3d ed. Tübingen 1964) 951–973, 1031. G. GERLEMANN, *Die Religion in Geschichte und Gegenwart,* 7 v. (3d ed. Tübingen 1957–65) 1:1193–1195. *Encyclopedic Dictionary of the Bible,* tr. and adap. L. HARTMAN (New York 1963) 2165–2171.

[P. W. SKEHAN]

SEPULCHER, HOLY

The present church of the Holy Sepulcher that houses the traditional sites of the Crucifixion and the Resurrection has had a long history of development. Although it is still essentially the Crusaders' basilica, it has suffered not only from centuries of neglect but also from earthquakes and fires, not to mention outrageous alterations. Yet in spite of its dilapidated condition it is one of the most sacred spots in the world.

The Constantinian Basilica. An archeological consideration of capital importance for the traditional identification of the Lord's tomb on this spot is the fact that the church was built on ground that already at the time of Our Lord had tombs hewn in it. One can still see inside the church, in the section reserved for the Syrian Jacobites, several ancient tombs of the *kôkîm* type that are purely Jewish in style. Moreover, it appears incredible that the first Christians would not have carefully preserved the memory of the site of the Resurrection.

When the Emperor Hadrian (A.D. 135) built his pagan Jerusalem, Colonia Aelia Capitolina, a high terrace was prepared and a sanctuary of Venus (Aphrodite) erected at the place where, according to Christian tradition, the sepulcher of Christ had stood. In 326, after nearly 200 years, at the command of Constantine this temple was demolished and the tomb of Christ again came to light. The Christian Emperor then instructed Macarius, Bishop of Jerusalem, to erect on the site at imperial expense an outstanding monument. The church was dedicated on Sept. 14, 335, and is described minutely by Eusebius, with whose help one can visualize what the building was like.

The propylaea, or entrance, was to the east, opening from the middle of the chief market street, the characteristic Roman colonnaded road that crossed the city north to south. A triple gateway forming an artistic façade was approached by a formal flight of steps and led into an atrium. This first court was surrounded by porticoes and left open to the sky. Passing through the atrium the visitor came to the basilica proper, which later was quite appropriately called the *Martyrium,* or the place of witnessing.

The basilica with its central nave and double side naves was similar to that of Bethlehem. The layout of the central nave was planned in relation to the chapel of St. Helena, which was and still is an elegant crypt. The cave of the Finding of the Cross was a sort of second crypt 13 steps lower. The crowning part of the basilica was the Hemisphere, as Eusebius calls it. This was a beautifully decorated semicircular apse at the western end and corresponded to the opening of the great nave.

Beyond the basilica was a second open court, where, to the south of the main axis, the rock of Calvary stood in the open air, surrounded by a grille and rising some 12 feet above the ground. The rock-cut tomb that had been the sepulcher of Christ was enclosed by a round domed building that became known as the *Anastasis* because it commemorated the place of the Resurrection.

Only a few fragmentary portions of these Constantinian structures remain today. However this general picture, primarily according to Eusebius but following also the indications of Cyril of Jerusalem and the description

Church of the Holy Sepulcher, c. 12th Century, Old City, Jerusalem. (©Carmen Redondo/CORBIS)

given in Itinerarium of EGERIA, is confirmed by two ancient representations of the Church of the Holy Sepulcher: the fourth-century mosaic in the apse of S. Pudenziana in Rome and the famous sixth-century mosaic map at Medaba.

Subsequent History. In 614, the Persians burned the Constantinian buildings. Restoration work was carried out soon after by the Patriarch Modestus in far simpler style but along the same general lines of the previous buildings. In 935 a mosque was built on the site of the exterior atrium of the church, and in 1009 Caliph Hakim destroyed the church itself. He ordered the demolition of the Holy Sepulcher, so that very little can have remained of Our Lord's tomb. Hakim's successors showed more tolerance, and Constantine Monomachus (1048) was able to reconstruct the cave in masonry, obliterating, however, the last trace of the natural state of the tomb.

The Crusaders found Monomachus's timber-domed rotunda over the Holy Sepulcher, an oratory on Golgotha where the summit of the rock was still bare and the crypt of St. Helena. Constantine's basilica had been left in ruins. They built a Romanesque church, which was consecrated on July 15, 1149. It covered beneath its roof both the rock of Calvary and the interior Constantinian court. The building was erected against the rotunda and the architects were scrupulously respectful of the vestiges of the past.

The present church of the Holy Sepulcher consists of two main sections: on the west the great dome that rises over the commemorative shrine of Our Lord's sepulcher and on the east the church proper with its many adjacent chapels. Every inch is divided up by centuries-old tradition among the Latins, the Greeks, the Armenians, the Syrians and the Copts. Certain areas, however, such as the chapel of the Holy Sepulcher, are common property. The Ethiopians have to be contented with the roof terraces. The Anglicans, through the kindness of the Orthodox, hold services in the so-called chapel of Adam that is below the chapel of Calvary. The long simmering distrust over control of the property has made doubly difficult the attempts at restoration.

The locality of the church within the present walls of the city is no argument against the traditional identification (Jn 19.20), for Jerusalem had different walls at different periods of its history. The so-called Garden Tomb, another site recently claimed to have been that of Jesus' tomb, has no archeological evidence to support it. Finally, it may be noted that specialists as different in outlook as L. H. Vincent, G. H. Dalman and J. Jeremias agreed in localizing Golgotha and the tomb of Jesus in the present church of the Holy Sepulcher.

Bibliography: L. H. VINCENT and F. M. ABEL, *Jérusalem Nouvelle,* v.2 of *Jérusalem: Recherches de topographie, d'archéologie et d'histoire,* 2 v. (Paris 1912–26) 2:1–300, with plates 12–29. D. BALDI, *Enchiridion locorum sanctorum* (2d ed. Jerusalem 1955). L. H. VINCENT et al., *Il santo sepolcro di Gerusalemme* (Bergamo 1949). A. PARROT, *Golgotha and the Church of the Holy Sepulcher,* tr. E. HUDSON (New York 1957). *Bible et Terre Sainte,* 55 (1963). L. H. VINCENT, "Garden Tomb: Histoire d'un Mythe," *Revue biblique* 34 (1925) 401–431. C. KOPP, *The Holy Places of the Gospels,* tr. R. WALLS (New York 1963) 374–394. K. J. CONANT, *The Original Buildings at the Holy Sepulchre in Jerusalem* (Cambridge, Mass. 1956). S. DE SANDOLI, *Calvary and the Holy Sepulchre: Historical Outline* (Jerusalem 1977). M. BIDDLE, *The Tomb of Christ* (Stroud, Gloucestershire, England 1999).

[E. LUSSIER/EDS.]

The Stone of Unction, in the Holy Sepulcher. (©Richard T. Nowitz/CORBIS)